■ THE RESOURCE FOR THE INDEPENDENT TRAVELER

"The guides are aimed not only at young budget travelers but at the indepedent traveler; a sort of streetwise cookbook for traveling alone."

—The New York Times

"Unbeatable; good sight-seeing advice; up-to-date info on restaurants, hotels, and inns; a commitment to money-saving travel; and a wry style that brightens nearly every page."

—The Washington Post

"Lighthearted and sophisticated, informative and fun to read. [Let's Go] helps the novice traveler navigate like a knowledgeable old hand."

—Atlanta Journal-Constitution

"A world-wise traveling companion—always ready with friendly advice and helpful hints, all sprinkled with a bit of wit."

—The Philadelphia Inquirer

■ THE BEST TRAVEL BARGAINS IN YOUR PRICE RANGE

"All the dirt, dirt cheap."

—People

"Anything you need to know about budget traveling is detailed in this book."

—The Chicago Sun-Times

"Let's Go follows the creed that you don't have to toss your life's savings to the wind to travel—unless you want to."

—The Salt Lake Tribune

■ REAL ADVICE FOR REAL EXPERIENCES

"The writers seem to have experienced every rooster-packed bus and lunar-surfaced mattress about which they write."

—The New York Times

"A guide should tell you what to expect from a destination. Here Let's Go shines."

—The Chicago Tribune

LET'S GO PUBLICATIONS

TRAVEL GUIDES

Alaska & the Pacific Northwest 2003
Australia 2003
Austria & Switzerland 2003
Britain & Ireland 2003
California 2003
Central America 8th edition
Chile 1st edition **NEW TITLE**
China 4th edition
Costa Rica 1st edition **NEW TITLE**
Eastern Europe 2003
Egypt 2nd edition
Europe 2003
France 2003
Germany 2003
Greece 2003
Hawaii 2003 **NEW TITLE**
India & Nepal 7th edition
Ireland 2003
Israel 4th edition
Italy 2003
Mexico 19th edition
Middle East 4th edition
New Zealand 6th edition
Peru, Ecuador & Bolivia 3rd edition
South Africa 5th edition
Southeast Asia 8th edition
Southwest USA 2003
Spain & Portugal 2003
Thailand 1st edition **NEW TITLE**
Turkey 5th edition
USA 2003
Western Europe 2003

CITY GUIDES

Amsterdam 2003
Barcelona 2003
Boston 2003
London 2003
New York City 2003
Paris 2003
Rome 2003
San Francisco 2003
Washington, D.C. 2003

MAP GUIDES

Amsterdam
Berlin
Boston
Chicago
Dublin
Florence
Hong Kong
London
Los Angeles
Madrid
New Orleans
New York City
Paris
Prague
Rome
San Francisco
Seattle
Sydney
Venice
Washington, D.C.

WESTERN EUROPE 2003

BRIANNA M. EWERT EDITOR

JENNIFER MAY-ANNE CHEN ASSOCIATE EDITOR
TABATHA L. GEORGE ASSOCIATE EDITOR
MATTHEW K. HUDSON ASSOCIATE EDITOR
KALEN J. S. INGRAM ASSOCIATE EDITOR
HANNAH J. TRIERWEILER ASSOCIATE EDITOR

GENEVIEVE A. CADWALADER RESEARCHER-WRITER

MARLA KAPLAN MANAGING EDITOR

JULIE STEPHENS MAP EDITOR
MATT DANIELS TYPESETTER

ST. MARTIN'S PRESS NEW YORK

HELPING LET'S GO If you want to share your discoveries, suggestions, or corrections, please drop us a line. We read every piece of correspondence, whether a postcard, a 10-page email, or a coconut. Please note that mail received after May 2003 may be too late for the 2004 book, but will be kept for future editions. **Address mail to:**

Let's Go: Western Europe
67 Mount Auburn Street
Cambridge, MA 02138
USA

Visit Let's Go at **http://www.letsgo.com,** or send email to:

feedback@letsgo.com
Subject: "Let's Go: Western Europe"

In addition to the invaluable travel advice our readers share with us, many are kind enough to offer their services as researchers or editors. Unfortunately, our charter enables us to employ only currently enrolled Harvard students.

Distributed outside the USA and Canada by Macmillan.

ISBN: 0-312-30600-8

First edition
10 9 8 7 6 5 4 3 2 1

Let's Go: Western Europe is written by Let's Go Publications, 67 Mount Auburn Street, Cambridge, MA 02138, USA.

Printed in the USA on recycled paper with soy ink.

HOW TO USE THIS BOOK

Things are changing in Western Europe. You can now move from country to country without pulling out your passport or changing deutschmarks to pesetas to francs. But Western Europe's appeal to travelers remains steadfast—which is where we come in. *Let's Go: Western Europe 2003* is up-to-date and ready to savvily guide you through the the ever-evolving world of Western Europe.

ORGANIZATION. *Let's Go: Western Europe 2003* is arranged to make the information you need easy to find. The **Discover** chapter offers highlights of the region, tips on when to travel (including a calendar of festivals), and suggested itineraries. **Quick History** provides an overview of the past of this wildly diverse and yet interconnected collection of countries. The **Essentials** chapter details the nitty gritty of passports, transportation, money, communications, and more—everything you'll need to plan your trip and stay safe on the road. **Alternatives to Tourism** gives advice on how to work or volunteer your way through your journey. Next come the 17 jam-packed **country chapters,** from Andorra to Switzerland; each country chapter begins with a Life and Times section, detailing history and culture, and an Essentials section with important travel information specific to that country. The **Heading East** chapter covers two cities, Prague and Budapest, as a sampling of the travel opportunities on the rest of the Continent. At the back of the book is a **language appendix** (p. 1017), a crash course in 10 European languages. The black tabs on the sides of the pages separate the chapters and will help you navigate your way through the book.

RANKINGS AND PRICE RANGES. We list establishments in order of value, and our absolute favorites are denoted by the *Let's Go* thumbs-up (☒). Since the best value does not always mean the cheapest price, we have incorporated a system of **price ranges** (❶❷❸❹❺) into our coverage of accommodations and restaurants. At a glance, you can compare the costs of a night's stay in towns a mile apart or halfway across the country. The price ranges for each country can be found in the introductory section of the country chapters.

NEW FEATURES. Long-time readers will notice a number of changes in *Let's Go: Western Europe 2003*, most notably the sidebars that accompany much of our coverage. At the end of the book, you'll find a series of longer **Feature Articles** focused on issues affecting Western Europe as a whole. These additions are meant to go beyond the practical details and help you understand the place you are going. Whether enjoyed on a long train ride or at a quiet hostel, we hope these articles will entertain you and inform your travels throughout Western Europe.

ENJOY YOUR TRIP. *Let's Go* can only take you so far. The rest is up to you. The very best parts of your trip will likely be the ones no traveler could anticipate and no travel guide can describe.

A NOTE TO OUR READERS The information for this book was gathered by *Let's Go* researchers from May through August of 2002. Each listing is based on one researcher's opinion, formed during his or her visit at a particular time. Those traveling at other times may have different experiences since prices, dates, hours, and conditions are always subject to change. You are urged to check the facts presented in this book beforehand to avoid inconvenience and surprises.

CONTENTS

RESEARCHER-WRITERS

Genevieve A. Cadwalader *Belgium, Luxembourg, Denmark*

Majoring in the history of art and architecture, Genevieve set off with a passion for exploration that even a bout with a stomach virus couldn't spoil. A world-class rower and former wilderness camp counselor, Genevieve tackled the outdoors of Luxembourg and the bike routes of Denmark with a vengeance. She found her second home amongst the Art Nouveau architecture, chocolate, and mussels of Belgium.

REGIONAL EDITORS & RESEARCHER-WRITERS

LET'S GO: AMSTERDAM 2003

Sarah E. Kramer *Editor*
Stefan Atkinson, **Catherine Burch**, **Ian MacKenzie** *Amsterdam & the Netherlands*

LET'S GO: AUSTRIA & SWITZERLAND 2003

Joanna Shawn Brigid O'Leary *Editor*
Deborah Harrison *Associate Editor*
Jocelyn Beh *Bernese Oberland, Italian Switzerland, Lucerne*
Alinna Chung *Zurich, Basel, Bern, Geneva, Northern Switzerland*
Tom Miller *Carinthia, Hohe Tauern Region, Tyrol, Vorarlberg*
Christine Peterson *Niederösterreich, Salzburgerland, Styria*
Lora Sweeney *Vienna, Burgenland, Oberösterreich*

LET'S GO: BARCELONA 2003

Anna Elizabeth Byrne *Editor*
Colleen Gargan, **Rei Onishi**, **Adam Weiss** *Barcelona*

LET'S GO: BRITAIN & IRELAND 2003

Sonja Nikkila *Editor*
Teresa Elsey *Associate Editor*
Jenny Pegg *Wales, Isle of Man, Midlands, Northwest England*
Angie Sun *Midlands; Southwest, Heart of, and Northern England*
Sarah A. Tucker *South and Heart of England, Midlands, East Anglia, Yorkshire*
John T. Witherspoon *Glasgow, Central Scotland, Highlands & Islands*
Daniel Zweifach *Northern England, Southern and Central Scotland*

LET'S GO: EASTERN EUROPE 2003

Jennifer Anne O'Brien *Editor*
Susan E. Bell, **Rochelle Lundy**, **Mahmoud Youssef** *Associate Editors*
Sandra Nagy *E. Slovak Republic, Hungary*
Dalibor Eric Snyder *Czech Republic*

LET'S GO: FRANCE 2003

Annalise Nelson *Editor*
Paul Eisenstein, **Sarah Levine-Gronningsater** *Associate Editors*
Emily Buck *Loire Valley, Poitou-Charentes, Berry-Limousin, Périgord*
Edward B. Colby *Provence, Lyon and the Auvergne, Burgundy*
Laure "Voop" de Vulpillières *Champagne, Alsace-Lorraine, Flanders, Languedoc*
Robert Madison *Côte d'Azure, Corsica, the Alps*
Genevieve Sheehan *Brittany and Normandy*
Julia Steele *Languedoc-Roussillon, Aquitane, Pays Basque*

LET'S GO: GERMANY 2003

Jesse Reid Andrews *Editor*
Karoun Demirjian *Associate Editor*
Charlotte Douglas *Rhineland-Palatine, Saarland, North Rhine-Westphalia, Lower Saxony, Bremen*
Deidre Foley-Mendelssohn *Berlin, Potsdam, Mecklenburg-Upper Pomerania*
Paul G. Kofoed *Schleswig-Holstein, Hamburg, Mecklenburg-Upper Pomerania*
Patrick Morrissey *Saxony-Anhalt, Lower Saxony, Hessen, Bavaria*
Andrew Price *Saxony, Thuringia, Brandenburg, Saxony-Anhalt*
Matej Sapak *Hessen (Frankfurt), Baden Württemberg, Bavaria, Rhineland-Palatine*
Becky Windt *Bavaria*

LET'S GO: GREECE 2003

Jonelle Lonergan *Editor*
Andrew Zaroulis *Associate Editor*
Kevin Connor *Central Greece, the Sporades, Saronic Gulf, Northeast Aegean Islands*
Gary Cooney *Central and Northern Greece*
Emily Ogden *Cyprus, the Dodecanese*
Geoffrey Reed *Crete, the Cyclades, Northeast Aegean Islands*
Jen Taylor *Peloponnese and Ionian Islands*
Scottie Thompson *Athens, the Cyclades*

LET'S GO: IRELAND 2003

David James Bright *Editor*
Kathleen Marie Rey *Associate Editor*
Chris Gregg *Dublin, Midlands, Southeast*
Jack Riccobono *The Southwest*
Abigail Shafroth *Belfast, Derry, Sligo, Galway*
Kira Whelan *The Northwest*

LET'S GO: ITALY 2003

Amber K. Lavicka *Editor*
Theadosia M. Howell
Irin Carmon *Associate Editors*
Julia Bozer *Calabria, Sicily*
Paul W. Guilianelli *Tuscany, Umbria*
Christopher Kukstis *Abruzzo, Molise, Campania, Basilicata, Apulia*
Melissa LaScaleia *Veneto, Emilia Romagna, The Marches*
Hunter Maats *Piedmont, Lombardy, Trentino-Alto Adige*
Laura A. Nevison *Liguria, Sardinia*

LET'S GO: LONDON 2003

Eustace Santa Barbara *Editor*
Nathaniel Popper
John Mazza
Andrew Sodroski *London*

LET'S GO: PARIS 2003

Sarah Robinson *Editor*
Sarah Eno
Dehn Gilmore
Nathaniel Mendelsohn *Paris*

LET'S GO: ROME

Shannon F. Ringvelski *Editor*
Katharine Burrage
Michael Marean
Michael Simonetti *Rome*

LET'S GO: SPAIN & PORTUGAL

Andrew M. Torres *Editor*
Lucy B. Ebersold
Irin Carmon *Associate Editors*
Sebastián Andrés Brown *Extremadura, Cantabria, Asturias, Galicia*
Nate Gray *La Rioja, Navarra, Pyrenees, País Vasco, Andorra*
Josh Ludmir *Murcia, Valencia, Balearic Islands*
Karen L. McCarthy *Andalucia, the Algarve*
Paul Rubio *Madrid, the Canary Islands*
Marie C. Scott *Portugal*
Mosi Secret *Morocco*

CONTRIBUTING WRITERS

Charles Elrich — *Reclaiming the Past (p. 966)*

Charles Ehrlich was a Researcher-Writer for *Let's Go: Spain & Portugal.* He is formerly a Senior Staff Attorney at the Claims Resolution Tribunal that adjudicates claims to Swiss bank accounts from the Nazi era.

Jeremy Faro — *With or Without EU (p. 1034)*

Jeremy Faro is a former Senior Consultant at Interbrand and has worked in the past on *Let's Go: Britain & Ireland.* He is currently a master's student in European Studies at Cambridge University.

Kathleen Holbrook — *Europe in Black and White (p. 1035)*

Kathleen Holbrook is doing her doctoral research on globalization and human values. For a course on Personal Choice and Global Transformation, she was voted Harvard's best teaching fellow.

Caitlin Hurley — *When in Rome (p. 664)*

Caitlin Hurley, a teacher at Marymount International School in Rome, was a Researcher-Writer for *Let's Go: USA 1994.*

Matthew Lazen — *Many Cultures, One Race (p. 303)*

Matthew Lazen spent two years in Brittany and Alsace on a Chateaubriand Fellowship for dissertation research on regional cultures in post-modern France, and is currently a History & Literature lecturer at Harvard University.

Brian C. W. Palmer — *Europe in Black and White (p. 1035)*

Brian Palmer, Ph.D., lectures on globalization at Harvard and in Sweden. For a course which the New York Times nicknamed "Idealism 101," he was voted Harvard's best young faculty member.

Tobie Whitman — *Got Change for a Euro? (p. 1033)*

Tobie Whitman was a Researcher-Writer for *Let's Go: London 1999* and *2000,* as well as *Let's Go: Britain and Ireland 1998.* After an internship with the EU, she entered Cambridge University to pursue a Master's Degree in European Studies.

ACKNOWLEDGMENTS

The WEUR team would like to thank: EEUR for their help in our quest for world (office) domination. Financial for playing great music, paying us, and always speaking your mind. Julie and all the mappers for showing us the way. Caleb, Clayton, and Muehlke for ruining Tabby's X-Box scam. All the Western Europe editors, AEs, and RWs for incredible copy and crunches. Marla for keeping us on track. Gibson and Walsh for envisioning the relaunch. Team WEUR 02 for a sound foundation. To everyone in the office who helped in the last minute push. To our readers, for giving us reason to get every last detail right.

Bri thanks: The amazing W/EUR Team—Hannah, Jen, Kalen, Matt, Tabby—your devotion to the job and incredible enthusiasm was an inspiration. To Marla and Celeste, for keeping us together. To Julie, for maps and her cheerfulness. To my roommates—Amara, Giulia, Rachelle, and Shannon—for brightening every day. To Matt G. for listening… and talking, too! To Adam, for still being there. To Keith, for the ☎ phone. To Mom, Dad, and Chad, for loving me and supporting me always.

Hannah thanks: Tabby for Santa Ana, Matt for conspiratorial confusion, Kalen for a.m. inspiration, Jen for "awww...," Bri for pats on the back, and Jeff for Kings of Convenience. Julie, Marla, Celeste, David, Kathleen, Sonja, Teresa, Jonelle, Andrew, and Eustace for your infinite wisdom. Lowell girls, H-West, Tess, Bennett, and Natalie for loving me anyway. Sarah for keeping my chin up until it's done and done. Mom, Gordon, Dad, Deanna, John, Megan, and David—I love you.

Jen thanks: Bri for hiring me and embracing a bit of EEUR in her book, and for being so encouraging and sweet. AEs, thanks for all the laughs, you're great. Noah (you can turn the AC up now, I don't mind) and Jeff for introducing me to new music! Yo, Abi, thanks for introducing me to the world of *Let's Go*, and for always being there. EEUR gets my loyalty—look, the "East" grew this year! Mommy, Daddy, Ian, Pete, and Julianne, thanks for all the love and support.

Kalen thanks: My fellow AEs—we make a great team. Bri, for catching all my sighs and making sure they were aimed only at Frame. Marla for keeping us on the ball. GER and A&S for your patience and help. The fat camp crew—Sean, Jody, Haigher, Space, Jim, Kat, Cull, and Ang—for keeping me energized. The McAuliffe family for your generosity. For a lifetime of support and love, Mom, Dad, David, and Kelsey—I've missed you this summer.

Matt thanks: Bri, for giving me the nod. Team Europe. Skramer, for more than you know (but less than you suspect). Scrobins, for hot gossip. Dave and Beechie, for getting me thus far. Kris, for putting up with my nonsense and keeping me grounded. Mom and Dad, Monty, Mikey, and Fat Mr. C (who will eat this book while I'm out), for giving me somewhere to come home to and the desire to do so. But this is for Nana, who, I figure, deserves to have a book dedicated to her.

Tabby thanks: Hannah for always being on my page (re: boys), Matt for eloquence under fire and for making me laugh (Boom.), Kalen for knowing good beer, Jen for late-night company, Marla for a fabulous job. Bri for so much hard work and for homemade cookies. Mom and Dad for love, and being so smart. Maggie and Elvis for love and speaking their mind. Christy, forever my best friend. Justin for constant support. Erik for being there when I fell in love with Europe.

Julie thanks: Team Europe for super map edits. Bri for being a pleasure to work with. Mapland for map raves and late-night camaraderie. The MEs for a year of fun. 7 Story St. for good times. Kuba for reminding me there is more to life than work. My family for their patience, love, and support.

Editor
Brianna M. Ewert
Associate Editors
Jennifer May-Anne Chen, Tabatha George, Matthew K. Hudson, Kalen J. S. Ingram, Hannah J. Trierweiler
Managing Editor
Marla Kaplan
Map Editor
Julie Stephens

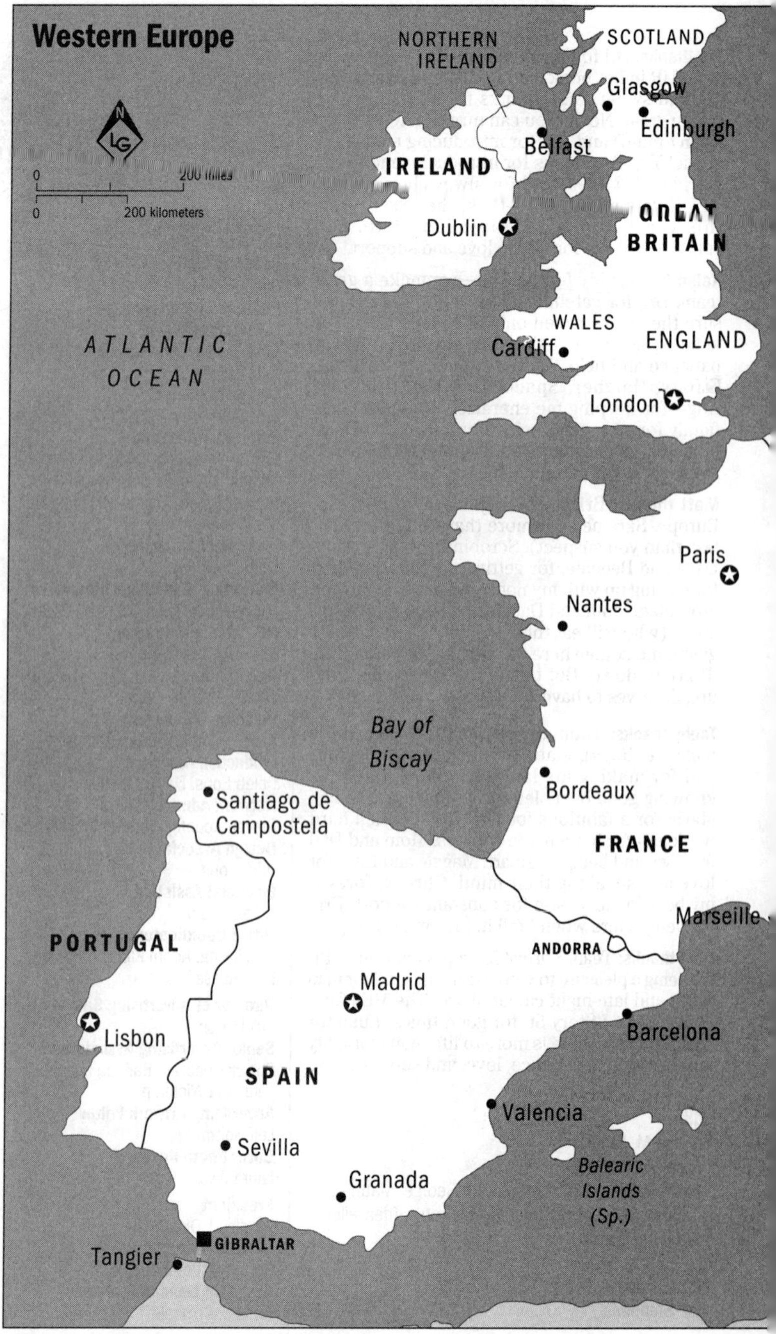
Western Europe
200 miles
200 kilometers
0
0
NORTHERN IRELAND
SCOTLAND
Glasgow
Edinburgh
Belfast
IRELAND
Dublin
GREAT BRITAIN
WALES
ENGLAND
Cardiff
London
ATLANTIC OCEAN
Paris
Nantes
Bay of Biscay
Bordeaux
FRANCE
Santiago de Campostela
Marseille
ANDORRA
PORTUGAL
Madrid
Barcelona
Lisbon
SPAIN
Valencia
Sevilla
Granada
Balearic Islands (Sp.)
Tangier
GIBRALTAR

NORWAY
North Sea
SWEDEN
DENMARK
Rīga
LATVIA
Baltic Sea
LITHUANIA
Copenhagen
RUSSIA
Hamburg
Gdańsk
NETHERLANDS
Amsterdam
Berlin
Warsaw
Brussels
GERMANY
POLAND
Bonn
BELGIUM
Frankfurt
Prague
Lux.City
Kraków
LUXEMBOURG
CZECH REPUBLIC
SLOVAKIA
Munich
Salzburg
Bratislava
Zurich
Vienna
SWITZERLAND
Bern
Budapest
Geneva
AUSTRIA
LIECHTENSTEIN
HUNGARY
Lyon
SLOVENIA
Ljubljana
Milan
Venice
CROATIA
Zagreb
Belgrade
Florence
BOSNIA-HERZEGOVINA
Nice
YUGOSLAVIA
MONACO
SERBIA
Sarajevo
SAN MARINO
Adriatic Sea
MONTENEGRO
KOSOVO
Corsica (Fr.)
Rome
FYR MACEDONIA
ITALY
Tiranë
Naples
ALBANIA
Sardinia (It.)
Tyrrhenian Sea
Mediterranean
Ionian Sea
Sicily

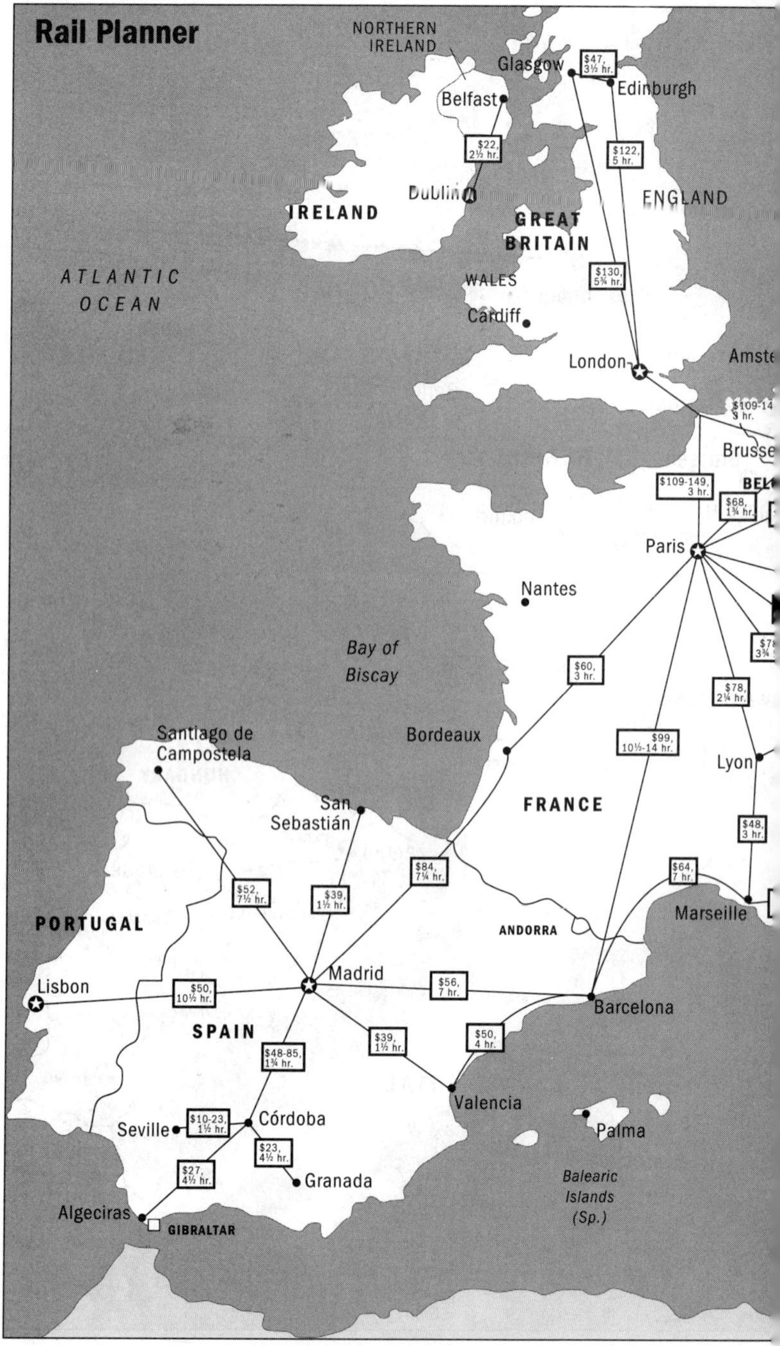

Rail Planner
NORTHERN IRELAND
Glasgow
$47, 3½ hr.
Edinburgh
Belfast
$22, 2½ hr.
$122, 5 hr.
Dublin
IRELAND
GREAT BRITAIN
ENGLAND
ATLANTIC OCEAN
WALES
$130, 5¾ hr.
Cardiff
London
$109-149, 3 hr.
Brussels
Paris
$68, 1¾ hr.
Nantes
Bay of Biscay
$60, 3 hr.
$78, 2¼ hr.
Bordeaux
$99, 10½-14 hr.
Lyon
Santiago de Compostela
San Sebastián
FRANCE
$48, 3 hr.
$84, 7¼ hr.
$64, 7 hr.
$52, 7½ hr.
$39, 1½ hr.
Marseille
PORTUGAL
ANDORRA
Madrid
Lisbon
$50, 10½ hr.
$56, 7 hr.
Barcelona
SPAIN
$39, 1½ hr.
$50, 4 hr.
$48-85, 1¾ hr.
Valencia
$10-23, 1½ hr.
Córdoba
Seville
Palma
$23, 4½ hr.
$27, 4½ hr.
Granada
Balearic Islands (Sp.)
Algeciras
GIBRALTAR

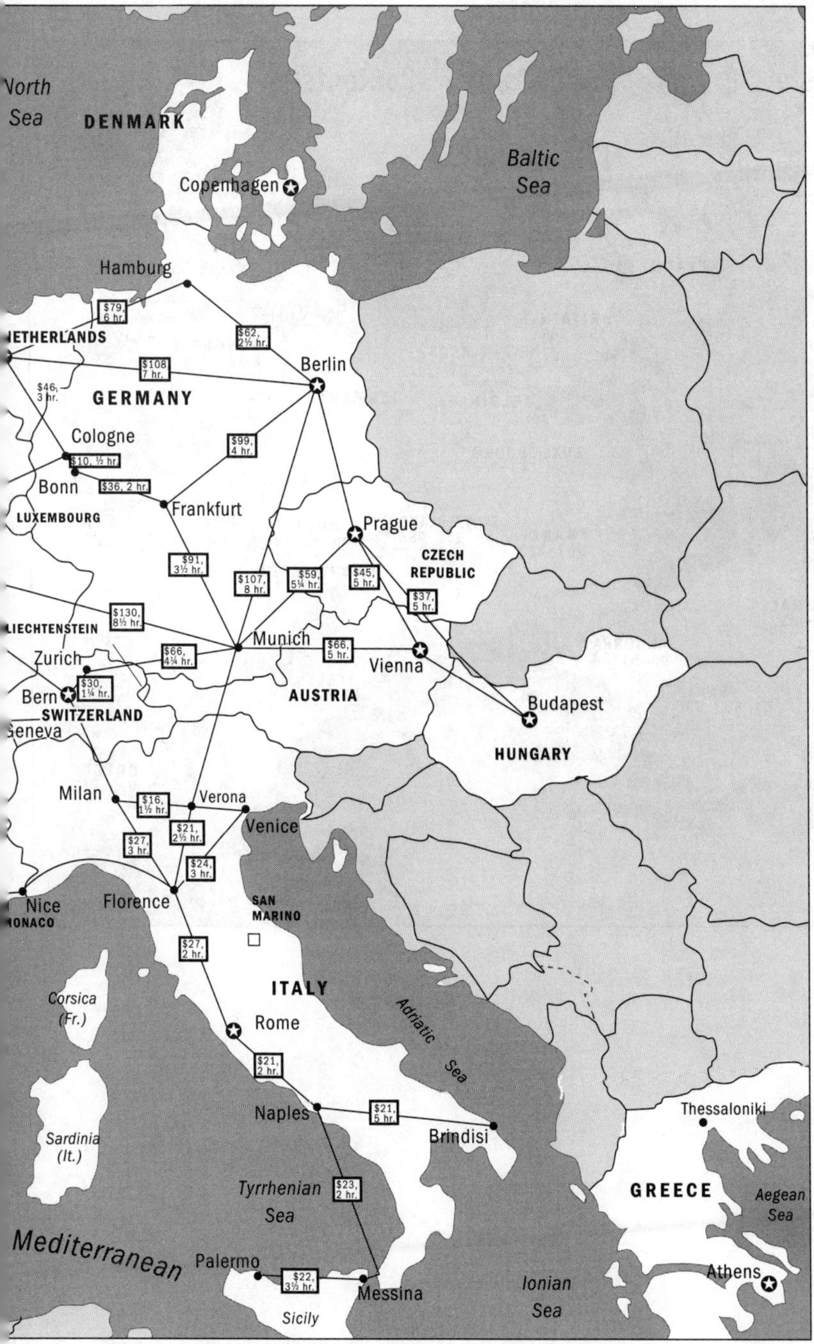
North Sea
DENMARK
Copenhagen
Baltic Sea
Hamburg
$79, 6 hr.
NETHERLANDS
$62, 2½ hr.
$108 7 hr.
Berlin
$46, 3 hr.
GERMANY
Cologne
$99, 4 hr.
$10, ½ hr.
Bonn
$36, 2 hr.
Frankfurt
LUXEMBOURG
Prague
$91, 3½ hr.
$107, 8 hr.
$59, 5¼ hr.
$45, 5 hr.
CZECH REPUBLIC
$37, 5 hr.
$130, 8½ hr.
LIECHTENSTEIN
Munich
$66, 5 hr.
Zurich
$66, 4¼ hr.
Vienna
$30, 1¼ hr.
Bern
AUSTRIA
SWITZERLAND
Budapest
Geneva
HUNGARY
Milan
$16, 1½ hr.
Verona
Venice
$21, 2½ hr.
$27, 3 hr.
$24, 3 hr.
Nice
Florence
MONACO
SAN MARINO
$27, 2 hr.
Corsica (Fr.)
ITALY
Adriatic Sea
Rome
$21, 2 hr.
Naples
$21, 5 hr.
Thessaloniki
Brindisi
Sardinia (It.)
$23, 2 hr.
Tyrrhenian Sea
GREECE
Aegean Sea
Mediterranean
Palermo
$22, 3½ hr.
Athens
Messina
Ionian Sea
Sicily

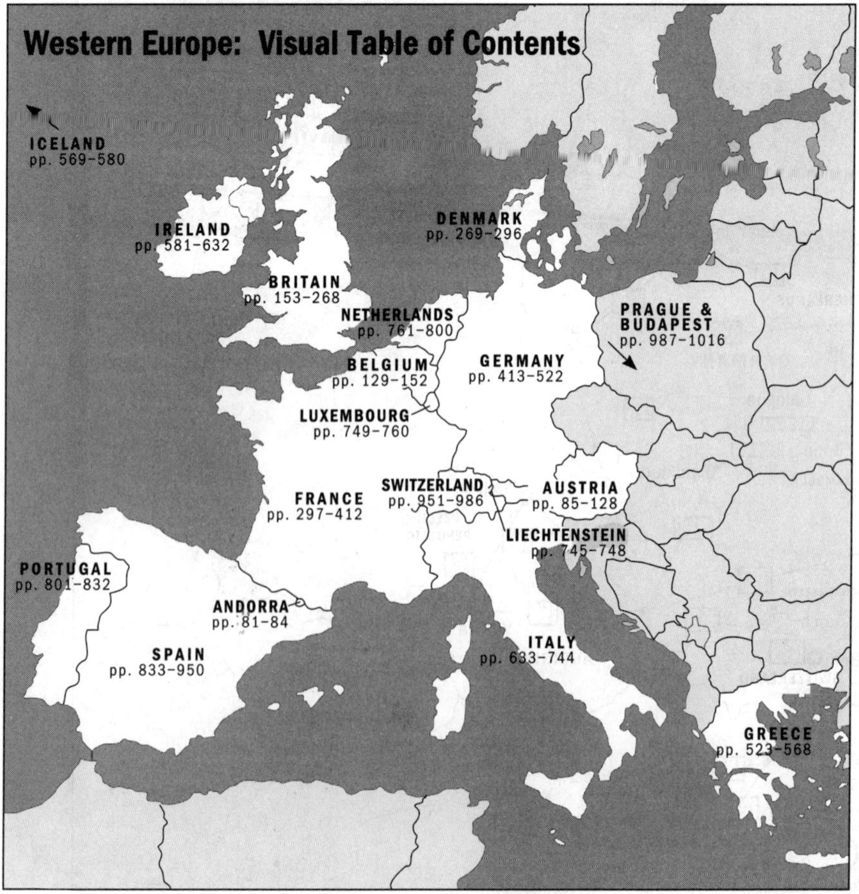

Western Europe: Visual Table of Contents
ICELAND
pp. 569-580
IRELAND
pp. 581-632
BRITAIN
pp. 153-268
DENMARK
pp. 269-296
NETHERLANDS
pp. 761-800
PRAGUE & BUDAPEST
pp. 987-1016
BELGIUM
pp. 129-152
GERMANY
pp. 413-522
LUXEMBOURG
pp. 749-760
SWITZERLAND
pp. 951-986
AUSTRIA
pp. 85-128
FRANCE
pp. 297-412
LIECHTENSTEIN
pp. 745-748
PORTUGAL
pp. 801-832
ANDORRA
pp. 81-84
SPAIN
pp. 833-950
ITALY
pp. 633-744
GREECE
pp. 523-568

DISCOVER WESTERN EUROPE

If you've made it this far, book in hand, then Western Europe has already captured a tiny corner of your imagination—the Continental foot in the door to your escape from banality. Over centuries and around the globe, Western Europe has ranked among the world's fantasy destinations: aspiring writers have spun romances in Parisian alleyways; budding sensualists have chased the legends of Dutch debauchery; and iconic treasures, from the tower at Pisa to the slabs at Stonehenge, cry out for discovery anew. And you lie awake in your sleepless desire to answer their summons. Well, you're not there yet, but you're real close...

Let's Go: Western Europe 2003 will lead you by the hand from well-photographed cultural troves to the obscure bistros and jazz dives that give Europe its pulse. We'll keep you abreast of a new Western Europe, changing faster than ever: an exploding economic community demolishing the barriers that have divided it for centuries. While some may fear that Western Europe risks losing its regional flavors, the perfect, satiny chocolates of the Swiss Alps and a sweet glass of *sangría* at twilight on the Plaza Mayor will put all such worries safely to rest. But don't take our word for it—go experience Western Europe for yourself.

FIGURES AND FACTS

POPULATION: 371,100,000.

LAND MASS: 2.5 million sq. km, almost equal to the Sahara Desert.

HIGHEST POINT: Mont Blanc, France (4807m above sea level).

LOWEST POINTS: Lemmefjord, Denmark and Prins Alexander Polder, The Netherlands (7m below sea level). Also, MC Solaar.

FACT: Every year the average Western European drinks 82L of beer and 17L of wine and consumes 19kg of cheese.

FACT: If a colony of honeybees has an average wing length of larger than 9.5mm, it is known as a European colony.

FACT: The world's largest pair of jeans (23m long) was created by Lee Jeans Europe and displayed at the Atomium in Brussels, Belgium in 1992.

WHEN TO GO

The Renaissance masterpieces of Italy, the ancient ruins of Greece, and the medieval castles of England know no season—they are timeless. However, more pragmatic concerns emerge regarding the most opportune time to visit Western Europe. Given that summer is the high-season for travel in Western Europe and throngs of tourists fill hostels and crowd museums, particularly during the months of July and August, you may find June or September a better time to travel. Additionally, climate can serve as a very good guide for the best time to travel in certain areas.

Av. Temp., Precipitation	January			April			July			October		
	°C	°F	in	°C	°F	in	°C	°F	in	°C	°F	in
Amsterdam	3	38	3.1	8	47	1.5	17	62	2.9	11	51	4.1
Athens	10	50	1.9	15	59	0.9	27	81	0.2	19	67	2.1
Berlin	-1	31	1.6	8	[illegible]	1.6	18	65	2.0	9	49	1.0
Copenhagen	1	33	1.7	6	43	1.6	17	62	2.6	9	49	2.1
Dublin	6	42	2.5	8	47	1.9	16	60	2.6	11	51	2.9
London	4	39	3.1	8	46	2.1	17	62	1.8	11	51	2.9
Madrid	6	42	1.8	12	53	1.8	24	76	0.4	14	58	1.8
Paris	4	39	0.2	10	50	0.2	19	67	0.2	12	53	0.2
Prague	-2	29	0.8	7	45	1.4	17	63	2.6	8	47	1.2
Rome	8	47	3.2	13	55	2.6	75	75	0.6	18	64	4.5
Vienna	0	32	1.5	9	49	2.0	20	68	2.9	11	51	1.9

THINGS TO DO

Western Europe can be as overwhelming as it is exciting. In hopes of making the planning stage more exciting than overwhelming, we've compiled a few launching pads from which you can start drawing up an itinerary: **themed categories** to let you know where to find your museums, your mountains, your madhouses; **Let's Go Picks** to point you toward some of the quirkiest gems you could uncover; and **suggested itineraries** to outline the common paths across Europe. Once you've cemented the basics of your trip, turn to the country-specific **Discover** sections at the beginning of each chapter to hammer out the details of your self-directed, nobody-but-you itinerary. But remember, on even the most meticulously planned itinerary, your greatest memories will likely be unexpected and intangible, like languorous evenings spent walking through a tiny coastal town whose name you hadn't known before you arrived.

MUSEUM MANIA

Europe's most precious artifacts reside in her museums; nearly every city houses a sculpture, a painting, or a relic recognized the world over. **London** (p. 164) is packed with artistic gems, not least of which are the imperialist booty at the British Museum and the striking Tate Modern Gallery. On the other side of the Channel, **Paris** (p. 311) is equally well-stocked—although you could spend half your life at the Louvre, you'd have to take some breaks to visit the Musée d'Orsay, the Musée Rodin, and the endearingly garish Pompidou Centre. For museums designed with as much artistic inspiration as their collections, try Spain's Guggenheim Museum in **Bilbao** (p. 942), and the Dalí Museum in **Figueres** (p. 930). **Madrid** (p. 846) preserves the world's largest collection of paintings in the Prado, while the Reina Sofía shelters Picasso's overpowering *Guernica.*

Florence (p. 711) was the home of the Renaissance and still retains many of its masterworks in the Uffizi and the Accademia. The Vatican Museum in **Rome** (p. 644) houses the Sistine Chapel and other priceless works of sculpture and art. Celebrate Germany's reunification at the East Side Gallery in **Berlin** (p. 426), built around the longest remaining stretch of the Wall. **Munich** boasts the technological Deutsches Museum and the twin Pinakotheks (p. 504); if those don't raise your spirits, try **Hamburg**'s Erotic Art Museum (p. 467). The biggest sin you could commit in **Amsterdam** (p. 769) would be to overlook the Rijksmuseum and the van Gogh Museum.

LET'S GO PICKS: AIR-CONDITIONED AND FULL OF ART.

BEST COLLEGE EXPERIENCE: You can tap into a wealth of knowledge at Amsterdam's **Cannabis College** (p. 783), where the basement gardener willingly shares venting, fertilization, and lighting tips.

BEST PLACE TO PUT YOUR BACK INTO IT: Roskilde, Denmark's **Viking Ship Museum** (p. 284), where a ride on a longboat will cost you 80kr and a share of sweat.

MOST PARANOID GALLERY: The **Collection de l'Art Brut** (p. 981) in Lausanne, Switzerland showcases works of institutionalized schizophrenics and convicted criminals.

RUINS AND RELICS

For those who prefer to meet history outside of a museum display case, Europe's castles, churches, and ruins are a dream come true. In **London** (p. 164), royals wander around Buckingham Palace, while choirboys croon at Westminster Abbey. Venture away from the city to ponder the mysteries of Stonehenge and scale the towers of magnificent Warwick Castle. Nobody could miss **Paris**'s breathtaking Cathédrale de Notre-Dame. Elsewhere in France, the *châteaux* of the **Loire Valley** (p. 355) and Normandy's fortified abbey of **Mont-St Michel** (p. 350) are must-sees, as is the fortress of **Carcassonne**. Manmade treasures are strewn throughout Spain, including the largest Gothic cathedral in the world in **Sevilla** (p. 879) and the luxurious Palacio Real in **Madrid** (p. 846). **Barcelona** (p. 907) sports fanciful Modernism, headlined by Antoni Gaudí's La Sagrada Família. Muslim-infused Andalucía offers the mosque in **Córdoba** (p. 889) and the Alhambra in **Granada** (p. 897).

Germany's marvels include the cathedral at **Cologne** (p. 481) and the pure gold tea house at **Potsdam**'s breathtaking Schloß Sans Souci (p. 452). Go a little crazy in Mad King Ludwig's castles (p. 521), or try to figure out Denmark's **Kværndrup** (p. 288) and the optical illusion that makes the castle of Egeskov Slot float on water. **Rome** (p. 644) practically invented architecture as we know it, beginning with the Pantheon, Colosseum, and Forum. In Greece, the crumbling Acropolis—the foundation of Western civilization—towers above **Athens** (p. 533). Journey to the navel of the ancient world to learn your fate from the oracle at **Delphi** (p. 541) or the temple of Apollo on **Delos** (p. 558).

LET'S GO PICKS: DEAD WHITE MEN AND THE STATUES THAT LOVE THEM

BEST PLACE TO FLEX YOUR MUSCLES: Forget the treadmill–take a lap around the millennia-old **stadium** at Ancient Olympia (p. 543).

BEST PLACE TO DECOMPOSE: Vienna's **Zentralfriedhof** (Central Cemetary; p. 106), where you'll find the final movements of Beethoven and Strauss, and an honorary monument to the absent Mozart.

LONGEST LEAK: Brussels's **Mannekin Pis** (p. 139) has urinated for visitors to the city for over 600 years, providing inspiration for lawn statues everywhere. Locals have made a tradition of decorating the boy statue in outlandish seasonal costumes; one on display in the nearby **Maison du Roi** was donated by King Louis XV of France.

THE GREAT OUTDOORS

When cosmopolitan life gets too dizzying, escape to the European outdoors. Britain brims with national parks; the **Lake District** (p. 239) is often considered the most beautiful. For starker beauty, head north to the Scottish Highlands; the **Outer Hebrides** (p. 267) are particularly breathtaking. Ireland's **Ring of Kerry** (p. 611) is home to quaint villages, and **Killarney National Park** (p. 610) features spectacular mountains. The majestic Pyrenees are the setting for Spain's **Parque Nacional de Ordesa** (p. 931). **Grenoble** (p. 392), in the French Alps, is full of hiking opportunities and tempts skiers with steep slopes. In Italy, the soaring **Dolomites** (p. 691) and their surrounding **Lakes** (p. 689) accommodate a wide range of activities. North of Sicily, the **Aeolian Islands** (p. 711) boast pristine beaches, bursting volcanoes, and bubbling thermal springs. In Greece, take a two-day hike to the summit of **Mt. Olympus** (p. 552), where the gods sipped ambrosia, and watch for endangered griffin vultures while trekking in the **Samaria Gorge** (p. 563). **Kitzbühel** (p. 120), in Austria, should quench your desire for world-class hiking and skiing. For fresh Swiss Alpine air, conquer the **Matterhorn** (p. 974) or take up adventure sports in **Interlaken** (p. 971). Soak up the scenery of Germany's **Saxon Switzerland** (p. 458), then hike through the eerie **Black Forest** (p. 502), which inspired the Brothers Grimm.

LET'S GO PICKS: LET'S TAKE THIS OUTSIDE!

BEST PLACE TO HUNT STUFF WITH SPEARS: Italy's **Tremeti Islands,** where popular spearfishing brings locals and tourists together to senselessly murder peaceful fish. *Let's Go* recommends you always point your speargun away from you.

BEST PLACE TO GET SKEWERED: On the horns of a stampeding bull in **Pamplona, Spain.** Alternatively, Italy's **Tremeti Islands,** where popular spearfishing occasionally goes horribly awry...

MOST LIKE YOUR WORST NIGHTMARE: Wander the damp caves under Budapest's **Buda Castle** (p. 1014) before hiking through the **Valley of Death** on Crete (p. 564).

WILD LIFE

When the museums close and the sun sets over the mountains, Europe's wildest parties are just beginning. **Edinburgh** (p. 249) has the highest concentration of pubs in Europe, but it's often overlooked for the pub crawls of **Dublin** (p. 591). There's nowhere sunnier and sexier than the Iberian Peninsula; soak up 3000 hours of sun and 365 nights of sin in **Lagos** (p. 824) on the Algarve coast of Portugal. Along Spain's **Costa del Sol,** hip clubs line the beaches of **Marbella** (p. 903), but it's the **Balearic Islands** that are an absolute must; **Ibiza** (p. 945) in particular is frenzied all hours of the day. Once you've eliminated each and every tan line, head inland to the festive cities of **Madrid** (p. 846) and **Barcelona** (p. 907) or flaunt your way to the one and only **Côte d'Azur** (p. 378). Dynamic **Milan** (p. 673) will introduce you to Italian style in a hurry. Most visitors to Italy don't venture south of Rome—a huge mistake, given the unspeakable beauty of the **Amalfi Coast** (p. 734), birthplace of the bikini. Bop down to the Greek islands for the beautiful beaches of **Corfu** (p. 554) volcanic **Santorini** (p. 561), and **Ios** (p. 560), a frat party run amok. **Prague** (p. 989) and **Munich** (p. 504) know that discriminating drinkers don't need a beach to get sloshed, and **Amsterdam** (p. 769)... trust us, it knows everything it needs to. For one final clubgasm, there's nowhere to go but uninhibited **Berlin** (p. 426).

LET'S GO PICKS: ALL THE NEWS THAT'S FIT TO DRINK.

WETTEST T-SHIRT CONTEST: The **Festival de Sant Joan** in Alicante, Spain (p. 904), when the whole city is doused with firehoses.

BEST PLACE TO GET HAMMERED: In a bar. Any bar. Perhaps in Western Europe.

BEST WAY TO SPEND OKTOBER: Festing on Munich's **Biergärten** (p. 512) bonanza of barley brews, bold, brown Bass, and big burly Brünhildas.

LIVLIEST WATERS: Midleton, Ireland's **Jameson Heritage Centre** (p. 609), where the secrets of the national elixir ("whiskey" is a translation of "water of life") are laid bare.

FÊTES! FESTAS! FESTIVALS!

COUNTRIES	APR. – JUNE	JULY – AUG.	SEPT. – MAR.
AUSTRIA & SWITZERLAND	**Vienna Festival** (May 9-June 15)	**Salzburger Festspiele** (late July to late Aug.) **Open-Air St. Gallen** (late June)	**Fasnacht** (Basel; Mar. 10-12) **Escalade** (Geneva; early Dec.)
BELGIUM	**Festival of Fairground Arts** (Wallonie; late May)	**International Bathtub Regatta** (Dinant; mid-Aug.)	**Gentse Feesten** (10 Days Off; Ghent; July 19-28)
BRITAIN & IRELAND	**Chelsea Flower Show** (London; late May) **Bloomsday** (Dublin; June 16) **Wimbledon** (London; late June)	**Edinburgh Int'l Festival** (Aug. 11-31) **Fringe Festival** (Aug. 4-26) **Mardi Gras** (Manchester; late Aug.)	**Matchmaking Festival** (Lisdoonvarna; Sept.) **Guiness Jazz Festival** (Cork; Oct.) **St. Patrick's Day** (Mar. 17)
DENMARK	**Roskilde Music Festival** (Late June)	**Copenhagen Jazz Festival** (Early July)	**Fastelavn (Carneval)** (Feb.-Mar.)
FRANCE	**Cannes Film Festival** (May14-24)	**Festival d'Avignon** (July) **Bastille Day** (July 14) **Tour de France** (July)	**Carnevale** (Nice, Nantes; Feb. 21-Mar. 5) **Vineyard Festival** (Nice; Sept.)
GERMANY	**May Day** (Berlin; May 1) **Christopher St. Day** (late June) **G-Move** (June 7)	**Love Parade** (Berlin; late July) **Rhine in Flames Festival** (Rhine Valley; Aug. 9)	**Fasching** (Munich; Jan. 7-Mar. 4) **Oktoberfest** (Munich; Sept. 20-Oct. 5)
GREECE	**St. George's Day** (Apr. 23)	**Feast of the Assumption of the Virgin Mary** (Aug. 15)	**Carnival** (Feb. 17-Mar. 10) **Feast of St. Demetrius** (Oct. 26)
ITALY	**Maggio Musicale** (Florence; May 11-Aug. 1) **Scoppio del Carro** (Florence; Easter Su)	**Il Palio** (Siena; Aug. 16) **Umbria Jazz Festival** (July 12-21)	**Carnevale** (Feb. 21-Mar. 5) **Festa di San Gennaro** (Naples; Dec. 16, Sept. 19, May 7) **Dante Festival** (Ravenna; mid-Sept.)
THE NETHERLANDS	**Queen's Day** (Apr. 30) **Holland Festival** (June)	**Gay Pride Parade** (Aug.)	**Flower Parade** (Aalsmeer; Sept.) **Cannabis Cup** (Nov.)
PORTUGAL	**Burning of the Ribbons** (Coimbra; May 6-7)	**Feira Internacional de Lisboa** (June) **Feira Popular** (mid-July)	**Carnival** (mid-Mar.) **Semana Santa** (Mar. 24-31)
SPAIN	**Feria de Abril** (Sevilla; Apr. 29-May 4)	**San Fermines** (Pamplona; July 6-14)	**Semana Santa** (Apr. 13-20) **Las Fallas** (Valencia; Mar. 15-18) **Carnival** (Feb. 21-Mar. 5)

SUGGESTED ITINERARIES

There is no formula for the perfect itinerary in Western Europe. Here we humbly suggest a few routes—just to give you an idea of what is possible. **The Basics** below outlines our skeletal suggestions for the best of Europe. We've also included some regional itineraries to help you plan a few extra forays. These other itineraries can be thought of as **Building Blocks** to tack onto a basic route. For more in-depth suggestions, see the **Suggested Itineraries** sections in individual country chapters.

THE BASICS

THE GRAND TOUR: BEST OF WESTERN EUROPE IN 1 MONTH Start out in **London,** spinning from theaters to museums to pubs (4 days, p. 164). Chunnel to the world-class galleries and chic shops of **Paris** (4 days, p. 311), and slip south to daring and colorful **Barcelona** (2 days, p. 907). Return to France for an all-night party in **Nice** (1 day, p. 381); recover in the blissful **Cinque Terre** on the Italian Riviera (1 day, p. 684). Prop up the leaning tower of **Pisa** (1 day, p. 725), be enchanted by Renaissance art in **Florence** (2 days, p. 711), and don your toga in **Rome** (3 days, p. 644). Float down the canals of **Venice** by gondola (2 days, p. 693) on your way to the opera in **Vienna** (2 days, p. 94). Sip absinthe in starlet **Prague** (2 days, p. 989) and sample the frothy brew in **Munich** (2 days, p. 504) before heading up to funky **Berlin** (2 days, p. 426). Indulge in **Amsterdam** (2 days, p. 769), and then relax with a day in the EU capital, **Brussels** (p. 135).

THE GRAND TOUR

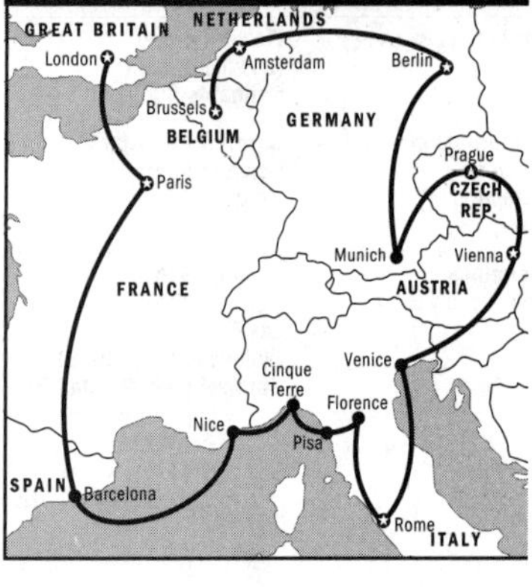

THE BEST OF WESTERN EUROPE

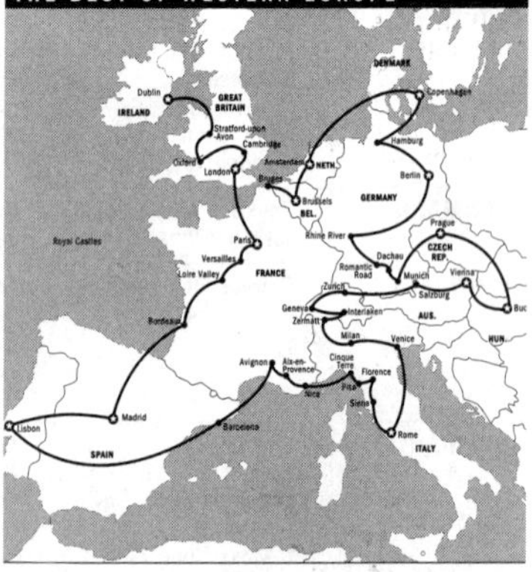

THE BEST OF WESTERN EUROPE IN 9 WEEKS From **London** (4 days, p. 164), meander the halls of **Cambridge** (1 day, p. 222) or **Oxford** (1 day, p. 213), then catch a play in Shakespeare's **Stratford-Upon-Avon** (1 day, p. 219), before heading to **Dublin,** home to Joyce and Guinness (2 days, p. 591). Chunnel from London to **Paris** (4 days, p. 311) and then gape at **Versailles** (1 day, p. 344). From the castle-dotted **Loire Valley** (1 day, p. 355), go test your taste buds in the vineyards of **Bordeaux** (1 day, p. 362). Proceed to the Iberian peninsula to rage in the clubs of **Madrid** (2 days, p. 846), and bask on the beaches of **Lisbon** (2 days, p. 808). After heading back east to **Barcelona** (3 days, p. 907), spend a day each in festive **Avignon** (p. 371), **Aix-en-Provence** (p. 373), and **Nice** (p. 381). Next replenish in the **Cinque Terre** (2 days, p. 684), send postcards from **Pisa** (1 day, p. 725), and continue on to **Florence** (2 days, p. 711). Stop at the stunning *duomo* in **Siena** (1 day, p. 724) en route to **Rome** (3 days, p. 644). Glide through **Venice** (2 days, p. 693) on your way to posh **Milan** (1 day, p. 673). Grapple the Matterhorn from **Zermatt** (1 day, p. 974), and conquer the Swiss Alps around **Interlaken** (1 day, p. 971). Be a diplomat for a day in **Geneva** (1 day, p. 976), and stock up on chocolate in **Zurich** (1 day, p. 964). Satiate your urge for *The Sound of Music* in **Salzburg** (1 day, p. 109) and waltz your way through **Vienna** (2 days, p. 94), then kick back for 2 days in either the baths of **Budapest** (p. 1005) or the bars of **Prague** (p. 989). From **Munich,** take a sobering daytrip to **Dachau** (3 days, p. 514). Move up the pastoral **Romantic Road** (2 days, p. 519), then cruise down the spectacular **Rhine River** (1 day, p. 492). From **Berlin** (2 days, p. 426) and reckless **Hamburg** (1 day, p. 467), head north to cosmopolitan **Copenhagen** (2 days, p. 275) and continue on to **Amsterdam** (3 days, p. 769). Spend a day each in **Brussels** (p. 135) and **Bruges** (p. 142) before heading home.

THE BEST OF THE MEDITERRANEAN IN 6 WEEKS Begin in the flower-filled *terrazas* of **Sevilla** (2 days, p. 879) before basking on the soft-sand beaches of **Cádiz** (2 days, p. 888). Stand on the imposing Rock of **Gibraltar** (1 day, p. 896) en route to partying with the beautiful people in the Costa del Sol resort town of **Marbella** (1 day, p. 903). Skip inland to **Granada** (2 days, p. 897), and wind your way through Moorish fortresses. From **Valencia** (2 days, p. 905), hop around the **Balearic Islands** between **Ibiza**'s foam parties and **Menorca**'s raw beaches (3 days, p. 946). Ferry to vibrant **Barcelona** (3 days, p. 907), before hitting the **Costa Brava** and the Dalí museum in **Figueres** (2 days, p. 930). Head to France's *provençal* **Nîmes** (1 day, p. 370) and follow van Gogh's traces through **Arles** (1 day, p. 372). More fun awaits in **Avignon** (1 day, p. 371), before you revel in **Aix-en-Provence** (1 day, p. 373). Taste the *bouillabaisse* in **Marseilles** (1 day, p. 374), and move on to all that glitters on the Côte d'Azur: **Cannes** (2 days, p. 379) is the star-studded diamond, and **Nice** (2 days, p. 381) is the party haven. Explore the gorgeous clifftop villages of the **Corniches** (1 day, p. 385) before hitting the world-famous casinos of **Monte-Carlo** (1 day, p. 386). Take a breather by relaxing in the placid waters of **Finale Ligure** (1 day, p. 683) and hiking through the colorful villages of Italy's **Cinque Terre** (1 day, p. 684). Admire the architecture of **Genoa** (1 day, p. 681) before oohing and aahing over **Florence**'s magnificent art collection (3 days, p. 711). Check out the two-toned *duomo* of **Siena** (2 days, p. 724) and indulge your gladiatorial fantasies in capital city **Rome** (4 days, p. 644).

THE BEST OF THE MEDITERRANEAN

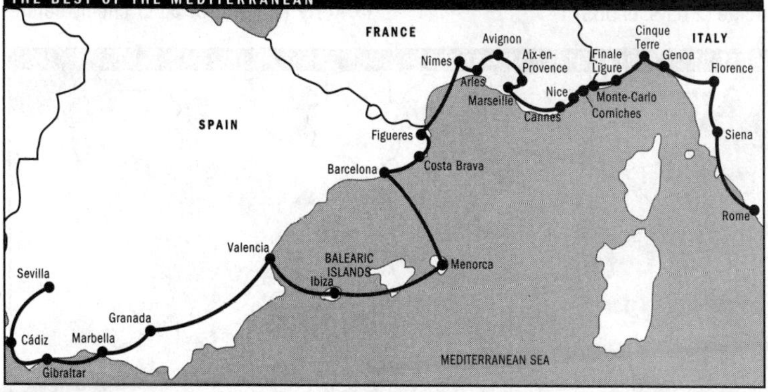

BUILDING BLOCKS

THE BEST OF SOUTHERN ITALY AND GREECE IN 4 WEEKS View the rubble of the toga-clad empire, the cathedrals of high Christianity, and the art of the Renaissance in **Rome** (5 days, p. 644). From **Naples** (2 days, p. 729), home to the world's best pizza and pickpockets, daytrip to **Pompeii** (1 day, p. 733) and check out lifelike Roman remains buried in AD 79. Then escape to the sensuous paradise of **Capri** (2 days, p. 735). Hop off the boot from **Bari** (p. 736) or **Brindisi** (p. 737), for which overnight ferries go to Greece (1 day). Get off at **Corfu** (1 day, p. 553), beloved by literary luminary Oscar Wilde and partiers alike, or continue on to **Patras** (1 day, p. 542). Wrestle in **Olympia** (1 day, p. 543) before beginning your Peloponnesian adventure with a survey of the ancient ruins in **Napflion, Mycenae,** and **Epidavros** (3 days, p. 546). Get initiated in the "mysteries of love" in equally ruinous **Corinth** (1 day, p. 547). On to chaotic **Athens,** a jumble of things ancient and modern (2 days, p. 533). Succumb to your longing in the Cyclades: party all night long on **Mykonos** (1 day, p. 558) and repent the morning after at the Temple of Apollo in **Delos** (1 day, p. 558), before continuing on to the earthly paradise of **Santorini** (2 days, p. 561). Catch the ferry to **Crete,** where chic **Iraklion** and **Knossos,** home to the Minotaur, await (2 days, p. 562). Base yourself in **Rethymno** or **Hania** and hike the **Samaria Gorge** (2 days, p. 563).

THE BEST OF BRITAIN AND IRELAND

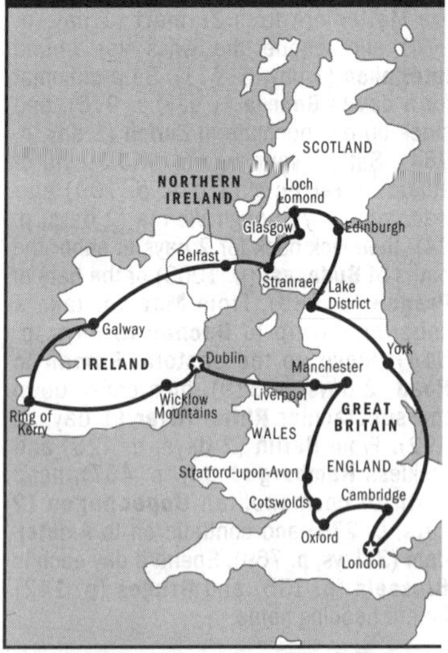

THE BEST OF BRITAIN AND IRELAND IN 3 WEEKS From **London** (4 days, p. 164), get studious in **Cambridge** (1 day, p. 222) and **Oxford** (1 day, p. 213), then take to the **Cotswolds** (1 day, p. 220). Love all things Shakespeare in **Stratford-Upon-Avon** (1 day, p. 219), and move on to party in **Manchester** (1 day, p. 227). Trip down Penny Lane in **Liverpool** (1 day, p. 229), home of the Beatles. Cross the Irish Sea to **Dublin** (3 days, p. 591), the latest international favorite, and daytrip to the **Wicklow Mountains** (1 day, p. 603). Run the **Ring of Kerry** (2 days, p. 611) circuit before

BEST OF SOUTHERN ITALY AND GREECE

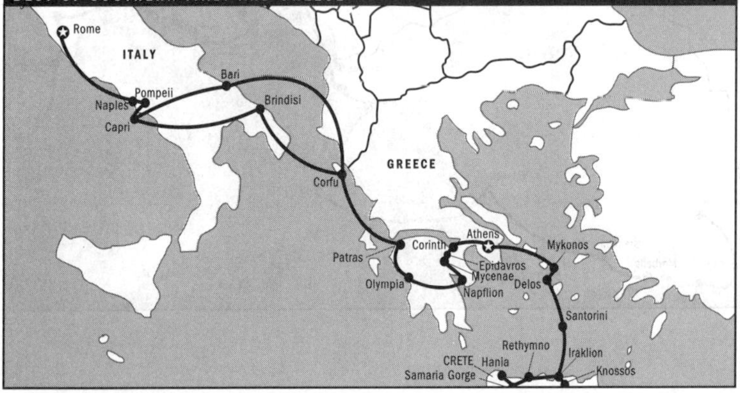

listening to *craic* in **Galway** (2 days, p. 615), the culture capital. Take in the murals at **Belfast** (2 days, p. 622) and from there it's back across the Irish Sea to **Stranraer,** energetic **Glasgow** (1 day, p. 257), and nearby **Loch Lomond.** Then jump over to historic and exuberant **Edinburgh** (3 days, p. 249). The **Lake District** (2 days, p. 239) offers scenic diversions, and historic **York** (1 day, p. 233) completes the journey. Return to London to kick back with a West End play and a glass of Tetley's bitter.

THE BEST OF SPAIN AND PORTUGAL IN 5 WEEKS Hop off the Paris-Madrid train at gorgeous **San Sebastián** (2 days, p. 937), and check out the new Guggenheim in **Bilbao** (1 day, p. 942) before heading to **Madrid** for urban fun (4 days, p. 846). Daytrip to the austere palace of **El Escorial** (1 day, p. 866) and the medieval streets of **Toledo** (1 day, p. 867). Visit the university town of **Salamanca** (1 day, p. 874) and then cross the border into Portugal, heading up to the unpretentious **Porto** (2 days, p. 830). Marvel at the painted tiles in **Lisbon** (3 days, p. 808) with a daytrip to the town of **Sintra** (1 day, p. 818). Bake in the sun along the Algarve in **Lagos** (3 days, p. 824), where hordes of visitors dance the night away. Sleep off your hangover on the 7hr. express bus from Lagos to **Sevilla** (2 days, p. 879) and prepare for a romantic stroll along the Guadalquivir River. Delve deeper into Arab-influenced Andalucía–don't miss the Mezquita in **Córdoba** (2 days, p. 889) and the Alhambra in **Granada** (2 days, p. 897). From Granada head up the Mediterranean Coast to stop in **Valencia** (1 day, p. 905) for the *paella* and oranges. Move on to northeastern Spain and hit sunny **Costa Brava** (2 days, p. 929), artsy **Figueres** (1 day, p. 930), and medieval **Girona** (1 day, p. 928). Finish up your journey in colorful **Barcelona** (4 days, p. 907).

THE BEST OF SPAIN AND PORTUGAL

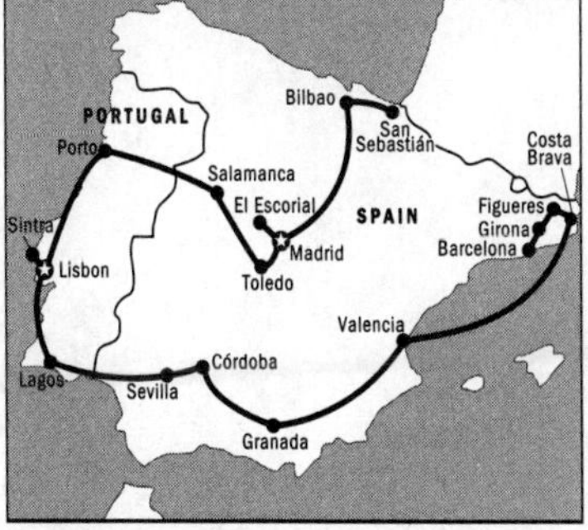

THE BEST OF FRANCE IN 3 WEEKS You'll need at least four days to see the sights and shops of **Paris** (p. 311)–make time for a daytrip to **Versailles** (p. 344). Then travel to **Tours** (2 days, p. 357) in the Loire Valley to explore beautiful châteaux. Next, head down to **Nantes** (1 day, p. 354) for medieval sights and modern nightlife, before soaking up the sun in beach-blessed **La Rochelle** (2 days, p. 359). For a change of pace, visit the 17,000-year-old cave paintings of **Les-Eyzies-de-Tayac** (1 day, p. 361) and stroll through the golden streets of **Sarlat** (1 day, p. 361). Sniff, swirl, and spit in **Bordeaux** (2 days, p. 362) before following the pilgrims to miraculous **Lourdes** (1 day, p. 365). Zip southward for some Franco-Spanish flavor in **Toulouse** (1 day, p. 366). Head east to reach the magnificent Roman ruins of **Nîmes** (1 day, p. 370), the birthplace of denim. The stunning Gothic fortifications of the Palais des Papes cast shadows over festive **Avignon** (1 day, p. 371). Students have been partying in elegant **Aix-en-Provence** (1 day, p. 373) for 600 years, but for non-stop action go to **Nice** (2 days, p. 381), undisputed capital

THE BEST OF FRANCE

of the Riviera. For a change of scenery, climb into the Alps to reach dynamic **Grenoble** (2 days, p. 392). **Strasbourg** (1 day, p. 403) offers a pleasant blend of French and German culture. Finish off in style with a tasting at one of the many champagne *caves* in **Reims** (1 day, p. 408).

THE BEST OF GERMANY, AUSTRIA, AND SWITZERLAND IN 5 WEEKS

Spend five days raging in **Berlin**'s chaotic nightclubs and recovering in the capital's museums and cafes (4 days, p. 426). Move north, where **Hamburg** fuses port town burliness with cosmopolitan flair (2 days, p. 467), before admiring Germany's greatest cathedral in **Cologne** (1 day, p. 481). Meander through **Bonn** (1 day, p. 486) and explore Germany's oldest university in **Heidelburg** (1 day, p. 496). Drool over Porsches and Mercedes-Benzes in ultramodern **Stuttgart** (1 day, p. 500), then relive your favorite Grimms' fairy tales in the **Black Forest** (1 day, p. 502). Cross into Switzerland and enjoy medieval sights in **Basel** (1 day, p. 961) before stopping for pastries in **Neuchâtel** (1 day, p. 984). Play world leader in **Geneva** (2 days, p. 976), shimmy over to capital city **Bern** (1 day, p. 958), and listen to jazz in **Montreaux** (1 day, p. 983). Ogle the Matterhorn from **Zermatt** (1 day, p. 974), and explore the Alps from **Interlaken** (2 days, p. 971). Take a train to the fairytale hamlet of **Lucerne** (1 day, p. 962) before tasting the nightlife in **Zurich** (1 day, p. 964). Skip over to Austria for skiing in **Innsbruck** (1 day, p. 121). Follow Mozart's footsteps in **Salzburg** (2 days, p. 109), then take in the enormous charm of **Vienna** (3 days, p. 94). Head back into Germany to **Munich** (1 day, p. 504) for boisterous beer halls and a daytrip to mad King Ludwig's Castles (1 day, p. 521). Admire the scenery along the **Romantic Road** (2 days, p. 519), but save the last dance for **Dresden** (1 day, p. 453).

BEST OF GERMANY, AUSTRIA, & SWITZ.

WESTERN EUROPE: A QUICK HISTORY

Western Europe arrests our adjective pool—ostentatious and elegant, tumultuous and serene. Underneath this multitude lies enough history to keep you busy for a lifetime and then some. During your travels, each country's political and cultural historics will emerge everywhere—from architecture to landscapes to the people. Below is a very brief primer on the major intellectual and political movements that forged four millennia of Western European identity. Use this abridged history along with the historical and cultural introductions at the beginning of each country chapter to truly partake in the delights of Western Europe.

IN THE BEGINNING... (2000 BC–AD 565)

From the din and tundra of the Paleolithic and Neolithic periods, some restless Indo-Europeans from the East migrated westward during the 18th and 17th centuries BC to the Aegean Sea. Inter-marriage with the natives gave rise to the **Greeks** and created the cornerstone of Western European civilization. Siege-happy, they overthrew the **Minoans** in the 15th century BC, and sacked Troy in the **Trojan War** (1500 BC). Between 337 and 323 BC, **Alexander the Great** expanded the Greek Empire across Europe, and autonomous **city-states** grew in size, power, and cultural influence with **Athens** (p. 533) and **Sparta** (p. 545) as the two dominant cities. At the height of **Classical Greece** (500–400 BC), Athens produced the art, literature, and philosophy that have been the keystone of Western culture ever since. Unable to withstand the military might of the **Romans,** by 133 BC Greece had all but fallen to the Roman empire. Rome expanded its empire over most of Western Europe through the **Punic Wars,** ruling the continent with its distinctive government and adopting (plagiarizing) Greek culture. Although there were no distinct nations, transportation arteries sprung up between cities and the empire kept general peace, **pax romana** style. **Diocletian** tried in AD 293 to strengthen his control over the empire by dividing East and West between himself and a co-emperor. Yet Emperor **Constantine the Great** revoked this agreement and reunited the Roman Empire between 306–337, moving its capital to Byzantium (a.k.a. Constantinople a.k.a. Istanbul) and declaring Christianity the new state religion.

EARLY MIDDLE AGES (AD 476–1000)

There's nothing like 200 years of **Huns, Visigoths,** and **Vandals** to spoil a perfectly good empire. In 476, the last Roman emperor was forced into retirement and the Germanic barbarians began a 150-year political renovation of the Roman Empire, reverting cities to tribal kingdoms. As life became increasingly localized, Western Europe tumbled into the poorly-lit **Dark Ages** (AD 500 to 1200). In 800AD, the Pope crowned Frankish king **Charlemagne** Holy Roman Emperor and united the divided East and West of Christian Europe. Following the death of Charlemagne's son, **Louis the Pious,** the Carolingian Empire was divided among his three sons, thus decentralizing power and leading to the rise of local lords. Europe was now divided into three parts: the **Byzantine Empire** (the East and parts of Italy), **Islamic Europe** (Spain and Portugal), and **Latin Christendom** (France, Belgium, Germany, Britain, and parts of Italy).

HIGH MIDDLE AGES (1000–1300)

When the millennial apocalypse didn't arrive in AD 1000, the first order of business was to establish a stable political system. Carolingian rulers established **feudalism,** a system of local government without a state that subjected agrarian **vassals** to the dictates of their **lords.** Above this political hierarchy, however, reigned the Church, an extremely wealthy and powerful institution that dictated law. Pope **Innocent III** financed and advised regional kings to advance his goal of Christian unification to the point that they viewed him as a feudal lord. The High Middle Ages were marked by costly and occasionally successful attempts to extend Christianity.

From 1095 to 1291, Western Europeans launched the **Holy War,** or the seven **Crusades,** against the Islamic East, although the most successful crusades attacked heathens within Europe itself. In the 13th century, Christianity claimed Spain, Italy, Prussia, and the Baltic regions. Overall, the wars both strengthened and demonstrated the might of Christian Europe.

THE RENAISSANCE (1350–1550)

In a fit of nostalgia for the Corinthian columns and toga parties of yore, 14th-century Italy helped Classicism stage a comeback with the **Renaissance** (literally, "rebirth"). Poets **Dante, Petrarch,** and **Boccaccio,** and the artist **Giotto,** set the stage during the 12th and 13th centuries with poetry and art that celebrated the inherent dignity and beauty of humankind. In the 14th century, sculptors and artists **Donatello, Michelangelo,** and **Da Vinci** provided the artistic apotheosis of **Humanism,** an outlook that treated rhetoric and the Classics as a celebration of human self-respect and preparation for a life of virtue. However, the **Black Death** (bubonic and pneumonic plague) devastated the continent, wiping out 25 million Europeans from 1347 to 1352.

The Renaissance also fostered the **Age of Exploration** that began in the 1490s, with the expansion of Spain's and Portugal's colonial empires. The period featured England's oddly-named **Hundred Years War** with France, which lasted from 1337 to 1453 but saw only 44 years of actual fighting. Although the English won early battles, they were eventually expelled from France. Squabbles within the Roman Catholic Church escalated into **The Great Schism,** during which multiple popes bickered over church power from 1378 to 1417. The election of an Italian Cardinal during the **Council of Constance** ended the schism, but papal authority remained weak.

PROTESTANT REFORMATION (1517–1555)

In 1517, **Martin Luther**'s *95 Theses* sparked the Protestant Reformation in Germany. The shocking treatise resulted in Luther's 1521 excommunication, and before the decade ended, the Holy Roman Empire was divided by the issue of reformation. **Henry VIII**'s divorce from **Catherine of Aragon** in 1534 to wed **Anne Boleyn** broke England from the Roman Catholic Church and caused a rift over which heads would (literally) roll for years. With the **Act of Supremacy** in 1534, Henry declared himself head of not only state, but of the new Protestant church as well, instigating the **English Reformation.** Later in the 16th century, **John Calvin** led the **Genevan Reformation** in Switzerland to establish too-late-you're-already-going-to-hell **Calvinism** as the dominant Protestant force in Europe.

Yet the movement toward Reformation did not go unchecked. The **Council of Trent** (1545–1563), the 19th ecumenical council of the Roman Catholic Church, formed the keystone of the **Counter-Reformation** argument. While the council refuted all criticism from Protestants, it also made sweeping reforms to correct the many abuses within the Church. Most importantly, the council halted the sale of **indulgences,** which forgave neglected penances or unrepented sins. In 1555, however, with the **Peace of Augsburg, Charles V** of the Holy Roman Empire granted the princes of Germany the right to establish the religion of their own people, whether that was Catholicism or Protestantism.

REVOLUTION IN THOUGHT (1555–1648)

Unwilling to witness the fracturing of his empire, Charles V abdicated all his titles in 1555. His brilliant solution to the lack of unity was to further divide power; his brother **Ferdinand I** gained control of the Austrian Habsburg lands, while his son **Philip II** ruled Spain and The Netherlands. Workaholic Philip II obsessed over the necessity for Catholic reform while propelling Spain into its Golden Age, **siglo de oro,** as the greatest power in Europe. Spanish troops and gold supported the Catholic cause in Western Europe, aiding rebellions against England's Protestant **Queen Elizabeth** and removing French Protestant **Huguenots** from power. The Spaniards were driven out of The Netherlands by **William of Orange** in the first phase of the **Eighty Years' War** (1568–1648). From 1618–1648, the **Thirty Years' War** made Germany a battlefield doormat as Protestant forces asserted their independence from the Roman Catholic Church and the Holy Roman Empire. The **Treaty of Westphalia** in 1648 reinforced the Peace of Augsburg's principle of *cuius regio eius religio* (whose region, his religion) and set European political geography for the next century. Calvinism was added to the list of (barely) tolerable religions, thus ensuring the safety of Calvinism in The Netherlands. In the aftermath, the Holy Roman Empire was severely weakened—Spain fell from her diva spotlight as Philip II's Catholic crusade crashed in flames, Queen Elizabeth restored the Protestant church, and a Huguenot sat on the throne in France.

The late 17th century exploded with political and intellectual revolutions. England plunged into civil war, and France, under the beaming "Sun King" **Louis XIV,** became the greatest power in Western Europe. The **Scientific Revolution** of the 17th century broke out of the medieval box to challenge traditional thought. **Galileo, Descartes, Newton,** and **Hobbes** were among the many whose works marked the revolution, each contributing to the belief in harmony, logic, and human abilities. The popularization of scientific thought and method and their increasing pertinence to everyday life, medicine, and politics formed the basis for the ideas of the **Age of Enlightenment**.

AGE OF ENLIGHTENMENT (1688–1789)

During the Enlightenment, thinkers such as **Voltaire, Charles-Louis Montesquieu, John Locke, Thomas Hobbes,** and **Jean-Jacques Rousseau** made the radical proposition that reason and science, rather than a mysterious God, could reveal the truth of life. By reasoning out the universal laws of nature, they claimed, one could achieve freedom and happiness. This age's questioning spirit also affected the conception of the state—**Frederick II** of Prussia, **Catherine the Great** of Russia, and **Joseph II** of the Habsburg empire were monarchs known as the **enlightened despots,** who combined liberal reforms with measures to maintain control over peasants.

Unfortunately, these utopian ideals didn't halt sparring monarchies. In the **War of the Spanish Succession** (1701–1714), Austria and Britain went to war to keep Louis XIV's son, Philip V, from the Spanish throne. This was settled by the **Treaty of Utrecht,** which allowed Philip to take the throne but forbade him from merging the empire with France. The **Seven Years' War** (1756–1763) saw Austria and France ally to fight Prussia and Britain over colonies. War eventually spread to North America, the Caribbean, and India, hinting at the impending wave of imperialism.

FRENCH REVOLUTION & NAPOLEON (1789–1814)

Louis XIV's full ascension to the French throne in 1661 ushered in an era of dictatorial, aristocratic **absolutism** and excess, perhaps best exemplified by the 14,000-room palace of **Versailles** (hey, everyone needs a little place in the country; see p. 344). Prompted by a financial crisis and a disgruntled population, **Louis XVI** called the first (and last) assembly of the **Estates General** in over 175 years, consisting of representatives from the three classes: nobility, clergy, and the common people. From this organization, the populace broke away, declaring itself the **National Assembly**. After chaos erupted, the radical **Jacobin** faction took control, abolished the monarchy, and declared France a Republic, symbolized by the storming of the **Bastille** on July 14, 1789 (see p. 332). The Revolution entered a more radical phase, dubbed the **Terror,** when counter-revolutionaries were weeded out and justice summarily dispensed by "Madame" Guillotine. The **Directory,** a second try at representative government, was established in 1794, but lasted only five years when a little man with a big ego, **Napoleon Bonaparte,** after waging victorious military campaigns in Italy and in Egypt, deposed the Directory and declared himself Emperor and "consul for life" in 1804. The **Napoleonic Code,** a direct result of the Age of Enlightenment ideals, defined property rights, declared all people equal before the law, and affirmed religious freedoms. Seeking to expand his control, he abolished the Holy Roman Empire and dismembered Prussia—by 1810, most of Europe was either annexed by or allied to France. After wars with Britain and Spain, Napoleon's **Grand Army** was disastrously defeated in Russia in 1812, after which he abdicated and was sent into luxurious exile on **Elba** to think up witty palindromes. Bourbon rule was restored in France in 1814 under Louis XVIII, but the **Congress of Vienna** in 1814 left France without Napoleon's land acquisitions.

INDUSTRIAL REVOLUTION (1760–1848)

With the invention of the steam engine, spinning mill, and **Spinning Jenny** (cotton spinning machine) in the 18th century, the Industrial Revolution was off to a running start, but still confined largely to Britain. From 1800 to 1850 it spread rapidly throughout Europe, bringing with it **urbanization** and greater life expectancy. **Factories,** especially for textiles and iron, were the Industrial Age's most visible symbol, but the period also saw heightened international trade and the birth of socialist ideology (**St. Simon, Marx,** and **Engels**). Heightened urbanization provided mobility for the peasant class, although conditions in slums remained deplorable, with rampant overcrowding and primitive sanitation tainting upper-class tennis matches and tea parties.

Industrial changes were harbingers of other social revolutions, as liberal revolts broke out in Spain, Italy, Portugal, Germany, Russia, and Poland from 1815 to 1848. The 19th century also brought new independence for several countries, as Belgium wrested autonomy from The Netherlands in 1830 and the Turks recognized Greek independence in 1832. An 18-year-old **Queen Victoria** ascended the British throne in 1837, giving rise to the era of her name.

NATIONAL UNIFICATION (1851–1867)

During the mid-19th century, European nations, inspired by the "survival of the fittest" ideology of **Social Darwinism,** consolidated land and power. Taking the lead from his dear old uncle, President Louis Napoleon dissolved the National Assembly and declared himself **Emperor Napoleon III.** In Italy, the efforts of **Victor Emmanuel II** and **General Giuseppe Garibaldi** from 1859 to 1870 managed to unify Italy despite longstanding regional tensions. Meanwhile, back in Prussia, newly appointed Prime Minister **Otto von Bismarck** unified the German Empire, including the new lands Prussia had garnered as spoils during the **Austro-Prussian** and **Franco-Prussian Wars** (1866 and 1870–71, respectively). As massive monarchal alliances became trendy, the **Dual Monarchy** of Austria-Hungary was created in 1867, the same year that the **British Reform Bill** doubled the number of English voters by granting suffrage to all household heads.

INVENTION AND IMPERIALISM (1870-1911)

Continuing innovation brought rapid industrialization to Europe with the spread of electricity and the invention of the sewing machine, telephone, and automobile. Railways surged across the continent, standards of living skyrocketed, and the service industry provided many women of the new and expanding middle class gainful employment. Chancellor Bismarck gave the **industrial bourgeoisie** something to cheer about as he enacted the world's first unemployment insurance in 1883. European powers, led by Germany and Britain, extended their long arms to Africa and Asia, establishing dominance during the **Age of Imperialism.** Explorers and missionaries were the first to introduce Europe to Africa, desiring to socialize an otherwise "primitive" continent. **King Leopold II** of Belgium was especially attracted to the potential wealth of Africa, while the British and French also ventured into the "dark continent" to secure political clout and plunder diamonds. The Dutch, British, and Russian imperialists also began to occupy parts of Asia, creating powerful empires while suppressing the revolts of native inhabitants.

WORLD WAR I (1914-1918)

The assassination of the Austro-Hungarian **Archduke Francis Ferdinand** in Serbia in 1914 was the straw that broke Europe's back. Through Bismarck's masterful diplomacy, the continent had become a mess of opposing alliances: Britain and France ended centuries of conflict in 1904 by forming the **Entente Cordiale,** an alliance which Russia later joined to create the **Triple Entente.** The assassination prompted Austria-Hungary to issue a military ultimatum to Serbia, backed by Germany's recently unified state and Turkey (forming an alliance of their own, the **Central Powers**). The standoff brought Russia into the conflict, prompting Germany to declare war against her. Germany, seeking to destroy the allied Franco-British threat, advanced quickly through Belgium and France before stalling at the **Battle of the Marne** in 1914, starting four long years of **trench** warfare. The United States was drawn into the war when Germany's practice of **unrestricted submarine warfare** became intolerable, and the American entry in 1917 was followed in short order by the Allied victory on November 11, 1918. In 1919, the **Big Four** (Orlando of Italy, Lloyd George of Britain, Clemenceau of France, and Wilson of the US) forced Germany to accept full responsibility for the Great War in the **Treaty of Versailles**—in the **war guilt clause,** the weak new **Weimar Republic** in Germany was forced to assume the financial burden of the war. The treaty also paved way for the **League of Nations.**

INTERWAR YEARS (1919-1938)

For Germany, the Treaty of Versailles was in many ways disastrous: the Allies demanded enormous reparations, apportioned significant German territory, stole all bratwurst, and limited the size of its standing military. This humiliation, combined with hyperinflation of the 1920s, the **Great Depression,** and alienating urbanization, set the stage for Austrian **Adolph Hitler**'s rise to power. As the leader of the **National Socialist German Workers' Party (NSDAP),** also known as the **Nazis,** Hitler pushed a program of Aryan supremacy (based on anti-Semitism and German racial purity), playing on the post-war insecurities of the Germans. By the 1930s, many European countries were dictatorships, most prominently fascist Italy under **Benito Mussolini,** autarchic Spain, commanded by **General Francisco Franco,** and of course, the newly-created Union of Soviet Socialist Republics, led by **Joseph Stalin.** By 1933, Hitler had been appointed chancellor of Germany; he banned all other parties and created a totalitarian state. The **Kristallnacht** (Night of Broken Glass), on November 9, 1938, saw the destruction of Jewish stores and homes throughout Germany, as well as attacks against and the imprisonment of thousands of Jews.

WORLD WAR II (1939–1945)

Continuing German expansion, Hitler, facilitated by British Prime Minister **Neville Chamberlain**'s naïve appeasement policy, moved into Czechoslovakia and then Poland, initiating WWII on September 1, 1939. Britain and France, bound by treaty to help Poland, declared war on Germany. As Germany overran Denmark, Norway, Luxembourg, Belgium, The Netherlands, and France with its **Blitzkrieg** (Lightning-War) offensives, Chamberlain resigned and **Winston Churchill** assumed the British helm. France, despite the elaborate fortifications of the **Maginot Line,** fell to the German offensive, leading to Nazi occupation and the formation of the puppet **Vichy** regime. Russia stayed neutral because of a secret non-aggression pact signed with Hitler. This short-lived treaty only lasted until the Nazis invaded the Soviet Union in 1941; however, German forces were unable to break through during the Russian winter. In the same year, the US, prompted by the Japanese bombing of Pearl Harbor, entered the fray. The Allied landings at **Normandy** (p. 346) on June 6, 1944 **(D-Day),** turned the war's tide and marked the beginning of a bloody, arduous advance across Western Europe. Paris was liberated by Allied forces in September 1944, and Berlin was captured by the Red Army in April 1945. Hitler's **Third Reich,** which he had boasted would last for a thousand years, was dissolved after just twelve. The **Holocaust,** Hitler's "final solution to the Jewish problem," involved establishing mass concentration camps, the most infamous being **Auschwitz-Birkinau.** German forces ultimately killed at least six million Jews and countless other "undesirables," including homosexuals, mentally disabled people, Gypsies, Slavs, and political dissidents.

COLD WAR (1946–1989)

In 1945, the US, Britain, and the USSR met at **Yalta** to lay the foundation of the **United Nations,** plan the occupation of Nazi Germany, and determine spheres of influence in post-war Europe. Three **occupation zones** were set up in Germany, with Berlin under joint control. Berlin became the symbol of mounting tension between the Western capitalist world, led by the US, and the communist sphere, controlled by the USSR. East Germany, under the USSR, became known as the **German Democratic Republic. Julius** and **Ethel Rosenberg** brought the secrets of the atomic bomb to Russia, initiating a 50-year American nuclear **arms race** with the USSR. In 1949, the American, British, and French zones became the **German Federal Republic.** Berlin itself was divided between the two opposing spheres, a division later marked by the construction of the **Berlin Wall** in 1961 (see p. 426). The **North Atlantic Treaty Organization (NATO)** was formed in 1949, by a band of 12 nations; it was countered by the Soviet alliance formed by the **Warsaw Pact** (1955). While the US was stricken with McCarthyism and anti-communist fervor, in Western Europe, the foundations for the now vibrant European Union (EU) were laid with the **European Economic Community** (EEC) in 1957—a tariff-free trading zone involving France, Belgium, The Netherlands, Luxembourg, Italy, and West Germany. Britain, Denmark, and Ireland joined in 1973, followed by Greece, Spain, Portugal, Eastern Germany, Austria, Sweden, and Finland over the next 20 years.

WESTERN EUROPE TODAY: EUROPEAN UNION

The fall of the Berlin Wall in November 1989 symbolized the fall of communism and the end Cold War in the Western world. At the **Treaty of Maastricht** in 1991, the **European Union** was created from the European Economic Community, eliminating national barriers for the movement of goods, services, workers, and capital (see p. 18). Twelve EU members—Austria, Belgium, Germany, Greece, Finland, France, Ireland, Italy, Luxembourg, The Netherlands, Portugal, and Spain—adopted the **euro (€)** as legal tender on January 1, 2002 (see p. 20). And while concerns over xenophobia have been rising, thirteen Eastern European countries are currently undergoing the application processes to join the EU, further signifying the general European movement toward integration.

ESSENTIALS

ENTRANCE REQUIREMENTS.

Passport (p. 17). Required of all foreigners visiting Western Europe.

Visa (p. 18). Most Western European countries require visas for citizens of South Africa, but not for citizens of Australia, Canada, Ireland, New Zealand, the UK, or the US. They are required for stays longer than three months.

Inoculations (p. 25). Travelers to Western Europe should be up to date on vaccines for measles, mumps, rubella, diptheria, tetanus, pertussis, polio, haemophilus influenza B, hepatitis B, and hepatitis A.

Work Permit (p. 18). Required of all foreigners planning to work in Western Europe, except for citizens of EU member countries.

Driving Permit (p. 56). An International Driving Permit is recommended for all those planning to drive.

DOCUMENTS AND FORMALITIES

Information on European **consular services** at home, as well as foreign consular services in Europe, is located in individual country chapters.

PASSPORTS

REQUIREMENTS. Citizens of Australia, Canada, Ireland, New Zealand, South Africa, the UK, and the US need valid passports to enter European countries and to reenter their own country. Most countries do not allow entrance if the holder's passport expires in fewer than six months. Returning home with an expired passport is illegal, and may result in a fine.

NEW PASSPORTS. Citizens of Australia, Canada, Ireland, New Zealand, the UK, and the US can apply for a passport at most post offices, passport offices, or courts of law. Citizens of South Africa can apply for a passport at any Home Affairs Office. Any new passport or renewal application must be filed well in advance of the departure date, although most passport offices offer rush services for a very steep fee.

PASSPORT MAINTENANCE. Be sure to photocopy the page of your passport with your photo, as well as your visas, traveler's checks' serial numbers, and any other important documents. Carry one set of copies in a safe place, apart from the originals, and leave another set at home. Consulates also recommend that you carry an expired passport or an official copy of your birth certificate in a part of your baggage separate from other documents.

If you lose your passport, immediately notify the local police and the nearest embassy or consulate of your home country. To expedite its replacement, you will need to know all information previously recorded and show ID and proof of citizenship. In some cases, a replacement may take weeks to process, and it may be valid only for a limited time. Any visas stamped in your old passport will be irretrievably lost. In an emergency, ask for immediate temporary traveling papers that will permit you to re-enter your home country.

ONE EUROPE. The idea of European unity has come a long way since 1958, when the European Economic Community (EEC) was created in order to promote solidarity and cooperation. Since then, the EEC has become the European Union (EU), with political, legal, and economic institutions spanning 15 member states: Austria, Belgium, Denmark, Finland, France, Germany, Greece, Ireland, Italy, Luxembourg, the Netherlands, Portugal, Spain, Sweden, and the UK.

What does this have to do with the average non-EU tourist? In 1999, the EU established **freedom of movement** across 15 European countries–the entire EU minus Ireland and the UK, but plus Iceland and Norway. This means that border controls between participating countries have been abolished, and visa policies harmonized. While you're still required to carry a passport (or government-issued ID card for EU citizens) when crossing an internal border, once you've been admitted into one country, you're free to travel to all participating nations. Britain and Ireland have also formed a **common travel area,** abolishing passport controls between the UK and the Republic of Ireland. This means that the only times you'll see a border guard within the EU are traveling between the British Isles and the continent.

For more important consequences of the EU for travelers, see **Customs in the EU** (p. 19) and **The Euro** (p. 20).

VISAS AND WORK PERMITS

VISAS. Some countries require a visa—a stamp, sticker, or insert in your passport specifying the purpose of your travel and the permitted duration of your stay—in addition to a valid passport for entrance. Most standard visas cost US$10-70, are valid for one to three months, and must be validated within six months to a year from the date of issue. Nearly all of the countries covered by *Let's Go: Western Europe* do not require visas for citizens of Australia, Canada, Ireland, New Zealand, the UK, or the US for stays shorter than three months; the exception being Australians and Canadians traveling to Prague or Budapest. All European countries, except for the UK, Ireland, and Switzerland, require visas for South African citizens. Travelers to Andorra should contact a French or Spanish embassy for more information, while those going to Liechtenstein should contact a Swiss embassy. In any case, check with the nearest embassy or consulate of your desired destination for up-to-date information. US citizens can consult www.travel.state.gov/foreignentryreqs.html and take advantage of the **Center for International Business and Travel** (☎800-925-2428), which secures visas for travel to almost all countries for a service charge.

The visa requirements above only apply to stays shorter than three months. If you plan to stay longer than 90 days, or if you plan to work or study abroad, your requirements will differ (see **Alternatives to Tourism,** p. 66).

IDENTIFICATION

When you travel, always carry two or more forms of identification on your person, including at least one photo ID; a passport combined with a driver's license or birth certificate is usually adequate. Never carry all your forms of ID together, split them up in case of theft or loss, and keep photocopies of them in your luggage and at home.

TEACHER, STUDENT & YOUTH IDENTIFICATION. The **International Student Identity Card (ISIC),** the most widely accepted form of student ID, provides discounts on sights, accommodations, food, and transport; access to 24hr. emergency helpline (call US collect ☎715-345-0505); and insurance benefits for US cardholders (see **Insurance,** p. 28). The ISIC is preferable to an institution-specific card (such as a university ID) because it is more likely to be recognized and honored abroad. Applicants must be degree-seeking students of a secondary or post-secondary school and must be of at least 12 years of age. Because of the proliferation of fake ISICs, some services (particularly airlines) require additional proof of student identity, such as a school ID or a letter attesting to your student status, signed by your registrar and stamped with your school seal.

The **International Teacher Identity Card (ITIC)** offers teachers the same insurance coverage as well as similar but limited discounts. For travelers who are 25 years old or under but are not students, the **International Youth Travel Card (IYTC;** formerly the **GO 25** Card) offers many of the same benefits as the ISIC.

Each of these identity cards costs US$22. ISIC and ITIC cards are valid for roughly one and a half academic years; IYTC cards are valid for one year from the date of issue. For a list of issuing agencies, or for more information, contact the **International Student Travel Confederation (ISTC),** Herengracht 479, 1017 BS Amsterdam, Netherlands (☎31 20 421 28 00; fax 421 28 10; istcinfo@istc.org; www.istc.org).

CUSTOMS

Upon entering a country, you must declare certain items from abroad and pay a duty on the value of those articles. Note that goods and gifts purchased at **duty-free shops** are not exempt from duty or sales tax upon return and must be declared; "duty-free" only means tax-free in the country of purchase. In order to expedite your return, make a list of any valuables brought from home and register them with customs before traveling abroad. Also be sure to keep receipts for all goods acquired abroad.

TAXES. The European Union imposes a **value-added tax (VAT)** on goods and services, usually included in the sticker price. Non-EU citizens may obtain a **refund** for taxes paid on retail goods, but not for taxes paid on services. As the VAT is 15-25%, it might be worthwhile to file for a refund. To do so, you must obtain **Tax-free Shopping Cheques,** available from shops sporting the Europe Tax-free Shopping logo, and save your receipts. Upon leaving the EU, present your goods, invoices, and passport to customs and have your Cheques stamped. Then go to an ETS cash refund office or file for a refund once back home. Keep in mind that goods must be taken out of the country within three months of the end of the month of purchase, and that some stores require minimum purchase amounts to become eligible for refund. For more information on tax-free shopping, visit www.globalrefund.com.

CUSTOMS IN THE EU. To compliment the free movement of people within the EU (see p. 18), travelers in member countries can take advantage of the free movement of goods. This means that there are no customs controls at internal EU borders (i.e., you can take the blue customs channel at the airport), and travelers are free to transport whatever legal substances they like as long as it is for their own personal (non-commercial) use—up to 800 cigarettes, 10L of spirits, 90L of wine (60L of sparkling wine), and 110L of beer. You should also be aware that duty-free was abolished on June 30, 1999 for travel between EU member states; however, travelers between the EU and the rest of the world still get a duty-free allowance when passing through customs.

MONEY

CURRENCY AND EXCHANGE

As a general rule, it's cheaper to convert money in Europe than at home. However, you should bring enough foreign currency for the first 24 to 72 hours of a trip to avoid being stuck if you arrive after bank hours or on a holiday. Travelers from the US can call **International Currency Express** (☎888-278-6628) which delivers foreign currency or traveler's checks 2nd-day (US$12) at competitive exchange rates.

When changing money abroad, try to go only to banks or change bureaus that have at most a 5% margin between their buy and sell prices. Since transactions typically have a service fee over and above the unfavorable exchange rate, convert large sums, but no more than you'll need.

If you use traveler's checks or bills, carry some in small denominations (the equivalent of US$50 or less) in case you must exchange money at disadvantageous rates, but bring a range of denominations since charges may be levied per check cashed. Store your money in a variety of forms; carry cash, traveler's checks, and an ATM and/or credit card. All travelers should also consider carrying about $50 worth of US dollars, which are often preferred by local tellers.

THE EURO. The official currency of 12 members of the European Union—Austria, Belgium, Finland, France, Germany, Greece, Ireland, Italy, Luxembourg, The Netherlands, Portugal, and Spain—is now the euro.

The currency makes for some important—and positive—developments for travelers hitting more than one euro-zone country. For one thing, money-changers across the euro-zone are obliged to exchange money at the official, fixed rate (see below), and at no commission (though they may still charge a small service fee). Second, euro-denominated travelers cheques allow you to pay for goods and services across the euro-zone, again at the official rate and commission-free.

At the time of printing, 1€ = US$1.02 = CAD$1.53 = AUD$1.78. For the latest exchange rates, check a currency converter, such as www.xe.com or www.oanda.com.

TRAVELER'S CHECKS

Traveler's checks are one of the safest and least troublesome means of carrying funds—American Express and Visa are the most widely recognized brands. Many banks and agencies sell them for a small commission. Check issuers provide refunds if the checks are lost or stolen, and many provide additional services, such as toll-free refund hotlines abroad, emergency message services, and stolen credit card assistance. They are readily accepted across Europe. Ask about toll-free refund hotlines and the location of refund centers when purchasing checks, and always carry emergency cash.

American Express: Checks available with commission at select banks and all AmEx offices. US residents can also purchase checks by phone (☎888-887-8986) or online (www.aexp.com). **AAA** offers commission-free checks to its members. Checks available in US, Australian, British, Canadian, Japanese, and Euro currencies. *Cheques for Two* can be signed by either of 2 people traveling together. For purchase locations or more information contact AmEx's service centers: in the US and Canada ☎800-221-7282; in the UK ☎0800 521 313; in Australia ☎800 25 19 02; in New Zealand 0800 441 068; elsewhere US collect ☎801-964-6665.

Visa: Checks available (generally with commission) at banks worldwide. For the location of the nearest office, call Visa's service centers: in the US ☎800-227-6811; in the UK ☎0800 89 50 78; elsewhere UK collect ☎+44 020 7937 8091. Checks available in US, British, Canadian, Japanese, and Euro currencies.

Travelex/Thomas Cook: In the US and Canada call ☎800-287-7362; in the UK call ☎0800 62 21 01; elsewhere call UK collect ☎+44 1733 31 89 50.

CREDIT, DEBIT, AND ATM CARDS

Where they are accepted, **credit cards** often offer superior exchange rates—up to 5% better than the retail rate used by banks and other currency exchange establishments. Credit cards may also offer services such as insurance or emergency help, and are sometimes required to reserve hotel rooms or rental cars. MasterCard and Visa are the most welcomed; American Express cards work at some ATMs and businesses as well as at AmEx offices and major airports.

ATM machines are often times the best way to get money—they are widespread in Europe and you can most likely access your personal bank account from abroad. ATMs get the same wholesale exchange rate as credit cards, but there is often a limit on the amount of money you can withdraw per day (around US$500), and the computer networks occasionally fail. While there is typically an international withdrawal surcharge of US$1-5, a growing number of banks waive this fee for the first few transactions each month. The two major international money networks are **Cirrus** (to locate ATMs, US ☎800-424-7787 or www.mastercard.com) and **Visa/PLUS** (to locate ATMs, US ☎800-843-7587 or www.visa.com). Most ATMs charge a transaction fee that is paid to the bank that owns the ATM.

Debit cards are a relatively new form of purchasing power that are as convenient as credit cards but require available funds. A debit card can be used wherever its associated credit card company (usually Mastercard or Visa) is accepted, yet the money is withdrawn directly from the holder's checking account. Debit cards often also function as ATM cards and can be used to withdraw cash from associated banks throughout Europe. Ask your local bank about obtaining one.

PIN NUMBERS& ATMS. To use a cash or credit card to withdraw money from an ATM in Europe, you must have a four-digit **Personal Identification Number (PIN).** If your PIN is longer than four digits, ask your bank whether you can just use the first four, or whether you'll need a new one. **Credit cards** don't usually come with PINs, so if you intend to hit up ATMs with a credit card to get cash advances, call your credit card company before leaving to request one.

People with alphabetic, rather than numerical, PINs may also be thrown off by the lack of letters on European cash machines. The corresponding numbers are: 1=QZ; 2=ABC; 3=DEF; 4=GHI; 5=JKL; 6=MNO; 7=PRS; 8=TUV; and 9=WXY. Note that if you mistakenly punch the wrong code into the machine three times, it will swallow your card for good.

GETTING MONEY FROM HOME

If you run out of money while traveling, the easiest and cheapest solution is to have someone back home make a deposit to your credit card or cash (ATM) account. Failing that, consider one of the following options.

WIRING MONEY. It is possible to arrange a **bank money transfer**, which means asking a bank back home to wire money to a bank in Europe. This is the cheapest way to transfer cash, but it's also the slowest, usually taking several days or more. Note that some banks may only release your funds in local currency, potentially sticking you with a poor exchange rate; inquire about this in advance. Money transfer services like **Western Union** are faster and more convenient than bank transfers—but also much pricier. To find one, visit www.westernunion.com, or call in the US ☎800-325-6000, in Canada ☎800-235-0000, in the UK ☎0800 83 38 33, in Australia ☎800 501 500, in New Zealand ☎800 27 0000, or in South Africa ☎0860 100031. Money transfer services are also available at **American Express** and **Thomas Cook.**

US STATE DEPARTMENT (US CITIZENS ONLY). In dire emergencies only, the US State Department will forward money within hours to the nearest consular office, which will then disburse it according to instructions for a US$15 fee. If you wish to use this service, you must contact the Overseas Citizens Service division of the US State Department (☎202-647-5225; nights, Sundays, and holidays ☎202-647-4000).

ESSENTIALS

COSTS

With so many options, the cost of your trip can be difficult to estimate. Your single biggest purchase will probably be your round-trip **airfare** to Europe (p. 39); a **railpass** can be another major pre-departure expense (p. 51). Before you go, calculate a reasonable per-day budget that will cover your needs without breaking the bank. To give you a general idea, the typical first-time, under-26 traveler planning to spend most of his or her time in Western Europe and then tack on a quick jaunt into Eastern Europe, sleeping in hostels and traveling on a two-month unlimited Eurail pass, can probably expect to spend about US$2000, plus cost of plane fare (US$300-800), railpass (US$882), and backpack (US$150-400). Also, don't forget emergency reserve funds (at least US$200).

TIPS FOR STAYING ON A BUDGET. Saving just a few dollars a day over the course of your trip might pay for days or weeks of additional travel, so learn to take advantage of freebies; for example, many museums are free once a week, and cities often host open-air concerts and cultural events. Bring a sleepsack (p. 29) to save on sheet charges in hostels, and do your **laundry** in the sink (unless you're explicitly prohibited from doing so). You can split **accommodations** costs with trustworthy fellow travelers; multi-bed rooms almost always are cheaper per person than singles. To cut down on the cost of **meals,** buy food in supermarkets instead of eating out; you'd be surprised how tasty a simple meal of bread, cheese, and fruit can be.

TIPPING AND BARGAINING

In most Western European countries, the 5-10% gratuity is already included in the food service bill, but an additional 5-10% tip for very good service is often also polite. Note that in Germany, the tip is handed directly to the server instead of being left on the table. For other services such as taxis or hairdressers, a 10-15% tip is recommended. Also, watch and learn from other customers to gauge what the appropriate actions are. Bargaining is an essential skill for shopping in Greece; otherwise, bargaining will be a very limited factor in your European shopping and will probably only be useful at places like outdoor markets in Italy, Britain, and Ireland. See individual country chapters for more specific information.

SAFETY AND SECURITY

PERSONAL SAFETY

EXPLORING. To avoid unwanted attention, try to blend in as much as possible. Respecting local customs (in many cases, dressing more conservatively) may placate would-be hecklers. Familiarize yourself with your surroundings before setting out. If you are traveling alone, never admit it, and be sure someone at home knows your itinerary. When walking at night, stick to busy, well-lit streets and avoid dark alleyways. If you feel uncomfortable, leave as quickly and directly as you can.

SELF DEFENSE. There is no sure-fire way to avoid all the threatening situations you might encounter when you travel, but a good self-defense course will give you concrete ways to react to unwanted advances. **Impact, Prepare, and Model Mugging** can refer you to local self-defense courses in the US (☎800-345-5425). Visit the website at www.impactsafety.org for a list of nearby chapters. Workshops (2-3hr.) start at US$50; full courses run US$350-500.

TERRORISM AND CIVIL UNREST. Use vigilance and caution to protect your personal security while traveling. Keep an eye on the news, heed travel warnings, steer clear of big crowds and demonstrations, and comply with security measures.

Overall, risks of civil unrest tend to be localized and rarely directed towards tourists. Though the peace process in Northern Ireland is progressing, tension tends to surround the July "marching season." Notoriously violent separatist movements include the ETA (a Basque group), which operates in France and Spain, and FLNC (embroiled over Corsica) in Italy. The November 17 group in Greece is known for anti-Western acts, though they do not target tourists. The box below will help you find an up-to-date list of your government's travel advisories.

TRAVEL ADVISORIES. The following government offices provide travel information and advisories by telephone, by fax, or via the web:

Australian Department of Foreign Affairs and Trade: ☎13 0055 5135; faxback service 02 6261 1299; www.dfat.gov.au.

Canadian Department of Foreign Affairs and International Trade (DFAIT): In Canada and the US call ☎800-267-6788; www.dfait-maeci.gc.ca. Call for their free booklet, *Bon Voyage...But.*

New Zealand Ministry of Foreign Affairs: ☎04 494 8500; fax 04 494 8506; www.mft.govt.nz/trav.html.

United Kingdom Foreign and Commonwealth Office: ☎020 7008 0232; fax 020 7008 0155; www.fco.gov.uk.

US Department of State: ☎202-647-5225, faxback service 202-647-3000; travel.state.gov. For *A Safe Trip Abroad,* call 202-512-1800.

FINANCIAL SECURITY

PROTECTING YOUR VALUABLES. There are a few steps you can take to minimize the financial risk associated with traveling. First, bring as little with you as possible. Second, buy a combination **padlock** to secure your belongings either in your pack or in a hostel or train station locker. Third, carry as little cash as possible. Keep your traveler's checks and ATM/credit cards in a **money belt**—not a "fanny pack"—along with your passport and ID cards. Fourth, keep a small cash reserve separate from your primary stash. This should be about US$50 sewn into or stored in the depths of your pack, along with your traveler's check numbers and important photocopies.

CON ARTISTS & PICKPOCKETS. In large cities **con artists** often work in groups, and frequently employ small children. Beware of certain classic scams, including sob stories that require money, rolls of bills "found" on the street, and mustard spilled (or saliva spit) onto your shoulder to distract you while they snatch your bag. Don't ever let your passport and your bags out of your sight. Beware of **pickpockets** in city crowds, especially on public transportation. Also, be alert in public telephone booths: if you must say your calling card number, do so very quietly; if you punch it in, make sure no one can look over your shoulder. Cities such as Rome, Paris, London, and Amsterdam have higher rates of petty crime.

ACCOMMODATIONS & TRANSPORTATION. Never leave your belongings unattended; crime occurs in even the most demure-looking hostel or hotel. Be particularly careful on **buses** and **trains,** as sleeping travelers are easy prey for thieves. Carry your backpack in front of you where you can see it. When traveling with others, sleep in shifts. When alone, use good judgement in selecting a train compartment: never stay in an empty one, and use a lock to secure your pack to the luggage rack. Try to sleep on top bunks with your luggage stored above you (if not in bed with you), and keep important documents and other valuables on your person. If traveling by **car,** don't leave valuables (such as radios or luggage) in sight while you are away.

DRUGS AND ALCOHOL

Drug and alcohol laws vary widely throughout Europe. In the Netherlands you can buy soft drugs on the open market; elsewhere drug possession may lead to a prison sentence. If you carry **prescription drugs,** it is vital to have both a copy of the prescriptions themselves and a note from a doctor, especially at border crossings. **Public drunkenness** is culturally unacceptable and against the law in many countries, and can also jeopardize your safety.

TROUBLE WITH THE LAW. Travelers who run into trouble with the law, both accidentally and knowingly, do not retain the rights of their home country; instead, they have the same rights as a citizen of the country they are visiting. The law mandates that police notify the embassy of a traveler's home country if he or she is arrested. In custody, a traveler is entitled to a visit from a consular officer. US citizens should check the Department of State's website (www.state.gov) for more information.

HEALTH

BEFORE YOU GO

In your **passport,** list any allergies or medical conditions, and write the names of any people you wish to be contacted in case of a medical emergency. While most prescription and over-the-counter **drugs** are available throughout Western Europe, matching a prescription to a foreign equivalent is not always easy, safe, or possible, so carry up-to-date, legible prescriptions or a statement from your doctor stating the medication's trade name, manufacturer, chemical name, and dosage. See www.rxlist.com to figure out what to ask for at the pharmacy counter. While traveling, be sure to keep all medication with you in your carry-on luggage. For tips on packing a basic **first-aid kit,** see p. 29.

IMMUNIZATIONS AND PRECAUTIONS

Travelers over two years of age should be sure that the following vaccines are up to date: MMR (for measles, mumps, and rubella); DTaP or Td (for diptheria, tetanus, and pertussis), OPV (for polio), HbCV (for haemophilus influenza B), and HBV (for hepatitis B). For travelers going to Western Europe, Hepatitis A vaccine and immune globulin is recommended. Those headed to Southern Europe should also consider the typhoid vaccine. Some countries may deny entrance to travelers arriving from South America and sub-Saharan Africa without a certificate of vaccination for yellow fever. For more **region-specific information** on vaccination requirements, as well as recommendations on immunizations and prophylaxis, consult the CDC (see below) in the US or the equivalent in your country.

USEFUL ORGANIZATIONS & PUBLICATIONS

The US **Centers for Disease Control and Prevention** (**CDC;** ☎877-FYI-TRIP; toll-free fax 888-232-3299; www.cdc.gov/travel) maintains an international travelers' hotline and an informative website. The CDC's comprehensive booklet *Health Information for International Travel*, an annual rundown of disease, immunization, and general health advice, is free online or US$25 for a paper copy via the Public Health Foundation (☎877-252-1200). Consult the appropriate government agency of your home country for consular information on health, entry requirements, and other issues for various countries (see the listings in the box on **Travel Advisories,** p. 23). For information on medical evacuation services and travel insurance firms, see the US government's website at travel.state.gov/medical.html or the **British Foreign and Commonwealth Office** (www.fco.gov.uk).

For detailed information on travel health, including a country-by-country overview of diseases, try the **International Travel Health Guide,** by Stuart Rose, MD (US$19.95; www.travmed.com). For general health info, contact the **American Red Cross** (☎800-564-1234; www.redcross.org).

MEDICAL ASSISTANCE ON THE ROAD

Overall, health care in Western Europe is of excellent quality and medical services are available in almost every town and city. Large cities and many smaller towns will have English-speaking doctors. Public hospitals are common and provide modern facilities and care. All EU citizens can receive free first-aid and emergency services with the presentation of an **E11 form** (available at post offices). Non-EU citizens should have good health insurance while traveling abroad; it is also advised to keep insurance information on-hand at all times in case of emergency.

If you are concerned about being able to access medical support while traveling, contact one of these two services: *MedPass*, from **GlobalCare, Inc.** (US ☎800-860-1111; fax 678-341-1800; www.globalems.com), which provides 24hr. international medical assistance, support, and medical evacuation resources, or the **International Association for Medical Assistance to Travelers** (**IAMAT;** US ☎716-754-4883, Canada ☎416-652-0137; www.iamat.org) which has free membership, lists English-speaking doctors worldwide, and offers detailed information on immunization requirements and sanitation.

Those with medical conditions (diabetes, allergies to antibiotics, epilepsy, heart conditions) may want to get a stainless-steel **Medic Alert** ID tag (first year US$35, US$20 thereafter), which identifies the condition and gives a 24hr.

collect-call number. Contact the Medic Alert Foundation (US ☎888-633-4298; www.medicalert.org).

In case of emergency, and for quick information on health and other travel warnings, contact a passport agency, embassy, or consulate abroad; US citizens can also call the **Overseas Citizens Services** (☎202-647-5225; after-hours 202-647-4000).

ONCE IN WESTERN EUROPE

ENVIRONMENTAL HAZARDS

Heat exhaustion and dehydration: Heat exhaustion can quickly overcome you while hiking around coastal and Mediterranean countries such as southern France, Spain, Portugal, Greece, and Italy, where temperatures easily soar over 90 degrees Fahrenheit (30 degrees Celsius) during the summer months. Heat exhaustion can lead to fatigue, headaches, and wooziness. Avoid it by drinking plenty of fluids, eating salty foods (e.g. crackers), and avoiding dehydrating beverages (e.g. alcohol and caffeinated drinks). Continuous heat stress can eventually lead to heatstroke, characterized by a rising temperature, severe headache, and cessation of sweating. Victims should be cooled off with wet towels and taken to a doctor.

High altitude: When hiking through mountainous areas like the Pyrenees or the Alps, allow your body a couple of days to adjust to less oxygen before exerting yourself. Note that alcohol is more potent and UV rays are stronger at high elevations.

Hypothermia and frostbite: A rapid drop in body temperature is the clearest sign of overexposure to cold. Victims may also shiver, feel exhausted, have poor coordination or slurred speech, hallucinate, or suffer amnesia. Do not let hypothermia victims fall asleep. To avoid hypothermia, keep dry, wear layers, and stay out of the wind. When the temperature is below freezing, watch out for frostbite. If skin turns white, waxy, and cold, do not rub the area. Drink warm beverages, get dry, and slowly warm the area with dry fabric or steady body contact until a doctor can be found.

INSECT-BORNE DISEASES

Many diseases are transmitted by insects—mainly mosquitoes, fleas, ticks, and lice—especially when hiking and camping in wet or forested areas. **Mosquitoes** are most active from dusk to dawn. Wear pants and long sleeves, tuck pants into socks, and sleep in a mosquito net. Use insect repellents such as DEET and soak or spray gear with permethrin (approved for use on clothing). **Ticks** can give you **Lyme disease.** If you find a tick attached to your skin, grasp the head with tweezers as close to the skin as possible and apply slow, steady traction. Removing a tick within 24hr. greatly reduces the risk of infection, which is marked by a 2in.-wide bull's-eye. Later symptoms include fever, headache, fatigue, and aches and pains. Left untreated, Lyme can cause problems in joints, the heart, and the nervous system. Antibiotics are effective if administered early. Ticks can also give you **encephalitis,** a viral infection. Symptoms can range from headaches and flu-like symptoms to swelling of the brain. The risk of contracting the disease is relatively low, especially if precautions are taken against tick bites. **Leishmaniasis,** a parasite transmitted by **sand flies,** can also occur in Europe. Common symptoms are fever, weakness, and swelling of the spleen. There is a treatment, but no vaccine.

FOOD- & WATER-BORNE DISEASES

Unpeeled fruit and vegetables and tap water should be safe throughout most of Western Europe. In Greece and other parts of Southern Europe, however, be cautious of ice cubes and anything washed in tap water, like salad. Other sources of illness include raw shellfish, unpasteurized milk, and sauces containing raw eggs. Buy bottled water, or purify your own water by bringing it to a rolling boil or treating it with **iodine tablets**.

Mad Cow Disease: The human variant is called Cruetzfeldt-Jakob disease (nvCJD), and involves invariably fatal brain diseases. Incidents in the United Kingdom have been tentatively linked to consuming infected beef, but the risk is calculated to be around 1 per 10 billion servings of meat. Information on nvCJD is not conclusive, but it is believed that milk and milk products do not pose a risk.

Parasites: Microbes, tapeworms, etc. that hide in unsafe water and food. **Giardiasis,** for example, is acquired by drinking untreated water from streams or lakes. Symptoms include swollen glands or lymph nodes, fever, rashes or itchiness, and digestive problems. Boil water, wear shoes, and eat only cooked food.

Traveler's diarrhea: Results from drinking untreated water or eating uncooked foods. Symptoms include nausea, bloating, and urgency. Try quick-energy, non-sugary foods with protein and carbohydrates to keep your strength up. Over-the-counter anti-diarrheals (e.g. Immodium) may counteract the problems. The most dangerous side effect is dehydration; drink 8 oz. of water with ½ tsp. of sugar or honey and a pinch of salt, try uncaffeinated soft drinks, and eat salted crackers. If you develop a fever or your symptoms don't go away after 4-5 days, consult a doctor. Consult a doctor immediately for treatment of diarrhea in children.

OTHER INFECTIOUS DISEASES

Foot and Mouth Disease (FMD): FMD experienced one of its worst outbreaks in 2001, largely in the United Kingdom and other Western European countries. FMD does not pose a health threat to humans but is devastating to animals. It can be transmitted by human as well as animal contact, and in the event of an outbreak, travel to farms and other rural areas may be restricted.

Hepatitis B: A viral infection of the liver transmitted via bodily fluids or needle-sharing. Symptoms may not surface until years after infection. A 3-shot vaccination sequence is recommended for health-care workers, sexually-active travelers, and anyone planning to seek medical treatment abroad; it must begin 6 mo. before traveling.

Hepatitis C: Like Hepatitis B, but the mode of transmission differs. IV drug users, those with occupational exposure to blood, hemodialysis patients, and recipients of blood transfusions are at the highest risk, but the disease can also be spread through sexual contact or sharing items like razors that may have traces of blood on them.

Rabies: Transmitted through the saliva of infected animals; fatal if untreated. By the time symptoms (thirst and muscle spasms) appear, the disease is in its terminal stage. If you are bitten, wash the wound thoroughly, seek immediate medical care, and try to have the animal located. A rabies vaccine, which consists of 3 shots given over a 21-day period, is available but is only semi-effective.

AIDS, HIV, AND STDS

For detailed information on **Acquired Immune Deficiency Syndrome (AIDS)** in Western Europe, call the CDC's 24hr. hotline at ☎800-342-2437, or contact the **Joint United Nations Programme on HIV/AIDS (UNAIDS)** (☎+41 22 791 3666; fax +41 22 791 4187; www.unaids.org). Some countries, like Cyprus, screen incoming travelers for HIV, primarily those planning extended visits for work or study, and deny entrance to those who test HIV-positive. Contact the country's consulate or the CDC in the US for information.

Sexually transmitted diseases (STDs) such as **gonorrhea, chlamydia, genital warts, syphilis,** and **herpes** are easier to catch than HIV and can be just as deadly. Hepatitis

B and C can also be transmitted sexually (see p. 27). Though condoms may protect you from some STDs, oral or even tactile contact can also lead to transmission. If you think you may have contracted an STD, see a doctor immediately.

WOMEN'S HEALTH

Women traveling in unsanitary conditions are vulnerable to **urinary tract** and **bladder infections,** common and very uncomfortable bacterial conditions that cause a burning sensation and painful (sometimes frequent) urination. Over-the-counter medicines can sometimes alleviate symptoms, but if they persist, see a doctor.

Vaginal yeast infections may flare up in hot and humid climates. Wearing loose-fitting trousers or a skirt and cotton underwear will help, as will over-the-counter remedies like Monistat or Gynelotrimin. Bring supplies from home if you are prone to infection, as they may be difficult to find on the road.

Tampons, pads, and reliable **contraceptives** can be hard to find in smaller towns; bring supplies with you.

INSURANCE

Travel insurance generally covers four basic areas: medical/health problems, property loss, trip cancellation/interruption, and emergency evacuation. Although your regular insurance policies may well extend to travel-related accidents, you should consider purchasing travel insurance if the cost of potential trip cancellation/interruption or emergency medical evacuation is greater than you can absorb. Prices for travel insurance purchased separately generally run about US$50 per week for full coverage, while trip cancellation/interruption may be purchased separately at a rate of about US$5.50 per US$100 of coverage.

Medical insurance (especially university policies) often covers costs incurred abroad; check with your provider. **US Medicare** does not cover foreign travel. Canadians are protected by their home province's health insurance plan for up to 90 days after leaving the country; check with the provincial Ministry of Health or Health Plan Headquarters for details. Australians traveling in the UK, the Netherlands, Sweden, Finland, Italy, or Malta are entitled to many of the services that they would receive at home as part of the Reciprocal Health Care Agreement. **Homeowners' Insurance** (or your family's coverage) often covers theft during travel and loss of travel documents (passport, plane ticket, railpass, etc.) up to US$500.

ISIC and **ITIC** (see p. 19) provide basic insurance benefits, including US$100 per day of in-hospital sickness for up to 60 days, US$3000 of accident-related medical reimbursement, and US$25,000 for emergency medical transport. Cardholders have access to a toll-free 24hr. helpline (run by the insurance provider **TravelGuard**) for medical, legal, and financial emergencies overseas (US and Canada ☎877-370-4742, elsewhere call US collect ☎+1 715-345-0505). **American Express** (US ☎800-528-4800) grants most cardholders automatic car rental insurance (collision and theft, but not liability) and ground travel accident coverage of US$100,000 on flight purchases made with the card.

INSURANCE PROVIDERS. Council and **STA** (see p. 41) offer a range of plans that can supplement your basic coverage. Other US and Canadian providers include **Access America** (☎800-284-8300) and **Berkely Group/Carefree Travel Insurance** (☎800-323-3149; www.berkely.com). The UK has **Columbus Direct** (☎020 7375 0011; www.columbusdirect.net), and Australia **AFTA** (☎02 9375 4955; www.afta.com.au).

PACKING

Pack light: Lay out only what you absolutely need, then take half the clothes and twice the money. If you plan to do a lot of hiking, also see the section on **Camping & the Outdoors,** p. 33.

LUGGAGE. If you plan to cover most of your itinerary by foot, a sturdy **frame backpack** is unbeatable. (For the basics on buying a pack, see p. 34.) Toting a **suitcase** or **trunk** is fine if you plan to live in one or two cities and explore from there, but a very bad idea if you're going to be moving around a lot. In addition to your main piece of luggage, a **daypack** (a small backpack or courier bag) is a must.

CLOTHING. No matter when you're traveling, it's always a good idea to bring a **warm jacket** or wool sweater, a **rain jacket** (Gore-Tex® is both waterproof and breathable), sturdy shoes or **hiking boots,** and **thick socks. Flip-flops** or waterproof sandals are must-haves for grubby hostel showers. You may also want to add one outfit beyond the jeans and t-shirt uniform, and maybe a nicer pair of shoes if you have the room. If you plan to visit any religious or cultural sites, remember that you'll need something besides tank tops and shorts to be respectful.

SLEEPSACK. Some hostels require that you either provide your own linen or rent sheets from them. Save cash by making your own sleepsack: Fold a full-size sheet in half the long way, then sew it closed along the long side and one short side.

CONVERTERS & ADAPTERS. In Europe, electricity is 220 volts AC, enough to fry any 110V North American appliance. Americans and Canadians should buy an **adapter** (which changes the shape of the plug) and a **converter** (which changes the voltage; US$20). Don't make the mistake of using only an adapter (unless appliance instructions state otherwise). New Zealanders, South Africans, and Australians won't need a converter, but still require an adapter to use anything electrical.

FIRST-AID KIT. For a basic first-aid kit, pack: bandages, pain reliever, antibiotic cream, a thermometer, a Swiss Army knife, tweezers, moleskin, decongestant, motion-sickness remedy, diarrhea or upset-stomach medication (Pepto Bismol or Imodium), an antihistamine, **sunscreen,** insect repellent, and burn ointment.

FILM. Film and developing in Europe are expensive, so consider bringing along enough film for your entire trip and developing it at home. Less serious photographers may want to bring **disposable cameras** rather than an expensive permanent one. Despite disclaimers, airport security X-rays *can* fog film, so buy a lead-lined pouch at a camera store or ask security to hand-inspect it. Always pack film in your carry-on luggage, since higher-intensity X-rays are used on checked luggage.

OTHER USEFUL ITEMS. For safety purposes, you should bring a **money belt** and small **padlock.** Basic **outdoors equipment** (water bottle, compass, waterproof matches, pocketknife, sunglasses, sunscreen) may also prove useful. Quick repairs of torn garments can be done on the road with a needle and thread; also consider bringing electrical tape for patching tears. Other things you're liable to forget: an **umbrella,** sealable **plastic bags** (for damp clothes, soap, food, etc.), an **alarm clock,** safety pins, rubber bands, a flashlight, **earplugs,** and garbage bags.

IMPORTANT DOCUMENTS. Don't forget your passport, traveler's checks, ATM card, credit cards, and adequate ID (see p. 18). Also be sure you have any of the following that might apply to you: a hosteling membership card (see p. 31); driver's license; travel insurance forms; and/or rail or bus pass (see p. 49).

ACCOMMODATIONS

HOSTELS

In the summer, Western Europe is overrun by young budget travelers. Hostels are the hub of this subculture, providing opportunities for young people from all over the world to meet, find travel partners, and learn about places to visit. Guests tend to be in their teens and 20s, but most hostels welcome travelers of all ages, though some hostels are only open to those under 26. In northern Europe, especially in Germany and Denmark, many hostels have special family rooms. In the average hostel, however, you and anywhere from one to 50 roommates will sleep on bunk beds in a gender-segregated room, with common bathrooms and a lounge down the hall. Other amenities may include kitchens for your use, bike or moped rentals, storage areas, internet access, and/or laundry facilities.

There can be drawbacks: Some hostels close during certain daytime "lockout" hours, have a curfew, don't accept reservations, impose a maximum stay, or, less frequently, require that you do chores. A bed in a hostel will average around US$10-25 in Western Europe.

HOSTELLING INTERNATIONAL

Joining the youth hostel association in your own country (listed below) automatically grants you membership privileges in **Hostelling International (HI)**, a federation of national hosteling associations. HI hostels are scattered throughout Western Europe, and are typically less expensive than private hostels. Many accept reservations via the **International Booking Network** (US ☎202-783-6161; www.hostelbooking.com). HI's umbrella organization's web page (www.iyhf.org), which lists the web addresses and phone numbers of all national associations, can be a great place to begin researching hostels in a specific region. Other comprehensive hostelling websites include www.hostels.com and www.hostelplanet.com.

Most HI hostels also honor **guest memberships**—you'll get a blank card with space for six validation stamps. Each night you'll pay a nonmember supplement (one-sixth the membership fee) and earn one guest stamp; get six stamps, and you're a member. Most student travel agencies (see p. 41) sell HI cards, as do all of the national hosteling organizations listed below. All prices listed below are valid for **one-year memberships** unless otherwise noted.

Australian Youth Hostels Association (AYHA), Level 3, 10 Mallett St., Camperdown NSW 2050 (☎02 9565 1699; fax 02 9565 1325; www.yha.org.au). AUS$52, under 18 AUS$16.

Hostelling International-Canada (HI-C), 400-205 Catherine St., Ottawa, ON K2P 1C3 (☎800-663-5777 or 613-237-7884; fax 613-237-7868; info@hostellingintl.ca; www.hihostels.ca). CDN$35, under 18 free.

Youth Hostels Association (England and Wales) Ltd., Trevelyan House, Dimple Road, Matlock, Devonshire, DE4 3YH, UK (☎01629 59 26 00; fax 01629 59 27 02; www.yha.org.uk). UK£13, under 18 UK£6.50, families UK£26.

An Óige (Irish Youth Hostel Association), 61 Mountjoy St., Dublin 7 (☎01 830 4555; fax 01 830 5808; anoige@iol.ie; www.irelandyha.org). IR£10, under 18 IR£4.

Youth Hostels Association of New Zealand (YHANZ), P.O. Box 436, 193 Cashel St., 3rd Floor Union House, Christchurch 1 (☎03 379 9970; fax 03 365 4476; info@yha.org.nz; www.yha.org.nz). NZ$40, under 17 free.

Hostelling International Northern Ireland (HINI), 22-32 Donegall Rd., Belfast BT12 5JN, Northern Ireland (☎02890 31 54 35; fax 02890 43 96 99; info@hini.org.uk; www.hini.org.uk). UK£10, under 18 UK£6.

Scottish Youth Hostels Association (SYHA), 7 Glebe Crescent, Stirling FK8 2JA (☎01786 89 14 00; fax 01786 89 13 33; www.syha.org.uk). UK£6.

Hostels Association of South Africa, 3rd fl. 73 St. George's House, P.O. Box 4402, Cape Town 8000 (☎021 424 2511; fax 021 424 4119; info@hisa.org.za; www.hisa.org.za). SAR55; under 18 SAR30.

Hostelling International-American Youth Hostels (HI-AYH), 733 15th St. NW, #840, Washington, D.C. 20005 (☎202-783-6161; fax 202-783-6171; hiayhserv@hiayh.org; www.hiayh.org). US$25, under 18 free.

ESSENTIALS

OTHER TYPES OF ACCOMMODATIONS

HOTELS, GUESTHOUSES, AND PENSIONS

In Britain, Switzerland, Austria, and northern Europe, **hotels** generally start at a hefty US$35 per person. Elsewhere, couples and larger groups can get by fairly well. You'll typically share a hall bathroom; a private bathroom will cost extra. Some hotels offer "full pension" (all meals) and "half pension" (no lunch). Smaller **guesthouses** and **pensions** are often cheaper than hotels. If you make reservations in writing, indicate your night of arrival and the number of nights you plan to stay. The hotel will send you a confirmation and may request payment for the first night. Not all hotels take reservations, and few accept checks in foreign currency. Enclosing two **International Reply Coupons** will ensure a prompt reply (each US$1.05; available at any post office).

BED & BREAKFASTS (B&Bs)

For a cozy alternative to impersonal hotel rooms, B&Bs (private homes with rooms available to travelers) range from the acceptable to the sublime. B&Bs are particularly popular in Britain and Ireland, where rooms average £20 per person. For more info on B&Bs, see **InnFinder** (www.inncrawler.com), or **InnSite** (www.innsite.com).

YMCAS & YWCAS

Young Men's Christian Association (YMCA) lodgings are usually cheaper than a hotel but more expensive than a hostel. Not all YMCA locations offer lodging; those that do are often located in urban downtowns. Many YMCAs accept women and families; some will not lodge those under 18 without parental permission. Book online at **Travel-Y's International** (www.travel-ys.com) for free. For a small fee ($3 in North America, $5 elsewhere), **Y's Way International** makes reservations between June and September for the YMCAs throughout Europe (224 E. 47th St., New York, NY 10017 USA; ☎212-308-2899; fax 212-308-3161).

UNIVERSITY DORMS

Many **colleges and universities** open their residence halls to travelers when school is not in session; some do so even during term-time. Getting a room may take a couple of phone calls and require advanced planning, but rates tend to be low, and the location is often great.

HOME EXCHANGES

Home exchange offers the traveler various types of homes (houses, apartments, condominiums, villas, even castles in some cases), plus the opportunity to live like a local and to cut down on accommodation fees. For more information, contact **HomeExchange.Com** (☎800-877-8723; www.homeexchange.com), **Intervac International Home Exchange** (www.intervac.com), or **The Invented City: International Home Exchange** (US ☎800-788-CITY, elsewhere US collect ☎+1 415-252-1141; www.invented-city.com).

CAMPING AND THE OUTDOORS

Organized campgrounds exist just outside most European cities. Showers, bathrooms, and a small restaurant or store are common; some have more elaborate facilities. Prices are low, at US$5-15 per person plus additional charges for tents and/or cars. While camping is a cheaper option than hostelling, the cost of transportation to the campsites can add up. Some parks or public land allow **free camping,** but check local regulations before you set up camp.

USEFUL PUBLICATIONS AND RESOURCES

An excellent resource for travelers planning on camping or spending time in the outdoors is the **Great Outdoor Recreation Pages** (www.gorp.com). Campers heading to Western Europe should consider buying an **International Camping Carnet.** Similar to a hostel membership card, it's required at a few campgrounds and provides discounts at others. It is available in North America from the **Family Campers and RVers Association** and in the UK from **The Caravan Club** (see below). For information about camping, hiking, and biking, write or call the publishers listed below to receive a **free catalog.**

Automobile Association, A. A. Publishing. Orders and inquiries to TBS Frating Distribution Centre, Colchester, Essex, CO7 7DW, UK (☎01206 255800; www.theaa.co.uk). Publishes *Caravan and Camping: Europe* and *Britain and Ireland* (UK£8) as well as *Big Road Atlases* for most European countries.

The Caravan Club, East Grinstead House, East Grinstead, West Sussex, RH19 1UA, UK (☎01342 326 944; fax 01342 410 258; www.caravanclub.co.uk). For UK£27.50, members receive equipment discounts, a 700-page directory and handbook, and a monthly magazine.

The European Federation of Campingsite Organizations, EFCO Secretariat, 6 Pullman Court, Great Western Road, Gloucester, GL 1 3 ND (UK ☎01452 526911; efco@bhpa.org.uk; www.campingeurope.com). The website has a comprehensive list of links to campsites in most European countries.

The Mountaineers Books, 1001 SW Klickitat Way, #201, Seattle, WA 98134, USA (☎800-553-4453 or 206-223-6303; fax 223-6306; www.mountaineersbooks.org). Over 400 titles on hiking, biking, mountaineering, natural history, and conservation.

CAMPING AND HIKING EQUIPMENT

WHAT TO BUY...

Good camping equipment is both sturdy and light. Camping equipment in Australia, New Zealand, and the UK is generally more expensive than in North America.

Sleeping Bag: Most sleeping bags are rated by season ("summer" means 30-40°F at night; "four-season" or "winter" often means below 0°F). They are made either of **down** (warmer and lighter, but miserable when wet, and more expensive) or of **synthetic**

material (heavier, more durable, and warmer when wet). Prices range US$80-210 for a summer synthetic to US$250-300 for a good down winter bag. **Sleeping bag pads** include foam pads (US$10-20), air mattresses (US$15-50), and Therm-A-Rest self-inflating pads (US$45-80). Bring a **stuff sack** to store your bag and keep it dry.

Tent: The best tents are free-standing (with their own frames and suspension systems), set up quickly, and only require staking in high winds. Low-profile dome tents are the best all-around. Good 2-person tents start at US$90, 4-person at US$300. Seal the seams of your tent with waterproofer, and make sure it has a rain fly. Other tent accessories include a **battery-operated lantern,** a **plastic groundcloth,** and a **nylon tarp.**

Backpack: Internal-frame packs mold better to your back, keep a lower center of gravity, and flex adequately to allow you to hike difficult trails. **External-frame packs** are more comfortable for long hikes over even terrain, as they keep weight higher and distribute it more evenly. Make sure your pack has a strong, padded hip-belt to transfer weight to your legs. Any serious backpacking requires a pack of at least 4000 cubic inches, plus 500 cubic inches for sleeping bags in internal-frame packs. Sturdy backpacks cost anywhere from US$125-420. This is one area in which it doesn't pay to economize. Fill up any pack with something heavy and walk around the store with it to get a sense of how it distributes weight before buying it. Either buy a **waterproof backpack cover,** or store all of your belongings in plastic bags inside your pack.

Boots: Be sure to wear hiking boots with good **ankle support.** They should fit snugly and comfortably over 1-2 pairs of wool socks and thin liner socks. Break in boots over several weeks first in order to spare yourself painful and debilitating blisters.

Other Necessities: Synthetic layers, like those made of polypropylene, and a **pile jacket** will keep you warm even when wet. A **"space blanket"** will help you to retain your body heat and doubles as a groundcloth (US$5-15). Plastic **water bottles** are virtually shatter- and leak-proof. Bring **water-purification tablets** for when you can't boil water. For those places that forbid fires or the gathering of firewood (virtually every organized campground in Europe), you'll need a **camp stove** (the classic Coleman starts at US$40) and a propane-filled **fuel bottle** to operate it. Also don't forget a **first-aid kit, pocketknife, insect repellent, calamine lotion,** and **waterproof matches** or a **lighter.**

...AND WHERE TO BUY IT

The mail-order/online companies listed below offer lower prices than many retail stores, but a visit to a local camping or outdoors store will give you a good sense of the look and weight of certain items.

Campmor, 28 Parkway, P.O. Box 700, Upper Saddle River, NJ 07458, USA (US ☎888-226-7667; elsewhere US ☎+1 201-825-8300; www.campmor.com).

Discount Camping, 880 Main North Rd., Pooraka, South Australia 5095, Australia (☎08 8262 3399; fax 08 8260 6240; www.discountcamping.com.au).

Eastern Mountain Sports (EMS), 1 Vose Farm Rd., Peterborough, NH 03458, USA (☎888-463-6367 or 603-924-7231; www.shopems.com).

L.L. Bean, Freeport, ME 04033 (US and Canada ☎800-441-5713; UK ☎0800 891 297; elsewhere, call US ☎+1 207-552-3028; www.llbean.com).

Mountain Designs, 51 Bishop St., Kelvin Grove, Queensland 4059, Australia (☎07 3856 2344; fax 07 3856 0366; info@mountaindesigns.com; www.mountaindesigns.com).

Recreational Equipment, Inc. (REI), Sumner, WA 98352, USA (☎800 426-4840 or 253-891-2500; www.rei.com).

YHA Adventure Shop, 152-160 Wardour St., London, WIF 8YA, UK (☎020 7025 1900; www.yhaadventure.com).

CAMPERS AND RVS

Renting an RV will always be more expensive than tenting or hosteling, but it's cheaper than staying in hotels and renting a car (see Renting a Car, p. 56), and the convenience of bringing along your own bedroom, bathroom, and kitchen makes it an attractive option, especially for older travelers and families with children. Rates vary widely by region, season (July and August are the most expensive months), and type of RV. **Motorhome.com** (www.motorhome.com/rentals.html) lists rental companies for several European countries. **Auto Europe** (US ☎800-223-5555; UK ☎0800 899 893; www.autoeurope.com) rents RVs in Britain, France, and Germany.

ORGANIZED ADVENTURE TRIPS

Organized adventure tours offer another way of exploring the wild. Activities include hiking, biking, skiing, canoeing, kayaking, rafting, climbing, photo safaris, and archaeological digs. Tourism bureaus can often suggest parks, trails, and outfitters; other good sources for information are stores and organizations that specialize in camping and outdoor equipment like REI and EMS (see above). The **Specialty Travel Index** (☎800-442-4922 or 415-459-4900; www.specialtytravel.com) compiles tours worldwide.

ENVIRONMENTALLY RESPONSIBLE TOURISM. The idea behind responsible tourism is to leave no trace of human presence behind. A campstove is the safer (and more efficient) way to cook than using vegetation, but if you must make a fire, keep it small and use only dead branches or brush rather than cutting vegetation. Make sure your campsite is at least 150 ft. (50m) from water supplies or bodies of water. If there are no toilet facilities, bury human waste (but not paper) at least four inches (10cm) deep and above the high-water line, and 150 ft. or more from any water sources and campsites. Always pack your trash in a plastic bag and carry it with you until you reach the next trash receptacle. For more information on these issues, contact one of the organizations listed below.

Earthwatch, 3 Clock Tower Place #100, Box 75, Maynard, MA 01754, USA (☎800-776-0188 or 978-461-0081; info@earthwatch.org; www.earthwatch.org).

International Ecotourism Society, 28 Pine St., Burlington, VT 05402, USA (☎802-651-9818; fax 802-651-9819; ecomail@ecotourism.org; www.ecotourism.org).

National Audubon Society, Nature Odysseys, 700 Broadway, New York, NY 10003 (☎212-979-3000; fax 212-979-3188; www.audubon.org).

Tourism Concern, Stapleton House, 277-281 Holloway Rd., London N7 8HN, UK (☎020 7753 3330; fax 020 7753 3331; info@tourismconcern.org.uk; www.tourismconcern.org.uk).

COMMUNICATION

BY MAIL

SENDING MAIL HOME FROM EUROPE

Airmail is the best way to send mail home from Europe. From Western Europe to North America, airmail averages seven days; from Central or Eastern Europe, allow anywhere from seven days to three weeks. **Aerogrammes,** printed sheets that fold into envelopes and travel via airmail, are available at post offices. Write "air mail" (or *par avion, por avion, mit Luftpost, via aerea,* etc.) on the front. Most post offices will charge exorbitant fees or simply refuse to send aerogrammes with enclosures. **Surface mail** is by far the cheapest and slowest way to send mail. It takes one to three months to cross the Atlantic and two to four to cross the Pacific—good for items you won't need to see for a while, such as souvenirs or other articles you've acquired along the way that are weighing down your pack.

SENDING MAIL TO EUROPE

Mark envelopes "par avion" or "airmail" in the appropriate language; otherwise, your letter or postcard will not arrive. In addition to the standard postal system, **Federal Express** (Australia ☎13 26 10; US and Canada ☎800-247-4747; New Zealand ☎0800 733 339; UK ☎0800 123 800; www.fedex.com) handles express mail services from most home countries to Europe.

Australia: Allow 5-6 days for regular **airmail** to Europe. Postcards and letters up to 20g cost AUS$1; packages up to 0.5kg AUS$9. **EMS** can get a letter there in 2-3 days for AUS$32. www.auspost.com.au/pac.

Canada: Allow 4-7 days for regular **airmail** to Europe. Postcards and letters up to 30g cost CDN$1.25; packages up to 0.5kg CDN$10.00. www.canadapost.ca/personal/rates/default-e.asp.

Ireland: Allow 2-3 days for regular airmail to the UK and Western Europe. Postcards and letters up to 25g cost €0.41 to the UK, €0.44 to the continent. **International Swiftpost** zips letters to some major European countries for an additional €3.40 on top of priority postage. www.letterpost.ie.

New Zealand: Allow 6-12 days for regular airmail to Europe. Postcards NZ$1.50. Letters up to 200g cost NZ$10; small parcels up to 0.5kg NZ$17.50, up to 2kg NZ$55.25. www.nzpost.net.nz/nzpost/control/ratefinder.

UK: Allow 2-3 days for airmail to Europe. Letters up to 20g cost UK£0.37; packages up to 0.5kg UK£2.73, up to 2kg UK£9.60. **UK Swiftair** delivers letters a day faster for an extra UK£2.85. www.royalmail.com/International/calculator.

US: Allow 4-7 days for regular **airmail** to Europe. Postcards/aerogrammes cost US$0.70; letters under 1oz. US$0.80; packages under 1lb. US$16.50; larger packages up to 5lb. $27.25). **Global Express Mail** takes 2-3 days; 0.5lb. costs US$23, 1lb. US$26. **US Global Priority Mail** delivers flat-rate envelopes to Europe in 3-5 days for US$5-9. http://ircalc.usps.gov.

RECEIVING MAIL IN EUROPE

There are several ways to arrange pick-up of letters sent to you by friends and relatives while you are abroad. Mail can be sent via **Poste Restante** (General Delivery; *Lista de Correos, Fermo Posta, Postlagernde Briefe,* etc.) to almost any city or town in Europe with a post office. See individual country chapters to see how to address *Poste Restante* letters. The mail will go to a special desk in the central post office, unless you specify a post office by street address or postal code. It's best to use the largest post office, since mail may be sent there regardless. It is usually safer and quicker, though more expensive, to send mail express or registered. Bring your passport (or other photo ID) for pick-up; there may be a small fee. If the clerks insist that there is nothing for you, check under your first name as well. *Let's Go* lists post offices in the **Practical Information** section for each city and most towns.

American Express travel offices offer a free **Client Letter Service** (mail held up to 30 days and forwarded upon request) for cardholders who contact them in advance.

Some offices offer these services to non-cardholders (especially AmEx Travelers Cheque holders), but call ahead. *Let's Go* lists AmEx office locations for most large cities in **Practical Information** sections; for a complete, free list, call US ☎800-528-4800; www.americanexpress.com.

BY TELEPHONE

CALLING HOME FROM EUROPE

A **calling card** is probably cheapest. Calls are billed collect or to your account. You can frequently call collect without even possessing a company's calling card just by calling their access number and following the instructions. **To obtain a calling card** from your national telecommunications service before leaving home, contact the appropriate company listed below:

AT&T (US): ☎800-361-4470.

British Telecom: ☎800 345144.

Bell Canada: ☎800-668-6878.

Ireland Direct: ☎800 400 000.

MCI (US): ☎800-444-3333.

Telecom New Zealand: ☎0800 000 000.

Sprint (US): ☎800-877-4646.

Telkom South Africa: ☎10 219.

Telstra Australia ☎132 200.

To **call home with a calling card,** contact the operator for your service provider in the country of your travel by dialing the appropriate toll-free access number (listed in the **Essentials** section of each country under Communications). You can usually make **direct international calls** from pay phones, but if you aren't using a calling card, you may need to drop your coins as quickly as your words. Where available, prepaid phone cards and occasionally major credit cards can be used for direct international calls, but they are still less cost-efficient. (See the box on **Placing International Calls** (p. 37) for directions on how to place a direct international call.) Placing a **collect call** through international operators is a more expensive alternative.

PLACING INTERNATIONAL CALLS. To call Europe from home or to call home from Europe, dial:

1. The **international dialing prefix.** To dial out of **Australia,** dial 0011; **Canada** or the **US,** 011; the **Republic of Ireland, New Zealand,** or the **UK,** 00; **South Africa,** 09. See the back cover for a full list of prefixes.
2. The **country code** of the country you want to call. To call **Australia,** dial 61; **Canada** or the **US,** 1; the **Republic of Ireland,** 353; **New Zealand,** 64; **South Africa,** 27; the **UK,** 44. Again, see the back cover for a full list.
3. The **city/area code.** *Let's Go* lists the city/area codes for cities and towns opposite the city or town name or at the end of a small town's write-up, next to a ☎. If the first digit is a zero (e.g., 020 for London), omit the zero when calling from abroad (e.g., dial 20 from Canada to reach London).
4. The **local number.**

STUDENT TRAVEL
how do you say
"please, no more sausage"
in German?
We've got the answer, and a whole lot more.
We specialize in one thing: HELPING STUDENTS TRAVEL BETTER by offering convenient one-stop access to the products and services they need to have a great travel experience.
(We'll even remind you to pack those all important antacid tablets.)
CST #1017560-40
(800) 777.0112
www.statravel.com
STA TRAVEL
ONLINE » ON THE PHONE » ON CAMPUS » ON THE STREET

CALLING WITHIN EUROPE

Much of Europe has switched to a prepaid phone card system. In some countries you may have a hard time finding any coin-operated phones at all. Prepaid phone cards (available at newspaper kiosks and tobacco stores), which carry a certain amount of phone time depending on the card's denomination, usually save time and money in the long run. The computerized phone will tell you how much time, in units, you have left on your card. Another kind of prepaid telephone card comes with a Personal Identification Number (PIN) and a toll-free access number. Instead of inserting the card into the phone, you call the access number and follow the directions on the card. These cards can be used to make international as well as domestic calls. Phone rates typically tend to be highest in the morning, lower in the evening, and lowest on Sunday and late at night

BY EMAIL AND INTERNET

Email is popular and easily accessible in most of Europe. Take advantage of free **web-based email accounts** (e.g., www.hotmail.com and www.yahoo.com); while it's sometimes possible to forge a remote link with your home server, in most cases this is a much slower and more expensive option. Travelers with laptops can call an Internet service provider via a **modem.** Long-distance phone cards specifically intended for such calls can defray normally high phone charges; check with your long-distance phone provider to see if it offers this option. **Internet cafes** and the occasional free Internet terminal at a public library or university are listed in the **Practical Information** sections of major cities. For lists of additional cybercafes in Europe, check out cybercaptive.com or netcafeguide.com.

GETTING TO WESTERN EUROPE

BY PLANE

When it comes to airfare, a little effort can save you a bundle. If your plans are flexible enough to deal with the restrictions, courier fares are the cheapest. Standby seats and tickets bought from consolidators are also good deals, but last-minute specials, charter flights, and airfare wars often generate even lower rates. The key is to hunt around, to be flexible, and to ask persistently about discounts. Students, seniors, and those under 26 should never pay full price for a ticket.

Timing: Airfares to Western Europe peak between mid-June and early Sept.; holidays are also expensive. The cheapest times to travel are Nov. to mid-Dec. and early Jan. to Mar. Midweek (M-Th morning) round-trip flights run US$40-50 cheaper than weekend flights, but they are generally more crowded and less likely to permit frequent-flier upgrades. An "open return" ticket can be pricier than fixing a return date and paying later to change it.

Route: Round-trip flights are by far the cheapest; "open jaw" (arriving in and departing from different cities, e.g. New York-Paris and Rome-New York) tickets tend to be pricier. Patching one-way flights together is the most expensive way to travel.

Round the World (RTW): If Western Europe is only one stop on a more extensive globe-hop, consider a round-the-world (RTW) ticket. Tickets usually include at least 5 stops and are valid for about a year; prices range US$1200-5000. Try **Northwest Airlines/KLM** (US ☎800-447-4747; www.nwa.com) or **Star Alliance,** a consortium of 22 airlines including United Airlines (US ☎800-241-6522; www.star-alliance.com).

Gateway Cities: Flights between capitals or regional hubs will offer the cheapest fares. The cheapest gateway cities to Western Europe are typically London, Paris, Amsterdam, and Frankfurt.

Boarding: Confirm international flights by phone within 72hr. of departure. Most airlines require that passengers arrive at the airport at least 2 to 3 hours before departure. One carry-on item and 2 checked bags is the norm for non-courier flights.

BUDGET AND STUDENT TRAVEL AGENCIES

While knowledgeable agents specializing in flights to Western Europe can make your life easy and help you save, they get paid on commission so they may not spend the time to find you the lowest possible fare. Travelers holding **ISIC and IYTC cards** (see p. 19) qualify for big discounts from student travel agencies. Most flights from budget agencies are on major airlines, but in peak season some may sell seats on less reliable chartered aircrafts.

Council Travel (www.counciltravel.com). Countless US offices, including branches in Atlanta, Boston, Chicago, L.A., New York, San Francisco, Seattle, and Washington, D.C. Check the website or call US ☎800-2-COUNCIL (226-8624) for the office nearest you. Also an office at 28A Poland St. (Oxford Circus), **London,** W1V 3DB (☎020 7437 7767). As of May, Council had declared bankruptcy and was subsumed under STA. However, their offices are still in existence and transacting business.

CTS Travel (www.ctstravelusa.com). Offices across Italy, in Paris, London, and now in New York. Call toll free US ☎877-287-6665. In UK, 44 Goodge St., **London** W1T 2AD (☎020 7636 0031; fax 637 5328; ctsinfo@ctstravel.co.uk).

STA Travel (www.sta-travel.com). A student and youth travel organization with over 300 offices worldwide, including over 100 US offices. Check their website for a listing of all their offices. Ticket booking, travel insurance, railpasses, and more. 24hr. reservations and info US ☎800-781-4040. In the UK, walk-in office 11 Goodge St., **London** W1T 2PF (☎020 7436 7779). In New Zealand, Shop 2B, 182 Queen St., **Auckland** (☎09 309 0458). In Australia, 366 Lygon St., **Carlton** Vic 3053 (☎03 9349 4344).

Travel CUTS (Canadian Universities Travel Services Limited), 187 College St., **Toronto,** ON M5T 1P7 (☎416-979-2406; fax 979-8167; www.travelcuts.com). 60 offices across Canada. Also in the UK, 295-A Regent St., **London** W1R 7YA (☎020 7255 1944).

usit world (www.usitworld.com). Over 50 **usit campus** branches in the UK, including 52 Grosvenor Gardens, **London** SW1W 0AG (☎0870 240 1010); **Manchester** (☎0161 273 1880); and **Edinburgh** (☎0131 668 3303). Nearly 20 **usit NOW** offices in Ireland, including 19-21 Aston Quay, O'Connell Bridge, **Dublin** 2 (☎01 602 1600; www.usitnow.ie), and **Belfast** (☎02 890 327 111; www.usitnow.com).

Wasteels, Skoubogade 6, 1158 **Copenhagen** (☎45 3314 4633; fax 3314 0865; www.wasteels.dk/uk). A huge chain with 165 locations across Europe. BIJ tickets discounted 30-45%. 2nd-class international point-to-point train tickets with unlimited stopovers for those under 26 (sold only in Europe).

COMMERCIAL AIRLINES

The commercial airlines' lowest regular offer is the **APEX** (Advance Purchase Excursion) fare, which provides confirmed reservations and allows "open-jaw" tickets. Generally, reservations must be made seven to 21 days ahead of departure, with seven- to 14-day minimum-stay and up to 90-day maximum-stay restrictions. These fares carry hefty cancellation and change penalties. Book peak-season APEX fares early; by May you will have a hard time getting your desired departure date. Use **Expedia** (www.expedia.com) or **Travelocity** (www.travelocity.com) to get an idea of the lowest published fares, then use the resources outlined here to try

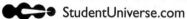

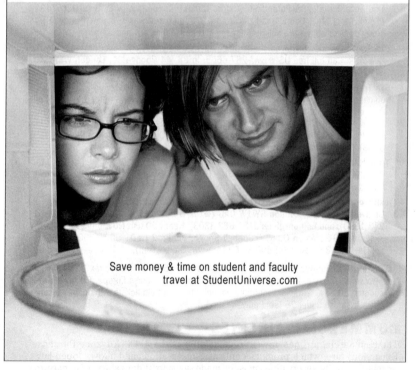

FLIGHT PLANNING ON THE INTERNET. The Internet is a great place to look for travel bargains—it's fast and convenient, and you can spend as long as you like exploring options without driving your travel agent insane.

Many airline companies offer special last-minute deals on the Web. Some require email addresses, so be wary of each site's privacy policy before you submit. Airlines like Continental (www.continental.com/cool) and United (www.united.com, click on "Special Deals") require membership logins or email subscriptions before allowing access to special prices. Other sites do the legwork and compile the deals for you; try www.bestfares.com, www.flights.com, www.hotdeals.com, www.onetravel.com, and www.travelzoo.com.

Student Universe (www.studentuniverse.com), **STA** (www.sta-travel.com), and **Orbitz** (www.orbitz.com) provide quotes on student tickets, while **Expedia** (www.expedia.com) and **Travelocity** (www.travelocity.com) offer full travel services. **Priceline** (www.priceline.com) allows you to specify a price, and obligates you to buy any ticket that meets or beats it; be prepared for antisocial hours and odd routes. **Skyauction** (www.skyauction.com) allows you to bid on both last-minute and advance-purchase tickets.

An indispensable resource on the Internet is the *Air Traveler's Handbook* (www.cs.cmu.edu/afs/cs/user/mkant/Public/Travel/airfare.html), a comprehensive listing of links to everything you need to know before you board a plane.

One last note: To protect yourself, make sure that the site you use has a secure server before handing over any credit card details.

and beat those fares. Low-season fares should be appreciably cheaper than the high-season (mid-June to August) ones listed here.

TRAVELING FROM NORTH AMERICA

Basic round-trip fares to Europe are roughly US$200-750. Standard commercial carriers like American (☎800-433-7300; www.aa.com) and United (☎800-241-6522; www.ual.com) will probably offer the most convenient flights, but they may not be the cheapest unless you grab a special promotion ticket. You might find flying one of the following airlines a better deal, if any of their limited departure points is convenient for you.

Icelandair: US ☎800-223-5500; www.icelandair.com. Stopovers in Iceland for no extra cost on most transatlantic flights. New York to Frankfurt May-Sept. US$500-780; Oct.-May US$390-$450.

Finnair: US ☎800-950-5000; www.us.finnair.com. Cheap return fares from San Francisco, New York, and Toronto to Helsinki. Connections throughout Europe.

Martinair: US ☎800-627-8462; www.martinairusa.com. Fly from California or Florida to Amsterdam mid-June to mid-Aug. US$880; mid-Aug. to mid-June US$730.

TRAVELING FROM THE UK AND IRELAND

Because many carriers fly from the British Isles to the continent, we only include discount airlines or those with cheap specials here. The **Air Travel Advisory Bureau** in London (☎020 7636 5000; www.atab.co.uk) provides referrals to travel agencies and consolidators that offer discounted airfares out of the UK.

Aer Lingus: Ireland ☎0818 365000; UK ☎0845 084 4444; www.flyaerlingus.com. Round-trip tickets from Dublin, Shannon, and Cork to Amsterdam, Brussels, Düsseldorf, Frankfurt, Madrid, Milan, Munich, Paris, Rome, Stockholm, and Zürich (€40-135).

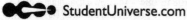

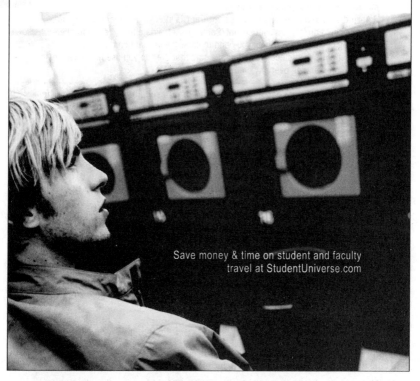

British Midland Airways: UK ☎0870 607 0555; www.flybmi.com. Departures from throughout the UK. Discounted online fares including London to Brussels (UK£83), Madrid (UK£118), Milan (£126), and Paris (UK£84).

buzz: UK ☎0870 240 7070; www.buzzaway.com. From London to Berlin, Frankfurt, and Paris (UK£30-35). Tickets cannot be refunded and flight changes cost UK£15.

easyJet: UK ☎0870 600 0000; www.easyjet.com. London to Amsterdam, Athens, Barcelona, Geneva, Madrid, Nice, and Zürich (from UK£30). On-line tickets.

Go-Fly Limited: UK ☎090 6302 0150, elsewhere call UK ☎4127 966 6388; www.go-fly.com. A subsidiary of British Airways. From London to Barcelona, Copenhagen, Edinburgh, Naples, Prague, Rome, and Venice (round-trip UK£50-180).

KLM: UK ☎0870 507 4074; www.klmuk.com. Cheap return tickets from London and elsewhere to Amsterdam, Brussels, Frankfurt, and Zürich; via Amsterdam Schiphol Airport to Düsseldorf, Milan, Paris, Rome, and elsewhere.

Ryanair: Ireland ☎0818 303 030, UK ☎0870 156 9569; www.ryanair.ie. From Dublin, London, and Glasgow to destinations in France, Germany, Ireland, Italy, Scandinavia, and elsewhere. Deals from as low as UK£9 on limited weekend specials.

ESSENTIALS

TRAVELING FROM AUSTRALIA AND NEW ZEALAND

Air New Zealand: New Zealand ☎0800 73 70 00; www.airnz.co.nz. From Melbourne, Auckland, and elsewhere to London, Paris, Rome, Frankfurt, and beyond.

Qantas Air: Australia ☎13 13 13; New Zealand ☎0800 808 767; www.qantas.com.au. Flights from Australia and New Zealand to London AUS$2400-3000.

Singapore Air: Australia ☎13 10 11; New Zealand ☎0800 808 909; www.singaporeair.com. Flies from Auckland, Sydney, Melbourne, and Perth to Amsterdam, Brussels, Frankfurt, London, Manila, and more.

Thai Airways: Australia ☎1300 65 19 60; New Zealand ☎09 377 02 68; www.thai-air.com. Connects Auckland, Sydney, and Melbourne to major European cities.

TRAVELING FROM SOUTH AFRICA

Air France: ☎011 770 16 01; www.airfrance.com/za. Johannesburg to Paris; connections throughout Europe.

British Airways: ☎0860 011 747; www.british-airways.com/regional/sa. Johannesburg to London direct, and connections to the rest of Western Europe from SAR3400.

Lufthansa: ☎0861 842 538; www.lufthansa.co.za. From Cape Town, Durban, and Johannesburg to Germany and elsewhere.

Virgin Atlantic: ☎011 340 34 00; www.virgin-atlantic.co.za. Flies to London from both Cape Town and Johannesburg.

AIR COURIER FLIGHTS

Those who travel light should consider courier flights. Couriers help transport cargo on international flights by using their checked luggage space for freight. Generally, couriers must travel with carry-ons only and must deal with complex flight restrictions. Most flights are return with short fixed-length stays (usually one week) and a limit of one ticket per issue. Most flights also operate only out of gateway cities, mostly in North America. Generally, you must be over 21 (in some cases 18).

In summer, popular destinations usually require advance reservation of about two weeks and you can usually book up to two months ahead. If you're willing to risk it, super-discounted fares are common for "last-minute" flights (three to 14 days ahead).

TRAVELING FROM NORTH AMERICA. Round-trip courier fares from the US to Europe run about US$200-500. Most flights leave from New York, Los Angeles, San Francisco, or Miami in the US; and from Montreal, Toronto, or Vancouver in Canada. The organizations below provide their members with lists of opportunities and courier brokers worldwide for an annual fee (typically US$50-60). Alternatively, you can contact a courier broker directly, most charge registration fees, but a few don't. Prices quoted below are round-trip.

Air Courier Association, 350 Indiana St., Suite 300, Golden, CO 80401 (☎800-282-1202, elsewhere call US ☎303-279-3600; www.aircourier.org). Ten departure cities throughout the US and Canada to London, Madrid, Paris, Rome, and throughout Western Europe (high-season US$150-360). One-year US$39.

International Association of Air Travel Couriers (IAATC), P.O. Box 980, Keystone Heights, FL 32656 (☎352-475-1584; fax 352-475-5326; www.courier.org). From 9 North American cities to Western European cities, including London, Madrid, Paris, and Rome. One-year US$45-50.

Global Courier Travel, P.O. Box 3051, Nederland, CO 80466 (☎866-470-3061, www.globalcouriertravel.com). Searchable on-line database. Departures from the US and Canada to Amsterdam, Athens, Brussels, Copenhagen, Frankfurt, London, Madrid, Milan, Paris, and Rome. Lifetime membership US$40, 2 people US$55.

FROM THE UK, IRELAND, AUSTRALIA, AND NEW ZEALAND. The minimum age for couriers from the **UK** is usually 18. **Brave New World Enterprises,** P.O. Box 22212, London SE5 8WB (info@courierflights.com; www.courierflights.com) publishes a directory of all the companies offering courier flights in the UK (UK£10, in electronic form UK£8). **Global Courier Travel** (see above) also offers flights from London and Dublin to continental Europe. **British Airways Travel Shop** (☎0870 240 0747; info@batravelshops.com; www.batravelshops.com) arranges some flights from London to destinations in continental Europe (specials may be as low as UK£60; no registration fee). From **Australia** and **New Zealand, Global Courier Travel** (see above) often has listings from Sydney and Auckland to London and occasionally Frankfurt.

STANDBY FLIGHTS

Traveling standby requires considerable flexibility in arrival and departure dates and cities. Companies dealing in standby flights sell vouchers rather than tickets, along with the promise to get to your destination (or near your destination) within a certain window of time (typically 1-5 days). You call in before your specific window of time to hear your flight options and the probability that you will be able to board each flight. You can then decide which flights you want to try to make, show up at the appropriate airport at the appropriate time, present your voucher, and board if space is available. Vouchers can usually be bought for both one-way and round-trip travel. You may receive a monetary refund only if every available flight within your date range is full; if you opt not to take an available (but perhaps less convenient) flight, you can only get credit toward future travel. Carefully read agreements with any company offering standby flights, as tricky fine print can leave you in a lurch. It is difficult to receive refunds, and clients' vouchers will not be honored when an airline fails to receive payment in time. To check on a company's service record in the US, call the Better Business Bureau (☎212-533-6200).

TICKET CONSOLIDATORS

Ticket consolidators, or "bucket shops," buy unsold tickets in bulk from commercial airlines and sell them at discounted rates. The best place to look is in the Sunday travel section of any major newspaper (such as the *New York Times*), where

many bucket shops place tiny ads. Call quickly, as availability is typically extremely limited. Not all bucket shops are reliable, so insist on a receipt that gives full details of restrictions, refunds, and tickets, and pay by credit card (in spite of the 2-5% fee) so you can stop payment if you never receive your tickets. For more information, see www.travel-library.com/air-travel/consolidators.html.

TRAVELING FROM THE US & CANADA

Travel Avenue (☎800-333-3335; www.travelavenue.com) searches for the best available published fares and then uses several consolidators to attempt to beat that fare. Other consolidators worth trying are **Interworld** (☎305-443-4929; fax 443-0351); **Pennsylvania Travel** (☎800-331-0947); **Rebel** (☎800-227-3235; travel@rebeltours.com; www.rebeltours.com); **Cheap Tickets** (☎800-377-1000; www.cheaptickets.com); and **Travac** (☎800-872-8800; fax 212-714-9063; www.travac.com). Consolidators on the web include the **Internet Travel Network** (www.itn.com); **Travel Information Services** (www.tiss.com); **TravelHUB** (www.travelhub.com); and **The Travel Site** (www.thetravelsite.com). Keep in mind that these are just suggestions to get you started in your research; *Let's Go* does not endorse any of these agencies. As always, be cautious, and research companies before you hand over your credit card number.

TRAVELING FROM THE UK, AUSTRALIA, & NEW ZEALAND

In UK, the **Air Travel Advisory Bureau** (☎0207-636-5000; www.atab.co.uk) can provide names of reliable consolidators and discount flight specialists. From Australia and New Zealand, look for consolidator ads in the travel section of the *Sydney Morning Herald* and other papers.

CHARTER FLIGHTS

Charters are flights a tour operator contracts with an airline to fly extra loads of passengers during peak season. Charter flights fly less frequently than major airlines, make refunds particularly difficult, and are almost always fully booked. Schedules and itineraries may also change or be cancelled at the last moment (as late as 48 hours before the trip, and without a full refund), and check-in, boarding, and baggage claim are often pretty slow. However, they can also be cheaper.

Discount clubs and **fare brokers** offer members savings on last-minute charter and tour deals. Study contracts closely; you don't want to end up with an unwanted overnight layover. **Travelers Advantage,** Trumbull, CT, USA (☎203-365-2000; www.travelersadvantage.com; US$60 annual fee includes discounts and cheap flight directories) specializes in European travel and tour packages.

BY CHUNNEL FROM THE UK

Traversing 27 mi. under the sea, the Chunnel is undoubtedly the fastest, most convenient, and least scenic route from England to France.

BY TRAIN. Eurostar, Eurostar House, Waterloo Station, London SE1 8SE (UK ☎0990 186 186; US ☎800-387-6782; elsewhere call UK ☎4020 7928 5163; www.eurostar.com; www.raileurope.com) runs frequent trains between London and the continent. Ten to twenty-eight trains per day run to Paris (3hr., US$75-159, 2nd class), Brussels (3hr., 50min., US$75-159, 2nd class), and Eurodisney. Routes include stops at Ashford in England, and Calais and Lille in France. Book at major rail stations in the UK, at the office above, by phone, or on the web.

BY BUS. Both **Eurolines** and **Eurobus** provide bus-ferry combinations (see p.33).

BY CAR. Eurotunnel (UK ☎ Customer relations, P.O. Box 2000, Folkestone, Kent CT18 8XY; www.eurotunnel.co.uk) shuttles cars and passengers between Kent and Nord-Pas-de-Calais. Return fares for vehicle and all passengers range from UK£100-210 with car, UK£259-636 with campervan. Same-day return costs UK£110-150, five-day return UK£139-195. Book online or via phone. Travelers with cars can also look into sea crossings by ferry (see below).

ESSENTIALS

BY BOAT FROM THE UK AND IRELAND

The fares below are **one-way** for **adult foot passengers** unless otherwise noted. Though standard return fares are usually just twice the one-way fare, **fixed-period returns** (usually within five days) are almost invariably cheaper. Ferries run **year-round** unless otherwise noted. **Bikes** are usually free, although you may have to pay up to UK£10 in high season. For a **camper/trailer** supplement, you will have to add UK£20-140 to the "with car" fare. If more than one price is quoted, the quote in UK£ is valid for departures from the UK, etc. A directory of ferries in this region can be found at www.seaview.co.uk/ferries.html.

P&O Stena Line: UK ☎ 087 0600 0611; from Europe UK ☎ 013 04 86 40 03; customer.services@posl.com; www.posl.com. **Dover** to **Calais** (1¼hr., 30 per day, UK£24).

Hoverspeed: UK ☎ 0870 240 8070; France ☎ 008 00 1211 1211; www.hoverspeed.co.uk. **Dover** to **Calais** (35-55min., every hr., UK£24) and **Ostend, Belgium** (2hr., 5-7 per day, UK£28). **Newhaven** to **Dieppe, France** (2¼-4¼hr., 1-3 per day, UK£28).

SeaFrance: UK ☎ 08705 711 711; France ☎ 08 03 04 40 45; www.seafrance.co.uk. **Dover** to **Calais** (1½hr., 15 per day, UK£15).

DFDS Seaways: UK ☎ 08705 333 000; www.dfdsseaways.co.uk. **Harwich** to **Hamburg** (20hr.) and **Esbjerg, Denmark** (19hr.). **Newcastle** to **Amsterdam** (14hr.); **Kristiansand, Norway** (19hr.); and **Gothenburg, Sweden** (22hr.).

Brittany Ferries: UK ☎ 08703 665 333; France ☎ 08 25 82 88 28; www.brittany-ferries.com. **Plymouth** to **Roscoff, France** (6hr., in summer 1-3 per day, off-season 1 per week, UK£19-40 or EUR€30-63) and **Santander, Spain** (24-30hr., 1-2 per week, return UK£73-95 or EUR€115-150). **Portsmouth** to **St-Malo** (8¾hr., 1-2 per day, UK£47-59 or EUR€74-93) and **Caen, France** (6hr, 1-3 per day, UK£29-44 or €46-69). **Poole** to **Cherbourg** (4¼hr., 1-2 per day, UK£29-43 or €45-68). **Cork** to **Roscoff, France** (13½hr., Apr.-Sept. 1 per week, €50-90).

P&O North Sea Ferries: UK ☎ 0870 129 6002; www.ponsf.com. Daily ferries from **Hull** to **Rotterdam, Netherlands** (13½hr.) and **Zeebrugge, Belgium** (14hr.). Both UK£38-48, students UK£24-31, cars UK£63-78. Online bookings.

Fjord Line: www.fjordline.no. Norway ☎ 55 54 88 00; UK ☎ 0191 296 1313; booking@fjordline.com. **Newcastle, England** to **Stavanger** (19hr.) and **Bergen, Norway** (26hr.; UK£50-110, students £25-110). Also between **Bergen** and **Egersund, Norway,** and **Hanstholm, Denmark.**

Irish Ferries: France ☎ 01 44 88 54 50; Ireland ☎ 1890 31 31 31; UK ☎ 08705 17 17 17; www.irishferries.ie. **Rosslare** to **Cherbourg** and **Roscoff** (17-18hr., Apr.-Sept. 1-9 per week, €60-120, students €48) and **Pembroke, UK** (3¾hr., €25-39/€19). **Holyhead, UK** to **Dublin** (2-3hr., round-trip UK£20-31/UK£15).

Stena Line: UK ☎ 4123 364 6826; www.stenaline.co.uk. **Harwich** to **Hook of Holland** (5hr., UK£26). **Fishguard** to **Rosslare** (1-3½hr., UK£18-21, students £14-17). **Holyhead** to **Dublin** (4hr., UK£23-27/£19-23) and **Dún Laoghaire** (1-3½hr., UK£23-27/£19-23). **Stranraer** to **Belfast** (1¾-3¼hr., UK£14-36/£10).

GETTING AROUND WESTERN EUROPE

Fares on all modes of transportation are either **single** (one-way) or **return** (round-trip). "Period returns" require that you return within a specific number of days. "Day returns" require you to return on the same day. Unless stated otherwise, *Let's Go* always lists single fares for trains and buses. Return fares on trains and buses in Europe are simply double the one-way fare.

BY PLANE

Flying is almost invariably more expensive than traveling by train. For lengthy trips, however, taking the time to research flight options can save on travel time and, in some circumstances, money. Student travel agencies sell cheap tickets, and budget fares are frequently available in the spring and summer on high-volume routes between northern Europe and resort areas in Greece, Italy, and Spain; consult budget travel agents and local newspapers. For information on cheap flights from Britain to the continent, see **Traveling from the UK,** p. 43.

The Star Alliance European Airpass offers low Economy Class fares for travel within Europe to more than 200 destinations in 43 countries. The pass is available to transatlantic passengers on Star Alliance carriers, including Air Canada, Austrian Airlines, BMI British Midland, Lufthansa, Mexicana, Scandinavian Airlines System, THAI, United Airlines, and Varig, as well as on certain partner airlines. Prices are based on mileage between destinations

In addition, a number of European airlines offer coupon packets that considerably discount the cost of each flight leg. Most are only available as tack-ons to their transatlantic passengers, but some are available as stand-alone offers. Most must be purchased before departure, so research in advance.

Austrian Airlines: US ☎800-843-0002; www.austrianair.com/greatdeals/europe_airpass.html. "European Airpass" is available in the US to Austrian Airlines transatlantic passengers (3 cities min., 10 max.). Price based on mileage between destinations.

Europe by Air: US ☎888-387-2479; www.europebyair.com. Coupons good on 30 partner airlines to 150 European cities in 30 countries. Must be purchased prior to arrival in Europe. US$99 each, excluding airport tax. Also offers 15- and 21-day unlimited passes; US$699-$899.

Iberia: US ☎800-772-4642; www.iberia.com. "EuroPass" allows Iberia passengers flying from the US to Spain to tack on additional destinations in Europe.

KLM/Northwest: US ☎800-800-1504; www.nwavacations.com. "Passport to Europe," available to US transatlantic passengers, connects 90 European cities (3 cities min., 12 max.). US$100 each.

Lufthansa: US ☎800-399-5838; www.lufthansa.com. "Discover Europe" available to US travelers on transatlantic Lufthansa flights (3 cities min., 9 max.). US$119 each for the first three cities, US$99 each for additional cities.

Scandinavian Airlines (SAS): US ☎800-221-2350; www.scandinavian.net. One-way coupons for travel within Scandinavia, the Baltics, or all of Europe. US$75-155, 8 coupons max. Most are available only to transatlantic SAS passengers, but some United and Lufthansa passengers also qualify.

BritRail
LETS GO READERS
EURAIL
Buy a Rail Pass
and get ALL this FREE...
Eurotrip Discount Coupons
Save at European shops, restaurants, museums and more.
One FREE night at The Pink Palace
Includes breakfast and dinner at the world famous youth resort in Corfu, Greece.
FREE Eurail timetable, guide & map
with every order.
Passes issued on the spot
Same day shipping! RUSH ORDERS are our specialty.
Expert Advice and Service
For over 20 years we have helped thousands of people travel Europe by rail. From Eurail to Britrail, we'll help you pick the perfect pass for your trip.
AND
Easy online ordering
Hundreds of passes to choose from
No handling fees
GUARANTEED BEST PRICES
ORDER ONLINE and SAVE
www.LETSRAIL.com
1-866-RAIL-PASS
(1-866-724-5727)
WINNER of the Eurail Award
Visit these helpful sites when planning your trip
EUROTRIP.com and RAILSAVER.com

BY TRAIN

Trains in Western Europe are generally comfortable, convenient, and reasonably swift. Second-class compartments, which seat two to six, are great places to meet others. For long trips, make sure you are on the correct car, as trains sometimes split at crossroads. Towns listed in parentheses on European train schedules require a train switch at the town listed immediately before the parenthesis.

You can either buy a **railpass,** which allows you unlimited travel within a particular region for a given period of time, or rely on buying individual **point-to-point** tickets as you go. Almost all countries give students or youths (usually defined as anyone under 26) direct discounts on regular domestic rail tickets, and many also sell a student or youth card that provides 20-50% off all fares for up to a year

RESERVATIONS. While seat reservations (usually US$3-10) are required only for selected trains, you are not guaranteed a seat without one. You should strongly consider reserving in advance during peak holiday and tourist seasons (at the very latest, a few hours ahead). You will have to purchase a **supplement** (US$10-50) or special fare for high-speed or high-quality trains such as Spain's AVE, Cisalpino, Finland's Pendolino S220, Italy's ETR500 and Pendolino, Germany's ICE, and certain French TGVs. InterRail holders must also purchase supplements (US$10-25) for trains like EuroCity, InterCity, Sweden's X2000, and many French TGVs.

OVERNIGHT TRAINS. On night trains, you won't waste valuable daylight hours traveling and you can avoid the added expense of staying at a hotel. However, the main drawbacks include discomfort, sleepless nights, and the lack of scenery. **Sleeping accommodations** on trains differ from country to country, but typically you can either sleep upright in your seat (for free) or pay for a separate space. **Couchettes** (berths) typically have four to six seats per compartment (about US$20 per person); **sleepers** (beds) in private sleeping cars offer more privacy and comfort, but are considerably more expensive (US$40-150). If you are using a railpass valid only for a restricted number of days, inspect train schedules to maximize the use of your pass: an overnight train or boat journey uses up only one of your travel days if it departs after 7pm.

SHOULD YOU BUY A RAILPASS? Railpasses were conceived to allow you to jump on any train in Europe, go wherever you want whenever you want, and change your plans at will. In practice, it's not so simple. You still must stand in line to validate your pass, pay for supplements, and fork over cash for seat and couchette reservations. More importantly, railpasses don't always pay off. Consult our railplanner (at the front of this book) to estimate the point-to-point cost of each leg of your journey; add them up and compare the total with the cost of a railpass. If you are planning to spend extensive time on trains, hopping between big cities, a railpass will probably be worth it. But in many cases, especially if you are under 26, point-to-point tickets may prove a cheaper option.

You may find it tough to make your railpass pay for itself in Belgium, Greece, Ireland, Italy, Luxembourg, the Netherlands, Portugal, Spain, Eastern Europe, or the Balkans, where train fares are reasonable, distances short, or buses preferable. If, however, the total cost of your trips nears the price of the pass, the convenience of avoiding ticket lines may be worth the difference.

MULTINATIONAL RAILPASSES

EURAIL. Eurail is valid in most of Western Europe: Austria, Belgium, Denmark, Finland, France, Germany, Greece, Holland, Hungary, Italy, Luxembourg, Norway, Portugal, the Republic of Ireland, Spain, Sweden, and Switzerland. It is not valid in

ESSENTIALS

the UK. Standard **Eurailpasses,** valid for a consecutive given number of days, are best for those planning on spending extensive time on trains every few days. **Flexipasses,** valid for any 10 or 15 (not necessarily consecutive) days within a two-month period, are more cost-effective for those traveling longer distances less frequently. **Saverpasses** provide first-class travel for travelers in groups of two to five (prices are per person). **Youthpasses** and **Youth Flexipasses** provide parallel second-class perks for those under 26. As of January 1, 2003, the Europass will be replaced by the **Selectpass,** which allows five to 15 travel days within a two-month period, in three to five pre-selected, contiguous countries. (For the purpose of the Selectpass, Belgium, The Netherlands, and Luxembourg are considered one country.) Youth and Saver Selectpasses are also available.

EURAILPASSES	15 DAYS	21 DAYS	1 MONTH	2 MONTHS	3 MONTHS
Eurailpass	US$588	US$762	US$946	US$1338	US$1654
Eurailpass Saver	US$498	US$648	US$804	US$1138	US$1408
Eurailpass Youth	US$414	US$534	US$664	US$938	US$1160

SELECTPASSES	5 DAYS	6 DAYS	8 DAYS	10 DAYS	15 DAYS
Selectpass: 3-country	US$356	US$394	US$470	US$542	N/A
4-country	US$398	US$436	US$512	US$584	N/A
5-country	US$438	US$476	US$552	US$624	US$794
Saver: 3-country	US$304	US$336	US$400	US$460	N/A
4-country	US$340	US$372	US$436	US$496	N/A
5-country	US$374	US$406	US$470	US$560	US$674
Youth: 3-country	US$249	US$276	US$329	US$379	N/A
4-country	US$279	US$306	US$359	US$409	N/A
5-country	US$307	US$334	US$387	US$437	US$556

FLEXIPASS	10 DAYS IN 2 MONTHS	15 DAYS IN 2 MONTHS
Flexipass	US$694	US$914
Flexipass Saver	US$592	US$778
Flexipass Youth	US$488	US$642

Passholders receive a timetable for major routes and a map with details on possible ferry, steamer, bus, car rental, hotel, and Eurostar (see p. 47) discounts. Passholders often also receive reduced fares or free passage on many bus and boat lines.

SHOPPING AROUND FOR A EURAIL OR EUROPASS. Eurailpasses and Europasses are designed by the EU itself, and can be bought only by non-Europeans almost exclusively from non-European distributors. These passes must be sold at uniform prices determined by the EU. However, some travel agents tack on a US$10 handling fee, and others offer certain bonuses with purchase, so shop around. Also, keep in mind that pass prices usually go up each year, so if you're planning to travel early in the year, you can save cash by purchasing before January 1 (you have three months from the purchase date to validate your pass in Europe). It is best to buy your Eurail- or Europass before leaving; only a few places in major European cities sell them, and at a marked-up price. You can get a replacement for a lost pass only if you have purchased insurance on it under the Pass Protection Plan (US$14). Passes are available through travel agents and student travel agencies like STA and Council (see p. 41). Several companies specialize in selecting and distributing appropriate railpasses; two to try are **Rail Europe** (US ☎888-382-7245; UK ☎0990 84 88 48; www.raileurope.com) and **Railpass.com** (US ☎877-724-5727; www.railpass.com/new).

OTHER MULTINATIONAL PASSES. If your travels will be limited to one area, regional passes are often good values. The new **France'n Italy Pass** lets you travel in France and Italy for 4 days in a 2 month period (standard US$239, under 26 US$199). If your travels will be limited to one area, regional passes are often good values. The **ScanRail Pass,** which covers rail travel in Denmark, Finland, Norway, and Sweden, is available both in the UK and the US (standard/under 26 passes for 5 days out of 1 month of 2nd-class travel US$214/161; 10 days out of 2 months US$288/216; 21 consecutive days US$332/249). The **Benelux Tourrail Pass** for Belgium, the Netherlands, and Luxembourg is available in the UK, in the US (5 days in 1 month 2nd-class US$155, under 26 US$104; discount for companion traveler), and at train stations in Belgium and Luxembourg (but not the Netherlands). The **Balkan Flexipass** is valid for travel in Bulgari a, Greece, Macedonia, Montenegro, Romania, Serbia, Turkey, and Yugoslavia (5 days in 1 month US$152, under 26 US$90). The **European East Pass** covers Austria, the Czech Republic, Hungary, Poland, and Slovakia (adults over 12 US$154 for 5 days in 1 month).

INTERRAIL PASS. **InterRail Passes** are another economical option, but can only be purchased if you have lived for at least six months in a European country. There are eight InterRail **zones.** The **Under 26 InterRail Card** allows either 21 consecutive days or one month of unlimited travel within one, two, three or all of the eight zones; the cost is determined by the number of zones the pass covers (UK£119-249). A card can also be purchased for 12 days of travel in one zone (119£). The **Over 26 InterRail Card** (UK£169-355) provides the same services as the Under 26 InterRail Card as does the new **Child Pass** (ages 4-11; UK£85-178). Passholders receive **discounts** on rail travel, Eurostar trains, and most ferries to Ireland, Scandinavia, and the rest of Europe. Most exclude **supplements** for high-speed trains. For info and ticket sales in Europe contact **Student Travel Centre,** 24 Rupert St., 1st fl., London W1V 7FN (☎020 7437 8101; fax 020 7734 3836; www.student-travel-centre.com). Tickets are also available from travel agents, at major train stations throughout Europe, or through on-line vendors (www.railpassdirect.co.uk)

DOMESTIC RAILPASSES

If you are planning to spend a significant amount of time within one country or region, a national pass—valid on all rail lines of a country's rail company—will probably be more cost-effective than a multinational pass. Several national and regional passes offer companion fares, allowing two adults traveling together to save about 50% on the price of one pass. However, many national passes are limited and don't provide the free or discounted travel on many private railways and ferries that Eurail does. Some of these passes can be bought only in Europe, some only outside of Europe; check with a railpass agent or with national tourist offices.

NATIONAL RAILPASSES. The domestic analogs of the Eurailpass, national railpasses (called "flexipasses" for some countries) are valid either for a given number of consecutive days or for a specific number of days within a given period. Usually, they must be purchased before you leave. Though national passes will usually save frequent travelers money, in some cases you may find that they are actually more expensive than point-to-point tickets. For more information, contact Rail Europe (see p. 52).

EURO DOMINO. Like the InterRail Pass, the Euro Domino pass is available to anyone who has lived in Europe for at least six months; however, it is only valid within the country that you designate upon buying the pass, which may not be your country of residence. The Euro Domino pass is available for 29 European countries including Morocco, for first- and second-class travel (with a special rate for those under 26). It can be used for three to eight days of unlimited travel within a one-month period, but is not valid on Eurostar or Thalys trains. **Supplements** for many high-speed (e.g., French TGV, German ICE, and Swedish X2000, but not the Spanish AVE) trains are included, though you must still pay for **reservations** where they are compulsory. The pass must be bought within your country of residence; each destination has a different price. Inquire with your national rail company for more information.

REGIONAL PASSES. When your main pass is not valid, regional passes are useful add-ons. Areas where regional passes are often used include **Prague, Copenhagen,** and **southeast England** (see country chapters for more information.)

RAIL-AND-DRIVE PASSES. In addition to simple railpasses, many countries (as well as Europass and Eurail) offer rail-and-drive passes, which combine car rental with rail travel—a good option for travelers who wish both to visit cities accessible by rail and to make side trips into the surrounding areas. Contact a budget travel agency for more information (see p. 41)

DISCOUNTED RAIL TICKETS

For travelers under 26, **BIJ** tickets (Billets Internationals de Jeunesse, i.e. **Wasteels, Eurotrain,** and **Route 26**) are a great alternative to railpasses. Available for international trips within Europe and for travel within France as well as most ferry services, they knock 20-40% off regular 2nd-class fares. Tickets are good for 60 days after purchase and allow a number of stopovers along the normal direct route of the train journey. Issued for a specific international route between two points, they must be used in the direction and order of the designated route and must be bought in Europe. The equivalent for those over 26, **BIGT** tickets provide a 20-30% discount on 1st- and 2nd-class international tickets for business travelers, temporary residents of Europe, and their families. Both types of tickets are available from European travel agents, at Wasteels or Eurotrain offices (usually in or near train stations), or directly at the ticket counter in some nations. For more info, see www.wasteels.com.

FURTHER RESOURCES ON TRAIN TRAVEL.

Point-to-point fares and schedules: www.raileurope.com/us/rail/fares_schedules/index.htm. Allows you to calculate whether buying a railpass would save you money. See also our **railmap** (p. xvi).

European Railway Servers: mercurio.iet.unipi.it/misc/timetabl.html. Links to rail servers throughout Europe.

Info on rail travel and railpasses: www.eurorail.com; www.raileuro.com.

Thomas Cook European Timetable, updated monthly, covers all major and most minor train routes in Europe. In the US, order it from Forsyth Travel Library (US$27.95; ☎800-367-7984; www.forsyth.com). In Europe, find it at any Thomas Cook Money Exchange Center. Alternatively, buy directly from Thomas Cook (www.thomascookpublishing.com).

Guide to European Railpasses, Rick Steves. Free on-line at www.ricksteves.com/subscribe/home.htm (US ☎425-771-8303).

On the Rails Around Europe: A Comprehensive Guide to Travel by Train, Melissa Shales. Thomas Cook Ltd. (US$18.95).

Europe By Eurail 2002, Laverne Ferguson-Kosinski. Globe Pequot Press (US$17.95).

BY BUS

Though European trains and railpasses are extremely popular, buses may prove a better option. In Spain, Hungary, and the Baltics, the bus and train systems are on par; in Britain, Greece, Ireland, Portugal, and Turkey, bus networks are more extensive, efficient, and often more comfortable. In the rest of Europe, scattered offerings from private companies can be inexpensive but sometimes unreliable. Often cheaper than railpasses, **international bus passes** typically allow unlimited travel on a hop-on, hop-off basis between major European cities. In general these services tend to be more popular among non-American backpackers. Note that **Eurobus,** a former UK-based bus service, is no longer in operation. **Contiki Holidays** (888-CONTIKI; www.contiki.com) offers a variety of European packages designed exclusively for 18- to 35-year-olds. For an average cost of $60 per day, tours include accommodations, transportation, guided sightseeing and some meals.

Eurolines, 52 Grosvenor Gardens, London SW1W 0AU (UK ☎ 1582 404 511; www.eurolines.co.uk or www.eurolines.com). The largest operator of Europe-wide coach services, Eurolines offers unlimited peak-season 30-day (UK£229, under 26 UK£186) or 60-day (UK£279/205) travel between 30 major European cities in 16 countries; off-season prices are lower. Euroexplorers mini-passes offer stops at select cities across Europe (UK£55 to UK£69).

Busabout, 258 Vauxhall Bridge Rd., London SW1V 1BS (☎ 207 950 1661; fax 950 1662; www.busabout.com). Offers 5 interconnecting bus circuits covering 60 cities and towns in Europe. Consecutive Day Passes and Flexi Passes both available. Consecutive Day standard/student passes range from US$269/239 for 2 weeks to US$1069/959 for a season pass.

BY CAR

Cars offer speed, freedom, access to the countryside, and an escape from the town-to-town mentality of trains. However, they also insulate you from the rail travel culture of Western Europe. A single traveler won't save by renting a car, but a group might. You can also combine train and car travel; RailEurope and other railpass vendors offer **rail-and-drive packages** for both individual countries and all of Europe. **Fly-and-drive packages** are also often available from travel agents or airline/rental agency partnerships.

Before setting off, know the laws of the countries in which you'll be driving (e.g., keep left in Ireland and the UK). Remember that in most of Europe **automatic transmission** is hard to find. Cheaper cars tend to be less reliable and harder to handle on difficult terrain. Less expensive 4WD vehicles in particular tend to be more top heavy and are more dangerous when navigating particularly bumpy roads. Western European roads are generally excellent, but keep in mind that each area has its own hazards. Even in areas with official speed limits, Europeans tend to drive *fast,* and roads are often curvy, particularly in mountainous areas. Road conditions fluctuate with the seasons; for instance, winter weather will make driving difficult in some countries, while summer weather causes flooding in others. For an informal primer on European road signs and conventions, check out www.travlang.com/signs. Additionally, the **Association for Safe International Road Travel (ASIRT),** 11769 Gainsborough Rd., Potomac, MD 20854, USA (☎ 301-983-5252; fax 983-3663; www.asirt.org), can provide more specific information about road conditions. ASIRT considers road travel (by car or bus) to be relatively **safe** in Denmark, Ireland, The Netherlands, Switzerland, and the UK. Western Europeans use **unleaded Petrol (gasoline)** almost exclusively. Carry emergency equipment with you and know what to do in case of a breakdown.

ESSENTIALS

> **DRIVING PRECAUTIONS.** When traveling in the summer, bring substantial amounts of water (5L of **water** per person per day) for drinking and for the radiator. For long drives to unpopulated areas, register with police before beginning your trek, and again upon arrival at the destination. Check with the local automobile club for details. When traveling for long distances, make sure tires are in good repair and have enough air, and **get good maps**. A **compass** and a **car manual** can also be very useful. You should always carry a **spare tire** and **jack, jumper cables, extra oil, flares, a flashlight,** and **heavy blankets** (in case your car breaks down at night or in the winter). If you don't know how to **change a tire,** learn before heading out, especially if you are planning on traveling in deserted areas. Blowouts on dirt roads are exceedingly common. If you do have a breakdown, **stay with your car;** if you wander off, there's less likelihood that trackers will find you.

DRIVING PERMITS AND CAR INSURANCE

INTERNATIONAL DRIVING PERMIT (IDP). If you plan to drive a car while abroad, you must be over 18 and have an **International Driving Permit (IDP),** though certain countries allow travelers to drive with a valid American or Canadian license for a limited number of months. It may be a good idea to get one anyway, in case you're in an accident or stranded in a smaller town where the police do not know English. Information on the IDP is printed in ten languages, including Spanish, French, Italian, Portuguese, and German.

Your IDP, valid for one year, must be issued in your own country before you depart. An application for an IDP usually needs to include one or two photos, a current local license, an additional form of identification, and a fee (about US$10). To apply, contact the national or local branch of your home country's automobile association.

CAR INSURANCE. If you rent, lease, or borrow a car, you will need a **green card,** or **International Insurance Certificate** to certify that you have liability insurance and that it applies abroad. Green cards can be obtained at car rental agencies, car dealers (for those leasing cars), some travel agents, and some border crossings. Rental agencies may require you to purchase theft insurance in countries that they consider to have a high risk of auto theft.

RENTING A CAR

You can rent a car from a US-based firm (Alamo, Avis, Budget, or Hertz) with European offices, from a European-based company with local representatives (Europcar), or from a tour operator (Auto Europe, Europe By Car, or Kemwel Holiday Autos) that will arrange a rental from a European company at its own rates. Multinationals offer greater flexibility, but tour operators often strike better deals. Rentals for smaller cars can vary from about US$100-300 per week, plus tax (5-25%). While price differences between countries are small overall, Denmark, Ireland, and Italy tend to be slightly more expensive, particularly during summer; Austria, Greece, and the Netherlands have the lowest rates.

Some chains allow you to choose a drop-off location different from your pick-up city, but there is often a minimum hire period and extra charge. Reserve ahead and pay in advance if possible. It is usually less expensive to reserve a car from the US than in Europe. Always check if prices quoted include tax and collision insurance; some credit card companies cover the deductible on collision insurance, allowing their customers to decline the collision damage waiver. Ask about discounts and check the terms of insurance, particularly the size of the deductible. Ask airlines about special fly-and-drive packages; you may get up to a week of free or discounted rental. Minimum age varies by country, but is usually 21 to 25. To rent a car, you will need a valid license and proof that you've had it for a year. European rental agencies include:

Auto Europe, US ☎888-223-5555; fax 207-842-2222; www.autoeurope.com.

Avis, US ☎800-230-4898; Canada ☎800-272-5871; UK ☎0870 606 0100; Australia ☎136 333; www.avis.com.

Budget, US ☎800-527-0700; international US ☎800-472-3325; www.budget.com.

Europe by Car, US ☎800-223-1516; www.europebycar.com.

Europcar, France ☎03 31 30 44 90 00; US ☎877-506-0070; www.europcar.com.

Hertz, US ☎800-654-3131; Canada ☎800-263-0600; UK ☎870 844 8844; Australia ☎613 9698 2555; www.hertz.com.

Kemwel Holiday Autos, US ☎877-820-0668; www.kemwel.com.

LEASING A CAR

For longer than 17 days, leasing can be cheaper than renting; it is often the only option for those ages 18 to 21. The cheapest leases are agreements to buy the car and then sell it back to the manufacturer at a prearranged price; as a lease, however, there won't really be any enormous financial transactions. Leases generally include insurance coverage and are not taxed. Leases are least expensive in France, with additional fees in other countries. Expect to pay around US$1100-1800 (depending on size of car) for 60 days. Contact **Auto Europe, Europe by Car,** or **Kemwel Holiday Autos** (see above) before you go.

BUYING A CAR

If you're brave and know what you're doing, **buying** a used car or van in Western Europe and selling it just before you leave can provide the cheapest wheels for longer trips. Check with consulates for import-export laws concerning used vehicles, registration, and safety and emissions standards. Camper-vans and motor homes give the advantages of a car without the hassle and expense of finding lodgings. Most of these vehicles are diesel-powered and deliver roughly 24 to 30 miles per gallon of diesel fuel, which is cheaper than regular gas.

BY FERRY

Most European ferries are quite comfortable; even the cheapest ticket typically includes a reclining chair or couchette. Fares jump sharply in July and August, but can be reduced—ISIC holders can often get student fares, and Eurailpass holders may get discounts or free trips. Occasional port taxes are less than US$10. For more info, consult the *Official Steamship Guide International* (available at travel agents) or www.youra.com/ferry.

ENGLISH CHANNEL AND IRISH SEA FERRIES. Ferries are frequent and dependable. The main route from England to France is **Dover-Calais**. The main ferry port on the southern coast of England is Portsmouth, with connections to France and Spain. Ferries also cross the **Irish Sea**, connecting Northern Ireland with Scotland and England and the Republic of Ireland with Wales (see p. 48).

NORTH AND BALTIC SEA FERRIES. Ferries in the **North Sea** are reliable and convenient. Those content with deck passage rarely need to book ahead. For ferries heading to and from the UK, see p. 49. **Baltic Sea** ferries service routes between Poland and Scandinavia.

Color Line: Norway ☎22 94 44 00; www.colorline.com. Offers ferries between Norway and Denmark, Sweden and Germany.

DFDS Seaways: US ☎800-533-3755; www.seaeurope.com. Offers routes within Scandinavia and between Scandinavia and England, Germany, Holland, and Poland.

Polferries: Sweden ☎84 11 49 80; www.polferries.com.pl/ieen. Ferries run from Poland to Sweden and Denmark.

Silja Line: US sales ☎800-323-7436, Finland ☎09 18041; www.silja.com. Helsinki to Stockholm (16hr.); Tallinn, Estonia (3hr., June to mid-Sept.); and Rostock, Germany (23-25hr., June to mid-Sept.). Also Turku to Stockholm (10hr.).

MEDITERRANEAN AND AEGEAN FERRIES. Mediterranean ferries, which run from France and Spain to Morocco, may be glamorous, but can also be the rockiest. Reservations are recommended, especially in July and August. Many companies operate on erratic schedules, with similar routes and varying prices; shop around, and beware of unreliable lines that don't take reservations. Bring toilet paper.

Companies such as **Superfast Ferries** (US ☎954-771-9200; www.superfast.com) offer routes across the **Adriatic and Ionian Seas** from Ancona and Bari, Italy, to Patras, and Igoumenitsa, Greece. **Eurail** is valid on certain ferries between Brindisi, Italy and Corfu, Igoumenitsa, and Patras, Greece. Countless ferry companies operate these routes simultaneously; websites such as www.ferries.gr list various schedules. See specific country chapters for more information.

BY BICYCLE

Biking is one of the key elements of the classic budget Eurovoyage. Many airlines will count your bike as your second free piece of luggage; a few charge extra (up to US$110 one-way). Bikes must be packed in a cardboard box with the pedals and front wheel detached; airlines often sell bike boxes at the airport (US$10). Most ferries let you take your bike for free or for a nominal fee, and you can always ship your bike on trains. If your touring will be confined to one or two regions, renting a bike beats bringing your own. Some youth hostels rent bicycles for low prices. In Switzerland, train stations rent bikes and often allow you to drop them off elsewhere; check train stations throughout Europe for similar deals.

In addition to **panniers** in which you can pack your luggage, you'll need a good **helmet** ($25-50) and a U-shaped **Citadel** or **Kryptonite lock** (from $30). For equipment, **Bike Nashbar,** 6103 State Rte. 446, Canfield, OH 44406 (☎800-627-4227; www.nashbar.com), ships anywhere in the US or Canada. For more country-specific books on biking through France, Germany, Ireland, or the UK, or to purchase *Europe by Bike*, by Karen and Terry Whitehall (US$14.95), try **Mountaineers Books,** (☎800 553-4453; www.mountaineersbooks.org).

BIKE TOURS. If you are nervous about striking out on your own, several companies lead European bike tours.

Bike Tours Ltd of Bath (UK ☎1225 310 859; www.biketours.co.uk) offers various 1- to 2-week tours throughout Europe.

Blue Marble Travel (US ☎215 923-3788; www.bluemarble.org) leads dozens of trips through Western Europe and Scandinavia that range from 6 days to 5 weeks.

CBT Tours (US ☎800-736-2453; www.cbttours.com) offers full-package 9- to 13-day biking, mountain biking, and hiking tours (around US$190 per day) in Western and Central Europe and the Netherlands.

EURO Bike and Walking Tours (US ☎800-321-6060; www.eurobike.com) gives dozens of 6- to 5-day bike tours across Central and Western Europe, and the Netherlands.

BY MOPED AND MOTORCYCLE

Motorized bikes (mopeds) use little gas, can be put on trains and ferries, and are a good compromise between the cost of car travel and the limited range of bicycles. However, they're uncomfortable for long distances, dangerous in the rain, and unpredictable on rough roads and gravel. Always wear a helmet and never ride with a backpack. If you've never been on a moped before, a twisting Alpine road is not the place to start. Expect to pay about US$20-35 per day; try auto repair or bike rental shops, and remember to bargain. Motorcycles can be much more expensive and normally require a license, but are better for long distances. Before renting, ask if the quoted price includes tax and insurance to avoid unexpected additional fees. Avoid offering your passport as a deposit; if you have an accident or mechanical failure you may not get it back until you cover all repairs. Pay ahead of time instead. For more information, try *Motorcycle Journeys through the Alps and Corsica*, by John Hermann (US$24.95), *Motorcycle Touring and Travel*, by Bill Stermer (US$19.95), both Whitehorse Press, or *Europe by Motorcycle*, by Gregory W. Frazier (Arrowstar Publishing, US$19.95).

BY FOOT

Europe's grandest scenery can often be seen only by foot. *Let's Go* describes many daytrips for those who want to hoof it, but locals, hostel proprietors, and fellow travelers are the best source of tips. Many European countries have hiking and mountaineering organizations; alpine clubs in Germany, Austria, Switzerland, and Italy, as well as tourist organizations in Scandinavia, provide simple accommodations in splendid settings.

BY THUMB

> **!** *Let's Go* strongly urges you to consider the risks before you choose to hitch. We do not recommend hitching as a safe means of transportation, and none of the information presented here is intended to do so.

Never hitch before carefully considering the risks involved. Hitching means entrusting your life to a random person that happens to stop beside you on the road, and risking theft, assault, sexual harassment, and unsafe driving. In spite of this, there are advantages to hitching when it is safe: it allows you to meet local people and get where you're going, especially in northern Europe and Ireland, where public transportation is poor. The choice, however, remains yours.

Safety-minded hitchers avoid getting in the back of two-door cars (or any car they wouldn't be able to get out of in a hurry) and never let go of their backpacks. If you ever feel threatened, insist on being let off immediately. Acting as if you are going to open the car door or vomit will usually get a driver to stop. Hitchhiking at night can be particularly dangerous; experienced hitchers stand in well-lit places and expect drivers to be leery of nocturnal thumbers.

Getting a lift in Britain and Ireland is easy. In Scandinavia, hitching is slow but steady. Hitching in Southern Europe is generally mediocre; France is the worst. Long-distance hitching in the developed countries of northwestern Europe demands close attention to expressway junctions, rest stop locations, and destination signs. For women traveling alone, hitching is just too dangerous. A man and a woman are a safer combination, but men traveling together may have a harder time getting a ride.

Experienced hitchers pick spots where drivers will have time to look over potential passengers as they approach; rest stops or entrance ramps to highways are common pick-up spots. Hitching on super-highways is usually illegal. In the **Practical Information** section of many cities, *Let's Go* lists the tram or bus lines that take travelers to strategic hitching points. Most Europeans signal with an open hand rather than a thumb; many write their destination on a sign in large, bold letters and draw a smiley-face under it. Drivers prefer hitchers who are neat and wholesome; rarely are people wearing sunglasses picked up.

RIDE SERVICES. Most Western European countries offer a ride service (listed in the **Practical Information** for major cities), a cross between hitchhiking and the ride boards common at many universities, which pairs drivers with riders; the fee varies according to destination. **Eurostop International** (**Verband der Deutschen Mitfahrzentralen** in Germany and **Allostop** in France) is one of the largest in Europe. Riders and drivers can register online at www.taxistop.be.

SPECIFIC CONCERNS

WOMEN TRAVELERS

Women exploring on their own inevitably face some additional safety concerns, but it's easy to be adventurous without taking undue risks. If you are concerned, consider staying in hostels which offer single rooms that lock from the inside or in religious organizations with rooms for women only. Stick to centrally located accommodations and avoid solitary late-night treks or metro rides.

Always carry extra money for a phone call, bus, or taxi. **Hitchhiking** is never safe for lone women, or even for two women traveling together. When on overnight or long train rides, if there is no women-only compartment, choose one that is occupied by women or couples. Look as if you know where you're going and approach older women or couples for directions if you're lost or uncomfortable.

Generally, the less you look like a tourist, the better off you'll be. Dress conservatively, especially in rural areas. Trying to fit in can be effective, but dressing to the style of an obviously different culture may cause you to be ill at ease and a conspicuous target. Wearing a conspicuous **wedding band** may help prevent unwanted overtures.

FURTHER READING: WOMEN TRAVELERS.

Active Women Vacation Guide, Evelyn Kaye. Blue Panda Publications (US$18).

A Foxy Old Woman's Guide to Traveling Alone: Around Town and Around the World, Jay Ben-Lesser. Crossing Press (US$11).

A Journey of One's Own: Uncommon Advice for the Independent Woman Traveler, Thalia Zepatos. Eighth Mountain Press (US$17).

Safety and Security for Women Who Travel, Sheila Swan. Travelers' Tales Guides, Inc. (US$13).

Your best answer to verbal harassment is no answer at all; feigning deafness, sitting motionless, and staring straight ahead at nothing in particular will do a world of good that reactions usually don't achieve. The extremely persistent can sometimes be dissuaded by a firm, loud, and very public "Go away!" in the appropriate language. Don't hesitate to seek out a police officer or a passerby if you are being harassed. Memorize the emergency numbers in places you visit, and consider carrying a whistle or airhorn on your keychain. A self-defense course will not only prepare you for a potential attack, but will also raise your level of awareness of your surroundings as well as your confidence (see **Self Defense**, p. 23). Also be sure you are aware of the health concerns that women face when traveling (see p. 28).

Journeywoman (www.journeywoman.com) posts an online newsletter and other resources providing female-specific travel tips. *Women Traveling Together* (www.women-traveling.com) places women in small groups to travel together.

TRAVELING ALONE

There are many benefits to traveling alone, including independence and greater interaction with locals. On the other hand, any solo traveler is a more vulnerable target of harassment and street theft. As a lone traveler, try not to stand out as a tourist, and be especially careful in deserted or very crowded areas. If questioned, never admit that you are traveling alone. Maintain regular contact with someone at home who knows your itinerary. For more tips, pick up *Traveling Solo* by Eleanor Berman (Globe Pequot Press, US$17), or subscribe to **Connecting: Solo Travel Network,** 689 Park Road, Unit 6, Gibsons, BC V0N 1V7, Canada (☎604-886-9099; www.cstn.org; membership US$35). Alternatively, several services will link solo travelers with companions who have similar travel habits and interests; **Travel Companion Exchange,** P.O. Box 833, Amityville, NY 11701 (☎800-392-1256; www.whytravelalone.com; US$48).

OLDER TRAVELERS

Senior citizens are eligible for a wide range of discounts on transportation, museums, movies, theaters, concerts, restaurants, and accommodations. If you don't see a senior citizen price listed, ask; you may be surprised. The books *No Problem! Worldwise Tips for Mature Adventurers*, by Janice Kenyon (Orca Book Publishers, US$16) and *Unbelievably Good Deals and Great Adventures That You Absolutely Can't Get Unless You're Over 50*, by Joan Rattner Heilman (NTC/Contemporary Publishing, US$13) are both excellent resources. For more information, contact one of the following organizations:

ElderTreks, 597 Markham St., Toronto, ON M6G 2L7, Canada (☎800-741-7956; www.eldertreks.com). Adventure travel programs for the 50+ traveler.

Elderhostel, 11 Ave. de Lafayette, Boston, MA 02111, USA (☎877-426-8056; www.elderhostel.org). Organizes 1- to 4-week "educational adventures" throughout Western Europe on varied subjects for those 55+.

The Mature Traveler, P.O. Box 15791, Sacramento, CA 95852, USA (☎800-460-6676). Deals, discounts, and travel packages for the 50+ traveler. Subscription US$30.

Walking the World, P.O. Box 1186, Fort Collins, CO 80522, USA (☎800-340-9255; www.walkingtheworld.com), organizes trips for 50+ travelers in many Western European countries.

BISEXUAL, GAY, & LESBIAN TRAVELERS

Attitudes toward bisexual, gay, and lesbian travelers are particular to each region in Western Europe. Consult the **Further Reading** box below for books that include individual country information. Acceptance is generally highest in large cities. Listed below are contact organizations, mail-order bookstores, and publishers that offer materials addressing some specific concerns. **Out and About** (www.outandabout.com) has a comprehensive website addressing travel concerns and ideas.

FURTHER READING: BISEXUAL, GAY, & LESBIAN.

Damron Men's Travel Guide, Damron Women's Traveller, Damron's Accommodations, and *Damron Amsterdam Guide.* Damron Travel Guides (US$10-19). For more info, call 800-462-6654 or visit www.damron.com.

Ferrari Guides' Gay Travel A to Z and Ferrari *Guides' Men's Travel in Your Pocket.* Ferrari Publications (US$19-20).

Odysseus International Gay Travel Planner, Eli Angelo and Joseph Bain. Odysseus Enterprises. (US$31).

Spartacus International Gay Guide 2002-2003, Bruno Gmunder Verlag (US$33).

Gay's the Word, 66 Marchmont St., London WC1N 1AB, UK (☎4420 7278 7654; www.gaystheword.co.uk). The largest gay and lesbian bookshop in the UK, with both fiction and non-fiction titles. Mail-order service available.

Giovanni's Room, 1145 Pine St., Philadelphia, PA 19107, USA (☎215-923-2960; www.queerbooks.com). An international lesbian/feminist and gay bookstore with mail-order service (carries many of the publications listed below).

International Gay and Lesbian Travel Association, International Lesbian and Gay Association (ILGA), 81 r. Marché-au-Charbon, B-1000 Brussels, Belgium (☎32 2 502 2471; www.ilga.org). Provides political information, such as homosexuality laws of individual countries.

TRAVELERS WITH DISABILITIES

Countries vary in accessibility to travelers with disabilities. Some national and regional tourist boards provide directories on the accessibility of various accommodations and transportation services. If these services are not available, contact institutions directly. Those with disabilities should inform airlines and hotels of their disabilities when making reservations; some time may be needed to prepare special accommodations. Call ahead to restaurants, museums, and other facilities to find out if they are handicapped-accessible. **Guide dog owners** should inquire as to the quarantine policies of each destination country.

Rail is probably the most convenient form of travel for disabled travelers in Europe: many stations have ramps, and some trains have wheelchair lifts, special seating areas, and specially equipped toilets. Greece and Spain's rail systems have limited resources for wheelchair accessibility. For those who wish to rent cars, some major car rental agencies (Hertz, Avis, and National) offer hand-controlled vehicles.

USEFUL ORGANIZATIONS

Mobility International USA (MIUSA), P.O. Box 10767, Eugene, OR 97440 (US ☎541-343-1284, voice and TDD; www.miusa.org). Sells *A World of Options: A Guide to International Educational Exchange, Community Service, and Travel for Persons with Disabilities* (US$35).

Moss Rehab ResourceNet, (www.mossresourcenet.org). An Internet information resource center on international travel accessibility and other travel-related concerns for those with disabilities.

Society for Accessible Travel & Hospitality (SATH), 347 Fifth Ave., #610, New York, NY 10016 (US ☎212-447-7284; www.sath.org). An advocacy group that publishes free online travel information and the travel magazine *OPEN WORLD* (US$18, free for members). Annual membership US$45, students and seniors US$30.

FURTHER RESOURCES: DISABILITIES.

The Guided Tour Inc., 7900 Old York Rd., #114B, Elkins, PA 19027 (☎800-783-5841 or 215-782-1370; www.guidedtour.com). Organizes travel programs for persons with physical challenges around London and Paris.

Around the World Resource Guide, Patricia Smither. Access for Disabled American Publishing (US$15).

Wheelchair Around the World, Patrick D. Simpson. Ivy House Publishing Group (US$25).

Wheelchair Through Europe, Annie Mackin. Graphic Language Press (US$13).

MINORITY TRAVELERS

In general, minority travelers will find a high level of tolerance in large cities; the small towns and the countryside are more unpredictable. *Romany* (Gypsies) encounter the most hostility throughout Eastern Europe, and travelers with darker skin might be mistaken for them and face unpleasant consequences. Other minority travelers, especially those of African or Asian descent, will usually meet with more curiosity than hostility; travelers of Arab ethnicity may be treated more suspiciously. Skinheads are on the rise in Europe, and minority travelers, especially Jews and blacks, should regard them with caution. Anti-Semitism is still a problem in many countries; it is generally best to be discreet about your religion. Still, attitudes will vary; travelers should use common sense—consult **Safety and Security** (see p. 23) for tips on how to avoid unwanted attention.

TRAVELERS WITH CHILDREN

Family vacations often require that you slow your pace and always require that you plan ahead. If you rent a car, make sure the rental company provides a car seat for younger children. **Be sure that your child carries some sort of ID** in case of an emergency or in case he or she gets lost. Museums, tourist attractions, accommodations, and restaurants often offer discounts for children. Children under two generally fly for 10% of the adult airfare on international flights (this does not necessarily include a seat). International fares are usually discounted 25% for children from two to 11.

FURTHER READING: TRAVELERS WITH CHILDREN.

Take Your Kids to Europe, Cynthia W. Harriman. Globe Pequot Press (US$18).

Have Kid, Will Travel: 101 Survival Strategies for Vacationing With Babies and

The Penny Whistle Traveling with Kids Book: Whether by Boat, Train, Car or Plane – How to Take the Best Trip Ever WIth Kids of All Ages, Meredith Brokaw. Fireside (US$14).

Young Children, Claire and Lucille Tristram. Andrews McMeel Publishing (US$9).

Adventuring with Children: An Inspirational Guide to World Travel and the Outdoors, Nan Jeffrey. Menasha Ridge Press (US$15).

Trouble Free Travel with Children, Vicki Lansky. Book Peddlers (US$9).

DIETARY CONCERNS

Vegetarians should have no problem finding suitable cuisine in most of Western Europe. Particularly in city listings, *Let's Go* notes many restaurants that cater to vegetarians or that offer good vegetarian selections. The North American Vegetarian Society, P.O. Box 72, Dolgeville, NY 13329, USA (☎518-568-7970; www.navs-online.org), publishes information about vegetarian travel, including *Transformative Adventures, A Guide to Vacations and Retreats* (US$15).

Travelers who keep **kosher** should contact synagogues in cities for information on kosher restaurants. Your own synagogue or college Hillel should have access to lists of Jewish institutions in Western Europe. If you are strict in your observance, you may have to prepare your own food on the road. A good resources is the *Jewish Travel Guide*, by Michael Zaidner (Vallentine Mitchell, US$17).

OTHER RESOURCES

Although *Let's Go* tries to cover all aspects of budget travel, we can't include *everything*. Listed below are books, organizations and websites for your own research.

TRAVEL PUBLISHERS AND BOOKSTORES

Adventurous Traveler Bookstore, 245 S. Champlain St., Burlington, VT 05401, USA (☎800-282-3963; www.adventuroustraveler.com), offers information and gear for outdoor and adventure travel.

Bon Voyage!, 2069 W. Bullard Ave., Fresno, CA 93711, USA (☎800-995-9716, elsewhere call US ☎559-447-8441; fax 447-8456; www.bon-voyage-travel.com), specializes in Europe and sells videos, travel gear, books, maps, and railpasses. Free newsletter.

Hippocrene Books, Inc., 171 Madison Ave., New York, NY 10016, USA (☎718-454-2366; www.hippocrenebooks.com). Publishes travel guides, as well as foreign language dictionaries and learning guides. Free catalog.

Hunter Publishing, 130 Campus Dr., Edison, NJ 08818, USA (☎800-255-0343; www.hunterpublishing.com). Has an extensive catalog of travel guides and diving and adventure travel books.

Rand McNally, 8255 N. Central Park Ave., Skokie, IL 60076, USA (☎800-275-7263; international 847-329-6656; fax 329-6659; www.randmcnally.com), publishes a number of comprehensive road atlases (from US$10).

WORLD WIDE WEB

Listed here are some budget travel sites to start off your surfing; other relevant web sites are listed throughout the book.

THE ART OF BUDGET TRAVEL

Backpacker's Ultimate Guide: www.bugeurope.com. Tips on packing, transportation, and where to go. Also tons of country-specific travel information.

Backpack Europe: www.backpackeurope.com. Helpful tips, online accommodation reservation, and links.

How to See the World: www.artoftravel.com. An online book with great travel tips, from cheap flights to self-defense to interacting with local culture.

Rec. Travel Library: www.travel-library.com. A fantastic set of links for general information and personal travelogues.

Eurotrip: www.eurotrip.com. Everything you need for backpacking trips including cheap flight tactics and hostel reviews.

INFORMATION ON WESTERN EUROPE

Atevo Travel: www.atevo.com/guides/destinations. Detailed introductions, travel tips, and suggested itineraries.

CIA World Factbook: www.odci.gov/cia/publications/factbook/index.html. Tons of vital statistics on Western European geography, government, economy, and people.

Foreign Language for Travelers: www.travlang.com. Provides free online translating dictionaries and lists of phrases in many Western European languages.

Geographia: www.geographia.com. Highlights, culture, and people of Western Europe.

Lycos: http://travel.lycos.com. General introductions to cities and regions throughout Western Europe, accompanied by links to histories, news, and local tourism sites.

MyTravelGuide: www.mytravelguide.com. Message boards and chat rooms where travelers share stories, photos, and advice from their journeys.

PlanetRider: www.planetrider.com. A subjective list of links to the "best" websites covering the culture and tourist attractions of Western Europe.

TravelPage: www.travelpage.com. Links to official tourist office sites in Western Europe.

Virtual Tourist: www.virtualtourist.com. Countless travel tips and tools, plus links to transportation and accommodation sites.

World Travel Guide: www.travel-guides.com/navigate/world.asp. Helpful practical info.

FURTHER READING: SURFING THE WEB.

Internet Travel Planner, Michael Shapiro. Globe Pequot Press (US$19)

Travel Planning Online for Dummies, Noah Vadnai. IDG Books (US$25).

Ten Minute Guide to Travel Planning on the Net, Thomas Pack. QUE. (US$15).

300 Incredible Things for Travelers on the Internet, Ken Leebow. 300 Incredible.com (US$9).

AND OUR PERSONAL FAVORITE...

Let's Go: www.letsgo.com. Our constantly expanding website features photos and streaming video, online ordering of all our titles, info about our books, a travel forum buzzing with stories and tips, and links that will help you find everything you ever wanted to know about Western Europe.

ALTERNATIVES TO TOURISM

Traveling from place to place around the globe may be a memorable experience. But if you are looking for a more rewarding and complete way to see the world, you may want to consider alternatives to tourism. Working, volunteering, or studying for an extended period of time can be a better way to understand life in a foreign country. This chapter outlines some of the different ways to get to know a new place, whether you want to fund your trip or just get the personal satisfaction that comes from studying and volunteering. In most cases, you will feel that you partook in a more meaningful and educational experience—something that the average budget traveler often misses out on.

There is a limitless range of opportunities for non-tourism travel in Western Europe—far more than we could sensibly list in this guide. We've compiled a diverse list of some of the most useful organizations to contact: education umbrellas, international work-placement firms, and volunteer companies. For more in-depth short-term work listings and extensive national information, pick up any of our European city or country guides.

WORK AND STUDY VISA INFORMATION

Work and study visas for most countries can only be acquired with the help of a sponsoring organization in that country; non-EU nationals looking for transient work will have a hard time getting a work visa. The organizations listed under Long-Term Work (see p. 74) may be able to find sponsors, while the **Center for International Business and Travel (CIBT;** see p. 77) can help expedite the visa process. Study-abroad programs or universities should have no problems sponsoring study visas; check before applying to any institution. Citizens of the EU are free to work in any EU member country, but they may need special permits. Contact the consulates of any countries in which you may seek work for further information.

STUDYING ABROAD

Study-abroad programs range from basic language and culture courses to college-level classes, and may count for credit at your university. In order to choose a program that best fits your needs, you will want to find out what kind of students participate in the program and what sort of accommodations are provided. In programs that have large groups of students who speak the same language, there is a trade-off. You may feel more comfortable in the community, but you will not have the same opportunity to practice a foreign language or to befriend other international students. For accommodations, dorm life provides a better opportunity to mingle with fellow students, but there is less of a chance to experience the local scene. If you live with a family, there is a potential to build lifelong friendships with natives and to experience day-to-day life in more depth, but conditions can vary greatly from family to family.

Those relatively fluent in the language of their destination country may find it cheaper to enroll directly in a university abroad, although getting college credit may be more difficult. Some American schools require students to pay them for credits they obtain elsewhere. Most university-level study-abroad programs are meant as language and culture enrichment opportunities, and therefore are conducted in the local language. Still, many programs do offer classes in English and beginner- and lower-level language courses.

STUDY ABROAD DIRECTORIES

The following websites are good resources for finding programs that cater to your particular interests. They each have links to various study-abroad programs broken down by a variety of criteria, including desired location and focus of study.

www.studyabroad.com. A great starting point for finding college- or high-school-level programs in foreign languages or specific subjects. Also maintains a page of links to several other useful websites.

www.petersons.com/stdyabrd/sasector.html. Lists summer and full-year study-abroad programs at accredited institutions that usually offer cross-credit.

www.westudyabroad.com/europe.htm. Lists language and college-level programs in a number of European countries.

AMERICAN PROGRAMS

The following organizations can help place students in university programs abroad, or have their own branches throughout Europe.

American Institute for Foreign Study, College Division, River Plaza, 9 West Broad St., Stamford, CT 06902, USA (☎800-727-2437, ext. 5163; www.aifsabroad.com). Organizes programs for high-school and college study in universities in Austria, Britain, the Czech Republic, France, Italy, The Netherlands, and Spain.

Arcadia University for Education Abroad, 450 S. Easton Rd., Glenside, PA 19038, USA (☎866-927-2234; www.arcadia.edu/cea). Operates programs in Britain, Greece, Ireland, Italy, and Spain. Costs range from US$2200 (summer) to US$29,000 (full-year).

Central College Abroad, Office of International Education, 812 University, Pella, IA 50219, USA (☎800-831-3629 or 641-628-5284; www.central.edu/abroad). Offers internships, as well as summer-, semester-, and year-long programs in Austria, Britain, France, The Netherlands, and Spain. US$25 application fee.

Council on International Educational Exchange (CIEE), 633 3rd Ave., 20th fl., New York, NY 10017, USA (☎800-407-8839; www.ciee.org/index/cfm). Sponsors work, volunteer, academic, and internship programs in Belgium, Britain, the Czech Republic, France, Hungary, Italy, The Netherlands, and Spain.

International Association for the Exchange of Students for Technical Experience (IAESTE), 10400 Little Patuxent Pkwy. Suite 250, Columbia, MD 21044, USA (☎410-997-2200; www.aipt.org). 8- to 12-week programs in Britain, France, Germany, Ireland, and Switzerland for college students who have completed 2 years of technical study. US$25 application fee.

School for International Training, College Semester Abroad, Admissions, Kipling Rd., P.O. Box 676, Brattleboro, VT 05302, USA (☎800-336-1616 or 802-257-7751; www.sit.edu). Semester- and year-long programs in the Czech Republic, France, Germany, Ireland, The Netherlands, Spain, and Switzerland run US$10,600-13,700. Also runs the **Experiment in International Living** (☎800-345-2929; fax 802-258-3428; www.usexperiment.org), 3- to 5-week summer programs that offer high-school students cross-cultural homestays, community service, ecological adventure, and language training in Britain, France, Germany, Ireland, Italy, Spain, and Switzerland and cost US$1900-5000.

AUSTRIA

Webster University in Geneva and Vienna, Study Abroad Office, Webster University, 470 E. Lockwood, St. Louis, MO, 63119, USA (☎800-984-6857 or 314-968-6900; fax 968-7119; worldview@webster.edu; www.webster.edu/worldwide_locations.html). International students come here to pursue full-degree programs or summer and semester sessions. All courses are taught in English and are fully accredited.

BRITAIN

University of North London, Office of International Programs, 228 Miller Bldg., Box 2000, SUNY Cortland, Cortland, NY 13045 (☎697-753-2209; www.cortland.edu/html/ipgms.html). Offers fall and spring internship openings in London. Students pay SUNY tuition costs plus program fees (US$4500-5500).

Hansard Scholar Programme, St. Philips, Building North, Sheffield St., London WC2 2EX (☎020 7955 7459; fax 7955 7492; www.hansard-society.org.uk). Combines classes at the London School of Economics with internships in British government.

FRANCE

Agence EduFrance, 173 bd. St-Germain, 75006 Paris (☎01 53 63 35 00; www.edufrance.fr), is a one-stop resource for North Americans thinking about studying for a degree in France. Info on courses, costs, grant opportunities, and related topics.

American University of Paris, 31 av. Bosquet, 75343 Paris Cedex 07 (☎01 40 62 06 00; www.aup.fr), offers US-accredited degrees and summer programs taught in English at its Paris campus. Intensive French language courses offered. Tuition US$9,000 per quarter, not including living expenses.

Université Paris-Sorbonne, 1 rue Victor Cousin, 75005 Paris Cédex 05 (☎01 40 46 25 42; www.paris4.sorbonne.fr), the grand-daddy of French universities, was founded in 1253 and is still going strong. Inscription into degree courses costs about €400 per year. Also offers 3- to 9-month programs for American students.

Grande Ecole des Arts Culinaires et de l'Hôtellerie de Lyon (Lyon Culinary Arts and Hotel Management School), Château de Vivier–BP25, 69131 Lyon-Ecully Cedex (☎04 72 18 02 20; fax 04 78 43 33 51; www.each-lyon.com; info@each-lyon.com). Premier school affiliated with Paul Bocuse, located in France's capital city of *haute cuisine.* 8- and 16-week summer courses in French and English for amateurs (€4200-7000). Offers individual day courses ranging €62-76.

Cordon Bleu Paris Culinary Arts Institute, 8 rue Léon Delhomme, 75015 Paris (☎01 53 68 22 50; fax 01 48 56 03 77; www.cordonbleu.edu; infoparis@cordonbleu.edu). M: Porte de la Chapelle. The *crème de la crème* of French cooking schools. A full-year diploma course will run you about €29,500, but Gourmet Sessions are also available, ranging from half-days to 4 weeks.

Pont Aven School of Art, 66 Commonwealth Ave., Concord, MA, USA (☎978-369-9740; fax 369-6954; www.pontavensa.org; artists@pontavensa.org) or in France, 5 pl. Paul Gaugin, 29930 Pont Aven (☎02 98 09 10 45; fax 02 98 06 17 38; psa.france@wanadoo.fr). English-speaking school in Brittany offers studio courses in painting and sculpture, art history, and French language. 4- and 6-week sessions €3200-6200, including room and board.

Lacoste School of Art, P.O. Box 3146, Savannah, GA 31401, USA (☎912-525-5803; www.scad.edu/lacoste; lacoste@scad.edu). Based in the tiny medieval town of Lacoste in Provence, this school is administered by the Savannah College of Art and Design. Summer and fall courses in architecture, painting, and historical preservation. Tuition €3850-5925; room and board €2350.

Painting School of Montmiral, rue de la Porte Neuve, 81140 Castelnau de Montmiral (☎/fax 05 63 33 13 11; www.painting-school.com; fpratt@painting-school.com). Teaches 2-week classes for student, amateur, teacher, and professional levels. In English or French. €1180, including accommodations and half-board.

GERMANY

Deutscher Akademischer Austauschdienst (DAAD), 950 3rd Ave., 19th fl., New York, NY 10022, USA (☎212-758-3223; daadny@daad.org; www.daad.org); in Germany, Kennedyallee 50, 53175 Bonn; mailing address Postfach 200404, 53134 Bonn. Information on language instruction, exchanges, and the wealth of scholarships for study in Germany. The place to contact if you want to enroll in a German university; distributes applications and the valuable *Academic Study in the Federal Republic of Germany.*

GREECE

College Year in Athens, P.O. Box 390890, Cambridge, MA 02139 (☎617-868-8200 from the US; fax 617-868-8207; ☎210 756 0749 from Greece; info@cyathens.org; www.cyathens.org). Runs semester-long, full-year, and summer programs for undergraduates (usually juniors), which includes travel as well as classroom instruction (all in English). The program has two tracks, one in Ancient Greek civilization and one in Mediterranean area studies. Scholarships available. Students are housed in apartments in Athens's Kolonaki district. College Year in Athens also offers summer programs, including a 3-week intensive course in modern Greek on Paros, a 6-week study-travel program, and two 3-week modules that cover different subjects every year.

American School of Classical Studies (ASCSA), Souidias 54, Athens (☎210 723 6313; info@ascsa.edu.gr). A highly competitive program open to graduate students. Degrees offered in archaeology, art history, and classical studies.

The Athens Centre, Archimidous 48, Athens 11636 (☎210 701 2268; fax 210 701 8603; info@athenscentre.gr; www.athenscentre.gr). Offers a Modern Greek Language program. Semester and quarter programs on Greek civilization in affiliation with US universities. Offers 4- to 6-week summer Classics programs, a yearly summer theater program, and Modern Greek Language programs in summer on the isle of Spetses.

Deree College, Gravias 6, GR-153 42 Agia Paraskevi, Athens (☎210 60 9 800; deree@acg.edu or info@acg.edu). Part of the American College of Greece. Bachelor's degree offered in a wide variety of subjects; classes taught in English. Open to students of all international backgrounds, including many Greek students.

Art School of the Aegean, P.O. Box 1375, Sarasota, FL 34230-1375 (☎941-351-5597; hera@artschool-aegean.com; www.artschool-aegean.com). Offers 2- to 3-week summer programs in painting and ceramics from US$1700.

IRELAND

Irish Studies Summer School, at **usit NOW,** 19-21 Aston Quay, O'Connell Bridge, Dublin (☎01 602 1600). 7-week program offering courses in Irish culture and history.

National University of Ireland, Galway, University Rd., Galway (☎091 524 411; www.nuigalway.ie). Offers half- and full-year opportunities for junior-year students who meet the college's entry requirements. **Summer school** courses offered July-Aug. include Irish studies, education, and creative writing.

Queen's University Belfast, University Rd., Belfast BT7 1NN (International Office ☎028 9033 5415; www.qub.ac.uk). Study abroad in Belfast for a semester or year. A 4-week **Introduction to Northern Ireland** program in January covers the political, social, and economic questions unique to the North.

Trinity College Dublin, Office of International Student Affairs (☎01 608 2011/2683; www.tcd.ie/isa). Offers a 1 year program of undergraduate courses for visiting students.

University College Cork. Students from around the world are encouraged to enroll through **Cultural Experiences Abroad** (☎800-266-4441; www.gowithcea.com) for semester- or year-long programs in various disciplines

University College Dublin, International Summer School, Newman House, 86 St. Stephen's Green, Dublin (☎01 475 2004; www.ucd.ie/summerschool). Offers a 2-week international summer course examining Irish culture and tradition.

University of Ulster, Shore Rd., Newtownabbey, Antrim, BT37 0QB, Northern Ireland (☎028 9036 6151; www.ulst.ac.uk). Offers semester- or year-long programs for visiting international students.

ITALY

John Cabot University, V. della Lungara, 233, 00165 Rome (☎39 06 681 9121; fax 683 2088; www.johncabot.edu). Offers a 4-year Bachelor of Arts degree and semester and summer courses. Tuition from US$5500 per semester.

American University of Rome, V. Pietro Roselli, 4, 00153 Rome (☎39 06 5833 0919; fax 5833 0992; www.aur.edu). Offers courses in English on international business, international relations, and Italian civilization and culture. US$4911 per semester; US$2830 for housing.

American Institute for Foreign Study: Richmond in Florence/Rome, College Division, River Plaza, 9 W. Broad St., Stamford, CT 06902, USA (☎800-727-2437, ext. 5163; www.aifsabroad.com). Programs in Florence and Rome. Homestay or student apartment included. 9-13 credits per semester. Semester US$11,495; year US$21,415.

Brown University: Study Abroad in Bologna, Office of International Programs, Brown University, Box 1973, RI 02912, USA (☎401-863-3555; fax 863-3311; www.brown.edu/Administration/OIP). Year-long program in which students take classes at the University of Bologna & *Accademia delle Belle Arti.* 4 full-year university classes required. Apartments with Italian students. Semester US$13,900; year US$27,000.

Institute for the International Education of Students: Study Abroad Italy, 33 N. LaSalle St., 15th fl., Chicago, IL 60602-2602, USA (☎800-995-2300; www.IESabroad.org). Milan-based program provides 15-19 credit hours (with option to take 1-2 courses at a local Italian university), housing (apartments with Italian students as well as homestays), and a cell phone. Semester US$10,500.

Study Abroad Italy, 7151 Wilton Ave., Ste. 202, Sebastopol, CA 95472, USA (☎707-824-0198; fax 824-0198; www.studyabroad-italy.com). Arranges enrollment in schools in Florence, Sicily, and Perugia, as well as travel, student visas, housing, and academic advising. Semester US$8000-10,000.

THE NETHERLANDS

University of Amsterdam (www.uva.nl/english). Programs for economics, philosophy, history, linguistics, film studies, international affairs. Open to college and graduate students. Students live either in university dormitories or apartments.

Amsterdam Maastricht Summer University, P.O. Box 53066, 1007 RB Amsterdam (☎620 02 25; fax 624 93 68; office@amsu.edu; www.amsu.edu). Located on Keizersgracht 324, the Summer University offers courses in cultural studies and art history, economics and politics, health sciences and medicine, language, law and public policy, media studies and information science, and performing arts.

Keizer Culinair, Keizergracht 376 (☎427 92 76; www.keizerculinair.nl). Choose between a sumptuous Dutch or Italian five-course feast–then learn to cook it and eat it–at this school in a lovely canal house (€53.50). An intensive workshop focuses on specialty skills (€59), while the extended course lasts five weeks (€235).

PORTUGAL

Universidade de Lisboa, Rectorate Al. da Universidade, Cidade Universitária, 1649-004 Lisbon, Portugal (☎217 96 76 24; fax: 217 93 36 24; www.ul.pt). Allows direct enrollment of foreign students in most of its divisions.

SPAIN

Universidad Complutense de Madrid, Vicerrectorado de Relaciones Internacionales, Isaac Peral, 28040 Madrid, Spain (☎913 94 69 20; fax 913 94 69 24; www.ucm.es). Largest university in Spain. Hosts 3500 foreign students annually. Opportunities for study in a variety of fields with or without a specific study abroad program.

SWITZERLAND

Webster University in Geneva and Vienna, see p. 68.

LANGUAGE SCHOOLS

Unlike American-affiliated universities, language schools are frequently independently-run international or local organizations or divisions of foreign universities that rarely offer college credit. Language schools are a good alternative to university study if you desire a deeper focus on the language or a slightly less rigorous course load. These programs are also good for younger high school students that might not feel comfortable with older students in a university program. Some good programs include:

Eurocentres, 101 N. Union St. Suite 300, Alexandria, VA 22314, USA (☎703-684-1494; www.eurocentres.com), or Head Office, Seestr. 247, CH-8038 Zurich, Switzerland (☎1 485 50 40; fax 1 481 61 24). Language programs for beginners to advanced students with homestays in Britain, France, Germany, Italy, Spain, and Switzerland.

Language Immersion Institute, 75 South Manheim Blvd., SUNY-New Paltz, New Paltz, NY 12561, USA (☎845-257-3500; www.newpaltz.edu/lii). 2-week summer language courses and some overseas courses in France, Italy, and Spain. Program fees are around US$1000 for a 2-week course.

LanguagesPLUS, 413 Ontario St., Toronto, Ontario M5A 2V9 (US ☎888-526-4758; international ☎416-925-7117; www.languagesplus.com), runs 1- to 36-week programs in Britain, France, Germany, Ireland, Italy, and Spain. US$350-3000; includes tuition and accommodations with host families or apartments. Minimum age 18.

AUSTRIA

Wiener Internationale Hochschulkurse, contact: Magister Sigrun Anmann-Trojer, Wiener Internationale Hochschulkurse, Universität, Ebendorserstr. 10, A-1010 Vienna, Austria (☎(01) 405 12 54; fax 405 12 54 10; www.univie.ac.at/wihok). Offers German courses for beginners and advanced students, as well as lectures on German and Austrian literature, music, linguistics, and Austrian culture, including exposure to the Vienna waltz and choir singing. Tuition for a 4-week summer course €338, with accommodations €736. Longer courses (trimesters and semesters) are also offered.

BRITAIN

Clì—The New Gaels, North Tower, The Castle, Inverness IV2 3EU (☎01463 226 710; www.cli.org.uk). Organization for the promotion of Scottish Gaelic culture. Language courses offered; searchable database of Gaelic centers and classes on their website.

Sabhal Mór Ostaig, Teangue, Isle of Skye, IV44 8RQ (☎01471 888 000; fax 01471 888 001; www.smo.uhi.ac.uk). College on the Isle of Skye, offering long- and short-term courses in Gaelic language and culture. Fees for short-term Gaelic classes £120-200.

The University of Edinburgh, Office of Lifelong Learning, 11 Buccleuch Pl., Edinburgh EH8 9LW (☎0131 650 4400 or 0131 662 0783; www.cce.ed.ac.uk). Has a wide range of short-term classes including language courses.

School of Welsh, Trinity College Carmarthen, Wales SA31 3EP (☎0126 676 746; www.trinity-cm.ac.uk). Offers Welsh language courses of varying intensity from 1 day to 30 weeks. Contact Dr. Lowri Lloyd for an application.

Acen, Ivor House, Bridge St., Cardiff, Wales CF10 2EE (☎029 2030 0808; www.acen.co.uk). Promotes the Welsh language through classes and publications; has contacts with organizations and schools throughout Wales.

DENMARK

AOF, Amager, 21 Lyongate, 2300 Copenhagen S (☎32 86 03 04 or 39 16 82 00). Non-Danes over 18 years of age living in Denmark are eligible for free language instruction. Also provides educational and vocational advisors to help you navigate Danish employment requirements and opportunities.

K.I.S.S., 2 Nørrebrogade, 2200 Copenhagen N (☎35 36 25 55). A super-efficient school that places emphasis on spoken communication and pronunciation. 3-week courses covering 10 levels of proficiency, and an 11th level culminating in the Danish Test 2 fluency exam. Instruction is free for non-native residents, but there is a waiting list.

H.O.F., 26 Købmagergade, 1150 Copenhagen K (☎33 11 88 33). Privately-run school offering morning, afternoon, and evening classes 2-3 times per week. 30 2-3hr. classes cost 775kr; basic instruction takes approximately 2 months and costs 1600kr.

FRANCE

Alliance Française, Ecole Internationale de Langue et de Civilisation Française, 101 bd. Raspail, 75270 Paris Cédex 06 (☎01 42 84 90 00; www.alliancefr.org). Instruction at all levels, with courses in legal and business French. Courses are 1-4 months in length, costing €267 for 16 2hr. sessions and €534 for 16 4hr. sessions.

Cours de Civilisation Française de la Sorbonne, 47 rue des Ecoles, 75005 Paris (☎01 40 46 22 11; www.fle.fr/sorbonne). Courses in the French language at all levels, along with a comprehensive lecture program of French cultural studies taught by Sorbonne professors. Must be at least 18 and at *baccalauréat* level. Semester- and year-long courses during the academic year and 4-, 6-, 8-, and 11-week summer programs.

Institut de Langue Française, 3 av. Bertie-Albrecht, 75008 Paris (☎01 45 63 24 00; fax 01 45 63 07 09; www.inst-langue-fr.com). M: Charles de Gaulle-Etoile. Language, civilization, and literature courses. Offers 4-week to year-long programs, 6-20hr. per week, starting at €185.

Institut Parisien de Langue et de Civilisation Française, 87 bd. de Grenelle, 75015 Paris (☎01 40 56 09 53; fax 01 43 06 46 30; www.institut-parisien.com). M: La Motte-Picquet-Grenelle. French language, fashion, culinary arts, and cinema courses. Intensive language courses for 10 (€95-117 per week), 15 (€143-177 per week), or 25 (€238-294 per week) hours per week.

GERMANY

Deutscher Akademischer Austauschdienst (DAAD), see page 69.

Goethe-Institut, Dachauer Str. 122, 80637 München, Germany (☎(089) 15 92 10; fax 15 92 14 50; mailing address Postfach 190419, 80604 München; for adult students esb@goethe.de, for students under 26 esj@goethe.de; www.goethe.de). Runs numerous German language programs in Germany and abroad; it also orchestrates high school exchange programs in Germany. For information on these programs and on their many cultural offerings, look on the web or contact your local branch (**Australia:** Canberra, Melbourne, Sydney; **Canada:** Montreal, Toronto, Vancouver; **Ireland:** Dublin; **New Zealand:** Wellington; **UK:** Glasgow, London, Manchester, York; **US:** New York, Washington, D.C., Boston, Atlanta, San Francisco, Los Angeles, Seattle) or write to the main office. 8-week intensive summer course €3350, with room €4550.

GREECE

School of Modern Greek Language at the Aristotle University of Thessaloniki, Thessaloniki 54006 (☎231 99 7571; fax 231 99 7573; thkaldi@auth.gr; www.auth.gr/smg). Summer, winter and intensive programs offered in conjunction with philosophy classes.

ITALY

Centro Fiorenza, V. S. Spirito, 14, 50125 Florence (☎39 055 239 8274; fax 28 71 48; www.centrofiorenza.com). Accommodations are homestays or student apartments (€16-67 per day). Also offers courses (with hotel accommodations) on the island of Elba, although these are considerably more expensive. 2- to 4-week courses, 20 lessons per wk., start at €270. €52 enrollment fee.

Istituto Zambler Venezia, Dorsoduro, 3116A, Campo S. Margherita, Venice (☎39 041 522 4331; fax 528 5628; www.istitutovenezia.com). 1- to 12-week language courses based in a 16th-century *palazzo* in the heart of Venice. €160-1240.

Italiaidea, P. della Cancelleria, 85, Rome (☎39 06 6830 7620; www.italiaidea.com). Italian language and culture courses, from €450. 4-week program, 60 total hr.

Koinè, V. de Pandolfini, 27, I-50122 Florence (☎39 055 21 38 81; fax 21 69 49; www.koinecenter.com). Language lessons (group and individual intensive), cultural lessons, wine tastings, and cooking lessons. Courses offered year-round in Florence, Lucca, and Bologna, summer programs in Cortona and Orbetello. Rates from €195 per week of 20 hr. group language lessons. Housing additional per week: €145 per person (single in a private home) to €372 (in a hotel).

PORTUGAL

CIAL Centro de Linguas, Av. de República, 41-8° Esq., 1050-187 Lisbon, Portugal (☎217 940 448; www.cial.pt). Portuguese language courses for all levels. Locations in Lisbon, Porto, and Faro.

SPAIN

Institute of Spanish Studies, 17303 Southwest 80st Place, Miami, FL 33157 (☎888-454-6777; www.spanish-studies.com). Located in Valencia. Offers a range of courses in history, Spanish language, and literature. Students live with host families.

Don Quijote, Plaza San Marcos 7, 37002 Salamanca, Spain (☎923 26 88 60; www.donquijote.org). Offers Spanish language courses for all levels in Barcelona, Granada, Madrid, Málaga, Salamanca, Sevilla, and Valencia.

SWITZERLAND

University of Geneva Summer Courses, contact: Mr. Gerard Benz, University of Geneva, summer courses, r. de Candolle 3, CH-1211 Geneva 4, Switzerland (☎(22) 750 74 34; fax 750 74 39; elcfete@uni2a.unige.ch). Teaches French language and civilization at all levels and offers excursions to Geneva and its surroundings. Tuition for a 3-week summer course 500SFr. Min. age 17.

WORKING

There are two main schools of thought. Some travelers want long-term jobs that allow them to get to know another part of the world in depth (e.g. teaching English, working in the tourist industry). Other travelers seek out short-term jobs to fund their travel. They seek usually employment in the service sector or in agriculture, working for a few weeks at a time to finance the next leg of their journey. This section discusses both short-term and long-term opportunities for working throughout Europe. Make sure you understand the relevant **visa requirements** for the country in which you are working (see p. 66 for more information).

LONG-TERM WORK

If you're planning on spending a substantial amount of time (more than three months) working abroad, search for a job well in advance. International placement agencies are often the easiest way to find employment abroad, especially for teaching English. **Internships,** usually for college students, are a good way to segue into working abroad, although they are often unpaid or poorly paid. Be wary of advertisements or companies that claim the ability to get you a job abroad for a fee—often their listings will have gone out of date or are easily available online or in newspapers. Some reputable organizations include:

Council Exchanges, 52 Poland St., London W1F 7AB, UK (☎020 7478 2000; US ☎888-268-6245; www.councilexchanges.org). Charges a US$300-475 fee for arranging three- to six-month working authorizations. They also provide extensive information on different job opportunities throughout Europe.

Escapeartist.com, 832-1245 World Trade Center, Panama, 832 (jobs.escapeartist.com). International employers post directly to this website; various European jobs advertised. No fee.

International Co-operative Education, 15 Spiros Way, Menlo Park, CA, 94025, USA (☎650-323-4944; www.icemenlo.com). Finds summer jobs for students in Belgium, Finland, Germany, and Switzerland. Costs include a US$200 application fee and a US$600 fee for placement.

International Employment Gazette, 423 Townes Street, Greenville, SC, 29601, USA (☎800-882-9188; www.intemployment.com). A biweekly publication that lists jobs in all sectors, including education, health care, social services, and agriculture. Six-month Internet subscription US$45.

BRITAIN

Anders Glaser Wills, 4 Maddison Ct., Southampton, SO1 0BU (☎0703 223 511; fax 227 911). An international job placement agency with 5 offices in Britain.

FRANCE

French-American Chamber of Commerce (FACC), International Career Development Programs, 1350 Avenue of the Americas, 6th fl., New York, NY 10019 (☎212-765-4598; fax 765-4650) has *Work In France* programs, internships, teaching, and public works.

L'Accueil Familial des Jeunes Etrangers, 23 rue du Cherche-Midi, 75006 Paris (☎01 42 22 50 34; fax 01 45 44 60 48; accueil@afje-paris.org). Arranges summer and 18-month au pair jobs (placement fee €108). Also arranges similar jobs for non-students which require 30hr. of work per week in exchange for room, board, employment benefits, and a métro pass.

Agence Nationale Pour l'Emploi (ANPE), 4 impasse d'Antin, Paris (☎01 43 59 62 63; www.anpe.fr). Has specific info on employment opportunities. Interested parties should bring a work permit and *carte de séjour.* Open M-W and F 9am-5pm, Th 9am-noon.

Centre d'Information et de Documentation Jeunesse (CIDJ), 101 quai Branly, 75740 Paris (☎01 44 49 12 00; fax 01 40 65 02 61; www.cidj.asso.fr). An invaluable state-run youth center provides info on education, résumés, employment, and careers. English spoken. Jobs are posted on the bulletin boards outside. Open M, W, F 10am-6pm; Tu and Th 10am-7pm; Sa 9:30am-1pm.

IRELAND

Working Ireland, 26 Eustace St., Dublin 2, Ireland (☎01 677 0300; www.workingireland.ie). Multi-tasking agency arranges accommodations and job placement throughout the country. They also help you collect tax refunds and arrange travel home.

ITALY

American Chamber of Commerce in Italy, V. Cantù, 1, 20123, Milan (☎39 02 869 0661; fax 05 77 37; www.amcham.it). Lists employment opportunities and allows job seekers to post résumés. Membership (US$400 for non-residents) gives access to networking, trade fairs, economics information, and professional discounts.

Italian Chambers of Commerce Abroad (www.italchambers.net). **Australia:** Adelaide, Brisbane, Melbourne, Perth, Sydney. **Canada:** Toronto, Winnipeg, Vancouver. **UK:** London. **US:** Chicago, Houston, Los Angeles, and New York.

Recruitaly (www.recruitaly.it). Directory of Italian corporations seeking to employ foreign college graduates. Useful information about labor laws and documentation.

Au Pair Italy, V. Demetrio Martinelli, 11/d, Bologna 40133 (☎39 05 138 3466; www.aupairitaly.com). Stays from 3 months to 2 years. Knowledge of Italian not required, but coursework while in Italy recommended. Stipends start at €60 per week.

Mix Culture Au Pair Service, V. Nazionale 204, Rome 00184 (☎39 06 4788 2289; fax 4782 6164; web.tiscali.it/mixcultureroma/index.htm). Minimum stay of 6 months to 1 year. Requires enrollment in a language school in order to obtain a student visa. €65 registration fee.

THE NETHERLANDS

Undutchables, P.O. Box 57204, 1040 BC Amsterdam (☎623 13 00; fax ☎428 17 81; office@amsterdam.undutchables.nl; www.undutchables.nl). The most useful job recruitment agency for foreigners, recruiting for jobs that require command of a language other than Dutch. Temporary and permanent jobs available.

Other temp agencies: Content, Van Baerlestraat 83 (☎676 44 41); **Manpower** (☎305 56 55); **Randstad,** Dam 4 (☎626 22 13).

SPAIN

Escape Artist (www.escapeartist.com/jobs/overseas1). Provides information on living abroad, including job listings for Spain, Portugal, and Morocco.

Go Jobsite (www.gojobsite.com). Lists jobs for European countries, including Spain.

Trabajos (www.trabajos.com). Provides job listings for all regions of Spain.

TEACHING ENGLISH

Teaching jobs abroad are rarely well-paid, although some elite private American schools pay competitive salaries. Volunteering as a teacher in lieu of getting paid is also a popular option; in those cases, teachers often get some sort of a daily stipend to help with living expenses. In almost all cases, you must have at least a bachelor's degree to be a full-fledged teacher, although college undergraduates can often get summer positions teaching or tutoring. Some schools prefer applicants from within the EU to simplify the work permit process; for this reason, non-EU citizens may have a harder time finding teaching jobs.

Many schools require teachers to have a **Teaching English as a Foreign Language (TEFL)** certificate. Not having one does not necessarily exclude you from finding a teaching job, but certified teachers often find higher paying jobs. Native English speakers working in private schools are most often hired for English-immersion classrooms where the local language is not spoken. Those volunteering or teaching in public or poorer schools are more likely to be working in both English and the local dialect. Placement agencies or university fellowship programs are the best resources for finding teaching jobs. The alternative is to make contacts directly with schools or just to try your luck once you get there. If you are going to try the latter, the best time of the year is several weeks before the start of the school year. The following organizations are extremely helpful in placing teachers.

Teaching English as a Foreign Language (TEFL), TEFL Professional Network Ltd., 72 Pentyla Baglan Rd., Port Talbot, SA12 8AD, UK (fax 020 7691 7074; info@tefl.com; www.tefl.com). Maintains the most extensive database of openings throughout Europe, as well as offering job training and certification.

International Schools Services (ISS), 15 Roszel Rd., Box 5910, Princeton, NJ 08543, USA (☎609-452-0990; fax 609-452-2690; www.iss.edu). Hires teachers for more than 200 schools worldwide; candidates should have experience teaching or with international affairs, 2-year commitment expected.

AU-PAIR WORK

Au pairs are typically women, aged 18-27, who work as live-in nannies, caring for children and doing light housework in foreign countries in exchange for room, board, and a small spending allowance or stipend. Most former au pairs speak favorably of their experience, and of how it allowed them to really get to know the country without the high expenses of traveling. Drawbacks, however, can include long hours of constantly being on-duty, and often mediocre pay. Much of the au-pair experience really does depend on the family you're placed with. The agencies below are a good starting point for looking for employment as an au pair.

Accord Cultural Exchange, 750 La Playa, San Francisco, CA 94121, USA (☎415-386-6203; www.cognitext.com/accord).

Au Pair Homestay, World Learning, Inc., 1015 15th St. NW, Suite 750, Washington, DC 20005, USA (☎800-287-2477; fax 202-408-5397).

Au Pair in Europe, P.O. Box 68056, Blakely Postal Outlet, Hamilton, Ontario, Canada L8M 3M7 (☎905-545-6305; fax 905-544-4121; www.princeent.com).

Childcare International, Ltd., Trafalgar House, Grenville Pl., London NW7 3SA (☎020 8906 3116; fax 020 8906 3461; www.childint.co.uk).

InterExchange, 161 Sixth Ave., New York, NY 10013, USA (☎212-924-0446; fax 212-924-0575; www.interexchange.org).

SHORT-TERM WORK

Traveling for long periods of time can get expensive; therefore, many travelers look for short-term jobs to fund the next leg of their travels. Hotels, resorts, and restaurants often have temporary work available. Usually, these can be found by word of mouth, or simply by talking to the owner of a hostel or restaurant. Many places, especially due to the high turnover in the tourism industry, are always eager for even temporary help. Jobs can usually be found quickly, but be aware that during busy times you may have to work long hours, and the pay can be low.

It is also possible to find unofficial temporary work, which means you can avoid the usual paperwork and hassle of getting employment in Europe; the disadvantage is that you won't be protected by the government's labor regulations. For example, agricultural work is often easy to find in the summer or fall. Such jobs may be advertised locally, but inquiring directly with farmers may uncover more opportunities. Such work, however, is often physically strenuous. Another popular option is to work several hours a day at a hostel in exchange for free or discounted room and/or board.

VOLUNTEERING

Volunteering can be one of the most fulfilling experiences you can have in life, especially if you combine it with the wonder of travel in a foreign land. Many volunteer services charge you a fee to participate in the program and to do work. These fees can be surprisingly hefty (although they frequently cover airfare and most, if not all, living expenses). Try to do research on a program before committing—talk to people who have previously participated and find out exactly what you're getting into, as living and working conditions can vary greatly. Different programs are geared toward different ages and levels of experience, so make sure that you are not taking on too much or too little. The more informed you are and the more realistic expectations you have, the more enjoyable the program will be.

Most people choose to go through a parent organization that takes care of logistical details and provides a group environment and support system. There are two main types of organizations—religious (often Catholic), and non-sectarian—although there are rarely restrictions on participation for either.

Though not quite as common as in the developing world, opportunities for volunteer work are abundant in Western Europe. Listed below are some of the organizations that provide volunteer opportunities in Western Europe.

Archaeological Institute of America, 656 Beacon St., Boston, MA 02215, USA (☎617-353-9361; www.archaeological.org). The *Archaeological Fieldwork Opportunities Bulletin*, available on the organization's website, lists field sites throughout Europe.

Earthwatch Institute, 57 Woodstock Rd., Oxford, UK OX2 6HJ (☎01865 318838; www.earthwatch.org). Arranges 1- to 3-week programs to promote conservation of natural resources. Fees vary, but costs average US$1700 plus airfare.

Global Volunteers, 375 E. Little Canada Rd., St. Paul, MN 55117, USA (☎800-487-1074). A variety of 1- to 3-week volunteer programs throughout Europe. Fees range from US$1295-2395, including room and board but not airfare.

Service Civil International Voluntary Service (SCI-IVS), SCI USA, 3213 W. Wheeler St., Seattle, WA 98199, USA (☎/fax 206-350-6585; www.sci-ivs.org). Arranges placement in work camps throughout Europe for those aged 18+. Registration fee US$125.

Volunteers for Peace, 1034 Tiffany Rd., Belmont., VT 05730, USA (☎802-259-2759; www.vfp.org). Arranges placement in work camps throughout Europe. Membership required for registration. Annual *International Workcamp Directory* US$20. Programs average US$200-500 for 2-3 weeks

BRITAIN

The National Trust, Volunteering and Community Involvement Office, 33 Sheep St., Cirencester GL7 1RQ, UK (☎01285 651 818; www.nationaltrust.org.uk/volunteers). Arranges numerous volunteer opportunities, including Working Holidays.

Royal Society for the Protection of Birds (RSPB), UK Headquarters, The Lodge, Sandy, Bedfordshire SG19 2DL (☎01767 680 551; www.rspb.org.uk). Hundreds of volunteer opportunities at sites throughout the UK–ranging from a day constructing nestboxes in East Anglia to week-long bird surveys off the Pembrokeshire coast to several months monitoring invertebrates in the Highlands. Work available for all levels of experience.

FRANCE

Club du Vieux Manoir, Abbaye Royale du Moncel, 60700 Pontpoint (☎03 44 72 33 98; cvmclubduvieuxmanoir.free.fr). Offers year-long and summer programs restoring castles and churches throughout France. €13.72 membership/insurance fee, €13.72 per day, including food and tent.

REMPART, 1 rue des Guillemites, 75004 Paris (☎01 42 71 96 55, www.rempart.com), enlists volunteers to care for endangered monuments. Membership fee €35; most projects charge €6-8 per day.

GREECE

The 2004 Summer Olympics and Paralympic Games are seeking upwards of 60,000 volunteers to assist with the running of the Games between May and September 2004. Placements are available at competition and non-competition venues; knowledge of foreign languages strongly desired.

Archelon Sea Turtle Protection Society, Solomou 57, GR-104 32, Athens (☎/fax 210 523 1342; stps@archelon.gr; www.archelon.gr). Non-profit group devoted to studying and protecting sea turtles on the beaches of Zakynthos, Crete, and the Peloponnese. Opportunities for seasonal field work and year-round work at the rehabilitation center. €70 participation fee includes lodging for work at the center. (Field volunteers stay at private campgrounds but must provide their own camping equipment.)

Conservation Volunteers Greece, Omirou 15, GR-14562, Kifissia, Greece (☎010 623 1120; cvgpeep@otenet.gr; users.otenet.gr/~cvgpeep). Young volunteers (ages 18-30) participate in 1- to 3-week community programs in remote areas of Greece. Projects range from reforestation to preserving archaeological sites. Lodging provided.

IRELAND

Mental Health Ireland, Mensana House, 6 Adelaide House, Dún Laoghaire, Co. Dublin, Ireland (☎01 284 1186; www.mentalhealthireland.ie). Volunteer activities include fundraising, housing, "befriending," and promoting mental health in various regions of Ireland. Opportunities listed in their newsletter, *Mensana News*, available online.

Northern Ireland Volunteer Development Agency, Annsgate House, 70-74 Anne St., Belfast, BT1 4EH (☎0232 236 100; info.nivda@cinni.org). Helps arrange individual and group volunteer efforts in Northern Ireland. IAVE membership fees for individuals US$30 per year; groups US$100.

Volunteering Ireland, Carmichael Centre for Voluntary Groups, Coleraine House, Coleraine St., Dublin 7, Ireland (☎01 872 2622; www.volunteeringireland.com). Offers opportunities for individuals or groups in various volunteering and advocacy settings.

ITALY

Italian League for the Protection of Birds (LIPU), V. Trento, 9-43100 Parma (☎0521 27 30 43; fax 27 34 19; www.lipu.it). Places 350-400 volunteers ages 18+ in data collection and research, conservation, nesting site surveillance, and environmental education work camps. Also offers 1000 administrative positions in 100 divisions throughout Italy. Programs from 1 week to 1 month in Apr., May, Sept., and Oct. Knowledge of Italian is useful. Required skills vary depending on assignment.

Agape Centro Ecumenico, 10060 Prali, Turin (☎3912 180 7690; fax 180 7514; www.chiesavaldese.org//agape). 12 volunteers age 18+ help run this international and national Christian conference center in the Italian Alps. Clean, cook, and maintain the center 6hr. per day, 6 days per week for at least 1 month. Work available June-Sept., Christmas, and Easter. Knowledge of Italian and any other languages a benefit. Free lodging provided. Travel costs not covered.

Italian Association for Education, Exchanges and Intercultural Activities (AFSAI), Viale Luigi Ronzoni, 91 - C/5, 00151 Rome (☎3906 537 0332; fax 5820 1442; www.afsai.it). The European Voluntary Service program, financed by the European Union, arranges for volunteers ages 16-25 to complete 6- to 12-month service projects in Italy. 2-week language course. Knowledge of Italian strongly encouraged.

Doctors Without Borders (Medicins Sans Frontieres/Medici Senza Frontiere), V. Volturno, 58, 00185 Rome (☎3906 448 6921; fax 448 6920; www.msf.it). The Italian branch coordinates volunteers over age 18 to provide health care for immigrants and asylum seekers. Project length from 6 months to 1 year. Brindisi center provides immigrants with shelter and health care. Rome center registers Italians with national health care system and free medical consultations. Emergency medical training provided for volunteers. Basic living expenses, round-trip airfare, health insurance, and other travel costs covered. First-time volunteers offered a US$700 stipend. In-person interview required.

THE NETHERLANDS

SIW Internationale Vjiwillgersprojekten, Willemstraat 7, Utrecht (☎231 77 21; info@siw.nl; www.siw.nl), organizes projects in The Netherlands for volunteers from other countries.

Vrijwilligers Centrale, Hartenstraat 16 (☎530 12 20). The main volunteer agency in Amsterdam.

FOR FURTHER READING ON ALTERNATIVES TO TOURISM

Alternatives to the Peace Corps: A Directory of Third World and U.S. Volunteer Opportunities, by Joan Powell. Food First Books, 2000 (US$10).

How to Get a Job in Europe, by Sanborn and Matherly. Surrey Books, 1999 (US$22).

How to Live Your Dream of Volunteering Overseas, by Collins, DeZerega, and Heckscher. Penguin Books, 2002 (US$17).

International Directory of Voluntary Work, by Whetter and Pybus. Peterson's Guides and Vacation Work, 2000 (US$16).

International Jobs, by Kocher and Segal. Perseus Books, 1999 (US$18).

Overseas Summer Jobs 2002, by Collier and Woodworth. Peterson's Guides and Vacation Work, 2002 (US$18).

Work Abroad: The Complete Guide to Finding a Job Overseas, by Hubbs, Griffith, and Nolting. Transitions Abroad Publishing, 2000 (US$16).

Work Your Way Around the World, by Susan Griffith. Worldview Publishing Services, 2001 (US$18).

ANDORRA

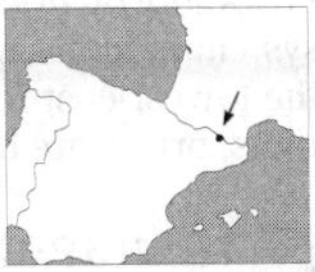

The forgotten country sandwiched between France and Spain, Andorra (pop. 65,000; 464 sq. km), has only had its democratic constitution for ten years; it spent its first 12 centuries caught in a tug-of-war between the Spanish Counts of Urgell, the Church of Urgell, and the French King. Catalán is the official language, but French and Spanish are widely spoken. All establishments were once required to accept *pesetas* and *francs*, but the country is now on the euro system. Because of Andorra's diminutive size, one day can include sniffing aisles of duty-free perfume, hiking through a pine-scented valley, and relaxing in a luxury spa.

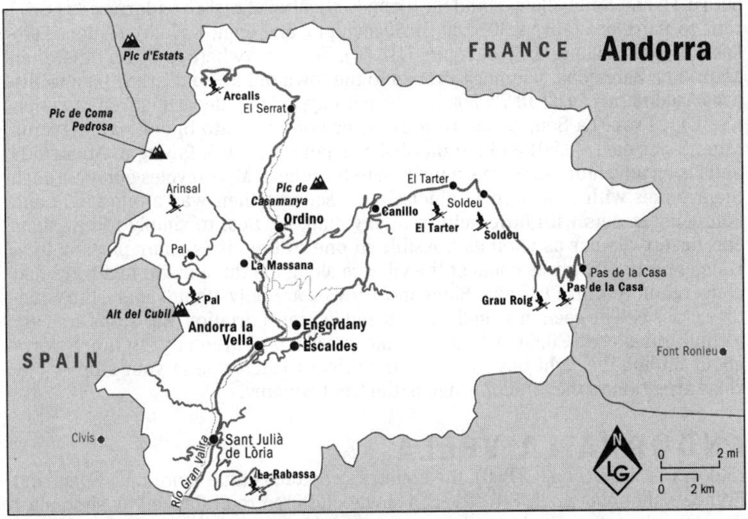

SUGGESTED ITINERARIES

THE BEST OF (OKAY, ALL OF) ANDORRA IN THREE DAYS

First, spend, spend, spend in the duty-free shops of **Andorra la Vella** (1 day, p. 82). Then hike Andorra's mountains, including its tallest peak, **Pic Alt de la Coma Pedrosa** (2946m) in nearby (and what isn't?) **La Massana.** (1 day, p. 83). Afterward, nurse sore muscles in **Escaldes-Engordany** (1 day, p. 83) at Europe's largest spa resort, Caldea-Spa.

SYMBOL	❶	❷	❸	❹	❺
ACCOMMODATIONS	under €15	€16-25	€26-35	€36-50	over €50
FOOD	under €6	€6-10	€11-15	€16-25	over €25

For Andorra, prices are indicated in food and accommodations listings using the system of icons and price ranges above. Prices for accommodations are based on the lowest cost for one person, excluding special deals or discounts. For restaurants, prices are based on the average entree price.

TRANSPORTATION

The only way to get to Andorra is by car or bus. All traffic from Spain enters through the town of La Seu d'Urgell; the gateway to France is Pas de la Casa. **Andor-Inter/Samar** buses (in Madrid ☎914 68 41 90; in Toulouse ☎561 58 14 53; in Andorra ☎82 62 89) run from Andorra la Vella to **Madrid** (9hr.; Tu and F-Su 11am, W-Th and Su 10pm; €33), as does **Eurolines** (Andorra ☎80 51 51; Madrid ☎915 06 33 60; Tu-Th and Su 11:30am; F and Su 10pm; €33). **Alsina Graells** (Andorra ☎82 65 67) runs to **Barcelona** (4hr.; 6:30, 7:30, 10:30am, 3pm, and 6pm; €17.25), as does **Eurolines** (3¼hr.; 6, 11am, 4, 6, and 8pm; €18.50). To go anywhere in Spain other than Madrid or Barcelona, you must first go to the town of La Seu d'Urgell on a **La Hispano-Andorra** bus (☎82 13 72; 30min., 5-7 per day, €2.50), departing from Av. Meritxell 11. From La Seu, Alsina Graells buses continue into Spain via Puigcerdà (1hr., 2 per day, €3.50) and Lérida (2½hr., 2 per day, €10). **Driving** in Andorra la Vella is an adventure for some, a nightmare for others. Motorcycles curve through the avenues with ease; larger vehicles must squeeze their way around tight and confusing streets with little help from any map. It's best to simply follow signs and desert the car as soon as possible in one of the city's many parking lots. Efficient intercity buses connect the villages along the three major highways that converge in Andorra la Vella. Since most towns are only 10min. apart, the country's cities can be seen in a single day via public transportation. **Bus** stops are easy to find; rides cost €0.60. All buses make every stop in the city, so don't worry about finding the right bus—just ask the driver to alert you at your stop or pay close attention to the direction sign in the front window.

ANDORRA LA VELLA

Andorra la Vella (pop. 23,000), the country's capital, is little more than Spain and France's shopping mall. Effectively a single cluttered road flanked by shop after duty-free shop, this city is anything but *vella* (old); most of the old buildings have been upstaged by shiny new electronics and sporting-goods stores. After doing a little shopping, you're best off escaping to the countryside.

PRACTICAL INFORMATION. The **tourist office** is on Av. Doctor Villanova. From the bus stop on Av. Princep Benlloch, continue away from the *Espanya* signs, past the *plaça* on your left, and take Av. Dr. Villanova as it curves to the right; the office is on the left. A multilingual staff offers the free *Sports Activities* and *Hotels i Restaurants* guides. (☎82 02 14. Open daily July-Aug. M-F 9am-1:30pm and 3-7pm; Sept.-June 10am-1pm and 3-7pm, Su 9am-1pm.) In a **medical emergency,** call ☎116 or the **police,** Prat de la Creu 16 (☎87 20 00). For **weather and ski conditions,** call Ski Andorra (☎86 43 89). For **taxi** service, call ☎86 30 00.

Making an international **telephone call** from Andorra is a chore. If you buy a cell phone in Spain, make sure to find out if you can call from within Andorra, as many plans do not service the area. Outside calling cards are just as futile; collect calls to most countries—including the US—are not possible from Andorra. You'll have to buy a STA *teletarjeta* (telecard) at the tourist office or the post office (€3 minimum). For directory assistance dial ☎111 or 119 (international). The **country code** is **376.** The **post office,** Carrer Joan Maragall 10, is across the river from Pl. Princep Benlloch. (☎902 19 71 97. **Lista de Correos** upstairs. Open M-F 8:30am-2:30pm, Sa 9:30am-1pm.) **Internet** access is available at **Future@Point,** C. de La Sardana 6, on the right down the street from the corner bus station. (☎82 82 02. €0.90 per 15min., €1.80 per 30min., €3 per hr. Open daily 10am-11pm. MC/V.)

ACCOMMODATIONS AND FOOD. From C. Major, turn left onto C. de la Vall to find **Hotel Viena ❸,** C. de la Vall 3. Its sunny doubles are a steal. (Doubles €30. MC/V.) To reach the inviting, spacious rooms of **Hostal del Sol ❶,** Pl. Guillemó, take a left onto C. Les Canals after the Pyrenees department store on the main road, then follow the signs for Spain until you reach the plaza with a water fountain. (☎82 37 01. €12 per person. MC/V.) You don't exactly rough it at shaded **Camping Valira ❶,** Av. Salou, behind the Estadi Comunal d'Andorra la Vella, which has video games, hot showers, and an indoor pool. (☎82 23 84. €4 per person, per tent, and per car.) Check out one of the three-story supermarket monstrosities in nearby Santa Coloma or the **Grans Magatzems Pyrénées,** Av. Meritxell 11, the country's biggest department store. (Open Sept.-July M-F 9:30am-8pm, Sa 9:30am-9pm, Su 9:30am-7pm.)

EXCURSIONS. The best thing to do in Andorra la Vella is to drop your bags in a hostel and get out. The **Caldea-Spa,** in nearby **Escaldes-Engordany,** is the largest in Europe, with luxurious treatments and prices to match. (☎80 09 95. Open daily 10am-11pm. €23 for 3hr., plus fees for each service.) The parish of **Ordino** bucks the Andorran trend of "bigger is better" with its quirky **Microminiature Museum,** Edifici Margada. Using yogic breathing to steady his hand, Nikolai Siadristy has created amazingly small, often microscopic objects, including the tiniest inscription ever made. A grain of rice has never been so enthralling. (☎83 83 38. Open Tu-Sa 9:30am-1:30pm and 3:30-7pm, Su 9:30am-1:30pm. €2.) If you have no patience for the miniscule, visit **Canillo** for some fun in the colossal **Palau de Gel D'Andorra,** a recreational complex complete with swimming pool, ice-skating rink ("ice disco" by night), and squash courts. (☎80 08 40. Palace open daily 10am-11:30pm; each facility has its own hours. Each €5, full palace €10. Equipment rental €2.50.)

HIKING AND THE OUTDOORS. An extensive network of hiking trails traverses Andorra. The free, multilingual, and extremely helpful tourist office brochure *Sports Activities* includes 52 suggested itineraries, as well as cabin and refuge locations within the principality. La Massana is home to Andorra's tallest peak, **Pic Alt de la Coma Pedrosa** (2946m). For organized hiking trips, try the **La Rabassa Sports and Nature Center** (☎32 38 68), in the parish of Sant Juliàde Lòria, in southwest Andorra. In addition to *refugio*-style accommodations, the center has mountain biking, guided hikes, horseback riding, archery, and other field sports.

SKIING. With five outstanding resorts, Andorra offers skiing opportunities galore during the Nov.-Apr. months; lift ticket prices range from €30-40. **Pal** (☎73 70 00), 10km from La Massana, is accessible by bus from La Massana (5 per day, last returning at 5pm, €1.50). Buses from La Massana also run to nearby **Arinsal** (7 per day, last return 6:45pm, €1). On the French border, **Pas de la Casa Grau Roig** (☎80 10 60) offers 600 hectares of skiable land, lessons, two medical centers, night skiing, and 27 lifts serving 48 trails for all levels of ability. **Soldeu-El Tarter** (☎89 05 00) occupies 840 hectares of skiable area between Andorra la Vella and Pas de la Casa. Free **buses** pick up skiers from their hotels in Canillo. The more horizontal **La Rabassa** (☎32 38 68) is Andorra's only cross-country ski resort, offering sleigh-ing, skiing, and horse rides. Call **SKI Andorra** (☎86 43 89; www.skiandorra.ad) or the tourist offices with any questions.

AUSTRIA (ÖSTERREICH)

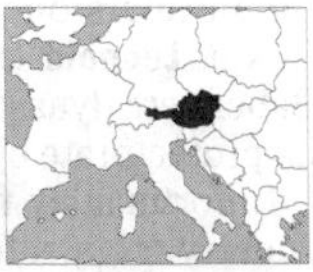

The mighty Austro-Hungarian Empire may have crumbled after World War I, but Austria remains a complex, multi-ethnic country with a fascinating history. Drawing on centuries of Habsburg political maneuvering, Austria has become a skillful mediator between Eastern and Western Europe. But Austria is renowned not so much for its strategic political situation as for its brilliant artists, writers, and musicians. From Gustav Klimt's colorful patterned paintings to Arthur Schnitzler's dark insights into imperial decadence to Beethoven's thundering symphonies, Austria has had an indelible impact on Western art. Austria owes its contemporary allure to a combination of its rich history and its overpowering Alpine landscape. A mention of Austria evokes images of onion-domed churches, snow-capped Alpine peaks, lush meadows of wildflowers, dark forests, and mighty castles.

SYMBOL	❶	❷	❸	❹	❺
ACCOMMODATIONS	under €9	€9-15	€16-30	€31-70	over €70
FOOD	under €5	€5-10	€11-16	€17-25	over €26

For Austria, prices are indicated in food and accommodations listings using the system of icons and price ranges above. Prices for accommodations are based on the lowest cost for one person, excluding special deals or discounts. For restaurants, prices are based on the average entree price.

SUGGESTED ITINERARIES

THREE DAYS Spend all three days in **Vienna** (p. 94), the Imperial headquarters of romance. From the stately **Staatsoper** to the glittering **Musikverein,** the majestic **Hofburg** to the simple **Kirche am Steinhof,** Vienna's attractions will leave you with enough sensory stimulation to last until your next vacation.

ONE WEEK Begin in the Western Austrian mountain town of **Kitzbühel** (1 day; p. 120) to enjoy an array of hiking and skiing opportunities. Stop in **Salzburg** (1 day; p. 109) to see the home of Mozart and *The Sound of Music.* Move on to the Salzkammergut region to hike in the **Echental Valley** (1 day; p. 116) and wonder at the **Dachstein Ice Caves** (1 day; p. 117). End by basking in the glory of **Vienna** (3 days).

TWO WEEKS Start in **Bregenz** for sublime views (1 day; p. 125). Take the train to **Innsbruck** to see museums and mountains (1 day; p. 121), then swing by the "Ski Circus" in **Kitzbühel** (2 days). Next, tour **Hallstatt,** famous for stunning hikes and nearby ice caves (2 days; p. 116). Follow your ears to the musically-inclined **Salzburg** (2 days), then check out rural Austria in **Grünau** (1 day; p. 117). Head to **Graz** (1 day; p. 126) for its Mediterranean feel and throbbing nightlife. Finally make your way to **Vienna** for a grand finale of romance and waltzes (4 days).

LIFE AND TIMES

HISTORY

THE HOLY ROMAN EMPIRE AND THE HABSBURGS (950-1740). Austria had its first taste of imperialism in the mid-9th century when **Charlemagne,** founder of the Holy Roman Empire, expanded his kingdom eastward. When he died, the kingdom collapsed and the eastern regions were overrun by pillaging tribes. After driving the invaders out, Holy Roman Emperor **Otto II** entrusted Margrave Liutpoldus (a.k.a. **Leopold of Babenberg**) with the defense of the eastern territories. The Babenberg dynasty concentrated on stabilizing the frontiers but also on extending its protectorate by shrewdness and strategic marriages.

Unfortunately for the dynasty, the last Babenberg died childless, leaving the country fragmented. Through a bloody conflict, **Rudolf of Habsburg** emerged with the crown, beginning six centuries of Habsburg rule in Austria. Gradually, they accumulated the various regions that make up modern Austria and then some. Friedrich III, for instance, strategically arranged the marriage of his son, **Maximilian I,** to gain Habsburg control of much of Western Europe. Another politically motivated marriage put **Charles V** in charge of a vast empire encompassing Austria, The Netherlands, and several Spanish holdings. Charles was then elected **Holy Roman Emperor** in 1519, gaining nominal control of Germany as well.

Despite their massive possessions and imperial veneer, the Habsburg ship hit rough waters in the 16th and 17th centuries as a result of Martin Luther's **Protestant Reformation.** Early victories over Protestant forces during the **Thirty Years' War** (1618-1648) restored Habsburg control of Bohemia, where they promptly and forcibly converted most of the peasants back to Catholicism. Soon after, the Ottoman Turks besieged Vienna until **Prince Eugene of Savoy** drove them out. The plucky Eugene came through again when he led the Habsburg troops to victory over the French in the **War of Spanish Succession,** which ended with a treaty that gave Spain to France, while the Habsburgs gained Belgium, Sardinia, and parts of Italy.

CASTLES CRUMBLE (1740-1914). Like a house of cards, the Habsburg empire teetered as it grew. When **Maria Theresa** ascended the throne in 1740, her neighbors were eager to see Habsburg power diminished. The marriage of her daughter **Marie Antoinette** to the future **Louis XVI** was a tragic attempt to forge an alliance with France that was quickly negated by the **French Revolution.** After the Revolution, **Napoleon Bonaparte** secured French possession of many Austrian territories. French troops even invaded Vienna, where Napoleon took up residence in Maria Theresa's favorite palace, Schönbrunn (see p. 106), and married her granddaughter.

Napoleon's success led to the official establishment of the Austrian empire. In 1804, Franz II renounced his claim to the now-defunct Holy Roman crown and proclaimed himself **Franz I,** Emperor of Austria. During the Congress of Vienna, which redrew the map of Europe after Napoleon's defeat, Austrian Chancellor **Clemens Wenzel Lothar von Metternich** tried to reconsolidate Austrian power. He managed to usher in a long peace of commerce and industry. In the spring of 1848, the French philosophy of **middle-class revolution** reached Austria. Students and workers revolted and took control of the palace, demanding a written constitution and freedom of the press. The movement was divided, and the rebellion was promptly quashed. Nevertheless, the emperor was eventually pressured to abdicate in favor of his nephew, **Franz Josef I,** whose 68-year reign was one of Austria's longest.

Austria's political status continued to shift throughout Franz Josef's life. Prussia, under **Otto von Bismarck,** dominated European politics, defeating Austria in 1866 and establishing a dual **Austro-Hungarian monarchy**. Unfortunately, burgeoning

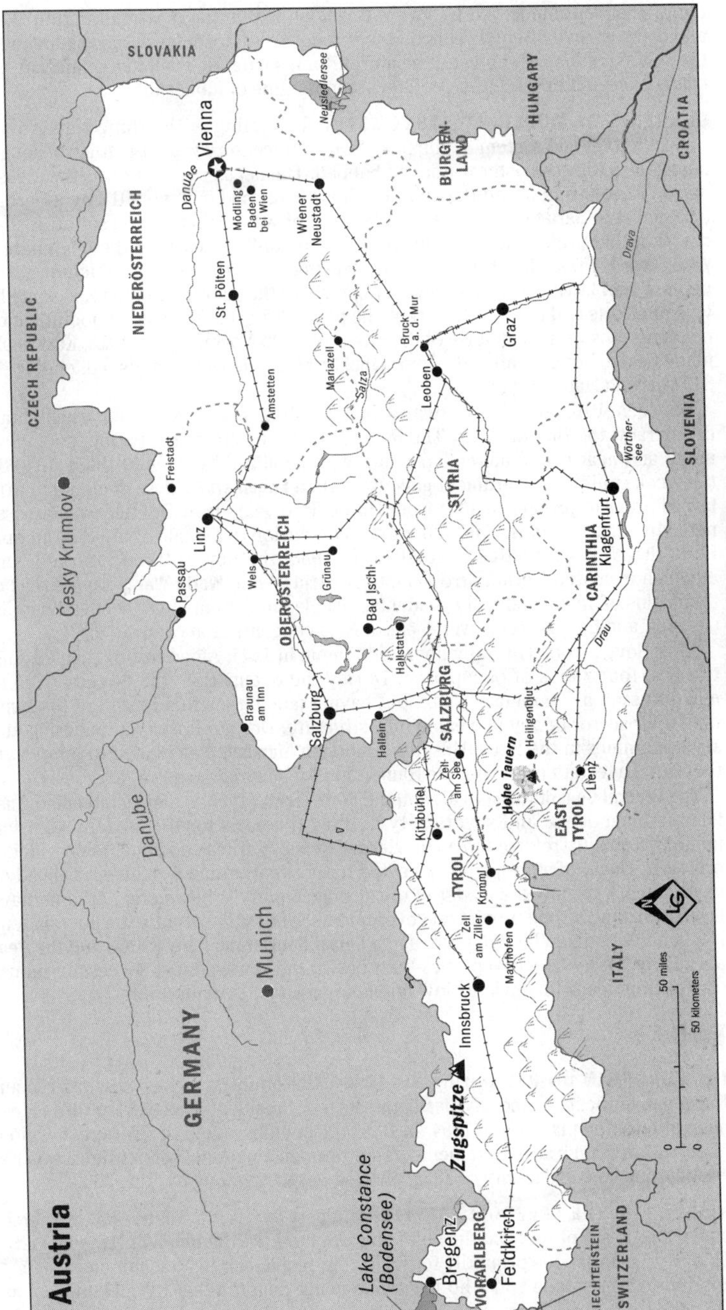
Austria
CZECH REPUBLIC
SLOVAKIA
HUNGARY
CROATIA
SLOVENIA
ITALY
SWITZERLAND
LIECHTENSTEIN
GERMANY
NIEDERÖSTERREICH
OBERÖSTERREICH
BURGEN-LAND
STYRIA
CARINTHIA
SALZBURG
TYROL
EAST TYROL
VORARLBERG
Vienna
Danube
Mödling
Baden bei Wien
Wiener Neustadt
Neusiedlersee
St. Pölten
Amstetten
Freistadt
Český Krumlov
Linz
Passau
Wels
Grünau
Bad Ischl
Hallstatt
Braunau am Inn
Salzburg
Hallein
Mariazell
Salza
Bruck a. d. Mur
Leoben
Graz
Drava
Wörther-see
Klagenfurt
Drau
Heiligenblut
Hohe Tauern
Lienz
Zell am See
Kitzbühel
Krimml
Zell am Ziller
Mayrhofen
Innsbruck
Munich
Zugspitze
Lake Constance (Bodensee)
Bregenz
Feldkirch
50 miles
50 kilometers
0
0

AUSTRIA

nationalist sentiments led to severe divisions within the new multination. Tired and disheartened after 50 years on the throne, Franz-Joseph was also saddened by the suicide of his only son and the murder of his wife. He wanted to maintain Austrian peace and order, but he couldn't stop the tide of modernity.

CURRENTS OF MODERNITY (1914-1945). Brimming with ethnic tension and locked into a rigid system of alliances from 19th-century wars, the Austro-Hungarian Empire was a disaster waiting to happen. The necessary spark was the assassination of Austrian archduke and heir **Franz Ferdinand** in June 1914 by a Serbian nationalist in Sarajevo. Austria's declaration of war against Serbia set off a chain reaction that pulled most of Europe into the conflict, marking the beginning of **World War I.** Franz Josef died in 1916, leaving the throne to his reluctant grand-nephew **Karl I,** who struggled in vain to preserve the Habsburg empire. Despite his valiant efforts and those of the army, the people's declarations of democratic independence ensured the demise of the monarchy. On November 11, 1918, Karl finally made peace, but only after the first **Republic of Austria** was established, ending the 640-year-old Habsburg dynasty.

Between 1918 and 1938, Austria had its first, bitter taste of parliamentary democracy, the **First Republic.** The Republic suffered massive inflation, unemployment, and near economic collapse, but was stabilized by the mid-1920s. In 1933, the weak coalition government gave way when **Engelbert Dollfuss** declared martial law in order to protect Austria from Hitler. Two years later Dollfuss was assassinated by Austrian **Nazis.** The well-known conclusion to the tale of the First Republic is the Nazi **annexation** of Austria. In 1938, the new Hitler-appointed Nazi chancellor invited German troops into Austria. While **World War II** raged, tens of thousands of Jews, political dissidents, disabled and mentally challenged people, Gypsies, and homosexuals were sent to Nazi concentration camps.

After Soviet troops brutally liberated Vienna in 1945, Allied troops divided Austria into four zones of occupation. During the occupation, the Soviets tried to make Austria a Communist state, but having failed, they finally settled for stripping their sector of any moveable infrastructure. Despite Russian plundering and severe famines in the late 1940s, the American **Marshall Plan** helped to jump-start the Austrian economy, laying the foundation for Austria's present prosperity.

The **Federal Constitution** (1945) and the **State Treaty** (1955) which established Austrian independence and sovereignty, formed the basis for the current Austrian nation, frequently referred to as the **Second Republic.** These documents provided a president (head of state), who is elected for six-year terms, a chancellor (head of government), usually the leader of the strongest party, a bicameral parliamentary legislature, and strong provincial governments. Until very recently the government has been dominated by two parties, the **Social Democratic Party** (SPÖ) and the **People's Party** (ÖVP). The two parties built one of the world's most successful industrial economies, with enviably low unemployment and inflation rates.

TODAY

THE EUROPEAN UNION. During the 1990s, the country moved toward closer European unification; **Thomas Klestil,** the current President, was elected on a European integration platform in 1994. In 1995, the country joined the European Union (EU), after citizens accepted membership through a national referendum. Austria adopted the **euro** in January of 2002, phasing out its schilling by July, 2002.

HAIDER AND THE FREEDOM PARTY. In the past few years Austria has garnered international attention from the political gains made by the far-right **Freedom Party.** This party is infamous primarily for its leader, **Jörg Haider,** who maintains a strong anti-immigrant stance and who has made many remarks that have been seen as sympathetic to Nazi beliefs. Haider euphemistically referred to the Nazi camps as "punishment camps" and also called for Austrian military members who fought for the Nazis to have pride in their work. In the November 1999 elections, Haider's party claimed 27% of the vote (second among all parties), effectively breaking the traditional two-party lock that the SPÖ and ÖVP held on the country's politics since WWII. Though Haider did not have a post in the new federal government, he remains governor of the province of Carinthia. One-hundred thousand protestors turned out on the day that members of the Freedom Party were sworn in, and the EU levied unprecendented political sanctions against Austria, which were lifted in 2000. The Freedom Party's success in 1999 should not be seen as the Austrian people's endorsement of Haider: the election had the lowest voter turnout in Austria's post-war history. In the 2001 elections the party slipped eight percent, which analysts see as the result of public disapproval of its policies. For more information on an interesting form of protest, see **Austrian Graffiti,** p. 104.

CULTURE

FOOD AND DRINK

Loaded with fat, salt, and cholesterol, traditional Austrian cuisine is a cardiologist's nightmare but a delight to the palate. Staple foods include pork, veal, sausage, eggs, cheese, bread, and potatoes. Austria's best known dish, **Wienerschnitzel,** is a breaded meat cutlet (usually veal or pork) fried in butter. Vegetarians should look for **Spätzle** (noodles), **Eierschwammerl** (yellow mushrooms), or anything with the word "Vegi" in it. The best supermarkets are Billa and Hofer, where you can buy cheap rolls, fruits, and veggies. Natives nurse their sweet tooths with **Kaffee und Kuchen** (coffee and cake). Try **Sacher Torte,** a rich chocolate cake layered with marmalade; **Linzer Torte,** a light yellow cake with currant jam; **Apfelstrudel;** or just about any pastry. Austrian beers are outstanding—try **Stiegl Bier,** a Salzburg brew; **Zipfer Bier** from upper Austria; and **Gösser Bier** from Styria.

AUSTRIA

CUSTOMS AND ETIQUETTE

In general, following good manners from your own country will take you far in German-speaking ones. The rules aren't too different in Austria, although there are a few ways you can disguise your tourist-side and impress the locals. For instance, most Germans and Austrians hold their fork in their left hand and knife in their right, but don't switch them after cutting something. Elbows on the table is fine. In fact they'll look at you a little funny if you have your hands under the table or in your lap. Meals in Europe are paced a bit slower, so take in the atmosphere and take your time. Menus will say whether service is included (*Preise inclusive* or *Bedienung inclusiv*); if it's not, leave up to a 10% tip. Austrian restaurants expect you to seat yourself, and servers will not bring the bill until you ask them to do so. Say "*Zahlen bitte*" (TSAHL-en BIT-uh) to settle your accounts, and don't leave tips on the table. Some restaurants charge for each piece of bread that you eat during your meal. Don't expect to bargain in shops or markets in Austria, except at flea markets and the Naschmarkt in Vienna.

THE ARTS

ART AND ARCHITECTURE. Landlocked in the middle of Europe and rolling with cash, the Habsburgs married into power and bought into art. Truly Austrian art emerged in the works of **Gustav Klimt** and his followers, who founded the **Secession movement.** Secessionists sought to create space and appreciation for symbolism, Impressionism, and other artistic styles. This can be seen in Klimt's later paintings, such as *The Kiss* (1907-08), which combine naturalistic portraits with abstractly patterned backgrounds. **Oskar Kokoschka** and **Egon Schiele** revolted against "art *qua* art," seeking to present the energy formerly concealed behind the Secession's surface. Schiele's works are still controversial today for their depictions of tortured figures destroyed by their own bodies or by debilitating sexuality.

In 1897, the new artists split from the old as proponents of modernism took issue with the Viennese Academy's conservatism. This gave rise to the **Jugendstil** (a.k.a. **Art Nouveau**) movement, which formulated the ethic of function over form, an idea embraced by Vienna's artistic elite and most notably by the guru of architectural modernism, **Otto Wagner.**

The emergence of architecture in Austria began with the extravagance of the **Baroque** style. With ornate forms orchestrated into a succession of grand entrances, dreamy vistas, and overwrought, cupid-covered facades, the Baroque invokes what was then the most popular art form in Europe, music. This style is exhibited exquisitely in the Schönbrunn (see p. 106) and Hofburg (see p. 105) palaces. Austria's 19th-century conservative modernism is showcased by the Ringstraße (see p. 95), the broad boulevard that encircles Vienna; this historicist taste came to be known as the **Ringstraße Style.** In the 1920s and early 1930s, the Social Democratic administration built thousands of apartments in large **municipal projects,** in a style reflecting the newfound assertiveness of workers' movement and the ideals of **urban socialism.** The most outstanding project of the era is the **Karl-Marx-Hof** in Vienna. The huge structure, completed in 1930, extends over 1km and consists of 1,600 apartments clustered around several courtyards.

LITERATURE. Many of Austria's great writers were immigrants, but native Austrians have made important contributions to the literary scene as well. The *Song of the Nibelungs* (c. 1200), of unknown authorship, is one of the most impressive heroic epics in German. In the 19th century, **Johann Nestroy** wrote biting comedies and satires that lampooned social follies, such as *The Talisman* (1840). **Adalbert Stifter,** often called Austria's greatest novelist, employed classical themes and strongly metaphysical descriptions of nature. His short stories and novels, such as *The Condor* (1840) and *Indian Summer* (1857), represent the height of Austria's classical style. A classicist with a more lyrical style, **Franz Grillparzer** penned pieces about the conflict between a life of thought and a life of action in such plays as *The Waves of the Sea and Love* (1831).

Around 1890, Austrian literature rapidly transformed in the heat of the "merry apocalypse" atmosphere that permeated society. The literature dating from this second heyday of Austrian culture, known as the **fin de siècle,** is legendary. **Karl Kraus** implacably unmasked the crisis, **Arthur Schnitzler** dramatized it, **Hugo von Hofmannsthal** ventured a cautious eulogy, and **Georg Trakl** commented on the collapse in feverish verse. The cafe provided the backdrop for the fin de siècle literary landscape. Meanwhile, the world's most famous psychoanalyst, **Sigmund Freud,** developed his theories of sexual repression and the subconscious—and no young man has looked at his mother in the same way ever since.

Many of Austria's literary titans, including **Marie von Ebner-Eschenbach** and **Franz Kafka,** lived within the Habsburg protectorate of Bohemia. Ebner-Eschenbach is often called the greatest female Austrian writer, known for her vivid individual portraits and her defense of women's rights. Kafka showed he was master of the surreal in *The Metamorphosis* (1915), a bizarre tale about waking up and really not feeling like yourself. Austrian literature today is still affected and informed by its literary tradition, but there is plenty of innovation as well. More recently, **Ingeborg Bachman** has sensitively examined the complexities of womanhood, while **Thomas Bernhard** has provided insightful critiques of Austrian society.

MUSIC. The first major musician of Viennese classicism was **Josef Haydn,** whose oratorio *The Creation* (1798) is a choral standard, but the work of **Wolfgang Ama-**

deus Mozart represents the pinnacle of the time period. A child prodigy and brilliant composer, he produced such well-known pieces as *A Little Night Music* (1787) and the unfinished *Requiem*. His work has been proclaimed to be "the culmination of all beauty in music." Although German-born, **Ludwig van Beethoven** lived in Vienna for much of his life and composed some of his most famous works there. In the 19th century, **Johannes Brahms** straddled musical traditions and **Anton Bruckner** created complicated orchestrations that earned him recognition as one of the world's greatest symphonic masters. Between **Johann Strauss the Elder** and his son, **Johann Strauss the Younger,** the Strauss family kept Vienna on its toes for much of the century by composing exhilarating **waltzes** that broke free from older, more formal dances. In the modern era, **Arnold Schönberg** rejected tonal keys, which produced a highly abstracted sound. **Anton von Webern** and **Alban Berg** were both students of Schönberg and suffered under Nazi occupation for their "degenerate art."

HOLIDAYS AND FESTIVALS

Holidays: Just about everything closes down on public holidays, so plan accordingly. Major holidays include: New Year's Day (Jan. 1); Epiphany (Jan. 6); Good Friday (Apr. 18); Easter Sunday and Monday (Apr. 20-21); Labor Day (May 1); Ascension (May 29); Whitmonday (June 9); Corpus Christi (June 19); Assumption Day (Aug. 15); Austrian National Day (Oct. 26); All Saints' Day (Nov. 1); Immaculate Conception (Dec. 8); Christmas (Dec. 25); Boxing Day (Dec. 26).

Festivals: Vienna celebrates **Fasching** (Carneval) during the first 2 weeks of February. Austria's most famous summer music festivals are the **Wiener Festwochen** (mid-May to mid-June) and the **Salzburger Festspiele** (late July to late Aug.).

AUSTRIA

ESSENTIALS

FACTS AND FIGURES

Official Name: Republic of Austria.
Capital: Vienna.
Major Cities: Salzburg, Innsbruck, Graz.
Population: 8,151,000.
Land Area: 83,857 sq. km.
Time Zone: GMT + 1.
Language: German.
Religions: Roman Catholic (78%), Protestant (5%), Muslim and other (3%).

WHEN TO GO

November to March is peak ski season; prices in western Austria double and travelers need reservations months in advance. The situation reverses in the summer, when the flatter, eastern half fills with vacationers. Sights and accommodations are cheaper and less crowded in the shoulder seasons (May-June and Sept.-Oct.), but some Alpine resorts close in May and June—call ahead. The Vienna State Opera, the Vienna Boys' Choir, and many major theaters throughout Austria don't perform during July and August.

! In August 2002, extreme weather conditions caused massive flooding in the area surrounding Salzburg. As of press time, the ultimate extent of the damage was not known. Many establishments we list may have been forced to shut down or may have altered opening times; additionally, train routes may be disrupted or changed. Make sure to check ahead thoroughly: call hostels and hotels in advance, and confirm the feasibility of your itinerary with Austria's National Tourist Office (www.austria-tourism.at).

DOCUMENTS AND FORMALITIES

Citizens of Australia, Canada, New Zealand, South Africa, and the US do not need a visa for stays up to three months.

Austrian Embassies at Home: Australia, 12 Talbot St., Forrest, Canberra ACT 2603 (☎00 62 95 15 33; austria@dynamite.com.au). **Canada,** 445 Wilbrod St., Ottawa, ON K1N 6M7 (☎613-789-1444; www.austro.org). **Ireland,** 15 Ailesbury Court, 93 Ailesbury Rd., Dublin 4 (☎01 269 45 77; dublin-ob@bmaa.gv.at). **New Zealand,** Level 2, Willbank House, 57 Willis St., Wellington (☎04 499 63 93). **South Africa,** 1109 Duncan St., Momentum Office Park, Brooklyn, Pretoria 0011 (☎012 45 29 155; autemb@mweb.co.az). **UK,** 18 Belgrave Mews West, London SW1 X 8HU (☎020 72 35 37 31; www.austria.org.uk). **US,** 3524 International Ct. NW, Washington, D.C. 20008-3035 (☎202-895-6700).

Foreign Embassies in Austria: All foreign embassies in Austria are in Vienna (see p. 98)

TRANSPORTATION

AUSTRIA

BY PLANE. The only major international airport is Schwechat Flughafen (VIE) in **Vienna.** European flights also land in Graz, Innsbruck, and Salzburg. From the UK, **buzz** (☎0870 240 70 70; www.buzzaway.com), a subsidiary of KLM, flies to Vienna.

BY TRAIN. The **Österreichische Bundesbahn (ÖBB),** Austria's federal railroad, operates an efficient system of fast and comfortable trains. **Eurail, InterRail,** and **Europe East** passes are valid in Austria; however, they do not guarantee a seat without a reservation (€12). The **Austrian Railpass** (2nd-class €110, each additional day €16) allows three days of travel within any 15-day period on all rail lines; it also entitles holders to 40% off bike rental at train stations.

BY BUS. The efficient Austrian bus system consists mainly of orange **Bundes-Buses,** which cover areas inaccessible by train. They usually cost about as much as trains; rail passes are not valid. Buy tickets at the station or from the driver. For bus information, dial ☎0222 711 01 within Austria from 7am-8pm.

BY CAR. Driving is a convenient way to see more isolated parts of Austria, but many small towns prohibit cars. The roads are generally very good and well-marked, and Austrian drivers are quite careful. **Mitfahrzentrale** (ride-sharing services) pair drivers with riders for a small fee. Riders then negotiate fares with the drivers. Be aware that not all organizations screen their drivers; ask in advance.

BY BIKE. Bikes are a great way to get around Austria; roads are generally level and safe. Many train stations rent bikes and allow you to return them to any participating station. Consult local tourist offices for bike routes and maps.

TOURIST SERVICES AND MONEY

EMERGENCY	**Police:** ☎133. **Ambulance:** ☎144. **Fire:** ☎122.

TOURIST OFFICES. Virtually every town in Austria has a **tourist office;** most marked by a green **"i"** sign. You may run into language difficulties in the small-town offices, but most brochures are available in English. Visit www.austria-tourism.at for more Austrian tourist information.

Tourist Boards at Home: Australia and New Zealand: Sydney, 1st Floor, 36 Carrington St., Sydney NSW 2000 (☎(02) 92 99 36 21; fax 92 99 38 08; oewsyd@world.net). **UK and Ireland:** London, 14 Cork St. GB-London W1X 1PF (☎(020) 76 29 04 61; fax 74 99 60 38; info@anto.co.uk). **US and Canada:** New York, 500 Fifth Ave., Suite 800, P.O. Box 1142, New York, NY 10110 (☎212-944-6880; fax 730-4568).

MONEY. The official currency of Austria is the **euro.** Austria formerly used the *Schilling* as its unit of currency, but as of July 2002, has completely switched over to the euro. For exchange rates and more information on the euro, see p. 20. If you stay in hostels and prepare most of your own food, expect to spend anywhere from €30-65 per person per day. Accommodations start at about €12, while a basic sit-down meal usually costs around €14. The European Union imposes a **value-added tax (VAT)** on goods and services purchased within the EU, which is included in the price (see p. 19).

ACCOMMODATIONS AND CAMPING

Always ask if your lodging provides a *Gästekarte* (guest card), which grants discounts on local activities, museums, and public transportation. The tax that most accommodations add to your bill funds these discounts—take advantage of them to get your money's worth.

HOSTELS. The *Österreiches Jugendherbergsverband-Hauptverband* (OJH) runs over 80 hostels in Austria. Because of the rigorous standards of the national organizations, hostels are usually as clean as any hotel. While the clientele of the hostels varies, HI hostels tend to be oriented toward families and school groups. Most hostels charge €13-22 a night for dorms. Non-HI members are frequently charged a surcharge.

HOTELS. Hotels are expensive (singles €40-100; doubles €80-150). The cheapest hotel-style accommodations have *Gasthof*, *Gästehaus*, or *Pension-Garni* in the name. Breakfast is almost always included.

PRIVATE ROOMS AND PENSIONS. Renting a *Privatzimmer* (room in a family home) is an inexpensive and friendly choice. Such rooms generally include a sink and use of a toilet and shower. Many places rent private rooms only for longer stays or levy a surcharge (10-20%) for stays less than three nights. Rooms range from €35-70 a night; breakfast is included. *Pensionen* (pensions) are slightly more expensive and similar to American and British bed-and-breakfasts. Contact the local tourist office for a list of private rooms.

CAMPING. Camping in Austria is less about getting out into nature and more about having a cheap place to sleep; most sites are large plots with many vans and cars. Campsites are usually only open in the summer. Prices run €4-6 per person.

COMMUNICATION

PHONE CODES	**Country code:** 43. **International dialing prefix:** 00 (900 in Vienna)

TELEPHONES. Whenever possible, use a calling card for international phone calls, as the long-distance rates for national phone services are often exorbitant. Prepaid phone cards and major credit cards can be used for direct international calls, but they are still less cost-efficient. Direct dial access numbers include: **AT&T,** ☎0800 20 02 88; **British Telecom,** ☎0800 20 02 09; **Canada Direct,** ☎0800 20 02 17; **Ireland Direct,** ☎0800 40 00 00; **MCI,** ☎0800 20 02 35; **Sprint,** ☎0800 20 02 36; **Telecom New Zealand,** ☎0800 20 02 22; **Telkom South Africa,** ☎0800 20 02 30.

MAIL. Letters take 1-2 days within Austria. Airmail to North America takes 4-7 days, but up to 9 days to Australia and New Zealand. Mark all letters and packages "mit Flugpost" or "par avion." Aerogrammes are the cheapest option. *Let's Go* lists the addresses for mail to be held in the **practical information** of major cities.

LANGUAGE. German is the official language. English is the most common second language, but outside of cities and among older residents, English is less common. For basic German words and phrases, see p. 1022.

VIENNA (WIEN) ☎0222

From its humble origins as a Roman camp along the Danube, Vienna became the cultural heart of Europe for centuries, the setting for fledgling musicians, writers, artists, philosophers, and politicians to achieve greatness—or infamy. Viennese satirist Karl Kraus once dubbed the city—the birthplace of psychoanalysis, atonal music, functionalist architecture, Zionism, and Nazism—a "laboratory for world destruction." During the height of its artistic ferment, at the turn of the century, the Viennese were already self-mockingly referring to their city as the "merry apocalypse." Its smooth veneer of waltzes and *Gemütlichkeit* (good nature) concealed a darker side expressed in Freud's theories, Kafka's dark fantasies, and Mahler's deathly beautiful music. Vienna has a reputation for living absent-mindedly in this grand past, but as the last fringes of the Iron Curtain have been drawn back, Vienna has tried to revitalize its political and cultural life to reestablish itself as the gateway to Eastern Europe and as a place where experimentalism thrives.

INTERCITY TRANSPORTATION

AUSTRIA

By Plane: The **Wien-Schwechat Flughafen** (VIE; ☎700 72 22 33) is home to **Austrian Airlines** (☎517 89). Daily flights to and from **New York** and frequent flights to **Berlin, London, Rome,** and most other major cities are available. The **airport** is 18km from the city center; the cheapest way to reach the city is S7 Flughafen/Wolfsthal, which stops at **Wien Mitte** (30min., every 30min. 5am-9:30pm, €3; Eurail not valid). The heart of the city, **Stephansplatz,** is a short metro ride from Wien Mitte on the U3 line. It's more convenient (but also more expensive) to take the **Vienna Airport Lines Shuttle Bus,** (☎93 00 00 23 00), which runs between the airport and the City Air Terminal, at the Hilton opposite Wien Mitte (every 20min. 6:30am-11:10pm, every 30min. midnight-6am; €5.80). **Buses** connect the airport to the **Südbahnhof** and **Westbahnhof** (see below) every 30min. from 8:55am-7:25pm and every hr. from 8:20pm-8:25am.

By Train: Vienna has two main train stations with international connections. For general train information, dial ☎17 17 (24hr.) or check www.bahn.at.

Westbahnhof, XV, Mariahilferstr. 132. Most trains head west, but a few go east and north. **Info counter** open daily 7:30am-8:40pm. To: **Amsterdam** (14½hr., 1 per day, €166); **Berlin Zoo** (11hr., 1 per day, €123); **Bregenz** (8hr., 9 per day, €58); **Hamburg** (9½hr., 2 per day, €176); **Innsbruck** (5-6hr., every 2hr., €48); **Munich** (4½hr., 5 per day, €60); **Paris** (14hr., 2 per day, €156); **Salzburg** (3½hr., every hr., €34); **Zurich** (9¼hr., 3 per day, €81).

Südbahnhof, X, Wiedner Gürtel 1a, on the D tram. To get to the city, take the tram (dir.: Nußdorf) to Opera/Karlspl. Trains generally leave for destinations south and east. **Info counter** open daily 6:30am-9:20pm. To: **Budapest** (3-4hr., 6 per day, €32); **Graz** (2¾hr., every hr., €23); **Krakow** (7-8hr., €37); **Prague** (4½hr., 3 per day, €39); **Rome** (14hr., 1 per day, €99); **Venice** (9-10hr., 3 per day, €64).

By Bus and Boat: Travel by bus in Vienna is seldom cheaper than travel by train; compare prices before buying a ticket. **City bus terminals** are located at Wien Mitte/Landstr., Hütteldorf, Heiligenstadt, Floridsdorf, Kagran, Erdberg, and Reumannpl. **BundesBuses** run from these stations to local and international destinations. Ticket counter is open M-F 6am-5:50pm, Sa-Su 6am-3:50pm. Many international bus lines also have agencies in the stations, each with different hours. For bus information, call BundesBus. (☎711 01. Operates daily 7am-7pm.)

Hitchhiking and Ride Sharing: While *Let's Go* does not recommend hitching, **hitchhikers** headed for Salzburg have been seen taking U4 to Hütteldorf; the highway leading to the Autobahn is 10km farther. Hitchers traveling south often ride tram #67 to the last stop and wait at the rotary near Laaerberg. A safer alternative is ride sharing; **Mitfahrzentrale Wien** pairs drivers and riders over the phone. Call to see what rides are available. (☎408 22 10. Open M-F 8am-noon and 2-7pm, Sa-Su 1-3pm.) A ride to **Salzburg** costs €16 and to **Prague** €33. Reservations 2 days in advance are recommended.

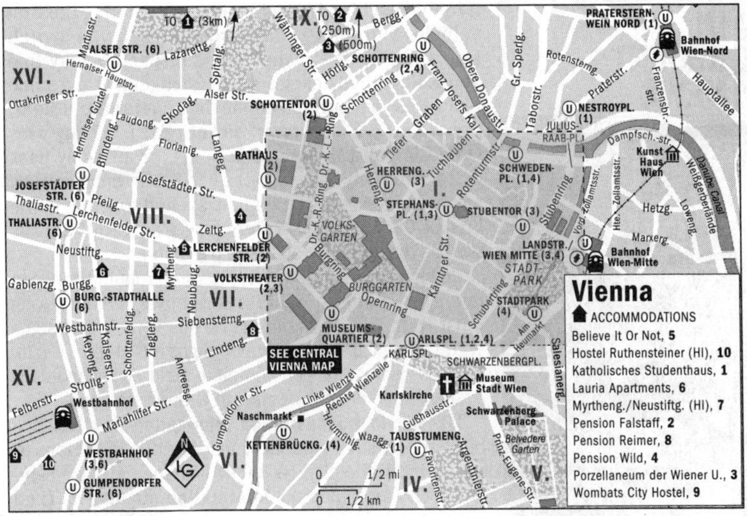

ORIENTATION

Vienna is divided into 23 **districts** *(Bezirke)*. The first is the *Innenstadt* (city center), defined by the **Ringstraße** on three sides and the Danube Canal on the fourth. The *Ringstraße* (or "Ring") consists of many different segments, each with its own name, including Opernring, Kärntner Ring, or Dr.-Karl-Lueger-Ring. Many of Vienna's major attractions are in District I and immediately around the *Ringstraße*. Districts II-IX spread out from the city center following the clockwise, one-way traffic of the Ring. The remaining districts expand from yet another ring, the **Gürtel** ("belt"). Like the Ring, this major two-way thoroughfare has numerous segments, including Margaretengürtel, Währinger Gürtel, and Neubaugürtel. Street signs indicate the district number in Roman or Arabic numerals before the street and number. ***Let's Go* includes district numbers for establishments in Roman numerals before the street address.**

LOCAL TRANSPORTATION

Public transportation in Vienna is extensive and dependable; call ☎580 00 for general information. The **subway** (U-Bahn), **tram** (Straßenbahn), **elevated train** (S-Bahn), and **bus** systems operate under one ticket system. A **single fare** (€1.80 on board, €1.50 in advance from a ticket machine, ticket office, or tobacco shop), lets you travel to any single destination in the city and switch from bus to U-Bahn to tram to S-Bahn, as long as your travel is uninterrupted. To **validate a ticket,** punch

LITTLE PIECES OF REVOLUTION Travelers may be perplexed by the little paper strips taped around columns in train stations, subway stops, and crowded streets. The slips, known as *Pflücktexte* (from *pflücken,* to pluck), contain short poems with vaguely anti-establishment messages and are meant to be "plucked" from the columns, whereupon they are mysteriously replaced. *Let's Go* sleuths have determined that the poems are composed by one Helmut Seethaler, Wasnerg. 43/8, 1200 Wien, who offers more insurgent poems via mail "for a small bill."

IN RECENT NEWS

THE TEURO

If everything seems more expensive in Austria, it may not be unfavorable exchange rates or faulty memories of the good old days when a schilling could buy a horse and a tankard of ale. The euro, (termed the "Teuro" by many Austrians, punning on *teurer*, German for "expensive"), may be, at least partly to blame.

Effective July 1, 2002, the schilling officially ceased to exist as currency and all transactions were carried out in euros. Though the transition went off without a major incident, it hasn't stopped people from grumbling. "It was bloody easy for the shopkeepers to make the switch," complains an Austrian expatriate. "They just rounded everything up."

While most people were content to pay a few extra cents here and there, some increases were harder to swallow. "In many places, they simply divided all the prices by 10 and called that the price in euros," explains a retired school teacher in Voralberg. What may seem like a reasonable solution is outrageous considering that the actual conversion rate was 13.7 schillings to the euro. Merchants who divided by 10 quietly upped prices 37% literally overnight.

Now that the logistical nightmare of refitting every vending machine, automat, and price tag is over, prices have finally stabilized. This means that while your money won't go quite as far as it used to, the runaway inflation of the first few months has come to a halt.

it in the machine immediately upon entering the first vehicle, but don't stamp it again when you switch trains. Otherwise, plain clothed inspectors may fine you €40. Other ticket options (available at the same places as pre-purchased single tickets) are a **24hr. pass** (€5), a **3-day "rover" ticket** (€12), a **7-day pass** (€11.20; valid M 9am to M 9am), or an **8-day pass** (€24; valid any 8 days, not necessarily consecutive; valid also for several people traveling together). The **Vienna Card** (€16.90) offers free travel for 72hr. as well as discounts at sights and events.

Regular trams and subway cars stop running between midnight and 5am. **Nightbuses** run every 30min. along most tram, subway, and major bus routes. "N" signs with yellow cat eyes designate night bus stops. (€1.10; day passes not valid.) A complete night bus schedule is available at bus info counters in U-Bahn stations.

The **public transportation information line** has live operators that give public transportation directions to any point in the city. (☎790 91 05. Open M-W, F 8am-3pm, Th 8am-5:30pm.) **Information stands** (marked with an "i") in many stations help with purchasing tickets and have an indispensable free pocket map of the U- and S-Bahn systems. Stands in the U-Bahn at Karlspl., Stephanspl., and the *Westbahnhof* are the most likely to have information in English. (Open M-F 6:30am-6:30pm, Sa-Su and holidays 8:30am-4pm.)

Taxis: (☎313 00, 401 00, 601 60, or 814 00). Stands at *Westbahnhof, Südbahnhof,* Karlspl. in the city center, and by the Bermuda *Dreieck* (Triangle) for late-night revelers. Accredited taxis have yellow and black signs on the roof. Rates generally run €2.20 per km; slightly more expensive Su, holidays, and 11pm-6am.

Car Rental: Avis, I, Opernring 3-5 (☎587 62 41). Open M-F 7am-8pm, Sa 8am-2pm, Su 8am-1pm. **Hertz** (☎700 73 26 61), at the airport. Open M-F 7:15am-11pm, Sa 8am-8pm, Su 8am-11pm.

Bike Rental: Pedal Power, II, Ausstellungsstr. 3 (☎729 72 34), rents bikes (€5 per hr., €32 for 24hr. with delivery) and offers bike tours (€19-23). Student and Vienna Card discounts. Open May-Sept. daily 8am-8pm. Pick up *Vienna By Bike* at the tourist office for details on the bicycle scene.

Central Vienna

ACCOMMODATIONS
- Hotel Zur Wiener Staatsoper, **17**

FOOD
- Centimeter, **15**
- DO&CO, **8**
- Korso, **18**
- Levante, **5**
- Margaritaville, **7**
- Maschu Maschu, **3**
- Trzesniewski, **6**
- University Mensa, **1**
- Yugetsu Saryo, **10**
- Zum Mogulhof, **12**

COFFEEHOUSES
- Café Central, **4**
- Café Sperl, **19**
- Hotel Sacher, **16**
- Kleines Café, **10**

NIGHTLIFE
- Das Möbel, **14**
- Mapitom der Bierlokal, **2**
- Objectiv, **12**
- Volksgarten Disco, **9**

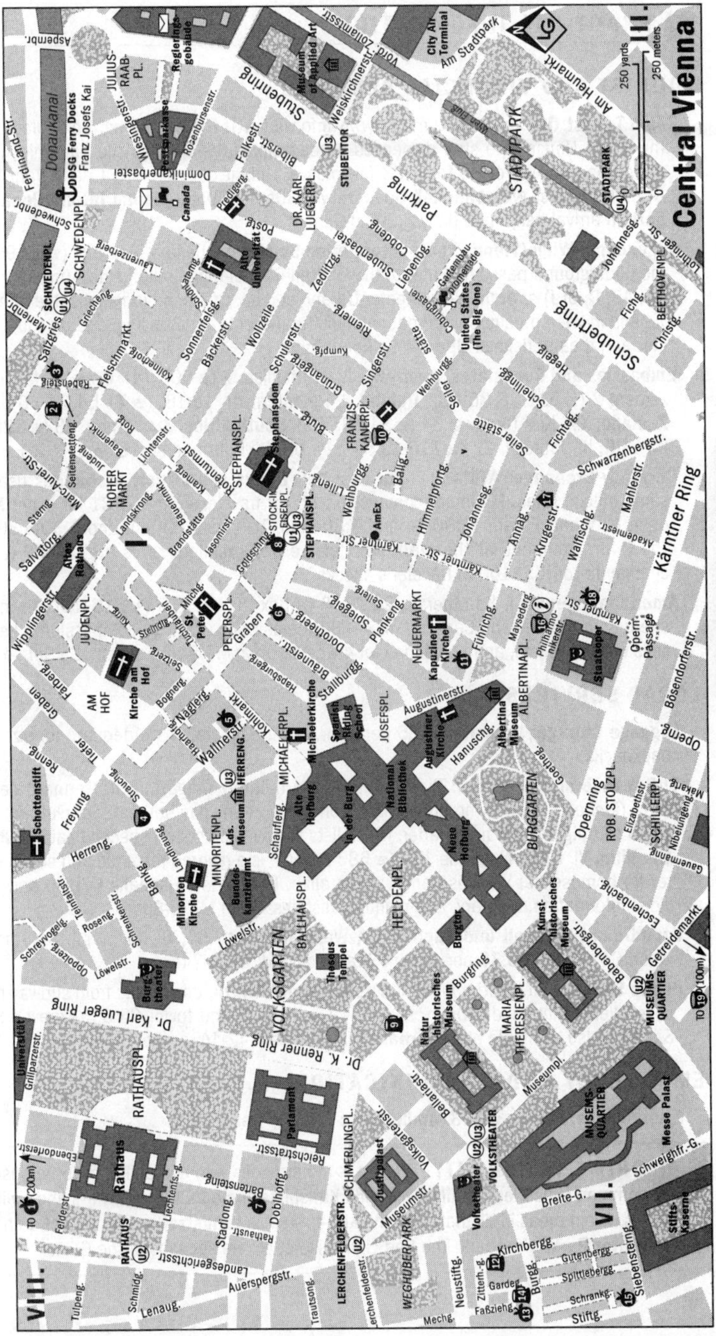
Central Vienna
250 yards
250 meters
I.
III.
VII.
VIII.
Donaukanal
DDSG Ferry Docks
Franz Josefs Kai
SCHWEDENPL.
JULIUS-RAAB-PL.
Stubenring
Museum of Applied Art
Regierungsgebäude
Postsparkasse
STUBENTOR
DR. KARL LUEGERPL.
Parkring
STADTPARK
City Air Terminal
Am Stadtpark
Am Heumarkt
Alte Universität
Canada
Wollzeile
Fleischmarkt
HOHER MARKT
Altes Rathaus
Salvatorg.
STEPHANSPL.
Stephansdom
STOCK-IM-EISENPL.
FRANZISKANERPL.
Singerstr.
Himmelpfortg.
Kärntner Str.
AmEx
United States (The Big One)
Schubertring
BEETHOVENPL.
Schwarzenbergstr.
Kärntner Ring
Staatsoper
Oper Passage
Philharmonikerstr.
NEUERMARKT
Kapuziner Kirche
Graben
PETERSPL.
St. Peter
JUDENPL.
AM HOF
Kirche am Hof
Wipplingerstr.
Freyung
Schottenstift
Herreng.
MINORITENPL.
Minoriten Kirche
Bundeskanzleramt
Lds. Museum
HERRENG.
Kohlmarkt
MICHAELERPL.
Michaelerkirche
Spanish Riding School
JOSEFSPL.
Alte Hofburg
In der Burg
National Bibliothek
Augustiner Kirche
Albertina Museum
ALBERTINAPL.
Neue Hofburg
BURGGARTEN
Opernring
ROB. STOLZPL.
SCHILLERPL.
Getreidemarkt
HELDENPL.
BALLHAUSPL.
VOLKSGARTEN
Theseus Tempel
Burgtor
Burgtheater
Dr. Karl Lueger Ring
RATHAUSPL.
Rathaus
Universität
Parlament
Dr. K. Renner Ring
Burgring
Natur-historisches Museum
Kunst-historisches Museum
MARIA THERESIENPL.
MUSEUMS-QUARTIER
Messe Palast
Justizpalast
SCHMERLINGPL.
VOLKSTHEATER
Volkstheater
WEGHUBERPARK
LERCHENFELDERSTR.
RATHAUS
Landesgerichtsstr.
Auerspergstr.
Stiftskaserne
Breite-G.
Kirchbergg.
Siebensterng.
Stiftg.

PRACTICAL INFORMATION

TOURIST AND FINANCIAL SERVICES

Main Tourist Office: I, Albertinapl. (www.info.wien.at). Follow Operng. up 1 block from the Opera House. The staff dispenses a free map of the city and the pamphlet *Youth Scene* and books rooms for a €3 fee plus a 1-night deposit. Open daily 9am-7pm. **Branch Offices: Westbahnhof,** open daily 7:30am-8:40pm; **Vienna International Airport**, in arrival hall, open daily 8:30am-9pm.

Jugend-Info Wien (Vienna Youth Information Service): I, Bellaria-Passage (☎17 99), in the underground passage. Enter at the Dr.-Karl-Renner-Ring/Bellaria stop (trams #1, 2, 46, 49, D, or J) or at the Volkstheater U-Bahn station. Offers the indispensable and free *Jugend in Wien* brochure, information on cultural events and housing, and discount concert and theater tickets. Open M-Sa noon-7pm.

Embassies and Consulates: Australia, IV, Mattiellistr. 2 (☎506 74). **Canada,** I, Laurenzerberg 2 (☎531 38 30 00). **Ireland,** I, Rotenturmstr. 16-18. (☎71 54 24 60). **New Zealand,** XIX, Karl-Tomay-g. 34 (☎318 85 05). **South Africa,** XIX, Sandg. 33 (☎320 64 93). **UK,** III, Jauresg. 12 (☎716 13 51 51). **US,** IX, Boltzmanng. 16 (☎313 39).

Currency Exchange: ATMs are your best bet. **Banks** and **airport exchanges** use the same official rates. Minimum commission €5 for traveler's checks, €1 for cash. Most open M-W and F 8am-12:30pm and 1:30-3pm, Th 8am-12:30pm and 1:30-5:30pm. The 24hr. exchange at the **main post office** has excellent rates and an €8 fee to change up to US$1100 in traveler's checks.

American Express: I, Kärntnerstr. 21-23, P.O. Box 28, A-1015 (☎515 40), down the street from Stephanspl. Cashes AmEx and Thomas Cook (min. €5 commission) checks, sells theater tickets, and holds mail for 4 weeks. Open M-F 9am-5:30pm, Sa 9am-noon.

AUSTRIA

LOCAL SERVICES

Luggage Storage: Lockers are €5 per 24hr. at all train stations. Adequate for sizeable backpacks.

Bi-Gay-Lesbian Resources: Pick up either the monthly magazine (in German) called *Extra Connect;* the free monthly publication *Bussi* at any gay bar, cafe, or club; or consult the straight *Falter* newspaper, which lists gay events under a special heading. **Rosa Lila Villa,** VI, Linke Wienzeile 102 (☎586 81 50), is a favored resource and social center for homosexual Viennese and visitors alike. Friendly staff speaks English and provides information, a library, and nightclub listings. Open M-F 5-8pm.

Laundromat: Schnell und Sauber, VII, Westbahnhofstr. 60; U6 to Burgg. Stadthalle. Wash €4.40, dry €0.75 per 15min. Soap included. Open 24hr.

Public Showers: At *Westbahnhof,* in **Friseursalon Navratil,** downstairs from subway passage. Well maintained. 30min. shower €4, with soap and towel €5.60 (extra on Su). Showers also available at **Jörgerbad,** XVII, Jörgerstr. 42-44, and at the **airport**.

EMERGENCY AND COMMUNICATION

Emergencies: Police: ☎133. **Ambulance:** ☎144. **Fire:** ☎122.

CRIME IN THE CITY. Vienna is a metropolis with crime like any other; use common sense, especially after dark. Karlspl. is home to many pushers and junkies. Avoid areas in districts V, X and XIV, as well as **Landstraßer Hauptstraße** and **Prater Park,** after dark. The Red Light District covers sections of the Gürtel.

Crisis Lines: All have English speakers. **Rape Crisis Hotline:** ☎523 22 22. Open M 10am-6pm, Tu 2-6pm, W 10am-2pm, Th 5-9pm. **24hr. immediate help:** ☎717 19.

24-Hour Pharmacy: ☎15 50. Consulates have lists of English-speaking doctors, or call **Fachärzte Zugeck** (☎512 18 18; 24hr.).

Medical Assistance: Allgemeines Krankenhaus (hospital), IX, Währinger Gürtel 18-20 (☎404 00 19 64). **Emergency care:** ☎141.

Internet Access: bigNET.internet.cafe, I, Kärntnerstr. 61 (☎503 98 44) or I, Hoher markt 8-9 (☎533 29 39). €3.65 per 30min. **Libro,** XXII, Donauzentrum (☎202 52 55), provides free access at 6 terminals. Open M-F 7am-7pm, Sa 9am-5pm. **Jugend-Info des Bundesministeriums,** I, Franz-Josefs-Kai 51 (☎533 70 30), has free access at 2 PCs. Open M-F 11am-6pm.

Post Offices: Hauptpostamt, I, Fleischmarkt 19. Open 24hr. Address mail to be held: Firstname SURNAME; Postlagernde Briefe; Hauptpostamt; Fleischmarkt 19; A-1010 Wien. Branches throughout the city and at the train stations; look for the yellow signs with the trumpet logo. **Postal Codes:** A-1XX0, where XX is the number of the district in Arabic numerals (ex.: District I: A-1010, District II: A-1020, District XVII: A-1170.)

ACCOMMODATIONS AND CAMPING

One of the few unpleasant aspects of visiting Vienna is the hunt for cheap rooms during peak tourist season (June-Sept.). Write or call for reservations at least five days in advance. Otherwise, plan to call from the train station between 6 and 9am to put your name down for a reservation. If your choice is full, ask to be put on a waiting list, or ask for suggestions. Those unable to find a hostel bed should consider a *Pension*. If you're staying for a longer period of time, try **Odyssee Reisen und Mitwohnzentrale,** VIII, Laudong. 7, which arranges apartments for about €90 per week, and a minimum of €150 per month. Bring your passport to register. (☎402 60 61. Open M-F 10am-2pm and 3-6pm.) **Arwag** offers similar services via the web (www.arwag.at) or its 24hr. hotline (☎79 70 01 18).

HOSTELS

Hostel Ruthensteiner (HI), XV, Robert-Hamerlingg. 24 (☎893 42 02). Exit *Westbahnhof* at the main entrance, turn right onto Mariahilferstr. and continue until Haidmannsg. Turn left, then take the 1st right on Robert-Hammerlingg. A top-notch hostel with a knowledgeable, English-speaking staff, spotless rooms, and a snack bar. Relax in their rose-filled courtyard. Internet access from €2. Breakfast €2.50. Sheets (except for 10-bed rooms) included. 4-night max. stay. Reception 24hr. Reservations recommended, but owners often hold beds for same-day arrivals. "The Outback" summer dorm €10.50; 3- to 10-bed dorms €12-13.50; singles €20-22; doubles €40-46. AmEx/MC/V. ❷

Wombats City Hostel, XIV, Grang. 6 (☎897 23 36). Exit *Westbahnhof* at the main exit and turn right onto Mariahilferstr., turn right onto Rosinag. and continue until Grang. (2nd left). While right next to the train tracks and near a number of auto-body shops, this superb modern hostel compensates with a pub and various other perks. Internet access €1 per 12min. Bike or in-line skate rental €8 per day. Breakfast €3. Laundry €4.50. 2- to 6-bed dorms €14-36 per person. ❷

Believe It Or Not, VII, Myrtheng. 10, Apt. #14 (☎526 46 58). From *Westbahnhof,* take U6 (dir.: Floridsdorf) to Burgg./Stadthalle, then bus #48A (dir.: Ring) to Neubaug. Walk back on Burgg. 1 block and take the 1st right on Myrtheng. Ring the bell. A converted apartment with kitchen and 2 co-ed bedrooms. Reception daily 8am until early afternoon—call early. Lockout 10:30am-12:30pm. Easter-Oct. €11.65; Nov.-Easter €8. ❶

Myrthengasse (HI), VII, Myrtheng. 7, across the street from Believe It or Not (above), and **Neustiftgasse (HI),** VII, Neustiftg. 85 (☎523 63 16). These simple, modern hostels, under the same management, are 20min. from the *Innenstadt*. Internet €4.40 for 30min. Breakfast included. Laundry €3.50. 5-day max. stay. Reception at Myrtheng. 24hr. Lockout 9am-2pm. Curfew 1am. Reservations recommended. Single-sex rooms. Jan. 7-Mar. 17 and Nov. 11-Dec. 22 4- to 6-bed dorms with shower €14; 2-bed dorms with shower €16. Rest of the year €15/€17. Nonmembers add €3.50. AmEx/MC/V. ❷

Turmherberge Don Bosco, III, Lechnerstr. 12 (☎713 14 94). Take U3 to Kardinal-Nagl-Pl., take the Kardinal-Nagl-Pl. exit facing the park, walk through the park, and turn right onto Erdbergstr.; Lechnerstr. is the 2nd left. The cheapest beds in town, in a bare former bell tower. Curfew 11:45pm. Open Mar.-Nov. Dorms €6, under 19 €5.85. ❶

HOTELS AND PENSIONS

The prices are higher here, but you pay for convenient reception hours, no curfews, and no lockouts.

Lauria Apartments, VII, Kaiserstr. 77, Apt. #8 (☎522 25 55). From *Westbahnhof,* take tram #5 to Burgg. Fully equipped kitchens. 2-night min. stay. Reception daily 8am-noon. Dorms €12.50; singles and twins €35; doubles €40, with shower €60; triples €45-70. AmEx/MC/V, except for dorm beds. ❷

Pension Wild, VIII, Langeg. 10 (☎406 51 74; fax 402 21 68). U2 to Lerchenfelderstr., and take the 1st right onto Langeg. Friendly, English-speaking staff and bright decorations. Kitchen access. Breakfast included. Reception daily 6am-10pm. Reservations by fax recommended. Singles €35-64; doubles €45-85; triples €75-120. AmEx/MC/V. ❹

Pension Reimer, IV, Kircheng. 18 (☎523 61 62), is centrally located and has huge, comfortable rooms that are always clean. Breakfast included. Singles €31-38; doubles €50-56, with bath €60-64. MC/V. ❹

Pension Falstaff, IX, Müllnerg. 5 (☎317 91 27). Take U4 to Roßauer Lände, cross Roßauer Lände, head down Grünentorg., and take the 3rd left onto Müllnerg. Breakfast included. Reception daily 7:30am-9pm. Singles €33, with shower €40; doubles €51-66. Reduced rates for stays of 1 week or more in off-season. MC/V. ❹

Hotel Zur Wiener Staatsoper, I Krugerstr. 11 (☎513 12 74 75). From Karlspl., exit Oper and follow Kärtnerstr. towards the city center; turn right on Krugerstr. This luxurious hotel offers simple elegance and a prime location. Breakfast included. Singles €76-88; doubles €109-124; triples €131-146. AmEx/MC/V. ❺

UNIVERSITY DORMITORIES

From July through September, many university dorms become hotels, usually with singles, doubles, and a few triples and quads. These rooms don't have much in the way of character, but showers and sheets are standard and their cleanliness and relatively low cost suffice for most budget travelers, particularly for longer stays.

Porzellaneum der Wiener Universität, IX, Porzellang. 30 (☎31 77 28 20). From *Südbahnhof,* take tram D (dir.: Nußdorf) to Fürsteng. From *Westbahnhof,* take tram #5 to Franz-Josefs *Bahnhof,* then tram D (dir.: Südbahnhof) to Fürsteng. Great location in the student district. Reception 24hr. Singles €16-18; doubles €30-35; quads €56-64. ❸

Katholisches Studentenhaus, XIX, Peter-Jordanstr. 29 (☎369 55 85). From *Westbahnhof,* take U6 (dir.: Heiligenstadt) to Nußdorferstr., then bus #35A or tram #38 to Hardtg. and turn left. From *Südbahnhof,* take tram D to Schottentor, then tram #38 to Hardtg. Reception daily until 10pm. Singles €18; doubles €30. ❸

Studentenwohnheim der Hochschule für Musik, I, Johannesg. 8 (☎514 84 48). Walk 3 blocks down Kärntnerstr. away from Stephansdom and turn left onto Johannesg. Unbeatable location and cheap meals. Breakfast included. Reception 24hr. Reserve well in advance. Singles €33-36; doubles €58-70; triples €66; quads €80; quints €100. Apartment with 2 double rooms, bathroom, kitchen, and living room €28.50 per person; €90 for entire apartment. ❹

CAMPING

Wien-West, Hüttelbergstr. 80 (☎914 23 14). Take U4 to Hütteldorf, then bus #14B or 152 (dir.: Campingpl.) to Wien West. 8km from the city center. Crowded, but grassy and pleasant. Laundry, grocery stores, wheelchair access, and cooking facilities. Reception daily 7:30am-9:30pm. Closed Feb. July-Aug. €6 per person, Sept.-June €5; €3 per tent. Electricity €3. ❶

Aktiv Camping Neue Donau, XXII, Am Kleehäufel 119 (☎202 40 10), is 4km from the city center and adjacent to Neue Donau beaches. Take U1 to Kaisermühlen and bus #91a to Kleehäufel. Laundry, supermarket, and kitchen. Showers included. Open mid-May to mid-Sept. July to mid-Aug. €5.50 per person; May-June, and Sept. €3.50 per person; €3 per tent. Electricity €3. ❶

FOOD

Vienna's restaurants are as varied as its cuisine. The restaurants near **Kärntnerstraße** are generally expensive—a better bet is the neighborhood north of the university and near the *Votivkirche* (take U2 to Schottentor), where **Universitätstraße** and **Währingerstraße** meet. Cafes with cheap meals also line **Burggasse** in District VI. The area radiating from the **Rechte** and **Linke Wienzeile** near Naschmarkt (take U4 to Kettenbrückeg.) houses a range of cheap restaurants, and the **Naschmarkt** itself contains open-air stands where you can purchase bread and a variety of ethnic foods. Almost all year long, **Rathausplatz** hosts food stands tied into the current festival. The open-air **Brunnenmarkt** (take U6 to Josefstädterstr., then walk up Veronikag. 1 block and turn right) is cheap and cheerful.

As always, supermarkets provide building blocks for cheap, solid meals. The lowest prices are on the shelves of **Zielpunkt, Hofer,** and **Spar.** Kosher groceries are available at the **Kosher Supermarket,** II, Hollandstr. 10 (☎216 96 75).

RESTAURANTS

INSIDE THE RING

DO&CO, I, Stephanspl. 12. Set above the Stephanspl. cathedral, this modern gourmet restaurant offers both traditional Austrian dishes as well as other international specialties like Thai noodles and Uruguay beef (€18.50-21.50). Prices are high, but so are the quality and location. Open daily noon-3pm and 6pm-midnight. ❹

Trzesniewski, I, Dorotheerg. 1, 3 blocks down the Graben from the Stephansdom. This unpronounceable but famous establishment has been serving petite open-faced sandwiches for over 80 years. A filling lunch–6 sandwiches and a mini-beer–costs about €5. This was Kafka's favorite place to eat. Open M-F 8:30am-7:30pm, Sa 9am-5pm. ❷

Levante, I, Wallnerstr. 2. Walk down Graben away from the Stephansdom, turn left on Kohlmarkt, and right onto Wallnerstr. Greek-Turkish franchise features street-side dining with some vegetarian dishes. Entrees €7-12. Open daily 11am-11pm. ❸

Margaritaville, I, Bartensteing. 3. U2 to Lerchenfelderstr., exit onto Museumstr., and cut across the triangular green to Bartensteing. Offers authentic Tex-Mex food among Spanish-speakers. Open M-Sa 4pm-2am, Su 4pm-midnight. MC/V. ❸

Korso, I, Mahlerstr. 2. Upon entering, you will find yourself overcome with gold and crystal opulence–as if you had been dropped directly into Rococo Vienna. The classic Viennese cuisine mirrors the surroundings. Open daily noon-3pm and 7pm-1am. ❹

Yugetsu Saryon, I, Fuhrichg. 10. Caters to your raw fish needs. At the sushi bar, have a full lunch (€23-25) or sample individual sushi items (€3.60-5.40). Upstairs, enjoy a full menu of Japanese cuisine (€30-63). Open daily noon-2:30pm and 6-11pm. ❹

Maschu Maschu, I, Rabensteig 8. In the Bermuda *Dreieck;* serves filling and super-cheap Israeli falafel (€3). Open M-W 11:30am-midnight, Th-Sa 11:30am-3am. ❶

OUTSIDE THE RING

Centimeter, IX, Liechtensteinstr. 42. Tram D to Bauernfeldpl. This chain offers huge portions of greasy Austrian fare and an unbelievable selection of beers. You pay by the centimeter. Open M-F 10am-2am, Sa 11am-2am, Su 11am-midnight. AmEx/MC/V. ❷

Elsäßer Bistro, IX, Währingerstr. 32. U2 to Schottentor. In the palace that houses the French Cultural Institute. Walk into the garden and follow your nose for an extravagant meal. Wonderful food, with prices hovering around €14, and exquisite French wines. Open M-F 11am-3pm and 6:30-11pm. ❹

Café Nil, VII, Siebensterng. 39. Enjoy vegetarian dishes with tortured writers and philosophers (€6-11). Breakfast until 3pm. Open daily 10am-midnight. ❷

OH Pot, OH Pot, IX, Währingerstr. 22. U2 to Schottentor. This adorable joint serves filling "pots," stew-like veggie or meat concoctions (€7-10). Open M-F, Su 11:30am-midnight, Sa noon-midnight. AmEx/MC/V. ❷

Blue Box, VII, Richterg. 8. U3 to Neubaug., turn onto Neubaug., and take the 1st left onto Richterg. Blue Box is a restaurant by day and a club by night. Dishes are fresh and original (€3.50-7.10), and DJs spin the latest trance and trip-hop. Open M 6pm-2am, Tu-Su 10am-2am. Visa. ❷

Zum Mogulhof, VII, Burgg. 12. Ample portions of delicious Indian food–both vegetarian and meat–served by candlelight amid crimson carpets and velvet wallpaper. Open daily 11:30am-2:30pm and 6-11:30pm. AmEx/MC/V. ❸

Fischerbräu, XIX, Billrothstr. 17. U6 to Nußdorfer Str., follow exit sign to Wahringer Gurtel. Continue on the gurtel until Döblinger Hauptstr. and take a left., then left again on Billrothstr. Popular spot for young locals with music, home-brewed beer (large €3-5), and delicious veal sausage (€4.65). Open M-F 4pm-1am, Sa-Su 11am-1am. ❷

University Mensa, IX, Universitätsstr. 7, on the 7th fl. of the university building, between U2 stops Rathaus and Schottentor. Ride the old-fashioned *Pater Noster* elevator (no doors and never stops, so jump in and out and say your prayers) to the 6th fl. and take the stairs up. Not much atmosphere, but the food is cheap. Typical cafeteria meals €3.85. Open M-F 11am-2pm, but snack bar open 8am-3pm; closed July-Aug. ❶

COFFEEHOUSES

There is an unwritten rule for the Vienna coffeehouse: the coffee matters, but the atmosphere matters more. The 19th-century coffeehouse was a haven for artists, writers, and thinkers who flocked there and stayed long into the night composing operettas, writing books, and cutting into each other's work. The bourgeoisie followed suit, and the coffeehouse became the living room of the city. The original literary cafes were **Café Griensteidl, Café Central,** and **Café Herrenhof.** Cafes still exist under all these names, but only Café Central looks like it used to. Delectable pastries round out the experience. To see a menu, ask for a *Karte.* Most cafes also serve hot food, but ordering anything but pastries with coffee just isn't done. The most serious dictate of coffeehouse etiquette is that you linger. The waiter (known as *Herr Ober*) will serve you as soon as you sit down, then leave you to sip, read, and brood. Newspapers and magazines, many in English, are neatly racked for patrons. When you are ready to leave, just ask to pay: "*Zahlen bitte!*" Vienna has dozens of coffeehouses; the best are below.

Kleines Café, I, Franziskanerpl. 3. Turn off Kärtnerstr. onto Weihburg. and follow it to the Franziskanerkirche. This tiny, cozy cafe features tables spilling out into the courtyard and salads that are minor works of art. Open M-Sa 10am-2am, Su 1pm-2am.

Café Central, I, at the corner of Herreng. and Strauchg. inside Palais Fers. Café Central has unfortunately surrendered to tourists because of its fame, but it is still definitely worth a visit. Open M-Sa 8am-10pm, Su 10am-6pm. AmEx/MC/V.

Hotel Sacher, I, Philharmonikerstr. 4, behind the opera house. This historic sight has served world-famous *Sacher Torte* (€3.65) in red velvet opulence for years. Cafe open daily 11am-11:30pm; bakery open 9am-11pm. AmEx/MC/V.

Café Sperl, VI, Gumpendorferstr. 11. U2 to Museumsquartier; exit to Mariahilferstr., walk 1 block on Getreidemarkt, and turn right on Gumpendorferstr. Built in 1880, Sperl is one of Vienna's oldest and most beautiful cafés. Open M-Sa 7am-11pm, Su 11am-8pm; July-Aug. closed Su.

SIGHTS

Vienna's streets are by turns startling, cozy, scuzzy, and grandiose; expect contrasts around every corner. To wander on your own, grab the brochure *Vienna from A to Z* (with Vienna Card €4; available at the tourist office). The range of available **tours** is overwhelming—there are 42 themed walking tours alone, detailed in the brochure *Walks in Vienna* from the tourist office. Contact **Vienna-Bike,** IX, Wasag. (☎319 12 58), for **bike rental** (€5) or a 2-3hr. **cycling tour** (€20). **Bus tours** are given by **Vienna Sight Seeing Tours,** III, Stelzhamerg. 4/11 (☎712 46 83), and **Cityrama,** I, Börgeg. 1 (☎534 13). Tours start at €30. The sights below are arranged for a do-it-yourself walking tour.

INSIDE THE RING

District I is Vienna's social and geographical epicenter as well as a gallery of the history of aesthetics, from Romanesque to *Jugendstil* (Art Nouveau).

STEPHANSPLATZ. *(Take U1 or 3 to Stephanspl.)* Right at the heart of Vienna, this square is home to the massive **Stephansdom,** Vienna's most treasured symbol. The North Tower was originally intended to match the South Tower, but construction ceased after a spooky tragedy. (See **A Pact with the Devil,** below.) The elevator in the North Tower leads to a view of the city. *(Open Apr.-June and Sept.-Oct. 8:30am-4pm; July-Aug. 9am-6:30pm; Nov.-Mar. 8:30am-5pm. €3.50).* The 343 steps of the South Tower climb to a 360-degree view. *(Open 9am-5:30pm. €2.50.)* Downstairs, the skeletons of thousands of plague victims fill the **catacombs.** The **Gruft** (vault) stores all of the Habsburg innards. *(Cathedral tours every 30min. M-Sa 10-11:30am and 1-4:30pm, Su and holidays 1:30-4:30pm. €3.)*

A PACT WITH THE DEVIL In the 16th century, during the construction of the North Tower of the Stephansdom, a young builder named Hans Puchsbaum wished to marry his master's daughter. The master promised his consent if Hans finished the entire North Tower, alone, within a year. Faced with this impossible task, Hans despaired until a stranger offered to help him—on condition that Hans not speak the name of God or any other holy name. The tower grew by leaps and bounds until the young mason spotted his love one day and called out her name, "Maria!" Unfortunately, Maria was also the name of the Blessed Virgin. The scaffolding collapsed and Hans plummeted to his death. Rumors of a satanic pact spread, and work on the tower ceased, leaving it in its present condition.

AUSTRIA

AUSTRIAN GRAFFITI Scratched into the stones near the entrance of the Stephansdom is the mysterious abbreviation "O5." It's not a sign of hoodlums up to no good, but rather a reminder of a different kind of subversive activity. During WWII, "O5" was the secret symbol of Austria's resistance movement against the Nazis. The capital letter "O" and the number "5," for the fifth letter of the alphabet, form the first two letters of "Oesterreich"—meaning Austria. Recently the monogram has received new life. Every time alleged Nazi collaborator and ex-president of Austria Kurt Waldheim attends mass, the symbol is highlighted in chalk. Throughout the city, "O5"s have also been appearing on buildings and flyers in protest against the anti-immigrant policies of Jörg Haider and the Freedom Party.

GRABEN AND PETERSPLATZ. *(From Stephanspl., follow Graben.)* Now closed to all traffic except feet and hooves, Graben was once a moat surrounding the Roman camp that became Vienna. The landscape of the boulevard is full of *Jugendstil* architecture, including the **Ankerhaus** (#10), the red marble **Grabenhof** by Otto Wagner, and the underground public toilet complex, designed by Adolf Loos. Two blocks down in **Petersplatz** stands the 1663 **Pestsaüle** (Plague Column), which was built in gratitude for the passing of the Black Death.

HOHER MARKT. *(Take Milchg. out of Peterspl., turn right, and go 3 blocks on Tuchlauben; Hoher Markt is on the right.)* Once both market and execution site, **Hoher Markt** was the heart of the Roman encampment, Vindobona. **Roman ruins** lie beneath the shopping arcade on its south side. *(Open Tu-Su 9am-12:15pm and 1-4:40pm. €1.85, students €0.75.)* The biggest draw is the 1914 *Jugendstil* **Ankeruhr** (clock). Twelve 3m tall historical figures—including Marcus Aurelius, Maria Theresa, and Joseph Haydn—rotate past the old Viennese coat of arms accompanied by music of their time period. *(1 figure per hr. At noon all figures appear in succession.)*

STADTTEMPEL. *(Follow Judeng. from Hoher Markt to Ruprechtspl.)* Almost hidden away in Ruprechtspl., at Seitenstetteng. 2-4, the 1826 **Stadttempel** (City Temple) was the only synagogue in Vienna to escape Nazi destruction during Kristallnacht because it was concealed from the street. *(Bring your passport. Open Su-F. Free.)*

ALTES RATHAUS. The government seat from 1316 to 1885, the *Altes Rathaus* is now home to the Austrian Resistance Museum, chronicling anti-Nazi activity during WWII. *(Backtrack to Hoher Markt and follow Wipplingerstr. Open M, W, Th 9am-5pm. Free.)*

AM HOF AND FREYUNG. *(From Judenpl., take Drahtg., which runs into Am Hof.)* The grand courtyard **Am Hof,** which was once a medieval jousting square, now houses the **Kirche am Hof** (Church of the Nine Choirs of Angels; built 1386-1662). In the middle of the square looms the black **Mariensäule** (Column to Mary), erected by Emperor Ferdinand III to thank the Virgin Mary for her protection during the Thirty Years' War. Just west of Am Hof, **Freyung** is an uneven square with the **Austriabrunnen** (Austria fountain) in the center. Freyung ("sanctuary") got its name from the **Schottenstift** (Monastery of the Scots) just behind the fountain. The square was once used for public executions, but the annual **Christkindl markt** (Christ Child market) held here in December blots out such unpleasant memories.

MICHAELERKIRCHE. *(From Freyung, follow Herreng. to Michaelerpl.)* **Michaelerplatz** is named for the **Michaelerkirche** occupying the block between Kohlmarkt and Habsburgerg. The church's foundation dates back to the early 13th century, but construction continued until 1792. *(Open May-Oct. M-F 11am-5pm. €1.85, students €0.75.)*

HOFBURG. *(Head through the half-moon-shaped Michaelertor in Michaelerpl.)* The sprawling **Hofburg** was the winter residence of the Habsburgs emperors. Construction began in 1279, and hodge-podge additions and renovations continued until the end of the family's reign in 1918. The Hofburg is divided into several sections:

In der Burg. When you come through the Michaelertor, you'll first enter the courtyard called In der Burg (within the fortress). On your left is the red-and-black-striped **Schweizertor** (Swiss Gate), erected in 1552. On the right side of the Michaelertor is the entrance to the **Kaiserappartements** (Imperial Apartments). They were once the private quarters of Emperor Franz Josef and Empress Elisabeth, but the rooms are disappointingly lifeless. The **Hofsilber und Tafelkammer** (Court Silver and Porcelain Collection), on the ground floor opposite the ticket office, displays examples of the ornate Imperial cutlery. *(Both open daily 9am-4:30pm. Combined admission €6.90, students €5.45.)*

Alte Burg. Behind the Schweizertor lies the **Schweizerhof,** the inner courtyard of the Alte Burg (Old Fortress), which stands on the same site as the original 13th-century palace. The stairs to the right of the Schweiztor lead to the Gothic **Burgkapelle** (chapel), where the members of the **Wiener Sängerknaben (Vienna Boys' Choir)** raise their heavenly voices every Su (see p. 108). Beneath the stairs is the entrance to the **Weltliche und Geistliche Schatzkammer** (Worldly and Spiritual Treasury), which contains Habsburg jewels, the crowns of the Holy Roman and Austrian Empires, the "horn of a unicorn" (really an 8ft. long narwhal's horn), and a tooth allegedly from the mouth of John the Baptist. *(Open W-M 10am-6pm. €7, students €5. Free audio guide available in English.)* Attached to the northeast side of the Alte Burg is the Renaissance Stallburg, the home base for the Royal Lipizzaner stallions. The cheapest way to get a glimpse of the famous steeds is to watch them train. *(From mid-Feb. to June and late Aug. to early Nov. Tu-F 10am-noon, except when the horses tour. €11.60.)*

Neue Burg. Built between 1881 and 1926, the Neue Burg (New Fortress) is the youngest wing of the palace. The double-headed golden eagle crowning the roof symbolizes the double empire of Austria-Hungary. Today, the Neue Burg houses Austria's largest library, the **Österreichische Nationalbibliothek.** *(Open Oct.-June M-F 9am-7pm, Sa 9am-12:45pm; July-Aug. and Sept. 23-30 M-F 9am-3:45pm, Sa 9am-12:45pm.)* The Neue Burg is also home to the fantastic Völkerkunde Museum (see p. 106).

Augustinerkirche. High masses are still held in the 14th-century **Augustinerkirche** (St. Augustine's Church). The hearts of the Habsburgs are stored in the **Herzgrüftel** (Little Heart Crypt). *(Open M-Sa 10am-6pm, Su 11am-6pm. Mass 11am.)*

NEUER MARKT. *(From Albertina in the Hofburg, walk down Tegetthoffstr.)* The spectacular Neuer Markt is centered around the **Donnerbrunnen,** a graceful fountain representing the Danube and her four tributaries. Inside the **Kapuzinerkirche** (Church of the Capuchin Friars), on the southwest corner of the Neuer Markt, is the **Kaisergruft** (Imperial Vault), which holds the remains of all Habsburg rulers since 1633, minus heart and entrails. *(Open daily 9:30am-4pm. €4, students €3.)*

OUTSIDE THE RING

Some of Vienna's most famous modern architecture is outside the Ring, where 20th-century designers found more space to build. This modern area is also home to a number of Baroque palaces and parks that were once beyond the city limits.

KARLSPLATZ AND NASCHMARKT. *(Take U1, 2, or 4 to Karlspl. Or, from Neuer Markt, follow Kärntnerstr. to Karlspl., on the left.)* **Karlsplatz** is home to Vienna's most beautiful Baroque church, the **Karlskirche,** an eclectic masterpiece combining a Neoclassical portico with a Baroque dome and towers on either side. *(Open M-F 7:30am-7pm, Sa 8:30am-7pm, Su 9am-7pm. Free.)* West of Karlspl., along Linke Wienzeile, is the **Naschmarkt,** a colorful food bazaar. On Saturdays, the Naschmarkt becomes a massive flea market. *(Open M-F 7am-6pm, Sa 7am-5pm.)*

SCHLOß BELVEDERE. *(Take tram #71 or tram D one stop past Schwarzenbergpl.)* **Schloß Belvedere** (Belvedere Castle) was originally the summer residence of Prince Eugène of Savoy, Austria's greatest military hero, and Archduke Franz Ferdinand lived here until his 1914 assassination. The grounds stretch from the Schwarzenberg Palace to the *Südbahnhof* and contain three spectacular sphinx-filled gardens and an equal number of excellent museums (see p. 106).

SCHLOß SCHÖNBRUNN. *(U4 to Schönbrunn.)* From its humble beginnings as a hunting lodge, **Schönbrunn** (beautiful brook) was Maria Theresia's favorite residence. Tours of some of the palace's 1500 rooms reveal the elaborate taste of her era. Both the Grand (44 rooms) and the Imperial (22 rooms) tours give you access to the **Great Gallery,** where the Congress of Vienna met, and the **Hall of Mirrors,** where 6-year-old Mozart played. *(Palace open daily July-Aug. 8:30am-7pm; Apr.-June and Sept.-Oct. 8:30am-5pm; Nov.-Mar. 8:30am-4:30pm. Imperial Tour €7.50, students €7. Grand Tour €10/€8. Audio guides included.)* Even more impressive than the palace itself are the classical **gardens** behind it, which extend nearly four times the length of the palace and contain a hodgepodge of attractions, including the world's oldest menagerie and the **Schmetterlinghaus** (Butterfly House). *(Park open daily 6am-dusk. Free.)*

ZENTRALFRIEDHOF. Tor I (Gate 1) leads to the **Jewish Cemetery**—many of the headstones are cracked and neglected because the families of most of the dead have left Austria. Behind **Tor II** (Gate 2) are Beethoven, Strauss, and an honorary monument to Mozart, whose true resting place is an unmarked paupers' grave in the **Cemetery of St. Mark,** III, Leberstr. 6-8. **Tor III** (Gate 3) leads to the Protestant section and the new Jewish cemetery. *(Tor II at XI, Simmeringer Hauptstr. 234. Take tram #71 from Schwarzenbergpl. or tram #72 from Schlachthaus. Open May-Aug. daily 7am-7pm; Mar.-Apr. and Sept.-Oct. 7am-6pm; Nov.-Feb. 8am-5pm.)*

MUSEUMS

Vienna owes its vast selection of masterpieces to the acquisitive Habsburgs and to the city's own crop of art schools and world-class artists. An exhaustive list is impossible to include here, but the tourist office's free Museums brochure lists all opening hours and admission prices. All museums run by the city of Vienna are **free on Friday** before noon (except on public holidays). If you're going to be in town for a while, invest in the **Museum Card** (ask at any museum ticket window).

Österreichische Galerie, III, Prinz-Eugen-Str. 27, in the Belvedere Palace behind Schwarzenbergpl. (p. 106). Walk up from the *Südbahnhof* and take tram D to Schloß Belvedere or tram #71 to Unteres Belvedere. The **Upper Belvedere** houses European art of the 19th and 20th centuries, including Klimt's *The Kiss*. The **Lower Belvedere** contains an extensive collection of sculptures, David's portrait of Napoleon on horseback, and the **Museum of Medieval Austrian Art.** Both Belvederes open Tu-Su 10am-6pm. Upper open Th until 9pm. €7.50, students €5.

Kunsthistorisches Museum. U2 to Museumsquartier or trams 1, 2, D, or J or U2 or 3 to Volkstheater. Across from the Burgring and Heldenpl. on Maria Theresia's right. The world's 4th-largest art collection, including Venetian paintings, Classical art, and an Egyptian burial chamber. Open Tu-Su 10am-6pm. €9, students €6.50. Audio guides €2.

Museum für Völkerkunde (Ethnology Museum), I, in the Neue Burg on Heldenpl. (p. 105). U2 to Museumsquartier or trams 1, 2, D, or J or U2 or 3 to Volkstheater. Collected here are Benin bronzes, Chinese paper kites, West African Dan heads, and a Japanese Doll Festival. The focal point, however, is undoubtedly the crown of Montezuma, still drawing a crowd of protesters demanding its return to Mexico. Open Apr.-Dec. W-M 10am-6pm. €7.50, students €5.50, free May 16, Oct. 26, Dec. 10 and 24.

Museumsquartier. U2 to Museumsquartier or trams 1, 2, D, or J or U2 or 3 to Volkstheater. A huge conglomeration of museums. **Kunsthalle Wien** features exhibitions of international contemporary artists. Open daily 10am-7pm, Th until 10pm. Hall 1 €6.50, students €5; Hall 2 €5/€3.50; both €8/€6.50. **Museum Moderner Kunst** holds Central Europe's largest collection of modern art. Open Tu-Su 10am-7pm, Th until 9pm. €8, students €6.50.

Jüdisches Museum (Jewish Museum), I, Dorotheerg. 11. From Stephanspl., off Graben. Jewish culture and history told through various media, including fragments of text stamped into the walls, holograms, and the traditional objects-in-a-glass-case. Open Su-F 10am-6pm, Th until 8pm. €5, students €2.90.

Kunst Haus Wien, III, Untere Weißgerberstr. 13. U1 or 4 to Schwedenpl., then tram N to Hetzg. This museum, built by artist and environmental activist Friedenreich Hundertwasser lacks straight lines, which Hundertwasser called "the Devil's work"; even the floor bends and swells. The Kunst Haus also hosts exhibits of contemporary art from around the world. Open daily 10am-7pm. €8, students €6; M half-price.

Historisches Museum der Stadt Wien, IV, Karlspl., to the left of the Karlskirche (see p. 105). This amazing collection of historical artifacts and paintings documents Vienna's evolution from a Roman encampment, through the Turkish siege of Vienna, to the subsequent 640 years of Habsburg rule. Open Tu-Su 9am-6pm. €3.50, students €1.50.

Sigmund Freud Haus, IX, Bergg. 19. U2 to Schottentor, then walk up Währingerstr. to Bergg or take tram D to Schlickg. The famed couch is not here, but this former Freud home provides lots of photos and documents, including his report cards and circumcision certificate. Open July-Sept. 9am-6pm; Oct.-June 9am-4pm. €5, students €3.

Lipizzaner Museum, I, Reitschulg. 2. If you ever liked horses, this is the place for you. What used to be the imperial pharmacy is now a museum dedicated to the imperial horses, featuring paintings, harnesses, video clips, and a small viewing window to the stables. Open daily 9am-6pm. €5.10, students €3.65.

ENTERTAINMENT

While Vienna offers all the standard entertainments in the way of theater, film, and festivals, the heart of the city beats to music. All but a few of classical music's marquee names lived, composed, and performed in Vienna. Mozart, Beethoven, and Haydn wrote their greatest masterpieces in Vienna, creating the **First Viennese School;** a century later, Schönberg, Webern, and Berg teamed up to form the **Second Viennese School.** Every Austrian child must learn to play an instrument during schooling, and the Vienna **Konservatorium** and **Hochschule** are world-renowned conservatories. All year, Vienna has performances ranging from the above-average to the sublime, with many accessible to the budget traveler. Note that the venues below have **no performances in July and August.**

Staatsoper, I, Opernring 2, is Vienna's premier opera, performing nearly every night Sept.-June. **Standing-room tickets** are the cheapest; 500 are available for every performance, but only 1 can be bought per person right before the performance (€2-3.50). Formal dress not necessary, but no shorts. **Box office tickets in advance:** purchase through the official ticket offices by phone, fax, or in person. The main office is the Bundestheaterkasse, I, Hanuschg. 3 (☎514 44 78 80; fax 514 44 29 69; www.wienerstaatsoper.at.), around the corner from the opera. Open M-F 8am-6pm, Sa-Su 9am-noon, 1st Sa of each month 9am-5pm. There is also a ticket office inside the Staatsoper, open during the same hours, but closed on Su and holidays. Tickets (€10-178) may be purchased 1 month before performance. **Web site:** www.bundestheater.at allows you to purchase tickets in advance; 20% commission.

Wiener Philharmoniker (Vienna Philharmonic Orchestra) plays in the **Musikverein,** Austria's premier concert hall. Write or visit the box office of the Musikverein for tickets, including standing room tickets well in advance (Gesellschaft der Musikfreunde, Bösendorferstr. 12, A-1010 Wien) or stop by the Bundestheaterkasse (see Staatsoper, above). Tickets are available at www.wienerphilharmoniker.at.

Wiener Sangerknaben (Viennese Boys' Choir) sings during mass every Su at 9:15am (mid-Sept. to May only) in the **Hofburgkapelle** (U3 to Herreng.). For more information, contact hofmusikkapelle@asn-wien.ac.at.

FESTIVALS

Vienna hosts an array of important annual festivals, mostly musical. The **Vienna Festival** (mid-May to mid-June) has a diverse program of exhibitions, plays, and concerts. (☎58 92 20; www.festwochen.or.at.) The Staatsoper and Volkstheater host the annual **Jazzfest Wien** during the first weeks of July, featuring many famous acts. (☎503 5647; www.viennajazz.org.) From mid-July to mid-August, the **Im-Puls Dance Festival** (☎523 55 58; www.impuls-tanz.com) attracts some of the world's great dance troupes and offers seminars to enthusiasts. In mid-October, the annual city-wide international film festival, the **Viennale,** kicks off.

AUSTRIA

NIGHTLIFE

With one of the highest bar-to-cobblestone ratios in the world, Vienna is a great place to party, whether you're looking for a quiet evening with a glass of wine or a wild night in a disco full of black-clad musclemen and drag queens. Take U1 or 4 to Schwedenplatz, which will drop you within blocks of the **Bermuda Dreieck** (Triangle), an area packed with lively, crowded clubs. If your vision isn't foggy yet, head down **Rotenturmstraße** toward Stephansdom or walk around the areas bounded by the Jewish synagogue and Ruprechtskirche. Slightly outside the Ring, the streets off **Burggaße** and **Stiftgaße** in the district VII and the **university quarter** (Districts VIII and IX) have tables in outdoor courtyards and loud, hip bars.

Viennese nightlife starts late, often after 11pm. For the scoop, pick up a copy of the indispensable **Falter** (€2), which prints listings of everything from opera and theater to punk concerts and updates on the gay/lesbian scene.

Objektiv, VII, Kirchbergg. 26. U2 or 3 to Volkstheater, walk down Burgg. 2 blocks, and turn right on Kirchbergg. to find one of the most eclectic bars in Vienna. A mellow atmosphere with cheap drinks. Happy Hour daily 11pm-1am. Open M-Sa 6pm-2am.

U-4, XII, Schönbrunnerstr. 222. U4 to Meidling Hauptstr. In the late 80s, U-4 hosted Nirvana, Mudhoney, and Hole before they were famous. 2 dance areas and multiple bars. Check in advance for information on theme nights. Cover €8. Open daily 10pm-5am.

Das Möbel, VII, Burgg. 10. U2 or 3 to Volkstheater. The metal couches, car seat chairs, and Swiss-army tables are in full use by a trendy crowd. Drinks €2.25. Open M-F noon-1am, Sa-Su 10-1am.

Mapitom der Bierlokal, I, Seitenstetteng. 1. Located in the center of the Bermuda Triangle, this bar has large tables clustered in a warehouse-style interior. Beer and mixed drinks about €3. Open Su-Th 5pm-3am, F and Sa 5pm-4am.

Volksgarten Disco, I, Volksgarten. U2 or 3 to Volkstheater. Hiphop/R&B and an adolescent crowd on F nights, house and a somewhat older crowd Sa. Cover €6-13. Open Th-Su 10pm-5am.

SALZBURGER LAND AND UPPER AUSTRIA

Salzburger Land derives its name from the German *Salz* (salt), and it was this white gold that first drew visitors to the region. Although tourism displaced the salt trade long ago, images of St. Barbara, the patron saint of salt miners, are everywhere. Combined with Upper Austria, this region encompasses the shining lakes and rolling hills of the Salzkammergut, where Hallstatt is among the more enticing destinations.

SALZBURG ☎0662

Wedged between mountains and graced with Baroque wonders, Salzburg offers both spectacular sights and a rich musical culture. Laying claim to Mozart's birthplace and *The Sound of Music*, Salzburg's streets resonate with plenty of melodies. The city's adulation for classical music and the arts in general reaches a dizzying climax every summer during the Salzburger Festspiele, a five-week music festival featuring hundreds of operas, concerts, plays, and open-air performances.

AUSTRIA

TRANSPORTATION

Trains: Hauptbahnhof, in Südtirolerpl. To: **Graz** (4hr., every 2hr., €33.40); **Innsbruck** (2hr., every 2hr., €27.60); **Munich** (2hr., 27 per day, €21.60); **Vienna** (3½hr., 29 per day, €33.40); **Zurich** (6hr., 3 per day, €63.40). Reservations (☎05 17 17). Regular ticket office open 24hr.

Public Transportation: Lokalbahnhof (☎44 80 61 66), next to the train station. Single tickets (€1.60) available at automatic machines or from the bus drivers. Books of **five tickets** (€6.50), **daypasses** (€2.90), and **week passes** (€9) available at machines, the ticket office, or *Tabak* shops (newsstand/tobacco shops). Punch your ticket when you board in order to validate it or risk a €36 fine. Buses usually make their last run at 10:30-11:30pm, but **BusTaxi** fills in when the public buses stop. Get on at Hanuschpl. or Theaterg. and tell the driver where you need to go (every 30min. Su-Th 11:30pm-1:30am, F-Sa 11:30pm-3am; €2.55 for anywhere within the city limits).

ORIENTATION AND PRACTICAL INFORMATION

Just a few kilometers from the German border, Salzburg covers both banks of the **Salzach River.** Two hills loom in the skyline: the **Monchsberg** over the *Altstadt* on the south side and the **Kapuzinerberg** by the *Neustadt* on the north side. The *Hauptbahnhof* is on the northern side of town beyond the Neustadt; buses #1, 5, 6, 51, and 55 connect it to downtown. From the bus, disembark at Mirabellplatz in the *Neustadt;* on foot, turn left out of the station onto Rainerstr. and follow it all the way (under the tunnel) to Mirabellpl.

Tourist Office, Mozartpl. 5 (☎88 98 73 30; www.salzburg.info.or.at), in the *Altstadt.* From the station, take bus #5, 6, 51, or 55 to Mozartsteg, head away from the river and curve right around the building into Mozartpl. The office gives out free hotel maps, offers guided tours of the city (daily 12:15pm, €8), and sells the **Salzburg Card,** which grants admission to all museums and sights as well as unlimited public transportation (24hr. card €18, 48hr. €26, 72hr. €32). Reservation service €2.20. Open daily 9am-6pm.

Consulates: South Africa, Buchenweg 14 (☎62 20 35). Open M-Th 3-5:30pm. **UK,** Alter Markt 4 (☎84 81 33). Open M-F 9-11:30pm. **US,** Alter Markt 1/3 (☎84 87 76), in the *Altstadt.* Open M, W-Th 9am-noon.

Currency Exchange: ReiseBank, Alter Markt 15, has extended exchange hours. Open daily 10am-2:30pm and 3-8pm.

American Express: Mozartpl. 5, A-5020 (☎80 80), near the tourist office. Provides all banking services; no commission on AmEx checks. Holds mail and books tours. Open M-F 9am-5:30pm, Sa 9am-noon.

Luggage Storage: At the train station. 24hr. lockers €2-3.50.

Bi-Gay-Lesbian Resources: Homosexual Initiative of Salzburg (HOSI), Müllner Hauptstr. 11 (☎43 59 27), hosts regular workshops and meetings, and has a **cafe-bar** open W from 7pm, F and Sa from 8pm.

Laundromat: Norge Exquisit Textil Reinigung, Paris-Lodronstr. 16 (☎87 63 81). Wash and dry €9 (including their soap, which must be used). Open M-F 7:30am-4pm, Sa 8-10am. Full-serve €14.20; next-day pickup. Open M-F 7:30am-6pm, Sa 8am-noon.

Emergencies: Police: ☎133. **Ambulance:** ☎144. **Fire:** ☎122.

Pharmacies: Elisabeth-Apotheke, Elisabethstr. 1a (☎87 14 84). Pharmacies in the city center open M-F 8am-6pm, Sa 8am-noon. There are always 3 pharmacies open for emergencies; check the list on the door of any closed pharmacy.

Medical Assistance: Call the **hospital,** Dr. Franz-Rebirl-Pl. 5 (☎658 00).

Internet Access: Internet Café, Mozartpl. 5 (☎84 48 22). €0.15 per minute. Open Sept.-May daily 9am-11pm; July-Aug. 9am-midnight.

Post Office: At the *Hauptbahnhof* (☎88 30 30). Address *Poste Restante*: Firstname SURNAME, *Postlagernde Briefe*, Bahnhofspostamt, **A-5020** Salzburg, AUSTRIA. Open M-F 7am-8:30pm, Sa 8am-2pm, Su 1-6pm.

ACCOMMODATIONS AND CAMPING

Salzburg has no shortage of hostels—then again, it has no shortage of tourists either. Housing in Salzburg is expensive; most affordable options lie on the outskirts of town. Be wary of hotel hustlers at the station; instead, ask for the tourist office's list of **private rooms** or consult the *Hotel Plan* (which has info on hostels). From mid-May to mid-September, hostels fill by mid-afternoon, so call ahead, and be sure to make reservations during the *Festspiele* (see p. 115).

HOSTELS, PENSIONS, AND CAMPING

Stadtalm, Mönchsberg 19c (☎/fax 84 17 29). Take bus #1 (dir.: Maxglan) to Mönchsbergaufzug, go down the street and through the stone arch on the left to the Mönchsberglift (elevator) and ride up (9am-11pm, round-trip €2.40). At the top, turn right, climb the steps, and follow signs for Stadtalm. A princely view on a pauper's budget. Breakfast included. Shower €0.80 per 4min. Reception daily 9am-9pm. Curfew 1am. Open Apr.-Sept. Dorms €12.50. AmEx/MC/V. ❷

Institut St. Sebastian, Linzerg. 41 (☎87 13 86). From the station, bus #1, 5, 6, 51, or 55 to Mirabellpl.; continue in same direction as the bus, turn left onto Bergstr., and left again onto Linzerg; the hostel is through the arch on the left. Rooftop terrace with postcard perfect views of the city. Breakfast included. Sheets €2 for dorms. Laundry €2.90. Reception daily 8am-noon and 4-9pm. Dorms €15; singles €21, with shower €33; doubles €40/€54; triples €60/€69; quads €72/€84. ❷

Pension Sandwirt, Lastenstr. 6a (☎fax 87 43 51). Exit the main train station from the platform #13 staircase, turn right on the footbridge, right again onto Lastenstr., and go behind the building with the Post sign. The down-to-earth hosts of this bed-and-breakfast speak excellent English. All rooms have TVs. Laundry included. Singles €21; doubles €35, with shower €42; triples €50; quads €64. ❸

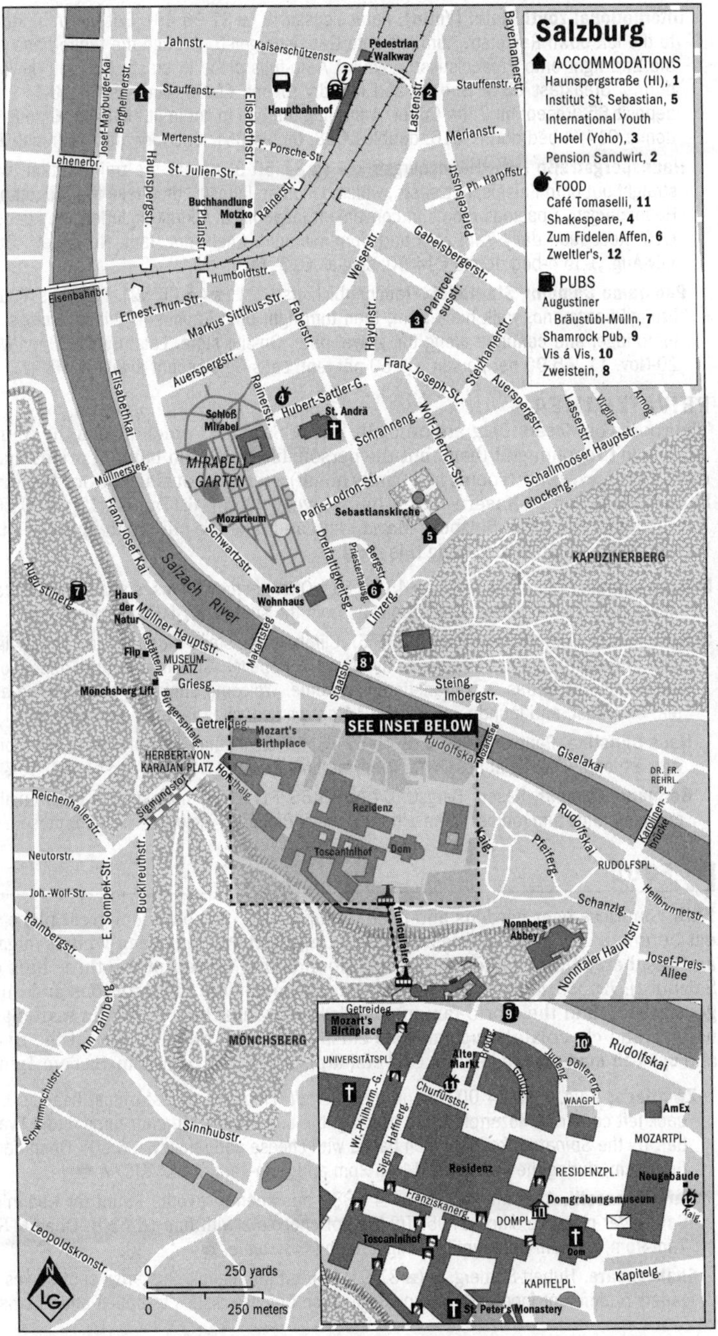
Salzburg
ACCOMMODATIONS
Haunspergstraße (HI), 1
Institut St. Sebastian, 5
International Youth Hotel (Yoho), 3
Pension Sandwirt, 2
FOOD
Café Tomaselli, 11
Shakespeare, 4
Zum Fidelen Affen, 6
Zweltler's, 12
PUBS
Augustiner Bräustübl-Mülln, 7
Shamrock Pub, 9
Vis á Vis, 10
Zweistein, 8
SEE INSET BELOW
Jahnstr.
Kaiserschützenstr.
Pedestrian Walkway
Stauffenstr.
Hauptbahnhof
Lastenstr.
Bayerhamerstr.
Josef-Mayburger-Kai
Bergheimerstr.
Mertenstr.
Elisabethstr.
F. Porsche-Str.
Merianstr.
Lehenerbr.
Haunspergstr.
St. Julien-Str.
Ph. Harpffstr.
Paracelsusstr.
Buchhandlung Motzko
Plainstr.
Rainerstr.
Humboldtstr.
Gabelsbergerstr.
Weiserstr.
Eisenbahnbr.
Ernest-Thun-Str.
Markus Sittikus-Str.
Faberstr.
Haydnstr.
Paracelsusstr.
Stelzhamerstr.
Auerspergstr.
Franz Joseph-Str.
Elisabethkai
Hubert-Sattler-G.
Schloß Mirabel
St. Andrä
Schranneng.
Wolf-Dietrich-Str.
Lasserstr.
Virgilg.
Arnog.
MIRABELL-GARTEN
Müllnersteg
Paris-Lodron-Str.
Schallmooser Hauptstr.
Glockeng.
Sebastianskirche
Mozarteum
Schwartzstr.
Dreifaltigkeitsg.
Priesterhausg.
Bergstr.
KAPUZINERBERG
Franz Josef Kai
Salzach River
Augustinerg.
Mozart's Wohnhaus
Linzerg.
Haus der Natur
Müllner Hauptstr.
Makartsteg
Flip
Gstätteng.
MUSEUM-PLATZ
Staatsbr.
Steing.
Imbergstr.
Mönchsberg Lift
Griesg.
Bürgerspitalg.
Getreideg.
Mozart's Birthplace
Rudolfskai
Mozartsteg
Giselakai
HERBERT-VON-KARAJAN PLATZ
Hofstallg.
Sigmundstor
Reichenhallerstr.
Rezidenz
DR. FR. REHRL. PL.
Karolinenbrücke
Toscaninihof
Dom
Kaig.
Pfeiferg.
Neutorstr.
Bucklreuthstr.
RUDOLFSPL.
Joh.-Wolf-Str.
Schanzlg.
Hellbrunnerstr.
funiculaire
E. Sompek-Str.
Rainbergstr.
Nonnberg Abbey
Nonntaler Hauptstr.
Josef-Preis-Allee
Am Rainberg
MÖNCHSBERG
Schwimmschulstr.
Sinnhubstr.
Leopoldskronstr.
0 250 yards
0 250 meters
Getreideg.
Mozart's Birthplace
UNIVERSITÄTSPL.
Alter Markt
Brodg.
Goldg.
Judeng.
Rudolfskai
Döllererg.
Churfürststr.
WAAGPL.
AmEx
Wr.-Philharm.-G.
Sigm. Haffnerg.
MOZARTPL.
Residenz
RESIDENZPL.
Neugebäude
Domgrabungsmuseum
Franziskanerg.
DOMPL.
Toscaninihof
Dom
Kapitelg.
KAPITELPL.
St. Peter's Monastery

AUSTRIA

International Youth Hotel (YoHo), Paracelsusstr. 9 (☎87 96 49). Exit the train station to the left down Rainerstr., turn left onto Gabelsbergerstr. through the tunnel, and take the 2nd right onto Paracelsusstr. (7min.) A no-frills place to crash. No room keys for dorms. Breakfast €3-4. Shower and laundry tokens €0.50. Lockers €0.10-1. Sheet deposit €5. Reception 24hr. Curfew 1am; ring the bell to get in at any time. 6- to 8-bed dorms €14; 4-bed dorms €16; doubles €38; triples €51. Cheaper after 1st night. ❷

Haunspergstraße (HI), Haunspergstr. 27 (☎87 50 30), near the train station. Walk straight out onto Kaiserschützenstr., which becomes Jahnstr., then take the 3rd left onto Haunspergstr. Spacious rooms in convenient location. Breakfast included. Key deposit €10. Reception daily 7am-2pm and 5pm-midnight. Check-out 9am. No curfew. Open July-Aug. 3- to 4-bed dorms €14.50; singles €19. ❷

Panorama Camping Stadtblick, Rauchenbichlerstr. 21 (☎45 06 52). Take bus #51 to Itzling-Pflanzmann, walk back 50m, then turn right onto Rauchenbichlerstr., cross the footbridge, and continue along the gravel path. On-site store. Laundry €5. Open Mar. 20-Nov. 11. €5.90 per person; €1.50 per tent. *Let's Go* discount available. ❶

PRIVATZIMMER

The rooms on **Kasern Berg** are officially out of Salzburg, which means the tourist office can't recommend them, but the personable hosts and bargain prices make these *Privatzimmer* (rooms in a family home) a terrific housing option. All northbound trains run to Kasern Berg (4min., every 30min. 6:17am-11:17pm, €1.60; Eurail valid). Get off at Salzburg-Maria Plain and take the only road uphill. All the Kasern Berg pensions are along this road.

Haus Lindner, Panoramaweg 5 (☎45 66 81). Offers homey rooms, some with mountain views. Breakfast included. Call for pickup from the station. €14-15 per person. ❷

Haus Moser, Turnerbühel 1 (☎45 66 76). Climb up the steep hidden stairs on the right side of Kasern Berg road across from Germana Kapeller. Charming couple offers comfortable rooms in this cozy, dark-timbered home. Welcome drink, unlimited coffee and tea, breakfast, and laundry included. €14 per person; cheaper after 1st night. ❷

Haus Christine, Panoramaweg 3 (☎45 67 73; haus.christine@gmx.at). Spacious rooms with a friendly, family atmosphere. Breakfast included. €14-15 per person. MC/V. ❷

Germana Kapeller, Kasern Bergstr. 64 (☎45 66 71). Lively host speaks good English and maintains trim rooms, some with balconies. Breakfast included. €15 per person. ❷

FOOD

With countless beer gardens and pastry-shop patios, Salzburg is a great place to eat outdoors. Local specialties include *Salzburger Nockerl* (egg whites, sugar, and raspberry filling baked into three mounds that represent the three hills of Salzburg), *Knoblauchsuppe* (a rich cream soup loaded with croutons and pungent garlic), and the world-famous **Mozartkugeln** (hazelnut coated in marzipan, nougat, and chocolate). **Supermarkets** cluster on the Mirabellpl. side of the river and **open-air markets** are held on Universitätpl. (Open M-F 6am-7pm, Sa 6am-1pm.)

Zweltler's, Kaig. 3 (☎84 00 44), in the *Altstadt*. From the tourist office, head to the back left corner of Mozartpl. In the evening, the cozy wooden interior turns into a lively bar. Try the *Spinatnockerl* (spinach baked with cheese and parsley; €6.50). Open daily 6pm-1am, during the *Festspiele* 11am-2pm and 6pm-1am. AmEx/MC/V. ❸

Café Tomaselli, Alter Markt 9 (☎84 44 88), has been a favorite haunt for wealthier Salzburger clientele since 1705. Try the hot chocolate with rum (€4.20). Open M-Sa 7am-9pm, Su 8am-9pm; until midnight during *Festspiele*. ❷

Shakespeare, Hubert-Sattlerg. 3 (☎87 91 06), off Mirabellpl. This artsy spot serves a variety of different foods, from surprisingly good Chinese dishes to Italian and Austrian ones. Large, spicy platter of Szechaun pork €8.45. Open daily 8am-2am. MC/V. ❸

Zum Fidelen Affen, Priesterhausg. 8 (☎87 73 61), off Linzerg. This popular restaurant serves hearty, honest Austrian food that keeps everyone coming back "To the Faithful Ape." Meals €8.50-17. Open M-Sa 5pm-11pm. ❸

SIGHTS

THE NEUSTADT

MIRABELL PALACE AND GARDENS. Mirabellpl. holds the marvelous **Schloß Mirabell,** which the supposedly celibate Archbishop Wolf Dietrich built for his mistress and their 10 children in 1606. Behind the palace, the delicately cultivated **Mirabellgarten** is a maze of seasonal flower beds and groomed shrubs. The Mirabellgarten contains a wooden, moss-covered shack called the **Zauberflötenhäuschen,** allegedly where Mozart composed *The Magic Flute* in just five months.

MOZARTS WOHNHAUS. Mozart moved here at age 17 with his family, staying from 1773-1780. See some Mozart memorabilia, and hear lots of excerpts from his music. The audio guides, however, tend to confuse more than enlighten. *(Makartpl. 8. Open daily 9am-6pm; July-Aug. until 7pm. €5.50, students €4.50.)*

SEBASTIANSKIRCHE AND MAUSOLEUM. A little way down Linzerg. from the river stands the 18th-century **Sebastianskirche,** with an Italian-style graveyard containing the impressive **mausoleum** of Prince Archbishop Wolf Dietrich. Ornate gravestones and frescoes line the walls. The tombs of Mozart's wife and father are along the main path. *(Linzerg. 41. Open Apr.-Oct. 9am-7pm; Nov.-Mar. 9am-4pm.)*

THE ALTSTADT

MOZARTS GEBURTSHAUS. Mozart's birthplace, on the 2nd floor of Getreideg. 9, holds an impressive collection of the child genius' belongings including his first viola and violin and a pair of keyboardish instruments. Several rooms recreate his young years as a traveling virtuoso. Come before 11am to avoid the crowd. *(Open July-Aug. daily 9am-6:30pm; Sept.-June 9am-5:30pm. €5.50, students and seniors €4.50.)*

TOSCANINIHOF, CATACOMBS, AND THE DOM. Steps lead from **Toscaninihof,** the courtyard of **St. Peter's Monastery,** up the Mönchesberg cliffs. **Stiftskirche St. Peter,** within the monastery, features a marble portal from 1244. In the 18th century, the

IN RECENT NEWS

MAKING MUSEUMS OUT OF MOUNTAINS

You've probably seen the fortress on the top of the Mönchsberg, but have you thought about what's inside that mountain? Salzburgers have been tunneling into it for centuries, starting from the catacombs behind St. Peter's cemetery and continuing into the busy traffic tunnel of the Sigmundstor. A new plan to build a museum of modern art inside the mountain has Salzburgers in a tizzy. The adventurous design first created more than 10 years ago involves a gallery located inside the mountain, lit by skylights from the surface.

Though the idea was rejected in 1990 for financial reasons, the debate is far from over. In 1998, a Europe-wide design competition was held, and the winning museum design was supposed to be finished in 2002. In 2002, however, there was nothing of the museum but a large gravel pit by the top of the Mönchsberg elevator. Dithering by the government and funding concerns have forced the project into limbo for years. The cost of the project has grown from 120 million Schillings in 1999 to 300 million Schillings (21.8 million euros, or 21.3 million US dollars). The date of completion has also been pushed back from 2002 to 2003 to 2004.

As a sort of penance for ripping apart the mountain even more, the museum is to incorporate many environmentally friendly features, such as utilization of the warmth coming from the underground garage in the Mönchsberg for heating.

building was remodeled in Rococo style. *(Open daily 9am-12:15pm and 2:30-6:30pm.)* Near the far end of the cemetery against the Mönchsberg is the entrance to the **Catacombs.** In the lower room (St. Gertrude's Chapel), a fresco commemorates the martyrdom of Thomas à Beckett. *(Open May-Sept. Tu–Su 10:30am-5pm; Oct.-Apr. W-Su 10:30am-4pm. €1, students €0.60.)* The exit at the other end of the cemetery leads to the immense Baroque **Dom,** where Mozart was christened in 1756 and later worked as *Konzertmeister* and court organist. The square leading out of the cathedral, **Domplatz,** features a statue of the Virgin Mary and figures representing wisdom, faith, the church, and the devil. Be prepared to give a small donation.

RESIDENZ. Salzburg's ecclesiastical elite have resided in the magnificent Residenz for the last 700 years. Stunning Baroque **Prunkräume** (state rooms) house gigantic ceiling frescoes, gilded furniture, Flemish tapestries from the 1600s, and ornate stucco work. A **gallery** exhibits 16th- to 19th-century art. *(Open daily 10am-5pm. €7.25, students €5.50; audio guide included.)*

FESTUNG HOHENSALZBURG. Built between 1077 and 1681, Festung Hohensalzburg (Hohensalzburg Fortress), which looms over Salzburg from atop Mönchesberg, is the largest completely preserved castle in Europe—probably because it was never successfully attacked. The castle contains formidable Gothic state rooms, the fortress organ (nicknamed the "Bull of Salzburg" for its off-key snorting), and a watchtower that affords an unmatched view of the city and mountains. The Burgmuseum inside the fortress displays medieval instruments of torture and has side-by-side histories of Salzburg, the Festung, and the world. *(Take the trail or the Festungsbahn funicular up to the fortress from the Festungsg. May-Sept. every 10min. 9am-9pm; Oct.-Apr. 9am-5pm. €5.55, round-trip €6.35; includes entrance to fortress. Grounds open mid-June to mid-Sept. 8:30am-8pm; mid-Sept. to mid-Mar. 9am-5pm; mid-Mar. to mid-June 9am-6pm. Interior open mid-June to mid-Sept. 9am-6pm; mid-Sept. to mid-Mar. 9:30am-5pm; mid-Mar. to mid-June 9:30am-5:30pm. If you make the steep 20min. walk up, entrance to fortress €3.55; combo ticket including fortress, castle interiors, and museum €7.10.)*

MUSEUMS

Salzburg's small, specialized museums often get lost in the shadow of the *Festung*, *The Sound of Music*, and the *Festspiele.* There are also private galleries on **Sigmund-Haffnergaße** that allow budget art viewing.

ART MUSEUMS. Museum Carolino Augusteum houses local Roman and Celtic artifacts on its ground floor, including mosaics and burial remains, naturally preserved thanks to the region's salt. *(Museumpl. 1. Open F-W 9am-5pm, Th until 8pm. €3.30, students €1.10.)* The Residenz Gallery, in the Orangerie of the Mirabellgarten, pays tribute to the aesthetic of 17th- and 18th-century Europe. *(Residenzpl. 1. Open Apr.-Sept. daily 10am-5pm; Oct.-Mar. closed M. €4.75, students €3.65.)*

OTHER MUSEUMS. The **Haus der Natur,** opposite the Carolino Augusteum, is an 80-room building with an eclectic collection, from live alligators and giant snakes to huge rock crystals. *(Museumpl. 5. Open daily 9am-5pm. €4.50, students €2.50.)* Just inside the main entrance to the *Dom*, the **Dom Museum** houses an unusual collection called the **Kunst- und Wunderkammer** (Art and Curiosity Cabinet) that includes old door locks, a big globe with men and beasts dancing across it, and a giant lobster claw, all collected by the archbishop to impress distinguished visitors. In the main museum, the gigantic Rupertskreuz (Cross of Rupert) stands guard over the back room. *(Open mid-May to mid-Oct. M-Sa 10am-5pm, Su 1pm-6pm. €4.50, students €1.50. Guided tours Sa 10:30am. €1.45.)* Down the stairs between Residenzpl. and Dompl., the **Domgrabungsmuseum** displays excavations of the Roman ruins under the cathedral, some of which date back as far as the 2nd century. *(Open May-Oct. W-Su 9am-5pm. €1.80, students €1.45.)*

ENTERTAINMENT

Max Reinhardt, Richard Strauss, and Hugo von Hofmannsthal founded the renowned **Salzburger Festspiele** in 1920. Ever since, Salzburg has become a musical mecca from late July to the end of August. On the eve of the festival's opening, over 100 dancers don regional costumes and perform a *Fackeltanz* (torchdance) on Residenzpl. Operas, plays, films, concerts, and tourists overrun every available public space. Information and tickets for *Festspiele* events are available through the *Festspiele Kartenbüro* (ticket office) and *Tageskasse* (daily box office) in Karajanpl., against the mountain and next to the tunnel. (Open M-F 9:30am-3pm; July 1-July 22 M-Sa until 5pm; July 23-end of festival daily until 6:30pm.)

Even when the *Festspiele* is not on, many other concerts and events occur around the city. The **Salzburg Academy of Music and Performing Arts** performs a number of concerts on a rotating schedule in the **Mozarteum** (next to the Mirabell gardens), and the **Dom** also has a concert program in July and August (Th-F 11:15am. €8.75, students €7.30). In addition, from May through August there are **outdoor performances,** including concerts, folk-singing, and dancing, around the Mirabellgarten. The tourist office has leaflets on scheduled events, but an evening stroll through the park might prove just as enlightening. **Mozartplatz** and **Kapitelplatz** are also popular stops for talented street musicians and touring school bands.

AUSTRIA

PUBS AND BEER GARDENS

Munich may be known as the world's beer capital, but a lot of that liquid gold flows south to Austria's pubs and **Biergärten** (beer gardens). These lager oases cluster in the city center by the Salzach River. *Altstadt* nightclubs (especially along Gstätteng. and near Chiemseeg.) attract a younger crowd and tourists; the other side of the river has a less juvenile atmosphere. **Augustiner Bräustübl-Mülln,** Augustinerg. 4, has been serving home-brewed beer since 1621. (From the *Altstadt,* follow the footpath from Hanuschpl. downstream along the river; take the stairs up to your left after the 1st bridge; cross the street and continue to your right along Muellner Haupstr.; turn left onto Augustinerg. Open M-F 3-11pm, Sa-Su 2:30-11pm.) Settle into an armchair with a brew at **Vis à Vis,** Rudolfskai 24. (Open daily from 8pm.) **Shamrock,** Rudolfskai 24, a relaxed and friendly Irish pub, has plenty of room and nightly live music. (Open Su-M 3pm-2am, Tu-W 3pm-3am, Th-Sa 3pm-4am.) **Zweistein,** Giselakai 9, is the place to come for Salzburg's gay and lesbian scene. (Open M-W 8pm-4am, Th 6pm-4am, F-Su 6pm-5am.)

DAYTRIPS FROM SALZBURG

LUSTSCHLOß HELLBRUNN AND UNTERSBERG PEAK

For Hellbrunn, take bus #55 (dir.: Anif) to Hellbrunn from the train station, Mirabellpl., or Mozartsteg. For Untersberg Peak, take bus #55 past Hellbrunn to St. Leonhard.

Just south of Salzburg lies the unforgettable Lustschloß Hellbrunn, a sprawling estate with a large palace, fish ponds, flower gardens, and the Wasserspiele, elaborate water-powered figurines and a booby-trapped table that could spout water on drunken guests. Pictures of you getting sprayed are available at the end of the tour. (Open July-Aug. 9am-10pm; May-June and Sept. 9am-5:30pm; Apr. and Oct. 9am-4:30pm. Mandatory castle tour €2.95, students €2.20. Wasserspiele tour €5.85, students €4.40. Combined tour €7.30, students €5.85.) Continue on bus #55 to St. Leonhard, where Charlemagne supposedly rests under luscious Untersberg Peak, prepared to return and reign over Europe when he is needed. A cable car glides over the rocky cliffs to the summit, and from there hikes lead off into the distance. On top is a memorial cross and some unbelievable mountain scenery. Don't leave your camera behind. (Open July-Sept. Th-Tu 8:30am-5pm; Mar.-June and Oct. 9am-5pm; Dec.-Feb. 10am-4pm. Round-trip €7.)

THE SALZKAMMERGUT

Every summer, bands of Austrian schoolchildren, tour groups of elderly Europeans, and tourists in-the-know come to the smooth lakes and furrowed mountains of the Salzkammergut. The region takes its name from the salt mines that, in their glory days, financed Salzburg's architectural treasures; today, the white gold of the Salzkammergut is no longer salt, but pure sunshine on sparkling water in summer and a quilt of fresh snow in winter. The area is easily navigable, with 2000km of footpaths and dozens of cable cars and chairlifts. **Buses** are the best way to travel into and through the region.

HALLSTATT ☎06134

Teetering on the banks of the Hallstättersee, tiny Hallstatt seems to defy gravity by clinging to the face of a stony slope. It is easily the most beautiful lakeside village in the Salzkammergut, if not in all of Austria.

TRANSPORTATION. **Buses** are the cheapest way to get to Hallstatt from Salzburg (€10.30) but require layovers in both Bad Ischl and Gosaumühle. The **train station,** on the other side of the lake, is not staffed to help travelers. All trains come from Attnang-Puchheim in the north or Stainach-Irdning in the south. **Trains** run hourly to Bad Ischl (30min., €2.75) and Salzburg via Attnang-Puchheim (€17).

AUSTRIA

PRACTICAL INFORMATION. The **tourist office,** Seestr. 169, finds rooms and offers help with the town's confusing system of street numbers. (☎82 08. Open July-Aug. M-F 9am-5pm, Sa 10am-4pm, Su 10am-2pm; Sept.-June M-Tu, Th-F 9am-noon and 2-5pm, W 9am-noon.) There is an **ATM** next to the post office. The **post office,** Seestr. 160, is below the tourist office. (Open M-Tu and Th-F 8am-noon and 2-5:30pm, W 8am-noon.) The **postal code** is A-4830.

ACCOMMODATIONS AND FOOD. To reach **Gästehaus Zur Mühle ❷,** Kirchenweg 36, from the tourist office, walk uphill, heading for a short tunnel at the upper right corner of the square; it's right at the end of the tunnel by the waterfall. (☎83 18. Breakfast €2.50. Reception 10am-2pm and 4-10pm. Closed Nov. Dorms €10.) **Frühstückspension Sarstein ❸,** Gosamühlstr. 83, offers glorious views as well as a beachside lawn. From the ferry landing, turn right on Seestr. and walk 10min. (Breakfast included. Showers €1 per 10min. Singles €18; doubles €38.) To get to **Camping Klausner-Höll ❷,** Lahnstr. 201, turn right out of the tourist office and follow Seestr. for 10min. (☎832 24. Breakfast €3.80-8. Showers included. Laundry €8. Gate closed daily noon-3pm and 10pm-7:30am. Open mid-Apr. to mid-Oct. €5.80; tent €3.70; electricity €2.90.) The cheapest eats are at the **Konsum supermarket** across from the bus stop; the butcher's counter prepares sandwiches on request. (Open M-Tu and Th-F 7:30am-12:30pm and 3-6pm, W and Sa 7:30am-noon.)

SIGHTS AND HIKING. Back when Rome was still a village, the "white gold" from the salt mines made Hallstatt a world-famous settlement. The 2500-year-old **Salzbergwerke** is the oldest salt mine in the world; zip down a wooden mining slide on a burlap sack to an eerie lake deep inside the mountain on a fascinating guided tour (1hr., in English and German). (☎(06132) 200 24 00. Open May-Sept. daily 9:30am-4:30pm; Oct. 9:30am-3pm. €14; guest card holders and students €9.20.) In the 19th century, Hallstatt was also the site of an immense and incredibly well-preserved Iron Age archaeological find. The **charnel house** next to St. Michael's Chapel is a bizarre repository filled with the remains of over 610 villagers dating from the 16th century on; the latest were added in 1995. The dead were previously buried in the mountains, but villagers soon ran out of space and transferred older bones to the charnel house to make room for more corpses. From the ferry dock, follow the signs marked K. Kirche. (Open June-Sept. daily 10am-6pm; May-Oct. 10am-4pm. €1.)

Hallstatt offers some of the most spectacular day hikes in the Salzkammergut. The tourist office offers an excellent Dachstein **hiking guide** in English (€6), which details 38 hikes in the area, as well as **bike** trail maps (€15). The **Salzbergwerk (salt mine) hike** is a simple 1½hr. gravel hike leading to the salt-mine tour; walk to the Salzbergbahn and take the road to the right upward, turning at the black and yellow Salzwelten sign. The **Waldbachstrub Waterfall hike** is a light 1¾hr. walk along a tumbling crystal-clear stream and up to a spellbinding waterfall. From the bus station, follow the brown sign reading Malerweg near the supermarket and continue to follow the Malerweg signs until the Waldbachstrub sign appears (about 40min.). The waterfall is in the **Echental,** a valley carved out a millennia ago by glaciers and now blazed with trails leading deep into the valley. The **Gangsteig,** a slippery, primitive stairway, carved into the side of a cliff, requires sturdy hiking shoes and a strong will to climb.

DAYTRIPS FROM HALLSTATT

DACHSTEIN ICE CAVES

From Hallstatt, walk to the Lahn bus station by heading down Seestr. with the lake to your left, and catch the bus to Obertraun (10min., every hr. 8:35am-4:50pm, €1.70). Stop at the Dachstein cable car station, then ride up to Schönbergalm to reach the ice and mammoth caves. (Every 15min. 8:40am-5:30pm, round-trip €13.) The Koppenbrüller cave is a 15min. walk from the Dachstein bus stop in Obertraun.

In **Obertraun,** at the other end of the lake, the magnificent **Dachstein Ice Caves** are proof of the region's geological hyperactivity. The eerie light of the caves casts fascinating shadows on the immense but intricate rock and ice formations. There are three sets of caves: the **Rieseneishöhlen** (Giant Ice Caves) and the **Mammuthöhlen** (Mammoth Caves), are up on the mountain, while the **Koppenbrüllerhöhle,** a giant spring, is in the valley near the village of Obertraun. Mandatory tours are offered in English and German; you'll be assigned to a group at the Schönbergalm station. The cave temperatures are near freezing, so wear good footwear and something warm. (☎(06131) 84 00. Open May to mid-Oct. daily 9am-5pm. Admission to each cave €8; children €4.80.)

GRÜNAU ☎07616

Grünau is a tiny community in a picturesque location, ideal for almost any kind of outdoor activity. The real reason to visit is **The Treehouse,** Schindlbachstr. 525, a backpacker's dream resort. The incredibly friendly staff will organize adventure tours, including **canyoning** (€50), **bungee jumping** (€95, only on weekends), and **horseback riding** (€9.50 per hr.). To strike out on your own, rent a **mountain bike** (€6 per day) or ask the staff about **hiking** trails. For winter visitors, the ski lift is a 5min. walk from the front door, and snow gear (jackets, snowsuits, gloves, etc.) is provided free of charge. Day ski-lift passes are €20.50, and **skis** and **snowboards** are available for rent (€9.50 and €13).

Regular **trains** service Grünau from Wels, on the Vienna-Salzburg rail line (1hr., 6:45am-8:45pm, €6). Call ahead to **The Treehouse** to be picked up free of charge. Rooms feature private showers and goosedown blankets, and resort amenities include a TV room with hundreds of English-language movies, book-exchange library, sauna, basketball and tennis courts, **Internet** (€0.10 per min.), and two in-house bars for nighttime revelry. (☎84 99. Breakfast included. 3-course dinners €6.90. 6-bed dorms €14; doubles €35; triples €51; quads €64. AmEx/MC/V. ❷)

AUSTRIA

FROM THE ROAD

LOVE THE STICK

As a veteran runner and former Boy Scout, I have, at times, felt entitled to break the common sense rules of Alpine hiking. I hiked alone (and got lonely), I hiked on glaciers in the afternoon (and sunk, getting snow in my underwear), and I hiked in sneakers (and rolled my ankles). I have, in fact, only done about two things right: I always carry a map, and I finally broke down and bought a walking stick.

I first saw them being used by an older couple, one in each hand, in the rolling hills of Bregenz. I thought they were primarily for older people who needed an extra boost. Then I saw people in their teens and 20s using them and figured walking sticks were accessories for weekend wanderers. Then I nearly fell off the Rotmoosferer glacier in Obergurgl, near Innsbruck, and decided I needed one.

I bought a close-out, half-price walking stick for €15 and couldn't tell the difference between mine and the model sold for €50. Like most walking sticks, the height is adjustable. As it was explained to me, the correct height for a stick when hiking uphill or over level ground is high enough so that the elbow forms a 90° angle when you hold it in front of you. When descending, add an extra couple of inches, since you'll be reaching down.

Does it work? It won't turn you into a *übermensch*, but it will improve your balance. If nothing else, it comes in handy fending off love-struck goats and bus drivers.

—Tom Miller

BAD ISCHL ☎06132

Bad Ischl was a salt-mining town for centuries until Dr. Franz Wirer arrived in 1821 to study the curative properties of the heated brine baths in the area. Today the bath facilities are mostly in the posh **Kaiser Therme,** Bahnhofstr. 1, a resort across from the tourist office. Splash around in the heated salt baths with whirlpool (9am-10pm, €9) or relax in the spacious sauna (daily 1:30-10pm, Tu men only, Th women only; €13 for 3hr.). Other than the salt baths, Bad Ischl's main attraction is the **Kaiservilla,** the summer palace of former Austro-Hungarian emperor Franz Josef. Inside is an eclectic collection of relics, including the desk where he signed the 1914 declaration of war against Serbia that led to WWI, and his extensive collection of mounted animal horns. Entrance is allowed only through a guided tour in German, with English text available. (☎232 41. Open May to mid-Oct. 9-11:45am and 1-5:15pm. €9.50.) Bad Ischl offers incredible **hiking** too; pick up a free trail map at the tourist office.

Only one **train** comes through the station, running between **Attnang-Puchheim** in the north (1hr., 4:40am-8:50pm, €6.50) and **Hallstatt** (30min., 6:15am-6:15pm, €6.50). **Buses** leave for Salzburg every hour (1½hr., 5am-7:15pm). To reach the **tourist office,** Bahnhofstr. 6, turn left onto Bahnhofstr. from the station and walk for 2min. (☎277 57. Open M-F 8:30am-noon and 1:30-5pm, Sa 9am-noon.) Every guest who stays the night in Bad Ischl must pay a **Kurtax** which entitles you to a **guest card** (June to mid-Sept. €1.85-€2.20 per person per night depending on proximity to the city center; mid-Sept. to May €0.95-1.10). To reach the **Jugendgästehaus (HI),** Am Rechensteg, from the tourist office, turn left on Bahnhofstr. then right on Kaiser-Franz-Josef-Str., and keep going until you see the sign on the left. The hostel offers mostly quads, each with their own bath. (☎265 77. Breakfast included. Reception 10am-1pm and 5-7pm. Checkout 9am. Reservations recommended. Dorms €16; singles €26; doubles €37. **HI membership required.** ❷) Restaurants are tucked into every possible niche in the pedestrian zone. Stop for a kebab (€3.30) at the nearby **Bistro Oriental,** Kreuzplatz 13—it's tiny but modern and very clean. (Open daily 10am-10pm. ❷) The **Konditorei Zauner,** Pfarrg. 7 (☎233 10 20), has an international reputation for heavenly sweets and tortes (€2.80) ❶. **Postal code:** A-4820.

HOHE TAUERN NATIONAL PARK

The enormous **Hohe Tauern** range, part of the Austrian Central Alps, boasts 246 glaciers and 304 mountains over 3000m. One of the park's goals is preservation, so there are no large campgrounds or recreation areas; most of it is pristine. The best way to explore this rare preserve is to **hike** one of the park's numerous trails, which range from pleasant ambles to difficult mountain ascents. *An Experience in Nature*, available at park offices and most area tourist offices, plots and briefly describes 84 different hikes. The center of the park is **Franz-Josefs-Höhe** and the **Pasterze glacier,** which sits right above the town of Heiligenblut. Aside from the skiing and hiking, the main tourist attractions are the **Krimml Waterfalls,** in the northwestern corner near Zell am See, and the **Großglocknerstraße,** a spectacular high mountain road that runs south from Zell am See through Franz-Josefs-Höhe.

TRANSPORTATION. Trains arrive in **Zell am See** from: Innsbruck (1½-2hr., 3:45am-9:25pm, €20); Kitzbühel (45min., 7:15am-11:30pm, €8.10); and Salzburg (1½hr., 1-2 per hr. 3am-10pm, €11). From Zell am See, a rail line runs west along the northern border of the park, terminating in Krimml (1½hr., 19 per day 6am-10:55pm, €6.80); a **bus** also runs directly to the Höhe (2hr.; 2 per day 11:45am-3:50pm; €10). The park itself is criss-crossed by bus lines which operate on a complicated timetable, with some buses running infrequently and others changing schedules in early summer; ask about specific connections at local tourist offices.

FRANZ-JOSEFS-HÖHE. This tourist center, stationed above the Pasterze glacier, has an amazing view of the Großglockner (3797m). The Höhe has its own **park office** and information center at the beginning of the parking area. (Open mid-May to mid-Oct. daily 10am-4pm; July-Aug. 9am-6pm.) The elevator next to the information center leads to the **Swarovski Observation Center,** a crystal-shaped building with binoculars for viewing the surrounding terrain. (Open daily 10am-4pm. Free.)

HEILIGENBLUT. The closest town to the highest mountain in Austria and a great starting point for most hikes, Heiligenblut also has convenient accommodations for those wishing to explore Franz-Josefs-Höhe and the Hohe Tauern Region. Heiligenblut can be reached by **bus** from Franz-Josefs-Höhe (30min.; July-Sept. 8:40am-4pm, May-Oct. daily at 4pm; €3.60) and Zell am See (2½hr., 3 per day 9:20am-12:20pm, €11.60; connect in Franz-Josefs-Höhe). The **tourist office,** Hof 4, up the street from the bus stop, dispenses information about accommodations and hiking. (☎20 01 21. Open July-Aug. M-F 8:30am-6pm, Sa 9am-noon and 4-6pm; Sept.-June M-F 8:30am-noon and 2:30-6pm, Sa 9am-noon and 4-6pm.) To reach **Jugendgästehaus Heiligenblut (HI)** ❸, Hof 36, take the path from the wall behind the bus stop parking lot. (☎22 59. Breakfast included. Reception July-Aug. daily 7-10am and 5-10pm; Sept.-June daily 7-10am and 5-9pm. Dorms €20, ages 19-27 €15, under 19 €10. Add €7.27 per person for a single, €3.63 for a double.)

KRIMML. Over 400,000 visitors per year arrive here to see the extraordinary **Krimml Waterfalls,** a set of three cascades spanning 380m. (8am-6pm €1.50; after 6pm free.) These waterfalls are usually enjoyed as a daytrip from Zell am See; **buses** run from Zell am See (1½hr., 11 per day 5:45am-8:55pm, €7.50) to Maustelle Ort, the start of the path to the falls. To reach the **tourist office,** Oberkrimml 37, follow the road from the Krimml Ort bus stop and turn right down the hill in front of the church. (☎72 39. Open M-F 8am-noon and 2:30-5:30pm, Sa 8:30-10:30am.)

TYROL (TIROL)

Tyrol's mountains overwhelm the average mortal with their superhuman scale and beauty. Although this topography has made it impossible for Tyrol to avoid becoming one of the primary mountain playgrounds for the world, this region has more to offer than just inclines. The urbane city of Innsbruck shows why it was a Habsburg favorite with a seamless blend of gilded houses and snowy mountains.

KITZBÜHEL ☎05356

Kitzbühel welcomes tourists with glitzy casinos and countless pubs, yet few visitors remain at ground level long enough to enjoy them. The mountains surrounding the city invite wealthy vacationers and ski bums alike. The Kitzbühel **ski area,** the "Ski Circus," is regarded as one of the best in the world. A one-day **ski pass** (€33) or a 3- or 6-day summer **vacation pass** (€35/€48) grants passage on all lifts and the shuttle buses that connect them; purchase either at any lift or the **Kurhaus Aquarena,** which offers free pool access with admission and sauna and solarium access for a fee. (☎643 85. Open daily 9am-8pm. €7.50, with guest card €6.50; free entry in winter with ski passes of 2 days or more, in summer with either vacation pass.) For summer visitors, more than 70 **hiking trails** snake up the mountains surrounding Kitzbühel, providing a variety of pleasurable day hikes and a wide range of difficulty levels. To avoid getting lost, pick up a free Hiking Trail Map at the tourist office. **Mountain bike trails** abound; rent a bike from **Stanger Radsport,** Josef-Pirchl-str. 42. (€18 per day. Open M-F 8am-noon and 1:15-6pm, Sa 9am-noon.) If you'd rather relax than hike, the **Kitzbüheler Hornbahn lift** (€14, with guest card €13) ascends to the **Alpenblumengarten,** where more than 120 different types of flowers blossom each spring. (Open late May to mid-Oct. daily 8:30am-5pm.) The **Schwarzsee,** near Camping Schwarzsee, is famed for its healing **mud baths.** (☎623 81. Open daily 8am-6pm. €3, after 4pm €1.) They also rent electric boats (€7 for 30min.) and rowboats (€3.70 per hr.).

AUSTRIA

Trains leave from the **Hauptbahnhof,** Bahnhofpl. 1, for: Innsbruck (1hr., every 2hr., €13.40); Salzburg (2½hr., 9 per day, €18.90); and Vienna (6hr., 6:25am-12:45am, €41.45). Buses depart regularly from the *Hauptbahnhof.* To reach the *Fußgängerzone* (pedestrian zone) from the *Hauptbahnhof,* head straight down Bahnhofstr., turn left at the main road, then right at the traffic light, and follow the road uphill. The **tourist office,** Hinterstadt 18, is near the *Rathaus* in the *Fußgängerzone.* (☎621 550. Open July-Aug. and Christmas to mid-Mar. M-F 8:30am-6:30pm, Sa 8:30am-noon and 4-6pm, Su 10am-noon and 4-6pm; Nov. to Christmas and mid-Mar. to June M-F 8:30am-12:30pm and 2:30-6pm, Sa 8:30am-noon.) Make sure to pick up a free **guest card,** which provides discounts, free **guided hikes** (June-Oct. M-F 8:45am), and free **informative tours** (M 10am), from the tourist office. For **Internet** access, try **Internet Café Videothek,** Schlosserg. 10. (€3.70 for 30min. Open daily 11am-9pm.) Exit the *Hauptbahnhof,* facing away from the tracks and turn left at the end of the street; look left for the clean and fuss-free **Pension Hörl ❷,** Josef-Pirchlstr. 60. (☎631 44. Breakfast included. Reception daily 7am-9pm. In summer €15-19 per person, with bath €17-22; in winter €20-25/€22-28.) **Hotel Haselberger ❹,** Maurachfeld 4, is one minute from the bottom station of the *Hahmennkammerbahn* ski lift. All rooms are equipped with TV, phone, and shower. (☎628 66. Breakfast included. In summer €31-35 per person; in winter €37-44. AmEx/MC/V.) Many of Kitzbühel's restaurants prepare gourmet delights at astronomical prices. Cheaper establishments pepper the area surrounding the *Fußgängerzone.* **SPAR supermarket,** Bichlstr. 22, is at the intersection with Ehrenbachg. (Open M-F 8am-7pm, Sa 7:30am-1pm.) **Postal Code:** A-6370.

ZILLER VALLEY (ZILLERTAL)

Extending from the Tuxer Alps, through the Zillertaler Alps, and to the Kitzbüheler Alps in the north, the Ziller Valley *(Zillertal)* provides spectacular, affordable, and easily accessible hiking and skiing away from crowds. The towns in the narrow valley offer some of the best hiking in western Austria, with more footpaths than roads and more trail guides than police officers.

TRANSPORTATION. The valley runs south from Jenbach through Zell am Ziller and Mayrhofen. Everyone entering the valley must go through Jenbach; you can get there easily from Innsbruck (20min.; €5.25, Eurail valid). From Jenbach, the **Zillertalbahn (Z-bahn),** an efficient network of private buses and trains, connects the towns. The Z-bahn has two types of trains: the **Dampfzug,** a more expensive, slower, touristy steam train; and the **Triebwagen,** which leaves daily every hour from 6am to 9pm. Note that travel on the Z-bahn is not covered by rail passes.

ZELL AM ZILLER. Zell am Ziller was founded by monks in the 8th century, but became a materialistic gold-mining town in the 1600s. Today, it offers skiing and hiking without resort-town hype. **Ski passes** are available at cable car stations. (1-day €28.50; 2-day €53; 3-day €75.) Two ski lifts take you into the alps for **hiking:** the **Kreuzjochbahn** (open daily 8:40am-12:10pm and 1-5:10pm; round-trip €13.20); and the **Gerlossteinbahn** (open daily 8:30am-12:15pm and 1-5pm; round-trip €8.80). For a look at Zell's history, take a tour of the nearby **gold mine,** which includes a scenic 45min. hike to the mine entrance. (Tours 2hr. May-Sept. every hr. 9am-6pm. €10.) The **tourist office,** Dorfpl. 3a, has maps and information on skiing and accommodations. From the rail station, head right along Bahnhofstr. and turn right at the end. (☎228 10. Open M-F 8:30am-12:30pm and 2:30-6pm, Sa-Su 9am-noon and 4-6pm; Nov.-June closed Su.) **Phone Code:** ☎05282.

MAYRHOFEN. Mayrhofen provides endless opportunities for hiking and skiing. The **Penkenbahn,** a lift system of gondolas right above the town, runs to the top of the 1850m Penkenberg and to several easy paths. (May 24 to Oct. 7 9am-5pm, €12.50.) The **Ahornbahn** lift ascends to a variety of easy and difficult hikes. (June 16 to Oct. 14 every 30min. 8:30am-noon and 12:30-5pm, €12.50.) In winter, **skiers** and **snowboarders** flock to the Ahorn, Penken, and Horberg ski areas above town, all of which are covered by the **Ski Zillertal 3000 pass** (1-day €31; 3-day €82). Mayrhofen is easily accessible via Z-Bahn from **Jenbach** (1hr., 24 per day 6am-9pm, €5.20) and **Zell am Ziller** (15min., 24 per day 6:35am-9:50pm, €1.80). The **tourist office,** Dursterstr. 225, has information on outdoor activities and accommodations and leads free **guided hikes and tours,** varying from short walks around town to 5hr. mountain hikes. (☎67 60. Hikes/tours mid-May to mid-Oct. M-F; call ahead for times. Open M-F 8am-6pm, Sa 9am-noon, Su 10am-noon; July-Aug. also Sa 2-6pm.)

INNSBRUCK ☎0512

The 1964 and 1976 winter Olympics were both held in Innsbruck, bringing international recognition to this beautiful mountain city. The nearby Tyrolean Alps await skiers and hikers, and the tiny cobblestoned streets of the *Altstadt* are peppered with fancy facades and remnants of the Habsburg Empire.

TRANSPORTATION AND PRACTICAL INFORMATION

Trains: Hauptbahnhof, Südtirolerpl. (☎05 17 17). To: **Munich** (2hr., 13 per day, €30); **Rome** (8½-9½hr., 2 per day, €60); **Salzburg** (2-2½hr., 13 per day, €27); **Vienna Westbahnhof** (5½-7hr., 10 per day, €48); **Zurich** (4hr., 4 per day, €43.50).

AUSTRIA

Public Transportation: For schedules and information on transportation in Innsbruck, head to the **IVB** Office, Stainerstr. 2 (☎530 17 99), near Maria-Theresien-Str. Open M-F 7:30am-6pm. The main bus station is in front of the main entrance to the train station. Buses stop running at 10:30 or 11:30pm; 3 *Nachtbus* lines run after hours.

Tourist Office: Innsbruck Tourist Office, Burggraben 3 (☎598 50), off the end of Museumstr., on the 3rd floor, sells maps (€1) and the **Innsbruck Card,** which provides free access to public transportation and many sights (24hr. €19; 48hr. €24; 72hr. €29). Open M-F 8am-6pm, Sa 8am-noon.

Laundromat: Bubblepoint Waschsalon, Brixnerstr. 1, or at Andreas-Hofer-Str. at the corner of Franz-Fischer-Str. Wash €4, dry €1 for 10min. **Internet** €0.10 per min. Open M-F 8am-10pm, Sa-Su 8am-8pm.

Emergency: Police: ☎133. **Ambulance:** ☎144 or 142. **Fire:** ☎122.

Internet Access: International Telephone Discount, Bruneckstr. 12 (☎59 42 72 61). Turn right from the *Hauptbahnhof;* it's on the left just past the end of Südtirolerpl. €0.11 per min. Open daily 9am-11pm.

Post Office: Maximilianstr. 2 (☎500 79 00). Open M-F 7am-11pm, Sa 7am-9pm, Su 8am-9pm. Address mail to be held: Postlagernde Briefe für Firstname SURNAME, Hauptpostamt, Maximilianstr. 2, **A-6020** Innsbruck AUSTRIA.

ACCOMMODATIONS

Inexpensive accommodations are scarce in June, when only two hostels are open. The opening of student dorms to backpackers in July and August somewhat alleviates the crush. Membership in the free **Club Innsbruck** gives discounts on skiing, bike tours, and the club's hiking program; join by registering at any of the below.

Haus Wolf, Dorfstr. 48 (☎54 86 73). Exit the train station through the main exit and walk straight to the traffic island next to streetcar tracks marked *Stubaitalbahn* (STB). Take the STB to Mutters, then walk toward the church and turn right onto Dorfstr. You'll be greeted by the warm hospitality of Titi and Georg Wolf, but call ahead—they are thinking of closing up shop after 30 years of true *gemütlichkeit.* €12-13 per person. ❷

Gasthof Innbruecke, Instr. 1 (☎28 19 34). From the *Altstadt,* cross the Innbruecke; the *gasthof* is at the corner of the intersection. The 575-year-old inn has a riverside and mountain view. Breakfast included. Singles €26-33; doubles €44-49; quads €109. ❸

Gasthof zur Stern, Schulstr. 17 (☎54 65 00). Take the *Stubaitalbahn* to Natters, then head uphill on Bahnhofstr. and turn left onto Schulstr. in front of the SPAR market. In the suburban village of Natters, for those looking to get away from the crowds. Breakfast included. All rooms with shower and toilet. €17-20 per person. ❸

Jugendherberge Innsbruck (HI), Reichenauer Str. 147 (☎34 61 79). From the train station, take tram 3 to Sillpark and bus O to Jugendherberge. Breakfast Included. Laundry €3.30. Reception July-Aug. daily 3-10pm; Sept.-June 5-10pm. Lockout 10am-5pm. Curfew 11pm. 6-bed dorms €12, after 1st night €9.50; 4-bed dorms €14.80/€12.25. Singles with shower €28; doubles with shower €41. Nonmembers add €3. ❷

Hostel Fritz Prior-Schwedenhaus (HI), Rennweg 17b (☎58 58 14). From the station, take bus A or tram 4 to Handelsakademie, continue to the end and across Rennweg to the river. Spacious, clean rooms with private shower and bathroom. No door locks, but closet keys available. Sheets €3.10. Laundry €5.50. Reception daily 7-9:30am and 5-10:30pm. Check-in before 6pm. Lockout 9:30am-5pm. Curfew 10:30pm. Open July-Aug. and Dec. 27-Jan. 5. Dorms €10; doubles €28; triples €42. ❷

Youth Hostel St. Niklaus (HI), Innstr. 95 (☎28 65 15). From the train station, take bus D to Schmelzerg. (€1.60) and cross the street. Small, crowded dorms are filled with English speakers. Breakfast included. Internet €0.15 per min. Reception daily 8am-2pm and 5-10pm. Lockout 10am-5pm. 6- to 8-bed dorms €13.80, €13 subsequent nights; 4-bed dorms €14.90. Doubles €36.40, with shower and toilet €43.60. ❷

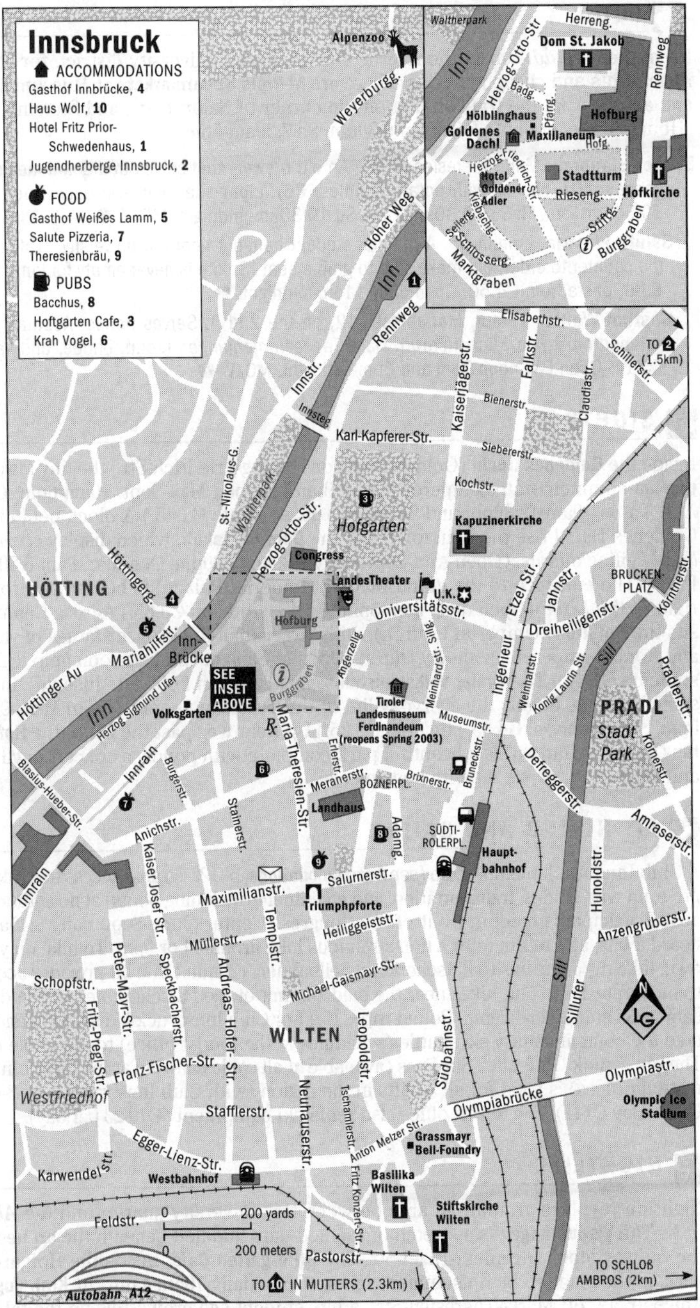
Innsbruck
ACCOMMODATIONS
Gasthof Innbrücke, 4
Haus Wolf, 10
Hotel Fritz Prior-Schwedenhaus, 1
Jugendherberge Innsbruck, 2
FOOD
Gasthof Weißes Lamm, 5
Salute Pizzeria, 7
Theresienbräu, 9
PUBS
Bacchus, 8
Hoftgarten Cafe, 3
Krah Vogel, 6
Alpenzoo
Weyerburgg.
Hoher Weg
Inn
Rennweg
Innstr.
Innsteg
Karl-Kapferer-Str.
Kaiserjägerstr.
Falkstr.
Elisabethstr.
Bienerstr.
Siebererstr.
Kochstr.
Claudiastr.
Schillerstr.
TO 2 (1.5km)
St.-Nikolaus-G.
Waltherpark
Herzog-Otto-Str.
Hofgarten
Congress
Kapuzinerkirche
LandesTheater
U.K.
Universitätsstr.
HÖTTING
Höttingerg.
Mariahilfstr.
Inn-Brücke
Höttinger Au
Herzog Sigmund Ufer
Volksgarten
SEE INSET ABOVE
Hofburg
Burggraben
Angerzellg.
Meinhardstr.
Sillg.
Tiroler Landesmuseum Ferdinandeum (reopens Spring 2003)
Museumstr.
Ingenieur Etzel Str.
Jahnstr.
Dreiheiligenstr.
BRUCKEN-PLATZ
Körntnerstr.
Weinhartstr.
Konig Laurin Str.
Sill
PRADL
Pradlerstr.
Stadt Park
Körnerstr.
Defreggerstr.
Amraserstr.
Maria-Theresien-Str.
Erlerstr.
Meranerstr.
BOZNERPL.
Brixnerstr.
Bruneckstr.
Landhaus
Innrain
Blasius-Hueber-Str.
Burgerstr.
Stainerstr.
Anichstr.
Adamg.
SÜDTI-ROLERPL.
Haupt-bahnhof
Kaiser Josef Str.
Salurnerstr.
Maximilianstr.
Triumphpforte
Templstr.
Heiliggeiststr.
Müllerstr.
Michael-Gaismayr-Str.
Schopfstr.
Peter-Mayr-Str.
Speckbacherstr.
Andreas-Hofer-Str.
Fritz-Pregl-Str.
WILTEN
Leopoldstr.
Südbahnstr.
Sillufer
Hunoldstr.
Anzengruberstr.
Franz-Fischer-Str.
Westfriedhof
Neuhauserstr.
Tschamlerstr.
Stafflerstr.
Olympiabrücke
Olympiastr.
Olympic Ice Stadium
Egger-Lienz-Str.
Anton Melzer Str.
Grassmayr Bell-Foundry
Karwendelstr.
Westbahnhof
Basilika Wilten
Stiftskirche Wilten
Fritz Konzert-Str.
Feldstr.
0 200 yards
0 200 meters
Pastorstr.
TO 10 IN MUTTERS (2.3km)
TO SCHLOß AMBROS (2km)
Autobahn A12
Waltherpark
Herreng.
Dom St. Jakob
Rennweg
Herzog-Otto-Str
Badg.
Pfarrg.
Hölblinghaus
Hofburg
Goldenes Dachl
Maxilianeum
Hofg.
Herzog-Friedrich-Str.
Hotel Goldener Adler
Stadtturm
Rieseng.
Hofkirche
Kiebachg.
Sellerg.
Schlosserg.
Stiftg.
Burggraben
Marktgraben

AUSTRIA

FOOD

From the *Altstadt*, cross the river to Innstr., in the university district, for ethnic restaurants and cheap pizzerias. There are **M-Preis Supermarkets** at Museumstr. 34 and across from the train station on the corner of Salurnerstr. and Sterzingerstr. (Hours are generally M-F 7:30am-6:30pm, Sa 7:30am-5pm.)

Theresianbrau, Maria-Theresienstr. 51. An old brewery that serves traditional meals like *kaesespatzl* (cheese with potato noodles; €6), alongside their own beer. Open M-W 10:30am-1am, Th-Sa 10:30am-2am, Su 10:30am-midnight. MC/V. ❷

Salute Pizzeria, Innrain 35. A popular student hangout near the university. Walk up to the counter to order, but make sure to grab a seat—Salute is never empty for long. Pizza €3-8, pasta from €4.50. Open daily 11am-midnight. ❷

Gasthof Weißes Lamm, Mariahilfstr. 12, on the 2nd fl. Serves honest Austrian fare, catering mostly to a local crowd. Daily *Tagesempfehlungen* (soup, entree, and salad) €6-14. Open F-W noon-2pm and 6pm-midnight. MC/V. ❸

SIGHTS

AUSTRIA

Inside the **Goldenes Dachl** (Golden Roof) on Herzog-Friedrich-Str., the tiny **Maximilianeum** commemorates emperor Maximilian I. (Open May-Sept. 10am-6pm; Oct.-Apr. Tu-Su 10am-12:30pm and 2-5pm. €3.65, students €1.45.) A block behind the Goldenes Dachl rise the twin towers of the **Dom St. Jakob,** which displays *trompe l'oeil* ceiling murals. (Open Apr.-Sept. daily 7:30am-7:30pm; Oct.-Mar. 8am-6:30pm. Free.) The entrance to the grand **Hofburg** (Imperial Palace) is behind and to the right of the *Dom*. (Open daily 9am-5pm. €5.45, students €3.65.) Across Rennweg sits the **Hofkirche** (Imperial Church), with larger-than-life bronze statues of saints and Roman emperors, some by Dürer. (Open M-Sa 9am-5pm, Su noon-5pm. €2.20, students €1.45.) The **Tiroler Volkskunstmuseum** (Tyrolean Folk Art Museum), in the same building, details the everyday life of the Tyrolean people. (Open M-Sa 9am-5pm, Su 9am-noon. €4.35, students €2.25.) Up Rennweg past the *Dom*, the **Hofgarten** (Imperial Garden) is a beautiful park complete with ponds, a concert pavilion, and an outdoor chess set with huge pieces.

HIKING AND SKIING

A Club Innsbruck membership (see **Accommodations,** p. 122) grants access to a hiking program with guides, transportation, and equipment (including boots) at no additional cost. Participants meet in front of the Congress Center (June-Sept. daily 8:45am), board a bus, and return after a non-strenuous hike around 4 or 5pm. To hike on your own, take the J-line bus to Patscherkofel Seilbahnen. (20min.) The lift provides access to moderate 1½ to 5hr. hikes near the bald summit of the Patscherkofel. (Open daily 9am-noon and 12:45-4:30pm. Round-trip €15.) For Club-Innsbruck-led ski excursions, take the complimentary ski shuttle (schedules at the tourist office) to any cable car. The Innsbruck Gletscher Ski Pass (available at all cable cars and at Innsbruck Information offices) is valid for all 59 lifts in the region (with Club Innsbruck card 3-day €80, 6-day €141). The tourist office also rents ski equipment (€19-23 per day).

NIGHTLIFE

Nightlife revolves around the area between the university quarter and the *Altstadt*. The **Viaduktbogen** is a stretch of themed bars huddled beneath the arches of the railway along Ingenieur-Etzel-Str. The **Hofgarten Café,** inside the Hofgarten park, is the place to be on summer nights. (Open daily 10am-4am.) At **Krah Vogel,** Anichstr. 12, off Maria-Theresien-Str., a hip, student-age crowd fills up the tables and small garden patio in the back. (Open daily 10am-2am.) **Bacchus,** Salurnerstr. 14, has an open-air cafe and basement disco for gays, lesbians, and transvestites. (Open M-Th 9pm-4am, F-Sa 9pm-6am.)

DAYTRIP FROM INNSBRUCK

SCHLOß AMBRAS

The castle stands in a park to the southeast of Innsbruck and is accessible by tram #6 (dir.: Igls) to Tummelplatz/Schloß Ambras (€1.60, 20min.). Follow the signs from the stop. Alternatively, take the shuttle that leaves every hr. from Maria-Theresien-Str., just opposite McDonald's. (Apr.-Oct every hr. 10am-5pm; round-trip €2.20.)

In the late 16th century, Archduke Ferdinand II transformed a royal hunting lodge into one of Austria's most beautiful castles, **Schloß Ambras,** and filled it with vast collections of art, armor, weapons, and trinkets, all of which are now on display. Across the grounds in the Hochschloß is the famous **Spanischer Saal** (Spanish Room), where light streams in from the windows onto portraits of the Habsburg rulers. Upstairs is the impressive three-floor **Portrait Gallery** (open only in summer). The **gardens** outside, which vary from manicured shrubs with modern sculptures to shady, forested hillsides, provide relief from the opulence, but keep an eye out for the **peacocks.** (Schloßstr. 20. Open Apr.-Oct. daily 10am-5pm; Dec.-Mar. closed Tu. Apr.-Oct €7.50, students €5.50; Dec.-Mar. €4.50/€3.)

AUSTRIA

VORALBERG

At the intersection of four nations, the residents of the Voralberg speak like the Swiss, eat like the Germans, and ski with the Liechtensteiners, yet are still true Austrians. Carry a passport at all times; foreign borders are never far away.

BREGENZ ☎05574

Bregenz's *Oberstadt* (high city) is dominated by the wooden **Martinturm,** Europe's largest onion dome. Next door is the **Martinskirche,** filled with 14th-century frescoes. Hike up Schloßbergstr. to the **St. Gallus Pfarrkirche,** a white stucco sanctuary that glows under lavish gold ornaments and a detailed painted ceiling. From the tourist office, walk down the *Fußgängerzone* (pedestrian zone) to reach the fantastically bizarre **Kunsthaus Bregenz,** which features outlandish modern art. (Open Tu-W and F-Su 10am-6pm, Th 10am-9pm. €5, students €3.50.) The **Strandweg** and **Seepromenade** follow the Bodensee from one end of town to the other. All along the waterfront, gardens and ice cream stands surround playgrounds and mini-golf courses. The concrete monstrosity on the edge of the lake is not a ski ramp gone awry but rather Europe's largest **floating stage** and the centerpiece for the annual **Bregenzer Festspiele,** held from mid-July to mid-August. In 2003, Leonard Bernstein's *West Side Story* will run from July 17-Aug. 17. Tickets go on sale in October (€22-124). For more info, call ☎40 76 or visit www.bregenzerfestspiele.com.

Trains go to: Feldkirch (30-45min., 2-4 per day, €4.50); Innsbruck (2¼hr., 8 per day, €23.30); Munich (2½hr., 4 per day, €31); and Zurich (1¾hr., 4 per day, €26.60). To reach the **tourist office,** Bahnhofstr. 14, from the train station, face away from the tracks and turn left; it will be on the right. The staff makes hotel reservations (€2.20 fee) and has *Privatzimmer* lists, hiking and city maps, and a free Internet terminal. (☎495 90. Open M-F 9am-noon and 1-5pm, Sa 9am-noon; during the *Festspiele* M-Sa 9am-7pm, Su 4-7pm.) At the **Jugendgästehaus (HI)** ❷, Mehrerauerstr. 3-5, all rooms have bathrooms and showers. From the station, cross the bridge over the tracks, walk left through the parking lot, and look for the yellow brick building on your left. (☎428 67. Internet €3 per hr. Breakfast included. Laundry €4.50. Reception daily 7am-10pm. Check-out 10am. Dorms €15.50-18.25; singles €22.50-25.25; doubles €41-51.50. For stays less than 3 nights, add €3. MC/V.) To reach **Pension Sonne ❸,** Kaiserstr. 8, go right from the station up Bahnhofstr. into the city, then turn right on Kaiserstr. (Breakfast included. Reception daily 7:30am-10pm. Singles €28, with bath €34; doubles €52/58; triples €49/55; quads €84—none with shower. MC/V.) **Zum Golden Hirschen ❸,** Kirchstr. 8, serves great local cuisine. (Open W-M 10am-midnight. AmEx/MC/V.) **SB Restaurant ❷,** on the first floor of the "GWL" mall building in the *Fußgängerzone,* has self-serve salad bars (€0.90 per 100g) and cafeteria-style entrees. (Open M-F 8:30am-5:30pm, Sa 8:30am-3pm.) Below the restaurant is a **SPAR Supermarkt.** (Open M-Th 8am-7pm, F 8am-7:30pm, Sa 8am-5pm.) **Postal Code:** A-6900.

STYRIA (STEIERMARK)

Styria, promoted by tourist offices as "the Green Heart of Austria," is the country's second largest province. The region has been spared from the tourist invasion, allowing for the preservation of many of Austria's folk traditions and ancient forests. Even its gem-like city, Graz, remains relatively untarnished by tourists.

GRAZ ☎0316

You'll definitely feel like you're in Austria's second largest city when you leave the train station and enter a mob of buses, streetcars, and busy locals. For a more relaxed pace, walk just a few minutes to the pedestrian district of the old city, where locals linger over coffee in one of the many cafes lining the narrow, cobblestoned, and relatively tourist-free streets of Graz's *Altstadt.*

TRANSPORTATION. Flights arrive at **Flughafen Graz** (GRZ; ☎290 20), 9km from the city center; take bus #631 from the airport into town (20min., every hr. 6:10am-11:30pm, €1.60). Trains run from the **Hauptbahnhof,** Europapl. (☎05 17 17 12; open daily 7am-8:45pm), for: Innsbruck (6hr., 4 per day, €42); Munich (6½hr., 4 per day, €57); Salzburg (4¼hr., €34); Vienna *Südbahnhof* (2½hr., 9 per day, €25); and Zurich (8½hr., 10pm, €108). The **Graz-Köflach Bus** (GKB), Köflacherg. 35-41 (☎59 87), runs daily 24hr.

IN RECENT NEWS

IMMIGRANT OUTCRY

Austria received a lot of international attention a few years ago for the anti-immigration stance of its Freedom Party. Although cutting off immigration entirely is no longer considered an option, there are still fierce debates in Austria about how to handle immigrants. Within the past year, a variety of proposals have been made in the Austrian parliament, including suggestions to provide social services to refugees only at the level of their home countries, or to require immigrants to attend German courses where failure to pass final exams would result in sanctions against them.

As a tourist, you can get involved in the campaign for minority rights by buying a copy of the non-profit monthly magazine *Das Megaphon.* On sale since 1995 on the streets of Graz and many other cities in Styria, *Das Megaphon* is primarily a forum for immigrant rights, but also serves the handicapped and the homeless. Half of the profits of each €2 issue sold go directly to the sellers, who are often of Nigerian descent, one of the two largest minority groups in Austria (the other is Turkish). After speaking to one seller in Bruck an der Mur, our *Let's Go* researcher learned that although he had been a biologist in his native Nigeria, he was now unemployed because of his inability to speak German. He summed up the inherent problem well in his complaint, "Everyone here, they want you to speak the Deutsch."

PRACTICAL INFORMATION. From the train station, go down Annenstr. and cross the *Hauptbrücke* to reach **Hauptplatz,** the center of town. Five minutes away is **Jakominiplatz,** the hub of the public transportation system. **Herrengaße,** a pedestrian street lined with cafes and boutiques, connects the two squares. The **tourist office,** Herreng. 16, has free city maps and a guide to walking the city. The staff offers English-language **tours** of the *Altstadt* (2hr.; Apr.-Oct. Tu-W, F-Su 2:30pm; €7.50) and makes room reservations for free. (☎807 50. Open June-Sept. M-F 9am-7pm, Sa 9am-6pm, Su 10am-4pm; Oct.-May M-F 9am-6pm, Sa 9am-3pm, Su 10am-3pm.) **Café Zentral,** Andreas-Hofer-Pl. 9, has **Internet** access. (€4.50 per hr. Open M-F 6am-midnight, Sa 6am-noon.) **Postal code:** A-8010.

ACCOMMODATIONS AND FOOD. In Graz, most budget hotels, guest houses, and pensions are pricey, and many are far from the city center. Luckily, the web of local transport provides a reliable and easy commute to and from the city center. To reach **Jugendgästehaus Graz (HI) ❷,** Idlhofg. 74, from the train station, cross the street, head right on Eggenberger Gürtel, turn left on Josef-Huber-G., then take the first right; the hostel is through the parking lot on your right. Buses #31 and 32 run here from Jakominipl. (☎71 48 76. Internet €1.50 per 20min. Breakfast included. Laundry €3. Reception daily 7am-10pm. Doors open every 30min. from 10pm-2am. All rooms with bath. 4-bed dorms €17; singles €24; doubles €40. €2.50 surcharge for stays of less than 3 nights. MC/V.) **Hotel zur Stadthalle "Johannes" ❹,** Munzgrabenstr. 48, has pleasant rooms close to the *Altstadt.* Take streetcar #6 to Neue Technik. The hotel is the pale yellow building close to the stop. (☎83 77 66. Breakfast, TV, and bath included. Singles €45; doubles €67.)

Find an inexpensive meal on **Hauptplatz,** where concession stands sell sandwiches, *Wurst* (€1.50-3), and other fast food. Cheap student hangouts line **Zinzendorfgaße** near the university, and a grocery store, **Merkur,** is to the left as you exit the train station. (Open M-Th 8am-7pm, F 7:30am-7:30pm.) There is also a **farmer's market** on Kaiser-Josef-Pl. and Lendpl. (Open M-Sa 7am-1pm.) **China Restaurant Mond ❷,** Harrachg. 12a, has an all-you-can-eat lunch buffet (M-F 11:30am-2:30pm) for a skinny €5.10, or try the daily menu for €3.80. (Open daily 11:30am-3pm and 5:30-10pm.) **Gasthaus "Alte Münze" ❸,** Schloßbergpl. 8, serves Styrian specialties in a traditional setting. (Open Su-M 10am-7pm, Tu-Sa 8am-midnight.)

SIGHTS AND ENTERTAINMENT. North of Hauptpl., the wooded **Schloßberg** (literally "Castle Mountain") rises 123m above Graz. The hill is named for the castle that stood there from 1125 until 1809, when it was destroyed by Napoleon's troops. Though the castle is mostly gone, the Schloßberg remains a beautiful city park. Climb the zigzagging stone steps of the **Schloßbergstiege,** built by Russian prisoners during WWI, for sweeping views of the vast Styrian plain. The **Landhaus,** which houses the tourist office, is a sight itself; the building was remodeled by architect Domenico dell'Allio in 1557 in Lombard style. The **Landeszeughaus** (Provincial Arsenal), Herreng. 16, details the history of Ottoman attacks on the arsenal. (Open Mar.-Oct. Tu-Su 9am-5pm; Nov.-Dec. Tu-Su 10am-3pm. €1.50.) The **Glockenspiel,** Glockenspielpl. off Engeg., opens its wooden doors every day, barring bad weather, to reveal life-size wooden figures spinning to a slow folk song. (Daily 11am, 3, and 6pm.)

The hub of after-hours activity is the so-called **Bermuda Triangle,** an area of the old city behind Hauptpl. and bordered by Mehlpl., Färberg., and Prokopig. At **Kulturhauskeller,** Elisabethstr. 30, a young crowd demands ever louder and more throbbing dance music, but the partying doesn't get started until 11pm on weekends. (No sports or military clothing. 19+. Cover €2. Open Tu-Sa from 9pm.) Have a chat over your beer at **Triangle,** Burgg. 15, a trendy, low-key bar. (No cover. Open Tu-Sa 9:30pm-4am.)

CARINTHIA (KÄRNTEN)

The province of Carinthia covers the southernmost part of Austria. The sunny climate, Italian architecture, and laid-back atmosphere give Carinthia a Mediterranean feel. Though foreigners take little notice of this part of the country, natives consider it a vacation paradise. If you'll be in Carinthia for a while, consider a **Kärnten Card,** good for up to three weeks of unlimited local transportation, free admission to area sights and museums, and many other discounts (€32).

KLAGENFURT ☎0463

Situated on the eastern edge of the idyllic Wörthersee, Klagenfurt (pop. 90,000) is a major summertime destination for Austrians. The Wörthersee is the warmest alpine lake in Europe and serves as Europe's largest skating arena in winter. Klagenfurt is home to no fewer than 23 castles and mansions; pick up the tourist office's free brochures *From Castle to Castle* and *A Walk Round Klagenfurt's Old Town* to help you explore. At the edge of Alterpl. stands the 16th-century **Landhaus,** originally an arsenal and later the seat of the provincial diet. (Open Apr.-Sept. M-F 9am-1pm and 2-5pm. €1.10, students €0.40.) **Strandbag Maria-Loretto** is a quiet beach on the southern side of the lake. (Open July-Aug. daily 9am-8pm; June 9am-7pm; May and Sept. 9am-6pm. €3.30, after 2:30pm €2.60.)

Trains leave the **Hauptbahnhof,** at the intersection of Südbahngürtel and Bahnhofstr., for: Graz (3hr., 16 per day 4:15am-8:30pm, €26.10); Salzburg (3½hr., 10 per day 5:25am-7:50pm, €26.10); and Vienna (4hr., 17 per day 1:45am-8:30pm, €24.80). The **tourist office** is on the 1st floor of the *Rathaus* in Neuer Pl.; from the station, go down Bahnhofstr. and left on Paradeiserg., which opens into Neuer Pl. (☎53 72 23. Open May-Sept. M-F 8am-8pm, Sa-Su 10am-5pm; Oct.-Apr. M-F 8am-5pm.) To get to **Jugendherberge Klagenfurt ❸,** Neckheimg. 6, at Universitätstr., take bus #40, 41, or 42 from the train station to Heiligengeistpl., then bus #10 or 11 to Neckheimg. from stand #2. (☎23 00 20. Breakfast included. Reception daily 7-11am and 5-10pm. Dorms €16.30; doubles €40. Nonmembers add €3.) **Neuer Platz, Kardinalplatz,** and **Burggasse** have cheap places to eat. The tourist office prints *Sonntagsbraten,* a pamphlet listing the addresses and hours of cafes, restaurants, clubs, and bars. **Postal Code:** A-9020.

BELGIUM (BELGIQUE, BELGIË)

Situated between France and Germany, little Belgium rubs shoulders with some of Western Europe's most powerful cultural and intellectual traditions. Travelers too often mistake Belgium's subtlety for dullness, but its cities offer some of Europe's finest art and architecture, and its castle-dotted countryside provides a beautiful escape for hikers and bikers. While Brussels, the nation's capital and home to the head offices of NATO and the European Union, buzzes with international decision-makers, regional tension persists within Belgium's borders between Flemish-speaking Flanders and French-speaking Wallonie. But some things transcend politics: from the deep caves of the Ardennes to the white sands of the North Sea coast, Belgium's diverse beauty is even richer than its chocolate.

SYMBOL	❶	❷	❸	❹	❺
ACCOMMODATIONS	under €9	€9-16	€17-25	€26-32	over €32
FOOD	under €5	€5-7.50	€8-9.50	€10-15	over €15

For Belgium, prices are indicated in food and accommodations listings using the system of icons and price ranges above. Prices for accommodations are based on the lowest cost for one person, excluding special deals or discounts. For restaurants, prices are based on the average entree price.

SUGGESTED ITINERARIES

THREE DAYS Spend all three days in **Brussels** (p. 135). The **Grand-Place,** the heart of the city, was declared by Victor Hugo to be "the most beautiful square in the world." Witness Brussels's most giggled-at sight, the **Mannekin Pis,** a statue of a cherubic boy continuously urinating. Visit the **Belgian Comic Strip Centre** and pick up the requisite **Tintin** paraphernalia. Check out the **Musées Royaux des Beaux Arts** and take a trip up to the **Atomium.**

ONE WEEK After three days in **Brussels,** head to **Antwerp** and stroll along the Meir for tasty beer and fine chocolates (1 day; p. 147). Move on to beautiful **Bruges** to climb the 366 steps of the Belfort (2 days; p. 142). Lay out on the beaches of the **North Sea coast,** parking your pack in **Ostend** (1 day; p. 146).

BEST OF BELGIUM, 11 DAYS After your week in **Brussels, Bruges,** and **Antwerp,** visit **Ypres** to remember victims of WWI (1 day; p. 149). Next, get chills in the medieval torture chamber of Gravensteen in **Ghent** (1 day; p. 148). Head south to explore the castle-dotted **Wallonie** region, where you can hike, bike, kayak, and spelunk (1 day; p. 150). Don't miss the glittering gold treasury in the cathedral of **Tournai** (1 day; p. 150).

LIFE AND TIMES

HISTORY

Belgium's strategic location between several European powers has long been coveted by military and political leaders, including **Julius Caesar** and **Charlemagne.** In 843, under the Treaty of Verdun, Flanders, the Dutch-speaking province in the north, and Wallonie, the French-speaking province in the south, were split. Commercial and urban development were at the core of both regions. The 14th century witnessed a golden period of prosperity in the Belgian region, with a boom in the cloth industry. Belgium was united again in the 15th century under control of the **Dukes of Burgundy.** Over the next several centuries, the territory passed through the hands of the Spanish, the Austrians, the French, and finally the Dutch. Only in 1830 did Belgium gain independence by popular **revolution** from the Kingdom of The Netherlands. The newly freed Belgians established a constitutional monarchy, selecting **Leopold I** of Saxe-Coburg as their first king. In 1839, the European powers declared Belgium a perpetually neutral state. After gaining its independence, Belgium was a pioneer in European industrialization; development of the coal and iron industries made salient once again the divide between regions, as the Walloon region had greater natural resources and thus prosperity. Other major projects in the 19th century included **colonial expansion** in Africa, most notably in the present-day **Congo.** Despite these international successes, Belgium experienced internal discontent due to poor labor conditions, prompting major social reforms under **King Leopold II.**

The Germans invaded during both World Wars, flagrantly violating Belgium's neutral status. In WWI, under **King Albert I,** the outmatched Belgian army courageously fought the German invaders for the entire four years of the war. The **Treaty of Versailles,** the settlement of WWI, granted Belgium monetary and territorial reparations as compensation for the widespread devastation resulting from German occupation. In WWII, **King Leopold III**'s rapid **surrender** shocked not only the Belgians, but the British and the French as well, as they were suddenly faced with the advancing German army. Belgium's post-war economic recovery was impressively swift, for its second wartime destruction was relatively limited. Of greater concern

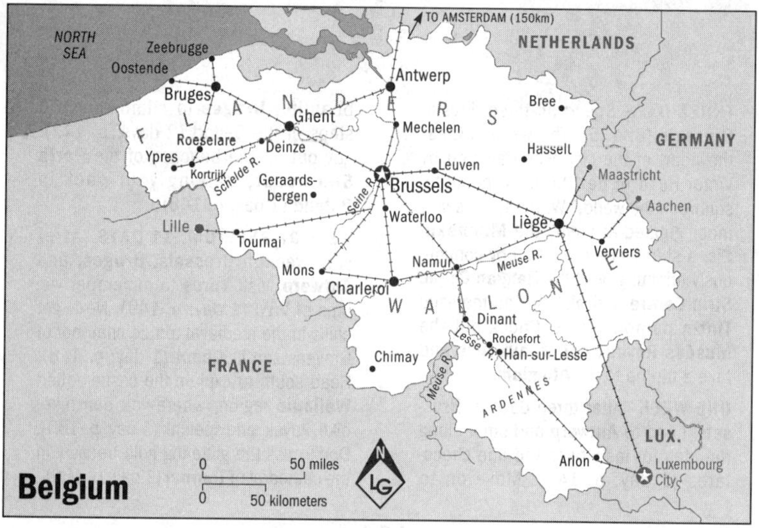

was the political disorganization upon the return of King Leopold III from Austria in 1950, where he had been sent during Nazi rule. Popular disapproval of his alleged defeatism led to his abdication in 1951.

TODAY

With the exception of the brief period after the Treaty of Versailles when Belgium was allied with France, the country has maintained a neutral political stance while remaining at the forefront of international affairs. Most significantly, Belgium is the seat of the **European Union.** Belgian government in the 19th and 20th centuries was largely dominated by the French-speaking minority, despite cries of injustice from the Flemish population. To ease tensions between these two groups, the constitution has undergone several revisions granting more autonomy to each of the three distinctive linguistic and cultural communities: **Flemish** in the north, **French** in the south, and **German** in the east. The Belgian king, currently **Albert II,** is the official head of state, but he is accountable to the democratically elected **parliament**. Day-to-day government is run by his appointed prime minister, **Guy Verhofstadt.**

CULTURE

FOOD AND DRINK

Belgian cuisine, a combination of French and German traditions, is praised throughout Western Europe, but a native meal may cost as much as a night in a decent hotel. Seafood, fresh from the coast, is served in a variety of dishes. **Moules** (steamed mussels), regarded as the national dish, are usually tasty and reasonably affordable (€14 is the cheapest, but they are usually €17-20). Belgians claim that they invented **frites** (potato fries), which they drown in mayonnaise and consume in abundance. Belgian **beer** is both a national pride and a national pastime; more varieties—over 300, ranging from ordinary **Pilsners** to religiously brewed **Trappist** ales—are produced here than in any other country. Prices range from as little as €1 for regular or quirky blonde up to €3 for other varieties. Leave room for Belgian **waffles** (*gaufres*)—soft, warm, glazed ones on the street (€1.50) and bigger, crispier ones piled high with toppings at cafes (€2-5)—and for the many famous brands of delectable **chocolates,** from Leonidas to Godiva.

BELGIUM

CUSTOMS AND ETIQUETTE

Restaurants and taxis usually include **service charges** (16%) in the price, but tip for exceptional service. Rounding up is also common practice. Give bathroom attendants €0.25-0.50 if there is not a posted price. **Banks** are generally open Monday through Friday 9am-4pm, but some take a lunch break noon-2pm. **Stores** are open Monday to Saturday 10am to 6 or 7pm; during summer some shops are open Sunday. Most **sights** are open Sundays but closed Mondays except in Bruges and Tournai, where museums are closed Tuesday or Wednesday. Most stores close on holidays; museums stay open during all except for Christmas, New Year's, and Armistice Day.

THE ARTS

PAINTING. Despite representing a school of painting known as the Flemish Primitives, **Jan van Eyck** in fact refined techniques of oil painting, working with layers of glaze to produce pieces of amazing detail. His most well-known painting is the *Adoration of the Mystic Lamb* (1432), the altarpiece of **St. Bavo's Cathedral** in **Ghent** (see p. 148). **Pieter Bruegel the Elder** shifted artistic focus from the sacred to the profane, choosing to depict commonplace scenes over legendary themes. **Peter Paul Rubens** was **Antwerp's** most famous artistic son; his paintings are distinctive for their religious symbolism, reflecting the turbulent climate of the **Counter-Reformation,** and for their fluid incorporation of the Italian Renaissance style. Ruben's assistant, **Anthony van Dyck,** was also a prominent member of the Flemish school of painting. Van Dyck's elegant portraits of the aristocracy gained him widespread renown and influenced **portraiture** style across the continent. In the 20th century, the leader of the **Surrealists** was **René Magritte,** who attempted to bring new and unusual meaning to ordinary household objects such as pipes, apples, instruments, and chairs. His most famous icon is probably the bowler-hatted man.

MUSIC. César Franck, the influential **Romantic** musician and organist, is Belgium's best-known composer. His symphonies and sonatas combined technical expertise with emotional energy. **Adolphe Sax,** born in **Dinant** (see p. 151), a musical instrument inventor, introduced the **saxophone** to the world. **Jacques Brel** was the voice of the nation; his most famous ballad, *Ne me quitte pas* (1959), has been covered by **Sting,** among countless other musicians.

COMIC STRIPS AND MYSTERIES. In the 20th century, Belgian talent made its presence known in the world of **comic strips** and **detective novels.** In Brussels, museums are dedicated to the history of cartooning, where tribute is paid to the work of **Georges Remi,** better-known as **Hergé,** creator of **Tintin** (see p. 139), and to **Peyo,** father of the **Smurfs.** The enigmatic **Georges Simenon** authored a 76-novel mystery series around the cunning **Commissaire Maigret,** another famous Belgian creation of the past century. **Henri Michaux** stretched the bounds by even Surrealist standards. His poetry explored the inner self and blurred the boundary between fantasy and reality.

HOLIDAYS & FESTIVALS

Holidays: New Year's Day (Jan. 1); Easter (Apr. 20); Easter Monday (Apr. 21); Labor Day (May 1); Ascension Day (May 29); Whit Sunday and Monday (June 8-9); Independence Day (July 21); Assumption Day (Aug. 15); All Saints Day (Nov. 1); Armistice Day (Nov. 11); Christmas (Dec. 25).

Festivals: Ghent hosts the **Gentse Feesten,** also know as 10 Days Off (July 19-28). Wallonie hosts a slew of quirky and creative carnival-like festivals, including the **Festival of Fairground Arts** (late May), **Les Jeux Nautiques** (early Aug.), the **International French-language Film Festival** (early Sept.) in Namur, and the **International Bathtub Regatta** (mid-Aug.) in Dinant.

ESSENTIALS

FACTS AND FIGURES

Official Name: Kingdom of Belgium.

Capital: Brussels.

Major Cities: Antwerp, Ghent, Charleroi, Liège.

Population: 10,259,000.

Land Area: 30,230 sq. km.

Time Zone: GMT +1.

Language: Flemish, French, German.

Religions: Roman Catholic (75%); Protestant, Muslim, Jewish, other (25%).

WHEN TO GO

Belgium, temperate and rainy, is best visited May to Sept., when temperatures average 13-21°C (54-72°F) and precipitation is the lowest. Winter temperatures average 0-5°C (32-43°F). Bring a sweater and umbrella whenever you go.

DOCUMENTS AND FORMALITIES

EU citizens may stay in Belgium for as long as they like. Citizens of Australia, Canada, New Zealand, South Africa, and the US do not need a visa for stays of up to 90 days.

Belgian Embassies at Home: Australia, 19 Arkana St, Yarralumla, Canberra ACT 2600 (☎(02) 62 73 25 01; fax 62 73 33 92). **Canada,** 80 Elgin St., 4th fl., Ottawa ON K1P 1B7 (☎613-236-7267; fax 236-7882. **Ireland,** 2 Shrewsbury Road, Ballsbridge, Dublin 4 (☎(353) 269 15 58; fax 283 84 88). **New Zealand,** Willis Corroon House, 12th fl., Willeston St. 1-3, PB 3379, Wellington (☎(04) 472 95 58; fax 471 27 64). **South Africa,** 625 Leyds St., Muckleneuk, Pretoria 0002 (☎(2712) 44 32 01; fax 44 32 16). **UK,** 103-105 Eaton Sq, London SW1W 9AB (☎(020) 470 37 00; fax 259 62 13; www.belgium-embassy.co.uk). **US,** 3330 Garfield St NW, Washington, D.C. 20008 (☎202-333-6900; fax 333-3079; www.diplobel.us).

Foreign Embassies in Belgium: All foreign embassies are in **Brussels** (see p. 136).

TRANSPORTATION

BY PLANE. Several major airlines fly into **Brussels** from Europe, North America, and Africa; many offer cheap deals. **SN Brussels Airlines** (Belgium ☎070 35 11 11, UK ☎0870 735 23 45; www.brussels-airlines.com) has taken over the service of Sabena airlines.

BY TRAIN AND BUS. The extensive and reliable **Belgian Rail** (www.b-rail.be) network traverses the country in 4hr. **Eurail** is valid in Belgium (see p. 51; US ☎877-456-RAIL, Canada ☎800-361-RAIL). A **Benelux Tourrail Pass** allows five days of unlimited **train** travel in a one-month period in Belgium, The Netherlands, and Luxembourg (€159, 50% companion discount; under 26 €106). The best deal for travelers under 26 may be the **Go Pass,** which allows 10 trips over one year in Belgium and may be used by more than one person (€39); the equivalent for travelers over 26 is the **Rail Pass** (€58). Because the train network is so extensive, **buses** are used primarily for municipal transport (€1-1.25).

BY FERRY. P&O European Ferries (UK ☎(01482) 795141, Belgium ☎(050) 54 34 30; www.ponsf.com) cross the Channel from **Zeebrugge,** north of Bruges, to **Hull, England** (14hr.; departures at 6:15pm; £38-48, under 26 £24-31). **Ostend Lines** (☎(059) 55 99 55) also crosses from Ostend to **Ramsgate, England,** 2hr. from London Victoria Station (6 per day, €39.70 round-trip). For info on Ostend, see p. 146.

BY CAR, BIKE, AND THUMB. Belgium honors most foreign driver's licenses, including those from Australia, Canada, the EU, and the US. **Speed limits** are 120kph on motorways, 90kph on main roads, and 50kph elsewhere. **Fuel** costs about €1 per liter. **Biking** is popular, and many roads have bike lanes (which you are required to use). In addition to being illegal, **hitchhiking** is not common in Belgium, nor does Let's Go recommend it as a safe means of transport.

TOURIST SERVICES AND MONEY

EMERGENCY	**Police:** ☎101. **Ambulance:** ☎105. **Fire:** ☎100.

TOURIST OFFICES. Bureaux de Tourisme, marked by green-and-white or blue signs labelled "i," are supplemented by **Infor-Jeunes/Info-Jeugd,** a service that helps young people secure accommodations. For info, contact the main office of the **Belgian Tourist Board,** 63 r. de Marché aux Herbes, B-1000 Brussels (☎(02) 504 03 90; fax 504 02 70; www.tourism-belgium.net; see p. 135). The weekly English-language *Bulletin* (€2.15 at newsstands) lists everything from movies to job openings.

Tourist Offices at Home: Canada, P.O. Box 760, Succursale NDG, Montreal, QU H4A 3S2 (☎514-457-2888; fax 457-9447) or 43 r. de Buade, Bureau 525, Quebec City, QU, G1R 4A2 (Wallonie office; ☎(418) 692-4939; fax 692-4974). **UK,** Brussels and

Wallonie office, 217 Marsh Wall, London E14 9FJ (☎(0906) 302 0245; fax (020) 7531 0393; www.belgiumtheplaceto.be), or Flanders and Brussels office, 31 Pepper St., London E14 9RW (☎(09001) 88 77 99; fax (020) 7458 0045; www.visitflanders.com; both http://antor.com/Belgium). **US,** 780 3rd Ave., Ste. 1501, New York, NY 10017 (☎212-758-8130; fax 355-7675; www.visitbelgium.com).

MONEY. The official currency of Belgium is the **euro.** The Belgian franc can still be exchanged at a rate of 44.34BF to €1. For exchange rates and more information on the euro, see p. 20. The European Union imposes a **value-added tax (VAT)** on goods and services purchased within the EU, which is included in the price (see p. 19). Belgium's VAT is generally 21%; refunds (usually 17% of purchase price) are available for purchases totaling over €123.95 at one establishment. Expect to pay €22-30 for a room, €12.50-16 for a hostel bed, €5-13 for a cheap restaurant meal, and €7-13 for a day's groceries. A barebones day in Belgium might cost €19-30; a slightly more comfortable day might cost €32-45.

ACCOMMODATIONS AND CAMPING

There is a wide range of accommodations throughout Belgium; however, **hotels** are fairly expensive, with "trench-bottom" singles from €22 and doubles around €30-35. Belgium's 31 **HI youth hostels,** which charge about €12.50 per night, are generally modern and many boast cheap bars. **Private hostels,** however, often cost about the same but are much nicer. Most receptionists speak at least some English, and reservations are a good idea, particularly in the summer and on weekends. Pick up a free copy of *Camping* at any tourist office for complete listings of hostels and campsites. **Campgrounds** charge about €3.25 per night. An **international camping card** is not required in Belgium.

BELGIUM

COMMUNICATION

PHONE CODES **Country code:** 32. **International dialing prefix:** 00.

TELEPHONES. Most phones require a phone card (€5), available at post offices, supermarkets, and magazine stands. Coin-operated phones are rare and more expensive. Calls are cheapest from 6:30pm to 8am and on weekends. For **operator assistance** within Belgium, dial ☎12 07 or 13 07; for **international assistance,** ☎12 04 or 13 04 (€0.25). **International direct dial** numbers include: **AT&T,** ☎0800 100 10; **British Telecom,** ☎0800 89 0032; **Canada Direct,** ☎0800 100 19 or 0800 700 19; **Ireland Direct,** ☎0800 10 353; **MCI,** ☎0800 100 12; **Sprint,** ☎0800 100 14; **Telecom New Zealand,** ☎0800 100 64; **Telkom South Africa,** ☎0800 100 27; **Telstra Australia,** ☎0800 100 61.

MAIL. A postcard or letter (up to 20g) sent to a destination within Belgium costs €0.42, within the EU €0.47-0.52, and to the rest of the world costs €0.74-0.84. Most post offices are open Monday to Friday 9am to 4 or 5pm (sometimes with a midday break) and sometimes on Saturdays 9 or 10am to noon or 1pm.

INTERNET ACCESS. There are cybercafes in the larger towns and cities in Belgium. For access to the web, expect to pay €2.50-3.25 per 30min. Many hostels have Internet access for around €0.07-0.10 per min.

LANGUAGES. Belgium is a multilingual nation, with several official languages. Flemish (a variation of Dutch) is spoken in Flanders, the northern half of the country; French is spoken in Wallonie, the southern region; and German is spoken in a small enclave in the west. Both Flemish and French are spoken in Brussels. Most people, especially in Flanders, speak English. For basic French words and phrases, see p. 1020; for German, see p. 1022.

BRUSSELS (BRUXELLES, BRUSSEL) ☎02

Beyond the international traffic resulting from the city's association with NATO and the EU, Brussels (pop. 1.1 million) has a relaxed and witty local character best embodied in its two boy heroes, Tintin and the Mannekin Pis. In the late 1920s, cartoonist Hergé created a comic strip hero, Tintin, who, followed by his faithful white dog, Snowy, righted international wrongs long before Brussels became the capital of the EU. The cherubic Mannekin Pis perpetually pees three blocks from the Grant Place, ruining any semblance of formality created by international politics. The museums of Brussels are rich with collections of Flemish masters, modern art, and antique sculptures, but you don't need to go inside for a visual feast—many of the city's restaurants, lounges, and movie theaters were built in the style of Art Nouveau architect Victor Horta.

TRANSPORTATION

Flights: Brussels International Airport (BRU; ☎753 42 21 or 723 31 11; www.brusselsairport.be) is 14km from the city. See p. 133 for information on **Sabena,** the Belgian national carrier. Trains run to the airport from Gare du Midi (25min., every 20min., €2.50), stopping at Gare Centraal and Gare du Nord.

Trains: Info ☎555 25 55. All international trains stop at **Gare du Midi;** most also stop at **Gare Centraal** (near Grand Place) or **Gare du Nord** (near the Botanical Gardens). To: **Amsterdam** (2½hr.; €32.50, under 26 €16); **Antwerp** (30min., €5); **Bruges** (45min., €9.70); **Cologne** (2¾hr.; €31.25, under 26 €22.35); **Luxembourg City** (1¾hr., €23); **Paris** (1½hr.; €54, under 26 €24.80). **Eurostar** goes to **London** (2¾hr.; from €140, discount for Eurail and Benelux rail pass holders; under 26 from €81).

Public Transportation: The **Métro (M), buses,** and **trams** run daily 6am-midnight. 1hr. ticket €1.40, day pass €3.60, 5 trips €6.20, 10 trips €9. All three are run by the **Société des Transports Intercommunaux Bruxellois (STIB),** Gare du Midi (☎515 20 00; www.stib.irisnet.be). Open M-F 7:30am-5pm, first and last Su of each month 8am-2pm. **Branch offices** at the Porte de Namur and Rogier Métro stops. Open M-F 8:30am-5:15pm.

Hitchhiking: Hitchhiking is illegal on highways and slip-roads in Belgium. *Let's Go* does not recommend hitchhiking.

ORIENTATION AND PRACTICAL INFORMATION

Most major attractions are clustered around **Grand Place,** between the **Bourse** (Stock Market) to the west and the **Parc de Bruxelles** to the east. Two **Métro** lines circle the city, while efficient trams run north to south. Signs in Brussels list both the French and Flemish street names. *Let's Go* gives the French name for all addresses. A **tourist passport** (*Carte d'un Jour;* €7.45), which includes two days of public transit, a map, and discounted museum admissions, is sold at the TIB and bookshops.

Tourist Offices: National, 63 r. du Marché aux Herbes (☎504 03 90; www.belgium-tourism.net), one block from Grand Place. Books rooms all over Belgium and offers the free weekly *What's On.* Open July-Aug. M-F 9am-7pm, Sa-Su 9am-1pm and 2-7pm; Sept.-June M-F 9am-6pm, Sa-Su 9am-1pm and 2-6pm; Nov.-Apr. closed Su afternoon. **Brussels International-Tourism and Congress** (TIB; ☎513 89 40; www.tib.be), on Grand Place, in the Town Hall, offers bus tours (3hr.; Apr.-Oct. 10, 11am, 2pm; Nov.-Mar. 10am, 2pm; €19.90, students €17), which leave from 8 r. de la Colline. Open Apr.-Oct. daily 9am-6pm; Nov.-Mar. M-Sa 9am-6pm, Su 10am-2pm.

Budget Travel: Infor-Jeunes Bruxelles, 155 r. Van Arteveld (☎514 41 11; bruxelles@inforjeunes.be). Budget travel info for young travelers. Open M-F 10am-5pm.

BELGIUM

Embassies: Australia, 6-8 r. Guimard, 1040 (☎286 05 00; fax 230 68 02). **Canada,** 2 av. Tervueren, 1040 (☎741 06 11; fax 448 00 00). **Ireland,** 89 r. Froissart, 1040 (☎230 53 37; fax 230 53 12). **New Zealand,** 1 de Meeussquare, 1000 (☎512 10 40). **South Africa,** 26 r. de la Loi (☎285 44 00). Generally open M-F 9am-5pm. **UK,** 85 r. d'Arlon, 1040 (☎287 62 11; fax 287 63 55). **US,** 27 bd. du Régent, 1000 (☎508 21 11; www.usinfo.be). Open M-F 9am-noon.

Currency Exchange: Many exchange booths near Grand Place stay open until 11pm. Most banks and booths charge a commission (€2.50-3.75) to cash checks. **CBC-Automatic Change,** 7 Grand-Place (☎547 12 11). Open 24hr. Exchange booths are also available in the train stations.

Bi-Gay-Lesbian Resources: Call ☎733 10 24 for info on local events. Staffed Tu 8-10pm, W and F 8-11pm. The tourist office offers a guide to gay establishments and nightlife.

Laundromat: Salon Lavoir, 62 r. Blaes, around the corner from the Jeugdherberg Bruegel (see below). M: Gare Centrale. Wash and dry €3.25. Open daily 7am-10pm.

Emergencies: Medical: ☎100. **Police:** ☎101.

Pharmacies: Neos-Bourse Pharmacie (☎218 06 40), bd. Anspach at r. du Marché aux Polets. M: Bourse. Open M-Sa 8:30am-6:30pm.

Medical Assistance: Free Clinic, 154a Chaussée de Wavre (☎512 13 14). Misleading name—you'll have to pay. Open M-F 9am-6pm. **Medical Services,** (☎479 18 18). Open 24hr.

Internet Access: easyEverything, (www.easyeverything.com) Place de Brouckère. Approx. €1.25 per hr., rate varies according to the time of day. Open 24hr.

Post Office: Pl. de la Monnaie, Centre Monnaie, 2nd fl. (☎226 21 11). M: de Brouckère. Open M-F 8am-7pm, Sa 9:30am-3pm. Address mail to be held: Firstname SURNAME, Poste Restante, pl. de la Monnaie, **1000** Bruxelles, Belgium.

BELGIUM

ACCOMMODATIONS

Accommodations can be difficult to find in Brussels, especially on weekends in June and July. In general, accommodations are well-kept and centrally located. If a hotel or hostel is booked, the staff will usually call other establishments on behalf of prospective guests.

Hotel Des Eperonniers, 1 r. des Eperonniers (☎513 53 66). Follow r. Inf. Isabelle from Gare Centraal into pl. Agora. Great location close to Grand Place. Well-kept rooms. Breakfast €3.75. Reception daily 7am-midnight. Singles €25-42; doubles €42-47. ❸

Hôtel Pacific, 57 r. Antoine Dansaert (☎511 84 59). M: Bourse. Follow the street in front of the Bourse, which becomes r. A. Dansaert after the intersection; it's on the right. Basic rooms in an excellent location. Breakfast included. Showers €5. Reception daily 7am-midnight. Curfew midnight. Singles €30; doubles €50; triples €70. ❹

Sleep Well, 23 r. du Damier (☎218 50 50; www.sleepwell.be), near Gare du Nord. M: Rogier. Exit onto r. Jardin Botanique, facing the pyramid, and go right; take the 1st right on r. des Cendres, then go slightly to the right at the intersection and continue onto r. du Damier. Breakfast included. Internet access. Curfew 3am. Lockout 10am-4pm. Dorms €16; singles €23.50; doubles €36. Reduced price after 1st night. ❷

Auberge de Jeunesse "Jacques Brel" (HI), 30 r. de la Sablonnière (☎218 01 87), on pl. des Barricades. M: Botanique. Take r. Royale, with the botanical gardens to your right, and take the 1st left onto r. de la Sablonnière. Clean, spacious rooms. Breakfast included. Sheets €3.25. Reception daily 8am-1am. HI members only. Dorms €12.50; singles €22.50; doubles €35; triples €43.50. ❷

Centre Vincent Van Gogh-CHAB, 8 r. Traversière (☎217 01 58; www.ping.be/chab). M: Botanique. Exit on r. Royale, head right, and turn right again. Newly renovated rooms. Internet

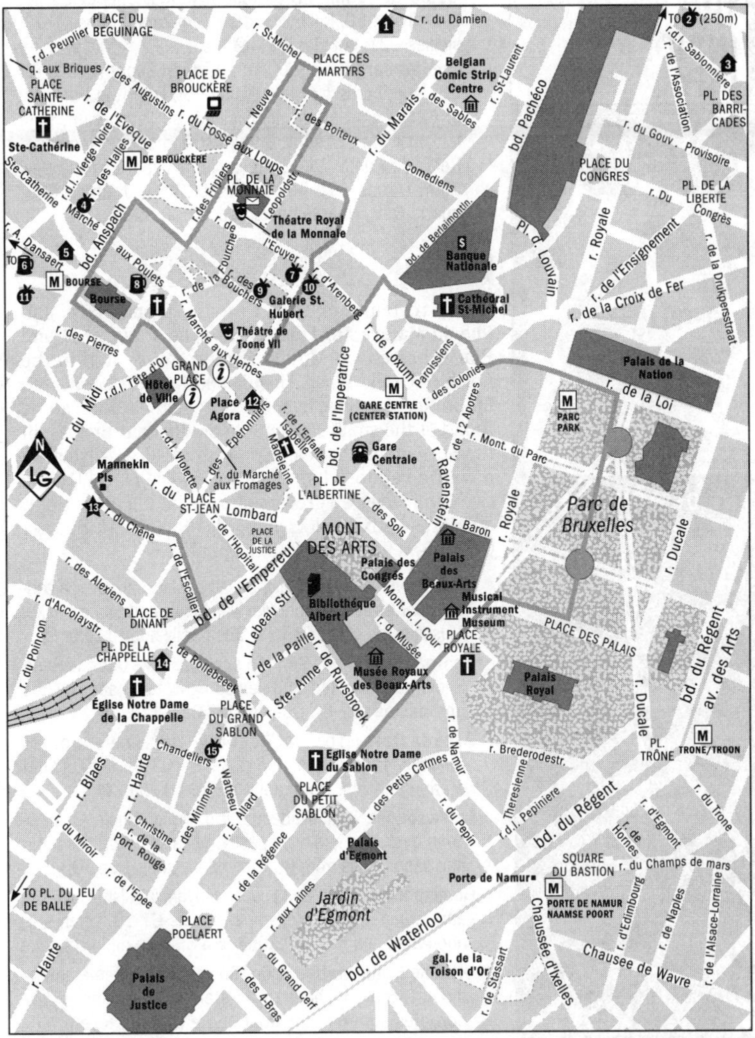

Brussels

ACCOMMODATIONS

Auberge de Jeunesse: "Jacques Brel" (HI), **3**
Hotel Des Eperonniers, **12**
Hôtel Pacific, **5**
Jeugdherberg Bruegel (HI), **14**
Sleep Well, **1**

FOOD

Arcadi Cafe, **10**
Chez Léon, **9**
Hemispheres, **7**
Le Perroquet, **15**
Super GB, **4**
Ultième Hallutinatie, **2**
Zebra, **11**

NIGHTLIFE

À La Bécasse, **8**
L'Archiduc, **6**

ENTERTAINMENT

Poechenellekelder, **13**

BELGIUM

THE INSIDER'S CITY

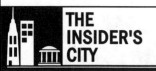

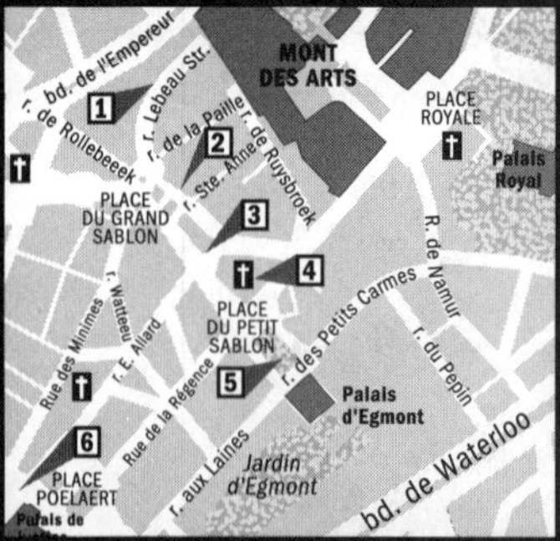

THE HEART OF BRUSSELS

This stroll past antique galleries, beautiful buildings, and the best chocolate shop in the city is a pleasant trip into a quintessentially Belgian neighborhood.

1. The splendid **Hotel Frison,** r. Lebeau 37, designed by Art Nouveau architect Victor Horta in 1894, now houses the **Gallery J. Visser.**

2. Splurge on some of the best chocolate in the city at **Wittamer,** pl. du Grand Sablon 6.

3. Surrounded by 16th- to 19th-century houses, the **Place du Grand Sablon** is enlivened every Saturday by an antique market.

4. View the splendid stained glass windows of the flamboyantly Gothic **Cathédral de Notre Dame du Sablon,** r. Bodenbroeck 6.

5. The bronze statues on the balustrades around **Place du Petit Sablon,** r. de la Régence, depict the ancient trades of Brussels, and the fountain memorializes the fight against Spanish tyranny.

6. The panoramic view from beside the immense **Palais de Justice** is worth the uphill walk.

€1.50 per 15min. Breakfast included. Sheets €3.50. Laundry €4.50. Reception daily 7am-2am. Dorms €9-12; singles €21; doubles €31. ❷

Jeugdherberg Bruegel (HI), 2 r. de St-Esprit (☎511 04 36; jeugdherberg.bruegel@ping.be). From the back exit of Gare Centraal, go right on bd. de l'Empereur, then left on r. de St-Esprit. Breakfast and sheets included. Reception daily 7am-1am. Lockout 10am-2pm. Curfew 1am. Dorms €12.50; singles €22.50; doubles €35; quads €58. Nonmembers add €2.50. ❷

FOOD

Cheap restaurants cluster around **Grand Place,** and **Rue du Marché aux Fromages,** to the south of Grand Place, has cheap Middle Eastern food. Just to the north of Grand Place, shellfish and *paella* are served up on **Rue des Bouchers,** but cheaper seafood can be found at the small restaurants on **Quai aux Briques,** in the Ste-Catherine area behind pl. St-Géry. **Belgaufras,** a waffle vendor chain, is everywhere (€1.40). The two-level **Super GB** grocery store is on the corner of r. du Marché aux Poulets and r. des Halles. (M: Bourse. Open M-Sa 9am-8pm, F until 9pm.)

Chez Léon, 18 r. des Bouchers. In business for over a century. Serves seafood popular with locals and tourists alike. Mussels and chips €15-22. Open daily noon-11pm. ❺

Zebra, 33-35 pl. St-Géry. This inexpensive but chic cafe is centrally located and serves light, tasty sandwiches and pastas (€2-6). Open daily 10am-1am. ❶

Arcadi Cafe, 1b r. d'Arenberg. Huge selection of quiches, sandwiches, and pastries (€3-6). Lots of vegetarian choices. Open daily 7:30am-11pm. ❶

Le Perroquet, 31 r. Watteau. Sit down for lunch, an afternoon beer, or a late-night pastry. Wide selection of salads and sandwiches from €5. Open daily noon-1am. ❷

Hemispheres, 65 r. de l'Ecuver. Libyan, Turkish, Chinese, and Indian cuisine. Vegetarian meals €7-10. Open M-F noon-3pm and 6:30-10:30pm, Sa 6:30pm-midnight. ❸

Ultième Hallutinatie, 316 r. Royale. Housed in a splendid Art Nouveau house with stained glass and a garden. Restaurant in the front and a cheaper tavern with an outdoor patio in back. Salads, pastas, and omelettes in the tavern from €6.20. Open M-F 11am-2:30pm and 7:30-10:30pm, Sa 4-10:30pm. ❷

Maison Antione, 1 pl. Jourdan. M: Schuman. Walk down r. Froissart; it's the brown kiosk in the middle of Place Jourdan. In business for over 50 years, it serves the best *frites* in town. A delicious cone of fries is €1.60-1.80; a huge selection of sauces are €0.50 each. Open Su-F 11:30am-1am, Sa 11:30am-2am. ❶

SIGHTS

GRAND PLACE AND ENVIRONS. Victor Hugo once called the gold-trimmed **Grand-Place** "the most beautiful square in the world." There is a flower market each morning, and at night the **Town Hall** is illuminated by 800 multi-colored floodlights while classical music plays. *(Apr.-Aug. and Dec. daily around 10 or 11pm. Tours available. Inquire at the Town Hall for info. ☎279 43 65.)* Three blocks behind the Town Hall, on the corner of r. de l'Etuve and r. du Chêne, is Brussels's most giggled-at sight, the **Mannekin Pis,** a statue of an impudent boy (with an apparently gargantuan bladder) steadily urinating. The most commonly told story claims that it commemorates a boy who ingeniously defused a bomb destined for Grand Place. In reality, the fountain was installed to supply the neighborhood with drinking water during the reign of Archduke Albert and Archduchess Isabelle. Locals have created hundreds of outfits for him, competitively dressing him with the ritual coats of their organization or region, each with a little hole for his you-know-what. His wardrobe is on display across from the Town Hall on the third floor of the **Museum of the City of Brussels (Maison de Roi),** which also gives the history of Brussels. *(Museum open Tu-F 10am-5pm, Sa-Su 10am-1pm. €2.50, students €2.)* In the glorious **Galerie Saint-Hubert** arcade, one block behind Grand Place, you can window-shop for everything from square umbrellas to marzipan frogs. Built over the course of six centuries, the magnificent **Cathédral Saint-Michel** is an excellent example of the Gothic style but mixes in a little Romanesque and modern architecture for good measure. *(Pl. St-Gudule, just north of Gare Centraal. Open M-F 7am-7pm, Sa-Su 8:30am-7pm. Free.)*

MONT DES ARTS. The **Musées Royaux des Beaux-Arts** houses the **Musée d'Art Ancien,** the **Musée d'Art Moderne,** a sculpture gallery, and temporary exhibitions. Together the museums house a huge collection of Belgian art spanning the centuries, including Bruegel the Elder's *Landscape with the Fall of Icarus* and pieces by Salle de Rubens and Brussels native Magritte. Other masterpieces not to be missed are David's *Death of Marat* and paintings by Ingres, Delacroix, Seurat, Gauguin, and Van Gogh. The panoramic view of Brussels's cityscape from the 4th floor of the 19th-century wing is alone worth the admission fee. *(3 r. de la Régence. M: Parc. ☎508 32 11. Open Tu-Su 10am-5pm. Some wings close noon-2pm. €5, students €3.50; 1st W of each month 1-5pm free.)* The **Musical Instrument Museum (MIM),** located in an Art Nouveau building in the beautifully restored Old England retail complex, houses over 1500 instruments. Headphones automatically play music from the instrument you are standing in front of. There is a fabulous panoramic view of the city from a corner turret on the third floor. *(2 r. Montagne de la Cour. One block from the Musées des Beaux-Arts. ☎545 01 30. Open Tu, W, F 9:30am-5pm; Th 9:30am-8pm; Sa-Su 10am-5pm. €5, students €3.50; headphones included.)*

BELGIAN COMIC STRIP CENTRE. This museum in the "Comic Strip Capital of the World" pays homage to *les bandes dessineés* with hundreds of Belgian comics.

INTERNATIONAL MAN OF MYSTERY Tintin (pronounced "tan-tan") is the greatest comic-strip hero in the French-speaking world. From Nice to Quebec City, he remains perpetually young to fans who play hardball at auctions for Tintin memorabilia. His creator, Georges Rémi (whose pen-name "Hergé," is his initials pronounced backwards) sent him to the Kremlin, Shanghai, the Congo, outer space, and the wilderness of... Chicago. Countless dissertations and novels have been written about Tintin's possible androgyny; many also say that Indiana Jones was Tintin made into a man. When former French president Charles de Gaulle was asked whom he feared the most, he replied, "Tintin is my only international competitor."

BELGIUM

THE LOCAL STORY

SOWING WILD YEAST

Jean-Pierre Van Roy is a brewer at the family-run Cantillon Brewery, which produces the distinctive Gueze blend of Lambic beer.

LG: What does Lambic mean?

JR: Lambic is a unique beer. It is the last beer in the world made from spontaneous fermentation, the last beer fermented with wild yeast.

LG: What is spontaneous fermentation?

JR: We don't use pure wheat like all the other beer producers in the world. We work only with wild yeast, we brew only in the winter, and the wort, the base of the beer, stays in contact with the air for one night for natural cooling. While cooling, the wort is inoculated with airborne wild yeast, so the beer takes a few years to produce, not a few weeks. And we don't control fermentation. Other beers take a few weeks because the breweries control fermentation.

LG: How long does the brewing process take?

JR: Just the brewing takes around one day, around 11 hours.

LG: And the fermentation takes how long?

JR: That depends, since it is uncontrolled. It begins a few days after the brewing if the weather is warm and a few weeks if the weather is cold. It is impossible to say exactly.

The Cantillon Brewery, 56 r. Gheude. M: Clemenceau. ☎521 49 28. Tours €2, includes tasting.

The **museum library,** in a renovated Art Nouveau warehouse, features a reproduction of Tintin's rocket ship and works by over 700 artists. For Tintin souvenirs, check out the museum store or the Tintin Boutique near Grand Place. *(20 r. des Sables. M: Rogier. From Gare Centraal, take bd. de l'Impératrice until it becomes bd. de Berlaimont, and turn left onto r. des Sables. ☎219 19 80. Open Tu-Su 10am-6pm. €6.20, students €5.)*

PARKS AND SQUARES. The charming hills around the **Place du Grand Sablon** are home to antique markets, art galleries, and cafes. Hidden behind the church lies the pastoral **Place du Petit Sablon.** Around **Place au Jeu de Balle,** you can practice the fine art of bargaining at the morning **flea market.** The **Botanical Gardens** on r. Royale are beautiful in summer. The **Parc de Bruxelles,** just behind Gare Centraal, and the **Parc Leopold,** amidst the EU buildings, are pleasantly green sanctuaries in otherwise urban surroundings.

OTHER SIGHTS. The enormous **Musée du Cinquantenaire (Musées Royaux d'Art et d'Histoire)** covers a wide variety of periods and parts—Roman torsos without heads, Syrian heads without torsos, and Egyptian caskets with feet. The eerily illuminated "Salle au Tresor" is one of the museum's main attractions. *(10 Parc du Cinquantenaire. M: Mérode. From the station, walk straight through the arch, turn left, go past the doors that appear to be the entrance, and turn left again for the real entrance. ☎741 72 11. Open Tu-F 9:30am-5pm, Sa-Su 10am-5pm. €4, students €3.)* Twentieth-century master architect Baron Victor Horta's graceful home, today the **Musée Horta,** is a skillful application of his Art Nouveau style to a domestic setting. *(25 r. Américaine. M: Horta. Take a right out of the stop, walking uphill on ch. de Waterloo (7min.), then turn right onto ch. de Charleroi and right onto r. Américaine. ☎543 04 90. Open Tu-Su 2-5:30pm. €5.)* The **European Parliament** has been called *Caprice des Dieux* ("Whim of the Gods"), perhaps because of its exorbitant cost. *(43 r. Wiertz. M: Schuman. ☎284 34 53; www.europarl.eu.int. Visits M-Th 10am and 3pm, F 10am; Apr. 14-Oct. 13 also Sa 10, 11:30am, 2:30pm.)* The **Atomium,** a shining 102m monument of aluminum and steel built for the 1958 World's Fair, represents an iron crystal molecule magnified 165 billion times. An elevator takes visitors to the very top for a view of the city. *(Bd. du Centenaire. M: Huysel. ☎475 47 77; www.atomium.be. Open Apr.-Aug. daily 9am-8pm; Sept.-Mar. 10am-6pm. €6.)* Nearby is the **Bruparck entertainment complex,** home of the **Kinepolis cinema** and **IMAX,** the largest movie theater in Europe, as well as **Mini-Europe** (a collection of European landmarks in miniature) and the **Oceade** water park. *(☎474 83 77; www.bruparck.com. Hours vary. Call or check website for info.)*

ENTERTAINMENT AND NIGHTLIFE

For information on events, check the weekly *What's On*, available from the tourist office. The flagship of Brussels's theater network is the beautiful **Théâtre Royal de la Monnaie,** on pl. de la Monnaie. (M: de Brouckère. Info ☎229 13 72, tickets 229 12 00; www.lamonnaie.be. Tickets €7.50-75). The theater is renowned throughout the world for its opera and ballet. Its performance of the opera *Muette de Portici* in August 1830 inspired the audience to take to the streets and begin the revolt that led to Belgium's independence. The **Théâtre Royal de Toone VII,** 21 petite r. des Bouchers, is a 170-year-old puppet theater that stages marionette performances, a distinctly Belgian art form. (☎513 54 86. Shows regularly in French; German, Flemish, and English available upon request. Usually Tu-Sa 8:30pm. €10, students €6.20.) In summer, **concerts** are held on **Grand Place,** on **Place de la Monnaie,** and in the **Parc de Bruxelles.**

On summer nights, **Grand Place** and the **Bourse** come to life with street performers and live concerts. Students crowd in bars around **Place Saint Géry**. The 19th-century puppet theater **Poechenellekelder,** 5 r. de Chêne, across from the Mannekin Pis, is today filled with lavishly costumed marionettes and a selection of Belgian beers. (Beer from €1.25. Open Su-Th noon-midnight, F-Sa noon to 1 or 2am.) **À La Bécasse,** 11 r. de Tabora, one of Brussels's oldest and best-known cafes, specializes in the local wheat beer. (Beer €1.25-2.25. Open daily 10am-midnight.) **L'Archiduc,** 6 r. A. Dansaert, is a pricey but casual Art Deco jazz bar. (Open daily 4pm-late.) **Le Fuse,** 208 r. Blaes, one of Belgium's trendiest clubs, plays techno. (Open daily 10pm-late.)

DAYTRIPS FROM BRUSSELS

WATERLOO

Bus W leaves Brussels's Gare du Midi (1¼hr., every hr., €2.70) and stops at Waterloo Church, across the street from Musée Wellington, at a gas station near Lion's Mound, and at the train station in Braine L'Alleud. Trains from Brussels's Gare du Midi run to Braine L'Alleud Station (45min., every hr., round-trip €3.60), near the Lion's Mound. It is more convenient to get off at Braine L'Alleud; the Waterloo stop is much farther from the town. There is a bus to the tourist office from the train station.

At Waterloo, site of the famous Napoleonic battle, the Allied troops, commanded by the Duke of Wellington, and the Prussians, led by Marshal Blucher, encountered the French army on June 18th, 1815. It took only nine hours to defeat Napoleon, but 50,000 men were killed in the process. **The Lion's Mound,** 5km outside of town, is a huge hill overlooking the battlefield. (Open Apr.-Sept. daily 9:30am-6:30pm; Oct. 9:30am-5:30pm; Nov.-Feb. 10:30am-4pm; Mar. 10am-5pm. €1.) In the center of Waterloo, the informative **Musée Wellington,** 147 ch. de Bruxelles, was the British general's headquarters and is now home to battle artifacts. (Open Apr.-Sept. daily 9:30am-6:30pm; Oct.-Mar. 10:30am-5pm. €5, students €4. Audio guide included.) Next door is the **tourist office,** 149 ch. de Bruxelles. (☎354 99 10. Open Apr.-Sept. daily 9:30am-6:30pm; Oct.-Mar. 10:30am-5pm.) There are several cheap restaurants along **Chaussée de Bruxelles.**

MECHELEN (MALINES)

Trains arrive from Brussels (15min., €3.20) and Antwerp (15min., €2.80).

Mechelen, historically the ecclesiastic capital of Belgium, is best known today for its abundance of treasure-filled churches and its grim role in the Holocaust. The stately **St. Rumbold's Cathedral,** down Consciencestr. from the station, features gorgeous stained-glass windows and the Gothic **St. Rumbold's Tower,** which rises 97m over **Grote Markt** and houses two carillons (sets of 49 bells). You can climb the tower with a guide (daily 2:15pm, M also 7:15pm; €2.50) or listen to one of the renowned **Carillon Recitals** (M and Sa 11:30am, Su 3pm; June-Sept. also M 8:30pm). Early Renaissance buildings, including the **Stadhuis** (city hall), line the Grote Markt. (Open M-Sa 8:30am-5:30pm, Su 2-5:30pm.) The 15th-century **Church of St. John** boasts Rubens's magnificent triptych *The Adoration of the Magi* (1619). The **Jewish Museum of Deportation and Resistance,** 153 Goswin de Stassartstr., is housed in the 18th-century military barracks used as a temporary camp for Jews en route to Auschwitz-Birkenau during the Holocaust. From the Grote Markt, follow Wollemarkt, which becomes Goswin de Stassartstr. (☎29 06 60. Open Su-Th 10am-5pm, F 10am-1pm. Free.) The **botanical gardens** along the Dilje River are a great place to stop for a picnic. The **tourist office** in the Stadhuis finds rooms for free. (☎29 76 55; www.mechelen.be. Open Easter-Oct. M-F 8am-6pm, Sa-Su 9:30am-12:30pm and 1:30-5pm; Nov.-Easter reduced hours.) There are several places to eat around the **Grote Markt.** *Asperge* (asparagus) appears on most menus, as Mechelen is in the center of the growing district; white asparagus is a regional specialty. **Postal Code:** 2800. **Phone code:** ☎015.

FLANDERS (VLAANDEREN)

In Flanders, the Flemish-speaking part of Belgium, you can boogie the night away in Antwerp, relax in beautiful Bruges, and sate your castle-cravings in Ghent. Historically, the delta of the Schelde River at Antwerp provided the region with a major port, and the production and trade of linen, wool, and diamonds created great prosperity. Flanders's Golden Age came during the 16th century, when its commercial centers were among the largest cities in Europe and its innovative artists motivated the Northern Renaissance. Today, the well-preserved Gothic cities of Flanders, rich in art and friendly people, are Belgium's biggest attractions.

BRUGES (BRUGGE) ☎050

Famed for its lace and native Jan van Eyck, Bruges is considered one of the most beautiful cities in Europe; it is also the most touristed city in Belgium. Canals carve their way through rows of stone houses and lead to the breathtaking Gothic Markt. The city remains one of the best-preserved examples of Northern Renaissance architecture. Its beauty, however, belies the destruction sustained in World War I; eight decades after the war, farmers still uncover 200 tons of artillery every year as they plough their fields.

TRANSPORTATION AND PRACTICAL INFORMATION

Bruges is enclosed by a circular canal, with the train station just beyond its southern extreme. Its historic district is entirely accessible on foot; the other mode of public transportation is the local bus system. The dizzying **Belfort** (belfry) towers high over the center of town, presiding over the handsome square of the **Markt.**

Trains: Leave from **Stationsplein** (☎38 23 82; open daily 7am-9pm), a 15min. walk south of the city, for: **Brussels** (1hr., €9.45); **Antwerp** (1hr., €9.80); **Ghent** (25min., €4.70); **Ostend** (17min., €2.90); **Zeebrugge** (10min., €2.10).

Bike Rental: At the train station (☎30 23 29). €6.30 per half-day, €8.80 per day. **'t Koffieboontje,** Hallestr. 4 (☎33 80 27), off the Markt by the belfry. €5.60 per half-day, €8.10 per day; student discount. Open daily 9am-10pm. Many hostels and hotels also rent bikes for around €7.50 per day.

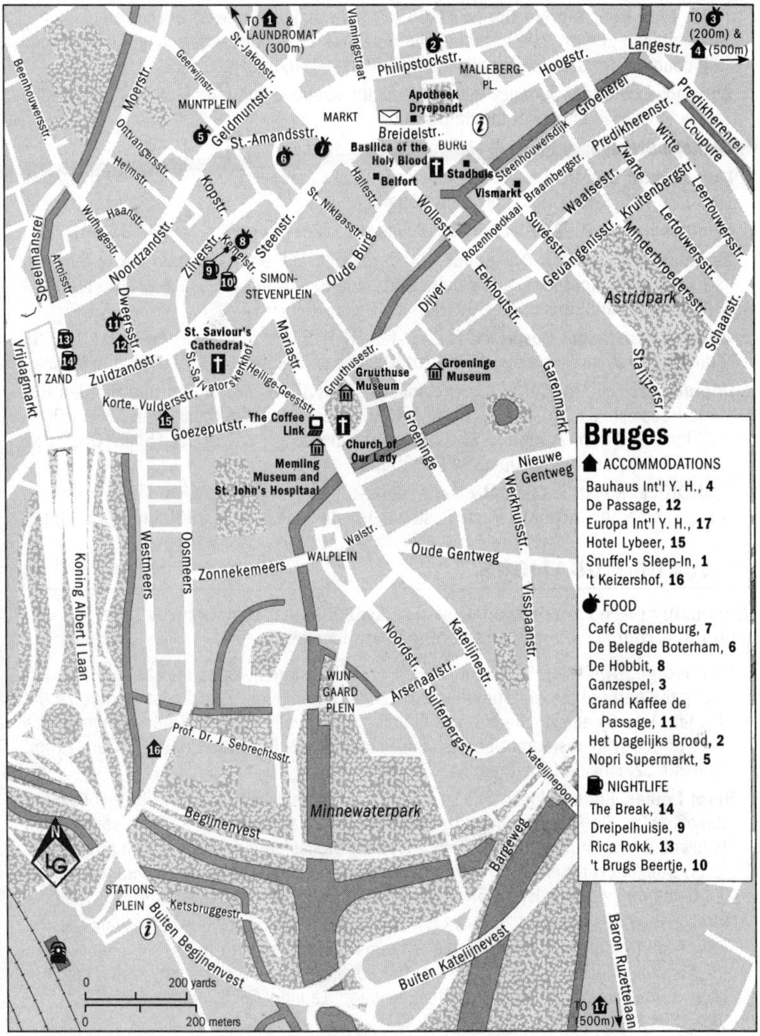

Tourist Office: Burg 11 (☎44 86 86; www.brugge.be), in Burg Square. From the station, head left to 't Zand Square, right on Zuidzandstr., and right on Breidelstr. through the Markt (15min.). Books rooms (€12.50 deposit and service fee) and sells maps (€0.65). Open Apr.-Sept. M-F 9:30am-6:30pm, Sa-Su 10am-noon and 2-6:30pm; Oct.-Mar. M-F 9:30am-5pm, Sa-Su 9:30am-1pm and 2-5:30pm. **Branch** office at the train station. Open M-Sa 10am-6pm.

Tours: Quasimodo Tours (☎37 04 70; www.quasimodo.be) leads excellent 25km bike and bus tours through the countryside to windmills, castles, and WWII bunkers. Bike tours depart mid-Mar. to Sept. daily from the tourist office at the Burg. €16, under 26

€13. **Pink Bear Bicycle Co.** (☎61 66 86; www.pinkbear.freeservers.com) guides two bike tours in English, one to the neighboring town of Damme and a longer one through the countryside; both leave daily from the Markt. €16, under 26 €13.

Currency Exchange: Currency exchanges fill the streets around the Markt, but there is no place to change money at the train station.

Luggage Storage: At the train station; €1.50-3.30. **Lockers** at the tourist office; €1.

Laundromat: Belfort, Ezelstr. 51, next to Snuffel's Sleep-In (see p. 144). Wash €2.50-3.50, dry €5-7.45. Open daily 7am-10pm.

Emergencies: ☎100. **Police:** ☎101. Police station at Hauwerstr. 7 (☎44 88 44).

Pharmacies: Apotheek Dryepondt, Markt 7. Open M-F 9am-12:30pm and 2-6:30pm, Sa until 6pm. **Apotheek K. Dewolf,** Zuidzandstr. 1. Open M-F 9am-12:30pm and 2-6:30pm, Sa until 6pm.

Medical Assistance: Hospitals: A. Z. St-Jan (☎45 21 11), St-Lucas (☎36 91 11), St-Franciscus Xaverivskliniek (☎47 04 70). Doctors on call: ☎81 38 99. F 8pm to M 8am.

Internet Access: The Coffee Link, Mariastr. 38 (☎34 99 73), in the Oud Sint-Jan Historic Hospital. €1.25 for first 15min., €0.07 per min. thereafter. Open M-Sa 10am-9:30pm, Su 10am-7:30pm. **KSI Online,** Katelijnestr. 67. €1.50 per 15min. Open Tu-F 9am-12:30pm and 2-6:30pm, Sa 2-6:30pm.

Post Office: Markt 5. Open M-F 9am-7pm, Sa 9:20am-12:30pm. Address mail to be held: Firstname SURNAME, Poste Restante, Hoedenmakerstr. 2, **8000** Brugge, Belgium.

ACCOMMODATIONS

Reasonably priced accommodations are available just blocks away from the city center, but rooms can be hard to come by on weekends.

De Passage, Dweersstr. 26 (☎34 02 32). From the station, cross the street and go left along the path; at the end, bear left on 't Zand, turn right on Zuidzandstr., and take the 1st left onto Dweersstr. Recently remodeled and ideally located. Offers guests a free beer at the lively restaurant downstairs. Breakfast €2. Reception daily 8:30am-11pm. Dorms €12; singles €22; doubles €35. ❷

Hotel Lybeer, Korte Vuldersstr. 31 (☎33 43 55; hotel.lybeer@pandora.be). Follow the directions for De Passage to Zuidzandstr.; take the 1st right onto Hoogste van Brugge, followed by an immediate left. Great location. Old-fashioned charm with modern comforts. Backpacker-friendly. Free Internet access. Breakfast included. Reception daily 7:30am-midnight. Singles €25; doubles €43; triples €57; quads €89. ❸

't Keizershof, Oostmeers 126 (☎33 87 28; hotel.keizershof@12move.be). From the station, walk to the traffic lights on the left, cross the street, and follow signs pointing to the Memling Museum and Oud St-Jan. The hotel is 80m up on the left. Pretty, comfortable rooms on a quiet street. Breakfast included. Laundry €7.55. Singles €24.50; doubles €36; triples €54; quads €64.50. ❸

Charlie Rockets, Hoogstr. 19 (☎33 06 60; info@charlierockets.com). From Markt, follow Breidelstr., which becomes Hoogstr. Central location. Packed restaurant-bar. Breakfast included. Reception daily 8am-4am. Dorms €13-16; doubles €46. ❷

Bauhaus International Youth Hotel, Langestr. 133-137 (☎34 10 93; info@bauhaus.be). Take bus #6 or 16 to Gerechtshof and go right about 50m; it's on the left. Cybercafe and popular bar. Nearby laundromat. Breakfast €2. Reception daily 8am-2am. Dorms €13.50-22.50; doubles €25-35. ❷

Snuffel's Sleep-In, Ezelstr. 49 (☎33 31 33). From Markt, follow St-Jakobsstr. (bearing right at Moerstr.), which becomes Ezelstr. (10min.). Or, take bus #3 or 13 from the station to Normaalschool. Internet access. Kitchen facilities. Breakfast and sheets included. Reception daily 8am-6am. Dorms €13. ❷

Europa International Youth Hostel (HI), Baron Ruzettelaan 143 (☎35 26 79; brugge@vjh.be). Quiet, away from the Markt and the nightlife. Turn right from the station and follow Buiten Katelijnevest to Baron Ruzettelaan (15min.). Or, take bus #2 to Wantestraat. Breakfast included. Sheets €3.10. Key deposit €2.50. Reception daily 7:30-10am and 1-11pm. Dorms €12.50; nonmembers add €2. ❷

Camping: St-Michiel, Tillegemstr. 55 (☎38 08 19). From the station, take bus #7 to Jagerstr. Go left on Jagerstr. and bear left at the 1st intersection, staying on Jagerstr. and going around the rotary to Tillegemstr. €2.85 per person, €3.35 per tent. ❶

FOOD

Inexpensive food can be hard to find in Bruges, but it is worth splurging at least once on Belgium's famous *mosselen* (mussels; usually €15-22). From the Burg, cross the river and turn left to buy fresh (raw) seafood at the **Vismarkt.** (Open Tu-Sa 8am-1pm.) For cheaper fare, head to **Nopri Supermarket,** Noordzandstr. 4, just off 't Zand. (Open M-Sa 9:30am-6:30pm.)

Ganzespel, Ganzestr. 37. Serves up generous portions of simple food. Pleasantly off the beaten track. From the Burg, turn up Hoogstr. and take the 2nd right after the river. Meals €6-15, quiche €6. Open W-F noon-2:30pm and 6-10pm, Su noon-10pm. ❹

De Hobbit, Kemelstr. 8. Big portions of hearty food. Meals from €6 for pasta to €15 for meat. Salads €8.90-13.65. Open daily 6pm-1am. ❹

Grand Kaffee de Passage, Dweerstr. 26-28. Traditional Belgian cuisine (€4.50-14). Attached to De Passage hotel. Open daily 5pm-1am. ❸

Café Craenenburg, Markt 16. Grab a quick bite to eat on the terrace (€9.70-12.30) and watch the passersby. Pricey, but has a great view. Open daily 7am-1am. ❹

Het Dagelijks Brood, Philipstockstr. 21. Sandwiches, quiches, salads, pastries, and organic yogurt. Great for breakfast and lunch. Everyone sits at a big wooden table. Open M and W-Sa 7am-6pm, Su 8am-6pm. ❷

De Belegde Boterham, Kleine St-Amandstr. 5. Salads €8-9.30, sandwiches €5-7.40. Open M-Sa noon-5pm. ❷

SIGHTS

Small enough to be explored on short walks and lined with gorgeous canals, Bruges is best seen on foot. The tourist office leads **walking tours** (July-Aug. daily 3pm, €3.75), and **boat tours** traverse Bruges's canals (every 30min., €5); ask at the tourist office or pick up tickets at the booth on the bridge between Wollestr. and Dijver. The combination ticket (€15) covers five sights of your choice, including the Gruuthuse, the Groeninge Museum, the Memling, the Belfort, and the Stadhuis.

MARKT AND BURG. Over the **Markt** looms the 88m medieval bell tower of the **Belfort.** During the day, climb its dizzying 366 steps for a great view; return at night, when the tower serves as the city's torch. *(Open daily 9:30am-5pm. Tickets sold until 4:15pm. Bell concerts M, W, Sa 9pm; Su 2:15pm. €5, students €3.)* Behind the Markt, the **Burg** square is dominated by the flamboyant Gothic facade of the medieval **Stadhuis** (City Hall), filled with paintings and wood carvings. Upstairs is a gilded hall where many Bruges residents still get married. *(Open daily 9:30am-5pm. €2.50, students €1.50. Audioguide included.)* Hidden in the corner of the Burg next to the Stadhuis, the **Basilica of the Holy Blood** houses a relic that allegedly holds the blood of Christ. *(Open Apr.-Sept. daily 9:30am-noon and 2-6pm; Oct.-Mar. 10am-noon and 2-4pm; closed W afternoon. Free. Worship of relic F 8:30-10am (ground floor), 10-11am, and 3-4pm (upstairs). €1.)*

MUSEUMS. From the Burg, follow Wollestr. left and then head right on Dijver to reach the **Groeninge Museum,** which has a comprehensive collection of Belgian and Dutch paintings from the last six centuries, featuring works by Bruges-based Jan Van Eyck, Bruges-born Hans Memling, and the master of medieval macabre, Hieronymous Bosch. *(Dijver 12. Open daily 9:30am-5pm; off-season closed Tu. €5, students €3.)* Next door, the **Gruuthuse Museum** houses an amazing collection of weapons, tapestries, musical instruments, and coins that date back to the 6th century. The small chapel, which protrudes into the Church of Our Lady (see below), was built so that the Palace residents could attend church services from the comfort of their own home. *(Dijver 17. Open daily 9:30am-5pm; Oct.-Mar. closed Tu. €5, students €3.)* Continue on Dijver as it becomes Gruuthusestr. and walk under the stone archway to enter the **Memling Museum,** housed in **St-Janshospitaal,** one of the oldest surviving medieval hospitals in Europe. The museum reconstructs everyday life in the hospital and has several paintings by Hans Memling. *(Mariastr. 38. Open Apr.-Sept. daily 9:30am-5pm; Oct.-Mar. Th-Tu 9:30am-12:30pm and 2-5pm. €7, students €3.)*

OTHER SIGHTS. The 13th- to 16th-century **Church of Our Lady,** at Mariastr. and Gruuthusestr., near the Groeninge Museum, contains Michelangelo's *Madonna and Child* as well as medieval frescoed tomb fragments and the 16th-century mausoleums of Mary of Burgundy and Charles the Bold. *(Open daily 9:30am-12:30pm and 1:30-5pm. Church free. Tomb fragment viewing €2.50, students €1.50.)* From the church, turn left, follow Mariastr., and turn right onto Stoofstr., where you will come to Walplein. Cross the footbridge to enter the Beguinage, a grassy cove encircled by picturesque medieval cloisters that are inhabited today by Benedictine nuns. *(Open Mar.-Nov. daily 10am-noon and 1:45-5:30pm; July-Aug. until 6pm. Gate closes at sunset. €1.50.)* The 230-year-old windmill **Sint-Janshuismolen** is still used to grind flour in the summer months. From the Burg, follow Hoogstr., which becomes Langestr., and turn left at the end onto Kruisvest. *(Open May-Sept. daily 9:30am-12:30pm and 1:30-5pm. €1, students €0.50.)* The **Minnewater** (Lake of Love), on the southern end of the city, has a less-than-idyllic history as the site of an ammunition dump, but you'd never know it from the picnickers lounging happily in the beautiful park.

BELGIUM

NIGHTLIFE

The best nighttime entertainment in Bruges is wandering through the city's romantic streets and over its cobblestoned bridges. Other options include the popular bar at the Bauhaus Hostel (see above) or the 300 varieties of beer at **'t Brugs Beertje,** Kemelstr. 5, off Steenstr. (Open M-Tu and Th 4pm-1am, F-Sa 4pm-2am, Su 4pm-1am.) Next door, the **Dreipelhuisje** serves tantalizingly fruity *jenever,* a flavored Dutch gin. Be careful—the flavors mask a very high alcohol content. (Open Tu-F 6pm-midnight, Sa-Su 6pm-2am.) **Rica Rokk,** 't Zand 6, is popular with local 20-somethings. (Beer from €1.80. Open daily 8am-5am.) **The Break,** 't Zand 9, has pulsing music. (Beer from €1.80. Open M-Sa 10am-late, Su 1pm-late.)

DAYTRIPS FROM BRUGES

OSTEND (OOSTENDE)

Trains run to Ostend from Bruges (15min., 3 per hr., €2.75). Get ferry tickets from travel agents, at ports, or in the Ostend train station. For info on ferries to the UK, see p. 57.

Ostend, along the coast of the North Sea, is a popular vacation spot with a crowded beach and a promenade lined with restaurants and bars. Once a stylish resort town, Ostend was heavily damaged by bombing during the World Wars and rebuilt itself in concrete highrises that now block the rest of the town's view. The pier and the

Viserkaai (Fishermans' Quay) mark the entrance to the harbor that brings in most of the fresh fish sold in the country. Near the bustling **Vitrap** (Fishmarket), vendors set up stands selling steaming bowls of *caricoles* (sea snails) and other seafood snacks. The **Casino-Kursaal,** Monacoplein, is currently undergoing renovations and is set to reopen in 2004. The **tourist office,** Monacoplein 2 (☎70 11 99; www.oostende.be), is across from the casino. To get from the Ostend train station to the **De Ploate Youth Hostel (HI) ❷,** Langestr. 82, cross the bridge directly in front of the station, turn right on Visserkaai, follow the Promenade for 10min., and turn left on Langestr. (☎(059) 80 52 97; http://travel.to/deploate. Reception daily 7:30am-midnight. Curfew midnight. Dorms €12.65, nonmembers €15.15.) Pick up *Oostende by Night* from the tourist office for listings of local bars and events.

ANTWERP (ANTWERPEN, ANVERS) ☎03

Antwerp (pop. 1.6 million) is distinctly cosmopolitan. Its main street, the **Meir,** proudly showcases trendy clothing, diamond jewelry, and delectable chocolate in its storefront windows. In the pubs at the end of the Meir, beer flows so cheaply that crowds pass another round in lieu of breakfast. Along the promenade by the **Schelde River** is the 13th-century **Steen Castle,** which houses the extensive collection of the National Maritime Museum. (Open Tu-Su 10am-5pm. €4, F free.) **Cogels Osylei** and the surrounding streets are famed for their fanciful and eclectic mansions, built in a variety of architectural styles; they are best reached by tram #11 or the Berchem train station. In the city's historic center, the cathedral bells chime along with the accordion music of the street performers. The **Cathedral of Our Lady,** Groenpl. 21, boasts a magnificent Gothic tower and Rubens's *Descent from the Cross.* (Open M-F 10am-5pm, Sa 10am-3pm, Su 1-4pm. €2.) Nearby, the dignified Renaissance **Stadhuis** (City Hall), in Grote Markt, is well worth visiting. (Tours ☎203 95 33. €0.75.) The **Mayer van den Bergh Museum,** Lange Gasthuisstr. 19, formerly a private collection with works from the 14th to 16th centuries, showcases Bruegel's *Mad Meg.* (Open Tu-Su 10am-5pm. €3, F free.) The **Rubens Huis,** Wapper 9-11, off Meir, was built by Antwerp's favorite son and is filled with his works. (Open Tu-Su 10am-5pm. €5, F free.) The **Royal Museum of Fine Arts,** Leopold De Waelpl. 1-9, has one of the world's finest collections of Old Flemish Master paintings. (Open Tu-Su 10am-5pm. €5, F free.) The newly opened **Diamant Museum,** Kon. Astridplein 19, follows Belgium's role in the history of the diamond industry and explains Antwerp's historic reputation as the world's diamond center. (Open Apr.-Oct. 10am-6pm; Nov.-Mar. 10am-5pm. €5, students €3. Audioguide included.) Get a copy of *Week Up* at the tourist office for information on Antwerp's nightlife. The streets behind the cathedral stay crowded at night, although many of the clubs are closer to the train station. **Bierland,** Korte Nieuwstr. 28, is a popular student hangout. (Open Su-Th 9am-noon, F-Sa 8am-2am.) Over 600 Flemish religious figurines hang out with drinkers at **Elfde Gebod,** Torfburg 10, next to the cathedral. (Beer €1.75-3. Open M-F noon-1am, Sa-Su noon-2am.) Sample the local *elixir d'Anvers* (a strong, sugary drink) in the candlelit, 15th-century **Pelgrom,** Pelgrimstr. 15. (Open daily noon-late.) Gay nightlife clusters on **Van Schoonhovenstraat,** just north of Centrale Station.

Trains go from Berchem Station to: Amsterdam (2hr., €24); Brussels (1hr., €5); and Rotterdam (1½hr., €17.35). To get from the station to the **tourist office,** Grote Markt 15, take tram #8 to Groenplaats. (☎232 01 03; www.visitantwerpen.be. Open M-Sa 9am-6pm, Su 9am-5pm.) The **New International Youth Hotel and Hostel ❷,** Provinciestr. 256, is about a 10min. walk from the train station, on the corner of De Boeystr. and Provinciestr. Take tram #2, 11, or 15 to Plantin, follow Plantin de Moretus under the bridge, and turn right on Baron Joostensstr., left on Van Den Nestlei, and right on De Boeystr. (☎230 05 22. Breakfast included. Sheets €3.

Reception daily 8am-11pm. No lockout. 8-bed dorms €13; singles €26; doubles €40-50; quads €65-77.) To get to **Scoutel ❹,** Stoomstr. 3, from the station, turn left on Pelikaanstr., left on Langekievitstr., and right on Stoomstr.; the entrance faces the bridge. (☎226 46 06; www.vvksm.be. Breakfast and sheets included. Reception daily 8am-7pm. Singles €27, under 26 €24; doubles €43/€38.50; triples €52.30/€45.70.) To reach **Jeugdherberg Op-Sinjoorke (HI) ❷,** Eric Sasselaan 2, take tram #8 or 11 to Groenplaats, then take tram #2 (dir.: Hoboken) to Bouwcentrum. From the tram stop, walk toward the fountain, take a left, and follow the yellow signs. (☎238 02 73; www.vjh.be. Breakfast included. Sheets €3.35. Lockout 10am-4pm. Dorms €12.50, nonmembers €15; doubles €17/€20.) You can **camp** near the Jeugdherberg Op-Sinjoorke at **Sted. Kamp Vogelzangan ❶.** Follow the directions to the hostel; when you get off the tram, face the Bouwventrum, turn right, walk away from the fountain, and cross the street to take the first left; the campground is on the left after the gates. (Open Apr.-Sept. €1.60 per person; €0.90 per car; €0.90 per tent, €2.10 per tent with electricity.) Numerous restaurants surround the **Grote Markt** and **Groenplaats.** There are loads of cheap Middle Eastern restaurants in the area. **Suikerrui,** off Grote Markt, is the street for those seeking seafood. **Gringos ❷,** Ernest van Dijckkaai 24, along the river, serves Mexican food and is always packed with a younger crowd. (Meals €5-10, margaritas €4.50. Open W-Su 6-11pm. No reservations or credit cards.) **Spaghettiworld ❸,** Oude Koornmarkt 3, has funky decor and a large selection of big and inexpensive pasta dishes. (Pasta €7-12. Open Tu-F 7am-11pm, Sa noon-11pm, Su 4-11pm.) The **GB Supermarkt** is off Groenpl. (Open M-Th and Sa 9am-8pm, F 9am-9pm.) **Postal Code:** 2000.

BELGIUM

GHENT (GENT) ☎09

Throughout the Middle Ages, Ghent prospered at the heart of the Flemish textile industry. Today, many of its buildings and monuments stand in proud testament to its former grandeur. The "10 Days Off" celebration, also known as the **Gentse Feesten,** commemorates the first vacation granted to laborers in 1860. During the festivities, the streets fill with performers, live music, carnival rides, and great food and beer; the celebration also brings 11 nights of international DJs. (July 19-28, 2003. ☎269 46 00.) The **Leie canal** runs through the center of the city and wraps around the **Gravensteen,** St-Veerlepl. 11, a medieval fortress whose shadowy halls and spiral staircases will give you chills before you even reach the crypt, dungeon, and torture chamber. (Open Apr.-Aug. daily 9am-5:15pm; Sept.-Mar. 9am-4:15pm. €6.20, students €1.20.) The castle is near the historic **Partershol** quarter, a network of well-preserved 16th- to 18th-century houses. Wind your way up the towering **Belfort** (Belfry) to experience some serious vertigo. (Open mid-Mar. to Nov. daily 10am-12:30pm and 2-5:30pm. €2.50, students €1.50.) The **Stadhuis** (Town Hall) is a mix of Gothic and Renaissance architecture. A block away on Limburgstr., the elaborately decorated 14th- to 16th-century **Saint Bavo's Cathedral** boasts van Eyck's *Adoration of the Mystic Lamb* and Rubens's *St. Bavo's Entrance into the Monastery of Ghent.* (Cathedral open Apr.-Oct. daily 8:30am-6pm; Nov.-Mar. M-Sa 8:30am-5pm, Su 2-7pm. Free. Crypt and *Mystic Lamb* open M-Sa 9:30am-5pm, Su 1-5pm. €2.50. Audioguide included.) Walk across **Saint Michael's Bridge** and along the **Graslei**, a medieval port-street, to see the handsomely preserved guild houses. **The Museum voor Sierkunst** (Museum of Decorative Arts), nearby on Jan Breydelstr., has a large collection of Art Nouveau designs as well as more contemporary furniture. (Open Tu-Su 9:30am-5pm. €2.50, students €1.20.) The **Museum voor Schone Kunsten** (Museum of Fine Arts), in Citadel Park, has a collection of 14th- to 16th-century Flemish works. (Open Tu-Su 10am-6pm. €2.50, students €1.20.) The **SMAK,** short for the **Stedelijk Museum voor Actuele Kunst** (Municipal Museum for Contemporary Art), is also located in Citadel Park. (Open Tu-Su 10am-6pm. €5, students €2.50).

Vooruit, a huge Art Deco bar and venue for visiting theater troupes on St-Pietersnieuwstr., was once the meeting place of the Socialist Party and was later occupied by Nazis in WWII. (Open M-Th 11:30am-2am, F-Sa 11:30am-3am, Su 4pm-2am.) Beer-lovers flock to **Dulle Grief,** in Vrijdagmarkt, for over 250 types of beer. (Open M 4:30pm-12:30am, Tu-Sa noon-12:30am, Su noon-7:30pm.)

Trains run from St-Pietersstation (accessible by tram #1 or 12) to: Antwerp (40min., €6.80); Brussels (40min., €6.10); and Bruges (20min., €4.70). The **tourist office** is in the crypt of the belfry, Botermarkt 17A. (☎266 52 32. Open Apr.-Oct. daily 9:30am-6:30pm; Nov.-Mar. 9:30am-4:30pm.) In the shadow of a castle, **De Draeke (HI)** ❷, St-Widostr. 11, blends into downtown Ghent despite its modernity. From the station, take tram #1, 10, or 11 to Gravensteen (15min.). Facing the castle, head left over the canal, then go right on Gewad and right again on St-Widostr. (☎233 70 50. Breakfast and sheets included. Internet access €0.07 per min. Reception daily 7:30am-11pm. Dorms €15; singles €22.50; doubles €36. Nonmembers add €2.50.) **The Hotel Flandria** ❺, Barrestr. 3, tucked away on a quiet road near Saint Bavo's Cathedral, is well-worth looking for. (☎223 06 26. Breakfast included. Reception 7am-9pm. Singles €33, with bath €41; doubles €38/€48.) To get to **Camping Blaarmeersen** ❶, Zuiderlaan 12, take bus #9 from St-Pietersstation and ask the driver to connect you to bus #38 to Blaarmeersen. When you get off, take the first street on your left to the end. (☎221 53 99. Open Mar. to mid-Oct. only. May-Aug. €4 per person and per tent; Mar.-Apr. and Sept.-Oct. €3.25 per person and per tent.) **Korenmarkt** and **Vrijdagmarkt** are surrounded by restaurants and pubs. **Oudburg,** near Patershol, has many inexpensive Turkish restaurants. Also try **St-Pietersnieuwstraat,** by the university. Students meet up at **Magazyne** ❶, on Penitentenstr., for cheap, hearty fare in the historic district. **Het Brood** ❷, Walpoortstr. 9, has sandwiches, salads, and omelets. (Open M-F 8:30am-6:30pm, Sa 9am-6:30pm, Su 9am-2:30pm.) **Postal Code:** 9000.

YPRES (IEPER) ☎57

"We are the dead. Short days ago/We lived, felt dawn, saw sunset glow/Loved and were loved, and now we lie/In Flanders fields." Canadian soldier John McCrae wrote these famous words during WWI at the Battle of Ypres Salient. Ypres, once a medieval textile center, was completely destroyed by the long combat; reconstruction took more than 40 years. Today, the town is surrounded by over 150 **British cemeteries** and filled with memorial sites, drawing victims' families as well as British tourists and school groups. In **Flanders Field Museum,** Grote Markt 34, documents and films attempt to convey the triumphs and the tribulations of the Great War. (Open Apr.-Sept. daily 10am-6pm; Oct.-Mar. Tu-Su 10am-5pm. €7.50.) The museum is housed in the **Cloth Hall,** a grand medieval building formerly used for textile production that presides over **Grote Markt,** the town center. Next door stands **Saint Martin's Cathedral,** another splendid example of the Gothic style. Cross the street in front of St. Martin's and head right to reach the Anglican **Saint George's Memorial Church,** Elverdingsestr. 1, constructed in 1928 as a tribute to war victims; each brass plaque and kneeling pillow commemorates a specific individual or unit. (Both churches free and open to the public except during services.) Diagonally across Grote Markt from St. Martin's is the somber **Menin Gate,** on Menenstr., upon which are inscribed the names of 54,896 British soldiers who were lost in the trenches and did not receive burial. At 8pm each evening, the **Last Post** bugle ceremony honors those who defended Ypres during the historic battle. You can easily walk the circumference of Ypres along the old ramparts. From Menin Gate, take the **Rose Coombs Walk** to visit the nearby **Ramparts Cemetery,** where row upon row of white crosses face the river. There are descriptions posted along the way; for more details, the tourist office has a brochure with explanations of the sights.

Trains run to Bruges via Courtrai (2hr., €8.80) and Ghent (1hr., €7.60). The **Visitors Center,** housed in the Cloth Hall in Grote Markt, has information on the cemeteries and memorials. To get there from the train station, head straight down Stationsstr., turn left onto Tempelstr., then turn right onto Boterstr. (☎22 85 84; www.ieper.be. Open Apr.-Sept. M-Sa 9am-6pm, Su 10am-6pm; Oct.-Mar. M-Sa 9am-5pm, Su 10am-5pm.) The **Old Tom** hotel ❺, Grote Markt 8, has charming but pricey rooms in an ideal location. (☎20 15 41. Singles €49; doubles €57; triples €78.) Many inexpensive restaurants line the **Grote Markt.** The **Tar Posterie ❷,** Rijelsestr. 57, although known for its beer selection, serves Flemish food. The **Super GB** grocery store is at Vandepeereboomplein 15. (Open M-Sa 9am-7pm.)

WALLONIE

The towns in the **Ardennes** offer a relaxing hideaway, with hiking trails that lead through deep forests to impressive citadels and cool caves. The most exceptional portion of the Belgian Ardennes lies in the southeast corner, where gorgeous train-rides sweep through peaceful farmland. Although nature-lovers will probably want to spend a night in this part of the Wallonie wilderness, urban addicts pressed for time can always enjoy the scenery on their way to Brussels, Paris, or Luxembourg.

TOURNAI ☎069

The first city liberated by Allied forces, Tournai's medieval old town escaped major damage in WWII. Once a Roman trading post and the original capital of France, Tournai is peaceful and less touristed than its Flemish counterparts. The city's most spectacular sight is the 800-year-old **Cathedral of Our Lady,** known for its five steeples, and its **treasure room,** which houses medieval goldware, reliquary shrines, and early-15th-century tapestries. (Treasure room open M-F 10:15am-12:30pm and 1:30-6pm, Sa 10:15am-12:30pm and 2-6pm, Su 11:15am-12:30pm and 2-6pm. €1.) The stunning Art Nouveau building of the **Museum of Fine Arts,** Enclos St-Martin, designed by Victor Horta, houses a fine collection of Flemish paintings. (Open W-M 10am-1pm and 2-5pm. €3, students €2.)

Trains arrive at pl. Cromberg (☎88 62 23) from Brussels's Gare du Midi (1hr., round-trip €11.60). To get to the **tourist office,** 14 Vieux Marché Aux Poteries, exit the station, walk straight to the city center (10min.), and go around the left side of the cathedral. (☎22 20 45; www.tournai.be. Open M-F 8:30am-6pm, Sa 10am-noon and 3-6pm, Su 2-6pm.) To get to the **Auberge de Tournai (HI) ❷,** 64 r. St-Martin, continue straight up the hill from the tourist office or take bus #7 or 88 (€1) from the station. (☎21 61 36. Breakfast and sheets included. Reception daily 9am-noon and 5-10pm. Closed Jan. Reservations required during off-season. Dorms €12.50; singles €22.50; doubles €17.50.) The area around the large, triangular **Grand Place** has plenty of options for cheap food.

NAMUR ☎081

The quiet and friendly city of **Namur,** in the heart of Wallonie, is the last sizable outpost before the wilderness of the Ardennes. Given the proximity of opportunities for **hiking, biking, caving,** and **kayaking,** it is the best base for exploring the area. The foreboding **citadel,** on top of a rocky hill to the south, was built by the Spanish in the Middle Ages, expanded by the Dutch in the 19th century, the site of a bloody battle in WWI, and occupied until 1978. Climb up or take a mini-bus from the tourist office at sq. Leopold and r. de Grognon; the bus will let you off at the Citadel, where you can join a tour of the fortress. (Mini-bus mid-June to mid-Sept. daily, Apr.-June Sa-Su; every hr.; €1. Citadel open daily 11am-5pm. €6, students €5.25.)

Trains link Namur to Brussels (1hr., €6.40). Two **tourist offices,** one a few blocks left of the train station at sq. Leopold (☎22 28 49; open daily 9:30am-6pm), and the other in **Hôtel de Ville** (☎24 64 44; www.ville.namur.be; open M-F 8:30am-4:30pm), help plan excursions. To reach the friendly **Auberge Félicien Rops (HI) ❷,** 8 av. Félicien Rops, take bus #3 directly to the door or take bus #4 and ask the driver to let you off. (☎22 36 88; namur@laj.be. **Bikes** €12.40 per day. Breakfast included. Sheets €2.75. Laundry €6.45. Reception daily 7:30am-1am. Lockout 11am-3pm. Dorms €11; singles €20; doubles €30. Nonmembers add €2.50.) To **camp** at **Les Trieux ❶,** 99 r. des Tris, 6km away in Malonne, take bus #6. (☎44 55 83. Open Apr.-Oct. €2.15 per person or per tent.) Restaurants cluster on the small streets around **Place Chanoine Deschamps** and **Rue Saint Jean. Brasserie Henry ❹,** 3 pl. St-Aubain, has a long menu of traditional French food and stays open late. (Entrees €7.50-12.50. Open daily noon-midnight.) For Italian, try the 15th-century cellar of **La Cava ❷,** 20 r. de la Monnaie. (Main dishes €5-10. Open daily noon-11pm.) Try the regional **Ardennes ham** (from €1.75) at one of the sandwich stands throughout the city.

DINANT ☎082

The tiny town of Dinant boasts wonders out of proportion to its size. The imposing **citadel** towers over the Meuse River. Ride the cable car up or brave the steep steps along the fortress. (☎22 36 70. Citadel open daily 10am-6pm. Mandatory tours in French and Dutch every 20min. €5.20.) Bring a sweater to the tour of the cascade-filled caves of **La Grotte Merveilleuse,** 142 rte. de Phillippeville. To reach the Grotte from the citadel, cross the bridge and take the second left onto rte. de Phillippeville. (Open July-Aug. daily 10am-6pm; Apr.-June and Sept.-Oct. daily 10am-5pm; Nov.-Mar. Sa-Su 1-4pm. Mandatory tours in French, Dutch, and English every hr. on the hr. €5, student €4.50.) Dinant is also a good base for **climbing** and **kayaking** excursions. **Dakota Raid Adventure,** 17 r. Saint Roch, leads rock-climbing daytrips in the area. (☎22 32 43. **Bikes** €12.40 per half-day, €20 per day. Open daily 9am-6:30pm.) Dinant is accessible by **train** from Brussels (1hr., €9:30) or by **bike** from Namur; on summer weekends, take a one-way river cruise from Namur (3hr.). The **tourist office,** Quai Cadoux 8 (☎22 28 70), helps plan outdoor activities (including kayaking trips) and books rooms. With your back to the train station, turn right, take the first left, and then the very next left.

BELGIUM

DAYTRIPS FROM NAMUR AND DINANT: ROCHEFORT AND HAN-SUR-LESSE. Rochefort, a charming town with welcoming residents, is hidden within the rolling hills and woods of the Lesse Valley. Hike up to the crumbled **Château Comtal** and its accompanying archaeological museum for a breathtaking view of the Northern Ardennes. (☎21 44 09. Site open Apr.-Oct. daily 10am-6pm. €1.80.) The town's other main sight is the **Grotte de Lorette,** a spectacular cave with an enormous main chamber. (☎21 20 80. Tours July-Aug. daily every 30-45min. 11am-5pm; May-June Th-Tu every 45min. 10am-5pm; Mar.-Apr. and Sept.-Oct. Th-Tu every 1½hr. 10am-4:30pm.) Signs from the center of town lead to both the chateau and the grotto. To reach Rochefort, take the **train** from Namur to Jemelle (40min., every 40min., €6.40) and then **bus** #29 from Jemelle (every hr., €1.10). The **tourist office,** 5 r. de Behogne, sells a map of hiking trails (€4) and provides information on package deals for sights in both Rochefort and Han-sur-Lesse. (☎34 51 72; rochefort.tourisme@skynet.be. Open M-F 8am-5pm, Sa-Su 9:30am-5pm.) If you decide to spend the night, try the pleasant **Gite d'Etape hostel ❷,** 25 r. du Hableau. (☎21 46 04; giterochefort@skynet.be. Breakfast included. Dorms €12.50, under 26 €10.) For something to eat, head to **Rue de Behogne,** the main street.

Nearby **Han-sur-Lesse** flourishes off the tourism generated by its famous grottoes, particularly the **Grotte de Han,** and its wild animal reserve. The grottoes boast large caverns with ancient rock formations. They can be seen on a combined tram-foot-boat trip. (€10.30. Small tip expected for English tours.) Tour the **Wild Animal Reserve** of a local Han estate, where you can see animals once typical in the Northern Ardennes (€7.80). Tickets for both expeditions are sold at the **Domain of the Grottoes** office, 2 r. J. Lamote (☎37 72 13). Tours depart from outside the office. (July-Aug. every 15-30min. 10am-noon and 1:30-5:30pm; May-June every 30min. 10am-noon and 1:30-4:30pm; Apr. every hr. 10am-noon and 1:30-4:30pm.) Across the street from the Domain, the **tourist office,** 1 pl. Theo Lannoy, sells maps of Han's six **hiking trails** (max. 2½hr.) for €2.50. The area is hilly, but all trails are manageable for able walkers. (☎37 75 96. Open M-F 9:30am-4:30pm, Sa-Su 9:30am-5:30pm; Jan. closed weekends) Han has neither a train station nor an ATM. To get to Han, take the **train** from Namur to Jemelle (40min., every 40min., €6.40) and then **bus** #29 from the Jemelle train station (every hr., €1.65). **Phone Code:** ☎084.

BRITAIN

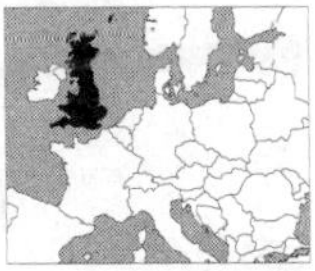

Having spearheaded the Industrial Revolution, colonized two-fifths of the globe, and won every foreign war in its history but two, Britain seems intent on making the world forget its tiny size. But this small island nation is just that: small. The rolling farms of the south and the rugged cliffs of the north are only a day's train ride apart, and peoples as diverse as London clubbers, Cornish miners, Welsh students, and Gaelic monks all occupy a land area half the size of Spain. Beyond the stereotypical snapshots of Merry Olde England—gabled cottages with flowery borders, tweed-clad farmers shepherding their flocks—Britain today is a cosmopolitan destination driven by international energy. Though the British Empire may have petered out, its legacy survives in multicultural urban centers and a dynamic arts and theater scene—the most accessible in the world, as long as English remains the planet's most widespread language. Brits eat kebab as often as they do lemon curd and scones, and five-story dance clubs in post-industrial settings draw as much attention as fairy-tale country homes with picturesque views.

Travelers should be aware that names hold political force. "Great Britain" refers to England, Scotland, and Wales; the political term "United Kingdom" refers to these nations as well as Northern Ireland. *Let's Go* uses the term "Britain" to refer to England, Scotland, and Wales because of legal and currency distinctions.

SYMBOL	❶	❷	❸	❹	❺
ACCOMMODATIONS	under £10	£10-19	£20-30	£31-59	over £60
FOOD	under £5	£5-9	£10-14	£15-20	over £21

SUGGESTED ITINERARIES

THREE DAYS Spend it all in **London** (p. 164), the city of tea, royalty, and James Bond. After a stroll through **Hyde Park,** head to **Buckingham Palace** for the changing of the guard. View the renowned collections of the **British Museum** and the **National Gallery.** Spend a night at the **Royal National Theatre** and have a drink or two in the **East End.**

ONE WEEK Begin in **Oxford** (1 day; p. 213) and travel north to Scotland for one day in **Glasgow** (p. 257). Head over for two days in lively **Edinburgh** (p. 249) before going to **London** (3 days).

BEST OF BRITAIN, THREE WEEKS Start in **London** (4 days), where you'll carouse the museums, theaters, and clubs. Tour the college greens in **Oxford** (1 day), then amble through the rolling hills of the **Cotswolds** (1 day; p. 220). Don't miss Shakespeare's hometown, **Stratford-upon-Avon** (1 day; p. 219), or that of the Beatles, **Liverpool** (2 days; p. 229). Head to **Manchester** for its nightlife (1 day; p. 227) before moving on to **Glasgow** (1 day) and nearby **Loch Lomond** (1 day; p. 262). Swing by the **Isle of Arran** (1 day; p. 261) for rural diversions; you'll need the rest before exuberant **Edinburgh** (3 days). Finally, enjoy the beautiful **Lake District** (2 days; p. 239), historic **York** (1 day, p. 233), and the hallowed halls of **Cambridge** (1 day; p. 222).

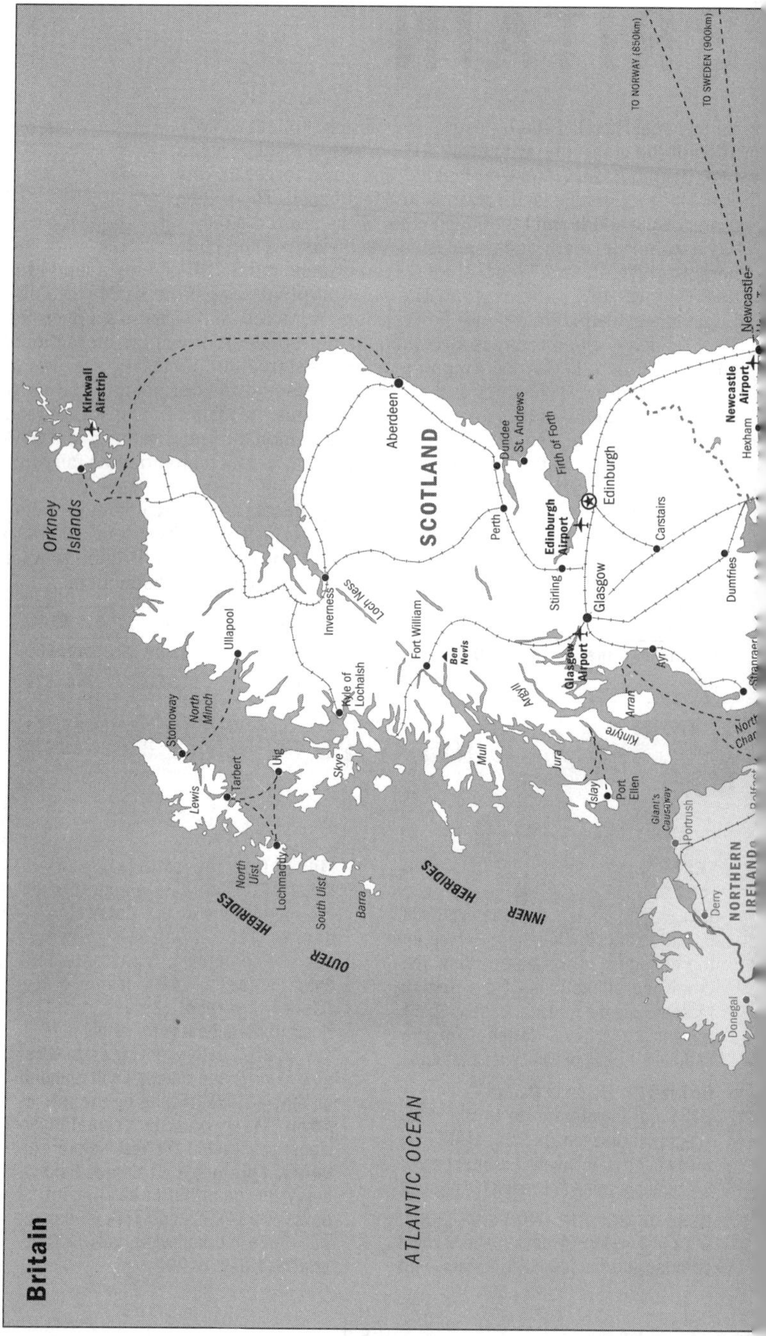

Britain
ATLANTIC OCEAN
Orkney Islands
Kirkwall Airstrip
SCOTLAND
Aberdeen
Dundee
St. Andrews
Firth of Forth
Perth
Edinburgh
Edinburgh Airport
Carstairs
Stirling
Glasgow
Glasgow Airport
Dumfries
Newcastle
Newcastle Airport
Hexham
Inverness
Loch Ness
Fort William
Ben Nevis
Ullapool
Kyle of Lochalsh
Stornoway
North Minch
Lewis
Tarbert
Uig
Skye
North Uist
Lochmaddy
South Uist
Barra
OUTER HEBRIDES
INNER HEBRIDES
Mull
Jura
Islay
Port Ellen
Argyll
Kintyre
Arran
Ayr
Stranraer
Giant's Causeway
Portrush
Derry
NORTHERN IRELAND
Donegal
TO NORWAY (850km)
TO SWEDEN (900km)

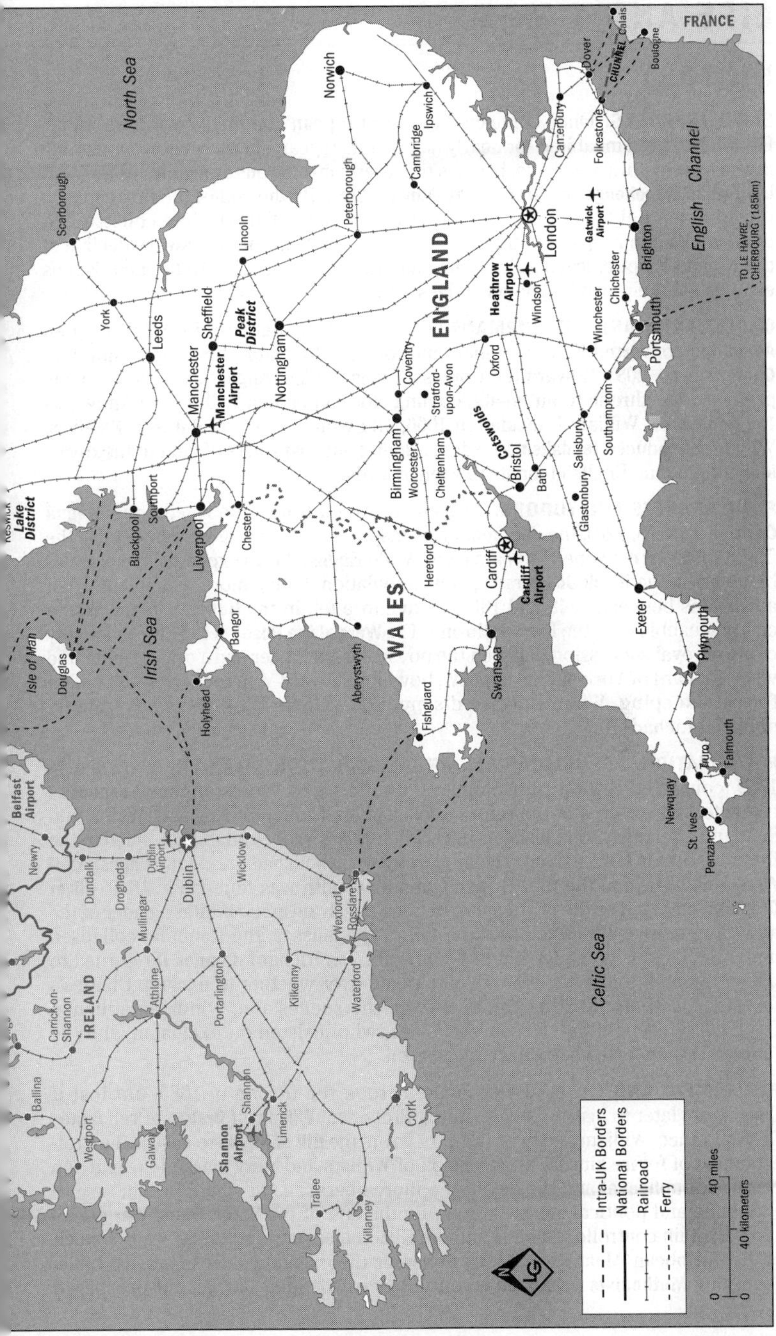
North Sea
Irish Sea
Celtic Sea
English Channel
FRANCE
ENGLAND
WALES
IRELAND
Isle of Man
Lake District
Peak District
Cotswolds
Scarborough
York
Leeds
Sheffield
Lincoln
Manchester
Manchester Airport
Nottingham
Norwich
Ipswich
Cambridge
Peterborough
Canterbury
Dover
Calais
Boulogne
CHUNNEL
Folkestone
London
Gatwick Airport
Brighton
Heathrow Airport
Windsor
Chichester
Winchester
Portsmouth
Southampton
Salisbury
Oxford
Coventry
Stratford-upon-Avon
Birmingham
Worcester
Cheltenham
Bristol
Bath
Glastonbury
Cardiff
Cardiff Airport
Hereford
Chester
Liverpool
Southport
Blackpool
Bangor
Holyhead
Aberystwyth
Fishguard
Swansea
Exeter
Plymouth
Truro
Falmouth
Newquay
St. Ives
Penzance
Douglas
TO LE HAVRE, CHERBOURG (185km)
Belfast Airport
Newry
Dundalk
Drogheda
Dublin Airport
Dublin
Wicklow
Wexford
Rosslare
Mullingar
Athlone
Carrick-on-Shannon
Portarlington
Kilkenny
Waterford
Ballina
Westport
Galway
Shannon
Shannon Airport
Limerick
Cork
Tralee
Killarney
Intra-UK Borders
National Borders
Railroad
Ferry
40 miles
40 kilometers

BRITAIN

LIFE AND TIMES

HISTORY

EARLY INVADERS. Once connected to the European continent by a land bridge, Britain has been inhabited for nearly half a million years. Little is known about the island's prehistoric residents, besides the utterly mysterious stone circles they left behind at **Stonehenge** (p. 208) and **Avebury** (p. 208). By the end of the first century, the Romans held all of "Britannia" (England and Wales); they constructed **Hadrian's Wall** to keep out unfriendly neighbors. The 4th century saw the decline of the Roman Empire, leaving Britannia vulnerable to raids. The Angles and Saxons established their own kingdoms in the south.

CHRISTIANITY AND THE NORMANS. Christianity caught on in AD 597 when **Augustine** converted King Æthelbert and founded England's first papal church at **Canterbury** (p. 203). Edward the Confessor was the last Anglo-Saxon king, having promised the throne to an up-and-coming Norman named Will. Better known as **The Conqueror,** William I invaded in 1066, and won the pivotal **Battle of Hastings.** William introduced **feudalism** to Britain, doling out vast tracts of land to the royals and subjugating English tenants to French lords.

PLANTAGENETS AND TUDORS. Noblemen forced King John to sign the **Magna Carta** in 1215 (p. 226), the document that inspired modern English democracy; the first **Parliament** convened 50 years later. While English kings expanded the nation's boundaries, the **Black Death** ravaged its population, killing more than one-third of all Britons between 1348 and 1361. Many more fell in the **Hundred Years' War,** a costly squabble over the French throne. The **Wars of the Roses** (1455-85)—a lengthy crisis of royal succession between the houses of Lancaster and York—culminated when Richard of York put his nephew, boy-king Edward V, in the Tower of London for safe-keeping. When Edward disappeared, Uncle Dick was conveniently crowned Richard III.

REFORMATION, REPUBLICANISM, AND RESTORATION. Henry VIII, crowned in 1509, converted Britain from Roman Catholicism to Protestantism; **Elizabeth I** cemented the success of the reformation. The first union of England, Wales, and Scotland effectively took place in 1603, when **James VI** of Scotland ascended to the throne as **James I** of England. The monarchy was abolished during the **English Civil Wars** (1642-51), and the first British Commonwealth was founded in 1649. **Oliver Cromwell** emerged as the charismatic but hopelessly despotic military leader of the new Commonwealth. Much to the relief of the masses, the Republic collapsed under the lackluster leadership of Cromwell's son Richard. **Charles II** returned to power unconditionally in 1660. Debate raged over whether to exclude Charles's fervently Catholic brother **James II** from the succession, which established England's first political parties: the **Whigs,** who insisted on exclusion, and the **Tories,** who supported hereditary succession.

PARLIAMENT AND THE CROWN. James II took the throne in 1685, but lost it three years later to his son-in-law, Dutch Protestant **William of Orange.** After James fled to France, William and his wife Mary wrote the **Bill of Rights** to ensure the Protestantism of future kings. The ascension of William and Mary marked the end of a century of upheaval and the debut of a more liberal age in which Britain rose to economic and political superstardom. By the end of the **Seven Years' War** (1756-1763), Britain controlled Canada and the 13 colonies to the south, as well as much of the Caribbean. Meanwhile, **Sir Isaac Newton** theorized the laws of gravity, bible-thumping **Methodists** preached to outdoor crowds, and Parliament prospered thanks to the ineffectual leadership of the Hanoverian kings, **Georges I, II, and III,** and the office of Prime Minister eclipsed the monarchy as the seat of power.

EMPIRE AND INDUSTRY. During the 18th and 19th centuries, Britain came to rule more than one quarter of the world's population and two-fifths of its land. The **Napoleonic Wars** (1800-15) revived the Anglo-French rivalry and racked up colonies, which by 1858 included India, South Africa, and Australia. The **Industrial Revolution** fueled Britain as a world power. Massive portions of the rural populace, pushed off their land and lured by growing opportunities in industrial employment, migrated to towns like **Manchester** (p. 227) and **Sheffield** (p. 231). The **Gold Standard,** which Britain adopted in 1821, established the pound's value with gold as an international financial system, securing Britain's economic supremacy.

THE VICTORIAN ERA. The long and stable rule of **Queen Victoria** (1837-1901) set the tone for foreign and domestic politics and even stylistic mores. A series of **Factory** and **Reform Acts** throughout the century limited child labor, capped the average workday, and made sweeping changes in voting rights. By 1906, trade unions found a political voice in the **Labour Party.** Yet pressures to alter the position of other marginalized groups proved ineffectual, as the rich and bohemian embraced *fin-de-siecle* decadence; women, for instance, would have to wait for the vote until after the trauma of **World War I.**

THE WORLD WARS. The **Great War,** as WWI was known until 1939, brought British military action back to the European stage, scarred the national spirit with the loss of a generation of young men, and dashed Victorian dreams of a peaceful, progressive society. The 1930s brought **depression** and mass unemployment, and tensions in Europe escalated once again with the German reoccupation of the Rhineland. Britain declared war on September 3, 1939. Even the Great War failed to prepare the British Isles for the utter devastation of **World War II.** German air raids began the prolonged **Battle of Britain** in the summer of 1940, and English cities were further demolished by thunderous **Blitzkriegs.** The fall of France precipitated the creation of a war cabinet, led by the eloquent **Winston Churchill.** With the 1944 **D-Day Invasion** of Normandy, the tide of the war changed; peace came to Europe in May 1945.

THE POST-WAR YEARS. With increasing immigration from former colonies and a growing rift between the rich and poor, post-war Britain faced economic and cultural problems that still rankle today. Britain joined the **European Economic Community (EEC)** in 1971, a move that received a rocky welcome from many Britons. It was against this backdrop that Britain grasped for change, electing "Iron Lady" **Margaret Thatcher** as Prime Minister. Her policies brought dramatic prosperity to many but sharpened the divide between the haves and have-nots. Aggravated by her resistance to the EEC, the Conservative Party conducted a vote of no confidence that led to Thatcher's 1990 resignation and the election of **John Major.** In 1993, the Major government suffered its first embarrassment when the British pound toppled out of the EEC's monetary regulation system. Major remained unpopular, and by 1995 his ratings were so low that he resigned as Party leader to force a leadership election. He won the election, but the Conservatives lost parliamentary seats and continued to languish in the polls.

TODAY

HOW BRITANNIA IS RULED. Since the 1700s the monarch has served in a purely symbolic role, leaving real power to **Parliament,** which consists of the **House of Commons,** with its elected Members of Parliament (MPs), and the **House of Lords,** most of whom are government-appointed Life Peers. All members of the executive branch, which includes the **Prime Minister** and the **Cabinet,** are also MPs; this fusing of legislative and executive functions, called the "efficient secret" of the British government, ensures the quick passage of the majority party's programs into bills. The two main parties are **Labour** and the **Conservatives,** representing roughly the left and the right respectively.

CURRENT EVENTS. Under the leadership of charismatic **Tony Blair,** the Labour Party reduced ties with unions, refashioned itself into the alternative for discontented voters, and finally began to rise in popularity. In 1999, however, Blair earned the title of "little Clinton" for his blind conformance to American foreign policy. After the September 11 attacks of 2002, Britain again gave its unilateral support to the US. Blair's detractors believe that Britain's refusal to adopt the **euro** is another sign that his sympathies with the US are greater than those with Europe. Throughout 2002, the British government prepared for the perhaps-inevitable currency switch-over, conducting five "tests" to see if Britain and the euro are compatible. The issue could go before the voters in a referendum in 2003.

Blair's Labour government has also initiated domestic devolution in Scotland and Wales. The Scots voted in a 1997 referendum to have their own Parliament, which opened in 1999, and the Welsh opened their National Assembly in 1999. Progress has been more halting in the latest attempts at Northern Irish autonomy; the British government suspended Belfast's **Stormont Assembly** in 2000, hoping to instigate the decommissioning of arms by the IRA and their Unionist counterparts. A lack of progress satisfactory to either side led to a year of violence throughout 2001 and into 2002. The Good Friday Agreement continues a precarious existence between cease-fires, election outcomes, and disarmament promises.

A ROYAL MESS? The spectacle of royal life took a tragic turn in 1997, when **Princess Diana** and **Dodi Al-Fayed** died in a car crash in a Paris tunnel. The immediate fate of the royals will depend on whether the monarchy embraces Diana's fervent populism or retreats with traditional aloofness to the private realm. **Charles** and his long-time paramour **Camilla Parker-Bowles** are making tentative steps toward public acceptance—royal-watchers were tittering over Camilla's seat in the Queen's box during the opening ceremonies of 2002's **Golden Jubilee** (a year-long bash celebrating the monarch's fifty years on the throne). A quick stop at a drug rehab clinic in 2002 heralded the onset of adult celebrity for **Harry,** the younger of Charles and Diana's sons. The spotlight, however, most often shines on **Prince William.** Whether "His Royal Sighness" will gracefully survive his trip to adulthood under the paparazzi's unforgiving lens remains to be seen.

CULTURE

FOOD AND DRINK

Britons like to start their day off heartily with the famous, cholesterol-filled, meat-anchored English breakfast, served in most B&Bs across the country. The best native dishes for lunch or dinner are roasts—beef, lamb, and Wiltshire hams—and puddings, including the standard Yorkshire. The ploughman's lunch, served in pubs, consists of cheese, bread, and pickles. Fish and chips (french fries) are traditionally drowned in vinegar and salt. To escape English food, try Chinese, Greek, or Indian cuisine. British "tea" refers to both a drink and a social ritual. The refreshment is served strong and milky. The ceremony might include cooked meats, salad, sandwiches, and pastries. Cream tea, a specialty of Cornwall and Devon, includes toast, shortbread, crumpets, scones, jam, and clotted cream.

CUSTOMS AND ETIQUETTE

BEING PROPER. English decorum is infamously reserved. Politeness, especially a simple thank-you (also expressed "ta" and "cheers"), is essential. Never jump the queue (line), be punctual, and keep a certain respectful distance—cheek-kissing and vigorous hand-shaking are continental trends that did not catch on in the Isles. The British sense of humor—fantastically wry, explicit, and even raunchy (witness the daily topless girl on page three of *The Sun*)—is somewhat at odds with any notion of reserve.

TIPPING AND BARGAINING. Tips are often included in the bill, sometimes as a "service charge." If gratuity is not included, you should tip 10-15%. Tipping the bartender is not expected, though a pub waiter should be tipped. Taxi drivers should receive a 10-15% tip, and bellhops and chambermaids usually expect somewhere between £1 and £3. Aside from open-air markets, don't expect to **bargain.**

THE ARTS

ARCHITECTURE. The cathedrals and castles of England's skyline trace a history of foreign conquests. Houses of worship began as stone, but gave way to cathedrals like **Winchester** (p. 206). The Normans introduced Romanesque architecture, and the Gothic period ushered in intricate buildings like the **Salisbury** (p. 207) cathedral and **King's College Chapel** in Cambridge (p. 222). Christopher Wren's dome on **St. Paul's Cathedral** (p. 183) attests to the capabilities of Renaissance architecture. Early domestic architecture progressed from the stone dwellings of pre-Christian folk to Roman forts and villas to squat Norman castles like the **Tower of London** (p. 184). The Renaissance was ushered in with sumptuous Tudor homes like Henry VIII's **Hampton Court** (p. 190). The **Arts and Crafts** movement was an architectural revival during the Victorian period that gave us the neo-Gothic **Houses of Parliament** (p. 181) and the neo-Classical **British Museum** (p. 191). Today, **Richard Rogers** and **Norman Foster** vie for bragging rights as England's most influential architect, littering London with several tributes to the millennium (p. 186).

ON THE CANVAS. Secular patronage and court painters followed Britain's early, religious-oriented art. Portrait artist **Thomas Gainsborough** propagated an interest in landscape painting, which peaked in the 19th century with his contemporaries **J.M.W. Turner** and **John Constable.** The Victorian era of revival saw movements like **Dante Gabriel Rossetti**'s (1828-82) Italian-inspired, damosel-laden Pre-Raphaelite school. Modernist trends from the Continent, like cubism and expressionism, were picked up by **Wyndham Lewis** (1882-1957) and **Henry Moore** (1898-1986). WWII inspired experimental works by **Francis Bacon** and **Lucian Freud.** The precocious **Young British Artists (YBAs)** of the 1990s include sculptor **Rachel Whitbread** and multi-media artist **Damien Hirst.**

LITERATURE. Geoffrey Chaucer tapped into the spirited side of Middle English; his *Canterbury Tales* (c. 1387) remain some of the funniest stories in the English canon. English literature flourished under the reign of Elizabeth I. The era's greatest contributions were dramatic, with the appearance of the first professional playwrights. The son of a glove-maker from Stratford-upon-Avon (p. 219), **William Shakespeare** looms over all of English literature. The British Puritans of the late 16th and early 17th centuries produced a huge volume of obsessive and beautiful literature, like **John Milton's** epic *Paradise Lost* (1667). In 1719, **Daniel Defoe** inaugurated the era of the English novel with his popular island-bound *Robinson Crusoe.* By the end of the century, **Jane Austen** had perfected the narrative technique; most of her great novels were written in a cottage near Winchester (p. 206).

The Romantic movement of the early 1800s found its greatest expression in poetry. The watershed *Lyrical Ballads* by **William Wordsworth** and **Samuel Taylor Coleridge** included classics like "Lines Composed a Few Miles above Tintern Abbey" (p. 244) and "The Rime of the Ancient Mariner." Victorian poverty and social change spawned the classic, sentimental novels of **Charles Dickens.** In the early 20th century, **Virginia Woolf** tried to capture the spirit of time and the mind in her novels; she and the Irish expatriate **James Joyce** were among the most groundbreaking practitioners of **Modernism.** One of Modernism's poetic champions was **T.S. Eliot;** his influential poem *The Waste Land* (1922) portrays London as a fragmented and barren desert awaiting redemption. The end of the Empire and the growing gap between the classes splintered British literature in a thousand directions. Postcolonial voices like **Salman Rushdie** and 2002 Nobel laureate **V.S. Naipaul** have become an important literary force, and England continues to produce acclaimed works from writers like **A.S. Byatt** and **Martin Amis.**

Britain has also produced volumes of children's literature. **Lewis Carroll's** *Alice's Adventures in Wonderland* (1865) and **C.S. Lewis's** *Chronicles of Narnia* (1950-56) have enchanted for generations. **J.R.R. Tolkien** wrote fanciful tales of elves, wizards, short folk, and rings (*The Hobbit*, 1934; *Lord of the Rings*, 1954-56), and recently, **J.K. Rowling** has swept the world with her tale of juvenile wizardry in the blockbuster *Harry Potter* series.

MUSIC. During the Renaissance, English ears were tuned to cathedral anthems, psalms, madrigals, and the odd lute performance. **Henry Purcell** (1659-1695) rang in the baroque with instrumental music for Shakespeare's plays as well as England's first great opera, *Dido and Aeneas*. The 18th century welcomed the visits of the foreign geniuses Mozart, Haydn, and **George Frideric Handel,** a German composer who wrote operas in the Italian style but spent most of his life in Britain. Today's audiences are probably familiar with the operettas of **W.S. Gilbert** (1836-1911) and **Arthur Sullivan** (1842-1900); the pair were rumored to hate each other, but managed to produce gems such as *The Mikado* and *The Pirates of Penzance*. The world wars provoked **Benjamin Britten**'s (1913-76) heartbreaking *War Requiem* and **Michael Tippett's** (1905-98) humanitarian oratorio, *A Child of Our Time*. Later 20th-century trends, including **Andrew Lloyd Webber's** blend of opera, popular music, and falling chandeliers, demonstrate the commercially lucrative shift of British musical influence.

The **British Invasion** groups of the 1960s infiltrated the world with daring, controversial sound. The **Beatles** were the ultimate trendsetters, still influential more than three decades after their break-up. The edgier lyrics and grittier sound of the **Rolling Stones** shifted teens' thoughts from "I Wanna Hold Your Hand" to "Let's Spend the Night Together." Over the next 20 years, England imported the Urban "mod" sound of **The Who** and guitar gurus Eric Clapton of **Cream** and Jimmy Page of **Led Zeppelin.** In the mid-1970s, British rock schismed, as the theatrical excesses of **glam rock** performers like **Queen, Elton John,** and **David Bowie** contrasted with the conceptual, album-oriented **art rock** emanating from **Pink Floyd** and Phil Collins's **Genesis.** Dissonant **punk rock** bands like **The Clash** emerged from Britain's industrial centers as a counter to self-indulgence. Meanwhile, the **Sex Pistols** stormed the scene with wildly successful antics—their angry 1977 single "God Save the Queen" topped the charts.

British bands continued to achieve popular success on both sides of the Atlantic thanks to the 1980s advent of America's Music Television. **Dire Straits** introduced the first computer-animated music video, while **Duran Duran,** the **Eurythmics, Boy George, Tears for Fears,** and the **Police** enjoyed many top-10 hits. Any clubber worth her tube-top can tell you about England's influence on dance music, from the **Chemical Brothers** to the Brighton-bred **Fatboy Slim.** Beatles-esque bands the **Verve** and **Oasis** cherish dreams of rock 'n' roll stardom, while the tremendous popularity of American grunge rock inspired a host of poseurs in the UK, reaching maturity with Oxford's conceptual innovators, **Radiohead.**

FILM. British film has endured an uneven history, marked by cycles of relative independence from Hollywood followed by increasing drains of talent to America. The Royal Shakespeare Company has produced a heavyweight set of alumni, like **Dame Judi Dench** and **Sir Ian McKellen,** who then made the transition to celluloid. Earlier Shakespeare impresario **Laurence Olivier** worked both sides of the camera in *Henry V* (1944); his *Hamlet* (1948) is still the hallmark Dane. Master of suspense **Alfred Hitchcock** snared audiences with films produced in both Britain and the US. The 1960s phenomenon of "swingin' London" created new momentum for the British film industry and jump-started international interest in British culture. American **Richard Lester** made pop stars into film stars in the Beatles' *A Hard Day's Night* (1963), and Scot **Sean Connery** downed the first of many martinis as James Bond in *Dr. No* (1962).

Elaborate costume drama and offbeat independent films have come to represent contemporary British film. **Kenneth Branagh** has focused his talents on adapting Shakespeare for the screen, with glossy, acclaimed works like *Hamlet* (1996). A new entry into the world of blockbusterdom is the *Harry Potter* franchise, which kicked off in 2001.

HOLIDAYS AND FESTIVALS

Holidays: New Year's Day (Jan. 1); Good Friday (Apr. 18); Easter Sunday and Monday (Apr. 20 and 21); May Day (May 5); Bank Holiday (May 26); and Christmas (Dec. 25).

Festivals: London's Chinatown celebrates **Chinese New Year** (Feb. 1) and Manchester's Gay Village hosts a vibrant **Mardi Gras** (late Aug.). Muddy fun abounds at the **Glastonbury Festival,** Britain's biggest homage to rocks (June 27-29). The **Royal Ascot** (June 17-20) brings hats and horses to London. The **National Eisteddfod** (www.eisteddfod.org.uk) is a competition of Welsh literature, music, and arts and crafts. One of the largest festivals in the world is the **Edinburgh International Festival** (Aug. 10-30); also highly recommended is the **Fringe Festival** (Aug. 3-25).

ESSENTIALS

FACTS AND FIGURES

Official Name: United Kingdom of Great Britain and Northern Ireland.

Capital: London.

Major Cities: Manchester, Liverpool, Cardiff, Glasgow, Edinburgh.

Population: 57,100,000.

Land Area: 244,110 sq. km.

Time Zone: GMT.

Language: English; also Welsh, Scottish, and Gaelic.

Religions: Anglican (68%), Roman Catholic (28%), other (4%).

WHEN TO GO

It may be wise to plan around the high season (June-Aug.). Spring or autumn (Apr.-May and Sept.-Oct.) are more appealing times to visit; the weather is still reasonable and flights are cheaper, though there may be fewer services in rural areas. If you intend to visit the large cities and linger indoors at museums and theaters, the off season (Nov.-Mar.) is most economical. Keep in mind, however, that sights and accommodations often close or run reduced hours, especially in rural regions. Another factor to consider is hours of daylight—in Scotland, summer light lasts almost to midnight, but in winter the sun may set as early as 3:45pm. Regardless of when you go, it will rain; have warm, waterproof clothing on hand.

DOCUMENTS AND FORMALITIES

EU citizens do not need a visa to enter Britain. Citizens of Australia, Canada, New Zealand, South Africa, and the US do not need a visa for stays up to six months.

British Embassies and High Comissions at Home: Australia, British High Commission, Commonwealth Ave., Yarralumla, Canberra, ACT 2606 (☎02 6270 6666; www.uk.emb.gov.au). **Canada,** British High Commission, 80 Elgin St., Ottawa, K1P 5K7 (☎613-237-1530; www.britain-in-canada.org). **Ireland,** British Embassy, 29 Merrion Rd., Ballsbridge, Dublin 4 (☎01 205 3700; www.britishembassy.ie). **New Zealand,** British High Commission, 44 Hill St., Thorndon, Wellington 1 (☎04 924 2888; www.britain.org.nz). **South Africa,** British High Commission, 91 Parliament St., Cape Town 8001 (☎021 405 2400). **US,** British Embassy, 3100 Massachusetts Ave. NW, Washington, D.C. 20008 (☎202-588-6500; www.britainusa.com).

Foreign Embassies in Britain: All foreign embassies are in **London** (p. 164).

TRANSPORTATION

BY PLANE. Most flights into Britain that originate outside Europe land at London's Heathrow and Gatwick airports (p. 165). Some fly directly to regional airports such as Manchester or Edinburgh (p. 249).

BY TRAIN. For info on getting to Britain from the Continent, see p. 47. Britain's train network is extensive. Prices and schedules often change; find up-to-date information from **National Rail Inquiries** (☎08457 484 950) or online at **Railtrack** (www.railtrack.co.uk; schedules only). The **BritRail Pass,** only sold outside Britain, allows unlimited travel in England, Wales, and Scotland (8-day US$270, under 26 US$220; 22-day US$500, under 26 US$360); in Canada and the US, contact **Rail Europe** (Canada ☎800-361-7245; US ☎800-456-7245; www.raileurope.com). Rail discount cards, available at rail stations and through travel agents, grant 33% off most fares and are available to those ages 16-25 and full-time students (£18), seniors (£18), and families (£20). **Eurail** is not valid in Britain.

BY BUS. The British distinguish between **buses,** which cover short local routes, and **coaches,** which cover long distances; *Let's Go* uses the term "buses" to refer to both. **National Express** (☎08705 808 080; www.gobycoach.co.uk) is the principal long-distance coach service operator in Britain, although **Scottish Citylink** (☎08705 505 050) has coverage in Scotland. **Discount Coachcards** (£9) are available for seniors over 50, students, and young persons ages 16-25; they reduce fares on National Express by about 30%. The **Tourist Trail Pass** offers unlimited travel for a number of days within a given period (2 days out of 3 £49, students, seniors, and children £39; 5 of 30 £85/£69; 8 of 30 £135/£99; 15 of 30 £190/£145).

BY FERRY. Several ferry lines provide service between Britain and the Continent. Ask for discounts; ISIC holders can sometimes get student fares, and Eurail passholders can get reductions and free trips. Book ahead June through August. For information on boats from Wales to Dublin and Rosslare, Ireland, see p. 241; from Scotland to Belfast, see p. 257; from England to the Continent, see p. 57.

BY CAR. To drive, you must be 17 and have a valid license from your home country. Britain is covered by a high-speed system of **motorways** ("M-roads") that connect London with other major cities. Visitors may not be accustomed to driving on the left, and automatic transmission is rare in rental cars. Roads are generally well-maintained, but parking in London is impossible and traffic is slow.

BY BIKE AND BY THUMB. Much of Britain's countryside is well suited for **biking.** Many cities and villages have bike rental shops and maps of local cycle routes. Large-scale Ordnance Survey maps, often available at tourist offices, detail the extensive system of long-distance **hiking** paths. Tourist offices and National Park Information Centres can provide extra information about routes. Hitchhiking is illegal on M-roads; *Let's Go* does not recommend hitchhiking.

TOURIST SERVICES AND MONEY

EMERGENCY	**Police:** ☎999. **Ambulance:** ☎999. **Fire:** ☎999.

TOURIST OFFICES. The **British Tourist Authority** (BTA; www.visitbritain.com) is an umbrella organization for four separate UK tourist boards outside the UK.

British Tourist Offices at Home: Australia, Level 16, Gateway, 1 Macquarie Pl., Circular Quay, Sydney NSW 2000 (☎02 9377 4400; www.visitbritain.com/au). **Canada,** 5915 Airport Rd., Ste. 120, Mississauga, ON L4V 1T1 (☎888-847-4885; www.visitbritain.com/ca). **New Zealand,** 151 Queen St., NZI House, 17th fl., Auckland 1 (☎09 303 1446; ww.visitbritain.com/nz). **South Africa,** Lancaster Gate, Hyde Park Ln., Hyde Park, 2196 (☎011 325 0343). **US,** 551 5th Ave., 7th fl., New York, NY 10176 (☎800-462-2748 or 212-986-2266; www.travelbritain.org).

MONEY. The **pound sterling** is the main unit of currency in the United Kingdom. It is divided into 100 pence, issued in standard denominations of 1p, 2p, 5p, 10p, 20p, 50p, and £1 in coins, and £5, £10, £20, and £50 in notes. Scotland has its own bank notes, which can be used interchangeably with English currency, though you may have difficulty using Scottish £1 notes outside Scotland. Expect to spend anywhere from £25-50 per day. London in particular is a budget-buster, with the bare minimum for accommodations, food, and transport costing £30-40. The European Union imposes a **value-added tax (VAT)** on goods and services purchased within the EU, which is included in the price (see p. 19).

BRITISH POUNDS (£)		
	AUS$1 = UK£0.36	UK£1 = AUS$2.77
	CDN$1 = UK£0.42	UK£1 = CDN$2.38
	EUR€1 = UK£0.64	UK£1 = EUR€1.56
	NZ$1 = UK£0.31	UK£1 = NZ$3.24
	ZAR1 = UK£0.06	UK£1 = ZAR16.15
	US$1 = UK£0.65	UK£1 = US$1.53

ACCOMMODATIONS AND CAMPING

Hostels are run by the **Youth Hostels Association (YHA) of England and Wales** (www.yha.org.uk) and the **Scottish Youth Hostels Association** (SYHA; www.syha.org.uk). Unless noted as "self-catering," the YHA hostels listed in *Let's Go* offer cooked meals at standard rates (breakfast £3.20, small/standard packed lunch £2.80/£3.65, evening meal £4.15, and children's meals £1.75-2.70). Hostel dorms will cost around £9 in rural areas, £13 in larger cities, and £15-20 in London. You can book **B&Bs** by calling directly, or by asking the local tourist office to help you find accommodations. Tourist offices usually charge a 10% deposit on the first night's or the entire stay's price, deductible from the amount you pay the B&B proprietor; often a flat fee of £1-3 is added on. **Campsites** tend to be privately owned and cost £3-10 per person per night. It is illegal to camp in national parks, since much of their land is privately owned.

COMMUNICATION

PHONE CODES	**Country code:** 44. **International dialing prefix:** 00. From outside Britain, dial int'l dialing prefix (see inside back cover) + 44 + city code + local number.

TELEPHONES. Most public pay phones in Britain are run by **British Telecom (BT).** The BT phonecard, available in denominations from £2-20, is a useful purchase, as BT phones are everywhere. Public phones charge a minimum of 10p and don't accept 1p, 2p, or 5p coins. For directory inquiries, which are free from payphones, call ☎192. International direct dial numbers include: **AT&T,** ☎0800 013 0011; **British Telecom,** ☎0800 345 144; **Canada Direct,** ☎0800 890 016; **MCI,** ☎0800 890 222; **Sprint,** ☎0800 890 877; and **Telkom South Africa,** ☎0800 890 027.

MAIL. To send a postcard or letter within Europe costs £0.37; a postcard to any other international destination costs £0.40, while a letter costs £0.65. Address mail to be held according to the following example: Firstname SURNAME, *Poste Restante,* New Bond St. Post Office, Bath BA1 1A5, UK.

INTERNET ACCESS. Britain is one of the world's most wired countries. Cybercafes can be found in larger cities. They cost £4-6 per hour, but you often pay for only the time used, not for the whole hour. Online guides to cybercafes in Britain and Ireland, updated daily, include the **Cybercafe Search Engine** (http://cybercaptive.com) and **Cybercafes.com** (www.cybercafes.com).

LANGUAGE. The official languages are English and Welsh. Scottish Gaelic, though unofficial, is spoken in some parts of Scotland along with English.

ENGLAND

In a land where the stately once prevailed, conservatism has been booted in two successive elections and a wild profusion of the avant-garde has emerged from hallowed academic halls. The country that once determined the meaning of "civilised" now takes many of its cultural cues from former fledgling colonies. The vanguard of art, music, film, and eclecticism, England is a youthful, hip nation looking forward. But traditionalists can rest easy; for all the moving and shaking in the large cities, around the corner there are handfuls of quaint towns, dozens of picturesque castles, and scores of comforting cups of tea.

LONDON ☎020

London defies easy categorization. Those expecting tea-drinking, Royal-loving, Kensington-bred green-thumbs will quickly find equal numbers of black-clad youth lounging in Soho bars, Indian takeaway owners in the East End, and pinstriped bankers in the City. While London abounds with remnants of Britain's long history, a trip to one of many futuristic boutiques will eclipse any impression that this city is chained to bygone days. Pubs may close early, but London roars on, full throttle, around the clock. One of the world's greatest centers for the arts, London dazzles with concert halls, theaters, museums, and bookshops. Despite the dismal reputation of British food, London has steadily gained status as a culinary center, in no small measure due to a diverse and ever-growing international population that infuses the metropolis with energy and optimism.

INTERCITY TRANSPORTATION

Flights: Heathrow (LON; ☎(0870) 000 0123) is London's main airport. The **Piccadilly Line** heads from the airport to central London (45min.-1hr.; every 4-5min.; £3.60, under 16 £1.50). The **Heathrow Express** train shuttles to Paddington (15min.; every 15min.; £11, round-trip £20). From **Gatwick Airport** (LGW; ☎(0870) 000 2468), the **Gatwick Express** heads to Victoria (30-35min.; 6am-8pm every 15min., 8pm-6am every 30min.; £11, round-trip £21), as do cheaper **Connex** commuter trains (35-45min.; £8.20, round-trip £16.40).

Trains: London has 8 major stations: **Charing Cross** (serves south England); **Euston** (the northwest); **King's Cross** (the northeast); **Liverpool St.** (East Anglia); **Paddington** (the west and south Wales); **St. Pancras** (the Midlands and the northwest); **Victoria** (the south); and **Waterloo** (the south, the southwest and the Continent). All stations are linked by the Underground (Tube). Itineraries involving a change of stations in London usually include a cross-town transfer by Tube. Get info at the station ticket office or from the **National Rail Inquiries Line** (☎(08457) 484 950; www.britrail.com).

Buses: Long-distance buses (known as **coaches** in the UK) arrive in London at **Victoria Coach Station,** 164 Buckingham Palace Rd. (☎7730 3466; Tube: Victoria). Some services stop at nearby **Eccleston Bridge,** behind Victoria train station.

ORIENTATION

The heart of London is the vaguely defined **West End,** which stretches east from Park Lane to Kingsway and south from Oxford St. to the River Thames; within this area you'll find aristocratic **Mayfair,** the shopping streets around **Oxford Circus,** the bars and clubs of **Soho,** and the street performers and boutiques of **Covent Garden.** Heading east of the West End, you'll pass legalist **Holborn** before hitting the ancient **City of London** (a.k.a. "the City"), the site of the original Roman settlement and home to St. Paul's Cathedral and the Tower of London. The City's eastern border jostles the ethnically diverse, working-class **East End.**

Westminster encompasses the grandeur of **Trafalgar Square,** extending south along the Thames; this is the heart of royal and political London, with the Houses of Parliament, Buckingham Palace, and Westminster Abbey. Farther west lies artsy, prosperous **Chelsea.** Across the river from Westminster and the West End, the **South Bank** has an incredible variety of entertainment and museums, from Shakespeare's Globe Theatre to the Tate Modern. The enormous expanse of **Hyde Park** lies to the west of the West End; along its southern border lies chic **Knightsbridge,** home to Harrods and Harvey Nicks, and posh **Kensington.** North of Hyde Park is the media-infested **Notting Hill** and the B&B-filled **Bayswater.** Bayswater, Mayfair, and **Marylebone** meet at Marble Arch, on Hyde Park's northeast corner; from there, Marylebone stretches west to meet academic **Bloomsbury,** north of Soho and Holborn. **Camden Town, Islington, Hampstead,** and **Highgate** lie to the north of Bloomsbury and the City. A good street atlas is essential for efficient navigation; the best is *London A to Z* (£5), available at bookstores and newsstands.

LOCAL TRANSPORTATION

Public Transportation: Run by Transport for London (TfL; 24hr. info ☎7222 1234; www.transportforlondon.gov.uk). Pick up maps at all Tube stations; TfL **Information Centres** at Euston, Heathrow Terminals 1, 2, and 3, Liverpool St., Oxford Circus, Paddington, Picadilly Circus, St. James's Park, and Victoria also offer guides.

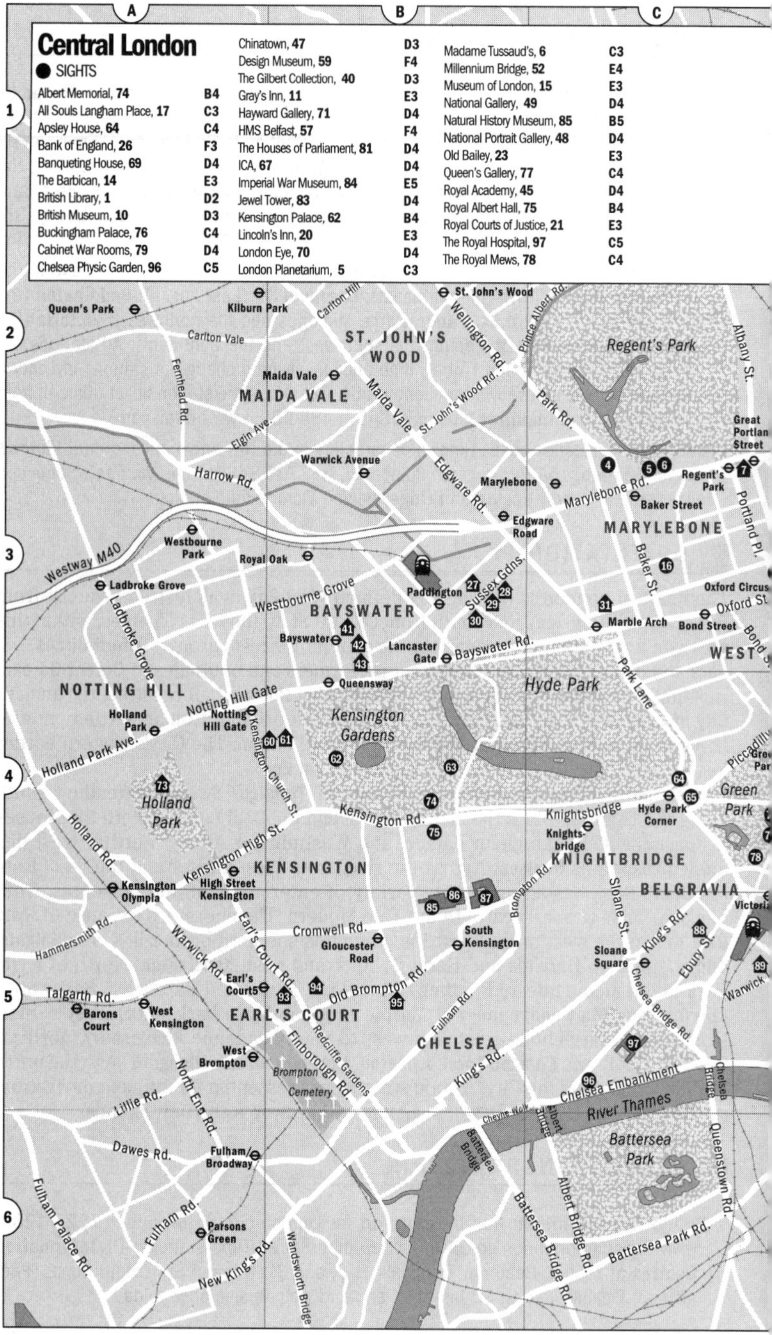
Central London
SIGHTS
Albert Memorial, 74 B4
All Souls Langham Place, 17 C3
Apsley House, 64 C4
Bank of England, 26 F3
Banqueting House, 69 D4
The Barbican, 14 E3
British Library, 1 D2
British Museum, 10 D3
Buckingham Palace, 76 C4
Cabinet War Rooms, 79 D4
Chelsea Physic Garden, 96 C5
Chinatown, 47 D3
Design Museum, 59 F4
The Gilbert Collection, 40 D3
Gray's Inn, 11 E3
Hayward Gallery, 71 D4
HMS Belfast, 57 F4
The Houses of Parliament, 81 D4
ICA, 67 D4
Imperial War Museum, 84 E5
Jewel Tower, 83 D4
Kensington Palace, 62 B4
Lincoln's Inn, 20 E3
London Eye, 70 D4
London Planetarium, 5 C3
Madame Tussaud's, 6 C3
Millennium Bridge, 52 E4
Museum of London, 15 E3
National Gallery, 49 D4
Natural History Museum, 85 B5
National Portrait Gallery, 48 D4
Old Bailey, 23 E3
Queen's Gallery, 77 C4
Royal Academy, 45 D4
Royal Albert Hall, 75 B4
Royal Courts of Justice, 21 E3
The Royal Hospital, 97 C5
The Royal Mews, 78 C4
ST. JOHN'S WOOD
MAIDA VALE
MARYLEBONE
BAYSWATER
NOTTING HILL
KENSINGTON
KNIGHTBRIDGE
BELGRAVIA
EARL'S COURT
CHELSEA
Regent's Park
Hyde Park
Kensington Gardens
Holland Park
Green Park
Battersea Park
River Thames
Brompton Cemetery
Queen's Park
Kilburn Park
St. John's Wood
Maida Vale
Warwick Avenue
Marylebone
Edgware Road
Baker Street
Regent's Park
Great Portland Street
Westbourne Park
Royal Oak
Ladbroke Grove
Paddington
Marble Arch
Bond Street
Oxford Circus
Bayswater
Lancaster Gate
Queensway
Notting Hill Gate
Holland Park
Knightsbridge
Hyde Park Corner
High Street Kensington
Kensington Olympia
Gloucester Road
South Kensington
Sloane Square
Earl's Court
Barons Court
West Kensington
West Brompton
Fulham Broadway
Parsons Green
Victoria
Westway M40
Harrow Rd.
Carlton Vale
Carlton Hill
Fernhead Rd.
Elgin Ave.
Wellington Rd.
Prince Albert Rd.
St. John's Wood Rd.
Park Rd.
Albany St.
Maida Vale
Edgware Rd.
Marylebone Rd.
Portland Pl.
Baker St.
Oxford St.
Sussex Gdns.
Westbourne Grove
Bayswater Rd.
Park Lane
Ladbroke Grove
Notting Hill Gate
Holland Park Ave.
Kensington Church St.
Kensington Rd.
Kensington High St.
Holland Rd.
Piccadilly
Knightsbridge
Brompton Rd.
Sloane St.
Hammersmith Rd.
Warwick Rd.
Earl's Court Rd.
Cromwell Rd.
Old Brompton Rd.
Fulham Rd.
King's Rd.
Ebury St.
Chelsea Bridge Rd.
Talgarth Rd.
Redcliffe Gardens
Finborough Rd.
North End Rd.
Lillie Rd.
Dawes Rd.
Fulham Rd.
Fulham Palace Rd.
New King's Rd.
Wandsworth Bridge
Chelsea Embankment
Cheyne Walk
Albert Bridge
Battersea Bridge
Chelsea Bridge
Battersea Bridge Rd.
Albert Bridge Rd.
Battersea Park Rd.
Queenstown Rd.
Warwick
A
B
C
1
2
3
4
5
6

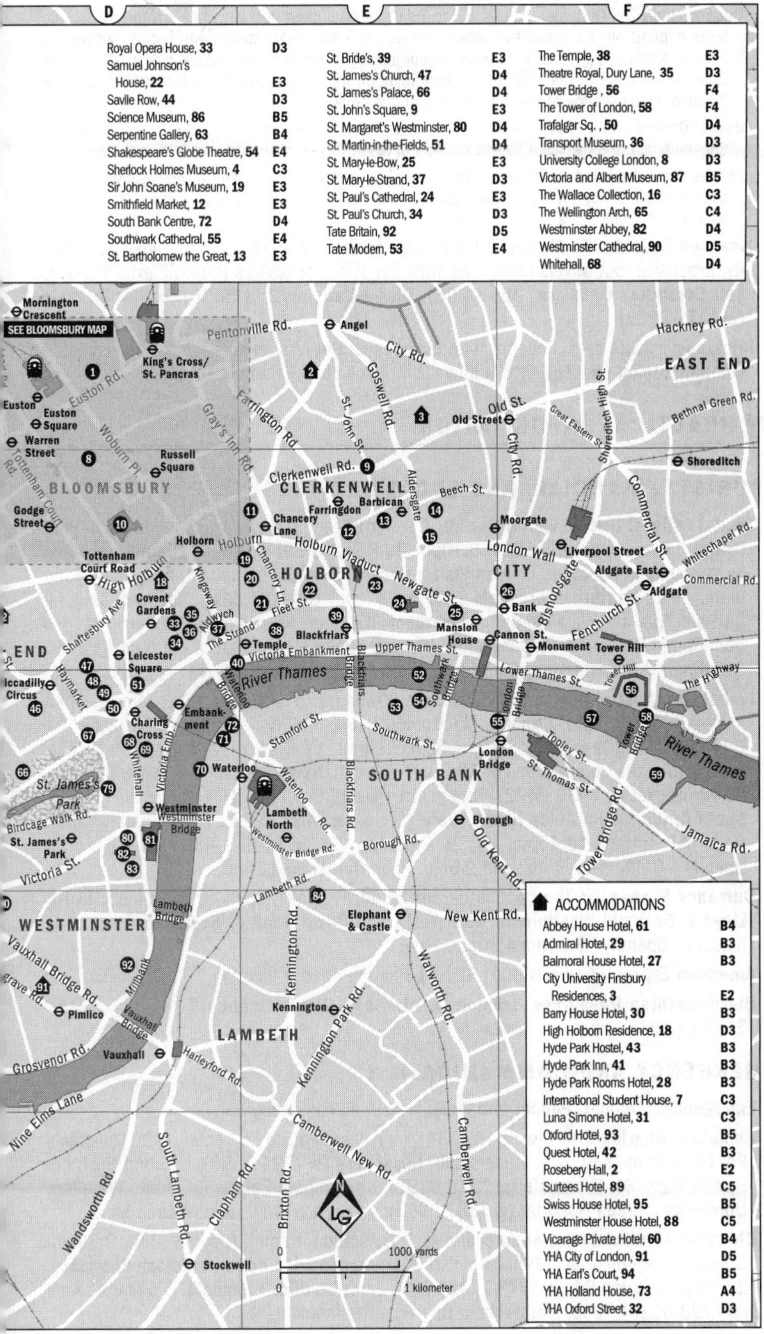

Royal Opera House, **33**	D3
Samuel Johnson's House, **22**	E3
Savile Row, **44**	D3
Science Museum, **86**	B5
Serpentine Gallery, **63**	B4
Shakespeare's Globe Theatre, **54**	E4
Sherlock Holmes Museum, **4**	C3
Sir John Soane's Museum, **19**	E3
Smithfield Market, **12**	E3
South Bank Centre, **72**	D4
Southwark Cathedral, **55**	E4
St. Bartholomew the Great, **13**	E3
St. Bride's, **39**	E3
St. James's Church, **47**	D4
St. James's Palace, **66**	D4
St. John's Square, **9**	E3
St. Margaret's Westminster, **80**	D4
St. Martin-in-the-Fields, **51**	D4
St. Mary-le-Bow, **25**	E3
St. Mary-le-Strand, **37**	D3
St. Paul's Cathedral, **24**	E3
St. Paul's Church, **34**	D3
Tate Britain, **92**	D5
Tate Modern, **53**	E4
The Temple, **38**	E3
Theatre Royal, Dury Lane, **35**	D3
Tower Bridge , **56**	F4
The Tower of London, **58**	F4
Trafalgar Sq. , **50**	D4
Transport Museum, **36**	D3
University College London, **8**	D3
Victoria and Albert Museum, **87**	B5
The Wallace Collection, **16**	C3
The Wellington Arch, **65**	C4
Westminster Abbey, **82**	D4
Westminster Cathedral, **90**	D5
Whitehall, **68**	D4

ACCOMMODATIONS

Abbey House Hotel, **61**	B4
Admiral Hotel, **29**	B3
Balmoral House Hotel, **27**	B3
City University Finsbury Residences, **3**	E2
Barry House Hotel, **30**	B3
High Holborn Residence, **18**	D3
Hyde Park Hostel, **43**	B3
Hyde Park Inn, **41**	B3
Hyde Park Rooms Hotel, **28**	B3
International Student House, **7**	C3
Luna Simone Hotel, **31**	C3
Oxford Hotel, **93**	B5
Quest Hotel, **42**	B3
Rosebery Hall, **2**	E2
Surtees Hotel, **89**	C5
Swiss House Hotel, **95**	B5
Westminster House Hotel, **88**	C5
Vicarage Private Hotel, **60**	B4
YHA City of London, **91**	D5
YHA Earl's Court, **94**	B5
YHA Holland House, **73**	A4
YHA Oxford Street, **32**	D3

Underground: The Underground (a.k.a. the Tube) network is divided into 6 concentric zones, and fares depend on the number of zones crossed. Buy your ticket before you board and pass it through automatic gates at both ends of your journey. A one-way trip in Zone 1 costs £1.60. The Tube runs approx. 5:30am-12:30am, depending on the line; always check last train times. See the color maps section at the front or back of this book.

Buses: Divided into 4 zones. Zones 1-3 are identical to the Tube zones. Fares £0.70-1. Buses run 6am-midnight, after which a limited network of **Night Buses,** prefixed by an "N," take over.

Passes: The **Travelcard** is valid for travel on all TfL services. Daily, weekend, weekly, monthly, and annual cards. 1-day Travelcard from £5.30 (Zones 1-2). Passes expire at 4:30am the morning after their printed expiration date.

Licensed Taxicabs: An illuminated "taxi" sign on the roof of a black cab signals availability. Expensive, but drivers know their stuff. Tip 10%. For pick-up (min. £2 extra charge), call **Computer Cabs** (☎7286 0286), **Dial-a-Cab** (☎7253 5000), or **Radio Taxis** (☎7272 0272).

Minicabs: Private cars. Cheaper than black cabs, but less reliable–stick to a reputable company. **Teksi** (☎7267 0267) offers 24hr. pick-up anywhere in London.

PRACTICAL INFORMATION

TOURIST, FINANCIAL, AND LOCAL SERVICES

Tourist Offices: Britain Visitor Centre, 1 Lower Regent St. (www.visitbritain.com). Tube: Oxford Circus. Open M 9:30am-6:30pm, Tu-F 9am-6:30pm, Sa-Su 10am-4pm; June-Sept. extended hours Sa. **London Visitor Centres** (www.londontouristboard.com). Tube branches at: **Heathrow Terminals 1, 2,** and **3** (open Oct.-Aug. daily 8am-6pm; Sept. M-Sa 9am-7pm and Su 8am-6pm); **Liverpool St.** (open June-Sept. M-Sa 8am-7pm, Su 8am-6pm; Oct.-May daily 8am-6pm); **Victoria** (open Easter-Sept. M-Sa 8am-8pm, Su 8am-6pm; Oct.-Easter daily 8am-6pm); **Waterloo** (open daily 8:30am-10:30pm).

Embassies: Australia, Australia House, The Strand (☎7379 4334). Tube: Temple. Open daily 9:30am-3:30pm. **Canada,** MacDonald House, 1 Grosvenor Sq. (☎7258 6600). Tube: Bond St. Open daily 8:30am-5pm. **Ireland,** 17 Grosvenor Pl. (☎7235 2171). Tube: Hyde Park Corner. Open M-F 9:30am-4:30pm. **New Zealand,** New Zealand House, 80 Haymarket (☎7930 8422). Tube: Leicester Sq. Open M-F 10am-noon and 2-4pm. **South Africa,** South Africa House, Trafalgar Sq. (☎7451 7299). Tube: Charing Cross. Open M-F 8:45am-12:45pm. **US,** 24 Grosvenor Sq. (☎7499 9000). Tube: Bond St. Open M-F 8:30am-12:30pm and 2-5pm. Phones answered 24hr.

Currency Exchange: The best rates are found at banks, such as **Barclays, HSBC, Lloyd's, National Westminster** (NatWest), and **Royal Bank of Scotland.** Most bank branches open M-F 9:30am-4:30pm.

American Express: Call ☎(0800) 521 313 for the nearest location.

Bi-Gay-Lesbian Resources: London Lesbian and Gay Switchboard (☎7837 7324). 24hr. advice and support service.

EMERGENCY AND COMMUNICATIONS

Emergency (Medical, Police, and Fire): ☎999; no coins required.

Hospitals: Charing Cross (☎8846 1234), on Fulham Palace Rd.; enter on St. Dunstan's Rd. Tube: Baron's Ct. or Hammersmith. **Royal Free** (☎7794 0500), on Pond St. Tube: Belsize Park. **St. Thomas's** (☎7928 9292), on Lambeth Palace Rd. Tube: Waterloo. **University College Hospital** (☎7387 9300), on Grafton Way. Tube: Warren St.

Chemists (Pharmacies): Most chemists keep standard hours (usually M-Sa 9:30am-5:30pm). Late-night and 24hr. chemists are rare; one 24hr. option is **Zafash Pharmacy,** 233 Old Brompton Rd. (☎7373 2798). Tube: Earl's Ct. **Bliss Chemists,** 5-6 Marble Arch (☎7723 6116). Tube: Marble Arch. Open daily 9am-midnight.

Police: London is covered by two police forces: the **City of London Police** (☎7601 2222) for the City, and the **Metropolitan Police** (☎7230 1212) for the rest. There is at least one police station in each borough open 24hr. Call to locate the nearest one.

Internet Access: Try the ubiquitous **easyInternet Cafe** (☎7241 9000). Locations include 9-16 Tottenham Court Rd. (Tube: Tottenham Court Rd.); 456-459 The Strand (Tube: Charing Cross); and 9-13 Wilson Rd. (Tube: Victoria). From £1 per hr.; min. charge £2. Prices vary with demand. All open 24hr.

Post Office: Post offices are everywhere; call ☎(08457) 740 740 for locations. When sending mail to London, be sure to include the full postal code, since London has 7 King's Roads, 8 Queen's Roads, and many other opportunities for misdirected mailings. The largest office is the **Trafalgar Square Post Office,** 24-28 William IV St. (☎7484 9304). Tube: Charing Cross. All mail sent *Poste Restante* to unspecified post offices ends up here. Open M-Th and Sa 8am-8pm, F 8:30am-8pm. **Postal Code:** WC2N 4DL.

ACCOMMODATIONS

No matter where you plan to stay, it is essential to plan ahead, especially in summer; London accommodations are almost always booked solid. Be sure to check the cancellation policy before handing over the deposit; some are non-refundable.

HOSTELS. Hostels are not always able to accommodate every written request for reservations, much less on-the-spot inquiries, but they frequently hold a few beds—it's always worth checking. Sheets are included at all YHA hostels, but towels are not; buy one from reception (£3.50). YHA hostels also sell discount tickets to theaters and major attractions. No YHA hostels have lockouts or curfews.

STUDENT RESIDENCE HALLS. The best deals in town are university residence halls, which often rent out rooms over the summer and, less frequently, Easter vacations—you can often get a single for a little more than the price of a hostel bed. Book as early as possible. Don't expect luxury, although rooms are generally clean and well equipped and the halls often have extra facilities such as bars, game rooms, and sports facilities.

BED AND BREAKFASTS. In London, the term "B&B" encompasses accommodations of wildly varying quality and personality, often with little relation to price. Be aware that in-room showers are often prefabricated units jammed into a corner.

WESTMINSTER

Quiet **Pimlico,** south of Victoria station, is full of budget hotels; **Belgrave Road** has the highest number. Quality tends to improve the farther you go from the station. Though the area is fairly close to major sights such as Parliament and Buckingham Palace, there's little in the way of restaurants and nightlife.

Westminster House Hotel, 96 Ebury St. (☎7730 7850). Tube: Victoria. The welcoming proprietors keep the 10 rooms spotless. All rooms with TV and almost all with private bath. English breakfast included. Singles £50, with bath £55; doubles £70/£80; triples with bath £90; quads with bath £100. AmEx/MC/V. ❹

Luna Simone Hotel, 47-49 Belgrave Rd. (☎7834 5897). Tube: Victoria. Modern rooms with TV and phone are concealed by a Victorian facade. English breakfast included. Singles £40, with bath £60; doubles £60/£80; triples with bath £110. Off-season discounts for longer stays. MC/V. ❹

Surtees Hotel, 94 Warwick Way (☎7834 7163). Tube: Victoria. Flowers create the atmosphere at this hospitable B&B. English breakfast included. Singles £30, with bath £50; doubles £55/£70; triples £70/£80; quads £80/£90; family suite with bath £100. ❸

THE WEST END

High Holborn Residence, 178 High Holborn (☎7379 5589). Tube: Holborn. Comfortable, modern student residence. Suites of 4-5 rooms share phone, kitchen, and bath. Continental breakfast included. Laundry. Open mid-June to late Sept. Singles £29-36; doubles £48-58, with bath £58-68; triples with bath £68-78. MC/V. ❸

YHA Oxford Street, 14-18 Noel St. (☎7734 1618). Tube: Oxford Circus. Limited facilities, but an unbeatable location for Soho nightlife. Continental breakfast £3.40. Reserve at least 1 month ahead. Dorms £22, under 18 £17.75; doubles £24. ❷

THE CITY OF LONDON

YHA City of London, 36 Carter Ln. (☎7236 4965). Tube: St. Paul's. In the frescoed former buildings of St. Paul's Choir School, within spitting distance of the cathedral. Single-sex dorms have sinks. English breakfast included. Internet access. Currency exchange and secure luggage storage. Reception 7am-11pm. Dorms £15-25, under 18 £15-22; private rooms £30-£148; family rooms £44-125. MC/V. ❷

BAYSWATER

The streets between **Queensway** and **Paddington** station house London's highest concentration of cheap accommodations, with countless hostels, B&Bs, and budget hotels. The neighborhood is fairly central, with plenty of nearby restaurants, but accommodations vary in quality—be sure to see a room first.

HOSTELS

Hyde Park Hostel, 2-6 Inverness Terr. (☎7229 5101). Tube: Queensway or Bayswater. Crowded women's and coed dorms. Private rooms are more spacious and the bathrooms are a cut above average. Continental breakfast included. Internet and kitchen access, bar, cafeteria, laundry, lounge, luggage room. Ages 16-35 only. Reserve at least 2 weeks ahead. Dorms £11-17.50; doubles £42-45. MC/V. ❷

Quest Hotel, 45 Queensborough Terr. (☎7229 7782). Tube: Queensway or Bayswater. Better beds and a more personal size than at Hyde Park Hostel, but dorms without bath could be 2 fl. from a shower. Continental breakfast and sheets included. Kitchen access and laundry. Reserve 2-3 weeks ahead. Dorms £14-17; doubles £42. MC/V. ❷

Hyde Park Inn, 48-50 Inverness Terr. (☎7229 0000). Tube: Queensway or Bayswater. Cheap and cheerful. Continental breakfast included. Internet and kitchen access. Laundry. Lockers £1. Luggage storage £1.50. Sheets and key deposit £10. Dorms £9-19; singles £29-32; doubles £36-42. MC/V (2.5% surcharge). ❶

B&BS AND HOTELS

Hyde Park Rooms Hotel, 137 Sussex Gdns. (☎7723 0225). Tube: Paddington. All rooms with sink and TV. June-Aug. reserve ahead. Singles £30, with bath £40; doubles £40-45/£50-55; triples £60/£72; quads £80/£96. AmEx/MC/V (5% surcharge). ❸

Admiral Hotel, 143 Sussex Gdns. (☎7723 7309). Tube: Paddington. Beautifully kept B&B. 19 summery, non-smoking rooms with bath, TV, and tea kettle. Singles £40-50; doubles £58-75; triples £75-90; quads £88-100; quints £100-130. MC/V. ❹

Barry House Hotel, 12 Sussex Pl. (☎7723 7340). Tube: Paddington. Bright, small rooms with phone, TV, kettle, and hair dryer; most with bath. Singles £38, with bath £52; doubles £75; triples £90; quads £105; quints £120. AmEx/MC/V. ❹

Balmoral House Hotel, 156-157 Sussex Gdns. (☎7723 4925). Tube: Paddington. Classy establishment with low prices. All rooms with bath, TV, and hair dryer. English breakfast included. Singles £40; doubles £65; triples £80; quads £100, quints £120. MC/V (5% surcharge). ❹

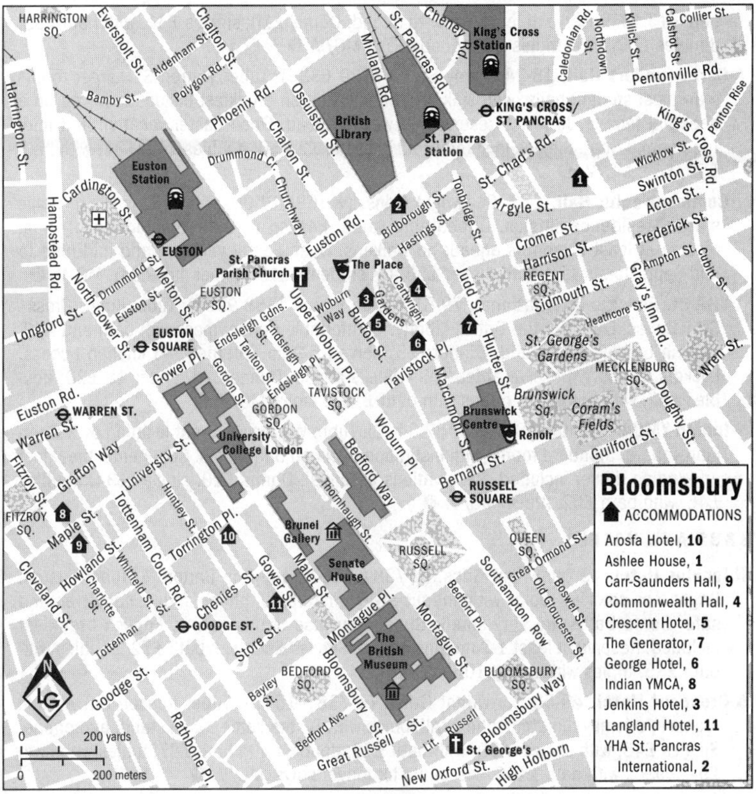

BLOOMSBURY AND MARYLEBONE

Bloomsbury's proximity to Soho makes it well suited for those who want to stay near nightlife. The neighborhood is also close to the British Museum and plenty of cheap restaurants. Many B&Bs are on busy roads, so be wary of noise levels. The area becomes seedier closer to King's Cross.

HOSTELS AND STUDENT RESIDENCES

The Generator, Compton Pl. (☎7388 7655), off 37 Tavistock Pl. Tube: Russell Sq. or King's Cross/St. Pancras. In a former police station, this hostel features cell-like units with metal bunks. Basement dorms have lockers and military-style bathrooms. Bar and cafeteria. Internet access. No noise after 9pm. Reserve ahead for weekends. Dorms £15-17; singles £42; doubles £53; triples £68; quads £90. MC/V. ❷

Ashlee House, 261-265 Gray's Inn Rd. (☎7833 9400; www.ashleehouse.co.uk). Tube: King's Cross/St. Pancras. Not the best neighborhood, but convenient to nightlife. Quiet and friendly. Steel bunks crammed into clean, bright rooms. Continental breakfast included. Sightseeing tours Th-Sa. TV room, Internet and kitchen access. Towels £1. Laundry. Dorms £15-£19; singles £36; doubles £48. ❷

International Student House, 229 Great Portland St. (☎7631 8300). Tube: Great Portland St. A thriving international metropolis. Continental breakfast included with private rooms; with dorms £2. 3 bars, cafeteria, fitness center. Internet access. Laundry. Key deposit £10. Reserve at least 1 month ahead. Dorms £10; singles £31, with bath £33; doubles £50/£52; triples £60; quads £70. MC/V. ❷

Carr-Saunders Hall, 18-24 Fitzroy St. (☎7580 6338). Tube: Warren St. Larger rooms than most student halls, with sink and phone. English breakfast included; served on a beautiful terrace. July-Aug. reserve 6-8 weeks ahead. Open Easter vacation and mid-June to mid-Sept. Singles in summer £27, Easter £23.50; doubles £45/£37, with bath £50/£42. MC/V. ❸

Commonwealth Hall, 1-11 Cartwright Gdns. (☎7685 3500). Tube: Russell Sq. Basic student-residence singles. Unbeatable value. English breakfast included. July-Aug. reserve at least 2 months ahead; no walk-ins. Open Easter vacation and mid-June to mid-Sept. Dorms £22, with dinner £26; UK students £19 (dinner included). MC/V. ❸

YHA St. Pancras International, 79-81 Euston Rd. (☎7388 9998). Tube: King's Cross/St. Pancras. Opposite the British Library. Comfortable dorms, most with bath and A/C. English breakfast included. Dinner (£5) served 6-9pm. Internet and kitchen access. Lockers. Laundry. Reserve at least 2-4 weeks ahead. Dorms £24, under 18 £20; doubles £52, with bath £58; quads with bath £104. AmEx/MC/V. ❸

Indian YMCA, 41 Fitzroy Sq. (☎7387 0411). Tube: Warren St. Great location by a Georgian square. Standard rooms with institutional shared bathrooms. Continental breakfast and Indian dinner included. Reservations essential. Dorms £20; singles £34; doubles £46, with bath £52. AmEx/MC/V. ❸

B&BS AND HOTELS

Jenkins Hotel, 45 Cartwright Gdns. (☎7387 2067); enter on Barton Pl. Tube: Euston. Bright, non-smoking rooms with antique-style furniture, TV, phone, fridge, hair dryer, and safe. Some baths are very small. Guests can use tennis courts. English breakfast included. Reserve at least 1-2 months ahead. Singles £52, with bath £72; doubles with bath £85; triples with bath £105. MC/V. ❹

Crescent Hotel, 49-50 Cartwright Gdns. (☎7387 1515). Tube: Russell Sq. Artistic rooms in a family-run atmosphere. All rooms with TV, tea kettle, wash stand, and phone. Singles £45, with shower £50, with bath £72; doubles with bath £87; triples with bath £97; quads with bath £106. Discounts for longer stays. MC/V. ❹

Langland Hotel, 29-31 Gower St. (☎7636 5801). Tube: Goodge St. Family atmosphere, sparkling bathrooms. All rooms with TV and fan. Singles £40, with bath £55; doubles £50/£75; triples £70/£90; quads £90/£110; quints £100. AmEx/MC/V. ❹

Arosfa Hotel, 83 Gower St. (☎7636 2115). Tube: Warren St. The owners ensure that this small, non-smoking B&B lives up to its Welsh name ("place to rest"). English breakfast included. Singles £37; doubles £50, with bath £66; triples £68/£79; quad with bath £92. MC/V. ❹

George Hotel, 58-60 Cartwright Gdns. (☎7387 8777). Tube: Russell Sq. Meticulous rooms with TV, kettle, phone, and sink. Front-facing 1st-floor rooms are best, with high ceilings and tall windows. Internet access. Singles £50, with shower £65, with bath £75; doubles £70/£77/£90; triples £83/£92/£105; quads £95. Nov.-June discounts for longer stays. MC/V. ❹

HOLBORN AND CLERKENWELL

City University Finsbury Residences, 15 Bastwick St. (☎7040 8811). Tube: Barbican. Student residence with a grim tower-block facade but renovated interior. Short walk to City sights, Islington restaurants, and Clerkenwell nightlife. English breakfast included. Dinner £4.70. Open late June to mid-Sept. £21 per person, students £19. MC/V. ❸

Rosebery Hall, 90 Rosebery Ave. (☎7278 3251). Tube: Angel. Exit left from the Tube, cross the street, and take the second right onto Rosebery Ave. (10min.). Modern student residence by a sunken garden. English breakfast included. Reserve at least 6 weeks ahead; cancellation fee £10. Open Easter vacation and mid-June to mid-Sept. Singles £26-31; doubles £35-46, with bath £58; triples £55. MC/V. ❸

KENSINGTON

Vicarage Private Hotel, 10 Vicarage Gate (☎7229 4030). Tube: High St. Kensington. Beautifully kept house with TV lounge and superb rooms. English breakfast included. Singles £46; doubles £76, with bath £100; triples £93; quads £100. ❹

Swiss House Hotel, 171 Old Brompton Rd. (☎7373 2769). Tube: Gloucester Rd. or South Kensington. Large rooms all with TV, phone, fan, and bath. Continental breakfast included; English breakfast £6.50. In summer reserve at least 1 month ahead. Singles £71; doubles £89-104; triples £120; quads £134. AmEx/MC/V. ❺

Abbey House Hotel, 11 Vicarage Gate (☎7937 0748). Tube: High St. Kensington. Spacious rooms with TV, desk, and sink. Very helpful staff. English breakfast included. Singles £45; doubles £74; triples £90; quads £100. ❹

YHA Holland House, Holland Walk (☎7937 0748). Tube: High St. Kensington or Holland Park. On the edge of Holland Park, this hostel has dorms in both a 17th-century mansion and a 1970s unit. Breakfast included. In summer reserve at least 1 month ahead. Dorms £21, under 18 £18.75. AmEx/MC/V. ❸

EARL'S COURT

West of fashionable Kensington, Earl's Court feeds on budget tourism. The area is especially popular with Australian travelers. Be careful at night, and be cautious of guides trying to lead you from the station to a hostel. Some B&Bs conceal grimy rooms behind fancy lobbies and well-dressed staff; always ask to see a room.

Oxford Hotel, 24 Penywern Rd. (☎7370 1161). 3min. from the Connex train to Heathrow or Gatwick. Large rooms with enormous windows afford grand views of the gardens. Continental breakfast included. Reserve at least 3-4 weeks ahead. Singles with shower £36, with bath £50; doubles £57/£67; triples £69/£79; quads £87/£93; quints £105/£115. Discounts for longer stays. AmEx/MC/V. ❹

YHA Earl's Court, 38 Bolton Gdns. (☎7373 7083). Tube: Earl's Court. Rambling Victorian townhouse, more casual than most YHAs. Garden. Single-sex dorms. Breakfast included for doubles. Sheets included. Reserve at least 1 month ahead. Dorms £16-19; doubles £52; quads £76. AmEx/MC/V. ❷

NORTH LONDON

YHA Hampstead Heath, 4 Wellgarth Rd. (☎8458 9054). Tube: Golders Green. From the Tube station, turn left onto North End Rd.; Wellgarth Rd. is a 10min. walk up on the left. Out-of-the-way location is main disadvantage of this manorial hostel with large garden. Breakfast included. Internet access and currency exchange. 24hr. reception. Dorms £20.40; doubles £47; triples £67; quads £84; quints £103. Discounts on larger rooms for families. AmEx/MC/V. ❸

FOOD

Forget stale stereotypes: in terms of quality and choice, London's restaurants offer a gastronomic experience as diverse, stylish, and satisfying as you'll find, albeit an expensive one. An entree under £10 is regarded as "cheap"; add drinks and service and you're nudging £15. The trick to eating cheaply and well is knowing where and when to eat. Special offers at lunchtime and in the early evening make it possible to dine in style and stay on budget. While pubs offers hearty staples, many of the best budget meals are found in the variety of ethnic restaurants. For the best ethnic food, head to the source: Whitechapel for Bengali *baltis*, Islington for Turkish *meze*, Marylebone for Lebanese *schwarma*, and Soho for Cantonese *dim sum*.

WESTMINSTER

Jenny Lo's Teahouse, 14 Eccleston St. (☎7259 0399). Tube: Victoria. Stripped-down Chinese fare at communal tables. *Cha shao* (pork noodle soup) £5. Teas, from £0.85, are blended in-house and served in hand-turned stoneware. £5 min. Open M-F 11:30am-3pm and 6-10pm, Sa noon-3pm and 6-10pm. ❷

Red Lion, 48 Parliament St. (☎7930 5826). Tube: Westminster. The MPs' hangout, where the Chancellor's press secretary was infamously overhead leaking information in 1998. A "division bell" alerts MPs to drink up when a vote is about to be taken. Entrees £3-6. Open M-Sa 11am-11pm, Su noon-7pm; food served daily noon-3pm. MC/V. ❷

THE WEST END

busaba eathai, 106-110 Wardour St. (☎7255 8686). Tube: Tottenham Court Rd. Wildly popular Thai eatery. Great food (£5-8) at shared, square tables in a cozy, wood-paneled room. Open M-Th noon-11pm, F-Sa noon-11:30pm, Su noon-10pm. AmEx/MC/V.❷

Mô, 23 Heddon St. (☎7434 3999). Tube: Piccadilly Circus. A "salad bar, tea room, and bazaar," Mô is functionally and aesthetically Marrakesh. Mix and match *tapas*-style dishes £6-7.50. Wash it down with sweet mint tea (£2). No reservations, but very popular–arrive early or late. Open M-W 11am-11pm, Th-Sa noon-midnight. AmEx/MC/V. ❷

Mr. Kong, 21 Lisle St. (☎7437 7341). You can't go wrong at Mr. Kong. Deep-fried Mongolian lamb £6.50, shark fin soup £6. £7 min. Open daily noon-3am. AmEx/MC/V. ❷

Pâtisserie Valerie, 44 Old Compton St. (☎7437 3466). Renowned goodies at this continental patisserie. Delicious croissants £0.90, cakes and pastries £1-3, sandwiches £3-6. Open M-F 7:30am-8pm, Sa 8am-8pm, Su 9:30am-7pm. AmEx/MC/V. ❶

Bar Italia, 22 Frith St. (☎7437 4520). Tube: Tottenham Court Rd. A fixture of the late-night Soho scene. Nothing stronger than an espresso here (£1.80), but it's *the* place for a post-club panini (£4-6). £10 min. Open 24hr. except M 3-7am. AmEx/MC/V. ❸

Bibo Cibo, 59 Endell St. (☎7240 3343). Downstairs bar and swanky-looking upstairs restaurant serve similar pub fare. Sausage and mash £7. Sa nights DJs play funk/soul/hip-hop. 2-for-1 bottled beers during Happy Hour (M all night, Tu-F 5:30-8:30pm). Open M-Sa 11:30am-midnight, Su 11:30am-10:30pm. AmEx/MC/V. ❷

THE CITY OF LONDON

Futures, 8 Botolph Alley (☎7623 4529), off Botolph Ln. Tube: Monument. Suits besiege this tiny takeaway for breakfast (pastries £0.80, porridge £1) and later for a variety of vegetarian dishes (£2-4). Open M-F 7:30-10am and 11:30am-3pm. ❶

Cafe Spice Namaste, 16 Prescot St. (☎7488 9242). Tube: Tower Hill. The standard-bearer for a new breed of Indian restaurants. Carnivalesque decoration brings an exotic feel to this old Victorian warehouse, as does the menu of Goan and Parsee specialities. Meat dishes are on the pricey side (£11-13), but vegetarian meals are a bargain (£7-8). Open M-F noon-3pm and 6:15-10:30pm, Sa 6:30-10pm. AmEx/MC/V. ❸

Simpson's, on Ball Court (☎7626 9985), off 38½ Cornhill. Tube: Bank. Established in 1757. Different rooms divide the classes: drinkers populate the basement wine bar (sandwiches £2-4) and ground-floor bar, diners the ground-floor and upstairs restaurants (entrees £6-7). Open M-F 11:30am-3:30pm.❶

BRITAIN

THE SOUTH BANK

Cantina del Ponte, 36c Shad Thames (☎7403 5403), Butler's Wharf. Tube: Tower Hill or London Bridge. Amazing riverside location and high-quality Italian food. Bargain fixed menu £10 for 2 courses, £12.50 for 3 (available M-F noon-3pm and 6-7:30pm). Pizzas £7-8, entrees £12-15. Live Italian music Tu and Th evenings. Open M-Sa noon-3pm and 6-10:45pm, Su noon-3pm and 6-9:45pm. MC/V. ❸

Tas, 72 Borough High St. (☎7403 7200; Tube: London Bridge) and 33 The Cut (☎7928 2111; Tube: Waterloo). Stylish and affordable Turkish food. Stews and baked dishes—many vegetarian—outshine the kebabs. Entrees £6-8. Live music from 7:30pm. Reservations essential. Open M-Sa noon-11:30pm, Su noon-10:30pm. AmEx/MC/V. ❷

BAYSWATER

Royal China, 13 Queensway (☎7221 2535). Tube: Bayswater. Renowned for London's best *dim sum* (£2-3 per dish; count on 3-4 dishes per person), served M-Sa noon-5pm, Su 11am-5pm. On weekends arrive early or expect to wait 30-45min. Open M-Th noon-11pm, F-Sa noon-11:30pm, Su 11am-10pm. AmEx/MC/V. ❷

BLOOMSBURY AND MARYLEBONE

Diwana Bhel Poori House, 121-123 Drummond St. (☎7387 5556). Tube: Euston Square. No frippery here—just great, cheap south-Indian vegetarian food. Filling *Paneer Dosa* (rice pancake stuffed with potato and cheese) £5. *Thali* fixed meals (£4-6) offer great value. Open daily noon-11:30pm. AmEx/MC/V. ❷

Mandalay, 444 Edgware Rd. (☎7258 3696). Tube: Edgware Rd. Looks ordinary, tastes extraordinary; this Burmese restaurant's wall is plastered with awards. Great lunch specials (curry and rice £3.70; 3 courses £5.90). Most dishes are not that spicy, but the charming owner will gladly increase the heat. Entrees £3-5. No smoking. Open M-Sa noon-2:30pm and 6-10:30pm. AmEx/MC/V. ❶

ICCo (Italiano Coffee Co.), 46 Goodge St. (☎7580 9250). 11-inch thin-crust pizzas, made to order, cost an incredible £3.50. Sandwiches and baguettes from £1.50, rolls from £0.50. Buy any hot drink before noon and get a fresh-baked croissant for free. Pizzas available after noon. Open M-Sa 7am-11pm, Su 9am-11pm. ❶

HOLBORN AND CLERKENWELL

Bleeding Heart Tavern (☎7404 0333), on the corner of Greville St. and Bleeding Heart Yard. Tube: Farringdon. Light, laid-back upstairs pub and cozy restaurant below. Restaurant decor provides a romantic backdrop to the hearty English fare, which includes spit-roasted pork with crackling. Entrees £8-10. Open M-F noon-10:30pm. AmEx/MC/V. ❷

St. John, 26 St. John St. (☎7251 0848). Tube: Farringdon. St. John has won countless prizes for its eccentric English cuisine. Prices in the posh restaurant are high (entrees from £14), but you can enjoy similar bounty (in smaller quantities) in the smokehouse, formerly used by the butchers at Smithfield Market. Excellent lamb sandwich £5, roast bone-marrow salad £6. A bakery at the back of the bar churns out fresh loaves for £2.50. Open M-F 11am-11pm, Sa 6-11pm. MC/V. ❷

Ye Olde Cheshire Cheese, 145 Fleet St. (☎7353 6170), in Wine Office Ct. Tube: Blackfriars. Dark labyrinth of oak-panelled rooms on 3 fl., dating from 1667; a one-time haunt of Johnson, Dickens, Twain, and Teddy Roosevelt. Multiple bars and restaurants dish out traditional English food at many price ranges. Food served M-F noon-9:30pm, Sa noon-2:30pm and 6-9:30pm, Su noon-2:30pm. Open M-F 11:30am-11pm, Sa 11:30am-3pm and 5:30-11pm, Su noon-3pm. AmEx/MC/V. ❸

Tinseltown 24-Hour Diner, 44-46 St. John St. (☎7689 2424). Tube: Farringdon. Cavernous underground haven for pre- and post-clubbers. Burgers (£5.50) and shakes (£3.50). Open 24hr. ❶

KENSINGTON AND EARL'S COURT

Zaika, 1 Kensington High St. (☎7795 6533). Tube: High St. Kensington. Arguably London's best Indian restaurant: elegant decor, attentive service, and sophisticated food. Appetizers £6-8, entrees £13-18, desserts £4-5. 2-course min. for dinner. Lunch fixed menu £12 for 2 courses, £14 for 3. 5-course dinner menu £33.50, with wine £40. Dinner reservations recommended. Lunch M-F noon-2:30pm, Su noon-2:45pm; dinner M-Sa 6:30-10:45pm, Su 6:30-9:45pm. MC/V. ❺

Raison d'Être, 18 Bute St. (☎7584 5008). Tube: South Kensington. Caters to the local French community with a bewildering range of filled *baguettes* (£2-5) and *salades* (£3.50-4.70). Open M-F 8am-6pm, Sa 9:30am-4pm. ❶

KNIGHTSBRIDGE AND BELGRAVIA

Stockpot, 6 Basil St. (☎7589 8627). Tube: Knightsbridge. Unbelievable value at this super-cheap stalwart. No-frills interior is the setting for bargains. Traditional menu focuses on roasted meats (£3.50-4) and pasta, with plenty of vegetarian options and big salads. Open M-Sa 7:30am-11pm, Su noon-10:30pm. ❷

NOTTING HILL

George's Portobello Fish Bar, 329 Portobello Rd. (☎8969 7895). Tube: Ladbroke Grove. Choose from the fillets on display or ask them to fry up a new one (£4-5), add a generous helping of chunky chips (£1), and wolf it down outside (no inside seating). Open M-F 11am-midnight, Sa 11am-9pm, Su noon-9pm. ❶

The Grain Shop, 269a Portobello Rd. (☎7229 5571). Tube: Ladbroke Grove. It's hard to ignore the aromatic invitation of this mini-bakery. The generous homemade pastries and salads are phenomenal; mix as many dishes as you like to make a small (£2.25), medium (£3.45), or gut-busting large (£4.60) takeaway box. The line is long but fast-moving. Organic breads baked on-site (£1-2). Open M-Sa 9:30am-6pm. MC/V. ❶

AFTERNOON TEA

Afternoon tea provides a great chance to lounge in sumptuous surroundings that at any other time would be beyond all but a Sultan's budget. Note that you'll often need to book in advance, especially for weekends, and that many hotels have a strict dress code.

The Lanesborough, Hyde Park Corner (☎7259 5599). Tube: Hyde Park Corner. For sheer opulence, the interior of The Lanesborough out-ritzes The Ritz. Set tea £23, champagne tea £27. A la carte, including scones with jam and clotted cream, £6.50. Dress code: smart casual. £9.50 per person min. ❸

The Orangery, Kensington Palace (☎7938 1406). Tube: High St. Kensington. Built for Queen Anne's dinner parties, this airy building is now a popular setting for light lunches (£7-8, set lunch £9) and afternoon teas (from £8). Open daily 10am-6pm. MC/V. ❷

The Ritz, on Piccadilly (☎7493 8181). Tube: Green Park. The world's most famous tea (£27). Reserve at least 1 month ahead for the weekday sittings, 3 months for weekends; alternatively, skip lunch and arrive at noon for an early tea. No jeans or sneakers; jacket and tie preferred for men. Sittings at 3:30 and 5pm daily. AmEx/MC/V. ❺

SIGHTS

ORGANIZED TOURS

The classic London **bus tour** is on an open-top double-decker; in good weather, it's undoubtedly the best way to get a good overview of the city. Tickets for the **Big Bus Company,** 48 Buckingham Palace Rd., are valid for 24hr. on three hop-on, hop-off routes, with 1hr. walking tours and a short Thames cruise included. (☎7233 9533; www.bigbus.co.uk. Tube: Victoria. £16, children £6.) For a more in-depth account, you can't beat a **walking tour** led by a knowledgeable guide. **Original London Walks** is the biggest walking-tour company, running 12-16 walks per day, from the "Magical Mystery Tour" to the nighttime "Jack the Ripper's Haunts" and guided visits to larger museums. Most walks last 2hr. and start from Tube stations. (☎7624 3978; www.walks.com. £5, students and seniors £4, under 16 free.)

WESTMINSTER

The City of Westminster, now a borough of London, has been the seat of British power for over a thousand years. William the Conqueror was crowned in Westminster Abbey on Christmas Day, 1066, and his successors built the Palace of Westminster that would one day house Parliament.

BUCKINGHAM PALACE

The Mall; entrance to State Rooms on Buckingham Palace Rd. Tube: Victoria, Green Park, or St. James's Park. ☎7839 1377. State Rooms open early Aug. to Sept. daily 9:30am-4:30pm. Tickets ☎7321 2233. Ticket Office in Green Park open late July to Sept. £11.

Originally built for the Dukes of Buckingham, Buckingham House was acquired by George III in 1762 and converted into a full-scale palace by George IV. The palace was found to be too small for Queen Victoria's growing brood; a solution was found by closing off the three-sided courtyard, concealing the best architecture with Edward Blore's uninspiring facade. During the summer opening of the **State Rooms,** visitors have access to the **Throne Room,** the **Galleries** (with works by Rubens, Rembrandt, and van Dyck), and the **Music Room,** where Mendelsohn played for Queen Victoria, among others. In the opulent **White Room,** the large mirrored fireplace hides a door used by the Royal Family at formal dinners. Since 2001, Queen Elizabeth has also allowed visitors to take a brief excursion into the **gardens.**

THE HIDDEN DEAL

WE'VE GOT YOUR CHEAP TICKET TO RIDE

If you're scorning the cost of an organized bus tour, keep in mind that an all-day pass on a regular bus costs just £2. Yes, you'll miss the commentary, but you can get on and off according to your own schedule, and you'll be riding the genuine thing. Here are two routes that will leave you with an appreciation for London *and* money in your pocket.

Bus #11 runs to: **Liverpool Street Station,** the financial center of London (p. 183); **St. Paul's,** Christopher Wren's masterpiece (p. 183); **Fleet Street,** London's home of journalism (p. 187); **The Strand,** the theatrical heart of the West End (p. 182); **Trafalgar Square,** featuring the National Gallery, Nelson, and pigeons (p. 181); and **Westminster,** a phenomenally royal stretch of sights (p. 177).

Bus #14 makes stops at: **South Kensington,** arguably the greatest concentration of museums in the world (p. 191); **Knightsbridge,** with high-brow Harrods and haughty Harvey Nick's (p. 198); **Hyde Park Corner,** the First Royal Park (p. 188); **Piccadilly Circus,** a jumble of neon signs and of tourists (p. 183); **Leicester Square,** where you can pick up discounts to West End shows (p. 194); and **Tottenham Court Road,** a shopping mecca (p. 197).

THE MILLENNIUM MILE: THE SOUTH BANK

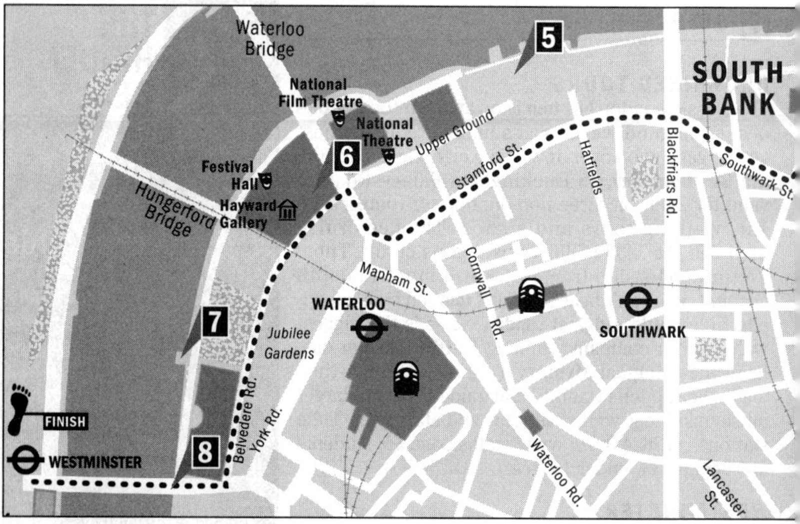

Time: 6hr.

Distance: 2.5mi. (4km)

When To Go: Start early morning

Start: London Bridge Underground

Finish: Westminster Underground

Call Ahead: 3,6,7.

The rejuvenation of the South Bank has by no means been brought about exclusively by the opening of Tate Modern in 2000. Shakespeare's Globe Theatre had its first season in 1997, and each subsequent season brings bolder interpretations of Will's works; more visitors has meant that The South Bank Centre has been able to expand its musical repertoire (without detracting from its quality); commercial Gabriel's Wharf thrives in the excitement of the area; fantastic city views from Tate Modern, OXO Wharf and, of course, London Eye, in addition to the understated beauty of a walk along the Thames, are constant draws. Meanwhile, the highly acclaimed Jubilee Line Extension—which includes a revamped interior at London Bridge—has greatly facilitated transportation to the South Bank and helped to transform the area into the cultural powerhouse it was originally intended to be.

1 OLD OPERATING THEATRE & HERB GARRET. Don't be fooled by preconceptions of show-stoppers at this "theatre," or of lavender, rosemary, and saffron at the "herb garret"; this first stop is not for the faint of heart. In the loft of an 18th century church, the oldest surviving operating theater in the world awaits. As if imagining what took place on the wooden operating table isn't chilling enough, the surrounding saws and knives hammer home the point. The herb garret was used by the hospital apothecary, but the soothing scent is fouled by old medical instruments. Victorian doctors couldn't reach for the aspirin bottle, and so opted for the trepanning drill—boring holes in patients' skulls was one remedy for a headache.

2 SOUTHWARK CATHEDRAL. Spare a thought (and say a prayer) for those operated on in the days before anesthesia. London's newest Anglican Cathedral illustrates how great the strides in medicine and technology have been in its hi-tech exhibits of "The Long View of London." An "X-ray" wall allows you to search for archaeological treasures.

3 SHAKESPEARE'S GLOBE THEATRE. "I hope to see London once ere I die," says Shakespeare's Davy in *Henry IV, Part II.* In time, he may see it from the beautiful recreation of Will's most famous theater. Excellent exhibits reveal how Shakespearean actors dressed and the secrets of Elizabethan special effects, and tell of the painstaking process involved in the rebuild-

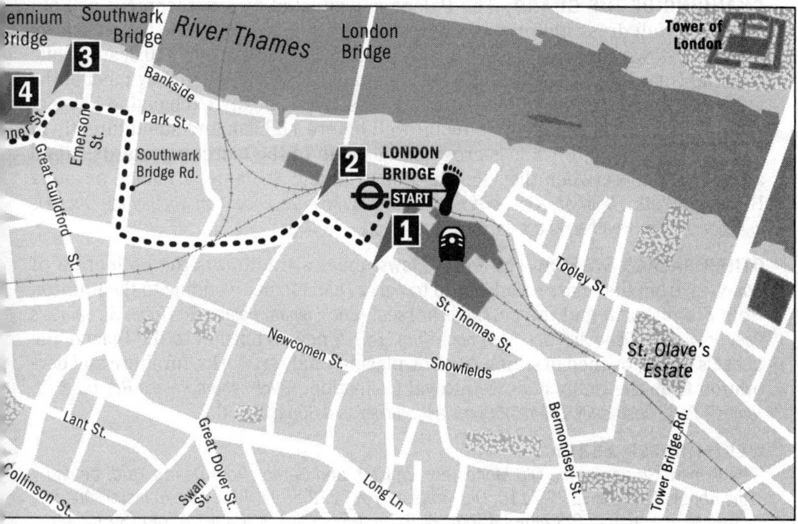

ing of the theater almost 400 years after the original burned down (see p. 186). *Call ahead to find out what time tours run that day.*

4 TATE MODERN. It's hard to imagine anything casting a shadow over Shakespeare's Globe Theatre, but the massive former Bankside Power Station does just that—at least in the physical sense. Having fulfilled your theatrical and artistic appetite, now may be a good time to have a quick bite. **Café 7** and the **East Room** of the Tate Modern (see p. 192) offer meals and snacks, respectively, not to mention fabulous views of the City of London. Alternatively, wait until the next stop for both food and view...

5 GABRIEL'S WHARF. Cafes, bars, and boutiques characterize colorful Gabriel's Wharf. The Art Deco OXO tower resembles the beginning of a stalemate in a giant game of "noughts and crosses" (tic-tac-toe). If you missed the top floor of the Tate Modern, go to the public viewing gallery on the 8th floor of the OXO Tower Wharf.

6 SOUTH BANK CENTRE. 1951—the year that the Royal Festival Hall was built and the South Bank was to be established as a primary culture center. If the architecture does not appeal to you today, consider what your sentiments would have been in the '50s. It gives me a headache, you say? Recall the trepanning drill; do you still have a headache? With a musical range from Philharmonic extravaganzas to low-key jazz, now is an ideal time to find out what's on and buy tickets. Having planned and timed things right, you could even catch one of the free lunchtime or afternoon events right now (see p. 186). *Call ahead to find out what's going on that day.*

7 LONDON EYE. Also known as the "Millennium Wheel," but given its siblings—the misbehaving "Bridge" and bloated ego of "Dome"—it's no surprise that the "Wheel" shed its Millennium maiden name at the first possible chance. Not that it can be too self-righteous; the Wheel had some early problems itself, as any Virgin will tell you (see p. 186). But it was all in the head—the London Eye has now firmly established itself as one of London's top attractions. *Call ahead to book in advance and avoid the long queues.*

8 WESTMINSTER BRIDGE. The bridge teasingly invites you to the Houses of Parliament, and although Waterloo Underground station is a little closer to The London Eye, you will probably want a first (or another) peek at Parliament's magnificence. Head to Westminster Underground Station, one of the four stations on the Jubilee Line Extension to have been especially commended for its innovative design. If you like this one, take the tour of the four (see p. 190).

CHANGING OF THE GUARD. The Palace is protected by a detachment of Foot Guards in full dress uniform. Accompanied by a band, the "New Guard" starts marching down Birdcage Walk from Wellington Barracks around 10:30am, while the "Old Guard" leaves St. James's Palace around 11:10am. When they meet at the gates of the palace, the officers touch hands, symbolically exchanging keys, *et voilà*, the guard is changed. Show up well before 11:30am and stand directly in front of the palace; for a less-crowded close-up of the marching guards, stand along the Mall between the Victoria Memorial and St. James's Palace or along Birdcage Walk. *(Daily Apr.-Oct., every other day Nov.-Mar. Dependent on whether the Queen is in residence, the weather, and state functions. Free.)*

OTHER PALACE SIGHTS. The **Royal Mews**' main attraction is the collection of coaches, from the "glass coach" used to carry Diana to her wedding to the four-ton Gold State Coach and the carriage horses. *(Buckingham Palace Rd. Tube: St. James's Park or Victoria. Open Apr.-Oct. M-Th noon-4pm. £4.)* A new extension to the Palace, the **Queen's Gallery** opened in spring 2002, displaying gaudy artworks, furniture and decoration from the richly endowed Royal Collection. *(Buckingham Palace Rd. Tube: St. James's Park. Open daily 10am-5:30pm; last admission 4:30pm. £6.50.)*

WESTMINSTER ABBEY

Parliament Sq.; enter the Old Monastery, Cloister, and Garden from Dean's Yard, behind the Abbey. Abbey ☎ 7222 7110; Old Monastery ☎ 7222 5897. Tube: Westminster. Abbey open M-Tu and Th-F 9:30am-3:45pm, W 9:30am-7pm, Sa 9:30am-1:45pm, Su for services only. Museum open daily 10:30am-4pm. Chapter House open Apr.-Oct. daily 9:30am-4:45pm; Nov.-Mar. 10am-4pm. Cloisters open daily 8am-6pm. Abbey £6, students £3; services free. Chapter House £1. Cloisters and Garden free.

On December 28, 1065, Edward the Confessor, the last Saxon King of England, was buried in the church of the West Monastery; a year later, the Abbey saw the coronation of William the Conqueror, thus establishing the Abbey's twin traditions as the figurative birthplace and literal resting place of royalty. It was this connection that allowed Westminster, uniquely among England's great monasteries, to escape wholesale destruction during Henry VIII's campaign against the Pope.

The **north transept** contains memorials to Victorian statesmen, including Prime Ministers Disraeli and Gladstone. Early English kings are buried around the Confessor's tomb in the **Shrine of St. Edward,** behind which the **Coronation Chair** stands at the entry to the Tudor **Lady Chapel.** Henry VII and his wife Elizabeth lie at the end of the chapel. Queen Elizabeth I and the cousin she beheaded, Mary Queen of Scots, are buried on opposite sides of the chapel. **Poet's Corner** begins with Geoffrey Chaucer, buried in 1400; plaques at his feet commemorate both poets and prose writers, as does the stained-glass window above. At the center of the Abbey, the **Sanctuary** holds the altar, where coronations and royal weddings are held. After a detour through the **Cloisters,** visitors re-enter the nave. At the western end is the **Tomb of the Unknown Warrior,** whose epitaph is inscribed in molten bullets; just beyond is the simple grave of **Winston Churchill.** The north aisle holds **Scientists' Corners,** with physicists and biologists resting around the tombs of Isaac Newton and Charles Darwin respectively. The **Old Monastery** houses the **Great Cloister,** festooned with monuments and plaques, from which passages lead to the **Chapter House,** the original meeting place of Parliament, the **Pyx Chamber,** formerly the Abbey treasury, and the **Abbey Museum,** which features an array of royal funeral effigies. The pleasant **Gardens** are reached from the Cloisters; concerts are occasionally held here in summer.

THE HOUSES OF PARLIAMENT

Parliament Sq. Tube: Westminster. ☎ 7219 4272. Debates open to all while Parliament is in session (Oct.-July). Advance tickets required for Prime Minister's Question Time (W 3-3:30pm). M-Th after 6pm and F are least busy. Lords usually sits M-W from 2:30pm, Th 3pm, occasionally F 11:30am; closing times vary. Commons sits M-W 2:30-10:30pm, Th 11:30am-7:30pm, F 9:30am-3pm. Free. Tours Aug.-Sept. M-Sa 9:15am-4:30pm; reserve through Firstcall (☎ 0870 906 3773). £7, students £3.50.

The Palace of Westminster, as the building in which Parliament sits is officially known, has been at the heart of English government since the 11th century, when Edward the Confessor established his court here. William the Conqueror found the site to his liking, and under the Normans the palace was greatly extended. Westminster Hall aside, little of the Norman palace remained after the massive fire of October 16, 1834; the rebuilding started in 1835 under the joint command of Charles Barry and Augustus Pugin.

OUTSIDE THE HOUSES. A statue of Oliver Cromwell, the sole survivor of the 1834 fire, stands in front of the midpoint of the complex, **Westminster Hall.** Unremarkable from the outside, the hall's chief feature is a magnificent hammer-beam roof, constructed in 1394 and considered the finest timber roof ever made. During its centuries as a court of law, famous defendants included Thomas More and Charles I. Today, it is used for public ceremonies and occasional exhibitions. The **Clock Tower** is universally miscalled **Big Ben,** which actually refers only to the bell within; it's named after the robustly proportioned Sir Benjamin Hall, who served as Commissioner of Works when the bell was cast in 1858.

DEBATING CHAMBERS. Visitors to the debating chambers first pass through **St. Stephen's Hall.** Formerly the king's private chapel, in 1550 St. Stephen's became the meeting place of the House of Commons. MPs have since moved down the corridor, but four brass markers indicate where the Speaker's Chair used to stand. At the end of the hall, the **Central Lobby** marks the separation between the two houses, with the Commons to the north and the Lords to the south. The ostentatious **House of Lords** is dominated by the **Throne of State,** under a gilt canopy. The Lord Chancellor presides over the Peers from the giant red **Woolsack.** In contrast is the restrained **House of Commons,** with simple green-backed benches under a plain wooden roof. The different decors are not entirely due to the difference in class—the Commons was bombed in 1941, and rebuilding took place during a time of post-war austerity. The **Speaker** sits at the rear of the chamber, with government MPs to his right and the opposition to his left. With seating for only 437 out of 635 MPs, things get hectic when all are present.

TRAFALGAR SQUARE AND THE STRAND

John Nash suggested the design of **Trafalgar Square** in 1820 to commemorate Nelson's 1805 victory over Napoleon's navy at the Battle of Trafalgar. But it took years to take on its current appearance: Nelson only arrived in 1843, the bronze lions in 1867. The reliefs at the column's base are cast from captured French and Spanish cannons. Every December the square hosts a giant **Christmas Tree,** donated by Norway to thank the British for assistance against the Nazis. (Tube: Charing Cross.)

ST. MARTIN-IN-THE-FIELDS. James Gibbs's 1720s creation was the model for countless Georgian churches in Britain and America. It's still the Queen's parish church; look for the royal box to the left of the altar. The **crypt** downstairs has a life of its own, home to a cafe, bookshop, art gallery, and the **London Brass Rubbing Centre.** *(St. Martin's Lane, in the northeast corner of Trafalgar Sq. Tube: Leicester Sq. Brass Rubbing Centre open daily 10am-7pm. Rubbings £3-15.)*

SOMERSET HOUSE. A magnificent Palladian structure completed in 1790, Somerset House was London's first intended office block. Originally home to the Royal Academy and the Royal Society, the building now harbors the magnificent **Courtauld Institute** (see p. 193). From mid-December to mid-January the central **Fountain Courtyard** is iced over to make an open-air rink. *(On the Strand. Tube: Charing Cross. Courtyard open daily 7:30am-11pm. Free. Tours Sa 1:30 and 3:45pm. £2.75.)*

OTHER WESTMINSTER SIGHTS

WHITEHALL. A long stretch of imposing facades housing government ministries, Whitehall is synonymous with the British civil service. From 1532 until a fire in 1698, Whitehall was the main royal palace. All that remains is Inigo Jones's **Banqueting House,** which features magnificent ceiling paintings by Rubens. Charles I was executed on a scaffold outside the house in 1649. *(Whitehall. Tube: Westminster. Open M-Sa 10am-5pm; last admission 4:30pm. £4, students and seniors £3.)* Opposite Banqueting House, tourists line up to be photographed with the Household Cavalry at **Horseguards;** the guard is changed Monday to Friday at 11am and Saturday at 10am. Just off Whitehall, King James St. leads to the **Cabinet War Rooms** (see p. 194). Current Prime Minister Tony Blair lives on **Downing Street,** separated from Whitehall by steel gates. The Prime Minister traditionally lives at #10, but Tony's family is so big that he's had to swap with the Chancellor, Gordon Brown, at #11.

WESTMINSTER CATHEDRAL. Westminster, London's first Catholic cathedral after Henry VIII espoused Protestantism, was started in 1887; in 1903, money ran out, leaving the interior only partially completed. The blackened brick domes contrast dramatically with the swirling marble of the lower walls and the magnificence of the side chapels. An elevator carries visitors up the striped 90m **bell tower.** *(Cathedral Piazza, off Victoria St. Tube: Victoria. Cathedral open daily 7am-7pm. Suggested donation £2. Bell tower open Apr.-Nov. daily 9am-5pm; Dec.-Mar. Th-Su 9am-5pm. £2, students £1.)*

THE WEST END

MAYFAIR AND ST. JAMES'S

Home to Prince Charles, the Ritz, and exclusive gentlemen's clubs, this is London's aristocratic quarter. On **Jermyn St.,** one block south of Piccadilly, stores cater to the tastes of the traditional English squire with hand-cut suits and hunting gear.

BURLINGTON HOUSE. The only one of Piccadilly's aristocratic mansions that stands today, Burlington House was built in 1665. Today, it houses numerous regal societies, including the **Royal Academy,** heart of the British artistic establishment and home to some excellent exhibitions (see p. 193).

ST. JAMES'S PALACE. Built in 1536, St. James's is London's only remaining purpose-built palace; Prince Charles lives here. The only part of the palace open to the public is the **Chapel Royal,** open for Sunday services from October to Easter at 8:30 and 11am. *(Between the Mall and Pall Mall. Tube: Green Park.)* From Easter to September, services are held in **Queen's Chapel,** across Marlborough Rd.

REGENT STREET. Originally designed by John Nash in the 19th century to link Regent's Park in the north to the Prince Regent's residence in St. James's, Regent St. is divided into two parts. "Upper" Regent St., between Oxford Circus and Piccadilly Circus, is known for its elegant shopping; "Lower" Regent St., running south from Picadilly Circus, terminates at **Waterloo Place,** where a column topped with the "Grand Old" Duke of York overlooks St. James's Park.

SOHO

Soho has a history of welcoming all colors and creeds to its streets. The first settlers were French Huguenots fleeing religious persecution in the 17th century.

These days, a concentration of gay-owned restaurants and bars has turned **Old Compton Street** into the heart of gay London.

PICCADILLY CIRCUS. In the glow of lurid neon signs, five of the West End's major arteries merge and swirl round the **statue of Eros,** dedicated to the Victorian philanthropist, Lord Shaftesbury. Eros originally pointed down Shaftesbury Ave., but recent restoration work has put his aim significantly off. *(Tube: Piccadilly Circus.)*

LEICESTER SQUARE. Amusements at this entertainment nexus range from London's largest cinema to the **Swiss Centre** glockenspiel, whose atonal renditions of Beethoven's *Moonlight Sonata* are enough to make even the tone-deaf weep. *(Rings M-F noon, 6, 7, and 8pm; Sa-Su noon, 2, 4, 5, 6, 7, and 8pm.)* Be true to your inner tourist by having your name engraved on a grain of rice and sitting for a caricature. *(Tube: Leicester Sq. or Piccadilly Circus.)*

CHINATOWN. The pedestrian, tourist-ridden **Gerrard Street,** with dragon gates and pagoda-capped phone booths, is the heart of London's tiny slice of Canton, but gritty **Lisle Street,** one block to the south, has a more authentic feel. Chinatown is most vibrant during the raucous Chinese New Year in February. *(Between Leicester Sq., Shaftesbury Ave., and Charing Cross Rd.)*

COVENT GARDEN

The Covent Garden piazza, designed by Inigo Jones in the 17th century, is one of the few parts of London popular with locals and tourists alike. On the very spot where England's first Punch and Judy show was performed, street entertainers delight the thousands who flock here year round. (Tube: Covent Garden.)

THE ROYAL OPERA HOUSE. The Royal Opera House reopened in 2000 after a major expansion. After wandering the ornate lobby of the original 1858 theater, head up to the enormous **Floral Hall.** From there, take the escalator to reach the **terrace,** which has great views of London. *(Bow St. Open daily 10am-3:30pm. 1¼hr. backstage tours M-Sa 10:30am, 12:30 and 2:30pm; reservations essential. £8, students £7.)*

THEATRE ROYAL DRURY LANE. Founded in 1663, this is the oldest of London's surviving theaters; David Garrick ruled the roost here in the 18th century. The theater even has a ghost—a corpse and dagger were found bricked up in a wall in the 19th century. This and other pieces of Drury Lane lore are brought back to life in the actor-led backstage tours. *(Entrance on Catherine St. Tours M-Tu and Th-F 2:15 and 4:45pm, W and Sa 10:15am and noon. £8.50, children £6.50.)*

THE CITY OF LONDON

Until the 18th century, the City *was* London; the rest was merely outlying villages. Yet its modern appearance belies a 2000-year history; what few buildings survived the Great Fire of 1666 and WWII bombings are now overshadowed by giant temples of commerce. The second half of the 20th century has had an even more profound effect on the City than the cosmetic rearrangement of the Blitz: as its power in international finance grew, the City's relevance to ordinary Londoners diminished. Nowadays, of the 300,000 who work here, only 8000 people call the City home. The **City of London Information Centre,** in St. Paul's Churchyard, offers acres of leaflets and maps, sells tickets to sights and shows, and provides info on a host of traditional municipal events. (☎7332 1456. Tube: St. Paul's. Open Apr.-Sept. daily 9:30am-5pm; Oct.-Mar. M-F 9:30am-5pm, Sa 9:30am-12:30pm.)

ST. PAUL'S CATHEDRAL

St. Paul's Churchyard. ☎7246 8348; www.stpauls.co.uk. Tube: St. Paul's. Open M-Sa 8:30am-4pm; open for worship daily 7:15am-6pm. £6, students £5; worshippers free. Audio tours £3.50, students £3. 1½hr. tours M-F 4 per day; £2.50, students £2.

Sir Christopher Wren's masterpiece is the fifth cathedral to occupy the site; the original was built in AD 604. Wren's succeeded "Old St. Paul's," begun in 1087, whose steeple was just one-third as high as the current 111m dome. By 1666, when the Great Fire swept it away, Old St. Paul's—used as a marketplace and barracks during the Civil War—was ripe for replacement. After three designs were rejected by the bishops, Wren, with Charles II's support, just started building—sneakily, he had persuaded the king to let him make "necessary alterations" as work progressed, and the building that emerged from the scaffolding in 1708 bore little resemblance to the "Warrant Model" Charles II had approved.

With space to seat 2500 worshippers, the **nave** is festooned with monuments to great Britons; however, unlike Westminster Abbey, no one is buried in the cathedral floor—the tombs, including those of Nelson, Wellington, and Florence Nightingale, are all downstairs, in the **crypt.** Surrounded by Blake, Turner, and Henry Moore, Christopher Wren lies beneath the epitaph *Lector, si monumentum requiris circumspice* ("Reader, if you seek his monument, look around"). To see the inside of the second-tallest freestanding **dome** in Europe (after St. Peter's in the Vatican), climb the 259 steps to the **Whispering Gallery.** The gallery is a perfect resounding chamber: whisper into the wall, and your friend on the opposite side should be able to hear you. From here, 119 more steps lead to **Stone Gallery,** on the outer base of the dome, and it's another 152 to the summit's **Golden Gallery.** Back inside, the mosaic of *Christ Seated in Majesty* overlooks the **High Altar.** The north quire aisle holds Henry Moore's *Mother and Child.* The statue of **John Donne** in the south quire aisle is one of the few monuments to survive from Old St. Paul's.

THE TOWER OF LONDON

Tower Hill. ☎ 7709 0765; www.hrp.org.uk. Tube: Tower Hill. Open Mar.-Oct. M-Sa 9am-5:30pm, Su 10am-5:30pm; Nov.-Feb. M 10am-4:30pm, Tu-Sa 9am-5:30pm. £11.50, students £8.75. Tickets also sold at Tube stations; buy them in advance to avoid horrendous lines. Audio tours £3. 1hr. tours M-Sa 9:30am-3:30pm, Su 10am-3:30pm; free.

The Tower of London, palace and prison of English monarchs for over 900 years, is steeped in blood and history. Conceived by William the Conqueror in 1067 to provide protection *from* rather than *to* his new subjects, the original wooden palisade was replaced by a stone structure in 1078 that over the next 20 years would grow into the **White Tower.** Colorfully dressed Yeomen Warders, or "Beefeaters" (a reference to their former daily allowance of meat), serve as guards and tourist guides; to be eligible for Beefeaterhood, candidates must have 20 years of distinguished service in the armed forces.

From the western entrance near the **Middle Tower,** you pass over the old moat, now a garden, entering the **Outer Ward** though **Byward Tower.** Just beyond Byward Tower is a massive **Bell Tower,** dating from 1190; the curfew bell has been rung nightly for over 500 years. The stretch of the Outer Ward along the Thames is **Water Lane,** which until the 16th century was adjacent to the river. **Traitor's Gate** was built by Edward I for his personal use, but it is now associated with the prisoners who passed through it on their way to execution at **Tower Green.** Some of the victims are buried in the **Chapel Royal of St. Peter and Vincula,** including Catholic martyr Sir Thomas More and Henry VIII's wives Catherine Howard and Anne Boleyn. The green abuts the White Tower, now home to a fearsome display of arms and armor from the Royal Armory; one look at Henry VIII's "generous" suit will show why he never had any trouble remarrying. Across the green is the **Bloody Tower,** so named because Richard III allegedly imprisoned and then murdered his nephews here before usurping the throne in 1483.

The most famous sights in the Tower are the **Crown Jewels;** moving walkways ensure no awestruck gazers hold up the queue. While the eye is naturally drawn to the **Imperial State Crown,** featuring the Stuart Sapphire along with 16 others, 2876 diamonds, 273 pearls, 11 emeralds, and a mere five rubies, don't miss the **Sceptre with the Cross,** topped with the First Star of Africa, the largest quality-cut diamond in the world. This was hewn from an even larger monster, the 3106-carat Cullinan diamond (the largest ever found); Scotland Yard mailed the stone third class from South Africa in an unmarked brown parcel. Other famous gems include the **Koh-i-Noor,** set into the **Queen Mother's Crown;** legend claims the stone will bring luck only to women. These jewels, along with numerous retired crowns and other treasures, are displayed in the **Martin Tower,** at the end of **Wall Walk.**

OTHER CITY OF LONDON SIGHTS

GUILDHALL. In this vast Gothic hall, representatives from the City's 102 guilds, from the Fletchers (arrow-makers) to the Information Technologists, meet at the **Court of Common Council,** under the Lord Mayor. The Court meets the third Thursday of every month. *(Off Gresham St. Tube: St. Paul's. Open May-Sept. daily 10am-5pm, Sa-Su 10am-4pm; Oct.-Apr. closed Su. Free.)*

BANK OF ENGLAND AND ENVIRONS. Government financial difficulties led to the founding of the **Bank of England** (a.k.a. "The Old Lady of Threadneedle St.") in 1694—the bank's creditors supplied £1.2 million, and the national debt was born. Other hallowed institutions stand on the streets nearby: the **Stock Exchange,** on Throgmorton St.; the **Royal Exchange,** between Cornhill and Threadneedle St., founded in 1566; and the 18th-century **Mansion House,** on Walbrook, the official residence of the Lord Mayor. The most famous modern structure in the City is **Lloyd's of London,** on Leadenhall, designed by Richard Rogers. With metal ducts, lifts, and chutes on the outside, it wears its heart on its sleeve. *(Tube: Bank.)*

MONUMENT. Raised in 1677, Christopher Wren's 202 ft. column stands exactly that distance from the bakery on Pudding Lane where the Great Fire started in 1666. *(Monument St. Tube: Monument. Open daily 9:30am-5pm. £1.50.)*

TOWER BRIDGE. This iconic symbol of London is often mistaken for its plain upriver sibling, London Bridge—the story goes that when an Arizona millionaire bought the previous London Bridge and shifted it stone-by-stone to the US, he thought he was getting Tower Bridge. The **Tower Bridge Experience** offers a cutesy introduction to the history and technology of the unique lifting mechanism, though the view isn't all it's cracked up to be. *(Tube: Tower Hill. Open daily 9:30am–6pm; last admission 5pm. £4.50, students £3.)*

WREN CHURCHES. Aside from St. Paul's Cathedral, the City's greatest architectural treasures are the 22 surviving churches designed by Christopher Wren to replace those lost in the Great Fire of 1666. The most famous is **St. Mary-le-Bow;** traditionally, the term "cockney" is reserved for those born within range of its bells. For the past 800 years, the Archbishop of Canterbury has sworn in bishops in the 11th-century crypt, whose "bows" (arches) gave the church its epithet. *(On Cheapside, near Bow Ln. Tube: St. Paul's. Open M-F 6:30am-6pm. Free.)* **St. Stephen Walbrook,** built 1672-79, was Wren's personal favorite. A plain exterior gives no inkling of the wide dome that floats above Henry Moore's 1985 mysterious free-form altar. *(39 Walbrook. Tube: Bank. Organ concert F 12:30pm. Open M-Th 9am-4pm. Free.)*

THE SOUTH BANK

From the Middle Ages until Cromwell's arrival, the South Bank was London's center of amusement; banished from the strictly regulated City, all manner of illicit attractions sprouted in "the Borough" at the southern end of London Bridge. Today, the South Bank is once again at the heart of London entertainment, with some of the city's top concert halls, theaters, cinemas, and galleries.

LONDON EYE. At 135m, the London Eye, also known as the Millennium Wheel, is the world's biggest observational wheel. The ellipsoid glass "pods" give uninterrupted views at the top of each 30min. revolution; on clear days, Windsor is visible to the west. *(Jubilee Gardens, between County Hall and the Festival Hall. Tube: Waterloo. Open late May to early Sept. daily 9:30am-10pm; Apr. to late May and late Sept. 10:30am-8pm; Oct.-Mar. 10:30am-7pm; the ticket office, in the corner of County Hall, opens 30min. earlier; advance booking recommended. May-Sept. £10.50; Oct.-June £9.50.)*

THE SOUTH BANK CENTRE. Sprawling on either side of Waterloo Bridge, this concrete complex is Britain's premier cultural center. Its nucleus is the **Royal Festival Hall,** a classic piece of white 1950s architecture. Nearby, the **Purcell Room** and **Queen Elizabeth Hall** host smaller concerts, while just behind, the spiky ceiling of the **Hayward Gallery** shelters excellent modern art exhibitions. The **National Film Theatre,** on the embankment beneath the bridge, offers London's most varied cinematic fare, while the **National Theatre** (see p. 195) looms past the bridge. To find out how one of the world's largest, most modern theaters operates, join a backstage tour. *(On the riverbank between Hungerford and Waterloo Bridges. Tube: Waterloo. Tours M-Sa 10:15am, 12:15 and 5:15pm. £5, students £4.25.)*

TATE MODERN AND THE MILLENNIUM BRIDGE. Squarely opposite each other on Bankside are the biggest success and most abject failure of London's millennial celebrations. **Tate Modern** (see p. 192), created from the shell of the Bankside power station, is as visually arresting as its contents are thought-provoking. The **Millennium Bridge,** built to link the Tate to the City, was completed six months too late for the Y2K festivities and, following a literally shaky debut, has only recently been stabilized. *(Queen's Walk, Bankside. Tube: Southwark.)*

SHAKESPEARE'S GLOBE THEATRE. In the shadow of Tate Modern, the half-timbered Globe, opened in 1997, sits just 200m from where the original burned down in 1613. Try to arrive in time for a tour of the theater itself, given on mornings during the performance season. *(Bankside. Tube: Southwark. Open May-Sept. daily 9am-noon and 1-4pm; Oct.-Apr. 10am-5pm. £8, students £6.50. See also* p. 195.*)* Nearby lie the ruins of the 1587 **Rose Theatre,** where both Shakespeare and Marlowe performed. The site was rediscovered in 1989; not much is left, though the outline is clearly visible. *(56 Park St. Open daily 11am-5pm. £4, students £3; £1 discount with same-day Globe ticket.)*

OTHER SOUTH BANK SIGHTS. The giant **HMS Belfast** was used in the bombardment of Normandy during D-Day and then to support UN forces in Korea before graciously retiring in 1965. Kids love clambering over the decks and aiming the anti-aircraft guns at dive-bombing seagulls. Dozens of narrow passages, steep staircases, and ladders make exploring the boat a physical challenge in itself. *(At the end of Morgans Ln., off Tooley St. Tube: London Bridge. Open Mar.-Oct. daily 10am-6pm; Nov.-Feb. 10am-5pm. £5.80, students £4.40.)* The giant curved facade of **County Hall,** almost opposite the Houses of Parliament, houses two of London's most-advertised and least-impressive sights, the **London Aquarium** and **Dalí Universe.** *(Westminster Bridge Rd. Tube: Westminster. Aquarium open daily 10am-6pm; last admission 5pm. £8.75, students £6.50. Dalí open daily 10am-5:30pm. £8.50, students £7.50.)* **Vinopolis** is a Dionysian fantasy land offering patrons an interactive tour of the world's wine regions. *(1 Bank End. Tube: London Bridge. Open M and Sa 11am-9pm, Tu-F and Su 11am-6pm. £11.50, seniors £10.50.)* The **London Dungeon** is always mobbed with thousands of children reveling in tasteful displays about Jack the Ripper, the Fire of London, and anything else remotely connected to British horror. *(28-34 Tooley St. Tube: London Bridge. Open mid-July to Aug. daily 10:30am-8pm; Apr. to mid-July and Sept.-Oct. 10:30am-5:30pm; Nov.-Mar. 10:30am-5pm. £11, students £9.50.)*

BLOOMSBURY AND MARYLEBONE

Marylebone's most famous resident (and address) never existed. 221b Baker St. was the fictional lodging house of Sherlock Holmes, but 221 Baker St. is actually the headquarters of the Abbey National Bank. A little farther down the street, the **Sherlock Holmes Museum** gives its address as 221b, although a little sleuthing will reveal that it in fact stands at #239. Bloomsbury's intellectual reputation was bolstered in the early 20th century when Gordon Sq., east of Marylebone, resounded with the philosophizing and womanizing of the **Bloomsbury Group,** an early 20th-century coterie of intellectuals that included Virginia Woolf, John Maynard Keynes, Lytton Strachey, and Bertrand Russell.

BRITISH LIBRARY. Since its 1998 opening, the new British Library has won acclamation from visitors and users alike. The 325km of underground shelving can hold up to 12 million books. The library also houses a dramatic glass cube containing the 65,000 volumes of George III's King's Library, and a stunning display of books, manuscripts, and artifacts, from the 2nd-century *Unknown Gospel* to Joyce's handwritten draft of *Finnegan's Wake. (96 Euston Rd. ☎7412 7332. Tube: King's Cross. Open M and W-F 9:30am-6pm, Tu 9:30am-8pm, Sa 9:30am-5pm, Su 11am-5pm. Free. Tours M, W, F-Sa 3pm, also Sa 10:30am. £5, students £3.50. Tours including one reading room Tu 6:30pm, Su 11:30am and 3pm. £6, £4.50. Reservations recommended for all tours.)*

ACADEMIA. The strip of land along **Gower Street** and immediately to its west is London's academic heartland. Established in 1828, **University College London** was the first in Britain to admit Catholics, Jews, and women. The embalmed body of founder **Jeremy Bentham** has occupied the South Cloister since 1850. *(Main entrance on Gower St. South Cloister entrance through the courtyard. Tube: Warren St.)* Now the administrative headquarters of the University of London, **Senate House** was the model for the Ministry of Truth in *1984;* George Orwell worked there as part of the BBC propaganda unit in WWII. *(At the southern end of Malet St. Tube: Goodge St.)*

HOLBORN AND CLERKENWELL

Squeezed between the capitalism of the City and the commercialism of the West End, Holborn is historically the home of two of the world's least-loved professions—lawyers and journalists.

INNS OF COURT. These venerable institutions house the chambers of practicing barristers and provide apprenticeships for law students. Most were founded in the 13th century when a royal decree barred the clergy from the courts, giving rise to a class of professional advocates. Most impressive of the four Inns are those of the **Middle** and **Inner Temple,** south of Fleet St. *(Between Fleet St., Essex St., Victoria Embankment, and Temple Ave./Bouvier St. Numerous passages lead from these streets into the Temple. Tube: Temple.)* The 12th-century **Temple Church** is the finest surviving round church in England. *(Open W-Th 11am-4pm, Sa 10am-2:30pm, Su 12:45-4pm. Free.)* Shakespeare premiered *Twelfth Night* in front of Elizabeth I in **Middle Temple Hall,** whose large wooden dining table is made from the hatch of Sir Francis Drake's *Golden Hinde.* According to Shakespeare's *Henry VI,* the red-and-white flowers of the War of the Roses were plucked in **Middle Temple Garden,** south of the hall. *(Garden open May-Sept. M-F noon-3pm. Free.)*

FLEET STREET. Named for the river (now underground) that flows from Hampstead to the Thames, Fleet Street's association with publishing goes back to the days when Wyken de Worde relocated from Westminster to the precincts of **St. Bride's** church, ever since known as "the printer's cathedral." Christopher Wren's odd steeple is the original inspiration for the tiered wedding cake, invented by a local baker. *(On St. Bride's Ave., just off Fleet St. Tube: Temple. Open daily 8am-4:45pm. Free.)*

ROYAL COURTS OF JUSTICE. This elaborate neo-Gothic structure—easily mistaken for a cathedral—straddles the official division between Westminster and the City of London; the courtrooms are open to the public during cases. *(Where the Strand becomes Fleet St. Tube: Temple. Open M-F 9am-6pm. Cases start 10am.)*

KENSINGTON

Nobody took much notice of Kensington before 1689, when the newly crowned William III and Mary II moved into Kensington Palace. Then, in 1851, the Great Exhibition brought in enough money to finance the museums and colleges of South Kensington. Now the neighborhood is home to London's most expensive stores, including Harrods and Harvey Nichols, and it's hard to imagine the days when the area was known for its taverns and its highwaymen.

KENSINGTON PALACE. Remodelled by Wren for William III and Mary II, parts of the palace are still in use today as a royal residence. Princess Diana lived here until her death. The **Royal Ceremonial Dress Collection** features 19th-century court costumes along with the Queen's demure evening gowns and some of Diana's sexier numbers. Hanoverian economy is evident in the *trompe l'oeil* decoration in the **State Apartment**, carried out by William Kent for George I. *(On the eastern edge of Kensington Gardens; enter through the park. Tube: High St. Kensington. Open Mar.-Oct. daily 10am-6pm; Nov.-Feb. 10am-5pm. £10, students £7.50.)*

HYDE PARK AND KENSINGTON GARDENS. Surrounded by London's wealthiest neighborhoods, giant Hyde Park has served as the model for city parks around the world, including Central Park in New York and Bois de Boulogne in Paris. **Kensington Gardens,** to the west, is contiguous with Hyde Park. The 41-acre **Serpentine** was created in 1730; innumerable people pay to row and swim here. At the northeastern corner of the park, near Marble Arch, proselytizers, politicos, and flat-out crazies dispense their knowledge to bemused tourists at **Speaker's Corner** on Sundays. *(Tube: Queensway, Lancaster Gate, Marble Arch, Hyde Park Corner, or High St. Kensington. Hyde Park open daily 5am-midnight. Kensington Gardens open dawn-dusk. Both free.)*

BRITAIN

KNIGHTSBRIDGE

APSLEY HOUSE AND WELLINGTON ARCH. Apsley House, with the convenient address of "No. 1, London," was bought in 1817 by the Duke of Wellington. On display is Wellington's outstanding collection of art, much of it given in gratitude by European royalty following the battle of Waterloo. The majority of the paintings hang in the **Waterloo Gallery,** where the Duke would hold his annual Waterloo banquet. *(Hyde Park Corner. Tube: Hyde Park Corner. Open Tu-Su 11am-5pm. £4.50, students £3.)* Across from Apsley House, the **Wellington Arch** was built in 1825. In 1838 it was dedicated to the Duke of Wellington; later, to the horror of its architect, Decimus Burton, a statue of the Duke was placed on top. The platforms inside the arch offer scenic views. *(Hyde Park Corner. Tube: Hyde Park Corner. Open Apr.-Sept. W-Su 10am-6pm; Oct. 10am-5pm; Nov.-Mar. 10am-4pm. £2.50, students £1.90.)*

NORTH LONDON

CAMDEN TOWN

An island of good, honest tawdriness in an increasingly affluent sea, Camden Town has effortlessly thrown off attempts at gentrification thanks to the ever-growing **Camden Markets** (see p. 199). On weekends, the market, London's fourth most popular tourist attraction, presents a variety of life unmatched even by **London Zoo,** just up the **Regent's Canal** from the market's nerve center in Camden Lock.

LONDON ZOO. Thousands of little critters from around the world run around freely, their guardians trying frantically to keep up, as the animals look on with indifference from their enclosures. Penguin feeding (daily 2:30pm) is always popular, as is the elephant washing (3:30pm); for other activities, check the *Daily Events* leaflet. *(Main gate on Outer Circle, Regent's Park. Tube: Camden Town. 12min. walk from Tube station or a quick jaunt on bus #274. Open Apr.-Oct. daily 10am-5:30pm, Nov.-Mar. 10am-4:30pm. £11, students £9.30.)*

HAMPSTEAD

Hampstead first caught the attention of well-heeled Londoners in the 17th century. In the 1930s, the neighborhood found itself at the forefront of a European avant-garde in flight from fascism. Residents such as Aldous Huxley, Piet Mondrian, Barbara Hepworth, and Sigmund Freud lent the area a cachet that grows to this day.

HAMPSTEAD HEATH. Hampstead Heath is one of the last remaining commons in England, open to all since 1312. **Parliament Hill** is the highest open space in London, with excellent views of the city. Farther north, **Kenwood** is a picture-perfect 18th-century country estate, designed by Robert Adams for the first Earl of Mansfield and home to the impressive **Iveagh Bequest** of Old Masters, including works by Rembrandt, Vermeer, Turner, and Botticelli. *(Tube: Hampstead. Rail: Hampstead Heath. A 20min. walk from the station. Kenwood open Apr.-Sept. daily 8am-8pm, Oct.-Mar. 8am-4pm.)*

EAST LONDON

THE EAST END AND DOCKLANDS

The boundary between the East End and the City of London is as sharp today as it was when Aldgate and Bishopsgate were literal gateways in the wall separating the rich and powerful City from the poorer quarters to the east. **Whitechapel** is the oldest part of the East End. In the 19th century it was thronged with Jewish refugees from Eastern Europe; today it's the heart of London's Bangladeshi community, which centers around the restaurants, spice shops, and markets of **Brick Lane.** The most recent wave of immigrants is made up of artists; the former **Truman Brewery** is now occupied by a cafe-bar-club trio that together form one of London's hottest nightspots. (Tube: Aldgate East or Liverpool St.) **Christ Church,** on Commercial St., opposite Spitalfields market, is Nicholas Hawksmoor's largest, and considered by many to be his masterpiece; it is slowly being restored to its former glory. (Tube: Liverpool St. Open M-F 12:30-2:30pm.) The area of the East End along the river is known as the **Docklands.** This man-made archipelago of docks was for centuries the commercial heart of the British Empire. In 1981, the Thatcher government decided to redevelop the area; the showpiece of the regeneration is **Canary Wharf,** with Britain's highest skyscraper, the 244m pyramid-topped **One Canada Square.** Under the tower, the **Canada Place** and **Cabot Square** malls suck in shoppers from all over London, while the dockside plaza is lined with corporate drinking and eating haunts. (Tube: Canary Wharf.)

GREENWICH

Greenwich's position as the "home of time" is connected to its maritime heritage—the Royal Observatory, site of the Prime Meridian, was founded to produce star-charts once essential to navigation. The most pleasant way of getting to Greenwich is by boat. **Westminster Passenger Association** boats head from Westminster Pier (1hr., every 3min., round-trip £6). TfL Travelcard holders get 33% off riverboat fares. "Sail&Rail" tickets combine a one-way boat trip with unlimited all-day travel on the Dockland's Light Railway (£8.75). The **Greenwich Tourist Information Centre** is in Pepys House, 2 Cutty Sark Gdns. (☎(0870) 608 2000. Open daily 10am-5pm.)

ROYAL OBSERVATORY. Charles II founded the Royal Observatory in 1675 to find a way of calculating longitude at sea; the **Prime Meridian** (which marks 0° longitude) started out as the axis along which the astronomers' telescopes swung. Next to the Meridian is Wren's **Flamstead House,** whose **Octagon Room** features long windows designed to accommodate telescopes. The **Observatory Dome,** next to the Meridian Building's telescope display, houses a 28" telescope constructed in 1893. It hasn't been used since 1954, but you can get a peek at the stars at the **Planetarium** in the South Building. *(Greenwich Park. Open daily 10am-5pm. Free.)*

ROYAL NAVAL COLLEGE. On the site of Henry VIII's Palace of Placentia, the Royal Naval College was founded by William III in 1694 as the Royal Hospital for Seamen. In 1998, the University of Greenwich moved in. Don't miss the **Painted Hall** and the **Chapel,** which shelters Benjamin West's painting of a shipwrecked St. Paul. *(King William Walk. Open daily 12:30-5pm. £3, students £2.)*

CUTTY SARK. Even landlubbers will appreciate the **Cutty Sark,** the last of the great tea clippers. Launched in 1869, she was the fastest ship of her time, making the trip to and from China in only 120 days. *(King William Walk, by Greenwich Pier. Open daily 10am-5pm; last admission 4:30pm. £3.90, students £2.90.)*

WEST LONDON

KEW GARDENS. The Kew Gardens (a.k.a. the Royal Botanic Gardens) feature thousands of flowers, fruits, trees, and vegetables from around the globe. The three **conservatories,** housing a staggering variety of plants ill-suited to the English climate, are the highlight of the gardens. Most famous is the steamy **Palm House,** home to "The Oldest Pot Plant In The World," which is not at all what it sounds like but interesting nonetheless. The **Temperate House** is the largest ornamental glasshouse in the world. The interior of the **Princess of Wales Conservatory** is divided into 10 different climate zones, including one entirely devoted to orchids. *(Main entrance at Victoria Gate. Tube: Kew Gardens. Open Apr.-Aug. M-F 9:30am-6:30pm, Sa-Su 9:30am-7:30pm; Sept.-Oct. daily 9:30am-6pm; Nov.-Jan. daily 9:30am-4:15pm; Feb.-Mar. daily 9:30am-5:30pm. Glasshouses close Feb.-Oct. 5:30pm, Nov.-Mar 3:45pm. £6.50, "late entry" (45min. before closing) £4.50; students £4.50.)*

HAMPTON COURT PALACE. Although a monarch hasn't lived here for 250 years, Hampton Court still exudes regal charm. Cardinal Wolsey built the first palace here in 1514, showing the young Henry VIII how to act the part of a splendid and powerful ruler. In 1689, William III and Mary II employed Christopher Wren to bring Hampton Court up to date. In addition to touring the sumptuous rooms of the palace, including Henry's **State Apartments** and William's **King's Apartments,** be sure to leave time for the vast

THE INSIDER'S CITY

THE JUBILEE LINE

While subway stations may not seem like worthy tourist destinations, London Underground's Jubilee Line is certainly an exception. The line was begun in 1977 to honor Queen Elizabeth's 25 years on the throne. In 2002, more stations were added to celebrate Liz's 50th anniversary as monarch. The phenomenal architecture of the stations combines with their proximity to London's aboveground sights for a fascinating tour.

1. **Westminster Underground:** Lots of glass and massive pillars, pipes, and escalators. **Overground:** State-of-the-art gives way to the stately British brilliance of Big Ben and Parliament.
2. **Southwark Underground:** Steep walls, high skylit ceilings, and daylight at the rotunda exit. **Overground:** Gleaming beams (the now-sturdy Millennium Bridge) and the big brick block Tate Modern.
3. **Canary Wharf Underground:** Precipitous escalator, arching overhang, and a sloping concrete ceiling. **Overground:** A financial mecca of glass skyscrapers and thriving urbanity.
4. **North Greenwich Underground:** Bold purple floods the walls, then yields to a cool breezeway. **Overground:** The Millennium Dome—an eye-catching, albeit hollow, testament to modern architecture.

gardens, including the devilishly difficult **maze.** Take the train from Waterloo (35min., every 30min., round-trip $4) or a boat from Westminster Pier (4hr.; 4 per day; $10, round-trip $14); to leave time to see the palace, take the boat one way and return by train. *(Open mid-Mar. to late Oct. M 10:15am-6pm, Tu-Su 9:30am-6pm; late Oct. to mid-Mar. closes 4:30pm. £11, students £8.25. Maze only £3. Gardens only free.)*

MUSEUMS

Centuries spent as the capital of an empire, together with a decidedly English penchant for collecting, have given London a spectacular set of museums. Art lovers, history buffs, and amateur ethnologists won't know which way to turn when they arrive. And there's even better news for museum lovers: the government now plans to return all major collections—once some of the capital's most expensive attractions—to free admission.

BRITISH MUSEUM

Great Russell St., Bloomsbury. Rear entrance on Montague St. ☎7323 8000; www.thebritishmuseum.ac.uk. Tube: Tottenham Court Rd., Russell Sq., or Holborn. Great Court open M 9am-6pm, Tu-W and Su 9am-9pm, Th-Sa 9am-11pm. Galleries open Sa-W 10am-5:30pm, Th-F 10am-8:30pm. Suggested donation £2. Temporary exhibitions average £7, students £3.50. Audio tours £2.50. 1½hr. highlights tour M-Sa 10:30am and 1pm, Su 11am, 12:30, 1:30, 2:30, and 4pm. £7, students £4.

The funny thing about the British Museum is that there's almost nothing British in it. The museum was founded in 1753 with the personal collection of Sir Hans Sloane; in 1824, work started on the current Neoclassical building, which took another 30 years to construct. The December 2000 opening of the **Great Court,** the largest covered square in Europe, finally restored to the museum its focal point; for the past 150 years the area was used as the book stacks of the British Library. The courtyard remains dominated by the enormous rotunda of the **Reading Room,** whose desks have shouldered the weight of research by Marx, Lenin, and Trotsky as well as almost every major British writer and intellectual.

The **Western Galleries** house the most famous items in the collection. Room 4 harbors Egyptian sculpture, including the **Rosetta Stone,** and Room 18 is entirely devoted to the Athenian **Elgin Marbles.** Other highlights include giant Assyrian and Babylonian **reliefs,** the Roman **Portland Vase,** and bits and bobs from two Wonders of the Ancient World, the **Temple of Artemis** at Ephesus and the **Mausoleum of Halikarnassos.** The **Northern Galleries** feature eight rooms of mummies and sarcophagi and nine of artifacts from the ancient Near East, including the **Oxus Treasure** from Iran. The northern wing also houses the excellent African and Islamic galleries, the giant Asian collections, and the Americas collection. The upper level of the **South** and **East Galleries** is dedicated to ancient and medieval Europe, some of which is actually British. Famous remains include the preserved body of **Lindow Man,** an Iron Age Celt (Room 50), along with treasures excavated from the **Sutton Hoo Burial Ship** (Room 41). Room 42 is home to the enigmatic **Lewis Chessmen,** an 800-year-old chess set mysteriously abandoned in Scotland.

NATIONAL GALLERY

Main entrance on north side of Trafalgar Sq., Westminster. ☎7747 2885; www.nationalgallery.org.uk. Tube: Charing Cross or Leicester Sq. Open Th-Tu 10am-6pm; W 10am-9pm, Sainsbury Wing exhibitions until 10pm. Free; some temporary exhibitions £5-7, students £2-3. Audio tours free; suggested donation £4. 1hr. gallery tours start at Sainsbury Wing info desk daily 11:30am and 2:30pm, W also 6:30pm. Free.

The National Gallery was founded by an Act of Parliament in 1824, with 38 paintings displayed in a townhouse; it grew so rapidly in size and popularity that a new

BRITAIN

gallery was constructed in 1838. The new **Sainsbury Wing** houses the oldest, most fragile paintings, including the 14th-century English *Wilton Diptych*, Botticelli's *Venus and Mars*, and the *Leonardo Cartoon*, a detailed preparatory drawing by Leonardo da Vinci for a never-executed painting. The **West Wing** displays paintings from 1510-1600 and is dominated by Italian High Renaissance and early Flemish art. Rome and Florence fight it out in Room 8, with versions of the *Madonna and Child* by Raphael and Michelangelo. The **North Wing** spans the 17th century, with an exceptional array of Flemish work. Room 23 boasts no fewer than 17 Rembrandts; the famous *Self Portrait at 63* gazes knowingly at his *Self Portrait at 34*. The **East Wing,** home to paintings from 1700-1900, is the most popular in the gallery, thanks to an array of Impressionist works including van Gogh's *Sunflowers* and Cézanne's *Bathers* in Room 45, and two of Monet's *Waterlilies* in Room 43. Room 34 serves as a reminder that there was art on the British side of the Channel, too, with six luminescent Turners.

TATE MODERN

Bankside, The South Bank. Main entrance on Holland St. ☎ 7887 8006; www.tate.org.uk. Tube: Blackfriars. Open Su-Th 10am-6pm, F-Sa 10am-10pm. Free. Special exhibitions £5-7; students £4-6. Audio tours £1. Free tours meet on the gallery concourses: Landscape/Matter/Environment 11am, level 3; Still Life/Object/Real Life noon, level 3; Nude/Body/Action 2pm, level 5; History/Memory/Society 3pm, level 5.

Since opening in May 2000, Tate Modern has been credited with single-handedly reversing the long-term decline in museum attendance in Britain. The largest modern art museum in the world, its most striking aspect is the building, formerly the Bankside power station. A conversion by Swiss firm Herzog and de Meuron added a seventh floor with wraparound views of north and south London, and turned the old **Turbine Hall** into an immense atrium that often overpowers the installations commissioned for it. For all its popularity, the Tate has been criticized for its controversial curatorial method, which groups works according to themes rather than period or artist: the four divisions are **Landscape/Matter/Environment** and **Still Life/Object/Real Life** on level 3 and **Nude/Body/Action** and **History/Memory/Society** on level 5. Even skeptics admit that this arrangement throws up some interesting contrasts, such as the nascent geometry of Cézanne's *Still Life with Water Jug* overlooking the checkerboard tiles of Carl André's *Steel Zinc Plain*, and the juxtaposition of Monet's *Waterlilies* with Richard Long's energetic *Waterfall Line*. The main achievement of the thematic display is that it forces visitors into contact with an exceptionally wide range of art. It's now impossible to see the Tate's more famous pieces, which include Marcel Duchamp's *Large Glass* and Picasso's *Weeping Woman*, without also confronting challenging and invigorating works by little-known contemporary artists.

TATE BRITAIN

Millbank, near Vauxhall Bridge, Westminster. Wheelchair access via Clore Wing. ☎ 7887 8008; www.tate.org.uk. Tube: Pimlico. Open daily 10am-5pm. Free. Special exhibitions £3-9. Audio tours £1. Highlights tour M-F 11:30am, Sa 3pm. Free.

The original Tate opened in 1897 as a showcase for modern British art. Before long, it had expanded to include contemporary art from all over the world, as well as British art from the Middle Ages on. Despite many expansions, it was clear that the dual role was too much for one building; the problem was resolved with the relocation of almost all the contemporary art to the new Tate Modern at Bankside (see above). At the same time, the original Tate was rechristened and rededicated to British art. The **Clore Gallery** continues to display the Turner Bequest of 282 oils and 19,000 watercolors; other painters featured heavily are William Blake, John Constable, Dante Gabriel Rossetti, Lucien Freud, and David Hockney. Despite the

Tate Modern's popular explosion, the annual **Turner Prize** for contemporary art is still held here. After a decade that saw Damien Hirst, Chris Ofili, and Rachel Whiteread take the prize, an apparent backlash started in 1999 when Tracey Emin's unmade bed famously failed to win. The short-listed works go on display from early November to mid-January every year.

VICTORIA AND ALBERT MUSEUM

Main entrance on Cromwell Rd., Kensington. ☎7942 2000; www.vam.ac.uk. Tube: South Kensington. Open Th-Tu 10am-5:45pm, W and last F of month 10am-10pm. Free; additional charge for some exhibitions. Free introductory tours daily 10:30, 11:30am, 1:30, 2:30pm; W also 4:30pm. Gallery talks daily 1pm. Free. Talks, tours, and live music W from 6:30pm; last F of month also fashion shows, debates, and DJs.

Founded in 1852 to encourage excellence in art and design, the V&A is the largest museum of the decorative arts in the world—as befits an institution dedicated to displaying "the fine and applied arts of all countries, all styles, all periods." The subject of a £31 million renovation, the vast **British Galleries** hold a series of recreated rooms from every period between 1500 and 1900, mirrored by the vast **Dress Collection,** a dazzling array of the finest *haute couture* through the ages. The ground-floor **European** collections range from 4th-century tapestries to Alfonse Mucha posters; if you only see one thing in the museum, make it the **Raphael Gallery,** hung with paintings commissioned by Leo X in 1515. The **Sculpture Gallery,** home to Canova's *Three Graces* (1814-17), is not to be confused with the **Cast Courts,** a plaster-cast collection of the world's sculptural greatest hits, from Trajan's Column to Michelangelo's *David.* The V&A's **Asian** collections are particularly formidable—if the choice of objects occasionally seems to rely on national cliches (Indian carvings, Persian carpets, Chinese porcelain, Japanese ceramics), it says more about how the V&A has formed opinion than followed it. In contrast to the geographically themed ground floor, the **upper levels** are mostly arranged in specialist galleries devoted to everything from jewelry to musical instruments to stained glass. An exception to the materially themed arrangements is the large **20th-century** collections, featuring design classics from Salvador Dalí's 1936 "Mae West" sofa lips to a pair of 1990s rubber hot pants. The six-level **Henry Cole wing** is home to a collection of **British paintings,** including some 350 works by Constable and numerous Turners. Also on display are a number of Rodin bronzes, donated by the artist in 1914, and a collection of **miniature portraits,** including Holbein's *Anne of Cleves.* The **Frank Lloyd Wright gallery** contains a full-size recreation of the office commissioned by Edgar J. Kauffmann for his Pittsburgh department store in 1935.

BRITAIN

OTHER MUSEUMS AND GALLERIES

Courtauld Institute, Somerset House, The Strand, Westminster (☎7848 2526). Tube: Charing Cross. Small, outstanding collection. 14th- to 20th-century abstractions, focusing on Impressionism. Manet's *A Bar at the Follies Bergères,* van Gogh's *Self Portrait with Bandaged Ear,* and Cézanne's *The Card Players.* Open M-Sa 10am-6pm. £5, students £4; free M 10am-2pm.

Natural History Museum, on Cromwell Rd., Kensington (☎7942 5000). Tube: South Kensington. Cathedral-like building home to an array of minerals and stuffed animals. Highlights include a frighteningly realistic T-Rex and the engrossing, interactive *Human Biology* gallery. Open M-Sa 10am-5:50pm, Su 11am-5:50pm. Free.

Royal Academy, Burlington House, Piccadilly, The West End (☎7300 8000). Tube: Piccadilly Circus. Founded in 1768 as both an art school and meeting place for Britain's foremost artists. Outstanding exhibitions on all manner of art. Open Sa-Th 10am-6pm, F 10am-10pm. Around £7; £1-4 student discounts.

Cabinet War Rooms, Clive Steps, Westminster (☎7930 6961). Tube: Westminster. The rooms where Churchill and his ministers, generals, and support staff lived and worked underground from 1939 to 1945. Highlights include the small room containing the top-secret transatlantic hotline—the official story was that it was Churchill's personal loo. Open Apr.-Sept. daily 9:30am-6pm; Oct.-Mar. 10am-6pm. £5.80, students £4.20.

London's Transport Museum, Covent Garden Piazza, The West End (☎7565 7299). Tube: Covent Garden or Charing Cross. Informative *and* fun. Kids and adults will find themselves engrossed in the history of London's public transportation system. Open Sa-Th 10am-6pm, F 11am-6pm. £6, students £4, under 16 free with adult.

Wallace Collection, Manchester Sq., Marylebone (☎7563 9500). Tube: Bond St. Palatial Hertford House holds a stunning array of porcelain, medieval armor, and weaponry. Open M-Sa 10am-5pm, Su noon-5pm. Free.

Imperial War Museum, Lambeth Rd., South London (☎7416 5320). Tube: Lambeth North. The commendably un-jingoistic exhibits follow every aspect of war from 1914 on, covering conflicts large and small. The largest and most publicized display, the Holocaust Exhibition, graphically documents Nazi atrocities. Open daily 10am-6pm. Free.

Institute of Contemporary Arts (ICA), Nash House, The West End (☎7930 3647). Tube: Charing Cross. Down the road from Buckingham Palace—convenient for questioning the establishment. Open M noon-11pm, Tu-Sa noon-1am, Su noon-10:30pm; galleries close 7:30pm. M-F £1.50, Sa-Su £2.50.

Sir John Soane's Museum, 13 Lincoln's Inn Fields, Holborn. Tube: Holborn. Architect John Soane built this intriguing museum for his own art collection. Open Tu-Sa 10am-5pm; first Tu of month also 6-9pm. Suggested donation £1.

Science Museum, Exhibition Rd., Kensington (☎(0870) 870 4868). Tube: South Kensington. A mix of state-of-the-art interactive displays and priceless historical artifacts, encompassing all forms of technology. Open daily 10am-6pm. Free.

Museum of London, London Wall, The City of London (☎7600 3699). Tube: Barbican. Enter through the Barbican. The engrossing collection traces the history of London from its foundations to the present day, with a particular focus on Roman objects. Open M-Sa 10am-6pm, Su noon-6pm; last admission 5:30pm. Free.

National Maritime Museum, Trafalgar Rd., Greenwich, East London (☎8858 4422). Docklands Light Railway: Cutty Sark. Broad-ranging, child-friendly displays cover almost every aspect of seafaring history. The naval portraits in the neighboring Queen's House take second place to Inigo Jones's architecture. Open June to early Sept. daily 10am-6pm; early Sept. to May 10am-5pm. Free.

National Portrait Gallery, St. Martin's Pl., Westminster (☎7312 2463). Tube: Charing Cross. The artistic *Who's Who* of Britain. Began in 1856 as "the fulfillment of a patriotic and moral ideal." Open Sa-W 10am-6pm, Th-F 10am-9pm. Free.

ENTERTAINMENT

On any given day or night in London, you can choose from the widest range of entertainment a city can offer. The West End could perhaps be called the world's theater capital; it is supplemented by an adventurous "fringe" and a justly famous National Theatre. New bands constantly emerge from London's many music venues. Dance, film, comedy, sports, and countless other happenings abound. *Time Out* (£2.20), which comes out every Wednesday and is available from newsstands, has indispensable listings.

THEATER

The stage for a national dramatic tradition over 500 years old, London theaters maintain an unrivaled breadth of choice. At a **West End** theater (a term referring to all the major stages, whether or not they're actually in the West End), you can expect a mainstream production, top-quality performers, and (usually) comfortable seats. **Off-West End** theaters usually present more challenging work, while remaining as professional as their West End brethren. The **Fringe** refers to the scores of smaller, less commercial theaters, often just a room in a pub basement with a few benches and a team of dedicated amateurs.

tkts, on the south side of Leicester Sq. (formerly the **Leicester Square Half-Price Ticket Booth**), releases half-price tickets on the day of the show. The catch is that you have to buy them in person, in cash, with no choice in seating (most expensive tickets sold first) and there's no way of knowing in advance what shows will have tickets available that day. Be prepared to wait, especially on Saturday. (Tube: Leicester Sq. £2.50 booking fee per ticket. Open M-Sa 10am-7pm, Su noon-3pm.)

Barbican Theatre, on Barbican (☎7638 8891), main entrance on Silk St. Tube: Barbican. A futuristic auditorium seating 1166 in steeply raked, forward-leaning balconies. The theater hosts touring companies and short-run shows. Tickets £6-30; cheapest M-F evening and Sa matinee. Student standbys from 9am day of performance. In the same complex, **The Pit** is an intimate 200-seat theater used primarily for new and experimental productions. Tickets £10-15.

National Theatre, just down river of Waterloo Bridge (info ☎7452 3400; box office ☎7452 3000). Tube: Waterloo. Since opening in 1963, the National has been at the forefront of British theater. The **Olivier** stage seats 10,800 in a fan-shaped open-stage layout. The **Lyttelton** is a proscenium theater with 890 seats. The 300-seat **Cottesloe** stages experimental dramas. Box office open M-Sa 10am-8pm. Tickets £10-33, students £8-15; same-day £10 from 10am, standby £15 2hr. before curtain.

Royal Court Theatre, Sloane Sq. (☎7565 5000). Dedicated to challenging new writing and innovative interpretations of classics. Experimental work runs in the intimate upstairs auditorium. Main stage £7-26, students £9; standing places £0.10 1hr. before curtain. Upstairs £12-15, students £9; M all seats £7.50.

Shakespeare's Globe Theatre, 21 New Globe Walk (☎7401 9919). Tube: London Bridge. A faithful reproduction of the original 16th-century playhouse where Shakespeare himself performed. Choose between the backless wooden benches or stand through a performance as a "groundling." For tours of the Globe, see **Sights,** p. 186. Performances mid-May to late Sept. Tu-Sa 7:30pm, Su 6:30pm; June to late Sept. also Tu-Sa 2pm, Su 1pm. Box office open M-Sa 10am-6pm, until 8pm on performance days. Seats £12-27, students £10-24; yard (standing) £5.

CINEMA

London's film scene offers everything. The heart of the celluloid monster is **Leicester Square** (p. 183), where the latest releases premiere a day before hitting the chains. The dominant mainstream cinema chain is **Odeon** (☎(0870) 505 000), while **The Empire** (☎(0870) 010 2030) is the most famous first-run theater. Tickets to West End cinemas cost £8-10; M-F screenings before 5pm are usually cheaper.

BFI London IMAX Cinema (☎7902 1234), at the south end of Waterloo Bridge, accessed via underground walkways. Tube: Waterloo. Stunning glass drum houses UK's biggest screen. £7.10, students and seniors £6, under 17 £5; additional film £4.20.

National Film Theatre (NFT) (☎7928 3232), on the south bank, right underneath Waterloo Bridge. Tube: Waterloo, Embankment, or Temple. One of the world's leading cinemas, with a mind-boggling array of films. 6 different movies hit the 3 screens every evening, starting around 6pm. £7.20, students £5.50.

The Prince Charles, Leicester Pl. (☎7957 4009). Tube: Leicester Sq. Features *Sing-a-long-a-Sound-of-Music*, where Von Trappists dress as everything from nuns to "Ray, a drop of golden sun" (F 7:30pm, Su 2pm; £12.50). Otherwise, screens second-run Hollywood and recent independent films. £3.50; M-F before 5pm £2, M evenings £2.

MUSIC

ROCK AND POP

Birthplace of the Rolling Stones, the Sex Pistols, and the Chemical Brothers, home to Madonna and Paul McCartney, London is a town steeped in rock 'n' roll history.

Borderline, Orange Yard (☎7395 0777), off Manette St. Tube: Tottenham Court Rd. Basement hosted secret REM gig years ago, now stages up-and-coming groups with a strong folk-rock flavor. Music M-Sa from 8pm. Box office open M-F 1-7:30pm. Tickets £5-10 in advance.

The Water Rats, 328 Grays Inn Rd. (☎7837 7269). Tube: King's Cross/St. Pancras. Pub-cafe by day, stomping venue for top new talent by night. Oasis was signed here after their first London gig. Cover £5, £4 with band's flyer. Open for coffee M-F 8am-noon, surprisingly good lunch (£5-6) served M-F noon-3pm, music M-Sa 8pm-11pm.

London Astoria (LA1), 157 Charing Cross Rd. (☎7344 0044). Tube: Tottenham Court Rd. Was a pickle factory, strip club, and music hall before turning into a full-time rock venue in the late 1980s. Hosts hip, not-quite-there-yet acts Su-W (£5-20). F-Sa hosts the popular G-A-Y club night (see p. 202).

Dublin Castle, 94 Parkway (☎8806 2668). There's music in the back every night, but Tu *Club Fandango* gets particularly intense when record execs and talent scouts descend looking for the next big thing. W-Sa after the bands play the room turns into a dance club until 1am. £5, students £4. 3 bands nightly 8:45-11pm; doors open 8:30pm.

CLASSICAL

Home to four world-class orchestras, three major concert halls, two opera houses, two ballet companies, and scores of chamber ensembles, London is center stage for serious music. To hear some of the world's top choirs for free, head to Westminster Abbey (p. 180) or St. Paul's Cathedral (p. 183) for Evensong.

English National Opera (☎7632 8300), at the Coliseum, St. Martin's Lane. Tube: Charing Cross or Leicester Sq. All the classics, plus contemporary and avant-garde work, sung in English. £6-60; under 18 half-price with adult. Same-day seats for the dress-circle (£31) and balcony (£3) released M-F 10am (12:30pm by phone). Standbys 3hr. before curtain; students £12.50, seniors £18.

Barbican Hall, same details as for Barbican Theatre (p. 195). One of Europe's leading concert halls. The resident **London Symphony Orchestra** plays throughout the year. Also hosts jazz, world musicians, and international orchestras. Tickets £6-35.

The Proms, at the Royal Albert Hall, Kensington Gore (www.bbc.co.uk/proms). Tube: Knightsbridge. Summer season of classical music, with concerts every night from mid-July to mid-Sept. "Promenade" refers to the tradition of selling dirt-cheap standing tickets; lines often start forming mid-afternoon. Tickets go on sale in mid-May (£5-30); standing places sold from 1½hr. before the concert (£4).

Royal Opera House, Bow St. (☎7304 4000). Tube: Covent Garden. Also home to the **Royal Ballet.** Productions tend to be conservative but lavish, like the wealthy patrons. Standing room and restricted-view seating in the upper balconies is under £5. Same-day seats £10-40 from 10am on performance day. Standby £12-15 4hr. before curtain.

Royal Festival Hall (☎7960 4242), on the south bank of the Thames between Hungerford and Waterloo Bridges. Tube: Waterloo or Embankment. 2700-seat concert hall with the best acoustics in London. The two resident orchestras, the **Philharmonic** and the **London Philharmonic,** predominate, but big-name jazz, Latin, and world-music groups also visit. Classical concerts £6-33; others £10-30.

JAZZ, FOLK, AND WORLD

London's jazz scene is small but serious; top clubs pull in big-name performers from around the world. Folk and world music keep an even lower profile, mostly restricted to pubs and community centers.

Ronnie Scott's, 47 Faith St. (☎7439 0747). Tube: Tottenham Court Rd. London's oldest and most famous jazz club. Music M-Sa 9:30pm-3am, Su 7:30-11:30pm. M-Th cover £15, F-Sa £25, Su £8-12; M-W students £10. Reservations recommended; if it's sold out, try coming back at midnight to catch the second set.

606 Club, 90 Lot's Rd. (☎7352 5953). Hard to find, but the intrepid will be rewarded with some of the best British and European jazz in a classic, smoky venue. M-W music 8-1:30am; Th doors open 8pm, music 9:30pm-1:30am; F-Sa doors open 8pm, music 10pm-2am; Su doors open 8pm, music 9pm-midnight.

SPECTATOR SPORTS

FOOTBALL. From late August to May, over half a million people attend professional football (soccer) matches every Saturday, dressed with fierce loyalty in team colors. Though violence at stadiums have plagued the game for years, the atmosphere has become much tamer now. The three major London teams are: **Arsenal,** Highbury Stadium, Avenell Rd. (☎7713 3366; Tube: Arsenal); **Chelsea,** Stamford Bridge, Fulham Rd. (☎7386 7799; Tube: Fulham Broadway); and **Tottenham Hotspur,** White Hart Lane (☎8365 5000; Tube: Seven Sisters).

RUGBY. Rugby was allegedly created when a confused Rugby School student picked up a regular football and ran it into the goal. The rugby season is from August to May; games are on weekend afternoons. The four major London teams are: **London Wasps** (☎8740 2545); **NEC Harlequins** (☎8410 6000); **Saracens** (☎(01923) 496 200); and **London Broncos** (☎8853 8800). International competitions, including the springtime **Six Nations Championship,** a contest between England, Scotland, Wales, Ireland, France, and Italy, are played at **Twickenham** (☎8831 6666; Rail: Twickenham); tickets are virtually impossible to get.

CRICKET. London's two cricket grounds stage both county and international contests. **Lord's,** on St. John's Wood Rd., is the home of the **Marylebone Cricket Club (MCC),** the established governing body of cricket. (☎7432 1066. Tube: St. John's Wood.) The **Oval,** on Kennington, also fields test matches. (☎7582 7764. Tube: Oval.) Every summer a touring nation plays England in a series of matches around the country, including a customary thrashing every four years at the hands of the **Australian Cricket Team.**

TENNIS. Every year for two weeks in late June and early July, tennis buffs the world over focus their attention on **Wimbledon.** Reserve months ahead or arrive by 6am (gates open 10:30am) to secure one of the 500 Centre and #1 court tickets sold every morning; otherwise, settle for a "grounds" ticket for the outer courts. (All England Lawn Tennis Club. ☎8971 2473. Tube: Southfields. Rail: Wimbledon. Grounds £9-11; after 5pm £5-7. Show courts £17-50.)

SHOPPING

From its earliest days, London has been a trading city, its wealth and power built upon almost two millennia of commerce. Today, even more so than at the height of the Empire, London's economy is truly international—and thanks to the fundamentally eclectic nature of Londoners' diverse tastes, the range of goods is unmatched anywhere. From Harrods's proud boast to supply "all things to all people" to outrageous club wear in Camden, you could shop for a lifetime.

DEPARTMENT STORES

Fortnum & Mason, 181 Piccadilly (☎7734 8040). Tube: Green Park. Founded in 1707. Famed for a sumptuous food hall with liveried clerks, chandeliers, and fountains. London's snootiest department store. Open M-Sa 10am-6:30pm. AmEx/MC/V.

Harrods, 87-135 Old Brompton Rd. (☎7730 1234). Tube: Knightsbridge. The only thing bigger than the store itself is the mark-up. No wonder only tourists and oil sheikhs actually shop here. Bewildering. Open M-Sa 10am-7pm. AmEx/MC/V.

Harvey Nichols, 109-125 Knightsbridge (☎7235 5000). Tube: Knightsbridge. Imagine Bond St., rue St-Honoré, and Fifth Avenue all rolled up into 5 fl. of the biggest names in fashion and the hippest contemporary unknowns. Open M-Tu and Sa 10am-7pm, W-F 10am-8pm, Su noon-6pm. AmEx/MC/V.

Selfridges, 400 Oxford St. (☎(0870) 837 7377). Tube: Bond St. With 14 cafes and restaurants, a hair salon, and a hotel, shopaholics need never leave. Open M-W 10am-7pm, Th-F 10am-8pm, Sa 9:30am-7pm, Su noon-6pm. AmEx/ MC/V.

CLOTHING AND FOOTWEAR

Cyberdog/Cybercity, Stables Market (☎7482 2842). Tube: Camden Town. Unbelievable club clothes for superior life forms. Alien goddesses will want to try on steel corsets with rubber breast hoses. Open M-F 11am-6pm, Sa-Su 10am-7pm. AmEx/MC/V.

Miss Sixty, 39 Neal St. (☎7836 3789). Tube: Covent Garden. The newest clothing craze. Bright, patterned, and skin-hugging female fashions in a laid-back and sexy style. Open M-W and F-Sa 10am-6:30pm, Th 10am-7:30pm, Su noon-6pm. AmEx/MC/V. Nearby is the recently opened men's equivalent, **Energie** (47-49 Neal St.).

Dr. Marten's Dept. Store, 1-4 King St. (☎7497 1460). Tube: Covent Garden. Tourist-packed 5-tiered megastore. Baby Docs, papa Docs, and the classic yellow-stitched boots. Open M-W and F-Sa 10am-7pm, Th 10:30am-8pm, Su noon-6pm. AmEx/MC/V.

Dolly Diamond, 51 Pembridge Rd. (☎7792 2479). Tube: Notting Hill Gate. Jackie Onassis or Audrey Hepburn? Choose your look from the great selection of classic 50s-70s clothes, along with some elegant 20s-40s evening gowns. Open M-F 10:30am-6:30pm, Sa 9:30am-6:30pm, Su noon-6pm.

BOOKSTORES

Even the chain bookstores are wonders in London. An exhaustive selection of bookshops lines Charing Cross Rd. between Tottenham Court Rd. and Leicester Sq.; many sell second-hand paperbacks. Establishments along Great Russell St., by the British Museum, and in Cecil Court, near Leicester Sq., stock esoteric and specialized books subjects from Adorno to the Zohar.

Sotheran's of Sackville Street, 2-5 Sackville St. (☎7439 6151). Tube: Piccadilly Circus. Hushed atmosphere gives an impression of exclusivity, but affordable books abound. Charming staff. Open M-F 9:30am-6pm, Sa 10am-4pm. AmEx/MC/V.

Waterstone's, 203-206 Piccadilly (☎7851 2400). Tube: Piccadilly Circus. Europe's largest bookstore. The 8 fl. house a cafe, Internet station, and posh basement restaurant. Open M-Sa 10am-11pm, Su noon-6pm. AmEx/MC/V.

RECORD STORES

London crawls with music junkies, and the city has a record collection to match. Don't expect any bargains; remember, when it comes to records, "import" means "rip-off." Megastores carry vinyl versions of most major-label releases, but to get rare promos, white labels, or collectibles, go to an independent record store.

HMV, 150 Oxford St. (☎7631 3423). Tube: Oxford Circus. 3 massive fl. Exceptional range. Open M-Tu and Th-Sa 9am-8pm, W 9am-7pm, Su noon-6pm. AmEx/DC/MC/V.

Rough Trade, 130 Talbot Rd. (☎7229 8541). Tube: Ladbroke Grove. **Branch** at 16 Neal's Yard (☎7240 0105; Tube: Covent Garden). Short, well-opinionated reviews tacked to most CDs and records. Open M-Sa 10am-6:30pm, Su 1-5pm. AmEx/MC/V.

Uptown Records, 3 D'Arblay St. (☎7434 3639). Tube: Oxford Circus. Ever wondered what DJs do in the daytime? You'll find lots of them working in this small all-vinyl store. Open M-W and F-Sa 10:30am-7pm, Th 10:30am-8pm. AmEx/MC/V.

STREET MARKETS

Camden Markets, off Camden High St. and Chalk Farm Rd. Tube: Camden Town. London's 4th-biggest tourist attraction. On Su the market fills with hordes looking for the latest mainstream, vintage, and off-beat fashions.

Stables Market, farthest from the station and the best of the bunch. The railway arches hold club wear and a good selection of vintage clothes. Open F-Sa, a few shops open M-Th.

Camden Lock Market, from the railway bridge to the canal. Arranged around food-filled courtyard. Indoor shops sell pricier items (carpets, household goods). Most stalls operate F or Sa-Su only.

Camden Canal Market, down tunnel opposite the Lock, starts promisingly (jewelry, watches), but degenerates (sub-par club wear, tourist trinkets). Good spot for a bite to eat, though. Open F-Su.

Brick Lane Market. Tube: Shoreditch or Aldgate East. Famous weekly market with a South Asian flair (food, rugs, spices, bolts of fabric, strains of sitar). Open Su 8am-2pm.

Petticoat Lane Market. Tube: Liverpool St., Aldgate, or Aldgate East. Block after block of cheap clothing, with lots of leather jackets around Aldgate East. The real action begins at about 9:30am. Open Su 9am-2pm; starts shutting down around noon.

OTHER SPECIALTY STORES

Lush (☎(01202) 668 545). 6 locations, including: 123 King's Rd. (Tube: Sloane Sq.); Covent Garden Piazza (Tube: Covent Garden); 40 Carnaby St. (Tube: Oxford Circus). All-natural cosmetics that look good enough to eat. Vegan cosmetics with a green dot.

Hamley's, 188-189 Regent St. (☎7734 3161). Tube: Oxford Circus. 7 fl. stuffed with every conceivable toy. Open M-F 10am-8pm, Sa 9:30am-8pm, Su noon-6pm.

Trainings, 216 Strand (☎7353 3511). Tube: Temple. London's narrowest shop sells noble tea blends. Tiny museum in the back. Open M-F 9:30am-4:45pm. AmEx/MC/V.

NIGHTLIFE

The **West End**—especially **Soho**—is the scene of most of London's after-dark action, from the glitzy Leicester Sq. tourist traps, like the Hippodrome and Equinox, to semi-secret underground clubs. The other major axis of London nightlife is East London's **Shoreditch** and **Hoxton** (known as Shoo).

THE WEST END

PUBS

Dog and Duck, 18 Batman St., Soho (☎7494 0697). The oldest and smallest pub in Soho. The name and decor serve as a reminder of the area's hunting past. Open M-F noon-11pm, Sa 2-11pm, Su 6-10:30pm.

Lamb and Flag, 33 Rose St., Covent Garden (☎7497 9504). Tube: Leicester Sq. Traditional dark-wood interior. Food daily noon-3pm. Live jazz upstairs Su 7:30pm. Open M-Th 11am-11pm, F-Sa 11am-10:45pm, Su noon-10:30pm.

BARS

Freud, 198 Shaftesbury Ave., Covent Garden (☎7240 9933). Invigorate your psyche in this off-beat underground hipster hangout. Occasional live music. Cheap cocktails (from £3.40). Light meals noon-4:30pm (£3.50-6). No cover. Open M-Sa 11am-11pm, Su noon-10:30pm. MC/V.

Point 101, 101 New Oxford St. (☎7379 3112), underneath the Centripetal office tower. Tube: Tottenham Court Rd. 1970s decor. Long vinyl booths line the balcony bar (accessed via a separate door). Nightly DJs tend toward jazz, Latin, and soul. Big crowds, but enough space for all. Open M-Th 8am-2am, F-Sa 8am-2:30am, Su 8am-11:30pm. AmEx/MC/V.

NIGHTCLUBS

Sound, 10 Wardour St., Soho (☎7287 1010). Tube: Leicester Sq. A real labyrinth, with rooms hidden over 4 fl. Music styles vary greatly; call ahead. Cover £8, before 11pm £6. Open daily 10pm-3am.

Velvet Room, 143 Charing Cross Rd., Soho (☎7734 4687). Tube: Tottenham Court Rd. Small, and showing its age, but packed even mid-week. Come here for the music, not the posing scene. Cover £5-10. M gay night, with R&B and hip-hop (10pm-3am). W *Swerve* with Brazilian-flavored drum and bass (10pm-2:30am). House and garage dominate the weekend (F-Sa 10pm-4am, Su 7pm-midnight).

BLOOMSBURY

PUBS

The Lamb, 94 Lamb's Conduit St. (☎7405 0713). Tube: Russell Sq. This old-fashioned pub is an actors' hangout. Peter Tooley is a regular, and fading daguerreotypes of past thespian tipplers line the walls. The "snob screens" around the bar originally provided privacy for "respectable" men meeting with ladies of ill-repute. Food served M-Sa noon-2:30pm and daily 6-9pm. Open M-Sa 11am-11pm, Su noon-10:30pm. MC/V.

BARS

AKA, 18 West Central St. (☎7419 9199). Tube: Tottenham Ct. Rd. There's nowhere like the candlelit island lounge for people watching. Cocktails £6-7. It's "members only," but you can join at the door. Casual to smart casual dress. Cover free-£10. Open Su-F 6pm-3am, Sa 7pm-7am; food served until 1am.

BRITAIN

CLERKENWELL

BARS

Match EC1, 45-47 Clerkenwell Rd. (☎7250 4002). Tube: Farringdon. A sign outside bemoans the "virus of trendy new bars." Match resists pretense with an emphasis on cocktails (£6). Lounge on the plush sofas, eat in one of the snug booths (entrees £6-11), or crush into the sunken bar. Open M-Sa 11am-midnight. AmEx/MC/V.

NIGHTCLUBS

Fabric, 77a Chartreuse St. (☎7336 8898). Tube: Farringdon. Bigger than a B52 and 100 times as loud. When they power up the underfoot suborder, lights dim across London. 3 dance fl., chill-out beds, multiple bars, and unisex toilets, all crammed with up to 2500 dance-crazed Londoners. Yow. F *Fabric Live* (hip-hop, break-beat; 9:30pm-5am), Sa mega dance fest *Fabric* (house, techno; 9:30pm-7am). Cover £10-15.

NOTTING HILL

BARS

Pharmacy, 150 Notting Hill Gate (☎7221 2442). Tube: Notting Hill Gate. This Domain First-designed joint is *so* aptly named, darling. Clinical environment of bright lights and medicine cabinets—though there'd be an outcry if drug companies charged this much (cocktails £6-7). The American-style Sunday brunch (£5-10) is increasingly popular. Bar open Su-Th noon-3pm and 5pm-1am, F-Sa noon-3pm and 5pm-2am. AmEx/MC/V.

NORTH LONDON

NIGHTCLUBS

Scala, 275 Pentagonal Rd. (☎7833 2022; tickets ☎(0870) 0600 100). Tube: Kings Cross. Huge main floor embraces its cinematic past: DJs spin from the projectionist's box, ramped balconies provide multiple levels, and a giant screen pulsates with visuals as 3m pyramids of speakers detonate the bass. F gay/mixed eclectica (10pm-5am); Sa blend of garage and R&B; every other Su *Latin 8* has 6 hours of salsa with a free dance workshop 8:30-9:30pm (8pm-2am). Dress code enforced. Cover £8-10.

EAST LONDON

BARS

Soshomatch, 2 Tabernacle St. (☎7920 0701). Tube: Moorgate. A 2-floor bar/restaurant that converts into a stylish club Th-Sa. DJ-driven atmosphere with acres of comfy leather couches. F-Sa cover £5. Open M-W 11am-midnight, Th-Sa 11am-2am. AmEx/MC/V.

Vibe Bar, 91-95 Brick Ln. (☎7247 3479). Tube: Aldgate East. Young, fun, clubby bar, with an interior straight out of a magazine. M-Sa DJs from 7:30pm, Su from 6:30pm. In summer, a second DJ works the shady courtyard. Tends towards soul/jazz/funk. Occasional cover £2. Open Su-Th noon-11pm, F-Sa noon-1am.

NIGHTCLUBS

93 Feet East, 150 Brick Ln. (☎7247 3293). Tube: Aldgate East. One of the hottest new clubs in East London. Barn-like main dance floor, sofa-strewn room upstairs. W salsa with a live Latin band (7-11pm); Th world-dance mixes (9pm-3am); F techno and house (9pm-3am); Sa anything from house to ska (9pm-2am). Cover £3-10.

Cargo, 83 Rivington St., Kingsland Viaduct (☎7739 3440). Tube: Old Street. Despite the superclub trimmings—two enormous arched rooms, fab acoustics, movie projectors, and an intimate candle-lit lounge—Cargo is crippled by a 1am license. On the plus side, the place is kicking by 9:30pm. Strong Latin lineup with mixing DJs and live music. Cover £3-7. Open M-F noon-1am, Sa 6pm-1am, Su noon-midnight.

SOUTH LONDON

BARS

The Dogstar, 389 Coldharbour Ln. (☎7733 7515). Tube: Brixton. At 9pm, the tables are cleared from the dance floor and the projectors turned on. House, hiphop, and dance music. Su-Th no cover; F before 10pm free, 10-11pm £4, after 11pm £5; Sa before 10pm free, 10-11pm £5, after 11pm £7. Open Su-Th noon-2am, F-Sa noon-4am.

NIGHTCLUBS

The Fridge, Town Hall Parade, Brixton Hill (☎7326 5100). Tube: Brixton. Turn left from the station and bear right at the fork onto Brixton Hill; it's opposite the church. Giant split-level dance floor. F trance glo-stick madness; Sa usually gay night. Cover £10-17;

sometimes less before 10:30pm. Open F-Sa 10pm-6am. After-parties start Sa-Su 5:30am at the neighboring **Fridge Bar;** cover £6.

Ministry of Sound, 103 Gaunt St. (☎ 7378 6528). Tube: Elephant and Castle. Take the exit for South Bank University. The granddaddy of serious clubbing. Arrive early or wait in line all night. Dress code generally casual, but famously unsmiling door staff makes it sensible to err on the side of dressy (no sneakers). F garage and R&B (10:30pm-5am); Sa US and vocal house (11pm-8am). Cover £12-15.

GAY AND LESBIAN NIGHTLIFE

London has a very visible gay scene, ranging from flamboyant to mainstream. *Time Out* devotes a section to gay listings, and gay newspapers include *Capital Gay*, *Pink Paper*, and *Shebang* (for women). *Boyz* magazine, free from gay bars, and the *Ginger Beer* website (www.gingerbeer.co.uk) track the gay and lesbian nightlife scene respectively. Soho—especially **Old Compton Street**—is the heart of gay London, with much smaller scenes in Islington, Earl's Court, and Brixton.

79CXR, 79 Charing Cross Rd. (☎ 7734 0769). Tube: Leicester Sq. This split-level gay bar is notable for its late hours. Happy Hour daily 8-10pm. Cover after 10:30pm £3. Open M 1pm-2am, Tu-Sa 1pm-3am, Su 1-10:30pm.

The Box, 32-34 Monmouth St. (☎ 7240 5828). Recently renovated, this spacious gay/mixed bar-brasserie is popular with a stylish media/fashion crowd. Daily food specials (entrees around £9). Also sells club tickets. Food served until 5pm. Open M-Sa 11am-11pm, Su 7-10:30pm. MC/V.

Comptons of Soho, 53 Old Compton St. (☎ 7479 7461). Tube: Leicester Sq. or Piccadilly Circus. Soho's "official" gay pub is always busy. Horseshoe bar encourages the exchange of meaningful glances, while upstairs (opens 6pm) offers a more mellow scene and a pool table. Open M-Sa 11am-11pm, Su noon-10:30pm. MC/V.

G-A-Y (☎ 7434 9592; www.g-a-y.co.uk). M and Th at the Mean Fiddler, 165 Charing Cross Rd.; F-Sa at the London Astoria, 157 Charing Cross Rd. Tube: Tottenham Court Rd. London's biggest gay and lesbian night, 4 nights a week. M *Pink Pounder* 90s classics with 70s-80s faves in the bar; F *Camp Attack* 70s and 80s cheese; Sa *G-A-Y* big night out, rocking the capacity crowd with commercial-dance DJs and live pop performances. Cover free-£10. Open M, Th, F until 4am, Sa until 5am.

Heaven, The Arches, Craven Terr. (☎ 7930 2020). Tube: Charing Cross or Embankment. Though running regular mixed nights, it's the self-proclaimed "world's most famous gay disco." Intricate interior rewards explorers. Fantastically lit main floor, second room upstairs, a coffee bar, and an elusive red-themed chill-out room. M mixed (chart-toppers, 70s-80s disco, house); W gay (house, garage, soul, and swing); F mixed (hard house trance); Sa gay/lesbian *Heaven* dance (trance, house, disco). Cover £4-12. Open daily 10:30pm-3am, Sa until 5:30am.

Vespa Lounge, St. Giles Circus (☎ 7836 8956). Tube: Tottenham Court Rd. Relaxed lesbian lounge bar with comfy seats, pool table. Thai food from downstairs Conservatory restaurant. First Su of month "Laughing Cows" comedy night (£4-6), plus occasional theme nights. Gay men welcome as guests. Open M-Sa 6-11pm.

DAYTRIPS FROM LONDON

OXFORD. This university town bustles with activity and overflows with grandeur. Enjoy the punting and the festivals (see p. 213).

STRATFORD-UPON-AVON. Stratford crawls with everything Shakespeare. Enjoy a show and explore the Bard's birthplace and various residences (see p. 219).

STONEHENGE. The incredible 7m high monoliths of Stonehenge, which date from 1500 BC, lie near Salisbury, less than 2hr. by train from London (see p. 207).

WINDSOR. **Windsor Castle** houses sumptuous rooms, rare artwork, and, on occasion, the Queen herself. And **Eton** educated those princes charming (see p. 218).

SOUTHERN ENGLAND

Southern England's history has deep continental roots. Early Britons settled the pastoral counties of Kent, Sussex, and Hampshire after crossing the Channel. Later, William the Conqueror left his mark in the form of awe-inspiring cathedrals, many built around settlements begun by Romans. During WWII, German bombings uncovered long-buried evidence of an invasion by Caesar. This historied landscape, so intertwined with that of continental Europe, has in turn had a profound influence on the country's national identity, inspiring such distinctly British literati as Geoffrey Chaucer, Jane Austen, and E.M. Forster. For detailed info on over- and underwater transport options to the Continent, see p. 47.

CANTERBURY ☎01227

Archbishop Thomas à Becket was beheaded at **Canterbury Cathedral** in 1170 after an irate Henry II asked, "Will no one rid me of this troublesome priest?" Later, in his famed *Canterbury Tales*, Chaucer captured the irony of tourists visiting England's most famous execution site. (☎762 862. Open M-Sa 9am-5pm, Su 12:30-2:30pm and 4:30-5:30pm. £3, students £2. Audio tour £2.50.) **The Canterbury Tales,** on St. Margaret's St., is a museum that simulates the journey of Chaucer's pilgrims. (☎479 227. Open July-Aug. daily 9am-5:30pm; Mar.-June and Sept.-Oct. daily 9:30am-5:30pm; Nov.-Feb. Su-F 10am-4:30pm, Sa 9:30am-5:30pm. £6, students £5.50.) On Stour St., the **Canterbury Heritage Museum** tells the history of Canterbury from medieval times to WWII. (☎452 747. Open June-Oct. M-Sa 10:30am-5pm, Su 1:30-5pm; Nov.-May M-Sa 10:30am-5pm. £2.60, students £1.70.) For a quiet break, walk to the riverside gardens of England's first Franciscan friary, **Greyfriars,** Stour St. (Open in summer M-F 2-4pm. Free.)

Trains from London Victoria arrive at Canterbury's **East Station** (1½hr., 2 per hr., £15.90), while trains from London Charing Cross and Waterloo arrive at **West Station** (1½hr., every hr., £15.90). National Express **buses** (☎(08705) 808 080) arrive from London at St. George's Ln. (2hr., every hr., £9.50). The **tourist office** is in The Buttermarket, 12-13 Sun St. (☎378 100. Open M-Sa 9:30am-5:30pm, Su 10am-4pm.) **B&Bs** cluster near West Station, around **High Street,** and on **New Dover Road.** The front rooms of **The Tudor House** ❷, 6 Best Ln., off High St., have incredible views of the cathedral. (☎765 650. Singles £18-22; doubles £36-38, with bath £44-45.) The **YHA Canterbury** ❷, 54 New Dover Rd., is in a beautiful old house. (☎462 911. Kitchen. Internet £2.50 per 30min. Reception 7:30-10am and 1-11pm. Dorms £11.25, under 18 £8.) **The Camping and Caravaning Club Site** ❶, on Bekesbourne Ln., has good facilities. (☎463 216. £5 per tent, plus £4-5.50 per person.) **Marlowe's** ❷, 55 St. Peter's St., serves an eclectic mix of English and Mexican food. (Entrees €7-10. Open daily 11:30am-10:30pm.) For groceries, head to **Safeway** supermarket, on St. George's Pl. (☎769 335. Open M-F 8am-8pm, Su 10am-4pm.) **Postal Code:** CT1 2BA.

DOVER ☎01304

While the city's tranquility is often disrupted by the puttering of ferries and the hum of hovercrafts, the splendor of this transportation hub survives in the magnificent **Dover Castle,** which reigns supreme over the famous **White Cliffs.** (Buses from the town center run Apr.-Sept. daily every hr., fare £0.55. Open Apr.-Sept.

BRITAIN

daily 10am-6pm; Oct. 10am-5pm; Nov.-Mar. 10am-4pm. £7.50, students £5.60, children £3.80, families £18.80.) **Trains** arrive at Dover's **Priory Station** from London Victoria, Waterloo East, London Bridge, and Charing Cross stations (2hr., 2 per hr., £21). National Express **buses** (☎(08705) 808 080) run from London Victoria to the bus station on Pencester Rd. and then on to the Eastern Docks (2¾hr., 23 per day, £10), where **ferries** and **hovercraft** depart from the Prince of Wales Pier for Calais (foot passengers £17-27). The **tourist office,** on Townwall St., has lodging info and ferry and hovercraft tickets. (☎205 108. Open daily 9am-6pm.) The **YHA Charlton House ❷,** 306 London Rd., is 800m from the train station; turn left onto Folkestone Rd., then left again at the roundabout onto High St., which becomes London Rd. (☎201 314. Kitchen. Lockout 10am-1pm. Curfew 11pm. Dorms £11, under 18 £7.80.) The **Gladstone Guest House ❸,** 3 Laureston Pl., offers wonderful views and tastefully decorated rooms with hand-crafted furniture. (☎208 457. Singles £25-28; doubles £44-48.) Cheap food is available on **London Road** and **Biggin Street,** home to many fish and chip shops. **Cullins Yard ❸,** 11 Cambridge Rd., is a nice seafood restaurant. (Entrees £10-20.) **Postal Code:** CT16 1PW.

BRIGHTON ☎01273

According to legend, the future King George IV scuttled into Brighton (pop. 250,000) for some decidedly common hanky-panky around 1784. Today, Brighton is still the unrivaled home of the "dirty weekend"—it sparkles with a tawdry luster all its own. Before indulging, check out England's long-time obsession with the Far East at the excessively ornate **Royal Pavilion,** on Pavilion Parade, next to Old Steine. (Open June-Sept. daily 10am-6pm, Oct.-May 10am-5pm. £5.20, students £3.75. Guided tours at 11:30am and 2:30pm, £1.25. Audio tour £1.) Around the corner on Church St. stands the **Brighton Museum and Art Gallery,** with paintings, English pottery, and a wild collection of Art Deco and Art Nouveau pieces—leer at Salvador Dalí's sexy red sofa, *Mae West's Lips.* (Open Tu 10am-7pm, W-Sa 10am-5pm, Su 2-5pm. Free.) Before heading out to the rocky **beach,** stroll the **Lanes,** a jumble of 17th-century streets forming the heart of Old Brighton.

Brighton has plenty of nightlife options; for tips, pick up *The Punter* or *What's On* at music stores, news agents, and pubs. Sample the hot chocolate and dark rum concoction at the trendy pub **Mash Tun,** 1 Church St., which attracts an eclectic student crowd. (Open M-Sa noon-11pm, Su noon-10:30pm.) Relax with a drink on the sand at **Fortune of War,** 157 King's Rd., the place to be at sunset. (Open M-Sa 10:30am-11pm, Su 11am-10:30pm.) Most clubs are open M-Sa 9pm-2am. Brighton native Fatboy Slim still mixes occasionally at **The Beach,** 171-181 King's Rd., a popular shore-side club. **Casablanca,** on Middle St., plays live jazz to a predominantly student crowd. **Event II,** on West St., is crammed with the down-from-London crowd looking for thrills. Gay clubbers flock to the zany **Zanzibar,** 129 James St., for drinks and nightly entertainment.

Trains (☎(0345) 484 950) leave from the station at the northern end of Queen's Rd. for London (1¼hr., 6 per hr., £11.90) and Portsmouth (1½hr., every hr., £11.70). National Express **buses** (☎(08705) 808 080) arrive at Pool Valley from London (2hr., 15 per day, round-trip £8). The **tourist office** is at 10 Bartholomew Sq. (☎(0906) 711 2255. Open M-F 9am-5pm, Sa 10am-5pm; Mar.-Oct. also Su 10am-4pm.) Rest at **Baggies Backpackers ❷,** 33 Oriental Pl., which has exquisite murals and frequent live music. Head west of West Pier along King's Rd., and Oriental Pl. is on the right. (☎733 740. Dorms £11; doubles £27.) The rowdy **Brighton Backpackers Hostel ❷,** 75-76 Middle St., features a downstairs lounge that functions as an all-night party spot. (☎777 717. Dorms £11-12; doubles £25-30.) Crowds pack **Food for Friends ❶,** 17a-18a Prince Albert St., a delicious vegetarian cafe. (Entrees £2-6. Open M-Sa 8am-10pm, Su 9:15am-10pm.) **Postal Code:** BN1 1BA.

CHICHESTER ☎01243

The remains of Roman walls and an imposing Norman cathedral provide the backdrop for Chichester's (pop. 30,000) superb theater, arts festivals, and gallery exhibits. The **cathedral,** built in 1091, houses a glorious stained glass window by Marc Chagall. (Open daily 7:30am-7pm; off-season 7:30am-5pm. £2 donation encouraged.) **Chichester Festival Theatre,** Oaklands Park, was founded by Sir Laurence Olivier, and has attracted artists such as Maggie Smith, Kathleen Turner, and Julie Christie. (Open M-Sa 9am-8pm. £15-20, same-day discounts.) The remarkably well-preserved **Roman Palace** in nearby **Fishbourne,** dating from AD 80, is the largest Roman residence ever excavated in Britain. Follow the signs from the end of Westgate St.; the palace is 3km west of town. (Open Mar.-July and Sept.-Oct. daily 10am-5pm; Aug. 10am-6pm; Feb. and Nov.-Dec. 10am-4pm; Jan. Su 10am-4pm. £4.70, students £4.) A gorgeous fairy-tale **castle,** one of the best in Britain, sits in nearby **Arundel.** (☎(01903) 882 173. Open Apr.-Oct. Su-F noon-5pm. £7.50, children £5, families £21.) Trains run to Arundel from Chichester (20min., 2 per hr., £3.40).

Trains (☎(08457) 484 950) run to: Brighton (50min., 2-3 per hr., round-trip £8.10); London Victoria (1½hr., 3 per hr., round-trip £17.20); and Portsmouth (40min., 2-3 per hr., round-trip £4.90). **Buses** (☎(01903) 237 661) depart from opposite the train station on Southgate. National Express runs to London (1 per day, round-trip £9). Coastline serves Brighton (#702; 3hr., 2 per hr., £4.60) and Portsmouth (#700 and 701; 1hr., 2 per hr., £4). To get to the **tourist office,** 29a South St., turn left as you exit the station onto Southgate, which becomes South St. (☎775 888. Open M-Sa 9:15am-5:15pm; July-Aug. also Su 10am-4pm.) **Bayleaf ❸,** 16 Whyke Rd., pampers guests with colorful geraniums and made-to-order breakfasts. (☎774 330. £23 per person.) Camp at **Southern Leisure Centre ❶,** on Vinnetrow Rd., a 15min. walk out of town. (☎787 715. Open Apr.-Oct. £3 per person, £8-10 per tent.) **Postal Code:** PO19 1AB.

PORTSMOUTH ☎023

Set Victorian seaside holidays against prostitutes, drunkards, and a lot of bloody cursing sailors, and the 900-year history of Portsmouth (pop. 190,500) will emerge. On the **seafront,** visitors relive D-Day, explore warships, and learn of the days when Britannia truly ruled the waves. War buffs and historians will want to plunge head first into the unrivaled ■**Portsmouth Historic Dockyard,** in the Naval Base, which houses a fleet of Britain's most storied ships, including Henry VIII's *Mary Rose,* the HMS *Victory,* and the HMS *Warrior.* The entrance is next to the tourist office on The Hard. (Ships open Mar.-Oct. daily 10am-5:30pm; Nov.-Feb. 10am-5pm. Individual site tickets £6. All-inclusive ticket £18, seniors and children £14.50.) The ■**D-Day Museum,** on Clarence Esplanade, leads visitors through life-size dioramas of the 1944 invasion. (Open Apr.-Sept. daily 10am-5:30pm; Oct.-Mar. 10am-5pm. £5, seniors £3.75, students £3, families £13.)

Trains (☎(0345) 484 950) run to Southsea Station, on Commercial Rd., from Chichester (40min., 2 per hr., £4) and London Waterloo (1½hr., 3 per hr., £20). National Express **buses** (☎(08705) 808 080) arrive from London (2½hr., every hr., £10.50) and Salisbury (2hr., every hr., £8.25). The **tourist office** is on The Hard, next to the dockyard. (☎9282 6722. Open daily 9:30am-5:45pm.) Moderately priced **B&Bs** (around £20) clutter **Southsea,** 2½km east of The Hard along the coast. Take any Southsea bus and get off at The Strand to reach the energetic ■**Portsmouth and Southsea Backpackers Lodge ❷,** 4 Florence Rd. (☎9283 2495. Internet £1 per 15min. Dorms £10; doubles £22.) **Birchwood Guest House ❷,** 44 Waverly Rd., offers bright, spacious rooms and an ample breakfast. (☎9281 1337. Singles £18; doubles £40.) The owner of the **Brittania Guest House ❸,** 48 Granada Rd., loves to share his mari-

BRITAIN

time interests with guests. (☎814 234. Full breakfast included. Singles £20; doubles £40-45.) **Country Kitchen ❶**, 59a Marmion Rd., serves savory vegetarian and vegan entrees. (£4-6. Open daily 9:30am-5pm.) **Pubs** near The Hard provide weary sailors with galley fare and jars of gin. **Postal Code:** PO1 1AA.

ISLE OF WIGHT ☎01983

Life on the Isle has softened the hardest of hearts through the centuries, from Queen Victoria to Karl Marx, who proclaimed the island "a little paradise!" The **Osborne House** was meant to serve as Queen Victoria's "modest" country home and refuge from affairs of state; she used it as a long-term retreat after Albert's death in 1861 and died here herself 40 years later. To reach Osborne House, take Southern Vectis bus #4 or 5 from **Ryde,** the best base town for the island. (Open Apr.-Sept. daily 10am-6pm; Oct. 10am-5pm; Nov. to mid-Dec. and Feb.-Mar. by tour only. House and grounds £7.50, students £5.60, under 16 £3.80. Grounds only £4/£3/£2.) On the western tip of the island, the white chalk **Needles** jut into a dark sea; cruises in **Alum Bay** afford a good view. (Purchase tickets at the Ryde bus station. £12, seniors £11, children £6.50; includes transport from Ryde). Explore the island's 800km of well-maintained footpaths during the annual **Walking Festival** (mid-May) and **Cycling Festival** (late Sept.), when participants pace along scenic routes or race over strenuous courses.

Wight Link (☎(0870) 582 7744) **ferries** go from the Portsmouth harbor to Ryde (15min., round-trip £11.70). The Ryde **tourist office** is on Western Esplanade, opposite Ryde Pier. (☎562 905. Open M-Sa 9:30am-5:30pm, Su 10am-4pm.) Accommodations on Wight usually require a two-night minimum stay. **Claverton House ❸,** 12 The Strand, Ryde, features lavishly appointed bedrooms and a breathtaking ocean view from the dining room. (☎613 015. £40 per person for 2 nights.) The friendly proprietor of **Seaward Guest House ❷,** 14-16 George St., Ryde, offers airy, pastel rooms and hearty breakfasts. (☎563 168. Singles £18-20; doubles £30-36, with bath £36-44.) Feast on gourmet baguettes and pastries (£1.30-3.30) from the **Baguette Factory ❶,** 24 Cross St., Ryde. (Open M-Sa 8:30am-4pm.)

WINCHESTER ☎01962

BRITAIN

The glory of Winchester (pop. 32,000) stretches back to Roman times, when William the Conqueror deemed it the center of his kingdom. Duck under the archway, pass through the square, and behold the 900-year-old **Winchester Cathedral,** 5 The Close. Famed for the small stone figure in its nave, the 169m long cathedral is the longest medieval building in Europe; the interior holds magnificent tiles and Jane Austen's tomb. The **Norman crypt,** supposedly the oldest in England, can be viewed only in the summer by guided tour. The 12th-century Winchester Bible resides in the library. (Open daily 7:15am-5:30pm; East End closes at 5pm. Free tours 10am-3pm. Suggested donation £3.50, students £2.30.) About 25km north of Winchester is the meek village of **Chawton,** where Jane Austen lived. It was in her cottage that she penned *Pride and Prejudice*, *Emma*, *Northanger Abbey*, and *Persuasion*, among others. Many of her manuscripts are on display. Take Hampshire **bus** #X64 (M-Sa 11 per day, round-trip £5.30), or the London and Country bus #65 from the bus station (Su); ask to be let off at the Chawton roundabout and follow the signs. (☎(01420) 83 262. Open Mar.-Dec. daily 11am-4:30pm; Jan.-Feb. Sa-Su 11am-4:30pm. £4, students £3, under 18 £0.50.)

Trains (☎(08547) 484 950) arrive at Winchester's Station Hill, at City Rd. and Sussex St., from London Waterloo (1hr., 2 per hr., £16.60) and Portsmouth (1hr., every hr., £7). National Express **buses** (☎(08705) 808 080) go to London (1½hr., 7 per day,

£12); Hampshire Stagecoach (☎(01256) 464 501) goes to Salisbury (#68, 45min., 7 per day, round-trip £4.45) and Portsmouth (#69, 1½hr., 12 per day, round-trip £4.45). The **tourist office,** The Guildhall, Broadway, is across from the bus station. (☎840 500; fax 850 348. Open May-Sept. M-Sa 9:30am-5:30pm, Su 11am-4pm; Oct.-Apr. M-Sa 10am-5pm.) The lovely home of **Mrs. P. Patton ❸,** 12 Christchurch Rd., between St. James Ln. and Beaufort Rd., is near the cathedral. (☎854 272. Singles £25-28; doubles £33-40.) Go past the Alfred statue and across the bridge to reach the **YHA Winchester ❶,** 1 Water Ln. (☎853 723. Lockout 10am-5pm. Curfew 11pm. Open from late Mar. to early Nov. daily; late Nov. to early Mar. weekends only. Dorms £9.50, students £8.25, under 18 £7.) **Royal Oak ❶,** on Royal Oak Passage, next to Godbegot House off High St., is yet another pub touting itself as the UK's oldest. The locally brewed hogshead cask ale (£1.75) is delicious. (Open daily 11am-11pm.) A **Sainsbury's** supermarket is on Middle Brook St., off High St. (Open M-Sa 7am-8pm, Su 11am-5pm.) **Postal Code:** SO23 8WA.

SALISBURY ☎01722

Salisbury (pop. 36,890) centers around **Salisbury Cathedral** and its astounding 123m spire. The bases of the pillars literally bend inward under the strain of 6400 tons of limestone; if a pillar rings when you knock on it, you should probably move away. (☎555 120. Open June-Aug. M-Sa 7:15am-8:15pm, Su 7:15am-6:15pm; Sept.-May daily 7:15am-6:15pm. Free tours May-Oct. M-Sa 9:30am-4:45pm, May-Sept. until 6:15pm; Nov.-Feb. M-Sa 10am-4pm. Donation £3.50, students and seniors £2.50.) The 1½hr. roof and tower tours are also worthwhile. (May-Sept. M-Sa 11am, 2, 3pm, Su 4:30pm; June-Aug. M-Sa 11am, 2, 3, 6:30pm, Su 4:30pm; winter hours vary. £3, students £2. Call ahead.) One of four surviving copies of the **Magna Carta** rests in the **Chapter House.** (Open June-Aug. M-Sa 9:30am-5:30pm, Su noon-5:30pm; Sept.-May M-Sa 9:30am-5:30pm, Su 1-3:15pm. Free.)

Trains arrive at South Western Rd. from London (1½hr., every hr., £22-30) and Winchester (1½hr., every hr., £11.50). National Express **buses** (☎08705 808 080) pull into 8 Endless St. from London Victoria (2¾hr., 4 per day, £12.20); Wilts & Dorset buses (☎336 855) arrive from Bath (#X4; every hour from 7am-6pm, £3.95). The **Tourist Information Centre** is on Fish Row in the Guildhall; from the train station, turn left on South Western Rd., bear right on Fisherton St., continue on Bridge St., cross the bridge onto High St., and walk straight down Silver St., which becomes Butcher Row, then Fish Row (10-15min.). From the bus station, head left on Endless St., which becomes Queen St. Turn right at the first old building on the right to enter Fish Row. (☎334 956. Open June-Sept. M-Tu 9:30am-5pm, W-Sa 9:30am-6pm, Su 10:30am-4:30pm; Oct.-Apr. M-Sa 9:30am-5pm; May M-Sa 9:30am-5pm, Su 10:30am-4:30pm.) From the TIC, head left on Fish Row, right on Queen St., left on Milford St., and under the overpass to find the **YHA Salisbury ❷,** in Milford Hill House, on Milford Hill. (☎327 572. Lockout 10am-1pm. Dorms £11.25.) **Matt and Tiggy's ❷,** 51 Salt Ln., a welcoming 450-year-old house with warped floors and exposed ceiling beams, is just up from the bus station. (☎327 443. Dorms £11-12.) At **Harper's "Upstairs Restaurant" ❷,** 6-7 Ox Rd., inventive international and English dishes (£6-10) make hearty meals and the "8B48" (2 courses for £8 before 8pm) buys a heap of food. (☎333 118. Open M-F noon-2pm and 6-9:30pm, Sa noon-2pm and 6-10pm, Su 6-9pm.) **Sainsbury's** supermarket is at The Maltings. (Open M-Th 8am-8pm, F 8am-9pm, Sa 7:30am-7pm, Su 10am-4pm.) **Postal Code:** SP1 1AB.

DAYTRIPS FROM SALISBURY

STONEHENGE

Wilts & Dorset buses (☎336 855) connect from Salisbury's center and train station (40min., round-trip £5.25).

A sunken colossus amid swaying grass and indifferent sheep, Stonehenge stands unperturbed by 80km/h whipping winds and legions of people who have visited for over 5000 years. The monument's present shape—once a complete circle of 7m-high stones weighing up to 45 tons—dates from about 1500 BC. Though fantastical attributions of Stonehenge ranging from Merlin to helpful extraterrestrials have helped build an attractive mythology around the site, the more plausible source—Neolithic builders—is perhaps the most astonishing of all. The laborers' technological capabilities were extremely advanced; their unknown methods continue to elude archaeologists. You may admire Stonehenge for free from nearby Amesbury Hill, 2½km up A303, or pay admission at the site. (Open June-Aug. daily 9am-7pm; mid-Mar. to May and Sept. to mid-Oct. 9:30am-6pm; mid-Oct. to mid-Mar. 9:30am-4pm. £4.20, students £3.20.)

AVEBURY

Take bus #5 or 6 from Salisbury to Avebury (1½hr., 6 per day, £3.90).

This hamlet sprouts from within a **stone circle** that is the third largest of its kind in Europe. Avebury's sprawling titans were constructed over 500 years before Stonehenge. Just outside the circle is **Silbury Hill,** built in 2660 BC; the curious man-made mound represents another archaeological mystery. The **tourist office** is near the car park. (☎01672 539 425. Open W-Sa 10am-5pm, Su 10am-4pm.)

BATH ☎01225

A visit to the elegant Georgian city of Bath (pop. 83,000) remains *de rigueur,* even if today it's more of a museum than a resort. But expensive trinkets can't conceal the fact that Bath, immortalized by Austen and Dickens, once stood second only to London as the social capital of England.

TRANSPORTATION AND PRACTICAL INFORMATION. **Trains** leave from Bath for: Bristol (15min., 4 per hr., £4.60); Exeter (1¼hr., every hr., £22); and London Paddington (1½hr., 2 per hr., £32). National Express **buses** (☎(08705) 808 080) run to London (3hr., every hr., £13) and Oxford (2hr., daily, £10.25). The train and bus stations are near the south end of Manvers St.; walk towards the town center and turn left on York St. to reach the **tourist office,** in Abbey Chambers. (☎477 221. Open May-Sept. M-Sa 9:30am-6pm, Su 10am-4pm; Oct.-Apr. M-Sa 9:30am-5pm, Su 10am-4pm.) **Postal Code:** BA1 1AJ.

ACCOMMODATIONS AND FOOD. **B&Bs** cluster on Pulteney Rd., Pulteney Gdns., and Crescent Gdns. The **International Backpackers Hostel ❷,** 13 Pierrepont St., which has whimsical, musically themed rooms, is up the street from the stations. (☎446 787. Internet. Laundry £2.50. Dorms £12.) To get to the friendly, well-priced **Toad Hall Guest House ❸,** 6 Lime Grove, go across Pulteney Bridge and through Pulteney Gardens. (☎423 254. Singles £22-25; doubles £42-45.) **The White Hart ❷,** Widcombe Hill, is friendly and has simple rooms. (☎313 985. Dorms £12.50; singles £20; doubles £40.) To reach **Newton Mill Camping ❶,** 4km west on Newton Rd., take bus #5 from the station to Twerton and ask to be let off at the campsite. (☎333 909. Tents £4.25-12.) **Demuths Restaurant ❸,** 2 North Parade Passage, has creative vegetarian and vegan dishes. (Entrees £8-11. Open daily 10am-10pm.) Fantastic pan-Asian noodles at **f.east ❷**, 27 High St., range from £5-8. (Open M-Sa noon-11pm, Su noon-5pm.) **Guildhall Market,** between High St. and Grand Parade, has fresh fruits and vegetables. (Open daily 9am-5:30pm.)

SIGHTS. For 400 years, Bath flourished as a Roman city, its bubbling hot springs making the city a pilgrimage site for those seeking religious miracles and physical healing. The **Roman Baths Museum** showcases the complexity of Roman architecture and engineering, which included central heating and internal plumbing. (Open Apr.-June and Sept. daily 9am-6pm; July-Aug. 9am-10pm; Oct.-Mar. 9:30am-5pm; last admission 1hr. before closing. Audio tour included. £8, seniors and students £7, children £4.) Next to the baths, the towering 15th-century **Bath Abbey** has a whimsical west facade with several angels climbing ladders up to heaven, and curiously enough, two climbing down. (Open Apr.-Oct. M-Sa 10am-6pm, Su 8am-8pm; Nov.-Mar. M-Sa 10am-4pm, Su 8am-8pm. £2.) Head north up Stall St., turn left on Westgate St., and turn right on Saw Close to reach Queen Sq.; Jane Austen lived at #13. Continue up Gay St. to **The Circus,** where Thomas Gainsborough, William Pitt, and David Livingstone lived. To the left down Brock St. is the **Royal Crescent,** a half-moon of Gregorian townhouses bordering **Royal Victoria Park.** The **botanical gardens** nurture 5000 species of plants. (Open M-Sa 9am-dusk, Su 10am-dusk. Free.) Backtrack down Brock St. and bear left at The Circus to reach Bennett St. and the dazzling **Museum of Costume,** which will satisfy any fashion fetish. (Open daily 10am-5pm. £5; joint ticket with Roman Baths £10.)

GLASTONBURY ☎01458

The reputed birthplace of Christianity in England and the seat of Arthurian myth, Glastonbury (pop. 6900) is an intersection of mysticism and religion. Present-day pagan pilgrimage destination **Glastonbury Tor** is supposedly the site of the mystical Isle of Avalon, where King Arthur is predicted to return. To reach the Tor, turn right at the top of High St. onto Lambrook, which becomes Chilkwell St.; turn left onto Wellhouse Ln. and follow the path up the hill (summer buses £1). On your way down, visit the **Chalice Well,** on Chilkwell St., the purported resting place of the Holy Grail. (Open Apr.-Oct. daily 10am-6pm; Nov. 11am-5pm; Dec.-Jan. 11am-4pm; Feb.-Mar. 11am-5pm. £1.60.) The annual summertime **Glastonbury Festival** is Britain's largest music event. (Tickets ☎(0115) 912 9129; www.glastonburyfestivals.co.uk.) No trains

THE BIG SPLURGE

THE CALORIE CRAWL

It's only appropriate to splurge in the resort town of Bath. This sumptuous trek will make you as fat and happy as the royalty that used to frequent the town.

Start at **Jim Garrahy's Fudge Kitchen,** 10 Abbey Churchyard. Mouthwatering handmade fudges, sold by the slice (£3), come in over a dozen flavors, including Coffee Walnut, Whiskey Cream, After-Dinner Mint, and the awesome Belgian Chocolate Swirl. *(Open daily 10am-5:30pm.)*

The next stop is **The Fine Cheese Co.,** 29/31 Walcot St., specializing in English and European cheeses. Prices range from Munster at £10 per kg to Roquefort at £27. The *Bath Box* gift set (£23.50) includes crackers, chutney, and local cheeses. *(Open M-F 9:30am-5:30pm, Sa 9am-5:30pm.)*

For your final indulgence, head to Whittard, 10 Stall St., which sells Lindor chocolates by the box (£4) in white, dark, and hazelnut. *(Open M-Sa 9am-5:30pm, Su noon-5pm.)* Don't forget to take something home—the kid in you will get a kick out of the full-sized chocolate rugby balls (£13) from Café Cadbury, 23 Union St. *(Open M-Sa 9am-7pm, Su 11am-4pm).*

serve Glastonbury, but First **buses** (☎(0870) 608 2608) run from Bath (1¼hr., £4; change at Wells). From the bus stop, turn right on High St. to reach the **tourist office,** The Tribunal, 9 High St. (☎832 954. Open Apr.-Sept. Su-Th 10am-5pm, F-Sa 10am-5:30pm; Oct.-Mar. Su-Th 10am-4pm, F-Sa 10am-4:30pm.) **Glastonbury Backpackers ❷,** at the corner of Magdalene St. and High St., has a fantastic location and an attached sandwich shop. (☎833 353. Free Internet access. Dorms £10; doubles £26-30.) **Postal Code:** BA6 9HG.

BOURNEMOUTH ☎01202

In the summer, daytrippers invade Bournemouth (pop. 150,000), a seaside resort made popular by its healing pine scents and curative sea-baths. Most visitors come for **Bournemouth Beach** (☎451 781), an 11.25km sliver of shoreline barely wide enough for its many inflatable slides. Cheap amusements have spoiled the area surrounding **Bournemouth Pier,** but a short walk takes sunbathers to quieter spots, where they can rent bungalows and deck chairs. Travel along the shore for more stunning sights: the 153km **Jurassic Coast** was recently named a World Heritage Site for its famous fossils and unique geology (www.jurassiccoast.com). Beautiful **Studland Beach** sits across the harbor, reachable by bus #150 (50min., every hr.); a **nude beach** awaits just down the shore. Take bus #150 or 151 (25min., 2 per hr.) to reach the themed landscapes of **Compton Acres,** featuring a stunning Italian garden with Roman statues and a sensory garden designed for the blind. (Open Mar.-Oct. daily 10am-7:30pm; Nov.-Feb. 9am-5:30pm. £6, seniors £5.45, children £3.25.) Most start their nights at the roundabout up the hill from **Firvale Road,** working their way downhill through the numerous bars on **Christchurch Road.** The bar **Circo** and downstairs club **Elements,** on Firvale Rd., attract large crowds. (Circo open M and W-Sa 7-11pm, Su 7pm-12:30am. Elements cover £3-7. Open M and W-Sa 9:30pm-2am.)

Trains (☎(08457) 484 950) arrive at Holdenhurst Rd. from Birmingham (3½hr., 8 per day) and London Waterloo (1¾hr., 2 per hr., £30.40). National Express **buses** (☎(08705) 808 080) arrive at The Square in Bournemouth from: Birmingham (5hr., 3 per day, £31); Bristol (3½hr., 1 per day, £12.50); and London (3hr., every hr., £11). Bournemouth's **tourist office** is on Westover Rd. (☎(0906) 802 0234. Open July-Aug. M-Sa 9:30am-7pm, Su 10:30am-4pm; Sept.-June M-Sa 9:30am-5:30pm.) The **Boscombe** neighborhood has many affordable B&Bs; follow signs from the train station (20min.). The friendly **Bournemouth Backpackers ❶,** 3 Frances Rd., has the most reasonable rates. (☎299 491. Kitchen. Reception June-Aug.; call ahead other months. Dorms £9-16; doubles £42. Discounts for longer stays.) **Christchurch Road** boasts diverse food offerings, and international students living north of Bournemouth make **Charminster Road** a center of great ethnic cuisine and cheap Internet cafes. **Postal Code:** BH1 2BU.

BRISTOL ☎0117

The southwest's largest city, Bristol (pop. 401,000) hums as a business center by day and jumps into energetic revelry by night. The **Bristol Cathedral,** overlooking the College Green, features a beautiful Norman Chapter House. (Open daily 8am-6pm. Donation £2.) **@Bristol,** Anchor Rd., educates all ages with interactive exhibits, wildlife, and multimedia presentations. (☎915 5000. Open daily 10am-6pm. £6.50-7.50.) **Trains** (☎(08457) 484 950) come to Bristol Temple Meads Station from: Bath (15min., 4 per hr., £4.80); Cardiff (50min., 2 per hr., £7.20); and London Paddington station (1¾hr., 2 per hr., £41). National Express **buses** (☎(08705) 808 080) arrive at Marlborough St. Station from London (2½hr., every hr., £13) and Manchester (5¾hr., 6-8 per day, £19). The **tourist office,** The Annex, Wildscreen Walk, Harbourside, is adjacent to @Bristol. (☎926 0767. Open Apr.-Oct. daily 10am-6pm; Nov.-Mar. M-Sa 10am-5pm, Su 11am-4pm.) **Bristol Backpackers ❷,** 17 St. Stephen's St., in an old newspaper building, is now a backpacker's dream. (☎925

7900. Internet £0.03 per min. Dorms £13.) **Glanville Guest House ❷,** 122 Coronation Rd., provides simple lodgings. (☎963 1634. Singles £16; doubles £27.) **Boston Tea Party ❷,** 75 Park St., has an exquisite selection of coffees and sandwiches for £4-7. (☎929 8601. Open M 7am-6pm, Tu-Sa 7am-10pm, Su 9am-7pm.) **Baldwin Street** and **St. Nicholas Street** are at the center of Bristol nightlife; also try **Frogmore Street,** home to the seductive and spacious club **Bristol Academy.** (☎927 9227. Cover £5-20. Open M-W 7-11pm, Th 10pm-3am, F-Sa 10pm-4am.)

DARTMOOR NATIONAL PARK

Dartmoor is strewn with remnants of the past, from oddly balanced granite *tors* to Neolithic rock formations. Visitors may also stumble upon the skeleton of a mining industry and the heavily guarded Princetown prison. Due to rough terrain and a harsh climate, Dartmoor has remained largely untouched, except by sheep and wild ponies. The Ministry of Defense uses the moor for target practice, and the boundaries of dangerous areas change yearly; consult your map and check weekly firing times at tourist offices. An Ordnance Survey Outdoor Leisure Map #28 (7), a compass, and waterproof garb are essential. Stick to the marked paths. *Dartmoor Visitor*, free at tourist offices, provides maps and information on accommodations and food. Tourist offices also offer detailed guides to hikes and walks (free to £10). The official **Dartmoor Rescue Group** is on call at ☎999.

Buses are infrequent; plan ahead, using the bus schedules available at tourist offices. A few bus routes run one or two more trips on Sundays. The **Sunday Rover** allows unlimited bus travel (£6). DevonBus #82, a.k.a. the **Transmoor Link** (late May to Sept. M-Sa 3 per day, Su 5 per day; £5), connects Plymouth in the southwest to Exeter in the northeast. Buses run from Plymouth to: Okehampton (#86 or 118; 1½-2hr.; M-Sa every hr., Su 5 per day) in the north and Tavistock (#83, 84, or 86; 1hr., 4 per hr.) in the west. For more info, call **Traveline** (☎0870 608 2608) which operates daily 7am-5pm. There is a **National Park Information Centre** in Postbridge, off the B3212 Moretonhampstead-Yelverton Rd. (☎01822 880 272. Open Easter-Oct. daily 10am-5pm; Nov.-Easter Sa-Su 10am-4pm.) Most villages in Dartmoor have **tourist offices.** The one in Okehampton is on 3 West St., adjacent to the White Hart Hotel. (☎01837 53 020. Open Easter-Oct. M-Sa 10am-5pm; Apr. and Sept.-Oct. daily 10am-5pm; Nov.-Easter M and F-Sa 10am-4:30pm.) The Tavistock tourist office is in Town Hall. (☎01822 612 938. Open Easter-Oct. M-Sa 9:30am-5pm; July-Aug. also Su 9:30am-5pm; Nov.-Easter M-Tu and F-Sa 10am-4pm.) Spend the night at **YHA Bellever ❷,** 1.5km southeast of Postbridge on bus #82 from Plymouth. (☎01822 880 227. Open July-Aug. daily; Sept.-Oct. and Mar.-June M-Sa. Dorms £10.25, under 18 £7.) Although official campsites exist, many travelers **camp** on the open moor. Dartmoor land is privately owned, so ask permission before crossing or camping on land. Camping is permitted on the non-enclosed moor land more than 1.2km away from the road or out of sight of inhabited areas. Campers may only stay for one night in a single spot. Don't build fires on the moors unless posted signs say you may do so. To camp at an official site, try **River Dart Country Park ❶,** Holne Park, Ashburton (☎01364 652 511; open Easter-Sept.; tent or caravan £9.50-14), or **Higher Longford Farm ❶,** Moorshop, Tavistock. (☎01822 613 360. Office open daily 10am-5pm. Tents and caravans £8-12.)

PLYMOUTH ☎01752

Plymouth (pop. 250,000) is a famed port—the English fleet sailed from here to defeat the Spanish Armada in 1588. It remains a useful hub for getting to the Continent. **Trains** (☎(08457) 484 950) run from **Plymouth Station,** on North Rd., to London Paddington (4hr., 2 per day, £58) and Penzance (2hr., 2 per hr., £14); take bus #5 or 6 to the city center—it's a long walk. **Buses** leave from **Bretonside Station,** near St. Andrew's Cross at the east end of Royal Parade; National Express (☎(08705) 808 080) goes to London (5hr., 7-8 per day, £23.50), and Stagecoach runs to Exeter (#X38, 39, and X39; 1¼hr., 12-13 per day, £5). For **ferries** (☎(08750) 360 360) departing from the Millbay Docks for France and Spain, see p. 48. The **tourist office** is in Island House, 9 The Barbican. (☎304 849. Open Easter-Oct. M-Sa 9am-5pm, Su 10am-4pm; Nov.-Easter M-F 9am-5pm, Sa 10am-4pm.) Inexpensive B&Bs grace **Citadel Road** and its side streets. **Seymour Guest House ❷,** 211 Citadel Rd. E., where Hoegate St. meets Lambhay Hill, has comfortable lodgings in a convenient location. (Singles £16; doubles £30.) **Sainsbury's** supermarket is in the Armada Shopping Centre. (Open M-Sa 8am-8pm, Su 11am-4pm.) **Postal Code:** PL1 1AB.

THE CORNISH COAST

With lush cliffsides stretching out into the Atlantic, Cornwall's terrain doesn't feel quite like England. Indeed, Cornwall's isolation made it a favored place for Celtic migration in the face of Saxon conquest; though the Cornish language is no longer spoken, the area remains protective of its distinctive past. England's southwest tip has some of the broadest, sandiest beaches in northern Europe, and the surf is up year-round, whether or not the sun decides to break through.

FALMOUTH. Seven rivers flow into the port of Falmouth (pop. 18,300), guarded against invaders by two spectacular castles. **Pendennis Castle,** built by Henry VIII to keep out French frigates, now features a walk-through diorama. (Open July-Aug. daily 9am-6pm; Apr.-June and Sept. 10am-6pm; Oct. 10am-5pm; Nov.-Mar. 10am-4pm. £4, students £3.) Across the channel lies another Henry VIII fortification, the magnificently preserved **St. Mawes Castle.** To reach the castle, take a ferry (20min., 2 per hr., round-trip £4.60) from Falmouth. (Open Apr.-Sept. daily 10am-6pm; Oct. daily 10am-5pm; Nov.-Mar. W-Su 10am-1pm and 2-4pm. 1hr. audio tour included. £2.90, students £2.20.) **The Lizard Peninsula,** near Falmouth, offers peaceful hiking trails. Truronian runs buses from Falmouth to Helston (T4; 70min., 4 per day) and from Helston to Lizard (T1; 40min., £1.90). **Trains** (☎(08475) 484 950) arrive in Falmouth from London Paddington (5½hr., 6-7 per day, £68) and Plymouth (2hr., 9-17 per day, £9.70). National Express (☎(08705) 808 080) **buses** arrive from London (8hr., 2 per day, £34.50) and Plymouth (2½hr., 2 per day, £5.25). The **tourist office** is at 28 Killigrew St., The Moor. (☎312 300. Open daily M-Sa 9:30am-5:30pm; July-Aug. also Su 10am-2pm.) Guest needs are always met at **Castleton Guest House ❸,** 68 Killigrew St. (☎311 072. Singles £22; doubles £36-46.) **Phone Code:** ☎01326.

NEWQUAY. An outpost of surfer subculture, Newquay lures the bald, the bleach-blond, and even the blue-haired to its waves and pubs. Winds descend on **Fistral Beach** with a vengeance, creating what some consider the best surfing conditions in Europe. The enticing **Lusty Glaze Beach** beckons from the bay side. Drink up at **The Red Lion,** on North Quay Hill, at Tower Rd. (open M-Sa 11am-11pm, Su 11am-10:30pm), then dance at **Bertie's,** on East St. (Cover £5-7. Open daily 9:30pm-2am.) All **trains** (☎(08457) 484 950) to Newquay come from **Par** (50min., 4-5 per day, £4.30). From Par, trains connect to Plymouth (1hr., 15 per day, £8.10) and Penzance (1¾hr., every hr., £10.30). First (☎(0870) 608 2608) runs **buses** to St. Ives (2hr., June-Sept. 1 per day, £5) and Falmouth (£3.30). National Express (☎(08705) 808 080) runs to London (6hr., 1-3 per day, £30.50). The **tourist office** is on Marcus Hill, a block from the bus station. (☎854 020. Open Easter-Oct. M-Sa 9:30am-5:30pm, Su 9:30am-4:30pm; Nov.-Easter M-F 9:30am-4:30pm, Sa 9:30am-12:30pm.) **Original Backpackers ❷,** 16 Beachfield Ave., has a fantastic location off Bank St. and near Central Sq., facing the beach. (☎874 668. £12 per person, £50 per week.) **Phone Code:** ☎01637.

PENZANCE. Penzance is the very model of an ancient English pirate town. A Benedictine monastery, **St. Michael's Mount,** was built on the spot where St. Michael appeared in AD 495. The interior is unspectacular, but the grounds are lovely and the 30-story views are captivating. (Open Apr.-Oct. M-F 10:30am-5:30pm; July-Aug. also most weekends; Nov.-Mar. M, W, F by guided tours only. £4.60.) During low tide, visitors can walk to the mount; during high tide, take ferry bus #2 or 2A to Marazion Sq. and catch a ferry (£1). Penzance boasts an impressive number of art galleries; pick up the *Cornwall Gallery Guide* (£1) at the tourist office. **Trains** (☎(08457) 484 950) go to London (5½hr., every hr., £56) and Plymouth (2hr., every hr., £10.30). National Express (☎(08705) 808 080) **buses** also run to London (8hr., 8 per day, £28.50) and Plymouth (3hr., 2 per hr., £6). The **tourist office** is between the train and bus stations on Station Rd. (☎362 207. Open May-Sept. M-Sa 9am-6pm, Su 10am-1pm; Oct.-Apr. M-F 9am-5pm, Sa 10am-1pm.) **Blue Dolphin Penzance Backpackers ❷,** on Alexandra Rd., is relaxed and well-kept. (☎363 836. Dorms £10; doubles £24.) The 13th-century **The Turk's Head,** 49 Chapel St., is a pub once sacked by Spanish pirates. **Phone Code:** ☎01736.

ST. IVES. St. Ives is 15km north of Penzance, on a spit of land edged by pastel beaches and azure waters. The town drew a colony of painters and sculptors in the 1920s; Virginia Woolf's *To the Lighthouse* is thought to refer to the Godrevy Lighthouse in the distance. The *Cornwall Gallery Guide* (£1) will help you navigate the dozens of galleries here, but St. Ives's real attractions are its beaches. **Porthminster Beach,** downhill from the train station, is a magnificent stretch of white sand and tame waves. **Trains** (☎(08457) 484950) arrive from Penzance (25min., 2 per hr., £3). National Express (☎(08705) 808 080) **buses** go to Plymouth (3hr., 4 per day) and Penzance (20min., 4 per day). First (☎(0870) 608 2608) buses #16, 16B, and 17 go to Penzance (30-40min., 2 per hr., £2.50); buses #57 and 57D run to Newquay (2¼hr., 3 per day, £2.50). The **tourist office** is in the Guildhall on Street-an-Pol. From the stations, walk down to the foot of Tregenna Hill and turn right. (☎796 297. Open Easter-Sept. M-Sa 9:30am-6pm, Su 10am-1pm; Oct.-Easter M-F 9am-5pm.) **St. Ives International Backpackers ❶,** The Stenmack, is in a 19th-century Methodist church. (☎799 444. Dorms £8-12.) **Phone Code:** ☎01736.

EAST ANGLIA AND THE MIDLANDS

The rich farmland and watery flats of East Anglia stretch northeast from London, cloaking the counties of Cambridgeshire, Norfolk, and Suffolk, as well as parts of Essex. Literally England's newest landscape, the vast plains of the fens were drained as late as the 1820s. Mention of The Midlands inevitably evokes grim urban images, but there is a unique heritage and quiet grandeur to this smoke-stacked pocket. Even Birmingham, the region's much-maligned center, has its saving graces, among them a lively nightlife and the Cadbury chocolate empire.

OXFORD ☎01865

Academic pilgrims to Oxford's university, founded in the 12th century, can delve into the basement room of Blackwell's Bookstore, explore the impeccable galleries of the Ashmolean Museum, or stroll through the perfectly maintained quadrangles of Oxford's 39 colleges. Secluded from the touring crowds, these quiet destinations reveal Oxford's history and irrepressible grandeur.

TRANSPORTATION

Trains: Botley Road (☎794 422), down Park End, west of Carfax. Ticket office open M-F 6am-8pm, Sa 6:45am-8pm, Su 7:45am-8pm. Trains (☎(08457) 484 950) from London Paddington Station (1hr., 2-4 per hr., round-trip £14.80).

Buses: Bus station, Gloucester Green. **Oxford CityLink** (☎785 400) goes to and from: **London Victoria** (1¾hr.; 3 per hr.; round-trip £9, students £7); **Gatwick airport** (2hr.; every hr. daytime, every 2 hr. at night; round-trip £22); **Heathrow airport** (1½hr., 2 per hr., round-trip £12). **National Express** (☎(08705) 808 080) offers national routes.

Public Transportation: Local services, including The **Oxford Bus Company** (☎785 400) and **Stagecoach** (☎772 250), board on streets around Carfax. Fares are low (most 80p).

ORIENTATION AND PRACTICAL INFORMATION

The easiest way to orient yourself in Oxford is to locate the colossal Carfax Tower. **Queen, High, St. Aldate's,** and **Cornmarket** streets intersect at **Carfax,** the town center. The colleges are all within 1½km of one another, mainly to the east of Carfax along **High Street** and **Broad Street.** The **bus station** and the **tourist office** lie to the west on Gloucester Green—from Carfax, follow Cornmarket St. to George St. and turn right onto Gloucester.

Tourist Office: TIC, 15-16 Broad St. (☎726 871; fax 240 261). Books rooms for a £3 fee and a 10% deposit. **Walking tours** depart 2-5 times per day (10:30am-2pm; £6-7). Open M-Sa 9:30am-5pm and Su 10am-3:30pm.

American Express: 4 Queen St. (☎207 101). Open M-F 9am-5:30pm, Sa 9am-5pm.

Police: Station on St. Aldates and Speedwell St. (☎260 000).

Internet Access: Pickwick Papers, 90 Gloucester Green (☎793 149). Located next to the bus station. £1 for 30min. Open M-Sa 5am-9pm, Su 8am-8pm.

Post Office: 102-104 St. Aldates St. (☎08457 223 344). Open M-Sa 9am-5:30pm, Sa 9am-6pm. **Bureau de change. Postal Code:** OX1.

BRITAIN

ACCOMMODATIONS

In summer, book at least a week ahead. **B&Bs** line the main roads out of town. The 300s on Banbury Road are reachable by buses #2A, 2C, or 2D. Cheaper ones are in the 200s and 300s on Iffley Road (bus #4) and on Abingdon Road in South Oxford (bus #16). Expect to pay £25 per person.

Oxford Backpacker's Hotel, 9a Hythe Bridge St. (☎721 761). Between the bus and train stations, a short walk away from most sights. Lively atmosphere with an inexpensive bar, a pool table, and constant music. Internet access £1 for 15min. Laundry £2. Dorms £12. ❷

YHA Youth Hostel, 2a Botley Rd. (☎767 275). Immediately to the right of the train station. Superb location and bright surroundings. Generous rooms and facilities include kitchen, laundry, and lockers. Most rooms have 4-6 bunks. Breakfast included. Dorms £18.50, under 18 £13.50. £1 discount for students. ❷

Heather House, 192 Iffley Rd. (☎249 757). Take the bus marked "Rose Hill" from the bus station, train station, or Carfax Tower. Sparkling, modern rooms. Singles £33; doubles £66. Cheaper for longer stays. ❹

Falcon Private Hotel, 88-90 Abingdon Rd. (☎511 122). Provides a great base for exploring Oxford. Singles £36; doubles £58-68. ❹

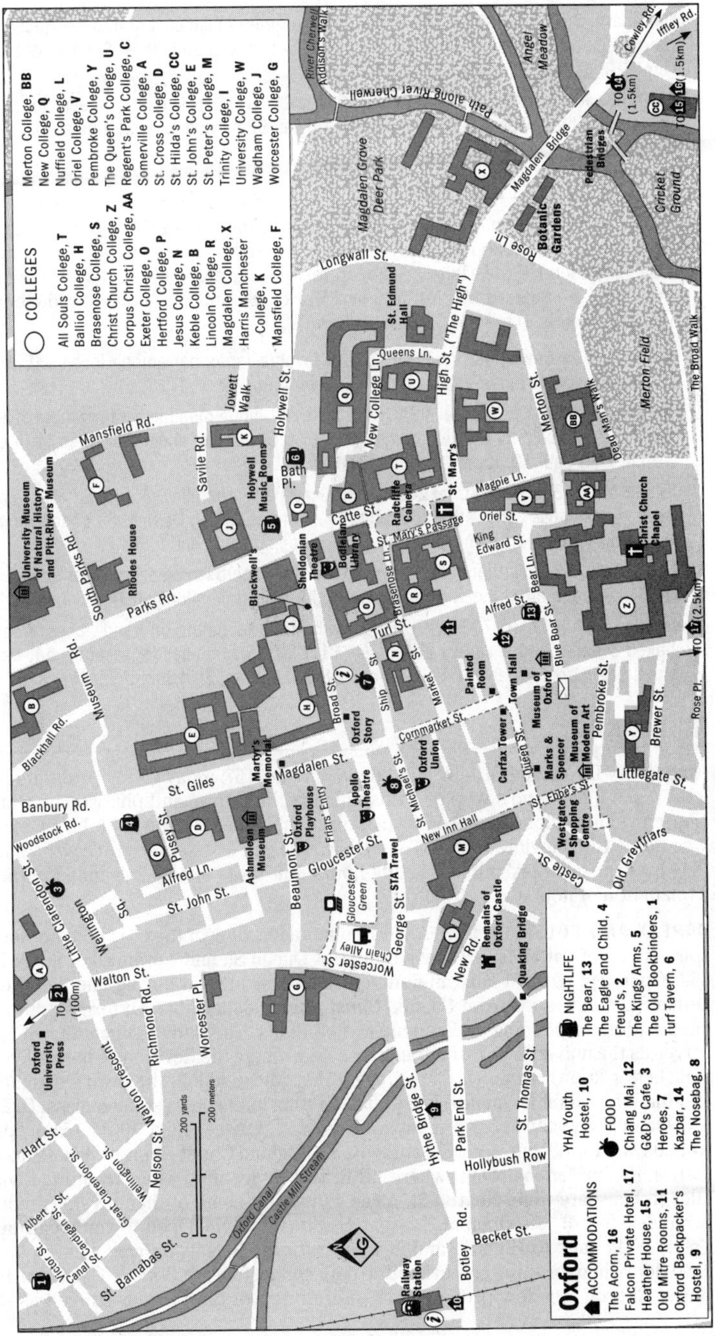

COLLEGES
All Souls College, T
Balliol College, H
Brasenose College, S
Christ Church College, Z
Corpus Christi College, AA
Exeter College, O
Hertford College, P
Jesus College, N
Keble College, B
Lincoln College, R
Magdalen College, X
Harris Manchester College, K
Mansfield College, F
Merton College, BB
New College, Q
Nuffield College, L
Oriel College, V
Pembroke College, Y
The Queen's College, U
Regent's Park College, C
Somerville College, A
St. Cross College, D
St. Hilda's College, CC
St. John's College, E
St. Peter's College, M
Trinity College, I
University College, W
Wadham College, J
Worcester College, G
Oxford
ACCOMMODATIONS
The Acorn, 16
Falcon Private Hotel, 17
Heather House, 15
Old Mitre Rooms, 11
Oxford Backpacker's Hostel, 9
YHA Youth Hostel, 10
FOOD
Chiang Mai, 12
G&D's Cafe, 3
Heroes, 7
Kazbar, 14
The Nosebag, 8
NIGHTLIFE
The Bear, 13
The Eagle and Child, 4
Freud's, 2
The Kings Arms, 5
The Old Bookbinders, 1
Turf Tavern, 6
Magdalen Grove Deer Park
Angel Meadow
Path along River Cherwell
River Cherwell
Addison's Walk
Cowley Rd.
Iffley Rd.
TO 14 (1.5km)
TO 15 16 (1.5km)
Magdalen Bridge
Pedestrian Bridges
Cricket Ground
Botanic Gardens
Rose Ln.
Longwall St.
High St. ("The High")
St. Edmund Hall
Queens Ln.
New College Ln.
Holywell St.
Jowett Walk
Mansfield Rd.
Savile Rd.
Holywell Music Rooms
Bath Pl.
Merton St.
Merton Field
Dead Man's Walk
The Broad Walk
Magpie Ln.
St. Mary's
Radcliffe Camera
Catte St.
Oriel St.
King Edward St.
St. Mary's Passage
Bodleian Library
Sheldonian Theatre
Brasenose Ln.
Christ Church Chapel
Bear Ln.
Alfred St.
Blue Boar St.
TO 17 (2.5km)
Rose Pl.
Brewer St.
Pembroke St.
Littlegate St.
Old Greyfriars
Turl St.
Market St.
Painted Room
Town Hall
Museum of Oxford
Blackwell's
Parks Rd.
Rhodes House
South Parks Rd.
University Museum of Natural History and Pitt-Rivers Museum
Museum Rd.
Blackhall Rd.
Broad St.
Ship St.
Oxford Story
Cornmarket St.
Carfax Tower
Queen St.
Marks & Spencer
Museum of Modern Art
St. Ebbe's St.
Westgate Shopping Centre
Castle St.
Martyr's Memorial
Magdalen St.
St. Giles
Banbury Rd.
Woodstock Rd.
Pusey St.
Ashmolean Museum
Beaumont St.
Oxford Playhouse
Friars' Entry
Apollo Theatre
St. Michael's St.
Oxford Union
New Inn Hall
Gloucester St.
STA Travel
Gloucester Green
Alfred Ln.
St. John St.
Little Clarendon St.
Wellington Sq.
Chain Alley
Worcester St.
George St.
Remains of Oxford Castle
New Rd.
Quaking Bridge
Walton St.
TO 2 (100m)
Oxford University Press
Richmond Rd.
Worcester Pl.
Walton Crescent
Nelson St.
Hythe Bridge St.
Park End St.
St. Thomas St.
Hollybush Row
Becket St.
Botley Rd.
Railway Station
Oxford Canal
Castle Mill Stream
Hart St.
Albert St.
Great Clarendon St.
Wellington St.
Cardigan St.
Canal St.
Victor St.
St. Barnabas St.
200 yards
200 meters
0

BRITAIN

The Acorn, 260 Iffley Rd. (☎247 998). About a quarter mile east of Heather House. The good price at this B&B makes up for the relative lack of amenities. Singles with wash bin £29; doubles £52. ❸

Old Mitre Rooms, 4b Turl St. (☎279 821; fax 279 963). Lincoln College dorms. All rooms with bath. Open July to early Sept. Singles £32; doubles £53; triples £63.50. ❹

FOOD

Oxford students bored with cafeteria food sustain a market for budget eats in town. After hours, **kebab vans** roam Broad St., High St., Queen St., and St. Aldates. Across Magdalen Bridge, there are cheap restaurants along the first four blocks of Cowley Rd. The **Covered Market** between Market St. and Carfax has produce, deli goods, and breads. (Open M-Sa 8am-5:30pm.)

Kazbar, 25-27 Cowley Rd. (☎202 920). A favorite *tapas* bar among locals. £5 lunch deal includes two *tapas* and a drink (M-F noon-4pm). ❷

The Nosebag, 6-8 St. Michael's St. (☎721 033). Unique menu served cafeteria-style in a quaint 15th-century building. Lunch under £6.50, dinner under £8. Open M-Th until 10pm, F-Sa until 10:30pm, Su until 9pm. ❷

Chiang Mai, 130a High St. (☎202 233), tucked down an alley. A popular Thai restaurant; try the jungle curry with wild rabbit (£7). Entrees £7-10. Open M-Sa noon-2pm and 6-11pm, Su noon-1pm and 6-10pm. Reservations recommended. ❷

G&D's Cafe, 55 Little Clarendon St. (☎516 652). Superb ice cream and sorbet (£1.65-3.45) served in a fun, noisy atmosphere. Open daily 8am-midnight. ❶

Heroes, 8 Ship St. (☎723 459). Filled with students dining on sandwiches, freshly-baked breads, and a variety of fillings (£1.90-3.65). Popular for takeout, but has a small eat-in area. Open M-F 8am-9pm, Sa 8:30am-6pm, Su 10am-5pm. ❶

SIGHTS

King Henry II founded Britain's first university in 1167; today Oxford's alumni register reads like a who's who of British history, literature, and philosophy. Christ Church College alone has produced 13 prime ministers, while St. John's College was home to collegiate rocker Tony Blair. The TIC's *Welcome to Oxford* guide (£1) lists the colleges' public visiting hours, but these can be rescinded without explanation or notice.

CARFAX AND SOUTH OF CARFAX. For a fantastic view of the city, hike up the 99 spiral stairs of **Carfax Tower,** at the corner of Queen St. and Cornmarket St. (☎792 653. Open Apr.-Oct. M-F 10am-5pm; closed Oct.-Apr. and during bad weather.) Down St. Aldate's St. from Carfax, **Christ Church College** has Oxford's grandest quad and its most socially distinguished students. The **Christ Church Chapel** also serves as the university's cathedral. It was here where the Reverend Charles Dodgson (better known as Lewis Carroll) first met Alice Liddell, the dean's daughter, and the White Rabbit can also be spotted fretting in the hall's stained glass. (☎286 573. Open M-Sa 9:30am-5:30pm, Su noon-5:30pm. Services Su 8, 10, 11:15am, 6pm; weekdays 7:15, 7:35am, 6pm. £4, students £3.) Behind Christ Church Chapel, up on Merton Rd., is **Merton College,** where J.R.R. Tolkien lectured while inventing Elvish tales in his spare time. Nearby **St. Alban's Quad** has some of the university's best gargoyles. (☎276 310. Open M-F 2-4pm, Sa-Su 10am-4pm. Open to guided groups. Free.) Walk back to High St. and head east for the **Botanic Garden,** where plants have flourished for three centuries. The path connecting the Botanic Garden to the Christ Church Meadow provides a beautiful view of the Thames as well as the cricket grounds on the opposite bank. (Open Apr.-Sept. daily 9am-5pm; Oct.-Mar. 9am-4:30pm. Greenhouses open daily 10am-4pm. Apr.-Aug. £2; Sept.-Mar. free.)

NORTH OF CARFAX. From Carfax, head up Cornmarket St., which becomes Magdalen St., and turn left onto Beaumont St. for the imposing **Ashmolean Museum**. It houses works by da Vinci, Monet, Manet, van Gogh, Michelangelo, Rodin, and Matisse. (☎278 000. Open Tu-Sa 10am-5pm, Su 2-5pm. Free.) The **Bodleian Library,** at Catte St., is Oxford's principal reading and research library, with over five million books. Take High St. and turn left on Catte. As a copyright library, it receives a free copy of every book printed in Great Britain. No one has ever been permitted to take out a book. (☎277 224. Open M-F 9am-6pm, Sa 9am-1pm. Tours £3.50.) The **Sheldonian Theatre,** on Broad St., beside the Bodleian, is a Romanesque auditorium designed by Christopher Wren. Graduation ceremonies are conducted here in Latin. The cupola of the theater affords an inspiring view of the spires of Oxford. (☎277 299. Open M-Sa 10am-12:30pm and 2-4:30pm. £1.50, children £1.) You could browse for days at **Blackwell's Bookstore,** on Broad St., which according to the *Guinness Book of Records* is the largest room devoted to bookselling in the world. (☎333 606. Open M and W-Sa 9am-6pm, Tu 9:30am-6pm, Su 11am-5pm.) **New College,** New College Ln., named because it was founded "only" in 1379, has become one of Oxford's most prestigious colleges. From Carfax, head down High St. and turn onto Catte St.; New College Ln. is to the right. The bell tower has gargoyles representing the seven deadly sins on one side, and the seven virtues on the other, all equally grotesque. Use the Holywell St. Gate. (☎279 555. Open Easter-Oct. daily 11am-5pm; Nov.-Easter 2-4pm. £1.50 in summer.)

ENTERTAINMENT AND NIGHTLIFE

PUNTING

A traditional pastime in Oxford is punting on the River Thames (known in Oxford as the Isis) or on the River Cherwell (CHAR-wul). Punters receive a tall pole, a small oar, and a travel advisory before venturing out in boats that resemble shallow gondolas—swimming in the canals can lead to a tetanus shot and stitches. You might come across **Parson's Pleasure,** a small riverside area where men sometimes sunbathe nude. **Magdalen Bridge Boat Co.,** just under Magdalen Bridge, rents boats. (☎202 643. Open Mar.-Nov. daily 10am-9pm. M-F £9 per hr., Sa-Su £10 per hr. Deposit £20 plus ID.)

FESTIVALS

The university celebrates **Eights Week** at the end of May, when all the colleges enter crews in the bumping races while others nibble strawberries and sip pim, a liqueur mixed with lemonade, on the banks. In early September, **St. Giles Fair** invades Oxford's main streets with an old-fashioned carnival, complete with Victorian roundabout and whirligigs.

CONCERTS AND THEATER

Music and drama at Oxford are cherished arts. Attend a concert or Evensong service at one of the colleges—the **New College Choir** is one of the best boy choirs around. The **Oxford Playhouse,** 11-12 Beaumont St, is a venue for bands, dance troupes, and both amateur and professional plays. (☎798 600. Standby tickets available for seniors and students.) The **Oxford Union,** St. Michael's St., also puts up consistently good theater productions (☎778 119. Tickets £8, students £5). The **City of Oxford Orchestra,** the professional symphony orchestra, plays a subscription series in the Sheldonian Theatre. (☎744 457. Tickets £10-15.)

PUBS AND NIGHTLIFE

Pubs far outnumber colleges in Oxford; many even consider them the city's prime attraction. The popular student bar **Turf's Tavern,** on 4 Bath Pl., off Holywell St., is a sprawling 13th-century pub tucked in an alleyway. (Open M-Sa 11am-11pm, Su noon-10:30pm. Kitchen open noon-7:30pm.) Walk up Walton St. and take a left at Jericho St. to reach **The Old Bookbinders,** 17-18 Victor St., a crowded little pub featuring low ceilings, a young crowd, and lots of noise. (☎553 549. Open M-Sa until 11pm.) **The Eagle and Child,** 49 St. Giles, quenched the thirsts of C.S. Lewis and J.R.R. Tolkien for a quarter-century—*The Chronicles of Narnia* and *The Hobbit* were first read aloud here. (Open M-Sa 11am-11pm, Su 11am-10:30pm.) **The Kings Arms,** 40 Holywell St., draws in a huge young crowd. The coffee room at the front of the bar lets quieter folk avoid the merry masses. (Open M-Sa 10:30am-11pm, Su 10:30am-10:30pm.) **The Bear,** 6 Alfred St., established in 1242, is covered with over 5000 ties from Oxford students and visiting celebrities. (Open M-Sa noon-11pm, Su noon-10:30pm.) Although pubs in Oxford tend to close down by 11pm, nightlife can last until 3am. Check *This Month in Oxford* (free at the TIC) for upcoming events. **Walton Street** and **Cowley Road** host late-night clubs, as well as a jumble of ethnic restaurants and offbeat shops. **Freud's,** 119 Walton St., in former St. Paul's Parish Church, is a cafe by day and collegiate cocktail bar by night. (Open M-Tu until midnight, W-Th until 1am, F-Sa until 2am, Su until 10:30pm.)

WINDSOR ☎01753

The town of Windsor and the attached village of Eton are consumed by their two bastions of the British class system, Windsor Castle and Eton College. In the Middle Ages, residential Windsor spread out from the castle; today it is filled with specialty shops, tea houses, and pubs. Within the ancient stone walls of **Windsor Castle** lie some of the most sumptuous rooms and rarest artwork in Europe. Built by William the Conqueror as a fortress rather than as a residence, the castle has expanded over the course of nine centuries. When the Queen is home, the Royal Standard flies in place of the Union Jack. As a practical consequence of the Royals' residence, large areas of the castle will be unavailable to visitors, usually without warning. The **Changing of the Guard** takes place in front of the Guard Room at 11am on most days; see them before and after the ceremony marching through the streets of Windsor proper. Passing through the Norman Tower and Gate (built by Edward III from 1359-60), you will come upon the **upper ward.** Many of its rooms are open to the public and are richly decorated with art from the massive Royal Collection, including works by Holbein, Rubens, Rembrandt, and van Dyck. The **middle ward** is dominated by the **Round Tower** and its surrounding moat-cum-rose garden. A stroll to the **lower ward** reveals **St. George's Chapel,** where 10 sovereigns rest eternally, including Queen Mary and Henry VI. (24hr. info ☎831 118. Open Apr.-Oct. daily 10am-5:30pm, last entry 4pm; Nov.-Mar. 10am-4pm, last entry 3pm. £11.50, over 60 £9.50, under 17 £6, families £29.) **Eton College,** founded by Henry VI in 1440, is still England's preeminent public (known as private in the US) school. The best way to see Eton is just to wander around the schoolyard, a central quad complete with a statue of Henry VI. (10min. down Thames St. from the town center, across the river. ☎671 177. Open July-Aug. and late Mar. to mid-Apr. daily 10:30am-4:30pm; other times 2-4:30pm. £3, under 16 £2.25. Tours daily 2:15 and 3:15pm. £4, under 16 £3.10.)

Windsor is best seen as a daytrip from London. Two train stations are near Windsor Castle; follow the signs. **Trains** (☎08457 484 950) pull into **Windsor and Eton Central** from London Victoria and London Paddington via **Slough** (50min., 2 per hr., round-trip £6.90). Trains arrive at **Windsor and Eton Riverside** from London Waterloo (50min., 2 per hr., round-trip £6.90). Green Line (☎8668 7261) **buses** #700 and 702 make the trip from London, leaving from Eccleston Bridge, behind Victoria station (1-1½hr., round-trip £5.50-6.70). **The Waterman's Arms ❶** (☎861 001), a traditional pub (c. 1542), is just over the bridge into Eton and to the left at Brocas St., next to the Eton College Boat House. It's a local favorite with delicious cod, chips, and salad for £4.50. (Open M-Sa noon-2:30pm and 6-11pm, Su noon-3pm and 7-10pm.)

STRATFORD-UPON-AVON ☎01789

Former native William Shakespeare is now the area's industry; you'll find even the most vague connections to the Bard exploited to their full potential. Of course, all the perfumes of Arabia will not sweeten the exhaust from tour buses, but beyond the "Will Power" t-shirts, the aura of Shakespeare does remain: in the grace of the weeping Avon and for the pin-drop silence before a soliloquy in the Royal Shakespeare Theatre.

TRANSPORTATION. Thames **trains** (☎(08457) 484 950) arrive from: London Paddington (2¼hr., 7 per day, £22.50); Birmingham (1hr., every hr., £3.80); and Warwick (25min., 7 per day, £2.80). National Express (☎(08705) 808 080) runs **buses** from London Victoria (3hr., 3 per day, £12).

PRACTICAL INFORMATION. The **tourist office,** Bridgefoot, across Warwick Rd. toward the waterside park, offers maps and a free accommodations guide. (☎293 127. Open Apr.-Oct. M-Sa 9am-6pm, Su 10:30am-4:30pm; Nov.-Mar. M-Sa 9am-5pm.) Surf the **Internet** at **Cyber Junction,** 28 Greenhill St. (£3 per 30min., £5 per hr.; students £2.50, £4.) **Postal Code:** CV37 6PU.

ACCOMMODATIONS. To B&B or not to B&B? B&Bs line **Evesham Place, Evesham Road, Grove Road,** and **Shipston Road,** but 'tis nobler in summer to make advance reservations. The **Stratford Backpackers Hotel ❷,** 33 Greenhill St., is conveniently located just across the bridge from the train station and has clean rooms, a common lounge, and a kitchen. (☎263 838. Dorms £12.) The friendly proprietress makes **Clodagh's ❷,** 34 Banbury Rd., difficult to leave. (☎269 714. Free internet access. Book early; only two rooms available. Singles £17; doubles £34.) A 10min. walk down Evesham, **Penhurst Guest House ❸,** 34 Evesham Pl., has clean and spacious rooms beneath a drab exterior. (☎205 259. Singles £18-24; doubles £30-46.) Warm and attentive proprietors consider **The Hollies ❹,** 16 Evesham Pl., their labor of love. (☎266 857. Doubles £35, with bath £45.) **Riverside Caravan Park ❶,** Tiddington Rd., 1½km east of Stratford on B4086, has **camping** with beautiful but crowded views of the Avon. (☎292 312. Open Easter-Oct. Tent and 2 people £8, each additional person £1.)

FOOD. Opposition ❸, 13 Sheep St., is a bistro that receives rave reviews from locals. (Entrees £8-12. Open M-Sa noon-2pm and 5-10pm, Su noon-2pm and 6-9 pm.) **Hussain's Indian Cuisine ❷,** 6a Chapel St., has fantastic chicken *tikka masala;* keep an eye out for regular Ben Kingsley. (Lunch £6, main dishes from £6.50. Open daily 5pm-midnight, also Th-Su 12:30-2:30pm.) A great place for breakfast or lunch is **Le Petit Croissant ❶,** 17 Wood St. (Baguettes from 80p. Open M-Sa 8am-6pm.) A **Safeway** supermarket is on Alcester Rd., just across the bridge past the train station. (Open M-W and Sa 8am-9pm, Th-F 8am-10pm, Su 10am-4pm.)

SIGHTS. Traffic at the Shakespeare sights peaks around 2pm, so try to hit them before 11am or after 4pm. Die-hard fans can buy a ticket for admission to all five official Shakespeare properties: Anne Hathaway's cottage, Mary Arden's House and Countryside Museum, Shakespeare's Birthplace, New Place and Nash's

House, and Hall's Croft (£12, students and seniors £11). You can also buy a ticket that covers only the latter three sights (£8.50, students and seniors £7.50). **Shakespeare's Birthplace,** on Henley St., is part period re-creation and part exhibition of Shakespeare's life and works. (Open summer M-Sa 9am-5pm and Su 9:30am-5pm; mid-season M-Sa 10am-5pm and Su 10:30am-5pm; winter M-Sa 10am-4pm and Su 10:30am-4pm.) **New Place,** on High St., was Stratford's finest address when Shakespeare bought it in 1597. Only the foundation remains—it can be viewed from **Nash's House,** which belonged to the husband of Shakespeare's granddaughter. **Hall's Croft** and **Mary Arden's House** also capitalize on connections to Shakespeare's extended family, but provide exhibits of what life was like in Elizabethan times. Pay homage to Shakespeare's grave in the **Holy Trinity Church,** on Trinity St. (£1).

ENTERTAINMENT. Get thee to a performance at the world-famous **Royal Shakespeare Company;** recent sons include Kenneth Branagh and Ralph Fiennes. Tickets for all three theaters—the Royal Shakespeare Theatre, the Swan Theatre, and The Other Place—are sold through the box office in the foyer of the Royal Shakespeare Theatre, on Waterside. (☎403 403. 24hr. ticket hotline ☎(0870) 609 1110. £5-40. Highly demanded student standbys £8-12. Open M-Sa 9:30am-8pm. Tours M-Sa 1:30, 5:30pm, Su noon, 1, 2, 3, 5:30pm. £4, students and seniors £3.)

DAYTRIP FROM STRATFORD: WARWICK CASTLE. Climb to the top of the towers of England's finest medieval castle and see the countryside unfold like a fairy tale kingdom of hobbits and elves. The castle dungeons are filled with life-size wax soldiers preparing for battle, while "knights" and "craftsmen" talk about their trades. (Open Apr.-Sept. daily 10am-6pm; Oct.-Mar. 10am-5pm. £13, students £9.80; early Sept. to early May £1-2 discount.) **Trains** arrive from Stratford (20-40min., every 2hr., £2.70) and Birmingham (40min., 2 every hr., £3.70).

CHELTENHAM ☎01242

BRITAIN

The spa town of Cheltenham (pop. 107,000) is a pleasant break from heavily touristed Bath and Stratford, as well as a useful starting point for visiting the Cotswolds. Residents sunbathe at the exquisite **Imperial Gardens,** five minutes north of the center of town. **Trains** (☎(08457) 484 950) arrive at the station on Queen's Rd. from: Bath (1½hr., every hr., £11); Exeter (2hr., every 2hr., £32.50); and London (2hr., every hr., £36.30). To reach the **tourist office,** 77 The Promenade, walk down Queen's Rd. and bear left onto Lansdown Road; head left again at the Rotunda onto Montpellier Walk, which leads to The Promenade. The staff posts accommodations vacancies after-hours. (☎522 878. Open M-Tu and Th-Sa 9:30am-5:15pm, W 10am-5:15pm.) **Benton's Guest House ❸,** 71 Bath Rd., has towel warmers, generous hospitality, and breakfasts that barely fit on the plates. (☎517 417. £25 per person.) The well-situated **YMCA ❷,** on Vittoria Walk, houses both men and women. At Town Hall, turn left onto The Promenade and walk three blocks; Vittoria Walk is on the right. (☎524 024. Breakfast included. Reception 24hr. £16 per person.) **Postal Code:** GL50 1AA.

THE COTSWOLDS

Stretching across western England—bounded by Cheltenham in the north, Banbury in the northeast, Malmesbury in the south, and Bradford-on-Avon in the southwest—the Cotswolds' verdant, vivid hills hide tiny towns barely touched by modern life. These old Roman settlements and tiny Saxon villages, hewn from the famed Cotswold stone, demand a place on any itinerary, although their relative inaccessibility via public transportation will necessitate extra effort to get there.

TRANSPORTATION. Useful gateway cities are Cheltenham, Oxford, and Bath. **Moreton-in-Marsh** is one of the bigger villages and has **trains** to Oxford (30min., every hr., £7.80) and London (1½hr., every hr., £23.90). It's much easier to reach the Cotswolds by **bus.** *Getting There*, a pamphlet that details bus information in The Cotswolds, is available free from the Cheltenham tourist office. **Pulham's Coaches** (☎(01451) 820 369) run from Cheltenham to Moreton-in-Marsh (1hr.; M-Sa 7 per day, Su 1 per day; £2) via Stow-on-the-Wold (50min., £1.55).

Local roads are perfect for biking. **The Toy Shop,** on High St. in Moreton-in-Marsh, rents bikes. (☎(01608) 650 756. Open M, W-Sa 9am-1pm and 2-5pm. £12 per day.) Visitors can also experience the Cotswolds as the English have for centuries by treading footpaths from village to village. **Cotswold Way,** spanning 160km from Bath to Chipping Camden, gives hikers glorious vistas of hills and dales. The *Cotswold Events* booklet lists anything from music festivals and antique markets to cheese-rolling and woolsack races along the Cotswold Way. A newer way of seeing the region, the **Cotswold Experience** is a full-day bus tour that starts in Bath and visits five of the most scenic villages. (☎(01225) 325 900. £23.50, students £19.50.)

WINCHCOMBE, MORETON-IN-MARSH, STOW-ON-THE-WOLD. 10km north of Cheltenham on the A46, **Sudeley Castle,** once the manor of King Ethelred the Unready, crowns the town of Winchcombe. (Open Mar.-Oct. daily 11am-5pm. £6.50.) The Winchcombe **tourist office** is in Town Hall. (☎(01242) 602 925. Open Apr.-Oct. M-Sa 10am-1pm and 2-5pm, Su 10am-1pm and 2-4pm.)

With a train station, relatively frequent bus service, and bike shop, Moreton-in-Marsh is a convenient base for exploring the Cotswolds. Three miles east of Moreton on the A24, visitors to the **Longborough Farm Shop** can pick fruit on 10 acres of farmland. (☎(01451) 830 413. Open M-Sa 9am-6pm, Su 10am-6pm. Self-picking June-Sept. £1-3 per basket.) The **tourist office** is in the District Council Building. (☎(01208) 650 881. Open Easter-Oct. M-F 9am-5pm.) **Warwick House B&B ❸,** on London Rd., offers many small luxuries, including access to a nearby gym. Book in advance. (☎(01608) 650 733. www.snoozeandsizzle.com. £25 per person, two nights or more £20.)

Stow-on-the-Wold, the self-proclaimed "Heart of the Cotswolds," quietly sleeps atop a hill, offering visitors fine views and a sense of the Cotswold pace of life. The **tourist office** is in Hollis House on The Square. (☎(01451) 831 082. Open Easter-Oct. M-Sa 9:30am-5:30pm, Su 10:30am-4pm; Nov.-Easter M-Sa 9:30am-4:30pm.) The **YHA youth hostel ❷** is near the tourist office on The Square. (☎(01451) 830 497. Open Apr.-Sept. Dorms £12.75, students £11.75.)

BIRMINGHAM ☎0212

As the industrial heart of the Midlands, Birmingham (pop. 1.2 million) is a resolutely modern transportation hub, its city center packed with convention-goers, cell phones, and three-piece suits. Twelve minutes south of town by rail lies **Cadbury World,** an unabashed celebration of the chocolate company. Take a train from New St. to Bournville, or bus #83, 84, or 85 from the city center. (☎451 4159. Open daily 10am-3pm; closed certain days Nov.-Feb. £8.25, students and seniors £6.75, children £6.25. Includes free chocolate bars.) The **Barber Institute of Fine Arts,** in the University of Birmingham on Edgbaston Park Rd., displays works by artists as diverse as Rubens, Gainsborough, and Magritte. Take bus #61, 62, or 63 from the city center. (☎414 7333. Open M-Sa 10am-5pm, Su noon-5pm. Free.) Pick up a copy of the bimonthly *What's On* to discover the latest hot spots. **Broad Street** is home to trendy cafe-bars and clubs. The **Birmingham Jazz Festival** (☎454 7020) brings over 200 jazz singers and instrumentalists to town during the first two weeks of July; book through the tourist office.

Birmingham is the center of a web of train and bus lines between London, central Wales, southwest England, and all points north. **Trains** arrive in New St. Station (☎(08457) 484 950) from: Liverpool Lime St. (1½hr., 1-2 per hr., £18.50); London Euston (2hr., 2 per hr., £29.60); Manchester Piccadilly (2½hr., every hr., £16.50); and Oxford (1¼hr., 1-2 per hr., £16.50). National Express **buses** (☎(08705) 808 080) arrive in Digbeth Station from: Cardiff (3hr., 3 per day, round-trip £17.80); Liverpool (2½hr., every hr., round-trip £11.75); London (3hr., every hr., round-trip £11.50); and Manchester (2½hr., every 2hr., round-trip £13). The **tourist office,** 2 City Arcade, makes room reservations. (☎643 2514. Open M-Sa 9:30am-5:30pm.) Despite its size, Birmingham has no hostels, and inexpensive B&Bs are rare; **Hagley Road** is your best bet for B&Bs. To reach **Grasmere Guest House ❷,** 37 Serpentine Rd., take bus #22, 23, or 103 from Colmore Row to the Harbourne swimming bath (20min.); turn right off Harborne Rd. onto Serpentine Rd. (☎/fax 427 4546. Singles £15, with bath £25; doubles £30.) **Warehouse Cafe ❶,** 54 Allison St., off Digbeth above the Friends of the Earth office, keeps locals satisfied with delicious veggie burgers. (£2. Open M-F noon-2:30pm, Sa noon-3pm.) **Postal Code:** B2 4AA.

CAMBRIDGE ☎01223

In contrast to museum-oriented, metropolitan Oxford, Cambridge is determined to retain its pastoral academic robes. As the tourist office will tell you, the city manages—rather than encourages—visitors. No longer the exclusive preserve of upper-class sons, the university has finally opened its doors to women and state-school pupils; during May Week, which marks the end of exams, Cambridge shakes off its reserve with gin-soaked glee.

TRANSPORTATION

Trains: (☎(08457) 484 950), Station Rd. Ticket office open daily 5am-11pm. To **London King's Cross** (45min., 2 per hr., £15.10) and **London Liverpool Street** (1¼hr., 2 per hr., £15.10).

Buses: Drummer St. **National Express** (☎(08705) 808 080) arrives from **London Victoria** (2hr., 17 per day, from £8). **Stagecoach** buses go to **Oxford** (2¾hr., 10-12 per day, from £6). **Cambus** (☎423 554) runs local routes (£1-2).

Bike Rental: Mike's Bikes, 28 Mill Rd. (☎312 591). £8 per day, £10 per week. Open M-Sa 9am-6pm, Su 10am-4pm.

ORIENTATION AND PRACTICAL INFORMATION

The city has two main avenues. One, a main shopping street, starts at **Magdalene** (MAUD-lin) **Bridge** and becomes **Bridge Street, Sidney Street, St. Andrew's Street, Regent Street,** and finally **Hills Road.** The other—first **St. John's Street,** then **Trinity Street, King's Parade,** and **Trumpington Street**—is the academic thoroughfare. The two streets cross at **St. John's College.** From the bus station at **Drummer Street,** a quick walk down **Emmanuel Street** will land you right in the shopping district near the tourist office. To get to the city center from the train station on **Station Road,** turn right onto Hills Rd., and continue straight ahead.

Tourist Office: (☎322 640), on Wheeler St., just south of Market Sq. Open Apr.-Oct. M-F 10am-5:30pm, Sa 10am-5pm, Su 11am-4pm; Nov.-Mar. closed Su.

American Express: 25 Sidney St. (☎(08706) 001 060). Open M-Tu and Th-F 9am-5:30pm, W 9:30am-5:30pm, Sa 9am-5pm.

Laundromat: Clean Machine, 22 Burleigh St. (☎578 009). Open daily 8am-8pm.

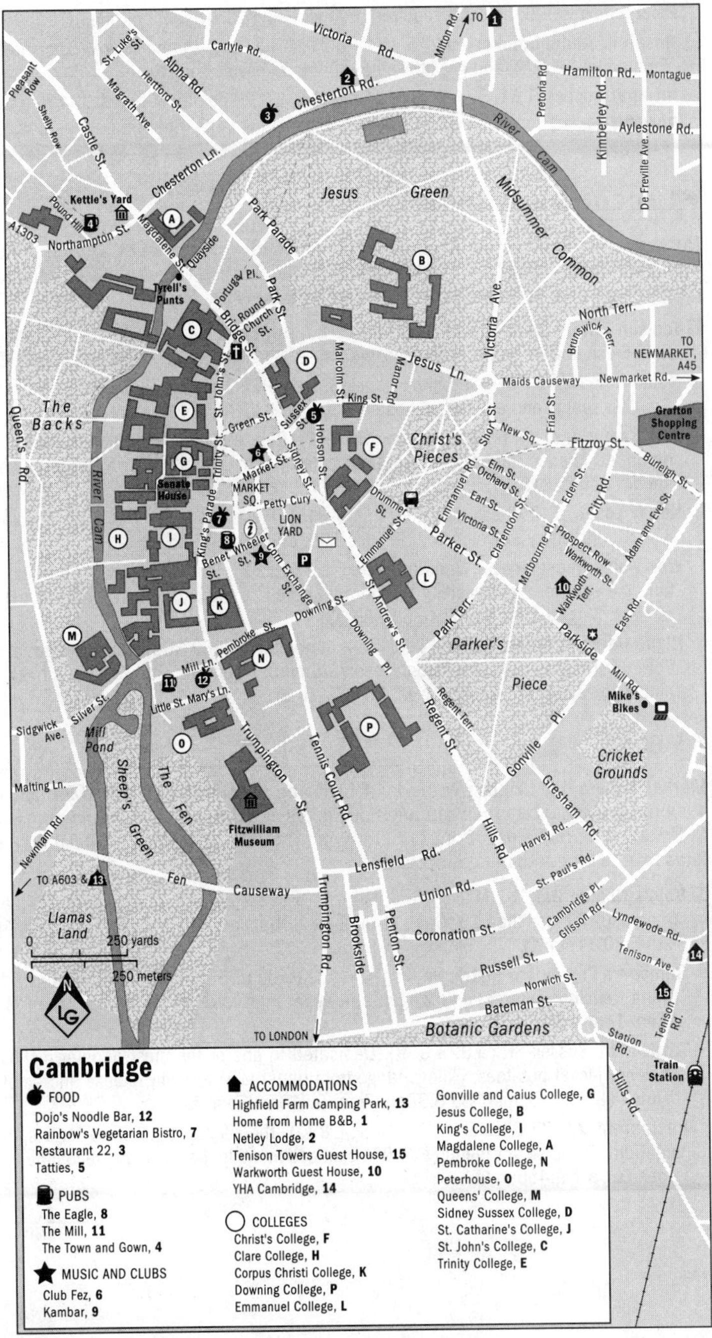

Cambridge

FOOD
- Dojo's Noodle Bar, **12**
- Rainbow's Vegetarian Bistro, **7**
- Restaurant 22, **3**
- Tatties, **5**

PUBS
- The Eagle, **8**
- The Mill, **11**
- The Town and Gown, **4**

MUSIC AND CLUBS
- Club Fez, **6**
- Kambar, **9**

ACCOMMODATIONS
- Highfield Farm Camping Park, **13**
- Home from Home B&B, **1**
- Netley Lodge, **2**
- Tenison Towers Guest House, **15**
- Warkworth Guest House, **10**
- YHA Cambridge, **14**

COLLEGES
- Christ's College, **F**
- Clare College, **H**
- Corpus Christi College, **K**
- Downing College, **P**
- Emmanuel College, **L**
- Gonville and Caius College, **G**
- Jesus College, **B**
- King's College, **I**
- Magdalene College, **A**
- Pembroke College, **N**
- Peterhouse, **O**
- Queens' College, **M**
- Sidney Sussex College, **D**
- St. Catharine's College, **J**
- St. John's College, **C**
- Trinity College, **E**

Emergency: ☎999; no coins required. **Police:** (☎358 966), on Parkside.

Hospital: Addenbrookes (☎245 151), on Hills Rd. Catch Cambus #4, 5, or 5a from Emmanuel St. (£1), and get off where Hill Rd. intersects Long Rd.

Internet Access: CB1, 32 Mill Rd. (☎576 306). £0.05 per min. Open daily 10am-8pm.

Post Office: 9-11 St. Andrew's St. (☎323 325). Open M-Sa 9am-5:30pm. **Postal Code:** CB2 3AA.

ACCOMMODATIONS

Rooms are scarce in Cambridge; book ahead. Many of the **B&Bs** around **Portugal Street** and **Tenison Road** are open only in July and August. Check the list at the tourist office, or pick up their guide to accommodations (£0.50).

Tenison Towers Guest House, 148 Tenison Rd. (☎566511). 2 blocks from the train station. Fresh flowers grace an impeccable house. Singles £20-25; doubles £40-50. ❸

Home from Home B&B, 39 Milton Rd. (☎323 555). A 20min. walk from the city center. Spotless rooms and a pleasant hostess. Singles £25-30; doubles £50-60. ❸

YHA Cambridge, 97 Tenison Rd. (☎354 601). Relaxed, welcoming atmosphere. Well-equipped kitchen, laundry, and a great cafeteria. In summer, reserve several weeks ahead. Dorms £15.10, under 18 £11.40. ❷

Netley Lodge, 112 Chesterton Rd. (☎363 845). Plush red carpets and a conservatory lush with greenery welcome you. Singles £28; doubles £45-55. ❸

Warkworth Guest House, Warkworth Terr. (☎363 682). Sunny rooms near the bus station; the spot for those wishing to skip a long walk to the city center. Packed lunch on request. Singles £35; doubles £55-£60. ❹

Highfield Farm Camping Park, Long Rd., Comberton (☎262 308). Take Cambus #118 from the Drummer St. bus station (every 45min.). Open Apr.-Oct. Call ahead. £7 per tent, with car £8.75; off-season £6.25/£7.25. ❶

BRITAIN

FOOD

Market Square has bright pyramids of fruit and vegetables. (Open M-Sa 9:30am-4:30pm.) Students buy their gin and cornflakes at **Sainsbury's,** 44 Sidney St. (Open M-F 8am-9pm, Sa 7:30am-9pm, Su 11am-5pm.) South of town, **Hills Road** and **Mill Road** brim with good, budget options.

Dojo's Noodle Bar, 1-2 Miller's Yard, Mill Ln. (☎363 471). Whips out enormous plates of noodles for less than £6. Open M-Th noon-2:30pm and 5:30-11pm, F-Su noon-4pm and 5:30-11pm. ❶

Rainbow's Vegetarian Bistro, 9a King's Parade (☎321 551). A tiny, creative burrow featuring delicious international vegan and vegetarian fare, all for £6.95. Open M-Sa 11am-11pm. ❷

Tatties, 11 Sussex St. (☎323 399). Dedicated to one of the most popular dishes in England, jacket potatoes. Fillings range from butter (£2) to Philly cheese and smoked salmon (£5.75). Open M-Sa 8:30am-7pm, Su 10am-5pm. ❶

Restaurant 22, 22 Chesterton Rd. (☎351 880). There's no better place for a special night out. 3-course set menu (£24.95) changes monthly. Reservations recommended. Open Tu-Sa 7-9:45pm. ❺

SIGHTS

Cambridge is an architect's fantasy—it packs some of the most breathtaking examples of English architecture into less than 3 square kilometers. If you have time for only a few colleges, **Trinity, King's, St. John's, Queens'** and **Christ's** should top your list. Cambridge is most exciting during the university's three eight-week terms: Michaelmas (Oct.-Dec.), Lent (Jan.-Mar.), and Easter (Apr.-June). Most of the colleges are open daily from 9am to 5:30pm, but hours vary often. A few are closed to sightseers during the Easter term, and virtually all are closed during exams (mid-May to mid-June).

TRINITY COLLEGE. Founded in 1546 by Henry VIII, the college is legendarily the wealthiest at Cambridge. Sir Isaac Newton, who lived in E-entry for 30 years, originally measured the speed of sound by stamping his foot in the cloister along the north side of the **Great Court**—the largest courtyard in Cambridge. The college also houses the stunning **Wren Library,** home to A.A. Milne's handwritten manuscript of *Winnie the Pooh* and Newton's own copies of his work. *(On Trinity St. ☎338 400. Chapel and courtyard open daily 10am-5pm. Library open M-F noon-2pm, Sa 10:30am-12:30pm. Easter-Oct. £1.75; Nov.-Easter free.)*

KING'S COLLEGE. E.M. Forster's alma mater dominates King's Parade St. from street level to skyline. Founded in 1441 by Henry VI, the college houses **King's College Chapel,** a spectacular Gothic monument with elaborately carved interiors. Rubens's magnificent *Adoration of the Magi* hangs behind the altar. *(On King's Parade. ☎331 100. Open M-Sa 9:30am-4:30pm, Su 9:30am-2:30pm. Tours arranged through the tourist office. £3.50, students £2.50, under 12 free.)*

ST. JOHN'S COLLEGE. Established in 1511 by Lady Margaret Beaufort, mother of Henry VIII, St. John's is one of the seven colleges founded by women. A copy of Venice's **Bridge of Sighs** connects the older part of the college to the neo-Gothic extravagance of **New Court.** The **School of Pythagoras,** a 12th-century pile of wood and stone, supposedly the oldest complete building in Cambridge, hides in St. John's Gardens. *(St. John's St. ☎338 600. Open daily 10am-4:45pm. £2, students £1.20.)*

QUEENS' COLLEGE. Queens' has the only unaltered Tudor courtyard in Cambridge. The **Mathematical Bridge,** despite rumors to the contrary, has always been supported by screws and bolts, not just mathematical principle. *(On Silver St. ☎335 511. Open Mar.-Oct. daily 10am-4:30pm. Closed during exams. £1.)*

CHRIST'S COLLEGE. Founded as "God's house" in 1448, Christ's has won fame for gorgeous gardens and its association with John Milton. Charles Darwin studied at Christ's before dealing a blow to its religious origins. *(On St. Andrews St. ☎334 900. Gardens open in summer M-F 9:30am-noon; term-time M-F 9am-4:30pm. Free.)*

FITZWILLIAM MUSEUM. A welcome break from academia, the Fitzwilliam Museum displays Egyptian, Chinese, Japanese, and Greek treasures, as well as an intimate collection of French Impressionist works. *(On Trumpington St. ☎332 900. Open Tu-Sa 10am-5pm, Su 2:15-5pm. Suggested donation £3. Guided tours Sa 2:30pm; £3.)*

KETTLE'S YARD. This museum used to be the home of Tate curator Jim Ede; now visitors wander through the house and admire his early 20th-century collection. The gallery rotates exhibits. *(☎352 124. House open Apr.-Sept. Tu-Sa 1:30-4:30pm, Su 2-4:30pm; Oct.-Mar. Tu-Su 2-4pm; gallery open year-round Tu-Su 11:30am-5pm. Free.)*

BRITAIN

ENTERTAINMENT AND NIGHTLIFE

The best source of info on student activities is the student newspaper *Varsity;* the tourist office also has useful brochures. **Punts** (gondola-like boats) are a favored form of entertainment in Cambridge. Beware that punt-bombing—jumping from bridges into the river alongside a punt, thereby tipping its occupants into the Cam—has evolved into an art form. **Tyrell's,** on Magdalene Bridge, rents boats. (☎(01480) 413 517. £10 per hr. plus a £40 deposit.) Even more traditional than punting is **pub-crawling;** most pubs stay open 11am-11pm. **The Eagle,** 8 Benet St., is the oldest pub in Cambridge. Watson and Crick once rushed in to announce their discovery of the DNA double helix—unimpressed, the barmaid insisted they settle their four-shilling tab before she'd serve them a toast. **The Mill,** 14 Mill Ln. off Silver St. Bridge, claims a riverside park as its own for punt- and people-watching. The gay crowd downs ale at **The Town and Gown,** on Poundhill off Northhampton. Late-night, the club **Kambar,** 1 Wheeler St., attracts crowds with the only regular indie night (Sa) as well as garage, goth, and electronica. (Open M-Sa 10pm-2:30am.) **Club Fez,** 15 Market Passage, offers music ranging from Latin to trance to dance in Moroccan-themed surroundings. (Cover Su-Th £2-5, F-Sa £7-8. Open M-Tu 9pm-2:30am, W-Sa 9pm-2am, Su 8pm-midnight.)

DAYTRIP FROM CAMBRIDGE

GRANTCHESTER

To reach Grantchester Meadows from Cambridge, take the path that follows the River Cam (45min. by foot). Grantchester itself lies about 1½km from the meadows; ask the way at a neighborhood shop. Stagecoach Cambus #118 also runs to Grantchester; get off at the town's bus stand (9-11 per day from Drummer St., round-trip £1.50).

Travelers searching for rejuvenation after the bustle of the college town head to the idyllic setting of Grantchester, once a stomping ground for Cambridge literati including Virginia Woolf, Rupert Brooke, E.M. Forster, and Ludwig Wittgenstein. Wander past the town to the idyllic **Orchard Tea Gardens,** on Mill Way. Outdoor plays are occasionally performed on summer evenings; ask at the Cambridge tourist office. (Open daily 10am-7pm.) The weathered 14th-century **Parish Church of St. Andrew and St. Mary,** on Millway, is beautifully intimate and not to be missed.

NORWICH ☎01603

Even though Norwich retains the hallmarks of an ancient city, its university and active art community ensure that it is thoroughly modern. The 11th-century **Norwich Cathedral** and the 12th-century **Norwich Castle,** where King John signed the Magna Carta in 1215, reign over puzzling, winding streets. (Cathedral open mid-May to mid-Sept. daily 7:30am-7pm; mid-Sept. to mid-May 7:30am-6pm. Suggested donation £3. Castle open July-Aug. M-Sa 10am-7pm, Su noon-5pm; Sept.-June M-Sa 10am-5pm, Su 2-5pm. £4.70, students £4.10.) **Trains** (☎(08457) 484 950) arrive at the corner of Riverside and Thorpe Rd. from London Liverpool St. (2hr., M-Sa 30 per day, £34.50). National Express **buses** (☎(08705) 808 080) also travel from London (3hr., 6 per day, £13.25). To get to the **tourist office** in The Forum, Millenium Plain, on Bethel Street, head right from the train station, take a left on Prince of Wales Rd., and cross the bridge to the castle; from the bus station, head left on Surrey St. and then right on St. Stephen's St. to the castle. (☎666 071. Open June-Sept. M-Sa 9:30am-5pm; Oct.-May M-Sa 9:30am-4:30pm.) **The Abbey Hotel ❸,** 16 Stracey Rd., 5min. from the train station up Thorpe Rd., is clean and quiet. (☎612 915. Singles £20-29; doubles £40-54.) In the heart of the city is one of England's largest and oldest open-air **markets** (open M-Sa 8:30am-4:30pm) as well as a trove of excellent restaurants. Nightlife abounds on **Tombland, Prince of Wales Road,** and **The Riverside.** **Postal Code:** NR1 3DD.

NOTTINGHAM ☎0115

Nottingham (pop. 262,000), home to the mythical Robin Hood and his band of merry men, lures visitors with a tourist industry that boasts little substance but plenty of thrill. **The Galleries of Justice,** High Pavement, is an interactive museum that puts tourists on trial, throws them behind bars, and lets them see the English prison system through the eyes of the convicted. (Open Tu-Su 10am-5pm. £7, students £6.) The remains of **Nottingham Castle,** originally constructed in 1068 by William the Conqueror, now house the **Castle Museum.** (Open Mar.-Oct. daily 10am-5pm; Nov.-Feb. Sa-Th 10am-5pm. M-Th free; Sa-Su £2, students £1.) **Trains** (☎(08457) 484 950) leave from Carrington St. for London (2hr., every hr., £42.50) and Sheffield (50min., every hr., £7.30). National Express **buses** (☎(08705) 808 080) leave from the station between Collin St. and Canal St. for London (3hr., 7 per day, £15) and Sheffield (1¼hr., every hr., £5.25). The **tourist office,** 1-4 Smithy Row, is just off Old Market Sq. (☎915 5330. Open M-F 9am-5:30pm, Sa 9am-5pm; Aug.-Sept. also Su 10am-3pm.) **Igloo ❷,** 110 Mansfield Rd., is a homey hostel run by an experienced backpacker. Take bus #90 from the train station to Mansfield Rd. (☎947 5250. Dorms £12.) **The Alley Cafe ❶,** 1a Cannon Court, Long Row West, is a delicious vegetarian restaurant and relaxed nightspot. (Entrees £4-5. Open M-Tu 11am-6pm, W-Sa 11am-11pm.) **Postal Code:** NG1 2BN.

NORTHERN ENGLAND

The north's innovative music and arts scenes are world-famous: Liverpool and Manchester alone produced four of *Q* magazine's ten biggest rock stars of the century. Its principal urban areas may have grown out of the wool and coal industries, bearing 19th-century scars to prove it, but their newly refurbished city centers have redirected their energies toward accommodating visitors. Find respite from city life in the Peak District to the east or the Lake District to the north.

MANCHESTER ☎0161

The Industrial Revolution transformed the once unremarkable village of Manchester into a northern hub, now Britain's second-largest urban area. With few attractive areas and fewer budget accommodations in the city center, Manchester proves that you don't have to be pretty to be popular, attracting thousands with its pulsing nightlife and vibrant arts scene.

TRANSPORTATION. **Trains** leave **Piccadilly Station,** on London Rd., and **Victoria Station,** on Victoria St., for: London Euston (2½hr., 1 per hr., £49); Birmingham (1¾hr., 2 per hr., £16.50); Chester (1hr., every hr., £8.95); Edinburgh (4hr., every hr., £45.90); Liverpool (50min., 2 per hr., £7.40); and York (40min., 2 per hr., £17.90). National Express **buses** (☎(08705) 808 080) go from Chorlton St. to London (4-5hr., 7 per day, £17) and Liverpool (50min., every hr., £4.75). **Piccadilly Gardens** is home to about 50 local bus stops; pick up a route map at the tourist office.

PRACTICAL INFORMATION. The **Manchester Visitor Centre,** in the Town Hall Extension on Lloyd St., provides maps and books accommodations for £2.50. (☎234 3157; info. (0891) 715 533. Open M-Sa 10am-5pm, Su 10:30am-4:30pm.) Check **email** at **Internet Exchange,** 1-3 Piccadilly Sq., on the 2nd fl. of Coffee Republic. (£1 per hr. with £2 membership, otherwise £1 per 15min. Open M-F 7:30am-6:30pm, Sa 8am-6:30pm, Su 9:30am-5:30pm.) **Postal Code:** M2 1BB.

ACCOMMODATIONS AND FOOD. The elegant **Jury's Inn Manchester ❺,** 56 Bridgewater St., offers enormous, economic triples, luxurious baths, and professional service. (☎953 8888. A double and single bed in each room; £65 per room. £45 weekend special subject to availability.) Take bus #33 from Piccadilly Gardens toward Wigan to reach the swanky **YHA Manchester ❷,** Potato Wharf, Castlefield. (☎839 9960. Lockers £1-2. Laundry £1.50. Internet access £0.50 per 6min. Reception 7am-11pm. Dorms £18.50, under 18 £13.50.) **Tampopo Noodle House ❷,** 16 Albert Sq., is a chic Manchester favorite (Dishes £3-8. Open M-Sa noon-11pm, Su noon-10pm.) At **Gaia ❸,** 46 Sackville St., skilled chefs fuse British and Mediterranean cuisines. (Entrees £8-13. Open Su-Th noon-midnight, F-Sa noon-2am.)

SIGHTS AND ENTERTAINMENT. The exception to Manchester's unspectacular buildings is the neo-Gothic **Manchester Town Hall,** behind the tourist office in St. Peter's Sq. Nearby is the domed **Central Library,** one of the largest municipal libraries in Europe. (Open M-Th 10am-8pm, F-Sa 10am-5pm.) In the **Museum of Science and Industry,** on Liverpool Rd. in Castlefield, working steam engines provide a dramatic vision of Britain's industrialization. (Open daily 10am-5pm. Free. Special exhibit £3-5.) The **Manchester United Museum and Tour Centre,** on Sir Matt Busby Way at the Old Trafford football stadium, revels in everything that is the football team Manchester United. Follow the signs up Warwick Rd. from the Old Trafford Metrolink stop. (Open daily 9:30am-5pm. Museum £5.50, seniors and children £3.75. Tours every 10min. 9:40am-4:30pm. £3, seniors and children £2.) One of Manchester's biggest draws is its artistic offerings, most notably its theater and music scenes; the **Royal Exchange Theatre,** on St. Ann's Sq., regularly puts on Shakespearean and original works. (☎833 9333. Box office open M-Sa 9:30am-7:30pm. £7-24. Student discounts when booked in advance.)

Come nightfall, try **The Lass O'Gowrie,** 36 Charles St., a lively pub with good food at even better prices. (Food served 9am-7pm, £2-5. Open M-Sa 11am-11pm, Su noon-10:30pm.) **Musicbox,** on Oxford Rd., is a popular underground warehouse club that hosts weekly events. (Cover £5-8. Open Th-Sa from 10pm.) Manchester's gay nightlife is centered around the vibrant **Gay Village,** northeast of Princess St.; bars line **Canal Street,** the center of the village. Enthusiastic crowds pack **Cruz 101,** 101 Princess St., the champion of Manchester's nightlife. (M, F, Sa cover £2-5, Tu-Th free. Open M-Sa 10:30pm-2:30am.)

CHESTER ☎01244

With fashionable stores behind mock-medieval facades, tour guides in Roman armor, a town crier in full uniform, and a Barclays bank in a wing of the cathedral, Chester at times resembles a theme park of Ye Olde English Towne. Originally built by frontier-forging Romans, the crowded but lovely town now maintains a pace to match the horse races at its internationally celebrated **Roodee racetrack.** The famous **city walls** completely encircle the town. Just outside Newgate lies the base of the largest Roman **amphitheater** in Britain. (Always open. Free.) **Chester Zoo** is one of Europe's largest; go on a weekday to avoid the crowds. Take Crosville bus #8 or 8x (£2) from the bus exchange behind the town hall. (Open in summer daily 10am-7pm, last entry 5pm; off-season until 5:30pm, last entry 3:30pm. £10.50, YHA members £9.50, seniors and children £8.50.) Intersecting stone arches, "The Crown of Stone," support the tower of **Chester Cathedral,** just off Northgate St., and stained-glass windows blaze throughout. (Open daily 8am-6pm. Suggested donation £3.) Pubs line **Lower Bridge Street** and **Watergate Street.**

Trains (☎(08457) 484 950) arrive from: Birmingham (1¾hr., 1-2 per hr., £10.90); Liverpool (1½hr., 1-2 per hr., £3.60); London Euston (2½hr., 1-2 per hr., £50); and Manchester Piccadilly (1hr., 1-2 per hr., £8.90). National Express (☎(08705) 808 080) **buses** arrive on Delamere St. from: Birmingham (2hr., 5 per day); London (5½hr., 5-6 per day, £16.50); and Manchester (1¼hr., 3 per day). The **tourist office** is in Town Hall, on Northgate St. (☎402 111. Open daily M-Sa 9am-5pm, Su 10am-4pm.) **B&Bs** (£20 and up) concentrate on **Hoole Road** and **Brook Street.** Bus #53 (6 per hr.) runs to the area from the city center. To get to the Victorian **YHA Chester ❷,** Hough Green House, 40 Hough Green, take bus #7 or 16 from the bus exchange. (☎680 056. Internet access. Laundry. Breakfast included. Reception 7am-10:30pm. Open mid-Jan. to mid-Dec. Dorms £15, under 18 £12.) **Laburnum Guest House ❸,** 2 St. Anne St., across from the bus station, offers sparkling rooms only a minute's walk from the town's north gate. (☎380 313. All rooms with bath. £22 per person.) **Philpotts ❶,** 2 Goss St., off Watergate St., stuffs baguettes with ingredients like tuna, sweet corn, and Somerset brie for £1.60-2.30. (Open M-Sa 8am-2:30pm.) **Postal Code:** CH1 1AA.

LIVERPOOL ☎0151

Free museums, a raucous nightlife, and restaurants on every block make Liverpool, hometown of the Beatles, a great destination for travelers. Scousers—as Liverpudlians are colloquially known—are usually happy to introduce you to their dialect and to discuss the relative merits of Liverpool's two football teams.

TRANSPORTATION AND PRACTICAL INFORMATION. Trains (☎(08457) 484 950) leave Lime St. for: Birmingham (1¾hr., 2-5 per day, £18.50); Chester (45min., 2 per hr., £3.20); London Euston (3hr., every hr., £48.40); and Manchester Piccadilly (1½hr., 2-3 per hr., £7.40). National Express **buses** (☎(08705) 808 080) go from Norton St. Coach Station to: Birmingham (2½hr., 5 per day); London (4½hr., 5 per day, £16.50); and Manchester (1hr., 1-2 per hr.). The Isle of Man Steam Packet Company (☎(08705) 523 523) runs **ferries** from Princess Dock to Dublin.

The main **tourist office,** in the Queen Square Centre, sells the handy *Visitor Guide to Liverpool and Merseyside* (£1) and books beds for a 10% deposit. (☎(0906) 680 6886; £0.25 per min. Open M and W-Sa 9am-5:30pm, Tu 10am-5:30pm, Su 10:30am-4:30pm.) Expert guide Phil Hughes runs excellent personalized **Beatles tours** (☎228 4565) for the lucky eight that fit in his van. Check **email** at the **Central Library,** William Brown St. (Free. Open M-Sa 9am-5pm, Su noon-5pm.) **Postal Code:** L1 1AA.

ACCOMMODATIONS AND FOOD. Budget hotels are mostly on **Lord Nelson Street,** next to the train station, and **Mount Pleasant,** one block from Brownlow Hill. Clean rooms await at **Aachen Hotel ❸,** 89-91 Mt. Pleasant, the winner of numerous awards. (☎709 3477. Singles £28-38; doubles £46-54.) **YHA Liverpool ❷,** 24 Tabley St., off The Wapping, is in an ideal location. (☎709 8888. Breakfast included. Dorms £19, under 18 £14.50.) The **International Inn ❷,** 4 South Hunter St., off Hardman St., is clean *and* fun, a rare hostel combo. (☎709 8135. Dorms £15; doubles £36.) The pleasant **Thistle Hotel ❹,** on Chapel St., is a short walk from downtown Liverpool. (☎227 4444. Singles £50-100. Call ahead for discounts.)

Trendy cafes and well-priced Indian restaurants line **Bold Street** and **Hardman Street,** while fast-food joints crowd **Hardnon Street** and **Berry Street.** Many eateries stay open until 3am. **Simply Heathcotes ❹,** 25 The Strand, Beetham Plaza, is simply elegant. Try the breaded veal escalope or seared fillet of salmon. (Entrees average £15. Open M-Sa noon-2:30pm and 6-10pm.) **Tavern Co. ❷,** in Queen Sq., near the tourist office, serves hearty burritos and creative taco salads (£5-7) in a popular

BRITAIN

wine-bar atmosphere. (Open M-Sa noon-11pm, Su 10:30am-10:30pm; food served until 10pm.) Candles and Spanish music set the mood at **La Tasca ❷,** on Queen St., a popular *tapas* bar. (*Tapas* £3-4. Open daily noon-11pm.)

SIGHTS. The tourist office's **Beatles Map** (£2.50) leads visitors through Beatles-themed sights, including **Strawberry Fields** and **Penny Lane.** At Albert Dock, **The Beatles Story** pays tribute to the group's work with a recreation of the Cavern Club and a yellow submarine. (Open Apr.-Oct. daily 10am-6pm; Nov.-Mar. 10am-5pm. £8, students £5.50.) Nearby, the **Merseyside Maritime Museum** details Liverpool's heyday as a major port. (Open daily 10am-5pm. Free.) The intimate Liverpool branch of the **Tate Gallery,** also on Albert Dock, contains a select range of 20th-century artwork. (Open Tu-Su 10am-6pm. Free; some special exhibits £4.) The Anglican **Liverpool Cathedral,** on Upper Duke St., boasts the highest Gothic arches ever built and the heaviest bells in the world. Climb to the top of the 100m tower for a view stretching to Wales. (Cathedral open daily 8am-6pm. Suggested donation £2.50. Tower open M-Sa 11am-4pm, weather permitting. £2.) Neon-blue stained glass casts a glow over the interior of the **Metropolitan Cathedral of Christ the King,** on Mt. Pleasant, and modern sculptures fill the chapels. (Open in summer M-F 8am-6pm, Sa-Su 8:30am-6pm; off-season M-F 8am-6pm, Sa 8:30am-6pm, Su 8:30am-5pm. Free.) The **Liverpool** and **Everton football clubs**—intense rivals—both offer tours of their grounds. Bus #26 runs from the city center to both stadiums. (Book in advance. Everton ☎330 2277; £5.50. Liverpool ☎260 6677; £8.50.)

NIGHTLIFE. Consult the *Liverpool Echo*, an evening paper sold by street vendors, for up-to-date information on nightlife. **Slater Street** in particular brims with £1 pints, while on weekend nights, the downtown area—especially **Mathew Street, Church Street,** and **Bold Street**—overflows with young clubbers. John Lennon once said that the worst thing about fame was "not being able to get a quiet pint at the Phil." Fortunately, the rest of us can sip in solitude at **The Philharmonic,** 36 Hope St. (Open M-Sa noon-11pm, Su noon-10:30pm.) **The Jacaranda,** on Slater St., the site of the Beatles' first paid gig, has live bands and a dance floor. (Open M-Sa noon-2am, Su noon-10:30pm.) **The Caledonia Laundromatic Super Pub,** on the corner of Catherine St. and Caledonia St., is half-launderette and half-pub, with nightly DJs and cheap food and pints. (Laundry £3. Free Internet. Open M-Sa noon-11pm, Su noon-10:30pm; food served noon-8pm.) **Medication,** in Wolstonholme Sq.,

THE LOCAL STORY

I ONCE HAD A BAND, OR SHOULD I SAY, THEY ONCE HAD ME

Alan Williams, owner of The Jacaranda Coffee Bar in Liverpool, was the first manager of the world's favorite mopheads. According to Williams, the Beatles were coffee bar bums who skipped lectures to hang out at The Jac, eating their beloved "bacon-butty" sandwiches and listening to the music they would come to dominate. Williams also recalled that when Pete Best kept the beat (not that interloper, Ringo), the group was smuggled into Hamburg as "students," then deported when a 17-year-old George Harrison was busted for hanging out at 18+ clubs. Here are a few more of Williams's memories.

LG: How did you meet the Beatles?
AW: My wife and I had a coffee bar club. Because I was a rock 'n' roll promoter, all the groups used to come to my place, mainly 'cuz I let them rehearse for free in the basement. I only knew [the Beatles] as coffee bar layabouts–they were always bummin' free coffee off of *anybody*... I had complaints about the obscene graffiti that the girls were writing about the groups, and here these lads were from the art school and they could paint. I said, "Will you decorate the ladies' toilets for me?" And the way they decorated them, I'd have preferred the graffiti, to be honest with you. They were just *throwing* paint on them as if they were Picassos.

offers the wildest student night in town, with house, pop, and indie rooms. (Students only; bring ID. Open W 10am-2am. Cover £5.) **The Cavern Club,** 10 Mathew St., is on the site where the Fab Four gained prominence; today it draws locals for live bands. (No cover until 10pm, 10-11pm £2, 11pm-2am £4. Live music Th-F 8pm-2am, Sa 2-11pm. Open Th-F 6pm-2am, Sa 6pm-3am; pub open M-Sa from noon, Su noon-11:30pm.)

SHEFFIELD ☎0114

Stainless steel was invented in Sheffield (pop. 530,000), a former center for the mass production of cutlery. As industry moved elsewhere, economic depression, made familiar in *The Full Monty*, set in. Like other post-industrial areas in Britain, Sheffield now offers its visitors numerous art galleries and vibrant nightlife, making it a nice stop before the pastoral Peak District. The **Millennium Galleries,** Arundel Gate, showcase both national and international exhibitions, with a focus on the relationship between art and industry. (Open M-Sa 10am-5pm, Su 11am-5pm. Free; special exhibits from £4.) The collection at **Graves Gallery,** on nearby Surrey St., above the public library, includes post-war British art as well as Romantic and Impressionist works. (Open in summer M-Sa 10am-5pm; off-season Tu-Sa 10am-5pm. Free.) Most clubs are in the southeast, near **Matilda Street.** Students pack **The Leadmill,** 6 Leadmill Rd. (Cover £2-5. Open M-Th 10pm-2am, F 10pm-2:30am, Sa 10pm- 3am.)

Trains (☎(08457) 484 950) leave from Sheaf St. for: Birmingham (1½hr., 1-2 per hr., £18.50); Liverpool (1¾hr., every hr., £13.90); London St. Pancras (2-3hr., 1-2 per hr., £46); Manchester (1hr., every hr., £10.75); and York (1¼hr., every hr., £12.80). National Express **buses** (☎(08705) 808 080) leave from the **Interchange,** between Pond St. and Sheaf St., for: Birmingham (2½hr., 6 per day, £13.25); London (3½hr., 8 per day, £12.75); and Nottingham (1¼hr., every hr., £5.25). The **tourist office** is at 1 Tudor Sq., off Surrey St. (☎221 1900. Open M-Th 9:30am-5:15pm, F 10:30am-5:15pm, Sa 9:30am-4:15pm.) **Rutland Arms ❸,** 86 Brown St., near the bus and train stations, offers clean rooms above a pub. (☎272 9003. Breakfast included. All rooms with bath. Singles £23.50; doubles £37.) **Havana Bistro ❶,** 32-34 Division St., is an Internet cafe with delicious food for under £5. (Internet £1 per 15min., £3 per hr. Open M-Th 10am-10pm, F-Sa 10am-7pm, Su 11am-6pm.) **Postal Code:** S1 1AB.

LG: Sort of Pollock-style...

AW: Heh. Yeah...

LG: And how did you become their manager?

AW: I put this big rock 'n' roll show on. They came and saw me the next day and said, "Hey Al? When are you going to do something for us like?" And I said to them, "Look, there's no more painting to be done." And they said, "No, we've got a *group*." I said, "I didn't know that." And they said, "Well, will you manage us?" By then I had got to know them, and they were quite nice personalities—very witty. And I go, "Oh yeah, this could be fun." And then I managed them.

Williams felt that it was their stint in Hamburg, and not Liverpool, that made the Beatles. He describes his falling out with the group as a disagreement over—what else?—contract disputes and general rock-star ingratitude.

AW: I wrote them a letter saying that they appeared to be getting more than a little swell-headed and "Remember, I managed you when nobody else wanted to know you. But I'll fix it now so that you'll never ever work again."

LG: Uh-oh.

AW: So that's my big mistake, yeah. Heh. And on that note, we'll finish.

PEAK DISTRICT NATIONAL PARK

A green cushion between England's industrial giants of Manchester, Sheffield, and Nottingham, Britain's first national park sprawls across 1400 sq. km of rolling hills and windswept moors, offering a playground for its 22 million urban neighbors. In the **Dark Peak** area to the north, deep groughs (gullies) gouge the hard peat moorland below gloomy cliffs, while friendlier footpaths criss cross the rocky hillsides and village clusters of the **Northern Peak** area. The rolls of the southern **White Peak** cradle abandoned millstones and stately country homes.

TRANSPORTATION AND PRACTICAL INFORMATION. The invaluable *Peak District Timetable* (£0.60), available at tourist offices, has transport routes and a map. Two **train** lines originate in Manchester and enter the park from the west: one stops at Buxton, near the park's edge (1hr., every hr., £5.70), and the other crosses the park (1½hr., 9-17 per day) via Edale (£6.70), Hope (near Castleton), and Hathersage, terminating in Sheffield (£11). Trent (☎01773 712 2765) **bus** TP, the "Transpeak," goes from Manchester to Nottingham (3hr.), stopping at Buxton, Bakewell, Matlock, Derby, and other towns in between. First PMT (☎01782 207 999) #X18 runs from Sheffield to Bakewell (45min., M-Sa 5 per day). First Mainline (☎01709 515 151) #272 and Stagecoach East Midland (☎01246 211 007) #273 and 274 run from Sheffield to Castleton (40-55min., 12-15 per day). The **Derbyshire Wayfarer,** available at tourist offices, allows one day of train and bus travel through the Peak District north to Sheffield and south to Derby (£7.25).

The **National Park Information Centres** (NPICs) at Bakewell, Castleton, and Edale offer walking guides. Info is also available at **tourist offices** in Buxton (☎01298 25 106) and Matlock Bath (☎01629 55 082). There are 20 **YHA youth hostels** ❷ in the park (£8-15); for Bakewell, Castleton, and Edale, see below, or try Buxton (☎01298 22 287) or Matlock (☎01629 582 983). To stay at the 13 **YHA Camping Barns** ❶ throughout the park (£3.60 per person), book ahead at the **Camping Barns Reservation Office,** 6 King St., Clitheroe, Lancashire BB7 2EP (☎01200 420 102). The park authority operates six **Cycle Hire Centres** (£12 per day); a free brochure, *Peak Cycle Hire*, available free at NPICs, includes phone numbers, hours, and locations.

BRITAIN

CASTLETON. The main attraction in **Castleton** (pop. 705) is **Treak Cliff Cavern.** Seams of Blue John, a semi-precious mineral found only in these hills, run along the walls of chambers filled with stalagmites and stalagtites. (40min. mandatory tours every 15-30min. Open Easter-Oct. daily 10am-4:45pm; Nov.-Feb. 10am-3:20pm; Mar.-Easter 10am-4:20pm. £5.50, students £4.50.) Hikers can set off southward from Castleton on the 42km **Limestone Way Trail** to Matlock. Castleton lies 3.2km west of the **Hope.** The Castleton **NPIC** is on Buxton Rd. (☎620 679. Open Apr.-Oct. daily 10am-5:30pm; Nov.-Mar. Sa-Su 10am-5pm.) **YHA Castleton** ❷ is in Castleton Hall, a pretty house in the heart of town. (☎620 235. Internet access. Open Feb. to late Dec. Dorms £11-14, under 18 £8-10.) **Phone Code:** ☎01433.

BAKEWELL AND EDALE. The town of **Bakewell,** 50km southeast of Manchester, is the best spot from which to explore the region. Located near several scenic walks through the White Peaks, the town itself is best known for its Bakewell pudding, created when a flustered cook inadvertently erred while making a tart. Take bus #179 (2 per day) to **Chartsworth House,** the beautifully decorated home of the Duke and Duchess of Devonshire. (Open Apr.-Dec. daily 11am-5:30pm; last admission 4:30pm. £7, students £5.50. 1½hr. audio tour £3.) Bakewell's **NPIC** is in Old Market Hall, at Bridge St. (☎813 227. Open Mar.-Oct. daily 9:30am-5:30pm; Nov.-Feb. 10am-5pm.) The cozy **YHA Bakewell** ❷, on Fly Hill, is 5min. from the town center. (☎812 313. Open Mar.-Oct. M-Sa; Nov.-Feb. daily. Dorms £10.25, under 18 £7.) **Phone Code:** ☎01629.

The northern Dark Peak area contains some of the wildest and most rugged hill country in England. The area around **Edale** is spectacular, and the National Park Authority's *8 Walks Around Edale* (£1.20) details nearby trails. The town offers little other than a church, cafe, pub, school, and the nearby **YHA youth hostel ❷.** (☎670 302. Dorms £11.25, under 18 £8.) **Phone Code:** ☎01433.

HAWORTH ☎01535

The childhood home of the Brontë family, Haworth's (HAH-wuth) *raison d'être*, sits atop the town's main hill. A cobbled main street milks all association with the ill-fated literary siblings, with numerous tearooms and souvenir shops lining the uphill climb to the **Brontë Parsonage,** whose exhibits detail the lives of Charlotte, Emily, Anne, Branwell, and their irascible father. Quiet rooms, including the dining room where the sisters penned *Wuthering Heights*, *Jane Eyre*, and *The Tenant of Wildfell Hall*, contain original furnishings and mementos like Charlotte's miniscule boots and mittens. (☎642 323. Open Apr.-Sept. daily 10am-5pm; Oct.-Mar. 11am-4:30pm; closed in Jan. £4.80, students £3.50, children £1.50.) The best way to reach Haworth is from Manchester. **Trains** go from Manchester to **Hebden Bridge** (every hr., £6.30); from there, take **Metroline bus** #500 to Haworth (30min., 4-5 per day, £1). You can also hike from Hebden Bridge to Haworth (6-8km); consult Haworth's **tourist office,** 2-4 West Ln., for info. (☎642 329. Open Easter-Oct. daily 9:30am-5:30pm; Nov.-Easter 9:30am-5pm.) **Ashmount ❸,** 5min. from the tourist office on Mytholmes Ln., is a B&B built by the doctor who attended to Charlotte Brontë during her death. Its rooms feature sweeping views of the countryside. (☎645 726. Singles £29; doubles £42; triples £55.) The elegant **YHA Haworth ❷** is in a Victorian mansion, a 15min. hike up Lees Ln.; turn left onto Longlands Dr. (☎642 234. Meals £3-5.25. Open mid-Feb. to Oct. daily; Nov. to mid-Dec. F-Sa. Dorms £10.25, under 18 £7.) Diverse restaurants line **Mill Hey,** just east of the train station; most are only open for dinner (5:30-11pm). **The Black Bull ❶,** a pub once frequented by the errant Branwell Brontë, is a stone's throw from the tourist office. (Open M-Sa noon-11pm, Su noon-10:30pm.) **Postal Code:** BD22 8DP.

YORK ☎01904

Although its well-preserved city walls have foiled many, York fails to impede its present-day hordes of visitors. Today's marauders brandish cameras instead of swords and are after York's compact collection of rich historical sights, including Britain's largest Gothic cathedral.

BRITAIN

TRANSPORTATION

Trains: York Station, Station Rd. Ticket office open M-Sa 5:45am-10:15pm, Su 7:30am-10:10pm. Trains (☎(08457) 484 950) from: **Edinburgh** (2-3hr., 2 per hr., £52.50); **London King's Cross** (2hr., 2 per hr., £65); **Manchester Piccadilly** (1½hr., 2 per hr., £16.10); **Newcastle** (1hr., 2 per hr., £15.50).

Buses: There are **bus stations** at Rougier St., Exhibition Sq., Station Rd., and on Piccadilly. **National Express** (☎(08705) 808 080) from: **Edinburgh** (5hr., 2 per day, £26.50); **London** (4½hr., 6 per day, £19.50); **Manchester** (3hr., 6 per day, £7.25).

Local Transportation: Call **First York** (☎622 992, bus times ☎551 400) for info. Ticket office open M-Sa 8:30am-4:30pm. **Yorkshire Coastliner** (☎(0113) 244 8976 or (01653) 692 556) runs buses from the train station to Castle Howard (see p. 236).

Bike Rental: Bob Trotter, 13 Lord Mayor's Walk (☎622 868). Open M-Sa 9am-5:30pm, Su 10am-4pm. From £8 per day, plus £50 deposit.

ORIENTATION AND PRACTICAL INFORMATION

York's streets are generally short, winding, and unlabeled, and the longer ones change names every block or so. Fortunately, most attractions lie within the city walls, so you can't get too lost, and the **Minster** (cathedral), visible from almost anywhere, provides an easy reference point. The **River Ouse** (OOZE) cuts through the city, curving from west to south. The city center lies between the Ouse and the Minster; **Coney Street, Parliament Street,** and **Stonegate** are the main thoroughfares.

Tourist Office: De Grey Rooms, Exhibition Sq. (☎621 756). The *York Visitor Guide* (£0.50) includes a detailed map. Sells *Snickelways of York* (£5), an off-beat self-tour guide. Open June-Oct. daily 9am-6pm; Nov.-May 9am-5pm. A **branch** is in the train station. Open June-Oct. M-Sa 9am-8pm, Su 9am-5pm; Nov.-May daily 9am-5pm.

American Express: 6 Stonegate (☎676 501). Open M-F 9am-5:30pm, Sa 9am-5pm; in summer **currency exchange** also open Su 10:30am-4:30pm.

Laundromat: Haxby Road Washeteria, 124 Haxby Rd. (☎623 379). Open M-F 8am-6pm, Sa 8am-5:30pm, Su 8am-4:30pm. Last wash 2hr. before closing.

Police: (☎631 321), on Fulford Rd.

Hospital: York District Hospital (☎631 313), off Wigginton Rd. Take bus #1, 2, 3, or 18 from Exhibition Sq. and ask for the hospital stop.

Internet Access: Cafe of the Evil Eye, 42 Stonegate (☎640 002). £2 per hr.

Post Office: 22 Lendal (☎617 285). **Currency exchange.** Open M-Tu 8:30am-5:30pm, W-Sa 9am-5:30pm. **Postal Code:** YO1 8DA.

ACCOMMODATIONS

B&Bs are concentrated on the side streets along **Bootham** and **Clifton,** in the **Mount** area down **Blossom Street,** and on **Bishopsthorpe Road,** south of town. Book ahead in summer, when competition for all types of accommodations can be fierce.

York Backpackers Hostel, 88-90 Micklegate (☎627 720). Fun atmosphere in an 18th-century mansion. Internet £2.50 per 30min. Kitchen and laundry facilities. "Dungeon Bar" open 3 nights per week, long after the pubs close. Dorms £9-14; doubles £30. ❶

Avenue Guest House, 6 The Avenue (☎620 575), off Clifton on a quiet, residential side street. Enthusiastic hosts provide immaculate rooms with soft beds. Singles £18-20; doubles £34-38, with bath £38-44. ❷

Alexander House, 94 Bishopthorpe Rd. (☎625 016), 5min. from the train station. Luxurious rooms have flowers and king-sized beds. Singles £55-60; doubles £64-70. ❹

Cornmill Lodge, 120 Haxby Rd. (☎620 566). From Exhibition Sq. go up Gillygate to Clarence St., which becomes Haxby Rd., or take bus #A1 from the station. A quiet, vegetarian B&B with clean, convivial rooms. Singles £20-30; doubles £40-60. ❸

Queen Anne's Guest House, 24 Queen Anne's Rd. (☎629 389), a short walk down Bootham from Exhibition Sq. Spotless rooms with TVs. Large breakfasts fit for a queen. Singles £18-20; doubles £32-40. ❷

YHA York (☎653 147), Water End, Clifton. From Exhibition Sq., walk about 1km on Bootham and take a left at Water End. Excellent facilities. Reception 7am-10:30pm. Lockout 10am-1pm. Open mid-Jan. to mid-Dec. Dorms £16, under 18 £12; singles £18.50; doubles £37; family rooms £52-£78. ❷

Riverside Caravan and Camping Park (☎705 812), York Marine Services, Ferry Ln., Bishopthorpe, 3km south of York off the A64. Take bus #23 from the bus station and ask the driver to let you off at the campsite (2 per hr., round-trip £1.30). Pleasant riverside site. July-Aug. £8 for tent and 2 people; Sept.-June £7. ❶

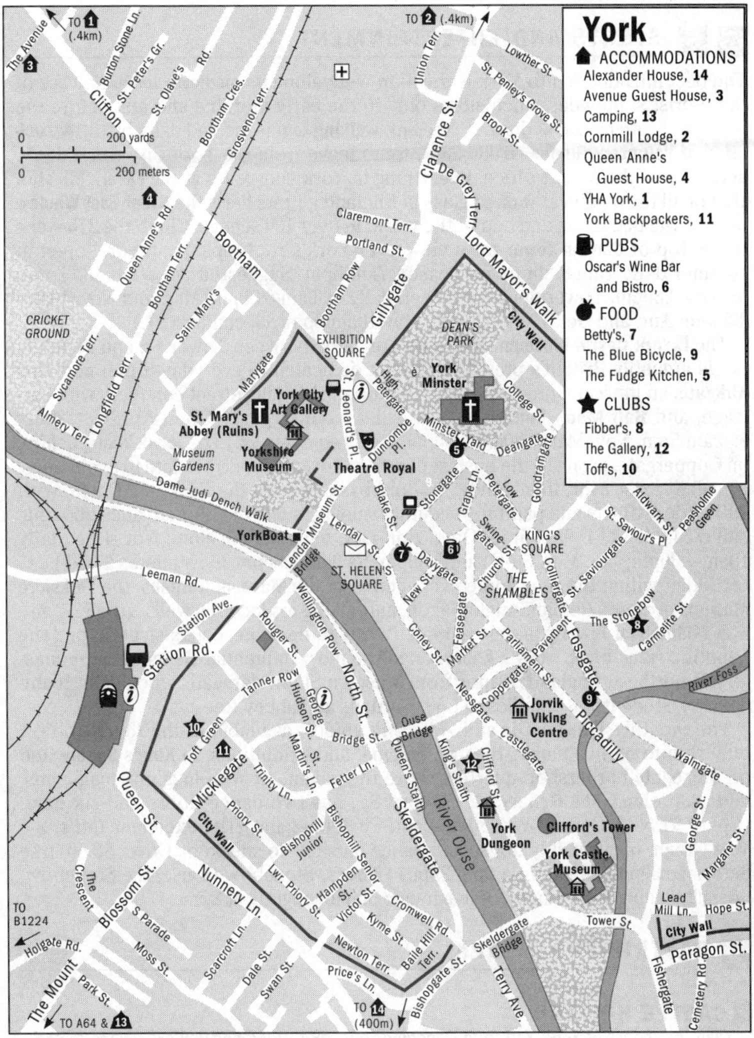

BRITAIN

FOOD

Fruits and veggies are at **Newgate market,** between Parliament St. and Shambles. (Open Apr.-Dec. M-Sa 9am-5pm, Su 9am-4:30pm; Jan.-Mar. M-Sa 9am-5pm.) **The Blue Bicycle ❹,** 34 Fossgate, serves light and delicious French food. (Entrees £11-18. Open daily noon-2:30pm and 6-10pm.) **Oscar's Wine Bar and Bistro ❷,** 8 Little Stonegate, stuffs patrons with massive portions of pub grub for £6-8. (Open daily 11am-11pm.) **Betty's ❷,** 6-8 St. Helen Sq., serves traditional cream teas (£5-9) in a terrifically refined atmosphere. (Open daily 9am-9pm.) **The Fudge Kitchen ❶,** 58 Low Petergate, sells over 20 scrumptious flavors of homemade fudge by the slice. (£2-3. Open M-Sa 10am-5:30pm.)

SIGHTS AND ENTERTAINMENT

The best introduction to York is the 4km walk along its **medieval walls.** Beware of the tourist stampede, which slows only in the early morning and just before the walls and gates close at dusk. A free 2hr. **walking tour** is offered daily by the **Association of Voluntary Guides** (☎630 284); tours leave from the York City Art Gallery, across from the tourist office. Everything in York converges at the **York Minster.** Half of all the medieval stained glass in England glitters here; the **Great East Window** depicts the beginning and end of the world in over 100 scenes. Climb the 275 steps to the top of **Central Tower** for a view over York's roof-tops. (Cathedral open in summer daily 7am-8:30pm; off-season 7am-6pm. Suggested donation £3. Tours 9:30am-3:30pm. Tower open June-Sept. daily 9:30am-6:30pm; Mar. and Nov. 10am-4:30pm; Apr. and Oct. 10am-5:30pm; May 10am-6pm. £3, children £1.)

The **York Castle Museum,** at the Eye of York, between Tower St. and Picadilly St., is arguably Britain's premier museum dedicated to everyday life. It contains **Kirkgate,** an intricately reconstructed Victorian shopping street complete with carriage, and **Half Moon Court,** its Edwardian counterpart. (Open Apr.-Oct. daily 9:30am-5pm; Nov.-Mar. 9:30am-4:30pm. £6.75, students £4.) The **Jorvik Viking Centre,** on Coppergate, is one of the busiest places in York; visit early or late to avoid lines, or call at least 24hr. in advance. Visitors pass through the York of AD 948, with authentic artifacts and painfully accurate smells. (☎643 211. For advance booking, call ☎543 403 M-F 9am-5pm. Open Apr.-Oct. daily 9am-5:30pm; Nov.-Dec. daily 10am-4:30pm; Jan.-Mar. Su-F 9am-3:30pm, Sa 9am-4:30pm. £9, students £7.50.)

Hidden within the four gorgeous hectares of the **Museum Gardens,** the **Yorkshire Museum** presents Roman, Anglo-Saxon, and Viking artifacts, as well as the £2.5 million **Middleham Jewel** from circa 1450. In the gardens, peacocks strut among the haunting ruins of **St. Mary's Abbey,** once the most influential Benedictine monastery in northern England. (Enter from Museum St. or Marygate. Open daily 10am-5pm. £4, students £3, families £11.50. Gardens and abbey free.)

The monthly *What's On* and *Artscene* guides, available at the tourist office, publish info on live music, theater, cinema, and exhibitions. In **King's Square** and on **Stonegate** barbershop quartets share the pavement with jugglers, magicians, and politicians. **The Gallery,** 12 Clifford St., has two dance floors and six bars. (Cover £1.50-4. Open F-W 9:30pm-2am, Th 10pm-2am.) The excellent **Toff's,** 3-5 Toft Green, plays mainly house and dance music. (No sneakers. Cover £3.50, free before 10:30pm. Open M-Sa 9pm-2am.) **Fibber's,** Stonebow House, the Stonebow, doesn't lie about the quality of live music playing nightly at 8pm.

BRITAIN

DAYTRIP FROM YORK

CASTLE HOWARD

24km northeast of York. Yorkshire Coastliner bus #842 runs half-day excursions to the castle (5 per day, round-trip £4.50); reduced admission with bus ticket. ☎(01653) 648 333. Open mid-Mar. to Nov. daily 11am-4:30pm; gardens mid-Mar. to Nov. daily 10am-6:30pm. £7.50, students £6.75. Gardens only £4.50.

The baroque Castle Howard, still inhabited by the Howard family, presides over 4 square kilometers of stunning grounds that teem with gardens, fountains, and lakes. The **long gallery** provides a dazzling and dwarfing promenade between enormous windows and shelves stuffed with books. Be sure to see the domed **Temple of the Four Winds,** with a hilltop perch that offers views of grassy fields, still waters, and lazy cows.

NORTH YORK MOORS NATIONAL PARK

The attractions of the North York Moors, 50km north of York, include heather-covered hills, deep-sided valleys, a superb scenic railway, and endearing towns, both country and seaside.

TRANSPORTATION. Trains run to Scarborough from York (45min., 2 per hr., £9.30). Yorkshire Coastliner (☎0113 244 8976) **bus** #840 travels between Leeds, York, Pickering, and Whitby (3hr., 5 per day), while bus #843 runs between Leeds, York, and Scarborough (3hr., every hr.). In summer, the **Moorsbus** (☎01845 597 426) runs throughout the park (day pass £2.50); schedules are available at tourist offices. Hiking is the best way to travel the moors. The 150km **Cleveland Way** wraps all the way around the park. Tourist offices have maps and information.

PICKERING AND THE NORTH YORKSHIRE MOORS RAILWAY. Pickering is the starting point for the North Yorkshire Moors Railway, which covers 30km of superb scenery. The train recently appeared as the "Hogwarts Express" in the first *Harry Potter* film. Hiking trails depart from stations along the way; pick up the guide at tourist offices. (Info ☎01751 472 508; timetable 01751 473 535. Late Mar. to Oct., most weekends Nov.-Dec., and select holidays Jan.-Feb. 3-7 round-trips per day. £10, children £5.) The Pickering **tourist office** is at The Ropery, beside the library. (☎01751 473 791. Open Mar.-Oct. M-Sa 9:30am-6pm, Su 9:30am-5:30pm; Nov.-Feb. M-Sa 10am-4:30pm.) The **YHA Old School ❶** is 6.5km north of Pickering off the Pickering-Whitby Rd. Take Coastliner bus #840. (☎01751 460 376. Open July-Aug. daily; June and Sept. M-Sa. Dorms £7.75; under 18 £5.50.)

WHITBY AND SCARBOROUGH. Straddling a harbor between two desolate headlands, the beautiful seaside town of **Whitby** has been home to more than its share of history-makers and literary greats, including Lewis Carroll, Bram Stoker, and Captain Cook. **Whitby Abbey** sits atop a hill buffeted by shrieking winds, and its graveyard is said to have inspired *Dracula*. The **tourist office** is at Station Sq., on Langborned Rd. (☎01947 602 674. Open May-Sept. daily 9:30am-6pm; Oct.-Apr. 10am-4:30pm.) The **YHA Whitby ❷**, next to the abbey, is in a 12th-century stone building. (☎01947 602 878. Lockout 10am-5pm. Curfew 11pm. Open Apr.-Aug. daily; Sept.-Oct. M-Sa; Jan.-Mar. and Nov. F-Sa. Dorms £10.25, under 18 £7.)

English families still flock to **Scarborough**, one of the country's first seaside resorts. The town is large and often tacky, but it is graced with a beautiful setting, a magnificent castle, and two grand stretches of beach. The **tourist office** is in Unit 3, Pavillion House, Valley Bridge Rd. (☎01723 373 333. Open May-Sept. daily 9:30am-6pm; Oct.-Apr. 10am-4:30pm.) The **YHA White House ❷**, 3km from Scarborough on Burniston Rd., resides in a former mill on the river. Take bus #3 from the train station. (☎01723 361 176. Lockout 10am-5pm. Open Mar.-Aug. daily; Sept.-Oct. M-Sa. Dorms £10.25, under 18 £7.)

BRITAIN

DURHAM ☎0191

Spiralling medieval streets, footbridges, and restricted vehicle access make clifftop Durham pedestrian-friendly. The magnificent **Durham Cathedral**, England's finest of the Norman era, houses the tomb of the Venerable Bede, author of *The Ecclesiastical History of the English People*. The view from the tower easily compensates for the 325-step climb. (Cathedral open June-Sept. M-Sa 9:30am-8pm, Su 12:30-8pm; Oct.-May M-Sa 9:30am-6pm, Su 12:30-5pm. Suggested donation £3. Tower open mid-Apr. to Sept. daily 9:30am-4pm; Oct. to mid-Apr. M-Sa 10am-3pm. £2.) Across the cathedral green, **Durham Castle** was once a key defensive fortress. (Mandatory tours Mar.-Sept. daily 10am-12:30pm and 2-4pm; Oct.-Feb. W and Sa-M

2-4pm. £3.) Nightlife starts up around 10pm; head to the intersection of **Crossgate** and **North Road,** across Framwellgate Bridge, where pubs await with open doors.

Trains (☎(08457) 484 950) run from the station west of town to: London (3hr., every hr., £83); Newcastle (20min., 2 per hr., £3.40); and York (1hr., 2 per hr., £15.50). **Buses** leave North Rd. for London (5½hr., 5-6 per day, £26.50). The **tourist office** is in Millennium Place, just north of Millburngate Bridge. (☎384 3720. Open July-Aug. M-Sa 10am-5:30pm, Su 11am-4pm; June and Sept. M-Sa 10am-5:30pm; Oct.-May M-Sa 10am-5pm.) A large supply of cheap **dormitory rooms** ❸ surrounds the cathedral; rooms start at £20 and are generally available July-Sept. and around Easter and Christmas. For more information, contact the **Durham University Conference and Tourism Office** (☎374 7360). **Mrs. Koltai's** ❷ is a comfortable B&B at 10 Gilesgate. (☎386 2026. Singles £16; doubles £32.) The crowded **Almshouse Cafe and Restaurant** ❷, 10 Palace Green, serves delicious specials for £4-6. (Open daily in summer 9am-8pm; in winter 9am-5:30pm.) **Postal Code:** DH1 3RE.

NEWCASTLE-UPON-TYNE ☎0191

Hardworking Newcastle is legendary for its pub and club scene, but ambitious building efforts have lent the city genuine daytime energy. Explore the masterful **Tyne Bridge** and neighboring **Castle Keep,** erected in the 12th century. (Open Apr.-Sept. daily 9:30am-5:30pm; Oct.-Mar. daily 9:30am-4:30pm. £1.50.) **LIFE Interactive World,** Times Sq., on Scotswood Rd., is an enjoyable hands-on science museum. (Open daily 10am-6pm. £6.95, seniors and students £5.50, children £4.50.) The **Laing Art Gallery,** on New Bridge St., showcases an excellent collection of local art. (Open M-Sa 10am-5pm, Su 2-5pm. Free.) Rowdy **Bigg Market** features the highest concentration of pubs in England, while **Quayside** (KEY-side) is slightly more relaxed and attracts local students. **Chase,** 10-15 Sandhill, is a flashy pub, while nearby **Offshore 44,** 40 Sandhill, has a tropical theme. (Both open M-Sa 11am-11pm and Su noon-6pm). The hottest dance club is **The Tuxedo Princess,** on a cruise ship under the Tyne Bridge. (Open M and W-Sa 7:30pm-2am.) Gays and lesbians flock to Waterloo St. to drink and dance at **The Powerhouse.** (Open M and Th 10pm-2am, Tu-W 11pm-1am, F-Sa 10pm-3am.)

Trains leave from Neville St. for London (3hr., every hr., £83) and Edinburgh (1½hr.; M-Sa 23 per day, Su 16 per day; £33.50). National Express **buses** (☎08705 808 080) leave Percy St. for London (6hr., 6 per day, round-trip £23) and Edinburgh (3hr., 3 per day,

FROM THE ROAD

SHOWER POWER

Most travel guides spend pages telling you how to purchase traveler's checks and keep clear of European stinging nettles, when, really, how to avoid exhibitionary nakedness and evade plumbing disasters are much more pertinent (and interesting) topics. In Britain, the bathing establishment has an unsettling habit of building showers in front of large windows. It also has a habit of "accidentally" forgetting to put curtains on those windows. Then there's the building code, which apparently says it's okay to build houses so close that you can inspect your neighbor's dental work without leaving home.

A B&B I stayed at recently (quite a nice one, mind you: big fluffy beds, an affectionate Burmese cat happily drooling on my hand, and a kindly owner plying me with tea and cakes) had one of these shameless showers. It was late evening and completely dark outside when I walked into the shower-room like the heroine of a decadently twisted film noir (okay, a lame, boring film noir). The shower was, as expected, in front of the window, and as usual, the window was curtainless.

Feeling terribly clever, I turned the light off and set about figuring out the shower. It featured two pull strings, two twisting knobs, one button, and one switch, as well as a soap dispenser I decided not to mess with. I turned the most likely looking knob and was pelted with icy cold water. Twisting the knob all the way to the right didn't change the temperature. I yanked one of the pull cords.

round-trip £13). The **tourist office** is on 132 Grainger St., facing Grey's Monument. (☎277 8000. Open M-W and F-Sa 9:30am-5:30pm, Th 9:30am-7:30pm; June-Sept. also Su 10am-4pm.) To get to the friendly **YHA youth hostel ❷,** 107 Jesmond Rd., take the Metro to Jesmond, turn left onto Jesmond Rd., and walk past the traffic lights (☎281 2570. Lockout 10am-5pm. Open Feb.-Dec. Dorms £11.25, under 18 £8.) **Portland Guest House ❸,** 134 Sandyford Rd., is cheap and convenient. From the Jesmond metro stop, turn left onto Jesmond Rd., then right onto Portland Terr.; the guest house is at the end. (☎232 7868. Breakfast included. Singles £18-30; doubles £36-40.) **Don Vito's ❶,** 82 Pilgrim St., stands out among the many Italian eateries. (☎232 8923. Entrees £4-6. Open M-F 11:45am-2pm and 5-10pm, Sa 11:45am-10:30pm.) **Postal Code:** NE1 7AB.

LAKE DISTRICT NATIONAL PARK

The Lake District was gouged by glaciers during the last ice age, creating the most dramatic landscape in all England. Jagged peaks and windswept fells stand in desolate splendor and water wends its way in every direction. Use Windermere, Ambleside, Grasmere, and Keswick as bases from which to ascend into the hills—the farther west you go from the **A591,** which connects these towns, the more countryside you'll have to yourself.

The **National Park Visitor Centre** is in **Brockhole,** halfway between Windermere and Ambleside. (☎015394 46 601. Open Easter-Oct. daily 10am-5pm; Nov.-Easter most weekends.) **National Park Information Centres** book accommodations and dispense free information and town maps. While B&Bs line every street in every town and there's a hostel around every bend, lodgings do fill up in summer; book ahead.

TRANSPORTATION. Trains (☎08457 484 950) run to Oxenholme from: Birmingham (2½hr., 1-2 per hr., £41.50); Edinburgh (2½hr., 6 per day, £41.50); London Euston (4-5hr., 11-16 per day, £101); and Manchester Piccadilly (1½hr., 5-7 per day, £17). A short line covers the 16km between Windermere and Oxenholme (20min., every hr., £3.10). There is also direct service to Windermere from Manchester Piccadilly (2hr., 3-4 per day, £19.80). National Express **buses** (☎08705 808 080) arrive in Windermere from Birmingham (4½hr., 1 per day, £24.50) and London (7½hr., 1 per day, £26), and continue north through Ambleside and Grasmere to Keswick. **Stagecoach in Cumbria** (☎0870 608 2608) is the primary operator of bus service in the

The entire tub began shaking violently and water spurted two feet up the sides. I yanked desperately at the other cord. The light burst on, the neighbor looked up, and I stopped, dropped, and rolled into a towel. Something under the tub made a high pitched, warning-like whistle. Envisioning my editors gaping at a bill for one new tub, one new shower head, one re-tiled wall, and one new ceiling, I jumped up and managed to turn the whole dang thing off. Travel writing is every bit as glamorous as they say.

How to avoid this sort of situation: In general, the pull cord farthest from the shower operates the fan and/or lightswitch. Closer pull cords often turn the hot water on. Turning the swivel-knob won't do a bit of good until the heat's on. Be sure NOT to turn it all the way on before turning on the hot water—third-degree burns aren't as cool as they sound. Some showers only have one pull cord, which might serve either function.

Other showers have a cord that turns on the tub jets, while a wall switch turns the light on. Still others possess small white boxes with a button that turns the shower on and off and two knobs, marked "temperature" and "pressure," but which may control the opposite features. Be wary of soap vs. shampoo dispensers—I have often Dove-soaped my hair.

One final word to the wise—many seemingly curtainless windows have small grooves along the top, concealing the elusive shade.

—Jenny Pegg

region; a complete timetable, *The Lakeland Explorer*, is available at tourist offices. An **Explorer** ticket offers unlimited travel on all area Stagecoach buses (1-day £7, children £5; 4-day £16/£12). The Ambleside YHA Youth Hostel offers a convenient **minibus** service (☎015394 32 304) between hostels (£2.50) as well as free service from the Windermere train station to the Windermere and Ambleside hostels. Cyclists can get **bike rental** information at tourist offices; the *Ordnance Survey Cycle Tours* (£10) has route maps.

WINDERMERE AND BOWNESS. Windermere and its sidekick **Bowness-on-Windermere** fill to the gills with vacationers in summer, when sailboats and waterskiers criss cross incessantly over Lake Windermere. At **Windermere Lake Cruises** (☎433 60), at the north end of Bowness Pier, boats are more frequent in summer and sail north to Waterhead Pier in Ambleside (30min., round-trip £6.20) and south to Lakeside (40min., round-trip £6.40). Lakeland Experience **buses** to Bowness (#599; 3 per hr., £1) leave from the train station. The **tourist office** is next door. (☎46 499. Open July-Aug. daily 9am-7:30pm; Easter-June and Sept.-Oct. 9am-6pm; Nov.-Easter 9am-5pm.) The local **National Park Information Centre**, on Glebe Rd., is beside Bowness Pier. (☎42 895. Open July-Aug. daily 9:30am-6pm; Apr.-June and Sept.-Oct. daily 9am-5:30pm; Nov.-Mar. F-Su 10am-4pm.) To get to the spacious **YHA Windermere ❷,** on High Cross in Troutbeck, 1.5km north of Windermere off A591, take the Ambleside bus to Troutbeck Bridge and walk 1.25km uphill, or catch the YHA shuttle from the train station. (☎43 543. Bike rental. Open mid-Feb. to Oct. daily; Nov. to mid-Feb. F-Sa. only. Dorms £11.25, under 18 £8.) **Camp** at **Park Cliffe ❷,** Birks Rd., 5km south of Bowness. Take bus #618 from Windermere station. (☎(015295) 31 344. £10-£13 per tent.) **Phone Code:** ☎015394.

AMBLESIDE. About 2km north of Lake Windermere, Ambleside is an attractive village with convenient access to the southern lakes. It's popular with hikers, who are drawn by its location—or perhaps by its absurd number of outdoors shops. Splendid views of higher fells can be had from the top of **Loughrigg** (a moderately difficult 11km round-trip hike); 1km from town is the lovely waterfall **Stockghyll Force.** The tourist office has guides to these and other walks. Lakeslink **bus** #555 (☎32 231) leaves from Kelsick Rd. for Grasmere, Keswick, and Windermere (every hr., £2-6.50). The **tourist office** is located in the Central Building on Market Cross. (☎31 576. Open daily 9am-5:30pm.) To reach the **National Park Information Centre**, on Waterhead, walk south on Lake Rd. or Borrans Rd. from town to the pier. (☎32 729. Open Easter-Oct. daily 9:30am-6pm.) Bus #555 also stops at the superb ■**YHA Ambleside ❷,** 1.5km south of Ambleside and 5km north of Windermere, on the north shore of Lake Windermere. (☎32 304. Bike rental. Mar.-Oct. no curfew; Nov.-Feb. midnight. Dorms £13.50, under 18 £9.50.) **Phone Code:** ☎015394.

GRASMERE. The peace that Wordsworth enjoyed in the village of Grasmere is still apparent on quiet mornings. The 17th-century ■**Dove Cottage,** 10 minutes from the center of town, was Wordsworth's home from 1799 to 1808 and remains almost exactly as he left it; next door is the outstanding **Wordsworth Museum.** (Both open mid-Feb. to mid-Jan. daily 9:30am-5pm. £5.50, students £4.70.) The **Wordsworth Walk** (9.5km) circumnavigates the two lakes of the Rothay River, passing the cottage, the poet's grave in St. Oswald's churchyard, and ■**Rydal Mount,** where Wordsworth lived until his death. (Rydal open Mar.-Oct. daily 9:30am-5pm; Nov.-Feb. W-M 10am-4pm. £3.75, students £3.25.) **Bus** #555 stops in Grasmere every hour on its way south to Ambleside or north to Keswick. The **National Park Information Centre** is on Redbank Rd. (☎35 245. Open Easter-Oct. daily 9:30am-5:30pm; Nov.-Easter Sa-Su 10am-4pm.) **The Hardwood ❸,** on Red Lion Sq., has eight comfortable rooms right in the center of town. (☎35 248. 2-night min. stay on weekends. £24.50-32.50

per person.) Sarah Nelson's famed Grasmere Gingerbread, a staple since 1854, is a bargain at £0.22 in **Church Cottage,** outside St. Oswald's Church. (Open Easter-Nov. M-Sa 9:15am-5:30pm, Su 12:30-5:30pm; Dec.-Easter M-Sa 9:15am-5pm, Su 12:30-5pm.) **Phone Code:** ☎015394.

KESWICK. Between towering Skiddaw peak and the north edge of Lake Derwentwater, Keswick (KEZ-ick) rivals Windermere as the Lake District's tourist capital but surpasses it in charm. A standout 6.5km day-hike from Keswick visits the **Castlerigg Stone Circle,** a 5000-year-old neolithic henge. Another short walk hits the beautiful **Friar's Crag,** on the shore of Derwentwater, and **Castlehead,** a viewpoint encompassing the town, the lakes, and the peaks beyond. Both of these walks are fairly easy, although they do have their more strenuous moments. Maps and information on these and a wide selection of other walks are available at the **National Park Information Centre,** in Moot Hall, Market Sq. (☎72 645. Open Aug. daily 9:30am-6pm; Sept.-July 9:30am-5:30pm.) **YHA Derwentwater ❷,** in Barrow House, Borrowdale, is in a 200-year-old house with its own waterfall. Take bus #79 (every hr.) 3km south out of Keswick. (☎77 246. Open Feb. to early Oct. daily; Dec.-Jan. F-Sa only. Dorms £11.25, under 18 £8.) **Phone Code:** ☎017687.

WALES

Wales may border England, but if many of the 2.9 million Welsh people had their way, it would be floating oceans away. Ever since England solidified its control over the country with the murder of Prince Llywelyn ap Gruffydd in 1282, relations between the two have been marked by a powerful unease. Wales clings steadfastly to its Celtic heritage, continuing a centuries-old struggle for independence, and the Welsh language endures in conversation, commerce, and literature. As coal, steel, and slate mines fell victim to Britain's faltering economy in the mid-20th century, Wales turned its economic eye from heavy industry to tourism. Travelers come for the sandy beaches, grassy cliffs, brooding castles, and dramatic mountains that typify the rich landscape of this corner of Britain.

FERRIES TO IRELAND

Irish Ferries (☎08705 171 717; www.irishferries.ie) run to Dublin, Ireland, from Holyhead (2-3hr., round-trip £20-31) and to Rosslare, Ireland, from Pembroke (4hr., round-trip £25-39). **Stena Line** (☎01233 646 826; www.stenaline.co.uk) runs from Holyhead to Dublin, Ireland (4hr., £23-27), and Dún Laoghaire, Ireland (1-3½hr., £23-27). **Swansea Cork Ferries** (☎(01792) 456 116) run from Swansea to Cork, Ireland (10hr., £24-34).

CARDIFF (CAERDYDD) ☎029

Formerly the main port of call for Welsh coal, Cardiff (pop. 325,000) is now the port of arrival for a colorful international population—you're as likely to hear Urdu on a street corner as you are to hear Welsh. Climb the Norman keep of the flamboyant **Cardiff Castle** for a sweeping view of the city, then tour its restored medieval interior. (Open Mar.-Oct. daily 9:30am-6pm; Nov.-Feb. 9:30am-4:30pm. £5.50, students £4.20.) At the **National Museum and Gallery,** in the Civic Centre across North Rd. from the castle, a dazzling audio-visual exhibit on the evolution of Wales speeds you through millennia of geological transformation. (Open Tu-Su 10am-5pm. Free.) **The Prince of Wales,** at the corner of St. Mary St. and Wood St., is a sprawling, boisterous pub. (Open M-Sa 11am-11pm, Su noon-10:30pm.) A colorful live-music venue, **The Toucan,** 95-97 St. Mary's St., features a wide variety of sounds, from hip-hop to salsa. (Open Tu-Su noon-2am.) **Clwb Ifor Bach** (the Welsh Club), 11 Womanby St., is a manic, three-tiered club with everything from Motown tunes to video games. (Cover £2-8. Open M-Th until 2am, F-Sa until 3am.)

Trains (☎(08457) 484 950) arrive at **Central Station,** Central Sq., from: Bath (1-1½hr., 1-3 per hr., £12.20); Edinburgh (7hr., 7 per day, £105); and London Paddington (2hr., every hr., £46.80). National Express **buses** (☎(08705) 808 080) leave from Wood St. for London Victoria (3½hr., 6 per day, £12.50) and Manchester (5½hr., 4 per day, £19.50). The **tourist office** is at 16 Wood St., across from the bus station. (☎2022 7281. Open July-Aug. M-Sa 9am-6pm, Su 10am-4pm; Sept.-June M-Sa 9am-5pm, Su 10am-4pm.) **Internet Exchange** is located at 8 Church St., by St. John's Church. (£4 per hr. Open M-Th 9am-9pm, F-Sa 9am-8pm, Su 11am-7pm.) The best **B&Bs** are on Cathedral Rd. (take bus #32 or walk 15min. from the castle). To get to the colorful **Cardiff International Backpacker ❷,** 98 Neville St., from the train station, go west on Wood St., turn right on Fitzham Embankment, and turn left onto Despenser St. (☎2034 5577. Kitchen access. Internet £1 per 15min. Dorms £14.50; doubles £35; triples £43.) **Anned Lon ❸,** 157-159 Cathedral Rd., provides a peaceful respite from the city. (☎2022 3349. No smoking. Singles £20-25; doubles £40-45.) For quick food and a wide variety of options, head to the Victorian **Central Market,** in the arcade between St. Mary St. and Trinity St. **Europa Cafe ❶,** 25 Castle St., across from the castle, is a comfortable coffeehouse. (Beverages £1-3. Open Su-Tu 11am-6pm, W-Sa 11am-11pm.) **Postal Code:** CF10 2ST.

DAYTRIPS FROM CARDIFF: CAERPHILLY CASTLE AND THE MUSEUM OF WELSH LIFE. Thirteen kilometers north of Cardiff, **Caerphilly Castle** will enchant romantics and history buffs alike. Begun in 1268 by Norman warlord Gilbert de Clare, its stone walls, catapults, and pivoting drawbridges made it the most technologically advanced fortification of its time. Take the **train** (30min., M-Sa 2 per hr., £2.60) or hourly **bus** #24 or 25 from Central Station stand C1. (☎2088 3143. Open June-Sept. daily 9:30am-6pm; Apr.-May and Oct. daily 9:30am-5pm; Nov.-Mar. M-Sa 9:30am-4pm, Su 11am-4pm. £2.50, students £2.) Lying 6.5km west of Cardiff, the open-air **Museum of Welsh Life** is home to more than 40 authentic buildings from all corners of Wales, reassembled into an interactive account of Welsh history. Bus #320 runs to the museum (20min., every hr., £1.20) from Central Station. (☎2057 3500. Open June-Sept. daily 10am-5pm. Free.)

WYE VALLEY ☎01291

Crossing and recrossing the oft-troubled Welsh-English border, the Wye River (Afon Gwy) cuts through a tranquil valley, its banks riddled with trails, abbeys, and castles rich in legend. The past is palpable in the towns and clusters of homes and farms, from Tintern Abbey to the George Inn Pub.

TRANSPORTATION. The valley is best entered from the south, at Chepstow. **Trains** go to Chepstow from Cardiff and Newport (40min., 7-8 per day). National Express **buses** (☎(08705) 808 080) arrive from Cardiff (50min., 7 per day) and London (2¼hr., 10 per day). There is little Sunday bus service in the valley. For schedules, pick up *Discover the Wye Valley on Foot and by Bus* in tourist offices.

Hiking grants the most stunning vistas of the valley. The 124km **Wye Valley Walk** treks north from Chepstow, through Hay-on-Wye, and on to Prestatyn along cliffs and farmland. **Offa's Dyke Path** consists of more than 285km of hiking paths along the length of the Welsh-English border. For information, consult the **Offa's Dyke Association** (☎(01547) 528 753).

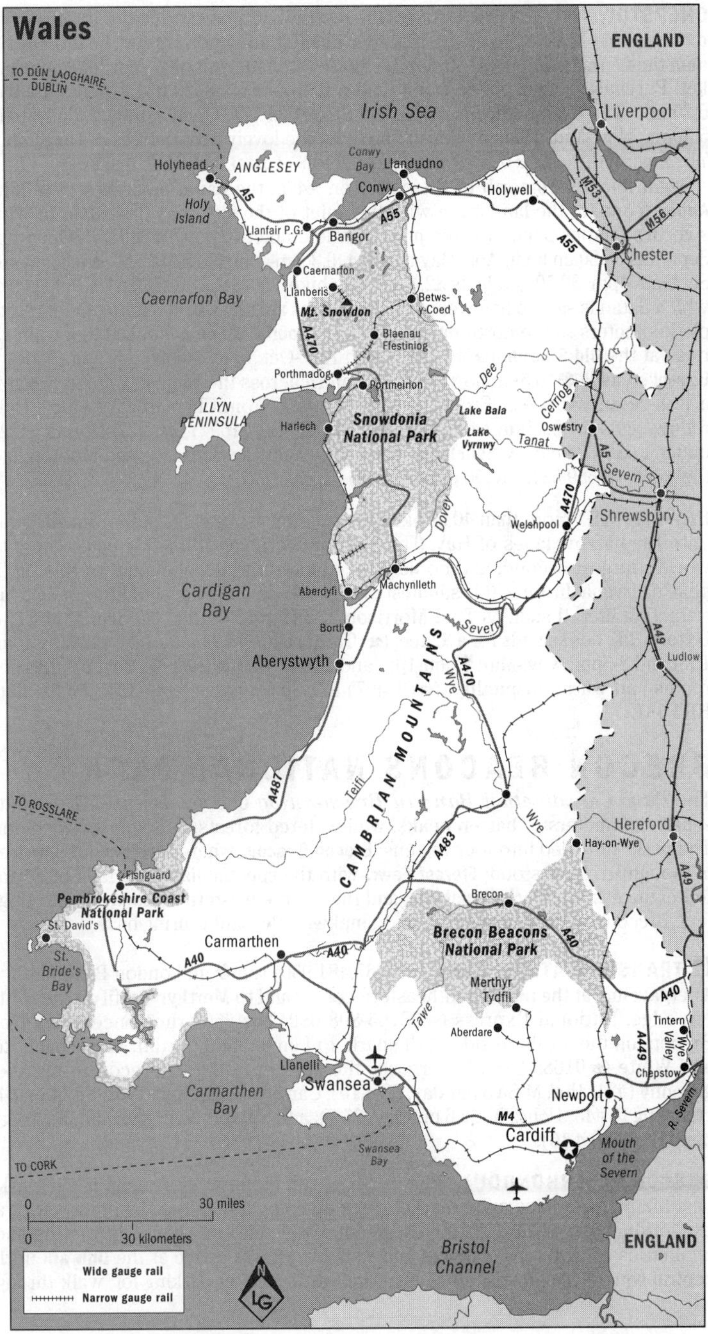
Wales
ENGLAND
TO DÚN LAOGHAIRE, DUBLIN
Irish Sea
Liverpool
Holyhead
ANGLESEY
Conwy Bay
Llandudno
Conwy
Holywell
Holy Island
A5
A55
M53
M56
Llanfair P.G.
Bangor
Chester
Caernarfon
Llanberis
Caernarfon Bay
Betws-y-Coed
Mt. Snowdon
A470
Blaenau Ffestiniog
Porthmadog
Portmeirion
Dee
LLŶN PENINSULA
Harlech
Snowdonia National Park
Lake Bala
Ceiriog
Oswestry
Lake Vyrnwy
Tanat
Severn
Shrewsbury
Dovey
Welshpool
Machynlleth
Cardigan Bay
Aberdyfi
Borth
Severn
A49
Aberystwyth
CAMBRIAN MOUNTAINS
Wye
Ludlow
A487
Teifi
TO ROSSLARE
Wye
Hereford
A483
Hay-on-Wye
Fishguard
Pembrokeshire Coast National Park
Brecon
St. David's
Brecon Beacons National Park
A40
Carmarthen
St. Bride's Bay
Merthyr Tydfil
Tintern
Aberdare
Tawe
Wye Valley
A449
Llanelli
Chepstow
Swansea
Carmarthen Bay
Newport
R. Severn
M4
Cardiff
Mouth of the Severn
Swansea Bay
TO CORK
0
30 miles
30 kilometers
Bristol Channel
Wide gauge rail
Narrow gauge rail
N
LG

BRITAIN

CHEPSTOW AND TINTERN. **Chepstow**'s strategic position at the mouth of the river and the base of the English border made it an important fortification in Norman times. **Trains** arrive on Station Rd.; **buses** stop in front of Somerfield supermarket. Purchase tickets at **The Travel House,** 9 Moor St. (☎623 031. Open M-Sa 9am-5:30pm.) The **tourist office** is on Bridge St. (☎623 772. Open Apr.-Oct. daily 10am-5:30pm; Nov.-Mar. 10am-4:30pm.) Stay with the lovely proprietress of **Langcroft ❸,** 71 Kingsmark Ave. (☎625 569. £20 per person.) **Postal Code:** NP16 5DA.

Eight kilometers north of Chepstow on A466, the haunting arches of **Tintern Abbey** "connect the landscape with the quiet of the sky"—as described in Wordsworth's famous poem, written just a few kilometers away. (☎689 251. Open June-Sept. daily 9:30am-6pm; Apr.-May and Oct. 9:30am-5pm; Nov.-Mar. M-Sa 9:30am-4pm, Su 11am-4pm. £2.50; students £2.) A 1½hr. hike will get you to **Devil's Pulpit,** from which Satan is said to have tempted the monks as they worked in the fields. A couple kilometers to the north on the A466, the **tourist office** is housed in a train carriage at the **Old Station.** (☎689 566. Open Apr.-Oct. daily 10:30am-5:30pm.) **YHA St. Briavel's Castle ❷,** 6.5km northeast of Tintern across the English Border, occupies a 12th-century fortress. From the A466 (bus #69 from Chepstow) or Offa's Dyke, follow signs for 3.25km from Bigsweir Bridge. (☎(01594) 530 272. Dorms £11.25, under 18 £8.) The cozy **Holmleigh House ❷** is near the Sixpence and Moon pub on the A466. (☎689 521. £16.50 per person.)

HAY-ON-WYE. More than 40 bookshops and numerous cafes spill from alleyways onto the narrow lanes of Hay. The 1961 appearance of **Booth's Books,** now the world's largest secondhand bookstore, sparked the development of this bibliophile's nirvana. In June, this smallest of towns hosts the largest of literary festivals, attracting literati such as Toni Morrison and Harold Pinter. The **tourist office,** on Oxford Rd., books beds for a £2 fee. (☎(01497) 820 144. Open Apr.-Oct. daily 10am-1pm and 2-5pm; Nov.-Mar. 11am-1pm and 2-4pm.) **The Bear ❸,** Bear St., has cozy rooms and warm hospitality. (☎(01497) 821 302. Singles from £24.) **Postal Code:** HR3 5AE.

BRECON BEACONS NATIONAL PARK

The *Parc Cenedlaethol Bannau Brycheiniog* encompasses 1344 dramatic square kilometers of barren peaks, well-watered forests, and windswept moors. The park is divided into four regions: **Brecon Beacon,** where King Arthur's fortress is thought to have stood; **Fforest Fawr,** with the spectacular waterfalls of Ystradfellte; the eastern **Black Mountains;** and the remote western **Black Mountain** (singular). Brecon, on the fringe of the park, makes a pleasant touring base.

TRANSPORTATION. **Trains** (☎08457 484 950) run from London Paddington to Abergavenny at the park's southeastern corner and to Merthyr Tydfil on the southern edge. National Express (☎08705 808 080) **bus** #509 runs once a day from Brecon, on the northern side of the park, to London and Cardiff. Stagecoach Red and White (☎01685 388 216) crosses the park en route to Brecon from: Abergavenny (#21; 1hr., M-Sa 5 per day, £3-4.10); Cardiff via Merthyr Tydfil (#X4 or X40, changing to #43; 1½hr., M-Sa 6 per day, £5-7); and Hay-on-Wye (#39; 45min., M-Sa 6 per day, £2.80-4.10).

BRECON (ADERHONDDU). Just north of the mountains, Brecon is the park's best hiking base. This quiet market town takes on a temporary vibrancy with an exceptional **jazz festival** during the second weekend in August, attracting such luminaries as Branford Marsalis and Keb' Mo'. **Buses** arrive at the **Bulwark** in the central square. The **tourist office** is in the Cattle Market parking lot; walk through

Bethel Square off Lion St. (☎622 485. Open daily 9:30am-5pm.) The **National Park Information Centre** (☎623 156) is in the same building. **Mulberry House ❷,** 3 Priory Hill, across from the cathedral, is in a former monks' habitation. (☎624 461. £18 per person.) Camp at **Brynich Caravan Park ❶,** 2.5km east on the A40, signposted from the A40-A470 roundabout. (☎623 325. Open Easter-Oct. £4.50 per person, £9.50 with car.) **Phone Code:** ☎01874.

FFOREST FAWR. Rivers tumble through rapids, gorges, and spectacular falls near Ystradfellte, about 11km southwest of the Beacons. **YHA Ystradfellte ❶** is a perfect launching pad. (☎01639 720 301. Open mid-July to Aug. daily; Apr. to mid-July and Sept.-Oct. F-Tu. Dorms £8.50, under 18 £5.75.) Less than 2km from the hostel at **Porth-yr-Ogof** the River Mellte ducks into a cliff cave and emerges as an icy pool. To the west near **Abercrave,** the **Dan-yr-Ogof Showcaves** impress with enormous stalagmites (24hr. info ☎01639 730 801). From YHA Ystradfellte, 16km of trails pass **Fforest Fawr,** the headlands of the Waterfall District, on their way to the caves. (Open Apr.-Oct. daily 10:30am-5pm. £7.80, children £4.80.) Stagecoach Red and White **bus** #63 (1½hr.; 2-3 per day) stops at the hostel and caves en route to Brecon.

THE BLACK MOUNTAINS. Located in the easternmost section of the park, the Black Mountains are a group of long, lofty ridges offering 130 square kilometers of solitude, linked by unsurpassed ridge-walks. Invest in the Ordnance Survey Outdoor Leisure Map #13 (£7). Begin forays from **Crickhowell,** or travel the eastern boundary along **Offa's Dyke Path,** which is dotted with a handful of impressive ruins. There is almost no public transportation along valley routes. The **YHA Capel-y-ffin ❶** (kap-EL-uh-fin), along Offa's Dyke Path, is 13km from Hay-on-Wye. Take Stagecoach Red and White **bus** #39 from Hereford to Brecon, stop before Hay, and walk uphill. (☎01873 890 650. Lockout 10am-5pm. Open July-Sept. daily; Oct.-Dec. and Mar.-June F-Tu. Dorms £8.75, students £7.75. Camping £5 per tent.)

THE BRECON BEACONS. These peaks at the center of the park lure hikers with pastoral slopes. A 1hr. walk from the Mountain Centre outside Libanus leads to the scant remains of an **Iron-Age fort.** The most convenient route to the top of **Pen-y-Fan** (pen-uh-van; 886m) begins at **Storey Arms,** a large parking lot and bus stop 8km south of Libanus on the A470. Unfortunately, frequent use has led to erosion of this trail. A more pleasant hiking route starts in **Llanfaes,** Brecon's western suburb, and passes **Llyn Cwm Llwch** (HLIN koom hlooch), a 600m deep glacial pool. Walk 5km from Llanfaes down Ffrwdgrech Rd. to the car park, taking the middle fork after the first bridge, where the trail begins.

ST. DAVID'S (TYDDEWI) ☎01437

An evening walk in St. David's (pop. 1700), medieval Wales's largest and richest diocese, inevitably leads to **St. David's Cathedral,** where visitors and locals gather to watch the sunset. (Cathedral open daily 6am-5:30pm. Suggested donation £2.) The **Bishop's Palace,** across a bridged brook, was built from 1328 to 1347 by Bishop Henry Gower. (☎720 517. Open June-Sept. daily 9:30am-6pm; Oct. and Apr.-May daily 9:30am-5pm; Nov.-Mar. M-Sa 9:30am-4pm, Su noon-2pm. £2.) To reach St. David's from Cardiff, take a **train** to Haverfordwest (2½hr., 2 per day), and then take Richards Bros. **bus** #411 (50min., 2-5 per day). The **tourist office** is on The Grove. (☎720 392. Open Easter-Oct. daily 9:30am-5:30pm; Nov.-Easter M-Sa 10am-4pm.) Beautiful **Alandale ❸,** 43 Nun St., has friendly proprietors whose warmth and filling breakfasts will make your stay worthwhile. (☎720 404. £25 per person.) For excellent Welsh food, head to **Cartref ❷,** in Cross Sq. (Lunch £3-4, dinner from £8. Open Mar.-May daily 11am-2:30pm and 6:30-8:30pm; June-Aug. 11am-3pm and 6-8:30pm.) **Postal Code:** SA62 6SW.

SNOWDONIA NATIONAL PARK

Rough and handsome, misty purple and mossy green, the highest mountains of England and Wales stretch across 2175 square kilometers, from forested Machynlleth to sand-strewn Conwy. Although these lands lie largely in private hands, endless public footpaths accommodate droves of visitors.

TRANSPORTATION AND PRACTICAL INFORMATION. **Trains** (☎08457 484 950) stop at several large towns on the park's outskirts, including Bangor (see p. 248) and Conwy (see p. 248). The **Conwy Valley Line** runs through the park from **Llandudno** through **Betws-y-Coed** to **Blaenau Ffestiniog** (1hr., 2-7 per day). At Blaneau Ffestiniog the Conwy Valley Line connects with the narrow-gauge Ffestiniog Railway (see p. 247), which runs through the mountains to Porthmadog, meeting the Cambrian Coaster to Llanberis and Aberystwyth. **Buses** run to the interior of the park from Bangor, Conwy, and Caernarfon; consult the *Gwynedd Public Transport Maps and Timetables*, available in all regional tourist offices. The **Snowdonia National Park Information Headquarters,** Penrhyndeudraeth, Gwynedd, Wales (☎01766 770 274), provides hiking info and Ordnance Survey Maps (£5-7), and can best direct you to the eight quality **YHA hostels** in the park as well as the region's other **tourist offices** (www.gwynedd.gov.uk).

OUTDOOR ACTIVITIES. The park's most popular destination and the highest peak in England and Wales is **Mount Snowdon** (*Yr Wyddfa;* "the burial place"), measuring 1085m. Six paths of varying difficulties wind their way up Snowdon; tourist offices and National Park Information Centres can provide guides on these ascents. Weather on Snowdonia's exposed mountains shifts unpredictably. No matter how beautiful the weather is below, it will be cold and wet in the high mountains. Pick up the Ordnance Survey Landranger Map #115 (£6) and Outdoor Leisure Map #17 (£7), as well as individual path guides at tourist offices, park centers, and bookstores. Contact **Mountaincall Snowdonia** (☎0891 500 449; £0.35-0.50 per min.) for the local forecast and ground conditions. Weather forecasts are also tacked outside Park Information Centres.

Beics Eryri Cycle Tours, 44 Tyddyn Llwydyn, leads guided trips from Caernarfon for multi-night forays into the park. (☎01286 676 637. From £42 per night, including bike rental and accommodations; groups only.) **Snowdonia Riding Stables,** 3mi. from Caernarfon, off the A4085 near Waunfawr, offers horse treks. Take Sherpa bus #95 or 95A (10min., 7-14 per day) and ask to be let out at the turn-off for the stables. (☎01286 650 342. £13 per hr., £28 per half-day, £48 per day.) The brave can paraglide off Snowdonia's peaks with the help of the Llanberis-based **Snowdonia Paragliding School.** (☎01248 602 103. Three flights with instruction £75. Call ahead.)

LLANBERIS. Llanberis owes its outdoorsy bustle to the popularity of Mt. Snowdon, whose ridges and peaks unfold just south of town. **Parc Padarn** holds a host of attractions, including tours of the **Welsh Slate Museum.** (Open Easter-Oct. daily 10am-5pm; Nov.-Easter Su-F 10am-4pm. Free.) To view the waterfall **Ceunant Mawr,** follow the well-marked 1km footpath from Victoria Terr., by the Victoria Hotel. The immensely popular **Snowdon Mountain Railway** whisks visitors to Snowdon's summit. (☎01286 870 223. Open mid-Mar. to Oct. only. Round-trip £18.) KMP (☎01286 870 880) **bus** #88 runs from Caernarfon (25min., 1-2 per hr.). The **tourist office** is at 41b High St. (☎01286 870 765. Open Easter-Oct. daily 10am-6pm; Nov.-Easter W and F-Su 11am-4pm.) Plenty of sheep keep hostelers company at the **YHA Llanberis ❷.** (☎0870 770 5990. Curfew 11:30pm. Open Apr.-Oct. daily; Nov.-Mar. Su-Th. Dorms £10.25, under 18 £7.) **Phone Code:** ☎01286.

HARLECH ☎ 01766

This tiny coastal town just south of the Llyn Peninsula commands panoramic views of sea, sand, and Snowdonian summits. High above the sea and sand dunes is ■**Harlech Castle,** another of Edward I's Welsh castles; this one served as the insurrection headquarters of Welsh rebel Owain Glyndŵr. (Open June-Sept. M-Sa 9:30am-6pm, Su 9:30am-5pm; May and Oct. daily 9:30am-5pm; Nov.-Mar. M-Sa 9:30am-4pm, Su 11am-4pm. £3, students £2.) Harlech lies midway on the Cambrian Coaster line; **trains** arrive from Machynlleth (1¼-1¾hr., 3-6 per day, £8.20) and connect to Pwllheli and other spots on the Llyn Peninsula. The **Day Ranger** pass allows unlimited travel on the Coaster line for one day (£4-7). The **tourist office,** 1 Stryd Fawr, doubles as a **Snowdonia National Park Information Centre.** (☎780 658. Open daily 10am-6pm.) Enjoy spacious rooms and Harlech's best views at **Arundel ❷,** Stryd Fawr. Call ahead for pick-up. (☎780 637. £15 per person.) At the **Plâs Cafe ❷,** Stryd Fawr, guests linger over afternoon tea (£1-4) and sunset dinners (from £7) while enjoying sweeping ocean views from the grassy patio. (Open Mar.-Oct. daily 9:30am-8pm; Nov.-Feb. 9:30am-5:30pm.) **Postal Code:** LL46 2YA.

LLYN PENINSULA ☎ 01766

The Llyn has been a hotbed of tourism since the Middle Ages, when crowds of religious pilgrims tramped through on their way to Bardsey Island, just off the western tip of the peninsula. Today, sun worshippers make the pilgrimage to the endless beaches that line the southern coast. **Porthmadog,** on the southeastern part of the peninsula, is the main gateway. This travel hub's principal attraction is the charming ■**Ffestiniog Railway** (☎516 073), which runs from Harbour Station on High St. into the hills of Snowdonia (1¼hr., 2-10 per day, round-trip £14). **Trains** run from Aberystwyth (1½-2hr., 3-6 per day). TrawsCambria **bus** #701 travels once a day to Aberystwyth (2hr.) and Cardiff (7hr.). Express Motors bus #1 stops in Porthmadog on its way from Blaenau Ffestiniog to Caernarfon (M-Sa every hr.). The **tourist office** is on High St. by the harbor. (☎512 981. Open Easter-Oct. daily 10am-6pm; Nov.-Easter 10am-5pm.) The birthplace of Lawrence of Arabia is now the huge and comfortable **Snowdon Backpackers Hostel ❷.** (☎515 354. Dorms £11-13; doubles £29-33.) **Postal Code:** LL49 9AD.

CAERNARFON ☎ 01286

Majestic and fervently Welsh, the walled city of Caernarfon (car-NAR-von) has a world-famous castle at its prow and mountains in its wake. Built by Edward I beginning in 1283, the ■**Caernarfon Castle** was left unfinished when Eddie ran out of money and became distracted by unruly Scots. (☎677 617. Open June-Sept. daily 9:30am-6pm; Apr.-May and Oct. daily 9:30am-5pm; Nov.-Mar. M-Sa 9:30am-4pm, Su 11am-4pm. £4.50, students £3.50.) Arriva Cymru (☎(08706) 082 608) **buses** #5 and 5x arrive from Conwy (1¼hr., 1-2 per hr.). Buses #5A and 5B arrive from Bangor (25min.; M-Sa 5-6 per hr., Su every hr.). TrawsCambria bus #701 arrives daily from Cardiff (7½hr.). National Express (☎(08705) 808 080) bus #545 arrives daily from London (9hr.). The **tourist office** is on Castle St. (☎672 232. Open Apr.-Oct. daily 10am-6pm; Nov.-Mar. Th-Tu 9:30am-4:30pm.) ■**Totter's Hostel ❷,** 2 High St., has huge rooms and a comfortable living room. (☎672 963. Dorms £12.) Try the Welsh lamb (£11) at **Stones Bistro ❸,** 4 Hole-in-the-Wall St., a crowded, candle-lit eatery near Eastgate. **Postal Code:** LL55 2ND.

BANGOR

☎02148

This Victorian port and university town is a convenient locale for exploring the nearby Isle of Anglesey. The wildly opulent **Penrhyn Castle** stands as a testament to the staggering wealth accumulated by Welsh slate barons over a century ago. To get there, walk up High St. toward the pier, turn right on the A5122 and head 1.5km north. (Castle open July-Aug. W-M 11am-4:30pm; late Mar. to June and Sept. to Oct. W-M noon-4:30pm. Grounds open July-Aug. W-M 10am-5:30pm; late Mar. to June and Sept. to Oct. W-M 11am-5pm. Castle and grounds £6, grounds only £3.) **Trains** arrive at Holyhead Rd., at the end of Deiniol Rd., from Chester (1hr., 1-2 per hr.). **Buses** arrive at Garth Rd., down the hill from the town clock, from: Beaumaris (#53, 57, and 58; 30min., 2-8 per day); Caernarfon (#5, 5A, 5B, and 5X; 25min., every hr.); Cardiff (#701; 7¾hr., 1 per day); Conwy (#5 and 5X; 40min., 1-2 per hr.); Holyhead (#4; 1¼hr., M-Sa 2 per hr.) via Llanfair P.G.; and London (8½hr., 1 per day). The **tourist office** is in the Town Hall on Deiniol Rd. (☎352 786. Open Easter-Sept. daily 10am-6pm; Oct.-Easter F-Sa 10am-6pm.) To reach the **YHA Bangor ❷**, in Tan-y-Bryn, 800m from the town center, follow High St. to the water, turn right at the end on A5122 (Beach Rd.), and turn right at the sign. (☎353 516. Internet £1 per 20min. Open Apr.-Sept. daily; Oct. and Mar. Tu-Sa; Nov. and Jan.-Feb. F-Sa. Dorms £11.25, under 18 £8.) **High Street** has many fruit shops, cafes, and a **Kwik Save** supermarket. (Open M-Sa 8am-10pm, Su 10am-4pm.) **Postal Code:** LL57 1AA.

DAYTRIP FROM BANGOR: ISLE OF ANGLESEY. The **Isle of Anglesey**'s old name, *Mona mam Cymru* ("Mona the Mother of Wales"), hints at the island's Celtic past. **Bryn Celli Ddu** (bryn kay-HLEE thee; "The Mound in the Dark Grove") is a burial chamber dating from the late Neolithic period and is the most famous of Anglesey's remains. Take **bus** #4 from Bangor to Llandaniel (M-Sa 9 per day) and walk 1.5km from the station. (Chamber free. Bring a flashlight.) The magnificent **Beaumaris Castle,** in Beaumaris off the A545, is the last of Edward I's Welsh fortresses and is now a World Heritage Site. **Buses** #53, 57, and 58 (30min.; 8-16 per day) go from Bangor to Beaumaris. (Castle open June-Sept. daily 9:30am-6pm; Apr.-May and Oct. 9:30am-5pm; Nov.-Mar. M-Sa 9:30am-4pm, Su 11am-4pm. £3, students £2.50.) Across the Britannia Bridge from Bangor sits the longest-named village in the world, **Llanfairpwllgwyngyllgogerychwyrndrobwllllantysiliogogogoch** (Llanfair P.G.), although there's little to see apart from the sign at the station. **Trains** (☎08457 484 950) run from Llanfair P.G. to Bangor (1-2 per hr., from £5).

CONWY

☎01492

The central attraction of this tourist mecca is the 13th-century **Conwy Castle,** another link in Edward I's chain of impressive North Wales fortresses. (Open June-Sept. daily 9:30am-6pm; Apr.-May and Oct. 9:30am-5pm; Nov.-Mar. M-Sa 9:30am-4pm, Su 11am-4pm. £3.50, students £3. Tours £1.) Other sights include Britain's **Smallest House,** on the Quay (open Easter-July and Sept.-Oct. daily 10am-6pm; Aug. 10am-9pm; £0.50), and the **Teapot Museum,** on Castle St (open Easter-Oct. M-Sa 10am-5:30pm, Su 11am-5:30pm; £1.50, students £1). Arriva Cymru (☎(08706) 082 608) **buses** #5 and 5X stop in Conwy on their way to Caernarfon from Bangor (1-2 per hr.). National Express (☎(08705) 808 080) buses arrive from: Liverpool (2¾hr., 1 per day); Manchester (4hr., 1 per day); and Newcastle (10hr., 1 per day). The **tourist office** is at the castle entrance. (☎592 248. Open Easter-Oct. daily 9:30am-6pm; Nov.-Easter Th-Sa 10am-4pm.) **Bryn Guest House ❸,** below the town wall's highest point, has big bedrooms and hearty breakfasts. (☎592 449. All rooms with bath. Singles £23; doubles £40.) A **Spar** supermarket is on High St. (Open daily 8am-10pm.) **Postal Code:** LL32 8DA.

SCOTLAND

A little over half the size of England but with just a tenth of the population, Scotland possesses open spaces and wild natural splendor its southern neighbor cannot hope to rival. The craggy, heathered Highlands, the silver beaches of the west coast, and the luminescent mists of the Hebrides elicit any traveler's awe, while farmlands to the south and peaceful fishing villages on the east coast harbor a gentler beauty. Scotland at its best is a world apart from the rest of the UK. Before reluctantly joining with England in 1707, the Scots defended their independence, bitterly and heroically, for hundreds of years. Since the union, they have nurtured a separate identity, retaining control of schools, churches, and the judicial system. In 1999, the Scots finally regained a separate parliament, which gave them more power over domestic tax laws and strengthened their national identity.

TRANSPORTATION

Bus travel from London is generally cheaper than **train** fares. **British Airways** (☎08457 773 3377) sells a limited number of APEX round-trip tickets from £70. **British Midland** (☎(08706) 070 555) also offers a round-trip Saver fare from London to Glasgow (from £70). Scotland is also linked by **ferry** to Northern Ireland (see Stranraer, p. 261).

In the **Lowlands** (south of Stirling and north of the Borders), train and bus connections are frequent. In the **Highlands,** trains snake slowly on a few restricted routes, bypassing the northwest almost entirely, and many stations are unstaffed or nonexistent—buy tickets on board. A great money-saver is the **Freedom of Scotland Travelpass.** It allows unlimited train travel as well as transportation on most Caledonian MacBrayne ferries, with discounts on some other ferry lines. Purchase the pass *before* traveling to Britain, at any BritRail distributor (see By Train, p. 162). Buses tend to be the best way to travel; **Scottish Citylink** (☎08705 505 050) provides most intercity service. **MacBackpackers** (☎0131 558 9900; www.macbackpackers.com) and **HAGGiS** (☎0131 557 9393; www.radicaltravel.com) run hop-on/hop-off tours that let you travel Scotland at your own pace.

BRITAIN

EDINBURGH ☎0131

A city of elegant stone amid rolling hills and ancient volcanoes, Edinburgh (ED-in-bur-ra; pop. 500,000) is the jewel of Scotland. Since David I granted it burgh (town) status in 1130, Edinburgh has been a site of cultural significance—the seeds of the Scottish Reformation were sown here, as well as the philosophies of the Scottish Enlightenment. The tradition lives on during the festivals each August, when the city becomes a theatrical, musical, and literary magnet, drawing international talent and enthusiastic crowds. Of late, tourism has motivated a flurry of construction, from hostels and museums to government buildings.

TRANSPORTATION

Flights: Edinburgh International Airport (EDI; ☎333 1000), 11.25km west of the city center. **Lothian Buses' Airlink** (☎555 6363) shuttles to the airport (25min., £3.30) from Waverley Bridge. **Airsaver** gives you 1 trip on Airlink plus 1 day unlimited travel on local Lothian Buses (£4.20, children £2.50).

Trains: Waverley Station straddles Princes St., Market St., and Waverley Bridge. Trains (☎(08457) 484 950) to: **Aberdeen** (2½hr.; M-Sa every hr., Su 8 per day; £31); **Glasgow** (1hr., 2 per hr., £7.40-8.40); **Inverness** (3½hr., every 2hr., £31); **London King's Cross** (4¾hr., 2 per hr., £90); **Stirling** (50min., 2 per hr., £5.30).

Buses: The **bus station** is on the east side of St. Andrew's Sq. **National Express** (☎(08705) 808 080) from **London** (10hr., 5 per day, £27). **Scottish Citylink** (☎(08705) 505 050) from: **Aberdeen** (4hr., every hr., £15); **Glasgow** (1hr.; M-Sa 4 per hr., Su 2 per hr.; £3.80); **Inverness** (4½hr., 8-10 per day, £14.70). A bus-ferry route via Stranraer goes to **Belfast** (2 per day, £29-33) and **Dublin** (1 per day, £41).

Public Transportation: Lothian Buses (☎555 6363; www.lothianbuses.co.uk) provide most services. Exact change required (£0.50-£1). Buy a 1-day **Daysaver** ticket (all day M-F £2.20; after 9:30pm M-F and all day Sa or Su £1.50) from any driver or from the **Travelshops** on Hanover St. and Waverley Bridge. **Night buses** cover selected routes after midnight (£2). **First Edinburgh** also operates locally. **Traveline,** 2 Cockburn St. (☎(0800) 232 323), has info on all public transport.

Bike Rental: Biketrax, 11 Lochrin Pl. (☎228 6633). Mountain bikes £15 per day. Open M-F 9:30am-6pm, Sa 9:30am-5pm, Su noon-5pm.

ORIENTATION AND PRACTICAL INFORMATION

Edinburgh is a glorious city for walking. **Princes Street** is the main thoroughfare in **New Town,** the northern section of Edinburgh. From there you can view the impressive stone facade of the towering **Old Town,** the southern half of the city. **The Royal Mile** (Castle Hill, Lawnmarket, High St., and Canongate) is the major road in the Old Town and connects **Edinburgh Castle** in the west to the **Palace of Holyroodhouse** in the east. **North Bridge, Waverley Bridge,** and **The Mound** connect Old and New Town. Greater Edinburgh stretches well beyond Old and New Town; **Leith,** 3.2km northeast, is the city's seaport on the Firth of Forth.

Tourist Office: 3 Princes St. (☎473 3800), Waverley Market, on the north side of the Waverley Station complex. **Currency exchange.** Books rooms (£4) and has excellent free maps and pamphlets. Open July-Aug. M-Sa 9am-8pm, Su 10am-8pm; May-June and Sept. M-Sa 9am-7pm, Su 10am-7pm; Oct.-Apr. M-W 9am-5pm, Th-Sa 9am-6pm, Su 10am-5pm. In summer, look for **City Centre Representatives,** wearing yellow, who can answer questions in several languages.

Budget Travel: STA Travel, 27 Forrest Rd. (☎226 7747). Open M-Th 9:30am-6pm, F 10am-5:30pm, Sa 11am-5pm.

American Express: 139 Princes St. (☎718 2503 or (08706) 001 600). Open M-F 9am-5:30pm, Sa 9am-4pm.

Bi-Gay-Lesbian Resources: Pick up *Gay Information* at the tourist office or drop by the **Centre for Lesbians, Gays, and Bisexuals,** 58a Broughton St. (☎557 2625).

Emergency: ☎999 or 112; no coins required. **Police:** 5 Fettes Ave. (☎311 3131).

Hospital: Royal Infirmary of Edinburgh, 1 Lauriston Pl. (emergencies ☎536 4000, otherwise 536 1000).

Internet Access: easyInternet Cafe, 58 Rose St. (☎220 3577). £1 per 30min.-3hr., price varies with demand. Open M-Sa 7am-11pm, Su 8am-11pm. **e-corner,** Platform 1, Waverley Station. £1 per 20min. Open M-F 7:30am-9:30pm, Sa-Su 8am-9pm.

Post Office: (☎556 9546), in the St. James Shopping Centre, New Town. Open M 9am-5:30pm, Tu-F 8:30am-5:30pm, Sa 8:30am-6pm. **Postal Code:** EH1.

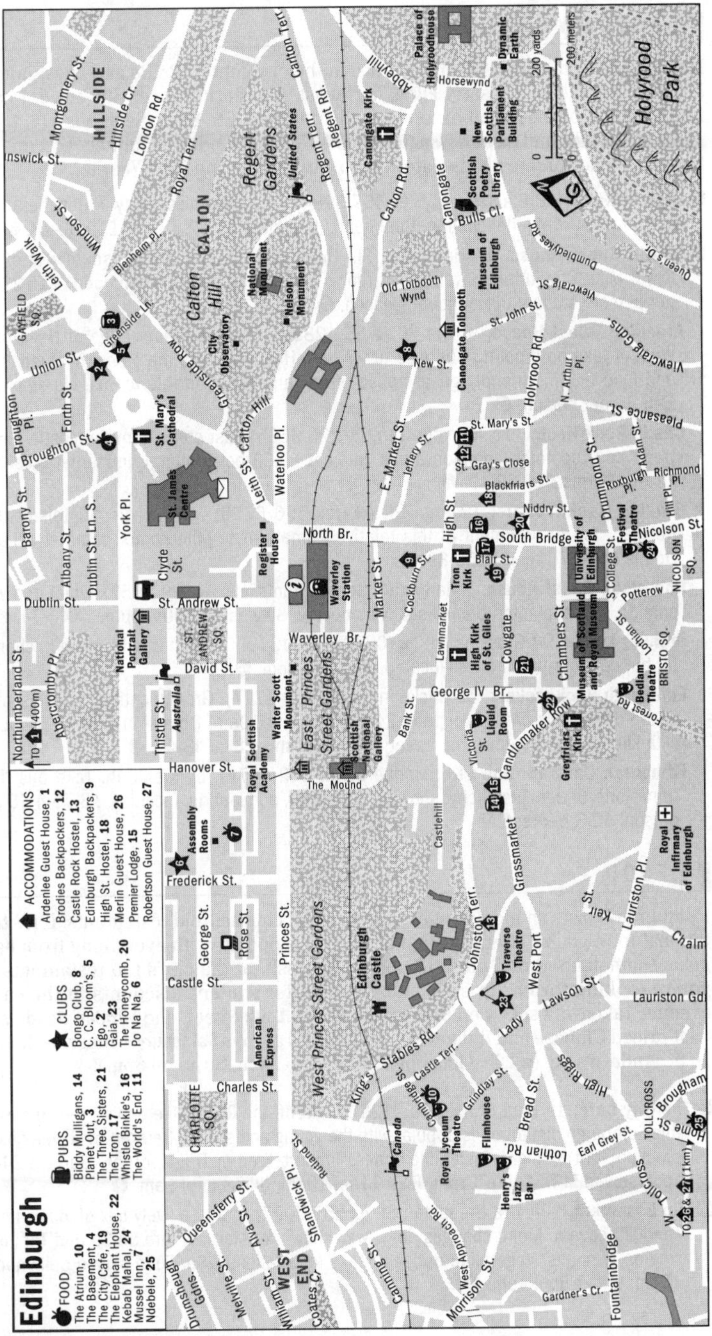
Edinburgh
FOOD
The Atrium, 10
The Basement, 4
The City Cafe, 19
The Elephant House, 22
Kebab Mahal, 24
Mussel Inn, 7
Ndebele, 25
PUBS
Biddy Mulligans, 14
Planet Out, 3
The Three Sisters, 21
The Tron, 17
Whistle Binkie's, 16
The World's End, 11
CLUBS
Bongo Club, 8
C. C. Bloom's, 5
Ego, 2
Gaia, 23
The Honeycomb, 20
Po Na Na, 6
ACCOMMODATIONS
Ardenlee Guest House, 1
Brodies Backpackers, 12
Castle Rock Hostel, 13
Edinburgh Backpackers, 9
High St. Hostel, 18
Merlin Guest House, 26
Premier Lodge, 15
Robertson Guest House, 27
TO 1 (400m)
TO 26 & 27 (1km)
HILLSIDE
CALTON
Calton Hill
Regent Gardens
Holyrood Park
Palace of Holyroodhouse
Dynamic Earth
New Scottish Parliament Building
Scottish Poetry Library
Museum of Edinburgh
Canongate Tolbooth
Canongate Kirk
National Monument
Nelson Monument
City Observatory
United States
St. Mary's Cathedral
St. James Centre
Register House
Waverley Station
National Portrait Gallery
ST. ANDREW SQ.
Australia
Walter Scott Monument
East Princes Street Gardens
Royal Scottish Academy
Scottish National Gallery
The Mound
Assembly Rooms
American Express
West Princes Street Gardens
Edinburgh Castle
Tron Kirk
High Kirk of St. Giles
Liquid Room
Greyfriars Kirk
Museum of Scotland and Royal Museum
University of Edinburgh
Festival Theatre
Bedlam Theatre
Royal Infirmary of Edinburgh
Traverse Theatre
Royal Lyceum Theatre
Filmhouse
Henry's Jazz Bar
Canada
CHARLOTTE SQ.
WEST END
NICOLSON SQ.
BRISTO SQ.
TOLLCROSS
GAYFIELD SQ.
Princes St.
George St.
Rose St.
Queen St.
Leith Walk
Leith St.
London Rd.
Royal Terr.
Regent Terr.
Regent Rd.
Calton Rd.
Canongate
High St.
Cowgate
Grassmarket
North Br.
South Bridge
George IV Br.
Waverley Br.
Lothian Rd.
Holyrood Rd.
Nicolson St.
Chambers St.
Lauriston Pl.
Candlemaker Row
0 200 yards
0 200 meters

BRITAIN

ACCOMMODATIONS

Hostels and hotels are the only options in the city center. B&Bs and guest houses begin on the outer edges; try **Pilrig,** northeast of eastern Princes St. (bus #11 east/northbound), or the neighborhoods south of Princes St., **Bruntsfield** (bus #11, 16, or 17 west/southbound) and **Newington** (bus #37, 7, or 31). It's absolutely essential to book ahead around festivals (late July to early Sept.) and New Year's.

High St. Hostel, 8 Blackfriars St. (☎557 3984). Good facilities, party atmosphere, and convenient Royal Mile location. Continental breakfast £1.60. Dorms £10.50-13. ❷

Merlin Guest House, 14 Hartington Pl., Bruntsfield (☎229 3864), southwest of the Royal Mile. Comfortable, well-priced rooms in a leafy-green neighborhood. £15-22.50 per person; student discounts off-season. ❷

Ardenlee Guest House, 9 Eyre Pl. (☎556 2838), at the northern edge of New Town. Walk or take northbound bus #23 or 27 from Hanover St. to the corner of Dundas St. and Eyre Pl. This friendly guest house offers large, comfortable rooms. No smoking. £26-35 per person. ❸

Castle Rock Hostel, 15 Johnston Terr. (☎225 9666), just steps from the castle. Regal views and top-notch common areas. Internet £0.80 per 30min. Continental breakfast £1.60. Dorms £10.50-13. ❷

Brodies Backpackers, 12 High St. (☎/fax 556 6770; www.brodieshostels.co.uk). Relaxed, fun environment at this relatively small Royal Mile hostel. Internet access. Dorms £10-17; weekly £59-89. ❷

Robertson Guest House, 5 Hartington Gdns., Bruntsfield (☎229 2652). Quiet and welcoming, with top-notch breakfasts. No smoking. Singles £22-50; doubles £44-74. ❸

Premier Lodge, 94 Grassmarket (☎(0870) 700 1370). A chain hotel lacking in character but comfortable and well-located. £50 per room. ❹

Edinburgh Backpackers, 65 Cockburn St. (☎220 1717). Great location. 10% discount at the downstairs cafe. Reception 24hr. Check-out 10am. Dorms £12.50-15. Doubles with kitchen access down the street at 34a Cockburn St. £43-49. ❷

Edinburgh Caravan Club Site, Marine Dr. (☎312 6874), by the Forth. Take bus #8A from North Bridge. Electricity, showers, hot water, and laundry facilities. £3.75-4.75 per person, £2-3 per tent. ❶

FOOD

Edinburgh boasts an increasingly wide range of cuisines and restaurants. If it's traditional food you're after, the capital won't disappoint, with everything from haggis at the neighborhood pub to "modern Scottish" at the city's top restaurants. If you're looking for cheap eats, many pubs offer student discounts in the early evening, takeaway shops on **South Clerk Street, Leith Street,** and **Lothian Road** have well-priced Chinese and Indian fare, and there's always **Sainsbury's** supermarket, 9-10 St. Andrews Sq. (☎225 8400; open M-Sa 7am-10pm, Su 10am-8pm).

The City Cafe, 19 Blair St. (☎220 0125). Right off the Royal Mile behind the Tron Kirk, this Edinburgh institution is popular with the young and stylish. Relaxed by day, a flashy pre-club spot by night. Incredible shakes immortalized in *Trainspotting*. Burgers £4-6. Food served M-Th 11am-11pm, F-Su 11am-10pm; drinks until 1am. ❷

The Basement, 10a-12a Broughton St. (☎557 0097). Draws a lively mix of locals to its candlelit cavern. Menu changes daily, well-known for Mexican fare Sa-Su and Thai cuisine on W nights. Vegetarian options. Make reservations F-Sa. Food served daily noon-10pm; drinks until 1am. ❷

Ndebele, 57 Home St. (☎221 1141), in Tolcross, 800m south of western Princes St. Named for a tribe from Swaziland, this atmospheric restaurant serves generous portions of African food for under £5. Open daily 10am-10pm. ❶

The Atrium, 10 Cambridge St. (☎228 8882). One of Edinburgh's hottest eateries, serving modern Scottish cuisine. Two courses about £28. Reservations essential. Open M-F noon-2pm and 6-10pm; Sa 6-10pm. ❹

Kebab Mahal, 7 Nicolson Sq. (☎667 5214). This hole-in-the-wall will stuff you with Indian food for under £5. Open Su-Th noon-midnight, F-Sa noon-2am. ❶

Mussel Inn, 61-65 Rose St. (☎225 5979). Fresh, expertly prepared seafood. Lunch under £10, dinner under £15. Open M-Sa noon-10pm, Su 1:30-10pm. ❸

The Elephant House, 21 George IV Bridge (☎220 5355). A perfect place to chill, chat, or smoke. Tea, coffee, delicious shortbread, and filling fare for less than £5. Happy Hour M-Sa 9-10pm. Live music Th 7pm. Open daily 8am-11pm. ❶

SIGHTS

A boggling array of tour companies tout themselves as "the original" or "the scariest," but the most worthwhile is the **Edinburgh Literary Pub Tour.** Led by professional actors, this alcohol-sodden 2hr. crash course in Scottish literature meets outside the Beehive Inn in the Grassmarket. (☎226 6665. July-Aug. daily 6 and 7:30pm; June and Sept. daily 7:30pm; Apr.-May and Oct. Th-Su 7:30pm; Nov.-Mar. F 7:30pm. £7, students £5.) Alternatively, consider a one-on-one encounter with the MacKenzie Poltergeist on the **City of the Dead Tour,** 40 Candlemaker Row. (☎225 9044. Daily 8:30 and 10pm. £5, children £4.)

THE OLD TOWN AND THE ROYAL MILE

Edinburgh's medieval center, the fascinating Royal Mile defines Old Town and passes many classic houses and attractions. The Old Town once packed thousands of inhabitants into a scant few square miles, with narrow shop fronts and slum buildings towering to a dozen stories.

EDINBURGH CASTLE. Perched atop an extinct volcano and dominating the city center, the castle is a testament to Edinburgh's past strategic importance. The castle is the result of centuries of renovation and rebuilding; the most recent additions date to the 1920s. The **One O'Clock Gun** fires daily (except Su) at 1pm. *(Open Apr.-Sept. daily 9:30am-6pm; Oct.-Mar. 9:30am-5pm. Last admission 45min. before closing. £8, seniors £6.50, children £2, under 5 free. Audio tours £3.)*

ALONG THE ROYAL MILE. Near the Castle, through Mylne's Close, the **Scottish Parliament** convenes in the **Church of Scotland Assembly Hall;** visitors are welcome to watch the MPs debate. *(☎348 5411. Sept.-June. Tickets must be reserved in advance. Free.)* The **Visitors Centre** is nearby, at the corner of the Royal Mile and the George IV Bridge. *(Open M-F 10am-5pm. Free.)* The 17th-century **Lady Stair's House** contains the **Writer's Museum,** featuring memorabilia and manuscripts belonging to three of Scotland's greatest literary figures: Robert Burns, Sir Walter Scott, and Robert Louis Stevenson. *(Through the passage at 477 Lawnmarket St. Open M-Sa 10am-5pm; during festival season also Su 2-5pm. Free.)* At the beautiful **High Kirk of St. Giles** (St. Giles Cathedral), Scotland's principal church, John Knox delivered the fiery Presbyterian sermons that drove Mary, Queen of Scots, into exile. Now it offers free concerts year-round. *(Where Lawnmarket becomes High St. Open Easter to mid-Sept. M-F 9am-7pm, Sa 9am-5pm, Su 1-5pm; mid-Sept. to Easter M-Sa 9am-5pm, Su 1-5pm. Suggested donation £1.)* The 17th-century **Canongate Kirk,** on the steep hill at the end of the Mile, is the resting place of Adam Smith; royals also worship here when in residence. *(Same hours as the High Kirk. Free.)*

THE INSIDER'S CITY

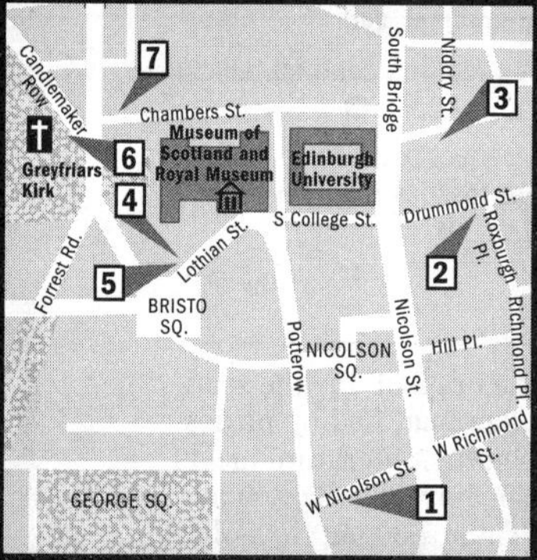

A FOUNTAIN OF KNOWLEDGE

***Let's Go* has rounded up the favorite watering holes of the students at the University of Edinburgh for your inebriated convenience.**

1. If the sun is shining, head to the beer garden at the **Pear Tree House.** (38 West Nicholson St. Open daily noon-midnight.)
2. **Brass Monkey** features a cinema lounge. Pair *Braveheart* with a pint of McEwan's. (14 Drummond St. Open daily 10am-1am.)
3. **Oxygen Bar** offers a chill atmosphere. (3-5 Infirmary St. Open M-Sa 10am-1am, Su noon-1am.)
4. Catch disco fever at **Iguana.** (41 Lothian St. Open daily 9am-3am.)
5. Laid-back **Negociants** has great food. (45-47 Lothian St. Open M-Sa 9am-3am, Su 10am-3am.)
6. There's no better spot than **Greyfriars Bobby** for a pint and a cheap meal. (34 Candlemaker Row. Open daily 11am-1am.)
7. **Beluga Bar** is *the* spot for stylish scholars. (30a Chambers St. Open daily 9am-1am.)

THE PALACE OF HOLYROODHOUSE. This Stewart palace abuts Holyrood Park and the peak of Arthur's Seat and dates from the 16th century. It remains Queen Elizabeth II's official Scottish residence. Once home to Mary, Queen of Scots, it was the site of the brutal murder of her secretary, David Rizzio. *(Open Apr.-Oct. daily 9:30am-6pm; Nov.-Mar. M-Sa 9:30am-4:30pm; last admission 45min. before closing. Closed during official residences. £6.50.)*

OTHER SIGHTS IN THE OLD TOWN. The **Museum of Scotland** and the connected **Royal Museum,** on Chambers St., just south of the George IV Bridge, are not to be missed. The former houses a definitive collection of Scottish artifacts in a stunning contemporary building; the latter contains a varied mix of art and natural history. *(Open M and W-Sa 10am-5pm, Tu 10am-8pm, Su noon-5pm. Free.)* Just across the street stands the statue of Greyfriar's loyal pooch, Bobby, marking the entrance to **Greyfriar's Kirk,** built in 1620 and surrounded by a beautiful and supposedly haunted churchyard. *(Off Candlemaker Row. Gaelic services Su 12:30pm, English 11am. Open Easter-Oct. M-F 10:30am-4:30pm, Sa until 2:30pm. Free.)*

THE NEW TOWN

Edinburgh's New Town is a masterpiece of Georgian design. James Craig, a 23-year-old architect, won the city-planning contest in 1767; his rectangular grid of three parallel streets (Queen, George, and Princes) linking two large squares (Charlotte and St. Andrew) reflects the Scottish Enlightenment's belief in order.

THE GEORGIAN HOUSE AND THE WALTER SCOTT MONUMENT. The elegantly restored **Georgian House** gives a picture of life 200 years ago. *(7 Charlotte Sq. From Princes St., turn right on Charlotte St. and take the second left. Open Apr.-Oct. daily 10am-6pm; Nov.-Mar. 11am-4pm. £5, students £3.75.)* The **Walter Scott Monument** is a Gothic "steeple without a church"; climb the 287-step staircase for far views stretching out to Princes St. Gardens, the castle, and Old Town's Market St. *(On Princes St., between The Mound and Waverley Bridge. Open June-Sept. M-Sa 9am-8pm, Su 10am-6pm; Mar.-May and Oct. M-Sa 9am-6pm, Su 10am-6pm; Nov.-Feb. M-Sa 9am-4pm, Su 10am-6pm. £2.50.)*

THE NATIONAL GALLERIES

Edinburgh's National Galleries of Scotland form an elite group, with excellent collections connected by a free shuttle every hr. The flagship is the **National Gallery of Scotland,** on the Mound, which houses a superb collection of works by Renaissance, Romantic, and Impressionist masters and a fine spread of Scottish art. The **Scottish National Portrait Gallery,** 1

Queen St., north of St. Andrew Sq., features the faces of famous Scots. Take the free shuttle, bus #13 from George St., or walk to the **Scottish National Gallery of Modern Art,** 75 Belford Rd., west of town, and the new **Dean Gallery,** 73 Belford Rd., specializing in Surrealist and Dadaist art. *(All open M-Sa 10am-5pm, Su noon-5pm; longer hours during festival season. Free.)*

GARDENS AND PARKS

Just off the eastern end of the Royal Mile, **Holyrood Park** is a true city oasis, a natural wilderness replete with hills, moorland, and lochs. **Arthur's Seat,** the park's highest point, affords stunning views of the city and countryside. The walk to the summit takes about 45min. The lovely **Royal Botanic Gardens** are north of the city center. Take bus #23 or 27 from Hanover St. *(Open Apr.-Aug. daily 9:30am-7pm; Mar. and Sept. 9:30am-6pm; Feb. and Oct. 9:30am-5pm; Nov.-Jan. 9:30am-4pm. Free.)*

ENTERTAINMENT

The summer sees an especially joyful string of events—music in the gardens, plays and films, and *ceilidhs*—even before the Festival comes to town. In winter, shorter days and the crush of students promote a flourishing nightlife. For the most up-to-date info on what's going on, check out *The List* (£2.20), a comprehensive biweekly guide to events, available from any local newsstand.

THEATER, FILM, AND MUSIC. The **Festival Theatre,** 13-29 Nicholson St., stages ballet and opera, while the affiliated **King's Theatre,** 2 Leven St., hosts comedy, drama, musicals, and opera. Same-day seats (£5.50) for the Festival Theatre go on sale daily at 10am. (☎529 6000. Box office open M-Sa 10am-6pm.) **The Stand Comedy Club,** 5 York Pl., has nightly acts. (☎558 7272. Tickets £1-7.) The **Filmhouse,** 88 Lothian Rd., offers quality European, arthouse, and Hollywood cinema. (☎228 2688. Tickets £3.20-5.20.) Thanks to an abundance of students, Edinburgh's live music scene is alive and well. For a run-down of upcoming acts, look to *The List* or *The Gig Guide.* Free live jazz can be found at **Henry's Jazz Bar,** 8 Morrison St. (Open W-Sa; performances around 8pm, doors open around 6pm.) **The Venue,** 15 Calton Rd., and **The Liquid Room,** 9c Victoria St., often host rock and progressive shows. **Whistle Binkie's,** 4 Niddry St., off High St., is a subterranean pub with live music most nights. (Open daily until 3am.)

NIGHTLIFE

PUBS

Edinburgh claims to have the highest density of pubs anywhere in Europe. Pubs directly on the Royal Mile usually attract an older crowd, while students tend to loiter in the Old Town just to the south.

The Tron, 9 Hunter Sq., behind the Tron Kirk. Wildly popular for its incredible deals. Frequent live music on three hopping fl. All pints under £2. June-Sept. students and hostelers get £1 drinks on W nights. Open daily 11:30am-1am.

The Three Sisters, 139 Cowgate. Copious space for dancing, drinking, and socializing. Three themed bars and an outdoor beer garden. Open daily 9am-1am.

Biddy Mulligans, 96 Grassmarket. An Irish-themed pub. Also serves big breakfasts. Open daily 9am-1am, food until 9pm.

The World's End, 4 High St. Frequented by locals. On open-mic night (Su 10pm-midnight), performers get a free pint.

CLUBS

Club venues are constantly closing down and reopening under new management; consult *The List* for updated info. Clubs cluster around the historically disreputable **Cowgate,** just downhill from and parallel to the Royal Mile; most close at 3am.

The Honeycomb, 15-17 Niddry St. Monthly theme nights and frequent guest DJs. Cover free-£10.

Bongo Club, 14 New St. Noted for hip-hop. Cover £4-6.

Le Belle Angele, 11 Hasties Close. Showcases hip-hop, trance, and progressive house. Cover £2-10.

Po Na Na, 26 Frederick St. Moroccan-themed and glamorous. Su-Th no cover, F-Sa £3.

GAY AND LESBIAN

The Broughton St. area of the New Town (better known as the **Broughton Triangle**) is the center of Edinburgh's gay community.

Planet Out, 6 Baxter's Pl. Start off the night at this mellow club. Open M-F 4pm-1am, Sa-Su 2pm-1am.

C.C. Bloom's, 23-24 Greenside Pl., on Leith St. A friendly gay club with no cover. M-Sa dancing, Su karaoke. Open M-Sa 6pm-3am, Su 8pm-3am.

Ego, 14 Picardy Pl. Hosts several gay nights, including the long-established **Joy** (1 Sa per month). Cover £10.

FESTIVALS

Edinburgh has special events year-round, but the real show is in August. What's commonly referred to as "the Festival" actually encompasses a number of independently organized events. For more information on all the festivals, check out www.edinburghfestivals.co.uk. The **Edinburgh International Festival** (Aug. 10-30 in 2003), the largest of them all, features a kaleidoscopic program of music, drama, dance, and art. Tickets (£5-80) are sold beginning in April, but you can usually get tickets at the door; look for half-price tickets starting at 9am on performance days at **The HUB,** Edinburgh's Festival Centre, Castlehill. (☎473 2000. Open M-Sa.) Around the established festival has grown a less formal **Fringe Festival** (Aug. 3-25 in 2003), which now includes over 600 amateur and professional companies presenting theater, comedy, children's shows, folk and classical music, poetry, dance, and opera events that budget travelers may find more suitable for their wallets (usually free-£11). Contact the **Fringe Festival Office,** 180 High St. (☎226 0000; www.edfringe.com. Open mid-June to mid-July M-F; mid-July to Aug. daily.) Another August festival is the **Military Tattoo**—a spectacle of military bands, bagpipes, and drums. For tickets (£9-28), contact the **Tattoo Ticket Sale Office,** 32 Market St. (☎225 1188; www.edintattoo.co.uk). The excellent **Edinburgh International Film Festival** is also in August at The Filmhouse (☎229 2550; tickets on sale starting late July), while the **Edinburgh Jazz and Blues Festival** is from late July to early August (☎467 5200; tickets on sale in June). The fun doesn't stop for the long, dark winter: **Hogmanay,** Edinburgh's traditional New Year's Eve festival, is a serious street party with a week of associated events (www.edinburghshogmanay.org).

DAYTRIP FROM EDINBURGH

ST. ANDREWS

Stagecoach Express Fife buses (☎01334 474 238) pull in from Edinburgh (bus #X59 or X60; 2hr.; M-Sa 2 per hr. until 6:45pm, fewer on Su; £5.70) and Glasgow (#X24, change at Glenrothes to #X59; 2½hr.; M-Sa every hr., fewer on Su; £5.50). Trains (☎08457 484 590) from Edinburgh stop 11km away at Leuchars (1hr., every hr., £8.10), where buses #94 and 96 (£1.60) depart for St. Andrews.

Golf overruns the small city of St. Andrews, where the rules of the sport were formally established. The **Old Course** is a frequent site of the British Open. (☎01334 466 666 for reservations or enter a same-day lottery for starting times. Apr.-Oct. £90 per round; Nov.-Mar. £56.) The budget option, still lovely, is the nine-hole **Balgove Course** for £7. If you're more interested in watching than playing, the **British Golf Museum,** next to the Old Course, details the ancient origins of golf. (Open Easter-Oct. daily 9:30am-5:30pm; Nov.-Easter Th-M 11am-3pm. £4, students £3.) **St. Andrews Cathedral** was the center of Scottish religion before and during the Middle Ages. The nearby **St. Andrews Castle** hides secret tunnels and bottle-shaped dungeons. (Cathedral and castle open Apr.-Sept. daily 9:30am-6:30pm; Oct.-Mar. 9:30am-4:30pm. Joint ticket £3.75.)

To get from the bus station to the **tourist office,** 70 Market St., turn right on City Rd. and take the first left. (☎01334 472 021. Open Apr.-June M-Sa 9:30am-5:30pm, Su 11am-4pm; July-Aug. M-Sa 9:30am-7pm, Su 10:30am-5pm; Sept. M-Sa 9:30am-6pm, Su 11am-4pm; Oct.-Mar. M-Sa 9:30am-5pm.) **Internet access** is across the street at **Costa Coffee,** 83 Market St. (£1 per 20min. Open M-Sa 8am-6pm, Su 10am-5:30pm.) B&Bs line **Murray Place** and **Murray Park** near the bus station. **St. Andrews Tourist Hostel ❷,** St. Mary's Pl., is in a great location and has sparkling facilities. (☎01334 479 911. Dorms £12; 4-bed family room £40-48.)

GLASGOW ☎0141

Scotland's largest metropolitan area, Glasgow (pop. 700,000) rose to prominence during the reign of Queen Victoria, exploiting heavy industry to become the world's leading center of shipbuilding and steel production, as evidenced by the cranes that litter the river Clyde. Across the river, however, the daring curves of a new multi-million pound Science Centre shimmer brilliantly, a bright spot southwest of the city center. Furthermore, dozens of free museums, excellent international cuisine, and shopping add cosmopolitan flair and separate the city from its industrial past. But the glamour wears off in Glasgow's bustling clubs and pubs, popular with the largest student population in Scotland and football-mad locals, which lie behind the city's national reputation for nighttime fun.

BRITAIN

TRANSPORTATION

Flights: Glasgow Airport (☎887 1111), 15km west in Abbotsinch. Citylink buses connect to **Buchanan Station** (20min., 6 per hr., £3.30).

Trains: Two main stations. Trains leave from **Central Station,** on Gordon St. (U: St. Enoch), for **London King's Cross** (5-6hr., every hr., £82) and **Stranraer** (2½hr., 3-8 per day, £15.50). From **Queen St. Station,** on George Sq. (U: Buchanan St.), trains go to: **Aberdeen** (2½hr., 11-24 per day, £31); **Edinburgh** (50min., 2 per hr., £7.40); **Inverness** (3¼hr., 5 per day, £31). Bus #88 runs between the two stations (£0.50).

Buses: Buchanan Station (☎(0870) 608 2608), on Hanover St., 2 blocks north of Queen St. Station. **Scottish Citylink** (☎(08705) 505 050) to: **Aberdeen** (4hr., every hr., £25.50); **Edinburgh** (1¼hr., 2-3 per hr., £5.50); **Inverness** (3½-4½hr., every hr., £25); **Oban** (3hr., 2-3 per day, £10.70). **National Express** (☎(08705) 808 080) buses arrive daily from **London** (8hr.; every hr.; £21.50, round-trip £28).

Public Transportation: The circular **Underground (U)** subway line, a.k.a. the "Clockwork Orange," runs M-Sa 6:30am-11pm, Su 11am-5:30pm. £0.90.

ORIENTATION AND PRACTICAL INFORMATION

George Square is the center of town. Sections of Sauchiehall St., Argyle St., and Buchanan St. are pedestrian areas. **Charing Cross,** where Bath St. crosses M8 in the northwest, is a useful landmark. The vibrant **West End** revolves around **Byres Road** and **Glasgow University,** 1½km northwest of the city center.

Tourist Office: 11 George Sq. (☎204 4400). South of Queen St. Station, northeast of Central Station. U: Buchanan St. Books rooms for £2 fee plus deposit. **Walking tours** depart M, Tu, Th, and F 2:30 and 6pm, Su 10:30am. (1½hr., £5.) Open July-Aug. M-Sa 9am-8pm, Su 10am-6pm; Sept.-June M-Sa 9am-7pm, Su 10am-6pm.

American Express: 115 Hope St. (☎(08706) 001 060). Open July-Aug. M-F 8:30am-5:30pm, Sa 9am-5pm; Sept.-June M-F 8:30am-5:30pm, Sa 9am-noon.

Laundromat: Coin-Op Laundromat, 39-41 Bank St. (☎339 8953). U: Kelvin Bridge. Wash £3, dry £1. Open M-F 9am-7:30pm, Sa-Su 9am-5pm.

Emergency: ☎999; no coins required.

Police: On Stewart St. (☎532 3000).

Hospital: Glasgow Royal Infirmary, 84-106 Castle St. (☎211 4000).

Internet Access: easyEverything Internet Cafe, 57-61 St. Vincent St. (☎222 2365). £1 buys 40min.-3hr. depending on time of day. Open daily 7am-10:45pm.

Post Office: 47 St. Vincent St. (☎204 3688). Open M-F 8:30am-5:45pm, Sa 9am-5:30pm. **Postal Code:** G2 5QX.

ACCOMMODATIONS

Reserve B&Bs and hostels in advance, especially in August. If rooms are booked in Glasgow, consider staying at the **SYHA Loch Lomond** (p. 262). Most B&Bs cluster on **Argyle St.** in the university area or near **Westercraigs Road,** east of the Necropolis.

Bunkum Backpackers, 26 Hillhead St. (☎581 4481). Minutes away from the West End. Spacious dorms with comfortable beds. Laundry. Dorms £10 per day, £50 per week. ❷

Berkeley Globetrotters Hostel, 56 Berkeley St. (☎221 7880), about 2 blocks west of Charing Cross, just south of Sauchiehall St. Clean, basic rooms at rock bottom prices. Free breakfast. Dorms £9.50; £8.50 per night for longer stays. ❶

Merchant Lodge, 52 Virginia St. (☎552 2424). Originally a tobacco store, this upscale B&B is convenient and fairly priced. Singles £35; doubles £55; triples £70. ❸

University of Glasgow, No. 3 The Square, Conference & Visitor Services (☎330 5385). Enter the University of Glasgow from University St. and turn immediately right into the square. Summer housing at several dorms. Office open M-F 9am-5pm. Student dorms £14; B&B £17.50. ❷

Alamo Guest House, 46 Gray St. (☎339 2395), across from Kelvingrove Park at its southern exit. Beautiful location in the West End. Family-run and on a quiet street. Singles £20-22; doubles from £34. ❸

SYHA Glasgow, 7-8 Park Terr. (☎332 3004). U: St. George's Cross. From Central Station, take bus #44 from Hope St.; ask for the first stop on Woodlands Rd., then follow the signs. This hostel maintains an air of luxury. All rooms with bath. TV and game rooms. Breakfast included. Laundry (£1 wash and dry). Dorms July-Aug. £12, under 18 £9.50; Sept.-Oct. £11/£9.50; Nov.-Feb. £10/£8.50; Apr.-June £11/£9.50. ❷

Glasgow
ACCOMMODATIONS
Alamo Guest House, 6
Berkeley Globetrotters, 8
Bunkum Backpackers, 2
Merchant Lodge, 13
SYHA Glasgow, 5
University of Glasgow, 1
NIGHTLIFE
Archaos, 14
Cathouse, 11
FOOD
Ashora, 10
Bay Tree Cafe, 4
Cul de Sac Restaurant, 15
Willow Tea Rooms, 9
PUBS
Babbity Bowster, 16
Horseshoe Bar, 12
Nice 'n' Sleazy, 7
Uisge Beatha, 3
Byres Rd.
Glasgow University Visitor's Center
Kelvingrove Museum & Art Gallery
Royal Infirmary
Glasgow Cathedral
CATHEDRAL SQ.
St. Mungo Museum
TO NECROPOLIS (700m)
High St. Station
Strathclyde University
Campus Village
City Hall/ Ticket Centre
City Chambers
GEORGE SQ.
Queen St. Station
Buchanan Bus Station
Glasgow Caledonian University
Stirling Library
Gallery of Modern Art
NELSON MANDELA PL.
Princes Sq. Shopping Centre
ST. ENOCH
Argyle St. Station
Central Station
Suspension Bridge
COWCADDENS
GARNETHILL
CHARING CROSS
ST. GEORGE'S CROSS
Glasgow School of Art
Anderston Cross Bus Station
KELVINGROVE PARK
Hunterian Museum and Art Gallery
Kelvingrove Art Gallery and Museum
Glasgow University
Kelvin Hall
see Byres' Rd. inset
River Clyde
River Kelvin
Sauchiehall St.
Argyle St.
St. Vincent St.
W. George St.
Bath St.
Hope St.
Union St.
Jamaica St.
Clyde St.
Broomielaw
Trongate
Gallowgate
George St.
Cathedral St.
Renfield St.
Buchanan St.
M8
TO GLASGOW AIRPORT (15km)
TO QUEEN'S CROSS
Clydeside Expwy.
500 yards
500 meters

FOOD

The area bordered by Otago St. in the west, St. George's Rd. in the east, and along Great Western Rd., Woodlands Rd., and Eldon St. brims with cheap kebab-and-curry joints. **Byres Road** and **Ashton Lane,** a tiny cobblestoned alley parallel to Byres Rd., thrive with cheap, trendy cafes.

Ashora, 108 Elderslie St. Just west of several hostels on Berkeley St., this award-winning restaurant features cheap, delicious Indian food. Lunch buffet £2.95, dinner buffet £5.95. Lunch served 11am-2pm. Open daily 11am-midnight. ❶

The Willow Tea Rooms, 217 Sauchiehall St. Upstairs from Henderson the Jewellers. A Glasgow landmark. Sip one of 31 kinds of tea. £1.60-1.70 per pot. High tea £8.75. Open M-Sa 9am-4:30pm, Su noon-4:15pm. ❷

Cul-De-Sac Restaurant, 44-46 Ashton Ln. Turn from Byres Rd. onto Ashton Ln., bear right. Three-course dinners include vegetable dishes, meat *cassoulet,* and the Scottish delicacy haggis (£13-20). Lunch M-Sa noon-5pm; brunch Su 12:30-4pm; dinner every-day until 10:30 pm. ❸

The Bay Tree Café, 403 Great Western Rd., at Park Rd. in the West End. Hummus with pita bread and salad £5.25. Open daily 10:30am-10pm. ❷

SIGHTS

Follow George St. from George Square and take a left on High St., which turns into Castle St., to reach the Gothic **Glasgow Cathedral,** the only full-scale cathedral spared the fury of the 16th-century Scottish Reformation. (Open Apr.-Sept. M-Sa 9:30am-6pm, Su 2-5pm; Oct.-Mar. M-Sa 9:30am-4pm, Su 2-4pm. Free.) On the same street is the **St. Mungo Museum of Religious Life and Art,** 2 Castle St., which surveys every religion from Islam to Yoruba. (Open M-Sa 10am-5pm, Su 11am-5pm. Free.) Behind the cathedral is the spectacular **Necropolis,** a terrifying hilltop cemetery filled with broken tombstones. (Open 24hr. Free.)

In the West End, **Kelvingrove Park** lies on the banks of the River Kelvin. In the southwest corner of the park, at Argyle and Sauchiehall St., sits the **Kelvingrove Art Gallery and Museum,** which shelters works by van Gogh, Monet, and Rembrandt. (U: Kelvin Hall. Open M-Th and Sa 10am-5pm, F and Su 11am-5pm. Free.) Farther west rise the Gothic edifices of the **University of Glasgow.** The main building is on University Ave., which runs into Byres Rd. While walking through the campus, stop by the **Hunterian Museum,** home to the death mask of Bonnie Prince Charlie, or see 19th-century Scottish art at the **Hunterian Art Gallery,** across the street. (U: Hillhead. Open M-Sa 9:30am-5pm. Free.) Several buildings designed by Charles Rennie Mackintosh, Scotland's most famous architect, are open to the public; the **Glasgow School of Art,** 167 Renfrew St., south of the river, reflects a uniquely Glaswegian Modernist style. (Tours M-F 11am and 2pm, Sa 10:30am; July-Aug. also Sa 11:30am and 1pm, Su 10:30, 11:30am, and 1pm. £5, students £3.)

ENTERTAINMENT AND NIGHTLIFE

Glaswegians have a reputation for partying hard. *The List* (£2.20 from newsagents) has detailed nightlife and entertainment listings for both Glasgow and Edinburgh. The infamous **Byres Road** pub crawl slithers past the Glasgow University area, starting at Tennant's Bar and proceeding toward the River Clyde. **Uisge Beatha,** 232 Woodlands Rd., serves over 100 kinds of malt whiskey. (£1.30-1.60. Open M-Th 11am-11pm, F-Sa 11am-midnight, Su 12:30-11pm.) Go to **Babbity Bowster,** 16-18 Blackfriar St., for football talk and good drinks. (Open M-Sa 10am-midnight, Su 11am-midnight.) At **Nice 'n' Sleazy,** 421 Sauchiehall St., enjoy eclectic live music downstairs and cheap food and drink upstairs. (Open M-Sa 11:30am-midnight, Su 12:30pm-midnight.) **Horseshoe Bar,** 17-21 Drury St., boasts the longest continuous bar in the UK, as well as karaoke. (Open M-Sa 11am-midnight, Su 12:30pm-midnight.) At the club **Archaos,** 25 Queen St., students drink two-for-one whiskeys. (Cover £3-7. Open Tu, Th-Su 11pm-3am.) Grunge and indie music pleases mostly younger crowds at **Cathouse,** 15 Union St., a three-story club. (Cover £3-5, £1-2 student discount. Open W-Su 11pm-3am.)

STRANRAER ☎01776

On the westernmost peninsula of Dumfries and Galloway, Stranraer provides ferry access to Northern Ireland. **Stena Line** (☎(08705) 707 070) sails to Belfast (1¾-3¼hr; 9 per day; £14-24, students and seniors £10-19, children £7-12). **Trains** (☎(08457) 484 950) arrive from Glasgow (2½hr., 2-7 per day, £15), as do Citylink **buses** (☎(08705) 505 050; #923; 2½hr., 2 per day, £8.50). National Express buses (☎(08705) 808 080) run from London (9hr., 2 per day, £33) and Manchester (5½hr., 1 per day, £27). The **tourist office** is on Harbour St. (☎702 595. Open June-Sept. M-Sa 9:30am-5:30pm, Su 10am-4:30pm; Apr.-May and Oct. M-Sa 10am-5pm; Nov.-Mar. M-Sa 11am-4pm.) If you're stranded, try the **Jan Da Mar Guest House ❷,** 1 Ivy Pl., on London Rd. (☎706 194. Singles £18-25; doubles £32-40.) The **Tesco supermarket** is on Charlotte St. at Port Rodie near the ferry terminal. (Open M-F 8:30am-8pm, Sa 8am-6pm, Su 10am-5pm.)

ISLE OF ARRAN ☎01770

With both gentle lowland hills and majestic highland peaks, the glorious Isle of Arran (AH-ren) justifiably bills itself as "Scotland in Miniature." In the north, the craggy peaks of Goatfell and the Caisteal range surge above the pine-filled foothills. Prehistoric stone circles rise suddenly out of the mist in the west, while the eastern coastline winds past meadows and white beaches. Arran is a popular destination for both **hikers** and **bikers.** Pedaling part or all of the 90km road around the island reveals splendid views, and the tourist office in Brodick has maps, leaflets, and information on high-season guided walks.

TRANSPORTATION. To reach Arran, take a **train** to Ardrossan from Glasgow Central (☎(08457) 484 950; 45min., 4-5 per day, £4.50). The Caledonian-MacIntyre **ferry** from Ardrossan to Brodick runs in sync with train schedules (☎302 166; 1hr., 4-6 per day, £4.60). On the island, the **Rural Day Card** grants a day of travel on Arran's buses (available on the bus; £3, children £1.50).

BRODICK. In addition to its major transportation connections, Arran's main town (pop. 2000) features a peaceful bay against a backdrop of rugged mountains. Four kilometers north of town, **Brodick Castle** sits above fantastic wild and walled gardens. Built on the site of an old Viking fort and the ancient seat of the Dukes of Hamilton, the castle contains a fine porcelain collection, paintings, and scores of dead animals. (☎302 202. Castle open Apr.-Oct. daily 10am-5pm, Nov.-Dec. Sa-Su 10am-4pm. Castle and gardens £6, students £4. Gardens only £2.50/£1.70.) The well-marked path up popular **Goatfell,** Arran's highest peak (1000m), begins on the road between the Arran Heritage Museum and Brodick Castle. The 11.2km round-trip hike averages 4-5hr., but the view from the cold and windy peak is worth it; on a clear day, it stretches from Ireland to the Isle of Mull.

The **tourist office** is across from the ferry pier. (☎302 140. Open June-Sept. M-Sa 9am-7:30pm, Su 10am-5pm; Oct.-May M-F 9am-5pm, Sa 10am-5pm.) The spacious, seafront **Glenfloral Guest House ❷** is on Shore Rd. (☎302 707. Singles £17; doubles £34-40.) **Camp** at **Glen Rosa Farm ❶,** 3.2km north of Brodick. (☎302 380. Toilets and cold water. £2.50 per person.) The **Co-op** sells groceries across from the ferry terminal. (☎302 515. Open M-Sa 8am-10pm, Su 9am-7pm.) **Stalkers Eating House ❷,** Shore Rd., has cheap pub grub. (☎302 579. Open Easter-Oct. daily 9am-9pm, Nov.-Easter M-Sa 10:30am-4:30pm.) **Postal Code:** KA27 8AA.

STIRLING ☎01786

The third point of a strategic triangle completed by Glasgow and Edinburgh, Stirling has historically presided over north-south movement in the region; it was once said that "he who controlled Stirling controlled Scotland." At the 1297 Battle of Stirling Bridge, **William Wallace** (of *Braveheart* fame) overpowered the English army; this enabled Robert the Bruce to finally overthrow the English at **Bannockburn,** 3.25km south of town. To reach Bannockburn, take bus #51 or 52 from Murray Pl. in Stirling. (Visitors center open Apr.-Oct. daily 10am-5:30pm; Mar. and Nov.-Dec. 10:30am-4:30pm. £2.50, children £1.70. Battlefield open year-round.) The **Stirling Castle** has prim gardens, superb views of the Forth Valley, and a militant history. (Open Apr.-Oct. daily 9:30am-6pm; Nov.-Mar. 9:30am-5pm. £6.50, children £2.) **Argyll's Lodging,** a 17th-century mansion on the castle's esplanade, has been impressively restored. (Open Apr.-Sept. daily 9:30am-6pm; Oct.-Mar. 9:30am-5pm. £3, children £1.40; free with castle admission.) The 19th-century **Wallace Monument Tower,** on Hillfouts Rd., 2.5km from town, offers incredible views. You can also admire the 1.5m sword William Wallace wielded against King Edward I. Take bus #62 or 63 from Murray Pl. (Open July-Aug. daily 9:30am-6:30pm; June and Sept. 10am-6pm; Mar.-May and Oct. 10am-5pm; Nov.-Feb. 10:30am-4pm. £4, students £3, seniors and children £2.75.)

Trains run from Goosecroft Rd. (☎(08457) 484 950) to: Aberdeen (2hr.; M-Sa every hr., Su 6 per day; £31); Edinburgh (50min., 2 per hr., £5.30); Glasgow (30min., 1-3 per hr., £5.40); Inverness (3hr., 3-4 per day, £31); and London King's Cross (5½hr., every hr., £44-84). **Buses** also run from Goosecroft Rd. to: Edinburgh (1¼hr., every hr., £4); Fort William (2¾hr., 1 per day, £13); Glasgow (40min., 2-3 per hr., £3.80); and Inverness (3¾hr., every hr., £11.80). The **tourist office** is at 41 Dumbarton Rd. (☎475 019. Open July-Aug. M-Sa 9am-7:30pm, Su 9:30am-6:30pm; June and Sept. M-Sa 9am-6pm, Su 10am-4pm; Oct.-May M-Sa 10am-5pm.) At the well-equipped **Willy Wallace Hostel ❷,** 77 Murray Pl., a delightful staff fosters a fun atmosphere. (☎446 773. Dorms £10-14.) The comfortable **Forth Guest House ❸,** 23 Forth Pl., is near the train station. (☎471 020. All rooms with bath. Singles £20-35; doubles £39-45.) **Barnton Bar & Bistro ❶,** 3½ Barnton St., serves delicious, light fare. (Open Su-Th 10:30am-midnight, F-Sa 10:30am-1am.) **Postal Code:** FK8 2BP.

LOCH LOMOND ☎01389

With Britain's largest lake as its base, the landscape surrounding Loch Lomond is filled with the lush bays, wooded islands, and bare hills immortalized in the famous ballad. Hikers adore the **West Highland Way,** which snakes along the entire eastern side of the Loch and stretches north 152km from Milngavie to Fort William. At the southern tip of Loch Lomond is **Balloch,** the area's largest tourism center. Attractions and services at the new **Loch Lomond Shores** in Balloch include a giant-screen film about the loch, a **National Park Gateway Centre,** a tourist office, and bike and canoe rentals. A shuttle runs from the train station every 30min. during the summer. (☎721 500. Open Apr.-Sept. daily 7am-7pm, Oct.-Mar. 10am-5pm. £6, students £3.75.) One of the best introductions to the area is a **Sweeney's Cruises** boat tour, which leaves from the tourist office's side of the River Leven in Balloch (1hr.; every hr. 10am-4pm; £4.80, children £2.50).

Trains arrive on Balloch Rd. from Glasgow Queen St. (45min., 2 per hr., £3.20). Scottish Citylink **buses** (☎(08705) 808 080) arrive from Glasgow (40min., 3-5 per day, £3.60). First (☎(01324) 613 777) buses arrive from Stirling (1½hr., 1-3 per day, £4.80). **Tourist offices** are at Loch Lomond Shores (see above) and in the Old Station Building. (☎753 533. Open June-Sept. daily 9:30am-6pm; Apr.-May and Oct. 10am-5pm.) The **SYHA Loch Lomond ❷,** 3km north of town, is one of Scotland's largest hostels. From the train station, follow the main road for 800m; at the roundabout, turn right, continue 2.5km, turn left at the sign for the hostel, and it's a short way up the hill. (☎850 226. Book ahead in summer. Dorms £10-12.50, under 18 £8.50-11.) **B&Bs** congregate on **Balloch Road;** among these, a good choice is **Norwood Guest House ❸,** overlooking Balloch Castle Country Park. (☎750 309. Singles £20-25; doubles £36-44.) Camp at the luxurious **Lomond Woods Holiday Park ❶,** on Old Luss Rd., up Balloch Rd. from the tourist office. (☎759 475. Spa facilities. Bikes £7.50 per 4hr., £10 per 8hr.; deposit £100. Reception 8:30am-10pm. Tent and two people £6-9, with car £8-13; additional guests £2, free off-season.)

THE TROSSACHS ☎01877

The gentle mountains and lochs of the Trossachs form the northern boundary of central Scotland and together with Loch Lomond have been designated Scotland's first national park. The A821 winds through the heart of the area between **Aberfoyle** and **Callander,** the region's main towns. It passes near majestic **Loch Katrine,** the Trossachs' original lure and the setting of Scott's "The Lady of the Lake." A road for walkers and cyclists traces the loch's shoreline, while the popular **Steamship Sir Walter Scott** cruises from the Trossachs Pier (2-3 per day; round-trip £5.50-6.50, children £3.60). Nearby hulks **Ben A'an'** (1207 ft.); the rocky 1hr. hike up begins a mile from the pier, along the A821. The Trossachs are known as "Rob Roy Country"; the **Rob Roy and Trossachs Visitor Centre** in Callander is a combined tourist office and exhibit on the 17th-century hero. (☎330 342. Open July-Aug. daily 9:30am-8pm; June daily 9:30am-6pm; Sept. daily 10am-6pm; Mar.-May and Oct.-Dec. daily 10am-5pm; Jan.-Feb. Sa-Su 11am-4:30pm. £3.25, children £2.25.)

From Callander, First (☎(01324) 613 777) **buses** run to Stirling (45min., 11 per day, £2.90) and Aberfoyle (45min., 4 per day, £3.40). **Postbuses** reach some remoter areas of the region; find timetables at tourist offices or call the **Stirling Council Public Transport Helpline** (☎(01786) 442 707). About 2km south of Callander on Invertrossachs Rd. is **Trossachs Backpackers ❷,** a comfortable hostel with an attractive setting. (☎331 200. Dorms £10-15.) Camp at **Trossachs Holiday Park ❶,** outside of Aberfoyle's town center. (☎382 614. Open Mar-Oct. £9 per person.)

BRITAIN

ABERDEEN ☎01224

The din of the student party scene, the hum of a vibrant arts community, and the swish of Britain's North Sea oil industry offset the perennial grayness of Aberdeen's skies. The **Aberdeen Art Gallery,** on Schoolhill, displays striking 20th-century art alongside a varied older collection. (Open M-Sa 10am-5pm, Su 2-5pm. Free.) The **Maritime Museum,** on Shiprow, provides a fascinating and comprehensive history of Aberdeen's affair with the sea. (Open M-F 8:15am-5:45pm, Sa 8:15am-4:30pm. Free.) Wander in the extensive rose gardens of **Duthie Park** (DA-thee), by the River Dee at Polmuir Rd. and Riverside Dr. The **Lemon Tree Café and Theatre,** 5 West North St., near Queen St., presents folk, jazz, drama, and dance. (☎642 230. Tickets £5-9, students and seniors £2-3.)

The **train** and **bus** stations are on Guild St. Trains arrive from: Edinburgh (2½hr., every hr., £21); Glasgow (2½hr., every hr., £28); and Inverness (2¼hr., every 1½hr., £18.20). Scottish Citylink buses (☎(08705) 505 050) come from Edinburgh (4hr., every hr., £15) and Glasgow (4hr., every hr., £15). Turn right on Guild St., left on Market St., and take the second left onto Union St. to get to the **tourist office,** 23 Union St., St. Nicholas House. (☎288 828. Open July-Aug. M-Sa 9:30am-7pm, Su

10am-4pm; Sept.-June M-Sa 9:30am-5pm.) Take bus #14 or 15 to Queen's Rd. to reach the **SYHA King George VI Memorial Hostel ❷,** 8 Queen's Rd. (☎646 988. Laundry £1 per wash/dry. Lockout 9:30am-1:30pm. Curfew 2am. Dorms £10-12.) **The Ashvale ❶,** 42-48 Great Western Rd., is a winner of Scotland's Fish-and-Chip Shop of the year award. (Lunch £4.50. Open daily 11:45am-1am.) **Postal Code:** AB1 6AZ.

CAIRNGORM MOUNTAINS ☎01479

The towering Cairngorms are real Scottish wilderness: misty, mighty, and arctic even in summer. The area is scheduled to become a national park in 2003. Outdoor enthusiasts converge at **Cairngorm Mountain** for skiing, hikes on the **Windy Ridge Trail,** and a trip on the newly unveiled **funicular railway.** Take Highland County bus #37 from Aviemore. (☎861 261. Railway ticket £7.50, students and seniors £6.50, children £5. Ski ticket £24, students £18, seniors and children £15.) Experienced hikers should consider taking the **Northern Corries Path** to the summit of Britain's second highest peak, **Ben MacDui.** Consult the **Cairngorm Rangers** (☎861 703) for trail and weather information. Down the hill, 3mi. west of the funicular, the **Cairngorm Reindeer Centre** is home to dozens of velvet-horned sled-pullers. (☎861 228. Call ahead. Open daily 10am-5pm. £6.)

Aviemore is a concrete roadstrip with several places to stay. **Trains** arrive at the station on Grampian Rd. from Inverness (45min., 7-8 per day, £7.20) and Edinburgh and Glasgow (2¼hr., 7 per day, £32). **Buses** stop north of the train station and run from: Inverness (40min., 15 per day, £4.70); Glasgow (3½hr., 15 per day, £12.50); and Edinburgh (3hr., 12 per day, £12.50). The **tourist office** is on Grampian Rd. near the train station. (☎810 363. Open July to mid-Sept. M-Sa 9am-6pm, Su 10am-4pm; mid-Sept. to June M-F 9am-5pm, Sa 10am-4pm.) **Lazy Duck Hostel ❶,** on Badanfhuarain just east of Nethy Bridge, is located in a snug cottage with a magical garden. Take Highland Country bus #334 (20min., 8 per day) from Aviemore. (☎821 642. Kitchen access. Dorms £8.50.)

INVERNESS AND LOCH NESS ☎01463

In AD 565, St. Columba repelled a savage sea beast as it attacked a monk; whether a prehistoric leftover or cosmic wanderer, the monster has captivated the world's imagination ever since. The **Loch Ness** guards its secrets 7.5km south of Inverness. Tour agencies are the most convenient ways to see the loch; **Guide Friday** offers a 3hr. bus and boat tour. (☎224 000. May-Sept. daily 10:30am and 2:30pm. £14.50, students and seniors £11.50, children £6.50.) Or, let **Kenny's Tours** take you around the entire loch and back to Inverness on a minibus. (☎252 411. Tours 10:30am-5pm. £12, students £10.) Three miles south on the A82, **Urquhart Castle** (URK-hart) was one of the largest in Scotland before it was blown up in 1692 to prevent Jacobite occupation; alleged photos of Nessie have since been taken from the ruins. (☎(01456) 450 551. Open June-Aug. daily 9:30am-6:30pm; Apr.-May and Sept. daily 9:30am-5:45pm; Oct.-Mar. M-Sa 9:30am-3:45pm. £5.) The Jacobite cause died in 1746 on **Culloden Battlefield,** east of Inverness; take **Highland County bus** #12 from the post office at Queensgate (round-trip £2). Just 2.5km south of Culloden, the stone circles and chambered cairns (mounds of rough stones) of the **Cairns of Clava** recall civilizations of the Bronze Age. Bus #12 will also take you to the **Cawdor Castle,** home of the Cawdors since the 15th century; don't miss the maze. (Open May-Sept. daily 10am-5pm. £6.10, students and seniors £5.10, children £3.30.)

Trains (☎(08457) 484 950) run from Academy St. in Inverness's Station Sq. to: Aberdeen (2¼hr., 7-10 per day, £18.80); Edinburgh (3½-4hr., 5-7 per day, £31); Glasgow (3½hr., 5-7 per day, £31); and London (8hr., 3 per day, £84-110). Scottish Citylink **buses** (☎(08705) 505 050) run from Farraline Park, off Academy St., to Edinburgh and Glasgow (both 4½hr., 10-12 per day, £14.70). To reach the **tourist**

office, Castle Wynd, from the stations, turn left on Academy St. and then right onto Union St. (☎234 353. Open mid-June to Aug. M-Sa 9am-7pm, Su 9:30am-5pm; Sept. to mid-June M-Sa 9am-5pm, Su 10am-4pm.) **Bazpackers Backpackers Hotel ❶,** 4 Culduthel Rd., has a homey atmosphere and great views of the city. (☎717 663. Reception 7:30am-midnight. Dorms £8.50-10; doubles £12-14.) A minute's walk from the city center, **Felstead ❸,** 18 Ness Bank, is a spacious B&B with comfortable beds. (☎321 634. £28-36 per person.)

FORT WILLIAM AND BEN NEVIS ☎01397

With a slew of beautiful lochs and valleys, **Fort William** makes an excellent base camp for mountain excursions to **Ben Nevis** (1342m), the highest peak in Britain. The walk up Ben Nevis (round-trip 15km) starts in **Glen Nevis,** a gorgeous glacial valley 2.5km from town. The **Glen Nevis Visitor Centre,** at the trailhead, provides info on Ben Nevis and other nearby hikes. (Open June-Sept. daily 9am-6pm; Apr.-May and Oct. 9am-5pm.) **Trains** arrive on High St. in Fort William from Glasgow Queen St. (3¾hr., 2-3 per day, £18) and London Euston (12hr., 1 per day, £70-97). Scottish Citylink (☎(08705) 505 050) **buses** go from High St. to: Edinburgh (3¾hr., 2 per day, £15.20); Glasgow (3hr., 4 per day, £11.90); Inverness (2hr., 5-6 per day, £7.20); and Kyle of Lochalsh (2hr., 3 per day, £10.70). The **tourist office** is in Cameron Sq., just off High St. (☎703 781. Open mid-July to Aug. M-Sa 9am-8:30pm, Su 9am-6pm; mid-June to mid-July M-Sa 9am-7pm, Su 10am-6pm; Mar. to mid-June M-Sa 9am-6pm, Su 10am-4pm; Sept.-Oct. M-Sa 9am-6pm, Su 10am-5:30pm; Nov.-Feb. M-Sa 9am-5pm, Su 10am-4pm.) At the comfortable **Farr Cottage Accommodation and Activity Centre ❷** in Corpach, the owners give Scottish history lessons and whiskey talks. Take Highland County bus #45 from Ft. William. (☎772 315. Laundry and kitchen. Dorms £11.) The **Rhu Mhor Guest House ❷,** on Alma Rd., offers rooms with fantastic sunset views of the Nevis Range. (☎702 213. Open Apr.-Oct. Book ahead July-Aug. £16-24 per person.) The **Glen Nevis Caravan & Camping Park ❶** is 5.5km east of town on Glen Nevis Rd. (☎702 191. Open mid-Mar. to Oct. Tent and two people £7.10, with car £12.) **Postal Code:** PH33 6AR.

GLEN COE ☎01855

Stunning in any weather, Glen Coe is best seen in the rain, when a web of mist laces the valley's innumerable rifts and silvery waterfalls that spill into the River Coe. Glen Coe is infamous as the site of a 1692 massacre, when a company of Campbell soldiers slaughtered their MacDonald hosts, violating the age-old tradition of Highland hospitality. Well-equipped, sure-footed hikers can scramble up the 1260m **Bidean nam Bian** or try the 6.5km traverse of the **Aonach Eagach** ridge on the north side of the glen. Easier walks are found in the **Lost Valley,** once the hiding place of the MacDonalds' pilfered goods. You can avoid the 350m climb by taking the **Glen Coe Ski Centre Chairlift,** off the A82 in the middle of Glen Coe. (Open June-Aug. daily 9:30am-4:30pm, weather permitting. £4, children £2.50. During ski season daily lift pass £17.50, children £9.50.)

Scottish Citylink (☎(08705) 505 050) **buses** arrive in **Glencoe Village,** at the edge of Loch Leven, from Fort William and Glasgow (4 per day). The **Glen Coe Visitor Centre,** off the A82 about 2km south of Glencoe Village, has films and displays on the area, as well as hiking info. (☎811 307. Open May-Oct. daily 10am-6pm. £3.50, students £2.60.) For bike rentals, try **Mountain Bike Hire,** at the Clachaig Inn, across the river from the Visitor Centre. (☎811 252. £8.50 per half-day, £12 per day.) The **SYHA Glencoe ❶** is 2.5km southeast of Glencoe Village. (☎811 219. Internet access. Reception 7am-midnight. Curfew midnight. Dorms £9-11, under 18 £6-10.) If the hostel is full, backtrack 500m to the **Leacantium Farm Bunkhouse ❶.** (☎811 256. Dorms £6.50-7.50.) The farm's riverside **Red Squirrel Camp Site ❶** is next door. (£4.50 per person, under 12 £0.50.)

BRITAIN

THE INNER HEBRIDES

ISLE OF SKYE

Often described as the shining jewel in the Hebridean crown, Skye radiates natural beauty, from the serrated peaks of the Cuillin Hills to the rugged northern tip of the Trotternish Peninsula. Though spotty public transportation may force you to concentrate your travels, Skye's lovely wilds and folk culture ensure that you won't be disappointed.

TRANSPORTATION. The tradition of ferries carrying passengers "over the sea to Skye" ended with the **Skye Bridge,** which links **Kyle of Lochalsh,** on the mainland, to **Kyleakin,** on the Isle of Skye. **Trains** (☎08457 484 950) arrive at Kyle of Lochalsh from Inverness (2½hr., 2-4 per day, £15). Skye-Ways (☎01599 534 328) runs **buses** from: Fort William (2hr., 3 per day, £11); Glasgow (5½hr., 3 per day, £19); and Inverness (2½hr., 2 per day, £10.90). **Pedestrians** can traverse the Skye Bridge's 2.5km footpath or take the **shuttle bus** (2 per hr., £1.70). Buses on the island are infrequent and expensive; pick up the handy *Public Transport Guide to Skye and the Western Isles* (£1) at a tourist office.

KYLE OF LOCHALSH AND KYLEAKIN. Kyle of Lochalsh and Kyleakin (Ky-LAACK-in) bookend the Skye Bridge. The former, on the mainland, has an ATM, tourist office, and train station, making it of practical value to travelers. Kyleakin is a backpackers' hub with three hostels and countless tours. **MacBackpackers Skye Trekker Tour,** departing from Kyleakin, offers one- or two-day historical and eco-conscious tours, with all necessary gear provided. (☎01599 534 510. Call ahead. 1-day £15, 2-day £45.) The picturesque **Eilean Donan Castle** is between Kyle of Lochalsh and Inverness; take a Scottish Citylink bus and get off at Dornie. (☎555 202. Open Apr.-Oct. daily 10am-5:30pm; Mar. and Nov. 10am-3pm. £4, students £3.20.) To enjoy the incredible sunset views from the quiet Kyleakin harbor, climb to the memorial on the hill behind the SYHA hostel. A slippery scramble to the west takes you to the small ruins of **Castle Moil.** Cross the little bridge behind the hostel, turn left, follow the road to the pier, and take the gravel path. The Kyle of Lochalsh **tourist office** is on the hill right above the train station. (☎534 276. Open May-Oct. M-Sa 9am-5:30pm.) The friendly owners of **Dun Caan Hostel ❷,** in Kyleakin, have masterfully renovated a 200-year-old cottage. (☎534 087. **Bikes** £10 per day. Book ahead. Dorms £10.) **Phone Code:** ☎01599.

BRITAIN

SLIGACHAN. The **Cuillin Hills** (COO-leen), the highest peaks in the Hebrides, are renowned for their cloud and mist formations and for hiking. *Walks from Sligachan and Glen Brittle* (£1), available at tourist offices, hotels, and campsites, suggests routes. West of Kyleakin, the smooth, conical Red Cuillin and the rough, craggy Black Cuillin Hills meet in Sligachan, a hiker's hub in a jaw-dropping setting. Your best bet is the **Sligachan Hotel ❹,** a classic hill-walker's and climber's haunt. (☎650 204. Breakfast included. £30-50 per person.) Campers should head to **Glenbrittle Campsite ❶,** in Glenbrittle at the foot of the Black Cuillins. Take bus #53 (M-Sa 2 per day) from Portree and Sligachan to Glenbrittle. (☎640 404. Open Apr.-Sept. £4 per person, children £2.) **Phone Code:** ☎01478.

PORTREE. The island's capital, **Portree,** has busy shops and an attractive harbor. Buses (1-3 per day) run from Portree to **Dunvegan Castle,** the seat of the clan MacLeod. The castle holds the **Fairy Flag,** a 1500-year-old silk. (☎521 206. Open Apr.-Oct. daily 10am-5:30pm; Nov.-Mar. 11am-4pm. £6. Gardens only £4.) **Buses** to Portree from Kyle of Lochalsh (5 per day, £7.80) stop at Somerled Sq. The **tourist office** is on Bayfield Rd. (☎612 137. Open July-Aug. M-Sa 9am-7pm, Su 10am-4pm;

Sept.-Oct. and Apr.-June M-F 9am-5pm, Su 10am-4pm; Nov.-Mar. M-Sa 9am-4pm.) The **Portree Independent Hostel ❷,** The Green, has a multitude of amenities. (☎613 737. Internet £1 per 20min. Dorms £10.50; doubles £23.) **Phone Code:** ☎01478.

THE OUTER HEBRIDES

The landscape of the Outer Hebrides is extraordinarily beautiful and astoundingly ancient. Much of its rock is more than half as old as the Earth itself, and long-gone inhabitants have left a collection of tombs, standing stones, and other antiquities. While television and tourism have diluted old ways of life, you're still more likely to get an earful of Gaelic here than anywhere else in Scotland. The Western Isles remain one of Scotland's most undisturbed and unforgettable realms.

TRANSPORTATION. Three major Caledonian MacBrayne (☎(01475) 650 100) **ferries** serve the Western Isles: from Ullapool to Lewis, from Skye to Harris and North Uist, and from Oban to South Uist and Barra. Find schedules in *Discover Scotland's Islands with Caledonian MacBrayne*, free from tourist offices. You'll also want to pick up the *Lewis and Harris Bus Timetables* (£0.40) and *Uist and Barra Bus Timetables* (£0.20). Inexpensive **car rental** (from £20 per day) is possible throughout the isles. The terrain is hilly but excellent for **cycling.**

LEWIS AND HARRIS. The island of **Lewis** is relentlessly desolate, the landscape flat, treeless, and speckled with quiet lochs. Drifting mists shroud miles of moorland and fields of peat, nearly hiding Lewis's many archaeological sites, most notably the **Callanish Stones,** an extraordinary and isolated Bronze Age circle. Buses on the W2 route from Stornoway (M-Sa 5 per day) stop at the stones. (☎621 422. Visitors center open Apr.-Sept. M-Sa 10am-7pm; Oct.-Mar. 10am-4pm. £1.75, students £1.25.) CalMac **ferries** sail from Ullapool, on the mainland, to **Stornoway** (pop. 8000), the largest town in northwestern Scotland (M-Sa 2 per day; £13.35, round-trip £22.85). To get to the Stornoway **tourist office,** 26 Cromwell St., turn left from the ferry terminal, then right onto Cromwell St. (☎703 088. Open Apr.-Oct. M-Sa 9am-6pm and to meet late ferries; Nov.-Mar. M-F 9am-5pm.) The best place to lay your head is **Fair Haven Hostel ❷,** over the surf shop at the intersection of Francis St. and Keith St. From the pier, turn left onto Shell St., which becomes South Beach, then turn right on Kenneth St. and right again onto Francis St. The meals here are better than the places in town. (☎705 862. Dorms £10, with three meals £20.) **Phone Code:** ☎01851.

Harris is technically the same island as Lewis, but they're entirely different worlds. The deserted flatlands of Lewis, in the north, give way to another, more rugged and spectacular kind of desolation—that of Harris's steely gray peaks. Toward the west coast, the **Forest of Harris** (ironically, a treeless, heather-splotched mountain range) descends to yellow beaches bordered by indigo waters and *machair*—sea meadows of soft grass and summertime flowers. Essential *Ordnance Survey* hiking maps can be found at the tourist office in **Tarbert,** the biggest town on Harris. **Ferries** arrive in Tarbert from Uig on Skye (M-Sa 2 per day; £8.70, round-trip £14.90). The **tourist office** is on Pier Rd. (☎502 011. Open Apr. to mid-Oct. M-Sa 9am-5pm and for late ferry arrivals; mid-Oct. to Mar. for arrivals only.) **Rockview Bunkhouse ❶,** on Main St., is less than 5min. west of the pier, on the north side of the street. (☎502 211. Dorms £9.) **Phone Code:** ☎01859.

BARRA. Barra, the most southern of the Outer Isles is gorgeous—a composite of moor, *machair*, and beach. **Kisimul Castle,** bastion of the MacNeil clan, sits in stately solitude in the middle of Castlebay harbor. Take a motorboat from the pier in front of the tourist office to the castle gate. (☎810 313. Open Apr.-Oct. M-Sa

9:30am-6:30pm. £3, students £2.30.) You can see almost all of Barra in a day; by far the best way to do so is by **bike.** To rent from **Castlebay Cycle Hire,** drop by the long wooden shed on the main road. (☎810 438. From £8 per day. Open daily 10am-1pm.) The road west from Castlebay passes an amazing white stretch of beach at **Halaman Bay.** There are numerous **standing stones** and **cairns** dotting the hills in the middle of the island, which can be found with the help of a detailed map from the tourist office. CalMac **ferries** arrive at **Castlebay** (Bagh A Chaisteil), Barra's main town, from Oban (5hr.; M, W-Th, Sa 1 per day; £19.20). The Castlebay **tourist office** is around the bend to the east of the pier. (☎810 336. Open Easter-Oct. M-Sa 9am-5pm, Su 10-11am; also open for late ferry arrivals.) Barra is home to the excellent **Dunard Hostel ❶,** a short walk uphill from the pier and around the bend to the west. (☎810 443. Dorms £10. **Camping** £7.) **Phone Code:** ☎01871.

DENMARK (DANMARK)

Like Thumbelina, the heroine of native son Hans Christian Andersen's fairy tales, Denmark (pop. 5.3 million; 43,094 sq. km) has a tremendous personality crammed into a tiny body. Danes delight in their eccentric traditions, such as burning witches in effigy on Midsummer's Eve and eating pickled herring on New Year's Day. Although the Danes are justifiably proud of their fertile farmlands and pristine beaches, their sense of self-criticism is reflected in the Danish literary canon: the more famous voices are Andersen, Søren Kierkegaard, and Karen Blixen. Located between Sweden and Germany, the country is the geographic and cultural bridge between Scandinavia and continental Europe, made up of the Jutland peninsula and the islands of Zealand, Funen, Lolland, Falster, and Bornholm, as well as some 400 smaller islands, some of which are not inhabited. With its Viking past behind it, Denmark now has one of the most comprehensive social welfare structures in the world, and liberal immigration policies have diversified the erstwhile homogeneous population. Today, Denmark has a progressive youth culture that beckons travelers to the hip pub scene in Copenhagen. Contrary to the suggestion of a certain English playwright, very little seems to be rotten in the state of Denmark.

SYMBOL	❶	❷	❸	❹	❺
ACCOMMODATIONS	under 76kr	76-95kr	96-130kr	131-200kr	over 200kr
FOOD	under 40kr	40-70kr	71-100kr	101-130kr	over 130kr

For Denmark, prices are indicated in food and accommodations listings using the system of icons and price ranges above. Prices for accommodations are based on the lowest cost for one person, excluding special deals or discounts. For restaurants, prices are based on the average entree price.

SUGGESTED ITINERARIES

THREE DAYS Explore chic and progressive **Copenhagen** (p. 275). Get your kicks in the **Tivoli** amusement park and delight in the **Little Mermaid** statue.

BEST OF DENMARK, 9 DAYS Start in wonderful **Copenhagen** (3 days). For the best beaches in Denmark, take a ferry to **Bornholm** island (1 day, p. 286). Shoot south to rockin' **Roskilde** (1 day, p. 284). Move west to catch some more rays on **Funen** island (1 day, p. 287); don't miss **Odense** (p. 287), hometown of Hans Christian Andersen. Then hop a ferry to the idyllic **Ærø** (1 day, p. 289), a throwback to the Denmark of several centuries ago. Cross the Lillebælt to **Jutland** to chill with laid-back students in **Århus** and play with blocks at **Legoland** (1 day, p. 290). On your way south, stop in **Ribe,** a well-preserved medieval town (1 day, p. 295).

LIFE AND TIMES

HISTORY

The former home base of raiding Vikings, Denmark has done its share of pillaging. Danes evolved from nomadic hunters to farmers during the Stone Age, and from the 8th to 11th centuries AD they proceeded to sack the English coast as Vikings. Denmark, then called **Jutland,** was Christianized in the 10th century under **King Harald the Bluetooth.** Under the rule of Harald's descendents, Denmark gained dynastic control over Norway, Iceland, and Sweden. However, various disputes plagued the Danish throne, and in 1282 regal power was ultimately made accountable to the **Danehof,** a council composed of high nobles and church leaders. In the 16th century, the **Protestant Reformation** swept through Denmark, and **Lutheranism** was established as the state denomination. The next several centuries were overall a disastrous period for Denmark; its involvement in the **Thirty Years War** (1618-1648), the **Napoleonic Wars** (1799-1815), and the **War of 1864,** as well as a prolonged squabble with Sweden, resulted in severe financial and territorial losses. Denmark's neutrality during **World War I** proved fiscally beneficial, as Denmark profited by trade with the warring nations. **World War II** saw the country occupied by Nazis, but Denmark refused to comply with pressure to persecute Jewish citizens. After World War II, Denmark took its place on the international stage, becoming a founding member of **NATO** (1949) and joining the **European Union** (1972).

TODAY

Denmark's support for the European Union has been lukewarm; the country has declined to accept common defense and single currency, among other EU policies. 20th-century Denmark has been plagued by periodic economic setbacks and a high budget deficit. Although Denmark's **social welfare system** has long been recognized as one of the world's best, the conservative **Danish People's Party** recently helped pass a controversial anti-immigration bill limiting spouse's rights of entry and eliminating welfare benefits to foreigners for their first seven years in residence. The government is a **constitutional monarchy** in which the monarch, **Queen Margrethe II,** is the nominal head of state, while major decision-making power is vested in the unicameral legislature, led by **Prime Minister Anders Fogh Rasmussen.**

CULTURE

FOOD AND DRINK

A "Danish" in Denmark is a *wienerbrød* ("Viennese bread"), found in bakeries alongside other flaky treats. For more substantial fare, Danes favor open-faced sandwiches called *smørrebrød.* Herring is served in various forms, though usually pickled or raw with onions or a curry mayonnaise. For cheap eats, look for lunch specials *(dagens ret)* and all-you-can-eat buffets (*spis alt du kan* or *tag selv buffet*). National beers are Carlsberg and Tuborg; bottled brew tends to be cheaper. A popular alcohol alternative is *snaps* (or *aquavit*), a clear distilled liquor flavored with fiery spices, usually served chilled and unmixed. Many vegetarian *(vegetarret)* options are the result of Indian and Mediterranean influences, but salads and veggies *(grønsager)* can be found on most menus.

CUSTOMS AND ETIQUETTE

There are no hard and fast rules for **tipping,** but it's always polite to round up to the nearest 10kr in restaurants and for taxis. In general, service at restaurants is included in the bill. Tipping up to 15% is becoming common in Copenhagen. **Shops** are normally open M-Th from about 9 or 10am to 6pm and F until 7 or 8pm; they are always open Sa mornings (Copenhagen shops stay open all day Sa). Regular **banking** hours are M-W and F 9:30am-4pm, Th 9:30am-6pm.

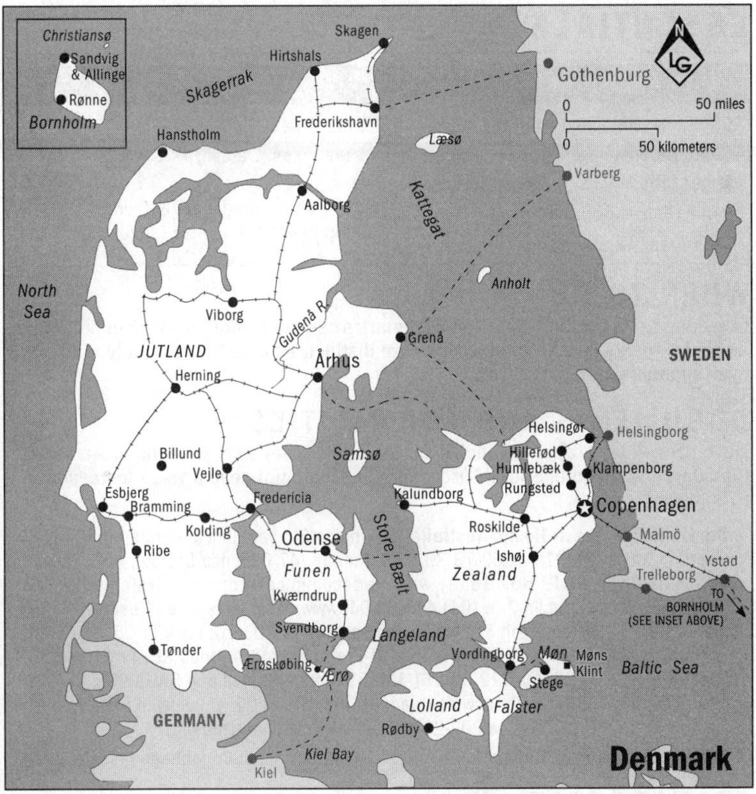

THE ARTS

The relatively small population of Denmark hasn't precluded the development of a rich cultural life. On the literary front, the fairy tales of **Hans Christian Andersen**—from the Little Mermaid to the Ugly Duckling—have delighted children throughout the world for generations. Philosopher and theologian **Søren Kierkegaard** developed the "leap of faith," the idea that religious belief is beyond the bounds of human reason. **Karen Blixen** gained fame under the name **Isak Dinesen,** detailing her life experiences in the book *Out of Africa* (1937). Denmark's most famous musician, **Carl Nielsen,** composed six symphonies with unusual tonal progressions that won him international recognition (see p. 287). Director **Carl Dreyer** explored complex religious themes in his films; the most well-known is *The Passion of Joan of Arc* (1928).

HOLIDAYS AND FESTIVALS

Holidays: New Year's (Jan. 1); Queen's Birthday (Apr. 16); Easter Holidays (Apr. 17-21); Worker's Day (May 1); Great Prayer Day (May 16); Ascension Day (May 29); Constitution Day (June 5); Whit Sunday and Monday (June 8-9); Midsummer Eve (June 24); Christmas (Dec. 24-26).

Festivals: Danes celebrate **Fastelavn** (Carneval) in Feb. and Mar. In early July, the **Copenhagen Jazz Festival** hosts a week of concerts, many free. The **Roskilde Festival** is an immense open-air music festival held in Roskilde in late June.

ESSENTIALS

FACTS AND FIGURES

Official Name: Kingdom of Denmark.
Capital: Copenhagen.
Major Cities: Aalborg, Århus, Odense.
Population: 5,360,000.
Land Area: 42,394 sq. km.
Time Zone: GMT +1.
Languages: Danish, Faroese, Greenlandic.
Religions: Evangelical Lutheran (91%), other Protestant/Roman Catholic (2%).

WHEN TO GO

Considering its northern location, Denmark's climate is more solar than polar and more dry than wet. The four seasons are distinct, winters are relatively mild, and even summers aren't very warm.

DOCUMENTS AND FORMALITIES

EU citizens may stay in Denmark for as long as they like. Citizens of Australia, Canada, New Zealand, South Africa, and the US do not need a visa for stays of up to 90 days.

Danish Embassies at Home: Australia, 19 Arkana St., Yarralumla, Canberra, ACT 2600 (☎(02) 62 73 25 01; fax 62 73 33 92). **Canada,** 47 Clarence St., Ste. 450, Ottawa, ON K1N 9K1 (☎613-562-1811; www.tradecomm.com/danish). **Ireland,** 121 St. Stephen's Green, Dublin 2 (☎(01) 475 64 04; www.denmark.ie). **New Zealand** (consulate), Level 7, 45 Johnston St., Wellington (☎(04) 471 05 20; fax 471 05 21). **South Africa,** 8th fl., Sanlam Centre, corner of Pretorius and Andries St., Pretoria 0002 (☎(012) 322 05 95; fax 322 05 96). **UK,** 55 Sloane St., London SW1X 9SR (☎(020) 7333 02 00; 7333 02 70; www.denmark.org.uk). **US,** 3200 Whitehaven St. NW, Washington, D.C. 20008-3683 (☎202-234-4300; www.denmarkemb.org).

Foreign Embassies in Denmark: All foreign embassies are in **Copenhagen** (see p. 275).

TRANSPORTATION

BY PLANE. The airport in Copenhagen (CPH; see p. 275) handles international flights from cities around the world, mostly by SAS, Delta, Icelandair, British Airways, Air France, KLM, Lufthansa, and Swiss. **Billund Airport** (BLL; ☎76 50 50 50; www.billund-airport.dk) in Jutland handles flights to other European cities. SAS (Scandinavian Airlines; US ☎800-437-5804; www.scandinavian.net), the national airline company, offers youth, spouse, and senior discounts to some destinations.

BY TRAIN AND BY BUS. **Eurail** is valid on all state-run **DSB** routes. The **Scanrail Pass,** when purchased outside Scandinavia, offers five days within two months (US$214, under 26 US$161), 10 days within two months (US$288/US$216), or 21 consecutive days (US$332/US$249) of unlimited rail travel through Denmark, Norway, Sweden, and Finland, as well as many discounted ferry and bus rides (from 50% off to free). The Scanrail Pass is also available for purchase within Scandinavia, with restrictions on the number of days spent in the country of purchase. Visit www.scanrail.com or www.railpass.com/eurail/passes/scanrail.htm for more info. Remote towns are typically served by **buses** from the nearest train station. The national **bus** network is also reliable and fairly cheap. You can take buses or trains over the new **Øresund bridge** from Copenhagen to Malmö, Sweden.

BY FERRY. Railpasses earn discounts or free rides on many Scandinavian ferries. The free *Vi Rejser* newspaper, at tourist offices, can help you sort out the dozens of smaller ferries that serve Denmark's outlying islands, although the best bet for overcoming language problems is just to ask at the station. For info on ferries from **Copenhagen** to **Norway, Poland,** and **Sweden,** see p. 275. For more on connections from **Bornholm** to **Germany** and **Sweden,** see p. 286, and from **Jutland** to **England, Norway,** and **Sweden,** see p. 290

BY CAR. Roads are toll-free, except for the **Storebæltsbro** (Great Belt Bridge; 210kr) and the **Øresund bridge** (around 220kr). **Car rental** is generally around US$75 per day, plus insurance and a per-kilometer fee; to rent a car, you must be at least 21 years old (in some cases even 25). Speed limits are 50kph (30mph) in urban areas, 80kph (50mph) on highways, and 110kph (68mph) on motorways. **Service centers** for motorists, called Info-terias, are spaced along Danish highways. **Gas** averages 6.50kr per liter. Watch out for bikes, which have the right-of-way. Driving in cities is discouraged by high parking prices and numerous one-way streets. For more info on driving in Denmark, contact the **Forenede Danske Motorejere (FDM),** Firskovvej 32, Box 500, 2800 Kgs. Lyngby (☎70 13 30 40; fax 45 27 09 33; www.fdm.dk).

BY BIKE AND BY THUMB. Flat terrain, well-marked bike routes, bike paths in the countryside, and raised bike lanes on most streets in towns and cities make Denmark a cyclist's dream. You can **rent bikes** (55-65kr per day) from some tourist offices, rental shops, and a few train stations. The **Dansk Cyklist Forbund** (Danish Cycle Federation), Rømersg. 7, 1362 Copenhagen K (☎33 32 31 21; fax 33 32 76 83; www.dcf.dk), can hook you up with longer-term rentals. For info on bringing your bike on a train (which costs 50kr or less), pick up *Bikes and Trains* at any train station. **Hitchhiking** is illegal on motorways and uncommon. *Let's Go* does not recommend hitchhiking.

TOURIST SERVICES AND MONEY

EMERGENCY	**Police, Ambulance,** and **Fire:** ☎112.

TOURIST OFFICES. Contact the main tourist board in Denmark at Vesterbrog. 6D, 1620 Copenhagen V (☎33 11 14 15; dt@dt.dk; www.visitdenmark.dt.dk).

Tourist Boards at Home: UK, 55 Sloane St., London SW1X 9SY (☎7259 5959; www.dtb.dt.dk). **US,** 18th fl., 655 3rd Ave., New York, NY 10017 (☎212-885-9700; www.goscandinavia.com).

MONEY. The Danish unit of currency is the **krone** (kr), divided into 100 *øre*. The easiest way to get cash is from **ATMs; Cirrus** and **PLUS** cash cards are widely accepted, and many machines give advances on credit cards. Denmark has a high cost of living; expect to spend from 226kr (hostels and supermarkets) to 490kr-566kr (cheap hotels and restaurants) per day. The European Union imposes a **value-added tax (VAT)** on goods and services purchased within the EU, which is included in the price (see p. 19). Denmark's **value-added tax (VAT)** is one of the highest in Europe (25%). You can get a VAT refund upon leaving the country for purchases in any one store that total over 300kr.

DANISH KRONE (KR)		
	AUS$1 = 4.17KR	10KR = AUS$2.40
	CDN$1 = 4.84KR	10KR = CDN$2.07
	EUR€1 = 7.43KR	10KR = EUR€1.35
	NZ$1 = 3.54KR	10KR = NZ$2.83
	ZAR1 = 0.71KR	10KR = ZAR14.04
	UK£1 = 11.71KR	10KR = UK£0.84
	US$1 = 7.54KR	10KR = US$1.33

ACCOMMODATIONS AND CAMPING

While Denmark's **hotels** are generally expensive (300-850kr per night), the country's more than 100 **HI youth hostels** *(vandrehjem)* are cheap (dorms less than 100kr per night; nonmembers add 25kr), are well-run, and have no age limit. They are also given an official ranking of one to five stars, based on facilities and service. Sheets cost about 45-50kr. Breakfasts usually run 45kr and dinners 65kr. Reception desks normally close for the day around 8 or 9pm, although some are open 24hr. Reservations are highly recommended, especially in summer and near beaches. Many Danish youth hostels are filled by school groups in summer, so it's important to make reservations well in advance. Make sure to arrive before check-in to confirm your reservation. For more info, contact the **Danish Youth Hostel Association,** Vesterbrog. 39, in Copenhagen. (☎31 31 36 12; www.danhostel.dk. Open M-Th 9am-4pm, F 9am-3pm.) Tourist offices offer the *Danhostel* booklet, which also has more information, and many book rooms in private homes (125-175kr).

Denmark's 525 official **campgrounds** (about 60kr per person) rank from one-star (toilets and drinking water) to three-star (showers and laundry) to five-star (swimming, restaurants, and stoves). You'll need either a **Camping Card Scandinavia,** available at campgrounds (1-year 80kr), or a **Camping Card International.** Campsites affiliated with hostels generally do not require this card. If you only plan to camp for a night, you can buy a 24hr. pass (20kr). The **Danish Camping Council** (*Campingradet;* ☎39 27 80 44) sells the campground handbook, *Camping Denmark,* and passes. Sleeping in train stations, in parks, or on public property is illegal.

COMMUNICATION

PHONE CODES	**Country code:** 45. **International dialing prefix:** 00.

TELEPHONES. There are no separate city codes; include all digits for local and international calls. Buy phone cards at post offices or kiosks (30 units 30kr; 53 units 50kr; 110 units 100kr). For **domestic directory info,** call ☎118; **international info,** ☎113; collect calls, ☎141. International direct dial numbers include: **AT&T,** ☎8001 0010; **Canada Direct,** ☎80 01 00 11; **Ireland Direct,** ☎80 01 03 53; **MCI,** ☎8001 0022; **Sprint,** ☎800 10 877; **Telecom New Zealand,** ☎80 01 0064; **Telkom South Africa,** ☎8001 0027; **Telstra Australia,** ☎80 88 0543.

MAIL. Mailing a postcard/letter to Australia, Canada, New Zealand, the US, or South Africa costs 5.50kr; to elsewhere in Europe 4.50kr. Domestic mail costs 4kr.

LANGUAGES. Danish. The Danish add *æ* (like the "e" in "egg"), *ø* (like the "i" in "first"), and å (sometimes written as *aa;* like the "o" in "lord") to the end of the alphabet; thus Århus would follow Viborg in an alphabetical listing of cities. *Let's Go* indexes these under "ae," "o," and "a." Knowing *ikke* ("not") will help you figure out such signs as "No smoking" *(ikke-ryger); aben/lukket* (O-ben/loock-eh) means open/closed. Nearly all Danes speak flawless English, but a few Danish words might help break the ice: try *skal* (skoal), or "cheers." Danish has a distinctive glottal stop known as a *stød.*

COPENHAGEN (KØBENHAVN)

Despite the swan ponds and cobblestone clichés that Hans Christian Andersen's fairy-tale imagery brings to mind, Denmark's capital is a fast-paced, modern city that offers cafes, nightlife, and style to rival those of the great European cities. But if you're still craving Andersen's Copenhagen, the *Lille Havfrue* (Little Mermaid), Tivoli, and Nyhavn's Hanseatic gingerbread houses are also yours to discover.

TRANSPORTATION

Flights: Kastrup Airport (CPH; ☎32 47 47 47). S-trains connect the airport to Central Station (12min., every 20min., 21kr).

Trains: Trains stop at **Central Station** (also called Hovedbanegården and København H). Domestic travel ☎70 13 14 15, international ☎70 13 14 16. To: **Berlin** (9hr.; 1 per day; 895kr, under 26 580kr); **Hamburg** (4½hr., 5 per day, 485kr/320kr); **Oslo** (9hr., 3 per day, 740kr/530kr); **Stockholm** (5½hr., 4-5 per day, 700kr/540kr). Reservations mandatory (20kr). For cheaper travel to **Oslo,** Norway, and **Gothenburg, Östersund,** and **Stockholm,** Sweden, buy a **Scanrabat** ticket a week ahead; you must reserve.

Ferries: Scandinavian Seaways (☎33 42 33 42) departs daily **Oslo** (16hr.; 5pm; 480-735kr, under 26 315-570kr; Eurail and ScanRail 50% off). Trains to **Sweden** cross over on the **Helsingør-Helsingborg** ferry at no extra charge. **Hydrofoils** (☎33 12 80 88) go to **Malmö,** Sweden from Havneg., at the end of Nyhavn (40min., every hr., 19-49kr). Both **Flyvebådene** and **Pilen** run hydrofoils to Malmö (45min., every hr. 9am-11pm, 50kr). **Polferries** (☎33 11 46 45) set out from Ndr. Toldbod, 12A (off Esplanaden) for **Świnoujście,** Poland (10hr.; Su-M and W 8am; Th-F 7:30pm; 340kr, with ISIC 285kr).

Public Transportation: Bus info ☎36 13 14 15 (daily 7am-9:30pm); **train** info ☎33 14 17 01 (daily 6:30am-11pm). **Buses** and **S-trains** (subways and suburban trains; M-Sa 5am-12:30am, Su 6am-12:30am) operate on a zone system; 2-zone **tickets** run 14kr, additional zones 7kr each. The cheaper **rabatkort** (rebate card), available from kiosks and bus drivers, gets you 10 "clips," each good for 1 journey within a specified number of zones. The blue 2-zone *rabatkort* (90kr) can be clipped more than once for longer trips. Tickets and clips allow 1hr. of transfers. The **24hr. pass** (85kr), available at the Tivoli tourist office or any train station, grants unlimited bus and train transport in greater Copenhagen. **Railpasses,** including Eurail, are good on S-trains but not buses. **Night buses,** marked with an "N," run 12:30-5:30am on limited routes and charge double fare; they also accept the 24hr. pass. Copenhagen's newly renovated **Metro** system, opening in three stages in 2002, 2003, and 2006, should make public transportation even more efficient.

Taxis: ☎35 35 35 35; 38 77 77 77; or 38 10 10 10. Base fare 22kr; add 9.50-12.50kr per km. Central Station to airport 150kr.

Bike Rental: City Bike lends bikes for free, within a designated area of the city. Deposit 20kr at any of 120 bike racks citywide; retrieve the coin upon return. **Københavns Cykler,** Reventlowsg. 11 (☎33 33 86 13; www.rentabike.dk), in Central Station. 50kr per day, 90kr for 2 days, 125kr for 3 days, 225kr per week; 300kr deposit. Open July-Aug. M-F 8am-5:30pm, Sa 9am-1pm, Su 10am-1pm; Sept.-June closed Su. Bikes are allowed on **trains** for an additional 10kr.

Hitchhiking and Ridesharing: Hitchhiking is illegal on motorways and is not common in Denmark. For info on ridesharing, check out **www.nice.person.dk** or links at the **Use It** website, www.useit.dk. *Let's Go* does not recommend hitchhiking.

ORIENTATION AND PRACTICAL INFORMATION

Copenhagen lies on the east coast of the island of **Zealand** (Sjælland), across the Øresund sound from Malmö, Sweden. The 28km **Øresund bridge and tunnel,** which opened July 1, 2000, established the first "fixed link" between the two countries. Copenhagen's **Central Station** lies near the city's heart. North of the station, **Vesterbrogade** passes **Tivoli** and **Rådhuspladsen,** the central square and terminus of most bus lines, then cuts through the city center as **Strøget** (STROY-yet), which is the world's longest pedestrian thoroughfare and goes through a series of names: **Frederiksberggade, Nygade, Vimmelskaftet, Amagertorv,** and **Østergade.** The main pedestrian areas are **Orstedsparken, Botanisk Have,** and **Rosenborg Have.**

TOURIST, FINANCIAL, AND LOCAL SERVICES

Tourist Offices: Wonderful Copenhagen, Bernstorffsg. 1 (☎70 22 24 42; www.visitcopenhagen.dk). Head out the main exit of Central Station and go left, past the back entrance to Tivoli. Open May-Aug. M-Sa 9am-8pm, Su 10am-6pm; Sept.-Apr. M-F 9am-4:30pm, Sa 9am-1:30pm. Consult website for separate accommodations service and info-line hours. **Use It,** Rådhusstr. 13 (☎33 73 06 20; www.useit.dk). From the station, follow Vesterbrog., cross Rådhuspladsen onto Frederiksbergg., and turn right on Rådhusstr. Indispensable and geared toward budget travelers. Pick up a copy of *Play Time,* a comprehensive budget guide to the city. Provides daytime luggage storage, has free Internet access, finds lodgings, and holds mail. Open mid-June to mid-Sept. daily 9am-7pm; mid-Sept. to mid-June M-W 11am-4pm, Th 11am-6pm, F 11am-2pm. The **Copenhagen Card,** sold in hotels, tourist offices, and train stations, grants unlimited travel in North Zealand, discounts on ferries to Sweden, and admission to most sights (24hr. 215kr; 48hr. 375kr; 72hr. 495kr), but may not be worth it unless you plan to ride the bus frequently and see several museums per day. Also check out **www.aok.dk,** a helpful English-language website.

Budget Travel: Wasteels Rejser, Skoubog. 6 (☎33 14 46 33). Open M-F 9am-7pm, Sa 10am-3pm. **Kilroy Travels,** Skinderg. 28 (☎33 11 00 44). Open M-F 10am-5:30pm, Sa 10am-2pm.

Embassies: Australia (consulate), Dampfaergevej 26, 2nd fl. (☎70 26 36 76). **Canada,** Kristen Bernikowsg. 1 (☎33 48 32 00; fax 33 48 32 21). **Ireland,** Østerbaneg. 21 (☎35 42 32 33; fax 35 43 18 58). **New Zealanders** should contact their embassy in Brussels (see p. 133). **South Africa,** Gammel Vartovvej 8 (☎39 18 01 55; www.southafrica.dk). **UK,** Kastelsvej 36-40 (☎35 44 52 00; fax 35 44 52 93). **US,** Dag Hammarskjölds Allé 24 (☎35 55 31 44; www.usembassy.dk).

Currency Exchange: Numerous locations, especially on Strøget. 25kr commission standard. **Forex,** in Central Station. 25kr commission on cash, 15kr per traveler's check. Open daily 8am-9pm. **The Change Group,** Østerg. 61. 25kr commission minimum. Open May-Sept. M-Sa 9am-10pm, Su 10am-8pm; Oct.-Apr. daily 10am-6pm.

Luggage Storage: Free at **Use It** (see tourist offices, above) and most hostels. At **Central Station,** 25-35kr per 24hr. Open M-Sa 5:30am-1am, Su 6am-1am.

Laundromats: Look for **Vascomat** and **Møntvask** chains. At Borgerg. 2, Nansensg. 39, and Istedg. 45. Wash and dry 40-50kr. Most open daily 7am-9pm.

Bi-Gay-Lesbian Resources: Landsforeningen for Bøsser and Lesbiske (National Assoc. for Gay Men and Women), Teglgårdsstr. 13 (☎33 13 19 48; www.lbl.dk). Open M-F 11am-4pm. The monthly *Gay and Lesbian Guide to Copenhagen,* which lists clubs, cafes, and organizations, is available at several gay clubs (see p. 283). Also check out www.copenhagen-gay-life.dk, www.gayonline.dk., or www.panbladet.dk. The city is home to the annual **Mermaid Pride Parade** (www.mermaidpride.dk) each August.

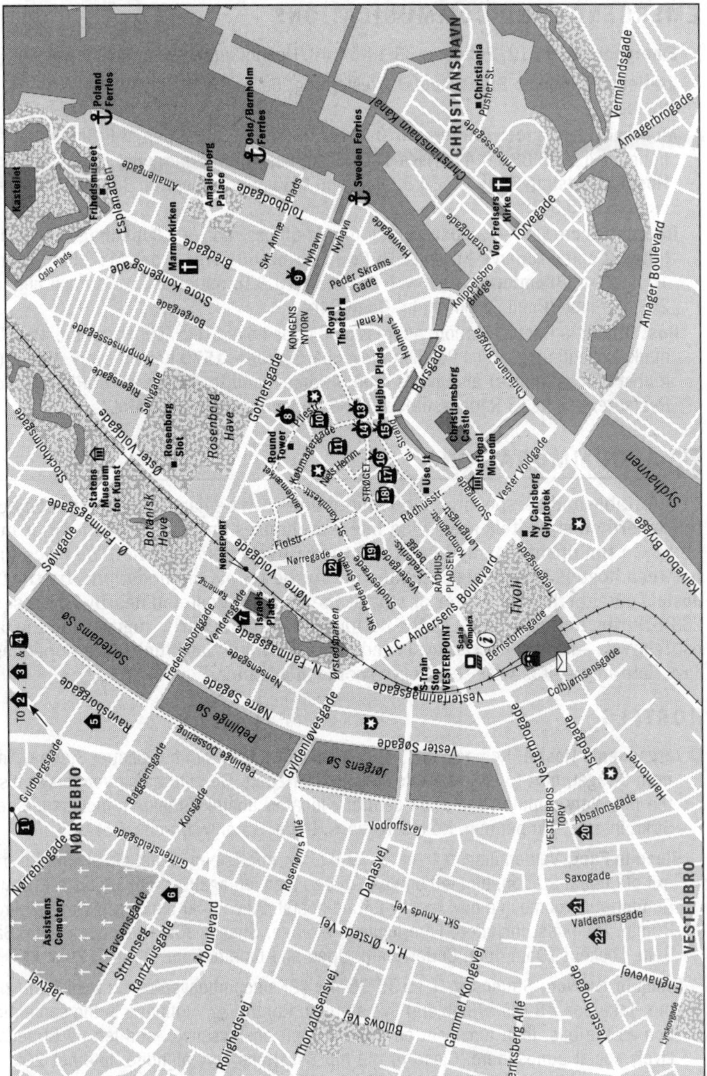
Copenhagen
ACCOMMODATIONS
City Public Hostel, 20
Hotel Jørgensen, 7
Hotel Rye, 3
Jørgensen's Hostel, 7
Mike's Guest House, 23
Sleep-In, 2
Sleep-In-Fact, 22
Sleep-In Green, 5
Sleep-In Heaven, 6
Vesterbros Interpoint, 21
FOOD
Café Europa, 14
Café Norden, 13
Den Grønne Kælder, 8
Kafe Kys, 15
Nyhavns Færgekro, 9
RizRaz, 16
NIGHTLIFE
Bombay, 12
IN Bar, 19
JazzHouse, 11
PAN Club and Café, 18
Park, 4
Rust, 1
Sebastian Bar and Disco, 17
Studenterhuset, 10
NØRREBRO
VESTERBRO
CHRISTIANSHAVN
Kastellet
Frihedsmuseet
Poland Ferries
Oslo/Bornholm Ferries
Sweden Ferries
Amalienborg Palace
Marmorkirken
Statens Museum for Kunst
Rosenborg Slot
Rosenborg Have
Botanisk Have
Round Tower
Royal Theater
Christiansborg Castle
National Museum
Ny Carlsberg Glyptotek
Tivoli
Christiania
Vor Frelsers Kirke
Assistens Cemetery
Frederiksberg Have
Carlsberg Brewery
KONGENS NYTORV
RÅDHUS PLADSEN
STRØGET
NØRREPORT
S-Train Stop VESTERPORT
Scala Complex
Israels Plads
VESTERBROS TORV
Sortedams Sø
Peblinge Sø
Sankt Jørgens Sø
Sydhavnen
Christianshavn Kanal
Nørrebrogade
Vesterbrogade
H.C. Andersens Boulevard
Amager Boulevard
Gammel Kongevej
Frederiksberg Allé
Torvegade
Bredgade
Store Kongensgade
Gothersgade
Nyhavn
Børsgade
Knippelsbro Bridge
Østerbrogade
Øster Voldgade
Nørre Voldgade
Nørre Søgade
Vester Søgade
Vesterfarimagsgade
Istedgade
Valdemarsgade
Saxogade
Absalonsgade
Åboulevard
Rantzausgade
Jagtvej
TO 2, 3 & 4
TO 23 (100m)

EMERGENCY AND COMMUNICATIONS

Emergencies: ☎112. **Police:** ☎33 14 14 48. Headquarters are at Polititorvet.

24-Hour Pharmacy: Steno Apotek, Vesterbrog. 6c (☎33 14 82 66). Open 24hr.; ring the bell.

Medical Assistance: Doctors on Call (☎33 93 63 00). Open M-F 8am-4pm; after hours, call ☎38 88 60 41. Visits 120-350kr, cash only. **Emergency rooms** at **Amager Hospital,** Kastrup 63 (☎32 34 32 34), and **Bispebjerg Hospital,** Bispebjerg Bakke 23 (☎35 31 35 31).

Internet Access: Free at **Use It** (see tourist offices, above). **Copenhagen Hovedbibliotek** (Central Library), Krystalg. 15 (☎33 73 60 60). Free. Open M-F 10am-7pm, Sa 10am-2pm. **Boomtown,** Axeltorv 1 (☎33 32 10 32), opposite Tivoli's main entrance. 20kr per first 30min., 30kr per hr. Open 24hr.

Post Office: In Central Station. Address mail to be held: SURNAME Firstname, Post Denmark, Hovedbanegårdens Posthus, Hovedbanegården, **1570** Kobenhavn V. **Use It** (see tourist offices, above) also holds mail. Address mail to: Firstname SURNAME, *Poste Restante,* Use It, 13 Rådhusstræde, **1466** Copenhagen K, DENMARK.

ACCOMMODATIONS

Comfortable and inexpensive accommodations can be hard to find in the city center, where most hostels are styled like warehouses and packed with 50 or more beds. On the upside, many hostels feature a lively social scene. The price jump between hostels and hotels is significant; for better accommodations, try the **Danhostels** outside the city center or stay at the five-star hostel in nearby Ishøj (see p. 283). During holidays (such as the national vacation in early August) and the largest festivals—especially Karneval (mid-May), Roskilde (late June), and Copenhagen Jazz (late July)—it is wise to reserve rooms in advance.

HOSTELS

Jørgensen's Hostel, Rømersg. 11 (☎33 13 81 86). 25min. from Central Station, 5min. from Strøget, next to Israels Plads. S-train: Nørreport. Go right along Vendersg.; it's on the left. Very popular; the most centrally located hostel. Breakfast included. Sheets 30kr. Internet 1kr per min. No reservations. Under 35 only. Dorms 125kr. ❸

Sleep-In-Fact, Valdemarsg. 14 (☎33 79 67 79; info@sleep-in-fact.dk). From the main exit of Central Station, turn left on Vesterbrog., then left again on Valdemarstr. (10min.). Comfortable rooms in a new factory-turned-hostel. Bikes 50kr per day. Internet 20kr per 30min. Breakfast included. Free luggage storage. Sheets 30kr. Reception daily 6am-3am. Lockout 10am-4pm. Curfew 3am. Open mid-June to Sept. Dorms 120kr. ❸

Sleep-In Heaven, Struenseg. 7 (☎35 35 46 48; sleepinheaven@get2net.dk), in Nørrebro. Take bus #8 (dir.: Tingbjerg) five stops to Rantzausg.; continue in the same direction as the bus, then turn right on Kapelvej, left on Tavsensg., and left on Struenseg. Lively social atmosphere. Close to the hip Skt. Hans Torv nightlife. Internet 20kr per 30min. Breakfast 40kr. Free lockers. Sheets 30kr. Reception daily 7:30am-2am. Dorms 110kr; doubles 450kr. ❸

Sleep-In, Blegdamsvej 132 (☎35 26 50 59). Bus #1, 6, or 14: Trianglen. S-train: Østerport. Facing the station, go left and walk 10min. up Hammerskjölds. Near the city center and Østerbro nightlife. This popular (and noisy) warehouse of a hostel favors quantity over privacy. Kitchen. Internet 6kr per 15min. Sheets 30kr. Reception 24hr. Lockout noon-4pm. Open June 28-Aug. No reservations. Dorms 90kr. ❷

Sleep-In Green, Ravnsborgg. 18, Baghuset (☎35 37 77 77). Take bus #16 from the station to Nørrebrog., and then walk down Ravnsborgg. Cozy, eco-friendly hostels outside the city center. Ragged on the outside, but clean inside. Internet 20kr per 30min. Bikes 30kr per day. Organic breakfast 30kr. Sheets 30kr. Reception 24hr. Check-out noon. Lockout noon-4pm. Open mid-May to mid-Oct. Dorms 95kr. ❷

Vesterbros Interpoint, Vesterbros KFUM (YMCA), Valdemarsg. 15 (☎33 31 15 74). Across the street from Sleep-In-Fact (see above). Super-friendly staff, homey atmosphere, and fewer beds per room than other area hostels. Breakfast 25kr. Sheets 15kr. Kitchen. Reception daily 8:30-11:30am, 3:30-5:30pm, and 8pm-12:30am. Curfew 12:30am. Open late June to early Aug. Dorms 85kr. ❷

City Public Hostel, Absalonsg. 8 (☎33 31 20 70; www.city-public-hostel.dk), in the Vesterbro Youth Center. From the station, walk away from the Rådhuspladsen on Vesterbrog. and turn left on Absalonsg. Breakfast 20kr. Lounge, BBQ, and kitchen. Sheets 30kr. Reception 24hr. Open early May to late Aug. Dorms 130kr. ❸

Ajax, Bavnehøj Allé 30 (☎33 21 24 56). S-train A: Sydhavn; walk north on Enghavevej with the train tracks on your right, turn left on Bavnehøj Allé, and look for signs on the right. Or, bus #10 (dir.: Vigerslev), then walk up Bavnehøj Allé. Kitchen and TV. Breakfast 25kr. Sheets 20kr. Reception daily 8am-midnight. Open July-Aug. Dorms 70kr; doubles 200kr; triples 300kr. **Camping** 50kr; tent rental 10kr. ❶

København Vandrerhjem Bellahøj (HI), Herbergvejen 8 (☎38 28 97 15; bellahoj@danhostel.dk), in Bellahøj. Take bus #11 (dir.: Bellahøj/Bronshøj Torv) from the station to Primulavej. Large, clean, and modern, but far from the city center. Bikes 60kr per day. Internet 1kr per min. Breakfast 40kr. Sheets 35kr. Laundry 30kr. Reception 24hr. Lockout 10am-2pm. Dorms 95kr; doubles 275kr. Nonmembers add 30kr. ❷

København Vandrerhjem Amager (HI), Vejlandsallé 200 (☎32 52 29 08). Take bus #46 (M-F 6am-5pm; night bus #96N) from Central Station; or catch the S-train to Valby, then take bus #100S (dir.: Svanemollen St.). Far from civilization in a huge nature reserve. Kitchen. Breakfast 40kr. Sheets 35kr. Laundry 25kr. Reception 24hr. Check-in 1-5pm. Open mid-Jan. to Nov. Dorms 95kr; nonmembers 125kr. ❷

HOTELS

Hotel Jørgensen, Rømersg. 11 (☎33 13 81 86; www.hoteljorgensen.dk). Same ownership as Jørgensen's Hostel (see above) and in the same location. Friendly staff. Breakfast included. Reception 24hr. Singles 475kr; doubles 575kr; triples 725kr. ❺

Hotel Rye, Ryesg. 115 (35 26 52 10, www.hotelrye.dk). Take bus #1, 6, 14, or 650 to Trianglen, then turn right off Osterbrog. onto Ryesg. Cozy hotel that provides a kimono and slippers in your room and homemade buns at breakfast. Breakfast included. Reception daily 8am-9pm. Singles 500kr; doubles 700kr; triples 900kr. ❺

Mike's Guest House, Kirkevænget 13 (☎36 45 65 40). Bus #6 from Central Station toward Valby Langg. (10min.). Call ahead. Four clean, spacious rooms, some with private balconies, in Mike's own home. Quiet neighborhood near the Carlsberg brewery. Singles 200kr; doubles 290kr; triples 400kr. ❹

CAMPING

Bellahøj Camping, Hvidkildevej 66 (☎38 10 11 50), 5km from the city center. Take bus #11 to "Bellahøj." Shower included. Kitchen, cafe and market. Reception 24hr. Open June-Aug. 58kr per person; tents available for extra charge. ❶

Absalon Camping, Korsdalsvej 132, Rødovre (☎36 41 06 00), 9km from the city center. From Central Station, take bus #550S to "Korsdalsvej/Roskildevej" and ask the driver to let you off at the campsite. Kitchen, laundry (30kr), and store. Reception daily 8am-10pm. 62kr per person, 20kr per tent; cabins 195kr plus 54kr per person. ❷

THE INSIDER'S CITY

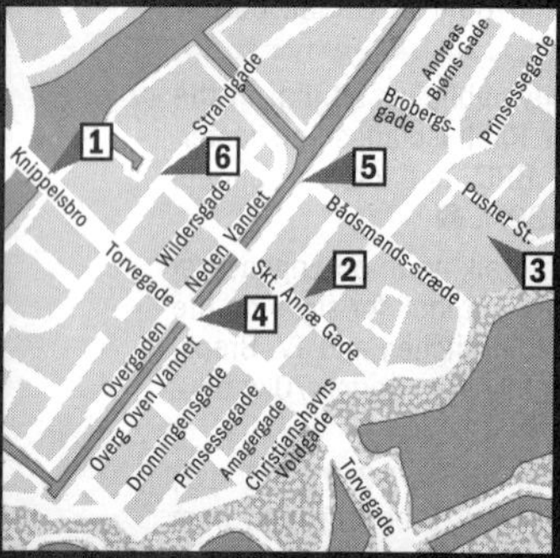

CHRISTIANSHAVN

Christianshavn was built on islets and earth filling by King Christian IV who wished to create a Dutch inspired town. A stroll through the cobbled streets and crooked, colorful houses reveal why the area is nicknamed "Little Amsterdam."

1 Walk across the **Knippelsbro bridge** over the fairway harbor from Slotsholm and continue down the main road, **Tovegade.**

2 For a spectacular view, climb up the spire of **Vor Frelsers Kirke** (The Church of Our Savior), 29 Sankt Annae G., built 1682-1696.

3 Visit the over 1000 self-governing residents of the "free state" of **Christiana.**

4 Stroll along the docked line canals of Sankt Annae G. and grab a quick bite to eat or rent a boat at **Christianshavn Cafe,** Overgaden Neden Vandet 29.

5 The **Royal Danish Naval Museum,** Vandet 58, houses an enormous collection of model ships.

6 **#32 Strandgade,** built in 1622, is the oldest house in Christianshavn.

FOOD

The Vikings left many legacies, pickled herring among them. Around **Kongens Nytorv,** elegant cafes serve *smørrebrød* (open-faced sandwiches) for about 40kr. All-you-can-eat buffets (40-70kr) are popular, especially at Turkish, Indian, and Italian restaurants. **Fakta** and **Netto supermarkets** are budget fantasies; there are several around the Nørreport area (S-train: Nørreport). Open-air **markets** provide fresh fruits and veggies; try the one at **Israels Plads** near Nørreport Station. (Open M-Th 9am-5:30pm, F 9am-6:30pm, Sa 9am-3pm.) **Fruit stalls** line Strøget and the side streets to the north.

Nyhavns Færgekro, Nyhavn 5. Upscale fisherman's cottage atmosphere along the canal. Lunch on 10 varieties of all-you-can-eat herring (89kr). Lunch served 11:30am-5pm. Dinner around 165kr. Open daily 9:30am-11:30pm. ❹

Café Norden, Østerg. 61, on Strøget and Nicolaj Plads, in sight of the fountain. A French-style cafe with the best vantage point on Strøget. Great for people-watching. Lots of good food for a good price. Nachos 45-79kr, sandwiches 62-69kr, salads 82-98kr, pastries 15-40kr, brunch 89kr. Open daily 9am-midnight. ❸

Café Europa, Amagertorv 1, on Nicolaj Plads opposite Café Norden. If Norden is the place to see, then trendy Europa is the place to be seen. Smaller and somewhat pricier. Sandwiches 45-65kr, gourmet salads 89-119kr. Beer 45kr per pint. Great coffee. Open M-W 9am-midnight, F-Sa 9am-1am, Su 10am-7pm. ❸

Kafe Kys, Læderstr. 7, on a quiet street running south of and parallel to Strøget. Vegetarian options, sandwiches, and salads 48-75kr. Beer 24kr. Open M-Th 11am-1am, F-Sa 11am-2am, Su noon-10pm. Kitchen closes daily at 10pm. ❷

Den Grønne Kælder, Pilestr. 48. Popular, classy vegetarian and vegan dining in a casual atmosphere. Hummus 35-45kr, veggie burgers 35kr, salad combo meals 35-80kr. Open M-Sa 11am-10pm. ❷

RizRaz, Kompagnistr. 20. Extensive mediterranean lunch buffet. Lots of vegetarian options. Lunch buffet 49kr. Dinner 59kr. ❷

SIGHTS

Compact Copenhagen is best seen by foot or bike. Various **tours** are detailed in Use It's *Play Time* and tourist office brochures. The squares along the lively pedestrian Strøget, which divides the city center, are Nytorv, Nicolaj Plads, and Kongens Nytorv. Opposite

Kongens Nytorv is Nyhavn, the "new port" where Hans Christian Andersen wrote his first fairy tale. There are several canal tours, but **Netto Boats** offers the best value and covers a lot of sights. (Every 20min. Apr. to mid-Sept. 10am-5pm, 20kr.) Bus #6 travels through Vesterbro and Rådhuspladsen, alongside Strøget, and on to Østerbro, acting as a sight-seeing guide to the city. Wednesday is a great day to visit museums, as most are free.

CITY CENTER. The first sight you'll see as you exit the train station is **Tivoli,** the famed 19th-century **amusement park,** which has botanical gardens, marching toy soldiers, and, of course, rides. Saturday nights and some Sunday and Wednesday nights culminate with music and fireworks. An increasingly popular Christmas market is open mid-November through mid-December. *(Vesterbrog. 3. www.tivoligardens.com. Open mid-June to mid-Aug. Su-Th 11am-midnight, F-Sa 11am-1am; Mid-Aug. to Sept. Su-Tu 11am-11pm, W-Th and Sa 11am-midnight, F 11am-1am. Rides open at 11:30am, children's rides open noon. Admission 55kr; ride tickets 10kr, 1-5 tickets per ride; 1-day admission and unlimited rides 180kr.)* From Central Station, turn right on Bernstorffsg. and left on Tietgensg. to get to the beautiful **Ny Carlsberg Glyptotek** with its collection of ancient and Impressionist art and sculpture and an enclosed Mediterranean garden. *(Dantes Plads 7. Open Tu-Su 10am-4pm. 30kr; free W and Su or with ISIC.)* Continue along Tietgensg., which becomes Stormg., to see Denmark's Viking treasures and other tidbits of cultural history at the **National Museum.** *(Ny Vesterg. 10. ☎33 13 44 11. Open Tu-Su 10am-5pm. 40kr, students 30kr; W free.)* **Christiansborg Castle,** Prins Jørgens Gård, features subterranean ruins, still-in-use royal reception rooms, and the *Folketing* (Parliament) chambers. To get there, continue down Tietgensg. from the city center and cross the canal. *(☎33 92 64 94. Tours of royal reception rooms June-Aug. daily 11am, 1, 3pm; May and Sept. 11am and 3pm; Oct.-Apr. Tu, Th, Sa-Su 11am and 3pm. 40kr, students 30kr. Palace ruins open May-Sept. daily 9:30am-3:30pm; Oct.-Apr. Tu-Th and Sa-Su 9:30am-3:30pm. 20kr. Ask for free Parliament tours.)*

CHRISTIANSHAVN. Climb the golden spire of **Vor Frelsers Kirke** (Our Savior's Church) for a great view of both the city and the water. *(Sankt Annæg. 29. Turn left off Prinsesseg.; or, take bus #8 from Central Station. Church open Mar.-Nov. daily 11am-4:30pm; Dec.-Feb. 10am-2pm. Free. Tower open Mar.-Nov. M-Sa 11am-4:30pm, Su noon-4:30pm. 20kr.)* In the southern section of Christianshavn, the "free city" of **Christiania,** which was founded in 1971 by youthful squatters in abandoned military barracks, is inhabited by a thriving group of artists and alterna-thinkers carrying 70s activism and free love into the new millennium. At Christmas, there is a fabulous **market** with curiosities from all over the world. Exercise caution in the aptly named **Pusher Street** area, the site of *many* hash and marijuana sales. Possession of even small amounts can get you arrested. Always ask before taking pictures, never take pictures on Pusher St. itself, and exercise caution in the area at night.

FREDERIKSTADEN. Edvard Eriksen's **den Lille Havfrue (The Little Mermaid),** the tiny but touristed statue at the opening of the harbor, honors Hans Christian Andersen. *(S-train: Østerport; turn left out of the station, left on Folke Bernadottes Allé, right on the path bordering the canal, left up the stairs, and then right along the street. Open daily 6am-dusk.)* Head back along the canal and turn left to cross the moat to **Kastellet,** a 17th-century fortress, now with a park. Cross through Kastellet to the **Frihedsmuseet** (Museum of Danish Resistance), a fascinating museum documenting Denmark's efforts to rescue its Jews during the Nazi occupation, as well as its earlier period of acceptance of German "protection." *(At Churchillparken. ☎33 13 77 14. Open May to mid-Sept. Tu-Sa 10am-4pm, Su 10am-5pm; mid-Sept. to Apr. Tu-Sa 11am-3pm, Su 11am-4pm. 30kr; W free.)* From the museum, walk south down Amalieng. to reach the lovely **Amalienborg Palace,** residence of Queen Margarethe II and the royal family; most of the interior is closed to the public, but the apartments of Christian VII are open. The changing of the palace guard takes place at noon on the brick plaza. *(☎33 12 21 86;*

www.ses.dk. Open May-Oct. daily 10am-4pm; Nov.-Apr. Tu-Su 11am-4pm. 40kr, students 25kr; combined ticket with Rosenborg Slot (see below) 70kr.) The 19th-century **Marmokirken** (Marble Church), opposite the palace, features an ornate interior and Europe's third-largest dome, which has a spectacular view of the city and neighboring sound. *(Fredriksg. 4. www.marmorkirken.dk. Open M-Tu and Th 10am-5pm, W 10am-6pm, F-Su noon-5pm. Free. Dome open mid-June to Aug. daily 1 and 3pm; Sept. to mid-June Sa-Su 1 and 3pm. 20kr.)* A few blocks north, **Statens Museum for Kunst** (State Museum of Fine Arts) displays an eclectic collection of Danish and Modern art in a beautifully designed building. From the church, head away from Amalienborg, go left on Store Kongensg., right on Dronningens Tværg., right on Borgerg., and left onto Sølvg. *(Sølvg. 48-50. S-train: Nørreport; walk up Øster Voldg. ☎33 74 84 94; www.smk.dk. Open Tu and Th-Su 10am-5pm, W 10am-8pm. 50kr, under 25 35kr; W free.)* Opposite the museum, **Rosenborg Slot** (Rosenborg Palace and Gardens) hoards royal treasures, including the **crown jewels.** *(Øster Voldg. 4A. S-train: Nørreport; walk up Øster Voldg.; it's on the left past the intersection. ☎33 15 32 86. Open June-Aug. daily 10am-5pm; May and Sept. 10am-4pm; Oct. 11am-3pm; Nov.-Apr. Tu-Su 11am-2pm. 60kr, students 30kr.)* Head across Øster Voldg. from the palace to stroll through the **Botanisk Have** (Botanical Gardens) and visit the indoor tropical Palm House. *(Open June-Aug. daily 8:30am-6pm, Sept.-May 8:30am-4pm. Palm House open year-round daily 10am-3pm. Free.)*

OTHER SIGHTS. A trip to the **Carlsberg Brewery** will reward you with a wealth of ale-related knowledge and, more importantly, free samples. *(Ny Carlsbergvej 140. Take bus #6 west from Rådhuspladsen to Valby Langg. ☎33 27 13 14; www.carlsberg.com. Open Tu-Su 10am-4pm. Free.)* If the breweries haven't completely confused your senses, go play at the hands-on **Experimentarium** (Danish Science Center). It's geared toward kids but is fun for everyone. *(Tuborg Havnevej 7. Take bus #6 north from Rådhuspladsen. ☎39 27 33 33; www.experimentarium.dk. Open late June to mid-Aug. daily 10am-5pm; late Aug. to early June M and W-F 9am-5pm, Tu 9am-9pm, Sa-Su 11am-5pm. 89kr, children 62kr.)*

ENTERTAINMENT AND FESTIVALS

For events, consult *Copenhagen This Week* (free at hostels and tourist offices), or pick up *Use It News* from Use It (see tourist offices, p. 276). The **Royal Theater** is home to the world-famous Royal Danish Ballet; the box office is located at Tordenskjoldsg. 7. (Open M-Sa 10am-6pm.) For same-day half-price tickets, head to the **Tivoli ticket office,** Vesterbrog. 3. (☎33 15 10 12. Open mid-Apr. to mid-Sept. daily 10am-8pm; mid-Sept. to mid-Apr. 9am-7pm. Royal Theater tickets available at 4 or 5pm, others at noon.) Call **Arte,** Hvidkildevej 64 (☎38 88 22 22), to ask about student discounts. Tickets for a variety of events are sold online at www.billetnet.dk. The relaxed **Kul-Kaféen,** Teglgårdsstr. 5, is a great place to see live performers, get info on music, dance, and theater, and grab some food. (Sandwiches 51kr. Open M-Sa 11am-midnight.) During the world-class **Copenhagen Jazz Festival** (☎33 93 20 13; www.cjf.dk) in mid-July, the city teems with free outdoor concerts as well as indoor shows. Other festivals include the **Swingin' Copenhagen** festival in late May (www.swinging-copenhagen.dk) and the **Copenhagen Autumn Jazz** festival in early November.

NIGHTLIFE

In Copenhagen, weekends often begin on Wednesday, nights rock until 5am, and "morning pubs" open when the clubs close so you can party around the clock. On Thursday, most bars and clubs have reduced covers and cheap drinks. The central **pedestrian district** reverberates with crowded bars and discos. **Kongens Nytorv** has fancier options, but many Danes just buy beer at a supermarket and head for the boats, cafes, and salty charisma of nearby **Nyhavn.** The **Scala** complex, opposite Tivoli, has many bars and restaurants, and students fill the cheaper bars in the **Nørrebro** area. Copenhagen's gay and lesbian scene is one of Europe's best.

Park, Østerbrog. 79, in the Østerbro. Buses #6 and 14. An enormous (and enormously popular) club with 2 packed dance floors, live music hall, and rooftop patio. Pints 40kr. Cover Th-Sa 60kr. Open Th-Sa 11am-5am, Su-M 11am-midnight, Tu-W 11am-2am.

Rust, Guldbergsg. 8, in the Nørrebro. Buses #3, 5, and 16. 20-somethings pack this lively disco. Has places to dance and to chill. Long lines by 1am. Cover 50kr; free before 11pm. Open W-Sa 10pm-5am.

Café Pavillionen, Borgmester Jensens Allé 45, in Fælleaparken. This summer-only outdoor cafe has local bands 8-10pm, plus a disco W-Sa 10pm-5am. On Mondays, enjoy a concert (2:30-5pm), tango lessons (7-8:15pm; 50kr), and dancing until midnight.

Bombay, Nørreg. 41. Soul, R&B, and Latin music. Oriental decor attracts a young stylish crowd. Dress code. Th 18+, F 20+, Sa 22+. Cover Th-F 50kr; Sa 60kr. Open Th 9pm-4am, F 9pm-5am, Sa 9pm-6am.

IN Bar, Nørreg. 1. Drink cheaply and then dance on the speakers. Th-Sa 20+. F-Sa cover 150kr, includes open bar. Open Su-Th 10pm-5am, F-Sa 10pm-10am.

JazzHouse, Niels Hemmingsens Gade 10 (www.jazzhouse.dk). Turn left off Strøget from Gammeltorv (closer to Råhuspladsen) and Nytorv. Copenhagen's premier jazz venue makes for a sophisticated and potentially expensive evening. Cover depends on performer. Concerts Su-Th 8:30pm, F-Sa 9:30pm. Dance club open daily midnight-5am.

PAN Club and Café, Knabrostr. 3. Gay cafe, bar, and disco. Homoguide available. Cover W 30kr, F-Sa 50kr; Th no cover. Cafe opens daily 8pm; disco opens 11pm and gets going around 1am. Both open late.

Sebastian Bar and Disco, Hyskenstr. 10, off Strøget. The city's best-known gay and lesbian bar. Relaxed, welcoming atmosphere. Homoguide available. Happy Hour 5-9pm. Open daily noon-2am.

Studenterhuset, Købmagerg. 52. Laid-back environment, popular with Copenhagen's students. Cheap bar with student discounts. W international, Th live jazz, F rock. Open M and Th noon-midnight, Tu noon-6pm, W noon-1am, F noon to 2 or 5am.

DAYTRIPS FROM COPENHAGEN

Stunning castles and white sand beaches hide in North and Central Zealand. Trains offer easy access to many attractive daytrips within an hour of Copenhagen.

ISHØJ. The small harbor town of Ishøj, just south of Copenhagen, is home to the **Arken Museum of Modern Art,** Skovvej 100, which features temporary exhibitions by notable artists; Edward Munch and Gerhard Richter have both been featured. (☎43 54 02 22; www.arken.dk. Open Tu and Th-Su 10am-5pm, W 10am-9pm. 55kr, students 35kr; extra for some exhibitions.) Take bus #128 from Ishøj Station (every hr., 14kr) or follow the signs from the station (45min. walk). From Copenhagen to Ishøj, take **S-train** lines A or E. To stay near the beach at **Ishøj Strand Vandrerhjem ❸,** Ishøj Strandvej 13, follow the signs from the station. (☎43 53 50 15. Breakfast 45kr. Sheets 40kr. Internet 2kr per min. Reception daily 8am-noon and 2-9:30pm. Dorms 100kr; singles and doubles 370-400kr. **Camping** 62kr per person.)

HUMLEBÆK AND RUNGSTED. Humlebæk distinguishes itself with the spectacular **Louisiana Museum of Modern Art,** 13 Gl. Strandvej, named for the three wives (all named Louisa) of the estate's original owner. The museum contains works by Picasso, Warhol, Lichtenstein, Calder, and other 20th-century masters; the building and its beautifully landscaped, sculpture-studded grounds overlooking the sea are themselves worth the trip. Follow signs 1.5km north from the Humlebæk station or take bus #388. (☎49 19 07 19. Open Th-Tu 10am-5pm, W 10am-10pm. 68kr, students 60kr.) The quiet harbor town of **Rungsted** is where Karen Blixen (pseudonym Isak Dinesen) wrote *Out of Africa.* The **Karen Blixen Museum,** Rungsted Strandvej 111, houses her abode, personal belongings, and grave. Follow the street leading out of the train station and turn right on Rungstedsvej, then right again on Rungsted Strandvej; or, take bus #388 (2 per hr.) and tell the driver your destination. (☎45 57 10 57. Open May-Sept. Tu-Su 10am-5pm; Oct.-Apr. W-F 1-4pm, Sa-Su 11am-4pm. 35kr.) The **tourist office** kiosk is on the corner by the museum. Both Humlebæk (45min., 38.50kr or 4 clips) and Rungsted (30min., 40kr or 4 clips on the blue *rabatkort*) are on the Copenhagen-Helsingør northern **train** line.

HILLERØD AND FREDENSBORG. **Hillerød** is home of the moated **Frederiksborg Slot;** with its exquisite Baroque gardens and brick ramparts spanning three islands, it is arguably the most impressive of North Zealand's castles. Free concerts are given Thursdays at 1:30pm on the famous 1610 **Esaias Compenius organ**. To get there from the station, cross the street onto Vibekeg. and follow the signs. (Castle open Apr.-Oct. daily 10am-5pm; Nov.-Mar. 11am-3pm. 50kr, students 40kr. Gardens open May-Aug. daily 10am-9pm; Sept. and Apr. 10am-7pm; Oct. and Mar. 10am-5pm; Nov.-Feb. 10am-4pm. Free.) A final stop on the northern castle tour is **Fredensborg Palace.** Built in 1722 as a hunting retreat for King Frederik IV, the castle still serves as the spring and fall royal residence. Follow the signs from the station. (☎33 40 31 87. Palace open only in July daily 1-4:30pm; mandatory tours every 15-30min.; call ahead about tours in English (2 per day). 30kr. Outlying gardens always open. Private gardens open July daily 9am-5pm. Free.) Hillerød is at the end of **S-train** lines A and E (40min., 42kr). Fredensborg is on the Lille Nord rail line connecting Hillerød and Helsingør. The **tourist office,** located in a kiosk down the hill from the palace, has information about seasonal boating on Lake Esrum. (☎48 48 21 00. Open June-Aug. M-F 10am-5pm, Sa 10am-3pm, Su 11am-3pm; Sept.-May M-F 10am-4pm, Sa 10am-1pm.) **Fredensborg Youth Hostel (HI)** ❷, Østrupvej 3, is 1km from the station. (☎48 48 03 15. Breakfast 45kr. Sheets 45kr. Reception daily 9am-noon and 4-9pm. Dorms 95kr; singles 185kr; doubles 325kr.)

ROSKILDE. Roskilde, in Central Zealand, served as Denmark's first capital when King Harald Bluetooth built the country's first Christian church here in AD 980. The ornate sarcophagi of the red-brick **Roskilde Domkirke** in Domkirkepladsen hold most of the Danish Kings and Queens since the Reformation. (☎46 35 27 00. Open Apr.-Sept. M-Sa 9am-4:45pm, Su 12:30-4:45pm; Oct.-Mar. Tu-Sa 10am-3:45pm, Su 12:30-3:45pm. 15kr, students 10kr. Free organ concerts June-Aug. Th 8pm.) The **Viking Ship Museum,** Vindeboder 12, near Strandengen along the harbor, houses remnants of five trade ships and warships sunk circa 1060 and salvaged in the late 1960s. From the tourist office, it is a pleasant walk to the cathedral and downhill through the park, or take bus #605 (dir.: Boserup). In summer, book a ride on a Viking longboat, but be prepared to take an oar—Viking conquest is no spectator sport. (☎46 30 02 00; www.vikingeskibsmuseet.dk. Museum open May-Sept. daily 9am-5pm; Oct.-Apr. 10am-4pm. May-Sept. 60kr; Oct.-Apr. 45kr. Boat trip 40kr, without museum ticket 80kr; book ahead.) Roskilde hosts one of Europe's largest **music festivals** (June 26-29, 2003; ☎46 36 66 13; www.roskilde-festival.dk), drawing over 90,000 fans with seven stages and big-name bands such as REM, U2, Radiohead, Smashing Pumpkins, and Metallica.

Roskilde is accessible by **train** from Copenhagen (25-30min., 38.50kr or 4 clips). The **tourist office,** Gullandsstr. 15, sells festival tickets and books rooms for a 25kr fee and a 10-15% deposit. From the train station, turn left on Jernbaneg., right on

Allehelgansg., and left again on Barchog.; it's on the left. (☎46 35 27 00. Open July-Aug. M-F 9am-6pm, Sa 10am-2pm; Apr.-June M-F 9am-5pm, Sa 10am-1pm; Sept.-Mar. M-Th 9am-5pm, F 9am-4pm, Sa 10am-1pm.) Although Roskilde is close enough to Copenhagen to be an easy daytrip, its accommodations are nice enough to make staying the night a tempting option. The **HI Youth Hostel ❸,** Vindeboder 7, is on the harbor next to the Viking Museum shipyard. The gorgeous, modern facility is always booked during the festival. (☎46 35 21 84; www.danhostel.dk/roskilde. Reception daily 8am-noon and 4-10pm. Open Feb.-Dec. Dorms 100kr, nonmembers 115kr.) **Roskilde Camping ❶,** Baunehøjvej 7, is on the beach, 4km north of town; take bus #603 toward Veddelev to Veddelev Byg. (☎46 75 79 96. Reception daily 8am-9pm. Open Apr. to mid-Sept. 62kr per person.)

CHARLOTTENLUND AND KLAMPENBORG. Charlottenlund and Klampenborg, on the coastal line, feature topless **beaches.** To get to the beach from the Charlottenlund station, follow the signs for the "Danmark Akvarium," which is next to the beach. (Public dock open June-Aug. daily 7am-6:30pm. 20kr.) The Klampenborg beach is somewhat bigger (free). Although less ornate than Tivoli, **Bakken,** the world's oldest amusement park, delivers more thrills. From the Klampenborg train station, turn left, cross the overpass, and head through the park. (☎39 63 73 00. Open July to early Sept. daily noon-midnight; mid-Sept. to Apr. M-F 2pm-midnight, Sa 1pm-midnight, Su noon-midnight. Entrance free. Rides open 2pm; 30-35kr each.) Bakken borders the **Jægersborg Deer Park,** the royal family's former hunting grounds. Still home to wooded paths, their **Eremitage** summer chateau, and over 2000 Red and Japanese sika deer, it is perfect for picnics and strolling. Charlottenlund and Klampenborg are both at the end of the **S-train** line C.

HELSINGØR AND HORNBÆK. Helsingør is evidence of the Danish monarchy's fondness for lavish architecture. The 15th-century **Kronborg Slot,** also known as **Elsinore,** is the setting for Shakespeare's *Hamlet* (although neither the historical "Amled" nor the Bard ever visited Kronborg). A statue of Viking chief Holger Danske sleeps in the castle's spooky casemates; according to legend, he will awake to face any threat to Denmark's safety. The castle also houses the **Danish Maritime Museum,** which contains a sea biscuit (the world's oldest, in fact) from 1852. From the train station, turn left and follow the signs along the waterfront to the castle. (☎49 21 30 78. Open May-Sept. daily 10:30am-5pm; Apr. and Oct. Tu-Su 11am-4pm; Nov.-Mar. Tu-Su 11am-3pm. 60kr.) Helsingør is at the end of the northern line (1hr.). The **tourist office,** Havnepladsen 3, is in the Kulturhuset, the large brick building across the street to the left of the station; the entrance is around the corner. (☎49 21 13 33. Open mid-June to Aug. M-Th 9am-5pm, F 9am-6pm, Sa 10am-3pm; Sept. to mid-June M-F 9am-4pm, Sa 10am-1pm.) To reach the gorgeous beachfront **Helsingør Vandrerhjem Hostel (HI) ❸,** Ndr. Strandvej 24, take bus #340 to Hojstrup and walk back along the street in the opposite direction. Or, take the train toward Hornbæk, get off at Hojstrup, and follow the path across the park; it's on the other side of the street. (☎49 21 16 40; www.helsingorhostel.dk. Breakfast 45k. Sheets 40kr. Reception daily 8am-noon and 3-9pm. Curfew 11pm. Open Feb.-Nov. Dorms 100kr; singles 250kr; doubles 250kr; triples 350-400kr. Nonmembers add 30kr.) Camp by the coast at **Helsingør Camping ❷,** Strandalleen 2; take the train toward Hornbæk and get off at Campingvej. (☎49 28 12 12; www.helsingorcamping.dk. 55kr per person, 35kr per tent.)

Hornbæk, a small, untouristed fishing town near Helsingør, offers beautiful beaches. The town hosts a wild **harbor festival** on the fourth weekend in July. Bus #340 runs from Helsingør to Hornbæk (20min., 20kr). The **tourist office,** Vestre Stejlebakke 2A, in the public library, has a listing of local B&Bs. Turn right from the station onto Havnevej, left onto Ndr. Strandvej, then right through the alley just before the Danske bank. (☎49 70 47 47; www.hornbaek.dk. Open M-Tu and Th 2-7pm, W and F 10am-5pm, Sa 10am-2pm.) **Camping Hornbæk ❷,** Planetvej 4, is within walking distance of the beach through the Hornbæk Plantation. Take bus #340 to Planetvej. (49 70 02 23; www.camping-hornbaek.dk. Open year-round. Reception 8am-noon and 2-10pm. 58kr per person, 20kr per tent.)

NEAR COPENHAGEN

MØN. To see what H.C. Andersen called one of the most beautiful spots in Denmark, head south of Copenhagen to the isle of Møn. Locals travel to Møn to explore the gorgeous chalk cliffs and the pastoral landscape. **Liselund Slot,** the only thatched castle in the world, is surrounded by a lush park with many hiking trails. To get there from **Stege,** take bus #632 (30min., 3 per day), which continues to the cliffs of **Møns Klint.** To get to Møn, take the train from Copenhagen to Vordingborg (1½hr.), then bus #62 or 64 to Stege (45min., 33kr). The **Møns Turistbureau,** Storeg. 2, is next to the bus stop in Stege. (☎55 86 04 00; www.moen-touristbureau.dk. Open June 15-Aug. M-F 10am-5pm, Sa 9am-6pm, Su 11am-1pm; Sept.-June 14 M-F 10am-5pm, Sa 9am-noon.) Stay at the lakeside **youth hostel (HI) ❸,** Langebjergvej 1. To reach the hostel, take bus #632 to the campsite stop, backtrack, then take the first road on the right. From Sept. to mid-July, take bus #62 to Magleby and walk 2.5km down the road. (☎55 81 20 30. Breakfast 45kr. Sheets 30-45kr. Reception daily 8am-noon and 4-8pm. Dorms 100kr; singles 225-280kr; doubles 270-280kr.)

BORNHOLM

In an area ideal for bikers and nature-lovers, Bornholm's red-roofed cliffside villas may seem Mediterranean, but the flowers and half-timbered houses are undeniably Danish. The unique round churches were both places of worship and fortresses for waiting out pirate attacks. The sandiest and longest **beaches** are at **Dueodde,** on the island's southern tip. For more info, check out www.bornholminfo.dk.

TRANSPORTATION. **Trains** from Copenhagen to **Ystad, Sweden** are timed to meet the ferry to **Rønne,** Bornholm's capital (train ☎70 13 14 15; 1¾hr., 5-6 per day; ferry 1½hr.; total trip 205kr, under 26 180kr.) A cheaper option is the combo bus/ferry trip (bus ☎56 95 18 66; 1½hr., 4-6 per day; ferry 1½hr.; total trip 195kr, under 26 145kr.) Overnight ferries from Copenhagen to Rønne leave at 11:30pm and arrive in Rønne at 6:30am (224kr). **Bornholmstrafikken** (Rønne ☎56 95 18 66, M-F 9am-5pm; Copenhagen ☎33 13 18 66; Ystad ☎+46 (411) 558 700; www.bornholm-ferries.dk) offers the combo train/ferry and bus/ferry route and also operates ferries from **Fährhafen Sassnitz** in **Germany** (☎+49 38392 64420; 3½hr., 1-2 per day, 90-130kr). Bornholm has an efficient local BAT **bus** service. (☎56 95 21 21; 34kr to Gudhjem or Sandvig-Allinge, 42.50kr to Svaneke; 24hr. pass 110kr.) There are numerous well-marked cycling paths between all the major towns; pick up a guide at the tourist office in Rønne (40kr). **Biking** from Rønne to Sandvig is about 28km.

RØNNE. Tiny but charming Rønne, on the southwest coast, is Bornholm's principal port of entry. The town serves mainly as an outpost for biking trips through the surrounding fields, forests, and beaches. Rent a **bike** from **Bornholms Cykeludlejning,** Ndr. Kystvej 5. (☎56 95 13 59. Reserve ahead. 60kr per day. Open May-Sept. daily 7am-4pm and 8:30-9pm.) The **tourist office,** Ndr. Kystvej 3, a mirrored-glass building behind the gas station by the Bornholmstrafikken terminal, books private rooms for free. (☎56 95 95 00. Open June-Aug. M-Sa 9:30am-5:30pm, Su 10am-4pm; Sept.-May M-F 9am-4pm, Sa 10am-1pm.) The **HI youth hostel ❸,** Arsenalvej 12, is in a quiet, wooded area near the coastline. From the ferry terminal, take the bus directly or walk 15min. along Munch Petersens Vej; when the road forks, go left up the hill, then turn left on Zahrtmannsvej, right at the roundabout on Søndre Allé, right again on Arsenalvej, and then follow the signs. (☎56 95 13 40. Breakfast 45kr. Sheets 55kr. Kitchen facilities. Reception daily 8am-noon and 4-5pm. Open mid-June to mid-Aug. Dorms 100kr, nonmembers add 30kr.) **Galløkken Camping ❶,** Strandvejen 4, is centrally located and near the beach. (☎56 95 23 20. **Bikes** 55kr per day. Reception 7:30am-noon and 2-9pm. Open mid-May to Aug. 56kr per person.) Get groceries at **Kvickly,** in the Snellemark Centret opposite the tourist office. (Open mid-June to late Aug. daily 9am-8pm; Sept. to early June M-F 9am-8pm, Sa 8am-5pm, Su 10am-4pm.)

SANDVIG AND ALLINGE. On the tip of the spectacular northern coast, the white-sand and rock beaches in these little towns attract bikers and bathers. A few kilometers from central Allinge down Hammershusvej, **Hammershus** is northern Europe's largest castle ruin. **Østerlars Rundkirke** is the largest of the island's four uniquely fortified round churches. Take bus #3 or 9 to Østerlars. The **Nordbornholms Turistbureau,** Kirkeg. 4, is in Allinge. (☎56 48 00 01. Open mid-June to mid-Aug. M-F 10am-5pm, Sa 10am-3pm; mid-Aug. to mid-June 10am-5pm, Sa 10am-noon.) Rent **bikes** at the **Sandvig Cykeludlejning,** Strandvejen 121. (☎56 48 00 60. 55kr per day. Open June-Aug. M-F 9am-4pm, Sa 9am-2pm, Su 10am-1pm.) Just outside Sandvig is the lakeside **Sandvig Vandrerhjem (HI) ❸,** Hammershusvej 94. (☎56 48 03 62. Breakfast 45kr. Sheets 60kr. Reception daily 9-10am and 4-6pm. Open Apr.-Oct. Dorms 100kr; singles 250kr; doubles 350kr.) **Hotel Nordland ❺,** Strandpromenaden 5, in Sandvig, overlooks the harbor and is within walking distance of the beach. (☎56 48 03 01; www.hotel-nordland.dk. Open Apr.-Oct. Doubles 600-720kr.) For longer stays, look into renting one of the numerous flats available in the town. **Sandvig Familie Camping ❶,** Sandlinien 5, has sites on the sea. (☎56 48 04 47. **Bikes** 50kr per day, 200kr per week. Reception daily 8am-11pm. Open Apr.-Oct. 50kr per person, 15kr per tent.)

FUNEN (FYN)

Situated between Zealand to the east and the Jutland Peninsula to the west, the island of Funen is Denmark's garden. This remote breadbasket is no longer isolated from the rest of Denmark—a bridge and tunnel now connect it to Zealand. Pick up maps of the bike paths covering the island at Funen tourist offices (75kr).

ODENSE

Though most tourists are drawn by the legacy of Hans Christian Andersen and his fairytales, modern Odense (OH-n-sa) has a network of lively pedestrian streets and a noteworthy venue for contemporary art and photography. The town can easily be covered on foot. At **H. C. Andersens Hus,** Hans Jensens Stræde 37-45, you can learn about the author's eccentricities and see free performances of his work. From the tourist office, walk right on Vesterg., then turn left on Torveg. and right on Hans Jensens Str. (☎66 14 88 14. Performances June 19-July 30 11am, 1, 3pm. Museum open mid-June to Aug. daily 9am-7pm; Sept. to mid-June Tu-Su 10am-4pm. 35kr.) A few scraps of Andersen's own ugly-duckling childhood are on display at **H. C. Andersens Barndomshjem** (Childhood Home), Munkemøllestr. 3-5. (☎66 14 88 14. Open mid-June to Aug. daily 10am-4pm; Sept. to mid-June Tu-Su 11am-3pm. 10kr.) At the **Carl Nielsen Museum,** Claus Bergs Gade 11, near the main H. C. Andersens Hus, don headphones and listen to the work of another great Dane.

(☎66 14 88 14. Open Jan.-Aug. Tu-Su noon-4pm; Sept.-Dec. Th-F 4-8pm, Su noon-4pm. 15kr.) Walk back to the tourist office and all the way down Vesterg. to the outstanding **Brandts Klædefabrik,** Brandts Passage 37 and 43, a former cloth mill that houses the **Museum of Photographic Art,** the **Danish Press/Graphic Arts Museum,** and a **contemporary art** gallery with changing exhibitions. (☎66 13 78 97. All open July-Aug. daily 10am-5pm; Sept.-June Tu-Su 10am-5pm. 25-30kr each, joint ticket 50kr.) The **Fyns Kunstmuseum** (Funen Art Gallery), Jernbaneg. 13, features Danish art. (☎66 14 88 14, ext. 4601. Open Tu-Su 10am-4pm. 25kr.)

Trains arrive from Copenhagen via Fredericia (2¼hr.) and from Svendborg via Kværndrup (1¼hr.). **Buses** depart from behind the train station. The **tourist office,** on Rådhuspladsen, books rooms for a 35kr fee and sells the **Odense Adventure Pass,** good for admission to museums, discounts on plays, and unlimited public transport (24hr. 100kr; 48hr. 140kr). From the train station, take Nørreg., which becomes Asylg., and turn left at the end on Vesterg.; it's on the right. (☎66 12 75 20; www.visitodense.com. Open June 15-Aug. M-F 9:30am-7pm, Sa 10am-5pm, Su 10am-4pm; Sept.-June 14 M-F 9:30am-4:30pm, Sa 10am-1pm.) The library in the station has free **Internet.** (Open Apr.-Sept. M-Th 10am-7pm, F 10am-4pm, Sa 10am-2pm; Oct.-Mar. M-Th 10am-7pm, Sa-Su 10am-4pm.) Rent **bikes** across the street at **Rolsted Cykler.** (85kr per day, 300kr deposit. Open M-Th 10am-5:30pm, F 10am-7pm, Sa 10am-2pm.) The brand-new **Danhostel Odense City (HI)** ❹ is attached to the station. (☎63 11 04 25. Internet access. Sheets 50kr. Laundry 40kr. Reception daily 8am-noon and 4-8pm. Call ahead. Dorms 145kr; singles 405kr; doubles 490kr; triples 535kr. Nonmembers add 30kr.) To camp next to the Fruens Boge park at **DCU Camping** ❷, Odensevej 102, take bus #41 or 81. (☎66 11 47 02. Pool. Reception daily 7am-10pm. Open late Mar. to Sept. 58kr per person, 20kr per tent.) Get groceries at **Aktiv Super,** at Nørreg. and Skulkenborgg. (Open M-F 9am-7pm, Sa 9am-4pm.)

DAYTRIP FROM ODENSE: KVÆRNDRUP. Just 30min. south of Odense on the Svendborg rail line is the town of **Kværndrup,** home to **Egeskov Slot,** a stunning 16th-century castle that appears to float on the surrounding lake but is actually supported by 12,000 oak pilings. Spend at least two hours in the magnificent Renaissance interior and the equally splendid grounds, which include a large bamboo labyrinth as well as a car and motorcycle museum. On summer Sundays at 5pm, classical concerts resound in the **Knight Hall.** (Castle open July daily 10am-7pm; Apr.-June and Aug.-Sept. 10am-5pm. Grounds open July daily 10am-8pm; June and Aug. 10am-6pm; Apr.-May and Sept. 10am-5pm. Grounds, maze, and museums 75kr, with castle 130kr. Ticket window closes 1hr. before castle.) Take the Svendborg-bound train to Kværndrup; from the station, go right and continue to Bøjdenvej, the main road. Wait for bus #920 (every hr., 18kr), or turn right and walk 2km through wheat fields to the castle. The **tourist office,** Egeskovg. 1, is up the street from the castle ticket window and books rooms for a 35kr fee. (☎62 27 10 46. Open July daily noon-8pm; June and Aug. noon-6pm; Sept. and Apr.-May noon-5pm.)

SVENDBORG AND TÅSINGE

On Funen's south coast, an hour from Odense by train, Svendborg is a beautiful harbor town and a departure point for ferries to the south Funen islands. On the adjacent island Tåsinge, the regal 17th-century estate of **Valdemars Slot,** built by Christian IV for his son, holds a yachting museum, Scandinavia's largest hunting museum, a toy museum, and a beach. (☎62 22 61 06. Open May-Aug. daily 10am-5pm; Sept. Tu-Su 10am-5pm; Apr. and Oct. Sa-Su 10am-5pm. Castle 55kr, castle and all museums 105kr.) Cruise there on the antique passenger steamer **M/S Helge,** which leaves from Jensens Mole, behind the Svendborg train station (55min., May-Aug. 5 per day, round-trip 65kr).

Ferries from Ærø (see below) arrive behind the train station. The **tourist office,** on the Centrum Pladsen, books ferries and accommodations. From the train station, go left on Jernbaneg., then right on Brog., which becomes Gerritsg., and right on Kyseborgstr.; it's in the plaza on the right. (☎62 21 09 80. Open late June to Aug. M-F 9:30am-6pm, Sa 9:30am-3pm; Sept. to late June M-F 9:30am-5pm, Sa 9:30am-1pm.) To get from the station to the **HI youth hostel ❸,** Vesterg. 45, a five-star on the Danhostel scale, turn left on Jernbaneg. and walk with the coast to your left, then go right onto Valdemarsg., which becomes Vesterg. (☎62 21 66 99; dk@danhostel-svenborg.dk. Bikes 50kr per day. Kitchen. Breakfast 45kr. Sheets 50kr. Laundry 30kr. Reception M-F 8am-6pm, Su 8am-noon and 4-6pm. Dorms 100kr; singles and doubles 330kr; overflow mattresses 50kr. Nonmembers add 30kr.) To get to **Carlsberg Camping ❶,** Sundbrovej 19, across the sound on the top of Tåsinge, take bus #800, 801, or 910 from the ferry terminal to Bregninge Tåsinge and walk up the street. (☎62 22 53 84; www.carlsbergcamping.dk. Reception daily 8am-10pm. Open Apr.-Sept. 57kr per person.) **Jette's Diner ❷,** Kullingg. 1, between the train station and the docks, puts a Danish spin on diner fare. (☎62 22 16 97. Open daily noon-9:30pm.) **Postal code :** 5700.

ÆRØ

The wheat fields, harbors, and hamlets of Ærø (EH-ruh), a small island off the south coast of Funen, quietly preserve an earlier era in Danish history. Cows, rather than real estate developers, lay claim to the beautiful land, and bikes are the ideal way to explore the three towns, Ærøskøbing, Marstal, and Søby.

TRANSPORTATION. Several **trains** from Odense to Svendborg are timed to meet the **ferry** (☎62 52 40 00) to Ærøskøbing (1¼hr.; 6 per day; one-way 77kr, round-trip 128kr; buy tickets on board). From Mommark, on Jutland, **Ærø-Als** (☎62 58 17 17) sails to Søby (1hr.; 2-5 per day, Oct.-Mar. Sa-Su only; 80kr), on Ærø's northwestern shore. **Bus** #990 travels between Ærøskøbing, Marstal, and Søby (16kr).

ÆRØSKØBING. Due to economic stagnation followed by conservation efforts, the town of Ærøskøbing appears today almost as it did 200 years ago. Rosebushes and half-timbered houses attract tourists from Sweden and Germany as well as vacationing Danes. The **tourist office,** Vesterg. 1, opposite the ferry landing, arranges rooms (170kr) in private homes. (☎62 52 13 00; www.aeroe-turistbureau.dk. Open mid-June to Aug. M-F 9am-5pm, Sa 9am-2pm, Su 9:30am-12:30pm; Sept. to mid-June M-F 9am-4pm, Sa 9:30am-12:30pm.) To get from the landing to the **HI youth hostel ❸,** Smedevejen 15, turn left on Smedeg., which becomes Nørreg., Østerg., and finally Smedevejen. The hostel's tree-lined lane leads to a small beach. (☎62 52 10 44. Breakfast 40kr. Sheets 35kr. Reception daily 8am-noon and 4-8pm. Check-in by 5pm or call ahead. Reserve far in advance. Open Apr. to mid-Oct. Dorms 100kr; nonmembers 130kr.) **Ærøskøbing Camping ❶,** Sygehusvejen 40b, is 10min. to the right along Sygehusvejen, off Vestre Allé as you leave the ferry. (☎62 52 18 54. Reception daily 8am-1pm and 3-9pm. Open May-Sept. 52kr per person, 20kr per tent.) To get to **Emerko supermarket,** Statene 3, walk uphill from the ferry on Vesterg., then turn right on Sluttergyden, which becomes Statene. (Open M-Th 9am-5pm, F 9am-6pm, Sa 9am-4pm, Su 10am-4pm.) **Postal Code:** 5970.

JUTLAND (JYLLAND)

The Jutland peninsula, homeland of the Jutes who joined the Anglos and Saxons in the conquest of England, is Denmark's largest landmass. Beaches and campgrounds mark the area as prime summer vacation territory, while rolling hills, marshland, and sparse forests add color and variety.

FERRIES TO ENGLAND, NORWAY, AND SWEDEN

From **Esbjerg** (see p. 295), on Jutland's west coast, **DFDF** sails to Harwich, England (18hr., 3-4 per week). From **Frederikshavn** (see p. 293), on the northern tip of Jutland, **Stena Line** ferries (☎96 20 02 00; www.stenaline.com) leave for Gothenburg, Sweden (2-3¼hr.; price varies, 50% off with Scanrail) and Oslo, Norway (8½hr.; 180kr, with Scanrail 90kr). **Color Line** (☎99 56 19 77; www.colorline.com) sails to Larvik, Norway (6¼hr.; 160-340kr, students and seniors 50% off). Color Line boats also go from Hirtshals, on the northern tip of Jutland, to Oslo (8-8½hr., 160-350kr) and Kristiansand, Norway (2½-4½hr., 160-350kr).

ÅRHUS

Århus (ORE-hoos), Denmark's second-largest city, bills itself as "the world's smallest big city." Studded with impressive museums and architectural gems, the city is a visual treat. Many travelers find this laid-back student and cultural center manageably sized.

TRANSPORTATION AND PRACTICAL INFORMATION. Trains run to Århus from: Aalborg (1¾hr.); Copenhagen (3hr.); Fredericia (2hr.); and Frederikshavn (2½hr.). Trains runs every 1-2hr. from Frederikshavn to Århus. Most public **buses** leave from the train station or from outside the tourist office. **Tourist passes** (see below) include unlimited bus transportation. The tourist office, in the city hall, books private rooms (125-175kr; no fee) and sells the Århus Pass, which includes unlimited public transit and admission to most museums and sights (1-day 88kr, 2-day 110kr). If you're not going to many museums, consider instead the **24hr. Tourist Ticket** (50kr), which provides unlimited bus transportation. To get to the office, exit the train station and go left across Banegardspladsen, then take the first right on Park Allé. (☎89 40 67 00; www.visitaarhus.com. Open late June to early Sept. M-F 9:30am-6pm, Sa 9:30am-5pm, Su 9:30am-1pm; May to late June M-F 9:30am-5pm, Sa 10am-1pm; early Sept. to Apr. M-F 9:30am-4:30pm, Sa 10am-1pm.) The main **library,** whose entrance is on Vesterg. 55 in Mølleparken, has free **Internet** access. From the center, walk away from the entrance to the cathedral on Store Torv, which becomes Vesterg. (Open May-Aug. M-Th 10am-7pm, F 10am-6pm, Sa 10am-2pm; Sept.-Apr. M 10am-10pm, Tu-Th 10am-8pm, F 10am-6pm, Sa 10am-3pm.) After hours, try **Net House,** Norre Allé 66a, in the city center. (☎87 30 00 96. Open daily noon-midnight. 20kr per hr.) The **post office,** Banegardspladsen 1A, is right next to the main entrance to the train station. (☎89 35 80 00. Open M-F 9:30am-6pm, Sa 10am-1pm.) **Postal Code:** 8000.

DENMARK

ACCOMMODATIONS AND FOOD. Popular with backpackers, **Århus City Sleep-In ❸**, Havneg. 20, is 10min. from the train station and in the middle of the city's nightlife. From the train station, follow Ryesg. (off of Banegardspladsen), which becomes Sønderg., all the way to the canal. Take the steps or elevator down to Aboulevarden, cross the canal, and turn right; at the end of the canal, turn left on Mindebrog., then left again on Havneg. (☎86 19 20 55; www.citysleep-in.dk. Kitchen. Internet. Bikes 50kr per day; deposit 200kr. Breakfast 35kr. Sheets 35kr; deposit 30kr. Laundry 25kr. Key deposit 50kr. Reception 24hr. Check-out noon.

Dorms 100kr; doubles 240-280kr.) **Hotel Guldsmeden ❺,** Guldsmedg. 40, is a small hotel with comfortable rooms in the center of town. The annex in the back has the cheapest rooms. From the tourist office, continue along Park Allé, which becomes Immervad, and veer left onto Guldsmedg. at the intersection of Vesterg. (☎86 13 45 50; www.hotelguldmeden.dk. Breakfast 60kr. Reception daily 7am-midnight. Singles 500-725kr; doubles 700-875kr.) **Pavillonen (HI) ❷,** Marienlundsvej 10, is in the Risskov forest, 3km north of the city center and 5min. from the beach. Take bus #1, 6, 9, 16, or 56 to Marienlund, then walk 300m into the park. (☎86 16 72 98; www.hostel-aarhus.dk. Breakfast 45kr. Sheets 30kr. Laundry. Reception daily 7:30-10am and 4-11pm. Dorms 95kr, nonmembers add 30kr; singles, doubles, and triples 285-400kr.) **Blommehavenn Camping ❶,** Ørneredevej 35, in the Marselisborg forest south of the city, is near the beach and the royal family's summer residence. In summer, take bus #19 from the station to the grounds; off-season, take bus #6 to Hørhavevej. (☎86 27 02 07; info@blommehaven.dk. Reception daily 7:30am-10pm. Open Apr.-Sept. 55kr per person.) The popular **Den Grønne Hjørne ❸,** Frederiksg. 60, has an all-you-can-eat Danish buffet (lunch 59kr, dinner 99kr). From the tourist office, turn left on Radhuspl. and then take an immediate right. (☎86 13 52 47. Open daily 11am-10pm.) Get groceries at **Fakta,** Østerg. 8-12. (Open M-F 9am-7pm, Sa 9am-4pm.)

SIGHTS AND ENTERTAINMENT. In the town center, the 13th-century **Århus Domkirke** (cathedral) dominates Bispetorv and the pedestrian streets. (☎86 12 38 45. Open May-Sept. M-Sa 9:30am-4pm; Oct.-Apr. 10am-3pm. Free.) Next door, the **Women's Museum,** Domkirkeplads 5, has thoughtful exhibits on women throughout time. (☎86 13 61 44; www.kvindemuseet.dk. Open June-Aug. daily 10am-5pm; Sept.-May Tu-Su 10am-4pm. 30kr.) Just west of the town center lies **Den Gamle By,** Viborgvej 2, an open-air museum displaying a collection of Danish buildings from the Renaissance through the 20th century. From the center, take bus #3, 14, 25, or 55. (☎86 12 31 88. Open June-Aug. daily 9am-6pm; Apr.-May and Sept.-Oct. 10am-5pm; Feb.-Mar. and Nov.-Dec. 10am-4pm; Jan. 11am-3pm. Apr.-Dec. 70kr; Jan.-Mar. 45kr. Grounds free after hours.) The **Århus Kunstmuseum,** on Vennelystparken, has a fine collection of Danish Golden Age paintings. (☎86 13 52 55. Open Tu-Su 10am-5pm, W until 8pm. 40kr, students 30kr.) Just outside town is the spectacular **Moesgård Museum of Prehistory,** Moesgård Allé 20, which chronicles Århus's history from 4000 BC through the Viking age. Two millennia ago, the casualties of infighting were entombed in a nearby bog and mummified by its acidity. Today the **Grauballe Man,** the only perfectly preserved bog person, is on display at the museum. Take bus #6 from the train station to the end. (Open Apr.-Sept. daily 10am-5pm; Oct.-Mar. Tu-Su 10am-4pm. 35kr, students 25kr.) The **Prehistoric Trail** is a beautiful walk that leads from behind the museum to a sandy **beach** (3km). In summer, bus #19 (last bus 10:18pm) returns from the beach to the Århus station. The exquisite rose garden of **Marselisborg Slot,** Kongevejen 100, Queen Margarethe II's summer getaway, is open to the public. From the train station, take bus #1, 18, or 19. (Palace and rose gardens closed in July and whenever the Queen is in residence. Changing of the guard daily at noon when the Queen is in residence.)

Åboulevarden, lined with trendy cafes and bars, is the heart of the town. Århus hosts an acclaimed **jazz festival** in late July (www.jazzfest.dk). The **Århus Festuge** (☎89 31 82 70; www.aarhusfestuge.dk), from late August to early September, is a rollicking celebration of theater, dance, and music. To get to **Tivoli Friheden,** Skovbrynet 1, a smaller version of Tivoli, take bus #1, 4, 6, 8, 18, or 19. (☎86 14 73 00. Open late June to mid-Aug. daily 1-11pm; early to mid-June F-Sa 2-11pm, Su-Th 1-10pm; late Apr.-May F-Sa 2-10pm, Su-M 1-9pm. 35kr.) Chill at the jazz club **Bent J,** Nørre Allé 66 (☎86 12 04 92), on every Monday evening and occasional other weekday evenings. The **Pan Club,** Jægergårdsg. 42, has a cafe, bar, and mainly gay and lesbian dance club. (☎86 13 43 80. Cafe open Tu-Th 7pm-6am, F-Sa 8pm-5am. Club cover F-Sa 50kr. Open Th-Sa 11pm-5am.)

BILLUND

Billund is renowned as the home of **Legoland**, an amusement park built constructed out of 40 million Lego pieces. "Lego" is an abbreviation of *leg godt* (have fun playing). Don't skip the impressive indoor exhibitions. To get there, take the train from Århus to **Vejle** (45min., every hr.), then bus #912 or 244 (dir.: Grindsted). (☎75 33 13 33; www.legoland.dk. Open July to mid-Aug. daily 10am-9pm; June and late Aug. daily 10am-8pm; Apr.-May and Sept.-Oct. M-F 10am-6pm, Sa-Su 10am-8pm. Rides close 2hr. before park. 1 day 160kr, under 13 140kr; 2 days 220kr.) **Billund airport** (BLL) is the terminus for many continental flights to Denmark (see p. 272). The Billund **tourist office,** by the entrance to Legoland, has information on accommodations and bus schedules. (☎76 50 00 55; www.billund.dk. Same hours as Legoland.) Bus #244 goes to the site shared by the high-quality **Billund Vandrerhjem (HI) ❸** and **Billund Camping ❶,** Ellehammers Allé 2; get off at Legoland, go back the way the bus came, and follow the footpath toward the hostel signs. In summer, book in advance. (Hostel ☎75 33 2777; www.sima.dk/billund. Kitchen. Breakfast 45kr. Sheets 50kr. Reception daily 8am-9pm. Dorms 100kr; singles and doubles 380-400kr. Camping ☎75 33 15 21; www.fdm.dk. 61kr per person, 15kr per tent.) **Postal Code:** 7190.

AALBORG

Aalborg (OLE-borg) is the site of the earliest known Viking settlement. **Lindholm Høje,** Vendilavej 11, has 700 Viking graves and a museum of Viking life; take bus #6 or 25 (13kr) from outside the tourist office. (☎96 31 04 28. Site open daily dawn-dusk. Museum open Apr. to mid-Oct. daily 10am-5pm; mid-Oct. to mid-Mar. Tu and Su 10am-4pm. 30kr.) The frescoed 15th-century **Monastery of the Holy Ghost,** on C.W. Obelsplads, is Denmark's oldest social institution. From the tourist office, cross the street and head down Adelg.; the monastery is on the right. (English tours late June to mid-Aug. Tu and Th-F 1:30pm. 40kr.) The **Budolfi Church,** on Alg., has a brilliantly colored interior. From the tourist office, turn left onto Østeråg. and right on Alg. (Open May-Sept. M-F 9am-4pm, Sa 9am-2pm; Oct.-Apr. M-F 9am-3pm, Sa 9am-noon.) At the corner of Alg. and Molleg., in front of the Sallig department store, an elevator goes down to the medieval ruins of the **Franciscan Friary.** (Open in summer daily 10am-5pm, in winter Tu-Su 10am-5pm. 20kr.) For serious rollercoasters, visit **Tivoliland,** on Karolinelundsvej. From the tourist office, turn right on Østeråg., right on Nytorv, and right on Kjellerupsg. (Open Apr.-Sept. daily noon-8pm. Entrance 40kr, rides 10-40kr.)

Trains arrive from Århus (1¾hr.) and Copenhagen. From the station, cross J.F.K. Plads and turn left on Boulevarden, which becomes Østeråg., to find the **tourist office,** Østeråg. 8. (☎98 12 60 22; www.visitaalborg.com. Open July M-F 9am-5:30pm, Sa 10am-4pm; late June and Aug. M-F 9am-5:30pm, Sa 10am-1pm; Sept. to mid-June M-F 9am-4:30pm, Sa 10am-1pm.) The public library has free **Internet** access. (☎99 31 44 00. Open June-Aug. M-F 10am-8pm, Sa 10am-2pm; Sept.-May M-F 10am-8pm, Sa 10am-3pm.) After hours, try **Net City,** Nytorv 13a. From the tourist office, turn right on Østeråg. and right again on Nytorv. (Open M-Th noon-midnight, F-Sa 11am-8am, Su 11am-midnight. 12kr per hour.) **Aalborg Vandrerhjem and Camping (HI) ❷,** Skydebanevej 50, has cabins with modern facilities next to a fjord. Take bus #2, 8, or 9 (dir.: Fjordparken) to the very end. (☎98 11 60 44. Laundry. Reception daily mid-June to mid-Aug. 7:30am-11pm; mid-Jan. to mid-June and mid-Aug. to mid-Dec. 8am-noon and 4-9pm. Dorms 85-100kr; singles 250-398kr; doubles 325-398kr. Camping 49kr.) Bars and restaurants line **Jomfru Ane Gade;** from the tourist office, turn right on Østeråg. and then left on Bispensg. Jomfru Ane G. will be on the right. **Postal code:** 9000.

VIBORG

Sights cluster around the cobblestoned center of this well-preserved provincial town. The mid-19th-century **Viborg Cathedral,** Sct. Mogensg. 4, contains enormous chalk reliefs depicting Bible scenes. (Open June-Aug. M-Sa 10am-5pm, Su noon-5pm; Apr.-May and Sept. M-Sa 11am-4pm, Su noon-4pm; Oct.-Mar. M-Sa 11am-3pm, Su noon-3pm.) Next door, the **Skovgaard Museum,** Domkirkestr. 2-4, houses an impressive collection of paintings by Danish Golden Age artists. (Open May-Sept. daily 10am-12:30pm and 1:30-5pm; Oct.-Apr. 1:30-5pm. 20kr.) The **Stifts Museum,** Hjultorvet 9, presents the history of the town and region. (Open June-Aug. daily 11am-5pm; Sept.-May Tu-F 2-5pm, Sa-Su 11am-5pm. 20kr.) Just outside of Viborg lie the limestone mines and subterranean rivers of **Monsted Kalkgruber,** Kalkvaerksvej 8. Though there is no direct public transportation, the visit is well worth the trek. Take the train (dir.: Stuer) to nearby Stoholm; from the station, turn right into town and continue straight about 3km, then turn left on Kalkvaerksvej and walk another 1km. Or, take bus #28 (every 1-2hr.) from Viborg to Monsted and follow the signs for 1.5km. (Open daily mid-May to Oct. 10am-5pm. 40kr.)

Viborg lies on the Århus-Struer railway line; **trains** run to Århus (1½hr., every hr.). To get to the **tourist office,** Nytorv 9, from the station, go straight across the roundabout and onto Jernebaneg., turn right onto Sct. Mathiasg., cross the plaza (Hjultorvet), and go left; it's in the main square. (☎86 61 16 66. Open mid-June to Aug. M-F 9am-5pm, Sa 9am-3pm; mid-May to mid-June M-F 9am-5pm, Sa 9:30am-12:30pm; Sept. to mid-May M-F 9am-4pm, Sa 9:30am-12:30pm.) Alongside a lake lie the **youth hostel (HI)** ❸ and **Viborg So Camping,** Vinkelvej 36. To get to either one, take bus #707 from the station to Vinkelvej and continue walking along the road (10min.). (Hostel ☎86 67 17 81; viborg@danhostel.dk. Kitchen. Breakfast 45kr. Laundry. Reception daily 7:30am-noon and 2-10pm. Dorms 100kr. Camping ☎86 67 13 11; viborg@dcu.dk. Same reception hours as hostel.) Viborg's charm is best experienced sitting outside and having a drink with the locals in the **Hjultorvet** area, in front of the Stifts Museum. For groceries, stop by the **Netto** on Vesterbrog. (☎43 56 88 11. Open M-F 9am-8pm, Sa 8am-5pm.)

FREDERIKSHAVN

Despite noble efforts to showcase its endearing streets and hospitality, Frederikshavn is best known for its **ferry** links (see p. 57). The **tourist office,** Skandia Torv 1, inside the Stena Line terminal south of the rail station, reserves rooms (125kr fee). (☎98 42 32 66; www.frederikshavn.dk. Open mid-June to mid-Aug. M-Sa 8:30am-7pm, Su 8:30am-5pm; mid-Aug. to mid-June M-Sa 9am-4pm.) From the tourist office, walk left 10min. to reach the bus and train stations. To get from the station to the **youth hostel (HI)** ❶, Buhlsvej 6, walk right on Skipperg. for 10min., then turn left onto Norreg., and follow the signs. (☎98 42 14 75; www.danhostel.dk/frederikshavn. Reception in summer daily 8am-noon and 4-9pm. Always call ahead. Open Feb.-Dec. Dorms 70-90kr; singles 150-200kr; doubles 210-270kr.) Take bus #4 from the station to Sinddallundvej/Campingpl. to get to **Nordstrand Camping** ❸, Apholmenvej 40. (☎98 42 93 50. Open Apr. to mid-Oct. 60kr per person, 40kr per tent; off-season 47kr/28kr.) **Postal code:** 9900.

SKAGEN

Perched on Denmark's northernmost tip, sunny Skagen (SKAY-en) is a beautiful summer retreat amid long stretches of sea and white sand dunes. The houses are all painted in deep "Skagen yellow" and the roofs are covered in red tiles with white edges—supposedly decorated to welcome local fisherman home from sea. The powerful currents of the North and Baltic Seas colliding is visible at **Grenen.** Stand with one foot in each ocean, but don't try to swim in these dangerous waters; every year people are carried out to sea. To get to Grenen, take bus #99 or 79 from the Skagen station to Gammel (11kr) or walk 3km down Fyrvej; turn left out of the train station and bear left when the road forks. In summer, you can climb the **lighthouse** tower for an amazing view of the rough seas at Grenen (5kr). The spectacular **Råberg Mile** sand dunes, formed by a 16th-century storm, migrate 15m east each year. Take bus #79 or the train from Skagen to Hulsig, then walk along Kandestedvej. From here, you can swim along 60km of **beaches,** where the endless summer light attracted Denmark's most famous late-19th-century painters. Their works are displayed in the wonderful **Skagen Museum,** Brøndumsvej 4. (☎98 44 64 44. Open June-Aug. daily 10am-6pm; May and Sept. 10am-5pm; Apr. and Oct. Tu-Su 11am-4pm; Nov.-Mar. W-F 1-4pm, Sa 11am-4pm, Su 11am-3pm. 50kr.) **Michael og Anna Archers Hus,** Markvej 2-4, is filled with the artists' works and set up as it was when they lived there. (☎98 44 30 09. Open mid-June to mid-Aug. daily 10am-6pm; May to mid-June and mid-Aug. to Sept. 10am-5pm; Apr. and Oct. 11am-3pm; Nov.-Mar. Sa-Su 11am-3pm. 40kr.) Equally impressive is **Holger Drachmanns Hus,** Hans Baghsvej 21. (☎98 44 51 88. Open July daily 10am-5pm; June and Aug. to mid-Sept. 11am-3pm; mid-Sept. to mid-Oct. and May Sa-Su 11am-3pm. 25kr). Skagen has a large annual **Dixieland music festival** in late June (up to 150kr); contact the tourist office for more info.

Nordjyllands Trafikselskab (☎98 44 21 33) runs **buses** and **trains** from Frederikshavn to Skagen (1hr.; 39kr, with ScanRail 20kr). Biking is the perfect way to see Skagen, including Grenen; rent **bikes** at **Skagen CykelUdlejning,** Banegardspladsen, next to the bus station. (☎98 44 10 70. 70kr per day.) The **tourist office** is in the train station. (☎98 44 13 77; www.skagen.dk. Open June-Aug. M-Sa 9am-7pm, Su 10am-2pm; Sept.-May reduced hours.) The only **Internet** access in town is free at the Skagen library, Sct. Laurentii Vej 23, across from the train station. (Open M and Th 10am-6pm; Tu, W, F 1-6pm; Sa 10am-1pm.) The **Skagen Ny Vandrerhjem ❸,** Rolighedsvej 2, has a friendly, helpful staff and is wildly popular among vacationing Danish families. From the station, turn right on Chr. X's Vej, which becomes Frederikshavnvej, then left on Rolighedsvej. (☎98 44 22 00; www.danhostel-nord.dk/skagen. Breakfast 45kr. Kitchen. Reception daily 9am-noon and 4-6pm. Open Mar.-Nov. Dorms 100kr; singles 250-400kr; doubles 300-500kr.) **Campgrounds** abound in the area, but most are open only early May to early September. Bus #79 passes by several sites. Try **Grenen ❶,** Fyrvej 16 (☎98 44 25 46; open May to mid-Sept.; 65kr) to the north, or **Øster Klit ❶,** Flagbakkevej 53 (☎98 44 31 23; open late Mar. to mid-Oct.; 65kr), to the south; both are near the city center and the beach.

FREDERICIA

Known primarily as a major railway junction, Fredericia is characterized by excessive military order, with perfectly straight streets set at right angles that date to the town's beginnings in the 17th century. The triangular center is bordered by coastlines on two sides and cannon-strewn **ramparts** on the third. Built between 1650 and 1657 by King Frederik III, the moated ramparts were the sight of the famed Battle of Fredericia in 1849. The most impressive parts lie on Vester Voldg., near the tourist office. For a great view of the ramparts, the city, and its coastlines, climb the **White Water Tower,** across the street from the tourist office. (Open mid-June to mid-Aug. 10am-5pm; May to mid-June and mid-Aug. to Sept. daily 11am-4pm. 10kr.) The **Fredericia Museum,** Jernbaneg. 10, chronicles the history of the town and the ramparts. From the train station, go right and follow Jernbaneg. (☎72 10 69 80. Open mid-June to Aug. daily 11am-4pm; Sept. to mid-June noon-4pm. 20kr.) The **Bunkermuseet,** Norre Voldg., at the end of Bjergeg., is in a World War II air raid shelter. From the tourist office, head right and walk along Norre Voldg. with the ramparts to your left; look closely—the entrance is just a hole in the ground. (☎72 10 69 80. Open mid-June to Aug. W and Sa-Su noon-4pm.)

Fredericia is located on the Esbjerg-Århus rail-line; **trains** arrive from: Århus (1¾hr.); Copenhagen (2hr.); Esbjerg (1hr.); and Hamburg (3hr.). To get to the **tourist office,** Danmarksg. 2A, from the station, go left across the plaza, and then turn right on Vesterbrog; at the roundabout, go right on Danmarksport. (☎75 92 13 77; www.visitfredericia.dk. Open June-Aug. M-F 9am-6pm, Sa 9am-2pm; Sept.-May M-F 10am-5pm, Sa 10am-1pm.) The lakeside **Fredericia Vandrerhjem and Kursuscenter (HI) ❸,** Vestre Ringvej 98, a five-star on the Danhostel scale, is a vacation spot in itself. From the station, go left across the plaza, left on Vejlevej, pass under the bridge, go right on the first road past the lake, and follow the path. (☎75 92 12 87; www.fredericia-danhostel.dk. Breakfast 45kr. Sheets 45kr. Reception daily 8am-noon and 4-9pm. Dorms 100kr; doubles 350-400kr.) To camp by the coast, take bus #6 to **Trelde-Naes Camping ❶,** Trelde Naesvej 297. (☎75 95 71 83; www.trelde.dk. Reception daily 8am-10:30pm. 60kr per person.) **Postal Code:** 7000.

ESBJERG

In a little over 100 years, Esbjerg has grown from a tiny port town to the bustling cultural, industrial, and commercial capital of West Jutland. The **Esbjerg Museum,** Torveg. 45, gives visitors a sense of the drastic changes that took place during this time of growth. The building also houses an exhibition on amber, the "Danish gold." From the tourist office, go right on Torveg. (☎75 12 78 11. Open daily 10am-4pm; Sept.-May closed M. 30kr.) For a glimpse of the latest in contemporary art, cross the square from the tourist office and follow Torvet to the end to reach the mirrored walls of the **Esbjerg Kunstmuseum,** Havneg. 20, designed by Jan and Jorn Utzon. (☎75 13 02 11. Open daily 10am-4pm. 30kr, students 25kr.) Next to the museum stands the city's symbol, a **water tower,** Havneg. 22, built in 1896 during the town's beginnings and modeled on medieval German architecture, with a great harbor view. (Open June to mid-Sept. daily 10am-4pm; Apr.-May and mid-Sept. to Oct. Sa-Su 10am-4pm; Nov.-Mar. by appointment only. 15kr.)

Trains (☎75 12 33 77) run to: Århus (2hr., every 2hr.); Copenhagen (2½hr., every 2hr.); and Fredericia (1hr., every hr.). **Ferries** head to Harwich, England (☎75 13 02 11; see p. 290). The **tourist office,** Skoleg. 33, is in the Old Courthouse in Market Square. From the station, go left on Jernbaneg. and right on Skoleg. (☎75 12 55 99; www.esbjerg.dk. Open in summer M-F 9am-5pm, Sa 9:30am-2:30pm; M-F 9am-5pm, Sa10am-1pm, Sa 9:30am-2:30pm.) The **Esbjerg Vandrerhjem (HI) ❸,** Gl. Vardevej 80, lies outside the city center, but is worth the trip. Take bus #4 from the station. (☎75 12 42 58; esbjerg@danhostel.dk. **Internet** 1kr per min. Breakfast 45kr. Sheets 48kr. Reception daily 8am-noon and 4-7pm. Dorms 100kr; singles 275kr; doubles 300-380kr. Nonmembers add 30kr.) The nearby **Svømmestadion,** Gl. Vardevej 60, Denmark's largest indoor bathing facility, has everything from Turkish baths to a wave pool and children's area. (☎76 11 42 40; www.svdk.dk. Open M-F 8am-9pm; Sa-Su and holidays 8am-7pm. 50kr per day; hostel guests 44kr.) **Postal Code:** 6710.

RIBE

Well aware of their town's historic value, the town government of Ribe forged preservation laws forcing residents to maintain the character of their houses and to live in them year-round. The result is a magnificently preserved medieval town, situated beautifully on the salt plains near Jutland's west coast. Ribe is particularly proud of the arrival of migratory storks who always roost on the roof of the town hall. For a great view of the birds and the surrounding landscape, climb the 248 steps through the clockwork and huge bells of the 12th-century **cathedral** tower._(☎75 42 06 19. Open July to mid-Aug. M-Sa 10am-5:30pm, Su noon-5:30pm; May-June and mid-Aug. to Sept. M-Sa 10am-5pm, Su noon-5pm; Apr. and Oct. M-Sa 11am-6pm, Su noon-4pm; Nov.-Mar. daily 11am-3pm. 12kr.) Next to the **Det Gamle Rådhus** (Old Town

Hall), Von Støckens Plads, a former debtor's prison houses a small museum on medieval torture. (☎76 88 11 22. Open June-Aug. daily 1-3pm; May and Sept. M-F 1-3pm. 15kr.) Follow the **night watchman** on his rounds for an English or Danish tour of town beginning in Torvet, the main square. (35min.; June-Aug. 8 and 10pm; May and Sept. 10pm. Free.) Across from the train station, **Museet Ribes Vikinger,** Odin Plads 1, houses artifacts recovered from an excavation of the town, once an important Viking trading post. (☎76 88 11 22. Open July-Aug. Th-Tu 10am-6pm, W 10am-9pm; Apr.-June and Sept.-Oct. daily 10am-4pm; Nov.-Mar. Tu-Su 10am-4pm. 50kr.) Next door, the **Ribe Kunst Museum,** Sct. Nikolaig. 10, presents Danish paintings from the Golden Age through the present in a house built in the Dutch Renaissance style. (☎75 42 03 62. Open mid-June to Aug. daily 11am-5pm; Sept. to mid-June Tu-Sa 1-4pm, Su 11am-4pm. 30kr, students 20kr.) South of town, the open-air **Ribe Viking-center,** Lustrupvej 4, recreates a Viking town, complete with farm and marketplace. (☎75 41 16 11. Open July-Aug. daily 11am-4:30pm; May-June and Sept. M-F 11am-4pm. 50kr.) Take bus #711 to the **Vadehavscentret** (Wadden Sea Center), Okholmvej 5 in Vestervedsted, which gives tours of the local marshes on the Mandobus (☎75 44 51 07; 50kr). Tours start from the Sea Center and cross to Mandø, an island, at low tide. (☎75 44 61 61. Open Apr.-Oct. daily 10am-5pm; Feb.-Mar. and Nov. 10am-4pm. 45kr. Mandobus runs May-Sept.; times depend on tides. Consult the tourist office. Bus and center 80kr.)

Trains to Ribe run from nearby Bramming (25min., 4-5 per day, 28kr) and Esbjerg (40min., every hr., 46kr). The **tourist office,** Torvet 3, has free maps and arranges accommodations for a 20kr fee. From the train station, walk down Dagmarsg. to the left of the Viking museum; it's on the right in the main square. (☎75 42 15 030; www.ribe.dk. Open July-Aug. M-F 9:30am-5:30pm, Sa 10am-5pm, Su 10am-2pm; Apr.-June and Sept.-Oct. M-F 9am-5pm, Sa 10am-1pm; Nov.-Mar. M-F 9am-4:30pm, Sa 10am-1pm.) Access the **Internet** at **Gamer's Gateway,** Saltg. 20. (☎76 88 03 37. 25kr per hr. Open daily noon-midnight.) The centrally located **Ribe Vandrerhjem (HI) ❸,** Sct. Pedersg. 16, offers **bike** rentals (50kr per day) and a gorgeous view of the flatlands. From the station, cross the Viking Museum parking lot, bear right, walk down Sct. Nicolajg. to the end, then turn right on Saltg. and immediately left on Sct. Petersg. (☎75 42 06 20. Breakfast 45kr. Sheets 38kr. Reception daily 8am-noon and 4-8pm; extended hours May-Sept. Open Feb.-Nov. Dorms 100kr; singles 250kr; doubles 295kr.) **Ribe Camping ❶,** Farupvej 2, is 1.5km from the town center. From the station, turn to face the Vikings Museum and go right on Rosen Allé until it becomes Norremarksvej. After the traffic light, go left along the bike path (Gronnestien) and cross onto Farupvej; it's on the second street on the right. Or, take bus #715 (every 1½hr.) from the station to Gredstedbro. (☎75 41 07 77. 50kr per person; 2-person cabins 175kr.) **Seminarievej** is home to a cluster of **supermarkets. Fakta** and **Netto** are budget grocery stores, while **Kvickly** has a much larger selection. From the hostel, follow Sct. Peders. to Saltg., turn left, and then right onto Seminarievej. (Most open M-F 9am to 6 or 7pm, Sa until 3 or 5pm.) Restaurants cluster around the Cathedral.

FRANCE

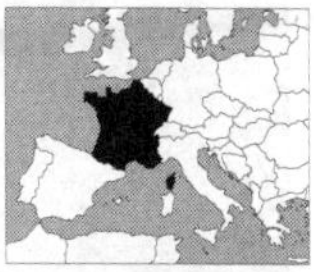

Given the vast cultural and geographic diversity of their homeland, the French have long celebrated the senses like no one else: the taste of the fruit of the vineyards of Bordeaux, the feel of hot Riviera sand underfoot, and the crisp smell of Alpine air all combine for an exhilarating experience. Superimposed on this reckless ride of sensation is the rationalism that has dominated French intellectual life for over 400 years. Sensuality and reason meet in neighborhood brasseries and cafes, where lively conversation is enjoyed no less than the *plat du jour*. While France no longer single-handedly controls the course of world events, it has secured a spot as one of the most influential forces in the course of Western history. As Napoleon once quipped, "'Impossible?' The word is not French."

SYMBOL	❶	❷	❸	❹	❺
ACCOMMODATIONS	under €15	€16-25	€26-35	€36-55	over €55
FOOD	under €5	€6-10	€11-15	€16-25	over €25

For France, prices are indicated in food and accommodations listings using the system of icons and price ranges above. Prices for accommodations are based on the lowest cost for one person, excluding special deals or discounts. For restaurants, prices are based on the average entree price.

SUGGESTED ITINERARIES

THREE DAYS Don't even think of leaving **Paris,** the City of Light (p. 311). Explore the shops and cafes of the **Latin Quarter,** then cross the **Seine** to reach **Ile de la Cité** to admire **Sainte Chapelle.** Visit the wacky **Centre National d'Art et de Culture Georges Pompidou** before seeing a hotspot of 1789, the **Bastille.** Then swing through **Marais** for food and fun. The next day, stroll down the **Champs-Elysées,** starting at the **Arc de Triomphe,** meander through the **Jardin des Tuileries,** and over the Seine to the **Musée d'Orsay.** Peruse part of the **Louvre** the next morning, then head out for an afternoon at **Versailles.**

ONE WEEK After three days in **Paris,** chug to **Tours** (2 days; p. 357) and explore the **castles** of the **Loire Valley** (1 day; p. 355). Bike or bus to **Chenonceau** (1 day; p. 358), **Chambord** (p. 356), and **Saumur** (1 day; p. 358). Then make your way to the waters of **La Rochelle** (2 days; p. 359), via **Poitiers** (1 day; p. 360).

BEST OF FRANCE, THREE WEEKS Whirl through the **Loire Valley** (3 days), before taking the train to the wine country of **Bordeaux** (2 days; p. 362). Check out **Toulouse** (2 days; p. 366) before sailing through **Avignon** (p. 371), **Aix-en-Provence** (p. 373), and **Nîmes** (p. 370) in sunny **Provence** (3 days; p. 370). Let loose your wild side in **Marseilles** and **Nice** (3 days; p. 381) on the **French Riviera** (p. 378). Show off your tan in the **Alps** (p. 392): scale the peaks near **Chamonix** (p. 393) and **Annecy** (2 days; p. 394). Party in **Lyon** (2 days; p. 395); and eat your fill in **Dijon** (1 day; p. 402). Return to Paris via the **Champagne** region (p. 408), visiting the *caves* of **Reims** (p. 408) and **Troyes** (2 days; p. 409).

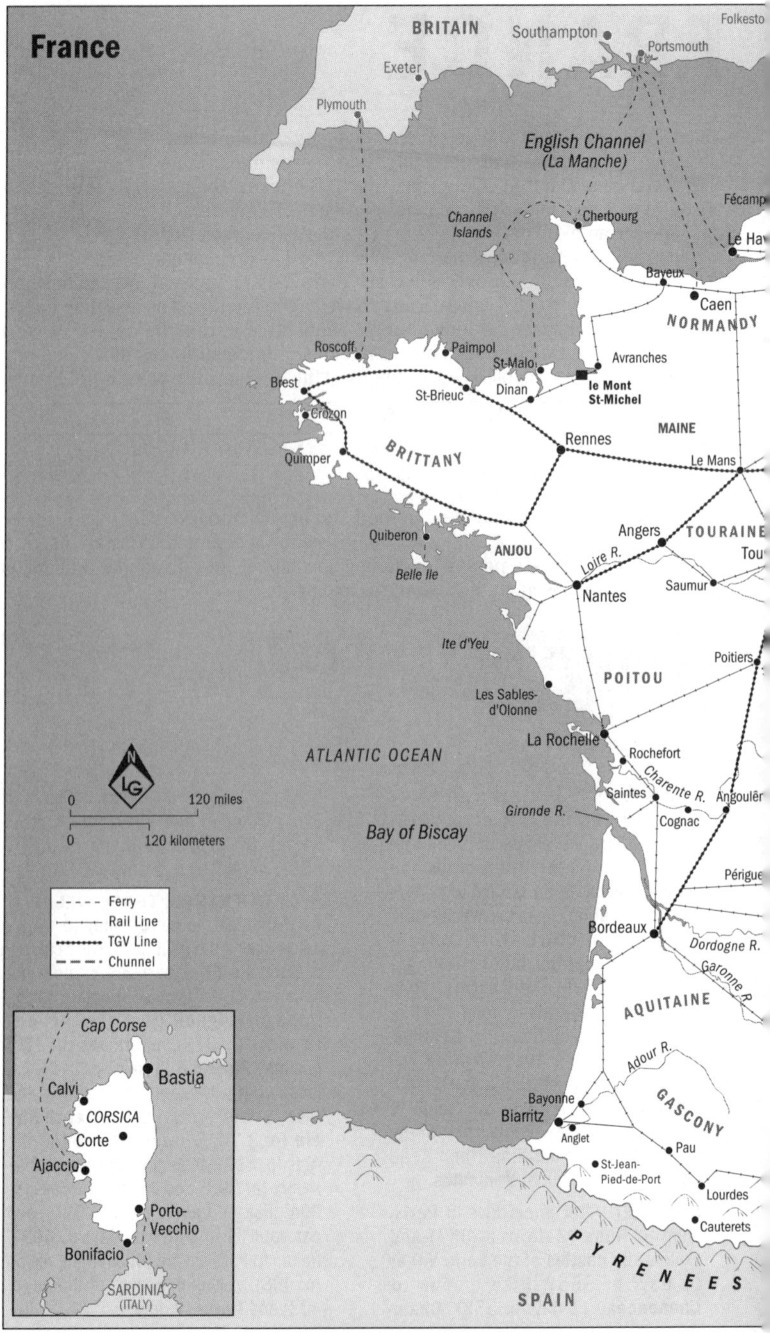
France
BRITAIN
Southampton
Folkesto
Portsmouth
Exeter
Plymouth
English Channel
(La Manche)
Fécamp
Channel
Islands
Cherbourg
Le Ha
Bayeux
Caen
NORMANDY
Roscoff
Paimpol
St-Malo
Avranches
Brest
St-Brieuc
Dinan
le Mont
St-Michel
Crozon
MAINE
Rennes
Quimper
BRITTANY
Le Mans
Angers
TOURAINE
Quiberon
ANJOU
Tou
Belle Ile
Loire R.
Nantes
Saumur
Ite d'Yeu
Poitiers
POITOU
Les Sables-
d'Olonne
La Rochelle
Rochefort
ATLANTIC OCEAN
Charente R.
Saintes
Angoulê
0
120 miles
Gironde R.
Cognac
0
120 kilometers
Bay of Biscay
Périgue
Ferry
Rail Line
TGV Line
Chunnel
Bordeaux
Dordogne R.
Garonne R.
AQUITAINE
Cap Corse
Bastia
Calvi
CORSICA
Corte
Ajaccio
Porto-
Vecchio
Bonifacio
SARDINIA
(ITALY)
Adour R.
GASCONY
Bayonne
Biarritz
Anglet
Pau
St-Jean-
Pied-de-Port
Lourdes
Cauterets
PYRENEES
SPAIN

FRANCE

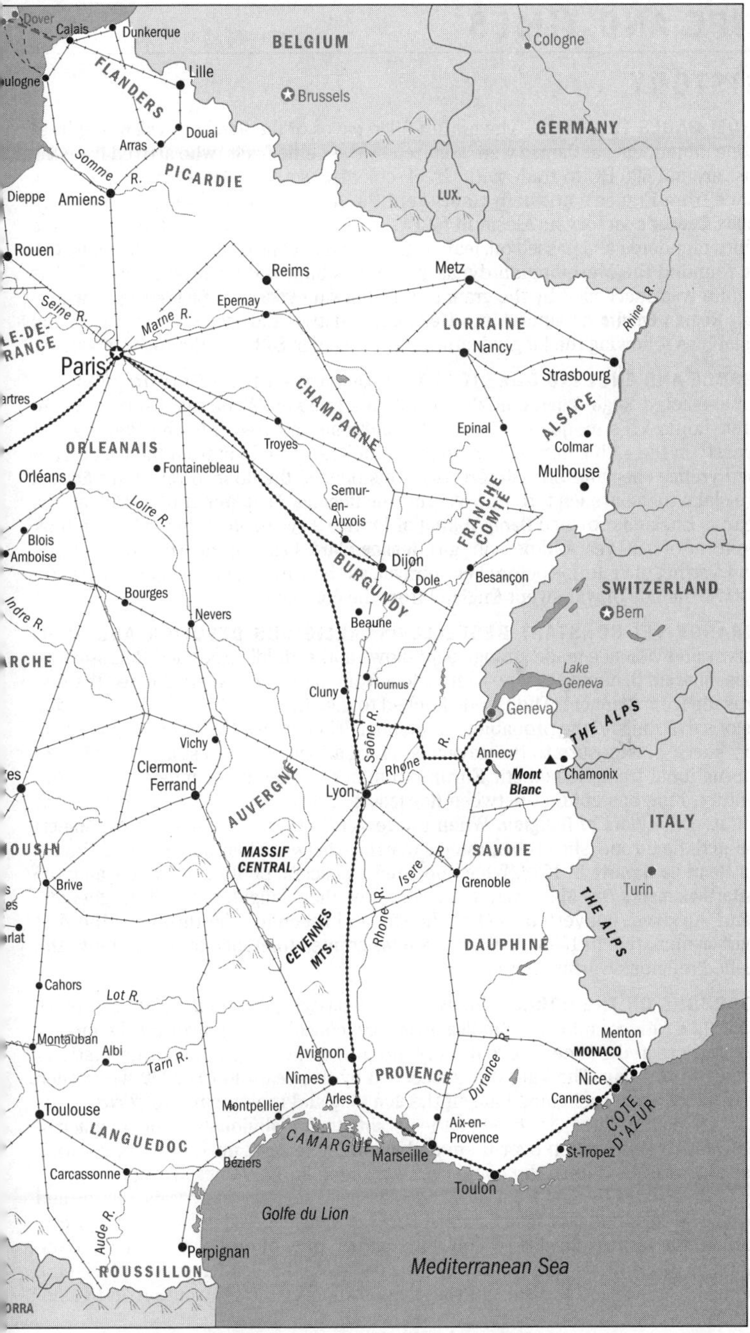
BELGIUM
Brussels
Cologne
GERMANY
LUX.
Calais
Dunkerque
Dover
FLANDERS
Lille
Douai
Arras
Somme R.
PICARDIE
Dieppe
Amiens
Rouen
Reims
Metz
Epernay
Seine R.
Marne R.
LORRAINE
Nancy
Rhine R.
Strasbourg
Paris
CHAMPAGNE
ALSACE
Epinal
Colmar
Mulhouse
ORLEANAIS
Troyes
Fontainebleau
Orléans
Loire R.
Semur-en-Auxois
FRANCHE COMTÉ
Blois
Amboise
Dijon
BURGUNDY
Dole
Besançon
SWITZERLAND
Bern
Bourges
Nevers
Indre R.
Beaune
Lake Geneva
Tournus
Cluny
Geneva
THE ALPS
Saône R.
Vichy
Annecy
Chamonix
Mont Blanc
Clermont-Ferrand
AUVERGNE
Rhone R.
Lyon
ITALY
MASSIF CENTRAL
SAVOIE
Isere R.
Brive
Grenoble
Turin
CEVENNES MTS.
Rhone R.
DAUPHINÉ
THE ALPS
Cahors
Lot R.
Montauban
Albi
Tarn R.
Avignon
Menton
MONACO
Nîmes
PROVENCE
Durance R.
Nice
Arles
Cannes
Toulouse
Montpellier
Aix-en-Provence
COTE D'AZUR
LANGUEDOC
CAMARGUE
Marseille
St-Tropez
Béziers
Carcassonne
Toulon
Golfe du Lion
Aude R.
Perpignan
Mediterranean Sea
ROUSSILLON

FRANCE

LIFE AND TIMES

HISTORY

FROM GAULS TO GOTHS. The graffiti-filled caves of the **Dordogne Valley** and huge stone monuments at **Carnac** were admired by the Celtic **Gauls,** who arrived from the east around 600 BC to trade with Greek colonists settling **Marseilles.** Fierce resistance from France's northern Gauls kept the Romans out of their territory until **Julius Caesar's** victory at Alesia in 52 BC. When Rome fell in AD 476, the Gothic tribes plundered and passed on, leaving the **Franks** in control. The Frankish king **Clovis** founded the Merovingian dynasty and was baptized a Christian in 507. His empire was succeeded by the grander Carolingian dynasty of **Charlemagne,** whose **Holy Roman Empire** expanded into Germany, Austria, and Switzerland. Territorial squabbles following the king's death were resolved in 843 with the **Treaty of Verdun.**

FRANCE AND ENGLAND DUKE IT OUT. In the wake of the Carolingians, the noble-elected **Hugh Capet** quickly consolidated power. When his distant descendant, Louis VII's ex-queen, **Eleanor of Aquitaine,** married into the Plantagenêt dynasty in the 12th century, a broad swath of land stretching from the Channel to the Pyrenees became English territory. This opened the door to England's **Edward III's** claim to the French throne, triggering the **Hundred Years War** in 1328. Defeat was near as England crowned **Henry VI** king of France 90 years later, but salvation took the form of a 17-year-old peasant girl, **Jeanne d'Arc.** Leading the French army, she won a string of victories before her betrayal; as she burned at the stake in **Rouen** (p. p. 347), the tide of war swept England from the continent.

STRANGE YET CONSTANT BEDFELLOWS: RELIGIOUS DEVOTION AND WAR. Fervor and violence made strange bedfellows in the Middle Ages and Renaissance. **Pope Innocent II**, hoping to wrest Jerusalem from the Saracens, proclaimed the first Crusade from **Clermont.** Thousands flocked to take the cross, swayed by the promise of salvation and the probability of plunder. Though few Crusades had any military success, exposure to the advanced civilizations of the East and a revival of international trade helped stir Europe from her intellectual slumber. In the 16th century, religious conflict between **Huguenots** (French Protestants) and **Catholics** initiated the **Wars of Religion.** When the fervently Catholic **Catherine de Médicis** claimed the throne, she orchestrated a marriage between her daughter and Huguenot **Henri de Navarre** in 1572. What appeared a peaceful political move became the **St-Bartholomew's Day Massacre,** a murder spree that slaughtered 2000 Huguenots. Henri survived, converted to Catholicism, and ascended the throne as the first **Bourbon** monarch. In 1598 the **Edict of Nantes** granted tolerance for Protestants and quelled religious warfare for a century.

BOURBONS ON THE ROCKS. The Bourbon dynasty peaked in the 17th century as **Louis XIII's** ruthless minister, **Cardinal Richelieu,** consolidated power for the monarchy and created the centralized, bureaucratic administration characteristic of France to this day. The king was succeeded by five-year-old **Louis XIV** who, when he came of age, proclaimed himself the **Sun King** and took the motto *"l'état, c'est moi"* ("I am the state"). He brought the nobility to the fabulously opulent palace of **Versailles** to keep watch over them and avoid unpleasant uprisings, yet growing resentment of the monarchy could not be avoided. In 1789 **Louis XVI** called a meeting of the **Estates General** from the three classes of society: aristocrats, clergy, and soon-to-be-revolutionary **Third Estate.** A Parisian mob, angered by high bread prices, stormed the fortress **Bastille** on July 14th, and an orgy of destruction engulfed the nation as peasants burned records of their debts. As the **First Republic** replaced the abolished monarchy, **Maximilien Robespierre** took over the Convention and guillotined the King and his cake-savoring Queen, **Marie-Antoinette.** The Revolution had taken a radical turn. Robespierre leveraged his influence into the **Reign of Terror,** executing rivals before falling to the guillotine in 1794. The Terror was over and power was entrusted to a five-man **Directory.**

THE LITTLE DICTATOR. Meanwhile, war continued as a young Corsican general, **Napoleon Bonaparte,** swept through northern Italy and into Austria. Riding a wave of public support, he deposed the Directory, ultimately crowning himself **Emperor** in 1804. After a disastrous invasion of Russia, Napoleon lost the support of a war-weary nation; in return for abdicating in 1814, he was given the Mediterranean island of **Elba.** The monarchy was reinstated under **Louis XVIII,** brother of his headless predecessor. The story has a final twist: Napoleon landed with an army at Cannes on March 26th, 1815, marching north as the king fled to England. The ensuing **Hundred Days' War** ended on the field of **Waterloo** in Flanders, Belgium, where the **Duke of Wellington** triumphed as much by luck as by skill. Napoleon was banished to remote **St. Helena** in the south Atlantic, where he died in 1821. Today, Napoleon is popularly regarded as a hero, and thousands pay their respects in his hometown of **Ajaccio.**

WAR AND PEACE. AND MORE WAR. Fifty years of revolution and instability left France with the **Third Republic.** Troubled by the shift in the European power balance from Germany's 1871 unification, a series of treaties forged the **Triple Entente** among France, Britain, and Russia to counter the **Triple Alliance** of Germany, Italy, and the Austro-Hungarian Empire. When **World War I** erupted in 1914, German armies swarmed to France, but a stalemate soon developed as the opposing armies dug trenches along the length of the country. The withdrawal of newly revolutionary Russia in 1917 was offset by the entry of the US, and victory for the West came in 1918. Devastated by four years of fighting and 1.3 million dead, France won crippling reparations from Germany; these and accompanying humiliations were often invoked by Adolf Hitler in his rise to power.

The 1930s found France ill-equipped to deal with Hitler's rise to power and mobilization across the Rhine. When **World War II** began with Germany's 1939 invasion of Poland, France declared war in response. In May 1940, Germany bypassed a string of fortresses, capturing the country by June. With the north under German occupation, and a puppet state in the south ruled from **Vichy,** those that escaped joined the French government-in-exile under **General Charles de Gaulle.** At his insistence French troops led the **liberation of Paris** on August 25th, 1944.

FOURTH REPUBLIC AND POST-COLONIAL FRANCE. De Gaulle's **Fourth Republic** was proclaimed in 1944, leading to female suffrage and nationalized energy companies. When he quit in 1946, the Fourth lacked a strong replacement, and the next 14 years saw 25 governments. The end of the war also signaled the end of France's 19th-century **colonial empire.** The 1950s witnessed the systematic dismantling of remaining colonies, despite de Gaulle's return to power. In 1962, with a new **constitution** in hand, the nation declared itself the **Fifth Republic.** In May 1968, what started as a student protest grew into a full-scale revolt as 10 million state workers went on strike in support of social reform. The government responded by deploying tank and commando units, and things looked to be heading for revolution yet again. The aging General had lost his magic touch, and he resigned following a referendum defeat in 1969.

THE 80S AND 90S. After de Gaulle's exit, France adopted a far less assertive foreign policy. In 1981, Socialist **François Mitterrand** assumed the presidency and the Socialists gained a majority in the Assemblée Nationale. Despite broad social programs created early in the administration, the political collapse of the left forced compromise with the right, and Mitterrand had to appoint the conservative **Jacques Chirac** as Prime Minister. **Jean-Marie Le Pen** formed the **Front National (FN)** on an anti-immigration platform to capitalize on blaming France's unemployment woes on foreigners. Meanwhile, in an unprecedented power-sharing relationship known as "cohabitation," Mitterrand withdrew to control foreign affairs, leaving Chirac domestic power. In 1995, Mitterrand chose not to seek reelection, and Chirac was elected president. Facing domestic and international pressure, he was forced to accept his former rival, Socialist **Lionel Jospin,** as Prime Minister in 1998.

Since the 1991 creation of the **European Union (EU),** the French have feared the loss of French national character and autonomy. The **Schengen Agreement** of 1995 created a six-nation zone without border controls, 1999 saw the extension of this zone to the entire EU (barring the UK, Ireland, and Denmark), and 2002 witnessed the birth of the **Euro** as the single European legal tender.

TODAY

The past has regularly seen France in the international limelight. The popularity of Le Pen's anti-immigrant Front National and France's continuing debate on gay rights has highlighted concerns of equality, ethics, and national identity. France's continuing struggle to formulate a just and EU-compatible immigration policy is the most visible indicator of its challenging role in an increasingly global society.

THE SHOCKING ELECTIONS OF 2002. While the 2002 presidential race was initially slated to be a lackluster showdown between the scandal-riddled Chirac and his innocuous prime minister Jospin, things got interesting when the far-right nationalist Jean-Marie Le Pen edged out Jospin in the preliminary elections in April. Throughout France, protesters took to the streets to condemn Le Pen's policies, citing his dismissive comments about the Holocaust as proof of his racism. On May 5, voters headed to the booths in droves, electing Chirac by a hefty 82% majority. The parliamentary elections on June 16 dramatically marked the end of cohabitation between President and Prime Minister. With a landslide victory for the center-right and the appointment of conservative Jean-Pierre Raffarin as Prime Minister, Chirac will face few barriers in fulfilling his pledges for tax cuts, institutional reform, and a crackdown on crime.

THE IMMIGRATION DEBATE. The steady popularity of Le Pen and his anti-immigration platform is only the most visible sign of the continuing national debate on immigration policy, a debate which has expanded in the last few years to encompass issues of national identity, migrant incorporation, and terrorism. France has passed a record amount of legislative change in its immigration policy, passing no less than seven reforms in the last 25 years. Anti-immigration sentiment increased substantially in 1993 when then-Interior Minister Charles Pasqua proposed "zero-immigration" and initiated the Law Pasqua, allowing police greater freeom to interrogate immigrants. Jospin's 1998 immigration law mitigated the effects of the Law Pasqua by allowing foreign scientists and scholars more relaxed conditions of entry.

GAY RIGHTS AND ADOPTION. In 1999, France became the first traditionally Catholic country to legally recognize homosexual unions. The Civil Solidarity Pact, known by its acronym PACS, was designed to extend to homosexual and unmarried heterosexual couples greater welfare, tax, and inheritance rights. While PACS has become so common a term in popular society that it has gained its own noun (*"pacser"*) and adjective (*"pacsé"*), it is has faced a number of detractors. Conservatives seek to keep PACS a strictly legal term, as gay marriage is still a concept unwelcome to many. Gay activists are currently struggling to attain the same rights to adoption and reproductive technologies that married couples enjoy.

CULTURE

FOOD AND DRINK

French chefs cook for the most finicky clients in the world—Charles de Gaulle once griped that no nation with 400 types of cheese could ever be united. The French breakfast *(le petit déjeuner)* is usually light, consisting of bread or sometimes croissants or *brioches* (pastry-like buttery breads), and espresso with hot milk *(café au lait)*. A full French dinner includes an **apéritif** (pre-dinner drink), an *entrée* (appetizer), *plat* (main course), salad, cheese, dessert, fruit, coffee, and *digestif* (after-dinner drink). Most restaurants offer **un menu à prix fixe** (fixed-price meal) that costs less than ordering *à la carte*. Odd-hour cravings can be satisfied at **brasseries,** the middle ground between cafes and restaurants. The French take **wine** with virtually every meal. Heed the tale of the famous director who dared to order a Coke with his €230 meal; he was promptly kicked out of the restaurant. Of him it was said, *"Il manque de savoir vivre"*—he doesn't know how to live. A warning to **vegetarians:** Trust no one. The concept of meatless life is foreign to most chefs; even a salad may have ham. You'll have more luck at **crêperies,** ethnic restaurants, and places catering to a younger crowd.

Cafes in France, haunts of intellectuals from Hemingway to Sartre, figure pleasantly in the daily routine. Prices are cheaper at the counter *(comptoir)* than in the seating area *(salle)*; outdoor seating *(la terrasse)* may be even more expensive. Coffee, beer, and (in the south) the anise-flavored *pastis* are staple cafe drinks. If you order *café*, you'll get espresso; for coffee with milk, ask for a *café crème*. *Bière à la pression*, or draft beer, is either pale *(blonde)* or dark *(brune)*. A glass of red is the cheapest wine in a cafe, often starting under €1.

CUSTOMS AND ETIQUETTE

BLENDING IN. The French are known for their conservative stylishness—and it's unlikely you'll be able to compete with them. Go for restrained sneakers or closed shoes, solid-color pants or jeans, and plain T-shirts or button-down shirts. If you choose to wear shorts, they shouldn't be too skimpy. For women, skirts or dresses are more appropriate, especially in summer. Blending in is a great excuse to shop for appropriate clothing. If you are traveling in January or August, be sure to take advantage of massive sales *(les soldes)*—prices are often slashed as much as 50%.

MANY CULTURES, ONE RACE France was forged pell-mell by annexation of ethnically diverse territories: parts of Catalonia and the Basque Country in the South; the ever-volatile island of Corsica in the Mediterranean, the rest of Southern France which goes by the name of Occitania, the Germanic regions of Alsace and part of Lorraine, Celtic Brittany, and the Flemish northern tip. Until the last century, these regions were like foreign countries on French soil.

The project of unifying French language and culture was not given much practical support until the institution of free and obligatory public schooling in the 1880s. In many schools, children caught speaking their local tongues anywhere on the school grounds were punished. As compensation, however, schools assigned readings on rural France like the enduring *Le Tour de la France par deux enfants*, a picaresque journey around France by two Alsatian orphans from which today's ultimate bike race derives its name.

ETAGES. The French call the ground floor the *rez-de-chaussée* and start numbering with the first floor above the ground floor *(premier étage)*. The button labeled "R," not "1," is typically the ground floor. The *sous-sol* is the basement.

HOURS. Most restaurants open at noon for lunch and then close for the afternoon before reopening for dinner. Some bistros and cafes will remain open throughout the afternoon. Small businesses, banks, and post offices close daily for "lunch" (noon-3pm). Many establishments shut down entirely on Sundays, and most museums are closed on Mondays. Calling ahead for hours is always a good idea.

LANGUAGE. Even if your French is near-perfect, waiters and salespeople who detect the slightest accent will often respond in English. If your language skills are good, continue to speak French; most will respect and appreciate your fortitude, and respond to you in kind.

MARKETS. Open-air markets are an institution in France, occuring at least once a week, usually on Sundays. In both large cities and small villages, vendors bring their produce to the regular *marché* street and families come to stock up on fresh food for the week. When purchasing goods, let the merchant pick out the products. Prices for food are usually set, although you may be able to find bargains towards the end of the day.

POLITESSE. The French put a premium on polite pleasantries. Always, always say "*Bonjour Madame/Monsieur*" when you come into a business, restaurant or hotel, and "*Au Revoir*" when you leave. The difference between getting good and bad service is the difference between a little meek politesse and careless rudeness. If you bump into someone on the street or while awaiting transportation, always say "*Pardon*" to excuse yourself. The proper way to answer the phone is "*Âllo,*" but if you use this on the street, you'll blow your cover. When meeting someone for the first time, a handshake is appropriate. However, friends and acquaintances greet each other with a kiss on each cheek (the exception is men kissing men). If you are unsure of how to appropriately greet someone, let them make the first move and gracefully follow. Don't use first names unless the person uses yours or is obviously younger than you.

PUBLIC RESTROOMS. The streetside public restrooms that have emerged all over France are worth the €0.30 they require. For this paltry sum, you are guaranteed a clean restroom, as these magic machines self-clean after each use. Toilets in train stations, major Métro stops, and public gardens generally cost €0.40-0.60.

TIPPING. Service is always included in meal prices in restaurants and cafes, and in drink prices at bars and clubs; look for the phrase *service compris* on the menu or just ask. If service is not included, tip 15-20%. Even when service is included, it is polite to leave a *pourboire* at a cafe, bistro, restaurant, or bar—up to 5%.

THE ARTS

ARCHITECTURE. Long before the arrival of the "civilizing" Greeks and Romans, Frenchmen were making their own impressive buildings. The prehistoric murals of **Lascaux** (p. 361) and **Les Eyzies-de-Tayac** (p. 362) testify to the presence of ancient and well-established peoples. No such monuments stand to the ancient Gauls, whose legacy was swept away by Roman conquerors. Rome's leavings are most visible in the arena and temple at **Nîmes** (p. 370). Romanesque churches, like the **Basilique St-Sernin** in Toulouse (p. 366), were designed to accommodate large crowds of worshippers and pilgrims, while the monastery of **Mont St. Michel** (p. 350) provided a secluded religious haven. Louis XIV commissioned the world's largest royal residence, the exorbitantly beautiful palace **Versailles** (p. 344); full of crystal, mirrors, and gold, and surrounded by formal gardens, it is the pinnacle of the Baroque style. Engineering came onto the architectural scene in the latter part of the 19th century, as Gustave Eiffel created the **Tour Eiffel** (p. 330), now the best-loved landmark in the country. Charles-Edouard Jeanneret, better known as **Le Corbusier,** was the interwar pioneer in reinforced concrete that dominated much of the rebuildinmg effort. In the 1980s, Paris became the hub of Mitterand's 15-billion-franc endeavor known as the *Grands Projets:* the construction of the **Musée d'Orsay,** the **Parc de la Villette,** the **Institut du Monde Arabe,** the **Opéra** at the Bastille, and **I.M. Pei's** glass pyramid at the **Louvre.**

FINE ARTS. France's surviving **medieval art** would instruct the average illiterate 12th-and 13th-century churchgoer on religious themes; stained glass and intricate stone facades, like those at **Chartres, Reims,** and **Sainte-Chapelle** in Paris, served as large reproductions of the Bible. The 11th-century **Bayeux tapestry** unravels a 70-meter-long narrative of the Battle of Hastings (p. 348). In 1515, **Leonardo da Vinci** trekked up from Florence bearing the smiling **Mona Lisa** in tow; his final home and a number of his sketches can be seen in **Amboise** (p. 357). The French Revolution inspired heroic scenes from their own time; **Jacques-Louis David's** *Death of Marat* paid gory tribute to the Revolutionary leader, while the paintings such as **Eugène Delacroix's** *Liberty Leading the People* (1830) shocked the salons of the 1820s and 1830s. **Edouard Manet** facilitated the transition to **Impressionism** by flattening the fine shading and sharp perspectives of academic art and turning his focus to texture and color; his portrait of a prostitute in *Olympia* scandalized his colleagues. **Claude Monet, Camille Pissarro,** and **Pierre-Auguste Renoir** began to explore Impressionist techniques in the 1860s; striving to attain a sense of immediacy, light became subject matter. Monet's garden at **Giverny,** which inspired his monumental Waterlilies series, remains a popular daytrip from Paris. **Post-Impressionist Paul Cézanne** created still-lifes, portraits, and geometric landscapes using bold, geometric blocks of color. **Georges Seurat** took fragmentation a step further with **Pointillism:** thousands of tiny dots merging to form a coherent picture. Dutchman **Vincent van Gogh migrated** to the south of France in search of new light, color, and imagery; the poverty and mental illness that plagued him throughout his short life are reflected in his work. Similarly tortured in his art and life, **Henri de Toulouse-Lautrec**'s vibrant posters capture the brilliant and lascivious nightlife of 19th-century Paris. Spanish-born **Pablo Picasso** developed **Cubism,** a technique of composing the canvas with shaded planes. By reducing everyday objects—fruits, glasses, vases, newspapers—Picasso became arguably the greatest artist of the 20th century, constantly innovating and breaking new ground; his career is chronicled at the **Musée Picasso** in Paris (p. 335) and at the beautiful **seaside Musée Picasso** in Antibes (p. 380). The loss and disillusionment that pervaded Europe after WWI prompted artists to reject the bourgeois culture that began the war. **Surrealism** and absurdity dominated 20th-century experiments in photography, installation, video, and sculpture; these can be seen in the collections and exhibitions of the **Centre Pompidou** and the **Fondation Cartier pour l'Art Contemporain.**

LITERATURE AND PHILOSOPHY. During the 13th century, popular satirical stories called **fabliaux** celebrated the bawdy with tales of cuckolded husbands, saucy wives, and shrewd peasants. **Calvin's** humanist treaties criticized the Catholic Church and opened the road to the ill-fated Protestant Reformation in France. In his 1637 *Discourse on Method,* **René Descartes** proved his own existence with the catchy deduction, "I think, therefore I am." **La Fontaine's** *Fables* and **Charles Perrault's** *Fairy Tales of Mother Goose* explored right and wrong in more didactic ways. **Molière,** the era's comic relief, satirized the social pretensions of his age, and his actors initiated the great **Comédie Française.** The Enlightenment in France was informed by advances in the sciences and aimed at the promotion of reason and tolerance in an often backward and bigoted world. **Denis Diderot's** *Encylopédie* (1752-1780) took no smaller ambition than to record the entire body of human knowledge. **Voltaire** gained fame with his satire *Candide* (1758), a refutation of the claim that "all is for the best in the best of all possible worlds." Voltaire's witticisms paled in comparison with **Jean-Jacques Rousseau's** *Confessions* (1769), which instructed readers to abandon society altogether rather than remaining in a corrupt world. The 19th century saw an emotional reaction against Enlightenment rationality; great novelists like **Stendhal** (*The Red and the Black*) and **Balzac** (*La Comédie Humaine*) penned their masterpieces, but it was **Victor Hugo** who dominated the **Romantic** age with his *The Hunchback of Notre Dame* (1831).The decadence and social snobbery of the turn of the century was captured by **Marcel Proust** in the seven volumes of *Remembrance of Things Past.* **Jean-Paul Sartre** dominated France's intelligentsia in the years following World War II; his theory of **Existentialism** held that life in itself was meaningless–only by committing yourself to a cause could existence take on a purpose. While Sartre worked under censorship in occupied Paris, Algerian-born **Albert Camus** edited the Résistance newspaper *Combat.* He achieved fame with his debut novel *The Outsider* (1942), in which a dispassionate social misfit is condemned to death for murder. Existentialist and feminist **Simone de Beauvoir** made waves with *The Second Sex* (1949), an essay attacking the myth of femininity. Its famous statement, "One is not born, but becomes a woman" inspired a generation of second-wave **feminism** in the 50s, 60s, and 70s. In turn, writers like **Marguerite Duras** *(The Lover)* explored gender identity, challenged Freudian 'penis envy,' and sparked feminist movements in France and abroad.

CINEMA. **François Truffaut**'s *The 400 Blows* (1959) and *Jules and Jim* (1961) paved the way for the New Wave movement that dominated French cinema though the 1970s. Recently, the *Three Colors* trilogy (1993-94), *Manon of the Spring* (1987), and *Goodbye Children* (1987) have moved movie-goers around the world. Actor **Gérard Depardieu** (*Cyrano de Bergerac*, 1990, *My Father the Hero*, 1993) is renowned for roles both serious and comic, but **Jean Reno** has had more luck making the transition into Hollywood following the success of **Luc Besson**'s *The Professional* (1994), *Fifth Element* (1997), and *Taxi* (1998). On the opposite end of the spectrum from the *belle de jour* fare is the recent spate of **cinéma beur,** second-generation North Africans' brutally honest documentation of life in the HLMs (municipal housing) of suburban Paris. These grafitti-decor films, such as **Mathieu Kassovitz**'s *The Hatred* (1995), confront the traumas of urban racism. **Claire Denis**'s *Chocolate* (1988) gives a voice to France's tumultuous history of colonialism. Art cinema continues to prosper under **Marcel Hanoun** (*Noise of Love and War*, 1997) and **Jacques Doillon** (*Ponette*, 1997), while the French flock to comedies like **Jean-Marie Poiré**'s *The Visitors* (1992). Most recently, the 1999 film *The Taste of Others* has made waves on both sides of the Atlantic, winning a César (French Oscar), several film festival awards, and a nomination for a 2000 Best Foreign Film Oscar.

HOLIDAYS AND FESTIVALS

The most important national holiday is **Bastille Day** *(La Fête Nationale)*, July 14, which commemorates the storming of the Bastille in 1789 and the birth of the French Republic. The day is celebrated with a solemn march up the Champs-Elysées followed by dancing, drinking, and fireworks all over the country. The 11 official national holidays are listed below. Note that the dates of many Catholic holidays change on a yearly basis; the dates listed are for 2003. Banks close at noon on the nearest working day before a national holiday.

Holidays: Le Jour de l'an St-Sébastian (New Year; Jan. 1); Le lundi de Pâques (Easter Monday; Apr. 5); La Fête du Travail (Labor Day; May 1); L'Anniversaire de la Liberation (celebrates the Liberation in 1944; May 8); L'Ascension (Ascension Day; June 1); Le lundi de Pentecôte (Whitmonday; June 12); La Fête Nationale (Bastille Day; July 14); L'Assomption (Feast of the Assumption; Aug. 15); La Toussaint (All Saints' Day; Nov. 1); L'Armistice 1918 (Armistice Day; Nov. 11); and Le Noël (Christmas; Dec. 25).

Festivals: Most festivals, like **fête du cinema** and **fête de la musique** (late June, when musicians rule the streets), are in summer. The **Cannes Film Festival** (May; www.festival-cannes.com) is mostly for directors and stars, but provides good people watching. The **Festival d'Avignon** (July-Aug.; www.festival-avignon.com/gbindex3.html) is famous for its theater. **Bastille Day** (July 14) is marked by military parades and fireworks nationwide. Although you may not be competing in the **Tour de France** (3rd and 4th week in July; www.letour.fr), you'll enjoy the hype. A **Vineyard Festival** (Sept., in Nice; www.nice-coteazur.org/americain/tourisme/vigne/index.html) celebrates the grape harvest with music, parades, and wine tastings. Nice and Nantes celebrate **Carnaval** in the last week or two before Ash Wednesday (culminating with Mardi Gras celebrations).

In addition to national holidays, there are numerous regional and city celebrations and festivals, especially throughout the summer. *Let's Go* provides coverage of these major *fêtes et manifestations* throughout the guide. For more information on specific events, from circuses in Aquitaine to fireworks in the Loire valley, check out the customized search engine on the French Government Tourist Office's website (www.franceguide.com, under "Culture and Art de vivre").

ESSENTIALS

FACTS AND FIGURES

Official Name: French Republic.
Capital: Paris.
Major Cities: Lyon, Nice, Marseilles.
Population: 60,000,000.
Land Area: 547,030 sq. km.
Time Zone: GMT +1.
Language: French.
Religions: Roman Catholic (90%).

WHEN TO GO

In July, Paris starts to shrink; by August it is devoid of Parisians, animated only by tourists and the pickpockets who love them. The Côte d'Azur fills with anglophones from June to September. On the other hand, the rest of France teems with Frenchmen during these months, especially along the Atlantic coast. Early summer and autumn are the best times to visit Paris—the city has warmed up, but not completely emptied out. The north and west have cool winters and mild summers, while the less-crowded center and east have a more continental climate. From December to February, the Alps provide some of the best skiing in the world, while the Pyrenees offer a calmer, if less climatically dependable, alternative.

DOCUMENTS AND FORMALITIES

Citizens of Australia, Canada, the EU, New Zealand, and the US do not need a visa for stays of up to 90 days. South Africans need a short-stay visa (*court séjour*; 30-day visas ZAR260.20; 90-day ZAR209.35-303.50). For stays longer than 90 days, all non-EU citizens need a long-stay visa (€95.20). Non-EU nationals cannot work in France without a **work permit,** which requires a job offer; nor can they **study** without a **student visa,** which requires proofs of admission to a French university, financial independence, and medical insurance. For **au pair** and **teaching assistant** jobs, special rules apply; check with your local consulate.

French Embassies at Home: Australia, Consulate General, Level 26 St. Martins Tower, 31 Market St., Sydney NSW 2000. (☎02 92 61 57 79; www.consulfrance-sydney.org. Open M-F 9am-1pm.) **Canada,** Consulate General, 1 pl. Ville-Marie, Suite 2601, 26th floor, Montréal, QC H3B 4S3. (☎514-878-4385; www.consulfrance-montreal.org.) **Ireland,** French Embassy, Consulate Section, 36 Ailesbury Rd., Ballsbridge, Dublin 4. (☎01 260 16 66; www.ambafrance.ie.) **New Zealand,** New Zealand Embassy and Consulate, 34-42 Manners St., P.O. Box 11-343, Wellington. (☎04 384 25 55; www.ambafrance-nz.org.) **South Africa,** Consulate General at Johannesburg, 191 Jan Smuts Ave., Rosebank, mailing address: PO Box 1027, Parklands 2121 (if you live in Gauteng, Kwazulu-Natal, Free State, Mpumalanga, Northern Province, North West Province or in Lesotho).

(☎011 778 56 00, visas ☎011 778 56 05; fax 011 778 56 01. Open M-F 8:30am-1pm. If you live in the Northern Cape, Eastern Cape or Western Cape, consult the Consulate General at Cape Town, 2 Dean St., Gardens, mailing address: P.O. Box 1702 Cape Town 8000. ☎021 423 15 75; www.consulfrance.co.za for both consulates.) **United Kingdom,** Consulate General, P.O. Box 520, 21 Cromwell Rd., London SW7 2EN. (☎020 7073 1200; www.ambafrance-uk.org. Visa service: P.O. Box 57, 6a Cromwell Pl., London SW7 2EW. ☎020 7073 1250.) **United States,** Consulate General, 4101 Reservoir Rd. NW, Washington D.C. 20007-2185. (☎202-944-6195; www.consulfrance-washington.org. Visa service: ☎202-944-6200.)

Foreign Embassies in France: All embassies are in **Paris** (see p. 311). There are **UK** consulates in Paris, Bordeaux, Lille, and Marseilles, and **US** consulates in Paris, Bordeaux, Lyon, Marseilles, Nice, Rennes, Strasbourg, and Toulouse.

TRANSPORTATION

BY PLANE. Airfares to France peak between June and September. The two major international airports in Paris are **Charles de Gaulle** and **Orly.** For info on cheap flights from the UK, see p. 43.

BY TRAIN. The French national railway company, **SNCF** (*Société Nationale de Chemins de Fer;* ☎08 36 35 35 35; www.sncf.fr), manages one of the most efficient transportation systems around. **TGV** (*train à grande vitesse,* or high-speed train), the fastest in the world, runs from Paris to major cities in France, as well as to Geneva and Lausanne, Switzerland. **Rapide** trains are slower, and local trains are the slowest of all, but are oddly called **Express** or **TER** *(Train Express Regional).* The **Eurostar** provides rapid connections to London and Brussels (see p. 47). SNCF offers a wide range of discounted round-trip tickets called **tarifs découvertes**—you should rarely have to pay full price. Get a calendar from a train station detailing **période bleue** (blue period), **période blanche** (white period), and **période rouge** (red period) times and days; blue gets the most discounts, while red gets none. Those under age 25 have two great options: the **Découverte 12-25** (€41.20) gives a 25% discount for any blue-period travel; and the **Carte 12-25** (€41.20), valid for a year, is good for 25-50% off all TGV trains, 50% off all other trips that started during a blue period, and 25% off those starting in a white period. Tickets must be validated in the orange machine at the entrance to the platforms at the *gare* (train station) and re-validated at any connections in your trip. Seat **reservations,** recommended for international trips, are mandatory on EuroCity (EC), InterCity (IC), and TGV trains. All three require a ticket supplement (travelers under 26 with ID are entitled to a discount) and reservation fee.

The **Eurailpass** is valid in France. The SNCF's **France Railpass** grants four days of unlimited rail travel in France in any 30-day period (€210, companion travelers €171 each; add up to 6 extra days for €30 each); the parallel **Youthpass** provides those under 26 with four days of unlimited travel within a one-month period (€148; up to 6 extra days €18 each). The **France Rail 'n Drive pass** combines three days of rail travel with two days of Avis car rental excluding insurance (€371-509 per person, depending on the type of car.).

BY BUS. Within France, long-distance buses are a secondary transportation choice; service is very infrequent compared to most other European countries. However, in some regions, buses can be indispensable for reaching out-of-the-way towns and sights. Bus services operated by the SNCF accept railpasses. Bus schedules usually indicate whether they run during "*période scolaire*" (school year), "*période de vacances*" (vacations), or both.

BY FERRY. Ferries across the English Channel *(La Manche)* link France to England and Ireland. The shortest and most popular route is between **Dover** (see p.

203) and **Calais** (see p. 411), and is run by **P&O Stena Line, SeaFrance,** and **Hoverspeed** (see p. 49). **Brittany Ferries** (☎08 03 82 88 28; www.brittanyferries.co.uk) travels from **Cherbourg** (see p. 349) to **Poole;** from **Caen** (see p. 348) to **Portsmouth;** and from **St-Malo** (see p. 352) to **Portsmouth. Irish Ferries** (☎01 44 94 20 40; www.irishferries.ie) has overnight ferries from **Cherbourg** and **Roscoff** to **Rosslare Harbour, Ireland** (see p. 604). **Eurailpass** is valid on boats to Ireland. On Brittany Ferries, students receive a 10% discount. For schedules and prices on English Channel ferries, see p. 49. For info on ferries from **Nice** and **Marseilles** to **Corsica,** see p. 388.

BY CHUNNEL. Traversing 27mi. under the sea, the Chunnel is undoubtedly the fastest, most convenient, least scenic route from England to France. There are two types of passenger service. **Eurostar** runs a frequent train service from London to Paris and Brussels, with stops at Ashford in England and Calais and Lille in France. Book reservations in UK, by phone, or over the web (UK ☎0990 18 61 86, US ☎800-387-6782, elsewhere ☎1233 61 75 75; www.eurostar.com, www.raileurope.com.) Eurostar tickets can also be bought at most major travel agents. **Eurotunnel** shuttles cars and passengers between Kent and Nord-Pas-de-Calais. (UK ☎0800 096 99 92, France ☎03 21 00 61 00; www.eurotunnel.co.uk.)

BY CAR. Unless you are traveling in a group of three or more, you won't save money traveling long distance by car rather than train, thanks to highway tolls, high gasoline costs, and rental charges. If you can't decide between train and car travel, get a **Rail 'n Drive pass** from railpass vendors (see above). The French drive on the right-hand side of the road; France maintains its roads well, but the landscape itself often makes the roads a menace, especially in twisting Corsica.

BY BIKE AND BY THUMB. Of all Europeans, the French may be alone in loving cycling more than football. Drivers usually accommodate bikers on the wide country roads, and many cities banish cars from select streets each Sunday. Renting a bike beats bringing your own if your touring will be confined to one or two regions (€7.65-18.30 per day). Many consider France the hardest country in Europe to get a lift. *Let's Go* does not recommend hitchhiking. In major cities ride-sharing organizations, such as **Eurostop International,** pair drivers and riders, though not all of them screen drivers (**Allostop** in France; www.ecritel.fr/allostop/).

TOURIST SERVICES AND MONEY

EMERGENCY	**Police:** ☎122. **Ambulance:** ☎123. **Fire:** ☎124.

TOURIST OFFICES. The extensive French tourism support network revolves around **syndicats d'initiative** and **offices de tourisme** (in the smallest towns, the **Mairie,** the mayor's office, deals with tourist concerns), all of which *Let's Go* labels "tourist office." All three distribute maps and pamphlets, help you find accommodations, and suggest excursions to the countryside. For up-to-date events and regional information, try www.francetourism.com.

MONEY. The official currency of France is the **euro.** The French Franc can still be exchanged at a rate of 6.56F to €1. For exchange rates and more information on the euro, see p. 20. The European Union imposes a **value-added tax (VAT)** on goods and services purchased within the EU, which is included in the price (see p. 19).

ACCOMMODATIONS AND CAMPING

Hostels generally offer dormitory accommodations in large single-sex rooms with four to 10 beds, though some have as many as 60. At the other end of the scale, many offer private singles and doubles. In France, a bed in a hostel averages around €7.65-15.25. The French **Hostelling International (HI)** affiliate is the **Fédération Unie des**

Auberges de Jeunesse (FUAJ) and it operates 178 hostels within France. Some hostels accept reservations through the **International Booking Network** (p. 31). Two or more people traveling together will often save money by staying in cheap **hotels** rather than hostels. The French government employs a four star hotel ratings system. Most hotels listed by *Let's Go* have zero stars or one, with a smattering of two stars. **Gîtes d'étapes** are rural accommodations for cyclists, hikers, and other ramblers, and are in less-populated areas. Expect *gîtes* to provide beds, a kitchen facility, and a resident caretaker. After 3000 years of settled history, true wilderness in France is hard to find. It's **illegal to camp** in most public spaces, especially in national parks. Instead, look forward to organized *campings* (campsites), where you'll share your splendid isolation with vacationing families and all manner of programmed fun. Most campsites have toilets, showers, and electrical outlets, though you may have to pay extra for such luxuries (€1.55-6.10); you'll often need to pay a supplement for your car, too (€3.05-7.65). Otherwise, expect to pay €7.65-13.75 per site.

COMMUNICATION

PHONE CODES	**Country code:** 33. **International dialing prefix:** 00. France has no city codes.

TELEPHONES. When calling from abroad, drop the leading zero of the local number. French pay phones only accept stylish phonecards called *Télécartes*, available in 50-unit (€7.50) and 120-unit (€15) denominations at train stations, post offices, and *tabacs*. *Décrochez* means pick up; you'll then be asked to *patientez* (wait) to insert your card; at *numérotez* or *composez* you can dial. Use only public France Télécom payphones, as privately owned ones charge more. An expensive alternative is to call collect *(faire un appel en PCV)*; an English-speaking operator can be reached by dialing the appropriate service provider listed below. The information number is ☎12; international operator, ☎00 33 11. International direct dial numbers include: **AT&T,** ☎0 800 99 00 11; **British Telecom,** ☎0 800 99 02 44; **Canada Direct,** ☎0 800 99 00 16 or 99 02 16; **Ireland Direct,** ☎0 800 99 03 53; **MCI,** ☎0 800 99 00 19; **Sprint,** ☎0 800 99 00 87; **Telecom New Zealand,** ☎0 800 99 00 64; **Telkom South Africa,** ☎0 800 99 00 27; **Telstra Australia,** ☎0 800 99 00 61.

MAIL. Airmail letters under 1 oz. between the US and France take 4 to 7 days and cost US$1. Letters from Canada cost CDN$0.95 for 20g. Allow at least 5 working days from Australia (postage AUS$1 for up to 20g) and 3 days from Britain (postage UK£0.30 for up to 20g). Envelopes should be marked *"par avion"* (airmail) to avoid having letters sent by sea. Mail can be held for pick-up through *Poste Restante* (General Delivery) to almost any city or town with a post office. Address letters to: SURNAME Firstname; *Poste Restante: Recette Principale;* [5-digit postal code] TOWN; FRANCE. Mark the envelope HOLD.

INTERNET ACCESS. Most major **post offices** and some branches now offer Internet access at special "cyberposte" terminals; you can buy a rechargeable card that gives you 50 minutes of access at the post office for €8. Note that *Let's Go* **does not list** "cyberposte" locations. Most large towns in France have a cybercafe. Rates and speed of connection vary widely; occasionally there are free terminals in technologically-oriented museums or exhibition spaces. **Cybercafé Guide** (www.cyberiacafe.net/cyberia/guide/ccafe.htm#working_france) lists cybercafes in France.

LANGUAGE. Contrary to popular opinion, even flailing efforts to speak French will be appreciated, especially in the countryside. Be lavish with your *Monsieurs*, *Madames*, and *Mademoiselles*, and greet people with a friendly *bonjour* (*bonsoir* in the evening). For basic French vocabulary and pronunciation, see p. 1020.

PARIS

City of light, of majestic panoramas and showy store windows, of the dark, and of the invisible—Paris (pop. 11,000,000) somehow manages to be it all. From twisting alleys that shelter the world's best bistros to broad avenues flaunting the latest in *haute couture*, from the ancient gargoyles of Notre Dame to the vibrant, modern Centre Georges-Pompidou, Paris is at once a bastion of tradition and a leader of the cutting edge. You can't conquer this city, but you can get acquainted in a few days, and after a week, you may find you're old friends.

INTERCITY TRANSPORTATION

Flights: Aéroport Roissy-Charles de Gaulle (CDG; ☎01 48 62 22 80; www.parisairports.com), 23km northeast of Paris, services most transatlantic flights. **Aéroport d'Orly** (ORY; ☎01 49 75 15 15), 18km south of Paris, is used by charters and many continental flights. The cheapest and fastest ways to get into the city are by **RER** or **bus.**

Transportation to and from Roissy-CDG: By **RER train,** take the free shuttle bus (*navette*) from Terminal 1 to the Roissy train station. From there, commuter rail line RER B will transport you to central Paris. To transfer to the métro, get off at Gare du Nord, Châtelet-Les-Halles, or St-Michel. To go to Roissy-CDG from Paris, take the RER B (30-35min.; every 15min.; €7.60, children €5.30) to Roissy, the end of the line. Then change to the free shuttle bus (every 10min.) to get to Terminal 1. **Roissybus** (☎01 49 25 61 87) leaves from 9 r. Scribe, near M: Opéra, and stops at Terminals 1, 2, and T9. Buy tickets on board (45min., every 15min., €8). **Air France buses** (☎08 92 35 08 20) run often into the city. Buy tickets on bus (30-35min., €10-20).

Transportation to and from Orly: From Orly Sud gate G or gate I, platform 1, or Orly Ouest level G, gate F, take the **Orly-Rail** shuttle bus (every 15min. 6am-11pm; €5.15, children €3.55) to Pont de Rungis/Aéroport d'Orly, where you can board the **RER C2** for several destinations in Paris. (English information ☎08 36 68 41 14. 35min., every 15min., €5.15.) The RATP **Orlybus** (☎01 40 02 32 94) runs to the airport from M: Denfert-Rochereau. Board at Orly Sud (30min., every 10-15min., €5.60). **Air France Buses** run between Orly and **Gare Montparnasse** (30min.; every 15min.; €7.50, round-trip €12.75).

Trains: There are 6 train stations in Paris. Each part of the Métro system services a different geographic region.

Gare du Nord: M: Gare du Nord. Serves Belgium, Britain, northern France, northern Germany, The Netherlands, and Scandinavia. To: **Amsterdam** (4-5hr., €73.30); **Brussels** (1½hr., €52); **Cologne** (4hr., €63). **Eurostar** departs for **London** (3hr., up to €255).

Gare de l'Est: M: Gare de l'Est. To Austria, eastern France, southern Germany, Luxembourg, and Switzerland. To: **Munich** (9hr., €99); **Vienna** (13hr., €161); **Zürich** (6-7hr., €70).

Gare de Lyon: M: Gare de Lyon. Serves southeastern France, Greece, Italy, and parts of Switzerland. To: **Geneva** (4hr., €65.40); **Nice** (6hr., €66); **Rome** (15hr., €160).

Gare d'Austerlitz: M: Gare d'Austerlitz. Serves southwestern France, the Loire Valley, Portugal, and Spain. To **Barcelona** (9hr., €94) and **Madrid** (12-13hr., €97).

Gare St-Lazare: M: Gare St-Lazare. Serves Normandy. To **Caen** (2hr., €26) and **Rouen** (2hr., €18).

Gare de Montparnasse: M: Montparnasse-Bienvenüe. Serves Brittany; also the departure point for **TGVs** to southwestern France. To **Rennes** (2-2½hr., €39).

Buses: Gare Routière Internationale du Paris-Gallieni, 28 av. du Général du Gaulle, just outside Paris in Bagnolet. M: Gallieni. **Eurolines** (☎01 43 54 11 99; www.eurolines.fr) sells tickets to most destinations in France and neighboring countries.

ORIENTATION

The **Ile de la Cité** and **Ile St-Louis** sit at the geographical center of the city, while the **Seine,** flowing east to west, splits Paris into two large expanses: the **Rive Gauche (Left Bank)** to the south and the **Rive Droite (Right Bank)** to the north. The Left Bank,

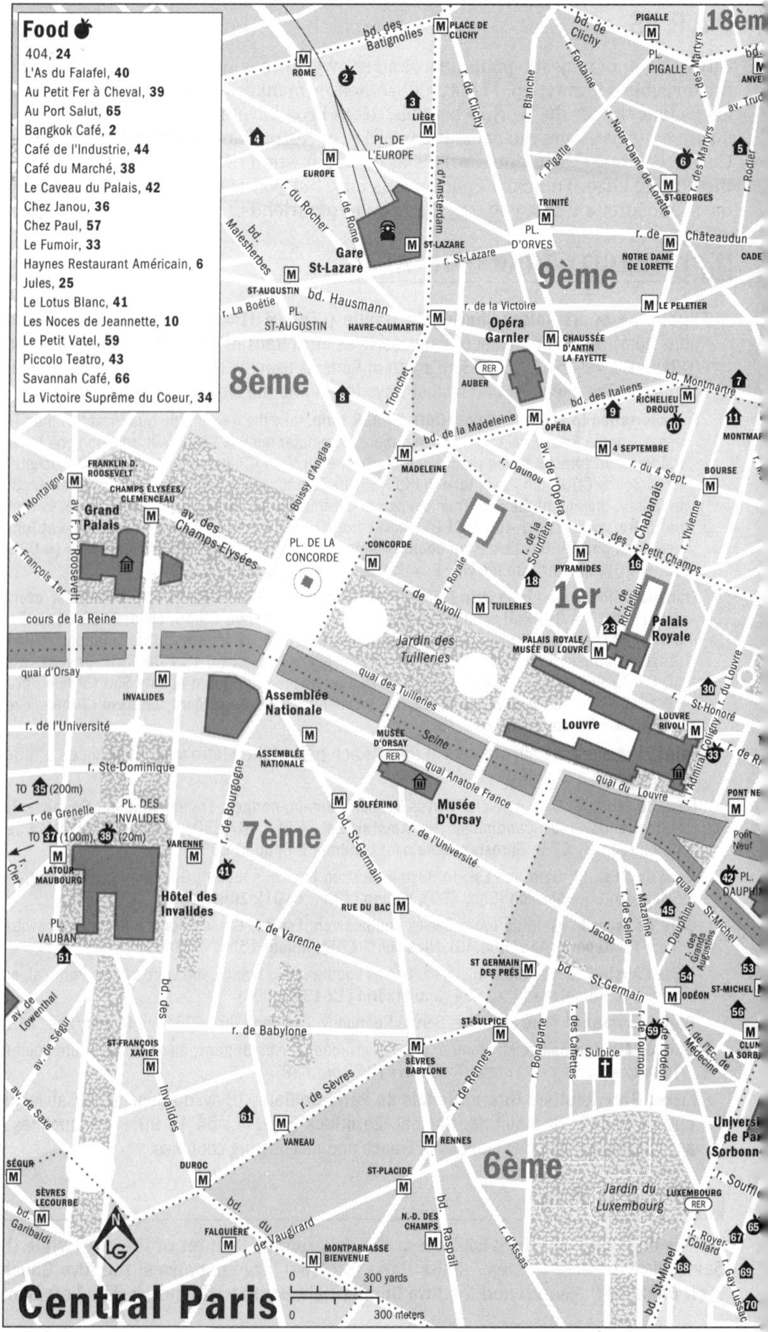
Central Paris
Food
404, 24
L'As du Falafel, 40
Au Petit Fer à Cheval, 39
Au Port Salut, 65
Bangkok Café, 2
Café de l'Industrie, 44
Café du Marché, 38
Le Caveau du Palais, 42
Chez Janou, 36
Chez Paul, 57
Le Fumoir, 33
Haynes Restaurant Américain, 6
Jules, 25
Le Lotus Blanc, 41
Les Noces de Jeannette, 10
Le Petit Vatel, 59
Piccolo Teatro, 43
Savannah Café, 66
La Victoire Suprême du Coeur, 34
8ème
9ème
7ème
1er
6ème
18ème
Gare St-Lazare
Opéra Garnier
Grand Palais
PL. DE LA CONCORDE
Jardin des Tuileries
Palais Royale
Louvre
Assemblée Nationale
Musée D'Orsay
Hôtel des Invalides
Jardin du Luxembourg
Université de Paris (Sorbonne)
Seine
bd. des Batignolles
bd. de Clichy
bd. Hausmann
bd. Montmartre
bd. des Italiens
bd. de la Madeleine
av. des Champs-Elysées
av. de l'Opéra
cours de la Reine
quai d'Orsay
quai des Tuilleries
quai Anatole France
quai du Louvre
r. de Rivoli
r. de l'Université
r. Ste-Dominique
r. de Grenelle
r. de Varenne
r. de Babylone
r. de Sèvres
bd. St-Germain
bd. Raspail
r. de Rennes
bd. du Vaugirard
PL. DE L'EUROPE
PL. ST-AUGUSTIN
PL. D'ORVES
PL. PIGALLE
PL. DES INVALIDES
PL. VAUBAN
TO 35 (200m)
TO 37 (100m), 38 (20m)
0 300 yards
0 300 meters

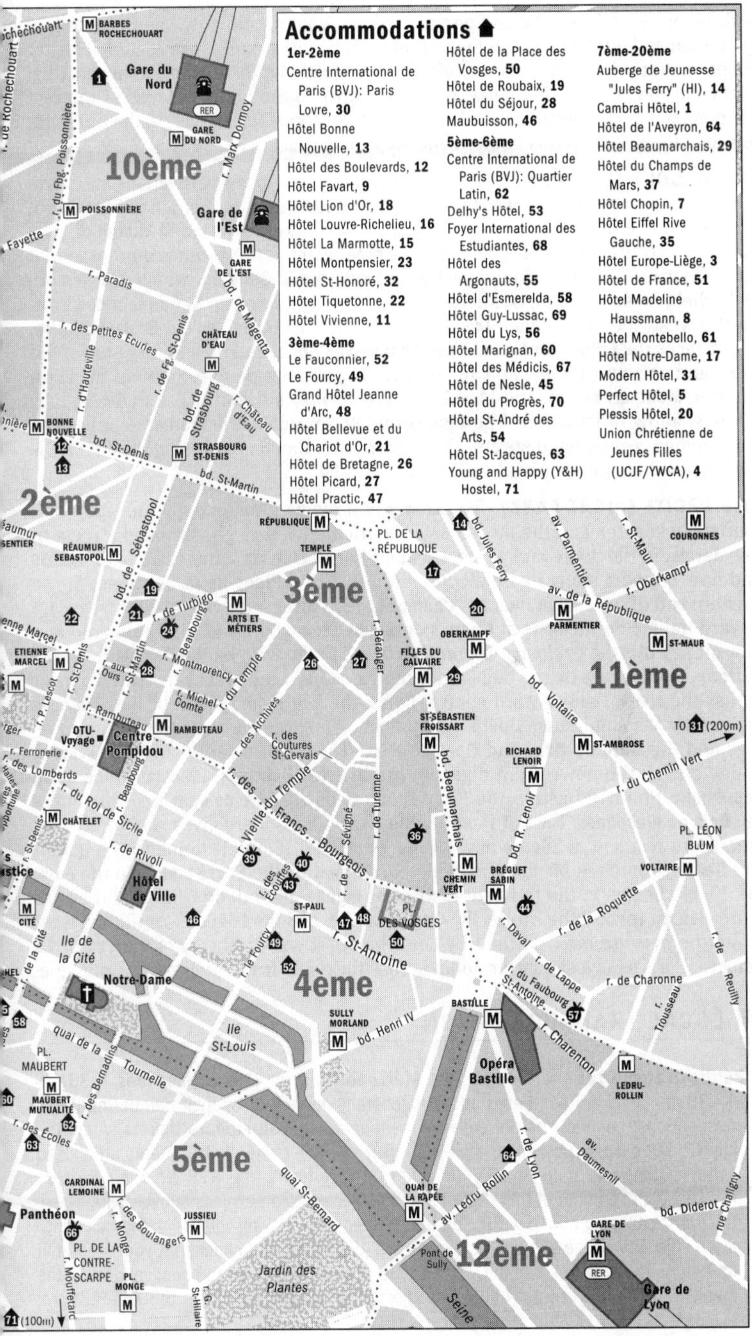
Accommodations
1er-2ème
Centre International de Paris (BVJ): Paris Lovre, 30
Hôtel Bonne Nouvelle, 13
Hôtel des Boulevards, 12
Hôtel Favart, 9
Hôtel Lion d'Or, 18
Hôtel Louvre-Richelieu, 16
Hôtel La Marmotte, 15
Hôtel Montpensier, 23
Hôtel St-Honoré, 32
Hôtel Tiquetonne, 22
Hôtel Vivienne, 11
3ème-4ème
Le Fauconnier, 52
Le Fourcy, 49
Grand Hôtel Jeanne d'Arc, 48
Hôtel Bellevue et du Chariot d'Or, 21
Hôtel de Bretagne, 26
Hôtel Picard, 27
Hôtel Practic, 47
Hôtel de la Place des Vosges, 50
Hôtel de Roubaix, 19
Hôtel du Séjour, 28
Maubuisson, 46
5ème-6ème
Centre International de Paris (BVJ): Quartier Latin, 62
Delhy's Hôtel, 53
Foyer International des Estudiantes, 68
Hôtel des Argonauts, 55
Hôtel d'Esmerelda, 58
Hôtel Guy-Lussac, 69
Hôtel du Lys, 56
Hôtel Marignan, 60
Hôtel des Médicis, 67
Hôtel de Nesle, 45
Hôtel du Progrès, 70
Hôtel St-André des Arts, 54
Hôtel St-Jacques, 63
Young and Happy (Y&H) Hostel, 71
7ème-20ème
Auberge de Jeunesse "Jules Ferry" (HI), 14
Cambrai Hôtel, 1
Hôtel de l'Aveyron, 64
Hôtel Beaumarchais, 29
Hôtel du Champs de Mars, 37
Hôtel Chopin, 7
Hôtel Eiffel Rive Gauche, 35
Hôtel Europe-Liège, 3
Hôtel de France, 51
Hôtel Madeline Haussmann, 8
Hôtel Montebello, 61
Hôtel Notre-Dame, 17
Modern Hôtel, 31
Perfect Hôtel, 5
Plessis Hôtel, 20
Union Chrétienne de Jeunes Filles (UCJF/YWCA), 4
10ème
2ème
3ème
4ème
5ème
11ème
12ème
Gare du Nord
Gare de l'Est
Centre Pompidou
Hôtel de Ville
Notre-Dame
Ile de la Cité
Ile St-Louis
Opéra Bastille
Jardin des Plantes
Panthéon
Gare de Lyon
Seine
PL. DE LA RÉPUBLIQUE
PL. DES VOSGES
PL. LÉON BLUM
PL. MAUBERT
PL. DE LA CONTRE-SCARPE
PL. MONGE
Pont de Sully
OTU-Voyage
BARBES ROCHECHOUART
GARE DU NORD
POISSONNIÈRE
GARE DE L'EST
CHÂTEAU D'EAU
BONNE NOUVELLE
STRASBOURG ST-DENIS
RÉPUBLIQUE
TEMPLE
RÉAUMUR-SEBASTOPOL
ARTS ET MÉTIERS
ETIENNE MARCEL
RAMBUTEAU
CHÂTELET
CITÉ
ST-PAUL
SULLY MORLAND
BASTILLE
MAUBERT MUTUALITÉ
CARDINAL LEMOINE
JUSSIEU
QUAI DE LA RAPÉE
GARE DE LYON
LEDRU-ROLLIN
FILLES DU CALVAIRE
OBERKAMPF
PARMENTIER
ST-MAUR
COURONNES
ST-SÉBASTIEN FROISSART
RICHARD LENOIR
ST-AMBROSE
CHEMIN VERT
BRÉGUET SABIN
VOLTAIRE
TO 31 (200m)
71 (100m)

with its older architecture and narrow streets, has traditionally been considered bohemian and intellectual, while the Right Bank, with grand avenues and designer shops, is more ritzy. Administratively, Paris is divided into 20 **arrondissements** (districts; e.g. *1er*, *6ème*) that spiral clockwise around the Louvre. Areas of interest are compact and central, and sketchier neighborhoods tend to lie on the outskirts of town. Refer also to this book's **color maps** of the city.

RIVE GAUCHE (LEFT BANK). The **Latin Quarter,** encompassing the *5ème* and parts of the *6ème* around the **Sorbonne** and the **Ecole des Beaux-Arts** (School of Fine Arts), has been home to students for centuries; the animated **Boulevard St-Michel** divides the two *arrondissements*. The lively **rue Mouffetard** in the *5ème* is quintessential Latin Quarter. The area around east-west **Boulevard St-Germain,** which crosses bd. St-Michel just south of pl. St-Michel in the *6ème*, is known as **St-Germain des Prés.** To the west, the gold-domed **Invalides** and the stern Neoclassical **Ecole Militaire,** which faces the **Eiffel Tower** across the **Champ-de-Mars,** recall the military past of the *7ème* and northern *15ème*, now full of traveling businesspeople. South of the Latin Quarter, **Montparnasse,** in the *14ème*, eastern *15ème*, and southwestern *6ème*, lolls in the shadow of its tower. The glamorous **Boulevard du Montparnasse** belies the surrounding residential districts. The eastern Left Bank, comprising the *13ème*, is Paris's new hotspot, centered on the **Place d'Italie.**

RIVE DROITE (RIGHT BANK). The **Louvre** and **rue de Rivoli** occupy the sight- and tourist-packed *1er* and the more business-oriented *2ème*. The crooked streets of the **Marais,** in the *3ème* and *4ème*, escaped Baron Haussmann's redesign of Paris and now support many diverse communities. From **Place de la Concorde,** at the western end of the *1er*, **Avenue des Champs-Elysées** bisects the *8ème* as it sweeps up toward the **Arc de Triomphe** at **Charles de Gaulle-Etoile.** South of the Etoile, old and new money fills the exclusive *16ème*, bordered to the west by the **Bois de Boulogne** park and to the east by the Seine and the **Trocadéro,** which faces the Eiffel Tower across the river. Back toward central Paris, the *9ème*, just north of the *2ème*, is defined by the sumptuous **Opéra.** East of the *9ème*, the *10ème* hosts cheap lodgings and the **Gare du Nord** and **Gare de l'Est.** The *10ème*, *3ème*, and the *11ème*, which claims the newest hip nightlife in Paris (in **Bastille**), meet at **Place de la République.** South of Bastille, the *12ème* surrounds the **Gare de Lyon,** petering out at the **Bois de Vincennes.** East of Bastille, the party atmosphere gives way to the quieter, more residential *20ème* and *19ème*, while the *18ème* is home to the quaint and heavily touristed **Montmartre,** which is capped by the **Sacré-Cœur.** To the east, the *17ème* begins in the red-light district of **Pigalle** and bd. de Clichy, and grows more elegant toward the Etoile, the **Opéra Garnier,** and the *16ème*. Continuing west along the *grande axe*, defined by the Champs-Elysées, the skyscrapers of **La Défense,** Paris's newest quarter, loom across the Seine from the Bois de Boulogne.

LOCAL TRANSPORTATION

Public Transportation: The efficient **Métropolitain,** or **Métro (M),** runs 5:30am-12:30am. Lines are numbered and are generally referred to by their number and final destinations; connections are called *correspondances*. **Single-fare tickets** within the city €1.30; ***carnet*** (packet) of 10 €9.30. Buy extras for when ticket booths are closed (after 10pm) and hold on to your ticket until you exit. The **RER** *(Réseau Express Régional),* the commuter train to the suburbs, serves as an express subway within central Paris; changing to and getting off the RER requires sticking your validated ticket into a turnstile. Watch the signboards next to the RER tracks and check that your stop is lit up before riding. **Buses** use the same €1.30 tickets (bought on the bus; validate in the machine by the driver), but transfer requires a new ticket. Buses run 6:30am-8:30pm,

Autobus de Nuit until 1am, and *Noctambus* (3-4 tickets) every hr. 1:30-5:30am at stops marked with the bug-eyed moon between the Châtelet stop and the *portes* (city exits). The **Mobilis** pass covers the Métro, RER, and buses only (€5 for a 1-day pass in Zones 1 and 2). A weekly pass *(carte orange hebdomadaire)* costs €13.75 and expires every Su; photo ID required. Refer to this book's **color maps** of Paris's transit network.

Taxis: Alpha Taxis (☎01 45 85 85 85); **Taxis 7000** (☎01 42 70 00 42). Cabs are expensive and take 3 passengers (there is a €2.45 surcharge for a fourth). The meter starts running when you phone. Cab stands are near train stations and major bus stops.

Car Rental: Rent-a-Car, 79 r. de Bercy (☎01 43 45 98 99). Open M-Sa 8:30am-6pm.

Bike Rental: Paris à velo, c'est sympa! 37 bd. Bourdon, 4*ème* (☎01 48 87 60 01; www.parisvelosympa.com). M: Bastille. Rentals available with a €305 or credit card deposit. 24hr. rental €16; 9am-7pm €12.50; half-day €9.15.

PRACTICAL INFORMATION

TOURIST AND FINANCIAL SERVICES

Tourist Offices: Bureau d'Accueil Central, 127 av. des Champs-Elysées, 8*ème* (☎08 36 68 31 12; www.paris-touristoffice.com). M: Georges V. English-speaking and enormous. Open daily 9am-8pm; off-season M-Sa 9am-8pm, Su 11am-6pm.

Embassies: Australia, 4 r. Jean-Rey, 15*ème* (☎01 40 59 33 00). M: Bir-Hakeim. Open M-F 9am-6pm. **Canada,** 35 av. Montaigne, 8*ème* (☎01 44 43 29 00). M: Franklin-Roosevelt or Alma-Marceau. Open M-F 9am-5pm. **Ireland,** 4 r. Rude, 16*ème* (☎01 44 17 67 00). M: Trocadéro. Open M-F 9:30am-1pm and 2:30-5:30pm. **New Zealand,** 7ter r. Leonardo de Vinci, 16*ème* (☎01 45 01 43 43). M: Victor-Hugo. Open July-Aug. M-Th 8:30am-1pm and 2-5:30pm, F 8:30am-2pm; Sept.-June M-F 9am-1pm and 2-5:30pm. **South Africa,** 59 quai d'Orsay, 7*ème* (☎01 53 59 23 23). M: Invalides. Open M-F 8:30am-5:15pm. **UK,** 18bis r. d'Anjou, 8*ème* (☎01 44 51 31 00). M: St-Augustin. Open M-F 9:30am-12:30pm and 2:30-5pm. **US,** 2 r. St-Forentin, 1*er* (☎01 43 12 22 22). M: Concorde. Open M-F 9am-12:30pm and 1-6pm.

Currency Exchange: Hotels, train stations, and airports offer poor rates but have extended hours; Gare de Lyon, Gare du Nord, and both airports have booths open 6:30am-10:30pm. Most **ATMs** accept **Visa** ("CB/VISA") and **MasterCard** ("EC"). Crédit Lyonnais ATMs take **AmEx;** Crédit Mutuel and Crédit Agricole ATMs are on the **Cirrus** network; and most Visa ATMs accept **PLUS**-network cards.

American Express: 11 r. Scribe, 9*ème* (☎01 47 14 50 00), opposite rear of the Opéra. M: Opéra or Auber. Mail held for cardholders and AmEx Travelers Cheques holders. Open M-Sa 9am-6:30pm, exchange counters open Su 10am-5pm.

LOCAL SERVICES

English-Language Bookstore: Shakespeare and Co., 37 r. de la Bûcherie, 5*ème*, across the Seine from Notre-Dame. M: St-Michel. A Paris fixture and a center for Anglos in the city, with a quirky selection of new and used books. Open daily noon-midnight.

Bi-Gay-Lesbian Organizations: Centre Gai et Lesbien, 3 r. Keller, 11*ème* (☎01 43 57 21 47). M: Ledru Rollin or Bastille. Info hub of all gay services and associations in Paris. English spoken. Open M-Sa 2-8pm, Su 2-7pm. **Les Mots à la Bouche,** 6 r. Ste-Croix de la Bretonnerie, 4*ème* (☎01 42 78 88 30; www.motsbouche.com), is Paris's largest gay and lesbian bookstore and serves as an unofficial information center for queer life. M: Hôtel-de-Ville. Open M-Sa 11am-11pm, Su 2-8pm.

Laundromats: Laundromats are everywhere, especially in the 5*ème* and 6*ème*. **Arc en Ciel,** 62 r. Arbre Sec, 1*er* (☎01 42 41 39 39), does dry cleaning. M: Louvre. Open M-F 8am-1:15pm and 2:30-7pm, Sa 8:30am-1:15pm.

EMERGENCY AND COMMUNICATIONS

Emergencies: Ambulance: ☎15. **Fire:** ☎18. **Police:** ☎17. For non-emergencies, head to the local *gendarmerie* (police force) in each *arrondissement.*

Crisis Lines: Rape, SOS Viol (☎0 800 05 95 95). Call free anywhere in France for counseling (medical and legal). Open M-F 10am-7pm. **SOS Help!** (☎01 47 23 80 80). Anonymous, confidential, English-speaking crisis hotline. Open daily 3-11pm.

Pharmacies: Every *arrondissement* should have a **pharmacie de garde** open 24hr. in case of emergencies. The locations change, but the name of the nearest one is posted on each pharmacy's door. **British & American Pharmacy,** 1 r. Auber, 9*ème* (☎01 42 65 88 29). M: Auber or Opéra. Open daily 8am-8:30pm.

Medical Assistance: Hôpital Américain de Paris, 84 bd. Saussaye, Neuilly (☎01 46 41 25 25). M: Port Maillot, then bus #82 to the end of the line. A private hospital. **Hôpital Franco-Britannique de Paris,** 3 r. Barbès (☎01 46 39 22 22), in the suburb of Levallois-Perret. M: Anatole-France. Some English spoken. **Hôpital Bichat,** 46 r. Henri Buchard, 18*ème* (☎01 40 25 80 80). M: Port St-Ouen. Emergency services.

Telephones: To use the phones, you'll need to buy a **phone card** *(télécarte),* available at post offices, Métro stations, and *tabacs.* For **directory info,** call ☎12.

Internet Access: **easyEverything,** 37 bd. Sébastopol, 1er (☎01 40 41 09 10). M: Châtelet-Les-Halles. Purchase a User ID for any amount (min. €3) and recharge the ID with €1.50 or more. Number of minutes depends on the time of day and how busy the store is. Open 24hr. **Le Jardin de l'Internet,** 79 bd. St-Michel, 5ème (☎01 44 07 22 20). RER: Luxembourg. 15min. minimum. €0.15 per min., €6.10 per hr., €29 for 5hr. Open daily 9am-11pm. **WebBar,** 32 r. de Picardie, 3ème (☎01 42 72 66 55). M: République. €1 per 15min. Open daily 8:30am-2am.

Post Office: Poste du Louvre, 52 r. du Louvre, 1*er* (☎01 40 28 20 40). M: Louvre. Open 24hr. Address mail to be held: SURNAME Firstname, *Poste Restante,* 52 r. du Louvre, 75001 Paris, France. **Postal Code:** 750XX, where "XX" is the *arrondissement* (e.g., 75003 for any address in the 3*ème*).

ACCOMMODATIONS

High season in Paris falls around Easter and from May to October, peaking in July and August. Paris's hostels skip many standard restrictions (sleep sheets, curfews, etc.) and they tend to have flexible maximum stays. The city's six HI hostels are for members only. The rest of Paris's dorm-style beds are either private hostels or quieter *foyers* (student dorms). Hotels may be the most practical accommodations for the majority of travelers. Expect to pay at least €25 for a single or €35 for a double in the cheapest, luckiest of circumstances. In cheaper hotels, few rooms have private baths; hall showers cost about €2.50 per use. Rooms fill quickly after morning check-out (10am-noon), so arrive early or reserve ahead. Many hotels accept reservations with a one-night credit card deposit. Most hostels and *foyers* include the **taxe de séjour** (€1-1.50 per person per day) in listed prices, but some do not. If you haven't reserved ahead, tourist offices (see p. 309) and other organizations (see below) can book rooms.

ACCOMMODATIONS SERVICES

La Centrale de Réservations (FUAJ-HI), 4 bd. Jules Ferry, 11ème (☎01 43 57 02 60; fax 01 40 21 79 92). M: République. Open daily 8am-10pm.

OTU-Voyage (Office du Tourisme Universitaire), 119 r. St-Martin, 4*ème* (☎08 20 81 78 17). €1.55 service fee. Full payment due with reservation. English spoken. Open M-F 9:30am-7pm, Sa 10am-noon and 1:30-5pm.

1ER AND 2ÈME: LOUVRE-PALAIS ROYAL

Central to the **Louvre,** the **Tuileries,** the **Seine,** and the ritzy **Place Vendôme,** this area still has some budget hotels. In general, avoid r. St-Denis.

Hôtel Montpensier, 12 r. de Richelieu (☎01 42 96 28 50; fax 01 42 86 02 70). M: Palais-Royal. Walk around the left side of the Palais-Royal to r. de Richelieu. Clean rooms, bright decor. Its good taste sets it apart from most hotels in this area and price range. Friendly English-speaking staff. Breakfast €6. Shower €4. Reserve 2 months in advance in high season. Singles and doubles with toilet €53; with toilet and shower €74; with toilet, bath, and sink €87. Extra bed €12. AmEx/MC/V. ❹

Hôtel Tiquetonne, 6 r. Tiquetonne (☎01 42 36 94 58; fax 01 42 36 02 94). M: Etienne-Marcel. Walk against traffic on r. de Turbigo; turn left on r. Tiquetonne. Clean 7-story hotel near Marché Montorgueil, the rowdy English bars near Etienne-Marcel, and r. St-Denis's sex shops—what more could you want? Elevator. Breakfast €5. Hall showers €5. Closed Aug. and 1 week at Christmas. Reserve 2 weeks in advance. Singles with shower €24-36; doubles with shower and toilet €41. AmEx/MC/V. ❷

Centre International de Paris (BVJ): Paris Louvre, 20 r. Jean-Jacques Rousseau (☎01 53 00 90 90; fax 01 53 00 90 91). M: Louvre or Palais-Royal. From M: Louvre, take r. du Louvre away from the river, turn left on r. St-Honoré and right on r. J.J. Rousseau. Large hostel that draws a very international crowd. Bright, dorm-style rooms with 4-10 beds per room. English spoken. Breakfast and showers included. Lockers €2. Reception 24hr. Reserve 1 week in advance by phone only. Rooms held for only 10-30min. after your expected check-in time; call if you'll be late. €24 per person. ❷

Hôtel Vivienne, 40 r. Vivienne (☎01 42 33 13 26; paris@hotel-vivienne.com). M: Grands Boulevards. Follow the traffic on bd. Montmartre past the Théâtre des Variétés, turn left on r. Vivienne. Elegant, with spacious rooms. Some rooms with balconies. Breakfast €6. Singles with shower €48, with shower and toilet €78; doubles €63/€78; 3rd person under 10 free, over 10 add 30%. MC/V. ❹

Hôtel Lion d'Or, 5 r. de la Sourdière (☎01 42 60 79 04; fax 01 42 60 09 14). M: Tuileries or Pyramides. From M: Tuileries, walk down r. du 29 Juillet away from the park and turn right on r. St-Honoré, then left on r. de la Sourdière. Clean and in a quiet area. Friendly, English-speaking staff. Breakfast €5. Reserve 1 month in advance in high season. Singles with shower, toilet, and double bed €58-74, with bath €68-80; doubles €74-85/€80-95; triples €84-95/€90-105. Extra bed €10. AmEx/MC/V. ❺

Hôtel St-Honoré, 85 r. St-Honoré (☎01 42 36 20 38; paris@hotelsainthonoré.com). M: Louvre, Châtelet, or Les Halles. From M: Louvre, cross r. de Rivoli onto r. du Louvre and turn right on r. St-Honoré. Friendly, English-speaking staff and young clientele. Breakfast area, sizable modern rooms. All rooms have shower, toilet, and TV. Breakfast €4.50. Reserve 3 weeks ahead. Singles €49; doubles €68, with bathtub €75; triples and quads €83. AmEx/MC/V. ❹

Hôtel des Boulevards, 10 r. de la Ville Neuve (☎01 42 36 02 29; fax 01 42 36 15 39). M: Bonne Nouvelle. Walk against traffic on av. Poissonnière and make a right on r. de la Ville Neuve. In a funky but slightly run-down neighborhood. Quiet, simple rooms with TVs, and phones. Friendly reception. Breakfast included. Reserve 2 weeks ahead, confirm with credit card deposit. Singles and doubles €39, with shower €49, with bath €53-55. Extra bed €10. 10% *Let's Go* discount. AmEx/MC/V. ❹

Hôtel Louvre-Richelieu, 51 r. de Richelieu (☎01 42 97 46 20; www.louvre-richelieu.com). M: Palais-Royal. See directions for Hôtel Montpensier. 14 large, clean rooms. English spoken. Reserve 3 weeks ahead in summer. Singles €45, with shower €60; doubles €55/€76; triples with shower and toilet €92. Extra bed €13. MC/V. ❹

Hôtel La Marmotte, 6 r. Léopold Bellan (☎01 40 26 26 51; fax 01 42 42 96 20). M: Sentier. Take r. Petit Carreaux (the street market) and then turn right at r. Léopold Bellan.

FRANCE

Quiet rooms with TVs, phones, and free safe-boxes. Breakfast €4. Shower €3. Reserve 1 month in advance. Singles and 1-bed doubles €28-35, with shower €42-53; 2-bed doubles €59. Extra bed €12. ❷

Hôtel Bonne Nouvelle, 17 r. Beauregard (☎01 45 08 42 42; www.hotel-bonne-nouvelle.com). M: Bonne Nouvelle. From the métro, follow traffic down r. Poissonnière and turn left on r. Beauregard. In a less-than-elegant neighborhood. Part Swiss chalet, part 70s motel. All rooms have bathrooms with toilet, shower, or bath. Reserve 1 month in advance. Singles €46; singles and doubles with bath €54-77; triples with bath €85-100; quads €100-115. MC/V. ❸

Hôtel Favart, 5 r. Marivaux, *2ème* (☎01 42 97 59 83; favart.hotel@wanadoo.fr). M: Richelieu Drouot. From the métro, turn left down bd. des Italiens and left on r. Marivaux. On a quiet, well-located street. Rooms are big and comfortable. One wheelchair accessible room on 1st fl. Breakfast included. Prices with *Let's Go:* singles €85; doubles €108. Extra bed €15.25. AmEx/MC/V. ❺

3ÈME AND 4ÈME: THE MARAIS

The Marais' 17th-century mansions now house budget hotels close to the **Centre Pompidou,** the **Ile St-Louis,** and bars. The area is convenient for sampling nightlife farther away, as Paris's night buses converge in the *4ème* at M: Châtelet.

Hôtel du Séjour, 36 r. du Grenier St-Lazare (☎/fax 01 48 87 40 36). M: Etienne-Marcel. Follow the traffic on r. Etienne-Marcel, which becomes r. du Grenier St-Lazare. One block from Les Halles and the Centre Pompidou, Clean, bright rooms. Reserve a week in advance. Showers €4. Reception daily 7am-10:30pm. Singles €30; doubles €43, with shower and toilet €54, third person €23 extra. ❷

Hôtel des Jeunes (MIJE) (☎01 42 74 23 45; www.mije.com). Books beds in Le Fourcy, Le Fauconnier, and Maubuisson (see below), 3 small hostels located on cobblestone streets in beautiful old Marais residences. English spoken. Ages 18-30 only. 7-day max. stay. Breakfast, shower, sheets included. Reception daily 7am-1am. Lockout noon-3pm. Curfew 1am. Reserve in advance and arrive before noon (call if you'll be late). Dorms €22; singles €38; doubles €54; triples €72. ❷

Le Fourcy, 6 r. de Fourcy. M: St-Paul or Pont Marie. From M: St-Paul, walk opposite the traffic for a few meters down r. François-Miron and turn left on r. de Fourcy. Hostel surrounds a large, social courtyard. The La Table d'Hôtes restaurant (at Le Fourcy) offers a main course with drink (€7.80) and coffee and 3-course "hosteler special" (€9.40).

Le Fauconnier, 11 r. du Fauconnier. M: St-Paul or Pont Marie. From M: St-Paul, take r. du Prevôt, turn left on r. Charlemagne, and turn right on r. du Fauconnier. Ivy-covered building steps away from the Seine and Île St-Louis.

Maubuisson, 12 r. des Barres. M: Hôtel-de-Ville or Pont Marie. From M: Pont Marie, walk opposite traffic on r. de l'Hôtel-de-Ville and turn right on r. des Barres. A half-timbered former girls' convent on a silent street by the St-Gervais monastery. Elevator.

Grand Hôtel Jeanne d'Arc, 3 r. de Jarente (☎01 48 87 62 11; www.hoteljeannedarc.com). M: St-Paul or Bastille. From M: St-Paul walk opposite traffic on r. de Rivoli and turn left on r. de Sévigné and right on r. de Jarente. Rooms have showers and toilets. 2 wheelchair-accessible rooms. Elevator. Reserve 2 months in advance. Singles €53-64; doubles €67-92; triples €107; quads €122. Extra bed €12. MC/V. ❹

Hôtel de Roubaix, 6 r. Greneta (☎01 42 72 89 91; fax 01 42 72 58 79). M: Réaumur-Sébastopol. From the métro, walk opposite traffic on bd. de Sébastopol and turn left on r. Greneta. Helpful staff, clean rooms. All rooms have shower, toilet, telephone, locker, and TV. Breakfast included. Reserve 1 week in advance. Singles €52-58; doubles €64-68; triples €78-81; quads €87; quints €92. MC/V. ❹

Hôtel Picard, 26 r. de Picardie (☎01 48 87 53 82; fax 01 48 87 02 56). M: Temple. From the métro, walk against traffic down r. du Temple, turn left on r. du Petit Thouars, and at the end of the street turn right. Not much English spoken. In a good location. Elevator. Breakfast €4.50. Hall showers €3. Reserve 2 weeks ahead from Apr. to Sept. 5% discount with *Let's Go*. Singles €33, with shower €41, with shower and toilet €51; doubles €40-43, with shower €52, with bath €63; triples €59-82. MC/V. ❸

Hôtel de la Place des Vosges, 12 r. de Birague (☎01 42 72 60 46; fax 01 42 72 02 64). M: Bastille. Take r. St-Antoine; r. de Birague is the third right. Steps away from pl. des Vosges. Beautiful interior with exposed beams and stone walls. Full bath in all rooms. Elevator. Breakfast €6. Reserve 2 months ahead with 1 night's deposit. Singles €76; doubles €101, with twin beds €106; triples €120; quads €140. AmEx/MC/V. ❺

Hôtel Bellevue et du Chariot d'Or, 39 r. de Turbigo (☎01 48 87 45 60; fax 01 48 87 95 04). M: Etienne-Marcel. From the métro, walk against traffic on r. de Turbigo. Clean, modern rooms with phones, toilets, and baths. Breakfast €5.25. Reserve 2 weeks in advance. Singles €51; doubles €57; triples €74; quads €91. AmEx/MC/V. ❹

Hôtel de Bretagne, 87 r. des Archives (☎01 48 87 83 14). M: Temple. Take r. du Temple against traffic and turn left onto r. de Bretagne; the hotel is on the right, at the corner with r. des Archives. Friendly reception and well-kept rooms. Breakfast €4.58. Reserve 1 week in advance. Singles €29, with shower and toilet €55; doubles €35-38, with full bath and toilet €61; triples €84; quads €92. ❸

Hôtel Practic, 9 r. d'Ormesson (☎01 48 87 80 47; fax 01 48 87 40 04). M: St-Paul. Walk against traffic on r. de Rivoli, turn left on r. de Sévigné, then right on r. d'Ormesson. A clean hotel in the heart of the Marais. Rooms are modest but bright, and all have TVs and hair dryers. English spoken. Breakfast €6. Reserve by fax 1 month in advance. Singles with toilet €49, with shower €75, with both €91; doubles €58/€80/€98; triples with both €112. Extra bed €12. MC/V. ❹

5ÈME AND 6ÈME: LATIN QUARTER AND ST-GERMAIN-DES-PRES

The lively *quartier latin* and St-Germain-des-Prés offer proximity to **Notre-Dame,** the **Panthéon,** the **Jardin du Luxembourg,** and the bustling student cafe-culture.

Young and Happy (Y&H) Hostel, 80 r. Mouffetard (☎01 45 35 09 53; fax 01 47 07 22 24). M: Monge. Cross r. Gracieuse and take r. Ortolan to r. Mouffetard. A lively hostel with laid-back staff, clean rooms. Breakfast included. Curfew 2am. 25 rooms. Doubles €50; triples €66; quads €88; Jan.-Mar. prices €2 less per night. ❷

Hôtel St-Jacques, 35 r. des Ecoles (☎01 44 07 45 45; fax 01 43 25 65 50). M: Maubert-Mutualité; RER: Cluny-La Sorbonne. Turn left on r. des Carmes, then left on r. des Ecoles. Spacious, faux-elegant rooms at reasonable rates, with balconies, bathrooms, and TVs. English spoken. Elevator. Internet access. Breakfast €6.50. Singles €44, with toilet and shower €68; doubles €77, with toilet and shower €102. AmEx/MC/V. ❹

Hôtel de Nesle, 7 r. du Nesle (☎01 43 54 62 41; www.hotelnesle.com). M: Odéon. Walk up r. Mazarine, turn right onto r. Dauphine, then left on r. du Nesle. Absolutely sparkling, the Nesle is a stand-out among budget hotels. Singles €50-70; doubles €70-100. Extra bed €12. AmEx/MC/V. ❹

Hôtel Marignan, 13 r. du Sommerard (☎01 43 54 63 81; www.hotel-marignan.com). M: Maubert-Mutualité. From the métro, turn left on r. des Carmes, then right on r. du Sommerard. Decent, amenable rooms and friendly owner. Breakfast €3. Reserve 2 months in advance. Singles €42-45; doubles €60, with shower and toilet €86-92; triples €100-110; quads €120-130. Mid-Sept. to Mar. 15% discount. AmEx/MC/V accepted for stays longer than 5 nights. ❹

Hôtel St-André des Arts, 66 r. St-André-des-Arts (☎01 43 26 96 16; fax 01 43 29 73 34). M: Odéon. From the métro, take r. de l'Ancienne Comédie, and take the first right on r. St-André-des-Arts. In the heart of St-Germain, with the feel of a country inn. New bathrooms and friendly owner. Breakfast included. Reservations recommended. Singles €52-62; doubles €76-80; triples €93; quads €104. MC/V. ❹

Delhy's Hôtel, 22 r. de l'Hirondelle (☎01 43 26 58 25; fax 01 43 26 51 06). M: St-Michel. Just steps from pl. St-Michel and the Seine. Modern facilities and quiet location. Breakfast and tax included. Hall showers €4. Reserve 2-3 weeks ahead with deposit. Singles €39-58, with shower €65-73; doubles €57-63/€71-79; triples €79-92/€92-115. Extra bed €15.25. MC/V. ❹

Hôtel d'Esmeralda, 4 r. St-Julien-le-Pauvre (☎01 43 54 19 20; fax 01 40 51 00 68). M: St-Michel. Walk along the Seine on quai St-Michel toward Notre Dame and turn right at Parc Viviani. Clean but creaky rooms. By a small park with views of the Seine. Singles €30, with shower and toilet €60; doubles €60-85; triples €95; quads €105. ❸

Hôtel des Argonauts, 12 r. de la Huchette (☎01 43 54 09 82; fax 01 44 07 18 84). M: St-Michel. With your back to the Seine, take the first left off bd. St-Michel onto r. de la Huchette. Ideally located in a bustling, Old Paris pedestrian quarter (a stone's throw from the Seine). Clean rooms. Breakfast €4. Reserve 3-4 weeks in advance in high season. Singles with shower €44; doubles with bath and toilet €63-71. AmEx/MC/V. ❹

Centre International de Paris (BVJ): Paris Quartier Latin, 44 r. des Bernardins (☎01 43 29 34 80; fax 01 53 00 90 91). M: Maubert-Mutualité. Walk with traffic on bd. St-Germain and turn right on r. des Bernardins. Boisterous if generic hostel. English spoken. Breakfast included. Showers in rooms. Reception 24hr. 97 beds. 5- and 6-bed dorms €25; singles €30; doubles €54; triples €81. ❸

Hôtel du Lys, 23 r. Serpente (☎01 43 26 97 57; fax 01 44 07 34 90). M: Odéon or St-Michel. From either subway stop, take r. Danton; r. Serpente is a side street. Feels like a French country B&B. All rooms have bath or shower. Breakfast included. Reserve 1 month ahead in summer. Singles €93; doubles €105; triples €120. MC/V. ❺

Foyer International des Etudiantes, 93 bd. St-Michel (☎01 43 54 49 63). RER: Luxembourg. Across from the Jardin du Luxembourg. Library, laundry facilities, and TV lounge. Kitchenettes, showers, and toilets on hallways. Breakfast included. July-Sept. hostel is coed, open 24hr. Reserve in writing as early as January for summer months; €30.50 deposit. Singles €27; doubles €39. Oct.-June hostel is women only, and rooms are for rent by the month—call or write for prices and availability. ❷

Hôtel du Progrès, 50 r. Gay-Lussac (☎01 43 54 53 18). M: Luxembourg. From the métro, walk away from Jardin du Luxembourg on r. Guy-Lussac. Fairly clean, sometimes noisy rooms. Elevator. Reserve 2-3 weeks ahead. Breakfast included. Singles €27-41, with shower and toilet €54; doubles €42-46/€57. Cash or traveler's checks only. ❸

Hôtel Gay-Lussac, 29 r. Gay-Lussac (☎01 43 54 23 96; fax 01 40 51 79 49). M: Luxembourg. Friendly owner and clean, old rooms. Near the Luxembourg gardens. Elevator. Reserve by fax 2 weeks in advance (1 month in summer). Singles €31, with toilet €47, with shower and toilet €60; doubles €52, with toilet €64; triples €53, with toilet €56, with shower and toilet €73; quads €95. ❸

Hôtel des Médicis, 214 r. St-Jacques (☎01 43 54 14 66). M: Luxembourg. From the métro, turn right on r. Gay-Lussac and left on r. St-Jacques. Rickety old place that shuns right-angles; Jim Morrison slummed here (room #4) for 3 weeks in 1971. 1 shower and toilet per floor. English spoken. Singles €16; doubles €31; triples €45. ❷

7ÈME: EIFFEL TOWER AND LES INVALIDES

With top-notch sights like the **Musée d'Orsay** and the **Eiffel Tower,** this *arrondissement* is not the best bet for a cheap room.

Hôtel du Champs de Mars, 7 r. du Champ de Mars (☎01 45 51 52 30; www.hotel-du-champs-de-mars.com). M: Ecole Militaire. Just off av. Bosquet. High quality, elegant rooms. Breakfast €6.50. Reserve 1 month in advance. Small elevator. Singles and doubles with shower €66-72; triples with bath €92. MC/V. ❺

Hôtel Montebello, 18 r. Pierre Leroux (☎01 47 34 41 18; fax 01 47 34 46 71). A bit far from the 7*ème*'s sights, but amazing prices for this upscale neighborhood. Behind the missable facade are clean, cheery rooms with full baths. Reserve at least 2 weeks in advance. Breakfast served 7:30-9:30am, €3.50. Singles €37; doubles €42-45. ❹

Hôtel Eiffel Rive Gauche, 6 r. du Gros Caillou (☎01 45 51 24 56; eiffel@easynet.fr). M: Ecole Militaire. Walk up av. de la Bourdonnais, turn right on r. de la Grenelle, and left on Gros-Caillou. A favorite of anglophone travelers. Rooms have cable TV, phone, and full baths. Dogs allowed. Breakfast €7. Rooms with double beds €76-85, with twin beds €80-92; triples €96-110. Extra bed €14. MC/V. ❺

Hôtel de France, 102 bd. de la Tour Maubourg (☎01 47 05 40 49; www.hotelde-france.com). M: Ecole Militaire. Clean rooms and amazing views. Multilingual staff. All rooms with phone and full bath. Reserve 1 month in advance. Breakfast €7. Singles €64; doubles €81; connecting rooms for 4-5 people available. AmEx/MC/V. ❺

8ÈME: CHAMPS-ELYSÉES

Full of expensive shops and restaurants, grand boulevards, and grandiose monuments, the 8*ème* is decidedly Paris's most glamorous *arrondissement.*

Hôtel Europe-Liège, 8 r. de Moscou (☎01 42 94 01 51; fax 01 43 87 42 18). M: Liège. From the métro, walk down r. d'Amsterdam and turn left on r. de Moscou. Very pleasant, quiet, and reasonably priced (for the 8*ème)* hotel with a friendly staff. Reserve 15 days in advance. All rooms have TV and shower or bath. 2 wheelchair-accessible rooms. Breakfast €6. Singles €65; doubles €80. AmEx/MC/V. ❺

Union Chrétienne de Jeunes Filles (UCJF/YWCA), 22 r. Naples (☎01 53 04 37 47; fax 01 53 04 37 54). M: Europe. From the métro, take r. de Constantinople and turn left onto r. de Naples. Also at **168 r. Blomet, 15*ème*** (☎01 56 56 63 00; fax 01 56 56 63 12); M: Convention. The UCJF has spacious and quiet (if a bit worn) rooms with sinks and large desks. June-Aug. 3-day minimum stay; Sept.-May longer stays for women ages 18-26. €5 YWCA membership fee, €8 for 1-week stays, €15.25 for stays of 1 month or more. Reception M-F 8am-12:25am, Sa 8:30am-12:25pm, Su 9am-12:25pm and 1:30pm-12:30am. Guests permitted until 10pm. Curfew 12:30am. Kitchen, laundry. Breakfast and dinner included; monthly rates include *demi-pension*. Singles €25.93, weekly €156, monthly €497; doubles €46/€250/€793; triples €23/€375/€1189. Men should contact the YMCA Foyer **Union Chrétienne de Jeunes Gens,** 14 r. de Trévise, 9*ème* (☎01 47 70 90 94). ❷

Hôtel Madeleine Haussmann, 10 r. Pasquier (☎01 42 65 90 11; www.3hotels.com). M: Madeleine. From the métro, walk up bd. Malesherbes and turn right on r. Pasquier. Centrally located, comfortable, and professional. Bathroom, TV, and safe box in every room. 1 room is wheelchair-accessible. Breakfast €7. Reserve 1 month in advance. Singles €100-120; doubles €120-130; triples €140; quads €180. ❺

9ÈME AND 10ÈME: OPÉRA AND GARE DE NORD

There are plenty of hotels in the 9*ème*, but many to the north are used for prostitution. Nicer but not-so-cheap hotels are available near the respectable and central bd. des Italiens and bd. Montmartre. A flock of inexpensive hotels roosts near the stations in the 10*ème*, but the area is far from the action and rather unsafe.

Hôtel Chopin, 46 passage Jouffroy (☎01 47 70 58 10; fax 01 42 47 00 70). M: Grands Boulevards. Walk west on bd. Montmartre and make a right into passage Jouffroy. Very clean, new rooms; a cut above most budget hotels. Elevator. Breakfast €7. Singles with shower €55, with shower and toilet €62-70; doubles with shower and toilet €69-80; triples with shower and toilet €91. AmEx/MC/V. ❺

Perfect Hôtel, 39 r. Rodier (☎01 42 81 18 86 or 01 42 81 26 19; perfecthotel@hotmail.com). Some rooms have balconies, and the upper floors have a beautiful view.

Phones, communal refrigerator and kitchen access, free coffee, beer vending machine (€1.50), and an English-speaking staff. Breakfast free with *Let's Go.* Singles €30, with shower and toilet €48; doubles €36/€48; triples €45/€60. MC/V. ❸

Cambrai Hôtel, 129bis bd. de Magenta (☎01 48 78 32 13; www.hotel-cambrai.com). M: Gare du Nord. Follow traffic on r. de Dunkerque to pl. de Roubaix and turn right on bd. de Magenta. Close to the Gare du Nord. Clean rooms with TVs. Breakfast €5. Showers €3. Singles €30, with toilet €35, with shower €41, with full bath €46; doubles with toilet €41, with shower €46, with full bath €52, with twin beds and full bath €58; triples €76; family suite €84. MC/V. ❸

11ÈME AND 12ÈME: BASTILLE AND RÉPUBLIQUE

A youthful and lively atmosphere pervades these *arrondissements*, but travelers should be cautious around pl. de la République and Gare de Lyon at night.

Hôtel de l'Aveyron, 5 r. d'Austerlitz (☎01 43 07 86 86; fax 01 43 07 85 20). M: Gare de Lyon. Walk away from the train station on r. de Bercy and take a right on r. d'Austerlitz. On a quiet street, with clean, unpretentious rooms. Downstairs lounge with TV. Helpful English-speaking staff. Breakfast €4. Reserve 1 month in advance. Singles and doubles €30, with shower €42; triples €39/€49. MC/V. ❸

Centre International du Séjour de Paris: CISP "Ravel," 6 av. Maurice Ravel (☎01 44 75 60 00; cisp@csi.com). M: Porte de Vincennes. Walk east on cours de Vincennes then take the first right on bd. Soult, left on r. Jules Lemaître, and right on av. Maurice Ravel. Large, clean rooms (most with fewer than 4 beds), auditorium, and outdoor public pool. Cafeteria open daily 7:30-9:30am, noon-1:30pm, and 7-8:30pm. Restaurant open noon-1:30pm. Breakfast, sheets, and towels included. 1-month max. stay. Reception daily 6:30am-1:30am. Reserve at least a few days ahead by phone. 8-bed dorm with shower and toilet in hall €15; 2-to 4-bed dorm €19; singles with shower and toilet €30; doubles with shower and toilet €24. AmEx/MC/V. ❶

Modern Hôtel, 121 r. de Chemin-Vert (☎01 47 00 54 05; www.modern-hotel.fr). M: Père Lachaise. A few blocks from the métro on r. de Chemin-Vert, on the right. Newly renovated, with modern furnishings and spotlessly clean marble bathrooms. All rooms have a hair dryer, modem connection, and safe-deposit box. Rooms are on the 6th fl.; no elevator. Breakfast €5. Singles €60; doubles €70; quads €95; extra bed €15. MC/V. ❺

Hôtel Beaumarchais, 3 r. Oberkampf (☎01 53 36 86 86; www.hotelbeaumarchais.com). M: Oberkampf. Exit on r. de Malte and turn right on r. Oberkampf. Newly renovated, with clean bathrooms. Elevator. A/C. Breakfast €6. Reserve 2 weeks ahead. Singles €69-85; doubles €99; suites €140. AmEx/MC/V. ❺

Plessis Hôtel, 25 r. du Grand Prieuré (☎01 47 00 13 38; fax 01 43 57 97 87). M: Oberkampf. From the métro, walk north on r. du Grand Prieuré. 5 floors of clean, bright rooms. Some rooms have showers, fans, TVs, and balconies. Breakfast €6. Open Sept.-July. Singles €36, with shower and toilet €60, with bath €63; doubles €36-63; twin beds with shower €63. AmEx/MC/V. ❹

Hôtel Notre-Dame, 51 r. de Malte (☎01 47 00 78 76; hotelnotredame@wanadoo.fr). M: République. Walk down av. de la République and go right on r. de Malte. Basic rooms. Elevator. Showers €3.50. Breakfast €6. Reserve 10 days ahead. Singles and doubles €35, with shower €42-55, with shower and toilet €56-67. AmEx/MC/V. ❸

Auberge de Jeunesse "Jules Ferry" (HI), 8 bd. Jules Ferry (☎01 43 57 55 60; auberge@easynet.fr). M: République. Walk east on r. du Faubourg du Temple and turn right on the far side of bd. Jules Ferry. Wonderful location in front of a park and next to pl. de la République. Clean rooms with sinks. Party atmosphere. Breakfast and shower included. 1 week max. stay. Reception and dining room 24hr. No reservations; arrive by 8am. 4- to 6-bed dorms €18.50; doubles €37. MC/V. ❷

13ÈME AND 14ÈME: MONTPARNASSE

While the 13*ème* has few established hotels, there are some hostels with reasonable prices and easy access to the Métro. Montparnasse mixes bohemian, intellectual charm with commercial centers and venerable cafes.

Hôtel de Blois, 5 r. des Plantes (☎01 45 40 99 48; fax 01 45 40 45 62). M: Mouton-Duvernet. From the métro, turn left on r. Mouton Duvernet then left on r. des Plantes. One of the best deals in Paris. Rooms have TVs, phones, hair dryers, and big, clean baths. Laundromat across the street. Breakfast €5. Free hall showers. Reserve 10 days ahead. Singles €39, with shower €43, with shower and toilet €45, with bath and toilet €51; doubles €41/€45/€47/€56; triples €61. Extra bed €12. AmEx/MC/V. ❹

Ouest Hôtel, 27 r. de Gergovie (☎01 45 42 64 99; fax 01 45 42 46 65). M: Pernety. Walk against traffic on r. Raymond Losserand and turn right on r. de Gergovie. A clean hotel with modest furnishings, outstanding rates, and friendly staff. Breakfast €5. Hall shower €5. Singles with small bed €22; singles with larger bed and doubles with 1 bed €28, with shower €37; 2-bed doubles €34, with shower €39. MC/V. ❷

FIAP Jean-Monnet, 30 r. Cabanis (☎01 43 13 17 17; www.fiap.asso.fr). M: Glacière. From the métro, walk straight down bd. Auguste-Blanqui, turn left on r. de la Santé, and then right on r. Cabanis. 500-bed international student center; spotless rooms with phone, toilet, and shower. The concrete complex has a game room, TV rooms, laundry, sunlit piano bar, restaurant, outdoor terrace, and disco. Breakfast included. Curfew 2am. Reserve 2-4 weeks in advance. Wheelchair accessible. Singles €49; doubles €62; triples €84. MC/V. ❹

Centre International du Séjour de Paris: CISP "Kellerman," 17 bd. Kellerman (☎01 44 16 37 38; www.cisp.asso.fr). M: Porte d'Italie. Cross the street and turn right on bd. Kellerman. 396-bed hostel with clean rooms. In a boring area close to Cité Universitaire and the métro. TV room, laundry, and cafeteria. Breakfast included. Wheelchair accessible. Reserve 2-3 weeks in advance. Free showers on floors with dorms. 8-bed dorms €15.40; 2- to 4-bed dorms €19.21; singles with shower and toilet €30; doubles with shower and toilet €48. AmEx/MC/V. ❶

15ÈME: INVALIDES AND ECOLE MILITAIRE

In the populous 15*ème*, hotels scramble for guests in the summer, and tourists can sometimes bargain for rates.

Hôtel Printemps, 31 r. du Commerce (☎01 45 79 83 36; fax 01 45 79 84 88). M: La Motte-Picquet-Grenelle. Clean rooms. Breakfast €4. Reserve 3-4 weeks ahead. Singles and doubles with sink €30, with shower €36, with shower and toilet €38. MC/V. ❸

Three Ducks Hostel, 6 pl. Etienne Pernet (☎01 48 42 04 05; www.3ducks.fr). M: Félix Faure. Walk against traffic on the left side of the church; the hostel is on the left. 15min. from the Eiffel Tower. Shower, breakfast included. 1 week max. stay. Reserve with credit card a week ahead. Mar.-Oct. dorms €21; doubles €48; triples €67.50. Nov.-Feb. dorms €19; doubles €22.50. MC/V. ❷

17ÈME TO 20ÈME: PIGALLE AND MONTMARTRE

Around Montmartre, in the 18*ème*, hotel rates rise as you climb up to the Basilique Sacré-Coeur. At night, avoid M: Pigalle and M: Barbès-Rochechouart; use M: Abbesses instead, and be careful on deserted side streets. The 19*ème* and 20*ème* are not central; major sights are at least a 30min. métro ride away.

Hôtel Caulaincourt, 2 sq. Caulaincourt, 18*ème* (☎01 46 06 46 06; bienvenue@caulaincourt.com). M: Lamarck-Caulaincourt. Walk up the stairs to r. Caulaincourt and go right. Big, simple rooms with great views. Breakfast €5. Reserve a month in advance. Singles €30, with shower €38, with shower and toilet €46; doubles €40-43/€47-50/€55-58; triples with shower €56-59, with shower and toilet €64-67. MC/V. ❸

Eden Hôtel, 7 r. Jean-Baptiste Dumay, 20*ème* (☎01 46 36 64 22; fax 01 46 36 01 11). M: Pyrénées. Turn right from the métro; off r. de Belleville. Clean rooms with toilets. Breakfast €4.50. Shower €4. Reserve 1 week in advance. Singles €35, with shower €48; doubles with shower €50-53. Extra bed €10. MC/V. ❸

Rhin et Danube, 3 pl. Rhin et Danube, 19*ème* (☎01 42 45 10 13; fax 01 42 06 88 82). M: Danube; or bus #75 from M: Châtelet. Just steps from the métro. Rooms are spacious and adequately clean. Each room has fridge, dishes, coffee maker, shower, toilet, and TV. Singles €46; doubles €61; triples €73; quads €83. MC/V. ❹

FOOD

In Paris, life is about eating. Scratch that—life *is* eating. Establishments range from the famous repositories of *haute cuisine* to corner *brasseries*. Inexpensive bistros and *crêperies* offer the breads, cheeses, wines, pâtés, *pôtages*, and pastries central to French cuisine. *Gauche* or gourmet, French or foreign, you'll find it in Paris. The specialty shops of the **Marché Montorgeuil,** 2*ème*, **Marché Mouffetard,** 5*ème*; the **Marché Bastille,** on bd. Richard-Lenoir, can help you assemble a picnic.

ILE DE LA CITE AND ILE ST-LOUIS

Le Caveau du Palais, 19 pl. Dauphine (☎01 43 26 04 28). M: Cité. A chic, intimate restaurant serving traditional, hearty French food. Basque specialties, which include lots of steak (€15-24) and fish (€19.50-24.40). A favorite with the locals. MC/V. ❸

Brasserie de l'Île St-Louis, 55 quai de Bourbon (☎01 43 54 02 59). M: Pont Marie. Known for its great cafe fare and for Alsatian specialities such as *choucroute garnie* (a mixture of sausages and pork on a bed of sauerkraut; €16). Open M-Tu and F-Su noon-1am, Th 5pm-1am. AmEx/MC/V. ❸

1ER AND 2ÈME: LOUVRE-PALAIS ROYAL

Cheap options surround **Les Halles,** 1*er* and 2*ème*. Near the **Louvre,** the small streets of the 2*ème* teem with traditional bistros.

Jules, 62 r. Jean-Jacques Rousseau (☎ 01 40 28 99 04). M: Les Halles. This restaurant feels like home, with a mantelpiece and blinds on the windows. Blend of modern and traditional French cooking from an award-winning chef. 4-course *menu* €21-29. Open M-F noon-2:30pm and 7-10:30pm. AmEx/MC/V. ❺

La Victoire Suprême du Coeur, 41 r. des Bourdonnais (☎01 40 41 93 95). M: Châtelet. All vegetarian, and all very tasty. All-day 3-course *formule* €16. *Entrées* €4-9. Open M-F 11:45am-2:45pm and 7-10pm, Sa noon-4pm and 7-10pm. MC/V. ❹

Le Fumoir, 6 r. de l'Amiral Coligny (☎01 42 92 05 05). M: Louvre. Close to the Louvre. Part bar, part tea house; decidedly untouristy in feel. Serves the best brunch in Paris (€19), coffee €2.40. Open daily 11am-2am. AmEx/MC/V. ❹

Les Noces de Jeannette, 14 r. Favart, and 9 r. d'Amboise (☎01 42 96 36 89). M: Richelieu-Drouot. *Menu du Bistro* (€27.50) with large salad *entrées,* roasted fish, duck, and grilled meat *plats.* Reserve ahead. Open daily noon-1:30pm and 7-9:30pm. ❺

Il Buco, 18 r. Léopold Bellan (☎01 45 08 50 10). M: Sentier. Serves fresh, flavorful Italian food to a hip local crowd. *Entrées* €9-10.50, *plats* €10-13. Reservations recommended. Open M-F noon-2:30pm and 8-11pm, Sa dinner only. MC/V. ❸

3ÈME AND 4ÈME: THE MARAIS

The Marais offers chic bistros, kosher delis, and cheap, couple-friendly cafes.

Chez Janou, 2 r. Roger Verlomme (☎01 42 72 28 41). M: Chemin-Vert. This hip and friendly restaurant is lauded for its reasonably priced gourmet food. The *ratatouille* *entrée* (€7) is delicious. Main courses like *thon à la provençale* €9.50-14. Open M-F noon-3pm and 7:45pm-midnight, Sa-Su noon-5pm and 7:45pm-midnight. ❸

Au Petit Fer à Cheval, 30 r. Vieille-du-Temple (☎01 42 72 47 47). M: Hôtel-de-Ville or St-Paul. An oasis of *chèvre, kir,* and *Gauloises,* and a loyal local crowd. *Filet mignon de veau* €15, excellent salads €3.50-10. Open daily noon-1:15am. MC/V. ❸

Piccolo Teatro, 6 r. des Ecouffes (☎01 42 72 17 79). M: St-Paul. A romantic vegetarian eatery. Weekday lunch *menus* €8.20-13.30. *Entrées* €3-7, *plats* €8-13. Open Tu-Sa noon-3pm and 7-11:30pm. AmEx/MC/V. ❷

L'As du Falafel, 34 r. des Rosiers (☎01 48 87 63 60). M: St-Paul. A kosher falafel stand and restaurant with arguably the best falafel in Paris (€4). Thimble-sized (but good) lemonade €2.50. Open Su-F 11:30am-11:30pm. MC/V. ❶

404, 69 r. des Gravilliers (☎ 01 42 74 57 81). M: Arts et Métiers. Classy but comfortable North African restaurant. Mouth-watering couscous (€13-23) and *tagines* (€13-19). Lunch *menu* €17. Open daily noon-2:30pm and 8pm-midnight. AmEx/MC/V. ❹

Georges, on the 6th fl. of the Centre Pompidou (☎01 44 78 47 99). M: Rambuteau. Ultra-sleek, Zen-cool, in-the-spotlight cafe; don't miss the terrace. Wine €8, champagne €10, gazpacho €8, fresh fruit salad €9.50. Open W-M noon-2am. ❸

Sacha Finkelsztajn, 27 r. des Rosiers (☎01 42 72 78 91). M: St-Paul. Sandwiches for around €5. Go with an open mind and come away with combos like smoked salmon and green olive paste. Open M and W-Th 10am-2pm and 3-7pm, F-Su 10am-7pm. ❶

5ÈME AND 6ÈME: LATIN QUARTER AND ST-GERMAIN-DES-PRÉS

The way to the Latin Quarter's heart is through its cafes. Here, eating is less about fine dining than about whiling away an afternoon and soaking up the atmosphere.

Savannah Café, 27 r. Descartes (☎01 43 29 45 77). M: Cardinal Lemoine. Lebanese food. *Entrées* €6-11.50, *menu gastronomique* €21.65. Open M-Sa 7-11pm. MC/V. ❹ Savannah's little sister is the **Comptoir Méditerranée,** 42 r. du Cardinal Lemoine (☎01 43 25 29 08), with takeout and much lower prices. Open M-Sa 11am-10pm. ❶

Au Port Salut, 163bis r. St-Jacques (☎01 46 33 63 21). M: Luxembourg. This former cabaret now houses 3 floors of traditional French gastronomic joy. 3-course *menus* €12 and €21. Open Tu-Sa noon-2:30pm and 7-11:30pm. MC/V. ❸

Le Petit Vatel, 5 r. Lobineau (☎01 43 54 28 49). M: Mabillon. This charming little home-run bistro serves Mediterranean French specialties, all €10. €11 lunch *menu* usually has a vegetarian option. Open Tu-Sa noon-2pm and 8-10:30pm. ❸

Les Editeurs, 4 carrefour d'Odéon (☎01 43 26 67 76). The newest and classiest cafe on the block. Jazz music and a piano upstairs. *Cafe* €2.50, *croque monsieur* €9.50. Happy Hour daily 6-8pm (cocktails €6-8). Open daily 8am-2am. AmEx/MC/V. ❷

Café de Flore, 172 bd. St-Germain (☎01 45 48 55 26). M: St-Germain-des-Prés. Sartre composed *Being and Nothingness* here; Apollinaire, Picasso, and Thurber sipped brew. Espresso €4, pastries €6-11. Open daily 7:30am-1:30am. AmEx/MC/V. ❹

Les Deux Magots, 6 pl. St-Germain-des-Prés (☎01 45 48 55 25). M: St-Germain-des-Prés. The other biggie (with Café de Flore), frequented by Mallarmé and Hemingway. Coffee €3.80, sandwiches €6.10-7.60. Open daily 7:30am-1:30am. AmEx/V. ❷

Le Sélect, 99 bd. du Montparnasse (☎01 45 48 38 24). M: Vavin. Trotsky, Satie, Breton, Cocteau, and Picasso all frequented this huge Art Deco cafe. Today, this "American Bar" draws a local crowd. *Cafe* €2.15-2.60. Open daily 7am-3am. MC/V. ❷

Le Perraudin, 157 r. St-Jacques (☎01 46 33 15 75). M: Cluny-La Sorbonne. A traditional French bistro that draws students and locals. Lunch *menu* €11.90, *menu gastronomique* €28. Open M-F noon-2:30pm and 7-11pm. ❹

Così, 54 r. de Seine (☎01 46 33 35 36). M: Mabillon. This hip *sandwicherie* sells enormous, tasty, inexpensive sandwiches on fresh, brick-oven bread; don't be detered by the lines. Sandwiches €5.20-7.60. Desserts €2.80-3.40. Open daily noon-11pm. ❶

7ÈME: EIFFEL TOWER AND LES INVALIDES

Café du Marché 38 r. Cler (☎01 47 05 51 27). M: Ecole Militaire. Good American-style food (caesar salad €8) along with customary French dishes (duck confit €9.50). Charming terrace. Open M-Sa 7am-1am, food served until 11pm; Su 7am-3pm. MC/V. ❷

Le Lotus Blanc, 45 r. de Bourgogne (☎01 45 55 18 89). M: Varenne. Vietnamese specialties. Lunch *menu* €9-29. Veggie *menu* €6.50-10.50. Reservations encouraged. Open M-Sa noon-2:30pm and 7-10:30pm. Closed 2 weeks in Aug. AmEx/MC/V. ❸

Au Pied de Fouet, 45 r. de Babylone (☎01 47 05 12 27). M: Vaneau. Small, bustling bistro that attracts both cigarette-puffing locals and Franglaisphone Americans. Appetizers €2-3, *entrées* €7-11. Open M-F noon-2:30pm and 7-9:30pm, Sa noon-2pm. ❷

8ÈME: CHAMPS-ELYSÉES

Bangkok Café, 28 r. de Moscou (☎01 43 87 62 56). M: Rome. Inventive Thai food, including seafood salads (€8-10) and meat cooked in coconut milk (€12-18). Vegetarian options. Open M-F noon-2:30pm and 7-11:30pm, Sa 7-11:30pm. AmEx/MC/V. ❸

Bagel & Co., 31 r. de Ponthieu (☎01 42 89 44 20). M: Franklin D. Roosevelt. One of the only cheap options in the *8ème*. A New York-inspired deli; bagel and specialty sandwiches (€3-5). Homemade dessert €2-3. Vegetarian and kosher options. Open M-F 7:30am-9pm, Sa 10am-8pm. AmEx/MC/V. ❶

Fouquet's, 99 av. des Champs-Elysées (☎01 47 23 70 60). M: George V. A Parisian institution, with stereotypical "French" snobbery. Coffee €4.60. *Entrées* €10-34. Food served all day in the cafe. Open daily 8am-2am. AmEx/MC/V. ❺

9ÈME AND 10ÈME: OPÉRA AND GARE DU NORD

Haynes Restaurant Américain, 3 r. Clauzel (☎01 48 78 40 63). M: St-Georges. The first African-American owned restaurant in Paris (1949), a center for expatriates, and a former hangout for the likes of Louis Armstrong. Ma Sutton's fried chicken €14. Regular jazz and funk concerts. Open Tu-Sa 7pm-12:30am. AmEx/MC/V. ❸

Au Bon Café, 2 bd. St-Marti (☎01 42 00 21 45). M: République. A haven from the frenzy of the pl. de la République, and a nice alternative to the *place's* pizza chain stores. Superb salads €9-10, quiches €6-8. AmEx/MC/V. ❷

Chartier, 7 r. du Faubourg-Montmartre (☎01 47 70 86 29). M: Grands Boulevards. This Parisian fixture has been French cuisine since 1896. *Entrées* €7-9.50. Side dishes of vegetables €2.20. Open daily 11:30am-3pm and 7-10pm. MC/V. ❷

11ÈME AND 12ÈME:BASTILLE AND RÉPUBLIQUE

Chez Paul, 13 r. de Charonne (☎01 47 00 34 57). M: Bastille. A worn exterior hides a kicking bistro. Peppercorn steak €12.50. Reservations a must. Open daily noon-2:30pm and 7pm-2am; food served until 12:30am. AmEx/MC/V. ❸

Café de l'Industrie, 16 r. St-Sabin (☎01 47 00 13 53). M: Breguet-Sabin. This hip cafe pays tribute to France's colonialist past with palm trees and weapons on the walls. Coffee €2, salads €7-7.50. Open Su-F 10am-2am; lunch served noon-1pm. ❷

13ÈME THROUGH 16ÈME: MONTPARNASSE

Scores of Asian restaurants cluster in Paris's **Chinatown,** south of pl. d'Italie on av. de Choisy. The *14ème* is bordered at the top by the busy **boulevard du Montparnasse,** which is lined with a wide range of restaurants. R. du Montparnasse, which intersects with the boulevard, teems with reasonably priced *crêperies*. R. Daguerre is lined with vegetarian-friendly restaurants. Inexpensive restaurants cluster on r. Didot, r. du Commerce, r. de Vaugirard, bd. de Grenelle, and Gare Montparnasse.

Café du Commerce, 39 r. des Cinq Diamants (☎01 53 62 91 04). M: Place d'Italie. A local establishment serving traditional food with a special, funky twist. Dinner *menu* €15.50, lunch *menu* €10.50. Options like spiced bloodwurst or steak with avocado and strawberries. Open daily noon-3pm (service until 2:30pm) and 7pm-2am (service until 1am). Sa and Su brunch until 4pm. Reserve ahead for dinner. AmEx/MC/V. ❸

Phinéas, 99 r. de l'Ouest, 14*ème* (☎01 45 41 33 50). M: Pernety. At this restaurant/comic book shrine, the chef makes *tartes salées* (€6.50-8) and *tartes sucrées* (€6-6.50), right before your eyes. Vegetarian options available. Open Tu-Sa 9am-noon for take-out, noon-11:30pm for dine-in. Su brunch 11am-3pm. AmEx/MC/V. ❸

La Coupole, 102 bd. du Montparnasse (☎01 43 20 14 20). M: Vavin. La Coupole's Art Deco chambers have hosted Lenin, Stravinsky, Hemingway, and Einstein. Coffee (€2), *croque monsieur* (€5). The outrageously expensive food proper is some of the best in Paris. Open M-F 8:30am-1am, Sa-Su 8:30am-1:30am. AmEx/MC/V. ❺

Aquarius Café, 40 r. de Gergovie (☎01 45 41 36 88). M: Pernety. A vegetarian oasis and celebrated local favorite. Tofu sausages, wheat pancakes, brown rice, and vegetables in a mushroom sauce €9.90. Open M-Sa noon-2:15pm and 7-10:30pm. Also in the 4*ème* (54 r. Ste-Croix de la Bretonnerie; ☎01 48 87 48 71). AmEx/MC/V. ❸

17ÈME AND 18ÈME: MONTMARTRE

Bistros are around **place du Tertre** and **place St-Pierre.** Be cautious at night. Charming bistros and cafes line **rue des Abbesses** and **rue Lepic.**

Le Patio Provençal, 116 r. des Dames, 17*ème* (☎01 42 93 73 73). M: Villiers. This rustic farmhouse-style restaurant serves staples of southern French fare. Glass of wine €3-4. Reservations a must. Open M-F noon-2:30pm and 7-11pm. MC/V. ❸

Le Soleil Gourmand, 10 r. Ravignan (☎01 42 51 00 50). M: Abbesses. A local favorite serving inventive *Provençale*. Try the specialty *bricks* (fried, stuffed filo dough; €11), 5-cheese *tartes* with salad (€10), and house-baked cakes (€4.50-7). Vegetarian options available. Evening reservations needed. Open daily 12:30-2:30pm and 8:30-11pm. ❸

THE INSIDER'S CITY

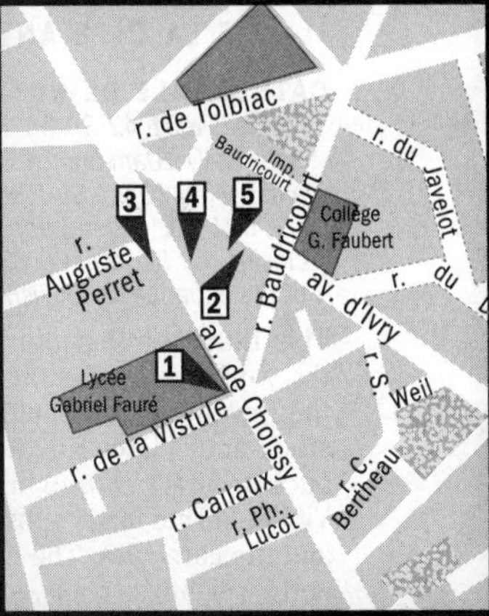

CHINATOWN'S BEST

While the edges of 13*éme* are pursuing a trendy rebirth, in its middle a pocket of tradition remains. Paris's take on Chinatown is actually multinational and largely culinary, with Thai, Vietnamese, and Chinese Restaurants. Here are some other reasons to stop by:

1. **Dong Nam A.** You'll be amazed by this store's selection of exotic produce.
2. **L'Empire des Thés.** (☎01 45 85 66 33). A delightful tea shop–eat in on sesame eclairs, or take home a pot.
3. **Ka Sun Sas** (☎01 56 61 98 89). You may just find a priceless Ming Vase here.
4. **Lycée Gabriel Faure.** Brilliant orange and blue tilings, and swirling statues decorate this neighborhood school.
5. **Ho A Ly** (☎01 45 83 96 63). Beautiful mandarin dresses, jackets and blouses.

SIGHTS

For its modest size, Paris is amazingly diverse. In a few hours, you can walk from the heart of the Marais in the east to the Eiffel Tower in the west, passing most major monuments along the way. A solid day of wandering will show you how close the medieval Notre-Dame is to the modern Centre Pompidou and the funky *Quartier Latin* to the Louvre, and why you came here in the first place.

ÎLE DE LA CITE AND ÎLE ST-LOUIS

CATHÉDRALE DE NOTRE DAME DE PARIS

M: Cité. ☎01 42 34 56 10; crypt ☎01 43 29 83 51. Open daily 8am-6:45pm. Towers open daily 10am-5pm. €5.50, ages 18-25 €3.50. Treasury open M-Sa 9:30am-12:30pm and 1:30-5:30pm, Su 1:30-5:30pm; last entrance 5pm. €2.50, students and ages 12-17 €2; 6-12 €1, under 6 free. Crypt open daily 10am-5:30pm; last ticket sold 30min. before closing. €3.30, over-60 €2.20, under 27 €1.60, under 13 free. Tours leave from the right of the entrance. In English W-Th noon, Sa 2:30pm; in French M-F noon, Sa 2:30pm.

This 12th- to 14th-century cathedral, begun under Bishop Maurice Sully, is one of the world's most famous and beautiful examples of medieval architecture. After the Revolution, the building fell into disrepair and was even used to shelter livestock until Victor Hugo's 1831 novel *Notre Dame de Paris* (a.k.a. *The Hunchback of Notre Dame*) inspired citizens to lobby for restoration. Architect Eugène Viollet-le-Duc made subsequent modifications, including the addition of the spire and the gargoyles. The intricately carved, apocalyptic facade and soaring, apparently weightless walls, effects produced by brilliant Gothic engineering and optical illusions, are inspiring even for the most church-weary. The cathedral's biggest draws are its enormous stained-glass **rose windows** that dominate the north and south ends of the transept. At the center of the 21m north window is the Virgin, depicted as the descendant of the Old Testament kings and judges who surround her. The base of the south window shows Matthew, Mark, Luke, and John on the shoulders of Old Testament prophets. In the central window, Christ is surrounded by the 12 apostles and the virgins and saints of the New Testament. A staircase inside the towers leads to a perch from which gargoyles survey the city.

OTHER SIGHTS

ÎLE DE LA CITÉ. If any place could be called the heart of Paris, it is this island in the river. In the 3rd century BC, when it was inhabited by the *Parisii*, a Gallic tribe of hunters, sailors, and fishermen, the Île de la Cité was all there was to Paris. Although the city has expanded in all directions, all distance-points in France are measured from *kilomètre zéro*, a sundial on the ground in front of Notre-Dame.

STE-CHAPELLE AND CONCIERGERIE. Within the courtyard of the **Palais de Justice,** which has housed Paris's district courts since the 13th century, the opulent, Gothic **Ste-Chapelle** was built by Saint Louis (Louis IX) to house his most precious possession, Christ's crown of thorns, now in Notre Dame. No mastery of the lower chapel's dim gilt can prepare the visitor for the **Upper Chapel,** where twin walls of stained glass glow and frescoes of saints and martyrs shine. *(4 bd. du Palais. M: Cité. ☎01 53 73 58 51 or 01 53 73 78 50. Open daily Apr.-Sept. 9:30am-5:30pm. Last admission 30min. before closing. €5.50, seniors and ages 18-25 €3.50, under 18 free. Twin ticket with Conciergerie €8, seniors and ages 18-25 €5, under 18 free.)* Around the corner is the **Conciergerie,** one of Paris's most famous prisons; Marie-Antoinette and Robespierre were imprisoned here during the Revolution. *(Entrance on bd. du Palais. M: Cité. ☎01 53 73 78 50. Open daily Apr.-Sept. 9:30am-6:30pm; Oct.-Mar. 10am-5pm. Last ticket 30min. before closing. €5.50, students €3.50. Tours in French, 11am and 3pm. For English tours, call ahead.)*

ÎLE ST-LOUIS. The Île St-Louis is home to some of Paris's most privileged elite, such as the Rothschilds and Pompidou's widow, and former home to other super-famous folks, including Voltaire, Baudelaire, and Marie Curie. At night, the island glows in the light of cast-iron lamps and candlelit bistros. Look for Paris's best ice cream at Île St-Louis's **Berthillon,** 31 r. St-Louis-en-Île. *(Walk across the Pont St-Louis from Notre-Dame; also across the Pont Marie from M: Pont Marie. Berthillon open Sept. to mid-July; take-out W-Su 10am-8pm; eat-in W-F 1-8pm, Sa-Su 2-8pm. Closed 2 weeks Feb. and Apr.)*

LATIN QUARTER AND ST-GERMAIN-DES-PRÉS: 5ÈME AND 6ÈME ARRONDISSEMENTS

The student population is the soul of the *Quartier Latin*, so named because prestigious *lycées* and universities taught in Latin until 1798. Since the violent student riots in May 1968, many artists and intellectuals have migrated to the cheaper outer *arrondissements*, and the *haute bourgeoisie* have moved in. The *5ème* still presents the most diverse array of bookstores, cinemas, bars, and jazz clubs in the city. Designer shops and cutting-edge art galleries lie near **St-Germain-des-Prés.**

CAFES. Cafes along bd. St-Germain have long been gathering places for literary and artistic notables. **Les Deux Magots,** 6 pl. St-Germain-des-Prés, named for two porcelain figures that adorned a store selling Chinese silk and imports on the same spot in the 19th century, was a favorite hangout of Verlaine and Rimbaud, and later Breton, Artaud, and Picasso. The **Café de Flore,** 172 bd. St-Germain, established in 1890, was made famous in the 1940s and 50s by Sartre and Camus, who lingered over cafe and their fair share of martinis. *(M: St-Germain-des-Prés.)*

BOULEVARD ST-MICHEL AND ENVIRONS. At the center of the Latin Quarter, bd. St-Michel, which divides the *5ème* and *6ème*, is filled with cafes, restaurants, bookstores, and clothing boutiques. **Place St-Michel,** to the north, is filled with students, often engaged in a protest of some sort, and lots of tourists. *(M: St-Michel.)*

RUE MOUFFETARD. South of pl. de la Contrescarpe, **rue Mouffetard** plays host to one of the liveliest street markets in Paris, and, along with **rue Monge,** binds much of the Latin Quarter's tourist and student social life. *(M: Cardinal Lemoine or Place Monge.)*

JARDIN DU LUXEMBOURG. South along bd. St-Michel, the formal French gardens of the Jardin du Luxembourg are perfect for strolling and reading; also the home of the most famous *guignol* puppet theater. *(RER: Luxembourg; main entrance is on bd. St-Michel. Open Apr.-Oct. daily 7:30am-9:30pm; Nov.-Mar. 8:15am-5pm.)*

PANTHÉON. The **crypt** of the Panthéon, which occupies the highest point on the Left Bank, houses the tombs of Louis Braille, Victor Hugo, Jean Jaurès, Rousseau, Voltaire, and Emile Zola; you can spy each tomb from behind locked gates. The Panthéon also houses **Foucault's Pendulum,** which proves the rotation of the earth (though Napoleon III begged to differ). *(Pl. du Panthéon. M: Cardinal Lemoine. From the métro, walk down r. Cardinal Lemoine and turn right on r. Clovis. ☎01 44 32 18 00. Open daily in summer 10am-6:30pm; in winter 10am-6:15pm; last admission 5:45pm. Admission €7, students €4.50, under 18 free; Oct.-Mar. free first Su of every month. Guided tours in French leave from inside the main door daily at 2:30 and 4pm.)*

EGLISE ST-GERMAIN-DES-PRÉS. Scarred by centuries of weather, revolution, and war, the Eglise St-Germain-des-Prés, begun in 1163, is the oldest standing church in Paris. *(3 pl. St-Germain-des-Prés. M: St-Germain-des-Prés. From the métro, walk into pl. St-Germain-des-Prés to enter the church from the front. ☎01 55 42 81 33. Open daily 8am-8pm. Info office open Tu-Sa 10:30am-noon and 2:30-6:45pm, M 2:30-6:45pm.)*

JARDIN DES PLANTES. Opened in 1640 to grow medicinal plants for King Louis XIII, the garden now features science museums, and roserie, and a **zoo,** which Parisians raided for food during the Prussian siege of 1871. *(M: Gare d'Austerlitz or Jussieu. ☎01 40 79 37 94. Open daily in summer 7:30am-8pm; in winter 7:30am-5:30pm.)*

7ÈME ARRONDISSEMENT

EIFFEL TOWER. Built in 1889 as the centerpiece of the World's Fair, the *Tour Eiffel* has come to symbolize the city. Despite criticism, tacky souvenirs, and Gustave Eiffel's own sentiment that "France is the only country in the world with a 300m flagpole," the tower is unfailingly elegant and commands an excellent view of the city. At night, when the lights are turned on, it will win over even the most jaded tourist. *(M: Bir-Hakeim or Trocadéro. ☎01 44 11 23 23; www.tour-eiffel.fr. Open mid-June through Aug. daily 9am-midnight; Sept.-Dec. 9:30am-11pm; Jan. through mid-June 9:30am-11pm. Elevator to 1st fl. €3.70, under 12 € 2.10; 2nd fl. €6.90/€3.80; 3rd fl. €9.90/€5.30. Stairs to 1st and 2nd fl. €3. Under 3 free. Last access to top 30min. before closing.)*

INVALIDES. The tree-lined **Esplanade des Invalides** runs from the impressive **Pont Alexandre III** to the gold-leaf domed **Hôtel des Invalides.** The Hôtel, built for veterans under Louis XIV, now houses the **Musée de l'Armée** and **Napoleon's Tomb.** The **Musée Rodin** (see p. 335) is nearby on r. Varenne. *(M: Invalides, Latour Maubourg, or Varenne.)*

LOUVRE AND OPÉRA: 1ER, 2ÈME, AND 9ÈME ARRONDISSEMENTS

AROUND THE LOUVRE. World-famous art museum and former residence of kings, the **Louvre** (see p. 334) occupies about one-seventh of the 1*er arrondissement*. **Le Jardin des Tuileries,** at the western foot of the Louvre, was commissioned by Catherine de Médici in 1564 and improved by André Le Nôtre (designer of the gardens at Versailles) in 1649. *(M: Tuileries. Open Apr.-Sept. daily 7am-9pm; Oct.-Mar. 7:30am-7:30pm. Free tours in English from the Arc de Triomphe du Carrousel.)* Three blocks north along r. de Castiglione, **Place Vendôme** hides 20th-century offices and luxury shops behind 17th-century facades. Look out for Napoleon on top of the column in the center of the *place*—he's the one in the toga. *(M: Tuileries or Concorde.)* The **Palais-Royal** was commissioned in 1632 by Cardinal Richelieu, who gave it to Louis XIII. In 1784, the buildings enclosing the palace's formal garden became *galeries*, the prototype of a shopping mall. The revolutions of 1789, 1830, and 1848 all began with angry crowds in the same garden. *(M: Palais-Royal/Musée du Louvre or Louvre-Rivoli.)*

OPÉRA. Located north of the Louvre in the 9*ème* arrondissement, Charles Garnier's grandiose **Opéra Garnier** was built under Napoleon III in the eclectic style of the Second Empire. Gobelin tapestries, gilded mosaics, a 1964 Marc Chagall ceiling, and a six-ton chandelier adorn the magnificent interior. *(M: Opéra. ☎08 36 69 78 68. Open Sept. to mid-July daily 10am-5pm, last entry 4:30pm; mid-July to Aug. 10am-6pm, last entry 5:30pm. €4.58; ages 10-16, students, and over 60 €3. English tours daily at noon and 2pm in summer; €10; students, ages 10-16, and over 60 €8; under 10 €4.)*

MARAIS: 3ÈME AND 4ÈME ARRONDISSEMENTS

The Marais became the most chic place to live with Henri IV's construction of the elegant **Place des Vosges** at the beginning of the 17th century; several remaining mansions, including Victor Hugo's former home, now house museums. Today, the streets of the Marais house the city's Jewish and gay communities as well as fun, hip restaurants and shops. The **rue des Rosiers** (M: St-Paul) is packed with kosher delis and falafel counters. At the confluence of the 1er, 2ème, 3ème, and 4ème, the **Centre Pompidou** (see p. 335), a museum and cultural center, looms like a colorful factory over the vast place, where artists, musicians, and pickpockets gather. Be

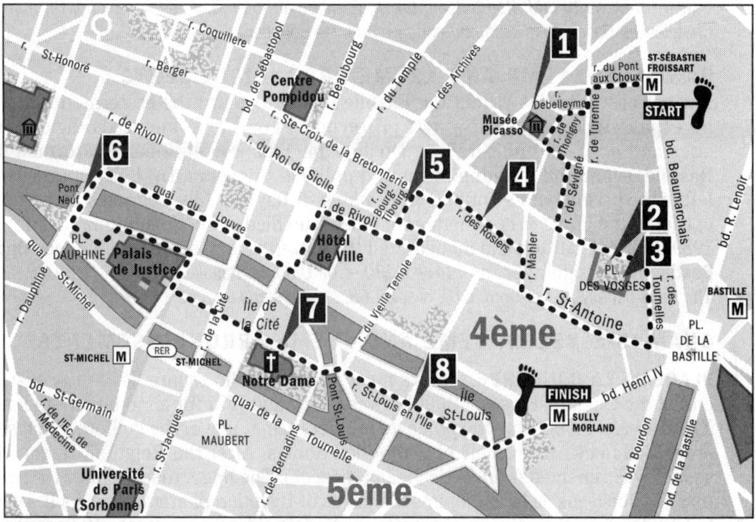

1 MUSÉE PICASSO. This museum traces Picasso's life and work chronologically, all the way from Paris to the Riviera, from blue to pink, from first mistress to last. (5, r. de Thorigny. Open Apr.-Sept. W-M 9:30am-6pm, Oct.-Mar. 9:30am-5pm. See p. 335.)

START: M: St-Sébastien Froissart

FINISH: M: Sully Morland

DISTANCE: 5.2km/3.2 mi.

DURATION: 3-4hr.

WHEN TO GO: Start in the late morning.

2 PL. DES VOSGES. This is Paris's oldest public square. Its exquisite manicured park has been tread by the likes of Molière and Victor Hugo, not to mention a good number of royals. An arcade runs around all four of its sides and houses several restaurants, art galleries, and shops. (See p. 330.)

3 MAISON DE VICTOR HUGO. The building where Victor Hugo lived from 1832 to 1848 is now a museum dedicated to the author's (and, it turns out, amateur painter's) life and work. (6, pl. des Vosges. Open Tu-Su 10am-5:40pm. See p. 330.)

4 RUE DES ROSIERS. This quintessential Marais street is filled with bakeries, off-beat boutiques, and kosher restaurants. You will regret not stopping at no. 34, the perpetually crowded **l'As du Falafel,** for a falafel sandwich. (See p. 330.)

5 MARIAGE FRÈRES. This classic and classy *salon de thé* has 500 varieties of tea to choose from. (30, r. du Bourg-Tibourg. Open daily 10:30am-7:30pm.)

6 PONT NEUF. By way of the very long, very straight, very fashionable r. de Rivoli and the scenic quai du Louvre, make your way to the Pont Neuf, Paris's oldest bridge (circa 1607). Its gargoyles have seen peddlers and pickpockets, and a whole lot of bubble wrap.

7 CATHÉDRALE DE NOTRE DAME. The postcard darling of Paris, the Notre Dame held Joan of Arc's heresy trial and saw the coronation of Napoleon. Not even the hordes of tourists can ruin the experience of visiting this newly restored Gothic masterpiece. Those who make the 422-step climb up the tower staircase are rewarded with a spectacular view. (See p. 328.)

8 BERTHILLON. The worst-kept secret in Paris, Berthillon has the uncontested title of best ice cream shop. Choose from dozens of flavors of ice cream and sorbet. (31, r. St-Louis-en-l'Île. Open Sept.-July 14: take-out W-Su 10am-8pm; eat-in 1-8pm, Sa-Su 2-8pm. See p. 329.)

cautious at night. *(M: Rambuteau; take r. Rambuteau to pl. Georges Pompidou. Or, from M: Chatelet-Les Halles, take r. Rambuteau or r. Aubry le Boucher.)*

BASTILLE: 11ÈME AND 12ÈME ARRONDISSEMENTS

Further east, Charles V built the Bastille prison to guard the eastern entrance to his capital. When it became a state prison under Louis XIII, it housed religious heretics and political undesirables. On July 14, 1789, revolutionaries stormed the Bastille, searching for gunpowder and political prisoners. By 1792, nothing was left of the prison but its outline on the *place*. Today, the July Column stands at one corner of the *place* to commemorate those who died in the Revolution. On July 14, 1989, François Mitterrand inaugurated the glittering and, some say, hideous **Opéra Bastille** to preside over the *place*. *(130, r. de Lyon. M: Bastille. ☎01 40 01 19 70. Daily 1hr. tours usually at 1 or 5pm. €10, over 60 €8, students and under 26 €5.)*

CHAMPS-ELYSÉES: 8ÈME AND 16ÈME ARRONDISSEMENTS

PLACE DE LA CONCORDE. Paris's most famous public square lies at the eastern end of the Champs-Elysées. Built between 1757 and 1777 for a monument to Louis X, the area soon became the *place de la Révolution*, site of the guillotine that severed 1343 necks from their blue-blooded bodies. After the Reign of Terror, the square was renamed (*concorde* means "peace"). The huge, rose-granite, 13th-century BC **Obélisque de Luxor** depicts the deeds of Egyptian pharaoh Ramses II. Given to Charles X by the Viceroy of Egypt, it is Paris's oldest monument. *(M: Concorde.)*

CHAMPS-ELYSÉES. Stretching west and anchored by the Arc de Triomphe on one end and the place de la Concorde on the other, the **Avenue des Champs-Elysées** is lined with luxury shops, *haute couture* boutiques, cafes, and cinemas. The avenue is the work of Baron Haussmann, who was commissioned by Napoleon III to convert Paris into a grand capital with broad avenues, wide sidewalks, new parks, elegant housing, and sanitary sewers.

ARC DE TRIOMPHE. Napoleon commissioned the **Arc de Triomphe,** at the western terminus of the Champs-Elysées, in 1806 in honor of his Grande Armée. In 1940, Parisians were brought to tears as Nazis goose-stepped through the Arc; on August 26, 1944, British, American, and French troops liberating the city from Nazi occupation marched through to the roaring cheers of thousands. The terrace at the top has a fabulous view. The **Tomb of the Unknown Soldier** has been under the Arc since

PARIS IS(N'T) BURNING As the Allied troops made their way to Paris after their successful landing on the beaches of Normandy, Hitler and the occupying Nazi forces in Paris prepared for a scorched-earth retreat. By August 23, 1944, following direct orders from Adolf Hitler, *Wehrmacht* engineers had placed mines at the base of every bridge in Paris. Despite Hitler's admiration of Napoleon's monumental tomb in the Invalides (see p. 330) during his smug visit in 1940, explosives were crammed into the basement of the Invalides, the Assemblée Nationale, and Notre Dame. The Opéra and Madeleine were to be destroyed, and the Eiffel Tower was rigged so that it would topple and prevent the approaching Allies from crossing the Seine. A brief order from German commander **Dietrich von Cholitz** would reduce every major monument in Paris—10 centuries of history—to heaps of rubble and twisted iron. Although in all other ways loyal to the Nazi party, von Cholitz simply couldn't oversee the destruction of a city such as Paris. Pestered by Hitler's incessant question, "Is Paris burning?" von Cholitz managed to stall until the Allies arrived. In 1968, he was awarded the French *Légion d'Honneur* for his bravery in the face of an irate Hitler.

November 11, 1920. It bears the inscription, "Here lies a French soldier who died for his country, 1914-1918," but represents the 1,500,000 men who died during WWI. *(On pl. Charles de Gaulle. M: Charles-de-Gaulle-Etoile. Open Apr.-Sept. daily 10am-11pm; Oct.-Mar. 10am-10:30pm. €7, ages 18-25 €4.50, under 17 free.)*

THE MADELEINE. Mirrored by the Assemblée Nationale across the Seine, the Madeleine—formally called **Eglise Ste-Marie-Madeleine** (Mary Magdalene)—was begun in 1764 by Louis XV and modeled after a Greek temple. Construction was halted during the Revolution, when the Cult of Reason proposed transforming the building into a bank, a theater, or a courthouse. Characteristically, Napoleon decreed that it should become a temple to the greatness of his army, but Louis XVIII shouted, "It shall be a church!" Completed in 1842, the structure stands alone in the medley of Parisian churches, distinguished by four ceiling domes that light the interior, 52 exterior Corinthian columns, and a curious altarpiece. *(Pl. de la Madeleine. M: Madeleine. ☎01 44 51 69 00. Open daily 7:30am-7pm.)*

MONTMARTRE AND PERE-LACHAISE: 18ÈME AND 20ÈME ARRONDISSEMENTS

MOUNTING MONTMARTRE. Montmartre, comprised mostly of one very large hill, is one of the few Parisian neighborhoods Baron Haussmann left intact when he redesigned the city and its environs. During its Belle Epoque heydey from 1875 to 1905, it attracted bohemians like Toulouse-Lautrec and Erik Satie as well as performers and impresarios like Aristide Bruant. Later, Picasso, Modigliani, Utrillo, and Apollinaire came into its artistic circle. Nowadays, Montmartre is a mix of upscale bohemia (above r. des Abbesses) and sleaze (along bd. de Clichy). The northwestern part of the area retains some village charm, with breezy streets speckled with interesting shops and cafes. *(Funicular runs cars up and down the hill every 2min. Open 6am-12:30am. €1.30 or métro ticket. M: Anvers or Abbesses.)*

BASILIQUE DU SACRE-COEUR. The Basilique du Sacré-Coeur crowns the butte Montmartre like an enormous white meringue. Its onion dome is visible from almost anywhere in the city, and its 112m bell tower is the highest point in Paris, offering a view that stretches up to 50km. *(35 r. du Chevalier de la Barre. M: Abbesses, Anvers, or Château-Rouge. From Anvers, take r. de Steinkerque off bd. de Rochechouart and climb the steps. Open daily 7am-11pm. Free. Dome and crypt open daily 9am-6pm. €5.)* Nearby, **Place du Tertre** features outdoor cafes and sketch artists.

CIMETIÈRE PÈRE LACHAISE. The Cimetière Père Lachaise, located in the *20ème*, holds the remains of Balzac, Sarah Bernhardt, Colette, Danton, David, Delacroix, La Fontaine, Haussmann, Molière, Proust, and Seurat within its peaceful, winding paths and elaborate sarcophagi. Foreigners buried here include Modigliani, Gertrude Stein, and Oscar Wilde, but the most visited grave is that of Jim Morrison. French Leftists make ceremonious pilgrimage to the **Mur des Fédérés** (Wall of the Federals), where 147 revolutionary *Communards* were executed and buried. *(16 r. du Repos. M: Père-Lachaise. Open Mar.-Oct. M-F 8am-6pm, Sa 8:30am-6pm, Su and holidays 9am-6pm; Nov.-Feb. M-F 8am-5:30pm, Sa 8:30am-5:30pm, Su and holidays 9am-5:30pm. Free.)*

PERIMETER SIGHTS: LA DÉFENSE AND BOIS DE BOULOGNE

LA DÉFENSE. Outside the city limits, west of the *16ème*, the skyscrapers and modern architecture of La Défense make up Paris's newest (unofficial) *arrondissement*, home to the headquarters of 14 of France's top 20 corporations. The **Grande Arche,** inaugurated in 1989, completes the *axe historique* running through the Louvre, pl. de la Concorde, and the Arc de Triomphe. There's yet another stunning view from the top. Trees, shops, and sculptures by Miró and

Calder line the esplanade. *(M/RER: La Défense; M, zone 2; RER, zone 3. Arch open daily 10am-8pm. €7; under 18, students, and seniors €5.50.)*

BOIS DE BOULOGNE. Popular by day for picnics, this 846-hectare (roughly 2,000-acre) park was until recently home to many drug dealers and prostitutes at night and is not the best bet for nightime entertainment. *(On the western edge of the 16ème. M: Porte Maillot, Sablons, Pont de Neuilly, or Porte Dauphine.)*

MUSEUMS

The **Carte Musées et Monuments** grants entry to 70 Paris museums without waiting in line and will save you money if you plan to visit three or more museums and major sights per day. It's available at major museums and Métro stations (1-day €15, 3-day €30, 5-day €45).

MUSÉE DU LOUVRE

1er. M: Palais-Royal/Musée du Louvre. ☎01 40 20 51 51. Open M and W 9am-9:30pm, Th-Su 9am-6pm. Last entry 45min. before closing, but people are asked to leave 15-30min. before closing. €7.50; M and W-Sa 9am-3pm €5.30; first Su of the month free. English tours M and W-Sa at 11am, 2, 3:45pm. €3.

A short list of its masterpieces includes the *Code of Hammurabi*, the *Venus de Milo*, the *Winged Victory of Samothrace*, Vermeer's *Lacemaker*, and Delacroix's *Liberty Leading the People*. Oh, yeah, and there's that lady with the mysterious smile, too—the *Mona Lisa*. Enter through I.M. Pei's controversial glass **Pyramid** in the Cour Napoléon, or skip lines by entering directly from the Métro. When visiting the Louvre, strategy is everything. The Louvre is organized into three different wings: Sully, Richelieu, and Denon. Each is divided into different sections according to the artwork's date, national origin, and medium. The color-coding and room numbers on the free maps correspond to the colors and numbers on the plaques at the entrances to every room within the wing.

The Italian Renaissance collection, on the first floor of the Denon wing, is rivaled only by that of the Uffizi museum in Florence. Look for Raphael's *Portrait of Balthazar Castiglione* and Titian's *Man with a Glove*. Titian's *Pastoral Scene* inspired Manet's *Déjeuner sur l'Herbe* (*Luncheon on the Grass;* see Musée d'Orsay, below). Bought by François I during the artist's visit to Paris, Leonardo da Vinci's *Mona Lisa* (or *La Joconde*, the Smiling One), smiles at millions each year. Nearby, da Vinci's *Virgin of the Rocks* displays the *sfumato* (smoky) technique for which he is famous. The *Venus de Milo* and the *Winged Victory of Samothrace* are just the tip of the Greek, Etruscan, and Roman antiquities iceberg. The painting collection begins with the Middle Ages and goes through the mid-19th century. Highlights include Hieronymous Bosch's *Ship of Fools* and Jan Van Eyck's *Madonna of Chancellor Rolin*, both in the Flemish gallery. The French works stretch through all three wings and include paintings from the Neoclassical, Rococo, and Romantic schools. Don't miss Jacques-Louis David's *Le serment de Horaces (The Oath of the Horatii)* and Delacroix's controversial *La Liberté guidant le peuple (Liberty Leading the People)*.

MUSÉE D'ORSAY

62 r. de Lille, 7ème. M: Solférino; RER: Musée d'Orsay. ☎01 40 49 48 14. Open mid-June to mid-Sept. Tu-W and F-Su 9am-6pm, Th 9am-9:45pm; mid-Sept to mid-June Tu-W and F-Su 10am-6pm, Th 10am-9:45pm. Last tickets 45min. before closing. €7, ages 18-25 and Su €5, under 18 free. 90min. tours in English Tu-Sa 11:30am and 2:30pm. €5.50. MC/V.

While it's considered the premier Impressionist museum, d'Orsay is dedicated to presenting all major artistic movements between 1848 and WWI. On the ground floor, works from Classicism and Proto-Impressionism are on display, and include Edouard Manet's *Olympia*, a painting that caused a scandal when it was unveiled in 1865. The first room of the upper level features Manet's controversial *Déjeuner sur l'Herbe (Luncheon in the Grass)*. Monet's *La Gare St-Lazare (St-Lazare Train Station)* and Renoir's *Le bal du Moulin de la Galette (Dance at the Moulin de la Galette)* capture the atmosphere of the industrialized Paris of the 1870s. Monet's experiments with light culminated in his *Cathédral de Rouen (Rouen Cathedral)* series. Paintings by Alfred Sisley, Camille Pissarro, and Berthe Morisot probe the allegorical beauty of the simple country life. Edgar Dégas examines the moods of dancers in *La classe de danse (The Dance Class)*. James Whistler, the American artist associated with French Realism, is represented by his *Portrait of the Artist's Mother*. Over a dozen diverse works by Vincent Van Gogh follow, including his tormented *Portrait de l'Artiste (Portrait of an Artist)*. Paul Cézanne's still lifes, portraits, and landscapes experiment with the soft colors and geometric planes that led to Cubism. Other highlights include Dégas's *L'absinthe*, and works by Rodin, Toulouse-Lautrec, Gaugin, and Seurat.

OTHER MUSEUMS

CENTRE NATIONAL D'ART ET DE CULTURE GEORGES-POMPIDOU. This inside-out building has inspired debate since its inauguration in 1977. The exterior is a sight, with chaotic colored piping and ventilation ducts (blue for air, green for water, yellow for electricity, red for heating). But the outside is an appropriate shell for the collection of Fauves, Cubists, and Pop and Conceptual works inside. Its exhibit halls, library, and superb museum collections (including the **Musée d'Art Moderne**) are excellent. *(Pl. Georges-Pompidou, 4ème. M: Rambuteau or Hôtel-de-Ville; RER: Châtelet-Les-Halles. ☎01 44 78 12 33, wheelchair info ☎01 44 78 49 54. Centre open W-M 11am-10pm; museum open W-M 11am-9pm, last tickets 8pm. Permanent collection €5.50, students and over 60 €3.50, under 13 free; 1st Su of month free.)*

MUSÉE RODIN. The 18th-century Hôtel Biron holds hundreds of sculptures by Auguste Rodin (and by his student and lover, Camille Claudel), including the *Gates of Hell*, *The Thinker*, *Burghers of Calais*, and *The Kiss*. *(77 r. de Varenne, 7ème. M: Varenne. ☎01 44 18 61 10. Open Apr.-Sept. Tu-Su 9:30am-5:45pm; Oct.-Mar. 9:30am-4:45pm. Last tickets 30min. before closing. €5; seniors, ages 18-25, and all on Su €3 Park open Apr.-Sept. Tu-Su 9:30am-6:45pm; Oct.-Mar. 9:30am-5pm. €1. Audio tour €4. MC/V.)*

MUSÉE PICASSO. This museum follows Picasso's career from his early work in Barcelona to his Cubist and Surrealist years in Paris and Neoclassical work on the Riviera. *(5 r. de Thorigny, 3ème. M: Chemin Vert. ☎01 42 71 63 15 or 01 42 71 25 21. Open Apr.-Sept. W-M 9:30am-6pm; Oct.-Mar. 9:30am-5:30pm; last tickets 30min. before closing. €5.50, Su and ages 18-25 €4, under 18 free.)*

MUSÉE DE CLUNY. One of the world's finest collections of medieval art, the Musée de Cluny is housed in a medieval monastery built on top of Roman baths. Works include *La Dame et La Licorne* (The Lady and the Unicorn), one of the world's most beautiful extant medieval tapestry series. *(6 pl. Paul Painlevé, 5ème. M: Cluny-Sorbonne. ☎01 53 73 78 00. Open W-M 9:15am-5:45pm, last tickets 5:15pm. €6.70; students, under 25, over 60, and all on Su €5.20; under 18 free.)*

MUSÉE MARMOTTAN MONET. Owing to generous donations by the families of Monet and others, this hunting-lodge-turned-mansion features an eclectic collection of Empire furniture, Impressionist Monet and Renoir canvases, and medieval illuminations. *(2 r. Louis-Boilly, 16ème. M: La Muette. Follow Chaussée de la Muette (it becomes av. Ranelagh), through the Jardin du Ranelagh. ☎01 44 96 50 33. Open Tu-Su 10am-6pm. €6.50, students €4, under 8 free.)*

IN RECENT NEWS

BEACH BUMMING

As the saying goes, if you can't stand the heat, then get the hell out of town. Among those who heed this mantra are the citizens of Paris, who, come August, flee their beloved city for the shores of Normandy and Côte d'Azur. But in the summer of 2002, the city figured out how to bring the beach to Paris. Bertrand Delanoe, the city's mayor, decided to transform 2km of Seine riverfront into "Paris Plage." The result was five patches of "beach"—one of sand, two of grass, and two of pebbles—that stretched from quai Tuileries to quai Henri IV. Equipped with lounge chairs, parasols, palm trees, and even a volleyball court, the beach drew hordes of sun-hungry citizens.

True, the *plage,* for which the city shelled out €1.5 million, fell short of paradise. Pollution by Parisians past, who failed to foresee the city's beach potential, makes the Seine unfit for swimming. More tragically, perhaps, the city discourages one of Europe's age-old customs, nude sunbathing. Despite these setbacks, the *plage* was a resounding success. With any luck, this year it will again be drawing crowds eager to, if not beat the summer heat, then at least get a tan for their trouble. Just not a seamless one.

LA VILLETTE. This vast urban renewal project encloses a landscaped park, a science museum, a planetarium, a conservatory, a concert/theater space, a high-tech music museum, and more. *(19ème. M: Porte de la Villette or Porte de Pantin. Music museum open Tu-Sa noon-6pm, Su 10am-6pm. €6.10, students €4.60, children 6-18 €2.30, under 6 free. Science museum open Tu-Sa 10am-6pm, Su 10am-7pm. €7.50, students €5.50, under 7 free.)*

INVALIDES MUSEUMS. The resting place of Napoleon also hosts the **Musée de l'Armée,** which celebrates French military history, and the **Musée de l'Ordre de la Libération,** on bd. de Latour-Maubourg, which tells the story of the Resistance fighters. *(Esplanade des Invalides, 7ème. M: Invalides. ☎01 47 05 04 10. Open Apr.-Sept. daily 10am-6pm; Oct.-Mar. 10am-5pm. €6.10, students under 26 and 12-18 €4.50, under 18 free.)*

MUSEE D'ART MODERNE DE LA VILLE DE PARIS. In the magnificent Palais de Tokyo, this museum contains one of the world's foremost collections of 20th-century art. Two stand out: Matisse's *La Danse Inachevée* and Dufy's fauvist epic of electricity, *La Fée Electricité.* *(11 av. du Président Wilson, 16ème. M: Iéna. From Iéna, follow av. du Président Wilson with the Seine on your right. ☎01 53 67 40 00. Open Tu-F 10am-5:30pm, Sa-Su 10am-6:45pm. Permanent exhibits free. Special exhibits €5, students €2.20-3.)*

INSTITUT DU MONDE ARABE. Featuring art from the Maghreb and the Near and Middle East, the riverside facade is shaped like a boat, representing the migration of Arabs to France. *(1 r. des Fossés St-Bernard 5ème. M: Jussieu. From the métro, walk down r. Jussieu away from the Jardin des Plantes. ☎01 40 51 38 38. M: Jussieu. Open Tu-Su 10am-7pm; €3.81, ages 12-18 €3.05, under 12 free.)*

MUSÉE DE L'ORANGERIE. L'Orangerie houses Renoirs, Cézannes, Rousseaus, Matisses, and Picassos, but is most famous for Monet's eight gigantic *Water Lilies.* Closed until 2004. *(1er. M: Concorde. ☎01 42 97 8 16.)*

MUSÉE DE LA MODE ET DU COSTUME. With 30,000 outfits and 70,000 accessories, the museum showcases fashions of the past three centuries. A fabulous place to see the history of Parisian fashion, society, and *haute couture.* *(10 av. Pierre I-de-Serbie, 16ème, in the Palais Galleria. M: Iéna. ☎01 56 52 86 00. Open Tu-Su 10am-6pm; last entry 5:30pm. €7, students and seniors €5.50, children €3.50)*

ENTERTAINMENT

Paris's cabarets, cinemas, theaters, and concert halls can satisfy all tastes and desires. The bibles of Paris entertainment, the weekly *Pariscope* and the *Officiel des Spectacles* (both €0.40), on sale at any kiosk or *tabac*, have every conceivable listing. *Pariscope* includes an English-language section. Some popular nightlife areas, such as Pigalle, Gare St-Lazare, and Beaubourg, are not always safe.

FREE CONCERTS. For listings of free concerts, check *Paris Selection*, free at tourist offices. Free concerts are often held in churches and parks, especially during summer festivals, and are extremely popular. The **American Church in Paris,** 65 quai d'Orsay, *7ème* (☎01 40 62 05 00; M: Invalides or Alma Marceau), sponsors free concerts (Sept.-May Su at 6pm). **Eglise St-Germain-des-Prés** (see **Sights,** p. 339) also has free concerts; check the information booth just inside the door for times. **Eglise St-Merri,** 78 r. St-Martin, *4ème* (M: Hôtel-de-Ville), is also known for its free concerts (Sept.-July Sa at 9pm, Su at 4pm); contact Accueil Musical St-Merri, 76 r. de la Verrerie, *4ème* (☎01 42 71 40 75 or 01 42 71 93 93; M: Châtelet). Concerts take place W-Su in the **Jardin du Luxembourg's** band shell, *6ème* (☎01 42 34 20 23); show up early for a seat or prepare to stand. Concerts in the **Musée d'Orsay,** 1 r. Bellechasse, *7ème* (☎01 40 49 49 66; M: Solférino), are sometimes free.

OPERA AND THEATER

Opéra de la Bastille, pl. de la Bastille, *12ème* (☎08 92 69 78 68; www.opera-de-paris.fr). M: Bastille. Opera and ballet with a modern spin. Because of acoustical problems, it's not the place to splurge for front row seats. Subtitles in French. Tickets can be purchased by Internet, mail, fax, phone (M-Sa 9am-7pm), or in person (M-Sa 11am-6pm). Tickets €57-105. Rush tickets for students under 25 and anyone over 65 15min. before show. For wheelchair access, call 2 weeks ahead (☎01 40 01 18 08). MC/V.

Opéra Garnier, pl. de l'Opéra, *9ème* (☎08 92 69 78 68; www.opera-de-paris.fr). M: Opéra. Hosts operas, symphonies, chamber music, and the Ballet de l'Opéra de Paris. Tickets available 2 weeks before shows. Box office open M-Sa 11am-6pm. Tickets usually €19-64. Last-minute discount tickets available 1hr. before showtime. For wheelchair access, call 2 weeks ahead (☎01 40 01 18 08). AmEx/MC/V.

La Comédie Française, 2 r. de Richelieu, *1er* (☎01 44 58 15 15; www.comedie-francaise.fr). M: Palais-Royal. Founded by Molière, now the granddaddy of all French theaters. Expect wildly gesticulated slapstick farce; you don't need to speak French to understand the jokes. This season: canonized plays by French greats Molière, Racine, and Corneille. Box office open daily 11am-6pm. Tickets €4.50-30, under 27 €4.50-7.50. Student rush tickets (€9) available 1hr. before showtime.

Odéon Théâtre de l'Europe, 1 pl. Odéon, *6ème* (☎01 44 41 36 36; www.theatre-odeon.fr). M: Odéon. Programs in this elegant Neoclassical building range from classics to avant-garde. 1042 seats. Also **Petit Odéon,** an affiliate with 82 seats, which in the past has presented the poetry of Lou Reed and *Medea* by Euripedes. Box office open daily 11am-7pm. Tickets €5-28 for most shows; under 27 rush tickets €7.50, available 90min. before showtime. Petit Odéon €10. Call ahead for wheelchair access. MC/V.

JAZZ AND CABARET

Au Duc des Lombards, 42 r. des Lombards, *1er* (☎01 42 33 22 88; www.jazzvalley.com/duc). M: Châtelet. The best in French jazz, with occasional American soloists. Cover €12-23, music students €7.40-18.60. Beer €5-8, mixed drinks €9. Music 9:30pm-1:30am. Open M-Sa 8pm-2am. MC/V.

Le Caveau de la Huchette, 5 r. de la Huchette, 5*ème* (☎01 43 26 65 05). M: St-Michel. Come prepared to listen, watch, and jitterbug, swing, and jive in this extremely popular club. Bebop dance lessons at 9:30pm; call ☎01 42 71 09 09. Cover Su-Th €10.50, F-Sa €13. Students €9 during the week. Dance School €8. Drinks €5.50-8.50. Open daily 9:30pm-2:30am, F untill 3:30am, Sa untill 4am. AmEx/MC/V.

Au Lapin Agile, 22 r. des Saules, 18*ème* (☎01 46 06 85 87). M: Lamarck-Coulaincourt. Turn right on r. Lamarck, then right up r. des Saules. Picasso, Verlaine, Renoir, and Apollinaire hung out here; now audiences crowd in for comical poems and songs. Shows Tu-Su 9pm-2am. Drinks €6-7. Cover €24, Su-F students €17.

CINEMA

There are scores of cinemas throughout Paris, particularly in the *Quartier Latin* and on the Champs-Elysées. The two big theater chains—**Gaumont** and **UGC**—offer *cartes privilèges* discounts for five visits or more. Most cinemas offer student, senior, and family discounts. On Monday and Wednesday, prices drop by about €1.50 for everyone. Check *Pariscope* or *l'Officiel des Spectacles* (available at any newsstand, €0.40) for weekly film schedules, prices, and reviews.

Musée du Louvre, 1*er* (info ☎01 40 20 53 17; schedules and reservations ☎01 40 20 52 99; www.louvre.fr). M: Louvre. Mainly art and silent films. Open Sept.-June. Free.

Les Trois Luxembourg, 67 r. Monsieur-le-Prince, 6*ème* (☎01 46 33 97 77). M: Cluny. Turn left on bd. St-Michel, right on r. Racine, and left on r. M-le-Prince. Independent, classic, and foreign films, all in original language. €6.40, students and seniors €5.

La Pagode, 57bis r. de Babylone, 7*ème* (☎01 45 55 48 48). M: St-François-Xavier. A Japanese pagoda built in 1895 and reopened as a cinema in 2000. Foreign and independent films, and the occasional American film. Stop in at the cafe between shows. Tickets €7; over 60, under 21, students, and M and W €5.50. MC/V.

Cinémathèque Française, pl. du Trocadéro, 16*ème* (☎01 45 53 21 86, schedule ☎01 47 04 24 24; www.cinemathequefrancaise.com). M: Trocadéro. At the Musée du Cinéma in the Palais de Chaillot. **Branch:** 18 r. du Faubourg-du-Temple, 11*ème*. M: République. Two to three classics, near-classics, or soon-to-be classics per day. Usually in original language. €4.70, students €3. Open W-Su 5-9:45pm.

SHOPPING

Like its food, nightlife, and conversation, Paris's fashion is an art. From the wild wear near r. Etienne-Marcel to the boutiques of the Marais to the upscale shops of St-Germain-des-Prés, everything Paris touches turns to gold (or, if we're talking about this year's runway looks, basic black). The great *soldes* (sales) of the year begin after New Year's and at the very end of June, with the best prices at the beginning of February and the end of July. And, if at any time of year you see the word *braderie* (clearance sale) in a store window, march in without hesitation.

BY NEIGHBORHOOD

ETIENNE-MARCEL AND LES HALLES (1ER AND 2EME). Fabrics here are a little cheaper, and the style is younger. The stores on r. Etienne-Marcel and r. Tiquetonne are best for clubwear and outrageously sexy outfits. *(M: Etienne-Marcel.)*

MARAIS (4EME AND THE LOWER 3EME). The Marais has a line-up of affordable, trendy boutiques, mostly mid-priced clothing chains, independent designer shops, and vintage stores that line **rue Vieille-du-Temple, rue de Sévigné, rue Roi de Sicile** and **rue des Rosiers.** Lifestyle shops line **rue de Bourg-Tibourg** and **rue des**

Francs-Bourgeois. The best selection of affordable-chic menswear in Paris can be found along **rue Ste-Croix-de-la-Bretonnerie.** *(M: St-Paul or Hôtel de Ville.)*

ST-GERMAIN-DES-PRES (6EME AND EASTERN BORDER OF 7EME). St-Germain-des-Prés, particularly the triangle bordered by **Boulevard St-Germain, rue St-Sulpice,** and **rue des Sts-Pères,** is saturated with high-budget names. **Paul and Joe** (men's; no. 40; ☎01 45 44 97 70; open daily 11am-7:30pm) and **Sinéquanone** (women's; no. 16; ☎01 56 24 27 74; open M-Sa 10am-7:30pm). Closer to the Jardin du Luxembourg, calm **rue de Fleurus** hosts **A.P.C.** as well as the interesting designs of **t***** at no. 7 (M: St-Placide). In the *7ème*, visit **rue de Pré-aux-Clercs** and check out the avant-garde jewelry at Stella Cadente, **no. 22, rue de Grenelle**. In general, the *7ème* is very expensive, but there are some impressive little boutiques around the Bon Marché department store on r. de Sèvres, and r. du Cherche-Midi. *(M: Vaneau, Duroc, Sèvres-Babylone, r. du Bac.)*

DEPARTMENT STORES

Au Bon Marché, 22 r. de Sèvres, *7ème*. M: Sèvres-Babylone. Paris's oldest department store, with everything from scarves to smoking accessories to home furnishings. Across the street is *La Grande Epicerie de Paris,* Bon Marché's celebrated gourmet food annex. Open M-W and F 9:30am-7pm, Th 10am-9pm, Sa 9:30am-8pm. AmEx/MC/V.

Au Printemps, 64 bd. Haussmann, *9ème*. M: Chaussée d'Antin-Lafayette or Havre-Caumartin. Also at **30 pl. d'Italie,** *13ème*, M: Place d'Italie; and 21-25, cours de Vincennes, *20ème*, M: Porte de Vincennes. One of the two biggies in the Parisian department store scene. Haussmann open M-W and F-Sa 9:30am-7pm, Th 9:30am-10pm. Other locations open M-Sa 10am-8pm. AmEx/MC/V.

Galeries Lafayette, 40 bd. Haussmann, *9ème* (☎01 42 82 34 56). M: Chaussée d'Antin. Also at **22 r. du Départ,** *14ème* (☎01 45 38 52 87), M: Montparnasse. Chaotic and crowded, with mini-boutiques of Kookaï, agnès b., French Connection, and Cacharel. *Lafayette Gourmet,* on the first floor, has everything from a sushi counter to a mini-*boulangerie.* Haussmann open M-W, F, Sa 9:30am-7:30pm, Th 9:30-9pm; Montparnasse open M-Sa 9:45am-7:30pm. AmEx/MC/V.

Samaritaine, 67 r. de Rivoli, on the quai du Louvre, *1er* (☎01 40 41 20 20). M: Pont Neuf, Châtelet-Les Halles, or Louvre-Rivoli. 4 large Art Deco buildings connected by tunnels and bridges. Not as chic as the bigger names–it dares to sell merchandise at reasonable prices. Open M-W and F-Sa 9:30am-7pm, Th 9:30am-10pm. AmEx/MC/V.

NIGHTLIFE

Though historically Parisians' nightlife involved provoking revolution and burning buildings, today, nighttime pleasures tend more toward drinking, relaxing, and people watching. Those looking for live music, especially jazz, are in heaven. Dancing kings and queens may be frustrated by Paris's rather exclusive club scene, but *Let's Go* tries to list places that are accepting of non-models. If you'd rather just watch the world go by, the city's many bars won't disappoint. In the *18ème*, the streets are lined with aggressive peep-show hawkers and prowling drug-dealers; avoid making eye contact with strangers and stay near well lit, heavily trafficked areas. Tourists, especially women, should avoid the areas around M: Pigalle, M: Anvers and M: Barbès-Rochechouart at night. Bisexual, lesbian, and gay entertainment is centered around the Marais in the fourth *arrondissement*, with most establishments clustered around r. du Temple, r. Ste-Croix de la Bretonnerie, r. des Archives, and r. Vieille du Temple.

LA REPUBLIQUE: 3ÈME, 4ÈME, AND 11ÈME

L'Apparemment Café, 18 r. des Coutures St-Gervais, 3*ème*. M: St-Paul. Beautiful wood-and-red lounge complete with games and a calm, young crowd. Late-night meals €10-13, served until closing.

Chez Richard, 37 r. Vieille-du-Temple, 4*ème*. M: Hôtel-de-Ville. An atmosphere reminiscent of Casablanca. Jumping on weekends but chill during the week. Beer €4-5, mixed drinks €8-9. Open daily 6pm-2am. AmEx/MC/V.

Lizard Lounge, 18 r. du Bourg-Tibourg, 4*ème*. M: Hôtel-de-Ville. A hot, split-level space for Anglo/Franco late 20-somethings. Cellar has DJ every night. Happy Hour 6-10pm (mixed drinks €4.60). Pint of lager €5.20. Food served noon-3pm and 7-10:30pm, weekend brunch noon-4pm. Open daily noon-2am. MC/V.

Café Charbon, 109 r. Oberkampf, 11*ème*. M: Parmentier or Ménilmontant. A spacious bar that bears traces of its dance hall days but still manages to pack in a crowd of young locals and artists. Beer €3. Happy Hour 5-7pm. Open daily 9am-2am. MC/V.

Villa Keops, 58 bd. Sébastopol. M: Etienne-Marcel. Stylish, candlelit couch bar decorated with beautiful people. Everyone comes here before heading to Les Bains. Open M-Th noon-2am, F-Sa noon-4am, Su 4pm-3am. AmEx/MC/V.

Les Etages, 35 r. Vieille-du-Temple. M: St-Paul. Set in an 18th-century hotel-turned-bar. Its 3 floors are filled with chill kids basking in dim lighting. Sangria €4.50. Brunch buffet €15, Su 11am-4pm. Open daily 3:30pm-2am. MC/V.

Amnésia Café, 42 r. Vieille-du-Temple. M: Hôtel-de-Ville. A largely gay crowd comes to lounge on plush sofas. This is one of the top spots in the Marais, especially on Sa nights. Espresso €2, *kir* €4. Open daily noon-2am. MC/V.

Mixer Bar, 23 r. Ste-Croix de la Brettonerie. M: St-Paul. Almost entirely a male crowd, though women are welcome. Always packed. DJs stationed above the doorway. Happy Hour 6-8pm. Beer €2.80-4.30, mixed drinks €7. Open daily 5pm-2am. AmEx/MC/V.

DANCE CLUBS

Les Bains, 7 r. du Bourg l'Abbé, 3*ème*. M: Etienne-Marcel or Réaumur-Sébastopol. Ultra-selective and super-crowded. Madonna and Mick Jagger have been spotted here. House and garage grunge, W is hip-hop. Cover and 1st drink Su-Th €16; F-Sa €19. Clubbing daily 11pm-6am; open for dinner until 9pm, reservations a must. AmEx/MC/V.

Le Dépôt, 10 r. aux Ours. A veritable pleasure complex for gay men. Women welcome upstairs after 11pm, and W is lesbian night. Disco M, House/Techno W, Latin Th, visiting DJ F, House Sa (called "*Putas* at Work"). Cover includes first drink; M-Th €7.50, F €10, Sa €12, Su €10; W free for ladies. Open daily 2pm-8am. V.

LEFT BANK: 5ÈME, 6ÈME, 7ÈME, 13ÈME

Le Reflet, 6 r. Champollion, 5*ème*. M: Cluny-La Sorbonne. Walk away from the river on bd. St-Michel, then make a left on r. des Ecoles. Take the first right. Small and low-key; crowded with students and younger Frenchies. Beer €1.90-2.70 at the bar, *kir* €2. Open M-Sa 10am-2am, Su noon-2am. MC/V.

Le Caveau des Oubliettes, 52 r. Galande, 5*ème*. M: St-Michel. Three entertainments in one: the bar upstairs has a real-live guillotine; downstairs, there's an outstanding jazz club; and beneath the club. Attracts a mostly local set. Jazz concerts every night; free jam session Su-Th from 10:30pm-1:30am; F-Sa concerts €7.50. Beer €3.70-4.10, rum cocktail €3.80. Happy Hour 5-9pm. Open daily 5pm-2am.

Le Bar Dix (Bar 10), 10 r. de l'Odéon, 6*ème*. M: Odéon. A classic student hangout with a tiny cellar for packing into; roomier upstairs. Sangria (€3) makes their great jukebox (everything from Edith Piaf to Aretha Franklin) even better. Open daily 5:30pm-2am.

Le Crocodile, 6 r. Royer-Collard, 6*ème*. M: Cluny-La Sorbonne. A lively crowd packs into this unassuming bar that lurks behind boarded-up windows on a quiet side street. Ring to be let in. 238 tasty cocktails (€8) to choose from. Pick a number from the menu or at random, write it down, and hand it across the bar. Open M-Sa 10:30pm-4am.

Le Club des Poètes, 30 r. de Bourgogne, 7*ème*. M: Varenne. For 40 years, Jean-Pierre Rosnay has been making "poetry contagious and inevitable." At 10pm, a troupe of readers transform this restaurant into a poetry salon. Drinks €9.15, for students €6.86. Open M-Sa noon-2:30pm and 8pm-1am; food served until 10pm. AmEx/MC/V.

O'Brien's, 77 r. St-Dominique, 7*ème*. M: Latour-Maubourg. A lively Irish pub drawing a mix of locals and tourists. Happy Hour M-F from opening time until 8pm, pints €5. Otherwise, beer €4-7, mixed drinks €7. Open M-Th 6pm-2am, F-Su 4pm-2am. MC/V.

DANCE CLUBS

Batofar, facing 11 quai François-Mauriac, 13*ème*. M: Quai de la Gare. This barge/bar/club on the Seine has made it big with the electronic music crowd but maintains a friendly vibe. Open Tu-Th 9pm-3am, F-Sa until 4am; hours change for film and DJ events. Cover €6.50-9.50, usually includes first drink. MC/V.

RIGHT BANK: 1ER, 2ÈME, AND 8ÈME

Banana Café, 13-15 r. de la Ferronnerie, 1*er*. M: Châtelet. From the métro, take r. Pierre Lescot to r. de la Ferronerie. This evening arena is the most popular gay bar in the 1*er*. Legendary theme nights. "Go-Go Boys" W-Sa midnight-dawn. Drinks 2-for-1 during Happy Hour (4-10pm). Beer €5-7. Open daily 4pm-dawn. AmEx/MC/V.

Le Champmeslé, 4 r. Chabanais. M: Pyramides or Quatre Septembre. This lesbian bar is Paris's oldest and most famous. Mixed crowd in the front, women-only in back. Beer €4. Cabaret show Th 10pm. Free drink during the month of your birthday. Monthly photo exhibits. Open M-Th 2pm-2am, F and Sa 2pm-5am. MC/V.

House of Live, 124 r. La Boétie, 8*ème*. M: Franklin D. Roosevelt. Formerly the Chesterfield Café. Friendly and happening American bar with first-class live music. A mix of Anglophones and Parisians. Snack bar has good ol' yankee fare. Beer €6, mixed drinks €8.10, coffee €2-4. No cover Su-Th. Open daily 10am-5am. AmEx/MC/V.

buddha-bar, 8 r. Boissy d'Anglas, 8*ème*. M: Madeleine or Concorde. Stereotypically snobbish, but you won't find a hotter place in the 8*ème*. Mixed drinks and martinis €11, the mysterious Pure Delight (€12) is indeed that. Open M-F noon-3pm, daily 6pm-2am.

The Flann O'Brien, 6 r. Bailleul, 1*er*. M: Louvre-Rivoli. Arguably the best Irish bar in Paris. Packed on live music nights (F, Sa, and Su). Great Guinness and reportedly good "crack" downstairs (Irish for good fun). Demi €3.40, full pint €6. Open daily 4pm-2am.

DANCE CLUBS

Latina Café, 114 av. des Champs-Elysées, 8*ème*. M: George V. Draws one of the largest nightclub crowds on the glitzy Champs-Elysées with an energetic world music mix. Mixed drinks €9-11. Live concerts Th. Cover €16 includes first 2 drinks. Cafe open daily 7:30pm-2am, club open daily 11:30am-6:30am.

Le Queen, 102 av. des Champs-Elysées, 8*ème*. M: George V. Her majesty is one of the most fashionable gay clubs in town. Mostly male crowd. M disco, Th-Sa house, Su 80s. Cover Su-Th €9, F-Sa €18. Mixed drinks €9. Open daily midnight to dawn. AmEx/MC/V.

Rex Club, 5 bd. Poissonnière. M: Bonne-Nouvelle. A non-selective club which presents the most selective of DJ line-ups. A casual, subterranean venue to hear cutting-edge techno, jungle, and house fusion. Large dance floor and lots of seats as well. Shots €4-5, beer €5-7. Cover €8-12.50. Open Th-Sa 11:30pm-6am.

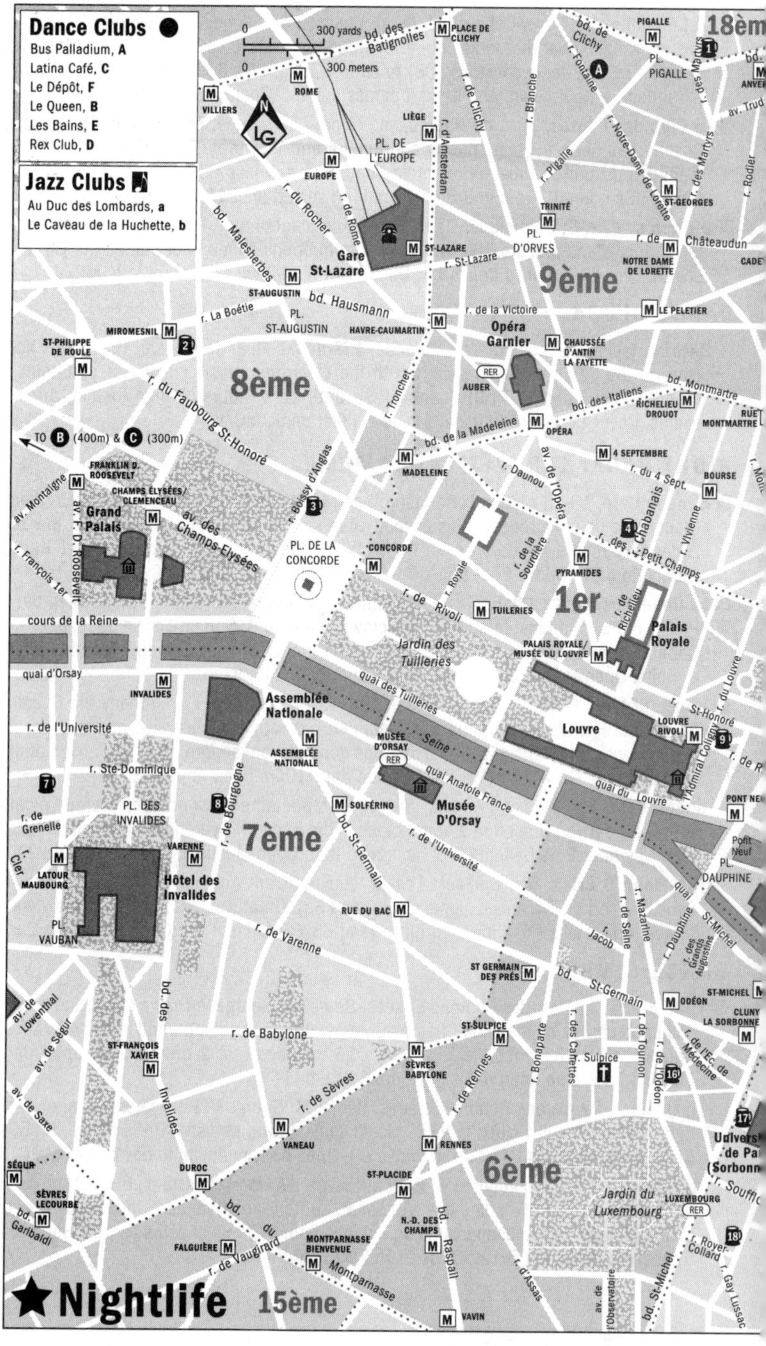
Dance Clubs
Bus Palladium, A
Latina Café, C
Le Dépôt, F
Le Queen, B
Les Bains, E
Rex Club, D
Jazz Clubs
Au Duc des Lombards, a
Le Caveau de la Huchette, b
0 300 yards
0 300 meters
TO B (400m) & C (300m)
Nightlife
8ème
9ème
1er
7ème
6ème
15ème
18ème
Gare St-Lazare
Opéra Garnier
Grand Palais
PL. DE LA CONCORDE
Jardin des Tuilleries
Palais Royale
Louvre
Assemblée Nationale
Musée D'Orsay
Hôtel des Invalides
Jardin du Luxembourg
Seine
PL. DE L'EUROPE
PL. ST-AUGUSTIN
PL. D'ORVES
PL. PIGALLE
PL. DES INVALIDES
PL. VAUBAN
PL. DAUPHINE
bd. des Batignolles
bd. de Clichy
bd. Malesherbes
bd. Hausmann
bd. des Italiens
bd. Montmartre
bd. de la Madeleine
bd. St-Germain
bd. Raspail
bd. du Montparnasse
bd. des Invalides
bd. St-Michel
r. du Faubourg St-Honoré
r. de Rivoli
r. St-Lazare
av. des Champs-Elysées
av. de l'Opéra
quai d'Orsay
quai des Tuilleries
quai Anatole France
quai du Louvre
cours de la Reine
r. de l'Université
r. de Varenne
r. de Babylone
r. de Sèvres
r. de Rennes
r. de Vaugirard
ST-LAZARE
MADELEINE
CONCORDE
TUILERIES
OPÉRA
INVALIDES
SOLFÉRINO
RUE DU BAC
ST GERMAIN DES PRÉS
ST-SULPICE
ODÉON
RENNES
VAVIN
LUXEMBOURG
RER

FRANCE

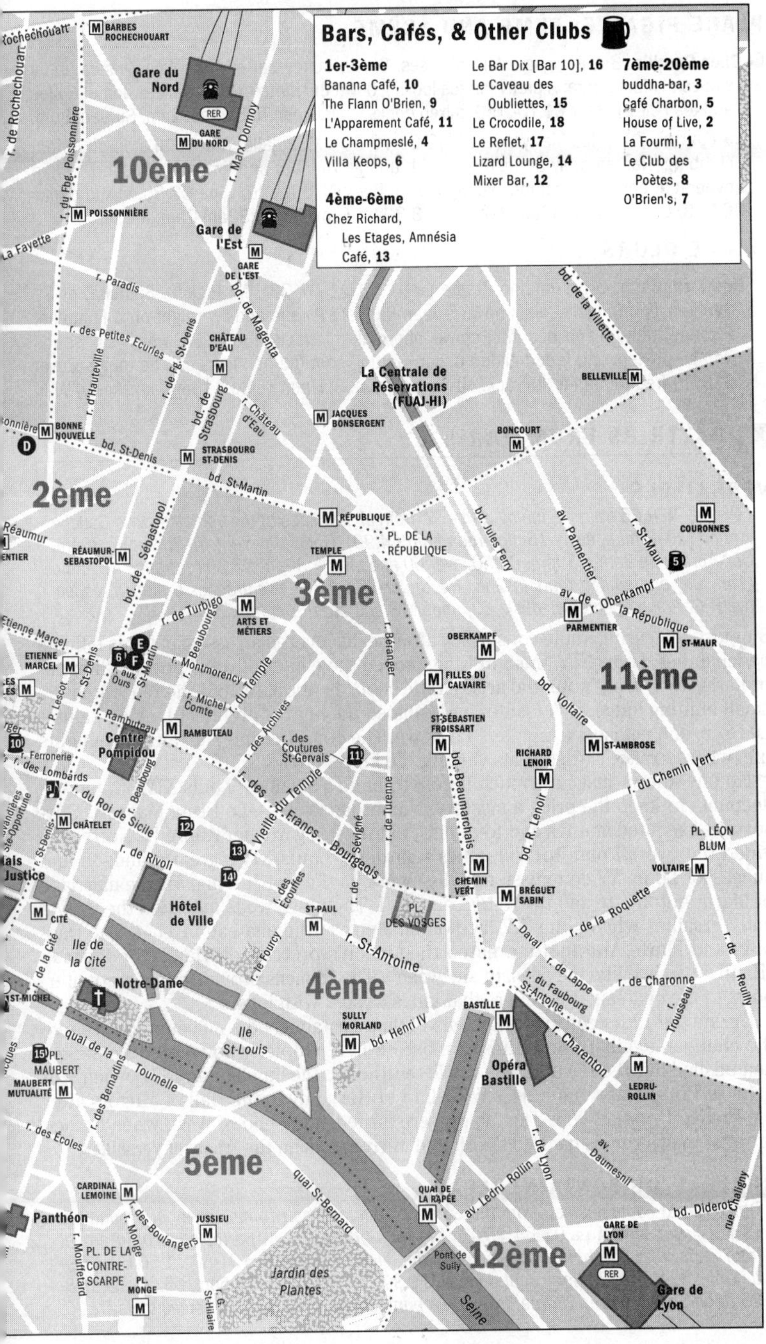
Bars, Cafés, & Other Clubs
1er-3ème
Banana Café, 10
The Flann O'Brien, 9
L'Apparement Café, 11
Le Champmeslé, 4
Villa Keops, 6
4ème-6ème
Chez Richard, Les Etages, Amnésia Café, 13
Le Bar Dix [Bar 10], 16
Le Caveau des Oubliettes, 15
Le Crocodile, 18
Le Reflet, 17
Lizard Lounge, 14
Mixer Bar, 12
7ème-20ème
buddha-bar, 3
Café Charbon, 5
House of Live, 2
La Fourmi, 1
Le Club des Poètes, 8
O'Brien's, 7
10ème
2ème
3ème
11ème
4ème
5ème
12ème
BARBES ROCHECHOUART
Gare du Nord
GARE DU NORD
Gare de l'Est
GARE DE L'EST
POISSONNIÈRE
CHÂTEAU D'EAU
La Centrale de Réservations (FUAJ-HI)
JACQUES BONSERGENT
BELLEVILLE
BONCOURT
BONNE NOUVELLE
STRASBOURG ST-DENIS
RÉPUBLIQUE
PL. DE LA RÉPUBLIQUE
TEMPLE
COURONNES
RÉAUMUR-SEBASTOPOL
ARTS ET MÉTIERS
PARMENTIER
OBERKAMPF
ST-MAUR
ETIENNE MARCEL
FILLES DU CALVAIRE
ST-SÉBASTIEN FROISSART
RAMBUTEAU
Centre Pompidou
ST-AMBROSE
RICHARD LENOIR
CHÂTELET
PL. LÉON BLUM
VOLTAIRE
CHEMIN VERT
BRÉGUET SABIN
Hôtel de Ville
CITÉ
ST-PAUL
PL. DES VOSGES
Ile de la Cité
Notre-Dame
ST-MICHEL
BASTILLE
SULLY MORLAND
Ile St-Louis
Opéra Bastille
LEDRU-ROLLIN
PL. MAUBERT
MAUBERT MUTUALITÉ
CARDINAL LEMOINE
QUAI DE LA RAPÉE
GARE DE LYON
Gare de Lyon
Panthéon
JUSSIEU
PL. DE LA CONTRESCARPE
PL. MONGE
Jardin des Plantes
Pont de Sully
Seine
r. de Rochechouart
r. du Fbg. Poissonnière
r. Marx Dormoy
r. Lafayette
r. Paradis
r. des Petites Ecuries
r. d'Hauteville
r. de Fg. St-Denis
bd. de Strasbourg
bd. de Magenta
r. Château d'Eau
bd. de la Villette
bd. St-Denis
bd. St-Martin
r. Réaumur
bd. de Sébastopol
bd. Jules Ferry
av. Parmentier
r. St-Maur
av. de la République
r. Oberkampf
r. de Turbigo
r. Beaubourg
r. Etienne Marcel
r. Montmorency
r. du Temple
r. Michel Comte
r. Béranger
bd. Voltaire
r. St-Denis
r. aux Ours
r. St-Martin
r. P. Lescot
r. Rambuteau
r. des Archives
r. des Coutures St-Gervais
bd. Beaumarchais
r. du Chemin Vert
r. Ferronerie
r. des Lombards
r. du Roi de Sicile
r. Vieille du Temple
r. des Francs Bourgeois
r. de Turenne
r. de Sévigné
bd. R. Lenoir
r. de Rivoli
r. des Ecouffes
r. de la Roquette
r. de la Cité
r. le Fourcy
r. St-Antoine
r. Daval
r. de Lappe
r. de Charonne
r. du Faubourg St-Antoine
r. Trousseau
r. de Reuilly
bd. Henri IV
r. Charenton
quai de la Tournelle
r. des Bernadins
r. des Écoles
quai St-Bernard
r. de Lyon
av. Daumesnil
av. Ledru Rollin
bd. Diderot
rue Chaligny
r. des Boulangers
r. Monge
r. Mouffetard
r. G. St-Hilaire

PLACE PIGALLE: 9ÈME AND 18ÈME

Chez Camille, 8 r. Ravignan. M: Abbesses. Small, trendy bar on the relatively safe upper slopes of Montmartre. A pretty terrace looking down the *butte* to the Invalides dome. Coffee and tea (€1-2). Beer €1.70-2.50, mixed drinks €3-8. Open Tu-Sa 9am-2am, Su 9am-8pm.

La Fourmi, 74 r. des Martyrs (☎01 42 64 70 35). M: Pigalle. A popular stop-off before clubbing. Has an artsy atmosphere, with a large zinc bar and industrial decor. Draws a hyper-hip, energetic, scrappy young crowd. Beer €2.30-3.20, wine €2.50, mixed drinks €7-10. Open M-Th 8:30am-2am, F-Sa 8:30am-4am, Su 10:30am-2am. MC/V.

DANCE CLUBS

Bus Palladium, 6 r. Fontaine, 9*ème* (☎01 53 21 07 33). M: Pigalle, Blanche, or St-Georges. From Pigalle, walk down r. Jean-Baptiste Pigalle and turn right on r. Fontaine. A young, trendy, and beautiful crowd who rock this rock 'n roll club, which still sports vintage posters and faded gilded decor. Getting past the bouncers can be tough. Cover €16. Tu free for ladies, Th rock. Mixed drinks €13. Open Tu-Sa 11pm-6am. AmEx/V.

DAYTRIPS FROM PARIS

VERSAILLES

Take any RER C5 train beginning with a "V" from M: Invalides to the Versailles Rive Gauche station (30-40min., every 15min., round-trip €4.90). Open May-Sept. Tu-Su 9am-6:30pm; Oct.-Apr. Tu-Su 9am-5:30pm. €7.50, over 60 and after 3:30pm €5.30 (entrance A). Audio (1hr., €4) and guided tours (1-2hr., €4, under 18 €2.70) at entrances C and D, respectively. Gardens open dawn-dusk; €3, under 18 and after 6pm free.

Supposedly fearing noble conspiracy after he discovered an assassin in his father's bedchamber, Louis XIV, the Sun King, moved the center of royal power 12km out of Paris, away from potential aristocratic subordination. In 1661, he renovated the small hunting lodge in Versailles and enlisted the help of architect Le Vau, painter Le Brun, and landscape architect Le Nôtre. The court became the nucleus of noble life, where France's aristocrats vied for the king's favor.

No one knows just how much it cost to build Versailles; Louis XIV burned the accounts to keep the price a mystery. Numerous artists—Le Brun, Mansart, Coysevox—executed statues and fountains, but master gardener André Le Nôtre provided the overall plan for Versailles's gardens. Louis XIV's great-grandson and successor Louis XV commissioned the Opéra, in the North Wing, for the marriage of Marie Antoinette and the to-be Louis XVI. The newlyweds inherited the throne and Versailles when Louis XV died of smallpox at the chateau in 1774. The Dauphin and Marie Antoinette created the Queen's pretend playland, the **Hameau** (Hamlet), to live like the peasant she wasn't. The **Trianons** provide a racier counterpoint to the chateau: it was here that kings trysted with lovers.

During the 19th century, King Louis-Philippe established a museum to preserve the chateau, against the wishes of most French people, who wanted Versailles demolished like the Bastille. The castle returned to the limelight in 1871, when Wilhelm of Prussia became Kaiser Wilhelm I of Germany in the Hall of Mirrors after the Franco-Prussian War. The tables were turned at the end of WWI, when France brought the Germans back to the Hall of Mirrors to sign the **Treaty of Versailles.**

CHÂTEAU DE FONTAINEBLEAU

Trains run to Fontainebleau from the Gare de Lyon in Paris (45min., every hr., round-trip €14.60). ***Car Vert A*** *(☎01 64 23 71 11) runs buses (€1.40) after each train arrival from Paris; take the bus in direction "Château-Lilas." Chateau ☎01 60 71 50 60. Open June-Aug. W-M 9:30am-6pm; Sept.-June W-M 9:30am-12:30pm and 2-5pm. €5.50, ages 18-25 or on Su €4, under 18 free. Invest in a printed guide (€7.50). 1hr. audio tours €2.20.*

Easier to take in all at once than Versailles, the Château de Fontainebleau achieves nearly the same grandeur with a unique charm. François I and Napoleon stand out among the parade of post-Renaissance kings who lived here; the first was responsible for the dazzling ballrooms lined with work of Michelangelo's school, the second restored the post-Revolution dilapidation to a home befitting of an emperor. The **Grands Appartements** provide a lesson in the history of French architecture and decoration. Dubreuil's **Gallery of Plates** tells the history of Fontainebleau on a remarkable series of 128 porcelain plates, fashioned in Sèvres between 1838 and 1844. In the long **Galerie de François I,** the most famous room at Fontainebleau, muscular figures by Il Rosso (known in French as Maître Roux) tell mythological tales of heroism. Decorated under Henri IV, the **King's Cabinet** (also known as the **Louis XIII Salon** because Louis XIII was born there) was the site of *le débotter*, the king's post-hunt boot removal. Napoleon pored over the volumes of the long, lofty, sunlit library known as the **Bibliothèque Diana.** Since the 17th century, every queen and empress of France has slept in the gold and green **Queen's Bed Chamber;** the bed was built for Marie-Antoinette. In the **Emperor's Private Room,** known today as the **Abdication Chamber,** Napoleon signed off his empire in 1814. The tour ends with the 16th-century, Italian-frescoed **Trinity Chapel.**

CHARTRES

Take a train from Paris's Gare Montparnasse (1hr.; every hr.; round-trip €22.70, under 26 and groups of 2-4 €17.20). From the train station, walk straight along r. Jehan de Beauce to pl. de Châtelet and turn left into the place, right onto r. Ste-Même, and left on r. Jean Moulin. ☎ 02 37 21 75 02. Open Easter through Oct. daily 8am-8pm, Nov. through Easter daily 8:30am-7pm. No visits during mass: M-F 11:45am and 6:15pm; Sa 11:45am and 6pm; Su 9:15am (Latin), 11am, and 6pm (in the crypt); May-Aug. M-Sa 9am-6pm, Su 1-6:30pm; Sept.-Oct. and Mar.-Apr. M-Sa 9:30-11:30am and 2-6:30pm, Su 2-5pm; Nov.-Feb. M-Sa 10-11:30am and 2-4pm, Su 2-4pm. €4, ages 18-25 €2.50, under 18 and some Su. free. Malcolm Miller's famous English tours during winter months. €8, students €5.

The **Cathédrale de Chartres** is the best-preserved medieval church in Europe, miraculously escaping major damage during the Revolution and WWII. A patchwork masterpiece of Romanesque and Gothic design, the cathedral was constructed by generations of unknown masons, architects, and artisans who labored for centuries. The year after he became emperor in 875, Charlemagne's grandson, Charles the Bald, donated to Chartres the **Sancta Camisia,** the cloth believed to be worn by the Virgin Mary when she gave birth to Christ. Although a church dedicated to Mary had existed on the site as early as the mid-700s, the emperor's bequest required a new cathedral to accommodate the growing number of pilgrims.

Most of the **stained glass** dates from the 13th century and was preserved through both World Wars by heroic town authorities, who dismantled over 2000 sq. m and stored the windows pane by pane in Dordogne. The medieval merchants who paid for each window are shown in the lower panels, providing a record of daily life in the 13th century. The center window shows the story of Christ from the Annunciation to the ride into Jerusalem. The windows of Chartres often distract visitors from the treasures below their feet. A winding **labyrinth** is carved into the floor in the rear of the nave. Designed in the 13th century, the labyrinth was laid out for pilgrims as a symbolic journey to the Holy Land. The adventurous climb the cathedral's north tower, **Tour Jehan-de-Beauce,** for a stellar view of the cathedral roof, the flying buttresses, and the city below. Parts of Chartres's **crypt,** such as a well down which Vikings tossed the bodies of their victims during raids, date back to the 9th century. You can enter the subterranean crypt as part of a tour that leaves from La Crypte, opposite the cathedral's south entrance.

DISNEYLAND PARIS

From Paris, take RER A4 Marne-la-Vallée to the last stop, Marne-la-Vallée/Chessy (45min., every 30min., round-trip €11); the last train back leaves at 12:22am but arrives after the Métro closes. Eurailers can take the TGV from Roissy/Charles de Gaulle Airport to the park in 15min. For more information, see www.disneylandparis.com. Open Apr.-Sept. 9am-11pm; Oct.-Apr. M-F 10am-9pm, Sa-Su 10am-10pm. Hours subject to change, especially during winter. Buy passeports (tickets) on Disneyland Hotel's ground floor, at the Paris tourist office, or at any major station on RER line A. Apr. to Dec. €38, ages 3-11 €29; Jan. to Mar. €29/€25; 2- and 3-day passeports also available.

It's a small, small world and Disney is hell-bent on making it even smaller. When Euro Disney opened on April 12, 1992, Mickey Mouse, Snow White, and friends were met by jeers of French intellectuals and the press, who called the Disney theme park a "cultural Chernobyl." Resistance seems to have subsided since Walt & Co. renamed it Disneyland Paris and started serving wine. Despite its small dimensions, this Disney park is the most technologically advanced yet, and the special effects on some rides will knock your socks off. Everything in Disneyland Paris is in English and French. The detailed guide called the *Park Guide Book* (free at Disney City Hall to the left of the entrance) has a map and info on everything from restaurants and attractions to bathrooms and first aid. The *Guests' Special Services Guide* has info on wheelchair accessibility throughout the park.

GIVERNY

Trains (☎08 36 35 35 35) run erratically from Gare St-Lazare to Vernon, the station nearest Giverny (round-trip €21). When you purchase your ticket from St-Lazare, check the timetables or ask for the bus schedules for travel from Vernon to Giverny (☎02 32 71 06 39; 10min., Tu-Su 4 per day, round-trip €4).

Today, Monet's house and gardens in Giverny are maintained by the Fondation Claude Monet. From April to July, Giverny overflows with roses, hollyhocks, poppies, and the heady scent of honeysuckle. The water lilies, the Japanese bridge, and the weeping willows look like, well, like Monets. Monet's thatched-roof house shelters his collection of 18th- and 19th-century Japanese prints. Near the foundation, the incongruously modern but respectfully hidden **Musée d'Art Américain** houses a small number of works by American impressionists.

OTHER DAYTRIPS FROM PARIS

THE LOIRE VALLEY. Between Paris and Brittany stretches the Loire Valley, where renowned chateaux line the celebrated Loire river. Visit Blois, Chambord, or Cheverny (see p. 355).

ROUEN. Visit the city of a hundred spires, and party with the students in the largest city in Normandy (see p. 347).

RENNES. If Parisian students will travel out to Rennes for the nightlife, then you should too (see p. 350).

NORMANDY (NORMANDIE)

Fertile Normandy is a land of fields, fishing villages, and cathedrals. Vikings first seized the region in the 9th century, and subsequent invasions have twice secured Normandy's place in military history: in 1066, William of Normandy conquered England; on D-Day, June 6, 1944, Allied armies began the liberation of France on Normandy's beaches.

ROUEN

Despite the criticisms Gustave Flaubert may have made of his home in *Madame Bovary*, Rouen (pop. 108,000) is no provincial town. The pathos of the Joan of Arc story and the Gothic splendor of Rouen's church have always entranced artists and writers, and today a hip, young crowd populates the *vieille ville*. The most famous of Rouen's "hundred spires" are those of the **Cathédrale de Notre-Dame,** in pl. de la Cathédrale, with the tallest spire in France (151m). The facade incorporates nearly every style of Gothic architecture; don't miss the stained glass in the **Chapelle St-Jean de la Nef.** (Open M-Sa 8am-7pm, Su 8am-6pm.) Behind the cathedral, at the poorly marked 186 r. de Martainville, is the **Aitre St-Maclou,** which served as the church's charnel house and cemetery through the later Middle Ages. Suspended behind a glass panel is the cadaver of a cat entombed alive to exorcise spirits. (Open daily 8am-8pm. Free.) Joan of Arc died on **place du Vieux Marché,** to the left as you exit the station on r. du Donjon. A 6½m cross marks the spot, near the unsightly **Eglise Ste-Jeanne d'Arc,** designed to resemble an overturned Viking boat. A block up r. Jeanne d'Arc, the **Musée des Beaux-Arts,** on pl. Verdrel, houses a worthwhile collection of European masters from the 16th to 20th centuries, including Monet and Renoir. (☎02 35 71 28 40. Open W-M 10am-6pm. €3, ages 18-25 and groups €2, under 18 free.) The **Musée Flaubert et d'Histoire de la Médecine,** 51 r. de Lecat, next to the Hôtel-Dieu hospital, showcases a gruesome array of medical instruments used by Gustave Flaubert's father, a physician. Some of Flaubert's possessions are also on display. (Open Tu 10am-6pm, W-Sa 10am-noon and 2-6pm. €2.20, ages 18-25 €1.50, seniors and students free.)

Trains leave r. Jeanne d'Arc for Lille (3hr., 5 per day, €25.30) and Paris (1½hr., every hr., €16.50). From the station, walk down r. Jeanne d'Arc and turn left on r. du Gros Horloge to get to the **tourist office,** 25 pl. de la Cathédrale. (☎02 32 08 32 40; fax 02 32 08 32 44. Open May-Sept. M-Sa 9am-7pm, Su 9:30am-12:30pm and 2-6pm; Oct.-Mar. M-Sa 9am-6pm, Su 9:30am-12:30pm and 2-6pm.) Check **email** at **Place Net,** 37 r. de la République, near the Eglise St-Maclou. (€4 per hr. Open M-Sa 11am-midnight, Su 2-10pm.) **Hôtel des Arcades ❸,** 52 r. de Carmes, is bright and clean. (☎02 35 70 10 30; www.hotel-des-arcades.fr. Singles and doubles €25, with shower €34-40. AmEx/MC/V.) Cheap eateries crowd place du Vieux-Marché. **Restaurant Punjab ❸,** 3 r. des Bons Enfants, just off r. Jeanne D'Arc, provides a taste of India. (☎02 35 88 63 48. €8 and €10 lunch menus. Dinner from €10, with €16 and €20 fixed menus. A wide vegetarian selection as well as a full bar and wine list. Open M-Su 11:30am-3pm and 7pm-11:30pm. MC/V.) Just a few feet from the side of the Cathédrale de Notre-Dame, the welcoming **Saint Romain Cafe Creperie,** 52 r. St.-Romain, offers sweet crepes and savory buckwheat *galettes* that satisfy both your hunger and your wallet. (☎02 35 88 90 36. Lunch €3, dinner €7. Open Tu-Sa noon-2pm; Th-Sa 7pm-10pm. MC/V. ❶) For groceries, **Monoprix** is at 73-83 r. du Gros Horloge. (Open M-Sa 8:30am-9pm.) **Postal Code:** 76000.

DAYTRIP FROM ROUEN: MONT-ST-MICHEL. Rouen is the perfect town from which to explore Mont-St-Michel (see p. 350).

NORMANDY COAST

LE HAVRE

An elegy to concrete, the hub Le Havre (pop. 200,000) can brag of being France's largest transatlantic port and little else. For information on **ferries** to Portsmouth, see p. 57. **Trains** leave from cours de la République for: Fécamp (1hr., 9 per day, €6.70) via Etretat; Paris (2hr., 8 per day, €23.70); and Rouen (50min., 13 per day,

€11.40). If you must stay in town, visit the spacious **Hôtel Le Monaco ❷**, 16 r. de Paris. (☎02 35 42 21 01. Reception daily 6:30am-11pm. Singles €22.90, with shower €28.30-33.55; doubles €26.70, with bath €33.10. AmEx/MC/V.) Get food for the ferry at **Super U,** bd. François 1*er*, near the tourist office. (Open M-Sa 8:30am-9pm.)

CAEN

Although Allied bombing leveled three-quarters of its buildings in World War II, Caen has skillfully rebuilt itself into a vibrant university town. Its biggest draw is the powerful **Mémorial de Caen,** the best of Normandy's World War II museums, which includes footage of the war, displays on pre-war Europe and the Battle of Normandy, a haunting testament to the victims of the Holocaust, and a new wing exploring the Cold War. Take bus #17 to Mémorial. (☎02 31 06 06 44; www.memorial-caen.fr. Open daily mid-July to Aug. 9am-8pm; Feb. to mid-July and Sept.-Oct. 9am-7pm; mid-Jan. to Feb. and Nov.-Dec. 9am-6pm. €16, students €14.) Flanking the ruined chateau of Caen's most famous denizen, the twin abbeys **Abbaye-aux-Hommes** (open 9:15am-noon and 2-6pm; €1.55, students €0.80.) off r. Guillaume le Conquérant, and **Abbaye-aux-Dames** (open M-Sa 8am-5:30pm, Su 9:30am-12:30pm. Free.) off r. des Chanoines, hold the tombs of William the Conqueror and his wife.

Trains (☎08 29 35 35 35) run to: Paris (2½hr., 12 per day, €44.60); Rennes (3hr., 3 per day, €25.70); Rouen (2hr., 5 per day, €18.20); and Tours (3½hr., 2 per day, €26.70). Located to the left of the station, **Bus Verts** (☎08 10 21 42 14) covers the region. The **tourist office,** pl. St-Pierre, offers free maps. (☎02 31 27 14 14; www.ville-caen.fr. Open July-Aug. M-Sa 9:30am-7pm, Su 10am-1pm and 2-5pm; Sept.-June M-Sa 9:30am-1pm and 2-6pm, Su 10am-1pm.) The social **Auberge de Jeunesse (HI) ❶**, 68bis r. Eustache-Restout, is at Foyer Robert Reme. Take a right from the train station, take your second right on r. de Vaucelles, walk one block, and catch bus #5 or 17 (dir.: Fleury or Grâce de Dieu) from the stop on your left to Lycée Fresnel. (☎02 31 52 19 96; fax 02 31 84 29 49. Breakfast €2. Sheets €2.30. Reception 5-10pm. Beds €9.45.) **Hôtel du Château ❹**, 5 av. du 6 juin, has large, bright rooms. (☎02 31 86 15 37; fax 02 31 86 58 08. Reception 24hr. Singles and doubles €35, with sink €45. Prices €3.05 lower Oct.-Easter. MC/V.) Ethnic restaurants, *crêperies*, and *brasseries* line the **quartier Vaugueux** near the chateau and the streets between **Eglise St-Pierre** and **Eglise St-Jean.** Get your groceries at **Monoprix supermarket,** 45 bd. du Maréchal Leclerc. (Open M-Sa 9am-8:30pm.) Caen's old streets pulsate by moonlight, especially around **rue de Bras, rue des Croisiers,** and **rue St-Pierre. Postal Code:** 14000.

BAYEUX

Relatively untouched by war, beautiful Bayeux (pop. 15,000) is an ideal base for exploring the nearby D-Day beaches. However, visitors should not overlook its 900-year-old **Tapisserie de Bayeux,** 70m of embroidery that relates the tale of William the Bastard's invasion of England and his earning of a more acceptable name—"the Conqueror." The tapestry is displayed in the **Centre Guillaume le Conquérant,** on r. de Nesmond. (Open daily May-Aug. 9am-7pm; mid-Mar. to Apr. and Sept. to mid-Oct. 9am-6:30pm; mid-Oct. to mid-Mar. 9:30am-12:30pm and 2-6pm. €6.40, students €2.60.) Nearby is the original home of the tapestry, the extraordinary **Cathédrale Notre-Dame.** (Open July-Aug. M-Sa 8am-7pm, Su 9am-7pm; Sept.-June M-Sa 8:30am-noon and 2:30-7pm, Su 9am-12:15pm and 2:30-7pm. Free.) The amazing **Musée de la Bataille de Normandie,** bd. Fabian Ware, recounts the D-Day landing and 76-day battle. (Open May to mid-Sept. 9:30am-6:30pm; mid-Sept. to Apr. 10am-12:30pm and 2-6pm; closed early Jan. €5.70, students €2.50.) The **British Cemetery** across the street provides a strikingly simple yet moving wartime record.

Trains (☎02 31 92 80 50) arrive at pl. de la Gare from: Caen (20min., 15 per day, €4.90); Cherbourg (1hr., 12 per day, €12.50); and Paris (2½hr., 12 per day, €26.55). To reach the **tourist office,** on pont St-Jean, turn left on the highway (bd. Sadi-Carnot), bear right, follow the signs to the *centre ville,* and follow r. Larcher to r. St-Martin. (☎02 31 51 28 28; fax 02 31 51 28 29. Open mid-June to mid-Sept. M-Sa 9am-7pm, Su 9:30am-12:30pm and 2:30-6:30pm; mid-Sept. to mid-June M-Sa 9am-noon and 2-6pm.) From the tourist office, turn right onto r. St-Martin, continue down through several name changes, and turn left onto r. General de Dais to reach the **Family Home/Auberge de Jeunesse (HI) ❶,** 39 r. General de Dais. (☎02 31 92 15 22; fax 02 31 92 55 72. Breakfast included. Dorms €16, nonmembers €18.) Follow r. Genas Duhomme to the right and continue straight for **Camping Municipal ❶,** on bd. d'Eindhoven. (☎02 31 92 08 43. Open May-Sept. €2.85 per person, €3.52 per tent and car.) Get **groceries** at **Champion,** on bd. d'Eindhoven. **Postal Code:** 14400.

D-DAY BEACHES

On June 6, 1944, over one million Allied soldiers invaded the beaches of Normandy in the first of a chain of events that liberated France and led to the downfall of Nazi Europe. Today, reminders of that first devastating battle can be seen in sobering gravestones, remnants of German bunkers, and the pockmarked landscape.

TRANSPORTATION. Most of the beaches and museums can be reached from Caen and Bayeux with **Bus Verts** (☎08 10 21 42 14); ask about the special "D-Day" line. You may want to buy a day pass (€17.50) if you plan to make many stops. **Utah Beach** is accessible only by car or by foot from **Ste-Mère-Eglise.** Take a **train** from Bayeux to Caretan (30min., 10 per day, €6.60) and then a **bus** from Caretan to Ste-Mère-Eglise (15min., 12:50pm, return 6:35pm; €2.90). **Victory Tours** leads four- and eight-hour tours in English that leave from behind the Bayeux tourist office. (☎02 31 51 98 14; www.victory-tours.com. 4hr. tour 12:30pm, €31; 8hr. tour 9:15am, €54. Reservations required.)

BEACHES NEAR BAYEUX. At **Utah Beach,** near Ste-Marie du Mont, the Americans headed the western flank of the invasion. The **Musée du Débarquement** here shows how 836,000 troops, 220,000 vehicles, and 725,000 tons of equipment came ashore. (☎02 33 71 53 35. Open June-Sept. daily 9:30am-7pm; Oct.-May reduced hours. €4.50.) The most difficult landing was that of the First US Infantry Division at **Pointe du Hoc.** The Pointe is considered a military cemetery because many who perished are still there, crushed beneath collapsed concrete bunkers. **Omaha Beach,** next to Colleville-sur-Mer and east of the Pointe du Hoc, is perhaps the most famous beach and is often referred to as "bloody Omaha." Overlooking the beach, 9387 American graves stretch across the American Cemetery. (Open daily mid-Apr. to Sept. 8am-6pm; Oct. to mid-Apr. 9am-5pm.) Ten kilometers north of Bayeux and just east of Omaha is **Arromanches,** a small town at the center of **Gold Beach,** where the British built the artificial Port Winston in a single day to provide shelter while the Allies unloaded their supplies. The Arromanches **360° Cinéma** combines images of modern Normandy with those of D-Day. Turn left on r. de la Batterie from the museum and climb the steps. (Open daily June-Aug. 9:40am-6:40pm; Sept.-May reduced hours; closed Jan. €3.65.)

CHERBOURG

On the northern tip of the Cotentin peninsula, Cherbourg (pop. 44,000) was the "Gateway to France," serving as the major supply port following the D-Day offensive of 1944. Today, the town's many ferry lines shuttle tourists from France to England and Ireland. **Ferries,** which leave from bd. Maritime, northeast of the *cen-*

tre ville, connect to Rosslare, Portsmouth, and Poole (p. 57). Make sure to **reserve ahead** and check the most up-to-date schedules. To get to the train station, go left at the roundabout onto av. A. Briand and follow it as it becomes av. Carnot; it's at the end of the canal right off av. Carnot on av. Millet (25min.). **Trains** go to: Bayeux (1hr., 8 per day, €12.80); Caen (1½hr., 10 per day, €15.70); Paris (3hr., 7 per day, €34.20); and Rouen (4½hr., 4 per day, €29.10). A **shuttle bus** connects the ferry terminal and train station. To reach the **tourist office,** 2 quai Alexandre III, turn right from the ferry terminal onto bd. Felix Amiot, go straight at the roundabout, and turn right to cross the canal; it will be on your left. (☎02 33 93 52 02; www.ot-cherbourg-cotentin.fr. Open 9am-12:30pm and 2-6pm.) **Postal Code:** 50100.

MONT-ST-MICHEL

Rising like a vision from the sea, the fortified island of Mont-St-Michel (pop. 42) is a dazzling labyrinth of stone arches, spires, and stairways that climb up to the **abbey.** Adjacent to the abbey church, **La Merveille,** a 13th-century Gothic monastery, encloses a seemingly endless web of passageways and chambers. (Open mid-July to Aug. daily 9am-7pm; Sept. to early July reduced hours. Admission €7, ages 18-25 €4.50.) The Mont is most stunning at night, but plan carefully—there is no late-night public transport off the island. Mont-St-Michel is best visited as a daytrip via Courriers Bretons **bus,** 104 r. Couesnon in Pontorson (☎02 33 60 11 43), from Rennes (1½hr., 3-6 per day, €11) or St-Malo (1½hr., 2-4 per day, €9). Hotels on Mont-St-Michel are expensive, starting at €45 a night. The **Pontorson tourist office,** pl. de l'Eglise, helps visitors find affordable accommodations (☎02 33 60 20 65; fax 02 33 60 85 67). The cheapest beds are at the **Centre Duguesclin (HI) ❶**, r. Général Patton. (☎/fax 33 60 18 65. Dorms €8.) **Postal Code:** 50116.

BRITTANY (BRETAGNE)

Lined with spectacular beaches, wild headlands, and cliffs gnawed by the sea into long crags and inlets, Brittany fiercely maintains its Celtic traditions despite Paris's age-old effort to Frenchify the province. Britons fled Anglo-Saxon invaders between the 5th and 7th centuries for this beautiful, wild peninsula and in the 800 years that followed, they defended their independence from Frankish, Norman, French, and English invaders. Breton traditions, dating from the Duchy's centuries of freedom, linger in the pristine islands off the Atlantic coast and lilting *Brezhoneg* (Breton) is heard at pubs and ports in the western part of the province.

RENNES

Rennes (pop. 210,000) tempers its Parisian sophistication with traditional Breton spirit. Its *vieille ville* of half-timbered medieval houses teems with hip cafes and bars so that by dusk, this youthful city—students comprise more than a quarter of its residents—invariably falls victim to the irresistible magnetism of its sizzling nightlife. A popular stopover between Paris and Mont-St-Michel, Rennes also makes for a packed weekend excursion of its own.

TRANSPORTATION. Trains leave from pl. de la Gare (☎02 99 29 11 92) for: Brest (2¼hr., every hr., €26.90); Caen (3hr., 8 per day, €25.70); Nantes (1¼-2hr., 7 per day, €17.40); Paris (2hr., every hr., €44.80); and St-Malo (1hr., 15 per day, €10.70). **Buses** (☎02 99 30 87 80) leave the train station for Angers (2½-3hr., 3-4 per day, €14.95) and Mont-St-Michel (2½hr., 1-2 per day, €11).

PRACTICAL INFORMATION. To get from the train station to the **tourist office,** 11 r. Saint-Yves, take av. Jean Janvier to quai Chateaubriand, turn left, walk along the river until you reach r. George Dottin, then turn right onto r. Saint-Yves. (☎02 99 67 11 11; fax 02 99 67 11 10. Open Apr.-Sept. M-Sa 9am-7pm, Su and holidays 11am-6pm.) Access the **Internet** at **Cybernet Online,** 22 r. St. Georges (☎99 36 37 41. €6 per hr. Open M 2-8pm, Tu-Sa 10am-8pm; closed Aug. 1-20.) The **post office** (☎02 99 01 22 11) is at 27 bd. du Colombier, near the train station. **Postal Code:** 35032.

ACCOMMODATIONS AND FOOD. The **Auberge de Jeunesse (HI) ❶,** 10-12 Canal St-Martin, provides cheap and decent lodging. From the train station, take av. Jean Janvier toward the canal (where it becomes r. Gambetta) for five blocks, turn left on r. des Fossés, take r. de la Visitation to pl. Ste-Anne, staying on the right; follow r. de St-Malo on your right until you cross the small canal; the hostel is on the right. (☎02 99 33 22 33; fax 02 99 59 06 21. Breakfast included. Reception 7am-11pm. Dorms €12.20; singles €21.20. MC/V.) **Hotel d'Angleterre ❷,** 19 r. Marechal Joffre, can't be beat for location. From the train station's north entrance, proceed along av. Jean Janvier to bd. de la Liberte; after three blocks, take a right on r. Marechal Joffre, and it's on the right. (☎02 99 79 38 61; fax 02 99 79 43 85. Breakfast €4.90. Reception 7am-10:30pm. Singles €22; doubles €31. MC/V.) **Camping Municipal des Gayeulles ❶,** deep within Parc les Gayeulles, is packed with activities. Take bus #3 (dir.: Gayeulles/St-Laurent) from pl. de la Mairie to the third stop after you reach the park. Follow the paths and the signs to the campgrounds. (☎02 99 36 91 22. Reception mid-June to mid-Sept. daily 7:30am-1pm and 2-8pm; mid-Sept. to mid-June 9am-12:30pm and 4:30-8pm. €3.05 per person, €1.55 per car. Electricity €2.60. MC/V.) Look for food on **rue St-Malo, rue St-Georges,** or **place St-Michel;** or, explore **place des Lices** and its Saturday market. The upscale **Café Breton ❷,** 14 r. Nantaise, serves Breton cuisine at reasonable prices. (☎02 99 30 74 95. Open M and Sa noon-4pm, Tu-F noon-3pm and 7-11pm.)

SIGHTS AND ENTERTAINMENT. Excellent examples of medieval architecture are near the tourist office on **rue de la Psalette** and **rue St-Guillaume**. At the end of St-Guillaume, turn left onto r. de la Monnaie to visit the imposing **Cathédrale St-Pierre,** which was begun in 1787. The center of attention is its carved and gilded altarpiece depicting the life of the Virgin. (Open daily 9:30am-noon and 3-6pm.) Across the street from the cathedral, the **Portes Mordelaises,** down an alley bearing the same name, are the former entrance to the city and the last vestiges of the medieval city walls. The **Musée des Beaux-Arts,** 20 quai Emile Zola, houses a collection that includes Pharoic Egyptian pieces, works by de la Tour and Picasso, and contemporary art. (☎02 99 28 55 85 40. Open W-M 10am-noon and 2-6pm. €4, students €2, under 18 free.) Across the river and up r. Gambetta is the lush **Jardin du Thabor,** considered to be among the most beautiful gardens in France. (Open June-Sept. 7:15am-9:30pm.) Next door is the magnificent 11th- to 19th-century **Eglise Notre Dame** where you can gaze at the remnants of a 15th-century fresco depicting the Baptism of Christ.

With enough bars for a city twice its size and a collection of clubs that draws students from Paris and beyond, Rennes is a partygoer's weekend Mecca. Look for action in **place Ste-Anne, place St-Michel,** and the radiating streets. **Le Zing,** 5 pl. des Lices, packs the house with the young and beautiful. (☎02 99 79 64 60. Open 2pm-2am.) **L'Espace,** 45 bd. La Tour d'Auvergne, pounds all night with writhers of all sizes, styles, and sexual orientations. Upstairs, **L'Endroit** attracts a more relaxed mixed crowd. (☎02 99 30 21 95. Cover €9. Both open Th 11pm-4am, F-Sa 11pm-5am, Su-W midnight-4am.)

THE LOCAL STORY

BROTHER, CAN YOU SPARE A WEB DESIGN?

Frère Tobie, age 25, is a native Breton and monk at Mont St-Michel. He is a serious-looking young man, thin with closely cropped red hair, and he wears a monk's full-length dark blue robe and simple sandals. Attached to his belt, along with his prayer beads, is a mobile phone.

Q: What is life like on Mont St-Michel?
A: It's an exceptional place. The condition of life is particular to the location, because this is not just a monastery but also a tourist site, a place of pilgrimage, and an ancient monument. Life varies each day, but for us essentially this is a place of sanctuary, even though almost three thousand people visit each year. Living in the midst of the sea, we have to pay attention to the tides, because they dictate when we can venture off the island. At night and in the early morning the Mont is completely deserted. When you look out on the bay, with 500km of sand, it is a great desert.

Q: And the monastic community?
A: We have two communities, who live in parallel and have liturgies together. We have four monks and seven nuns. We hope to become more numerous over time, with more brothers and sisters from other communities.

Q: What is a normal day for you?
A: Our day begins at 6am. At 6:30 we have a half-hour of silent prayer and

ST-MALO

St-Malo (pop. 52,000) is the ultimate oceanside getaway, combining miles of warm, sandy beaches and crystal blue waters with a historic *centre ville*. To the east of the city is the **Grand Plage,** the most popular beach. The best view of St-Malo is from its **ramparts**—enter the walled city through Porte St-Vincent and follow the stairs up on the right. **Trains** run from pl. de l'Hermine to: Dinan (1hr., 5 per day, €7.30); Paris (5hr., 3 per day, €49.60); and Rennes (1hr., 8-12 per day, €10.70). As you exit the station, cross bd. de la République and follow esplanade St-Vincent to the **tourist office,** near the entrance to the old city. (☎02 99 56 64 48; www.saint-malo-tourisme.com. Open July-Aug. M-Sa 8:30am-8pm, Su 10am-7pm; Sept.-June reduced hours.) The 247-bed **Auberge de Jeunesse (HI) ❶,** 37 av. du Révérend Père Umbricht, is near the beach. From the train station, take bus #5 (dir.: Parame or Davier) or bus #1 (dir.: Rotheneuf) to Auberge de Jeunesse. (☎02 99 40 29 80; fax 02 99 40 29 02. Reception 24hr. Dorms €12.20.) To reach the simple-yet-spotless **Hôtel Avenir ❷,** 31 bd. de la Tour d'Auvergne, from the station, turn right onto bd. de la République and then right onto bd. de la Tour d'Auvergne; the hotel is on your left. (☎02 99 56 13 33. Breakfast €4. Singles €20; doubles €21.50.) **Champion supermarket,** on av. Pasteur, is near the hostel. (Open M-F 8:30am-1pm and 3-7:30pm, Sa 8:30am-7:30pm, Su 9:30am-noon.) **Postal Code:** 35400.

DINAN

Perhaps the best-preserved medieval town in Brittany, Dinan (pop. 10,000) sports cobblestone streets lined with 15th-century houses inhabited by artisans. On the ramparts, the 13th-century **Porte du Guichet** is the entrance to the **Château de Dinan,** also known as the Tour de la Duchesse Anne. Climb to the terrace to look over the town or inspect the galleries of the 15th-century **Tour de Coëtquen,** which houses a collection of funerary ornaments. (Open June-Sept. daily 10am-6:30pm; Oct.-May reduced hours. €3.90, ages 12-18 €1.50.) On the other side of the ramparts from the chateau is the **Jardin du Val Cocherel,** which holds bird cages and a chessboard for life-sized pieces. (Open daily 8am-7:30pm.)

Trains run from the pl. du 11 novembre 1918 to Paris (3hr., 8 per day, €49.60) and Rennes (1hr., 8 per day, €11.20). To get from the station to the **tourist office,** r. du Château, bear left across pl. 11 novembre to r. Carnot, turn right on r. Thiers, turn left into the old city, and bear right onto r. du Marchix, which becomes r. de la Ferronnerie; it will be on your right. (☎02 96 87 69 76; www.dinan-tourisme.com. Open mid-June to mid-Sept. M-Sa 9am-7pm, Su 10am-12:30pm and 2:30-6pm; mid-Sept. to mid-June M-Sa 9am-12:30pm and 2-6:15pm.) To walk to the **Auberge de Jeunesse (HI) ❶,** in Vallée de la Fontaine-des-Eaux, turn left as you exit the station and cross the tracks; turn right, and follow the tracks and signs downhill for 1km before turning right again; it will be on your right. (☎02 96 39 10 83; fax 02 96 39 10 62. Reception 8am-noon and 5-8pm. Curfew 11pm. Dorms €8.50.) **Hôtel du Théâtre ❶,** 2 r. Ste-Claire, is in the heart of the *vieille ville.* (☎02 96 39 06 91. Singles €14.50; doubles €20.50; triples €36.) Get groceries at **Monoprix** on r. de la Ferronnerie. (Open M-Sa 9am-7:30pm.) Inexpensive *brasseries* lie on **rue de la Cordonnerie** and near **rue de la Ferronnerie** and **place des Merciers.** **Postal Code:** 22100.

ST-BRIEUC. Situated between the Côte d'Emeraude and the Côte de Granite Rose, St-Brieuc is a perfect base for daytrips to the scenic countryside. **Trains** arrive from Dinan (1hr., 2-3 per day, €8.60) and Rennes (1hr., 15 per day, €14.40). From the station, on bd. Charner, walk straight down r. de la Gare and bear right at the fork to reach pl. de la Résistance and the **tourist office,** 7 r. St-Gouéno. (☎02 96 33 32 50; www.baiesaintbrieuc.com. Open July-Aug. M-Sa 9am-12:30pm and 2-7pm, Su 10am-1pm; Sept.-June M-Sa 9am-12:30pm and 2-6pm.) The **youth hostel ❶** is in a 15th-century house 3km from town; take bus #2 (dir.: Centre Commercial les Villages) and get off at the last stop. From the stop, turn right on bd. de l'Atlantique, take the 2nd left onto r. du Vau Meno, and turn right on r. de la Ville Guyomard; it will be on the left. (☎02 96 78 70 70. Breakfast included. Reception 8am-noon, 2-4pm and 8-10pm. Dorms €12.20. MC/V.) **Postal Code:** 22000.

CAP FRÉHEL. The rust-hued cliffs of **Cap Fréhel** mark the northern point of the Côte d'Emeraude. Catch a CAT **bus** from St-Brieuc (1½hr.; 3-4 per day; €7.20, students €5.80) and follow the red- and white-striped markers along the well-marked **GR34 trail** on the edge of the peninsula. There's also the scenic 90min. walk to **Fort La Latte,** a 13th-century castle complete with drawbridges. To reach the **Auberge de Jeunesse Cap Fréhel (HI) ❶,** in La Ville Hadrieux in Kerivet, get off the bus one stop after Cap Fréhel at Auberge de Jeunesse, take the only road that branches from the stop, and follow the fir-tree hostel signs. (☎02 96 41 48 98; mid-Sept. to Apr. ☎02 98 78 70 70. Breakfast €2.90. Open May-Sept. Dorms or camping €6.90.)

then *laudes,* the first services of the day. After breakfast we have *lectio divino*, a reading from the Bible, because the word of God is the basis of our life. We eat lunch in silence. In the afternoon we work. At 6:30pm, we have the adoration of the sacrement for an hour and then vespers, in which the public can participate. Later we eat dinner, also in silence.

Q: What kind of work do you do?
A: Our vocation is being monks in the town, among people. Here at Mont St-Michel, we divide up our daily tasks: we have one brother who cooks, one brother who cleans and gardens, and our superior who coordinates the masses. And I am the webmaster, so I develop Internet sites.

Q: What drew you to a monastic life?
A:The monastic life is chosen in response to a call from God. This is our answer. In the community, we have all possible routes: there is one brother who converted after spending 20 years as a communist, because he had such a strong personal experience. There are also those from devout families, who joined very young, just after finishing high school.

Q: How do you feel about all the tourists who come to the Mont?
A: For us, it's not difficult, because we need to interact with people. We have a mission here, and it allows this place to touch the hearts of those who come.

PAIMPOL. Paimpol, northwest of St-Brieuc at the end of the Côte de Granite Rose, offers easy access to nearby islands, beaches, and hiking. The **train** (1hr., 4-5 per day, €10) and CAT buses (1¼hr.; 8 per day; €7.20, students €5.80) leave av. Général de Gaulle for St-Brieuc. From the station, turn right onto ave. de Général de Gaulle. Bear left at the roundabout; the **tourist office** will be on the left, and the port will be to the right. (☎02 96 20 83 16; fax 02 96 55 11 12. Open July-Aug. M-Sa 10am-7pm, Su 10am-1pm; Sept.-June Tu-Sa 10am-12:30pm and 2:30-6pm.) The blue "H" signs guide you to the comfortable rooms of the **Hôtel Berthelot ❷,** 1 r. du Port. (☎02 96 20 88 66. Singles and doubles €26. MC/V) **Postal Code:** 22500.

BREST

Brest (pop. 156,000) slowly rose from the ashes of WWII to become a metropolis that blends the prosperity of a major port with the youthful energy of a university town. Brest's **château** was the only building in the town to survive WWII, and is now the world's oldest active military institution, as well as home to the **Musée de la Marine,** off r. de Château, which highlights the local maritime history. (Open Apr.-Sept. daily 10am-6:30pm; Oct-Mar. W-M 10am-noon and 2-6pm. €4.60, students €3.) The newly renovated **Océanopolis Brest,** at port de Plaisance, has tropical, temperate, and polar pavilions and a coral reef accessible by a glass elevator. From the Liberty terminal, take bus #7 (dir.: Port de Plaisance; M-Sa every 30min. until 7:30pm, €1) to Océanopolis. (☎02 98 34 40 40. Open Apr.-Aug. daily 9am-6pm; Sept.-Mar. Tu-Sa 10am-5pm and Su 10am-6pm. €13.50.)

Trains (☎02 98 31 51 72) leave pl. du 19*ème* Régiment d'Infanterie for: Nantes (4hr., 6 per day, €33.80) and Rennes (1½hr., 15 per day, €25.30). From the station, av. Georges Clemenceau leads to the intersection of r. de Siam and r. Jean Jaurès, and the **tourist office,** at pl. de la Liberté. (☎98 44 24 96. Open July-Aug. M-Sa 9:30am-7pm, Su 2-4pm; Sept.-June M-Sa 10am-12:30pm and 2-6pm.) Access the **Internet** at **@cces.cibles,** 31 av. Clemenceau. (☎02 98 33 73 07. €3 per hr. Open M-Sa 11am-1am, Su 2-11pm.) To get to the luxurious **Auberge de Jeunesse (HI) ❶,** 5 r. de Kerbriant, 4km away near Océanopolis, take bus #7 (dir.: Port de Plaisance) from opposite the station to its final stop (M-Sa until 7:30pm, Su until 6pm; €1); with your back to the bus stop, go left toward the beach, take an immediate left, and follow the signs to the hostel. (☎02 98 41 90 41. Breakfast included. Reception M-F 7-9am and 5-8pm, Sa-Su 7-10am and 6-8pm. Curfew July-Aug. midnight, Sept.-June 11pm; ask for a key. Dorms €11.30.) To reach **Camping du Goulet ❶,** 7km from Brest, take bus #14 (dir.: Plouzane) to Le Cosquer. (☎02 98 45 86 84. Shower included. €3.40 per person, €3.90 per tent. Electricity €1.70-2.50.) For groceries, visit **Monoprix,** 49 r. de Siam. (Open M-Sa 8:30am-7:30pm.) **Postal Code:** 29200.

NANTES

Nantes (pop. 550,000) tastefully blends the distinct flavors of a modern high-tech industry, a classy pedestrian district, and historical sights reminiscent of its glorious, if gory, past. At the imposing **Château des Ducs de Bretagne,** Henri IV composed the **Edict of Nantes,** which granted considerable religious liberties to the Huguenots. The interim **Musée du Château des Ducs de Bretagne** hosts temporary exhibits. (☎02 40 41 56 56. Courtyard open for free visits July-Aug. daily 10am-7pm; Sept.-June 10am-6pm. Museum open July-Aug daily 10am-6pm; Sept.-June closed on Tu. €3, students €1.50.) Go inside the **Cathédrale St-Pierre** to gape at the soaring 38m Gothic vaults and the largest stained-glass window in the country. (Open daily 10am-7pm.) For fans of Captain Nemo, the **Musée Jules Verne,** 3 r. de L'Hermiage, on the opposite side of town, is a small museum with tons of information about the *Nantais* author and scientist. (☎02 40 69 72 52. Open M and W-Sa 10am-noon and 2-5pm, Su 2-5pm. €1.50, students €0.75; Su free.)

Trains run from 27 bd. de Stalingrad to: Bordeaux (4hr., 6-8 per day, €35); La Rochelle (2hr., 8-11 per day, €17); Paris (2-4hr., 20 per day, €46); Rennes (2hr., 3-10 per day, €17); and Saumur (1¼hr., 7 per day, €16). To get from the train station to the **tourist office,** pl. du Commerce, turn left out of the north entrance to the train station *(accés nord)*, continue straight along allée du Charcto, which becomes cours John Kennedy, and after the chateau, it will be up on your right in the FNAC building. (☎02 40 20 60 00; www.reception.com/Nantes. Open M-Sa 10am-7pm.) Check your **email** and grab a falafel at **Cyberkebab,** 30 r. de Verdun. (€3 per hr. Open 11am-2am.) To get from the train station to the 200-bed **Foyer des Jeunes Travailleurs, Beaulieu (HI)** ❶, 9 bd. Vincent Gâche, take the #10 bus (dir.: Francois Mitterand) from opposite the south entrance to Pl. du Commerce; switch to the tramway #2 (dir.: Trocardinet) to Vincent Gache, and bd. Vincent Gache is just ahead on the left. (☎02 40 12 24 00; fax 02 51 82 00 05. Breakfast €2.20. Reception 8am-9pm, call ahead for late night check-in. €9.50, nonmembers €20.) The **Hôtel St-Daniel** ❷, 4 r. du Bouffay, is just off pl. du Bouffay. (☎02 40 47 41 25. Breakfast €3.85. Singles €24; doubles €24-28; triples and quads €36. AmEx/MC/V.) **Marché de Talensac** is on r. de Bel-Air, behind the post office. (Open Tu-Sa 9am-1pm.) **Monoprix** is at 2 r. de Calvaire, off cours de 50 Otages. (Open M-Sa 9am-9pm.) **Quartier St-Croix,** near pl. Bouffay, and **rue Scribe** have cafes and bars. **Postal Code:** 44000.

LOIRE VALLEY (VAL DE LOIRE)

The Loire, France's longest and most celebrated river, meanders to the Atlantic through a valley overflowing with gentle vineyards and majestic chateaux. Loire vineyards produce some of France's best wines, and the soil is among the country's most fertile. It is hardly surprising that a string of French (and English) kings chose to station themselves in opulent chateaux by these waters rather than in the dirt and noise of their capital cities.

TRANSPORTATION

Faced with such widespread grandeur, many travelers plan over-ambitious itineraries—two chateaux a day is a reasonable limit. Bike is the best way to explore the region, since trains to chateaux are infrequent. The city of Tours is the region's best rail hub, although the chateaux Sully-sur-Loire, Chambord, and Cheverny aren't accessible by train. Many stations distribute the invaluable *Châteaux pour Train et Vélo* booklet with train schedules and bike and car rental information.

ORLÉANS

A pleasant gateway from Paris into the Loire, Orléans (pop. 117,000) clings tightly to its historical claim to Joan of Arc's fame. Most of Orléans's historical and architectural highlights are near **Place Ste-Croix.** Joan of Arc triumphantly marched down nearby **rue de Bourgogne,** the city's oldest street, in 1429; the scene is vividly captured in *Jeanne d'Arc*, at the **Musée des Beaux-Arts,** 1 r. Ferdinand Rabier. (☎02 38 79 21 55. Open M 1:30-6pm, Tu-Sa 10am-noon and 1:30-6pm. €3, students €1.50.) The **Église St-Paterne,** pl. Gambetta, is a massive showcase of modern stained glass. The stunning windows of **Cathédrale Ste-Croix,** pl. Ste-Croix, depict Joan's dramatic story. (Open July-Aug. daily 9:15am-6:45pm; Sept.-June reduced hours. Free.) Forty-two kilometers from Orléans, the imposing 14th-century fortress **Sully-sur-Loire** dominates the southern bank of the Loire. Catch the bus at 2 r. Marcel Proust (1hr., 5 per day, €7.30).

Trains arrive at the Gare d'Orléans on pl. Albert 1*er* from: Blois (30min., every hr. 7am-9pm, €8.30); Paris (1¼hr., 3 per hr., €14.60) and Tours (1hr., 12 per day,

€14.10). To get from the station to the **tourist office,** 6 pl. Albert 1*er*, go left under the tunnel to pl. Jeanne d'Arc; it's across the street. (☎02 38 24 05 05; www.tourismloiret.com. Open Apr.-Sept. M-Sa 10am-1pm and 2-7pm, Su 10am-noon. Oct.-Mar. reduced hours.) To get to the spacious and clean **Auberge de Jeunesse (HI) ❶,** 1 bd. de la Motte Sanguin, take bus RS (dir.: Rosette) or SY (dir.: Concyr/La Bolière) from pl. d'Arc to Pont Bourgogne; follow bd. de la Motte and it'll be up on the right. (☎02 38 53 60 06. Reception M-F 8am-7pm, Sa-Su 9-11am and 5-7pm. Dorms €8; singles €14.) Get **groceries** at **Carrefour** at pl. d'Arc. (Open M-Sa 8:30am-9pm.) **Rue de Bourgogne** has a variety of inexpensive eateries. **Postal Code:** 45000.

BLOIS

Blois (pop. 50,000) welcomes visitors to the Loire Valley with imperial grandeur and pastoral charm. Home to monarchs Louis XII and François I, Blois's **château** was the Versailles of the late 15th and early 16th centuries; today it is decorated with François I's painted and carved salamanders and exemplifies the progression of French architecture from the 13th to the 17th century. Housed in the castle are excellent museums: the recently renovated **Musée de Beaux-Arts,** featuring a 16th-century portrait gallery; the **Musée d'Archéologie,** showcasing locally excavated glass and ceramics; and the **Musée Lapidaire,** preserving sculpted pieces from nearby chateaux. (☎02 54 78 06 62. Open July-Aug. daily 9am-7:30pm; Apr.-June and Sept. 9am-6pm; Oct.-Mar. 9am-12:30pm and 2-5:30pm. €6, students €4.) When the sun goes down, crowds move from the cafes of **Place de la Résistance** to **Z 64,** r. Maréchal de Tassigny, for cocktails, dancing, and karaoke. (☎02 54 74 27 76. Open Tu-Su 8:30pm-4am.)

Trains leave pl. de la Gare for: Orléans (30min., 14 per day, €8.30); Paris (1¾hr., 8 per day, €20) via Orléans; Tours (1hr., 10 per day, €8). **Transports Loir-et-Cher (TLC)** (☎02 54 58 55 44) sends buses from the station and pl. Victor Hugo to nearby chateaux (1¼hr., 4 per day, €5.35). Or, rent a **bike** from **Cycles Leblond,** 44 levée des Tuileries, for the hour-long ride to the valley. (☎02 54 74 30 13. €12.20 per day. Open daily 9am-9pm.) The **tourist office,** 3 av. Jean Laigret, can point the way. (☎02 54 90 41 41; www.loiredeschateaux.com. Open mid-Apr. to mid-Oct. Tu-Sa 9am-7pm, Su-M and holidays 10am-7pm; Oct-Mar. M 10am-12:30pm and 2-6pm, Tu-Sa 9am-12:30pm and 2-6pm, Su 9:30am-12:30pm.) Five kilometers west is the **Auberge de Jeunesse (HI) ❶,** 18 r. de l'Hôtel Pasquier. To get there from the tourist office, follow r. Porte Côté, bear right along r. Denis Papin to the river, and take bus #4 (dir.: Les Grouets) to "Auberge de Jeunesse." (☎/fax 02 54 78 27 21. Reception 6:45-10am and 6-10:30pm. Lockout 10am-6pm. Curfew 10:30pm. Open Mar. to mid-Nov. Dorms €7.) **Le Pavillon ❸,** 2 av. Wilson, has clean and bright rooms. (☎02 54 74 23 27; fax 02 54 74 03 36. Breakfast €5. Singles €20-36; quads €48. MC/V.) Fragrant *patisseries* entice from **rue Denis Papin,** while **rue Drussy, rue St-Lubin,** and **place Poids du Roi** have a wide variety of eateries. **Postal Code:** 41000.

DAYTRIPS FROM BLOIS: CHAMBORD AND CHEVERNY. Built between 1519 and 1545 to satisfy François I's egomania, **Chambord** is the largest and most extravagant of the Loire chateaux. With 440 rooms, 365 fireplaces, and 83 staircases, the chateau rivals Versailles in grandiosity. To cement his claim, François stamped 700 of his trademark stone salamanders throughout this "hunting lodge" and built a spectacular double-helix staircase in the center of the castle. (☎02 54 50 40 00. Open July-Aug. 9am-6:45pm; Sept.-June reduced hours. €7, ages 18-25 €4.50.) Take **TLC bus #2** from Blois (45min., €3.20) or **bike** south from Blois on D956 for 2-3km, and then turn left on D33 (1hr.).

Cheverny and its manicured grounds are unique among the major chateaux. Its magnificent furnishings include elegant tapestries and delicate Delft vases. Fans

FRANCE

of Hergé's *Tintin* books may recognize Cheverny's Renaissance facade as the inspiration for Marlinspike, Captain Haddock's mansion. The **kennels** hold 70 mixed English Poitevin hounds who stalk stags in hunting expeditions (Oct.-Mar. Tu and Sa). (☎02 54 79 96 29. Open July-Aug. daily 9:15am-6:45pm. Reduced hours off season. €5.80, students €2.60.) Cheverny is 45min. south of Blois by bike and on the route of TLC bus #2 (see above).

AMBOISE

The battlements of the 15th-century **château** at Amboise (pop. 11,000) that six paranoid French kings called home, stretch protectively above the town. In the **Logis de Roi,** the main part of the chateau, intricate 16th-century Gothic chairs stand over 2m high to prevent surprise attacks from behind. The jewel of the grounds is the 15th-century **Chapelle St-Hubert,** the final resting place of **Leonardo da Vinci.** (☎02 47 57 00 98. Open Apr.-Nov. daily 9am-6pm; Dec.-Mar. reduced hours. €6.50, students €5.50.) Four hundred meters away is **Clos Lucé** manor, where Leonardo da Vinci spent the last three years of his life. Check out the collection of 40 unrealized inventions. (☎02 47 57 62 88. Mar.-Oct. 9am-7pm; Nov.-Feb. reduced hours. €6.50, students €5.50.) **Trains** leave bd. Gambetta for: Blois (20min., 15 per day, €5.35); Orléans (1hr., 14 per day, €11.60); Paris (2¼hr., 5 per day, €23); Tours (20min., 14 per day, €4.30). The **Centre International de Séjour (HI) Charles Péguy ❶,** on Ile d'Or, sits on an island in the middle of the Loire. (☎02 47 30 60 90; fax 02 47 30 60 91. Sheets €3. Reception M-F 3-7pm. Dorms €8.40.) **Postal Code:** 35400.

TOURS

Tours (pop. 250,000) works best as a base for visiting nearby Loire chateaux, but its fabulous nightlife and collection of sights should not be missed. The **Cathédrale St-Gatien,** on r. Jules Simon, has dazzling stained glass. (Open daily 9am-7pm. Free.) At the **Musée du Gemmail,** 7 r. du Murier, works of *gemmail* (a fusion of enameled shards of brightly colored glass) by Picasso and Braque glow in rooms of dark velvet. (Open Apr. to mid-Nov. Tu-Su 10am-noon and 2-6:30pm; mid-Nov. to Mar. W-Su only. €4.60, students €3.05.) Stroll past the twin **Tours (towers) of Tours,** flanking r. des Halles, which are fragments of the huge 5th-century Romanesque Basilique St-Martin. **Place Plumereau** is the *place* to be: party with an older crowd at **Louis XIV,** or go upstairs to chill in the **Duke Ellington.** (Both open daily until 2am; Duke Ellington closed July-Aug.)

Trains leave 3 r. Édouard Vaillant for Bordeaux (2½hr., 6 per day, €35.50) and Paris (2¼hr., 7 per day, €24.20). The **tourist office,** 78/82 r. Bernard Palissy, distributes free maps and books rooms. (☎02 47 70 37 37; www.ligeris.com. Open mid-Apr. to mid-Oct. M-Sa 8:30am-7pm, Su 10am-12:30pm and 2:30-5pm; mid-Oct. to mid-Apr. M-Sa 9am-12:30pm and 1:30-6pm, Su 10am-1pm.) **Internet** access is available at the **Cyber Gate,** 11 r. de Président Merville. (☎47 05 95 94. €1 for 15min. Open M 1-10pm, Tu-Sa 11am-10pm, Su 2-10pm.) **Foyer des Jeunes Travailleurs ❷,** 24 r. Bernard Palissy, is centrally located. (☎02 47 60 51 51. Singles €15.25; doubles €24.40.) The owners of **Hôtel Regina ❸,** 2 r. Pimbert, make you feel like family. It's near beautiful river strolls and good restaurants. (☎02 47 05 25 36; fax 02 47 66 08 72. Breakfast €4.15. Singles €20-26; doubles €26-30. MC/V.) **Place Plumereau** offers an amazingly diverse array of restaurants, cafes, and bars with *menus* from €11. **Le Charolais Chez Jean Michel ❷,** 123 r. Colbert, serves local cuisine with regional wines. (3-course lunch *menus* €10.50 and €13. Open M 7:30-10:30pm, Tu-Sa noon-2pm and 7:30-10:30pm.) **Postal Code:** 37000.

DAYTRIPS FROM TOURS

CHENONCEAU. Perhaps the most exquisite chateau in France, Chenonceau arches gracefully over the Cher river. A series of women created the beauty that is the chateau: first Catherine, the wife of a tax collector; then Diane de Poitiers, the lover of Henri II; and then Henri's widowed wife, Catherine de Médici. The part of the chateau bridging the Cher marked the border between occupied and Vichy France during WWII. *(Trains from Tours roll into the station 2km away from the castle (45min., 8 per day, €5.50). Fil Vert buses also connect Tours with Chenonceau (25min., 2 per day, €2). Chateaux ☎47 23 90 07; www.chenonceaux-sa.fr. Open mid-Mar. to mid-Sept. daily 9am-7pm; reduced hours off season. €7.65, students €5.)*

LOCHES. Surrounded by a walled medieval town that merits a visit in itself, the chateau of Loches consists of two distinct structures at opposite ends of a hill. To the north, the 11th-century keep and watchtowers changed roles from keeping enemies out to keeping them in when Charles VII turned it into a state prison, complete with suspended cages. The Logis Royal honors the famous ladies who held court here, including Agnès Sorel, the first Mistress of the King of France. *(Trains and buses run from Tours to Loches (50min., 13 per day, €7.50). Chateau open Apr.-Sept. daily 9am-7pm; Oct.-Mar. 9:30am-12:30pm and 2-5pm. Logis Royal €3.80.)*

SAUMUR

Saumur (pop. 30,000) is a refreshing break from the usual castle-heavy Loire fare, with many other attractions and an enchanting old quarter. The 14th-century **château** is best known for its cameo appearance in the famous medieval manuscript *Les très riches heures du duc de Berry;* it contains the **Musée des Arts Décoratifs,** with medieval and Renaissance works, and the horse-crazy **Musée du Cheval.** (☎02 41 40 24 40. Open June-Aug. daily 9:30am-6pm; Sept.-May reduced hours. €6, students €4; gardens only €2.) **Gratien et Meyer,** on r. de Montsoreau, gives tours of its wine *cave* and offers tastings. Take bus D from pl. Bilange to Beaulieu. (☎02 41 83 13 32. Open Apr.-Nov. daily 9am-noon and 2-6pm. Dec.-Mar. reduced hours. Tour €2.30.) The **Musée de Champignon,** on rte. de Gennes in St-Hilaire-St-Florent, is a mushroom *cave* that traces the history of the mushroom industry in France. (☎41 50 31 55. Open Feb.-Nov. daily 10am-7pm. €6.50.)

Trains leave av. David d'Angers for: Angers (30min., 15 per day, €6.55); Paris (1½hr., 7:50pm. €29.20.); and Tours (45min., 21 per day, €8.80). The **tourist office,** pl. Bilange, next to pont Cessart, books beds (€1 fee). Exit to the right of the station on av. David d'Angers, turn right onto pont des Cadets, and it will be on your left, at the corner of quai Lucien Gautier. (☎02 41 40 20 60; fax 02 41 40 20 69. Open May-Sept. M-Sa 9:15am-7pm, Su 10:30am-5:30pm; Oct.-Apr. M-Sa 9:15am-12:30pm and 2-6pm, Su 10-noon.) The modern **Centre International de Séjour ❶,** r. de Verdun (*not* bd. de Verdun), is on Ile d'Offard. From the station, follow the directions above to pont des Cadets, turn left on r. Roi de Sicile after crossing the bridge, continue straight for 10min., and it's on the left. (☎02 41 40 30 00; fax 02 41 67 37 81. Reception 8:30am-12:30pm and 2-8pm. 2- to 8-bed dorms €13.30.) **Le Volney ❸,** 1 r. Volney, is a fresh, beautiful B&B on a quiet side street. (☎02 41 51 25 41; fax 02 41 38 11 04. Singles and doubles €25-€49. MC/V.) Get **groceries** at **Atac supermarket,** 6 r. Franklin D. Roosevelt, inside a shopping center. (Open M-F 9am-1pm and 2:15-7:30pm, Sa-Su 9am-12:30pm.) **Postal Code:** 49400.

DAYTRIP FROM SAUMUR: FONTEVRAUD ABBEY. Fourteen kilometers east of Saumur lies the **Abbaye de Fontevraud,** the largest existing monastic complex in Europe. The 12th-century abbey church serves as a Plantagenêt necropolis;

Eleanor of Aquitaine, who lived out her days here after being repudiated by her second husband, **Henry II,** now lies next to him along with their son **Richard the Lionheart.** The **tourist office** offers free maps of the town. (☎ 02 41 51 79 45. Open Apr. to mid-Oct. 10:30am-12:30pm and 2:30-5:30pm.) *(Bus #16 leaves from Saumur's train station (25min., 3-5 per day, €2.15). Abbey ☎ 02 41 51 71 41. Open June to mid-Sept. daily 9am-6:30pm; mid-Sept. to May 9:30am-12:30pm and 2-5pm. Tours €1.50.)*

ANGERS

From behind the massive stone walls of the **Château d'Angers,** on pl. Kennedy, the Dukes of Anjou ruled the surrounding area and a certain island across the Channel. The 13th-century chateau remains a well-preserved haven of medieval charm in a city filled with shops and sights. Inside the chateau is the 14th-century **Tapisserie de l'Apocalypse,** the world's largest tapestry. (Open May to mid-Sept. daily 9:30am-7pm; mid-Sept. to Apr. 10am-5:30pm. €5.50, students €3.50.) Angers's other woven masterpiece is the 1930 **Chant du Monde** ("Song of the World"), in the **Musée Jean Lurçat,** 4 bd. Arago. (☎ 02 41 24 18 45. Open mid-June to mid-Sept. daily 9:30am-6:30pm; late Sept. to mid-June Tu-Su 10am-noon and 2-6pm. €3.50.) In the *vieille ville* is the 12th-century **Cathédrale St-Maurice,** home to another impressive collection of tapestries. The tourist office sells a €4.50 admission to 5 museums and an €8 *billet jumelé,* which also includes the chateau.

From r. de la Gare, **trains** leave for: Nantes (1hr., 15 per day, €12); Paris (2-4hr., 3 per day, €39-49); and Tours (1hr., 7 per day, €13). **Buses** run from pl. de la République to Rennes (3hr., 2 per day, €15). To get from the station to the **tourist office,** at pl. du Président Kennedy, exit straight onto r. de la Gare, turn right at pl. de la Visitation on r. Talot, and turn left on bd. du Roi-René; it's on the right, across from the chateau. (☎ 02 41 23 50 00; accueil@angers-tourisme.com. Open June-Sept. M-Sa 9am-7pm, Su 10am-6pm; Oct.-May M-Sa 9am-6pm.) Access the **Internet** at **Cyber Espace,** 25 r. de la Roë. (☎ 02 41 24 92 71. €3.85 per hr. Open M-Th 10am-10pm, F-Sa 10am-midnight.) To get to the **Centre d'Accueil du Lac de Maine (HI)** ❷, 49 av. du Maine, take bus #6 or 16 to Accueil Lac de Maine, cross the road, and follow the signs. (☎ 02 41 22 32 10; infos@lacdemaine.fr. Breakfast included. HI members only. Singles and doubles with shower €24.) Walk straight down r. de la Gare for the spacious **Royal Hôtel** ❷, 8bis pl. de la Visitation. (☎ 02 41 88 30 25; fax 02 41 81 05 75. Breakfast €4.60. Singles and doubles €24-41; quads €55. AmEx/MC/V.) Grab groceries in **Galeries Lafayette,** at r. d'Alsace and pl. du Ralliement. (Open M-Sa 9:30am-7:30pm.) **Postal Code:** 49052.

POITOU-CHARENTES

Poitou-Charentes, on the western shore of France, boasts sun-drenched beaches, sedate canals, craggy cliffs, fertile plains, and a rich history. The *Côte d'Azur* may be tops in topless beaches, and the Loire Valley may be the king of chateaux, but no other region of France has so impressive a collection of both.

LA ROCHELLE

La Rochelle (pop. 100,000) has one great claim to fame—fish, and lots of it. As one of France's best-sheltered seaports, it was fought over by France and England during the Hundred Years' War. A magical world awaits in La Rochelle's popular **aquarium,** across from the Musée Maritime in Bassin des Grande Yacht. Hundreds of exotic fish, an octopus, and piranhas swim through realistic exhibits. (☎ 05 46 34 00 00. Open July-Aug. daily 9am-11pm; Apr.-June and Sept. 9am-8pm; Oct.-Mar. 9am-8pm. €10, students and children €7.) Climb up the fortifications of **Tour St-**

Nicolas and **Tour de la Chaîne,** to the left as you face the harbor. (St-Nicolas ☎05 46 41 74 13; Chaîne ☎06 46 34 11 81. Open Apr.-Sept. daily 10am-7pm; Oct.-Mar. W-M 10am-1pm and 2-6pm. €4, ages 18-25 €2.50, under 18 free.)

Trains leave bd. Maréchal Joffre for: Bordeaux (2hr., 5 per day, €21.10); Nantes (2hr., 5 per day, €19.80); Paris (3hr., 5 per day, €50.60); and Poitiers (2hr., 8 per day, €17.10). The **tourist office,** pl. de la Petite Sirène, is in the quartier du Gabut. (☎05 46 41 14 68; www.larochelle-tourisme.com. Open July-Aug. M-Sa 9am-8pm, Su 11am-5pm; Sept.-June reduced hours.) **Internet access** is available at **Centre Départemental d'Information Jeunesse (CDIJ),** 2 r. des Gentilshommes. (☎05 46 41 16 36. €1.60 per hr. Open M 2-6pm, Tu-F 10am-12:30pm and 1:30-6pm.) Take bus #10 (dir.: Port des Minimes; every 20min., €1.20) from av. de Colmar, near the train station, to Lycell Hotelier; go left at the rotary and walk down the road for 15min. **Centre International de Séjour (HI) ❶,** av. des Minimes, will be on the right. (☎05 46 44 43 11; fax 05 46 45 41 48. Breakfast included. Reception July-Aug. daily 8:30am-11pm; Sept.-June reduced hours. Dorms €13; singles €18.) **Postal Code:** 17000.

POITIERS

The renowned churches of Poitiers (pop. 83,000) were witness to the growth of Church power in the early Middle Ages. Facades in the 12th-century Romanesque **Notre-Dame-la-Grande,** pl. de Gaulle, off Grand Rue, display the story of Christianity, while the massive **Cathédrale St-Pierre,** in pl. de la Cathédrale, off r. de la Cathédrale, contains an elaborate 18th-century Cliquot classical organ. Nearby is the oldest Christian edifice in France, the 4th-century **Baptistère St-Jean,** on r. Jean Jaurès. (Open daily 10am-12:30pm and 3-6pm. €0.80.)

Trains run from the station at bd. du Grand Cerf to: Bordeaux (2hr., 8 per day, €25); La Rochelle (1¾hr., 8 per day, €17); Paris (2½hr., 6 per day, €41); and Tours (1hr., 5 per day, €13). The **tourist office,** 45 pl. Charles de Gaulle, is across from Notre Dame. (☎05 49 41 21 24; fax 05 49 88 65 84. Open mid-June to mid-Sept. M-Sa 9:30am-7:30pm, Su 10am-6pm; late Sept. to June M-Sa 10am-6pm.) For the **Auberge de Jeunesse (HI) ❶,** 1 allée Tagault, catch bus #3 (dir.: Pierre Loti; every 30min., €1), by the station, to Cap Sud. (☎05 49 58 03 05. Breakfast €2.70. Reception daily 7am-noon and 4pm-midnight. HI members only. Dorms €8.50.) **Postal Code:** 86000.

PÉRIGORD AND AQUITAINE

Périgord and Aquitaine present seductive images: green countryside splashed with yellow sunflowers, white chalk cliffs, golden white wine, plates of black truffles, and the smell of warm walnuts. First settled 150,000 years ago, the area around Les Eyzies-de-Tayac has produced more stone-age artifacts than anywhere on earth.

PÉRIGUEUX

The towering steeple and five massive cupolas of the **Cathédrale St-Front** dominate Périgueux (pop. 32,300) from above the Isle river. 1500 years of rebuilding, restoration, rethinking, and revision have produced the largest cathedral in southwestern France. (Open daily 8am-noon and 2:30pm-7pm.) Just down r. St-Front, the **Musée du Périgord,** 22 cours Tourny, houses one of France's most important collections of prehistoric artifacts, including 2m-long mammoth tusks and an Egyptian mummy whose toes peek out from crusty coverings, conspicuoulsy mixed with works by local middle schoolers. (☎05 53 06 40 70. Open M and W-F 11am-6pm, Sa-Su 1-6pm. €3.50, students €1.75; Sept. 15-June M-F noon-2pm 15 free.)

Trains leave r. Denis Papin for: Bordeaux (1½hr., 7 per day, €15.40); Paris (4-6hr., 12 per day, €42.80); and Toulouse (4hr., 8 per day, €26.80). The **tourist office,**

26 pl. Francheville, has free maps. From the station, turn right on r. Denis Papin, bear left on r. des Mobiles-de-Coulmierts, which becomes r. du Président Wilson; take the next right after passing r. Guillier; it will be on the left. (☎05 53 53 10 63; fax 05 53 09 02 50. Open July-Aug. M-Sa 9am-7pm, Su 10am-6pm; Sept.-June M-Sa 9am-6pm.) Across from the train station, **Hôtel des Voyageurs ❶**, 26 r. Denis Papin, has clean, bright rooms. (☎/fax 05 53 53 17 44. Breakfast €3.20. Singles €12.50; doubles €14, with shower €17.) Your stomach will thank you for visiting **Au Bien Bon ❸**, 15 r. Aubergerie, serving cuisine at the height of regional cooking with design-your-own lunch *formules*. (☎05 53 09 69 91. Entrees €10-13. Open M 7:30-10pm, Tu-Sa noon-2pm and 7:30-10pm.) **Monoprix supermarket** is on pl. de la République. (Open M-Sa 8:30am-8pm.) **Postal Code:** 24070.

SARLAT

The golden medieval *vieille ville* of Sarlat (pop. 11,000) has been the focus of both tourist and movie cameras—Gérard Depardieu's *Cyrano de Bergerac* was filmed here. Today, its narrow 14th- and 15th-century streets fill with flea markets, dancing violinists, and purveyors of *gâteaux aux noix* (cakes with nuts) and golden Monbazillac wines. **Trains** go to Bordeaux (2½hr., 4 per day, €18.60) and Périgueux (3hr., 2 per day, €11.40). The **tourist office,** r. Tourny in the Ancien Eveche, can arrange accommodations. (☎53 31 45 45. Open Apr.-Oct. M-Sa 9am-7pm, Su 10am-noon and 2-6pm; Nov.-Mar. M-Sa 9am-noon and 2-6pm.) You can rent **bikes** at **Cycles Sarlandais,** 36 av. Thiers. (☎05 53 28 51 87. €11 per day. Open Tu-Sa 9:30am-7pm. MC/V.) Sarlat's **Auberge de Jeunesse ❶**, 77 av. de Selves, is 40min. from the train station but only 10min. from the *vieille ville*. From the *vieille ville*, go straight on r. de la République, which becomes av. Gambetta, and bear left at the fork onto av. de Selves. (☎05 53 59 47 59. Reception daily 6-8:30pm. Open mid-Mar. to Nov. Reserve ahead. Dorms €10. **Camping** €6.) **Champion supermarket** is near the hostel on rte. de Montignac; continue following av. de Selves away from the *centre ville*. (Open M-Sa 9am-7:30pm, Su 9am-noon.) **Postal Code:** 24200.

DAYTRIPS FROM SARLAT AND PÉRIGUEUX

CAVE PAINTINGS

CFTA (☎05 55 86 07 07) runs buses to the Caves of Lascaux, near Montignac, from Périgueux (1½hr., 1 per day, €5.35). Buses also run every morning from Sarlat (20min., 3 per day, €6.10). Trains run to Les Eyzies-de-Tayac from Périgueux (30min., 45 per day, €6.10) and Sarlat (1hr.; 3 per day, change at Le Buisson; €7.20).

The most spectacular cave paintings ever discovered line the **Caves of Lascaux,** near the town of **Montignac,** 25km north of Sarlat. They were discovered in 1940 by a couple teenagers, but were closed in 1963—the oohs and aahs of tourists fostered algae and micro-stalactites that ravaged the paintings. **Lascaux II** duplicates the original cave in the same pigments used 17,000 years ago. Although they may lack ancient awe and mystery, the new caves—filled with paintings of 5m tall bulls, horses, and bison—manage to inspire a wonder all their own. The **ticket office** (☎53 35 50 10) shares a building with Montignac's **tourist office** (☎53 51 82 60), on pl. Bertram-de-Born. (Ticket office open 9am to sold out. €7.70.)

At the **Grotte de Font-de-Gaume,** 1km outside **Les Eyzies-de-Tayac** on D47 (10min. by foot), amazing 15,000-year-old paintings are still open for viewing. (☎05 53 06 86 00; www.leseyzies.com/grottes-ornees. Open Apr.-Sept. Th-Tu 9am-noon and 2-6pm; Mar. and Oct. Th-Tu 9:30am-noon and 2-5:30pm; Nov.-Feb. Th-Tu 10am-noon and 2-5pm. Reserve in advance. €5.50, ages 18-25 €3.50, under 18 free. Tours available in English.) Get more information at the **Point Accueil Prehistoire,** across from the post office, on the main street through town. (☎06 86 66 54 43. Open daily 9:15am-1:30pm and 3-7pm.) The **tourist office** is located at pl. de la Mairie, before the Point Accueil. (☎05 53 06 97 05; www.leseyzies.com. Open July-Aug. M-Sa 9am-8pm, Su 10am-noon and 2-6pm; Sept.-June reduced hours.)

THE DORDOGNE VALLEY

To get to and around the valley, you'll need to rent a car or be prepared for a good bike workout—the hills are steep but manageable. To paddle down the Dordogne River, rent canoes from Saga Team's Canoe. (☎05 55 28 84 84. Half-day €10, whole day €14.)

Steep, craggy cliffs and poplar tree thickets overlook the slow-moving turquoise waters of the Dordogne River, 15km south of Sarlat. The town of **Castelnaud-La Chapelle,** 10km southwest of Sarlat, snoozes in the shadow of its pale yellow **chateau.** (☎05 53 31 30 00. Open July-Aug. daily 9am-8pm; May-June and Sept. 10am-6pm; mid-Nov. to Feb. Su-F 2-5pm. €6.40.) **Domme** was built by King Philippe III (Philippe the Bold) in 1280 on a dome of solid rock. Over 70 Templar Knights were imprisoned by King Philip IV in the **Porte des Tours.** The graffiti they scrawled upon the walls with their bare hands and teeth still remains. Consult the **tourist office,** on pl. de la Halle (☎05 53 31 71 00), for daily tours (1hr.; €5.60, students €4.80).

BORDEAUX

Enveloped by emerald vineyards, Bordeaux (pop. 714,000) toasts the violet wine that made it famous. Not just a temple to wine connoisseurs, the city also has spirited nightclubs, a stunning opera house, and some of France's best food.

TRANSPORTATION AND PRACTICAL INFORMATION. **Trains** leave Gare St-Jean, r. Charles Domercq (☎05 56 33 11 83), for: Nice (9-10hr., 5 per day, €66.90); Paris (TGV; 3-4hr., 15-25 per day, €55.10); and Toulouse (2-3hr., 11 per day, €27.30). From the train station, take bus #7 or 8 (dir.: Grand Théâtre) to pl. Gambetta and walk toward the Monument des Girondins for the **tourist office,** 12 cours du 30 juillet, which arranges winery tours. (☎05 56 00 66 00; www.bordeaux-tourisme.com. Open May-Oct. M-Sa 9am-7pm, Su 9:30am-6:30pm; Nov.-Apr. M-Sa 9am-6:30pm, Su 9:45am-4:30pm.) Walk away from the river up r. Judaique for **Internet** access at **France Telecom,** 2 r. Château d'Eau, near pl. Gambetta. (€4.50 per hr., students €3. Open M-F noon-7pm.) **Postal Code:** 33065.

ACCOMMODATIONS AND FOOD. The newly renovated **Auberge de Jeunesse (HI) ❶,** 22 cours Barbey, is in a seedy area near the train station and 30min. from the *centre ville.* (☎56 33 00 70; fax 56 33 00 71. Breakfast €2.30. HI members only. Dorms €12.20.) For the **Hôtel Boulan ❷,** 28 r. Boulan, take bus #7 or 8 from the station to cours d'Albret; it's around the corner from the museum. (☎05 56 52 23 62; fax 05 56 44 91 65. Breakfast €3.50. Singles €17, with shower €20-23; doubles €20/€25. MC/V.) **Hôtel Studio ❷,** 26 r. Huguerie, with sunny rooms and lots of amenities, is a backpacker fave for good reason. (☎05 56 48 00 14; fax 05 56 81 25 71. Singles and doubles €16-24; triples €30.50. MC/V.)

Bordelais take their food as seriously as their wine. Hunt around **rue St-Remi** and **place St-Pierre** for splendid regional specialties, including oysters, beef braised in wine sauce, and the cake *canelé de Bordeaux.* **La Casuccia,** 49 r. Saint Rémi, is perfect for an intimate dinner or a casual outing. (☎05 56 51 17 70. Open daily 11:30am-midnight. MC/V.) Stock up at **Auchan supermarket,** at the Centre Meriadeck on r. Claude Bonnier. (☎05 56 99 59 00. Open M-Sa 8:30am-10pm.)

SIGHTS AND ENTERTAINMENT. Near the tourist office, on pl. de Quinconces, the elaborate fountains of the **Monument aux Girondins** commemorate revolutionary leaders from towns bordering the Gironde river. Retrace your steps to the breathtaking **Grand Théâtre,** on pl. de la Comédie, to see a performance or take a tour. (Tours €4.80, students €4.) Follow r. Ste-Catherine from the pl. de la Comédie, facing the theater, to reach the Gothic **Cathédrale St-André,** in pl. Pey-Berland. (Open Apr.-Oct. daily 7:30-11:30am and 2-6:30pm; Nov.-Mar. M-F only. €4, under 25 and seniors €2.50.) Walking toward the river along cours d'Alsace, turn left onto quai Richelieu for the **place de la Bourse,** whose pillars and fountains reflect Bordeaux's grandeur. On the left is the surprisingly interesting **Musée National des Douanes.** (Open Apr.-Sept. daily 10am-noon and 1-6pm; Oct.-Mar. M-Sa 10am-noon and 1-5pm. €3, students and seniors €1.50.) Near the river, just off quai des Chartrons, **Vinorama de Bourdeaux,** 12 cours du Médoc, features elaborate dioramas and wine samples. (Open June-Sept. Tu-Sa 10:30am-12:30pm and 2:30-6:30pm, Su 2-6:30pm; Oct.-May Tu-F 2-6:30pm, Sa 10:30am-12:30pm and 2:30-6:30pm. €5.50; students and seniors €2.50.)

For an overview of Bordeaux nightlife, pick up a copy of *Clubs and Concerts* at the tourist office, or purchase the magazine *Bordeaux Plus* (€0.30). **Place de la Victoire** and **place Gambetta** are year-round hotspots. **El Che,** 34 cours de l'Argonne, offers free Afro-Cuban salsa lessons. (W and F 8pm. Open Tu-Sa 7pm-2am.)

DAYTRIP FROM BORDEAUX: ST-ÉMILION. Just 35km northeast of Bordeaux, St-Émilion is home to viticulturists who have been refining their techniques since Roman times. Today, they gently crush hectares of grapes to produce 23 million liters of wine annually. Vineyards aside, the medieval-style village itself is a pleasure to visit, with its winding narrow streets and cafe-lined square. The **Eglise Monolithe** is the largest subterranean church is Europe. The **tourist office,** at pl. des Créneaux, near the church tower, rents **bikes** (€14 per day) and offers guided tours to the local chateaux. (☎05 57 55 28 28. Open July-Aug. daily 9:30am-8pm; Sept.-June approx. 9:30am-12:30pm and 1:45-6pm.) **Trains** run from Bordeaux to St-Émilion (30min., 2 per day, €10.10; the only return train leaves at 6:30pm).

THE PAYS BASQUE AND GASCONY

South of Aquitaine, the forests recede and the mountains of Gascony begin, shielded from the Atlantic by the Basque Country. Long renowned as fierce fighters, the Basques continue to struggle today, striving to win independence for their long-suffering homeland. Unlike the separatist Basques, Gascons have long considered themselves French. Today, people come to Gascony to be healed: millions of believers descend on Lourdes hoping for miracle cures while thousands of others undergo barely more scientific treatments in the *thermes* of the Pyrenees.

BAYONNE

Bayonne (pop. 43,000) is a city where the pace of life has not changed for centuries. Here, the word for walk is *flaner*, meaning "to stroll," rather than *marcher* or even *se promener*. Towering above it all, the grand Gothic 13th-century **Cathédrale Ste-Marie** marks the leisurely passing of time with the tolling of its bells. (Open M-Sa 7am-noon and 3-7pm, Su 3:30-10pm. Free.) The **Musée Bonnat,** 5 r. Jacques Laffitte, in Petit-Bayonne, contains works by Degas, El Greco, and Goya. (Open W-M 10am-6:15pm. €5.50, students €3.) The **Harmonie Bayonnaise orchestra** holds traditional Basque concerts in pl. de Gaulle. (July-Aug. Th at 9:30pm. Free.)

Trains depart from the station in pl. de la République, running to: Bordeaux (2hr., 9 per day, €20); Toulouse (4hr., 5 per day, €31); and San Sebastián, Spain (1½hr., 6 per day, €24). Trains run between Bayonne and Biarritz (10min., 11 per day, €2), but the local bus network is more extensive and cheaper than regional transit.

Local STAB **buses** depart from the Hôtel de Ville for Anglet and Biarritz (every 30min.; €1.15). The **tourist office,** on pl. des Basques, finds rooms. From the train station, take the middle fork onto pl. de la République, veer right over pont St-Esprit, pass through pl. Réduit, cross pont Mayou, turn right on r. Bernède and turn left for a 15min. walk down pl. des Basques. (☎05 59 46 01 46; www.bayonne-tourisme.com. Open July-Aug. M-Sa 9am-7pm, Su 10am-1pm; Sept.-June M-F 9am-6:30pm, Sa 10am-6pm.) Decent lodgings are near the train station and pl. Paul Bert, but the closest hostel is in Anglet. The **Hôtel Paris-Madrid ❷,** on pl. de la Gare, has cozy rooms. (☎05 59 55 13 98. Breakfast €4. Reception 6am-12:30am. Singles and doubles €15-20; triples and quads €39-42.) Get groceries at **Monoprix supermarket,** 8 r. Orbe. (Open M-Sa 8:30am-7:30pm.) **Postal Code:** 64100.

DAYTRIP FROM BAYONNE: ST-JEAN-PIED-DE-PORT. The Pyrenean village of St-Jean-Pied-de-Port (pop. 1600) epitomizes the spicy splendor of the Basque interior. The narrow streets ascend through the *haute ville* to the dilapidated fortress, which hovers over the calm Nive. This medieval capital of Basse-Navarre still hosts a procession of pilgrims on their way to Santiago de Compostela, Spain, 900km away. **Trains** arrive from Bayonne (1hr., 5 per day, €7.20) at the station on av. Renaud. **Rent bikes** at **Garazi Cycles,** 1 pl. St-Laurent. (☎05 59 37 21 79. Passport deposit. €18.50 per day, €23 per weekend. Open M-Sa 8:30am-noon and 3-6pm.) From the station, turn right on av. Renaud, follow it up to av. de Gaulle, and turn right to reach the **tourist office,** 14 av. de Gaulle. (☎05 59 37 03 57; fax 05 59 37 34 91. Open July-Aug. M-Sa 9am-12:30pm and 2-7pm, Su 10:30am-12:30pm and 3-6pm; Sept.-June M-F 9am-noon and 2-7pm, Sa 9am-noon and 2-6pm.) **Postal Code:** 64220.

BIARRITZ

Biarritz (pop. 29,000) is not a budget traveler's dream, but its free **beaches** make a daytrip *de luxe.* Surfers fill the **Grande Plage,** while just to the north at the less-crowded **Plage Miramar,** bathers repose *au naturel.* A short **hike** to **Pointe St-Martin** affords a priceless view of the water. **BASC Subaquatique,** near Plateau de l'Atalaye (☎05 59 24 80 40), organizes **scuba** excursions in summer for €17-28.

Trains leave from **Biarritz-la-Négresse** (☎05 59 23 04 84), 3km from town, for Bordeaux (2hr., 7 per day, €20.30) and Paris (5hr., 5 TGVs per day, €61.10). STAB **bus** #1 or 2 goes to the central Hôtel de Ville (1hr., €1.15). The **tourist office,** 1 sq. d'Ixelles, finds accommodations. (☎05 59 22 37 00. Open July-Aug. daily 8am-8pm; Sept.-June daily 9am-6pm.) The **Auberge de Jeunesse (HI) ❶,** 8 r. de Chiquito de Cambo, has a friendly staff and lakefront location, at the Bois de Boulogne stop on bus line #2. (☎05 59 41 76 00. Sheets €2.70. HI members only. Dorms €12.20.) **Hôtel Barnetche ❷,** 5bis r. Charles-Floquet, is in *centre ville.* (☎05 59 24 22 25. Breakfast included. In Aug., obligatory half-*pension* €15.25. Reception daily 7:30am-10:30pm, July-Aug. until 11pm. Open May-Sept. Dorm €17; doubles €58.) **Shopi supermarket,** 2 r. du Centre, is just off r. Gambetta. (Open M-Sa 8:45am-12:25pm and 3-7:10pm.) **Postal Code:** 64200.

ANGLET

Anglet's *raison d'être* is its beaches, which range from the perfect waves of the **Plage Les Cavaliers** to the topless **Plage des Sables d'Or.** Anglet hosts a number of professional surfing championships during the summer (free to spectators), including the **O'Neill Surf Challenge** and the **Europe Surfing Championship.** The **Rip Curl/Ecole Française de Surf,** av. des Dauphins, rents boards and arranges surfing lessons. (☎05 59 23 15 31. Boards €15.25 per day with passport deposit. 2hr. lessons €34. Open Apr.-Oct. daily 9:30am-7pm.) STAB **buses** connect Anglet to Bayonne and Biarritz (every 15min., €1.15). The **tourist office,** 1 av. de Chambre d'Amour, in pl. Leclerc, has information on surfing contests. (☎05 59 03 77 01. Open July-Sept. M-Sa 9am-7pm; Oct.-June M-F 9am-12:45pm and 1:45-6pm, Sa 9am-12:15pm.) The carefree **Auberge de Jeunesse (HI) ❶,** 19 rte. de Vignes, is just 600m uphill from the beach. From the Hôtel de Ville in Biarritz, take bus #4 (dir.: Bayonne Sainsontain) to Auberge. From the train station in Bayonne, take bus #4 to La Barre, then bus #9 or C to Auberge. (☎05 59 58 70 00. Sheets €2.60. Reception 8:30am-10pm. Dorms €11.45.) The central **Camping Fontaine Laborde ❶,** 17 allée Fontaine Laborde, caters to young surfers. Take bus #4 to Fontaine Laborde, down the road from the hostel. (☎05 59 03 48 16. €5 per person or site, €3 per car.) The strip behind the **Plage des Sables d'Or,** along **avenue des Dauphins,** offers many eateries. **Postal Code:** 64600.

LOURDES

In 1858, 14-year-old Bernadette Soubirous saw the first of 18 visions of the Virgin Mary in the Massabielle grotto in Lourdes (pop. 16,300). Today five million rosary-toting faithful annually make the pilgrimage. To get to **La Grotte de Massabielle** and the three **basilicas,** follow av. de la Gare, turn left on bd. de la Grotte, and follow it to the right and across the river Gave. Processions depart daily from the grotto at 5pm and 8:45pm. (No shorts or tank tops. Grotto open daily 5am-midnight. Basilicas open Easter to Oct. daily 6am-7pm; Nov.-Easter 8am-6pm.)

Trains leave the station, 33 av. de la Gare, for: Bayonne (2hr., 5 per day, €16.60); Bordeaux (3hr., 7 per day, €26.90); Paris (7-9hr., 5 per day, €79.80); and Toulouse (2½hr., 8 per day, €19.50). To get from the train station to the **tourist office,** on pl. Peyramale, turn right onto av. de la Gare, bear left onto av. Marasin, cross a bridge above bd. du Papacca, and climb uphill. The office is to the right. (☎05 62 42 77 40; lourdes@sudfr.com. Open May-Oct. M-Sa 9am-7pm; Nov.-Apr. 9am-noon and 2-6pm.) The newly-renovated **Hotel du Commerce ❸,** 11 r. Basse, faces the tourist office. Bright, newly renovated rooms all have showers and toilets, while those in the back have a view of the chateau. (☎05 62 94 59 23; hotel-commerce-et-navarre@wanadoo.fr. Pizzeria on the first floor. Breakfast €3.80. July-Oct. singles €31.20; doubles €37.40; triples €44.60. MC/V.) **Camping de la Poste ❶,** 26 r. de Langelle, is 2min. from the post office. (☎05 62 94 40 35. Open Easter to mid-Oct. €2.50 per person, €3.60 per site. Electricity €2.45. Showers €1.30.) You can find groceries at **Prisunic supermarket,** 9 pl. du Champ-Commun. (Open M-Sa 8:30am-12:30pm and 2-7:30pm, Su 8am-noon.) **Postal Code:** 65100.

CAUTERETS

Nestled in a narrow, breathtaking valley on the edge of the **Parc National des Pyrenees Occidentales** is tiny, friendly Cauterets. Cauterets's hot sulfuric *thermes* have long been instruments of healing; for more information, contact **Thermes de Cesar,** av. Docteur Domer. (☎05 62 92 51 60. Open M-F 9am-12:30pm and 1:30-6pm, Sa 9am-12:30pm and 3-6pm.) Today, most visitors come for the skiing and hiking. The **tourist office,** on pl. Foch, has free maps of ski trails. (☎05 62 92 50 27; www.cauterets.com. Open daily 9:30am-12:30pm and 1:30-7pm.) For more **hiking** information and advice, head to **Parc National des Pyrenees** (see below). **Skilys,** rte. de Pierrefitte, on pl. de la Gare, rents **bikes** and **skates.** (☎05 62 92 52 10. Bikes €15.25 per day. Open daily 9am-7pm; off-season 8am-7:30pm.)

SNCF **buses** run from pl. de la Gare to Lourdes (1hr., 6 per day, €5.90). The **Hôtel Bigorre ❷,** 15 r. de Belfort, has spacious rooms with views of the mountains. (☎05 65 92 52 81. Singles €20, with shower €28; doubles €31/40; triples and quads €44-61.) The **Halles market,** on av. du Général Leclerc, has fresh produce. (Open daily 8:30am-12:30pm and 2:30-7:30pm.) **Postal Code:** 65110.

DAYTRIP FROM CAUTERETS: THE PYRENEES. The striking **Parc National des Pyrenees** shelters thousands of endangered animals in its snow-capped mountains and lush valleys. Touch base with the friendly and helpful **Parc National Office,** Maison du Parc, pl. de la Gare, before braving the wilderness. They have tons of information on the park and the 15 trails beginning and ending in Cauterets. The trails in the park are designed for a range of aptitudes, from rugged outdoorsman to novice hiker. From Cauterets, the **GR10** winds through **Luz-St-Saveur,** over the mountain, and then on to **Gavarnie,** another day's hike up the valley; this is also known as the **"circuit de Gavarnie."** One of the most spectacular trails follows the GR10 to the turquoise **Lac de Gaube** and then to the end of the glacial valley (2hr. past the lake) where you can spend the night at the **Refuges Des Oulettes ❶,** the first shelter past the lake. (☎05 62 92 62 97. Open June-Sept. €12.50.) Dipping into the Vallée Lutour, the **Refuge Estom ❷** rests near Lac d'Estom. (Summer ☎05 62 92 72 93, off-season ☎05 62 92 75 07. €8.50, demi-pension €26.)

LANGUEDOC-ROUSSILLON

A region called Occitania once stretched from the Rhône Valley to the foothills of the Pyrenees. It was eventually integrated into the French kingdom, but nationalism still lingers: many speak Catalán, a relative of the *langue d'oc;* the occitan banner, with its black cross against yellow and red stripes, is displayed throughout the region; and locals look to Barcelona, instead of Paris, for inspiration.

TOULOUSE

When all of France starts to look alike, rose-tinted Toulouse, or *la ville en rose* (city in pink) provides a breath of fresh air with its stately architecture and vibrant twenty-something scene. A rebellious city during the Middle Ages, Toulouse has always retained an element of independence, pushing the frontiers of knowledge as a university town and the prosperous capital of the French aerospace industry.

TRANSPORTATION AND PRACTICAL INFORMATION. Trains leave **Gare Matabiau,** 64 bd. Pierre Sémard, for: Bordeaux (2-3hr., 14 per day, €26.10); Lyon (6½hr., 3-4 per day, €47.30); Marseilles (4½hr., 8 per day, €37.55); Paris (8-9hr., 4 per day, €68.65). To get from the station to the **tourist office,** r. Lafayette, in sq. Charles de Gaulle, turn left along the canal, turn right on allée Jean Jaurès, bear right around pl. Wilson, and turn right on r. Lafayette; it's in a park near r. d'Alsace-Lorraine. (☎05 61 11 02 22. www.mairie-toulouse.fr. Open Jun.-Sept. M-Sa 9am-7pm, Su 10am-1pm and 2-6pm; Oct.-May M-F 9am-6pm, Sa 9am-12:30pm and 2-6pm, Su 10am-12:30pm and 2-5pm.) Surf the **Internet** at **Espace Wilson Multimedia,** 7 allée du Président Roosevelt, at pl. Wilson. (€3.05 per hr. Open M-F 10am-7pm, Sa 10am-6pm.) **Postal Code:** 31000.

ACCOMMODATIONS AND FOOD. Antoine de St-Exupéry stayed in room #32 at the **Hôtel du Grand Balcon ❸,** 8 r. Romiguières, the official hotel of the French airborne postal service. (☎/fax 05 61 62 77 59. Breakfast €4. Singles and doubles €24.40, with bath €35.10; triples €41.20; quads €35.10.) **Hôtel Beauséjour ❷,** 4 r. Caffarelli, sports bright, clean rooms and easy access to the train station. (☎05 61 23 19 96; fax 05 61 21 47 66. Singles and doubles €20, with bath €25.) Take bus #59 (dir.: Camping) to **camp** at **Pont de Rupé ❶,** 21 chemin du Pont de Rupé. (☎05 61 70 07 35. €9, €3 per additional person.) **Markets** line **place des Carmes, place Victor Hugo,** and **boulevard de Strasbourg** (open Tu-Su 6am-1pm). Cheap eateries line **rue du Taur** and **place Wilson.**

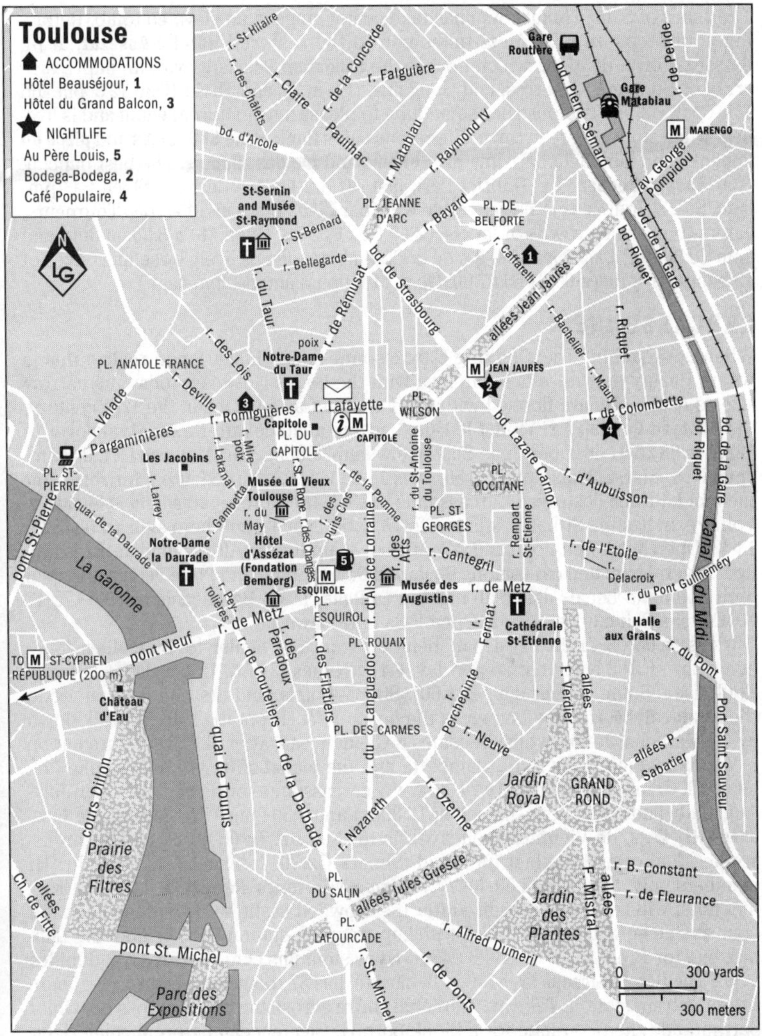

SIGHTS AND ENTERTAINMENT. The brick palace **Capitole** next door to the tourist office is the city's most prominent monument. (Open M-F 8:30am-noon and 1:30-7pm, Sa-Su 10am-noon and 2-6pm. Free.) The r. du Taur leads to the **Basilique St-Sernin,** the longest Romanesque structure in the world; its **crypt** houses ecclesiastical relics gathered from Charlemagne's time. (☎05 61 20 70 18. Open July-Sept. M-Sa 8:30am-6:15pm, Su 8:30am-7:30pm; Oct.-June reduced hours. Free. Crypt open July-Sept. M-Sa 10am-6pm, Su 11:30-6pm; Oct.-June M-Sa reduced hours. €2.) Backtrack to the pl. du Capitole, take a right on r. Romiguières, and turn left on r. Lakanal to get to the 13th-century **Les Jacobins,** built in the Southern Gothic style. (☎05 61 22 21 92. www.jacobins.mairie-toulouse.fr. Open daily 10am-7pm. €5.)

The ashes of Saint Thomas Aquinas take center stage in an elevated tomb. Retracing your steps on r. de Metz takes you to the restored **Hôtel d'Assézat,** at pl. d'Assézat on r. de Metz, which houses the **Fondation Bemberg,** with an impressive array of Bonnards, Pisarros, and Gauguins. (Open Tu and Th-Su 10am-12:30pm and 1:30-6pm. €2.75.) Toulouse has something to please any nocturnal whim and is liveliest when students are in town. Numerous cafes flank **place St-Georges** and **place du Capitole,** and late-night bars line **rue St-Rome** and **rue des Filatiers.** The best dancing is at **Bodega-Bodega**, 1 r. Gabriel Péri, just off bd. Lazare Carnot. (Open Sa 7pm-6am, Su-Fri 7pm-2am.) The venerable wine bar **Au Père Louis,** 45 r. des Tourneurs, caters to upscale crowds of locals. (☎05 61 21 33 45. Open M-Sa 8:30am-3pm and 5pm-10:30pm.) **Cafe Populaire,** 9 r. de la Colombette, keeps lively by selling boxes of 13 beers for €19. (☎05 61 63 07 00. Open M-F 9pm-2am, Sa 2pm-4am.)

CARCASSONNE

When approaching breathtaking Carcassonne (pop. 45,000), you realize this is where Beauty may have fallen in love with the Beast. However, today the narrow streets of the *cité* are flooded with tourists. Built as a palace in the 12th century, the **Château Comtal,** 1 r. Viollet-le-Duc, became a citadel after a royal takeover in 1226. (☎68 25 01 66. Open June-Sept. daily 9am-7:30pm; Apr.-May and Oct. 9:30am-6pm; Nov.-Mar. 9:30am-5pm. €5.50, ages 18-25 €3.50.) Turned into a fortress after the Black Prince destroyed Carcassonne in 1355, the Gothic **Cathédrale St-Michel,** r. Voltaire, in bastide St-Louis, still has fortifications on its southern side. (☎05 68 25 14 48. Open M-Sa 7am-noon and 2-7pm, Su 9:30am-noon.) Although nightlife is limited, several bars and cafes along **Boulevard Omer Sarraut** and **Place Verdun** are open until midnight. Locals dance all night at **La Bulle,** 115 r. Barbacane. (☎05 68 72 47 70. Cover €9, includes 1 drink. Open F-Sa until dawn.)

Trains (☎05 68 71 79 14) depart behind Jardin St-Chenier to: Marseilles (3hr., every 2hr., €31); Nice (6hr., 5 per day, €47); Nîmes (2½hr., 12 per day, €22); and Toulouse (50min., 24 per day, €11.60). Shops, hotels, and the train station are in the **bastide St-Louis,** once known as the *basse ville.* From the station, walk down av. de Maréchal Joffre, which becomes r. Clemenceau; after pl. Carnot, turn left on r. Verdun, which leads to pl. Gambetta and the **tourist office,** 15 bd. Camille Pelletan, pl. Gambetta. (☎05 68 10 24 30; www.carcassonne-tourisme.com. Open July-Aug. daily 9am-7pm; Sept.-June 9am-12:30pm and 1:30-6pm.) The **Auberge de Jeunesse (HI) ❶,** r. de Vicomte Trencavel, is in the *cité.* (☎05 68 25 23 16; carcassonne@fuaj.org. Breakfast included. Sheets €2.70. Internet €4.70 per hr. HI members only. Dorms €12.50. MC/V.) **Sidmum's Travelers' Retreat ❶,** 11 de la Croix d'Achille, will seem like paradise after the crowded castle walls with its beautiful countryside surroundings. Call for pickup from the station (€5) or take the Limoux bus for Preixan. (☎04 68 26 94 49; www.sidmums.com. Dorms €15; doubles €30.) The **Hôtel St-Joseph ❷,** 81 r. de la Liberté, has 37 rooms on a calm street 5min. from the train station. Take av. Maréchal Joffre across the canal, across bd. Omer Sarraut, and then continue for a block on r. G. Clemenceau before turning right. (☎05 68 71 96 89; fax 05 68 74 36 28. Breakfast €5. Singles €23, with shower €28; doubles €28. MC/V.) **Camping de la Cité ❶,** rte. de St-Hilaire, 2km from town across the Aude, has a pool and grocery store. A shuttle can take you there from the train station. (☎05 68 25 11 77. Reception 8am-9pm. Open Mar.-Oct. €12.20-16.80 per site.) The regional speciality is *cassoulet* (a stew of white beans, herbs, and meat). Restaurants on **rue du Plo** have €9 *menus*, but save room for dessert at one of the *crêperies* in **place Marcou.** Eat like a king at **Les Fontaines du Soleil,** 32 r. du Plo. (☎05 68 47 87 06. Open daily 11:30am-3pm and 7-10:30pm.) **Postal Code:** 11000.

FOIX

Il était une fois, as French fairy tales begin, that a town grew up at the base of large castle. The fantastic **Château de Foix** towers over Foix's busy markets. (☎05 61 65 56 05. Open July-Aug. daily 9:45am-6:30pm; June and Sept. daily 9:45am-noon and 2-6pm; Oct.-May W-Su 10:30am-noon and 2-5:30pm. €4.) A one-hour boat ride winds through the caves on the **Labouiche,** the longest navigable underground river in Europe. There is no public transport to this sight—consider biking the 6km from Foix. (☎05 61 65 04 11. Open July-Aug. daily 9:30am-6pm; Sept.-June reduced hours. €7.10.) The **Grotte de Niaux,** 20km south of Foix, has 13,000-year-old paintings of leaping bison, deer, and horses. (☎05 61 05 88 37. Reservations only. Open Apr.-Oct. daily; Nov.-Mar. Tu-Su. €9, students €5.50.)

The **train station,** on av. Pierre Sémard, is north of the town, off the N20. (☎05 61 02 03 64. Open M-Sa 8:10am-12:20pm and 1:25-8:30pm, Su 8:15am-1:55pm and 2:15-10:20pm.) **Trains** go to Toulouse (1hr., 10 per day, €10.80). Salt Autocars **buses,** 8 allées de Villote (☎05 61 65 08 40), also run to Toulouse (1¼hr., 2 per day, €8). For the **tourist office,** 29 r. Théophile Delcassé, leave the train station and turn right; follow the street until you reach the main road (N20), continue to the second bridge, cross it, and follow cours G. Fauré for three blocks. The tourist office is on the corner. (☎05 61 65 12 12; www.mairie-foix.fr. Open July-Aug. M-Sa 9am-7pm, Su 9am-noon and 2-6pm; June and Sept. M-Sa 9am-noon and 2-6pm, Su 10am-12:30pm; Oct.-May M-Sa 9am-noon and 2-6pm.) To get to the comfortable beds of **Foyer Léo Lagrange ❶,** 16 r. Peyrevidal, turn right on cours Gabriel Fauré out of the tourist office and turn right again on r. Peyrevidal just after the Halle Aux Grains; it's on your right. (☎05 61 65 09 04; fax 05 61 02 63 87. Reception 8am-11pm. Dorms €14.) **Casino** supermarket is on r. Laffont. (Open M-Sa 9am-7pm.) **Postal Code:** 09000.

PERPIGNAN

Brilliant "blood and gold" flags line Perpignan's (pop. 130,000) bustling streets, testifying to its Catalan heritage. Guarding the entrance to the *vieille ville,* **Le Castillet** holds the small **Casa Pairai,** a museum of Catalan history. (☎04 68 35 42 05. Open mid-June to mid-Sept. W-M 10am-7pm; mid-Sept to mid-June W-M 10am-5:30pm. €4, students €2.) At pl. Gambetta is the **Cathédrale St-Jean,** an impressive example of Gothic architecture. (☎04 68 51 33 72. Open daily 9am-noon and 3-7pm. Free.) The **Musée Hyacinthe Rigaud,** 16 r. de l'Ange, contains a small but impressive collection of 13th-century Spanish and Catalan paintings and works by Ingres, Picasso, Miró, and Dalí. (☎04 68 35 43 40. Open W-M noon-7pm. €3.) An uphill walk across the *vieille ville* leads to the 15th-century Spanish **citadelle.** Traditional Catalonian dancing in front of Le Castillet makes for a colorful scene around pl. de Verdun, especially in summer (Tu, Th, Sa).

Trains leave the station on r. Courteline, off av. de Gaulle, for: Carcassonne (1½hr., 2 per day, €12.20) via Narbonne; Nice (6hr., 3 per day, €45.60); Paris (6-10hr., 4 per day, €78.20); and Toulouse (2½-3hr., 15 per day, €21.90) via Narbonne. **Buses** leave 17 av. Général Leclerc for the beaches. The small *vieille ville*, just past the red **castillet** tower, makes a triangle bounded by the regional tourist office, **Place de la Victoire** (farther up the canal), and the **Palais des Rois de Majorque.** To get from the train station to the **tourist office,** Palais de Congrès, pl. Armand Lanoux, follow av. du Gaulle to pl. de Catalogne, then take bd. Georges Clemenceau across the canal past Le Castillet as it becomes bd. Wilson. Follow the signs along the promenade des Platanes. (☎04 68 66 30 30; www.perpignantourisme.com. Open June-Sept. M-Sa 9am-7pm, Su 10am-noon and 2-5pm; Oct.-May M-Sa 9am-noon and 2-6pm.) The central **Hôtel de l'Avenir ❷,** 11 r. de l'Avenir, welcomes visitors with its cheery and colorful interior. (☎04 68 34 20 30; avenirhotel@aol.com. Breakfast €4. Shower €2.75. Singles €15.25; doubles €18.30-29; quads €38.15. AmEx/MC/V.)

A block from the train station, **Hôtel Express ❷,** 3 av. de Gaulle, has clean, functional rooms. (☎04 68 34 89 96. Breakfast €3.05. Shower €2.30. Reserve ahead. Singles and doubles €15.25; triples and quads €28.05-38.75. MC/V.) To get to **Camping Le Catalan ❶** from the train station, take the bus (dir.: Bompas; 15min., 2 per day, €1.80) and to camping Catalan. (☎04 68 63 16 92. July-Aug. €14 for 2 people; Mar.-June €10 for 2 people; additional person €2.50.) **Casino supermarket** is on bd. Félix Mercader. (☎04 68 34 74 42. Open M-Sa 8:30am-8pm.) **Postal Code:** 66000.

DAYTRIPS FROM PERPIGNAN

COLLIOURE

Trains (☎04 68 82 05 89) arrive at av. Aristide Maillol from: Barcelona (3½hr., 5 per day, €12.10); Narbonne (1hr., 12 per day, €11.50); Perpignan (20min., 15 per day, €4.40).

Nestled where the Pyrenees tumble into the Mediterranean, tiny Collioure (pop. 2770) captured the fancy of Greeks and Phoenicians long before enrapturing Dalí, Picasso, and Matisse. The view of the harbor from the hulking stone **Château Royal,** stretching from pl. du 8 mai 1945 to the port, is worth the climb. (☎04 68 82 06 43. Open June-Sept. daily 10am-5:15pm; Oct.-May 9am-4:15pm. €3.05.) The **tourist office,** on pl. du 18 Juin, has info on day hikes and coastal bus routes. (☎04 68 82 15 47; www.collioure.com. Open July-Aug. daily 9am-8pm; Sept.-June M-Sa 9am-noon and 2-6:30pm.) **Hôtel Triton ❸,** 1 r. Jean Bart, is on the waterfront. (☎04 68 98 39 39; fax 04 68 82 11 32. Doubles €31, with toilet €44. AmEx/MC/V.)

CÉRET

Car Inter 66 (☎04 68 39 11 96) runs buses from Perpignan (45min., 1 per hr., €5.90).

In the early 20th century, a series of artists that included Picasso, Chagall, Manolo, and Herbin discovered Céret (pop. 8000), in the foothills of the Pyrenees, and created a "Cubist Mecca." Some of their works are housed in the impressive **Musée d'Art Moderne,** 8 bd. Maréchal Joffre, up the hill and to the right of the tourist office. (☎04 68 87 27 76. Open mid-June to mid-Sept. daily 10am-7pm.) From the bus stop on av. George Clemenceau, the **tourist office,** 1 av. Clemenceau, is two blocks up the hill on the right. (☎04 68 87 00 53. Open July-Aug. M-Sa 9am-12:30pm and 2-7pm, Su 10am-12:30pm; Sept.-June M-F 10am-noon and 2-5pm, Sa 10am-noon.)

PROVENCE

Carpets of olive groves and vineyards unroll along hills dusted with lavender, sunflowers, and mimosa, while the fierce winds of the *mistral* carry the scent of sage, rosemary, and time well-spent. Generations of writers have rhapsodized about Provence's fragrant and varied landscape—from the Roman arena and cobblestoned elegance of Arles to the lingering footsteps of Cézanne in Aix-en-Provence, life unfolds along Provence's shaded paths like a bottomless glass of *pastis*.

NÎMES

Southern France flocks to Nîmes (pop. 132,000) for the *férias*, celebrations featuring bullfights, flamenco dancing, and other hot-blooded fanfare. Yet Nîmes's star attractions are its incredible Roman structures. The magnificent **Les Arènes** is a well-preserved first-century Roman amphitheater that still holds bullfights and concerts. (☎04 66 76 72 77. Open daily 10am-6pm. €4.30, students €3.) North of the arena stands the exquisite **Maison Carrée,** a rectangular temple built in the first century BC. (☎04 66 36 26 76. Open daily June-Sept. 9am-7pm, Oct.-May 10am-

6pm. Free.) Across the square, the **Carrée d'Art** houses an excellent collection of contemporary art. (☎04 66 76 35 70. Open Tu-Su 10am-6pm. €4.30, students €3.) Along the canals to the left, off pl. Foch, the **Jardins de la Fontaine** hold the Roman ruins of the **Temple de Diane** and the **Tour Magne.** (Garden open daily Apr.-Sept. 7:30am-10pm; Oct.-Mar. 8am-6:30pm. Free. Tour Magne open daily July-Aug. 9am-7pm; Sept.-June 9am-5pm. €2.40, students €1.90.)

Trains go from bd. Talabot to: Arles (25min., 8 per day, €6.30); Marseilles (1¼hr., 11 per day, €11.30); and Toulouse (3hr., 8 per day, €29.30). **Buses** (☎04 66 29 52 00) depart from behind the train station for Avignon (1½hr., 2-8 per day, €6.70). The **tourist office** is at 6 r. Auguste, just off pl. Comédie and near the Maison Carrée. (☎04 66 58 38 00; fax 04 66 58 38 01. Open July-Aug. M-F 8am-8pm, Sa 9am-7pm, Su 10am-6pm; May and Sept. reduced hours.) The newly renovated **Auberge de Jeunesse (HI) ❶,** 257 chemin de l'Auberge de la Jeunesse, is 4½km from quai de la Fontaine, off chemin de la Cigale. Take bus #2 (dir.: Alès or Villeverte) to Stade, Route d'Alès and follow the signs uphill; after buses stop running, call for pick-up. (☎04 66 68 03 20; fax 04 66 68 03 21. Breakfast €3.20. Sheets €2.70 per week. Reception Mar.-Sept. 24hr. 4- to 6-bed dorms €8.65. **Camping** €4.95. MC/V.) Stock up at **Marché U supermarket,** 19 r. d'Alès, downhill from the hostel. (Open M-Sa 8am-12:45pm and 3:30-8pm.) **Postal Codes:** 30000 and 30900.

DAYTRIP FROM NÎMES: PONT DU GARD. In 19 BC, Augustus's close friend and advisor Agrippa built an aqueduct to channel water 50km to Nîmes from the Eure springs near Uzès. The architectural fruit of this 15-year project remains in the Pont du Gard, spanning the gorge of the Gardon River, towering over sunbathers and swimmers. A great way to see the Pont du Gard is to start from **Collias,** 6km toward Uzès. Here, **Kayak Vert** rents two-person canoes, solo kayaks, and bikes. (☎04 66 22 80 76. Canoes and kayaks €14 per day; kayak/canoe rental and shuttle €16; bikes €17 per day. 15% discount for students or with stay at the hostel in Nîmes.) **STDG buses** (☎04 66 29 27 29) run to the Pont du Gard from Avignon (45min., 7 per day, €5) and Nîmes (30min., 2-5 per day, €4.75). **Camping le Barralet ❶,** r. des Aires in Collias, offers a pool and hot showers. (☎04 66 22 84 52; fax 04 66 22 89 17. Closed Oct.-Feb. 1 person €6-7.40; 2 people €11-13.50; 3 people €13.50-16.50. Lower prices Mar.-June and Sept. MC/V.)

AVIGNON

Avignon (pop. 100,000) is chiefly known for the **Festival d'Avignon,** a huge theatrical celebration. The 14th-century golden **Palais des Papes** launches gargoyles out over the city and the Rhône. Its walls are oddly cut with the tall, ecclesiastical windows of the **Grande Chapelle** and the dark cross of arrow-loops. In the **Grand Tinel,** a banquet hall 45m long, blue canvas flecked with gold stars deck the arched ceiling. (☎04 90 27 50 74. Open July-Sept. daily 9am-8pm; Apr.-June and Oct. 9am-7pm; Nov. to Mar. 9:30am-5:45pm. €7.50.) Near the Palais des Papes, the **Pont St-Bénézet** steps into the Rhône and stops partway with four arches. Housed on the second arch is the **St-Nicolas Chapel,** dedicated to the patron saint of mariners. (Open Apr.-Nov. daily 9am-7pm; July-Sept. 9am-8pm; Nov.-Mar. 9:30am-5:45pm.) The riotous **Festival d'Avignon,** also known as the **IN,** goes from early July to early August, as Gregorian chanters rub shoulders with *Odyssey*-readers and African dancers. (☎04 90 14 14 14. Reservations accepted from mid-June. Tickets range from free to €30. Tickets available 45min. before shows; 50% student discount.) **Place des Corps Saints** has a few lively bars.

Trains (☎90 27 81 89) run from porte de la République to: Arles (30min., 19 per day, €5.50); Marseilles (1¼hr., 8 per day, €14.60); Nîmes (30min., 12 per day, €7.10); and Paris (TGV; 3½hr., 13 per day, €79.20). **Buses** leave from bd. St-Roch, to the right of the train station for Arles (45min., 5 per day, €7.80) and Marseilles (2hr., 5 per day, €15.20). From the train station, walk through porte de la République to cours Jean Jaurès to reach the **tourist office,** 41 cours Jean Jaurès (☎04 32 74 32 74; fax 04 90 82 95 03. Open July M-Sa 9am-7pm, Su 10am-5pm; Apr.-June and Aug.-Sept. M-Sa 9am-6pm; Oct.-Mar. M-F 9am-6pm, Sa 9am-5pm, Su 10am-noon.) Take an Internet break at **Webzone,** 3 r. St. Jean le Vieux, at pl. Pie (☎32 76 29 47. €4.50 per hr. Open M-F 9am-noon, Sa 11am-midnight, Su noon-8pm). Avignon's hotels and *foyers* usually have room outside of festival season. The **Foyer YMCA/UCJG ❶,** 7bis chemin de la Justice, is across the river in Villeneuve. From the station, turn left and follow the city wall, cross pont Daladier and Ile Barthelasse, walk straight ahead, and turn left on chemin de la Justice; it will be up the hill on your left. (☎04 90 25 46 20; info@ymca-avignon.com. Reception 8:30am-noon and 1:30-6pm. *Demi-pension* obligatory in July. Dorms €15. AmEx/MC/V.) The **Hôtel Splendid ❸,** 17 r. Perdiguier, near the tourist office, lives up to its name. (☎04 90 82 71 55; fax 04 90 85 64 86. Breakfast €5. Reception 7am-11pm. Singles €30-34; doubles €40-46. MC/V.) **Camp** at **Pont d'Avignon ❶,** 300 Ile de la Barthelasse, 10min. past Foyer Bagatelle. (☎04 90 80 63 50; fax 04 90 85 22 12. Reception daily 8am-10pm. Open Mar. 27-Oct. 28. €13.45 per person with tent or car, €19.65 per couple with tent or car.) **Rue des Teinturiers** bustles with restaurants. A **Petit Casino** supermarket is on r. St-Agricol. (Open M-F 8am-8pm, Su 9am-8pm.) **Postal Code:** 84000.

DAYTRIP FROM AVIGNON: THE VAUCLUSE. The Vaucluse is where all those perfect postcards of Provence come from. Tiny medieval villages perch on rocky escarpments and ochre hills burn in the sunset. This mini-Eden has been home and inspiration to writers from Petrarch to the Marquis de Sade to Samuel Beckett. The region is most accessible by car; **Voyages Arnaud buses** (☎04 90 38 15 58) run from Avignon to Fontaine de Vaucluse (55min., 4 per day, €4).

ARLES

The beauty and ancient history of Arles (pop. 35,000) have made it a Provence favorite. The streets of Arles all seem to lead to or from the great Roman arena, **Les Arènes,** which is still used for bullfights. (€4, students €3.) The city's Roman past comes back to life in the excellent **Musée d'Arles Antique,** on av. de la 1ère D.F.L. (Open Mar.-Oct. daily 9am-7pm; Nov.-Feb. 10am-5pm. €5.35, students €3.85.) The **Fondation Van Gogh,** 26 Rond-Point des Arènes, houses tributes to the master painter by artists, poets, and composers. (Open daily 10am-7pm. €5, students €3.50.) The contemporary **Musée Réattu,** r. du Grand Prieuré, houses 57 drawings with which Picasso honored Arles in 1971. (Open May-Sept. daily 10am-noon and 2-6:30pm; Oct.-Mar. reduced hours. €4, students €3.) The city celebrates **Fête d'Arles** in costume the last weekend in June and the first in July.

Trains leave av. P. Talabot for: Avignon (30min., 17 per day, €5.50); Marseilles (1hr., 23 per day, €11.20); Montpellier (1hr., 6 per day, €11.80); and Nîmes (30min., 8 per day, €6.30). **Buses** (☎04 90 49 38 01) depart from next to the station for Avignon (45min., M-Sa 7 per day, €8.10) and Nîmes (1hr., M-Sa 4 per day, €5.20). To get to the **tourist office,** esplanade Charles de Gaulle on bd. des Lices, turn left from the station, walk to pl. Lamartine, turn left and follow bd. Emile Courbes to the big intersection, and then turn right on bd. des Lices. (☎04 90 18 41 20; fax 04 90 18 41 29. Open Apr.-Sept. daily 9am-6:45pm; Oct.-Mar. M-Sa 9am-5:45pm, Su 10am-2:30pm.) To get from the tourist office to the **Auberge de Jeunesse (HI) ❶,** on av. Maréchal Foch, cross bd. des Lices and follow the signs down av. des Alyscamps. (☎04 90 96 18 25; fax 04 90 96 31 26. Breakfast included. Reception 7-10am and 5-11pm. Lockout 10am-5pm. Curfew midnight; in winter 11pm. Reserve ahead Apr.-June. Bunks €13.50.) The friendly **Hôtel Mirador ❸,** 3 r. Voltaire, is centrally located. (☎04 90 96 28 05; fax 04 90 96 59 89. Breakfast €4.30. Reception 7am-11pm. Singles and doubles €30-38. AmEx/MC/V.) Take the Starlette bus to Clemencau and then take bus #2 (dir.: Pont de Crau) to Hermite for **Camping-City ❶,** 67 rte. de Crau. (☎04 90 93 08 86. Reception 8am-8pm. Open Apr.-Sept. €6.20 per person.) **Monoprix** supermarket is on pl. Lamartine by the station. (Open M-Sa 8:30am-8pm.) Try the cafes in **place du Forum** or **place Voltaire. Postal Code:** 13200.

DAYTRIP FROM ARLES: THE CAMARGUE. Between Arles and the Mediterranean coast stretches the Camargue. Pink flamingos, black bulls, and the famous white Camargue horses roam freely across this flat expanse of protected wild marshland. Stop at the **Centre d'Information de Ginès,** along D570, for more information. (☎04 90 97 86 32. Open Apr.-Sept. daily 10am-6pm; Oct.-Mar. Sa-Th 9:30am-5pm.) Next door, the **Parc Ornithologique de Pont de Gau** offers views of birds and grazing bulls. (Open Apr.-Sept. daily 9am-dusk; Oct.-Mar. 10am-dusk. €5.50.) The best way to see the Camargue is on horseback; call the **Association Camarguaise de Tourisme Equestre** (☎04 90 97 58 45) for more information. Other options include jeep safaris (☎04 90 97 89 33; 2hr. trips €31, 4hr. trips €37) and boat trips (☎04 90 97 84 72; 1½hr., 3 per day, €10). Biking is another way to see the area, and informative trail maps are available from the Stes-Maries-de-la-Mer **tourist office,** 5 av. Van Gogh. (☎04 90 97 82 55. Open daily July-Aug. 9am-8pm; Apr.-June reduced hours.) Arles runs **buses** to Stes-Maries-de-la-Mer (1hr., 5 per day, €6), the region's largest town.

AIX-EN-PROVENCE

Famous for festivals, fountains, and former residents Paul Cézanne and Victor Vasarely, Aix (pop. 150,000) caters to tourists without being ruined by them. The **Chemin de Cézanne,** 9 av. Paul Cézanne, features a self-guided walking tour, including the artist's studio. (☎04 42 21 06 53. Open June-Sept. daily 10am-6:30pm; Oct.-May reduced hours. €5.50.) The **Fondation Vasarely,** av. Marcel-Pagnol, in Jas-de-Bouffan, designed by artist Victor Vasarely, is a must-see for modern art fans. (☎04 42 20 01 09. Open July-Sept. daily 10am-7pm; Oct.-June 10am-1pm and 2-6pm. €7.) **Cathédrale St-Sauveur,** r. Gaston de Saporta, on pl. de l'Université, is a dramatic mix of Romanesque, Gothic, and Baroque carvings and reliefs. (☎04 42 23 45 65. Open daily 9am-noon and 2-6pm.) In June and July, Aix's **International Music Festival** brings in operas and concerts. (☎04 42 17 34 34; www.aix-en-provence.com/festartlyrique. Tickets from €6.) Aix also hosts a two-week **dance festival.** (☎04 42 23 41 24. Tickets €7-38.) The **Office des Fêtes et de la Culture,** Espace Forbin, 1 pl. John Rewald (☎04 42 63 06 75), has festival information. Bars and clubs line **rue Verrerie.** House and club music pulsate at **Le Richelm,** 24 r. de la Verrerie. (☎04 42 23 49 29. Cover Tu-Th €9.15, women free; F €12.20; Sa €15.25. Open Tu-Sa 11:30pm-dawn includes 1 drink.) **Bistro Aixois,** 37 cours Sextius, off La Rotonde, packs in students. (☎04 42 27 50 10. Open daily 6:30pm-4am.)

Trains, at the end of av. Victor Hugo, run almost exclusively through Marseilles (35min., 21 per day, €5.70). **Buses** (☎04 42 91 26 80), av. de l'Europe, run to Avignon (2hr., M-Sa 5 per day, €13.50) and Marseilles (30min., every 10min., €4). From the train station, follow av. Victor Hugo, bearing left at the fork, until it feeds into La Rotonde. On the left is the **tourist office,** 2 pl. du Général de Gaulle, which books rooms for free, sells a city museum pass (€6.10-9.15), and stocks maps and guides. (☎04 42 16 11 61; fax 04 42 16 11 62. Open July-Aug. daily 8:30am-8pm; Sept.-June M-Sa 8:30am-7pm, Su 8:30am-1pm and 2-6pm.) You can surf the Internet at **Millenium,** 6 r. Mazarine, off cours Mirabeau. (☎04 42 27 39 11. €3 per hr. Open daily 10am-midnight.) The excellent **Hôtel du Globe ❸,** 74 cours Sextius, is 5min. from *centre ville.* (☎42 26 03 58; fax 42 26 13 68. Singles €32, with bath €35;

doubles €48; triples €66; quads €77.) **Hôtel des Arts ❸,** 69 bd. Carnot, has compact modern rooms. (☎04 42 38 11 77; fax 04 42 26 77 31. Breakfast €4.30. Singles and doubles €30-35. MC/V.) To **camp** at **Arc-en-Ciel ❶,** on rte. de Nice, take bus #3 from La Rotonde to Trois Sautets or Val St-André. (☎04 42 26 14 28. €5.20 per person, €5.80 per tent.) The roads north of **cours Mirabeau** and **rue Verrerie,** off Cordiliers, are packed with reasonable restaurants. You can choose from three **Petit Casinos supermarkets** at: 3 cours d'Orbitelle (open M-Sa 8am-1pm and 4-7:30pm); 16 r. Italie (open M-Sa 8am-7:30pm, Su 8:30am-12:30pm); and 5 r. Sapora (open M and W-Sa 8:30am-7:30pm, Su 8:30am-12:30pm). **Postal Code:** 13100.

MARSEILLES (MARSEILLE)

France's third-largest city, Marseilles (pop. 900,000) is like the *bouillabaisse* dish for which it is famous: steaming hot and pungently spiced, with a little bit of everything mixed in. A blend of wild nightclubs, beaches, islands, gardens, and big-city adventure, Marseilles bites its thumb at the manicured nails of Monaco and struts a true, gritty urban intensity.

TRANSPORTATION

Flights: Aéroport Marseille-Provence (MRS; ☎04 42 14 14 14). Flights to **Lyon** and **Paris.** Buses connect airport to Gare St-Charles (3 per hr. 5:30am-9:50pm, €7.65).

Trains: Gare St-Charles, pl. Victor Hugo (☎08 36 35 35 35). To: **Lyon** (3½hr., 2-3 per day, €38.10); **Nice** (2¾hr., 13 per day, €23.50); **Paris** (4¾hr., 17 per day, €66.60).

Buses: Gare des Autocars, pl. Victor Hugo (☎04 91 08 16 40), half a block from the train station. Open M-Sa 6:30am-6:30pm, Su 7:30am-6:30pm. To: **Avignon** (2hr., 5 per day, €15); **Cannes** (2¼-3hr., 4 per day, €21); **Nice** (2¾hr., 1 per day, €22.50).

Ferries: SNCM, 61 bd. des Dames (☎08 91 70 18 01). Ferries to **Corsica** (€98) and **Sardinia** (€114).

Local Transportation: RTM, 6-8 r. des Fabres (☎04 91 91 92 10). Tickets sold at bus and Métro stations (day pass €3.85, 6- to 12-ride **Carte Liberté** €6.50-13). **Métro** runs M-Th 5am-9pm and F-Su 5am-12:30am.

Taxis: (☎04 91 02 20 20). €20-30 from the train station to hostels.

ORIENTATION AND PRACTICAL INFORMATION

Although the city is divided into 16 *arrondissements*, Marseilles is understood by neighborhood names and major streets. **La Canebière** divides the city into north and south, funneling into the **vieux port,** with its upscale restaurants and nightlife, to the east. North of the *vieux port*, working-class residents pile into the hilltop neighborhood of **Le Panier,** east of which lies **Quartier Belsunce,** the hub of the city's Arab and African communities. A few blocks to the southeast, **Cours Julien** has a younger, countercultural feel to it. Both **Métro** lines go to the train station; line #1 (blue) goes to the *vieux port*. The thorough **bus** system is essential to get to beaches, stretching along the coast southwest of the *vieux port*.

Tourist Office: 4 La Canebière (☎04 91 13 89 00; fax 04 91 13 89 20). Has brochures of walking tours, free maps, accommodations service, and RTM day pass. Offers city tours (€6.50) daily at 10am and 2pm, as well as frequent special excursions. Open July-Aug. M-Sa 9am-8pm, Su 10am-6pm; Oct.-June M-Sa 9am-7pm, Su 10am-5pm.

Currency exchange: La Bourse, 3 pl. Général de Gaulle (☎04 91 13 09 00). Good rates and no commission. Open M-F 8:30am-6:30pm, Sa 9am-5:30pm.

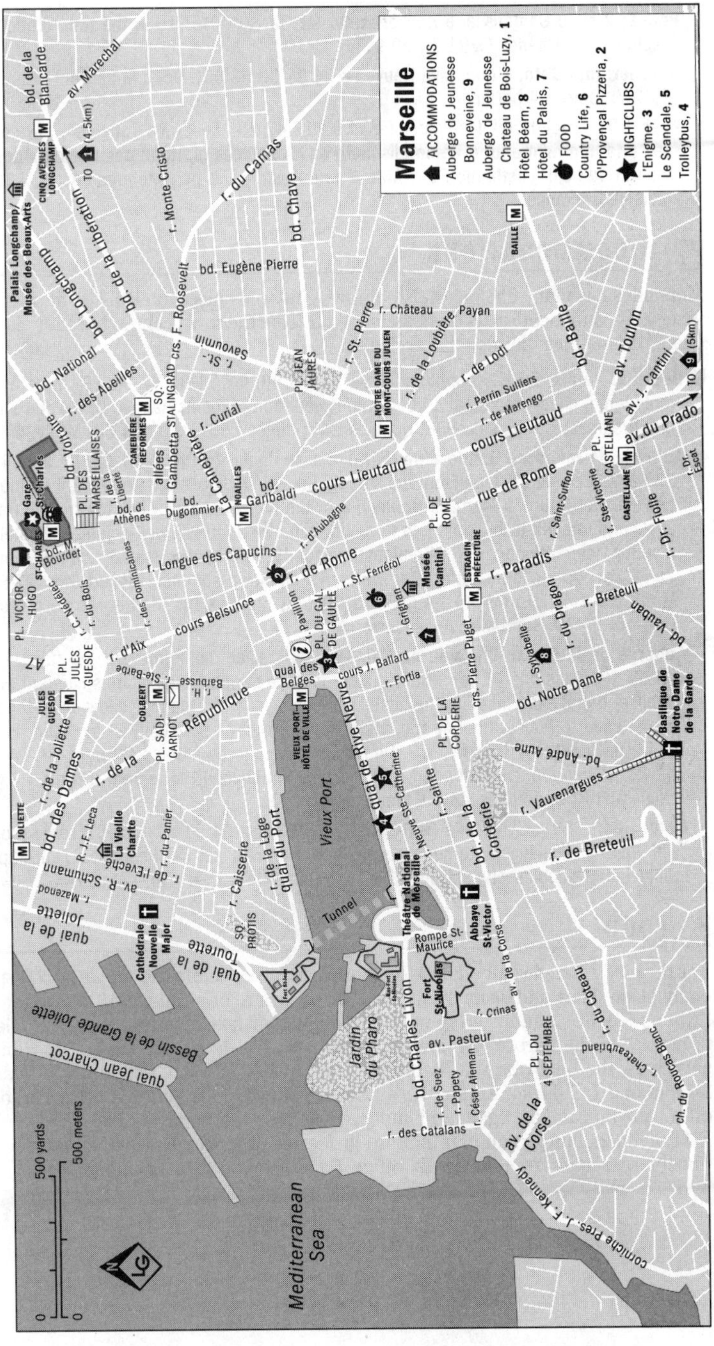
Marseille
ACCOMMODATIONS
Auberge de Jeunesse Bonneveine, 9
Auberge de Jeunesse Chateau de Bois-Luzy, 1
Hôtel Béarn, 8
Hôtel du Palais, 7
FOOD
Country Life, 6
O'Provençal Pizzeria, 2
NIGHTCLUBS
L'Enigme, 3
Le Scandale, 5
Trolleybus, 4
500 yards
500 meters
Mediterranean Sea
Vieux Port
Bassin de la Grande Joliette
quai Jean Charcot
quai de la Joliette
quai de la Tourette
Tunnel
Jardin du Pharo
Fort St-Nicolas
Abbaye St-Victor
Théâtre National de Marseille
Cathédrale Nouvelle Major
La Vieille Charité
Basilique de Notre Dame de la Garde
Palais Longchamp / Musée des Beaux-Arts
Gare St-Charles
Musée Cantini
La Canebière
quai de Rive Neuve
quai du Port
quai des Belges
r. de la République
cours Belsunce
r. de Rome
rue de Rome
cours Lieutaud
r. Paradis
bd. de la Corderie
r. de Breteuil
bd. Notre Dame
bd. Charles Livon
av. Pasteur
av. de la Corse
Corniche Pres. J. F. Kennedy
av. du Prado
av. Toulon
bd. Baille
bd. Longchamp
bd. de la Libération
bd. National
bd. Voltaire
bd. des Dames
r. du Camas
bd. Chave
bd. Eugène Pierre
r. Château Payan
r. de la Loubière
r. de Lodi
PL. CASTELLANE
PL. JEAN JAURÈS
PL. JULES GUESDE
PL. DU GAL. DE GAULLE
PL. SADI-CARNOT
PL. DU 4 SEPTEMBRE
VIEUX PORT-HÔTEL DE VILLE
JOLIETTE
COLBERT
NOAILLES
ESTRAGIN PRÉFECTURE
CASTELLANE
BAILLE
NOTRE DAME DU MONT-COURS JULIEN
CINQ AVENUES LONGCHAMP
TO 1 (4.5km)
TO 9 (5km)

FRANCE

Police: 2 r. du Commissaire Becker (☎04 91 39 80 00). Also in the train station on esplanade St-Charles (☎91 14 29 97).

Internet: Info Café, 1 quai Rive Neuve (☎04 91 33 53 05). Open M-Sa 9am-10pm, Su 2:30-7:30pm. €4 per hr.

Post Office: 1 pl. Hôtel des Postes (☎04 91 15 47 20). Follow La Canebière toward the sea and turn right onto r. Reine Elisabeth as it becomes pl. Hôtel des Postes. Address mail to be held: Firstname SURNAME, *Poste Restante,* 1 pl. Hotel des Postes, **13001** Marseilles, France.

ACCOMMODATIONS

Marseilles has many cheap hotels but few reputable ones. Hotels listed here prioritize safety and location. Both hostels are far from the town center, but there is frequent, if time-consuming, bus service.

Hôtel du Palais, 26 r. Breteuil (☎04 91 37 78 86; fax 04 91 37 91 19). Kind owner rents large, cheery rooms at a good value. Soundproof rooms have A/C, TV, and showers. Breakfast €5. Singles €38; doubles €45; triples €53. Extra bed €8. MC/V. ❹

Auberge de Jeunesse Bonneveine (HI), impasse Bonfils (☎04 91 17 63 30; fax 04 91 73 97 23), off av. J. Vidal. From the station, take Métro line #2 to Rond-Point du Prado, and transfer to bus #44 to pl. Bonnefon. At the bus stop, walk back toward the traffic circle and turn left at J. Vidal, then turn onto impasse Bonfils. A well-organized hostel for a young, international crowd. Breakfast included. July-Aug max. stay 6 days. Reception 7am-1am. No lockout. Curfew 1am. Reserve ahead in summer. Closed Dec. 22-Feb. Members only. Dorms Apr.-Aug. €13.60 first night, €11.90 thereafter; doubles €16.40/14.70. Sept.-Mar. prices lower. MC/V. ❷

Auberge de Jeunesse Château de Bois-Luzy (HI), allée des Primevères (☎/fax 04 91 49 06 18). Take bus #8 (dir.: Saint-Julien) from La Canebière to Felibres Laurient, walk uphill and make the first left; the hostel will be on your left. The big yellow tower-topped hostel used to house a count and countess, or so they say. Mostly 3- to 6-bed dorms and a few doubles. Breakfast €3. Dinner €7.50. Luggage storage €2 per bag. Sheets €1.80. Reception 7:30am-noon and 5-10:30pm. Lockout noon-5pm. Dorms €7.65; singles €11.50; doubles €8.40. Members only. ❶

Hôtel Béarn, 63 r. Sylvabelle (☎04 91 37 75 83; fax 04 91 81 54 98). Large rooms with high, airy ceilings. Internet access €4 per hr. Breakfast €4. Reception 7am-11pm. Singles and doubles with shower €23-34; triples with bath €41-42. AmEx/MC/V. ❷

FOOD

For the city's famed seafood and North African fare, explore the *vieux port,* especially **place Thiers** and **cours d'Estienne d'Orves,** where one can eat *al fresco* for as little as €9. For a more artsy crowd and cheaper fare, head up to **cours Julien,** northeast of the harbor. **O'Provençal Pizzeria** ❷, 7 r. de la Palud, off r. de Rome, serves up the best pizza in Marseilles. (☎04 91 54 03 10. Open M-Sa 11:30am-2:15pm and 7:30-11pm. AmEx/MC/V.) **Country Life** ❶, 14 r. Venture, off r. Paradis, offers all-you-can-eat vegan food under a huge skylight. (☎04 96 11 28 00. Open M-F 11:30am-2:30pm.) You can pick up groceries at **Monoprix supermarket,** on La Canebière, across from the AmEx office. (Open M-Sa 8:30am-8:30pm.)

SIGHTS

Marseilles in all its glory can be seen from the steps of the **Basilique de Notre Dame de la Garde.** Its golden statue of the Madonna, affectionately known as *"la bonne mère,"* towers 230m above the city. (☎04 91 13 40 80. Open in summer 7am-8pm; off-season 7am-7pm. Free.) The chilling catacombs of the fortified **Abbaye St-Victor,** on r. Sainte at the end of quai de Rive Neuve, contain an array of pagan and Christian relics, including the remains of 3rd-century martyrs. (☎04 96 11 22 60. Open daily 9am-7pm. Crypts €2.) Take a boat out to the **Château D'If,** the sun-blasted dungeon immortalized in Dumas's *Count of Monte Cristo*, or explore the wind-swept quarantine island of **Île Frioul.** (Boats ☎04 91 55 50 09. Depart from quai des Belges (20min., both islands €13). Chateau ☎04 91 59 02 30. Boats leave for the chateau June-Aug. daily 9am-5pm; Sept.-May Tu-Su 9am-3:30pm. €4, under age 25 €2.50.) The remains of the original port of Marseilles rest peacefully in the **Jardin des Vestiges.** Your ticket to the garden also admits you to the **Musée d'Histoire de Marseille.** (Museum ☎04 91 90 42 22. Garden and museum open M-Sa noon-7pm. €2, students €1, over 65 and under 10 free.) Also worth a visit is **La Vieille Charite,** 2 r. de la Charite, an old poorhouse and orphanage that now shelters Egyptian, prehistoric, and classical collections. (☎04 91 14 58 80. Open June-Sept. Tu-Sa 11am-6pm. Temporary exhibits €3, permanent €4.50, students with ID half-price.) Bus #83 (dir.: Rond-Point du Prado) takes you from the *vieux port* to Marseilles's **public beaches.** Catch it on the waterfront side of the street and get off at the statue of David (20-30min.). Both **Plage du Prado** and **Plage de la Corniche** offer wide beaches, clear water, and plenty of grass for impromptu soccer matches.

NIGHTLIFE

People-watching and nightlife center around **place Thiers** and **cours Julien.** Local and international DJs spin at **Trolleybus,** 24 quai de Rive Neuve, a mega-club in an 18th-century warehouse. (☎04 91 54 30 45. Beer from €5, drinks €6. Sa cover €10, includes 1 drink. Open W-Sa 11pm-7am.) The vibrant **Le Scandale,** 16 quai de Rive Neuve, is packed with locals and travelers. (☎04 91 54 46 85. Pints for €5. Happy Hour 6-10:30pm. Open daily 1pm-5am.) The friendly **L'Enigme,** 22 r. Beauvau, is one of the few gay/lesbian places around. (☎04 91 33 79 20. Open daily 7pm-5am.)

DAYTRIPS FROM MARSEILLES

CASSIS. Twenty-three kilometers from Marseilles is the charming resort town of Cassis. Follow the signs to the **Calanque de Port-Pin,** 1hr. east of town. From there it's a 30min. hike to the popular **En Vau** *calanque* and beach. A **bus** runs from Marseilles to Cassis (1hr., 4 per day, €3.20). Two blocks down from the bus stop, turn right into the Jardin Public. The **tourist office** is on the left as you leave the park. (☎04 42 01 71 17; fax 04 42 01 28 31. Open July-Aug. daily 9am-7pm; Sept.-June reduced hours.) The **Auberge de Jeunesse de la Fontasse (HI) ❶,** off D559 near En Vau, is a sweaty 4km climb from the Cassis tourist office (1hr.). From Cassis's port, follow signs for the *calanques* and when the road ends at a fork, take the steep right path and look for signs engraved in rocks. (☎04 42 01 02 72. Reception daily 8-10am and 5-9pm. Closed Jan.-Mar. HI members only. Dorms €8.30.)

AIX-EN-PROVENCE. Just 35min. away is festive Aix-en-Provence, the cultural capital of Provence (see p. 373).

FRENCH RIVIERA. Mug for the camera at **Cannes** (see p. 379), toss some dice at the **Monte-Carlo casino** in **Monaco** (see p. 386), or just hit one of the beaches.

FRENCH RIVIERA (CÔTE D'AZUR)

Between Marseilles and the Italian border, the sun-drenched beaches and warm waters of the Mediterranean form the backdrop for this fabled playground of the fab and famous—F. Scott Fitzgerald, Cole Porter, Picasso, Renoir, and Matisse are among those who flocked to the coast in its heyday. Despite the Riviera's glorious past, today this choice stretch of sun and sand is a curious combination of high-handed millionaires and low-budget tourists. High society steps out yearly for the Cannes Film Festival and the Monte-Carlo Grand Prix, both in May. Less exclusive are Nice's raucous *Carnaval* in February and various summer jazz festivals.

> **!** Every woman who has traveled on the Riviera has a story to tell about men in the big beach towns. Unsolicited pick-up techniques range from subtle invitations to more, uh, bare displays of interest. Brush them off with a biting *"laissez-moi tranquille!"* ("leave me alone") or stony indifference, but don't be shy about enlisting the help of passersby or the police to fend off Mediterranean Don Juans.

ST-TROPEZ

Nowhere does the glitz and glamour of the Riviera shine more than in St-Tropez. The "Jewel of the Riviera" unfailingly attracts Hollywood stars and curious backpackers with its exclusive clubs and nude beaches. **Plage Tahiti,** the first of the famous **plages des Pampelonne,** and **Les Salins,** a more secluded sunspot, can be reached via the free **shuttle** *(navette municipale)* that leaves pl. des Lices four times a day. Take a break from the sun at **La Musée de l'Annonciade,** pl. Grammont, with Fauvist and neo-Impressionist paintings. (Open W-M June-Sept. 10am-noon and 3-7pm; Oct.-May 10am-noon and 2-6pm. Closed Nov. €5.35, students €2.30.)

Les Bateaux de St-Raphaël **ferries** (☎04 94 95 17 46), at the old port, sail to St-Tropez from St-Raphaël (1hr., 2-5 per day, €10). Sodetrav **buses** (☎04 94 97 88 51) leave av. Général Leclerc for St-Raphaël. (2hr., 8-14 per day, €8.30.) The **tourist office,** on quai Jean Jaurès, has schedules of the shuttle transport and a *Manifestations* guide that lists local events. (☎04 94 97 45 21; www.saint-tropez.st. Open daily July-Aug. 9:30am-8:30pm, Sept.-June reduced hours.) Budget hotels do not exist in St-Tropez, and the closest youth hostel is in Fréjus (see below). **Camping** is the cheapest option—a ferry (€9 round trip) to Port Grimaud and **Les Prairies de la Mer ❶** leaves St-Tropez every hour. (☎04 94 79 09 09; prairies@campazur.com. Open Apr.-Oct. €20 per two people and tent.) The **vieux port** and the streets behind the waterfront are lined with expensive restaurants, so create your own meal at **Monoprix supermarket,** 9 av. du Général Leclerc. (July-Aug. 8am-10pm, Sept.-June 8am-7:50pm.) The restaurant-bar **Bodega de Papagayo,** on the old port, and nightclub **Le Papagayo** are magnets for tanned youth. (Open daily June-Sept. 11:30pm-5am; May and Oct. F-Su 11:30pm-5am. Cover €25.)

ST-RAPHAËL AND FRÉJUS

The twin cities of St-Raphaël and Fréjus provide an excellent base for exploring the Riviera with cheap accommodations, convenient transport, and proximity to the sea. In **St-Raphaël,** the **boardwalk** turns into a carnival and golden **beaches** stretch along the coast. The first weekend in July brings the **Compétition Internationale de Jazz New Orleans** (☎04 98 11 89 00). In Fréjus, the **Roman Amphitheater,** on r. Henri Vadon, holds rock concerts and bullfights. (Open Apr.-Oct. M and W-Sa 10am-1pm and 2:30-6:30pm; Nov.-Mar. M and W-F 10am-noon and 1:30-5:30pm, Sa 9:30am-12:30pm and 1:30-5:30pm. Bullfights €22-61.) The **Musée Archeologique Municipal,** on pl. Calvini, houses Fréjus' city emblem, a stunning double-headed sculpture. (Open Apr.-Oct. M and W-Sa 10am-1pm and 2:30-6:30pm; Nov.-Mar. 10am-noon and 1:30-5:30pm. Free.)

St-Raphaël sends trains every 30 minutes to Cannes (25min., €5.30) and Nice (1hr., €8.80). Buses leave from behind the train station in St-Raphaël for Cannes (1¼hr., 8 per day, €5.50) and Nice (2¼hr., 2 per day, €8.80). The **tourist office,** on r. Waldeck Rousseau, is opposite the train station. (☎04 94 19 52 52; www.saint-raphael.com. July-Aug. open daily 9am-7pm; Sept.-June M-Sa 9am-12:30pm and 2-6:30pm.) Take bus #6 from St-Raphaël to pl. Paul Vernet to get to the tourist office in Fréjus, 325 r. Jean Jaurès. (☎04 94 51 83 83; www.ville-frejus.fr. Open M-Sa 9am-7pm, Su 10am-noon and 3pm-6pm; Sept.-June M-Sa 9am-noon and 3-6pm.) Take av. du 15*ème* Corps d'Armée from the tourist office and turn left on chemin de Councillier after the next roundabout to reach the **Auberge de Jeunesse de St-Raphaël-Fréjus (HI) ❶,** chemin du Counillier. (☎04 94 52 93 93; youth.hostel.frejus.st.raphael@wanadoo.fr. Breakfast included. Sheets €2.70. Reception 8-10am and 6-8pm. Closed Dec.-Jan. Dorms €12. Camping €8 per person with tent.) To reach the rooms at **Le Touring ❸,** in St-Raphaël at 1 quai Albert 1*er*, take your 3rd right after the train station. (☎04 94 95 01 72; fletouring@wanadoo.fr. Closed mid-Nov. to mid-Dec. Singles and doubles €32-58; triples €58-68. AmEx/MC/V.) From St-Raphaël, a shuttle bus (€1.30) leaves quai #7 of the bus station for the hostel. St-Raphaël's **Monoprix** is on 14 bd. de Félix Martin, off av. Alphonse Karr near the train station. (Open M-Sa 8:30am-7:30pm.) **Postal Codes:** St-Raphaël 83700; Fréjus 83600.

CANNES

With its renowned annual film festival in May, the **Festival International du Film,** Cannes (pop. 78,000) has more associations with stardom than any other place on the coast. None of the festival's 350 screenings are open to the public, but the sidewalk show is free. Yet for the other 11 months, Cannes is one of the most accessible of the Riviera's glam-towns. A palm-lined boardwalk, gorgeous sandy beaches, and innumerable boutiques ensure that anyone can sport the famous Cannes style. The best window-shopping in the Riviera lies along **rue d'Antibes** and **Boulevard de la Croisette.** Farther west, the **Eglise de la Castre** and its courtyard stand on the hill on which *vieux Cannes* was built. Of Cannes's three **casinos,** the least expensive is **Le Casino Croisette,** 1 jetée Albert Edouard, next to the Palais des Festivals, with slots, blackjack, and roulette. (Gambling daily 8pm-4am; open for

THE BIG SPLURGE

LA GROSSE TARTINE

Staring at celebrity handprints, you may get the urge to live it up in Cannes. For a wonderful meal, pass on the tourist-saturated r. du Suquet and head over to **La Grosse Tartine ❺.** The friendly manager will greet and usher you to a table on the year-round terrace or to a cozy yellow interior with tropical hints and old French posters.

Though the restaurant offers a budget-oriented selection of *tartines,* including lamb confit, chicken, goat cheese, and foie gras *poêlé (€11-18.50),* you should consider splurging on three courses from the main menu. To begin, try the house speciality: homemade, patê de foie gras (€17), accompanied by grapes and figs. For a main course, the chef proposes fish dishes (€16-30) from saumon tartare to royal king prawns, and a varied listing of meats (€18-30), including beef, lamb, steak tartare, and duck. For dessert (€8-9), do not miss the chocolate fondue.

Three courses and wine may force you to ration for a few days, but the generous portions and lingering pleasure are worth it. (9 r. du Batéguier. ☎93 68 59 28. Open M-Sa 7pm-midnight. AmEx/MC/V.)

slots at 10am. No shorts, jeans, or t-shirts. Jackets required for men. 18+ with ID. Cover €10.) A cheaper way to lose your shirt is dancing until dawn at Cannes's favorite discothèque, **Jane's,** at 38 r. des Serbes. (Cover €10; includes 1st drink. Open Th-Su 11pm-dawn.) **Cat Corner,** 22 r. Macé, is a magnet for Cannes's coolest, with DJs spinning house, R&B, and funk. (Cover €16. Open daily 11:30pm-5am.)

Coastal **trains** depart from 1 r. Jean-Jaurès, every 30 min. to: Antibes (15min., €2.10); Marseilles (2hr., €15.25); Monaco (1hr., €7.10); Nice (40min., €5); St-Raphaël (25min., €5.30). The **tourist office,** 1 bd. de la Croisette, helps find accommodations. (☎04 93 39 24 53; www.cannes-online.com. Open July-Aug. daily 9am-8pm; Sept.-June M-F 9am-7pm.) **Branch** office at the train station. (Open M-Sa 9am-7pm.) Access the **Internet** at **CyberCafé Institut Riviera Langue,** 26 r. de Mimont. (€4.60 per hr. Open daily 9am-10pm.) Hostels are 10-20min. farther from the beach than other lodgings, but are the cheapest options in town. The **Hostel Les Iris ❷,** 77 bd. Carnot, thrives under the care of friendly English-speaking owners who have converted an old hotel into a clean, bright hostel. (☎04 93 68 30 20; lesiris@hotmail.com. Rooms of 2-6 have firm beds, with terrace lounge for dining, and TV. Breakfast €4.50, dinner €7-8. No curfew. Dorms €16. MC/V.) **Hotel Mimont ❸,** 39 r. de Mimont, is two streets behind the train station, off bd. de la République. (☎04 93 39 51 64; fax 04 93 99 65 35. Singles €29; doubles €36.50; triples €51. AmEx/MC/V.) **Camp** at **Parc Bellevue ❶,** 67 av. M. Chevalier, in La Bocca. Take the #9 bus to the La Boissière stop (30min.) and walk for 100m; it's on the right. (☎04 93 47 28 97. With tent: €13; €2 per car.) Reasonably priced restaurants abound in the pedestrian zone around **rue Meynadier. Monoprix** supermarket, 6 r. Meynadier, is located in Champion. (Open M-Sa 8:30am-7:30pm.) **Postal Code:** 06400.

ANTIBES-JUAN-LES-PINS

Although officially one city, Antibes and Juan-Les-Pins are 2km apart, with separate train stations and tourist offices. Blessed with beautiful beaches and a charming *vieille ville*, Antibes remains less touristy than Nice and more relaxed than St-Tropez. The **Musée Picasso,** in the Château Grimaldi, on pl. Mariejol, displays works by the master and his contemporaries. (☎04 92 90 54 20. Open Tu-Su June-Sept. 10am-6pm; Oct.-May 10am-noon and 2pm-6pm. Audioguide €3. €4.60, students €2.30.) **Musée Peynet,** pl. Nationale, has over 300 colorful *naïf* drawings by local artist Raymond Peynet. (☎04 92 90 54 30. Open June-Sept. Tu-Su 10am-6pm; Oct.-May 10am-noon and 2-6pm. €3, students €1.5.) **Trains** leave av. Robert Soleau for: Cannes (15min., every hr., €2.10); Marseilles (2½hr., every hr., €21.80); Nice (30min., every hr., €3.30). **Buses** (station open M-F 8am-noon and 2-6pm, Sa 9am-noon and 2-5pm) leave from 200 pl. de Gaulle for: Cannes (25min., every 20min., €2.40) and Nice (1hr., every 20min., €4.10). Exit the station, turn right on av. Robert Soleau, and follow the signs to the **tourist office,** 11 pl. de Gaulle. (☎04 92 90 53 00; www.antibes-juanlespins.com. Open July-Aug. daily 9am-7pm; Sept.-June M-F 9am-6pm, Sa 9am-noon and 2-6pm.) For the distant but beautiful **Relais International de la Jeunesse (Caravelle 60) ❶,** take bus #2A (every 40min., €1.15) from pl. Guynemer in Antibes. (☎04 93 61 34 40. Reception 5:30-10:30pm. No curfew. Dorms €14.)

Come summer, the young and hip **Juan-Les-Pins** is synonymous with wild nightlife. Boutiques remain open until midnight, cafes until 2am, and nightclubs past dawn. **Discothèques** are generally open from 11pm to 5am. (Cover approx. €15, usually includes 1st drink.) **Pulp,** at av. Gallice, fills with a hip crowd. (Cover €15.25, F ladies free. Open July-Aug. daily midnight-5am; Sept.-June F-Sa midnight 5am.) In the psychedelic **Whisky à Gogo,** 5 r. Jacques Leonetti, a young crowd dances the night away to house, hiphop, and Latino beats amid water-filled columns. (☎04 93 61 26 40. Cover €15.25. Open July-Aug. daily midnight-6am; Sept.-

June F-Sa midnight-6am.) **Trains** depart av. l'Esterel for: Antibes (5min., €1.20); Cannes (10min., €1.90); Nice (30min., €3.60). From the station, walk striaght on av. du Maréchal Joffre and turn right onto av. Guy de Maupassant for the **tourist office** at 51 bd. Guillaumont. To get from Antibes's pl. du Général de Gaulle to Juan-Les-Pins on foot, follow bd. Wilson, which runs right into the center of town (about 1½km). Rather than make the post-party trek back to Antibes, crash at **Hôtel Trianon ❸,** 14 av. de L'Estérel. (☎/fax 04 93 61 18 11. Breakfast €4. Singles €25; doubles €37; triples €45.) **Postal Codes:** Antibes: 06600; Juan-Les-Pins: 06160.

NICE

Sun-drenched and spicy, Nice (pop. 380,000) is the unofficial capital of the Riviera. Its pumping nightlife, top-notch museums, and bustling beaches are unerring tourist magnets. During the annual three-week February **Carnaval,** visitors and *Niçois* alike go wild with revelry, grotesque costumes, and raucous song and dance.

TRANSPORTATION

Flights: Aéroport Nice-Côte d'Azur (☎08 20 42 33 33). **Air France,** 10 av. Félix Faure (☎08 02 80 28 02), serves **Paris** (€283, under 25 €40).

Trains: Gare SNCF Nice-Ville (☎04 92 14 81 62), on av. Thiers. Open 5am-12:15am. To: **Cannes** (45min., every 15-45min., €5); **Marseilles** (2¾hr., every 30-90min., €24); **Monaco** (15min., every 10-30min., €2.90); **Paris** (5½hr., 6 per day, €75-91).

Buses: 5 bd. Jean Jaurès (☎93 85 61 81). Open M-Sa 8am-6:30pm. To **Cannes** (1½hr., every 20 min., €6) and **Monaco** (40min., every 15 min., €3.40).

Ferries: SNCM, quai du Commerce (☎04 93 13 66 66. www.corsicaferries.com). Dock open M-F 6am-7pm. Take bus #1 (dir.: Port) from pl. Masséna. To **Corsica** (€35-45).

Public Transportation: Sunbus, 10 av. Félix Faure (☎04 93 16 52 10), near pl. Leclerc and pl. Masséna. Long treks to museums, the beach, and hostels make the €8.30 8-ticket *carnet,* €4 day pass, €13 5-day pass, or €17 7-day pass well worth it. Individual tickets €1.30. The tourist office provides **Sunplan** bus maps, schedules, and route info.

Bike and Scooter Rental: JML Location, 34 av. Auber (☎04 93 16 07 00), opposite the train station. Bikes €11 per day, €42 per week; credit card deposit required. Open June-Sept. daily 8am-6:30pm; Oct.-May M-F 8am-1pm and 2-6:30pm, Sa 8am-1pm, Su 9am-1pm and 4-6:30pm.

ORIENTATION AND PRACTICAL INFORMATION

As you exit the train station, **Avenue Jean-Médecin,** on the left, and **Boulevard Gambetta,** on the right, run directly to the beach. **Place Masséna** is 10min. down av. Jean-Médecin. Along the coast, **Promenade des Anglais** is a people watching paradise. To the southeast, past av. Jean Médecin and toward the bus station, is **Vieux Nice.** Women should not walk alone after sundown, and everyone should exercise caution at night around the train station, *Vieux Nice*, and Promenade des Anglais.

Tourist Office: Av. Thiers (☎08 92 70 74 07; www.nicetourism.com), by the train station. Makes same-day hotel reservations; best chance of getting a room is between 9 and 11am. Ask for *Nice: A Practical Guide, Museums and Churches of Nice,* and a map. Open June-Sept. M-Sa 8am-8pm, Su 9am-6pm; Oct-May M-Sa 8am-7pm.

Consulates: Canada, 10 r. Lamartine (☎04 93 92 93 22). Open M-F 9am-noon. **UK,** 26 av. Notre Dame (☎93 62 13 56). Open M, W, and F 9:30-11:30am. **US,** 7 av. Gustave V (☎04 93 88 89 55). Open M-F 9-11:30am and 1:30-4:30pm.

American Express: 11 promenade des Anglais (☎04 93 16 53 53). Open 9am-8:30pm.

Laundromat: Laverie Niçoise, 7 r. d'Italie (☎04 93 87 56 50). Next to Basilique Notre-Dame. Open M-Sa 8:30am-12:30pm and 2:30-7:30pm.

Police: (☎04 93 17 22 22) At the opposite end of bd. M. Foch from bd. Jean Médecin.

Hospital: St-Roch, 5 r. Pierre Devoluy (☎04 92 03 33 75).

Internet Access: Organic CyberCafé, 16 r. Paganini. Mention *Let's Go* and pay €4.50 per hr. Open daily 9am-9pm. **Urgence Informatique,** 26 r. Pertinax (☎04 93 62 07 60), closes late. €5 per hr. Open July-Aug. M-Sa 9am-midnight, Sept.-June 9am-9pm.

Post Office: 21 av. Thiers (☎93 82 65 22) Near the train station. Open M-F 8am-7pm, Sa 8am-noon. 24hr. **ATM.** Address mail to be held: Firstname SURNAME, *Poste Restante, Recette Principale,* Nice 06000, France. **Postal Code:** 06033.

ACCOMMODATIONS

To sleep easy, come to Nice with reservations. Affordable places surround the train station, but without reservations (made at least 2-3 weeks ahead in the summer), you'll be forced to risk a night on the beach or outside the train station. The city has two clusters of budget hotels: ones by the station are newer but poorly located; those nearer to *Vieux Nice* are more convenient but less modern.

Relais International de la Jeunesse "Clairvallon," 26 av. Scudéri (☎04 93 81 27 63; clajpaca@cote-dazur.com), in Cimiez, 4km out of town. Take bus #15 to "Scudéri" (dir.: "Rimiez," 20min., every 10min.). In a pretty, residential neighborhood, you'll find this luxurious villa of a deceased marquis. TV, swimming pool (open 5-7pm). Laundry €4. 4- to 10-bed rooms. Breakfast included. 5-course dinner €8.50. Check-in 5pm. Lockout 9:30am-5pm. Curfew 11pm. Dorms €13. No reservations. ❶

Hôtel Baccarat, 39 r. d'Angleterre (☎04 93 88 35 73), 2nd right off r. de Belgique. Large rooms in homey, secure atmosphere. 3- to 5-bed dorms €14; singles €29; doubles €36; triples €44. AmEx/MC/V. ❸

Hôtel Little Masséna, 22 r. Masséna (☎04 93 87 72 34). Small but functional rooms. Singles and doubles €28-48, extra person €6.10. Oct.-May prices lower. MC/V. ❸

Hôtel des Flandres, 6 r. de Belgique (☎04 93 88 78 94). Large rooms with high ceilings and private bathrooms. Breakfast €5. Dorms €17; singles €35-45; doubles €45-51; triples €60; quads €67. Extra bed €12. MC/V. ❹

Hôtel Notre Dame, 22 r. de la Russie (☎04 93 88 70 44), 1 block west of av. Jean Médecin. Spotless, quiet rooms. Reception 24hr. Singles €31; doubles €42; triples €54; quads €67. Extra bed €9.15. MC/V. ❸

Hôtel Belle Meunière, 21 av. Durante (☎04 93 88 66 15), on a street facing the train station. Lively backpacker atmosphere in an elegant converted mansion. Breakfast included. 4- to 5-bed co-ed dorms €13; doubles €45.50; triples €40-54. ❶

Hôtel Les Orangiers, 10bis av. Durante (☎04 93 87 51 41). Bright rooms, all with showers and fridges. Free luggage storage. Closed Nov. Dorms €14; singles €16-25; doubles €36-38; triples €46-48; quads €60. MC/V. ❷

Les Mimosas, 26 r. de la Buffa (☎04 93 88 05 59). Close to the beach and r. Massena. Renovated homey rooms. Singles €31; doubles €37-46; triples €46-53; quads €54-64. Oct.-Mar. prices €5 lower. ❸

Hôtel Petit Trianon, 11 r. Paradis (☎04 93 87 50 46), off r. Massena. Humble but elegant rooms. Singles €15; doubles €31; triples €50. Extra bed €8. MC/V. ❶

Hôtel Au Picardy, 10 bd. Jean-Jaurès (☎04 93 85 75 51), across from the bus station. Near *Vieux Nice.* Breakfast €3. Singles €19, with shower €27.30; doubles €24-27; triples €34-38; quads €38-48. Extra bed €5. ❷

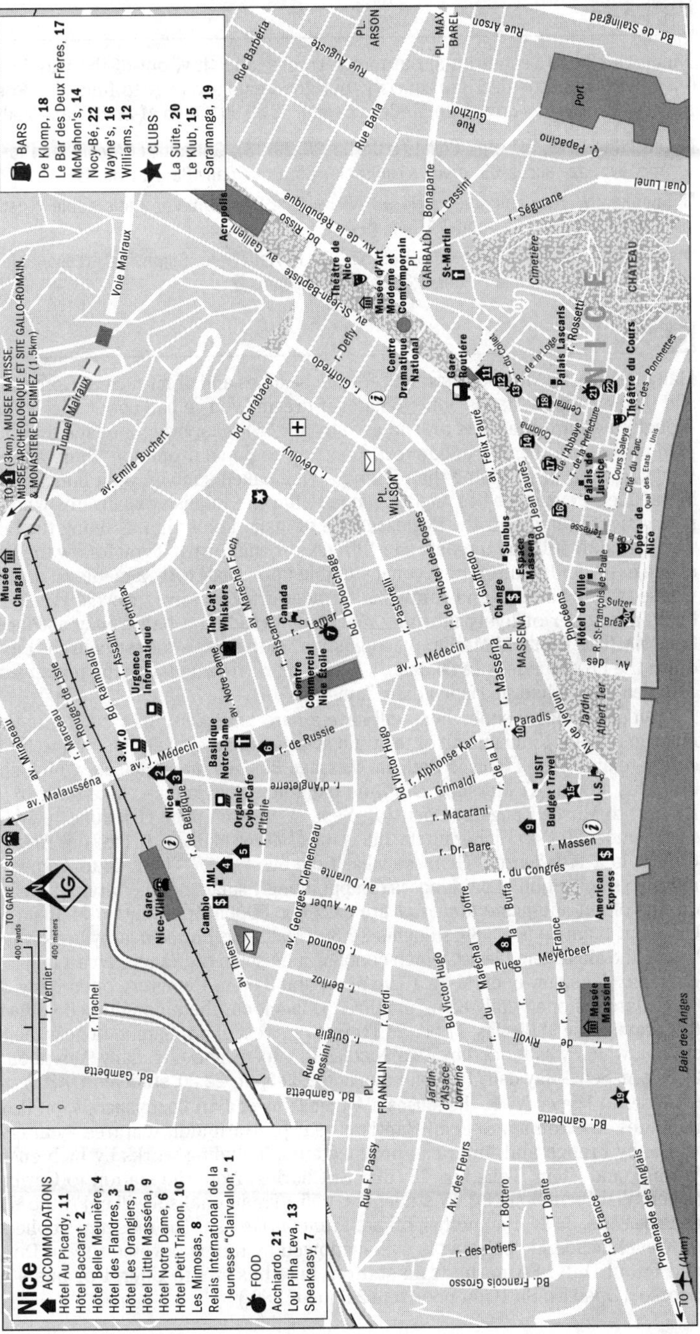
Nice
ACCOMMODATIONS
Hôtel Au Picardy, 11
Hôtel Baccarat, 2
Hôtel Belle Meunière, 4
Hôtel des Flandres, 3
Hôtel Les Orangiers, 5
Hôtel Little Masséna, 9
Hôtel Notre Dame, 6
Hôtel Petit Trianon, 10
Les Mimosas, 8
Relais International de la Jeunesse "Clairvallon," 1
FOOD
Acchiardo, 21
Lou Pilha Leva, 13
Speakeasy, 7
BARS
De Klomp, 18
Le Bar des Deux Frères, 17
McMahon's, 14
Nocy-Bé, 22
Wayne's, 16
Williams, 12
CLUBS
La Suite, 20
Le Klub, 15
Saramanga, 19
TO GARE DU SUD
TO 1 (3km), MUSEE MATISSE, MUSEE ARCHEOLOGIQUE ET SITE GALLO-ROMAIN, & MONASTERE DE CIMIEZ (1.5km)
Musée Chagall
Gare Nice-Ville
Basilique Notre-Dame
Centre Commercial Nice Étoile
Théâtre de Nice
Musée d'Art Moderne et Contemporain
Centre Dramatique National
Acropolis
Gare Routière
St-Martin
Palais Lascaris
Théâtre du Cours
Palais de Justice
Opéra de Nice
Hôtel de Ville
Musée Masséna
CHATEAU
Cimetière
VIEUX NICE
Port
Baie des Anges
Promenade des Anglais
Quai des Etats - Unis
Jardin Albert 1er
Jardin d'Alsace-Lorraine
PL. MASSENA
PL. WILSON
PL. GARIBALDI
PL. FRANKLIN
PL. ARSON
PL. MAX BAREL
American Express
Cambio
Change
Budget Travel
USIT
U.S.
Sunbus
Espace Masséna
Organic CyberCafe
3.W.O
Urgence Informatique
The Cat's Whiskers
Canada
IML
Nicea
TO (4km)
av. Malausséna
av. J. Médecin
av. Jean Médecin
av. Thiers
av. Georges Clemenceau
av. Notre Dame
av. Maréchal Foch
av. Félix Faure
av. de la République
av. St-Jean-Baptiste
av. Gallieni
av. Emile Buchert
av. Mirabeau
av. Durante
av. Auber
Av. de Verdun
Av. des Fleurs
Bd. Gambetta
Bd. Victor Hugo
bd. Dubouchage
bd. Carabacel
bd. Risso
Bd. Raimbaldi
Bd. Jean Jaurès
Bd. François Grosso
Bd. de Stalingrad
Voie Malraux
Tunnel Malraux
Quai Lunel
Q. Papacino
Rue Arson
Rue Barla
Rue Auguste
Rue Barbéria
Rue Guizhol
Rue Bonaparte
Rue Rossini
Rue F. Passy
Rue du Maréchal Joffre
Rue de la Buffa
Rue de Rivoli
Rue de France
Rue Meyerbeer
r. Vernier
r. Trachel
r. Marceau
r. Rouget de Lisle
r. Assalit
r. Pertinax
r. de Belgique
r. d'Italie
r. d'Angleterre
r. de Russie
r. Biscarra
r. Lamar
r. Gioffredo
r. Defly
r. Dévoluy
r. Pastorelli
r. de l'Hôtel des Postes
r. Masséna
r. Paradis
r. Alphonse Karr
r. Grimaldi
r. de la Liberté
r. Macarani
r. Dr. Baréty
r. Massenet
r. du Congrès
r. Gounod
r. Berlioz
r. Guiglia
r. Verdi
r. Dante
r. Bottero
r. des Potiers
r. Cassini
r. Ségurane
r. du Collet
R. de la Loge
r. Rossetti
r. Centrale
r. Colonna
r. de l'Abbaye
r. de la Préfecture
Cours Saleya
Cité du Parc
r. des Ponchettes
r. de la Terrasse
R. St-François de Paule
r. Sulzer
r. Bréa
Av. des Phocéens
400 yards
400 meters
0

FRANCE

FOOD

Nice is a city of restaurants, outdoor terraces, and tiny, out-of-the-way bistros. *Vieux Nice* is crowded and touristy, but good eats are easy to find. The **Prisunic** supermarket is at 42 av. Jean Médecin. (☎93 62 38 90. Open M-Sa 8:30am-8:30pm.)

Lou Pilha Leva, 13 r. du Collet (☎04 93 80 29 33). Get a lot of *Niçois* food for little money. Pizza slices €3, *moules* (mussels) €5. Open daily 8am-11pm. ❶

Speakeasy, 7 r. Lamartine (☎04 93 85 59 50). Delectable and affordable vegetarian options. Open M-Sa noon-2:15pm. ❷

Acchiardo, 38 r. Droite (☎04 93 85 51 16), in *Vieux Nice.* Surprisingly reasonable pastas from €6. Open M-F noon-1:30pm and 7-10pm. ❶

SIGHTS

Many visitors to Nice head straight for the beaches and don't retreat from the sun and water until the day is done. Whatever dreams you've had about Nice's beach, though, the hard reality is an endless stretch of rocks; bring a beach mat if you plan to soak up the sun in comfort. Contrary to popular opinion, there are more things in Nice worth doing than taking a long naked sunbath on a bunch of pebbles. Nice's **Promenade des Anglais,** named after the English expatriates who built it, is a sight in itself. At the **Négresco,** one of many luxury hotels lining the boulevard, the staff still don top-hats and 19th-century uniforms. If you follow the Promenade east of bd. Jean Jaurès, you'll stumble upon **Vieux Nice,** a medieval *quartier* whose twisting streets and sprawling terraces draw massive crowds. *Vieux Nice* hosts a number of lively morning markets, including a fish frenzy at **Place St-François.** The **Eglise St-Martin,** pl. Augustine, is the city's oldest church. Further down the Promenade is **Le Château,** a hillside park crowned with the remains of an 11th-century cathedral. (Open daily 7am-8pm.)

Even professional sunbathers will have a hard time passing by Nice's first-class museums. Walk 15min. north of the train station onto av. du Dr. Ménard to find the concrete and glass **Musée National Message Biblique Marc Chagall,** which showcases his moving 17 *Message Biblique* paintings. You can also take bus #15 (dir.: Rimiez) to Musée Chagall. (Open July-Sept. W-M 10am-6pm; Oct.-June 10am-5pm. €5.50, under 26 €4.) Higher up the hill is the **Musée Matisse,** 164 av. des Arènes de Cimiez, in a 17th-century Genoese villa. Take bus #15, 17, 20, or 22 to Arènes. The museum's collection of paintings is disappointingly small, but the bronze reliefs and dozens of cut-and-paste *tableaux* are dazzling. (Open Apr.-Sept. W-M 10am-6pm; Oct.-Mar. 10am-5pm. €3.80, students €2.30.) Matisse is buried nearby in a cemetery beside the **Monastère Cimiez,** which contains a museum of Franciscan art and lovely gardens. (Museum open M-Sa 10am-noon and 3-6pm. Cemetery open daily 8am-6pm. Gardens open daily 8am-7pm. Free.) Check out the onion-domed **Cathédrale Orthodoxe Russe St-Nicolas,** 17 bd. du Tzarevitch, west of bd. Gambetta near the train station, which was funded by Tsar Nicolas II. (Open June-Aug. daily 9am-noon and 2:30-6pm, Sept.-May daily 9:30am-noon and 2:30-5pm. €2.30, students €1.85.)

Closer to *Vieux Nice*, the **Musée d'Art Moderne et d'Art Contemporain,** on Promenade des Arts, on av. St-Jean Baptiste near pl. Garibaldi, features avant-garde works by French and American provocateurs, including works by Lichtenstein, Warhol, and Klein. Take bus #5 (dir.: St-Charles) from the station to Garibaldi. (Open W-M 10am-6pm. €3.05, students €1.55.) Traditionalists will enjoy the **Musée de Beaux Arts,** 33 av. Baumettes, off bd. Francois Grosso. The museum's collection of French academic painting is overshadowed by rooms devoted to Van Dongen and Raoul Dufy. From the train station, take bus #38 to Chéret or bus #12 to Grosso. (Open Tu-Su 10am-noon and 2-6pm. €1.80.)

NIGHTLIFE

FNAC, 24 av. Jean Médecin, in the Nice Etoile shopping center, sells tickets for performances around town. (☎04 92 17 77 77; www.fnac.com.) Nice's **Jazz Festival,** in mid-July at the Parc et Arènes de Cimiez near the Musée Matisse, attracts world-famous jazz and non-jazz musicians. (☎08 20 80 04 00; www.nicejazzfest.com. €30.) Nice's **Carnaval** in late February gives Rio a run for its money with two weeks of parades, outlandish costumes, fireworks, and parties. The party crowd here swings long after the folks in St-Tropez and Antibes have called it a night. The bars and nightclubs around r. Masséna and *Vieux Nice* pulsate with dance, jazz, and rock. The dress code at all bars and clubs is simple: look good. Most pubs will turn you away if you're wearing shorts, sandals, or a baseball cap.

BARS

De Klomp, 6 r. Mascoinat (☎04 93 92 42 85). 40 types of whiskey (from €6.50) and 18 beers on tap (pint €7). A variety of live music from salsa to jazz every night. Happy Hour 5:30-9:30pm. Open M-Sa 5:30pm-2:30am, Su 8:30pm-2:30am.

Le Bar Des Deux Frères, 1 r. du Moulin (☎04 93 80 77 61). A young crowd tosses back tequila (10 for €22) and beer (€5). Open T-Sa 6pm-3:30am, Su-M 10pm-2:30am.

Wayne's, 15 r. de la Préfecture (☎04 93 13 46 99). Common denominators for this wild, crowded bar: young, Anglo, and on the prowl. Open noon-1am.

McMahon's, 50 bd. Jean Jaurès (☎04 93 13 84 07). Join the locals and expats who lap up Guinness at this low-key pub. Happy Hour daily 4-9pm. Open daily 8am-2am.

Williams, 4 r. Centrale (☎04 93 62 99 63). When other bars close up, Williams keeps the kegs flowing. Karaoke nights M-Th. Live music F and Sa. Open 9pm-7am.

Nocy-Bé, 4-6 r. Jules Gilly (☎04 93 85 52 25). Take a time-out at this mellow Indian tearoom with one of 45 different teas or a heady fruit pipe. Open W-M 4pm-12:30am.

CLUBS

Saramanga, 45-47 Promenade des Anglais (☎04 93 96 68 00). A tropical theme reigns in Nice's hottest club, replete with exotic drinks, Hawaiian shirts, and fire-juggling showgirls. Cover €15. Open F-Sa 11pm-5am.

La Suite, 2 r. Brea (☎04 93 92 92 91). This *petite boite* attracts a funky, well-dressed, moneyed crowd. Cover €13. Open T-Su 11pm-2:30am.

Le Klub, 6 r. Halévy (☎04 60 55 26 61). A golden-tanned set populates this successful gay club. Cover €11. Open T-Su 11:30pm-6am.

DAYTRIPS FROM NICE

THE CORNICHES

Trains and buses between Nice and Monaco serve most of the Corniche towns frequently. Hourly ***trains*** *from Nice to Monaco stop at: Beaulieu-sur-Mer (7min., €1.30); Cap d'Ail (20min., €2.40); Eze-sur-Mer (16min., €2); Villefranche-sur-Mer (7min., €1.30). Also departing from the train station are numerous numbered* ***RCA buses*** *(☎04 93 85 64 44), which run between Nice and Monaco, making different stops along the way. Bus* ***#111*** *leaves Nice, stopping in Villefranche-sur-Mer (M-Sa 9 per day). 3 buses continue on to St-Jean-Cap-Ferrat. Bus* ***#112*** *travels from Nice to Monte-Carlo, stopping in Eze-le-Village (7 per day).* ***RCA*** *and* ***Broch buses*** *(☎04 93 85 61 81) run every hr. from Nice to: Beaulieu-sur-Mer (20min., €2); Cap d'Ail (30min., €3.20); Eze-le-Village (25min., €2.40); Monaco-Ville (40min., €3.70); Monte-Carlo (45min., €3.70); Villefranche-sur-Mer (15min., €1.60).*

Rocky shores, pebble beaches, and luxurious villas glow along the Corniches, between hectic Nice and high-rolling Monaco. More relaxing than their glam-fab neighbors, these tiny towns have interesting museums, ancient ruins, and breathtaking countryside. The train offers a glimpse of the coast up close, while bus rides on the high roads allow bird's-eye views of the steep cliffs and crashing sea below.

VILLEFRANCHE-SUR-MER. The town's narrow streets and pastel houses have enchanted Aldous Huxley, Katherine Mansfield, and many other artists. Strolling from the train station along quai Ponchardier, a sign to the *vieille ville* points to the spooky 13th-century Rue Obscure, the oldest street in Villefranche. At the end of the quai is the Chapelle St-Pierre, decorated by Jean Cocteau, former resident, film-maker, and jack-of-all-arts. (☎04 93 76 90 70. Call ahead for hours. €2.) To get to the tourist office from the train station, exit on quai 1 and head inland on av. G. Clemenceau, continue straight when it becomes av. Sadi Carnot, and it will be at the end of the street. (☎04 93 01 73 68. Open July-Aug. daily 9am-7pm; mid-Sept. to June M-Sa 9am-noon and 2-6pm.)

ST-JEAN-CAP-FERRAT. A lovely town with an even lovelier beach, St-Jean-Cap-Ferrat is the trump card of the Riviera. The **Fondation Ephrussi di Rothschild,** just off av. D. Semeria, is a stunning Italian villa that houses the collections of the Baroness de Rothschild, including Monet canvases, Gobelins tapestries, and Chinese vases. The seven lush gardens reflect different parts of the world. (Open July-Aug. daily 10am-7pm; Sept.-Nov. 1 and Feb. 15-June daily 10am-6pm; Nov. 2-Feb. 14 M-F 2-6pm, Sa-Su 10am-6pm. €8, students €6.) The town's beautiful **beaches** merit the area's nickname *"presqu'île des rêves"* (peninsula of dreams).

EZE. Three-tiered Eze owes its fame to the pristine medieval town in the middle tier. It features the **Porte des Maures,** which served as a portal for a surprise attack by the Moors, and the **Eglise Paroissial,** containing sleek Phoencian crosses mixed with Catholic gilt. (Open daily 9am-7pm.) The best views are 40min. up the **Sentier Friedrich Nietzsche,** a windy trail where its namesake found inspiration; the path begins in **Eze Bord-du-Mer,** 100m east of the train station and tourist office, and ends near the base of the medieval city, by the **Fragonard parfumerie.**

CAP D'AIL. With 3km of cliff-framed foamy seashore, Cap d'Ail's **Les Pissarelles** draws hundreds of nudists, while **Plage Mala** is frequented by more modest folk. To get from the station to the **tourist office,** 87bis av. de 3 Septembre, turn right at the village, continue on av. de la Gare, and turn left on r. du 4 Septembre. (☎04 93 78 02 33; www.monte-carlo.mc/cap-d'ail. Open July-Aug. M-Sa 9am-noon and 2-6pm, Su 9am-noon; Sept.-June M-F 9am-noon and 2-6pm, Sa 9am-noon.) The **Relais International de la Jeunesse ❶,** on bd. F. de May, has a waterfront location. (☎04 93 78 18 58; clajpaca@cote-dazur.com. Breakfast included. Open Apr.-Oct. €13.)

MONACO AND MONTE-CARLO

Monaco (pop. 7,160) has money—lots of it—invested in ubiquitous surveillance cameras, high-speed luxury cars, and sleek yachts. At Monaco's spiritual heart is its famous casino in Monte-Carlo, a magnet for the wealthy and dissolute since 1885. The sheer spectacle of it all is worth a daytrip from Nice.

PHONING TO AND FROM MONACO	Monaco's country code is 377. To telephone Monaco from France, dial 00377, then the 8-digit Monaco number. To call France from Monaco, dial 0033, and drop the first zero of the French number.

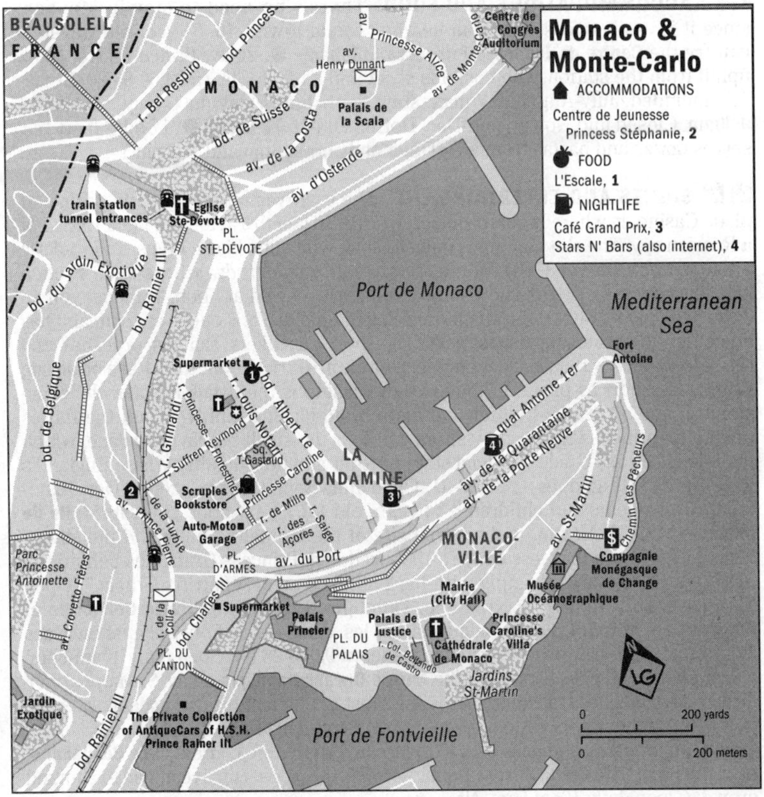

TRANSPORTATION. Trains (☎08 36 35 35 35) run to: Antibes (1hr., every 30min., €6.40); Cannes (65min., every 30min., €7.10); and Nice (25min., every 30min., €2.90). **Buses** (☎04 93 85 61 81) leave pl. d'Armes or pl. du Casino for Nice (45min., every 15min., €3.70).

PRACTICAL INFORMATION. Follow the signs in the new train station for Le Rocher and Fontvieille to the **avenue Prince Pierre** exit; it's close to the **La Condamine** quarter, Monaco's port and nightlife hub. To the right of La Condamine rises the *vieille ville*, **Monaco-Ville.** Leaving the train station onto bd. Princess Charlotte or pl. St-Devote leads to **Monte-Carlo** and the casino. **Bus #4** links the train station to the casino in Monte-Carlo. (Buy tickets on board. €1.30, €3.30 for a *carte* of 4.) At the **tourist office,** 2a bd. des Moulins, a friendly, English-speaking staff provides city plans, a monthly events guide, and hotel reservations free of charge. (☎92 16 61 16; www.monacotourisme.com. Open M-Sa 9am-7pm, Su 10am-noon.) Stop by the lively **fruit and flower market** on pl. d'Armes, on av. Prince Pierre (open daily 6am-1pm) or the huge **Carrefour supermarket** in Fontvieille's plaza (open M-Sa 8:30am-10pm). Access the **Internet** at **Stars 'N' Bars,** 6 quai Antoine 1*er*. (Open daily 10am-midnight. €6 per 30min.) **Postal Code:** 06500.

ACCOMMODATIONS AND FOOD. There's no need to stay in Monaco, since it is easily accessible from nearby coastal towns. 16- 31-year-old travelers can try the **Centre de Jeunesse Princesse Stéphanie ❶,** 24 av. Prince Pierre, 100m uphill from the station. The hostel is strict and a bit sterile. (☎93 50 83 20. Breakfast included. July-Aug. 5-day max. stay; Sept.-June 7-day max. stay. Check-out 9:30am. Closed mid-Nov. to mid-Dec. Dorms €14-16.) **L'Escale ❷,** 17 bd. Albert 1*er*, serves pizzas and pastas from €7. (Open daily noon-3pm and 7-11pm.)

SIGHTS AND ENTERTAINMENT. The extravagant **Monte-Carlo Casino,** at pl. de Casino, is where Richard Burton wooed Elizabeth Taylor and Mata Hari shot a Russian spy. The slot machines open at 2pm, while blackjack, craps, and roulette open at noon (cover €10). The exclusive *salons privés*, where such French games as *chemin de fer* and *trente et quarante* begin at noon, will cost you an extra €10 cover. Next door, the more relaxed **Café de Paris** opens at 10am and has no cover. All casinos have **dress codes** (no shorts, sneakers, sandals, or jeans), and the *salons privés* require coat and tie. Guards are strict about the **21 age minimum;** bring a passport as proof. High above the casino is the **Palais Princier,** the occasional home of Prince Rainier and his tabloid-darling family. When the flag is down, the prince is away and visitors can tour the small but lavish palace, which includes Princess Grace's official state portrait and the chamber where England's King George III died. (☎93 25 18 31. Open June-Sept. 9:30am-6:20pm; Oct. 10am-5pm. €6, students and children 8-14 years old €3.) Next door, the **Cathédrale de Monaco,** at pl. St-Martin, is the burial site of the Grimaldi family and the site of Prince Rainer and Princess Grace's 1956 wedding; Princess Grace lies behind the altar in a tomb marked simply with her Latinized name, "Patritia Gracia." (Open Mar.-Oct. daily 7am-7pm; Nov.-Feb. 7am-6pm. Free.) The **Private Collection of Antique Cars of H.S.H. Prince Rainier III,** on les Terraces de Fontvielle, showcases 105 of the most glamorous cars ever made. (☎92 05 28 56. Open daily 10am-6pm. €6, students and ages 8-14 €3.) The **Musée Océanographique** on av. St-Martin, once directed by Jacques Cousteau, holds the most exotic and bizarre oceanic species. (☎93 15 36 00; www.oceano.mc. Open Apr.-Sept. daily 9am-7pm; Oct.-Mar. 10am-6pm. €11, students and ages 6-18 €6.) Monaco's nightlife centers in **La Condamine,** near the port. **Café Grand Prix,** at 1 quai Antoine 1*er*, serves up live music to a mixed crowd. (Open daily 10am-5am. No cover.)

CORSICA (LA CORSE)

An island of paradisiacal escape, Corsica thrives on tourism. From mid-June to August, flocks of mainland French and global comfort-seekers retreat to the island's renowned beaches and pricey resorts. The summer climaxes in a nationalistic blast on August 15, when France celebrates the Fête de l'Assomption, and Corsicans observe hometown-boy **Napoleon's birthday.** Tourists depart by September, when the weather is at its best and the waters their warmest. Winter visitors can explore sleepy coastal towns or head inland to ski.

TRANSPORTATION

Air France, 3 bd. du Roi Jérôme in Ajaccio (☎08 20 82 08 20), and its subsidiary **Compagnie Corse Méditerranée (CCM)** fly to Bastia and Ajaccio from: Paris (€170, students €140); Nice (€120, students €98); Marseilles (€128, students €104); and Lyon (€142, students €114). There's also a direct link from Lille to Bastia (€196, students €178). **Air Liberté** services Calvi from Nice and Marseilles. Air France/CCM offices are at the airports in Ajaccio (p. 389) and Bastia (p. 391). **Ferry** travel between the mainland and Corsica can be a rough trip, and in some circumstances not much cheaper than a plane. High-speed ferries run between Nice and Corsica (3½hr.). Overnight ferries from Toulon and Marseilles take upwards of 10 hours. The **Société National Maritime Corse Méditerranée (SNCM)** (☎08 91 70 18 01; www.sncm.fr) sends ferries from Marseilles (€43-60, under 25 €34-48) and Nice (€38-48, under 25 €23-33). SNCM schedules and fees are listed in a booklet available at travel agencies and ports. **SAREMAR** (☎04 95 73 00 96) and **Moby Lines** (☎04 95 73 00 29; www.mobylines.de) run from Santa Teresa in Sardinia to Bonifacio. (3-10 per day depending on the season, €7-15.) **Corsica Ferries** (☎08 25 095 095; www.corsicaferries.com) crosses from Livorno and Savona in Italy to Bastia (€23-38). **Train** service in Corsica is slow and limited to the half of the island north of Ajaccio; **railpasses** are not valid. **Buses** aren't much better but provide more comprehensive service; call **Eurocorse Voyages** (☎04 95 21 06 30) for more info.

HIKING

Hiking is the best way to explore the island's mountainous interior. The **GR20** is an extremely difficult 14- to 15-day 200km trail that crosses the island. The popular **Mare e Monti** (10 days) and **Da Mare a Mare Sud** (4-6 days) trails are shorter and less challenging. The **Parc Naturel Régional de la Corse,** 2 Sargent Casalonga, in Ajaccio (☎04 95 51 79 10), publishes maps and a guide to *gîtes d'étapes*.

AJACCIO (AIACCIU)

Swinging Ajaccio (pop. 60,000) often trades in Corsican nationalism for the *français* flavor of life. Celebrating their diminutive native son is also a regular pastime, starting with the **Musée National de la Maison Bonaparte,** r. St-Charles, between r. Bonaparte and r. Roi-de-Rome. (☎04 95 21 43 89. Open Apr.-Sept. M 2-6pm, Tu-Su 9am-noon and 2-6pm; Oct.-Mar. Tu-Su 10am-noon and 2-4:45pm, M 2-4:45pm. €4, ages 18-25 €2.60, under 18 free.) Inside the **Musée Fesch,** 50-52 r. Cardinal Fesch, you'll find an impressive collection of 14th- to 19th-century Italian paintings gathered by Napoleon's uncle Fesch. Also within the complex is the **Chapelle Impériale,** the final resting place of most of the Bonaparte family: Napoleon himself, however, is buried in a modest Parisian tomb. (☎04 95 21 48 17. Open July-Aug. M 1:30-6pm, Tu-Th 9am-6:30pm, F 9am-6:30pm and 9pm-midnight, Sa-Su 10:30am-6pm; Sept.-June reduced hours. Museum €5.35, students €3.85. Chapel €1.55/€0.75.) Southwest of Ajaccio,

IN RECENT NEWS

A POLITICAL OBSTACLE *CORSE*

Despite their politically volatile reputation, fully 80% of Corsicans subscribe to traditional French parties; a mere 20% supports nationalist parties. Though there are ten major nationalist parties, only one favors immediate independence: the *FLNC*, which is the political wing of *Indipendenza*, a clandestine organization that has been linked to terrorism. The other nationalist parties believe the island must experience political and economic autonomy before complete independence: a trial and error period.

If the FLNC has any center of support, it is Corte. After all, it served as capital to the shot-lived independent Corsican state under Paoli. This maverick spirit has lingered in the Cortenais, but the political reality has changed. Since 1983, the mayor of Corte has always been affiliated with the RPR, not known for warmth towards the independence cause. This rather illogical status quo stems from the fact that on the local articular political affiliation. Corte's current mayor, for instance, received overwhelming support from the right, left, *and* nationalists.

Regardless of individual relations and party affiliations, Corsicans are anxious to see how the new Interior Minister, Nicolas Sarkozy, will treat the island. Thus far, he seems more Corsica-friendly than his predecessor, but the question remains: in whose interests will he work when Corsica stands apart from the rest of France?

the striking black cliffs of **Îles Sanguinaires** loom over the sea. Nave Va **ferries,** at a kiosk on the port, run to the largest island. (☎04 95 51 31 31. Apr.-Oct. daily. €20.)

Trains (☎04 95 23 11 03) leave pl. de la Gare, for Bastia (4hr., 4 per day, €23.10) and Calvi (4½hr., 2 per day, €26.90). Eurocorse Voyages **buses** (☎04 95 21 06 30) go to Bastia (3hr., 2 per day, €19) via Corte (1½hr., €10.50); Autocars SAIB (☎95 22 41 99) runs to Porto (2hr., 1-3 per day, €11). The **tourist office** is at 3 bd. du Roi Jérôme. (☎04 95 51 53 03; www.tourisme.fr/ajaccio. Open July-Aug. M-Sa 8am-8:30pm, Su 9am-1pm and 4-7pm; Apr.-June and Sept.-Oct. M-Sa 8am-7pm, Su 9am-1pm; Nov.-Mar. reduced hours.) The serene **Hôtel Kallisté ❹** is at 51 cours Napoléon. (☎04 95 51 34 45; www.cyrnos.com. Singles €45; doubles €52; triples €69. AmEx/MC/V.) **Hôtel le Dauphin ❹,** 11 bd. Sampiero, is halfway between the station and port. (☎04 95 21 12 94; fax 04 95 21 88 69. Singles and doubles €49-60; triples €69. AmEx/MC/V.) Get groceries at **Monoprix** supermarket, 31 cours Napoléon. (Open M-Sa 8am-7:40pm.) **Postal Code:** 20000.

BONIFACIO (BONIFAZIU)

The fortified city of Bonifacio (pop. 3000) rises like a majestic sand castle atop jagged limestone cliffs. **Marina Croisères** offers **boat tours** of the hidden coves and grottoes. (☎04 95 73 09 77. €11-21.) All the companies by the port run frequent ferries (30min.) to the pristine sands of **Îles Levezzi,** a nature reserve with beautiful reefs just off its coast perfect for **scuba diving.** To explore the *haute ville,* head up the steep montée Rastello, the wide staircase halfway down the port, where excellent views of the ridged cliffs to the east await. Continue up montée St-Roch to the lookout at **Porte des Gênes,** a drawbridge built by invaders. Then walk to the **place du Marche** to see Bonifacio's famous cliffs and the **Grain de Sable.**

Eurocorse Voyages (☎04 95 21 06 30) runs **buses** to Ajaccio (3½hr., 2 per day, €20.50) as well as Porto Vecchio (30min., 1-4 per day, €6.50), where connections can be made to Bastia. To reach the **tourist office,** at the corner of av. de Gaulle and r. F. Scamaroni, walk along the port and then up the stairs before the *gare maritime.* (☎04 95 73 11 88; www.bonifacio.com. Open May to mid-Oct. daily 9am-8pm; mid-Oct. to Apr. M-F 9am-noon and 2-6pm, Sa 9am-noon.) Finding affordable rooms is difficult in summer; avoid visiting in August, when prices soar. Try **Hôtel des Étrangers ❹,** av. Sylvère Bohn. (☎04 95 73 01 09; fax 04 95 73 16 97. Singles and doubles €40-71; triples €62; quads €74. MC/V.) **Postal Code:** 20169.

CALVI

Known as Corsica's Côte d'Azur, Calvi offers a lively port as well as gorgeous beaches, turquoise waters, and mountains. six kilometers of **public beaches** dotted by rocky coves wind around the coast. Visit the **citadel** and bask in the setting sun. **Trains** (☎04 95 65 00 61) leave pl. de la Gare, on av. de la République near Port de Plaisance, for Bastia (3hr., 2 per day, €17.50) and Corte (2½hr., 2 per day, €14.60). Les Beaux Voyages **buses** (☎04 95 65 15 02) leave pl. Porteuse d'Eau, by the taxi stand, for Ajaccio (4¾hr., 1 per day, €20.60) and Bastia (4hr., M-Sa 1 per day, €22). To reach the **tourist office,** Port de Plaisance, exit from the back of the train station (facing the beach), turn left, and follow the signs. (☎04 95 65 16 67; www.tourisme.fr/calvi. Open June-Sept. M-Sa 8:30am-1pm and 2:30-7pm; reduced hours off season.) The central **BVJ Corsotel "Hôtel des Jeunes" ❷,** on av. de la République, is opposite the train station. (☎04 95 65 14 15; fax 04 95 65 33 72. Open Apr.-Oct. Dorms €20.) The plush **Il Tramonto ❹,** rte. d'Ajaccio R.N. 199, is near the town center. (☎04 95 65 04 17; www.hotel-iltramonto.com. Open Apr.-Oct. Singles and doubles €49. MC/V.) **Camping International ❶,** on RN 197, is 1km from town, past Super U. (☎04 95 65 01 75; fax 04 95 65 36 11. Open Apr.-Oct. July-Aug. €5 per person, €3 per tent, €1.50 per car; reduced prices off season.) **Postal Code:** 20260.

BASTIA

Corsica's second largest city and a major transport hub, Bastia (pop. 40,000) is a good base from which to explore Cap Corse; with the frenetic new port encompassing the bulk of its coast, it may seem as if the entire city is waiting to move elsewhere. The 14th-century **Citadel,** also called Terra Nova, has beautiful views of the sea. The **Oratoire de St-Roch,** on r. Napoleon, is a jewel-box of a church with crystal chandeliers and meticulous *trompe l'oeil* decoration. The neoclassical towers of the **Eglise St-Jean Baptiste,** pl. de l'Hôtel de Ville, cover an immense interior with gilded domes. **Shuttle buses** leave pl. de la Gare for the **Bastia-Poretta airport** (30min., €8). **Trains** (☎04 95 32 80 61) also leave pl. de la Gare for Ajaccio (4hr., 4 per day, €23.10) and Calvi (3hr., 2 per day, €17.50). **Eurocorse buses** (☎04 95 21 06 30) leave r. Nouveau Port for Ajaccio (3hr., 2 per day, €17). The **tourist office** is on pl. St-Nicholas. (☎04 95 54 20 40; fax 04 95 31 81 34. Open July-Sept. daily 8am-8pm; Oct.-June M-Sa 8:30am-6pm.) **SPAR supermarket** is at 14 r. César Campinchini. (Open M-Sa 8:30am-12:30pm and 4-8:30pm.) The **Hôtel Central ❷,** 3 r. Miot, has large, well-kept rooms. (☎04 95 31 71 12; fax 04 95 31 82 40. Breakfast €5.50. Singles €35-50; doubles €40-68. AmEx/MC/V.) **Les Orangiers camping ❶** is 4km north in Miomo. (☎04 95 33 24 09. Open May. to mid-Oct. €4 per person, €2 per tent, €1.60 per car.) Inexpensive cafes crowd **place St-Nicolas.**

DAYTRIP FROM BASTIA: CAP CORSE. North of Bastia stretches the gorgeous Cap Corse peninsula, a necklace of tiny former fishing villages strung together by a narrow road of perilous curves and breathtaking views. The Cap is a dream for **hikers;** every jungle, forest, and cliff lays claim to some decaying Genoese tower or hilltop chapel. The cheapest and most convenient way to see Cap Corse is to take **bus #4** from pl. St-Nicolas in Bastia, which goes to: Erbalunga (20min., €2); Macinaggio (50min., €6.40); and Marina di Siscu (30min., €2.30). Ask the driver to drop you off wherever you feel the urge to explore. However, most buses serve only the coast; you'll have to hike or hitch to the inland villages.

CORTE

The heart of Corsica, Corte combines breathtaking natural scenery with an intellectual flair. Resting between sheer cliffs and snow-capped peaks, Corte houses the island's only university, whose students keep prices thankfully low. The town's *vieille ville,* with its steep streets and stone **citadel,** has always been a bastion of fierce Corsican patriotism. At the top of r. Scolisca, the **Musée de la Corse** displays a detailed history of Corsica. Entrance includes a visit to the only inland citadel. (☎04 95 45 25 45. Museum open June 20-Sept. 20 daily 10am-8pm; Sept. 21-Nov. Tu-Su 10am-6pm; Dec.-Mar. Tu-Sa 10am-6pm; Apr.-June 19 T-Su 10am-6pm. Citadel closes 1hr. earlier than museum. €5.30, students €3.) Corte's mountains and valleys feature numerous spectacular trails. Choose from **hiking** (call tourist office for maps and info; call 08 92 68 02 20 for weather), **biking,** and **horseback riding.** Rent **horses** at **Ferme Equestre Albadu,** 1.5km from town on N193. (☎04 95 46 24 55. €14 per hr., €38 per half-day, €61 per day.)

Trains (☎04 95 46 00 97) leave from the rotary, where av. Jean Nicoli and the N193 meet, for: Ajaccio (2hr., 4 per day, €12.30); Bastia (1½hr., 4 per day, €10.80); Calvi (2½hr., 2 per day, €14.60) via Ponte-Leccia. Eurocorse Voyages runs **buses** to Ajaccio (1¾hr., M-Sa 2 per day, €11.50) and Bastia (1¼hr., M-Sa 2 per day, €10). To reach the *centre ville* from the train station, turn right on D14 (av. Jean Nicoli), cross two bridges, and follow the road until it ends at **Cours Paoli,** Corte's main drag. A left turn leads to **Place Paoli,** the town center; at the *place*'s top right corner, climb the stairs of r. Scolisca for the citadel and the **tourist office.** (☎04 95 46 26 70; www.corte-tourisme.com. Open July-Aug. daily 9am-8pm; May-June and

Sept. M-Sa 9am-1pm and 2-7pm; Oct.-Apr. M-F 9am-noon and 2-6pm.) The youthful **Hôtel-Residence Porette (H-R) ❷,** 6 allée du 9 Septembre, offers lots of amenities. Bear left from the train station to the stadium and follow it around for another 100m. (☎04 95 45 11 11; fax 04 95 61 02 85. Breakfast €5. Reception 24hr. Singles €21, with bath €31; doubles €23-25/€27-35; triples €51; quads €54.) The huge **Casino supermarket** is near the train station, on allée du 9 Septembre. (Open mid-June to Aug. daily 8:30am-7:45pm; Sept. to mid-June M-F 8:30am-12:30pm and 3-7:30pm, Sa 8:30am-7:30pm.) **Postal Code:** 20250.

THE ALPS (LES ALPES)

The curves of the Chartreuse Valley rise to rugged Alpine crags in the Vercors Range and ultimately crescendo into Europe's highest peak, Mont Blanc (4807m). Winter skiers enjoy some of the most challenging slopes in the world; in summer, hikers take over the same mountains for endless vistas and clean air. Hiking trails are clearly marked but consider investing in a *Topo-Guide* (hiking map). Skiing arrangements should be made in advance; Chamonix and Val d'Isère are the easiest bases. TGV trains will whisk you from Paris to Grenoble and Annecy; from there, Alpine towns are serviced by scenic trains and slower buses.

GRENOBLE

Grenoble's (pop. 156,000) charming *vieille ville* hosts the eccentric cafes, dusty bookshops, and shaggy radicals found in any university town, but its snow-capped peaks and sapphire-blue lakes are cherished by athletes and aesthetes alike.

TRANSPORTATION AND PRACTICAL INFORMATION. Trains arrive in Grenoble at pl. de la Gare from: Annecy (2hr., 18 per day, €14.10); Lyon (1½hr., 27 per day, €15.40); Marseilles (2½-4½hr., 15 per day, €32.30); Nice (5-6½hr., 5 per day, €47.20); and Paris (3hr., 6 per day, €58.80). **Buses** leave from the left of the station for Geneva (3hr., 1 per day, €25.50). From the station, turn right into pl. de la Gare, take the third left on av. Alsace-Lorraine, and follow the tram tracks on r. Félix Poulat and r. Blanchard to reach the **tourist office,** 14 r. de la République. (☎04 76 42 41 41; www.grenoble-isere.info. Open M-Sa 9am-6:30pm, Su 10am-1pm and 2-5pm.) **Postal Code:** 38000.

ACCOMMODATIONS AND FOOD. To get from the station to the **Auberge de Jeunesse (HI) ❶,** 3 av. Victor Hugo, 4km from Grenoble in Echirolles, take bus #16 from Docteur Martin in the *centre ville* (dir.: Le Canton) to Monmousseau. From the stop, turn around and walk along av. Victor Hugo for about 50m. A temporary location (a new hostel is being built for 2004), the two buildings bring an industrial feel to a quiet green space. (☎04 76 09 33 52; grenoble-echirolles@fuaj.org. Sheets €2.70. Reception M-Sa 7:30am-11pm, Su 7:30-10am and 5:30-11pm. Lockout 10am-5:30pm. No curfew. Dorms €9. MC/V.) **Hôtel de la Poste ❷,** 25 r. de la Poste, near the pedestrian zone, has amazing rooms. (☎/fax 04 76 46 67 25. Singles €22; doubles €28; triples €32; quads €37. MC/V.) To reach **Camping Les 3 Pucelles ❶,** 58 r. des Allobroges in Seyssins, take tram A (dir.: Fontaine-La Poya) to Louis Maisonnat, then take bus #51 (dir.: Les Nalettes) to Mas des Iles; it's on the left. (☎04 76 96 45 73; fax 04 76 21 43 73. €7.50 per person, tent, and car.) **University Restaurants (URs) ❶** sell meal tickets in *carnets* of 10 to those with a student ID. (☎04 76 57 44 00. Open during the school year. €2.40.) The two URs in Grenoble are **Restaurant d'Arsonval,** 5 r. d'Arsonval (open M-F 11:30am-1:30pm and 6:30-7:45pm) and **Restaurant du Rabot,** r. Maurice Gignoux. (Open daily noon-1:15pm and 6:30-7:50pm.) **Monoprix,** opposite the tourist office, stocks groceries. (Open M-Sa 8:30am-7:30pm.)

SIGHTS AND THE OUTDOORS. *Téléphériques* (lifts) depart from quai Stéphane-Jay every 10min. for the 16th-century **Bastille,** a fort that hovers above town. Enjoy the views from the top, then descend via the **Parc Guy Pape,** which criss-crosses through the fortress and deposits you just across the river from the train station. (Open July-Aug. M 11am-12:15am, Tu-Su 9:15am-12:15am; Sept.-June reduced hours.) Cross the Pont St-Laurent and go up Montée Chalemont for the **Musée Dauphinois,** 30 r. Maurice Gignoux, with its futuristic exhibits. (Open June-Sept. W-M 10am-7pm; Oct.-May 10am-6pm. €3.20, under 25 free.) Grenoble's major attraction is its proximity to the slopes. The biggest and most developed **ski areas** are to the east in **Oisans;** the **Alpe d'Huez** boasts 220km of trails. (Tourist office ☎04 76 11 44 44. €33 per day, €171 per week.) The **Belledonne** region, northeast of Grenoble, has lower elevation and prices. **Chamrousse,** its biggest and most popular ski area (lift tickets €23 per day, €79-113 per week), has a **youth hostel** (☎04 76 89 91 31; fax 04 76 89 96 96). Only 30min. from Grenoble by **bus** (€8.70), the resort also makes for a hiker's ideal daytrip in summer. Grenoble boasts plenty of funky cafes and bars; most nightspots are between **Place St-André** and **Place Notre-Dame.**

CHAMONIX

The site of the first winter Olympics in 1924, Chamonix (pop. 10,000) is the ultimate ski town, with soaring mountains and the toughest slopes in the world. The town itself combines the dignity of Mont Blanc, Europe's highest peak (4807m), with the exuberant spirit of the numerous Anglo travelers.

TRANSPORTATION AND PRACTICAL INFORMATION. Trains leave av. de la Gare (☎04 50 53 12 98) for: Annecy (2½hr., 7 per day, €16.80); Geneva (2½hr., 7 per day, €20.80); Lyon (4hr., 6 per day, €29.60); and Paris (6½hr., 9 per day, €50-70). Société Alpes Transports **buses** (☎04 50 53 01 15) leave the train station for Annecy (2¼hr., 1 per day, €15) and Geneva (1½hr., 2 per day, €29-32). **Local buses** connect to ski slopes and hiking trails (€1.50). From the station, follow av. Michel Croz, turn left on r. du Dr. Paccard, and take the first right to reach pl. de l'Eglise and the **tourist office,** 85 pl. du Triangle de l'Amitié. (☎04 50 53 00 24; fax 04 50 53 58 90. Open daily July-Aug. 8:30am-7:30pm; Dec.-Feb. 8:30am-7pm; Mar.-June and Sept.-Nov. 9am-noon and 2-6pm.) Across from the tourist office, **Compagnie des Guides,** in Maison de la Montagne, leads ski trips and hikes. (☎04 50 53 22 88; www.cieguides-chamonix.com. Open daily Jan.-Mar. and July-Aug. 8:30am-noon and 3:30-7:30pm; Sept.-Dec. and Apr.-June reduced hours.) **Postal Code:** 74400.

ACCOMMODATIONS AND FOOD. *Gîtes* (mountain hostels) and dorms are cheap, but they fill up fast; call ahead. The **Auberge de Jeunesse (HI) ❶,** 127 montée Jacques Balmat, in Les Pèlerins at the base of the Glacier de Bossons, offers all-inclusive winter **ski packages** (€389-481 per week). Take the bus from the train station or pl. de l'Eglise (dir.: Les Houches) to Pèlerins Ecole (€0.60) and follow the signs uphill; by train, get off at Les Pèlerins and follow the signs. (☎04 50 53 14 52; www.aj-chamonix.fr.st. Breakfast included. Reception daily 8am-noon and 5-10pm. Dorms €13; singles €15.25; doubles €30.50. MC/V.) **Gîte le Vagabond ❶,** 365 av. Ravanel le Rouge, is near the center of town. (☎04 50 53 15 43; www.limelab.com/vagabond. Reception daily 8-10:30am and 4:30pm-1am. 4- to 8-bed dorms €12.50.) Turn left from the base of the Aiguille du Midi *téléphérique*, continue past the main roundabout, and look right to **camp** at **L'Ile des Barrats ❶,** on rte. des Pélerins. (☎/fax 04 50 53 51 44. Reception daily July-Aug. 8am-10:30pm;

May-June and Sept. 8am-noon and 4-7pm. Open May-Sept. €5 per person, €3.60 per tent, €2 per car.) Get groceries at **Super U,** 117 r. Joseph Vallot. (Open M-Sa 8:15am-7:30pm, Su 8:30am-noon.)

HIKING AND SKIING. Whether you've come to climb up the mountains or to ski down them, you're in for a challenge. But wherever you go, be cautious—on average, one person a day dies on the mountains. The **l'Aiguille du Midi** *téléphérique* offers a pricey, knuckle-whitening ascent over forests and snowy cliffs to a needlepoint peak at the top; the ride to the top reveals a fantastic panorama from 3842m. (☎04 50 53 40 00. €32.) Bring your passport to continue by gondola to **Helbronner, Italy** for views of three countries and the **Matterhorn** and **Mont Blanc peaks;** pack a picnic to eat on the glacier (round-trip €50). Hike or take a train to the **ice cave** carved afresh every year by **La Mer de Glace,** a glacier that slides 30m per year. Special trains (☎04 50 53 12 54) run from a small station next to the main one. (Daily July-Aug. Every 20min. 8am-6pm; May-June and early Sept. to mid-Sept. every 30min. 8:30am-5pm; mid-Sept. to Apr. every 30min. 10am-4pm; round-trip €13.) Sunken in a valley, Chamonix is surrounded by mountains ideal for skiing. To the south, **Le Tour-Col de Balme** (☎04 50 54 00 58), above the village of **Le Tour,** is ideal for beginner and intermediate skiers (day-pass €24.60). On the northern side of the valley, **Les Grands Montets** is the *grande dame* of Chamonix skiing, with advanced terrain and remodeled **snowboarding** facilities. (☎04 50 53 13 18. €32 per day.)

ANNECY

With narrow cobblestone streets, winding canals, and a turreted castle, Annecy appears more like a fairy-tale fabrication than a modern city. The **Palais de l'Isle** is a 13th-century fortress that served as a prison for Resistance fighters during World War II. (Open daily June-Sept. 10am-6pm; Oct.-May 10am-noon and 2-6pm. €3.10, students €0.80.) The shaded **Jardins de l'Europe** are Annecy's pride and joy. Although it may be hard to tear yourself away from the city's charming **vieille ville,** Annecy's Alpine forests boast excellent **hiking** and **biking trails.** One of the best hikes begins at the **Basilique de la Visitation,** near the hostel. An exquisite 16km scenic *piste cyclable* (bike route) hugs the lake shore along the eastern coast.

Trains (☎08 36 35 35 35) arrive at pl. de la Gare from: Chamonix (2½hr., 7 per day, €16.70); Grenoble (2hr., 12 per day, €14.10); Lyon (2hr., 9 per day, €18); Nice (7hr., 2 per day, €54.20); and Paris (4hr., 8 per day, €57.60). Autocars Frossard **buses** (☎04 50 45 73 90) leave from next to the station for Geneva (1¼hr., 6 per day, €9) and Lyon (3½hr., 2 per day, €16.40). From the train station, take the underground passage to r. Vaugelas, follow the street left for four blocks, and enter the Bonlieu shopping mall to reach the **tourist office,** 1 r. Jean Jaurès, in pl. de la Libération. (☎04 50 45 00 33; www.lac-annecy.com. Open July-Aug. M-Sa 9am-6:30pm, Su 9am-12:30pm and 1:45-6:30pm; Sept.-June daily 9am-12:30pm and 1:45-6pm.) In summer, you can reach the **Auberge de Jeunesse "La Grande Jeanne" (HI) ❶,** on rte. de Semnoz, via the *ligne d'été* (dir.: Semnoz) from the station (€1); otherwise, take bus #1 (dir.: Marquisats) from the station to Hôtel de Police, turn right on av. du Tresum, and follow signs pointing to Semnoz. (☎04 50 45 33 19; fax 04 50 52 77 52. Breakfast included. Sheets €2.70. Reception daily 8am-10pm. Dorms €12.70. AmEx/MC/V.) **Camp** at **Camping Bélvèdere ❶,** 8 rte. de Semnoz, near the youth hostel. (☎04 50 45 48 30. Reception daily July-Aug. 8am-9pm; mid-Apr. to June and Sept to mid-Oct 8am-8pm. Open mid-Apr. to mid-Oct. €13 for 2 people, tent and car.) A **Monoprix supermarket** fills the better part of pl. de Notre-Dame. (Open M-Sa 8:30am-7:30pm.) **Postal Code:** 74000.

LYON

World-renowned culinary capital, former center of the silk trade, and home to the French Resistance, Lyon (pop. 1.2 million) is a world-class city friendlier and more relaxed than Paris, with a few centuries' more history. While the narrow, twisting streets of *vieux Lyon* are lined with elegant 16th-century townhouses, Lyon is a modern city, with every urban comfort imaginable, from skyscrapers and cafes to speedy transport systems and lush parks to concert halls and *discothèques*.

TRANSPORTATION

Flights: Aéroport Lyon-Saint-Exupéry (LYS; ☎04 72 22 72 21), 25km east of Lyon. The TGV, which stops at the airport, is cheaper than the 50 daily flights to Paris. **Satobuses/ Navette Aéroport** (☎04 72 68 72 17) shuttle to Gare de Perrache, Gare de la Part-Dieu, and subway stops Jean Mace, Grange-Blanche, and Mermoz Pinel (every 20min. until 9pm, €8.20). **Air France** is at 17 r. Victor Hugo, 2*ème* (☎04 20 82 08 20).

Trains: Trains passing through Lyon stop only at **Gare de la Part-Dieu,** bd. Marius Vivier-Merle (M: Part-Dieu), in the business district on the east bank of the Rhône. Trains terminating at Lyon stop also at **Gare de Perrache,** pl. Carnot (M: Perrache). TGV trains to Paris stop at both. **SNCF** info and reservation desk at Part-Dieu open M-F 9am-7pm, Sa 9am-6:30pm; Perrache open M-F 9am-7pm, Sa 9am-6:30pm. To: Dijon (2hr., 6 per day, €21.20); Geneva, Switzerland (2hr., 13 per day, €18.80); Grenoble (1¼hr., 21 per day, €15.40); Marseilles (3hr., 17 per day, €32.90); Nice (6hr., 12 per day, €47.70); Paris (2hr., 26 TGVs per day, €53); Strasbourg (5½hr., 9 per day, €38.40).

Buses: On the lowest level of the Gare de Perrache (☎04 72 77 63 03), and also at Gare de Part-Dieu (**Allô Transports** ☎04 72 61 72 61). Domestic companies include **Philibert** (☎04 78 98 56 00) and **Transport Verney** (☎78 70 21 01). **Eurolines** (☎72 56 95 30) travels out of France. Ask about student prices. Station open M-Sa 8am-8:30pm.

Local Transportation: TCL (☎04 78 71 70 00), has info offices at both train stations and major *Métro* stops. Pocket maps are available from the tourist office or any TCL branch. Tickets are valid for all methods of mass transport, including the Métro, buses, funiculars, and trams. 1hr. **single-fare tickets** €1.40; **carnet of 10** €10.60, students €9.10. The *Ticket Liberté* day pass (€3.80) allows unlimited use of all mass transit for the day. The efficient **Métro** runs 5am-midnight. **Buses** run 5am-9pm (a few until midnight).

Taxis: Taxi Radio de Lyon (☎04 72 10 86 86). To airport from either train station 7am-7pm €36, 7pm-7am €49.

ORIENTATION AND PRACTICAL INFORMATION

Lyon is divided into nine *arrondissements* (districts). The 1*er*, 2*ème*, and 4*ème* lie on the **presqu'île** (peninsula), which juts south toward the confluence of the Saône and Rhône rivers. The **2ème** *(centre ville)* includes the **Perrache** train station and **Place Bellecour.** In the **1er** is the nocturnal **Terraux** neighborhood with cafes and bars. Further north, is the **4ème** and the **Croix-Rousse.** The main pedestrian arteries of the *presqu'île* are **rue de la République,** northeast of pl. Bellecour, and **rue Victor Hugo,** to the south of pl. Bellecour. West of the Saône is Vieux Lyon and **Fourvière Hill.** East of the Rhône (3*ème* and 6-8*ème*) lies the **Part-Dieu** train station, the commercial complex, and most of the city's population. Fourvière and its **Tour Metallique** are to the west, and the **Tour du Crédit Lyonnais** is to the east. Lyon's safe and simple **Métro** is the fastest way to reach the tourist office. From Perrache, take line A (dir.: Bonnevay); from Part-Dieu, take B (dir.: Charpennes) and then line A (dir.: Perrache); get off at Bellecour for the town center.

Tourist Office: In the Tourist Pavilion, at pl. Bellecour, 2*ème* (☎04 72 77 69 69; fax 04 78 42 04 32). M: Bellecour. Free, indispensable **Map and Guide,** hotel reservation office, SNCF desk, and city tours (€6.50-9). The **Lyon City Card** (€13.75-30.50) authorizes unlimited public transport along with admission to the 14 biggest museums and various tours. 1 day €15, 2 days €25, or 3 days €30. Open May-Oct. M-Sa 9am-6pm; Nov.-Apr. daily 10am-6pm.

Consulates: Canada, 21 r. Bourgelat, 2*ème* (☎04 72 77 64 07). 1 block west of Ampere *Métro* stop. Open M-F 9am-noon. **Ireland,** 58 r. Victor Lagrange, 7*ème* (☎06 85 23 12 03). Open M-F 9am-noon. **UK,** 24 r. Childebert, 2*ème* (☎04 72 77 81 70). M: Bellecour. Open M-F 9am-12:30pm and 2-5:30pm. **US,** 16 r. de République, 2*ème* (☎04 78 38 33 03), in the World Trade Center. Open daily 9am-noon and 2-6pm.

Emergency: ☎17.

Police: 47 r. de la Charité (☎04 78 42 26 56).

Hospital/Medical Service: Hôpital Hôtel-Dieu, 1 pl. de l'Hôpital, 2*ème* (☎04 72 41 30 00), near quai du Rhône.

Internet Access: Station-Internet, 4 r. du President Carnot, 2*ème*. €7 per hr., students €5 per hr. Open M-Sa 10am-7pm. Also **Connectix Café,** 19 quai St-Antoine, 2*ème*. €7 per hr. Open M-Sa 11am-7pm.

Post Office: Pl. Antonin Poncet, 2*ème* (☎04 72 40 65 22), near pl. Bellecour. Currency exchange. Open M-F 8am-5pm, Su 8am-12:30pm. Address mail to be held: SURNAME FirstName, *Poste Restante,* pl. Antonin Poncet, **69002** Lyon, France. **Postal Codes:** 69001-69009; last digit indicates *arrondissement.*

ACCOMMODATIONS

As a financial center, Lyon has few empty beds during the work week but plenty of openings on the weekends. Fall is the busiest season; it's easier and cheaper to find a place in the summer, but making reservations is still a good idea. Budget hotels cluster east of **Place Carnot,** near Perrache. Prices rise as you approach **Place Bellecour,** but there are less expensive options north of **Place des Terreaux.**

Hôtel de Paris, 16 r. de la Platière, 1*er* (☎04 78 28 00 95; fax 04 78 39 57 64). Bursting with color and character, Hôtel de Paris has rooms ranging from the classic to the futuristic. Breakfast €6.50. Reception 24hr. Singles €42, doubles €49-75, triples €78. AmEx/MC/V. ❹

Hôtel St-Vincent, 9 r. Pareille, 1*er* (☎04 78 27 22 56; fax 04 78 30 92 87). Just off the Quai St-Vincent, north of passerelle St-Vincent. Hôtel St-Vincent has simple, elegant rooms. Breakfast €5.50. Reception 24hr. Reserve ahead. Singles with shower €31; doubles €38. MC/V. ❸

Auberge de Jeunesse (HI), 41-45 montée du Chemin Neuf, 5*ème* (☎04 78 15 05 50; fax 04 78 15 05 51). Or take the funicular from Vieux Lyon to Minimes, walk down the stairs and go left down the hill for 5min. Breakfast included. Reception 24hr. HI members only. 4- to 8-bed dorms €12.20. ❶

Hôtel Vaubercour, 28 r. Vaubecour, 2*ème* (☎04 78 37 44 91; fax 04 78 42 90 17), on the east bank of the Saône. Elegantly furnished rooms. Breakfast included. Reception 24hr. Reserve ahead. Singles from €23; doubles from €26; triples and quads from €54.15. Extra bed €12.20. MC/V. ❷

Camping Dardilly, 10km from Lyon in a suburb (☎04 78 35 64 55). From the Hôtel de Ville, take bus #19 (dir.: Ecully-Dardilly) to Parc d'Affaires. Pool, TV, and restaurant. Reception 8am-10pm. Electricity €3. €3 per person; €6 per tent; car free. MC/V. ❶

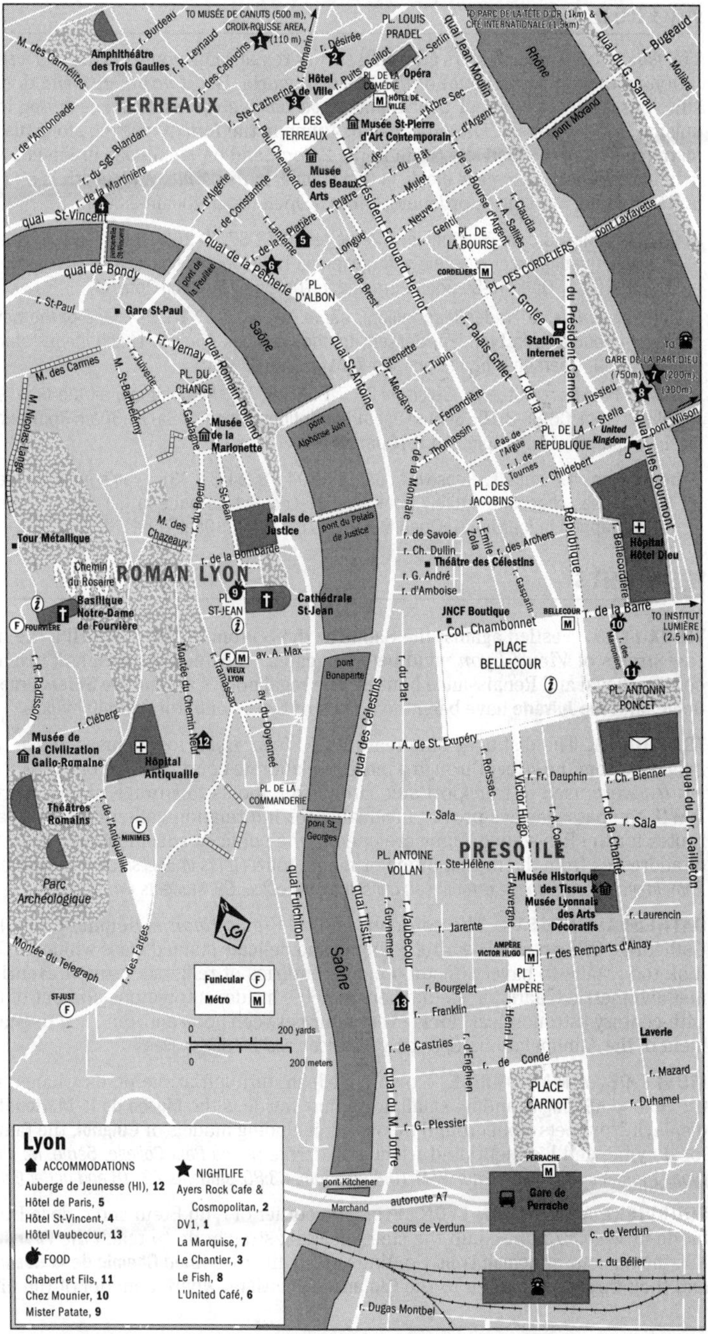
Lyon
ACCOMMODATIONS
Auberge de Jeunesse (HI), 12
Hôtel de Paris, 5
Hôtel St-Vincent, 4
Hôtel Vaubecour, 13
FOOD
Chabert et Fils, 11
Chez Mounier, 10
Mister Patate, 9
NIGHTLIFE
Ayers Rock Cafe & Cosmopolitan, 2
DV1, 1
La Marquise, 7
Le Chantier, 3
Le Fish, 8
L'United Café, 6
Funicular
Métro
0 200 yards
0 200 meters
TO MUSÉE DE CANUTS (500 m), CROIX-ROUSSE AREA, (110 m)
TO PARC DE LA TÊTE D'OR (1km) & CITÉ INTERNATIONALE (1.5km)
TO GARE DE LA PART DIEU (750m) (200m) (300m)
TO INSTITUT LUMIÈRE (2.5 km)
TERREAUX
ROMAN LYON
PRESQU'ILE
Amphithéâtre des Trois Gaules
Hôtel de Ville
Opéra
PL. LOUIS PRADEL
PL. DE LA COMÉDIE
HÔTEL DE VILLE
PL. DES TERREAUX
Musée St-Pierre d'Art Contemporain
Musée des Beaux Arts
PL. DE LA BOURSE
CORDELIERS
PL. DES CORDELIERS
PL. D'ALBON
Gare St-Paul
Station-Internet
PL. DU CHANGE
Musée de la Marionette
Palais de Justice
Tour Métallique
Basilique Notre-Dame de Fourvière
FOURVIÈRE
PL. ST-JEAN
Cathédrale St-Jean
VIEUX LYON
PL. DE LA RÉPUBLIQUE
United Kingdom
PL. DES JACOBINS
Hôpital Hôtel Dieu
Théâtre des Célestins
JNCF Boutique
BELLECOUR
PLACE BELLECOUR
PL. ANTONIN PONCET
Musée de la Civilization Gallo-Romaine
Hôpital Antiquaille
Théâtres Romains
MINIMES
Parc Archéologique
PL. DE LA COMMANDERIE
PL. ANTOINE VOLLAN
Musée Historique des Tissus & Musée Lyonnais des Arts Décoratifs
AMPÈRE VICTOR HUGO
PL. AMPÈRE
Laverie
PLACE CARNOT
ST-JUST
PERRACHE
Gare de Perrache
Rhône
Saône
pont Morand
pont Lafayette
pont Wilson
pont de la Feuillée
passerelle St-Vincent
pont Alphonse Juin
pont du Palais de Justice
pont Bonaparte
pont St. Georges
pont Kitchener Marchand
autoroute A7
cours de Verdun
c. de Verdun
r. du Bélier
r. Dugas Montbel
quai St-Vincent
quai de Bondy
quai de la Pêcherie
quai St-Antoine
quai Romain Rolland
quai des Célestins
quai Fulchiron
quai Tilsitt
quai du M. Joffre
quai Jean Moulin
quai du G. Sarrail
quai Jules Courmont
quai du Dr. Gailleton
r. du Président Edouard Herriot
r. du Président Carnot
r. de la République
r. Victor Hugo
r. Bugeaud
r. Molière
r. Burdeau
M. des Carmélites
r. R. Leynaud
r. des Capucins
r. Romarin
r. Désirée
r. Puits Gaillot
r. J. Serlin
r. de l'Arbre Sec
r. d'Argent
r. Ste-Catherine
r. de l'Annonciade
r. du Sgt. Blandan
r. de la Martinière
r. Paul Chenavard
r. d'Algérie
r. de Constantine
r. Lanterne
r. de la Platière
r. Plâtre
r. du Bât
r. Mulet
r. Neuve
r. Gentil
r. de la Bourse
r. d'Argent
r. Claudia
r. A. Sallès
r. Longue
r. de Brest
r. Grolée
r. St-Paul
r. Fr. Vernay
r. Juiverie
M. des Carmes
M. St-Barthélemy
M. Nicolas Lange
r. Gadagne
r. Grenette
r. Tupin
r. Mercière
r. Palais Grillet
r. Ferrandière
r. Thomassin
Pas de l'Argue
r. J. de Tournes
r. Jussieu
r. Stella
r. Childebert
r. de la Monnaie
r. du Boeuf
r. St-Jean
M. des Chazeaux
Chemin du Rosaire
r. de la Bombarde
r. de Savoie
r. Ch. Dullin
r. G. André
r. d'Amboise
r. Emile Zola
r. des Archers
r. Gasparin
r. Bellecordière
r. de la Barre
r. Col. Chambonnet
r. des Marronniers
av. A. Max
r. Tramassac
av. du Doyenné
Montée du Chemin Neuf
r. R. Radisson
r. Cléberg
r. de l'Antiquaille
r. du Plat
r. A. de St. Exupéry
r. Roissac
r. Fr. Dauphin
r. Ch. Bienner
r. Sala
r. de la Charité
r. A. Comte
r. Ste-Hélène
r. d'Auvergne
r. Laurencin
r. Guynemer
r. Vaubecour
r. Jarente
r. des Remparts d'Ainay
r. Bourgelat
r. Franklin
r. Henri IV
r. de Castries
r. d'Enghien
r. de Condé
r. Mazard
r. Duhamel
r. G. Plessier
Montée du Telegraph
r. des Farges

FOOD

The galaxy of *Michelin* stars adorning Lyon's restaurants confirms the city's reputation as the culinary capital of the Western world. But if *haute cuisine* doesn't suit your wallet, try one of Lyon's many **bouchons,** cozy restaurants serving local cuisine for low prices. *Bouchons* can be found in the **Terraux** district, along **rue des Marronniers** and **rue Mercière** (both in the *2ème*), and on **rue St-Jean** in Vieux Lyon. Ethnic restaurants are near **rue de la République,** in the *2ème*. A **Monoprix** is on r. de la République, at pl. des Cordeliers, *2ème*. (Open M-Sa 8:30am-9:30pm.)

Chez Mounier, 3 r. des Marronniers, 2*ème* (☎04 78 37 79 26). This tiny place satisfies a discriminating local clientele with generous traditional specialties. 4-course *menus* €9.60-15.10. Open Tu-Sa noon-2pm and 7-10:30pm, Su noon-2pm. ❸

Chabert et Fils, 11 r. des Marronniers, 2*ème* (☎04 78 37 01 94). One of the better-known *bouchons* in Lyon. For dessert, try the delicious *Guignol*. Lunch *menùs* start at €8-12.50. Open daily noon-2pm and 7-11pm. MC/V. ❷

Mister Patate, pl. St-Jean, 5*ème* (☎04 78 38 18 79). All potatoes, all the time, with plates from €6.80-8.10. Some vegetarian options. Open M-Sa 11:30am-3pm and 6-11:30pm, Su 11:30-3pm and 6-10pm. ❷

Bernachon, 42 cours F. Roosevelt, 6*ème* (☎04 78 24 37 98). Lyon's grandest *pâtisserie* makes chocolate entirely from scratch. Locals take pride in the *cocons* (chocolates wrapped in marzipan). Open M-F 9am-7pm, Sa 8:30am-7pm.

SIGHTS

VIEUX LYON. Nestled against the Saône at the bottom of Fourvière Hill, the narrow streets of *Vieux Lyon* wind between cafes, tree-lined squares, and magnificent medieval and Renaissance houses. The regal homes around **rue St-Jean, rue du Boeuf,** and **rue Juiverie** have been the homes of Lyon's elite for over 400 years.

TRABOULES. The distinguishing feature of *Vieux Lyon* townhouses, these tunnels lead from the street through a maze of elaborate courtyards. At one time, *traboules* were used to transport silk safely from looms to storage rooms. During WWII, the passageways proved invaluable for information gathering and escape routes for the Resistance. Many are open to the public at specific hours; get a list of addresses from the tourist office or take a tour. *(Tours in English daily in summer at 2pm, irregular hours during rest of year; consult tourist office. €9, students €4.50.)*

CATHEDRALE ST-JEAN. The southern end of *Vieux Lyon* is dominated by the Cathédrale St-Jean, with soaring columns and delicate stained-glass windows that look too fragile to have withstood eight centuries of religious turmoil. Henri IV met and married Maria de Médici here in 1600. Inside, automatons pop out of the 14th-century astronomical clock, every hour between noon and 4pm, in a re-enactment of the Annunciation. *(Open daily 8am-noon and 2-7:30pm. Free.)*

MUSÉE DE LA MARIONETTE. Down r. St-Jean, turn left at the pl. du Change for the **Hôtel de Gadagne** and its small museums. Inside is the **Musée de la Marionette,** displaying puppets from around the world, including models of **Guignol,** the famed local cynic, and his inebriated friend, Gnaffron. *(Pl. du Petit College, 5ème. M: Vieux Lyon. 1hr. tours on request. Open W-M 10:45am-6pm. €3.80, students €2, 18 and under free.)*

FOURVIERE AND ROMAN LYON. From the corner of r. du Bœuf and r. de la Bombarde in *Vieux Lyon*, climb the stairs heading straight up to reach the **Fourvière Hill,** the nucleus of **Roman Lyon.** Continue up via the rose-lined **Chemin de la Rosaire,** and then through a garden to the **Esplanade Fourvière,** where a model of the cityscape points out local landmarks. *(Open daily 6:30am-9:30pm.)* Most prefer to take the less strenuous **funicular** *(la ficelle)* from the head of av. A. Max in Vieux Lyon, off pl. St-Jean, to the top of the hill. The **Tour de l'Observatoire** offers an incredible view—on a clear day, look for Mont Blanc, about 200km east. *(Open daily 6:30am-9:30pm. Tour: Open W-Su 10am-noon and 2-6:30pm. €2, children 14 and under €1.)*

BASILIQUE NOTRE-DAME DE FOURVIÈRE. When the city was spared attack during the Franco-Prussian War, Lyon's archbishop made good on his promise to build a church. Inside the white, meringue-like exterior, the walls are decked with gigantic, gilded mosaics depicting religious scenes, including Joan of Arc at Orléans and the naval battle of Lepante. *(Behind the Esplanade. Open daily 8am-7pm.)*

MUSÉE GALLO-ROMAIN. Almost invisible from the outside, circling deep into the historic hillside of Fourvière, the five levels of this brilliant museum hold a huge collection of arms, pottery, statues, and jewelry. Highlights include six brilliant mosaics and a bronze tablet inscribed with a speech by Lyon's native son, the Roman Emperor Claudius. *(17 r. Cléberg, 5ème. Open Mar.-Oct. Tu-Su 10am-6pm; Nov.-Feb. 10am-5pm. €3.80, students €2.30. Free Th.)*

LA PRESQU'ÎLE AND LES TERREAUX. Monumental squares, statues, and fountains highlight the Presqu'île, a lively area between the Rhône and the Saône. Its heart is **place Bellecour,** an expanse of red gravel lined with shops and flower stalls. The pedestrian **rue Victor Hugo** runs south from Bellecour, lined with boutiques and rollerbladers. To the north, the crowded **rue de la République** is the urban aorta of Lyon. It runs through **place de la République** and terminates at **place Louis Pradel** in the 1*er*, at the tip of the chic and bustling Terreaux district. Nearby, at **place Louis Pradel,** is the 17th-century **Hôtel de Ville.** The **Opéra,** pl. Louis Pradel, is a 19th-century neoclassical edifice supporting what looks like an airplane hangar.

MUSÉE DES BEAUX-ARTS. Second only to the Louvre, this museum includes a comprehensive archeological wing, a distinguished collection of French paintings, works by Spanish and Dutch masters, a wing devoted to the Italian Renaissance, and a lovely sculpture garden. Even the more esoteric works are delightful. Be sure to visit Maillol's bronze *Venus*, whose classic composure is disrupted by a single displaced lock of hair. *(Pl. des Terreaux. Open W-Th and Sa-M 10am-6pm, F 10:30am-8pm. Sculptures closed noon-1pm, paintings closed 1-2pm. €3.80, students €2.)*

CROIX-ROUSSE DISTRICT. Begun in the 15th century, Lyon's silk industry operated 28,000 looms by the 18th century, mainly in the Croix-Rousse district. Mass silk manufacturing is based elsewhere today, and Lyon's few remaining silk workers perform delicate handiwork of reconstructing and replicating rare patterns for museum and chateau displays.

MUSÉE HISTORIQUE DES TISSUS. It's not in the Croix-Rousse quarter, but textile and fashion fans—along with anyone else who's ever worn clothes—will have a field day here. This world-class collection includes wonderfully preserved examples of 18th-century elite garb and luminous silk wall hangings that look like stained glass windows. Included with admission is the neighboring **Musée des Arts Décoratifs,** housed in an 18th-century *hôtel*, with a comprehensive collection of period porcelain, furniture, and ornamental excess. *(34 r. de la Charité, 2ème. Open Tu-Su 10am-noon and 2-5:30pm. Maps in English. Tour in French Su 3pm. €4.60, students €2.30.)*

MODERN LYON. Lyon's newest train station and monstrous space-age mall form the core of the ultra modern **Part-Dieu** district. Many see the place as an eyesore and consider its shops to be its greatest virtue—they are perhaps the only ones in France open between noon and 2pm. Locals call the **Tour du Crédit Lyonnais,** on the other end of the mall, *"Le Crayon"* (the pencil). Next to it, the shell-shaped **Auditorium Maurice Ravel** hosts major cultural events.

CENTRE D'HISTOIRE DE LA RESISTANCE ET DE LA DEPORTATION. The center is housed in a building in which Nazis tortured detainees during the Occupation. Here you'll find assembled documents, photos, and films of the Resistance, which was based in Lyon. The museum forces upon its visitors a haunting awareness of the context of genocide and resistance in France. *(14 av. Bertholet, 7ème. Open W-Su 9am-5:30pm. €3.80, students €2. Admission includes an audio guide in French or English.)*

MUSÉE D'ART CONTEMPORAIN. In the super-modern **Cité International de Lyon** commercial complex, you'll find this extensive and entertaining mecca of modern art. All the museum's exhibits are temporary; the walls themselves are built anew each time. *(Quai Charles de Gaulle 6ème, next to Parc de la Tête d'Or. Bus #4 from M: Foch. Open W noon-10pm, Th-Su noon-7pm. €3.80, students €2.)*

PARC DE LA TÊTE D'OR. The massive park, one of the biggest in Europe, owes its name to a legend that a golden head of Jesus lies buried somewhere within its grounds. The park sprawls over 105 hectares, and you can rent paddle boats to explore its artificial lake and artificial island. Thousands of animals fill the zoo, and the 60,000-bush rose gardens are stunning in summer. *(Open daily Apr. 15-Oct. 14 6am-11pm, Oct. 15-Apr. 14 6am-9pm.)*

NIGHTLIFE

At the end of June is the two-week **Festival du Jazz à Vienne,** which welcomes jazz masters to Vienne, a medieval town south of Lyon, accessible by bus or train. (☎04 74 85 00 05. Tickets €26, students €24.) **Les Nuits de Fourvière** is a two-month summer music festival held in the ancient Théâtre Romain and Odéon. (☎04 72 32 00 00. Tickets and info at the Théâtre Romain and the FNAC shop on r. de la Republique.) The biennial **Festival de Musique du Vieux Lyon,** 5 pl. du Petit Collège, *5ème*, draws artists worldwide between mid-Nov. and mid-Dec. to perform in the churches of Vieux Lyon. (☎04 78 42 39 04. Tickets €10-35.)

Nightlife in Lyon is fast and furious. Students congregate in a series of bars on **rue Ste-Catherine** (*1er*) until 1am before heading to the clubs. There's a whole row of semi-exclusive joints off the Saône, on **Quais Romain Rolland, de Bondy,** and **Pierre Scize** in Vieux Lyon (*5ème*). The city's best and most accessible late-night spots are a strip of riverboat dance clubs by the east bank of the Rhône.

Le Fish, across from 21 quai Augagneur (☎04 72 87 98 98). Has theme nights with salsa, jungle, groove, hip-hop and disco. Cover €11-13, includes first drink, F-Sa free before 11pm. Open W-Sa 10pm-5am.

Le Chantier, 20 r. Ste-Catherine, *1er*. Slip down the spiral slide to reach the dance floor downstairs. Open Tu-Sa 9pm-3am.

Ayers Rock Café, 2, r. Desiree (☎04 78 29 13 45), and the **Cosmopolitan** (☎04 72 07 09 80), next door. A hotspot for students, with lots of drinking (shooters €3) and fun bartenders. Open M-Sa 6pm-3am.

La Marquise (☎04 78 71 78 71), next to Le Fish. Draws big-name DJs for jungle and house. Cover €6. Open W-Sa 11pm-dawn.

L'United Café, impasse de la Pêcherie (☎04 78 29 93 18), in an alley off of quai de la Pêcherie. Plays American and Latino dance hits and the occasional slow song for a mixed gay-lesbian crowd. No cover. Mixed drinks from €3. Open daily 10:30pm-5am.

DV1, 6 r. Violi (☎04 72 07 72 62), off r. Royale. Gay club with drag queens nightly on the huge dance floor. A mostly male, mid-20s to mid-30s crowd. Mixed drinks €3.50-4. Open W-Th and Su 10pm-3am, F-Sa 10pm-5am.

DAYTRIPS FROM LYON

ANNECY. A 2hr. train ride will take you into the fairytale city of Annecy, nestled in the French Alps (see p. 394).

BEAUJOLAIS

Guided bus tours in English are available from Lyon. ☎04 78 98 56 98. Apr.-Oct. Th-F and Su; tours leave at 1:15pm, return to Lyon at 7pm. €34.

The very mention of Beaujolais provokes a thirst for the cool, fruity wine that it exports. Beaujolais lies roughly between the Loire and the Saône, with Lyon and Mâcon on either end. The tourist offices dotting the countryside can provide suggested bike or car routes that wind through vineyards, sleepy villages, and medieval chateaux, with a few *dégustations* (tastings) thrown in for good measure.

BERRY-LIMOUSIN

Too often passed over for beaches and big cities, Berry-Limousin offers peaceful countryside, quaint villages, and fascinating towns. Bourges served as the capital of France and benefited from King Charles VII's financier, Jacques Coeur, who built a lavish string of chateaux. The region later became an artistic and literary breeding ground, home to Georges Sand, Auguste Renoir, and Jean Giraudoux.

BOURGES

In 1433, Jacques Coeur chose Bourges (pop. 80,000) as the site for one of his many chateaux. You'll see more of the unfurnished **Palais Jacques-Coeur** than he ever did, for he was imprisoned for embezzlement before its completion. (Open July-Aug. daily 9am-6pm; Apr.-June and Sept. 9am-noon and 2-6pm; Nov.-Mar. 9am-noon and 2-5pm. €5.50, ages 18-24 €3.50, under 18 free.) The **Cathédrale St-Etienne** has stunning 13th-century handiwork in the **tower** and **crypt,** a dramatic Gothic facade, and stained-glass windows. (Open daily Apr.-Sept. 8:30am-7:15pm; Oct.-Mar. 9am-5:45pm. Closed Su morning. €5.50, students €3.50.) As you exit the cathedral, head right on r. des 3 Maillets and turn left on r. Molière for the **promenade des Remparts,** which offers a quiet stroll past ramparts and flowery gardens.

Trains leave from the station at pl. Général Leclerc (☎02 48 51 00 00) for Paris (2½hr., 5-8 per day, €24) and Tours (1½hr., 10 per day, €17). From the station, follow av. H. Laudier, which turns into av. Jean Jaurès, bear left onto r. du Commerce, and continue down r. Moyenne to reach the **tourist office,** 21 r. Victor Hugo. (☎02 48 23 02 60; www.ville-bourges.fr. Open M-Sa 9am-7pm, Su 10am-7pm.) To get to the **Auberge de Jeunesse (HI) ❶,** 22 r. Henri Sellier, bear right from r. du Commerce on to r. des Arènes, which becomes r. Fernault, cross at the intersection to r. René Ménard, follow it to the right, and turn left at r. Henri Sellier. (☎02 48 24 58 09. Reception M-F 8am-noon and 2pm-1am, Sa-Su 8am-noon and 5-10pm. 3- to 8-bed dorms €8.) For the **Centre International de Séjour, "La Charmille" ❶,** 17 r. Félix-Chédin, cross the footbridge from the station over the tracks. (☎02 48 23 07 40. Singles €15; doubles €22; triples €33. MC/V.) **Place Gordaine, rue des Beaux-Arts, rue Moyenne,** and **rue Mirabeau** are lined with eateries. The **Leclerc supermarket** is on r. Prado off bd. Juraville. (Open M-F 9:15am-7:20pm, Sa 8:30am-7:20pm.) **Le Phénicien ❷,** 13 r. Jean Girard, off pl. Gordaine, offers decent Middle Eastern cuisine. (Open M-Sa 11am-11pm.) **Postal Code:** 18000.

BURGUNDY (BOURGOGNE)

What the Loire Valley is to chateaux, Burgundy is to churches. During the Middle Ages, the duchy was the heart of the religious fever sweeping Europe: abbeys swelled in size and wealth, and towns eager for pilgrim traffic built magnificent cathedrals. Today, Burgundy's production of some of the world's finest wines and delectable dishes, like *coq au vin* and *bœuf bourguignon*, have made this region the homeland of epicures worldwide.

DIJON

Dijon (pop. 160,000) isn't just about the mustard. The capital of Burgundy is a charming city with gardens, a couple of good museums, and fine wines. The diverse **Musée des Beaux-Arts** occupies the east wing of the colossal **Palais des Ducs de Bourgogne,** in pl. de la Libération, at the center of the *vieille ville.* (☎80 74 52 70. Open W-M 10am-6pm. €3.40, students €1.60.) The **Horloge à Jacquemart,** ticking above the tower of **Eglise Notre-Dame,** in pl. Notre-Dame, is worth the maneuevering to see. The brightly tiled **Cathédrale St-Bénigne,** in pl. St-Bénigne, has a spooky circular crypt. (☎03 80 30 14 90. Open daily 9am-6:30pm. Crypt €1.) Next door, the **Musée Archéologique,** 5 r. Dr. Maret, features Gallo-Roman sculpture and Neolithic house wares. (☎03 80 30 88 54. Open June-Sept. Tu-Su 9am-6pm; Oct.-May Tu-Su 9am-noon and 2-6pm. €2.20, students free, Su everyone free.) Get your **Grey Poupon** at the Maille Boutique 32, r. de la Liberté, where *moutarde au vin* has been made since 1747. (☎03 80 30 41 02. Open M-Sa 9am-7pm.)

From the train station at cours de la Gare, at the end of av. Maréchal Foch, **trains** chug to: Lyon (2hr., 7 per day, €21); Nice (7-8hr., 6 per day, €57); and Paris (1½hr., 20 per day, €26). The **tourist office,** on pl. Darcy, is a straight shot down av. Maréchal Foch from the station. (☎03 80 44 11 44. Open July-Aug. daily 9am-8pm; Sept.-June 9am-7pm.) To get to the huge **Auberge de Jeunesse (HI), Centre de Rencontres Internationales ❶,** 1 av. Champollion, take bus #5 (or night bus A) from pl. Grangier to Epirey. (☎03 80 72 95 20; fax 03 80 70 00 61. Breakfast included. Dorms €15; singles €27.50. MC/V.) **Hôtel Montchapet ❸,** 26-28 r. Jacques Cellerier, north of av. Première Armée Française off pl. Darcy, is bright and comfortable. (☎03 80 53 95 00; fax 03 80 58 26 87. Breakfast €5. Reception daily 7am-10:30pm. Check-out 11am. Singles €24-39; doubles €36-46.) **Rue Berbisey** and **rue Monge** host a wide variety of low- to mid-priced restaurants. Fend for yourself at the the **Galeries Lafayette,** 41 r. de la Liberté. (Open M-Sa 9am-7:15pm.) **Postal Code:** 21000.

DAYTRIP FROM DIJON: BEAUNE. Wine has poured out of the well-touristed town of **Beaune,** just south of Dijon (25min., 37 trains per day, €5.70), for centuries. Surrounded by the famous Côte de Beaune vineyards, the town itself is packed with wineries offering free *dégustations* (tastings). The largest of the cellars belongs to **Patriarche Père et Fils,** 5-7 r. du Collège, a labyrinth of 5km of corridors packed with over four million bottles. (☎03 80 24 53 78. Open daily 9:30-11:30am and 2-5:30pm. €9.) The **tourist office,** 1 r. de l'Hôtel-Dieu, lists *caves* (cellars) in the region offering tours. (☎03 80 26 21 30; fax 03 80 26 21 39. Open mid-June to mid-Sept. M-Sa 9:30am-8pm, Su 9:30am-6pm; Oct.-June reduced hours.)

AVALLON AND VÉZELAY

High atop a hillside, the village of Vézelay (pop. 497) watches over dense forests and the misty gold of wheat. The houses, covered with red tile roofs and wild roses, seem lost in time. Vézelay lives up to its billing as one of the most beautiful villages in France. The town has been a major pilgrimage destination since the 11th century, thanks to the relics of Saint Mary Magdelene held within the **basilica.**

The main attraction is the array of grotesque, lyrical carved capitals, which depict Biblical monsters and tales of violence. (Open daily 8am-7:30pm. Suggested donation €4.60.) **Avallon** (pop. 8560) is poor on museums and monuments but can be used as a base from which to explore nearby Vézelay.

Avallon has one of the region's few train stations. **SNCF trains** run to Dijon (2-3hr., 2 per day, €14.90) and Paris (2½-3hr., 4 per day, €24.60). On Saturdays, a **bus** (☎03 86 33 35 95) runs between Vézelay and Avallon. In summer, an **SNCF bus** leaves the train station at Avallon for Vézelay (22min., €3.30). The tiny **tourist office,** r. St-Pierre, just down the street from the church, offers free maps and a *guide pratique* with accommodations listings. (☎03 86 33 23 69. Open June-Oct. daily 10am-1pm and 2-6pm; Nov.-May closed Th.) The closest bank is in Avallon, but the **post office,** r. St-Etienne, has an **ATM.** (☎03 86 33 26 35. Open M-F 8:30am-12:30pm and 1:30-5pm, Sa 8:30-noon.) **Postal Code:** 89450.

ALSACE, LORRAINE, AND FRANCHE-COMTÉ

As first prize in the endless Franco-German border wars, France's northeastern frontier has long been a bloody battlefield. Given its ping-pong history, it's not surprising that the region's cuisine, architecture, and *patois* vary area to area. Germanic influences are most apparent in its cuisine, pairing *baguettes* and wine with sauerkraut and heavy German meats, adding heartiness to traditional delicacies.

STRASBOURG

Just a few kilometers from the Franco-German border, Strasbourg (pop. 260,000) has spent much of its history being annexed by one side or another. Today the city serves as a symbol of French-German *détente*, with as many *winstubs* as *pâtisseries* lining its squares. Strasbourg is also the joint center of the European Union, along with Brussels. This quaint and charming city makes a fantastic stopover.

TRANSPORTATION AND PRACTICAL INFORMATION. Strasbourg is a major rail hub. **Trains** (☎03 88 22 50 50) go to: Luxembourg (2½hr., 14 per day, €25.20); Frankfurt, Germany (3hr., 18 per day, €36.60); Paris (4hr., 16 per day, €34.50); and Zürich, Switzerland (3hr., 18 per day, €39). The **tourist office,** 17 pl. de la Cathédrale, makes hotel reservations for €1.60 plus deposit. (☎03 88 52 28 28. Open June-Sept. M-Sa 9am-7pm, Su 9am-6pm; Oct.-May. daily 9am-6pm.) Rent **bikes** at **Vélocation,** at 4 r. du Maire Kuss, near the train station. (€4.50 per day. €45 deposit and copy of ID.) Access the **Internet** at **Net computer,** 14 quai des Pêcheurs. (☎03 88 36 46 05. €3 per hr. Open M-F 9am-10pm, Sa and Su 11am-10pm.)

ACCOMMODATIONS AND FOOD. Make reservations or arrive early to find reasonable accommodations. **CIARUS (Centre International d'Accueil de Strasbourg) ❷,** 7 r. Finkmatt, has large, spotless facilities with an international atmosphere. From the train station, take r. du Maire-Kuss to the canal, turn left, and follow quais St-Jean, turn left on r. Finkmatt, and it's on the left. (☎03 88 15 27 88; www.ciarus.com. Breakfast included. Reception 24hr. Check-in 3:30pm. Check-out 9am. Curfew 1am. Dorms €16; singles €38; doubles €42. MC/V.) **Hôtel de Bruxelles ❸,** 13 r. Kuhn, is up the street from the train station. Ask to see your room in advance. (☎03 88 32 45 31; fax 03 88 32 22 01. Breakfast €5.30. Singles and doubles €27-44; triples and quads €44-65. MC/V.) **Auberge de Jeunesse, Centre International de Rencontres du parc du Rhin (HI) ❶,** r. des Cavaliers, is 7km from the station and

1km from Germany. From the station, take bus #2 (dir.: Pond du Rhin) to Parc du Rhin. Facing the tourist office, go to the left and look for the flashing red lights. (☎03 88 45 54 20; fax 03 88 45 54 21. Breakfast included. Reception daily 7am-12:30pm, 2-7:30pm, and 8:30pm-1am. Curfew 1am. Dorms €13. MC/V.)

Winstubs are informal places that serve Alsatian specialties such as *choucroute garnie* (spiced sauerkraut served with meats); try the **La Petite France** neighborhood, especially along **rue des Dentelles** and petite **rue des Dentelles.** Explore **place de la Cathédrale, rue Mercière,** or **rue du Vieil Hôpital** for restaurants, and **place Marché Gayot,** off r. des Frères, for lively cafes. For groceries, swing by the **ATAC,** 47 r. des Grandes Arcades, off pl. Kléber. (Open M-Sa 8:30am-8pm.)

SIGHTS AND ENTERTAINMENT. The ornate Gothic **Cathédrale de Strasbourg** sends its tower 142m skyward. Inside, the **Horloge Astronomique** demonstrates the wizardry of 16th-century Swiss clockmakers. While you wait for the clock to strut its stuff—daily at 12:30pm, apostles troop out of the clockface while a cock crows to greet Saint Peter—check out the **Pilier des Anges** (Angels' Pillar), a masterpiece of Gothic sculpture. You can climb the **tower** in front of the clock like the young Goethe, who scaled its 330 steps regularly to cure his fear of heights. (Cathedral open M-Sa 7-11:40am and 12:45-7pm, Su 12:45-6pm. Tickets for the clock on sale 8:30am in cathedral and 11:45am at south entrance. €0.80. Tower open daily 9am-6:30pm. €3; children €1.50.) **Palais Rohan,** 2 pl. du Château, houses three small but excellent museums: the **Musée des Beaux-Arts, Musée des Arts Décoratifs,** and **Musée Archéologique.** (Open Tu-Su 10am-6pm. €3 each; students €1.50.) Take bus #23, 30, or 72 to **L'Orangerie,** Strasbourg's most spectacular park; free concerts play in the summer at the Pavilion Joséphine (Th-Tu 8:30pm).

LA ROUTE DU VIN (WINE ROUTE)

The Romans were the first to ferment Alsatian grapes; today over 150 million bottles are sold yearly. The Alsatian vineyards flourish along a 170km corridor known as **La Route du Vin** (Wine Route), which stretches south along the foothills of the Vosges through 100 towns between **Strasbourg** (see p. 403) and **Mulhouse** (see p. 405). Hordes of tourists are drawn each year to explore the medieval villages and the numerous free *dégustations* (tastings) along the route. Accommodations tend to be expensive and transportation is infrequent in smaller towns; **Colmar** and **Sélestat** are excellent bases from which to explore the Route. Information can be found at the **Centre d'Information du Vin d'Alsace,** 12 av. de la Foire aux Vins (☎03 89 20 16 20), at the Maison du Vin d'Alsace in Colmar, and **tourist offices** in Strasbourg.

SÉLESTAT

Sélestat (pop. 17,200), between Colmar and Strasbourg, is a charming town often overlooked by tourists on their way to larger Route cities. The **Bibliothèque Humaniste,** 1 r. de la Bibliothèque, founded in 1452, contains a fascinating collection of ancient documents produced during Sélestat's 15th-century humanistic boom. (Open July-Aug. M and W-F 9am-noon and 2-6pm, Sa 9am-noon and 2-5pm, Su 2-5pm; Sept.-June closed Su. €3.50.) The **tourist office,** 10 bd. Gén. Leclerc, in the Commanderie St-Jean, rents **bikes.** (☎03 88 58 87 20; www.selestat-tourisme.com. €12.50 per day. Open May-Sept. M-F 9am-12:30pm and 1:30-7pm, Sa 9am-noon and 2-5pm, Su 9am-3pm; Oct.-Apr. M-F 8:30am-noon and 1:30-6pm, Sa 9am-noon and 2-5pm.) The **Hôtel de l'Ill ❷,** 13 r. des Bateliers, has bright rooms. (☎03 88 92 91 09. Breakfast €4.60. Reception daily 7am-3pm and 5-11pm. Singles €23; doubles €37; triples €53. MC/V.) **Camping Les Cigognes ❶** is on the south edge of the *vieille ville.* (☎03 88 92 03 98. Reception July-Aug. daily 8am-noon and 3-10pm; May-June and Sept.-Oct 8am-noon and 3-7pm. Open May-Oct. July-Aug. €9.15 per person; reduced prices Sept.-June.) You'll find food on **rue des Chevaliers** and **rue de l'Hôpital. Postal Code:** 67600.

COLMAR

Colmar's (pop. 65,000) bubbling fountains, crooked lanes, and pastel houses evoke an intimate charm despite packs of tourists. The collection of **Musée Unterlinden,** 1 r. d'Unterlinden, ranges from Romanesque to Renaissance, with Grünewald's *Issenheim Altarpiece.* (Open daily Apr.-Oct. 9am-6pm; Nov.-Mar. W-M 10am-5pm. €7, students €5.) The **Eglise des Dominicains,** on pl. des Dominicains, has Colmar's other major masterpiece, Schongauer's *Virgin in the Rose Bower.* (Open Apr.-Dec. daily 10am-1pm and 3-6pm. €1.30, students €1.)

To get to the **tourist office,** 4 r. d'Unterlinden, from the train station, turn left on av. de la République (which becomes r. Kléber) and follow it to the right to pl. Unterlinden. (☎03 89 20 68 92; info@ot-colmar.fr. Open July-Aug. M-Sa 9am-7pm, Su 9:30am-2pm; Apr.-June and Sept.-Oct. M-Sa 9am-6pm, Su 10am-2pm; Nov.-Mar. M-Sa 9am-noon and 2-6pm, Su 10am-2pm.) To reach the **Auberge de Jeunesse (HI) ❶,** 2 r. Pasteur, take bus #4 (dir.: Logelbach) to Pont Rouge. (☎03 89 80 57 39. Breakfast included. Sheets €3.50. Reception daily July-Aug. 7-10am and 5pm-midnight; Sept.-June 5-11pm. Lockout 10am-5pm. Curfew midnight. No reservations. Open mid-Jan. to mid-Dec. Dorms €12; singles €17; doubles €29. MC/V.) Take bus #1 (dir.: Horbourg-Wihr) to Plage d'Ill for **Camping de l'Ill ❶,** on rte. Horbourg-Wihr. (☎03 89 41 15 94. Reception daily July-Aug. 8am-10pm; Feb.-June and Sept.-Nov. 8am-8pm. Open Feb.-Nov. €2.90 per person, €1.70 per child, €3.05 per site. Electricity €2.40.) **Monoprix** is on pl. Unterlinden. (Open M-F 8am-8pm, Sa 8am-8pm.) *Brasseries* are in **La Petite Venise** and the **Quartier des Tanneurs. Postal Code:** 68000.

MULHOUSE

A bustling city of 110,000, Mulhouse boasts a plethora of fabulous museums on its periphery. Its historical district centers around the festive **Place de la Réunion,** which commemorates the "reunion" of Mulhouse with distant Paris in 1798 and 1918. Nearby is the **Temple de St-Etienne,** one of France's few Protestant Gothic cathedrals. (☎03 89 66 30 19. Open May-Sept. M and W-Su 10am-noon and 2-6pm.) The **Musée Français du Chemin de Fer,** 2 r. Alfred de Glehn, maintains a stunning collection of gleaming engines and railway cars. Take bus #17 (dir.: Musées) from Porte Jeune Place. (☎03 89 42 25 67. Open May.-Sept. daily 9am-6pm, Oct.-Apr. 9am-5pm. €7.60, students €4.) Over 500 cars in mint condition are on display at the **Musée National de l'Automobile,** 192 av. de Colmar. Take buses #1, 4, 11, 13, or 17 north to Musée Auto. (☎03 89 33 23 23. Open July-Aug. daily 9am-6:30pm; Sept.-June reduced hours. €10, students €7.50.) **Trains** run from bd. Général Leclerc to Paris (4½hr., 9 per day, €42.70) and Strasbourg (1hr., 14 per day, €13.30). The **tourist office,** 9 av. Foch, is two blocks up from the right end of the train station. (☎89 35 48 48; www.ot.ville-mulhouse.fr. Open July-Aug. M-F 10am-7pm, Su 10am-noon; Sept.-June reduced hours.) To get to the newly renovated **Auberge de Jeunesse (HI) ❶,** 37 r. d'Ilberg, take bus #2 (bus S1 after 8:30pm; dir.: Loteaux) to Salle des Sports. (☎03 89 42 63 28. Sheets €2.70. Reception daily 8am-noon and 5-11pm, until midnight in summer. HI members only. Dorms €8.10. MC/V.) Numerous eateries line **rue de l'Arsenal,** or buy **groceries** at **Monoprix,** on the corner of r. du Sauvage and r. des Maréchaux. (Open M-F 8:15am-8pm, Sa 8:15am-7pm.) **Crampous Mad ❶,** 14 impasse des Tondeurs, serves crepes (€2-7) on a bright terrace. (Open M-F 11:30am-10pm, Sa 11:30am-11pm. MC/V.) **Postal Code:** 68100.

BESANÇON

As far back as 58 BC, when Julius Caesar founded a military post here, Besançon (pop. 120,000) has intrigued military strategists because of its prime geographic location. Today, Besançon boasts a smart, sexy student population and an impressive number of museums and discos. See the city's well-preserved Renaissance buildings from high up in the Vauban's **citadel,** at the end of r. des Fusilles de la Résistance. Within the citadel, the **Musée de la Résistance et de la Déportation** (☎81 65 07 55) chronicles the Nazi rise to power and the German occupation of France. Other sights include a natural history museum, a zoo, an aquarium, and a folk arts museum. (☎03 81 65 07 50. Grounds open July-Aug. daily 9am-7pm; Apr.-June and Sept.-Oct. 9am-6pm; Nov.-Mar. 10am-5pm. Museums open Apr.-Oct. daily 9am-6pm; Nov.-Mar. 10am-5pm. €7, students €6.) The **Cathédrale St-Jean,** beneath the citadel, holds two treasures: the white marble **Rose de St-Jean** and the intricate 19th-century **Horloge Astronomique.** (Open W-M 9am-7pm. Free.) The **Musée des Beaux-Arts et d'Archéologie,** on pl. de la Révolution, houses an exceptional collection ranging from ancient Egyptian mummies to works by Matisse. (☎03 81 87 80 49. Open W-M 9:30am-6pm. €4, students free; Su and holidays free.) The area between **rue C. Pouillet** and **rue Pont Battant** buzzes with nightlife. **Madigan's,** pl. 8 Septembre, is packed every night with a young crowd. (Open Su-Th 7pm-1am, F-Sa until 2:30am.) Shoot pool at the surprisingly hip **Pop Hall,** 26 r. Proudhon. (Open Su-Th 6pm-1am, F-Sa until 2am.)

Trains pull up at the station on av. de la Paix (☎08 36 35 35 35) from: Dijon (1hr., 25 per day, €11.70); Paris Gare de Lyon (2hr., 8 per day, €42.50); and Strasbourg (3hr., 10 per day, €25.70). **Monts Jura buses,** 9 r. Proudhon (☎03 81 21 22 00), go to Pontarlier (1hr., 6 per day, €7.80). From the station, walk downhill; turn onto av. Maréchal Foch, and continue to the left as it becomes av. de l'Helvétie, until you reach pl. de la Première Armée Française. The *vieille ville* is across the pont de la République; the **tourist office,** 2 pl. de la Première Armée Française, is in the park to the right. (☎03 81 80 92 55; www.besancon.com. Open Apr.-Sept. M 10am-7pm, Tu-Sa 9:30am-7pm; mid-June to mid-Sept. also open Su 10am-noon and 3-5pm; Oct.-Mar. M 10am-6pm, Tu-Sa 9am-6pm.) Surf the **Internet** for free at **Centre Information Jeunesse (CIJ),** 27 r. de la République. (Open M and Sa 1:30-6pm, Tu-F 10am-noon and 1:30-6pm.) Cheap beds can be found at the **Centre International de Séjour ❷,** 19 r. Martin-du-Gard. Take bus #8 (dir.: Campus) from the Foch stop near the station, in front of a gas station, to Intermarché. (☎03 81 50 07 54. Reception 7am-1pm. Singles €17.50; doubles €26.60; triples €30.) A variety of restaurants line **rue Claude-Pouillet.** Buy groceries at **Monoprix,** 12 Grande Rue. (Open M-Sa 8:30am-8pm.) **La Boîte à Sandwiches ❶,** 21 r. du Lycée, off r. Pasteur, serves sandwiches and salads. (Open M-Sa 11:30am-2pm and 7pm-midnight.) **Postal Code:** 25000.

DAYTRIP FROM BESANÇON: PONTARLIER AND THE JURA. The sedate town of **Pontarlier** is a good base from which to explore the oft-overlooked **Haut-Jura mountains.** The Jura are best known for cross-country **skiing;** eight trails cover every skill level. (Day pass €5, under 17 €2; available at the **Le Larmont** and **Le Malmaison** trails.) Le Larmont is the closest Alpine ski area (☎03 81 46 55 20). **Sport et Neige,** 4 r. de la République (☎03 81 39 04 69), rents skis (€38 per week). In summer, **fishing, hiking,** and **mountain biking** are popular sports. Rent a **bike** from **Cycles Pernet,** 23 r. de la République. (☎03 81 46 48 00. €15 per day with passport deposit. Open Tu-Sa 9am-noon and 2-7pm.) Monts Jura **buses** (☎03 81 39 88 80) run to Besançon (1hr., 6 per day, €7.30). The **tourist office,** 14bis r. de la Gare, has free regional guides and sells maps. (☎03 81 46 48 33; fax 03 81 46 83 32.) **L'Auberge de Pontarlier (HI) ❶,** 2 r. Jouffroy, is clean and central. (☎03 81 38 54 54. Breakfast €3. Sheets €2.70. Reception 8am-noon and 5:30-10pm. Dorms €8.) **Postal Code:** 25300.

NANCY

Nancy (pop. 100,000) has always been passionate about beauty: the town that spawned the art-nouveau "Nancy school" is today the artistic and intellectual heart of modern Lorraine. The elaborate **Place Stanislas** houses three neoclassical pavilions separated by gilt iron fences, with *son-et-lumière* spectacles held nightly at 10pm in July and August. The collection in the **Musée des Beaux-Arts,** 3 pl. Stanislas, spans from the 14th century to the present. (☎03 83 85 30 72. Open W-M 10am-6pm. €4.60, students €2.30; W and 1st Su students free.) Pass through the five-arch **Arc de Triomphe** to the tree-lined **Place de la Carrière.** Portals of pink roses lead into the aromatic **Roseraie,** in the relaxing **Parc de la Pépinière,** just north of pl. de la Carrière. (Open May-Sept. 6:30am-11:30pm; Oct.-Apr. reduced hours. Free.)

Trains (☎03 83 22 12 46) depart from the station at pl. Thiers to: Metz (40min., 24 per day, €8); Paris (3hr., 14 per day, €35); and Strasbourg (1hr., 17 per day, €19). Head left from the station and turn right on r. Raymond Poincaré, which leads straight to pl. Stanislas, the center of the city, and the **tourist office.** Ask for the invaluable *Le Fil d'Ariane* guide. (☎03 83 35 22 41; www.ot-nancy.fr. Open Apr.-Sept. M-Sa 9am-7pm, Su 10am-5pm; Oct.-Mar. M-Sa 9am-6pm, Su 10am-1pm.) Access the Internet at **E-café,** on r. des Quatre Eglises. (☎03 83 35 47 34. €5.40 per hr. Open M-Sa 9am-9pm, Su 2-8pm.) **Centre d'Accueil de Remicourt (HI) ❶,** 149 r. de Vandoeuvre, is in Villiers-lès-Nancy, 4km away. From the station, take bus #122 to St-Fiacre (dir.: Villiers Clairlieu; 2 per hr., last bus 8pm; confirm direction with the driver); head downhill from the stop, and turn right on r. de la Grange des Moines, which turns into r. de Vandoeuvre. Look for signs pointing to Château de Remicourt. (☎03 83 27 73 67; fax 03 83 41 41 35. Breakfast included. Reception daily 9am-9pm. 3- to 4-bed dorms €12.50; doubles €29. MC/V.) **Hôtel Flore ❸,** 8 r. Raymond, is bright and homey. (☎03 83 37 63 28. Reception daily 7:30am-2am. Singles €26-32; doubles €37-40; triples €43. AmEx/MC/V.) Restaurants line **rue des Maréchaux, place Lafayette,** and **place St-Epvre.** A **SHOPI** market sits at 26 r. St-Georges. (Open M-Sa 9am-8pm) **Postal Code:** 54000.

METZ

Modern Metz (pop. 200,000) is a stroller's city, a place of classic fountains, sculptured gardens, and golden cobblestoned streets that reflect the town's mixed Franco-German heritage. The golden **Cathédrale St-Etienne,** pl. d'Armes, is the third-tallest nave in France. Marvel at its 6500m of stained-glass windows, including some by Marc Chagall. (Open M-Sa 9am-7pm, Su 1pm-7pm. Free.) At the other end of the r. des Clercs from pl. d'Armes lies the **Esplanade,** a broad formal garden accented by leisurely promenades. Down the steps from the Esplanade, shady paths wind through wooded parkland along the **Lac aux Cygnes.** Afterward, get down in the student-packed bars and cafes in **Place St-Jacques.**

Trains leave pl. du Général de Gaulle for: Luxembourg (45min., 1 per hr., €10.20); Nancy (40min., 31 per day, €8); Paris (3hr., 10 per day, €33); and Strasbourg (1½hr., 12 per day, €18). To get from the station to the **tourist office,** on pl. d'Armes, turn right and then left onto r. des Augustins; at pl. St-Simplice, turn left onto r. de la Tête d'Or, and right on r. Fabet. Or, take bus #11 (dir.: St-Eloy) or #9 (dir.: J. Bauchez) from pl. Charles de Gaulle to pl. d'Armes. (☎03 87 55 53 76. Open July-Aug. M-Sa 9am-9pm, Su 11am-5pm; Mar.-June and Sept.-Oct. M-Sa 9am-7pm, Su 11am-5pm; Nov.-Feb. M-Sa 9am-6:30pm, Su 11am-5pm.) Surf the Internet for free at the tourist office, or for free at **Espace Multimédia,** 6 r. Four de Cloitre, near the cathedral. (☎03 87 36 56 56. Open M 1-6pm and T-Fr 9am-6pm.) Take bus #3 (dir.: Metz-Nord) or 11 (dir.: St-Eloy) to Pontiffroy to reach the well-run **Auberge de Jeunesse (HI) ❶,** 1 allée de Metz Plage. (☎03 87 30 44 02; fax 03 87 33 19 80. Breakfast included. Reception daily 7:30-10am and 5-10pm. 2- to 6-bed dorms €11.30 per person. Nonmembers add €2.90. MC/V.) Cheap eateries lie on **rue du Pont des Morts,** in the pedestrian district, and toward the station on **rue Coisin.** The **ATAC supermarket** is in the Centre St-Jacques. (Open M-Sa 8:30am-7:30pm.) **Postal Code:** 57000.

VERDUN

Reminders of the Battle of Verdun, one of the worst battles of World War I, are everywhere in the town, from the many war memorials to the pockmarked surface of the land. Despite Verdun's painstaking efforts to rebuild, this city's main draw will always be its tragic history. Built in 1200, the **Porte Chaussée,** on the quai de Londres, served as a prison and guard tower, and later as the entrance for troops during World War I. At the other end of the r. Frères Boulhaut, Rodin's bronze **Victory** guards the Port St-Paul. Marking the edge of the *haute ville*, the **Monument à la Victoire** rises above a flight of 72 granite steps. This tower stands atop the remains of the **Eglise de la Madeleine,** built in 1049 and bombed beyond recognition in 1916. (Open daily 9am-noon and 2-6pm.) The 4km of underground galleries in the massive **Citadelle Souterraine,** down r. de Rû, held supplies for the 10,000 soldiers sheltered there on their way to the front. (Open July-Aug. daily 9am-6:30pm; Apr.-June and Sept. 9am-6pm; Nov.-Mar. 9:30am-noon and 1-5pm. €5.40.)

Trains leave from pl. Maurice Genovoix for Metz (1½hr., 5 per day, €11). **Buses** run from pl. Vauban to Metz (2hr., 8 per day, €11). To get to the **tourist office,** pl. de la Nation, from the train station, take av. Garibaldi until you reach the bus station, turn left onto r. Frères Boulhaut, and continue until you reach the Port Chaussée. Turn left again, cross the bridge onto pl. de la Nation and the office will be on your right. (☎03 29 86 14 18; fax 03 29 84 22 42. Open July-Aug. M-Sa 8:30am-7:30pm, Su 9am-5pm; May-June and Sept. M-Sa 8:30am-6:30pm, Su 9am-5pm; Mar.-Apr. and Oct.-Feb. reduced hours.) The **Auberge de Jeunesse (HI) ❶,** pl. Monseigneur Ginisty, next to the cathedral at the Centre Mondial de la Paix, has simple, renovated rooms. From the train station, cross to the island with the Match supermarket in front of the station and turn right onto r. Louis Maury; continue up on r. de la Belle Vierge and the hostel is at the end of the cathedral. (☎03 29 86 28 28; fax 03 29 86 28 82. Reception M-F 8am-1pm and 5pm-11pm; Sa-Su 8-10am and 5-9pm. No curfew. Bunks €8.85. Nonmembers add €2.90. MC/V.) **Postal Code:** 55107.

CHAMPAGNE AND THE NORTH

John Maynard Keynes once remarked that his major regret in life was not having consumed enough champagne; a trip through the rolling vineyards and fertile plains of Champagne promises many opportunities to avoid his mistake. The term *champagne* is fiercely guarded; the name can only be applied to wines made from regional grapes and produced according to a rigorous, time-honored method. To the north, Flanders, the coastal Pas de Calais, and Picardy remain the final frontiers of tourist-free France. As you flee the ferry ports, don't overlook the intriguing Flemish culture of Arras and the world-class art collections of Lille.

REIMS

Reims (pop. 185,000) delights in the bubbly champagne of its famed *caves* and the beauty of its architectural masterpieces. The **Cathédrale de Notre-Dame,** built with golden limestone quarried in the Champagne *caves*, features sea-blue stained-glass windows by Marc Chagall. (☎03 26 77 45 25. Open daily 7:30am-7:30pm. Tours daily 2:30pm; less frequently in Oct. and late Mar. to mid-June. €5.35, students €3.05.) Enter the adjacent **Palais du Tau,** at pl. du Cardinal Luçon, for dazzling 16th-century tapestries. (☎03 26 47 81 79. Open July-Aug. daily 9:30am-

6:30pm; Sept. to mid-Nov and mid-Mar. to June daily 9:30am-12:30pm and 2-6pm; mid-Nov. to mid-Mar. M-F 10am-noon and 2-5pm, Sa-Su 10am-noon and 2-6pm. €5.50, students €3.50.) The firm of **Champagne Pommery,** 5 pl. du Général Gouraud, boasts the largest *tonneau* (vat) in the world. (☎03 26 61 62 56. Tours daily Apr.-Oct. 11am-7pm. €7, students €3.50.) For good deals on champagne, look for sales on local brands and check prices at Monoprix. Good bottles start at €9.15.

Trains (☎26 88 11 65) leave bd. Joffre for Paris (1½hr., 11 per day, €18.75). To get from the train station to the **tourist office,** 2 r. Guillaume de Machault, follow the right-hand curve of the rotary to pl. Drouet d'Erlon, turn left onto r. de Vesle, and turn right on r. du Tresor; it's on the left before the cathedral. (☎03 26 77 45 25; fax 03 26 77 45 27. Open mid-Apr. to mid-Oct. M-Sa 9am-7pm, Su 10am-6pm; mid-Oct. to mid-Apr. M-Sa 9am-6pm, Su 10am-5pm.) Inexpensive hotels cluster west of pl. Drouet d'Erlon, above the cathedral, and near the *mairie.* The sunny and spotless **Au Bon Accueil ❷,** 31 r. Thillois, is just off the central pl. d'Erlon. (☎03 26 88 55 74; fax 03 26 05 12 38. Breakfast €4.50. Reception 24hr. Reserve ahead. Singles €18-21; doubles €36-44. MC/V.) **Place Drouet d'Erlon** is crowded with cafes, restaurants, and bars. Relax at **Le Kraft ❸,** 5 r. Salin, which includes restaurant, bar, and lounge. (☎03 26 05 29 29. Open M-F 11am-3am, Sa 6pm-3am.) **Monoprix supermarket** is at r. de Vesle and r. de Talleyrand. (Open M-Sa 8:30am-9pm.) **Postal Code:** 51100.

DAYTRIP FROM REIMS: ÉPERNAY. Épernay (pop. 30,000), at the juncture of three wealthy grape-growing regions, is appropriately ritzy. **Avenue de Champagne** is distinguished by its palatial mansions, lush gardens, and swanky champagne firms. Both tours below offer a *petite dégustation* (tasting) for those over 16. **Moët & Chandon,** 20 av. de Champagne, produces the king of all wines: **Dom Perignon.** (☎03 26 51 20 20. Open Apr. 1-Nov. 11 daily 9:30-11:30am and 2-4:30pm; Nov. 12-Mar. M-F only. 1hr. tour with one glass €6.) Ten minutes away is **Mercier,** 70 av. de Champagne, the self-proclaimed "most popular champagne in France," who gives tours in roller-coaster-like cars. (☎26 51 22 22. Open Mar.-Nov. M-F 9:30-11:30am and 2-4:30pm, Sa-Su 9:30-11:30am and 2-5pm; Dec. 1-19 and Jan. 13-Feb. Th-M only. 30min. tours €4.) **Trains** leave cour de la Gare for Paris (1¼hr., 18 per day, €16.60) and Reims (25min., 16 per day, €5.20). From the station, walk straight ahead through pl. Mendès France, go one block up r. Gambetta to **Place de la République,** and turn left on av. de Champagne to reach the **tourist office,** 7 av. de Champagne. (☎03 26 53 33 00. Open Easter-Oct. 15 M-Sa 9:30am-noon and 1:30-7pm, Su 11am-4pm; Oct. 16-Easter M-Sa 9:30am-5:30pm.) **Postal Code:** 51200.

TROYES

While the city plan of Troyes resembles a champagne cork, this city shares little with its grape-crazy northern neighbors. Gothic churches, 16th-century mansions, and an abundance of museums attest to the city's colorful role in French history, dating back to the Middle Ages. The **Musée d'Art Moderne,** on pl. St-Pierre, has over 2000 modern works by French artists, including Rodin, Degas, and Seurat. (Open Tu-Su 11am-6pm. €6, students €0.80; W free.) Cinemas and pool halls rub elbows with chic boutiques on **rue Emile Zola.** On warm evenings, *Troyens* fill the cafes and taverns of **rue Champeaux** and **rue Mole** near pl. Alexandre Israel.

Trains run from av. Maréchal Joffre to Paris (1½hr., 14 per day, €8.60) and Mulhouse (3hr., 9 per day, €31.80). The **tourist office,** 16 bd. Carnot, near the station, helps reserve rooms. (☎03 25 82 62 70; www.tourisme-troyes.fr. Open M-Sa 9am-12:30pm and 2-6:30pm.) **Les Comtes de Champagne ❸,** 56 r. de la Monnaie, sports large and airy rooms. (☎03 25 73 11 70; fax 03 25 73 06 02. Reception 7am-10:30pm. Call ahead. Singles €25-31; doubles €28-34; triples €44-55; quads €49-58.) **Camping Municipal ❶,** 2km from Troyes, on N60, has showers and laundry. Take bus #1 (dir.: Pont St-Marie) and ask to be let off at the campground. (☎03 25 81 02 64. €4 per person, €4.60 per tent or car. Open Apr. to mid-Oct.) *Crêperies* and inexpensive eateries lie near r. Champeaux, in *quartier* St-Jean, and on **rue de la Cité,** near the cathedral. You can stock up at **Monoprix supermarket,** 78 r. Emile Zola. (Open M-Sa 8:30am-8pm.) **Postal Code:** 10000.

DAYTRIPS FROM TROYES: LES GRANDS LACS. About 30km from Troyes are the freshwater lakes of the **Forêt d'Orient. Lake Orient** welcomes sunbathers, swimmers, and windsurfers; **Lake Temple** is reserved for fishing and bird-watching; and **Lake Amance** roars with speedboats from **Port Dierville.** The **Comité Départmental du Tourisme de l'Aube,** 34 quai Dampierre, provides information on hotels and restaurants. (☎03 25 42 50 00; fax 03 25 42 50 88. Open M-F 8:45am-noon and 1:30-6pm.) The Troyes tourist office has bus schedules for routes to the Grands Lacs.

LILLE

A longtime international hub with a rich Flemish ancestry and exuberant nightlife, Lille (pop. 175,000) exudes big-city charm without the hassle. The impressive **Musée des Beaux-Arts,** on pl. de la République (M: République), boasts a wide display of 15th- to 20th-century French and Flemish masters. (☎03 20 06 78 00. Open M 2-6pm, W-Th and Sa-Su 10am-6pm, F 10am-7pm. €4.60, students €3.05.) The **Musée d'Art Moderne,** 1 allée du Musée, in the suburb of Villeneuve d'Ascq, showcases Cubist and postmodern art, including works by Braque, Picasso, Léger, Miró, and Modigliani. Take the tram (dir.: 4 Cantons) to Pont du Bois, then take bus #41 (dir.: Villeneuve d'Ascq) to Parc Urbain-Musée. (☎03 20 19 68 68. Open W-M 10am-6pm; free 1st Su of every month 10am-2pm. €6.55, students €1.55.) The **Vieille Bourse** (Old Stock Exchange), on pl. Général de Gaulle, epitomizing the Flemish Renaissance, houses flower and book markets. (Markets Tu-Su 9:30am-7:30pm.) Head down r. de Paris for the 14th- to 19th-century **Eglise St-Maurice.** (M: Rihour. Open M-F 7:15am-7pm, Sa 8am-7pm.)

Trains leave from **Gare Lille Flandres,** on pl. de la Gare (M: Gare Lille Flandres), for Brussels, Belgium (1½hr., 20 per day, €21) and Paris (1hr., 21 per day, €32-46). **Gare Lille Europe,** on r. Le Corbusier (M: Gare Lille Europe; ☎03 36 35 35 35), sends **Eurostar** trains to London, Brussels, and Paris and all **TGVs** to the south of France and Paris. From Gare Lille Flandres, walk straight down r. Faidherbe and turn left through pl. du Théâtre and pl. de Gaulle; behind the huge war monument is the castle housing the **tourist office,** pl. Rihour (M: Rihour), which offers free maps and currency exchange. (☎03 20 21 94 21; fax 03 20 21 94 20. Open M-Sa 9:30am-6:30pm, Su 10am-noon and 2-5pm.) To reach the **Auberge de Jeunesse (HI) ❶,** 12 r. Malpart (M: Mairie de Lille), from Gare Lille Flandres, circle left around the station, turn right onto r. du Molinel, take the second left on r. de Paris, and take the 3rd right onto r. Malpart. (☎03 20 57 08 94; fax 03 20 63 98 93. Breakfast included. Sheets €2.75. Reception 7am-noon and 2pm-1am. Check-out 10:30am. Curfew 2am. Open Feb.-Dec. 17. 3- to 6-bed dorms €11.45; deposit of ID or €7.65 required.) The spotless **Hôtel Faldherbe ❸,** 42 pl. de la Gare (M: Gare Lille Flandres), is noise-proof. (☎03 20 06 27 93; fax 03 20 55 95 38. Reception 24hr. Singles and doubles €26-40. 10% discount with *Let's Go.* AmEx/MC/V.) Restaurants and markets line **rue de Béthune** and **rue Léon Gambetta.** A huge **Carrefour supermarket** is next to the Eurostar train station. (Open M-Sa 9am-10pm.) Pubs and bars line **rue Solférino** and **rue Masséna.** The intimate **Le Clave,** 31 r. Massena, (☎03 20 30 09 61) serves tropical drinks (from €3.85) and Afro-Cuban jazz. **Postal Code:** 59000.

DAYTRIPS FROM LILLE: ARRAS AND VIMY. The town hall of **Arras,** housed in the gorgeous **Hôtel de Ville,** is built over the eerie **Les Boves** tunnels, which have sheltered both medieval chalk miners and British WWI soldiers. (€3.85, students €2.30.) Bars and cafes line the lively **Place des Héros. Trains** leave pl. Maréchal Foch for Lille (45min., 20 per day, €8.80). From the train station, walk across pl. Foch to r. Gambetta, turn left on r. Desire Delansorne, turn left, and walk two blocks to reach the **tourist office,** on pl. des Héros, in the Hôtel de Ville. (☎03 21 51 26 95. Open May-Sept. M-Sa 9am-6:30pm, Su 10am-1pm and 2:30-6:30pm; Oct.-Apr. M-Sa 9am-noon and 2-6pm, Su 10am-12:30pm and 3-6:30pm.) Stay at the central **Auberge de Jeunesse (HI) ❶,** 59 Grand'Place. (☎03 21 22 70 02; fax 03 21 07 46 15. Reception daily 8am-noon and 5-11pm. Curfew 11pm. Open Feb.-Nov. Dorms €8.)

The countryside surrounding Arras is dotted with war cemeteries and unmarked graves. The vast limestone **Vimy Memorial,** 12km from Arras, honors the more than 66,000 Canadians killed in WWI. The morbidly beautiful park, whose soil came from Canada, is dedicated to the crucial victory at Vimy Ridge in April 1917. The kiosk by the trenches is the starting point for an **underground tour** of the crumbling tunnels dug by British and Canadian soldiers. (☎03 21 59 19 34. Memorial open dawn-dusk. Free tunnel tours Apr. to mid-Nov. 10am-6pm.) The memorial is 3km from the town of **Vimy. Buses** run from Arras to Vimy (20min., 8 per day, €2.40).

CALAIS

Calais (pop. 80,000) is the liveliest of the Channel ports, and with the Chunnel next door, English is spoken as often as French. Rodin's famous sculpture **The Burghers of Calais** stands in front of the **Hôtel de Ville,** at the juncture of bd. Jacquard and r. Royale. Follow r. Royale to the end of r. de Mer for Calais's wide, gorgeous **beaches.** For schedules and prices to **Dover, England,** see p. 49. During the day, free **buses** connect the ferry terminal and train station, **Gare Calais-Ville,** on bd. Jacquard, from which **trains** leave for: Boulogne (45min., 8 per day, €6.30); Lille (1¼hr., 8 per day, €13.40); and Paris-Nord (3¼hr., 6 per day, €40). To reach the **tourist office,** 12 bd. Clemenceau, from the train station, turn left, cross the bridge, and it's on your right. (☎03 21 96 62 40; fax 03 21 96 01 92. Open M-Sa 9am-7pm, Su 10am-1pm.) **Morning markets** are held on pl. Crèvecoeur (Th and Sa) and on pl. d'Armes (W and Sa); or look for **Prisunic,** 17 bd. Jacquard. (Open M-Sa 8:30am-7:30pm, Su 10am-7pm.) The renovated **Centre Européen de Séjour/Auberge de Jeunesse (HI) ❶,** av. Maréchal Delattre de Tassigny, is near the beach. (☎03 21 34 70 20. Check-out 11am. Dorms €14.50.) The quiet **Hotel Bristol ❸,** 13-15 r. du Duc de Guise, is off the main road. (☎03 21 34 53 24. Singles and doubles €31-36. MC/V.) **Postal Code:** 62100.

BOULOGNE-SUR-MER

With its refreshing sea breeze and lavish floral displays, Boulogne is by far the most attractive Channel port. The huge **Château-Musée,** r. de Bernet, houses an eclectic art collection that includes Napoleon's second-oldest hat. (☎03 21 10 02 20. Open M and W-Sa 10am-12:30pm and 2-5pm, Su 10am-12:30pm and 2:30-5:30pm. €3.05.) Just down r. de Lille, the 19th-century **Basilique de Notre-Dame** sits above 12th-century labyrinthine crypts. (Open Apr. to mid-Sept. daily 9am-noon and 2-6pm; mid-Sept. to Mar 10am-noon and 2-5pm. Crypt open M-Sa 2-5pm, Su 2:30-5pm. €1.55.) **Trains** leave **Gare Boulogne-Ville,** bd. Voltaire, for: Calais (30min., 18 per day, €6.40); Lille (2½hr., 11 per day, €16.50); and Paris-Nord (2-3hr., 11 per day, €26-45). From the train station, turn right on bd. Voltaire, turn left on bd. Danou, and follow it to pl. Angleterre; continue past pl. de France and pl. Frédéric Sauvage onto r. Gambetta and look right for the **tourist office,** 24 quai Gambetta. (☎03 21 10 88 10; fax 03 21 10 88 11. Open July-Aug. M-Sa 9am-7pm, Su 10am-1pm and 3-6pm; Sept.-June reduced hours.) The fantastic **Auberge de Jeunesse (HI) ❶**, 56 pl. Rouget de Lisle, is across from the station. (☎03 21 99 15 30; fax 03 21 80 45 62. Breakfast included. Internet €4.60 per 30min. Reception daily 8am-1am; in winter until midnight. Curfew 1am. Dorms €13; nonmembers €3 extra per night up to 6 nights. MC/V.) **Champion supermarket,** on r. Daunou, is in the Centre Commercial de la Liane mall. (Open M-Sa 8:30am-8pm.) **Postal Code:** 62200.

GERMANY (DEUTSCHLAND)

Germany is a nation saddled with an incredibly fractured past. Steeped deeply in Beethoven's fiery orchestration and Goethe's Faustian whirlwind, modern Germany must also contend with the legacy of xenophobia and genocide left by Hitler and the Nazis. Even now, more than a decade after the fall of the Berlin Wall, Germans are still fashioning a new identity for themselves. After centuries of fragmentation, Germany finds itself a wealthy nation at the forefront of both European and global politics. Its medieval castles, snow-covered mountains, and funky metropolises make Germany well worth a visit.

SYMBOL	❶	❷	❸	❹	❺
ACCOMMODATIONS	under €14	€14-19	€20-35	€36-60	over €60
FOOD	under €4	€4-6	€7-12	€13-20	over €20

For Germany, prices are indicated in food and accommodations listings using the system of icons and price ranges above. Prices for accommodations are based on the lowest cost for one person, excluding special deals or discounts. For restaurants, prices are based on the average entree price.

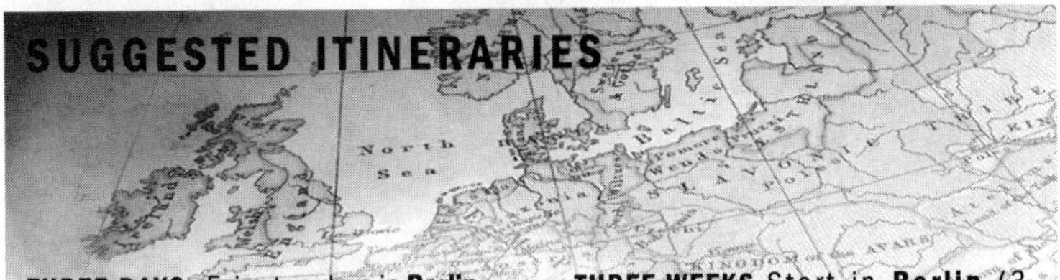

SUGGESTED ITINERARIES

THREE DAYS Enjoy two days in **Berlin** (p. 426): stroll along **Unter den Linden** and the **Ku'damm,** gawk at the **Brandenburger Tor** and the **Reichstag,** and explore the **Tiergarten.** Walk along the **East Side Gallery** and visit **Checkpoint Charlie** for a history of the Berlin Wall, then spend an afternoon at **Schloß Sans Soucci** (p. 452). Overnight it to Bavarian **Munich** (p. 504) for a beer-filled last day.

ONE WEEK After scrambling through **Berlin** (3 days), head north to racy **Hamburg** (1 day; p. 467). Take in the splendor of **Cologne** (1 day; p. 481) before heading to the former West German capital **Bonn** (1 day; p. 486). End your trip in true Bavarian style with castles, churches, and beer in **Munich** (1 day).

THREE WEEKS Start in **Berlin** (3 days). Party in **Hamburg** (2 days), stop by **Lübeck** for marzipan (1 day; p. 475), and zip to **Köln** (1 day). Peek at Charlemagne's remains in **Aachen** (1 day; p. 488) and explore **Bonn** (1 day). Spend a day in glitzy **Frankfurt** (p. 488), visit Germany's oldest university in **Heidelberg** (1 day; p. 496), then zoom to **Stuttgart** (2 days; p. 500). Get lost in a fairy tale world by daytripping through the **Schwarzwald** (1 day; p. 502), listening to the Glockenspiel in **Munich** (1 day), and marvelling at **Neuschwanstein** (1 day; p. 521). Take in the view along the **Romantic Road** (2 days; p. 519) and in the **Saxon Switzerland** (1 day; p. 458) before ending your trip in **Dresden** (2 days; p. 453).

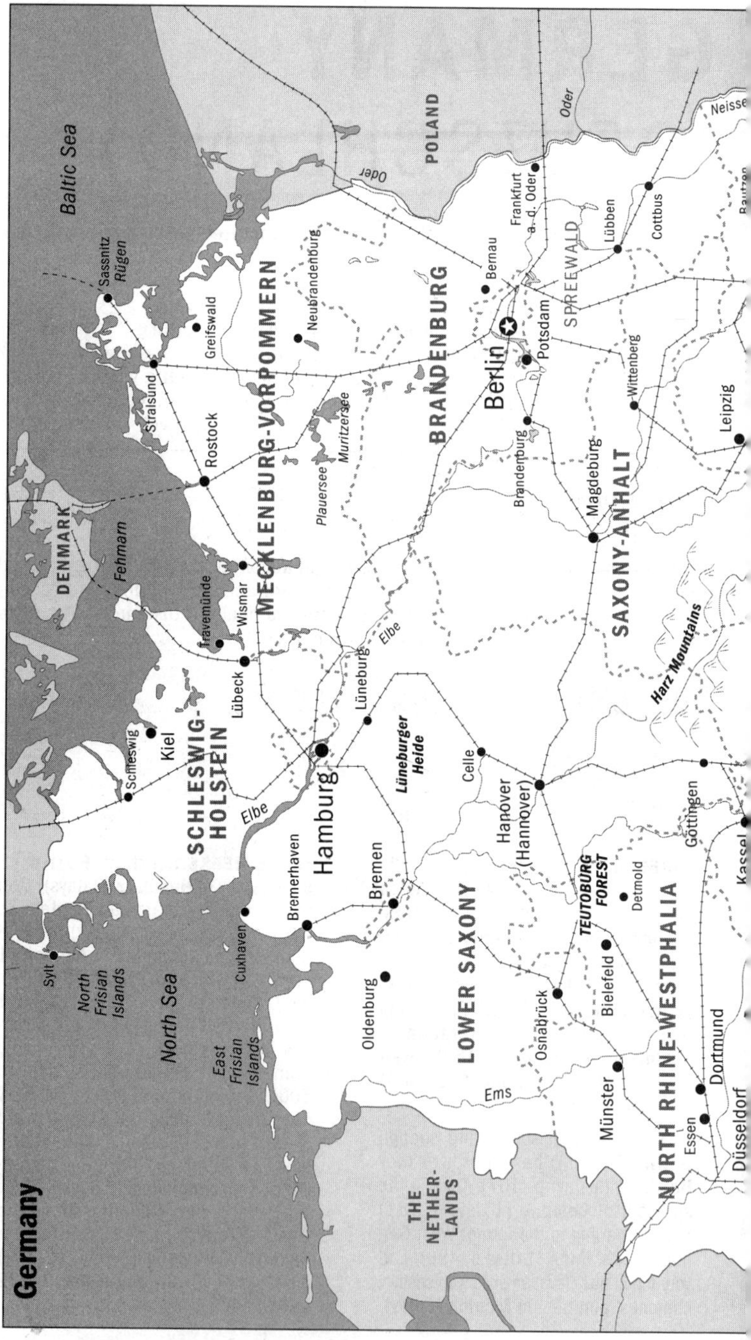
Germany
Baltic Sea
North Sea
North Frisian Islands
East Frisian Islands
DENMARK
POLAND
THE NETHERLANDS
Fehmarn
Rügen
Sassnitz
Stralsund
Greifswald
Rostock
Neubrandenburg
Wismar
Travemünde
Lübeck
Kiel
Schleswig
Sylt
Cuxhaven
Bremerhaven
Bremen
Hamburg
Oldenburg
Lüneburg
Lüneburger Heide
Celle
Hanover (Hannover)
Osnabrück
Bielefeld
Detmold
Münster
Dortmund
Essen
Düsseldorf
Göttingen
Kassel
Magdeburg
Brandenburg
Berlin
Potsdam
Bernau
Frankfurt a. d. Oder
Lübben
Cottbus
Wittenberg
Leipzig
SPREEWALD
Plauersee
Muritzersee
Harz Mountains
TEUTOBURG FOREST
SCHLESWIG-HOLSTEIN
MECKLENBURG-VORPOMMERN
BRANDENBURG
SAXONY-ANHALT
LOWER SAXONY
NORTH RHINE-WESTPHALIA
Elbe
Ems
Oder
Neisse

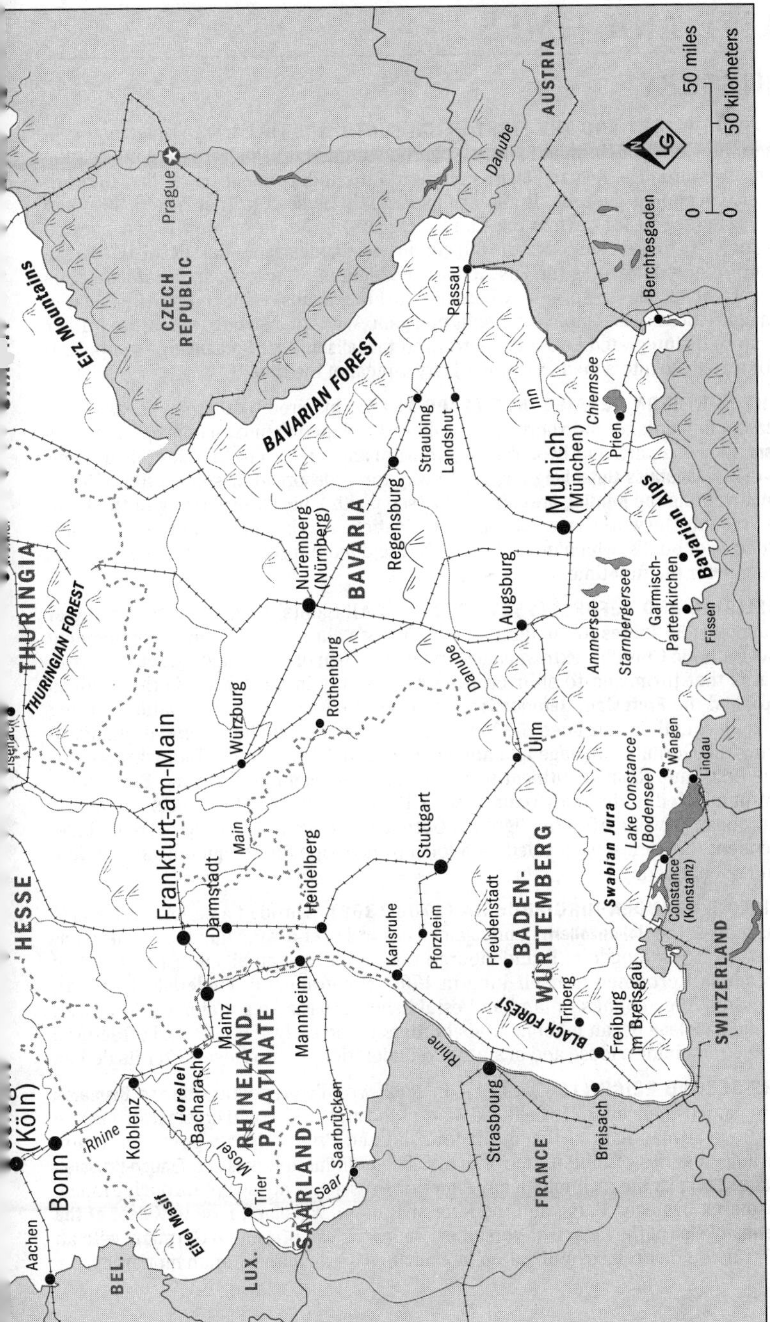
(Köln)
Bonn
Aachen
BEL.
LUX.
Eifel Massif
Koblenz
Rhine
Mosel
Trier
Saar
SAARLAND
Saarbrücken
RHINELAND-PALATINATE
Lorelei
Bacharach
Mainz
Mannheim
HESSE
Frankfurt-am-Main
Darmstadt
Heidelberg
Main
Karlsruhe
Pforzheim
Stuttgart
Strasbourg
FRANCE
Breisach
Freiburg im Breisgau
Triberg
BLACK FOREST
BADEN-WÜRTTEMBERG
Freudenstadt
Swabian Jura
Lake Constance (Bodensee)
Constance (Konstanz)
SWITZERLAND
Lindau
Wangen
Ulm
Danube
Würzburg
Rothenburg
Eisenach
THURINGIA
THURINGIAN FOREST
Nuremberg (Nürnberg)
BAVARIA
Regensburg
Augsburg
Ammersee
Starnbergersee
Garmisch-Partenkirchen
Füssen
Bavarian Alps
Munich (München)
Chiemsee
Prien
Inn
Straubing
Landshut
Passau
BAVARIAN FOREST
CZECH REPUBLIC
Prague
Erz Mountains
AUSTRIA
Berchtesgaden
0 50 miles
0 50 kilometers

LIFE AND TIMES

HISTORY

EARLY HISTORY AND THE FIRST REICH (UNTIL 1400). Early German history—actually, most of German history—can be summed up as alternating unification and fracture. The **Roman Empire** conquered the independent tribes that had formerly occupied the area; Roman ruins can still be seen in **Trier** (see p. 494) and **Cologne** (see p. 481). When the Empire collapsed, the Germanic tribes separated again, only to be reunified in the 8th century by **Charlemagne** (Karl der Große) in an empire now known as the **First Reich,** or kingdom. Charlemagne established his capital at **Aachen** (see p. 488), where his earthly remains reside today. After Charlemagne's death, the empire was split up again. Without a strong leader, the former empire disintegrated into a decentralized **feudalism.** Visit **Rothenburg** (see p. 520) for a glimpse into a medieval walled city typical of the time.

THE NORTHERN RENAISSANCE (1400-1517). Inspired by the new ideas of the Italian Renaissance, northern philosophers developed their own concept of **humanism,** focusing particularly on religious reform and a return to Classics (virtues and works). **Johannes Gutenberg** paved the way for widespread dissemination of ideas by inventing the **printing press** in Mainz (see p. 492); his Latin printing of the Bible is arguably the world's most seminal publication. This invention allowed rapid production of books, which increased literacy and put information in the hands of the people for the first time.

RELIGION AND REFORM (1517-1700). On All Saints' Day, 1517, **Martin Luther** nailed his **95 Theses** to the door of Wittenberg's church (see p. 462), condemning the Catholic Church's extravagance and its practice of selling **indulgences**—certificates that promised to shorten the owner's stay in purgatory. Luther's ideas sparked the **Protestant Reformation,** a period of intense religious conflict. During this time, Luther translated the New Testament from Latin into German, standardizing the German language and allowing lay-people to read the Bible directly for the first time. Rising continent-wide tensions between Catholics and Protestants eventually led to the **Thirty Years' War** (1618-1648), a series of conflicts among the European powers. After the fighting, Germany emerged as a group of small, independent territories, each ruled by a local prince, ripe for conquering, separation, and re-conquering.

RISE OF BRANDENBURG-PRUSSIA (1700-1862). Through a series of strategic marriages, the **Hohenzollern** family gained control over a large number of these territories. Their kingdom, Brandenburg-Prussia, became an absolutist state when **Frederick I** crowned himself king in 1701. His grandson, **Frederick the Great,** acquired huge chunks of land and established Prussia as a major world power. When **Napoleon** began nibbling at its borders in the early 1800s, Prussia fractured again, remaining a loose and unstable confederation of states even after its defeat.

THE SECOND REICH (1862-1914). In 1862, worldly aristocrat **Otto von Bismarck** was named chancellor. He believed that "blood and iron" could create a strong and unified German nation. Bismarck consolidated Prussia into a powerful nation through a series of military movements. The culmination was the **Franco-Prussian War** in 1870, as the technologically superior Prussian army swept through France. Bismarck besieged Paris, and the king of Prussia, **Wilhelm I,** rose to **Kaiser of the German Reich** at the Palace of Versailles. Bismarck had presented Germany with an offer it couldn't refuse: unification in exchange for an authoritarian monarchy.

WORLD WAR I (1914-1918). On the eve of **WWI,** Europe was entangled in a complex web of precarious alliances. In 1914, when a Serbian nationalist assassinated **Archduke Franz-Ferdinand,** heir to the Austrian throne, Austria declared war on Serbia. Germany jumped in to help Austria, and the rest of Europe was soon drawn into full-blown war. After four agonizing years of trench warfare, Germany and its allies were defeated. Germany's aggressiveness in France, along with its use of **unrestricted submarine warfare,** allowed the victors to place responsibility for WWI on Germany's shoulders.

THE WEIMAR REPUBLIC (1918-1933). France insisted on a harsh peace in the **Treaty of Versailles,** which imposed staggering reparation payments, drastically reduced the German army, and officially ascribed the blame for the war to Germany. The defeated Germans had little choice but to accept the humiliating terms, and a new republic was set up in **Weimar** (see p. 462). Outstanding war debts and the burden of reparations produced staggering hyperinflation in 1922-23; paper money was worth more as fireplace fuel than currency. Already smarting from Versailles, the German people needed stability and relief from the post-war hardships, which a charismatic Austrian named **Adolf Hitler** seemed to promise. His party, the National Socialists (**Nazis**), was increasingly associated with German ultra-nationalist ideals.

Hitler's first attempt to seize power, the **Beer Hall Putsch** in Munich (1923), was unsuccessful. As economic troubles worsened, more and more Germans were drawn to the Nazis and their promises of prosperity and community. Party membership increased to more than a million by 1930. Hitler failed in a presidential bid against the nearly senile war-hero **Paul von Hindenburg** in 1932, but since elections made the Nazis the dominant party in the legislature, Hindenburg reluctantly appointed Hitler chancellor on January 30, 1933.

BEGINNING OF THE THIRD REICH (1933-39). Hitler's platform, crystallized in his book, **Mein Kampf** *(My Struggle)*, provided a scapegoat for WWI losses—the Jews—and played on centuries-old feelings of anti-Semitism. The new government quickly instituted a boycott of Jewish enterprises and expelled Jews from professional and civil service; rival parties that might have opposed the Nazis were outlawed or dissolved. In 1934, after Hindenburg's death, Hitler appropriated presidential powers for himself; that year, the first of the **Nürnberg Laws** were passed, depriving Jews of German citizenship and preventing intermarriage between Aryan and Jewish Germans—it was felt that the "debased" Jews would taint the pure and "superior" German blood. Nazis destroyed thousands of Jewish businesses, burned synagogues, and killed and deported thousands of Jews on **Kristallnacht** (Night of Broken Glass), November 9, 1938. With the help of **Joseph Goebbels,** his minister of propaganda, Hitler consolidated his power by saturating mass culture—from art to literature to movies to music—with Nazi ideology: the Nazis burned books by Jewish and "subversive" authors at Bebelplatz in Berlin (see p. 440), banned American films and music, and destroyed "degenerate" art in favor of propagandist paintings and statues.

Hitler was also busy mounting a war effort. He first freed Germany from making reparations payments by abrogating the Treaty of Versailles. Next, he annexed Austria in an infamous attack known as the **Anschluß** (1938). Other nations, hoping that Hitler would be satisfied with these new acquisitions, followed a policy of **appeasement,** led by British Prime Minster Neville Chamberlain, and allowed Germany to take over the Sudetenland region (now in the Czech Republic). However, it soon became clear that Hitler was after more than small territorial gains.

WORLD WAR II (1939-1945). On September 1, 1939, German tanks rolled into Poland. Britain and France, bound by treaty to defend Poland, immediately declared war on Germany, and the rest of Europe was again dragged into global conflict. Germany's new tactic of **Blitzkrieg** (literally, "lightning war") quickly crushed Poland. Denmark, Norway, Belgium, The Netherlands, and France were soon overwhelmed as well.

The Nazis then began a two-front war, attacking westward with an air-borne offensive in the **Battle of Britain** and eastward in the **invasion of the USSR.** However, daily air raids spurred the British to fight harder rather than submit. Meanwhile, the *Blitzkrieg* faltered in the Russian winter and Hitler sacrificed thousands of German soldiers in his adamant refusal to retreat. The bloody **Battle of Stalingrad** (1942-43) marked a critical turning point in the East as the Soviets gained the upper hand. Soon Germany was retreating on all fronts. The Allied landing in Normandy on **D-Day** (June 6, 1944) preceded an arduous eastward advance across Europe; the Soviet Army rolled westward and took Berlin in April 1945. The Third Reich, which Hitler had boasted would endure for 1000 years, had lasted only 12.

THE HOLOCAUST. By the outbreak of WWII, Jews had lost virtually all rights and and were forced to identify themselves with a yellow Star of David patch. The Nazis portrayed Jews as the ultimate influence corrupting the German soul, and Hitler was fixated on his **Final Solution:** genocide. Seven death camps, including **Buchenwald** (see p. 463), were designed for mass extermination; dozens of "labor" camps such as **Dachau** (see p. 514) were operating before war's end. Nearly six million Jews—two-thirds of Europe's Jewish population—mostly from Poland and the Soviet Union, were gassed, shot, starved, worked to death, or killed by exposure. Millions of other victims, including prisoners of war, Slavs, gypsies, homosexuals, the mentally disabled, and political disidents, also died in Nazi camps.

OCCUPATION AND DIVISION (1945-1949). In July 1945, the United States, Great Britain, and the Soviet Union met at **Potsdam** to partition Germany into zones of occupation: the east under the Soviets, the west under the British and Americans, and Berlin under divided control. The Allied program for the **Occupation**—democratization, demilitarization, and de-Nazification—proceeded, but growing animosity between the Soviets and the Western Allies made joint control of Germany increasingly difficult. In 1947, the Allies merged their occupation zones into a single economic unit and began to rebuild a market economy with huge cash infusions under the American **Marshall Plan.** East and West Germany became increasingly distant, especially after the Western Allies introduced the **Deutschmark** into their zones.

THE FEDERAL REPUBLIC OF GERMANY (1949-1989). The Federal Republic of Germany *(Bundesrepublik Deutschland)* was established as the provisional government of Western Germany on May 24, 1949. **Basic Law** safeguarded individual rights and established a system of freely elected parliamentary assemblies. One of the most visionary paragraphs established a **Right of Asylum,** guaranteeing refuge to any person fleeing persecution.

As the only party untainted by the Third Reich, the Social Democratic Party seemed poised to dominate postwar German politics, but the **Christian Democratic Union (CDP)** provided some competition by uniting Germany's historically fragmented conservatives and centrists under a nondenominational platform. With former Cologne mayor **Konrad Adenauer** at the helm, the CDU won a small majority of seats in the Federal Republic's first general election. As chancellor, Adenauer unflaggingly pursued the integration of Germany into a unified Europe; West Germany was aligned with **NATO** (North Atlantic Treaty Organization) in 1955 and became one of the charter members of the European Economic Community (later the **European Union**) in 1957. Speedy fiscal recovery secured the future dominance of the CDU party. In 1982, Christian Democrat **Helmut Kohl** became chancellor and pursued a policy of welfare state cutbacks, tight monetary policy, and military cooperation with the US.

MEANWHILE... IN THE GERMAN DEMOCRATIC REPUBLIC. In spite of pledges to the contrary, the Soviets stopped holding free elections in their sector by 1949. On October 7, 1949, they declared the establishment of the **German Democratic Republic,** with the national capital in Berlin. Constitutional promises of civil liberties and democracy were empty: East Germany became unquestioningly subservient to the Soviet Union. The **Stasi,** or secret police, maintained a network of agents that strove to monitor every citizen from their headquarters in Berlin (see p. 444)—one in seven East Germans was a paid informant.

Many East Germans chose to escape oppression by emigrating to West Germany. By 1961, more than three million had illegally crossed the border, and the East German government decided to stop the exodus of young skilled workers. Overnight on August 12, the first barriers of the **Berlin Wall** were laid, and barbed wire and guns dissuaded further attempts to escape, making for a confusing and dangerous barrier between the two halves.

REUNIFICATION (1989). When **Mikhail Gorbachev** took the helm of the USSR in 1985, liberalizing reform spread throughout the Eastern Bloc under his policy of *glasnost* (openness). East Germany, however, remained under tight control. The turning point came in May 1989 when Hungary dismantled its barbed-wire border with Austria, giving East Germans an escape route to the West. In October, Gorbachev announced that the USSR would not interfere with East Germany's domestic affairs, and citizens began to demand free elections, freedom of press, and freedom of travel. The entire East German government resigned on November 8, and a day later, a Central Committee spokesperson announced the opening of all borders to the West.

The destruction of the Wall was the most symbolically significant event for Germans since the end of WWII. The signing of the **Four-Plus-Two Treaty** by the two Germanies and the four occupying powers on September 12, 1990, signaled the **end of a divided Germany.** On October 3, 1990, the Allies forfeited their occupation rights, East Germany ceased to exist, and Germany became one united sovereign nation for the first time in 45 years. However, East and West Germany did not come together on equal terms. The collapse of East Germany's inefficient industries and institutions led to massive unemployment and the Federal Republic's worst-ever recession. Many Westerners resented the inflation and taxes brought on by reunification, while Easterners missed the generous social benefits that communism had afforded them. Economic frustrations led to the scapegoating of foreigners, especially asylum-seekers from Eastern Europe and immigrant workers. Thankfully, violence has decreased greatly over the past few years.

TODAY

After the dramatic fall of the Berlin Wall in 1989, Helmut Kohl and his CDU party seemed insurmountable. Carrying their momentum into the first all-German elections, the CDU scored a stunning victory. However, Kohl found it difficult to manage the reunification, and his popularity plummeted to the point where Easterners pelted him with rotten vegetables during one visit. In 1998, left-wing parties ousted the CDU, electing **Gerhard Schroeder** chancellor.

Germany's new place within Europe remains a great political question. The burden of the past makes everyone, including Germans themselves, nervous about Germany's participation in international military operations. In the summer of

2001, the government overwhelmingly voted to distribute 10 million DM (€5.32 million) among Nazi-era slave-laborers as belated compensation, signalling that Germany has come to grips, at least partially, with its Nazi past. Recently, Germany has begun to redefine its international role; in the **Kosovo** crisis, for example, Germany played a pivotal role in negotiating a peace accord, and German forces were present both at peacekeeping missions in Yugoslavia and flood relief operations in Africa. The persistent feeling among Germans now is that they should stay out of foreign policy, acting instead as a large, benign economic machine at the heart of the European Union, but such a neutral stance may not be possible in the long run for Europe's most populous and economically powerful nation.

CULTURE

FOOD AND DRINK

German cooking has a robust charm that is especially satisfying for meat-and-potato lovers. German delights include **Schnitzel** (a lightly fried veal cutlet), **Spätzle** (a southern noodle), and **Kartoffeln** (potatoes). The typical German **Frühstück** (breakfast) consists of coffee or tea with rolls, bread, cold sausage, eggs, and cheese. The main meal of the day, **Mittagessen** (lunch), includes soup, broiled sausage or roasted meat, potatoes or dumplings, and a salad or vegetable side dish. **Abendessen** or **Abendbrot** (dinner) is a reprise of breakfast, only beer replaces coffee and the selection of meats and cheese is wider. Many older Germans indulge in a daily ritual of **Kaffee und Kuchen** (coffee and cakes) at 3 or 4pm.

To eat on the cheap, stick to the daily **Tagesmenü** (fixed-price menu), buy food in supermarkets, or, if you have a student ID, head to a university **Mensa** (cafeteria). *Imbiß* (fast food stands) also provide inexpensive fare; try the delicious Turkish *Döner* (something like a gyro). In small towns, buy bread at a *Bäckerei* (bakery) and add sausage from a butcher (*Fleischerei* or *Metzgerei*).

German beer is maltier and more "bread-like" than other beers. One exception is **Pils,** or *Pilsner*, popular in the north; its clarity and bitter taste comes from extra hops. In the south, try **Weißbier,** a smooth refreshing wheat brew. Also sample the largely overlooked German **wines,** particularly the sweet (*Lieblich* or *Süß*) whites of the Rhine and Mosel valleys.

CUSTOMS AND ETIQUETTE

The multiple rules surrounding German etiquette usually only apply among older Germans and in rural areas. Germans are incredibly big on punctuality. An invitation to a German home is a major courtesy; you should bring a gift for the hostess. Try to use the formal *Sie* for "you" when addressing others as in the question *Sprechen Sie Englisch?* Addressing a woman as *Fraulein* is inappropriate in most instances; use *Frau* (followed by the name) instead. Germans will be more receptive to a traveler who knows at least a little German.

Everything you've heard about the Germans' compulsive abidance of the law is true. Jay-walking and littering are two of the petty offenses that will mark you as a foreigner. Many tourists also do not realize that the bike lanes marked in red between the sidewalk and the road are not for pedestrians. The drinking age is 16 for beer and wine, 18 for hard liquor—neither are strictly enforced. Driving under the influence, however, is a severe offense. Drug use has yet to become publicly acceptable, even where legal—and barely legal, at that.

Most Germans just round up €1 in restaurants and bars, or when they receive a service, such as a taxi ride. Note that tips in Germany are not left lying on the table, but handed directly to the server. If you don't want any change, say "*Das stimmt so*" (das SHTIMMT zo). Germans rarely bargain except at flea markets.

THE ARTS

VISUAL ART. In the Renaissance, **Albrecht Dürer** emerged as a master of engraving and draftsmanship. His *Adam and Eve* still peppers advertisements today, and his *Self-Portrait at 20* (1500), was one of the first self-portraits in Europe. In the 19th century, **Caspar David Friedrich** painted dramatic mountain scenes and billowing landscapes that exemplify the Romantic style. However, it was in the 20th century that German art truly blossomed. The deliberate anti-realism of **German Expressionism** intensified color and object representation to project deeply personal emotions. A 1911 exhibition in Munich entitled **Der Blaue Reiter** (The Blue Rider), led by Russian emigré **Wassily Kandinsky,** displayed some of the first totally non-representational paintings in Western art. In the period between the wars, artists became increasingly political in reaction to the rise of Fascism: **Max Beckmann** painted posed figures whose gestures and symbolism expressed a tortured view of man's condition, and **Max Ernst** started a **Dadaist** group in Cologne, conveying artistic nihilism through collage. During the Nazi era, almost all art was controlled by the state for propagandistic purposes, featuring idealized images of workers, soldiers, and citizens. Nevertheless, the German art scene bounced back after the war's end. **Anselm Kiefer** examines Germany's previously unapproachable past in his paintings, while **Josef Beuys**'s innovative art objects and performances challenge artistic conventions.

ARCHITECTURE AND DESIGN. Outstanding **Romanesque** cathedrals, featuring a clover-leaf floor plan, numerous towers, and a mitre-like steeple, can be found along the Rhine at **Trier** (see p. 494) and **Mainz** (see p. 492). The **Gothic** style, with its pointed spires and vaulted roofs, gradually replaced the Romanesque form between 1300 and 1500; stained glass windows fill otherwise gloomy interiors with divine light. The cathedral at **Cologne** (see p. 481) is one of the most famous German gothic structures. Secular architecture at the end of the Middle Ages was dominated by the **Fachwerk** (half-timbered) houses that can still be seen in the *Altstadt* ("old-town") sections of many German cities. In the 17th century, the **Baroque** style emerged with ostentatious decorations and sinuous contours; the **Zwinger** (see p. 456) in Dresden is a magnificent example. Baroque developed into the highly decorative **Rococo** style with ornately garnished buildings like **Schloß Sanssouci** (see p. 452). A simpler movement, **Neoclassicism,** arose in reaction to the frou-frou Rococo facades; the **Brandenburger Tor** (see p. 440) and the buildings along Unter den Linden in Berlin (see p. 439) use stylistic elements of Classical Greece and Rome. In 1919, Weimar saw the birth of the boxy **Bauhaus** style of architecture, which emphasized form based on function. The movement later moved to **Dessau**, where a school for design still flourishes.

LITERATURE. The first significant German novel, **Hans J. C. von Grimmelshausen**'s roguish series *Simplicissimus*, was written during the chaos of the Thirty Years' War, a period that saw little literary development due to political turmoil. By the 18th century, however, the German literary scene was flourishing. **Johann Wolfgang von Goethe** exemplified the Romantic era with emotional, dramatic masterpieces such as *Faust* (1832; see p. 460), while the **Brothers Grimm** transformed folk tales from an oral tradition into morbid, child-scaring (but classic) literature in the 19th century. A rush of realistic political literature emerged in the turbulent mid-19th century; **Heinrich Heine** was the one of the finest, writing witty satires as well as romantic poems. In the early 20th century, **Thomas Mann** carried the modern novel to a high point with *The Magic Mountain* (1924) and *Doctor Faustus* (1947), while **Hermann Hesse** experimented with Eastern motifs in the quasi-Buddhist novel *Siddhartha* (1922). **Rainer Maria Rilke,** living in Austria-Hungary, produced some of Germany's most enduring poems, and **Franz Kafka** examined the complications of modern existence in *The Metamorphosis* (1915).

Despite the disruption of WWI, the **Weimar era** was a period of active artistic production. **Erich Maria Remarque**'s *All Quiet on the Western Front* (1929), a blunt account of war's horrors, became an international bestseller. **Bertolt Brecht**'s dramas and poems presented humankind in all its grotesque absurdity (see p. 442). To nurse German literature back to health after the Nazi book-burning years, several writers, including **Günter Grass** and poet **Paul Celan,** joined to form **Gruppe 47,** named after the year of its founding. The group coined the term *Nullstunde* ("Zero Hour") to signify that after WWII, culture had to begin again. Much of the ensuing literature dealt with the problem of Germany's Nazi past; the novels of Grass and **Heinrich Böll** and the poetry of **Hans Magnus Enzensberger** turned a critical eye to post-war West Germany's repressive, overly organized tendencies.

PHILOSOPHY. Germany's philosophical tradition is one of the most respected in the world. Initially, philosophy dealt only with religion. In 1517, **Martin Luther**'s *95 Theses* denied papal infallibility, claiming that only scripture was holy and thus advocating a direct relationship with God; **Gottfried Wilhelm Leibnitz** thought of God as a watchmaker who set the individual's body and soul in motion like two synchronized clocks. In the **Enlightenment,** reason was the key word: **Immanuel Kant,** the foremost German thinker of the time, argued that ethics can be rationally deduced. **Georg W. F. Hegel** proposed that world history and the development of the individual consciousness could be understood as a thesis and antithesis, respectively, combining to form a new synthesis.

The 19th century brought several controversial but highly influential theories. The founder of modern socialism, **Karl Marx** (see p. 494) asserted that class conflict was the driving force of all history. **Friedrich Nietzsche** developed the idea of the *Übermensch,* a super-man so wise and self-mastered that he could enjoy life even to the point of eternal repetition. **Max Weber** created the idea of the "Protestant Ethic," which related Protestantism to capitalism. In the interwar period, **Martin Heidegger** became one of the main exponents of Existentialism; his *Being and Time* (1927) examines the crisis of alienation in a world of technical development. After the fall of the Third Reich, thinkers **Theodor Adorno** and **Max Horkheimer** penned the classic *Dialectic of Enlightenment* (1947), which suggests that civilization ultimately culminates in fascism. More recently, **Jürgen Habermas** has criticized German reunification, citing the danger of joining two nations that have adopted very different cultures.

MUSIC. Johann Sebastian Bach was one of the first great German composers. Bach and his contemporary **Georg Friedrich Händel** composed during the Baroque period of the 17th century, which was known for its extravagant decoration and popularized the theme-and-variation pattern. Händel's *Messiah* (1741) is still widely performed today—Hallelujah!

The 19th century was an era of German musical hegemony. **Ludwig van Beethoven**'s symphonies and piano sonatas bridged Classicism and Romanticism with rhythmic drives and intense emotional expressionism; he is perhaps best known in popular culture for his dramatic *Fifth* and *Ninth Symphonies* (1808 and 1824, respectively). Meanwhile, **Felix Mendelssohn-Bartholdy** wrote more ethereal works, such as his musical interpretation of Shakespeare's *A Midsummer Night's Dream* (1826). The second generation of Romantic composers included **Johannes Brahms,** who imbued Classical forms with Romantic emotion. *Tristan and Isolde* (1859), *Lohengrin* (1850), and the other (interminably long) operas of **Richard Wagner** express the nationalist sentiments rising in the mid-19th century.

Germany's postwar music scene is mostly transnational; Germans are more likely to listen to American pop than their own countrymen. Nevertheless, they have made important contributions to the field. Germany is best known internationally for pioneering **techno** with bands like **Kraftwerk,** to the delight of clubgoers worldwide. Rap and hip-hop have become quite popular since the rise of **Die fantastischen Vier,** the first German rap group.

HOLIDAYS AND FESTIVALS

Holidays: Epiphany (Jan. 6); Good Friday (Apr. 18); Easter Sunday and Monday (Apr. 20-21); Labor Day (May 1); Ascension Day (May 29); Whit Sunday and Monday (June 8-9); Corpus Christi (June 19); Assumption Day (Aug. 15); Day of German Unity (Oct. 3); All Saint's Day (Nov. 1); and Christmas (Dec. 25-26). Expect changes in the opening hours of most establishments.

Festivals: Check out the **Fasching** in Munich (Jan. 7-Mar. 4; see p. 504); **Berlinale Film Festival** (Feb. 5-16; see p. 448); **Karneval** in Cologne (Feb. 27-Mar. 3; see p. 485); **Christopher St. Day** in Berlin and other major cities (late June to early July); **Love Parade** in Berlin (late July); **Oktoberfest** in Munich (Sept. 20-Oct. 5; see p. 506); and **Christmas Market** in Nuremberg (see p. 519).

ESSENTIALS

FACTS AND FIGURES

Official Name: Federal Republic of Germany.

Capital: Berlin.

Major Cities: Munich, Frankfurt, Cologne, Hamburg.

Population: 83,030,000.

Land Area: 357,021 sq. km.

Time Zone: GMT + 1.

Language: German.

Religions: Protestant (38%), Roman Catholic (34%), Muslim (1.7%), unaffiliated or other (26.3%).

WHEN TO GO

Germany's climate is temperate, with rain year-round (especially in summer). The cloudy, temperate months of May, June, and September are the best time to go, as there are fewer tourists and the weather is pleasant. Germans head to vacation spots en masse in early July with the onset of school vacations. Winter sports gear up November to April; skiing high season is mid-December to March.

! In August 2002, extreme weather conditions caused massive flooding along the Elbe and Danube, especially in eastern Germany and its neighbors further east. As of press time, the ultimate extent of the damage was not known. Many establishments we list may have been forced to shut down or may have altered opening times; additionally, train routes may be disrupted or changed. Make sure to check ahead thoroughly: call hostels and hotels in advance, and confirm the feasibility of your itinerary with Germany's National Tourist Board (www.germany-tourism.de).

DOCUMENTS AND FORMALITIES

Citizens of Australia, Canada, the EU, New Zealand, and the US do not need a visa for stays up to 90 days. Germany requires visas of South Africans.

German Embassies at Home: Australia, 119 Empire Circuit, Yarralumla, Canberra, ACT 2600 (☎02 62 70 19 11). **Canada,** 1 Waverly St., Ottawa, ON K2P 0T8 (☎613-232-1101). **Ireland,** 31 Trimleston Ave., Booterstown, Blackrock, Co. Dublin (☎01 269 30 11). **New Zealand,** 90-92 Hobson St., Thorndon, Wellington (☎04 473 60 63). **South Africa,** 180 Blackwood St., Arcadia, Pretoria, 0083 (☎012 427 89 00). **UK,** 23 Belgrave Sq., London SW1X 8PZ (☎020 7824 1300). **US,** 4645 Reservoir Rd., Washington, D.C. 20007 (☎202-298-4393).

Foreign Embassies in Germany: All foreign embassies are in **Berlin** (p. 426).

TRANSPORTATION

BY PLANE. Most flights land in Frankfurt (FRF); Berlin (3 airports), Munich (MUC), and Hamburg (HAM) also have international airports. **Lufthansa,** the national airline, has the most flights in and out of the country, but they're not always the cheapest option. Flying within Germany is usually more expensive and less convenient than taking trains.

BY TRAIN. The **Deutsche Bahn (DB)** network (in Germany ☎0180 599 66 33; www.bahn.de) is among Europe's best but also one of the most expensive. **RE** (RegionalExpress) and the slightly slower **RB** (RegionalBahn) trains include a number of rail networks between neighboring cities. **IR** (InterRegio) trains, covering larger networks between cities, are speedy and comfortable. **D** trains are foreign trains that serve international routes. **EC** (EuroCity) and **IC** (InterCity) trains zoom along between major cities every hour from 6am-10pm. You must purchase a **Zuschlag** (supplement) for IC or EC trains (€3.60). **ICE** (InterCityExpress) trains approach the luxury and kinetics of an airplane running at speeds up to 280km per hour. On all trains, second-class compartments are clean and comfortable.

Designed for tourists, the **German Railpass** allows unlimited travel for four to 10 days within a four-week period. Non-Europeans can purchase German Railpasses in their home countries and—with a passport—in major German train stations (2nd-class 5-day €202, 10-day €316). The **German Rail Youth Pass** is for those under 26 (5-day €156, 9-day €216). The **Twin Pass** is for two adults traveling together (2nd-class 5-day €303, 10-day €474). Travelers ages 12-25 can purchase **TwenTickets,** which knock 20% off fares. A **Schönes-Wochenende-Ticket** (€21) gives up to five people unlimited travel on any of the slower trains (*not* ICE, IC, EC, D, or IR) from 12:01am Saturday or Sunday until 3am the next day. The **Guten-Abend-Ticket** allows travel anywhere (*not* on InterCityNight or CityNightLines) in Germany between 7pm (2pm Saturdays) and 3am (2nd-class M-Th €30, F-Su €38.10). The **Bahncard** is valid for one year and gives a 50% discount on all trains. Passes are available at major train stations and require a passport-sized photo and mailing address in Germany (2nd-class €140; ages 18-22, over 60, or students under 27 €35.)

Eurail is valid in Germany and provides free passage on urban S-Bahns and DB buses, but not U-Bahns. **Public transport** is excellent, and comes in four variations: the **Straßenbahn** (streetcar), **S-Bahn** (surface commuter rail), **U-Bahn** (underground subway), and regular **buses.** Consider buying a *Tageskarte* (day card) or *Mehrfahrkarte* (multiple-ride ticket); they usually pay for themselves quickly.

BY BUS. Bus service between cities and to outlying areas runs from the local **Zentralomnibusbahnhof (ZOB),** which is usually close to the main train station. Buses are often slightly more expensive than trains for comparable distances. Railpasses are not valid on any buses other than a few run by Deutsche Bahn.

BY CAR. German road conditions are generally excellent. It's true—there is no set speed limit on the *Autobahn,* only a recommendation of 130kph (80mph). Germans drive fast. Watch for signs indicating right-of-way (usually designated by a yellow triangle). The *Autobahn* is indicated by an intuitive "A" on signs; secondary highways, where the speed limit is usually 100kph, are accompanied by signs bearing a "B." Germans drive on the right side of the road. In cities and towns, speed limits hover around 30-60kph (20-35mph). Germans use mainly unleaded gas; prices run around €4.30 per gallon, or €1.10 per liter. **Mitfahrzentralen** are agencies that pair up drivers and riders for a small fee; riders then negotiate payment for the trip with the driver.

BY BIKE. Germany's wealth of trails make bikes sightseeing power tools. Cities and towns usually have designated bike lanes and biking maps. *Germany by Bike,* by Nadine Slavinski (Mountaineers Books, 1994; US$15), details 20 tours throughout the country.

TOURIST SERVICES AND MONEY

EMERGENCY **Police:** ☎110. **Ambulance** and **Fire:** ☎112.

TOURIST OFFICES. Every city in Germany has a tourist office, usually near the *Hauptbahnhof* (main train station) or *Marktplatz* (central square). All are marked by a thick lowercase "i" sign. The offices often book rooms for a small fee. The tourist information website for Germany is www.germany-tourism.de.

Tourists Boards at Home: Australia: Sydney, c/o German-Australian Chamber of Industry and Commerce, P.O.Box A980, Sydney South, N.S.W. 1235 (☎(02) 92 67 81 48; fax 92 67 90 35; gnto@germany.org.au). **Canada:** Toronto, P.O.Box 65162, Ontario M4K 3Z2 (☎877-315-6237 within Canada, 212-661-7200 from outside of Canada; fax 416-968-1986; gnto-toronto@look.ca). **South Africa:** Johannesburg, c/o Lufthansa German Airlines, P.O. Box 10883, Johannesburg 2000 (☎11 643 16 15; fax 484 2750; claudia.walther@dlh.de). **UK:** London, P.O. Box 2695, W1A 3TN (☎20 73 17 09 08; fax 495 61 29; gntolon@d-z-t.com). **US:** New York, 122 E. 42nd Street, 52nd Floor, New York, NY 10168 (☎212-661-7200; fax 661-7174; gntonyc@d-z-t.com; www.visits-to-germany.com). **Los Angeles,** 8484 Wilshire Blvd. Suite. 440, Beverly Hills, CA 90211 (☎323-655-6085; fax 655-6086; GNTOLAX@aol.com). **Chicago,** P.O. Box 59594, Chicago, IL 60659 (☎773-539-6303; fax 539-6378; gntoch@aol.com).

MONEY. The official currency of Germany is the **euro** which replaced the **Deutschmark** (abbreviated DM). For more information on the euro, see p. 20. As a general rule, it's cheaper to exchange money in Germany than at home. If you stay in **hostels** and prepare your own food, expect to spend anywhere from €20-40 per person per day. The EU imposes a **value-added tax (VAT)** on goods and services purchased within the EU, which is included in the price (see p. 19).

ACCOMMODATIONS AND CAMPING

HOSTELS. Germany currently has about 600 **hostels**—more than any other nation. Hostelling in Germany is overseen by **Deutsches Jugendherbergswerk (DJH),** Bismarckstr. 8, 32756 Detmold, Germany (☎05231 740 10; www.djh.de). DJH has recently initiated a growing number of **Jugendgästehäuser,** youth guest-houses that have more facilities and attract slightly older guests than traditional hostels. DJH publishes *Jugendherbergen in Deutschland*, a guide to their German hostels.

HOTELS. The cheapest **hotel-style** accommodations are places with *Pension*, *Gasthof*, *Gästehaus*, or *Hotel-Garni* in the name. Hotel rooms start at €20 for singles and €25 for doubles; in large cities, expect to pay nearly twice as much. Breakfast *(Frühstück)* is almost always available and often included.

PRIVATE ROOMS. The best bet for a cheap bed is often a **Privatzimmer** (a room in a family home). This option works best if you have at least a rudimentary knowledge of German. Prices generally run €15-30 per person. Travelers over 26 who would otherwise pay higher prices at youth hostels will find these rooms within budget range. Reservations are made through the local tourist office or through a private *Zimmervermittlung* (room-booking office) for free or a €1-4 fee.

CAMPING. Germans love camping; over 2600 campsites dot the outskirts of even the most major cities. Facilities are well maintained and usually provide showers, bathrooms, and a restaurant or store. Camping costs €3-6 per person, with additional charges for tents and vehicles. Blue signs with a black tent on a white background indicate official sites. Deutscher Camping-Club (DCC), Mandlstr. 28, 80802 München (☎(089) 380 14 20), has more information, and the National Tourist Office distributes a free map, *Camping in Germany*.

COMMUNICATION

PHONE CODES	**Country code:** 49. **International dialing prefix:** 00.

TELEPHONES. Most public phones only accept *Telefonkarte* (telephone cards) which you can pick up in post offices, at kiosks, or at selected Deutsche Bahn counters in major train stations. There is no standard length for telephone numbers. The smaller the city, the more digits in the city code, while telephone numbers tend to have three to 10 digits. International direct dial numbers include: **AT&T,** ☎(800) 22 55 288; **British Telecom,** ☎800 89 00 49; **Canada Direct,** ☎800 888 00 14; **Ireland Direct,** ☎08000 800 353; **MCI,** ☎800 88 88 000; **Sprint,** ☎800 888 00 13; **Telecom New Zealand,** ☎800 080 00 64; **Telkom South Africa,** ☎800 180 00 27; **Telstra Australia,** ☎800 08 00 061.

MAIL. Mail can be sent via *Postlagernde Briefe* (Poste Restante) to almost any German city or town with a post office. The mail will go to the main post office unless you specify a post office by street address or postal code. Air mail usually takes 3-7 days to North America, Europe, and Australia; 6-12 days to New Zealand.

INTERNET ACCESS. Most German cities (as well as a surprising number of smaller towns) have at least one Internet cafe with web access for about €1-5 per 30min. Some German universities have banks of computers hooked up to the Internet in their libraries, ostensibly for student use only.

LANGUAGE. Many people in Western Germany speak English; this is less common in the East. For basic German words and phrases, see p. 1022.

BERLIN ☎030

Don't wait any longer to see Berlin. The city is nearing the end of a massive transitional phase, developing from a newly reunited metropolis reeling in the aftermath of the Cold War to the epicenter of the European Union—and the Berlin of five or even two years from now will be radically different from the Berlin of today. Germany is the industrial leader of the continent, and when the Lehrter *Stadtbahnhof* (Europe's largest train station) opens in 2004, this capital city will essentially become the capital of Europe. However, in the wake of the Nazi regime and the Holocaust, Germans question their own ability—and right—to govern. The problem of "*Mauer im Kopf*" ("wall in the head"), the still-existing feelings of division between East and West Germany is more prevalent here than anywhere else. Indeed, the concept of a divided city is quite familiar to Berliners; Berlin is built not around a single center but around many colorfully varied neighborhoods. As a result, the atmosphere is the most diverse and tolerant of any of Germany's cities, with a world-famous gay and lesbian scene and an almost non-existent racial crime rate. But the real reason to visit is the city's exquisite tension between past and future, conservation and modernization. No other city is currently poised to attain such geopolitical importance, and the air is taut with hope and foreboding.

INTERCITY TRANSPORTATION

Berlin is rapidly becoming the hub of the international rail network, with rail and air connections to most other European capitals. Almost all European airlines have service to one of Berlin's three airports.

Flights: For information on all 3 airports, call ☎(0180) 500 01 86. Currently, the city is making the transition from 3 airports to 1 (Flughafen Schönefeld), but for now,

Flughafen Tegel (TXL) will remain Western Berlin's main airport. Express bus #X9 from Bahnhof Zoo, bus #109 from Jakob-Kaiser-Pl. on U7, bus #128 from Kurt-Schumacher-Pl. on U6, or bus TXL from Potsdamer Platz. **Flughafen Tempelhof** (THF), Berlin's smallest airport, has intra-German and intra-European flights. U6 to Pl. der Luftbrücke. **Flughafen Schönefeld** (SXF), southeast of Berlin, has intercontinental flights. S45 or S9 to Flughafen Berlin Schönefeld.

Train Stations: Trains to and from Berlin are serviced by **Zoologischer Garten** (almost always called **Bahnhof Zoo**) in the West and **Ostbahnhof** (formerly the *Hauptbahnhof*) in the East. Most trains go to both stations, but some connections to cities in the former GDR only stop at *Ostbahnhof.* For **info,** call ☎(0180) 599 66 33 or visit www.bahn.de. Trains run to: **Cologne** (4¼hr., every hr., €98); **Dresden** (2¼hr., every 2hr., €22); **Frankfurt** (4hr., every hr., €106); **Hamburg** (2½hr., every hr., €45); **Leipzig** (2-2¾hr., every hr., €26-34); **Munich** (6½-7hr., every hr., €102). **International connections** to most major European cities. Times and prices change frequently—check at the train stations.

Buses: ZOB, the central bus station (☎301 03 80), is by the *Funkturm* near Kaiserdamm. U2 to Kaiserdamm or S4, 45, or 46 to Witzleben. Open daily 6:30am-9pm. Check *Zitty* and *Tip* for deals on long-distance buses, or call **Gulliver's** travel agency, Hardenbergpl. 14 (☎311 02 11 or (00800) 4855 4837), at the far end of the bus parking lot in Bahnhof Zoo. Open M-F 8am-8pm, Sa-Su 10am-8pm. To **Paris** (14hr., €59) and **Vienna** (10½hr., €49).

Mitfahrzentralen (Ride Sharing): *Let's Go* does not recommend hitchhiking as a safe mode of transportation. **City Netz,** Joachimstaler Str. 17 (☎194 44), has a computerized ride-share database. U9 or 15 to Kurfürstendamm. **Mitfahr2000,** Yorckstr. 52 (☎194 20 00; www.mitfahr.de), formerly the *Mitfahrtelefon für Schwule und Lesben* (Ride Sharing for Gays and Lesbians). Open daily 8am-8pm.

ORIENTATION

Berlin is an immense conglomeration of what were once two separate and unique cities. The former East contains most of Berlin's landmarks and historic sites, as well as an unfortunate number of pre-fab concrete socialist architectural experiments. The former West functioned for decades as a small, isolated, Allied-occupied state and is still the commercial heart of united Berlin. The situation is rapidly changing, however, as businesses and embassies move their headquarters to Potsdamer Pl. and Mitte in the East.

The vast **Tiergarten,** Berlin's beloved park, lies in the center of the city; the grand, tree-lined **Straße des 17. Juni** runs through it from west to east and becomes **Unter den Linden** at the **Brandenburg Gate.** North of the Gate is the **Reichstag,** while south of the Gate **Ebertstraße** winds to glitzy **Potsdamer Platz.** Unter den Linden continues east through **Mitte,** the location of countless historical sites. The street changes names once again, to **Karl-Liebknecht-Straße,** before emptying into **Alexanderplatz,** home to Berlin's most visible landmark, the **Fernsehturm** (TV tower). At the east end of Mitte is the **Museumsinsel** ("Museum Island"). Cafe- and shop-lined **Oranienburgerstraße** cuts through the area of northeastern Mitte known as **Scheunenviertel,** historically Berlin's center of Jewish life.

The commercial district of West Berlin lies at the southwest end of the Tiergarten, centered around **Bahnhof Zoo** and the **Kurfürstendamm** (**Ku'damm** for short). To the east is **Breitscheidplatz,** marked by the bombed-out **Kaiser-Wilhelm-Gedächtniskirche,** and **Savignyplatz,** one of many pleasant squares in **Charlottenburg,** which is home to cafes, restaurants, and *Pensionen.* Southeast of the Ku'damm, **Schöneberg** is a pleasant residential neighborhood and the traditional nexus of the city's gay and lesbian community. At the southeast periphery of Berlin lies **Kreuzberg,** a district home to an exciting mix of radical leftists and punks as well as

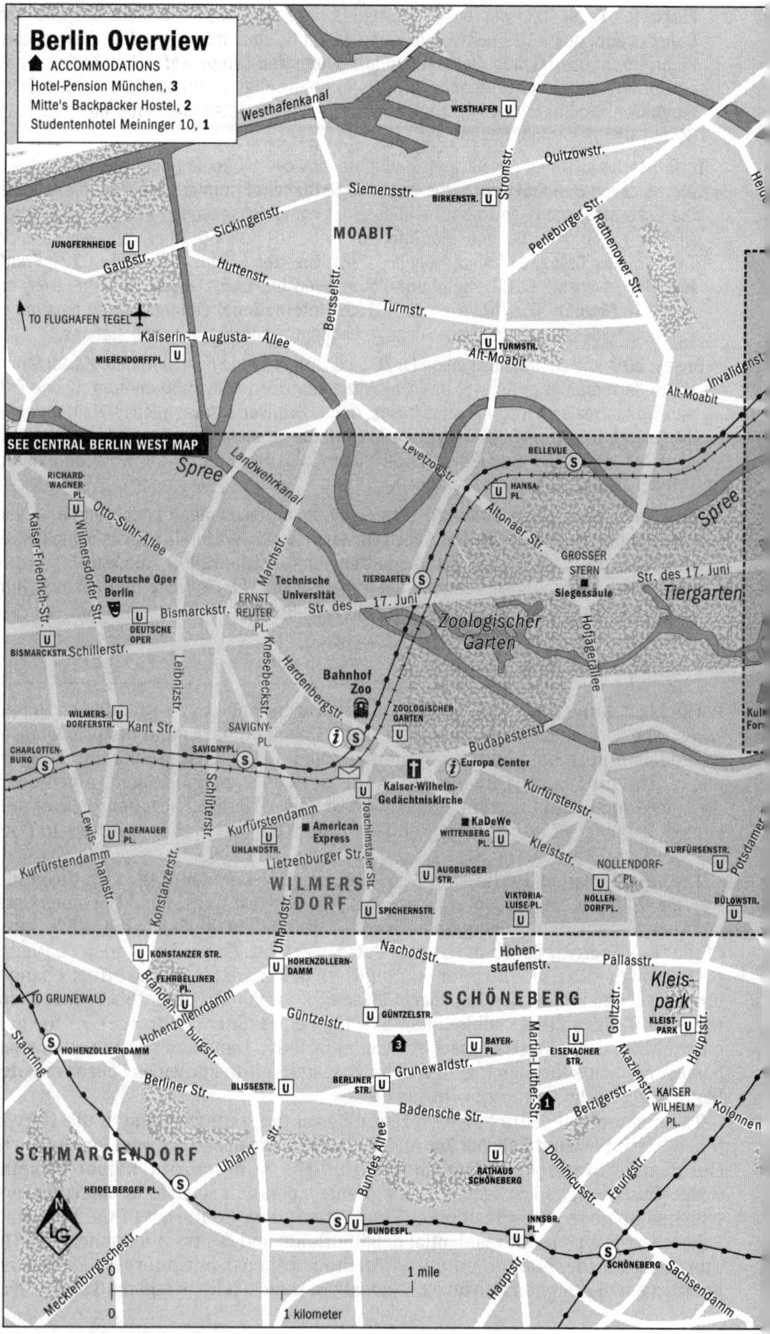
Berlin Overview
ACCOMMODATIONS
Hotel-Pension München, 3
Mitte's Backpacker Hostel, 2
Studentenhotel Meininger 10, 1
SEE CENTRAL BERLIN WEST MAP
MOABIT
WILMERSDORF
SCHÖNEBERG
SCHMARGENDORF
Tiergarten
Zoologischer Garten
Spree
Westhafenkanal
Landwehrkanal
TO FLUGHAFEN TEGEL
TO GRUNEWALD
Bahnhof Zoo
Technische Universität
Deutsche Oper Berlin
Kaiser-Wilhelm-Gedächtniskirche
Europa Center
KaDeWe
American Express
Siegessäule
Kleistpark
0
1 mile
0
1 kilometer

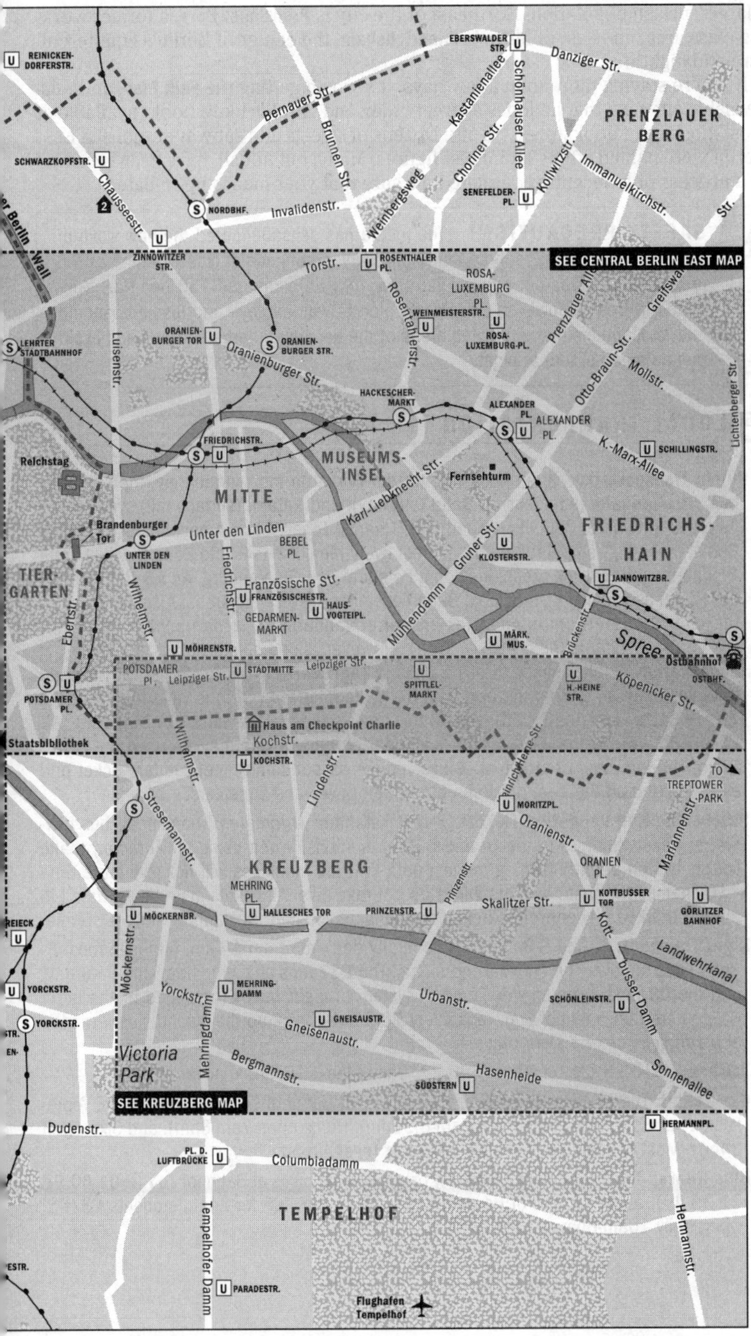
REINICKEN-DORFERSTR.
EBERSWALDER STR.
Danziger Str.
Bernauer Str.
Kastanienallee
Schönhauser Allee
PRENZLAUER BERG
SCHWARZKOPFSTR.
Chausseestr.
Brunnen Str.
Choriner Str.
Immanuelkirchstr.
Weinbergsweg
SENEFELDER-PL.
Kollwitzstr.
NORDBHF.
Invalidenstr.
Berlin Wall
ZINNOWITZER STR.
ROSENTHALER PL.
SEE CENTRAL BERLIN EAST MAP
Torstr.
ROSA-LUXEMBURG PL.
Rosenthalerstr.
WEINMEISTERSTR.
ROSA-LUXEMBURG-PL.
Prenzlauer Allee
Greifswalder
LEHRTER STADTBAHNHOF
Luisenstr.
ORANIEN-BURGER TOR
ORANIEN-BURGER STR.
Oranienburger Str.
Otto-Braun-Str.
Mollstr.
Lichtenberger Str.
HACKESCHER-MARKT
ALEXANDER PL.
ALEXANDER PL.
FRIEDRICHSTR.
Reichstag
MUSEUMS-INSEL
K.-Marx-Allee
SCHILLINGSTR.
MITTE
Fernsehturm
Karl-Liebknecht Str.
Brandenburger Tor
Unter den Linden
UNTER DEN LINDEN
BEBEL PL.
Friedrichstr.
Gruner Str.
KLOSTERSTR.
FRIEDRICHS-HAIN
TIER-GARTEN
Französische Str.
FRANZÖSISCHESTR.
HAUS-VOGTEIPL.
Wilhelmstr.
GEDARMEN-MARKT
Mühlendamm
JANNOWITZBR.
Ebertstr.
MÖHRENSTR.
MÄRK. MUS.
Brückenstr.
Spree
Ostbahnhof
OSTBHF.
POTSDAMER PL.
Leipziger Str.
STADTMITTE
Leipziger Str.
SPITTEL-MARKT
H.-HEINE STR.
Köpenicker Str.
POTSDAMER PL.
Haus am Checkpoint Charlie
Kochstr.
Staatsbibliothek
Wilhelmstr.
KOCHSTR.
Lindenstr.
Heinrich-Heine-Str.
TO TREPTOWER PARK
Stresemannstr.
MORITZPL.
Oranienstr.
Mariannenstr.
ORANIEN PL.
KREUZBERG
MEHRING PL.
Prinzenstr.
KOTTBUSSER TOR
GÖRLITZER BAHNHOF
Skalitzer Str.
MÖCKERNBR.
HALLESCHES TOR
PRINZENSTR.
Möckernstr.
Kottbusser Damm
Landwehrkanal
YORCKSTR.
MEHRING-DAMM
Yorckstr.
Urbanstr.
SCHÖNLEINSTR.
YORCKSTR.
GNEISAUSTR.
Gneisenaustr.
Mehringdamm
Victoria Park
Bergmannstr.
Hasenheide
SÜDSTERN
Sonnenallee
SEE KREUZBERG MAP
HERMANNPL.
Dudenstr.
PL. D. LUFTBRÜCKE
Columbiadamm
TEMPELHOF
Hermannstr.
Tempelhofer Damm
PARADESTR.
Flughafen Tempelhof

a large Turkish population. Northeast of the city is **Prenzlauer Berg,** a former working-class area, and east of Mitte is **Friedrichshain,** the center of Berlin's counterculture and nightlife.

If you're staying more than a few days, it's worth getting the **Falk Plan**, an indispensable city map that includes a street index and unfolds like a book (available at most kiosks and bookstores; €6.50). Dozens of streets and subway stations in East Berlin were named after Communist figures. Many, but not all, have been renamed in a process only recently completed; be sure that your map is up-to-date.

SAFETY PRECAUTION! The media has sensationalized the new wave of Nazi extremism perhaps more than necessary; among major cities, Berlin has the fewest hate crimes per capita. There are only an estimated 750 neo-Nazi skinheads in Berlin. However, people of color as well as gays and lesbians should take precautions in the outlying areas of the eastern suburbs and perhaps avoid them altogether late at night.

LOCAL TRANPORTATION

Public Transportation: It is impossible to tour Berlin on foot—fortunately, the extensive **bus, Straßenbahn** (streetcar), **U-Bahn** (subway), and **S-Bahn** (surface rail) systems will take you anywhere. Berlin is divided into 3 transit zones. **Zone A** encompasses central Berlin, including Tempelhof airport. Almost everything else falls into **Zone B,** while **Zone C** contains the outlying areas, including Potsdam and Oranienburg. An **AB ticket** is the best deal, as you can buy regional Bahn tickets for the outlying areas. A single ticket for the combined network is good for 2hr. after validation (*Eizelfahrschein* AB or BC, €2.10; or *Eizelfahrschein* ABC, €2.45). However, since single tickets are pricey, it almost always makes sense to buy a pass: a **Tageskarte** (AB €6, ABC €6.50) is good from validation until 3am the next day; the **WelcomeCard** (€17) is valid for 72hr.; the **7-Tage-Karte** (€22, ABC €28) is good for 7 days; and the **Umweltkarte Standard** (AB €56, ABC €69.50) is valid for one calendar month. Tickets may be used on any S-Bahn, U-Bahn, bus, or streetcar. **Bikes** require an additional, reduced-fare ticket and are permitted on the U- and S-Bahn but not on buses and streetcars.

Purchasing and Validating Tickets: Buy tickets from *Automaten* (machines), bus drivers, or ticket windows in the U- and S-Bahn stations. When using an *Automat,* make your selection before inserting money; note that the machines will not give more than €10 change and that some machines do not take bills. All tickets must be validated in the box marked hier entwerfen before boarding, or you may be slapped with a €30 fine.

Night Transport: U- and S-Bahn lines generally don't run from 1-4am, although most S-Bahn lines run every hr. on weekend nights. The **U12** runs all night Friday and Saturday, and the **U9** runs 24hr. all week long. A system of **night buses** (preceded by the letter N), centered on Bahnhof Zoo, runs every 20-30min.; pick up the *Nachtliniennetz* map at a *Fahrscheine und Mehr* office.

Taxis: ☎26 10 26, 21 02 02, or 690 22. Call at least 15min. in advance.

Car Rental: The **Mietwagenservice,** counter 21 in Bahnhof Zoo's *Reisezentrum*, represents Avis, Europacar (both open 7am-6:30pm), Hertz (open 7am-8pm), and Sixt (open 24hr.). Most companies also have offices in Tegel Airport.

Bike Rental: The government's **Bikecity** program rents bikes at Bahnhof Zoo (☎01 60 98 21 35 49), at the far end of Hardenbergpl. €5 for 4hr., €8 for 24hr.; students €3/€5. Open daily 10am-6pm.

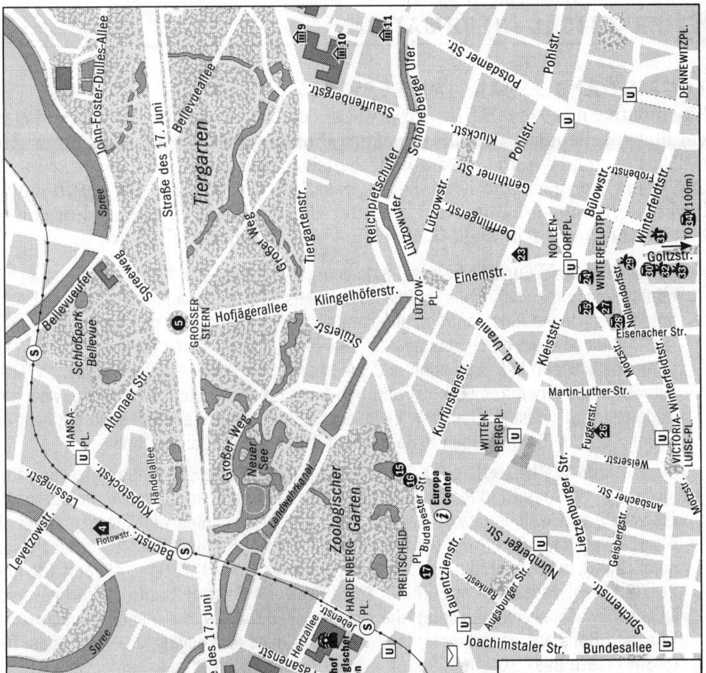
Central Berlin West
ACCOMMODATIONS
Art Hotel Connection, 26
Charlottenburger Hof, 21
CVJM-Haus, 23
Hotel-Pension Cortina, 20
Hotel-Pension Hansablick, 4
Hotel Sachsenhof, 27
Jugendgästehaus am Zoo, 8
Pension Knesebeck, 13
FOOD
Ali Baba, 22
Baharat Falafel, 31
Filmbühne am Steinplatz, 12
Fish and Vegetables, 33
Mensa TU, 7
Schwarzes Café, 19
Sushi am Winterfeldtplatz, 32
Tim's Canadian Deli, 29
NIGHTLIFE
A-Trane, 14
Metropol, 24
Mister Hu, 34
Omnes, 25
Quasimodo, 18
Scheune, 28
Slumberland, 30
ENTERTAINMENT
Deutsche Oper, 6
SIGHTS
Aquarium, 15
Elefantentor, 16
Kaiser-Wilhelm-Gedächtniskirche, 17
Siegessäule, 5
MUSEUMS
Ägyptisches Museum, 2
Gemäldegalerie, 10
Kunstgewerbemuseum, 9
Neue Nationalgalerie, 11
Sammlung Berggruen, 3
Schloß Charlottenburg, 1
Tiergarten
Straße des 17. Juni
Zoologischer Garten
Neuer See
Landwehrkanal
Spree
CHARLOTTENBURG
Technische Universität
Bahnhof Zoologischer Garten
Europa Center
GROSSER STERN
Schloßpark Bellevue
Kurfürstenstr.
Kantstr.
Hardenbergstr.
Tauentzienstr.
Joachimstaler Str.
Bundesallee
Nürnberger Str.
Lietzenburger Str.
Potsdamer Str.
Bülowstr.
Goltzstr.
Winterfeldtstr.
Kaiser-Friedrich-Str.
Otto-Suhr-Allee
Bismarckstr.
Kaiserdamm
Spandauer Damm
Schloßstr.
TO FUNKTURM & (700m)
TO 34 (100m)

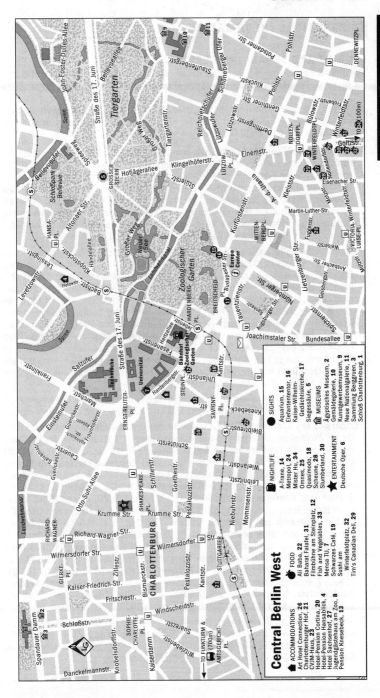

PRACTICAL INFORMATION

TOURIST AND FINANCIAL SERVICES

The monthly magazine *Berlin Programm* (€1.50) lists opera, theater, and classical music schedules. German-speakers should spring for *Tip* (€2.50) or *Zitty* (€2.30), which have the most comprehensive listings for film, theater, concerts, and clubs. For gays and lesbians, *Siegessäule*, *Sergej*, and *Gay-yellowpages* have entertainment listings and are offered in most tourist offices. For comprehensive information in English, check out www.berlin.de.

Tourist Offices: EurAide (www.euraide.com), in Bahnhof Zoo, has excellent travel information, recommends hostels for free, and makes train and hotel reservations (€4 fee for hotels). Facing the Reisezentrum, head left and down the corridor on your right; it's on the left. Come early—the office gets packed, and like all Berlin tourist offices, they don't take phone calls. Open M-F 8am-noon and 1-4pm, Sa 8am-noon. **Europa-Center,** on Budapester Str., has city maps (€0.50) and free transit maps. From Bahnhof Zoo, walk along Budapester Str. past the Kaiser-Wilhelm-Gedächtniskirche; the office is on the right after about 2 blocks (5min.). Open M-Sa 8:30am-8:30pm, Su 10am-6:30pm.

Tours: Berlin Walks (☎301 91 94) offers a range of English-language walking tours, including Infamous Third Reich Sites, Jewish Life in Berlin, and Discover Potsdam. Their Discover Berlin Walk is one of the best ways to get acquainted with the city. Tours (2½-6hr.) leave daily 10am from the taxi stand in front of Bahnhof Zoo (Discover Potsdam meets 9am); in summer, the Discover Berlin Walk also meets 2:30pm. All tours €9, under 26 €8. Tickets available at EurAide. **Terry Brewer's Best of Berlin** (info@brewersberlin.com; www.brewersberlin.com) offers info-packed tours with a personal touch: guides Terry and Boris are legendary for their vast knowledge and engaging personalities. Tours (5-8hr.) leave daily 10:30am from the Neue Synagoge on Oranienburger Str. (S1, 2, or 25 to Oranienburger Str.). €10, under 14 free. **Insider Tour** (☎692 31 49) has enthusiastic guides. Tours last 4hr. and leave from the *McDonald's* by Bahnhof Zoo daily at 10am. In summer an additional tour runs at 2:30pm (€9).

Budget Travel: STA, Dorotheenstr. 30 (☎20 16 50 63) at the corner of Charlottenstr. U6 or S3, 5, 7, 9, or 75 to Friedrichstr. Open M, Th-F 10am-6pm, Tu-W 10am-8pm.

Embassies and Consulates: Berlin is building a new embassy complex. As of press time, the locations of the embassies and consulates remain in a state of flux. For the latest information, call the **Auswärtiges Amt Dienststelle Berlin** (☎20 18 60) or visit its office on the Werderscher Markt. U2 to Hausvogteipl. **Australian Embassy,** Friedrichstr. 200 (☎880 08 80). U2 or 6 to Stadtmitte. Open M-F 8:30am-1pm and 2-5pm; closes F at 4:15pm. Also Uhlandstr. 181-183 (☎880 08 80). U15 to Uhlandstr. Open M-F 8:30am-1pm. **Canadian Embassy,** Friedrichstr. 95 (☎20 31 20), on the 12th fl. of the International Trade Center. U6 or S1, 2, 3, 5, 7, 9, 25, or 75 to Friedrichstr. Open M-F 9-11am. **Irish Embassy,** Friedrichstr. 200 (☎22 07 20). Open M-F 9:30am-12:30pm and 2:30-4:45pm. **New Zealand Embassy,** Friedrichstr. 60 (☎20 62 10). Open M-F 9am-1pm and 2-5:30pm; closes F at 4:30pm. **South African Embassy,** Friedrichstr. 60 (☎22 07 30). South African Consulate: Douglasstr. 9 (☎82 50 11 or 825 27 11). S7 to Grunewald. Open M-F 9am-noon. **UK Embassy,** Wilhelmstr. 70-71 (☎20 18 40). S1, 2, 3, 5, 7, 9, 25, or 75 or U6 to Friedrichstr. Open M-F 9am-4pm. **US Citizens Service/ US Consulate,** Clayallee 170 (☎832 92 33). U1 to Oskar-Helene-Heim. Open M-F 8:30am-noon. Advice M-F 2-4pm; after hours, call ☎830 50.

Currency Exchange: Geldwechsel, Joachimstaler Str. 1-3 (☎882 63 71), has decent rates and no commission. **ReiseBank,** at Bahnhof Zoo (☎881 71 17; open daily 7:30am-10pm) and *Ostbahnhof* (☎296 43 93; open M-F 7am-10pm, Sa 8am-8pm, Su 8am-noon, 12:30-4pm), is conveniently located but has worse rates.

Central Berlin East

ACCOMMODATIONS
Circus, **8**
Clubhouse Hostel, **10**
Honigmond, **3**

NIGHTLIFE
Hackesche Höfe, **12**
Tresor, **37**
VEB-OZ, **6**
Zosch, **7**

ENTERTAINMENT
Ber. Philharmonisches Orchester, **38**
Konzerthaus, **32**

FOOD
Assel, **11**
Beth Café, **5**
Cafeteria Charlottenstr., **33**
Mensa der Humboldt-U, **19**
Taba, **4**

CHURCHES
Berliner Dom, **18**
Deutscher Dom, **34**
Französischer Dom, **31**
St.-Hedwigs-Kathedrale, **30**

MUSEUMS
Alte Nationalgalerie, **14**
Altes Museum, **17**
Deutsche Guggenheim Berlin, **27**
Deutsches Hist. Museum, **23**
Gemäldegalerie, **39**
Hamburger Bahnhof, **2**
Neue Nationalgalerie,**40**
Pergamonmuseum, **13**

SIGHTS
Alte Bibliothek, **29**
Bertolt-Brecht-Haus, **1**
Brandenburger Tor, **25**

SIGHTS (CONT.)
Deutsche Staatsbibliothek, **20**
Deutsche Staatsoper, **28**
Fernsehturm, **15**
Führerbunker, **35**
Haus am Checkpoint Charlie, **41**
Hotel Adlon, **26**
Humboldt-Universität, **21**
Neue Synagogue, **9**
Neue Wache, **22**
Rathaus Schöneberg, **24**
Reichstag, **16**
Russian Embassy, **36**

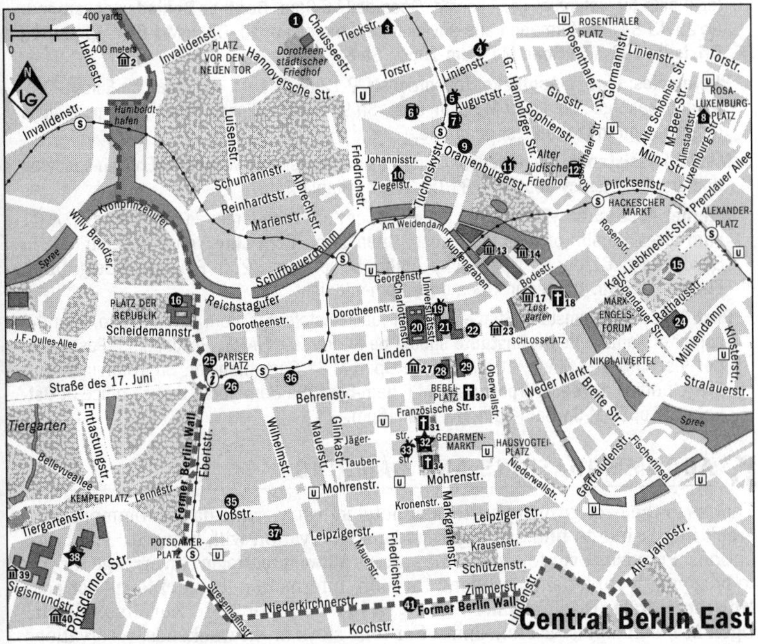

American Express: Main Office, Bayreuther Str. 37 (☎21 49 83 63). U1, 2, or 15 to Wittenbergpl. Holds mail, offers banking services and cashes AmEx Travelers Cheques with no commission. Expect long lines F and Sa. Open M-F 9am-7pm, Sa 10am-1pm. **Branch office,** Friedrichstr. 172 (☎20 17 40 12). U6 to Französische Str. Offers the same services and same hours.

LOCAL SERVICES

Luggage Storage: In **Bahnhof Zoo.** Lockers €0.50-2 per day, depending on size. 72hr. max. Open 24hr. If all lockers are full, try **Gepäckaufbewahrung,** the next window over (€2 per piece per day). Open daily 6:15am-10:30pm. 24hr. lockers are available at **Ostbahnhof** and **Alexanderplatz.**

Bi-Gay-Lesbian Resources: Lesbenberatung, Kulmer Str. 20a (☎215 20 00), offers counseling on lesbian issues. U7 to Kleistpark. Open M-Tu and Th 4-7pm, F 2-5pm. **Mann-o-Meter,** Motzstr. 5 (☎216 80 08), off Nollendorfpl., has information on gay nightlife and accommodations. Open M-F 5-10pm, Sa-Su 4-10pm.

Laundromat: Waschcenter Schnell und Sauber has locations in **Charlottenburg,** Leibnizstr. 72 (S3, 5, 7, 9, or 75 to Savignypl.); **Schöneberg,** Wexstr. 34 (U9 to Bundespl.); **Kreuzberg,** Mehringdamm 32 (U6 or 7 to Mehringdamm); **Mitte,** Torstr. 115 (U8 to Rosenthaler Pl.). Wash €2-4 for 6kg, dry €0.51 per 15min. Open daily 6am-11pm.

EMERGENCY AND COMMUNICATIONS

Emergency: Police: ☎110. **Ambulance and Fire:** ☎112.

Crisis Lines: English spoken at most crisis lines. **Sexual Assault Hotline** (☎251 28 28). Open Tu and Th 6-9pm, Su noon-2pm. **Schwules Überfall** (☎216 33 36), hotline and legal help for victims of gay bashing. Open daily 6-9pm. **Berliner Behindertenverband,** (☎20 43 847), information and advice for the handicapped. Open M-F 8am-4pm. **Drug Crisis** (☎192 37). Open M-F 8am-10pm, Sa-Su 2-9:30pm.

Pharmacies: Europa-Apotheke, Tauentzienstr. 9-12 (☎261 41 42), near the Europa-Center and Bahnhof Zoo. Open M-F 9am-8pm, Sa 9am-4pm. Closed pharmacies post signs directing you to the nearest open one.

Medical Assistance: The American and British embassies have a list of English-speaking doctors. **Emergency doctor** (☎31 00 31). Available 24hr.

Internet Access: easyEverything, the corner of Kurfürstendamm and Meineckestr. A €1 card gives 25min. of Internet access. Open 24hr. **Com Line,** Innsbrückerstr. 56, in Schöneberg. €1 per hr. Open 24hr. **Alpha,** Dunckerstr. 72, in Prenzlauer Berg. U2 to Eberswalder Str. €4 per hr. Open daily 2pm-midnight.

Post Office: Joachimstaler Straße 7, down Joachimstaler Str. from Bahnhof Zoo, near the corner of Kantstr. **Poste Restante** should be addressed: NAME, Postlagernd, Postamt in der Joachimstaler Str. 7, 10706 Berlin. Open M-Sa 8am-midnight, Su 10am-midnight. Branch office at **Tegel Airport** open M-F 8am-6pm, Sa 8am-noon; branch office at **Ostbahnhof** open M-Sa 8am-8pm, Su 10am-6pm.

ACCOMMODATIONS AND CAMPING

Thanks to the ever-growing hostel and hotel industry, same-day accommodations aren't impossible to find. Failing to make a reservation will, however, limit your options. For visits over four days, the various **Mitwohnzentralen** can arrange for you to housesit or sublet an apartment; for more information, contact **Home Company Mitwohnzentrale,** Joachimstaler Str. 17. (☎194 45. U9 or 15 to Kurfürstendamm. Open M-F 9am-6pm, Sa 11am-2pm.) For long stays or on weekends, reservations are essential. During the **Love Parade** (see p. 450), call at least two months ahead for a choice of rooms and at least two weeks ahead for any bed at all. Some hostels increase prices that weekend by up to €10 per night.

HOTELS, HOSTELS, AND PENSIONEN

MITTE

Mitte's Backpacker Hostel, Chausseestr. 102 (☎262 51 40). U6 to Zinnowitzer Str. Friendly English-speaking staff, themed rooms, and a relaxed atmosphere. Bikes €5 per day. Internet access. Kitchen available. Sheets €2.50. Laundry €5. Reception 24hr. Dorms €13-15; doubles €44-46; triples €57-60; quads €68-72. ❶

Circus, Rosa-Luxemburg-Str. 39-41 (☎28 39 14 33). U2 to Rosa-Luxemburg-Pl. Bikes €6 per day. Sheets €2. Reception 24hr. Reservations should be reconfirmed 1 day before

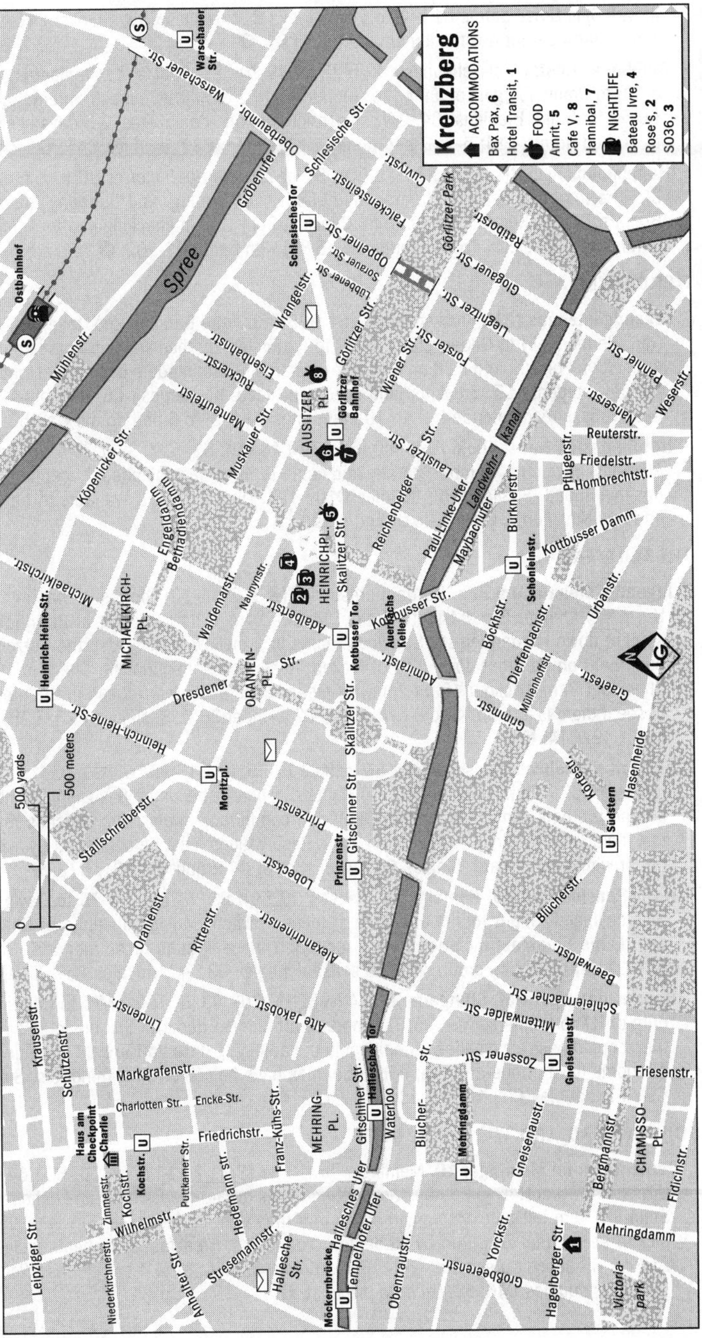
Kreuzberg
ACCOMMODATIONS
Bax Pax, 6
Hotel Transit, 1
FOOD
Amrit, 5
Cafe V, 8
Hannibal, 7
NIGHTLIFE
Bateau Ivre, 4
Rose's, 2
SO36, 3
500 yards
500 meters
Spree
Landwehr-kanal
Görlitzer Park
Ostbahnhof
Warschauer Str.
Schlesisches Tor
Görlitzer Bahnhof
Kottbusser Tor
Moritzpl.
Heinrich-Heine-Str.
Prinzenstr.
Hallesches Tor
Kochstr.
Möckernbrücke
Mehringdamm
Gneisenaustr.
Südstern
Schönleinstr.
Zossener Str.
LAUSITZER PL.
HEINRICHPL.
ORANIEN-PL.
MICHAELKIRCH-PL.
MEHRING-PL.
CHAMISSO-PL.
Haus am Checkpoint Charlie
Victoria-park
Hasenheide
Auerbachs Keller

arrival. 6- to 8-bed dorms €14; 4- to 5-bed dorms €17; singles €30; doubles €46; triples €60. Apartment for 4 with kitchen and bath €92. ❷

Clubhouse Hostel, Kalkscheunestr. 2 (☎28 09 79 79). S1, 2, or 25 to Oranienburger Str. or U6 to Oranienburger Tor. Enter from Johannisstr. 2 or Kalkscheunestr. Internet access €0.50 for 5min. Breakfast €4. 24hr. reception and bar. Call at least 2-3 days ahead. 8- to 10-bed dorms €14; 5- to 7-bed dorms €17; singles €32; doubles €45. ❷

Honigmond, Tieckstr. 12 (☎284 45 50). S1 or 2 to *Nordbahnhof* or U6 to Zinnowitzer Str. The romantic decor features canopy beds, iron grating, and bubbling fountains. Breakfast €3-9. Reception 9am-6pm. Check-in 3pm-1am; if checking in after 8pm, call beforehand. Singles €45-70; doubles €65-85, with bath €71-102. ❹

TIERGARTEN

Jugendgästehaus (HI), Kluckstr. 3 (☎257 998 08). From Bahnhof Zoo, take bus #129 (dir.: Hermannpl.) to Gedenkstätte or U1 to Kurfürstenstr., then walk up Potsdamer Str., turn left on Pohlstr., and right on Kluckstr. Clean rooms and modern decor. Bike rental €8 per day, students €5. Breakfast and sheets included. Key deposit €5. Reception 24hr. Reservations recommended. 6- to 10-bed dorms €14, 3- to 5-bed dorms €18.50. ❷

Hotel-Pension Hansablick, Flotowstr. 6 (☎390 48 00). S3, 5, 7, 9, or 75 to Tiergarten. All rooms have bath, minibar, phone, and cable TV. Breakfast included. Reception 24hr. Reserve ahead. Singles €82; doubles €101-121. Discount rates available in July-Aug. and mid-Nov.-Feb. 5% *Let's Go* discount. ❺

CHARLOTTENBURG

Jugendgästehaus am Zoo, Hardenbergstr. 9a (☎312 94 10), opposite the Technical University *Mensa.* Bus #145 to Steinpl., or walk from the back exit of Bahnhof Zoo straight down Hardenbergstr. Spacious rooms in a mellow setting. Use the buzzer and push hard on the front door; it's not locked. Reception 9am-midnight. Check-in 10am. Check-out 9am. Lockout 10am-2pm. No reservations accepted but call in the morning to see if there is a room. 4- to 8-bed dorms €21, under 26 €18; singles €28/€25; doubles €49/€44. ❸

Pension Knesebeck, Knesebeckstr. 86 (☎312 72 55; fax 313 95 07). S3, 5, 7, 9, or 75 to Savignypl. Follow Knesebeckstr. to Kantstr., where it becomes Savignypl.; continue around the park semicircle. Friendly staff and comfortable rooms with couches. Breakfast included. Laundry €4. Reception 24hr. Reservations must be confirmed by fax, letter, or with a credit card. Singles €39, with shower €43; doubles €61/€72. ❹

Hotel-Pension Cortina, Kantstr. 140 (☎313 90 59). S3, 5, 7, 9, or 75 to Savignypl. High-ceilinged, bright rooms and a great location within walking distance of Bahnhof Zoo. Large breakfast included. 24hr. reception. Reservations recommended. Dorms €20-31 depending on group size and season; singles €31-47; doubles €47-77. ❸

Charlottenburger Hof, Stuttgarter Pl. 14 (☎32 90 70). S3, 5, 7, 9, or 75 to Charlottenburg or U7 to Wilmersdorfer Str. The modern art-themed decor of this hostel is so chic that it could pass for a gallery. Breakfast in the adjoining **Café Voltaire** €4. Laundry €4. All rooms have phone and TVs; pricier doubles have balconies and whirlpools. Singles €61-77; doubles €81-103; quads €112-123. ❺

SCHÖNEBERG AND WILMERSDORF

Studentenhotel Meininger 10, Meininger Str. 10 (☎78 71 74 14 or (0800) 634 64 64). U4, bus #146 or N46 to Rathaus Schöneberg. Walk toward the *Rathaus* on Freiherr-vom-Stein-Str., turn left onto Martin-Luther-Str. and then right on Meininger Str. Free shuttle pickup at Bahnhof Zoo. Run by students, for students. Breakfast and sheets included. Lockers €5 deposit. Reception 24hr. Co-ed dorms €12.50; 3- to 4-bed dorms €21; singles €33; doubles €46; 5% *Let's Go* discount. ❶

CVJM-Haus, Einemstr. 10 (☎264 91 00). U1, 2, 4, or 15 to Nollendorfpl. Popular with school groups, and host to a surprisingly young crowd. One block from the gay nightlife of Nollendorfpl. Breakfast included. Sheets €4. Reception 24hr. Book in advance. €21 per person for dorms, singles, and doubles. ❸

Hotel-Pension München, Güntzelstr. 62 (☎857 91 20). U9 to Güntzelstr. Gracefully-decorated white-walled rooms with cable TV and phones, in a peaceful, relaxing part of Wilmersdorf. Breakfast €5. Parking €5. Check-out 11am. Written reservations recommended. Singles €33-36, with shower €48-57; doubles €40-47, with bath €58-72. Ask about *Mehrbettzimmer.* ❸

Art Hotel Connection, Fuggerstr. 33 (☎217 70 28). U1, 2, or 15 to Wittenbergpl., on a side street off Martin-Luther-Str. For gay and lesbian guests only (though mostly men stay here). Artsy rooms come with phones, TVs, and alarm clocks. Breakfast included. Reservations for weekends required at least 1 month in advance. Singles €60-80; doubles €100; cheaper in winter. ❹

Jugendhotel Berlin City. Crellestr. (☎78 70 21 30). U7 to Kleistpark. This hotel provides simple, clean rooms and is popular with school groups, so book ahead. Breakfast included. 6-bed dorms €26-28; singles €38-46; doubles €60-80. ❹

Hotel Sachsenhof, Motzstr. 7 (☎216 20 74). U1, 2, 4, or 15 to Nollendorfpl. Small, well-furnished rooms with phone and TV. Surrounded by the myriad cafes and gay nightlife of Nollendorfpl. Breakfast €6. Reception 24hr. Singles €30, with shower €35; doubles €51/€65; new double with shower €69, with full bath €80. ❸

KREUZBERG

Bax Pax, Skalitzer Str. 104 (☎69 51 83 22). U1 or 15 to Görlitzer Bahnhof. Great location at the mouth of mighty Oranienstr. Fuzzy blue carpets and one room with a bed inside a VW Bug make this a unique hostelling experience. Sheets €2.50. Reception 7am-10pm. Dorms €15-18; singles €30; doubles €46; triples €60. ❷

Hotel Transit, Hagelberger Str. 53-54 (☎789 04 70). U6 or 7 or bus #N19 to Mehringdamm. Modern rooms and a sleek lounge with big-screen TV and well-stocked bar. Breakfast included. Reception 24hr. Dorms €19; singles €52; doubles €60; triples €78; quads €104. ❷

CAMPING

Deutscher Camping-Club runs the following campgrounds. Reservations are recommended. Call ☎218 60 71 or 218 60 72. All sites €5.10 per person, €3.80 per tent.

Dreilinden, Albrechts-Teerofen (☎805 12 01). S7 to Griebnitzsee, then turn right out of the station onto Rudolf-Breitschied-Str., take another right on Bäkestr. and follow to campground (40min.). Isolated location, just off the river. Open Mar.-Oct. ❶

Kladow, Krampnitzer Weg 111-117 (☎365 27 97). U7 to Rathaus Spandau, then bus #135 (dir.: Alt-Kladow) to the end and bus #234 to Krampnitzer Weg/Selbitzerstr. Swimmable lake, store, and restaurant on premises. ❶

FOOD

Berlin defies all expectations with both tasty home-grown options and terrific ethnic food from its Turkish, Indian, Italian, and Thai immigrants. Typical Berlin street food is Turkish; most *Imbiße* (fast-food snack stands) are open late. The *Döner kebap*, a sandwich of lamb or chicken and salad, has cornered the fast-food market, with *falafel* running a close second; either makes a small meal for €1.50-3. Berlin's numerous relaxed cafes, restaurants, and *kneipen* are budget friendly and usually offer meals of many sizes.

THE HIDDEN DEAL

BABEL

Schwarma, falafel, and thou. An Elysian field of eating, this crowded locale serves excellent Lebanese specialties on a pleasant Prenzlauer Berg boulevard.

The interior is a mish-mash of intensely orange walls, bundles of fresh flowers, eclectic chairs, and paintings of Mediterranean seascapes. Lush plants climb the walls, while the display reveals an awe-inspiring feast of rainbow-colored veggies, rotund pots of hummus, and delectable spinach-stuffed pastries.

The ingredients are superb–the fluffy falafel balls are stuffed with spices and the schwarma comes with mint and potatoes. A falafel or schwarma by itself makes a surprisingly filling meal (€3), while the plate option allows you to indulge in literally mountains of food without taking a bite out of your budget (most €5).

To avoid the temptation of ordering multiple meals, pick up your food at the counter and eat at the spacious sidewalk tables among salivating Prenzlauer Berg hipsters.

(☎440 313 18. Kastanienallee 33. U2 to Eberswalderstr. Open daily 11am-midnight.) ❷

Aldi, Plus, Edeka, and **Penny Markt** are the cheapest supermarket chains. Supermarkets are usually open Monday to Friday 9am-6pm and Saturday 9am-4pm. At Bahnhof Zoo, **Nimm's Mit** near the Reisezentrum is open 24hr. The best **open-air market** fires up Saturday mornings on Winterfeldtpl.

MITTE

Mensa der Humboldt-Universität, Unter den Linden 6, behind the university's main building. The cheapest *Mensa* in Berlin, conveniently located amidst Mitte's many stellar sights. Meals €1.80-3. Student ID required. Open M-F 11:30am-2:30pm. ❶

Cafeteria Charlottenstraße, Charlottenstr. 55, at the Hochschule für Musik, near the Gendarmenmarkt. U6 to Französische Str. or U2 or 6 to Stadtmitte. The entrance is in a corridor accessible from Taubenstr. or Charlottenstr. Salads and grill items available. Meals €1.90, students €1.20. Open M-F 8:30am-3pm. ❶

Assel, Oranienburgerstr. 21. S1, 2, or 25 to Oranienburgerstr. A rotating menu has everything from Tex-Mex to pasta. (Entrees €5-8). Open daily 10pm-late. ❸

Taba, Torstr. 164. U6 to Rosenthaler Pl. Meals are pricey, but the vast buffet W-Th (€6.50) is a filling and tasty option at this festive Brazilian eatery. Buy a Brazilian cigar or listen to the live music F-Su. Open Tu-Su from 7pm. ❸

Beth Café, Tucholskystr. 40, just off Auguststr. S1, 2, or 25 to Oranienburger Str. Kosher restaurant in the heart of the Scheunenviertel. Open M-Th and Su 11am-10pm, F 11am-5pm; in winter closes F 3pm. ❷

CHARLOTTENBURG

Mensa TU, Hardenbergstr. 34. Bus #145 to Steinpl., or walk 10min. from Bahnhof Zoo. Meals (including a variety of vegetarian dishes) €2-3 for students, others €2-4. Cafeteria downstairs has longer hours but slightly higher prices. *Mensa* open M-F 11am-2:15pm. Cafeteria open M-F 8am-5pm. ❶

Filmbühne am Steinplatz, Hardenbergstr. 12. This cafe at Berlin's oldest independent cinema has an unhurried atmosphere. Entrees €3-11, drinks €3. Open M-Sa 9am-3am, Su 9am-2am. Films (usually subtitled) €6. Call ☎312 90 12 for film info. ❸

Schwarzes Café, Kantstr. 148. S3, 5, 7, 9, or 75 to Savignypl. This cafe is always open, except Tu 3am-10am. Prices are a bit high (a milkshake is €3), but breakfast is served around the clock. ❸

Ali Baba, Bleibtreustr. 45. S3, 5, 7, 9, or 75 to Savignypl. A faithful sect of followers crowds the outdoor seating to enjoy the mountainous servings of spaghetti (€4) and the crunchy personal pizzas (€4), baked fresh every day. Open daily 11:30am-3am. ❷

SCHÖNEBERG

Baharat Falafel, Winterfeldtstr. 37. U1, 2, 4, or 15 to Nollendorfpl. Falafel with veggies and heavenly hummus from €6. Open daily 11am-3am; closed last week in July. ❷

Fish and Vegetables, Goltzstr. 32. U1, 2, 4, or 15 to Nollendorfpl. A no-nonsense do-it-yourself Thai restaurant, bustling around lunchtime and during the evening. Entrees from €3. Open daily noon-midnight. Next door, **Rani** serves Indian food in a similar fashion. ❷

Sushi am Winterfeldtplatz, Goltzstr. 24. U1, 2, 4, or 15 to Nollendorfpl. Standing-room only Japanese cuisine in the heart of Schöneberg. Sample the fresh sushi for €2-7. Open M-Sa noon-midnight, Su 3pm-midnight. Delivery until 1hr. before closing. ❷

Tim's Canadian Deli, Maaßenstr. 14. U1, 2, 4, or 15 to Nollendorfpl. With 3 menu pages devoted to bagels, Tim's is much more than a respite for the homesick Canadian. Open M-F 8am-1am, Sa-Su 9am-3am. ❶

KREUZBERG

Amrit, Oranienstr. 202-203. U1 or 15 to Görlitzer Bahnhof. Serves up generous, but pricey, dishes of colorful Indian food. Open Su-Th noon-1am, F-Sa noon-2am. ❹

Hannibal, at the corner of Wienerstr. and Skalitzerstr. Bus N29 or U1, 12, or 15 to Görlitzer Bahnhof. A unique spot for a leisurely breakfast or for scarfing down a massive Hannibal-burger (€6). Open M-Th 8am-3am, F-Sa 8am-4am, Su 9am-3am. ❷

Cafe V, Lausitzer Pl. U1 or 15 to Görlitzer Bahnhof. Berlin's oldest vegetarian restaurant. Top-of-the-line, bottom-of-the-food-chain. Open daily 10am-1am. ❸

PRENZLAUER BERG

Osswald, Göhrener Str. 5. U2 to Eberswalder Str. This restaurant/bar caters to locals with simple but tasty German dishes. A staggering breakfast buffet packs the place until 5pm on Sunday (€7). Open daily 9am-4am. ❸

Im Nu, Lychnerstr. 41. U2 to Eberswalderstr. Eclectic decor complements crunchy salads (€3-5) and sumptuous baguettes (€3). Open daily 8am-1am. ❷

SIGHTS

Berlin's sights cover an area eight times the size of Paris. For a guide to the city's major neighborhoods, see **Orientation,** p. 427. Below, the sights are organized by *Bezirk* (district), beginning with Mitte and spiralling outward. Many of central Berlin's major sights lie along the route of **bus #100,** from Bahnhof Zoo to Prenzlauer Berg; consider a day pass (€6.10) or a 7-day pass (€22).

MITTE

Formerly the heart of Imperial Berlin, Mitte contains some of Berlin's most magnificent sights and museums. Much of the neighborhood languished in disrepair during GDR (East German) days, but now that the government is back in town, the district is once again living up to its name (*Mitte* means center), as embassies and national institutes pour back into the area's rapidly-renovating streets.

UNTER DEN LINDEN

This area is best reached by taking S1, 2, or 25 to Unter den Linden; alternatively, bus #100 runs the length of the boulevard every 4-6min.

THE INSIDER'S CITY

GALLERIES OF MITTE

Mitte is home to a plethora of galleries—mostly small, cutting-edge exhibition spaces inconspicuously located in courtyards set back from the street. While walking through the area around Auguststraße will inevitably lead to a number of good finds, many of the more established galleries are within a few blocks of one another and can easily be seen on a short walking tour.

1. Large-scale photography at **Kicken Berlin,** Linienstr. 155.
2. **Wohnmaschine,** Tucholskystr. 35, is Mitte's oldest, wackiest gallery.
3. Sepia-toned vintage photographs at **Bodo Niemann,** Auguststr. 19.
4. Ultra-hip, trend-setting works at **EIGEN+ART,** Auguststr. 26.
5. Representatives of the local scene at **Zwinger Galerie,** Gipsstr. 3.
6. Young international artists' electric, paint-spattered work at **griedvonputtkamer,** Sophienstr. 25.
7. Steaming coffee and rich, layered cakes facilitate recovery at **Barcomi's Deli.**

BRANDENBURGER TOR AND PARISER PLATZ. For decades a barricaded gateway to nowhere, the **Brandenburg Gate** is the most powerful emblem of reunited Germany. Standing right in the center of the city, it was in no-man's land during the time of the wall; today it opens east onto **Pariser Platz** and Unter den Linden and west onto the Tiergarten and Str. des 17. Juni. All but a few of the venerable buildings near the gate were destroyed in WWII, but a massive reconstruction effort has already revived such pre-war staples as the Hotel Adlon, once the premier address for visiting dignitaries and celebrities.

RUSSIAN EMBASSY. Rebuilding the edifices of the rich and famous wasn't a huge priority in the workers' state, but one exception was this imposing *Palais*, Unter den Linden 55. The massive building, which takes up an entire block, reverted to an ordinary embassy at the end of the Cold War, and the huge bust of Lenin that once graced its red star-shaped topiary was quietly removed in 1994.

DEUTSCHE STAATSBIBILIOTHEK AND HUMBOLDT-UNIVERSITÄT. The library's shady, ivy-covered courtyard provides respite from the surrounding urban bustle. *(Unter den Linden 8. Library open M-F 9am-9pm, Sa 9am-5pm. €0.50.)* Just beyond is the H-shaped main building of Humboldt University, Unter den Linden 6, whose alumni include Einstein, the Brothers Grimm, Bismarck, and Karl Marx. In the street, a triumphant Friedrich the Great stands guard on horseback.

NEUE WACHE. During the GDR era, the "New Guardhouse" was known as the "Memorial to the Victims of Fascism and Militarism" and, ironically, was guarded by East German soldiers. It was reopened in 1993 as a war memorial. The remains of an unknown soldier and an unknown concentration camp victim are buried inside with earth from Nazi concentration camps as well as from the battlefield at Stalingrad. *(Unter den Linden 4. Open daily 10am-6pm.)*

BEBELPLATZ. On May 10, 1933, Nazi students burned nearly 20,000 books here, all written by "subversive" authors such as Heinrich Heine and Sigmund Freud—both Jews. A plaque in the center of the square is engraved with Heine's eerily prescient 1820 quote: *Nur dort wo man Bücher verbrennt, verbrennt man am Ende auch Menschen.* ("Wherever books are burned, ultimately people are burned as well.") Look down into the glass-covered opening a few yards away.

The building with the curved façade is the **Alte Bibliothek,** once the royal library. On the other side of the square is the **Deutsche Staatsoper** (opera house), fully rebuilt after the war from original sketches. The distinctive blue dome at the end of the square belongs to the **St.-Hedwigs-Kathedrale.** Built in 1773 as the first Catholic church in Berlin after the Reformation, it was destroyed by American bombers in 1943 and then rebuilt in the 1950s. *(Cathedral open M-Sa 10am-5pm, Su 1-5pm. Free.)*

AROUND POTSDAMER PLATZ

POTSDAMER PLATZ. Built under Friedrich Wilhelm I with the primary purpose of moving troops quickly, Potsdamer Platz was chosen to become the new commercial center of Berlin after reunification. Completion is now in sight, and the cutting-edge, wildly ambitious architectural designs make for some spectacular sight-seeing. *(U2 or S1, 2, or 25 to Potsdamer Pl.)*

FÜHRERBUNKER. Near Potsdamer Pl., unmarked and inconspicuous, lies the site of the bunker where Hitler married Eva Braun and then ended his life. Tourists looking for it often mistakenly head for the visible bunker at the southern edge of Potsdamer Platz; it's actually on the street In den Ministergärten, off Eberstr., behind a playground. Plans to restore the bunker were shelved amid fears that the site would become a shrine for the radical right.

GENDARMENMARKT

Several blocks south of Bebelplatz, **Gendarmentmarkt** is home to some of Berlin's most impressive 19th-century buildings. During the last week of June and the first week of July, the square transforms into an outdoor stage for classical concerts.

DEUTSCHER DOM. Gracing the southern end of the square, the *Dom* is not used as a church but instead houses **Fragen an die deutsche Geschichte** ("Questions asked of German History"), a government-sponsored exhibition on German political history. *(Gendarmenmarkt 5. Open June-Aug. W-Su 10am-7pm, Tu 10am-10pm; Sept.-May W-Su 10am-6pm, Tu 10am-10pm. Free.)*

FRANZÖSISCHER DOM. At the opposite end of the square from the Deutscher Dom, the Französischer Dom (French Cathedral) is now home to a restaurant and a small museum chronicling the French Huguenot diaspora. The tower offers a 360-degree panorama of the city. *(Gendarmenmarkt 5. Museum open Tu-Sa noon-5pm, Su 11am-5pm. €2, students €1. Tower open M-Sa 9am-7pm. €2, students €1.50.)*

KONZERTHAUS AM GENDARMENMARKT. The Konzerthaus in between the two churches was badly damaged by World War II bombings. It reopened in 1984 as the most elegant concert venue in Berlin and hosts a variety of performances from chamber music to international orchestras. *(Gendarmenmarkt 2. ☎ 203 09 21 01.)*

MUSEUMSINSEL AND ALEXANDERPLATZ

After crossing over the Spree, Unter den Linden becomes Karl-Liebknecht-Str. and cuts through the **Museumsinsel** (Museum Island), home to five major museums and the **Berliner Dom.** (For information on the museums of Museumsinsel, see p. 445.) Karl-Liebknecht-Str. continues into the monolithic **Alexanderplatz.**

BERLINER DOM. This multiple-domed cathedral, one of Berlin's most recognizable landmarks, was built during the reign of Kaiser Wilhelm II and recently emerged from 20 years of restoration after being damaged in a 1944 air raid. *(Open M-Sa 9am-7pm, Su noon-7pm. Dom and crypt €4, students €2. Free organ recitals W-F at 3pm.)*

ALEXANDERPLATZ. Formerly the heart of Weimar Berlin, the plaza was transformed in East German times into an urban wasteland of fountains and pre-fab office buildings. In the 1970s, enormous neon signs like "Medical Instruments of the GDR—Distributed in All the World!" were added to satisfy the people's need for bright lights. Today the signs have vanished, and the square is filled with bourgeois German shoppers, tourists, and dog-walkers.

FERNSEHTURM. The TV tower, the tallest structure in Berlin, was originally intended to showcase East Germany's technological prowess. The windows have a crucifix-shaped glint pattern known as the *Papsts Rache* ("pope's revenge") when the sun is out. *(Open Mar.-Oct. daily 9am-1am; Nov.-Feb. 10am-midnight. €6.)*

SCHEUNENVIERTEL AND ORANIENBURGER STRAßE

Northwest of Alexanderpl., around Oranienburger Str. and Große Hamburger Str., lies the **Scheunenviertel,** once the center of Berlin's Orthodox Jewish community. Take S1, 2, or 25 to Oranienburger Str. or U6 to Oranienburger Tor. Today the Scheunenviertel is better known for its outdoor cafes than for its historical significance as Berlin's Jewish center, but the past few years have seen the opening of several Judaica-oriented bookstores and kosher restaurants.

NEUE SYNAGOGE. This huge building survived *Kristallnacht* when a local police chief, realizing that the building was a historic monument, ordered it spared. The synagoge was later destroyed by bombing but was restored in 1995. The interior, too big for Berlin's remaining Jewish community, now houses an exhibit chronicling the synagogue's history and temporary exhibits on the history of Berlin's Jews. *(Oranienburger Str. 30. Open Su-M 10am-8pm, Tu-Th 10am-6pm, F 10am-2pm. Museum €5, students €3. Entry to the dome €1.50, students €1.)*

TIERGARTEN

Once a hunting ground for Prussian monarchs, the lush **Tiergarten** is now a vast landscaped park in the center of Berlin stretching from Bahnhof Zoo to the Brandenburg Gate. **Straße des 17. Juni** bisects the park from west to east, connecting Ernst-Reuter-Pl. to the Brandenburg Gate.

SIEGESSÄULE. In the heart of the Tiergarten, the slender 70m "victory column" commemorates Prussia's humiliating defeat of France in 1870. The gilded statue on top—Victoria, the goddess of victory—is made of melted-down French cannons. The 285 steps lead to a panoramic view of the city. *(Bus #100 or 187 to Großer Stern. Open Apr.-Nov. M 1-6pm, Tu-Su 9am-6pm. €1.20, students €0.60.)*

THE REICHSTAG. Just north of the gate is the current home of Germany's governing body, the *Bundestag.* The glass dome on top is built around an upside-down solar cone that powers the building. A walkway spirals up the inside of the dome, leading visitors around a panoramic view to the top of the cone. *(Open daily 8am-midnight; last entrance 10pm. Free.)*

OTHER SIGHTS IN MITTE

BERTOLT-BRECHT-HAUS. If any single man personifies the maelstrom of political and aesthetic contradictions that is Berlin, it is **Bertolt Brecht,** who lived and worked in this house from 1953 to 1956. *(Chausseestr. 125. U6 to Zinnowitzer Str. Mandatory German tours every 30min. Tu-F 10-11:30am, Th also 5-6:30pm, and Sa 9:30am-1:30pm; every hour Su 11am-6pm. €3, students €1.50.)* Brecht is buried in the attached **Dorotheenstädtischer Friedhof.** *(Open daily Apr.-Sept. 7am-7pm and Oct.-Mar. 8am-4pm.)*

CHARLOTTENBURG

BAHNHOF ZOO

During the city's division, West Berlin centered around Bahnhof Zoo, the station which inspired U2's "Zoo TV" tour. (The U-Bahn line with the same name as the band runs through the station. Clever.) The area surrounding the station is packed with department stores and peep shows intermingled with souvenir shops and G-rated attractions.

ZOOLOGISCHER GARTEN AND AQUARIUM. Located across from Bahnhof Zoo and through the corral of bus depots, the Zoo is one of the best in the world, with many animals displayed in open-air habitats instead of cages. The second entrance, across from Europa-Center, is the famous **Elefantentor,** Budapester Str. 34, a decorated pagoda of pachyderms. *(Open May-Sept. daily 9am-6:30pm; Oct.-Feb. 9am-5pm; Mar.-Apr. 9am-5:30pm. €8, students €6.50.)* Within the walls of the Zoo, but independently accessible, is the excellent **Aquarium,** which houses broad collections of insects and reptiles as well as endless tanks of rainbow-colored fish. Its pride and joy is the 450kg **Komodo dragon,** the world's largest reptile. *(Budapester Str. 32. Open daily 9am-6pm. Aquarium €8, students €6.50. Combination ticket to zoo and aquarium €13, students €10.50, children €6.50.)*

KAISER-WILHELM-GEDÄCHTNISKIRCHE. Nicknamed "the rotten tooth" by Berliners, the jagged edges of this shattered church stand as a reminder of the destruction caused by WWII. Built in 1852 in a Romanesque-Byzantine style, the church has an equally striking interior, with colorful mosaics covering the ceiling, floors, and walls. The exhibit displays shocking photos of the entire city in ruins just after the war. *(Exhibit open M-Sa 10am-4pm. Church open daily 9am-7pm.)*

SCHLOß CHARLOTTENBURG. The broad Baroque palace commissioned by Friedrich I for his second wife, Sophie-Charlotte, sprawls over a park on the northern edge of Charlottenburg. The Schloß's many buildings include the **Neringbau,** or Altes Schloß, the palace proper *(open Tu-F 9am-5pm, Sa-Su 10am-5pm; €8, students €5)*; the **Neuer-Pavillon,** a museum dedicated to Prussian architect Karl Friedrich Schinkel *(open Tu-Su 10am-5pm; €2, students €1.50)*; **Belvedere,** a small building housing the royal family's porcelain collection *(open Apr.-Oct. Tu-Su 10am-5pm, Nov.-Mar. Tu-F noon-4pm and Sa-Su noon-5pm; €2, students €1.50)*; and the **Mausoleum,** the final resting spot for most of the family *(open Apr.-Oct. Tu-Su 10am-noon and 1-5pm; €2, students €1.50)*. The **Schloßgarten,** *(open Tu-Su 6am-9pm; free)*, behind the main buildings, is a paradise of small lakes, fountains, and carefully planted rows of trees. *(Bus #145 from Bahnhof Zoo to Luisenpl./Schloß Charlottenburg or U7 to Richard-Wagner-Pl. and walk 15min. down Otto-Suhr-Allee. Entire complex €7, students €5.)*

OLYMPIA-STADION. At the western edge of Charlottenburg, the Olympic Stadium was erected for the 1936 Olympic Games, in which Jesse Owens, an African-American, triumphed over Nazi racial theories by winning four golds. There is now a Jesse-Owens Allee to the south of the stadium. The stadium is currently under construction until 2004, but the bell tower provides a great view. *(S5 or 75 to Olympiastadion or U2 to Olympia-Stadion (Ost).)*

FUNKTURM. Erected in 1926 to herald the radio age, the Funkturm offers a stunning view of the city from its observation deck. The world's first television transmission was made here in 1931. *(Take S45 or 46 to Witzleben or U2 to Kaiserdamm. Panorama deck open M 11am-9pm, Tu-Su 11:30am-11pm. €3.60, students €1.80.)*

GEDENKSTÄTTE PLÖTZENSEE. Housed in the terrifyingly well-preserved former execution chambers of the Third Reich, this memorial documents death sentences of "enemies of the people," including the officers who attempted to assassinate Hitler in 1944. More than 2500 people were murdered within this small, stark red brick complex. Still visible are the hooks from which victims were hanged. English literature is available. *(Off the main road where the bus stops, down Emmy-Zehden-Weg on Hüttigpfad. Take U9 to Turmstr., then bus #123 (dir.: Saatwinkler Damm) to Gedenkstätte Plötzensee. Open daily Mar.-Oct. 9am-5pm; Nov.-Feb. 9am-4pm. Free.)*

SCHÖNEBERG AND WILMERSDORF

South of the Ku'damm, Schöneberg and Wilmersdorf are pleasant, middle-class residential districts noted for their shopping streets, lively cafes, and good restaurants. Schöneberg is also home to the more affluent segments of Berlin's gay and lesbian community (see **Gay and Lesbian Nightlife,** p. 451).

RATHAUS SCHÖNEBERG. West Berlin's city government met here until the Wall fell in 1989. On June 26, 1963, 15 years after the beginning of the Berlin Airlift, 1.5 million Berliners swarmed the streets beneath to hear John F. Kennedy reassure them of the Allies' commitment to the city in a speech with the now-famous words "*Ich bin ein Berliner.*" Today, the fortress is home to Schöneberg's municipal government. *(John-F.-Kennedy-Pl. U4 to Rathaus Schöneberg. Open daily 9am-6pm.)*

GRUNEWALD. This 745-hectare birch forest is home to the **Jagdschloß,** a restored royal hunting lodge containing a worthwhile collection of European paintings, including works by Rubens, van Dyck, and Cranach. The one-room hunting museum in the same building houses knives, guns, spears, crossbows, and racks of antlers and mounted wild boars. *(Am Grunewaldsee 29. U1 or 7 to Fehrbelliner Pl., then bus #115 (dir.: Neuruppiner Str.) to Pücklerstr. Walk west 15min. on Pücklerstr. Open Tu-Su 10am-1pm and 1:30-5pm. €2, students €1.)*

KREUZBERG

If you find the Ku'damm's consumerism nauseating, Kreuzberg provides the perfect dose of counter-culture relief as the indisputable center of Berlin's alternative *Szene*—it's filled with diverse ethnic groups, revolutionary graffiti, punks, and a large gay and lesbian community. Kreuzberg's anti-government demonstrations are still frequent and intense. The most prominent is the annual May 1st parade, a series of chaotic riots focused mostly on venting steam against the Man.

HAUS AM CHECKPOINT CHARLIE. A fascinating exhibition at the location of the famous border-crossing point, the Checkpoint Charlie is one of Berlin's most popular tourist attractions. A strange mix of eastern sincerity and western salesmanship, the museum contains all types of devices used to get over, under, or through the wall. *(Friedrichstr. 43-45. U6 to Kochstr. Open daily 9am-10pm. €7, students €4.)*

ORANIENSTRAẞE. This was the site of frequent riots in the 1980s. Today, it is the starting point for the May Day parades. The rest of the year, revolution-minded radicals rub shoulders with tradition-oriented Turkish families, while an anarchist punk faction and a boisterous gay and lesbian population make things interesting after hours. Restaurants, clubs, and shops of all possible flavors make it a great place to wander. *(U1 or 15 to Kottbusser Tor or Görlitzer Bahnhof.)*

FRIEDRICHSHAIN AND LICHTENBERG

EAST SIDE GALLERY. The longest remaining portion of the Wall, the 1.3km stretch of cement and asbestos slabs also serve as the world's largest open-air art gallery. The murals are the efforts of an international group of artists who gathered here in 1989 to celebrate the end of the city's division. In 1999, the same artists came together to repaint their work and cover the scrawlings of later tourists; however, would-be artists are rapidly defacing the wall once again. *(Along Mühlenstr. U1 or 15 or S3, 5, 6, 7, 9, or 75 to Warschauer Str. and walk back toward the river.)*

FORSCHUNGS- UND GEDENKSTÄTTE NORMANNENSTRAẞE. In the suburb of Lichtenberg stands perhaps the most feared building of the GDR regime—the headquarters of the East German secret police, the **Staatssicherheit** or **Stasi.** Since a 1991 law opened the records to the public, the "Horror-Files" have rocked Germany, exposing informants—and wrecking careers, marriages, and friendships—

WALKING MAN In east Berlin, you may notice that the crossing-light figures are thicker, bolder, and more eye-catching than those in west Berlin. The *Ampel-Männchen* ("little traffic-light guy") of east Berlin was drawn by cartoonist Karl Peglau during the days of the GDR. The *Ampel-Männchen*'s simple, cheerful design and easy visibility are supposed to appeal to children and the elderly, but he's beloved by just about everyone. When the city was reunified and the government planned to standardize the lights to the boring western design, east Berliners protested. Now, the *Ampel-Männchen* is a favorite figure for Berliners and tourists alike and has spawned his own line of t-shirts, mouse pads, key-chains, and strings of lights. Ah, capitalism.

at all levels of society. Today, German-language exhibits display tiny microphones and hidden cameras used for surveillance, a GDR shrine full of Lenin busts, and countless other bits of bizarre memorabilia. *(Ruschestr. 103, Haus 1. U5 to Magdalenenstr. Open Tu-F 11am-6pm, Sa-Su 2-6pm. €3, students €1.50.)*

PRENZLAUER BERG

Northeast of Mitte lies Prenzlauer Berg, a former working-class district largely neglected by East Germany's reconstruction efforts. Many of the older buildings are crumbling at the edges, resulting in a charming state of age and graceful decay. Unlike the loud, raucous scene in Kreuzberg and Mitte, Prenzlauer Berg's streets are studded with trendy but casual cafes and bars.

KOLLWITZPLATZ. The heart of Prenzlauer Berg's cafe scene, Kollwitzpl. offers a little triangle of greenery centered around a statue of the square's namesake, artist **Käthe Kollwitz.** The monument has been painted a number of times—most notably with big pink polka-dots—in acts of affectionate vandalism. *(U2 to Senefelderpl.)*

JÜDISCHER FRIEDHOF. Prenzlauer Berg was one of the major centers of Jewish Berlin, especially during the 19th and early 20th centuries. The Jewish cemetery on Schönhauser Allee contains the graves of composer Giacomo Meyerbeer and painter Max Liebermann. *(Men must cover their heads before entering the cemetery. Open M-Th 8am-4pm, F 8am-3pm.)* Nearby stands one of Berlin's loveliest synagogues, **Synagoge Rykestraße,** which was spared on *Kristallnacht* due to its inconspicuous location in a courtyard.

MUSEUMS

Berlin is one of the world's great museum cities, with collections of artifacts encompassing all subjects and eras. The **Staatliche Museen zu Berlin (SMB)** runs over 20 museums located in several regions—**Museumsinsel**, **Kulturforum, Mitte/Tiergarten, Charlottenburg,** and **Dahlem.** A single admission to any of these museums is €2, students €1; admission is free the first Sunday of every month. A *Tageskarte* (€4, students €2) is valid for all SMB museums on the day of purchase; the *Drei-Tage-Karte* (€8, students €4) is valid for three consecutive days. Either can be bought at any SMB museum. Non-SMB-affiliated museums tend to be smaller and quirkier.

SMB MUSEUMS

MUSEUMSINSEL (MUSEUM ISLAND)

Museumsinsel contains five separate museums, although several are undergoing extensive renovation. Take S3, 5, 7, 9, or 75 to Hackescher Markt or bus #100 to Lustgarten. All museums offer free audio tours in English.

Pergamonmuseum, Kupfergraben. One of the world's great ancient history museums, it's named for Pergamon, the Turkish city from which the enormous Altar of Zeus (180 BC) in the main exhibit hall was taken. The museum features pieces of ancient Mediterranean history from as far back as 10th century BC. Open Tu-Su 10am-6pm. SMB prices.

Alte Nationalgalerie, Am Lustgarten. Attracts eager art-lovers, who come to see everything from German realism to French impressionism. Casper Friedrich and Karl Schinkel are but two names in an all-star cast on display. Open Tu-Su 10am-6pm. SMB prices.

Altes Museum, Am Lustgarten. The museum contains the *Antikensammlung,* an excellent permanent collection of Greco-Roman art. Open Tu-Su 10am-6pm. SMB prices.

TIERGARTEN-KULTURFORUM

The **Tiergarten-Kulturforum (TK)** is a complex of museums at the eastern end of the Tiergarten, near Potsdamer Pl. Take S1, 2, or 25 or U2 to Potsdamer Pl. and walk down Potsdamer Str.; the museums will be on your right on Mattäikirchplatz. All museums are open Tu-F 10am-6pm, Th until 10pm, Sa-Su 11am-6pm.

Gemäldegalerie. One of Germany's most famous museums, and rightly so. It houses a stunning and enormous collection by Italian, German, Dutch, and Flemish masters, including Dürer and Rembrandt. SMB prices.

Hamburger Bahnhof/Museum für Gegenwartkunst, Invalidenstr. 50-51. U6 to Zinnowitzer Str. or S3, 5, 7, 9, or 75 to Lehrter Stadtbahnhof. Berlin's foremost collection of contemporary art, housed in a converted train station, features works by Warhol, Beuys, and Kiefer as well as in-your-face temporary exhibits. €6, students €3. Tours Su at 4pm.

Neue Nationalgalerie, Potsdamer Str. 50. This sleek building contains both interesting temporary exhibits and a formidable permanent collection, including works by Warhol, Kirchner, and Ernst. Never has roadkill looked so cool. SMB prices for permanent collection; €6, students €3 for the whole museum.

CHARLOTTENBURG

The area surrounding **Schloß Charlottenburg** is home to a number of excellent museums. Take bus #145 to Luisenpl./Schloß Charlottenburg or U7 to Richard-Wagner-Pl. and walk about 15min. down Otto-Suhr-Allee.

Ägyptisches Museum, Schloßstr. 70. This stern Neoclassical building contains a famous collection of ancient Egyptian art: animal mummies, elaborately-painted coffins, a magnificent temple gateway, papyrus scrolls, and the famous bust of **Queen Nefertiti**. Open Tu-Su 10am-6pm. €6, students €3.

Sammlung Berggruen, Schloßstr. 1, across from the Egyptian museum in an identical building. Three floors house a substantial collection of Picasso's work, including pieces that influenced him. The top floor exhibits Paul Klee paintings and Alberto Giacometti sculptures. Open Tu-Su 10am-6pm. €6, students €3.

DAHLEM

Ethnologisches Museum. The Ethnological Museum alone makes the trek to Dahlem worthwhile. The exhibits range from beautiful ancient Central American stonework to ivory African statuettes to enormous boats from the South Pacific. The **Museum für Indisches Kunst** (Museum for Indian Art) and the **Museum für Ostasiatisches Kunst** (Museum for East Asian Art), housed in the same building, are smaller but no less fascinating. Take U1 to Dahlem-Dorf and follow the Museen signs. Open Tu-F 10am-6pm, Sa-Su 11am-6pm. SMB prices.

INDEPENDENT (NON-SMB) MUSEUMS

EASTERN BERLIN

Deutsche Guggenheim Berlin, Unter den Linden 13-15. Located in a newly renovated building across the street from the Deutsche Staatsbibliothek, the museum features changing exhibits of contemporary avant-garde art. Open daily 11am-8pm, Th until 10pm. €3, students €2, M free.

Filmmuseum Berlin, Potsdamer Str. 2, 3rd and 4th fl. of the Sony Center. This brand-spanking-new museum shows the development of German film. The exhibits (with good English captions) are fascinating, and the ultra-futuristic entrance is a mind-altering experience. U2 or S1, 2, or 25 to Potsdamer Pl. Open Tu-Su 10am-6pm, Th until 8pm. €6, students €4.

Deutsches Historisches Museum, Unter den Linden 1, in the Kronprinzenpalais. Exhibits trace German history until the Nazis, while rotating exhibitions examine the last 50 years. S3, 5, 7, 9, or 75 to Hackescher Markt. Open Th-Tu 3-6pm. Free.

ENTERTAINMENT

Berlin has one of the most vibrant cultural scenes in the world: exhibitions, concerts, plays, and dance performances abound. Despite recent cutbacks, the city still has a generously subsidized art scene, and tickets are usually reasonable, especially with student discounts. Numerous festivals celebrating everything from Chinese film to West African music spice up the regular offerings; posters proclaiming special events festoon the city well in advance.

CONCERTS, OPERA, AND DANCE

Berlin reaches its musical zenith during the fabulous **Berliner Festwochen,** lasting almost all of September and drawing the world's best orchestras and soloists. The **Berliner Jazztage** in November, featuring top-notch jazz musicians, also brings in the crowds. For more information about either, call or write to Berliner Festspiele (☎654 890; www.berlinerfestspiele.de). In mid-July, the **Bachtage** offers an intense week of classical music, while every Saturday night in August, the **Sommer Festspiele** turns the Ku'damm into a concert hall with punk, steel-drum, and folk groups competing for attention. Look for concert listings in the monthly pamphlets *Konzerte und Theater in Berlin und Brandenburg* (free) and *Berlin Programm* (€1.50), as well as in the biweeklies *Zitty* and *Tip* (all available at newsstands or tourist offices).

Berliner Philharmonisches Orchester, Matthäikirchstr. 1 (☎25 48 81 32; kartenbuero@philharmonic.sireco.de). Take U2 or S1, 2, or 25 to Potsdamer Pl. then walk up Potsdamer Str. The *Berliner Philharmoniker* is one of the world's finest orchestras, but it's almost impossible to get a seat; check an hour before concert time or write at least 8 weeks in advance. Tickets start at €7 for standing room, €15 for seats. Box office open M-F 3-6pm, Sa-Su 11am-2pm. Closed from the end of June until the start of Sept.

Konzerthaus (Schauspielhaus am Gendarmenmarkt), Gendarmenmarkt 2 (☎203 09 21 01). U2 or 6 to Stadtmitte. The opulent home of Berlin's symphony orchestra. Last-minute tickets are sometimes available. Box office open M-Sa 11am-7pm, Su noon-4pm. The orchestra goes on vacation mid-July through Aug.

Deutsche Oper Berlin, Bismarckstr. 35 (☎341 02 49 for info, ☎343 84 01 for tickets; toll-free ☎(0 800)248 98 42). U2 to Deutsche Oper. Berlin's best and youngest opera, featuring newly commissioned works as well as all the German and Italian classics. Tickets €10-110. 25% student discount available 1 week before performance. Box office open M-Sa 11am until 1hr. before performance, Su 10am-2pm. For program information, write to Deutsche Oper Berlin, Bismarckstr. 35, 10627 Berlin. Closed July-Aug.

Deutsche Staatsoper, Unter den Linden 7 (☎20 35 45 55; www.staatsoper-berlin.de). U6 to Französische Str. Eastern Berlin's leading opera company. Tickets €5-200. Student tickets €10 1hr. before show. Box office open M-F 11am-6pm, Sa-Su 2pm-7pm, and 1hr. before performance. Closed mid-July to Aug.

THEATER

Theater listings are available in the monthly pamphlets *Kultur!news* and *Berlin Programm,* as well as in *030, Zitty,* and *Tip* (all available at newsstands). In addition to the world's best German-language theater, Berlin has a lively English-language scene; look for listings that say *in englischer Sprache* ("in English").

Deutsches Theater, Schumannstr. 13a (☎28 44 12 25). U6 or S1, 2, 3, 5, 7, 9, 25, or 75 to Friedrichstr. or bus #147 to Albrechtpl. Walk north on Friedrichstr., turn left on Reinhardtstr., and then right on Albrechtstr., which turns into Schumannstr. The best theater in the country, with innovative productions of the classics and newer works from Büchner to Mamet to Ibsen. Box office open M-Sa 11am-6:30pm, Su 3-6:30pm. Tickets €4-36, students €8.

Hebbel-Theater, Stresemannstr. 29 (☎25 90 04 27). U1, 6, or 15 to Hallesches Tor. The most avant of the avant-garde theaters in Berlin, drawing cutting-edge talent from all over the world. Order tickets at the box office on Stresemannstr., by phone daily 4-7pm, or show up 1hr. before performance. Tickets €11-23.

Berliner Ensemble, Bertolt-Brecht-Pl. 1 (☎28 40 81 55). U6 or S1, 2, 3, 5, 7, 9, 25, or 75 to Friedrichstr. Hip repertoire, including Heiner Müller, young American playwrights, and Brecht. Box office open M-Sa 8am-6pm, Su 11am-6pm, and 1hr. before performance. Tickets €6-24, students €5.

FILM

Berlin is a movie-loving town—it hosts the international **Berlinale** film festival (Feb. 5-16, 2003), and on any night you can choose from over 150 different films, many in the original languages. *O.F.* next to a movie listing means original version (i.e., not dubbed); *O.m.U.* means original version with German subtitles. Check *Tip, Zitty,* or the ubiquitous blue *Kinoprogramm* posters plastered throughout the city. Mondays, Tuesdays, or Wednesdays are *Kinotage* at most movie theaters, with reduced prices. Bring a student ID for discounts. Potsdamer Platz, home to **Filmhaus** and **Cinemaxx,** has the most options for English films. **Freiluftkino Hasenheide,** at the Sputnik in Hasenheide park, has open-air screenings of everything from silent films to last year's blockbusters. (U7 or 8 to Hermannpl.)

SHOPPING

The seven-story **KaDeWe department store** on Wittenbergpl. at Tauentzienstr. 21-24, is the largest department store in mainland Europe. The name is an abbreviation of *Kaufhaus des Westens* (Department Store of the West); for product-starved East Germans who flooded Berlin in the days following the opening of the Wall, KaDeWe *was* the West. (☎212 10. Open M-F 9:30am-8pm, Sa 9am-4pm.) The food department, on the 6th floor, has to be seen to be believed. The **Kurfürstendamm,** near Bahnhof Zoo, has almost every kind of shop imaginable. **Bleibtreustraße** has stores closer to the budget traveler's reach. On the other side of town, **Friedrichstraße,** especially south of Unter den Linden, also has a respectable shopping district. In addition, the new **Daimler-Benz** complex on **Potsdamer Platz** has more than 100 new shops and many restaurants, cafes, and pubs. There is a typical German *Fußgängerzone* (pedestrian zone) on **Wilmersdorfer Straße,** where bakeries, *Döner* joints, trendy clothing shops, and department stores abound. (U7 to Wilmersdorfer Str. or S3, 5, 7, 9, or 75 to Charlottenburg.)

At Berlin's **flea markets,** you can usually find a fantastic bargain. The market on **Straße des 17. Juni** has the best selection, but the prices are higher. (S3, 5, 7, 9, or 75 to Tiergarten. Open Sa-Su 10am-5pm.) The **Trödelmarkt** on Nostitzstr. 6-7 in Kreuzberg aims to help the homeless of Berlin. (U6 or 7 to Mehringdamm. Open Tu 5-7pm, Th 11am-1pm and 3-6pm, Sa 11am-3pm.) Other markets are located near **Ostbahnhof** in Friedrichshain (by Erich-Steinfurth-Str.; S3, 5, 7, 9, or 75 to *Ostbahnhof.* Open Sa 9am-3pm, Su 10am-5pm) and on **Am Weidendamm** in Mitte (U2 or S1, 2, 3, 5, 7, 9, 25, or 75 to Friedrichstr. Open Sa-Su 11am-5pm).

NIGHTLIFE

Berlin's nightlife is absolute madness. Bars typically open around 6pm and get going around 10pm, just as the clubs are opening their doors. Bar scenes wind down between midnight and 6am, while club dance floors fill up around 1am and groove till dawn. A variety of after-parties and 24hr. cafes keep up this seemingly perpetual motion. It's completely possible (if you can live without sleep) to party non-stop Friday night through Monday morning. The best sources of information about bands and dance venues are the bi-weekly magazines *Tip* (€2.20) and the superior *Zitty* (€2.40), available at all newsstands, or the free and highly comprehensive *030*, distributed in hostels, cafes, and bars.

In west Berlin, **Savignyplatz,** near Zoologischer Garten, offers refined, laid-back cafes and jazz clubs. Gay life in Berlin centers around **Nollendorfplatz,** where the crowds are usually mixed and establishments range from the friendly to the cruisey. **Gneisenaustraße,** on the western edge of Kreuzberg, offers a variety of ethnic restaurants and some good bars. Closer to the former Wall, a dizzying array of clubs and bars on and around **Oranienstraße** rage all night, every night, with a superbly mixed crowd of partygoers both gay and straight. In East Berlin, Kreuzberg's reputation as dance capital of Germany is challenged as clubs sprout up in **Mitte, Prenzlauer Berg,** and near **Potsdamer Platz.** Berlin's largest bar scene sprawls down **Oranienburger Straße** in Mitte; it's pricey, but never boring. **Prenzlauer Berg,** originally the edgy alternative to Mitte's trendier repertoire, has become a bit more classy and established, especially around **Kollwitzplatz.** South of it all, **Friedrichshain** has developed a reputation for lively, quirky nightlife, with a terrific group of bars along **Simon-Dach-Str.** and more on **Gabriel-Max-Str.**

If at all possible, try to hit (or, if you're prone to claustrophobia, avoid) Berlin during the **Love Parade,** usually held in the third weekend of July, when all of Berlin says "yes" to everything (see below). Prices hit astronomical heights during this weekend of hedonism and insanity, making it something of a rich kids' festival. It's also worth mentioning that Berlin has **de-criminalized marijuana possession** of up to eight grams, although the police can arrest you for any amount if they feel the need to, so exercise some discretion. Smoking in public is not officially accepted but is becoming more common in some clubs—you'll know which ones.

BARS AND CLUBS

MITTE

Tresor, Leipziger Str. 126a. U2 or S1, 2, or 25 or bus #N5, N29 or N52 to Potsdamer Pl. One of the most rocking techno venues in Berlin. Open W and F-Sa 11pm-6am. Cover W €3, F €7, Sa €7-11.

VEB-OZ, Auguststr. 92, at the corner of Oranienburgerstr. S1, 2, or 25 to Oranienburger Str. Late hours make it a good weekday watering hole. Open daily 6pm until 2 or 3am.

Zosch, Tucholskystr. 30 (☎280 76 64). U6 to Oranienburger Tor. Relaxed bar on the ground floor, live music in the basement. Open M-F from 4pm, Sa-Su from midnight.

THE LOVE PARADE Every year during the third weekend in July, the Love Parade brings Berlin to its knees—its trains run late, its streets fill with litter, and its otherwise patriotic populace scrambles to the countryside in the wake of a wave of German teenagers dying their hair, dropping ecstasy, and getting down *en masse*. What started in 1988 as a DJ's birthday party has mutated into the world's only 1.5 million-person rave, dubbed *Die Größte Partei der Welt*, "the biggest party in the world." The city-wide party turns the Str. des 17. Juni into a riotous dance floor and the Tiergarten into a garden of iniquity. The BVG offers a "No-Limit-Ticket," useful for getting around from venue to venue during the weekend's **54 hours of nonstop partying** (€5, condom included). Club prices skyrocket for the event as the best DJs from Europe are imported for a frantic weekend of beat-thumping madness. It's an experience that you won't forget, unless of course, you party *too* hard. Then again, as far as the Love Parade goes, there's no such thing.

Hackesche Höfe, Rosenthaler Str. 40-41. S3, 5, 7, 9, or 75 to Hackescher Markt. A series of interconnected courtyards containing restaurants, cafes, clubs, galleries, shops, and a movie theater. The **Sophienclub,** Sophienstr. 6, is a smaller club more focused on having fun than on being trendy. Features soul, funk, house, and Britpop. Cover €5. Open Tu and Th-Sa from 10pm.

CHARLOTTENBURG (SAVIGNYPLATZ)

A-Trane, Bleibtreustr. 1. S3, 5, 7, 9, or 75 to Savignypl. Known chiefly to a sizable crowd of jazz-loving locals, this club attracts quality musicians and showcases them in a mellow, intimate setting. Cover €7-21 (usually about €13 on weekends). Club open daily 10pm-2am, later on weekends.

Quasimodo, Kantstr. 12a. U2 or 12 or S3, 5, 7, 9, or 75 to Zoologischer Garten. A smoky basement jazz venue with a wide variety of artists from disco to swing. Cover Tu and W €5-6; on weekends, cover depends on performance, ranging from free to €27. Concert tickets available after 5pm at the cafe upstairs or at Kant-Kasse ticket service (☎313 45 54). Open Tu, W, F, Sa from 9pm; occasionally open Su-M.

SCHÖNEBERG

Slumberland, Winterfeldtpl. U1, 2, 4, 12, or 15 to Nollendorfpl. An African motif with R&B and Bob Marley tunes. Open Su-Th 6pm-2am, F 6pm-5am, Sa 11am-5am.

Mister Hu, Goltzstr. 39. U1, 2, 4, or 15 to Nollendorfpl. Happy Hour 5-8pm, Su all cocktails €5. Open daily 5pm-late, Sa 11am-late.

KREUZBERG

SO36, Oranienstr. 190. U1, 12, or 15 to Görlitzer Bahnhof or bus #N29 to Heinrichpl. Berlin's only truly mixed club (see p. 451), with all orientations grooving to a number of wild genres. Open 11pm-late. Cover for parties €4-8, concerts €7-18.

Bateau Ivre, Oranienstr. 18. Locals sit back and relax over coffee or beer at this friendly bistro-bar before shakin' that thing across the street at SO36. Open daily from 9am.

FRIEDRICHSHAIN

Euphoria, Grünbergerstr. 60, on the corner of Simon-Dach Str. U5 to Frankfurter Tor. Serves perhaps the best mixed drinks in Berlin. Happy Hour 6-8pm. Wide selection of Italian entrees and Sunday brunch (€8.50) also served. Open daily from 9am.

Dachkammer Bar (DK), Simon-Dach Str. 39. The bright, friendly, and rustic feel of the ground floor complements the mellow music and lively crowd. Sip cocktails (€5-7) with appetizers (from €4). Open M-F from noon, Sa-Su from 10am.

Zehn Vorne, Simon-Dach Str. 9. A jam-packed little bar based mainly on Star Trek. Don't let the theme scare you off–this place is weird and fun. Open daily from 3pm.

PRENZLAUER BERG

KulturBrauerei, Knaackstr. 97 (☎441 92 69). U2 to Eberswalder Str. In a former brewery; houses everything from the highly popular clubs **Soda** and **Kesselhaus** to a Russian theater to an art school. Venues include everything from disco to techno and reggae; cover and opening times vary, so it's best to call ahead.

Pfefferberg, Schönhauser Allee 176. U2 to Senefelderpl. or bus #N58. Features a slightly younger crowd and a rooftop garden. Techno and world music rotate weekly. Cover free to €15. Garden open in summer M-F from 3pm, Sa-Su from noon.

GAY AND LESBIAN NIGHTLIFE

Berlin is one of the most gay-friendly cities on the continent. All of **Nollendorfpl.** is a gay-friendly environment. The main streets, including **Goltzstraße, Akazienstraße,** and **Winterfeldtstraße,** tend to contain mixed bars and cafes. The **"Bermuda Triangle"** of **Motzstr., Fuggerstr.,** and **Eisenacherstr.** is more exclusively gay. For up-to-date events listings, pick up a copy of the amazingly comprehensive *Siegessäule* (free).

SCHÖNEBERG

Metropol, Nollendorfpl. 5. U1, 2, 4, or 15 to Nollendorfpl., or buses #N5, 19, 26, 48, 52, or 75. The Metropol contains 3 dance venues: **Tanz Tempel, West-Side Club,** and **Love Lounge.** This club has only recently come out, and many of its parties are still mixed–every other F the Tanz Tempel and Love Lounge team up to host the heterosexual *Fisch Sucht Fahrrad* party ("Fish seeks bicycle", for you Gloria Steinem fans). West-Side Club holds the infamous Naked Sex Party, as well as numerous other naked parties. Hours and cover vary–check *Siegessäule* for details.

Omnes, Motzstr. 8. U1, 2, 4, or 15 to Nollendorfpl. A mainly male gay cafe/bar, Omnes accommodates late-night revelers. Open 24hr.

Anderes Ufer, Hauptstr. 157. U7 to Kleistpark. A quieter, more relaxed *Kneipe* (tavern) away from the club scene. Open M-Th and Su 11am-1am, F-Sa 11am-2am.

Scheune, Motzstr. 25. U1, 2, 4, or 15 to Nollendorfpl. A dimly lit popular bar that increases the mystique by making you ring the bell to enter. Men only. Open Su-Th 9pm-7am, F-Sa 9pm-9am.

KREUZBERG

Rose's, Oranienstr. 187. A mixed gay and lesbian clientele packs this intense and claustrophobic party spot, marked only by "Bar" over the door. Open daily 10pm-6am.

SO36, while usually a mixed club (p. 450), sponsors three predominantly gay events: **Hungrige Herzen** (W from 10pm), a jam-packed gay and (somewhat) lesbian trance and drum 'n' bass party; **Café Fatal** (Su from 5pm) with ballroom dancing; and **Gayhane** (last Sa of the month), a self-described "HomOrientaldancefloor" for a mixed crowd of Turks and Germans.

FRIEDRICHSHAIN

Die Busche, Mühlenstr. 12. East Berlin's largest gay disco, with an incongruous rotation of techno, Top-40, and *Schlager.* Open W and F-Su from 9:30pm. The party gets going around midnight. It *really* gets going around 3am. Cover €4-5.

PRENZLAUER BERG

Schall und Rauch, Gleimstr. 23 (☎448 07 70). U2 or S4, 8, or 85 to Schönhauser Allee. Sizable, popular spot, with a glossier classy feel. Ridiculously well-stocked bar and friendly waitstaff ensure drinking bliss. Highly popular brunch Sa and Su for €7.50; reservations a must. Open daily 9am-late.

Café Amsterdam, Gleimstr. 24 (☎44 00 94 54). U2 or S4, 8, or 85 to Schönhauser Allee. Next to Schall und Rauch. Amidst silver curtains and glitzy paintings, Amsterdam's clientele down cheap drinks and challenge each other to games of backgammon. Open daily 4pm-6am.

DAYTRIPS FROM BERLIN

KZ SACHSENHAUSEN

Take Berlin's S1 (dir.: Oranienburg) to the end (40min.). The camp is a 20min. walk from the station. Follow the signs from Straslunderstr., turning right on Bernauer Str., left on Str. der Einheit, and right on Str. der Nationen.

The small town of Oranienburg, just north of Berlin, was home to the Nazi concentration camp Sachsenhausen, in which more than 100,000 Jews, communists, intellectuals, gypsies, and homosexuals were killed between 1936 and 1945. The Gedenkstätte Sachsenhausen was opened by the GDR in 1961. Parts of the camp have been preserved in their original forms, including sets of cramped barracks, but only the foundations of Station Z (where prisoners were methodically exterminated) remain. Barracks 38 and 39 feature displays on daily life in the camp during the Nazi period and on the lives of specific prisoners. The jail block contains a museum detailing its uses along with rotating exhibits on individual inmates. Broader exhibits on Sachsenhausen and the concentration camp experience reside in the museum buildings and *Industriehof*. The exhibits, however, aren't nearly as expressive of the desperation and despair of Sachsenhausen as the camp itself; its brutally blunt gray buildings, barbed-wire fencing, and vast, bleak spaces testify to the hopelessness that was life here. *(Str. der Nationen 22. ☎(03301) 20 00. Open Apr.-Sept. Tu-Su 8:30am-6pm; Oct.-Mar. Tu-Su 8:30am-4:30pm. Last entry 30min. before closing. Free. Audio tour rental €3.50.)*

POTSDAM

Berlin's S7 runs from Bahnhof Zoo to Potsdam (30min., €2.50).

Visitors disappointed by Berlin's distinctly unroyal demeanor can get their Kaiserly fix in nearby Potsdam, the glittering city of Friedrich II (the Great). The 245-hectare **Park Sanssouci** is Friedrich's testament to the size of his treasury and the diversity of his aesthetic tastes. For information on the park, stop by the **Visitors Center** at the windmill. **Schloß Sanssouci,** the park's main attraction, was built in 1747 to allow Friedrich to escape his wife. German tours are limited to 40 people and leave every 20min., but the final tour (5pm) usually sells out by 2pm, so come early. The tourist office leads English-language tours of the main Schloß only. *(Open Apr.-Oct. Tu-Su 9am-5pm; Nov.-Mar. Tu-Su 9am-4pm. €8, students €5.)* The exotic gold-plated **Chinesisches Teehaus,** complete with a rooftop Buddha toting a parasol, contains 18th-century *chinoiserie* porcelain. (€1.05.) Next door is the **Bildergalerie,** whose collection of Caravaggio, van Dyck, and Rubens (some of them copies—but still impressive) recently opened after extensive restoration. *(Open mid-May to mid-Oct. Tu-Su 10am-12:30pm and 1-5pm. €2, students €1.50; tour €1 extra.)* The nearby **Sizilianischer Garten** is perhaps the park's most stunningly beautiful garden. At the opposite end of the park is the largest of the castles, the 200-room **Neues Palais.** *(Open Apr.-Oct. Sa-Th 9am-5pm; Nov.-Mar. 9am-4pm. €6, students €5; €1 less in off-season.)*

Potsdam's second park, **Neuer Garten,** contains several royal residences; to get there, take bus #692 to Schloß Cecilienhof. At **Schloß Cecilienhof,** built in the style of an English Tudor manor, exhibits document the **Potsdam Treaty,** which was signed here in 1945. It was supposed to be the "Berlin Treaty," but the capital was too bombed-out to house the Allies' head honchos. *(Open Tu-Su 9am-12:30 and 1-5pm. €3, students €2; tour €1 extra.)* The garden also contains the **Marmorpalais,** a huge marble-intensive palace, as well as many other odd little buildings, including a replica of an Egyptian pyramid. *(Marmorpalais open Apr.-Oct. Tu-Su 10am-5pm; Nov.-Mar. Sa-Su 10am-4pm. €2, students €1.50; tour €1 extra.)*

EASTERN GERMANY

Saxony *(Sachsen)* is known primarily for Dresden and Leipzig, but the entire region offers a fascinating historical and cultural diversity that reveals a great deal about life in the former East. West of Saxony, Thuringia *(Thüringen)*, the "Green Heart of Germany," is a hilly and mostly pastoral land where Bach, Goethe, Schiller, Luther, and Wagner all left their mark. It's arguably the most beautiful landscape in Germany. North of Thuringia and Saxony, the endless grass plains of Saxony-Anhalt offer one of the region's more tranquil landscapes. Its high unemployment rate mirrors the economic woes of Eastern Germany as a whole, but many construction sites mushrooming across the *Land* point toward the future.

DRESDEN ☎0351

The stunning buildings of Dresden's *Altstadt* look ancient, but most are newly reconstructed—the Allied bombings of February 1945 that claimed over 50,000 lives destroyed 75% of the city center. Today, Dresden pulses with a historical intensity, engaging visitors with world-class museums and partially reconstructed palaces and churches. However, Dresden is not all nostalgic appeals to the past; the city has entered the new millennium as a young, dynamic metropolis propelled by a history of cultural turbulence.

TRANSPORTATION

Flights: Dresden's **airport** (DRS; ☎881 33 60) is 9km from town; the S2 makes the 20min. trip from both train stations (2 per hr., 4am-10:30pm, €1.50).

Trains: From the **Dresden Hauptbahnhof,** in the *Altstadt*, and **Bahnhof Dresden Neustadt,** across the Elbe, travelers zoom to **Berlin** (3hr., every hr., €30); **Budapest** (11hr., every 2hr., €64); **Frankfurt** (7hr., 2 per hr., €70); **Leipzig** (1½hr., 1-2 per hr., €17); **Munich** (7hr., 24 per day, €27); **Prague** (2½hr., 12 per day, €20); **Warsaw** (8hr., 8 per day, €27). Buy tickets from the machines in the main halls of both stations or from the staff at the *Reisezentrum* desk.

Public Transportation: Dresden's **streetcars** are efficient and cover the whole city. Single-ride €1.50; 4 or fewer stops €1. Day-pass €4; weekly pass €13. Most major lines run every hr. after midnight. Tickets are available from *Fahrkarten* dispensers at major stops, on the streetcars, and from **Verkehrs-Info** stands in front of the *Hauptbahnhof* or at Postpl. (Info stands open M-F 7am-7pm, Sa 8am-6pm, Su 9am-6pm).

ORIENTATION AND PRACTICAL INFORMATION

Dresden is bisected by the **Elbe.** The **Altstadt** lies on the same side as the *Hauptbahnhof.* **Neustadt,** to the north, escaped most of the bombing, paradoxically making it one of the oldest parts of the city. Many of Dresden's main attractions are centered between the **Altmarkt** and the Elbe, 5min. from the *Neustadt.*

TOURIST, FINANCIAL, AND LOCAL SERVICES

Tourist Office: Prager Straße 3, near the *Hauptbahnhof* (open M-F 9am-7pm, Sa 9am-4pm), and **Theaterplatz,** in the *Schinkelwache,* in front of the Semper-Oper (☎49 19 20; open M-F 10am-6pm, Sa-Su 10am-4pm). Sells city maps (€2.50) and the **Dresden Card,** which includes 48hr. of public transit, free or reduced entry at many museums, and city tours (€14).

Currency Exchange: ReiseBank, in the *Hauptbahnhof.* 1-3% commission, depending on the amount; 1-1.5% for traveler's checks. Open M-F 8am-7:30pm, Sa 12:30pm-4pm, Su 9am-1pm. A self-service exchange machine is available, but rates are poor.

Luggage Storage: At both train stations. Lockers €1-2 for 24hr. storage.

Bi-Gay-Lesbian Resources: Gerede-Dresdner Lesben, Schwule und alle Anderen, Prießnitzstr. 18 (☎802 22 51; 24hr. hotline ☎802 22 70). From Albertpl., walk up Bautzner Str. and turn left onto Prießnitzstr. Open M-F 3-5pm.

Laundromat: Groove Station, Katharinenstr. 11-13. Wash (€2.50) and dry (€1.50), while browsing the tattoo and piercing studio. Open daily 3pm-late.

EMERGENCY AND COMMUNICATIONS

Police: ☎110. **Ambulance and Fire:** ☎112.

Pharmacy: Apotheke Prager Straße, Prager Str. 3 (☎490 30 14). Open M-F 8:30am-7pm, Sa 8:30am-4pm.

Internet Access: Internet Cafe Netzstatt, Schandauerstr. 64. €3 per hr. Open M-Su 1pm-midnight.

Post Office: Hauptpostamt, Königsbrücker Str. 21/29 (☎819 13 73), in *Neustadt.* Open M-F 8am-7pm, Sa 9am-1pm. Address mail to be held: *Postlagernde Briefe* für Firstname SURNAME, Hauptpostamt, **D-01099** Dresden, Germany.

ACCOMMODATIONS AND CAMPING

If there's one thing that attests to Dresden's status as a city on the rise, it's the state of its accommodations. New hotels and hostels are constantly being opened, but on weekends it's still hard to get a spot in a good location—call ahead.

Mondpalast Backpacker, Katharinenstr. 11-13 (☎/fax 804 60 61). From *Bahnhof Neustadt,* walk down Antonstr. toward Albertpl., turn left onto Königsbrücker Str., then right on Katharinenstr. Located in the heart of the *Neustadt* scene, it's the hippest place in town. Breakfast €4.50. Sheets €2.50. Key deposit €5. Reception 24hr. 8-bed dorms €13.50; 5- to 7-bed dorms €15; 3- to 4-bed dorms €16; doubles €34. ❷

Jugendgästehaus Dresden (HI), Maternistr. 22 (☎49 26 20). Take the Prager Str. exit from the *Hauptbahnhof* and turn left on Ammonstr., turn right on Rosen Str., and then take a left onto Maternistr. This sleek hostel has newly renovated rooms with more than 400 beds. Breakfast included. Reception 24hr. Check-in after 4pm. Check-out 9:30am. 2- to 4-bed dorms €17.50, with shower €21; singles €25/€28.50. ❷

Lollis Homestay, Seitenstr. 2A (☎819 84 58). From the *Neustadt* station, turn left along Dr.-Friedrich-Wolf-Str., follow it for 10min. to Bischofsweg and turn left. After the tracks,

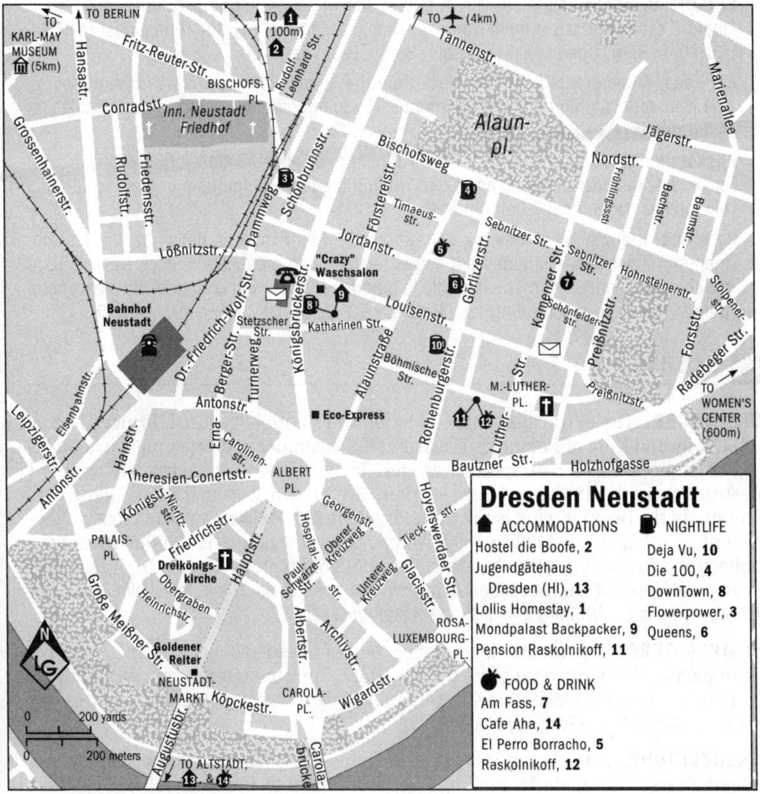

take a right on Rudolf Leonardstr., and then a quick left and right after the park. Bear right, the hostel is directly ahead. A small and comfortably furnished hostel that feels like home. Breakfast €3. Laundry free. 6-bed dorms €13; singles €25; doubles €34. ❶

Pension Raskolnikoff, Böhmische Str. 34 (☎804 57 06). Located right in the middle of the *Neustadt,* this 6-room pension is the perfect way to escape the hostel scene. Singles €31; doubles €41; each extra person €8. ❸

Hostel Die Boofe, Hechtstr. 10 (☎801 33 61). From the *Neustadt,* take a left and walk parallel to the tracks on Dr.-Friedrich-Wolf-Str; turn left onto Bischofsweg and then right onto Hechtstr. A pristine, yet funky hostel that is quieter than Mondpalast. Breakfast €4.60. Sheets €2.75. Reception daily 6pm-midnight. Reservations recommended. 2- to 5-bed dorms €14.50; singles with breakfast €29; doubles €44. ❷

FOOD

Unfortunately, the surge in Dresden's tourism has raised food prices, particularly in the *Altstadt.* The cheapest eats in the *Altstadt* are at supermarkets or *Imbiß* stands along **Prager Straße.** The **Neustadt** spawns a new bar every few weeks and rules the roost of quirky ethnic and student-friendly restaurants.

El Perro Borracho, Alaunstr. 70. A tiny sparkle of sunny Spain. Try the tasty "mix & match" *tapas* and wash them down with sangria. Entrees €7. Buffet breakfast (€8) Sa-Su 10am-3pm. Open M-F 11am-2am, Sa-Su 10am-1am. ❸

Am Fass, Kammenzerstr. 28, set back from the street behind a grafitti-covered sign in the *Neustadt.* A unique dining experience; the menu features Hungarian specialties for great prices (€3-€8.50). Open M-F 11am-late. ❷

Raskolnikoff, Böhmische Str. 34. Savory fare from all over the globe (€3-14.50). A local crowd fills the cozy dining room or eats around the unusual fountain in the back among tiki-torches. Open daily 10am-2am. ❸

Café Aha, Kreuzstr. 7, across the street from the Kreuzkirche. A haven for the environmentally conscious, the restaurant serves healthy food produced by ecologically sound means and changes its menu monthly to introduce foods from countries that can't compete in the world market. Entrees €3.50-€8.50. Open daily 10am-midnight. ❷

SIGHTS

ZWINGER. The extravagant art collection of Friedrich August I, Prince Elector of Saxony and King of Poland, is housed in the magnificent **Zwinger** palace, a building championed as a triumph of Baroque design. The palace narrowly escaped destruction in the 1945 bombings; workers are busy restoring it to aesthetic perfection. In the Semper wing is the **Gemäldegalerie Alte Meister,** a world-class collection of paintings from 1400 to 1800. Across from the gallery is the **Rüstkammer,** a collection of courtly toys including silver- and gold-plated suits for both man and horse and a set of toddler-sized armor. *(Both open Tu-Su 10am-6pm. Joint admission €3.60, students €2.10. Tours F and Su 11am and 4pm. €0.50)*

SEMPER-OPER. This famed opera house, one of Dresden's major attractions, has been painstakingly restored to its original state. Tour the interior any day—or just go to an opera. *(Theaterplatz 2. ☎491 14 96. Check the main entrance for tour times, usually M-F every 30min. 11am-3pm. €5, students €3.)*

KREUZKIRCHE. After being leveled four times—in 1669 by fire, in 1760 by the Seven Years War, again in 1897 by fire, and finally in February 1945 by Allied bombing—the interior remains in a damaged state. The tower offers a bird's eye view of downtown Dresden. *(An der Kreuzkirche 6. Open in summer M-Tu and Th-F 10am-5:30pm, W and Sa 10am-4:30pm, Su noon-4:30pm; in winter M-Sa 10am-3:30pm, Su noon-4:30pm. Free. Tower closes 30min. before the church. €1.)*

DRESDENER SCHLOß. Once the proud home of August the Strong, this palace was ruined in the Allied firebombing of 1945, but a good deal of its restoration is nearly complete. The 100m tall **Hausmannsturm** hosts fascinating but sobering photographs and texts discussing the Allied bombings, and the top floor offers a 360-degree view of the city. *(Across from the Zwinger on Schloßpl. Open Tu-Su 10am-6pm. €3.50, students €2.)* Stop by the **Fürstenzug** (Procession of Electors), along Augustusstr., a 102m mural made of 24,000 tiles of Meißen china for a history lesson on the rulers of Saxony from 1123 to 1904.

NEUSTADT. Across the magnificent **Augustusbrücke,** Hauptstr. is home to the **Goldener Reiter,** a gold-plated statue of August the Strong atop a steed in pompous glory. August's nickname reputedly paid homage to his remarkable virility; legend has it he fathered 365 children, though the official tally is 15. At the other end of Hauptstr., **Albertplatz** is the gateway to the *Neustadt* scene.

SCHLACHTHOFRINGE. The **Schlachthofringe** (Slaughterhouse Circle), a 1910 housing complex in a more dismal part of Dresden, was used during WWII as a P.O.W.

camp. Its buildings have since been left to waste away. Novelist Kurt Vonnegut was imprisoned here during the bombing of Dresden, inspiring his masterpiece *Slaughterhouse Five*. *(Take bus #82 (dir.: Dresden Messe) to Ostragehege.)*

ALBERTINUM. The Albertinum holds the **Gemäldegalerie der Neuen Meister,** which combines an ensemble of German and French Impressionists with a collection of Expressionists and Neue Sachlichkeit modernist works, including Otto Dix's renowned *War* triptych. *(Open F-W 10am-6pm. €4.50, students €2.50.)*

DEUTSCHES HYGIENEMUSEUM. This ill-named museum long celebrated the health and cleanliness of East Germans. Now that the Party's over, the rather bizarre, interactive, and playful collection includes optical illusions, a hallway of condom propaganda, and a glass cow whose innards light up. *(Lingnerpl. 1, enter from Blüherstr. Open Tu-F 9am-5pm, Sa-Su 10am-6pm. €2.50, students €1.50.)*

ENTERTAINMENT AND NIGHTLIFE

For centuries, Dresden has been a focal point for theater, opera, and music. The superb **Semper-Oper,** Theaterpl. 2 (☎491 17 05) premiered many of Strauss and Wagner's greatest pieces—today, tickets are hard to come by. Dresden's nightlife scene is young and dynamic; the **Neustadt,** roughly bounded by Königsbrückerstr., Bischofsweg, Kamenzerstr., and Albertpl., is its pulsing heart. Over 50 bars pack the area; *Kneipen Surfer* (free at *Neustadt* hostels) lists all of them.

DownTown, Katharinenstr. 11-13, below the Mondpalast hostel. Caters to those wanting something more lively than witty conversations at a bar. The music is loud and seating is rare. Cover €3.50, students €2.50. Open Tu and Th-Sa 10pm-5am.

Die 100, Alaunstr. 100. An unpolished and relaxed atmosphere in a dimly lit coal cellar. With over 300 wines, Die 100 is first and foremost a *weinkeller*. Open daily 5pm-3am.

Deja Vu, Rothenburgerstr. 37. If you're tired of German beer and bar stools, head to this "milk bar" for a milkshake (alcoholic or non) and creamy, blue-lit decor. Open M-F 10am-3am, Sa-Su 10am-5am.

Flowerpower, Eschenstr. 11. From Albertpl., walk up Konigsbrückerstr. and take a left on Eschenstr.; it's on the left. The club is packed with 20-somethings sitting around the colorful bar or getting down to popular tunes. M "student day," with beer and wine half-price. No cover. Open daily 8pm-5am.

Queens, Görlitzer Str. 3. A popular gay bar with plenty of sparkle to go around. Drinks (€2.50-€7), music, and occasional special entertainment. Open daily from 8pm.

DAYTRIP FROM DRESDEN

MEIßEN ☎03521

(Reach Meißen from Dresden by train. 35min., €4.50).

Meißen, 30km from Dresden, is another testament to the frivolity of August the Strong. In 1710, the Saxon elector contracted severe *Porzellankrankheit* (the porcelain "bug," which still afflicts tourists today) and turned the city's defunct castle into Europe's first porcelain factory. The building was once more tightly guarded than KGB headquarters to prevent competitors from learning its techniques; today, anyone can tour the **Staatliche Porzellan-Manufaktur,** Talstr. 9. Peruse finished products in the **Schauhalle** (€4.50, students €4), but the real fun lies in the high-tech tour of the **Schauwerkstatt** (show workshop), which demonstrates the manufacturing process. (Open May-Oct. daily 9am-6pm; Nov.-Apr. 9am-5pm. €3. English headsets available.) Narrow, romantic alleyways lead up to the

Albrechtsburg castle and cathedral. (Open Mar.-Oct. daily 10am-6pm; Nov.-Feb. 10am-5pm. Last entry 30min. before closing. €3.50, students €2.50.) From the train station, walk straight onto Bahnhofstr. and follow it over the Elbbrücke. Cross the bridge, continue straight to the Markt, and turn right onto Burgstr. At the end of Burgstr., on Holweg, take the *Schloßstufen* (castle stairs) on your right, which lead up to Albrechtsburg. Next door looms the **Meißener Dom,** a Gothic cathedral featuring four 13th-century statues by the Naumburg Master, a triptych by Cranach the Elder, and the metal grave coverings of the Wettins. (Open Apr.-Oct. daily 9am-6pm; Nov.-Mar. 10am-4pm. €2, students €1.50.) The **tourist office,** Markt 3, is across from the church, and finds private rooms for a €3 fee. (☎419 40. Open Apr.-Oct. M-F 10am-6pm, Sa-Su 10am-4pm; Nov.-Mar. M-F 10am-5pm, Sa 10am-3pm.) **Postal Code:** 01662.

SAXON SWITZERLAND

Formerly one of East Germany's most beloved holiday destinations, Saxon Switzerland *(Sächsische Schweiz)*—so dubbed because of its stunning, Swiss-like landscape—is now one of unified Germany's favorite national parks. Its sandstone cliffs, sumptuous summits, and breathtaking hikes should be temptation enough to lure anyone off the path and into the hills for a few days.

TRANSPORTATION. Dresden's S1 (dir.: Schöna) runs from the Dresden *Hauptbahnhof* to Wehlen, Rathen, Königstein, and Bad Schandau. The S-Bahn stops just across the river from each of these towns; hop on a ferry to get to the sights (€0.70). Since *Wanderwege* (footpaths) crisscross the area, you can also easily hike from town to town if you're sick of being on the train. Wehlen is probably the ideal jumping-off point to explore other towns in Saxon Switzerland. From Bad Schandau at the end of the line, ride the S-Bahn back to Dresden (50min., every 30min., €4.50) or continue to Prague (2hr., every 2hr., €16).

RATHEN. Two beautiful hikes through the Bastei cliffs run from Wehlen to Rathen. One of the paths climbs up the cliffs and was a favorite of August the Strong; the other path—shorter and easier but much less impressive—is along the Elbe (45min., turn right after the ferry ramp). Rathen makes a good starting point for hikes of any length because of its location on the edge of the **Sächsische Schweiz National Park.** The town also boasts the **Felsenbühne,** a beautiful open-air theater; its 2000 seats are carved into a cliff, and stone pillars loom over the stage. (Open 8am until 2hr. before rehearsal/event and 1hr. after rehearsal/event.) To get there, follow the signs from the ferry landing. Tickets and schedules are available from the **Theaterkasse,** on the way to the theater. (☎77 70. €6-20.)

The **tourist office** gives advice on hiking and finds rooms for free. From the ferry landing, take the main road, Zum Grünbar, for 5min.; it's on the left. (☎704 22. Open Apr.-Oct. M-F 9am-noon and 1-6pm, Sa-Su 9am-1pm; Nov.-Mar. M-F 10am-noon and 1-3pm.) For a knightly night, try **Burg Altrathen ❶,** Am Grünbach 10 um 11, in a castle perched above the Elbe. Take a right up the narrow path to the left after the ferry landing, just past the Hotel Erbgericht. (☎76 00. Dorms €13; singles €22-52; doubles €44-104.) For good eats and an even better view, hit the aptly-named **Pension Panoramo ❷,** a bright pink building up the right-hand slope. (Open M-F 5pm-11pm, Sa noon-11pm. Entrees €3-8.) **Phone Code:** ☎035024.

HOHNSTEIN. The small village of Hohnstein ("high stone" in old Saxon) is linked to Rathen by two beautiful hikes through one of the national park's most stunning valleys. Starting at Rathen, follow the shorter, more challenging red-striped path (2hr.), or the longer green-striped path (3hr.). On your way, be sure to stop at the

Hockstein, an isolated outcropping with a spectacular view of the valley below. Alternatively, you can reach Hohnstein by taking Dresden's S-Bahn to Pirna (40min.) and then bus #236 or 237 from the *Bahnhof* (€3).

The **tourist office,** Rathausstr. 10, in the *Rathaus*, doles out info on trails and finds rooms for free. (☎194 33. Open M and W-F 9am-noon and 12:30-5pm, Tu 9am-noon and 12:30-6pm.) **Naturfreundehaus Burg Hohnstein ❷,** Am Markt 1, is a hostel in a fortress that also houses a nature and history museum, lookout tower, and cafe. (☎812 02. Breakfast included. Reception daily 7:30am-8pm. 6- to 18-bed dorms, singles, doubles, and quads all €18.80 per person.) **Phone Code:** ☎035975.

KÖNIGSTEIN. Above the town looms the impressive fortress Festung Königstein, whose huge walls are built right into the same stone spires that made the Sächsische Schweiz famous. Complete with drawbridges and impenetrable stone walls, the fortress was later converted into a feared state prison. From the city, it's a 40min. uphill struggle, but the view atop the fortress wall is worth sweating for; follow the signs to the well-worn path. (Open Apr.-Sept. daily 9am-8pm; Oct. 9am-6pm; Nov.-Apr. 9am-5pm. €4, students €3.) The touristy Festungs Express is an option for those too tired to make the trek; rides leave from Reißigerpl., just to the right down Bahnhofstr. from the S-Bahn station. (Apr.-Oct. every 30min. 9am-6pm; €3, round-trip €4.)

The **tourist office,** Schreiberberg 2, books rooms and houses the **post office.** It also has a list of available rooms, vacation houses, and *Pensionen;* prices are posted on a bulletin board outside when they're closed. From Reißigerpl., take Hainstr., turn left on Pirnaerstr., then right on Schreiberberg. (☎682 61. Open Apr.-Oct. M-F 9am-6pm, Sa 9am-noon; Nov.-Mar. M-F 9am-noon and 2-6pm; Sa 9-10:30am.) To reach **Naturfreundehaus ❸,** Halbestadt 13, take the ferry across the river and turn right; the hostel is on the right about 10min. down. (☎(035022) 994 80. Breakfast included. Reception daily 8am-7:30pm. €22.50-32 per person; €5.50 added per person for single rooms.) **Schräger's Gasthaus ❸,** Kirchgasse 1, has antlers on the walls and hearty food (€4.50-9) on the table. **Phone Code:** ☎035021.

BAD SCHANDAU. The biggest town in the Sächsische Schweiz, Bad Schandau takes advantage of its location between the two halves of the national park by offering plenty of hiking opportunities. Take the *Kirnitzschtalbahn* trolley car (Mar.-Oct. every 30min. 9:30am-5:30pm; €3, round-trip €4) to the Lichtenhain waterfall, a favorite starting point for three- and four-hour hikes on the Schrammsteine. Bad Schandau is more of a family vacation spot than other towns in the area, so hotels fill up quickly when the weather is good.

The S-Bahn runs to Dresden (50min., every 30min., €4.50). The **tourist office,** Markt 12, finds rooms, suggests hikes, and offers city tours and trips to the Czech Republic. (☎900 30. Open Apr.-Oct. M-F 9am-7pm, Sa 9am-4pm, Su 9am-1pm; Nov.-Apr. M-F 9am-6pm.) To rent a bike, try **Rund Um's Fahrradverleih,** Poststr. 14. (€7.50-9 per day. Open M-F 9am-noon and 2-6pm, Sa 9am-noon.) In a town that shuts down before 11pm, **Sigl's ❸,** Kirnitzschtalstr. 17, a bar-bistro, offers food and a wide selection of beers until 2am and doubles as a cheap hotel. (☎407 02. Singles €34; doubles €100-120.) **Phone Code:** ☎035022.

LEIPZIG ☎0341

Leipzig's *Innenstadt* is small in size, though anything but small in energy and style. Bursting with museums, monuments to Bach, cafes, and bars, Leipzig's appeal can be felt from almost any angle. As in much of former East Germany, unemployment still poses a problem, but Leipzig's fascinating role in history, from the time of Napoleon to the present day, makes it well worth the visit.

THE BIG SPLURGE

AUERBACHS KELLER

It was in this 16th-century tavern that Mephistopheles, the most notorious of evil spirits, tricked some drunkards in Goethe's *Faust* before disappearing in a puff of smoke.

Since then, the Auerbachs Keller has become Leipzig's most famous restaurant and one of the best known eateries in all of Europe. Check out the scenes from *Faust* on the walls of the barrel cellar over a long lunch or dinner in this elegant and atmospheric, yet somehow unpretentious restaurant.

Each of the restaurant's several different eating areas has its own atmosphere and name. The Luther room reminds guests of one of the early patrons of the restaurant. The old Leipzig room dates back to the "good times" in the late 19th century. The Goethe room keeps the legend of their most famous guest alive with pictures and documents on the wall. The barrel cellar, a more relaxed eating location, is where the alleged disappearance took place.

Their extensive menu includes duck, salmon, and steak entrees from €18 to 35. Their dessert menu featuring sorbet, crêpes, and chocolate parfait should also not be missed.

(☎21 61 00. Grimmaische Str. 2-4. Across from the Altes Rathaus, inside the Mädlerpassage. Open daily 11:30am-midnight. MC/V.) ❸

TRANSPORTATION AND PRACTICAL INFORMATION. Leipzig lies on the Berlin-Munich line, with regular service to Frankfurt. **Trains** run to: Berlin (2-3hr., 3 per hr., €26); Dresden (1½hr., 3 per hr., €17); Frankfurt (5hr., 2 per hr., €62); and Munich (7hr., 3 per hr., €68). To reach the **tourist office,** Richard-Wagner-Str. 1, cross Willy-Brandt-Pl. in front of the station and turn left at Richard-Wagner-Str. (☎710 42 60. Open M-F 9am-7pm, Sa 9am-4pm, Su 9am-2pm.) The **post office** is at Augustusplatz 1-4, **04109** Leipzig. (Open M-F 8am-8pm, Sa 9am-4pm.)

ACCOMMODATIONS AND FOOD. To reach **Hostel Sleepy Lion ❷,** Käthe-Kollwitz-Str. 3, take streetcar #1 (dir.: Lausen) or #14 (dir.: S-Bahnhof Plagwitz) to Gottschedstr. Conveniently located next to the city's night scene, the Sleepy Lion draws an international crowd. All rooms have shower and bathroom. (☎993 94 80. Internet €2 per hr. Breakfast €3. Sheets €2. Reception 24hr. 6- to 8-bed dorms €14; singles €24; doubles €36; quads €60.) **Kosmos Hotel ❸** is a 12min. walk from the train station. From the *Hauptbahnhof,* cross the street and turn right onto Richard-Wagner-Str.; when it ends cut left through the parking lot and small park. At the end of the park, keep left on Dittrichring and it'll be ahead on the right. This funky hotel is part of a complex that includes a nightclub and restaurant. (☎233 44 20. Breakfast €5. Reception daily 8am-11pm. Singles from €30; doubles from €50; all with private bathrooms.) Camping is available at **Campingplatz Am Auensee ❶,** Gustav-Esche-Str. 5, in the nearby suburb of Wahren. From the train station, take streetcar #10 or 11 to Wahren. Turn left before the *Rathaus* onto Linkelstr. and follow the main road for 10min.; it will be on your right. (☎465 16 00. Showers €0.50. Reception M-Sa 6am-9:30pm, Su 6am-8pm. €4 per person, €3-5 per tent.)

The *Innenstadt,* especially **Grimmaischestraße,** has *Imbiß* stands, bistros, and bakeries. Just outside the city center, **Karl-Liebknecht-Straße** (streetcar #10 or 11 to Kochstr.) is packed with cheap *Döner* stands and cafes that double as bars come nighttime. **Avocado ❸,** Karl-Liebknecht-Str. 79, has vegetarian and vegan options. (Open M-Th, Su 11:30am-1am, F 11:30am-2am, Sa 4pm-2am.) **Zur Pleißenburg ❷,** Schulstr. 2, just down Burgstr. from the Thomaskirche, is popular with locals and serves hearty fare. (Open daily 9am-5am.) A **market** on Richard-Wagner-Pl. at the end of the Brühl sells fresh goodies. (Open Tu and F 9am-5pm.)

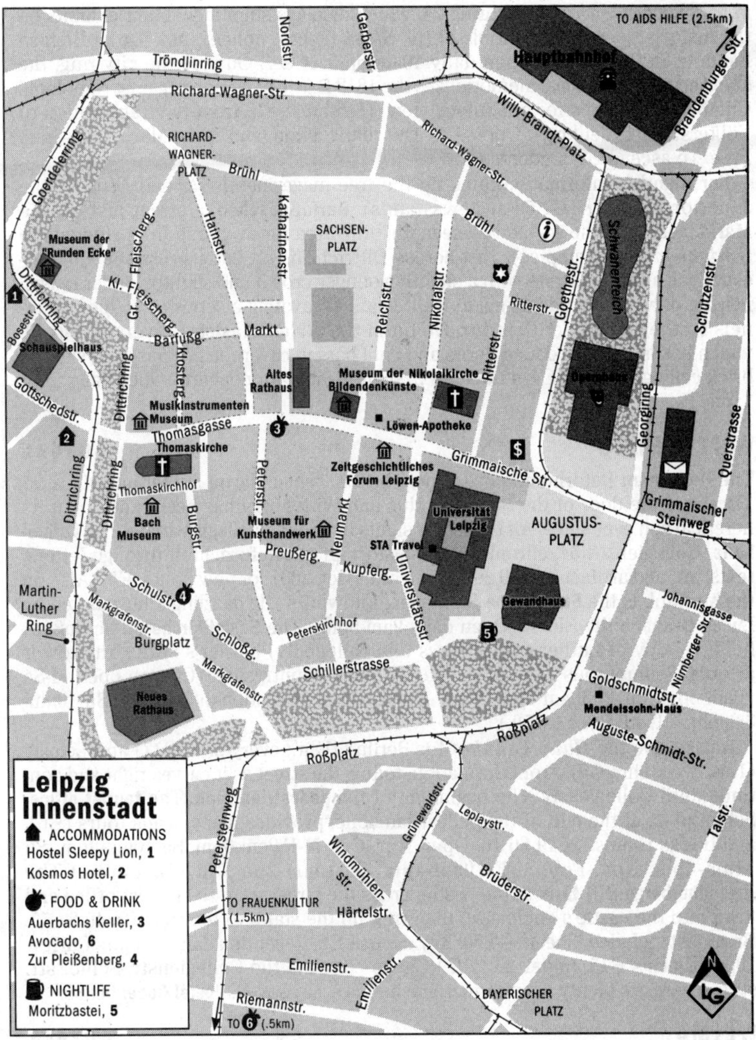

SIGHTS AND ENTERTAINMENT. The heart of Leipzig is the **Marktplatz,** a cobblestoned square guarded by the slanted 16th-century **Altes Rathaus.** Head down Grimmaischestr. to the **Nikolaikirche,** where massive weekly demonstrations led to the fall of the GDR. (Open M-Sa 10am-6pm, Su after services. Free.) Backtrack to the *Rathaus* and follow Thomasg. to the **Thomaskirche;** Bach's grave lies beneath the floor in front of the altar. (Open daily 9am-6pm. Free.) Just behind the church is the **Johann Sebastian Bach Museum,** Thomaskirchhof 16. (Open daily 10am-5pm. €3, students €2. Free English audio tours.) Head back to Thomasg., turn left, then turn right on Dittrichring to reach Leipzig's most fascinating museum, the **Museum**

in der "Runden Ecke," Dittrichring 24, which displays stunningly blunt exhibits on the history, doctrine, and tools of the *Stasi* (secret police). Ask for an English handout in the office. (Open daily 10am-6pm. Free.) Outside the city ring, the **Völkerschlachtdenkmal** memorializes the 1813 Battle of Nations against Napoleon. Climb the 500 steps for a fabulous view. (Streetcar #15 from the train station to Völkerschlachtdenkmal. Open Apr.-Oct. daily 10am-6pm; Nov.-Mar. 10am-5pm. Free. To ascend €3, students €2.)

For nightlife information, pick up the free magazines *Fritz* and *Blitz* or the superior *Kreuzer* (€1.50 at newsstands). **Barfußgäschen,** a street just off the Markt, serves as the see-and-be-seen nightlife area for everyone from students to *Schicki-mickis* (yuppies). Just across Dittrichring on **Gottschedstraße** and **Bosestraße** is a similar scene with a slightly younger crowd and slightly louder music. Leipzig university students spent eight years excavating a series of medieval tunnels so they could get their groove on in the **Moritzbastei,** Universitätsstr. 9, which has multi-level dance floors and chill bars in cavernous rooms with vaulted brick ceilings. (Cover €4, students €2; slightly more for concerts. Open daily from 11pm.)

WITTENBERG ☎03491

The Protestant Reformation began here in 1517 when Martin Luther nailed his *95 Theses* to the door of the Schloßkirche, and Wittenberg has been nuts about its heretical son ever since. All the major sights lie around **Collegienstraße.** The **Lutherhalle,** Collegienstr. 54, chronicles the history of the Reformation through letters, texts, art, and artifacts. (☎40 26 71. Call after Oct. 2002 for new hours. €5.) Also on the Marktpl. is the **Stadtkirche St. Marien,** known for the dazzling altar painted by Lucas Cranach the Elder. (Open daily 9am-5pm.) The **Schloßkirche** on Schloßstr. holds a copy of Luther's *95 Theses* and (allegedly) Luther's body. The tower affords a sumptuous view of the surrounding countryside. (Church open M-Sa 10am-5pm, Su 11:30am-5pm. Free. Tower open M-F noon-3:30pm, Sa-Su 10am-3:30pm. €1, students €0.50.)

Trains leave the *Hauptbahnhof* for Berlin (1½hr., every 2hr., €17) and Leipzig (1hr., every 2hr., €9). From the station, follow the street as it curves right and continue until Collegienstr., the beginning of the **pedestrian zone.** The **tourist office,** Schloßpl. 2, at the end of the pedestrian zone, provides maps, leads tours (€6), and books rooms. (☎49 86 10. Open Mar.-Oct. M-F 9am-6pm, Sa 10am-3pm, Su 11am-4pm; Nov.-Feb. M-F 10am-4pm, Sa 10am-2pm, Su 11am-3pm.) The **Jugendherberge (HI)** ❷ is in the castle; cross the street from the tourist office and head into the castle's enclosure, then trek up the stairs to the right. (☎40 32 55. Breakfast included. Sheets €3.50. Key deposit €5. Reception daily 3-10pm. Curfew 10pm. Dorms €15, under 26 €12.) Cheap eats line the Collegienstr.-Schloßstr. strip. There are plenty of supermarkets in this area as well. **Postal Code:** 06886.

WEIMAR ☎03643

While countless German towns leap at any excuse to build memorial *Goethehäuser* (proclaiming that Goethe slept here, Goethe ate here, Goethe once asked for directions here, etc.), Weimar features the real thing: the **Goethehaus** and **Goethe-Nationalmuseum,** Frauenplan 1, present the preserved private chambers where the poet entertained, wrote and ultimately died after 50 years in Weimar. (Open mid-Mar. to mid-Oct. Tu-Su 9am-6pm; mid-Oct. to mid-Mar. Tu-Su 10am-4pm. Expect a wait of up to 2hr. on summer afternoons. €6, students €4.50.) Weimar's other pride and joy is the *Bauhaus* architectural movement, which began here. The **Bauhaus-Museum,** Theaterpl., showcases its history. (Open Apr.-Oct. Tu-Su 10am-6pm; Nov.-Mar. 10am-4:30pm. €3, students €2.) The **Neuesmu-**

seum, Weimarpl. 4, hosts fascinating rotating exhibits of modern art, including an interactive "Terrororchestra," composed of knives, nails, and a hammer and sickle. (Open Apr.-Sept. Tu-Su 10am-6pm. Oct.-Mar. 10am-4:30pm. €3, students €2.) South of the town center in the **Historischer Friedhof,** Goethe and Schiller rest together in the basement of the **Fürstengruft** (Ducal Vault). Schiller, who died in an epidemic, was originally buried in a mass grave. Later, Goethe combed through the remains until he identified Schiller and had him interred in a tomb. Skeptics argued that Goethe was mistaken, but in the 1960s a team of Russian scientists determined that Goethe was right after all. (Cemetery open Mar.-Sept. daily 8am-9pm; Oct.-Feb. 8am-6pm. Tomb open mid-Mar. to mid-Oct. W-M 9am-1pm and 2-6pm; mid-Oct. to mid-Mar. W-M 10am-1pm and 2-4pm. Tomb €2, students €1.50.)

Trains run to: Dresden (3½hr., 2 per hr., €30); Frankfurt (3hr., 1 per hr., €40); and Leipzig (1½hr., 2 per hr., €21.20). To reach **Goetheplatz** (the center of the *Altstadt*) from the station, follow Carl-August-Allee downhill to Karl-Liebknecht-Str. which leads into Goethepl. (15min.) The **tourist office,** Marktstr. 10, across from the *Rathaus*, hands out free maps, books rooms (€2.55 fee), and offers German-language **walking tours.** The Weimarer Wald desk has lots of info on **outdoor activities** in the area. (☎240 00. Open Apr.-Oct. M-F 9:30am-6pm, Sa 9:30am-4pm, Su 9:30am-3pm; Nov.-Mar. M-F 10am-6pm, Sa-Su 10am-2pm.) To get to the student-run **Hababusch Hostel ❶,** Geleitstr. 4, follow Geleitstr. from Goethepl.; after it takes a sharp right, you'll come to a statue on your left; the entrance to the Hababusch is tucked in the ivied corner behind the statue. Conveniently located in the heart of Weimar, the hostel has a laid-back, communal atmosphere. (☎85 07 37. Kitchen access. Reception 24hr. Dorms €10; singles €15; doubles €24.) **Gästehaus Appartements am Theater ❸,** Heinrich-Heine-Str. 16, has apartment-style rooms each with a full kitchen and bathroom. From the station, walk down Carl-August-Allee, turn right at Rathenau-Pl. and keep heading south on Karl-Leibknecht-Str.; it turns into Heinrich-Heine-Str. (☎50 41 66. Call ahead. Singles €28; doubles €38.) A combination cafe and gallery, **ACC ❸,** Burgpl. 1-2, is popular with students. (Open daily noon-1am.) The daily **produce market,** at Marktpl., has groceries (M-Sa 7am-5pm).

DAYTRIP FROM WEIMAR: BUCHENWALD. During World War II, over 250,000 Jews, Gypsies, homosexuals, communists, and political prisoners were imprisoned at the labor camp of Buchenwald. Although it was not intended as an extermination camp, over 50,000 died here due to the harsh treatment of the SS. The **Nationale Mahnmal und Gedenkstätte Buchenwald** (National Monument and Memorial) has two principal sights. The **KZ-Lager** refers to the remnants of the camps itself ("Konzentration-Lager" means "concentration camp" in German); the large storehouse building documents both the history of Buchenwald (1937-1945) and the general history of Nazism, including German anti-Semitism. The East-German-designed **Mahnmal** (monument) is on the other side of the hill; go straight up the main road which bisects the two large parking lots, or take the footpath uphill from the old Buchenwald *Bahnhof* and then continue on the main road. Many simple memorials for different groups are scattered around the camp, and the camp **archives** are open to anyone searching for records of family and friends between 1937 and 1945. Schedule an appointment with the curator. (Archives ☎(03643) 43 01 54, library ☎(03643) 43 01 60. Outdoor camp area open daily until sundown.) Ironically, suffering in Buchenwald did not end with liberation—Soviet authorities used the site as an internment camp, **Special Camp No. 2,** where more than 28,000 Germans, mostly Nazi war criminals and opponents of the Communist regime, were held until 1950; an exhibit detailing this period opened in 1997.

The best way to reach the camp is by bus #6 from Weimar's train station or Goethepl. (20min. M-F 1 per hr., Sa-Su every 2hr.) Check the schedule carefully; some #6 buses go to Ettersburg rather than Gedenkstätte Buchenwald. Buses back to

Weimar stop at the *KZ-Lager* parking lot and at the road by the *Glockenturm* (belltower). There is an **information center** near the bus stop at Buchenwald, which offers a walking tour (€3, students €2), and shows an excellent video with English subtitles on the hour. (Open May-Sept. Tu-Su 9am-6pm; Oct.-Apr. 8:30am-4:30pm.)

EISENACH ☎03691

Birthplace of Johann Sebastian Bach, Eisenach is also home to one of Germany's most treasured national symbols, **Wartburg castle.** In 1521, the castle sheltered Martin Luther (disguised as a bearded noble named Junker Jörg) after his excommunication. Much of the castle's interior is not authentically medieval, but the Wartburg is still enchanting, and the view from the south tower is spectacular. From the station, Wartburger Allee leads to the foot of the hill on which the castle stands. Tour buses run between the station and the castle. (Every hr. 9am-5pm, €0.75 one-way. Castle open Mar.-Oct. daily 8:30am-5pm; Nov.-Feb. 9am-3:30pm. Mandatory German tour €6, students and children €3.) According to local tradition, the location of Bach's birth in 1685 was the **Bachhaus,** Frauenplan 21. Every 40min. a guide gives a presentation on Bach's life in German and English, complete with musical interludes. (Open Apr.-Sept. M noon-5:45pm, Tu-Su 9am-5:45pm.; Oct.-Mar. M 1-4:45pm, Tu-Su 9am-4:45pm. €2.50, students €2.) Bach was baptized at the 800-year-old **Georgenkirche,** just off the Markt. (Open M-Sa 10am-12:30pm and 2-5pm, Su after services.) Just up the street sits the latticed **Lutherhaus,** Lutherpl. 8, young Martin's home in his school days. (Open Apr.-Oct. daily 9am-5pm; Nov.-Mar. 10am-5pm. €2.50, students €2.)

Trains run frequently to Weimar (1hr., 2 per hr., €11). The **tourist office,** Markt 2, sells maps (€2), offers daily city tours (2pm, €3), and books rooms for free. From the train station, follow Bahnhofstr. through the tunnel and veer left, then turn right onto the pedestrian Karlstr. (☎194 33. Open M 10am-6pm, Tu-F 9am-6pm, Sa-Su 10am-2pm.) To reach the recently renovated **Jugendherberge Arthur Becker (HI) ❷,** Mariental 24, take Bahnhofstr. from the station to Wartburger Allee, which runs into Mariental. (☎74 32 59. Breakfast included. Sheets €3.30. Reception daily 8am-11pm. No curfew. Dorms €17, under 26 €14.) For groceries, head to **Edeka supermarket** on Johannispl. (Open M-F 8am-6:30pm, Sa 8am-12:30pm.) Near the train station, **Café Moritz ❷,** Bahnhofstr. 7, serves Thüringer specialities (€3-9) and sinful ice cream delicacies. (Open May-Oct. M-F 8am-9pm, Sa-Su 10am-9pm; Nov.-Apr. M-F 8am-7pm, Sa-Su 10am-7pm.) The pizza and pasta at the centrally-located **La Fontana ❶,** Georgenstr. 22, are a steal at €3. (Open Su-Th 11:30am-2:30pm and 5-9pm, F-Sa 11:30am-2:30pm and 5pm-midnight.) **Postal Code:** 99817.

NORTHERN GERMANY

Although once a favored vacation spot for East Germans, Mecklenburg-Vorpommern, the northeasternmost portion of Germany, has unfortunately suffered in recent years from economic depression. Just to the west, Schleswig-Holstein, which borders Denmark, has always been driven by its port towns and retains close cultural and commercial ties with Scandinavia. To the west, Bremen (along with Bremerhaven) constitutes Germany's smallest *Land*.

HANOVER (HANNOVER) ☎0511

Despite its relatively small size, Hanover proves itself a rival of any European city in the realms of art, culture, and landscape. Its broad avenues, enormous pedestrian zones, and endless square kilometers of parks and gardens make Hanover an example of all that is good in urban planning. Add to that a famed opera house, museums that exhibit the finest art of the last several thousand years, an endless summer of outdoor festivals, and a vibrant scene of bars and discos, and you've got a cosmopolitan dream boat on the river Leine.

TRANSPORTATION. **Trains** leave at least every hour for: Amsterdam (4½-5hr., €40); Berlin (2½hr., €40); Cologne (2hr., €50); Frankfurt (3hr., €80); Hamburg (1½hr., €25); and Munich (9hr., €130). **ÜSTRA,** Hanover's **public transportation** system, is thorough and fast. Tickets are available from machines or drivers (*Kurzstrecke* (3 stops) €1; single ride €1.50-3 depending on zone; day ticket €3-5.) Remember to punch your ticket at the blue machines, or risk a €30 fine. For more info and maps, call the **ÜSTRA customer service office** in the Kröpcke station. (☎166 822 38. Open M-W and F 8am-6pm, Th 8am-7pm, Sa 9am-2pm.)

PRACTICAL INFORMATION. To reach the **tourist office,** Ernst-August-Pl. 2, head out the main exit of the train station; facing the large rear of the king's splendid steed, turn right. (☎168 497 00. Open M-F 9am-6pm, Sa 9am-2pm.) For **currency exchange, ReiseBank,** inside the train station, has decent rates. (Open M-Sa 7am-10pm, Su 9am-10pm.) Get on the **Internet** at **Das Netz,** at the intersection of Gustav-Bratke-Allee and Humboldt. (€3 per hr. Open daily noon-midnight.) The **post office** is in the same building as the tourist office. (Open M-F 9am-8pm, Sa 9am-4pm.) **Postal Code:** 30159.

ACCOMMODATIONS AND FOOD. **Jugendherberge Hannover (HI) ❷,** Ferdinand-Wilhelm-Fricke-Weg 1, is far from the city center, but definitely worth the trek. Take U3 or 7 (dir.: Wettbergen) to Fischerhof/Fachhochschule. From the stop, backtrack 10m, turn right, cross the tracks, and walk on the path through the school's parking lot; follow the path as it curves, and cross the street. Go over the enormous red footbridge and turn right. The hostel is 50m down on the right, within walking distance of the Maschsee and Schützenffestpl. (☎131 76 74. Breakfast included. Reception 7:30am-11:30pm. Dorms €19-30, under 26 €16-28.) To reach **Naturfreundehaus Stadtheim ❸,** Hermann-Bahlsen-Allee 8, take U3 (dir.: Lahe) or U7 (dir.: Fasanenkrug) to Spannhagengarten, walk 15m back to the intersection, turn left on Hermann-Bahlsen-Allee, and follow the signs. (☎691 493. Breakfast included. Reception 8am-noon and 3-10pm. Dorms €25.) To reach **Hotel am Thielenplatz ❺,** Thielenpl. 2, take a left onto Joachimstr. from the station and go one block to Thielenpl. (☎327 691 93. Breakfast included. Check-out 11:30am. Singles with shower €66-76; doubles with shower €92-112; weekends cheaper.)

Jalda ❷, Limmerstr. 97, serves a combination of Italian, Greek, and Arabic dishes for €4-8. (Open M-Th and Su 11:30am-midnight, F-Sa noon-1am.) **Uwe's Hannenfaß Hanover ❷,** Knochenhauerstr. 36, in the center of the *Altstadt*, serves traditional German fare (€5-7) and great brews. (Open Su-F 4pm-2am, Sa noon-3am.) **Spar supermarkets** sit by the Lister Meile and Kröpcke U-Bahn stops. (Open M-F 7am-7pm, Sa 8am-2pm.)

SIGHTS AND ENTERTAINMENT. With great economic vigor, a wealth of museums, and a tradition of popular festivals, Hanover reigns as the political and cultural capital of Lower Saxony. Many sights stand in the **Altstadt;** from the train station, walk down Bahnhofstr. and continue along as it becomes Karmarschstr., then take a right on Knochenhauer Str. The brick 14th-century **Marktkirche,** will be on your left. (Open daily 10am-4pm; check for concerts.) Used for official purposes until 1913, Hanover's former **Rathaus** has become a shopping area and cafe. Just gawk at the lovely exterior; everything inside is pricey. On the outskirts of the *Altstadt* stands the spectacular **Neues Rathaus;** take the elevator (€2, students €1.50) up the tower for a great view of the city. (Open May-Sept. M-F 8am-10pm,

Sa-Su 10am-10pm.) Right next door, the **Kestner-Museum,** Trammpl. 3, features medieval, Renaissance, and ancient arts. (Open Tu and Th-Su 11am-6pm, W 11am-8pm. €2.60, students €1.50; F free.) The nearby **Sprengel Museum,** Kurt-Schwitters-Pl., at the corner of the Maschsee and Maschpark, near the *Neues Rathaus*, is a 20th-century art-lover's dream with works by James Turrell, Henry Moore, Dalí, and Picasso. (Open Tu 10am-8pm, W-Su 10am-6pm. Permanent collection €3.30, students €2; with special exhibits €6, students €3.50.) The gems of Hanover are the three paradisiacal **Herrenhausen gardens.** The largest, the geometrically trimmed **Großer Garten,** holds the **Große Fontäne,** Europe's highest fountain, which shoots an astounding 80m. (Fountain spurts M-F 11am-noon and 3-5pm, Sa-Su 11am-noon and 2-5pm. Garden open Apr.-Oct. 8am-8pm; Nov.-Mar. 8am-dusk. €2.50.) The **Georgengarten** (open 24hr.) is a maze of open fields, while the **Berggarten** showcases an indoor rain forest. (Open Su-Tu and Th-Sa 10am-6pm, W 10am-9pm. €8.50, students €4.50.)

When the sun goes down, the university crowds flock to the area of **Linden-Nord,** between **Goetheplatz** and **Leinaustraße. The Loft,** Georgstr. 50b, is packed with students on the weekends. (Disco night F and ladies night Sa have €3.50 covers. Open W-Sa from 8pm.) **Osho Disco,** Raschpl. 7L, is a great place to meet (pick up) folks. Every Wednesday is "Forever Young" night—no cover for anyone over 30. (Cover €3-5. Open W-Su from 10pm.)

BREMEN ☎0421

Bremen may be best known as the setting of the Grimm's fairy tale "The Bremen Town Musicians," but its most enduring trait is a strong desire for independence. Today, Bremen has given over its medieval ambience to a thriving cosmopolitan swirl in which cathedrals compete with video art for tourists' attention. The *Altstadt* revolves around the ornate **Rathaus,** which was spared during WWII by a bomber pilot who deliberately missed the target. (Mandatory tours M-Sa 11am, noon, 3, and 4pm; Su 11am and noon. €4, students €2.) Just to the left of the *Rathaus* is a sculpture of the Brothers Grimm's **Die Bremer Stadtmusikanten** (The Bremen Town Musicians)—a donkey, dog, cat, and rooster who terrified a band of robbers with their off-key singing en route to Bremen. Also next to the *Rathaus* is **Saint Petri Dom,** Sandstr. 10-12, with a mosaic exterior and frescoed ceilings; its first stone was laid by Charlemagne in AD 798. Once you've seen the inside, climb the tower to gaze down upon the hubbub of the market square below. (Cathedral open M-F 10am-5pm, Sa 10am-2pm, Su 2-5pm. Free. Tower open Easter-Oct. same hours. €0.70.) **Beck's Brewery,** Am Deich 18/19, provides 2hr. tours complete with samples. (Open M-Sa 11am-5pm, Su 10am-3pm. English tours daily 1:30pm. €3.) The **Neues Museum Weserburg Bremen,** Teerhof 20, off the Bürgermeister-Schmidt Brücke (bridge), displays a constantly evolving array of contemporary artists. (Open Tu-F 10am-6pm, Sa-Su 11am-6pm. €5, students €3.)

Trains run to Hamburg (1½hr., 2-3 per hr., €17) and Hanover (1¼hr., 1-2 per hr., €17). The **tourist office,** in front of the train station, sells the **Erlebnis Card Bremen** (prices for one adult and two children: 1-day €5.50, 2-day €8.50), which provides free local transportation and 20-50% discounts on shows and museums. (☎308 00 51. Open M-W 9:30am-6:30pm, Th 9:30am-8pm, Sa-Su 9:30am-4pm.) **Hotel-Pension Garni Weidmann ❸,** Am Schwarzen Meer 35, provides pampering at bargain prices. Take S2 or 3 to St. Jürgen-Str. and continue on the same road for two blocks. (☎498 44 55. Singles from €21; doubles from €42.) To reach the sleek **Jugendgästehaus Bremen (HI) ❷,** Kalkstr. 6, from the station, take Bahnhofstr. to Herdentorsteinweg, go right at Am Wall, then left on Bürgermeister-Smidt-Str. and right along the water. (☎17 13 69. Breakfast included. Reception 24hr. Check-in 2pm. Check-out 10am. Dorms €20, under 27 €17.) Take-out cafes on **Sögerstraße,** in the Marktpl., sell everything from chocolate truffles to fish sandwiches. The **Schlachte**

is overrun at all hours with people sipping cocktails and enjoying river panoramas. **Auf den Häfen** is a tiny cobblestoned alley crammed with gourmet restaurants and trendy *kneipes* (taverns). Cheap pubs cluster farther east in the **Viertel,** an area filled with hip students and clubs. **Postal Code:** 28195.

HAMBURG ☎040

The largest port city in Germany, Hamburg radiates an inimitable recklessness. Hamburg gained the status of Free Imperial City in 1618 and proudly retains its autonomy as one of Germany's 16 *Länder* and one of only three German city-states. Restoration and riots determined the post-World War II landscape, but today Hamburg has become a haven for contemporary artists and intellectuals as well as party-goers who live it up in Germany's self-declared "capital of lust."

TRANSPORTATION

Flights: Lufthansa (☎01 803 803 803) and **Air France** (☎50 75 24 59) are the 2 main airlines at **Fuhlsbüttel Airport** (HAM; ☎507 50). **Jasper buses** (☎227 10 60) run to the airport from the Kirchenallee exit of the *Hauptbahnhof* (20min.; every 20min. 5am-9:30pm, €5). Or, take U1 or S1 to Ohlsdorf, then take an **express bus** to the airport (every 10min. 4:30am-1am, €2).

Trains: The **Hauptbahnhof** handles most traffic to: **Amsterdam** (5½hr., 3 per day, €68.60); **Berlin** (2½hr., every hr., €45); **Copenhagen** (4½hr., €67.20); **Frankfurt** (3¾hr., every hr., €98); **Hanover** (1¼hr., 3 per hr., €25.60); **Munich** (5½hr., every hr., €133). Two other stations, **Dammtor** (near the university) and **Altona** (in the west) service the city; frequent trains and the S-Bahn connect the 3 stations. 24hr. **lockers** available for €1-2 per day; follow the overhead signs.

Buses: The **ZOB** is on Steintorpl. across from the *Hauptbahnhof*, between McDonald's and the Museum für Kunst und Gewerbe. To: **Berlin** (3¼hr., 8 per day, €22); **Copenhagen** (5½hr., 2 per day, €30); **Paris** (12½hr., 1 per day, €56). Open M-F 9am-8pm, Sa 9:30am-1:30pm and 4-8pm, Su 4-8pm.

Public Transportation: HVV operates an efficient U-Bahn, S-Bahn, and bus network. Most single tickets within the downtown area cost €1, but can vary depending on where you go and what transport you take. 1-day ticket €5, 3-day ticket €12.30. All tickets can be bought at orange *Automaten*, but consider buying a **Hamburg Card** instead (see **Tourist Offices,** below).

Car Rental: Hertz, Kirchenallee 34-36 (☎533 35 35), has cars from €40 per day and €150 per week without insurance, €64 per day with insurance. **Avis** (☎32 87 38 00), in the *Hauptbahnhof*'s Reisebank, has cars from €237 per week with insurance.

ORIENTATION AND PRACTICAL INFORMATION

Hamburg's city center sits between the Elbe River and the two city lakes, **Außenalster** and **Binnenalster.** Most major sights lie between the **St. Pauli Landungsbrücken** port area in the west and the *Hauptbahnhof* in the east. Both the *Nordbahnhof* and *Südbahnhof* U-Bahn stations exit onto the *Hauptbahnhof*. The **Hanseviertel** is crammed with banks, shops, and art galleries. North of downtown, the **university** dominates the **Dammtor** area and sustains a vibrant community of students and intellectuals. To the west of the university, the **Schanzenviertel** is a politically active community home to artists, squatters, and a sizeable Turkish population. At the south end of town, an entirely different atmosphere reigns in **St. Pauli,** where the raucous **Fischmarkt** (fish market) is juxtaposed by the equally wild **Reeperbahn,** home to Hamburg's infamous sex trade.

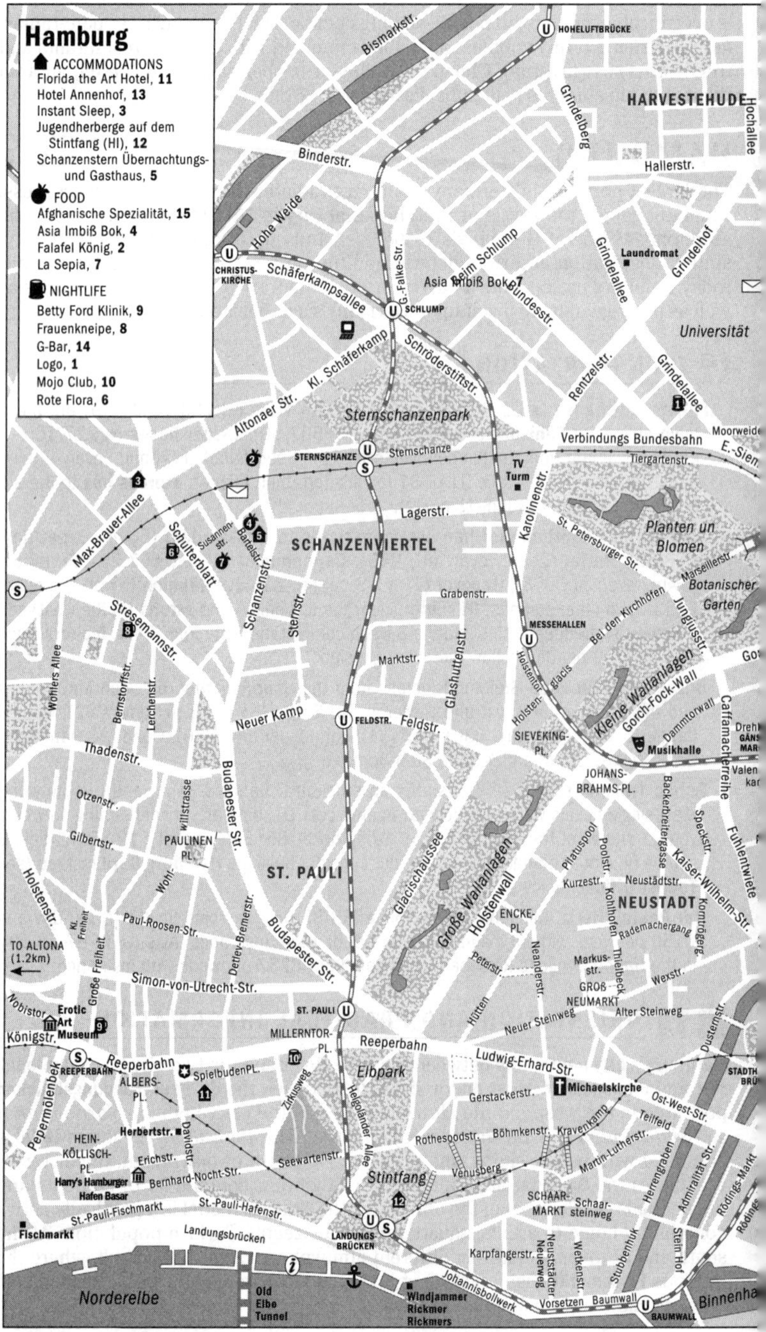
Hamburg
ACCOMMODATIONS
Florida the Art Hotel, 11
Hotel Annenhof, 13
Instant Sleep, 3
Jugendherberge auf dem Stintfang (HI), 12
Schanzenstern Übernachtungs- und Gasthaus, 5
FOOD
Afghanische Spezialität, 15
Asia Imbiß Bok, 4
Falafel König, 2
La Sepia, 7
NIGHTLIFE
Betty Ford Klinik, 9
Frauenkneipe, 8
G-Bar, 14
Logo, 1
Mojo Club, 10
Rote Flora, 6
HARVESTEHUDE
Universität
SCHANZENVIERTEL
ST. PAULI
NEUSTADT
Sternschanzenpark
Planten un Blomen
Botanischer Garten
Kleine Wallanlagen
Große Wallanlagen
Elbpark
Stintfang
Norderelbe
HOHELUFTBRÜCKE
CHRISTUSKIRCHE
SCHLUMP
STERNSCHANZE
MESSEHALLEN
FELDSTR.
ST. PAULI
REEPERBAHN
LANDUNGSBRÜCKEN
BAUMWALL
TO ALTONA (1.2km)
Erotic Art Museum
Harry's Hamburger Hafen Basar
Michaelskirche
Musikhalle
TV Turm
Laundromat
Fischmarkt
Old Elbe Tunnel
Windjammer Rickmer Rickmers
Reeperbahn
Budapester Str.
Simon-von-Utrecht-Str.
Ludwig-Erhard-Str.
Schanzenstr.
Schulterblatt
Max-Brauer-Allee
Stresemannstr.
Altonaer Str.
Schäferkampsallee
Grindelallee
Bundesstr.
Karolinenstr.
Feldstr.
Neuer Kamp
Lagerstr.
Helgoländer Allee
Johannisbollwerk
St.-Pauli-Hafenstr.
Landungsbrücken
Holstenwall
Glacischaussee
Gorch-Fock-Wall
Ost-West-Str.
Kaiser-Wilhelm-Str.
Caffamacherreihe

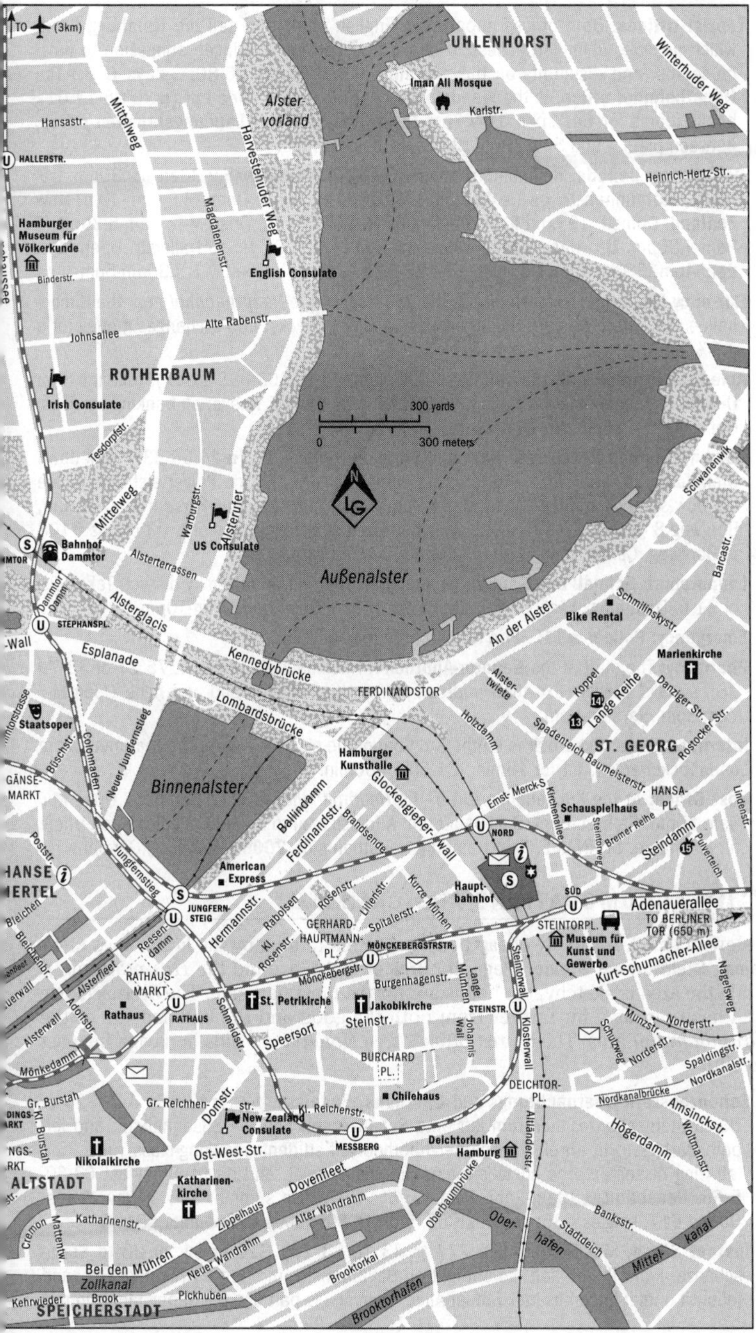
TO (3km)
UHLENHORST
Iman Ali Mosque
Karlstr.
Winterhuder Weg
Alster-vorland
Hansastr.
Mittelweg
Harvestehuder Weg
HALLERSTR.
Heinrich-Hertz-Str.
Hamburger Museum für Völkerkunde
Binderstr.
Magdalenenstr.
English Consulate
Alte Rabenstr.
Johnsallee
ROTHERBAUM
Irish Consulate
0 300 yards
0 300 meters
Tesdorpfstr.
Schwanenwik
Mittelweg
Warburgstr.
Alsterufer
US Consulate
Bahnhof Dammtor
Alsterterrassen
Außenalster
Barcastr.
Dammtor Damm
STEPHANSPL.
Alsterglacis
Schmilinskystr.
Bike Rental
An der Alster
Esplanade
Kennedybrücke
Marienkirche
Alster-twiete
Koppel
Lange Reihe
FERDINANDSTOR
Danziger Str.
Lombardsbrücke
Staatsoper
Holzdamm
Rostocker Str.
Spadenteich
ST. GEORG
Büschstr.
Colonnaden
Neuer Jungfernstieg
Hamburger Kunsthalle
Baumeisterstr.
GÄNSE-MARKT
Binnenalster
Glockengießer-wall
HANSA-PL.
Ballindamm
Ernst-Merck-Str.
Kirchenallee
Schauspielhaus
Lindenstr.
Poststr.
Ferdinandstr.
Brandsende
Steintorweg
Bremer Reihe
HANSE VIERTEL
Jungfernstieg
American Express
NORD
Steindamm
Pulverteich
Bleichen
Hermannstr.
Raboisen
Rosenstr.
Lilienstr.
Kurze Mühren
Haupt-bahnhof
SÜD
Adenauerallee
JUNGFERN-STEIG
GERHARD-HAUPTMANN-PL.
Spitalerstr.
STEINTORPL.
TO BERLINER TOR (650 m)
Kl. Rosenstr.
MÖNCKEBERGSTRSTR.
Museum für Kunst und Gewerbe
Reesen-damm
Alsterfleet
RATHAUS-MARKT
Mönckebergstr.
Burgenhagenstr.
Lange Mühren
Steintorwall
Kurt-Schumacher-Allee
Nagelsweg
Rathaus
RATHAUS
Schmiedestr.
St. Petrikirche
Jakobikirche
STEINSTR.
Alsterwall
Adolfsbr.
Steinstr.
Speersort
Johannis Wall
Klosterwall
Münzstr.
Norderstr.
Schultzweg
Norderstr.
Mönkedamm
BURCHARD PL.
Spaldingstr.
Nordkanalstr.
Chilehaus
DEICHTOR-PL.
Nordkanalbrücke
Gr. Burstah
Gr. Reichhen-str.
Domstr.
Kl. Reichenstr.
Amsinckstr.
New Zealand Consulate
Högerdamm
Kl. Burstah
MESSBERG
Deichtorhallen Hamburg
Nikolaikirche
Ost-West-Str.
Altländerstr.
Wolmanstr.
ALTSTADT
Katharinen-kirche
Dovenfleet
Oberbaumbrücke
Alter Wandrahm
Zippelhaus
Katharinenstr.
Banksstr.
Cremon
Mattentw.
Ober-hafen
Stadtdeich
Neuer Wandrahm
Bei den Mühren
Brooktorkai
Mittel-kanal
Zollkanal
Kehrwieder
Brook
Pickhuben
Brooktorhafen
SPEICHERSTADT

Tourist Offices: Both offices supply free English maps and sell the **Hamburg Card,** which provides unlimited access to public transportation, reduced admission to most museums, and discounts on bus and boat tours. (1-day €6.80; 3-days €13.) The **Hauptbahnhof office,** in the Wandelhalle near the Kirchenallee exit (☎30 05 12 01), books rooms for €4. Open daily 7am-11pm. The **St. Pauli Landungsbrücken office,** between piers 4 and 5 (☎300 512 03), is less crowded.

Consulates: Canada, Ballindamm 35 (☎460 02 70). Open M-F 9:30am-12:30pm. **Ireland,** Feldbrunnenstr. 43 (☎441 81 14); U1 to Hallerstr. Open M-F 9am-1pm. **New Zealand,** Domstr. 19, 2nd fl. of Zürich-haus (☎442 55 50). Open M-Th 9am-5:30pm, F 9am-4:30pm. **UK,** Harvestehuder Weg 8a (☎448 03 20); U1 to Hallerstr. Open M-Th 9am-4pm, F 9am-3pm. **US,** Alsterufer 26-8 (☎411 710). Open M-F 8:30am-5pm.

Currency Exchange: ReiseBank, on the 2nd floor of the *Hauptbahnhof* near the Kirchenallee exit, offers Western Union, cashes traveler's checks, and exchanges money for a 4.5% fee. Open daily 7:30am-10pm.

American Express: Ballindamm 39, 20095 Hamburg (☎303 938 11 12). Take the S- or U-Bahn to Jungfernstieg. Letters held for members up to 5 weeks; all banking services. Open M-F 9am-6pm, Sa 10am-1pm.

Gay and Lesbian Resources: Hein und Fiete, Pulverteich 21 (☎24 03 33). Walk down Steindammstr. away from the *Hauptbahnhof* and turn right on Pulverteich; it's in the rainbow-striped building. Open M-F 4-9pm, Sa 4-7pm. **Magnus-Hirschfeld-Centrum,** Borgweg 8 (☎279 00 69), offers daily films and counseling sessions. U3 or bus #108 to Borgweg. Center open M and F 2-6pm, Tu-W 7-10pm.

Laundromat: Schnell und Sauber, Grindelallee 158, in the university district. Take S21 or 31 to Dammtor. Wash €3.50, dry €1 for 15min. Open daily 7am-10pm.

Emergency: Police: ☎110. **Fire** and **Ambulance:** ☎112.

Pharmacy: The staff at the **Senator-Apotheke,** Hachmannpl. 14 (☎32 75 27 or 33 79 76), speaks English. Exit the *Hauptbahnhof* on Kirchenallee and turn right. Open M-F 7am-8pm, Sa 8am-6pm.

Internet Access: Cyberb@r is on the 3rd floor of the gigantic **Karstadt** department store on Mönckebergstr. €1 for 15min., €1.50 for 30min.

Post Office: At the Kirchenallee exit of the *Hauptbahnhof,* 20097 Hamburg. Open M-F 8am-10pm, Sa 9am-6pm, Su 10am-6pm. Address mail to be held: Postlagernde Briefe für Firstname, SURNAME, Post Hamburg-Hauptbahnhof, **20099** Hamburg, Germany.

ACCOMODATIONS AND CAMPING

A slew of small, relatively cheap pensions (often renting by the hour) lines **Steindamm, Steintorweg, Bremer Weg,** and **Bremer Reihe,** around the *Hauptbahnhof.* While the area is sketchy, the hotels are for the most part safe. The Sternschanze area has options a bit farther from both the good and the bad aspects of the *Hauptbahnhof* area. The tourist office's free *Hotelführer* aids in navigating past the filth.

Schanzenstern Übernachtungs-und Gasthaus, Bartelsstr. 12 (☎439 84 41). S21 or U3 to Sternschanze, then turn left onto Schanzenstr., right on Susannenstr., and left onto Bartelsstr. In an electrifying neighborhood of students, working-class Turks, and left-wing dissenters, the hostel's rooms are clean, quiet, and bright. Breakfast €3.60-5.65. Reception 6:30am-2am. Reservations a must in summer and at New Year's. Dorms €17; singles €35; doubles €50; triples €60; quads €73; quints €91. ❷

Instant Sleep, Max-Brauer-Allee 277 (☎43 18 23 10). S21 or 31, or U3 to Sternschanze. From the station, go straight on Schanzenstr., turn left on Altonaer Str., and follow it until it becomes Max-Brauer-Allee. Everyone is part of a big happy family in this backpacker hostel; rooms are often left open while guests lounge together or cook dinner in the communal kitchen. Sheets €3. Internet €1 for 15min. Reception 9am-2pm. Call ahead. Dorms €15; singles €26; doubles €42; triples €57. ❷

Florida the Art Hotel, Spielbudenpl. 22 (☎31 43 93). U3 to St. Pauli, or S1 or 3 to Reeperbahn. Each room in this immaculate hotel reflects the work of a different artist. Breakfast included. Check-out 4pm. Call ahead. Singles €57; doubles €85. ❹

Hotel Annenhof, Lange Reihe 23 (☎24 34 26). From the train station's Kirchenallee exit, turn left onto Kirchenallee. Pass the Schauspielhaus on your right, then turn left on Lange Reihe. Simple rooms and soft beds. Breakfast €4. Singles €27; doubles €43. ❸

Jugendherberge auf dem Stintfang (HI), Alfred-Wegener-Weg 5 (☎31 34 88). Take U3 or S1, 2, or 3, to Landungsbrücke, then head up the hill on the wooded path. Clean and well-furnished rooms look out on the woods or the harbor. Breakfast included. Laundry €3.50. Reception 11:30am-2am. Curfew 2am. Call ahead. Dorms €19.30, under 26 €16.60; doubles €47.60/€42.20. ❷

Camping: Campingplatz Rosemarie Buchholz, Kieler Str. 374 (☎540 45 32). From Altona train station, take bus #182 or 183 to Basselweg, then walk 100m in the same direction as traffic. Breakfast €4. Showers €1. Reception 8am-noon and 2-10pm. Check-out noon. Call ahead. €4 per person, €6 per tent. ❶

FOOD

Seafood abounds in Hamburg, as you'd expect in a port city. The most interesting part of town from a culinary standpoint is **Sternschanze,** where Turkish fruit stands, Asian *imbiße,* and avant-garde cafes entice hungry passersby with good food and great atmosphere. **Schulterblatt, Susannenstraße,** and **Schanzenstraße** host funky cafes and restaurants, while slightly cheaper establishments abound in the **university** area, especially along **Rentzelstraße, Grindelhof,** and **Grindelallee.** In **Altona,** the pedestrian zone leading up to the train station is packed with ethnic food stands and produce shops. Check out the market inside Altona's massive **Mercado** mall, which includes everything from sushi bars to Portuguese fast food.

La Sepia, Schulterblatt 36, is a fine Portuguese restaurant with the city's best-prepared and most reasonably priced seafood. Dinner €8-14. Open daily 10am-3am. ❸

Asia Imbiß Bok, Bartelstr. 28. To call this merely an *imbiß* is misleading—this joint serves real restaurant food. Join the Bok's thrilled customers for some spicy Thai noodles or roasted duck (€7-9). Open daily 11am-11:30pm. ❸

Falafel König, Schanzenstr. 115. An excellent option for vegetarians. Made individually upon order, the falafel is fresh and sumptuous. Open Su-Th 9am-4am, F-Sa 24hr. ❶

Afghanische Spezialität, on the corner of Steindamm and Polverteich. While the name's not creative, the cooks are. This simple Afghan grill and goods shop serves a variety of kebabs and rice dishes. Open daily 9am-9pm. ❷

SIGHTS

ALTSTADT

Historical sites and modern commercialism abound in Hamburg's *Altstadt.* Within walking distance of each other are imposing churches, government buildings, and winding roads with boutiques to sate the casual browser and the serious shopper.

GROßE MICHAELSKIRCHE. The gargantuan 18th-century Michaelskirche is the symbol of Hamburg, and with good reason. The turning times that raised the city razed the church as well: lightning, accidents, and Allied bombs destroyed the church again and again. Renovated in 1996 along old designs, the church's interior and scalloped walls are reminiscent of a concert hall. The tower, accessible by foot or elevator, is the only one of the city's six spires that may be climbed. On weekends, it is used to project a multimedia presentation about Hamburg's millennial existence onto a 5m-high screen. *(Screenings Th-Su every hr. 12:30-3:30pm. Organ music Apr.-Aug. daily at noon and 5pm. Church open May-Oct. M-Sa 9am-6pm, Su 11:30am-5:30pm; Nov.-Apr. M-Sa 10am-4:30pm, Su 11:30am-4:30pm. Tower €3, students €1.)*

RATHAUS. The town hall, a copper-spired neo-Renaissance monstrosity, serves as the political center of Hamburg. Inside, one can browse through displays of the city's history. The Rathausmarkt in front hosts festivities from political demonstrations to medieval fairs. *(Tours of the Rathaus in German every 30min. M-Th 10am-3pm, F-Su 10am-1pm. Tours in English every hr. M-Th 10:15am-3:15pm, F-Su 10:15am-1:15pm. €1.)*

NIKOLAIKIRCHE. Devastated by an Allied bomb in 1943, the spire of this hallowed (and hollowed) neo-Gothic cathedral pierces the heavens as a reminder of war. *(Exhibition of its history open M-F 10am-5pm, Sa-Su 11am-4pm. €1.50.)* The buildings along nearby **Trostbrücke** sport huge copper models of clipper ships on their spires—a testament to Hamburg's sea-trade wealth. *(Just south of the Rathaus, off Ost-West-Str.)*

SPEICHERSTADT. East of the docks near the copper dome of the **St. Katherinenkirche** lies the historic warehouse district of *Speicherstadt*. These elegant, late-19th-century brick storehouses are filled with cargo, spices, and other sea-faring goods. *(Church open daily 9am-5pm; free organ concerts W 12:30pm.)*

MÖNKEBERGSTRAẞE. Mönkebergstr., Hamburg's shopping zone, stretches from the *Rathaus* to the *Hauptbahnhof* and is punctuated by two spires. The first belongs to the **St. Petrikirche,** the oldest church in Hamburg. *(Open M-Tu and Th-F 10am-6:30pm, W 10am-7pm, Sa 10am-5pm, Su 9am-9pm. Free concerts W 5:15pm.)* The second tower belongs to **St. Jakobikirche,** known for its 14th-century Arp-Schnittger organ. *(Open M-Sa 10am-5pm. Services Su.)*

BEYOND THE ALTSTADT

ST. PAULI LANDUNGSBRÜCKEN. Hamburg's harbor lights up at night with ships from all over the world. Take the elevator from the building behind Pier 6 to the old **Elbtunnel,** which was built from 1907 to 1911 and runs 1200m under the Elbe—it's still used by commuters. At the **Fischmarkt,** charismatic vendors haul in and hawk huge amounts of fish, produce, and other goods. Don't shy away if you dislike fish—about 90% of the goods come in another variety. *(U- or S-Bahn to Landungsbrücken or S-Bahn to Königstr. Open Su 6-10am.)*

PLANTEN UN BLOMEN AND ALSTER LAKES. To the west of the Alster lies **Planten und Blomen,** a huge expanse of manicured flower gardens and trees. *(Open 7am-11pm.)* Daily performances ranging from Irish step-dancing to Hamburg's police orchestra shake the outdoor **Musikpavillon** from May to September at 3pm. There are also nightly **Wasserlichtkonzerte,** in which the fountains are bathed in rainbows of light. *(May-Aug. 10pm, Sept. 9pm.)* North of the city center, the two Alster lakes, bordered by tree-lined paths, provide further refuge from crowded Hamburg.

BEYOND THE CENTER

Though not in the city center, two very different testaments to the atrocities of the Nazi regime are accessible by public transportation.

GEDENKSTÄTTE BULLENHUSER DAMM UND ROSENGARTEN. Surrounded by warehouses, the schoolhouse serves as a memorial to 20 Jewish children brought here from Auschwitz for "testing" and murdered by the S.S. only hours before

Allied troops arrived. Visitors are invited to plant a rose for the children in the flower garden behind the school, where plaques with the children's photographs line the fence. *(Bullenhuser Damm 92. S21 to Rothenburgsort. Follow the signs to Bullenhuser Damm along Ausschlaeger Bildeich and across a bridge; the school is 200m down. Open Su 10am-5pm and Th 2-8pm. Free.)*

KZ NEUENGAMME. An idyllic agricultural village east of Hamburg provided the backdrop for the Neuengamme concentration camp, where Nazis killed 55,000 prisoners through slave labor. In 1989, the Hamburg senate built a memorial on the site. Banners inscribed with the names and death-dates of the victims, along with four 500-page books listing their names, hang in the **Haus des Gedenkens.** *(Jean-Doldier-Weg. S21 to Bergedorf, then bus #227 to Jean-Doldier-Weg. Open May-Oct. Tu-F 10am-5pm, Sa-Su 10am-6pm.)*

MUSEUMS

The one- or three-day **Hamburg Card** (see p. 467) provides access to most of these museums, with the exception of the Deichtorhallen and the Erotic Art Museum. The free newspaper *Museumswelt Hamburg* lists museum exhibitions and events and can be picked up at the tourist offices.

Hamburger Kunsthalle, Glockengießerwall 1. Turn left from the City exit of the *Hauptbahnhof* and cross the street. This sprawling first-rate art museum requires many hours to appreciate in full. The lower level presents the Old Masters, classical modern art, and extensive temporary displays of private collections. Open Tu-W and F-Su 10am-6pm, Th 10am-9pm. €7.50, students €5.

Deichtorhallen Hamburg, Deichtorstr. 1-2. U1 to Steinstr. Follow signs from the subway station; look for two entwined iron circles. Hamburg's contemporary art scene resides here in two buildings that were once fruit market halls. New exhibits each season showcase up-and-coming artists. Open Tu-Su 11am-6pm. Each building €6, students €4.

Erotic Art Museum, Nobistor 10a. S1 or 3 to Reeperbahn. The silver sperm painted on the floor lead you through mazes of rooms full of pictures and figurines of people in sexual contortions. Going up the stairs, the exhibitions move from the Kama Sutra and aristocratic displays of lust towards modernity, interchanging pornographic photos with impressionistic art. Open Su-Th noon-midnight, F-Sa noon-2am. €8. Under 16 not admitted.

Hamburger Museum für Völkerkunde, Rothenbaumchaussee 64. U1 to Hallerstr. Diverse world cultures unravel their ancient tales through traditional attire, weaponry, and religious artifacts. Egyptian mummies preserve a view of long-dead customs while stunning photographs attempt to capture the character of a modern European. Open Tu-Su 10am-6pm, Th 10am-9pm. €5, students €2; F half-price.

ENTERTAINMENT AND NIGHTLIFE

MUSIC AND FESTIVALS

The **Staatsoper,** Große Theaterstr. 36, houses one of the best opera companies in Germany; the associated ballet company is the acknowledged dance powerhouse of the nation. (☎356 80. U1 to Stephanspl. Open M-F 10am-6:30pm, Sa 10am-2pm.) **Orchestras** abound—the Philharmonie, the Norddeutscher Rundfunk Symphony, and Hamburg Symphonia all perform at the **Musikhalle** on Johannes-Brahms-Pl. (☎34 69 20. U2 to Gänsemarkt or Messehallen.) Live music prospers in Hamburg, satisfying all tastes. Superb traditional **jazz** swings at the **Cotton Club** and **Indra** (see Nightlife, below). On Sunday mornings, good and bad alike play at the **Fischmarkt.** The **West Port Jazz Festival,** Germany's largest, runs in mid-July;

call the Koncertskasse (☎ 32 87 38 54) for information. The most anticipated festival is the **G-Move** (June 7, 2003), dubbed the "Love Parade of the North." Check www.g-move.com for the dates and performers.

NIGHTLIFE

The Sternschanze and St. Pauli areas host Hamburg's unrepressed nightlife scene. The infamous **Reeperbahn,** is the spinal cord of **St. Pauli;** it's lined with sex shops, strip joints, peep shows, and other establishments seeking to satisfy every lust. Though the Reeperbahn is reasonably safe for both men and women, it is not recommended for women to venture into the adjacent streets. **Herbertstraße,** Hamburg's only remaining legalized prostitution strip, runs parallel to the Reeperbahn, and is open only to men over 18. The prostitutes flaunting their flesh on Herbertstr. are licensed professionals required to undergo health inspections, while the streetwalkers elsewhere are venereal roulette wheels.

Students trying to avoid the hypersexed Reeperbahn head north to the trendy streets of the **Schanzenviertel.** Unlike St. Pauli, these areas are centered around cafes and weekend extravaganzas of an alternative flavor. Much of Hamburg's **gay scene** is located in the **St. Georg** area of the city, near Berliner Tor. Gay and straight bars in this area are more welcoming and classier than those in the Reeperbahn. In general, clubs open late and close late, with some techno and trance clubs remaining open until noon the following day. *Szene*, available at newsstands (€2.50), lists events and parties, while the gay magazine *hinnerk* lists gay and lesbian events and is available for free at the tourist offices.

Rote Flora, Schulterblatt 71. Held together both figuratively and literally by the spray paint and posters that cover all its vertical surfaces, this looming mansion of graffiti serves as the nucleus of the Sternschanze scene. Weekend cover from €4. Cafe open M-F 6-10pm. Club opening times vary.

Betty Ford Klinik, Große Freiheit 6. Rehab never hurt so good. Chat on the couches lining the hall lit by black chandeliers, or head to the atomic den of the most creative DJs and dancers in town. Cover €10. Open Th 9pm-5am, F-Sa 11pm-6am.

Mojo Club, Reeperbahn 1. This club is adorned with artsy paper lamps and filled with stylish students. The attached **Jazz Café** attracts the trendy. €5 cover on weekends. Open daily 11pm-4am.

Logo, Grindelallee 5. Keeps the college crowd cultured with its eclectic lineup of folk, rock, and samba. Cover €5-15. Open daily from 8pm; music from 9pm.

Lehmitz, Reeperbahn 22. Friendly students and hardcore punks gather around the clock for €2 beers. Live, thrashing music W and weekends. Open 24hr.

G-Bar, Lange Reihe 81. Men in skin-tight shirts serve beer (€2-3) and cocktails (€7) with a smile in this comfortable, neon-lit, gay bar. Open daily noon-2am.

Frauenkneipe, Stresemannstr. 60. Visitors disconcerted by the Reeperbahn and its objectification of women will find another option here. For women only, gay or straight. Open Su-M and W-F from 8pm, Sa from 9pm.

DAYTRIPS FROM HAMBURG

LÜNEBURG HEATH (LÜNEBURGER HEIDE)

To see the Heide, a bike is your best bet. Check the bookstore for extensive and detailed maps of major bike tours in the area. The most popular route is an 80km tour leaving from Luneburg that winds along main roads and through the endless woods and pastures of the suburbs and countryside.

The shrub-covered Lüneburger Heide stretches between the Elbe and Aller rivers. In the undulating countryside, green gives way to purple from July to Sept., when the bushes flower. All of Germany comes here to bike, hike, motor, and frolic in the late summer. The most important regional towns are **Lüneburg** and **Celle.** The staff at the **AG Urlaub und Freizeit auf dem Lande,** Lindrooperstr. 63, Verden-Aller 272380 (☎(04231) 966 50), in Lüneberg provides information on Heu-Hotels ("hay hotels"), functioning barns with rooms for travelers for around €10. You sleep in the hay (hence the name), so bring a sleeping bag, but all Heu-Hotels have showers and toilets, and many are surprisingly luxurious.

LÜBECK ☎0451

Lübeck is easily Schleswig-Holstein's most beautiful city—you'd never guess that the greater part of the city was razed in World War Two. In its heyday, Lübeck was the capital of the Hanseatic league, controlling trade across Northern Europe. Though no longer a center of political and commercial influence, Lübeck remains home to stunning churches, unusual cultural sites, and delicious, sugary marzipan.

TRANSPORTATION AND PRACTICAL INFORMATION. **Trains** depart frequently for Berlin (3¼hr., every hr., €38) and Hamburg (45min., every 30min., €10.80). Avoid the privately owned, expensive tourist office in the train station and head for the **city tourist office** in the *Altstadt*, Breite Str. 62. (☎122 54 13. Open M-F 9:30am-7pm, Sa-Su 10am-3pm.) **Postal Code:** 23552.

ACCOMMODATIONS AND FOOD. To reach **Rucksack Hotel ❶,** Kanalstr. 70, walk past the *Holstentor* from the station, turn left on An der Untertrave, right on Beckergrube and keep going for 20min.; the hostel is on the corner of Kanalstr. Alternatively, take bus #1, 11, 13, 21, or 31 from the station to Pfaffenstr., and turn right at the church on Glockengießerstr. (☎70 68 92 or 261 87 92. Breakfast €3. Sheets €3. Reception daily 9am-1pm and 4-10pm. 10-bed dorms €12; 6-bed dorms €13; doubles with bath €40; quads €60, with bath €68.) **Jugendherberge Lübeck-Altstadt (HI) ❷,** Mengstr. 33, is found in a stately building, seconds away from Lübeck's sights. From the station, head for the *Holstentor*, cross the river, make a left on An der Untertrave and turn right on Mengstr. (☎702 03 99. Breakfast included. Reception daily 7:30am-noon, 1:15-6pm, and 7:15pm-midnight. Dorms €20, under 26 €17.40; doubles €44/34.) The bright and clean **Baltic Hotel ❹,** Hansestr. 11, is across the street from the bus station, 5min. from the *Altstadt*. (☎855 75. Breakfast included. Reception 7am-10pm. Singles €35-45; doubles €58-65; triples from €80.) Lübeck's specialty is **marzipan,** a delectable candy made from almonds. Stop by the famous confectionery **I.G. Niederegger Marzipan Café ❶,** Breitestr. 89, for marzipan in the shape of pigs, jellyfish, and even the town gate. **Tipasa ❷,** Schlumacherstr. 12-14, serves pizza, pasta, and vegetarian dishes, and there's a *Biergarten* in back. (Open M-Th and Su noon-1am, F-Sa noon-2am.) Sample *Pfanne*, pan-cooked ingredients with melted cheese, under oak rafters at **Kurbis ❸,** Mühlenstr. 9. (Open Su-Th 11am-1am, F-Sa 11am-2am.)

SIGHTS. Between the station and the *Altstadt* stands the massive **Holstentor,** one of Lübeck's four 15th-century gates and the symbol of the city; the museum inside displays armor and torture implements. (Open daily 10am-5pm; Oct.-Mar. closed M. €5, students €3.) The city skyline is dominated by the twin brick towers of the **Marienkirche,** a gigantic church housing the largest mechanical organ in the world. Photographs of the destroyed medieval masterpiece **Totentanzbild** ("Dance of the Dead") remind viewers that everything—even paintings—must die. (Open in summer daily 10am-6pm; in winter 10am-4pm. Short organ concerts daily at noon, Th at 6:30pm. €1 donation suggested.) The **Dom,** on Domkirchhof, shelters a majestic crucifix and is guarded by the trademark lion statue. (Open Apr.-Sept. daily 10am-6pm; Mar. and Oct. 10am-5pm; Nov. 10am-4pm; Dec.-Feb. 10am-3pm.

Free.) The floor of the Gothic **Katharinenkirche,** Königstr. 27, is lined with gravestones; formerly a Franciscan monastery, it was used as a stable by Napoleon. (Open Tu-Su 10am-1pm and 2-5pm. €0.50.) For a sweeping view of the *Altstadt,* take the elevator to the 50.5m steeple of the **Petrikirche.** (Church open daily 11am-4pm. Free. Tower open Apr.-Oct. 9am-7pm. €2, students €1.)

MUSEUMS. The largest private puppet collection in the world, the **Museum für Puppentheater,** Kolk 16, displays fascinating hand and string puppets from around the globe. Call for info on shows. (☎786 26. Open daily 10am-6pm. €3, students €2.50.) In the **Museum Behn- und Drägerhaus,** Königstr. 11, Neoclassical landscapes, portraits, and religious works decorate already exquisitely painted walls. The artists' cooperative in the **sculpture garden** outside showcases local artists. (☎122 41 48. Open Apr.-Sept. Tu-Su 10am-5pm; Oct.-Mar. 10am-4pm. €3, students €1.50. 1st F of every month free. Sculpture garden free.)

SCHLESWIG ☎04621

With a harbor full of sailboats and waterside promenades sprinkled with cafes, Schleswig holds both the air of a sea town and the artistic interest of a big city. Scale the 237 steps of the **St. Petri Dom** for a striking birds-eye view of the town. (Open May-Sept. M-Sa 9am-5pm, Su 1:30-5pm; Oct.-Apr. M-Sa 10am-4pm, Su 1:30-5pm. €1.) By the harbor, the 16th-century **Schloß Gottorf** houses the **Landesmuseen,** a treasure trove of Dutch, Danish, and Art Deco pieces. On the other side of the *Schloß*, the **Kreuzstall** houses the **Museum des 20. Jahrhunderts,** devoted to artists of the Brücke school. The surrounding park contains an **outdoor sculpture museum.** (All museums open Apr.-Oct. daily 10am-6pm; Nov.-Mar. Tu-F 9:30am-4pm, Sa-Su 10am-5pm. €5, students €2.50.)

Schleswig centers around its **bus terminal** rather than its train station. Single rides on the bus network cost €2. The **train station** is 20min. south of the city center; take bus #1, 2, 4, or 5 from the stop outside the bus station. Consider buying a **Schleswig Card** (1-day €8, 3-day €11), valid for public transit and admission to most sights. The **tourist office,** Plessenstr. 7, is up the street from the harbor; from the bus station, walk down Plessenstr. toward the water. The staff books rooms. (☎98 16 16; room reservations ☎98 16 17. Open May-Sept. M-F 9:30am-5:30pm, Sa 9:30am-12:30pm; Oct.-Apr. M-Th 10am-4pm, Fri 10am-1pm.) The **Jugendherberge (HI) ❶,** Spielkoppel 1, is close to the center of town. Take bus #2 (dir.: Hühnhauser Schwimmhalle) from either the train or bus station to Schwimmhalle; the hostel is across the street. (☎238 93. Breakfast included. Sheets €3.60. Reception daily 7am-1pm and 5-11pm. Curfew 11pm. Dorms €15, under 26 €12.30.) A windswept little **Hafen Pavilion ❷,** at the harbor, sells fresh seafood. (Open daily 9am-8pm.)

CENTRAL AND WEST GERMANY

Lower Saxony (*Niedersachsen*), which stretches from the North Sea to the hills of central Germany, has foggy marshland and broad agricultural plains inland. Just south of Lower Saxony, North Rhine-Westphalia is the most heavily populated and economically powerful area in Germany. While the region's squalor may have inspired the philosophy of Karl Marx and Friedrich Engels, the area's natural beauty and the intellectual energy of Cologne and Düsseldorf inspired the muses of Goethe, Heine, and Böll. Right in the center of Germany is the region of Hesse. Before the 20th century it was mostly known as a source for mercenary soldiers (many hired by King George III to put down an unruly gang of colonials in 1776); today it's the busiest commercial center in Germany.

DÜSSELDORF ☎0211

As Germany's fashion hub and multinational corporation base, as well as the capital of densely populated Nordrhein-Westfalen, the rich city of Düsseldorf crawls with German patricians and wannabe aristocrats. Set on the majestic Rhine, Germany's *"Hautstadt"* (a pun on *Hauptstadt* (capital) and the French *haute,* as in *haute culture*) is a stately, modern metropolis with an *Altstadt* that hosts the best nightlife along the Rhine in authentic German style.

TRANSPORTATION

Trains: Run to: **Amsterdam** (3hr., every hr., €39); **Berlin** (4½hr., 1-2 per hr., €93); **Frankfurt** (2½hr., 3 per hr., €32); **Hamburg** (3½hr., 2 per hr., €63); **Munich** (6hr., 2-3 per hr., €98); **Paris** (4½hr., 7 per day, €87). The S-Bahn is the cheapest way to get to **Aachen** and **Cologne.**

Public Transportation: Single tickets €1-7, depending on distance traveled. The *Tagesticket* (€6.35-17.50) lets up to 5 people travel for 24hr. on any line. Tickets are sold by vending machine; pick up the *Fahrausweis* brochure in the tourist office for instructions. Düsseldorf's S-Bahn is integrated into the mammoth regional **VRR** *(Verkehrsverbund Rhein-Ruhr)* system, which connects most surrounding cities. For schedule information, call ☎582 28.

PRACTICAL INFORMATION

Tourist Office: Immermannstr. 65 (☎17 20 20). Head straight and to the right from the train station and look for the Immermanhof building. Books rooms for €4 (M-Sa 8am-8pm, Su 2-8pm). Sells the **Düsseldorf WelcomeCard** (24hr. €9; 48hr. €14; 76hr. €19), which includes entrance to major museums as well as free public transportation and additional discounts. Open M-F 8:30am-6pm, Sa 9am-12:30pm.

Currency Exchange: ReiseBank, in the train station. Open M-F 7am-10pm, Sa 7am-9pm, Su 8am-9pm.

Laundromat: Wasch Center, Friedrichstr. 92, down the street from the Kirchpl. S-Bahn stop. Wash €3, dry €0.50 per 15min. Open M-Sa 6am-11pm.

Post Office: Hauptpostamt, Konrad-Adenauer-Pl., **40210** Düsseldorf, just to the right of the tourist office. Open M-F 8am-6pm, Sa 9am-2pm.

ACCOMMODATIONS AND CAMPING

It's not unusual for hotels in Düsseldorf to double their prices during a convention. Call at least one month ahead if possible.

Jugendgästehaus Düsseldorf (HI), Düsseldorfer Str. 1 (☎55 73 10), is just over the Rheinkniebrücke from the *Altstadt.* U70, 74, 75, 76, 77 to Luegpl., then walk 500m down Kaiser-Wilhelm-Ring. Reception daily 7am-1am. Curfew 1am, doors open every hr. on the hr. 2-6am. Dorms €20. ❷

Hotel Schaum, Gustav-Poengsen Str. 63 (☎31 16 510). From the main train station, exit going left on Graf-Adolf-Str., take the 1st left, and follow the tracks to Gustav-Poengsen-Str. Large rooms and a welcoming staff. Call for pickup from the train station. Breakfast included. Singles from €30; doubles from €50. ❸

Hotel Komet, Bismarckstr. 93 (☎17 87 90), straight down Bismarckstr. from the train station. Offers bright but snug rooms 10min. from the *Altstadt.* Singles with showers €48; doubles from €55. ❹

Camping: Kleiner Torfbruch (☎899 20 38). S-Bahn to Düsseldorf Geresheim, then bus #735 (dir.: Stamesberg) to Seeweg. €4 per person, €5 per tent. ❶

FOOD

For a cheap meal, the endless eateries in the *Altstadt* can't be beat; rows of pizzerias, *Döner* stands, and Chinese diners reach from Heinrich-Heine-Allee to the banks of the Rhine. **Otto Mess** is a popular **grocery** chain; the most convenient location is at the eastern corner of Karlspl. in the *Altstadt*. (Open M-F 8am-8pm, Sa 8am-4pm.)

A Tavola, Wallstr. 11. Score a seat on the attractive outdoor patio as you delight in bottomless bread baskets, meticulously prepared pasta dishes, and an Italian-speaking waitstaff. Open daily noon-3pm and 6-11pm. ❸

Pilsener Urquell, Grabenstr. 6. This local outlet of the Czech brewery specializes in European cuisine. Open M-Sa noon-1am, Su 4pm-midnight. ❷

Im Füchschen, Ratingerstr. 28. A favorite for all the local delicacies, including *Blutwurst* (blood sausage), Mainz hand cheese, and delicious *Füchsenbier* (brewed on premises). Open daily 9am-midnight. ❷

Zum Csikos, Andreasstr. 9. This colorful little tavern is bursting with character and Hungarian food and drink. Open Tu-Su 6pm-3am. ❸

SIGHTS

KÖNIGSALLEE. The glitzy Kö—properly called the Königsallee—just outside the *Altstadt*, embodies the vitality and glamor of wealthy Düsseldorf. Stone bridges span the little river that runs through the middle and trickles to a stop at the toes of a statue of the sea god Triton. Midway up is the awesome **Kö-Galerie,** a marble-and-copper shopping mall showcasing one haughty store after another. *(10min. down Graf-Adolf-Str. from the train station.)*

SCHLOß BENRATH. This Baroque palace in the suburbs of Düsseldorf was built 200 years ago as a pleasure palace and hunting grounds for Elector Karl Theodor. The architect used strategically placed mirrors and false exterior windows to make the castle appear larger than it is, but the enormous French gardens temper the effect. *(S6 (dir.: Köln) to Schloß Benrath. Open Tu-Su 10am-6pm, W until 8pm. Tours every 30min. €4, students €1.75.)*

HEINRICH-HEINE-INSTITUT. Beloved poet Heinrich Heine is Düsseldorf's melancholic son. This institute is the official shrine, with a collection of manuscripts, Lorelei paraphenalia, and an unsettling death mask. *(Bilker Str. 12-14. Open Tu-Su 11am-5pm, Sa 1-5pm. €2, students €1.)*

HOFGARTEN AND GOETHEMUSEUM. At the upper end of the Kö, the Hofgarten park is the oldest public park in Germany. At the east end, the 18th-century **Schloß Jägerhof** houses the **Goethemuseum,** where 30,000 souvenirs memorialize the poet. *(Jakobistr. 2. Streetcar #707 or bus #752 to Schloß Jägerhof. Open Tu-F and Su 11am-5pm, Sa 1-5pm. €2, students and children €1.)*

KUNSTSAMMLUNG NORDRHEIN-WESTFALEN. The black glass edifice west of the Hofgarten houses works by Matisse, Picasso, Surrealists, Expressionists, and hometown boy Paul Klee, as well as many changing exhibits of modern art and film. *(Grabbepl. 5. U70, 75, 76, 78, or 79 to Heinrich-Heine-Allee; walk north 2 blocks. Open Tu-F 10am-6pm, Sa-Su 11am-6pm, first W of every month until 10pm. €3, students €1.50.*

KUNSTHALLE. Across the square from the Kunstsammlung Nordrhein-Westfalen, this building stands as a forum for modern exhibits of every shape and size. Exhibits rotate every 2-3 months. *(Open Tu-Sa noon-8pm, Su 11am-6pm. Grabbepl. 4. Admission depends on the exhibit; usually €5, students €4.)*

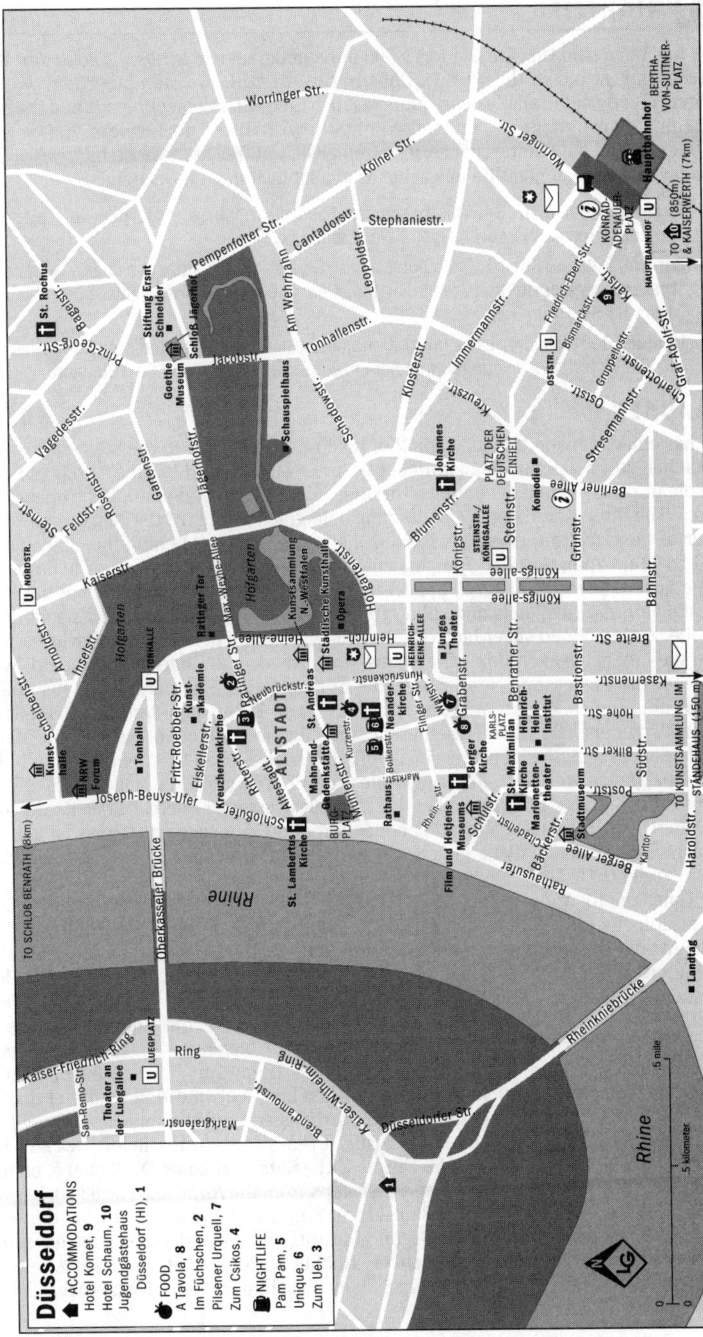
Düsseldorf
ACCOMMODATIONS
Hotel Komet, 9
Hotel Schaum, 10
Jugendgästehaus Düsseldorf (HI), 1
FOOD
A Tavola, 8
Im Füchschen, 2
Pilsener Urquell, 7
Zum Csikos, 4
NIGHTLIFE
Pam Pam, 5
Unique, 6
Zum Uel, 3
Rhine
ALTSTADT
Hofgarten
Hauptbahnhof
KONRAD-ADENAUER-PLATZ
BERTHA-VON-SUTTNER-PLATZ
TO 10 (850m) & KAISERWERTH (7km)
TO SCHLOß BENRATH (8km)
TO KUNSTSAMMLUNG IM STÄNDEHAUS (150 m)
St. Lambertus Kirche
St. Andreas
Kunstsammlung N. Westfalen
Städtische Kunsthalle
Opera
Schauspielhaus
Goethe Museum
Schloß Jägerhof
Stiftung Ernst Schneider
St. Rochus
Johannes Kirche
Kunsthalle
NRW Forum
Tonhalle
Kunstakademie
Kreuzherrenkirche
Ratinger Tor
Mahn-und-Gedenkstätte
Rathaus
Neanderkirche
Junges Theater
Film und Hetjens-Museums
Berger Kirche
St. Maximilian Kirche
Marionetten-theater
Heinrich-Heine-Institut
Stadtmuseum
Komodie
Landtag
Theater an der Luegallee
Oberkasseler Brücke
Rheinkniebrücke
Königsallee
Worringer Str.
Kölner Str.
Pempelforter Str.
Kaiserstr.
Joseph-Beuys-Ufer
Berliner Allee
Graf-Adolf-Str.
.5 mile
.5 kilometer

NIGHTLIFE

It has been said that Düsseldorf's 500 pubs make up *die längste Theke der Welt* (the longest bar in the world). Pubs in the *Altstadt* are standing-room-only by 6pm, and by nightfall it's nearly impossible to see where one pub ends and the next begins. **Bolkerstraße** is jam-packed nightly with street performers. *Prinz* (€3) gives tips on happening scenes; it's often given out free at the hostel. *Facolte* (€2), a gay and lesbian nightlife magazine, is available at most newsstands.

Pam-Pam, Bolkerstr. 34. This basement disco plays house, rock, pop, and plenty of American music. No cover. Open F-Sa 10pm-dawn.

Zur Uel, Ratinger Str. 16. The quintessential German tavern attracts a largely local crowd that congregates out front, rendering the street impassable most nights. Open M-F 9am-1am, Sa-Su 10am-3am.

Unique, Bolkerstr. 30. Lives up to its name, at least in Düsseldorf's *Altstadt.* This red-walled club draws a younger, trendier crowd. Cover €5. Open W-Sa 10pm-late.

AACHEN ☎0241

Charlemagne made this the capital of his Frankish empire in the 8th century, and Aachen still maintains its historical treasures—from Charlemagne's body parts to Roman ruins—while becoming a thriving forum for up-and-coming European artists. The three-tiered dome and dazzling blue-gold mosaics of the **Dom** is in the center of the city; Charlemagne's remains lie in the reliquary behind the altar. (Open M-Sa 11am-7pm, Su 12:30-7pm, except during services.) Just around the corner is the **Schatzkammer,** Klosterpl. 2, a treasury of reliquaries containing John the Baptist's hair and ribs, nails and splinters from the true cross, and Christ's scourging robe. A gold-plated silver bust of Charlemagne, which holds his skull, was carried to the city gates each time a new king was crowned so Charlemagne could "welcome" his successors. Nearby, a statue of a gigantic golden arm holds his radius and ulna bones. (Open M 10am-1pm, Tu-W and F-Su 10am-6pm, Th 10am-9pm. €2.50, students €2.) The 14th-century stone **Rathaus,** which looms over the Marktpl., contains magnificent frescoes depicting scenes from Charlemagne's military campaigns as well as a glittering collection of crown jewels. (Open daily 10am-1pm and 2-5pm. €1.50, students €1.) The **Ludwigforum für Internationale Kunst,** Jülicherstr. 97-109, houses a rotating collection of cutting-edge art. (Open Tu and Th 10am-5pm, W and F 10am-8pm, Sa-Su 11am-5pm. Free tours Su 11:30am and 3pm. €3, students €1.50.)

Trains run to: Amsterdam (4hr., 1-2 per hr., €34); Brussels (2hr., every 2hr., €20); and Cologne (1hr., 2-3 per hr., €11). The **tourist office,** on Friedrich-Wilhelm-Pl. in the Atrium Elisenbrunnen, runs tours and finds rooms for free. From the train station, cross the street and head up Bahnhofstr., turn left onto Theaterstr., which becomes Theaterpl., then right onto Kapuzinergraben, which becomes Friedrich-Wilhelm-Pl. (☎180 29 60. Open M-F 9am-6pm, Sa 9am-2pm.) **Internet** access is available at the city library, **Öffentliche Bibliothek,** Couvenstr. 15. (€3 per hr. Open Tu-W and F 11am-5:45pm, Th 1:15-8pm, Sa 10am-1pm.) The **Euroregionales Jugendgästehaus (HI) ❸,** Maria-Theresia-Allee 260, feels more like a hotel than a hostel. From the station, walk left on Lagerhausstr. until it intersects Karmeliterstr. and Mozartstr., then take bus #2 (dir.: Preusswald) to Ronheide. (☎71 10 10. Breakfast included. Curfew 1am. Dorms €21.) **Hotel Drei König ❸,** Büchel 5, on the corner of Marktpl., has clean rooms just steps from the *Rathaus.* (☎483 93. Breakfast included. Reception daily 8am-11pm. Singles €34, with bath €65; doubles €54/€75; triples €100.) **Pontstraße,** off Marktpl., and the pedestrian zone have lots of great restaurants. **Van den Daele ❷,** Büchel 18-20, just off the *Markt,* serves Aachen delicacies. (Open M-Sa 9am-6:30pm, Su 11am-6:30pm.) **Postal code:** 52064.

COLOGNE (KÖLN) ☎0221

Although most of the inner city was destroyed in World War II, Cologne's magnificent Gothic *Dom* survived its 14 bombings and remains the city's main attraction. Today, the city is the largest in the North Rhine-Westphalia and its most important cultural center, with a full range of world-class museums and theatrical offerings.

TRANSPORTATION

Flights: Flights depart from **Köln-Bonn Flughafen** (CGN). A shuttle to **Berlin** leaves 24 times per day. Bus #170 to the airport leaves from stop 3 at the train station. (20min.; every 30min. 5:30-6:30am and 8-11pm, every 15min. 6:30am-8pm; €4.80.)

Trains: The trains in the northern part of the *Innenstadt* depart for: **Amsterdam** (4hr., €44); **Berlin** (6½hr., 1-2 per hr., €98); **Brussels** (2½hr., €43); **Düsseldorf** (30min., 5 per hr., €6.50); **Frankfurt** (2hr., 3 per hr., €32); **Hamburg** (5hr., 3 per hr., €67); **Munich** (6½hr., 3-4 per hr., €102).

Ferries: Köln-Düsseldorfer (☎208 83 18) begins its popular Rhine cruises here. Sail upstream to **Koblenz** (€33) or **Bonn** (€10.40). Eurail valid on most trips.

Public Transportation: VRS (Verkehrsverbund Rhein-Sieg) offices have free maps of the S- and U-Bahn, bus, and streetcar lines; there is one downstairs in the train station.

ORIENTATION AND PRACTICAL INFORMATION

Although the Rhine stretches along Cologne's eastern side, nearly all sights and the city center can be found on the western side. The train station is in the northern part of the **Innenstadt** (town center). The *Altstadt* is split into **Altstadt-Nord,** near the **Hauptbahnhof,** and **Altstadt-Süd,** south of the **Severinsbrücke** (bridge).

Tourist Office: Verkehrsamt, Unter Fettenhennen 19 (☎22 12 33 45), across from the entrance to the *Dom*, provides free city maps and books rooms for €3. Open May-Oct. M-Sa 8am-10:30pm, Su 9am-10:30pm; Nov.-Apr. M-Sa 8am-9pm, Su 9:30am-7pm.

Currency Exchange: An office at the train station is open daily 7am-9pm.

Bi-Gay-Lesbian Resources: Schulz Schwulen-und Lesbenzentrum, Kartäuserwall 18 (☎93 18 80 80), near Chlodwigpl. Info, advice, and cafe. The tourist office also offers a Gay City Map with listings of gay-friendly hotels, bars, and clubs.

Laundry: Eco-Express Waschsalon, at the corner of Richard-Wagner-Str. and Händelstr. Wash €2.50-3; dry €0.50 for 10min. Soap included. Open M-Sa 6am-11pm.

Emergency: Police: ☎110. **Fire** and **ambulance:** ☎112.

Pharmacy: Apotheke im Hauptbahnhof, Gleisaufgang 10 (☎139 11 12), in the train station. Open M-F 6am-8pm, Sa 8am-4pm.

Internet Access: FuturePoint, Richmodstr. 13 (☎206 72 06). €2 for 30min. ID required. Open daily 10:30am-11:30pm.

Post Office: At the corner of Breite Str. and Tunisstr. in the *WDR-Arkaden* shopping gallery. Address mail to be held: Postlagernde Briefe für Firstname SURNAME, Hauptpostamt, **50667** Köln, Germany. Open M-F 8am-8pm, Sa 8am-4pm.

ACCOMMODATIONS

Most hotels fill up in spring and fall when conventions come to town; the two hostels are also nearly always booked from June to September—call ahead. The main hotel haven centers around **Brandenburgerstraße,** on the less interesting side of the train station. Scrounging for a last minute room during Karneval is futile.

Jansen Pension, Richard-Wagner-Str. 18 (☎25 18 75). U1, 6, 7, 15, 17, or 19 to Rudolfpl. Owned by a welcoming English couple and featuring high-ceilinged rooms in a Victorian-style building. Breakfast included. Singles €31-36; doubles €57-62. ❸

Station Hostel and Bar, Rheing. 34-36 (☎23 02 47). Across from the Rhine, it's 10min. from the *Dom.* Clean rooms and English-speaking staff. Free Internet access. Reception 24hr. Reservations held until 6pm. Singles €25; doubles €40; triples €54. ❸

Jugendgästehaus Köln-Riehl (HI), An der Schanz 14 (☎76 70 81), on the Rhine, north of the zoo. U16 (dir.: Ebertplatz/Mülheim) to Boltensternstr. Breakfast included. Reception 24hr. Call ahead. 4- to 6-bed dorms €21; singles €34. ❸

Jugendherberge Köln-Deutz (HI), Siegesstr. 5a (☎81 47 11), just over the *Hohenzollernbrücke.* S6, 11, or 12 to Köln-Deutz. Exit the station, walk down Neuhöfferstr., and take the 1st right; the hostel is in a courtyard. Newly renovated rooms. Breakfast and laundry included. Reception 11am-1am. Curfew 1am. Call ahead. Dorms €20. ❸

Das Kleine Stapelhäus'chen, Fischmarkt 1-3 (☎257 78 62). Cross the Altenmarkt from the back of the *Rathaus* and take Lintg. to the Rischmarkt. An old-fashioned and elegant inn overlooking the river. Breakfast included. Singles €39-41, with shower €52-64, with full bath €64-74; doubles €64-74/€90-97/€100-121. ❹

Hotel Im Kupferkessel, Probsteig. 6 (☎13 53 38). From the *Dom,* follow Dompropst-Ketzer-Str. as it becomes An der Dominikan, Unter Sachenhausen, Gereonstr., and finally Christophstr.; Probsteig. is on the right. Cozy rooms with TV and telephone. Breakfast included. Singles €30-41; doubles from €66. ❸

Campingplatz Poll, Weidenweg (☎83 19 66), on the Rhine, southeast of the *Altstadt.* U16 to Marenberg and cross the Rodenkirchener Brücke. Reception daily 8am-noon and 5-8pm. Open mid-Apr. to Oct. €4.50 per person, €2.50 per tent or car. ❶

FOOD

Cologne cuisine includes scrumptious *Rievekoochen* (slabs of fried potato dunked in applesauce) and smooth *Kölsch* beer. Cheap restaurants line **Zülpicherstraße** (U7 or 9 to Zülpicher Pl.). Mid-priced ethnic restaurants lie around the perimeter of the *Altstadt,* particularly from **Hohenzollernring** to **Hohenstaufenring;** the city's best cheap eats are on **Weideng** in the Turkish district. An open-air **market** on **Willhelmsplatz** takes over the neighborhood in the mornings. (Open M-Sa 8am-1pm.)

Brauhaus Früh am Dom, Am Hof 12-14. Enjoy hearty regional specialties with a tall glass of Cologne's finest *Kölsch,* served here since the early 19th century. Entrees €4-18. Open daily 8am-midnight. ❸

Päffgen-Brauerei, Friesenstr. 64-66. A local favorite since 1883. Legendary *Kölsch* is brewed on the premises and consumed in cavernous halls or in the *Biergarten.* Hearty meals €2-16. Open daily 10am-midnight. Kitchen open 11am-11pm. ❸

Café Magnus, Zülpicherstr. 48. Funky indoor/outdoor cafe with beautifully presented meals. Pizzas and salads from €4, pasta from €5. Open daily 8am-3am. ❷

SIGHTS

DOM. Whether illuminated in a pool of eerie blue lighting or eclipsing the sun with its colossal spires, the *Dom,* Germany's greatest cathedral, is the first thing to greet travelers as they enter the city. A chapel to the right of the choir houses a 15th-century **triptych,** representing the city's five patron saints. In the center of the choir, behind the altar, is the **Shrine of the Magi,** which reportedly holds the remains of the Three Kings, and is the most sacred element of the cathedral. Before exiting the choir, stop in the **Chapel of the Cross** to admire the 10th-century

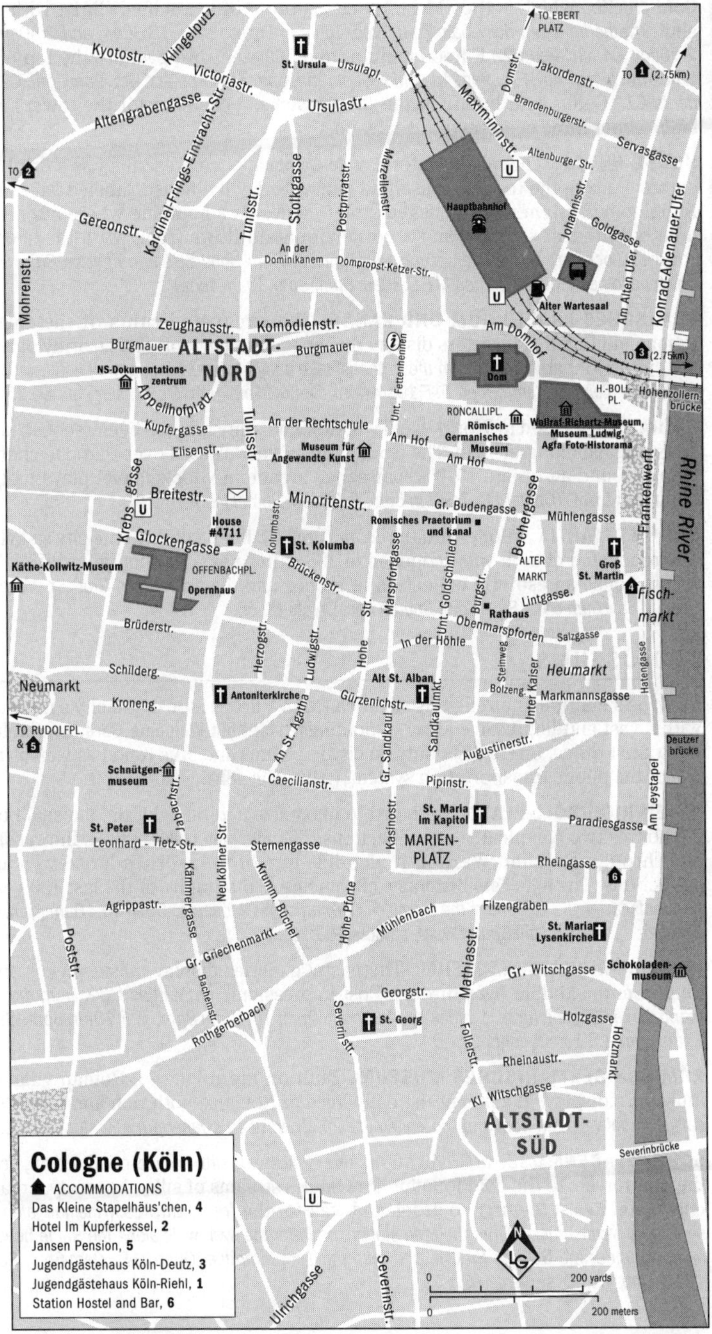
Cologne (Köln)
ACCOMMODATIONS
Das Kleine Stapelhäus'chen, 4
Hotel Im Kupferkessel, 2
Jansen Pension, 5
Jugendgästehaus Köln-Deutz, 3
Jugendgästehaus Köln-Riehl, 1
Station Hostel and Bar, 6
ALTSTADT-NORD
ALTSTADT-SÜD
Rhine River
Hauptbahnhof
Dom
Alter Wartesaal
St. Ursula
Wallraf-Richartz-Museum, Museum Ludwig, Agfa Foto-Historama
Römisch-Germanisches Museum
Museum für Angewandte Kunst
NS-Dokumentations-zentrum
House #4711
St. Kolumba
Romisches Praetorium und kanal
Groß St. Martin
Rathaus
Opernhaus
Käthe-Kollwitz-Museum
Antoniterkirche
Alt St. Alban
Schnütgen-museum
St. Peter
St. Maria im Kapitol
MARIEN-PLATZ
St. Maria Lysenkirche
Schokoladen-museum
St. Georg
Neumarkt
Heumarkt
Fischmarkt
ALTER MARKT
OFFENBACHPL.
RONCALLIPL.
H.-BÖLL-PL.
Hohenzollernbrücke
Deutzer brücke
Severinbrücke
TO EBERT PLATZ
TO RUDOLFPL. & 5
TO 1 (2.75km)
TO 3 (2.75km)
TO 2
0 200 yards
0 200 meters

Gero crucifix, which is the oldest intact sculpture of a crucified Christ with eyes shut. *(Cathedral open daily 6am-7pm. Free. Tours in English M-Sa 10:30am and 2:30pm, Su 2:30pm. €4, children €2.)* Fifteen minutes and 509 steps bring you to the top of the **Südturm.** *(Open Nov.-Feb. 9am-4pm; May-Sept. 9am-6pm; Mar.-Apr. and Oct. 9am-5pm. €2, students €1.)* Catch your breath at the **Glockenstube,** a chamber for the tower's nine bells, about three quarters of the way up.

HOUSE #4711. The magic water **Eau de Cologne,** once prescribed as a drinkable curative, made the town a household name. Today the house, labeled #4711 by a Napoleonic system that abolished street names, is a boutique where attendants dole out modest samples and a corner fountain flows freely with the scented water. *(Glockeng., at the intersection with Tunisstr. From Hohe Str., turn right on Brückenstr., which becomes Glockeng. Open M-F 9:30am-8pm, Sa 9:30am-4pm.)*

RÖMISCHES PRAETORIUM UND KANAL. The excavated ruins of the former Roman military headquarters display remains of Roman idols and an array of rocks left by early inhabitants. *(From the Rathaus, take a right toward the swarm of hotels and then a left onto Kleine Budeng. Open Tu-F 10am-4pm, Sa-Su 11am-4pm. €1.50, students €0.75.)*

RATHAUS. Bombed in World War Two, Cologne's city hall has been reconstructed in its original mongrel style. The Gothic tower stands guard over Baroque cherubs flying around an ornate 1570 Renaissance arcade. A Glockenspiel plays daily at noon and 5pm. *(Open M-Th 7:30am-5pm, F 7:30am-2pm. Free.)*

GROß ST MARTIN. Along with the *Dom*, **Groß St. Martin** defines the city's skyline. The renovated church was reopened in 1985 after near-destruction in WWII. The crypts house an esoteric collection of stones and diagrams. *(An Groß St. Martin 9. Open M-Sa 10am-6pm, Su 2-4pm. Church free. Crypts €0.50.)*

MUSEUMS

Cologne's cultural and religious significance in Europe stocks the city's museums with a vast and impressive array of holdings. The **Köln Welcome Card,** available at the tourist office, offers discounts on city museums and bike rental as well as free use of the public transportation system. (24hr. €9; 48hr. €14.)

HEINRICH-BÖLL-PLATZ. Designed to maximize natural light, the unusual building houses two complementary collections. The **Museum Ludwig** spans Impressionism through Dalí and Warhol; it also has one of the world's largest Picasso collections. The **Agfa Foto-Historama** chronicles photography of the last 150 years. *(Bischofsgartenstr. 1. Behind the Römisch-Germanisches Museum. Open Tu 10am-8pm, W-F 10am-6pm, Sa-Su 11am-6pm. €6.40, students €3.20.)*

WALLRAF-RICHARTZ MUSEUM. The pastel galleries display masterpieces spanning from the Middle Ages through Post-Impressionism. *(Martinstr. 39. From the Heumarkt, take Gürzenichtstr. 1 block to Martinstr. Open Tu 10am-8pm, W-F 10am-6pm, Sa-Su 11am-6pm. €5.10, students €2.60.)*

RÖMISCH-GERMANISCHES MUSEUM. Built on the ruins of a Roman villa, the museum's displays document the daily lives of Romans, both rich and poor. *(Roncallipl. 4, between the Dom and Diözeansmuseum. Open Tu-Su 10am-5pm. €3, students €2.)*

SCHOKOLADENMUSEUM. Salivate at every step of chocolate production, from the rain forests to the gold fountain that spurts streams of silky, heavenly, creamy chocolate. Resist the urge to drool, and wait for the free samples. *(Rheinauhafen 1a, near the Severinsbrücke. From the train station, head for the river, walk along the Rhine heading right, go under the Deutzer Brücke, and take the 1st footbridge. Open M-F 10am-6pm, Sa-Su 11am-7pm. €5.50, students €3.)*

KÄTHE-KOLLWITZ-MUSEUM. The world's largest collection of sketches, sculptures, and prints by the brilliant 20th-century artist-activist Käthe Kollwitz. *(Neumarkt 18-24. On the top floor in the Neumarkt-Passage. U12, 14, 16, or 18 to Neumarkt. Open Tu-F 10am-6pm, Sa-Su 11am-6pm. €2.50, students €1.)*

NS-DOKUMENTATIONS-ZENTRUM. Once Cologne's Gestapo headquarters, the museum portrays the city as it was during the Nazi regime, including a display of the 1200 wall inscriptions made by political prisoners kept in the basement prison cells. All displays in German. *(Appellhofpl. 23-25. At the corner of Elisenstr., on the far side from the Dom. Open Tu-F 10am-4pm, Sa-Su 11am-4pm. €2.50, students €1.)*

ENTERTAINMENT AND NIGHTLIFE

Cologne explodes in celebration during **Karneval,** a week-long pre-Lent festival that begins on Ash Wednesday (Feb. 27, 2003) when the mayor abdicates leadership of the city to the women; the women then find their husbands at work and chop off their ties. The festivities build up to an out-of-control parade on **Rosenmontag** (Mar. 3, 2003). For more information, pick up the Karneval booklet at the tourist office.

Cologne has over 30 theaters: **KölnTicket,** a ticket agent in the same building as the Römisch-Germanisches Museum (see above), sells tickets for the opera, the world-class **Philharmonie** (orchestra), open-air rock concerts, and everything in between. (☎28 01. Open M-F 9am-6:30pm, Sa 9am-2pm.)

Partying has long been a favorite pastime in Cologne. Today, Cologne focuses on a sophisticated bump-and-grind. At the various *Brauhaüser*, waiters will greet you with a friendly "*Kölsch*?" and bring one glass after another until you fall under the table or you place your coaster over your glass. Many bars and clubs change their music nightly; the best way to know what you'll get is to pick up the monthly magazine *Kölner* (€1). The closer to the Rhine or *Dom* you venture, the more quickly your wallet gets emptied. Students congregate in the **Bermuda-Dreieck** (Bermuda Triangle), bounded by Zülpicherstr., Zülpicherpl., Roonstr., and Luxemburgstr. The center of **gay nightlife** runs up Matthiasstr. to Mühlenbach, Hohe Pforte, and Marienpl., and to the Heumarkt area by the *Deutzer Brücke.*

Papa Joe's Jazzlokal, Buttermarkt 37, is the oldest jazz club in Germany and has a worthy reputation for great music and good times. No cover. Open M-Sa 7pm-2am, Su 3:30pm-midnight.

Alter Wartesaal, Johannisstr. 11. In the basement of the train station, with an enormous dance floor and an impressively hip crowd. Cover €6-12. Opening hours vary.

M20, Maastrichterstr. 20. This small bar plays some of the city's best drum 'n bass to crowds of locals. No cover. Open M-F 8pm-1am, Sa 8pm-2am.

Stadtgarten, Venloerstr. 40. The upstairs has occasional jazz recordings; downstairs spins techno and house. Cover €4-5. Open M-Th 9pm-1am, F-Sa 9pm-3am.

GAY AND LESBIAN NIGHTLIFE

Vampire, Rathenaupl. 5. A gay and lesbian bar with a mellow atmosphere, dark interior, and plenty of delicious holy water. Open Tu-Th and Su 9pm-2am, F-Sa 9pm-3am.

Hotel Timp, Heumarkt 25. This outrageous gay-friendly club attracts crowds by hosting nightly cabaret shows for no cover. Hours vary. Shows daily 1-4am.

Gloria, Apostelnstr. 11. This popular cafe and club is at the nexus of Cologne's gay and lesbian scene. Cover around €7. Open daily 10am-1am.

BONN

☎0228

Once derisively called *Hauptdorf* (capital village) just because it wasn't Berlin, Bonn became capital of West Germany by chance because Konrad Adenauer, the first chancellor, resided in the suburbs. In 1999, the *Bundestag* packed up and moved back to Berlin, allowing Bonn to be itself again. Today, the sparkling streets of the *Altstadt* bustle with notable energy. The well-respected university and excellent museums bolster a thriving cultural scene, and Bonn is fast becoming a center for Germany's computer technology industry.

TRANSPORTATION. **Trains** run to: Cologne (20min., 5 per hr., €5); Frankfurt (1½hr., 2 per hr., €27) and Koblenz (1hr., 3 per hr., €8). The S-Bahn and U-Bahn network, **VRS** (Verkehrsverbund Rhein-Sieg), links Bonn to Cologne and other riverside cities. Areas are divided into **Tarifzonen;** the farther you go, the more you pay. Single tickets (€1.20-7.85) and day tickets (€5.15-19.25) are available at *Automaten* and designated vending stations.

PRACTICAL INFORMATION. The **tourist office** is at Windeckstr. 2, near the cathedral on Münsterpl. (☎194 33. Open M-F 9am-6:30pm, Sa 9am-4pm, Su 10am-2pm.) Consider buying the **Bonn Regio Welcome Card** (1 day €9, 2 days €14, 3 days €19), which covers transportation costs after 9am (all day Sa-Su) and admission to more than 20 museums in Bonn and the surrounding area. **Schwulen- und Lesbenzentrum (Gay and Lesbian Center)** is at Am Frankenbad 5. From Münsterpl., follow Windeckstr. to Berliner Pl., cross to Bornheimer Str., and take a right on Adolfstr.; Am Frankenbad is two blocks down the street and to the left. (☎63 00 39. Open M-Tu and Th 8pm-midnight, W 7pm-midnight.) Mail letters from the **post office,** Münsterpl. 17. (Open M-F 8:30am-8pm, Sa 8:30am-4pm.) Address mail to be held: Postlagernde Briefe für Firstname SURNAME, **53111** Bonn, Germany.

ACCOMMODATIONS. Take bus #621 (dir.: Ippendorf Altenheim) to Jugendgästehaus for the sparkling, super-modern **Jugendgästehaus Bonn-Venusberg (HI) ❷,** Haager Weg 42. (☎28 99 70. Breakfast included. Laundry €5. Curfew 1am. Dorms €21; singles €34; doubles €48.) For a splurge, try **Hotel Hofgarten ❹,** Fritz-Tillman-Str. 7. From the station, turn right onto Maximilianstr., continue on Kaiserstr., and then turn left on Fritz-Tillman-Str. (☎22 34 82. Breakfast included. Call ahead. Singles €41-74; doubles €66-95.) To reach **Campingplatz Genienaue ❶,** Im Frankenkeller 49, take U16 or 63 to Rheinallee, then bus #613 (dir.: Giselherstr.) to Guntherstr. Turn left on Guntherstr. and right on Frankenkeller. (☎34 49 49. Reception daily 9am-noon and 3-10pm. €5.20 per person, €3-5 per tent.)

FOOD. The pedestrian zone in the center of the city and the area around the university are both packed with restaurants. Cheap eats are available at **Mensa ❶,** Nassestr. 11, a 15min. walk from the station along Kaiserstr. (Open M-Th 11:30am-2:15pm and 5:30-7:30pm, F 11:30am-2pm and 5:30-7:30pm, Sa noon-1:45pm.) The food at **Cafe Blau ❷,** Franziskanerstr. 5, across from the university, is cheap, inexpensive and filling. (Chicken or pasta entrees €3-5. Open daily 9am-1am.) The **market** on Münsterpl. teems with vendors selling meat, fruit, and vegetables. (Open M-F 9:30am-8pm, Sa 9am-4pm.) There's a **supermarket** in the basement of the Kaufhof department store on Münsterpl. (Open M-F 9:30am-8pm, Sa 9am-4pm.)

SIGHTS AND MUSEUMS. Bonn's old town center winds into a lively pedestrian zone littered with historic niches. **Beethoven Geburtshaus** (Beethoven's birthplace), Bonng. 20., hosts a fantastic collection of his personal effects, from his primitive hearing aids to his first violin. (Open Apr.-Oct. M-Sa 10am-6pm, Su

11am-4pm; Nov.-Mar. M-Sa 10am-5pm, Su 11am-4pm. €4, students €3.) The **Münster,** Münsterpl., holds three stories of arches within arches leading to a gorgeous gold-leaf mosaic; a 12th-century cloister laced with crossways and latticed passages branches off under the doorway labeled Kreuzgang. (Cloister open M-Sa 9am-5:30pm, Su 1:30-6pm.) In its governmental heyday, the transparent walls of the **Bundestag** were meant to symbolize the government's responsibility to the public. (Take U16, 63, or 66 to Heussallee/Bundeshaus or bus #610 to Bundeshaus.) Forty thousand students study within the **Kurfürstliches Schloß,** the huge 18th-century palace now serving as the center of Bonn's **Friedrich-Wilhelms-Universität;** through the *Schloß* are the student- and punk-filled **Hofgarten** and **Stadtgarten.** To find Bonn's other palace, follow Poppelsdorfer Allee to the 18th-century **Poppelsdorfer Schloß,** which boasts beautifully manicured **botanical gardens.** (Gardens open Apr.-Oct. M-F 9am-6pm, Su 10am-5pm; Nov.-Mar. M-F 9am-4pm. Free.)

The **Welcome Card** (see **Practical Information,** above) provides admission to most of Bonn's **"Museum Mile."** To start your museum-crawl, take U16, 63, or 66 to Heussallee or Museum König. **Haus der Geschichte** (House of History), Adenauerallee 250/Willy-Brandt 4, examines post-WWII German history through interactive exhibits. (Open Tu-Su 9am-7pm. Free.) One block away, **Kunstmuseum Bonn,** Friedrich-Ebert-Allee 2., houses a superb selection of Expressionist and modern German art. (Open Tu and Th-Su 10am-6pm, W 10am-9pm. €5, students €2.50.)

NIGHTLIFE. Bonn's bombastic and versatile nightlife forcefully debunks myths suggesting that the city is boring. Pick up *Schnüss* (€1.05) for club listings. The **Jazz Galerie,** Oxfordstr. 24, is a hub for jazz and rock concerts as well as a jumping bar and disco. (Cover varies. Open Tu-Th and Su 9pm-3am, F-Sa 9pm-4am.) **Pantheon,** Bundeskanzlerpl., caters to eclectic tastes with a disco, concerts, and stand-up comedy; follow Adenauerallee out of the city until you reach Bundeskanzlerpl. (Cover €6.50-8. Open M-Sa 11pm-4am.) Bonn has an active gay scene; **Boba's Bar,** Josephstr. 17, is popular with both gays and lesbians. (Open Tu-Su 8pm-3am.)

KASSEL ☎0561

Napoleon III was dragged to Kassel as a prisoner of Prussian troops, but today, hordes of tourists visit this ultra-sophisticated city of their own free will. From *Bahnhof* Wilhelmshöhe, take streetcar #1 to **Wilhelmshöhe,** a weirdly fascinating hillside park.

IN RECENT NEWS

GOLDEN GOAL, COPPER WIRING

It seems as though Germans have discovered yet another means of assuaging an insatiable appetite for football. This time, however, the game is unspoiled by poor conditions, unhindered by broken bones, and uninterrupted by a flash of red cards.

The key: teams of fine-tuned two-wheelers. Since its birth in the early 1990s, robot soccer has flourished into an international enterprise. The mechanized sport consists of five leagues, including a simulation league, a small-size league, a medium-size league, a four-legged league, and a humanoid league.

Typically, teams of up to five robots are coached by university specialists, trained in the art of artificial intelligence. As one might expect, Germany has quickly become a dominant participant; since the first RoboCup in 1997, the same German team has rolled away with three world championships in the middle-size division, which features a playing field the size of nine ping-pong tables.

While these machines can't match the spectacular saves of Oliver Kahn, newer models are not without superhuman qualities, including special lasers and a reflex speed that clearly surpasses human capabilities. At this rate, competition with humans is not far off. Indeed, by 2050, robot soccer advocates hope to organize a team of humanoid robots that can contend with the real-life football superstars. And with so long to wait before the next World Cup, this sport is due to gather a greater German following.

Inside, **Schloß Löwenburg** was built by Wilhelm in the 18th century with stones deliberately missing to look like a crumbling medieval castle—he was obsessed with the year 1495 and fancied himself to be a time-displaced knight. (Open Mar.-Oct. Tu-Su 10am-5pm; Nov.-Feb. Tu-Su 10am-4pm. Mandatory tours every hr. €3.50.) All of the park's paths lead up to **Herkules,** Kassel's emblem; visitors can climb up onto Herkules's pedestal and, if they're brave enough, into his club. (Access to the base of the statue free. Pedestal and club open mid-Mar. to mid-Nov. daily 10am-5pm. €2, students €1.25.) The **Brüder-Grimm-Museum,** Schöne Aussicht 2, exhibits Jacob's and Wilhelm's handwritten copy of *Kinder- und Hausmärchen* and artistic interpretations of their tales. (Open daily 10am-5pm. €1.50, students €1.) The **Museum für Sepulkralkultur,** Weinbergstr. 25-27, will satisfy your morbid fixations with death-related paraphernalia; its intent is to "arrest the taboo process which surrounds the subject of 'death and dying' in today's world and open it to public discussion." (Open Tu-Su 10am-5pm, W 10am-8pm. €4, students €3.)

Kassel has two train stations, **Bahnhof Wilhelmshöhe** and the **Hauptbahnhof;** but most trains stop only at Wilhelmshöhe. Trains run to: Düsseldorf (3½hr., 1 per hr., €37); Frankfurt (2hr., 3 per hr., €27); Hamburg (2½hr., 3 per hr., €51); Munich (4hr., 1 per hr., €88). The **tourist office,** in *Bahnhof* Wilhelmshöhe, has free maps and books rooms for a €4 fee. (☎70 77 07. Open M-F 9am-6pm, Sa 9am-1pm.) To reach **Jugendherberge am Tannenwäldchen (HI) ❷,** Schenkendorfstr. 18, take streetcar #4 from *Bahnhof* Wilhelmshöhe to Annastr., backtrack on Friedrich-Ebert-Str., and make a right on Querallee, which becomes Schenkendorfstr. (☎77 64 55. Breakfast included. Sheets €4. Reception daily 9am-11:30pm. Curfew 12:30am. €19, under 26 €17. HI members only.) For **Hotel Kö78 ❸,** Kölnische Str. 78, follow the directions to the *Jugendherberge*, then walk up Annastr. from the train stop and turn right onto Kölnische Str. (☎716 14. Breakfast included. Reception daily 7am-10pm. Singles €32, with shower €41-51; doubles €51/€56-75.) **Friedrich-Ebert-Straße,** the upper part of **Wilhelmshöher Allee,** and the area around **Königsplatz** all have supermarkets, food stands, and cafes sprinkled among clothing stores and boutiques.

FRANKFURT AM MAIN ☎069

Frankfurt's integral economic role as home to the central bank of the European Union lends it a glitzy vitality—international offices, shiny skyscrapers, and expensive cars lie at every intersection. Equally important is its role as a transportation hub for all of Europe. Indeed, Frankfurt was initially used as a crossing point for the Main River—the Franks forded the river in early times and the city's name literally means "ford of the Franks." Today, the city spends more on cultural attractions and tourism than any other German city. Visitors are drawn by the selection of museums and exhibits, while the highly trafficked train station and airport make Frankfurt a likely stop on your journey.

TRANSPORTATION

Flights: The airport, **Flughafen Rhein-Main** (FRF; ☎69 00), is connected to the *Hauptbahnhof* by S8 and 9 (every 15min; €3; buy tickets from the green machines marked *Fahrkarten* before boarding).

Trains: Frequent trains leave the **Hauptbahnhof** for: **Amsterdam** (5hr., 2 per hr., €76, under 26 €61); **Berlin** (5-6hr., 2 per hr., €107/€86); **Cologne** (2½hr., 3 per hr., €39/€32); **Hamburg** (5hr., 2 per hr., €98/€79); **Munich** (3½-4½hr., 2 per hr., €76/€61); **Paris** (6-8hr., 2 per hr., €73/€59); **Rome** (15hr., every hr., €144/€111). Call ☎(0180) 599 66 33 for schedules, reservations, and information.

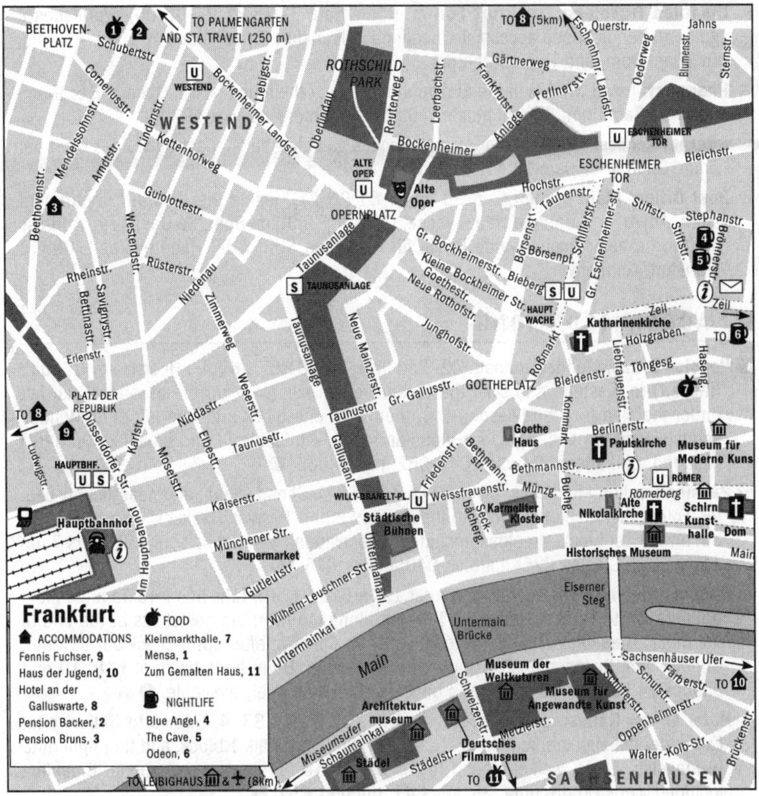

Public Transportation: Runs daily until about 1am. Single-ride tickets (€1.60, rush hour €1.90) are valid for 1hr. in one direction, transfers permitted. **Eurail** valid only on S-Bahn. The **Tageskarte** (day pass, valid until midnight of the day of purchase) provides unlimited transportation on the S-Bahn, U-Bahn, streetcars, and buses; buy from machines in any station (€4.45, children €2.70).

ORIENTATION AND PRACTICAL INFORMATION

The train station lies at the end of Frankfurt's red light district; from the station, the **Altstadt** is a 20min. walk down Kaiserstr. or Münchener Str. To the north, the commercial heart of Frankfurt lies along **Zeil.** Cafes, stores, and services cluster in **Bockenheim** (U6 or 7 to Bockenheimer Warte). Across the Main River, **Sachsenhausen** draws pub-crawlers and museum-goers (U1, 2, or 3 to Schweizer Pl.).

Tourist Office: (☎21 23 88 00), in the *Hauptbahnhof.* Open M-F 8am-9pm, Sa-Su and holidays 9am-6pm. Sells the **Frankfurt Card** (1-day €6.15, 2-day €9.75), which allows unlimited travel on all trains and buses and gives 50% off admission to many museums and attractions.

Laundromat: Schnell & Sauber, Wallstr. 8, near the hostel in Sachsenhausen. Wash €3, dry €0.50 per 15min., soap included. Open daily 6am-11pm.

Emergency: Police: ☎110. **Fire** and **ambulance:** ☎112.

Disabled Travelers: Frankfurt Forum, Römerberg 32 (☎21 24 00 00). Publishes a guide to handicapped-accessible locations in Frankfurt. Open M and W 10am-4:30pm, Tu 10am-6pm, and Th-F 10am-2pm.

Pharmacy: (☎23 30 47) In the Einkaufs passage of the train station. Open M-F 6:30am-9pm, Sa 8am-9pm, Su and holidays 9am-8pm. Emergencies ☎192 92.

Internet Access: Alpha, in the *Hauptbahnhof*'s gambling salon, past track 24. €0.50 per 5min. Open M-Sa 6am-12:45am, Su 8am-12:45am.

Post Office: Main branch, Zeil 90 (☎13 81 26 21), inside the *Karstadt* department store. Any U- or S-Bahn to Hauptwache. Open M-F 9:30am-8pm, Sa 9am-4pm. Address mail to be held: Postlagernde Briefe für Firstname SURNAME, Hauptpostamt, 60313 Frankfurt, Germany.

ACCOMMODATIONS

Pension Bruns, Mendelssohnstr. 42, 2nd fl. (☎74 88 96). U6 (dir.: Heerstr.) or U7 (dir.: Hausen) to Westend and take the Siesmayerstr. exit. Once up the escalator, exit left under the sign for Mendelssohn Str., then walk one block and turn left onto Mendelsohnstr. Ring the bell. Spacious Victorian rooms with cable TV and breakfast (in bed!) included. Call ahead. Doubles €46-€52; triples €63. ❹

Pension Backer, Mendelssohnstr. 92 (☎74 79 92). Cheap, clean, and near the city center. Follow the directions above to the Pension Bruns; Pension Backer is also on the left, but on the 1st block. Breakfast included. Reservations with deposit only. Showers 7am-10pm (€2). Singles €25; doubles €40; triples €45. ❸

Haus der Jugend (HI), Deutschherrnufer 12 (☎610 01 50). Take bus #46 from the main train station to Frankensteiner Pl. Turn left along the river; the hostel sits at the end of the block. Breakfast included. Reception 24hr. Check-in after 1pm. Check-out 9:30am. Curfew 2am. Reservations by phone recommended. Dorm beds begin at €18, 19 and under €14.50. Singles (€29) and doubles (€48) are rarely available. ❷

Hotel an der Galluswarte, Hufnagelstr. 4 (☎73 39 93). S3, 4, 5, or 6 to Galluswarte. Exit under the sign marked Mainzer Landstr., turn right, walk 1 block, and turn right onto Hufnagelstr. Large, well-equipped rooms each have TV, shower, and phone. Breakfast included. *Let's Go* discount. Singles €41; doubles €52. ❹

Fennis Fuchser, Mainzer Landstr. 95 (☎25 38 55). Near the *Hauptbahnhof,* it is a convenient place to crash. From the station, take a left on Düsseldorf Str., walk two blocks and take a left onto Mainzer Landstr.; the hotel is one block down on the left. Enter through the restaurant downstairs. Singles €25; doubles €50; triples €62. ❸

FOOD

The cheapest meals surround the university in **Bockenheim** and the nearby parts of Westend, and many of the pubs in **Sachsenhausen** serve food at a decent price. (For directions, see **Orientation,** above.) Just a few blocks from the youth hostel is a fully stocked **HL Markt,** Dreieichstr. 56 (open M-F 8am-8pm, Sa 8am-4pm), while an **Alim Markt,** Münchener Str. 37, is close to the *Hauptbahnhof* (open M-F 8:30am-7:30pm, Su 8am-2pm).

Mensa, U6 (dir.: Heerstr.) or U7 (dir.: Hausen) to Bockenheimer Warte, follow signs for Palmengarten Universität, then use the exit labeled Mensa. Take the 1st left, just before the STA office; the mensa will be inside the courtyard to your right. Two floors of cheap cafeteria fare. Show your ISIC. Open M-F 11:30am-3pm. ❶

Zum Gemalten Haus, Schweizer Str. 67 (☎61 45 59), is a Sachsenhausen institution that has seen generations of talkative locals treat themselves to *wurst, kraut,* and home-brewed wine (€7). Open W-Su 10am-midnight. ❸

Kleinmarkthalle, on Haseng. between Berliner Str. and Töngesg., is a 3-story warehouse with bakeries, butchers, and produce stands. Cutthroat competition between the many vendors pushes prices way down. Open M-F 7:30am-6pm, Sa 7:30am-4pm. ❶

SIGHTS

Much of Frankfurt's historic splendor lives on only in memories and in reconstructed monuments, since Allied bombing left everything but the cathedral completely destroyed. At the center of the *Altstadt* is **Römerberg Square** (U-Bahn to Römer), home to half-timbered architecture and a medieval fountain of Justice that once spouted wine. At the west end of the Römerberg, the gables of **Römer** have marked the site of Frankfurt's city hall since 1405; upstairs, the **Kaisersaal,** a former imperial banquet hall, is adorned with portraits of the 52 German emperors from Charlemagne to Franz II. (Open daily 10am-1pm and 2-5pm. €1.50, students €0.50.) Next to the Römerberg stands the only building that survived the bombings, the red sandstone **Dom,** which contains several elaborate altarpieces. A new viewing tower is scheduled to open sometime this year. (Open daily 9am-noon and 2:30-6pm.) Across Braubachstr. from the Römerberg, **Paulskirche** holds a political memorial to the trials and tribulations of German democracy. (Open daily 10am-5pm. Free.) A few blocks away is the **Museum für Moderne Kunst,** a triangular building (dubbed "the slice of cake") displaying an array of modern art. (Domstr. 10. Open Tu and Th-Su 10am-5pm, W 10am-8pm. €5, students €2.50, W free.) The **Städel,** Schaumainkai 63, has important paintings from nearly every period in the western tradition. (Open Tu and F-Su 10am-5pm, W-Th 10am-8pm. €6, students €5, Tu free.) Only Goethe-fanatics will be awestruck by his reconstructed first house, the **Goethehaus.** (Großer Hirschgraben 23-25, a few blocks northwest of the Römer. Open Apr.-Sept. M-F 9am-6pm, Sa-Su 10am-4pm; Oct.-Mar. M-F 9am-4pm, Sa-Su 10am-4pm. Tours must be arranged in advance. €5, students €2.50.) Tired of churches and museums? Take refuge in the **Palmengarten,** in the northwest part of town. (Siesmayerstr. 61-63. U6 or 7 to Bockenheimer Warte. Open daily Mar.-Oct. 9am-6pm; Nov.-Jan. 9am-4pm; Feb. 9am-5pm. €3.50, students €1.50.)

ENTERTAINMENT AND NIGHTLIFE

Frankfurt's ballet, theater, and opera are first-rate. The **Alte Oper,** Opernpl. (☎134 04 00; U6 or 7 to Alte Oper), offers a full range of classical music, while the **Städtische Bühne,** Untermainanlage 11 (☎2123 71 33; U1, 2, 3, or 4 to Willy-Brandt-Pl.), hosts ballets and operas. The **English Theatre,** Kaiserstr. 52 (☎24 23 16 20), near the *Hauptbahnhof,* puts on comedies and musicals in English. Shows and schedules are listed in *Fritz* and *Strandgut* (free). For information on tickets at almost any venue, call **Frankfurt Ticket** (☎134 04 00).

Frankfurt has a number of thriving discos and prominent techno DJs, mostly in the commercial district between **Zeil** and **Bleichstraße.** Wear something dressier than jeans if you plan to get past the picky bouncers. **Odeon,** Seilerstr. 34, packs its two floors with students dancing to house, soul, and hip hop. (Cover €5, students €3; Th drinks half-priced until midnight and free buffet from 11:30pm. Open Tu-Sa from 10pm.) **The Cave,** Brönnerstr. 11, features hip-hop, house, and reggae every night in a catacomb-like locale. (Cover €5.15. Open M-Th 10pm-4am, Sa-Su 10pm-6am.) **Blue Angel,** Brönnerstr. 17, is a Frankfurt institution and one of the liveliest gay men's clubs around. Ring the bell to be let in. (Cover €5. Open daily 11pm-4am.) For more drinks and less dancing, head to the **Alt-Sachsenhausen** district between Brückenstr. and Dreieichstr., home to a huge number of rowdy pubs and taverns. The complex of cobblestoned streets centering on **Grosse** and **Kleine Rittergaße** teems with cafes, bars, restaurants, and Irish pubs.

GERMANY

SOUTHWEST GERMANY

A trip to the Rhineland-Palatinate (Rheinland-Pfalz) to see the castles and wine towns along the Rhine and Mosel rivers is an obligatory tourist tromp. The region is a visual feast—the Mosel curls downstream to the Rhine Gorge, a soft shore of castle-backed hills. But it also provides a gustatory feast; the region grows abundant fresh fruits and vegetables, and vineyards in the Rhine and Mosel Valleys produce sweet, delicious wines. Just to the south, the bucolic, traditional hinterlands of the Black Forest contrast with the region's modern, industrial cities.

RHINE VALLEY (RHEINTAL)

The Rhine River runs from Switzerland to the North Sea, but in the popular imagination it exists only in the 80km Rhine Valley, a region prominent in historical legends, sailors' nightmares, and poets' dreams. The river flows north from **Mainz** (easily accessible from Frankfurt) through **Bacharach** and **Koblenz** to **Bonn.**

TRANSPORTATION. Two different **train** lines (one on each bank) traverse the Rheintal; the line on the west bank stays closer to the water and provides superior views. If you're willing to put up with lots of tourists, **boats** are probably the best way to see the sights; the **Köln-Düsseldorfer (KD) Line** covers the Mainz-Koblenz stretch four times per day in summer.

MAINZ. Once the greatest Catholic diocese north of the Alps, Mainz's colossal sandstone **Martinsdom** stands as a memorial to its former ecclesiastic power. (Open Mar.-Oct. M-F 9am-6:30pm, Sa 9am-4pm, Su 12:45-3pm and 4-6:30pm; Nov.-Feb. M-F 9am-5pm, Sa 9am-4pm, Su 12:45-3pm and 4-5pm. Free.) The Gothic **Stephanskirche,** south of the Dom, holds stunning stained-glass windows created by artist Marc Chagall. (Stephansberg. Open daily 10am-noon and 2-5pm.) Johannes Gutenberg, the father of movable type, is immortalized at the **Gutenberg-Museum,** which contains a replica of his original press. (Liebfrauenpl. 5, across from the Dom. Open Tu-Sa, 9am-5pm, Su 11am-3pm. €3.10.)

Trains run to: Frankfurt (30min., €6); Heidelberg (1hr., €17); and Koblenz (1hr., €17). **KD ferries** (☎23 28 00) depart from the wharves on the other side of the *Rathaus.* The **tourist office** arranges **tours** (2hr., July-Aug. daily 2pm, Sept.-Jun. W, F, Sa 2pm. €5.15) and gives free maps. (☎28 62 10. Open M-F 9am-6pm, Sa 9am-4pm.) To reach the **Jugendgästehaus (HI) ❶,** Otto-Brunfels-Schneise 4, take bus #62 (dir.: Weisenau), 63 (dir.: Laubenheim), or 92 (dir.: Ginsheim) to Viktorstift/Jugendherberge and follow the signs. All rooms are clean and come with a private bath. (☎853 32. Breakfast included. Reception daily 7am-10pm. Dorms €16.10; doubles €21.20.) On the edge of the *Altstadt,* **Der Eisgrub-Bräu ❷,** Weißliliengaße 1a., brews its own beer and serves breakfast (€2.90) and lunch buffets (€5.10). (Open Su-Th 9am-1pm, F-Sa 9am-2pm. MC/V.) For groceries, try **Supermarkt 2000,** Am Brand 41, under the Sinn-Leffers department store (open M-F 9:30am-8pm, Sa 9am-4pm). **Postal Code:** 55001. **Phone Code:** ☎06131.

BACHARACH. Bacharach lives up to its name ("Altar of Bacchus") with many *Weinkeller* and *Weinstuben* (wine cellars and pubs). **Die Weinstube,** Oberstr. 63, is a family-owned pub that makes its own wine on the premises. Nearby is the 14th-century **Wernerkapelle,** the remains of a red sandstone chapel that took 140 years to build but only a few hours to destroy in the Palatinate War of Succession of 1689. The **tourist office,** Oberstr. 45, and the *Rathaus* share a building at one end of the town center. (☎91 93 03. Open Apr.-Oct. M-F 9am-5pm, Sa 10am-4pm; Nov.-Mar. M-F 9am-noon.) Hostels get no better than **Jugendherberge Stahleck (HI) ❷,** a gorgeous 12th-century castle that provides a panoramic view of the Rhine Valley. The steep 15min. hike to the hostel is worth every step. Call ahead; they're usually full by 6pm. Make a right out of the station pathway, turn left at the Peterskirche, and take any of the marked paths leading up the hill. (☎12 66. Breakfast included. Curfew 10pm. Dorms €14.20; doubles €35.) At **Café Restaurant Rusticana ❸**, Oberstr. 40, a lovely German couple serves up three-course meals (€6-11) and lively conversation. (Open May-Oct. daily 11:30am-9:30pm.) **Phone Code:** ☎06743.

LORELEI CLIFFS AND CASTLES. Whereas sailors were once lured to these cliffs by the infamous Lorelei maiden, her hypnotic song is now superfluous; today, hordes of travelers are seduced by the amazing scenery alone. The charming towns of **St. Goarshausen** and **St. Goar,** on either side of the Rhine, host the spectacular firework-filled **Rhein in Flammen** celebration at the end of every summer (September 20, 2003). St. Goarshausen, on the east bank, provides access by foot to the Lorelei statue and the infamous cliffs. Directly above the town, the fierce **Burg Katz** (Cat Castle) eternally stalks its prey, the smaller **Burg Maus** (Mouse Castle). Burg Maus offers daily falconry demonstrations at 11am and 2:30pm; call ☎76 69 for information or visit St. Goarshausen's **tourist office,** Bahnhofstr. 8. (☎(06771) 76 69. Open M-F 9am-1pm and 2-5:30pm, Sa 9:30am-12:30pm.) The **"Lorelei V" ferry** (M-F 6am-11pm, Sa-Su from 7am; €1, round-trip €1.50) crosses the river to **St.Goar,** from which the view is spectacular. St. Goar's **tourist office,** Heerstr. 6, is in the pedestrian zone. (☎(06741) 333. Open M-F 8am-12:30pm and 2-5pm, Sa 10am-noon.) To reach **Jugendheim Loreley ❶,** on the St. Goarshausen side of the Rhine, walk from the cliffs past the red-and-white parking gate down the road a few hundred meters and turn left. (☎(06771) 26 19. Breakfast €4.10. Curfew 10pm. Dorms €7.) **Postal code:** 56329.

KOBLENZ ☎0261

Koblenz has long been a strategic hotspot—in the 2000 years since its birth, the city has hosted every empire seeking to conquer Europe. The city centers around the **Deutsches Eck** (German Corner), a peninsula at the confluence of the Rhine and Mosel Rivers that purportedly witnessed the birth of the German nation in 1216. The **Mahnmal der Deutschen Einheit** (Monument to German Unity) to the right is a tribute to Kaiser Wilhelm I. The **Museum Ludwig im Deutschherrenhaus,** behind the Mahnmal, features contemporary French art. (Danziger Freiheit 1. Open Tu-Sa 10:30am-5pm, Su 11am-6pm. €2.50, students €1.50.) Head across the river to the **Festung Ehrenbreitstein,** a fortress at the highest point in the city. Today, it's a youth hostel. (Non-hostel guests €1.05; students €0.60. Tours €2.10.)

Trains run to: Bonn (30min., 4 per hr, €8); Cologne (1hr., 2-4 per hr., €13.50); Frankfurt (2hr., 1-2 per hr., €18.20); Mainz (1hr., 3 per hr., €13.50); and Trier (2hr., 1-2 per hr., €15.60). Directly across from the station is the **tourist office,** Bahnhofpl. 7. (☎303 880; open May-Oct. M-F 9am-8pm, Sa-Su 10am-8pm; Nov.-Apr. M-F 9am-6pm, Sa-Su 10am-6pm.) **Jugendherberge Koblenz (HI) ❷,** within the fortress, offers breathtaking views of the Rhine and Mosel. Take bus #9 or 10 from the stop on Löhrstr. (just left of the train station) to Charlottenstr. Then take the chairlift up (operates Mar.-Sept. daily 9am-5:50pm; €4, round-trip €5.60), or continue along the Rhine side of the mountain on the main road, following the DJH signs, and take the footpath up. (☎972 870. Breakfast included. Reception daily 7:15am-10pm. Curfew 11:30pm. Dorms €15; doubles €37.) **Ferries** (€1) cross the Mosel to **Campingplatz Rhein-Mosel ❶,** Am Neuendorfer Eck. (☎827 19. Reception 8am-10pm. Open Apr.-Oct. 15. €4 per person, €2.50 per tent.) **Marktstübchen,** Am Markt 220, at the bottom of the hill from the hostel, serves authentic German food at budget prices. (Open M-Tu, Th, and Su 11am-midnight, W 11am-2pm, F 4pm-1am, Sa 11am-1am.) **Postal code:** 56329.

MOSEL VALLEY (MOSELTAL)

As if trying to avoid its inevitable surrender to the Rhine, the Mosel river meanders slowly past sun-drenched hills, picturesque towns, and ancient castles. The headwaters of the Mosel flow from the Vosges Mountains of France, following a northeasterly course that winds over 200km of German territory from Trier to Koblenz.

TRANSPORTATION

The Mosel Valley runs northeast from **Trier** through **Cochem** and **Beilstein** to **Koblenz,** where it bisects the Rhine Valley (see p. 493). The best way to view the scenery is by boat, bus, or bicycle, since the train line between Koblenz and Trier runs through unremarkable countryside. If you're starting in Koblenz, try taking the train to Cochem, then pop by Beilstein (a short distance upstream) and Trier before taking the train (2hr., 1-2 per hr., €15.60) or a boat back. To really soak up the scenery, consider renting a bike in Koblenz or Trier and biking along the river.

COCHEM AND BEILSTEIN

Busloads of city-dwellers devour the quintessential quaintness of Cochem, yet the impressive vineyard-covered hills and majestic **Reichsburg Castle,** perched high on a hill above town, simply can't be cheapened. The 11th-century castle was destroyed in 1689 by French troops led by Louis XIV but was rebuilt in 1868. (Open daily Mar.-Jan. 9am-5pm. Mandatory 40min. tours on the hr.; written English translation available. €3.60, students €3.10.) The **Weinwoche** (wine week) begins a week and a half after Pfingsten (Pentecost) and showcases some of the Mosel's best vintages (June 18-22, 2003). On the last weekend of August, the **Heimat-und-Weinfest** culminates in a dramatic fireworks display. Cochem is easily accessible by **train** from Koblenz (1hr., 2-3 per hr., €7) and Trier (1hr., 2 per hr., €9); the Koblenz route is prettier and hugs the Mosel. The **tourist office,** Endertpl. 1., next to the bus station, books rooms for free. (☎(02671) 600 40. Open Apr.-Oct. M-Th 9am-5pm, F 9am-6pm; Nov.-Mar. M-F 9am-1pm and 2-5pm.) **Hotel Holl ❹,** Endertstr. 54, combines large, bright, and comfortable rooms with good food. (☎(02671) 43 23. Breakfast included. Doubles €36.) **Campingplatz am Freizeitzentrum ❶,** on Stadionstr., rents bikes for €7.50 per day. (Laundry €1.60. Reception 9am-9pm. Open Easter-Oct. €4 per person, €4 per tent.) **Café-Restaurant Mosella ❸,** on the Marktplatz next to the bridge, offers hearty meals. (Open Apr.-Oct. daily 9am-10pm.)

Beilstein, the smallest official town in Germany, can be reached from Cochem by taking bus #8060 (15min; M-F 14 per day, Sa 5 per day, Su 3 per day; €3). A tiny hamlet of half-timbered houses, crooked cobblestone streets, and about 170 residents, Beilstein was spared in WWII and its untarnished beauty has made it the idyllic backdrop of several movies and political summits. **Burg Metternich** is the resident castle; the French sacked it in 1689, but the ruins and the view from the tower are still spectacular. (Open Apr.-Oct. daily 9am-6pm. €2, students €1.) The recently repainted Baroque **Karmelitenkirche** contains an intricately carved wooden altar and the famous 16th-century **Schwarze Madonna von Beilstein** sculpture. (Open daily 9am-8pm.) The **Klostercafé ❷** outside offers traditional food, fantastic Mosel wine, and a view that beats them both. (Open daily 9am-7pm.)

TRIER ☎0651

The oldest town in Germany, Trier was founded by the Romans during the reign of Augustus and had its heyday in the 4th century as the capital of the Western Roman Empire. A one-day **combination ticket** (€6.20, students €3.10) provides access to all of the city's Roman monuments. The most impressive is the massive 2nd-century **Porta Nigra** (Black Gate), which got its name from the centuries of grime that turned its sandstone face gray. It once served as the strongest line of defense against attacks on the city—now throngs of tourists penetrate the barrier everyday. (Open Apr.-Sept. daily 9am-6pm; Oct.-Mar. 9am-5pm. €2.10, students €1.60.) A short stroll away, the 11th-century **Dom** (cathedral) shelters what is reputedly the Tunica Christi (Holy Robe of Christ) and the tombs of archbishops. (Open Apr.-Oct. daily 6:30am-6pm; Nov.-Mar. 6:30am-5:30pm. Free.) The enormous **Basilika** was originally the location of Emperor Constantine's throne room. (Open M-Sa 10am-6pm, Su noon-6pm. Free.) Near the southeast corner of the city walls, the 4th-century **Kaiserthermen** (Emperor's baths) are most memorable for their gloomy underground passages remaining from the ancient sewer network—avoid contact with the walls. (Open Apr.-Sept. 9am-6pm; Oct.-Mar. 9am-5pm. €2.15, students €1.60.) A 10min. walk uphill along Olewiger Str. brings you to the **amphitheater;** once the site for bloody gladiatorial games, it's now a stage for city productions. (Admission and times same as Porta Nigra above.)

Trains go to Koblenz (1¾hr., 2 per hr., €16) and Luxembourg (45min., 1 per hr., €8). From the station, walk down Theodor-Haus-Allee or Christophstr. to reach the **tourist office,** under the shadow of the Porta Nigra. (☎97 80 80. Open Apr.-Oct. M-Sa 9am-6pm, Su 10am-3pm; Nov.-Dec. and Mar. M-Sa 9am-6pm, Su 10am-1pm; Jan.-Feb. M-F 10am-5pm, Sa 10am-1pm. English tours daily 1:30pm; €6, students €5.) The staff at nearby **Vinothek,** Margaritengässchen 2a, can give information on **wine tasting** in the region. (☎978 08 34. Open M-Sa 10am-6pm.) The **Jugendhotel/ Jugendgästehaus Kolpinghaus ❶,** Dietrichstr. 42, one block off the Hauptmarkt, has well-used rooms in an unbeatable location. (☎97 52 50. Breakfast included. Sheets €2.50 for dorms. Dorms €13.50; singles €22; doubles €44.) **Casa Chiara ❹,** Engelstr. 8, has sunny rooms with private baths and cable TV. (☎27 07 30. Breakfast inlcuded. Reception 6:30am-late. Singles €50; doubles €80; triples €110.) **Astarix ❶,** Karl-Marx-Str. 11, serves excellent food at unbelievable prices (under €5). It's squeezed into a passageway next to Miss Marple's; if you get to a big white fence on the left, you've gone too far. (Open M-Th 11:30am-1am, F-Sa 11:30am-2am, Su 2pm-1am.) There's a **Plus supermarket,** Brotstr. 54, near the Hauptmarkt. (Open M-F 8:30am-7pm, Sa 8:30am-4pm.)

WORMS ☎06241

This town has forever been immortalized in the minds of English-speaking students by the unfortunate spelling of "the Diet of Worms" (pronounced DEE-ET OF VOHRMS). Few remember what the Diet of Worms actually was; it was the imperial council which sent Martin Luther into exile for refusing to renounce his heretical doctrine that religious truth existed only in scripture, not in popes. The sight of Luther's confrontation is memorialized at the **Lutherdenkmal,** a large statue three blocks southeast of the station along Wilhelm-Leuschner-Sr. Crowning Worms with its distinctive Romanesque spirals is the **Dom St. Peter.** (Open daily Apr.-Oct. 9am-6pm; Nov.-Mar. 9am-5pm.) The nearby **Nibelungen Museum** offers an interactive glimpse into the magnificent Nibelunglied; to get there, follow Petersstr. until you reach the town wall and turn right. (Open Tu-Su 10am-5pm, F until 10pm. €5.50, students €4.50.) Though remembered internationally for its Christian ties, Worms was actually a cultural center for Jews in Europe before the Holocaust. The 900-year-old **Heiliger Sand,** Europe's oldest Jewish cemetery, and the **Synagogue** are a testament to Worms' Jewish heritage. (Enter the cemetery from Willi-Brandt-Ring, just south of Andreasstr. Synagogue open Apr.-Oct. daily 10am-12:30pm and 1:30-5pm; Nov.-Mar. 10am-noon and 2-4pm. Required yamulkes available at the door.)

Trains go to Mainz (45min., 2 per hr., €7). The **tourist office** is in a shopping complex across the street from the Dom St. Peter. (☎250 45. Open Apr.-Oct. M-F 9am-

6pm, Sa 9:30am-2:30pm; Nov.-Mar. closed Sa.) To get to the **Jugendgästehaus (HI)** ❷, Dechaneig. 1, follow Bahnhof right from the station, turn left on Adreasstr.; the hostel will be on your right, across from the Dom. (☎257 80. Reception 7am-11pm. Curfew 11pm. Dorms €16.60; doubles €43.60.)

HEIDELBERG ☎06221

This sunlight-coated town by the Neckar river and its crumbling castle has lured writers and artists—including Twain, Goethe, and Hugo—for years; today it draws in roughly 32,000 tourists each summer day. However, the incessant buzz of mass tourism is worth enduring to experience Heidelberg's beautiful hillside setting, famous university, and lively nightlife.

TRANSPORTATION

Trains run to Frankfurt (50min., 2 per hr., €12) and Stuttgart (40min., 1 per hr., €31); other trains run regularly to towns in the Neckar Valley. On Heidelberg's **public transportation** system, single-ride tickets cost €2; day passes (€5) are available from the tourist office. Rent bikes at **Per Bike,** Bergheimer Str. 125. (€10 per day. Open M-F 9am-6pm.) *Let's Go* does not recommend **hitchhiking,** but hitchers are known to wait at the western end of Bergheimerstr. The Rhein-Neckar-Fahrgastschiffahrt (☎201 81), in front of the *Kongresshaus*, runs **ferries** all over Germany and provides round-trip Neckar cruises to Neckarsteinach (1½hr., Easter-Oct. 9:30am-3:30pm, €9.50).

ORIENTATION AND PRACTICAL INFORMATION

Most of Heidelberg's attractions are in the eastern part of the city, along the south bank of the Neckar. From the train station, take any bus or streetcar to Bismarckpl., then walk east down **Hauptstraße** to the **Altstadt.** The **tourist office,** in front of the station, books rooms for a €2.50 fee and a small deposit. (☎13 88 121. Open Apr.-Oct. M-Sa 9am-7pm, Su 10am-6pm; Nov.-Mar. M-Sa 9am-6pm.) They also sell the 2-day **Heidelberg Card,** which includes unlimited public transit and admission to most sights (€12). In an **emergency,** call ☎110; for **fire** or an **ambulance,** call ☎112. Check your **email** at **Mode Bredl,** Hauptstr. 90, near Bismarckpl. (Open M-F 9:30am-7:30pm, Sa 9:30am-4pm. €3 per 30min.) The **post office,** Sofienstr. 8-10, **69155** Heidelberg, is open M-F 9am-6:30pm and Sa 9:30am-1pm.

ACCOMMODATIONS

Jugendherberge (HI), Tiergartenstr. 5 (☎41 20 66). From Bismarckpl. or the station, bus #33 (dir.: Zoo-Sportzentrum) to Jugendherberge. One of the largest hostels in Europe with 584 beds and 150 rooms. Basement pub serves cheap beer from 7pm-midnight. In peak season, call at least a week ahead. Sheets €3. Reception daily until 11:30pm. Lockout 9am-1pm. Curfew 11:30pm; stragglers admitted every 30min. until 2am. **HI members only.** Partial wheelchair access. Dorms €17.60, under 26 €14.90. ❷

Pension Jeske, Mittelbadg. 2 (☎237 33). From the station, bus #33 (dir.: Ziegelhausen) or 11 (dir.: Karlstor) to Rathaus/Kornmarkt; Mittelbadg. is the 2nd left off the square. Great value with an ideal location. 5-bed dorms €20; doubles €50; triples €60. ❸

Hotel-Pension Elite, Bunsenstr. 15 (☎257 34). From Bismarckpl., follow Rohrbacher Str. away from the river and turn right on Bunsenstr. From the train station, take streetcar #1 to Poststr.; the hotel is on the 2nd street behind the Holiday Inn. Comfortable and spacious rooms with bath and TV. Breakfast included. *Let's Go* discounts. Singles €51; doubles €61; triples €77; quads €87. MC/V. ❹

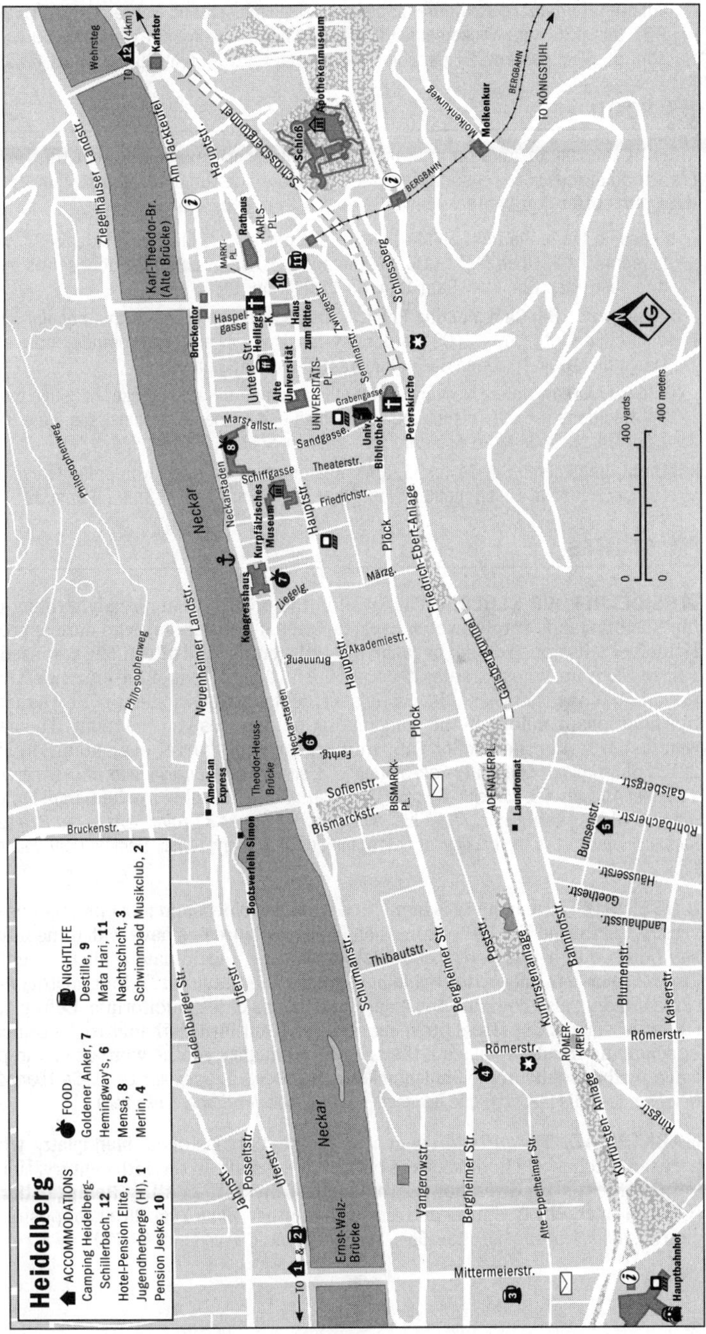
Heidelberg
ACCOMMODATIONS
Camping Heidelberg-Schillerbach, 12
Hotel-Pension Elite, 5
Jugendherberge (HI), 1
Pension Jeske, 10
FOOD
Goldener Anker, 7
Hemingway's, 6
Mensa, 8
Merlin, 4
NIGHTLIFE
Destille, 9
Mata Hari, 11
Nachtschicht, 3
Schwimmbad Musikclub, 2
Neckar
Karl-Theodor-Br. (Alte Brücke)
Theodor-Heuss-Brücke
Ernst-Walz-Brücke
Schloß
Apothekenmuseum
Karlstor
Molkenkur
TO KÖNIGSTUHL
BERGBAHN
Rathaus
MARKT-PL.
KARLS-PL.
Brückentor
Heiliggeist-K.
Haus zum Ritter
Alte Universität
UNIVERSITÄTS-PL.
Univ. Bibliothek
Peterskirche
Kurpfälzisches Museum
Kongresshaus
American Express
Bootsverleih Simon
Laundromat
BISMARCK-PL.
ADENAUERPL.
RÖMER-KREIS
Hauptbahnhof
Hauptstr.
Plöck
Friedrich-Ebert-Anlage
Schlossberg
Schlossbergtunnel
Gaisbergtunnel
Neckarstaden
Neuenheimer Landstr.
Ziegelhäuser Landstr.
Philosophenweg
Sofienstr.
Bismarckstr.
Bergheimer Str.
Kurfürstenanlage
Römerstr.
Mittermeierstr.
Ladenburger Str.
Uferstr.
Posseltstr.
Jahnstr.
Vangerowstr.
Schurmanstr.
Thibautstr.
Poststr.
Bahnhofstr.
Blumenstr.
Kaiserstr.
Rohrbacherstr.
Gaisbergstr.
Ringstr.
Bunsenstr.
Alte Eppelheimer Str.
Bruckenstr.
Wehrsteg
Am Hackteufel
Untere Str.
Marstallstr.
Sandgasse
Schiffgasse
Theaterstr.
Friedrichstr.
Märzg.
Akademiestr.
Brunneng.
Ziegelg.
Fahrtg.
Seminarstr.
Zwingerstr.
Grabengasse
Haspelgasse
Molkenkurweg
TO 1 & 2
TO 12 (4km)
400 yards
400 meters

Camping Heidelberg-Schlierbach, between Ziegelhausen and Neckargemünd (☎80 25 06). Bus #35 (dir.: Neckargemünd) to Im Grund. Check-in 8am-10pm. €5.50 per person, €2.50-6 per tent, €2 per car. Rent caravan €12.50, tent €8; breakfast €3.50. ❶

FOOD

Most of the restaurants on and around Hauptstr. are expensive, but the *Imbiße* (fast food stands) are reasonably priced. Just outside the central area, historic student pubs offer good values as well.

Mensa, in the red fortress on Marstallstr. Take bus #35 to Marstallstr. Meals €4, with a student ID €2. Open M-F 11:30am-2pm and 6-10pm. A **cafe** next door serves snacks and beer (€2). Open M-F 9am-1am, Sa 11am-1am. ❶

Hemingway's Bar-Café-Meeting Point, Fahrtgasse 1. The mood of this popular joint is embodied in its "Ernie" (€5)—a dessert consisting of a shot of brandy and a cigar. Lunch menu €4.10. Open Su-Th 9am-1am, F-Sa 9am-3am. ❷

Goldener Anker, Untere Neckar 52, near the river and the Alte Brücke. Although most of the traditional German dishes are on the high end of the price scale, some are affordable (€4-8). Open M-Sa 6pm-midnight, kitchen closes 10:30pm. MC/V. ❸

Merlin, Bergheimer Str. 71 (☎252 34). A good place for those who prefer to avoid the touristy Hauptstr. Lunch menu €5.50. Open Su-Th 9am-1am, F-Sa 9am-2am. ❷

SIGHTS

HEIDELBERGER SCHLOß. The jewel in the crown of an already striking city, the Schloß stands careful watch over the armies (of tourists) who dare approach Heidelberg. Its construction began in the 14th century and after 1329, it housed the Prince Electors, whose statues decorate the facade in front of the entrance. Over a period of almost 400 years, the castle's residents commissioned their own distinctive additions, resulting in the conglomeration of styles you see today. The castle **wine cellar** holds the **Großer Faß,** the largest wine barrel ever made, holding 221,726L. *(Grounds open daily 8am-5:30pm. €2, students €1. English tours of castle every hr. 11:15am-4:15pm. €3, students €1.50.)* The *Schloß* is accessible by the **Bergbahn,** Germany's oldest cable car. *(Take bus #11 (dir.: Köpfel) or 33 (dir.: Karlstor) to Bergbahn/Rathaus. Trams leave the parking lot next to the bus stop every 10min. 9am-8:20pm, round-trip €3.)*

UNIVERSITÄT. Heidelberg is home to Germany's oldest and most prestigious university, established in 1368. More than 20 Nobel laureates have called the university home, and it was here that sociology became a legitimate academic subject. The **Museum der Universität Heidelberg** traces the university's long history—the same building also contains **Alte Aula,** Heidelberg's oldest auditorium. Before 1914, students were exempt from prosecution by civil authorities thanks to the principle of academic freedom; instead, the crimes of naughty youths were tried and punished by the faculty in the **Studentenkarzer.** *(Grabeng. 1. Open Apr.-Oct. M-Sa 10am-4pm, Nov.-Mar. Tu-F 10am-2pm. €2.50, students €2, also includes Studentenkarzer.)*

MARKTPLATZ. The *Altstadt*'s center is the cobblestoned **Marktplatz,** where accused witches and heretics were burned at the stake in the 15th century. Heidelberg's oldest structures border the square: the 14th-century **Heiliggeistkirche** (Church of the Holy Spirit) and the 16th-century **Haus Zum Ritter,** opposite the church. *(Church open M-Sa 11am-5pm, Su 1-5pm. Free. Church tower €0.50.)*

KURPFÄLZISCHES MUSEUM. Artifacts on display include: the jawbone of a *homo Heidelbergensis*, a.k.a. "Heidelberg man," one of the earliest humans ever discovered; art by Dürer; and a fascinating archaeology exhibit. *(Hauptstr. 97. Open Tu and Th-Su 10am-5pm, W 10am-9pm. €2.50, students €1.50; Su €1.50, students €1.)*

PHILOSOPHENWEG. A high path opposite the Neckar from the *Altstadt*, the Philosophenweg (Philosopher's Way) offers the best views of the city. On the top of Heiligenberg (Holy Mountain) lie the ruins of the 9th-century **St. Michael Basilika,** the 13th-century **Stefanskloster,** and an **amphitheater** built under Hitler in 1934 on the site of an ancient Celtic gathering place. *(Take streetcar #1 or 3 to Tiefburg to begin the hike upwards, or use the footpath 10m west of the Karl-Theodor-Brücke.)*

ENTERTAINMENT AND NIGHTLIFE

The first Saturday in June and September and the second Saturday in July draw giant crowds to the front of the Schloß for fireworks. The **Faschingsparade** (carnival) struts through the city on Shrove Tuesday (Tuesday before Lent), and the **Schloßfestspiele Heidelberg** features a series of concerts and plays at the castle in August (☎583 52 for tickets). The *Altstadt* hosts the **Heidelberger Herbst** (a medieval market) for the last weekend in September and the **Weihnachtsmarkt** ("Christmas Market") in December.

The **Marktplatz** is the hub of the city's action; the most popular nightspots fan out from here. **Unter Straße,** on the Neckar side of the Heiliggeistkirche, boasts the most prolific—and often congested—conglomeration of bars in the city. **Hauptstraße** also harbors a fair number of venues.

Nachtschicht, in Landfried-Komplex. From the train station, take Mittermaierstr. past the post office; take the 1st left onto Alte Eppenheimerstr. and enter the parking lot on the right. University students jam to a variety of music. Open M 8pm-3am, W 10pm-3am, Th-Sa 10pm-4am. Cover €3.50; W and F students €1.50.

Destille, Unterstr. 16. Regular patrons gather here for a game of Yahtzee!© in the afternoon and for beers in the evening (Pils €3). Open Su-Th noon-2am, F-Sa noon-3am.

Schwimmbad Musikclub, Tiergartenstr. 13, across the river. Conveniently up the street from the *Jugendherberge,* but a trek otherwise. W is independent alternative night. Open W-Th 8pm-3am, F-Sa 8pm-4am.

Mata Hari, on Zwingerstr. near Oberbadg. A small gay and lesbian bar. Tu men only. Beer €3. Open Tu-Su 10pm-3am.

DAYTRIP FROM HEIDELBERG

THE NECKAR VALLEY

Trains connecting Heidelberg to Heilbronn run through the Neckar valley (Neckartal), a thickly-forested stretch running north through Bad Wimpfen, Burg Guttenberg, Hirschhorn am Neckar, and Neckarsteinach. Castles dot the hilltops of the valley and form part of the Burgenstraße (Castle Road), which stretches from Mannheim to Prague. Each town has its own tourist office, and local buses make town-hopping an easy and pleasant daytrip.

BAD WIMPFEN. The fairy tale demeanor of Bad Wimpfen was once one of the best-kept secrets in southwest Germany. The **Altstadt** is a 10min. walk from the train station; follow Karl-Ulrich-Str. or take the steep hiking trail to the right of the station. Laid out along the northern side of town, easily accessible points on the ancient battlements offer incredible views of the valley. The **Roter Turm** (Red Tower; open Sa-Su 10am-1pm and 2-5pm; €0.50) and the **Blauer Turm** (Blue Tower; open Tu-Su 10am-6pm; €1) display the medieval character of the town. Bad Wimpfen is also home to the world's only **Pig Museum,** Kronengäßchen 2, which details the role of swine (considered a good luck symbol in Germany) in pop culture. (Open daily 10am-5pm. €2.60, students €1.30.) The friendly **tourist office,** in the train station, finds **private rooms** for good prices. (☎972 00. Open M-F 9am-7pm; Easter to mid-Oct. also open Sa-Su 10am-noon and 2-4pm.) **Phone code: ☎07063**

NECKARSTEINACH. At the north end of the valley, Neckarsteinach's four **castles** lord over the village below. The two westernmost castles stand in romantic ruin, while the two to the east are privately occupied and not open to visitors. All lie within 3km of one another along the north bank of the Neckar river and can be reached by foot via the **Burgenweg** (castle path): from the train station, turn right on Bahnhofstr., turn left on Hauptstr., and follow the bend in the road; a red stone cross marks the beginning of the *Schloßsteige* (Castle Stairs), a brick path leading upward to the Burgenweg. The **tourist office,** Hauptstr. 7, inside *Schreibwaren Petter*, has a list of **private rooms.** (☎920 00. Open M-Tu, Th-F 8:30am-12:30pm and 2:30-6pm, W 8:30am-12:30pm, Sa 8:30am-1pm.)

STUTTGART ☎0711

Forget about *lederhosen*—Porsche, Daimler-Benz, and a host of other corporate thoroughbreds keep Stuttgart speeding along in the fast lane. After almost complete destruction in World War II, Stuttgart was rebuilt in a thoroughly modern, functional, and uninspiring style, but the surrounding forested hills provide welcome tranquility to the busy capital of Baden-Württemberg.

TRANSPORTATION AND PRACTICAL INFORMATION. Stuttgart has direct **trains** to most major German cities, including: Berlin (5½-12hr., 2 per hr., €98-132); Frankfurt (1½-4½hr., 2 per hr., €28-44); and Munich (2½-3½hr., 2-3 per hr., €33-45). The tourist office, **tips 'n' trips,** Lautenschlagerstr. 20, has **Internet** access and resources on the Stuttgart scene. (☎222 27 30. Internet €3 per hr. W free. Open M-F noon-7pm, Sa 10am-2pm.) The **post office** is in the train station. (Open M-F 8:30am-6pm, Sa 8:30am-12:30pm.) **Postal Code:** 70173.

ACCOMMODATIONS AND FOOD. To reach the **Jugendherberge Stuttgart (HI) ❷,** Haußmannstr. 27, take streetcar #15 to Eugenspl. and go downhill on Kernerstr.; the entrance is up the stairs with the red handrail. (☎24 15 83; jh-stuttgart@t-online.de. Breakfast included. Sheets €3.10. Reception 24hr. Lockout 9:30am-1pm. Reserve at least a week ahead by mail or email. Dorms €16, under 26 €14.) **Hotel Espenlaub ❹,** Charlottenstr. 27, has pricey but well-equipped rooms. Take streetcar #15 or U5, 6, or 7 to Olgaeck. (☎21 09 10. Breakfast included. Singles €44, with bath €59; doubles €59/€79; triples €74/€92. MC/V.) The pedestrian zone between Pfarrstr. and Charlottenstr. is home to many reasonably priced restaurants, while Rotebühlpl. is filled with *imbiße* and fast food joints.

SIGHTS. Stuttgart harbors amazing **Mineralbäder** (mineral baths)—the perfect remedy for traveler-exhaustion. **Mineralbad Leuze,** Am Leuzebad 2-6, has indoor, outdoor, and thermal therapy pools. Take U1 or 14, or streetcar #2 to Mineralbäder. (☎216 42 10. Open daily 6am-9pm. 2hr. soak €6.40, students €4.80.) The superb **Staatsgallerie Stuttgart,** Konrad-Adenauer-Str. 30-32, houses an excellent collection of modern art in the new wing. (Open Tu-W and F-Su 10am-6pm, Th 10am-9pm. €4.50, students €2.50; W free.) The **Mercedes-Benz Museum,** Mercedesstr. 137, is a must for car-lovers. Take S1 to Daimlerstadion. (Open Tu-Su 9am-5pm. Free.) The **Schloßgarten,** Stuttgart's principal park, is crammed with fountains and beautiful flower gardens. At the north end is the **Wilhelma,** a large garden that holds 9000 species of animals and plants. Take U14 to Wilhelma.

(Open daily Mar. and Oct. 8:15am-5pm; Nov.-Feb. 8:15am-4pm; May-Aug. 8:15am-6pm; Apr. and Sept. 8:15am-5:30pm. €9, students €4.) Nearby **Ludwigsburg** has a trio of luxurious palaces that are well worth the visit. Take S4 (dir.: Marbach) or 5 (dir.: Bietigheim) to Ludwigsburg (20min., 4 per hr., €2.60). The 1½hr. guided tour is the best way to see the lavish gold, marble, and velvet interior of Ludwigsburg's **Residenzschloß.** (Open mid-Mar. to mid-Oct. daily 9am-noon and 1-5pm, mid-Oct. to mid-Mar. 10am-noon and 1-4pm. €3.50, students €1.70.)

TÜBINGEN ☎07071

With nearly half its residents affiliated with the 500-year-old university, Tübingen is an academic town and proud of it. The chancel of the 15th-century **Stiftskirche** contains the tombs of 14 members of the former House of Württemberg, and the tower provides a lovely view. (Church open daily 9am-5pm. Chancel and tower open Oct.-July F-Su 11:30am-5pm, Aug.-Sept. Tu-Su 11:30am-5pm. €1, students €0.50.) Atop the hill in the center of town, **Schloß Hohentübingen** offers breathtaking views of the surrounding valleys. (Castle grounds open daily 7am-8pm. Free.) Inside, the excellent **Museum Schloß Hohentübingen** features what is purportedly the oldest surviving example of handiwork, a 35,000-year-old ivory horse sculpture. (Open May-Sept. W-Sa 10am-6pm; Oct.-Apr. W-Su 10am-5pm. €3, students €2.) Head down Kirchg. to the old market square to see the ornate painted facade of the **Rathaus.** A block below Marktpl., on Kronenstr., is the **Evangelisches Stift,** which was once a monastery and is now a dorm for theology students; its alumni include such academic luminaries as Kepler and Hegel.

Trains run to Stuttgart (1hr., 3-4 per hr., €9). Turn right from the station and take a left on Karlstr. to reach the **tourist office,** on the Neckarbrücke, which books rooms for free. (☎913 60. Open M-F 9am-7pm, Sa 9am-5pm; May-Sept. also Su 2-5pm.) To reach the **Jugendherberge (HI)** ❷, Gartenstr. 22/2, cross the bridge past the tourist office and make a right; the entrance is on Herman-Kurz-Str. (☎230 02. Internet €1 per 10min. Breakfast included. Sheets €3.10. Reception daily 5-8pm and 10-11pm. Dorms €17.60, under 26 €14.90; singles €27.60/€24.90; doubles €45.20/€39.80.) **Hotel am Schloß** ❸, Burgsteige 18, on the hill leading to the Schloß, has well-equipped rooms in a picturesque location. (☎929 40. Breakfast included. Singles €30, with bath €51-67; doubles with bath €76-86.) Most inexpensive eateries cluster around **Metzgerg.** and **Am Lustnauer Tor,** while modern *Imbiße* crowd **Kornhausg.** For fresh falafel and vegetarian sandwiches, head to **Die Kichererbse** ❷, Metzgerg. 2. (Open M-F 11am-8pm, Sa 11am-4pm.) Buy groceries at **HL-Markt,** Europapl. 8, across from the post office (open M-F 7am-8pm, Sa 7am-4pm), or at the **market** on Am Markt. (Open M, W, and F 7am-1pm.) **Postal Code:** 72072.

BADEN-BADEN ☎07221

If you dream of leading an Old World aristocrat's pampered life, you'll have a ball in Baden-Baden. Although the spa town has declined somewhat since its 19th-century heyday, it remains a playground where minor royalty and the well-to-do bathe in the curative mineral spas and drop fat sums of money in the casino. Baden-Baden's history as a resort town goes back nearly two millennia, to when the Romans started soaking themselves in the town's first **thermal baths.** The **Friedrichsbad,** Römerpl. 1, is a beautiful 19th-century bathing palace where visitors are soaked, scrubbed, doused, and pummeled by trained professionals. (☎27 59 20. Open M-Sa 9am-10pm, Su noon-8pm. Standard Roman-Irish bath €21, with soap and brush massage €29.) Budget-minded cure-seekers should head next door to **Caracalla-Thermen,** Römerpl. 1, where pools, whirlpools, and solaria of varying sizes and temperatures soothe the weary traveler. (☎27 59 40. Open daily 8am-10pm. 2hr. €11; 3hr. €13; 4hr. €15.)

The **train station** is 5km out of town; take bus #201 to Hindenburgpl. to reach the **tourist office,** inside the Trinkhalle on Kaiserallee, which has free maps and a list of hotels. (☎27 52 00. Open M-Sa 10am-5pm, Su 2-5pm.) The cheapest beds in town are at the **Werner-Dietz-Jugendherberge (HI) ❷,** Hardenbergstr. 34, between the station and the town center. Take bus #201, 205, or 216 to Grosse-Dollen-Str. (€2) and follow the signs uphill. (☎522 23; jh-baden-baden@t-online.de. Sheets €3. Reception every hr. on the hour 5-11pm. Curfew 11:30pm. Write in advance for reservations. Dorms €16, under 26 €14.) **Hotel am Markt ❸,** Marktpl. 18, is between the Friedrichsbad and the Stiftskirche. (☎270 40. Breakfast included. Reception 7am-10pm. Singles €30, with shower €42-45; doubles €59-61/€73-76.) Most restaurants in Baden-Baden are too pricey for the budget traveler; your best bet is to pick up **groceries** at **Pennymarkt,** near the hostel. (Open M-F 8am-8pm, Sa 8am-4pm.)

BLACK FOREST (SCHWARZWALD)

The Black Forest owes its name to the eerie gloom that prevails under its evergreen canopy. Once inspiration for "Hansel and Gretel," the region now attracts hikers and skiers with more than just gingerbread.

TRANSPORTATION. The main entry point to the Black Forest is **Freiburg,** which is accessible by **train** from Stuttgart and Basel, Switzerland. Most visitors use a bike to explore the area, as public transportation is sparse. Rail lines encircle the perimeter, with only two **train** lines cutting through the region. **Bus** service is more thorough, albeit slow and less frequent.

FREIBURG IM BREISGAU. Freiburg may be the metropolis of the Schwarzwald, but it has yet to succumb to the hectic pace of city life. Its pride and joy is the majestic **Münster,** a stone cathedral with a 116m spire and a tower with the oldest bell in Germany. (Open M-Sa 10am-6pm, Su 1-6pm. Tower open M-Sa 9:30am-5pm, Su 1-5pm. Tower €1, students €0.50.) The surrounding hills brim with fantastic **hiking** trails; maps are available in the tourist office or at most bookstores, and all trails are clearly marked. **Mountain biking** trails also traverse the hills; look for signs with bicycles to guide you. (Maps €3.50-6 at the tourist office.)

Trains run to Basel (30min.-1hr., 1-2 per hr., €9-16) and Stuttgart (2-3hr., 2 per hr., €32-35). The **tourist office,** Rotteckring 14, two blocks down Eisenbahnstr. from the station, has maps and books **Privatenzimmer** (rooms in private homes); these are usually the most affordable accommodations in Freiburg, since most hotels and *Pensionen* are outside the city center. (Open June-Sept. M-F 9:30am-8pm, Sa 9:30am-5pm, Su 10am-noon; Oct.-May M-F 9:30am-6pm, Sa 9:30am-2pm, Su 10am-noon.) To reach the **Jugendherberge (HI) ❷,** Kartäuserstr. 151, take S1 to Römerhof, backtrack and take the next right down Fritz-Geiges-Str., cross the stream, and follow the footpath for 5min. to the right. (Breakfast included. Sheets €3.10. Dorms €18, under 26 €15; doubles €25/€22.) The **Freiburger Markthalle ❷,** next to the Martinstor, is home to food stands serving ethnic specialties for €3-8. The entrance is on Grünwälderstr. (Open M-F 7am-7pm, Sa 7am-4pm.) **Brennessel ❸,** Eschholzstr. 17, behind the train station, fills the empty gullet without emptying the wallet. (Open M-Sa 8am-1am, Su 5pm-1am.) **Phone code:** ☎0761.

TITISEE AND SCHLUCHSEE. The more scenic and touristed **Titisee** (TEE-tee-zay) is only 30min. by train (2 per hr., €4.35) from Freiburg via the scenic **Höllental** (Hell's Valley). The **tourist office,** Strandbadstr. 4, books rooms for a small fee, rents **bikes** (€12 per day), and dispenses maps of the 130km of nearby **hiking** trails. From the station, take a right onto Parkstr., left across the square, and another on Strandbadstr. (☎(07651) 980 40. Open May-Oct. M-F 8am-noon and 1:30-5:30pm, Sa

11am-1pm, Su 10am-noon; Nov.-Apr. M-F 8am-noon and 1:30-5:30pm.) **Schluchsee,** to the south, also has a slew of first-rate **hiking** trails. The simple **Seerundweg** (19km, about 4hr.) circles the lake; follow the markers with red dots. More difficult and rewarding trails depart from the Sportplatz parking lot, a 15min. walk up Dresselbacher Str. past the huge resort hotel. To reach the **tourist office,** a block into the pedestrian zone, turn right from the train station, walk through the underpass, and turn left up the brick sidewalk; it's at the corner of Fischbacher Str. and Lindenstr., in the *Kurhaus*. The staff books rooms for free and has hiking maps. (☎(07656) 77 32. Open May-Sept. M-Th 8am-6pm, F 9am-6pm, Sa 10am-noon; July-Aug. also Su 10am-noon; Oct.-Apr. M-F 8am-noon and 2-6pm.)

ST. PETER AND ST. MÄRGEN. Just north of Titisee and 17km east of Freiburg, twin villages St. Peter and St. Märgen lie between cow-speckled hills. **Bus** #7216 runs from **Freiburg** to **St. Peter** (25min.); get off at Zähriger Eck to reach St. Peter's **tourist office,** in the Klosterhof, which has a list of affordable rooms. (☎(07660) 91 02 24. Open M-F 9am-noon and 2-5pm; July-Aug. also Sa 10am-noon.) Many hiking paths—most well marked—begin at the tourist office. An easy and very scenic 8km path leads to **St. Märgen;** follow the blue diamonds of the **Panoramaweg.** Alternatively, **bus** #7216 continues on to St. Märgen about half the time; check with the driver. With links to all major Black Forest trails and a number of gorgeous **day hikes,** St. Märgen rightfully calls itself a *Wanderparadies* (hiking paradise). Most of the trails are marked from Hotel Hirschen, uphill from the bus stop. The **tourist office,** in the *Rathaus*, 100m from the bus stop, provides good hiking and biking maps (€2.60-3.50) and books **rooms** for free. (☎(07669) 91 18 17. Open M-Th 9am-4:30pm, F 9am-2pm; July-Sept. also Sa 10am-noon.)

TRIBERG. The residents of touristy Triberg brag about the **Gutacher Wasserfall,** the highest in Germany, a series of bright cascades tumbling over moss-covered rocks for 163m. It's more of a mountain stream than a waterfall, but the idyllic hike through the lush park makes up for the unimpressive trickle. (Park open 9am-7pm. €1.50, students €1.20.) The signs for **Wallfahrtskirche** lead to the small pilgrim church, where the pious have, according to legend, been miraculously cured since the 17th century. The area around town offers several beautiful hikes—ask at the tourist office for information and maps.

Trains run to Freiburg (1¾-2½hr., 1-2 per hr., €16-25). The **tourist office,** Luisenstr. 10, is on the ground floor of the local *Kurhaus;* from the station, turn right and follow the signs, or take bus #7265, which runs every hour to Marktpl. The staff has a catalog of all hotels, *Pensionen*, and private rooms. (☎95 32 30. Open M-F 9am-5pm; May-Sept. also Sa 10am-noon.) Grab groceries for a picnic at **Plus market,** Schulstr. 5. (Open M-F 8:30am-6:30pm, Sa 8am-2pm.) **Phone code:** ☎07722.

CONSTANCE (KONSTANZ) ☎07531

Located on the **Bodensee** (Lake Constance), the charming city of Constance has never been bombed; part of the city extends into Switzerland, and the Allies were leery of accidentally striking neutral territory. Now one of Germany's favorite vacation spots, its narrow streets wind around beautiful Baroque and Renaissance facades, gabled and turreted 19th-century houses gleam with a confident gentility along the river promenades, and a palpable jubilation fills the streets. The **Münster** has a 76m Gothic spire and a display of ancient religious objects, but it's being renovated through 2003. (Open M-Sa 10am-6pm, Su noon-6:30pm.) Wander down **Seestraße,** near the yacht harbor on the lake, or **Rheinsteig,** along the Rhine, for picturesque promenades. Constance boasts a number of **public beaches;** all are free and open May to September **Freidbad Horn** (bus #5), the largest and most crowded, sports a nude sunbathing section modestly enclosed by hedges.

Trains run from Constance to most cities in southern Germany. **BSB** ships leave hourly from Constance for all ports around the lake. Buy tickets on board or in the building, Hafenstr. 6, behind the train station. (☎28 13 89. Open Apr.-Oct. daily 7:45am-6:35pm.) The friendly but tiny **tourist office,** Bahnhofspl. 13, to the right of the train station, provides free walking maps and finds rooms for a €2.50 fee. (☎13 30 30. Open Apr.-Oct. M-F 9am-6:30pm, Sa 9am-4pm, Su 10am-1pm; Nov.-Mar. M-F 9:30am-12:30pm and 2-6pm.) In the center of town, **Pension Gretel ❸,** Zollernstr. 6-8, offers bright rooms. In summer, call at least a month ahead. (☎45 58 25. Breakfast included. Singles €29-36; doubles €49-64, with bath €59-75; triples €75-95; quads €87-113; extra bed €18.) To reach the newly renovated **Jugendherberge "Otto-Moericke-Turm" (HI) ❷,** Zur Allmannshöhe 18, take bus #4 from the train station to Jugendherberge; turn back and head uphill on Zur Allmannshöhe. (☎322 60. Breakfast included. Sheets €3.10. Reception Apr.-Oct. daily 3-10pm; Nov.-Mar. 5-10pm. Lockout 9:30am-noon. Call ahead. HI members only. Dorms €17.60, under 26 €14.90.) Camp by the waterfront at **DKV-Campingplatz Bodensee ❶,** Fohrenbühlweg 45. Take bus #1 to Staad and walk for 10min. with the lake to your left. (☎330 57. Reception closed daily noon-2:30pm. Warm showers included. €4 per person, €4 per tent.) For groceries, head to the basement of the **Karstadt** department store, on Augustinerpl. (Open M-F 9:30am-8pm, Sa 9am-4pm.)

BAVARIA (BAYERN)

Bavaria is the Germany of Teutonic myth, Wagnerian opera, and the Brothers Grimm's fairy tales. From the Baroque cities along the Danube to King Ludwig's castles high in the Alps, the region draws more tourists than any other part of the country. Most foreigners' notions of Germany are tied to this land of *Biergartens* and *Lederhosen*. Mostly rural, Catholic, and conservative, it contrasts sharply with the rest of the country. Local authorities still use Bavaria's proper name, *Freistaat Bayern* (Free State of Bavaria), and its traditions and dialect have been preserved. Residents have always been Bavarians first and Germans second.

REMINDER. HI-affiliated hostels in Bavaria generally do not admit guests over age 26 except in families or groups of adults with young children.

MUNICH (MÜNCHEN) ☎089

The capital and cultural center of Bavaria, Munich is a sprawling, relatively liberal island metropolis in the midst of conservative southern Germany. World-class museums, handsome parks and architecture, a rambunctious arts scene, and an urbane population collide to create a city of astonishing vitality. *Müncheners* party zealously during *Fasching* (Carnival; Jan. 7-Mar. 4, 2003), shop with abandon during the *Christmas Market* (Nov. 28-Dec. 24, 2003), and consume unbelievable quantities of beer during the legendary *Oktoberfest* (Sept. 20-Oct. 5, 2003).

TRANSPORTATION

Flights: Flughafen München (MUC; ☎97 52 13 13). S8 runs between the airport and the *Hauptbahnhof* (40min., every 20min., €8 or 8 stripes on the *Streifenkarte*).

Trains: Munich's **Hauptbahnhof** (☎22 33 12 56) is the transportation hub of Southern Germany, with connections to: **Amsterdam** (9hr.; 1 per hr.; €143); **Berlin** (8hr.; 1 per hr.; €141, or €103 via Leipzig); **Cologne** (6hr.; 1 per hr.; €101); **Frankfurt** (3½hr.; 1 per hr.; €76); **Hamburg** (6hr.; 1 per hr.; €138); **Paris** (10hr.; 3 per day; €105); **Prague**

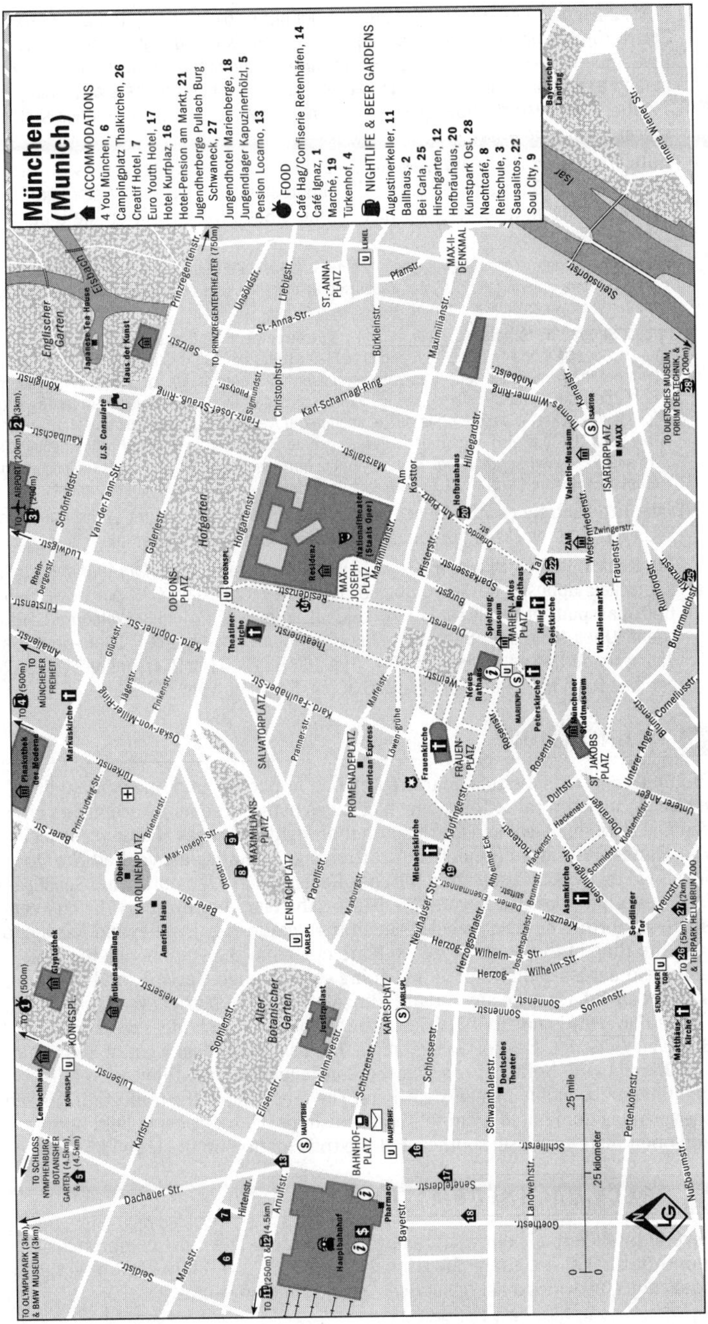
München (Munich)
ACCOMMODATIONS
4 You München, 6
Campingplatz Thalkirchen, 26
Creatif Hotel, 7
Euro Youth Hotel, 17
Hotel Kurfplaz, 16
Hotel-Pension am Markt, 21
Jugendherberge Pullach Burg Schwaneck, 27
Jungendhotel Marienberge, 18
Jungendlager Kapuzinerhölzl, 5
Pension Locarno, 13
FOOD
Café Hag/Confiserie Retenhäfen, 14
Café Ignaz, 1
Marché, 19
Türkenhof, 4
NIGHTLIFE & BEER GARDENS
Augustinerkeller, 11
Ballhaus, 2
Bei Carla, 25
Hirschgarten, 12
Hofbräuhaus, 20
Kunstpark Ost, 28
Nachtcafé, 8
Reitschule, 3
Sausalitos, 22
Soul City, 9
Englischer Garten
Hofgarten
Residenz
Nationaltheater (Staats Oper)
MAX-JOSEPH-PLATZ
ODEONSPLATZ
MARIEN-PLATZ
Neues Rathaus
Frauenkirche
FRAUEN-PLATZ
Viktualienmarkt
KARLSPLATZ
KAROLINENPLATZ
MAXIMILIANSPLATZ
LENBACHPLATZ
BAHNHOF-PLATZ
Hauptbahnhof
Alter Botanischer Garten
Glyptothek
Antikensammlung
KÖNIGSPL.
ISARTORPLATZ
Isar
Deutsches Theater
Sendlinger Tor
.25 mile
.25 kilometer

(7hr.; 2 per day; €60); **Salzburg** (1¾hr.; 1 per hr.; €25); **Vienna** (5hr.; 1 per hr.; €59); **Zurich** (5hr.; 4 per day; €61). For 24hr. schedules, fare information, and reservations (in German), call ☎(01805) 99 66 33. **EurAide,** in the station, provides free train information and books train tickets. **Reisezentrum** information counters open daily 6am-10:30pm. As of Dec. 2002, Deutsche Bahn will be instituting a new price system so expect changes to existing fares.

Public Transportation: MVV, Munich's public transport system, runs Su-Th 5am-12:30am, F-Sa 5am-2am. S-Bahn to the airport starts running at 3:30am. Eurail, InterRail, and German railpasses are valid on the S-Bahn (S) but *not* on the U-Bahn (U), streetcars, or buses.

Tickets: Buy tickets at the blue vending machines and **validate them** in the blue boxes marked with an "E" before entering the platform. Disguised agents check for tickets sporadically; if you jump the fare (known as *schwarzfahren*), you risk a €30 fine.

Prices: Single ride tickets (€2, valid for 3hr.). **Kurzstrecke** (short trip) tickets are good for 2 stops on U or S, or 4 stops on a streetcar or bus (€1). A **Streifenkarte** (10-strip ticket, €9) can be used by more than 1 person. Cancel 2 strips per person for a normal ride, or 1 strip per person for a *Kurzstrecke;* beyond the city center, cancel 2 strips per additional zone. A **Single-Tageskarte** (single-day ticket) is valid for one day of unlimited travel until 6am the next day (€4.50). The **3-Day Pass** (€11) is also a great deal. Passes can be purchased at the **MVV office** behind tracks 31 and 32 in the *Hauptbahnhof,* or at any of the *Kartenautomats*. Ask at tourist offices about the **Munich Welcome Card,** which gives public transportation and various other discounts.

Taxis: Taxi-Zentrale (☎216 11 or 194 10) has large stands in front of the train station and every 5-10 blocks in the central city. Women can request a female driver.

Bike Rental: Radius Bikes (☎59 61 13), at the far end of the *Hauptbahnhof,* behind the lockers opposite tracks 30-36. €3 per hr., €13 per day, €43 per week. Deposit €50, passport, or credit card. 10% student, Eurail, and Munich Welcome Card discount. Open May-June, Sept.-Oct. M-F 10am-6pm; July-Aug. M-F 10am-6pm, Sa-Su 9am-8pm. **Aktiv-Rad,** Hans-Sachs-Str. 7 (☎26 65 06). U1 or 2: Fraunhofer Str. €12-20 per day. Open M-F 10am-1pm and 2-6:30pm, Sa 10am-1pm.

ORIENTATION

Munich's center is a circle quartered by one horizontal and one vertical line. The circle is the main traffic Ring, which changes names frequently around its circumference. The east-west and north-south thoroughfares cross at Munich's epicenter, the **Marienplatz,** and connect the traffic rings at **Karlsplatz** (called *Stachus* by locals) in the west, **Isatorplatz** in the east, **Odeonsplatz** in the north, and **Sendliger Tor** in the south. In the east beyond the Isartor, the **Isar River** flows by the city center, south to north. The **Hauptbahnhof** (main train station) is just beyond Karlspl. outside the Ring in the west. To get to Marienpl. from the station, use the main exit and head across Bahnhofpl., keep going east through Karlspl., and Marienpl. is straight ahead. Or, take any S-Bahn (dir.: Marienpl.) to Marienpl.

The **University** is north of Munich's center, next to the budget restaurants of the **Schwabing** district. East of Schwabing is the **English Garden;** west of Schwabing is the **Olympiapark.** South of town is the **Glockenbachviertel,** filled with all sorts of night hotspots, including many gay bars. The area around the train station is rather seedy and is dominated by hotels and sex shops. Oktoberfest is held on the large and open **Theresienwiese,** southeast of the train station on the U4 and 5 lines.

PRACTICAL INFORMATION

Several publications help visitors navigate Munich. The most comprehensive, the monthly English-language *Munich Found* (€3), available at newsstands and bookshops, provides a list of services, events, and museums.

TOURIST, FINANCIAL, AND LOCAL SERVICES

Tourist Offices:

Main Tourist Office (☎233 96 500), on the front (east) side of the train station, next to the SB-Markt on Bahnhofpl. They do speak English, but for more in-depth questions, EurAide (see below) will probably better suit your needs. The office **books rooms** for free with a 10-15% deposit, sells English city maps (€0.30), and offers the **Munich Welcome Card**. Open M-Sa 9am-8pm, Su 10am-6pm. **Branch office** just inside the entrance to the *Neues Rathaus* on Marienpl. Open M-F 10am-8pm, Sa 10am-4pm.

EurAide (☎59 38 89), along track 11 (room 3) of the *Hauptbahnhof*, near the Bayerstr. exit. Books train tickets, explains the public transport, and sells maps (€1) and tickets for English tours of Munich. Offers the free brochure *Inside Track*. Open daily June-Sept. 7:45am-12:45pm and 2-6pm; Oct. 7:45am-12:45pm and 2-4pm; Nov.-Apr. 8am-noon and 1-4pm; May 7:45am-12:45pm and 2-4:30pm.

Discover Bavaria (☎25 54 39 88), Hochorückenstr., near the rear entrance of the Haufbrau Haus. Helps find rooms for free, rents bikes, and dispenses coupons for a variety of activities. Also sells tickets for the hugely popular Mike's Bike Tours of Munich, Neuschwanstein, and Dachau. Open daily 8:30am-9pm; closed Oct.-Mar.

Consulates: Canada, Tal 29 (☎219 95 70). S-Bahn to Isartor. Open M-Th 9am-noon and 2-5pm, F 9am-noon and 2-3:30pm. **Ireland,** Dennigerstr. 15 (☎2080 5990). Open M-F 9am-noon. **South Africa,** Sendlinger-Tor-Pl. 5 (☎2311 6337). U1, 2, 3 or 6 to Sendlinger Tor. Open M-F 9am-noon. **UK,** Bürkleinstr. 10, 4th fl. (☎21 10 90). U4 or 5 to Lehel. Open M-Th 8:30am-noon and 1-5pm, F 8:30am-noon and 1-3:30pm. **US,** Königinstr. 5 (☎288 80). Open M-F 8-11am.

Bi-Gay-Lesbian Resources: Gay Services (☎260 30 56). **Lesbian information** and the **LeTra Lesbentraum,** Angertorstr. 3 (☎725 42 72). Telephone times M and W 2:30-5pm, Tu 10:30am-1pm, Th 7-9pm. See also **Gay and Lesbian Nightlife** (see p. 514).

Disabled Resources: Info Center für Behinderte, Schellingstr. 31 (☎211 70; www.vdk.de/bayern), has a list of Munich's resources for disabled persons. Open M-Th 9am-noon and 12:30-6pm, F 9am-5pm.

Laundromat: SB Waschcenter, Paul-Heyse-Str. 21, near the train station. Turn right on Bayerstr., then left on Paul-Heyse-Str. Wash €4, dry €0.60 per 10min. Open daily 7am-11pm. **Kingsgard Waschsalon,** Amalienstr. 61, near the university. Wash €3, dry €1.50. Open M-F 8am-6:30pm, Sa 9am-1pm.

EMERGENCY AND COMMUNICATIONS

Police: ☎110. **Ambulance** and **Fire:** ☎112. **Medical service:** ☎192 22.

Pharmacy: Bahnhofpl. 2 (☎59 41 19 or 59 81 19), on the corner outside the train station. Open M-F 8am-6:30pm, Sa 8am-2pm. 24hr. service rotates among the city's pharmacies–check the window of any pharmacy for a list.

Internet Access: EasyEverything (The Internet Shop), on Bahnhofspl. next to the post office. Prices depend on demand (max. €3 per hr.) Open 24hr. **Savic Internet Point,** Schillerstr. 15, is slightly more expensive. Open daily 10am-midnight.

Post Office: Bahnhofpl., **80335 Munich.** It's the yellow building across the street from the main train station exit. Open M-F 7am-8pm, Sa 9am-4pm, Su 10am-3pm.

ACCOMMODATIONS AND CAMPING

Munich's accommodations usually fall into one of three categories: seedy, expensive, or booked solid. During times like Oktoberfest, when prices usually jump 10-15%, only the last category exists. In summer, start calling before noon or book a few weeks in advance. At most of Munich's hostels you can check in all day, but try to start your search before 5pm. Don't even think of sleeping in any public area, including the *Hauptbahnhof;* police patrol frequently all night long.

HOSTELS AND CAMPING

Euro Youth Hotel, Senefelderstr. 5 (☎599 088 11, 599 088 71, or 599 088 72). From the Bayerstraße exit of the *Hauptbahnhof,* make a left on Bayerstr. and a right on Senefelderstr. Friendly and well-informed English-speaking staff. Breakfast buffet €4.90. Wash €2.80, dry €1.30. Reception 24hr. Dorms €17.50; doubles €48, with private shower, telephone, and breakfast €72; triples €63; quads €84. Inquire about their new location scheduled to open early in 2003. ❷

4 You München, Hirtenstr. 18 (☎552 16 60), 200m from the *Hauptbahnhof.* Exit at Arnulfstr., go left, and take an immediate right onto Pfefferstr., then hang a left onto Hirtenstr. Ecological youth hostel with restaurant and bar. Wheelchair-accessible. Breakfast €4.35. 12-bed dorms €17.50; 4-, 6,- or 8-bed dorms €20-22; singles €35, with bath €43.50; doubles €52/€68.50. 15% surcharge for ages 27+. ❷

Jugendhotel Marienherberge, Goethestr. 9 (☎55 58 05), less than a block from the train station. Take the Bayerstr. exit and walk down Goethestr. **Open only to women.** Reduced prices for those 25 and under. Staffed by merry nuns, the rooms are spacious, cheery, and spotless. Breakfast included. Kitchen, laundry, and television facilities. Wash €1.50. Reception daily 8am-midnight. Curfew midnight. 6-bed dorms €25; singles €31; doubles €50; triples €75. ❸

Jugendherberge Pullach Burg Schwaneck (HI), Burgweg 4-6 (☎793 06 43), in a castle 12km outside the city center. S7 (dir.: Wolfratshausen) to Pullach. Exit the station from the Munich side, walk toward the huge soccer field down Margarethenstr., and follow the signs. Caters largely to an under 18 crowd. Breakfast and sheets included. Reception daily 11am-11pm. Curfew 11:30pm. Make reservations 9am-1pm. 6- to 8-bed dorms €15.50; singles €23.50; doubles €42; quads €66. ❷

Jugendlager Kapuzinerhölzl ("The Tent"), In den Kirschen 30 (☎141 43 00). Streetcar #17 from the *Hauptbahnhof* (dir.: Amalienburgstr.) to Botanischer Garten (15min.). Follow the signs straight on Franz-Schrank-Str. and turn left at In den Kirschen. Sleep with 250 fellow campers under a big tent on a wooden floor. Laundry €2. Lockers €4. Internet €1 for 15min. Kitchen facilities available. 24hr. reception. Reservations only for groups over 15, but rarely full. Open June-Aug. €8.50 gets you a foam pad, blankets (you can use your sleeping bag also), a shower, and breakfast. Actual beds €11. **Camping** available for €5.50 per campsite plus €5.50 per person. ❶

Campingplatz Thalkirchen, Zentralländstr. 49 (☎723 17 07). U1 or 2 to Sendlinger Tor, then U3 to Thalkirchen, and change to bus #57 (20min). From the bus stop, cross the busy street on the left and take a right onto the footpath next to the road. The entrance is down the tree-lined path on the left. Well-run crowded grounds with jogging and bike paths, TV lounge, groceries, and a restaurant. Showers €1. Wash €4, dry €0.25 for 11min. Open mid-Mar. to late Oct. €4.40 per person, €8 per tent. ❶

HOTELS AND PENSIONS

Hotel Helvetia, Schillerstr. 6 (☎590 68 50), at the corner of Bahnhofspl., just beyond the Vereinsbank, to the right as you exit the station. A friendly hotel with newly renovated rooms. Free Internet. Breakfast included. Laundry €6. Reception 24hr. Singles €30-35; doubles €40-55, with shower €50-65; triples €55-69; quads €72-90. ❸

Pension Locarno, Bahnhofspl. 5 (☎55 51 64). Cozy rooms, all with cable TV and phone. Reception daily 7:30am-5pm. Singles €38; doubles €57; triples €69; quads €81. ❸

Creatif Hotel, Lammerstr. 6 (☎55 57 85). Take the Arnulfstr. exit out of the station, hang a quick right, then left on Hirtenstr., and then a right on Lammerstr. Uniquely modern rooms, all with bath, telephones and TVs. Internet €1 per 30min. Reception 24hr. Singles €30-40; doubles €40-65. Extra bed €10. ❸

Hotel Kurpfalz, Schwanthaler Str. 121 (☎540 98 60). Exit on Bayerstr. from the station, turn right and walk 5-6 blocks down Bayerstr., veer left onto Holzapfelstr., and make a right onto Schwanthaler Str. Or take streetcar #18 or 19 to Holzapfelstr. and walk from there. TVs, phones, and baths in all rooms. Breakfast included. Free email; Internet €3 per 30min. Reception 24hr. Singles from €50; doubles from €100. ❹

Hotel-Pension am Markt, Heiliggeiststr. 6 (☎22 50 14), smack dab in the city center, off the Viktualienmarkt. Take any S-Bahn to Marienpl., then walk past the *Altes Rathaus* and turn right down the little alley behind the Heiliggeist Church. Small but spotless rooms are wheelchair-accessible. Breakfast included. Reception (3rd floor) daily 7am-9pm. Singles €38, with shower €66; doubles €68/€87-92; triples €100/€123. ❹

Pension Frank, Scheillingstr. 24 (☎28 14 51). U3 or 6 to Schellingstr. Rooms with balconies. In a great location for cafe and bookstore afficionados. Breakfast included. Reception daily 7:30am-10pm. Dorms €25; singles €35-40; doubles €52-55. ❸

FOOD

For an authentic Bavarian lunch, grab a *Brez'n* (pretzel) and spread it with *Leberwurst* (liverwurst) or cheese. **Weißwürste** (white veal sausages) are another native bargain, served in a pot of hot water with sweet mustard and a soft pretzel on the side. Don't eat the skin of the sausage; just slice it open and eat the tender meat. **Leberkäs** is a slice of a pinkish, meatloaf-like compound of ground beef and bacon. **Leberknödel** are liver dumplings, usually served in soup. **Kartoffelknödel** (potato dumplings) and **Semmelknödel** (made from white bread, egg, and parsley) are eaten along with a hearty chunk of German meat.

The vibrant **Viktualienmarkt,** 2min. south of Marienpl., is Munich's gastronomic center, offering both basic and exotic foods and ingredients. It's fun to browse, but don't plan to do any budget grocery shopping here. (Open M-F 10am-8pm, Sa 8am-4pm.) The ubiquitous **beer gardens** serve savory snacks along with booze. The university district off **Ludwigstraße** is Munich's best source of filling meals in a lively, unpretentiously hip scene. Many reasonably-priced restaurants and cafes cluster on **Schellingstraße, Amalienstraße,** and **Türkenstraße** (U3 or 6 to "Universität").

Marché, Neuhauser Str., between Karlspl. and Marienpl. The top floor offers cafeteria-style food; downstairs, chefs prepare a variety of food, including great vegetarian selections. You'll get a food card that will be stamped for each item taken; pay at the end. Bottom floor open daily 11am-10pm, top floor open 8am-10pm; 11pm in summer. ❷

Cafe Hag/Confiserie Retenhäfer, Residenzstr. 25-26, across from the Residenz. Specializes in cakes and sweets (€2-4). Serves breakfast (€4-8) and entrees (€5-8). Open M-F 8:45am-7pm, Sa 8am-6pm. ❷

News Bar, Amalienstr. 55 (☎28 17 87), at the corner of Schellingstr. Trendy cafe teeming with students; serves large meals at reasonable prices. Open daily 7:30am-2am. ❸

Türkenhof, Türkenstr. 78 (☎280 02 35), offers a wide selection of global cuisine, from Middle Eastern to Mexican to Thai. Variable daily menu with numerous veggie options. Entrees €6-9. Open M-Th and Su 11am-1am, F-Sa 11am-2am. ❸

Café Ignaz, Georgenstr. 67. U2 to Josephspl. Take Adelheidstr. 1 block north and turn right on Georgenstr. Earth-friendly cafe with a nutritious, inexpensive vegetarian menu. Lunch buffet M-F noon-2pm €7.50, brunch buffet Sa-Su 9am-1:30pm €8. Open M-F 8am-10pm, Sa-Su 9am-10pm. ❷

SIGHTS

MARIENPLATZ. The **Mariensäule,** an ornate 17th-century monument to the Virgin Mary, was built to commemorate the city's survival during the Thirty Years' War. At the neo-Gothic **Neues Rathaus,** the **Glockenspiel** chimes with a display of jousting knights and dancing coopers. *(Daily 11am and noon; in summer also 5pm.)* At 9pm, a mechanical watchman marches out and the Guardian Angel escorts the *Münchner Kindl* (Munich Child, the town's symbol) to bed. The *Neues Rathaus* tower offers a sweeping view. *(Tower open M-F 9am-7pm, Sa-Su 10am-7pm. €1.50.)* On the face of the **Altes Rathaus** tower, to the right of the *Neues Rathaus,* are all of Munich's coats of arms since its inception as a city but one: the local government refused to include the swastika-bearing arms from the Nazi era.

PETERSKIRCHE AND FRAUENKIRCHE. Across from the *Neues Rathaus* is the 12th-century **Peterskirche,** the city's oldest parish church. More than 300 steps lead to the tower and its spectacular view of Munich. *(Open daily 10am-7pm. €1.50, students €1.)* From the Marienpl., walk one block toward the *Hauptbahnhof* on Kaufingerstr. to the onion-domed towers of the 15th-century **Frauenkirche,** one of Munich's most notable landmarks and now the symbol of the city. *(Towers open Apr.-Oct. M-Sa 10am-5pm. €3, students €1.50.)*

RESIDENZ. Down the pedestrian zone from Odeonspl., the richly decorated rooms of the **Residenz** (Palace), built from the 14th to 19th centuries, form the material vestiges of the Wittelsbach dynasty. The beautifully landscaped **Hofgarten,** behind the Residenz, shelters the lovely temple of Diana. The **Schatzkammer** (treasury) contains jeweled baubles, crowns, swords, china, ivory work, and other trinkets. *(Open Apr. to mid-Oct. daily 9am-6pm; mid-Oct. to Mar. 10am-4pm. €4, students €3.)* The **Residenzmuseum** is comprised of the former Wittelsbach apartments and State Rooms, a collection of European porcelain, and a 17th-century court chapel. The 120 portraits in the **Ahnengalerie** trace the royal lineage in an unusual manner back to Charlemagne. *(Max-Joseph-pl. 3. U3-6 to Odeonspl. Same hours and admission as Schatzkammer. Combination ticket €7, students €5.50.)*

ENGLISCHER GARTEN. Extending from the city center is the vast **Englischer Garten** (English Garden), Europe's largest metropolitan public park. On sunny days, all of Munich turns out to bike, fly kites, play badminton, ride horseback, swim or sunbathe. The garden includes a Japanese tea house, a Chinese pagoda, a Greek temple, and a few beer gardens. **Nude sunbathing** areas are designated FKK *(Frei-Körper-Kultur)* on signs and park maps. Daring Müncheners surf the rapids of the Eisbach, which flows artificially through the park.

SCHLOß NYMPHENBURG. After 10 years of trying for an heir, Ludwig I celebrated the birth of his son in 1662 by erecting an elaborate summer playground. **Schloß Nymphenburg,** in the northwest of town, hides a number of treasures. Check out Ludwig's "Gallery of Beauties"—whenever a woman caught his fancy, he would have her portrait painted (a scandalous hobby considering many of the women were commoners). A few lakes and four manors also inhabit the grounds. The **Marstallimuseum** displays various means of 17th-century royal travel. *(Streetcar #17 to Schloß Nymphenburg. Museum and Schloß open Tu-Su 9am-noon and 1-5pm. Schloß €3.50, students €2.50. Each manor €3/€2. Museum €2.50/€2. Entire complex €7.50/€6.)*

OLYMPIAPARK. Built for the 1972 Olympic Games in Munich, the **Olympiapark** contains the architecturally daring, tent-like **Olympia-Zentrum** and the **Olympia Turm**

(tower), the highest building in Munich at 290m. Two tours in English are available: the "Adventure Tour" of the entire park (Apr.-Oct. daily 2pm, €7) or a tour of just the soccer stadium (Mar.-Oct. daily 11am, €5). The Olympiapark hosts various events all summer, ranging from concerts to flea markets to bungee jumping. *(U3 to Olympiazentrum. Tower open daily 9am-midnight. €3, students €2. Info Pavillion (besucherservice) open M-F 10am-6pm, Sa 10am-3pm.)*

TIERPARK HELLBRUN. Animals are allowed to roam (relatively) freely and interact with each other in Munich's large **zoo,** which has been around since 1911. There are no fences to obstruct the view; the animals are kept in by large ditches. An excellent place for children, with petting zoos, pony rides, clowns, and ice cream wagons. Don't miss the vulgar talking raven. *(Tierparkstr. 30. U3 to Thalkirchen, then follow the signs. Open Apr.-Sept. daily 8am-6pm; Oct.-Mar. 9am-5pm. €6.)*

MUSEUMS

Munich is a superb museum city—many of the city's offerings would require days for exhaustive perusal. The *Münchner Volkshochschule* (☎480 062 29 or 480 062 30) offers tours of many city museums for €6. A **day pass** to all of Munich's state-owned museums is sold at the tourist office and many larger museums (€15). All state owned museums are **free on Sunday.**

DEUTSCHES MUSEUM. One of the world's largest and best museums of science and technology, with fascinating exhibits, including a mining exhibit that winds through a labyrinth of recreated subterranean tunnels. The museum's 50+ departments cover 17km. Grab an English guidebook for €4. *(Museuminsel 1. S1 or 8 to Isartor or street car #18 to Deutsches Museum. Open daily 9am-5pm. €6, students €2.50.)*

ALTE PINAKOTHEK AND NEUE PINAKOTHEK. Commissioned in 1826 by King Ludwig I, this world-renowned hall houses Munich's most precious art, including works by da Vinci, Rembrandt, and Rubens. *(Barerstr. 27. U2 to Königspl. Open Tu-Su 10am-5pm, Th until 10pm. €5, students €3.50.)* The **Neue Pinakothek** next door displays paintings and sculptures from the 19th and 20th centuries, including work by van Gogh, Cézanne, and Manet. *(Barerstr. 29. Open W-M 10am-5pm, Th until 8pm. Same prices as the Alte Pinakothek; combination ticket for Alte and Neue Pinakotheken €6, students €3)* The **Pinakothek Der Moderne** was under construction at the time of publication; it will eventually house the **Staatsgalerie Moderner Kunst.**

BMW-MUSEUM. The ultimate driving museum features a fetching display of past, present, and future BMW products. The English brochure *Horizons in Time* guides you through the spiral path to the top of the museum. *(Petuelring 130. U3: Olympiazentrum. Take the Olympiaturm exit and walk a block up Lerchenauer Str., the museum will be on your left. Open daily 9am-5pm. €3, students €2.)*

ZENTRUM FÜR AUSSERGEWÖHNLICHE MUSEEN (ZAM). Munich's Center for Unusual Museums brazenly corrals—under one roof—such treasures as the Peddle-Car Museum, and the Museum of Easter Rabbits. *(Westenriederstr. 41. Any S-Bahn or streetcar #17 or 18 to Isartor. Open daily 10am-6pm. €4, students €3.)*

MÜNCHENER STADTMUSEUM. A collection of exhibitions on Munich's city life and history, including film, musical instruments, weapons, and more. *(St.-Jakobs-pl. 1. U3 or 6 or any S-Bahn to Marienplatz. Open Tu-Su 10am-6pm. Museum €3, students €2.)*

THE INSIDER'S CITY

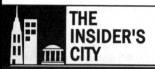

THE MANY NECTARS OF MUNICH

Small beer gardens and street-side cafes pepper Munich's *Altstadt*, offering up an array of local beverages to suit any palette.

1. Sample the many faces of *Hacker-Pschorr* at *Donisl.*
2. Think Germans only drink beer? Think again. Local wines await in the medieval winery in the Ratskeller beneath the *Neues Rathaus.*
3. Down an *Augustiner* at the *Wirthaus zur Weißblauen Rose.*
4. Make merry with hundreds of tourists and locals in *Lederhosen* at the *Hofbräuhaus.*
5. Try out *Schneider Weiße,* at the *Weißes Bräuhaus.*
6. Look for the barrel-table of the *Imbiß* to try the taste of *Paulaner.*
7. Roar like a lion at the *Löwe am Markt,* home of *Löwenbräu.*
8. Revisit favorites at the *Münchener Bier* gardens: *Augustiner, Hacker-Pschorr, Hofbräu, Löwenbräu, Paulanerbräu,* and *Spatenbräu.*

ENTERTAINMENT

Munich's cultural cachet rivals the world's best. Sixty theaters of various sizes are scattered throughout the city; styles range from dramatic classics at the **Residenztheater** and **Volkstheater** to comic opera at the **Staatstheater am Gärtnerplatz** to experimental works at the **Theater im Marstall** in Nymphenburg. Munich's **opera festival** (in July) is held in the **Bayerische Staatsoper** (Bavarian National Theater), Max-Joseph-pl. 2. (U3, 4, 5, or 6 to Odeonspl. or streetcar #19 to Nationaltheater. Tickets ☎21 85 19 20; recorded info ☎21 85 19 19. Standing-room and student tickets €4-10, sold 1hr. before performance at the side entrance on Maximilianstr. Box office open M-F 10am-6pm, Sa 10am-1pm. No performances Aug. to mid-Sept.) *Monatsprogramm* (€1.50) and *Munich Found* (€3) both list schedules for Munich's stages, museums, and festivals. Munich shows its bohemian face with small fringe theaters, cabaret stages, art cinemas, and artsy pubs in **Schwabing.**

NIGHTLIFE

Munich's nightlife is a curious collision of Bavarian *Gemütlichkeit* ("camaraderie") and trendy cliquishness. The odyssey begins at one of Munich's beer gardens or beer halls, which generally close before midnight and are most crowded in the early evening. The alcohol keeps flowing at cafes and bars, which, except for Friday and Saturday nights, close their taps at 1am. Discos and dance clubs, sedate before midnight, throb relentlessly until 4am. The trendy bars, cafes, cabarets, and discos along **Leopoldstraße** in **Schwabing** attract tourists from all over Europe. Many of these venues require you to at least attempt the jaded hipster look, and the Munich fashion police generally frown on shorts, sandals, and T-shirts.

BEER GARDENS

The six great Munich labels are *Augustiner*, *Hacker-Pschorr*, *Hofbräu*, *Löwenbräu*, *Paulaner*, and *Spaten-Franziskaner*, but most restaurants and *Gaststätte* pick a side and only serve one brewery's beer. There are four main types of beer served in Munich: **Helles** (light), **Dunkles** (dark), **Weißbier** (cloudy blond beer made from wheat instead of barley), and **Radler** (cyclist's brew; half beer and half lemon soda). Saying *"Ein Bier, bitte"* will get you a liter, known as a *Maß* (€4-6). Specify if you want only a half-*Maß* (€3-4). Since the time of King Ludwig I, patrons have been permitted to bring their own food to many of the gardens; to make sure that your chow is welcome, ask a server or check for tables without tablecloths, as bare tables usually indicate self-service.

Augustinerkeller, Arnulfstr. 52, at Zirkus-Krone-Str. Any S-Bahn to Hackerbrücke. Founded in 1824, *Augustiner* is viewed by most *Müncheners* as the finest beer garden in town. Lush grounds, 100-year-old chestnut trees, and the delicious, sharp *Augustiner* beer (*Maß* €5.70) support their assertion. Open daily 10:30am-1am.

Hirschgarten, Hirschgarten 1. Streetcar #17 (dir.: Amalienburgstr.) to Romanpl. Walk south to the end of Guntherstr. to enter the Hirschgarten. The largest beer garden in Europe (seating 9000) is boisterous and pleasant but somewhat remote, near Schloß Nymphenburg. *Maß* €5.30. Open daily 9am-midnight.

Hofbräuhaus, Platzl 9, 2 blocks from Marienpl. Walk past the *Altes Rathaus* and take an immediate left onto Sparkassenstr. Turn right onto Lederstr.; and then take the 1st left onto Orlandostr.; Hofbräuhaus is ahead on the right. Many tables are reserved for locals—some even keep their personal steins in the hall's safe. To avoid tourists, go in the early afternoon. *Maß* €6. *Weißwürste* with pretzel €3.70. Open daily 9am-midnight.

Taxisgarten, Taxisstr. 12. U1 to Gern, then walk one block east on Tizianstr. This beer garden's small size (1500 chairs) has kept it a favorite of locals and students. *Maß* €5.70. Open daily 11am-11pm.

BARS

Nachtcafe, Maximilianspl. 5. U4 or 5 or any S-Bahn to Karlspl. Live jazz, funk, soul, and blues until the wee hours. Very *schicki-micki* (yuppie). Things don't get rolling until midnight. No cover, but outrageous prices, so do your drinking beforehand. Very picky on weekends—you'll have to look the part. Open daily 9pm-6am; live music 11pm-4am.

Reitschule, Königinstr. 34. U3 or 6 to Giselastr. A sleek bar with marble tables. Also a cafe with a beer garden out back. *Weißbier* €3. Open daily 9am-1am.

Sausalitos, Im Tal 16. Any U-Bahn to Marienpl. Mexican bar and restaurant hopping with a 20-something crowd. Mixed drinks €6-9. Open daily 11am-late.

Kilian's Irish Pub and **Ned Kelly's Australian Bar**, Frauenplatz 11. U-Bahn to Marienpl., bars are behind the Frauenkirche. Two venues in one, with live music, Irish and Australian beer and food, and live sports coverage. Kilian's also features an outdoor beer garden. Kilian's open daily 11am-1am, Ned Kelly's 5pm-1am.

CLUBS

Kunstpark Ost, Grafinger Str. 6. U5 or any S-Bahn to *Ostbahnhof;* follow signs for the Kunstpark Ost exit, turn right onto Friedenstr., and then left onto Grafinger Str. The newest and biggest addition to the Munich nightlife scene, this huge complex has 40 different venues swarming with young people. Try the hip **MilchBar** (open M and W-F) with modern hits and old favorites, the psychedelic-trance **Natraj Temple** (open F-Sa), or the alternative cocktail and disco joint **K41** (open daily; Th 80s night). Hours, cover, and themes vary—check *Kunstpark* for details on specific club nights and specials. The entire venue will be moving to Frottmaning, outside the city center, sometime in 2003. Check their website (www.kunstpark.de) for details about the move.

Nachtwerk, Club, and Tanzlokal, Landesberger Str. 185. Streetcar #18 or 19 or bus #83 to Lautensackstr. **Nachtwerk** spins mainstream dance tunes for sweaty crowds in a packed warehouse; Sa "Best of the 50s to the 90s" night. **Club** offers a 2-level dance floor just as tight and swinging as its neighbor. **Tanzlokal** (open F-Sa) has hip-hop on F. Beer €2.50 at all venues. Cover €5.50. Open daily 10pm-4am.

Ballhaus, Domagkstr. 33, in the Alabamahalle. U6 to Heide. Free shuttle from there to the club. On a former military base in Schwabing with 3 other discos. Start out in the beer garden, which opens 8pm. Try **Alabama** for German oldies (F 9pm-4am, drinks free until 1am) and hits from the 60s to the 90s (Sa 10pm-5am, free drinks all night). **Tempel Club** has typical pop music (open Sa 10pm-4am), and **Schwabinger Ballhouse** plays international jams (F-Sa 10pm-5am; cover €8, drinks €1.50-3).

GAY AND LESBIAN NIGHTLIFE

Although Bavaria has the reputation of being less welcoming to homosexuality, Munich sustains a respectably vibrant gay nightlife. The center of Munich's gay scene is in the **Glockenbachviertel,** stretching from the area south of the Sendlinger Tor through the Viktualienmarkt/Gärtnerpl. to the Isartor. *Our Munich*, Munich's gay and lesbian leaflet, is available at the tourist office. Pick up *Sergej*, for details on Munich's gay and lesbian scene at **Max&Milian Bookstore,** Ickstattstr. 2 (open M-F 10:30am-2pm and 3:30-8pm, Sa 11am-4pm), or at any gay locale.

Bei Carla, Buttermelcherstr. 9. Any S-Bahn to Isartor. Walk 1 block south on Zweibrueckenstr., take a right on Rumfordstr., turn left on Klenzestr., then left again onto Buttermelcherstr. One of Munich's best-kept secrets. Open M-Sa 4pm-1am, Su 6pm-1am.

Soul City, Maximilianspl. 5, at the intersection with Max-Joseph-Str. Purportedly the biggest gay disco in Bavaria; music ranges from disco to Latin to techno. Straights always welcome. Cover €5-13. Open W-Sa 10pm-late.

DAYTRIPS FROM MUNICH

DACHAU ☎08131

From Munich, take S2 (dir.: Petershausen) to Dachau (20min., €4, or 4 stripes on the Streifenkarte), then bus #724 (dir.: Kraütgarten) or 726 (dir.: Kopernikusstr.) to KZ-Gedenkstätte (10min., €1 or one stripe on the Streifenkarte). Informative but lengthy (2hr.) tours of the camp in English leave from the museum July-Aug. daily 12:30pm; Sept.-June Sa-Su and holidays 12:30pm. Free, but donation requested. Call ☎08131 17 41 for more information. Camp open Tu-Su 9am-5pm.

"*Arbeit Macht Frei*" ("work will set you free") was the first thing prisoners saw as they entered Dachau; it's written over the gate of the **Jourhaus,** formerly the only entry to the camp. Dachau was primarily a work camp (rather than a death camp, like Auschwitz). During the war, prisoners made armaments in Dachau because the SS knew that the Allies would not bomb a concentration camp. Although Dachau has a **gas chamber,** it was never actually used because the prisoners purposely made mistakes and worked slowly in order to delay completion. The once tightly-packed **barracks** are now, for the most part, only foundations. However, survivors ensured that at least two barracks would be reconstructed to teach future generations about the 206,000 prisoners who were interned here from 1933 to 1945. The walls, gates, and crematorium have been restored since 1962 in a chillingly sparse memorial to the victims of Dachau. The **museum,** located in the former administrative buildings, examines pre-1930s anti-Semitism, the rise of Nazism, the establishment of the concentration camp system, and the lives of prisoners through photographs, documents, and artifacts. The thick **guide** (€26) translates the propaganda posters, SS files, documents, and letters. Most exhibits are accompanied by short captions in English. A short **film** (22min.) is screened in English at 11:30am, 2pm, and 3:30pm. A new display in the **bunker,** the concentration camp's prison and torture chamber, chronicles the lives and experiences of the camp's special prisoners and the barbarism of SS guards.When you visit, it is important to remember that, while the concentration camp is treated as a tourist attraction by many, it is first and foremost a memorial.

GARMISCH-PARTENKIRCHEN ☎08821

The **Zugspitze** (2964m), Germany's tallest mountain, is the main attraction in town, and there are two ways to conquer it, though they should only be attempted in fair weather. You can take the **cog railway** from the *Zugspitzbahnhof* (50m behind the Garmisch main station) to the *Zugspitzplatt* outlook (1¼hr., every hr. 7:35am-2:35pm), then continue on the **Gletscherbahn** cable car to the top. (Round-trip with train and cable car €42.) You can also get off the cog railway at Eibsee and take the **Eibsee Seilbahn,** one of the steepest cable car runs in the world, all the way to the top (1½hr., every hr. 8am-4:15pm, round-trip with train and cable car €42).

Garmisch-Partenkirchen is accessible by train from Innsbruck (1½hr., 1 per hr., €10) or Munich (1½hr., 1 per hr., €14), and by bus #1084 and 9606 from Füssen (2hr., 6-7 per day, €7). To get to the tourist office, Richard-Strauss-Pl. 2, from the train station, turn left on Bahnhofstr., and left again onto Von-Brug-Str.; the office faces the fountain on the square. The staff distributes maps and finds rooms for free. (☎18 07 00. Open M-Sa 8am-6pm, Su 10am-noon.) To reach **Naturfreundehaus** ❶, Schalmeiweg 21, from the station, walk straight on Bahnhofstr. as it becomes Ludwigstr.; follow the bend to the right and turn left on Sonnenbergstr. Continue straight as this becomes Prof. Michael-Sachs-Str. and then Schalmeiweg (25min.). Sleep in attic lofts with 16 other backpackers. (☎43 22. Kitchen use €1. Reception 6-8pm. Loft beds €8; 3- to 5-bed dorms €10.) HL Markt, at the intersection of Bahnhofstr. and Von-Brug-Str., sells groceries. (Open M-F 8am-8pm, Sa 7:30am-4pm.)

THE CHIEMSEE

With picturesque islands, pastures, forests, marshland, and a dramatic crescent of mountains, the Chiemsee region has been luring visitors for 2000 years. Although the area has been overrun by resorts, don't expect to find many foreigners—Chiemsee is where the German *nouveaux riches* vacation.

PRIEN AM CHIEMSEE. On the southwestern corner of the Chiemsee, Prien is a good base for exploring the islands. **Trains** depart from the station, a few blocks from the city center, for Munich (1hr., every hr., €12.40) and Salzburg (50min., every hr., €9). **Ferries** run from Prien to Herreninsel and Fraueninsel (every 40min., 6:40am-7:30pm, €5.50-6.60). To get to the ferry port, turn right from the main entrance of the Prien train station and follow Seestr. for 20min., or hop on the green *Chiemseebahn* steam train from the station (9:40am-6:15pm, round-trip including ship passage €8.50). The **tourist office,** Alte Rathausstr. 11, dispenses maps and books private rooms for free. (☎690 50. Open M-F 8:30am-6pm, Sa 8:30am-noon.) The **Jugendherberge (HI)** ❷, Carl-Braun-Str. 66, is a 15min. walk from the station: go right on Seestr. and turn left on Staudenstr., which becomes Carl-Braun-Str. (☎687 70. Breakfast, showers, and lockers included. Reception 8-9am, 5-7pm, and 9:30-10pm. Open early Feb. to Nov. 4- to 6-bed dorms €15.50.) To reach **Campingpl. Hofbauer** ❶, Bernauer Str. 110, from the station, turn left on Seestr., then left again at the next intersection, and walk 25min. along Bernauerstr. heading out of town. (☎41 36. Showers included. Reception 7:30-11am and 2-8pm. Open Apr.-Oct. €6 per person, €5.10 per campsite.) Grab a cheap meal at **Bäckerei/Cafe Müller** ❷, Marktpl. 8. (Open M-F 6:30am-6pm, Sa 6:30am-12:30pm, Su 7:30-10:30am.) Try **Weininger Bräu** ❸, Bernauerstr. 13b, for excellent *Bayerische Käsespätzli* (Bavarian cheese noodles €9) and Lederhosen-clad waitstaff. (☎610 90. Open M and W-F 10am-midnight, Su 9am-midnight.) **Phone code:** ☎08051.

HERRENINSEL AND FRAUENINSEL. Ludwig's palace on **Herreninsel** (Gentlemen's Island), **Königsschloß Herrenchiemsee,** is a shameless attempt to be larger and more extravagant than Louis XIV's Versailles. Ludwig bankrupted Bavaria building this place—a few unfinished rooms (abandoned after funds ran out) contrast greatly with the completed portion of the castle. (Open Apr.-Sept. daily 9am-6pm; Oct. 9:40am-5pm; Nov.-Mar. 9:40am-4pm. Mandatory tour €5.50, students €4.50.) **Fraueninsel** (Ladies' Island), is home to the **Klosterkirche** (Island Cloister), the nunnery that complemented the monastery on Herreninsel. The nuns make their own marzipan, beeswax candles, and five kinds of liqueur, for sale in the convent shop. The 8th-century **Cross of Bischofhofen** and other artifacts are displayed in the Michaelskapelle above the **Torhalle** (gate), the oldest surviving part of the cloister. (Open May-Oct. 11am-5pm. €2, students €1.50.) **Phone code:** ☎08054.

BERCHTESGADEN ☎08652

The area's natural beauty and the sinister attraction of Hitler's mountaintop retreat, **Kehlsteinhaus** ("Eagle's Nest"), draw world travelers to the town. The stone resort house, now a restaurant, has a spectacular view from the 1834m peak. (Open daily May-Oct. except heavy snow days.) From the train station, take bus #38 to Obersalzburg/Hintereck (June-Oct. every 45min., Nov.-May much less regularly; round-trip €3); at Hintereck, catch bus #49 to Kehlstein Parkpl./Eagle's Nest (June-Oct. every 30min. 9:30am-4pm, Nov.-Mar. much less regularly; €12). Be sure to reserve your spot for the return bus when you get off. **Trains** run hourly to Munich (3hr., €24.80) and Salzburg (1hr., €6.60). The **tourist office,** Königsseerstr. 2, opposite the station, has tips on **hiking** trails in the Berchtesgaden National Park. (☎96 71 50. Open mid-June to Oct. M-F 8:30am-6pm, Sa 9am-5pm, Su 9am-3pm; Nov. to mid-June M-F 8:30am-5pm, Sa 9am-noon.) To get to the **Jugendherberge (HI)** ❷, Gebirgsjägerstr. 52, turn right from the station, left on Ramsauer Str., right on Gmündbrücke, and left up the steep gravel path. You can also take bus #39 (dir.: Strub Kaserne) to Jugendherberge. (☎943 70. Breakfast and sheets included. Reception 6:30-9am and 5-7pm. Check-in until 10pm. Curfew midnight. Closed Nov.-Dec. 26. 10-bed dorms €15.40.) For groceries, stop by the **Edeka Markt,** Königsseer Str. 22. (Open M-F 7:30am-6pm, Sa 7:30am-noon.) The nearby **Bäckerei-Konditorei Ernst,** Königseer Str. 10, sells fresh bread and pastries. (Open M-F 6:30am-6pm, Sa 6:30am-noon.) **Postal Code:** 83471.

HIKING NEAR BERCHTESGADEN. From Berchtesgaden, the 5.5km path to the Königssee—which winds through fields of flowers, across bubbling brooks, and past several beer gardens—affords a heart-stopping view of the Alps. From the train station, cross the street, turn right, and take a quick left over the bridge. Walk to the right of and past the green-roofed building (but not up the hill) and take a left onto the gravel path near the stone wall, then follow the "Königssee" signs. Alternatively, take bus #41 from the bus station to Königssee (round-trip €3.40). Once you arrive in Königstein, walk down Seestr. and look for the Nationalpark Informationstelle to your left, which has hiking information. To explore the **Berchtesgaden National Park,** take bus #46 from Berchtesgaden (15min., 6:10am-7:25pm., €2.10). Get off at the Neuhausenbrücke stop in Ramsau, then visit the Ramsau **tourist office,** Im Tal 2, for trail maps and hiking information. (☎(08657) 98 89 20. Open Oct.-Jun. M-F 8am-noon and 1:15-5pm; Jul.-Sept. M-Sa 8am-noon and 1:15-5pm, Su 9am-noon and 2-5pm.)

PASSAU ☎0851

This beautiful 2000-year-old city embodies the ideals of Old World Europe. Passau's Baroque architecture peaks at the sublime **Stephansdom,** Domplatz, where cherubs sprawl across the ceiling and the world's largest church organ looms above the choir. (Open daily in summer 6:30am-7pm; in winter 6:30am-6pm. Free. Organ concerts May-Oct. M-F noon, Th 7:30pm. €3, students €1; Th €5, students €3.) Behind the cathedral is the **Residenz,** home to the **Domschatz,** an extravagant collection of gold and tapestries. (Enter through the back of the Stephansdom, to the right of the altar. Open Easter-Oct. M-Sa 10am-4pm. €1.50, students €0.50.) The heights of the river during various floods are marked on the outside wall of the 13th-century Gothic **Rathaus.** (Open Apr.-Oct. daily 10am-4pm. €1.50, students €1.) Over the Luitpoldbrücke bridge is the former palace of the bishopric, now home to the **Cultural History Museum.** (Open Apr.-Oct. M-F 9am-5pm, Sa-Su 10am-6pm; Nov.-Mar. Tu-Su 9am-5pm. €4, students €2.50.)

Trains depart the **Hauptbahnhof** for: Frankfurt (4½hr., every 2hr., €64); Munich (2hr., every 2 hr., €27); Nuremberg (2hr., every 2hr., €31); and Vienna (3½hr., 1 per hr., €31). To get to the **tourist office,** Rathauspl. 3, follow Bahnhofstr. from the train station to Ludwigspl., bear left downhill across Ludwigspl. to Ludwigstr., which becomes Rindermarkt, Steinweg, and finally Große Messerg.; continue straight on Schusterg. when the street ends and turn left on Schrottg. (☎95 59 80. Open Easter to mid-Oct. M-F 9am-5pm, Sa-Su 9am-1pm.) To reach **Pension Rößner ❸,** Bräug. 19, from the *Rathaus*, walk downstream along the Danube. These homey rooms are the cheapest in the *Altstadt.* (☎93 13 50. Breakfast included. Singles €35; doubles €50-60.) The **Jugendherberge (HI) ❷,** Veste Oberhaus 125, is perched high above the Danube. Hop on the *Pendelbus* (shuttle bus), from Rathauspl., bound for the museum adjacent to the hostel. (Easter to mid-Oct. every 30min. M-F 10:30am-5pm, Sa-Su 11:30am-6pm; €1.50, same-day round-trip €2.) The clean, elegant hostel has a pretty location. (☎413 51. Breakfast included. Reception 7am-1pm and 1:30-11:30pm. Dorms €15.70.) The student district centers on **Innstraße.,** which runs parallel to the Inn River, and is lined with good, cheap places to eat. Pick up groceries at **Edeka supermarket,** Ludwigstr. 2, at the intersection with Grabeng. (Open M-F 8am-8pm, Sa 8am-4pm.) Get fruit, meat, baked goods, sandwiches, and salad by weight at **Schmankerl Passage ❷,** Ludwigstr. 6. (Open M-F 7:30am-6pm, Sa 7:30am-2pm.) **Postal Code:** 94032.

REGENSBURG ☎0941

Regensburg is alive with students and with places that cater to their appetites for food, drink, and fun. The city is reputed to have more cafes and bars per square meter than any other city in Europe. The **Dom St. Peter** dazzles with richly colored stained glass. Inside, the **Domschatz** (Cathedral Treasury) displays gold and jewels purchased by the bishops, as well as the preserved hand of Bishop Chrysostomus, who died in AD 407. (Open Apr.-Oct. daily 6:30am-6pm; Nov.-Mar. 6:30am-5pm. Free. Wheelchair-accessible.) A few blocks away, the **Rathaus** served as the capital of the Holy Roman Empire until 1803. The *Rathaus* also houses the **Reichstagsmuseum,** which details the history of the town. (English tours May-Sept. M-Sa 3pm. €2.50, students €1.25.)

Trains head to: Munich (1½hr., every hr., €19.20); Nuremberg (1-1½hr., 1-2 per hr., €14); and Passau (1-1½hr., every hr., €16.60). The **tourist office** is in the *Altes Rathaus* on Rathauspl. From the station, walk down Maximilianstr., turn left on

Grasg., turn right at the end onto Obere Bachg., and follow it for five blocks. (☎507 44 10. Open M-F 8:30am-6pm, Sa 9am-4pm, Su 9:30am-2:30pm; Apr.-Oct. open Su until 4pm.) To get from the station to the **Jugendherberge (HI) ❷,** Wöhrdstr. 60, walk to the end of Maximilianstr., turn right at the *Apotheke* onto Pflugg., and turn left immediately at the *Optik* sign onto tiny Erhardig.; at the end, take the steps down and walk left over the bridge, and veer right onto Wöhrdstr. The hostel is on the right. Or, take bus #3, 8, or 9 (€1.50) from the station to Eisstadion. (☎574 02. Breakfast included. Reception daily 6am-1am. Check-in until 1am. Dorms €17.) **Spitalgarten ❸,** St.-Katharinen-Pl. 1, has inexpensive rooms in a convenient location. Take bus #12 from the station to Stadtamhof. (☎847 74. Breakfast included. Reception daily until midnight. Reserve well in advance. Singles €22; doubles €44.) **Hinterhaus ❷,** Rote-Hahnen-Gasse 2, serves both vegetarian (from €4) and meat (from €5) dishes. (Open daily 6pm-1am.) **Historische Wurstküche,** Thundorfer Str., an 850-year-old beer garden, is ideal for sipping brews while watching ships drift by on the Danube. There's a **supermarket** in the basement of Galeria Kaufhof, on Neupfarrpl. (Open M-F 9am-8pm, Sa 9am-4pm.) **Postal Code:** 93047.

NUREMBERG (NÜRNBERG) ☎0911

Nuremberg served as the site of massive annual Nazi rallies; Allies later chose it as the site of the postwar crime trials to foster a sense of justice. Today, the townspeople are working to forge a new image for their city as the *Stadt der Menschenrechte* (City of Human Rights). While physical remnants of Nazi rule remain, Nuremberg's cultural aspects outweigh the bitter memories, and today the city is known for its Christmas market and sausages as much as for its ties to Nazism.

TRANSPORTATION AND PRACTICAL INFORMATION. Trains go to: Berlin (6hr., every 2hr., €78-120); Frankfurt (3½hr., 2 per hr., €36-55); Munich (2½hr., 2 per hr., €38); and Stuttgart (2¾hr., 6 per day, €28). **DB Reisezentrum,** located in the central hall of the station, sells tickets. (Open daily 6am-9:30pm.) The **tourist office,** Königstr. 93, books rooms for free. Walk through the tunnel from the station to the *Altstadt* and take a right. (☎233 61 31. Open M-Sa 9am-7pm.) **Internet** access is available at **Flat-s,** on the second floor of the train station. (€1 for 15min. Open M-Th 7am-11pm and continuously from F 7am to Su 11pm.) **Postal Code:** 90402.

ACCOMMODATIONS AND FOOD. Jugendgästehaus (HI) ❷, Burg 2, is in a castle above the city. From the tourist office, follow Königstr. through Lorenzerpl. and over the bridge to the Hauptmarkt. Head towards the fountain on the left and bear right on Burgstr., then head up the hill. (☎230 93 60. Reception daily 7am-1am. Curfew 1am. 4- to 6-bed dorms €18.) For **Gasthof Schwänlein ❸,** Hintere Sterng. 11, take the underground passage from the station to Königstr. and immediately turn left on Frauentormauerstr; follow the town wall and bear right onto Hintere Sterng. (☎22 51 62; fax 241 90 08. Breakfast included. Reservations by fax or mail only. Singles €26-28, with shower €30-33, with bath €36-38; doubles €41-43/€46-49/€52-57.) **Sushi Glas ❸,** Kornmarkt 7, next to the Nationalmuseum, attracts a chic yuppie crowd with delicious Japanese specialties. (Open M-W noon-11pm, Th-Sa noon-midnight, Su 6-11pm). Try Nuremberg's famous *Rostbratwurst* (sausage) at the **Bratwursthäusle ❷,** Rathauspl. 1, next to the Sebalduskirche. (Open M-Sa 10am-10:30pm.) **Edeka,** Hauptmarkt 12, near the Frauenkirche, sells **groceries.** (Open M-F 8:30am-7pm, Sa 8am-3pm.)

SIGHTS AND ENTERTAINMENT. Allied bombing left little of Nuremberg intact; its churches, castle, and other buildings have all been reconstructed. The walled-in Handwerkerhof market near the station is a tourist trap masquerading as a historical attraction; head up Königstr. for the real sights. Take a detour to the left for the pillared **Straße der Menschenrechte** ("Avenue of Human Rights") as well as the **Germanisches Nationalmuseum,** Kartäuserg. 1, which chronicles German art from pre-history to the present. (Open Tu and Th-Su 10am-5pm, W 10am-9pm. €4, students €3; free W 6-9pm.) Head on to the Gothic **Lorenzkirche,** on Lorenzpl., which features a 20m tabernacle. (Open M-Sa 9am-5pm, Su noon-4pm. Free German tours; in summer M-Sa 11am and 2pm, Su 2pm; in winter M-F 2pm.) Across the river are the **Frauenkirche** (open M-Sa 9am-6pm, Su 12:30-6pm) and the **Hauptmarktplatz,** the site of the annual **Christmas market.** Hidden in the fence of the **Schöner Brunnen** (Beautiful Fountain), in the northwest corner of the Hauptmarkt, is a seamless gold-colored ring. If you can find it, spinning it will supposedly bring good luck. Walk uphill to the **Rathaus;** the **Lochgefängnisse** (dungeons) beneath contain medieval torture instruments. (Open Tu-Su 10am-4:30pm. Mandatory tours every 30min. €2, students €1.) Across from the *Rathaus* is the **Sebalduskirche,** which houses the remains of St. Sebaldus for 364 days a year; on the 365th, they're paraded around town. (Open June-Sept. daily 9:30am-8pm; Mar.-May and Oct.-Dec. 9:30am-6pm; Jan.-Feb. 9:30am-4pm.) Atop the hill, the **Kaiserburg** (Emperor's fortress), Nuremberg's symbol, offers the best vantage point of the city. (Open Apr.-Sept. daily 9am-6pm; Oct.-Mar. 10am-4pm. Mandatory tours every 30min. €5, students €4.)

The ruins of **Dutzendteich Park,** site of the Nazi Party Congress rallies, remind visitors of Nuremberg's darker history. On the far side of the lake is the **Tribüne,** the marble platform where throngs gathered to hear Hitler. The exhibit "Fascination and Terror," in the **Kongresshalle,** at the north end of the park, covers the rise of the Third Reich and the war crimes trials. (Open M-F 9am-6pm, Sa-Su 10am-6pm. €5, students €2.50.) To reach the park, take S2 (dir.: Freucht/Altdorf) to Dutzendteich, then take the middle of three exits, head down the stairs, and turn left. Walk past the lake on your left and turn left, then right after it to reach the Kongresshalle. On the other side of town, Nazi leaders faced Allied judges during the infamous Nuremberg war crimes trials, held in room 600 of the **Justizgebäude.** (Fürtherstr. 110. U1 (dir.: Stadthalle) to Bärenschanze and continue on Fürtherstr. Tours Sa-Su 1, 2, 3, and 4pm. €2, students €1.)

Nuremberg's nightspots are clustered around the *Altstadt;* the best are in the west, near the river. **Cine Città,** Gewerbemuseumspl. 3, has 16 bars and cafes, 21 cinemas, an IMAX theater, and a disco. (Open M-Th and Su until 3am, F-Sa until 4am.) **Frizz,** Weißgerberg. 37, is a hip bar that sweats to the oldies and 80s rock. (Cover for men €2, women no cover. Open M and Th 8pm-2am, F-Sa 8pm-4am.) Mellow and dimly-lit, **Cafe Ruhestörung,** Tetzelg. 21, draws a large number of 20-somethings. (Open M-W 7:30am-1am, Th-F 7:30am-2am, Sa 9am-2am, Su 9am-1am.)

ROMANTIC ROAD

Between Würzburg and Füssen lies a beautiful countryside of colorful castles, walled cities, elaborate churches, and dense forests. In 1950, the German tourist industry christened these bucolic backwaters the Romantic Road (Romantische Straße), and the region has since become the most visited in Germany.

☐ TRANSPORTATION. Europabus runs daily at 10am from bus platform #13 in Würzburg through Rothenburg ob der Tauber to Füssen. Students receive a 10% discount, Eurail and German Rail Pass holders 60%. For reservations or additional information, contact **EurAide.** (☎ (089) 59 38 89; www.euraide.de/romantic.) A more flexible and economical way to travel the Romantic Road is by the frequent **trains** that connect all the towns.

WÜRZBURG. Surrounded by vineyard slopes and bisected by the Main River, Würzburg is a famous university town. In 1895 Wilhelm Conrad Röntgen discovered X-rays here and was awarded the first Nobel Prize. Inside the striking **Fortress Marienburg** are the 11th-century **Marienkirche**, the 40m Bergfried watchtower under which lies the **Hole of Fear** (dungeon), and the **Fürstengarten,** built to resemble a ship. Outside the main fortress is the castle arsenal, which now houses the **Mainfränkisches Museum.** Take bus #9 from the station to Festung, or walk toward the castle on the hill. (40min. tours depart from the main courtyard Apr.-Oct. Tu-F 11am, 2, and 3pm; Sa-Su every hr. 10am-4pm. €2, students €1.50. Museum open Apr. to mid-Oct. Tu-Su 9am-6pm; mid-Oct. to Mar. 10am-4pm. €2.50/€2.) The **Residenz,** on Residenzpl., houses the largest ceiling fresco in the world, and the **Residenzhofkirche** inside is a Baroque fantasy of gilding and pink marble. (Open Apr. to mid-Oct. daily 9am-6pm, Th until 8pm; mid-Oct. to Mar. 10am-4pm. €4, students €3. English tours Sa-Su 11am and 3pm.) Trains head to: Frankfurt (2hr., 2 per hr., €19); Munich (3hr., 1 per hr., €39); Nuremberg (1hr., 2 per hr., €15); and Rothenburg ob der Tauber (1hr., 1 per hr., €9). The **tourist office,** in the Haus zum Falken on the Marktpl., provides maps and helps find rooms. (☎37 23 98. Open M-F 10am-6pm, Sa-Su 10am-2pm; Nov.-Mar. closed Su.) The **Jugendgästehaus (HI) ❷,** Burkarderstr. 44, is housed in a villa with views of the fortress and river. Take streetcar #3 or 5 to Löwenbrücke, and backtrack. (☎425 90. Breakfast included. Check-in 5-10pm. Curfew 1am. Dorms €18.) **Phone code: ☎**0931.

ROTHENBURG OB DER TAUBER. After the Thirty Years' War, Rothenburg had no money to modernize; it remained unchanged for 250 years. When it became a tourist destination at the end of the 19th century, new laws protected the integrity of the medieval *Altstadt.* Today, Rothenburg is probably your only chance to see a walled medieval city without a single modern building. After the war, the conquering general promised to spare the town from destruction if any local could chug a wine keg—3.25L of wine. The mayor successfully met the challenge, then passed out for several days. The **Meistertrunk** is reenacted each year, and the town clock performs a slow motion version every hour over the Marktpl. For many other fascinating tidbits of Rothenburg history, take the 1hr. English tour led by the ☒**night watchman,** which starts from the *Rathaus.* (Easter-Christmas daily 8pm. €3.) The 60m tower of the Renaissance **Rathaus,** on Marktpl., provides a panoramic view of the town. (Open Apr.-Oct. daily 9:30am-12:30pm and 1-5pm; Nov.-Mar. noon-3pm, Dec. closed M-F. €1.) The ☒**Medieval Crime Museum,** Burgg. 3, exhibits torture instruments for anyone who can stomach the thought of iron-maiden justice. (Open Apr.-Oct. daily 9:30am-6pm; Nov. and Jan.-Feb. 2-4pm; Dec. and Mar. 10am-4pm. €3, students €2.) Head to **Christkindlmarkt** (Christ Child Market), Herrng. 2, and **Weihnachtsdorf** (Christmas Village), Herrng. 1, which houses a **Christmas Museum** documenting the evolution of gift-giving. (Open M-F 9am-6:30pm, Sa 9am-4pm, Su 11am-6pm; Jan. to mid-May closed Su.)

Trains run to and from Steinach (15min., €1.75), where you can transfer to trains for Würzburg and Munich. The **Europabus** leaves from the *Busbahnhof,* next to the train station. The **tourist office,** Marktpl. 2, books rooms. (☎404 92. Open M-F 9am-noon and 1-6pm, Sa 10am-3pm; Nov.-Apr. M-F 9am-noon and 1-5pm, Sa 10am-1pm.) There are also many **private rooms** not registered with the tourist office; look for *Zimmer frei* signs and knock on the door to inquire. **Phone code: ☎09861.**

FÜSSEN. At the foot of the Romantic Road, nestled in the foothills of the Bavarian Alps, the name Füssen (feet), is apt for this little town. Füssen's main attraction is its easy access to Ludwig's famed **Königsschlösser** (see p. 521). Within the town, the inner walls of the **Hohes Schloß** (High Castle) courtyard feature arresting *trompe-l'oeil* windows and towers; the **Staatsgalerie** in the castle shelters a collection of regional late Gothic and Renaissance art. (Open Apr.-Oct. Tu-Su 11am-4pm; Nov.-Mar. 2-4pm. €2.50, students €2.) Inside the **Annenkapelle,** macabre paintings depict everyone from the Pope and Emperor to the smallest child engaged in the *Totentanz* (death dance), a public frenzy of despair that overtook Europe during the plague. (Open Apr.-Oct. Tu-Su 11am-4pm, Nov.-Mar. 2-4pm. €2.50, students €2.) **Trains** run to **Munich** (2hr., every 2hr., €18). Füssen can also be reached by **bus** #1084 or 9606 from **Garmisch-Partenkirchen** (2¼hr., €7). To get from the train station to the **tourist office,** Kaiser-Maximilian-Pl. 1, walk the length of Bahnhofstr. and head across the round-about to the big yellow building on your left. The staff finds rooms for free. (☎938 50. Open Apr.-Sept. M-F 8:30am-6:30pm, Sa 9am-12:30pm, Su 10am-noon; Oct.-Mar. M-F 9am-5pm, Sa 10am-noon.) To reach the **Jugendherberge (HI) ❷,** Mariahilfer Str. 5, turn right from the station and follow the tracks for 10min. (☎77 54. Reception 7am-noon and 5-10pm. Closed Nov. Dorms €14.) **Phone code: ☎08362.**

KÖNIGSSCHLÖßER (ROYAL CASTLES)

King Ludwig II, a zany visionary and fervent Wagner fan, used his cash to create fantastic castles. In 1886, a band of nobles and bureaucrats deposed Ludwig, had him declared insane, and imprisoned him. Three days later, the King and a loyal advisor were mysteriously discovered dead in a nearby lake. The fairy tale castles that framed Ludwig's life and the enigma of his death still captivate tourists today.

NEUSCHWANSTEIN AND HOHENSCHWANGAU. The glitzy **Schloß Neuschwanstein** is now Germany's most clichéd tourist attraction and was the inspiration for Disney's Sleeping Beauty Castle. The completed chambers (63 remain unfinished) include a Byzantine throne room, a small artificial grotto, and an immense *Sängersaal* (singer's hall) built expressly for Wagnerian opera performances. Ludwig grew up in the bright yellow, neo-Gothic **Schloß Hohenschwangau** across the way. (Both open Apr.-Sept. daily 9am-6pm, Th until 8pm; Oct.-Mar. 10am-4pm. Mandatory tours €7 per castle; combination ticket €13.) Tickets can be purchased at the Ticket-Service Center, Alpseestr. 12 (☎(08362) 93 08 30), about 100m south of the Hohenschwangau bus stop. From Füssen, hop on **bus** #73 or 78, marked Königsschlösser, which departs from the train station (10min., 2 per hr., €1.40). It will drop you in front of the information booth (open daily 9am-6pm); the Ticket-Service Center is a short walk uphill on Alpseestr. Separate paths lead up to both Hohenschwangau and Neuschwanstein. A *Tagesticket* (€5.60, from the bus driver) gives castle-hoppers unlimited regional bus use.

LINDERHOF. East of Neuschwanstein and Hohenschwangau lies **Schloß Linderhof,** Ludwig II's hunting palace. The royal bedchamber, the largest room in the castle, is covered with gold leaf and contains a colossal 454kg crystal chandelier. Even more impressive is the surrounding **park.** Paths originating at the swan lake at the park entrance weave through the ornately landscaped grounds, which include an enormous, artificial **grotto** bathed in red and blue floodlights and the **Hunding-Hütte,**

modeled after a scene from Wagner's Die Walküre. (Open Apr.-Sept. daily 9am-6pm, Th until 8pm; Oct.-Mar. 10am-4pm. Apr.-Sept. mandatory castle tour €6, students €5; Oct.-Mar. €4/€3. Park open Apr.-Sept. Free.) **Bus** #9622 connects to Linderhof from Oberammergau (20min., every hr. 9:50am-4:55pm, round-trip €5; last return bus 6:40pm). Oberammergau is accessible by **bus** #1084 from Füssen (1¾ hr., 8 per day, €7) or by **train** from Munich (1¾hr., 1 per hr., €13).

GREECE (Ελλας)

A land where sacred monasteries are mountainside fixtures, three-hour seaside siestas are standard issue, and dancing on tables until daybreak is a summer rite— Greece's treasures are impossibly varied. Much of the history of the Western world owes its character to the philosophical, literary, artistic, and athletic mastery of the ancient Greeks, and schoolkids still dream of Hercules and Medusa, only to long later for Greece's beaches and the gorgeous natural landscape, once the playground of a pantheon of gods. The all-encompassing Greek lifestyle is a mix of high speed and sun-inspired lounging: old men hold lively debates in town *plateias*, mopeds skid through the streets around the clock, and unpredictable schedules force a go-with-the-flow take on life.

SYMBOL	❶	❷	❸	❹	❺
ACCOMMODATIONS	under €10	€10-24	€25-40	€40-70	over €70
FOOD	under €5	€5-9	€10-15	€16-24	over €25

For Greece, prices are indicated in food and accommodations listings using the system of icons and price ranges above. Prices for accommodations are based on the lowest cost for one person, excluding special deals or discounts. For restaurants, prices are based on the average entree price.

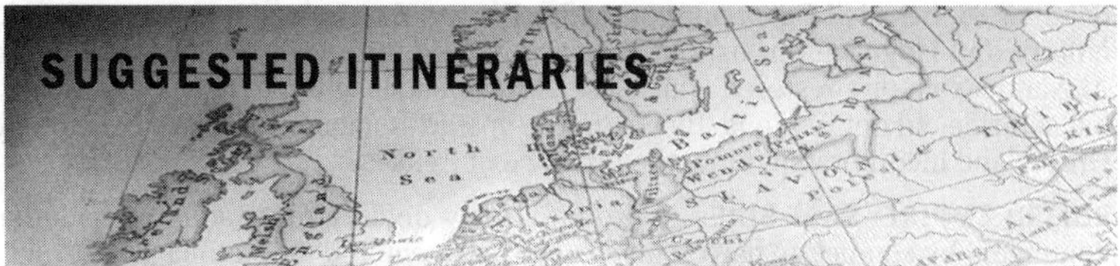

SUGGESTED ITINERARIES

THREE DAYS Spend it all in **Athens** (p. 533). Roam the **Acropolis,** gaze at the treasures of the **National Archaeological Museum,** and pay homage to the gods in the fabulous **Parthenon.** Visit the ancient Athenian **Agora,** and run a lap in the **Panathenaic Olympic Stadium.**

ONE WEEK Begin your week with a sojourn in **Athens** (3 days). Move on to **Corinth** to wander through the 6th-century **Temple of Apollo** (1 day; p. 547). Sprint to **Olympia** to see where the games began–check out the immense **Temple of Zeus** (1 day; p. 543). Take the ferry to **Corfu** (1 day; p. 553) and then soak up Byzantine history in **Thessaloniki** (1 day; p. 548). Ask the **Oracle at Delphi** how to top off your week (1 day; p. 541).

BEST OF GREECE, THREE WEEKS Explore **Athens** (4 days) before strolling among the mansions of **Nafplion** (1 day; p. 546). Race west to **Olympia** (1 day), and then take a ferry from Patras to the immortalized beaches of **Corfu** (2 days). Back on the mainland, wander the streets of **Thessaloniki** (2 days), and then climb to the cliffside monasteries of **Meteora** (1 day, p. 552). Be sure to consult the gods at **Mt. Olympus** (1 day; p. 552). and the **Oracle of Delphi** (1 day). A ferry from Athens to **Crete** (3 days; p. 562) will let you discover Europe's largest gorge. Seek respite on **Santorini** (1 day; p. 561), debauchery on **Ios** (1 day; p. 560), and suntanning on **Mykonos** (1 day; p. 558). Finally, repent at the famous temples on **Delos** (1 day; p. 558).

LIFE AND TIMES

HISTORY

THE RISE OF THE CITY-STATE. In the aftermath of Dorian invasion of Mycenaen cities in 1000 BC, the **polis,** or city-state, rose as the major Greek political structure. The heart of the city was the **acropolis,** a fortified citadel and religious center atop the highest point, and the **agora,** the marketplace and the center of commercial and social life. During the **Persian Wars** (490-477 BC), the Greeks overcame overwhelming odds to defeat the Persians in the legendary battles at Marathon, Salamis, and Plataea. The victories ushered in a period of unprecedented prosperity and artistic, commercial, and political success.

CLASSICAL GREECE. At the end of the Persian Wars, Athens established itself as the head of the **Delian League,** an organization of Greek city-states formed to defend against Persian aggression that actually acted as an Athenian empire. Athens, which prided itself in its commercial, democratic, and cultural achievements, rivaled the agricultural, oligarchical, and military Sparta in controlling Greece. The competition erupted into violence during the **Peloponnesian War** (431-404 BC), which ended in total defeat for Athens.

MACEDONIAN RULE. The period after the Peloponnesian War was marked by a gradual devolution of city-state power. Macedonia's **King Phillip** seized control in 338 BC. After Philip's assassination in 336 BC, his 20-year-old son, Alexander, later known as **Alexander the Great,** took the throne. Alexander ruled Greece with an iron fist and consolidated control of his father's empire. By the time of his sudden death at 33, he ruled Egypt and the entire Persian Empire and had spread Greek culture and language throughout the eastern Mediterranean. The dissolution of Alexander's empire restored a measure of independence to the Greek city-states, but self-rule did not last long. By 27 BC, the upstart Roman Empire had conquered Greece and incorporated it into the province of Achaea.

ROMAN EMPIRE: EAST SIDE. As Rome slowly declined, the empire became dominated by competing halves: an eastern half, centered in Anatolia, the Levant, and Greece, and a western half, centered at Rome. The unusual political arrangement ended in a scramble for power, finally won by **Constantine** in AD 312, who later legalized Christianity within his empire. He gave the Roman Empire a new capital in 324 by founding **Constantinople,** built over the ancient city of Byzantium. While Western Europe was overrun by barbarian invaders, the eastern **Byzantine Empire** became a center of learning, trade, and influence, unrivaled in its time.

NETTLESOME NEIGHBORS. During the 6th century, **Emperor Justinian**'s battles against the Sassanians of Persia overstretched the empire's strength. Power waned under the force of constant raids by Slavs, Mongols, and Avars, and in many areas of the mainland and Peloponnese, Greek culture was wiped out entirely. From 1200 to 1400, the Byzantine Empire was plagued by Norman and Venetian crusaders, who conquered and looted Constantinople in 1204 and imposed western Catholic culture upon the city. On May 29, 1453, the Ottoman Turks overran the much-reduced city, renaming it **İstanbul.** The Muslim Turkish rulers treated their Greek subjects as a **millet**—a separate community ruled by its own religious leaders. The Orthodox Greek church became the moderator of culture and tradition and the foundation of Greek autonomy. By the 19th century, Greeks were pushing for complete independence from the empire.

GREEK NATIONALIST REVOLT. On March 25, 1821, Bishop Germanos of Patras raised a Greek flag at the monastery of Agia Lavra and sparked an empire-wide

rebellion. Disorganized but impassioned guerrillas in the Peloponnese and Aegean islands waged sporadic war on the Turkish government for years. Finally, in 1829, with great support from European powers, Greece won its independence. The borders of the new Greece were narrow, including only a fraction of the six million Greeks living under Ottoman rule. For the next century, Greek politics centered around freeing İstanbul from the Turks and uniting all Greeks into one sovereign state, a project called the *Megali Idhea* (the Great Idea).

EXPAND AND CONTRACT. In 1833, the European powers declared Greece a monarchy and handed the crown to a succession of Germanic princes. The 1864 constitution, however, downplayed the power of the king and emphasized the importance of the elected prime minister. In 1919, Prime Minister **Eleftherios Venizelos** ordered an outright invasion of Turkey, but a young Turkish general, Mustafa Kemal, later called **Atatürk,** crushed the invasion. The **Treaty of Lausanne,** signed in 1923, enacted a population exchange that sent a million Greeks living in Asia Minor to Greece, and 400,000 Turkish Muslims from Greece to Turkey. This ended the *Megali Idhea* but began a series of economic problems for Greece.

THE SECOND WORLD WAR AND THE MODERN GREEK STATE. The 1930s were rocked by political turmoil, as Greeks lived through brief intervals of democracy amid a succession of monarchies and military rule. Although the nation defeated the Italian forces, Greece fell to Germany in 1941 and endured four years of bloody and brutal Axis occupation. The communist-led resistance received broad popular support, and many resistance fighters received aid from the Western powers, which were eager to prevent a communist Greece.

Civil war broke out in 1944. The left-wing, Soviet-backed Democratic Army eventually lost to the US-supplied anti-communist coalition government. Keeping a visible hand in Greek politics, the US helped place **General Papagos, Constantine Karamanlis,** and the right-wing **Greek Rally Party** in power. When Karamanlis resigned in 1963, left-wing **George Papandreou** came to power, but the right-wing respite was short-lived; the army staged a coup on April 21, 1967, which resulted in rule by a military junta for seven years. The junta ultimately fell in 1973 after a Turkish invasion of Cyprus and a nationwide student uprising.

Karamanlis returned to power in 1975, instituting parliamentary elections and organizing a referendum on the form of government. Monarchy was defeated by a two-thirds vote, and a new constitution was drawn up in 1975, calling for a parliamentary government with a ceremonial president appointed by the legislature—the system still in use today.

TODAY

In the 1980s, **Andreas Papandreou,** founder of the leftist **Panhellenic Socialist Movement (PASOK),** steered Greece into the European Economic Community (EEC) and pioneered the passage of women's rights legislation. Fellow socialist **Costas Simitis** took control of the party after the unpopular tenure of **Constantine Mitsotakis,** and has since pursued economic reforms in an attempt to meet the qualifying standards for entry into the **European Union (EU),** which became a reality in January 2001. Also in January 2001, Foreign Minister **George Papandreou** traveled to Turkey, the first such visit in 37 years. While there, he signed four cooperation agreements concerning tourism, the environment, the protection of investments, and terrorism. Talks have even begun regarding Cyprus, which remains divided into Turkish and Greek Cypriot states. Though the discussions have been fruitless so far, the dialogue has brought the nations closer and helped guarantee an extended peace in the Aegean. In the summer of 2004, the **Olympic Games** will return to their birthplace as Athens plays host to the world's athletes and spectators.

CULTURE

FOOD AND DRINK

Penny-pinching carnivores will thank Zeus for lamb, chicken, or beef *souvlaki*, stuffed into a pita to make *gyros* (yi-ROS). Vegetarians can also eat their fill on the cheap, with *horiatiki* (Greek salad) and savory pastries like *tiropita* (cheese pie) and *spanakopita* (spinach and feta pie). Frothy, iced coffee *frappés* take an edge off the heat in the summer. *Ouzo*, a powerful, licorice-flavored spirit, is served with *mezedes*, which are snacks of octopus, cheese, and sausage.

Breakfast, served only in the early morning, is generally very simple: a piece of toast with *marmelada* or a pastry. Lunch, a hearty and leisurely meal, can begin as early as noon but is more likely eaten sometime between 2 and 5pm. Dinner is a drawn-out, relaxed affair served late. A Greek restaurant is known as a *taverna* or *estiatorio;* a grill is a *psistaria.* Many restaurants don't offer printed menus.

CUSTOMS AND ETIQUETTE

BUSINESS HOURS. Normal business hours in Greece include a break from about 2 until 6pm or so. Hours vary, but banks are normally open M-F 8am-1:30pm, and also 3:30-6pm in some larger cities.

CONVERSATION. Personal questions aren't considered rude in Greece, and pointed inquires from locals can be a bit disconcerting. Expect to be asked about family, career, salary, and other personal information by people you've just met. Returning questions in kind is expected and appreciated.

LOCAL LIFE. Greek hospitality is legendary. From your first days in the country, you will be invited to drop by a stranger's home for coffee, share a meal at a local *taverna* or attend a engagement party or a baptism. The invitations are genuine; it's impossible to spend any length of time in the country and not have some friendly interaction with locals. Greet new acquaintances, shopkeepers, and waiters with *"kalimera"* (good morning) or *"kalispera"* (good evening).

PHOTOGRAPHY. Take signs forbidding photography seriously, especially in Cyprus. Never photograph anything having to do with the military. Even if photography isn't specifically forbidden in a particular church or monastery, avoid using a flash and taking pictures of the main altar.

TIPPING AND BARGAINING. There is no tipping anywhere except restaurants. Service is typically included in the bill, but leave an extra euro or two. Generally, bargaining is expected for street wares and in other informal venues, but shop owners whose goods are tagged will consider bargaining rude and disrespectful.

ART HISTORY

It is impossible to overestimate how much Western culture owes to the architectural and artistic achievements of the ancient Greeks—Augustus Caesar, Michelangelo, Jacques-Louis David, Thomas Jefferson, Constantine Brancusi, and even Salvador Dalí found inspiration in Greek works.

ART AND ARCHITECTURE. After the Dark Ages that followed the collapse of Mycenaean civilization, a new artistic style emerged with ceramics as its primary medium and Athens as its major cultural center. During the **Archaic Period** (700-480 BC), artists decorated clay figurines and pottery with geometrical motifs reminiscent of basket-weaving patterns. The Archaic Period also saw the innovation of the **Doric** and **Ionic** architectural orders. Ionic columns were distinguished from their more austere Doric predecessors by their twin **volute** (scrolled spiral) capitals, and their slender, fluted shafts.

The arts flourished as Athens reached the pinnacle of its political and economic power, in what is known as the **Classical Period** (480-323 BC). The peerless Athenian **Acropolis** (p. 538), built during this era, embodied "classic" for the entire world; its crown, the **Parthenon,** demonstrates the Greek aesthetic of perfect proportions. Sculptors mastered the representation of the human form during the Classical Period. By the middle of the 5th century BC, they had developed the **severe style,** which elevated the human form to a plane of universal physical perfection, idealizing the athletic heroism praised by Pindar's Olympic odes.

After the death of Alexander the Great, the flamboyant **Hellenistic Period** rose out of the ashes of Classical Greece. Scuttling the simpler Doric and Ionic styles, Eastern Greeks designed ornate, flower-topped **Corinthian** columns. Hellenistic architects worked on a monumental scale, building huge complexes of temples and palaces. Astoundingly precise acoustics graced the enormous amphitheaters like the one at **Epidavros** (p. 547); a coin dropped onstage is audible from the most distant seat. Hellenistic sculpture exuded passion, testing the aesthetic value of ugliness. With the arrival of the Roman Empire, styles shifted to suit Roman tastes.

The art and architecture in Greece under **Byzantine** and **Ottoman** rule belonged more to those imperial cultures than to Greece. Religious Byzantine artistry saw the creation of magnificent mosaics, iconography, and church architecture. Mosaics were composed of **tesserae,** small cubes of stone, glass-covered ceramic, or metallic foil. Sparkling examples can be seen in the churches of **Thessaloniki** (p. 548) and **Meteora** (p. 552) and at the **Monastery of Osios Loukas** (p. 542).

After Greek independence, nationalist sentiment led the government to subsidize Greek art. King Otto encouraged young artists to study their craft in Munich, and the **Polytechneion,** Greece's first modern art school, was established in 1838. While sculptors still looked to Classical Greece for inspiration, the first wave of post-independence painters showed strong evidence of their German training. Many 20th-century Greek artists contended with European trends, including Impressionism, Expressionism, and Surrealism. Other painters rejected foreign influence, among them the much-adored **Theophilos Chatzimichael** (1873-1934).

LITERATURE AND DRAMA. The first written Greek did not appear until the 8th century BC, but the Greek literary tradition may have begun as much as 150 years earlier, with the epic songs of **Homer,** including the *Iliad* and *Odyssey,* which most scholars believe survived through oral tradition alone. During the 7th century BC, **Archilochus** of Paros made what is believed to be the first contributions to written poetry in the form of anti-heroic, anti-Homeric elegies.

The foundation for modern drama was laid in the 5th century BC, in the *tragodoi* (goat songs) dedicated to the god **Dionysus.** Greek drama began as a religious rite in which all attendants performed in the chorus. Individual acting began when, at a public competition of masked choruses in Dionysus's honor, young **Thespis** stepped out of the crowd to become Athens's first actor—hence the word "thespian." By adding other characters, **Aeschylus** composed the *Oresteia* (458 BC), a trilogy about Agamemnon's ruinous return home from the Trojan War. **Sophocles**'s *Oedipus* trilogy (c. 444-401 BC) arguably founded modern dramatic tragedy.

Greek independence gave rise to the **Ionian School** of modern literature, which dealt with the political and personal issues of the Greek revolution. **Dionysios Solomos** (1798-1857), whose *Hymn to Liberty* became the Greek national anthem, is still referred to as the National Poet.

ARTS TODAY

ART AND ARCHITECTURE. Modern Greek art unfortunately tends to be overshadowed by its Classical roots. Current notable artists include **Yiannis Psychopedis** (b. 1945), whose paintings combine social and aesthetic criticism, and the painter **Opy Zouni** (b. 1941), who has won much international acclaim for her geometric art.

LITERATURE AND DRAMA. Twentieth-century poets alternately denounced and celebrated nationalism and politics. **Odysseas Elytis,** winner of a 1979 Nobel Prize in Literature, felt that French Surrealism was an integral part of national redemption. **Nikos Kazantzakis** (1883-1957) may be the best-known modern Greek author. His many novels include *Zorba the Greek* and *The Last Temptation of Christ,* both of which were made into successful films.

Contemporary playwrights like **Iakovos Kambanellis** (b. 1922), **Demitris Kehadis** (b. 1933), and Symiot writer **Eleni Haviara** have delighted audiences with their portrayals of Greek life. Taking advantage of the international attention of the Olympic Games, the **Greek Playwrights Society** (www.eeths.gr) is organizing a May 2003 festival of modern plays from local writers. But classical theater still dominates, especially at the **Athens Festival** (p. 540) and the **Epidavros Festival** (p. 547).

MUSIC. *Rembetika* (gutsy blues music with folk influences) first made its appearance in Greece in the late 19th century. After decades of inauthentic performances, interest in traditional *rembetika* has resurfaced, and musicians strumming *bouzouki* (a traditional Greek instrument similar to a mandolin) can be found in several clubs. Trendier venues offer a playlist saturated with Western music, but local band **Pyx Lax** is gaining something of an international following.

FILM. After suffering under the colonels' junta, the Greek film industry rebuilt itself throughout the 1980s and has recently emerged as a distinguished and prolific presence in the international arena. The 1982 reestablishment of the **Greek Film Center,** a state-supported institute, aided this revitalization by funding and producing many of the most highly regarded modern Greek films, including works by **Nikos Perakis, Pantelis Vougaris,** and **Nikos Panayotopoulos,** Greece's most acclaimed filmmaker and winner of the 1998 Cannes Palme d'Or.

HOLIDAYS AND FESTIVALS

Holidays: Feast of St. Basil/New Year's Day (Jan. 1); Epiphany (Jan. 6); 1st Monday in Lent (Mar. 10); Greek Independence Day (Mar. 25); St. George's Day (Apr. 23); Easter (Apr. 27); Labor Day (May 1); Ascension (June 5); Pentecost (June 15); Feast of the Assumption of the Virgin Mary (Aug. 15); The Virgin Mary's Birthday (Sept. 8); Feast of St. Demetrius (Oct. 26); Ohi Day (Oct. 28); Christmas (Dec. 25).

Festivals: Three weeks of **Carnival** feasting and dancing (Feb. 17-Mar. 10) precede Lenten fasting. April 23 is **St. George's Day,** when Greece honors the dragon-slaying knight with horse races, wrestling matches, and dances. The **Feast of St. Demetrius** (Oct. 26) is celebrated with particular enthusiasm in Thessaloniki.

ESSENTIALS

FACTS AND FIGURES

Official Name: Hellenic Republic.	**Land Area:** 131,940 sq. km.
Capital: Athens.	**Time:** GMT.
Major Cities: Thessaloniki.	**Language:** Greek.
Population: 10,600,000.	**Religion:** Eastern Orthodox (98%).

WHEN TO GO

June through August is high season in Greece; consider visiting during May or September, when the weather is equally beautiful but the crowds thinner. The off season, from mid-September through May, offers cheaper airfares and lodging, but many sights and accommodations have shorter hours or close altogether. Ferries and trains run considerably less frequently, although ski areas at Mt. Parnassos, Mt. Pelion, and Metsovo beckon winter visitors.

DOCUMENTS AND FORMALITIES

South Africans need a visa for stays of any length. Citizens of Australia, Canada, the EU, New Zealand, and the US do not need a visa for stays of up to 90 days, though they are ineligible for employment. Apply for visa extensions at least 20 days prior to the three-month expiration date at the **Aliens Bureau,** Alexandras 173, Athens 11522 (☎210 770 5711), or check with a Greek embassy or consulate.

Greek Embassies at Home: Australia, 9 Turrana St., Yarralumla, Canberra, ACT 26000 (☎02 6273 3011). **Canada,** 80 MacLaren St., Ottawa, ON K2P 0K6 (☎613-238-

6271; www.greekembassy.ca); **Ireland,** 1 Upper Pembroke St., Dublin 2 (☎01 6767 2545). **South Africa,** 1003 Church St., Hatfield, Pretoria 0028 (☎12 437 351). **UK,** 1a Holland Park, London W11 3TP (☎0171 229 3850). **US,** 2221 Massachusetts Ave. N.W., Washington, D.C. 20008 (☎202-939-5800; www.greekembassy.org).

Foreign Embassies in Greece: All embassies are located in **Athens** (see p. 533).

TRANSPORTATION

BY PLANE. Basic round-trip fares from North America to Athens range from €600-1100. Flights from London average €320. The domestic service of **Olympic Airways,** Syngrou 96-100, Athens 11741 (☎2810 114 4444), has increased greatly. A 1hr. flight from Athens (€60-90) can get you to almost any island in Greece. Even in the off season, remote destinations are serviced several times per week, while developed areas may have several flights per day.

BY TRAIN. Greece is served by a number of international train routes that connect Athens, Thessaloniki, and Larissa to most European cities. Train service within Greece, however, is limited and sometimes uncomfortable, and no lines go to the western coast. The new express, air-conditioned intercity trains, while slightly more expensive and infrequent, are worth the price. **Eurail** passes are valid on all Greek trains. **Hellenic Railways Organization** (OSE; www.osenet.gr) connects Athens to major Greek cities; from Greece, call ☎145 or 147 for schedules and prices.

BY BUS. There are almost no buses running directly from any European city to Greece. **Busabout,** 258 Vauxhall Bridge Rd., London (☎0171 950 1661; www.busabout.com), is one of the few European bus companies that runs to Greece. Domestic bus service is extensive and fares are cheap. **KTEL** (www.ktel.org) runs most domestic buses; always check with an official source about scheduled departures, as posted schedules are often outdated. Smaller towns may use cafes as bus stops. Confirm your destination with the driver; signs may be wrong. If your stop is passed, yell *"Stasi!"* (STASH; "Stop!"). Intercity buses are usually blue.

BY FERRY. The most popular way of getting to Greece is by ferry from Italy. Boats travel from Brindisi, Italy (p. 737), to Patras (p. 542), Corfu (p. 554), and Kephalonia (p. 555), and from Ancona, Italy (p. 728), to Patras and Corfu. Ferries also run from Greece to various points on the Turkish coast (p. 565). There is frequent ferry service to the Greek islands, but schedules are irregular and faulty information is common. Check schedules posted at the tourist office or the *limenarcheio* (port police), or at www.ferries.gr. Make reservations and arrive at least 1-2hr. before your departure time. **Flying Dolphins** (www.dolphins.gr) provides extensive hydrofoil service between the islands at twice the cost and speed as ferries; their routes are listed in the **Transportation** sections where appropriate.

BY CAR. Cars are a luxury in Greece, a country where public transportation is nonexistent after 7pm. Ferries charge a transport fee for cars. Rental agencies may quote low daily rates that exclude the 20% tax and **Collision Damage Waiver (CDW)** insurance; expect to pay €20-40 per day for a rental. Foreign drivers are required to have an **International Driving Permit** and an **International Insurance Certificate** to drive in Greece. The **Automobile and Touring Club of Greece (ELPA),** Messogion 395, Athens 11527, provides assistance and offers reciprocal membership to foreign auto club members. (☎01 606 8800. 24hr. emergency roadside assistance ☎104. Info line for Athens ☎174; elsewhere 01 606 8838. Open M-F 7am-3pm.)

BY BIKE, MOPED, AND THUMB. The mountainous terrain and unpaved roads make **cycling** in Greece difficult. **Mopeds** can be great for exploring, but they also make you extremely vulnerable to the carelessness of other drivers; wear a helmet. Greeks are not eager to pick up foreigners. Sparsely populated areas have little or no traffic. Visitors who choose to **hitchhike** write their destination on a sign in both Greek and English. Women should not hitch alone in Greece. *Let's Go* does not recommend hitchhiking.

TOURIST SERVICES AND MONEY

EMERGENCY	**Police:** ☎100. **Hospital:** ☎106. **Ambulance:** ☎166.

TOURIST OFFICES. Tourism in Greece is overseen by two national organizations: the **Greek National Tourist Organization (GNTO)** and the **tourist police** *(touristiki astinomia)*. The GNTO, Amerikis 2, Athens (☎01 327 1300), known as the **EOT** in Greece, can supply general information about sights and accommodations throughout the country. The tourist police (24hr. info ☎171) deal with local and immediate problems: bus schedules, accommodations, lost passports, etc. They are open long hours and are willing to help, although their English is often limited.

GNTO Offices at Home: Australia, 51 Pitt St., 3rd fl., Sydney, NSW 2000 (☎02 9241 166; hto@tpg.com.au). **Canada,** 91 Scollard St., 2nd fl., Toronto, ON M5R 1G4 (☎416-968-2220; grnto@tor.sympatico.ca); 1170 Place du Frère André, Suite 300, Montréal, QC, H3B 3C6 (☎514-871-1535). **UK,** 4 Conduit St., London W1S ODJ (☎207 734 5997; www.tourist-offices.org.uk). **US,** Head Office, Olympic Tower, 645 5th Ave., 9th fl., New York, NY 10022 (☎212-421-5777; www.greektourism.com).

MONEY. The official currency of Greece is the **euro.** The Greek drachma can still be exchanged at a rate of 340.75dr to €1. For exchange rates and more information on the euro, see p. 20. If you're carrying more than €1000 in cash when you enter Greece, you must declare it upon entry. A bare-bones day in Greece, staying at hostels, campgrounds, or *domatia* (rooms to let), and buying food at supermarkets or outdoor food stands, costs about €35. A day with more comforts, like accommodation in a nicer *domatia* or budget hotel, and eating one meal per day in a restaurant, runs €50. The European Union imposes a **value-added tax (VAT)** on goods and services purchased within the EU, included in the price (see p. 19).

ACCOMMODATIONS AND CAMPING

Lodgings in Greece are a bargain. Tourist offices usually maintain lists of inexpensive accommodations. A bed in a **hostel** averages around €7. Those not currently endorsed by HI are in most cases still safe and reputable. In many areas, **domatia** (rooms to let) are an attractive and perfectly dependable option. Often you'll be approached by locals as you enter town or disembark from your boat, a practice that is theoretically illegal, but common. Prices are quite variable; expect to pay €12-20 for a single and €25-35 for a double. Always negotiate with *domatia* owners before settling a price, and never pay more than you would for a hotel in town. If in doubt, ask the tourist police; they may set you up with a room and conduct the negotiations themselves. **Hotel** prices are regulated, but proprietors may try to push you to take the most expensive room. Budget hotels start at €15 for singles and €25 for doubles. Check your bill carefully, and threaten to contact the tourist police if you think you are being cheated. Greece hosts plenty of official **campgrounds,** which run about €4.50 per person, plus €3 per tent. Discreet freelance camping on beaches—though illegal—is common in July and August but may not be the safest way to spend the night.

GREECE

COMMUNICATION

PHONE CODES	**Country code:** 30. **International dialing prefix:** 00. The city code must always be dialed, even when calling from within the city. From outside Greece, dial int'l dialing prefix (see inside back cover) + 30 + local number.

TELEPHONES. The only way to use the phone in Greece is with a prepaid phone card. You can buy the cards at *peripteros* (streetside kiosks) in denominations of €3, €12, and €25. Time is measured in minutes or talk units (100 units=30min. of domestic calling). A calling card is the cheapest way to make international phone calls. To place a call with a calling card, contact your service provider's Greek operator: **AT&T,** ☎00 800 1311; **British Telecom,** ☎00 800 4411; **Canada Direct,** ☎00 800 1611; **Ireland Direct,** ☎00 155 1174; **MCI,** ☎00 800 1211; **Sprint,** ☎00 900 1411.

> Throughout 2002, Greece was changing its phone code system. In January, most numbers gained an additional "0" at the end of the local code; as of fall 2002, it was proposed that in November, the leading "0" of most phone numbers would become a "2." In addition, all local calls in Greece must now include the area code. Phone numbers in *Let's Go: Greece* reflect the proposed November changes, but as of press time further changes were still possible. Contact the Greek National Tourist Organization (see **Tourist Offices**) for further info.

MAIL. To send a letter weighing up to 50g within Europe costs €0.85; anywhere else in the world costs €0.90. Mail sent to Greece from the Continent generally takes at least 3 days to arrive; from the US, South Africa, and Australia airmail will take 5-10 days. Address *Poste Restante* according to the following example: Firstname SURNAME, Corfu Town Post Office, Corfu, Greece 8900, POSTE RESTANTE. The mail will go to a special desk in the central post office, unless you specify otherwise.

INTERNET ACCESS. The availability of the Internet in Greece is rapidly expanding. In all big cities, most small cities and large towns, and most of the touristed islands, you will able to find Internet access. Expect to pay between €3-6 per hour.

LANGUAGE. Although many Greeks in Athens and other heavily touristed areas—particularly young people—speak English, rural Greeks rarely do. Greek body language will help you avoid misunderstandings. To say no, Greeks lift their heads back abruptly while raising their eyebrows; they emphatically nod once to say yes. A hand waving up and down that seems to say "stay there" actually means "come." For the Greek alphabet and basic words and phrases, see p. 1024.

ATHENS (Αθηνα) ☎210

Ancient ruins sit quietly amid hectic modern streets as tacit testaments to Athens's rich history, while the Acropolis looms larger than life, a perpetual reminder of ancient glory. Byzantine churches recall an era of foreign invaders, when the city was ruled from Macedonia, Rome, and Constantinople. But the packs of mopeds in Pl. Syndagma prove that Athens refuses to become a museum—over the past two centuries, democracy has revived the city in a wave of madcap construction.

TRANSPORTATION

Flights: El. Venizelou (ATH; ☎210 353 0000), Greece's new international airport, is one massive, easily navigable terminal. Arrivals are on the ground floor, departures are on the 2nd fl. 4 bus lines run from the airport to Athens, Piraeus, and Rafina.

Trains: Hellenic Railways (OSE), Sina 6 (☎210 362 4402; www.ose.gr). **Larissis Train Station** (☎210 529 8837) serves northern Greece and Europe. Open 24hr. Take trolley #1 from El. Venizelou (also known as Panepistimiou) in Pl. Syndagma (every 10min. 5am-midnight, €0.45). Trains depart for **Thessaloniki** (7hr., 4 per day, €14.10) and **Prague, Czech Republic** (€128.60). **Peloponnese Train Station** (☎210 513 1601) serves **Patras** (4¼hr., €5.30) as well as major towns in the Peloponnese. From Larissis, exit to your right and go over the footbridge.

Buses: Terminal A: Kifissou 100 (☎210 512 4910). Take blue bus #051 from the corner of Zinonos and Menandrou near Pl. Omonia (every 15min., €0.45). Buses to: **Corinth** (1½hr., 1 per hr., €5.70); **Corfu** (10hr., 4 per day, €28); **Patras** (3hr., 30 per day, €12.25); **Thessaloniki** (6hr., 11 per day, €28). **Terminal B:** Liossion 260 (☎210 831 7153, M-F only). Take blue bus #024 from Amalias outside the National Gardens (45min., every 20min., €0.45). Buses to **Delphi** (3hr., 6 per day, €10.20).

Public Transportation: KTEL (KTEΛ) **buses** around Athens and its suburbs are blue or orange and designated by 3-digit numbers. Buy bus/trolley tickets at any street kiosk. Hold on to your ticket–you can be fined €18-30 by police if caught without one. **Trolleys** are yellow and crowded, sporting 1- or 2-digit numbers; they are distinguished from buses by their electrical antennae. **Subway:** The Athens **Metro** consists of 3 lines. **M1** runs from northern Kifissia to the port of Piraeus. **M2** runs from Ag. Antonios to Dafni. **M3** runs from Ethniki Amyna to Pl. Syndagma in central Athens. Trains run 5am-midnight. Buy tickets (€0.60) in any station.

Car Rental: Try the places on **Singrou.** €30-50 for a small car with 100km mileage (including tax and insurance). Student discounts up to 50%. Prices rise in summer.

Taxis: Meters start at €0.75, with an additional €0.25 per km; midnight-5am €0.45 per km. There's a €1.20 surcharge from the airport and a €0.60 surcharge for trips from bus and railway terminals, plus €0.30 for each piece of luggage over 10kg.

PIRAEUS PORT: FERRIES FROM ATHENS

The majority of ferries from Athens leave from the town of Piraeus Port. Ferries sail to nearly all Greek islands (except the Sporades and Ionian Islands). Ferries to Crete: **Hania** (9½hr., 1 per day, €17.60); **Iraklion,** (14hr., 3 per day, €21-26); and **Rethymno** (11hr., 1 per day, €21.40). Additional ferries to: **Chios** (9hr., 1 per day, €18.10); **Hydra** (3hr., every hr., €14.30); **Ios** (7½hr., 2-5 per day, €16.70); **Lesvos** (12hr., 1 per day, €22.40); **Milos** (7hr., 2-5 per day, €15.80); **Mykonos** (6hr., 2-5 per day, €16.30); **Naxos** (6hr., 2-5 per day, €16.10); **Paros** (6hr., 2-5 per day, €16.10); **Poros** (2½hr., every hr., €13.20); **Rhodes** (15hr., 2-5 per day, €26.80); **Santorini** (9hr., 2-5 per day, €18.70); and **Spetses** (4½hr., every hr., €20.50).

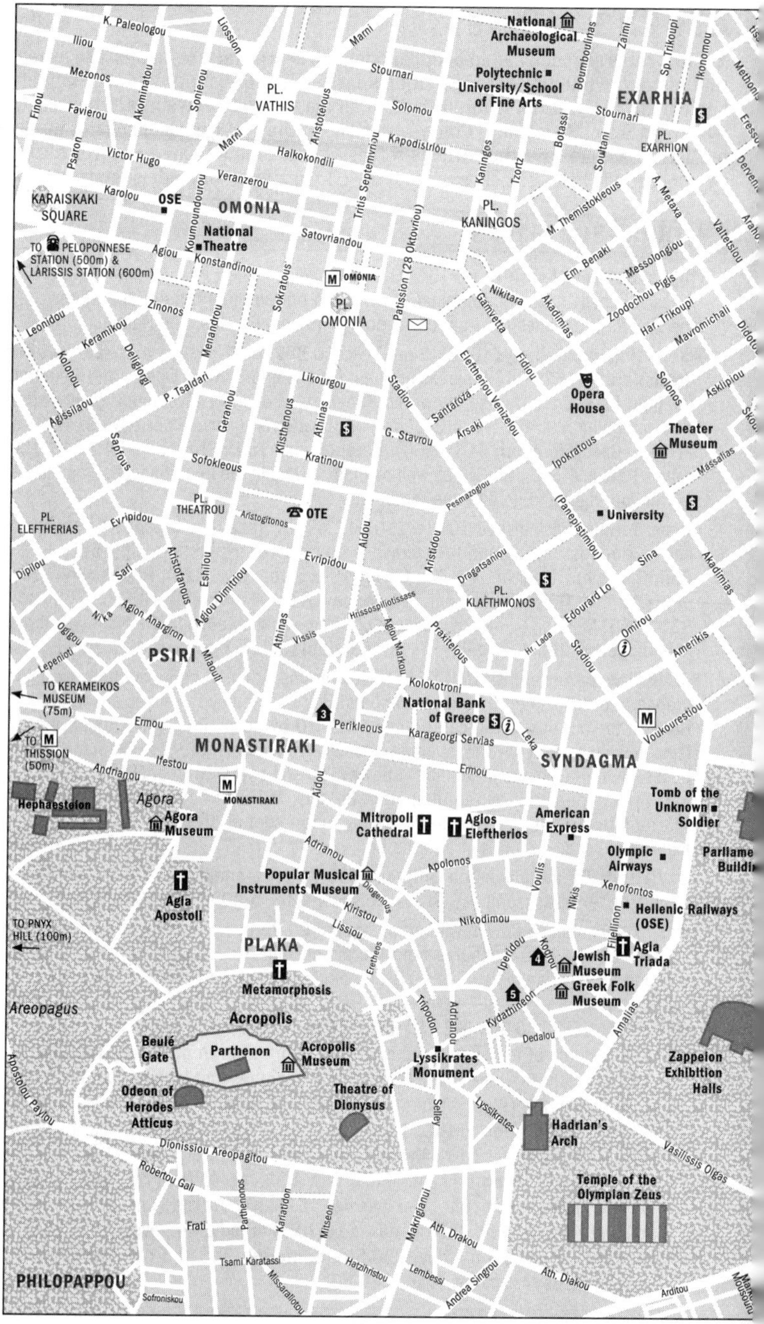
National Archaeological Museum
Polytechnic University/School of Fine Arts
EXARHIA
PL. EXARHION
PL. VATHIS
OMONIA
OSE
KARAISKAKI SQUARE
National Theatre
TO PELOPONNESE STATION (500m) & LARISSIS STATION (600m)
PL. KANINGOS
OMONIA
PL. OMONIA
Opera House
Theater Museum
PL. THEATROU
OTE
PL. ELEFTHERIAS
University
PL. KLAFTHMONOS
PSIRI
TO KERAMEIKOS MUSEUM (75m)
National Bank of Greece
TO THISSION (50m)
MONASTIRAKI
SYNDAGMA
Agora
Hephaesteion
Agora Museum
MONASTIRAKI
Mitropoli Cathedral
Agios Eleftherios
American Express
Tomb of the Unknown Soldier
Olympic Airways
Popular Musical Instruments Museum
Agia Apostoli
Hellenic Railways (OSE)
TO PNYX HILL (100m)
PLAKA
Agia Triada
Jewish Museum
Greek Folk Museum
Metamorphosis
Areopagus
Acropolis
Beulé Gate
Parthenon
Acropolis Museum
Lyssikrates Monument
Zappeion Exhibition Halls
Odeon of Herodes Atticus
Theatre of Dionysus
Hadrian's Arch
Temple of the Olympian Zeus
PHILOPAPPOU

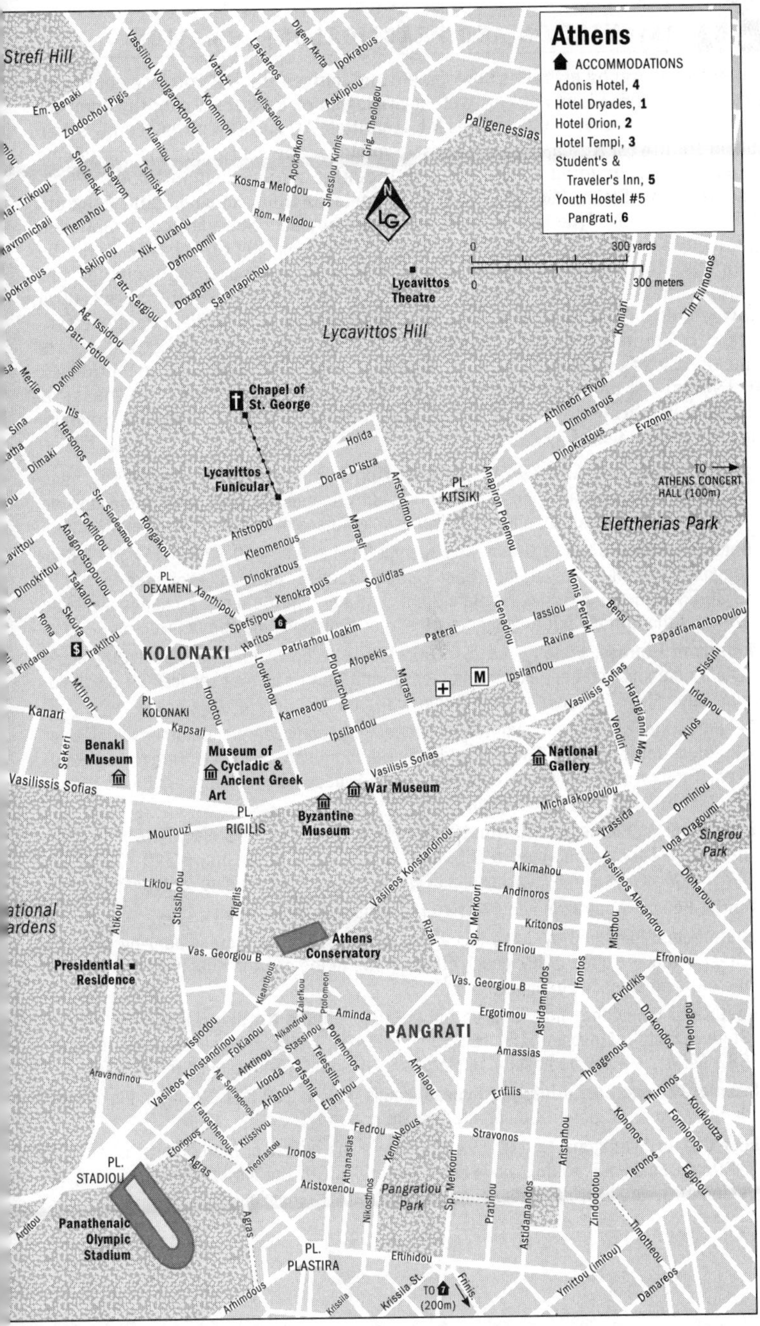
Athens
ACCOMMODATIONS
Adonis Hotel, 4
Hotel Dryades, 1
Hotel Orion, 2
Hotel Tempi, 3
Student's & Traveler's Inn, 5
Youth Hostel #5 Pangrati, 6
300 yards
300 meters
Lycavittos Theatre
Lycavittos Hill
Chapel of St. George
Lycavittos Funicular
Strefi Hill
KOLONAKI
PL. KOLONAKI
PL. DEXAMENI
PL. KITSIKI
TO ATHENS CONCERT HALL (100m)
Eleftherias Park
Benaki Museum
Museum of Cycladic & Ancient Greek Art
War Museum
Byzantine Museum
National Gallery
PL. RIGILIS
Singrou Park
Athens Conservatory
Presidential Residence
PANGRATI
Pangratiou Park
PL. STADIOU
Panathenaic Olympic Stadium
PL. PLASTIRA
TO 7 (200m)
Vasilissis Sofias
Vas. Georgiou B
Vasileos Konstandinou
Vassileos Alexandrou
Michalakopoulou
Papadiamantopoulou
Paligenessias
Kosma Melodou
Rom. Melodou
Sarantapichou
Xanthipou
Spefsipou
Haritos
Patriarhou Ioakim
Karneadou
Ipsilandou
Kanari
Kapsali
Mourouzi
Likiou
Aravandinou
Eftihidou
Krissila St.
Ymittou (Imitou)
Damareos
Efroniou
Ergotimou
Amassias
Stravonos
Aristoxenou
Ironos

GREECE

ORIENTATION AND PRACTICAL INFORMATION

Athenian geography mystifies newcomers and natives alike. If you lose your bearings, ask for directions back to well-lit **Syndagma** or look for a cab; the **Acropolis** serves as a reference point, as does **Mt. Lycavittos.** Athens's suburbs occupy seven hills in southwest Attica, near the coast. Syndagma, the central *plateia* containing the Parliament building, is encircled by the other major neighborhoods. Clockwise, they are **Plaka, Monastiraki, Psiri, Omonia, Exarhia, Kolonaki,** and **Pangrati.** Plaka, the center of the old city and home to many accommodations, is bounded by the city's two largest ancient monuments—the **Temple of Olympian Zeus** and the Acropolis. Monastiraki's frenetic flea market is home to vendors who sell rugs, furniture, leather, and all varieties of souvenirs. Omonia is the site of the city's central subway station. Two parallel avenues, **Panepistimiou** and **Stadiou,** connect Syndagma to Omonia. Omonia's neighbor to the east, progressive Exarhia, sports some of Athens's most exciting nightlife, while nearby Kolonaki, on the foothills of Mt. Lycavittos, has plenty of glitz and swanky shops. Pangrati, southeast of Kolonaki, is marked by several Byzantine churches, a park, the **Olympic Stadium,** and the **National Cemetery.**

GREECE

Tourist Office: Amerikis 2 (☎210 331 0565), off Stadiou near Pl. Syndagma. Bus, train, and ferry schedules and prices; lists of museums, embassies, and banks; brochures on travel throughout Greece; and an indispensable Athens map. Open M-F 9am-4:30pm.

Banks: National Bank of Greece, Karageorgi Servias 2 (☎210 334 0015), in Pl. Syndagma. Open M-Th 8am-2pm, F 8am-1:30pm; open for **currency exchange** only M-Th 3:30-5:20pm, F 3-6:30pm, Sa 9am-3pm, Su 9am-1pm. Currency exchange available 24hr. at the **airport,** but exchange rates and commissions may be unfavorable.

American Express: Ermou 7 (☎210 322 3380), in Pl. Syndagma. Cashes traveler's checks commission-free, exchanges money, and provides travel services for cardholders. Open M-F 8:30am-4pm, Sa 8:30am-1:30pm.

Laundromats: Most *plintirios* have signs reading "Laundry." A grandmother who lives at **Angelou Geront 10,** in Plaka, provides full laundry service for €8. Open M-Sa 8am-7pm, Su 9am-2pm. **National,** Apollonos 17, in Syndagma. Wash and dry €4.50 per kg. Open M-Th 8am-5pm, F 8am-8pm.

Emergencies: Police, ☎100. **Doctor,** ☎105 from Athens, 101 elsewhere; line open daily 2pm-7am. **Ambulance,** ☎166. **Fire,** ☎199. **AIDS Help Line,** ☎210 722 2222. *Athens News* lists emergency hospitals. Free emergency health care for tourists.

Tourist Police: Dimitrakopoulou 77 (☎171). English spoken. Open 24hr.

Pharmacies: Identified by a **red** (signifying a doctor) or **green cross** hanging over the street. Many are open 24hr.; check *Athens News* or the chart in pharmacy windows for the day's emergency pharmacy.

Hospitals: Emergency hospitals on duty ☎106. **Geniko Kratiko Nosokomio** (Public State Hospital), Mesogion 154 (☎210 777 8901). **Ygeia,** Erithrou Stavrou 4 (☎210 682 7904), is a private hospital in Maroussi. "Hospital" is *nosokomio* in Greek.

Internet Access: Berval Internet Access, Voulis 44A (☎210 331 1294), in Plaka near Pl. Syndagma. €5 per hr. Open daily 9am-9pm.

Post Office: Syndagma (☎210 322 6253), on the corner of Mitropoleos. Open M-F 7:30am-8pm, Sa 7:30am-2pm. **Postal Code:** 10300. Branch offices in **Omonia,** at Aiolou 100, and **Exarhia,** at the corner of Zaimi and K. Deligiani.

ACCOMMODATIONS

The **Greek Youth Hostel Association,** Damareos 75, lists hostels in Greece. (☎210 751 9530. Open daily M-F 9am-3pm.) The **Hellenic Chamber of Hotels,** Karageorgi Servias 2, provides info and makes reservations for all types of hotels throughout Greece. Reservations require a cash deposit; you must contact them at least one month in advance and know the length of your stay and the number of people. (☎210 323 7193. Open May-Nov. M-Th 8:30am-2pm, F 8:30am-1:30pm, Sa 9am-12:30pm.)

Student's and Traveler's Inn, Kydatheneon 16 (☎21 324 4808), in Plaka. Unrivaled location and lively atmosphere. Bring your own sheets and towel, and ask for toilet paper at the desk. Midnight curfew. Reserve ahead and arrive on time. Co-ed dorms €15-20; doubles €30-47; triples €45-60; quads €75-80. ❷

Adonis Hotel, Kodrou 3 (☎210 324 9737), in Plaka. From Syndagma, follow Filellinon; turn right on Nikodimou and left onto Kodrou. A family hotel with a delightful rooftop lounge. Reserve far in advance. All rooms with bath. Singles €27-39; doubles €56; triples €74. A/C €10 extra per person. Discounts for longer stays. ❸

Hotel Tempi, Aiolou 29 (☎210 321 3175), in Monastiraki. Simple rooms with ceiling fans. Ask for a brighter, front-facing room. Free luggage storage. Laundry service available. Check-out 11am. Singles €30; doubles €40, with bath €48; triples €55. Off-season 20% discount. ❸

Pella Inn, Karaiskaki 1 (☎210 325 0598), in Monastiraki. Walk 10min. down Ermou from Pl. Syndagma; it's two blocks from the Monastiraki subway station. Features a large terrace with impressive views of the Acropolis. Free luggage storage. Dorms €10-12; doubles €30-35; triples €36-55; quads €48-60. ❷

Hotel Dryades, Dryadon 4 (☎210 382 7116), in Exarhia. Elegant Dryades offers some of Athens's nicest budget accommodations, with large rooms and private baths. Internet €2 per 30min. Singles €35-40; doubles €44-53; triples €50-65. ❸

Hotel Orion, Em. Benaki 105 (☎210 382 7362), in Exarhia. From Pl. Omonia, walk up Em. Benaki or take bus #230 from Pl. Syndagma. Orion rents small rooms with shared baths. Sunbathers relax on the rooftop. Internet €2 per hr. Laundry €3. Singles €20-30; doubles €30-36; triples €36-40. Bargain for better prices. ❷

Youth Hostel #5 Pangrati, Damareos 75 (☎210 751 9530). From Omonia or Pl. Syndagma, take trolley #2 or 11 to Filolaou. There's no sign for this cheery hostel, just a green door. Owner speaks English. Hot showers €0.50 for 5min. Sheets €0.75; pillowcases €0.50. Laundry €3. Quiet hours 2-5pm and 11pm-7am. Dorms €7.50. Bring a sleeping bag to stay on the roof (€6). ❶

Hotel Omiros, Apollonos 15 (☎210 323 4486), near Pl. Syndagma. Relatively spacious rooms have A/C and private baths. Breakfast included. Call ahead. Singles €50; doubles €75; triples €93; quads €111. Bargain for student discounts. ❹

FOOD

Athens offers a mix of fast-food stands, open-air cafes, side-street *tavernas,* and intriguing restaurants. Cheap food abounds in **Syndagma** and **Omonia.** Pick up groceries at the markets on **Nikis.**

Pluto, Plutarchou 38 (☎210 724 4713), in Kolonaki. Chic, warm ambience with an international menu. Try the grilled eggplant with feta and tomatoes (€8.50) or strawberry meringue (€9). Open daily 11am-3pm. ❸

Eden Vegetarian Restaurant, Lysiou 12 (☎210 324 8858), in Plaka. Fantastic dishes like *boureki* pie (zucchini with feta; €4.90), as well as flavorful mushroom *stifado* with onions and peppers (€8.80). Open W-M noon-midnight. ❷

Dragon Palace, Andinoros 1 (☎210 724 2795), in Pangrati. Delicious Chinese food €7-12. Open daily 6:30pm-midnight; also open noon-1pm in winter. ❷

Kallimarmaron, Eforionos 13 (☎210 701 9727), in Pangrati. Serves some of the best traditional Greek food in the city. Entrees €10-20. ❹

Yiantes, Valtetsiou 44 (☎210 330 1369), in Exarhia. A vine-covered oasis that serves a complete Greek meal for €15. Fresh fish €6. Open daily 1pm-1am. ❷

Jungle Juice, Aiolou 21, under the Acropolis (☎210 331 6739). A fresh-squeezed smoothie and sandwich stand. Snag a turkey sandwich (€1.50) and a "Leone Melone," a blend of cantaloupe, mango, and pineapple (€3). Open daily 8am-9pm. ❶

GREECE

SIGHTS

ACROPOLIS

☎210 321 0219. Open in summer daily 8am-7:30pm; off-season 8am-2:30pm. Admission includes access to all of the sights below the Acropolis (including Hadrian's Arch, the Olympian Temple of Zeus, and the Agora) within a 48hr. period; tickets can be purchased at any of the sights. €12, students €6.

Looming majestically over the city, the Acropolis complex has been the heart of Athens since the 5th century BC. Although each Greek *polis* had an *acropolis* ("high point of the city"), the buildings atop Athens's central peak outshone their imitators and continue to awe visitors today. Visit as early in the day as possible to avoid crowds and the broiling midday sun.

TEMPLE OF ATHENA NIKE. This tiny cliff-side temple was raised during the Peace of Nikias (421-415 BC), a respite from the Peloponnesian War. The temple, known as the "jewel of Greek architecture," is ringed by eight miniature Ionic columns and once housed a statue of the winged goddess of victory, Nike. One day, in a paranoid frenzy, the Athenians were seized by a fear that Nike would flee the city and take peace with her, so they clipped the statue's wings. The remains of the 5m-thick **Cyclopean wall,** predating the Classical Period, lie below the temple.

PARTHENON. The **Temple of Athena Parthenos** (Athena the virgin), more commonly known as the Parthenon, keeps vigil over Athens and the modern world. Ancient Athenians saw their city as the capital of civilization, and the **metopes** (scenes in the open spaces above the columns) on the sides of the Parthenon celebrate Athens's rise. On the far right of the south side—the only side that has not been defaced—the Lapiths battle the Centaurs; on the east side, the Olympian gods defeat the giants; the north depicts the victory of the Greeks over the Trojans; and the west depicts their triumph against the Amazons.

ERECHTHEION. The Erechtheion, to the left of the Parthenon, was completed in 406 BC, just before Sparta defeated Athens in the Peloponnesian War. The building takes its name from the snake-bodied Erechtheus; the eastern half is devoted to the goddess of wisdom, Athena, the western half to the god of the sea, Poseidon.

ACROPOLIS MUSEUM. The museum, which neighbors the Parthenon, houses a superb collection of sculptures, including five of the original Caryatids that supported the south side of the Erechtheion. The statues seem to be replicas, but a close look at the folds of their drapery reveals individualized detail. *(Open in summer M 11am-7:30pm, Tu-Su 8am-7:30pm; off-season M 11am-2pm, Tu-Su 8am-2pm.)*

ELSEWHERE ON THE ACROPOLIS. The southwest corner of the Acropolis looks down over the **Odeon of Herodes Atticus,** a theater dating from the Roman period (AD 160). See the *Athens News* for a schedule of events. *(Entrance on Dionissiou Areopagitou. ☎210 322 1459. Purchase tickets at the door or by phone.)*

OTHER SIGHTS

AGORA. The Agora served as the city's marketplace, administrative center, and center of daily life from the 6th century BC to AD 500. Here, the debates of Athenian democracy raged; Socrates, Aristotle, Demosthenes, Xenophon, and St. Paul all preached here. Today, visitors have free reign over what is now an archaeological site. The 415 BC **Hephaesteion,** on a hill in the northwest corner of the Agora, is the best-preserved classical temple in Greece, flaunting **friezes** depicting Hercules's labors and Theseus's adventures. The **Stoa of Attalos** was a multi-purpose building filled with shops and home to informal gatherings of philosophers. Reconstructed in the 1950s, it now houses the **Agora Museum,** which contains relics from the site. According to Plato, Socrates's first trial was held at the recently excavated **Royal Stoa,** to the left of the Adrianou exit. *(Enter the Agora off Pl. Thission, from Adrianou, or as you descend from the Acropolis. Open Tu-Su 8:30am-3pm. €4, students and EU seniors €2, under 18 and EU students free.)*

KERAMEIKOS. The Kerameikos's geometric design is clearly visible from above, even before entering the grounds; the site includes a large-scale cemetery and a 40m-wide boulevard that ran through the Agora and the Diplyon Gate and ended at the sanctuary of **Akademos,** where Plato founded his academy. The **Oberlaender Museum** displays finds from the burial sites; it houses an excellent collection of highly detailed pottery and sculpture. *(Ermou 48, northwest of the Agora. From Syndagma, walk toward Monastiraki on Ermou for 25min. Open Tu-Su 8:30am-3pm. €2, students and EU seniors €1, under 18 and EU students free.)*

TEMPLE OF OLYMPIAN ZEUS AND HADRIAN'S ARCH. In the middle of downtown Athens, you'll spot what's left of the largest temple ever built in Greece: fifteen Corinthian columns of the Temple of Olympian Zeus. Started in the 6th century BC, it was completed 600 years later by Roman emperor Hadrian, who attached his name to the centuries-long effort by adding an arch to mark the boundary between the ancient city of Theseus and Hadrian's own new city. *(Vas. Olgas at Amalias, next to the National Garden. Open Tu-Su 8:30am-3pm. Temple €2, students and EU seniors €1, under 18 and EU students free. Arch free.)*

IN RECENT NEWS

STARTING BLOCKS

Throughout 2002, extensive preparations were underway in Athens in anticipation of the 2004 Olympic Games. Cranes towered over the city, and scaffolding blanketed buildings everywhere. The seemingly endless projects gave the appearance that all was running smoothly—but the reality was that the clock was ticking and funds were quickly disappearing. In July 2002, Gianna Angelopoulos-Daskalaki, the president of the Organizing Committee (ATHOC), announced that budget cuts were being implemented in order to decrease construction time and costs.

When Athens won the bid for the Olympics in 1997, the city and the IOC allotted a budget of €2.5 billion; as of August 2002, the city expected their costs would total almost €4.4 billion. The remodeling of the Olympic Stadium alone had already exceeded the original estimate by €119 million. ATHOC decided to cut back on spending by cancelling the construction of facilities that would have the least pertinence in the aftermath of the games. Plans to build a new football stadium were all but dropped, and the committee scrambled for an alternative venue for this popular event. Despite the financial difficulties, ATHOC remains adamant that Athens would be prepared to host the 2004 Olympic Games, over a century since the city first welcomed international athletes in the world's inaugural modern games.

OLYMPIC STADIUM. The Panathenaic Olympic Stadium is wedged between the National Gardens and Pangrati, carved into a hill. The site of the first modern Olympic Games in 1896, the stadium is now being refurbished in preparation for the **2004 Summer Olympics.** A new Olympic stadium sits in the northern suburb of Irini; take the M1 Metro line right to it. *(On Vas. Konstantinou. From Syndagma, walk up Amalias 15min. to Vas Olgas, then follow it left. Alternatively, take trolley #2, 4, or 11 from Syndagma. Open daily 8am-8:30pm. Free.)*

AROUND SYNDAGMA. Be sure to catch the changing of the guard in front of the **Parliament** building. Every hour on the hour, two *evzones* (guards) wind up like toy soldiers, kick their tasselled heels in unison, and fall backward into symmetrical little guardhouses on either side of the **Tomb of the Unknown Soldier.** Athens's endangered species—greenery and shade—are preserved in the **National Gardens.** Women should avoid strolling here alone.

MT. LYCAVITTOS. Of Athens's seven hills, Lycavittos is the largest and most central. Ascend at sunset to catch a glimpse of Athens's densely packed rooftops in waning daylight and watch the city light up for the night. At the top is the **Chapel of St. George,** a popular spot for weddings. A leisurely stroll around the church provides a view of Athens's panoramic expanse.

NATIONAL ARCHAEOLOGICAL MUSEUM. This astounding collection deserves a spot on even the most packed itinerary. The museum's highlights include the archaeologist Heinrich Schliemann's treasure, the **Mask of Agamemnon,** a death mask of a king who lived at least three centuries earlier than Agamemnon himself. *(Patission 44. Take trolley #2, 4, 5, 9, 11, 15, or 18 from the uphill side of Syndagma, or trolley #3 or 13 from the north side of Vas. Sofias. Open Apr.-Oct. M 12:30-7pm, Tu-Su 8am-7pm; Nov.-Mar. 8am-5pm; holidays 8:30am-3pm. €6, students and EU seniors €3; Nov.-Mar. free Su and holidays.)*

NATIONAL GALLERY. The National Gallery (a.k.a. Alexander Soutzos Museum) exhibits the work of Greek artists, with periodic international displays. The permanent collection includes works by El Greco, as well as drawings, photographs, and sculpture gardens. *(Vas. Konstantinou 50. Set back from Vas. Sofias, by the Hilton. ☎210 723 5857. Open M and W-Sa 9am-3pm, Su 10am-2pm. €6.50, students and seniors €3.)*

ENTERTAINMENT AND NIGHTLIFE

The weekly *Athens News* (€1) gives locations, hours, and phone numbers for events, as well as news and ferry information. The **Athens Flea Market,** adjacent to Pl. Monastiraki, is a jumble of second-hand junk and valuable antiques. Sunday is the best day, when it is open from 8am-1pm. Summertime performances are staged in **Lycavittos Theater** as part of the **Athens Festival,** which has included acts from the Greek Orchestra to Pavarotti to the Talking Heads. The **Festival Office,** Stadiou 4, sells tickets. (☎210 322 1459. Open M-F 9:30am-4pm, Sa-Su 9:30am-2pm. Tickets €10-16. Student discounts.) The cafe/bar flourishes throughout Athens, especially in **Kolonaki.** In summertime, chic Athenians head to the seaside clubs of **Glyfada,** past the airport. **Privilege, Venue,** and **Prime,** all along Poseidonos, are perfect places to enjoy the breezy night air. (Dress well; no shorts. Drinks €4-10. Cover €10-15.) Take the A3 or the B3 bus from Vas. Amalias to Glyfada (€0.75), and then catch a cab from there to your club. Taxis to Glyfada run about €8, but the return trip typically costs more.

Vibe, Aristophanous 1 (☎210 324 4794), just beyond Plateia Iroön in Monastiraki. Unusual lighting makes a great atmosphere.

Bee (☎210 321 2624), at the corner of Miaoli and Themidos, off Ermou; a few blocks from the heart of Psiri in Monastiraki. DJs spin while the friendly staff keeps the booze flowing. Drinks €3-9. Open daily 9pm-late.

Cafe 48, Karneadou 48 (☎210 725 2434). Classicists and students exchange stories at the bar and practice their dart game in the back room. With a student ID, beer costs €3. Free shot with each drink on Tu and Th. Open M-Sa 9am-2am, Su 4pm-2am.

The Daily, Xenokratous 47 (☎210 722 3430). Kolonaki's chic student population converges here to imbibe, listen to Latin and reggae, and watch sports on TV. Fabulous outdoor seating and open-air bar. Drinks €3-6. Open daily 9am-2am.

GREECE

DAYTRIPS FROM ATHENS

TEMPLE OF POSEIDON

Two buses travel to Cape Sounion from Athens: the shorter and more scenic route leaves from the Mavromateon 14 bus stop near Areos Park (2hr., every hr., €4.10). Get off the bus at the last stop and head up to the right past the cafeteria to a ticket booth. ☎22320 39 363. Open daily 10am-sunset. €4, students €2, EU students free.

Gracing the highest point on **Cape Sounion,** 65km from Athens, the Temple of Poseidon has been a dazzling white landmark for sailors at sea for millennia. The original temple was constructed around 600 BC, destroyed by the Persians in 480 BC, and rebuilt by Pericles in 440 BC; there are 16 remaining Doric columns.

MARATHON

The bus from the Mavromateon 29 station in Athens heads to Marathon (1½hr., every hr. 5:30am-10:30pm, €2.45); look for the bus's "Marathon" label. Sit in front and remind the driver of your destination, and flag the bus down on the way back.

Immediately after running 42km to spread word of the Athenian victory in the 490 BC battle of Marathon, **Phidippides** collapsed and died. Today, runners trace the route between Athens and Marathon twice per year, beginning at a commemorative plaque. With a car, you can explore nearby sights and beaches. At **Ramnous,** 15km northeast, lie the ruins of the **Temple of Nemesis,** goddess of divine retribution, and **Thetis,** goddess of law and justice. **Schinias** to the north and **Timvos Marathonas** to the south are popular beaches.

DELPHI

Buses leave Athens for Delphi from Terminal B, Liossion 260 (3hr., 6 per day, €10.20).

As any Delphinian will proudly attest, Delphi (pop. 2500) marks the *omphalos* (belly button) of the earth. According to the ancients, Zeus discovered this fact by releasing two eagles, one toward the east and one toward the west. They collided, impaling each other with their beaks, directly over Delphi. A sacred stone marks the spot. Troubled denizens of the ancient world journeyed to the **Oracle of Delphi,** where the priestess of Apollo related the god's cryptic advice. The **Temple of Apollo** is the centerpiece of the oracle site; other attractions include an ancient theater and stadium. Head east out of town to reach the site. (Open 7:30am-6:45pm. Museum and site €9, students and seniors €5, EU students free; museum or site only €6/3/free.) The **tourist office,** Friderikis 12, is in the town hall. (☎22650 82 900. Open M-F 8am-2:30pm.) If you spend the night, stay at **Hotel Sibylla ❷,** Pavlou 9, which has wonderful views and private baths at the best prices in town. (☎22650 82 335. Singles €15; doubles €20; triples €27.)

OSIOS LOUKAS

Take the Delphi Bus from Terminal B to Arahova (2hr., 6 per day, €10.30). From there, you'll need to hire a taxi (☎22670 31 566; €15-20 each way). Monastery open May 3-Sept. 15 daily 8am-2pm and 4-7pm; Sept. 16-May 2 8am-5pm. €3, seniors €2, students and under 18 free.

Mountain vistas and stunning Byzantine architecture delight visitors to Osios Loukas. The exquisite monastery, built in the 10th and 11th centuries and still in use today, overlooks Boeotia and Phokis from the green slopes of Mt. Elikon more than 1700m above sea level. When visiting, dress modestly. There are two churches at the site. The **Katholikon,** on the right after the museum, is the most impressive of the monastery's jewels. Built on the classic "Greek cross" basilica plan, the church features brilliant mosaics. The smaller **Church of Panagia** holds the dried body of saint Osios Loukas, as well as a **crypt** with stunning frescoes that should not be missed.

THE PELOPONNESE (Πελοποννεσος)

A hand-shaped peninsula stretching its fingers into the Mediterranean, the Peloponnese is steeped in history and folklore that contribute to its otherworldly atmosphere. The majority of Greece's top archaeological sites are here, including Olympia, Mycenae, Messene, Corinth, Mystras, and Epidavros. A world apart from the islands, the serenely beautiful and sparsely populated Peloponnese has been continuously inhabited for 5000 years, making it a bastion of Greek village life.

FERRIES TO ITALY AND CRETE

Boats go from Patras to destinations in Italy, including Brindisi, Trieste, Bari, Ancona, and Venice. **Manolopoulous,** Othonos Amalias 35, in Patras, sells tickets. (☎2610 223 621. Open M-F 9am-8pm, Sa 10am-3pm, Su 5pm-8pm.) Questions about departures from Patras should be directed to the Port Authority (☎2610 341 002). Ferries also sail from Gythion to Crete (7hr., Tu and Sa 1 per day, €18).

PATRAS (Πατρας) ☎2610

Sprawling Patras, Greece's third-largest city, serves primarily as a transport hub for island-bound tourists; during **Carnival** (mid-Jan. to Ash Wednesday), however, the port becomes one gigantic dance floor consumed by pre-Lenten madness. Follow the water to the west end of town to reach **Agios Andreas,** the largest Orthodox cathedral in Greece, which holds magnificent frescoes and St. Andrew's holy head. (Dress modestly. Open daily 9am-dusk.) Sweet black grapes are transformed into *Mavrodaphne* wine at the **Achaïa Clauss Winery,** the country's most famous vineyard. Take bus #7 (30min., €0.85) from the intersection of Kolokotroni and Kanakari. (Open May-Sept. daily 11am-8pm; Oct.-Apr. 9am-8pm. In summer free tours every hr. noon-5pm. Free samples.)

Trains (☎2610 639 110) leave from Othonos Amalias for: Athens (3½-5hr., 8 per day, €5.50-10); Kalamata (5½hr., 2 per day, €5); and Olympia (1½hr., 8 per day, €3-6) via Pyrgos. **KTEL buses** (☎2610 623 886) leave from Othonos Amalias for: Athens (3hr., 33 per day, €12.25); Ioannina (4hr., 4 per day, €14.55); Kalamata (4hr., 2 per day, €14); Thessaloniki (8hr., 3 per day, €28.25); and Tripoli (4hr., 2 per day, €10.45). **Ferries** go to: Corfu (6-8hr., 1 per day, €19-22); Ithaka (2½hr., 1 per day, €11) via Kephalonia (€10); and Italy (see above). The **tourist office** is on Othonos

Amalias, between 28 Octovriou and Astingos. (☎2610 461 740. Open daily 7:30am-12:30am.) The **Youth Hostel ❶**, Iroon Polytechniou 62-68, occupies a creaky turn-of-the-century mansion. (☎2610 427 278. Dorms €9.) The friendly, cafeteria-style **Europa Center ❶**, on Othonos Amalias between the customs exit and the bus station, serves cheap, large portions. (Entrees €3-5.50.) **Postal Code:** 26001.

OLYMPIA (Ολυμπια) ☎26240

Set among meadows and shaded by cypress and olive trees, modern Olympia is a friendly town whose mega-attraction—the ancient **Olympic arena**—draws hordes of tourists. The gigantic **Temple of Zeus** dominates **Ancient Olympia,** although **Hera's Temple,** dating from the 7th century BC, is better preserved. The **Archaeological Museum** has an impressive sculpture collection that includes the **Nike of Paionios** and the **Hermes of Praxiteles.** Maps, available at the site (€2-4), are essential for navigation. (Site open in summer daily 8am-7pm. Museum open M noon-3pm, Tu-Su 8am-7pm. Site or museum €6, both €9; students and seniors €3/€5; under 18 and EU students free.)

Buses run to Tripoli (4hr., 3 per day, €7.80). The **tourist office,** on Kondili, is on the east side of town toward the ruins. (☎26240 23 100. Open M-F 8am-3pm, Sa reduced hours.) **Zounis Rooms ❷,** two blocks uphill from Kondili, between the National Bank and Pirgos, has pleasant rooms with balconies. (☎26240 22 644. No reception, ask for the proprietor at the Anesi Cafe-Tavern, 13 Avgerinou. Singles €15; doubles €25; triples €30.) **Camping Diana ❶** is uphill from Kondili, past the Sports Museum. (☎26240 22 314. €5 per person, children €3.50; €3.50 per car, €3.50-5 per tent. 10% student discount.) **Minimarkets** along **Kondili** sell picnic fixings. Restaurants on Kondili are overpriced, but a walk toward the railroad station or up the hill leads to inexpensive *tavernas*. **Postal Code:** 27065.

TRIPOLI (Τριπολη) ☎2710

The transportation hub of Arcadia, Tripoli is crowded and fast-paced; the *plateias* and huge city park are a break in the city's otherwise urban landscape. The **Archaeological Museum** on Evangelistrias, Pl. Ag. Vasiliou, has a large prehistoric collection, including pottery, jewelry, and weaponry from the Neolithic to the Mycenaean periods. **Trains** arrive from: Athens (4hr., 4 per day, €8); Corinth (2½hr., 3 per day, €4.50); and Kalamata (2½hr., 4 per day, €4.50). **Buses** arrive at Pl. Kolokotronis, east of the center of town, from Athens (3hr., 14 per day, €15.50) and Nafplion (1hr., 4 per day, €3.50). Buses arrive at the KTEL Messenia and Laconia depot, across from the train station, from Kalamata (1½hr., 12 per day, €5.20) and Sparta (1hr., 10 per day, €3.40). **Hotel Alex ❸,** Vas. Georgiou 26, between Pl. Kolokotronis and Pl. Agios Vasiliou, has spacious, spotless rooms. (☎2710 223 465. Singles €30; doubles €50; triples €60.) Try the goat with mushrooms in egg and lemon sauce (€8.20) at **Klimataria ❸,** on Eth. Antistasis, four blocks past the park as you walk from Pl. Petriou. (Entrees €10-12.) **Postal Code:** 22100.

DIMITSANA AND STEMNITSA ☎27950

The villages of Dimitsana (Δημητσανα) and Stemnitsa (Στεμνιτσα), west of Tripoli, are excellent bases for excursions into the idyllic, rugged countryside. Arcadian **Dimitsana** clings to a steep, rocky mountainside covered with pines; every turn in the road reveals another spectacular vista. The **Lousios River** is popular for swimming and rafting in the summer and fall, but winter snows bring the most visitors to the village. **Bus** service is erratic, but buses are scheduled to leave each day for Olympia (1hr., 1 per day, €4.30) and Tripoli (1½hr., 2 per day, €3.60). *Domatia* are really the only lodging option; most establishments are beautifully furnished. Try above the **grocery store ❸.** (☎27950 31 084. Singles €30; doubles €38.)

FROM THE ROAD

DOMATIAN NATION

Getting a room in a *domatia* at a fair price can be quite an ordeal. Once, two men offered to drive me to the next village and "fix me up" with a room for the night. In Greece, "fix you up" often translates to "do my uncle a favor and pass you off to him." Sure enough, my "friends" delivered me to an older gentleman and then took off with hardly a farewell.

It's customary to try and bargain with *domatia* owners, but this man was a force to be reckoned with. He drew the same figure on the table in front of him again and again, refusing to budge. I was tired, hungry, and weighed down by my heavy pack–and the old man knew it. At a bus stop or ferry dock, multiple offers make bargaining much easier. But once you're in the *domatia,* owners know you just want to take a load off and settle down right there. I had walked right into a trap and we both knew it.

Luckily, I hadn't parted with any cash when the owner threw me out a few hours later for turning on the heat in my room. Another man who lived in the house walked me out, telling me the proprietor was "very difficult." This man then promised to "fix me up" at a place down the road. Alarms went off, but I decided to take a chance. I took one look at the beautiful room, heard the indecently low price, and immediately scrapped the hasty resolution I'd made moments ago to never trust the kindness of strangers.

–Kevin Connor

A lengthy but beautiful 11km stroll (taxi €4) along the road from Dimitsana will bring you to **Stemnitsa,** whose narrow cobblestone streets recall the village's medieval roots. Many consider the town the most beautiful in Greece. **Buses** allegedly arrive daily from Tripoli and Dimitsana, but service is irregular. The splendid **Hotel Triokolonion ❸** is on the left side of the main road from Dimitsana. Its terrace offers a relaxing place to unwind after a day of hiking. (☎27950 81 297. Breakfast included. Reserve ahead. Singles €25-30; doubles €40; triples €53.)

KALAMATA (Καλαματα) ☎27210

Kalamata, the second-largest Peloponnesian city, flourishes as a port and beach resort, and also serves as a useful transportation hub. Take a bus from Kalamata (1hr., M-Sa 2 per day, €1.50) to **Ancient Messene** in nearby **Mavromati,** one of Greece's most impressive archaeological sites. The remains of a theater, stadium, gymnasium, public baths, and nine different temples have been uncovered, but the city's **defensive walls** usually receive the most attention. The 3m thick walls circle a 9km perimeter. (Open daily 24hr. Free.) To reach the train station, walk toward the waterfront in Pl. Georgiou, turn right on Frantzi at the far end of the *plateia,* and walk a few blocks to Sideromikou Stathmou. **Trains** run to: Athens (6½hr., 4 per day, €7) via Tripoli (2½hr., €2.80); Corinth (5¼hr., €5.60); and Patras (5½hr., 4 per day, €5). **Buses** leave from the station on Artemidos to: Athens (4hr., 11 per day, €14); Patras (4hr., 2 per day, €13.50); Sparta (2hr., 2 per day, €3); and Tripoli (2hr., €4.50). **Tourist information** is available at **D.E.T.A.K.,** Polivou 6, just off Aristomenous near the Old Town. (☎27210 21 700. Open M-F 7am-2:30pm.) **Hotel George ❷,** on Dagre near the train station, is convenient, clean, and comfortable. (☎27210 27 225. Singles €20; doubles €26.) Good meals can be found along the waterfront. Before leaving town, sample the famous Kalamata olives and figs. The immense **New Market,** across the bridge from the bus station, has an assortment of meat, cheese, and fruit shops, as well as a daily farmer's market.

KARDAMYLI (Καρδαμυλη) ☎27210

Kardamyli's gorgeous white pebble beach and views of the surrounding mountains captivate an increasing number of foreign visitors. One kilometer along the waterfront towards Kalamata is the magnificent **Ritsa Beach,** on an enormous natural bay encircled by barren mountains. Trail maps for the nearby **Taygetus Mountains,** a limestone range home to the rare *testudo marninata* turtle, can be found in many of

Kardamyli's tourist shops and bookstores. A popular 1½hr. hike begins in town; the trail has black and yellow markers. **Buses** leave from the *plateia* and go to: Athens (6hr., 1 per day, €19); Kalamata (1hr., 5 per day, €2.40); and Itilo (30min., 4 per day, €2.40), where you can switch to the Areopolis bus (20min., €0.80). *Domatia* are everywhere, but start with the excellent, cheap rooms let by **Olympia Domatia ❷.** To get there, turn right off the main road across from the post office. (☎27210 73 623. Singles €17; doubles €24; triples €30.) Two **supermarkets** are just past the *plateia* towards Kalamata.

PYLOS (Πυλος) AND METHONI (Μεθωνη) ☎27230

The town of Pylos is wonderfully and mystifyingly untouristed. At **Neocastro,** a right off the road to Methoni, well-preserved walls enclose a fast-decaying church and citadel. (☎27230 22 010. Open Tu-Su 8:30am-3pm. €3, seniors and students €2, children and EU students free.) The beautiful **Yialova Beach** is 6km north of town; unfortunately, only the Athens bus goes there, so it's better to find your own transportation. In Homer's *Odyssey*, Nestor met Telemachus at **Nestor's Palace,** built in the 13th century BC. Take one bus from Pylos to Kyparissia (1½hr., 5 per day, €3.60) and then another (30min., €1) to the site. (Open daily 8:30am-3pm. €2, seniors and students €1, children and EU students free.) From Pylos, **buses** (☎27230 22 230) go to: Athens (6½hr., 2 per day, €17.50); Kalamata (1½hr., 9 per day, €3); and Methoni (15min., 6 per day, €0.80). The Pylos **tourist police** are in the same building as the police, on the left side of the *plateia* as you face inland. (☎27230 23 733. Open daily mornings only.) There are several signs for *domatia* as the bus descends into Pylos. The **Pension ❷,** off Nileos by the post office, is cheap for the area and has high-ceilings, private baths, and A/C. (☎27230 22 748. Singles €20; doubles €25; triples €29.) Pylos's waterfront restaurants cook up *taverna* staples accompanied by sunset views of the sea. **Postal Code:** 24001.

Just 15min. from Pylos by bus, Methoni's hibiscus-lined streets and relaxed atmosphere are a reprieve from the bustle of Kalamata. No visitor should miss the **☑Venetian fortress,** a 13th-century mini-city. (Open M-Sa 8:30am-7pm, Su 9am-7pm. Free.) **Buses** from Methoni run to: Athens (6hr., 2 per day, €15.40); Kalamata (2hr., €3.65); and Pylos (15min., 7 per day, €0.80). **Hotel Galini ❷** is near the end of the lower road to the left of the small *plateia*. (☎27230 31 467. A/C. Private baths. Singles €20-34; doubles €33-44). **Seaside Camping Methoni ❶** is a 5min. walk down the Methoni beach to the right of the *plateia*. (☎27230 31 228. €3.40 per person, €2.05 per car, €2.35 per small tent.) In the *plateia*, **Meltemi ❷** serves excellent traditional entrees. (*Moussaka* €4.) **Postal Code:** 24006.

SPARTA (Σπαρτη) AND MYSTRAS (Μυστρας) ☎27310

With public gardens, palm-lined boulevards, and citizens who now make olive oil instead of war, Sparta is a hospitable place to visit and makes a great base for exploring the impressive Byzantine ruins of Mystras. A public park, **Ancient Sparta** is only a 1km walk north down Paleologou. The ruins, including the last rows of one of the larger theaters of antiquity, lie in a scenic olive grove. **Buses** from Sparta go to: Areopolis (1½hr., 2 per day, €4.80); Athens (3½hr., 9 per day, €12.65) via Corinth (2½hr., €7.60) and Tripoli (1hr., €3.40); Gythion (1hr., 5 per day, €2.60); and Monemvasia (2hr., 3 per day, €6.15). To reach the town center from the bus station, walk about 10 blocks west on Lykourgou; the **tourist office** is to the left of the town hall. (☎27310 24 852. Open daily 8am-2pm.) **Hotel Apollon ❸,** Thermopilion 84, across Paleologou from Hotel Cecil, is wackily decorated but clean. (☎27310 22 491. Private baths. Breakfast €4.50. Singles €25-30; doubles €35-44.)

Mystras, 4km from Sparta, was once the religious center of all Byzantium and the locus of Constantinople's rule over the Peloponnese. Its extraordinary hillside ruins comprise a city of Byzantine churches, chapels, and monasteries. At the extreme left of the lower tier as you face the hillside is the **Church of Peribleptos,** whose exquisite religious paintings remain Mystras's most stunning relics despite Ottoman vandalization. Slightly higher is the **Pantanassa,** a still-operating convent with beautiful frescoes and flowers. Modest dress is required. Finally, at the top of the hill is the **castle,** with magnificent views of the surrounding countryside. (Open in summer daily 8am-7pm; in winter 8:30am-3pm. €5, children and EU students free.) **Buses** from Sparta to the top of the ruins leave from the station and from the corner of Lykourgou and Leonidou (20min., 9 per day, €0.80).

GYTHION (Γυθειο) AND AREOPOLIS (Αρεοπολη) ☎27330

Near sand and stone beaches, **Gythion** is the liveliest town in Mani and a good base for visiting other villages. A tiny causeway to the left of the waterfront as you face inland connects it to the island of **Marathonisi,** where Paris and Helen consummated their ill-fated love. **Buses** in Gythion leave from the north end of the waterfront, to the right as you face inland, for: Athens (4hr., 6 per day, €15.10) via Tripoli (2hr., €6); Corinth (3hr., €10.95); Kalamata (2hr., 2 per day, €6.20); and Sparta (1hr., €2.60). **Moto Makis Rent-A-Moped,** on the waterfront near the causeway, will rent you wheels for exploring. (☎27330 25 111. €20 per day. Open daily 8:30am-8:30pm.) **Xenia Karlaftis Rooms ❷,** on the water 20m from the causeway, rents spacious rooms with private baths. (☎27330 22 719. Singles €15; doubles €22; triples €30.) **Postal Code:** 23200.

Although **Areopolis** neighbors both the sea and the mountains, its buildings dominate the scenery: stone tower houses and cobbled streets are framed by the dramatic purple peaks of the Taygetus. Just 11km from Areopolis, the unusual **Vlihada Cave,** part of a subterranean river, is cool, quiet, and strung with tiny crystalline stalagmites. (Open daily 8am-3pm. Mandatory 30min. tours. €14; students €7. A bus runs from Areopolis at 11am and returns at 12:45pm; €0.80.) **Buses** stop in Areopolis's main *plateia* and go to Athens (6hr., 4 per day, €20) via Gythion (30min., €1.70) and Sparta (2hr., €6.30). To reach **Tsimova ❷,** which rents narrow rooms with tiny doors and windows typical of tower houses, turn left at the end of Kapetan Matapan, the road leading to the Old Town. (☎27330 51 301. Singles €20; doubles €40.) **Postal Code:** 23062.

MONEMVASIA (Μονεμβασια) AND GEFYRA (Γεφυρα) ☎27320

The island of Monemvasia, despite being one of the major tourist destinations on the Peloponnese, has an other-worldly quality. No cars or bikes are allowed on the island, and horses bear groceries into the city. Narrow streets hide child-sized doorways and flowered courtyards. The 12th-century **Agia Sofia** is on the edge of the cliffs; to get there, navigate through the maze of streets to the inland edge of town, where a path climbs the side of the cliff to the tip of the rock. Stay in more modern and less expensive **Gefyra,** a 15min. walk down the main road and across the causeway from Monemvasia. An **orange bus** runs between the causeway and Monemvasia's gate (every 15min., €0.29). Three **buses** per day leave for: Athens (6hr., €18.65); Corinth (5hr., €14); Sparta (2½hr., €6.15); and Tripoli (4hr., €9.70). **Hotel Akrogiali ❷,** across from Malvasia Travel at Iouliou 23, has glowing white rooms with private baths. (☎27320 61 360. Singles €20-23; doubles €26-33.) **To Limanaki ❶** in Gefyra serves an excellent *pastitsio* (€4).

NAFPLION (Ναυπλιο) ☎27520

Beautiful old Nafplion glories in its fortresses, beaches, and Venetian architecture. The town's crown jewel is the 18th-century **Palamidi Fortress,** with its spectacular views of the town and harbor. To get there, walk or take a taxi (€3) up the 3km road, or climb the grueling 999 steps up from Polizoidhou, across the park from the bus station. (Open daily 8am-6:45pm; off-season daily 8:30am-5:45pm. €4, students €2.) **Arvanitia,** Nafplion's small, pebbly beach, is away from town on Polizoidhou with Palimidi on your left; follow the footpath for lovely private coves. **Buses** leave from Singrou, off Pl. Kapodistrias, for Athens (3hr., every hr., €8.50) via Corinth (2hr., €3.80). To reach **Bouboulinas,** the waterfront promenade, from the station, go left and follow Singrou to the harbor and the **Old Town.** The **tourist office** is on 25 Martiou across from the telephone office. (☎27520 24 444. Open daily 9am-1pm and 4-8pm.) For the rooftop views from **Dimitris Bekas' Domatia** ❷ in the Old Town, turn up the stairs on Kokkinou, off Staikopoulou; climb to the top, turn left, and go up another 50 steps. (☎27520 24 594. Singles €13-16; doubles €18-20.) **To Fanaria** ❷, above the *plateia* on Staikopoulou in an alleyway, serves tantalizing entrees in an intimate atmosphere. (Soups €2.50-3, fish dishes €6-8.)

GREECE

DAYTRIPS FROM NAFPLION: MYCENAE AND EPIDAVROS. The supreme city of Greece from 1600 to 1100 BC, **Mycenae** (Μυκηνες) was once ruled by Agamemnon, leader of the attacking forces in the Trojan War. Excavations of ancient Mycenae have continued over the 126 years since Heinrich Schliemann first turned a spade here. Now Ancient Mycenae is one of the most visited sites in Greece, and mobs head to the famed Lion's Gate and Tomb of Agamemnon. (Both sites open Apr.-Sept. daily 8am-7pm; Oct.-Mar. 8am-5pm. €6, students €3. Keep your ticket or pay twice for both sites.) Join the illustrious ranks of Virginia Woolf, Claude Debussy, William Faulkner, and Allen Ginsberg, who have all stayed at **Belle Helene Hotel** ❸, which doubles as a bus stop on the main road. (☎207510 76 225. Singles €25, doubles €40.) The only direct **bus** to Mycenae is from Nafplion (45min., 4 per day, €1.90) via Argos (20min., €0.80).

The grandest structure at the ancient site in **Epidavros** (Επιδαυρος) is the **Theater of Epidavros,** built in the early second century BC with a capacity of 14,000. The incredible acoustics allow you to stand at the top row of seats and hear a match lit on stage. Near the theater on the road to the sanctuary's ruins is Epidavros's **museum.** (☎27520 22 009. Open daily 8am-7pm. Ticket office open daily 7:30am-7pm, F-Sa 7:30am-9pm during festival season. €6, students €3.) Late June to mid-Aug., the **Epidavros Theater Festival** brings performances of classical Greek plays on F and Sa nights. Shows are at 9pm; purchase tickets at the site or in advance by calling the Athens Festival Box Office. (☎210 322 1459. €12, students €6.) **Buses** arrive in Epidavros from Nafplion (45min., 4 per day, €1.90).

CORINTH (Κορινθος) ☎27410

Most visitors come to gaze on the ruins of **Ancient Corinth,** at the base of the **Acrocorinth.** Majestic columns and pediments lie around the courtyard of the **Temple of Apollo,** down the stairs to the left of the excellent **archaeological museum.** The **fortress** at the top of Acrocorinth is a tough 2-3hr. hike, but there is always the option of a taxi to the summit (€6) and back down (€9). At the top, explore the surprisingly intact remains of the **Temple to Aphrodite,** where disciples were initiated into the mysteries of love. (☎27410 31 207 for museum. Open 8am-7pm, off-season 8am-5pm. Museum and site €6, students €3.)

In **New Corinth,** the logical base for visiting the ruins, **buses** leave from station B, on Koliatsou, halfway through the park, to Ancient Corinth (20min., 15 per day 7am-9pm, €.80). Buses leave station A, behind the train station, for Athens (1½ hr., 30 per day, €5.07). Buses leave station C, **Argolis Station** (☎27410 24 403), at the intersection of Eth. Antistasis and Aratou, every hour for Argos (€3), Mycenae (€2.40), and Nafplion (€3.80). **Trains** go from the station on Demokratias to Athens (2hr., 14 per day, €2.60) and Patras (2½hr., 8 per day, €3.20). The **tourist police,**

Ermou 51, will provide tourists with maps, brochures, and other assistance. (☎27410 23 282. Open daily 8am-2pm.) In New Corinth, **Hotel Akti ❷,** Eth. Antistasis 3, is the best bet for accommodations, with simple, utilitarian bedrooms and a convenient location. (☎27410 23 337. Singles €12-15; doubles €25-30.) When mealtime comes, **AXINOS ❶,** Damaskinou 41, offers cheery *al fresco* dining by the waterfront. (☎27410 28 889. *Moussaka* €4.70. Feta in olive oil €2.35.)

NORTHERN AND CENTRAL GREECE

Under 19th-century Ottoman rule, Macedonia, Thessaly, and Thrace acquired a Byzantine aura. It's still discernible along forgotten mountain-goat paths that lead to the treasures of the era, with glorious vistas overlooking silvery olive groves, fruit-laden trees, and patchwork farmland.

THESSALONIKI (Θεσσαλονικη) ☎2310

Thessaloniki, a jumble of ancient, Byzantine, European, Turkish, Balkan, and contemporary Greek culture and history, fans out from its hilltop fortress toward the Thermaic Gulf. From its peak, the fortress oversees the Old Town's placid streets stretching down to the city's long, congested avenues. Among both glitzy and lackluster concrete facades, fashion-conscious young Salonicans rub shoulders with long-bearded monks and old women in mourning clothes. Golden mosaics, frescoes, and floating domes still gleam in the industrial city's Byzantine churches. Most travelers spend a couple of days in Thessaloniki going to clubs, checking out the sights, and enjoying the tranquility of countryside hikes.

TRANSPORTATION

Trains: Main Terminal (☎2310 517 517), on Monastiriou in the western part of the city. Take any bus down Egnatia (€0.44). To **Athens** (6-8hr., 10 per day, €15). The **Travel Office** (☎2310 598 112) can provide updated schedules.

Buses: Most **KTEL** buses leave from one central, dome-shaped bus station west of the city center. To: **Athens** (☎2310 595 495; 6hr., 11 per day, €28); **Corinth** (☎2310 595 405; 7½hr., 11:30am, €32); **Patras** (☎2310 595 419; 7hr., 3 per day, €32.55).

Ferries: Buy tickets at **Karacharisis Travel and Shipping Agency,** Koundouriotou 8 (☎2310 524 544). Open M-F 8:30am-8pm, Sa 8:30am-2:30pm. To **Chios** (20hr., Sa 1am, €27) via **Limnos** (8hr., €17) and **Lesvos** (14hr., €27), and to **Mykonos** (15hr., 1 per day, €31). **Crete Air Travel,** Dragoumi 1 (☎2310 534 376), operates daily ferries to **Skiathos** (4½hr., €31) and **Skopelos** (5½hr., €31). Open M-F 8am-9pm.

Public Transportation: Local buses cost €0.44 and run throughout the city. Buses #10, #11, and #31 run up and down Egnatia. Buy tickets at *periptera* or at major stations.

ORIENTATION AND PRACTICAL INFORMATION

Running from the shore inland, the main streets are **Nikis, Mitropoleos, Tsimiski, Ermou, Egnatia,** and **Agios Dimitriou.** Intersecting these streets and running from the water into town are (west to east) **Dragoumi, El. Venizelou, Aristotelous, Agios Sophias,** and **Eth. Aminis.** Tsimiski, Mitropoleos, Ag. Sophias, and streets between Aristotelous and Ipodromiou are the main shopping streets. The cheaper hotels are on Egnatia, with waterfront bars and cafes on Nikis. The roads north of Ag. Dimitriou get smaller and steeper and lead into the **Old Town.** Facing inland, go left on Mitropoleos to reach **Ladadika,** a pocket of turn-of-the-century bars and *tavernas*.

Tourist Office: EOT, Pl. Aristotelous (☎2310 271 888). Open M-Sa 7:30am-3pm.

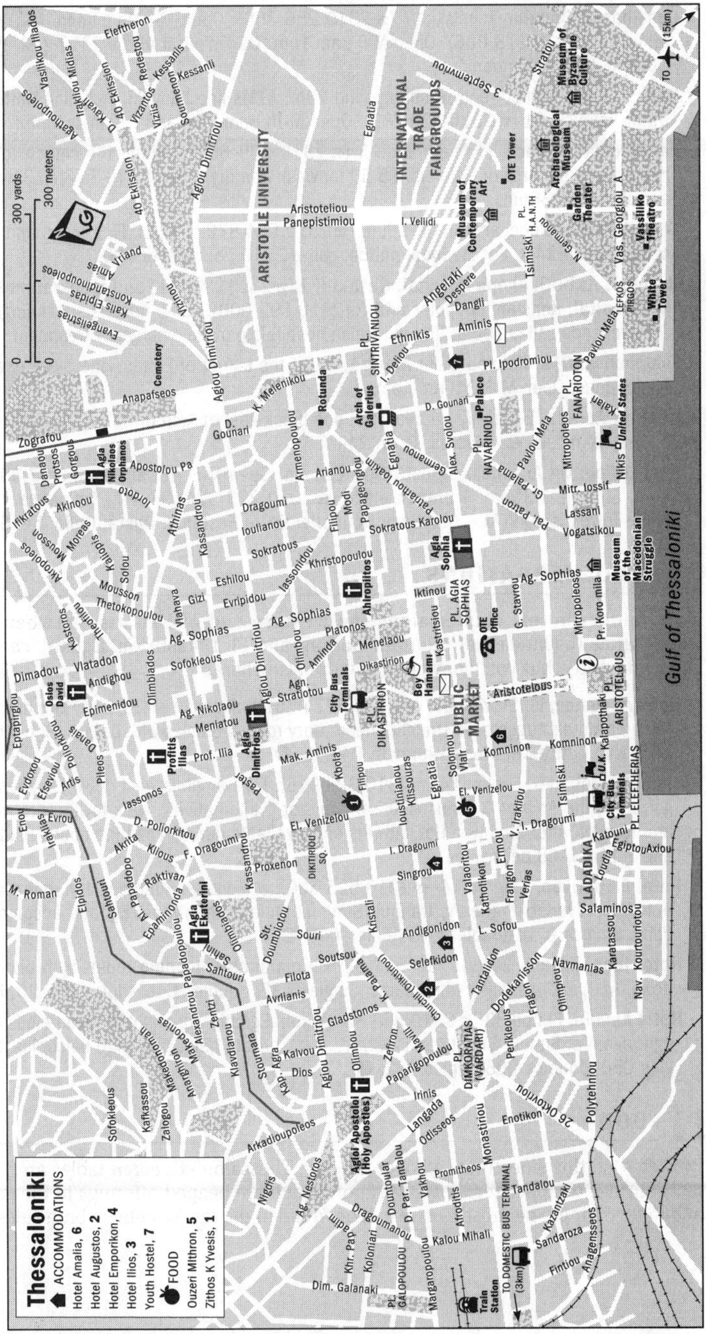
Thessaloniki
ACCOMMODATIONS
Hotel Amalia, 6
Hotel Augustos, 2
Hotel Emporikon, 4
Hotel Ilios, 3
Youth Hostel, 7
FOOD
Ouzeri Mithron, 5
Zithos K Yvesis, 1
0 300 yards
0 300 meters
ARISTOTLE UNIVERSITY
INTERNATIONAL TRADE FAIRGROUNDS
Museum of Byzantine Culture
Archaeological Museum
OTE Tower
Museum of Contemporary Art
PL. H.A.N.TH
Garden Theater
Vassiliko Theatro
White Tower
LEFKOS PIRGOS
Rotunda
Arch of Galerius
PL. SINTRIVANIOU
Palace
PL. NAVARINOU
PL. FANARIOTON
United States
Agia Nikolaos Orphanos
Cemetery
Agia Sophia
PL. AGIA SOPHIAS
Ahiropiitos
OTE Office
Museum of the Macedonian Struggle
Gulf of Thessaloniki
Osios David
Agia Dimitrios
City Bus Terminals
PL. DIKASTIRION
Bey Hamami
PUBLIC MARKET
PL. ARISTOTELOUS
Aristotelous
Profitis Ilias
U.K.
PL. ELEFTHERIAS
LADADIKA
DIKITIRIOU SQ.
Agia Ekaterini
PL. DIMKORATIAS (VARDARI)
Agioi Apostoloi (Holy Apostles)
TO DOMESTIC BUS TERMINAL (3km)
Train Station
PL. GALOPOULOU
TO (15km)
Egnatia
Ag. Sophias
Tsimiski
Mitropoleos
Nikis
El. Venizelou
Agiou Dimitriou
Vas. Georgiou A
Pavlou Mela
3 Septemvriou
26 Oktovriou
Monastiriou
Kassandrou
Olimbiados
Ethnikis Aminis
Angelaki
Komninon
Kalapothaki
Dodekanisson
Polytehniou
Navmanias
Salaminos
Katouni
Egiptou
Axiou
Anagennseos
Sandaroza
Langada
Filota
Sahtouri
Stournara
Eptapirgiou
Anapafseos
Zografou

Consulates: Canada, Tsimiski 17 (☎2310 256 350). Open M-F 9am-noon. **UK,** Venizelou 8 (☎2310 278 006). Open M-F 8am-1pm. **US,** Tsimiski 43 (☎2310 242 900). Open M, W, F 9am-noon.

Banks: Banks with currency exchange and 24hr. **ATMs** line Tsimiski, including **National Bank,** Tsimiski 11 (☎2310 230 783). Open M-Th 8am-2pm and F 8am-1:30pm.

Laundromat: Bianca, L. Antoniadou 3 (☎2310 209 602), behind the church to the right, facing the Arch of Galerius. €5.50 for wash and dry. Open M, W, Sa 8am-3pm; Tu and Th 8am-8:30pm.

Tourist Police: Dodekanissou 4, 5th fl. (☎2310 554 870 or 871). Free maps and brochures. Open 24hr. For the **local police,** call ☎2310 553 800 or 100.

Hospital: At both **Ahepa Hospital,** Kiriakidi 1 (☎2310 993 111) and **Ippokration Public Hospital,** Konstantinoupoleos 49 (☎2310 892 000), some doctors speak English. On weekends call ☎106 to find out which hospitals provide emergency treatment.

Telephones: OTE, Karolou Diehl 27 (☎134), at the corner of Ermou, one block east of Aristotelous. Open M-F 7:10am-1pm.

Internet Access: E-Global, Egnatia 105, one block east of Arch of Galerius, sports over 50 fast terminals. €2-3 per hr. Open 24hr.

Post Office: On Aristotelous, just below Egnatia. Open M-F 7:30am-8pm, Sa 7:30am-2pm, Su 9am-1:30pm. A **branch** office (☎2310 229 324), on Eth. Aminis near the White Tower, is open M-F 7am-8pm. Both offer *Poste Restante.* **Postal Code:** 54101.

ACCOMMODATIONS

Most budget hotels cluster along the western end of Egnatia, between Pl. Dimokratias (500m east of the train station) and Pl. Dikastiriou. Egnatia can be noisy and gritty, but you'll have to pay more elsewhere.

Hotel Augustos, El. Svoronou 4 (☎2310 522 955). Walking down Egnatia, turn north at the Argo Hotel; Augustos is straight ahead. Cozy rooms. Singles with bath €18; doubles €25, with bath €38; triples with bath €48.15. ❷

Youth Hostel, Alex. Svolou 44 (☎2310 225 946). Take any bus west down Egnatia and get off at the Arch of Galerius (the Kamara stop); alternatively, walk toward the water and turn left after 2 blocks. Hot showers only available during reception hours, 9-11am and 7-11pm. €8 per person. ❶

Hotel Emporikon, Singrou 14 (☎2310 525 560), at Egnatia. Simple, clean rooms with balconies overlooking leafy, tranquil Singrou. Quieter than most Egnatia accomodations. Singles €20; doubles €43; triples €40. ❷

Hotel Ilios, Egnatia 27 (☎2310 512 620). Comfortable, modern rooms with big windows, A/C, and gleaming white baths. Singles €32; doubles €46; triples €55.20. ❸

Hotel Amalia, Ermou 33 (☎2310 268 321). From Egnatia, turn right at Aristotelous and right again at Ermou. Bright rooms with TV, A/C, private bath, and large balconies. Singles €50; doubles €68; triples €82. ❹

FOOD

Pocketed on tiny sidestreets all over the city, Thessaloniki's **ouzeri** tables are veritable shrines to appetizer *mezedes*, upon which are heaped offerings to the gods of budget dining. The most *ouzeri* can be found in the tiny streets on both sides of

Aristotelous, while more innovative establishments are down from Egnatia between **Dragoumi** and **El. Venizelou.** The **Old Town** district brims with inexpensive, family *tavernas.*

Ouzeri Melathron, in an alley at 23 El. Venizelou. From Egnatia, walk past the Ottoman Bedesten on El. Venizelou and make a right into the passage. Witty 1.25m long menu features snails and a spicy dish called "Lonely Nights." Entrees €3.50-12. ❷

Zithos K Yvesis, near El Venizelou and Filipou (☎2310 268 746). Head up Tositsa; look for an alleyway entrance. Delicious meat and vegetarian dishes. Entrees €2.50-€6. ❶

SIGHTS AND ENTERTAINMENT

The streets of modern Thessaloniki are littered with the remnants of its significance during both the Byzantine and Ottoman empires. **Agios Dimitrios,** on Ag. Dimitriou north of Aristotelous, is the city's oldest and most famous church. Although most of its interior was gutted in a 1917 fire, some lovely mosaics remain. (Open daily 8am-8pm.) South of Egnatia, on the square that bares its name, the magnificent domed **Agia Sophia** features a splendid ceiling mosaic of the Ascension. (Open daily 7am-1pm and 5-7pm.) Originally part of a palatial complex designed to honor the Roman Emperor, the **Rotunda** became a church under the Byzantines. Its walls were once plastered with some of the city's most brilliant mosaics, but sadly very few remain. (Open daily 7am-2:30pm.) A colonnaded processional once led south to the **Arch of Galerius,** on the eastern end of Egnatia, which was built in the 4th century AD by Emperor Galerius. Returning west down Egnatia, don't miss **Bey Hamami,** a perfectly preserved 15th-century bath house that served the Ottoman governor and his retinue. (Open daily 9am-9pm. Free.) The **Heptapyrgion,** a 5th-century Byzantine fortress, is the main attraction of the city's modest acropolis. From 1890 to 1989, it replaced the White Tower as the city's prison; modern prison buildings remain both inside and outside the fortress ramparts. (Open M 12:30-7pm, Tu-Su 8am-7pm. Museum open daily 10:30am-5pm.)

Thessaloniki's **Archaeological Museum,** at the western end of Tsimiski, across from the International Helexpo Fairgrounds, is full of discoveries gleaned from Neolithic tombs, mosaics from Roman houses, and a dazzling display of Macedonian gold. Gold death masks and weapons can be seen in the graves of Sindos. (Open M 12:30-7pm, Tu-Su 8am-7pm; reduced hours in winter. €4, students €2, EU students free.) Just across the street on 3 Septemvriou, the **Museum of Byzantine Culture** displays an impressive array of artifacts from both the Early and Middle Byzantine eras, including church mosaics, elaborate tombs, and 1500-year-old personal effects. (Open M 12:30-7pm, Tu-Su 8am-7pm; reduced hours in winter. €4, students and seniors €2, EU students and under 18 free.) All that remains of a 15th-century Venetian seawall, the **White Tower** presides over the eastern edge of the waterfront like an overgrown chess piece. *Wandering Byzantine Thessaloniki,* a guide available at the tower for a pricey (but well-deserved) €18, will satisfy history buffs. (Tower open M 12:30-7pm, Tu-Su 8am-3pm. Free.)

There are three main hubs for late-night fun: the bars and cafes of the **Ladadika** district, the waterfront, and the open-air discos that throb near the airport exit (€8-9 by taxi). **Podon 2000,** 11km east of the city along the main highway, is a sophisticated hot spot that will introduce you to Greek music. (€10 cover includes 1 drink.) Nearby **Decadence** and **Mousis** are other popular discos. (Cover €10.)

DAYTRIP FROM THESSALONIKI: VERGINA

The tombs of Vergina (Βεργινα), final home to ancient Macedonian royalty, lie only 30km from Thessaloniki. The principal sight is the **museum,** while the intricate gold work and brilliant frescoes of the tombs themselves are under the **Great Tumulus,** a huge, man-made mount 12m tall and 110m wide. Check out the bones of **Alexander IV,** son of Alexander the Great, as well as the magnificent **Tomb of Philip II,** Alexander's father. (Open M noon-7pm, Tu-Su 8am-7pm; in winter Tu-Su 8am-7pm. €8, students €4.) **Buses** run from Thessaloniki (55min., every hr., €4.40) to Veria. From Veria take the bus to Vergina (20min., 11 per day, €0.95). Buses drop passengers off in the Vergina *plateia;* follow the signs to the sights.

MOUNT OLYMPUS (Ολιμποσ) ☎23520

The impressive height (nearly 3000m) and formidable slopes of the Thermaic Gulf's Mt. Olympus so awed the ancients that they proclaimed it the divine dwelling place of the gods. A network of well-maintained **hiking** trails now makes the summit accessible to just about anyone with sturdy legs and a taste for adventure. Two approaches to the peaks begin near **Litohoro** (280m); the first and most popular starts at **Prionia** (1100m), 18km from the village, and takes one full day round-trip. The second, a longer and more picturesque route, begins at **Diastavrosi** (also called **Gortsia;** 1300m), 14km away. There is no bus to the trailheads from Litohoro, so you'll have to walk, drive, or take a taxi (Prionia €20; Diastavrosi €8). Unless you're handy with a crampon and an ice axe, make your ascent between May and October. **Mytikas,** the tallest peak, is inaccessible without special equipment before June. The EOS-run **Spilos Agapitos** ❷ ("Refuge A") is about 800m below **Skala** and Mytikas peaks. The English-speaking staff dispenses hiking info over the phone to prospective hikers and can also help reserve spots in other refuges. (☎23520 81 800. Meals 6am-9pm. Lights out 10pm. Open mid-May to late-Oct. €10, €8 for members of mountain clubs. €4.20 to **camp** nearby and use facilities.)

Trains (☎23520 22 522) run to the Litohoro station from Athens (6hr., 4 per day, €15) and Thessaloniki (1½hr., 4 per day, €3); a **taxi** from the train station to the town center should cost around €6. KTEL **buses** (☎23520 81 271) run from Athens (5½hr., 3 per day, €24.70) and Thessaloniki (1½hr., 17 per day, €5.90). The **tourist office** is on Ag. Nikolaou by the park. (☎23520 83 100. Open July-Nov. 8:30am-2:30pm and 5-9pm.) If you're not bedding down in one of the refuges (see above), the most convenient place to stay is the **Hotel Park** ❷, Ag. Nikolaou 23, down from the *plateia* in Litohoro. (☎23520 812 52. Singles €20; doubles €30; triples €40.) **Camp** at **Olympus Zeus** ❶ (☎23520 22 115) or **Olympus Beach** ❶ (☎23520 22 112), both on the beach about 5km from town; expect to pay at least €8 for a site.

METEORA (Μετεωρα) ☎24230

The iron-gray pinnacles of the Meteora rock formations are stunning, offering astonishing views of fields, mountains, and monolithic stone. These wonders of nature are bedecked by 24 exquisite, gravity-defying Byzantine monasteries. Dress modestly: long skirts for women, long pants for men, and no bare shoulders. (Open Apr.-Sept. Sa-Su and W 10am-12:30pm and 3:30-5pm; hours vary during the rest of the week. €2 per monastery.) The **Grand Meteoron Monastery** is the oldest, largest, and most touristed of the monasteries. It houses a **folk museum** and the 16th-century **Church of the Transfiguration,** whose dome features a *Pantokrator* (a central image of Christ). To escape the hordes of tourists, venture to **Roussanou,** to the right after the fork in the road. Visible from most of the valley, it is one of the most spectacularly situated monasteries in the area. Buses leave for Meteora from the fountain in **Kalambaka,** the most popular base for exploring the sight (2 per day, €0.80). **Trains** leave Kalambaka for Athens (4hr., 3 per day, €19.10) and Thessaloniki (5hr., 3 per day, €10.50). **Buses** depart for Athens (5hr., 3 per day, €19.70) and Patras (6hr., Tu and Th 9am, €17.50). The rooms at **Koka Roka** ❷ offer awe-inspiring views of Meteora; from the central square, follow Vlachara until it ends, bear left, and follow the signs to Kanari. (☎24230 24 554. Singles €15; doubles €27, with bath €32; triples with bath €42.) Many of the **campsites** that line the roads out of town also rent cheap rooms. **Postal Code:** 42200.

IOANNINA (Ιωαννινα) ☎26510

The region's largest city, Ioannina, lies on the shores of Lake Pamvotis. Ioannina itself might not captivate you for long, but it is a useful transport hub if traveling between Greece and Italy. Aside from local finds, the highlights of the city's **Archaeological Museum,** off Averof, near the city center, are the lead tablets used by ancients to inscribe their questions to the oracle at Dodoni. (Open Tu-Su 8:30am-3pm. €2, students free.) Catch a boat from the waterfront (10min., €1) for **To Nisi** ("The Island") to explore Byzantine monasteries and the **Ali Pasha Museum.**

Buses run from the terminal at Zossimadon 4 to Athens (6½hr., 11 per day, €24.90) and Thessaloniki (7hr., 6 per day, €20.50). The **tourist office** is about 500m down Leoforis Dodoni on the left, immediately after the playground. (☎26510 46 662. Open July-Sept. M-F 7:30am-2:30pm and 5-8:30pm, Sa 9am-1pm; Oct.-June M-F 7:30am-2:30pm.) **Hotel Metropolis** ❷, Kristali 2, on the corner of Averof toward the waterfront, is conveniently located and has spacious rooms. (☎26510 26 207. Singles €20; doubles €25.) **Hotel Olympic** ❹, Melandis 2, is beautifully decorated and fully equipped. Take the second left off Averof as you walk towards the waterfront. (☎26510 22 233. Singles €50; doubles €70; triples €80.) Several *souvlaki* stands are at the end of Averof near the Frourio, and seafood restaurants line the waterfront. **Filippas** ❷, on the waterfront, has delicious specials; the chicken with honey and yogurt (€6.50) is a real treat. (Entrees €4.50-7.) **Postal Code:** 45110.

DAYTRIP FROM IOANNINA: DODONI. Ancient Dodoni (Δωδωνη), the site of mainland Greece's oldest oracle, is at the base of a mountain 22km southeast of Ioannina. According to myth, **Zeus** answered queries here from the roots of a giant oak tree. There is also a large 3rd-century **amphitheater** at the site. (Open daily 8am-5pm. €2, students €1, EU students free.) **Buses** to Dodoni run from Ioannina's smaller station at Bizaniou 21 (M, W, F 6:30am and 3:30pm; €1.35). Ask to be let off at the theater. The return bus passes by at about 4:45pm; alternatively, you can hire a **taxi** (at least €15 round-trip).

IONIAN ISLANDS (Νησια Του Ιουιου)

Just to the west of mainland Greece, the Ionian Islands are renowned for their medley of rugged mountains, rolling farmland, shimmering olive groves, and pristine beaches, all surrounded by a seemingly endless expanse of clear, blue water. The islands are a favorite among vacationing Brits, Italians, and Germans, as well as ferry-hopping backpackers heading to Italy.

FERRIES TO ITALY

To catch a ferry to Italy, buy your ticket at least a day ahead; be sure to find out if the port tax (€5-6) is included. **Corfu Mare** (☎26610 32 467), beneath the Ionian Hotel, sells tickets. Ferries go from Corfu to: Ancona (20hr., 1 per day, €56); Bari (9hr., 1 per day, €22); Brindisi (6-7hr., 3 per day, €30); Trieste (24hr., 4 per week, €38); and Venice (24hr., 1 per day, €42). Schedules vary by season; check before planning your trip.

GREECE

CORFU (KERKYRA; Κερκυρα) ☎26610

Ever since Homer's Odysseus washed ashore and praised its lush beauty, the seas have brought a multitude of conquerors, colonists, and tourists to verdant Corfu. Those who stray from the beaten path, however, will encounter unspoiled, uncrowded beaches.

CORFU TOWN AND ENVIRONS. Corfu Town enchants with its two fortresses, various museums, and winding streets. The lovely **Paleokastritsa beach,** where Odysseus supposedly landed, lies west of town; take a KTEL bus to Paleokastritsa (45min., 9 per day, €1.50). A 90min. walk from there will bring you to the mountaintop monastery **Panagia Theotokos.** KTEL buses also run from Corfu Town to **Agios Gordios** (45min., 7 per day, €1.25), 10km south of Pelekas, home to impressive rock formations, a beach, and the **Pink Palace Hotel ❷,** which is immensely popular with American and Canadian backpackers. The Palace has an impressive list of amenities, including tennis courts, a nightclub, massages (€11), clothing-optional cliff-diving (€15), and other water sports. They also run buses to Athens (€38-47) that bypass Patras. (☎26610 53 024. Internet €3 per 30min. Breakfast, dinner, and ferry pick-up included. Dorms €19, with A/C and bath €25.)

Ferries run from Corfu Town to Italy (see above) and Patras (6-7hr., 1-2 per day, €20), and high-speed **catamarans** run to Kephalonia (3hr., W and Sa 9am, round-trip €62). KTEL runs **bus/ferry combos** to Athens (9hr., 3 per day, €27.90) and Thessaloniki (9hr., 2 per day, €27). KTEL inter-city green buses depart from between I. Theotaki and the New Fortress; blue municipal buses leave from Pl. Sanrocco. The **EOT Tourist Office** is at the corner of Rizospaston Voulefton and I. Polila. (☎26610 37 520. Open M-F 8am-2pm.) **The Association of Owners of Private Rooms and Apartments,** I. Polila 24 (☎26610 26 133), has a complete list of rooms in Corfu. To get to **Hotel Europa ❸,** Giantsilio 10, from the port customs house, cross the main street and make a sharp right; Giantsilio is a tiny road on your left after the road turns sharply left and becomes Napoleonta. Rooms are white and airy, and the cheapest in Corfu Town. (☎26610 39 304. Singles €25, with bath €30; doubles €30/€35; triples €36.) **Restaurant Rex ❸,** Kapodistriou 66, one block back from the Spianada, has long been famed as one of Corfu's best. (Entrees €7.40-12.60.) The undisputed focus of Corfu Town's nightlife is the **Disco Strip,** on Eth. Antistaseos at the waterfront. **Postal Code:** 49100.

PELEKAS AND GLYFADA. The village of **Pelekas** (bus #11 from Corfu Town; 30min., 7 per day, €0.75) has some of the best of Corfu's offerings: sandy beaches, great food, and fun bars. The long **beach** is a pleasant 30min. walk from town down a very steep road. The beaches at **Glyfada,** 5km from Pelekas Town, are more touristed; water spouts abound. Free shuttles run between Glyfada and Pelekas (10min., 6 per day). Glyfada is also accessible by green KTEL **buses** from Corfu Town (45min., 10 per day, €1.25). North of Glyfada, accessible by a dirt path off the main Pelekas road, lie the isolated beaches of **Moni Myrtidion** and **Myrtiotissa** (the unofficial nude beach). While lodging is available in Glyfada, Pelekas is your best bet for a cheap night's stay—try **Pension Tellis and Brigitte ❷,** down the hill from the bus stop. (☎26610 94 326. Singles €18; doubles €20-25.)

KEPHALONIA (Κεφαλονια) ☎26710

Mountains, subterranean lakes and rivers, caves, forests, and more than 250km of sand-and-pebble coastline make Kephalonia a nature lover's paradise. **Argostoli,** the capital of Kephalonia and Ithaka, is a lively city packed with pastel buildings that climb the hills from the calm waters of the harbor. Argostoli offers good shopping and nightlife, as well as easy access to other points on the island. **Buses** leave from the south end of the waterfront for Sami (4 per day, €2) and Fiskardo (2hr., 2 per day, €3.30). **Hotel Tourist ❷,** on the waterfront near the bus station, is a great deal. (☎26710 22 510. All rooms have balconies. Singles €24-36; doubles €37-52.)

Sami is 24km from Argostoli on the east coast. Amazing views stretch in every direction, from the waves crashing on the beach to the green hills cradling the town. Sami is close to the underground **Melissani Lake** and **Drogarati Cave,** a large cavern filled with stalactites and stalagmites. (Cave open daily until nightfall. €3, children €1.50.) **Fiskardo,** at the northern tip of the island, is the most beautiful of Kephalonia's towns; take a bus from either Sami (1hr., 2 per day, €2.70) or Argostoli (1½-2hr., 2 per day, €3.40). Buses from Fiskardo stop at the turn-off for **Myrtos Beach,** one of Europe's best. (Beach 4km from turn-off.) **Ferries** run from Sami to: Ithaka (40min., 3 per day, €1.70); Patras (2½hr., 2 per day, €10.70); and Brindisi, Italy (July-Sept. 1 per day, €35). **Hotel Kyma ❷,** in Sami's main *plateia*, has spectacular views. (☎(26740) 22 064. Singles €17-26; doubles €30-46.)

ITHAKA (Ιθακη) ☎26740

The least-touristed of the Ionian Islands, Ithaka is all too often passed over for Lefkada and Kephalonia. Those who do discover the island delight in its pebbled beaches, rocky hillsides, and terraced olive groves. Ithaka was the kingdom that Odysseus left behind while he fought in the Trojan War. Its capital, **Vathy,** wraps around a bay skirted by steep, green hills. **Dexa** is the closest beach to Vathy, a 20min. walk along the main road out of town with the water on your right. The **Sarakiniko** and **Filiatro** beaches, towards the mountain to the left of town as you are facing inland (about a 40min. walk), are more rewarding. Homer fans can climb (4km; about 1hr.) up to the **Cave of the Nymphs,** where Odysseus supposedly hid his treasure. (On the road out of town to Stavros; look for signs. Bring a flashlight.) In summer, the bus to Frikes (45min., €1.20) stops at the scenic village of **Stavros,** allegedly the former home of **Odysseus's Palace;** follow signs to a small museum filled with excavated items from the site. (Hours vary. A small tip is expected.)

Ferries connect Ithaka to Kephalonia (45min., 2-3 per day, €1.70) and to Patras, in the Peloponnese (4½hr., 2 per day, €11.50). Boats depart from Piso Aetos, near Vathy, and from Frikes. Schedules vary; check with **Delas Tours** (☎26740 32 104; open daily 9am-2pm and 3:30-9:30pm) or **Polyctor Tours** (☎26740 33 120; open daily 9:30am-1:30pm and 3:30-9pm), both in the main *plateia*. Private *domatia* are your best option for affordable accommodations; check with Delas Tours to see what they have available. **Andriana Domatia ❸,** on the far right of the waterfront as you are facing inland, has immaculate rooms with A/C. (☎26740 32 387. All rooms with bath. Singles €25-30; doubles €40-47.) **Taverna To Trexantiri ❷,** one block behind the post office off the *plateia*, is a favorite restaurant among locals. (Entrees under €6.) **Postal Code:** 28300.

GREECE

THE SPORADES (Σποραδες)

Circling into the azure Aegean, the Sporades form a family of enchanting sea maidens. From wild Skiathos to sophisticated Skopelos to quiet Alonnisos and Skyros, the islands have beckoned visitors for millennia. Ancient Athenians and Romans, early Venetians, and modern-day tourists have all basked on their sun-lit shores and trod their shaded forests.

TRANSPORTATION

To get to most of the Sporades from Athens, take the bus to Agios Konstantinos (2½hr., every hr., €10.20), where **Hellas Lines** (☎22 209) operates **ferries** to: Alonnisos (5½hr., 2 per week, €13.40); Skiathos (2hr., 2 per day, €20.20); and Skopelos (3hr., 2 per day, €26.90). **Flying Dolphins** leave Agios Konstantinos for: Alonnisos (2¾hr., 1-5 per day, €26.90); Skiathos (1½hr., 1-5 per day, €20.30); and Skopelos (2½hr., 1-5 per day, €26.80). Ferries also shuttle between the islands (see below).

SKIATHOS (Σκιαθος) ☎24270

Having grown up almost overnight from an innocent island daughter to a madcap dancing queen, Skiathos is the tourism hub of the Sporades. Buses leave the port in Skiathos Town for the southern beaches (every 30min., €1). The bus route ends in Koukounaries, near the lovely, pine-wooded **Koukounaries Beach and Biotrope** and the nude **Banana Beach** and **Little Banana Beach.** Indulge at the countless bars in **Plateia Papadiamantis** or along **Polytechniou** or **Evangelista,** then dance all night long at the clubs on the eastern side of the waterfront. Hellas Lines (☎24270 22 209) runs **ferries** to Alonnisos (2hr., 1-2 per day, €6) and Skopelos (1½hr., 1-3 per day, €4.40). *Domatia* are the best deal in town. The **Rooms to Let Office,** in the wooden kiosk by the port, provides a list of available rooms. (☎24270 22 990. Open daily 9am-8pm.) The rooms at **Australia Hotel ❷,** in an alley on Evangelistra off Papadiamantis, have A/C, private baths, fridges, and balconies. (Sept.-July singles €20; doubles €25-30; triples €36; Aug. prices increase.) **Primavera ❷** has delicious Italian food. (Entrees €5-10. Open daily 6:30pm-12:30am.) **Postal Code:** 37002.

ALONNISOS (Αλοννησος) ☎24240

Of the 20-odd islands within Greece's new **National Marine Park,** only Alonnisos is inhabited. Hikers take to the highland trails in the north; pick up *Alonnisos on Foot* (€9) in **Patitiri** for walking routes. In the south, endless beaches satisfy less adventurous souls; many are accessible from the island's main road. A 1½hr. walk from Patitiri takes you to **Votsi;** locals dive off the 15-20m cliffs near **Votsi Beach.** Beautiful **Hora** (Χωρα; Old Town) is ideal for both hikers and beachgoers. The island's only **bus** runs between Hora and Patitiri (every hr., €1). **Ferries** run to Skiathos (2hr., 1-2 per day, €6) and Skopelos (30min., 1-2 per day, €5). **Alonissos Travel,** in the center of the waterfront, exchanges currency, finds rooms, books excursions, and sells ferry tickets. (☎24240 65 188. Open daily 8am-11pm.) **Panorama ❷,** down the first alley on the left from Ikion Dolophon, rents bright rooms and studios. (☎24240 65 240. All rooms with bath. Singles €15-30; doubles €25-45; triples €35-50.) Locals adore the *ouzeri* **To Kamaki ❶,** on the left side of Ikion Dolophon, past the National Bank. The warm octopus salad (€5) is delicious. (Open daily 11am-2am.) **Postal Code:** 37005.

SKOPELOS (Σκοπελος) ☎24240

Skopelos sits between the whirlwind of Skiathos and the wilderness of Alonnisos and features the best elements of both. Hikes and moped rides lead to numerous monasteries, bright beaches, and white cliffs. Buses leave from the right of the waterfront (as you face the sea) for beaches near **Stafylos, Milia,** and **Loutraki.** At night, the waterfront strip closes to traffic and crowds swarm the streets in search of the tastiest *gyros* and the most authentic Greek *taverna.* Up the whitewashed stairs at the far right of the waterfront, **Anatoli** is the haunt of one of the world's last great *rembetika* (folk music) singers, Giorgos Xintaris. (Mixed drinks €3-7. Open daily 8pm-2am.) Hellas Lines (☎24240 22 767) runs **ferries** to: Alonnisos (30min., 1-2 per day, €3.40); Skiathos (1hr., 3-4 per day, €3.10); and Thessaloniki (2 per week, €39). **Thalpos Travel Agency,** 5m to the right of Galanatsiou along the waterfront, provides tourist information. (☎24240 22 947. Open May-Oct. daily 10am-2pm and 6-10pm; Nov.-Apr. info available by phone.) The **Rooms and Apartments Association** can provide a list of current *domatia.* (☎24240 24 567. Open daily 10am-2pm and 6-10pm.) **Pension Sotos ❷,** on the waterfront at the corner of Galanatsiou, is in a fantastic location. (☎24240 22 549. Singles €17-35; doubles €24-35.) **Plateia Platanos** abounds with fast, cheap food. **Postal Code:** 37003.

SKYROS (Σκυρος) ☎22220

Tourism and local tradition genuinely coexist in Skyros—the island's inaccessibility from elsewhere in the Sporades ensures that visitors are in the market for more than just a whirlwind beach and bar tour. **Skyros Town,** the island's capital, stands out in bright white contrast to the hills that surround it. The superb **Faltaits Museum,** just past Pl. Rupert Brooke in Skyros Town, boasts an incredible folk art collection. (Open daily 10am-2pm and 6-9pm. €2.) The best way to get to Skyros is to take the **bus** from Athens to Kimi, on Evia (3½hr., 2 per day, €10). Then take a **ferry** to Skyros from Kimi (2 per day, €7.25). Ferries arrive in **Linaria,** the tiny western port; there are buses to Skyros Town (20min., 3 per day, €0.80). **Skyros Travel,** past the central *plateia* on Agoras, is a de facto tourist office, organizing excursions and helping with lodgings. (☎22220 91 123. Open daily 9am-2:30pm and 6:30-11pm.) For the full Skyrian experience, bargain to stay in a **domatia ❷.** The thick-walled houses are brimming with Delft ceramics and Italian linens, purchased from pirates who looted much of the known world; you'll be met at the bus stop by old women offering rooms. Expect to pay €15-35. The incredible **O Pappou Kai Ego ❷,** toward the top of Agoras on the right, serves Skyrian specialties, including nanny-goat with lemon. (Entrees €4-8. Open daily 7pm-late.) **Postal Code:** 34007.

THE BIG SPLURGE

TASIA'S

Good seafood restaurants aren't hard to come by in Greece, but **Tasia's** rises above the rest. This taverna, in the tiny village of Steni Vala on Alonnisos, is a family operation from start to finish.

Tasia Malamatenios, who inherited the business from her mother, prepares and serves the food with the help of her son and four daughters. Tasia's husband George, the family fisherman, is crucial to the taverna's distinctive appeal—instead of getting the fish from Volos, like most tavernas on Alonnisos, Tasia's is supplied exclusively by his rig. While the selection is not always as wide as that of other tavernas, the fish is as fresh as it gets. You can sit down to lunch here and eat fish that was caught hours (and never more than a day) before.

Seafood this fresh comes at a high price; the fish costs anywhere from €30-55 per kg. The delicious lobster (€51 per kg) with spaghetti, however, is worth every cent. Tasia's also has inexpensive options, such as fried fish (€5) and typical Greek fare, from stuffed tomatoes (€4) to *moussaka* (€5.50).

(The island's bus stops in Steni Vala; Tasia's is the first taverna you come to in the tiny harbor. Open daily noon-midnight.) ❹

THE CYCLADES (Κυκλαδες)

When people wax rhapsodic about the Greek islands, chances are they're talking about the Cyclades. Whatever your idea of Greece—peaceful cobblestone streets and whitewashed houses, breathtaking sunsets, scenic hikes, all-night revelry—you'll find it here. Although most islands are mobbed by tourists in the summer, each has quiet villages and untouched spots.

TRANSPORTATION

Ferries run from: Athens to Mykonos, Naxos, Folegandros, and Santorini; Crete to Naxos and Santorini; and Thessaloniki to Naxos and Ios. Frequent ferries also run between each of the islands in the Cyclades. See below for all ferry information. High-speed ferries and **hydrofoils** cover similar routes at twice the cost and speed.

MYKONOS (Μυκονος) ☎22890

Coveted by pirates in the 18th century, Mykonos is still lusted after by those seeking revelry and excess. Nightlife, both gay and straight, abounds; the island is also the expensive playground of chic sophisticates. Ambling in colorful alleyways at dawn or dusk is the cheapest and most exhilarating way to experience the island, especially **Mykonos Town.** All of Mykonos's beaches are nudist, but the degree of bareness varies. **Plati Yialos, Paradise Beach,** and **Super Paradise Beach** are the most daring; **Elia** is a bit tamer. Buses run south from South Station to Plati Yialos (every 30min., €0.80), where *caïques* (little boats) go to the other beaches (around €1.50); direct buses also run to Paradise from South Station (every 30min., €0.80) and to Elia from North Station (30min., 8 per day, €1). After 11pm, wild dancing and irresistible hedonism are the norm at **Pierro's** on Matogianni (beer €5). The **Skandinavian Bar** on the waterfront has something for everyone in its two-building party complex. (Beer and shots €3-4. Open Su-F 8:30pm-3am, Sa 8:30pm-4am.)

Ferries run to: Athens (6hr., 2-3 per day, €17); Naxos (3hr., 1-2 per day, €6.30); Santorini (6hr., 3 per week, €11); and Tinos (45min., 3 per day, €3.50). The helpful **tourist police** are located at the ferry landing. (☎22890 22 482. Open daily 8am-11pm.) Most budget travelers bed down at Mykonos's several festive campsites, which offer a myriad of sleeping options beyond the standard plot of grass. There are **information offices** on the dock, one for **hotels** (☎22890 24 540; open daily 9am-midnight) and one for **camping** (☎22890 23 567; open daily 9am-midnight). **Hotel Apollon ❹,** on the waterfront, is an antique-laden house with a view of the harbor. (☎22890 22 223. Singles and doubles €42-50; doubles with bath €50-65.) The lively **Paradise Beach Camping ❶,** 6km from the village, is directly on the beach; the round-trip bus costs €0.80. (☎22890 22 852. €5-7 per person; €2.50-3 per tent; 2-person beach cabin €20-45.) Cheap creperies and *souvlaki* joints are on nearly all of Mykonos's streets. **Appaloosa ❸,** one block from Taxi Square on Mavrogeneous, has an eclectic mix of food; Mexican selections are its best. (Entrees €9-11. Open daily 8pm-1:30am.) **Postal Code:** 84600.

DAYTRIP FROM MYKONOS: DELOS. Delos (Δηλος) is the sacred center of the Cyclades. The **archaeological site,** which occupies much of the small island, takes several days to explore completely, but the highlights can be seen in about three hours. From the dock, head straight to the **Agora of the Competaliasts;** continue in the same direction and go left onto the wide **Sacred Road** to reach the **Sanctuary of Apollo,** a collection of temples built from Mycenaean times onward. On the right is the biggest and most famous, the **Great Temple of Apollo.** Continue 50m past the end of the Sacred Road to the beautiful **Terrace of the Lions.** The **museum,** next

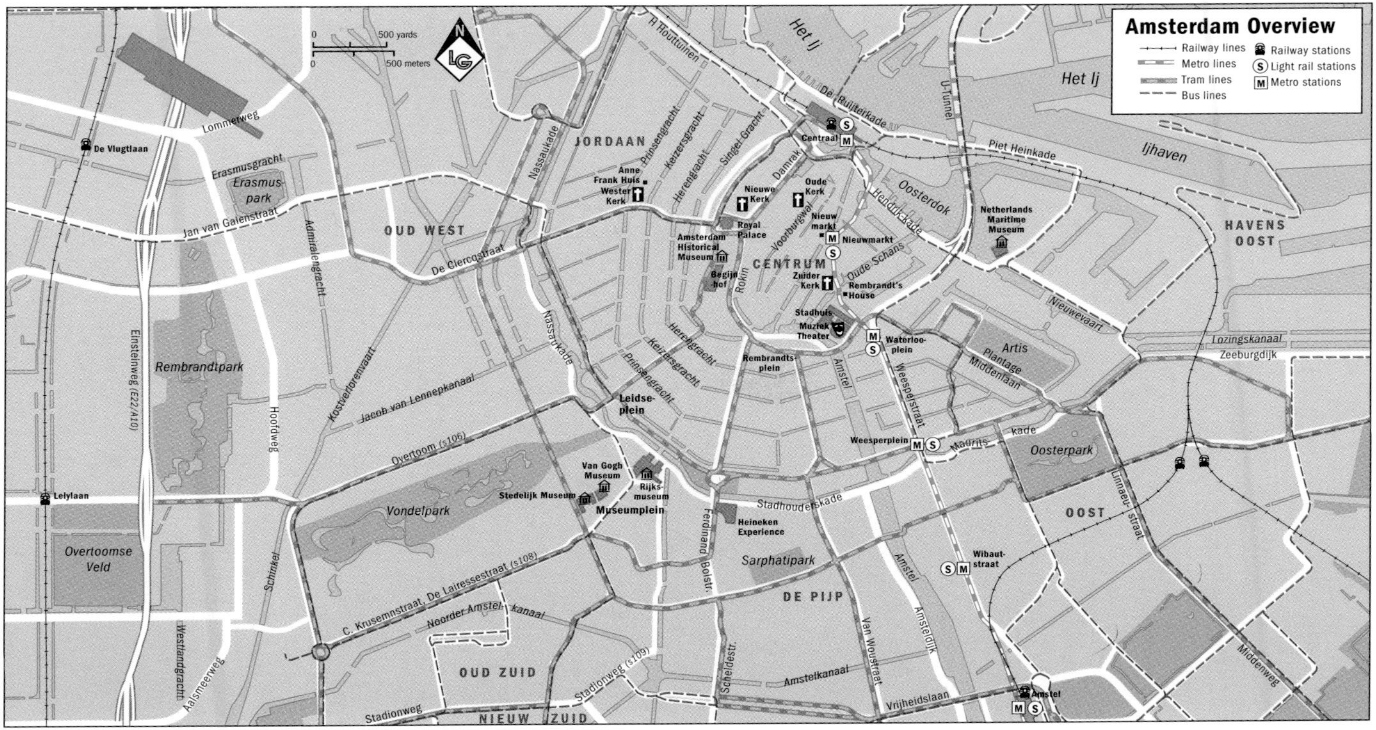

Amsterdam Overview
Railway lines
Metro lines
Tram lines
Bus lines
Railway stations
Light rail stations
Metro stations
0 500 yards
0 500 meters
N
LG
Het Ij
Ijhaven
HAVENS OOST
Lommerweg
De Vlugtlaan
Erasmusgracht
Erasmus-park
Jan van Galenstraat
OUD WEST
Admiralengracht
De Clercqstraat
Nassaukade
JORDAAN
H Houttuinen
Prinsengracht
Keizersgracht
Herengracht
Singel Gracht
Anne Frank Huis
Wester Kerk
Damrak
De Ruijterkade
Centraal
Nieuwe Kerk
Oude Kerk
Royal Palace
Voorburgwal
Nieuw markt
Nieuwmarkt
Amsterdam Historical Museum
Begijn-hof
Rokin
CENTRUM
Zuider Kerk
Oude Schans
Rembrandt's House
Stadhuis Muziek Theater
Waterloo-plein
U-Tunnel
Piet Heinkade
Oosterdok
Hendrikkade
Netherlands Maritime Museum
Nieuwevaart
Lozingskanaal
Zeeburgdijk
Artis
Plantage Middenlaan
Einsteinweg (E22/A10)
Rembrandtpark
Kostverlorenvaart
Jacob van Lennepkanaal
Hoofdweg
Leidse-plein
Rembrandts-plein
Amstel
Weesperstraat
Weesperplein
Mauritskade
Oosterpark
Overtoom (s106)
Van Gogh Museum
Rijks-museum
Stedelijk Museum
Museumplein
Lelylaan
Vondelpark
Stadhouderskade
Ferdinand Bolstr.
Heineken Experience
Sarphatipark
Wibaut-straat
OOST
Linnaeu-straat
Overtoomse Veld
Schinkel
C. Krusemnstraat, De Lairessestraat (s108)
Noorder Amstel-kanaal
DE PIJP
Westlandgracht
Aalsmeerweg
OUD ZUID
Stadionweg (s109)
Stadionweg
NIEUW ZUID
Scheldestr.
Amstelkanaal
Van Woustraat
Amsteldijk
Vrijheidslaan
Amstel
Middenweg

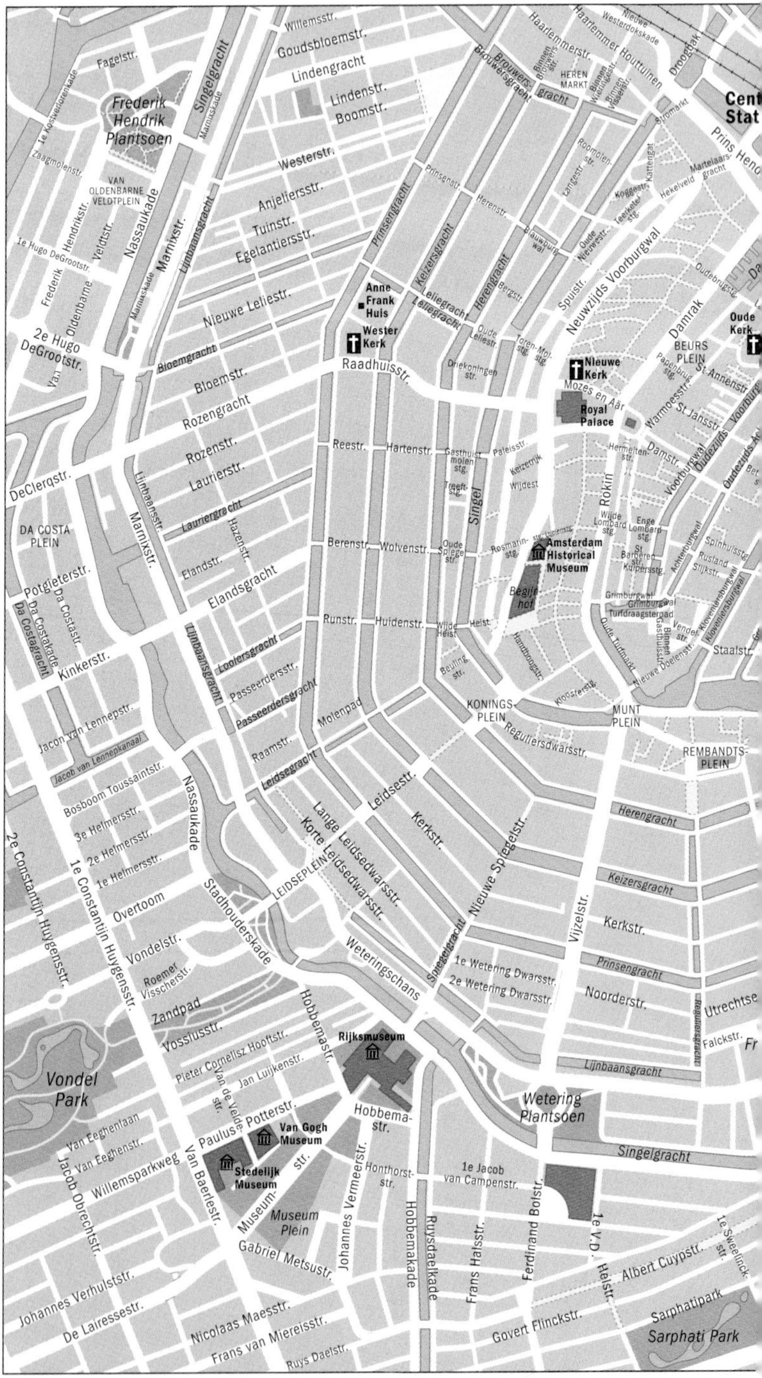

Willemsstr.
Goudsbloemstr.
Lindengracht
Lindenstr.
Boomstr.
Westerstr.
Anjeliersstr.
Tuinstr.
Egelantiersstr.
Nieuwe Leliestr.
Bloemgracht
Bloemstr.
Rozengracht
Rozenstr.
Laurierstr.
Lauriergracht
Elandstr.
Elandsgracht
Hazenstr.
Looiersgracht
Passeerdersstr.
Passeerdersgracht
Raamstr.
Leidsegracht
Molenpad
Fagelstr.
Frederik Hendrik Plantsoen
1e Kostverlorenkade
Zaagmolenstr.
VAN OLDENBARNE VELDTPLEIN
Nassaukade
Marnixstr.
Singelgracht
Marnixkade
Lijnbaansgracht
Hendrikstr.
Veldtstr.
1e Hugo DeGrootstr.
Frederik
Oldenbarne
2e Hugo DeGrootstr.
Van
DeClerqstr.
DA COSTA PLEIN
Potgieterstr.
Da Costastr.
Da Costakade
Da Costagracht
Kinkerstr.
Lijnbaansstr.
Jacob van Lennepstr.
Jacob van Lennepkanaal
Bosboom Toussaintstr.
3e Helmersstr.
2e Helmersstr.
1e Helmersstr.
Overtoom
2e Constantijn Huygensstr.
1e Constantijn Huygensstr.
Vondelstr.
Roemer Visscherstr.
Zandpad
Vossiusstr.
Vondel Park
Stadhouderskade
LEIDSEPLEIN
Pieter Cornelisz Hooftstr.
Jan Luijkenstr.
Van de Velde str.
Paulus Potterstr.
Van Eeghenlaan
Van Eeghenstr.
Willemsparkweg
Jacob Obrechtstr.
Van Baerlestr.
Van Gogh Museum
Stedelijk Museum
Museumstr.
Museum Plein
Gabriel Metsustr.
Johannes Verhulststr.
De Lairessestr.
Nicolaas Maesstr.
Frans van Mierisstr.
Ruys Daelstr.
Johannes Vermeerstr.
Hobbemastr.
Rijksmuseum
Hobbemakade
Honthorststr.
Ruysdaelkade
Frans Halsstr.
Ferdinand Bolstr.
1e Jacob van Campenstr.
1e V.D. Helststr.
Albert Cuypstr.
Govert Flinckstr.
1e Sweelinckstr.
Sarphatipark
Sarphati Park
Wetering Plantsoen
Singelgracht
Lijnbaansgracht
Weteringschans
1e Wetering Dwarsstr.
2e Wetering Dwarsstr.
Spiegelgracht
Nieuwe Spiegelstr.
Lange Leidsedwarsstr.
Korte Leidsedwarsstr.
Leidsestr.
Kerkstr.
Noorderstr.
Prinsengracht
Keizersgracht
Herengracht
Vijzelstr.
Utrechtse
Falckstr.
Reguliersgracht
REMBANDTS-PLEIN
Reguliersdwarsstr.
KONINGSPLEIN
MUNT PLEIN
Kloveniersburgwal
Staalstr.
Nieuwe Doelenstr.
Oude Turfmarkt
Binnen Gasthuisstr.
Turfdraagsterpad
Grimburgwal
Kloosterstg.
Handboogstr.
Heiligeweg
Beulingstr.
Wijde Heist
Begijnhof
Amsterdam Historical Museum
Rosmarijnstg.
Oude Spiegelstr.
Kalverstr.
Wijdest.
Treeftstg.
Gasthuismolenstg.
Paleisstr.
Keizerrijk
Singel
Rokin
Wijde Lombardstg.
Enge Lombardstg.
St. Barberenstr.
Kuipersstg.
Achterburgwal
Spinhuissteeg
Rusland
Slijkstr.
Hermeitenstr.
Damstr.
Voorburgwal
Oudezijds
St Jansstr.
Warmoesstr.
Royal Palace
Mozes en Aär
Nieuwe Kerk
Papenbrugstg.
St Annenstr.
BEURS PLEIN
Damrak
Oude Kerk
Oudebrugstg.
Neuwzijds Voorburgwal
Spuistr.
Torenstg.
Molstg.
Driekoningenstr.
Oude Leliestr.
Leliegracht
Bergstr.
Herengracht
Keizersgracht
Prinsengracht
Prinsenstr.
Herenstr.
Blauwburgwal
Oude Nieuwstr.
Teerketelstg.
Koggestr.
Kattengat
Hekelveld
Martelaarsgracht
Langestr.
Roomolenstr.
Anne Frank Huis
Wester Kerk
Raadhuisstr.
Reestr.
Hartenstr.
Berenstr.
Wolvenstr.
Runstr.
Huidenstr.
Brouwersgracht
HEREN MARKT
Binnen Brouwersstr.
Binnen Wieringerstr.
Binnen Visserstr.
Haarlemmerstr.
Haarlemmer Houttuinen
Nieuwe Westerdokskade
Droogbak
Stromarkt
Prins Hend
Cent Stat

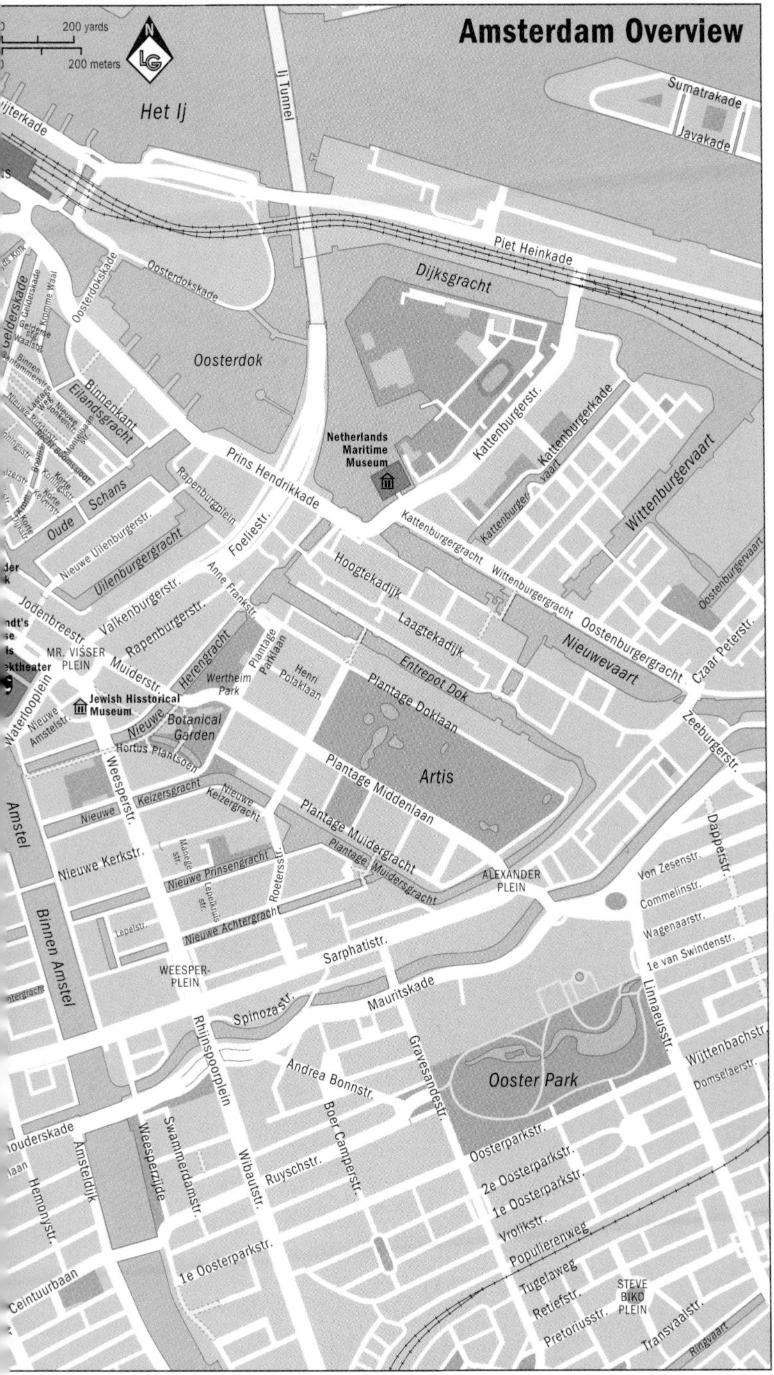

Amsterdam Overview
200 yards
200 meters
Het Ij
Ij Tunnel
Sumatrakade
Javakade
Piet Heinkade
Dijksgracht
Oosterdokskade
Oosterdok
Netherlands Maritime Museum
Kattenburgerstr.
Kattenburgerkade
Kattenburgervaart
Wittenburgervaart
Prins Hendrikkade
Rapenburgplein
Binnenkant
Eilandsgracht
Schans
Oude
Nieuwe Uilenburgerstr.
Uilenburgergracht
Foeliestr.
Kattenburgergracht
Wittenburgergracht
Oostenburgergracht
Oostenburgervaart
Hoogtekadijk
Laagtekadijk
Entrepot Dok
Nieuwevaart
Czaar Peterstr.
Anne Frankstr.
Valkenburgerstr.
Rapenburgerstr.
Jodenbreestr.
MR. VISSER PLEIN
Muiderstr.
Herengracht
Wertheim Park
Plantage Parklaan
Henri Polaklaan
Plantage Doklaan
Jewish Hisstorical Museum
Nieuwe
Botanical Garden
Hortus Plantsoen
Waterlooplein
Nieuwe Amstelstr.
Artis
Plantage Middenlaan
Zeeburgerstr.
Weesperstr.
Nieuwe Keizersgracht
Plantage Muidergracht
Amstel
Nieuwe Kerkstr.
Nieuwe Prinsengracht
Roetersstr.
ALEXANDER PLEIN
Dapperstr.
Von Zesenstr.
Commelinstr.
Wagenaarstr.
1e van Swindenstr.
Lepelstr.
Nieuwe Achtergracht
Binnen Amstel
Sarphatistr.
WEESPER-PLEIN
Mauritskade
Spinozastr.
Linnaeusstr.
Rhijnspoorplein
Gravesandestr.
Andrea Bonnstr.
Boer Camperstr.
Ooster Park
Wijttenbachstr.
Domselaerstr.
Amsteldijk
Weesperzijde
Swammerdamstr.
Wibautstr.
Ruyschstr.
Oosterparkstr.
2e Oosterparkstr.
1e Oosterparkstr.
Vrolikstr.
Populierenweg
Hemonystr.
1e Oosterparkstr.
Ceintuurbaan
Tugelaweg
Retiefstr.
Pretoriusstr.
STEVE BIKO PLEIN
Transvaalstr.
Ringvaart

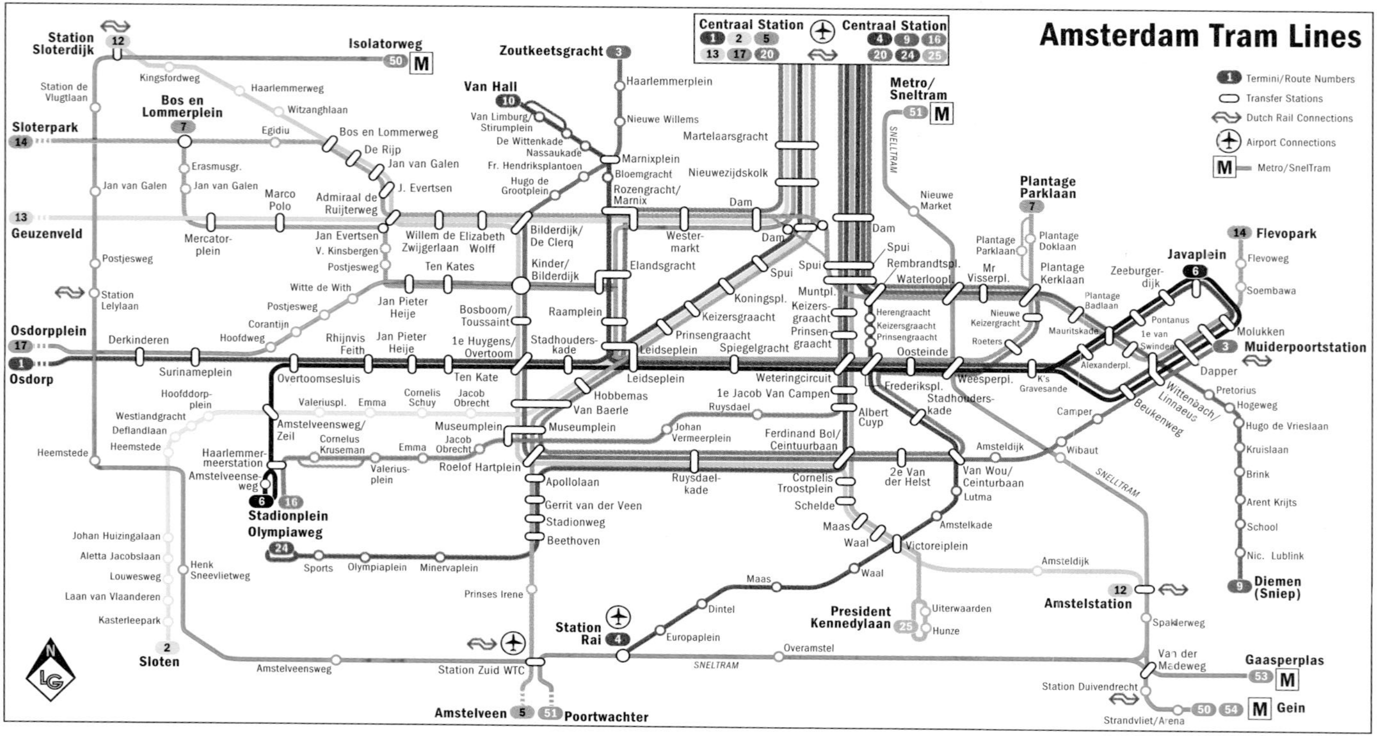
Amsterdam Tram Lines
Centraal Station 1 2 5 13 17 20
Centraal Station 4 9 16 20 24 25
Termini/Route Numbers
Transfer Stations
Dutch Rail Connections
Airport Connections
Metro/SnelTram
Station Sloterdijk 12
Isolatorweg 50 M
Zoutkeetsgracht 3
Van Hall 10
Metro/Sneltram 51 M
Plantage Parklaan 7
14 Flevopark
Javaplein 6
3 Muiderpoortstation
9 Diemen (Sniep)
Sloterpark 14
Bos en Lommerplein 7
13 Geuzenveld
Osdorpplein 17
1 Osdorp
Stadionplein 6
16
Olympiaweg 24
Sloten 2
Amstelveen 5
51 Poortwachter
Station Rai 4
President Kennedylaan 25
12 Amstelstation
Gaasperplas 53 M
50 54 M Gein
Station de Vlugtlaan
Kingsfordweg
Haarlemmerweg
Witzanghlaan
Egidiu
Bos en Lommerweg
De Rijp
Jan van Galen
J. Evertsen
Admiraal de Ruijterweg
Erasmusgr.
Jan van Galen
Marco Polo
Mercator-plein
Jan Evertsen
V. Kinsbergen
Postjesweg
Willem de Zwijgerlaan
Elizabeth Wolff
Ten Kates
Witte de With
Jan Pieter Heije
Postjesweg
Station Lelylaan
Corantijn
Hoofdweg
Derkinderen
Surinameplein
Rhijnvis Feith
Jan Pieter Heije
1e Huygens/ Overtoom
Bosboom/ Toussaint
Overtoomsesluis
Ten Kate
Hoofddorp-plein
Westlandgracht
Deflandlaan
Heemstede
Heemstede
Valeriuspl.
Emma
Cornelis Schuy
Jacob Obrecht
Amstelveensweg/ Zeil
Cornelus Kruseman
Emma
Jacob Obrecht
Museumplein
Valerius-plein
Haarlemmer-meerstation
Amstelveense-weg
Roelof Hartplein
Johan Huizingalaan
Aletta Jacobslaan
Louwesweg
Laan van Vlaanderen
Kasterleepark
Henk Sneevlietweg
Sports
Olympiaplein
Minervaplein
Prinses Irene
Amstelveensweg
Station Zuid WTC
Haarlemmerplein
Nieuwe Willems
Van Limburg/ Stirumplein
De Wittenkade
Nassaukade
Fr. Hendriksplantoen
Hugo de Grootplein
Marnixplein
Bloemgracht
Rozengracht/ Marnix
Martelaarsgracht
Nieuwezijdskolk
Dam
Bilderdijk/ De Clerq
Wester-markt
Dam
Kinder/ Bilderdijk
Elandsgracht
Spui
Raamplein
Koningspl.
Keizersgracht
Prinsengraacht
Stadhouders-kade
Leidseplein
Spiegelgracht
Leidseplein
Hobbemas
Van Baerle
Museumplein
Apollolaan
Gerrit van der Veen
Stadionweg
Beethoven
Dam
Spui
Rembrandtspl.
Waterloopl.
Muntpl.
Keizers-graacht
Prinsen-graacht
Herengraacht
Keizersgraacht
Prinsengraacht
Weteringcircuit
1e Jacob Van Campen
Ruysdael
Johan Vermeerplein
Albert Cuyp
Ferdinand Bol/ Ceintuurbaan
Ruysdael-kade
Cornelis Troostplein
Schelde
Maas
Waal
Victoreiplein
Waal
Maas
Dintel
Europaplein
Overamstel
SNELTRAM
Nieuwe Market
SNELLTRAM
Plantage Parklaan
Plantage Doklaan
Mr Visserpl.
Plantage Kerklaan
Nieuwe Keizergracht
Roeters
Oosteinde
Frederikspl.
Stadhouders-kade
Weesperpl.
K's Gravesande
Plantage Badlaan
Mauritskade
Zeeburger-dijk
Pontanus
1e van Swinden
Alexanderpl.
Flevoweg
Soembawa
Molukken
Dapper
Pretorius
Hogeweg
Wittenbach/ Linnaeus
Beukenweg
Hugo de Vrieslaan
Kruislaan
Brink
Arent Krijts
School
Nic. Lublink
Camper
Wibaut
Amsteldijk
2e Van der Helst
Van Wou/ Ceinturbaan
Lutma
Amstelkade
SNELLTRAM
Amsteldijk
Uiterwaarden
Hunze
Spaklerweg
Van der Madeweg
Station Duivendrecht
Strandvliet/Arena
N
LG

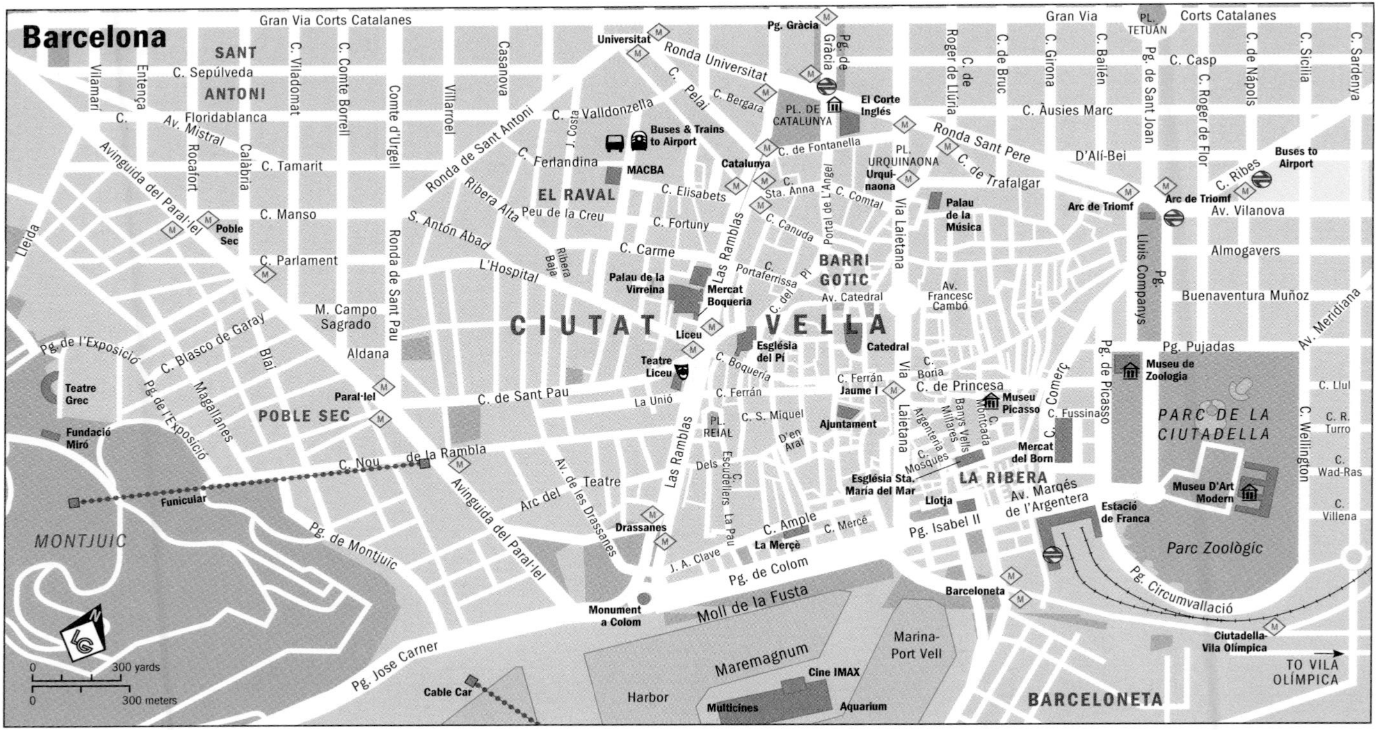
Barcelona
SANT
ANTONI
EL RAVAL
BARRI GOTIC
CIUTAT VELLA
LA RIBERA
POBLE SEC
BARCELONETA
MONTJUIC
PARC DE LA CIUTADELLA
Parc Zoològic
Gran Via Corts Catalanes
Gran Via
Corts Catalanes
PL. TETUAN
C. Sepúlveda
Floridablanca
Av. Mistral
Rocafort
Calàbria
C. Tamarit
C. Manso
C. Parlament
C. Viladomat
C. Comte Borrell
Comte d'Urgell
Villarroel
Casanova
Vilamarí
Entença
Avinguda del Paral·lel
Lleida
Ronda de Sant Antoni
Ronda de Sant Pau
Ronda Universitat
C. Pelai
C. Bergara
C. Valldonzella
J. Costa
C. Ferlandina
Ribera Alta
Peu de la Creu
S. Antón Abad
L'Hospital
Ribera Baja
C. Elisabets
C. Fortuny
C. Carme
Las Ramblas
C. Portaferrissa
C. del Pi
C. Canuda
C. Sta. Anna
Portal de L'Angel
C. Comtal
C. de Fontanella
PL. DE CATALUNYA
PL. URQUINAONA
Via Laietana
Ronda Sant Pere
C. de Trafalgar
Pg. de Gràcia
C. de Roger de Llúria
C. de Bruc
C. Girona
C. Bailén
Pg. de Sant Joan
C. Casp
C. Roger de Flor
C. de Nápols
C. Sicilia
C. Sardenya
C. Àusies Marc
D'Alí-Bei
C. Ribes
Av. Vilanova
Almogavers
Buenaventura Muñoz
Av. Meridiana
Pg. Lluis Companys
Pg. Pujadas
Pg. de Picasso
C. Wellington
C. Llul
C. R. Turro
C. Wad-Ras
C. Villena
Av. Catedral
Av. Francesc Cambó
C. Boria
C. de Princesa
C. Comerç
C. Fussina
C. Montcada
Banys Vells
Millares
Argenteria
C. Mosques
C. Boquería
C. Ferrán
C. S. Miquel
D'en Arai
PL. REIAL
Dels Escudellers
C. Escudellers
La Pau
C. Ample
C. Mercè
J. A. Clave
Pg. de Colom
Moll de la Fusta
Pg. Isabel II
Av. Marqués de l'Argentera
Pg. Circumvallació
La Unió
C. de Sant Pau
Av. de les Drassanes
Arc del Teatre
C. Nou de la Rambla
Aldana
M. Campo Sagrado
Blai
C. Blasco de Garay
Magallanes
Pg. de l'Exposició
Pg. de Montjuïc
Pg. Jose Carner
Universitat
Pg. Gràcia
El Corte Inglés
Buses & Trains to Airport
MACBA
Catalunya
Urquinaona
Palau de la Música
Arc de Triomf
Buses to Airport
Palau de la Virreina
Mercat Boqueria
Liceu
Teatre Liceu
Església del Pí
Catedral
Jaume I
Ajuntament
Museu Picasso
Mercat del Born
Església Sta. María del Mar
Llotja
Estació de Franca
Museu de Zoologia
Museu D'Art Modern
La Mercè
Drassanes
Monument a Colom
Barceloneta
Ciutadella-Vila Olímpica
TO VILA OLÍMPICA
Marina-Port Vell
Maremagnum
Cine IMAX
Aquarium
Multicines
Harbor
Cable Car
Funicular
Paral·lel
Poble Sec
Teatre Grec
Fundació Miró
0 300 yards
0 300 meters

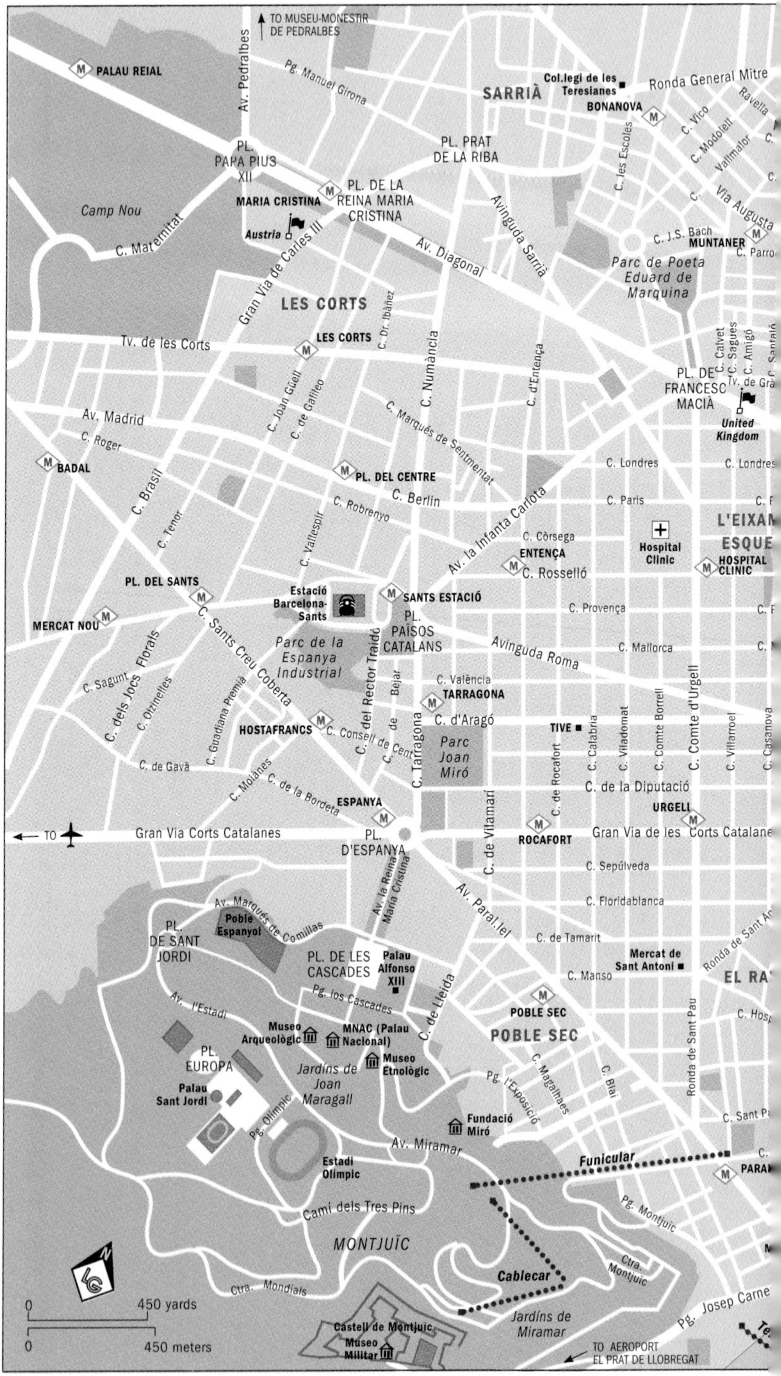

TO MUSEU-MONESTIR DE PEDRALBES
PALAU REIAL
Av. Pedralbes
Pg. Manuel Girona
SARRIÀ
Col.legi de les Teresianes
Ronda General Mitre
BONANOVA
C. Vico
C. Modolell
Vallmajor
Ravella
C. les Escoles
PL. PRAT DE LA RIBA
PL. PAPA PIUS XII
Via Augusta
MARIA CRISTINA
PL. DE LA REINA MARIA CRISTINA
Camp Nou
Austria
C. J.S. Bach
MUNTANER
C. Parro
C. Maternitat
Gran Via de Carles III
Av. Diagonal
Avinguda Sarrià
Parc de Poeta Eduard de Marquina
LES CORTS
C. Dr. Ibáñez
C. Numància
C. d'Entença
C. Calvet
C. Sagues
C. Amigó
Tv. de les Corts
LES CORTS
C. Joan Güell
C. de Galileo
PL. DE FRANCESC MACIÀ
Tv. de Grà
United Kingdom
Av. Madrid
C. Roger
C. Marquès de Sentmenat
BADAL
PL. DEL CENTRE
C. Londres
C. Londres
C. Berlin
C. Paris
C. Brasil
C. Robrenyo
Av. la Infanta Carlota
L'EIXAM
ESQUE
C. Tenor
C. Vallespir
C. Còrsega
Hospital Clinic
ENTENÇA
HOSPITAL CLINIC
C. Rosselló
PL. DEL SANTS
Estació Barcelona-Sants
SANTS ESTACIÓ
MERCAT NOU
C. Provença
C. Sants Creu Coberta
PL. PAÏSOS CATALANS
C. dels Jocs Florals
Parc de la Espanya Industrial
C. del Rector Triadó
Avinguda Roma
C. Mallorca
C. Sagunt
C. Olzinelles
C. Bejar
C. València
C. Guadiana Premia
TARRAGONA
C. d'Aragó
HOSTAFRANCS
C. Consell de Cent
C. Tarragona
TIVE
Parc Joan Miró
C. de Rocafort
C. Calabria
C. Viladomat
C. Comte Borrell
C. Comte d'Urgell
C. Villarroel
C. Casanova
C. de Gavà
C. Moianès
C. de la Bordeta
C. de la Diputació
ESPANYA
URGELL
TO
Gran Via Corts Catalanes
PL. D'ESPANYA
C. de Vilamarí
ROCAFORT
Gran Via de les Corts Catalane
Av. la Reina Maria Cristina
C. Sepúlveda
Av. Paral.lel
C. Floridablanca
Av. Marquès de Comillas
Poble Espanyol
PL. DE SANT JORDI
C. de Tamarit
PL. DE LES CASCADES
Palau Alfonso XIII
Mercat de Sant Antoni
Ronda de Sant An
C. Manso
EL RA
Pg. los Cascades
C. de Lleida
Av. l'Estadi
POBLE SEC
C. Hosp
Museo Arqueològic
MNAC (Palau Nacional)
POBLE SEC
PL. EUROPA
Museo Etnològic
C. Magalhaes
C. Blai
Ronda de Sant Pau
Jardins de Joan Maragall
Pg. l'Exposició
Palau Sant Jordi
Pg. Olímpic
Fundació Miró
C. Sant Pa
Av. Miramar
Funicular
Estadi Olímpic
PARA
Pg. Montjuïc
Camí dels Tres Pins
MONTJUÏC
Ctra. Montjuïc
Cablecar
Ctra. Mondials
Pg. Josep Carne
0
450 yards
0
450 meters
Jardins de Miramar
Castell de Montjuïc
Museo Militar
TO AEROPORT EL PRAT DE LLOBREGAT

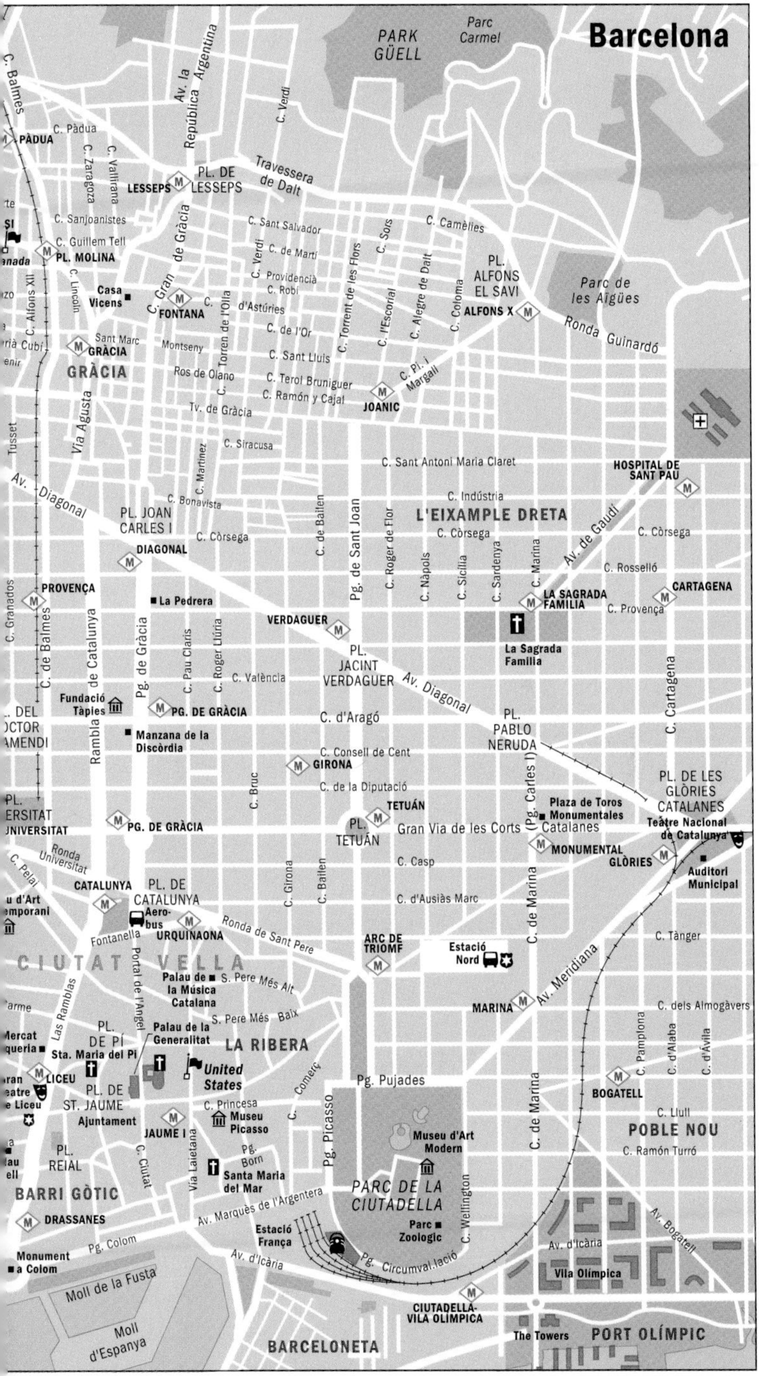
Barcelona
PARK GÜELL
Parc Carmel
C. Balmes
Av. la República Argentina
C. Verdi
C. Pàdua
PÀDUA
C. Zaragoza
C. Vallirana
PL. DE LESSEPS
LESSEPS
Travessera de Dalt
C. Sanjoanistes
C. Guillem Tell
PL. MOLINA
C. Sant Salvador
C. de Martí
C. Verdi
C. Camèlies
C. Sors
C. Torrent de les Flors
C. Alegre de Dalt
PL. ALFONS EL SAVI
Parc de les Aïgües
C. Gran de Gràcia
Casa Vicens
C. Lincoln
C. Alfons XII
Providència
C. Robí
d'Astúries
FONTANA
C. Torren de l'Olla
C. de l'Or
C. l'Escorial
C. Coloma
ALFONS X
Ronda Guinardó
Sant Marc
GRÀCIA
Montseny
C. Sant Lluís
C. Pi. i Margall
Ros de Olano
C. Terol Bruniguer
C. Ramón y Cajal
JOANIC
GRÀCIA
Via Augusta
Tv. de Gràcia
C. Siracusa
Tusset
C. Martínez
C. Sant Antoni Maria Claret
HOSPITAL DE SANT PAU
Av. Diagonal
C. Bonavista
C. Indústria
PL. JOAN CARLES I
L'EIXAMPLE DRETA
C. Còrsega
C. Còrsega
C. Còrsega
Av. de Gaudí
C. de Bailen
Pg. de Sant Joan
C. Roger de Flor
C. Nàpols
C. Sicília
C. Sardenya
C. Marina
DIAGONAL
C. Rosselló
PROVENÇA
La Pedrera
LA SAGRADA FAMILIA
CARTAGENA
C. Provença
C. Granados
C. de Balmes
Rambla de Catalunya
Pg. de Gràcia
C. Pau Claris
C. Roger Llúria
VERDAGUER
PL. JACINT VERDAGUER
La Sagrada Familia
C. València
Av. Diagonal
C. Cartagena
Fundació Tàpies
PG. DE GRÀCIA
C. d'Aragó
PL. PABLO NERUDA
Manzana de la Discòrdia
C. Consell de Cent
GIRONA
C. de la Diputació
C. Bruc
TETUÁN
(Pg. Carles I)
Plaza de Toros Monumentales Catalanes
PL. DE LES GLÒRIES CATALANES
Teatre Nacional de Catalunya
PG. DE GRÀCIA
PL. TETUÁN
Gran Via de les Corts Catalanes
MONUMENTAL
GLÒRIES
Ronda Universitat
C. Pelai
C. Girona
C. Bailen
C. Casp
Auditori Municipal
CATALUNYA
PL. DE CATALUNYA
C. d'Ausiàs Marc
Aero-bus
URQUINAONA
Ronda de Sant Pere
Fontanella
C. de Marina
ARC DE TRIOMF
Estació Nord
C. Tànger
CIUTAT VELLA
Portal de l'Àngel
Palau de la Música Catalana
S. Pere Més Alt
Av. Meridiana
MARINA
C. dels Almogàvers
Las Ramblas
S. Pere Més Baix
PL. DE PÍ
Palau de la Generalitat
LA RIBERA
C. Pamplona
C. d'Alaba
C. d'Àvila
Sta. Maria del Pi
LICEU
United States
C. Comerç
Pg. Pujades
BOGATELL
PL. DE ST. JAUME
C. Princesa
Ajuntament
Museu Picasso
Pg. Picasso
Museu d'Art Modern
C. de Marina
C. Llull
POBLE NOU
JAUME I
C. Ramón Turró
PL. REIAL
C. Ciutat
Via Laietana
Pg. Born
Santa Maria del Mar
PARC DE LA CIUTADELLA
BARRI GÒTIC
Av. Marquès de l'Argentera
C. Wellington
DRASSANES
Estació França
Parc Zoològic
Av. Bogatell
Pg. Colom
Av. d'Icària
Monument a Colom
Av. d'Icària
Pg. Circumval.lació
Vila Olímpica
Moll de la Fusta
CIUTADELLA-VILA OLIMPICA
Moll d'Espanya
BARCELONETA
The Towers
PORT OLÍMPIC

Barcelona Metro

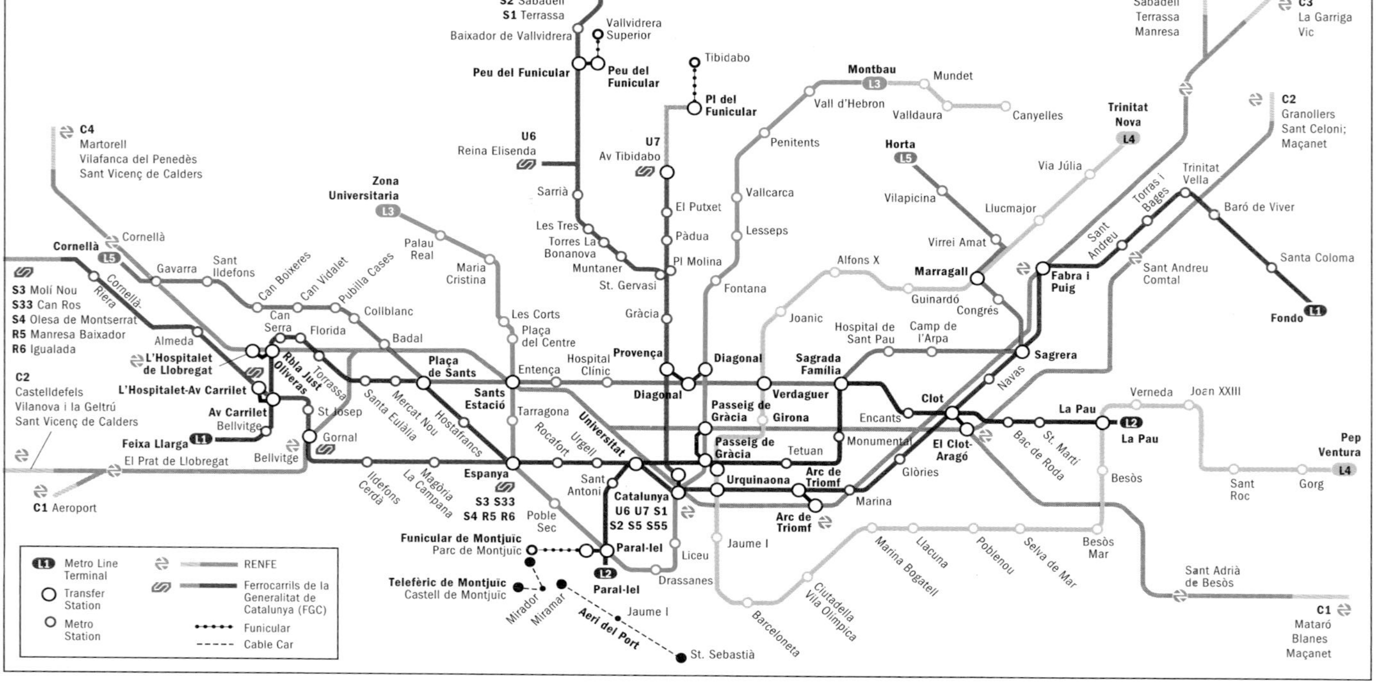

Berlin Transit

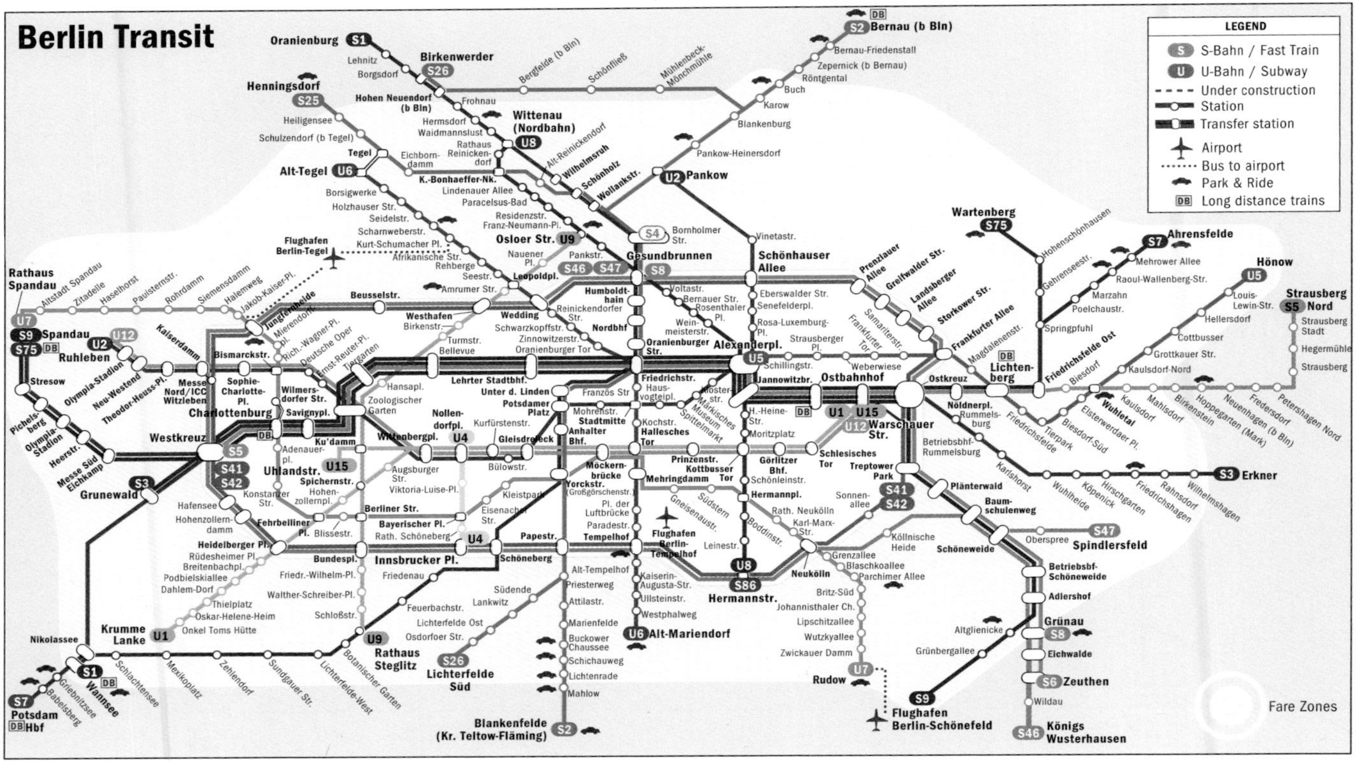

Berlin Overview

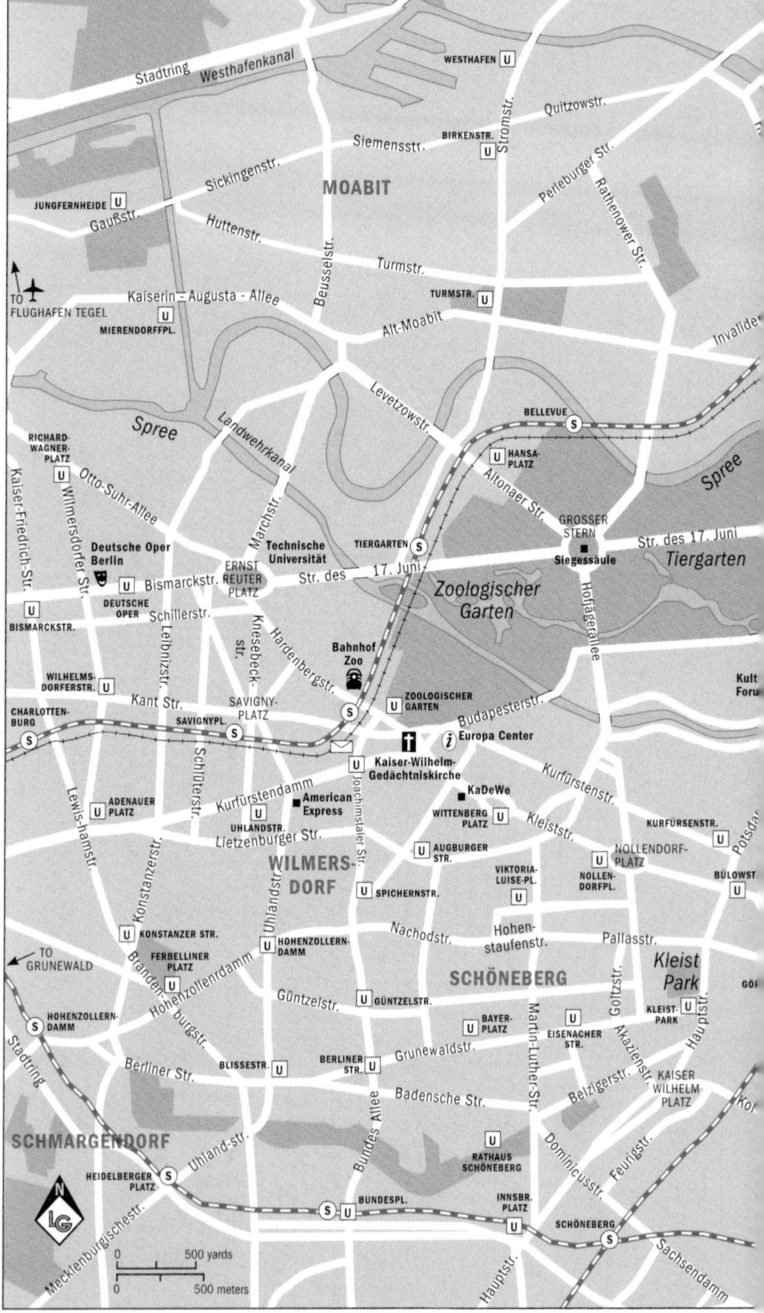

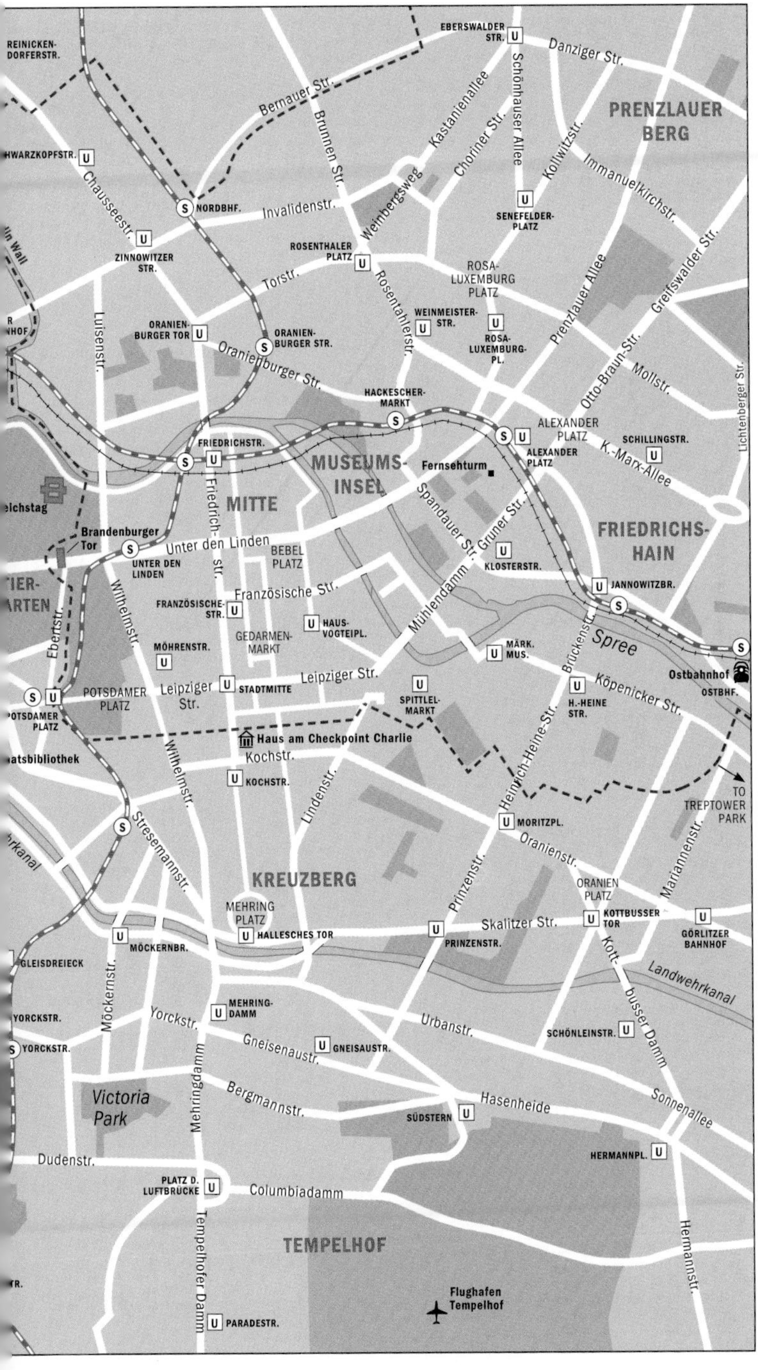

EBERSWALDER STR.
REINICKEN-DORFERSTR.
Danziger Str.
PRENZLAUER BERG
Bernauer Str.
Brunnen Str.
Kastanienallee
Schönhauser Allee
Choriner Str.
Kollwitzstr.
Immanuelkirchstr.
HWARZKOPFSTR.
Chausseestr.
NORDBHF.
Invalidenstr.
Weinbergsweg
SENEFELDER-PLATZ
ZINNOWITZER STR.
ROSENTHALER PLATZ
Greifswalder Str.
Torstr.
ROSA-LUXEMBURG PLATZ
Prenzlauer Allee
Rosentahlerstr.
Luisenstr.
ORANIEN-BURGER TOR
ORANIEN-BURGER STR.
WEINMEISTER-STR.
ROSA-LUXEMBURG-PL.
Otto-Braun-Str.
Oranienburger Str.
Mollstr.
Lichtenberger Str.
HACKESCHER-MARKT
ALEXANDER PLATZ
SCHILLINGSTR.
FRIEDRICHSTR.
ALEXANDER PLATZ
K.-Marx-Allee
MUSEUMS-INSEL
Fernsehturm
MITTE
Friedrich-str.
Spandauer Str.
Gruner Str.
FRIEDRICHS-HAIN
Brandenburger Tor
Unter den Linden
BEBEL PLATZ
KLOSTERSTR.
UNTER DEN LINDEN
Französische Str.
JANNOWITZBR.
FRANZÖSISCHE-STR.
Mühlendamm
HAUS-VOGTEIPL.
Spree
GEDARMEN-MARKT
MÄRK. MUS.
Ebertstr.
MÖHRENSTR.
Brückenstr.
Wilhelmstr.
Ostbahnhof
Leipziger Str.
STADTMITTE
Köpenicker Str.
OSTBHF.
POTSDAMER PLATZ
Leipziger Str.
SPITTEL-MARKT
H.-HEINE STR.
POTSDAMER PLATZ
Heinrich-Heine-Str.
Haus am Checkpoint Charlie
atsbibliothek
Kochstr.
KOCHSTR.
Lindenstr.
TO TREPTOWER PARK
Wilhelmstr.
MORITZPL.
Stresemannstr.
Oranienstr.
Mariannenstr.
rkanal
KREUZBERG
Prinzenstr.
ORANIEN PLATZ
MEHRING PLATZ
Skalitzer Str.
KOTTBUSSER TOR
GÖRLITZER BAHNHOF
MÖCKERNBR.
HALLESCHES TOR
PRINZENSTR.
Kott-busser Damm
GLEISDREIECK
Landwehrkanal
Möckernstr.
MEHRING-DAMM
YORCKSTR.
Yorckstr.
Urbanstr.
YORCKSTR.
Gneisenaustr.
GNEISAUSTR.
SCHÖNLEINSTR.
Mehringdamm
Victoria Park
Bergmannstr.
Hasenheide
Sonnenallee
SÜDSTERN
Dudenstr.
HERMANNPL.
PLATZ D. LUFTBRÜCKE
Columbiadamm
Tempelhofer Damm
TEMPELHOF
Hermannstr.
Flughafen Tempelhof
PARADESTR.

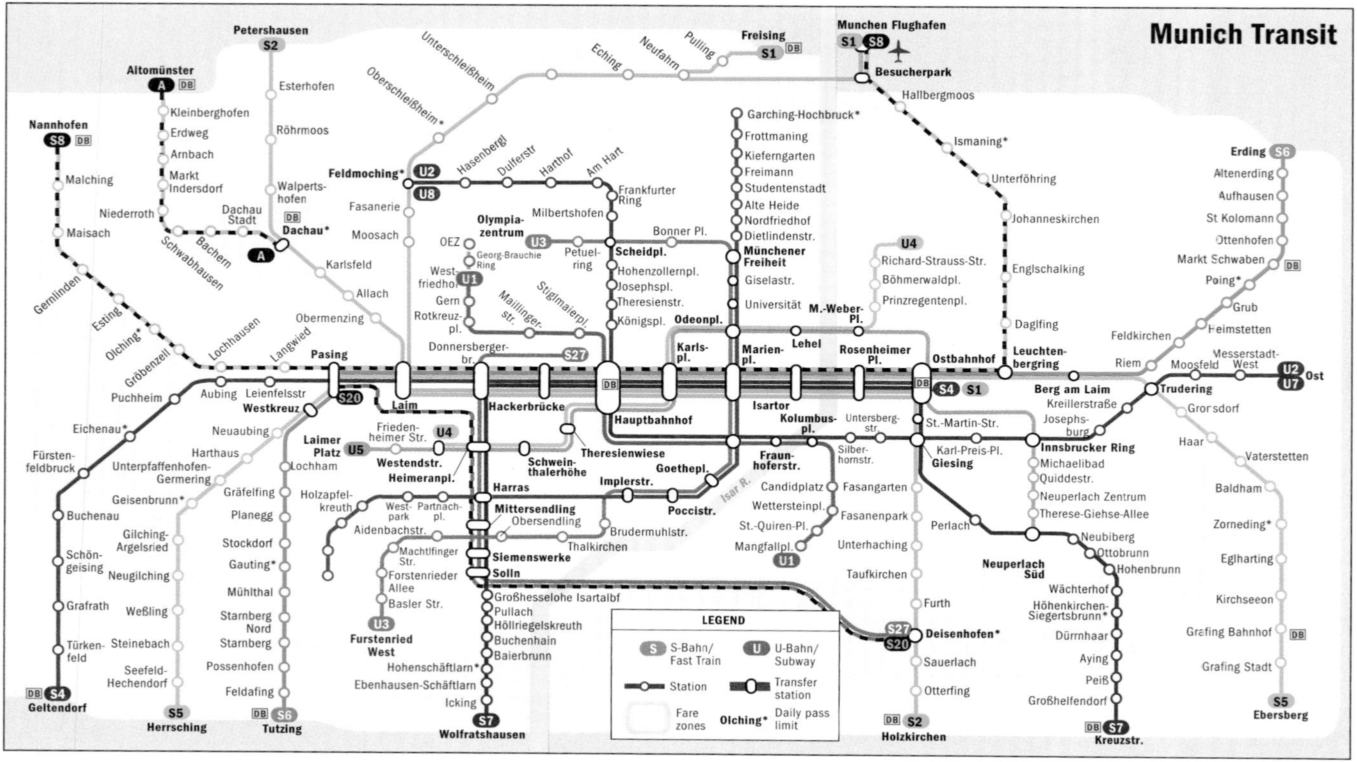

Munich Transit
Petershausen
S2
Esterhofen
Röhrmoos
Walperts-hofen
Dachau*
Dachau Stadt
Altomünster
A
Kleinberghofen
Erdweg
Arnbach
Markt Indersdorf
Niederroth
Schwabhausen
Bachern
Nannhofen
S8
Malching
Maisach
Gernlinden
Esting
Olching*
Gröbenzell
Lochhausen
Langwied
Pasing
Puchheim
Aubing
Leienfelsstr
Westkreuz
S20
Eichenau*
Fürsten-feldbruck
Buchenau
Schön-geising
Grafrath
Türken-feld
Geltendorf
S4
Neuaubing
Harthaus
Unterpfaffenhofen-Germering
Geisenbrunn*
Gilching-Argelsried
Neugilching
Weßling
Steinebach
Seefeld-Hechendorf
S5
Herrsching
Lochham
Gräfelfing
Planegg
Stockdorf
Gauting*
Mühlthal
Starnberg Nord
Starnberg
Possenhofen
Feldafing
S6
Tutzing
Oberschleißheim*
Unterschleißheim
Eching
Neufahrn
Pulling
Freising
S1
Munchen Flughafen
Besucherpark
Hallbergmoos
Ismaning*
Unterföhring
Johanneskirchen
Englschalking
Daglfing
Leuchten-bergring
Feldmoching*
U2
U8
Hasenbergl
Dulferstr
Harthof
Am Hart
Frankfurter Ring
Milbertshofen
Fasanerie
Moosach
Karlsfeld
Allach
Obermenzing
Laim
Olympia-zentrum
OEZ
Georg-Brauchie Ring
U3
Petuel-ring
West-friedhof
U1
Gern
Rotkreuz-pl.
Maillinger-str.
Stiglmaierpl.
Donnersberger-br.
S27
Hackerbrücke
Scheidpl.
Bonner Pl.
Hohenzollernpl.
Josephspl.
Theresienstr.
Königspl.
Hauptbahnhof
DB
Karls-pl.
Odeonpl.
Garching-Hochbruck*
Frottmaning
Kieferngarten
Freimann
Studentenstadt
Alte Heide
Nordfriedhof
Dietlindenstr.
Münchener Freiheit
Giselastr.
Universität
Marien-pl.
Isartor
Lehel
M.-Weber-Pl.
U4
Richard-Strauss-Str.
Böhmerwaldpl.
Prinzregentenpl.
Rosenheimer Pl.
Ostbahnhof
S4
S1
Berg am Laim
Riem
Feldkirchen
Heimstetten
Grub
Poing*
Markt Schwaben
Ottenhofen
St Kolomann
Aufhausen
Altenerding
Erding
S6
Moosfeld
Messerstadt-West
U2
U7
Ost
Trudering
Kreillerstraße
Josephs-burg
Innsbrucker Ring
Michaelibad
Quiddestr.
Neuperlach Zentrum
Therese-Giehse-Allee
Neuperlach Süd
Neubiberg
Ottobrunn
Hohenbrunn
Wächterhof
Höhenkirchen-Siegertsbrunn*
Dürrnhaar
Aying
Peiß
Großhelfendorf
S7
Kreuzstr.
Gronsdorf
Haar
Vaterstetten
Baldham
Zorneding*
Eglharting
Kirchseeon
Grafing Bahnhof
Grafing Stadt
S5
Ebersberg
St.-Martin-Str.
Karl-Preis-Pl.
Giesing
Perlach
Untersberg-str.
Silber-hornstr.
Kolumbus-pl.
Fraun-hoferstr.
Candidplatz
Fasangarten
Wettersteinpl.
Fasanenpark
St.-Quiren-Pl.
Mangfallpl.
U1
Unterhaching
Taufkirchen
Furth
Deisenhofen*
S27
S20
Sauerlach
Otterfing
S2
Holzkirchen
Isar R.
Goethepl.
Poccistr.
Implerstr.
Theresienwiese
Schwein-thalerhöhe
Laimer Platz
U5
Frieden-heimer Str.
U4
Westendstr.
Heimeranpl.
Harras
Mittersendling
Obersendling
Siemenswerke
Solln
Holzapfel-kreuth
West-park
Partnach-pl.
Aidenbachstr.
Brudermuhlstr.
Thalkirchen
Machtlfinger Str.
Forstenrieder Allee
Basler Str.
U3
Furstenried West
Großhesselohe Isartalbf
Pullach
Höllriegelskreuth
Buchenhain
Baierbrunn
Hohenschäftlarn*
Ebenhausen-Schäftlarn
Icking
S7
Wolfratshausen
LEGEND
S S-Bahn/ Fast Train
U U-Bahn/ Subway
Station
Transfer station
Fare zones
Olching* Daily pass limit

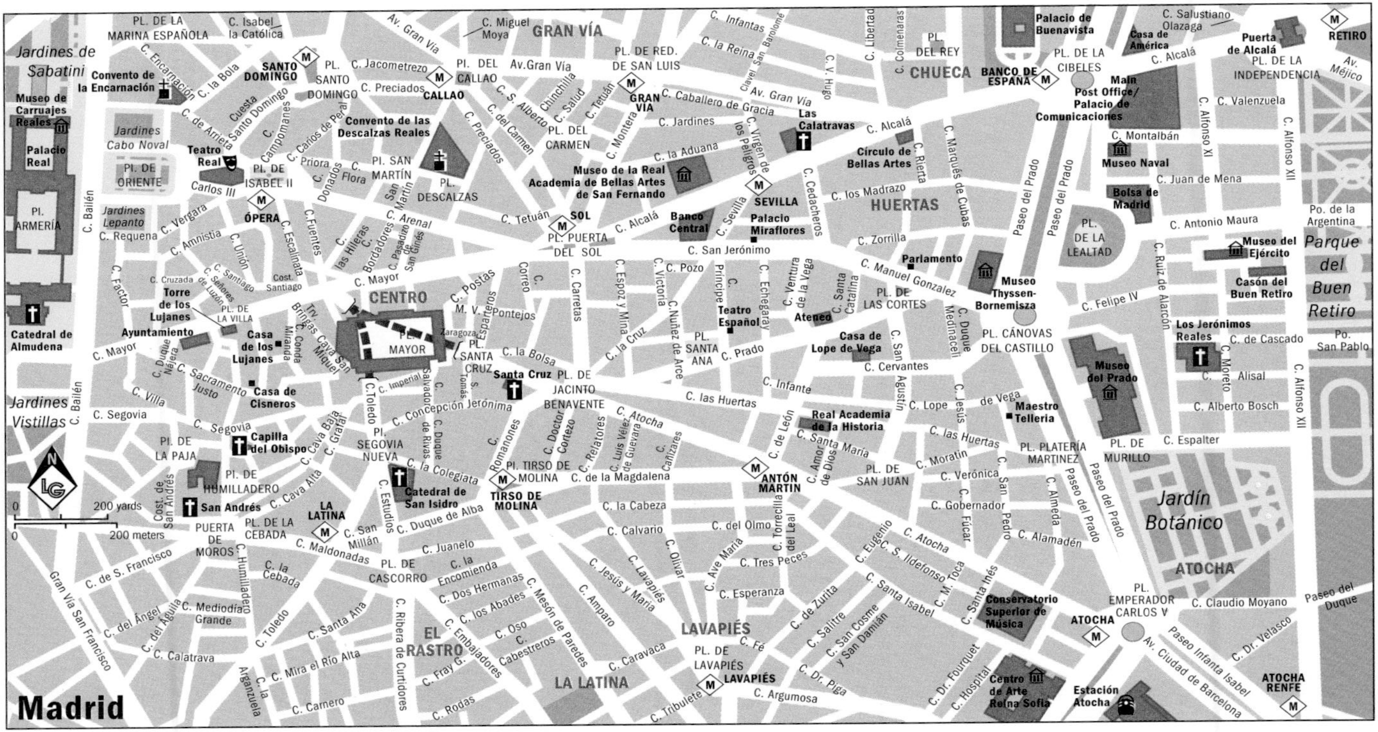

Madrid
Jardines de Sabatini
Museo de Carruajes Reales
Palacio Real
PL. ARMERÍA
Catedral de Almudena
Jardines Vistillas
C. Bailén
PL. DE LA MARINA ESPAÑOLA
C. Isabel la Católica
Convento de la Encarnación
C. Encarnación
C. la Bola
SANTO DOMINGO
PL. SANTO DOMINGO
Cuesta Santo Domingo
C. de Arrieta
C. Campomanes
Jardines Cabo Noval
PL. DE ORIENTE
Teatro Real
PL. DE ISABEL II
Carlos III
ÓPERA
Jardines Lepanto
C. Requena
C. Vergara
C. Amnistía
C. Unión
C. Escalinata
C. Fuentes
C. las Hileras
C. Bordadores
C. Pasadizo de San Ginés
C. Arenal
C. Donados
C. Flora
Priora
C. Caños de Peral
PL. SAN MARTÍN
San Martín
Convento de las Descalzas Reales
PL. DESCALZAS
C. Preciados
C. Jacometrezo
CALLAO
PL. DEL CALLAO
Av. Gran Vía
C. Miguel Moya
GRAN VÍA
C. S. Alberto
C. del Carmen
PL. DEL CARMEN
C. Chinchilla
C. Salud
C. Tetuán
C. Montera
PL. DE RED. DE SAN LUIS
GRAN VÍA
C. Caballero de Gracia
C. Jardines
C. la Aduana
Museo de la Real Academia de Bellas Artes de San Fernando
C. Tetuán
SOL
PL. PUERTA DEL SOL
C. Alcalá
Banco Central
C. Sevilla
SEVILLA
Palacio Miraflores
C. Virgen de los Peligros
Las Calatravas
C. Infantas
C. la Reina
Clavel
San Bartolomé
C. V. Hugo
C. Libertad
C. Colmenaras
PL. DEL REY
CHUECA
C. Cedacheros
Círculo de Bellas Artes
C. Rierta
C. los Madrazo
HUERTAS
C. Marqués de Cubas
BANCO DE ESPAÑA
Palacio de Buenavista
PL. DE LA CIBELES
Main Post Office/ Palacio de Comunicaciones
Casa de América
C. Salustiano Olazaga
Puerta de Alcalá
PL. DE LA INDEPENDENCIA
RETIRO
Av. Méjico
C. Valenzuela
C. Alfonso XI
C. Alfonso XII
C. Montalbán
Museo Naval
C. Juan de Mena
Bolsa de Madrid
C. Antonio Maura
Po. de la Argentina
Parque del Buen Retiro
Museo del Ejército
Casón del Buen Retiro
PL. DE LA LEALTAD
Paseo del Prado
C. Ruiz de Alarcón
C. Felipe IV
Los Jerónimos Reales
C. de Cascado
C. Moreto
Alisal
Po. San Pablo
C. Alberto Bosch
C. Espalter
Museo del Prado
PL. DE MURILLO
Jardín Botánico
ATOCHA
C. Claudio Moyano
Paseo del Duque
PL. EMPERADOR CARLOS V
Paseo Infanta Isabel
Av. Ciudad de Barcelona
C. Dr. Velasco
ATOCHA RENFE
Estación Atocha
Museo Thyssen-Bornemisza
PL. CÁNOVAS DEL CASTILLO
C. Duque Medinaceli
Parlamento
C. Manuel Gonzalez
C. Zorrilla
C. San Jerónimo
PL. DE LAS CORTES
C. Santa Catalina
C. Ventura de la Vega
Ateneo
C. Echegaray
Teatro Español
C. Príncipe
PL. SANTA ANA
C. Prado
Casa de Lope de Vega
C. Cervantes
C. San Agustín
C. Lope de Vega
C. Jesús
Maestro Tellería
C. las Huertas
PL. PLATERÍA MARTINEZ
C. Moratín
C. Verónica
C. San Pedro
C. Fúcar
C. Gobernador
C. Almeda
C. Alamadén
C. Infante
C. las Huertas
Real Academia de la Historia
C. de León
C. Santa María
C. Amor de Dios
PL. DE SAN JUAN
ANTÓN MARTÍN
C. Torrecilla del Leal
C. del Olmo
C. Tres Peces
C. Ave María
C. Esperanza
C. Olivar
C. Lavapiés
LAVAPIÉS
PL. DE LAVAPIÉS
C. Fé
C. de Zurita
C. Salitre
C. San Cosme y San Damián
C. Dr. Piga
C. Argumosa
C. Tribulete
C. Caravaca
C. Eugenio
C. Atocha
C. S. Ildefonso
C. M. Toca
C. Santa Isabel
C. Santa Inés
Conservatorio Superior de Música
C. Dr. Fourquet
C. Hospital
Centro de Arte Reina Sofía
C. Pozo
C. Victoria
C. Nuñez de Arce
C. Espoz y Mina
C. la Cruz
C. Carretas
C. Correo
M. V. Pontejos
C. Postas
C. Esparteros
CENTRO
PL. MAYOR
Zaragoza
PL. SANTA CRUZ
C. la Bolsa
Santa Cruz
PL. DE JACINTO BENAVENTE
S. Tomás
C. Concepción Jerónima
C. Imperial
C. Toledo
C. Salvador
C. Duque de Rivas
C. Romanones
C. Doctor Cortezo
C. Relatores
C. Luis Velez de Guevara
C. Cañizares
C. Atocha
PL. TIRSO DE MOLINA
TIRSO DE MOLINA
C. de la Magdalena
C. la Cabeza
C. Calvario
C. Jesús y María
C. Amparo
C. Mayor
C. Cruzada
C. Santiago
C. Señores de Luzón
Cost. Santiago
Torre de los Lujanes
PL. DE LA VILLA
Ayuntamiento
Casa de los Lujanes
C. Conda Miranda
Trv. Bringas
Cava San Miguel
C. Duque Nájera
C. Sacramento
Justo
Casa de Cisneros
C. Villa
C. Segovia
C. Factor
C. Cava Baja
C. Grafal
Capilla del Obispo
PL. SEGOVIA NUEVA
C. la Colegiata
Catedral de San Isidro
C. Estudios
PL. DE LA PAJA
PL. DE HUMILLADERO
C. Cava Alta
San Andrés
Cost. de San Andrés
LA LATINA
C. San Millán
C. Duque de Alba
PL. DE LA CEBADA
PUERTA DE MOROS
C. Maldonadas
C. Juanelo
PL. DE CASCORRO
C. la Encomienda
C. Dos Hermanas
C. los Abades
C. Mesón de Paredes
C. Oso
C. Cabestreros
C. Embajadores
EL RASTRO
C. Ribera de Curtidores
C. Fray G.
C. Rodas
LA LATINA
C. Humilladero
C. la Cebada
C. de S. Francisco
Gran Vía San Francisco
C. del Ángel
C. del Águila
C. Mediodía Grande
C. Toledo
C. Santa Ana
C. Calatrava
C. Mira el Río Alta
C. la Arganzuela
C. Carnero
0
200 yards
200 meters

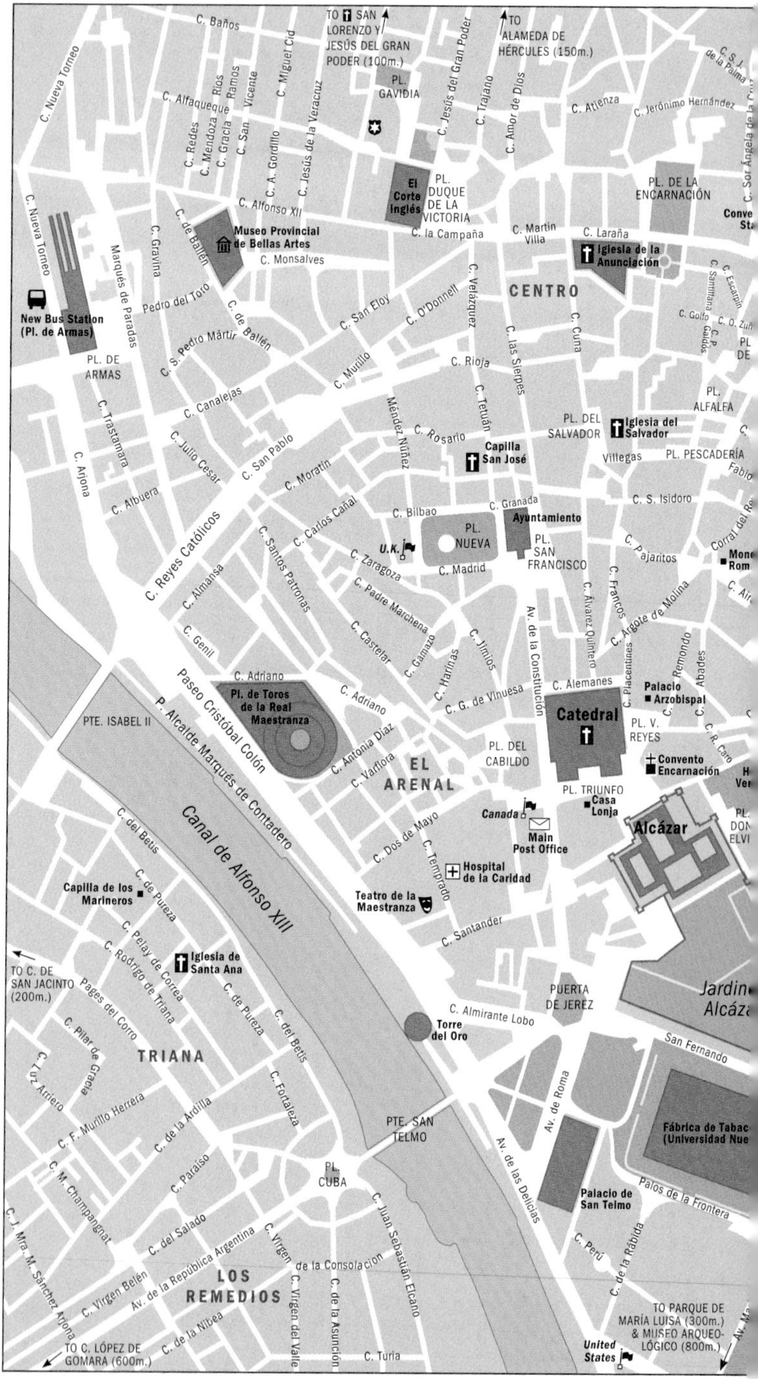

TO SAN LORENZO Y JESÚS DEL GRAN PODER (100m.)
TO ALAMEDA DE HÉRCULES (150m.)
C. Baños
C. Nueva Torneo
C. Alfaqueque
PL. GAVIDIA
El Corte Inglés
PL. DUQUE DE LA VICTORIA
PL. DE LA ENCARNACIÓN
C. Alfonso XII
Museo Provincial de Bellas Artes
C. Monsalves
C. la Campaña
C. Martin Villa
C. Laraña
Iglesia de la Anunciación
CENTRO
New Bus Station (Pl. de Armas)
PL. DE ARMAS
C. Rioja
C. Tetuán
C. las Sierpes
PL. DEL SALVADOR
Iglesia del Salvador
PL. ALFALFA
Capilla San José
Villegas
PL. PESCADERÍA
C. S. Isidoro
PL. NUEVA
Ayuntamiento
PL. SAN FRANCISCO
U.K.
C. Reyes Católicos
Av. de la Constitución
C. Alemanes
Catedral
PL. V. REYES
Palacio Arzobispal
Convento Encarnación
Pl. de Toros de la Real Maestranza
PTE. ISABEL II
Paseo Cristóbal Colón
P. Alcalde Marqués de Contadero
EL ARENAL
PL. DEL CABILDO
PL. TRIUNFO
Casa Lonja
Alcázar
Canada
Main Post Office
Hospital de la Caridad
Teatro de la Maestranza
Canal de Alfonso XIII
Capilla de los Marineros
Iglesia de Santa Ana
TO C. DE SAN JACINTO (200m.)
TRIANA
Torre del Oro
C. Almirante Lobo
PUERTA DE JEREZ
Jardines Alcázar
San Fernando
PTE. SAN TELMO
PL. CUBA
Av. de Roma
Av. de las Delicias
Fábrica de Tabaco (Universidad Nueva)
Palacio de San Telmo
Palos de la Frontera
LOS REMEDIOS
Av. de la República Argentina
C. Juan Sebastián Elcano
TO PARQUE DE MARÍA LUISA (300m.) & MUSEO ARQUEOLÓGICO (800m.)
United States
TO C. LÓPEZ DE GOMARA (600m.)
C. Turia

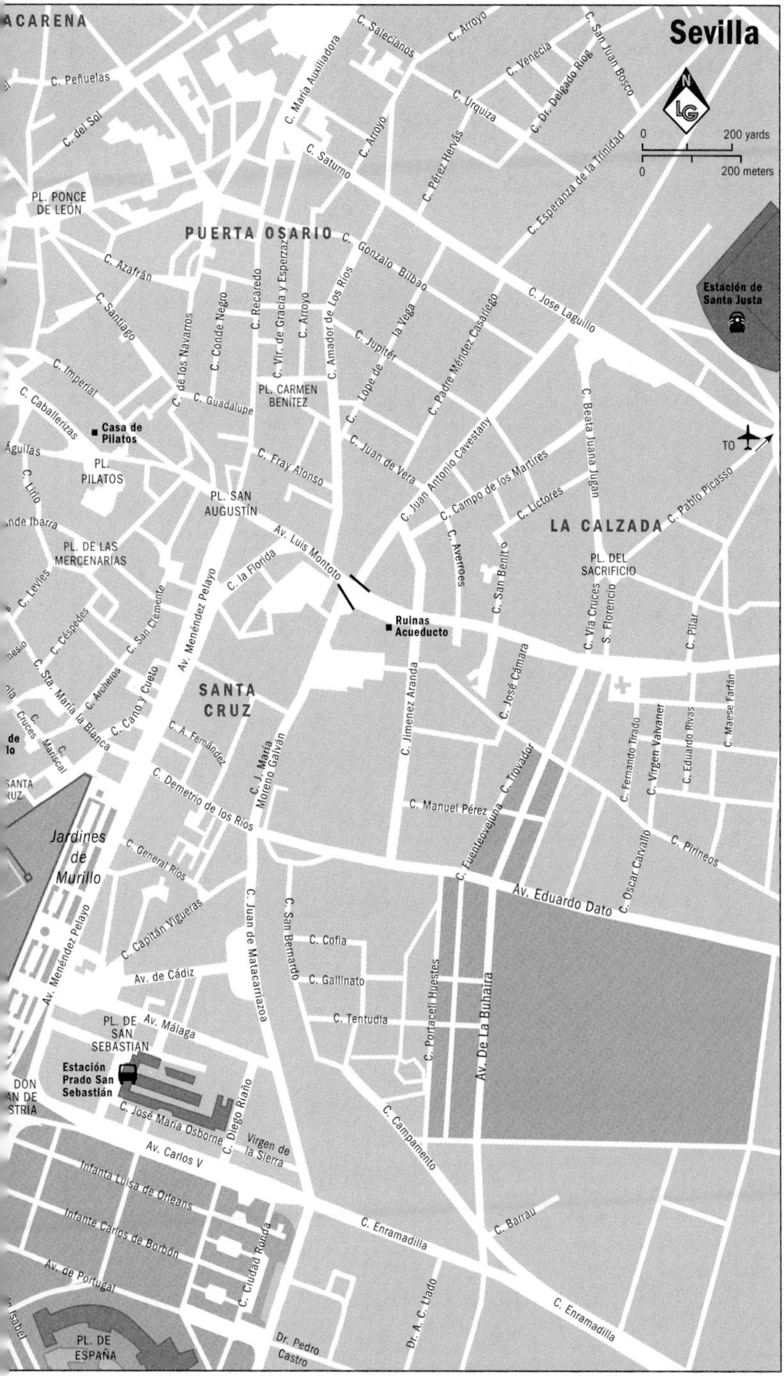

Sevilla
0
200 yards
0
200 meters
ACARENA
C. Peñuelas
C. del Sol
PL. PONCE DE LEÓN
PUERTA OSARIO
C. Salecianos
C. Arroyo
C. San Juan Bosco
C. Venecia
C. Dr. Delgado Riog
C. Urquiza
C. María Auxiliadora
C. Arroyo
C. Saturno
C. Pérez Hervás
C. Esperanza de la Trinidad
C. Gonzalo Bilbao
C. Jose Laguillo
Estación de Santa Justa
C. Azafrán
C. Santiago
C. Recaredo
C. Vir. de Gracia y Esperaz
C. Arroyo
C. Amador de Los Ríos
C. Lope de la Vega
C. Jupiter
C. Padre Méndez Casariego
C. de los Navarros
C. Conde Negro
C. Imperial
C. Caballerizas
PL. CARMEN BENÍTEZ
C. Guadalupe
Casa de Pilatos
Águilas
PL. PILATOS
C. Lirio
C. Fray Alonso
C. Juan de Vera
C. Juan Antonio Cavestany
C. Campo de los Martires
C. Beata Juana Jugan
TO
C. Lictores
C. Pablo Picasso
PL. SAN AUGUSTÍN
LA CALZADA
ande Ibarra
PL. DE LAS MERCENARIAS
Av. Luis Montoto
C. Averroes
C. San Benito
PL. DEL SACRIFICIO
C. la Florida
C. Levíes
C. San Clemente
Av. Menéndez Pelayo
C. Céspedes
Ruinas Acueducto
C. Vía Cruces
S. Florencio
C. Pilar
C. Archeros
C. Sta. María la Blanca
C. Cano y Cueto
SANTA CRUZ
C. Jimenez Aranda
C. José Cámara
C. Maese Farfán
C. Eduardo Rivas
C. Virgen Valvaner
C. Fernando Tirado
C. Cruces
C. Mariscal
C. A. Fernández
C. J. María Moreno Galván
C. Trovador
C. Demetrio de los Ríos
C. Manuel Pérez
C. Fuenteovejuna
Jardines de Murillo
C. General Ríos
C. Oscar Carvallo
C. Pirineos
Av. Eduardo Dato
C. Juan de Matacarriazoa
C. San Bernardo
C. Capitán Vigueras
C. Cofia
Av. Menéndez Pelayo
Av. de Cádiz
C. Gallinato
C. Portaceli Huestes
Av. De La Buhaira
C. Tentudia
PL. DE SAN SEBASTIAN
Av. Málaga
Estación Prado San Sebastián
C. Diego Riaño
C. José María Osborne
Virgen de la Sierra
C. Campamento
Av. Carlos V
Infanta Luisa de Orleans
C. Barrau
Infante Carlos de Borbón
C. Enramadilla
C. Ciudad Ronda
Av. de Portugal
Dr. A. C. Llado
C. Enramadilla
PL. DE ESPAÑA
Dr. Pedro Castro

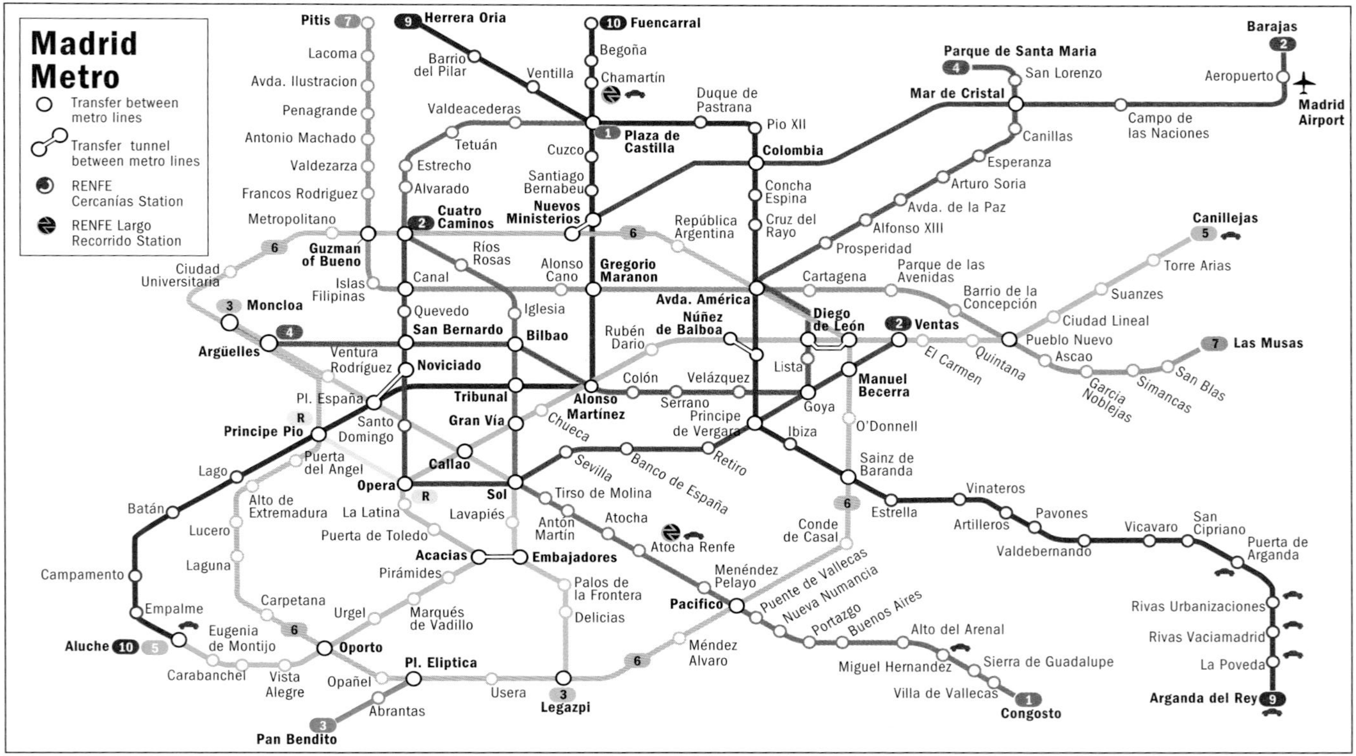
Madrid Metro
Transfer between metro lines
Transfer tunnel between metro lines
RENFE Cercanías Station
RENFE Largo Recorrido Station
Pitis 7
Lacoma
Avda. Ilustracion
Penagrande
Antonio Machado
Valdezarza
Francos Rodriguez
Metropolitano
Ciudad Universitaria
Guzman of Bueno
Islas Filipinas
3 Moncloa
Argüelles
4
9 Herrera Oria
Barrio del Pilar
Ventilla
Valdeacederas
Tetuán
Estrecho
Alvarado
2 Cuatro Caminos
Ríos Rosas
Canal
Quevedo
San Bernardo
Iglesia
Bilbao
Ventura Rodríguez
Noviciado
Pl. España
R
Principe Pio
Santo Domingo
Tribunal
Gran Vía
Callao
Opera
Sol
Lago
Puerta del Angel
Batán
Alto de Extremadura
Lucero
La Latina
Lavapiés
Puerta de Toledo
Laguna
Campamento
Acacias
Embajadores
Pirámides
Empalme
Carpetana
Urgel
Marqués de Vadillo
Palos de la Frontera
Delicias
Aluche 10 5
Eugenia de Montijo
6
Oporto
Carabanchel
Vista Alegre
Opañel
Pl. Eliptica
Usera
3 Legazpi
Abrantas
3 Pan Bendito
10 Fuencarral
Begoña
Chamartín
Duque de Pastrana
Pio XII
1 Plaza de Castilla
Cuzco
Santiago Bernabeu
Nuevos Ministerios
Colombia
Concha Espina
Cruz del Rayo
República Argentina
Alonso Cano
Gregorio Maranon
Avda. América
Rubén Dario
Núñez de Balboa
Diego de León
Lista
Colón
Velázquez
Serrano
Alonso Martínez
Chueca
Principe de Vergara
Goya
Ibiza
Retiro
Banco de España
Sevilla
Tirso de Molina
Antón Martín
Atocha
Atocha Renfe
Menéndez Pelayo
Pacifico
Méndez Alvaro
Conde de Casal
Puente de Vallecas
Nueva Numancia
Portazgo
Buenos Aires
Alto del Arenal
Miguel Hernandez
Sierra de Guadalupe
Villa de Vallecas
1 Congosto
O'Donnell
Manuel Becerra
Sainz de Baranda
Estrella
Vinateros
Artilleros
Pavones
Valdebernando
Vicavaro
San Cipriano
Puerta de Arganda
Rivas Urbanizaciones
Rivas Vaciamadrid
La Poveda
Arganda del Rey 9
2 Ventas
El Carmen
Quintana
Pueblo Nuevo
Ascao
Garcia Noblejas
Simancas
San Blas
7 Las Musas
Ciudad Lineal
Suanzes
Torre Arias
Canillejas 5
Cartagena
Parque de las Avenidas
Barrio de la Concepción
Prosperidad
Alfonso XIII
Avda. de la Paz
Arturo Soria
Esperanza
Canillas
Mar de Cristal
Parque de Santa Maria 4
San Lorenzo
Campo de las Naciones
Aeropuerto
Barajas 2
Madrid Airport

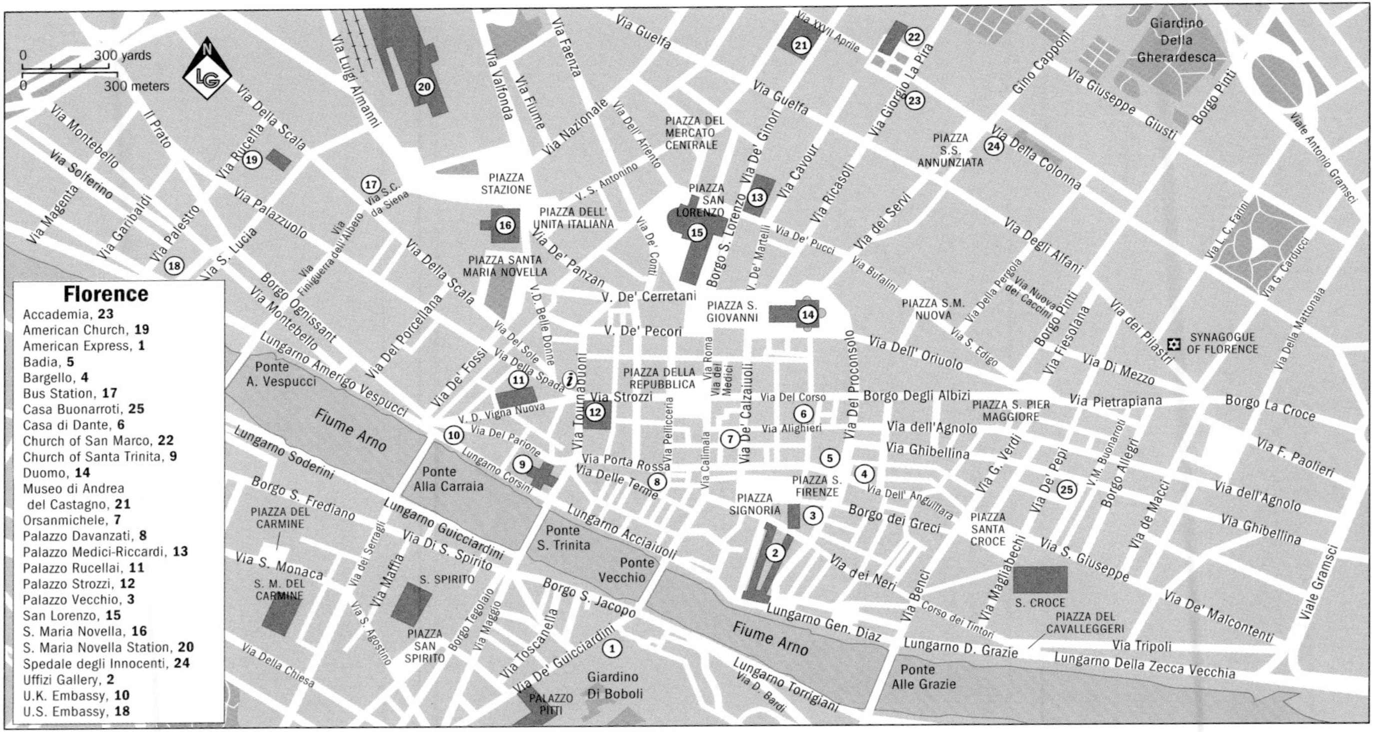
Florence
Accademia, 23
American Church, 19
American Express, 1
Badia, 5
Bargello, 4
Bus Station, 17
Casa Buonarroti, 25
Casa di Dante, 6
Church of San Marco, 22
Church of Santa Trinita, 9
Duomo, 14
Museo di Andrea del Castagno, 21
Orsanmichele, 7
Palazzo Davanzati, 8
Palazzo Medici-Riccardi, 13
Palazzo Rucellai, 11
Palazzo Strozzi, 12
Palazzo Vecchio, 3
San Lorenzo, 15
S. Maria Novella, 16
S. Maria Novella Station, 20
Spedale degli Innocenti, 24
Uffizi Gallery, 2
U.K. Embassy, 10
U.S. Embassy, 18
0 300 yards
0 300 meters
N
LG
Via Luigi Almanni
Via Valfonda
Via Fiume
Via Faenza
Via Guelfa
Via XXVII Aprile
Via Giorgio La Pira
Gino Capponi
Giardino Della Gherardesca
Via Giuseppe Giusti
Borgo Pinti
Viale Antonio Gramsci
Via Della Scala
Via Montebello
Il Prato
Via Solferino
Via Magenta
Via Garibaldi
Via Palestro
Via Rucella
Via Palazzuolo
Via S. Lucia
Via S.C. da Siena
Via Finiguerra dell'Albero
Borgo Ognissant
Via Montebello
Via Del Porcellana
Via Nazionale
Via Dell' Ariento
V. S. Antonino
PIAZZA STAZIONE
PIAZZA DELL' UNITA ITALIANA
PIAZZA SANTA MARIA NOVELLA
PIAZZA DEL MERCATO CENTRALE
PIAZZA SAN LORENZO
Via De' Ginori
Via Cavour
Via Ricasoli
Via dei Servi
PIAZZA S.S. ANNUNZIATA
Via Della Colonna
Via Degli Alfani
Via L. C. Farini
Via G. Carducci
Via Della Mattonaia
Via De' Panzan
Via De' Conti
Borgo S. Lorenzo
V. De' Martelli
Via De' Pucci
Via Bufalini
V. De' Cerretani
V. De' Pecori
PIAZZA S. GIOVANNI
PIAZZA S.M. NUOVA
Via Della Pergola
Via Nuova dei Caccini
Via S. Edigo
Borgo Pinti
Via Fiesolana
Via dei Pilastri
SYNAGOGUE OF FLORENCE
Via Dell' Oriuolo
Via Di Mezzo
Lungarno Amerigo Vespucci
Ponte A. Vespucci
Via De' Fossi
Via Del Sole
V.D. Belle Donne
Via Della Spada
PIAZZA DELLA REPUBBLICA
Via Roma
Via del Medici
Via Del Proconsolo
Borgo Degli Albizi
PIAZZA S. PIER MAGGIORE
Via Pietrapiana
Borgo La Croce
Fiume Arno
Via Tournabuoni
Via Strozzi
V. D. Vigna Nuova
Via Del Parione
Via Pellicceria
Via De' Calzaiuoli
Via Del Corso
Via Alighieri
Via dell'Agnolo
Via F. Paolieri
Lungarno Soderini
Ponte Alla Carraia
Lungarno Corsini
Via Porta Rossa
Via Delle Terme
Via Calimala
Via Ghibellina
Via G. Verdi
Via De' Pepi
V.M. Buonarroti
Borgo Allegri
PIAZZA S. FIRENZE
Via Dell' Anguillara
Borgo S. Frediano
PIAZZA DEL CARMINE
Lungarno Guicciardini
Ponte S. Trinita
Lungarno Acciaiuoli
PIAZZA SIGNORIA
Borgo dei Greci
PIAZZA SANTA CROCE
Via de Macci
Via dell'Agnolo
Via Ghibellina
Via S. Monaca
S. M. DEL CARMINE
Via dei Serragli
Via Maffia
Via Di S. Spirito
S. SPIRITO
Ponte Vecchio
Via dei Neri
Via Magliabechi
Via S. Giuseppe
Viale Gramsci
Via S. Agostino
Borgo Tegolaio
Via Maggio
PIAZZA SAN SPIRITO
Borgo S. Jacopo
Via Toscanella
Lungarno Gen. Diaz
Via Benci
Corso dei Tintori
S. CROCE
PIAZZA DEL CAVALLEGGERI
Via De' Malcontenti
Via Della Chiesa
Via De' Guicciardini
Giardino Di Boboli
PALAZZO PITTI
Lungarno Torrigiani
Via D. Bardi
Lungarno D. Grazie
Via Tripoli
Lungarno Della Zecca Vecchia
Ponte Alle Grazie

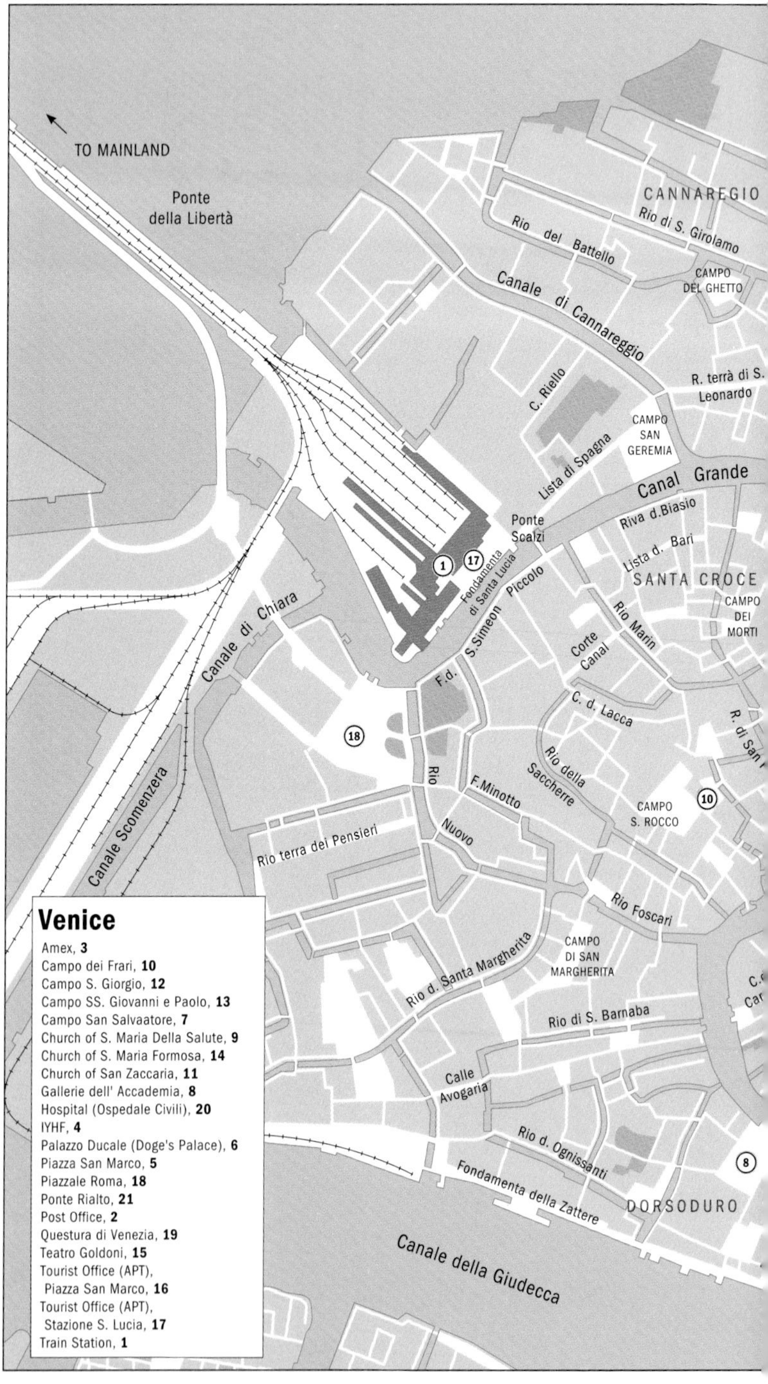
TO MAINLAND
Ponte
della Libertà
CANNAREGIO
Rio di S. Girolamo
Rio del Battello
CAMPO
DEL GHETTO
Canale di Cannareggio
R. terrà di S.
Leonardo
C. Riello
CAMPO
SAN
GEREMIA
Lista di Spagna
Canal Grande
Ponte
Scalzi
Riva d.Biasio
Lista d. Bari
SANTA CROCE
CAMPO
DEI
MORTI
1
17
Fondamenta
di Santa Lucia
Piccolo
S.Simeon
F.d.
Canale di Chiara
Rio Marin
Corte
Canal
C. d. Lacca
R. di San
18
Rio
F.Minotto
Nuovo
Rio della
Saccherre
CAMPO
S. ROCCO
10
Canale Scomenzera
Rio terra dei Pensieri
Rio Foscari
CAMPO
DI SAN
MARGHERITA
Rio d. Santa Margherita
Rio di S. Barnaba
Calle
Avogaria
Rio d. Ognissanti
8
Fondamenta della Zattere
DORSODURO
Canale della Giudecca
Venice
Amex, 3
Campo dei Frari, 10
Campo S. Giorgio, 12
Campo SS. Giovanni e Paolo, 13
Campo San Salvaatore, 7
Church of S. Maria Della Salute, 9
Church of S. Maria Formosa, 14
Church of San Zaccaria, 11
Gallerie dell' Accademia, 8
Hospital (Ospedale Civili), 20
IYHF, 4
Palazzo Ducale (Doge's Palace), 6
Piazza San Marco, 5
Piazzale Roma, 18
Ponte Rialto, 21
Post Office, 2
Questura di Venezia, 19
Teatro Goldoni, 15
Tourist Office (APT),
Piazza San Marco, 16
Tourist Office (APT),
Stazione S. Lucia, 17
Train Station, 1

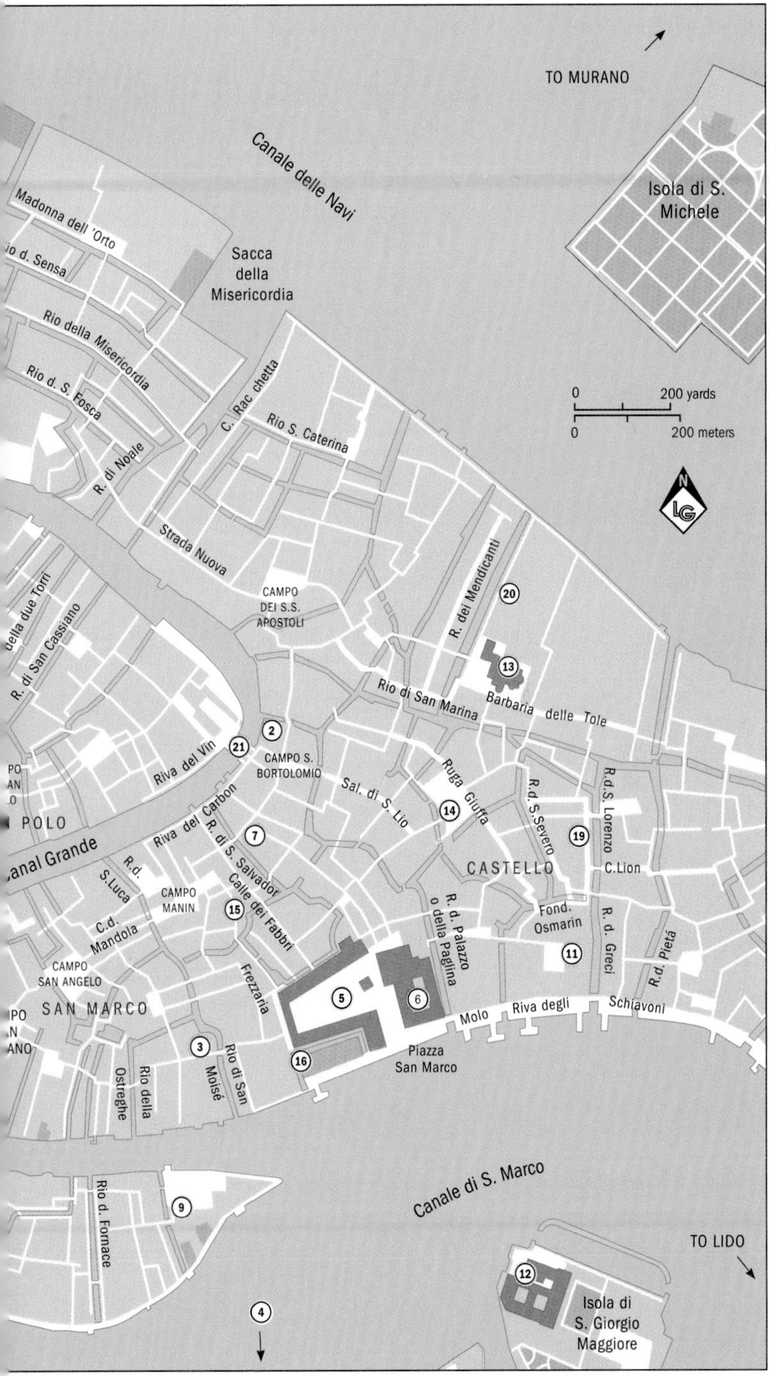
TO MURANO
Canale delle Navi
Isola di S. Michele
Madonna dell 'Orto
io d. Sensa
Sacca della Misericordia
Rio della Misericordia
Rio d. S. Fosca
C. Rac chetta
Rio S. Caterina
R. di Noale
0
200 yards
0
200 meters
N
LG
Strada Nuova
R. dei Mendicanti
CAMPO DEI S.S. APOSTOLI
della due Torri
R. di San Cassiano
Rio di San Marina
Barbaria delle Tole
Riva del Vin
CAMPO S. BORTOLOMIO
Sal. di S. Lio
Ruga Giuffa
R.d. S.Severo
R.d.S. Lorenzo
POLO
Riva del Carbon
R. di S. Salvador
Canal Grande
R.d. S.Luca
CAMPO MANIN
Calle dei Fabbri
CASTELLO
C.Lion
R. d. Palazzo o della Paglina
Fond. Osmarin
R. d. Greci
R.d. Pietá
C.d. Mandola
CAMPO SAN ANGELO
Frezzaria
SAN MARCO
Molo
Riva degli
Schiavoni
Piazza San Marco
Rio di San Moisé
Rio della Ostreghe
Canale di S. Marco
Rio d. Fornace
TO LIDO
Isola di S. Giorgio Maggiore
1
2
3
4
5
6
7
9
11
12
13
14
15
16
19
20
21

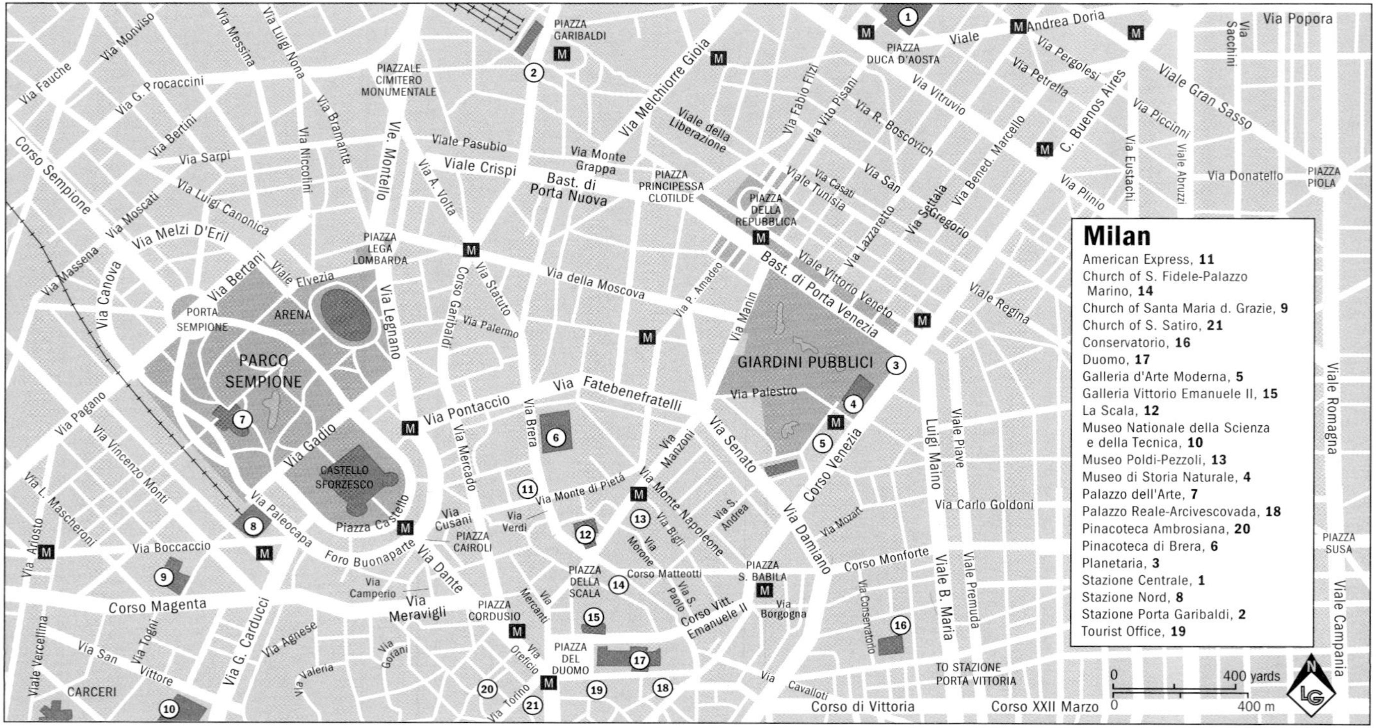
Milan
American Express, 11
Church of S. Fidele-Palazzo Marino, 14
Church of Santa Maria d. Grazie, 9
Church of S. Satiro, 21
Conservatorio, 16
Duomo, 17
Galleria d'Arte Moderna, 5
Galleria Vittorio Emanuele II, 15
La Scala, 12
Museo Nationale della Scienza e della Tecnica, 10
Museo Poldi-Pezzoli, 13
Museo di Storia Naturale, 4
Palazzo dell'Arte, 7
Palazzo Reale-Arcivescovada, 18
Pinacoteca Ambrosiana, 20
Pinacoteca di Brera, 6
Planetaria, 3
Stazione Centrale, 1
Stazione Nord, 8
Stazione Porta Garibaldi, 2
Tourist Office, 19
0 400 yards
0 400 m
PARCO SEMPIONE
GIARDINI PUBBLICI
CASTELLO SFORZESCO
ARENA
PIAZZA GARIBALDI
PIAZZA DUCA D'AOSTA
PIAZZALE CIMITERO MONUMENTALE
PIAZZA PRINCIPESSA CLOTILDE
PIAZZA DELLA REPUBBLICA
PIAZZA LEGA LOMBARDA
PIAZZA CAIROLI
PIAZZA CORDUSIO
PIAZZA DELLA SCALA
PIAZZA DEL DUOMO
PIAZZA S. BABILA
PIAZZA PIOLA
PIAZZA SUSA
PORTA SEMPIONE
CARCERI
TO STAZIONE PORTA VITTORIA
Corso Sempione
Corso Magenta
Corso Venezia
Corso di Vittoria
Corso XXII Marzo
Viale Romagna
Viale Campania
Via Popora

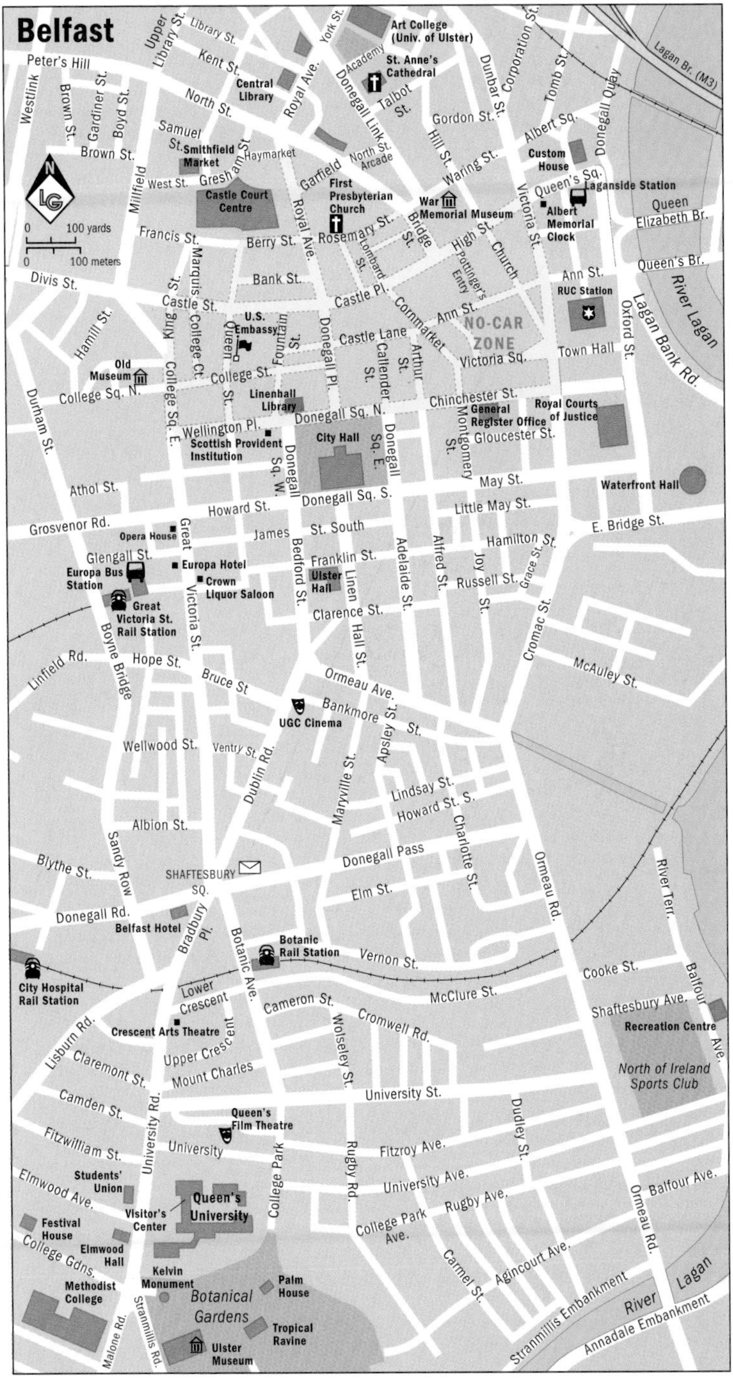
Belfast
0 100 yards
0 100 meters
Peter's Hill
Westlink
Brown St.
Gardiner St.
Boyd St.
Upper Library St.
Library St.
Kent St.
North St.
Samuel St.
Smithfield Market
Haymarket
Gresham St.
West St.
Castle Court Centre
Millfield
Francis St.
Berry St.
Divis St.
Bank St.
Castle St.
Marquis St.
King St.
College Ct.
College St.
Hamill St.
Old Museum
College Sq. N.
College Sq. E.
U.S. Embassy
Queen St.
Fountain St.
Linenhall Library
Wellington Pl.
Scottish Provident Institution
Durham St.
Central Library
Royal Ave.
York St.
Academy
Art College (Univ. of Ulster)
St. Anne's Cathedral
Donegall Link
Talbot St.
Garfield
North St. Arcade
First Presbyterian Church
Rosemary St.
Lombard St.
Bridge St.
Castle Pl.
Castle Lane
Donegall Pl.
Callender St.
Arthur St.
Cornmarket
Ann St.
NO-CAR ZONE
Victoria Sq.
Chinchester St.
Gordon St.
Hill St.
Dunbar St.
Corporation St.
Tomb St.
Waring St.
War Memorial Museum
High St.
Pottinger's Entry
Church
Victoria St.
Albert Sq.
Custom House
Queen's Sq.
Laganside Station
Albert Memorial Clock
Donegall Quay
Lagan Br. (M3)
Queen Elizabeth Br.
Queen's Br.
River Lagan
Ann St.
RUC Station
Oxford St.
Lagan Bank Rd.
Town Hall
Royal Courts of Justice
General Register Office
Montgomery St.
Gloucester St.
Donegall Sq. N.
City Hall
Donegall Sq. W.
Donegall Sq. E.
Donegall Sq. S.
May St.
Waterfront Hall
Little May St.
Athol St.
Howard St.
Grosvenor Rd.
Opera House
Great Victoria St.
James St. South
Hamilton St.
E. Bridge St.
Glengall St.
Europa Bus Station
Europa Hotel
Crown Liquor Saloon
Great Victoria St. Rail Station
Bedford St.
Franklin St.
Ulster Hall
Linen Hall St.
Adelaide St.
Alfred St.
Joy St.
Russell St.
Grace St.
Clarence St.
Cromac St.
McAuley St.
Linfield Rd.
Boyne Bridge
Hope St.
Bruce St.
Ormeau Ave.
Bankmore St.
UGC Cinema
Apsley St.
Wellwood St.
Ventry St.
Dublin Rd.
Maryville St.
Lindsay St.
Howard St. S.
Charlotte St.
Albion St.
Sandy Row
Blythe St.
SHAFTESBURY SQ.
Donegall Pass
Elm St.
Ormeau Rd.
River Terr.
Donegall Rd.
Belfast Hotel
Bradbury Pl.
Botanic Ave.
Botanic Rail Station
Vernon St.
City Hospital Rail Station
Lower Crescent
Cameron St.
Cromwell Rd.
McClure St.
Cooke St.
Balfour Ave.
Shaftesbury Ave.
Recreation Centre
North of Ireland Sports Club
Crescent Arts Theatre
Lisburn Rd.
Claremont St.
Upper Crescent
Mount Charles
Wolseley St.
University St.
Camden St.
University Rd.
Queen's Film Theatre
Fitzwilliam St.
University
College Park
Rugby Rd.
Fitzroy Ave.
Dudley St.
University Ave.
Elmwood Ave.
Students' Union
Visitor's Center
Queen's University
College Park Ave.
Rugby Ave.
Ormeau Rd.
Balfour Ave.
Festival House
Elmwood Hall
College Gdns.
Carmel St.
Agincourt Ave.
Kelvin Monument
Methodist College
Botanical Gardens
Palm House
Tropical Ravine
Ulster Museum
Malone Rd.
Stranmillis Rd.
Stranmillis Embankment
Annadale Embankment
River Lagan

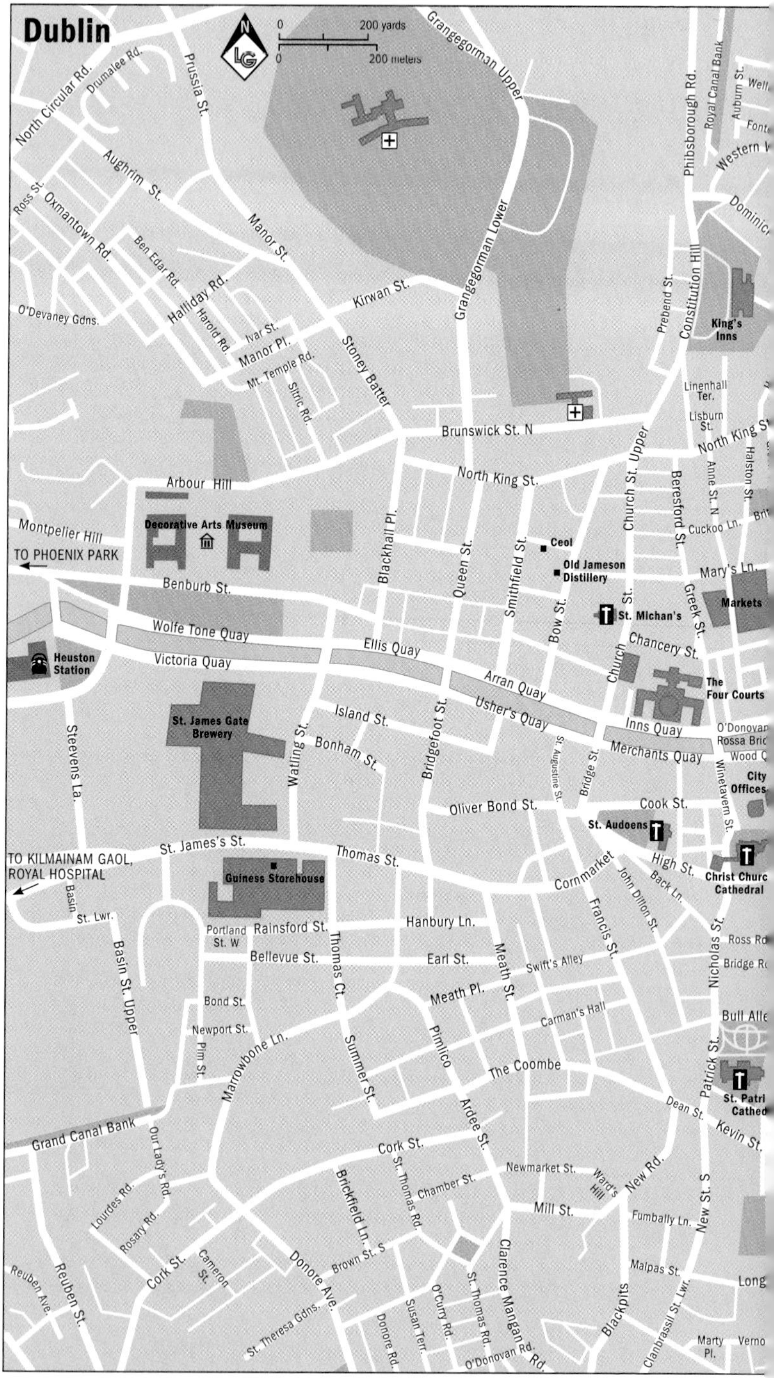
Dublin
0
200 yards
200 meters
Grangegorman Upper
Grangegorman Lower
Phibsborough Rd.
Royal Canal Bank
Auburn St.
Western Way
Dominick St.
Constitution Hill
Prebend St.
King's Inns
North Circular Rd.
Drumalee Rd.
Prussia St.
Aughrim St.
Ross St.
Oxmantown Rd.
Manor St.
Ben Edar Rd.
Halliday Rd.
Harold Rd.
O'Devaney Gdns.
Kirwan St.
Ivar St.
Manor Pl.
Mt. Temple Rd.
Sitric Rd.
Stoney Batter
Brunswick St. N
Linenhall Ter.
Lisburn St.
North King St.
Anne St. N
Halston St.
Church St. Upper
Beresford St.
Arbour Hill
Cuckoo Ln.
Montpelier Hill
Decorative Arts Museum
TO PHOENIX PARK
Blackhall Pl.
Queen St.
Smithfield St.
Ceol
Old Jameson Distillery
Mary's Ln.
Benburb St.
Bow St.
Church St.
St. Michan's
Markets
Greek St.
Wolfe Tone Quay
Ellis Quay
Chancery St.
Heuston Station
Victoria Quay
Arran Quay
The Four Courts
Island St.
Usher's Quay
Inns Quay
St. James Gate Brewery
Watling St.
Bonham St.
Bridgefoot St.
St. Augustine St.
Bridge St.
Merchants Quay
O'Donovan Rossa Bridge
Wood Quay
Winetavern St.
City Offices
Steevens La.
Oliver Bond St.
Cook St.
St. Audoens
St. James's St.
Thomas St.
TO KILMAINAM GAOL, ROYAL HOSPITAL
Guiness Storehouse
Cornmarket
John Dillon St.
High St.
Back Ln.
Christ Church Cathedral
Basin St. Lwr.
Francis St.
Portland St. W
Rainsford St.
Hanbury Ln.
Nicholas St.
Ross Rd.
Bellevue St.
Thomas Ct.
Earl St.
Meath St.
Swift's Alley
Bridge Rd.
Basin St. Upper
Bond St.
Meath Pl.
Bull Alley
Newport St.
Carman's Hall
Pim St.
Marrowbone Ln.
Summer St.
Pimlico
The Coombe
Patrick St.
St. Patrick's Cathedral
Dean St.
Grand Canal Bank
Ardee St.
Kevin St.
Our Lady's Rd.
Cork St.
St. Thomas Rd.
Newmarket St.
Ward's Hill
New Rd.
Brickfield Ln.
Chamber St.
New St. S
Lourdes Rd.
Rosary Rd.
Mill St.
Fumbally Ln.
Cork St.
Cameron St.
Donore Ave.
Brown St. S
Clarence Mangan Rd.
Malpas St.
Reuben Ave.
Reuben St.
O'Curry Rd.
St. Thomas Rd.
Blackpits
Clanbrassil St. Lwr.
Long
St. Theresa Gdns.
Donore Rd.
Susan Terr.
O'Donovan Rd.
Marty Pl.
Verno

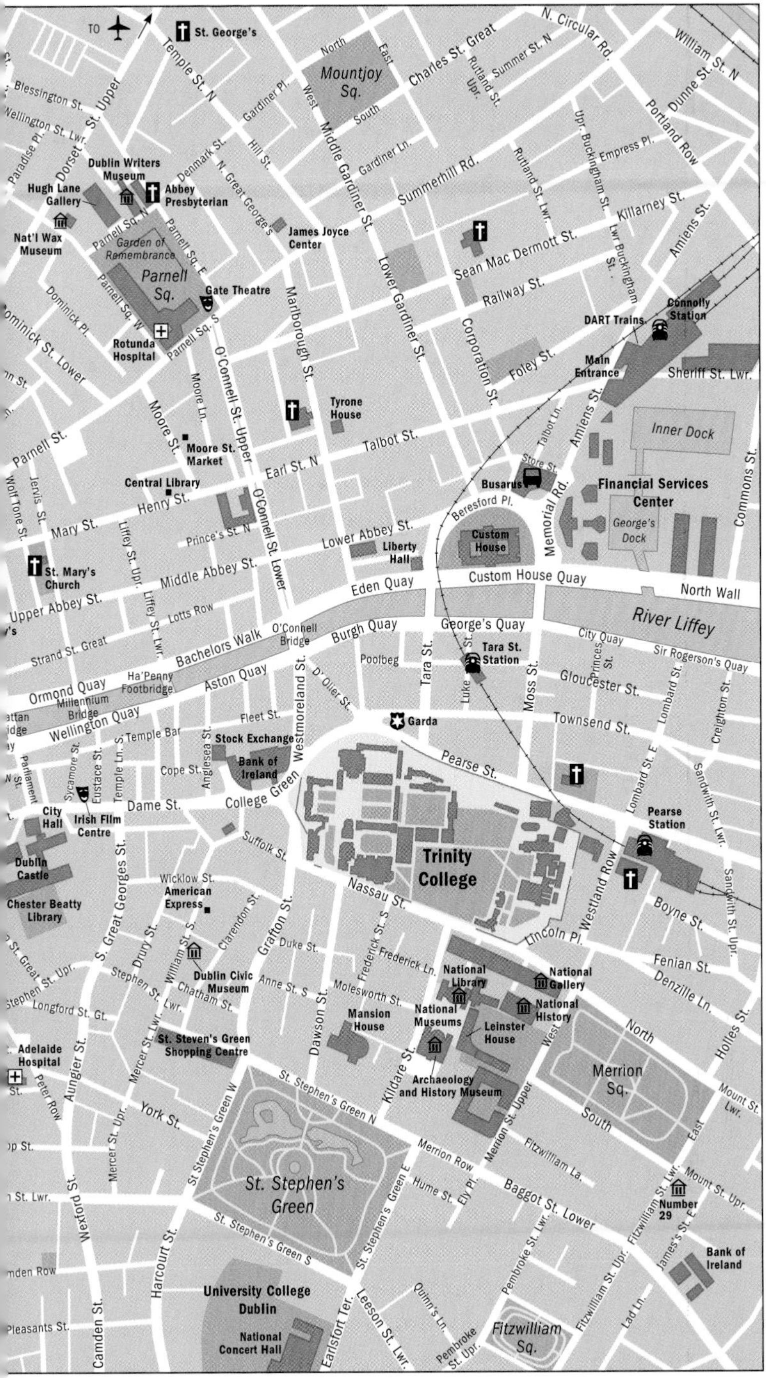
TO
St. George's
Temple St. N
Blessington St.
Wellington St. Lwr.
St. Upper
Dorset St.
Paradise Pl.
North
East
Mountjoy Sq.
West
South
N. Circular Rd.
Charles St. Great
Rutland St. Upr.
Summer St. N
William St. N
Dunne St.
Portland Row
Gardiner Pl.
Hill St.
Denmark St.
N. Great George's
Gardiner Ln.
Middle Gardiner St.
Summerhill Rd.
Rutland St. Lwr.
Upr. Buckingham St.
Empress Pl.
Killarney St.
Amiens St.
Dublin Writers Museum
Hugh Lane Gallery
Abbey Presbyterian
Nat'l Wax Museum
Parnell Sq. N
Garden of Remembrance
Parnell Sq. E
Parnell Sq.
James Joyce Center
Lower Gardiner St.
Sean Mac Dermott St.
Lwr Buckingham St.
Railway St.
Connolly Station
DART Trains
Dominick Pl.
Parnell Sq. W
Gate Theatre
Dominick St. Lower
Parnell Sq. S
Rotunda Hospital
Marlborough St.
Corporation St.
Foley St.
Main Entrance
Sheriff St. Lwr.
Moore Ln.
O'Connell St. Upper
Moore St.
Tyrone House
Talbot Ln.
Amiens St.
Inner Dock
Parnell St.
Moore St. Market
Talbot St.
Store St.
Earl St. N
Busarus
Financial Services Center
Commons St.
Jervis St.
Wolf Tone St.
Central Library
Henry St.
Beresford Pl.
Memorial Rd.
Mary St.
Liffey St. Upr.
Prince's St. N
O'Connell St. Lower
Lower Abbey St.
Custom House
George's Dock
Liberty Hall
St. Mary's Church
Middle Abbey St.
Custom House Quay
Eden Quay
North Wall
Upper Abbey St.
Liffey St. Lwr.
Lotts Row
River Liffey
O'Connell Bridge
Burgh Quay
George's Quay
City Quay
Strand St. Great
Bachelors Walk
Tara St.
Luke St.
Tara St. Station
Princes St.
Sir Rogerson's Quay
Poolbeg
Westmoreland St.
D'Olier St.
Moss St.
Gloucester St.
Lombard St.
Creighton St.
Ormond Quay
Ha'Penny Footbridge
Aston Quay
Millennium Bridge
Wellington Quay
Fleet St.
Garda
Townsend St.
Temple Bar
Stock Exchange
Pearse St.
Parliament St.
Sycamore St.
Eustace St.
Temple Ln. S
Cope St.
Anglesea St.
Bank of Ireland
College Green
Lombard St. E
Sandwith St. Lwr.
Dame St.
City Hall
Irish Film Centre
Pearse Station
Suffolk St.
Trinity College
Westland Row
Dublin Castle
Chester Beatty Library
S. Great Georges St.
Wicklow St.
American Express
Nassau St.
Boyne St.
Sandwith St. Upr.
Clarendon St.
Grafton St.
Frederick St. S
Lincoln Pl.
Drury St.
William St. S.
Duke St.
Frederick Ln.
National Library
National Gallery
Fenian St.
Great St. Upr.
Stephen St. Lwr.
Dublin Civic Museum
Anne St. S
Chatham St.
Molesworth St.
Denzille Ln.
Stephen St.
Longford St. Gt.
Mansion House
Dawson St.
National Museums
National History
Leinster House
North
Holles St.
West
Merrion Sq.
Mercer St. Lwr.
St. Steven's Green Shopping Centre
Adelaide Hospital
Aungier St.
Peter Row
Kildare St.
Archaeology and History Museum
St. Stephen's Green N
Merrion St. Upper
Mount St. Lwr.
York St.
St. Stephen's Green W
South
East
Mercer St. Upr.
Merrion Row
Fitzwilliam La.
Fitzwilliam St. Lwr.
Mount St. Upr.
St. Stephen's Green
Hume St.
Ely Pl.
Baggot St. Lower
Number 29
Wexford St.
St. Stephen's Green E
St. Stephen's Green S
James's St. E
Harcourt St.
Pembroke St. Lwr.
Fitzwilliam St. Upr.
Bank of Ireland
Camden Row
University College Dublin
Leeson St. Lwr.
Quinn's Ln.
Lad Ln.
Camden St.
Pleasants St.
National Concert Hall
Earlsfort Ter.
Pembroke St. Upr.
Fitzwilliam Sq.

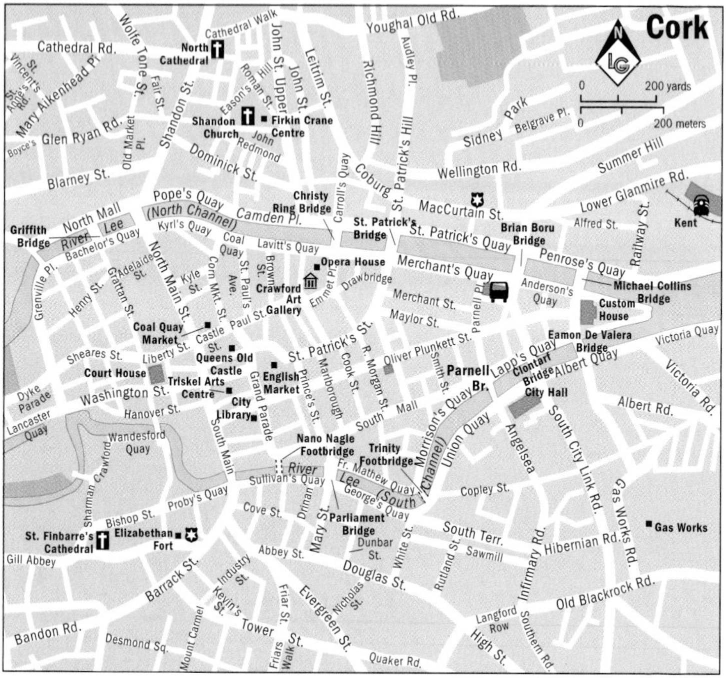
Cork
0 200 yards
0 200 meters
Cathedral Walk
Cathedral Rd.
Youghal Old Rd.
North Cathedral
Wolfe Tone St.
John St. Upper
John St.
Leitrim St.
Richmond Hill
Audley Pl.
St. Patrick's Hill
St. Vincent's Rd.
St. Anne's Rd.
Mary Aikenhead Pl.
Fair St.
Shandon St.
Eason's Hill
Roman St.
Shandon Church
Firkin Crane Centre
John Redmond
Glen Ryan Rd.
Boyce's
Old Market Pl.
Dominick St.
Sidney Park
Belgrave Pl.
Summer Hill
Wellington Rd.
Blarney St.
Carroll's Quay
Coburg St.
MacCurtain St.
Lower Glanmire Rd.
Kent
Pope's Quay
(North Channel)
Camden Pl.
Christy Ring Bridge
North Mall
Lee
River
Griffith Bridge
Bachelor's Quay
Kyrl's Quay
Coal Quay
Lavitt's Quay
St. Patrick's Bridge
St. Patrick's Quay
Brian Boru Bridge
Alfred St.
Railway St.
Penrose's Quay
Opera House
Merchant's Quay
Grenville Pl.
Henry St.
Grattan St.
Adelaide St.
North Main St.
Kyle St.
Corn Mkt. St.
St. Paul's Ave.
Brown St.
Crawford Art Gallery
Emmet Pl.
Drawbridge
Merchant St.
Parnell Pl.
Anderson's Quay
Michael Collins Bridge
Custom House
Maylor St.
Coal Quay Market
Castle St.
Paul St.
Liberty St.
Sheares St.
Queens Old Castle
St. Patrick's St.
Cook St.
R. Morgan St.
Oliver Plunkett St.
Smith St.
Eamon De Valera Bridge
Victoria Quay
Court House
English Market
Marlborough
Prince's St.
Grand Parade
Parnell Br.
Lapp's Quay
Clontarf Bridge
Albert Quay
Victoria Rd.
Triskel Arts Centre
Dyke Parade
Washington St.
City Library
South Mall
Morrison's Quay
City Hall
Albert Rd.
Lancaster Quay
Hanover St.
South Main St.
Union Quay
Wandesford Quay
Nano Nagle Footbridge
Trinity Footbridge
(Channel)
Angelsea
South City Link Rd.
Crawford
Sharman
River
Sullivan's Quay
Fr. Mathew Quay
Lee (South
George's Quay
Copley St.
Gas Works Rd.
Proby's Quay
Cove St.
Drinan
Mary St.
Parliament Bridge
Bishop St.
Gas Works
St. Finbarre's Cathedral
Elizabethan Fort
White St.
South Terr.
Dunbar St.
Rutland St.
Sawmill
Hibernian Rd.
Infirmary Rd.
Gill Abbey
Abbey St.
Douglas St.
Industry St.
Barrack St.
Kevin's St.
Nicholas St.
Old Blackrock Rd.
Evergreen St.
Langford Row
Bandon Rd.
Tower St.
Friar St.
Southern Rd.
Desmond Sq.
Mount Carmel
Friars Walk
Quaker Rd.
High St.

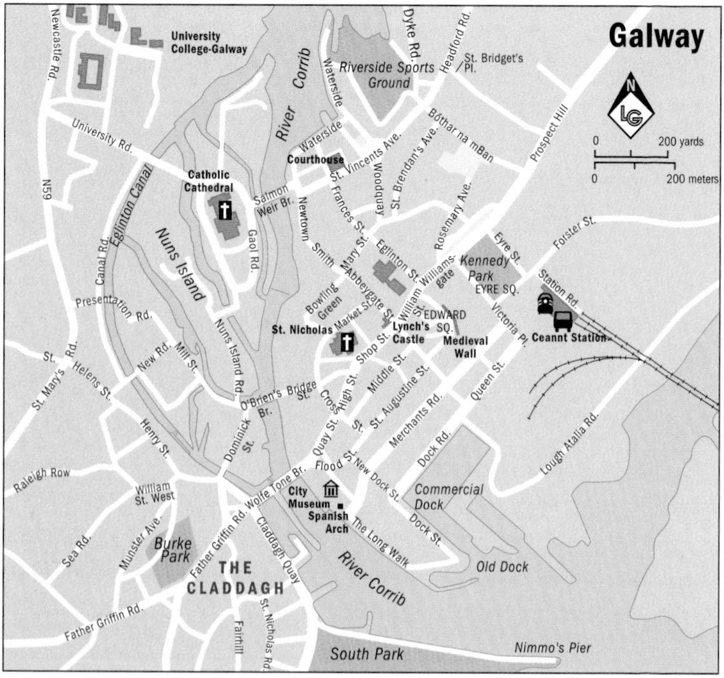
Galway
0 200 yards
0 200 meters
Newcastle Rd.
University College-Galway
Dyke Rd.
Headford Rd.
St. Bridget's Pl.
Riverside Sports Ground
River Corrib
Waterside
University Rd.
Bóthar na mBan
Prospect Hill
Courthouse
St. Vincents Ave.
St. Brendan's Ave.
Catholic Cathedral
Salmon Weir Br.
Woodquay
N59
Eglinton Canal
Frances St.
Rosemary Ave.
Gaol Rd.
Newtown Smith
Forster St.
Nuns Island
Canal Rd.
Mary St.
Eglinton St.
Eyre St.
Kennedy Park
EYRE SQ.
William Williamsgate
Abbeygate St.
Station Rd.
Bowling Green
Presentation Rd.
Market St.
William St.
EDWARD SQ.
Victoria Pl.
St. Nicholas
Lynch's Castle
Medieval Wall
Ceannt Station
Nuns Island Rd.
Shop St.
Mill St.
New Rd.
St. Mary's Rd.
St. Helens St.
Middle St.
Queen St.
High St.
St. Augustine St.
O'Brien's Bridge
Br.
Cross St.
Merchants Rd.
Henry St.
Dominick St.
Quay St.
Dock Rd.
Lough Atalia Rd.
Flood St.
New Dock St.
Raleigh Row
Wolfe Tone Br.
Commercial Dock
William St. West
City Museum
Spanish Arch
Dock St.
Sea Rd.
Munster Ave.
Father Griffin Rd.
Claddagh Quay
The Long Walk
Burke Park
Old Dock
THE CLADDAGH
River Corrib
Father Griffin Rd.
St. Nicholas Rd.
Fairhill
South Park
Nimmo's Pier

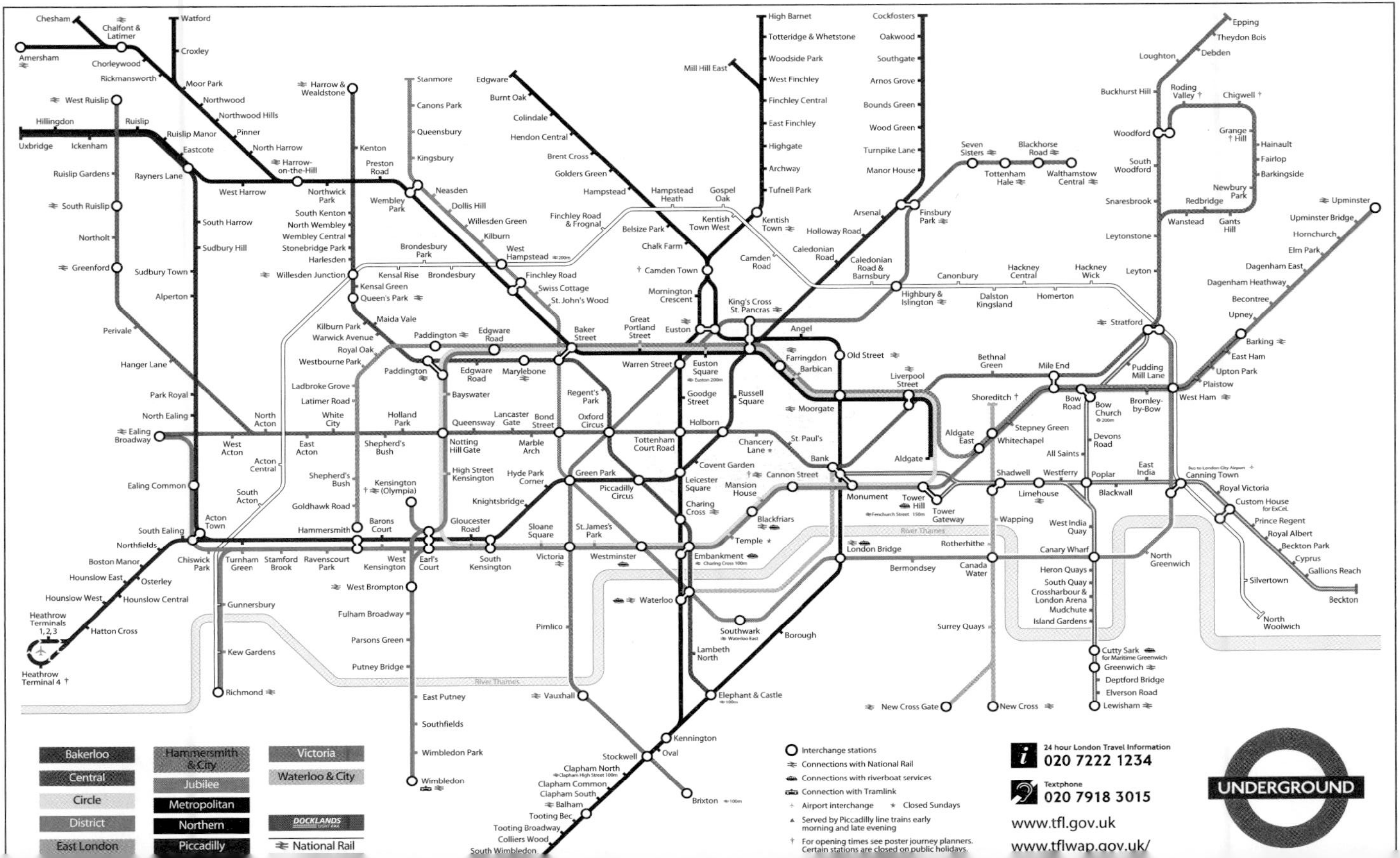

Chesham
Chalfont & Latimer
Watford
Amersham
Croxley
Chorleywood
Rickmansworth
Moor Park
Northwood
Northwood Hills
Pinner
North Harrow
Harrow-on-the-Hill
West Harrow
West Ruislip
Hillingdon
Ruislip
Ruislip Manor
Uxbridge
Ickenham
Eastcote
Rayners Lane
Ruislip Gardens
South Ruislip
Northolt
Greenford
Perivale
Hanger Lane
Park Royal
North Ealing
Ealing Broadway
Ealing Common
South Ealing
Northfields
Boston Manor
Hounslow East
Osterley
Hounslow West
Hounslow Central
Hatton Cross
Heathrow Terminals 1,2,3
Heathrow Terminal 4 †
South Harrow
Sudbury Hill
Sudbury Town
Alperton
Harrow & Wealdstone
Kenton
Preston Road
Northwick Park
Wembley Park
South Kenton
North Wembley
Wembley Central
Stonebridge Park
Harlesden
Willesden Junction
Kensal Green
Queen's Park
Kensal Rise
Brondesbury Park
Brondesbury
Stanmore
Canons Park
Queensbury
Kingsbury
Neasden
Dollis Hill
Willesden Green
Kilburn
West Hampstead
Finchley Road
Swiss Cottage
St. John's Wood
Edgware
Burnt Oak
Colindale
Hendon Central
Brent Cross
Golders Green
Hampstead
Finchley Road & Frognal
Belsize Park
Chalk Farm
Hampstead Heath
Gospel Oak
Kentish Town West
Camden Town †
Mornington Crescent
Camden Road
High Barnet
Totteridge & Whetstone
Woodside Park
Mill Hill East
West Finchley
Finchley Central
East Finchley
Highgate
Archway
Tufnell Park
Kentish Town
Holloway Road
Caledonian Road
Caledonian Road & Barnsbury
Cockfosters
Oakwood
Southgate
Arnos Grove
Bounds Green
Wood Green
Turnpike Lane
Manor House
Arsenal
Finsbury Park
Seven Sisters
Tottenham Hale
Blackhorse Road
Walthamstow Central
Highbury & Islington
Canonbury
Dalston Kingsland
Hackney Central
Hackney Wick
Homerton
Stratford
Epping
Theydon Bois
Loughton
Debden
Buckhurst Hill
Roding Valley †
Chigwell †
Grange Hill †
Hainault
Fairlop
Barkingside
Woodford
South Woodford
Snaresbrook
Newbury Park
Redbridge
Wanstead
Gants Hill
Leytonstone
Leyton
Upminster
Upminster Bridge
Hornchurch
Elm Park
Dagenham East
Dagenham Heathway
Becontree
Upney
Barking
East Ham
Upton Park
Plaistow
West Ham
Bromley-by-Bow
Pudding Mill Lane
Bow Road
Bow Church
Mile End
Bethnal Green
Stepney Green
Whitechapel
Devons Road
All Saints
Shoreditch †
Aldgate East
Aldgate
Liverpool Street
Old Street
Moorgate
Angel
King's Cross St. Pancras
Euston
Euston Square
Farringdon
Barbican
Great Portland Street
Baker Street
Warren Street
Goodge Street
Russell Square
Regent's Park
Oxford Circus
Tottenham Court Road
Holborn
Chancery Lane
St. Paul's
Bank
Monument
Cannon Street
Mansion House
Blackfriars
Temple
Covent Garden
Leicester Square
Charing Cross
Embankment
Piccadilly Circus
Green Park
Bond Street
Marble Arch
Lancaster Gate
Queensway
Notting Hill Gate
Bayswater
Edgware Road
Marylebone
Paddington
Maida Vale
Kilburn Park
Warwick Avenue
Royal Oak
Westbourne Park
Ladbroke Grove
Latimer Road
White City
Holland Park
Shepherd's Bush
East Acton
North Acton
West Acton
Acton Central
South Acton
Acton Town
Chiswick Park
Turnham Green
Stamford Brook
Ravenscourt Park
Hammersmith
Goldhawk Road
Barons Court
West Kensington
Kensington (Olympia)
Earl's Court
West Brompton
Fulham Broadway
Parsons Green
Putney Bridge
East Putney
Southfields
Wimbledon Park
Wimbledon
Gunnersbury
Kew Gardens
Richmond
Gloucester Road
South Kensington
High Street Kensington
Hyde Park Corner
Knightsbridge
Sloane Square
Victoria
St. James's Park
Westminster
Pimlico
Vauxhall
Waterloo
Southwark
Lambeth North
Elephant & Castle
Borough
London Bridge
Kennington
Oval
Stockwell
Brixton
Clapham North
Clapham Common
Clapham South
Balham
Tooting Bec
Tooting Broadway
Colliers Wood
South Wimbledon
Tower Hill
Tower Gateway
Shadwell
Limehouse
Westferry
Poplar
Blackwall
East India
Wapping
Rotherhithe
Canada Water
Surrey Quays
Bermondsey
New Cross Gate
New Cross
West India Quay
Canary Wharf
Heron Quays
South Quay
Crossharbour & London Arena
Mudchute
Island Gardens
Cutty Sark for Maritime Greenwich
Greenwich
Deptford Bridge
Elverson Road
Lewisham
North Greenwich
Canning Town
Royal Victoria
Custom House for ExCeL
Prince Regent
Royal Albert
Beckton Park
Cyprus
Gallions Reach
Beckton
Silvertown
North Woolwich
River Thames
Bakerloo
Central
Circle
District
East London
Hammersmith & City
Jubilee
Metropolitan
Northern
Piccadilly
Victoria
Waterloo & City
DOCKLANDS
National Rail
Interchange stations
Connections with National Rail
Connections with riverboat services
Connection with Tramlink
Airport interchange
Closed Sundays
Served by Piccadilly line trains early morning and late evening
For opening times see poster journey planners. Certain stations are closed on public holidays.
24 hour London Travel Information
020 7222 1234
Textphone
020 7918 3015
www.tfl.gov.uk
www.tflwap.gov.uk/
UNDERGROUND

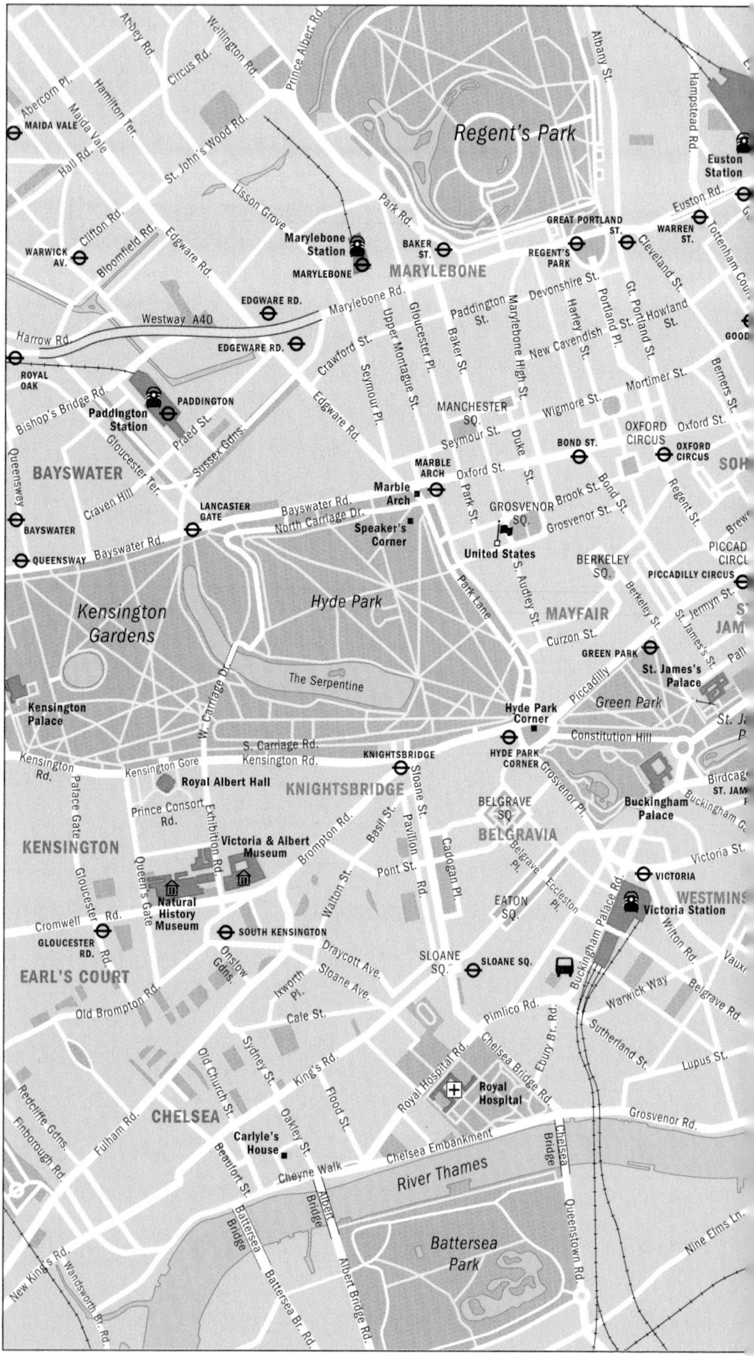

Regent's Park
MAIDA VALE
WARWICK AV.
Marylebone Station
MARYLEBONE
BAKER ST.
MARYLEBONE
GREAT PORTLAND ST.
REGENT'S PARK
WARREN ST.
Euston Station
EDGWARE RD.
EDGEWARE RD.
ROYAL OAK
PADDINGTON
Paddington Station
BAYSWATER
MANCHESTER SQ.
OXFORD CIRCUS
BOND ST.
MARBLE ARCH
Marble Arch
LANCASTER GATE
Speaker's Corner
GROSVENOR SQ.
United States
BERKELEY SQ.
PICCADILLY CIRCUS
QUEENSWAY
Kensington Gardens
Hyde Park
The Serpentine
MAYFAIR
GREEN PARK
St. James's Palace
Green Park
Hyde Park Corner
Kensington Palace
KNIGHTSBRIDGE
HYDE PARK CORNER
Royal Albert Hall
KNIGHTSBRIDGE
BELGRAVE SQ.
BELGRAVIA
Buckingham Palace
KENSINGTON
Victoria & Albert Museum
VICTORIA
Natural History Museum
EATON SQ.
Victoria Station
GLOUCESTER RD.
SOUTH KENSINGTON
SLOANE SQ.
SLOANE SQ.
EARL'S COURT
Royal Hospital
CHELSEA
Carlyle's House
River Thames
Battersea Park

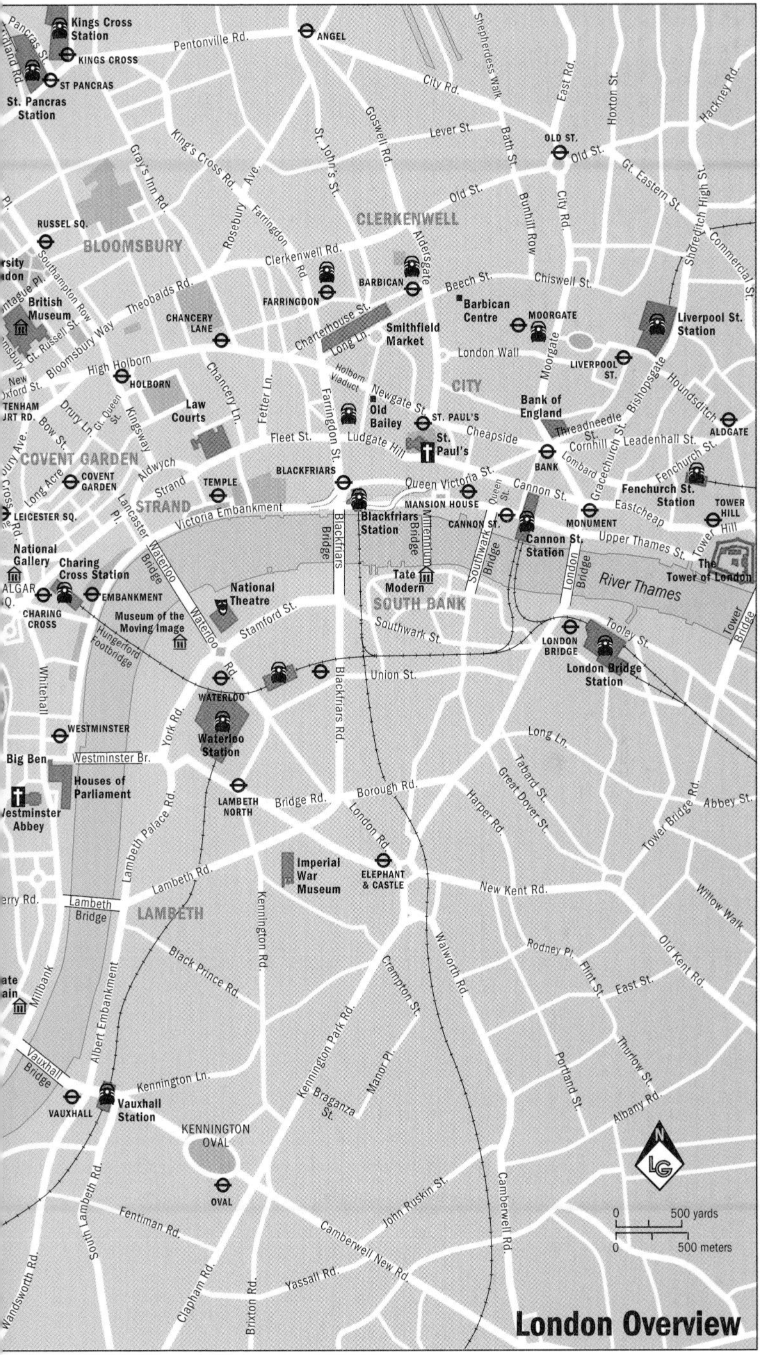

London Overview

London: Westminster

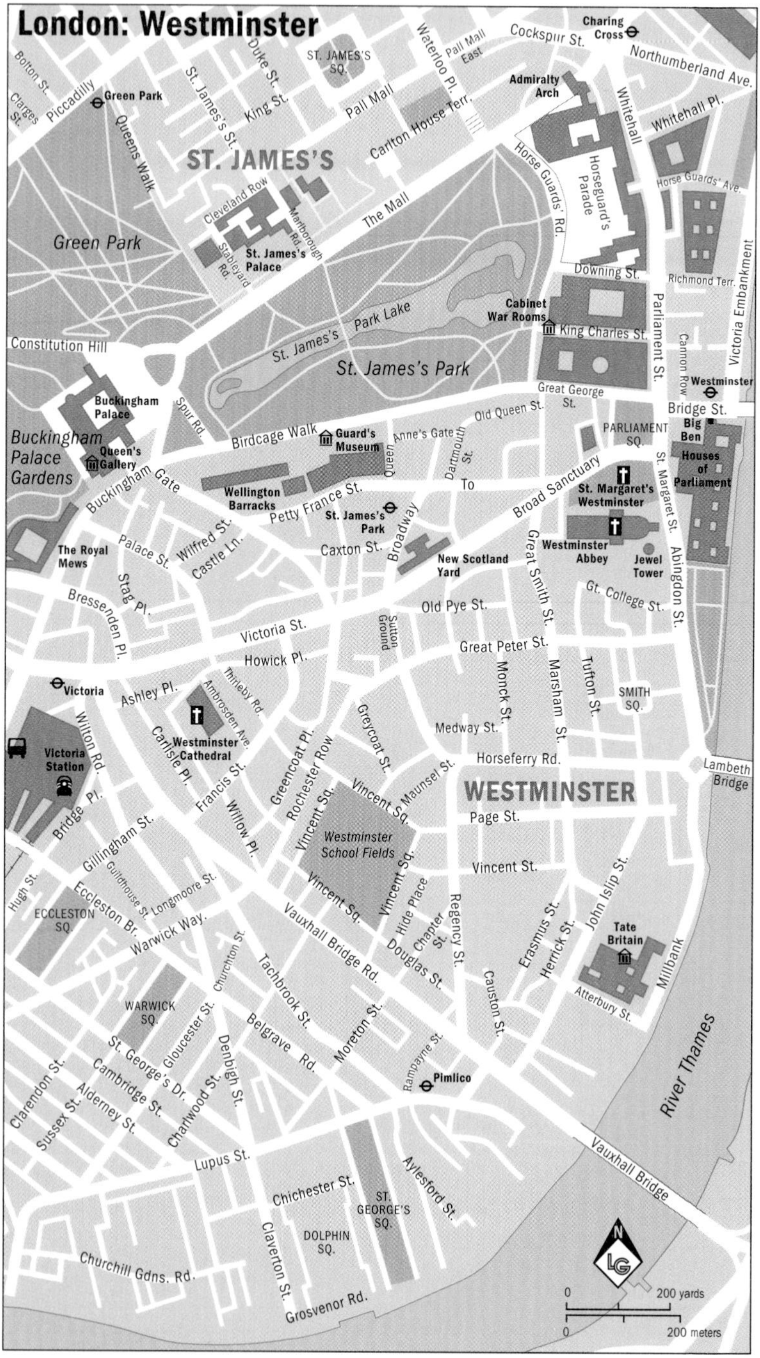

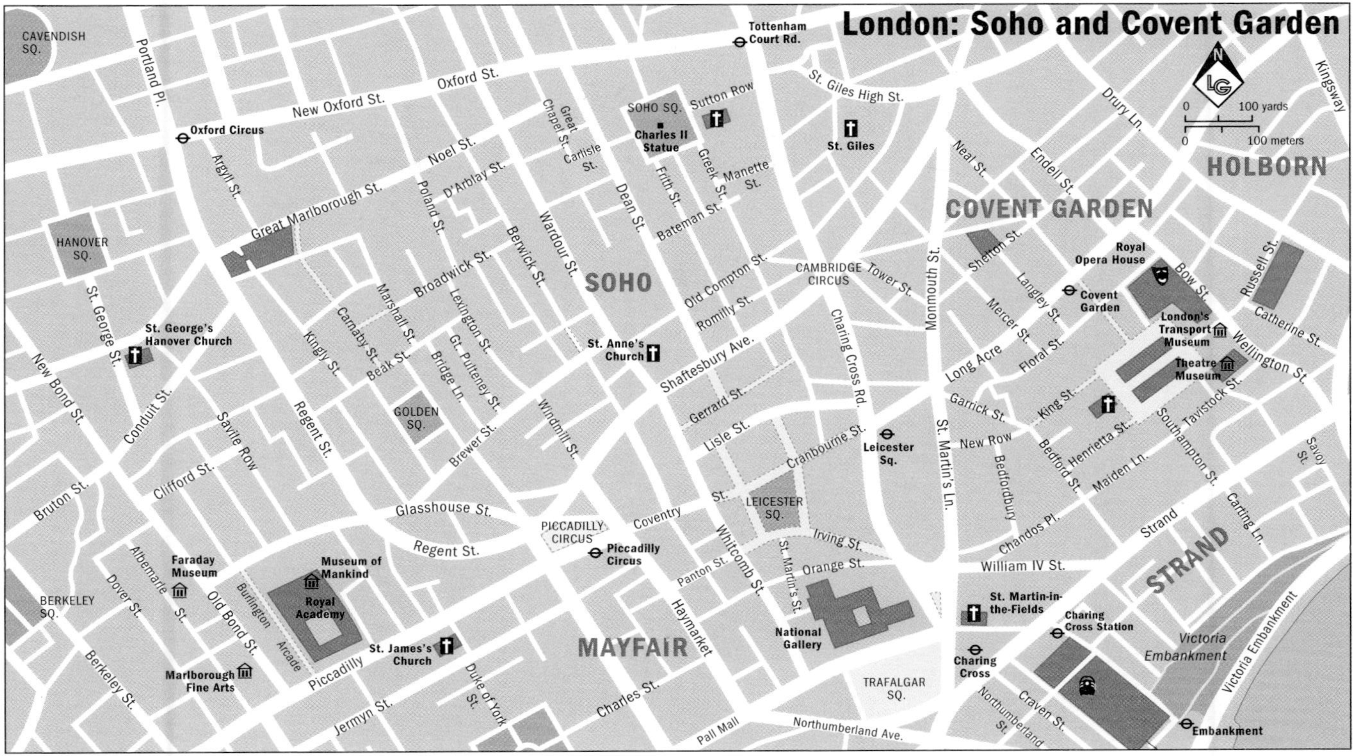
London: Soho and Covent Garden
N
0
100 yards
0
100 meters
CAVENDISH SQ.
Portland Pl.
Oxford Circus
Oxford St.
New Oxford St.
Tottenham Court Rd.
St. Giles High St.
St. Giles
Drury Ln.
Kingsway
HOLBORN
Argyll St.
Noel St.
Great Chapel St.
Carlisle St.
SOHO SQ.
Charles II Statue
Sutton Row
Greek St.
Manette St.
Frith St.
Dean St.
Bateman St.
Neal St.
Endell St.
COVENT GARDEN
HANOVER SQ.
Great Marlborough St.
D'Arblay St.
Poland St.
Berwick St.
Wardour St.
SOHO
Old Compton St.
CAMBRIDGE CIRCUS
Tower St.
Monmouth St.
Shelton St.
Royal Opera House
Bow St.
Russell St.
Broadwick St.
Marshall St.
Lexington St.
Carnaby St.
Kingly St.
St. George St.
St. George's Hanover Church
Romilly St.
Charing Cross Rd.
Langley St.
Covent Garden
Mercer St.
London's Transport Museum
Catherine St.
Wellington St.
Beak St.
Bridge Ln.
Gt. Pulteney St.
St. Anne's Church
Shaftesbury Ave.
Long Acre
Floral St.
Theatre Museum
New Bond St.
Conduit St.
Savile Row
Regent St.
GOLDEN SQ.
Windmill St.
Brewer St.
Gerrard St.
Lisle St.
Cranbourne St.
Leicester Sq.
St. Martin's Ln.
Garrick St.
King St.
New Row
Bedfordbury
Bedford St.
Henrietta St.
Southampton St.
Tavistock St.
Maiden Ln.
Savoy St.
Bruton St.
Clifford St.
Glasshouse St.
PICCADILLY CIRCUS
Coventry St.
LEICESTER SQ.
Irving St.
Chandos Pl.
Strand
STRAND
Carting Ln.
Regent St.
Piccadilly Circus
Faraday Museum
Museum of Mankind
Royal Academy
Albemarle St.
Dover St.
Old Bond St.
Burlington Arcade
Panton St.
Whitcomb St.
St. Martin's St.
Orange St.
William IV St.
St. Martin-in-the-Fields
Charing Cross Station
Victoria Embankment
BERKELEY SQ.
Berkeley St.
Marlborough Fine Arts
Piccadilly
St. James's Church
Duke of York St.
MAYFAIR
Haymarket
National Gallery
Charing Cross
Jermyn St.
Charles St.
Pall Mall
Northumberland Ave.
TRAFALGAR SQ.
Northumberland St.
Craven St.
Embankment

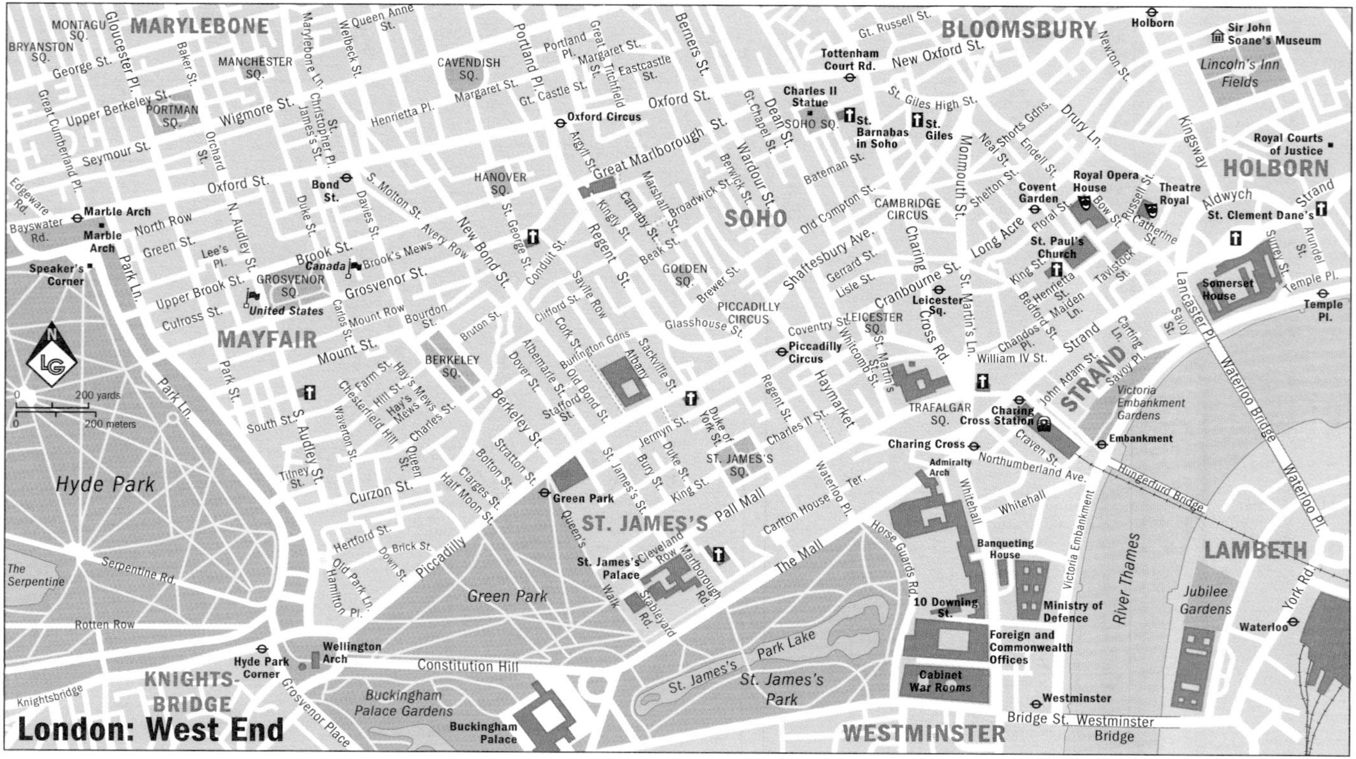
London: West End
MARYLEBONE
BLOOMSBURY
HOLBORN
SOHO
MAYFAIR
STRAND
ST. JAMES'S
LAMBETH
WESTMINSTER
KNIGHTS-
BRIDGE
MONTAGU SQ.
BRYANSTON SQ.
MANCHESTER SQ.
CAVENDISH SQ.
PORTMAN SQ.
HANOVER SQ.
GROSVENOR SQ.
BERKELEY SQ.
GOLDEN SQ.
SOHO SQ.
LEICESTER SQ.
TRAFALGAR SQ.
ST. JAMES'S SQ.
CAMBRIDGE CIRCUS
PICCADILLY CIRCUS
Holborn
Sir John Soane's Museum
Lincoln's Inn Fields
Royal Courts of Justice
Tottenham Court Rd.
Charles II Statue
St. Barnabas in Soho
St. Giles
Oxford Circus
Bond St.
Marble Arch
Speaker's Corner
Covent Garden
Royal Opera House
Theatre Royal
St. Clement Dane's
St. Paul's Church
Somerset House
Temple Pl.
Leicester Sq.
Piccadilly Circus
Charing Cross
Charing Cross Station
Embankment
Victoria Embankment Gardens
Admiralty Arch
Banqueting House
Ministry of Defence
10 Downing St.
Foreign and Commonwealth Offices
Cabinet War Rooms
Westminster
Waterloo
Jubilee Gardens
River Thames
Green Park
St. James's Palace
St. James's Park
Park Lake
Buckingham Palace
Buckingham Palace Gardens
Wellington Arch
Hyde Park Corner
Hyde Park
The Serpentine
Serpentine Rd.
Rotten Row
Knightsbridge
Canada
United States
Albany
Gloucester Pl.
George St.
Baker St.
Upper Berkeley St.
Great Cumberland Pl.
Seymour St.
Edgeware Rd.
Bayswater Rd.
North Row
Green St.
Park Ln.
Upper Brook St.
Culross St.
Lee's Pl.
N. Audley St.
Orchard St.
Oxford St.
Wigmore St.
Marylebone Ln.
Welbeck St.
Queen Anne St.
James's St.
St. Christopher Pl.
Duke St.
Davies St.
S. Molton St.
Brook St.
Brook's Mews
Grosvenor St.
Avery Row
Carlos St.
Mount Row
Mount St.
Bourdon St.
Park St.
South St.
S. Audley St.
Farm St.
Hay's Mews
Hill St.
Chesterfield Hill
Waverton St.
Charles St.
Queen St.
Tilney St.
Curzon St.
Hertford St.
Brick St.
Down St.
Old Park Ln.
Hamilton Pl.
Piccadilly
Half Moon St.
Clarges St.
Bolton St.
Stratton St.
Berkeley St.
Dover St.
Albemarle St.
Stafford St.
Old Bond St.
Burlington Gdns.
Cork St.
Clifford St.
Bruton St.
New Bond St.
St. George St.
Conduit St.
Savile Row
Regent St.
Henrietta Pl.
Margaret St.
Portland Pl.
Gt. Castle St.
Great Portland St.
Margaret St.
Great Titchfield St.
Eastcastle St.
Berners St.
Argyll St.
Great Marlborough St.
Kingly St.
Carnaby St.
Marshall St.
Beak St.
Broadwick St.
Berwick St.
Brewer St.
Glasshouse St.
Wardour St.
Gt. Chapel St.
Dean St.
Bateman St.
Old Compton St.
Shaftesbury Ave.
Gerrard St.
Lisle St.
Coventry St.
Whitcomb St.
St. Martin's St.
Cranbourne St.
Charing Cross Rd.
Gt. Russell St.
New Oxford St.
St. Giles High St.
Monmouth St.
Neal St.
Shorts Gdns.
Endell St.
Shelton St.
Drury Ln.
Newton St.
Kingsway
Aldwych
Long Acre
Floral St.
Bow St.
Russell St.
Catherine St.
King St.
Henrietta St.
Maiden Ln.
Tavistock St.
Bedford St.
Chandos Pl.
St. Martin's Ln.
William IV St.
Strand
Carting Ln.
Savoy St.
Savoy Pl.
John Adam St.
Craven St.
Northumberland Ave.
Lancaster Pl.
Surrey St.
Arundel St.
Temple Pl.
Waterloo Bridge
Waterloo Pl.
Hungerford Bridge
Victoria Embankment
Whitehall
Horse Guards Rd.
Bridge St.
Westminster Bridge
York Rd.
Haymarket
Charles II St.
Jermyn St.
Duke of York St.
Sackville St.
Duke St.
Bury St.
King St.
St. James's St.
Pall Mall
Waterloo Pl.
Carlton House Ter.
The Mall
Cleveland Row
Marlborough Rd.
Queen's Walk
Stableyard Rd.
Constitution Hill
Grosvenor Place
St. James's
200 yards
200 meters
0
N
LG

London: Kensington

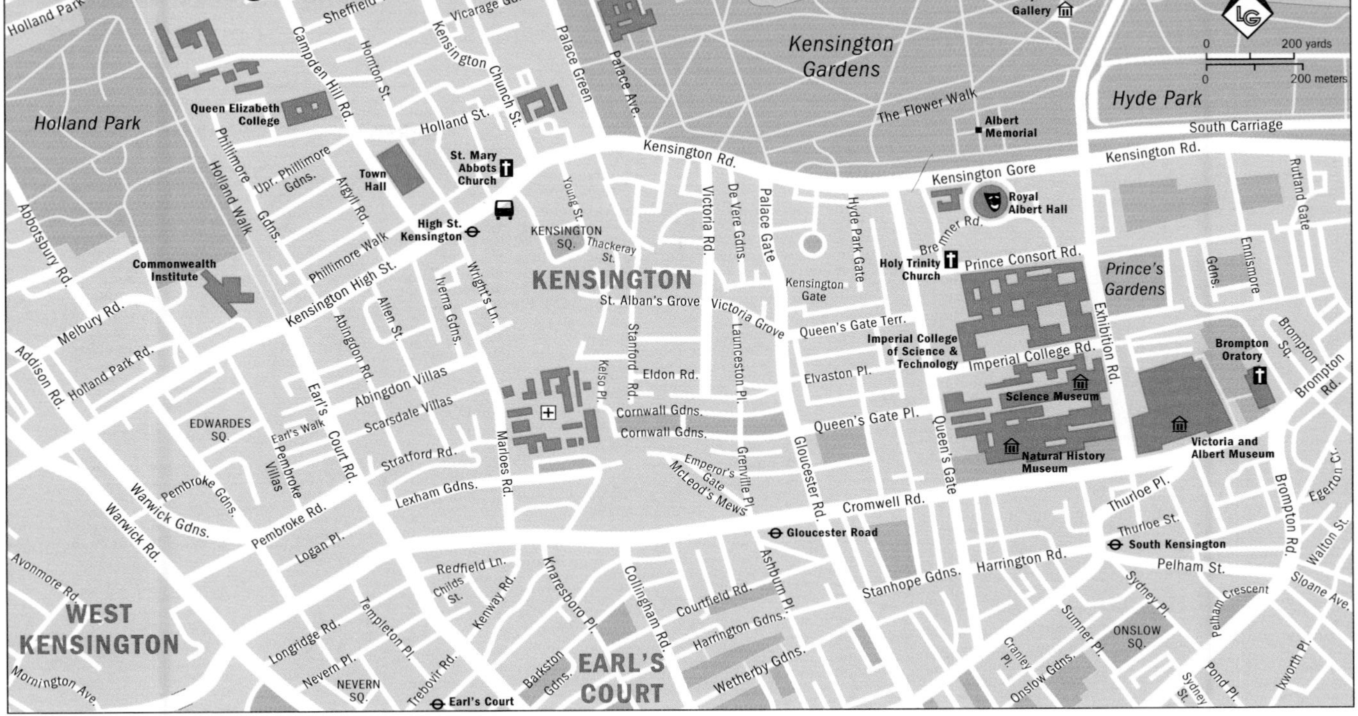

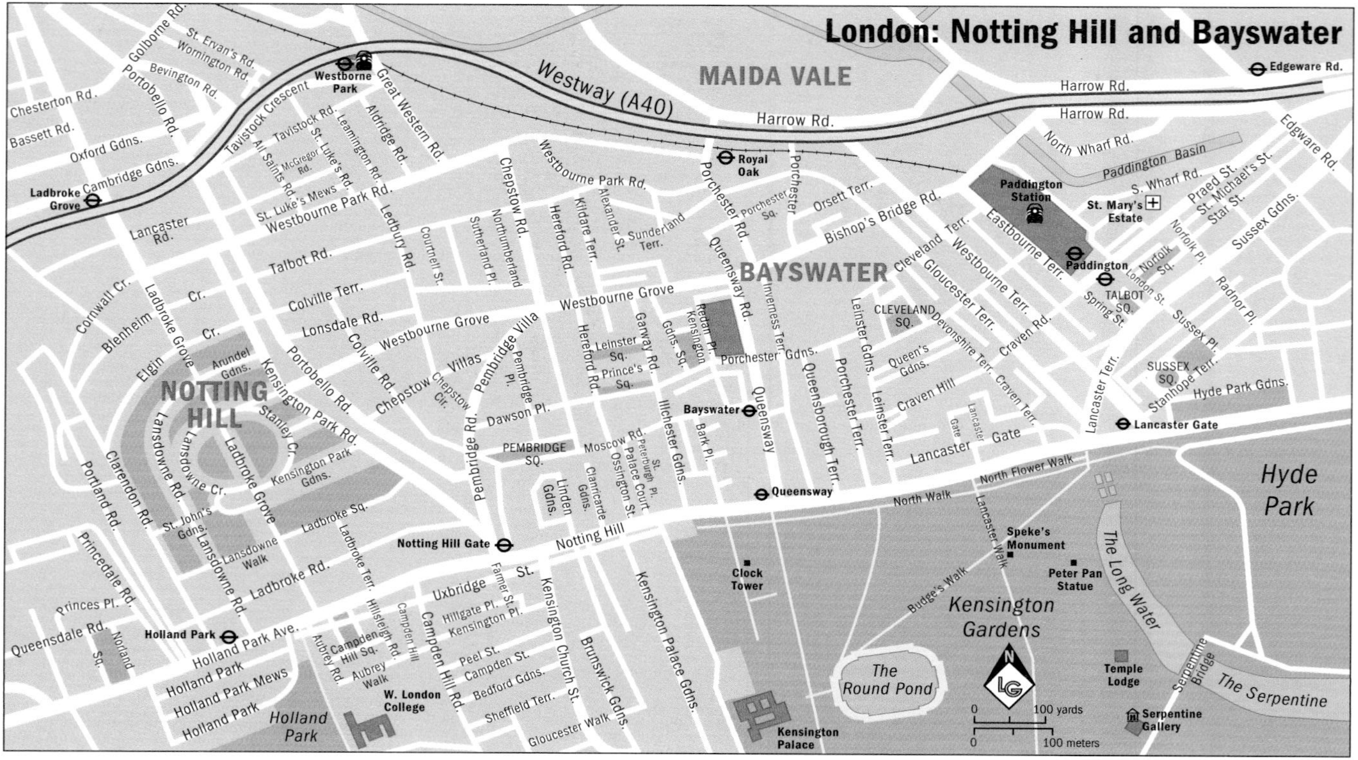

London: Notting Hill and Bayswater
MAIDA VALE
BAYSWATER
NOTTING HILL
Westway (A40)
Harrow Rd.
Edgeware Rd.
Paddington Station
Paddington
St. Mary's Estate
Paddington Basin
North Wharf Rd.
S. Wharf Rd.
Praed St.
St. Michael's St.
Star St.
Sussex Gdns.
Norfolk Pl.
Norfolk Sq.
London St.
TALBOT SQ.
Spring St.
Radnor Pl.
Sussex Pl.
SUSSEX SQ.
Stanhope Terr.
Hyde Park Gdns.
Lancaster Terr.
Lancaster Gate
Eastbourne Terr.
Westbourne Terr.
Gloucester Terr.
Cleveland Terr.
Craven Rd.
Craven Terr.
Devonshire Terr.
CLEVELAND SQ.
Queen's Gdns.
Craven Hill
Leinster Gdns.
Leinster Terr.
Porchester Terr.
Queensborough Terr.
Queensway
Inverness Terr.
Porchester Gdns.
Queensway Rd.
Bishop's Bridge Rd.
Orsett Terr.
Porchester
Porchester Sq.
Porchester Rd.
Royal Oak
Westbourne Park Rd.
Alexander St.
Sunderland Terr.
Kildare Terr.
Hereford Rd.
Chepstow Rd.
Northumberland
Sutherland Pl.
Courtnell St.
Ledbury Rd.
Redan Pl.
Kensington Gdns. Sq.
Garway Rd.
Leinster Sq.
Prince's Sq.
Westbourne Grove
Bayswater
Bark Pl.
Ilchester Gdns.
St. Peterburgh Pl.
Palace Court
Ossington St.
Moscow Rd.
Clanricarde Gdns.
Linden Gdns.
PEMBRIDGE SQ.
Dawson Pl.
Pembridge Pl.
Pembridge Villa
Pembridge Rd.
Chepstow Villas
Chepstow Cir.
Notting Hill Gate
Notting Hill
Great Western Rd.
Aldridge Rd.
Leamington Rd.
St. Luke's Rd.
Tavistock Rd.
McGregor Rd.
All Saints Rd.
St. Luke's Mews
Westbourne Park
Tavistock Crescent
Talbot Rd.
Colville Terr.
Lonsdale Rd.
Colville Rd.
Portobello Rd.
Kensington Park Rd.
Kensington Park Gdns.
Stanley Cr.
Ladbroke Grove
Ladbroke Sq.
Ladbroke Terr.
Ladbroke Rd.
Lansdowne Walk
Lansdowne Rd.
Lansdowne Cr.
St. John's Gdns.
Arundel Gdns.
Elgin Cr.
Blenheim Cr.
Cornwall Cr.
Clarendon Rd.
Portland Rd.
Princedale Rd.
Princes Pl.
Queensdale Rd.
Norland Sq.
Holland Park
Holland Park Ave.
Holland Park Mews
Aubrey Rd.
Aubrey Walk
Campden Hill Sq.
Hillsleigh Rd.
Campden Hill
Campden Hill Rd.
W. London College
Uxbridge St.
Farmer St.
Hillgate Pl.
Kensington Pl.
Peel St.
Campden St.
Bedford Gdns.
Sheffield Terr.
Gloucester Walk
Kensington Church St.
Brunswick Gdns.
Kensington Palace Gdns.
Kensington Palace
Lancaster Rd.
Cambridge Gdns.
Oxford Gdns.
Bassett Rd.
Chesterton Rd.
Ladbroke Grove
Golborne Rd.
St. Ervan's Rd.
Wornington Rd.
Bevington Rd.
Hyde Park
North Flower Walk
North Walk
Lancaster Walk
Budge's Walk
Clock Tower
Speke's Monument
Peter Pan Statue
The Long Water
Kensington Gardens
The Round Pond
Temple Lodge
Serpentine Bridge
The Serpentine
Serpentine Gallery
N
LG
0
100 yards
0
100 meters

Paris Metro

*The stations Liège and Rennes are closed after 8pm and on Sundays and holidays.

Beyond the city limits, *Métro Urbain* tickets are not valid on the RER

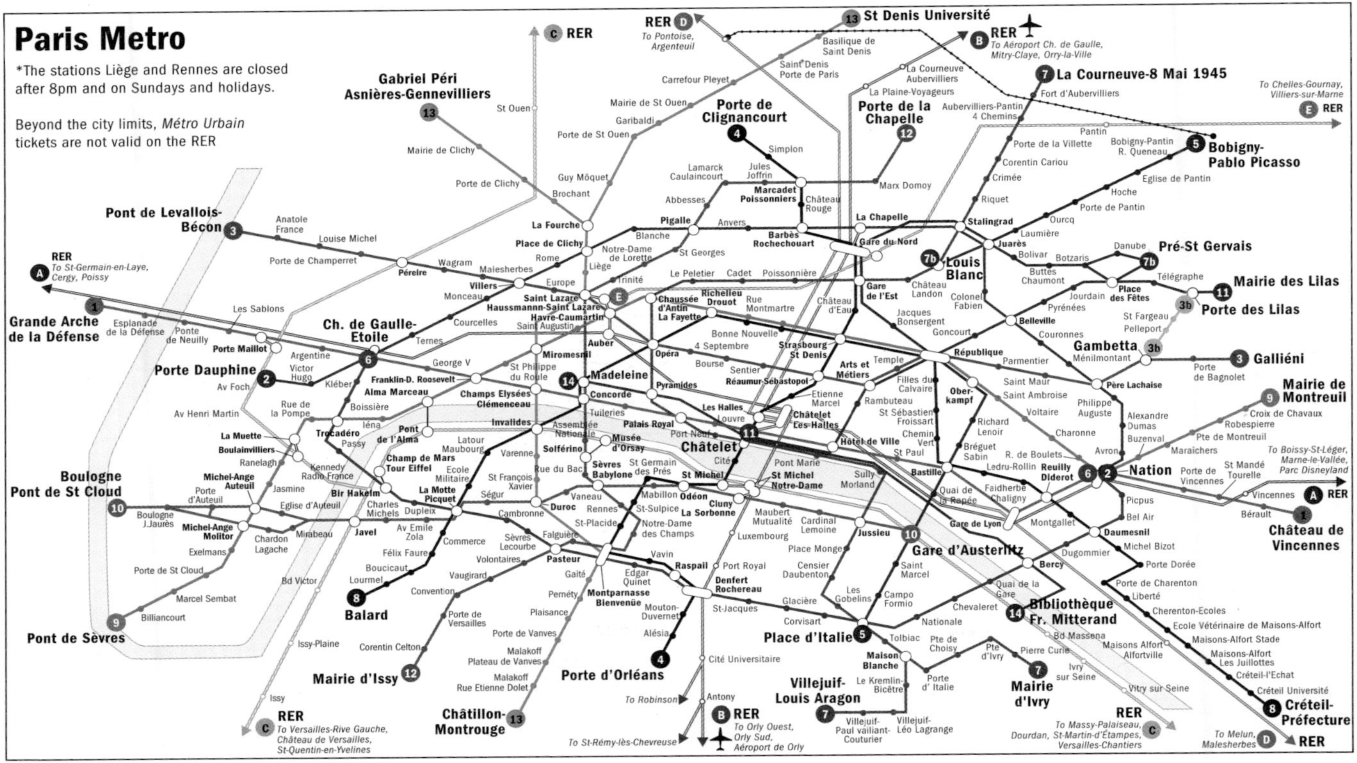

Paris: Overview and Arrondissements

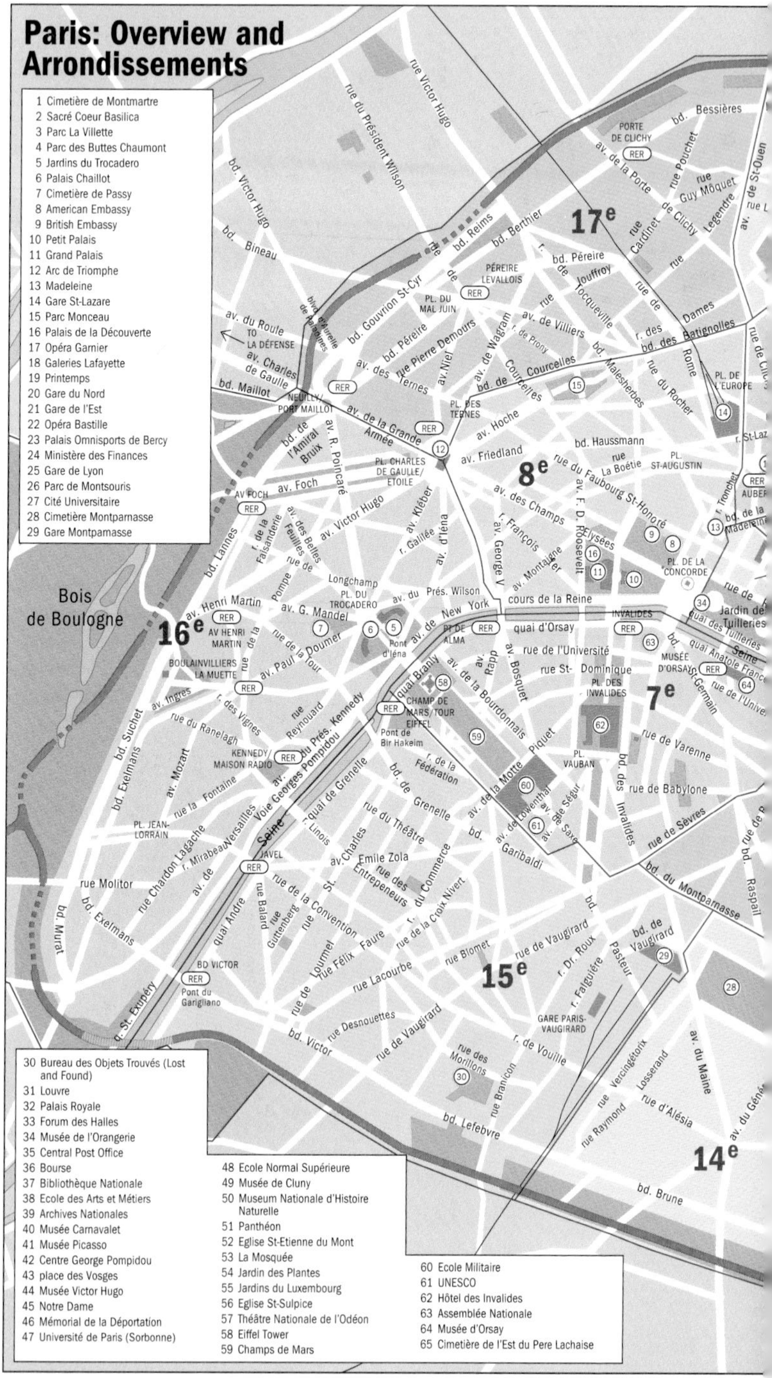

1 Cimetière de Montmartre
2 Sacré Coeur Basilica
3 Parc La Villette
4 Parc des Buttes Chaumont
5 Jardins du Trocadero
6 Palais Chaillot
7 Cimetière de Passy
8 American Embassy
9 British Embassy
10 Petit Palais
11 Grand Palais
12 Arc de Triomphe
13 Madeleine
14 Gare St-Lazare
15 Parc Monceau
16 Palais de la Découverte
17 Opéra Garnier
18 Galeries Lafayette
19 Printemps
20 Gare du Nord
21 Gare de l'Est
22 Opéra Bastille
23 Palais Omnisports de Bercy
24 Ministère des Finances
25 Gare de Lyon
26 Parc de Montsouris
27 Cité Universitaire
28 Cimetière Montparnasse
29 Gare Montparnasse
30 Bureau des Objets Trouvés (Lost and Found)
31 Louvre
32 Palais Royale
33 Forum des Halles
34 Musée de l'Orangerie
35 Central Post Office
36 Bourse
37 Bibliothèque Nationale
38 Ecole des Arts et Métiers
39 Archives Nationales
40 Musée Carnavalet
41 Musée Picasso
42 Centre George Pompidou
43 place des Vosges
44 Musée Victor Hugo
45 Notre Dame
46 Mémorial de la Déportation
47 Université de Paris (Sorbonne)
48 Ecole Normal Supérieure
49 Musée de Cluny
50 Museum Nationale d'Histoire Naturelle
51 Panthéon
52 Eglise St-Etienne du Mont
53 La Mosquée
54 Jardin des Plantes
55 Jardins du Luxembourg
56 Eglise St-Sulpice
57 Théâtre Nationale de l'Odéon
58 Eiffel Tower
59 Champs de Mars
60 Ecole Militaire
61 UNESCO
62 Hôtel des Invalides
63 Assemblée Nationale
64 Musée d'Orsay
65 Cimetière de l'Est du Pere Lachaise
17e
8e
16e
7e
15e
14e
Bois de Boulogne
Seine
PORTE DE CLICHY
PÉREIRE LEVALLOIS
PL. DU MAL JUIN
TO LA DÉFENSE
NEUILLY/ PORT MAILLOT
PL. DES TERNES
PL. CHARLES DE GAULLE/ ETOILE
AV FOCH
PL. DU TROCADERO
AV HENRI MARTIN
BOULAINVILLIERS LA MUETTE
KENNEDY/ MAISON RADIO
PL. JEAN-LORRAIN
JAVEL
BD VICTOR
Pont du Garigliano
Pont d'Iéna
PT DE ALMA
CHAMP DE MARS/ TOUR EIFFEL
Pont de Bir Hakeim
INVALIDES
PL. DES INVALIDES
MUSÉE D'ORSAY
PL. VAUBAN
PL. DE LA CONCORDE
PL. ST-AUGUSTIN
PL. DE L'EUROPE
GARE PARIS-VAUGIRARD
RER
bd. Bessières
bd. Berthier
bd. Péreire
bd. de Courcelles
bd. Malesherbes
bd. des Batignolles
bd. Haussmann
av. de la Grande Armée
av. Foch
av. Victor Hugo
av. Kléber
av. d'Iéna
av. des Champs Elysées
av. Montaigne
av. George V
cours de la Reine
quai d'Orsay
rue de l'Université
rue St- Dominique
rue de Varenne
rue de Babylone
rue de Sèvres
bd. du Montparnasse
bd. Raspail
av. de New York
av. Henri Martin
av. G. Mandel
av. Paul Doumer
rue de Passy
av. Mozart
bd. Exelmans
bd. Suchet
bd. Murat
rue Molitor
av. de Versailles
quai de Grenelle
bd. de Grenelle
av. de la Motte Piquet
bd. Garibaldi
rue de la Convention
rue de Vaugirard
rue Lecourbe
bd. Victor
bd. Lefebvre
bd. Brune
av. du Maine
rue d'Alésia
bd. Pasteur

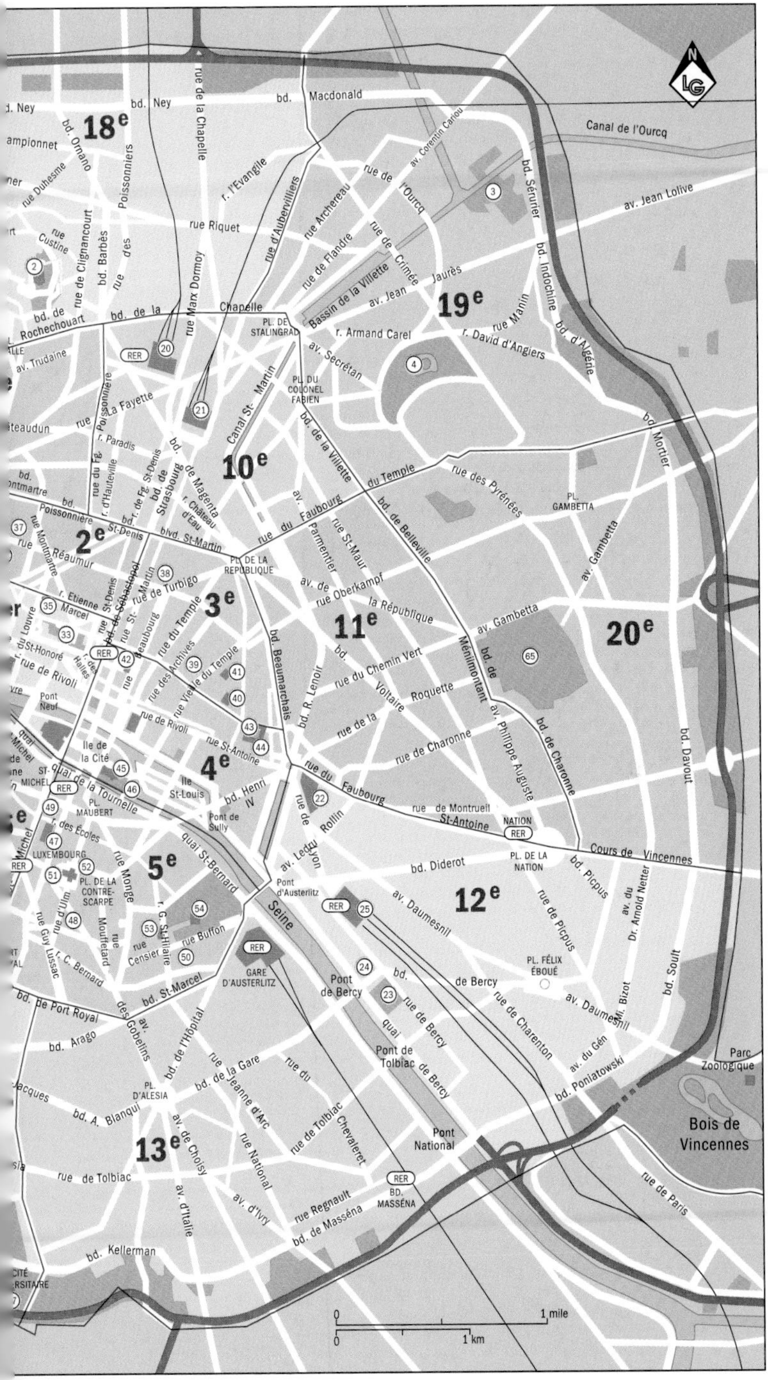

LG
18e
19e
10e
2e
3e
11e
20e
4e
5e
12e
13e
bd. Ney
bd. Macdonald
Canal de l'Ourcq
bd. Ornano
Poissonniers
rue de la Chapelle
r. l'Evangile
rue d'Aubervilliers
rue Archereau
av. Corentin Cariou
rue de l'Ourcq
bd. Sérurier
av. Jean Lolive
rue Duhesme
rue Custine
rue Riquet
rue de Clignancourt
bd. Barbès
rue des
rue Marx Dormoy
rue de Flandre
rue de Crimée
Bassin de la Villette
av. Jean Jaurès
bd. Indochine
bd. de Rochechouart
bd. de la Chapelle
PL. DE STALINGRAD
r. Armand Carel
rue Manin
r. David d'Angiers
bd. d'Algérie
RER
av. Trudaine
av. Secrétan
Canal St-Martin
PL. DU COLONEL FABIEN
rue La Fayette
rue Poissonnière
r. Paradis
rue du Fg. Poissonnière
r. d'Hauteville
r. de Fg. St-Denis
bd. de Strasbourg
bd. de Magenta
r. Château d'Eau
bd. de la Villette
rue du Faubourg du Temple
rue des Pyrénées
PL. GAMBETTA
bd. Mortier
bd. Montmartre
bd. Poissonnière
bd. St-Denis
blvd. St-Martin
PL. DE LA RÉPUBLIQUE
av. Parmentier
rue St-Maur
bd. de Belleville
av. Gambetta
rue Montmartre
rue Réaumur
bd. de Sébastopol
rue St-Martin
rue de Turbigo
av. de la République
rue Oberkampf
r. Etienne Marcel
rue du Louvre
rue St-Honoré
rue de Rivoli
r. des Halles
rue Beaubourg
rue du Temple
rue des Archives
rue Vieille du Temple
bd. Beaumarchais
bd. Voltaire
rue du Chemin Vert
Ménilmontant
bd. de Ménilmontant
Pont Neuf
rue de Rivoli
rue St-Antoine
bd. R. Lenoir
rue de la Roquette
rue de Charonne
av. Philippe Auguste
bd. de Charonne
bd. Davout
quai St-Michel
Ile de la Cité
Ile St-Louis
ST-MICHEL
quai de la Tournelle
bd. Henri IV
rue du Faubourg St-Antoine
rue de Montreuil
NATION
PL. MAUBERT
Pont de Sully
rue de Lyon
rue Rollin
av. Ledru
bd. St-Michel
r. des Écoles
quai St-Bernard
Cours de Vincennes
LUXEMBOURG
rue Monge
bd. Diderot
PL. DE LA NATION
bd. Picpus
PL. DE LA CONTRE-SCARPE
Pont d'Austerlitz
av. Daumesnil
av. du Dr. Arnold Netter
rue d'Ulm
rue Guy Lussac
rue Mouffetard
r. G. St-Hilaire
rue Buffon
rue Censier
Seine
rue de Picpus
r. C. Bernard
GARE D'AUSTERLITZ
Pont de Bercy
bd. de Bercy
PL. FÉLIX ÉBOUÉ
bd. Soult
bd. St-Marcel
av. des Gobelins
rue de Bercy
rue de Charenton
Mt. Bizot
bd. de Port Royal
bd. Arago
quai de Bercy
Pont de Tolbiac
av. du Gén
Parc Zoologique
bd. de l'Hôpital
bd. de la Gare
rue du Chevaleret
bd. Poniatowski
PL. D'ALESIA
rue Jeanne d'Arc
bd. A. Blanqui
rue de Tolbiac
Bois de Vincennes
av. de Choisy
rue Nationale
Pont National
rue de Paris
rue de Tolbiac
av. d'Italie
av. d'Ivry
rue Regnault
BD. MASSÉNA
bd. de Masséna
bd. Kellerman
0
1 mile
1 km

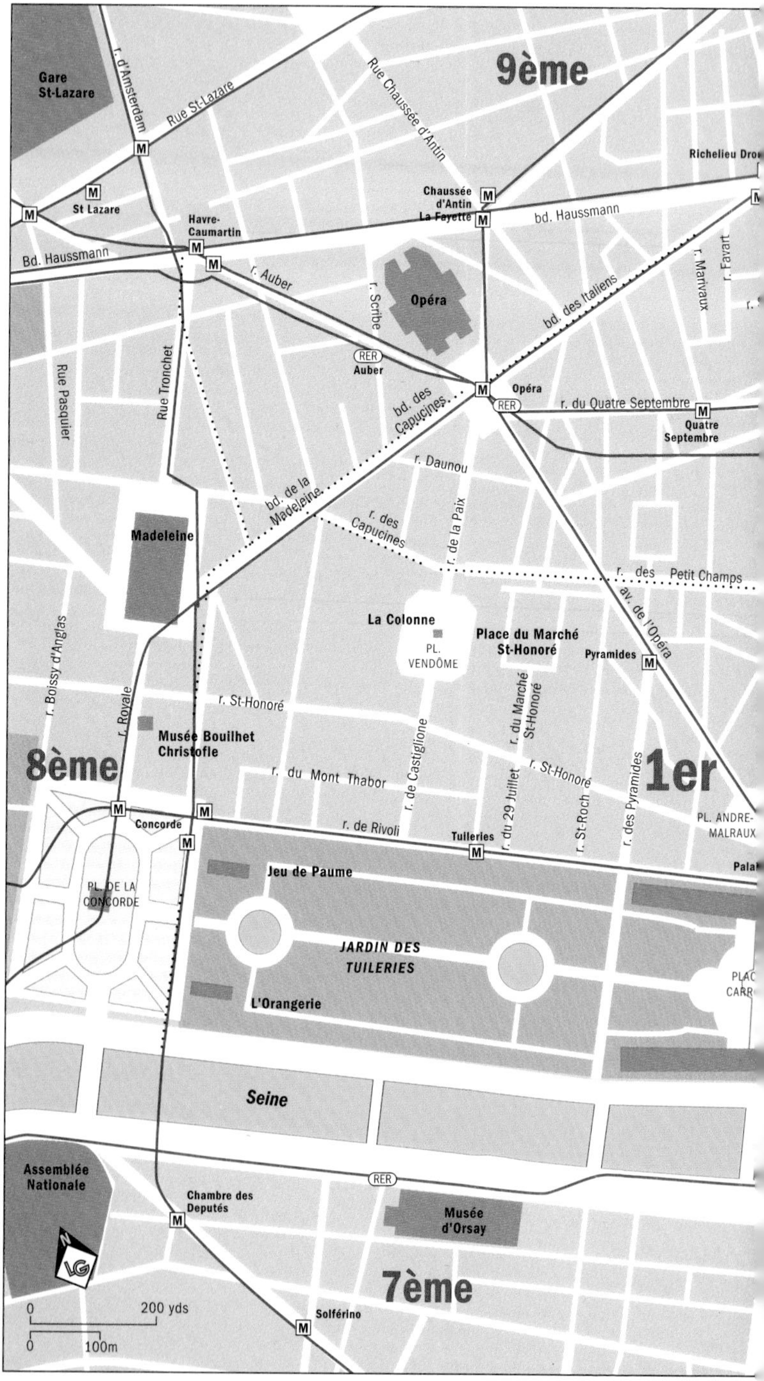

9ème
Gare St-Lazare
r. d'Amsterdam
Rue St-Lazare
Rue Chaussée d'Antin
Richelieu Drouot
St Lazare
Chaussée d'Antin La Fayette
bd. Haussmann
Havre-Caumartin
Bd. Haussmann
r. Auber
r. Scribe
Opéra
r. Marivaux
r. Favart
bd. des Italiens
Rue Pasquier
Rue Tronchet
RER
Auber
Opéra
RER
bd. des Capucines
r. du Quatre Septembre
Quatre Septembre
r. Daunou
bd. de la Madeleine
r. des Capucines
r. de la Paix
Madeleine
r. des Petit Champs
av. de l'Opéra
La Colonne
Place du Marché St-Honoré
PL. VENDÔME
Pyramides
r. Boissy d'Anglas
r. Royale
r. St-Honoré
Musée Bouilhet Christofle
r. du Marché St-Honoré
8ème
r. du Mont Thabor
r. de Castiglione
r. St-Honoré
r. du 29 Juillet
r. St-Roch
r. des Pyramides
1er
Concorde
r. de Rivoli
Tuileries
PL. ANDRE-MALRAUX
Jeu de Paume
PL. DE LA CONCORDE
JARDIN DES TUILERIES
L'Orangerie
Seine
Assemblée Nationale
RER
Chambre des Deputés
Musée d'Orsay
7ème
Solférino
0
200 yds
0
100m

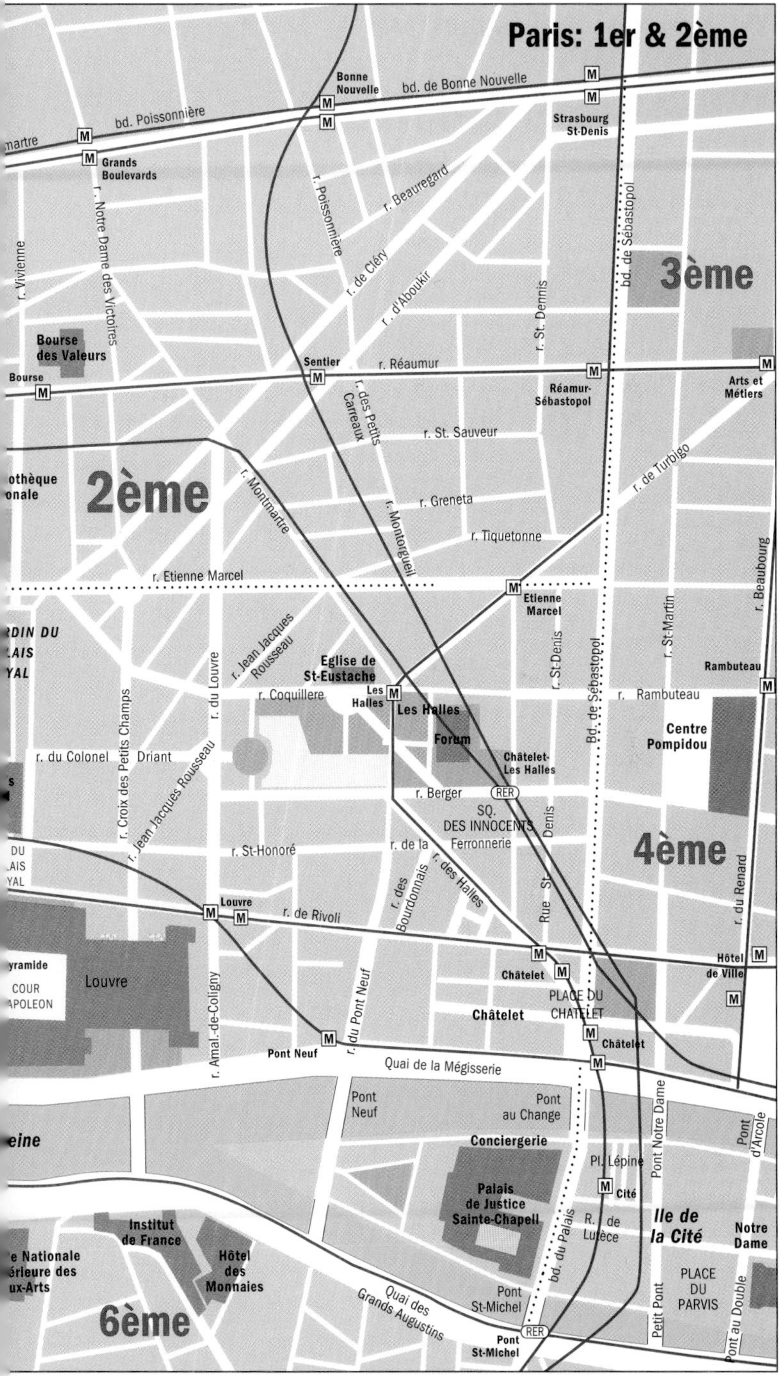

Paris: 1er & 2ème
bd. de Bonne Nouvelle
Bonne Nouvelle
bd. Poissonnière
Grands Boulevards
Strasbourg St-Denis
r. Notre Dame des Victoires
r. Poissonnière
r. Beauregard
r. de Cléry
r. d'Aboukir
r. Vivienne
Bourse des Valeurs
Bourse
Sentier
r. Réaumur
Réaumur-Sébastopol
Arts et Métiers
r. des Petits Carreaux
r. St. Sauveur
r. St. Dennis
bd. de Sébastopol
3ème
2ème
r. Montmartre
r. Greneta
r. Montorgueil
r. Tiquetonne
r. de Turbigo
r. Etienne Marcel
Etienne Marcel
r. Jean Jacques Rousseau
Eglise de St-Eustache
r. du Louvre
r. Coquillere
Les Halles
Forum
r. St-Denis
Bd. de Sébastopol
r. St-Martin
r. Beaubourg
Rambuteau
r. Rambuteau
Centre Pompidou
r. du Colonel Driant
r. Croix des Petits Champs
Châtelet-Les Halles
r. Berger
RER
SQ. DES INNOCENTS
r. de la Ferronnerie
Rue St Denis
4ème
r. du Renard
r. St-Honoré
r. des Bourdonnais
r. des Halles
Louvre
r. de Rivoli
Hôtel de Ville
Pyramide
COUR NAPOLEON
r. Amal.-de-Coligny
r. du Pont Neuf
Châtelet
PLACE DU CHATELET
Pont Neuf
Quai de la Mégisserie
Pont Neuf
Pont au Change
Conciergerie
Pl. Lépine
Pont Notre Dame
Pont d'Arcole
Palais de Justice Sainte-Chapell
Cité
R. de Lutèce
Ile de la Cité
Notre Dame
Institut de France
Hôtel des Monnaies
bd. du Palais
PLACE DU PARVIS
Petit Pont
Pont au Double
Quai des Grands Augustins
Pont St-Michel
6ème

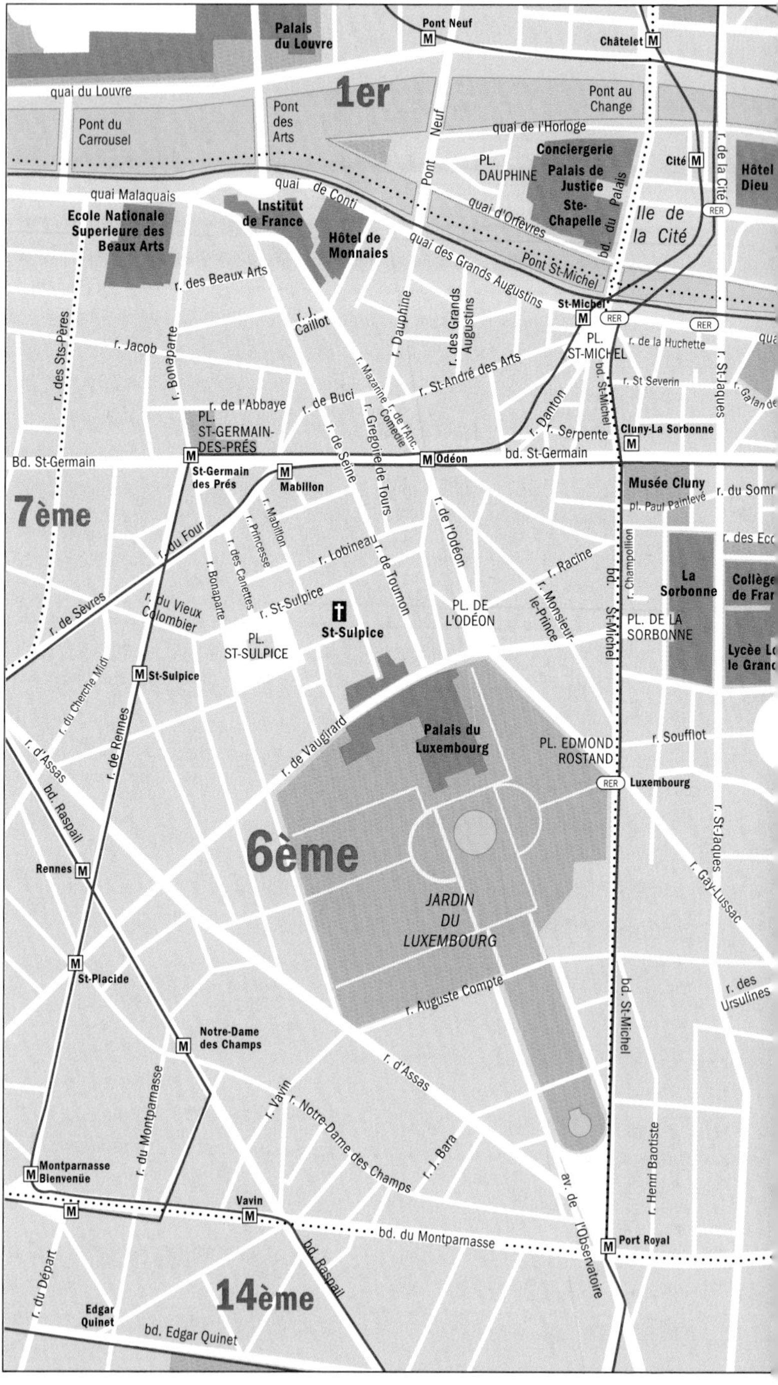
Palais du Louvre
Pont Neuf
Châtelet
1er
quai du Louvre
Pont du Carrousel
Pont des Arts
Pont Neuf
Pont au Change
quai de l'Horloge
Conciergerie
PL. DAUPHINE
Palais de Justice
Ste-Chapelle
Cité
r. de la Cité
Hôtel Dieu
Ile de la Cité
bd. du Palais
quai Malaquais
quai de Conti
Institut de France
Ecole Nationale Superieure des Beaux Arts
Hôtel de Monnaies
quai d'Orfèvres
quai des Grands Augustins
Pont St-Michel
r. des Beaux Arts
r. J. Caillot
St-Michel
RER
r. Dauphine
r. des Grands Augustins
PL. ST-MICHEL
r. de la Huchette
r. des Sts-Pères
r. Jacob
r. Bonaparte
r. St-André des Arts
r. St Severin
r. St-Jaques
r. Galande
r. de l'Abbaye
r. de Buci
r. Mazarine
r. de l'Anc. Comedie
bd. St-Michel
PL. ST-GERMAIN-DES-PRÉS
r. de Seine
r. Gregoire de Tours
r. Danton
r. Serpente
Cluny-La Sorbonne
Bd. St-Germain
St-Germain des Prés
Mabillon
Odéon
bd. St-Germain
Musée Cluny
pl. Paul Painlevé
r. du Somm
7ème
r. Mabillon
r. Princesse
r. des Canettes
r. de l'Odéon
r. des Eco
r. du Four
r. Lobineau
r. de Tournon
r. Racine
r. Champollion
La Sorbonne
Collège de Fran
r. de Sèvres
r. du Vieux Colombier
r. Bonaparte
r. St-Sulpice
St-Sulpice
PL. DE L'ODÉON
r. Monsieur-le-Prince
PL. DE LA SORBONNE
PL. ST-SULPICE
St-Sulpice
Lycée Lo le Granc
r. du Cherche Midi
r. de Vaugirard
Palais du Luxembourg
PL. EDMOND ROSTAND
r. Soufflot
r. d'Assas
r. de Rennes
bd. Raspail
Luxembourg
6ème
Rennes
JARDIN DU LUXEMBOURG
r. Gay-Lussac
St-Placide
r. Auguste Compte
r. des Ursulines
Notre-Dame des Champs
r. du Montparnasse
r. d'Assas
r. Vavin
r. Notre-Dame des Champs
r. J. Bara
Montparnasse Bienvenüe
av. de l'Observatoire
r. Henri Baotiste
Vavin
bd. du Montparnasse
Port Royal
bd. Raspail
r. du Départ
14ème
Edgar Quinet
bd. Edgar Quinet

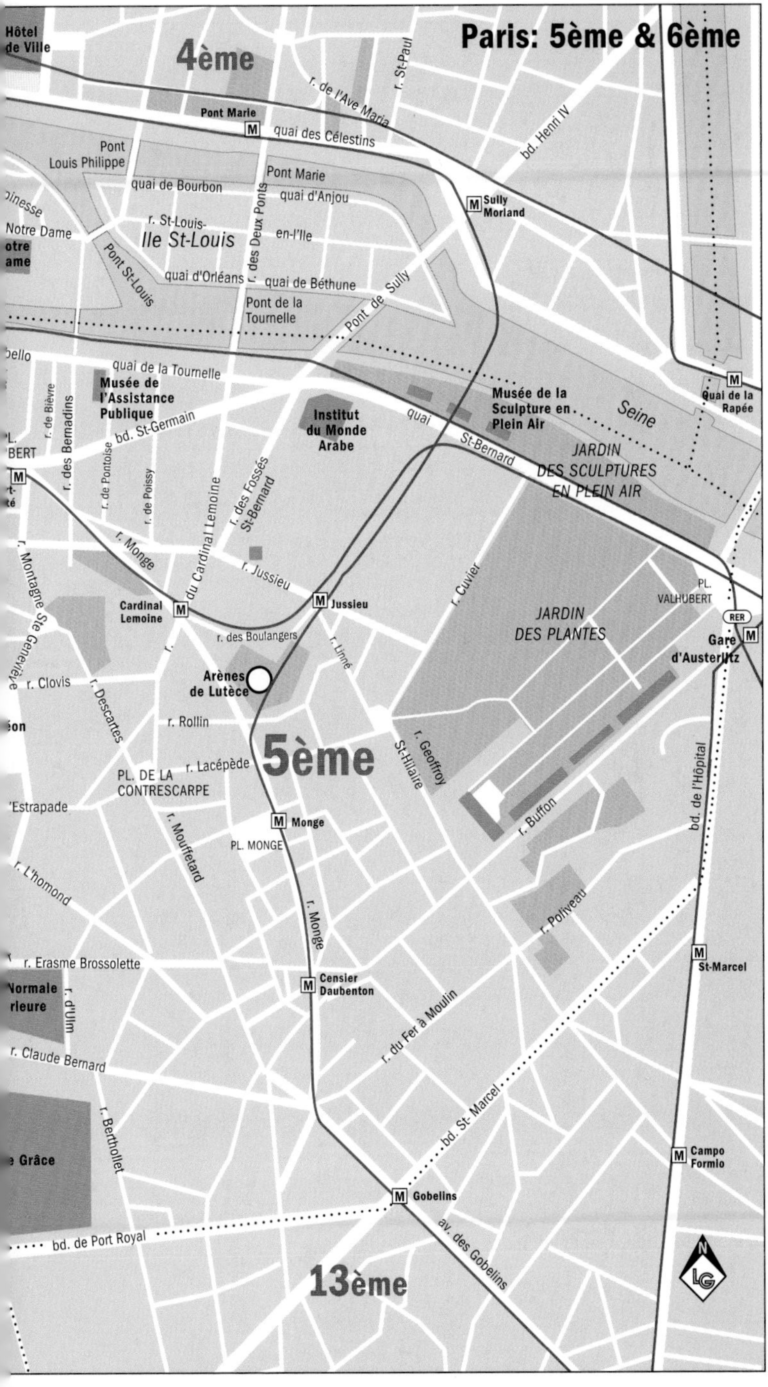

Paris: 5ème & 6ème
4ème
5ème
13ème
Hôtel de Ville
Pont Marie
quai des Célestins
r. de l'Ave Maria
r. St-Paul
bd. Henri IV
Sully Morland
Pont Louis Philippe
quai de Bourbon
Pont Marie
quai d'Anjou
Notre Dame
r. St-Louis-en-l'Ile
Ile St-Louis
Pont St-Louis
r. des Deux Ponts
quai d'Orléans
quai de Béthune
Pont de la Tournelle
Pont de Sully
quai de la Tournelle
Musée de l'Assistance Publique
Institut du Monde Arabe
Musée de la Sculpture en Plein Air
Seine
Quai de la Rapée
quai St-Bernard
JARDIN DES SCULPTURES EN PLEIN AIR
r. de Bièvre
r. des Bernadins
r. de Pontoise
bd. St-Germain
r. de Poissy
r. du Cardinal Lemoine
r. des Fossés St-Bernard
r. Monge
r. Jussieu
r. Cuvier
PL. VALHUBERT
RER
Gare d'Austerlitz
JARDIN DES PLANTES
r. Montagne Ste Geneviève
Cardinal Lemoine
Jussieu
r. des Boulangers
r. Linné
Arènes de Lutèce
r. Clovis
r. Descartes
r. Rollin
r. Lacépède
PL. DE LA CONTRESCARPE
r. Geoffroy St-Hilaire
r. Buffon
bd. de l'Hôpital
Monge
PL. MONGE
r. Mouffetard
r. L'homond
r. Poliveau
r. Monge
St-Marcel
r. Erasme Brossolette
Censier Daubenton
r. d'Ulm
r. du Fer à Moulin
r. Claude Bernard
bd. St-Marcel
r. Berthollet
Campo Formio
Gobelins
bd. de Port Royal
av. des Gobelins
N
LG

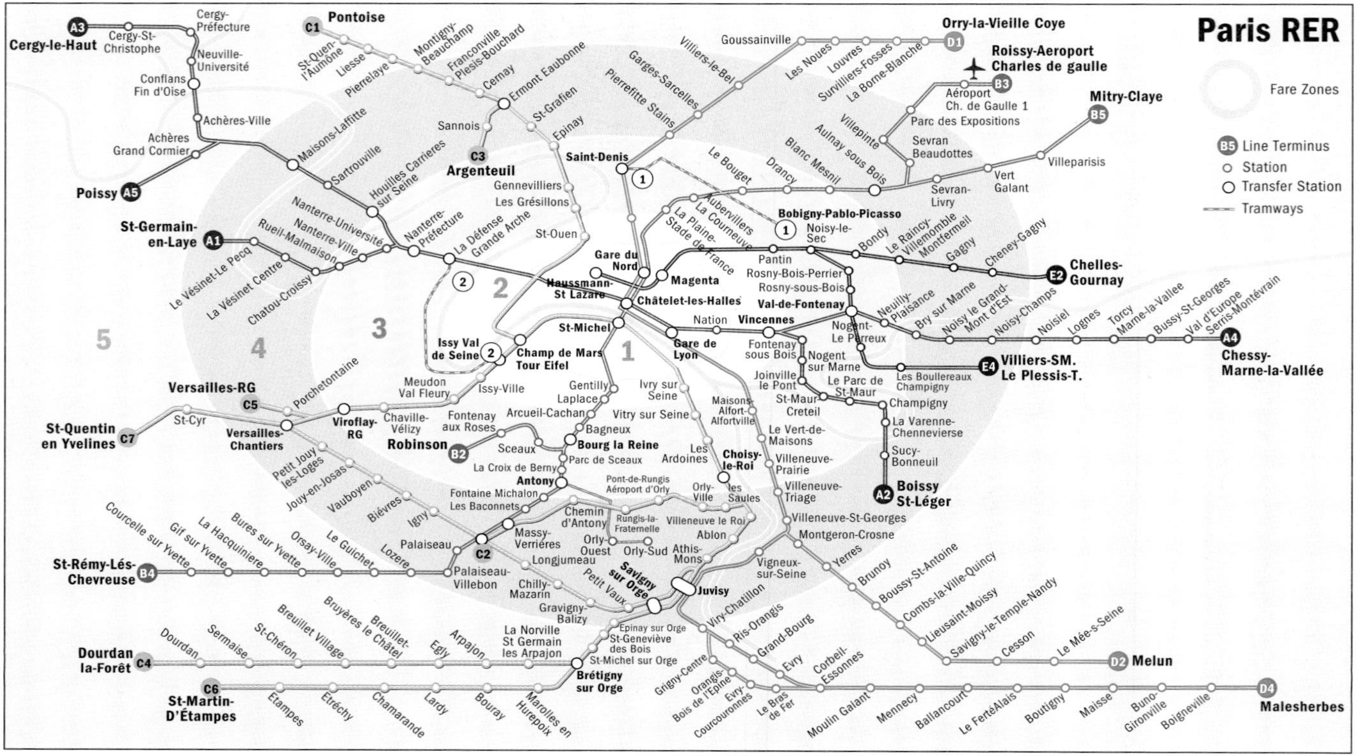

Paris RER
Fare Zones
Line Terminus
Station
Transfer Station
Tramways
1
2
3
4
5
Cergy-le-Haut
Cergy-St-Christophe
Cergy-Préfecture
Neuville-Université
Conflans Fin d'Oise
Achères-Ville
Achères Grand Cormier
Poissy
Maisons-Laffitte
Sartrouville
Houilles Carrieres sur Seine
Nanterre-Université
Nanterre-Préfecture
La Défense Grande Arche
St-Germain-en-Laye
Le Vésinet-Le Pecq
La Vésinet Centre
Chatou-Croissy
Rueil-Malmaison
Nanterre-Ville
Pontoise
St-Ouen-l'Aumône
Liesse
Pierrelaye
Montigny-Beauchamp
Franconville Plesis-Bouchard
Cernay
Ermont Eaubonne
St-Grafien
Epinay
Sannois
Argenteuil
Gennevilliers
Les Grésillons
St-Ouen
Saint-Denis
Goussainville
Villiers-le-Bel
Garges-Sarcelles
Pierrefitte Stains
Les Noues
Louvres
Survilliers-Fosses
La Borne-Blanche
Orry-la-Vieille Coye
Roissy-Aeroport Charles de gaulle
Aéroport Ch. de Gaulle 1
Parc des Expositions
Villepinte
Sevran Beaudottes
Mitry-Claye
Villeparisis
Vert Galant
Sevran-Livry
Aulnay sous Bois
Blanc Mesnil
Drancy
Le Bouget
La Plaine-Stade de France
La Courneuve Aubervilliers
Bobigny-Pablo-Picasso
Noisy-le-Sec
Bondy
Le Raincy-Villemomble Montfermeil
Gagny
Cheney-Gagny
Chelles-Gournay
Pantin
Rosny-Bois-Perrier
Rosny-sous-Bois
Val-de-Fontenay
Gare du Nord
Magenta
Haussmann-St Lazare
Châtelet-les-Halles
St-Michel
Nation
Vincennes
Gare de Lyon
Neuilly-Plaisance
Bry sur Marne
Noisy le Grand-Mont d'Est
Noisy-Champs
Noisiel
Lognes
Torcy
Marne-la-Vallee
Bussy-St-Georges
Val d'Europe
Serris-Montévrain
Chessy-Marne-la-Vallée
Nogent-Le Perreux
Les Boullereaux Champigny
Villiers-SM. Le Plessis-T.
Fontenay sous Bois
Nogent sur Marne
Joinville le Pont
Le Parc de St-Maur
St-Maur-Creteil
Champigny
La Varenne-Chennevierse
Sucy-Bonneuil
Boissy St-Léger
Issy Val de Seine
Champ de Mars Tour Eifel
Issy-Ville
Meudon Val Fleury
Chaville-Vélizy
Viroflay-RG
Porchetontaine
Versailles-RG
Versailles-Chantiers
St-Cyr
St-Quentin en Yvelines
Gentilly
Laplace
Arcueil-Cachan
Bagneux
Bourg la Reine
Fontenay aux Roses
Sceaux
Robinson
Parc de Sceaux
La Croix de Berny
Antony
Fontaine Michalon
Les Baconnets
Massy-Verrières
Palaiseau
Palaiseau-Villebon
Lozere
Le Guichet
Orsay-Ville
Bures sur Yvette
La Hacquinière
Gif sur Yvette
Courcelle sur Yvette
St-Rémy-Lés-Chevreuse
Petit Jouy les-Loges
Jouy-en-Josas
Vauboyen
Bièvres
Igny
Chemin d'Antony
Longjumeau
Chilly-Mazarin
Gravigny-Balizy
Petit Vaux
Savigny sur Orge
Juvisy
Ivry sur Seine
Vitry sur Seine
Les Ardoines
Choisy-le-Roi
Maisons-Alfort-Alfortville
Le Vert-de-Maisons
Villeneuve-Prairie
Villeneuve-Triage
Villeneuve-St-Georges
Montgeron-Crosne
Pont-de-Rungis Aéroport d'Orly
Rungis-la-Fraternelle
Orly-Ouest
Orly-Sud
Orly-Ville
les Saules
Villeneuve le Roi
Ablon
Athis-Mons
Vigneux-sur-Seine
Yerres
Brunoy
Boussy-St-Antoine
Combs-la-Ville-Quincy
Lieusaint-Moissy
Savigny-le-Temple-Nandy
Cesson
Le Mée-s-Seine
Melun
Viry-Chatillon
Ris-Orangis
Grand-Bourg
Evry
Corbeil-Essonnes
Grigny-Centre
Orangis-Bois de l'Epine
Evry-Courcouronnes
Le Bras de Fer
Moulin Galant
Mennecy
Ballancourt
Le FertéAlais
Boutigny
Maisse
Buno-Gironville
Boigneville
Malesherbes
Epinay sur Orge
St-Geneviève des Bois
St-Michel sur Orge
Brétigny sur Orge
La Norville St Germain les Arpajon
Arpajon
Egly
Breuillet-Bruyères le Châtel
Breuillet Village
St-Chéron
Sermaise
Dourdan
Dourdan la-Forêt
Marolles en Hurepoix
Bouray
Lardy
Chamarande
Etréchy
Etampes
St-Martin-D'Étampes
A1
A2
A3
A4
A5
B2
B3
B5
C1
C2
C3
C4
C5
C6
C7
D1
D2
D4
E2
E4

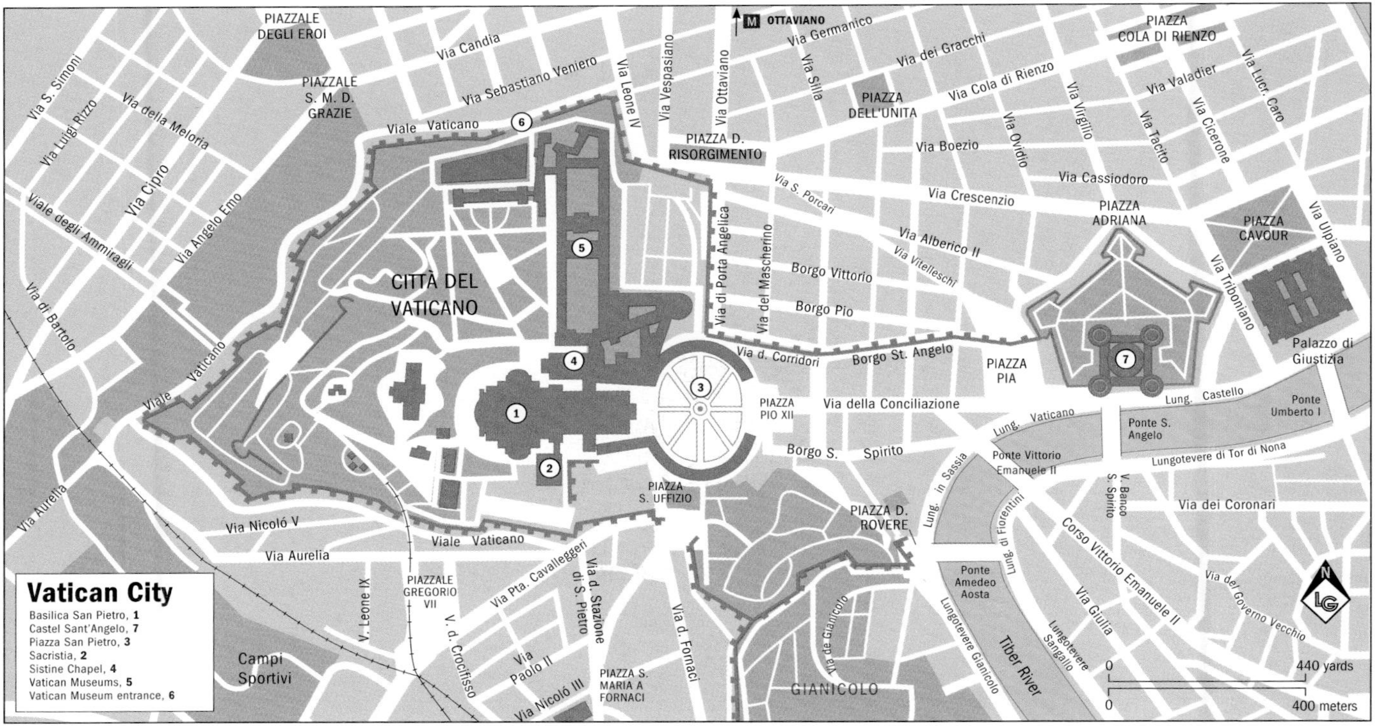
Vatican City
Basilica San Pietro, 1
Castel Sant'Angelo, 7
Piazza San Pietro, 3
Sacristia, 2
Sistine Chapel, 4
Vatican Museums, 5
Vatican Museum entrance, 6
CITTÀ DEL VATICANO
OTTAVIANO
PIAZZALE DEGLI EROI
PIAZZALE S. M. D. GRAZIE
PIAZZA D. RISORGIMENTO
PIAZZA DELL'UNITA
PIAZZA COLA DI RIENZO
PIAZZA ADRIANA
PIAZZA CAVOUR
PIAZZA PIA
PIAZZA PIO XII
PIAZZA S. UFFIZIO
PIAZZA D. ROVERE
PIAZZALE GREGORIO VII
PIAZZA S. MARIA A FORNACI
Palazzo di Giustizia
Via Candia
Via Sebastiano Veniero
Viale Vaticano
Via Leone IV
Via Vespasiano
Via Ottaviano
Via Germanico
Via Silla
Via dei Gracchi
Via Cola di Rienzo
Via Valadier
Via Lucr. Caro
Via Virgilio
Via Ovidio
Via Tacito
Via Cicerone
Via Boezio
Via Cassiodoro
Via Crescenzio
Via S. Porcari
Via Alberico II
Via Vitelleschi
Via Ulpiano
Via Triboniano
Via di Porta Angelica
Via del Mascherino
Borgo Vittorio
Borgo Pio
Via d. Corridori
Borgo St. Angelo
Via della Conciliazione
Borgo S. Spirito
Lung. Castello
Lung. Vaticano
Ponte Umberto I
Ponte S. Angelo
Lungotevere di Tor di Nona
Ponte Vittorio Emanuele II
Lung. in Sassia
Lung. di Fiorentini
V. Banco S. Spirito
Via dei Coronari
Corso Vittorio Emanuele II
Via del Governo Vecchio
Via Giulia
Lungotevere Sangallo
Ponte Amedeo Aosta
Lungotevere Gianicolo
Tiber River
Via de Gianicolo
GIANICOLO
Via d. Fornaci
Via d. Stazione di S. Pietro
Via Pta. Cavalleggeri
Via Paolo II
Via Nicoló III
V. d. Crocifisso
V. Leone IX
Via Aurelia
Via Nicoló V
Campi Sportivi
Via S. Simoni
Via Luigi Rizzo
Via della Meloria
Via Cipro
Via Angelo Emo
Viale degli Ammiragli
Via di Bartolo
0
440 yards
400 meters

Rome Overview

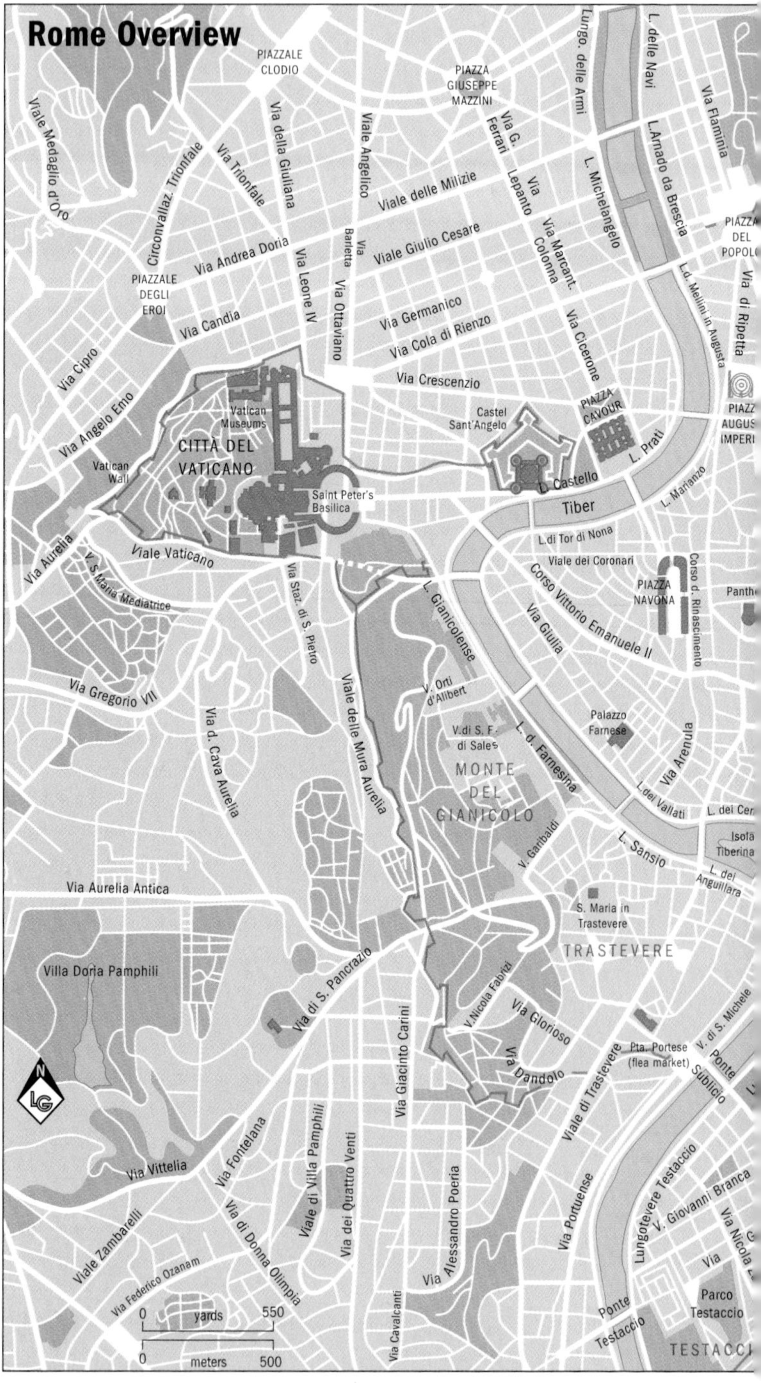

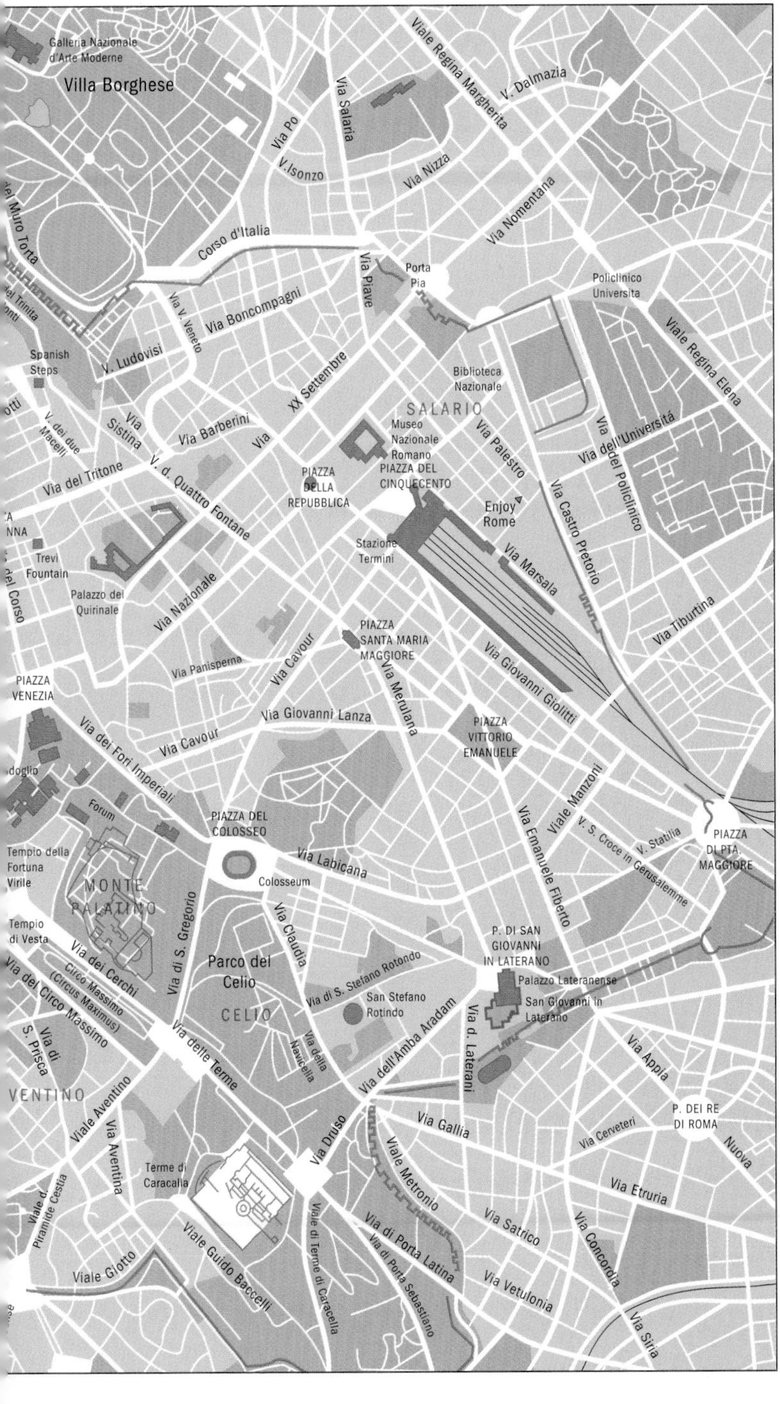

Galleria Nazionale d'Arte Moderne
Villa Borghese
Viale Regina Margherita
V. Dalmazia
Via Salaria
Via Po
V.Isonzo
Via Nizza
Via Nomentana
Corso d'Italia
Porta Pia
Via Piave
Policlinico Universita
Viale Regina Elena
Via Boncompagni
Via V. Veneto
V. Ludovisi
Spanish Steps
Via XX Settembre
Biblioteca Nazionale
SALARIO
Museo Nazionale Romano
PIAZZA DEL CINQUECENTO
PIAZZA DELLA REPUBBLICA
Via Palestro
Via dell'Università
Via del Policlinico
Via Castro Pretorio
Via Sistina
V. dei due Macelli
Via Barberini
Via del Tritone
V. d. Quattro Fontane
Enjoy Rome
Stazione Termini
Via Marsala
Trevi Fountain
Palazzo del Quirinale
Via Nazionale
Via Tiburtina
PIAZZA SANTA MARIA MAGGIORE
Via Cavour
Via Panisperna
Via Merulana
Via Giovanni Giolitti
PIAZZA VENEZIA
Via Giovanni Lanza
PIAZZA VITTORIO EMANUELE
Via dei Fori Imperiali
Forum
PIAZZA DEL COLOSSEO
Viale Manzoni
Via Emanuele Fiberto
V. S. Croce in Gerusalemme
V. Statilia
PIAZZA DI PTA. MAGGIORE
Tempio della Fortuna Virile
MONTE PALATINO
Via Labicana
Colosseum
Via di S. Gregorio
Via Claudia
Tempio di Vesta
Via dei Cerchi
Circo Massimo (Circus Maximus)
Via del Circo Massimo
Parco del Celio
CELIO
Via di S. Stefano Rotondo
San Stefano Rotindo
P. DI SAN GIOVANNI IN LATERANO
Palazzo Lateranense
San Giovanni in Laterano
Via d. Laterani
Via dell'Amba Aradam
Via della Navicella
Via Appia
S. Prisca
Via delle Terme
VENTINO
Viale Aventino
Via Aventina
P. DEI RE DI ROMA
Via Gallia
Via Cerveteri
Nuova
Terme di Caracalla
Via Druso
Viale Metronio
Via Etruria
Viale d. Piramide Cestia
Viale di Terme di Caracella
Via di Porta Latina
Via di Porta Sebastiano
Via Satrico
Via Concordia
Viale Guido Baccelli
Viale Giotto
Via Vetulonia
Via Siria

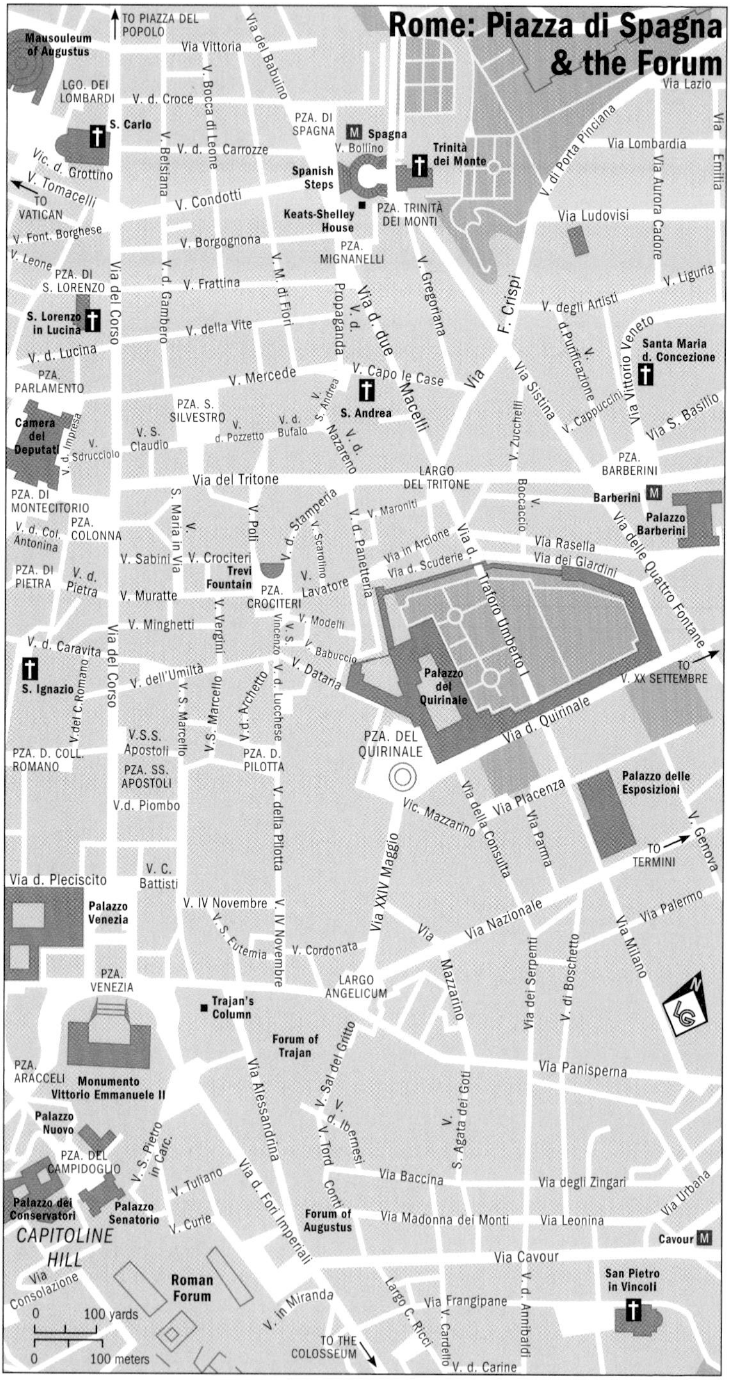
Rome: Piazza di Spagna & the Forum
TO PIAZZA DEL POPOLO
Mausouleum of Augustus
Via Vittoria
Via del Babuino
LGO. DEI LOMBARDI
V. d. Croce
V. Bocca di Leone
S. Carlo
V. Belsiana
V. d. Carrozze
PZA. DI SPAGNA
Spagna
Trinità dei Monte
V. Bollino
Spanish Steps
Vic. d. Grottino
V. Tomacelli
TO VATICAN
V. Condotti
Keats-Shelley House
PZA. TRINITÀ DEI MONTI
V. Font. Borghese
V. Borgognona
PZA. MIGNANELLI
V. Leone
PZA. DI S. LORENZO
Via del Corso
V. d. Gambero
V. Frattina
V. M. di Fiori
V. d. Propaganda
Via d. due Macelli
V. Gregoriana
S. Lorenzo in Lucina
V. della Vite
V. d. Lucina
PZA. PARLAMENTO
V. Mercede
V. Capo le Case
S. Andrea
V. S. Andrea
Camera dei Deputati
V. d. Impresa
PZA. S. SILVESTRO
V. S. Claudio
V. Sdrucciolo
V. d. Pozzetto
V. d. Bufalo
V. d. Nazareno
Via del Tritone
LARGO DEL TRITONE
PZA. DI MONTECITORIO
V. d. Col. Antonina
PZA. COLONNA
V. S. Maria in Via
V. Poli
V. d. Stamperia
V. Scarolino
V. d. Panetteria
V. Maroniti
Via in Arcione
Via d. Scuderie
Via d. Traforo Umberto I
V. Sabini
V. Crociteri
Trevi Fountain
PZA. DI PIETRA
V. d. Pietra
V. Muratte
PZA. CROCITERI
V. Lavatore
V. Minghetti
V. Vergini
V. S. Vincenzo
V. Modelli
V. Babuccio
V. d. Caravita
Via del Corso
S. Ignazio
V. dell'Umiltà
V. Dataria
V.del C.Romano
V. S. Marcello
V.S. Marcello
V. d. Archetto
V. d. Lucchese
Palazzo del Quirinale
V.S.S. Apostoli
PZA. D. COLL. ROMANO
PZA. SS. APOSTOLI
PZA. D. PILOTTA
PZA. DEL QUIRINALE
Via d. Quirinale
V.d. Piombo
V. della Pilotta
Vic. Mazzarino
Via della Consulta
Via Placenza
Via Parma
Palazzo delle Esposizioni
V. Genova
TO TERMINI
V. C. Battisti
Via d. Pleciscito
Palazzo Venezia
V. IV Novembre
V. S. Eutemia
V. IV Novembre
V. Cordonata
Via XXIV Maggio
Via Nazionale
Via Mazzarino
Via dei Serpenti
V. di Boschetto
Via Milano
Via Palermo
PZA. VENEZIA
LARGO ANGELICUM
Trajan's Column
Forum of Trajan
Monumento Vittorio Emmanuele II
PZA. ARACCELI
Via Alessandrina
V. Sal del Gritto
Via Panisperna
Palazzo Nuovo
PZA. DEL CAMPIDOGLIO
V. S. Pietro in Carc.
V. d. Ibernesi
V. Tord Conti
V. S. Agata dei Goti
Via Baccina
Via degli Zingari
V. Tuliano
Via d. Fori Imperiali
Palazzo dei Conservatori
Palazzo Senatorio
V. Curie
Forum of Augustus
Via Madonna dei Monti
Via Leonina
Via Urbana
Cavour
CAPITOLINE HILL
Via Cavour
Via Consolazione
Roman Forum
V. in Miranda
Largo C. Ricci
Via Frangipane
V. d. Annibaldi
San Pietro in Vincoli
0
100 yards
0
100 meters
TO THE COLOSSEUM
V. Cardello
V. d. Carine
Via Lazio
Via Emilia
Via Lombardia
V. di Porta Pinciana
Via Aurora Cadore
Via Ludovisi
Via F. Crispi
V. Liguria
V. degli Artisti
V. d.Purificazione
Via Vittorio Veneto
Santa Maria d. Concezione
Via Sistina
V. Cappuccini
Via S. Basilio
V. Zucchelli
PZA. BARBERINI
Barberini
Palazzo Barberini
V. Boccaccio
Via Rasella
Via dei Giardini
Via delle Quattro Fontane
TO V. XX SETTEMBRE

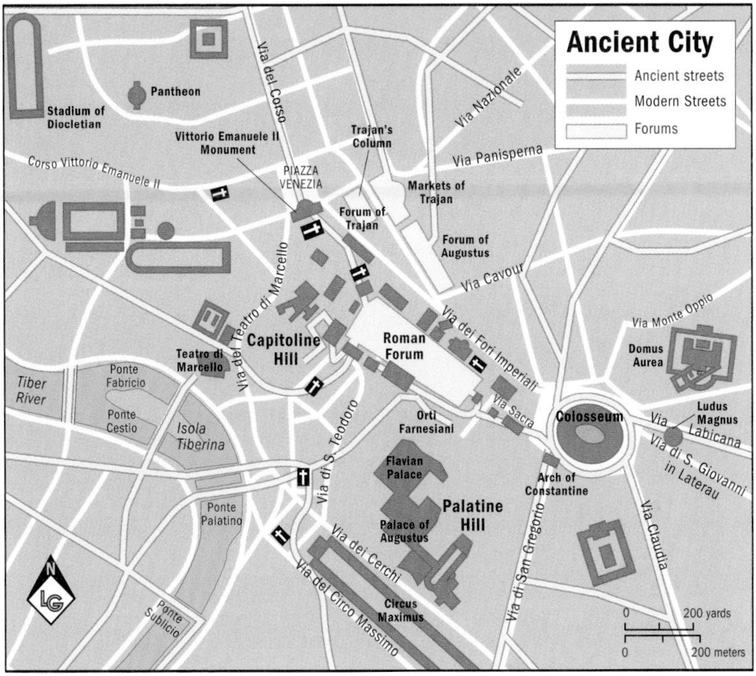

Ancient City
Ancient streets
Modern Streets
Forums
Pantheon
Stadium of Diocletian
Vittorio Emanuele II Monument
Trajan's Column
Via del Corso
Via Nazionale
Via Panisperna
Corso Vittorio Emanuele II
PIAZZA VENEZIA
Markets of Trajan
Forum of Trajan
Forum of Augustus
Via Cavour
Via del Teatro di Marcello
Capitoline Hill
Roman Forum
Via dei Fori Imperiali
Via Monte Oppio
Domus Aurea
Teatro di Marcello
Ponte Fabricio
Tiber River
Ponte Cestio
Isola Tiberina
Via di S. Teodoro
Orti Farnesiani
Via Sacra
Colosseum
Ludus Magnus
Via Labicana
Via di S. Giovanni in Laterau
Flavian Palace
Palatine Hill
Arch of Constantine
Ponte Palatino
Palace of Augustus
Via dei Cerchi
Via di San Gregorio
Via Claudia
Via del Circo Massimo
Circus Maximus
Ponte Sublicio
0 200 yards
0 200 meters

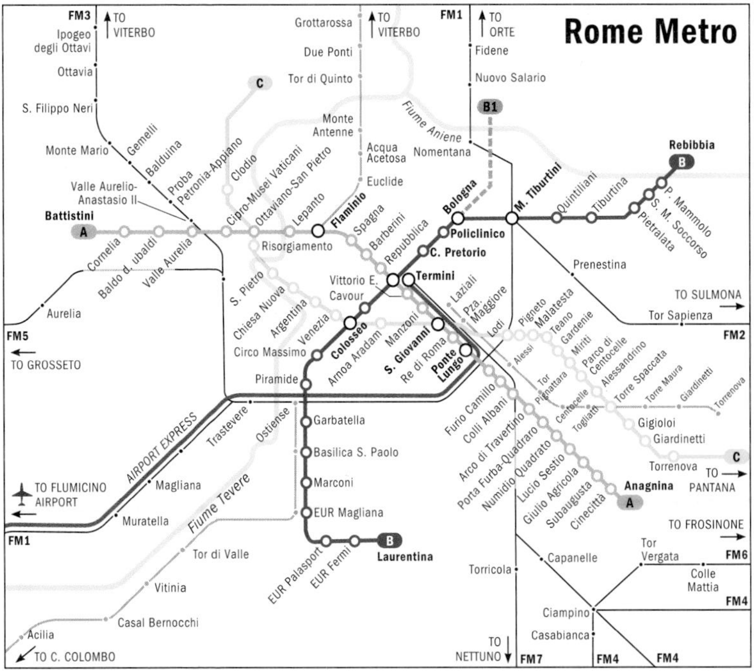

Rome Metro
FM3
TO VITERBO
Ipogeo degli Ottavi
Ottavia
S. Filippo Neri
Monte Mario
Gemelli
Balduina
Proba Petronia-Appiano
Valle Aurelio-Anastasio II
Battistini
A
Cornelia
Baldo d. ubaldi
Valle Aurelia
Aurelia
FM5
TO GROSSETO
C
Clodio
Cipro-Musei Vaticani
Ottaviano-San Pietro
Lepanto
Flaminio
Risorgimento
Grottarossa
Due Ponti
Tor di Quinto
Monte Antenne
Acqua Acetosa
Euclide
FM1
TO ORTE
Fidene
Nuovo Salario
Fiume Aniene
Nomentana
B1
Bologna
Policlinico
M. Tiburtini
Quintiliani
Tiburtina
Pietralata
S. M. Soccorso
P. Mammolo
Rebibbia
B
Spagna
Barberini
Repubblica
C. Pretorio
Termini
Vittorio E.
Cavour
S. Pietro
Chiesa Nuova
Argentina
Venezia
Colosseo
Circo Massimo
Piramide
Arnoa Aradam
Manzoni
S. Giovanni
Re di Roma
Ponte Lungo
Laziali
Pza. Maggiore
Lodi
Prenestina
TO SULMONA
Tor Sapienza
FM2
Pigneto
Malatesta
Teano
Gardenie
Mirti
Parco di Centocelle
Alessandrino
Torre Spaccata
Torre Maura
Giardinetti
Torrenova
Gigioloi
Giardinetti
Torrenova
TO PANTANA
Alessi
Tor Pignattara
Centocelle
Togliatti
Furio Camillo
Colli Albani
Arco di Travertino
Porta Furba-Quadraro
Numidio Quadrato
Lucio Sestio
Giulio Agricola
Subaugusta
Cinecittà
Anagnina
Trastevere
Ostiense
Garbatella
Basilica S. Paolo
Marconi
EUR Magliana
EUR Palasport
EUR Fermi
Laurentina
AIRPORT EXPRESS
TO FLUMICINO AIRPORT
Magliana
Muratella
Fiume Tevere
FM1
Tor di Valle
Vitinia
Casal Bernocchi
Acilia
TO C. COLOMBO
Torricola
TO NETTUNO
FM7
Capanelle
Ciampino
Casabianca
FM4
TO FROSINONE
Tor Vergata
FM6
Colle Mattia

Central Rome
Ara Pacis, 3
Campo dei Fiori, 27
Capitoline Hill and Museums, 22
Castel Sant' Angelo, 9
Chiesa Nuova, 10
Il Gesu, 23
Galleria Corsini, 31
Galleria Doria Pamphilj, 19
Galleria Spada, 28
Mausoleum of Augustus, 4
Museo Barrocco, 26
Museo Mario Praz, 7
Museo Napoleonico, 7
Museo di Palazzo Venezia, 18
Palazzo di Giustizia, 8
Pantheon, 13
P. Farnese, 29
P. Navona, 11
P. del Popolo, 2
P. della Rotonda, 13
P. di Spagna, 5
P. Venezia, 20
Sant' Agnesi in Agone, 11
Sant' Andrea delle Valle, 25
Sant' Antonio dei Portoghesi, 6
Santi Apostoli, 17
Sant' Ignazio, 15
San Luigi dei Francesi, 12
San Marcello, 16
Santa Maria sopra Minerva, 14
Santa Maria del Popolo, 1
Spanish Steps, 5
Theater of Marcellus, 24
Trevi Fountain, 16
Villa Farnesina, 30
Vittorio Emanuele II Monument, 27
VILLA BORGHESE
VILLA MEDICI
PIAZZA DEL POPOLO
PIAZZA D. LIBERTA
PIAZZA CAVOUR
PIAZZA ADRIANA
PIAZZA DEI TRIBUNALI
PIAZZA AUGUSTO IMPERATORE
PIAZZA D. PORTO DI RIPETTA
PIAZZA DI SPAGNA
PIAZZA TRINITÀ D. MONTE
PIAZZA S. SILVESTRO
PIAZZA DEL PARLIAMENTO
PIAZZA PIA
SPAGNA
M
Tiber River
Ponte Margherita
Ponte Cavour
Ponte Umberto I
Ponte S. Ange
Via degli Scipioni
Via Germanico
Via Orsini
Via dei Gracchi
Via Cola di Rienzo
Via Valadier
Via E. Q. Visconti
Via Cicerone
Via Lucr. Caro
Via Feder. Cesi
Via G. Belli
Via P. Cossa
Via M. Clementi
Via M. Dionigi
Via V. Colonna
Via Ulpiano
Via Triboniano
Lung. dei Mellini
Lung. Prati
Lung. in Augusta
Lungotevere Marzio
Lungotevere Castello
Lungotevere Vaticano
Via Boezio
Via Ovidio
Via Virgilio
Via Cassiodoro
Via Orazio
Via Tacito
Via Crescenzio
Via Alberico II
Via Vitelleschi
Via Porta Castello
Via Campanile
V. d. Conciliazione
TO ST. PETER'S
V. M. Cristina
Via Adelaide
Via F. di Savoia
Passeggiata di Ripetta
Via Brunetti
Via del Vantaggio
Via di Ripetta
Via del Corso
Via Canova
V. d. Frezza
Via Tomacelli
Via dell' Arancio
Via Borghese
Lgo Fontanella Borghese
Via Clementino
Via della Scrofa
Via M. Brianzo
Via dell'Orso
Via Prefetti
Campo Marzio
Via in Lucina
Viale G. d'Annunzio
Via Belvedere
Via Trinità dei Monti
V. del Muro Torto
Via Margutta
Via del Babuino
Via Laurina
Via Gesù e Maria
V. S. Giacamo
Via dei Greci
Via Vittorio
Via Belsiana
Via della Croce
Via della Carozze
Via d. Condotti
Via Borgogna
Via Frattina
Via delle Vite
Via della Mercede
Via del Pozzetto
Via Mario de Fiori
Via Propaganda
Via d. Due Macelli
Via Sistina
Via Claudio
Via del Tritone
LARGO

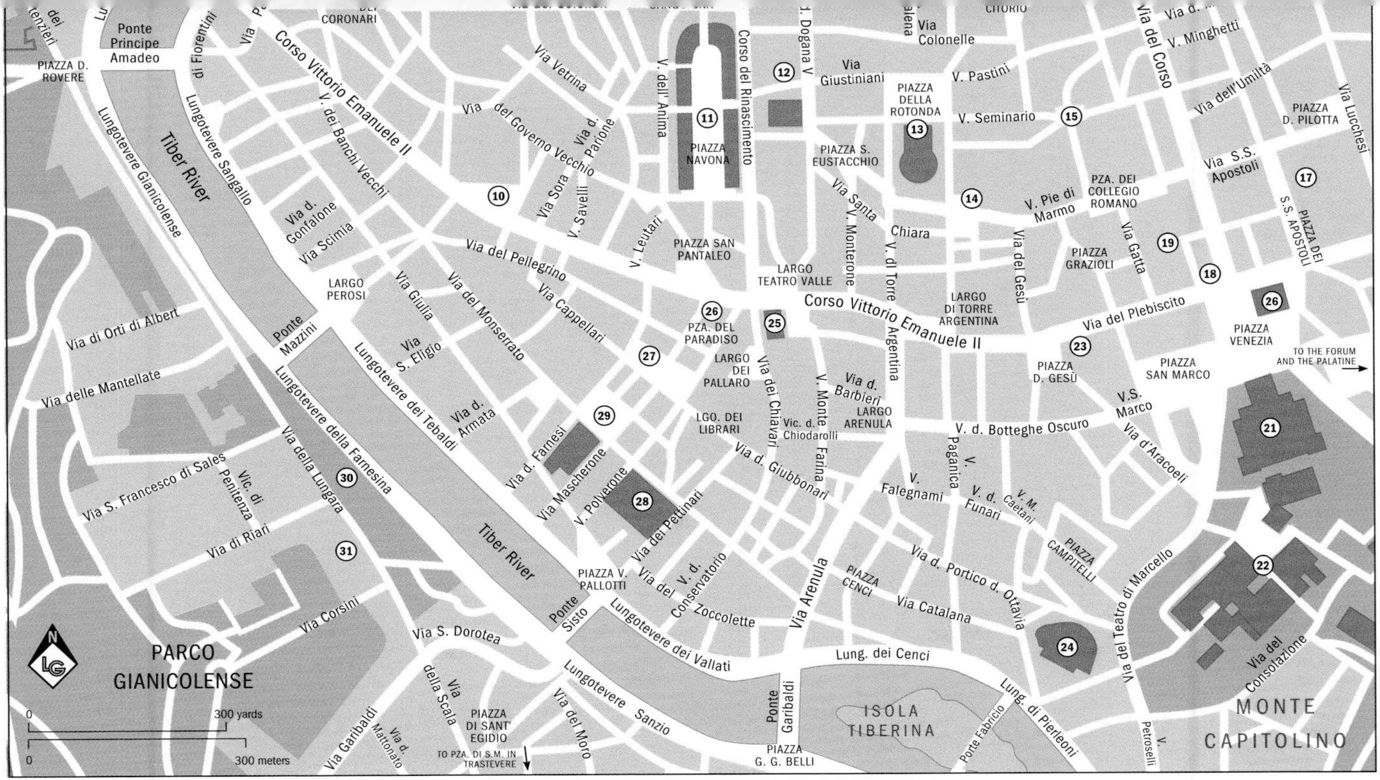
Ponte Principe Amadeo
PIAZZA D. ROVERE
CORONARI
Corso Vittorio Emanuele II
V. dei Banchi Vecchi
Lungotevere Sangallo
Lungotevere Gianicolense
Tiber River
Via Vetrina
Via del Governo Vecchio
Via d. Parione
V. dell' Anima
Corso del Rinascimento
PIAZZA NAVONA
Via Sora
V. Savelli
V. Leutari
PIAZZA SAN PANTALEO
Via d. Gonfalone
Via Scimia
Via del Pellegrino
Via Cappellari
Via Giulia
Via del Monserrato
LARGO PEROSI
Ponte Mazzini
Via di Orti di Albert
Via delle Mantellate
Lungotevere della Farnesina
Lungotevere dei Tebaldi
Via S. Eligio
Via d. Armata
Via della Lungara
Via S. Francesco di Sales
Vic. di Penitenza
Via di Riari
Via Corsini
PARCO GIANICOLENSE
Via S. Dorotea
Via della Scala
PIAZZA DI SANT' EGIDIO
TO PZA. DI S.M. IN TRASTEVERE
Via Garibaldi
Via d. Mattonato
Via del Moro
Lungotevere Sanzio
Ponte Sisto
PIAZZA V. PALLOTTI
Via d. Farnesi
Via Mascherone
V. Polverone
Via dei Pettinari
Via del Zoccolette
V. d. Conservatorio
Lungotevere dei Vallati
Ponte Garibaldi
PIAZZA G. G. BELLI
ISOLA TIBERINA
Lung. dei Cenci
Ponte Fabricio
Lung. di Pierleoni
V. Petroselli
MONTE CAPITOLINO
Via del Consolazione
Via del Teatro di Marcello
PIAZZA CAMPITELLI
Via Catalana
Via d. Portico d. Ottavia
PIAZZA CENCI
Via Arenula
Via d. Giubbonari
LGO. DEI LIBRARI
LARGO DEI PALLARO
PZA. DEL PARADISO
Via dei Chiavari
Vic. d. Chiodarolli
V. Monte Farina
Via d. Barbieri
LARGO ARENULA
V. Falegnami
V. Paganica
V. d. Funari
V. M. Caetani
V. d. Botteghe Oscuro
Via d'Aracoeli
V.S. Marco
PIAZZA D. GESÙ
PIAZZA SAN MARCO
Via del Plebiscito
PIAZZA VENEZIA
TO THE FORUM AND THE PALATINE
Corso Vittorio Emanuele II
LARGO TEATRO VALLE
LARGO DI TORRE ARGENTINA
V. dI Torre Argentina
V. Monterone
Via Santa Chiara
PIAZZA S. EUSTACCHIO
Via del Gesù
V. Pie di Marmo
PIAZZA GRAZIOLI
PZA. DEI COLLEGIO ROMANO
Via Gatta
Via S.S. Apostoli
PIAZZA DEI S.S. APOSTOLI
d. Dogana V
Via Giustiniani
PIAZZA DELLA ROTONDA
V. Seminario
V. Pastini
Via Colonelle
Via del Corso
V. Minghetti
Via dell'Umiltà
PIAZZA D. PILOTTA
Via Lucchesi
di Fiorentini
10
11
12
13
14
15
17
18
19
21
22
23
24
25
26
26
27
28
29
30
31
0
300 yards
0
300 meters
N

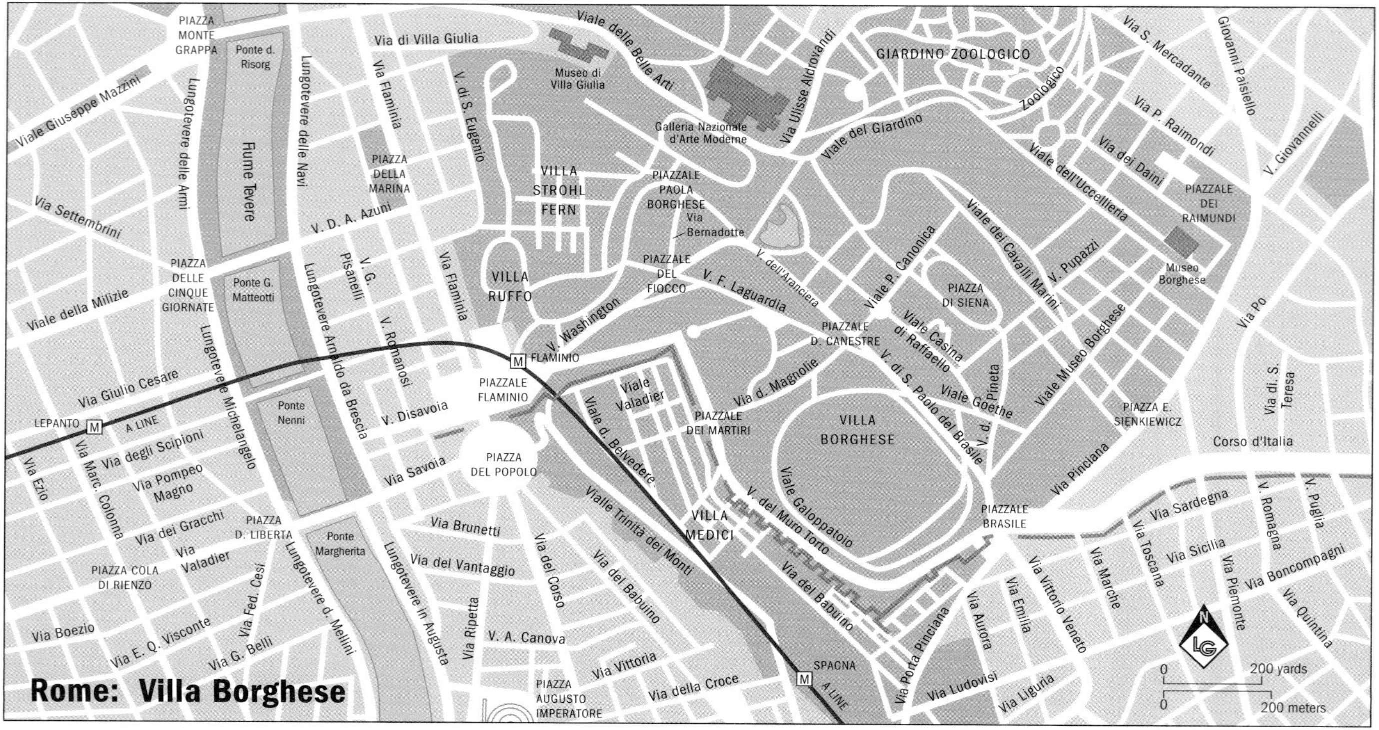
Rome: Villa Borghese
PIAZZA MONTE GRAPPA
Ponte d. Risorg
Fiume Tevere
Ponte G. Matteotti
Ponte Nenni
Ponte Margherita
Viale Giuseppe Mazzini
Lungotevere delle Armi
Lungotevere delle Navi
Via di Villa Giulia
Via Flaminia
V. di S. Eugenio
Museo di Villa Giulia
Viale delle Belle Arti
Galleria Nazionale d'Arte Moderne
Via Ulisse Aldrovandi
GIARDINO ZOOLOGICO
Zoologico
Viale del Giardino
Via S. Mercadante
Giovanni Paisiello
Via P. Raimondi
Via dei Daini
Viale dell'Uccellieria
V. Giovannelli
PIAZZALE DEI RAIMUNDI
Museo Borghese
PIAZZA DELLA MARINA
Via Settembrini
V. D. A. Azuni
VILLA STROHL FERN
PIAZZALE PAOLA BORGHESE
Via Bernadotte
PIAZZALE DEL FIOCCO
V. F. Laguardia
V. dell'Aranciera
Viale P. Canonica
Viale dei Cavalli Marini
V. Pupazzi
PIAZZA DI SIENA
Via Po
PIAZZA DELLE CINQUE GIORNATE
Viale della Milizie
V. G. Pisanelli
V. Romanosi
Lungotevere Arnaldo da Brescia
VILLA RUFFO
V. Washington
PIAZZALE D. CANESTRE
Viale Casina di Raffaello
Viale Museo Borghese
Via di. S. Teresa
M FLAMINIO
Via Giulio Cesare
PIAZZALE FLAMINIO
V. Disavoia
Viale Valadier
Via d. Magnolie
V. di S. Paolo del Brasile
Viale Goethe
V. d. Pineta
PIAZZA E. SIENKIEWICZ
Corso d'Italia
LEPANTO M
A LINE
Via Ezio
Via Marc. Colonna
Via degli Scipioni
Lungotevere Michelangelo
Via Pompeo Magno
Via Savoia
PIAZZA DEL POPOLO
Viale d. Belvedere
PIAZZALE DEI MARTIRI
VILLA BORGHESE
Viale Galoppatoio
Via Pinciana
PIAZZALE BRASILE
Via Sardegna
V. Romagna
V. Puglia
Via dei Gracchi
PIAZZA D. LIBERTA
Via Valadier
PIAZZA COLA DI RIENZO
Via Brunetti
Vialle Trinità dei Monti
VILLA MEDICI
V. del Muro Torto
Via Toscana
Via Sicilia
Via Boncompagni
Via del Vantaggio
Via del Corso
Via del Babuino
Via Marche
Via Vittorio Veneto
Via Emilia
Via Piemonte
Via Quintina
Via Boezio
Via E. Q. Visconte
Via Fed. Cesi
Via G. Belli
Lungotevere d. Mellini
Lungotevere in Augusta
Via Ripetta
V. A. Canova
Via Vittoria
PIAZZA AUGUSTO IMPERATORE
Via della Croce
SPAGNA
M
Via Porta Pinciana
Via Aurora
Via Ludovisi
Via Liguria
N
LG
0
200 yards
0
200 meters

to the cafeteria, contains an assortment of archaeological finds. (Open Tu-Su 8:30am-3pm. €5, students €2.) A path from the museum leads to the summit of **Mt. Kythnos** (112m), from which Zeus watched Apollo's birth. Excursion **boats** leave the dock near Mykonos Town for Delos (35min., 3 per day, round-trip €6).

TINOS (Tηνος) ☎22830

Beautiful Tinos spreads out from the summit of hulking **Mt. Exobourgo.** For the thousands of pilgrims who have flocked here each year since 1812, however, the island's allure lies not in its scenery but in the **Panagia Evangelistira Church,** home to the **Icon of the Annunciation,** one of the most sacred relics of the Greek Orthodox Church. The pilgrimage site is in **Tinos Town** (Hora), the island's capital. (Modest dress required. Open July-Aug. daily 7am-8pm; Sept.-June 7am-6pm. Free.) Beaches surround Tinos Town; **Kardiani** and **Agios Petros,** situated at the base of the mountains, are among the islands' most spectacular, while **Stavros** beach, a 2km walk out of town, is more touristy. For the best of the best, head east to **Agios Sostis** and **Porto;** take the KTEL bus from Tinos Town (3-5 per day, €0.60). Many hikes lead up **Mt. Exobourgo,** 14km north of Tinos Town, the site of the Venetian fortress **Xombourgo;** consult the agents at Windmills Travel (see below) for details.

Ferries (☎22830 22 348) run to Mykonos (30min., 4-5 per day, €3.50). **Windmills Travel,** opposite the park by the port, can help you find accommodations. (☎22830 23 398. Open daily 9am-3pm and 6-9pm.) **Vidalis,** Zanaki Alavanou 16, on the road inland from the right of the waterfront, rents **mopeds.** (☎22830 23 400. €10-13 per day. Open daily 8:30am-9pm.) **Dimitris-Maria Thodosis ❸,** Evangelistrias 33, is midway up the road on the left, on the second floor. The comfortable rooms have flower-laced balconies. (☎22830 24 809. Open Mar.-Oct. Doubles €30.) **Tinos Camping ❶** is 10min. from the waterfront to the right; follow the signs. (☎22830 22 344. July-Aug. €6 per person; May-June and Sept.-Oct. €4 per person. €2-3 per tent. Bungalows for 1-5 people with kitchen and bath €30-45.) **Postal Code:** 84200.

PAROS (Παρος) ☎22840

Paros is famed for its slabs of pure white marble, used for many of the great statues and buildings of the ancient world. Today's visitors know the island for its tall mountains and long, golden beaches. Behind the commercial surface of **Paroikia,** Paros's port and largest city, flower-filled streets wind through archways and past one of the most treasured basilicas of the Orthodox faith, the **Panagia Ekatontapiliani** (Church of Our Lady of 100 Gates). Tradition holds that only 99 of the church's 100 doors are visible—when the 100th appears, Constantinople will again belong to the Greeks. (Dress modestly. Open daily 8:30am-10:30pm. Free.) Just 10km south of town is the cool, spring-fed **Valley of the Butterflies** (a.k.a. **Petaloudes**), where rare *Panaxiaquadripunctaria* moths congregate in massive numbers during the mating season from June to late Sept. Take the bus from Paroikia to Aliki (10min., 8 per day, €0.80) and ask to be let off at Petaloudes. Follow the signs 2km up the road. (Open M-Sa 9am-8pm. €1.50.) At night, **Pirate Blues and Jazz** in the Old Town has eclectic music. (Beer €3, cocktails €7. Open daily 7pm-3am.)

Ferries sail to Ios (2½hr., 7-9 per day, €8) and Santorini (3½hr., 7-9 per day, €10.10). The **tourist police** are on the *plateia* behind the telephone office. (☎22840 21 673. Open daily 8am-2pm.) Turn left at the dock and take a right after the ancient cemetery ruins to reach the pleasant **Rena Rooms ❷.** (☎22840 22 220. Doubles €18-39; triples €27-45. 20% discount for *Let's Go* readers.) The psychedelic **Happy Green Cow ❸,** a block off the *plateia* behind the National Bank, serves tasty vegetarian fare. (Entrees €8-12. Open daily 7pm-midnight.) **Postal Code:** 84400.

GREECE

GREECE

NAXOS (Ναξος) ☎22850

The ancients believed Naxos, the largest of the Cyclades, was the home of Dionysus. Olive groves, wineries, small villages, and chalky white ruins fill its interior, while sandy beaches line its shores. **Naxos Town,** the capital, is crowned by the **Castro,** a Venetian castle now home to two museums. The **Venetian Museum** features evening concerts with traditional Greek music, dancing, and shadow theater. (Open daily 10am-4pm and 7-11pm. €5, students and seniors €3.) The **Archaeological Museum** occupies the former Collège Français, which educated Nikos Kazantzakis, author of *The Last Temptation of Christ* and *Zorba the Greek*. (Open Tu-Su 8:30am-2pm. €3, students €2.) The **Mitropolis Museum,** next to the Orthodox Church, is an architectural achievement in itself, built around the excavated site of a 13th-century BC civilization. (Open Tu-Su 8:30am-3pm. Free.) The 6th-century BC **Portara** archway, visible from the waterfront, is one of the few archaeological sites in Greece where you can actually climb all over the ruins. But to experience the island fully, it's essential to escape Naxos Town. A bus goes from the port to the beaches of **Agia Georgios, Agios Prokopios, Agia Anna,** and **Plaka** (every 30min., €1.10). Buses also run from Naxos Town to **Apollonas,** a fishing village on the northern tip of the island (2hr., €3.50). To get to the **Tragea** highland valley, an enormous, peaceful olive grove, take a bus from Naxos Town to Halki (15-20min.).

Ferries go from Naxos Town to: Athens (6½hr., 2 per day, €16.80); Crete (7hr., 3-5 per week, €16.30); Ios (1½hr., 2 per day, €6.90); Kos (7hr., 1 per week, €14.20); Mykonos (1½hr., 1 per day, €6.30); Paros (1hr., 2 per day, €4.50); Rhodes (13hr., 1 per week, €19.10); Santorini (3hr., 2 per day, €9.40); and Thessaloniki (14hr., 1-3 per week, €29). The **tourist office** is 300m up from the dock, by the bus station. (☎22850 24 358. Open daily 8am-11pm.) **Irene's Pension ❷,** about 100m from Ag. Giorgios, is near the center of the town. (☎22850 23 169. All rooms with A/C. Call ahead. Singles €15; doubles €20-30; triples €25-35.) **Panorama ❸,** in Old Naxos, has rooms with fans and fridges. (☎22850 22 330. Doubles from €25; triples from €30.) Naxos has three **camping ❶** options along the beach; see their representatives along the dock. (€4-6 per person, plus a small tent fee.) **Postal Code:** 84300.

IOS (Ιος) ☎22860

Ios has everything your mother warned you about—swimming less than 30 minutes after a meal, dancing in the streets, and drinking games all day long on the beach. If you're not drunk when you arrive, you will be when you leave. The **port,** Yialos, is at one end of the island's sole paved road; the **village,** Hora, sits above it on a hill; but the beaches are the place to be. Most spend their days at **Mylopotas Beach;** walk 20min. downhill from Ios Town or take a bus from the port or village (every 10-20min. 7am-midnight, €0.80). Sunning is typically followed by drinking; **Dubliner,** near the basketball courts, is a good place to start. On Thursday nights, €23.50 buys you pizza, a drink, and cover immunity at five bars that comprise the ultimate pub crawl. Head up from the *plateia* to reach the **Slammer Bar** for "tequila slammers" (€3), then run with the pack to **Red Bull** to get plastered on shots (€2.40). Then find techno at **Scorpion Disco,** the island's largest club, as you stumble your way back to the beach. (Cover after 1am.) After 2am, people dance on the tables at **Sweet Irish Dream,** near the "donkey steps." Take some aspirin in the morning and head down to the beach, where **Mylopotas Water Sports Center** offers rental and lessons for windsurfing, water-skiing, and snorkeling (€14-40).

Ferries go to: Mykonos (4hr., 1 per day, €11.64); Naxos (1¾hr., at least 3 per day, €7.32); and Santorini (1¼hr., 3 per day, €5.62). Once a week, ferries go to Thessaloniki (€31.06) and Tinos (€12.66). The main **tourist office** is next to the bus stop. (☎22860 91 343. Open daily 8am-midnight.) In the village, take the uphill steps to the left in the *plateia* and take the first left to reach **Francesco's ❷** for spectacular harbor views and a terrace bar. (☎22860 91 706. Dorms €7-15; doubles €10-25.)

On the end of Mylopotas Beach, **Far Out Camping ❶** has a pool, plenty of tents, parties, and activities, including bungee jumping. (☎22860 92 301. Open Apr.-Sept. Tent rental €4-7.50; small cabins €5 and up; bungalows €7-18.) **Ali Baba's ❷,** next to Ios Gym, offers delicious pad thai (€8.50) and burgers (€5.50). Around the corner from the church, **Lord Byron's ❸** serves a unique blend of Greek and Smirniki food. (Entrees €12-15.) **Postal Code:** 84001.

FOLEGANDROS (Φολεγανδρος) ☎22860

The island of Folegandros is a blissfully peaceful alternative to the other more hectic Cyclades. The dry, rocky hills are terraced with low, snaking stone walls worn by centuries of fierce wind. Don't miss the sunset view from the **Church of Panagia,** above the town of **Hora** on Paleocastro hill. **Agali** beach, accessible by foot (1hr.) on the road from Hora to **Ano Meria,** is lined with several *tavernas;* climb up past the first one on the right and continue on the rocky trail to reach **Agios Nikolaos** beach (30min.), or continue along the main road to get to the tiny old settlement of Ano Meria, where you can examine Ottoman artifacts at the superb **Folklore Museum.** (Open June-Aug. daily 5-8pm. Guidebook €5.90.) Infrequent **ferries** run from: Ios (1½hr., 4 per week, €4.70); Naxos (3hr., 2 per week, €7.70); Paros (4hr., 2 per week, €6.30); Piraeus (10-12hr., 1 per day, €16.50); and Santorini (1½hr., 6 per week, €5.60). A **bus** runs from Hora to the port, **Kararostassi,** 45min. before each ferry and returns with new arrivals (€0.80). The **Sottovento Travel Center** is near the post office, to the left as you enter town. (☎22860 41 444. Open daily 9am-1pm and 6-10pm.) **Pavlo's Rooms ❷** is about 200m from the post office, toward the port. They offer simple rooms in a charming converted stable. Call ahead; Folegandros has a shortage of accommodations. (☎22860 41 232. Doubles €10-25, with bath €25-50; triples €30-56; quads €40-50. **Camp** on the roof for €6.) **Livadi Camping ❶** is another option; call for a shuttle from the port. (☎22860 41 204. €5 per person, €2.50 per tent.) **Postal Code:** 84011.

SANTORINI (Σαντορινη) ☎22860

Whitewashed towns balanced on cliffs, black-sand beaches, and deeply scarred hills make Santorini's landscape nearly as dramatic as the volcanic explosion that created it. Despite all the kitsch in touristy **Fira,** the island's capital, nothing can ruin the pleasure of wandering the town's cobblestoned streets, browsing its craft shops, and taking in the sunset from its western edge. On the southwestern part of the island, the excavations at **Akrotiri,** a late Minoan city, are preserved under layers of volcanic rock. (Open Tu-Su 8:30am-3pm. €5, students €3.) Buses run to Akrotiri from Fira (30min., 16 per day, €1.20). Frequent buses also leave Fira for the black-sand **beaches** of Perissa (15min., 30 per day, €1.40) and Kamari (20min., 2-3 per hr., €0.80) to the southeast. The bus stops before Perissa in Pyrgos; from there, you can hike to the **Profitias Ilias Monastery** (40min.; open daily 8am-1pm), and continue to the ruins of **Thira** (an extra 1½hr.; open Tu-Su 8am-2pm).

Ferries from Fira run to: Athens (9hr., 4-8 per day, €20.20); Ios (1½hr., 3-5 per day, €5.80); Iraklion (4hr., 1 per day, €12.60); Naxos (4hr., 4-8 per day, €10); Mykonos (7hr., 2 per week, €11.20); and Paros (4½hr., 3-5 per day, €10). Most ferries depart from Athinios harbor; frequent buses (30min., €1.50) connect to Fira. Head 300m north from the *plateia* in Fira to reach the **Thira Youth Hostel ❶,** in an old monastery. (☎22860 22 387. Open Apr.-Oct. Dorms €7.50-10; doubles €20-40.) Take a bus from Fira to **Oia** (25min., 30 per day, €0.85) for more options; the clean rooms at **Youth Hotel Oia ❷** are a good choice. (☎22860 71 465. Breakfast included. Open May-Oct. Dorms €14.) **Chelidonia ❺,** 100m to the left of Oia's church, rents traditional cave houses, with beds built into the wall. (☎22860 71 287. Kitchens and baths. Doubles €115; triples €147; quads €170.) **Mama's Cyclades Cafe ❷,** north of Fira on the road to Oia, serves up a big breakfast special. (☎22860 24 211. Entrees €5-8. Open daily 7am-midnight.) **Postal Code:** 84700.

CRETE (Κρητη)

According to a Greek saying, a Cretan's first loyalty is to his island, his second to his country. Since 3000 BC, Crete has maintained an identity distinct from the rest of Greece, first expressed in the language, script, and architecture of the ancient Minoans. Despite this insular mindset, residents are friendly to visitors who come to enjoy their island's inexhaustible trove of mosques, monasteries, mountain villages, gorges, grottoes, and beaches. Crete is divided into four main prefectures: Iraklion, Hania, Rethymno, and Lasithi.

TRANSPORTATION

Olympic Airways and **Air Greece** connect Athens to: Sitia (2-3 per week, €83) in the east; Iraklion (45min., 13-15 per day, €84) in the center; and Hania (4 per day, €53) in the west. **Boats** run to Iraklion from: Athens (14hr., 3 per day, €27.50); Mykonos (8½hr., 5 per week, €20); Naxos (7hr., 3 per week, €17.10); Paros (9hr., 7 per week, €21); and Santorini (4hr., 2 per day, €12.60).

IRAKLION (Ηρακλιον) ☎2810

Iraklion is Crete's capital and primary port. The chic locals live life in the fast lane, which translates into the most diverse nightlife on the island and an urban brusqueness unique among the cities of Crete. Iraklion's main attraction after Knossos (see below) is the superb **Archaeological Museum,** off Pl. Eleftherias. By appropriating major finds from all over the island, the museum has amassed a comprehensive record of the Neolithic and Minoan stages of Crete's history. (Open M 12:30-7pm, Tu-Su 8am-7pm. €6, students €3, EU students free.) A maze of streets between **Pl. Venizelou** and **Pl. Eleftherias** houses Iraklion's night spots.

At **Terminal A,** between the old city walls and the harbor, **buses** leave for Agios Nikolaos (1½hr., 20 per day, €4.70) and Malia (1hr., 2 per hr., €2.50). Buses leave opposite Terminal A for Hania (1½hr., 17 per day, €10.50) and Rethymno (1½hr., 18 per day, €5.90). The **tourist police** are at Dikeosinis 10. (☎2810 283 190. Open daily 8am-10pm.) **Gallery Games Net,** Korai 14, has **Internet** access. (☎2810 282 804. €3 per hr.) **Rent a Room Hellas ❶,** Handakos 24, two blocks from El Greco Park, has large dorm rooms and a garden bar. (☎2810 288 851. Dorms €8; doubles €24; triples €34.) **Ilaria Hotel ❸,** at Epimenidou and Ariandis, has basic rooms in an ideal location. Walking toward the water on 25 Augustou, make a right onto Epimendou and walk three blocks. (☎2810 227 103. Singles €35; doubles €50.) The **open-air market** near Pl. Venizelou has stalls piled high with fruits, vegetables, cheeses, and meats. (Open M-Sa 8am-2pm, Tu and Th-F 5-9pm.) **Prassein Aloga ❷,** Handakos 21, blends a variety of Mediterranean tastes. (Entrees €6-10. Open in summer M-Sa noon-midnight, Su 7pm-midnight; off-season M-Sa noon-4pm and 7pm-midnight.) **Postal Code:** 71001.

DAYTRIP FROM IRAKLION: KNOSSOS. At Knossos (Κνωσσος), the most famous archaeological site in Crete, excavations have revealed the remains of the largest and most complicated of Crete's **Minoan palaces.** Sir Arthur Evans, who financed and supervised the excavations, eventually restored large parts of the palace in Knossos; his work often crossed the line from preservation to artistic interpretation, but the site is nonetheless impressive. (Open in summer daily 8am-7pm; off-season 8am-5pm. €6, students €3; off-season Su free.) To reach Knossos from Iraklion, take **bus** #2 from 25 Augustou or Pl. Eleftherias (€0.85).

RETHYMNO (Pεθυμνο) ☎28310

Crete's many conquerors—Venetians, Ottomans, and even Nazis—have had a profound effect in Rethymno. Arabic inscriptions adorn the walls of the narrow streets, minarets highlight the skyline, and Greek music spills out of cafes. The 16th-century **Venetian Fortezza** stands watch over the scenic harbor; bring a picnic and explore the fortress ruins. (Open Tu-Su 9am-6pm. €2.90, children €2.30.) Fine sand and large waves await in the nearby town of **Plakias.** (Buses from Rethymno, 4 per day, €3.10). The **Rethymno-Hania bus station** (☎28310 22 212) is south of the fortress on the water, with service to Hania (1hr., 16 per day, €5.55) and Iraklion (1½hr., 17 per day, €5.90). Climb the stairs behind the bus station, turn left on Ig. Gavriil, which becomes Kountouriotou, and turn left on Varda Kallergi to reach the waterfront and the **tourist office,** on El. Venizelou. (☎28310 29 148. Open M-F 8am-2:30pm.) To get from the station to the cheerful **Youth Hostel ❶,** Tombazi 41-45, walk down Ig. Gavriil, take a left at the park traffic light, walk through the gate, and take your first right. (☎28310 22 848. Breakfast €1.70. Internet €1 per 15 min. Reception 8am-noon and 5-9pm. Dorms €6.) **Postal Code:** 74100.

GREECE

HANIA (Χανια) ☎28210

The **Venetian lighthouse,** an odd tower of stone, guards the entrance to Hania's stunning architectural relic, the **Venetian Inner Harbor.** The inlet has retained its original breakwater and Venetian arsenal, and the Egyptians restored the lighthouse during their occupation of Crete in the late 1830s. Narrow Venetian buildings and Ottoman domes mingle in Hania's lively waterfront area, where a day is best spent sitting or meandering. **Ferries** arrive in the nearby port of Souda; buses connect from the port to Hania's supermarket on Zymvrakakidon (15min., €0.85). **Buses** (☎28210 93 306) leave from the station on the corner of Kydonias and Kelaidi for Rethymno (17 per day, €5.55). Turn right on Kidonias then turn left on Pl. 1866 to reach the **tourist office,** Kriairi 40. (☎28210 92 624. Open M-F 9am-2pm.) To get to **Hotel Fidias ❷,** Sarpaki 6, walk toward the harbor on Halidon and turn right onto Athinagora, which then becomes Sarpaki. (☎28210 52 494. Singles €12; doubles €12-18.) **Anaplous ❷** (☎28210 41 320), near the harbor on Sifaka, is an open-air bistro serving *pilino*, a pork and lamb creation enjoyed by locals (€23.50, serves three. Other dishes €6-8. Open daily 10am-1am.) **Postal Code:** 73100.

HIKING NEAR RETHYMNO AND HANIA: SAMARIA GORGE. The most popular excursion from Hania, Rethymno, and Iraklion is the 5-6hr. hike down Samaria Gorge (Φαραγγι τηϖ Σαμαριαϖ), a spectacular 16km long ravine extending through the White Mountains. Sculpted by rainwater over 14 million years, the gorge—the longest in Europe—retains its allure despite having been trampled by thousands of visitors. Rare native plants peek out from sheer rock walls, wild *agrimi* goats clamber about the hills, and golden eagles and endangered griffin vultures circle overhead. The trail starts in **Xyloskalo** and ends in **Agia Roumell.** (Open May to mid-Oct. daily 6am-6pm. €3, children under 15 and organized student groups free.) For more information, call **Hania Forest Service** (☎28210 92 287). Take the 6:15am or 8:30am **bus** from Hania to Xyloskalo (1½hr., €5 one-way) for a day's worth of hiking. The 1:45pm bus from Hania will put you in **Omalos,** near Xyloskalo, ready for the next morning. From Agia Roumell, you can hop on a **boat** to **Hora Sfakion** (1¼hr., 3-4 per day, €4.40) or take a return bus to Hania (€5.10). In Omalos, you can rest up at **Gigilos Hotel ❷** on the main road. (☎28210 67 181. Singles €12-15; doubles €20.)

AGIOS NIKOLAOS (Αγιοσ Νικολαοσ) ☎28410

Agios Nikolaos, in Crete's northeast, is a chic resort town where vacationers huff and puff their way up steep, boutiqued streets. Although there are few bargains here, nearby beaches and islands make it a worthy destination. **Almiros Beach,** 1.5km east of town, is the area's best. Hot springs hidden under the ocean surface mix with the cold rush of a river that comes through the beach's neighboring **wildlife reserve,** creating the possibility for a titillating hot-cold swim. Nostos Tours has **boats** departing from the town harbor for guided tours of the small, striking **Spinalonga Island,** formerly a leper colony (2 per day, €15). Upscale clubs in Agios Nikolaos can be found near the harbor on **I. Koundourou. Ferries** go to: Karpathos (7hr., 4 per week, €17.60); Piraeus (12hr., 5 per week, €25); Rhodes (12hr., 3 per week, €20.60); and Sitia (1hr., 5 per week, €5.90). **Buses** (☎28410 22 234) depart from Pl. Atlantidos. To reach the **tourist office,** S. Koundourou 21A, head right from the station, make your first right, follow Venizelou and then R. Koundourou to the harbor, and then bear left and across the bridge. (☎28410 22 357. Open Apr.-Nov. daily 8am-9:30pm.) To get to the pleasant **Christodoulakis Pension ❷,** Stratigou Koraka 7, turn away from the water at the tourist office and turn right onto the street behind the taxi stand. (☎28410 22 525. Singles €15; doubles €18.) **Sarri's ❶,** Kuprou 15, serves food from the owner's farm. (Entrees €4-5. Open 8:30am-4pm and 6pm-midnight.) **Postal Code:** 72100.

SITIA (Σητεια) ☎28430

Sitia makes a great base for exploring Crete's east coast. Skip the town's own beach and head to the beautiful **Vai Beach** and its palm tree forest, a one-hour bus ride away via Palaikastro (€2). Also near Sitia is the **Valley of Death,** a Minoan burial ground that's great for hiking. The **Minoan Palace** of Kato Zakros rests at the end of the valley. (Open daily 8am-5pm. €3, students and seniors €2.) After midnight, everyone in Sitia heads to **Hot Summer,** 1km down the road to Palaikastro, where a swimming pool replaces the traditional dance floor. To reach the valley, take a bus from Sitia via Palaikastro and Zakros (1hr., 2 per day, €3.75.) **Ferries** leave Sitia for: Athens (16-17hr., 5 per week, €23.50) via Agios Nikolaos (1½hr., €5.60); Karpathos (5hr., 3 per week, €11.20); and Rhodes (12hr., 3 per week, €18.80). From the center of town, head east along the water; the **tourist office** will be on your left. (☎28430 28 300. Open M-F 9:30am-2:30pm and 5:30-8:30pm.) **Venus Rooms to Let ❷,** Kondilaki 60, looks out on scenic views; walk up on Kapetan Sifi from the main *plateia* and turn right after the telephone office. (☎28430 24 307. Doubles €21; triples €25.) **Cretan House ❶,** K. Karamanli 10, off the *plateia*, serves Cretan meals for €4-5. (Open daily 9am-1am.) **Postal Code:** 72300.

EASTERN AEGEAN ISLANDS

The intricate, rocky coastlines and unassuming port towns of the **Northeast Aegean Islands** enclose thickly wooded mountains and unspoiled villages and beaches. Despite their proximity to the Turkish coast and a noticeable military presence, the Northeast Aegean Islands dispense a taste of undiluted Greek culture. **The Dodecanese** are the farthest Greek island group from the mainland. Closer to Asia Minor than to Athens, these islands have experienced more invasions than the central parts of the country—eclectic architecture is the most visible legacy of these comings and goings.

FERRIES TO TURKEY

Ferries run from Samos to Kuşadası (1¼hr., 5 per week, €30); from Chios to Çeşme (45min., 1 per day, €50); and from Kos to Bodrum (1 per day, round-trip €35-40). Citizens of Australia, Canada, Ireland, New Zealand, South Africa, the UK, and the US require a visa to enter Turkey. Port taxes average €8-10.

SAMOS (Σαμος) ☎22730

Visitors frequently stop in Samos en route to Kuşadası and the ruins of Ephesus on the Turkish coast. Palm trees shade quiet inland streets and red roofs speckle the hillsides of **Vathy (Samos Town),** one of the Aegean's most attractive port cities. The phenomenal **Archaeological Museum** is behind the municipal gardens. (Open Tu-Su 8:30am-3pm. €3, seniors and students €2, EU students free.) The ancient city of **Pythagorion,** once the island's capital, is 14km south of Vathy. Near the town are the magnificent remains of Polykrates's 6th-century BC engineering project, the **Tunnel of Eupalinos,** which diverted water to the city from a natural spring 1.3km away. (Open Tu-Su 8:45am-2:45pm. €4, students €2, EU students free.) Buses go from Samos Town to Pythagorion (20min., €1.10). Polykrates's greatest feat was the **Temple of Hera,** in Heraion, a 30min. bus ride (€1.51) from Pythagorion. (Open Tu-Su 8:30am-3pm. €3, students €2.)

Ferries arrive in Vathy from: Athens (12hr., 1 per day, €22.10); Chios (5hr., 2 per week, €9.30); Mykonos (6hr., 6 per week, €16); Naxos (6hr., 3 per week, €16.70) via Paros (€14.10); and Rhodes (2 per week, €30). The **tourist office** is on a side street a block before Pl. Pythagoras. (☎22730 28 530. Open July-Aug. M-Sa 7am-2:30pm.) **Medousa Hotel ❷,** Sofouli 25, is on the waterfront between the port and Pl. Pythagoras. (☎22730 23 501. Doubles €15-30.) **Postal Code:** 83100.

CHIOS (Χιος) ☎22710

The lack of mass tourism on Chios (HEE-os) seems like an anomaly given its volcanic beaches, cypress-covered hills, and medieval villages. **Pyrgi,** 25km from Chios Town, is one of Greece's most striking villages, with fantastic black-and-white geometric designs covering its buildings. Farther south lies **Emborio** beach, where beige cliffs contrast with the black stones and blue water below. **Buses** run from Chios Town to Pyrgi (5-8 per day, €2.20) and Emborio (4 per day, €2.50). **Ferries** go from Chios Town to: Athens (8hr., 1-2 per day, €19); Mykonos (3 per week, €13); Rhodes (1 per week, €27); Samos (4hr., 3 per week, €10); and Tinos (3 per week, €13.50). To reach the **tourist office,** Kanari 18, turn off the waterfront onto Kanari and walk toward the *plateia.* (☎22710 44 344. Open May-Oct. daily 7am-10pm; Nov.-Mar. M-F 7am-2:30pm.) The hospitable owners at **Chios Rooms ❷,** Leofores 114, offer large rooms with hardwood floors. (☎22710 20 198. Singles €18-22; doubles €23-25, with bath €30; triples with bath €35.) **Postal Code:** 82100.

LESVOS (Λεσβος) ☎22510

Lesvos's cosmopolitan, off-beat culture incorporates horse breeding, *ouzo,* and leftist politics. Huge, geographically diverse, and far from the mainland, the island attracts visitors who spend weeks exploring its therapeutic hot springs, monasteries, petrified forest, sandy beaches, mountain villages, and seaside cliffs. Most travelers pass through the modern **Mytilini,** the capital and central port city. At the new **Archaeological Museum,** on 8 Noemvriou, visitors can walk on preserved mosaic floors from ancient Mytilini. (Open daily 8am-7pm. €3, students €2, under 18 and EU students free.) Only 4km south of Mytilini along El. Venizelou, the village of **Varia** is home to two excellent museums. **Theophilos Museum** features the work of the neo-primitivist Greek painter Theophilos Hadzimichali. (Open May-Sept. Tu-Su 9am-2:30pm and 6-8pm. €2, students and under 18 free.) **Musée Tériade** displays Picasso, Miró, Chagall, and Matisse lithographs. (Open Tu-Su 9am-2pm and 5-8pm. €2, students and under 18 free.) The artist colonies of **Petra** and **Molyvos** have a quiet charm and more reasonable prices than the capital; take a bus from Mytilini (2hr., 4-5 per day, €4.50). **Eftalou** has beautiful black-sand and pebble beaches, accessible by frequent buses from Molyvos. **Skala Eressou,** in the south, is home to more lovely beaches; buses run from Mytilini (3hr., 2-3 per day, €6.70).

Ferries go from Mytilini to: Athens (12hr., 1-2 per day, €24); Chios (3hr., 1-2 per day, €11.20); Limnos (5hr., 6 per week, €15); and Thessaloniki (13hr., 1 per week, €12). Book ferries at **NEL Lines,** Pavlou Koudourioti 67 (☎22510 22 220), on the east side of the waterfront. The **tourist police,** on Aristarchou near the ferry docks, offer maps and advice. (☎22510 22 776. Open daily 7:15am-10pm.) Mytilini *domatia* are plentiful and well advertised. Be sure to negotiate; doubles should cost €20-23. **Nassos Guest House ❷,** on the hill just into Molyvos, offers cheerful rooms with balconies. (☎(22530) 71 432. Doubles €20-28; triples €24-34; discounts for longer stays.) **Postal Code:** 81100.

RHODES (Ροδος) ☎22140

Although Rhodes is the undisputed tourism capital of the Dodecanese, it has retained a sense of serenity in the sandy beaches along its east coast, the jagged cliffs skirting its west coast, and the green mountains dotted with villages in the interior. The island's most famous sight is one that doesn't exist, the **Colossus of Rhodes,** a 35m bronze statue of Helios and one of the seven wonders of the ancient world. It supposedly straddled the island's harbor until it was destroyed by an earthquake in 237 BC. The **Old Town,** constructed by the Knights of St. John, lends **Rhodes Town** a medieval flair. At the top of the hill, a tall, square tower marks the entrance to the pride of the city, the **Palace of the Grand Master,** which features moats, drawbridges, battlements, and 300 rooms. (Open M 12:30-7pm, Tu-Su 8am-7pm. €6, students €3.) The beautiful halls and courtyards of the **Archaeological Museum,** dominating the **Plateia Argykastrou,** shelter small treasures, including the exquisite *Aphrodite Bathing* from the first-century BC. (Open Tu-Su 8:30am-7pm. €3, students €1.50.) Nightlife in Old Town focuses around **Militadou,** off Apellou. **Orfanidou,** in New Town, is popularly known as **Bar Street.** Fifteen kilometers south of the city, **Faliraki** is frequented by rowdy drinkers and beach bathers. Buses run to Faliraki from Rhodes Town (17 per day, €1.90).

Ferries leave Rhodes Town for: Athens (1-4 per day, €30); Karpathos (3 per week, €15); Kos (1-2 per day, €11); Patmos (1-2 per day, €17.10); Samos (1 per week, €21.10); and Sitia, Crete (3 per week, €19.40). There is a **Greek National Tourist Office (EOT)** up Papgou, a few blocks from Pl. Rimini, at Makariou. The **Rhodes Youth Hostel ❶,** Ergiou 12, has a cool, quiet courtyard. Turn onto Fanouriou from Sokratous and follow the signs. (☎22410 30 491. Free luggage storage. Dorms €7; doubles and triples €20. Sleep on the roof for €5.) **Hotel Andreas ❸,** Omirou 28D, boasts spectacular views of the city. Ask for a room with a private balcony. (☎22410 34 156. Singles and doubles €30-52.) Fresh shellfish is the specialty at **Nireas ❷,** Sophocleous 22, in Old Town. (Entrees €6-8. Open daily 7:30-11pm.)

KARPATHOS (Καρπαθος) ☎22450

Halfway between Rhodes and Crete, windy Karpathos often receives no more than a passing glance from the deck of an overnight ferry, but the charming island and its gorgeous towns are well worth a stop. Isolation and insularity are the defining characteristics of **Olympus,** where centuries-old customs make the town itself the greatest sight. Chrisovalandu Lines and Karpathos 1 run **buses** to Olympus (depart 8:30am, return 6pm; €1); find them near the ferry docks or make reservations through Possi Travel (☎(22450) 22 235). **Ferries** arrive in Pigadia from Rhodes (5hr., 3 per week, €15) and Santorini (12hr., 1 per week, €25). From the bus station, walk past the supermarket to reach **Elias Rooms for Rent ❷,** which has a central location and quiet rooms. (☎22450 22 446. Singles €20; doubles €25-30.) The best dinner options lie along the waterfront. **Postal Code:** 85700.

GREECE

KOS (Κως) ☎22420

While the beaches of **Kos Town** draw a young party crowd, rural Kos attracts the traveler in search of serene mountain villages. At the sanctuary of **Asclepion,** 3.5km northwest of Kos Town, Hippocrates opened the world's first medical school in the 5th century BC. In summer, buses (15min.) run there from Kos Town. (Open Tu-Su 8am-6:30pm. €3, students €2.) The island's best beaches stretch along Southern Kos to Kardamene and are all accessible by bus; stops are by request. **Agios Theologos,** south of Limionas, is a pebbly beach perfect for night swimming. Most bars are located in **Exarhia,** in the Old City past Pl. Platonos, or along **Porfirou,** between Averof and Zouroundi. Runway models loom on giant television screens at the **Fashion Club,** Kanari 2, the hottest spot in town. (Cover €8, includes 1 drink.) The **Hamam Club,** inland from the Pl. Diagoras taxi station, is a former bathhouse that is now a dance club. **Heaven,** on Zouroudi, opposite the beach, is a large, popular disco. (Open Su-Th 10am-4am, F-Sa 10am-dawn.)

Ferries run to: Athens (11-15hr., 2-3 per day, €15.30); Patmos (4hr., 1-2 per day, €9.45); and Rhodes (4hr., 2-3 per day, €12.35). The **Greek National Tourist Office (EOT)** is at Vas. Georgiou 1. (☎22420 24 460. Open M-F 8am-8pm, Sa 8am-3pm.) Take the first right off Megalou Alexandrou to get to **Pension Alexis ❷,** Herodotou 9, where the hospitable owners offer their guests every service. (☎22420 28 798. Doubles €18-20; triples €25-30). **Studios Nitsa ❸,** Averof 47, has small rooms with baths and kitchenettes. Take Averof inland from Akit Koundourioti. (☎22420 25 810. Doubles €30; triples €35-45.) **Postal Code:** 85300.

PATMOS (Πατμος) ☎22470

Given that it has lately become a favorite destination of the rich and famous and has also been declared the "Holy Island" by ministerial decree, Patmos has an interesting blend of visitors. The white houses of **Hora** and the majestic walls of the sprawling **Monastery of St. John the Theologian** are visible from all over the island. (Dress modestly. Monastery open daily 8am-1pm; also Tu, Th, Su 4-6pm. Free.) Buses from **Skala,** the port town, run to Hora (10min., 11 per day, €1); alternatively, take a taxi (€3) or tackle the steep hike. The **Apocalypsis Monastery,** between Skala and Hora, is built on the site where St. John stayed while on Patmos. Most visitors come to Patmos to see the **Sacred Grotto of the Revelation,** the cave where St. John dictated the *Book of Revelation*. (Dress modestly. Open daily 8am-1pm; also T, Th, Su 4-6pm. Free.)

Ferries arrive in Skala from: Athens (10-12hr., 6 per week, €20); Kos (4hr., 2-3 per day, €7.15); Rhodes (9hr., 1 per day, €21); Samos (3 per week, €11); and Thessaloniki (22hr., 1 per week, €37). The **tourist office** is opposite the dock. (☎22470 31 666. Open daily 7am-2:30pm and 4-9pm.) *Domatia* are offered by locals who meet the ferries; expect to pay €15-20 for singles and €20-30 for doubles. To reach **Flower Stefanos Camping at Meloi ❶,** 2km northeast of Skala, follow the waterfront road past Apollon Travel as it wraps along the port. The campground is on the left at the bottom of the hill. (☎22470 31 821. €5 per person.) **To Kyma ❸,** near the campground at Meloi Beach, serves freshly prepared fish. (Fish €20-40 per kg. Open daily noon-midnight.) **Postal Code:** 85500.

ICELAND (ÍSLAND)

Iceland's landscape is uniquely warped and contorted, having been forged by the tempers of still-active volcanoes and raked by the slow advance and retreat of timeless glaciers. Nature is the country's greatest attraction—few other places allow visitors to walk across lava-filled moonscapes, dodge warm water shooting from geysers, and sail across a glacial lagoon filled with icebergs. Civilization has made a powerful mark on Iceland; the geothermal energy that causes numerous earthquakes also provides hot water and electricity to Iceland's settlements, and a network of roads carved through seemingly inhospitable terrain connects even the smallest villages to larger cities. A booming tourist industry attests to the fact that physical isolation has not set the country behind the rest of Europe. However, Iceland's island status has allowed it to achieve a high standard of living without damaging its pristine natural surroundings and deeply rooted sense of community.

ICELAND

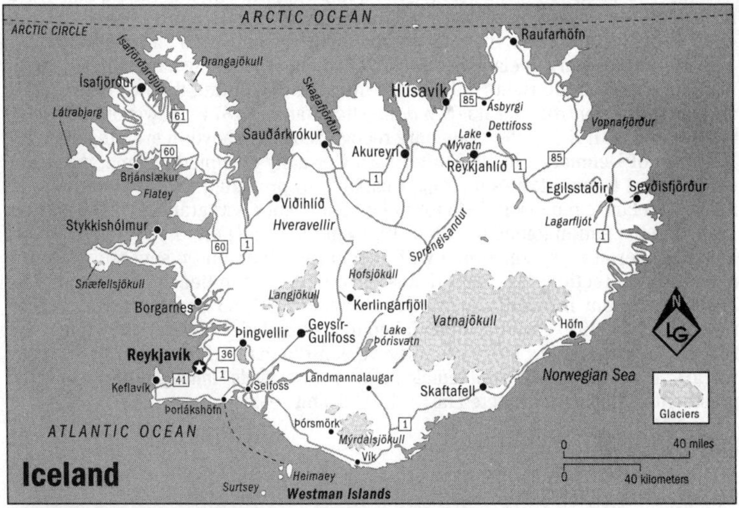

SUGGESTED ITINERARIES

BEST OF ICELAND, TWO DAYS. Spend a day exploring the heart of **Reykjavík** (p. 574), then daytrip to the peerless wonders of **Gullfoss, Geysir,** and **Blue Lagoon** (p. 579). Return to the city as the sun attempts to set, enjoying an intimate cafe or the never-ending Icelandic nightlife.

SYMBOL	❶	❷	❸	❹	❺
ACCOMMODATIONS	500-1500Ikr	1500-3000Ikr	3000-5000Ikr	5000-10000Ikr	over 10000Ikr
FOOD	under 800Ikr	800-1200Ikr	1200-2000Ikr	2000-3500Ikr	over 3500Ikr

For Iceland, prices are indicated in food and accommodations listings using the system of icons and price ranges above. Prices for accommodations are based on the lowest cost for one person, excluding special deals or discounts. For restaurants, prices are based on the average entree price.

LIFE AND TIMES

HISTORY

The modern settlement of Iceland began in the 9th century when **Norse settlers** displaced the Irish monks who were visiting the island. In the 1200s, as Iceland developed into a **feudal state,** the people were subject to heavy taxes and an externally imposed judicial system under Norwegian leadership. Disgruntlement escalated after **Denmark** gained control of Iceland in 1380, and over the next 400 years, the country was plagued with diseases, economic exploitation, starvation, and volcanic eruptions. The combination of these tragic events nearly resulted in its demise: by the late 1700s, the total population had plummeted below 40,000.

In the 19th century, Iceland completed an about-face: rising nationalism and the introduction of trade rights culminated in Iceland adopting its own constitution and obtaining control over its own domestic affairs in 1874. However, autonomy was limited until 1918, when Denmark recognized it as a sovereign state within the Kingdom of Denmark. In 1940, after Nazi Germany occupied Iceland, it became evident that Denmark was no longer capable of presiding over its international affairs. Iceland's request in 1943 for full independence was granted by Denmark in 1944, and the nation joined the **UN** in 1946. In the same period, the American and British governments, concerned with Iceland's vulnerability, sent troops to the island for protection. The Americans have remained in peace, if not complete acceptance, but intermittent battles between Iceland and Britain occurred throughout the 1970s, when Britain failed to acknowledge Iceland's newfound territorial fishing rights. More recently, Iceland became the proud home of the world's first popularly elected female head of state: **Vigds Finnbogadttir** was elected president in 1980 and reelected in 1984, 1988, and 1992.

CULTURE

FOOD AND DRINK

Traditional foods include *lundi* (puffin) on the Westman Islands, *rjúpa* (ptarmigan) around Christmas, and *selshreifar* (seal flippers) during the *Þorra matur* (Thorri or Mid-Winter Feast). Fish, lamb, and chicken are the most common components of authentic dishes, although more adventurous diners can try *svið* (singed and boiled sheep's head), *hrútspungur* (ram's testicles), or *hákarl* (rotten shark meat that has been buried underground), all of which are traditional dishes consumed during the Thorri Feast. International cuisine also has a strong presence in Iceland, and Italian, American, and Asian fare can usually be found even in smaller towns. Food is very expensive in Iceland; a *cheap* restaurant meal will cost at least 800Ikr. Grocery stores are the way to go; virtually every town has a couple of them. Gas stations usually run a grill and sell snacks. Bonus and Netto are cheaper alternatives to the more ubiquitous Hagkaup and 10-11. Iceland has some of the purest water in Europe. Beer costs 500-600Ikr at most pubs, cafes, and restaurants. The national drink is *Brennivín,* a type of schnapps known as "the Black Death." The rarely enforced drinking age is 20.

CUSTOMS & ETIQUETTE

Stores are generally open Monday to Friday 9am-5pm (6pm in summer) and Saturday mornings.

HOLIDAYS

Holidays: New Year's (Jan. 1); Good Friday (Apr. 18); Easter (Apr. 20-21); Labor Day (May 1); Ascension Day (May 29); National Day (June 17); Whit Sunday and Monday (Seventh Sunday and Monday after Easter); Commerce Day (Aug. 5); Christmas Eve and Day (Dec. 24-25); Boxing Day (Dec. 26); New Year's Eve (Dec. 31).

ESSENTIALS

FACTS AND FIGURES

Official Name: Ísland.	**Land Area:** 103,000 sq. km.
Capital: Reykjavík.	**Time Zone:** GMT
Major Cities: Hafnarfjörður, Höfn, Ísafjörður, Vík.	**Language:** Icelandic; English is widely spoken.
Population: 275,000.	**Religions:** Evangelical Lutheran (93%).

ICELAND

WHEN TO GO

High season hits in July, when the interior opens up, snow almost disappears, and all the bus lines are running. In summer, the sun dips below the horizon for a few hours each night, but the sky never truly gets dark and it's warm enough to camp and hike. With warm clothing you could travel as late as October, but in winter there is very little sun. The temperature rarely gets higher than 60°F (16°C) in summer or dips below 20°F (-6°C) in winter.

DOCUMENTS AND FORMALITIES

South Africans need a visa for stays of any length. Citizens of Australia, Canada, the EU, New Zealand, and the US do not need a visa for stays of up to 90 days, but this three-month period begins upon entry into any Nordic country; for more than 90 days in any combination of Denmark, Finland, Iceland, Norway, and/or Sweden, you will need a visa.

Iceland Embassies at Home: Canada, 360 Albert St., Suite 710, Ottawa, ON KIR 7X7 (☎613-482-1944; fax 613-482-1945); **UK,** 2A Hans St., London SW1X OJE (☎020 7259 3999; www.iceland.org.uk); and **US,** 1156 15th St. NW, Suite 1200, Washington, D.C. 20005 (☎202-265-6653; www.iceland.org).

Foreign Embassies in Iceland: All foreign embassies are in Reykjavik (p. 574).

TRANSPORTATION

BY PLANE. Icelandair (US ☎800-223-5500; UK ☎020 7874 1000; www.icelandair.net) flies to Reykjavík year-round from the US and Europe. Icelandair provides free stopovers of up to three days on all transatlantic flights; it also offers some student discounts, including half-price standby flights. Domestic **Flugfélag Islands** (☎750 30 30; eyjaflug.is) flies between Reykjavík and Iceland's other major towns; tickets can be issued at BSÍ Travel (see p. 574). Another option is the **Air/Bus Rover** (fly one way, bus the other), offered jointly by the domestic air carriers and BSÍ Travel (June-Sept.; from 8000Ikr). Weather can ground flights; leave yourself time for delays.

BY BUS. Iceland has no trains; although flying is faster and more comfortable, buses are usually cheaper and provide a closer look at the terrain. One tour company, **Destination Iceland** (☎591 10 00; www.dice.is), which has offices in the Reykjavík bus terminal, coordinates all schedules and prices. Schedules are available at hostels and tourist offices. Their main brochure lists all bus schedules and is a must for anyone traveling the **Ring Road,** the loop that circles Iceland. Buses run daily on each segment from mid-June to August, but frequency drops dramatically in the off season. The going is slow, since some roads are unpaved. The circle can be rushed through in three days, but ten days is a much more adequate time frame.

The **Full Circle Passport** lets travelers circle the island at their own pace on the Ring Road (available mid-May to Sept.; 21,000Ikr). It allows travel only in a continuous direction, so travelers must move either clockwise or counter-clockwise around the country. For an extra 10,000Ikr, the pass (which has no time limitation) provides access to the Westfjords in the island's extreme northwest. The **Omnibus Passport** gives a period of unlimited travel on all scheduled bus routes, including non-Ring roads (1-week 23,000Ikr, 2-week 33,000Ikr, 3-week 42,500Ikr, 4-week 47,000Ikr; off-season prices lower). Both passes give 5% discounts on many ferries, campgrounds, farms, *Hótel Edda* sleeping-bag dorms, and guided bus tours.

BY FERRY. The best way to see Iceland's rugged shores is on the **Norröna** car and passenger ferry (☎562 63 62; fax 552 94 50) that circles the North Atlantic via: Seyðisfjörður, East Iceland; Tórshavn in the Faroe Islands; and Hanstholm, Denmark (runs mid-May to Aug.; 7 days, students 42,500Ikr). From Tórshavn, you can continue on to Bergen or return to Seyðisfjörður. **Eimskip** (reservations ☎585 4070) offers more expensive ferry rides on cargo ships from Reykjavík to Immingham, Rotterdam, and Hamburg.

BY CAR. Travelers using cars have the most freedom. Iceland is overflowing with car rental *(bílaleiga)* companies. Prices average about 5000Ikr per day and 40Ikr per km after the first 100km for smaller cars, but are substantially higher for 4-wheel-drive vehicles (ask about special package deals). **Ragnar Bjarnason,** Staðarbakka 2 (☎557 42 66; fax 557 42 33), offers the lowest rates. You are required to keep your headlights on at all times, wear a seatbelt, and drive only on marked roads. Iceland recognizes foreign driver's licenses, but you may need to purchase insurance for the rented car (750-2000Ikr).

BY BIKE AND BY THUMB. Cycling is gaining popularity, but ferocious winds, driving rain, and nonexistent road shoulders make it difficult. Buses will carry bikes for a 5000-7000Ikr fee, depending on the distance covered. Trekking is extremely arduous; well-marked trails are rare, but several suitable areas await the truly ambitious. Ask the tourist office in Reykjavík for maps and more info. Determined hitchers try the roads in summer, but sparse traffic and harsh weather exacerbate the inherent risks. Nevertheless, for those who last, the ride usually does come (easily between Reykjavík and Akureyri; harder in the east and the south). *Let's Go* does not recommend hitchhiking.

TOURIST SERVICES AND MONEY

EMERGENCY	**Police:** ☎112. **Ambulance:** ☎112. **Fire:** ☎112.

TOURIST OFFICES. Tourist offices in large towns have schedules, maps, and brochures; check at hotel reception desks in smaller towns for local information. The free brochure *Around Iceland* (accommodation, restaurant, and museum listings for every town in the country), *The Complete Iceland Map*, and the BSÍ bus schedule are all must-haves. Reykjavík's tourist office maintains a helpful website (www.tourist.reykjavik.is), as does the US tourist board (www.goiceland.org).

MONEY. Iceland's monetary unit is the **króna,** which is divided into 100 *aurar.* There are 1Ikr, 5Ikr, 10Ikr, 50Ikr, and 100Ikr coins; notes are in denominations of 500Ikr, 1000Ikr, 2000Ikr, and 5000Ikr. Costs are high: on average, a night in a hostel might cost you 1750Ikr, a budget hotel 6500-8500Ikr, and a budget restaurant meal 1000-2000Ikr. Tipping is not customary in Iceland. **Value-added tax (VAT)** is included in all posted prices; refunds are available upon departure for purchases of 4000Ikr or more (see p. 19).

ICELANDIC KRÓNUR (IKR)		
	AUS$1 = 46.98IKR	100IKR = AUS$2.12
	CDN$1 = 55.39IKR	100IKR = AUS$2.12
	EUR€1 = 83.89IKR	100IKR = EUR€1.20
	NZ$1 = 40.32IKR	100IKR = NZ$2.48
	ZAR1 = 7.97IKR	100IKR = ZAR12.54
	UK£1 = 131.16IKR	100IKR = UK£0.76
	US$1 = 86.26IKR	100IKR = US$1.15

ACCOMMODATIONS AND CAMPING

Iceland's 27 HI youth hostels, invariably clean and always with kitchens, are uniformly priced at 1500Ikr for members, 1850Ikr for nonmembers. Pick up the free *Hostelling in Iceland* brochure at tourist offices. Sleeping-bag accommodations *(svefnpokapláss)*—available on farms, at summer hotels, and in guesthouses *(gistiheimili)*—are relatively cheap (see p. 576). In early June, many schoolhouses become *Hótel Eddas,* which have sleeping-bag accommodations (no kitchens; 950-1500Ikr, 5% discount with bus pass). Most also offer breakfast and beds, both quite expensive. Staying in a tiny farm or hostel can be the highlight of a trip, but the nearest bus may stop 20km away and run once a week. Many remote lodgings will pick up tourists in the nearest town for a small fee. In cities and nature reserves, camping is permitted only at designated campsites. Outside of official sites, camping is free but discouraged; watch out for *Tjaldstæði bönnuð* (No Camping) signs, and always ask at the nearest farm before you pitch a tent. Use gas burners; Iceland has no firewood, and it is illegal to burn the sparse vegetation. Official campsites (summer only) range from rocky fields with cold water taps to the sumptuous facilities in Reykjavík (around 700Ikr). Many offer discounts for students and bus-pass holders.

COMMUNICATION

PHONE CODE	
	Country code: 354. **International dialing prefix:** 00. There are no city codes in Iceland. From outside Iceland, dial int'l dialing prefix (see inside back cover) + 354 + local number.

TELEPHONES. Telephone *(sími)* offices are often in the same building as post offices. Pay phones take phone cards or 10Ikr, 50Ikr, or 100Ikr pieces; local calls cost 20Ikr. For the best prices, make calls from telephone offices; next best is a prepaid phone card. To make an international call, insert a phone card or dial direct (see numbers below). To reach the operator, call ☎118 (59Ikr per minute). International direct dial numbers include: **AT&T,** ☎800 90 01; **British Telecom,** ☎800 90 44; **Canada Direct,** ☎800 90 10; **Ireland Direct,** ☎800 93 53; **MCI,** ☎800 90 02; **Sprint,** ☎800 90 03; **Telecom New Zealand Direct,** ☎800 199 64; **Telkom South Africa,** ☎800 199 27; and **Telstra Australia,** ☎800 199 61.

MAIL. Mailing a postcard or letter from Iceland costs 80Ikr to Australia, Canada, New Zealand, the US, or South Africa; to Europe, 55Ikr. Post offices *(póstur)* are generally open M-F 9am-4:30pm. See p. 576 for information on *Poste Restante.*

INTERNET ACCESS. Internet access is widespread in Iceland, although in small towns it may only be available in public libraries.

REYKJAVÍK

Reykjavík's character more than makes up for its modest size. Bold, modern architecture complements a backdrop of snow-dusted purple mountains, and the city's refreshingly clear air is matched by its sparkling streets and gardens. Although quiet during the week, the world's smallest metropolitan capital comes alive on weekends. Inviting and virtually crime-free, Reykjavík's only weaknesses are its often-frigid weather and its high cost of living.

TRANSPORTATION

Flights: All international flights arrive at **Keflavík Airport** (KEF), 55km from Reykjavík. From the main exit, catch a **Flybus** (☎562 10 11, departs 30min. after every arrival, 900lkr) to the domestic **Reykjavík Airport** (REK) or Hótel Loftleiðir; from the hotel, you can take Flybus minivans to your hostel or hotel (free of charge) or bus #7 (every 20min. until 7pm, every hr. after 7pm; 200lkr) downtown to Lækjartorg. Flybuses back to the airport stop at Hótel Loftleiðir (2hr. before each departure), Grand Hótel Reykjavík (2½hr. before), and the youth hostel (June-Aug. 4:45am and 1:15pm). Most hostels and guesthouses can arrange for their guests to be picked up by Flybus at no extra charge. The **Omnibus Pass** (but not Full Circle Passport; see p. 572) covers Flybus; get a refund at Destination Iceland (see below) or Reykjavík Excursions (in the Hótel Loftleiðir; open 24hr.).

Buses: Umferðarmiðstöð (also known as **BSÍ Station**), Vatnsmýrarvegur 10 (☎552 23 00), off Hringbraut near Reykjavík Airport. Walk 15-20min. south along Tjörnin from the city center, or take bus #7 or 8 (every 20-30min., 200lkr). Open daily 7am-midnight; tickets sold 7:30am-10pm. **Destination Iceland** (☎591 10 20; www.dice.is), inside the bus terminal, sells bus passes and tour packages. Open June-Aug. M-F 7:30am-7pm, Sa-Su 7:30am-5pm; Sept.-May M-F 9am-5pm.

Public Transportation: Strætisvagnar Reykjavíkur (**SVR;** ☎551 27 00) operates yellow city buses (200lkr). Pick up SVR's helpful city map and bus schedule at its terminals. Tickets are sold at four terminals; the two major terminals are **Lækjartorg** in the center of town (open M-F 7am-11:30pm, Sa 8am-11:30pm, Su 10am-11:30pm) and **Hlemmur,** farther east on Hverfisg. (open M-Sa 8am-11:30pm, Su 10am-11:30pm). Either buy packages of 10 adult fares (1000lkr) or 20 senior fares (1600lkr) beforehand or buy tickets on the bus (exact change only). Ask the driver for a free transfer ticket (*skiptimiði;* valid for 45min.). Buses run M-Sa 7am-midnight, Su and holidays 10am-midnight. Night buses #125, 130, and 135 run limited routes F-Sa until 4:30am.

Taxis: BSR, Skolatröð 18 (☎561 00 00). 24hr. service. Tipping not customary. City center to: BSÍ Station 600-700lkr; Keflavík Airport 7200lkr; and Reykjavík Airport 700-800lkr. Other companies: **Hreyfill** (☎588 55 22); **BSH** (☎555 08 88).

Car Rental: Hertz (☎505 06 00), in the Reykjavík Airport. 3510-11440lkr per day. Also at the **youth hostel** (see p. 576). 4900-12500lkr per day.

Bike Rental: At the **youth hostel campsite** (see p. 577). 800lkr per 6hr., 1500lkr per day. Also at **Central Reykjavik Travel Service** (see Tourist Office). 1600lkr per day.

Hitchhiking: Hitchhiking is uncommon but not difficult in Iceland. Those looking for a ride generally head to the east edge of town. *Let's Go* does not recommend hitchhiking.

ORIENTATION AND PRACTICAL INFORMATION

Lækjartorg is Reykjavík's main square and a good base for navigation. **Lækjargata** leads from the southern end of Lækjartorg to **Tjörnin** (the pond), which lies halfway between the square and BSÍ Station. Reykjavík's main thoroughfare extends east

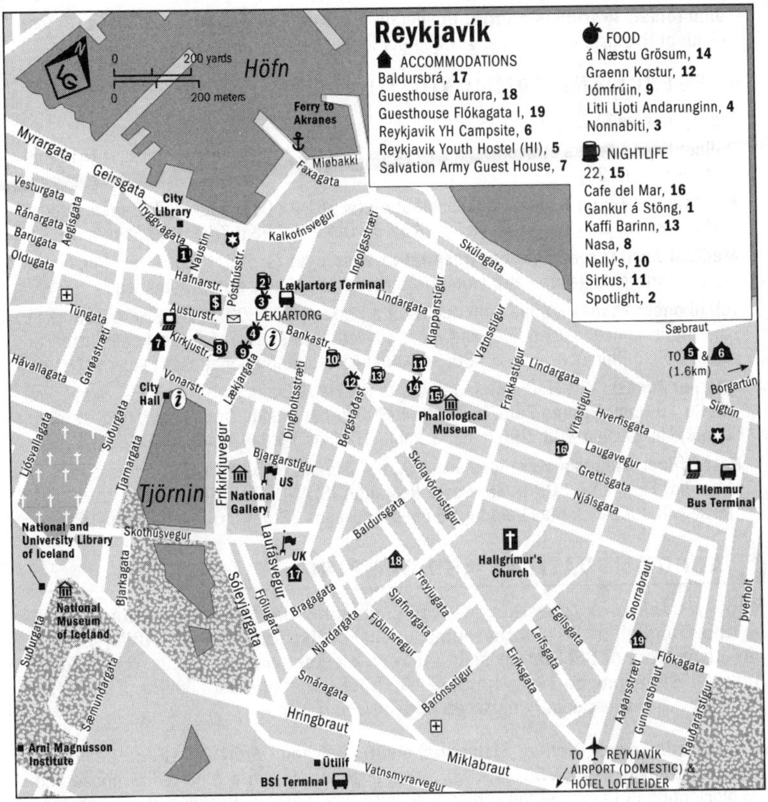

and west from Lækjartorg, changing names from **Austurstræti** to **Bankastræti** and then **Laugavegur** as it moves west to east. City maps are available at the tourist office or around town, and the monthlies *What's On in Reykjavík* and *Reykjavík This Month* provide information about exploring the city (all free).

TOURIST, FINANCIAL, AND LOCAL SERVICES

Tourist Office: Upplýsingamiðstöð Ferðamála í Íslandi, Bankastr. 2 (☎562 30 45; www.tourist.reykjavik.is), at Lækjartorg and Bankastr. **Branches** at the airport and City Hall. Open June-Aug. daily 8:30am-6pm; Sept.-May M-F 9am-5pm, Sa-Su 10am-2pm. All sell the **Reykjavík Card,** which allows unlimited public transportation and free entry to several museums and sights. (1-day 1000lkr, 2-day 1500lkr, 3-day 2000lkr. See p. 577 for participating establishments.) **Central Reykjavík Travel Service,** Lækjarg. 2 (☎511 24 42; www.travelservice.is), provides personal attention, rents **bikes,** and has **Internet** access (250lkr per 30min.). Open M-F 8am-10pm, Sa-Su 10am-10pm.

Embassies: Canada, Túngata 14 (☎533 55 50; fax 568 08 99). Open M-F 8am-4pm. **UK,** Laufásvegur 31 (☎550 51 00; fax 550 51 05). Open M-F 9am-noon. **US,** Laufásvegur 21 (☎562 91 00; fax 562 91 10). Open M-F 8am-12:30pm and 1:30-5pm.

Luggage Storage: At BSÍ Station, next to ticket window. 300lkr per day. Open daily 7:30am-7pm.

Laundromat: Þvottahusið Drifa, Hringbraut 19. **Þvottahusið Emla,** Barónsstíg. 3, just south of Hverfisg. Full service. 1700lkr per load. Open M-F 8am-6pm.

EMERGENCY AND COMMUNICATIONS

Emergency: ☎112.

Police: Headquarters at Hverfisg. 113-115 (☎569 90 20). Downtown office at Tryggvag. 19 (☎569 90 25).

Pharmacies: Lyf og Heilsa, Haaleitisbraut 68 (☎581 21 01). Open daily 8am-midnight. **Lyfja Apótek,** Laugavegur 16 (☎552 40 45). Open M-F 9am-7pm, Sa 10am-4pm.

Medical Assistance: National Hospital at Fossvogur (☎525 17 00), on Hringbraut, has a 24hr. emergency ward. From the center of town, take bus #3 southeast.

Telephones: Phones require either coins or a phone card (500 or 1000lkr; available at the tourist office, post office, and most convenience stores). For local calls insert at least 20lkr. Phones accept 10, 50, or 100lkr coins. International assistance: ☎1811.

Internet Access: City Hall cafe, north of Tjörnin. Free 20min. slots. Open M-F 8am-7pm, Sa-Su 10-6pm. **Ground Zero,** Vallarstr. 4. 300lkr per 30min. Open daily 10am-1am. **K-Lanið,** Laugavegur 103. 250lkr per 30min., 1000lkr per day. Open daily 10am-11pm.

Post Office: Íslandspóstur, Pósthússtr. 5, at Austurstr. (☎580 11 01). Address mail to be held: Firstname SURNAME, Poste Restante, ÍSLANDSPÓSTUR, Pósthússtr. 5, 101 Reykjavík, ICELAND. Mail held for 56 days, packages 28 days. Open M-F 9am-4:30pm.

ICELAND

ACCOMMODATIONS AND CAMPING

Many *gistiheimili* (guesthouses) offer "sleeping-bag accommodations" (bed, mattress, and pillow in a dorm room; add 300-500Ikr for a blanket). **Útilíf,** located directly in front of BSÍ Station, sells and rents sleeping bags and tents. (Open June-Aug. M-F 9am-6pm, Sa 10am-4pm.) Cheap hotels cost at least 5500Ikr. Call ahead for reservations, especially between mid-June and August.

Hjálpræðisherinn Gisti-og Sjómannaheimili (Salvation Army Guest and Seamen's Home), Kirkjustr. 2 (☎561 32 03; www.guesthouse.is), in a pale yellow house one block north of Tjörnin, at the corner of Kirkjustr. and Tjarnarg. Bustles with backpackers enjoying the fantastic location and friendly staff. Kitchen. Breakfast 800lkr. Laundry 700lkr. May-Sept. sleeping-bag accommodations 1800lkr; singles 4000lkr; doubles 5500lkr; triples 7000lkr; quads 8500lkr. Oct.-Apr. reduced prices. ❷

Guesthouse Flókagata 1, Flókag. 1 (☎552 11 55; guesthouse@eyjar.is). From Hallgrímur's Church, head down Egilsg. and turn left onto Snorrabraut. The guesthouse is on the corner on the right. Pristine rooms. Breakfast included. Reception 24hr. May-Sept. sleeping-bag accommodations 2500lkr; singles 6900lkr; doubles 9900lkr. Extra bed 3200lkr. Oct.-Apr. prices drop 10%. ❷

Reykjavík Youth Hostel (HI), Sundlaugavegur 34 (☎553 81 10; info@hostel.is). Take bus #5 from Lækjarg. to Sundlaugavegur. Far from the center of town, but next to Laugardalslaug (see p. 577). Kitchen. Laundry 300lkr. Internet 200lkr per 15min. Flybus pickup 900lkr. Reception 8am-11pm; ring bell after hours. Sleeping bag accommodations 1500lkr; singles 1500lkr; doubles 2800lkr. Nonmembers add 350lkr. ❶

Guesthouse Aurora, Freyjug. 24 (☎552 55 15; fax 551 48 94). Head south on Njarðarg. from Hallgrímur's Church and turn right onto Freyjug.; Aurora is the purple house on the left-hand corner. In a quiet neighborhood 10min. from the city center. Rustically homey, perfect for couples. Kitchen. Breakfast included. Laundry 250lkr. July-Aug. singles 5500lkr; doubles 7000lkr; triples 9500lkr. Sept.-June reduced prices. ❹

Baldursbrá, Laufásvegur 41 (☎552 66 46; heijfis@centrum.is), 10min. north of BSÍ Station, 5-10min. south of city center. Family-run guesthouse in a quiet residential neighborhood. Reserve ahead. Kitchen and sauna 300Ikr. May-Sept. singles 6500Ikr; doubles 8500Ikr. Oct.-Apr. singles 4350Ikr; doubles 7000Ikr. 10% cash discount. ❷

Reykjavík Youth Hostel Campsite (☎568 69 44), next to the youth hostel. Take bus #5 from city center. Campsite in a huge field next to Laugardalslaug (see p. 577). Friendly staff. Free bus from the campsite to BSÍ Station at 7:30am. Laundry 300Ikr. Free showers. Open mid-May to mid-Sept. 700Ikr per person; 2-bed cabins 3800Ikr. ❶

FOOD

An authentic Icelandic meal featuring seafood, lamb, or puffin will cost at least 1000Ikr and is worth splurging on at least once. Otherwise, buy fresh food at a market and take advantage of the kitchen in your hostel or guesthouse. Many supermarkets are on **Austurstræti, Hverfisgata,** and **Laugavegur.** Cheap fast-food joints are easy to find in the area west of Lækjartorg, especially on **Hafnarstræti** and **Tryggvagata.** The best of them is **Nonnabiti ❶,** Hafnarstr. 18, an Icelandic-style sandwich shop. (550-640Ikr. Open Su-Th 10am-2am, F-Sa 10am-5:30am.)

á Næstu Grösum (One Woman Restaurant), Laugavegur 20B, at the intersection with Klapparstígur. Delicious vegetarian fare, soothing environment. Daily special 600-900Ikr. Open M-Sa 11:30am-2pm and 5-10pm, Su 5-10pm. ❶

Jómfrúin, Lækjarg. 4. Casual Danish restaurant serves delectable open sandwiches (530-1680Ikr) that are almost too pretty to eat. Outdoor seating available. Beer 200-500Ikr. Open Apr.-Sept. daily 11am-10pm; Oct.-Mar. 11am-6pm. ❷

Litli Ljoti Andarunginn, Lækjarg. 6B. Litli's fish buffet (1990Ikr, available after 6pm), is the most affordable way to sample the Arctic's delicacies. Catch of the day 1090Ikr. Wine 650Ikr, beer 350Ikr. Open Su-Th 11am-1am, F-Sa 11am-3am. ❷

Grænn Kostur, Skólavörðustígur 8B. Two daily vegetarian specials (800Ikr) and luscious dessert cakes (450Ikr). Open M-Sa 11:30am-9pm, Su 1pm-9pm. ❶

SIGHTS AND HIKING

SIGHTS. Laugardalslaug is the largest of Reykjavík's geothermally heated pools. It boasts a giant slide and a series of jacuzzis, each one hotter than the last. (On Sundlaugavegur, next to the youth hostel campground. Bus #5. Open M-F 6:50am-9:30pm, Sa-Su 8am-8pm. 200Ikr.) A stunning domed gallery houses the **Ásmundur Sveinsson Sculpture Museum,** on Sigtún. (Bus #5. Open May-Sept. daily 10am-4pm; Oct.-Apr. 1-4pm. 500Ikr.) **Listasafn Íslands** (National Gallery of Iceland), Fríkirkjuvegur 7, on the east shore of Tjörnin, displays small exhibits of traditional Icelandic art, while the **Reykjavík Art Museum,** on Sigtún, focuses on more modern painting and sculpture. (Listasafn open Tu-Su 11am-5pm, Th until 10pm. 400Ikr, seniors 250; W free. Reykjavík Art open daily 11am-6pm, Th until 7pm. Free Internet in cafe. 500Ikr.) Laugardalslaug and these three museums are among the sights covered by the **Reykjavík Card** (see p. 575); ask for a list other participating institutions when you purchase the card.

Some of the city's must-sees are free or not covered by the Reykjavík Card. **City Hall,** on the north end of Tjörnin, is home to a raised relief map of Iceland as well as rotating exhibits. (Open M-F 8am-7pm, Sa-Su 10am-6pm. Free.) East of Lækjartorg is the world's only **Phallological Museum,** Laugavegur 24, a collection of Arctic and Icelandic mammal members sure to humble any man. Look for the sign and turn right through the yellow corridor. (Open Tu-Sa 2-5pm. 400kr.) Turn off

Laugavegur onto Skólavörðustígur to reach **Hallgrímskirkja** (Hallgrímur's Church), whose soaring steeple is the highest point in the city. A trip to the top provides a spectacular view and a good sense of Reykjavík's layout. (Open daily 9am-6pm. Services Su 11am. Elevator to the top 200Ikr.)

HIKING. South of the city lies the **Heiðmörk Reserve,** a large park and sports complex. Heiðmörk has the best hiking trails and picnicking spots in the Reykjavík area; however, there is no public transportation directly to the park. Pleasant **Viðey Island,** home to Iceland's second-oldest church, has been inhabited since the 10th century. (Ferry schedules are available at tourist offices and BSÍ Station.) Across the bay from Reykjavík looms **Mt. Esja,** which you can ascend via a well-maintained trail (2-3hr.). While the trail is not difficult, hikers are often assaulted by rain, hail, and snow, even in summer. (Take bus #10 or #110 to Artún and transfer to bus #20, exiting at Mógilsá. Bus #20 runs only once every 1-2hr.; consult SVR city bus schedule before departing.)

NIGHTLIFE

Although quiet on weeknights, Reykjavík reasserts its reputation as a wild party town each weekend; nowhere else on earth can you step out of a club at 3am to a sky that has barely dimmed to twilight. To avoid vicious drink prices and cover charges, most Icelanders pregame at home and then hit the clubs just before covers kick in. Only designated liquor stores can sell alcohol; **Nelly's,** Þingholtsstr. 2, sells the cheapest beer in town. (Open Su-Th noon-1am, F-Sa noon-6am.) Most cafes turn into boisterous bars on weekend nights, and crowds happily bar-hop along the vibrant streets **Austurstræti, Tryggvagata,** and **Laugavegur.**

CAFES

Kaffi Barinn, on Bergstaðastr. near Laugavegur. Cafe by day, bar by night, madhouse on weekends. Coffee 200-250Ikr, beer 550Ikr. Food served noon-6pm. Live DJ Th-Sa. Open M-Th 11am-1am, F 11am-4am, Sa noon-5am, Su 2pm-1am.

Sirkus, Klapparstígur 30. Outside patio and upstairs room make Sirkus the undisputed place to relax in Reykjavík. They've got the barbecue and basketball hoop if you've got beef or a ball. Beer 550Ikr. Open M-Th 5pm-1am, F-Sa 5pm-5:30am, Su 7pm-1am.

Cafe del Mar, Vitastígur 10A. One of the only cafes that keeps the coffeepot full after other cafes tap the keg. Live DJ Th. Pot of coffee 600Ikr. Open M-Sa 10:30am-1am, Su 2-11:30pm.

PUBS AND CLUBS

Gaukur á Stöng, Tryggvag. 22. Iceland's first pub and the most popular spot for live music. Schedules on www.gaukurinn.is. Open Su-Th 9pm-1am, F-Sa 9pm-5:30am.

22, Laugavegur 22. Upstairs disco, downstairs bar. A solid starter for your Laugavegur bar-hopping. 500Ikr cover after 1am. Open Su-Th 11:30am-1am, F-Sa noon-5:30am.

Nasa, Viðausturvöll 18. Reykjavík's most all-out dance club. Open F-Sa 11pm-4am.

Spotlight, Hafnarstr. 17, just down from the SVR Lækjartorg bus station. A self-proclaimed "straight-friendly" bar, Spotlight welcomes anyone and everyone to its all-night raves. Beer 600Ikr. Open Su-Th 9pm-1am, F-Sa 9pm-6am.

DAYTRIPS FROM REYKJAVÍK

Reykjavík is nice and all, but Iceland's true attractions are its mesmerizing natural wonders. Renting a car may be the best approach for groups (see p. 572); the comprehensive **bus tours** are more economical for solo travelers. **Iceland Excursions** runs the popular **Golden Circle** guided tour, stopping at Hveragerði, Kerið, Skálholt, Geysir, Gullfoss, and Þingvellir National Park. (Departs from Hótel Loftleiðir daily at 8:30am. 8hr. 5200Ikr). Book ahead in the tourist office or by phone (☎562 10 11). Free pickup at a number of other hotels and hostels in Reykjavík is available.

BLUE LAGOON. Southwest of Reykjavík lies paradise: a vast pool of geothermally heated water in the middle of a lava field. The lagoon is alongside a natural power plant that provides Reykjavík with electricity and heat by harnessing geothermal steam. Though the lagoon attracts a few too many tourists, its unique concentrations of silica, minerals, and algae are soothing enough to rejuvenate any crowd-weary traveler. Once inside the misty blue waters, bathers may further indulge in a steam bath, a skin-soothing mud facial, or a massage (1200Ikr per 10min.). The lagoon rents towels (300Ikr) and bathing suits (250Ikr) if you've forgotten your own. (3hr. admission 880Ikr; locker included.) **Buses** run from BSÍ Station in Reykjavík to the Blue Lagoon. (Daily 10am, 1:30, 5:15, and 6pm; return 12:40, 4, 6, and 8pm. 850Ikr each way.) Most hostels and hotels can arrange for pickup if you call ahead.

GULLFOSS AND GEYSIR. A glacial river plunging over 30m creates Gullfoss, the "Golden Falls." The greatest attraction of Gullfoss, besides the falls themselves, is the stunning view of the surrounding mountains, plains, and glaciers from atop the hill adjacent to the falls. Only 9km away is the **Geysir** area, a rocky, rugged tundra with steaming pools of hot water every few meters. The energetic **Strokkur** erupts every 5-10min., reaching heights of up to 25-35m. BSÍ runs a round-trip **bus** to both sites, stopping at Gullfoss for 1hr. and Geysir for 1-2hr. The ride is lengthy and roundabout, but the beautiful destinations are worth it. (Departs Reykjavík daily June-Aug. 8:30am and 12:30pm; Sept.-May M-Sa 9:30am, Su 12:30pm. 3800Ikr.)

ÞINGVELLIR NATIONAL PARK. Straddling the divide between the European and North American tectonic plates, Þingvellir National Park features impressive scenery. The **Öxará River,** slicing through lumpy lava fields and jagged fissures, leads to the **Drekkingarhylur** (Drowning Pool), where adulterous women were once drowned, and to **Lake Þingvallavatn,** the largest lake in Iceland. Not far from the Drekkingarhylur lies the site of **Alþing,** the ancient parliament of the first Icelandic democracy in AD 930. For almost nine centuries, Icelanders gathered once a year in the shadow of the Lögberg (Law Rock) to discuss matters of blood, money, and justice. A **bus** runs from Reykjavík to Þingvellir, dropping visitors off at an **information center.** (☎482 26 60. Open May-Sept. daily 8:30am-8pm. Bus May 20-Sept. 10 daily 1:30pm, return 4:50pm. 850Ikr, round-trip 1700Ikr.) Ask for directions for the 30-45min. walk along the road to reach the lake or the main historical sites. The **campground** by the information center has showers and laundry machines (500Ikr).

ICELAND

WESTMAN ISLANDS (VESTMANNAEYJAR)

Vaulting boldly from the depths of the North Atlantic, the black cliffs off the Westman Islands are the most recent products of the volcanic fury that created Iceland. Heimaey, the only inhabited island, is one of the most important fishing ports in the country. The three-day **Þjóðhátíð** (People's Feast) draws a hefty percentage of Reykjavík's livelier citizens to the island's shores for an annual festival of drinking and dancing (Aug. 1-3); the rest of the year, Heimaey is quiet and subdued.

TRANSPORTATION AND PRACTICAL INFORMATION. Getting to and from the Westman Islands is relatively easy. Flugfélag Islands (Air Iceland) has daily **flights** from Reykjavík Airport. (☎570 30 30. One-way from 5865Ikr.) A slower but much cheaper option is the Herjólfur **ferry** (☎481 28 00) departing from Þorlákshöfn. (3hr. In summer, daily at noon, Su-F also 7:30pm; return M-Sa 8:15am, Su 2pm, F also 4pm. In winter, M-Sa noon, Su 6pm, F also 7:30pm; return daily 8:15am, Su-F also 4pm. 1500Ikr.) Buses go from BSÍ Station in Reykjavík to the dock in Þorlákshöfn 1hr. before departure (750Ikr). The **tourist office** is on Básaskersbryggin, right in the central harbor. (☎481 35 55; www.eyjar.is. Open May-Sept. M-F 8am-5pm, Sa 10am-4pm, Su 10am-4pm; Oct.-May M-F 8am-5pm.) Ask about island **bus tours** (daily 8am and noon, or upon request; 1800Ikr) and **boat tours** (daily 10:30am and 3:30pm, 2000Ikr).

ACCOMMODATIONS AND FOOD. **Guesthouse Hreiðreið and Bolið ❶,** Faxastigur 33, is just past the Volcanic Show cinema on Heiðarvegur. (☎699 89 45. Sleeping-bag accommodations 1500Ikr; singles 3200Ikr; doubles 5200Ikr.) **Guesthouse Sunnoholl ❷,** Vestmannabraut 28, houses visitors in a white house behind Hótel Þorshamar. (☎481 29 00. Sleeping-bag accommodations 2700Ikr, 1800Ikr per person if two or more; singles 3900Ikr.) The **campground ❶,** 10min. west of town on Dalvegur, near the golf course, has showers and cooking facilities. (☎692 69 52. 500Ikr.) Get groceries at **Krónan** on Strandavegur. (Open daily 11am-7pm.)

SIGHTS. In 1973, the fiery **Eldfell** volcano tore through the northern section of Heimaey island, spewing glowing lava and hot ash in a surprise eruption that forced the population to flee in a dramatic overnight evacuation. When the eruption finally ceased five months later, a third of the town's houses had been destroyed but the island itself had grown by the same amount. Nearly all of its former inhabitants returned, rebuilding a more modern Heimaey. Today, visitors can feel the heat of the still-cooling lava, hike among the black and green mountains that shelter its harbor, and observe the chilling remnants of buildings half-crushed by the lava. The **Volcanic Show** cinema runs a fascinating but slow documentary about the eruption's full effects on the Westman Islands. (Shows daily at 11am and 3:30pm. 400Ikr.)

Hiking in the area is encouraged; the tourist office distributes a free map outlining hiking trails. Spectacular spots include the cliff's edge at **Há** and the puffin colony at **Stórhöfði.** Há provides a stunning view of the town, the twin volcanic peaks, and the snow-covered mainland. Both volcanic peaks also await intrepid hikers, but strong winds often make for rough going over the summits. Head to the **aquarium** on Heiðarvegur, near the gas station, to see some of the island's strange and wonderful sea creatures. (Open May-Sept. daily 11am-5pm; Sept.-Apr. Sa-Su 3-5pm; also upon request. 300Ikr.)

REPUBLIC OF IRELAND & NORTHERN IRELAND

Travelers who come to Ireland with their heads filled with poetic imagery will not be disappointed—this largely agricultural and sparsely populated island still looks as it did when Celtic bards roamed the land. Windswept scenery is found all along the coast, and untouched mountain chains stretch across the interior bogland. Dublin and Belfast are cosmopolitan centers whose international populations influence their immediate surroundings. Some fear this threatens the native culture, but the survival of traditional music, dance, and storytelling proves otherwise. The Irish language lives on in small, secluded areas known as *gaeltachts*, as well as on road signs, in national publications, and in a growing body of modern literary works. While non-violence usually prevails in Northern Ireland, recent negotiations hope to ensure peace for future generations. Although the Republic and Northern Ireland are grouped together in this chapter for geographical reasons, no political statement is intended.

THE REPUBLIC	❶	❷	❸	❹	❺
ACCOMMODATIONS	under €15	€15-24	€25-39	€40-54	over €55
FOOD	under €5	€5-9	€10-14	€15-19	over €20
NORTHERN IRELAND	❶	❷	❸	❹	❺
ACCOMMODATIONS	under £12	£12-19	£20-29	£30-44	over £45
FOOD	under £3	£3-5	£6-9	£10-14	over £15

SUGGESTED ITINERARIES

THREE DAYS Spend it all in **Dublin** (p. 591). Wander through **Trinity College,** admire the **Book of Kells,** then have a drink at the **Guinness Hopstore** or the **Old Jameson Distillery.** Take a day at to visit the **National Museums,** stopping to relax on **St. Stephen's Green.** Get smart at the **James Joyce Centre** and then work your pubbing potential in **Temple Bar** and on **Grafton Street.**

ONE WEEK From **Dublin** (2 days) head to historic **Belfast** (1 day; p. 622). Don't miss the beautiful **Giant's Causeway** (1 day; p. 632) before heading to artsy **Galway** (1 day; p. 615). Admire the romantic countryside in the **Ring of Kerry** (1 day; p. 611) and return to civilization in **Cork** (1 day; p. 606).

BEST OF IRELAND, THREE WEEKS Land in **Dublin** (4 days) before taking the train up to **Belfast** (3 days). Catch the bus to **Giant's Causeway** (1 day), and stop at **Derry** (2 days, p. 628). From **Donegal Town** (1 day, p. 620), climb **Slieve League** (1 day, p. 620), the highest seacliffs in Europe. Use **Sligo** (3 days; p. 619) as a base for visiting County Sligo's lakes and mountains. From there, head to **Galway** (2 days), the **Ring of Kerry** (2 days), **Killarney National Park** (1 day; p. 610), and **Cork** (1 day). On your way back to Dublin, take a detour to medieval **Kilkenny** (1 day; p. 604).

LIFE AND TIMES

HISTORY

EARLY CHRISTIANS AND VIKINGS (450-1200). Ireland was Christianized in a piecemeal fashion by a series of hopeful missionaries starting with **St. Patrick** in the 5th century. After the **Dal Cais** clan defeated the Vikings in the epic **Battle of Clontarf,** Ireland was divided between chieftains **Rory O'Connor** and **Dermot MacMurrough,** who then fought for the crown between themselves. Dermot ill-advisedly sought the assistance of Richard de Clare, known popularly as **Strongbow,** who arrived in 1169 and cut a bloody swath through Leinster (eastern and southeastern Ireland). Strongbow married Dermot's daughter Aoife after Dermot's death in 1171 and seemed ready to proclaim an independent Norman kingdom in Ireland. Instead, the turncoat affirmed his loyalty to King Henry II and offered to govern Leinster on England's behalf. Thus began English domination over Irish land.

FEUDALISM (1200-1641). The subsequent feudal period saw constant struggles between English lords of Gaelic and Norman descent. When **Henry VIII** created the Church of England, the Dublin Parliament passed the 1537 **Irish Supremacy Act,** which declared Henry head of the Protestant **Church of Ireland** and effectively made the island property of the Crown. In defiance of the monarchy, **Hugh O'Neill,** an Ulster earl, raised an army of thousands in open rebellion in the late 1590s, supported by Gaelic lords. Their forces were soon demolished, and the rebels left Ireland in 1607 in what is now known as the **Flight of the Earls.** The English took control of land, and parceled it out to Protestants.

PLANTATION AND CROMWELL (1641-1688). The English project of dispossessing Catholics of their land and "planting" Ireland with Protestants was most successful in Ulster, which became known as the **Ulster Plantation.** In response, the now landless Irish natives rebelled in 1641 under a loose-knit group of Gaelic-Irish leaders. In 1642 the rebels formed the **Confederation of Kilkenny,** an uneasy alliance of the Church and Irish and Old English lords. Negotiations between the Confederation and King Charles ended with **Oliver Cromwell**'s victory in England and his arrival in Ireland. Cromwell's army destroyed everything it came across, divvying up confiscated lands among Protestants and soldiers. By 1660, the vast majority of Irish land was owned, maintained, and policed by Protestant immigrants.

THE PROTESTANT ASCENDANCY (1688-1798). Thirty years after the English Civil War, English political disruption again resulted in Irish bloodshed. Deposed Catholic monarch **James II,** driven from England by the "Glorious Revolution" of 1688, came to Ireland to gather military support and reclaim his throne. A war between James and **William of Orange,** the new Protestant king, ended on July 12, 1690 at the **Battle of the Boyne** with James's defeat and exile. The term **"Ascendancy"** was coined to describe the social elite whose distinction depended upon Anglicanism. **Trinity College** was the quintessential institution of the Ascended Protestants.

UNION AND THE FAMINE (1798-1847). The 1801 **Act of Union** dissolved the Dublin Parliament and created The United Kingdom of Great Britain and Ireland; the Church of Ireland was subsumed by the "United Church of England and Ireland." During this time, the potato was the wonder-crop of the rapidly growing Irish population. The potato blight of the **Great Famine** (1847-51) killed an estimated two to three million people; a million more emigrated. In 1858, James Stephens founded the Irish Republican Brotherhood (IRB), commonly known as the **Fenians,** a secret society aimed at the violent removal of the British.

CULTURAL NATIONALISM (1870-1914). In 1870, Isaac Butt founded the **Irish Home Rule Party,** bent on securing autonomous rule for Ireland. Meanwhile, various groups tried to revive an essential "Gaelic" culture, unpolluted by foreign influence; **Arthur Griffin** began a fledgling movement by the name of **Sinn Féin** (SHIN FAYN; "Ourselves Alone"). As the Home Rule movement grew, so did resistance to it. Between 1910 and 1913, thousands of Northern Protestants opposing Home Rule joined a quasi-militia named the **Ulster Volunteer Force (UVF).** Nationalists led by **Eoin MacNeill** responded by creating the **Irish Volunteers.**

THE EASTER RISING (1914-1919). During **World War I,** British Prime Minister Henry Asquith passed a **Home Rule Bill** on the condition that Irishmen would fight for the British army. The Irish Volunteers that remained behind were led by MacNeill, who did not know that Fenian leaders were plotting to receive a shipment of German arms for use in a nationwide revolt on **Easter Sunday, 1916.** Although the arms arrived a day too early and were never picked up, Fenian leaders continued to muster support from the Volunteers. On Monday, April 24, about 1000 rebels seized the Dublin **General Post Office** on O'Connell St., holding on through five days of fighting. Fifteen ringleaders then received the death sentence, causing the public to grow increasingly anti-British and sympathetic to the rebels. In 1917, the Volunteers reorganized under Fenian bigwig **Michael Collins.** Collins brought the Volunteers to Sinn Féin, and **Éamon de Valera** became the party president.

INDEPENDENCE AND CIVIL WAR (1919-1922). Extremist Irish Volunteers became known as the **Irish Republican Army (IRA).** The IRA functioned as the military arm of Sinn Féin, winning the **War of Independence** (1919-1921) against the British. Hurried negotiations produced the **Anglo-Irish Treaty,** which created a 26-county Irish Free State, while still recognizing British rule over the northern counties. Sinn Féin, the IRA, and the population split on whether to accept the treaty. Collins said yes; de Valera said no. When the representative parliament voted in favor, de Valera resigned from the presidency and **Arthur Griffith** assumed the position. The capable Griffith and Collins government began the business of setting up a nation. A portion of the IRA, led by **General Rory O'Connor,** opposed the treaty. O'Connor's Republicans occupied the Four Courts in Dublin, took a pro-treaty Army general hostage, and were attacked by the forces of Collins's government. Two years of **civil war** followed. The pro-treaty government won, but Griffith died from the strain of the struggle and Collins was assassinated.

THE DE VALERA ERA (1922-1960). In 1927 de Valera broke with Sinn Féin and the IRA and founded his own political party, **Fianna Fáil.** The party won the 1932 election, and de Valera held power for much of the next 20 years. In 1937, de Valera and the voters approved the Irish Constitution. It declared the state's name to be **Éire,** and established the country's legislative structure, consisting of two chambers with five-year terms. Ireland stayed neutral during **World War II,** despite German air raids on Dublin. Many Irish citizens identified with the Allies, and approximately 50,000 served in the British army. In 1948, the Fine Gael government under **John Costello** had the honor of officially proclaiming "The Republic of Ireland" free, supposedly ending British Commonwealth membership. Britain recognized the Republic in 1949 but declared that the UK would maintain control over Ulster until the Parliament of Northern Ireland consented to join the Republic.

RECENT HISTORY (1960-1990). Ireland's post-war boom didn't arrive until the early 1960s, and economic mismanagement and poor governmental policies kept it short. In an effort to revitalize the nation, the Republic entered the European Economic Community, now the **European Union (EU),** in 1973. EU funds proved crucial to helping Ireland out of a severe mid-80s recession and reducing its dependence on the UK. In 1990, the Republic broke social and political ground when it elected its first female president, **Mary Robinson.**

TODAY

Social reform made further gains when the small, leftist **Labour Party** enjoyed unexpected success in the 1992 elections. The new Taoiseach, or Prime Minister, **Albert Reynolds,** declared that his priority was to stop violence in Northern Ireland. In August 1994, he announced a cease-fire agreement with Sinn Féin and the IRA. In April of 1998, Taoiseach **Bertie Ahern** helped to produce the **Northern Ireland Peace**

Agreement. In May of 1998, in the first island-wide election since 1918, 94% of voters in the Republic voted for the enactment of the Agreement.

The **euro** was formally introduced into the Republic on January 1, 2002. With the money garnered from the EU over the years, increased foreign investment and computer software development, and a flourishing tourism industry, the Irish economy is thriving like never before. According to a 1999 report, the unemployment rate should be reduced to three percent by the year 2005. With each boom comes a bust, however, and some fear the roar of the **Celtic Tiger,** a nickname for the Irish economy, will soon be reduced to a purr.

CULTURE

FOOD AND DRINK

Food in Ireland is expensive, but the basics are simple and filling. Find quick and greasy staples at **chippers** (fish 'n' chip shops) and **takeaways** (takeout joints). Most pubs serve food like Irish stew, burgers, soup, and sandwiches. Soda bread is delicious and keeps well, and Irish cheeses are addictive. Guinness, a rich, dark stout, is revered in Ireland with a zeal usually reserved for the Holy Trinity. Known as "the dark stuff" or "the blonde in the black skirt," it was once recommended as food for pregnant mothers, and its head is so thick its rumored that you can stand a match in it. Irish whiskey, which Queen Elizabeth once claimed was her only true Irish friend, is sweeter than its Scotch counterpart. Irish monks invented whiskey, calling it *uisce beatha*, meaning "water of life."

CUSTOMS AND ETIQUETTE

BUSINESS HOURS. Most banks are open Monday to Friday 9am-4:30pm, sometimes later on Thursdays. Pubs are usually open Monday to Saturday 10:30am to 11 or 11:30pm, Sundays 12:30 to 2pm and 4 to 11pm.

GIVING THE BIRD. The Irish flip people off with both their middle and index fingers, forming a V shape with their palm facing inward. *Let's Go* does not recommend making this gesture.

PUB LIFE. Ordering at an Irish pub can be a complex affair. When in a small group, one individual will usually approach the bar and buy a round of drinks for everyone. Once those drinks are downed, another individual will buy the next round. This continues until everyone has bought a round. It's considered poor form to refuse someone's offer to buy you a drink.

SAY WHAT. Try to avoid jokes or references to leprechauns, Lucky Charms, pots of gold, and the "wee" people. Likewise, abortion, divorce, gay marriages, and the Troubles up North do not make for casual conversation; these topics are largely avoided in pubs and public places.

TIPPING. Some restaurants in Ireland figure a service charge into the bill; some even calculate it into the cost of the dishes themselves. The menu often indicates whether or not service is included. Most people working in restaurants, however, do not expect a tip, unless the restaurant is targeted exclusively toward tourists. In those incidences, consider leaving 10-15%, depending upon the quality of the service. Tipping is very uncommon for other services, such as taxis and hairdressers, especially in rural areas. In most cases, people are usually happy if you simply round up the bill to the nearest euro.

ART HISTORY

LITERATURE. In the 17th century, wit and satire began to characterize emerging Irish literature. **Jonathan Swift** wrote some of the most sophisticated, misanthropic, and marvelous satire in the English language. Besides his masterpiece *Gulliver's Travels* (1726), Swift wrote political essays decrying English cruelty to the native Irish. While Dublin managed to breed talent, gifted young writers like **Oscar Wilde** often headed for London in order to make their names. Wilde wrote many delightful works; his best-known play is *The Importance of Being Earnest* (1895). Fellow playwright **George Bernard Shaw** also moved to London, where he became an active socialist, winning the Nobel Prize for Literature in 1925.

Towards the end of the 19th century, a crop of young Irish writers began to turn to Irish culture for inspiration; this period is known as the **Irish Literary Revival.** The poems of **William Butler Yeats** created an Ireland of loss and legend that won him worldwide fame and a 1923 Nobel Prize. Yet many authors still found Ireland too insular to suit their literary aspirations. **James Joyce** (1882-1942) is without a doubt Ireland's most famous expatriate, and yet his writing never escaped the island. His first novel, *A Portrait of the Artist as a Young Man* (1914), uses the protagonist Stephen Daedalus to describe Joyce's own youth in Dublin. Daedalus reappears in *Ulysses*, Joyce's revolutionary novel of 1922, loosely based on Homer's *Odyssey.* **Samuel Beckett**'s world-famous plays, including *Waiting for Godot* and *Endgame*, both written between 1946-1950, convey a deathly pessimism about language, society, and life. Beckett won the Nobel Prize in 1969, but refused acceptance because Joyce had never received it.

MUSIC. Traditional Irish music, commonly called *trad*, is an array of dance rhythms, cyclical melodies, and embellishments passed down through countless generations of musicians. A traditional musician's training consists largely of listening to and innovating from the work of others. A typical pub session will sample from a variety of styles, including reels, jigs, hornpipes, and slow airs. Different artists will put a unique spin on the same basic tune each time it's played.

Best-selling *trad* recording artists include **Altan, De Danann,** and the **Chieftains.** Equally excellent groups include the **Bothy Band** and **Planxty** of the 1970s, and, more recently, **Nomos, Solas, Dervish,** and **Deanta.** These bands have brought Irish music into international prominence, starting with the early recordings of the Chieftains and their mentor **Sean O'Riada,** who fostered the resurrection of *trad* from near-extinction to a national art form. For the best *trad*, find a *fleadh* (FLAH), a musical festival at which musicians' officially scheduled sessions often spill over into nearby pubs. **Comhaltas Ceoltóirí Éireann** (☎ 01 280 0295; www.comhaltas.com), the national *trad* music association, organizes *fleadhs.*

FILM. Hollywood discovered Ireland in John Wayne's 1952 film *The Quiet Man*, giving an international audience of millions their first view of the island's beauty, albeit through a stereotypical lens Irish film has long struggled to change. Aside from the garish green of Hollywood technicolor, art-filmmakers have also tried to capture Ireland, including **Robert Flaherty,** who created cinematic Realism in his classic documentary about coastal fishermen, *Man of Aran* (1934).

ARTS TODAY

LITERATURE. The dirt of Dublin continues to provide fodder for generations of writers. Mild-mannered schoolteacher **Roddy Doyle** wrote the well-known Barrytown trilogy about family life in down-and-out Dublin, as well as the acclaimed *The Woman Who Walked Into Doors* (1996). Doyle won the Booker Prize in 1994 for *Paddy Clarke Ha Ha Ha.* **Frank McCourt** won the Pulitzer Prize in 1996 for a memoir about his poverty-stricken childhood, *Angela's Ashes*, and followed up with a sequel, *'Tis* (2000). Not to be outdone, **Malachy McCourt,** Frank's brother, recently published his own memoir, *A Monk Swimming* (1999). Born in rural County Derry, **Seamus Heaney** was awarded the Nobel Prize for literature in 1995, and is the most prominent living Irish poet. His subject matter ranges from bogs to bombings to archeological remains.

MUSIC. Ireland's biggest rock export is **U2.** From the adrenaline-soaked promise of 1980's *Boy,* the band ascended into the stratosphere, culminating in international fame with *The Joshua Tree* (1987). After a brief turn to techno dance tunes (1997's *Pop*), the recent *All That You Can't Leave Behind* (2000) has been heralded as the band's triumphant return to its roots. **Boyzone** has recently conquered the UK charts and the hearts of millions of pre-adolescent girls; similar magic is practiced on the opposite sex by their sisters in the girl-group **B*witched.**

FILM. In the last decade, the government has encouraged a truly Irish film industry. **Jim Sheridan** helped kick off the Irish cinematic renaissance with his universally acclaimed adaptation of Christy Brown's autobiography, *My Left Foot* (1991). More recently, Sheridan has worked with actor Daniel Day-Lewis in two films that take a humanitarian approach to the lives of Catholics and Protestants during the Troubles with *In the Name of the Father* (1993) and *The Boxer* (1997). Based on Roddy Doyle's Barrytown Trilogy, *The Commitments* (1991), *The Snapper* (1993), and *The Van* (1996) follow a family from the depressed North Side of Dublin as its members variously form a soul band, have a kid, and get off the dole by running a chipper. Dublin native **Neil Jordan** has become a much-sought-after director thanks to the success of *The Crying Game* (1992), *Michael Collins* (1996), and *The Butcher Boy* (1998). Most recently, the appeal of Irish scenery and accents was demonstrated in the production of two highly Irish sounding and looking films by non-Irish filmmakers: Hollywood produced a film version of Donegal playwright Brian Friel's *Dancing at Lughnasa* (1998), and the government of the Isle of Man sponsored *Waking Ned Devine* (1998), which describes the antics of a village of rustic eccentrics.

HOLIDAYS AND FESTIVALS

Holidays: Holidays for the Republic of Ireland include: New Year's Day (Jan. 1); St. Patrick's Day (Mar. 17); Good Friday; Easter Monday (Apr. 21); and Christmas (Dec. 25-26). There are Bank Holidays in the Republic and Northern Ireland during the summer months; check at tourist offices for dates. Northern Ireland has the same national holidays as the Republic; it also observes Orange Day (July 12).

Festivals: All of Ireland goes green for **St. Patrick's Day** (Mar. 17th). On **Bloomsday** (June 16), Dublin celebrates James Joyce's *Ulysses* (p. 601). In mid-July, the **Galway Arts Festival** hosts theater, *trad,* rock, and film (p. 616). Many return home happy from the **Lisdoonvarna Matchmaking Festival** in early September (p. 614).

FACTS AND FIGURES: REPUBLIC OF IRELAND

Official Name: Éire.
Capital: Dublin.
Major Cities: Cork, Limerick.
Population: 3,800,000.
Land Area: 70,280 sq. km.
Time Zone: GMT.
Languages: English, Irish.
Religion: Roman Catholic (91.6%).

ESSENTIALS

WHEN TO GO

Irish weather is subject to frequent changes but relatively constant temperatures. The southeastern coast is the driest and sunniest, while western Ireland is considerably wetter and cloudier. May and June are the sunniest months, July and August the warmest. December and January have the worst weather. Take heart when you wake to clouded, foggy mornings—the weather usually clears by noon.

DOCUMENTS AND FORMALITIES

Citizens of Australia, Canada, the EU, New Zealand, South Africa, and the US do not need a visa for stays of up to 90 days.

Irish Embassies at Home: Australia, 20 Arkana St., Yarralumla, Canberra ACT 2600 (☎062 73 3022). **Canada,** Suite 1105, 130 Albert St., Ottawa, ON K1P 5G4 (☎613-233-6281; emb.ireland@sympatico.ca). **New Zealand,** Honorary Consul General, 6th fl., 18 Shortland St. 1001, Auckland 1 (☎09 997 2252, www.ireland.co.nz). **South Africa,** 1st fl., Southern Life Plaza, 1059 Shoeman St., Arcadia 0083, Pretoria (☎012 342 5062). **UK,** 17 Grosvenor Pl., London SW1X 7HR (☎020 7235 2171). **US,** 2234 Massachusetts Ave. NW, Washington, D.C. 20008 (☎202-462-3939).

Foreign Embassies in Ireland: All embassies for the Republic of Ireland are in **Dublin** (see p. 591). The US has a consulate in **Belfast,** Queen's House, 14 Queen St., Belfast BT1 6EQ (☎028 9032 8239).

TRANSPORTATION

BY PLANE. Flying to London and connecting to Ireland is often easier and cheaper than flying direct. A popular carrier to Ireland is its national airline, **Aer Lingus** (☎01 886 8888; US ☎800-IRISHAIR; www.aerlingus.ie), which has direct flights to the US, London, and Paris. **Ryanair** (☎01 609 7900; www.ryanair.ie) is a smaller airline that offers a "lowest-fare guarantee." The web-based phenomenon **easyJet** (UK☎08706 000 000; www.easyjet.com) has recently begun flying from Britain to Belfast. **British Airways** (UK ☎0845 773 3377; Republic ☎800 626 747; US ☎800-AIRWAYS; www.british-airways.com) flies into most Irish airports daily.

BY TRAIN. Iarnród Éireann (Irish Rail; ☎01 836 3333; www.irishrail.ie) is useful only for travel to urban areas. The **Eurail** pass is accepted in the Republic but not in Northern Ireland. The BritRail Pass does not cover travel in Northern Ireland or the Republic, but the month-long **BritRail+Ireland** pass works in both the North and the Republic, with rail options and round-trip ferry service between Britain and Ireland (€400-570). **Northern Ireland Railways** (☎028 9066 6630; www.nirailways.co.uk) is not extensive but covers the northeastern coastal region well; the major line connects Dublin to Belfast. A valid **Northern Ireland Travelsave** stamp (UK£6), affixed to the back of an ISIC card, will get you up to 33% off all train fares and 15% off bus fares over UK£1.45 within Northern Ireland. The **Freedom of Northern Ireland** ticket allows unlimited travel by train and Ulsterbus (1-day UK£11, 3-day UK£27.50, 7-day UK£40).

BY BUS. Bus Éireann (☎01 836 6111; www.buseireann.ie), the national bus company, reaches Britain and the Continent by working in conjunction with ferry services and the bus company **Eurolines** (www.eurolines.com). Most buses leave from Victoria Station in London (to Belfast: 15hr., €49/UK£31, round-trip €79/UK£51; Dublin: 12hr., €42/UK£27, round-trip €69/UK£45); other major city stops include

Birmingham, Bristol, Cardiff, Glasgow, and Liverpool. Services run to Cork, Derry, Galway, Limerick, Waterford, and Tralee, among others. Discounted fares are available in the off-season, as well as for people under 26 or over 60. Tickets can be booked through usit, any Bus Éireann office, Irish Ferries, Stena Line, or any Eurolines office or National Express (☎08705 808 080) office in Britain.

Buses in the Republic of Ireland reach many more destinations and are less expensive than trains. Bus Éireann operates both long-distance Expressway buses, which link larger cities, and local buses, which serve the countryside and smaller towns. Bus Éireann's **Rambler** pass offers unlimited bus travel within Ireland. (3 of 8 consecutive days €45, under 16 €25; 8 of 15 €100/€55; 15 of 30 €145/€80), but is generally less cost-effective than buying individual tickets. A combined **Irish Explorer Rail/Bus** pass allows unlimited travel on trains and buses (8 of 15 consecutive days €145, under 16 €72). Passes can be purchased at Bus Éireann terminals in large cities.

Ulsterbus (☎028 9033 3000; Belfast ☎028 9032 0011; www.ulsterbus.co.uk) runs extensive and reliable routes throughout Northern Ireland, where there are no private bus services. The **Irish Rover** pass covers both Bus Éireann and Ulsterbus services. It sounds ideal for visitors intending to travel in both the Republic and Northern Ireland, but unless you plan to travel extensively on the bus, its true value is debatable (3 of 8 consecutive days €60/UK£90, children €33/UK£50; 8 of 15 €135/UK£200, children €75/UK£113; 15 of 30 €195/UK£293, children €110/UK£165). The **Emerald Card** offers unlimited travel on Ulsterbus, Northern Ireland Railways, Bus Éireann Expressway, and many local services; for more info, see www.buseireann.ie (8 of 15 consecutive days €168/UK£108, children €84/UK£54; 15 of 30 €290/UK£187, children €145/UK£94).

BY FERRY. Ferries, more economical than air travel, journey between Britain and Ireland several times per day (€28-55/UK£18-35). Weeknight travel promises the cheapest fares. An Óige (HI) members receive up to a 20% discount on fares from Irish Ferries and Stena Sealink, while ISIC cardholders with the TravelSave stamp receive a 15-17% discount on Stena Line and Irish Ferries. Ferries run from Cork to South Wales and Roscoff, France (see p. 606), and from Rosslare Harbour to Pembroke, Wales, and Roscoff and Cherbourg, France (see p. 603).

BY CAR. Drivers in Ireland use the left side of the road, and their steering wheels are on the right side of the car. Petrol (gasoline) prices are high. Be particularly cautious at roundabouts—give way to traffic from the right. Irish law requires drivers and passengers to wear seat belts. For insurance reasons, most companies require renters to be over 23 and under 70. **Dan Dooley** (☎062 53103, UK ☎0181 995 4551, US ☎800-331-9301; dandooley.com) is the only company in Ireland that will rent to drivers between 21 and 24, though such drivers incur an added daily surcharge. Prices are €150-370/UK£95-235 (plus VAT) per week, including insurance and unlimited mileage. If you plan to drive a car while in Ireland for longer than 90 days, you must have an **International Driving Permit (IDP).** If you rent, lease, or borrow a car, you will need a **green card** or **International Insurance Certificate** to certify that you have liability insurance and that it applies abroad.

BY BIKE, FOOT, AND THUMB. Much of the Ireland's countryside is well suited for **biking,** as many roads are not heavily traveled. Single-digit N roads in the Republic and M roads in the North are more busily trafficked; try to avoid these. Ireland's mountains, fields, and heather-covered hills make **walking** and **hiking** an arduous joy. The **Wicklow Way** has hostels within a day's walk of each other. Locals do not recommend **hitchhiking** in Northern Ireland, where it is illegal along motorways; some caution against it in Co. Dublin, as well as the Midlands. *Let's Go* does not recommend hitchhiking.

TOURIST SERVICES AND MONEY

EMERGENCY	Police: ☎999. Ambulance: ☎999. Fire: ☎999.

TOURIST OFFICES. Bord Fáilte (the Irish Tourist Board; ☎01850 230 330; www.ireland.travel.ie) operates a nationwide network of offices. Most tourist offices book rooms for a small fee and a 10% deposit, but many fine hostels and B&Bs are not on the board's central list. The **Northern Ireland Tourist Board** (☎028 9023 1221; www.discovernorthernireland.com) offers similar services.

Irish Tourist Boards at Home: Australia, Level 5, 36 Carrington St., Sydney NSW 2000 (☎02 299 6177). **Canada,** 120 Eglington Ave. E., Ste. 500, Toronto, ON, M4P 1E2 (☎800-223-6470). **New Zealand,** Dingwall Building, 2nd fl., 87 Queen St., Auckland (☎09 379 8720). **South Africa,** Everite House, 7th fl., 20 De Korte St., Braamfontein, 2001, Johannesburg (☎011 339 4865). **UK,** 150 New Bond St., London W1Y 0AQ (☎020 7493 3201). **US,** 345 Park Ave., New York, NY 10154 (☎800-223-6470; www.irelandvacations.com).

Northern Ireland Tourist Boards at Home: Australia, 36 Carrington St., 5th fl., Sydney NSW 2000 (☎02 299 6177; info@tourismireland.com.au). **Canada,** 2 Bloor St., Ste. 1501, Toronto, ON, M4W 3E2 (☎800-223-6470). **New Zealand,** 18 Shortland St., Private Bag 92136, Auckland 1 (☎09 379 3708). **UK,** 24 Haymarket, London SW1 4DG (☎020 7766 9920). **US,** 551 5th Ave., #701, New York, NY 10176 (☎800-326-0036 or 212-922-0101).

IRELAND

MONEY. The official currency of the Republic is the **euro.** The Irish pound can still be exchanged at a rate of IR£0.79 to €1. For exchange rates and more information on the euro, see p. 20. Legal tender in Northern Ireland is the **British pound;** for more info, see p. 163. Northern Ireland has its own bank notes, identical in value to English and Scottish notes of the same denominations. Although all of these notes are accepted in Northern Ireland, Northern Ireland notes are not accepted in Britain. If you stay in hostels and prepare your own food, expect to spend anywhere from €20-34/UK£12-22 per person per day. The European Union imposes a **value-added tax (VAT)** on goods and services purchased within the EU, which is included in the price; for more info, see p. 19.

ACCOMMODATIONS AND CAMPING

A **hostel** bed will average €12-18 in the Republic and UK£7-12 in the North. **An Óige** (an OYJ), the **HI** affiliate, operates 32 hostels countrywide. (☎01 830 4555; www.irelandyha.org. One-year membership €15, under 18 €7.50.) Many An Óige hostels are in remote areas or small villages and were designed primarily to serve hikers, long-distance bicyclists, anglers, and others seeking nature, and do not offer the social environment typical of other European hostels. The North's HI affiliate is **HINI** (Hostelling International Northern Ireland; formerly known as **YHANI**). It operates only eight hostels, all comfortable. (☎028 9031 5435; www.hini.org.uk. One-year membership UK£10, under 18 UK£6.) A number of hostels in Ireland belong to **Independent Holiday Hostels** (IHH; ☎01 836 4700; www.hostels-ireland.com). Most of the 140 IHH hostels have no lockout or curfew, accept all ages, require no membership card, and have a comfortable atmosphere that generally feels less institutional than that at An Óige hostels; all are Bord Fáilte-approved. Numerous **B&Bs,** in virtually every Irish town, can provide a luxurious break from hostelling; expect to pay €20-30/UK£12-20 for singles and €35-50/UK£22-32 for doubles. "Full Irish breakfasts" are often filling enough to get you through to dinner. **Camping** in Irish State Forests and National Parks is not allowed; camping on public land is permissible only if there is no official campsite nearby. Sites cost €5-13, depending on the level of luxury. Northern Ireland treats its campers royally; there are well-equipped campsites throughout (UK£3-8).

COMMUNICATION

PHONE CODES	**Country codes:** 353 (Republic); 44 (Northern Ireland; dial 048 from the Republic). **International dialing prefix:** 00. From outside the Republic of Ireland, dial int'l dialing prefix (see inside back cover) + 353 + city code + local number.

TELEPHONES. Both the Irish Republic and Northern Ireland have public phones that accept coins (€0.20/UK£0.15 for about 4min.) and pre-paid phone cards. In the Republic, dial ☎114 for an international operator, 10 for a national operator, or 11850 for a directory. International direct dial numbers in the Republic include: **AT&T,** ☎800 550 000; **British Telecom,** ☎800 550 144; **Canada Direct,** ☎800 555 001; **MCI,** ☎800 551 001; **New Zealand Direct,** ☎800 550 064; **Telkom South Africa,** ☎800 550 027; and **Telstra Australia,** ☎800 550 061. In Northern Ireland, call ☎155 for an international operator, 100 for a national operator, or 192 for a directory. International direct dial numbers in Northern Ireland include: **AT&T,** ☎0800 013 0011; **Canada Direct,** ☎0800 890 016; **MCI,** ☎800 551 001; **New Zealand Direct,** ☎0800 890 064; **Telkom South Africa,** ☎0800 890 027; **Telstra Australia,** ☎0800 856 6161. For more info on making calls to and from Northern Ireland, see p. 622.

MAIL. In the Republic, postcards and letters up to 25g cost €0.40 domestically and to the UK, €0.45 to the Continent, and €0.60 to any other international destination. Airmail letters take about 6-9 days between Ireland and North America and cost €0.80. Dublin is the only place in the Republic with postal codes. Even-numbered codes are for areas south of the Liffey, odd-numbered are for those north. The North has the same postal system as the rest of the UK (p. 164). Address *Poste Restante* according to the following example: Firstname SURNAME, Poste Restante, Enniscorthy, Co. Wexford, Ireland. The mail will go to a special desk in the central post office, unless you specify otherwise.

INTERNET ACCESS. Internet access is available in cafes, hostels, and most libraries. One hour of web time costs about €4-6; an ISIC card often earns you a discount. Look into a county library membership in the Republic (€2.50-3), which gives unlimited access to participating libraries and their Internet terminals.

DUBLIN ☎01

In a country known for its relaxed pace and rural sanctity, Dublin stands out for its boundless energy and international flair. The city and its suburbs, home to one-third of Ireland's population, are at the vanguard of the country's rapid social change. In an effort to stem international and rural emigration, vast portions of the city have undergone renovation and redevelopment, funded by the deep pockets of the EU. Dublin may hardly look like the rustic "Emerald Isle" promoted on tourist brochures, but its people and history still embody the charm and warmth that have made the country famous.

TRANSPORTATION

Flights: Dublin Airport (DUB; ☎844 4900). **Dublin buses** #41, 41B, and 41C run from the airport to Eden Quay in the city center with stops along the way (every 20min., €1.50). The **Airlink shuttle** (☎844 4265) runs non-stop to Busáras Central Bus Station and O'Connell St. (20-25min., every 10-15min., €3.85) and on to Heuston Station (50min., €4.50). A **taxi** to the city center costs roughly €15-20.

Trains: The **Iarnród Éireann** travel center, 35 Lower Abbey St. (☎836 6222), sells tickets for **Irish Rail.** Open M-F 9am-5pm, Sa 9am-1pm. **Connolly Station,** Amiens St. (☎702 2358), is north of the Liffey and close to Busáras Central Bus Station. Buses #20, 20A, and 90 go from the station to destinations south of the river, and the DART (see below) runs to Tara on the south quay. Trains to **Belfast** (2hr., 5-8 per day, €27) and **Sligo** (3½hr., 3-4 per day, €19). **Heuston Station** (☎703 2132) is south of Victoria Quay, west of the city center (25min. walk from Trinity College). Buses #26, 51, 90, and 79 go to the city center. Trains to: **Cork** (3½hr., 6-11 per day, €43); **Galway** (2½hr., 4-5 per day, €21); **Limerick** (2½hr., 9 per day, €34); **Tralee** (4hr., 4-7 per day, €44); **Waterford** (2½hr., 3-4 per day, €16.50).

Buses: Info available at the **Dublin Bus Office,** 59 O'Connell St. (☎872 0000); the Bus Éireann window is open M-F 9am-5:30pm, Sa 9am-1pm. Buses arrive at **Busáras Central Bus Station** (☎836 6111), on Store St., directly behind the Customs House and next to Connolly Station. Bus Éireann runs to: **Belfast** (3hr., 6-7 per day, €16.50); **Derry** (4¼hr., 4-5 per day, €16.50); **Donegal Town** (4¼hr., 5-6 per day, €13.50); **Galway** (3½hr., 13 per day, €13.30); **Limerick** (3½hr., 7-13 per day, €13.30); **Rosslare Harbour** (3hr., 7-10 per day, €12.70); **Sligo** (4hr., 4-5 per day, €12.10); **Waterford** (2¾hr., 5-7 per day, €8.90).

Ferries: Irish Ferries (☎638 3333) has an office off St. Stephen's Green at 2-4 Merrion Row. Open M-F 9am-5pm, Sa 9:15am-12:45pm. Ferries arrive from **Holyhead, UK** at the **Dublin Port** (☎607 5665), from which buses #53 and 53A run every hr. to Busáras (€1). **Norse Merchant Ferries** also dock at the Dublin Port and run a route to **Liverpool, UK** (7½hr.; 1-2 per day; from €63.50, car from €215); booking for Norse Merchant is only available from **Gerry Feeney,** 19 Eden Quay (☎819 2999). **Stena Line** ferries arrive from Holyhead at the Dún Laoghaire ferry terminal (☎204 7777); DART (see below) trains run from Dún Laoghaire to the Dublin city center. Dublin Bus also runs connection buses timed to fit the ferry schedules (€2.50-3.20).

Public Transportation: Dublin Bus, 59 O'Connell St. (☎873 4222). Open M 8:30am-5:30pm, Tu-F 9am-5:30pm, Sa 9am-1pm. The smaller **City Imp** buses run every 8-15min. Dublin Bus runs the **NiteLink** service to the suburbs (M, W at 12:30am and 2am; Th-Sa nights at 12:30, 1:30, 2:30, and 3:30am; €3.80). **Travel Wide** passes offer unlimited rides for a day (€4.50) or a week (€16.50). **DART** trains serve the suburbs and the coast (every 10-15min., 6:30am-11:30pm, €0.75-1.40).

Taxis: National Radio Cabs, 40 James St. (☎677 2222). €2.75 plus €1.35 per mi. before 10pm, €1.80 per mi. after 10pm.; €1.50 call-in charge.

Car Rental: Budget, 151 Lower Drumcondra Rd. (☎837 9611), and at the airport. In summer from €40 per day, €158 per week; off-season €38/€138. Min. age 23.

Bike Rental: Cycle Ways, 185-6 Parnell St. (☎873 4748). Open M-W and F-Sa 10am-6pm, Th 10am-8pm. €20 per day, €80 per week; deposit €80.

ORIENTATION AND PRACTICAL INFORMATION

The **River Liffey** is the natural divide between Dublin's North and South Sides. Heuston Station and the more famous sights, posh stores, and upscale restaurants are on the **South Side.** Connolly Station and the majority of hostels and the bus station cling to the **North Side.** The streets running alongside the Liffey are called **quays** (KEYS); each bridge over the river has its own name, and streets change names as they cross. If a street running parallel to the river is split into "Upper" and "Lower," then the "Lower" is always the part of the street closer to the mouth of the Liffey. **O'Connell Street,** three blocks west of the Busáras Central Bus Station, is the primary link between north and south Dublin. **Fleet Street** becomes **Temple Bar** one block south of the Liffey. **Dame Street** runs parallel to Temple Bar until **Trinity College,** which defines the southern edge of the district. Trinity College is the nerve center of Dublin's cultural activity, with legions of bookshops and student-oriented pubs. The North Side hawks merchandise cheaper than in the more touristed South. **Henry Street** and **Mary Street** comprise a pedestrian shopping zone that intersects with O'Connell after the **General Post Office (GPO),** two blocks from the Liffey. The North Side has the reputation of being rougher, especially after sunset.

TOURIST, FINANCIAL, AND LOCAL SERVICES

Tourist Information: Main Office, Suffolk St. (☎(1850) 230 330). From Connolly Station, turn left down Amiens St., take a right onto Lower Abbey St., and continue until O'Connell St. Turn left, cross the bridge, and walk past Trinity College; Suffolk St. is on the right. Books rooms for €4 plus a 10% non-refundable deposit. Open July-Aug. M-Sa 9am-8:30pm, Su 11am-5:30pm; Sept.-June M-Sa 9am-5:30pm. The **Northern Ireland Tourist Board,** 16 Nassau St. (☎679 1977 or (1850) 230 230), books accommodations in the North. Open M-F 9:15am-5:30pm, Sa 10am-5pm.

Embassies: Australia, 2nd fl., Fitzwilton House, Wilton Terr. (☎676 1517; www.australianembassy.ie); **Canada,** 65/68 St. Stephen's Green (☎478 1988); **South Africa,** 2nd fl., Alexandra House, Earlsfort Terr. (☎661 5553); **United Kingdom,** 29 Merrion Rd., Ballsbridge (☎205 3700; www.britishembassy.ie); **United States,** 42 Elgin Rd. (☎668 8777). **New Zealanders** should contact their embassy in London.

Banks: Bank of Ireland, AIB, and **TSB** branches with currency exchange and 24hr. **ATMs** cluster on Lower O'Connell St., Grafton St., and in the Suffolk and Dame St. areas. Most bank branches are open M-F 10am-4pm.

American Express: 43 Nassau St. (☎679 9000). Currency exchange; no commission for AmEx Traveler's Cheques. Mail held. Open M-F 9am-5pm.

Luggage Storage: Connolly Station. €2.50 per item per day. Open M-Sa 7:40am-9:20pm, Su 9:10am-9:45pm. **Heuston Station.** €1.90-5.10 per item, depending on size. Open daily 6:30am-10:30pm.

Laundry: The Laundry Shop, 191 Parnell St. (☎872 3541), near Busáras. Wash and dry €8-12. Open M-F 8am-7pm, Sa 9am-6pm, Su 11am-5pm.

EMERGENCY AND COMMUNICATIONS

Emergency: ☎999 or 112; no coins required.

Police *(Garda)*: Dublin Metro Headquarters, Harcourt Terr. (☎666 9500); Store St. Station (☎666 8000); Fitzgibbon St. Station (☎666 8400).

Pharmacy: O'Connell's, 55 Lower O'Connell St. (☎873 0427). Open M-Sa 7:30am-10pm, Su 10am-10pm. Branches throughout the city, including two on Grafton St.

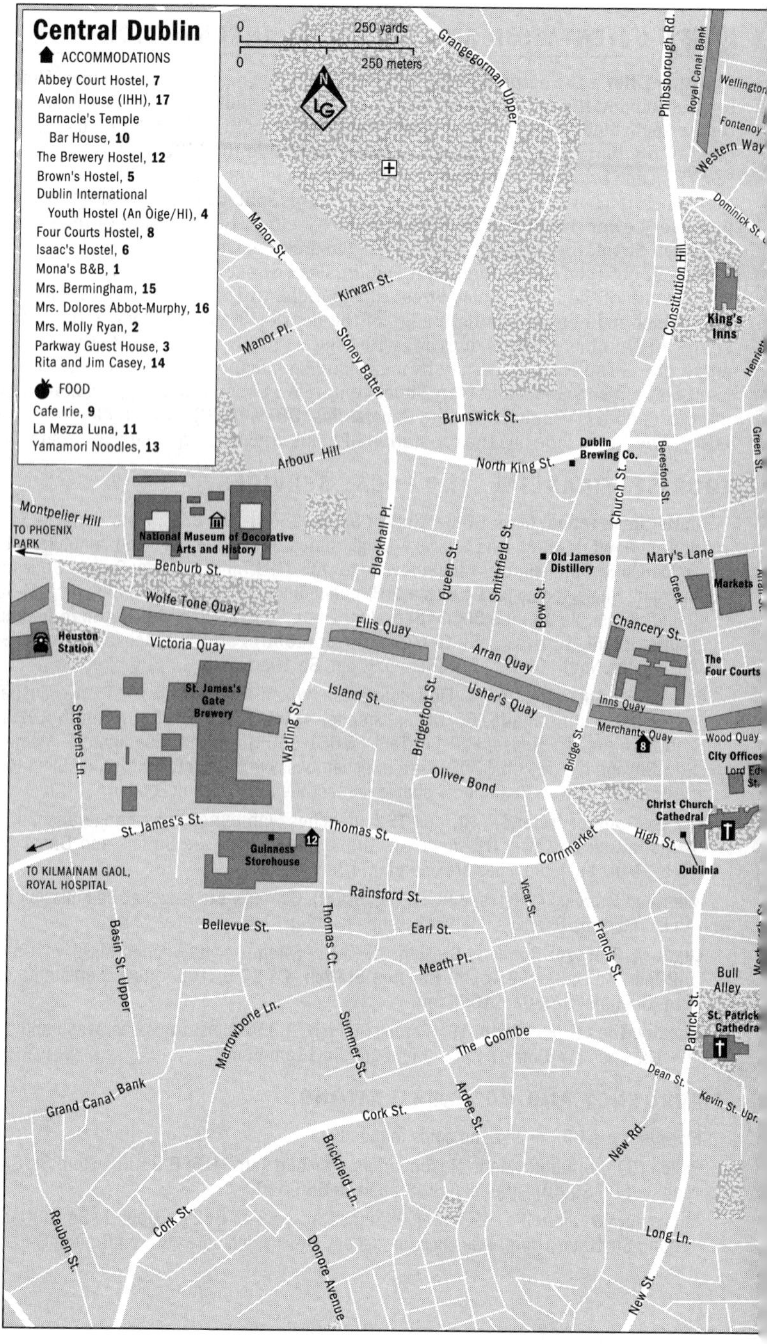

Central Dublin
ACCOMMODATIONS
Abbey Court Hostel, 7
Avalon House (IHH), 17
Barnacle's Temple Bar House, 10
The Brewery Hostel, 12
Brown's Hostel, 5
Dublin International Youth Hostel (An Òige/HI), 4
Four Courts Hostel, 8
Isaac's Hostel, 6
Mona's B&B, 1
Mrs. Bermingham, 15
Mrs. Dolores Abbot-Murphy, 16
Mrs. Molly Ryan, 2
Parkway Guest House, 3
Rita and Jim Casey, 14
FOOD
Cafe Irie, 9
La Mezza Luna, 11
Yamamori Noodles, 13
0 250 yards
0 250 meters
Grangegorman Upper
Phibsborough Rd.
Royal Canal Bank
Wellington
Fontenoy
Western Way
Dominick St.
Manor St.
Kirwan St.
Constitution Hill
King's Inns
Manor Pl.
Stoney Batter
Brunswick St.
Arbour Hill
North King St.
Dublin Brewing Co.
Beresford St.
Green St.
Church St.
Montpelier Hill
TO PHOENIX PARK
National Museum of Decorative Arts and History
Blackhall Pl.
Queen St.
Smithfield St.
Old Jameson Distillery
Mary's Lane
Benburb St.
Bow St.
Greek
Markets
Wolfe Tone Quay
Ellis Quay
Chancery St.
Heuston Station
Victoria Quay
Arran Quay
The Four Courts
St. James's Gate Brewery
Island St.
Usher's Quay
Inns Quay
Steevens Ln.
Watling St.
Bridgefoot St.
Bridge St.
Merchants Quay
8
Wood Quay
City Offices
Lord Edward St.
Oliver Bond
Christ Church Cathedral
St. James's St.
Thomas St.
12
Guinness Storehouse
High St.
Cornmarket
Dublinia
TO KILMAINAM GAOL, ROYAL HOSPITAL
Rainsford St.
Vicar St.
Basin St. Upper
Bellevue St.
Thomas Ct.
Earl St.
Francis St.
Meath Pl.
Bull Alley
Marrowbone Ln.
Summer St.
Patrick St.
St. Patrick's Cathedral
The Coombe
Dean St.
Grand Canal Bank
Ardee St.
Kevin St. Upr.
Cork St.
New Rd.
Brickfield Ln.
Cork St.
Long Ln.
Reuben St.
Donore Avenue
New St.

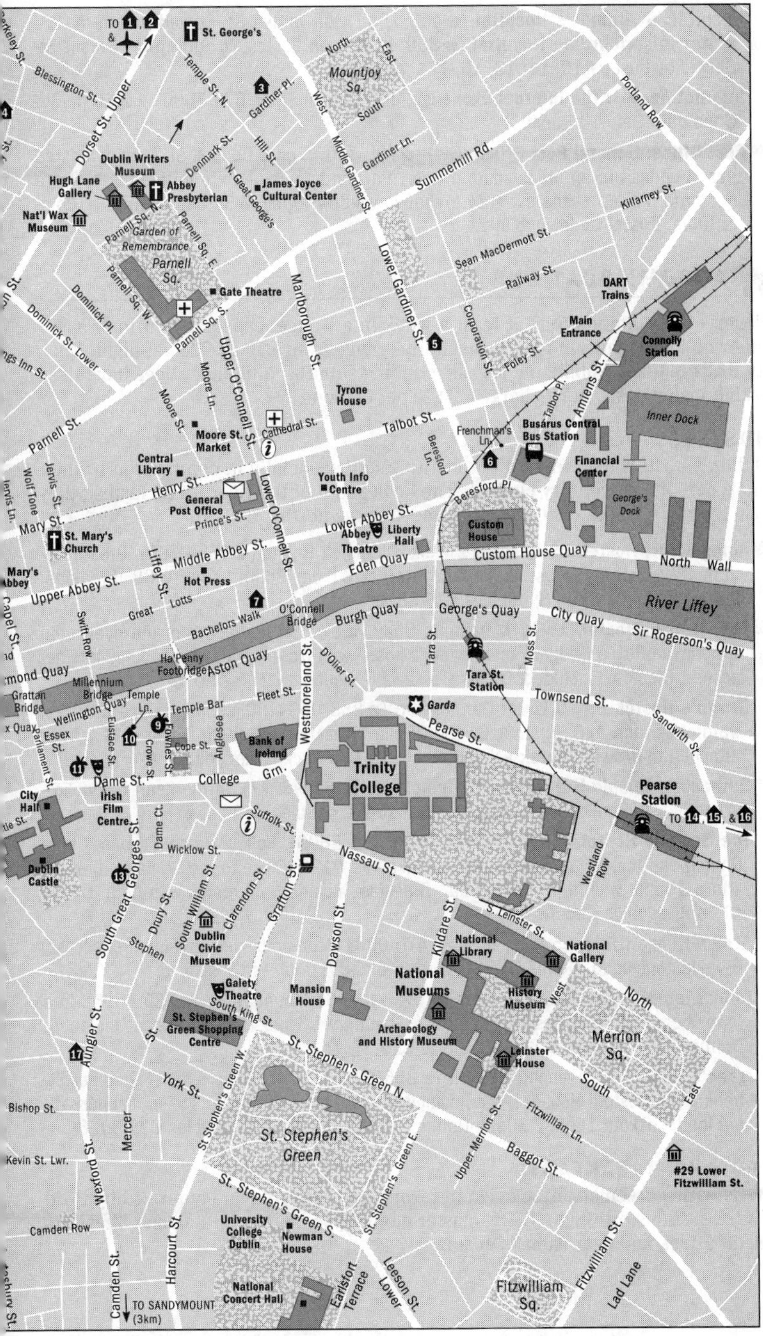
TO 1, 2 &
St. George's
Blessington St.
Dorset St. Upper
Temple St. N.
Gardiner Pl.
North
East
Mountjoy Sq.
West
South
Portland Row
Denmark St.
Hill St.
N. Great George's
Middle Gardiner St.
Gardiner Ln.
Summerhill Rd.
Dublin Writers Museum
Hugh Lane Gallery
Abbey Presbyterian
James Joyce Cultural Center
Nat'l Wax Museum
Parnell Sq. N.
Garden of Remembrance
Parnell Sq. E.
Parnell Sq.
Parnell Sq. W.
Killarney St.
Sean MacDermott St.
Lower Gardiner St.
Railway St.
Gate Theatre
Marlborough St.
Dominick Pl.
Dominick St. Lower
Parnell Sq. S.
DART Trains
Main Entrance
Connolly Station
Corporation St.
Foley St.
Upper O'Connell St.
Moore Ln.
Moore St.
Tyrone House
Amiens St.
Talbot Pl.
Inner Dock
Parnell St.
Moore St. Market
Cathedral St.
Talbot St.
Frenchman's Ln.
Busárus Central Bus Station
Beresford Ln.
Central Library
Financial Center
Henry St.
Lower O'Connell St.
Youth Info Centre
Beresford Pl.
General Post Office
George's Dock
Jervis St.
Wolf Tone St.
Mary St.
Prince's St.
Lower Abbey St.
Custom House
St. Mary's Church
Abbey Theatre
Liberty Hall
Middle Abbey St.
Custom House Quay
North Wall
Mary's Abbey
Liffey St.
Eden Quay
Hot Press
Upper Abbey St.
River Liffey
Capel St.
Great
Lotts
Bachelors Walk
O'Connell Bridge
Burgh Quay
George's Quay
City Quay
Swift Row
Sir Rogerson's Quay
Tara St.
Moss St.
Ha'Penny Footbridge
Aston Quay
Westmoreland St.
D'Olier St.
Tara St. Station
Millennium Bridge
Grattan Bridge
Wellington Quay
Temple Ln.
Temple Bar
Fleet St.
Garda
Townsend St.
Essex St.
Parliament St.
Eustace St.
Crowe St.
Fownes St.
Cope St.
Anglesea
Bank of Ireland
Pearse St.
Sandwith St.
Trinity College
Dame St.
College Grn.
City Hall
Irish Film Centre
Dame Ct.
Suffolk St.
Pearse Station
TO 14, 15, & 16
Wicklow St.
Nassau St.
Westland Row
Dublin Castle
South Great Georges St.
Drury St.
South William St.
Clarendon St.
Grafton St.
Dawson St.
Kildare St.
S. Leinster St.
Stephen
Dublin Civic Museum
National Library
National Gallery
Galety Theatre
Mansion House
National Museums
History Museum
West
North
South King St.
St. Stephen's Green Shopping Centre
Archaeology and History Museum
Leinster House
Merrion Sq.
Aungier St.
St. Stephen's Green N.
York St.
St. Stephen's Green W.
South
East
Bishop St.
Fitzwilliam Ln.
Upper Merrion St.
Mercer
St. Stephen's Green
St. Stephen's Green E.
Baggot St.
Kevin St. Lwr.
Wexford St.
St. Stephen's Green S.
#29 Lower Fitzwilliam St.
Camden Row
University College Dublin
Newman House
Fitzwilliam St.
Harcourt St.
National Concert Hall
Earlsfort Terrace
Leeson St. Lower
Fitzwilliam Sq.
Lad Lane
Camden St.
TO SANDYMOUNT (3km)

IRELAND

Hospital: St. James's Hospital (☎453 7941), on James St. Served by bus #123. **Mater Misericordiae Hospital** (☎830 1122), on Eccles St., off Lower Dorset St. Served by buses #10, 11, 13, 16, 121, and 122.

Internet Access: The Internet Exchange, 146 Parnell St. (☎670 3000). €2.50 per hr. Open daily 9am-10:30pm.

Post Office: General Post Office (GPO; ☎705 7000), on O'Connell St. Even-numbered postal codes are for areas south of the Liffey, odd-numbered are for the north. *Poste Restante* pick-up at the currency exchange window. Open M-Sa 8am-8pm, Su 10am-6:30pm. **Postal Code:** Dublin 1.

ACCOMMODATIONS

Reserve accommodations at least a week in advance, especially during Easter, other holidays, and summer. **Hostel** dorms range from €10 to €24 per night. Quality **B&Bs** blanket Dublin and the surrounding suburbs, although prices have risen with housing costs; most charge €20-40 per person.

HOSTELS

Dublin's hostels lean toward the institutional, especially in comparison to their more personable country cousins. The beds south of the river fill up fastest; they also tend to be more expensive than those to the north.

Abbey Court Hostel, 29 Bachelor's Walk, O'Connell Bridge (☎878 0700). Great location. Clean rooms, most with bath. Internet €1 per 8min. Laundry €8. Breakfast included. Dorms €17-28; doubles €76-88. ❷

Four Courts Hostel, 15-17 Merchants Quay (☎672 5839), south of the river, near O'Donovan Rossa Bridge. First-rate mega-hostel with clean rooms and parking. Internet access. Breakfast included. Dorms €15-21.50; doubles €27-32.50. ❷

Brown's Hostel, 89-90 Lower Gardiner St. (☎855 0034). Glistening rooms with TVs, wardrobes, and A/C. Internet €1 per 20min. Breakfast included. Dorms €12.50-25. Attached to **Brown's Hotel;** ask for the hotel's €75 backpacker special. ❶

Barnacle's Temple Bar House, 19 Temple Ln. (☎671 6277). In the heart of Dublin—expect noise. Breakfast included. Dorms €15-23; doubles €62-74. ❷

The Brewery Hostel, 22-23 Thomas St. (☎453 8600). Follow Dame St. past Christ Church and through name changes, or take bus #123. Close to the Guinness brewery and a 15min. walk from Temple Bar. Breakfast included. All rooms with bath. Dorms €16-28; doubles €65-78. ❷

Avalon House (IHH), 55 Aungier St. (☎475 0001). Top-notch security. Internet access. Breakfast included. Dorms €15-30; singles €30-37; doubles €28-35. ❷

Dublin International Youth Hostel (An Óige/HI), 61 Mountjoy St. (☎830 4555). In a former convent. Shuttles to Temple Bar. Laundry €5 per load. Breakfast included. Dorms €19-20; doubles €26-28; triples €25-27. ❷

Isaac's Hostel, 2-5 Frenchman's Ln. (☎855 6215), off the lower end of Gardiner St. behind the Custom House. Large hostel with cafe. Internet €1 per 15min. Laundry €8 per load. Lockout 11am-2:30pm. Dorms €12-20; singles €32; doubles €28.50. ❶

BED AND BREAKFASTS

B&Bs with a green shamrock sign out front are registered and approved by Bord Fáilte. On the North Side, B&Bs cluster along **Upper** and **Lower Gardiner Street,** on **Sheriff Street,** and near **Parnell Square.**

Parkway Guest House, 5 Gardiner Pl. (☎874 0469), just off Gardiner St. Clean rooms in an excellent location. Singles €32; doubles €52-60, with bath €60-70. ❸

Mona's B&B, 148 Clonliffe Rd. (☎837 6723). Gorgeous house. Full Irish breakfasts. Open May-Oct only. Singles €35; doubles €66. ❸

Mrs. Bermingham, 8 Dromard Terr. (☎668 3861), on Dromard Ave. Take the #2 or 3 bus and get off at Tesco. Soft, comfortable beds. Open Feb.-Nov. only. Singles €28; doubles with bath €52. ❸

Mrs. Dolores Abbot-Murphy, 14 Castle Park (☎269 8413). Take the #3 bus to Sandymount Green. Continue past Browne's Deli and take the 1st left; it's on the right at the end of the road. A 5min. walk from Sandymount DART stop. Cheerful rooms in a charming cul-de-sac. Open May-Oct. only. Singles €28; doubles €56. ❸

Rita and Jim Casey, Villa Jude, 2 Church Ave. (☎668 4982), off Beach Rd. Bus #3 to the 1st stop on Tritonville Rd.; Church Ave. is back a few yards. Call for directions from the Lansdowne Rd. DART stop. Clean rooms and big breakfasts. Doubles €22.50. ❷

Mrs. Molly Ryan, 10 Distillery Rd. (☎837 4147), off Clonliffe Rd. Small rooms, small prices, no breakfast. Singles €15; doubles €30. ❷

CAMPING

Most campsites are far away from the city center, and while it may be convenient, camping in **Phoenix Park** is both illegal and unsafe.

Camac Valley Tourist Caravan & Camping Park (☎464 0644), Naas Rd., Clondalkin, near Corkagh Park. Accessible by bus #69 (35min. from city center, €1.50). Food shop and kitchen facilities. Laundry €4.50. Hikers/cyclists €7; 2 people with car €14. ❶

Shankill Caravan and Camping Park (☎282 0011). The DART and buses #45 and 84 from Eden Quay run to Shankill, as does bus #45A from the Dún Laoghaire ferryport. Showers €1. €2 per adult, €1 per child; €9 per tent. ❶

FOOD

Dublin's **open-air markets** sell fresh and cheap fixings. On Saturdays, a gourmet open-air market takes place in Temple Bar in Meeting House Square. The cheapest **supermarkets** around Dublin are the **Dunnes Stores** chain, with branches at St. Stephen's Green (open M-W and F-Sa 8:30am-7pm; Th 8:30am-9pm; Su noon-6pm), the ILAC Centre off Henry St., and North Earl St. **Temple Bar** has creative eateries catering to every budget.

La Mezza Luna, 1 Temple Ln. (☎671 2840), on the corner of Dame St. Refined but not pretentious. Try the wok-fried chicken (€8.25). Entrees €5-10. Open M-Th 8am-11pm, F-Sa 9:30am-11:30pm, Su 9:30am-10:30pm. ❷

Cafe Irie, 11 Fownes St. (☎672 5090), above the clothing store Sé Sí Progressive. A small eatery with an impressive selection of sandwiches under €4. Great coffee. Vegan-friendly. Open M-Sa 9am-8pm, Su noon-6pm. ❶

Zaytoons, 14-15 Parliament St. (☎677 3595). Persian food served on big platters of warm bread. Excellent chicken kebab €6.50. Open M-Sa noon-4am. ❷

Queen of Tarts, 3 Cork Hill (☎670 7499). This little gem offers homemade pastries, scones, cakes, and coffee. Desserts from €3.75; continental breakfast €4-6. Open M-F 7:30am-6pm, Sa 9am-6pm, Su 10am-6pm. ❶

Yamamori Noodles, 71-72 S. Great Georges St. (☎475 5001). Exceptional Japanese cuisine. Entrees €12-14. Open Su-W and Su 12:30-11pm, Th-Sa 12:30-11:30pm. ❸

THE HIDDEN DEAL

THE EMERALD ISLE'S GOLDEN EGG

Many of Ireland's most touristed sights—its national parks, museums, monuments and gardens—are owned and operated by the Irish Department of Arts and Heritage. While the price of admission to these sights is typically quite low, the accumulated cost of visiting each may start to overwhelm the budget traveler.

Recently, the Department of Heritage began to offer the **Dúchas Heritage Discount Card,** perhaps Ireland's greatest hidden deal. The card grants access to all of the sights owned and operated by the Department of Heritage for one full year. At €19, the card is worthwhile even for those in Ireland for a short time; the savings start to accrue after visiting only three or four Heritage sights, whose individual admissions average €5-7.

The card will prove valuable for most Irish itineraries. It covers sights across the isle, including Kilmainham Gaol in Dublin, Kilkenny Castle, the Brú na Bóinne Visitors Centre in Newgrange, and Reginald's Tower in Waterford. The card can be purchased online and at Dúchas Heritage sights.

(Info ☎1850 600 601; international ☎01 647 2461; www.heritageireland.ie/en/HeritageCard. €19, students and children €7.60, seniors €12.70, families €45.75.)

SIGHTS

Most of Dublin's sights lie less than 2km from O'Connell Bridge. The **Historical Walking Tour** provides a 2hr. crash course in Irish history. Meet at Trinity College's front gate. (☎878 0227. Tours May-Sept. M-F 11am and 3pm; Sa-Su 11am, noon, and 3pm. Oct.-Apr. F-Su noon. €10, students €8.)

TRINITY COLLEGE AND ENVIRONS

TRINITY COLLEGE. Ancient walls surround Trinity's expanse of stone buildings, cobblestone walks, and green grounds. The British built Trinity in 1592 as a Protestant religious seminary that would "civilize the Irish and cure them of Popery." Jonathan Swift, Robert Emmett, Thomas Moore, Edmund Burke, Oscar Wilde, and Samuel Beckett are just a few of the famous Irishmen who studied here. Until the 1960s, the Catholic church deemed it a cardinal sin to attend Trinity; once the church lifted the ban, the size of the student body more than tripled. *(Between Westmoreland and Grafton St. The main entrance is on College Green. Pearse St. runs along the north edge of the college, Nassau St. to its south. Grounds open 24hr. Free.)* **Trinity College Walking Tour** is run by students and concentrates on University lore. *(June-Sept. daily 10:15am–3:40pm; Mar.-May weekends only. Tours leave roughly every 45min. from the info booth inside the front gate. €7, students €6; includes admission to the Old Library.)*

THE OLD LIBRARY. This 1712 chamber holds a priceless collection of ancient manuscripts, including the magnificent **Book of Kells.** Around AD 800, Irish monks squeezed multicolored ink from plants to illuminate this four-volume edition of the Gospels. *(From Trinity's main gate, go straight; the library is on the south side of Library Sq. Open June-Sept. M-Sa 9:30am-5pm, Su noon-4:30pm; Oct.-May M-Sa 9:30am-5pm, Su noon-4:30pm. €6, students and seniors €4.)*

GRAFTON STREET. The area south of College Green, off-limits to cars, is a haven for tourists and residents alike. Grafton's **street performers** range from string octets to jive limboists. Upstairs at the Grafton St. branch of Bewley's, a coffee chain, is the **Bewley's Museum,** located inside the company's former chocolate factory. Tea-tasting machines and a display on Bewley's Quaker heritage are among the curiosities. *(Open daily 7:30am-11pm. Free.)*

KILDARE STREET AND NATIONAL MUSEUMS

General information for all three National Museums ☎677 7444. All open Tu-Sa 10am-5pm, Su 2-5pm. Free.

The Museum Link runs from the Natural History and Archeology museums to Collins Barracks roughly once an hour. One-way €1; all-day pass €2.50.

The **National Museum of Archaeology and History** is Dublin's largest museum and has extraordinary artifacts spanning the last two millennia, including the **Tara Brooch,** the **Ardagh Hoard,** and other Celtic gold work. *(Kildare St., adjacent to Leinster House.)* The **Natural History Museum** displays fascinating examples of classic taxidermy. *(Upper Merrion St.)* The Collins Barracks are home to the **National Museum of Decorative Arts and History,** which features an impressive collection of furniture, textiles, costumes, and silver. *(On Benburb St., off Wolfe Tone Quay. Take the Museum Link, or bus #10 from O'Connell. Bus #90 to Heuston Station stops across the street.)* The **National Gallery** has a collection of over 2400 paintings, including canvases by Bruegel, Goya, Caravaggio, Vermeer, Rembrandt, and El Greco. *(Merrion Sq. West. Open M-W and F-Sa 9:30am-5:30pm, Th 10am-8:30pm, Su noon-5pm. Free.)* The **National Library** chronicles Irish history and exhibits literary curios in its entrance room. A genealogical research room can help families trace the thinnest tendrils of their Irish family tree. *(On Kildare St. Open M-W 10am-9pm, Th-F 10am-5pm, Sa 10am-1pm. Free.)*

TEMPLE BAR

West of Trinity, between Dame St. and the Liffey, the Temple Bar neighborhood has rapidly become one of Europe's hottest night spots. Narrow neo-cobblestone streets link cheap cafes, hole-in-the-wall theaters, rock venues, and used clothing stores. The government-sponsored Temple Bar Properties spent over IR£30 million to build a fleet of arts-related attractions. Among the most inviting are: **The Irish Film Centre,** 6 Eustace St., which screens specialty and art house film; Ireland's only **Gallery of Photography,** in Meeting House Sq.; and the **Temple Bar Gallery & Studios,** 5-9 Temple Bar.

IRELAND

DAME STREET AND THE CATHEDRALS

DUBLIN CASTLE. King John built the castle in 1204 on top of the Viking settlement of Dubh Linn and for 700 years, it was the seat of British rule in Ireland. Since 1938, presidents of Ireland have been inaugurated here. *(On Dame St., at the intersection of Parliament and Castle St. Open M-F 10am-5pm, Sa-Su 2-5pm. €4.50, students and seniors €3.50. Grounds free.)*

ST. PATRICK'S CATHEDRAL. Ireland's largest cathedral dates to the 12th century, although Sir Benjamin Guinness remodeled much of it in 1864. St. Patrick allegedly baptized converts in nearby park. Jonathan Swift was the Dean of St. Patrick's; his crypt is above the south nave. *(On Patrick St. Take bus #49, 49A, 50, 54A, 56A, 65, 65B, 77, or 77A from Eden Quay. Open Mar.-Oct. daily 9am-6pm; Nov.-Feb. Sa 9am-5pm, Su 9am-3pm. €4, students, seniors, and children free.)*

CHRIST CHURCH CATHEDRAL. Sitric Silkenbeard, King of the Dublin Norsemen, built a church on this site around 1038; Strongbow rebuilt it in stone in 1169. Further additions were made in the following century and again in the 1870s. Stained glass sparkles above the raised crypts, and fragments of ancient pillars are scattered about like bleached bones. *(At the end of Dame St., across from the castle. Take bus #50 from Eden Quay or 78A from Aston Quay. Open daily 9:45am-5:30pm except during services. Suggested donation €3.)*

GUINNESS BREWERY AND KILMAINHAM

GUINNESS STOREHOUSE. Guinness brews its black magic at the St. James Gate Brewery. Farsighted Arthur Guinness signed a 9000-year lease in 1759 for the original building. The lease is displayed in the atrium of the nearby Storehouse, an architectural triumph that rises seven floors and has a center shaped like a pint

THE LOCAL STORY

THE PERFECT PINT

Bartender Glenn, of a local Dublin pub, helps Let's Go *answer the most significant question of all...*

LG: Tell us, what's the most important thing about pouring a pint?
BG: The most important thing is to have the keg as close to the tap as possible. The closer, the better.
LG: And why's that?
BG: Well, you don't want the Guinness sitting in a long tube while you wait to pour the next pint. You want to pull it straight out of the keg, without any muck getting in between.
LG: Does stopping to let the Guinness settle make a big difference?
BG: Well, you can top it straight off if you want, but you might get too big a head with that. You don't want too small or big a head, so if you stop ¾ of the way, you can adjust the pint until the head is perfect. A true Guinness lover will taste the difference.
LG: Because of the head?
BG: No, because of the gas. If you pull the Guinness straight from the tap and get a big head, it means you've gotten too much gas. It kills the taste. Thats why you have to tilt the glass.
LG: Anything else to look for?
BG: Well what you don't want is a window-clean glass; you don't want a glass that you can see through when you're done. Good Guinness leaves a healthy film on the glass. If it doesn't, you didn't get a good Guinness.
LG: Well, Glenn, you sure make pouring pints sound like an art form.
BG: Oh aye, but only with Guinness—everything else you just chuck into a glass and hand out.

glass. View the exhibit on Guinness's infamously clever advertising—and then drink, silly tourist, drink. *(On St. James's Gate. From Christ Church Cathedral, follow High St. west through its name changes: Cornmarket, Thomas, and James. Take bus #51B or 78A from Aston Quay or #123 from O'Connell St. Open Apr.-Sept. daily 9:30am-7pm; Oct.-Mar. 9:30am-5pm. €12, students €8, seniors and children €5.30.)*

KILMAINHAM GAOL. Almost all of the rebels who fought in Ireland's struggle for independence from 1792 to 1921 spent time in this prison. Tours wind through the chilly limestone corridors and end in the haunting execution yard. *(On Inchicore Rd. Take bus #51 from Aston Quay, #51A from Lower Abbey St., or #79 from Aston Quay. Open Apr.-Sept. daily 9:30am-4:45pm; Oct.-Mar. M-F 9:30am-4pm, Su 10am-4:45pm. €4.40, seniors €3.10, students and children €1.90.)*

O'CONNELL ST. AND PARNELL SQUARE

HUGH LANE MUNICIPAL GALLERY OF MODERN ART. In the early 20th century, Dubliners refused to finance a gallery to hold Lane's collection of French Impressionist paintings; although the gallery was eventually constructed, Yeats lamented his city's provincial attitude in a string of poems. *(Buses #3, 10, 11, 13, 16, and 19 all stop near the gallery, in Parnell Sq. Open Tu-Th 9:30am-6pm, F-Sa 9:30am-5pm, Su 11am-5pm. Free; occasional special exhibits may charge.)*

THE DUBLIN WRITERS' MUSEUM. The city's literary heritage comes to life at this museum, which displays rare editions and memorabilia of Swift, Shaw, Wilde, Yeats, Beckett, Brendan Behan, Patrick Kavanagh, and Sean O'Casey. *(18 Parnell Sq. North. Open June-Aug. M-F 10am-6pm, Sa 10am-5pm, Su 11am-5pm; Sept.-May M-Sa 10am-5pm. €5.50, students and seniors €5. Combined ticket with James Joyce Centre €9/€8.)*

JAMES JOYCE CULTURAL CENTRE. This museum features a wide range of Joyceana, including portraits of the individuals who inspired his characters. Call for info on lectures, walking tours, and Bloomsday events. *(35 N. Great Georges St., past Parnell St. ☎878 8547. Open July-Aug. M-Sa 9:30am-5pm, Su 11am-5pm; Sept.-June M-Sa 9:30am-5pm, Su 12:30-5pm. €4, students and seniors €3.)*

ELSEWHERE

OLD JAMESON DISTILLERY. Learn how science, grain, and tradition come together to create the golden fluid called **whiskey.** The experience ends with a free glass of the stuff. *(On Bow St. From O'Connell St., turn onto Henry St. and continue straight as the street dwin-*

dles to Mary St., then Mary Ln., then May Ln.; the warehouse is on a cobblestone street on the left. Tours daily 9:30am-5:30pm. €6.50, students and seniors €3.80.)

PHOENIX PARK. Europe's largest enclosed public park is most famous for the 1882 "Phoenix Park murders." The Invincibles, a tiny nationalist splinter group, stabbed the Chief Secretary of Ireland, Lord Cavendish, and his Undersecretary 180m from the **Phoenix Column.** The 712-hectare park incorporates the President's residence *(Áras an Uachtaraín)* and **Dublin Zoo,** Europe's largest. It contains 700 animals and the world's biggest egg. *(Take bus #10 from O'Connell St. or #25 or 26 from Middle Abbey St. Park always open. Free. Zoo open June-Aug. M-Sa 9:30am-6pm, Su 10:30am-6pm. Closes at sunset in winter. €8, students €6.)*

ENTERTAINMENT AND NIGHTLIFE

Whether you fancy poetry or punk, Dublin is equipped to entertain you. The free *Event Guide* is available at the tourist office and Temple Bar restaurants. The **Abbey Theatre,** 26 Lower Abbey St., was founded in 1904 by Yeats and Lady Gregory to promote Irish culture and modernist theater. (☎878 7222. Box office open M-Sa 10:30am-7pm. Tickets €12-25; M-Th student rate €10.) **St. Patrick's Day** (Mar. 17) and the half-week leading up to it host a carnival of concerts, fireworks, street theater, and intoxicated madness. (☎675 3205; www.paddyfest.ie.) Dublin returns to 1904 on **Bloomsday** (June 16), the day of Leopold Bloom's journey in Joyce's *Ulysses*. The James Joyce Cultural Centre (☎873 1984) sponsors a reenactment of the funeral and wake, a lunch at Davy Byrne's, and a Guinness breakfast.

Trad (traditional music) is an important element of the Dublin music scene—some pubs in the city center have sessions nightly. The best pub for *trad* is **Cobblestones** (☎872 1799), on King St. North, in Smithfield. James Joyce once proposed that a "good puzzle would be to cross Dublin without passing a pub." A radio station once offered IR£100 to the first person to solve the puzzle. The winner explained that you could take any route—you'd just have to visit them all on the way. *Let's Go* recommends beginning your journey at the gates of Trinity College, moving onto Grafton St., stumbling onto Camden St., teetering down S. Great Georges St., and, finally, triumphantly crawling into the Temple Bar area.

PUBS

The Celts, 81-82 Talbots St. Step into Olde Ireland. A welcoming pub with nightly *trad.* Open Su-W 10:30am-11:30pm, Th-Sa 10:30am-12:30am.

Zanzibar, at the Ha'Penny Bridge. A hot spot with dancing. DJ M-Th from 10pm, F-Sa from 9pm. Open M-Th 5pm-2:30am, F-Sa 4pm-2:30am, Su 4pm-1am.

Whelan's, 25 Wexford St., down S. Great Georges St. The stage venue in back hosts big-name *trad* and rock, with live music every night at 9:30pm (doors open 8pm). Cover €7-12. Open for lunch daily 12:30-2:30pm; pub open W-Sa until late.

The Stag's Head, 1 Dame Ct. This beautiful Victorian pub has a largely student crowd. Excellent food. Entrees about €10. Food served M-F noon-3:30pm and 5-7pm, Sa 12:30-2:30pm. Open M-W 11:30am-11:30pm; Th-Sa 11:30am-12:30am.

The Long Stone, 10-11 Townsend St. Hand-carved banisters and old books give the place a rustic feel. Lots of interesting rooms; the largest has an enormous carving of a bearded man whose mouth serves as a fireplace. Lunch 12:30-2:30pm. Open M-W noon-11:30pm, Th-F 10am-12:30am, Sa 3pm-12:30am, Su 4-11pm.

Messrs. Maguire, on Burgh Quay. Homemade microbrews. *Trad* Su-Tu 9:30-11:30pm. Open Su-Tu 10:30am-12:30am, W-Th 10:30am-1:30am, F 10:30am-2am, Sa 12:30pm-2am.

CLUBS

The PoD, 35 Harcourt St. Spanish-style decor meets hard core dance music. The brave venture upstairs to **The Red Box** (☎478 0225), a separate club with a warehouse atmosphere. Often hosts big-name DJs, when cover charges skyrocket. Cover €10-20; Th and Sa €7 with ISIC; Th ladies free before midnight. Open until 3am.

Rí-Rá, 1 Exchequer St. Good music that steers clear of pop and house extremes. Two floors, several bars, lots of nooks and crannies. Cover €7-10. Open daily 11pm-2am.

Gaiety, S. King St., just off Grafton St. This elegant theater shows its wild side late night, with DJs and live music from salsa to soul. Cover from €10. Open F-Sa midnight-4am.

The George, 89 S. Great Georges St. Dublin's first and most prominent gay bar. All ages gather throughout the day to chat and drink. The attached nightclub is open W-Su until 2am. Frequent theme nights. Dress well—no effort, no entry. Cover €8-10 after 10pm.

DAYTRIPS FROM DUBLIN

HOWTH

Take a northbound DART train to the end of the line (30min., 6 per hr., €1.50).

Howth (rhymes with "both") dangles from the mainland in Edenic isolation, less than 16km from Dublin. A 3hr. **cliff walk** circles the peninsula, passing heather and thousands of seabird nests. The best section of the walk is a 1hr. hike between the harbor and the lighthouse at the southeast tip. To get to the trailhead from town, turn left at the DART station and follow Harbour Rd. around the coast for about 20min. Just offshore is **Ireland's Eye,** a former sanctuary for monks that has become an avian refuge. **Ireland's Eye Boat Trips,** on the East Pier, jets passengers across the water. (☎01 831 4200. €8 round-trip, students and children €4.) To reach the private **Howth Castle,** which features a curiously charming patchwork of architectural styles, turn right as you exit the DART station and then left after 400m, at the entrance to the Deer Park Hotel. Turn left out of the station to get to the **tourist office,** in the Old Courthouse on Harbour Rd. (☎01 832 0405. Open May-Aug. M-F 11am-1pm, also Tu-F 1:30-5pm.)

BOYNE VALLEY

From Dublin, Bus Éireann shuttles to the Brú na Bóinne Visitors Centre (1½hr., 1-4 per hr., €12.70 round-trip) and Trim Castle (1hr.; M-Sa every hr., Su 3 per day; €10.20).

The thinly populated Boyne Valley hides Ireland's greatest archaeological treasures. Along the curves of the river between Slane and Drogheda lie no fewer than 40 crypt-like passages constructed by the Neolithics around the 4th millenium BC. **Newgrange** is the most spectacular; a roof box over the entrance allows a solitary beam of sunlight to shine directly into the tomb for 17min. on the winter solstice, a breathtaking experience simulated on the tour. You may only enter Newgrange by admission at **Brú na Bóinne Visitors Centre,** near Donore on the south side of the River Boyne, across from the tombs. (☎041 988 0300. Open June to mid-Sept. daily 9am-7pm; May and late Sept. 9am-6:30pm; Mar.-Apr. and Oct. 9:30am-5:30pm; Nov.-Feb. 9:30am-5pm. Center and 1hr. tour €5, students €2.50.) A group of well-preserved Norman castles—including **Trim Castle,** conquered by Mel Gibson in *Braveheart*—overlooks **Trim** proper on the River Boyne. (Open May-Oct. 10am-6pm. Tours every 45min. Limited to 15 people; sign up upon arrival in Trim. Grounds only €1.20. Tour and grounds €3.10, students €1.20.) The Trim **visitors center** is on Mill St. (☎046 37 227. Open M-W and F-Sa 10am-5pm; Su noon-5:30pm.)

DÚN LAOGHAIRE

Reach Dún Laoghaire by DART from Dublin (£1.40).

As one of County Dublin's major ferry ports, Dún Laoghaire (dun-LEER-ee) is many tourists' first peek at Ireland. Fortunately, it makes a good spot to begin a ramble along the coast south of Dublin. The **harbor** itself is a sight, filled with yachts, boat tours, car ferries, fishermen, and a new marina. **James Joyce Tower** in Sandycove is a fascinating retreat. From the Sandycove DART station, go left at Eagle House down to the coast, turn right and continue to the Martello tower; alternatively, take bus #8 from Burgh Quay in Dublin to Sandycove Ave. James Joyce stayed in the tower for a tense six days in August 1904 as a guest of Oliver St. John Gogarty. The infamous Gogarty was immortalized in Chapter One of *Ulysses*. The two-room museum contains Joyce's death mask, a draft page of *Finnegan's Wake*, and several editions of *Ulysses*, including one illustrated by Henri Matisse. (☎280 9265. Open Apr.-Oct. M-Sa 10am-1pm and 2-5pm, Su 2-6pm; Nov.-Mar. by appointment. €5.50, students and seniors €5.) The **tourist office** is in the ferry terminal. (Open M-Sa 10am-6pm.) **Belgrave Hall ❷,** 34 S. Belgrave Sq., is a top-tier hostel that feels old but not run-down. (☎284 2106. Breakfast included. Laundry €7. F-Su dorms €25; M-Th €20. Off-season €2 less.)

IRELAND

SOUTHEAST IRELAND

A base first for the Vikings and then the Normans, the Southeast echoes a fainter Celtic influence than the rest of Ireland. Town and street names in this region reflect Norse, Norman, and Anglo-Saxon influences rather than Gaelic ones. The Southeast's busiest attractions are its beaches, which draw admirers to the coastline stretching from Kilmore Quay to tidy Ardmore.

FERRIES TO FRANCE AND BRITAIN

Irish Ferries (☎053 33 158) sails from Rosslare Harbour to Pembroke, Wales (4hr., every day, €28-38) and Roscoff and Cherbourg, France (18hr., every other day). **Eurail** passes grant passage on ferries to France. **Stena Line** (☎053 61 567) runs from Rosslare Harbour to Fishguard, Wales (3½hr., €28-35).

THE WICKLOW MOUNTAINS ☎0404

Over 600m high, carpeted in fragrant heather, and pleated by sparkling rivers, the Wicklow summits are home to grazing sheep and scattered villages. Smooth glacial valleys embrace the two lakes and the monastic ruins. Public transportation is severely limited, so driving is the easiest way to get around. The lush, blessed valley of **Glendalough** draws a steady summertime stream of coach tours filled with hikers and ruin-oglers. The **National Park Information Office,** between the two lakes, is the best source for hiking advice. (☎45 425. Open May-Aug. daily 10am-6pm; Apr. and Sept. Sa-Su 10am-6pm.) **St. Kevin's Bus Service** (☎(01) 281 8119) arrives in town from St. Stephen's Green in Dublin (2 per day, €13 round-trip). The **tourist office** is across from the Glendalough Hotel. (☎45 688. Open from mid-June to Sept. M-Sa 10am-1pm and 2-6pm.) Good beds are at **The Glendaloch Hostel (An Óige/HI) ❷,** 5min. up the road from the tourist office. (☎45 342. Internet €2 per 20min. Bike rental. Laundry €5. Dorms €19.50; doubles €43; off-season €2 less.) For more affordable food, B&Bs, and groceries, head to **Laragh,** 1.5km up the road.

ROSSLARE HARBOUR
☎ **053**

Rosslare Harbour is a useful departure point for Wales or France. **Trains** run from the ferry port to Dublin (3hr., 3 per day, €14.50) and Limerick (2½hr., 1-2 per day, €13.50) via Waterford (1¼hr., €8.50). **Buses** run from the same office to: Dublin (3hr., 10-12 per day, €12.70); Cork (3-5 per day, €17); Galway (4 per day, €22) via Waterford; Limerick (3-5 per day, €17); and Tralee (2-4 per day, €13). The Rosslare-Kilrane **tourist office** is 1.5km from the harbor on the Wexford road in Kilrane. (☎ 33 622. Open daily 10:15am-8pm.) If you need to stay overnight before catching a ferry, try the seaside ■**Mrs. O'Leary's Farmhouse** ❷, off N25 in Kilrane, a 15min. drive from town. Call for pickup. (☎ 33 134. Singles €23, with bath €25.50.)

KILKENNY
☎ **056**

Ireland's best-preserved medieval town, Kilkenny (pop. 25,000), is also a center of great nightlife; nine churches share the streets with 80 pubs. **Tynan Walking Tours** provide the down-and-dirty on Kilkenny's folkloric tradition; hour-long tours depart from the tourist office. (☎ 65 929. €5, students €4.50.) The 13th-century **Kilkenny Castle** housed the Earls of Ormonde from the 1300s until 1932. The basement shelters the **Butler Gallery**'s modern art exhibitions. (☎ 21 450. Open June-Sept. daily 9:30am-7pm; Oct.-Mar. 10:30am-12:45pm and 2-5pm; Apr.-May 10:30am-5pm. Mandatory guided tour €4.40, students €1.90.) Climb the narrow 30m tower of **St. Canice's Cathedral,** up the hill off Dean St., for a panoramic view of town and its surroundings. (☎ 64 971. Open Easter-Sept. M-Sa 9am-6pm, Su 2-6pm; Oct.-Easter M-Sa 10am-4pm, Su 2-4pm. Donation requested.) Start your pub crawl at either the top of **John Street** or the end of **Parliament Street;** outstanding *trad* can be found at **Anna Conda,** on Parliament St.

 Trains (☎ 22 024) arrive at Dublin Rd. from Dublin (2hr., €15.90) and Waterford (45min., €7). **Buses** (☎ 64 933) arrive at Dublin Rd. and the city center from: Cork (3hr., 2-3 per day, €15.20); Dublin (2hr., 5-6 per day, €9); Galway (5hr., 3-5 per day, €19); Limerick (2½hr., 1-5 per day, €13.30); Rosslare Harbour (2hr., 3-6 per day, €13.40); and Waterford (1½hr., 1-2 per day, €6.40). The **tourist office** is on Rose Inn St. (☎ 51 500. Open July-Aug. M-Sa 9am-7pm, Su 11am-5pm; Apr.-June and Sept. M-Sa 9am-6pm, Su 11am-5pm; Oct.-Mar. M-Sa 9am-5pm.) **B&Bs** are concentrated on **Waterford Road** and the more remote **Castlecomer Road.** Stay in former royal quarters at the 15th-century ■**Foulksrath Castle (An Óige/HI)** ❶, in Jenkinstown, 12.5km north of town on the N77. Buggy's Buses run to the hostel from the Parade (20min., M-Sa 2 per day, €2) in Kilkenny. (☎ 67 674. Sheets €2. Dorms €12-14.) **Pordylo's** ❹, on Butterslip Ln. between Kieran St. and High St., has excellent world cuisine, including many vegetarian options. (Entrees €10-23. Open daily 6-11pm.) A **Dunnes** supermarket is on Kieran St. (☎ 61 655. Open M-Tu and Sa 8:30am-7pm, W-F 8:30am-10pm, Su 10am-6pm.)

WATERFORD
☎ **051**

The highlight of Waterford, Ireland's oldest city, is the ■**Waterford Crystal Factory,** 3km away on the N25 (the Cork road). One-hour tours allow you to witness the transformation of molten glass into polished crystal. Catch the City Imp minibus outside Dunnes on Michael St. and request a stop at the factory (10-15min., every 15-20min., €1) or take city bus #1 (2 per hr., €1.10), which leaves across from the Clock Tower. (☎ 373 311. Gallery open Mar.-Dec. daily 8:30am-6pm; Jan. M-F 9am-5pm; Feb. daily 9am-5pm. Tours Mar.-Oct. daily 8:30am-4pm; Nov.-Dec. M-F 9am-3:15pm; Jan.-Feb. M-F 9am-5pm. Tours €6, students €3.50.) **Reginald's Tower,** at the end of The Quay, has guarded the city's entrance since the 12th century. (☎ 873 501. Open June-Sept. daily 9:30am-6:30pm; Oct.-May 10am-5pm. €1.90, students

€0.70.) The Quays are crowded with pubs; try **T&H Doolan's,** on George's St., which has been serving crowds for 300 years.

Trains (☎876 243) leave across the bridge from The Quay for: Dublin (2½hr., 5-6 per day, €17-22); Kilkenny (40min., 3-5 per day, €7); Limerick (2½hr., M-Sa 2 per day, €13.40); and Rosslare Harbour (1hr., M-Sa 2 per day, €8.25). **Buses** depart from The Quay for: Cork (2½hr., 10-13 per day, €13.30); Dublin (2¾hr., 6-12 per day, €9); Galway (4¾hr., 5-6 per day, €17.10); Kilkenny (1hr., 1 per day, €7); Limerick (2½hr., 6-7 per day, €13.30); and Rosslare Harbour (1¼hr., 3-5 per day, €11.60). The **tourist office** is on The Quay, across from the bus station. (☎875 823. Open July-Aug. M-Sa 9am-6pm, Su 11am-5pm; Sept.-Oct. and Apr.-June M-Sa 9am-6pm; Nov.-Mar. M-Sa 9am-5pm.) There are no hostels in town. **The Anchorage ❸,** 9 The Quay, is a conveniently located B&B. (☎854 302. Singles €35-40; doubles €65-75.) **Haricot's Wholefood Restaurant ❷,** 11 O'Connell St., serves healthy and innovative home-cooked meals. (Entrees €8-10. Open M-F 9am-8pm, Sa 9am-6pm.)

CASHEL ☎062

Cashel sits at the foot of the 90m **Rock of Cashel** (a.k.a. **St. Patrick's Rock**), a huge limestone outcropping topped by medieval buildings. (Open mid-June to mid-Sept. daily 9am-7:30pm; mid-Sept. to mid-Mar. 9:30am-4:30pm; mid-Mar. to mid-June 9:30am-5:30pm. €4.40, students €1.90.) Down the cow path from the Rock lie the ruins of **Hore Abbey,** built by Cistercian monks and presently inhabited by sheep. The **GPA-Bolton Library,** on John St., houses ecclesiastical texts and rare manuscripts, including a 1550 edition of Machiavelli's *Il Principe* and the world's smallest book. The internationally acclaimed **Brú Ború Heritage Centre,** at the base of the Rock, stages traditional music and dance performances; participation is encouraged. (☎61 122. Performances mid-June to mid-Sept. Tu-Sa 9pm. €13, with dinner €35.) **Bus Éireann** (☎62 121) leaves from the Bake House on Main St. for: Cork (1½hr., 6 per day, €12); Dublin (3hr., 6 per day, €15.40); and Limerick (1hr., 5 per day, €12). The **tourist office** is in the City Hall on Main St. (☎61 333. Open M-Sa 9:15am-6pm.) Just out of town on Dundrum Rd. is the outstanding **O'Brien's Farmhouse Hostel ❶.** (☎61 003. Laundry €8-10. Dorms €13-15; doubles €40-45. **Camping** €6, plus €15 for a car with two people.)

SOUTHWEST IRELAND

With a dramatic landscape that ranges from lakes and mountains to stark, ocean-battered cliffs, Southwest Ireland is a land rich in storytellers and history-makers. Outlaws and rebels once lurked in the hidden coves and glens now overrun by visitors. If the tourist mayhem is too much for you, you can always retreat to the placid stretches along the Ring of Kerry and Cork's southern coast.

FERRIES TO FRANCE AND BRITAIN

Swansea-Cork Ferries (☎021 427 1166) go between Cork and Swansea, South Wales (10hr., 1 per day, €30-43). **Brittany Ferries** (☎021 427 7801) sail from Cork to Roscoff, France (14hr., €50-100).

CORK CITY

☎021

Cork (pop. 150,000), the country's second-largest city, serves as the center of the sports, music, and arts scenes in Ireland's southwest. Cork is a great place to eat and sleep for those who want to explore the surrounding countryside.

TRANSPORTATION AND PRACTICAL INFORMATION

Cork is compact and pedestrian-friendly. **St. Patrick Street** becomes **Grand Parade** to the west; to the north it crosses **Merchant's Quay,** home of the bus station. North across **St. Patrick's Bridge, McCurtain Street** runs east to **Lower Glanmire Road** and the train station, before becoming the N8 to Dublin, Waterford, and Cobh. Downtown action concentrates on the vaguely parallel **Paul Street, Oliver Plunkett Street,** and St. Patrick Street. Their connecting north-south avenues are shop-lined and largely pedestrian.

Trains: Kent Station (☎450 6766), on Lower Glanmire Rd., across the river from the city center. Open M-Sa 6:35am-8:30pm, Su 7:50am-8pm. Connections to: **Dublin** (3hr., 5-7 per day, €45); **Killarney** (2hr., 4-7 per day, €18); **Limerick** (1½hr., 4-7 per day, €18); **Tralee** (2½hr., 3 per day, €23).

Buses: (☎450 8188), Parnell Pl., 2 blocks east of Patrick's Bridge on Merchants' Quay. Info desk open daily 9am-6pm. To: **Dublin** (4½hr., 5-6 per day, €19); **Galway** (4hr., 4-7 per day, €16); **Killarney** (2hr., 10-13 per day, €12); **Limerick** (2hr., 14 per day, €12.10); **Rosslare Harbour** (4hr., 3 per day, €17.10); **Sligo** (7hr., 5 per day, €21.40); **Tralee** (2½hr., 12 per day, €13); **Waterford** (2¼hr., 13 per day, €13.30).

Public Transportation: City buses criss cross the city and its suburbs every 10-30min. (M-Sa 7:30am-11:15pm, Su 10am-11:15pm; from €0.95). From downtown, catch buses along St. Patrick St., across from the Father Matthew statue.

Tourist Office: (☎427 3251), on Grand Parade, near the corner of South Mall, along the Lee's south channel. Open June-Aug. M-F 9am-6pm, Sa 9am-5:30pm; Sept.-May M-Sa 9:15am-5:30pm.

Banks: TSB, 40 Patrick St. (☎427 5221). Open M-W and F 9:30am-5pm, Th 9:30am-7pm. **Bank of Ireland,** 70 Patrick St. (☎427 7177). Open M 10am-5pm, Tu-F 10am-4pm. Patrick St. has plenty of **24hr. ATMs.**

Emergency: ☎999; no coins required. **Police** *(Garda)*: (☎522 000), on Anglesea St.

Pharmacies: Regional Late Night Pharmacy, (☎434 4575), on Wilton Rd., opposite the Regional Hospital on bus #8. Open M-F 9am-10pm, Sa-Su 10am-10pm. **Phelan's Late Night,** 9 Patrick St. (☎427 2511). Open M-Sa 9am-10pm, Su 10am-10pm.

Hospital: Mercy Hospital (☎427 1971), on Grenville Pl. €25.40 fee for emergency room access. **Cork Regional Hospital** (☎454 6400), on Wilton St., on the #8 bus.

Internet Access: Web Workhouse (☎434 3090), on Winthrop St., near the post office. €2.50-5 per hr. Open M-Th and Su 8am-3am, F and Sa 24hr.

Post Office: (☎427 2000), on Oliver Plunkett St., at the corner of Pembroke St. Open M-Sa 9am-5:30pm.

ACCOMMODATIONS

B&Bs are clustered along **Patrick's Hill,** rising upward from St. Patrick's Bridge above Glanmire Rd., and on **Western Road** near University College.

Sheila's Budget Accommodation Centre (IHH), 4 Belgrave Pl. (☎450 5562), at the intersection of Wellington St. and York St. Helpful, energetic staff. Internet €1 per 15min. Breakfast €3.20. 24hr. reception desk is also a general store. Check-out 10:30am. Key deposit €2. Dorms €13-16; singles €30; doubles €20-25. ❶

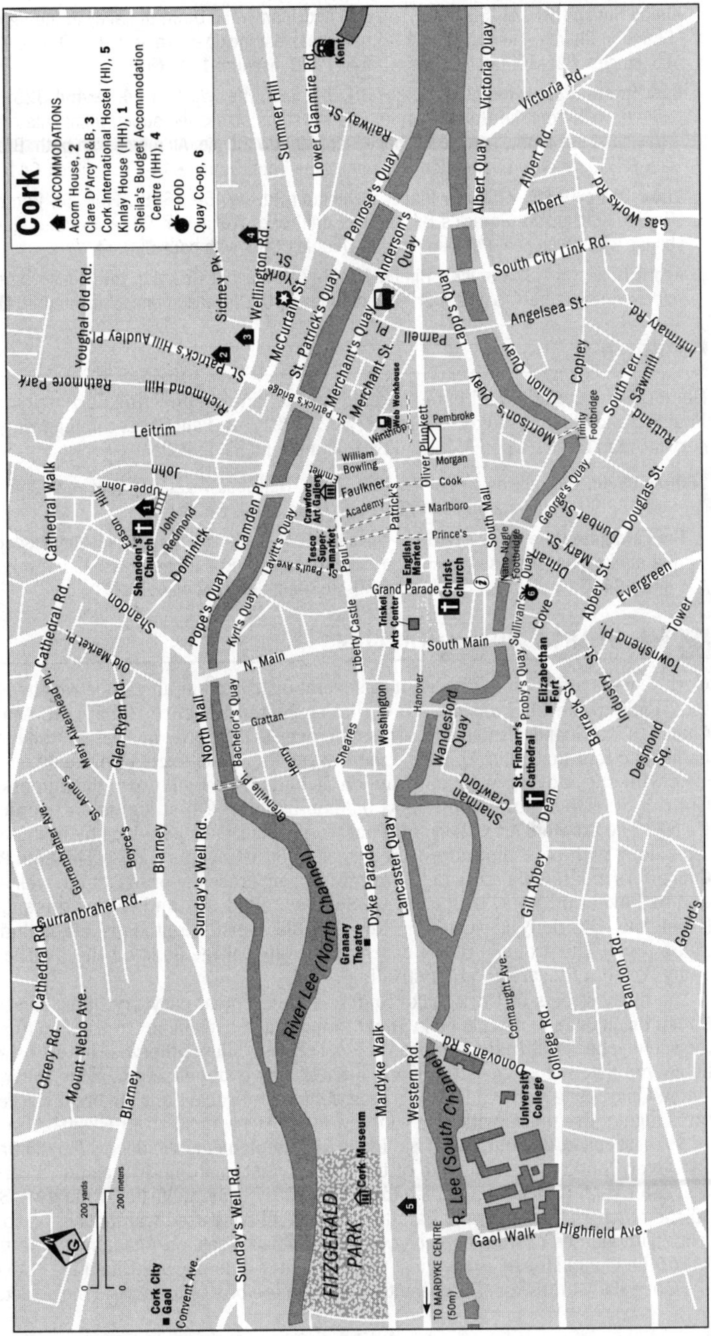
Cork
ACCOMMODATIONS
Acorn House, 2
Clare D'Arcy B&B, 3
Cork International Hostel (HI), 5
Kinlay House (IHH), 1
Sheila's Budget Accommodation Centre (IHH), 4
FOOD
Quay Co-op, 6
200 yards
200 meters
Cork City Gaol
Convent Ave.
Sunday's Well Rd.
FITZGERALD PARK
Cork Museum
River Lee (North Channel)
R. Lee (South Channel)
TO MARDYKE CENTRE (50m)
Gaol Walk
Highfield Ave.
University College
Donovan's Rd.
College Rd.
Connaught Ave.
Western Rd.
Mardyke Walk
Granary Theatre
Dyke Parade
Lancaster Quay
Bandon Rd.
Gould's
Gill Abbey
Dean
St. Finbarr's Cathedral
Elizabethan Fort
Proby's Quay
Sullivan's Quay
Crawford
Sharman
Wandesford Quay
Hanover
Washington
Sheares
Henry
Grenville Pl.
Bachelor's Quay
Grattan
North Mall
Blarney
Boyce's
St. Anne's
Mary Aikenhead Pl.
Glen Ryan Rd.
Gurranbraher Ave.
Gurranbraher Rd.
Cathedral Rd.
Orrery Rd.
Mount Nebo Ave.
Old Market Pl.
Cathedral Walk
Shandon
Shandon's Church
Eason Hill
Upper John
John
John Redmond
Dominick
Pope's Quay
Kyrl's Quay
N. Main
South Main
Liberty
Castle
Triskel Arts Center
Grand Parade
Christ-church
English Market
Paul
St. Paul's Ave.
Tesco Super-market
Lavitt's Quay
Camden Pl.
Crawford Art Gallery
Emmet
Faulkner
Academy
Patrick's
William Bowling
Winthrop
Web Workhouse
Oliver Plunkett
Pembroke
Morgan
Cook
Marlboro
Prince's
South Mall
Nano Nagle Footbridge
Cove
Dinan
Mary St.
Dunbar St.
George's Quay
Douglas St.
Abbey St.
Evergreen
Tower
Townshend Pl.
Industry St.
Barrack St.
Desmond Sq.
Rutland
Sawmill
South Terr.
Trinity Footbridge
Copley
Morrison's Quay
Union Quay
Lapp's Quay
Parnell Pl.
Merchant St.
Merchant's Quay
St. Patrick's Quay
St. Patrick's Bridge
Anderson's Quay
Angelsea St.
Infirmary Rd.
South City Link Rd.
Gas Works Rd.
Albert
Albert Rd.
Albert Quay
Victoria Rd.
Victoria Quay
Penrose's Quay
Railway St.
Lower Glanmire Rd.
Kent
Summer Hill
McCurtain St.
York St.
Wellington Rd.
Sidney Pk.
St. Patrick's Hill
Audley Pl.
Youghal Old Rd.
Rathmore Park
Richmond Hill
Leitrim

IRELAND

Kinlay House (IHH; ☎450 8966), on Bob and Joan Walk. Down the alley to the right of Shandon Church. Internet €1 per 15min. Breakfast included. Laundry €7. Dorms €14-16; singles €25-30; family rooms €70-80. ISIC discount 10%. ❷

Cork International Hostel (An Óige/HI), 1-2 Redclyffe, Western Rd. (☎454 3289), a 15min. walk from the Grand Parade. Bus #8 stops across the street. Immaculate and spacious bunk rooms in a stately brick Victorian townhouse. All rooms with bath. Breakfast €3.50. Check-in 8am-midnight. Open June-Sept. Dorms €14-17; doubles €41. ❷

Clare D'Arcy B&B, 7 Sidney Place, Wellington Rd. (☎450 4658). From St. Patrick's Bridge, start up St. Patrick's Hill, turning right onto Wellington Rd. A luxurious guesthouse with an elegant Parisian interior. Doubles €80, with bath €90. ❺

Acorn House, 14 St. Patrick's Hill (☎450 2474). Elegant Georgian townhouse. Street-side rooms are best. Singles €40-52; doubles €90. Off-season prices negotiable. ❹

FOOD

Delicious restaurants and cafes abound on the lanes connecting St. Patrick St., Paul St., and Oliver Plunkett St. **Tesco** (☎427 0791), on Paul St., is the biggest grocery store in town. (Open M-W and Sa 8:30am-8pm, Th-F 8:30am-10pm.)

Quay Co-op, 24 Sullivan's Quay (☎431 7660). Delicious vegetarian and vegan meals. Soup €2.80. Entrees around €6.50. Open M-Sa 9am-9pm. ❷

The Farmgate Cafe (☎427 8134), above the English Market. Balcony seating overlooks the market. Baguette sandwiches, excellent soups, and the best desserts in Cork, all under €4. Open daily for breakfast 8:30-10:30am, lunch noon-4pm. ❶

SIGHTS AND NIGHTLIFE

Cork's sights are loosely divided into several districts, but all can be reached by foot. Pick up the *Cork Area City Guide* at the tourist office (€1.90). **St. Anne's Church** (a.k.a. **Shandon's Church**), across the river to the north, has earned the nickname "the four-faced liar," because the tower's four clocks are notoriously out of sync with one another. Walk up Shandon St. and take a right down the unmarked Church St. (Open June-Sept. M-Sa 9:30am-5:30pm. €4, students and seniors €3.50.) The **Crawford Art Gallery,** off Paul St., specializes in paintings by Irish masters, along with contemporary work. (Open M-Sa 10am-5pm. Free.) The **Cork City Gaol** offers multimedia tours of the former prison; cross the bridge at the western end of Fitzgerald Park, turn right on Sunday's Well Rd., and follow the signs. (Open Mar.-Oct. daily 9:30am-6pm; Nov.-Feb. 10am-5pm. €5, students €4; includes audio tour.) The grounds of the nearby **University College Cork,** on the riverbank along Western Rd., are good for strolling.

The lively streets of Cork make finding entertainment easy; try **Oliver Plunkett Street, Union Quay,** and **South Main Street** for pubs and live music. To keep on top of the scene, check out *List Cork*, free at local shops. Unless otherwise noted, establishments listed close M-Th 11:30pm, F-Sa 12:30am, and Su 11pm. **The Lobby,** 1 Union Quay, gave some of Ireland's most famous folk acts their big breaks; it features nightly live music with a view of the river. (Occasional cover €2.50-6.50.) At **An Spailpín Fanac,** 28 South Main St., live *trad* complements the decor. **The Old Oak,** on Oliver Plunkett St., wins one of the "Best Traditional Pub in Ireland" awards year after year. (Open F-Sa until 1:45am.) At classy **Bodega,** 46-49 Cornmarket St., off the northern end of Grand Parade in a striking converted warehouse, patrons relax with glasses of wine on velvet couches. **Half Moon,** on Academy Ln. to the left of the Opera House, is the most popular dance club in Cork City. (18+. Cover €9. Open daily until 2am. Purchase tickets from the box office across the street.)

DAYTRIPS FROM CORK

BLARNEY (AN BHLARNA)

Buses run from Cork to Blarney (10-16 per day, round-trip €4.10). ☎ *438 5252. Castle open June-Aug. M-Sa 9am-7pm, Su 9:30am-5:30pm; Sept. M-Sa 9am-6:30pm, Su 9:30am-dusk; Oct.-Apr. M-Sa 9am-6pm* or *dusk, Su 9:30am-5pm* or *dusk; May M-Sa 9am-6:30pm, Su 9:30am-5:30pm. €4.50, students €3, children €1.50.*

Busloads of tourists eager for quintessential Irish scenery and a cold kiss head northwest of Cork to see **Blarney Castle** and its legendary **Blarney Stone,** which confers the gift of gab upon those who smooch it while leaning over backwards. The top of the castle provides an airy and stunning view of the countryside. Try to go early in the morning to avoid the crowds.

COBH AND FOTA ISLANDS

Trains run from Cork to Cobh (25min., 8-19 per day, €4 round-trip) via Fota; you can get off at Fota and re-board for free.

The island of **Cobh** is little more than a slumbering harbor village today, but it was Ireland's main transatlantic port until the 1960s, and notably, the *Titanic's* last stop before its watery doom. **The Queenstown Story,** next to the railway station, traces the port's past. (Open Mar.-Nov. daily 10am-6pm; Dec.-Feb. 10am-5pm. €5, students €4). **Fota** is home to the extraordinary **Fota Wildlife Park,** where penguins, peacocks, cheetahs, and giraffes roam free. (Open Apr.-Oct. M-Sa 10am-6pm, Su 11am-6pm. Last admission 5pm. €7, students €4.20.)

MIDLETON

Buses run from Cork (30min.; M-Sa 13-18 per day, Su 4 per day; €4.90). Heritage Centre (☎ 461 3594) open Mar.-Oct. daily 10am-6pm. Call ahead Nov.-Feb. €5.70, students €5, children €2.50. Tours every 30-45min.

Midleton beckons visitors to the **Jameson Heritage Centre** with the water of life (a literal translation of **whiskey**). The center takes visitors through a 1hr. tour detailing the craft and history of whiskey production—a glass of the stuff is included.

KINSALE ☎ 021

Affluent tourists come to eat at Kinsale's expensive, famed restaurants, known as the "Good Food Circle," but the town's best attractions are cheap. Follow the coastal **Scilly Walk** 30min. from the end of Pearse St. to reach the star-shaped, 17th-century **Charles Fort,** which offers spectacular views of the town and its watery surroundings. (Open mid-Mar. to Oct. M-F 10am-6pm; Nov. to mid-Mar. Sa-Su 10am-5pm, M-F by appointment. €4, students €1.50.) **Buses** arrive on the pier, at the Esso station, from Cork (40min., 5-11 per day, round-trip €6.50). The **tourist office,** on Emmet Pl., is on the waterfront. (☎ 477 2234. Open Mar.-Nov. M-Sa 9am-6pm.) Budget beds abound at **Guardwell Lodge ❷,** on Guardwell St., a newly opened hostel. (☎ 477 4686. Dorms €17; singles €15-25; doubles €30-50. 10% *Let's Go* discount.) **O'Donovan's B&B ❸,** on Guardwell Rd., has comfortable rooms. (☎ 477 2428. €24-28 per person.) Local fishermen roast their catch at **The Spaniard ❸,** a pub with delicious food. (Entrees €7-14.)

SCHULL AND THE MIZEN HEAD PENINSULA ☎ 028

The seaside hamlet of **Schull** is an ideal base for exploring the craggy and beach-laden southwest tip of Ireland. A calm harbor and numerous shipwrecks make it a diving paradise; the **Watersports Centre** rents gear. (☎ 28 554. Open M-Sa 9:30am-6pm.) The coastal road winds past the **Barley Coast Beach** and continues on to

IRELAND

Mizen Head. The Mizen becomes more scenic and less populated the farther west you go from Schull; **Betty Johnson's Bus Hire** offers tours of the area. (☎28 410. Call ahead. €12.) In summer, **ferries** (☎28 138) depart from Schull for Cape Clear Island (Jun.-Sept. 2-3 per day, round-trip €12). **Buses** arrive in Schull from Cork (1-3 per day, €12) and Goleen (1-3 per day, €3.10). There is no other public transportation on the peninsula. Confident **cyclists** can daytrip to Mizen Head (29km from Schull). The immaculate **Schull Backpackers' Lodge (IHH) ❶,** on Colla Rd., has **hiking** and **biking** maps and info. (☎28 681. Bike rental €11 per day, €50 per week. Dorms €10.50-11.50; doubles €32-33.) **The Courtyard ❶,** on Main St., has delicious options for breakfast and lunch; the fruit scones (€0.55) and the sandwiches on fresh ciabatta (€7-9.50) are both worth a try. (Open M-Sa 9:30am-6pm.)

CAPE CLEAR ISLAND ☎028

Although the scenery visible from the ferry landing at Cape Clear Island *(Oileán Chléire)* is desolate and foreboding, the main industry of this beautiful island is farming. Cape Clear provides asylum for gulls, petrels, cormorants, and their attendant flocks of ornithologists; the **Cape Clear Bird Observatory** (☎39 181), on North Harbour, has bird-watching and ecology courses. At **Cléire Goats** (☎39 126), on the steep hill between the harbor and the heritage center, sample rich goat's milk ice cream (€1.50). **Ferries** (☎28 138) go to Schull (45min., 1-3 per day, round-trip €11.50). There is an **information office** is in the pottery shop to the left of the pier. (☎39 100. Open July-Aug. 11am-1pm and 3-6pm; June and Sept. 3-6pm.) **Cléire Lasmuigh (An Óige/HI) ❶** is a 10min. walk from the pier; follow the main road and keep left. (☎39 198. June-Sept. dorms €11; Oct.-May €9.) To reach **Cuas an Uisce Campsite ❶,** on the south pier, walk 5min. uphill from the harbor and bear right before Ciarán Danny Mike's; it's 400m down on the left. (☎39 136. Open June-Sept. €5 per person, under 16 €2.50.) Groceries are available at **An Siopa Beag,** on the pier. (Open July-Aug. daily 11am-9pm; June 11am-6pm; Sept.-May 11am-4:30pm.)

KILLARNEY AND KILLARNEY NATIONAL PARK ☎064

The town of Killarney is just minutes from some of Ireland's most glorious natural scenery. The 95 square-kilometer national park outside town blends forested mountains with the famous **Lakes of Killarney.** Five kilometers south of Killarney on Kenmare Rd. is **Muckross House,** a massive 19th-century manor with a garden that blooms brilliantly each year. A path leads to the 20m high **Torc Waterfall.** (Open July-Aug. daily 9am-7pm; Sept.-Oct. and mid-Mar. to June 9am-6pm. €5.10, students €2.) Walk or drive to the 14th-century **Ross Castle** by taking a right on Ross Rd. off Muckross Rd., 3km from Killarney; the footpaths from Knockreer (out of town on New St.) are more scenic. (Open June-Aug. daily 9am-6:30pm; May and Sept. 10am-6pm; Oct. and mid-Mar. to Apr. 10am-5pm. €3.80, students €1.60.) Bike around the **Gap of Dunloe,** which borders **Macgillycuddy's Reeks,** Ireland's highest mountain range. Hop on a boat from Ross Castle to the head of the Gap (1½hr., €12; book at the tourist office). From **Lord Brandon's Cottage,** on the Gap, head left over the stone bridge, continue 3km to the church, and turn right onto a winding road. Huff the 2km to the top, and your reward is an 11km coast downhill through the park's most breathtaking scenery. The 13km ride back to Killarney (bear right after Kate Kearney's Cottage, turn left on the road to Fossa, and turn right on Killorglin Rd.) passes the ruins of **Dunloe Castle,** demolished by Cromwell's armies.

Trains (☎31 067) arrive at Killarney station, off East Avenue Rd., from: Cork (2hr., 4 per day, €17.80); Dublin (3½hr., 4 per day, €45); and Limerick (3hr., 4 per day, €19.70). **Buses** (☎30 011) leave from Park Rd. for Cork (2hr., 10-14 per day, €12) and Dublin (6hr., 5-6 per day, €19). **O'Sullivan's,** on Bishop's Ln., rents **bikes.** (☎31 282. Free locks and maps. Open daily 8:30am-6:30pm. €12 per day, €70 per week.) The **tourist office** is on Beech St., off New St. (☎31 633. Open July-Aug. M-Sa 9am-8pm, Su 10am-6pm; June and Sept. M-Sa 9am-6pm, Su 10am-6pm; Oct.-May M-Sa 9:15am-5:30pm.) The immense and immaculate **Neptune's (IHH) ❶**, on Bishop's Ln., is up the first walkway off New St. on the right. (☎35 255. Dorms €11-12; doubles €34.) **Orchard House B&B ❸**, on Fleming's Ln., is near the town center and an unbeatable bargain. (☎31 879. Singles €25-30; doubles €45-60.) A **Tesco** grocery store is in the arcade off New St. (Open M-W 8:30am-8pm, Th-F 8:30am-9pm, Sa 8:30am-7pm.) **The Grand,** on High St., brings together locals and tourists for fantastic live music. (No cover before 11pm. Open daily 7pm-3am.)

RING OF KERRY ☎066

The Southwest's most celebrated peninsula holds picturesque villages, fabled ancient forts, and rugged mountains. Although tour buses often hog the roads, rewards await those who take the time to explore the landscape on foot or by bike.

TRANSPORTATION. The term "Ring of Kerry" usually describes the entire **Iveragh Peninsula,** though it technically refers to the ring of roads circumnavigating it. Hop on the circuit run by **Bus Éireann,** based in Killarney and stopping at the major towns on the Ring (mid-June to Aug. 2 per day), including Cahersiveen (from Killarney 2½hr., €11.50) and Caherdaniel (from Cahersiveen 1hr., €4.25).

CAHERSIVEEN. Although best known as the birthplace of patriot Daniel O'Connell, Cahersiveen (CAR-sah-veen) serves as an excellent base for jaunts to Valentia Island, the Skelligs, and local archeological sites. The ruins of **Ballycarbery Castle,** once held by O'Connell's ancestors, are past the barracks on Bridge St. and the bridge, off the main road to the left. About 200m past the castle turn-off stands a pair of Ireland's best-preserved stone forts, **Cahergall Fort** and **Leacanabuaile Fort.** The **tourist office** is directly across from the bus stop, next to the post office. (☎947 2589. Open June to mid-Sept. M-F 9:30am-1pm and 2-5:30pm.) The welcoming **Sive Hostel (IHH) ❶** is at 15 East End, Main St. (☎947 2717. Dorms €10.50; doubles €25-32; **camping** €5 per person.) **O'Shea's B&B ❸,** next to the post office on Main St., boasts comfortable rooms, some with impressive views. (☎947 2402. Singles €25-30; doubles €50.) **Main Street** has several pubs that harken back to the early 20th century, when establishments served as both watering holes and the proprietor's main business, be it general store, blacksmith, or leather shop.

The quiet **Valentia Island** is a fantastic daytrip. The little roads of this unspoiled gem are perfect for biking or light hiking. Bridges on either end of the island connect it to the mainland; alternatively, a **ferry** runs during the summer (3min., May-Oct. 8:15am-10pm; €2, with bike €3) from **Reenard Point,** 5km west of Cahersiveen. A taxi to the ferry dock from Cahersiveen is about €7. Another recommended daytrip is to the **Skellig Rocks,** about 13km off the shore of the Iveragh Peninsula. From the boat, **Little Skellig** may appear snow-capped; it's actually covered with 24,000 pairs of crooning birds. Climb 630 steps to reach a **monastery** built by 6th-century Christian monks, whose beehive-like dwellings are still intact. The hostel and campground in Cahersiveen can arrange the **ferry** ride (about 1hr.) for €32-35, including a ride to the dock.

CAHERDANIEL. There's little in the village of **Caherdaniel** to attract the Ring's droves of buses. But nearby **Derrynane National Park,** 2.5km along the shore from the village, holds 3km of gorgeous beach ringed by picture-perfect dunes. Follow the signs for **Derrynane House,** once the residence of Daniel O'Connell. (Open May-Sept. M-Sa 9am-6pm, Su 11am-7pm; Apr. and Oct. Tu-Su 1-5pm; Nov.-Mar. Sa-Su 1-5pm. €3, students €1.50.) Guests are made to feel at home at **The Travellers' Rest Hostel ❶.** (☎947 5175. Breakfast €4. Dorms €12; singles €15.)

IRELAND

DINGLE PENINSULA ☎066

For decades, the Ring of Kerry's undertouristed counterpart has remained more congested with ancient sites than with tour buses; the Ring's tourist blitz has only just begun to encroach upon the spectacular cliffs and sweeping beaches of the Irish-speaking Dingle peninsula. Many visitors explore the area by bike, an especially attractive option given the scarcity of public transportation.

TRANSPORTATION. Dingle Town is most easily reached by **Bus Éireann** from Tralee (1¼hr., 4-6 per day, €7.90); other routes run from Dingle to Ballydavid (Tu and F 3 per day, €4 round-trip), Ballyferriter (M and Th 3 per day; €3.20), and Dunquin (1-5 per day, €3.15). In summer, additional buses tour the south of the peninsula beginning in Dingle (June-Sept. M-Sa 2 per day).

DINGLE TOWN. Lively Dingle Town, adopted home of **Fungi the Dolphin** (now a major focus of the tourist industry), is a good base for exploring the peninsula. **Sciúird Archaeology Tours** leave from the pier for 3hr. whirlwind bus tours of the area's ancient spots. (☎915 1606. 2 per day, €15; book ahead.) **Moran's Tours** runs great trips to Slea Head, passing through majestic scenery and stopping at historical sites. (☎915 1155. 2 per day, €10.20; book ahead.) The **tourist office** is on Strand St. (☎915 1188. Open July-Aug. M-Sa 9am-7pm, Su 10am-5pm; Sept.-Oct. and mid-Mar. to June M-Sa 9:30am-6pm, Su 9:30am-5pm.) The laid-back **Grapevine Hostel ❶** is on Dykegate St., off Main St. (☎915 1434. Dorms €10.80-13.35.) **Ballintaggart Hostel (IHH) ❶,** 25min. east on Tralee Rd. in a stone mansion, is supposedly haunted by the murdered wife of the Earl of Cork. (☎915 1454. Free shuttle to town. Dorms €12.50-15; doubles €43; off-season €1.30-2.50 less. **Camping** €11.)

SLEA HEAD AND DUNQUIN. Green hills interrupted by stone walls and occasional sheep break off into the sea near scenic Slea Head and Dunquin. *Ryan's Daughter* and parts of *Far and Away* were filmed in this appropriately melodramatic scenery. By far the most rewarding way to see Slea Head and Dunquin's cliffs and crashing waves is to **bike** along the predominantly flat **Slea Head Drive.** Past Dingle Town toward Slea Head sits the village of **Ventry** (Ceann Trá), home to a sandy beach and the marvelous **Ballybeag Hostel ❷;** a regular shuttle runs from Dingle Town. (☎915 9876. Bike rental €7. Laundry €2. €20 per person.) The **Celtic and Prehistoric Museum,** 3km farther down the road, is a must-see—the collection ranges from prehistoric sea worm fossils to Millie, a 50,000-year old woolly mammoth. (☎915 9931. Open from Mar. to mid-Nov. daily 10am-5pm; call ahead from mid-Nov. to Feb. €5, students €3.50.) North of Slea Head, the scattered settlement of Dunquin (Dún Chaoin) boasts **Kruger's ❸,** purportedly the westernmost pub in Europe. Come for the spontaneous music sessions and superlative views. (☎915 6194. Entrees €7-13.) Past Dunquin on the road to Ballyferriter, the **Great Blasket Centre** has outstanding exhibits about the isolated Blasket Islands. (☎915 6444. Open July-Aug. daily 10am-7pm; Easter-June and Sept.-Nov. 10am-6pm. €3.10, students €1.20.) At **An Óige Hostel (HI) ❶,** on the Dingle Way across from the turnoff to the Blasket Centre, each bunk has its own ocean view. (☎915 6121. Reception 9-10am and 5-10pm. Lockout 10am-5pm. Dorms €9-12; doubles €26.)

TRALEE. Tralee (pop. 20,000), a good departure point for the Ring of Kerry or the Dingle Peninsula, has a hustle and bustle appropriate for the economic and residential capital of County Kerry. **Kerry the Kingdom,** in Ashe Memorial Hall on Denny St., features a high-tech history of Ireland from 8000 BC to the present. (☎712 7777. Open mid-Mar. to Oct. daily 10am-6pm; Nov. noon-4:30pm. €8, students €6.50.) During the last week of August, the nationally-known **Rose of Tralee Festival** brings a horde of lovely Irish lasses to town to compete for the title "Rose of Tralee." **Trains** go from the station on Oakpark Rd. to: Cork (2½hr., 3-4 per day, €23); Galway (5-6hr., 3 per day, €45.10); and Killarney (40min., 4 per day, €7.50). **Buses** leave from the train station for: Cork (2½hr., 10-14 per day, €12.70); Galway (5-6hr., 9-11 per day, €17.10); Killarney (40min., 5-14 per day, €5.85); and Limerick (2¼hr., 7-8 per day, €12.20). To get from the station to the **tourist office** in Ashe Memorial Hall, head down Edward St., turn right on Castle St., and then left on Denny St. (☎712 1288. Open July-Aug. M-Sa 9am-7pm, Su 9am-6pm; May-June and Oct. M-Sa 9am-6pm; Nov.-Apr. M-F 9am-5pm.) **Courthouse Lodge (IHH) ❶**, 5 Church St., has a great location. (☎712 7199. Internet €1 per 10min. Dorms €14; doubles €32.) After a comfortable night's sleep at **Castle House ❹**, 27 Upper Castle St., don't miss the great pancakes. (☎712 5167. Singles €40; doubles €65.)

WESTERN IRELAND

Even Dubliners will tell you that the west is the "most Irish" part of Ireland. The potato famine that plagued the island was most devastating in the west—entire villages emigrated or died. The region still has less than half of its 1841 population. Though miserable for farming, the land from Connemara north to Ballina is great for hikers and cyclists who enjoy the isolation of mountainous landscapes.

LIMERICK ☎061

What little attention Limerick received in the 20th century focused on its squalor—a tradition exemplified by Frank McCourt's celebrated memoir, *Angela's Ashes*. Despite the stigma, Limerick is a city on the rise and a fine place to stay en route to points west. The **Hunt Museum,** in Custom House on Rutland St., has been recognized for its outstanding, diverse collection; visitors browse through drawers to find surprises like the world's smallest jade monkey. (Open M-Sa 10am-5pm, Su 2-5pm. €7, students and seniors €4.) Limerick's student population adds spice to the pub scene. **Dolan's ❷,** on Dock Rd., hosts nightly *trad* and rambunctious local patrons. **Trains** (☎315 555) leave Parnell St. for: Cork (2½hr., 5-6 per day, €18); Dublin (2hr., 9-10 per day, €33.10); Ennis (2 per day, €7); Killarney (2½hr., 3-4 per day, €20); and Waterford (2hr., 1-2 per day, €23). **Buses** (☎313 333) leave the train station for: Cork (2hr., 14 per day, €12.10); Derry (6½hr., 3 per day, €23); Donegal (6hr., 4 per day, €20.20); Dublin (3½hr., 13 per day, €13.30); Ennis (45min., 14 per day, €6.70); Galway (2hr., 14 per day, €12.10); Killarney (2½hr., 3-6 per day, €12.40); Rosslare Harbour (4hr., 3-4 per day, €15-16); Tralee (2hr., 7 per day, €12.10); and Waterford (2½hr., 6-7 per day, €13.30). The **tourist office** is on Arthurs Quay. From the station, walk down Davis St., turn right on O'Connell St., then left at Arthurs Quay Mall. (☎317 522. Open July-Aug. M-F 9am-6:30pm, Sa-Su 9am-6pm; May-June and Sept.-Oct. M-Sa 9:30am-5:30pm; Nov.-Apr. M-F 9:30am-5:30pm, Sa 9:30am-1pm.) **Summerville Holiday Hostel ❷,** past Dolan's on Dock Rd., is a brick complex of university dormitory singles. Take the Raheen bus (€0.95) from Williams St. (☎302 500. Continental breakfast included. Laundry €2. Check-out 10:30am. Open June-Aug. Dorms €16; singles €22; doubles €38; triples €50.) Close to the city center, **Alexandra House B&B ❸,** on O'Connell St. south of the Daniel O'Connell statue, is one of the better B&B values in Limerick. (☎318 472. Singles €26; doubles €48-64.) Dolan's (see above) is Limerick's best choice for evening meals. (Entrees €5-9.)

ENNIS AND DOOLIN ☎065

Ennis's proximity to Shannon Airport and The Burren make it a common stopover for tourists, who come for a day of shopping followed by a night of pub crawling. Sixty pubs line the streets of Ennis. At **Cruises Pub,** on Abbey St., local musicians appear nightly for cozy *trad* sessions. **Glor** is a newly opened, state-of-the-art music center that features nightly performances of both *trad* and more contemporary music, along with film, theater, and dance. (☎684 3103. Box office open M-Sa 9:30am-5:30pm. Tickets €12-22.) **Trains** leave from Station Rd. for Dublin (1-2 per day, €26.60). **Buses** also leave from Station Rd. for: Cork (3hr., every hr., €13.90); Doolin (1hr., 2 per day, €4.70); Dublin (4hr., every hr., €13.30); Galway (1hr., 5 per day, €9.80); Limerick (40min., every hr., €6.70); and Shannon Airport (40min., every hr., €6.10). The **tourist office** is on Arthur's Row, off O'Connell Sq. (☎28 366. Open July-Sept. daily 9am-6pm; Apr.-June and Oct. M-Sa 9:30am-6pm; Nov.-Mar. M-F 9:30am-6pm.) The recently renovated **Abbey Tourist Hostel** ❶ is on Harmony Row. (☎682 2620. Breakfast included. Internet €0.10 per 10min. Curfew Su-W 1:30am, Th 2:30am, F-Sa 3am. Dorms €13-15; singles €25; doubles €38.)

Something of a shrine to Irish music, the little village of **Doolin** draws thousands every year to its three pubs. The pubs are commonly known by the mnemonic **MOM: McDermott's** (in the Upper Village), **O'Connor's** (in the Lower), and **McGann's** (Upper). All have *trad* sessions nightly at 9:30pm. The **Cliffs of Moher,** 10km south of town, feature a 200m vertical drop into the sea. Take the bus from Doolin (#50; 15min., 1-3 per day). **Buses** leave from Doolin Hostel for Dublin via Ennis and Limerick (#15; 2 per day) and Galway (#50; 1½hr., 1-5 per day). Almost every house on the main road is a **B&B. Aille River Hostel (IHH)** ❶, between the Upper and Lower Villages, has a friendly atmosphere and a gorgeous location. (☎707 4260. Internet €6 per hr. Dorms €12; doubles €27. **Camping** €6.)

THE BURREN ☎065

If there were orchids, cows, and B&Bs on the moon, it would probably look a lot like The Burren, which covers 260 sq. km—almost one-third of Co. Clare's coastline. Limestone, butterflies, ruined castles, and labyrinthine caves make the region a unique geological fairyland. **Burren Exposure,** between Kinvara and Ballyvaughn on N67, gives a soaring introduction to The Burren through films shown on a wall-to-wall screen. (☎707 7277. €5, children €2.50.) For expansive views of town and countryside, climb up the narrow, winding staircase in **Dungaire Castle,** just outside of Kinvara. (☎(091) 637 108. €4, students €3.50. Open May-Sept. daily 9:30am-5pm.) The Burren town of **Lisdoonvarna** is synonymous with its **Matchmaking Festival,** a month-long *craic*-and-snogging celebration that attracts over 10,000 singles each September.

THE LOCAL STORY

HELLO, DALY

Let's Go *interviews Willie Daly, the Lisdoonvarna "matchmaker."*

LG: So people fill out a form about themselves and then they receive phone numbers?

WD: Aye, they do. They give us the form and we give them the names of people we think would be suitable.

LG: Have any marriages resulted?

WD: Well, I get invited to some, but I don't attend in case it embarrasses them, since people know what I do.

(Mr. Daly takes a phone call.)

WD: ...I'll send you a form and you can put in a little bit about yourself. Write down the sorts of things that you desire... When did you get the last one, John? Was there not anything in it that was suitable for you, then? Hmmm. Have you got a pen with you, and I'll give you the name of a nice girl I have now.

(The phone cuts off.)

LG: So, what is the most important advice you have?

WD: A woman needs to be treated with respect. She needs be made to feel important and wanted. You can't take her for granted. That's the key.

(The phone rings again.)

WD: Sorry, okay John. So here's another number for you... You've got a good attitude, you'll be fine. You have the number now, so you have no excuse. Okay John, good luck. You're welcome. It's not a problem, I do this all the time. It's me job.

The **Hydro Hotel ❹** has info on the festival and its own nightly music. (☎707 4005. Wheelchair-accessible. Open Mar.-Oct. €45 per person.)

The Burren is notoriously difficult to get around; the surrounding tourist offices (at Kilfenora, Ennis, and the Cliffs of Moher) have detailed maps of the region. Hikers can set out on the 40km **Burren Way,** a trail from Liscannor to Ballyvaughan marked by yellow arrows. **Bus Éireann** (☎682 4177) connects Galway to towns in and near the Burren a few times a day during summer but infrequently during winter. In **Kinvara,** stay at **Fallon's B&B ❹,** next to the market. (☎(091) 637 483. €40 per person, all with bath.) **Cois Cuain B&B ❸,** also in Kinvara on the Quay, is quaint and good for couples. (☎(091) 637 119. Open Apr.-Nov. €26.50 per person.)

DAYTRIP FROM THE BURREN: COOLE PARK AND THOOR BALLYLEE. Two of W. B. Yeats's favorite retreats lie about 32km south of Galway near **Gort,** where N18 meets N66. **Coole Park** is now a ruin and national park; **Thoor Ballylee** has been restored to appear as it did when Yeats lived there. The Coole Park nature reserve was once the estate of Lady Augusta Gregory, a friend and collaborator of Yeats. In the picnic area, a great copper beech known as the "autograph tree" bears the initials of some important Irish figures: George Bernard Shaw, Sean O'Casey, Douglas Hyde (the first president of Ireland), and Yeats himself. (☎091 631 804. Visitors center open Easter-Sept. daily 9:30am-6:30pm. Last admission 15min. before closing. €2.50, students €1.20.) A couple kilometers from the garden, **Coole Lake** is where Yeats watched "nine-and-fifty swans... all suddenly mount/ And scatter wheeling in great broken rings/ Upon their clamorous wings." Five kilometers north of Coole Park, a road turns off Galway Rd. and runs to Thoor Ballylee, a tower built in the 13th and 14th centuries. In 1916, Yeats bought it for £35 (€44.50), renovated it, and lived here with his family off and on from 1922 to 1928. A film on Yeats's life plays at the **visitors center.** (☎091 631 436. Open Easter-Sept. M-Sa 10am-6pm. €5, students €4.50.)

GALWAY CITY ☎091

Galway (pop. 70,000) has a mix of over 13,000 university students, a transient population of 20-something Europeans, and waves of international backpackers. Its main attractions are its nightlife and setting—it's a convenient starting point for trips to the Clare Coast or Connemara.

TRANSPORTATION AND PRACTICAL INFORMATION. Trains (☎561 444) leave for Dublin (3hr., 4-5 per day, €20-30) via Athlone (€10-15). Transfer at Athlone for lines to all other cities. **Bus Éireann** (☎562 000) leaves from Eyre Sq. for: Belfast (7hr., 2-3 per day, €27.50); Cork (4¼hr., 13 per day, €15.80); Donegal (4hr., 4 per day, €15.20); and Dublin (4hr., every hr., €12). The main **tourist office,** on Forster St., is a block south of Eyre Sq. (☎537 700. Open July-Aug. daily 9:30am-7:45pm; May-June and Sept. 9am-5:45pm; Oct.-Apr. Su-F 9am-5:45pm, Sa 9am-12:45pm.) Check email at **Neatsurf,** 7 St. Francis St. (☎533 976. €0.75 per 10min.)

ACCOMMODATIONS AND FOOD. Sleepzone ❷, Bóthar na mBán, northwest of Eyre Sq., takes the "s" out of "hostel." (☎566 999. Internet €4.50 per hr. Breakfast included. All rooms with bath. July-Aug. M-F dorms €16-20; singles €40; doubles €54. Weekend and off-season rates vary.) **Salmon Weir Hostel ❶,** 3 St. Vincent's Ave., is very homey. (☎561 133. Laundry €6. Curfew 3am. Dorms €10-15; doubles €35.) The conveniently located B&B **St. Martin's ❸,** 2 Nuns Island Rd., has a gorgeous riverside garden. (☎568 286. All rooms with bath. Singles €32; doubles

€60.) **Bananaphoblacht ❶,** on Dominick St., is an outstanding cafe. (Baked goods €2-5; beverages €2-3. Open M-F 8:30am-2am, Sa 10:30am-2am, Su noon-2am.) **The River God Cafe ❸,** on High St., combines French and Asian flavors in seafood and tofu dishes. (Entrees €10-14. Open daily 5-10pm.) On Saturdays, an **open-air market** sets up in front of St. Nicholas Church on Market St. (Open Sa 8am-1pm.)

SIGHTS AND NIGHTLIFE. The **Nora Barnacle House,** 8 Bowling Green, was once the home of James Joyce's life-long companion. Today, a friendly staff happily discusses their favorite author while pointing out his original love letters to Ms. Barnacle. (Open mid-May to mid-Sept. W-F 10am-1pm and 2-5pm; off-season by appointment. €2.50.) The Lynch family ruled Galway from the 13th to the 18th century; their 1320 mansion, **Lynch's Castle,** now houses the Allied Irish Bank. A small display recalls the story of an elder Lynch who hung his own son, thus giving his name to executions performed without legal authority. The castle is in front of the Church of St. Nicholas on Market St. (Exhibit open M-W and F 10am-4pm, Th 10am-5pm. Free.) Drift down the **Corrib** for views of the city, the countryside, and nearby castles. Frank Dolan rents **rowboats** at 13 Riverside, Woodquay (€4 per hr.). In mid-July, the **Galway Arts Festival** (☎583 800) attracts *trad* musicians, rock groups, theater troupes, and filmmakers.

The pubs along **Quay Street** tend to cater to tourists and students, while the pubs on **Dominick Street** (across the river from the Quay) are popular with locals. **The King's Head,** on High St., has three floors and nightly rock. Galway's best live music is hidden at the back of **Roisín Dubh** ("The Black Rose"), on Dominick St. (Occasional cover €5-20.) **The Crane,** 2 Sea Rd., is a great place to hear nightly *trad.*

ARAN ISLANDS (OILEÁIN ÁRANN) ☎099

Twenty-four kilometers off the western edge of Co. Galway, the Aran Islands feel like the edge of the world. Their green fields are hatched with a maze of limestone—the result of centuries of farmers piling stones into thousands of meters of walls. The tremendous cliff-top forts of the early islanders give the illusion of having sprung from the limestone itself. Of the dozens of ruins, forts, churches, and holy wells that rise from the stony terrain of **Inishmore** (Inis Mór; pop. 900), the most amazing is the **Dún Aengus** ring fort, where concentric stones circle a sheer 100m drop. The **Inis Mór Way** is a mostly paved route that passes the majority of the island's sights and is great for biking; pick up a map at the tourist office (€2). Windswept **Inishmaan** (Inis Meáin; pop. 300) elevates solitude to an art form; it too has a path, the **Inishmaan Way,** that passes the majority of the island's ruins. The **Inis Oírr Way** on **Inisheer** (Inis Oírr; pop. 300), the smallest island, goes past **Cnoc Raithní,** a bronze-age tumulus, and **An Loch Mór,** an inland lake brimming with wildfowl and ringed by wild leeks.

Island Ferries (☎(091) 561 767) go from **Rossaveal,** west of Galway, to Inishmore (40min., 2-3 per day, round-trip €20) and Inisheer (40min., 2 per day, round-trip €20). **Queen of Aran II** (☎566 535), based in the islands, also leaves from Rossaveal for Inishmore (4 per day, round-trip €19). Both companies run **buses** to Rossaveal, departing from Kinlay House, on Merchant St. in Galway, 1½hr. before ferry departure (€6, students €5). Ferries to Inishmore arrive at **Kilronan.** The **tourist office** there stores luggage (€0.95), changes money, and finds accommodations. (☎61 263. Open July-Sept. daily 10am-6:45pm; Oct. 10am-5pm; Nov.-Mar. 10am-4pm.) **Mainistir House (IHH) ❶,** less than 2km from town on the main road, is a sprawling hostel that was once a haven for musicians and writers. Don't miss the nightly

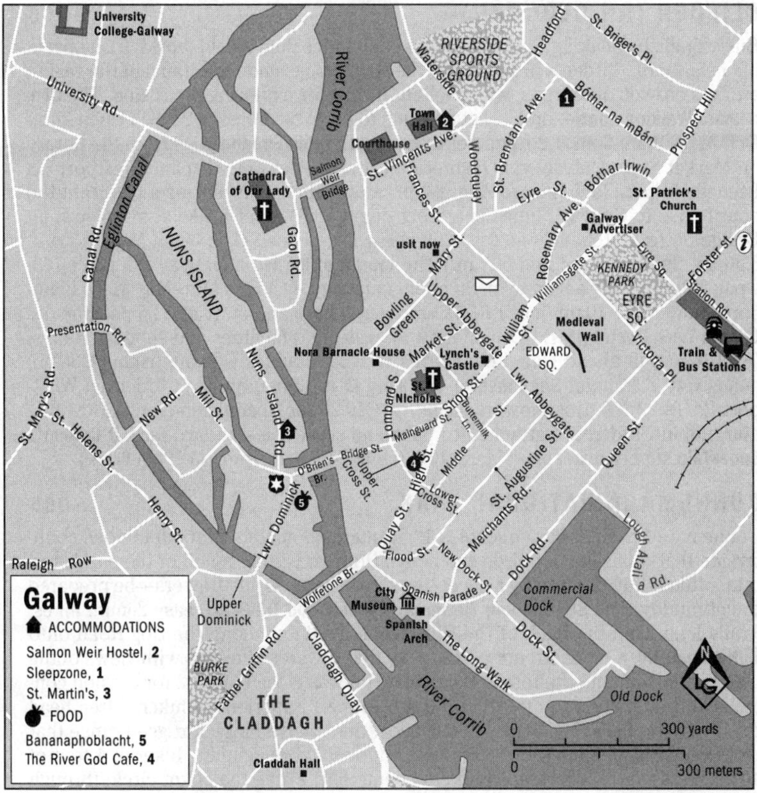

vegetarian buffet (€12), an excellent place to meet other travelers. (☎61 169. Bike rental €10 per day. Laundry €6. Dorms €12; singles €20; doubles €32.) The colorful and ivy-covered **St. Brendan's House ❷,** immediately to the left off the entrance to the main road, is across from the ocean. (☎61 149. Singles €18-22, with bath €20-25; doubles €36-44/40-50.) The **Spar Market** in Kilronan functions as an unofficial community center. (Open in summer M-Sa 9am-8pm, Su 10am-6pm; off-season M-Sa 9am-8pm, Su 10am-5pm.)

CONNEMARA

Connemara, a largely Irish-speaking region, is comprised of a lacy net of inlets and islands, a gang of inland mountains, and desolate stretches of bog. This thinly populated region of northwest County Galway harbors some of Ireland's most breathtaking scenery, from rocky offshore islands to the green slopes of the area's two major mountain ranges, the Twelve Bens and the Maamturks.

CLIFDEN (AN CLOCHÁN) ☎095

Busy, English-speaking Clifden has more amenities than its old-world, Irish-speaking neighbors. Clifden's proximity to the scenic bogs and mountains of the region attracts crowds of tourists, who use it as a base for exploring the region. The **Connemara Walking Centre,** on Market St., runs tours of the bogs. (☎21 379. Open Mar.-Oct. M-Sa 10am-6pm. 1-2 tours per day; €20-32.) **Bus Éireann** goes from the library on Market St. to Galway via Oughterard (2hr., 1-6 per day, €9) and Westport via Leenane (1½hr., late June to Aug. 1-3 per day). Michael Nee runs a bus from the courthouse to Galway (June-Sept. 2 per day, €7.60). Rent a **bike** at **Mannion's,** on Bridge St. (☎21 160. €9 per day, €60 per week; deposit €20. Open M-Sa 9:30am-6:30pm, Su 10am-1pm and 5-7pm.) The **tourist office** is on Galway Rd. (☎21 163. Open July-Aug. M-Sa 9am-6pm, Su noon-4pm; Sept.-Oct. and Mar.-May M-Sa 10am-5pm; June M-Sa 10am-6pm.) **B&Bs** are everywhere and start at €25 per person. **Clifden Town Hostel (IHH) ❶,** on Market St., has great facilities and spotless rooms. (☎21 076. Call ahead Dec.-Feb. Dorms €10.20; doubles €30.50; triples €38-42; quads €46.) Tranquil **Shanaheever Campsite ❶** is 1.5km outside Clifden on Westport Rd. (☎22 150. Hot showers. Laundry. €10.20 for 2 people and tent.) Most restaurants in Clifden are attached to pubs and serve the standard fare. **O'Connor's SuperValu** supermarket is on Market St. (Open M-F 9am-7pm, Su 10am-6pm.)

IRELAND

CONNEMARA NATIONAL PARK ☎095

Connemara National Park occupies 12.5 square kilometers of mountainous countryside that thousands of birds call home. Bogs constitute much of the park's terrain, often thinly covered by a deceptive screen of grass and flowers—be prepared to get muddy. The **Snuffaunboy Nature** and **Ellis Wood Trails** are easy 20min. hikes. Trails lead from the back of the Ellis Wood Trail and along the Bog Road onto **Diamond Hill,** a more strenuous 2hr. hike that rewards climbers with views of the bog, the harbor, and the forest. (Diamond Hill was closed in 2002 for erosion control; call the Visitors Centre to confirm opening.) Experienced hikers often head for the **Twelve Bens** (Na Benna Beola, a.k.a. the Twelve Pins), a rugged range that reaches 2200m heights (not recommended for solo or beginning hikers). A tour of all 12 Bens takes experienced hikers about 10hr. **Biking** the 65km circle through Clifden, Letterfrack, and the Inagh Valley is truly captivating, but only appropriate for fit bikers. A guidebook mapping out 30min. walks (€6.35) is available at the **Visitors Centre,** where the staff helps plan longer hikes. They'll also explain the differences between hummocks and tussocks. (☎41 054. Open June daily 10am-6:30pm; July-Aug. 9:30am-6:30pm; May and Sept. 10am-5:30pm. €2.60, students €1.25.) Hikers often base themselves at the **Ben Lettery Hostel (An Óige/HI) ❶,** in Ballinafad, 13km east of Clifden. (☎51 136. Dorms €10.20-11.45.)

Tiny **Letterfrack** is the gateway to the park. The Galway-Clifden **bus** (mid-June to Aug. 11 per week, Sept. to mid-June 4 per week; no buses on Su) and the summertime Clifden-Westport bus (1-2 per day) stop at Letterfrack. The **Old Monastery Hostel ❶** is one of Ireland's finest. (☎41 132. Bike rental €9 per day. Internet €4 per hr. Breakfast included. Dorms €10.20-12.70. **Camping** €6.40.)

BALLINA ☎096

Armies of fishermen invade Ballina each year during the salmon season (Feb.-Sept.). The town also attracts visitors and locals alike for its boisterous nightlife. The **Belleek Woods** surround the **Belleek Castle** and are filled with almost too-idyllic glades. Jolly drinkers head to **The Parting Glass,** on Tolan St. (☎72 714), for live music; call ahead for the schedule. **Trains** leave from Station Rd., near the bus station, for Dublin (3 per day, €21). **Buses** arrive at Kevin Barry St. from: Donegal (1-3 per day, €13.30); Galway (2hr., 5-6 per day, €11.50); and Dublin (4hr., 6 per day, €12.10). The **tourist office** is on Cathedral Rd. (☎70 848. Open June-Aug. daily 10am-5:30pm; May and Sept. 10am-1pm and 2-5:30pm.) **Fishing permits** and **licenses** are available at the **Northwest Regional Fisheries Board** from the angling officer. (☎22 788. Open daily 9:30am-11:30am.) There are no hostels in Ballina. Dozens of nearly identical B&Bs line the main roads into town; try the **Lismoyne House ❸,** on Kevin Barry St., for a good night's rest and some fishing tips. (☎70 582. Singles €35; doubles €70.) There is a **Quinnsworth** supermarket on Market Rd. (Open M-W and Sa 8:30am-7pm, Th-F 8:30am-9pm, Su noon-6pm.)

WESTPORT ☎098

Palm trees and steep hills lead down to Westport's busy Georgian streets. Nearby, the conical **Croagh Patrick** rises 650m over Clew Bay. The summit has been revered as a holy site for thousands of years. St. Patrick worked here in AD 441, praying for 40 days and nights to banish snakes from Ireland. Climbers start their excursion from the 15th-century **Murrisk Abbey,** several kilometers west of Westport on R395 toward Louisburgh. Buses go to Murrisk (2-3 per day); for groups, cabs (☎27 171) are cheaper and more convenient. Sheep calmly rule **Clare Island,** a desolate but beautiful speck in the Atlantic. Take a bus to Roonah Pier, 29km from Westport, and then a ferry to the island. (Bus departs Westport's tourist office at 10am and returns by 6pm; €25 for bus and ferry combined.) **Matt Molloy's,** on Bridge St., is owned by a member of the Irish band the Chieftains and has nightly *trad.* (Open M-W 12:30-11:30pm, Th-Sa 12:30pm-12:30am, Su 12:30-11pm.)

Trains arrive at the **Altamont St. Station** (☎25 253), a 5min. walk up the North Mall, from Dublin (2-3 per day, €21-23) via Athlone. **Buses** leave Mill St. for Galway (2hr., 4-8 per day, €11.60). The **tourist office** is on James St. (☎25 711. Open July-Aug. M-Sa 9am-6:45pm, Su 10am-6pm; Apr.-June and Sept.-Oct. M-Sa 9am-5:45pm.) **B&Bs** cluster on **Altamont Road** and **The Quay.** A conservatory and garden grace **The Granary Hostel ❶,** a 25min. walk from town, just at the bend in The Quay. (☎25 903. Open Apr.-Sept. Dorms €10.) Restaurants are concentrated on **Bridge Street.** The **SuperValu** supermarket is on Shop St. (Open M-Sa 8:30am-9pm, Su 10am-6pm.)

IRELAND

NORTHWEST IRELAND

The farmland of the upper Shannon stretches northward into Co. Sligo's mountains, lakes, and ancient monuments. A mere sliver of land connects Co. Sligo to Co. Donegal, the second-largest and most remote of the Republic's counties. Donegal's *gaeltacht* is a storehouse of genuine, unadulterated Irish tradition.

SLIGO ☎071

Since the beginning of the 20th century, Sligo has seen a literary pilgrimage of William Butler Yeats devotees; the poet spent summers in town as a child and set many of his poems around Sligo Bay. **Sligo Town,** the commercial center, is an excellent base from which to explore Yeats's haunts. The well-preserved 13th-century **Sligo Abbey** is on Abbey St. (Open Apr.-Oct. daily 10am-6pm; Nov.-Mar. call for hours. €1.90, students €0.70.) **The Model Arts Centre and Niland Gallery,** on the Mall, houses one of the finest collections of modern Irish art. (Open Tu-Sa 10am-5:30pm. Free.) Yeats is buried in **Drumcliffe Churchyard,** on the N15, 6.5km northwest of

Sligo. Buses from Sligo to Derry stop at Drumcliffe (10min., 3-7 per day, round-trip €4). Over 70 pubs crowd the main streets of Sligo. The trendy **Shoot the Crows,** on Grattan St., has fairies and skulls dangling from the ceiling.

Trains (☎69 888) go from Lord Edward St. to Dublin via Carrick-on-Shannon and Mullingar (3hr., 4 per day, €19). From the same station, **buses** (☎60 066) head to: Belfast (4hr., 2-3 per day, €22); Derry (3hr., 4-7 per day, €13.30); Dublin (3-4hr., 4-5 per day, €12.40); Galway (2½hr., 4-6 per day, €11.40); and Westport (2½hr., 1-4 per day, €12.70). Turn left on Lord Edward St., then follow the signs right onto Adelaid St. and around the corner to Temple St. to find the **tourist office.** (☎61 201. Open June-Aug. M-Sa 9am-7pm, Su 10am-6pm; Oct.-May M-F 9am-5pm.) **B&Bs** cluster on **Pearse Road,** on the south side. **Eden Hill Holiday Hostel (IHH) ❶,** off Pearse Rd., has Victorian decor and a friendly staff. From the town center, follow Pearse Rd., turn right at the Marymount sign, and take another right after one block. (☎43 204. Laundry. Dorms €11.) A **Tesco** supermarket is on O'Connell St. (☎62 788. Open M-Tu and Sa 8:30am-7pm, W-F 8:30am-9pm, Su 10am-6pm.)

COUNTY DONEGAL AND SLIEVE LEAGUE ☎073

Tourists are a rarity in County Donegal. Its geographic isolation in the northwest has spared it from the widespread deforestation of Ireland; vast wooded areas engulf many of Donegal's mountain chains, while the coastline alternates between beaches and cliffs. Travelers use **Donegal Town** as the gateway to the county. **Buses** (☎21 101) stop outside the Abbey Hotel on The Diamond and run to Dublin (4hr., 5-6 per day, €13.40) and Galway (4hr., 3-5 per day, €13.40). With your back to Abbey Hotel, turn right; the **tourist office,** on Quay St., is just outside of The Diamond. (☎21 148. Open July-Aug. M-Sa 9am-6pm, Su noon-4pm; Sept.-Oct. and Easter-June M-F 9am-5pm, Sa 10am-2pm.) **Donegal Independent Town Hostel (IHH) ❶,** on Killybegs Rd., is family-run and has a homey atmosphere. (☎22 805. Call ahead. Dorms €10.50; doubles €24. **Camping** €6.)

The **Slieve League Peninsula**'s rocky cliffs, Europe's highest, jut to the west of Donegal Town. The cliffs and mountains of this sparsely-populated area harbor coastal hamlets, untouched beaches, and dramatic scenery. **Glencolmcille** (glen-kaul-um-KEEL), on the western tip of the peninsula, is a parish of several tiny villages wedged between two monstrous cliffs. The villages are renowned for their handmade products, particularly sweaters. On sunny days, visitors to the **Silver Strand** are rewarded with stunning views of the gorgeous beach and rocky cliffs; the trek along the Slieve League coastline begins here. **Bus Éireann** runs from Donegal Town to Glencolmcille and Dungloe, stopping in tiny **Kilcar** (1-3 per day), the gateway to Donegal's *gaeltacht* and a commercial base for many Donegal tweed weavers. Many Slieve League hikers stay in Kilcar, where they can comfortably drive, bike, or hike to the mountains. The fabulous **Derrylahan Hostel (IHH) ❶** is 3km from Kilcar on the coast road to Carrick; call for pickup. (☎38 079. Laundry €7. Dorms €10; singles €14; doubles €28. **Camping** €6.) In Glencolmcille, sleep at the hillside **Dooey Hostel (IHO) ❶,** which has an ocean view and a beautiful garden. (☎30 130. Dorms €9.50; doubles €21. **Camping** €5.50.)

DERRYVEAGH MOUNTAINS ☎075

Beaches are separated by boglands in the eerie stillness of the Derryveagh Mountains. On the eastern side of the mountains is **Glenveagh National Park,** 60 sq. km of forest glens, bogs, and herds of red deer. (On the R251, east of Dunlewy. ☎(074) 37 090. Open Mar. to early Nov. daily 10am-5pm. Free.) **Crolly,** a village at the intersection of N56 and R259, and **Dunlewy,** off the R251, are excellent bases for exploring

Mount Errigal. From Crolly, Feda O'Donnell (☎48 114) runs daily **buses** to Galway and Donegal Town via Letterkenny; Swilly (☎21 380) passes Crolly on its Dungloe-Derry route; John McGinley Coaches (☎(074) 35 201) goes to Dublin; and O'Donnell Trans-Ulster Express (☎48 356) goes to Belfast via Derry. Buses don't travel near Dunlewy; you'll need a car to get around. **Errigal Youth Hostel (An Óige/HI) ❶,** off the R251 in Dunlewy, is clean and basic. (☎31 180. Lockout 10am-5pm. Curfew 1am. Dorms €9-11.) **Screagan an Iolair Hill Hostel ❶** (SCRAG an UH-ler) is in Tor, 6.5km outside Crolly. It's close to many Derryveagh hikes, if you can bear to leave it; each room has its own decor and the common room is very cozy. (☎48 593. Dorms €12.50; singles €15.)

LETTERKENNY ☎074

Letterkenny, while difficult to navigate, is a lively place to make bus connections to the rest of Donegal, the Republic, and Northern Ireland. **Buses** leave from the junction of Port Rd. and Pearse Rd., in front of the shopping center. Bus Éireann (☎21 309) runs to: Derry (30min., 3-6 per day, €6.35); Dublin (4½hr., 5-6 per day, €12.70); Galway (4¾hr., 4 per day, €15.25) via Donegal Town (50min., €6.35); and Sligo (2hr., 3-5 per day, €11.50). Lough Swilly (☎22 863) runs to Derry (M-Sa 11 per day, €5.60) and the Inishowen Peninsula (3-4 per day, €5.70). The **Chamber of Commerce Visitors Information Centre** is at 40 Port Rd. (☎24 866. Open M-F 9am-5pm.) **The Port Hostel (IHO) ❶,** Orchard Crest, is convenient to the city center. (☎25 315. Dorms €12; singles €13-16.) There is a **Tesco** supermarket behind the bus station. (Open M-Tu and Sa 8:30am-7pm, W 8:30am-8pm, Th-F 8:30am-9pm, Su noon-6pm.)

INISHOWEN PENINSULA AND MALIN HEAD ☎077

Brochures trumpet the Inishowen Peninsula as the "crown of Ireland." It combines rocky grasslands and bogs with the barren beauty that pervades much of Donegal. The clearly marked **Inish Eoghain 100** road winds around the peninsula's perimeter. The peninsula's most popular attraction is **Malin Head,** remarkable for its rocky, wave-tattered coast and sky-high sand dunes, reputedly the highest in Europe (up to 30m). The raised beaches around Malin Head are covered with semi-precious stones; walkers sifting through the sands may find jasper, quartz, small opals, or amethyst. **Bamba's Crown** is the northernmost tip of Ireland, a tooth of dark rock rising up from the ocean spray. Lough Swilly **buses** (☎61 340) run from Derry, the nearest city to Inishowen, to points on the peninsula including Malin Head (1½hr., 2-3 per day). To reach the **Sandrock Holiday Hostel (IHO/IHH) ❶,** on Port Ronan Pier, take the left fork off the Inish Eoghain 100 at the Crossroads Inn (also a bus stop). The friendly owners provide maps and walking tours. (☎70 289. Sheets €1.25. Wash €4, dry €2. Dorms €10.)

NORTHERN IRELAND

FACTS AND FIGURES: NORTHERN IRELAND

Official Name: Northern Ireland.
Capital: Belfast.
Population: 1,700,000.
Land Area: 14,160 sq. km.
Time Zone: GMT.
Language: English.
Religions: Protestant (56%), Roman Catholic (44%).

The calm tenor of life in the North has been overshadowed internationally by concerns about riots and bombings. But acts of violence and extremist fringe groups are less prominent than the division in civil society that sends Protestants and Catholics to separate neighborhoods, separate stores, separate pubs, and often separate schools, with separate, though similar, traditional songs and slang. The 1998 Good Friday Agreement, which granted Home Rule to Northern Ireland with the hope of resolving some of the region's struggles, has been struggling itself. Home Rule was suspended and reinstated in February 2000, and by the summer of 2001 a lack of progress on paramilitary promises to "put weapons beyond use" brought the Good Friday government to a frustrated halt. London took the reins again, if only briefly, and both sides renewed their efforts to make their country as peaceful as it is beautiful. While everyday life in Northern Ireland may be divided, its landscape and society are for the most part quiet and peaceful.

PHONE CODE	Northern Ireland is reached by using the UK **country code 44;** from the Republic dial **048.** The **phone code** for every town in the North is **028.**

BELFAST ☎028

Belfast (pop. 330,000), the second-largest city on the island, is the focus of the North's cultural, commercial, and political activity. Acclaimed writers and the annual arts festival in November support Belfast's reputation as a thriving artistic center. The bar scene, a mix of Irish and British pub culture, entertains locals, foreigners, and students alike. West Belfast's famous sectarian murals are perhaps the most informative source on the effects of what locals call "the Troubles." Despite the violent associations conjured by the name Belfast, the city feels more neighborly than most international—and even Irish—visitors expect.

TRANSPORTATION

Flights: Belfast International Airport (BFS; ☎9442 2888), in Aldergrove. **Airbus** (☎9033 3000) runs from the airport to the Europa and Laganside bus stations (M-Sa every 30min., Su about every hr.; £5). **Trains** connect the **Belfast City Airport** (Sydenham Halt), at the harbor, to Central Station (£1).

Trains: Central Station (☎9066 6630), on E. Bridge St. To **Derry** (2hr., 3-9 per day, £6.70) and **Dublin** (2hr., 5-8 per day, £20). **Centrelink** buses run from the station to the city center (free with rail tickets).

Buses: Europa Station (☎9066 6630), off Great Victoria St. Serves the north coast, the west, and the Republic. Buses to **Derry** (1¾hr., 6-19 per day, £7.50) and **Dublin** (3hr.,

5-7 per day, £10.40). **Laganside Station** (☎9066 6630), Donegall Quay, serves Northern Ireland's east coast. The **Centrelink** bus connects both stations with the city center.

Ferries: SeaCat (☎(08705) 523 523; www.seacat.co.uk) leaves for: **Heysham, England** (4hr., Apr.-Nov. 1-2 per day); the **Isle of Man** (2¾hr., Apr.-Nov. 1-2 per day); **Troon, Scotland** (2½hr., 2-3 per day). Fares £10-30 without car.

Local Transportation: The red **Citybus Network** (☎9024 6485) is supplemented by **Ulsterbus**'s suburban "blue buses." Travel within the city center £1.10, students and children £0.50. **Centrelink** buses traverse the city (every 12min. M-F 7:25am-9:15pm, Sa 8:35am-9:15pm; £1.10, free with bus or rail ticket). Late **Nightlink** buses shuttle to small towns outside the city (F-Sa 1 and 2am; £3, payable on board).

Taxis: Value Cabs (☎9080 9080). Residents of West and North Belfast use the huge **black cabs;** some are metered, and some follow set routes.

ORIENTATION AND PRACTICAL INFORMATION

Buses arrive at the Europa bus station on **Great Victoria Street.** To the northeast is the **City Hall** in **Donegall Square.** South of the bus station, Great Victoria St. meets **Dublin Road** at **Shaftesbury Square;** this stretch of Great Victoria St. between the bus station and Shaftesbury Sq. is known as the **Golden Mile** for its high-brow establishments and Victorian architecture. **Botanic Avenue** and **Bradbury Place** (which becomes **University Road**) extend south from Shaftesbury Sq. into the **Queen's University** area, where cafes, pubs, and budget lodgings await. To get to Donegall Sq. from Central Station, turn left, walk down East Bridge St., turn right on Oxford St., and make your first left on May St., which runs into Donegall Sq.; or, take the Centrelink bus. Divided from the rest of Belfast by the Westlink Motorway, working-class **West Belfast** is more politically volatile; the area is best seen by day. The Protestant neighborhood stretches along **Shankill Road,** just north of the Catholic neighborhood, which is centered around **Falls Road.** The two are separated by the **peace line.** During the week, the area north of City Hall is essentially deserted at night, and it's a good idea to use taxis after dark.

Tourist Office: The Belfast Welcome Centre, 47 Donegall Pl. (☎9024 6609). Has a great booklet on Belfast and info on surrounding areas. Open June-Sept. M-Sa 9am-7pm, Su noon-5pm; Oct.-May M-Sa 9am-5:30pm.

Banks: Banks and **ATMs** are on almost every corner. **Bank of Ireland,** 54 Donegall Pl. (☎9023 4334). Open M-F 9am-4:30pm.

Currency Exchange: Thomas Cook, 10 Donegall Sq. W. (☎9088 3800). Cashes Thomas Cook traveler's checks with no commission; others 2%. Open M-W and F 5:30am-10pm, Th 9am-6pm, Sa 10am-5pm.

Luggage Storage: For security reasons, there is no luggage storage at airports, bus stations, or train stations. All 4 **hostels** will hold bags during the day for guests.

Bi-Gay-Lesbian Resources: Rainbow Project N.I., 33 Church Ln. (☎9031 9030). Open M-F 10am-5:30pm.

Pharmacy: Boot's, 35-47 Donegall Pl. (☎9024 2332). Open M-W and F-Sa 8:30am-6pm, Th 8:30am-9pm, Su 1-6pm. Also on Great Victoria St. and Castle Pl.

Laundry: Globe Drycleaners & Launderers, 37-39 Botanic Ave. (☎9024 3956). About £3-4 per load. Open M-F 8am-9pm, Sa 8am-6pm, Su noon-6pm.

Emergency: ☎999; no coins required. **Police,** 65 Knock Rd. (☎9065 0222).

Hospitals: Belfast City Hospital, 9 Lisburn Rd. (☎9032 9241). From Shaftesbury Sq., follow Bradbury Pl. and take a right at the fork. **Royal Victoria Hospital,** 12 Grosvenor Rd. (☎9024 0503). From Donegall Sq., take Howard St. west to Grosvenor Rd.

Internet Access: Belfast Central Library, 122 Royal Ave. (☎9050 9150). £1.50 per 30min. Open M and Th 9am-8pm, Tu-W and F 9am-5:30pm, Sa 9:30am-1pm.

Post Office: Central Post Office, 25 Castle Pl. (☎9032 3740). *Poste Restante* mail comes here. Open M-Sa 9am-5:30pm. **Postal Code:** BT1 1NB. Branch offices: **Botanic Garden,** 95 University Rd., across from the university (☎9038 1309; **postal code:** BT7 1NG); **Botanic Avenue,** 1-5 Botanic Ave. (☎9032 6177; **postal code:** BT2 7DA). Branch offices open M-F 8:45am-5:30pm, Sa 10am-12:30pm.

ACCOMMODATIONS

Despite a competitive hostel market, Belfast's fluctuating tourism and rising rents have shrunk the number of available cheap digs. Nearly all are located near Queen's University, south of the city center, which is convenient to pubs and restaurants; this area is by far the best place to stay in the city. Take **Citybus** #69, 70, 71, 83, 84, or 86 from Donegall Sq. to areas in the south. A walk to these accommodations takes 10-20min. from the bus or train station. Hostels and B&Bs are busy in the summer; reservations are recommended.

HOSTELS AND UNIVERSITY HOUSING

The Ark (IHH), 18 University St. (☎9032 9626). A 10min. walk from Europa Bus Station on Great Victoria St. Take a right and head away from the Europa Hotel; at Shaftesbury Sq., take the right fork on Bradbury Pl., then fork left onto University Rd. University St. is the fourth left. Community feel. Weekend luggage storage. Internet £1 per 20min. Laundry £4. Curfew 2am. Dorms Su-Th £8.50, F-Sa £9.50; doubles £32. ❶

Arnie's Backpackers (IHH), 63 Fitzwilliam St. (☎9024 2867). From Bradbury Pl. (see The Ark, above), fork left onto University Rd.; Fitzwilliam St. is on the right. Friendly atmosphere. Key deposit £2. Luggage storage. 8-bed dorms £7-8.50. ❶

Belfast Hostel (HINI), 22 Donegall Rd. (☎9031 5435), off Shaftesbury Sq. Clean and inviting interior despite the concrete facade. Books tours of Belfast and Giant's Causeway. Breakfast £2. Laundry £3. Reception open 24hr. Dorms £8.50-10.50. ❶

The Linen House Youth Hostel (IHH), 18-20 Kent St. (☎9058 6400), in West Belfast. Across from the main entrance to City Hall, turn left onto Donegall Pl., which becomes Royal Ave. Take a left onto Kent St. just before the Belfast Library. This converted 19th-century linen factory now houses scores of weary travelers. 24hr. secure parking. Laundry £3. Internet £1 per 20min. 18-bed dorms £6.50-7; 6- to 10-bed dorms £8.50-9; 8-bed dorms with bath £8.50-9; singles £15-20; doubles £24-30. ❶

Queen's University Accommodations, 78 Malone Rd. (☎9038 1608). Take bus #71 from Donegall Sq. East; a 35min. walk from Europa. University Rd. runs into Malone Rd.; the residence halls are on your left. Undecorated, institutional dorms. Open mid-June to Aug. and Christmas and Easter vacations. Free laundry. Singles £8.50 for UK students, £10 for international students, £12.40 for non-students; doubles £21.40. ❶

BED AND BREAKFASTS

B&Bs occupy virtually every house between **Malone** and **Lisburn Roads,** just south of Queen's University. Calling ahead is generally a good idea; most owners, however, will refer you to other accommodations if necessary.

Camera Guesthouse, 44 Wellington Park (☎9066 0026). A family-run guesthouse with fabulous breakfasts. Singles £25, with bath £37; doubles £50/£55. July discounts. ❸

Botanic Lodge, 87 Botanic Ave. (☎9032 7682), at the intersection with Mt. Charles Ave. A short walk to the city center. Singles £25, with bath £35; doubles £40/£45. ❸

Marine House, 30 Eglantine Ave. (☎9066 2828). Housekeeping standards are as high as the ceilings in this airy mansion. All rooms with bath. Singles £35; doubles £48. ❹

All Seasons B&B, 365 Lisburn Rd. (☎9068 2814). Further out from the city center, this is a great choice for those with cars. Free secure parking. All rooms with bath. Singles £25; doubles £40. ❸

Avenue Guest House, 23 Eglantine Ave. (☎9066 5904). Large rooms with comfortable beds and expansive views. Singles £35; doubles £45. ❹

FOOD

Belfast's eateries assume a cosmopolitan character, with flavors from around the globe. **Dublin Road, Botanic Road,** and the **Golden Mile** have the highest concentration of restaurants. For fruits and vegetables, head to the lively **St. George's Market,** East Bridge St., in the enormous warehouse between May St. and Oxford St. (Open Th 3-9pm and F 6am-1pm.) **Lisburn Road,** which runs parallel to University Rd., has bakeries and fruit stands.

Azzura, 8 Church Ln. (☎9024 2444), north of Donegall Square. This tiny cafe has gourmet pizzas, pastas, soups, and sandwiches for under £4. Open M-Sa 9am-5pm. ❷

Maggie May's Belfast Cafe, 50 Botanic Ave. (☎9032 2622). In the Queen's University Area. Boasts some of the best breakfasts around. Pancakes £1.75. Entrees £4-6. Open M-Sa 8am-10:30pm, Su 10am-10:30pm. ❷

Bookfinders, 47 University Rd. (☎9032 8269). Atmospheric bookstore/cafe with mismatched dishes and counter-culture paraphernalia. Art gallery upstairs. Veggie options. Soup and bread £2.25, sandwiches £2.20-2.50. Open M-Sa 10am-5:30pm. ❶

The Moghul, 62A Botanic Ave. (☎9032 6677), overlooking the street from 2nd floor corner windows. Outstanding Indian lunch for carnivores or vegetarians M-Th noon-2pm £3. Open for dinner M-Th 5-11:30pm, F-Sa 5-11:45pm, Su 5-10:30pm. ❷

SIGHTS

DONEGALL SQUARE. After Queen Victoria made Belfast a city in 1888, the green copper-domed **Belfast City Hall** was built on the site of demolished linen warehouses. Neoclassical marble columns and arches figure prominently in A. Brunwell Thomas's 1906 design. Directly in front of the main entrance, an enormous marble **Queen Victoria statue** stares down at visitors with a formidable grimace, as bronze figures representing shipbuilding and spinning writhe at her feet. The interior of City Hall is accessible only by guided tour. *(☎9027 0456. 1hr. tours June-Sept. M-F 10:30, 11:30am, and 2:30pm; Sa 2:30pm. Oct.-May M-Sa 2:30pm. Free.)* One of Belfast's oldest establishments is the **Linen Hall Library.** The red hand of Ulster decorates the top of its street entrance. The library contains a renowned collection of political documents relating to Northern Ireland. *(Enter via 52 Fountain St. ☎9032 1707. Open M-F 9:30am-5:30pm, Sa 9:30am-4pm.)*

THE INSIDER'S CITY

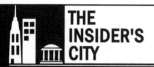

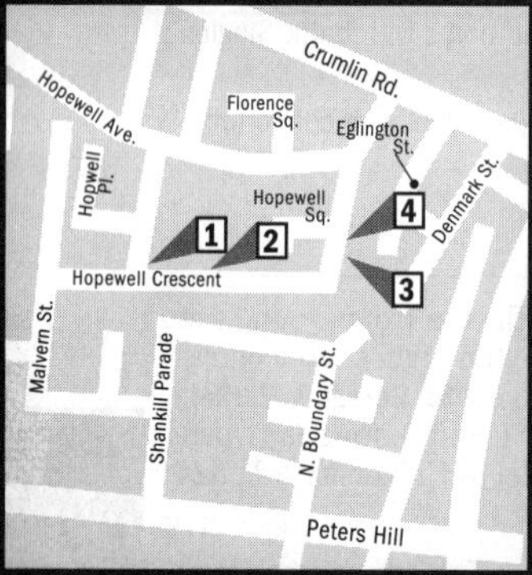

THE CATHOLIC MURALS

The following is a tour of Catholic Belfast's more important murals, as well as other sights related to Northern Ireland's Troubles centered on Falls Rd.

1 A mural on the side of the library illustrating the **Hunger Strikes of 1981,** when several Catholic prisoners died in protest of the conditions of their detainment.

2 Murals on the walls opposite the old **Sein Féin Office,** once used as the North's national headquarters.

3 A portrait of **Bobby Sands,** on the Sevastopol St. side of the Sinn Féin Office. Sands, elected to British Parliament during the height of the Troubles, was one of the first hunger strikers to die. He is the North's most legendary martyr.

4 **Northern Ireland's National RUC Headquarters.** The most bombed police station in England, the Republic, and the North, with a fortified, barb-wired facade.

CORNMARKET AND ST. ANNE'S CATHEDRAL. Just north of the city center, a shopping district envelops eight blocks around Castle St. and Royal Ave. This area, known as Cornmarket after one of its original commodities, has been a marketplace since Belfast's early days. Relics of old Belfast remain in the **entries,** or tiny alleys, that connect major streets. Belfast's newspapers all set up shop around **St. Anne's,** also known as the **Belfast Cathedral.** Each of the cathedral's 10 interior pillars names one of Belfast's fields of professionalism: Science, Industry, Healing, Agriculture, Music, Theology, Shipbuilding, Freemasonry, Art, and Womanhood. *(Donegall St., a few blocks from the city center. Open M-Sa 10am-4pm. Free.)*

THE DOCKS AND EAST BELFAST. Although the docks were once the heart of Belfast, continued commercial development made the area more suitable for industrial machinery than for people. However, Belfast's newest mega-attraction, **Odyssey,** a gigantic center that houses five different science attractions, promises to bring back the hordes. *(2 Queen's Quay. ☎9045 1055.)* The best of these is the **W5 Discovery Centre,** a top-of-the-line science and technology museum that beckons geeks of all ages to play with pulley chairs and robots. *(Open M-Sa 10am-6pm, Su noon-6pm; last admission 5pm. £5.50, students and seniors £4, children £3.50, families £15.)*

THE GOLDEN MILE. "The Golden Mile" refers to the strip along Great Victoria St. home to the jewels in the crown of Belfast's establishment. The **Grand Opera House,** the pride and joy of Belfast, was cyclically bombed by the IRA, restored to its original splendor at enormous cost, and then bombed again. *(☎9024 0411. Tours Sa 11am; £3, seniors and children £2. Office open M-W 8:30am-8pm, Th 8:30am-9pm, F 8:30am-6:30pm, Sa 8:30am-5:30pm.)* **The Grand Opera House Ticket Shop** sells tickets for performances, including operas, ballets, and concerts. *(2-4 Great Victoria St. 24hr. info ☎9024 9129. Tickets from £12.50)* The National Trust has restored the highly frequented **Crown Liquor Saloon,** 46 Great Victoria St, to make it a showcase of carved wood, gilded ceilings, and stained-glass. Damaged by 32 blasts in its history, the **Europa Hotel** has the dubious distinction of being "Europe's most bombed hotel."

QUEEN'S UNIVERSITY AREA. Charles Lanyon designed the Tudor-revival brick campus of **Queen's University** in 1849, modeling it after Magdalen College, Oxford. The **Visitors Centre** is in the Lanyon Room to the left of the main entrance. *(University Rd. Visitors Centre ☎9033 5252. Open May-Sept. M-Sa 10am-4pm; Oct.-Mar. M-F 10am-4pm.)* Bask in Belfast's occasional sun in the

Botanic Gardens behind the university. *(☎9032 4902. Open daily 8am-dusk. Free.)*

NORTH BELFAST. In 1934, the Earl of Shaftesbury presented the **Belfast Castle** to the city. The ancient King Matudan had his McArt's Fort here, at the top of **Cave Hill** where the more modern United Irishmen plotted rebellion in 1795. The summit is nicknamed "Napoleon's Nose." Marked trails lead north from the fort to five caves in the area; only the lowest is accessible. *(Open M-Sa 9am-10:30pm, Su 9am-6pm. Free.)*

WEST BELFAST AND THE MURALS

West Belfast is not a "sight" in the traditional sense. You will come across political **murals** as you wander among the houses. Be discreet if photographing the murals. It is illegal to photograph military installations; do so and your film may be confiscated. The Protestant Orangemen's **marching season** (July 4-12) is a risky time to visit the area, since the parades are underscored by mutual antagonism and can lead to violence. Taxi tours provide a fascinating commentary detailing the murals, paraphernalia, and sights on both sides of the peace line. Michael Johnston of **Black Taxi Tours** has made a name for himself with his witty, objective presentations. (☎0800 052 3914; www.belfasttours.com. £9 per person.)

THE FALLS. On **Divis Street,** a high-rise apartment building marks the site of the **Divis Tower,** an ill-fated housing development built by optimistic social planners in the 1960s. This project soon became an IRA stronghold and saw some of the worst of Belfast's Troubles in the 1970s. The British army still occupies the top three floors, and Shankill residents refer to it as "Little Beirut." Continuing west, Divis St. turns into **Falls Road.** The **Sinn Féin** office is easily spotted: one side of it is covered with an enormous portrait of Bobby Sands and an advertisement for the Sinn Fein newspaper, *An Phoblacht.* Continuing down the Falls there are a number of other murals, generally on side streets and on Beechmont.

SHANKILL. North Street turns into **Shankill Road** as it crosses the **Westlink** and then arrives in Protestant Shankill, once a thriving shopping district. Turning left (coming from the direction of North St.) onto most side roads leads to the peace line. The side streets on the right guide you to the **Shankill Estate** and more murals. **Crumlin Road,** through the estate, is the site of the oldest Loyalist murals.

THE INSIDER'S CITY

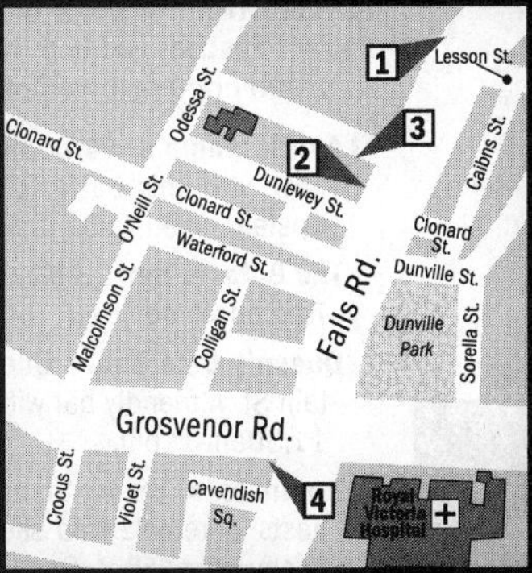

THE PROTESTANT MURALS

Most Protestant murals are found in the Shankill area of West Belfast, which is to the north of Shankill Rd., near Hopewell St. and Hopewell Crescent, and down Shankill Parade.

1. A mural of a **Loyalist martyr,** killed in prison in 1997, remembers those who have died fighting for British-Ulster rule.

2. A depiction of the **Grim Reaper** with a gun and British flag. Beside him are crosses with the names of three IRA men who set off a bomb in the Shankill area in 1993.

3. A collage representing Northern Ireland's **Loyalist militant groups**: the UFF, the UDU, and the UDA.

4. The large black silhouette on this orange-and-yellow mural represents the **Scottish Brigade,** a symbol illustrative of the connection Protestant Loyalists feel to their brethren across the way.

ENTERTAINMENT AND NIGHTLIFE

Belfast's many cultural events and performances are covered in the monthly *Arts Council Artslink*, which is free at the tourist office. Daily listings appear in the *Belfast Telegraph* as well as in Thursday's issue of the *Irish News*. For more information on pub entertainment, pick up the free, biweekly bulletin *The List*, available at the tourist office, hostels, and many pubs. Belfast reigns supreme in the art world for three weeks each November during the annual **Queen's University Belfast Festival** (☎9066 7687). Over 300 separate performances of opera, ballet, film, and comedy invade the city, drawing groups of international acclaim.

Auntie Annie's, 44 Dublin Rd. (☎9050 1660). Live music and a relaxed atmosphere have won this bar a following among all ages. Open M-Sa noon-1am; Su 6-12am. Upstairs open Th-Sa until 2am; cover £3.

The Botanic Inn, 23 Malone Rd. (☎9066 0460). A popular student bar. Pub grub £4-5. *Trad* on W; no cover. Th-Sa DJs; cover £2. 21+. Open daily until 1am.

Queen's Cafe Bar, 4 Queen's Arcade (☎9032 1347), between Donegall Pl. and Fountain St. A friendly bar with a mixed, gay-friendly crowd. Open M-W 11:30am-9pm, Th-Sa 11:30am-11pm.

Robinson's, 38-40 Great Victoria St. (☎9024 7447). **Fibber McGee's,** in the back, hosts incredible *trad* sessions Tu-Su 10pm, Sa 5-7pm; no cover. Nightclubs on top 2 floors; cover £5-8. Open M-Sa 11:30am-1am, Su noon-midnight.

The Empire, 42 Botanic Ave. (☎9024 9276). This 120-year-old building was once a church, but its 2 stories have been revamped to resemble Belfast's music halls. Tu comedy, Th-Su live bands. Cover M-Th and Su £3, F-Sa £3-7. Open daily 11:30am-1am.

The Kremlin, 96 Donegall St. (☎9080 9700). Look for the imposing statue of Stalin above the entrance. Belfast's newest and hottest gay nightspot with foam parties and internationally-renowned drag queens. Cover varies, but free Su, M, and before 9pm. Bar open M-Th 6pm-3am, F-Su 1pm-3:30am. Club open Th-Su.

DAYTRIP FROM BELFAST

ULSTER FOLK AND TRANSPORT MUSEUM

☎9042 8428. Open Mar.-June M-F 10am-5pm, Sa 10am-6pm, Su 11am-6pm; July-Sept. M-Sa 10am-6pm, Su 11am-6pm; Oct.-Feb. M-F 10am-4pm, Sa 10am-5pm, Su 11am-5pm. Each museum £4, students £2.50. Combined ticket £5/£3. Buses and trains stop here on the way to Bangor.

The **Ulster Folk Museum** and **Transport Museum** stretch over 71 hectares in **Holywood.** Established by an Act of Parliament in the 1950s, the Folk Museum aims to preserve the way of life of Ulster's farmers, weavers, and craftspeople, with over 30 buildings from the past three centuries. Across the road in the Transport Museum is a *Titanic* exhibit that includes original blueprints and traces the Belfast-built ship and its fate. The **Railway Museum** next door is stuffed with 25 old railway engines, including the largest locomotive built in Ireland.

DERRY (LONDONDERRY) ☎028

Modern Derry is in the middle of a determined and largely successful effort to cast off the legacy of its political Troubles. Although the landscape was razed by years of bombings and violence still erupts occasionally during the marching season (July 4-12), recent years have been relatively peaceful, and today's rebuilt city looks sparklingly new. Derry's **city walls,** 5.5m high and 6m thick, erected between

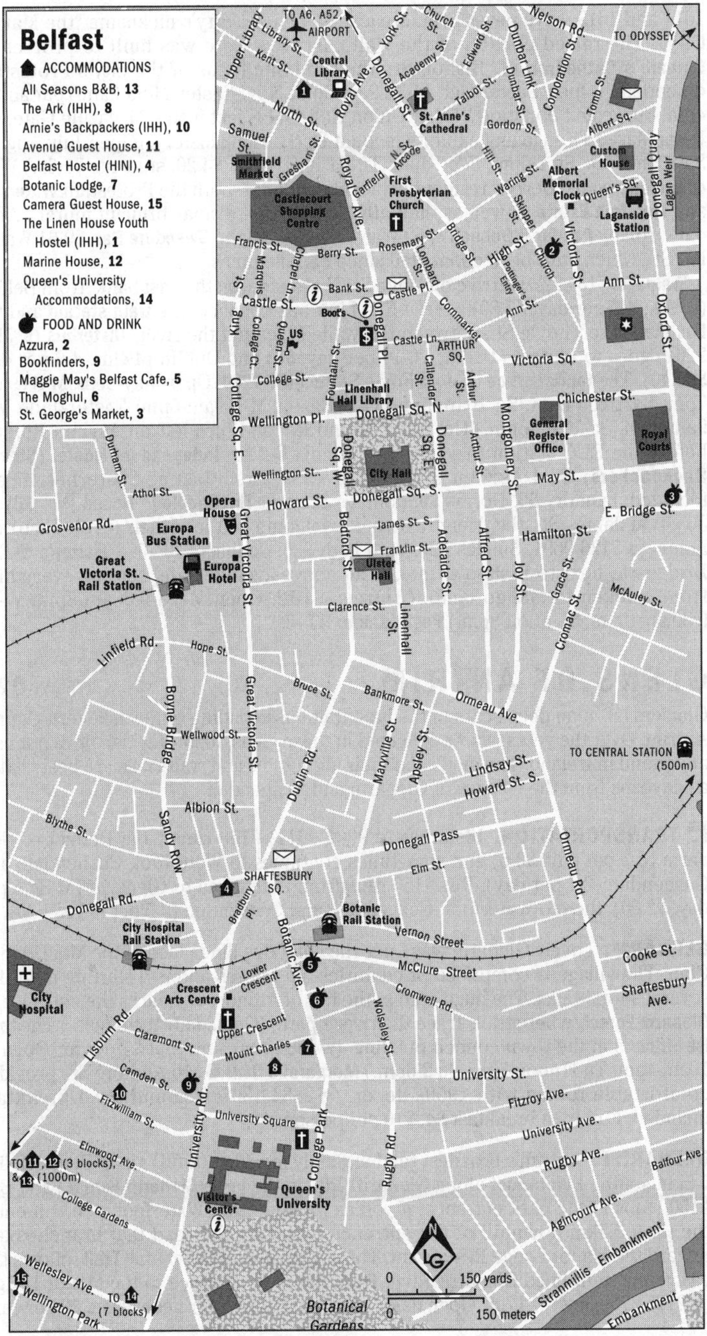
Belfast
ACCOMMODATIONS
All Seasons B&B, 13
The Ark (IHH), 8
Arnie's Backpackers (IHH), 10
Avenue Guest House, 11
Belfast Hostel (HINI), 4
Botanic Lodge, 7
Camera Guest House, 15
The Linen House Youth Hostel (IHH), 1
Marine House, 12
Queen's University Accommodations, 14
FOOD AND DRINK
Azzura, 2
Bookfinders, 9
Maggie May's Belfast Cafe, 5
The Moghul, 6
St. George's Market, 3
TO A6, A52, AIRPORT
TO ODYSSEY
Central Library
St. Anne's Cathedral
Smithfield Market
Castlecourt Shopping Centre
First Presbyterian Church
Albert Memorial Clock
Custom House
Laganside Station
Linenhall Library
City Hall
General Register Office
Royal Courts
Opera House
Europa Bus Station
Europa Hotel
Great Victoria St. Rail Station
Ulster Hall
TO CENTRAL STATION (500m)
SHAFTESBURY SQ.
Botanic Rail Station
City Hospital Rail Station
City Hospital
Crescent Arts Centre
Queen's University
Visitor's Center
Botanical Gardens
TO 11, 12 (3 blocks), & 13 (1000m)
TO 14 (7 blocks)
ARTHUR SQ.
US
Boots
150 yards
150 meters
Donegall Rd.
Donegall Pass
Ormeau Rd.
Ormeau Ave.
Great Victoria St.
Botanic Ave.
University Rd.
Lisburn Rd.
Sandy Row
Royal Ave.
Donegall Pl.
High St.
Victoria St.
Oxford St.
Donegall Quay
Chichester St.
May St.
Howard St.
Wellington Pl.
Castle St.
North St.
Ann St.
Stranmillis Embankment
University St.
Malone Rd.

IRELAND

1614 and 1619, have never been breached—hence Derry's nickname "the Maiden City." The raised portion of the wall past New Gate was built to protect **St. Columb's Cathedral,** off Bishop St., the symbolic focus of the city's Protestant defenders. (Open Easter-Oct. M-Sa 9am-5pm; Nov.-Easter M-Sa 9am-1pm and 2-4pm. Suggested donation £1.) At Union Hall Place, just inside Magazine Gate, the **Tower Museum**'s engaging exhibits recount Derry's long history. (Open July-Aug. M-Sa 10am-5pm, Su 2-5pm; Sept.-June Tu-Sa 10am-5pm. £4.20, students £1.60.) West of the city walls, Derry's residential neighborhoods—both the Protestant **Waterside** and **Fountain Estate** as well as the Catholic **Bogside**—display brilliant murals. After dark, roll by **Peadar O'Donnell's,** 53 Waterloo St., and the **Gweedore Bar,** 59-61 Waterloo St., which have been connected since Famine times.

Trains (☎7134 2228) arrive on Duke St., Waterside, on the east bank, from Belfast (2½hr., 4-7 per day, £7.80). A free Rail-Link bus connects the **train station** and the **bus station,** on Foyle St., between the walled city and the river. **Ulsterbus** (☎7126 2261) goes to Belfast (1½-3hr., 6-16 per day, £8) and Dublin (4¼hr., 4-6 per day, £10.40). The **tourist office** is at 44 Foyle St. (☎7126 7284. Open July-Sept. M-Sa 9am-7pm, Sa 10am-6pm, Su 10am-5pm; Oct.-Easter M-F 9am-5pm; Easter-June M-F 9am-5pm, Sa 10am-5pm.) Go down Strand Rd. and turn left on Asylum Rd. just before the RUC station to reach the friendly **Derry Independent Hostel (Steve's Backpackers) ❶,** 4 Asylum Rd. (☎7137 7989. Breakfast and Internet access included. Laundry £3. Dorms £9; doubles £24.) At **The Saddler's House (No. 36) ❸,** 36 Great James St., the friendly owners welcome you into their lovely Victorian home. (☎7126 9691. Singles £20, with bath £25; doubles £40/£50.) **Fitzroy's ❸,** 2-4 Bridge St., next to Bishop's Gate, is an above-average cafe, serving everything from chicken to mango lamb. (Entrees £4-12. Open M-Tu 9:30am-8pm, W-Sa 9:30am-10pm, Su noon-8pm.) **Postal Code:** BT48.

IRELAND

GLENS OF ANTRIM ☎028

Glaciers left nine deep scars in the mountainous coastline of northeastern County Antrim. Over the years, water collected in these glens, fostering lush flora not usually found in Ireland. The glens and their mountains and waterfalls are best visited as daytrips from the villages of Glenarm and Cushendall.

TRANSPORTATION. **Ulsterbus** (☎9032 0011) #156 runs from Belfast to Glenarm (3-7 per day, £3-6) and sometimes continues to Waterfoot, Cushendall, and Cushendun (2-4 per day). Bus #150 runs from Ballymena to Glenariff (M-Sa 5 per day, £2.60), then to Waterfoot, Cushendall, and Cushendun (3-5 per day, £4.30).

GLENARM. Lovely Glenarm was once the chief dwelling place of the MacDonnell Clan. The village is comprised of centuries-old houses and is a starting point for several short walks. The huge arch at the top of Altmore St. marks the entrance to **Glenarm Forest,** where trails trace the river's path. (Open daily 9am-dusk.) The **tourist office** is in the town council building. (☎2884 1087. Internet £4 per hr. Open M 10am-4pm, Tu-F noon-7pm, Su 2-6pm.) **Margaret's B&B ❶,** 10 Altmore St., provides comfortable rooms with 1950s decor. (☎2884 1307. Tea and toast breakfast included. Full Irish breakfast £4. £10 per person.)

GLENARIFF. Antrim's broadest (and arguably most beautiful) glen, Glenariff, lies 6.5km south of **Waterfoot** along Glenariff Rd., in the large **Glenariff Forest Park.** Bus #150 stops at the park entrance; if you're walking from Waterfoot, you can enter the park 2.5km downhill of the entrance by taking the road that branches left toward the Manor Lodge Restaurant. The stunning 5km **Waterfall Trail** follows the cascading, fern-lined Glenariff River from the park entrance to the Manor Lodge. (☎2175 8769 or 2177 1796. Open daily 10am-dusk. £1.50 per pedestrian, £3 per car.)

CUSHENDALL. Cushendall, nicknamed the capital of the Glens, houses a variety of goods, services, and pubs unavailable elsewhere in the region. The **tourist office,** 25 Mill St., is near the bus stop at the northern end of town. (☎2177 1180. Open July-Sept. M-F 10am-5:30pm, Sa 10am-4:30pm; Oct. to mid-Dec. and Feb.-June Tu-Sa 10am-1pm.) A warm welcome and huge rooms await at **Glendale ❷,** 46 Coast Rd., south of town overlooking the sea. (☎2177 1495. £17 per person.)

CUSHENDUN. This minuscule, picturesque seaside village is 8km north of Cushendall on the A2. Its white-washed and black-shuttered buildings sit next to a vast beach with wonderful, murky **caves** carved within red sea cliffs. Visitors can choose between the immaculate **B&B ❸** and **camping barn ❶** at **Drumkeerin,** just west of town on the A2 at 201a Torr Rd. (☎2176 1554. B&B singles £20; doubles £35. Camping barn £8.) **Mary McBride's ❷,** 2 Main St., used to hold the *Guinness Book of World Records* title "smallest bar in Europe"—until it expanded. (☎2176 1511. Steak-and-Guinness pie £5. Food served daily noon-9pm.)

CAUSEWAY COAST ☎028

Past Cushendun, the northern coast becomes even more dramatic. Sea-battered cliffs tower 185m over white beaches before giving way to the spectacular geology of **Giant's Causeway,** for which the region is named. Thousands of visitors swarm to the site today, but few venture beyond the visitors center to the stunning and easily-accessible coastline that stretches beyond.

TRANSPORTATION. **Ulsterbus** (☎7043 334) #172 runs between Ballycastle and Portrush along the coast (1hr., 4-6 per day, £3.70). The Antrim Coaster #252 runs from Belfast to Portstewart via most small towns along the coast (2 per day). The open-topped Bushmills Bus traces the coast between Coleraine, 8km south of Portrush, and the Causeway (July-Aug. 7 per day).

BALLYCASTLE AND ENVIRONS. The Causeway Coast leaves the sleepy glens behind when it hits **Ballycastle,** a bubbly seaside town that shelters tourists bound for Giant's Causeway. **Ulsterbus** #162A goes to Cushendall via Cushendun (50min., M-F 1 per day, £3), and #131 goes to Belfast (3hr., M-Sa 5-6 per day, £6.10). The **tourist office** is in Sheskburn House, 7 Mary St. (☎2076 2024. Open July-Aug. M-F 9:30am-7pm, Sa 10am-6pm, Su 2-6pm; Sept.-June M-F 9:30am-5pm.) Sleep at **Castle Hostel (IHH) ❶,** 62 Quay Rd. (☎2076 2337. Dorms £7.)

Just off the coast of Ballycastle, bumpy, boomerang-shaped **Rathlin Island** ("Fort of the Sea") is home to more puffins (pop. 20,000) than people (pop. 100). A minibus drives to the **Kebble Bird Sanctuary** at the western tip of the island, 7km from the harbor (20min., every 45min., £2.50). Caledonian MacBrayne (☎2076 9299) **ferries** run to the island from the pier at Ballycastle, up the hill from Quay Rd. (45min., 2-4 per day, round-trip £8.40).

Eight kilometers west of Ballycastle, the modest village of **Ballintoy** attracts the crowds on their way to the tiny **Carrick-a-rede Island.** From the mainland, cross the fishermen's rope bridge (about 2m wide) over the dizzying 30m drop to rocks and sea below; be extremely careful in windy weather. A sign marks the turn-off for the bridge from the coastal road east of Ballintoy. The island's **Larrybane sea cliffs** are home to a variety of species of gulls. The **Sheep Island View Hostel (IHH) ❶** is at 42A Main St. in Ballintoy. (☎2076 9391. Continental breakfast £3. Laundry £2. Dorms £10. **Camping** £5 per person.)

GIANT'S CAUSEWAY. Geologists believe that the unique rock formations found at **Giant's Causeway** were formed some 60 million years ago. Comprised of over 40,000 perfectly symmetrical hexagonal basalt columns, the site resembles a large descending staircase that leads out from the cliffs to the ocean's floor below. Ulsterbuses #172 to Portrush, the #252 Antrim Coaster, and the Bushmills Bus all drop off visitors at the **Giant's Causeway Visitors Centre.** A minibus (£1.20) runs from the center to the columns. (Causeway always open and free to pedestrians. Visitors Centre open July-Aug. daily 10am-6pm; June 10am-5pm; Sept.-May 10am-4:30pm. Parking £5.)

ITALY (ITALIA)

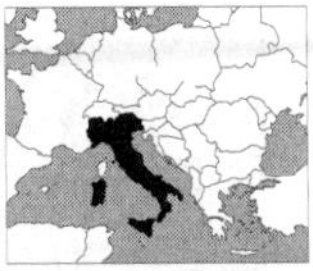

At the crossroads of the Mediterranean, Italy has served as the home of powerful empires, eccentric leaders, and great food. The country burst on stage as the base for the ambitious Roman empire; then it was persecutor and popularizer of an upstart religion called Christianity; next, Italy became the center of the artistic and philosophical Renaissance; it finally emerged as a world power that has changed governments more than 50 times since World War II. Countless invasions have left the land rich with examples of nearly every artistic era: Egyptian obelisks, Etruscan huts, Greek temples, Augustan arches, Byzantine mosaics, Renaissance *palazzi*, Baroque fountains, and post-modern superstructures sprawl across the 20 regions. From perfect pasta to the creation of pizza, Italy knows that the quickest way to a country's happiness is through its stomach. Italy is also the champion of romance—passionate lovers express their *amore* from the rooftops of southern Italy and Venice. Somewhere between the leisurely gondola rides and the frenetic nightclubs, you too will proclaim your love for Italy.

SYMBOL	❶	❷	❸	❹	❺
ACCOMMODATIONS	under €15	€16-25	€26-35	€36-60	over €60
FOOD	under €5	€6-10	€11-15	€16-25	over €25

SUGGESTED ITINERARIES

THREE DAYS Spend it all in the Eternal City of **Rome** (p. 644). Go back in time at the **Ancient City:** be a gladiator in the **Colosseum,** explore the **Roman Forum** and stand in the well-preserved **Pantheon.** Spend the next day admiring the fine art in the **Capitoline Museums** and the **Galleria Borghese,** then satiate your other senses in a disco. Redeem your debauched soul in **Vatican City** (p. 663), gazing at the ceiling of the **Sistine Chapel,** gaping at **St. Peter's Cathedral** and enjoying the **Vatican Museums.**

ONE WEEK Spend 3 days taking in the sights in **Rome** before heading north to **Florence** (2 days; p. 711) to immerse yourself in Italy's amazing Renaissance art at the Uffizi Gallery. Move to **Venice** (2 days; p. 693) to float through the canals and explore lagoon islands.

BEST OF ITALY IN 3 WEEKS Begin in **Rome** (4 days), then move to **Florence** (3 days). Cheer on horses in **Siena** (1 day; p. 724) before sailing to the isle of **Elba** (1 day; p. 726). Move up the coast to **Finale Ligure** (1 day; p. 683), and visit the fishing villages of **Cinque Terre** (2 days; p. 684). Move on to cosmopolitan **Milan** (2 days; p. 673) and visit **Lake Como** for hiking (1 day; p. 689). Spend some time in **Venice** (2 days; p. 693) before flying south to **Naples** (2 days; p. 729). Hike and swim along the **Amalfi Coast** (1 day; p. 734), and see the Grotto Azzura on the island of **Capri** (1 day; p. 735). End by visiting **Stromboli**'s live volcano (1 day; p. 742).

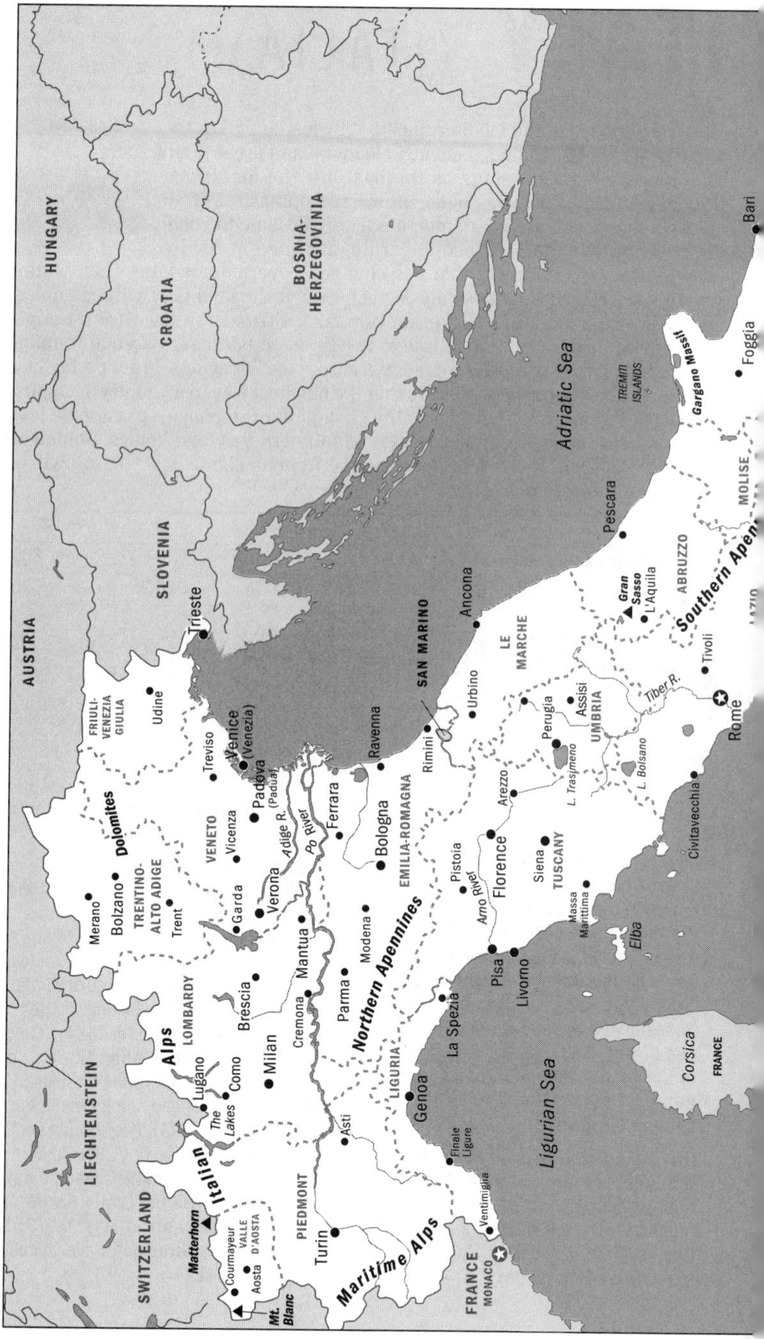
HUNGARY
CROATIA
BOSNIA-
HERZEGOVINIA
SLOVENIA
AUSTRIA
LIECHTENSTEIN
SWITZERLAND
FRANCE
MONACO
SAN MARINO
Adriatic Sea
Ligurian Sea
TREMITI
ISLANDS
Gargano Massif
Foggia
Bari
MOLISE
Pescara
ABRUZZO
Gran
Sasso
L'Aquila
Southern Apen
LAZIO
Ancona
LE
MARCHE
Tivoli
Tiber R.
Rome
Urbino
Assisi
Perugia
UMBRIA
L. Trasimeno
L. Bolsano
Civitavecchia
Trieste
FRIULI-
VENEZIA
GIULIA
Udine
Venice
(Venezia)
Treviso
Padova
(Padua)
Ravenna
Rimini
Arezzo
Dolomites
VENETO
Vicenza
Adige R.
Po River
Ferrara
Bologna
EMILIA-ROMAGNA
Florence
Pistoia
Arno River
Siena
TUSCANY
Massa
Marittima
Elba
Merano
Bolzano
TRENTINO-
ALTO ADIGE
Trent
Garda
Verona
Mantua
Modena
Northern Apennines
Pisa
Livorno
Corsica
FRANCE
Brescia
LOMBARDY
Alps
Cremona
Parma
La Spezia
Milan
Lugano
Como
The
Lakes
LIGURIA
Genoa
Asti
Finale
Ligure
Italian
Matterhorn
PIEDMONT
VALLE
D'AOSTA
Courmayeur
Aosta
Turin
Maritime Alps
Ventimiglia
Mt.
Blanc

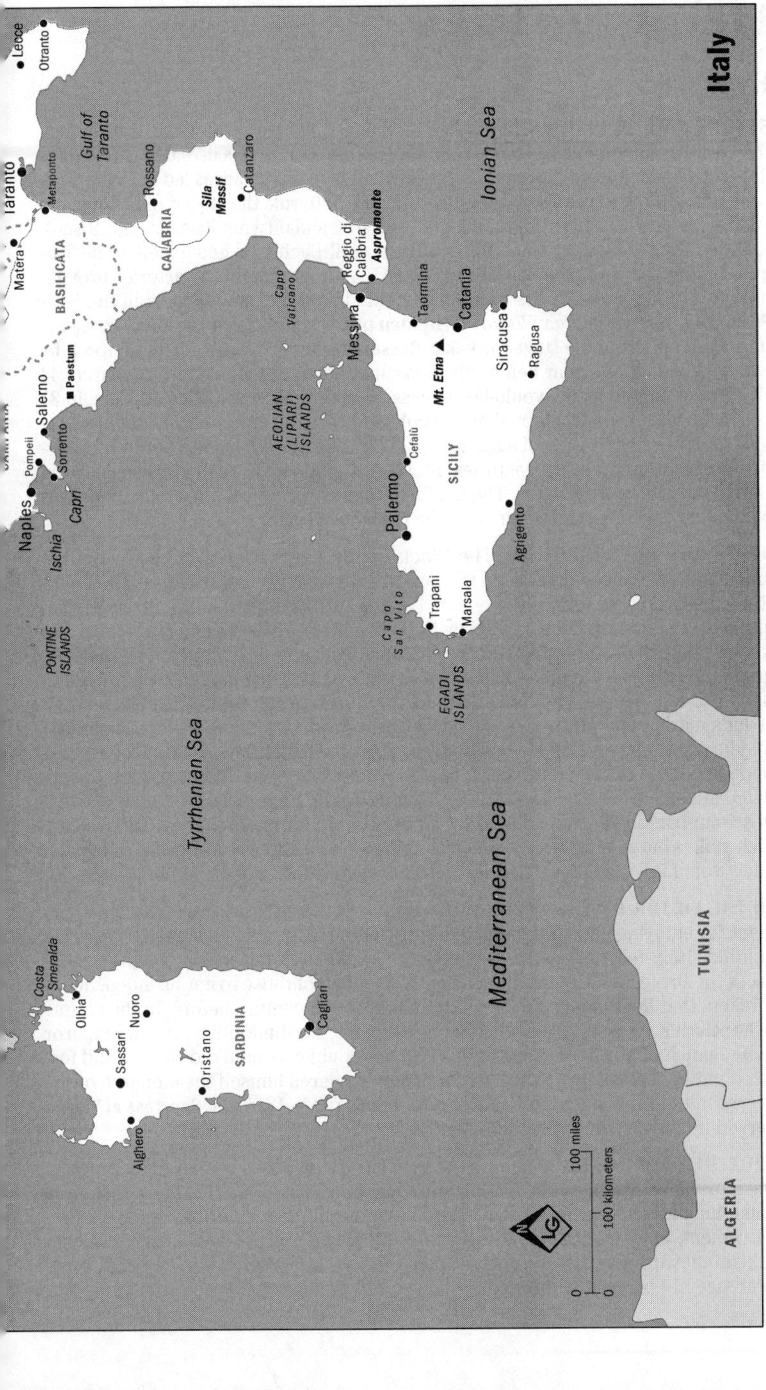
Italy
Lecce
Otranto
Taranto
Metaponto
Gulf of Taranto
Matera
BASILICATA
CALABRIA
Rossano
Sila Massif
Catanzaro
Aspromonte
Reggio di Calabria
Capo Vaticano
Ionian Sea
Messina
Taormina
Catania
Mt. Etna
Siracusa
Ragusa
SICILY
Cefalù
Palermo
Agrigento
Trapani
Marsala
Capo San Vito
EGADI ISLANDS
AEOLIAN (LIPARI) ISLANDS
Paestum
Salerno
Pompeii
Sorrento
Naples
Capri
Ischia
PONTINE ISLANDS
Tyrrhenian Sea
Mediterranean Sea
TUNISIA
ALGERIA
Costa Smeralda
Olbia
Nuoro
Sassari
Oristano
SARDINIA
Cagliari
Alghero
0
100 miles
0
100 kilometers

LIFE AND TIMES

HISTORY

BEFORE YOU WERE BORN. Although archaeological excavations at Isernia date the earliest inhabitants of Italy to the Paleolithic Era (100,000-70,000 BC), things didn't get swinging until around 1200 BC, when legendary **Aeneas** led his tribe from the ruins of Troy to the Tiber valley, settling down to rule the city of Alba Longa. In 753 BC, two of Aeneas's "descendants," the fratricidal twins **Romulus** and **Remus,** founded Rome. Tryanny ruled for centuries until Lucius Brutus expelled the Tarquins and established the **Republic** in 509 BC. A string of military victories brought near total unification of the Italian peninsula in 396 BC, and victory in the later **Punic Wars** spread the *Pax Romana* (Roman peace) throughout the Mediterranean. Internal conflict set the stage for **Julius Caesar** to name himself Dictator for Life, which lasted all of a year before his assassination on the Ides (15th) of March, 44 BC. Power eluded many would-be successors, like Brutus and Mark Antony. In 31 BC, Octavian, Caesar's adopted heir, a cold and calculating politician, emerged victorious, assuming the title of **Augustus** by 27 BC. The Empire made a hobby of Christian persecution for a few centuries until Constantine's 313 **Edict of Milan** declared Christianity the state religion. The fall finally came in 476, ushering in the **Dark Ages** while the East continued to thrive as the **Byzantine Empire.**

DEATH AND RESURRECTION. The Black Death and the struggle between monarchs and the Papacy dominated the period aptly called the Dark Ages. The fall of Rome had taken its toll on the region, but the 14th century saw a cultural revival unlike any before or since. Fueled by the rediscovery of Greek and Latin texts, the Renaissance exposed Italians to the Classical conception of education (rhetoric, grammar, logic) as the monopoly on knowledge held by the medieval church gradually eroded. Those who had survived the Black Death found themselves in a seller's market and profited from the labor shortage, producing the first merchant middle class. The exalted Medici family in Florence rose from obscurity, boasting a pope, a couple of cardinals, and a queen or two. Power in Florence was consolidated under Cosimo and Lorenzo (il Magnifico), who broadened the family's activities from banking and warring to the patronization of the arts. They engaged in a high-stakes battle with Pope Julius II to bring Michelangelo to Florence, and would have won if it weren't for that little matter of the Sistine Chapel.

TO THE VICTOR GO THE SPOILS. The 16th to 18th centuries were Italy's punishment for enjoying herself too much during the Renaissance. Weakened by internal conflict, Italy fell to Spanish conquerors. The **Spanish Inquisition** sought to suppress the Protestant Reformation and stamp out all of those irritating independent thinkers that the humanist movement had created a century before. In the course of **Napoleon's** 19th-century march through Europe, the diminutive French Emperor united much of northern Italy into the Italian Republic, conquered Naples, and fostered national sovereignty. In 1804, Napoleon declared himself the monarch of the newly united Kingdom of Italy. After Napoleon's fall in 1815, the **Congress of Vienna** carved up Italy, ceding control to Austria.

TOGETHER AGAIN. Reaction against the arbitrary divisions of Italy culminated in the nationalist **Risorgimento,** a unification movement in 1870. This bit of history is something Italian tourists cannot afford to ignore; the three primary leaders in the movement, **Giuseppe Mazzini, Giuseppe Garibaldi,** and **Camillo Cavour,** have a namesake boulevard in nearly every city. Once the elation of unification wore off, however, age-old provincial differences reasserted themselves. The North wanted to protect its money from the needs of the agrarian South, and cities were wary of surrendering power to a central administration. The Pope, who had lost power to the kingdom, threatened Catholics who participated in politics with excommunication. Disillusionment increased as Italy became involved in **World War I,** paving the way for the rise of fascism under the control of **Benito Mussolini,** "Il Duce," who promised strict order and stability for the young nation. Mussolini established the world's first Fascist regime in 1924 and expelled all opposition parties. As Mussolini initiated domestic development programs and aggressive foreign policy, support for the Fascist leader ran from intense loyalty to increasing discontent. In 1940, Italy entered **World War II** on the side of its Axis ally, Germany. Success came quickly but was short-lived; the Allies landed in Sicily in 1943, prompting Mussolini's fall from power. As a final indignity, he and his mistress were captured and executed by infuriated citizens, their naked bodies left hanging upside down in the public square. By the end of 1943, Italy had formally withdrawn its support from Germany. The Nazis responded by promptly invading and occupying their former ally. In 1945, the entirety of Italy was freed from German domination, and the country was divided between those supporting the monarchy and those favoring a return to Fascism.

POST-WAR POLITICS AND RECOVERY. The end of World War II did little but highlight the intense factionalism of the Italian peninsula. The **Constitution,** adopted in 1948, established the **Republic,** with a caesar, an augustus, and a committee of warring landlords known as a "senate"—or, a president, a prime minister (the chief officer), a bicameral parliament, and an independent judiciary. The **Christian Democratic Party (DC),** bolstered by Marshall Plan money and American military aid (as well as rumored Mafia collusion), soon overtook the **Socialist Party (PSI)** as the primary player in the government of the new Republic, as prominent members of the PSI were found to be sleeping with the fishes. Over 300 parties fought for supremacy; none could claim a majority, so they formed tenuous party coalitions. Italy has changed governments 58 times since World War II, none of which has lasted longer than four years.

Italian economic recovery began with 50s industrialization—skylines of northern cities were quickly dotted with Fiat and Lamborghini billboards and factory smokestacks, along with old cathedral spires and large glowing crucifixes. Despite the **Southern Development Fund,** which was established to build roads, construct schools, and finance industries, the South has lagged behind. Italy's economic inequality has contributed to much of the regional strife that persists today.

Economic success gave way to late-60s unrest. The *autunno caldo* (hot autumn) of 1969, a season of strikes, demonstrations, and riots (mainly by university students and factory workers) foreshadowed 70s violence. Perhaps the most shocking episode was the 1978 kidnapping and murder of ex-Prime Minister **Aldo Moro** by a group of left-wing militant terrorists, the *Brigate Rosse* (Red Brigade). Some positive reforms, however, accompanied the horror of the 70s: divorce was legalized and rights for women expanded. The events of the 70s had challenged the conservative Social Democrats, however, and **Bettino Craxi** became Italy's first Socalist premier in 1983.

TODAY

As far as politically stable countries go, Italy doesn't. Centuries of flux and internal tension have created a tradition of revolution, violent and non-, that has found a home in the rapidly changing Italian government. Facing the difficult transition into the interdependent European Union, Italy will have to maintain a greater degree of national consistency than ever before if it is to thrive in the new economic system spreading across Europe.

CORRUPTION AND GRAFT. It's no secret that Italian government officials have never been adverse to a little grease on their palms. Yet **Oscar Luigi Scalfaro,** elected in 1992, only realized the extent of this when the noticed that his secretary owned a Mercedes and wore a €20,000 diamond-studded Cartier watch. Shortly thereafter, in the *mani pulite* (clean hands) campaign, Scalfaro and **Judge Antonio di Pietro** managed to uncover the **"Tangentopoli"** (Kickback City) scandal. This unprecedented political crisis implicated over 2600 politicians and businessmen in corruption charges. Reactions to the investigation have included the May 1993 bombing of the Uffizi (Florence's premier art museum), the "suicides" of 10 indicted officials, and the murders of anti-Mafia judges and investigators.

"STABILITY" AND REFORM. The elections of 1996 brought the center-left coalition, the **Olive Tree** (l'Ulivo), to power, with **Romano Prodi,** a Bolognese professor, economist, and non-politician, as Prime Minister. Prodi helped stabilize Italian politics. For the first time in modern history, Italy was dominated by two stable coalitions: the center-left l'Ulivo and the center-right **Il Polo.** Despite high hopes for Prodi's government, his coalition lost a vote of confidence in October 1998; by the end of the month, his government collapsed, and former Communist **Massimo D'Alema** was sworn in as prime minister. D'Alema and Carlo Ciampi created fiscal reforms and pushed a "blood and tears" budget that qualified Italy for entrance into the European Monetary Union (EMU) in January 1999.

STATUS QUID PRO QUO. Despite D'Alema's fleeting success, he stepped down in May 2000 and was replaced by former Treasury Minister, **Giuliano Amato,** one of few to emerge unscathed from the corruption crack-downs of the early 90s. As the top untainted Socialist, Amato heads a 12-party coalition, Italy's 58th government since World War II. The real escape artist is **Silvio Berlusconi,** whose economic and media power managed, despite convictions for corruption and budget fraud, to secure his election as Prime Minister in May 2001. Winning 30% of the popular vote, Berlusconi's center-right Forza Italia became Italy's main political party.

Several organizations for foreign travelers in Italy immediately issued warnings about the conservative prime minister's agenda and tendency to support insular nationalism. In reality, the fractured nature of Italian politics will probably not allow Berlusconi total(itarian) freedom when it comes to parliament. But with Berlusconi's known preference for the corrupt political system that brought him to his current status, democratic reform is nowhere in sight. Projecting his self-confident image throughout Italy, via ownership of Mediaset and Mondadori, Berlusconi has successfully returned fascism to a government struggling to find itself.

CULTURE

FOOD & DRINK

Breakfast in Italy often goes unnoticed; lunch is the main feast of the day. A *pranzo* (full meal) consists of an *antipasto* (appetizer), a *primo* (first course of pasta or soup), a *secondo* (meat or fish), a *contorno* (vegetable side dish), and then finally *dolce* (dessert or fruit), a *caffè*, and often an after-dinner liqueur. If you don't have a big appetite, you can buy authentic snacks for a picnic at *salumeria* or *alimentari* (meat and grocery shops). A bar is an excellent place to grab coffee or a quick snack. They usually offer *panini* (hot and cold sandwiches), drinks with or without alcohol, and *gelato*. Grab a lighter lunch at an inexpensive *tavola calda* (hot table), *rosticceria* (grill), or *gastronomia* (serving hot prepared dishes). *Osterie, trattorie*, and *ristoranti* are, in ascending order, fancier and more expensive. Many restaurants offer a fixed-price tourist menu *(menù turistico)* that includes *primo, secondo*, bread, water, and wine. Italian dinner is a lighter meal, often a snack. In the north, butter and cream sauces dominate, while Rome and central Italy are notoriously spicy regions. Farther south, tomatoes play a more significant role. Coffee is another rich and varied focus of Italian life; for a standard cup of *espresso*, request a *caffè; cappuccino* is the breakfast beverage. *Caffè macchiato* (spotted coffee) has a touch of milk, while *latte macchiato* is heavier on the milk and lighter on the coffee. Wines from the north of Italy, such as the Piedmont's *Asti Spumante* or Verona's *Soave*, tend to be full-bodied; stronger, fruitier wines come from southern Italy and the islands. Almost every shop sells Italy's greatest contribution to civilization: *gelato*.

CUSTOMS & ETIQUETTE

Ah, Italian. Language of lovers, of mafiosi, and Dante's eternal damnation. One of the six surviving romance languages, it has long inspired everything from Petrarch's passionate ramblings to Calvino's insane ramblings. As a result of the country's fragmented history, variations in **dialect** are strong. The throaty **Neapolitan** can be difficult for a Northerner to understand; **Ligurians** use a mix of Italian, Catalán, and French; **Sardo,** spoken in Sardinia, bears little resemblance to standard Italian; and many **Tuscan** dialects differ from Italian in pronunciation. Some inhabitants of the northern border regions don't speak Italian at all: the population of Val d'Aosta speaks mainly French, and the people of Trentino-Alto Adige harbor a German-speaking minority. In the southern regions of Apulia, Calabria, and Sicily, entire villages speak Albanian and Greek. In order to facilitate conversation, all natives do their best to employ standard Italian when speaking with a foreigner. Nearly everything closes from around 1 to 3 or 4pm for *siesta*. Most museums are open 9am-1pm and 3-6pm; some are open through lunch. Monday is often their *giorno di chiusura* (day of closure).

THE ARTS

In Rome, the Colosseum hovers above a city bus stop; in Florence, young men and women meet in front of the *duomo* to flirt and gossip; in Sicily, remnants from Greek columns are used as dining tables. Italy is a country in which daily life and artistic masterpieces are inextricably woven together. The artistic tradition is prolific and varied—to visit only the most famous pieces would be to misunderstand the pervasive presence of art in everyday Italian settings.

FINE ARTS. The Greeks peppered southern Italy with a large number of **temples** and **theaters.** The best-preserved Greek temples in the world today are found not in Greece, but in Sicily. Most Roman houses incorporated **frescoes,** Greek-influenced paintings on plaster. **Mosaic** was another popular medium. The arch, along with the invention of **concrete,** revolutionized the Roman conception of architecture and made possible such monuments as the **Colosseum** (see p. 660) and the **Pantheon** (see p. 661), as well as public works like **aqueducts** and **thermal baths.** For fear of persecution, early Christians fled underground to worship; their **catacombs** (see p. 665) are now among the most haunting and intriguing of Italian monuments. In the Renaissance, **Filippo Brunelleschi** and **Donatello** revolutionized architecture and sculpture, respectively. Brunelleschi's (see p. 720) mathematical studies of ancient Roman architecture became the cornerstone of all later Renaissance building. In sculpture, Donatello (see p. 703) built upon the realistic articulation of the human body in motion. The torch was passed to three exceptional men: Leonardo da Vinci, Michelangelo Buonarroti, and Raphael Santi. **Leonardo** (see p. 677) was not only an artist but a scientist, architect, engineer, musician, and weapon designer. **Michelangelo** created the illusion of vaults on the flat ceiling of the **Sistine Chapel** (1473-81; see p. 664), which remains his greatest surviving achievement in painting. Sculpture, however, was his favorite mode of expression, the most classic example being *David* (1501-04; see p. 721). **Raphael** created technically perfect figures in his paintings (see p. 666). The Italians started to lose their artistic dexterity in the 18th and 19th centuries. **Antonio Canova** explored the formal **Neoclassical** style, which professed a return to the rules of Classical antiquity, while the **Macchiaioli** group, spearheaded by **Giovanni Fattori,** revolted with a unique technique of "blotting." The Italian **Futurist** artists of the 1910s used machines to bring Italy back to the cutting edge of artistry. **Amadeo Modigliani** crafted figures famous for their long oval faces.

LITERATURE. **Virgil** wrote and wrote and never finished the epic *Aeneid* about the godly origins of Rome. **Horace**'s (65-8 BC) texts gave powerful voice to his personal experiences. It is primarily through **Ovid**'s various works that we learn the gory details of Roman mythology: Usually disguised as animals or humans, these gods and goddesses often descended to earth to intervene romantically or combatively in human affairs. The Dark Ages put a stop to most literary musings, but three Tuscan writers reasserted the art in the late 13th century. **Dante Alighieri** was one of the first Italian poets to write in the *volgare* (common Italian) instead of Latin. In his infamous epic poem, *The Divine Comedy* (1308-21), Dante explores the various fires of the afterlife. **Petrarch** restored the popularity of ancient Roman writers by writing love sonnets to a married woman, compiled in *Songbook* (1350). **Giovanni Boccaccio,** a close friend of Petrarch's, composed a collection of 100 bawdy stories in *The Decameron* (1348-53). Paralleling the scientific exploration of the time, 15th- and 16th-century Italian authors explored new dimensions of the human experience. **Alberti** and **Palladio** wrote treatises on architecture and art theory. **Baldassare Castiglione**'s *The Courtier* (1528) instructed the fastidious Renaissance man on deportment, etiquette, and other fine points of behavior. **Niccolò Machiavelli**'s *The Prince* (1513) gives a timeless sophisticated assessment of climbing the political ladder. The 1800s were an era primarily of *racconti* (short stories) and poetry. **Pellegrino Artusi**'s 1891 cookbook *Science in the Kitchen and the Art of Eating Well* was the first attempt to assemble recipes from regional traditions into a unified Italian cuisine. The 20th century saw a new tradition in Italian literature as Nobel Prize-winning author and playwright **Luigi Pirandello** explored the relativity of truth in works like *Six Characters in Search of an Author* (1921). Literary production slowed in the years preceding WWII, but the conclusion of the war ignited an explosion in antifascist fiction. **Primo Levi** wrote *If This is a Man* (1947) about his experiences in Auschwitz. Mid-20th-century poets include Nobel Prize winners **Salvatore Quasimodo** and **Eugenio Montale,** who founded the "hermetic movement," characterized by an intimate poetic vision and allusive imagery. More recently, internationally known playwright and satirist **Dario Fo** claimed the 1997 Nobel Prize for literature.

MUSIC. A medieval Italian monk, **Guido d'Arezzo,** is regarded as the originator of musical notation. Religious strains held the day until the 16th century ushered in a new musical extravaganza: **opera.** Italy's most cherished art form was born in Florence, nurtured in Venice, and revered in Milan. Conceived by the **Camerata,** a circle of Florentine writers, noblemen, and musicians, opera originated as an attempt to recreate the dramas of ancient Greece by setting lengthy poems to music. **Jacobo Peri** composed *Dafne*, the world's first complete opera, in 1597. The first successful opera composer, **Claudio Monteverdi,** drew freely from history, juxtaposing high drama, love scenes, and bawdy humor. **Baroque** music, known for its literal and figurative hot air, took the 17th and 18th centuries by storm. During this period, two main instruments saw their popularity mushroom: the violin, the shape of which was perfected by Cremona families, including the **Stradivari,** and the piano, created in about 1709 by members of the Florentine **Cristofori** family. **Antonio Vivaldi,** who composed over 400 concertos, triumphed with *The Four Seasons* (1725). With convoluted plots and strong, dramatic music, 19th-century Italian opera continues to dominate modern stages. **Gioacchino Rossini** was the master of the *bel canto* ("beautiful song"), which consists of long, fluid, melodic lines. **Giuseppe Verdi** remains the transcendent musical and operatic figure of 19th-century Italy. Verdi produced the touching, personal dramas and memorable melodies of *Rigoletto* (1851), *La Traviata* (1853), and *Il Trovatore* (1853) and the grand and heroic conflicts of *Aida* (1871). At the turn of the century, **Giacomo Puccini** created *Madame Butterfly* (1904), *La Bohème* (1896), and *Tosca* (1900).

FILM. In the early 20th century, Mussolini created the *Centro Sperimentale della Cinematografia*, a national film school that stifled any true artistic development. The fall of Fascism allowed the explosion of **Neorealist cinema** (1943-50), which rejected contrived sets and professional actors and sought to produce a candid look at post-war Italy. This new style caught the world's attention and Rome soon became a hotspot for the international jet set. On the heels of these celebrities also came a certain set of photographic stalkers called **paparazzi.** The works of **Roberto Rossellini** and **Vittorio de Sica** best represent *Neorealismo*, with de Sica's 1945 film *The Bicycle Thief* as perhaps the most famous and successful Neorealist film. In the 1960s, post-Neorealist directors like **Federico Fellini** rejected plots and characters for a visual and symbolic world. Fellini's *La Dolce Vita* (*The Sweet Life*, 1960), which was banned by the Pope, is an incisive film scrutinizing 1950s Rome. In a similar vein, **Pier Paolo Pasolini** explored Italy's infamous underworld in films like *Accatone* (*The Beggar*, 1961). Although Italian cinema has fallen into a recent slump, **Bernardo Bertolucci**'s *The Last Emperor* (1987) and Oscar-winners **Giuseppe Tornatore** and **Gabriele Salvatore** have garnered the attention of US and international audiences. Enthusiastic sparkplug **Roberto Benigni** became one of Italy's leading cinematic personalities when his *La Vita e Bella (Life is Beautiful)* gained international fame, receiving Best Actor and Best Foreign Film Oscars and a Best Picture Oscar nomination at the 1999 Academy Awards.

HOLIDAYS & FESTIVALS

From the number of festivals commemorating an appearance of the Virgin Mary in Italy, it's easy to reach the conclusion that she has found *bella Italia* so appealing that she has decided never to leave. **Carnevale,** a brilliant invention held in February during the 10 days before Lent, energizes Italian towns; in Venice, costumed Carnevale revelers fill the streets and canals. During **Scoppio del Carro,** held in Florence's Piazza del Duomo on Easter Sunday, Florentines set off a cart of explosives, following a tradition dating back to medieval times. Festivals in smaller towns are less touristed and much quirkier. For a complete list of festivals, write the **Italian Government Travel Office** (www.italiantourism.com/html/event_en.html).

Holidays: New Year's Day (Jan. 1); Epiphany (Jan. 6); Easter Sunday and Monday (Mar. 31 and Apr. 1); Liberation Day (Apr. 25); Labor Day (May 1); Assumption of the Virgin (Aug. 15); All Saints' Day (Nov. 1); Immaculate Conception (Dec. 8); Christmas Day (Dec. 25); and Santo Stefano (Dec. 26).

FACTS AND FIGURES

Official Name: Italian Republic.

Capital: Rome.

Major Cities: Florence, Venice, Milan, Naples.

Population: 57,000,000. Urban 67%, rural 33%.

Land Area: 301,230 sq. km.

Time Zone: GMT +1.

Language: Italian; some German, French and Slovenian.

Religions: Roman Catholic (98%).

ITALY

ESSENTIALS

WHEN TO GO

Traveling to Italy in late May or early September, when the temperature drops to a comfortable 25°C (77°F), will assure a calmer and cooler vacation. Also keep weather patterns, festival schedules, and tourist congestion in mind. Tourism enters overdrive in June, July, and August, and almost all hotels are booked solid. During *Ferragosto*, a national holiday in August, all Italians take their vacations and flock to the coast like well-dressed lemmings. Northern cities become ghost towns or tourist-infested infernos. Though many visitors find the larger cities enjoyable even during the holiday, most agree that June and July are better months for a trip to Italy.

DOCUMENTS AND FORMALITIES

VISAS. EU citizens may stay in Italy for as long as they like. Citizens of Australia, Canada, New Zealand, South Africa, and the US do not need visas for up to three months. Those wishing to stay in Italy for more than three months must apply for a *permesso di soggiorno* (residence permit) at a police station *(questura)*.

Italian Embassies at Home: Australia, 12 Grey St., Deakin, Canberra ACT 2600 (☎02 6273 3333; www.ambitalia.org.au). **Canada,** 275 Slater St., 21st fl., Ottawa, ON K1P 5H9 (☎613-232-2401; www.italyincanada.com). **Ireland,** 63 Northumberland Rd., Dublin (☎01 660 1744; homepage.eircom.net/~italianembassy). **New Zealand,** 34 Grant Rd., Wellington (☎(006) 4473 5339; www.italy-embassy.org.nz). **South Africa,** 796 George Ave., Arcadia 0083, Pretoria (☎012 43 55 41; www.ambital.org.za). **UK,** 14 Three Kings Yard, London W1Y 2EH (☎020 73 12 22 00; www.embitaly.org.uk). **US,** 1601 Fuller St. NW, Washington, D.C. 20009 (☎202-328-5500; www.italyemb.org).

Foreign embassies in Italy: are in **Rome** (p. 648).

ITALY

TRANSPORTATION

BY PLANE. Rome's international airport, known as both Fiumicino and Leonardo da Vinci, is served by most major airlines. You can also fly into Milan's Malpensa or Linate airports or Florence's Amerigo Vespucci airport. **Alitalia** (US ☎800-223-5730; (UK ☎870 544 8259; www.alitalia.it/eng) is Italy's national airline.

BY TRAIN. The Italian State Railway **Ferrovie dello Stato** (**FS** ☎147 88 80 88; www.fs-on-line.com), offers inexpensive and efficient service. There are several types of trains: the *locale* stops at every station on a particular line; the *diretto* makes fewer stops than the *locale;* and the *espresso* stops only at major stations. The air-conditioned *rapido*, an **InterCity (IC)** train, zips along but costs a bit more. Tickets for the fast, pricey **Eurostar** trains require reservations. If you are under 26 and plan to travel extensively in Italy, the **Cartaverde** should be your first purchase. The card (€20.65) is valid for one year and gives a 20% discount on state train fare. **Eurail** passes are valid without a supplement on all trains except Eurostar. For a couple or a family, an **Italian Kilometric Ticket** (€103.30-174.45; good for 20 trips or 3000km), can pay off. Otherwise, railpasses are seldom cost-effective, since regular fares are cheap.

BY BUS. Intercity buses serve countryside points inaccessible by train and occasionally arrive in more convenient places in large towns. For city buses, buy tickets in *tabacchi* or kiosks, and validate them on board to avoid a fine.

BY FERRY. Ferry services at the ports of Bari, Brindisi, and Ancona (p. 728) connect Italy to Greece. Boats from Trieste (p. 709) serve the Istrian Peninsula down to Croatia's Dalmatian Coast. Ferries link Italy's islands to the mainland, and boats go to Sardinia from Genoa (p. 681), La Spezia (p. 685), and Naples (p. 729). Travelers to Sicily (p. 738) take the ferry from Naples (p. 729) or Reggio di Calabria.

BY CAR OR MOPED. There are four kinds of roads: *Autostrada* (superhighways; mostly tollroads); *strade statali* (state roads); *strade provinciali* (provincial); and *strade communali* (local). Italian driving is frightening; congested traffic is common in large cities and in the north. On three-lane roads, be aware that the center lane is for passing. **Mopeds** (€20-31 per day) can be a great way to see the islands and the more scenic areas of Italy, but can be disastrous in the rain and on rough roads. Call **Automobile Club Italiano (ACI)** at ☎116 if you break down.

BY BIKE. Bicycling is a popular national sport, but bike trails are rare, drivers often reckless, and, except in the Po Valley, the terrain challenging.

TOURIST SERVICES AND MONEY

EMERGENCY	**Police:** ☎112. **Ambulance:** ☎113. **Fire:** ☎115.

TOURIST OFFICES. In provincial capitals, look for the **Ente Provinciale per il Turismo (EPT)** or **Azienda di Promozione Turistica (APT)** for information on the entire province and the town. Local tourist offices, **Informazione e Assistenza ai Turisti (IAT)** and **Azienda Autonoma di Soggiorno e Turismo (AAST),** are generally the most useful.

Tourist Boards at Home: Australia, Level 26, 44 Market St., Sydney NSW 2000 (☎(02) 9262 1666; fax 9262 5745). **Canada,** 175 E. Bloor St., #907 South Tower, Toronto, ON M4W 3R9 (☎416-925-4887; initaly@ican.net). **UK,** 1 Princes St., London WIR 9AY (☎(020) 7355 1439; www.enit.it). **US,** 630 5th Ave., #1565, New York, NY 10111 (☎212-245-5618; www.italiantourism.com).

MONEY. The official currency of Italy is the **euro.** The Italian Lire can still be exchanged at a rate of L1,9628 to €1. For exchange rates and more information on the euro, see p. 20. The European Union imposes a **value-added tax (VAT)** on goods and services purchased within the EU, which is included in the price (see p. 19).

ITALY

ACCOMMODATIONS AND CAMPING

Associazione Italiana Alberghi per la Gioventù (AIG), the Italian hostel federation, is a Hosteling International (HI) affiliate, though not all Italian hostels *(ostelli per la gioventù)* are part of AIG. A full list is available from most **EPT** and **CTS** offices and from many hostels. Prices start at about €13 per night for dorms. Hostels are the best option for solo travelers (single rooms are relatively scarce in hotels), but curfews, lockouts, distant locations, and less-than-perfect security detract from their appeal. For more information, contact the AIG office in Rome, V. Cavour 44 (☎06 487 11 52; www.hostels-aig.org). Italian hotel rates are set by the state; hotel owners will need your passport to register you, don't be afraid to hand it over for a while (usually overnight), but ask for it as soon as you think you will need it. Hotel singles *(camera singola)* usually start at around €26-31 per night, and doubles *(camera doppia)* start at €36-41. A room with a private bath *(con bagno)* usually costs 30-50% more. Smaller *pensioni* are often cheaper than hotels. Be sure to confirm the charges before checking in; Italian hotels are notorious for tacking on additional costs at check-out time. The **Azienda di Promozione Turismo (APT)**, provides lists of hotels that have paid to be listed; some of the hotels we recommend may not be on the list. **Affittacamere** (rooms for rent in private houses) are another inexpensive option. For more information, inquire at local tourist offices. There are over 1700 campsites in Italy; the **Touring Club Italiano**, Corso Italia, 10-20122 Milano (☎02 852 61; fax 53 59 95 40) publishes numerous books and pamphlets on the outdoors. Rates average €4 per tent, and €3.50 per car.

COMMUNICATION

PHONE CODE	**Country code:** 39. **International dialing prefix:** 00. The city code must always be dialed, even when calling from within the city. From outside Italy, dial int'l dialing prefix + 39 + local number (drop the leading zero).

TELEPHONES. Pre-paid phone cards, available from *tabacchi*, vending machines, and phone card vendors, carry a certain amount of time depending on the card's denomination (€2.60, €5.20, or €7.75). International calls start at €1.05, and vary depending on where you are calling. A collect call is a *contassa a carico del destinatario* or *chiamata collect.* International direct dial numbers: **AT&T,** ☎172 10 11; **British Telecom,** ☎172 00 44; **Canada Direct,** ☎172 10 01; **Ireland Direct,** ☎172 03 53; **MCI,** ☎172 10 22; **Sprint,** ☎172 18 77; **Telecom New Zealand,** ☎172 10 64; **Telkom South Africa,** ☎172 10 27; **Telstra Australia,** ☎172 10 61.

MAIL. Airmail letters sent from North America, United Kingdom, or Australia to Italy take anywhere from 3 to 7 days. Since Italian mail is notoriously unreliable, it is usually safer and quicker to send mail express *(espresso)* or registered *(raccomandata)*. *Fermo Posta* is Italian for *Poste Restante.*

INTERNET ACCESS. Though Italy had initially lagged behind in building ramps and turnpikes on the information superhighway, it's now playing the game of catch-up like a pro. While Internet cafes are still rare in rural and industrial cities, "Internet points" such as bars and even laundromats appear at an alarming rate in well-touristed areas. Rates range from €5-8 per hour. For free Internet access, try the local universities and libraries.

LANGUAGE. Any knowledge of Spanish, French, Portuguese, or Latin will help you understand Italian. The tourist office staff usually speaks some English. For a traveler's survival kit of basic Italian, see p. 1027.

ROME (ROMA)

Centuries of sporadic growth transformed Rome from a fledgling city-state to the capital of the Western world. At its zenith, the glory of Rome transcended human imagination and touched upon the divine; from legendary founding in the shadows of pre-history, to the demi-god emperors who reveled in human form, to the modern papacy's global political influence, earthly ideas have proved insufficient to capture the Eternal City. Looking at Rome today, the phrase "decline and fall" seems preposterous—though, perhaps, Rome no longer dictates the course of Western history, its claim upon the modes of culture remains firmly intact. Style. Art. Food. Passion. These are Rome's new empire, tying the city to the living moment, rather than relegating it to stagnate in a museum case.

Today, while the Colosseum crumbles from industrial pollution, Romans celebrate their city: concerts animate the ancient monuments, designer boutiques call the faithful to worship at the temples of capitalism, children play football around the Pantheon, and august *piazze* serve as movie houses for the latest Hollywood costume dramas. In a city that has stood for nearly three thousand years, Rome's glory is not dimmed, merely altered.

INTERCITY TRANSPORTATION

Flights: da Vinci International Airport (FCO; ☎066 59 51) known as **Fiumicino,** handles most flights. The **Termini line** runs nonstop to Rome's main station, **Termini Station** (30min., 2 per hr., €20). After hours, take the blue **COTRAL bus** to Tiburtina from the ground floor outside the main exit doors after customs (€4.50). From Tiburtina, take bus #40N to Termini. Most charter flights arrive at **Ciampino** (CIA; ☎06 79 49 41). To get to Rome, take the COTRAL bus (every 30min., €1) to Anagnina station on Line A .

Trains: From Termini Station to: **Bologna** (2¾-4¼hr., €19); **Florence** (2-3hr., €22); **Milan** (4½-8hr., €26); **Naples** (2-2½hr., €10); **Venice** (5hr., €34). Trains arriving in Rome between midnight and 5am arrive at **Stazione Tiburtina** or **Stazione Ostiense,** which are connected to Termini by the #40N and 20N-21N buses, respectively.

ORIENTATION

From the **Termini** train station, **Via Nazionale** is the central artery connecting **Piazza della Repubblica** with **Piazza Venezia,** home to the immense wedding-cake-like **Vittorio Emanuele II monument.** West of P. Venezia, **Largo Argentina** marks the start of C. V. Emanuele, which leads to Centro Storico, the medieval and Renaissance tangle of sights around the **Pantheon, Piazza Navona, Campo dei Fiori,** and **Piazza Farnese.** From P. Venezia, V. dei Fori Imperiale leads southeast to the **Forum** and **Colosseum,** south of which are the ruins of the **Baths of Caracalla** and the **Appian Way,** and the neighborhoods of southern Rome: the Aventine, Testaccio, Ostiense, and EUR. **Via del Corso** stretches from P. Venezia north to **Piazza del Popolo.** East of the Corso, fashionable streets border the **Piazza di Spagna** and, to the northeast, the **Villa Borghese.** South and east are the **Fontana di Trevi, Piazza Barberini,** and the **Quirinal Hill.** Across the Tiber to the north is **Vatican City,** and to the south **Trastevere** is the best neighborhood for wandering. It's impossible to navigate Rome without a map. Pick up a free one from a tourist office. The invaluable **Roma Métro-Bus map** (€4) is available at newsstands.

LOCAL TRANSPORTATION

Public Transportation: The 2 **Metropolitana** subway lines (A and B) meet at Termini and run 5:30am-11:30pm. **Buses** run 6am-midnight (with limited, unreliable late-night routes); board at the front or back and validate your ticket in the machine. Buy **tickets** (€0.80) at *tabacchi,* newsstands, and station machines; they're valid for 1 Métro ride or unlimited bus travel within 1¼hr. of validation. **BIG daily tickets** (€4.15) and **C.I.S. weekly tickets** (€16.35) allow unlimited public transport, including Ostia but not Fiumicino. **Pickpocketing is rampant on buses and trains.**

Taxis: Easily located at stands, or flag them down in the street. Ride only in yellow or white taxis, and make sure your taxi has a meter (if not, settle on a price before you get in the car). **Surcharges** at night (€2.55), on Su (€1), and when heading to or from Fiumicino (€7.25) or Ciampino (€5.20). Fares run about €9 from Termini to the Vatican; between the city center and Fiumicino around €35.

Bike and Moped Rental: Bikes generally cost €2.50 per hr. or €8 per day, but the length of a "day" varies according to the shop's closing time. In summer, try the stands on V.d. Corso at P.d. San Lorenzo and V. di Pontifici. 16+. Open daily 10am-7pm.

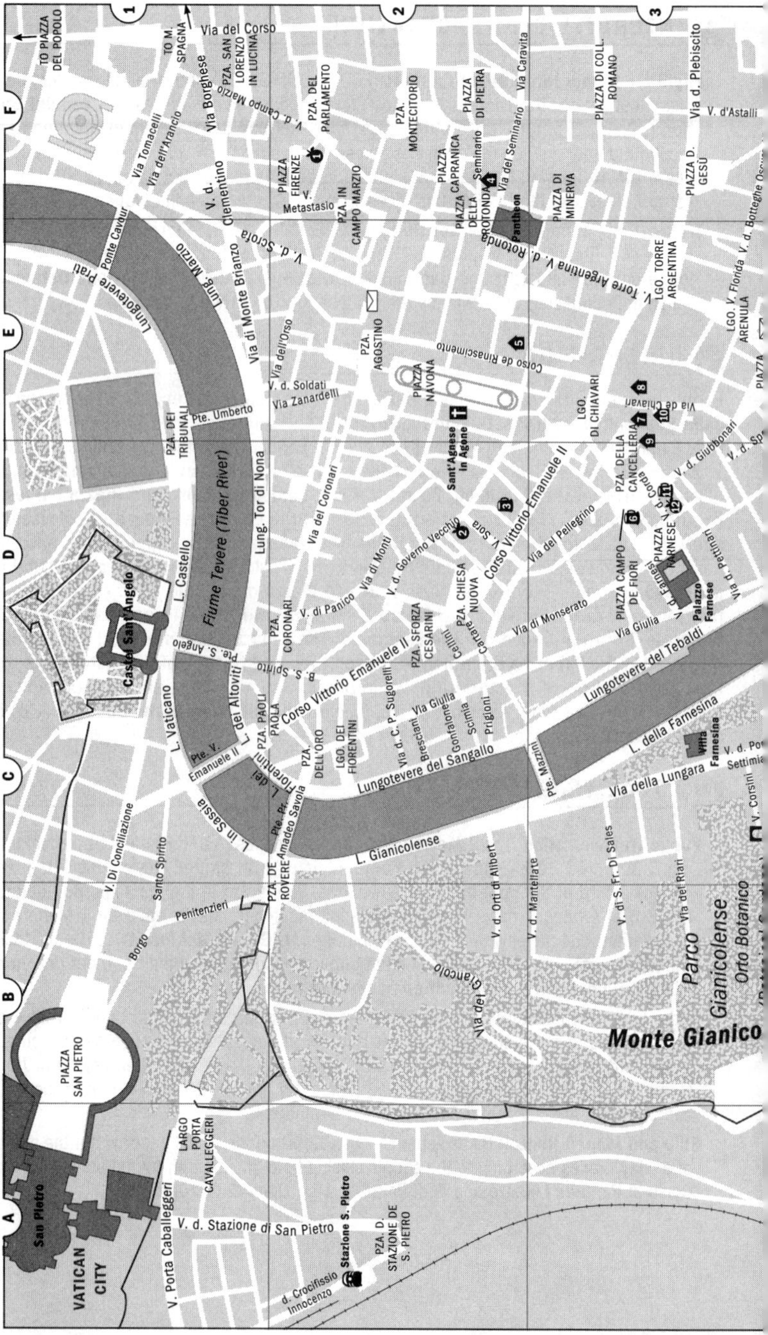
TO PIAZZA DEL POPOLO
TO M. SPAGNA
Via del Corso
PZA. SAN LORENZO IN LUCINA
Via Borghese
V. d. Campo Marzio
PZA. DEL PARLAMENTO
PZA. MONTECITORIO
PIAZZA DI PIETRA
Via Caravita
PIAZZA DI COLL. ROMANO
Via d. Plebiscito
V. d'Astalli
Via Tomacelli
Via dell'Arancio
V. d. Clementino
PIAZZA FIRENZE
V. Metastasio
PZA. IN CAMPO MARZIO
PIAZZA CAPRANICA
Seminario
Via del Seminario
PIAZZA DELLA ROTONDA
Pantheon
PIAZZA DI MINERVA
PIAZZA D. GESÙ
Via d. Botteghe Oscure
Ponte Cavour
Lungotevere Prati
Lung. Marzio
V. d. Scrofa
V. d. Rotonda
V. Torre Argentina
LGO. TORRE ARGENTINA
V. Florida
LGO. V. ARENULA
Via di Monte Brianzo
Via dell'Orso
PZA. AGOSTINO
Corso de Rinascimento
V. d. Soldati
Via Zanardelli
PIAZZA NAVONA
Sant'Agnese in Agone
LGO. DI CHIAVARI
Via de Chiavari
PZA. DEI TRIBUNALI
Pte. Umberto
Fiume Tevere (Tiber River)
Lung. Tor di Nona
Via del Coronari
Corso Vittorio Emanuele II
PZA. DELLA CANCELLERIA
V. d. Giubbonari
V. d. Sp
L. Castello
Castel Sant'Angelo
Via di Monti
V. d. Governo Vecchio
V. Sora
Via del Pellegrino
V. Corda
PIAZZA FARNESE
PIAZZA CAMPO DE FIORI
V. d. Farnesi
Palazzo Farnese
Via d. Pettinari
Pte. S. Angelo
PZA. CORONARI
V. di Panico
PZA. CHIESA NUOVA
Cellini
Carrozze
Via di Monserrato
Via Giulia
Lungotevere del Tebaldi
B. S. Spirito
PZA. SFORZA CESARINI
L. Vaticano
L. dei Altoviti
PZA. PAOLI PAOLA
Via d. C. P. Sugarelli
Via Giulia
Bresciani
Gonfalone
Scimia
Prigioni
Pte. V. Emanuele II
L. dei Fiorentini
PZA. DELL'ORO
LGO. DEI FIORENTINI
Lungotevere del Sangallo
Pte. Mazzini
L. della Farnesina
Villa Farnesina
V. d. Po
Settimia
Via della Lungara
V. Corsini
V. Di Conciliazione
Santo Spirito
L. in Sassia
Pte. Pr. Amadeo Savoia
PZA. DE ROVERE
L. Gianicolense
V. d. Orti di Alibert
V. d. Mantellate
V. di S. Fr. Di Sales
Via dei Riari
Penitenzieri
Borgo
Via del Gianicolo
Parco Gianicolense
Orto Botanico
Monte Gianicolo
PIAZZA SAN PIETRO
San Pietro
VATICAN CITY
LARGO PORTA CAVALLEGGERI
V. Porta Cavalleggeri
V. d. Stazione di San Pietro
Stazione S. Pietro
PZA. D. STAZIONE DE S. PIETRO
d. Crocifissio Innocenzo
1
2
3
A
B
C
D
E
F

ITALY

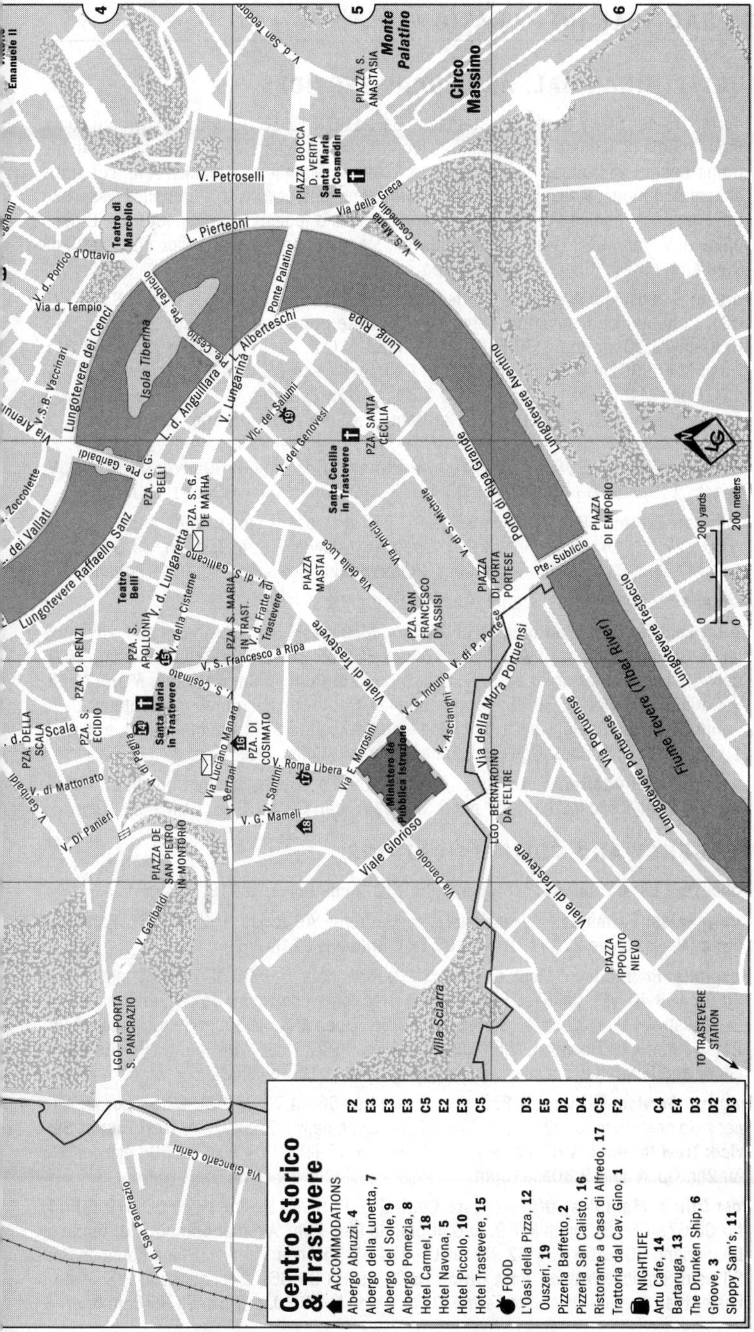
Centro Storico & Trastevere
ACCOMMODATIONS
Albergo Abruzzi, 4 F2
Albergo della Lunetta, 7 E3
Albergo del Sole, 9 E3
Albergo Pomezia, 8 E3
Hotel Carmel, 18 C5
Hotel Navona, 5 E2
Hotel Piccolo, 10 E3
Hotel Trastevere, 15 C5
FOOD
L'Oasi della Pizza, 12 D3
Ouszeri, 19 E5
Pizzeria Baffetto, 2 D2
Pizzeria San Calisto, 16 D4
Ristorante a Casa di Alfredo, 17 C5
Trattoria dal Cav. Gino, 1 F2
NIGHTLIFE
Artu Cafe, 14 C4
Bartaruga, 13 E4
The Drunken Ship, 6 D3
Groove, 3 D2
Sloppy Sam's, 11 D3
Monte Palatino
Circo Massimo
Teatro di Marcello
Isola Tiberina
Santa Maria in Cosmedin
Santa Cecilia in Trastevere
Santa Maria in Trastevere
Ministero da Pubblica Istruzione
Villa Sciarra
Fiume Tevere (Tiber River)
Lungotevere Raffaello Sanz
Lungotevere dei Cenci
Lungotevere Aventino
Lungotevere Testaccio
Lungotevere Portuense
Viale di Trastevere
Via della Mura Portuensi
Viale Glorioso
Ponte Palatino
Pte. Sublicio
Pte. Garibaldi
PIAZZA DI EMPORIO
PIAZZA IPPOLITO NIEVO
PIAZZA DI PORTA PORTESE
PZA. SAN FRANCESCO D'ASSISI
PIAZZA MASTAI
PZA. SANTA CECILIA
PIAZZA BOCCA D. VERITA
PIAZZA S. ANASTASIA
PIAZZA DE SAN PIETRO IN MONTORIO
LGO. D. PORTA S. PANCRAZIO
LGO. BERNARDINO DA FELTRE
TO TRASTEVERE STATION
200 yards
200 meters

ITALY

PRACTICAL INFORMATION

TOURIST, FINANCIAL, AND LOCAL SERVICES

Tourist Office: Enjoy Rome, V. Marghera 8a (☎06 445 18 43; www.enjoyrome.com). From middle concourse of Termini (between trains and ticket booths), exit right, with the trains behind you; cross V. Marsala and follow V. Marghera 3 blocks. Arranges hotel accommodations, walking and bicycle tours, and bus service to Pompeii. Full-service travel agency, booking transportation worldwide and lodgings throughout Italy. Branch office at V. Varese 39 (walk 1 block down V. Marghera and go right). Open M-F 8:30am-2pm and 3:30-6:30pm, Sa 8:30am-2pm.

Foreign Embassies: Australia, V. Alessandria 215 (☎06 85 27 21; fax 06 85 27 23 00). Consular and passport service around the corner at C. Trieste 25. Open M-F 8:30am-12:30pm and 1:30-5:30pm. **Canada,** V.G.B. De Rossi 27 (☎06 44 59 81). Open M-F 8:30am-4:30pm. **Ireland,** P. Campitelli 3 (☎06 697 91 21; fax 06 69 79 12). Open M-F 10am-12:30pm and 3-4:30pm. **New Zealand,** V. Zara 28 (☎06 441 71 71; fax 06 440 29 84). Open M-F 8:30am-12:45pm and 1:45-5pm. **South Africa,** V. Tanaro 14 (☎06 85 25 41; fax 06 85 25 43). Open M-F 8:30am-4:30pm. **UK,** V. XX Settembre 80/A (☎06 482 54 41; www.grbr.it). Open M-F 8:30am-4:30pm. **US,** V. Veneto 119/A (☎06 467 41; fax 06 488 26 72). Open M-F 8:30am-10:30am.

American Express: P. di Spagna 38 (☎06 676 41; lost or stolen cards and/or checks ☎06 722 82; fax 06 67 64 24 99). Open Sept.-July M-F 9am-7:30pm, Sa 9am-3pm; Aug. M-F 9am-6pm, Sa 9am-12:30pm. **Holds mail:** P. di Spagna 38; 00187 Roma.

Luggage Storage: In train station Termini, by track 1.

Bi-Gay-Lesbian Organizations: ARCI-GAY and **ARCI-Lesbica** share offices at V. Orvinio 2 (☎06 86 38 51 12) and V. Lariana 8 (☎06 855 55 22). ARCI-GAY membership (€10 per yr.) gives admission to all gay clubs. **Circolo di Cultura Omosessuale Mario Mieli,** V. Corinto 5 (☎06 541 39 85; www.mariomieli.it), provides information about gay life in Rome. M: B-San Paolo, walk 1 block to Largo Beato Placido Riccardi, turn left, and walk 1½ blocks to V. Corinto. Open M-F 9am-1pm and 2-6pm; closed Aug.

Laundromat: OndaBlu, V. La Mora 7 (☎800 86 13 46). Locations throughout Rome. Wash €3 per 6.5kg load; dry €3 per 6.5kg load; soap €0.75. Open daily 8am-10pm.

ITALY

EMERGENCY AND COMMUNICATIONS

Police: ☎113. **Carabinieri** (civil corps): ☎112. **Ambulance:** ☎118. **Fire:** ☎115.

Pharmacies: Farmacia Internazionale, P. Barberini 49 (☎06 482 54 56). **Farmacia Piram,** V. Nazionale 228 (☎06 488 07 54). Both open 24hr.

Hospitals: International Medical Center, V.G. Amendola 7 (☎06 488 23 71; nights and Su 06 488 40 51). Call first. Prescriptions filled, paramedic crew on call, referral service to English-speaking doctors. General visit €68. Open M-Sa 8:30am-8pm. On-call 24hr. **Rome American Hospital,** V.E. Longoni 69 (☎06 225 51; www.rah.it). Private emergency and laboratory services. HIV and pregnancy tests. On-call 24hr.

Internet Service: Marco's Bar, V. Varese 54 (☎06 44 70 35 91). €2.50 per hr. with *Let's Go* or student ID, otherwise €4 per hour. Open daily 5:30am-2am. **Trevi Tourist Service: Trevi Internet,** V.d. Lucchesi 31-32 (☎/fax 06 69 20 07 99). €2.50 per hour, €4 for 2hr. Open daily 9:30am-10pm.

Post Office: Main Post Office (Posta Centrale), P. San Silvestro 19 (☎06 679 50 44; fax 06 678 66 18). Open M-F 9am-6:30pm, Sa 9am-2pm. Another **branch,** V.d. Terme di Diocleziano 30 (☎06 481 82 98; fax 06 474 35 36), near Termini. Same hours as San Silvestro branch. **Vatican Post Office** (☎06 69 88 34 06), 2 locations in P.S. Pietro. Faster than postal service. No *Fermo Posta.* Open M-F 8:30am-7pm, Sa 8:30am-6pm.

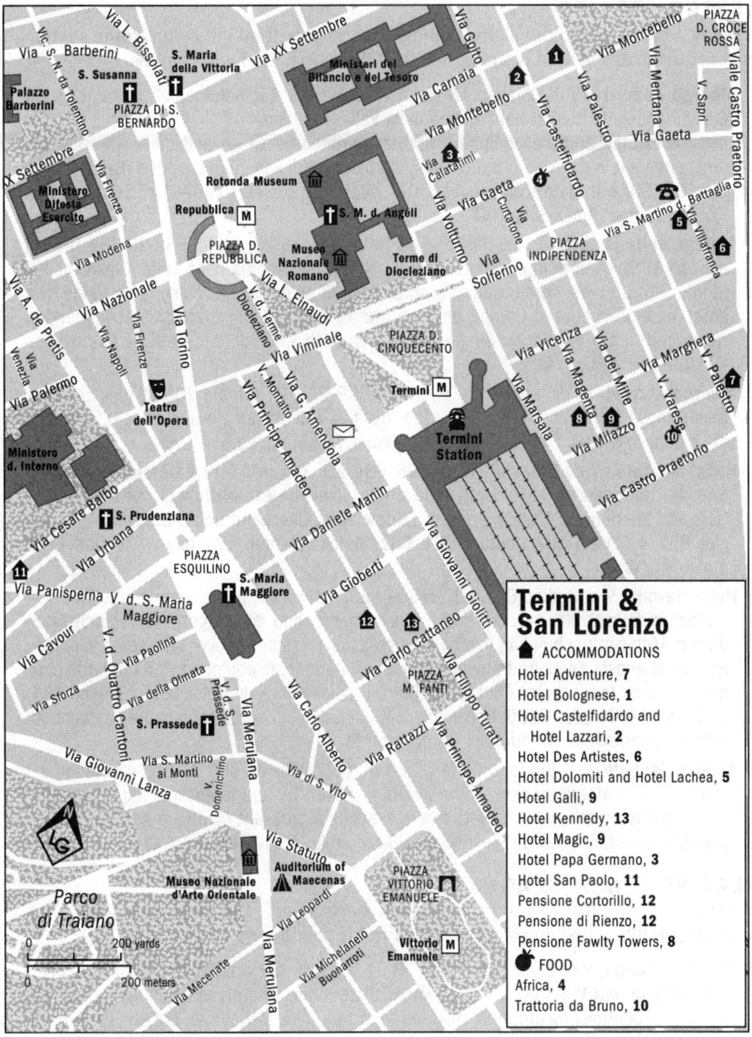

ACCOMMODATIONS

Rome swells with tourists around Easter, from May through July, and in September. Prices vary widely with the time of year, and a proprietor's willingness to negotiate increases with length of stay, number of vacancies, and group size. Termini is swarming with hotel scouts. Many are legitimate and have IDs issued by tourist offices; however, some imposters have fake badges and direct travelers to rundown locations with exorbitant rates, especially at night.

CENTRO STORICO

If being a bit closer to the sights is important to you, then choosing Rome's medieval center over the area near Termini may be worth the higher prices.

Albergo Pomezia, V.d. Chiavari 13 (☎/fax 06 686 13 71; hotelpomezia@libero.it). Off C.V. Emanuele II, behind Sant'Andrea della Valle. The rooms on all 3 floors have recently been renovated and are equipped with new bathrooms. Clean and quiet with phones, fans, and heat in the winter. Breakfast in the pleasant dining room included (8-10:30am). Singles €50, with bath €60; doubles €77.50/€110; triples €120/€127.50. Extra bed 35% surcharge. AmEx/MC/V. ❹

Albergo della Lunetta, P. del Paradiso 68 (☎06 686 10 80; fax 06 689 20 28). The 1st right off V. Chiavari from C.V. Emanuele II behind Sant'Andrea della Valle. Clean, well-lit rooms with phones; some around a small, fern-filled courtyard. Fairly good value in a great location (between Campo dei Fiori and P. Navona). Reservations recommended (with credit card or check). Singles €52, with bath €62; doubles €83/€109; triples €112/€147). MC/V. ❹

Albergo Abruzzi, P. della Rotonda 69 (☎06 679 20 21). A mere 200 ft. from the Pantheon, these are rooms with a view. The facilities aiding your viewing are old-fashioned but clean. A/C €10. Singles €43-65; doubles €73-95; triples €125. ❹

Hotel Piccolo, V.d. Chiavari, 32 (☎06 689 23 30), off C.V. Emanuele II behind Sant'Andrea della Valle. Recently renovated, family-run establishment. All rooms have fans and telephones. English spoken. Curfew 1am. Check-out noon. Breakfast €4. Singles €52, with bath €62; doubles €62/€82; triples with bath €88; quads with bath €90. AmEx/MC/V. ❹

Hotel Navona, V.d. Sediari 8, 1st fl. (☎06 686 42 03; www.hotelnavona.com). Take V.d. Canestrari from P. Navona, cross C.d. Rinascimento, and go straight. This recently refurbished 16th-century building has been used as a *pensione* for over 150 years, counting among its guests Keats and Shelley. Brand-new bathrooms equipped with the added luxury of heated towel racks. Check-out 10am. Breakfast included. A/C €15. Singles €84; doubles €110; triples €150. Reservations with credit card and first night pre-payment. All other payments in cash (euros or US dollars). ❺

Albergo del Sole, V.d. Biscione 76 (☎06 68 80 68 73; fax 06 689 37 87), off Campo dei Fiori. 61 comfortable modern rooms with phone, fan, TV, and fantastic antique furniture. Some rooms on the rowdy street; others overlook a pleasant courtyard garden. Parking garage €18-23. Singles €65, with bath €83; doubles €95/€110-125. ❺

NEAR PIAZZA DI SPAGNA

These accommodations might cost a few euros more, but can you really put a price tag on living just a few steps from Prada? John Keats couldn't.

Pensione Panda, V.d. Croce 35 (☎06 678 01 79; www.webeco.it/hotelpanda), between P.d. Spagna and V.d. Corso. Lovely, immaculate rooms and arched ceilings (some with frescoes). Centrally located but shielded from the noise. Always an English speaker on staff. Check-out 11am. Reservations recommended. Mar-Dec. singles €42, with bath €62; doubles with bath €83; triples with bath €124; quads with bath €168. Jan.-Feb. singles €37, with bath €57; doubles with bath €83; triples with bath €109; quads with bath €145. Jan.-Feb. *Let's Go* discount 5%. AmEx/MC/V. ❹

Hotel Pensione Suisse S.A.S., V. Gregoriana 54 (☎06 678 36 49; info@HotelSuisseRome.com). Turn right at the top of the Spanish Steps. Impeccable service, sleek, old-fashioned furniture, comfortable beds, phone and fan in every room. Internet access, TV available. Continental breakfast included. All rooms with bath. Singles €88; doubles €134; triples €184; quads €208. MC/V. ❺

Daphne B&B, V.d. Avignonesi 20 (☎/fax 06 47 82 35 29; www.daphne-rome.com), off the P. Barberini. Friendly English-speaking owner and a substantial list of amenities just steps from P.d. Spagna and the Trevi Fountain make these rates exceptional for Rome. A/C, daily maid service, common bathrooms. Check-out 10am. Reservations strongly recommended. Singles €100; doubles €110; triples €165; quads €220. Jan.-Feb. and Nov.-Dec. 26 as much as 40% cheaper. MC/V. ❺

Hotel Boccaccio, V.d. Boccaccio 25 (☎/fax 06 488 59 62; www.hotelboccaccio.com). M: A-Barberini. Off V.d. Tritone. This quiet, well-situated hotel offers 8 elegantly furnished rooms near many sights. Reception daily 9am-11pm, late-night key, no deposit. Singles €42; doubles €62, with bath €84; triples €84/€112. AmEx/MC/V. ❹

Pensione Jonella, V. d. Croce 41 (☎06 679 79 66), between P.d. Spagna and V.d. Corso. 4 beautiful rooms. Quiet, roomy, and cool in summer. No reception: call to arrange for someone to meet you when you arrive. 4th fl. location; no elevator. No private bathrooms. Doubles Jul.-Aug. €62; Mar.-Jun., Nov. 10-Mar. and Dec. 24-Jan. 2 €68. ❸

BORGO AND PRATI (NEAR VATICAN CITY)

Home to lots of priests and nuns, the Vatican and environs are pretty quiet at night.

Colors, V. Boezio 31 (☎06 687 40 30; www.colorshotel.com). M: A-Ottaviano, or take a bus to P. Risorgimento. Take V. Cola di Rienzo to V. Terenzio. Located in the elegant Prati area, Colors offers rooms painted with a bravado that would put Caravaggio to shame. Kitchen, hair dryers. Internet €3 per hr. Laundry service €2.10 per load. Beautiful terrace and kitchen open 7:30am-11pm. Dorms €20; doubles €67.50-83; triples €77.50-98.50. Credit card for private room reservations. ❷

Pensione Ottaviano, V. Ottaviano 6 (☎06 39 73 72 53; www.pensioneottaviano.com), just north of P.d. Risorgimento. A few blocks from the Métro stop of the same name. Satellite TV, fridges, a microwave, hot showers, free linens, and free Internet access for guests. Lockout 11:30am-2:30pm. 6-8 bed dorms. Oct.-June €15, July-Sept., and winter holidays €18; doubles €62/€50; one triple €70/€62. ❶

Hotel Lady, V. Germanico 198, 4th fl. (☎06 324 21 12; venneri@libero.it), between V. Fabbio Massimo and V. Paolo Emilio. The 8 rooms, some with beautiful loft-style open wood-work ceilings and tile floors, lack A/C but are miraculously cool in the middle of summer. All rooms with sinks and desks. With *Let's Go* discount: singles €65; doubles €82, with bath €100; triples €106/€130. AmEx/MC/V. ❺

Hotel Florida, V. Cola di Rienzo 243 (☎06 324 18 72; www.hotelfloridaroma.it), on the 1st-3rd floors, reception on 2nd fl. Floral carpets, floral bedspreads, floral wall decorations. TV, phone, and hair dryers in each of the 18 rooms. A/C €10. 1 single with sink €31, with bath €72; doubles €68/€103; triples with bath €134; quads with bath €155. Ask about discounts. 5% discount if you pay in cash. AmEx/MC/V. ❸

Hotel Isa, V. Cicerone 39 (☎06 321 26 10; www.hotelisa.com). 1 block north of P. Cavour. 3-star hotel with A/C, full bath, and chandeliers. Private terraces, telephone, TV, and minibar. Breakfast included. 24hr. English-speaking reception. May-Sept. singles €163, doubles €212; Oct.-Apr. €114/€145. Extra bed €20. AmEx/MC/V. ❺

TRASTEVERE

Hotels here are scattered, most of them too pricey for budget travelers, but the area does offer great nightlife and a location near the Vatican.

Hotel Carmel, V.G. Mameli 11 (☎06 580 99 21; hotelcarmel@hotmail.com). Take a right on V.E. Morosini (V.G. Mameli) off V.d. Trastevere. Though a short walk from the heart of Trastevere, this simple hotel offers 9 no-frills, smallish rooms for reasonable prices. All with bath. Breakfast included. Singles €75; doubles €85; triples €110; quads €130. AmEx/MC/V. ❺

ITALY

Hotel Trastevere, V. Luciano Manara 25 (☎06 581 47 13; fax 06 588 10 16). Take a right off V.d. Trastevere onto V.d. Fratte di Trastevere, which becomes V. Luciano Manara. Neighborhood murals give way to 9 simple and airy rooms with bath, TV, and phone. English spoken. Breakfast included. Singles €77; doubles €98-103; triples €129; quads €154. Short-term apartments for 2-6 people with small kitchens and loft beds available. AmEx/MC/V. ❺

TERMINI AND SAN LORENZO

This is budget-traveler central. Rooms range from ultra-cheap to moderate, but beware of *pensioni* that agree to reserve you a room and, when you arrive, offer you accommodations in a "sister" hotel. The rates will usually be twice as high.

NORTH OF TERMINI

Although this region has its fair share of tourist traps, it's cheaper than the historical center and is considerably nicer than seedy Esquilino to the south.

Pensione Fawlty Towers, V. Magenta 39 (☎/fax 06 445 03 74; www.fawltytowers.org). Exit Termini to the right from the middle concourse, cross V. Marsala onto V. Marghera, and turn right onto V. Magenta. An extremely popular 15-room hotel/hostel. Common room with satellite TV, library, refrigerator, microwave, and free Internet access. Frequently full, but the reception will help you find a room elsewhere, usually at one of the other 2 hotels that the proprietors own. Check-out 9am for dorms and 10am for private rooms. Reservations possible a week in advance; confirm all reservations 48 hr. before arrival. €23; 4-bed dorms €18 (no children); singles €44, with shower €51; doubles €62, with shower €67, with bath €77. ❷

Hotel Des Artistes, V. Villafranca 20 (☎06 445 43 65; www.hoteldesartistes.com). From the middle concourse of Termini, exit right, turn left onto V. Marsala, right onto V. Vicenza, and then left onto the 5th cross-street. 3-star hotel with clean, elegant rooms. Free Internet access. Breakfast included with rooms with a bathroom, otherwise €4.50. Reception 24hr. Cancel reservations 5 days before. Check-out 11am. Singles €39-57, with bath €98-140; doubles €46-85/€103-150; triples €57-114/€103-150; quads €72-130/€146-195. €15 discount with cash payment. AmEx/MC/V. ❹

Hotel Papa Germano, V. Calatafimi 14a (☎06 48 69 19; www.hotelpapagermano.com). From the middle concourse of Termini, exit right, and turn left onto V. Marsala, which shortly becomes V. Volturno; V. Calatafimi is the 4th cross-street on your right. Clean rooms, all with TV and telephone, and outstanding service. English, French, and Spanish spoken. Internet access €2.60 per hr. Check-out 11am. Dorms €18-25. Singles €23-40; doubles €42-70, with bath €52-93; triples €54-78, with bath €72-105. Nov.-Mar. 10% discount. AmEx/MC/V. ❷

Hotel Dolomiti and **Hotel Lachea,** V.S. Martino della Battaglia 11 (☎06 495 72 56; www.hotel-dolomiti.it). From the middle concourse of Termini, exit right, turn left onto V. Marsala and right onto V. Solferino (V.S. Martino della Battaglia). Aging 19th-century *palazzo* houses sparkling new 3-star hotels, with the same reception (on 2nd fl.) and management. Bar, breakfast room, and Internet access (€2.60 per 30min.). Breakfast €6. A/C €13 per night. Check-out 11am. Check-in 1pm. Singles €52-67; doubles €73-93; triples €83-108; quads €114-135; quints €145-155. ❹

Hotel Cathrine, V. Volturno 27 (☎06 48 36 34). From the middle concourse of Termini, exit right, and turn left onto V. Marsala (V. Volturno). 2 common bathrooms serve the 8 spacious singles and doubles with sinks. More rooms at the modern **Affitacamere Aries** at V. XX Settembre 58a. Breakfast €2. *Let's Go* discount available. Singles €35-45; doubles €47-62, with bath €52-72; Extra bed €15. ❸

Hotel Adventure, V. Palestro 88 (☎06 446 90 26; www.hoteladventure.com). From the middle concourse of Termini, exit right, cross V. Marsala onto V. Marghera, and take the 4th right onto V. Palestro. Newly renovated rooms, all with bath, satellite TV, telephone, and fridge. Breakfast included. Check-out 11am. A/C €13. Singles €100; doubles €120; triples €140. AmEx/MC/V. ❺

Hotel Bolognese, V. Palestro 15 (☎/fax 06 49 00 45). From the middle concourse of Termini, exit right. Walk down V. Marghera and take your 4th left on V. Palestro. In a land of run-of-the-mill *pensioni,* this place is spruced up by the artist-owner, whose impressive paintings decorate all the rooms. Probably the only hotel near Termini to have won an award from the Knights of Malta for hospitality. Check-out 11am. Singles €31, with bath €43; doubles €47-60/€72; triples €62-77.50. ❸

Hotel Magic, V. Milazzo, 20 (☎06 495 98 80; fax 06 444 14 08). From the middle concourse of Termini, exit right. Take a right on V. Marsala and your first left on V. Milazzo. The owners of Hotel Magic will make a clean, modern room and a bar appear before your very eyes. All rooms include private baths, TVs, hair-dryers, and in-room safes. A/C €10. Singles €52; doubles €77; triples €103; quads €118. MC/V. ❹

Hotel Galli, V. Milazzo 20 (☎06 445 68 59; www.albergogalli.com). From the middle concourse of Termini, exit right. Take a right on V. Marsala and your first left on V. Milazzo. Offers clean and modern rooms with tile floors and wrought-iron beds. All 12 rooms have bath, TV, mini-bar, and safe. Breakfast, A/C included. Singles €50; doubles €80; triples €90; quads €120. Winter 10-15% lower. AmEx/MC/V. ❹

VIA XX SETTEMBRE

Dominated by government ministries and private apartments, this area is less noisy than nearby Termini.

Pensione Tizi, V. Collina 48 (☎06 482 01 28; fax 06 474 32 66). A 10min. walk from the station. Take V. Goito from P. dell'Indipendenza, cross V. XX Settembre onto V. Piave, then go left on V. Flavia and right on V. Collina. Or take bus #319 or 270 from Termini. Marble floors and inlaid ceilings adorn spacious and recently renovated rooms. Check-out 11am. Singles €42; doubles €52, with bath €62; triples €80/€90; quads €100/€110. AmEx/MC/V. ❹

Hotel Castelfidardo and **Hotel Lazzari,** V. Castelfidardo 31 (☎06 446 46 38; www.castelfidardo.com). Two blocks off V. XX Settembre. Both run by the same friendly family. Renovated rooms with spanking clean floors. 3 floors of modern, shiny comfort and plenty of bathroom space. Hall bathrooms shared by 3 rooms at most. Check-out 10:30am. English spoken. Singles €42, with bath €52; doubles €60/€70; triples €77/€93; quads with bath €108. AmEx/MC/V. ❹

Hotel Baltic, V. XX Settembre 89 (☎06 481 47 75; fax 06 48 55 09). Sleek and well maintained. Quiet rooms with high ceilings are more like those in a business hotel than the typical *pensione;* all have phone, TV, microfridge, and safe. Breakfast €5. Check-out 11am. A/C €10. Singles €45; doubles €62; triples €77; quads €100. AmEx/MC/V. ❹

Pensione Monaco, V. Flavia 84 (☎/fax 06 42 01 41 80). From V. XX Settembre, turn left onto V. Quinto Sellia and right onto V. Flavia. Friendly Italian woman and English-speaking children keep these 11 sunlit rooms, all with bathroom. Comfortable mattresses, bright courtyard. Check-out 9am. With *Let's Go* discount: singles €35; doubles €56; triples and quads €25 per person. Winter prices about 10% lower. ❸

SOUTH OF TERMINI (ESQUILINO)

Women might feel uncomfortable walking in this area at night.

Pensione di Rienzo, V. Principe Amedeo 79a (☎06 446 71 31; fax 06 446 69 80). A tranquil, family-run retreat with spacious, newly renovated rooms. Plain and cheap. 20 rooms with balconies, TVs, and baths. Breakfast €7. Check-out 10am. Singles without bath €19-47; doubles €23-57, with bath €26-67. Prices vary by season. MC/V. ❷

Pensione Cortorillo, V. Principe Amedeo 79a, 5th fl. (☎06 446 69 34; fax 06 445 47 69). This small *pensione* has TVs and A/C in all 14 rooms, and a cheap lobby phone. English, French, and Spanish spoken. Breakfast included. Check-out 10am. Singles €30-70; doubles €40-100; rooms can be made into triples and quads for an additional €10 per person. Prices depend on season. AmEx/MC/V. ❸

Hotel Kennedy, V. Filippo Turati 62-64 (☎06 446 53 73; www.hotelkennedy.net). Ask not what you can do for Hotel Kennedy, ask what Hotel Kennedy can do for you. Classical music in the bar, leather couches, and a large color TV in the lounge. Private bath, satellite TV, phone, and A/C. Hearty all-you-can-eat breakfast included. English, French, Spanish, and Portugese spoken. Check-out 11am. Reservations by fax/email only. Singles €45-88; doubles €70-139; triples €80-159; quads €90-258. 10% *Let's Go* discount. AmEx/D/MC/V. ❹

Hotel Il Castello, V. Vittorio Amedeo II 9 (☎06 77 20 40 36; www.ilcastello.com). M: A-Manzoni. Beyond Termini, but well within the backpacker's budget. Walk down V. San Quintino and take the first left. Housed in a castle with smallish rooms and eager serving knaves (mostly native English speakers). Breakfast €3. Check-out 10:30am. Dorms €17; singles €42; doubles €57, with bath €68; triples €65-95. MC/V. ❷

WEST OF TERMINI

Close by the bustle of Termini, this area houses more restaurants and shops.

Hotel San Paolo, V. Panisperna 95 (☎06 474 52 13; www.hotelsanpaoloroma.com). Exiting from the front of the train station, turn left onto V. Cavour. After you pass Santa Maria Maggiore (on the left), bear right onto V.d. Santa Maria Maggiore (V. Panisperna). 10min. from Termini; housed in a bright little *palazzo* with whimsically decorated rooms. Hall baths are clean and private. English spoken. Breakfast €5. Check-out 11am. Singles €39; doubles €57, with bath €78; triples €78. 6-10 person suite €26 per person. AmEx/MC/V. ❹

Pensione Sandy, V. Cavour 136 (☎06 488 45 85; www.sandyhostel.com), just past the intersection with V. S. Maria Maggiore. No sign; look for the Hotel Valle, Sandy is next door to the right. 4th fl., no elevator (ouch). Under the same ownership as Pensione Ottaviano, but not quite as nice. Free Internet access and individual lockers (bring your own lock) in each room. No curfew, no lock-out. Simple, hostel-style rooms, usually for 3-5 people, €18. ❷

ITALY

RELIGIOUS ACCOMMODATIONS

Don't automatically think cheap when you think religion. Nuns and priests in Rome skin tourists to the tune of €30 a night, usually for rooms with a strict curfew and some light housework associated with them. The best ones provide quiet rooms, usually in lovely surroundings. Most are open to people of all religions.

Domus Nova Bethlehem, V. Cavour 85/A (☎06 478 24 41; www.suorebambinogesu.it/DNB). Walk down V. Cavour from Termini. Pass P.d. Esquilino on the right. A clean, modern, and centrally located hotel that happens to carry a religious name, decorations, and a 1am curfew along with it. Alas. The newly-renovated rooms come with A/C, baths with showers, TV and phone. Singles €67; doubles €47 per person; triples €41 per person; quads €36 per person. AmEx/MC/V. ❺

Santa Maria Alle Fornaci, P. S. Maria alle Fornaci 27 (☎06 39 36 76 32; ciffornaci@tin.it). Facing St. Peter's Basilica, take a left (through the basilica walls) onto V.d. Fornace. Take your 3rd right onto V. d. Gasperi, which leads to P. S. Maria alle Fornaci. Just south of the Vatican, this *casa per ferie,* in the Trinitarian tradition of hospitality, offers 54 rooms, each with a private bath and phone. Simple, small, and clean. No curfew. Breakfast included. Singles €47; doubles €78; triples €104. AmEx/MC/V. ❹

FOOD

Ancient Roman dinners were lavish, festive affairs lasting as long as 10 hours. Peacocks and flamingos were served with their full plumage, while acrobats and fire-eaters distracted guests between their courses of camels' feet and goats' ears. Food orgies went on *ad nauseam*, literally—after gorging themselves, guests would retreat to a special room called the *vomitorium*, throw it all up, and return to the party. Meals in Rome are still lengthy affairs. Restaurants tend to close between 3 and 7pm, so plan accordingly.

RESTAURANTS

ANCIENT CITY

Despite its past glory, this area has yet to discover the noble concept of "affordable food." But along **Via dei Fori Imperiali,** several restaurants offer decent prices.

I Buoni Amici, V. Aleardo Aleardi 4 (☎06 70 49 19 93). From the Colosseum, take V. Labicana to V. Merulana. Turn right, then left onto V.A. Aleardi. A long walk, but the cheap and excellent food is well worth the hike. Choices include the *linguine all'astice* (linguini with lobster sauce; €6.50), *risotto con i funghi* (€5.50), and *penne alla vodka* (€5.50). Cover €1.29. Open M-Sa noon-3pm and 7-11:30pm. AmEx/D/MC/V. ❶

Taverna dei Quaranta, V. Claudia 24 (☎06 700 05 50), off P.d. Colosseo. Shaded by the trees of the Celian Park, outdoor dining at this corner *taverna* is a must. The menu changes weekly, and in summer often features the sinfully good *oliva ascolane* (olives stuffed with meat and fried; €3.87) and *ravioli all'Amalfitana* (€7.75). 0.5L of house wine €2.85. Cover €1.29. Reservations suggested, especially for a table outside. Open daily 12:30-3:30pm and 7:45-11:30pm. AmEx/D/MC/V. ❷

CENTRO STORICO

The twisting streets of Rome's historic center offer many hidden gems, especially just off the main *piazze*.

Pizzeria Baffetto, V.d. Governo Vecchio 114 (☎06 686 16 17). At the intersection of V. d. Governo Vecchio and V. Sora. Once a meeting place for 60s radicals, Baffetto now overflows with hungry Romans. It's gotten famous–be prepared to wait a long time. Pizza €4.50-7.50. Open daily 8-10am and 6:30pm-1am. ❶

L'Oasi della Pizza, Via della Corda 3-5 (☎06 687 28 76). The *capricciosa* (tomato, mozzarella, ham, eggs, and mushrooms; €8) is great; you'll get your vegetables with the leafy *margherita* (€6). Basket of bread €2. A logical first stop before a beer in the Campo. Open Th-Tu noon-3pm and 7-11:30pm. ❶

Trattoria dal Cav. Gino, V. Rosini 4 (☎06 687 34 34). Off V. d. Campo Marzio across from P. del Parlamente. The sign above the door announces that *tonnarelli alla ciociala* (€6.20) is the house specialty. *Primi* €5.15-6.20; *secondi* €7.20-9.30. Reservations accepted. Open M-Sa 1-3:45pm and 8-10:30pm. ❷

CAMPO DEI FIORI AND THE JEWISH GHETTO

Trattoria da Sergio, V.d. Grotte 27 (☎06 654 66 69). Take V.d. Giubbonari and your 1st right. Sergio offers an authentic Roman ambience and hearty portions. Try the *spaghetti Matriciana* (with bacon and spicy tomato sauce; €6)–a front-runner for the city's best plate of pasta–and the *Straccetti* (shredded beef with arugula salad; €8). Reservations suggested. Open M-Sa 12:30-3pm and 6pm-midnight. MC/V. ❷

Hostaria Grappolo d'Oro, P. della Cancelleria 80-81 (☎06 689 70 80), between C.V. Emanuele II and the Campo. A Roman legend, it's running out of space in its front window to plaster all the awards it's won over the years. The small menu changes daily. *Primi* €7-

8; *secondi* €12-13; dessert around €4.50. Cover €1. Open M-Sa noon-2:30pm and 7:30-11pm. Closed M lunch. AmEx/MC/V. ❸

Trattoria Da Luigi, P.S. Cesarini 24 (☎06 686 59 46), near Chiesa Nuova. Enjoy inventive cuisine such as the delicate *carpaccio di salmone fresco con rughetta* (€8), as well as simple dishes like *vitello con funghi* (veal with mushrooms; €9.50). Bread €1. Open Tu-Su noon-3pm and 7pm-midnight. AmEx/MC/V. ❷

Trattoria da Giggetto, V.d. Portico d'Ottavio 21-22 (☎06 686 11 05). Their *carciofi alla Giudia* (€4.50) are legendary, but be daring and go for the *fritto di cervello d'abbacchino, funghi, zucchine* (fried brains with mushrooms and zucchini; €11.50). Reservations necessary for dinner. Open Tu-Su 12:30-3pm and 7:30-11pm. AmEx/MC/V. ❸

PIAZZA DI SPAGNA

Although the upscale P. d. Spagna might appear to have little in common with Termini, they both share one thing in common: tons of bad, bad food. The difference is that you'll pay €10 more for the atmosphere here. The best food is closer to the Ara Pacis, across V. d. Corso, away from the throngs of tourists.

Trattoria da Settimio all'Arancio, V.d. Arancio 50-52 (☎06 687 61 19). Take V.d. Condotti from P.d. Spagna; take the 1st right after V.d. Corso, then the 1st left. Order the fried artichokes (€4.50), although the less inhibited might try the squid's ink risotto (€7.50). No meal is complete without *panna cotta,* the Italian cream custard with fresh fruit. Bread €1. Open M-Sa 12:30-3pm and 7:30-11:30pm. AmEx/D/MC/V. ❷

Vini e Buffet, P. Torretta 60 (☎06 687 14 45). From V.d. Corso, turn into P.S. Lorenzo in Lucina. Take a left on V. Campo Marzio and a quick right onto V. Toretta. Popular salads are creative and fresh—the *insalata con salmone* (€8.50/€10 *gigante*) is delightful. Don't leave without getting one of their signature yogurt, almond, and cassis combination bowls (€4). Reservations recommended. Open M-Sa 12:30-3pm and 7-11pm. ❷

Il Brillo Parlante, V. Fontanella, 12 (☎06 324 33 34), near P. del Popolo. The wood-burning pizza oven, fresh ingredients, and excellent wine attract many lunching Italians. Pizza €5-7.75. Restaurant open Tu-Su noon-3pm and 7:30pm-1am; *enoteca* (wine bar) open Tu-Su 11am-2am. MC/V. ❷

ITALY

BORGO AND PRATI (NEAR VATICAN CITY)

Establishments near the Vatican serve mediocre sandwiches at hiked-up prices, but just a few blocks northeast is better and much cheaper food.

Franchi, V. Cola di Rienzo 204 (☎06 687 46 51). Delicacies include various croquettes (€1.29), marinated munchies (anchovies, peppers, olives, and salmon, all sold by the kilo), and pastas (vegetarian lasagna and *cannellini* stuffed with ricotta and beef €5 per generous portion). Open M-Sa 8:15am-9pm. AmEx/MC/V. ❷

Guido, V. Borgo Pio 13 (☎06 687 54 91). There's no sign, but you can recognize it by the men playing cards in the sun. Guido holds court behind a counter filled with all the makings of a beautiful *tavola calda.* Prices vary, but a full meal (*primi, secondi,* and all the wine you want) will run you less than €8. Usually open M-Sa 9am-8pm. ❷

TRASTEVERE

Perhaps one of the best places to enjoy a meal in Rome, with fabulous, largely undiscovered restaurants.

Pizzeria San Calisto, P.S. Calisto 9a (☎06 581 82 56). Right off P.S. Maria in Trastevere. Simply the best damn pizza in Rome. Gorgeous thin crust pizzas so large they hang off the plates (€4.15-7.75). Open Tu-Su 7pm-midnight. MC/V. ❷

Ristorante a Casa di Alfredo, V. Roma Libera 5-7 (☎06 588 29 68). Try the *gnocchi tartufo e gamberi* (€9.30) or tonarelli with tomatoes, sausage, porcini mushrooms, and arugula (€10.33) to start and the grilled calamari (€10.33) or the *filetto a pepe verde* (€12.40) as a main dish. Open daily noon-3pm and 7:30-11:30pm. ❸

Ouszeri, V.d. Salumi 2 (☎06 581 82 56). Either go left off V.d. Trastevere or take V. Vascellari from Lungotevere Ripa and then go right onto V.d. Salumi. Ouszeri advertises itself as a "Taverna Greca," but the waiters will tell you it is actually a Greek Cultural Association, complete with Greek dancing lessons. Food is out of this world—share the *piatto misto* with a friend (€7-15). Ring the doorbell. €1.50 membership required. ❸

TERMINI

Tourist traps abound; avoid the torturous €8 "quick lunch" advertised in windows.

Africa, V. Gaeta 26-28 (☎06 494 10 77), near P. Independenza. Excellent Eritrean/Ethiopian food. The meat-filled *sambusas* (€2.50) are a flavorful starter; both the *zighini beghi* (roasted lamb in a spicy sauce; €7) and the *misto vegetariano* (mixed veggie dishes; €6) make fantastic entrees, while the thick yogurt (€1.55) goes well with spicy dishes. Open M-Sa 8pm-midnight. AmEx/MC/V. ❷

Trattoria da Bruno, V. Varese 29 (☎06 49 04 03). From V. Marsala, next to the train station, walk 3 blocks down V. Milazzo and turn right onto V. Varese. Start with the *tortellini con panna e funghi* (with cream and mushrooms; €6.50) or the tasty homemade *gnocchi* (€6) and continue with the delicious *ossobuco* (€7.80). Open daily noon-3:30pm and 7-10:15pm. Closed Aug. AmEx/MC/V. ❷

SAN LORENZO

Rome's funky university district, San Lorenzo, offers many good, cheap eateries. From Termini, walk south on V. Pretoriano to P. Tiburtino, or take bus #492. Women may find the walk a little uncomfortable at night.

Il Pulcino Ballerino, V. d. Equi 66-68 (☎06 494 12 55). Take a right off V. Tiburtina. The cook stirs up dishes like *conchiglione al "Moby Dick"* (shells with tuna, cream, and greens) and *risotto* (various types; €5.16-6.20). Excellent vegetarian dishes. Cover €1. Open M-Sa 1-3:30pm and 8pm-midnight. Closed mid-Aug. AmEx/MC/V. ❷

Arancia Blu, V. d. Latini 65 (☎06 445 41 05), off V. Tiburtina. Enjoy elaborate dishes like *tonnarelli con pecorino romano e tartufo* (pasta with sheep cheese and truffles; €6.20) or fried ravioli stuffed with eggplant and smoked *caciocavallo* with pesto sauce (€8.50). Open daily 8:30pm-midnight. ❷

Il Capellaio Matto, V.d. Marsi 25. From V. Tiburtina, take the 4th right off V.d. Equi. Pasta and rice dishes like *risotto al pepe verde* (with green peppercorn; €5), imaginative salads like *insalata di rughetta, pere, e parmigiano* (arugula, pears, and parmesan; €3.75), and a variety of crepes (€3.62-4.65). Cover €1. Open W-M 8pm-midnight. ❶

TESTACCIO

This working-class southern neighborhood is the center of Roman nightlife, and eateries here offer food made of just about every animal part imaginable.

La Cestia, V. di Piramide Cestia 69. M: B-Piramide. Walk across P. di Porta San Paolo to V. di Piramide Cestia; restaurant is on the right. La Cestia's offerings, particularly their fish, are so fresh that employees of the Food and Agriculture Organization make the trek from their headquarters to grab lunch. Pasta €4.20-7.20, pizza €4.20-7.80, *secondi* €6.20-11, fish €6.20-15. Open Tu-Su 12:30-3pm and 7:30-11pm. D/MC/V. ❸

Trattoria da Bucatino, V. Luca della Robbia 84-86 (☎06 574 68 86). Take V. Luigi Vanvitelli off V. Marmorata, then the first left. The animal entrails you know and love, and plenty of gut-less dishes as well. Heaping, delicious mounds of *tripe alla romana* (€7) stay true to the traditions of Testaccio. Try the daily specials. Pizza €4-7. Cover €1.50. Open Tu-Su 12:30-3:30pm and 6:30-11:30pm. Closed Aug. D/MC/V. ❷

DESSERT AND COFFEE

Cheap *gelato* is as plentiful on Roman streets as leather pants. Look for *gelato* with very muted (hence natural) colors. Coffee (*espresso*) is Italian for "wash away those early morning hostel lock-out blues" and "drink that goes well with pastry/*gelati*/wine/beer."

San Crispino, V. d. Panetteria 42 (☎06 679 39 24), very near the Trevi Fountain. Crispino is almost universally acknowledged as the best *gelato* in Rome. Every flavor made from scratch. Don't miss the honey infused "gelato di San Crispino." Cups €1.70-6.30. Open M, W-Th, Su noon-12:30am, F-Sa noon-1:30am.

The Old Bridge, Vle. dei Bastioni di Michelangelo (☎06 39 72 30 26), off P. del Risorgimento, perpendicular to Vatican museum walls. Huge cups and cones (€1.50-3) filled with your choice of 20 homemade *gelato* flavors, some of the best in the city. Open M-Sa 9am-2am, Su 3pm-2am.

Pasticceria Ebraica Boccione, Portico d'Ottavia 1 (☎06 687 86 37). Little fanfare, just long queues of locals who line up for what they all acknowledge to be the best pastry in Rome. *Torta Riccotta Vicciole* and *Torta Ricotta Cioccolate* are the most in famous of their creations, both sold at excellent prices (€10.33/kg). Open Su-Th 8am-8pm, F 8am-5:30pm (1hr. before sundown).

Bar Giulia (a.k.a. Caffe Peru), V. Giulia 84 (☎06 686 13 10), near P. V. Emmanuele II. No other bar is crazy enough to open near this 50-year-old institution. Giulia serves what may be the cheapest (and most delicious) coffee in Rome (€0.60 at bar, €0.75 sitting) and they'll even add your favorite liqueur. Open M-Sa 4am-9:30pm.

ENOTECHE (WINE BARS)

Roman wine bars range from laid-back and local to chic and international. They often serve excellent food to accompany your bottle.

Bar Da Benito, V.d. Falegnami 14 (☎06 686 15 08), off P. Cairoli in the Jewish Ghetto. A *tavola calda* lined with bottles and hordes of hungry workmen. Glasses of wine from €1; bottles from €6. One hot pasta prepared daily (€4), along with fresh *secondi* like *prosciutto* with vegetables (€5). Open M-Sa 6:30am-7pm; lunch noon-3:30pm. Closed Aug.

Cul de Sac, P. Pasquino 73 (☎06 68 80 10 94), off P. Navona. House specialty *pate* (such as pheasant and mushroom; €5.10) is exquisite, as are the scrumptious *escargot alla bourguigonne* (€4.50). Open M 7pm-12:30am, Tu-Sa noon-4pm and 6pm-12:30am. MC/V.

Enoteca Cavour 313, V. Cavour 313 (☎06 678 54 96). A short walk from M: B-Cavour. Wonderful meats and cheeses (€8-9 for a mixed plate) listed by region or type, many fresh salads (€5-7), and rich desserts (€4-5). Massive wine list (€11-€260). M-Sa 12:30-2:30pm and 7:30pm-1am (kitchen closes 12:30am). Closed Aug.

SIGHTS

Rome wasn't built in a day, and it's not likely that you'll see any substantial portion of it in 24 hours, either. Ancient temples and forums, Renaissance basilicas, 280 fountains, and 981 churches--there's a reason, according to Robert Browning, that "everyone sooner or later comes 'round by Rome."

ANCIENT CITY

What Rome lacks in a "downtown" it more than makes up for in ruins—the downtown Cicero and Catullus knew. The **Umbilicus Urbis,** literally "navel of the world," marked the center of the known universe. And who said Romans were egocentric?

ROMAN FORUM

M: B-Colosseo, or bus to P. Venezia. Main entrance is on V.d. Fori Imperiali (at Largo C. Ricci, between P. Venezia and the Colosseum). Open in summer daily 9am-6:30pm; in winter 9am-3:30pm. Free. Guided tours €3.50; audioguides in English, French, German, Italian, Japanese, or Spanish available at main entrance. €4.

Here the pre-Romans founded a thatched-hut shantytown in 753 BC. The entrance ramp leads to **Via Sacra,** Rome's oldest street, near the **Basilica Aemilia,** built in 179 BC, and the area once known as the **Civic Forum.** Next to the Basilica stands the **Curia** (Senate House); it was converted to a church in AD 630 and restored by Mussolini. The broad space in front of the Curia was the **Comitium,** where male citizens came to vote and representatives of the people gathered for public discussion. Bordering the Comitium is the large brick **Rostrum** (speaker's platform) erected by Julius Caesar in 44 BC, just before his death. The hefty **Arch of Septimius Severus,** to the right of the Rostrum, was dedicated in AD 203 to celebrate Caesar's victories in the Middle East. The **market square** holds a number of shrines and sacred precincts, including the **Lapis Niger** (Black Stone), where Romulus was supposedly murdered by Republican senators. Below the Lapis Niger are the underground ruins of a 6th-century BC altar and the oldest known Latin inscription in Rome. In the square, the **Three Sacred Trees** of Rome—olive, fig, and grape—have been replanted by the Italian state. The newest part of the Forum is the **Column of Phocas,** erected in AD 608. The three great temples of the **Lower Forum** have been closed off for excavations; however, the eight columns of the 5th-century BC **Temple of Saturn,** next to the Rostrum, have been restored. Around the corner, rows of column bases are all that remain of the **Basilica Julia,** a courthouse built by Julius Caesar in 54 BC. At the far end, three marble columns mark the massive podium of the recently restored **Temple of Castor and Pollux,** built to celebrate the Roman defeat of the Etruscans. The circular building is the **Temple of Vesta,** where Vestal Virgins tended the city's sacred fire, keeping it lit for more than a thousand years.

In the **Upper Forum** lies the **House of the Vestal Virgins.** For 30 years, the six virgins who officiated over Vesta's rites lived in seclusion here from the ripe old age of seven. As long as they kept their vows of chastity, they remained among the most respected people in ancient Rome. Near here, V. Sacra runs over the **Cloaca Maxima,** the ancient sewer that still drains water from the otherwise marsh-like valley. V. Sacra continues out of the Forum proper to the **Velia** and the gargantuan **Basilica of Maxentius** (also known as the Basilica of Constantine). The middle apse of the basilica once contained a gigantic statue of Constantine with a bronze body and marble head, legs, and arms. The uncovered remains, including a 2m foot, are displayed at the **Palazzo dei Conservatori** on the Capitoline Hill (see p. 661). V. Sacra leads to an exit on the other side of the hill to the Colosseum; the path that crosses before the **Arch of Titus** heads to the Palatine Hill.

THE PALATINE HILL

The Palatine rises to the south of the Forum. Open in summer daily 9am-6:30pm; in winter M-Sa 9:30am to 1hr. before sunset, Su 9am-3:30pm; sometimes closes M-F 3pm, Su and holidays noon. Last entrance 45min. before closing. Ticket to the Palatine Hill and the Colosseum €8, EU citizens 18-24 €4, EU citizens under 18 and over 65 free. 7-day ticket book good for entrance to the 4 Musei Nazionali Romani, the Colosseum, the Palatine Hill, the Terme di Diocleziano, and the Crypti Balbi €20, EU citizens 18-24 €10.

The best way to attack the Palatine is from the stairs near the Forum's **Arch of Titus.** The hill, actually a plateau between the Tiber and the Forum, was home to the she-wolf that suckled Romulus and Remus. Throughout the garden complex, terraces

ITALY

provide breathtaking views. Lower down, excavations continue on the 9th-century BC village, the **Casa di Romulo.** To the right of the village is the podium of the 191 BC **Temple of Cybele.** The stairs to the left lead to the **House of Livia,** which is connected to the **House of Augustus** next door. Around the corner, the long, spooky **Cryptoporticus** connected Tiberius's palace with the buildings nearby. The path around the House of Augustus leads to the vast ruins of a giant palace and is divided into two wings. The solemn **Domus Augustana** was the private space for the emperors; the adjacent wing, the sprawling **Domus Flavia,** once held a gigantic octagonal fountain. Between the Domus Augustana and the Domus Flavia stands the **Palatine Antiquarium,** the museum that houses the artifacts found during the excavations of the Palatine Hill. *(30 people admitted every 20min. starting at 9:10am. Free.)* Outside on the right, the palace's east wing contains the curious **Stadium of Domitian,** or *Hippodrome*, a sunken oval space once surrounded by a colonnade but now decorated with fragments of porticoes, statues, and fountains. The **Arch of Constantine** lies between the Colosseum and the Palatine Hill, marking the tail end of the V. Sacra. One of the best-preserved monuments in the area, it commemorates Constantine's victory over Maxentius at the Milvian Bridge in AD 315.

OTHER SIGHTS

FORI IMPERIALI. Across the street from the Ancient Forum are the **Fori Imperiali,** a conglomeration of temples, basilicas, and public squares constructed in the 1st and 2nd centuries. Excavations will proceed through 2003, so the area is closed off, but you can still get free views by peering over the railing from V.d. Fori Imperiali or V. Alessandrina. Built between AD 107 and 113, the **Forum of Trajan** included a colossal equestrian statue of Trajan and an immense triumphal arch. At one end of the now-decimated forum, 2500 carved legionnaires march their way up the almost perfectly preserved **Trajan's Column,** one of the greatest extant specimens of Roman relief-sculpture. The crowning statue is St. Peter, who replaced Trajan in 1588. The gray tufa wall of the **Forum of Augustus** commemorates Augustus' victory over Caesar's murderers in 42 BC. The aptly named **Forum Transitorium** (also called the **Forum of Nerva**) was a narrow, rectangular space connecting the Forum of Augustus with the Republican Roman Forum. The only remnant of **Vespatian's Forum** is the mosaic-filled **Church of Santi Cosma e Damiano** across V. Cavour, near the Roman Forum. *(Open daily 9am-1pm and 3-7pm.)*

THE COLOSSEUM. This enduring symbol of the Eternal City—a hollowed-out ghost of marble that dwarfs every other ruin in Rome—once held as many as 50,000 spectators. Within 100 days of its opening in AD 80, some 5000 wild beasts perished in the arena (from the Latin word for sand, *harena*, which was put on the floor to absorb blood). The floor (now partially restored) covers a labyrinth of brick cells, ramps, and elevators used to transport wild animals from cages up to arena level. Beware the men dressed as gladiators: they want to take a picture with you for a cool €5. *(M: B-Colosseo. Open daily May-Oct. 9am-6:30pm; Nov.-Apr. 9am-3:30pm.)*

DOMUS AUREA. This park houses just a portion of Nero's "Golden House," which once covered a huge chunk of Rome. After deciding that he was a god, Nero had architects build a house worthy of his divinity. The Forum was reduced to a vestibule of the palace; Nero crowned it with the 35m Colossus, a huge statue of himself as the sun. Nero committed suicide only five years after building his gargantuan pleasure garden, and later emperors tore down his house and replaced all traces of the palace with monuments built for the public good. *(On the Oppian Hill. From the Colosseum, walk through the gates up V.d. Domus Aurea and make the 1st left. Open daily 9am-6:45pm, closed Tu. Groups of 30 admitted every 20min. €5, EU citizens 18-24 €2.50.)*

ITALY

VELABRUM. The **Velabrum** is a flat flood plain south of the Jewish Ghetto. At the bend of V. del Portico d'Ottavia, a shattered pediment and a few ivy-covered columns are all that remain of the once-magnificent **Portico d'Ottavia.** The stocky, gray **Teatro di Marcello** next door is named for Augustus's nephew, whose early and sudden death remains a mystery. Farther down V. di Teatro di Marcello, **Chiesa di San Nicola in Carcere** incorporates three Roman temples originally dedicated to Juno, Janus, and Spes. *(☎06 686 99 72; call to visit the interior. Open Sept.-July M-Sa 7:30am-noon and 4-7pm.)* Across the street, the **Chiesa di Santa Maria in Cosmedin** harbors some of Rome's most beautiful medieval decorations. The Audrey Hepburn film *Roman Holiday* made the portico's relief, the **Bocca della Verità,** famous; according to legend, the hoary face will chomp on the hand of a liar. *(Church open daily 10am-1pm and 3-7pm. Portico open daily 9am-7pm.)*

CAPITOLINE HILL. Home to the original capitol, the **Monte Capitolino** still serves as the seat of the city government. Michelangelo designed its crowning **Piazza di Campidoglio,** now home to the **Capitoline Museums** (see p. 666). Stairs lead up to the rear of the 7th-century **Chiesa di Santa Maria in Aracoeli.** The gloomy **Mamertine Prison,** consecrated the **Church of San Pietro in Carcere,** lies down the hill from the back stairs of the Aracoeli. Saint Peter, imprisoned here, baptized his captors with the waters that flooded his cell. *(Open daily 9am-noon and 2:30-6pm. Donation requested.)* At the far end of the *piazza*, opposite the stairs, lies the turreted **Palazzo dei Senatori,** the home of Rome's mayor. *(To get to the Campidoglio, take any bus that goes to P. Venezia. From P. Venezia, face the Vittorio Emanuele II monument, walk around to the right to P. d'Aracoeli, and take the stairs up the hill.)*

CENTRO STORICO

PIAZZA VENEZIA AND VIA DEL CORSO. The **Via del Corso** takes its name from its days as Rome's premier racecourse, running between P. del Popolo and the rumbling P. Venezia. **Palazzo Venezia** was one of the first Renaissance *palazzi* built in the city; Mussolini used it as an office and delivered his famous orations from its balcony, but today it's little more than a glorified traffic circle dominated by the **Vittorio Emanuele II monument.** Off V. del Corso, the picturesque **Piazza Colonna** was named for the colossal **Colonna di Marco Aurelio,** designed in imitation of Trajan's column. Off the northwest corner of the *piazza* is the **Piazza di Montecitorio,** dominated by Bernini's **Palazzo Montecitorio,** now the seat of the Chamber of Deputies. The opulent **Il Gesu,** mother church of the Jesuit order, makes few concessions towards poverty, chastity, or obedience. *(Take V.C. Battisti from P. Venezia, which becomes V.d. Plebiscito before entering P.d. Gesu. Open daily 6am-12:30pm and 4-7:15pm.)*

THE PANTHEON. Architects still wonder how this 2000-year-old temple was erected; its dome—a perfect half-sphere made of poured concrete without the support of vaults, arches, or ribs—is the largest of its kind. The light that enters the roof was used as a sundial to indicate the passing of the hours and the dates of equinoxes and solstices. In AD 606, it was consecrated as the **Church of Santa Maria ad Martyres.** *(In P. della Rotonda. Open M-Sa 8:30am-7:30pm, Su 9am-6pm. Free.)*

PIAZZA NAVONA. Originally a stadium built in AD 86, the *piazza* once hosted wrestling matches, track and field events, and mock naval battles (in which the stadium was flooded and filled with fleets skippered by convicts). Each of the river god statues in Bernini's **Fountain of the Four Rivers** represents one of the four continents of the globe (as known then): the Ganges for Asia, the Danube for Europe, the Nile for Africa (veiled, since the source of the river was unknown), and the Rio de la Plata for the Americas. At the ends of the *piazza* are the **Fontana**

ITALY

del Moro and the **Fontana di Nettuno,** designed by Giacomo della Porta in the 16th century and renovated by Bernini in 1653. The **Church of Sant'Agnese in Agone** dominates the *piazza*'s western side. *(Open daily 9am-noon and 4-7pm.)*

OTHER SIGHTS. In front of the temple, the *piazza* centers on Giacomo della Porta's late-Renaissance fountain and an Egyptian obelisk added in the 18th century. Around the left side of the Pantheon, another obelisk marks the center of tiny **Piazza Minerva.** Behind the obelisk, the **Chiesa di Santa Maria sopra Minerva** hides some Renaissance masterpieces, including Michelangelo's **Christ Bearing the Cross, Annunciation** by Antoniazzo Romano, and a statue of St. Sebastian recently attributed to Michelangelo. The south transept houses the famous **Carafa Chapel,** home to a brilliant fresco cycle by Filippino Lippi. Catherine of Siena's body also rests here. *(Open M-Sa 7am-7pm, Su 7am-1pm and 3:30-7pm.)* From the upper left-hand corner of P. della Rotonda, V. Giustiniani goes north to intersect V. della Scrofa and V. della Dogana Vecchia at the **Church of San Luigi dei Francesi,** home to three of Caravaggio's most famous paintings: **The Calling of St. Matthew, St. Matthew and the Angel,** and **Crucifixion.** *(Open F-W 7:30am-12:30pm and 3:30-7pm, Th 7:30am-12:30pm.)*

CAMPO DEI FIORI

Campo dei Fiori lies across C.V. Emanuele II from P. Navona. During papal rule, the area was the site of countless executions; now the only carcasses that litter the *piazza* are the fish in the colorful produce **market** (M-Sa 6am to 2pm). South of the Campo lie P. Farnese and the huge, stately **Palazzo Farnese,** the greatest of Rome's Renaissance *palazzi*. To the east of the *palazzo* is the Baroque facade of the **Palazzo Spada** and the collection of the **Galleria Spada** (see p. 591).

THE JEWISH GHETTO. The Jewish community in Rome is the oldest in Europe—Israelites came in 161 BC as ambassadors from Judas Maccabei, asking for Imperial help against invaders. The Ghetto, the tiny area to which Pope Paul IV confined the Jews in 1555, was closed in 1870, but is still the center of Rome's vibrant Jewish population of 16,000. In the center of the ghetto are **Piazza Mattei** and the 16th-century **Fontana delle Tartarughe.** Nearby is the **Church of Sant'Angelo in Pescheria;** Jews were forced to attend mass here every Sunday and quietly resisted by stuffing their ears with wax. *(Toward the eastern end of V.d. Portico d'Ottavia. Prayer meetings W 5:30pm, Sa 5pm.)* The **Sinagoga Ashkenazita,** on the Tiber near the Theater of Marcellus, was bombed in 1982; guards now search all visitors. *(Open for services only.)*

IN RECENT NEWS

FISHING IN THE TREVI

Roberto Cercelletta was no stranger to the Roman *carabinieri*, who affectionately called him by his nickname, D'Artagnan, and looked the other way as the otherwise unemployed, mentally unstable man looted about €1000 per day from the Trevi Fountain. Six mornings a week, clad in galoshes and armed with a large magnet on a pole, he carried away the coins tossed into the fountain by tourists hoping for a return visit to the Eternal City and intended for a number of Roman charities. On the seventh day, he rested, watching from afar the civic officials who came to collect the money, which, somehow, was always less than they expected.

For 34 years, it wasn't clear that Cercelletta was actually breaking any laws. The coins didn't belong to anyone, not even the city of Rome. An ordinance passed in 1999 to protect city monuments, however, hefted a fine upon anyone who waded in the fountain. Cercelletta was charged several times, but police found no indication, despite his staggering daily take, that he was able to pay. He owned a moped and a cell phone, but little else. In August 2002, after the Italian media made his crime public, he was arrested after one of his early morning wades and charged.

PIAZZA DI SPAGNA AND ENVIRONS

THE SPANISH STEPS. Designed by an Italian, funded by the French, named for the Spaniards, occupied by the British, and currently under the sway of American ambassador-at-large Ronald McDonald, the **Scalinata di Spagna** exude an international air. The pink house to the right of the Steps was the site of John Keats's 1821 death; it's now the **Keats-Shelley Memorial Museum.**

FONTANA DI TREVI. The extravagant **Fontana di Trevi** emerges from the back wall of **Palazzo Poli.** Legend says that a traveler who throws a coin into the fountain is ensured a speedy return to Rome; a traveler who tosses two will fall in love there. Forget about funding your vacation with an early morning treasure hunt: several homeless men were arrested in the summer of 2003 and fined €500. Opposite is the Baroque **Chiesa dei Santi Vincenzo e Anastasio,** rebuilt in 1630. The crypt preserves the hearts and lungs of popes from 1590-1903. *(Open daily 8am-7:30pm.)*

PIAZZA DEL POPOLO. P. del Popolo, once a favorite venue for public executions of heretics, is now the lively "people's square." In the center is the 3200-year-old **Obelisk of Pharaoh Ramses II,** which Augustus brought back as a souvenir from Egypt in the first century BC. Behind an early-Renaissance shell, the **Church of Santa Maria del Popolo** contains several Renaissance and Baroque masterpieces. Two exquisite Caravaggios, *The Conversion of St. Paul* and *Crucifixion of St. Peter*, are found in the **Cappella Cerasi.** Raphael designed the **Cappella Chigi** for the great Renaissance financier Augustino Chigi. *(Open M-Sa 7am-noon and 4-7pm, Su and holidays 8am-1:30pm and 4:30-7:30pm.)*

VILLA BORGHESE. To celebrate his purchase of a cardinalship, Scipione Borghese built the **Villa Borghese** north of P.d. Spagna and V.V. Veneto. Its huge park houses three art museums: world-renowned **Galleria Borghese,** stark **Galleria Nazionale d'Arte Moderna,** and the intriguing **Museo Nazionale Etrusco di Villa Giulia.** North of the Borghese are the **Santa Priscilla catacombs.** *(M: A-Spagna and follow the signs. Open M-F 9:30am-5pm, Sa-Su 9:30am-6pm. €8.)*

VATICAN CITY

M: A-Ottaviano, A-Cipro/Musei Vaticani, bus #64, 492 from Termini or Largo Argentina #62 from P. Barberini, or #23 from Testaccio. ☎06 69 82.

Vatican City—almost 0.5 sq. km of independent territory entirely within the boundaries of Rome—is the seat of the Catholic Church and was once the mightiest power in Europe. The nation preserves its independence by running a separate postal system and maintaining an army of Swiss Guards.

BASILICA DI SAN PIETRO (ST. PETER'S). A colonnade by Bernini leads from **Piazza San Pietro** to the church. The **obelisk** in the center is framed by two fountains; stand on the round disks set in the pavement and the quadruple rows of the colonnade will visually resolve into one perfectly aligned row, courtesy of the Reformation popes' battery of architects. Above the colonnade are 140 statues; those on the basilica represent Christ, John the Baptist, and the Apostles (except for Peter, naturally). The pope opens the **Porta Sancta** (Holy Door) every 25 years by knocking in the bricks with a silver hammer; the last opening was in 2000, so don't hold your breath. The basilica itself rests on the reputed site of St. Peter's tomb. To the right, Michelangelo's *Pietà* has been protected by bullet-proof glass since 1972, when an axe-wielding fiend smashed Christ's nose and broke Mary's hand. Arnolfo di Cambio's *Peter*, in the central nave of the basilica, was not originally malformed, but centuries' worth of pilgrims rubbing his foot have crippled him. The climb to the top of the **Dome** might very well be worth the heart attack it will undoubtedly cause. An elevator will take you up about 300 of the 330 stairs. *(Dress* *modestly–no shorts, skirts above the knee, sleeveless shirts, or sundresses allowed, although jeans and a t-shirt is fine. Multi-lingual confession available. Open daily 7am-7pm. Mass M-Sa 9, 10, 11am, noon, 5pm; Su 9, 10:30, 11:30am, 12:10, 1, 4, 5:30pm. Dome: From inside the basilica, exit the building, and re-enter the door to the far left with your back to the basilica. €4, by elevator €5. Open Apr.-Sept. daily 7am-5:45pm; Oct.-Mar. 7am-4:45pm.)*

SISTINE CHAPEL. Ever since its completion in the 16th century, the **Sistine Chapel** (named for its founder, Pope Sixtus IV) has served as the chamber in which the College of Cardinals elects new popes. The frescoes on the side walls predate Michelangelo's ceiling; on the right, scenes from the life of Moses complement parallel scenes of Christ's life on the left. The simple compositions and vibrant colors of Michelangelo's unquestioned masterpiece hover above, each section depicting a story from Genesis. The ceiling appears vaulted but is actually flat; contrary to legend, Michelangelo painted not flat on his back but standing up and craning backwards, and he never recovered from the strain to his neck and eyes. In his *Last Judgement*, on the altar wall, the figure of Christ as judge hovers in the upper center. *(Included with admission to Vatican Museums.)*

CASTEL SANT'ANGELO. Built by **Hadrian** (AD 117-138) as a mausoleum for himself, this hulking mass of brick and stone has served the popes as a fortress, prison, and palace. When the city was wracked with plague in 590, Pope Gregory saw an angel sheathing his sword at the top of the complex; the plague abated soon after, and the edifice was rededicated to the angel. It now contains a **museum of arms and artillery** and offers an incomparable view of Rome and the Vatican. *(Walk along the river with St. Peter's behind you and the towering castle to your left; follow the signs the entrance. Open Tu-Su 9am-7pm. €5, EU citizens under 18 and over 65 free.)*

TRASTEVERE

Right off the **Ponte Garibaldi** stands the statue of the famous dialect poet G. G. Bellie. On V. di Santa Cecilia, behind the cars, through the gate, and beyond the courtyard full of roses, is the **Basilica di Santa Cecilia in Trastevere;** Carlo Maderno's famous statue of Santa Cecilia lies under the altar. *(Open M-Sa 8am-12:30pm and 4:15-6:30pm; Su 9:30-10am, 11:15-noon, and 4:15-6:30pm.)* From P. Sonnino, V. della Lungaretta leads west to P. di S. Maria in Trastevere, home to numerous stray dogs, expatriates, and the **Chiesa di Santa Maria in Trastevere,** built in the 4th century. *(Open M-Sa 9am-5:30pm, Su 8:30-10:30am, noon-5:30pm.)* North of the *piazza* are the Rococo **Galleria Corsini,**

FROM THE ROAD

WHEN IN ROME

Here are a few tips to help travelers survive their first trip to Rome:

First, finding your *albergo* or *ostello* can be a harrowing experience, and many wily cabbies possess the innate ability to identify confused and weary travelers. Don't let your guard down, or you might find yourself on the receiving end of a €150 fare. Some will attempt to charge you for their return to wherever they picked you up, so make sure you agree upon the terms before you get taken for a ride.

If you are so foolhardy as to attempt to cross the *corso*, seize any break in traffic to edge into the street, staring the oncoming driver in the eye. He may accelerate for a perilous moment, but will, theoretically, *not* hit you. This tactic is helpful while trolling for souvenirs along one of Rome's impossibly narrow sidewalks; when a harried motorist attempts to park on you, hold your ground. However, if it's you vs. the car, the car wins.

Lines and queues are decidedly *not* Italian. If and when you make your way across the street, you may want to grab a bite, yet a group of ravenous tourists will doubtlessly be waiting in what you (newcomer that you are) naively assume to be a line. As locals brush past, it will become clear that they are taking advantage of your patience. After a couple of such waits, you too will push your way in, past the unfortunates in "line".

Armed with such wisdom, all you'll need is a good pair of walking shoes and a love of fine wine to capture the Eternal City. Just like the Gauls.

— Caitlin Hurley

V. della Lungara 10, (see **Museo Nazionale dell'Arte Antica,** p. 667) and, across the street, the **Villa Farnesina,** the jewel of Trastevere. Atop the Gianicolo hill is the **Chiesa di San Pietro in Montorio,** built on the spot once believed to be the site of St. Peter's upside-down crucifixion. Next door in a small courtyard is Bramante's tiny **Tempietto,** constructed to commemorate the site of Peter's martyrdom. *(Church and Tempietto open daily 9:30am-12:30pm and 4-6:30pm.)*

NEAR TERMINI

The sights in this urban part of town are concentrated northwest of the station and to the south, near P. Vittorio Emanuele II.

PIAZZA DEL QUIRINALE AND VIA XX SETTEMBRE. Several blocks south of P. Barberini and northeast of P. Venezia, the statues of Castor and Pollux, Rome's protectors, flank yet another obelisk that served as part of Sixtus V's redecoration plan for city. The **Church of Sant'Andrea al Quirinale,** full of Bernini's characteristic jolly cherubs, highlights the artist's ability to combine architecture and painting for a single, coherent effect—even if that effect is as overdone as most Baroque work. *(Open W-M 8am-noon and 4-7pm; Aug. W-M 8am-noon.)* A Counter-Reformation facade by Maderno marks **Santa Susanna,** the American parish in Rome. The Mannerist frecoes by Croce are worth a look. *(Open daily 9am-noon and 3:30-7pm.)*

BASILICA OF SANTA MARIA MAGGIORE. As one of the five churches in Rome granted extraterritoriality, this basilica, crowning the Esquiline Hill, is officially part of Vatican City. To the right of the altar, a marble slab marks the **tomb of Bernini.** The 14th-century mosaics in the **loggia** recount the story of the August snowfall that showed the pope where to build the church. *(Open daily 7am-7pm. Loggia open daily 9:30am-noon and 2-5:30pm. Tickets in souvenir shop €2.70. Dress code strictly enforced.)*

CHURCH OF SAN PIETRO IN VINCOLI. Michelangelo's imposing **statue of Moses** presides over this 4th-century church. *(M: B-Cavour. Walk southwest on V. Cavour, down toward the Forum, and take the stairs on the left. Open daily 7am-12:30pm and 3:30-7pm.)*

SOUTHERN ROME

The area south of the center is a great mix of wealthy and working-class neighborhoods, and is home to the city's best nightlife and some of its grandest churches.

CAELIAN HILL. Southeast of the Colosseum, the Caelian, along with the Esquiline, is the biggest of Rome's seven original hills and home to some of the city's greatest chaos. Split into three levels, each from a different era, the **Church of San Clemente** is one of Rome's most intriguing churches. A fresco cycle by Masolino dating from the 1420s graces the **Chapel of Santa Caterina.** *(M: B-Colosseo. Turn left out of the station and walk east on V. Fori Imperiali. Open M-Sa 9am-12:30pm and 3-6pm, Su and holidays 10am-12:30pm and 3-6pm. €3.)* The immense **Chiesa di San Giovanni in Laterano** was the seat of the pope until the 14th century; founded by Constantine in AD 314, it's Rome's oldest Christian basilica. The two golden reliquaries over the altar contain the heads of **St. Peter and St. Paul.** Across the street is the **Scala Santa,** which houses the *acheropite* image—a depiction of Christ supposedly not created by human hands—and what are believed to be the 28 steps used by Jesus outside Pontius Pilate's house. *(M: A-San Giovanni or bus #116 from Termini. Open daily 7am-7:30pm. €2; museum €1. Dress code enforced.)*

APPIAN WAY. Since burial inside the city walls was forbidden during ancient times, fashionable Romans made their final resting places along the Appian Way. At the same time, early Christians secretly dug maze-like catacombs under the ashes of their persecutors. *(M: A-San Giovanni. Take bus #218 from P. di S. Giovanni to the intersection of V. Ardeatina and V. delle Sette Chiese. €4.15.)* **San Callisto,** V. Appia Antica,

ITALY

110, is the largest catacomb in Rome, with nearly 22km of subterranean paths. Its four levels once held 16 popes, St. Cecilia, and 500,000 other Christians. *(Take the private road that runs northeast to the entrance to the catacombs. Open M-Tu and Th-Su 8:30am-5:30pm; in winter Th-Su 8:30am-noon and 2:30-5pm; closed Feb.)* **Santa Domitilla** houses an intact 3rd-century portrait of Christ and the Apostles. *(Facing V. Ardeatina from the exit of S. Callisto, cross the street and walk up V. delle Sette Chiese. Open W-M 8:30am-5:30pm; in winter W-M 8:30am-5pm; closed Jan.)* **San Sebastiano,** V. Appia Antica 136, once housed the bodies of Peter and Paul. *(Open Tu-Su 9am-7pm. €2.60, EU residents 18-24 €1.55.)*

AVENTINE HILL. The **Roseto Comunale,** Rome's official rose garden, is host to the annual Premio Roma, the worldwide competition for the best blossom. Entries are sent in May. *(On both sides of V.d. Valle Murcia, across the Circus Maximus from the Palatine Hill. Open daily 8am-7:30pm.)* The **Giardini degli Aranci** nearby is also a pleasant place for an afternoon stroll. *(Open daily dawn to dusk.)* The church of Santa Sabina and its accompanying monastery were home to St. Dominic, Pius V, and St. Thomas Aquinas, and dates from the 5th century. *(At the southern end of Parco Savello. Open daily 6:30am-12:45pm and 3:30-7pm.)*

EUR. EUR (AY-oor) is an Italian acronym for the 1942 Universal Exposition of Rome, which Mussolini planned as a showcase of Fascist achievement. (The achievement was apparently Rome's ability to build lots of identical square buildings.) The center of the area is **Piazza Guglielmo Marconi.** According to legend, when St. Paul was beheaded at the **Abbazia delle Tre Fontane (Abbey of the Three Fountains),** his head bounced three times, creating a fountain at each bounce. *(M: B-Laurentina. Walk north on V. Laurentina and turn right on V. di Acque Salve; the abbey is at the bottom of the hill. Or, take bus #761 north from the Laurentina stop; ask to get off at V. di Acque Salve. Open daily 9am-noon and 3-6pm.)*

ITALY

MUSEUMS

Etruscans, emperors, popes, and *condottiere* have been busily stuffing Rome's belly full with artwork for several millennia, leaving behind a city teeming with galleries. Museums are generally closed holidays, Sunday afternoons, and all day Mondays.

VATICAN MUSEUMS. More or less the content of every art book you've ever seen. The four color-coded routes displayed at the entrance are the only way to see the museums, but route C is the most comprehensive. The **Egyptian Museum** contains a small, high-quality sample of Egyptian and pseudo-Egyptian statuary and paintings. The walk through the entire gallery comes out in the **Belvedere Courtyard,** with its gigantic bronze pinecone, and a view of the **Tower of the Winds,** where Queen Christina of Sweden lived briefly before insisting on more comfortable accommodations. The **Pio-Clementine Museum** is the western world's finest collection of antique sculpture, and features, among other wonders, the Apollo Belvedere. Minor galleries (Gallery of the Candelabra, Gallery of the Tapestries, Gallery of the Maps) abound—a trip to the Vatican without a sojourn in the **Raphael Rooms** is no trip at all. The **Stanza della Segnatura** and its companions hold the *School of Athens* and a number of famous frescoes. The **Pinacoteca,** the Vatican's painting collection, spans eight centuries. *(Walk north from the right hand side of P.S. Pietro along the wall of the Vatican City for about 10 blocks. ☎06 69 88 49 47. Open M-F 8:45am-3:30pm, Sa 8:45am-1:30pm. Last entrance 1hr. before closing. €10, with ISIC card €7, children under 1m tall free; free last Su of the month 8:45am-1:45pm. Most of the museum is wheelchair-accessible. Plan to spend at least 4-5hr.)*

GALLERIA BORGHESE. One of the most important and enjoyable art collections in Rome, the collection attests to the buying power of Cardinal Scipione Borghese, nephew to Paul V. **Room 1** on the ground floor is home to Canova's seductive statue of Pauline Bonaparte Borghese, thought so luscious by contemporaries that it was hidden from view for years. In **Room 3,** *Apollo and Daphne* was sculptured by Bernini when he was only 24. The Pinacoteca at the Galleria Borghese is accessible from the gardens in back of the gallery. It contains primarily Renaissance work, and a few genuinely famous paintings, like Raphael's *Deposition* in **Room 9.** If the face of Christ looks familiar, it's because he was modeled on Michelangelo's *Pieta*, which Raphael greatly admired. *(M: A-Spagna; take the exit labeled Villa Borghese, walk to your right past the Métro stop to V. Muro Torto and P. Porta Pinciana; Viale del Museo Borghese will be in front of you. Open daily 9am-7pm. Entrance on the hr., visits limited to 2hr.; last entrance 30min. before closing. €7, EU citizens under 18 and over 65 €4.25.)*

CAPITOLINE MUSEUMS. Founded in 1471 by Sixtus IV, the Capitoline Museums are the world's oldest public art collection. The Palazzo Nuovo is home to the original 2nd-century copy of the equestrian statue of Marcus Aurelius, much imitated during the Renaissance. The Palazzo dei Conservatori, reached by underground passage from the Palazzo Nuovo, is a walk through the ancient myths about the founding of Rome. The Capitoline She-Wolf, a 6th-century BC Etrsucan bronze, resides in Room IV. *(On top of the Capitoline Hill, behind the Vittorio Emanuele II monument. Open Tu-Su 9:30am-7pm. Ticket office closes 1hr. before. €7.75, with ISIC €5.70.)*

EUR MUSEUMS. All of the museums are splayed around Mussolini's obelisk, are small and manageable, and serve as a break from the usual decadent Classical and Renaissance offerings of Rome's more popular museums. The intimidating facade of the **Museo della Civilita Romana** gives way to a number of scale models of life in ancient Rome. Come see how the Longobards overran the remains of the Empire in the **Museo dell'Alto Medioevo,** a collection of weapons, jewelry, and household items from Late Antiquity. The **Museo Nazionale delle Arti e Tradizioni Popolari** contains such incongruent items as a Carnevale costume and a wine press. The skull of the famous Neanderthal Guattari Man, discovered near Circeo, is found at the **Museo Preistorico ed Etnografico Luigi Pigorini.** *(M: B-EUR-Palasport or B-EUR-Fermi. Walk north up V. Cristoforo Colombo. Civilita Romana: Open Tu-Sa 9am-6:45pm, Su and holidays 9am-1:30pm. €4.15. Alto Medioevo: Open Tu-Su 9am-8pm. €2. Nazionale delle Arti e Tradizioni Popolari: Open Tu-Su 9am-8pm. Closed holidays. €4. Preistorico ed Etnografico Luigi Pigorini: Open daily 9am-8pm. €4. All museums: under 18 and over 65 free.)*

OTHER RECOMMENDED COLLECTIONS. Montemartini, Rome's first power plant, was converted to hold displaced sculpture from the Capitoline Museums in the 1990s. *(V. Ostiense 106. M: B-Piramide. Open Tu-Su 9:30am-7pm. €4; EU citizens ages 18-24 €3.)* The **Doria Pamphilj** family, whose relations with Pope Innocent X coined the term "nepotism," still owns their stunning private collection. Titian's *Salome* and Velasquez's portrait of Innocent X alone are worth the visit. *(P. del Collegio Romana 2. Open F-W 10am-5pm. €7.30, students and seniors €5.70. Audioguide included.)* After overdosing on "artwork" and "culture," get your aesthetic stomach pumped at the one museum dedicated to crime and punishment. Etchings like *A Smith Has His Brains Beaten Out With a Hammer* hang on the walls along with terrorist, spy, and druggie paraphernalia. *(V. del Gonfalone 27. Open Tu-Th 9am-1pm and 2:30-6:30pm, F-Sa 9am-1pm. €2; under 18 and over 65 €1.)*

ENTERTAINMENT

Unfortunately, Roman entertainment just ain't what it used to be. Back in the day, you could swing by the Colosseum to watch a man get mauled by a bear; today, Romans seeking diversion are more likely to go to a nightclub than fight some hairy beast to the death. Check *Roma C'è* (which has an English-language section) or *Time Out*, available at newsstands, for club, movie, and events listings.

THEATER AND CINEMA. The **Festival Roma-Europa** in late summer brings a number of world-class acts to Rome (consult www.romace.it for more information), but for year-round performances of classic Italian theater, **Teatro Argentina,** Largo di Torre Argentina 52, is the grand matriarch of all Italian venues. (☎06 68 80 46 01. Box office open M-F 10am-2pm and 3-7pm, Sa 10am-2pm. Tickets around €20.60, depending on performance; students €15.50. AmEx/D/MC/V.) **Teatro Colosseo,** V. Capo d'Africa 5a, usually features work by foreign playwrights translated into Italian, but also hosts an English theater night. Call for details. (☎06 7004932. M: B-Colosseo. Box office open Tu-Sa 6-9:30pm. Tickets €5-15.50. Student discount €7.75. Closed in summer.)

Most English-language films are dubbed into Italian, so unless you speak Italian or enjoy hearing Woody Allen speak it, you'll have a definite obstacle when it comes to your Roman cinematic enjoyment. Check newspapers or *Roma C'è* for listings with a **v.o.** or **l.o,** which indicate that the film is in the original language. For a sure bet, pay a visit to **Il Pasquino,** P. Sant-Egidio 10, off P.S. Maria in Trastevere. Three different screens show English films, and the program changes daily. (☎06 58 33 33 10. €6.20, students €4.13.)

MUSIC. Founded by Palestrina in the 16th century, **Accademia Nazionale di Santa Cecilia** remains the only name in classical music performances. Concerts are held at the **Auditorio Pio,** V.d. Conciliazione 4. (☎06 361 10 64; www.santacecilia.it. Box office at the Auditorio Pio open Th-Tu 11am-7pm, and until showtime on concert days.) Free classical music concerts are organized frequently during the summer months by **Amici di Castel Sant'Angelo,** Lungotevere Castello. (☎32 94 14 01 66; www.santangeloestate.it.)

Rome is no New Orleans. It's not Chicago. It's not even Paris. But it does have the **Alexanderplatz Jazz Club,** V. Ostia 9, current residence of that *je ne sais quoi* that was expatriate life in Italy during the '50s. Read messages on the wall from old jazz greats, and be prepared to move outside during the summer to the Villa Celimontana. (☎06 39 74 21 71. M: A-Ottaviano, near the Vatican City. Cocktails €6.20; *tessera* required (€6.20, good for two months). Open Sept.-June daily 9pm-2am. Shows start at 10pm.)

Big name American and European pop acts perform at the Palazzo dello Sport in EUR, and will inevitably have massive poster campaigns. The **Cornetto Free Music Festival Roma Live** attracts acts like Pink Floyd, the Cure, and the Backstreet Boys at a number of venues throughout the city during the summer. (☎06 592 21 00; www.bbecom.it. Shows start at 9:30pm.)

SPECTATOR SPORTS. While other spectator sports may exist in Rome (and the key word is "may"), it's *calcio* (soccer) that brings the scantily clad fans and the large-scale riots that the world knows and loves. Rome has two teams in Italy's Serie A: **A.S. Roma** and **S.S. Lazio.** Games are played at the Stadio Olimpico in the Foro Italico (M: A-Ottaviano to bus #32). *Tifosi,* as hardcore fans are called, arrive hours or sometimes days ahead of time for big games, to drink, sing, and taunt rivals. Tickets can be bought at the stadium box office, but are easier to obtain at the **A.S. Roma Store,** P. Colonna 360. (☎06 678 65 14; www.asroma.it. Open daily 10am-10pm, tickets sold 10am-6:30pm. Tickets start at €15.50. AmEx/MC/V.)

SHOPPING

Everything you need to know about Italian fashion is summed up in one simple phrase: *la bella figura.* It describes a beautiful, well-dressed, put-together woman, and it is very, very important in Rome. Think whole picture: tinted sunglasses, Ferragamo suit, Gucci pumps with six-inch heels, and, stuffed in your Prada bag, a *telefonino* with a signature ring. For men, a single gorgeous black suit will do the trick.

If you're not a telecom heir or heiress, there are still ways to purchase grace and aplomb. Sales happen twice a year, in mid-January and mid-July, and a number of boutiques, while not as fashionable as their counterparts on the Via Condotti, won't require the sale of a major organ.

BOUTIQUES

No matter what anti-capitalist mantra you may espouse, you know you've secretly lusted after that Versace jacket. So indulge. If you happen to spend over €155 at one store, you are eligible for a tax refund. As if you needed another incentive to splurge.

Dolce & Gabbana, V.d. Condotti 52 (☎06 69 92 49 99). Who wouldn't kill for their suits? Open M-Sa 10am-7:30pm.

Prada, V.d. Condotti 88-95 (☎06 679 08 97). Open M-Sa 10am-7pm, Su 2-8pm.

Salvatore Ferragamo, Men: V.d. Condotti 64-66 (☎06 678 11 30). Women: V. d. Condotti, 72-74 (☎06 679 15 65). Open M 3-7pm, Tu-Sa 10am-7pm; June and July M-F 10am-7pm, Sa 9am-1pm.

Bruno Magli, V.d. Gambero 1 (☎06 679 38 02). Open M-Sa 10am-7:30pm.

Emporio Armani, V.d. Babuino 140 (☎06 36 00 21 97). Houses the less expensive end of the Armani line. Same hours as Armani.

Giorgio Armani, V.d. Condotti 75 (☎06 699 14 60). Open M-Sa 10am-7pm.

Gucci, V.d. Condotti 8 (☎06 678 93 40). Open Tu-F 10am-7pm, Sa 9:30am-1:30pm.

CHEAP AND CHIC

Designer emporiums such as **David Cenci,** V. Campo Marzio 1-7 (☎06 699 06 81; open M 4-8pm, Tu-F 9:30am-1:30pm and 4-8pm, Sa 10am-8pm); **Antonelo & Fabrizio,** C.V. Emanuele 242-243 (☎06 68 80 27 49; open daily 9:30am-1:30pm and 4-8pm; in winter 3:30-7:30pm); and **Discount dell'alta Moda,** V. Agostino Depretis 87, stock many lines of designer clothes and shoes at sometimes half the prices. (☎06 47 82 56 72; open M 2:30-7:30pm, Tu-Sa 9:30am-7:30pm.)

Diesel, V.d. Corso 186 (☎06 678 39 33). Off V.d. Condotti. Also at V.d. Babuino, 95. *The* label in retro fashion is surprisingly high-octane. Prices are cheaper than elsewhere in the world, so it's worth the visit. Open M-Sa 10:30am-8pm, Su 3:30-8pm.

Mariotti Boutique, V.d. Frezza 20 (☎06 322 71 26). This elegant boutique sells modern, sophisticated clothes in gorgeous materials. Open M-Sa 10am-1:30pm and 3:30-8pm; in winter closed M morning.

MISCELLANEOUS

Alcozer, V.d. Carozze 48 (☎06 679 13 88). Near P. di Spagna. Gorgeous old-world jewelry at decent prices. Earrings €22; a jeweled crucifix Lucrezia Borgia would've been proud of for €65. Open M 2-7:30pm, Tu-Sa 10am-7:30pm.

Materozzoli, P.S. Lorenzo in Lucina 5, (☎06 68 89 26 86), off V.d. Corso. This old-world *profumeria* carries everything from the exclusive Aqua di Parma line to shaving brushes. Hard to find perfumes and colognes. Open M 3:30-7:30pm, Tu-Sa 10am-1:30pm and 3:30-7:30pm. Closed Aug 10-28.

Campo Marzio Penne, V. Campo Marzio 41 (☎06 68 80 78 77). Fountain pens (€26+) and leather goods, in addition to brightly-colored journals and photo albums (€25+). The small address books (€6) make great presents. Open M-Su 10am-1pm and 2-7pm.

Disfunzioni Musicali, V. degli Etruschi 4 (☎06 446 19 84; fax 06 445 17 04), in San Lorenzo. CDs, cassettes, and LPs available, including excellent selections of rock, avant-garde classical, jazz, and ethnic. Open M-Sa 10:30am-8pm. Closed major holidays and Ferragosto. MC/V.

ITALY

Don Chisciotte, V.A. Brunetti 21a (☎06 32 24 55; www.gallerisdonchisciotte.com). Near P.d. Popolo. A bit like walking into Alice's Wonderland, Giuliano de Marsanich's store sells marionettes, puppet theaters, and a wide selection of lead soldiers. Marionettes and soldiers start at €15. Open M-Sa 10am-1:30pm and 4-7:30pm. Closed Aug.

UPIM, V. Nazionale 215; V.C. Alberto 53 (P. S. Maria Maggiore); V. Tritone 173, between V.d. Corso and Barberini (☎800 82 40 40). UPIM is the bargain basement of department stores in Rome, and their goods tend to run towards the uninspiring. But if you need a pair of socks, UPIM's a cheap, solid option. Open daily 9am-8pm.

NIGHTLIFE

CLUBS

Although Italian discos can be a flashy, sweaty good time, the scene changes as often as Roman phone numbers. Check *Roma C'è* or *Time Out.* Rome has fewer gay establishments than most cities its size, but those it has are solid and keep late hours. Many gay establishments require an **ARCI-GAY pass** (€13 yearly), available from **Circolo di Cultura Omosessuale Mario Mieli** (☎06 541 39 85).

Chic and Kitsch, V.S. Saba 11a. Uniting the elegant with the ecletic; music (often House or a variant) is selected by resident DJ Giuliano Marchili. Cover: men €13, women €10 includes 1 drink. Open Th-Sa 11:30pm-4am. Closed Aug.

Groove, V. Savelli 10. Head down V.d. Governo Vecchio from P. Pasquino and take the 2nd left. Look for the black door. Lose it to acid jazz, funk, soul, and disco. F and Sa 1-drink minimum (€5). Open W-Su 10pm-2am. Closed most of Aug.

Alien, V. Velletri 13-19. One of the biggest discos in Rome. As of this writing, the comfy chill-out room had not yet reached 1987. Cover varies (about €15, including 1 drink). Open Tu-Su 11pm-5:30am. In summer, moves to Fregene.

Piper, V. Tagliamento 9. From V. XX Settembre, take V. Piave (V. Salaria). Take a right on V. Po (V. Tagliamento). Alternatively, take bus #319 from Termini to Tagliamento. A popular club that occasionally hosts gay nights. 70s, rock, disco, as well as the standard house and underground. Very gay friendly all the time. Cover €10-18, includes 1 drink. Open F-Sa 11pm-4:30am; in summer Sa and Su 11pm-4:30am.

Il Giardini di Adone, V.d. Reti 38a. Off V.d. Sabelli. Though it fancies itself a "spaghetti-pub," the happy students who frequent this little place would remind you that tables are properly used for dancing, not for eating linguini. Cover €6, includes 1 drink. Open Tu-Su 8pm-3am. Closed late July-Aug.

Charro Cafe, V. di Monte Testaccio 73. So you wanted to go to Tijuana, but got stuck in Rome. Weep no more, *mis amigos*—make a run for Charro, home of the €2.60 tequila *bum bum.* Open daily midnight-3am.

Aquarela, V. di Monte Testaccio 64. You want pottery shards? You got pottery shards. A fine example of urban renewal, Roman style. Cover €10, includes 1 drink. Open Tu-Su 8:30pm-3am.

Caruso Caffe, V. di Monte Testaccio 36. 5 rooms of tropical decor, packed with writhing Latino wannabes on Saturday nights. Live music F. Cover €7-10, includes 1 drink. Open Tu-Sa 11:30pm-3am.

Radio Londra Caffè, V. di Monte Testaccio 65b. Packed with an energetic, good-looking, young crowd. Pint of Carlsberg €3.60. Pizza, *panini,* and hamburgers €4-6. 1 year membership €5. Open M-Sa 9pm-3am.

Classico Village, V. Libetta 3. M: B-Garbatella. Exit onto V. Argonauti and take a left on V. Libetta. Women probably don't want to travel alone in this area at night. One of the best-known *centri sociali* in Rome—your one-stop shop for all things counter-cultural. Hosts live music, films, art exhibits, poetry readings, African cuisine tastings, and more. Cover €8-10. Hours vary.

PUBS

For organized, indoor drunkenness, stop into any of Rome's countless pubs, many of which have some sort of Irish theme. Drink prices often increase after 9pm.

Jonathan's Angels, V.d. Fossa 14-16, west of P. Navona. Take V. Pasquino (V. Governo Vecchio) from the southwest end of P. Navona, a right on V. Parione, a left on V.d. Fossa, and head for the lights. Not since Pope Julius II has there been a case of Roman megalomania as severe as that of Jonathan, whose face serves as the theme for the decor in this bar. Medium beer on tap €5; delicious cocktails/long drinks €8. Open daily 9:30am-2am.

Trinity College, V.d. Collegio Romano 6. Off V.d. Corso near P. Venezia. Offers degrees in such diverse curricula as Guinness, Harp, and Heineken. Tuition €3-4.50. Happy Hour noon-8pm. Classes held every day noon-3am. AmEx/MC/V.

Il Simposio, V. d. Latini 11. Off V. Tiburtina. Chances are good that on any given night a splattered painter will be hard at work beautifying a discarded refrigerator. With cocktails from €3.50 and a glass of *fragolino* for €2.75, even starving artists can afford the place. Open daily 9pm-2am. Closed late July-Aug.

The Nag's Head, V. IV Novembre 138b. Dance floor inside; live music twice a week. Guinness €5; mixed drinks €8. Cover (imposed by bouncers with gratutious ear pieces) €5, F and Sa men €7.75, free Su. Open daily 8pm-2am; winter noon-2am. MC/V.

Nuvolari, V. degli Ombrellari 10. Off V. Vittorio. This cocktail bar (serving beer and tropical drinks) also functions as an *enoteca* with wine by the glass (€3.50), a diverse wine list, and the usual salads (choose from 30 at €6 each) and meat and cheese platters (€7.50). Open M-Sa 8pm-2am.

Artu Cafe, Largo Fumasoni Biondi 5. Good selection of drinks (beer €4.50; wine €3-5.50 per glass; mixed driniks €6.20-7.20). Enjoy specialy cocktails made with fresh juices. Free *apertivi* buffet 6:45-9pm. Open Tu-Su 6pm-2am. MC/V.

Pub Hallo'Ween, P. Tiburtino 31, at the corner of V. Tiburtina and V. Marsala. The plastic skulls and fake spiders and spiderwebs confirm your suspicions: this is indeed a gateway to the darkest pits of Hell. Draft beer €3.70-4.20, bottles €3.70. Mixed drinks €4.20-5.20. Open daily 8:30pm-2:30am, Su 5pm-2:30am. Closed Aug.

Il Barone Rosso, V. Libetta 13. M: B-Garbatella. Left on V. Ostiense, then left at V. Libetta, and take it to the end. Worth the short trek from Mt. Testaccio. Plenty of room on the 2 floors and outdoor patio, plenty of snacks (€3-5.50), and plenty of beer (€4). Open Tu-Su 8pm-3am. Dinner served until 9:30pm. Closed Aug.

ketumbar, V. Galvani 24. A taste of New York decadence in the middle of Italy. It even doubles as a Japanese restaurant (sushi plates €18-36). Wear black; everyone else will. Open M-Sa 8pm-3am. Closed Aug. AmEx/MC/V.

Mount Gay Music Bar, V. Galvani 54. Named for the rum and not the crowd (although the W evening drag show attracts more diverse patrons). Open daily 11pm-6am. MC/V.

The Proud Lion Pub, Borgo Pio 36. The outside of the pub says "Rome, Borgo Pio," but the beer and scotch says "Hey, I don't forget my Highland roots." Beer and mixed drinks €4; single malts €4.50-5. Open M-Sa 8:30-late.

The Drunken Ship, Campo dei Fiori 20-21. Because you're tired of meeting Italians. Because you feel the need to have an emotion-free fling with a kindred spirit. Because you're proud to be an American, dammit. Happy Hour daily 5-8pm. W 9-10pm power hour (all you can drink; €6). Open daily 11am-2am. AmEx/MC/V.

Sloppy Sam's, Campo dei Fiori 9-10. The identical twin of the Drunken Ship. Note that once home, wistful stories about that "special someone" you "befriended" at Sloppy Sam's will probably be regarded somewhat cynically. Beer €3; shots €2.50. Ask about student discounts and theme nights. Happy Hour 5-8pm. Open M-F 4pm-2am, Sa-Su 11am-2am. AmEx/MC/V.

Night and Day, V.d. Oca 50, off V. di Ripetta near P. del Popolo. Don't even think of coming until the rest of the bars close. At 2am, Italians who don't let dawn stop their fun stream in. Buy a membership card (€5) for discounts on drinks. Beer €3-5, Guinness €4.50. Happy Hour until midnight. Open daily 7pm-6am. Closed part of Aug.

Bartaruga, P. Mattei 7/8, in the Jewish Ghetto. A surreal drinking experience in a myriad of Murano glass, light blue and pink sofas, and tasseled drapery. Wide variety of cocktails available; beer €4. Open M-Sa 3pm-2am.

DAYTRIPS FROM ROME

PONZA

From Rome, take the train from Termini to Anzio (1hr., every hr. 6am-11pm, €2.90) and then the Linee Vetor hydrofoil from Anzio to Ponza (1hr.; 3-5 per day 8:10am-5:15pm, return 9:50am-7pm; M-F €20, Sa-Su and Aug. €23.) Ticket office in Anzio is on the quay. (☎06 984 50 85; www.vetor.it.) To navigate Ponza, Autolinee Isola di Ponza buses leave from V. Dante (every 15-20min. until 1am; buy tickets from driver for €1). Follow C. Pisacane until it become V. Dante, past the tunnel; stop is to your left. Buses stop by request; flag them down at stops. Pro Loco Tourist Office, V. Molo Musco, is at the far right of the port, next to the lighthouse, in the long red building. Offers tours of archaeological sights. ☎07 718 00 31; prolocoponza@liberto.it. Open in summer M-Sa 9am-1pm and 4-8:30pm, Su 9am-1pm and 5-8:10pm.

As the largest of the Pontine Islands, Ponza was also the one most susceptible to pirate attacks, which were frequent until the arrival of the fierce and wealthy Bourbon monarchs in 1734. Pirates aside, *dunque, tutti siamo in vacanza:* we're all equal in the eyes of the sun gods. The laid-back island lifestyle has resulted in a happy disregard for signs, street names, or maps. The only streets you'll ever need to know are **Via Banchina Nuova,** which runs along the docks and changes into **Via Dante** on the other side of the **Sant'Antonio tunnel; Corso Piscane,** which runs along the port above the docks; **Via Molo Muscolo,** jutting out along the pier to your right as you face the water; and **Piazza Carlo Pisacane,** where V. Molo Muscolo meets C Pisacane. *Isole Pontine,* a comprehensive guide to the islands, is available at newstands for €6.20.

ITALY

Beaches are the reason for the season in Ponza. **Cala dello Schiavone** and **Cala Cecata** (on the bus line) are the best and most accessible spots. The most spectacular views on the island are available at **Chiaia di Luna,** an expansive, rocky beach set at the bottom of a 200m *tufo* cliffside. Another point of sunbathing interest are the **Piscine Naturale,** just a quick ride through Ponza's lovely hillside. *(Take the bus to Le Foma and ask to be let off at the Piscine; cross the street and make your way down the long, steep path. Spiny sea urchins line the rocks, so take caution.)*

Hotel rooms in Ponza hover somewhere around the €100 mark, so Let's Go recommends forgoing hotels entirely and checking out one of the many *immobiliare vacanze* (vacation property) offices instead. The folks at **Isotur ❹,** Corso Pisacane 18 can set you up with a double room with a bath, kitchen, terrace, and beautiful views of the port. (☎07 718 03 39; agenzia.isotur@tin.it; www.isotur.it. Open May M- 9:30am-12:30pm and 4:30-8pm, Sa 9:15am-1pm and 4-8:30pm; June-August daily 9:15am-8:30pm. €45 in June; €60 in August.)

Restaurants are also on the expensive side, but **Ristorante da Antonio ❹** (☎07 71 80 98 32), on the water at V. Dante, has seafood and view well worth the splurge.

FRASCATI

A 15min. bus ride from Anagnina Station; the bus driver will let you off at the depot in P. Marconi, the town center. I.A.T. Tourist Office, P. Marconi 1 is across the street, next to the town hall. Open M and W 9am-1pm; Tu, Th-Sa 9am-1pm and 4-7pm.

Patrician villas dotting the hillside are a testament to the peculiar power of Frascati, and, possibly, of its superb dry white wines. The sculpture-filled gardens of the **Villa Aldobrandini** dominate the hills over P. Marconi, while a 1km walk up on F. Massaia leads to the tiny **Chiesa dei Cappuccini.** A sign above the door announces that you need reservations for marriages, but the **Ethiopian Museum** next door requires no such foresight. It houses a collection of weapons, handmade crafts, and the death mask of the cardinal who collected the artifacts while doing missionary work. *(Open daily 9am-noon and 4-6pm. Free.)*

The town of **Tusculum** was an ancient resort for the who's who of Roman society, including Cicero and Cato. From the entrance of the Villa Aldobrandini, turn right onto V. Tusculo, which climbs 5km over winding country roads to reach the ruins of the collection of villas. Death masks and Republican judges notwithstanding, the primary attraction here is still the wine. **Bar Baioni,** V.C. Battisti 22, to the right of the cathedral, is where locals flock for both wine and pastries. (☎06 942 22 05. *Pannini* €1.55, *cappuccino* €1. Open M-Sa 6:30am-11pm, Su 6:30am-4pm.)

LOMBARDY (LOMBARDIA)

Over the centuries, Roman generals, German emperors, and French kings have all vied for control of Lombardy's fertile soil. Today, business and employment opportunities have made Lombardy an even more vital cornerstone of the Italian economy. Milan may drive the mighty engine of progress, but don't let its exhaust fumes blind you to the beauty of Bergamo, Mantua, and the foothills of the Alps.

MILAN (MILANO) ☎02

Milan has always been the *bella* of the Italian ball: once the capital of the Roman Empire, today it is the most cutting-edge of major Italian cities. The pace of life in Milan is dizzying, and a stream of well-dressed Italians blurs the panorama of tree-lined boulevards and graceful architecture darkened by omnipresent urban graffiti. A regional expression sums up the nature of this fashionable beast succinctly: "*Milano l'e Milano*" (Milan is just Milan).

TRANSPORTATION

Flights: Malpensa Airport (MXP; ☎02 74 85 22 00), 45km from town. Handles intercontinental flights. Malpensa Express leaves Cadorna Métro station for the airport (45min., €9). **Linate Airport** (LIN; ☎02 74 85 22 00), 7km away. Flights within Europe. Take bus #73 from MM1: P.S. Babila (€1).

Trains: Stazione Centrale (☎(01) 47 88 80 88), in P. Duca d'Aosta on MM2. Info office open daily 7am-9:30pm. Every hour to: **Florence** (2½hr., €22); **Genoa** (1½hr., €8); **Rome** (4½hr., €28); **Turin** (2hr., €8); and **Venice** (3hr., 21 per day, €13).

Buses: Stazione Centrale. Intercity buses tend to be less convenient and more expensive than trains. **SAL, SIA, Autostradale,** and other carriers leave from P. Castello and nearby (MM1: Cairoli) for Bergamo, the Lake Country, and Turin.

Public Transportation: The **subway** (Metropolitana Milanese, or **MM**) runs daily 6am-midnight. The **buses** (Azienda Trasporti Muncipali or **ATM**), in the P. del Duomo station, handle local transportation. Info and ticket booths (toll-free ☎800 01 68 57) are open M-Sa 7:15am-7:15pm. Single-fare tickets (€1) are good for 75min. of surface transportation. Day passes €3, 2-day €5.50.

ORIENTATION AND PRACTICAL INFORMATION

The layout of the city resembles a giant target, encircled by a series of ancient concentric city walls. In the outer rings lie suburbs built during the 1950s and 60s to house southern immigrants. Within the inner circle are four central squares: **Piazza Duomo,** at the end of V. Mercanti; **Piazza Cairoli,** near the Castello Sforzesco; **Piazza Cordusio,** connected to Largo Cairoli by V. Dante; and **Piazza San Babila,** the business and fashion district along Corso Vittorio Emanuele. The **duomo** and **Galleria Vittorio Emanuele** comprise the bull's-eye, roughly at the center of the downtown circle. Radiating from the center lie two large parks, the Giardini Pubblici and the Parco Sempione. From the colossal **Stazione Centrale** train station, farther northeast, you can take a scenic ride on bus #60 or the more efficient commute on subway line #3 to the downtown hub. **Via Vito Pisani,** which leads to the mammoth **Piazza della Repubblica,** connects the station to the downtown area.

TOURIST, FINANCIAL, AND LOCAL SERVICES

Tourist Office: APT, V. Marconi 1 (☎02 72 52 43 00; www.milanoinfotourist.com), in the Palazzo di Turismo in P. del Duomo. Pick up the comprehensive **Milano: Where, When, How,** as well as *Milano Mese* for info on activities and clubs. Open M-F 8:30am-8pm, Sa 9am-1pm and 2-7pm, Su 9am-1pm and 2-5pm.

American Express: V. Brera 3 (☎02 72 00 36 93), on the corner of V. dell'Orso. Walk through the Galleria, across P. Scala, and up V. Verdi. Holds mail free for AmEx members for 1 month, otherwise €5 per month. Sends and receives wired money for AmEx cardholders. Also **exchanges currency.** Open M-F 9am-5:30pm.

Lost Property: Ufficio Oggetti Smarriti Comune, V. Fruili 30 (☎02 546 81 18). Open M-F 8:30am-4pm.

ITALY

EMERGENCY AND COMMUNICATIONS

Emergencies: ☎118. **Toll-free Operator:** ☎12. **Medical Assistance:** ☎38 83.

Police: ☎113 or 02 772 71. **Carabinieri** (civil corps): ☎112.

Hospital: Ospedale Maggiore di Milano, V. Francesco Sforza 35 (☎(025) 50 31).

Late-Night Pharmacy: *Galeria* of the Stazione Centrale never closes (☎(026) 69 07 35).

Internet Access: Manhattan Lab, in the Università Statale, formerly the Ospedale Maggiore, on V. Festa del Perdono. Use the entrance opposite V. Bergamini. Take the stairs on the right to the 3rd fl. Turn left, and walk to the end of the corridor. Take 2 lefts; it's the 3rd door on your left. Microsoft workstations are only for Easmus students, but at the far end are computers for the public. Free. Open M-F 8:15am-6pm.

Post Office: V. Cordusio 4 (☎02 72 48 22 23). Address mail to be held: FirstName SURNAME, *In Fermo Posta,* Ufficio Postale Centrale di Piazza Cordusio 4, Milano **20100,** Italia. Open M-F 8:30am-7:30pm, Sa 8:30am-1pm. **Postal Code:** 20100.

ACCOMMODATIONS

Every season in Milan is high season, except August—go figure. A single room in a decent establishment for under €35 is a real find. For the best deals, try the city's southern periphery or areas south and east of the train station. When possible, make reservations well ahead of time.

Hotel Sara, V. Sacchini 17 (☎02 20 17 73). MM1/2: Loreto. From Loreto, take V. Porpora; the 3rd street on the right is V. Sacchini. Recently renovated on a peaceful street. Singles €42-48; doubles €65-72; triples €88-93. ❹

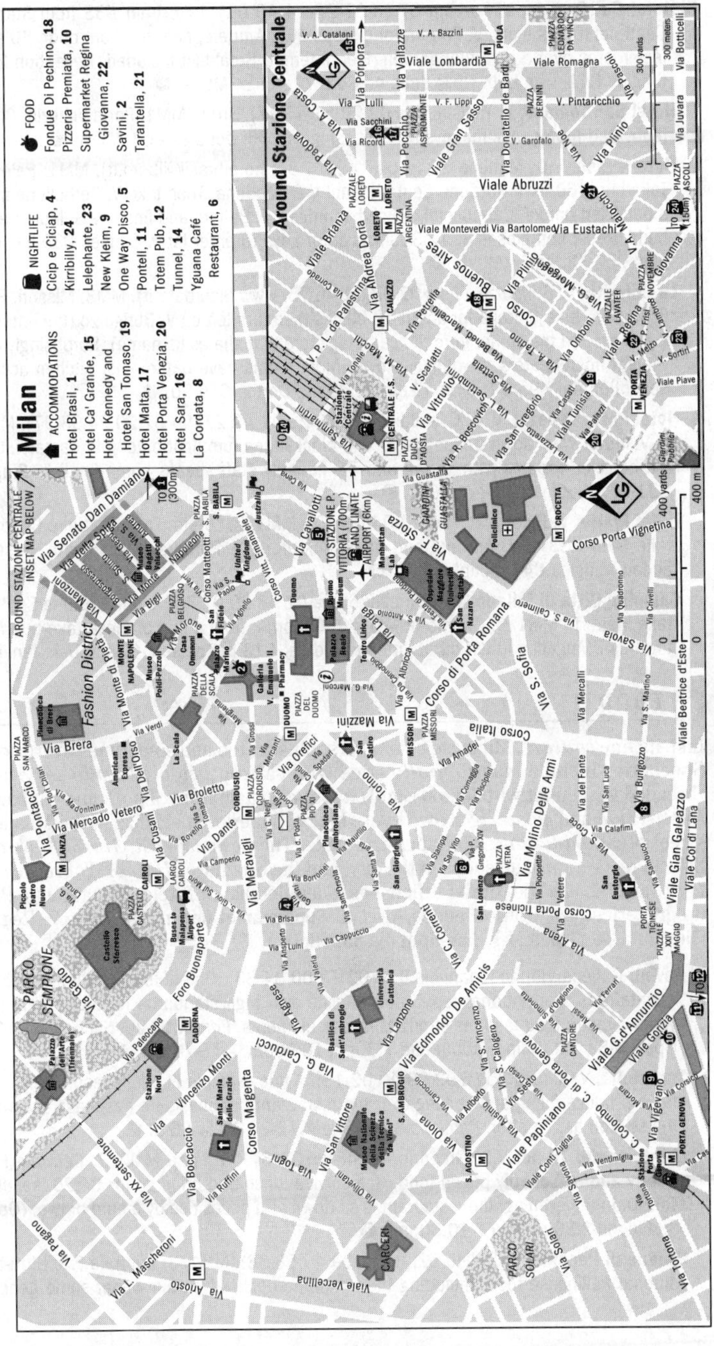
Milan
ACCOMMODATIONS
Hotel Brasil, 1
Hotel Ca' Grande, 15
Hotel Kennedy and Hotel San Tomaso, 19
Hotel Malta, 17
Hotel Porta Venezia, 20
Hotel Sara, 16
La Cordata, 8
NIGHTLIFE
Cicip e Ciciap, 4
Kirribilly, 24
Lelephante, 23
New Kleim, 9
One Way Disco, 5
Pontell, 11
Totem Pub, 12
Tunnel, 14
Yguana Café Restaurant, 6
FOOD
Fondue Di Pechino, 18
Pizzeria Premiata, 10
Supermarket Regina Giovanna, 22
Savini, 2
Tarantella, 21
Around Stazione Centrale
AROUND STAZIONE CENTRALE INSET MAP BELOW
Fashion District
PARCO SEMPIONE
PARCO SOLARI
CARCERI

ITALY

Hotel Ca' Grande, V. Porpora 87 (☎02 26 14 40 01). Take tram #33 from Stazione Centrale; it runs along V. Porpora and stops at V. Ampere, near the front door. 20 spotless rooms over a beautiful garden. Free Internet. Breakfast included. Reception 24hr. Singles €41, with bath €51; doubles €62/72. AmEx/MC/V. ❹

Hotel San Tomaso, V. Tunisia 6 (☎02 29 51 47 47), 3rd fl. MM1: Porta Venezia. Clean, renovated rooms. Ask for keys at night. Singles €35; doubles €62. MC/V. ❸

Hotel Brasil, V.G. Modena 20 (☎027 49 24 82; hotelbrasil@libero.it). MM1: Palestro. Take bus #60 from Stazione Centrale until V.G. Modena. Then take V. Serbelloni, make a quick left onto V. Cappuccini, which becomes V.F. Bellotti and finally V.G. Modena. 20 beds. Reception closes at 12:30am; ask for keys to enter later. Singles €39-57; doubles €52-72. AmEx/MC/V. ❹

La Cordata, V. Burigozzo 11 (☎02 58 31 46 75; www.lacordata.it). MM3: Missori. From P. Missori, take C. Italia for about 10 blocks then turn left on V. Burigozzo (the entrance is just around the corner from the camping store that shares its name). Surprisingly convenient hostel caters to younger crowd. Most rooms have bathrooms. Kitchen access. Reception daily 9am-1pm and 2pm-12:30am. Dorms €15.50. ❷

Hotel Porta Venezia, V. P. Castaldi 26 (☎02 29 41 42 27; fax 02 20 24 93 97). MM1: P. Venezia. Walk down C. Venezia for two blocks then turn right onto V. P. Castaldi. Simple but clean rooms with phone and TV. Friendly staff speaks some English. Singles €31-47; doubles €41-77. MC/V. ❸

Hotel Malta, V. Ricordi 20 (☎022 04 96 15). MM1/2: Loreto. From Stazione Centrale, take tram #33 to V. Ampere and backtrack along V. Porpora to V. Ricordi. Reserve ahead. Singles €47; doubles €73. ❹

Camping Citta di Milano, V. G. Airaghi 61 (☎02 48 20 01 34). From Stazione Centrale take Métro to MM1/3: Duomo or MM1/2: Cadorna; from either of these take bus #62 towards D'Angelli and get off at Vittoria Caldera. €13 per person. Closed Dec.-Jan. ❶

ITALY

FOOD

Like its fine *couture*, Milanese cuisine is sophisticated and sometimes overpriced. Specialties include *risotto giallo* (rice with saffron), *cotoletta alla milanese* (breaded veal cutlet with lemon), and *cazzouela* (a mixture of pork and cabbage). *Pasticcerie* and *gelaterie* crowd every block. Bakeries specialize in the Milanese sweet bread *panettone*, an Italian fruitcake. The newspaper *Il Giornale Nuovo* lists all restaurants and shops in the city, and the brochure *Milano: Where, When, How*, available at the tourist office, has a detailed list of foreign restaurants. Pick up groceries near Corso Buenos Aires at **Supermarket Regina Giovanna,** V. Regina Giovanna 34. (Open M-F 8am-9pm, Sa 8am-8pm.)

Savini, Galleria Vittorio Emanuele II (☎02 72 00 34 33). One of few restaurants able to maintain an international reputation and its own high standards for more than 100 years. Superb food features strong Milanese elements. *Primi* €13-20. *Secondi* €21-29. Open M-Sa 12:30pm-2:30pm and 7:30pm-10:30pm. AmEx/MC/V. ❺

Tarantella, V. Abruzzi 35 (☎02 29 40 02 18). A fine example of a Milanese eatery, with fresh produce filling and spilling over the restaurant. Emphasis on freshness and what the season has to offer. *Primi* €5-8. *Secondi* €12-20. Pizza €6-8. ❸

L'Osteria del Treno, V.S. Gregorio 46/48 (☎02 67 00 479). MM2/3: Centrale F.S. Hearty and reasonably priced food. Self-service lunch and *primi* go for €4.20, *secondi* €6.50. In the evening, the restaurant is sit down and prices rise by a euro or two. (Open Su-F noon-2:30pm and 7-10:30pm.) ❶

Fondue di Pechino, V. Tadino 52, (☎02 29 40 58 38). MM1/3: Centrale F.S. Ultra-traditional Pekingese food, including the infamous duck. Give your waiter some general guidelines, and let them take you on a gastronomic whirlwind. Open daily noon-3pm and 6pm-midnight. Lunch *menu* €7.50. *Primi* €1-3.50. *Secondi* €3.50-8. MC/V. ❷

Pizzeria Premiata, V. Alzaia Naviglio Grande 2. MM2: Porto Genova. Serves hearty portions. Pizza from €4.50, *primi* around €7.75. Open daily noon-2am. ❶

SIGHTS

DUOMO. The looming Gothic cathedral is the geographical and spiritual center of Milan and makes a good starting point for a walking tour of the city. The *duomo* is the third-largest church in the world, after St. Peter's in the Vatican and the Seville Cathedral. Gian Galeazzo Visconti founded the cathedral in 1386, hoping to flatter the Virgin into granting him a male heir. Construction proceeded sporadically over the next four centuries and was finally completed at Napoleon's command in 1809. The imposing 16th-century marble tomb of Giacomo de Medici, in the south transept of the cathedral, was inspired by the work of Michelangelo. *(MM1: Duomo. Modest dress. Open daily 9am-5:30pm. Free. Roof access €3.50, with elevator €5.)* The **Museo del Duomo**, across the *piazza*, to the right as you face the *duomo*, in the Palazzo Reale at P. del Duomo 14, explains the construction of the *duomo* with its display of artifacts. *(☎02 86 03 58. Open M-Su 10am-1:15pm 3pm-6pm. €6.)*

TEATRO ALLA SCALA. Known simply as La Scala, this is the world's most renowned opera house. Singer Maria Callas became a legend in this 18th-century Neoclassical building. Enter through the **Museo Teatrale alla Scala,** which includes such memorabilia as Verdi's famous top hat. *(P. della Scala, at the opposite end of galleria from the duomo. Open daily 9am-noon and 2-5:30pm. €5.)*

MUSEO POLDI PEZZOLI. The museum contains an outstanding private art collection bequeathed to the city by Poldi Pezzoli in 1879. Famous paintings include Bellini's *Ecce Homo*, and the museum's signature piece, Antonio Pollaiuolo's *Portrait of a Young Woman*. *(V. Manzoni 12, on the right of La Scala. ☎02 79 48 89. Open Tu-Su 10am-6pm. €6, seniors and students €3.60.)*

PINACOTECA DI BRERA. The Brera Art Gallery presents one of the most impressive collections of paintings in Italy, with works that range from the 14th to the 20th century. Works include Bellini's *Pietà*, Andrea Mantegna's brilliantly foreshortened *Dead Christ*, Raphael's *Marriage of the Virgin*, Caravaggio's *Supper at Emmaus*, and Piero della Francesca's 15th-century *Sacra Conversazione*. A limited collection of works by modern masters includes pieces by Modigliani and Carlo Carrà. *(V. Brera 28. Open daily 8:30am-7:30pm. €6.20.)*

GALLERIA VITTORIO EMANUELE II. To the left as you face the *duomo*, this monumental glass barrel vault with a beautiful glass *cupola* (48m) is five stories of overpriced cafes and shops. Mosaics representing different continents sieged by the Romans adorn the floors and the central octagon's upper walls. Once considered the drawing room of Milan, the Galleria is now home to the icons of commercialism. *(☎02 06 46 02 72. Open M-Sa 10am-11pm, Su 10am-8pm.)*

CASTELLO SFORZESCO. Restored after heavy bomb damage in 1943, the Castello Sforzesco is one of Milan's best-known monuments and a great place for a picnic. The Castello houses the **Musei Civici,** which includes the **Musical Instruments Museum** and the **Applied Arts Museum.** The ground floor contains a sculpture collection famous for Michelangelo's unfinished *Pietà Rondanini*, his last work. *(MM1: Cairoli. ☎02 62 36 39 47. Open Tu-Su 9:30am-7:30pm. Free.)*

CHIESA DI SANTA MARIA DELLE GRAZIE. Once a 15th-century convent, the church's Gothic nave is dark and elaborately patterned with frescoes. Next to the church entrance, in what was once the dining hall, is the **Cenacolo Vinciano (Vinciano Refectory),** one of Milan's most famous sites, and home to one of the most important pieces of art in the world, **Leonardo da Vinci's Last Supper.** *(P. di S. Maria delle Grazie, 2, on Corso Magenta, off V. Carducci below MM1: Cadorna Cairoli. ☎02 89 42 11 46. Arrive early or late to avoid a long wait. Open Tu-Su 8am-7:30pm, Sa 8am-11pm. €6.50.)*

STADIO GIUSEPPE MEAZZA. The true *duomo* of Milanese youth, the *Stadio* is one of the most famous soccer arenas on the planet. The tour of the stadium includes visits to the locker rooms and a museum dedicated to the two local teams. *(V. Piccolomini, 5. MM2: Lotto. Walk along V. Fed. Caprilli and you can't miss it. Tours M-Sa 10am-6pm. €10. Under 18 or over 65 €7.)*

MUSEO NAZIONALE DELLA SCIENZA E DELLA TECNICA LEONARDO DA VINCI. Quirky ancestral artifacts of modern technology fill this museum—an attendant will turn on the machines to show their ingenuity. *(V.S. Vittore 21, off V. Carducci. MM2: San Ambrogio. ☎02 48 55 51. Open Tu-F 9:30am-4:50pm, Sa-Su 9:30am-6:20pm. €6.20, children and seniors €4.20.)*

BASILICA DI SANT'AMBROGIO. A prototype for Lombard-Romanesque churches throughout Italy, the *basilica* is the most influential medieval building in Milan. The tiny 4th-century **Cappella di San Vittore,** with exquisite 5th-century mosaics, lies through the seventh chapel on the right. *(MM1: Sant'Ambrogio. Open M-Sa 7:30am-noon and 2:30-7pm, Su 3-7pm. Free.)*

NAVIGLI DISTRICT. The Venice of Lombardy, the Navigli district comes alive at night (see p. 678). Complete with canals, small footbridges, open-air markets, cafes, alleys, and trolleys, this area constitutes part of a medieval canal system with original locks that were designed by Leonardo da Vinci. *(Outside the MM2: Porta Genova station, through the Arco di Porta Ticinese.)*

CHIESA DI SAN LORENZO MAGGIORE. The oldest church in Milan, it is a testament to the city's 4th-century greatness. To its right sits the 14th-century **Cappella di Sant'Aquilino.** Inside is a 5th-century mosaic of a beardless Christ among his apostles. A staircase behind the altar leads to a Roman amphitheater's remains. *(On Corso Ticinese. MM2: Porta Genova, then tram #3 from V. Torino. Open daily 7:30am-6:45pm. Cappella €1.)*

BASILICA DI SANT'EUSTORGIO. Founded in the 4th century to house the bones of the Magi, the church lost its original function when the dead wise men were spirited off to Cologne in 1164. The triumph of this church, and one of the great masterpieces of early Renaissance art, is the **Portinari Chapel,** attributed to the Florentine Michelozzo. *(P.S. Eustorgio 3. Farther down Corso Ticinese from San Lorenzo Maggiore. Tram #3. Open W-M 9:30am-noon and 3:30-6pm.)*

PINACOTECA AMBROSIANA. The Ambrosiana's 23 rooms display exquisite works from the 14th through 19th centuries, including works by Botticelli, Leonardo, Raphael, Caravaggio, Tizian, and Breugel. *(P. Pio XI 2. Follow V. Spadari off V. Torino and make a left onto V. Cantù. ☎02 86 46 29 81. Open Tu-Su 10am-5:30pm. €7.50.)*

ENTERTAINMENT AND NIGHTLIFE

Ciak, V. Sangallo 33, near P. Gorini Argonne, southeast of the *duomo,* offers cabaret popular with young Milanese. Take tram #5 from Stazione Centrale to V. Beato Angelico Argonne. (☎02 76 11 00 93. Cover €12.95-20.70.) The **Teatri d'Italia di Porta Romana,** Corso di Porta Romana 124 (☎02 58 31 58 96), puts on experimental productions and first-rate plays (€14.50). **Milan Oltre** is a festival of drama, dance, and music; call the **Ufficio Informazione del Comune** (☎02 86 46 40 94) for more details.

If Milan's status as a world-famous fashion capital has lured you here for shopping, don't despair about the prices. If you can tolerate the stigma of being an entire season behind, purchase your famous designer duds from *blochisti* (wholesale clothing outlets) such as **Monitor,** on V. Monte Nero (MM3: Porta Romana, then tram #9 or 29), or the well-known **Il Salvagente,** V. Bronzetti 16, off Corso XXII Marzo (bus #60 from MM1: Lima or MM2/3: Stazione Centrale). The clothing sold along **Corso Buenos Aires** is more affordable—all the stores are open daily 10am-12:30pm and 2:30-7pm. Winter sales begin January 10. Shop in late July for end-of-the-summer sales (20-50% off) and a glimpse of the new fall lines. The brochure *Milano: Where, When, How,* available at the tourist office, has a great list of markets and second-hand stores. Hard-core window shoppers should head to the world-famous **fashion district** between **Corso Vittorio Emanuele** near the *duomo* and **Via Monte Napoleone** off P. San Babila. The dresses come straight from the designers and the selection is more up-to-date than anywhere else in the world, including New York and Tokyo. Expect to find high-class places to buy perfume, glasses, leather goods, shoes, and jewelry.

Le Trottoir, near V. Brera. From MM2: Lanza, take V. Tivoli to the Corso Garibaldi intersection. A lively atmosphere with live bands nightly. Open daily 7pm-2:30am.

Yguana Cafe Restaurant, V. P. Gregorio XIV 16 (☎033 81 09 30 97). Gorgeous but relatively down-to-earth natives sip cocktails next to their scooters. Happy Hour daily 5:30pm-9pm. Su brunch 12:30pm-3pm. Open daily 5pm-2am.

New Kleim, V. Vigevano 8. MM2: Porta Genova is 3 blocks from Blue Kleim's unmistakable trendy funk. Dedicated to the author Irwin Kleim. Open Tu-Su 7:30pm-4am.

Pontell, on V. Navigli Pavese. Serves beer quite creatively. Always crowded with a mix of locals and foreigners. Open daily 6pm-2am.

Cafe Capoverde, V. Leoncavallo 16 (☎02 26 82 04 30). MM1/2: Loreto. Cocktails dominate, but decent food is available. *Primi* €6. Open 12:30-2:30pm and 6pm-2am.

Totem Pub, at V. Naviglio Pavese and V.E. Gola (☎028 37 50 98). For a more head-banging sort. Be prepared to hear anything from Metallica to reggae. Serves beer in huge mugs for €8. Open daily 8:30pm-2:30am.

Rock: Hollywood, Corso Como 15 (☎026 59 89 96). One of the only discos in the city to select from the crowd at the door. Hip-hop, house, and commercial music. Cover €13-16. Open Tu-Su 11pm-4am.

Tunnel, V. Sammartini 30 (☎02 66 71 13 70), near V. Giuseppe Bruscetti, bordering Stazione Centrale. Underground rock and various indie bands frequent this train tunnel converted into a bandshell. Cover €3-10. Hours vary.

Kirribilly, V. Castel Morone 7 (☎02 70 12 01 51). MM1: Porta Venezia. Cheery Australian pub with good beer. Try Cuban rum and kangaroo meat. Open M-F noon-3pm and 6pm-3am, Sa-Su 6pm-3am.

GAY BARS AND CLUBS

Lelephante, V. Melzo 22 (☎02 29 51 87 68). From MM2: Porta Venezia, walk up Corso Bueno Aires 3 blocks and turn right on V. Melzo. Across from Artdecothe. Mixed gay and straight crowd. Open Tu-Su 6:30pm-2am.

Cicip e Ciciap, V. Gorani 9 (☎02 86 72 02). From MM1: Cairoli, take V.S. Giov. sul Muro which turns into V. Brisa. V. Gorani is the 2nd left. Attracts a women-only crowd. Open only Sa 8:30pm-3am.

One Way Disco, V. Cavallotti 204 (☎022 42 13 41). MM2: Sesto FS. Disco and leather. Membership card required. Open F and Sa 10:30pm-3:30am, Su 3:30-7pm.

DAYTRIPS FROM MILAN

GENOA. Stroll by gorgeous *palazzia* on V. Garibaldi and gaze at the fish in the fabulous aquarium (see p. 681).

TURIN. Pay a visit to the home of both the Fiat auto-company and one of Christianity's most famous relics, the Shroud of Turin (see p. 710).

MANTUA (MANTOVA) ☎0376

Mantua owes its literary fame to its most famous son, the poet Virgil. Its grand *palazzi* and graceful churches come thanks to the Gonzaga family, who, after ascending to power in 1328, imported well-known artists to change Mantua's small-town image. Today, Mantua is a bustling city with easy passage to the surrounding lakes. Once the largest palace in Europe, the opulent **Palazzo Ducale** towers over **Piazza Sordello,** sheltering the Gothic **Magna Domus** *(duomo)* and **Palazzo del Capitano.** Inside, check out a breathtaking array of frescoes, gardens, and facades. Outside the *palazzo*, signs point to the **Castello di San Giorgio** (1390-1406), once a formidable fortress before its absorption into the *palazzo* complex. (Open Tu-Su 8:45am-6:30pm. €6.50, students €3.25, children and seniors free.) In the far south of the city, down V.P. Amedeo, through P. Veneto, and down Largo Parri, lies the opulent **Palazzo di Te,** built by Giulio Romano in 1534 as a suburban retreat for Federico II Gonzaga. It is widely considered the finest building in the Mannerist style. (☎0376 32 32 66. Open Tu-Su 9am-6pm, M 1-6pm. €8, students €2.50, under 11 free.) Just south of P. Sordello is the 11th-century Romanesque **Piazza delle Erbe;** opposite the *piazza* is Leon Alberti's **Chiesa di Sant'Andrea,** Mantua's greatest contribution to the Italian Renaissance. (*Piazza* open daily 10am-12:30pm and 2:30-6:30pm. Free.) Walk from P. dell'Erbe to P. Broletto and then take V. Accademia to the end to reach the lovely **Teatro Bibiena,** one of Italy's few theaters *not* modeled on Milan's La Scala. (☎0376 32 76 53. Open Tu-Su 9:30am-12:30pm and 3-6:30pm. €2.10, students €1.05.)

Trains (☎0376 84 88 88 088) go from P. Don E. Leoni to Milan (2hr., 9 per day, €7.90) and Verona (40min., every hr., €2.30). From the train station, head left on V. Solferino, through P.S. Francesco d'Assisi to V. Fratelli Bandiera, and right on V. Verdi to reach the **tourist office,** P. Mantegna 6, next to Chiesa Sant'Andrea. (☎32 82 53; fax 36 32 92. Open M-Sa 8:30am-12:30pm and 3-6pm.) Charming **Hotel ABC ❸,** P. Don E. Leoni 25, is opposite the station. (☎0376 32 33 47; fax 0376 32 23 29. Breakfast included. Singles €40-67; doubles €65-88; triples €90-118.) **Antica Osteria ai Ranari ❷,** V. Trieste 11, near Porta Catena, specializes in regional dishes. (☎0376 32 84 31. *Primi* €4.50-6, *secondi* €4.50-9. Closed for 3 weeks late July to early Aug. Open Tu-Su noon-2:30pm and 7-11:30pm.) **Postal Code:** 46100.

BERGAMO ☎035

Bergamo's two sections reflect its colorful history: while the *città alta* (upper city) reveals its origins as a Venetian outpost, the *città bassa* (lower city) is a modern metropolis packed with Neoclassical buildings. **Via Pignolo,** in the *città bassa*, winds past a succession of handsome 16th- to 18th-century palaces. Turning left onto V.S. Tomaso and then right brings you to the astounding **Galleria dell'Accademia Carrara,** which holds works by Titian, Rubens, Breughel, and van Dyck. (Open W-M 9:30am-12:30pm and 2:30-5:30pm. €2.60, under 18 and over 60 free.) From the Galleria, the terraced **Via Noca** ascends to the medieval *città alta* through the 16th-century **Porta S. Agostino** gate. Stroll down V. Porta Dipinta to V. Gambito, which ends in **Piazza Vecchia,** an ensemble of medieval and Renaissance buildings flanked by restaurants and cafes at the heart of the *città alta.* Head through the archway flanking P. Vecchia to P. del Duomo, and see the fresco-laden **Cappella Colleoni.** (Open daily Mar.-Oct. 9am-12:30pm and 2-6:30pm; Nov.-Feb. 9am-12:30pm and 2:30-4:30pm. Free.) Immediately left of the Cappella Colleoni is the **Basilica di Santa Maria Maggiore,** a 12th-century basilica with an ornate Baroque interior and tapestries depicting biblical scenes. (Open daily Apr.-Oct. 9am-12:30pm and 2:30-6pm; Nov.-Mar. reduced hours. Free.) Climb the **Torre Civica** (Civic Tower) for a marvelous view of Bergamo and the hills (€1).

The train station, bus station, and many budget hotels are in the *città bassa.* **Trains** (1hr., every hr., €3.65) and **buses** (every 30min., €4.10) pull into P. Marconi from Milan. To get to the **tourist office,** V. Aquila Nera 2, in the *città alta,* take bus #1a to the top of the *città alta.* (☎035 24 22 26; www.apt.bergamo.it. Open daily 9am-12:30pm and 2-5:30pm.) To get from the train station to **Ostello della Gioventù di Bergamo (HI) ❶,** V.G. Ferraris 1, take bus #9 to Comozzi, then take bus #14 to Leonardo da Vinci, and walk up the hill. (☎/fax 035 36 17 24. Breakfast included. HI members only. Dorms €13.50. MC/V.) **Locanda Caironi ❷,** V. Torretta 6B, off V. Gorgo Palazzo, is in a quiet residential neighborhood. Take bus #5 or 7 from V. Angelo Maj. (☎035 24 30 83. Singles €15.50; doubles €28.50. MC/V.) **Trattoria Casa Mia ❷,** V.S. Bernardino 20A, provides full meals from €11. (☎035 22 06 76. Open M-Sa noon-2pm and 7-10pm.) **Postal Code:** 24122.

ITALIAN RIVIERA (LIGURIA)

The Italian Riviera stretches 350km along the Mediterranean between France and Tuscany, forming the most famous and touristed area of the Italian coastline. Genoa divides the crescent-shaped strip into the **Riviera di Levante** ("rising sun") to the east and the **Riviera di Ponente** ("setting sun") to the west. The elegant coast beckons with lemon trees, almond blossoms, and turquoise seas. Especially lovely is the **Cinque Terre** area, just to the west of **La Spezia.**

TRANSPORTATION

The coastal towns are linked by the main **rail** line, which runs west to Ventimiglia (near the French border) and east to La Spezia (near Tuscany), but slow local trains can make short trips take hours. Frequent intercity **buses** pass through all major towns, and local buses run to inland hill-towns. **Boats** connect most resort towns. **Ferries** go from Genoa to Olbia, Sardinia and Palermo, Sicily.

GENOA (GENOVA) ☎010

Genoa, city of grit and grandeur, has little in common with its resort neighbors. A Ligurian will tell you, *"Si deve conosceria per amaria"*—you have to know her to love her. If lacking in the laid-back intimacy and friendliness of a small-town resort, Genoa more than makes up for it in its rich cultural history and bewitching sights. Since falling into decline in the 18th century, modern Genoa has turned its attention from industry and trade to the restoration of its bygone splendor.

TRANSPORTATION. The **C. Columbo Internazionale** (GOA) airport, in Sesti Ponente, services European destinations. Take **Volabus #100** from Stazione Brignole to the airport (every 30min., €2) and get off at Aeroporto. Most visitors arrive at one of Genoa's two **train stations: Stazione Principe,** in P. Acquaverde, or **Stazione Brignole,** in P. Verdi. **Trains** go to Rome (5hr., 14 per day, €23.50) and Turin (2hr., 19 per day, €8.70). **AMT buses** (☎558 24 14) run throughout the city. One-way tickets (€0.80) are valid for 1½hr.; 24hr. tourist passes cost €3. **Ferries** depart from the Ponte Assereto arm of the port; buy tickets at **Stazione Marittima** in the port.

ORIENTATION AND PRACTICAL INFORMATION. To get to the center of town, **Piazza de Ferrari,** from Stazione Principe, take **Via Balbi** to **Via Cairoli,** which becomes **Via Garibaldi,** and turn right on **Via XXV Aprile** at P. delle Fontane Marose. From Stazione Brignole, turn right onto **Via Fiume,** and right onto **Via XX Settembre.** Or, take bus #19, 20, 30, 32, 35, or 41 from Stazione Principe or bus #19 or 40 from Stazione Brignole to Piazza de Ferrari in the center of town. The **centro storico** (historic center) contains many of Genoa's monuments. The **tourist office** is on Porto Antico, in Palazzina S. Maria. From the aquarium, walk toward the complex of buildings to the left. (☎24 87 11. Open daily 9am-1pm and 2-6pm.) Log on at **Internet Village,** at V. Brigata Bisagno and C. Buenos Aires, across from P. Vittoria. (€7.75 per hr. Open M-Sa 9am-1pm and 3-7pm.) **Postal Code:** 16121.

ACCOMMODATIONS AND FOOD. Ostello per la Gioventù (HI) ❶, V. Costanzi 120, has a cafeteria, TV, and a view of the city far below. From Stazione Principe, take bus #35 to V. Napoli and #40 to the hostel. From Stazione Brignole, pick up bus #40 (every 15min.) and ask to be let off at the *ostello.* (☎/fax 010 242 24 57. Breakfast included. Reception 7-11am and 3:30pm-12:30am. No curfew. HI card available at hostel. Dorms €13.) **Albergo Carola ❸,** V. Gropallo 4/12, has elegant rooms overlooking a garden. From Stazione Brignole, turn right on V. de Amicis, and continue into P. Brignole; turn right when facing Albergo Astoria, and walk 15m. Go 2 flights up from Albergo Argentina. (☎010 839 13 40. Singles €26; doubles €42.) **Hotel Balbi ❸,** V. Balbi 21/3, offers large, ornate rooms. (☎/fax 010 25 23 62. Breakfast €4. With *Let's Go:* singles €25-32; doubles €45-55. AmEx/MC/V.) **Camping** is popular; check the tourist office for availability, or try **Genova Est ❶,** on V. Marcon Loc Cassa. Take the train from Stazione Brignole to the suburb of Bogliasco (10min., 6 per day, €1); a free bus (5min., every 2hr. 8:10am-6pm) will take you from Bogliasco to the campsite. (☎347 20 53. Electricity €1.60 per day; laundry €3.50 per load. €4.65 per person, €9.30 per large tent.) **Trattoria da Maria ❷,** V. Testa d'Oro 14r, off V. XXV Aprile, has a new menu every day, with the *pranzo turistico* (set-price lunch) for €6.75. (☎010 58 10 80. Open Su-F noon-2:30pm and 7-9:30pm.)

SIGHTS. Genoa boasts a multitude of *palazzi* built by its famous merchant families. These are best seen along **Via Garibaldi,** on the edge of *centro storico,* and **Via Balbi,** in the heart of the university quarter. The 17th-century **Palazzo Reale,** V. Balbi 10, 10min. west of V. Garibaldi, is filled with Rococo rooms bathed in gold and upholstered in red velvet. (Open M-Tu 9am-3:30pm, W-Su 8:15am-7:15pm. €4, ages 18-25 €2, under 18 and seniors free.) Follow V. Balbi through P. della Nunziata and continue to L. Zecca, where V. Cairoli leads to **Via Garibaldi,** the most impressive street in Genoa, bedecked with elegant *palazzi* that once earned it the names "Golden Street" and "Street of Kings." The **Galleria di Palazzo Bianco,** V. Garibaldi 11, exhibits Ligurian, Dutch, and Flemish paintings. Across the street, the 17th-century **Galleria Palazzo Rosso,** V. Garibaldi 18, has magnificent furnishings in a lavishly frescoed interior. (Both open Tu-Sa 9am-7pm, Su 10am-6pm. €3.10 each, €5.20 together; Su free.) The **Villetta Di Negro,** on the hill further down V. Garibaldi, contains waterfalls, grottoes, and terraced gardens. From P. de Ferrari, take V. Boetto to P. Matteotti for the ornate **Chiesa di Gesù.** (Open daily 7:15am-12:30pm and 4-7:30pm. Free.) Head past the Chiesa di Gesù down V. di Porta Soprana to V. Ravecca to reach the medieval twin-towered **Porta Soprana,** the supposed boyhood home of **Christopher Columbus.** Off V.S. Lorenzo lies the **San Lorenzo Duomo,** a church in existence since the 9th century, which boasts a striped Gothic facade with a copiously decorated main entrance and 9th-century carved lions. (Open M-Sa 8am-7pm, Su 7am-7pm. Free.) The **centro storico,**

the eerie and beautiful historical center, is a mass of winding and confusing streets bordered by the port, V. Garibaldi, and P. Ferrari. Due to an extremely dangerous night scene, the center is only safe during weekdays when stores are open. It is, however, home to some of Genoa's most memorable monuments, including the **duomo** and the medieval **Torre Embraici.** Once you're back on P. Matteotti, go down V.S. Lorenzo toward the water, turn left on V. Chiabrera and left on V. di Mascherona to reach the **Chiesa S. Maria di Castello,** a labyrinth of chapels, courtyards, cloisters, and cruxifices. (Open daily 9am-noon and 3-6pm. Free.) Kids and ocean-lovers will adore the massive **aquarium,** on Porto Antico to the right of the APT tourist office. (Open M-F 9:30am-7:30pm, Sa-Su 9:30am-8:30pm; in summer Th until 11pm. €12.)

FINALE LIGURE ☎019

A beachside plaque proclaims the town of Finale Ligure the place for "*Il riposo del popolo*" (the people's rest). Whether your idea of *riposo* involves bodysurfing in the choppy waves near Torrente Porra, browsing through Finalmarina's chic boutiques, or scaling Finalborgo's looming 15th-century Castello di San Giovanni, the *popolo* have many options. The city is divided into three sections: **Finalpia** to the east, **Finalmarina** in the center, and **Finalborgo** further inland. The train station and most sights are in Finalmarina. Skip the packed beaches in town and walk east along V. Aurelia through the first tunnel, turning right for a less populated **free beach.** Climb the tough trail to the ruins of **Castel Govone** for a spectacular view of Finale. Enclosed within ancient walls, **Finalborgo,** the historic quarter of Finale Ligure proper, is a 1km walk or short bus ride up V. Bruneghi from the station. **Pilade,** V. Garibaldi 67, features jazz on Friday nights. (☎019 69 22 20. Open daily 10am-2am; off-season closed Th.) The towns near Finale Ligure are also worth exploring. SAR **buses** run from the train station to **Borgo Verezzi** (10min., 8 per day, €0.80).

Trains leave from P. Vittorio Veneto for Genoa (1hr., every hr., €3.70). The IAT **tourist office,** V.S. Pietro 14, gives out free maps. (☎019 68 10 19; fax 019 68 18 04. Open M-Sa 9am-12:30pm and 3:30-6:30pm, Su 9am-noon.) **Castello Wuillerman (HI) ❶,** on V. Generale Caviglia, is well worth the hike. From the station, take a left onto V. Mazzini, which becomes the narrow V. Torino, turn left on V. degli Ulivi, and trudge up the daunting steps. (☎019 69 05 15; hostelfinaaleligure@libero.it. Breakfast and sheets included. Reception 7-10am and 5-10pm. Curfew 11:30pm. Email reservations. €11.) **Albergo Carla ❷,** V. Colombo 44, offers a bar and a restaurant. (☎69 22 85; fax 68 19 65. Breakfast €3.70. Singles €23-29; doubles €44-49. AmEx/MC/V.) **Camping Del Mulino ❶,** on V. Castelli, has a restaurant and mini-market on the premises. Take the Calvisio bus from the station to the Boncardo Hotel and follow the brown and yellow signs to the campsite entrance. (☎019 60 16 69. Laundry €5. Reception Apr.-Sept. 8am-8pm. €7 per person, €7 per tent.) Cheap restaurants lie inland along **Via Rossi** and **Via Roma. Ferinata e Vino ❷,** V. Roma 25, serves up homestyle cooking. (☎692 562. *Primi* €4.65-7.25; *secondi* €6.20-9.30. Open daily 12:30-2pm and 7:30-9pm.) **Coop supermarket** is at V. Dante Alighieri 7. (Open M-Sa 8:30am-7:30pm, Su 9am-1pm. MC/V.) **Postal Code:** 17024.

CAMOGLI ☎0185

Postcard-perfect Camogli shimmers with color. Sun-faded peach houses crowd the hilltop, red and turquoise boats bob in the water, piles of fishing nets cover the docks, and bright umbrellas dot the dark stone beaches. **Trains** run on the Genoa-La Spezia line to Genoa (20min., 32 per day, €1.50) and La Spezia (1½hr., 21 per day, €3.50). Golfo Paradiso **ferries,** V. Scalo 3 (☎77 20 91; www.golfoparadiso.it), near P. Colombo, go to Portofino (€8) and Cinque Terre (€12). Buy tickets on the dock. Head right from the station to find the **tourist office,** V. XX Settembre 33, which can help find rooms. (☎0185 77 10 66. Open M-Sa 9am-12:30pm and 3:30-7pm, Su 9am-1pm.) Exit the train station, walk down the stairway to the right, and look for the large blue sign for the ■**Albergo La Camogliese ④**, V. Garibaldi 55. (☎0185 77 14 02; fax 0185 77 40 24. Reserve ahead. Singles €51-59; doubles €69-75. 10% *Let's Go* discount with cash. AmEx/MC/V.) **Postal Code:** 16032.

SANTA MARGHERITA LIGURE ☎0185

Santa Margherita Ligure led a calm existence as a fishing village until the early 20th century, when it fell into favor with Hollywood stars. Today, grace and glitz paint the shore, but the serenity of the town's early days still lingers. If ocean waves don't invigorate your spirit, try the holy water in seashell basins at the **Basilica di Santa Margherita,** at P. Caprera. **Trains** along the Pisa-Genoa line go from P. Federico Raoul Nobili, at the top of V. Roma, to Genoa (40min., 2-3 per hr., €2) and La Spezia (2 per hr., €3.80). Tigullio **buses** (☎0185 28 88 34) go from P.V. Veneto to Camogli (30min., every hr., €1.20) and Portofino (20min., 3 per hr., €1.50). Tigullio **ferries,** V. Palestro 8/1b (☎0185 28 46 70), have tours to Cinque Terre (July-Sept. W and Sa-Su 1 per day; €20) and Portofino (every hr., €3.20). Turn right from the train station on V. Roma, left on Corso Rainusso, turn left and take a hard right onto V. XXV Aprile from Largo Giusti to find the **tourist office,** V. XXV Aprile 2b, which arranges lodging. (☎0185 28 74 85; fax 0185 28 30 34. Open M-Sa 9am-12:30pm and 3-7:30pm, Su 9:30am-12:30pm and 4:30-7:30pm.) ■**Hotel Nuova Riviera ④**, V. Belvedere 10, has spacious rooms. (☎/fax 0185 28 74 03. Breakfast included. Singles €55-75; doubles €62-92; triples €90-120. MC/V.) ■**La Piadineria and Creperia ❷**, V. Giuncheto 5, off P. Martiri della Libertà, serves large portions. (Sandwiches from €5. Open daily 5pm-3am.) **Postal Code:** 16038.

PORTOFINO ☎0185

As long as you don't buy anything, princes and paupers alike can enjoy the curved shores and tiny bay of Portofino. A one-hour walk along the ocean road offers the chance to scout out small rocky **beaches. Njasca** offers boat rental in the summer months (€6-13 per hr.); **Paraggi** (where the bus stops) is the area's only sandy beach, but only a small strip is free. In town, follow the signs uphill from the bay to escape to the cool interior of the **Chiesa di San Giorgio.** A few minutes up the road toward the **castle** is a serene garden with sea views. (Open in summer daily 10am-7pm; in winter 10am-5pm. €2.50.) To get to town, take the bus to Portofino Mare (*not* Portofino Vetta). From P. Martiri della Libertà, Tigullio **buses** go to Santa Margherita (3 per hr., €1); buy tickets at the green kiosk. **Ferries** also go to Camogli (2 per day, €7) and Santa Margherita (every hr. 9am-7pm, €3.50). The **tourist office,** V. Roma 35, is on the way to the waterfront from the bus stop. (☎0185 26 90 24. Open daily 10:30am-1:30pm and 2:30-7pm.)

CINQUE TERRE ☎0187

The five bright fishing villages of Cinque Terre cling to a stretch of terraced hillsides and steep crumbling cliffs, with the dazzling turquoise sea lapping against their shores. You can hike through all five—Monterosso, Vernazza, Corniglia, Manarola, and Riomaggiore—in a few hours. **Monterosso** is the most developed, with sandy beaches and exciting nightlife; **Vernazza** has a seaside *piazza* with colorful buildings and a busy harbor; **Corniglia** hovers high above the sea in peaceful solitude; **Manarola** has quiet streets and a spectacular swimming cove; and **Riomaggiore** has a tiny harbor and lots of rooms for rent. The best views are from the narrow goat paths that link the towns, winding through vineyards, streams, and dense foliage. The best hike lies between Monterosso and Vernazza (1½hr.); the trail between Vernazza and Corniglia (2hr.) also winds through spectacular scenery.

The largest **free beach** lies directly below the train station; get there early to reserve a space. Alternatively, follow V. Fegina through the tunnel to get to another free beach. **Guvano Beach,** a pebbly strip frequented by nudists, is through the tunnel at the base of the steps leading up to Corniglia (€2.60). Tiny trails off the road to Vernazza lead to popular hidden coves.

The Genoa-La Spezia rail line connects the five towns; Monterosso is the most accessible. From V. Fegina, at the north end of town, **trains** run to: Pisa (2½hr., every hr.); Genoa (1½hr., every hr.); La Spezia (20min., every 30min.); and Rome (7hr., every 2hr.). Trains also connect the five towns (5-20min., every 50min., €1). Reserve rooms several weeks in advance. Private rooms *(affittacamere)* are the most plentiful and economical options. To find Manarola's hostel, **Albergo Della Gioventù-Ostello "Cinque Terre" ❷,** V.B. Riccobaldi 21, turn right from the train station and go uphill 300m to discover more fabulous amenities than can be believed. (☎92 02 15; www.cinqueterre.net. Breakfast €3.50. Reception daily 2am-1pm and 5pm-1am. Reserve 1 month ahead. Dorms €16-19; quads €64-76. AmEx/MC/V.) In Vernazza, ask in Trattoria Capitano about **Albergo Barbara ❸,** P. Marconi 30, top floor, at the port. (☎/fax 81 23 98. 2-night min. stay for a reservation. Doubles €43-55; triples €65; quads €70.) In Monterosso, try the **tourist office** (☎0185 81 75 06) or **Hotel Souvenir ❸,** V. Gioberti 24, the best deal in town. (☎0185 81 75 95. Breakfast €5. Singles €35, students €30.) For private rooms in Riomaggiore, call **Robert Fazioli ❸,** V. Colombo 94. (☎0185 92 09 04. Rooms €20-50.) Get supplies for a romantic picnic at **Cantina di Sciacchetrà,** V. Roma 7, in Monterosso. (Open Mar.-Oct. daily 9am-11pm; closed Nov.; Dec-Feb. open only on weekends.)

LA SPEZIA ☎0187

A departure point for Corsica and an unavoidable transport hub for Cinque Terre, La Spezia is among Italy's most beautiful ports, with regal palms lining the promenade and citrus trees growing throughout the parks. La Spezia lies on the Genoa-Pisa **train** line. **Happy Lines,** with a ticket kiosk on V. Italia, sends **ferries** to Corsica (round-trip €44-64). **Navigazione Golfo dei Poeti,** V. Mazzini 21, run ferries to: each village in Cinque Terre and Portovenereo (€11); Capraia (5hr., €41); and Elba (3½hr., €41). The **tourist office,** V. Mazzini 45, is at the port. (☎0187 77 09 00. Open M-Sa 9:30am-12:30pm and 3:30-7:30pm.) **Albergo Ilsole ❹,** V. Cavalloti, off V. Prione, offers rooms with couches and high ceilings. (☎73 51 64. Doubles €39-47; triples €52-62. MC/V.) **Postal Code:** 19100.

ITALY

EMILIA-ROMAGNA

Go to Florence, Venice, and Rome to sightsee; come to Emilia-Romagna to eat. Italy's wealthy wheat- and dairy-producing region covers the fertile plains of the Po River Valley, and celebrates the finest culinary traditions on the peninsula. The Romans originally settled here, but the towns later fell under the rule of great Renaissance families whose names adorn every *palazzo* and *piazza* in the region.

BOLOGNA ☎051

Bright facades line the cobblestone roads that twist by churches, but the city's appeal extends far beyond aesthetics. Blessed with prosperity and Europe's oldest university, which counts Dante, Petrarch, and Copernicus among its graduates, Bologna has developed an open-minded atmosphere with strong minority and gay political activism. The city also prides itself on a great culinary heritage.

EAT YOUR HEART OUT, CHEF BOYARDEE

In Italy, the desecration of pasta is a mortal sin. Pasta must be chosen correctly and cooked *al dente* (firm, literally "to the tooth"). To avoid embarrassment, get to know the basics. The *spaghetti* family includes all variations that require twirling, from hollow cousins *bucatini* and *maccheroni* to the more delicate *capellini*. Flat *spaghetti* include *fettuccini, taglierini,* and *tagliatelle*. Short pasta tubes can be *penne* (cut diagonally and occasionally *rigate,* or ribbed), *sedani* (curved), *rigatoni* (wider), or *cannelloni* (usually stuffed). *Fusilli* (corkscrews), *farfalle* (butterflies or bow-ties), and *ruote* (wheels) are fun as well as functional. Don't be alarmed if you see pastry displays labeled "pasta"; the Italian word refers to anything made of dough.

TRANSPORTATION AND PRACTICAL INFORMATION. Bologna is a rail hub for all major Italian cities and the Adriatic coast. **Trains** leave the northern tip of the walled city for: Florence (1½hr., every 2hr., €5); Milan (3hr., 2 per hr., €10); Rome (4hr., 1 per hr., €21); and Venice (2hr., every hr., €10). Take caution, especially at night, as the area near the station is not the safest. **Buses** #25 and 30 run between the train station and the historic center at **Piazza Maggiore** (€1). The **tourist office,** P. Maggiore 1, is next to the Palazzo Comunale. (☎051 648 76 07; www.prenotabologna.it. Open M-Sa 10am-2pm and 3-7pm.) **Postal Code:** 40100.

ACCOMMODATIONS AND FOOD. The sparklingly clean **Albergo Panorama ❹,** V. Livraghi 1, 4th fl., has a prime location. Follow V. Ugo Bassi from P. Maggiore and take the third left. (☎051 22 18 02; fax 051 26 63 60. Singles €47; doubles €62; triples €78. AmEx/MC/V.) **Ostello due Torre San Sisto (HI) ❶,** V. Viadagola 5, is off V. San Donato in the Località di San Sisto, 6km from the center of town. Walk down V. dell'Indipendenza from the station, turn right on V. della Mille, and take bus #93 from across the street to San Sisto. (☎/fax 051 50 18 10. Breakfast included. Reception daily 7am-midnight. Lockout 10am-3:30pm. Curfew midnight. Dorms €12; family rooms €13-14 per person.) For the clean **Pensione Marconi ❸,** V. Marconi 22, turn right from the train station and then turn left on V. Amendola, which becomes V. Marconi. (☎26 28 32. Singles €34-43; doubles €53-68; triples €90.)

Don't leave without sampling Bologna's signature *spaghetti alla bolognese*. Scout **Via Augusto Righi, Via Piella,** and **Via Saragozza** for traditional *trattorie*. A **PAM** supermarket, V. Marconi 26, is by the intersection of V. Riva di Reno. (Open M-W and F-Sa 7:45am-7:45pm, Th 7:45am-1pm.) Locals chat over regional dishes like *tagliatelle* at **Trattoria Da Maro ❸,** V. Broccaindosso 71b, between Strada Maggiore and V.S. Vitale. (☎051 22 73 04. *Primi* €5-6, *secondi* €5-7. Open M 8-10:15pm, Tu-Sa noon-2:30pm and 8-10:15pm.) Savor hearty food in **Antica Trattoria Roberto Spiga ❸,** V. Broccaindosso, 21a. (☎051 23 00 63. *Primi* €6-8, *secondi* €8-10. Open Sept.-July M-Sa noon-3pm and 7:30-10pm.) **Il Gelatauro,** V.S. Vitale 82/b, uses only fresh fruit to create delicious sorbets. Cones start at €2. (Open June-Aug. daily 11am-11pm; Sept.-May Tu-Su 11am-11pm.)

SIGHTS AND ENTERTAINMENT. Forty kilometers of porticoed buildings line the streets of Bologna in a mix of Gothic, Renaissance, and Baroque styles. The tranquil **Piazza Maggiore** flaunts both Bologna's historical and modern wealth. The cavernous Gothic interior of the city's *duomo*, **Basilica di San Petronio,** was meant to be larger than Rome's St. Peter's, but the jealous Church ordered that the funds be used instead to build the nearby Palazzo Archiginnasio. It hosted both the Council of Trent (when it wasn't meeting in Trent) and the 1530 ceremony in which Pope Clement VII gave Italy to the German king Charles V. The pomp and pageantry of the exercises at the church allegedly inspired a disgusted Martin

Luther to reform religion in Germany. (Open M-Sa 7:15am-1pm and 2-6pm, Su 7:30am-1pm and 2-6:30pm. Sacristy open daily 8am-noon and 4-6pm.) The **Palazzo Archiginnasio,** behind S. Petronio, was once a university building; the upstairs theater was built in 1637 to teach anatomy to students. (☎051 23 64 88. Open M-F 9am-7pm, Sa 9am-2pm. Theater open M-Sa 9am-1pm. Both closed 2 weeks in Aug. Free.) On the northern side of P. Maggiore is the **Palazzo de Podestà,** remodeled by Fioravanti's son Aristotle, who later designed Moscow's Kremlin. Next to P. Maggiore, **Piazza del Nettuno** contains Giambologna's famous 16th-century fountain, *Neptune and Attendants*. From P. Nettuno, go down V. Rizzoli to **Piazza Porta Ravegana,** where seven streets converge to form Bologna's **medieval quarter.** Two towers that constitute the city's emblem rise magnificently from the *piazza;* you can climb the **Torre degli Asinelli.** (Open daily May-Aug. 9am-6pm; Sept.-Apr. 9am-5pm. €3.) From V. Rizzoli, follow V.S. Stefano to **Piazza Santo Stefano,** where four of the original seven churches of the Romanesque **Piazza Santo Stefano Church Complex** remain. Bologna's patron saint, San Petronio, lies buried under the pulpit of the **Chiesa di San Sepolcro.** (Open daily 9am-noon and 3:30-6pm.) Take Strada Maggiore to P. Aldrovandi to reach the remarkably intact **Chiesa di Santa Mari dei Seru,** whose columns support an unusual combination of arches and ribbed vaulting. The **Pinacoteca Nazionale,** V. delle Belle Arti, 56, off V. Zamboni, traces the history of Bolognese artists. (☎051 24 32 22. Open Tu-Su 9am-6:30pm. €7.)

Bologna's hip student population ensures raucous nighttime fun. **Cluricaune,** V. Zamboni 18/b, is an Irish bar packed with students who flock to its pool table and dart boards. (Pints €4.20. Happy Hour 5-8:30pm; drinks €3.10. Open Su-F 11pm-3am, Sa 4pm-3am.) **Cassero,** in the Porta Saragozza, is a lively gay bar packed with men and women. (Open daily 10pm-2am.)

PARMA ☎0521

Parma maintains an artistic and culinary elegance from its rich past, while vibrating with youthful energy from the nearby university. From P. Garibaldi, follow Strada Cavour toward the train station and take the third right on Strada al Duomo to reach the 11th-century Romanesque **duomo,** in P. del Duomo, which is filled with masterpieces. Most spectacular is the dome, where Correggio's *Virgin* ascends to a golden heaven in a spiral of white robes, pink *putti*, and blue sky. The pink-and-white marble **baptistery** was built between the Romanesque and Gothic periods. (*Duomo* open daily 9am-noon and 3-7pm. Baptistery open daily 9am-12:30pm and 3-7pm. €2.70, students €1.50.) Behind the *duomo* is the frescoed dome of the **Chiesa di San Giovanni Evangelista,** P.S. Giovanni, designed by Correggio. (Open daily 9am-noon and 3-7pm.) From P. del Duomo, follow Strada al Duomo across Strada Cavour, walk one block down Strada Piscane, and cross P. della Pace to reach the 17th-century **Palazzo della Pilotta,** Parma's artistic treasure chest, which houses the **Galleria Nazionale.** (Open daily 9am-2pm. €6.)

Parma is on the Bologna-Milan rail line. **Trains** go from P. Carlo Alberto della Chiesa to: Bologna (1hr., 2 per hr., €4); Florence (3hr., 7 per day, €14.20); and Milan (1½hr., every hr., €7). Walk left from the station, turn right on V. Garibaldi, and turn left on V. Melloni to reach the **tourist office,** V. Melloni 1a. (☎0521 21 88 89; fax 0521 23 47 35. Open M-Sa 9am-7pm, Su 9am-1pm.) From the station, take bus #9 (€0.75) and get off when the bus turns left on V. Martiri della Libertà for the **Ostello Cittadella (HI) ❶,** on V. Passo Buole, in a corner of a 15th-century fortress. (☎96 14 34. 3-night max. stay. Lockout 9:30am-5pm. Curfew 11pm. Open Apr.-Oct. HI members only. Dorms €9. **Camping** open Apr.-Oct. €6 per person, €11 per site.) **Albergo Leon d'Oro ❸,** V. Fratti 4, off V. Garibaldi, is two blocks from the train station. (☎0521 77 31 82. Singles €30; doubles €47. AmEx/MC/V.) Look for fragrant Parma cuisine along **Via Garibaldi. Le Sorelle Picchi,** Strada Farini 27, is a traditional

ITALY

salumeria and *trattoria*. (☎0521 23 35 28. *Primi* €5-6, *secondi* €7-8. *Trattoria* open M-Sa noon-3pm; *salumeria* open 8:30am-7pm.) **K2,** Borgo Cairoli 23, next to the Chiesa di San Giovanni Evangelista, has great *gelato*. (Cones from €1.50. Open Th-Tu 11am-midnight.) **Supermarket 2B** is at V. XXII Luglio 27c. (Open M-W and F-Sa 8:30am-1pm and 4:30-8pm, Th 8:30am-1pm.) **Postal Code:** 43100.

RAVENNA ☎0544

Ravenna's 15min. of historical superstardom came and went 14 centuries ago when Justinian and Theodora, rulers of the Byzantine Empire, headquartered their campaign here to restore order in the anarchic west. Take V. Argentario from V. Cavour to reach the 6th-century ■**Basilica di San Vitale,** V.S. Vitale 17. An open courtyard overgrown with greenery leads to the brilliant, glowing mosaics inside; those of the Emperor and Empress adorn the lower left and right panels of the apse. Behind S. Vitale, the city's oldest and most intriguing mosaics cover the glittering interior of the **Mausoleo di Galla Placidia.** (☎0544 21 62 92. Open Apr.-Sept. daily 9am-7pm; Oct.-Mar. 9:30am-4:30pm. Joint ticket €3.10.) Take bus #4 or 44 (€0.70) across from the train station to Classe, south of the city, to see the astounding mosaics at the ■**Chiesa di Sant'Apollinare in Classe.** (Open M-Sa 8:30am-7:30pm, Su 9am-1pm. €2.10, Su free.) Much to Florence's dismay, Ravenna is also home to the **Tomb of Dante Alighieri.** In the adjoining **Dante Museum,** his heaven and hell come alive in etchings, paintings, and sculptures. From P. del Popolo, cut through P. Garibaldi to V. Alighieri. (☎0544 302 52. Tomb open daily 9am-7pm. Free. Museum open Apr.-Sept. Tu-Su 9am-noon and 3:30-6pm. €2.)

Trains (☎0544 21 78 84) leave P. Farini for Ferrara, Florence, and Venice (1hr., every 2hr., €4.50) via Bologna (1hr., every 1-2hr., €4). Follow Viale Farini from the station to V. Diaz, which runs to the central P. del Popolo and the **tourist office,** V. Salara 8. (☎0544 354 04; fax 0544 48 26 70. Open M-Sa 8:30am-7pm, Su 10am-4pm.) Take bus #1 or 70 from V. Pallavicini at the station (every 15min.-1hr., €0.70) to reach **Ostello Dante (HI) ❶,** V. Nicolodi, 12. (☎/fax 0544 42 11 64. Breakfast included. Reception daily 7-10am and 5-11:30pm. Lockout 10am-5pm. Curfew 11:30pm. 4- to 6-bed dorms €12.50. MC/V.) Walk down V. Farini, and go right at P. Mameli for the renovated **Albergo Al Giaciglio ❸,** V. Rocca Brancaleone 42. (☎0544 394 03. Breakfast €2-5. Singles €28-32; doubles €35-45; triples €45-60. MC/V.)

FERRARA ☎0532

Rome has its mopeds, Venice its boats, and Ferrara its bicycles. Old folks, young folks, and babies perched precariously on handlebars whirl through Ferrara's jumble of major thoroughfares and twisting medieval roads. Take a deep breath of fresh air, hop on a bike, and head for the giant castle.

▐ TRANSPORTATION. Ferrara **trains,** on the Bologna-Venice line, go to: Bologna (30min., 1-2 per hr., €2.75); Padua (1hr., every hr., €4); Ravenna (1hr., 1-3 per hr., €4); Rome (3-4hr., 7 per day, €31); and Venice (2hr., 1-2 per hr., €6). ACFT (☎59 94 92) and GGFP **buses** leave V. Rampari S. Paolo or the train station for Bologna (1½hr., 15 per day, €3.30) and Ferrara's beaches (1hr., 12 per day, €4-5).

▐ PRACTICAL INFORMATION. To get to the center of town, turn left out of the train station and then veer right on **Viale Costituzione.** This road becomes Viale Cavour and runs to the **Castello Estense** at the center of town (1km). Or, take bus #2 to the Castello stop or bus #1 or 9 to the post office (every 15-20min., €0.85). The **tourist office** is in Castello Estense. (☎0532 20 93 70. Open daily 9am-1pm and 2-6pm.) Rent cheap **bikes** at P. le Stazione 2. (€7 per day. Open daily 6:30am-1pm and 3:30-7pm.) **Postal Code:** 44100.

ACCOMMODATIONS AND FOOD. Walk down Corso Ercole I d'Este from the *castello*, or take bus #4c from the station and ask for the *castello* stop to reach the central **Ostello della Gioventu Estense (HI) ❶**, Corso B. Rossetti 24, with simple dorm rooms. (☎/fax 0532 20 42 27. Reception daily 7-10am and 5-11:30pm. Lockout 10am-3:30pm. Curfew 11:40pm. Dorms €13.) **Casa degli Artisti ❷**, V. Vittoria 66, near P. Lampronti, is in the historic center of Ferrara. (☎76 10 38. Singles €21; doubles €38.) The **Albergo Nazionale ❹**, Calle Porta Reno 32, is on a busy street right off the *duomo*. (☎/fax 0532 20 96 04. Curfew 12:30am. Singles €40; doubles with bath €65; triples €78. AmEx/MC/V.) In Ferrara, gorge on delicious triangular meat *ravioli* served in a broth or the traditional *Ferrarese* dessert of luscious *pampepato*, chocolate-covered almond and fruit cake. Try delicious *panini* with one of 600 varieties of wine at the oldest *osteria* in Italy, **Osteria Al Brindisi 11 ❷**, V.G. degli Adelardi 9b. (☎0532 20 91 42. Open Tu-Su 8:30am-1am.) For picnic supplies, stop by the **Mercato Comunale**, on V. Mercato, next to the *duomo*. (Open M-W 7am-1:30pm and 4:30-7:30pm, F 4:30-7:30pm, Th and Sa 7am-1:30pm.)

SIGHTS AND ENTERTAINMENT. **Bike** the tranquil, wooded concourse along the city's well-preserved 9km **medieval wall**, which begins at the far end of Corso Giovecca. The imposing **Castello Estense** stands precisely in the center of town. Corso della Giovecca lies along the former route of the moat's feeder canal, separating the medieval section from the part planned by the d'Este's architect. (☎0532 29 92 33. Open Tu-Su 9:30am-5pm. €4.10, students €3.) From the *castello*, take Corso Martiri della Libertà to P. Cattedrale and the **Duomo San Romano**, which contains the **Museo della Cattedrale**. (Cathedral open M-Sa 7:30am-noon and 3-6:30pm, Su 7:30am-12:30pm and 4-7:30pm. Museum ☎0532 20 74 49. Open Tu-Sa 10am-noon and 3-5pm, Su 10am-noon and 4-6pm.) From the *castello*, cross Largo Castello to Corso Ercole I d'Este and walk to the corner of Corso Rossetti to reach the gorgeous **Palazzo Diamanti**, built in 1493. Inside, the **Pinacoteca Nazionale** holds many of the best works of the Ferrarese school. (Open Tu-W and F-Sa 9am-2pm, Th 9am-7pm, Su and holidays 9am-1pm. €4.) Follow Corso Ercole I d'Este behind the *castello* and go right on Corso Porta Mare to find the **Palazzo Massari**, Corso Porta Mare 9, which houses both the **Museo d'Arte Moderna e Contemporanea "Filippo de Pisis,"** and, upstairs, the spectacular **Museo Ferrarese dell'Ottocentro/Museo Giovanni Boldini.** (Both open daily 9am-1pm and 3-6pm. Joint ticket €6.70.) In July and August, a free **Discobus** (☎0532 59 94 11) runs every Saturday night between Ferrara and the hottest clubs; pick up flyers in the train station. **Postal Code:** 44100.

ITALY

THE LAKE COUNTRY

When Italy's monuments and museums start blurring together, escape to the natural beauty of the northern Lake Country, where clear waters lap the encircling mountains. A young crowd descends upon Lake Garda for its watersports by day and thriving club scene at night; palatial hotels line Lake Maggiore's sleepy beaches, while Lake Como's urbane shore hosts three excellent hostels.

LAKE COMO (LAGO DI COMO)

Although a heavenly magnificence lingers over the reaches of Europe's deepest lake (410m), peaceful Lake Como is more than a figment of your imagination. *Bougainvillea* and lavish villas adorn the lake's craggy backdrop, warmed by the sun and cooled by lakeside breezes. Como, the largest city on the lake, makes an ideal transportation hub. Menaggio, one of the three smaller Centro Lago towns, is an alternate base for exploring the lake, and makes for a more relaxing stay.

TRANSPORTATION. The only town on the lake accessible by train is Como, on the southwestern tip. **Trains** roll into Stazione San Giovanni (☎0147 88 80 88) from Milan (1hr., every 30min. 4:45am-11:35pm, €4.85) and Venice (4hr., every hr. 4:45am-7:55pm, €21.33). **Buses** leave P. Matteotti for Bergamo (C46, 2hr., every hr. 6:45am-6:30pm, €4.30). From Como, take the C10 near Ferrovia Nord to Menaggio or Domaso (1hr., every hr. 7:10am-8:30pm, €2.43). Hourly C30 buses also serve Bellagio (1hr., 6:34am-8:14pm, €2.72). Spend the day zipping between stores, gardens, villas, and wineries of the remaining towns by **ferry** (day pass €7-17).

COMO. Situated on the southwest tip of the lake, at the receiving end of the Milan rail line, Como is the lake's token semi-industrial town. For excellent **hiking** and stunning views, head from the far end of Lungo Lario Trieste up to **Brunate.** To get from the train station to the **tourist office,** P. Cavour 16, walk down the steps, turn left on V. Fratelli Ricchi after the little park, and turn right on Viale Fratelli Roselli, which leads to P. Cavour via Lungo Lario Trento. (☎031 26 97 12; www.lakecomo.org.) **Ostello Villa Olmo (HI) ❶,** V. Bellinzona, 2, behind Villa Olmo, offers clean rooms, great food, and discounts on various sights in Como. From the train station, walk 20min. down V. Borgo Vico, which becomes V. Bellinzona. (☎/fax 031 57 38 00. hostellocomo@tin.it. Breakfast included. Lockout 10am. Strict curfew 11:30pm. Reserve ahead. Open daily Mar-Nov. 7-10am and 4-11:30pm. Dorms €11.50.) **In Riva al Lago ❷,** P. Matteotti, 4, is centrally located with immaculate rooms. (☎031 30 23 33. www.inrivallago.com. Breakfast €2-4. Singles €24, with bath €39; doubles €36.) The **G.S. supermarket** is at V. Recchi and V. Fratelli Roselli. (Open M 9am-9:30pm, Tu-F 8am-8:30pm, Sa 8am-8pm.) **Postal Code:** 22100.

ITALY

MENAGGIO. Menaggio is home to historic streets, stunning scenery, and a youth hostel that makes it a perfect northern getaway. From the top of **Rifugio Menaggio,** 1400m above the lake, hikers can make trips to **Monte Grona** and the **Chiesa di S. Amate.** A 1-2hr. hike (each way) leads to the spectacular **Sass Corbee Gorge;** inquire at the **tourist office** for directions and maps. (☎034 43 29 24. infomenaggio@tiscalinet.it. Open M-Sa 9am-noon and 3-6pm.) To get to the resort-like **Ostello La Prinula (HI) ❶,** V. IV Novembre, 86, walk along the shore to the main thoroughfare, go past the gas station, and walk up the less steep incline on the right. (☎034 43 23 56; www.menaggiohostel.com. Breakfast included. Lockout 10am-5pm. Curfew 11:30pm. Call ahead to reserve. Open Mar.-Nov. Dorms €11.50. Family rooms of 4-6 beds and private bath €12 per person.)

LAKE MAGGIORE (LAGO MAGGIORE)

Lacking the frenzy of its eastern neighbors, Lake Maggiore combines similar temperate mountain waters and idyllic shores. The romantic resort town **Stresa** is only an hour from Milan by **train** (every hr., €5.10). The local **tourist office** is in the ferry building at the dock, in P. Martini. (☎/fax 0323 30 150 or 31 308. Open daily 10am-12:30pm and 3-6:30pm.) To find comfy beds at **Hotel Mon Toc ❹,** V. Duchessa di Genova 67/69 in Stresa, turn right from the station and then right again at the intersection under the tracks. (☎0323 302 82; fax 0323 93 38 60. info@hotelmontoc.com. Breakfast included. Singles €45; doubles €78. AmEx/DC/MC/V.)

DAYTRIP FROM LAKE MAGGIORE: BORROMEAN ISLANDS. Stresa is a perfect stepping-stone to the gorgeous Borromean Islands. Daily excursion tickets (€10) allow you to hop back and forth between Stresa and the three islands—**Isola Bella, Isola Superiore dei Pescatori,** and **Isola Madre.** The islands boast lush, manicured botanical gardens, elegant villas, and an opulent Baroque palace.

LAKE GARDA (LAGO DI GARDA)

Garda has staggering mountains and breezy summers. **Desenzano,** the lake's southern transport hub, is only 30min. from Verona, 1hr. from Milan, and 2hr. from Venice. Sirmione and Gardone Riviera, easily accessible by bus and boat, are best explored as daytrips, as accommodations are scant and pricey.

SIRMIONE. Sirmione's beautiful 13th-century castle and Roman ruins make for a leisurely day or a busy afternoon. **Buses** run every hour from: Brescia (1hr., €3.10); Desenzano (20min., €1.45); and Verona (1hr., €2.65). *Battelli* (water steamers) run until 8pm to: Desenzano (20min., €3); Gardone (1¼hr., €6); and Riva (4hr., €8.50). The **tourist office,** V. Guglielmo Marconi 2, is in the disc-shaped building. (☎030 91 61 14. Open Apr.-Oct. daily 9am-9pm; Nov.-Mar. reduced hours.) The **Albergo Grifone ❸,** V. Bocchio 4, has a prime location. (☎030 91 60 14; fax 030 91 65 48. Reserve ahead. Singles €32; doubles €55.) **Postal Code:** 25019.

GARDONE RIVIERA. Formerly the playground of the rich and famous, this town is now home to Lake Garda's most famous sight: the villa of 20th-century poet and latter-day Casanova Gabriele D'Annunzio. His quirky mansion, **Il Vittoriale,** sprawls above Gardone, off V. Roma and V. dei Colli. (Villa open Apr.-Sept. Tu-Su 8:30am-8pm. Gardens open Oct.-Mar. Tu-Su 9am-5pm. €11.) **Buses** (☎0365 210 61) run to Desenzano (30min., 6 per day, €2.40) and Milan (3hr., 2 per day, €8). The **APT tourist office,** V. Repubblica 8, is in the center of Gardone Sotto. (☎/fax 0365 203 47. Open M-Sa 9am-1pm and 3:30-6:30pm, Su 9am-1pm.) **Postal Code:** 25083.

RIVA DEL GARDA. Riva's calm pebble beaches are Lake Garda's compromise for the budget traveler. Travelers **swim, windsurf, hike,** and **climb** near the most stunning portion of the lake, where cliffs crash into the water. Riva is accessible by **bus** (☎0464 55 23 23) from Trent (2hr., 6 per day, €3.20) and Verona (2hr., 11 per day, €5). **Ferries** (☎030 914 95 11) leave from P. Matteoti for Gardone (€6.60). The **tourist office,** Giardini di Porta Orientale 8, is near the water. (☎0464 55 44 44; fax 52 03 08. Open M-Sa 9am-noon and 3-6pm, Su 10am-noon and 4-6:30pm.) Snooze at the fabulous **Locanda La Montanara ❷,** V. Montanara 20, off V. Florida. (☎/fax 0464 55 48 57. Breakfast €5. Singles €16; doubles €32.) **Postal Code:** 38066.

THE DOLOMITES

With their sunny skies and powdery, light snow, the Dolomites offer immensely popular downhill skiing. These amazing peaks, which start west of Trent and extend north and east to Austria, are also fantastic for hiking and rock climbing.

TRENT ☎0461

Between the Dolomites and the Veneto, Trent offers an affordable sampling of northern Italian life with superb restaurants and hikes against dramatic scenery. The **Piazza del Duomo,** Trent's center and social heart, contains the city's best sights. The **Fontana del Nettuno** stands, trident in hand, in the center of the *piazza*. Nearby is the **Cattedrale di San Vigilio,** named for the patron saint of Trent. (Open daily 6:40am-12:15pm and 2:30-7:30pm. Free.) Walk down V. Belenzani and head right on V. Roma to reach the well-preserved **Castello del Buonconsiglio.** (Open daily 10am-6pm. €5, students and seniors €2.50.) **Monte Bondone** rises majestically over Trent, making a pleasant daytrip or overnight excursion. Catch the **cable car** (☎0461 38 10 00; every 30min., €0.80) to **Sardagna** on Mt. Bondone from V. Lung'Adige Monte Grappa, between the train tracks and the river.

Trains (☎0461 98 36 27) leave V. Dogana for: Bologna (3hr., 13 per day, €10.15); Bolzano (45min., 2 per hr., €2.90); Venice (3hr., 5 per day, €10.15); and Verona (1hr., every hr., €4.65). Atesina **buses** (☎0461 82 10 00) go from V. Pozzo, next to the train station, to Riva del Garda (1hr., every hr., €2.80). The **tourist office,** V. Alferi 4, offers advice on biking, skiing, and hiking. (☎0461 98 38 80; www.apt.trento.it. Open daily 9am-7pm.) The central **Hotel Venezia** ❹ is at P. Duomo 45. (☎/fax 23 41 14. Breakfast €5.20. Singles €40; doubles €59. MC/V.) From the station, turn right on V. Pozzo and left on V. Torre Vanga to get to **Ostello Giovane Europa (HI)** ❶, V. Torre Vanga 11. (☎0461 26 34 84; fax 0461 22 25 17. Breakfast and sheets included. Reception daily 7:30am-11pm. Check-out 9:30am. Curfew 11:30pm. Dorms €13; singles €21.) **Ristorante Al Vo** ❸, V. del Vo 11, gives new meaning to "family-run restaurant," with 650 years of Trentino cooking to back it up (Open M-Sa 11:30am-3pm, Th-F 7-9:30pm. AmEx/MC/V.). **Postal Code:** 38100.

BOLZANO (BOZEN) ☎0471

In the tug-of-war between Austrian and Italian cultural influences, Bolzano pulls on Austria's side. The town's prime location beneath vineyard-covered mountains makes it a splendid base for hiking or skiing in the Dolomites. Artwork and numerous frescoes fills the Gothic **duomo,** off P. Walther. (Open M-F 9:45am-noon and 2-5pm, Sa 9:45am-noon. Free.) The fascinating **South Tyrol Museum of Archaeology,** V. Museo 43, near Ponte Talvera, houses the actual 5000-year-old **Ice Man.** (☎0471 98 06 48. Open Tu-W and F-Su 10am-6pm, Th 10am-8pm. €6.70, students €3.60.) **Trains** (☎0471 97 42 92) leave P. Stazione for: Milan (3hr., 3 per day, €21); Trent (45min., 2 per hr., €3); and Verona (2hr., 1-2 per hr., €6.80). Walk up V. Stazione from the train station to reach the **tourist office,** P. Walther 8. (☎0471 30 70 00; fax 0471 98 01 28. Open M-F 9am-6:30pm, Sa 9am-12:30pm.) **Croce Bianca** ❸, P. del Grano 3, is around the corner from P. Walther. (☎0471 97 75 52. Breakfast €4.15. Singles €28; doubles €47.) **Casa al Torchio** ❷, V. Museo 2c, just off P. Erbe, serves up great food. (Open M-F noon-2pm and 7-11pm, Su 7-11pm.) **Postal Code:** 39100.

AOSTA ☎0165

Aosta is the geographical and financial center of a region increasingly dependent upon tourism for economic livelihood. Aosta makes a good base for explorations in the area, but be aware that daytrips to the valleys often require tricky train and bus connections—if you hope to return before nightfall, plan ahead. **Valle del Gran San Bernardo** links Aosta to Switzerland via the Great St. Bernard Pass, which incorporates a 5854m tunnel through the mountains. Napoleon trekked through the pass with 40,000 soldiers in 1800. The area is better known for the 1505 **Hospice of St-Bernard,** home to the patron saint of man's best friend. The highest mountain in Switzerland, **The Matterhorn (Il Cervino)** looms majestically over the nondescript town of **Breuil-Cervinia** in Valtournenche. However, many fresh-air fiends consider the economic deterrents a small price to pay for the opportunity to climb up and glide down one of the world's most famous mountains. A cable car provides year-round service to **Plateau Rosà** (round-trip €23.25), where summer skiers tackle the slopes in lighter gear. Hikers can forgo the lift tickets and attempt the three-hour ascent to **Colle Superiore delle Cime Bianche** (2982m), with tremendous views of Val d'Ayas to the east. A shorter trek (1½hr.) on the same trail leads to the emerald waters of **Lake Goillet.** The **Società Guide** (☎(0166) 94 81 69) arranges group outings. Don't forget your **passport**—many trails cross into Switzerland.

Trains leave P. Manzetti for Milan (4hr., 12 per day, €10.15) and Turin (2hr., every hr., €6.85). To get from the train station to the **tourist office,** P. Chanoux 8, go straight down av. du Conseil des Commis. (☎0165 23 66 27; fax 0165 346 57. Open M-Sa 9am-1pm and 3-8pm, Su 9am-1pm.) To get to **Hotel Turin** ❷, V. d'Avise 18, from the train station turn left down the V. Giorgio, then right onto the V. Vevey, then right onto the V. Torino. (☎0165 44 55 93. Singles €21-48; doubles €62-72.) Savor great food at the classy **Trattoria Praetoria,** V. Sant'Anselmo 9, just past the Porta Praetoria. (☎0165 443 56. *Primi* €6-7.50, *secondi* €6.50-12. Open daily 12:15-2:30pm and 7:15-9pm.) **Postal Code:** 11100.

DAYTRIP FROM AOSTA: VAL D'AYAS. Budget-minded sports enthusiasts should consider bypassing the pleasure grounds to the west and stopping here instead. Val d'Ayas has the same outdoor activities as its flashy neighbors—skiing, hiking, and rafting—without the hype. **Trains** run to Verrès from Aosta (40min., 17 per day, €2.60) and Turin (1½hr.). **Buses** run from the train station at Verrès to Champoluc (1hr., 4 per day, €2.20). The **tourist office** in **Champoluc,** V. Varase 16 (☎(0125) 30 71 13; fax 30 77 85), also has branches in **Brusson** (☎(0125) 30 02 40; fax 30 06 91) and **Antagnod** (☎(0125) 30 63 35). They speak English and provide trail maps and hotel information. (Open daily 9am-12:30pm and 3-6pm.)

THE VENETO

From the rocky foothills of the Dolomites to the fertile valleys of the Po River, the Veneto region has a geography as diverse as its historical influences. Once loosely linked under the Venetian Empire, these towns retained their cultural independence, and visitors are more likely to hear regional dialects than standard Italian when neighbors gossip across their geranium-bedecked windows. The sense of local culture and custom that remains strong within each town may surprise visitors lured to the area by Venice, the *bella* of the north.

VENICE (VENEZIA) ☎041

There is a mystical quality to Venice's decadence: her lavish palaces stand proudly on a steadily sinking network of wood, treading in the clouded waters of age-old canals lapping at the feet of her abandoned front doors. Venice's labyrinthine streets lead to a treasury of Renaissance art, housed in scores of palaces, churches, and museums that are themselves architectural delights. But the same streets that once earned the name *La Serenissima* (Most Serene) are now saturated with visitors, as Venice grapples with an economy reliant on the same tourism that forces more and more of the native population away every year. Still, Romanticism dies hard, and the sinking city persists beyond the summer crowds and polluted waters, united by winding canals and the memory of a glorious past.

TRANSPORTATION

The **train station** is on the northwest edge of the city; be sure to get off at **Santa Lucia,** *not* Mestre on the mainland. **Buses** and **boats** arrive at **Piazzale Roma,** just across the Canal Grande from the train station. To get from either station to **Piazza San Marco** or the **Ponte di Rialto** (Rialto Bridge), take *vaporetto* #82 or follow the signs for the 40min. walk—exit left from the train station on Lista di Spagna.

Flights: Aeroporto Marco Polo (VCE; ☎041 260 61 11; www.veniceairport.it), 10km north of the city. Ticket office open daily 5:30am-9:30pm. Take the **ATVO shuttlebus** (☎041 520 55 30) from the airport to Piazzale Roma (30min., 2 per hr., €2.70).

Trains: Stazione Venezia Santa Lucia, northwest corner of the city. Open daily 3:45am-12:30am. **Info office** at the left as you exit the platforms, open daily 7am-9pm. To: **Bologna** (2hr., 1 per hr., €7.90-18.33); **Florence** (3hr., every 2hr., €26.60); **Milan** (3hr., 1-2 per hr., €12.40); and **Rome** (4½hr., 5 per day, €45).

ITALY

Buses: ACTV, on Piazzale Roma (☎041 528 78 86). The local line for buses and boats. Long-distance carrier buses run to nearby cities. Ticket office open daily 6:30am-11pm. ACTV offers a 3-day **discount vaporetto pass** (€13) to Rolling Venice cardholders.

Public Transportation: The **Canal Grande** can be crossed on foot only at the Scalzi, Rialto, and Accademia *ponti* (bridges). Most **vaporetti** (water buses) run 5am-midnight, the *Notte* line 11:30pm-5:30am. Single-ride €3.10. 24hr. *biglietto turistico pass* €9.30, 3-day €18.10 (€13 with Rolling Venice Card), 7-day €31. Buy tickets from booths in front of *vaporetto* stops, self-serve dispensers at the ACTV office in Piazzale Roma and the Rialto stop, or from the conductor. Pick up extra *non timbrati* (non-validated) tickets for when the booths aren't open. Validate them yourself before boarding to avoid a fine. Lines #82 (faster) and #1 (slower) run from the station down Canale Grande and Canale della Giudecca; line #52 goes from the station through Canale della Giudecca to Lido and along the city's northern edge, then back to the station; line #12 runs from Fond. Nuove to Murano, Burano, and Torcello.

ORIENTATION AND PRACTICAL INFORMATION

Venice spans 118 bodies of land in a lagoon and is connected to the mainland by a thin causeway. A veritable labyrinth, Venice can confuse even its natives, most of whom simply set off in a general direction and then patiently weave their way through the city. If you follow their example by ungluing your eyes from your map and going with the flow, you'll discover some of the unexpected surprises that make Venice spectacular. A few tips will help you to orient yourself. Locate the following landmarks on a map: **Ponte di Rialto** (the bridge in the center), **Piazza San Marco** (central south), the **Ponte Accademia** (bridge in the southwest), **Ferrovia** (the train station, in the northwest), and **Piazzale Roma** (directly south of the station). The Canal Grande snakes through the city, creating six *sestieri* (sections): Cannaregio, Castello, Santa Croce, San Polo, San Marco, and Dorsoduro. Within each *sestiere,* there are no street numbers—door numbers in a section form one long, haphazard set, consisting of around 6000 numbers. While these boundaries are nebulous, they can give you a general sense of location. **Cannaregio** is in the north and includes the train station, Jewish ghetto, and Cà d'Oro; **Castello** extends east toward the Arsenale; **San Marco** fills in the area between the Ponte di Rialto and Ponte Accademia; **Dorsoduro,** across the bridge from S. Marco, stretches the length of Canale della Giudecca and up to Campo S. Pantalon; **San Polo** runs north from Chiesa S. Maria dei Frari to the Ponte di Rialto; and **San Croce** lies west of S. Polo, across the Canal Grande from the train station. If *sestiere* boundaries prove too vague, Venice's **parrochie** (parishes) provide a more defined idea of where you are; *parrochia* signs, like *sestiere* signs, are painted on the sides of buildings.

TOURIST, FINANCIAL, AND LOCAL SERVICES

Tourist Office: APT, Calle della Ascensione, P.S. Marco, 71/F (☎/fax 041 529 87 40; www.tourismovenezia.it), directly opposite the Basilica. Open M-Sa 9:30am-3:30pm. The APT desk at the nearby **Venice Pavilion,** Giardini E Reali, S. Marco 2 (☎041 522 51 50) sells ACTV tickets. Open daily 9am-6pm. **AVA** (☎041 171 52 88), in the train station, to the right of the tourist office. Makes same-day reservations for €0.55. Open in summer daily 9am-10pm. Offices also in Piazzale Roma (☎041 523 13 79) and the airport (☎041 541 51 33). Call for advance reservations.

Rolling Venice Card: Offers discounts at over 200 restaurants, cafes, hotels, museums, and shops. Ages 14-29 only. Tourist office provides list of participating vendors. Cards cost €2.60 and are valid for one year from date of purchase. The card is sponsored by

ACTV and can be purched at the **ACTV VeLa** office (☎274 7650) in the Piazzale Roma, open daily 8:30am-6pm. The card is also available at any APT tourist office, and ACTV VeLa kiosks next to the Ferrovia, Rialto, S. Marco, and Vallaresso *vaporetto* stops.

Budget Travel: CTS, Fondamenta Tagliapietra, Dorsoduro, 3252 (☎041 520 5660; www.cts.it). From Campo S. Barnaba, cross the bridge and follow the road through the piazza. Turn left at the foot of the large bridge. Sells discounted student plane tickets, and issues ISIC cards. English spoken. Open M-F 9:30am-1:30pm and 2:30-6pm.

Currency Exchange: Money exchangers charge high prices for service. Use banks whenever possible and inquire about fees beforehand. The streets around S. Marco and S. Polo are full of banks and ATMs. Many 24hr. automatic change machines, outside banks and next to ATMs, offer low commissions and decent rates.

EMERGENCY AND COMMUNICATIONS

Emergency: ☎113. **First Aid:** ☎118.

Police: ☎113. **Carabinieri** (civil corps): ☎112. Campo S. Zaccaria, Castello, 4693/A. **Questura,** V. Nicoladi 24 (☎041 271 55 11). Contact the Questura if you have a serious complaint about your hotel.

Pharmacy: Farmacia Italo Inglese, Calle della Mandola, S. Marco, 3717 (☎041 522 4837), Follow C. Cortesia out of Campo Manin. Open M-F 9am-12:30pm and 3:45-7:30pm, Sa 9am-12:30pm. Late-night and weekend pharmacies rotate; check the list posted in the window of any pharmacy.

Hospital: Ospedale Civile, Campo S.S. Giovanni e Paolo, Castello (☎041 529 4111).

Internet Access: The NetGate, Crosera S. Pantalon, Dorsoduro, 3812/A (☎041 244 0213), From Santa Frari, take C. Scalater to C. Pantalon and follow signs for C. Margherita. €4 per hr. Open M-F 10am-8pm, Sa 10am-10pm, Su 2:15-10pm. AmEx/MC/V.

Post Office: Poste Venezia Centrale, Salizzada Fontego dei Tedeschi, S. Marco, 5554 (☎041 271 7111), off Campo S. Bartolomeo. Open M-Sa 8:30am-6:30pm.

Postal Codes: S. Marco: 30124; Castello: 30122; S. Polo, S. Croce, and Canareggio: 30121; Dorsoduro: 30123.

ACCOMMODATIONS

Plan to spend more for a room in Venice than you would elsewhere in Italy. Always agree on what you will pay before you take a room, and if possible, make reservations at least one month in advance. Dormitory-style arrangements are sometimes available without reservations, even in summer.

Religious institutions around the city offer both dorms and private rooms during the summer for about €25-70. Options include **Casa Murialdo,** Fondamenta Madonna dell'Orto, Cannaregio 3512 (☎041 719 933); **Casa Capitania,** S. Croce 561 (☎041 520 3099; open June-Sept.); **Patronato Salesiano Leone XIII,** Calle S. Domenico, Castello 1281 (☎240 3611); **Domus Cavanis,** Dorsoduro 896 (☎041 528 7374), near the Accademia Bridge; **Ostello Santa Fosca,** Cannaregio 2372 (☎041 715 775); **Instituto Canossiano,** F. delle Romite, Dorsoduro 1323 (☎041 240 9711); and **Instituto Ciliota,** Calle Muneghe S. Stefano, S. Marco 2976 (☎041 520 4888).

CANNAREGGIO AND SANTA CROCE

The station area, around the Lista di Spagna, has some of the best budget accomodations in Venice. At night the streets bustle with young travelers and students, even though the area is a 20-minute *vaporetto* ride from most major sights.

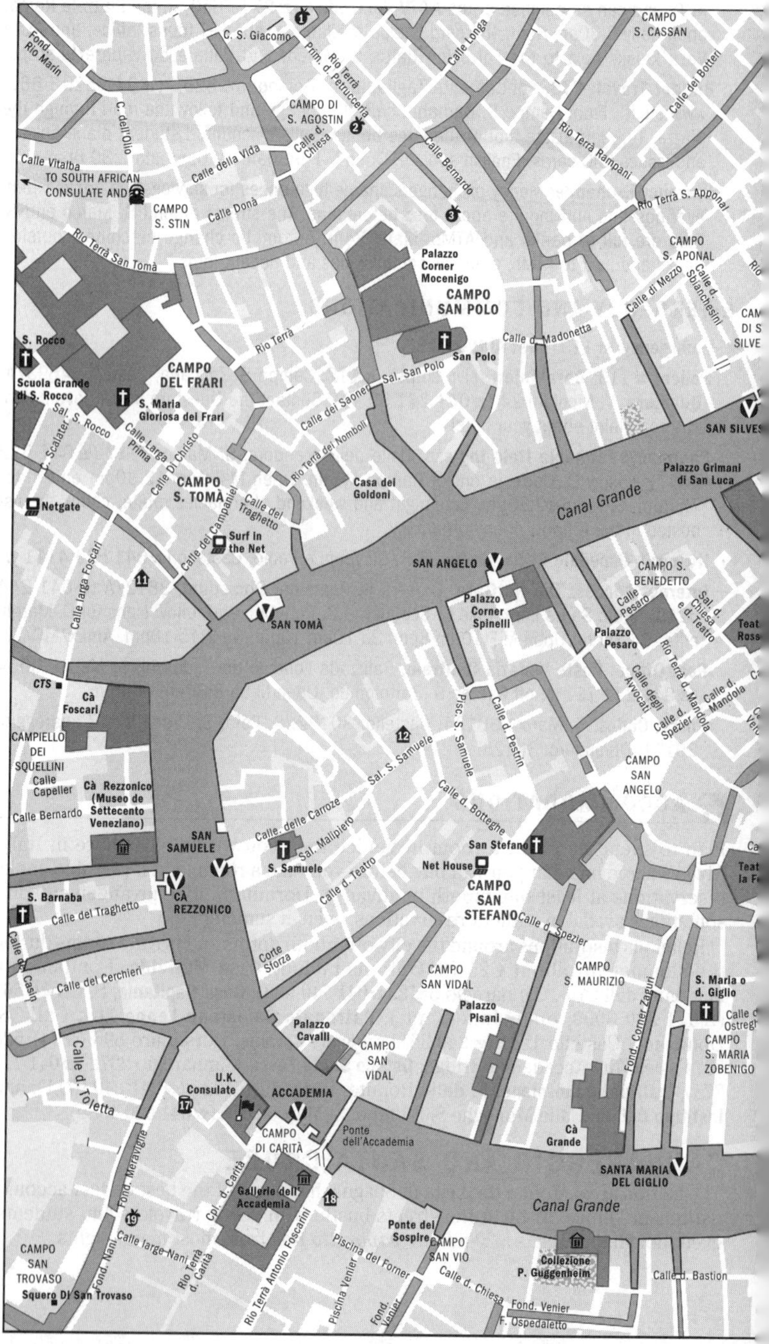
CAMPO S. CASSAN
C. S. Giacomo
Fond. Rio Marin
Rio Terrà Prim. d. Petrucceria
Calle Longa
Calle dei Botteri
CAMPO DI S. AGOSTIN
Calle d. Chiesa
C. dell'Olio
Calle della Vida
Rio Terrà Rampani
Calle Vitalba
TO SOUTH AFRICAN CONSULATE AND
CAMPO S. STIN
Calle Donà
Calle Bernardo
Rio Terrà S. Aponal
Rio Terrà San Tomà
Palazzo Corner Mocenigo
CAMPO SAN POLO
CAMPO S. APONAL
Calle di Mezzo
Calle d. Sbianchesini
Calle d. Madonetta
Rio Terrà
S. Rocco
CAMPO DEL FRARI
San Polo
Sal. San Polo
Scuola Grande di S. Rocco
S. Maria Gloriosa dei Frari
Calle dei Saoner
Sal. S. Rocco
C. Scalater
Calle Larga Prima
Calle Di Christo
Rio Terrà dei Nomboli
SAN SILVES
Palazzo Grimani di San Luca
CAMPO S. TOMÀ
Casa del Goldoni
Netgate
Calle del Traghetto
Calle dei Campaniel
Canal Grande
Surf in the Net
Calle larga Foscari
SAN ANGELO
CAMPO S. BENEDETTO
Palazzo Corner Spinelli
Calle Pesaro
Sal. d. Chiesa e d. Teatro
SAN TOMÀ
Palazzo Pesaro
CTS
Cà Foscari
Rio Terrà d. Mandola
Calle degli Avvocati
Calle d. Mandola
Calle d. Spezier
Pisc. S. Samuele
Calle d. Pestrin
CAMPIELLO DEI SQUELLINI
Calle Capeller
Calle Bernardo
Cà Rezzonico (Museo de Settecento Veneziano)
Sal. S. Samuele
CAMPO SAN ANGELO
Calle d. Botteghe
SAN SAMUELE
Calle. delle Carroze
Sal. Malipiero
S. Samuele
San Stefano
Net House
CAMPO SAN STEFANO
S. Barnaba
CÀ REZZONICO
Calle d. Teatro
Calle del Traghetto
Calle d. Spezier
Calle d. Casin
Calle del Cerchieri
Corte Sforza
CAMPO SAN VIDAL
CAMPO S. MAURIZIO
S. Maria o d. Giglio
Palazzo Pisani
Fond. Corner Zaguri
Calle d. Ostreghe
CAMPO S. MARIA ZOBENIGO
Palazzo Cavalli
CAMPO SAN VIDAL
Calle d. Toletta
U.K. Consulate
ACCADEMIA
Cà Grande
CAMPO DI CARITÀ
Ponte dell'Accademia
SANTA MARIA DEL GIGLIO
Fond. Meravigie
Cpl. d. Carità
Gallerie dell' Accademia
Canal Grande
Ponte del Sospiro
CAMPO SAN VIO
Calle large Nani
Rio Terrà d. Carità
Rio Terrà Antonio Foscarini
Piscina del Forner
Collezione P. Guggenheim
Calle d. Bastion
CAMPO SAN TROVASO
Fond. Nani
Squero Di San Trovaso
Piscina Venier
Fond. Venier
Calle d. Chiesa
Fond. Venier
F. Ospedaletto

ITALY

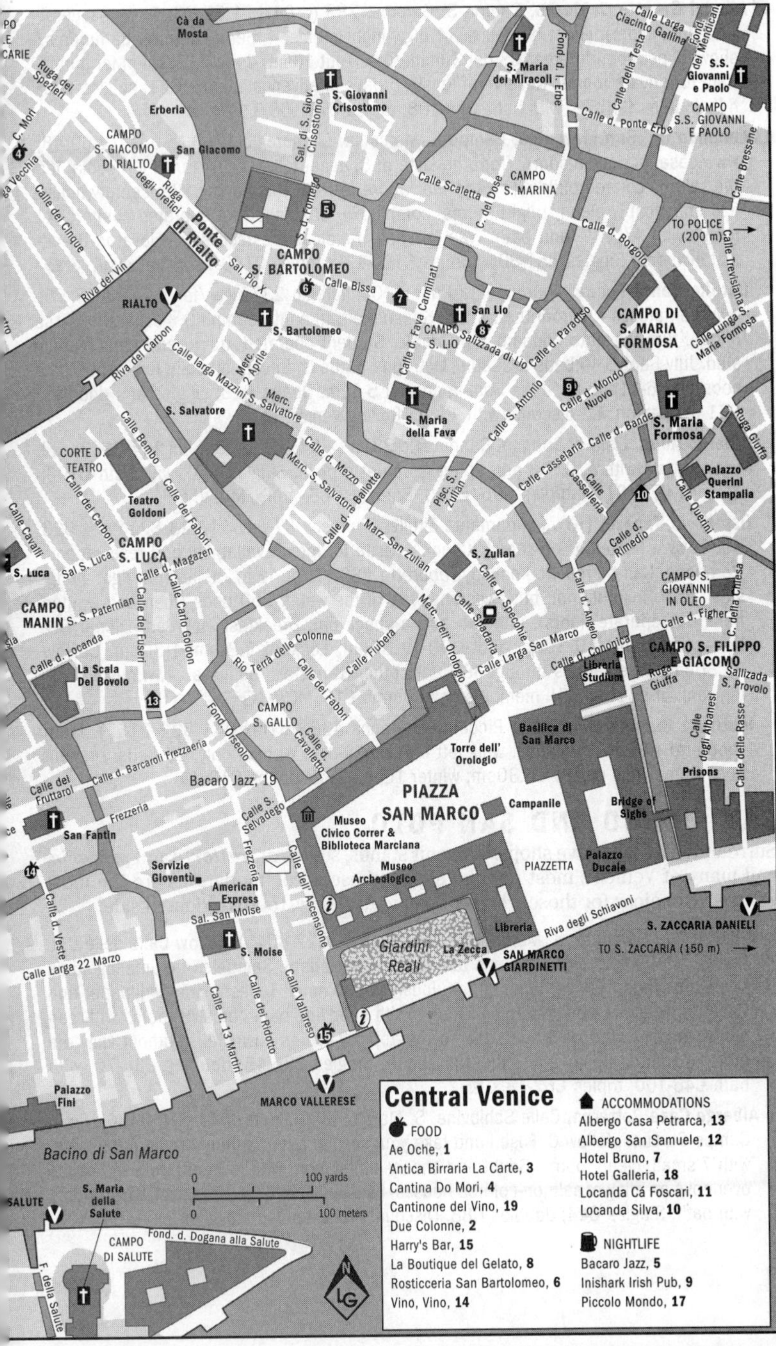
Cà da Mosta
Ruga del Speziali
C. Mori
Erberia
CAMPO S. GIACOMO DI RIALTO
San Giacomo
Ruga degli Orefici
Calle dei Cinque
Ponte di Rialto
Riva del Vin
RIALTO
Riva del Carbon
S. Giovanni Crisostomo
Sal. di S. Giov. Crisostomo
S. d. Fontego
CAMPO S. BARTOLOMEO
Sal. Pio X
Calle Bissa
S. Bartolomeo
S. Maria dei Miracoli
Fond. d. l. Erbe
Calle Larga Giacinto Gallina
Calle della Testa
Fond. dei Mendicanti
S.S. Giovanni e Paolo
CAMPO S.S. GIOVANNI E PAOLO
Calle d. Ponte Erbe
Calle Bressana
Calle Scaletta
C. del Dose
CAMPO S. MARINA
Calle d. Borgolo
TO POLICE (200 m)
Calle Trevisiana
CAMPO DI S. MARIA FORMOSA
Calle Lunga S. Maria Formosa
Calle d. Fava Carminati
CAMPO S. LIO
San Lio
Salizzada di Lio
Calle d. Paradiso
S. Maria della Fava
Calle S. Antonio
Calle d. Mondo Nuovo
Calle d. Bande
S. Maria Formosa
Ruga Giuffa
Palazzo Querini Stampalia
Calle Querini
Calle Casselaria
Calle Casselleria
Calle d. Rimedio
Calle larga Mazzini
Merc. 2 Aprile
Merc. S. Salvatore
S. Salvatore
Calle d. Mezzo
Calle d. Ballotte
Marz. San Zulian
Pisc. S. Zulian
S. Zulian
Calle d. Specchieri
Calle Spadaria
Merc. dell' Orologio
Calle Larga San Marco
Calle d. Angelo
Calle d. Canonica
Libreria Studium
CAMPO S. GIOVANNI IN OLEO
Calle d. Figher
C. della Chiesa
CAMPO S. FILIPPO E GIACOMO
Ruga Giuffa
Sallizada S. Provolo
Calle degli Albanesi
Calle delle Rasse
Prisons
Bridge of Sighs
Palazzo Ducale
Basilica di San Marco
Torre dell' Orologio
Campanile
PIAZZA SAN MARCO
PIAZZETTA
Museo Civico Correr & Biblioteca Marciana
Museo Archeologico
Libreria
La Zecca
Giardini Reali
Riva degli Schiavoni
S. ZACCARIA DANIELI
TO S. ZACCARIA (150 m)
SAN MARCO GIARDINETTI
CORTE D. TEATRO
Calle Bembo
Teatro Goldoni
Calle del Carbon
Calle dei Fabbri
Calle Cavalli
CAMPO S. LUCA
S. Luca
Sal S. Luca
Calle d. Magazen
CAMPO MANIN
S. S. Paternian
Calle dei Fuseri
Calle Carlo Goldon
Calle d. Locanda
La Scala Del Bovolo
Rio Terrà delle Colonne
Calle dei Fabbri
Calle Fiubera
CAMPO S. GALLO
Fond. Orseolo
Calle d. Cavalletto
Calle d. Barcaroli Frezzaria
Calle del Fruttarol
Bacaro Jazz, 19
Frezzeria
San Fantin
Calle S. Selvadego
Frezzeria
Calle dell' Ascensione
Servizie Gioventù
American Express
Sal. San Moise
S. Moise
Calle d. Veste
Calle Larga 22 Marzo
Calle d. 13 Martiri
Calle del Ridotto
Calle Vallaresso
Palazzo Fini
MARCO VALLERESE
Bacino di San Marco
0 100 yards
0 100 meters
S. Maria della Salute
SALUTE
CAMPO DI SALUTE
Fond. d. Dogana alla Salute
F. della Salute
LG
Central Venice
FOOD
Ae Oche, 1
Antica Birraria La Carte, 3
Cantina Do Mori, 4
Cantinone del Vino, 19
Due Colonne, 2
Harry's Bar, 15
La Boutique del Gelato, 8
Rosticceria San Bartolomeo, 6
Vino, Vino, 14
ACCOMMODATIONS
Albergo Casa Petrarca, 13
Albergo San Samuele, 12
Hotel Bruno, 7
Hotel Galleria, 18
Locanda Cá Foscari, 11
Locanda Silva, 10
NIGHTLIFE
Bacaro Jazz, 5
Inishark Irish Pub, 9
Piccolo Mondo, 17

ITALY

Alloggi Gerotto Calderan, Campo S. Geremia 283 (☎041 71 55 62; www.casagerottocalderan.com). Great bargains. 34 big, bright rooms. 4 clean common bathrooms/showers per floor. Internet €3 per 30min. Check-out 10am. Curfew 12:30am for dorms, 1am for private rooms. Reserve at least 15 days in advance. Dorms €21; singles €31-41; doubles €46-72, with bath €78-108; triples €78-108/€120. ❷

Locanda Ca' San Marcuola, Campo S. Marcuola, Cannaregio 1763 (☎041 71 60 48; www.casanmarcuola.com). From the Lista di Spagna, follow signs for S. Marcuola; it's the salmon-colored building next to the *vaporetto* stop. This homey 17th century house has impeccably clean, bright rooms, completely refurbished for supreme comfort. All rooms with A/C, TV, and bath. Free Internet. Handicapped-accessible elevator. Breakfast included. Singles €51-80; doubles €100-130; triples €140-180. AmEx/MC/V. ❹

Ostello Santa Fosca, Fondamenta Canale, Cannaregio 2372 (☎/fax 041 71 57 75; www.santafosca.it). From the Lista di Spagna left, turn into Campo S. Fosca. Cross 1st bridge, turn left onto Fondamenta Canale. Student operated, quiet, and church-affiliated. July-Sept. 140 beds available; Oct.-June 31 beds. Reception daily July-Sept. 7am-noon and 6-11pm; Oct-June 8am-noon and 5-8pm. Dorms €18; singles and doubles, €21 per person. €2 discount with ISIC or Rolling Venice. ❷

Albergo Adua, Lista di Spagna, Cannaregio 233a (☎041 71 61 84; fax 244 0162). 22 basic rooms with A/C, TV, and phone come at a price. Singles €70, with bath €100; doubles €78/€114; triples €95/€150. Breakfast €6. AmEx/MC/V. ❹

Ostello di Venezia (HI), Fondamenta Zitelle, Giudecca 87 (☎041 523 8211; fax 523 5689; www.hostelbooking.com). Check website for room availability and reservations. No phone. Can be reached only by *vaporetto* #82, 41 or 42 to Zitelle. Turn right alongside canal. Institutional, but sweeping view of the water. 250 beds (men and women bunk on separate floors), Internet, and a snack bar. Breakfast included. Dinner €8. Reception daily 7-9:30am and 1:30-11:30pm. Lockout 9:30am-1:30pm. Curfew 11:30pm. Reservations through IBN from other HI hostels, online at www.hostelbooking.com, or by phone. HI members only. Dorms €16. MC/V. ❷

Instituto Cannosiano, Ponte Piccolo, Giudecca 428 (☎/fax 041 522 2157). From *vaporetto* #82, 41: Palanca, walk left over the bridge. Women only. 35 beds. Lockout noon-3pm. Strict curfew 10:30pm; winter 10pm. Large dorms €13. ❶

ITALY

SAN MARCO AND SAN POLO

Surrounded by exclusive shops, souvenir stands, scores of *trattorie* and *pizzerie*, and many of Venice's most popular sights, these accommodations are the most expensive choices for those who seek Venice's showy, tourist-oriented side.

Albergo San Samuele, S. Marco, 3358 (☎/fax 041 522 8045). Follow Calle delle Botteghe from Campo S. Stefano and turn left on Salizzada S. Samuele. A crumbling stone courtyard leads to this charming, fabulously priced hotel. Tapestry-print wallpaper and Italian art decorate colorful, clean rooms with sparkling bathrooms. 8 rooms with gorgeous balcony view of S. Marco's red roof-tops. 2 rooms downstairs without view are more spacious. Reserve 1-2 months ahead. Singles €26-45; doubles €36-70, with bath €46-100; triples €62-135. ❸

Albergo Casa Petrarca, Calle Schiavine, S. Marco, 4386 (☎/fax 041 520 0430). From Campo St. Luca, follow C. Fuseri and take your second left and then a right. A tiny hotel with 7 small, clean rooms. Bright and cheery sitting room with rows of books in English overlooks an alley of salmon-colored houses. Fans in each room. Breakfast €7. 4 rooms with bath. Singles €44; doubles €88. Discounts for extended stays. ❹

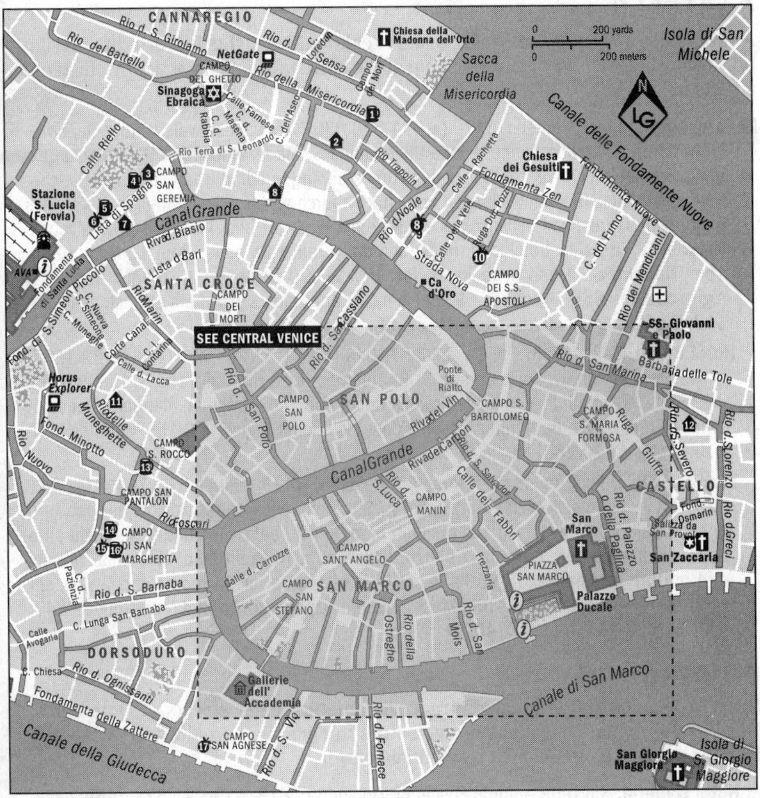

Venice

ACCOMMODATIONS
- Albergo Adua, **7**
- Allogi Gerotto Calderan, **3**
- Domus Civica (ASISJF), **11**
- Foresteria Valdese, **12**
- Locanda San Marcuola, **8**
- Ostello Santa Fosca, **2**

FOOD
- Gelateria Nico, **17**
- Pizza al Volo, **15**
- Ristorante Brek, **6**
- Standa Supermarket, **9**
- Trattoria da Bepi, **10**

NIGHTLIFE
- Bar Santa Lucia, **4**
- Café Blue, **13**
- Casanova, **5**
- Duchamp, **16**
- Il Caffé, **14**
- Paradiso Perduto, **1**

Domus Civica (ACISJF), Campiello Chiovere Frari, S. Polo, 3082 (☎041 72 11 03; fax 522 7139). From the station, cross the Scalzi Bridge and turn right. Turn left on Fondamenta dei Tolentini, then left through the courtyard onto Corte Amai. The hostel is the building with the rounded facade on the right, directly after the bridge. Simple student housing. 75 beds, TV room, and piano. Check-in 7:30am-2pm. Strict curfew 11:30pm. Open mid-June to Sept. Singles €28.50, Rolling Venice and ISIC €23; doubles and triples €26/€21. ❸

CASTELLO

A room with a view of red rooftops and breakthtaking sights is worth the inevitability of losing your way amongst some of the narrowest and most tightly clustered streets in Venice.

Foresteria Valdesi, Castello, 5170 (☎041 528 6797; www.chiesavaldese.org/venezia). From Campo S. Maria Formosa take Calle Lunga S. Maria. Housed in the Palazzo Cavagnis, immediately over the 1st bridge. This stunning building was once the 18th-century guest house of Venice's largest Protestant church and is a 2min. walk from Venice's major sights. Frescoed ceilings grace the dorms (with 33 beds) and the private rooms (all with TV). Breakfast included. Reception daily 9am-1pm and 6-8pm. Lockout 10am-1pm. No curfew. Closed 3 weeks in Nov. Dorms €20 first night, €19 each additional night; doubles €54-70; quads €98. Also has 2 apartments with bath and kitchen €99-110. €1 Rolling Venice discount. MC/V. ❷

Hotel Bruno, Salizzada S. Lio, Castello, 5726/A (☎041 523 0452; fax 041 522 1157; www.hoteldabruno.it). From Campo S. Bartolomeo, take the Salizzada S. Lio, crossing the bridge. Beautiful high-ceilinged rooms decorated in the original, elaborate Venetian style. All rooms with bath and A/C. Breakfast included. Singles €60-155; doubles €80-210; triples €120-260. MC/V. ❺

Locanda Silva, Fondamenta del Rimedio, Castello, 4423 (☎041 522 7643; fax 041 528 6817; albergosilva@libero.it). From P. S. Marco, walk under clock tower and turn right on Calle Larga S. Marco and then left on d. Angelo before the bridge and right onto Calle d. Rimedio before the next bridge. Follow straight to the end. This hotel with its odd mixture of Asian and 1950's decor has 24 sparse, clean rooms and 2 resident cats. All rooms with phone. Breakfast included. Open Feb. to mid-Nov. Singles €47; doubles €78-104; triples €140. ❹

ITALY

DORSODURO

Spartan facades and still canals trace the quieter, wider streets of Dorsoduro. Here, numerous art museums draw visitors to canal-front real estate, while the interior remains a little-visited residential quarter.

Hotel Galleria, Rio Terra Antonio Foscarini, Dorsoduro, 878/A (☎041 523 2489; galleria@tin.it; www.hotelgalleria.it), on the left as you face the Accademia museum. Sumptuous oriental rugs and tasteful art prints lend the Galleria an elegance appropriate to its location on the Grand Canal. Stunning views in some of the 10 rooms compensate for their small size. Breakfast, served in rooms, included. Singles €62; doubles €88-135. Extra bed 30% more. AmEx/MC/V. ❺

Locanda Ca' Foscari, Calle della Frescada, Dorsoduro, 3887b (☎041 71 04 01; valtersc@tin.it), in a quiet neighborhood near the *vaporetto*. From *vaporetto:* "San Tomà," turn left at the dead end, cross the bridge, turn right, and then take a left into the little alleyway. Murano glass chandeliers and Venetian Carnival masks embellish this simple hotel operated by a warm older couple. Breakfast included. Curfew 1am. Book 2 or 3 months in advance. Closed 1st wk. of Aug, and end of Nov.-Jan. 1. Singles €60; doubles €70-90; triples €87-110; quads €108-130. MC/V. ❹

CAMPING

If camping, plan on a 20min. boat ride to Venice. In addition to these listings, the **Litorale del Cavallino,** on the Lido's Adriatic side, has endless beach campsites.

Camping Miramare, Lungomare Dante Alighieri 29 (☎041 96 61 50; www.camping-miramare.it). A 40min. boat ride (*vaporetto* #14) from P. S. Marco to "Punta Sabbioni." Campground is 700m along the beach to your right. 3-night min. stay in high-season.

Open mid-Mar. to Dec. €3.60-5.85 per person, €3.25-14.20 per tent. Bungalows €23.20-58.50. 15% Rolling Venice discount. ❶

Camping Fusina, V. Moranzani 79 (☎041 547 0055; www.camping-fusina.com), in Malcontenta. From Mestre, take bus #1. Call ahead. €6 per person, €8-13 per tent and car, €11 to sleep in car. ❶

FOOD

In Venice, dining well on a budget requires exploration. The best and most affordable restaurants are hidden in the less-traveled alleyways. For an inexpensive and informal option, visit any *osteria* or *bacario* in town for the chance to create a meal from the vast array of meat- and cheese-filled pastries, tidbits of seafood, rice, meat, and *tramezzini* (triangular slices of soft white bread with every imaginable filling). These tasty treats are known as **cicchetti** and cost about €1.30-2.60. The key ingredients of Venetian cuisine come fresh from the sea. *Spaghetti al vongole* (pasta with fresh clams and spicy vegetables) is served on nearly every menu. Good local wines include the sparkling *prosecco della Marca* white wine or the red *valpolicella*. **STANDA supermarket,** Strada Nuova, Cannaregio 3650, near Campo S. Felice, has a large grocery store in the back, behind the clothing. (Open M-Sa 8:30am-7:20pm, Su 9am-7:20pm.)

RESTAURANTS

Trattoria da Bepi, Cannaregio 4550 (☎041 528 5031; fax 041 241 7245). From Campo SS. Apostoli, turn left onto Salizzade del Pistor. Traditional Venetian restaurant with copper pots dangling from the ceiling. Huge bread baskets and authentic cuisine. *Primi* €7-10.50, *secondi* €9.50-18. Open F-W noon-2:30pm, 7-10pm. MC/V. ❸

Ristorante Brek, Lista di Spagna, Cannaregio 124A (☎041 244 0158). From the station, turn left. Italian fast food chain whips up fresh pasta and salad dishes from an extensive aray of ingredients that you pick out. Perfect for a cheap meal on the go. Menu and prices change daily. Most items €2-8. Open daily 11:30am-10:30pm. ❷

Vino, Vino, Ponte delle Veste, S. Marco 2007a (☎041 241 7688). From Calle Larga XXII Marzo, turn onto Calle delle Veste. Dark, no-frills wine bar has over 350 varieties of wine. Seafood-focused menu changes daily. *Primi* €5, *secondi* €9. Cover €1. Open W-M 10:30am-midnight. Sa open till 1am. 15% Rolling Venice discount. ❸

Rosticceria San Bartomoleo, Calle della Bissa, S. Marco 5424/A (☎041 522 3569). Offers a smorgasbord of sandwiches, pasta, and *cicchetti* to be enjoyed on the go or while seated at a window booth. The full-service restaurant upstairs is open for lunch. Entrees start €4.90. Cover €1.30. Open Tu-Su 9:30am-9:30pm. AmEx/MC/V. ❶

Harry's Bar, Calle Vallaresso, S. Marco 1323 (☎041 528 5777). Around the corner from the Venice Pavilion. This cafe pours pricey drinks to tourists and such notables as Ernest Hemingway, Catherine Hepburn, Robert Deniro, and Tom Cruise. *Bellini* €13. Service 15%. Open daily 10:30am-10:55pm. MC/V. ❹

Pizza al Volo, Campo S. Margherita, Dorsoduro 2944 (☎041 522 5430). Serves delicious, cheap pizza. The tasty house specialty is a sauceless pie topped with mozzarella, *grado,* and eggplant. Slices start at €1.30. Large pizzas start at €3.40. Take-out only. Open daily 11:30am-4pm and 5:30pm-1:30am. ❶

Cantinone del Vino, Fondamente Meraviglie, Dorsoduro 992 (☎041 523 0034). A spectacular display of wines, featured in *Gourmet Magazine,* line the walls (€3-€200 per bottle). Enjoy a glass at the bar with some *cichetti* (starting at €1). Open M-Sa 8am-2:30pm and 3:15-8:30pm. ❷

Ae Oche, Santa Croce, 1552a/b (☎041 524 1161). From Campo S. Giacomo da L'Orio, take Calle del Trentor. Join all the Venetians at their local hangout. Choose from 100 different types of huge pizzas (€4-7). Open daily noon-3pm and 7pm-midnight. ❷

Antica Birraria La Carte, Campo S. Polo, S. Polo 2168 (☎041 275 0570). This restuarant is the site of a lively scene of students and native Venetians. Musicians play nightly on their accordians just outside. Beer €1.50-4.30, pizzas €4-8. Open Tu-Su noon-3pm and 6pm-midnight. AmEx/MC/V. ❷

Due Colonne, Campo S. Agostin, S. Polo 2343 (☎041 524 0685). Students, families, and tourists crowd the large indoor booths and the *campo* seating to sample the variety of pizzas (€3.50-7.50). Cover €0.80. Service 10%. Closed Aug. Open M-Sa 8am-3pm and 7-11pm. Kitchen closes 10pm. ❶

Cantina Do Mori, Calle due Mori, S. Polo, 429 (☎041 522 5401). Venice's oldest wine bar may be a tourist attraction, but it is still an elegant place to grab a a few *cicchetti* (from €1.50) or a superb glass of local wine. No seating. Open M-Sa 9am-9pm. ❷

GELATERIE

La Boutique del Gelato, Salizzada S. Lio, Castello, 5727 (☎041 522 3283). From Campo Bartolomeo, walk under the Sotoportego de la Bissa, go straight, cross the bridge into Campo S. Lio. Follow Salizada S. Lio; it is on the left. Large cones with the cheapest prices. Single scoop €0.80. Open daily 10am-8pm.

Gelateria Nico, Fondamenta Zattere, Dorsoduro, 922 (☎041 522 5293). Near *vaporetto*: "Zattere" with a great view of the Giudecca Canal. Gelato €0.80-6.50. Try the Venetian specialty *gianduiotto al passagetto* (a slice of dense chocolate-hazelnut ice cream dunked in whipped cream, €2.30). Open daily 6:45am-11pm.

SIGHTS

AROUND THE RIALTO BRIDGE

CANAL GRANDE. The Canal Grande loops through Venice and the splendid facades of the *palazzi* that crown its banks testify to the city's history of immense wealth. Although their external decorations vary, the palaces share the same basic structure. A **nighttime tour** reveals the startling beauty of the *palazzi*. *(Vaporetto #82 or 1 to P.S. Marco.)*

PONTE DI RIALTO. The Ponte di Rialto (1588-91) arches over the Canal Grande and symbolizes Venice's commercial past. Antonio da Ponte created this image that graces postcards throughout the city. *(Vaporetto: Rialto.)*

CHIESA DI SAN GIACOMO DI RIALTO. Between the Ponte di Rialto and the markets stands Venice's first church, diminutively called "San Giacometto." The bent stone statue was once the finish line for convicted thieves after they had run naked from P.S. Marco and were lashed all the way by bystanders. *(Vaporetto: Rialto. Cross the bridge and head right. Open daily 10am-5pm. Free.)*

AROUND PIAZZA SAN MARCO

BASILICA DI SAN MARCO. The interior of this glittering church sparkles with both 13th-century Byzantine and 16th-century Renaissance mosaics. Behind the altar screen is the **Pala D'Oro,** a gem-encrusted relief covering the tomb of Saint Mark. To the right of the altar is the **tesoro** (treasury), a hoard of gold and relics from the Fourth Crusade. Steep stairs in the atrium lead to the **Galleria della Basilica,** which offers a staggering perspective on the interior mosaics, a tranquil vista of the exterior *piazza*, and an intimate view of the original bronze *Horses of St.*

Mark. St. Mark's is worth the long lines; try to time your visit for the shortest wait, in the early morning, or best natural illumination of the mosaics at dusk. *(Basilica open daily 9:30am-4:30pm. Illuminated 11:30am-12:30pm. Dress code enforced; shoulders and knees must be covered. Free. Pala D'Oro open daily 9:45am-5pm. €1.50. Treasury open M-Sa 9:45am-5pm, €2. Galleria open daily 9:45am-5pm. €1.50.)*

PALAZZO DUCALE (DOGE'S PALACE). Once the home of Venice's mayor, or *doge*, the Palazzo Ducale now houses one of Venice's best museums—its collection combines historical artifacts with spectacular artwork. Within the palace lie the *doge*'s private apartments and the magnificent state rooms of the Republic. Climb the richly decorated **Scala d'Oro** (Golden Staircase) to reach the Sala del Maggior Consiglio (Great Council Room), dominated by Tintoretto's *Paradise*, the largest oil painting in the world. Passages lead through the courtrooms of the much-feared **Council of Ten** and the even-more-feared **Council of Three,** crossing the **Ponte dei Sospiri** (Bridge of Sighs) and continuing into the prisons. *(☎041 520 9070; mkt.musei@comune.venezia.it. Open Nov.-Apr. daily 9am-3:30pm, Apr.-Oct. 9am-5:30pm. €9.50, student €5.50, ages 6-14 €3. Includes entrance to Museo Correr, Biblioteca Nazionale Marciana, Museo Archeologico, Museo di Palazzo Mocenigo, Museo del Vetro di Murano, and Museo del Merletto di Burano. Pass for above museums and Casa Rezzonico and Casa di Goldoni €15.50, students €10. Audio guides €5.50. Wheelchair accessible.)*

PIAZZA SAN MARCO. In contrast to the narrow, labyrinthine streets that wind through most of Venice, P.S. Marco (Venice's only official *piazza*) is a magnificent expanse of light and space. Enclosing the *piazza* are the unadorned 16th-century Renaissance **Procuratie Vecchie (Old Treasury Offices),** the more ornate 17th-century Baroque **Procuratie Nuove (New Treasury Offices),** and the smaller Neoclassical **Ala Napoleonica,** sometimes called the *Procuratie Nuovissime* (Really New Treasury Offices), which Napoleon constructed when he took the city in 1797. The brick **campanile** (96m) across the *piazza* stands on Roman foundations. *(Campanile open daily 9am-9pm. €6. Audioguide for 1 €3, for 2 €4.)*

CHIESA DI SAN ZACCARIA. Dedicated to the father of John the Baptist and designed by (among others) Coducci in the late 1400s, this Gothic-Renaissance church holds one of the masterpieces of Venetian Renaissance painting, **Giovanni Bellini's** *Virgin and Child Enthroned with Four Saints. (Vaporetto: S. Zaccaria. From P.S. Marco, turn left along the water, cross the bridge, and turn left on Calle Albanesi. Take a right and go straight. ☎041 522 1257. Open daily 10am-noon and 4-6pm. Free.)*

> **!** **MINI-SKIRTS, MINI-PASSES, AND MINI-DISCOUNTS** Mini-skirts are verboten in many Venetian churches, which enforce a strict dress code that calls for the coverage of shoulders and knees. Mini-passes to visit Venice's churches are sold by the Foundation for the Churches of Venice. A three-day mini-pass (€8, students €5) for all 15 of Venice's churches, including S. Maria dei Miracoli, S. Maria Gloriosa dei Frari, S. Polo, Madonna dell'Orto, Il Redentore, and S. Sebastiano, is available at all participating churches (except S. Maria Gloriosa dei Frari). For information call ☎275 0462.

SAN POLO

BASILICA DI SANTA MARIA GLORIOSA DEI FRARI (I FRARI). Within the cavernous brick walls of this church rest outstanding paintings by masters of the Renaissance. **Titian**'s *Assumption* (1516-18) on the high altar marks the height of the Venetian Renaissance. In the Florentine chapel to the right is Donatello's *St. John the Baptist* (1438), a wooden Renaissance sculpture. *(Vaporetto: S. Tomà. Follow signs back to Campo dei Frari. Open M-Sa 9am-6pm, Su 1-6pm. €2.)*

ITALY

THE LOCAL STORY

UNREAL RELICS?

Dr. Luigi Garlaschelli is an organic chemist at the University of Pavia who investigates the authenticity of religious blood relics in his spare time.

LG: Can you explain the ubiquitousness of relics in Italian churches?

Dr. LG: In the Middle Ages, it was believed that they would protect the city from its enemies. [Relics include] the last breath of St. Joseph, the feather of the Archangel Michael, the milk of the Virgin Mary, and the fingernails and blood of Christ.

LG: What was your first project?

Dr. LG: My first work was on the blood of St. Januarius, which is contained in a small vial kept in the duomo in Naples. Saint Januarius was beheaded in 305 AD. The relic only appeared in the Middle Ages, 1000 years later, contemporary to the appearance of the shroud of Turin. Normally blood taken from a living body will clot only once; the "miracle" of this blood is that it turns from solid to liquid and back again twice a year during religious ceremonies.

LG: How does that work?

Dr. LG: Well, using only ferric chloride (an iron salt), which exists naturally near active volcanoes (like Vesuvius, near Naples, active at the time of the discovery of the blood), calcium carbonate (for example, crushed eggshells), kitchen salt, and techniques available in the Middle Ages, we were able to make a substance of the same color and properties as the reputed blood of St. Januarius. The matter would be closed were we to open the vial and take a sample. But, of course, the vial is sealed.

See http://chifis.unipv.it/garlaschelli for more information on Dr. Garlaschelli's research.

SCUOLA GRANDE DI SAN ROCCO. Venice's most illustrious *scuola*, or guild hall, stands as a monument to painter Jacopo Tintoretto. The *scuola* commissioned Tintoretto to complete all of the building's paintings, a task that took 23 years. *(Behind Basilica dei Frari in Campo S. Rocco. ☎523 4864. Open Nov.-Mar. M-F 10am-1pm, Sa-Su 10am-4pm. €5.50, students €3.75. Audioguides free.)*

DORSODURO

GALLERIE DELL'ACCADEMIA. The Accademia houses the most extensive collection of Venetian art in the world. At the top of the double staircase, **Room I,** topped by a ceiling full of cherubim, houses Venetian Gothic art, with a luxurious use of color that influenced Venetian painting for centuries. Among the enormous altarpieces in **Room II,** Giovanni Bellini's *Madonna Enthroned with Child, Saints, and Angels* stands out for its lush serenity. **Rooms IV** and **V** display more Bellinis and **Giorgione's** enigmatic *La Tempesta*. On the opposite wall is Titian's last painting, a brooding *Pietà*. In **Room XX,** works by Gentile Bellini and Carpaccio display Venetian processions and cityscapes so accurately that scholars use them as "photos" of Venice's past. *(Vaporetto: Accademia. ☎522 2247. Open M 8:15am-2pm, T-Su 9:15am-7:15pm. €6.50. Guided tours free for group.)*

COLLEZIONE PEGGY GUGGENHEIM. Ms. Guggenheim's Palazzo Venier dei Leoni now displays works by Brancusi, Marini, Kandinsky, Picasso, Magritte, Rothko, Ernst, Pollock, and Dalí. The Marini sculpture *Angel in the City*, in front of the *palazzo*, was designed with a detachable penis. Ms. Guggenheim occasionally modified this sculpture so as not to offend her more prudish guests. *(Calle S. Cristoforo, Dorsoduro, 710. Vaporetto: Accademia. Turn left and follow the yellow signs. ☎240 5411. Open Su-M and W-F 10am-6pm, Sa 10am-10pm. €8, under 12 free. Audio guides €4.)*

CHIESA DI SANTA MARIA DELLA SALUTE. The dramatically designed **Salute,** poised at the tip of Dorsoduro, is a prime example of the Venetian Baroque. Next to the Salute stands the **Dogana,** the old customs house, where ships sailing into Venice were required to stop and pay appropriate duties. Stand at the doors for a marvelous view of the city. *(Vaporetto: Salute. ☎522 5558. Open daily 9am-noon and 3-5:30pm. The Dogana is closed to the public. Free. Entrance to sacristy with donation.)*

CHIESA DI SAN SEBASTIANO. The painter Veronese hid here when he fled Verona in 1555 after reputedly killing a man, and filled the church with some of his finest works. His breathtaking *Stories of Queen Esther* covers the ceiling. *(Vaporetto: S. Basilio. Open M-Sa 10am-5pm, Su 3-5pm. €2.)*

CASTELLO

CHIESA DI SANTISSIMI GIOVANNI E PAOLO (SAN ZANIPOLO). This immense church is the final resting place of 25 *doges*, with monuments to them and other honored citizens lining the walls. Outside stands the bronze **statue of Bartolomeo Colleoni,** a mercenary who left his inheritance to the city on the condition that a monument to him be erected in front of S. Marco. The city, unwilling to honor him in such a grand space, decided to pull a fast one and place the statue in front of the Scuola di San Marco. *(Vaporetto: Fond. Nuove. Turn left and then right onto Fond. dei Mendicanti. ☎523 5913. Open M-Sa 7:30am-12:30pm and 3:30-7pm, Su 3-6pm. Free)*

CHIESA DI SANTA MARIA DEI MIRACOLI. Among the most stunning Venetian churches, this Renaissance jewel was designed by the Lombardos in the late 1400s. *(From S.S. Giovanni e Paolo, cross Ponte Rosse. Open M-Sa 10am-5pm, Su 1-5pm. €2.)*

SCUOLA DALMATA SAN GIORGIO DEGLI SCHIAVONI. Between 1502 and 1511, Carpaccio decorated the ground floor with some of his finest paintings, depicting episodes from the lives of Saint George, Jerome, and Tryfon. *(Castello, 3259/A. Vaporetto: S. Zaccaria. From the Riva Schiavoni, take Calle Dose up to C. Bandiera e Moro. Follow it to S. Antonin to Fon. Furlani. Open Tu-Sa 9:30am-12:30pm and 3:30-6:30pm, Su 9:30am-12:30pm. Shoulders and knees must be covered. €2.)*

GIARDINI PUBLICI AND SANT'ELENA. Longing for trees and grass? Stroll through the Public Gardens, installed by Napoleon, or bring a picnic lunch to the shady lawns of Sant'Elena. *(Vaporetto: Giardini or S. Elena. Free.)*

CANNAREGIO

JEWISH GHETTO. In 1516 the *doge* forced Venice's Jewish population into the old cannon-foundry area, creating the first Jewish ghetto in Europe; the word "ghetto" is the Venetian word for "foundry." The oldest synagogue, the **Schola Grande Tedesca** (German Synagogue), shares a building with the **Museo Ebraica di Venezia** (Hebrew Museum of Venice) in the Campo del Ghetto Nuovo. *(Cannaregio, 2899/B. Vaporetto: S. Marcuola. Follow the signs straight ahead and then turn left into Campo del Ghetto Nuovo. ☎041 71 53 59. Hebrew Museum open June-Sept. Su-F 10am-7pm. €3, students €2. Entrance to synagogue by guided tour only (40min). English tours leave from the museum every hr. from 10:30am-4:30om. Museum and tour €8, students €6.50.)*

CÀ D'ORO AND GALLERIA GIORGIO FRANCHETTI. The most spectacular facade on the Canal Grande and the premiere example of Venetian Gothic, the Cà d'Oro, built between 1425 and 1440, now houses the Giorgio Franchetti collection. For the best view of the palace, take the *traghetto* across the canal to the Rialto Markets. *(Vaporetto: Ca' d'Oro. ☎523 8790. Open M-Su 9am-2pm. €3.50.)*

GIUDECCA AND SAN GIORGIO MAGGIORE

BASILICA DI SAN GIORGIO MAGGIORE. Standing on its own monastic island, S. Giorgio Maggiore contrasts sharply with most other Venetian churches. Palladio ignored the Venetian fondness for color and decorative excess, and constructed an austere church of simple dignity. Ascend the elevator to the top of the **campanile** for a breathtaking view. *(Vaporetto: S. Giorgio Maggiore. ☎041 522 7827. Open M-Sa 10am-12:30pm and 2:30-4:30pm. Basilica free. Campanile €3. Pay the Brother in the elevator.)*

ISLANDS OF THE LAGOON

BURANO. In this traditional fishing village, fishermen haul in their catch every morning as their wives, black-clad, sit in the doorways of the fantastically colored houses, creating unique knots of Venetian lace. See their handiwork in the small-lace museum, the Scuola di Merletti di Burano. *(A 40min. boat ride from Venice. Vaporetto #12: Burano from either S. Zaccaria or Fond. Nuove. Museum in P. Galuppi. ☎ 73 00 34. Open W-M 10am-5pm. €4. Included on combined Palazzo Ducale ticket or full museum pass.)*

MURANO. Famous for its glass since 1292, the island of Murano affords visitors the opportunity to witness the glass-blowing process. The **Museo Vetrario** (Glass Museum) houses a splendid collection that includes pieces from Roman times. Farther down the street is the 12th-century **Basilica di Santa Maria e San Donato.** *(Vaporetto #12 or 52: Faro from S. Zaccaria. Museo Vetrario, Fond. Giustian 8. ☎ 041 73 95 86. Open Th-Tu 10am-5pm. €5, students €3. Basilica ☎ 73 90 56. Open daily 8am-noon and 4-7pm.)*

TORCELLO. Torcello boasts a lovely cathedral, **Santa Maria Assunta,** which contains 11th- and 12th-century mosaics of the Last Judgment and the Virgin Mary. *(A 45min. boat ride from Venice. Vaporetto #12: Torcello from either S. Zaccaria or Fond. Nuove. Cathedral ☎ 041 73 00 84. Open daily 10:30am-12:30pm and 2-6:30pm. €2.)*

LIDO. The Lido is now mostly a summer beach town, complete with cars, blaring radios, and beach bums. Head for the **public beach,** which features an impressive shipwreck at the southern end. *(Vaporetto: Lido.)*

ISOLA DI SAN MICHELE. Venice's cemetery island, marked by the first Renaissance church in Venice, is the resting place of poet Ezra Pound, composer Igor Stravinsky, and Russian choreographer Sergei Diaghilev. *(Vaporetto: Cimitero.)*

NIGHTLIFE

The weekly booklet, **A Guest in Venice** (free at hotels and tourist offices or online at www.unospitedivenezia.it), lists current festivals, concerts, and gallery shows. The famed **Biennale di Venezia,** a world-wide contemporary art exhibition, covers the *Giardini Publici* and the Arsenal in provocative international art every odd-numbered year. (☎ 241 1058; www.labiennale.org.) Venice's famous **Carnevale** draws masked figures and camera-happy tourists during the 10 days before Ash Wednesday, doubling the city's population by Mardi Gras.

Venetian nightlife is quieter and more relaxed than other major Italian cities. **P. S. Marco** is always a favorite destination from which to hear string quartets. For most locals, nighttime action means an evening spent sipping wine or beer rather than gyrating in a disco. But Venice does have a few hot dance spots. Student nightlife is concentrated around **Campo Santa Margherita** in Dorsoduro and the areas around the **Lista di Spagna** in Cannaregio.

Paradiso Perduto, Fondamenta della Misericordia 2540 (☎ 041 72 05 81). From Strada Nuova, cross Campo S. Fosca, cross bridge, and continue in same direction, crossing 2 more bridges. Students and locals flood this unassuming bar with conversation and laughter, while the young, casually dressed waitstaff doles out large portions of *cichetti* (mixed plate, €11.36). Live jazz Su 9pm. Open Th-Su 7pm-2am.

Piccolo Mondo, Accademia, Dorsoduro 1056/A (☎ 041 520 0371). With your back to the canal, facing the Accademia, turn right and follow the street around. Join in with the dance-happy students, locals, and tourists at this small but pumping *discotecca* where such notables as Shaquille O'Neil and Prince Albert of Monaco have strutted their stuff. Mick Jagger comes to visit every year when he's in town. No cover. Mixed drinks start at €7. Open nightly 10pm-4am. AmEx/MC/V.

Duchamp, C. Santa Margherita 3019 (☎041 528 6255). Lively place with students and tourists noisily congregating. Outdoor seating. Beer €4.30 for a pint. Wine €1.10. Open nightly 9pm-2am, Sa 5pm-2am.

Casanova, Lista di Spagna, Cannaregio 158/A (☎041 275 0199; www.casanova.it). There's always plenty of room on the floor for the tourists and locals to dance to the perpetual strobe light and beats of house and techno music at Casanova. But dance lovers make up for the lack of numbers with their enthusiasm, staying long into the night until closing. Open daily 10pm-4am. Cover €10 F-Sa includes 1 drink. AmEx/MC/V.

Inishark Irish Pub, Calle Mondo Novo, Castello 5787 (☎041 523 5300). Off C. S. Maria Formosa. Most creative Irish pub in Venice, with themed decorations. Guinness €4.65, Harp €4.50. Open Tu-Su 6pm-1:30am.

Il Caffè, C. Santa Margherita, Dorsoduro 2963 (☎041 528 7998). Music pumps at the door and people are stuffed inside of this tiny, non-descript bar. Outdoor seating. Wine €0.80, beer €1.36. Open M-Sa 8am-2am.

Bacaro Jazz, C.S. Bartolmeo, S. Marco 5546 (☎041 528 5249). From post office, follow red lights and sounds of jazz across the street. At this chic restaurant and evening haunt, 20- and 30-somethings share big, expensive plates of *cicchetti* (€13). Jazz paraphernalia lines wood-paneled walls. Drinks are more affordable during Happy Hour (3-7pm), when you get two drinks for the price of one. Open Th-Tu 11am-2am.

Café Blue, S. Pantalon, Dorsoduro 5778 (☎041 71 02 27). From S. Maria Frari, take Calle Scalater and turn right at the end. Bright, noisy, and crowded American bar with droves of expats and exchange students. Free email kiosk. Afternoon tea in winter 3:30-7:30pm. Bar open M-Sa 9:30pm-2am, all drinks half price 8:30-9:30pm.

Bar Santa Lucia, Lista di Spagna, Cannareggio 282/B (☎041 524 2880), near the train station. This tiny bar stays crowded and noisy long into the night with American travelers and the locals who want to meet them. Good selection of Irish beers. Pint of Guinness €5. Wine €2.10. Open M-Sa 6pm-2am.

PADUA (PADOVA) ☎049

Book-toting students walk through sculpture-lined *piazze* in Padua, epitomizing the city's unique blend of ancient and modern culture. The **Cappella degli Scrovegni** (Arena Chapel), P. Eremitani 8, contains Giotto's breathtaking 38-panel fresco cycle, illustrating the lives of Mary, Jesus, and Mary's parents. Buy tickets at the adjoining **Musei Civici Eremitani,** which features a restored Giotto crucifix. (☎049 820 45 50. Open Feb.-Oct. Tu-Su 9am-7pm; Nov.-Jan. Tu-Su 9am-6pm. Chapel open Feb.-Dec. daily 9am-7pm. €9, students €4.) Thousands of pilgrims are drawn to Saint Anthony's jawbone and well-preserved tongue at the **Basilica di Sant'Antonio,** in P. del Santo, a medieval conglomeration of eight domes filled with beautiful frescoes. (Dress code enforced. Open daily Apr.-Sept. 6:30am-8pm; Nov.-Mar. daily 6:30am-7pm. €2.) From the basilica, follow signs to V. Orto Botanico 15, for **Orto Botanico,** which tempts visitors with water lilies, medicinal herbs, and a 417-year-old palm tree that still offers shade. (☎049 65 66 14. Open daily 9am-1pm and 3-6pm; in winter M-F 9am-1pm. €2.60, students €1.55.) Next to the **duomo,** in P. Duomo, lies the 12th-century **Battistero,** the jewel of Padua, with a dome of highly concentrated frescoes. (☎049 66 28 14. Open M-Sa 7:30am-noon and 3:45-7:45pm, Su 7:45am-1pm and 3:45-8:30pm. €2.50, students €1.50.) Ancient university buildings are scattered throughout the city, centered in **Palazzo Bó.** For nighttime action, **Lucifer Young,** V. Altinate 89, near the university, is a hip young bar. (☎049 66 55 31. Open Su-Tu and Th 7pm-2am, F-Sa 7pm-4am.)

Trains depart from P. Stazione for: Bologna (1½hr., 1-2 per hr., €6); Milan (2½hr., 1-2 per hr., €17); Venice (30min., 3-4 per hr., €2.30); and Verona (1hr., 1-2 per hr., €7). **Buses** (☎049 820 68 11) leave from P. Boschetti for Venice (45min., 2 per hr.,

€3.25). The **tourist office,** in the train station, sells the one-year **Biglietto Unico,** valid at most of Padua's museums. The *biglietto* is also available at participating sights. (☎049 875 20 77. Biglietto €7.75, students €5.20. Open M-Sa 9am-7pm, Su 9:30am-12pm.) Take bus #18 from the station to the stop after Prato della Valle; then walk two blocks, turn right on V. Marin, turn left on V. Torresino, turn right on V. Aleardi, and **Ostello Città di Padova (HI) ❶,** V. Aleardi 30, will be on the left. (☎049 875 22 19. Breakfast, sheets, and shower included. Reception daily 7-9:30am and 2:30-11pm. Curfew 11pm. Reserve 1 week in advance. Dorms €13.) **Hotel Al Santo ❹,** V. del Santo 147, near the basilica, rents airy, well-kept rooms. (☎049 875 21 31. Breakfast included. Open Feb.-Dec. Singles €52; doubles €90; triples €130. MC/V.) Join a lively crowd at **Pizzeria Al Borgo ❷,** V.L. Belludi 56, near the Basilica di S. Antonio. (Pizzas €3.50. Open W-Su noon-3pm and 7-11:30pm.) **Postal Code:** 35100.

VERONA ☎045

A glorious combination of majestic Roman ruins, colorful Venetian facades, and orange rooftops, Verona is one of the most beautiful cities in Northern Italy. Gazing at the town from one of its many bridges at sunset sets the tone for romantic evenings befitting the home of *Romeo and Juliet.* Meanwhile, its artistic and historical treasures fill days with rewarding sightseeing.

TRANSPORTATION AND PRACTICAL INFORMATION. **Trains** (☎045 800 08 61) go from P. XXV Aprile to: Bologna (2hr., every hr., €5.75); Milan (2hr., every hr., €6.85); and Venice (1¾hr., every hr., €5.75). The **tourist office,** in P. Brà, is on the left of the *piazza.* (☎045 806 86 80. Open daily 10am-7pm.) Check **email** at the **Internet Train,** V. Roma 17/a, past P. Brà. Go right on V. Roma and it's two blocks ahead. (☎803 41 00. €5 per hr. Open M-F 10am-10pm, Sa noon-8pm, Su 4-8pm.) To reach the **post office,** P. Viviani 7, follow V. Cairoli from P. delle Erbe. (☎045 800 39 38. Open M-Sa 8:10am-7pm.) **Postal Code:** 37100.

ACCOMMODATIONS AND FOOD. Reserve lodgings ahead, especially in opera season (June-Sept.). The **Ostello della Gioventù (HI) ❶,** Villa Francescatti, Salita Fontana del Ferro 15, is in a renovated 16th-century villa with gorgeous gardens; from the station, take bus #73 or night bus #90 to P. Isolo, turn right, and follow the yellow signs uphill. (☎045 59 03 60. Breakfast included. 5-night max. stay. Check-in 5pm. Check-out 7-9am. Lockout 9am-5pm. Curfew 11pm; flexible for opera-goers. No reservations. Dorms €12.50.) Women can also try the beautiful **Casa della Giovane (ACISJF) ❶,** V. Pigna 7. (☎045 59 68 80. Reception 9am-11pm. Curfew 11pm; flexible for opera-goers. Dorms €11.50; singles €16.50; doubles €26.) To get to **Locanda Catullo ❹,** Vco. Catullo 1, walk to V. Mazzini, turn onto V. Catullo, and turn left on Vco. Catullo. (☎045 800 27 86. July-Sept. 3-night min. stay. Singles €37; doubles €52-62; triples €78-93.) Verona is famous for its wines, such as the dry white *soave* and red *valpolicella.* Prices in **Piazza Isolo** are cheaper than those in P. delle Erbe. **Cantore,** V.A. Mario 2, has cheap, delicious food. (Pizzas from €4.30. Open Th-Tu noon-3pm and 4pm-midnight.) **Pam supermarket** is at V. dei Mutilati 3. (Open M-Sa 8:30am-8pm and Su 9am-1pm.)

SIGHTS. The physical and emotional heart of Verona is the majestic, pink-marble, first century **Arena** in P. Brà. (Open Tu-Su 8:30am-7:30pm. €3.10, students €2.10.) From P. Brà, V. Mazzini leads to the markets and stunning medieval architecture of **Piazza delle Erbe,** the former Roman forum. The 83m **Torre dei Lambertini,** in P. dei Signori, offers a stunning view of Verona. (Open Tu-Su 9:30am-6pm. Elevator €2.60, students €2.10. Stairs €2.60.) The **Giardino Giusti,** V. Giardino Giusti 2, is a magnificent 16th-century garden with a labyrinth of mythological statues. (Open Apr.-Sept. daily 9am-8pm; Oct.-Mar. 9am-dusk. €4.50, students €3.50.) The della Scala fortress, the **Castelvecchio,** down V. Roma from P. Brà, is filled with walkways, parapets, and an art collection including Pisanello's *Madonna and Child.* (Open Tu-Su 8:30am-7:30pm. €4.20, students €3.10; first Su of each month free.) Thousands of tourists have immortalized **Casa di Giulietta** (Juliet's House), V. Cappello 23, where the Capulet family never really lived. Avoid wasting money to stand on the balcony. (Open Tu-Su 8:30am-7:30pm. €3.10, students €2.10.) From late June to early September, tourists and singers from around the world descend on the Arena for the city's annual **Opera Festival.** (☎045 800 51 51. General admission Su-Th €19.50, F-Sa €21.50.)

FRIULI-VENEZIA GIULIA

Friuli-Venezia Giulia traditionally receives less than its fair share of recognition, but this region has served as inspiration to a number of prominent literary figures. James Joyce lived in Trieste for 12 years, during which he wrote most of *Ulysses;* Ernest Hemingway drew part of the plot for *A Farewell to Arms* from the region's role in WWI, and Freud and Rilke both worked and wrote here. The city of Trieste attracts large numbers of tourists to the cheapest beach resorts on the Adriatic.

TRIESTE (TRIEST) ☎040

In the post-Napoleonic real estate grab, the Austrians snatched Trieste (pop. 230,000); after a little more ping-pong, the city became part of Italy in 1954, but it still remains divided between its Slavic and Italian origins. While Trieste's fast-paced center, with Gucci-clad locals and bustling quays, is undeniably urban, the colors of the surrounding Carsoian hillside and the tranquil Adriatic Sea temper the metropolis with stunning natural beauty. The **Città Nuova,** a grid-like pattern of streets lined with crumbling Neoclassical palaces, centers around the **Canale Grande.** Facing the canal from the south is the striking Serbian Orthodox **Chiesa di San Spiridione.** (Dress modestly. Open Tu-Sa 9am-noon and 5-8pm.) The ornate **Municipio** complements the **Piazza dell'Unità d'Italia,** the largest *piazza* in Italy. Take bus #24 to the last stop (€0.90) to reach the 15th-century Venetian **Castello di San Giusto,** which presides over **Capitoline Hill,** south of P. Unità, the city's historical center, and includes a museum. From P. Goldoni, you can ascend the hill by the daunting 265 Steps of the Giants, **or Scala dei Giganti.** (☎040 31 36 36. Castle open daily 9am-sunset. Museum €1.55.) **Piazza della Cattedrale** overlooks the sea and downtown Trieste. The archaeological **Museo di Storia e d'Arte,** V. Cattedrale 15, is down the hill past the *duomo.* (☎040 37 05 00. Open Tu-Su 9am-1pm. €1.55.)

Trains (☎379 47 37) leave P. della Libertà 8, down Corso Cavour from the quays, for Budapest (12hr., 2 per day, €71) and Venice (2hr., 2 per hr., €8.15). The **APT tourist office** is at P. dell'Unita d'Italia 4/E. (☎040 347 83 12; fax 040 347 83 20. Open M-Sa 7:30am-8:30pm.) **Hotel Alabarda ❸,** V. Valdirivo 22, is near the city center. From P. Oberdan, head down V. XXX Ottobre, and turn right onto V. Valdirivo. (☎040 63 02 69; fax 040 63 92 84. Singles €31-33; doubles €43-48. AmEx/MC/V.) To get from the station to **Ostello Tegeste (HI) ❶,** V. Miramare 331, 6km away just south from Castle Miramare, take bus #36 (€0.90), which leaves from across V. Miramare, and ask for the Ostello stop. From there, walk along the Barcola, following the seaside road toward the castle. (☎/fax 040 22 41 02. Breakfast included. Reception daily 8am-11:30pm. HI members only. Dorms €12.) For cheap food, stop by **Euro Spesa** supermarket at V. Valdirivo 13/F, off Corso Cavour. (Open M-Sa 8am-8pm.) **Pizzeria Barattolo ❶,** P.S. Antonio 2, along the canal, has delicious pizza crust. (☎040 63 14 80. Pizza €4-9. Open daily 8:30am-midnight.) **Postal Code:** 34100.

PIEDMONT (PIEMONTE)

Piedmont has been a politically influential region for centuries, as well as a fountainhead of fine food, wine, and nobility. After native-born Vittorio Emanuele II and Camillo Cavour united Italy, Turin served as the capital from 1861 to 1865.

TURIN (TORINO) ☎011

Turin's elegance is the direct result of centuries of urban planning–graceful, church-lined avenues lead to spacious *piazze*. At the same time, Turin vibrates with the economic energy of the modern era as it continues to provide a reliable headquarters for the **Fiat Auto Company** and prepares to host the **2006 Winter Olympics.** The city is also home to one of the more famous relics of Christianity: the **Holy Shroud of Turin** is housed in the **Cattedrale di San Giovanni,** behind the **Palazzo Reale.** The church is undergoing restoration, but remains open. (Open daily 7am-12:30pm and 3-7pm. Free.) The **Museo Egizio,** in the **Palazzo dell'Accademia delle Scienze,** V. dell'Accademia delle Scienze 6, boasts a collection of Egyptian artifacts second only to the British Museum, including several copies of the Egyptian Book of the Dead. (Open Tu-F and Su 8:30am-7:30pm, Sa 8:30am-11pm. €6.50, ages 18-25 €3, under 18 and over 65 free.) The **Museo dell'Automobile,** Corso Unita d'Italia, 40, documents the evolution of the automobile, including prototype models of the Ford, Benz, Peugeot, and the homegrown Fiat. From the station, head south along V. Nizza. (Open Tu-Su 10am-7pm. €2.70.) One of Guarini's great Baroque palaces, the **Palazzo Carignano,** V. dell'Accademia delle Scienze 5, houses the **Museo Nazionale del Risorgimento Italiano,** commemorating the 1706-1846 unification of Italy. (Open Tu-Su 9am-7pm. €4.25, students €2.50, under 10 and over 65 free.)

Trains leave **Porta Nuova** on Corso Vittorio Emanuele (☎011 531 327) for: Genoa (2hr., every hr., €7.90); Milan (2hr., every hr., €7.90); Rome (4½hr., 5 per day, €32.60); Venice (4½hr., 2 per day, €27.70). **Buses** leave Turin for Aosta (3½hr., 6 per day, €6.28) and Milan (2hr., every hr., €5.70). The **tourist office,** P. Castello 161, has free maps. (☎011 53 51 81. Open M-Sa 9:30am-7pm, Su 9:30am-3:30pm.) To get to the clean and comfortable **Ostello Torino (YHI) ❶,** V. Alby 1, take bus #52 (bus #64 on Su) from Stazione Porto Nuova to the 2nd stop past the Po river. Turn right onto Corso Lanza and look for the Ostello sign on the corner. Follow the signs to V. Gatti and then climb up 200m up a winding road. (☎011 660 29 39; hostelto@tin.it. Reception 7-10am and 3:30-11pm. Curfew 11:30pm; ask for a key if you go out. Closed Dec. 20-Feb. 1. Dorms €12; doubles €13.) To **camp** at **Campeggio Villa Rey ❶,** Strada Superiore Val S. Martino 27, take bus #61 from Porta Nuova until P. Vittorio and then take bus #56 and follow the signs after the last stop.

ITALY

HOLY SHROUD, BATMAN! Called a hoax by some and a miracle by others, the holy shroud of Turin (a 1m-by-4.5m piece of linen) was supposedly wrapped around Jesus' body in preparation for burial after his crucifixion. Visible on the cloth are outflows of blood: around the head (supposedly from the Crown of Thorns), all over the body (from scourging), and, most importantly, from the wrists and feet (where the body was nailed to the cross). Although radiocarbon dating places the piece in the 12th century AD, the shroud's uncanny resemblance to that of Christ precludes its immediate dismissal. Scientists agree that the shroud was wrapped around the body of a 5'7" man who died by crucifixion, but whether it was the body of Jesus remains a mystery. For Christian believers, however, the importance of this relic is best described by Pope Paul VI's words: "The Shroud is a document of Christ's love written in characters of blood."

(☎011 819 01 17. €3 per person; €2 for 1 tent.) Cheap fruit, cheese, and bread shops are on **Via Mazzini** and at **Di Per Di,** V. Carlo Alberto at the corner of V. Maria Vittoria. (Open daily 8am-1pm and 3:30-7:30pm.) **Postal Code:** 10100

ASTI ☎0141

Asti sparkles, just like its intoxicating progeny, the famous *Asti Spumante* wine. More than a hundred 13th-century edifices have survived the city's tumultuous history, lending it a medieval air. The **Cattedrale d'Asti,** in P. Cattedrale, is one of Piedmont's most noteworthy Gothic cathedrals. Walk down Corso Alfieri and turn right on V. Mazzini. (Open daily 7am-12:30pm and 3-7pm.) From the last week of June through the first week of July, **Asti Teatro,** the oldest Italian theatrical festival, puts on numerous performances of theatrics, music, and dance. Call the **Teatro Alfieri,** V. al Teatro 1 (☎0141 35 39 88). Beginning on the second Friday in September, Asti's agricultural side revels in the **Douja d'Or,** a week-long exposition of wines.

Trains head from P. Marconi, just a few blocks south of P. Alfieri, to Milan (2hr., 1 per day, €7) and Turin (1hr., 2 per hr., €3.10). The **tourist office,** P. Alfieri 29, helps find accommodations. (☎0141 53 03 57; fax 0141 53 82 00. Open M-Sa 9am-1pm and 2:30-6:30pm, Su 10am-1pm.) **Hotel Cavour ❹,** P. Marconi 18, is across from the train station and has immaculate rooms with TVs and phones. (☎/fax 0141 53 02 22. Reception 6am-1am. Closed in Aug. Singles €39; doubles €55. AmEx/MC/V.) *Astigiano* cuisine is truly a treat, famous for its simplicity, using only a few crucial ingredients and pungent cheeses to create culinary masterpieces. The extensive fruit and vegetable **markets** in P. Alfieri and Corso del Palio provide great snacks. (Open W and Sa 7:30am-1pm.) **Postal Code:** 14100.

TUSCANY (TOSCANA)

The vision that is Tuscany has inspired countless artists, poets, and hordes of tourists. Its rolling hills, prodigious olive groves, and cobblestone streets beg visitors to slow their frenetic pace, sip some wine, and relax in fields of brilliant sunflowers. Tuscany fostered some of Italy's, and the world's, greatest cultural achievements under the tender care—and devious machinations—of the powerful Medici family, gaining eternal eminence in the arts for its staggering accomplishments during a scant half-century. Today, tourists flock to Tuscany to witness the glory that was, and the wonder that still is *Toscana.*

FLORENCE (FIRENZE) ☎055

In the early 14th century, Florence's Dante Alighieri bitterly bemoaned his hometown's infamous mercenary greed and political ferocity. Yet since then, numerous visitors have walked the city's cobblestone streets to fall under its spell of Renaissance mystique. Cosmopolitan Henry James, lonely Albert Camus, sensitive E. M. Forster, and cranky Mark Twain were all taken in by the city's beauty. Today's Florence blends the ancient and modern as Florentine students quote Marx and Malcolm X in street graffiti, colorful windows prophesy the latest looks, businessmen whiz by on Vespas, and children play soccer in the P. del Duomo.

TRANSPORTATION

Flights: Amerigo Vespucci Airport (FLR; ☎055 31 58 74), in Peretola. The **ATAF** bus #62 connects the train station to the airport (€1). **Galileo Galilei Airport** (PSA; ☎(050) 50 07 07), in Pisa. Take airport express from the train station (1¼hr., €4.85).

ITALY

Trains: Santa Maria Novella Station, across from S. Maria Novella. Trains depart for: **Bologna** (1hr., every hr., €7.75), **Milan** (3½hr., every hr., €22), and **Rome** (3½hr., every hr., €15-22); **Siena** (2hr., 10 per day, €5.30) and **Venice** (3hr., 4 per day, €19).

Buses: SITA, V.S. Caterina da Siena 15r (☎28 46 61). Runs to: **Arezzo** (2½hr., 3 per day, €4.10); **San Gimignano** (1½hr., 14 per day, €5.70); and **Siena** (1½hr., 2 per day, €6.50). **LAZZI,** P. Adua, 1-4r (☎055 35 10 61) sends buses to **Pisa** (every hr., €5.80).

Public Transportation: ATAF (☎055 565 02 22), outside the train station, runs orange city buses (6am-1am). 1hr. tickets €1; 3hr. €1.80; 24hr. €4; 3-day €7.20. Buy tickets at any newsstand, *tabacchi,* or automated ticket dispenser before boarding. Validate your ticket using the orange machine on board or risk a €50 fine.

Taxis: (☎055 43 90, 055 47 98, or 055 42 42). Outside the train station.

Bike/Moped Rental: Alinari Noleggi, V. Guelfa 85r (☎055 28 05 00). Bikes €12-18 per day, mopeds €28-55 per day.

ORIENTATION AND PRACTICAL INFORMATION

From the train station, a short walk on **Via de' Panzani** and a left on **Via de' Cerretani** leads to the **duomo,** the center of Florence. Major arteries radiate from the *duomo* and its two *piazze.* A bustling walkway, **Via de' Calzaiuoli** runs south from the *duomo* to the **Piazza Signoria.** V. Roma leads from P.S. Giovanni through **Piazza della Repubblica** to the **Ponte Vecchio** (Old Bridge), which spans the Arno River to the **Oltrarno** district. Note that most streets change names unpredictably. For guidance through Florence's tangled center, grab a **free map** from the tourist office. Sights are scattered throughout Florence, but few lie beyond walking distance.

STENDHAL WOULD BE PROUD. Florence's streets are numbered in red and black sequences. Red numbers indicate commercial establishments and black numbers denote residential addresses (including most sights and hotels). Black addresses appear in *Let's Go* as a numeral only, while red addresses are indicated by a number followed by an "r." If you reach an address and it's not what you're looking for, you've probably got the wrong color sequence.

TOURIST, FINANCIAL, AND LOCAL SERVICES

Tourist Office: Informazione Turistica, P. della Stazione 4 (☎055 21 22 45), across the *piazza* from the main exit. Info on entertainment and cultural events. Be sure to ask for a **free map** with a street index. Open daily 8:30am-7pm.

Tours: **Enjoy Florence** (☎055 167 27 48 19; www.enjoyflorence.com). Gives fast-paced, informative walking tours of the old city center. Tours meet daily in summer at 10am in front of the Thomas Cook office at the Ponte Vecchio. €16, under 26 €13.

Consulates: UK, Lungarno Corsini 2 (☎055 28 41 33). Open M-F 9:30am-12:30pm and 2:30-4:30pm. **US,** Lungarno Amerigo Vespucci 38 (☎055 239 8276), at V. Palestro, near the station. Open M-F 9am-12:30pm. **Canadians, Australians,** and **New Zealanders** should contact their consulates in Rome or Milan.

Currency Exchange: Local banks offer the best rates. Most are open M-F 8:20am-1:20pm and 2:45-3:45pm, some also Sa morning. 24hr. **ATMs** abound.

American Express: V. Dante Alighieri 20-22r (☎055 509 81). From the *duomo,* walk down V. dei Calzaiuoli and turn left on V. dei Tavolini. Mail held free for AmEx members and check customers, otherwise €1.55. Open M-F 9am-5:30pm, Sa 9am-12:30pm.

EMERGENCY AND COMMUNICATIONS

Emergency: ☎113. **Fire:** ☎115. **Police:** V. Zara 2 (☎055 497 71).

24-Hour Pharmacies: Farmacia Comunale (☎055 28 94 35), at the train station by track #16. **Molteni,** V. dei Calzaiuoli, 7r (☎055 28 94 90).

Medical Emergency: ☎118.

Internet Access: Walk down almost any busy street and you'll find an Internet cafe. Try **Internet Train:** 15 locations listed on www.internettrain.it/citta.isp. Adults €4 per hr., students €3 per hr. Most open M-F 9am-midnight, Sa 10am-8pm, Su noon-9pm.

Post Office: V. Pellicceria (☎055 21 61 22), off P. della Repubblica. Address mail to be held: Firstname SURNAME, *In Fermo Posta*, L'Ufficio Postale, V. Pellicceria, Firenze, **50100** ITALY. Open M-F 8:15am-7pm, Sa 8:15am-noon.

ACCOMMODATIONS

As the astute reader will discern from the abundance of ❹s and ❺s, accommodations in Florence don't come cheap. **Consorzio ITA,** in the train station by track #16, can find cheap rooms for a €2.50-7.75 commission. (☎055 28 28 93. Open daily 8:45am-8pm.) Because of the constant stream of tourists in Florence, it is best to make reservations in advance, especially if you plan to visit during summer.

HOSTELS

Ostello Archi Rossi, V. Faenza 94r (☎055 29 08 04; fax 055 230 26 01). Exit left from the station on V. Nazionale and take the 2nd left on V. Faenza. A patio brimming with young travelers. Wheelchair accessible. Breakfast €1.60. Laundry €5.20. Lockout 11:30am-2pm. Curfew 1am. No reservations; in summer, arrive before 8am. 4- to 9-bed dorms €17-23; rooms for handicapped €26. ❷

Istituto Gould, V. dei Serragli, 49 (☎055 21 25 76), in the **Oltrarno.** Exit the station by track 16, head right to P. della Stazione, walk to the left of the church, and continue through the P.S. Maria Novella and down V. dei Fossi (15min.). Spotless rooms. Reception M-F 9am-1pm and 3-7pm, Sa 9am-1pm. No check-in or check-out Sa afternoons or Su. Singles €30; doubles €44; triples €56. ❸

Ostello Santa Monaca, V.S. Monaca 6 (☎055 26 83 38). Exit the station by track #16, head right to P. della Stazione, walk to the left of the church, continue through P.S. Maria Novella and down V. dei Fossi, and turn right onto V.S. Monaca off V. dei Serragli. 7-night max. stay. Reception 6am-1pm and 2pm-1am. Curfew 1am. Reserve 3 days in advance, in writing. Dorms €16. AmEx/MC/V. ❷

Pensionato Pio X, V. dei Serragli 106 (☎/fax 055 22 50 44). Past the Istituto Gould in Oltrarno. Quiet, clean rooms and comfortable lounges. 2-night min. stay. Check-out 9am. Curfew midnight. No reservations—arrive before 9am. Dorms €15. ❶

OLD CITY (NEAR THE DUOMO)

Though flooded by tourists, this area has a surprising array of budget accommodations. Many provide great views of Florence's monuments, while others lie hidden in Renaissance *palazzi*. Follow V. de' Panzani from the train station and take a left on V. de' Cerretani to reach the *duomo*.

Locanda Orchidea, Borgo degli Albizia 11 (☎055 248 03 46). Turn left off V. Proconsolo from the *duomo*. Dante's wife was born in this 12th-century *palazzo*. Some of the rooms open onto a garden. Singles €45; doubles €65; triples €90. ❹

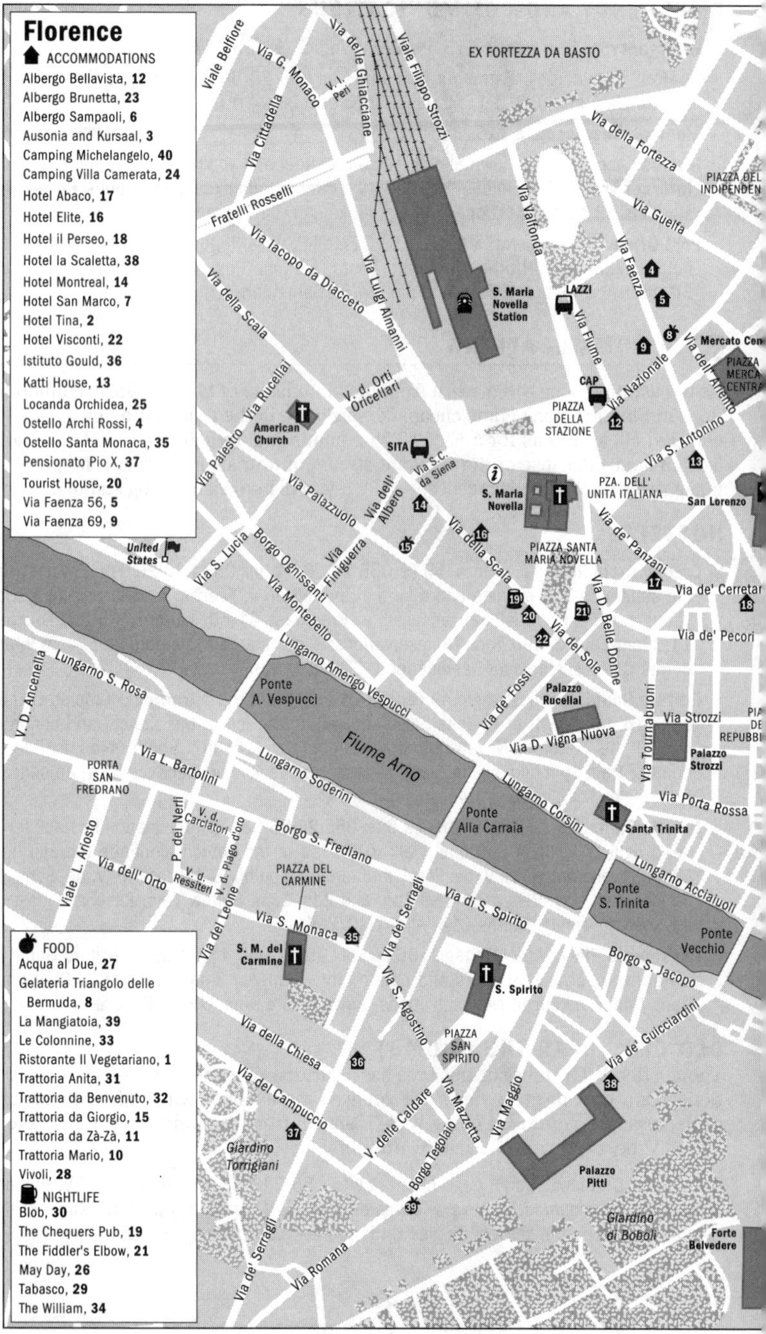

Florence
ACCOMMODATIONS
Albergo Bellavista, 12
Albergo Brunetta, 23
Albergo Sampaoli, 6
Ausonia and Kursaal, 3
Camping Michelangelo, 40
Camping Villa Camerata, 24
Hotel Abaco, 17
Hotel Elite, 16
Hotel il Perseo, 18
Hotel la Scaletta, 38
Hotel Montreal, 14
Hotel San Marco, 7
Hotel Tina, 2
Hotel Visconti, 22
Istituto Gould, 36
Katti House, 13
Locanda Orchidea, 25
Ostello Archi Rossi, 4
Ostello Santa Monaca, 35
Pensionato Pio X, 37
Tourist House, 20
Via Faenza 56, 5
Via Faenza 69, 9
FOOD
Acqua al Due, 27
Gelateria Triangolo delle Bermuda, 8
La Mangiatoia, 39
Le Colonnine, 33
Ristorante Il Vegetariano, 1
Trattoria Anita, 31
Trattoria da Benvenuto, 32
Trattoria da Giorgio, 15
Trattoria da Zà-Zà, 11
Trattoria Mario, 10
Vivoli, 28
NIGHTLIFE
Blob, 30
The Chequers Pub, 19
The Fiddler's Elbow, 21
May Day, 26
Tabasco, 29
The William, 34
EX FORTEZZA DA BASTO
Viale Belfiore
Via G. Monaco
V. l. Peri
Via delle Ghiacciane
Viale Filippo Strozzi
Via della Fortezza
PIAZZA DELL' INDIPENDEN
Via Cittadella
Fratelli Rosselli
Via Valfonda
Via Guelfa
Via Faenza
Via Iacopo da Diacceto
Via Luigi Alamanni
Via della Scala
S. Maria Novella Station
LAZZI
Via Fiume
Mercato Cen
PIAZZA MERCA CENTRA
Via dell' Ariento
Via Nazionale
CAP
PIAZZA DELLA STAZIONE
V. d. Orti Oricellari
Via Rucellai
American Church
Via Palestro
SITA
Via S.C. da Siena
Via S. Antonino
S. Maria Novella
PZA. DELL' UNITA ITALIANA
San Lorenzo
Via Palazzuolo
Via dell' Albero
Via de' Panzani
PIAZZA SANTA MARIA NOVELLA
United States
Via S. Lucia
Borgo Ognissanti
Via Finiguerra
Via della Scala
Via de' Cerretani
Via Montebello
Via D. Belle Donne
Via del Sole
Via de' Pecori
Lungarno Amerigo Vespucci
Via de' Fossi
Palazzo Rucellai
Via Strozzi
Via Tornabuoni
Lungarno S. Rosa
V. D. Ancenella
Ponte A. Vespucci
Fiume Arno
Via D. Vigna Nuova
REPUBBLI
Palazzo Strozzi
PORTA SAN FREDRANO
Via L. Bartolini
Lungarno Soderini
Lungarno Corsini
Via Porta Rossa
Ponte Alla Carraia
Santa Trinita
P. dei Nerli
V. d. Carciatori
V. d. Piago d'oro
Borgo S. Frediano
Viale L. Ariosto
Via dell' Orto
V. d. Ressiteri
PIAZZA DEL CARMINE
Lungarno Acciaiuoli
Via di S. Spirito
Ponte S. Trinita
Via del Leone
Via S. Monaca
Via dei Serragli
Ponte Vecchio
S. M. del Carmine
Borgo S. Jacopo
S. Spirito
Via S. Agostino
Via de' Guicciardini
PIAZZA SAN SPIRITO
Via della Chiesa
Via del Campuccio
V. delle Caldaie
Via Mazzetta
Via Maggio
Giardino Torrigiani
Borgo Tegolaio
Palazzo Pitti
Giardino di Boboli
Forte Belvedere
Via de' Serragli
Via Romana

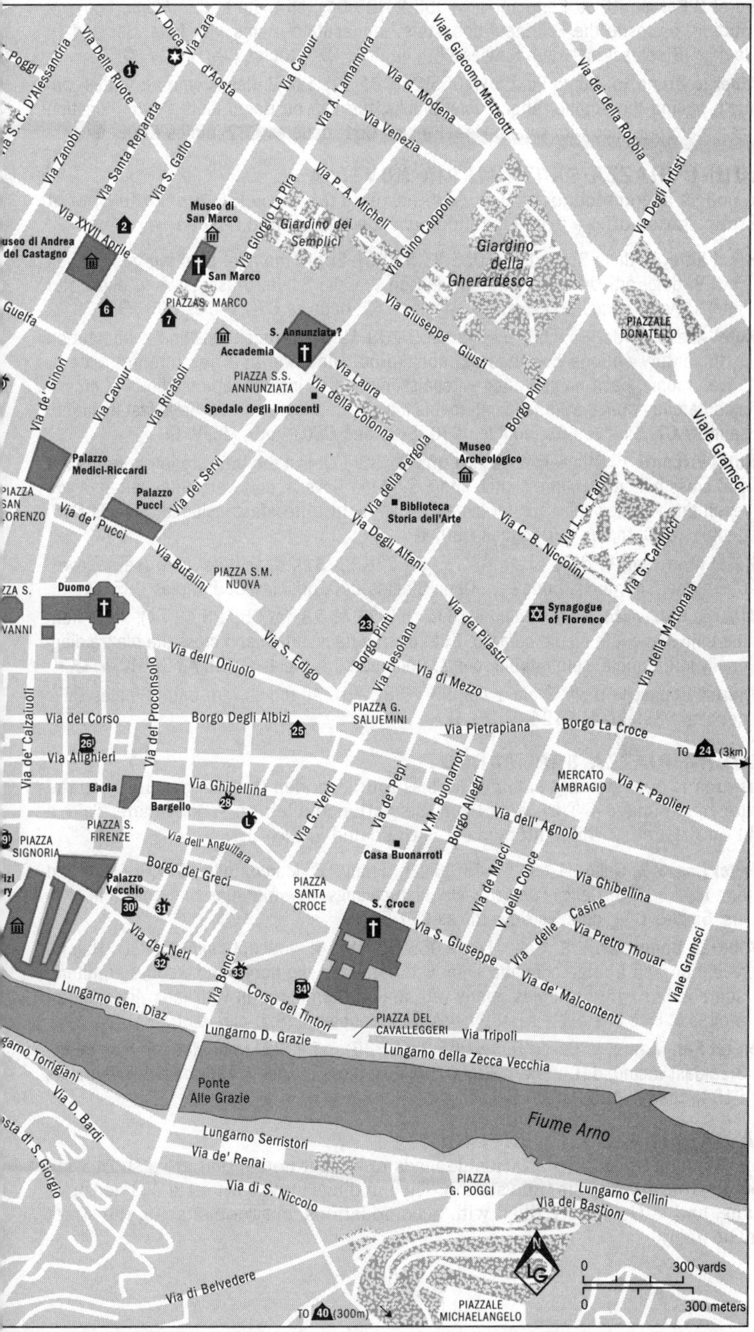
Via Delle Ruote
V. Duca d'Aosta
Via Zara
Via S. C. D'Alessandria
Via Zanobi
Via Santa Reparata
Via S. Gallo
Via Cavour
Via A. Lamarmora
Via G. Modena
Viale Giacomo Matteotti
Via dei della Robbia
Via Venezia
Via P. A. Micheli
Via Giorgio La Pira
Giardino dei Semplici
Via Gino Capponi
Giardino della Gherardesca
Via Degli Artisti
Via XXVII Aprile
Museo di San Marco
Museo di Andrea del Castagno
San Marco
PIAZZA S. MARCO
Guelfa
Via Giuseppe Giusti
PIAZZALE DONATELLO
S. Annunziata?
Accademia
PIAZZA S.S. ANNUNZIATA
Via Laura
Via della Colonna
Spedale degli Innocenti
Borgo Pinti
Via de' Ginori
Via Cavour
Via Ricasoli
Viale Gramsci
Palazzo Medici-Riccardi
Museo Archeologico
Via dei Servi
Via della Pergola
Via L. C. Farini
Palazzo Pucci
PIAZZA SAN LORENZO
Via de' Pucci
Biblioteca Storia dell'Arte
Via Degli Alfani
Via C. B. Niccolini
Via G. Carducci
Via Bufalini
PIAZZA S.M. NUOVA
Duomo
Synagogue of Florence
Via dei Pilastri
Via della Mattonaia
Via S. Edigo
Borgo Pinti
Via Fiesolana
Via dell' Oriuolo
Via di Mezzo
Via del Proconsolo
Via de' Calzaiuoli
Via del Corso
Borgo Degli Albizi
PIAZZA G. SALUEMINI
Via Pietrapiana
Borgo La Croce
TO 24 (3km)
Via Alighieri
Badia
Bargello
Via Ghibellina
MERCATO AMBRAGIO
Via F. Paolieri
Via G. Verdi
Via de' Pepi
V.M. Buonarroti
Borgo Allegri
Via dell' Agnolo
PIAZZA SIGNORIA
PIAZZA S. FIRENZE
Via dell' Anguillara
Casa Buonarroti
Via de Macci
V. delle Conce
Borgo dei Greci
Palazzo Vecchio
PIAZZA SANTA CROCE
S. Croce
Via Ghibellina
Via delle Casine
Via Pietro Thouar
Via dei Neri
Via S. Giuseppe
Via de' Malcontenti
Viale Gramsci
Via Benci
Corso dei Tintori
Lungarno Gen. Diaz
PIAZZA DEL CAVALLEGGERI
Via Tripoli
Lungarno D. Grazie
Lungarno della Zecca Vecchia
Lungarno Torrigiani
Ponte Alle Grazie
Via D. Bardi
Fiume Arno
Costa di S. Giorgio
Lungarno Serristori
Via de' Renai
Via di S. Niccolo
PIAZZA G. POGGI
Lungarno Cellini
Via dei Bastioni
N
LG
0 300 yards
0 300 meters
Via di Belvedere
TO 40 (300m)
PIAZZALE MICHAELANGELO

ITALY

Hotel Il Perseo, V. de Cerretani 1 (☎055 21 25 04), en route to the *duomo* from the station, opposite the Feltrinelli bookstore. Immaculate rooms with fans. Bar and TV lounge. Breakfast included. Singles €50; doubles €70; triples €93. MC/V. ❹

Albergo Brunetta, Borgo Pinti 5 (☎055 247 81 34). Exit P. del Duomo on V. dell' Oriuolo behind the *duomo*. After 2 long blocks, turn left on Borgo Pinti. Central location and rooftop terrace with superb view. Singles €51; doubles €82; triples €103. ❹

AROUND PIAZZA SANTA MARIA NOVELLA

The budget accommodations that cluster around this attractive *piazza* in front of the train station offer a prime location near the *duomo* and the *centro*.

Hotel Elite, V. della Scala 12 (☎055 21 53 95). Exit to the right from the train station onto V. degli orti Oricellari, and turn left on V. della Scala. Brass glows in this 2-star hotel's lovely rooms. Breakfast €6. Singles €52; doubles €70; triples €95. ❹

Hotel Abaco, V. dei Banchi 1 (☎/fax 055 238 19 19; abacohotel@tin.it). Immitation 17th-century antique headboards, noise-proof windows, and free Internet access. Seven rooms, each named after a Renaissance artist, include reproductions of artist's most famous work on the walls. All rooms have A/C, phone, and TV. Breakfast included. Laundry €7. Singles €63; doubles €70. Extra bed €10. AmEx/MC/V. ❺

Hotel Visconti, P. Ottaviani 1 (☎/fax 055 21 38 77). Exit the train station from the left and cross behind S. Maria church into P.S. Maria Novella, and walk to the left until you reach tiny P. Ottaviani. Look for huge Grecian nudes. Breakfast included. Singles €40; doubles €60; triples €80; quads €90. ❹

Hotel Montreal, V. della Scala 43 (☎055 238 23 31), near Hotel Elite (see above). Clean, modern rooms. Curfew 1:30am. Singles €40; doubles €65; triples €85. ❹

Albergo Bellavista, Largo F. Alinari 15 (☎055 28 45 28; fax 055 28 48 74), steps from the train station, in an old *palazzo*. Exit from the train station and cross the *piazza* diagonally left. Simple, comfortable rooms. Doubles €98; triples €139. AmEx/MC/V. ❺

Tourist House, V. della Scala 1 (☎055 26 86 75). All rooms with bath. Singles €67; doubles €83; quads €124. MC/V. ❺

ITALY

AROUND PIAZZA SAN MARCO

This area is considerably calmer and less tourist-ridden than its proximity to the center might suggest. Turn right from the station and left on V. Nazionale. Take a right on V. Guelfa, which intersects V.S. Gallo and V. Cavour.

Hotel Tina, V.S. Gallo 31 (☎055 48 35 19). From P.S. Marco, follow V. XXII Aprile and turn right on V.S. Gallo. *Pensione* with high ceilings, new furniture, and amicable owners. Singles €44; doubles €62; triples €77.50. ❹

Albergo Sampaoli, V.S. Gallo 14 (☎055 28 48 34; www.hotelsampaoli.it). Helpful reception and a large common area with patterned tile floors and wooden furniture. Some rooms with balconies, many with antique furniture, all with fans. Refrigerator available. Free Internet access. Singles €45; doubles €58; triples €110. ❹

Hotel San Marco, V. Cavou 50 (☎055 28 42 35), off P.S. Marco. Modern, airy rooms. Breakfast included. Curfew 1:30am; ask for a key. Singles €42; doubles €7; triples €104; quads €135. MC/V. ❹

VIA NAZIONALE AND ENVIRONS

From P. della Stazione, V. Nazionale leads to budget hotels that are a short walk from the *duomo* and the train station. The buildings on V. Nazionale, V. Faenza, V. Fiume, and V. Guelfa are filled with accomodations, but rooms facing the street may be noisy.

Katti House, V. Faenza 21 (☎055 21 34 10; www.kattihouse.com). Exit train station onto V. Nazionale. Walk 1 block on V. Nazionale and turn right onto V. Faenza. Private dwelling, lovingly renovated by the proprietors, with hand-made drapes, 400-year-old antiques and attentive service. Large rooms with A/C and TV. Prices drop significantly Nov.-Mar. Doubles with bath €95; triples with bath €105; quads with bath €105. ❺

Via Faenza 56 houses six separate *pensioni*, among the best deals in the city. From the train station, exit left onto V. Nazionale, walk 1 block, and turn left on V. Faenza. The prices and amenities for the Azzi, Anna, and Paola are listed under the Azzi.

Pensione Azzi (☎055 21 38 06) has large rooms and a terrace. Breakfast included. Singles €41; doubles €62; triples €77.50. AmEx/MC/V. ❹

Albergo Anna (☎055 239 83 22) has lovely singles and doubles with frescoes and fans. ❹

Locanda Paola (☎055 21 36 82) has spartan doubles with views of the surrounding hills. ❹

Albergo Merlini (☎055 21 28 48; www.hotelmerlini.it) has some rooms with views of the *duomo*. Curfew 1am. Doubles €69; triples €80. AmEx/MC/V. ❺

Albergo Marini (☎055 28 48 24) boasts spotless rooms. Breakfast €5.15. Singles €47; doubles €62; triples €82.65; quads €103.30; quints €123.95. ❹

Albergo Armonia (☎055 21 11 46) decorates its rooms with film posters. Singles €42; doubles €65; triples €90; quads €100. ❹

Via Faenza 69 houses no-frills hotels. Same directions as for Via Faenza 56.

Locanda Giovanna (☎055 238 13 53) 4th fl., has basic, well-kept rooms with garden views. Singles €37.40; doubles €57. ❹

Hotel Nella/Pina (☎055 265 43 46) 1st and 2nd fl., has 14 basic rooms and Internet. Singles €47; doubles €62. AmEx/MC/V. ❹

Ausonia and Kursaal, V. Nazionale 24 (☎055 49 65 47). Exit train station to the left and turn left on V. Nazionale. Lots of amenities. Wheelchair-accessible. Breakfast included. No curfew. Doubles €82-116; triples €109-143; quads €170. MC/V. ❺

IN THE OLTRARNO

Only a 10min. walk across the Arno from the *duomo*, this area and its *pensione* offer a respite from Florence's bustling hubs.

Hotel La Scaletta, V. Guicciardini 13b (☎055 28 30 28). Turn right onto V. Roma from the *duomo*, cross Ponte Vecchio and walk on V. Guicciardini. Has views of Boboli gardens. Breakfast included. Reception open until midnight. Singles €40; doubles €100; triples €154; quads €170. 10% *Let's Go* discount when you pay cash. MC/V. ❹

CAMPING

Campeggio Michelangelo, V. Michelangelo 80 (☎055 681 19 77), beneath Piazzale Michelangelo. Take bus #13 from the bus station (15min.; until 11:25pm). Crowded, but has a great view of Florence. Open Apr.-Nov. €7.50 per person, €5 per tent. ❶

Villa Camerata, V. A. Righi 2-4 (☎055 60 03 15), same entrance as the HI hostel on the #17 bus route. Breakfast €1.30. Reception daily 1pm-midnight. Check-out 7-10am. €6 per person, €5 per tent. ❶

FOOD

Florence's hearty cuisine originated from the peasant fare of the surrounding countryside. Specialties include *bruschetta* (grilled bread soaked with olive oil and garlic and topped with tomatoes and basil, anchovy, or liver paste) and *bistecca alla Fiorentina* (thick sirloin steak). Wine is a Florentine staple, and genuine *chianti classico* commands a premium price; a liter costs €3.65-5.20 in

Florence's *trattorie,* while stores sell bottles for as little as €2.60. The local dessert is *cantuccini di prato* (almond cookies made with egg yolks) dipped in *vinsanto* (a rich dessert wine made from raisins). Florence's own Buontalenti family supposedly invented *gelato* centuries ago; true or not, you must sample it. For lunch, visit a *rosticceria gastronomia,* peruse the city's pushcarts, or pick up fresh produce or meat at the **Mercato Centrale,** between V. Nazionale and S. Lorenzo. (Open June-Sept. M-Sa 7am-2pm; Oct.-May M-F 7am-2pm, Sa 7am-2pm and 4-8pm.) To get to **STANDA supermarket,** V. Pietrapiana 1r, turn right on V. del Proconsolo, take the 1st left on Borgo degli Albizi, continue straight through P.G. Salvemini, and it's on the left. (Open M 2-9pm, Tu-Su 8:30am-9pm.)

OLD CITY (THE DUOMO)

Trattoria Anita, V. del Parlascio 2r (☎055 21 86 98), just behind the Bargello. Dine by candlelight, surrounded by expensive wine bottles on wooden shelves. Traditional Tuscan fare–filling pastas and an array of meat dishes from roast chicken to beefsteak Florentine. *Primi* €4.70-5.20; *secondi* from €5.20. Fantastic lunch *menu* €5.50. Cover €1. Open M-Sa noon-2:30pm and 7-10pm. AmEx/MC/V. ❷

Acqua al Due, V. Vigna Vecchia 40r, behind the Bargello. Popular with young Italians. Serves Florentine specialties, including an excellent *assaggio* (€7.50). *Primi* €6.70, *secondi* €7-19. Cover €1. Reserve ahead. Open daily 7:30pm-1am. ❸

Le Colonnine, V. dei Benci 6r, north of the Ponte alle Grazie. Delicious traditional fare. Pizza €4.70; pasta *secondi* from €7. Famous *paella* could feed a small army (€18). Open daily noon-3:30pm and 6:30pm-midnight. ❷

Trattoria da Benvenuto, V. della Mosca 16r, on the corner of V. de' Neri. Wonderfully fresh *spaghetti alle vongole* (with clams) for €5.50. Cover €1.50. Open M-Sa 11am-3pm and 7pm-midnight. ❸

ITALY

SANTA MARIA NOVELLA AND ENVIRONS

Trattoria da Giorgio, V. Palazzuolo, 100r. Generous portions. *Menu* €8-9. Expect a wait. Open M-Sa noon-3:30pm and 7pm-12:30am. ❷

Ristorante Il Vegetariano, V. delle Ruote 30r, off V.S. Gallo. Fresh, inventive meat-free dishes. Smoke-free. *Primi* from €4.65; *secondi* from €5.70. Open Tu-F 12:30-3pm and 7:30pm-midnight, Sa-Su 8pm-midnight. ❸

THE STATION AND UNIVERSITY QUARTER

Trattoria da Zà-Zà, P. del Mercato Centrale 26r (☎055 21 54 11). Heavy wooden beam ceilings, brick archways, and wine racks on the wall. Bustles with a mixed crowd of Italians and foreigners. Try the *tris* (a mixed bean, tomato, and vegetable soup; €6) or the *tagliata di manzo* (house beef speciality; €12-15.50). Outdoor seating available. Cover €1.55. Open M-Sa noon-3pm and 7-11pm. Reservations suggested. AmEx/MC/V. ❸

Trattoria Mario, V. Rosina 2r (☎055 21 85 50), right around the corner from P. del Mercato Centrale. Share small wooden tables with the local crowd in this informal lunch spot. Order at your table from a paper menu on the wall that lists the days offerings in English as well as Italian. Incredible pasta, cheap meat dishes. *Primi* €3.10-3.40; *secondi* €3.10-10.50. Cover €0.50. Open M-Sa noon-3:30pm. ❸

THE OLTRARNO

Il Borgo Antico, P.S. Spirito 6r (☎055 21 04 37). *Mangia* outside listening to the street sounds settling on the *piazza,* or inside to the equally soothing ambient world beats. The *antipasti* are wonderful (tomato and basil salad; €7). The bread comes with a small dish of black olives in oil with a touch of hot pepper. *Antipasti* €5-10; *primi* €6; *secondi*

€10-15. Cover €2. Open June-Sept. daily 1pm-12:30am; Oct.-May daily 12:45-2:30pm and 7:45pm-1am. Reservations recommended. AmEx/MC/V. ❸

La Mangiatoia, P.S. Felice 8r (☎055 22 40 60). Continue straight on V. Guicciardini from Ponte Vecchio, and pass P. dei Pitti. Quality Tuscan fare. Grab a table in back dining room, or sit at stone counter in front to watch them make pizza in the brick oven. Try the pesto gnocchi (€4). Pizza €4-7.50; *primi* €3.50-5.50; *secondi* €3-9. Cover €1 in dining room only. Open Tu-Su noon-3pm and 7-10pm. AmEx/MC/V. ❷

GELATERIE

Florence's own Buontalenti family supposedly invented *gelato;* as a tourist, it's your duty to sample this creamy manifestation of the city's culture.

Vivoli, V. della Stinche 7, behind the Bargello. A renowned Florentine *gelateria* with a huge selection of the self-proclaimed "best ice cream in the world." Cups from €1.50. Open T-Sa 7:30am-1am; Su 9:30-1am. ❶

Gelateria Triangolo delle Bermuda, V. Nazionale, 61r. Blissful *crema venusiana* has hazelnut, caramel, and meringue. Cones €1.60. Open daily 11am-midnight. ❶

SIGHTS

Florence's museums have recently doubled their prices (now €3.10-6.20 per venue) and no longer offer student discounts. In summer, watch for **Sere al Museo,** evenings when certain museums are free from 8:30-11pm. Also, many of Florence's churches are free treasuries of great art.

PIAZZA DEL DUOMO

DUOMO. The red brick of Florence's *duomo*, the **Cattedrale di Santa Maria del Fiore,** at the center of P. del Duomo, is visible from virtually every part of the city. Filippo Brunelleschi drew from long-neglected classical methods to come up with his revolutionary double-shelled construction that utilized self-supporting interlocking bricks. Today the *duomo* claims the world's third longest nave. *(Open M-Sa 10am-4:45pm, Su 1:30-4:45pm. Mass daily 7am-12:30pm and 5-7pm.)* Climb the 463 steps inside the dome to **Michelangelo's lantern,** or cupola, which offers an unparalleled view of the city. *(Open M-F 8:30am-7pm. Sa 8:30am-5:40pm. €6.)* The top of the 82m high **campanile** next to the *duomo* also has beautiful views. *(Open daily 8:30am-7:30pm. €6.)*

BATTISTERO. The *battistero* (baptistry) next to the *duomo*, built between the 5th and 9th centuries, was the site of Dante's christening; its Byzantine-style mosaics inspired the details of his *Inferno*. The famous **bronze doors** were a product of intense competition among Florentine artists; Ghiberti was commissioned to forge the last set of doors. The products, reportedly dubbed the **Gates of Paradise** by Michelangelo, exchanged his earlier 28-panel design for 10 large, gilded squares, each of which employs mathematical perspective to create the illusion of deep space. Under restoration since a 1966 flood, they will soon be housed in the Museo dell'Opera del Duomo. *(Open M-Sa noon-7pm, Su 8:30am-2pm. €3.)*

MUSEO DELL'OPERA DEL DUOMO. Most of the *duomo's* art resides behind the cathedral in the Museo dell'Opera del Duomo. Up the first flight of stairs is a late *Pietà* by Michelangelo, who, according to legend, destroyed Christ's left arm with a hammer in a fit of frustration; soon after, a diligent pupil touched up the work, leaving visible scars on parts of Mary Magdalene's head. The museum also houses four frames from the baptistery's *Gates of Paradise*. *(P. del Duomo 9, behind the duomo. ☎264 7287 Open M-Sa 9am-6:30pm, Su 9am-1pm. €6.)*

PIAZZA DELLA SIGNORIA AND ENVIRONS

From P. del Duomo, the bustling **Via dei Calzaiuoli,** one of the city's oldest streets, runs south through crowds and chic shops to P. della Signoria.

PIAZZA DELLA SIGNORIA. The destruction of powerful Florentine families' homes in the 13th century created a empty space that cried out *"piazza!"*. With the construction of the Palazzo Vecchio in 1299, the square became Florence's civic and political center. In 1497, religious leader and social critic Savonarola convinced Florentines to light the **Bonfire of the Vanities,** a grand roast in the square that consumed some of Florence's best art. A year later, disillusioned citizens sent Savonarola up in smoke on the same spot, marked today by a granite disc. Monumental sculptures cluster in front of the *palazzo*, including a copy of Michelangelo's *David.* The awkward *Neptune* to the left of the Palazzo Vecchio so revolted Michelangelo that he insulted the artist: "Oh Ammannato, Ammannato, what lovely marble you have ruined!" The graceful 14th-century **Loggia dei Lanzi,** built as a stage for civic orators, contains world-class sculpture free of charge.

PALAZZO VECCHIO. Arnolfo del Cambio designed this fortress-like *palazzo* in the late-13th century as the governmental seat. It later became the Medici family home, and in 1470 Michelozzo decorated the **courtyard** in Renaissance style. Inside are works by Michelangelo, da Vinci, and Bronzino. *(Open June-Aug. M and F 9am-11pm, Tu-W and Sa 9am-7pm, Th and Su 9am-2pm; Sept.-May M-W and F-Sa 9am-7pm, Th 9am-2pm, Su 9am-2pm. €9.20.)*

THE UFFIZI. Vasari designed this palace in 1554 for the offices *(uffizi)* of Duke Cosimo's administration; today, it houses more first-class art per square inch than any other museum in the world. Botticelli, da Vinci, Michelangelo, Raphael, Titian, Giotto, Fra Angelico, Caravaggio, Bronzino, Cimabue, della Francesca, Bellini, even Dürer, Rubens, and Rembrandt—you name it, they have it. *(From P. della Signoria to the Arno River. ☎055 21 83 41. Open Tu-Su 8:15am-6:50pm. €8.50.)*

ITALY

PONTE VECCHIO. From the Uffizi, follow V. Georgofili left and turn right along the river to reach the nearby **Ponte Vecchio** (Old Bridge). The oldest bridge in Florence, it replaced an older Roman version in 1345. In the 1500s, the Medici kicked out the butcheries and tanneries that lined the bridge and installed goldsmiths and diamond-carvers instead. The view of the bridge from the neighboring Ponte alle Grazie at sunset is breathtaking, and the bridge itself buzzes with pedestrians and street performers, particularly at night.

BARGELLO. The heart of medieval Florence lies in this 13th-century fortress between the *duomo* and P. della Signoria. Once the residence of the chief magistrate and later a brutal prison with public executions in the courtyard, it was restored in the 19th century and now houses the sculpture-filled **Museo Nazionale.** Donatello's bronze *David*, the first freestanding nude since antiquity, stands opposite the two bronze panels of the *Sacrifice of Isaac*, submitted by Ghiberti and Brunelleschi in the baptistery door competition. Michelangelo's early works, including *Bacchus*, *Brutus*, and *Apollo*, are on the ground floor. *(V. del Proconsolo, 4, between duomo and P. della Signoria. ☎055 238 86 06. Open daily typically 8:15am-1:50pm; closed 2nd and 4th M of each month, though hours and off days vary by month. €4.)*

SAN LORENZO AND FARTHER NORTH

BASILICA DI SAN LORENZO. The Medici, who lent the city the funds to build the church (designed in 1419 by Brunelleschi), retained artistic control over its construction. The family cunningly placed Cosimo Medici's grave in front of the high altar, making the entire church his personal mausoleum. Michelangelo designed the exterior but, disgusted by Florentine politics, he abandoned the project to study architecture in Rome. *(☎055 21 66 34. Open daily M-Sa 10am-5pm. €2.50.)*

To reach the **Cappelle dei Medici** (Medici Chapels), walk around to the back entrance on P. Madonna degli Aldobrandini. The **Cappella dei Principi** (Princes' Chapel) is a rare Baroque moment in Florence, while the **Sacrestia Nuova** (New Sacristy) shows Michelangelo's work and holds two Medici tombs. *(Open daily 8:15am-5pm; closed the 2nd and 4th Su and the 1st, 3rd, 5th M of every month. €6.)*

ACCADEMIA. Michelangelo's triumphant **David** stands in self-assured perfection in a rotunda designed specifically for it. In the hallway stand Michelangelo's four *Prisoners;* the master left these intriguing statues intentionally unfinished, chipping away just enough to liberate the "living stone." *(V. Ricasoli 60, between churches of S. Marco and S.S. Annunziata. Wheelchair accessible. Open Tu-Su 8:15am-6:50pm. €6.50.)*

PIAZZA SANTA CROCE AND ENVIRONS

CHIESA DI SANTA CROCE. The thrifty Franciscans ironically built the city's most splendid church. Among the luminaries buried here are Machiavelli, Galileo, Michelangelo, who rests at the front of the right aisle in a tomb designed by Vasari, and humanist Leonardo Bruni, shown holding his precious *History of Florence.* Note also Donatello's gilded *Annunciation.* *(Open M-Sa 9:30am-5:30pm, Su and holidays 3-5:30pm.)* Intricate *pietra serena* pilasters and statues of the evangelists by Donatello grace Brunelleschi's small **Cappella Pazzi,** at the end of the cloister next to the church. *(Enter through the Museo dell'Opera. Open Th-Tu 10am-7pm. €2.60.)*

THE OLTRARNO

Historically disdained by downtown Florentines, the far side of the Arno remains a lively and unpretentious quarter, even in high season.

PALAZZO PITTI. Luca Pitti, a nouveau-riche banker of the 15th century, built his *palazzo* east of Santo Spirito against the Boboli hill. The Medici acquired the *palazzo* and the hill in 1550 and enlarged everything possible. Today, it houses six museums, including the **Galleria Palatina.** The Galleria was one of only a few public galleries when it opened in 1833, and today houses Florence's most important art collection after the Uffizi. Works by Raphael, Titian, Andrea del Sarto, Caravaggio, and Rubens line the walls. Other museums display Medici family treasures, costumes, porcelain, carriages, and *Apartamenti Reale* (royal apartments)—lavish reminders of the time when the *palazzo* was the royal House of Savoy's living quarters. *(Open Tu-Su 8:30am-6.50pm. €6.50)*

BOBOLI GARDENS. With geometrically sculpted hedges, contrasting groves of holly and cypress trees, and bubbling fountains, the elaborate gardens are an exquisite example of stylized Renaissance landscaping. A large oval lawn is just up the hill from the back of the palace, with an Egyptian obelisk in the middle and marble statues in free-standing niches dotting the hedge-lined perimeter. *(Open daily Nov.-Feb. 9am-4:30pm, Mar.-May and Sept.-Oct. 9am-5:30pm, June-Aug. 9am-7:30pm.*

CHIESA DI SANTA MARIA DEL CARMINE. Inside, the **Brancacci Chapel** holds Masaccio's 15th-century frescoes, declared masterpieces even in their time. With such monumental works as the *Tribute Money,* this chapel drew many artists, including Michelangelo. *(Open M and W-Sa 10am-5pm, Su 1-5pm. €3.10.)*

NIGHTLIFE

For information on what's hot in the nightlife scene, consult the monthly *Firenze Spettacolo* (€2). Begin your nighttime *passeggiata* along V. dei Calzaiuoli and end it with coffee or *gelato* in a ritzy cafe on P. della Repubblica, where singers prance about the stage in front of **Bar Concerto.** In the Oltrarno, **Piazza San Spirito** has plenty of bars and restaurants, and live music in summer.

In June, the *quartieri* of Florence turn out in costume to play their own medieval version of soccer, known as **calcio storico,** in which two teams of 27 players face off over a wooden ball in one of the city's *piazze.* These games often blur between athletic contest and riot. Tickets (from €12.40) are sold at the box office. The **Festival of San Giovanni Battista,** on June 24, features a tremendous fireworks display in P. le Michelangelo (easily visible from the Arno) starting around 10pm. May starts the summer music festivals with the classical **Maggio Musicale.** The **Estate Fiesolana** (June-Aug.) fills the Roman theater in nearby Fiesole with concerts, opera, theater, ballet, and film. September brings the **Festa dell'Unità,** a concert series at Campi Bisenzia (take bus #30). On the first Sunday after Ascension Day is the **Festa del Grillo** (Festival of the Cricket), when crickets in tiny wooden cages are sold in the Cascine park and then released into the grass.

BARS

The William, V. Magliabechi 7/9/11r (☎055 263 83 57). Rowdy on weekends, mellow on weeknights. Serves Bass Ale (€4.50). Open daily 12:30pm-1:30am.

May Day Lounge, V. Dante Alighieri 16r. Aspiring artists display their work on the walls of this eclectic lounge. Play pong on the circa 1980 gaming system or sip mixed drinks (€4.50) to the beat of background funk. Happy Hour 8-10pm. Open daily 8pm-2am.

The Fiddler's Elbow, P.S. Maria Novella 74r (☎055 21 59 56). An authentic Irish pub that serves cider, Guinness, and various other draught beers to a crowd of foreign tourists. €4.20 per pint. Open Su-Th 3pm-1am, F-Sa 2pm-2am.

The Chequers Pub, V. della Scala, 7/9r (☎055 28 75 88). This bar attracts a large and lively Italian crowd with its range of beers and typical pub grub. Happy Hour daily 6:30-8pm. Open daily 6pm-1:30am.

DISCOS

Rio Grande, V. degli Olmi 1, near Parco delle Cascinè. Among locals and tourists alike, this is the most popular of Florence's discos. Cover €16, includes 1 drink. Special nights include soul, hip-hop, house, and reggae. Open Tu-Sa 11pm-4am. AmEx/MC/V.

Blob, V. Vinegia 21r, behind the Palazzo Vecchio. DJs, movies, foosball, and an evening bar buffet. Mixed drinks €6. Open daily 6pm-3:30am.

Yab, V. Sassetti 5. Another dance club seething with American students and locals. With classic R&B and reggae on M. A very large dance floor, mercifully free of strobe lights, is packed come midnight. Mixed drinks €5.20. Open daily 9pm-1am.

Tabasco Gay Club, P.S. Cecilia 3r from Palazzo Vecchio. Smoke machines and strobe lights on dance floor. Florence's popular gay disco. Caters primarily to men. 18+. Cover €13, includes first drink. Open Tu-Su 10pm-4am. AmEx/MC/V.

DAYTRIPS FROM FLORENCE

FIESOLE

No trains run to Fiesole, but the town is a 25min. bus ride away; catch the ATAF city bus #7 from the train station near track #16, P.S. Marco. It runs throughout the day (less frequently at night) and drops passengers at P. Mino da Fiesole in the town center.

Older than Florence itself, Fiesole is the site of the original Etruscan settlement that farmed the rich flood plain below. Florence was actually colonized and settled as an off-shoot of this Etruscan town. Fiesole has long been a welcome escape from the sweltering summer heat of the Arno Valley and a source of inspiration for numerous famous figures, including Alexander Dumas, Marcel Proust, Gertrude Stein, and Frank Lloyd Wright. Leonardo da Vinci even used the town as a testing ground for his famed flying machine. Fiesole's location provides incomparable views of both Florence and the rolling countryside to the north—it's a perfect place for a picnic or a daylong *passeggiata.* Outside the bus stop, up the hill to the left, is the fascinating **Missionario Francesco,** the public gardens, and spectacular views of the Florentine sprawl. Half a block off P. Mino da Fiesole is the **Museo Civico.** One ticket gains admission to its three constituent museums. The **Teatro Romano,** or Roman amphitheater, includes Etruscan thermal baths and temple ruins. The amphitheater grounds lead to the **Museo Civico Archeologico,** which houses an extensive collection of Etruscan artifacts. Then breeze through the **Museo Bandini,** a small collection of 14th- and 15th-century Italian paintings. (Open Apr.-Oct. daily 9:30am-6:30pm; Sept.-Mar. W-M 9:30am-6:30pm. €6.20, students and over 65 €4.15.)

The **tourist office,** P. Mino da Fiesole 37, is in the yellow building facing the *piazza.* (☎59 94 78. Open M-Sa 8:30am-7:30pm, Su 10am-7pm.). Accommodations in Fiesole are expensive compared to the budget options in nearby Florence, but the town is a great place to stop for a leisurely lunch. **Pizzeria Etrusca ❷,** in P. Mina da Fiesole, has delicious pizza at reasonable prices. (☎59 94 84. Pizza €4.65-6.75; *primi* from €4.65; *secondi* from €8.26. Open noon-3pm and 7pm-1am.)

ITALY

AREZZO

Trains arrive from Florence (1½hr., 2 per hr., €5) and Rome (2hr., every 1-2hr., €11). Buses pull in from Siena (1½hr., 7 per day, €4.60.)

The poet Petrarch, native son Michelangelo, and, most recently, Roberto Benigni of the film *Life is Beautiful* have all found inspiration in the streets of Arezzo. The town's most famous treasure is the magnificent fresco cycle **Leggenda della Vera Croce** (Legend of the True Cross) by **Piero della Francesca,** which portrays the story of the crucifix. It is housed in the extraordinary 14th-century **Basilica di San Francesco,** P.S. Francesco, up V.G. Monaco from the train station. (Open daily 8:30am-noon and 2-7pm. €5, students €3.) Seven 6m high circular stained-glass windows let light into the massive **duomo,** up V. Andrea Cesalpino from P.S. Francesco. (Open daily 7am-12:30pm and 3-6:30pm.) Down Corso Italia, the **Piazza Grande** showcases Arezzo's most impressive examples of architecture, including the spectacular **Chiesa di Santa Maria della Pieve.** (Open M-Sa 8am-noon and 3-7pm, Su 8:30am-noon and 4-7pm.) The **tourist office,** P. della Repubblica 22, is to the right as you exit the train station. (☎0575 37 76 78; fax 0575 208 39. Open Apr.-Sept. M-Sa 9am-1pm and 3-7pm, Su 9am-1pm; Oct.-Mar. M-Sa 9am-1pm and 3-6:30pm.)

SIENA ☎0577

Many travelers rush from Rome to Florence, ignoring gorgeous, medieval Siena. The Sienese have a rich history in arts, politics, and trade; one of their proudest celebrations is the semiannual **Palio,** a wild horse race among the city's 17 competing *contrade* (districts).

TRANSPORTATION AND PRACTICAL INFORMATION. Trains (☎0577 28 01 15) leave P. Rosselli hourly for Florence (1½hr., 12 per day, €5) and Rome (3hr., 16 per day, €16.25) via Chiusi. **TRA-IN/SITA buses** (☎0577 20 42 45) depart from P. Gramsci and the train station for Florence (every hr., €6) and San Gimignano (8 per day, €5). From the train station, cross the street and take **TRA-IN/SITA buses** #3, 4, 7-10, 14, 17, or 77 into the center of town at **Piazza del Sale** or **Piazza Gramsci** (€0.80). The central **APT tourist office** is at Il Campo 56. (☎0577 28 05 51; fax 0577 27 06 76. Open daily mid-Mar. to mid-Nov. 8:30am-7:30pm; mid-Nov. to mid-Mar. 8:30am-1pm and 3-7pm.) **Prenotazioni Alberghiere,** in P.S. Domenico, finds rooms for €2. (☎0577 28 80 84. Open M-Sa 9am-7pm.) Check email at **Internet Train,** V. di Citta 121. (€5 per hr. Open daily 10am-8pm.) **Postal Code:** 53100.

ACCOMMODATIONS AND FOOD. Finding a room in Siena can be difficult from Easter to October. Book months ahead if coming during *Il Palio.* The tastefully furnished **Albergo Tre Donzelle ❸** is at V. Donzelle 5. (☎0577 28 03 58; fax 0577 22 39 38. Curfew 1am. Singles €31; doubles €44-57. MC/V.) Take bus #15 from P. Gramsci to reach the **Ostello della Gioventù "Guidoriccio" (HI) ❶,** V. Fiorentina 89, in Località Lo Stellino. (☎0577 522 12. Curfew midnight. Reserve ahead. Dorms €13. MC/V.) **Santvario S. Caterina Alma Domus ❹,** V. Camporegio 37, behind S. Domenico, has spotless rooms with views of the *duomo.* (☎0577 441 77; fax 0577 476 01. Curfew 11:30pm. Singles €42; doubles €55; triples €70; quads €85.) To **camp** at **Colleverde ❶,** Strada di Scacciapensieri 47, take bus #3 or 8 from P. del Sale. (☎0577 28 00 44. Open mid-Mar. to mid-Nov. €8 per adult, including tent; €4.15 per child.)

Siena specializes in rich pastries, of which the most famous is *panforte,* a confection of honey, almonds, and citron; indulge in this serious pastry at **Bar/Pasticceria Nannini,** V. Banchi di Sopra 22-24, the oldest *pasticceria* in Siena. Next to Santuario di S. Caterina is the divine **Osteria La Chiacchera ❷,** Costa di S. Antonio 4. (☎0577 28 06 31. *Secondi* €4.65-6.75. Open W-M 12:30-3pm and 7-10:30pm.) **Consortio Agrario supermarket,** V. Pianigiani 5, is off P. Salimberi. (Open M-F 8am-7:30pm.)

ITALY

SIGHTS AND ENTERTAINMENT. Siena offers two *biglietto cumulativi* (cumulative tickets)—the first is good for five days (€7.50) and allows entry into the Museo dell'Opera Metropolitana, baptistery, and Piccolomini library; the second is valid for seven days (€16) and covers four more sights, including the Museo Civico. Both may be purchased at any of the included sights. Siena radiates from **Piazza del Campo (Il Campo),** a shell-shaped brick square designed for civic events. At the top of Il Campo is the **Fonte Gaia,** still fed by the same aqueduct used in the 1300s. At the bottom, the **Torre del Mangia** clock tower looms over the graceful Gothic **Palazzo Pubblico.** Inside the *palazzo,* the **Museo Civico** contains excellent Gothic and early Renaissance paintings; also check out the **Sala del Mappamondo** and the **Sala della Pace.** (*Palazzo,* museum, and tower open Mar.-Oct. daily 10am-7pm; Nov.-Feb. 10am-4pm. Tower €5.50; museum €6.50, students €4; combined ticket with tower €9.50.) From the *palazzo,* take the right-side stairs and cross V. di Città for Siena's Gothic **duomo.** The apse would have been left hanging in mid-air save for the construction of the lavishly decorated **baptistery** below. (Open mid-Mar. to Oct. daily 9am-7:30pm; Nov. to mid-Mar. 10am-1pm and 2:30-5pm. Free except when floor is uncovered in Sept. €4-5.50.) The **Libreria Piccolomini,** off the left aisle, holds frescoes and 15th-century scores. (Same hours as *duomo*. €1.50.) The **Museo dell'Opera della Metropolitana,** to the right of the *duomo*, houses overflow art. (Open Apr.-Oct. daily 9am-7:30pm; Nov.-Mar. 9am-1:30pm. €5.50.)

Siena's **Il Palio** occurs twice a year, July 2 and Aug. 16, and is a traditional bareback horse race around the packed P. del Campo. Arrive three days earlier to watch the five trial runs and to pick a *contrada* to root for. At *Il Palio*, the jockeys take about 90 seconds to tear around Il Campo three times. To stay in Siena during the Palio, book rooms at least four months in advance, especially budget accommodations—write the APT in March or April for a list of rented rooms.

DAYTRIP FROM SIENA: SAN GIMIGNANO. The hilltop village of San Gimignano looks like an illumination from a medieval manuscript. The city's famous 14 towers, which are all that survive of its original 72, earned San Gimignano its nickname as the *Città delle Belle Torri* (City of Beautiful Towers). Not for the faint of heart, **Museo Della Tortura,** V. del Castello 1, just off P. Cisterna, offers a morbidly fascinating history of torture from Medieval Europe to the present. (Open Apr.-Oct. 10am-8pm; Nov.-Mar. 10am-6pm. €8, students €5.50.) The **Museo Civico,** on the second floor of **Palazzo del Popolo,** houses an amazing collection of Sienese and Florentine artwork. Within the museum is the entrance to the **Torre Grossa,** the tallest remaining tower; climb its 218 steps for a panorama of Tuscany. (Palazzo open Tu-Su 9am-7:30pm. Museum and tower open Mar.-Oct. daily 9:30am-7:20pm; Nov.-Feb. Sa-Th 10:30am-4:20pm. Museum and tower €7.50, €5.50.)

TRA-IN buses leave P. Montemaggio for Siena (1hr., every hr., €5) and Florence (1½hr., every hr., €5.70) via Poggibonsi (20min., €1.35). From the bus station, pass through the *porta*, climb the hill, following V.S. Giovanni to the city center **Piazza della Cisterna,** which runs into P. del Duomo and the **tourist office,** P. del Duomo 1. (☎0577 94 00 08; fax 0577 94 09 03. Open Mar.-Oct. daily 9am-1pm and 3-7pm; Nov.-Feb. 9am-1pm and 2-6pm.) Accommodations are pricey in San Gimignano—*affitte camere* (private rooms) are a good alternative at about €40. The **Associazione Strutture Extralberghiere,** P. della Cisterna 6, finds private rooms. (☎94 08 09. Open Mar.-Nov. daily 9:30am-7:30pm.) From the bus stop, enter through Porta S. Giovanni for the quaint **Camere Cennini Gianni ❺,** V.S. Giovanni 21. The reception is at the *passticceria* at V.S. Giovanni 88. (☎0577 94 10 51; www.sangiapartments.com. Reserve ahead. Doubles €55; triples €65; quads €75.) **Camp at Il Boschetto ❶,** at Santa Lucia, a 2.5km bus ride (€0.80) from Porta S. Giovanni. (☎94 03 52. Reception daily 8am-1pm and 3-10pm. Open Apr.-Oct. €5 per person, €5 per tent.) **La Bettola del Grillo ❸,** V. Quercecchio 33, off V.S. Giovanni, opposite P. della Cisterna, serves traditional Tuscan delights. The *menù* (€13) includes wine and dessert. (*Primi* €5-7, *secondi* €7.50. Open Tu-Su 12:30-3pm and 7:30-11pm.)

PISA ☎050

Tourism hasn't always been Pisa's prime industry: during the Middle Ages, the city was a major port with a Mediterranean empire. But when the Arno River silted up and the tower started leaning, the city's power and wealth declined accordingly. Today the city seems resigned to welcoming tourists and myriad t-shirt and ice cream vendors to the **Piazza del Duomo,** also known as the **Campo dei Miracoli** (Field of Miracles), a grassy expanse enclosing the tower, *duomo*, baptistry, Camposanto, Museo delle Sinopie, and Museo del Duomo. An **all-inclusive ticket** to the Campo's sights–excluding the tower–costs €10.50. Begun in 1173, the famous **Leaning Tower** began to tilt when the soil beneath suddenly shifted. In June of 2001, a multi-year stabilization effort was completed and the tower is now considered stable at its present inclination. Guided tours of 40 visitors are permitted to ascend the 300 steps once every 40 minutes. The dazzling **duomo** is a treasury of fine art, and one of the finest Romanesque cathedrals in the world. (Open daily 10am-

7:30pm. €2.) Next door is the **baptistry,** with precise acoustics that allow an non-amplified choir to be heard 2km away. (Open late Apr. to late Sept. daily 8am-7:30pm; Oct.-Mar. 9am-6pm. €6 includes 1 other museum or monument.) The adjoining **Camposanto,** a cloistered cemetery, has Roman sarcophagi and a series of haunting frescoes by an unidentified 14th-century artist known only as the "Master of the Triumph of Death." (Open late-Apr. to late-Sept. daily 8am-7:30pm; Mar. and Oct. 9am-5:40pm; Nov.-Feb. 9am-4:40pm. €6.20 includes 1 other museum or monument.) The **Museo delle Sinopie,** across the *piazza* from the Camposanto, displays preliminary fresco sketches discovered during post-WWII restoration. Behind the tower is the **Museo dell'Opera del Duomo.** (Both open late Apr. to late Sept. daily 8am-7:20pm; Mar. and Oct. 9am-5:20pm; Nov.-Feb. 9am-4:20pm. €6.20 includes 1 other museum or monument.) From the Campo, walk down V.S. Maria and over the bridge to the Gothic **Chiesa di Santa Maria della Spina,** whose tower allegedly holds a thorn from Christ's crown.

Trains (☎050 147 808 88) leave **Piazza della Stazione,** in the southern part of town, to Florence (1hr., every hr., €4.85); Genoa (2½hr., €7.90); and Rome (3hr., €23.50). To reach the Campo from the train station, take **bus** #3 (€0.75). The **tourist office** is to the left as you exit the station. (☎050 422 91; www.turismo.toscana.it. Open M-Sa 9am-7pm, Su 9:30am-3:30pm.) The **Albergo Helvetia ❸,** V. Don G. Boschi 31, 2min. from the *duomo*, off P. Archivescovado, has large, clean rooms. (☎55 30 84. Singles €32; doubles €42.) The **Hotel Galileo ❹,** V.S. Maria 12, has spacious, simple rooms with tiled floors. (☎406 21. Singles and doubles €42; triples €57.) Try the heavenly *risotto* at the lively **Il Paiolo ❶,** V. Curtatone e Montanara 9. (*Menù* with *primi* and *secondi* €4-6. Open M-F noon-10pm, Sa 5-10pm.) **Trattoria da Matteo ❷,** V. l'Aroncio 46, serves authentic cuisine and 40 types of pizza. (☎410 57. *Menù* €12.Open Su-F 9am-3pm and 6-11pm.) Get **groceries** at **Superal,** V. Pascoli 6, off C. Italia. (Open M-Sa 8am-8pm.) **Postal Code:** 56100.

ITALY

ELBA ☎0565

Napoleon spent his exile here—all would-be conquerors of Europe should be so lucky. Elba's turquoise waters, dramatic mountains, velvety beaches, and diverse attractions accommodate almost any interest. While families lounge in **Marina di Campo** and **Marciana Marina,** party-hard beach fanatics waste away in **Capoliveri,** yacht-club members gallivant in **Porto Azzurro,** and nature-loving recluses gravitate to the mountainous northeast tip, between **Cavi** on the beach and **Rio nell'Elba** in the interior. Elba is one of the best places in Italy to bike or scooter, with roads that wind through the island's mountainous terrain, affording stupendous views of the ocean. **Ferries** go from **Piombino Marittima** (or *Piombino Porto*) on the mainland to **Portoferraio,** Elba's largest city. Although **trains** on the Genoa-Rome line travel to Piombino Marittima, most stop at **Campiglia Marittima** (from Florence, change at Pisa), where a *pullman* (intercity bus; 30min., €1) meets trains and connects to ferries in Piombino Marittima. Both Toremar (☎311 00; 1hr., €6) and Moby Lines (☎0565 22 52 11; 1hr., €8) run to Elba. The **tourist office,** Calata Italia 32, 1st fl., across from the Toremar boat landing, helps with rooms and transport. (☎91 46 71. Open daily 9am-1pm and 2:30-7:30pm; off-season 9am-1pm and 3-7pm.) **Ape Elbana,** Salita Cosimo de' Medici 2, overlooks the main *piazza* of the *centro storico*. (☎0565 91 42 45. Singles €50; doubles €62.)

UMBRIA

Umbria is known as the "Green Heart of Italy," a land rich in natural beauty, encompassing wild woods, fertile plains, craggy gorges, and tiny villages. Christianity transformed Umbria's architecture and regional identity, turning it into a breeding ground for saints and religious movements; it was here that St. Francis of Assisi shamed the extravagant church with his humility.

PERUGIA ☎075

Between Perugia's art and architecture and its big-city vitality and gorgeous countryside, there's no reason not to visit this gem of a city. The city's most popular sights frame **Piazza IV Novembre.** In the center of the *piazza*, the **Fontana Maggiore** is adorned with sculptures and bas-reliefs by Nicolà and Giovanni Pisano. At the end of the *piazza*, the imposing Gothic **duomo** houses the Virgin Mary's purported wedding ring. (Open daily 8am-noon and 4pm-dusk.) The 13th-century **Palazzo dei Priori** presides over the *piazza* and houses the impressive **Galleria Nazionale dell'Umbria,** Corso Vannucci 19. (Open daily 8:30am-7:30pm; closed 1st M each month. €6.50.) At the end of town past the Porta S. Pietro, the **Basilica di San Pietro,** on Corso Cavour, has a beautiful garden. (Open daily 8am-noon and 3:30pm-dusk.)

Trains leave P.V. Veneto, Fontiveggio, for: Assisi (25min., every hr., €1.60); Florence (2½hr., 7 per day, €7.90); and Rome (direct 2½hr., €10.15) via Terontola or Foligno. From the station, take bus #6, 7, 9, 13d, or 15 to the central P. Italia (€0.80), then walk down Corso Vannucci to P. IV Novembre and the **tourist office,** P. IV Novembre 3. (☎075 572 33 27; fax 075 573 93 86. Open M-Sa 8:30am-1:30pm and 3:30-6:30pm, Su 9am-1pm.) To get from the tourist office to **Ostello della Gioventù/Centro Internazionale di Accoglienza per la Gioventù ❶,** V. Bontempi 13, walk down Corso Vannucci past the *duomo* and P. Danti, take the farthest street right through P. Piccinino, and turn right on V. Bontempi. (☎/fax 075 572 28 80; www.perugia.it. Sheets €1.50. Lockout 9:30am-4pm. Curfew midnight. Open mid-Jan. to mid-Dec. Dorms €12.) **Albergo Anna ❹,** V. dei Priori 48, off Corso Vannucci, has cozy 17th-century rooms with great views. (☎/fax 075 573 63 04. Singles €40, with bath €45; doubles €46/60; triples €70/85. AmEx/MC/V.) **Ristorante da Gianocarlo ❸,** V. dei Priori 36, two blocks off Corso Vannucci, is full of locals dining on delicious food. (*Primi* €6-14; *secondi* from €9-21. Open Sa-Th noon-3pm and 6-10pm.) The **COOP,** P. Matteotti 15, has **groceries.** (Open M-Sa 9am-8pm.) **Postal Code:** 06100.

ASSISI ☎079

The undeniable jewel of Assisi is the 13th-century **Basilica di San Francesco.** Giotto's renowned *Life of St. Francis* fresco cycle decorates the walls of the upper church, paying tribute to his sainthood and consecration. From P. del Commune, take V. Portica. (Dress code strictly enforced. Lower basilica open daily 6:30am-7pm. Upper basilica open daily 8:30am-7pm.) The dramatic fortress **Rocca Maggiore** towers above town, offering panoramic views. (Open daily 10am-dusk. €1.70, students €1.) The pink and white **Basilica of Santa Chiara** houses St. Francis's tunic, sandals, and crucifix. (Open M-F daily 9am-noon and 2-7pm.)

From the station near the Basilica Santa Maria degli Angeli, **trains** go to: Ancona (8 per day, €6.85); Florence (7 per day, €9); and Rome (5 per day, €9); more frequent trains go to Rome via Foligno and to Florence via Ternotola. **Buses** run from P. Unita D'Italia to Florence (2½hr., 1 per day, €6.40) and Perugia (1hr., 11 per day, €2.70). From P. Matteotti, follow V. del Torrione, bear left on P.S. Rufino, and take V.S. Rufino to **Piazza del Comune,** the town center, and the **tourist office,** in P. del Comune. (☎079 81 25 34; www.umbria2000.it. Open M-F 8am-2pm and 3:30-6:30pm,

ITALY

Sa 9am-1pm and 3:30-6:30pm, Su 9am-1pm.) Perhaps the cleanest hostel you'll find, the lovely **Camere Annalisa Martini ❷,** V.S. Gregorio 6, has lots of amenities and a friendly atmosphere. (Singles €22; doubles €32; triples €48-52; quads €57.) For **Ostello della Pace (HI) ❶,** V. di Valecchi 177, turn right out of the station, then left at the intersection on V. di Valecchi. (☎/fax 079 81 67 67. Breakfast included. Reception daily 7-9am and 3:30-11:30pm. Check-out 9:30am. Reserve ahead. Dorms €14, with bath €16. MC/V.) **Postal Code:** 06081.

THE MARCHES (LE MARCHE)

In the Marches, green foothills separate the gray shores of the Adriatic from the Apennine peaks and the traditional hill towns from the umbrella-laden beaches. Inland towns, easily accessible by train, rely on agriculture and preserve the region's historical legacy in the architectural remains of Gauls and Romans.

URBINO ☎0722

Urbino's fairy-tale skyline, scattered with humble stone dwellings and an immense turreted palace, has changed little over the past 500 years. The city's most remarkable monument is the imposing Renaissance **Palazzo Ducale** (Ducal Palace), in P. Rinascimento, though its facade is more thrilling than its interior. The central courtyard is the essence of Renaissance balance and proportion; to the left, stairs lead to the former private apartments of the Duke, which now house the **National Gallery of the Marches.** (Open M 8:30am-2pm, Tu-F 8:30am-7:15pm, Sa 8:30am-10:30pm, Su 8:30am-7:15pm. €4.) Walk back across P. della Repubblica and continue onto V. Raffaello to Raphael's birthplace, the **Casa di Rafaele,** V. Raffaello 57, now a museum that contains a reproduction of his earliest work, *Madonna e Bambino.* (Open M-Sa 9am-1pm and 3-6pm, Su 10am-1pm. €3.)

ITALY

Bucci **buses** (☎0722 13 24 01) go from Borgo Mercatale to Rome (5hr., 1 per day, €18.50). Blue SOBET **buses** (☎0722 223 33) run to P. Matteotti and the train station in Pesaro (1hr., 4-10 per day, €2.10; buy tickets on the bus). From there, a short walk uphill on V.G. Mazzini leads to **Piazza della Repubblica,** the city center. The **tourist office,** P. Rinascimento 1, is opposite the palace. (☎0722 328 568; fax 0722 309 457. Open mid-June to mid-Sept. M-Sa 9am-1pm and 3-7pm, Su 9am-1pm; in winter 9am-1pm and 3-6pm.) **Hotel San Giovanni ❷,** V. Barocci 13, has simple, clean rooms. (☎0722 28 27. Open Aug.-June. Singles €22, with bath €27; doubles €38/48; triples €57.) **Camping Pineta ❶,** on V.S. Donato, is 2km away in Cesane; take bus #4 or 7 from Borgo Mercatale to camping. (☎0722 47 10. Reception daily 9-11am and 3-10pm. Open Apr. to mid-Sept. €6 per person, €12 per tent.) **Margherita supermarket** is at V. Raffaello 37. (Open M-Sa 7:30am-2pm and 3-8pm.) **Postal Code:** 61029.

ANCONA ☎071

Ancona is the epicenter of Italy's Adriatic Coast—a major port in a small, whimsical, largely unexplored city. **Piazza Roma** is dotted with yellow and pink buildings, and **Piazza Cavour** is the heart of the town. Ancona has **ferry service** to Greece, Croatia, and northern Italy. **Adriatica** (☎071 20 49 15; www.adriatica.it), **Jadrolinija** (☎20 43 05; www.jadrolinija.tel.hr/jadrolinija), and **SEM Maritime Co.** (☎071 20 40 90; www.sem.hr) run to Croatia (from €45). **ANEK** (☎207 23 46; www.anek.gr) and **Blue Star (Strintzis)** (☎071 207 10 68; www.strinzis.gr) ferries go to Greece (from €50). Schedules and tickets are available at the Stazione Marittima; reserve ahead in July or August. **Trains** arrive at P. Rosselli from: Bologna (2½hr., 1-2 per hr., €12); Milan (5hr., 24 per day, €21); Rome (3-4hr., 9 per day, €15); and Venice (5hr., 3 per day, from €15). Take bus #1/4 (€0.80) along the port past **Stazione Marittima** and up Corso Stamira to reach P. Cavour. A branch of the **tourist office** is located in

Stazione Marittima and provides ferry information. (☎071 20 11 83. Open June-Sept. Tu-Sa 8am-8pm, Su-M 8am-2pm.) From the train station, cross the *piazza*, turn left, then take the first right, and make a sharp right behind the newsstand to reach the new **Ostella della Gioventù ❶**, V. Lamaticci 7. (☎/fax 071 422 57. Reception 6:30-11am and 4:30pm-midnight. Dorms €13.) **CONAD supermarket** is at V. Matteotti 115. (Open M-Sa 8am-1:30pm and 5-7:30pm.) **Postal Code:** 60100.

SOUTHERN ITALY

South of Rome, the sun gets brighter, the meals longer, and the passion more intense. The introduction to the *mezzogiorno* (Italian South) begins in Campania, the fertile cradle of the Bay of Naples and the Gulf of Salerno. The shadow of Mt. Vesuvius hides the famous ruins of Pompeii, lost to time and a river of molten lava, while the Amalfi Coast cuts a dramatic course down the lush Tyrrhenian shore. The region remains justly proud of its open-hearted populace, strong traditions, classical ruins, and relatively untouristed beaches.

NAPLES (NAPOLI) ☎081

Italy's third-largest city is also its most chaotic: shouting merchants flood markets and summer traffic jams clog the broiling city. The city's color and vitality, evident in the street markets and family-run pizzerias, have gradually overcome its traditionally rough-edged image. In recent years, aggressive restoration has opened monuments for the first time, revealing exquisite architectural works of art.

ITALY

TRANSPORTATION

Flights: Aeroporto Capodichino, V. Umberto Maddalena (☎081 789 61 11), northwest of the city. Connects to all major Italian and European cities. A CLP **bus** (☎531 16 46) leaves from P. Municipio (20min., 6am-10:30pm, €1.55).

Trains: Ferrovie dello Stato goes from Stazione Centrale to: **Brindisi** (5hr., 5 per day, €18.85); **Milan** (8hr., 13 per day, €50); **Rome** (2hr., 34 per day, €9.60). **Circumvesuviana** (☎081 772 24 44) heads for **Herculaneum** (€1.55) and **Pompeii** (€1.90).

Ferries: Depart from **Molo Angioino** and **Molo Beverello,** at the base of P. Municipio. From P. Garibaldi, take tram #1; from P. Municipio, take the R2 bus. **Caremar,** Molo Beverello (☎081 551 38 82), goes frequently to **Capri** and **Ischia** (both 1½hr., €5). **Tirrenia Lines,** Molo Angioino (☎081 720 11 11), goes to **Palermo, Sicily,** and **Cagliari, Sardinia.** Schedules and prices change frequently, so check *Qui Napoli*.

Public Transportation: Giranapoli tickets (1½hr.; €0.80, full-day €2.35) are valid on **buses, Métro** (subway), **trams,** and **funiculars.**

Taxis: Cotana (☎081 570 70 70) or **Napoli** (☎081 556 44 44). Take metered taxis.

ORIENTATION AND PRACTICAL INFORMATION

The main train and bus terminals are in the immense **Piazza Garibaldi** on the east side of Naples. From P. Garibaldi, broad **Corso Umberto I** leads southwest to P. Bovi, from which V. Depretis leads left to **Piazza Municipio,** the city center, and **Piazza Trieste e Trento** and **Piazza Plebiscito.** Below P. Municipio lie the **Stazione Marittima** ferry ports. From P. Trieste e Trento, **Via Toledo** (also known as **Via Roma**) leads through the Spanish quarter to **Piazza Dante.** Make a right into the historic **Spaccanapoli** neighborhood, which follows **Via dei Tribunali** through the middle of town. While violence is rare in Naples, theft is relatively common. Always be careful.

Tourist Offices: EPT (☎081 26 87 79), at Stazione Centrale. Helps with hotels and ferries. Has copies of *Qui Napoli,* a monthly tourist publication full of schedules and listings. Open M-Sa 9am-7pm. **Branches** at P. dei Martiri 58 and Stazione Mergellina.

Consulates: Canada, V. Carducci 29 (☎081 40 13 38). **South Africa,** Corso Umberto 1 (☎551 75 19). **UK,** V. dei Mille 40 (☎081 423 89 11). **US,** P. della Repubblica (☎081 583 81 11, emergency ☎03 37 94 50 83), at the west end of Villa Comunale.

Currency Exchange: Thomas Cook, at the airport (☎081 551 83 99). Open M-F 9:30am-1pm and 3-6:30pm.

Emergency: ☎113. **Police:** ☎113 or 081 794 11 11. English spoken.

Hospital: Cardarelli (☎081 747 28 59), on the R4 line. **Ambulance:** ☎081 752 06 96.

Internet Access: Internetbar, P. Bellini 74. €2.50 per hr. Open M-Sa 9am-2am, Su 8am-2am. **Internet Multimedia,** V. Sapienza 43. €1.55 per hr. Scanning and printing available. Open daily 9:30am-9:30pm.

Post Office: P. Matteotti (☎081 552 42 33), at V. Diaz (R2 line). Address mail to be held: Firstname SURNAME, *In Fermo Posta,* P. Matteotti, Naples **80100,** ITALY. Open M-F 8:15am-6pm, Sa 8:15am-noon.

ACCOMMODATIONS

Although Naples has some fantastic bargain lodgings, especially near **Piazza Garibaldi,** be cautious when choosing a room. Avoid hotels that solicit customers at the station, never give your passport until you've seen the room, and gauge how secure a lodging seems. The **ACISJF/Centro D'Ascolto,** at Stazione Centrale, helps women find safe rooms. (☎081 28 19 93. Open M-Tu and Th 3:30-6:30pm.) Rooms are scarce in the historic district between P. Dante and the *duomo.*

Casanova Hotel, C. Garibaldi 333 (☎081 26 82 87). From P. Garibaldi, continue down C. Garibaldi and turn right before V. Casanova. Clean, airy rooms, and a rooftop terrace. Breakfast €4. Reserve ahead. Singles €20, with bath €26; doubles €36/€46; triples €49/€57; quads €69. 10% *Let's Go* discount. AmEx/MC/V. ❷

Soggiorno Imperia, P. Miraglia 386 (☎081 45 93 47). Take the R2 from the train station, walk up V. Mezzocannone through P.S. Domenico Maggiore, and enter the 1st set of green doors to the left on P. Miraglia. Clean rooms in a 16th-century *palazzo.* Call ahead. Dorms €16; singles €30; doubles €42; triples €60. ❶

Hotel Eden, C. Novara 9 (☎081 28 53 44). Convenient for backpackers arriving without reservations. With *Let's Go:* singles €30; doubles €40; triples €60. AmEx/MC/V. ❸

6 Small Rooms, V. Diodato Lioy 18 (☎081 790 13 78), up from P. Monteolovieto. Big rooms in a friendly atmosphere. Dorms €16; singles €20.70. ❶

FOOD

Pizza-making is an art born in Naples. **Pizzeria Di Matteo ❷,** V. Tribunali 94, draws a crowd of students and pizza connoisseurs to this small, pre-eminent eatery. (Open M-Sa 9am-midnight.) **Pizzeria Brandi ❷,** Salita S. Anna di Palazzo 1, counts Luciano Pavarotti and Isabella Rossellini among its patrons. (Cover €1.55. Open M-Su noon-3pm and 7pm-midnight.) To get to **Antica Pizzeria da Michele ❷,** V. Cesare Sersale 1-3, walk up C. Umberto I from P. Garibaldi and take the first right. Get a slice of *marinara* (tomato, garlic, oregano, and oil) or *margherita* (tomato, mozzarella, and basil) and a beer for €4.15. (Open M-Sa 8am-11pm.) Some of the best pizza in Naples is at **Pizzeria Trianon da Ciro ❶,** V. Pietro Colletta 44, a block off C. Umberto I. (Pizza €3-7. Open daily 10am-3:30pm and 6:30-11pm.) For excellent waterfront seafood, take the C25 bus to P. Amedeo.

ITALY

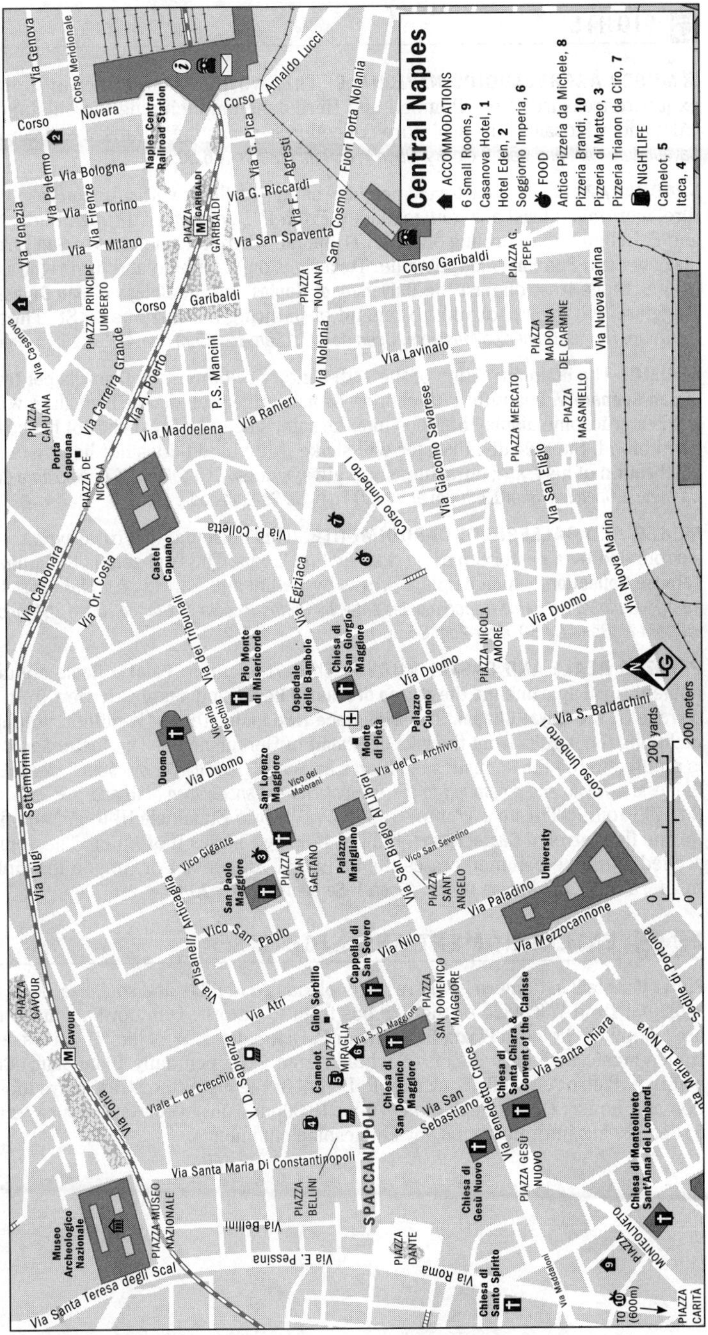
Central Naples
ACCOMMODATIONS
6 Small Rooms, 9
Casanova Hotel, 1
Hotel Eden, 2
Soggiorno Imperia, 6
FOOD
Antica Pizzeria da Michele, 8
Pizzeria Brandi, 10
Pizzeria di Matteo, 3
Pizzeria Trianon da Ciro, 7
NIGHTLIFE
Camelot, 5
Itaca, 4
Naples Central Railroad Station
PIAZZA GARIBALDI
GARIBALDI
Via Genova
Corso Meridionale
Corso Novara
Arnaldo Lucci
Corso
Via Bologna
Via Palermo
Via Torino
Via Firenze
Via Milano
Via Venezia
Via G. Pica
Via G. Riccardi
Via F. Agresti
Fuori Porta Nolania
Via San Spaventa
San Cosmo
Corso Garibaldi
PIAZZA G. PEPE
PIAZZA NOLANA
Via Nolania
PIAZZA PRINCIPE UMBERTO
Via Casanova
Corso Garibaldi
Via Carreira Grande
Via A. Poerio
P.S. Mancini
Via Ranieri
Via Lavinaio
PIAZZA MADONNA DEL CARMINE
Via Nuova Marina
PIAZZA CAPUANA
Porta Capuana
PIAZZA DE NICOLA
Via Maddelena
PIAZZA MERCATO
PIAZZA MASANIELLO
Via Giacomo Savarese
Corso Umberto I
Castel Capuano
Via P. Colletta
Via San Eligio
Via Carbonara
Via Or. Costa
Via del Tribunali
Via Egiziaca
Pio Monte di Misericorde
Chiesa di San Giorgio Maggiore
Ospedale delle Bambole
PIAZZA NICOLA AMORE
Via Duomo
Via S. Baldachini
Vicaria Vecchia
Duomo
Monte di Pietà
Palazzo Cuomo
Settembrini
San Lorenzo Maggiore
Vico dei Maiorani
Via del G. Archivio
Al Librai
200 yards
200 meters
Via Luigi
Vico Gigante
PIAZZA SAN GAETANO
Palazzo Marigliano
Via San Biagio
Vico San Severino
University
San Paolo Maggiore
PIAZZA SANT' ANGELO
Via Paladino
Via Pisanelli Anticaglia
Vico San Paolo
Cappella di San Severo
Via Nilo
Via Mezzocannone
PIAZZA CAVOUR
CAVOUR
Via Atri
Gino Sorbillo
PIAZZA SAN DOMENICO MAGGIORE
Sedile di Portone
PIAZZA MIRAGLIA
Via S. D. Maggiore
Chiesa di San Domenico Maggiore
Chiesa di Santa Chiara & Convent of the Clarisse
Via Santa Chiara
Via Maria La Nova
Camelot
Viale L. de Crecchio
V. D. Sapienza
Via San Sebastiano Croce
Via Benedetto Croce
Via Foria
SPACCANAPOLI
Via Santa Maria Di Constantinopoli
PIAZZA BELLINI
Chiesa di Gesù Nuovo
PIAZZA GESÙ NUOVO
Chiesa di Monteoliveto Sant'Anna dei Lombardi
Museo Archeologico Nazionale
PIAZZA MUSEO NAZIONALE
Via Bellini
PIAZZA DANTE
PIAZZA MONTEOLIVETO
Via Santa Teresa degli Scal
Via E. Pessina
Via Roma
Via Maddaloni
Chiesa di Santo Spirito
TO 10 (600m)
PIAZZA CARITÀ

ITALY

SIGHTS

MUSEO ARCHEOLOGICO NAZIONALE. This world-class collection houses exquisite treasures from Pompeii and Herculaneum, including the outstanding "Alexander Mosaic." The sculpture collection is also quite impressive. *(From M: P. Cavour, turn right and walk 2 blocks. Open W-M 9am-7:30pm. €6.50.)*

SPACÇANAPOLI. This east-west neighborhood overflows with gorgeous architecture, meriting at least a 30min. meander. From P. Dante, walk through Porta Alba and P. Bellini before turning on V. dei Tribunali, where the churches of **San Lorenzo Maggiore** and **San Paolo Maggiore** lie. Turn right on V. Duomo and turn right again on V.S. Biago to stroll past the **University of Naples** and the **Chiesa di San Domenico Maggiore,** where, according to legend, a painting once spoke to St. Thomas Aquinas. *(In P.S. Domenico Maggiore. Open daily 7:15am-12:15pm and 4:15-7:15pm. Free.)*

DUOMO. The main attraction of the 14th-century *duomo* is the **Cappella del Tesoro di San Gennaro.** A beautiful 17th-century bronze grille protects the high altar, which holds a gruesome display of relics like the saint's head and two vials of his coagulated blood. Supposedly, disaster will strike if the blood does not liquefy on the celebration of his *festa*; miraculously, it always does. *(3 blocks up V. Duomo from Corso Umberto I. Open M-F 8am-12:30pm and 4:30-7pm, Sa-Su 9am-noon. Free.)*

MUSEO AND GALLERIE DI CAPODIMONTE. This museum, in a royal *palazzo*, is surrounded by a pastoral park and sprawling lawns. The true gem is the amazing **Farnese Collection,** which displays works by Bellini and Caravaggio. *(Take bus #110 from P. Garibaldi to Parco Capodimonte; enter by Portas Piccola or Grande. Open Tu-F and Su 8:30am-7:30pm, €7.50, after 2pm €6.50.)*

PALAZZO REALE AND CASTEL NUOVO. The 17th-century **Palazzo Reale** contains opulent royal apartments, the **Museo di Palazzo Reale,** and a fantastic view from the terrace of the **Royal Chapel.** The **Biblioteca Nazionale** stores 1½ million volumes, including the scrolls from the **Villa dei Papiri** in Herculaneum. The **Teatro San Carlo** is reputed to top the acoustics in Milan's La Scala. *(Take the R2 bus from P. Garibaldi to P. Trieste e Trento and go around to the P. Plebiscito entrance. Open M-Tu and Th-F 9am-8pm. €4.15.)* From P. Trieste e Trento, walk up V. Vittorio Emanuele III to P. Municipio for the five-turreted **Castel Nuovo,** built in 1286 by Charles II of Anjou. The double-arched entrance commemorates the arrival of Alphonse I of Aragon in Naples. Inside, admire the **Museo Civico.** *(Open M-Sa 9am-7pm. €5.20.)*

ITALY

ENTERTAINMENT AND NIGHTLIFE

Piazza Vanvitelli in Vomero is where the cool kids go to relax and socialize. Take the funicular from V. Toledo or the C28 bus from P. Vittoria. Outdoor bars and cafes are a popular choice in **Piazza Bellini,** near P. Dante. **Itaca,** P. Bellini 71, mixes eerie trance music with dark decor. (Cocktails from €6. Open daily 10am-3am.) **Camelot,** V.S. Pietro A Majella 8, just off P. Bellini in the historic district, plays mostly pop and house. (Open Sept.-June Tu-Su 10:30pm-5am.) **ARCI-Gay/Lesbica** (☎081 551 82 93) has information on gay and lesbian club nights.

✦ DAYTRIPS FROM NAPLES

Mount Vesuvius, the only active volcano on the European continent, looms over the area east of Naples. Its infamous eruption in AD 79 buried the nearby Roman city of **Ercolano** (Herculaneum) in mud and neighboring **Pompei** (Pompeii) in ashes.

POMPEII. Since 1748, excavations have unearthed a stunningly well-preserved picture of Roman daily life. The site hasn't changed much since then, and neither have the victims, whose ghastly remains were partially preserved by plaster casts in the hardened ash. Walk down V.D. Marina to reach the colonnaded ■**Forum,** which was once the commercial, civic, and religious center of the city. Exit the Forum through the upper end by the cafeteria, and head right on V. della Fortuna to reach the ■**House of the Faun,** where a bronze dancing faun and the spectacular Alexander Mosaic (today in the Museo Archeologico Nazionale) were found. Continue on V. della Fortuna and turn left on V. dei Vettii to reach the **House of the Vettii,** on the left, and the most vivid frescoes in Pompeii. Back down V. dei Vettii, cross V. della Fortuna to V. Storto, turn left on V. degli Augustali, and take a quick right to reach a small **brothel** (the Lupenar). After 2000 years, it's still the most popular place in town. V. dei Teatri, across the street, leads to the oldest standing **amphitheater** in the world (80 BC), which once held up to 12,000 spectators. To get to the ■**Villa of the Mysteries,** the complex's best-preserved villa, head west on V. della Fortuna, right on V. Consolare, and all the way up Porta Ercolano. *(Pompeii open daily 8:30am-7:30pm. €10.)* Take the Circumvesuviana **train** (☎081 772 24 44) from Naples's Stazione Centrale to Pompeii *(dir.: Sorrento; 2 per hr., €1.90).* To reach the site, head downhill and take your first left to the west (Porta Marina) entrance. To get to the **tourist office,** V. Sacra 1, walk right from the station and continue to the bottom of the hill. *(Open M-F 8am-3:30pm, Sa 8am-2pm.)* Food at the on-site cafeteria is expensive, so bring lunch.

HERCULANEUM. Herculaneum is 500m downhill from the Ercolano stop on the Naples Circumvesuviana train *(dir.: Sorrento; 20min., €1.90).* Stop at the **tourist office,** V. IV Novembre 84 *(☎081 88 12 43),* to pick up a free **map.** The city is less excavated than Pompeii. *(Open daily 8:30am-7:30pm. €10.)*

MT. VESUVIUS. You can peer into the only active volcano on mainland Europe at Mt. Vesuvius. Trasporti Vesuviani **buses** (buy ticket on board; roundtrip €3.10) run from the Ercolano Circumvesuviana station to the crater. Although Vesuvius hasn't erupted since March 31, 1944 (and scientists say volcanoes should erupt every 30 years), experts deem the trip safe.

AMALFI COAST. The dramatic scenery and pulsing nightlife of the towns on the Amalfi Coast are easily accessible from Naples by train, ferry, and bus (p. 734).

BAY OF NAPLES. Only an hour away from Naples by ferry, the islands of Capri and Ischia tempt travelers with luscious beaches and enchanting grottos (p. 735).

AMALFI COAST

The beauty of the Amalfi coast rests in immense, rugged cliffs plunging downward into calm azure waters and coastal towns climbing the sides of narrow ravines. The picturesque villages provide stunning natural panoramas, delicious food, and throbbing nightlife.

TRANSPORTATION. The coast is accessible from Naples, Sorrento, Salerno, and the islands by **ferry** and blue SITA **buses. Trains** run directly to Salerno from Naples (45min., 29 per day, €5-10); Rome (2½-3hr., 19 per day, €20-30); and Venice (9hr., 1am, €35). **Buses** also link Paestrum and Salerno (1hr., every hr. 7am-7pm, €2.50). From Salerno, Travelmar (☎089 87 31 90) runs **ferries** to Amalfi (35min., 6 per day, €3.50) and Positano (1¼hr., €5). From Sorrento, Linee Marittime Partenopee **ferries** (☎081 807 18 12) run to Capri (40min., 5 ferries per day 8:30am-4:50pm, €6.50; 20min., 17 hydrofoils per day 7:20am-5:40pm, €8.50).

AMALFI AND ATRANI. Breathtaking natural beauty surrounds the narrow streets and historic monuments of **Amalfi.** Visitors crowd the P. del Duomo to admire the elegant 9th-century **Duomo di Sant'Andrea** and the nearby **Fontana di Sant'Andrea,** a marble nude with water spouting from her breasts. **A'Scalinatella ❶,** P. Umberto 12, has hostel beds and regular rooms all over Amalfi and Atrani. (☎089 87 19 30. Dorms €10.25; doubles €26.45. **Camping** €7.75 per person.) The tiny beachside village of **Atrani** is a 10min. walk around the bend from Amalfi. **Path of the Gods,** a spectacular 3hr. hike, runs the coast from Bomerano to Positano.

RAVELLO. Perched atop 330m cliffs, Ravello has provided a haven for many celebrity artists over the years. The Moorish cloister and gardens of **Villa Rufolo,** off P. Duomo, inspired Boccaccio's *Decameron* and Wagner's *Parsifal.* (Open daily 9am-8pm. €4.) The small road to the right leads to the impressive **Villa Cimbrone,** whose floral walkways and gardens hide temples and statue-filled grottoes. (Open daily 9am-7:30pm. €4.50.) **Classical music concerts** are performed in the gardens of the Villa Rufolo; call the *Società di Concerti di Ravello* (☎089 85 81 49) for more info. All 10 rooms at the **Albergo Garden,** V.G. Boccaccio 4, have a great view of the cliffs. (☎089 85 72 26; www.starnet.it/hgarden. Breakfast included. Reserve ahead. Doubles €77-88. Closed Nov. 15-Feb. 15. AmEx/MC/V.)

POSITANO. Today, Positano's most frequent visitors are the wealthy few who can afford pricey *Positanese* culture, yet the town has its picturesque charms. To see the large *pertusione* (hole) in **Montepertuso,** one of three perforated mountains in the world, hike 45 min. uphill or take the bus from P. dei Mulini. Positano's **beaches** are also popular, and although boutiques may be a bit pricey, no one charges for window-shopping. The **tourist office,** V. del Saraceno 4 (☎089 87 50 67), is below the *duomo.* **Ostello Brikette ❷,** V.G. Marconi 358, 100m up the main coastal road to Sorrento from Viale Pasitea, has incredible views from two large terraces. (☎089 87 58 57. Breakfast and sheets included. Dorms €20; doubles €65.) **Casa Guadagno ❸,** V. Fornillo 22, has 15 spotless rooms. (☎089 87 50 42; fax 81 14 07. Breakfast included. Reserve ahead. With *Let's Go:* doubles €85; triples €95. MC/V.) Prices in the town's restaurants reflect the high quality of the food. For a sit-down dinner, thrifty travelers head toward the beach at **Fornillo.**

SORRENTO. The most heavily touristed town on the peninsula, lively Sorrento makes a convenient base for daytrips around the Bay of Naples. Caremar **ferries** (☎081 807 30 77) go to Capri (20min., €5.70). The **tourist office,** L. de Maio 35, is off P. Tasso. (☎081 807 40 33. Open Apr.-Sept. M-Sa 8:45am-7:45pm; Oct.-Mar. M-Sa 8:30am-2pm and 4-6:15pm.) Halfway to the free **beach** at **Punta del Capo** (bus A), **Hotel Elios ❷,** V. Capo 33, has comfy rooms. (☎081 878 18 12. Singles €25-30; doubles €40-50.) For extensive amenities, stay at **Hotel City ❸,** C. Italia 221; turn left on C. Italia from the station. (☎081 877 22 10. Singles €37-46; doubles €40-50.) It's easy to find good, affordable food in Sorrento. **Davide ❶,** V. Giuliani 39, off Corso Italia, two blocks from P. Tasso, has divine *gelato* and masterful *mousse* (60 flavors. Open daily 10am-midnight.) After 10:30pm, a crowd gathers in the rooftop lemon grove above **The English Inn,** C. Italia 56. (Open daily 9am-1am.)

SALERNO AND PAESTUM. Industrial **Salerno** is best used as a base for daytrips to nearby **Paestum,** the site of three spectacularly preserved **Doric buildings,** including the **Temple of Ceres,** the **Temple of Poseidon,** and the **basilica.** (Temples open daily 9am-6:30pm. Closed 1st and 3rd M each month. €4.) To sleep at **Ostello della Gioventù "Irno" (HI) ❶,** in Salerno at V. Luigi Guercio 112, go left from the station on V. Torrione, then left under the bridge on V. Mobilio. (☎089 79 02 51. Breakfast included. Curfew 1:30am. Dorms €10.)

BAY OF NAPLES ISLANDS ☎081

Off the shores of the Bay of Naples, the pleasure islands **Capri** and **Ischia** beckon weary travelers with promises of breathtaking natural sights, comfortable accommodations, and gorgeous beaches. The islands can be reached by ferries *(traghetti)* or the faster, more expensive hydrofoils *(aliscafi)*. For trips to Capri, Sorrento is the closest starting point. The busiest route to Capri and Ischia is through Naples's Mergellina and Molo Beverello ports. To reach Molo Beverello from Naples's Stazione Centrale, take tram #1 from P. Garibaldi to P. Municipio on the waterfront. Ferries and hydrofoils also run between the islands.

ITALY

CAPRI. Visitors flock to the renowned **Blue Grotto,** a sea cave whose waters shimmer with neon-blue light. (Open daily 9am-5pm. Boat tour €8.10.) In the summer months crowds and prices increase, so the best times to visit are in the late spring and early fall. Capri proper sits above the port, and buses departing from V. Roma make the trip up the mountain to Anacapri every 15 min. until 1:40am. Away from the throngs flitting among Capri's expensive boutiques, Anacapri is home to budget hotels, spectacular vistas, and empty mountain paths. Upstairs from P. Vittoria in Anacapri, **Villa San Michele** sports lush gardens, ancient sculptures, and a remarkable view of the island. (Open daily 9:30am-6pm. €5.) To appreciate Capri's Mediterranean beauty from higher ground, take the chairlift up **Monte Solaro** from P. Vittoria. (Open Mar.-Oct. daily 9:30am-4:45pm. Round-trip €5.50.) For those who prefer cliff to coastline, Capri's hiking trails lead to some stunning panoramas; take a short but very uphill hike to the magnificent ruins of Emperor Tiberius's **Villa Jovis,** the largest of his 12 Capri villas. Always the gracious host, Tiberius tossed those who displeased him over the precipice. The view from the **Cappella di Santa Maria del Soccorso,** built onto the villa, is unrivaled.

Caremar (☎ 081 837 07 00) **ferries** run from Marina Grande to Naples (1¼hr., 6 per day) and Sorrento (50min., 3 per day, €5.68). **LineaJet** (☎ 081 837 08 19) runs hydrofoils to Naples (40min., 10 per day 8:30am-6:25pm, €11) and Sorrento (20min., €7.23). Ferries and hydrofoils to Ischia and Amalfi run with much less frequency and regularity; check with the lines at Marina Grande for details. The Capri **tourist office** (☎ 081 837 06 34) sits at the end of Marina Grande; in Anacapri, it's at V. Orlandi 59 (☎ 837 15 24), to the right of the P. Vittoria bus stop. (Both open June-Sept. M-Sa 8:30am-8:30pm; Oct.-May M-Sa 9am-1:30pm and 3:30-6:45pm.) For quick access to the beach and center of Capri, stay at the **Bed and Breakfast Tirrenia Roberts ❸,** V. Mulo 27. Walk away from P. Umberto on V. Roma and take the stairs on your right just before the fork. (☎ 081 837 61 19; bbtirreniaroberts@iol.it. Reserve well in advance. 3 rooms, all doubles, €80-105.) Another good option is **Pensione 4 Stagioni ❸,** V. Marina Piccola 1. From P. Umberto, walk 5 min. down V. Roma, turn left at the triple fork, and look for the green gate on the left. (☎ 081 837 00 41; www.hotel4stagionicapri.com. Breakfast included. Doubles €110; in winter €90. AmEx/MC/V.) Bear right at the fork to reach **Dimeglio supermarket.** (Open M-Sa 8:30am-1:30pm and 5-9pm.) At night, dressed-to-kill Italians come out for Capri's *passegiatta;* bars around **Piazza Umberto** keep the music pumping late, but Anacapri is cheaper and more fun. **Postal Code:** Capri: 80073; Anacapri: 80021.

ISCHIA. Augustus fell in love with Capri's fantastic beauty in 29 BC, but swapped it for its more fertile neighbor, Ischia. Just across the bay, edenic Ischia offers sandy beaches, natural hot springs, ruins, forests, vineyards, and lemon groves. Orange SEPSA **buses** #1, CD, and CS (every 20 min.; €1, day pass €2.75) depart from the ferry landing and follow the coast in a circular route, stopping at: **Ischia Porto,** a port formed by the crater of an extinct volcano; **Casamicciola Terme,** with a crowded beach and legendary thermal waters; **Lacco Ameno,** the oldest Greek settlement in the western Mediterranean; and popular **Forio,** home to lively bars. **Caremar ferries** (☎ 081 98 48 18) arrive from Naples (1½hr., 14 per day, €5.06) and Alilauro (☎ 081 99 18 88, www.alilauro.it) runs hydrofoils to Sorrento (6 per day).

Stay in Ischia Porto only if you want to be close to the ferries and nightlife—most *pensioni* are in Forio. **Pensione Di Lustro ❸,** V. Filippo di Lustro 9, is near the beach. (☎ 081 99 71 63. Breakfast included. Doubles €45-62.) The **Ostello "Il Gabbiano" (HI) ❷,** Strada Statale Forio-Panza, 162, is accessible by buses #1, CS, or CD, and near the beach. (☎ 081 90 94 22. Breakfast included. Lockout 10am-1pm. Curfew 12:30am. Open Apr.-Sept. Dorms €16.) **Camping Internazionale ❶** is at V. Foschini 22, 15 min. from the port. Take V. Alfredo de Luca from V. del Porto; bear right on V. Michele Mazzella at P. degi Eroi. (☎ 081 99 14 49; fax 081 99 14 72. Open May-Sept. €6-9 per person, €3-10 per tent. 2-person bungalows €26-39.)

BARI

☎ 080

Most tourists stay in Bari only long enough to buy a ferry ticket to Greece, but Apulia's capital is a vibrant and grittily modern city that thrives in the scorching southern sun. The **Basilica di San Nicola** houses the remains of Saint Nicolas, which were stolen by 11th-century *Baresi* sailors from Turkey. (Open daily 7am-noon and 4-7:30pm.) To reach the broad range of art exihibits at the majestic **Castel del Monte,** take the Ferrotramviara Bari Nord **train** (☎ 0883 59 26 84) to Andria (1¼hr., 19 per day, €2.65) and then a bus (30min., 2 per day, €1).

FS **trains** go to: Brindisi (1-1¾hr., 26 per day, €6.20-10.35); Naples (4½hr., 1 per day, €14.30); and Rome (5-7hr., 6 per day, €26-36). Bari is an important port for **ferries** to Albania, Greece, Israel, and Turkey. **InterRail** and **Eurail** pass holders get no discounts on ferries from Bari (see **Brindisi,** below), but some ferries have student rates. **Ventouris Ferries,** V. Piccinni 133 (☎080 521 76 99; www.ventouris.gr), goes to **Corfu** (11hr.; June-Sept. 1 per day, Oct.-May M and W; €22-42) and **Igoumenitsa** (13hr.; mid-June to mid-Sept. 1 per day, mid-Sept. to mid-June 4 per week; €22-42). **Marlines** (☎080 523 18 24; fax 080 523 02 87) go to **Kotor, Montenegro** (8hr.; July-Aug. 5 per week; Sept.-Dec 4 per week; €39). **Superfast Ferries** (☎080 528 28 28; fax 080 528 24 44) runs to **Igoumenitsa** (9½hr.; June 28-July 24 3 per week; July 25-Aug 11 1 per day; €42-52); and **Patras** (15½hr.; June 28-July 24 3 per week, June 25-Aug 11 1 per day; €42-52). **Adriatic Shipping Company** (☎080 527 54 52; fax 080 575 10 89) goes to **Dubrovnik** (9hr.; July 5-June 24 and Aug. 29-Sept. 13 2 per week, June 25-Aug. 28 3 per week; €43). **Albergo Serena ❷,** V. Imbriani 69, has 14 spacious rooms. (☎080 554 09 80; fax 080 558 66 13. Singles €25.85; doubles €51.65.) **Pensione Giulia ❹,** V. Crisanzio 12, has 13 rooms. (☎080 521 66 30; fax 080 521 82 71. Singles €40; doubles €50. AmEx/MC/V.)

BRINDISI ☎0831

Everyone comes to Brindisi to leave Italy—here Pompey fled from Caesar's armies and Crusaders set forth to retake the Holy Land. If you're a more peaceful traveler heading for Greece, arrive in the afternoon, as ferries leave in the evening. In August, consider arriving early or departing from Ancona or Bari instead. **Trains** arrive in P. Crispi from: Bari (1½ hr., 31 per day, €6-10); Milan (10hr., 6 per day, €41-65); and Rome (6-9hr., 4 per day, €27-45). **Ferries** leave for: Cephalonia (16½hr.); Corfu (8hr.); Igoumenitsa (10hr.); and Patras (17hr.). All passengers leaving from Brindisi pay a **port tax** (€6) in addition to regular fare. **Deck passage** *(passagio semplice;* sleeping on the deck) is the cheapest option. **Strintzis Lines,** C. Garibaldi 65 (☎0831 56 22 00); **Med Link Lines,** C. Garibaldi 49 (☎0831 52 76 67); and **Fragline,** V. Spalato 31 (☎0831 54 85 34) all run reputable, well-established ferries. InterRail and Eurail passes are valid on **Hellenic Mediterranean Lines,** C. Garibaldi 8 (☎0831 52 85 31; www.hml.it), for deck passage; a seat inside costs €15. Eurail pass holders must pay a €10 fee for travel between June 10 and September 30; InterRail passholders are exempt from this fee. Those without passes will have to shop for cheap fares—tickets are around €25 for deck passage. Most companies offer a 10-20% discount on round-trip tickets, youth/student fares, and bargain tickets on certain days. Check in **two hours** before departure, wear warm clothes, and bring your own food.

Corso Umberto runs from the train station to the port, becoming Corso Garibaldi. From Corso Garibaldi, turn left onto V. Regina Margherita for the *stazione marittima* and **tourist office,** V. Regina Margherita 5. (☎0831 52 30 72. Open daily 8am-2pm and 3-8pm.) If you're staying in town, try **Hotel Venezia ❶,** V. Pisanelli 4. After the fountain, take the second left off Corso Umberto onto V.S. Lorenzo da Brindisi, then turn right onto V. Pisanelli. (☎0831 52 75 11. Reserve ahead. Singles €13; doubles €25.) Get food for the ferry at **Gulliper supermarket,** Corso Garibaldi 106. (Open M-Sa 8am-1:30pm and 4:30-8:30pm, Su 9am-1pm.)

ITALY

SICILY (SICILIA)

With a history so steeped in chaos, catastrophe, and conquest, it's no wonder that the island of Sicily possesses such passionate volatility. The tempestuousness of Sicilian history and political life is matched only by the island's dramatic landscape, which is dominated by craggy slopes. Entire cities have been destroyed in seismic and volcanic events, but those that have survived have lived up to the cliché and grown stronger; Sicilian pride is a testament to the resilience they have shown during centuries of occupation and destruction.

TRANSPORTATION

Tirrenia ferries (☎091 33 33 00) offers extensive service. From southern Italy, take a **train** to **Reggio di Calabria,** then a NGI or Meridiano **ferry** (40min.; NGI 10-12 per day, €0.55; Meridiano 11-15 per day, €1.55) or Ferrovie Statale **hydrofoil** (☎(096) 586 35 40) to Messina, Sicily's transport hub (25min., 12 per day, €2.60). Ferries also go to Palermo from Sardinia (14hr., €42) and Naples (10hr., 2 per day, €38). **SAIS Trasporti** (☎(091) 617 11 41) and SAIS **buses** (☎(091) 616 60 28) serve destinations throughout the island. **Trains** head to Messina directly from Naples (4½hr., 7 per day, €22) and Rome (9hr., 7 per day, €30). Trains continue west to Palermo (3½hr., 15 per day, €10.10) via Milazzo (45min., €2.35) and south to Syracuse (3hr., 14 per day, €6.75) via Taormina (1hr., €2.85).

PALERMO ☎091

From twisting streets lined by ancient ruins to the symbolic marionette strings of Italian organized crime, gritty urban Palermo is a city tied both to the past and present. To get to the magnificent **Teatro Massimo,** where the climactic opera scene of *The Godfather: Part III* was filmed, walk up V. Maqueda past the intersection of Quattro Canti and Corso Vittorio Emanuele. (Open Tu-Su 10am-5:30pm for 20min. tours.) Up Corso Vittorio Emanuele, the **Palazzo dei Normanni** contains the **Cappella Palatina,** with incredible golden mosaics. (Open M-Sa 9am-noon and 3-4:45pm, Su 9-10am and noon-1pm.) The morbid **Cappuchin Catacombs,** in P. Cappuccini, are only for the strong of stomach. Eight thousand corpses and twisted skeletons line the underground labyrinth. To get there, take buses #109 or 318 from Stazione Centrale to P. Indipendenza and then transfer to bus #327. (Open M-Su 9am-noon and 3-5pm. €1.50.)

Trains leave Stazione Centrale, in P. Giulio Cesare, at V. Roma and V. Maqueda, for Milan (19½hr., 2 per day, €50) and Rome (11hr., 7 per day, €53). All four **bus** lines run from V. Balsamo, next to the train station. After purchasing tickets, ask exactly where your bus will arrive and its logo. Ask an **AMAT** or **Métro** information booth for a combined Métro and bus map. The **tourist office,** P. Castelnuovo 34, is opposite Teatro Politeama; from the train station, take a bus to P. Politeama, at the end of V. Maqueda. (☎091 605 83 51; fax 091 58 63 38. Open daily 8am-5pm.) Homey **Hotel Regina ❷,** Corso Vittorio Emanuele 316, is off V. Maqueda. (☎091 611 42 16; fax 091 612 21 69. Kitchen. Singles €18; doubles €34.) Grab a bite to eat at **Pizzeria Bellini ❶,** P. Bellini 6. (Pizza from €3.10. Open W-M 6am-1am.) Elegant **Hotel del Centro ❺,** V. Roma 72, is five blocks up V. Roma from the train station, on the second floor. (☎091 617 03 76; fax 091 617 36 54. Singles €62; doubles €80.) For **camping,** take bus #101 from the train station to P. de Gasperi, and then take bus #628 to V. S. Ferracavallo. Walk downhill one block, turn right on V. dei Manderini after the post office, and **Campeggio dell'Ulivi ❶,** V. Pegaso 25, is on the right.

(☎/fax 091 53 30 21. €6.50 per person and tent.) Palermo's specialty is *arancini* (fried balls filled with rice, spinach, or meat); indulge at **Lo Sparviero ❸**, V. Sperlinga 23, a block from the Teatro Massimo. (Pizza from €3, *primi* from €6.50. Open daily noon-3pm and 6:30pm-midnight.) **Postal Code:** 90100.

DAYTRIPS FROM PALERMO

MONREALE

Bus #389 leaves Palermo's P. Indipendenza for Monreale's P. Vittorio Emanuele (40min., 3 per hr., €0.80). To get to P. Indipendenza, take bus #109 or 118 from Palermo's Stazione Centrale. Dress modestly. Cathedral open daily 8am-noon and 3:30-6pm. Free. Cloister open M-Sa 9am-7pm, Su 9am-1pm. €2.10.

Eight kilometers outside of Palermo, Monreale's magnificent Norman-Saracen **cathedral** glistens with 6430 square meters of golden mosaics and 130 panels depicting Bible scenes. Next door, the **cloisters** house a renowned Sicilian sculpture collection in their serene courtyard, surrounded by 228 tiled columns.

CEFALÙ ☎0921

Trains arrive at P. Stazione 1 (☎0921 42 11 69) from Palermo (1hr., 36 per day, €3.60). Open daily 6:45am-8:50pm.

Tiny Cefalù is a labyrinth of cobblestone streets winding along the sea. The dramatic 11th-century **duomo** combines Norman, Byzantine, and Roman architectural styles, with elegant arches and dazzling Byzantine mosaics. (Dress modestly. Open daily 8am-noon and 3:30-7pm.) The centerpiece of the eclectic collection in the **Museo Mandralisca,** V. Mandralisca 13, is the *Ritratto di un Ignoto (Portrait of an Unknown)* by Sicilian master Antonello da Messina. (☎0921 42 15 47. Open daily 9am-7pm. €4.15.) For amazing views and ruins, hike up to the Rocca by way of the Salita Saraceni; from P. Garibaldi, follow the signs for *Pedonale Rocca* (30min.). From the train station, V. Aldo Moro leads to the **tourist office,** Corso Ruggero 77. (☎0921 42 10 50; fax 0921 42 23 86. Open M-Sa 8am-2:30pm and 3:30-8pm, Su 9am-1:30pm.)

AGRIGENTO ☎0922

The five elevated temples composing the majestic **Valle dei Tempii** at Agrigento offer breathtaking vistas from every angle. Further along, the **Tempio della Concordia,** one of the world's best-preserved Greek temples, owes its survival to consecration by the archbishop of Agrigento. One kilometer uphill from the ruins, the excellent **Museo Nazionale Archeologico di San Nicola** houses a fabulous collection of

LA FAMIGLIA Pinstriped suits, machine guns, and *The Godfather* are a far cry from the reality of the **Sicilian Mafia.** The system has its roots in the *latifondi* (agricultural estates) of rural Sicily, where land managers and salaried militiamen (a.k.a. landlords and bouncers) protected their turf and people. Powerful because people owed them favors, strong because they supported one another, and feared because they did not hesitate to kill offenders, they founded a tradition that has dominated Sicilian life since the late 19th century. Since the mid-1980s, the Italian government has worked to curtail Mafia influence. Today Sicilians shy away from any Mafia discussion, referring to the system as *Cosa Nostra* (our thing).

Greek vases and relics from the area's necropolis. To reach the Valley of Temples, take bus #1 or 2 (€0.80) from the train station. (Open M-Sa 8am-12:30pm. €4.) Literature aficionados will want to visit the birthplace of **Luigi Pirandello,** now a small museum of books, notes, and family photographs. For the Pirandello museum, take Lumia bus #1 to P. Kaos. (☎0922 51 11 02. Open daily 8am-1:30pm. €2.10.) **Trains** arrive in P. Marconi, below P. Moro, from Palermo (2hr., 11 per day, €6.60). **Buses** run from P. Roselli, left of P. Vittorio, to Palermo (2hr., M-Sa 7 per day, €6.50). The **tourist office,** V. Battista 13, is the first left off V. Atenea. (☎204 54. Open M-F 9am-1:30pm.) **Trattoria Atenea ❶,** V. Ficani 32, off V. Atenea from P. Moro, has extensive seafood offerings. Try *grigliata mista di pesce* (mixed grilled fish) for €4.65. (☎0922 202 47. Open M-Sa noon-3pm and 7pm-midnight.) **Postal Code:** 92100.

SYRACUSE (SIRACUSA) ☎0931

Never having regained the glory of its golden Grecian days, the super-modern city of Syracuse places its pride upon its extraordinary Greek ruins. Syracuse's past role as one of the most powerful cities in the Mediterranean is still evident in the **Archaeological Park,** on the north side of town. The enormous **Greek theater** is where 20,000 spectators watched Aeschylus premiere his *Persians.* The amazing acoustics of the **Orecchio di Dionigi** (Ear of Dionysius) spawned the legend that the tyrant Dionysius put prisoners here to eavesdrop on them. For the well-preserved 2nd-century **Roman amphitheater,** follow Corso Gelone until it meets Viale Teocrito, then walk left down V. Augusto. (Open daily 9am-7pm. €4.50.) More Greek ruins lie over the Ponte Umbertino on **Ortigia,** the serene island on which the Greeks first landed. The ruined **Temple of Apollo** has a few columns still standing, but those at the **Temple of Diana** are much more impressive. Integrated into the cathedral, the temple's columns line the walls of the **duomo.** Down V. Picherale from P. Duomo, the **Fonte Aretusa** reflects self-admirers. Back on the mainland, off Viale Teocrito from Corso Gelone, near the tourist office, is the **Catacombe di San Giovanni.** (Open daily 9am-12:30pm and 2-5pm. €3.50.) Those who prefer tans to temples should take bus #21, 22, or 24 18km to **Fontane Bianche,** a glitzy beach with plenty of discos.

Trains leave V. Francesco Crispi for Messina (3hr., 16 per day, €8.30) and Rome (12hr., 5 per day, €38). Interbus **buses,** V. Trieste 28 (☎0931 667 10), leave for Palermo (3hr., 5 per day, €13.40) and Taormina (2hr., 1 per day, €13.40). To get from the train station to the **tourist office,** V.S. Sebastiano 43, take V.F. Crispi to Corso Gelone, turn right on Viale Teocrite, turn left on V.S. Sebastianoi; it's on the left. (☎0931 48 12 32. Open M-Sa 8:30am-1:30pm and 3:30-6:30pm, Su 8:30am-1:30pm.) **Hotel Centrale ❷,** C. Umberto I 141, has clean, air-conditioned rooms with astounding sea views. (☎0931 605 28. Singles €17; doubles €26; triples €37.) **Spaghetteria do Scugghiu ❶,** V.D. Sciná 11, off P. Archimede, on Ortigia, serves 20 delicious types of spaghetti. (From €5.20. Open Tu-Su noon-3pm and 7-11pm.) For more budget eats, try places on **Via Savoia** and **Via Cavour,** or the open-air **market** in Ortigia, on V. Trento, off P. Pancali. (Open M-Sa 8am-1pm.)

TAORMINA ☎0942

From the high cliffs of Mt. Tauro, the serene buildings of beautiful Taormina overlook a spectacular panorama that includes the simmering Mt. Etna. The 3rd-century **Greek theater,** at the cliff's edge, has a view more dramatic than most Greek tragedies. To get there, walk up V. Teatro Greco; it's off Corso Umberto I at P. Vittorio Emanuele. (Open daily 9am-dusk. €4.15.) Cable cars leave every 15min. from V. Pirandello for **Lido Mazzarò** beach (€1.60), just below town. **Gole Alcantara** is a nearby haven of stunning gorges, roaring waterfalls, and crystal rapids. (☎0942 98 50 10. €4.15; wetsuit €7.75.)

Taormina is accessible by **bus** from Messina (10 per day, €2.50). **Trains** (€2.85) are more frequent, but the station is far from Taormina. The **tourist office,** P. Corvaja, is off Corso Umberto across from P. Vittorio Emanuele. (☎0942 232 43; fax 0942 249 41. Open M-Sa 8am-2pm and 4-7pm.) **Pensione Svizzera ❹,** V. Pirandello 26, has coastal views and clean rooms. (☎0942 237 90; www.tao.it/svizzera. Reserve ahead. Open Feb.-Nov. Singles €52; doubles €80; triples €108. MC/V.) Nearby **Inn Piero ❹,** V. Pirandello 20, has 10 rooms with a sea view. (☎231 39. Reserve ahead. Singles €50; doubles €64. AmEx/MC/V.) You can buy groceries at **STANDA supermarket,** V. Apollo Arcageta 49, at the end of Corso Umberto. (Open M-Sa 8:30am-1pm and 5-9pm.) **Bella Blu ❸,** V. Pirandello 28, serves delicious food. (*Primi* from €4.50, *secondi* from €6.50. Open daily 10am-3:30pm and 6pm-late. MC/V.)

AEOLIAN ISLANDS (ISOLE EOLIE)

Homer thought the **Aeolian Islands** to be the second home of the gods, and indeed, these last few stretches of unspoiled seashore border on the divine. Sparkling seas, smooth beaches, and fiery volcanoes testify to the area's stunning beauty.

TRANSPORTATION

The archipelago lies off the Sicilian coast, north of **Milazzo,** the principal and least expensive departure point. Hop a **train** from Messina (30min., €2.35) or Palermo (2½hr., €9) and onto an orange AST **bus** for the port (10min., every hr., €0.75). Siremar (☎98 60 11) and Navigazione Generale Italiana (☎98 30 03) **ferries** depart for Lipari (2hr., €5.45-5.95); Stromboli (5hr., €8.55-9.85); Vulcano (1½hr., €5.20-5.70). **Hydrofoils** *(aliscafi)* make the trip in half the time, but cost twice as much. All three have ticket offices on V. Dei Mille facing the port in Milazzo. **Ferries** leave for the islands less frequently from **Naples'** Molo Beverello port. Lipari sends ferries to Vulcano (€2.35) and Stromboli (€13.20).

LIPARI ☎090

Lipari, the largest and most developed of the islands, is renowned for its amazing beaches and stunning hillside views. To reach the popular beaches of **Porticello** and **Spiaggia Bianca,** *the* spot for topless (and sometimes bottomless) sunbathing, take the Lipari-Cavedi bus a few kilometers north to Canneto. Lipari's other offerings include a splendidly rebuilt medieval **castello,** occupying the site of an ancient Greek acropolis. The fortress shares its hill with an **archaeological park,** the **San Bartolo church,** and the superb **Museo Archeologico Eoliano,** up the stone steps off V. Garibaldi. (☎090 988 01 74. Open May-Oct. M-Su 9am-1:30pm and 4-7pm; Nov.-Apr. M-Su 9am-1:30pm and 3-6pm. €4.30.)

ITALY

The **AAST delle Isole Eolie tourist office,** Corso Vittorio Emanuele 202, is near the ferry dock. (☎090 988 00 95; www.net-net.it/aasteolie. Open July-Aug. M-Sa 8am-2pm and 4-10pm, Su 8am-2pm; Sept.-June M-F 8am-2pm and 4:30-7:30pm, Sa 8am-2pm.) When bedtime nears, **Casa Vittorio ❶,** Vico Sparviero 15, is on a quiet side street in the center of town. Rooms range from intimate singles to a five-person penthouse. (☎090 981 15 23. €16-37 per person.) The elegant **Pensione Enso il Negro ❷,** V. Garibaldi 29, is 20m up V. Garibladi and three flights of stone stairs. (☎981 31 63. Singles €30-47; doubles €50-80.) **Hotel Europeo ❸,** Corso Vittorio Emanuele 98, has small, modest rooms in a great location. (☎090 981 15 89. Open July-Aug. €30 per person.) **Camp** at **Baia Unci ❶,** V. Marina Garibaldi 2, 2km from Lipari at the entrance to the hamlet of Canneto. (☎090 981 19 09; www.campeggitalia.it/sicilia/baiaunci. Reserve in Aug. Open mid-Mar. to mid-Oct. €6.20-11 per person, with tent.) Stock up at **UPIM supermarket,** Corso Vittorio Emanuele 212. (Open M-Sa 8:30am-1:30pm and 4-9:30pm.) **Da Gilberto ❶,** V. Garibaldi 22-24, is famous for delicious sandwiches starting at €2.60. (☎090 981 27 56. Open 7pm-midnight, though closing time may vary.)

VULCANO ☎090

Black beaches, bubbling seas, and natural mud spas attract visitors worldwide to this island. A steep 1hr. **hike** to the inactive **Gran Cratere** (Grand Crater) snakes between the volcano's noxious yellow fumaroles. On a clear day, you can see all the other islands from the top. The allegedly therapeutic **Laghetto di Fanghi** (mud pool) is just up V. Provinciale to the right from the port. If you would prefer not to bathe in sulfuric radioactive mud, you can step gingerly into the scalding waters of the **acquacalda,** where underwater volcanic outlets make the sea percolate like a jacuzzi, or visit the black sands and clear waters of **Sabbie Nere,** just down the road from the *acquacalda*. Follow the signs off V. Ponente. To get to Vulcano, take the 30min. **ferry** from the port at nearby Lipari (30min., 2 per day, €1.30). For more info, the **tourist office,** is at V. Provinciale 41. (☎090 985 20 28. Open May-Aug. daily 8am-1:30pm and 3-5pm.) For **rented rooms** *(affittacamere)*, call ☎090 985 21 42.

STROMBOLI ☎090

If you find luscious beaches and hot springs a bit tame, a visit to Stromboli's active **volcano,** which spews orange cascades of lava and molten rock about every 10min. each night, will quench your thirst for adventure. A guided hike to the crater rewards diligent climbers with a view of the nightly eruptions. **Hiking** the *vulcano* on your own is **illegal** and **dangerous,** but **Magmatrek** offers tours. (☎/fax 090 986 57 68. Tours depart from Via Vittorio Emanuele. Departure times vary. €21-34.) Bring sturdy shoes, a flashlight, snacks, water, and warm clothes; don't wear contact lenses, as the wind sweeps ash and dust everywhere. From July to September, forget finding a room unless you have a reservation; your best bet may be one of the non-reservable *affittacamere*. Expect to pay €15-25 for a room. The best value is **Casa del Sole ❷,** on V. Giuseppe Cincotta, off V. Regina at the end of town. At St-Bartholomew's Church, take a right down the stairs and go down the alley. Large rooms face a communal terrace. (☎090 98 60 17. June €18; July-Aug. €20.)

SARDINIA (SARDEGNA)

When the boyish vanity of over-cultivated mainland Italians starts to wear thin, and when one more church interior will send you into the path of the nearest speeding Fiat, Sardinia's savage coastline and rugged people will be a reality check for your soul. D. H. Lawrence sought respite from the "deadly net of European civilization," and he found his escape among the wild horses, wind-carved rock formations, and pink flamingos of this remote island. The ancient feudal civilizations that settled in Sardinia some 3500 years ago left about 8000 *nuraghe* ruins, cone-shaped stone tower-houses assembled without mortar.

TRANSPORTATION

Tirrenia **ferries** (☎1678 240 79) run to **Olbia,** on the northern tip of Sardinia, from Civitavecchia, just north of Rome (6hr., 4 per day, from €17), and Genoa (9hr., 6 per week, from €28). They also chug to southern **Cagliari** from Civitavecchia (15-18hr., 2 per day, from €26); Genoa (20hr., July-Sept. 2 per week, from €45); Naples (16hr., Jan.-Sept. 1 per week, €26); and Palermo (13½hr., 1 per week, from €24). **Trains** run from Cagliari to Olbia (4hr., €13) via Oristano (1½hr., €4.55), and Sassari (4hr., 2 per day, from €12.10). From Sassari, trains run to **Alghero** (40min., 11 per day, €3.10). PANI **buses** connect Cagliari to Oristano (1½hr., €5.85).

CAGLIARI ☎070

Cagliari combines the bustle and energy of a modern Italian city with the endearing rural atmosphere of the rest of the island. Its Roman ruins, medieval towers, and cobblestone streets contrast with the regal tree-lined streets and sweeping beaches downtown. Climb Largo Carlo Felice to reach the city's impressive **duomo,** P. Palazzo 3, with dazzling gold mosaics topping each of its entryways. (☎070 66 38 37. Open daily 8am-12:30pm and 4-8pm.) The 2nd-century **Roman ampitheater** comes alive with concerts, operas, and classic plays during the summer **arts festival.** If you prefer to worship the sun, take city **bus** P, PQ, or PF to **Il Poetto** beach (20min., €0.80), with pure white sand and turquoise water. The **tourist office** is on P. Matteotti. (☎070 66 92 55; fax 070 66 49 23. Open in summer M-Sa 8:30am-1:30pm and 2:30-7:30pm.) The elegant **Hotel Aer Bundes Jack Vittoria ❹** is at V. Roma 75. (☎070 65 79 70. Singles €36-43; doubles €60-65.) **Postal Code:** 09100.

ALGHERO ☎079

Vineyards, ruins, and horseback rides are all a short trip away from Alghero's palm-lined parks and twisting medieval streets. The nearby **Grotte di Nettuno,** an eerie stalactite-filled 60- to 70-million-year-old cavern complex, in Capo Caccia, can be reached by **bus** (1hr., 3 per day, round-trip €1.75). Visitors descend 632 steps between massive white cliffs. (Open Apr.-Sept. daily 9am-7pm; Oct. 10am-5pm; Nov.-Mar. 9am-2pm. €10.) The **tourist office,** P. Porta Terra 9, is to the right of the bus stop. (☎079 97 90 54. Open Apr.-Oct. M-Sa 8am-8pm, Su 9am-1pm; Nov.-Mar. M-Sa 9am-1pm.) To get to **Hotel San Francisco ❹,** V. Machin 2, walk straight from the tourist office and take the 3rd right. (☎079 98 03 30; hotsfran@tin.it. Singles €36-43; doubles €62-77. MC/V.) **Postal Code:** 07041.

ORISTANO AND THE SINIS PENINSULA ☎0783

The town of **Oristano** is an excellent base for excursions to the nearby Sinis Peninsula. From the train station, follow V. Vittorio Veneto straight to P. Mariano, then take V. Mazzini to P. Roma to reach the town center (25min.). Rent a moped or car to explore the tranquil beaches, stark white cliffs, and ancient ruins on the mystical Sinis Peninsula. At the tip, 17km west of Oristano, lie the ruins of the ancient Phoenician port of **Tharros.** Take the ARST bus to San Giovanni di Sinis (dir.: Is Arutas; 40min., 5 per day, €1.45). Slightly to the north off the road to Cuglieri is **S'Archittu,** where youths leap from a 15m limestone arch into the waters of a rocky inlet. ARST **buses** go to S'Archittu (30min., 7 per day, €1.45). The secluded white quartz sands of **Is Arutas** are well worth the trip. The ARST bus to Is Arutas runs only during July and August (50min., 5 per day, €1.45). The **tourist office,** V. Vittorio Emanuele 8, provides maps. (☎/fax 0783 30 32 12. Open M-F 9am-12:30pm and 4:30-8pm, Sa 9am-12:30pm.) To get some rest at **ISA ❹,** P. Mariano 50, exit from the back of the ARST station, turn left, turn right on V. Vittorio Emanuele, walk through P. D'Aborea and P. Martini, and follow V. Lamarmora to its end. Turn right, turn left, and take the first right down V. Mazzini to P. Mariano. (☎/fax 0783 36 01 01. Singles €50; doubles €83. AmEx/MC/V.) **Postal Code:** 09170.

LIECHTENSTEIN

A recent tourist brochure amusingly mislabeled the already tiny 160 sq. km country as an even tinier 160 sq. m. That's just about how much most tourists see of the world's only German-speaking monarchy, but the cliff-hugging roads are gateways to unspoiled mountains with great biking and hiking. Above the valley towns, cliff-hanging roads lead to places truly worth visiting—the quiet mountains offer hiking and skiing without the touristy atmosphere of many other alpine resorts.

SYMBOL	❶	❷	❸	❹	❺
ACCOMMODATIONS	under 16SFr	16-35SFr	36-60SFr	61-120SFr	over 120SFr
FOOD	under 9SFr	9-15SFr	16-24SFr	25-34SFr	over 34SFr

For Liechtenstein, prices are indicated in food and accommodations listings using the system of icons and price ranges above. Prices for accommodations are based on the lowest cost for one person, excluding special deals or discounts. For restaurants, prices are based on the average entree price.

SUGGESTED ITINERARIES

BEST OF (OKAY, ALL OF) LIECHTENSTEIN, TWO SHORT DAYS. Scope out the art collection at the **Staatliche Kunstmuseum** and compare stamps in the **Briefmarken-museum** in capital city **Vaduz** (1 day, p. 746), then scan the Alps from the **Pfälzerhütte** on the sharp ridge above **Malbun** (1 day, p. 748).

HISTORY

Liechtenstein's miniscule size and minute population (31,320) belies its long and rich history. The **Romans** invaded in 15 BC, but with the coming of Christianity in the 4th century AD, **Germanic tribes** pushed the Romans out, bringing the area under the control of the German dukedom. Prince **Johann Adam** of Liechtenstein purchased the land and created the Principality of Liechtenstein in 1719, which **Napoleon** conquered in 1806. After the defeat, Liechtenstein became part of the **German Confederacy** in 1815 and was granted a constitution in 1862. It separated from Germany for good in 1866 when the German Confederation dissolved. Two years later Liechtenstein disbanded its army—an intimidating 80-man juggernaut—which it has not re-formed since. In 1938, Prince **Franz Josef** ascended the throne and continued the transformation of Liechtenstein from an impoverished nation into one of the wealthiest (per capita) in Europe. Following the example of the Swiss, Liechtenstein established itself as an extremely desirable tax haven for international companies with its strict banking secrecy policies. The country joined the United Nations in 1990 and the European Economic Area in 1995.

ESSENTIALS

FACTS AND FIGURES

Official Name: Principality of Liechtenstein.
Capital: Vaduz.
Major Cities: Malbun, Schaan.
Population: 32,550.
Land Area: 160 sq. km.
Time Zone: GMT + 1.
Language: German (see p. 1022).
Religions: Roman Catholic (80%), Protestant (7.4%), unknown (7.7%), other (4.9%).

DOCUMENTS AND FORMALITIES. Citizens of Australia, Canada, the EU, New Zealand, South Africa, and the US do not need a visa for stays up to 90 days.

TRANSPORTATION. To enter Liechtenstein, catch a **bus** from **Sargans** or **Buchs** in Switzerland, or from **Feldkirch** just across the Austrian border (20min., 3.60SFr). Although trains from Austria and Switzerland pass through the country, Liechtenstein itself has no rail system. Instead, it has a cheap, efficient **Post Bus** system that links all 11 villages (short trips 2.40SFr; long trips 3.60SFr, students half-price; SwissPass valid). A **one-week bus ticket** (10SFr, students and seniors 5SFr) covers all (and we mean *all*) of Liechtenstein as well as buses to Swiss and Austrian border towns. **Bicycles** are a great way to get around Lower Liechtenstein; see below for rental information. Remember to keep a passport on you when traveling.

PHONE CODES **Country code:** 0423. **International dialing prefix:** 00.

EMERGENCY. Police: ☎117. **Ambulance:** ☎144. **Fire:** ☎118.

MONEY. Liechtenstein uses the **Swiss Franc (SFr)** (see p. 956). For currency exchange at acceptable rates, go to Switzerland. (Really.)

SWISS FRANC (SFR)		
	AUS$1 = 1.51SFR	1SFR = AUS$1.21
	CDN$1 = 0.97SFR	1SFR = CDN$1.03
	EUR€1 = 1.47SFR	1SFR = EUR€0.68
	NZ$1 = 0.71SFR	1SFR = NZ$1.41
	ZAR1 = 0.14SFR	1SFR = ZAR7.12
	US$1 = 1.51SFR	1SFR = US$0.66
	UK£1 = 2.41SFR	1SFR = UK£0.43

VADUZ AND LOWER LIECHTENSTEIN

A handful of museums await in Liechtenstein's capital, but not much else; Vaduz rarely requires more than one day. Lower Liechtenstein refers to the elevation; it's actually in the north. Campers and bikers will enjoy the flat ground here; hikers should consider heading for the hills in Upper Liechtenstein, particularly Malbun.

PRACTICAL INFORMATION. Liechtenstein's **national tourist office,** Städtle 37, one block up the hill from the Vaduz Post Bus stop, will stamp your passport with Liechtenstein's bi-colored seal (2SFr). It also sells hiking maps (15.50SFr), locates rooms free of charge, and distributes free city maps and advice on outdoor activities. (☎232 14 43. Open July-Sept. M-F 8am-5:30pm, Sa-Su 9am-5pm; Oct.-June M-F 8am-noon and 1:30-5:30pm; Apr. and Oct. M-F 8am-noon and 1:30-5:30pm, Sa 9am-noon and 1:30-5pm; May also Su 9am-noon and 1:30-5:30pm.) Rent **bicycles** at **Bike-Garage** in nearby Triesen. (35SFr per day. Open M-F 8am-noon and 1:30-6pm, Sa 8am-2pm.) The main **post office** is near the tourist office and has an amazing selection of postage stamps. (Open M-F 7:45am-6pm, Sa 8-11am.) **Postal code:** FL-9490.

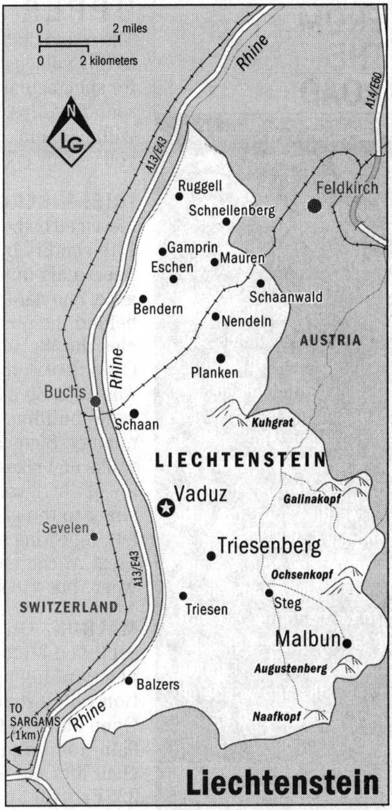

ACCOMMODATIONS, CAMPING, AND FOOD. Budget housing options in Vaduz are few and far between, but nearby **Schaan** is more inviting and contains Liechtenstein's only **Jugendherberge (HI)** ❷, Untere Rüttig. 6. From Vaduz, take bus #1 (dir.: Schaan) to Mühleholz, walk toward the intersection, turn left down Marianumstr., and follow the signs. (☎232 50 22. Breakfast included. Laundry 8SFr. Reception daily 5-10pm. Check-out 10am. Open Feb.-Oct. HI members only. Dorms 28.60SFr; doubles 37.10SFr.) **Hotel Post** ❸, Bahnhofstr. 14, faces the back of the Schaan post office and offers reasonably priced rooms, but it's near a busy bus stop. (☎232 17 18. Breakfast included. Reception daily 8am-11pm. 40SFr per person, with shower 50SFr.) For **Camping Mittagspitze** ❶, take bus #1 (dir.: Sargans) to Säga, cross the street, and walk toward the mountains, following the signs. Located at the foot of the *Mittagspitze*, this campground provides great scenery and a pool to splash in. (☎392 26 86. Showers included. Laundry 4.50SFr. Reception June-Aug. daily 8-10am and 5-8pm; Sept.-May 7-8am and 5-6pm. 8.50SF per person, 5SFr per tent; 0.30SFr tax.) Groceries are available at **Migros**, Aulestr. 20, across from the tour bus parking lot. (Open M-F 8am-1pm and 1:30-6:30pm, Sa 8am-4pm.)

SIGHTS. The 12th-century **Schloß Vaduz,** the regal home of Hans Adam II, Prince of Liechtenstein, presides over the town. The interior is off-limits to the masses; however, you can hike up to the castle for a closer look and a phenomenal view of the whole country. The 15min. trail begins down the street from the tourist office, heading away from the post office. Across the street from the tourist office is the **Kunstmuseum Liechtenstein,** Städtle 32. Mostly for modern art, the museum boasts paintings by Dalí, Kandinsky, and Klee, as well as rotating special exhibits and installations. The prince's collection of Renaissance and Romantic masterpieces is also displayed here. (Open Tu-W and F-Su 10am-5pm, Th until 8pm. 8SFr, students and seniors 5SFr.)

UPPER LIECHTENSTEIN

The roads that snake their way up the mountainsides to tiny villages, such as **Triesenberg** and **Malbun,** allow for spectacular views of the Rhine Valley and the surrounding Alps. Buses make the short run from Vaduz within 30min., and the trips are well worth it even if you're only spending one day in the country.

TRIESENBERG. The first town up the mountain (serviced by bus #10), Triesenberg was founded in the 13th century by the Walsers, a Swiss group forced to flee Valais due to overpopulation, religious intolerance, and natural disaster. The **Walser Heimatmuseum,** behind the post office right by the bus stop, chronicles the Walsers' customs and crafts. (☎262 19 26. Open Sept.-May Tu-F 1:30-5:30pm, Sa 1:30-5pm; June-Aug. also Su 2-5pm. 2SFr.) The **tourist office** is in the same building and has the same hours and phone number. Signs at the post office point to a variety of walks and **hikes.** For stunning views of the Rhine Valley (1½hr.), take bus #34 to **Gaflei,** head across the street to the gravel path and look for the trail on the left, following signs to Silum and then to Ob. Tunnel, Steg. At the end, walk through the tunnel to Steg, where bus #10 runs back to Vaduz or Schaan every hr.

MALBUN. On the other side of the mountain, secluded Malbun offers affordable ski slopes and plenty of hiking. The **tourist office** provides information on all that Malbun has to offer. (☎263 65 77. Open June to Oct. and mid-Dec. to mid-Apr. M-Sa 9am-noon and 1:30-5pm.) During the winter, two chair lifts and four T-bars are in operation. (Day pass 33SFr.) Right in the middle of town, **Malbun A.G.** (☎263 97 70 or 262 19 15) offers 1-day classes (65SFr), 3-day classes (155SFr), and private ski lessons (230SFr per day). **Malbun Sport** rents skis and snowboards in winter and bikes in summer. (☎263 37 55. Open M-F 8am-6pm, Sa 8am-5pm, Su 9am-5pm.) In summer, try the round-trip hike to **Pfälzerhütte,** which leads over the Augustenberg and culminates in fine views of the Alps (5hr.). It's doable even if you're not into hiking. Take the only chairlift open in the summer, the **Sareiserjoch** (7.50SFr, round-trip 11.70SFr; open daily 8-11:50am and 1-4:50pm) and follow signs for Pfälzerhütte (be sure to turn left off the main trail after 5min.). To get back, head toward Gritsch and then Tälihöhi. **Hotel Alpen ❸,** close to the bus stop and tourist office, includes a restaurant and a large common room with TV. The more expensive rooms have cable TV, phone, shower, and a stocked fridge. (☎263 11 81. Reception daily 8am-10pm. Open mid-May to Oct. and mid-Dec. to Apr. In summer 45-65SFr per person. In winter, add 20SFr.)

FROM THE ROAD

A SIX-HOUR TOUR

Though we joke about being able to see all of Liechtenstein in a day, it's actually possible to see the entire nation in a little under six hours. The LGT-Alpin Marathon runs 42km from just outside of Schaan to Malbun.

The course began in a relatively flat farmland near the Rhine. The smell of cow manure was overwhelming at times as we ran past farmers harvesting hay. When we hit Vaduz, the next 11km were entirely uphill, rising over 1000m. Most of us slowed to a walk, but the enthusiastic Liechtensteiners were out in force chanting, "Haub! Haub! Bravo!" as we lumbered past.

Coming around a corner, I heard dozens of ringing bells and wondered if a local church had decided to ring its bells for us. As I came around the hairpin turn, I found 400 cows, all wearing bells. To my left, I had a perfect view of the yellow and green rolling hills in the Rhine valley below and straight ahead of the snow-covered peaks of the Alps. A paraglider chose this moment to fly overhead and I wondered if I hadn't stumbled into a picture postcard by mistake.

The final 8km were all downhill, as we circled Malbun's valley at reckless speeds. I finished in 5 hours and 40 minutes, almost 2½ hours behind the winner, having crossed the entire country and ascended 1800m in the process. The mountain goats didn't seem too impressed though—they've been doing the same thing for years.

—Tom Miller

LUXEMBOURG

Too often overlooked by budget travelers, the tiny Grand Duchy of Luxembourg boasts impressive fortresses and castles as well as beautiful hiking trails. Established in 963, the original territory was called *Lucilinburhuc*, named for the "little fortresses" that saturated the countryside after successive waves of Burgundians, Spaniards, French, Austrians, and Germans had receded. Today, Luxembourg has become a notable European Union member and a prominent international financial center. Judging by their national motto, *"Mir welle bleiwe wat mir sinn"* ("We want to remain what we are"), it seems that the Luxembourgians are pleased with their accomplishments.

SYMBOL	❶	❷	❸	❹	❺
ACCOMMODATIONS	under €12	€13-16	€17-30	€31-40	over €40
FOOD	under €5	€6-9	€10-14	€15-20	over €21

For Luxembourg, prices are indicated in food and accommodations listings using the system of icons and price ranges above. Prices for accommodations are based on the lowest cost for one person, excluding special deals or discounts. For restaurants, prices are based on the average entree price.

SUGGESTED ITINERARIES

THREE DAYS Spend all of it in **Luxembourg City,** arguably one of Europe's most beautiful capitals (p. 753). Marvel at the **Grand Ducal Palace** and wander underground through the **Casemates.**

BEST OF LUXEMBOURG, ONE WEEK Enjoy **Luxembourg City** (2 days; p. 753). Visit the gorgeous château in **Vianden** (2 days; p. 758), hike or bike around the rock formations and view the illuminated manuscripts in **Echternach** (1 day; p. 759), and then canoe down the Sûre River in **Diekirch** (1 day; p. 758). Finally, check out the Family of Man exhibit in little **Clervaux** (1 day; p. 759).

LIFE AND TIMES

HISTORY

The Grand Duchy of Luxembourg has a long history of occupation and domination by its larger European neighbors. Ancient history saw Luxembourg inhabited by Belgic tribes and controlled by Romans. In the early Middle Ages, the territory was annexed by the Franks as part of Austrasia, and then claimed by **Charlemagne** as part of the Holy Roman Empire. Luxembourg became an independent region in AD 963, under the control of **Siegfried, Count d'Ardennes.** Siegfried's descendents ruled Luxembourg, eventually adopting the title of Count of Luxembourg. The region became a duchy in 1354 by edict of Emperor Charles IV, but in 1443, the Duchess of Luxembourg was forced to give up the property to the Duke of Burgundy. Luxembourg passed into the hands of the Spanish **Habsburgs** in the early 16th century, only to be conquered by France after the devastating **Thirty Years' War** (1618-1648). During the 17th and 18th centuries, Luxembourg was tossed between France, Spain, and Austria. The year after the fall of **Napoleon** at Waterloo in 1814, the **Congress of Vienna** made Luxembourg a grand duchy and gave it to **William I,** King of The Netherlands. After the 1830 Belgian revolt against William, part of Luxembourg was ceded to Belgium, and the remainder was recognized as a sovereign and independent state. A subsequent economic union with Prussia brought industrialization to the previously agrarian country. In 1867, the **Treaty of London** reaffirmed Luxembourg's autonomy and declared its neutrality. Yet the 20th century found Luxembourg occupied by Germany during both world wars. After being liberated by the Allied powers in 1944, Luxembourg became a member of the **Benelux Economic Union,** along with The Netherlands and Belgium. It relinquished its neutral status in 1948 in order to join various international economic, political, and military institutions, including **NATO** and the **United Nations**. It was also one of the six founding members of the **European Economic Community,** which later became the **European Union.**

TODAY

Luxembourg is one of the world's most industrialized countries, and it enjoys an economic security evidenced by the highest purchasing power and per capita income in Western Europe. The country is governed by a **constitutional monarchy,** in which the Grand Duke, currently **Henri I,** holds formal authority. The major executive and legislative power is vested in the prime minister, currently **Jean-Claude Juncker,** appointed by the Grand Duke, and in the Chamber of Deputies, elected by popular vote. Luxembourg has the greatest proportion of foreign residents of any Western European country. The Luxembourgian people have been significantly influenced by both German and French culture, but they maintain a distinct national identity.

CULTURE

CUSTOMS & ETIQUETTE

Service (15-20%) is included in the price; tipping extra for exceptional service is optional. Tip taxi drivers 10%. Most **banks** are open M-F 8:30am-4:30pm, and most **shops** are open M-Sa 10am-6pm and some open shorter hours on Su. However, many banks and shops close at noon for two hours, especially in the countryside.

HOLIDAYS & FESTIVALS

Holidays: New Year's Day (Jan. 1); Carnival (Mar. 3); Easter (Apr. 20); Easter Monday (Apr. 21); May Day (May 1); Ascension Day (May 29); Whit Sunday and Monday (June 8-9); National Holiday (June 23); Assumption Day (Aug. 15); All Saints' Holiday (Nov. 1); Christmas (Dec. 25); and Saint Stephen's Day (Dec. 26).

Festivals: Luxembourg City hosts the **Luxembourg City Fete** (Sept. 1).

ESSENTIALS

FACTS AND FIGURES

Official Name: Grand Duchy of Luxembourg.
Capital: Luxembourg City.
Population: 415,870.
Land Area: 2586 sq. km.
Time Zone: GMT +1.
Languages: French, German, Luxembourgian.
Religions: Roman Catholic (90%).

WHEN TO GO

Luxembourg has a temperate climate with less moisture than Belgium. Anytime between May and mid-Oct. is a good time to visit.

DOCUMENTS & FORMALITIES

South Africans need a visa for stays of any length. Citizens of Australia, Canada, the EU, New Zealand, and the US do not need a visa for stays of up to 30 days. Contact your embassy for more information.

Luxembourg Embassies at Home: Australia (consulate), Level 18, Royal Exchange Bldg., 56 Pitt St., Sydney NSW 2000 (☎(02) 92 41 43 22; fax 92 51 11 13). **Canada** (honorary consulate), 3706 St. Hubert St., Montréal, PQ H2L 4A3 (☎514-849-2101). **South Africa** (honorary consulate), P.O. Box 357, Lanseria 1748 (☎(011) 659 09 61). **UK,** 27 Wilton Crescent, London SW1X 8SD (☎(020) 7235 6961; fax 7235 9734). **US,** 2200 Massachusetts Ave. NW, Washington, D.C. 20008 (☎202-265-4171; fax 328-8270).

Foreign Embassies in Luxembourg: All foreign embassies are in **Luxembourg City** (see p. 754).

TRANSPORTATION

The Luxembourg City airport (LUX) is serviced by **Luxair** (☎479 81, reservations ☎4798 42 42) and by flights from the UK and throughout the continent. Cheap last-minute flights on Luxair are available at www.luxair.lu. A **Benelux Tourrail Pass** allows five days of unlimited **train** travel in a one-month period in Belgium, The Netherlands, and

Luxembourg (€159, 50% companion discount; under 26 €106). The **Billet Réseau** (€4.50, book of 5 €17.50), a network ticket, is good for one day of unlimited bus and train travel. Even better is the **Luxembourg Card** (see below), which includes unlimited transportation. International train routes to Luxembourg include: Brussels (1¾hr.; see p. 135) and Liège (2½hr.) in Belgium; Koblenz (2¼hr.; see p. 493) and Trier (45min., see p. 494) in Germany; and Metz in France (45min.; see p. 407). **Hiking** and **biking trails** run between Luxembourg City and Echternach, from Diekirch to Echternach and Vianden, and elsewhere. **Bikes** aren't permitted on buses, but are allowed on many trains for free.

TOURIST SERVICES AND MONEY

EMERGENCY	**Police:** ☎112. **Ambulance:** ☎112. **Fire:** ☎112.

TOURIST OFFICES. For general information, contact the **Luxembourg National Tourist Office,** P.O. Box 1001, L-1010 Luxembourg (☎(352) 42 82 82 10; www.etat.lu/tourism). The **Luxembourg Card,** available from Easter to October at tourist offices, hostels, and many hotels and public transportation offices, provides unlimited transportation on national trains and buses and includes admission to 32 tourist sites (1-day €9, 2-day €16, 3-day €22).

Tourist Boards at Home: UK, 122 Regent St., London W1R 5FE (☎(020) 7434 2800; www.luxembourg.co.uk). **US,** 17 Beekman Pl., New York, NY 10022 (☎212-935-8888; www.visitluxembourg.com).

MONEY. The official currency of Luxembourg is the **euro.** The Luxembourg franc can still be exchanged at a rate of 40LF to €1. For exchange rates and more information on the euro, see p. 20. The European Union imposes a **value-added tax (VAT)** on goods and services purchased within the EU (see p. 19). Luxembourg's VAT (15%) is already included in most prices. Luxembourg's refund threshold (US$85) is lower than most other EU countries; refunds are usually 13% of the purchase price. The cost of living in Luxembourg is moderate to high. Expect to pay €30-45 for a hotel room, €13.60-15.50 for a hostel bed, and €8-11 for a restaurant meal.

ACCOMMODATIONS AND CAMPING

Luxembourg's 12 **HI youth hostels** *(Auberges de Jeunesse)* are often filled with school groups. Check the sign posted in any hostel to find out which hostels are full or closed each day. Prices range from €13.60-15.50; nonmembers pay €2.75 extra. Breakfast and sheets are included, a packed lunch costs €3.80, and dinner €7.10. Half of the hostels close from mid-November to mid-December, and the other half close from mid-January to mid-February. Contact **Centrale des Auberges de Jeunesse Luxembourgeoises** (☎26 29 35 00; www.youthhostels.lu) for information. **Hotels** advertise €25-50 per night, depending on amenities; make sure you clarify the price you will pay. Luxembourg is a **camping** paradise; most towns have campsites close by. Two people with a tent will typically pay €5-9 per night.

COMMUNICATION

PHONE CODES	**Country code:** 352. **International dialing prefix:** 00. Luxembourg has no city codes.

TELEPHONES. There are no city codes; just dial 352 plus the local number. Most public phones accept phone cards, which are sold at post offices and newspaper stands. International direct dial numbers include: **AT&T,** ☎8002 0111; **British Telecom,** ☎0800 89 0352; **Canada Direct,** ☎800 2 0119; **Ireland Direct,** ☎0800 353; **MCI,** ☎8002 0112; **Sprint,** ☎0800 0115; **Telecom New Zealand,** ☎800 20064.

MAIL. Mailing a postcard or a letter (up to 20g) from Luxembourg costs €0.55 to the UK and Europe and €0.75 anywhere else.

LANGUAGES. French and German are the administrative languages, and, since a referendum in 1984, *Letzebuergesch*, a mixture of the other two that sounds a bit like Dutch, is the national language. French is most common in the city, while German is more common in smaller towns. For basic phrases in French and German, see p. 895. English is also commonly spoken.

LUXEMBOURG CITY

With a medieval fortress perched on a cliff that overlooks lush green river valleys, and high bridges stretching all over the downtown area, Luxembourg City (pop. 81,800) is one of the most attractive and dramatic capitals in Europe. As an international banking capital, it is home to thousands of frenzied foreign business executives; even so, most visitors find it surprisingly relaxed and idyllic.

TRANSPORTATION

Flights: Findel International Airport (LUX), 6km from the city. **Bus #9** (€1.10) is cheaper than the Luxair bus (€3.75) and runs the same route every 10-20min.

Trains: Gare CFL, av. de la Gare (toll-free info ☎49 90 49 90; www.cfl.lu), near the foot of av. de la Liberté, 10min. south of the city center. To: **Amsterdam** (5¾hr.; €42, under 26 €34.20); **Brussels** (2¾hr., round-trip €39/€13.30); **Frankfurt** (5hr., €43.20/€38.20); **Paris** (3½-4hr., €39.20/€31.30).

Buses: Buy a **billet courte distance** (short-distance ticket) from the driver (single-fare €1.10, full-day €4.40), or pick up a package of 10 (€7.95) at the train station. Tickets also valid on **local trains.** Buses run until midnight; night buses offer limited service.

Taxis: ☎48 22 33. €0.87 per km. 10% premium 10pm-6am; 25% premium on Su. €17-20 from the city center to the airport.

Bikes: Rent from **Velo en Ville,** 8 r. Bisserwé (☎47 96 23 83). Open daily 10am-noon and 1-8pm. €12.50 per half-day, €20 per day, €37.50 per weekend, €75 per week. Under 26 20% discount.

ORIENTATION AND PRACTICAL INFORMATION

Five minutes by bus and 15min. by foot from the train station, Luxembourg City's historic center revolves around the **Place d'Armes.** Facing the municipal tourist office, located in the commemorative Town Hall, turn right down r. Chimay to reach **Boulevard Roosevelt.**

Tourist Offices: Grand Duchy National Tourist Office (☎42 82 82 20; www.etat.lu/tourism), in the train station, has tons of info and lacks the long lines of the office in town. Open July-Sept. 9am-7pm; Oct.-June 9:15am-12:30pm and 1:45-6pm. **Municipal Tourist Office,** pl. d'Armes (☎22 28 09; www.luxembourg-city.lu/touristinfo). Open Apr.-Sept. M-Sa 9am-7pm, Su 10am-6pm; Oct.-Mar. M-Sa 9am-6pm, Su 10am-6pm. Also, look for the helpful, yellow-shirted **"Ask Me"** representatives all over the city; they give out free tourist info. **Center Information Jeunes,** 26 pl. de la Gare (☎26 29 32 00), inside Galerie Kons across from the train station, is a great service for young travelers, offering information on everything from hostels to finding jobs as well as free **Internet** access for students (1hr. max.). Open M-F 10am-6pm.

Budget Travel: SOTOUR, 15 pl. du Théâtre (☎46 15 14). Sells BIJ and other discount tickets for international flights; makes train reservations that begin or end in Luxembourg. Open M-F 9am-6pm, Sa 9am-noon.

Embassies: Ireland, 28 r. d'Arlon (☎45 06 10; fax 45 88 20). Open M-F 10am-12:30pm and 2:30-5pm. **UK,** 14 bd. Roosevelt (☎22 98 64; fax 22 98 67). Open M-F 9am-12:30pm. **US,** 22 bd. Emmanuel Servais (☎46 01 23; www.amembassy.lu). Open M-F 8:30am-12:30pm. **Australians, Canadians, New Zealanders,** and **South Africans** should contact their embassies in France or Belgium.

Currency Exchange: Banks are the only option for changing money or cashing traveler's checks. Most are open M-F 8:30am until 4 or 4:30pm. All are closed on weekends. Expect to pay a commission of €5 for cash and €8.30 for traveler's checks.

Luggage Storage: In train station. €2.50 per day (1-month max.); 2-day lockers €2-4.

Laundromat: Quick Wash, 31 r. de Strasbourg, near the station. Wash and dry €10. Open M-F 8:30am-6:30pm, Sa until 6pm. Cheaper at the HI hostel (see below).

Emergency: Police: ☎113. **Ambulance:** ☎112.

Pharmacy: Pharmacie Goedert, 5 pl. d'Armes (☎22 39 91). Open M 1-6:15pm, Tu-F 8am-6:15pm, Sa 8am-12:30pm. Check any pharmacy window for night info.

Medical Services: Doctors and pharmacies on call: ☎112. **Clinique Ste-Therese,** (☎49 77 61 or 49 78 81), Rue Ste-Zithe.

Internet Access: Center Information Jeunes (see above) has free Internet for students. **Sparky's,** 11a av. Monterey (☎620 12 23), at the pl. d'Armes. €0.10 per min. Open M-F 8am-8pm, Sa 11am-8pm.

Post Office: 38 pl. de la Gare, across the street and left of the train station. Open M-F 6am-7pm, Sa 6am-noon. Address mail to be held: Firstname SURNAME, *Poste Restante,* Recette Principale, **L-1009** Luxembourg City, Luxembourg. **Branch office,** 25 r. Aldringen, near the pl. d'Armes. Open M-F 7am-7pm, Sa 7am-5pm.

ACCOMMODATIONS

Budget travelers have two basic options in Luxembourg City—the city's hostel, often filled with school and tour groups in the summer, or the relatively inexpensive accommodations near the train station. Prices in the city center are about €50 higher than those around the train station.

Auberge de Jeunesse (HI), 2 r. du Fort Olisy (☎22 19 20 or 22 68 89; luxembourg@youth.hostels.lu). Take bus #9 and ask to get off at the hostel stop; head under the bridge and turn right down the steep path. Low security; lock up your valuables. Breakfast and sheets included. Laundry €7.50. 6-night max. stay in high season. Reception daily 7am-1am. Curfew 2am. Dorms €15.50; singles €23; doubles €36. Nonmembers add €2.75. ❷

Bella Napoli, 4 r. de Strasbourg (☎48 46 29). Simple rooms with hardwood floors and full bath. Breakfast included. Reception daily 7am-midnight. Singles €38; doubles €45; triples €60. ❹

Hotel Schintgen, 6 r. Notre Dame (☎22 28 44; schintgn@pt.lu). One of the cheapest hotels in the Old Center. Breakfast included. Reception daily 7am-11pm. Singles €50-65; doubles €75-85; triples €87. ❺

Hotel Carlton, 9 r. de Strasbourg (☎29 96 60; www.carlton.lu). Clean and freshly renovated rooms in an old marble building. Free Internet access. All rooms with bath and TV. Breakfast included. Singles €69; doubles €83. ❺

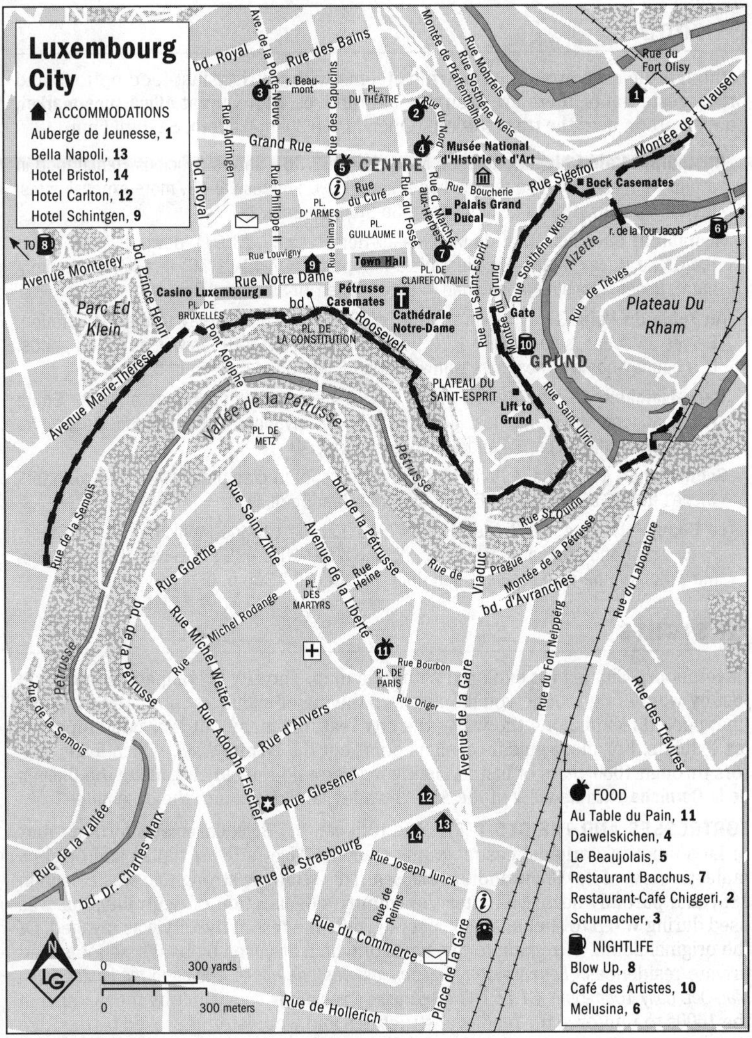

Hotel Bristol, 11 r. de Strasbourg (☎48 58 29). Comfy rooms, some with showers. Breakfast included. Singles €40-65; doubles €45-75. ❹

Camping: Kockelscheuer (☎47 18 15), outside Luxembourg City. Take bus #5 to Kockelscheuer-Camping from the station. Showers included. Open Easter-Oct. €3.50 per person, €4 per tent. ❶

FOOD

Although the area around pl. d'Armes teems with touristy fast-food options and pricey restaurants, there are desirable alternatives. Stock up at **Alima supermarket,** on r. Bourbon near the train station. (Open M-F 8:30am-6:30pm, Sa until 6pm.)

Restaurant-Café Chiggeri, 15 r. du Nord (☎22 82 36). Serves delicious French food in a funky atmosphere. The terrace has a great view. Entrees €9-13; more expensive restaurant upstairs. Open M-F noon-1am, Sa-Su noon-3am. ❸

Restaurant Bacchus, 32 r. du Marché-aux-Herbes (☎47 13 97), down the street from the Grand Ducal palace. Excellent pizza and pasta (€7.40-11.70) in a homey environment. Reservations recommended 7-10pm. Open Tu-Su noon-10pm. ❷

Au Table du Pain, 37 av. de la Liberté (☎29 56 63), on the way to the train station. Serves up soups, salads (€8-11.20), and sandwiches (€4-8), as well as baked goods, in a country-home atmosphere with wooden tables. Open daily 8am-6pm. ❷

Daiwelskichen, 4 Grand Rue (☎22 15 08). A great but out-of-the-way place for South American food and margaritas. Meals €10-20. Reservations recommended. Open M-Sa noon-3pm and 7-11pm; M and Sa closed midday. ❹

Schumacher, 18 av. de la Porte-Neuve. Popular spot to grab a sandwich and go. Sandwiches from €1.75. Open M-F 7am-6pm, Sa 7am-5pm. ❶

Le Beaujolais, 2a r. des Capucins (☎47 45 12), next to the Municipal Tourist Office. Tasty pasta and pizza at reasonable prices (€7.20-10.20). Sit in velvet booths or people watch on the pl. d'Armes. Open daily 11:30am-11:30pm. ❷

SIGHTS

Luxembourg City is best explored without a map. The city is compact enough that just by wandering around you'll bump into the major sights. Be prepared for some unexpected treats along the way—the city features many outdoor contemporary art exhibits. For more guidance, signs point out the **Wenzel Walk,** which leads visitors through 1000 years of history as it winds around the old city, along the **Chemin de la Corniche** with its view of the Alzette valley, and down into the casemates.

FORTRESSES AND THE OLD CITY. The 10th-century **Bock Casemates** fortress, part of Luxembourg's original castle, looms over the Alzette River Valley and offers a fantastic view of the **Grund** and the **Clausen.** This strategic stronghold was closed in 1867 and partially destroyed after the country's declaration of neutrality, but was used during WWII to shelter 35,000 people while the rest of the city was ravaged. Of the original 23km, 17 remain today, parts of which are used by banks, schools, and private residences. *(Entrance on r. Sigefroi, just past the bridge leading to the hostel. Open Mar.-Oct. daily 10am-5pm. €1.75.)* The **Pétrusse Casemates** were built by the Spanish in the 1600s to reinforce the medieval structures and were later improved by the Austrians. In the 19th century, a second ring was extended and a third began around the city, giving Luxembourg the nickname "Gibraltar of the North." *(On pl. de la Constitution. Open July-Sept. €1.75, students €1.50. Tours every hr. 11am-4pm.)* The view from the nearby **Place de la Constitution** is incredible. Stroll down into the lush green valley, or catch one of the little green tourist trains that run down from pl. de la Constitution into the valley and back up to the **Plateau du Rham.** *(Trains ☎651 16 51. Mid-Mar. to Oct. every 30min. 10am-6pm except 1pm. €6.50.)*

MUSEUMS. The **Luxembourg Card** (see p. 751) covers entrance to all museums in the city. The **All-in-One Ticket** covers five museums over two days (€8.70 at the Municipal Tourist Office). The eclectic collection at the **Musée National d'Histoire et**

d'Art chronicles the influences of the various European empires, from ancient to contemporary, that controlled Luxembourg. *(Marché-aux-Poissons, at r. Boucherie and Sigefroi. ☎479 33 01; www.mnha.lu. Open Tu-Su 10am-5pm. €5, students €3.)* The **Casino Luxembourg** houses changing exhibitions of contemporary art. *(41 r. de Notre Dame, near pl. de la Constitution. ☎22 50 45. Open M, W, F-Su 11am-6pm; Th 11am-8pm. €4.)* The **Musée d'Histoire de la Ville de Luxembourg** features quirky exhibits that allow you to view the history of the city through photographs, films, and music clips. *(14 r. du St-Esprit. ☎47 96 30 61. Open Tu-Su 10am-6pm, Th until 8pm. €5, students €3.70.)*

OTHER SIGHTS. Built as the city hall in 1574, the Renaissance **Palais Grand Ducal** became the official city residence of the Grand Duke in 1890. To reach the palace from the info office, walk straight ahead on r. du Curé and turn right on r. du Marché-aux-Herbes. *(Mandatory tours mid-July to Aug. M-F afternoons and Sa mornings; tickets sold at the Municipal Tourist Office. Reservations ☎22 28 09; English-language tours available. €5.45.)* Nearby, the 7th-century **Cathédrale de Notre Dame,** which incorporates features of the Dutch Renaissance and early Baroque styles, houses the tomb of John the Blind, the 14th-century King of Bohemia and Count of Luxembourg. *(Entrance at bd. Roosevelt. Open daily 10am-noon and 2-5:30pm. Free.)*

ENTERTAINMENT AND NIGHTLIFE

At night, the **Place d'Armes** comes to life with free concerts and stand-up comedy. Pick up *La Semaine à Luxembourg* at the tourist office for a list of events. On the **Grand Duke's birthday** (June 23), the city shuts down to host a large military and religious procession. Nightlife centers on the valley in the **Grund** (by the bottom of the elevator lift on pl. du St-Esprit) and the **Clausen** area. Check the monthly *Nightlife.lu*, available at most cafes and newsstands. Dance the night away at **Melusina,** 145 r. de la Tour Jacob (☎43 59 22), a popular student nightspot, which is also open for lunch and dinner (M-Sa; €7.40-17). To get there, cross the bridge from the Grund lift and follow r. de Trèves until it becomes r. de la Tour Jacob. At **Blow Up,** 14 av. de la Faiencerie, three rooms pump house, 80s, and Latin music late into the night. (☎43 34 86. Cover €10; W free for women. Open W-Sa nights.) For a more relaxed and slightly older crowd, warm up in the Grund at the candle-lit piano bar **Café des Artistes,** 22 Montée du Grund. (☎52 34 46. Beer €2.50. Piano W-Su 10:30pm-2am. Open daily 2:30pm-late.)

THE ARDENNES

Almost six decades ago, the Battle of the Bulge (1944) mashed Luxembourg into slime and mud. Today, the forest is verdant again, and the quiet towns, looming castles, and pleasant hiking trails are powerful draws.

ETTELBRÜCK. Ettelbrück's position on the main railway line between Liège, Belgium, and Luxembourg City makes it a transportation hub of the Ardennes. To get to the city center from the train station, go left on r. du Prince Henri, continue right on the same street, then turn left on Grand Rue and follow it to pl. de l'Église. The **General Patton Memorial Museum,** 5 r. Dr. Klein, commemorates the liberation of Luxembourg during WWII. To get there, walk back along the Grand Rue, away from pl. de l'Église, and go left onto r. Dr. Klein. (☎81 03 22. Open July to mid-Sept. daily 10am-5pm; mid-Sept. to June Su 2-5pm. €2.50.) The **tourist office** at the train station has information about excursions to the surrounding Ardennes towns. (☎81 20 68; site@pt.lu. Open M-F 9am-noon and 1:30-5pm, July-Aug. also Sa 10am-noon and 2-4pm.) To get to the **Ettelbrück Hostel (HI) ❷,** r. G. D. Josephine-Charlotte, follow signs from the station. (☎81 22 69; ettelbruck@youthhostels.lu. Lockout 10am-5pm. Breakfast and sheets included. Dorms €13.60.) **Camping Kalkesdelt**

❶ is located at 22 r. du Camping. (☎81 21 85. Open Apr.-Oct. Reception daily 7:30am-noon and 2-10pm. €3.80 per person, €4 per tent.) The huge **Delhaize grocery** is close to the hostel and the center of town. Follow r. G. D. Josephine-Charlotte and then r. M. Weber into pl. Marie-Adelaide. (Open M-F 8am-7pm, Sa 8am-6pm.)

VIANDEN. The village of Vianden, in the dense Ardennes woods along the Our River, is home to one of the most impressive castles in Western Europe. Backpackers **hike** and **kayak** along the Sûre River, just south of Vianden, or **bike** to Diekirch (15-20min.) and Echternach (30min.). The **château,** a mix of Carolingian, Gothic, and Renaissance architecture, is filled with medieval armor, 16th-century furniture, and 17th-century tapestries. From March to October, the château hosts classical concerts each weekend. Walk uphill from the town or downhill from the *télésiège* (chairlift) to get to the château. (☎83 41 08. Open Apr.-Sept. daily 10am-6pm.; Mar. and Oct. M-F 10am-5pm, Sa 10am-5:30pm, Su 10am-6pm; Nov.-Feb. daily 10am-4pm. €4.50, students €3.50. Concerts €7.45-12.40.) For a stellar view of the château, ride the *télésiège*, 39 r. de Sanatorium. From the tourist office, cross the river, go left on r. Victor Hugo, then left again on r. de Sanitorium. (☎83 43 23. Open July-Aug. daily 10am-6pm; Easter-June and Sept.-Oct. 10am-5pm. €2.75; round-trip €4.25.) The **Maison Victor Hugo,** 37 r. de la Gare, former home of the famous French writer, documents his life and works. (26 87 40 88; www.victorhugo.lu. Open Apr.-Nov. Tu-Su 11am-5pm; Dec.-Mar. Sa 11am-5pm.)

Buses arrive from Ettelbrück (#570; 2 per hr., €2.25) via Diekirch. The **tourist office,** 1 r. du Vieux Marché, next to the main bus stop, sells trail maps (€2.30) and gives info on kayaking and private rooms. (☎83 42 57; www.tourist-info-vianden.lu. Open M-F 8am-noon and 1-6pm, Sa 10am-2pm, Su 2-4pm.) To reach the **HI youth hostel ❷,** 3 Montée du Château, from the bus stop or tourist office, follow Grande Rue away from the river and head up the hill; bear onto Montée du Château and follow the signs. (☎83 41 77; vianden@youthhostels.lu. Sheets €3.10. Reception daily 8-10am and 5-9pm. Lockout 10am-5pm. Curfew 11pm. Open mid-Mar. to mid-Nov. Call ahead. Dorms €13.60, nonmembers add €2.75.) Relax by the fountain at **Hotel Berg en Dal ❸,** 3 r. de la Gare. (☎83 41 27; info@hotel-bergendal.com. Breakfast included. Singles €27-50; doubles €38-44.) **Camp op dem Deich ❶,** r. Neugarten, alongside the Our river, is 5min. downstream from the tourist office. (☎83 43 75. Open Easter-Oct. €4 per person, €3.50 per tent.)

DIEKIRCH. Diekirch is a convenient outpost for biking and canoeing. The **National Museum of Military History,** 10 Bamertal, presents a comprehensive exhibit of relics from WWII's Battle of the Bulge. Highlights include pictures taken by a German propaganda unit at the Battle of the Bulge showing captured US infantry. (☎80 89 08. Open Apr.-Oct. daily 10am-6pm; Nov.-Mar. 2-6pm. €5, students €3.) The nearby **Municipal Museum,** on pl. Guillaume, houses three Roman mosaics found in the area. (Open Easter-Oct. daily 10am-noon and 2-6pm. €1.25.) The 15th-century **Église Saint-Laurent,** in the *Zone Pietone* (pedestrian area), is built upon Roman ruins. (Open Easter-Oct. Tu-Su 10am-noon and 2-6pm.)

Trains arrive from Ettelbrück hourly, while the more scenic **bus** rolls in every 15min. Buses run from Echternach hourly and drop you off on the Esplanade in front of the Municipal Museum. Buses headed for Vianden stop in the center of Diekirch, just off the Esplanade at the end of the *Zone Pietone* (#570; every 30min.). To get to the **tourist office,** 3 pl. de la Liberation, from the station, take the underground stairs to r. St. Antione and walk to the end; it's directly across the Place. (☎80 30 23; www.diekirch.lu. Hiking maps €2.30, mountain-biking maps €5. Open July-Aug. M-F 9am-5pm, Sa-Su 10am-noon and 2-4pm; Sept.-June M-F

9am-noon and 2-5pm, Sa 2-4pm. Free guided tours daily 3pm.) Rent **bikes** at **Speicher Sport,** 56 r. Clairefontaine (☎80 84 38; speibike@pt.lu; €10 per half-day, €15 per day), or **canoes** at **Outdoor Center,** 10 r. de la Sure (☎86 91 39). Stay at the conveniently located **Au Beau-Sejour ❸,** 12 Esplanade. (☎80 34 03; hotelbeausejour@hotmail.com. All rooms have shower and TV. Reception daily 8am-midnight. Singles €52; doubles €72.) Pitch your tent at **Camping de la Sûre ❶,** 34 rte. de Gilsdorf. (☎80 94 25; tourisme@diekirch.lu. Open Apr.-Sept. €3.50 per person, €3.75 per tent. Showers €0.75.) Restaurants line **Grand Rue.** The **Match** grocery store is just off r. Alexis Heck. (Open M-Th 8:30am-7:30pm, F 8:30am-8pm, Sa 8am-6pm.)

CLERVAUX. Little Clervaux's **château** houses the striking **Family of Man** exhibition, compiled in 1955 by Luxembourgian photographer Edward Steichen. The exhibition contains 500 pictures depicting every facet of human life in 68 countries. It was displayed worldwide before being permanently installed in Clervaux. (☎92 96 57. Open Mar.-Dec. Tu-Su 10am-6pm. €3.75, students €2.) To get to the château and the **Benedictine Abbey,** turn left from the train station and walk straight. (Abbey open daily 9am-7pm. Free.) Clervaux lies right on the main **railway** line that connects Luxembourg City, Ettelbrück, and Liège, Belgium. The **tourist office,** in the castle, books private rooms at Clervaux's B&Bs. (☎92 00 72; www.tourisme-clervaux.lu. Open July-Oct. daily 9:45am-11:45am and 2-6pm, Sept.-Oct. closed Su; Apr.-June M-Sa 2-5pm.) **Camping Officiel ❶,** 33 Klatzewe, is situated alongside the river. (☎92 00 42. Open Apr.-Nov. €4.30 per person, €4.30 per tent.)

ESCH-SUR-SÛRE. Surrounded by the majestic Ardennes and the placid Sûre River, the tiny town of Esch-sur-Sûre (pop. 235) is one the most outstanding in the country. So small you hardly need a map, this is the perfect place for those seeking beautiful scenery. The narrow streets wind up toward the crumbling **château,** dating to 927, where visitors are free to climb around and marvel at the panaromic view from all sides. Just outside the town is the **Upper Sûre Lake,** the country's largest lake as well as its drinking water reservoir. For a break from the greenery, head to the **candle factory,** 1 r. du Moulin. (☎89 91 97. Open M-F 8am-noon and 2-5pm.) The **Maison du Parc,** 15 rte. de Lultzhausen, is the reception center for the town and the **Nature Parc,** which includes the Lake of the Upper Sûre. The Maison du Parc has information on leisure activities in and around the lake and houses a permanent exhibition on wool spinning. (☎89 93 311; www.naturpark-sure.lu. Open M-Tu and Th-F 10am-noon and 2-6pm, Sa-Su 2-6pm.) Take bus #535 from Ettelbruck to the base of town (5 per day). Stay right across from the bus stop at **Hotel Le Postillon ❸,** 1 r. de l'Eglise. (☎89 90 33 or 89 90 35; www.lepostillon.lu. Doubles €74, demi-pension €65 per person.) **Camping im Aal ❶,** r. du Mouln, is on the banks of the Sûre near town. (☎83 95 14. €5 per person, €5 per site.)

LITTLE SWITZERLAND (LE MULLERTHAL)

In the eastern corner of Luxembourg, the region known as Little Switzerland, provides the ideal setting for hiking and rock-climbing. The unusual sandstone rock formations and numerous paths are the main attraction for visitors to the area.

ECHTERNACH. A favorite vacation spot of European families, the Lower-Sûre village of **Echternach** is known for its millennial rock formations and 7th-century monastic center. In the Middle Ages, the monastic center was known for its **illuminated manuscripts;** several are at the 18th-century **Benedictine Abbey.** From the bus station, go left at the marketplace on r. de la Gare, take the last left, and walk past the basilica. (☎72 74 72. Open July-Aug. daily 10am-6pm; Sept.-June 10am-noon and 2-5pm. €2, students €1.) Rent **bikes** at **Trisport,** 31 rte. de Luxembourg. (☎72 00 86. €2.50 per hr., €10 per half-day, €15 per day. Open Tu-Th 9am-noon and 2-6pm, F until 7pm, Sa until 5pm.) Echternach is accessible by **bus** from Ettelbrück and Luxembourg City. The **tourist office** is next to the abbey on Porte St-Willibrord. (☎72 02 30. Open in summer daily 9am-5pm; off-season M-F 9am-5pm.) To get from the bus station to the centrally located **youth hostel (HI) ❷,** 9 r. André Drechscher, turn left on av. de la Gare and take the last right. (☎72 01 58; echternach@youthhostels.lu. Breakfast and sheets included. Reception daily 5-11pm. Lockout 10am-5pm. Open Feb.-Dec. Dorms €13.60; nonmembers add €2.75.)

THE NETHERLANDS (NEDERLAND)

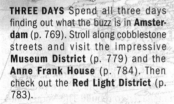

The Dutch say that although God created the rest of the world, *they* created The Netherlands. The country is a masterful feat of engineering; since most of it is below sea level, vigorous pumping and many dikes were used to create dry land. What was once the domain of seaweed is now packed with windmills, bicycles, tulips, and wooden shoes. The Netherlands' wealth of art and canal-lined towns draw as many travelers as do the unique hedonism and perpetual, indulgent partying of Amsterdam.

SYMBOL	❶	❷	❸	❹	❺
ACCOMMODATIONS	under €20	€20-34	€35-49	€50-65	over €65
FOOD	under €10	€10-15	€15-20	€20-30	over €30

For The Netherlands, prices are indicated in food and accommodations listings using the system of icons and price ranges above. Prices for accommodations are based on the lowest cost for one person, excluding special deals or discounts. For restaurants, prices are based on the average entree price.

SUGGESTED ITINERARIES

THREE DAYS Spend all three days finding out what the buzz is in **Amsterdam** (p. 769). Stroll along cobblestone streets and visit the impressive **Museum District** (p. 779) and the **Anne Frank House** (p. 784). Then check out the **Red Light District** (p. 783).

ONE WEEK Begin with **Amsterdam** (2 days), then head to charming **Haarlem** (1 day; p. 789). Stop by the world's largest flower auction in nearby **Aalsmeer** (1 day; p. 788) or tan your whole self on the beaches in **Zandvoort** (1 day; p. 790). From capital city **The Hague** (1 day; p. 792), make your way to student center **Utrecht** (1 day; p. 795).

BEST OF THE NETHERLANDS, TWO WEEKS Chill in **Amsterdam** (4 days). Then take the train to **Haarlem** (1 day) before heading on to **Aalsmeer** (1 day). Catch some rays in **Zandvoort** (1 day), and make your way to **The Hague** (1 day). Swing by ultra-modern **Rotterdam** (1 day; p. 794) and then relax in **Utrecht** (2 days). Visit artsy **Maastricht** (1 day; p. 797) and then head north to hike in **Hoge Veluwe National Park,** using **Arnhem** as your base (1 day; p. 797), before trekking up to trendy **Groningen** (1 day; p. 798).

LIFE AND TIMES

HISTORY AND POLITICS

FROM ROMANS TO HABSBURGS (100 BC TO AD 1579). Julius Caesar, leader of the Roman Empire, invaded the region in the first century BC, displacing obviously disgruntled Celtic and Germanic tribes. The native Germanic tribes had the last laugh in the 4th century as their reconquest swept across the Low Countries—The Netherlands, Belgium, and Luxembourg. Freedom was brief, however; the **Franks** took the place of the Romans from the 5th to the 8th century AD. During this period, towns rose as powerful centers only vaguely connected to each other. The **House of Burgundy** infiltrated the region in the 14th century to establish a more centralized monarchy. By 1482, the Austrian **Habsburgs** had managed to marry into the throne, beginning the long and volatile modern history of The Netherlands. The area quickly came under Spanish control after **Philip I** of the Habsburgs inherited the Spanish crown in 1493.

UTRECHT AND THE WAR WITH SPAIN (1579-1651). The Netherlands was officially founded in 1579 with the **Union of Utrecht,** which aimed to form an independent group of provinces and cities led by a **States-General.** Under Prince **William of Orange,** the Dutch declared independence from Spain in 1580, sparking prolonged struggle with Spanish forces. The conflict was settled in 1609 with the **Twelve Years' Truce,** which included recognition of The Netherlands' sovereignty. Unfortunately, this peace was short-lived; Spain resumed hostilities in 1621. **Frederick Henry** of the House of Orange led the Dutch to stunning victories, while the Dutch navy trounced the Spanish in battles near Cuba and along the English coast. Shamed by losing to such a tiny country, Spain quickly offered the **Peace of Westphalia** (1648), which not only acknowledged Dutch independence, but also pushed for friendship in order to hedge the growing power of France.

During the **Age of Exploration** in the 17th century, Dutch conquerors fanned out over the globe and gained control of all the major trade routes across Europe. This created incredible wealth for the Dutch—mostly generated by the **Dutch East India Company**—but it also trod on the toes of the British, who resented invasion of their commercial spheres. To protect its trade routes, the company colonized the Cape of Good Hope and other strategic posts to protect its trade routes. Meanwhile, the **Dutch West India Company** was exploring the New World, creating colonies such as New Amsterdam (modern-day New York). All of this activity created unprecedented growth in Amsterdam, which served as the chief port for The Netherlands.

WAR GAMES AND POWER STRUGGLES (1651-1795). Neighboring European powers resented the success and power of The Netherlands, causing an almost constant period of war and changing alliances for The Netherlands. England began by passing the **Navigation Act,** limiting Dutch involvement in English trade, and then by attacking the Dutch navy. The vastly stronger Brits prevailed forced peace and secretly drafted the **Act of Seclusion,** forever banning the Prince of Orange from Dutch politics. Councillor **Johan de Witt** managed to rebuild The Netherlands' military and economy, but when the restored King **Charles II** of England decided to re-start the war, the Dutch instantly negotiated an alliance with the French and sabotaged the English fleet.

In 1667, France invaded The Netherlands, threatening both the English and the Dutch, which caused them to form an alliance. This infuriated King **Louis XIV** of France, as he believed the Dutch had betrayed him, so he offered the English a highly subsidized alliance in return. In 1672, The Netherlands found itself in a full-scale war against both countries, but under the leadership of **William III,** it managed

to defeat the Franco-English fleets repeatedly. Ironically, William was crowned King of England in 1688, only 14 years after defeating it in battle, and The Netherlands found itself subordinated to English will. The Dutch grip on international trade quickly eroded with the expansion of French and English colonialism throughout the 18th century.

FRENCH RULE AND INDEPENDENCE (1795-1914). In 1795, **Napoleon Bonaparte** continued the Dutch doormat syndrome by invading and establishing French rule over the country. After Napoleon's defeat at Waterloo, the **Treaty of Vienna** (1815) established the Kingdom of The Netherlands, which included Belgium and Luxembourg. King **William I of Orange** managed to rebuild the economy and trade routes, but Belgium soon revolted against Dutch rule and gained independence in 1839. Under **William III,** the Dutch created a constitution establishing The Netherlands as a **constitutional monarchy** in which Parliament held most of the power, and the formation of modern political parties began. William's death in 1890 lead to the end of male succession as **Wilhelmina** became queen.

THE WORLD WARS (1914-1945). The outbreak of **World War I** posed a serious threat to The Netherlands, but it managed to remain neutral while focusing its attention on maintaining its trade and economy. After the war, The Netherlands strictly reaffirmed its neutrality despite Belgian attempts to cede Dutch lands (the issue was settled by the **Treaty of Versailles**). The Dutch did not fare as well in **World War II.** Without warning, the Nazis invaded in May 1940 and occupied the nation for almost five years. The Dutch suffered horribly—all acts of resistance were punished, Dutch Jews were sent to concentration camps, and the general population was in near-famine conditions.

THE POSTWAR ERA (1945-1990). After the war, Wilhelmina supported sweeping democratic changes for the nation, granting universal suffrage and proportional representation. The nation also abandoned its policy of neutrality, joining NATO and creating a "closer union" with Belgium and Luxembourg. In order to recover from WWII destruction, the government began an economic policy that focused on industrial and commercial expansion.

While the nation experienced relative peace through the 1950s, the 1960s brought years of rioting students and workers in response to economic and political problems. In the 1980s, Dutch politics saw the disintegration of old parties and old alliances. The recent rise of the **Christian Democratic Appeal** (CDA) has provided a new outlet for the major Christian factions. While the established **Labour Party** (PvdA) has managed to avoid ties with extreme leftist groups, it had to form a coalition government with the CDA in 1989.

TODAY

The Netherlands is an integral member of the **European Union (EU)** and has adopted the **euro** as legal tender. The government remains a constitutional monarchy: Parliament holds legislative power while the monarchy **(Queen Beatrix)** retains a symbolic role. Recently, The Netherlands has seen the rise of the conservative Christian Democratic party (CDA). In July of 2002, CDA's **Prime Minister Jan Peter Balkenende** was sworn into office. Among other things, his party is opposed to the country's more liberal sex and drug policies.

CULTURE

FOOD & DRINK

Traditional Dutch cuisine is hearty, heavy, meaty, and wholesome. Expect a lot of bread and cheese for breakfast and lunch, and generous portions of meats and fish for dinner. Popular seafood choices include all sorts of grilled fish and shellfish, fish stews, and raw herring. To round out a truly authentic Dutch meal, ask (especially in May and June) for white asparagus, which can be a main dish on its own, served with potatoes, ham, and eggs. Early on, the Dutch appropriated dishes from their nearby neighbors, the Swiss, including fondue, a delicious, though not health-conscious option. The Dutch conception of a light snack often includes **tostjes,** piping hot grilled cheese or ham and cheese sandwiches, **broodjes** (sandwiches), **olie-bollen** (doughnuts), or **poffertjes** (small pancakes). Colonial history has brought Surinamese and Indonesian cuisine to The Netherlands, followed closely by near-relatives from other South American and Asian countries. Indonesian cuisine is probably one of the safest bets for vegetarians and vegans. Wash it all down with a small, foamy glass of domestic beer: **Heineken** or **Amstel.**

CUSTOMS & ETIQUETTE

DRUGS. Refrain from smoking up outside; not only will this give you away as a tourist, but it can be seen as offensive. Be sure to ask if it's okay to smoke before lighting up. You may only carry up to 5g of soft drugs on you at one time.

LOVE FOR HIRE. A walk in the Red Light District will make it abundantly clear that prostitution is legal in Amsterdam. All of the prostitutes you see belong to a union called "The Red Thread" and are tested for HIV and STDs, although testing is on a voluntary basis. Do not take photos unless you want to explain yourself to the angriest—and largest—man you'll ever see. Keep in mind that prostitution is an entirely legal enterprise, and windows are a place of business. Show up clean and sober. Prostitutes reserve the right to refuse service to anyone. Specifically state what you get for the money you're paying—that means which sex acts, in what positions, and especially how much time you have in which to do it. Always practice safe sex. A prostitute will not even touch an uncondomed penis.

BUSINESS HOURS. Most shops are open M-F 9am-6pm, and generally open late at night on the weekends. Post offices close at noon on Saturdays and remain closed on Sundays. Lunch is typically served starting at 11am and ends at 3pm; dinner is served from 5:30pm to 11pm.

TAX AND TIP. The value added tax and service charges are always included in bills for hotels, shopping, taxi fares, and restaurants. If you buy an expensive item like a diamond, you are probably eligible for a tax refund. Keep your receipt and fill out a form at the airport. Tips for services are accepted and appreciated but not necessary. No waiter expects a 15% tip in Amsterdam, though it would most likely be appreciated. Ten percent is more normal; taxi drivers generally get tipped that much as well. Bouncers in clubs are often tipped €1-2 as patrons leave the club.

THE ARTS

VISUAL ARTS. The monumental genius of **Rembrandt** made him a legend in the art world. He made his living as a renowned portrait artist in the 1620s in Amsterdam, but he began to break new artistic ground with **chiaroscuro**—painting in light and dark. His paintings are characterized by rich, luxuriant color and texture and sensual brushwork, evidenced in *Judas Returning the Thirty Pieces of Silver* (1629). Later in the 17th century, **Jan Vermeer** explored bold perspectives and aspects of light. In the 19th century, ear-butcher **Vincent van Gogh,** perhaps the most famous **Post-Impressionist** artist, created a masterful collection of paintings in his own intensely personal style, characterized by bright, vibrantly contrasting colors and thick brush strokes, as can be seen in his *Starry Night* (1889). **Piet Mondrian,** the founder of the influential *De Stijl* magazine, formulated the theory of **neoplasticism**, which held that art should not attempt to recreate real life but should instead express universal absolutes. His signature works, characterized by black grids over primary-color blocks, have made their mark all over popular culture, from fashion to interior design.

LITERATURE. Dutch literature runs back to the 10th century when the Old Dutch *Wachtendonck Psalm Fragments* were written. The most influential works, however, didn't come until the Dutch **Golden Age** in the early 17th century. The primary author of the time was **Henric Laurenszoon Spieghel,** whose *Heart-Mirror* (1614) was the first philosophical work written in Dutch. The Reformed Church commissioned the *States Bible* (1620), the first translation of the Bible into Dutch, which further legitimized the language. **Joost van den Vondel** firmly placed the Dutch in the literary world with his dramatic tragedies and satirical treatment of the church and government; his *Lucifer* (1654) depicts an imagined conflict between the angels and God. Dutch literature took a back seat to Dutch imperialism in the 18th century, but in 1839 **Nicolaas Beets** led the recovery with *Camera Obscura,* drawing on the humor of Charles Dickens and Laurence Sterne. With the terror of **World War I** and **World War II** came a new focus on social and philosophical questions. **Willem Frederik Hermans** examines the hostile environment in *The Dark Room of Damocles* (1958). **Anne Frank** recorded her experience hiding from Nazi soldiers in *The Diary of Anne Frank.*

HOLIDAYS & FESTIVALS

Holidays: New Year's Day (Jan. 1); Good Friday (Apr. 18); Easter Monday (Apr. 20); Liberation Day (May 5); Ascension Day (May 9), Whitsunday and Whitmonday (June 3-4); Christmas Day (Dec. 25); Boxing Day (Dec. 26; also called Second Christmas Day).

Festivals: Koninginnedag (Queen's Day; Apr. 30) turns the country into a huge carnival. The **Holland Festival** (in June) features more than 30 productions in a massive celebration of the arts. **Bloemen Corso** (Flower Parade; first Sa in Sept.) runs from Aalsmeer to Amsterdam. Many historical canal houses and windmills are open to the public for **National Monument Day** (2nd Sa in Sept.). The **Cannabis Cup** (November) celebrates the magical mystery weed that brings millions of visitors to Amsterdam every year.

ESSENTIALS

FACTS AND FIGURES

Official Name: The Kingdom of The Netherlands.

Capital: Amsterdam.

Major Cities: Maastricht, Rotterdam, The Hague, Utrecht.

Population: 16 million.

Land Area: 41,526 sq. km.

Time Zone: 1hr. ahead of GMT.

Language: Dutch.

Religions: Catholic (34%), Protestant (25%), Muslim (3%).

WHEN TO GO

The ideal time to visit is between mid-May and early October, when day temperatures are generally 20-31°C (70-80°F), with nights around 10-20°C (50-60°F). It can be quite rainy; bring an umbrella. The tulip season runs from April to mid-May.

DOCUMENTS AND FORMALITIES

South Africans need a visa for stays of any length. Citizens of Australia, Canada, the EU, New Zealand, and the US do not need a visa for stays of up to 90 days.

Dutch Embassies at Home: Australia, 120 Empire Circuit, Yarralumla Canberra, ACT 2600 (☎02 62 73 31 11; www.netherlandsembassy.org.au). **Canada,** 350 Albert St., Ste. 2020, Ottawa ON K1R 1A4 (☎613 237 5030; www.netherlandsembassy.ca). **Ireland,** 160 Merrion Rd., Dublin 4 (☎012 69 34 44; www.netherlandsembassy.ie). **New Zealand,** P.O. Box 840, at Ballance and Featherston St., Wellington (☎04 471 63 90; http://netherlandsembassy.co.nz). **South Africa,** 825 Arcadia St., Pretoria, P.O. Box 117, Pretoria (☎012 344 3910; www.dutchembassy.co.za). **UK,** 38 Hyde Park Gate, London SW7 5DP (☎020 75 90 32 00; www.netherlands-embassy.org.uk). **US,** 4200 Linnean Ave., NW, Washington D.C. 20008 (☎202-244-5300; www.netherlands-embassy.org).

Foreign Embassies in The Netherlands: All foreign embassies and most consulates are in **The Hague** (p. 792). The US has a consulate in **Amsterdam** (p. 769).

TRANSPORTATION

BY PLANE. KLM/Northwest, Martinair, Continental, Delta, United, and **Singapore Airlines** serve Amsterdam's sleek, glassy Schiphol Airport.

BY TRAIN. The national rail company is the efficient **Nederlandse Spoorwegen** (**NS**; Netherlands Railways; www.ns.nl). Train service tends to be faster than bus service. *Sneltreins* are the fastest; *stoptreins* make the most stops. One-way tickets are called *enkele reis;* normal round-trip tickets, *retour;* and same-day round-trip tickets (valid only on day of purchase, but cheaper than normal round-trip tickets), *dagretour.* **Eurail** and **InterRail** are valid in The Netherlands. The **Holland Railpass** (US$52-98) is good for three or five travel days in any one-month period. Although available in the US, the Holland Railpass is cheaper in The Netherlands at DER Travel Service or RailEurope offices. **One-day train passes** cost €35, which is about the equivalent of the most expensive one-way fare across the country. The fine for a missing ticket on one of The Netherlands' trains is a whopping €90.

BY BUS. A nationalized fare system covers city buses, trams, and long-distance buses. The country is divided into zones; the number of strips on a **strippenkaart** (strip card) required depends on the number of zones through which you travel. A trip between destinations in the same zone costs one strip; a trip that traverses two zones requires two strips. On buses, tell the driver your destination and he or she will cancel the correct number of strips; on trams and subways, stamp your own *strippenkaart* in either a yellow box at the back of the tram or in the subway station. Train and bus drivers sell tickets, but it's cheaper to buy in bulk at public transit counters, tourist offices, post offices, and some tobacco shops and newsstands. *Dagkarten* (day passes) are valid for unlimited use in any zone (€5.20, children and seniors €3.60). Unlimited-use passes are valid for one week in the same zone (€21, seniors and children €13; requires a passport photo and picture ID). Riding without a ticket can result in a €30 fine.

BY CAR. The Netherlands have well-maintained roadways. North Americans and Australians need an International Driver's License; if your insurance doesn't cover you abroad, you'll also need a green insurance card. Fuel comes in two types; some cars use benzene (€1.50 per liter), while others use gasoline (€0.50 per liter). The **Royal Dutch Touring Association** (ANWB; ☎0800 08 88.) offers roadside assistance to members. For more information, contact the ANWB at Wassenaarseweg 220, 2596 EC The Hague (☎070 314 71 47), or Museumsplein 5, 1071 DJ Amsterdam (☎0800 05 03).

BY BIKE AND BY THUMB. Cycling is the way to go in The Netherlands—distances between cities are short, the countryside is absolutely flat, and most streets have separate bike lanes. Bikes run about €7 per day or €30 per week. Bikes are sometimes available at train stations and hostels, and *Let's Go* also lists bike rental shops in many towns. For more information, try www.visitholland.com. Hitchhiking is somewhat effective, but on the roads out of Amsterdam there is cut-throat competition. For more information on hitching, visit www.hitchhikers.org. *Let's Go* does not recommend hitchhiking.

TOURIST SERVICES AND MONEY

EMERGENCY	**Police, Ambulance,** and **Fire:** ☎112.

TOURIST OFFICES. VVV (vay-vay-vay) tourist offices are marked by triangular blue signs. The website www.goholland.com is also a useful resource.

MONEY. A bare-bones day traveling in The Netherlands will cost €30-35; a slightly more comfortable day will run €50-60. Service charges are always included in bills for hotels, shopping, and restaurants. Tips for services are accepted and appreciated but not necessary. Taxi drivers are generally tipped 10% of the fare.

ACCOMMODATIONS AND CAMPING

VVV offices supply accommodation lists and can nearly always reserve rooms in local and other areas for a €2 fee. **Private rooms** cost about two-thirds as much as hotels, but they are hard to find; check with the VVV. During July and August, many cities add a tourist tax of €1.15 to the price of all rooms. The country's best values are the 34 **HI Youth Hostels,** run by the **NJHC (Dutch Youth Hostel Federation).** Hostels are divided into four price categories based on quality. Most are exceedingly clean and modern. The VVV has a hostel list, and the useful *Jeugdherbergen* brochure describes each one (both free). For more information, contact the NJHC at P.O. Box 9191, 1006 AD Amsterdam (☎010 264 60 64; www.njhc.org). **Camping** is available across the country, but many sites are crowded in summer.

COMMUNICATION

PHONE CODES	**Country code:** 31. **International dialing prefix:** 00. From outside the Netherlands, dial int'l dialing prefix (see inside back cover) + 31 + city code + local number.

TELEPHONES. Pay phones require a Chipknip card, which can be bought at hostels, train stations, and tobacconists for as little as €4.50. Even when using a calling card, a chipknip card is necessary to gain access to the phone system. For directory assistance, dial ☎09 00 80 08; for collect calls, dial ☎06 04 10. International dial direct numbers include: **AT&T** ☎0800 022 91 11; **Sprint** ☎0800 022 91 19; **Australia Direct** ☎0800 022 20 61; **BT Direct** ☎0800 022 00 44; **Canada Direct** ☎0800 022 91 16; **Ireland Direct** ☎0800 02 20 353; **MCI WorldPhone Direct,** ☎0800 022 91 22; **NZ Direct** ☎0800 022 44 64; **Telekom South Africa Direct** ☎0800 022 02 27.

MAIL. Post offices are generally open Monday to Friday 9am-6pm, and some are also open Saturday 10am to 1:30pm; larger branches may stay open later. Mailing a postcard or letter (up to 20g) in the EU or a postcard outside of Europe costs €0.54; letters to outside of Europe cost €0.75. Mail takes 3 days to the UK, 4 to 6 to North America, 6 to 8 to Australia and New Zealand, and 8 to 10 to South Africa.

INTERNET ACCESS. Email is easily accessible within The Netherlands. In small towns, if Internet access is not listed, try the library or even your hostel.

LANGUAGE. Dutch is the official language of The Netherlands; however, most natives speak English fluently. Dutch uses a gutteral "g" sound for both "g" and "ch." "J" is usually pronounced as the English "y"; e.g., *hofje* is "hof-YUH." "Ui" is pronounced "ow," and the dipthong "ij" is best approximated in English as "ah" followed by a long "e." For basic Dutch words and phrases, see p. 1019.

AMSTERDAM ☎020

Some say the best vacation to Amsterdam is one you can't remember. The city lives up to its reputation as a never-never land of bacchanalian excess: the aroma of cannabis wafts through public parks, and the city's infamous sex scene swathes itself in red lights. But a large array of coffeeshops isn't the only thing that will take your breath away—the Golden Age of art flourished here, and troves of Rembrandts, Vermeers, and van Goghs remain as a result. Moreover, a walk down the city's endless cobblestone streets or a stroll along its sparkling canals will prove that the beauty of the city isn't limited to its museums. A land of substance in more ways than one, any visit to Amsterdam makes for quite a trip.

INTERCITY TRANSPORTATION

Flights: Schiphol Airport (AMS; ☎0800 7244 74 65). **Trains** connect the airport to Centraal Station (20min., every 10min., €3).

Trains: Centraal Station, Stationspl. 1, at the end of Damrak (☎0900 92 92, €0.30 per min.; www.ns.nl). International reservations daily 6:30am-11:30pm. To: **Brussels** (3-4hr., 10-28 per day, €120-250); **Groningen** (2-3hr., every 30min., €24); **Haarlem** (20min., €3); **Leiden** (20min., every 30min. until 2:45am, €11); **Paris** (8hr., 10-28 per day, €120-250); **Rotterdam** (1hr., €11); **The Hague** (50min., €8); **Utrecht** (30min., 3-6 per hr., same day round-trip €10).

ORIENTATION

A series of roughly concentric canals ripple out around the **Centrum** (city center), resembling a giant horseshoe opening to the northeast. Emerging from Centraal Station, at the top of the horseshoe, you'll hit **Damrak,** a key thoroughfare leading to **Dam Square.** Just east of Damrak in the Centrum is Amsterdam's infamous **Red Light District,** bounded by Warmoestr., Zeedijk, Damstr., and Klovenniersburgwal. Don't head into the area until you've locked up your bags at the train station or a hostel. South of the Red Light District, but still within the horseshoe, lies the **Rembrandtplein.** The canals radiating around the Centrum (lined by streets of the same names) are **Singel, Herengracht, Keizergracht,** and **Prinsengracht.** West of the Centrum, beyond Prinsengracht, lies the **Jordaan,** an attractive residential neighborhood. Moving counterclockwise around Prinsengracht, you'll hit the **Leidseplein,** which lies just across the canal from **Vondelpark** and the **Museumplein,** followed by **De Pijp,** another less crowded residential neighborhood.

LOCAL TRANSPORTATION

Buses: Trains are quicker, but the **GVB** (see below) will direct you to a bus stop for domestic destinations not on a rail line. **Muiderpoort** (2 blocks east of Oosterpark) sends buses east; **Marnixstation** (at the corner of Marnixstr. and Kinkerstr.) west; and the **Stationsplein depot** north and south.

Public Transportation: GVB (☎0900 92 92, €0.30 per min.), in Stationspl., In front of Centraal Station. Open M-F 7am-9pm, Sa-Su 8am-9pm. **Tram, metro,** and **bus** lines radiate from Centraal Station. Trams are most convenient for inner-city travel; the metro leads to farther-out neighborhoods. The last trams leave Centraal Station M-F at midnight, Sa-Su at 12:25am. Pick up a ***nachtbussen*** (night bus) schedule from the GVB office. Single bus or train ticket €1.40. The 45-strip *strippenkaart* is the best deal; it can be used on trams and buses throughout The Netherlands and is available at the VVV, the GVB, and newsstands.

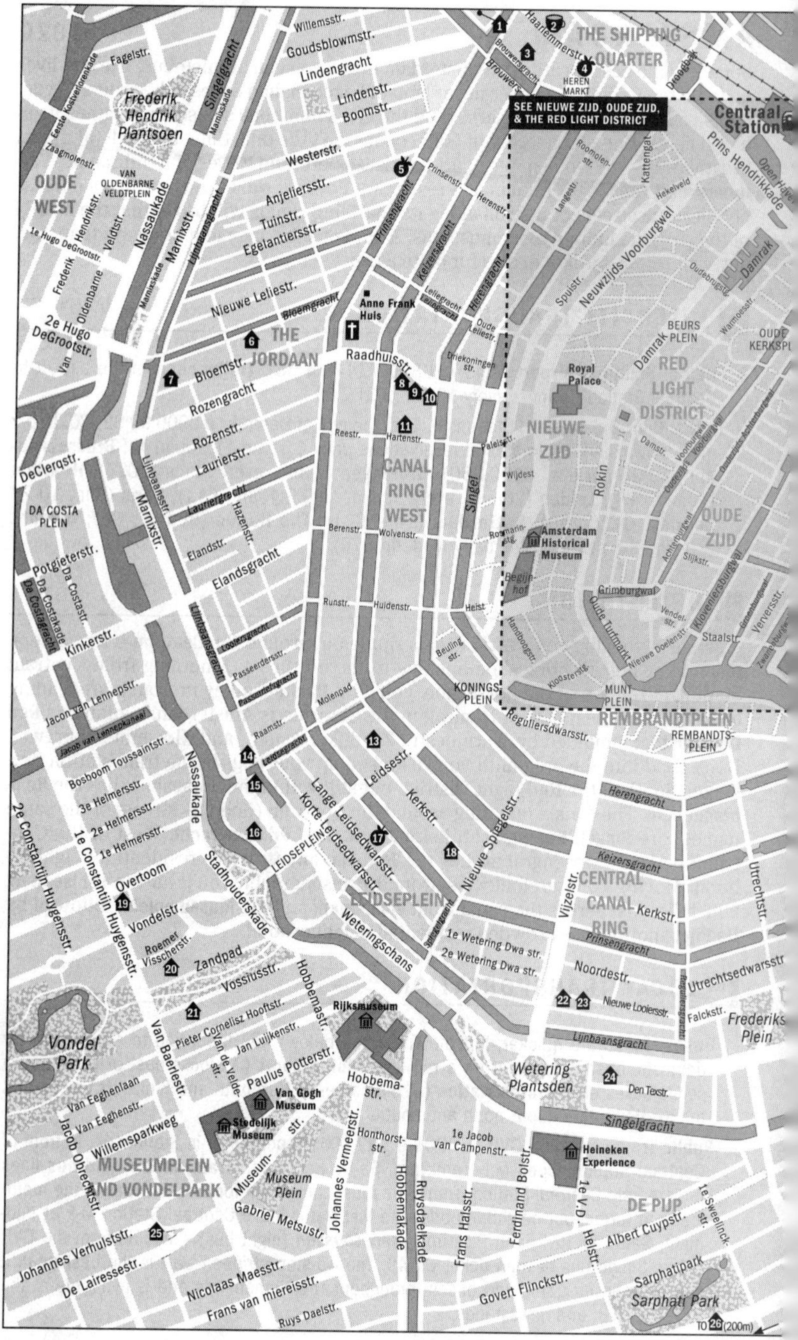

THE NETHERLANDS

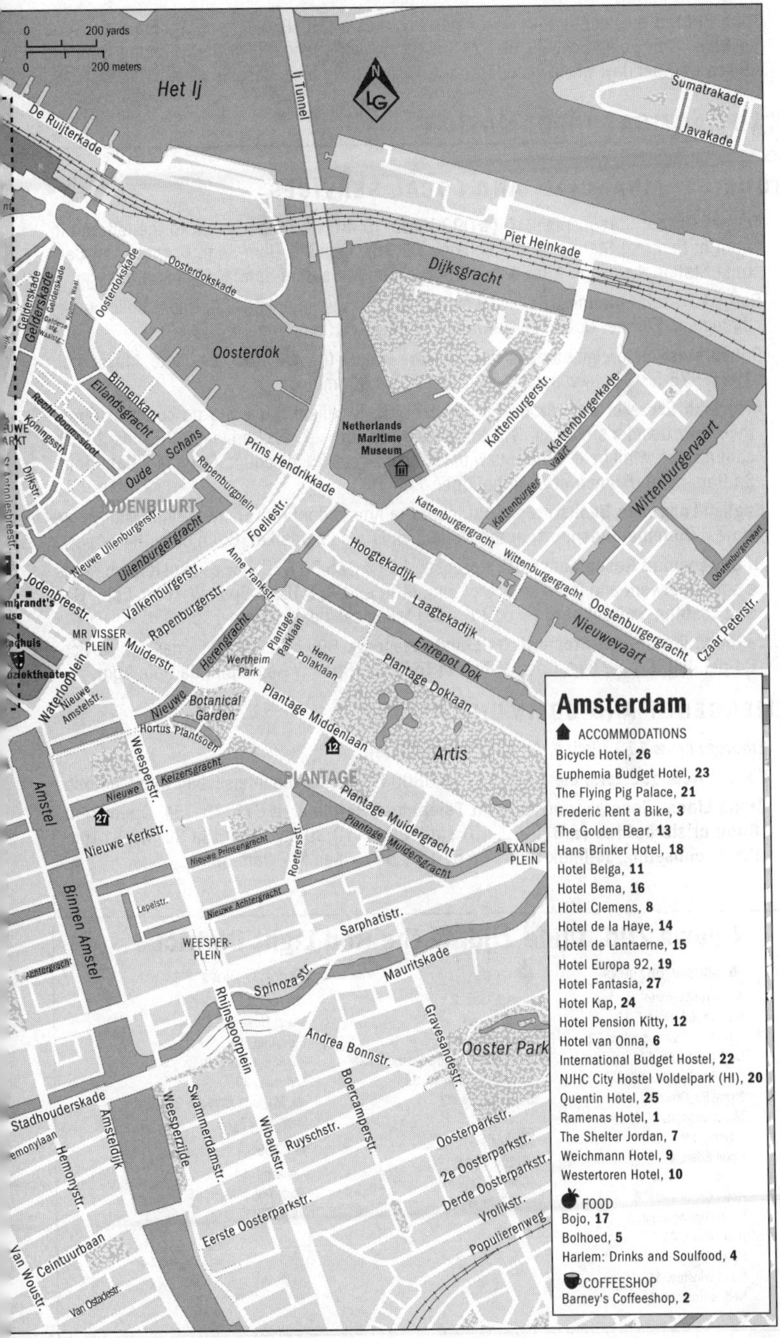
0 200 yards
0 200 meters
N
LG
Het Ij
Ij Tunnel
De Ruijterkade
Sumatrakade
Javakade
Piet Heinkade
Dijksgracht
Oosterdokskade
Oosterdok
Netherlands Maritime Museum
Kattenburgerstr.
Kattenburgerkade
Wittenburgervaart
Kattenburger vaart
Kattenburgergracht
Wittenburgergracht
Oostenburgergracht
Oostenburgervaart
Nieuwevaart
Czaar Peterstr.
Gelderskade
Binnenkant
Eilandsgracht
Recht Boomssloot
Koningsstr.
Dijkstr.
Oude Schans
Prins Hendrikkade
Rapenburgplein
Foeliestr.
Nieuwe Uilenburgerstr.
Uilenburgergracht
Anne Frankstr.
Hoogtekadijk
Laagtekadijk
Entrepot Dok
Jodenbreestr.
Valkenburgerstr.
Rapenburgerstr.
Herengracht
Plantage Parklaan
Henri Polaklaan
Plantage Doklaan
MR VISSER PLEIN
Muiderstr.
Wertheim Park
Waterlooplein
Nieuwe Amstelstr.
Botanical Garden
Hortus Plantsoen
Plantage Middenlaan
Artis
Weesperstr.
Nieuwe Keizersgracht
PLANTAGE
Plantage Muidergracht
Plantage Muidersgracht
ALEXANDER PLEIN
Amstel
Nieuwe Kerkstr.
Nieuwe Prinsengracht
Roeterstr.
Binnen Amstel
Lepelstr.
Nieuwe Achtergracht
Sarphatistr.
WEESPER-PLEIN
Achtergracht
Mauritskade
Spinozastr.
Rhijnspoorplein
Andrea Bonnstr.
Gravesandestr.
Ooster Park
Stadhouderskade
Amsteldijk
Weesperzijde
Swammerdamstr.
Wibautstr.
Boerecamperstr.
Ruyschstr.
Oosterparkstr.
2e Oosterparkstr.
Derde Oosterparkstr.
Vrolikstr.
Populierenweg
Eerste Oosterparkstr.
Hemonylaan
Hemonystr.
Ceintuurbaan
Van Woustr.
Van Ostadestr.
Amsterdam
ACCOMMODATIONS
Bicycle Hotel, 26
Euphemia Budget Hotel, 23
The Flying Pig Palace, 21
Frederic Rent a Bike, 3
The Golden Bear, 13
Hans Brinker Hotel, 18
Hotel Belga, 11
Hotel Bema, 16
Hotel Clemens, 8
Hotel de la Haye, 14
Hotel de Lantaerne, 15
Hotel Europa 92, 19
Hotel Fantasia, 27
Hotel Kap, 24
Hotel Pension Kitty, 12
Hotel van Onna, 6
International Budget Hostel, 22
NJHC City Hostel Voldelpark (HI), 20
Quentin Hotel, 25
Ramenas Hotel, 1
The Shelter Jordan, 7
Weichmann Hotel, 9
Westertoren Hotel, 10
FOOD
Bojo, 17
Bolhoed, 5
Harlem: Drinks and Soulfood, 4
COFFEESHOP
Barney's Coffeeshop, 2

Bike Rental: Bikes run about €5-12 per day, plus a €30-100 deposit. Try **Frederic Rent a Bike,** Brouwersgracht 78 (☎624 55 09; www.frederic.nl), in the Shipping Quarter. Bikes €10 per day, which includes lock and theft insurance. Reserve online. AmEx/MC/V.

PRACTICAL INFORMATION

TOURIST, FINANCIAL, AND LOCAL SERVICES

Tourist Office: Stationsplein 10 (☎0900 400 40 40; €0.55 per min.), to the left and in front of Centraal Station. Room booking €2.75. Open M-F 9am-5pm. **Branches** at Centraal Station, Leidsepl. 1, and the airport. Open M-Sa 8am-8pm, Su 9am-5pm.

Budget Travel: Eurolines, Rokin 10 (☎560 87 88; www.eurolines.nl). Books coach travel throughout Europe. Open M-F 9:30am-5:30pm, Sa 10am-4pm.

Consulates: All foreign embassies are in **The Hague** (p. 792). **US** consulate, Museumpl. 19 (☎575 53 09; www.usemb.nl). Open M-F 8:30am-noon.

American Express: Damrak 66 (☎504 87 70). Excellent rates and no commission on their own traveler's checks, 3% commission for others'. Exchange €2.25 plus 2.25% commission. Mail held. Students with ISIC card get 25% discount. Open M-F 9am-5pm, Sa 9am-noon. **Branch** at Schiphol open 24hr.

English-Language Bookstores: Spui, near the Amsterdam University, is lined with bookstores. **Oudemanhuispoort,** in the Oude Zijd, is a book market. Open daily; times vary.

Bi-Gay-Lesbian Resources: COC, Rozenstr. 14 (☎626 30 87; www.cocamsterdam.nl), is a social network and main source of info. M-Tu and Th-F 10am-5pm, W 10am-8pm. **Gay and Lesbian Switchboard** (☎623 65 65) takes calls daily 10am-10pm.

Laundry: Wasserette-Stomerij 'De Eland,' Elandsgr. 59 (☎625 07 31), has self-service. €4 per 4kg, €6 per 6kg. Open M-Tu and Th-F 8am-8pm, W 8am-6pm, Sa 9am-5pm.

EMERGENCY AND COMMUNICATIONS

Emergency: ☎112 (Police, Ambulance, and Fire).

Police: Headquarters, Elandsgr. 117 (☎0800 88 44), at the intersection with Marnixstr.

Crisis Lines: General counseling at **Telephone Helpline** (☎675 75 75). Open 24hr. **Rape crisis hotline** (☎612 02 45) staffed M-F 10:30am-11pm, Sa-Su 3:30-11pm. **Drug counseling, Jellinek Clinic** (☎570 23 55). Open M-F 9am-5pm.

Nieuwe Zijd, Oude Zijd, & the Red Light District

ACCOMMODATIONS
- Anna Youth Hostel, **2**
- Bob's Youth Hostel, **12**
- City Hostel Stadsdoelen, **32**
- De Oranje Tulp, **11**
- De Witte Tulp Hostel, **13**
- Flying Pig Downtown, **3**
- The Greenhouse Effect Hotel, **10**
- Hotel Brian, **6**
- Hotel Brouwer, **4**
- Hotel Continental, **8**
- Hotel Groenendael, **1**
- Hotel Nova, **25**
- Hotel Rokin, **26**
- Hotel Winston, **16**
- Nelly's Hostel, **15**
- Old Quarter, **5**

FOOD
- Aneka Rasa, **7**
- Foodism, **18**
- In de Waag, **17**
- Pannenkoekenhuis Upstairs, **33**
- Ristorante Caprese, **29**
- Stereo Sushi, **22**

BARS
- Absinthe, **21**
- Cafe de Engelbewaarder, **28**
- The Tara, **31**

COFFEESHOPS
- Abraxas, **23**
- Dutch Flowers, **34**
- Grey Area, **19**
- Hill Street Blues, **9**
- Kadinsky, **30**
- The Magic Mushroom, **24**
- Rusland, **27**

CLUBS
- Cockring, **14**
- Danse Bij Jansen, **35**
- Item, **20**

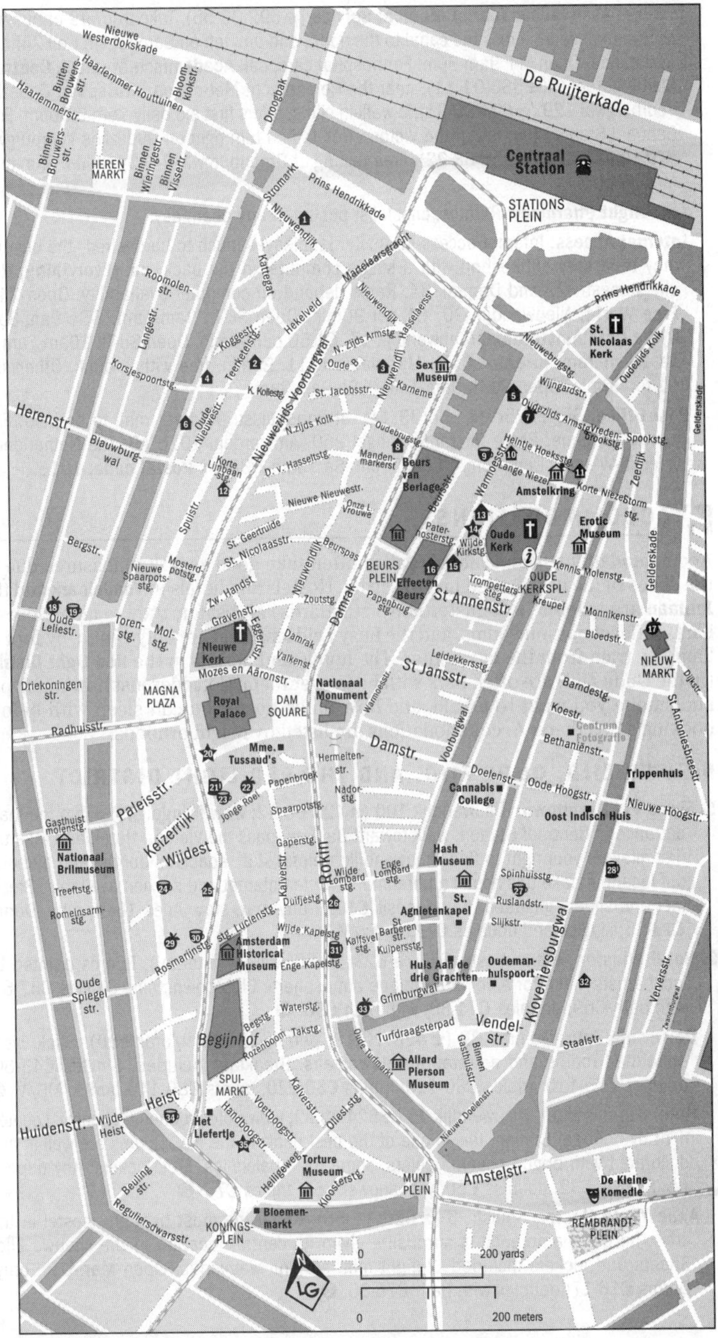

THE NETHERLANDS

Medical Assistance: Tourist Medical Service (☎592 33 55). Take tram #9 or bus #22 to Tropenmuseum, cross the canal to the north, and turn left on Sarphatistr. Call 24hr. for assistance. Open M-F 9am-5pm. For hospital care, call **Academisch Medisch Centrum,** Meibergdreef 9 (☎566 91 11), near the Holendrecht Metro stop. **Kruispost,** Oudezijds Voorburgwal 129 (☎624 90 31), a walk-in clinic, offers first aid daily 7am-9:30pm. From Centraal Station, turn left at the Victoria Hotel, then turn right on Oudezijds Voorburgwal. **STD Line** (hotline ☎555 58 22). Free testing at Groenburgwal 44. Open M-F 8am-noon and 1-4pm.

Late-Night Pharmacy: Rotates; check list posted at any pharmacy.

Internet Access: Internet access in Amsterdam leaves much to be desired—the best bet may be a cozy coffeeshop with a single computer in the back. **easyEverything,** Reguliersbreestr. 22 and Damrak 34. Rates depend on computer availability. Open 24hr. **Free World,** Nieuwendijk 30. €1 per 30min. Open Su-Th 9am-1am, F-Sa 9am-3am. **Cyber Cafe Amsterdam,** Nieuwendijk 17. €1.50 per 30min. Open Su-Th 10am-1am, F-Sa 10am-2am. **Internet Cafe,** Martelaarsgr. 11. 20min. free with a drink. Otherwise, €1 for 30min. Open Su-Th 9am-1am, F-Sa 9am-2am.

Post Office: Singel 250 (☎556 33 11), at Raadhuisstr. Address mail to be held: First name, Surname, *Poste Restante,* Singel 250, Amsterdam 1016 AB, The Netherlands. Open M-W and F 9am-6pm, Th 9am-9pm, Sa 10am-1:30pm. **Postal code:** 1016.

ACCOMMODATIONS

Accommodations near **Centraal Station** often take good security measures due to the chaos of the nearby Red Light District. Hostels and hotels in **Vondelpark** and the **Jordaan** are quieter (by Amsterdam's standards) and safer; they're also close to bars, coffeeshops, museums, and the busy Leidsepl., and are only 15min. by foot or 2min. by train from the city center. The hotels and hostels in the **Red Light District** (in the Oude Zijd) are often bars with beds over them. Consider just how much pot and smoke you want to inhale, and how much noise you can sleep with before booking a bed there. Accommodations are listed by neighborhoods.

NIEUWE ZIJD, OUDE ZIJD, AND THE RED LIGHT DISTRICT

Flying Pig Downtown, Nieuwendijk 100 (☎420 68 22; www.flyingpig.nl). From the main entrance of Centraal Station, walk toward Damrak, pass the Victoria Hotel, and take the first alley on your right to find Nieuwendijk. Helpful staff, spacious dorms, and a knockout location make this hostel a perennial favorite. Internet and kitchen available. Breakfast and sheets included. Key deposit €10. 7-day max. stay. Ages 18-35 only. Dorms €19-25; singles and doubles €72. AmEx/MC/V. ❷

Hotel Winston, Warmoesstr. 125 (☎623 13 80; www.winston.nl). Rooms painted by local artists make for a colorful, unique atmosphere. Club downstairs. Singles €57-61, with bath €69; doubles €71-80, with bath €90. ❹

De Oranje Tulp, Damrak 32 (☎428 16 18; people.a2000.nl/oranje00). Slick, well-appointed rooms and a restaurant downstairs. Breakfast included. Singles €45-60; doubles €75-110; triples €80-110; quads €80-120; quints €80-140. AmEx/MC/V. ❹

Hotel Groenendael, Nieuwendijk 15 (☎624 48 22; www.hotelgroenendael.com). Located right by Centraal Station, this is one of the best deals in the city. Rooms are well-lit and decorated with bright, cheerful colors; some have balconies. Free lockers. Key deposit €5. Singles €32; doubles €50, with shower €55; triples €75. ❷

Anna Youth Hostel, Spuistr. 6 (☎620 11 55). By far the most beautiful hostel in the city. The quiet ambience is surprising given its central location in the Nieuwe Zijd. Sheets and lockers included. 2-night min. stay on weekends. Open Mar.-Dec. only. Dorms €16-17; doubles with bath €75-80. ❶

Hotel Brouwer, Singel 83 (☎624 63 58; www.hotelbrouwer.nl). Eight gorgeous, restored rooms, each with private bathroom and canal view. Breakfast included. Singles €45; doubles €80. ❸

City Hostel Stadsdoelen (HI), Kloveniersburgwal 97 (☎624 68 32; www.njhc.org). Take tram #4, 9, 16, 20, 24, or 25 to Muntplein. From Muntplein, proceed down Nieuwe Doelenstr. (which is just off Muntplein); Kloveniersburgwal will be over the bridge on your right. Sleeps 170 and provides clean, drug-free lodgings for very reasonable prices. Plain dorms get the job done. Internet (€1 per 12min.) and kitchen facilities. Breakfast, lockers, and sheets included. Reception daily 7am-1am. Book through website. Dorms €18.50; nonmembers add €2.50. MC/V. ❶

Bob's Youth Hostel, Nieuwezijds Voorburgwal 92 (☎623 00 63). Well-known among European backpackers, Bob's provides the bare necessities. Young clientele relaxes in the underground reception area, the only place where drugs are permitted. Breakfast and sheets included. Locker deposit €10. Key deposit €10. 2-night min. stay on weekends, 7-day max. stay. Reception daily 8am-3am. No reservations; arrive before 10am. Dorms €17; doubles €70, additional person €10. ❶

Old Quarter, Warmoesstr. 20-22 (☎626 64 29; info@oldquarter.a2000.nl). Modern rooms; some with canal view. Downstairs *bruine cafe* is a great place to watch a football game (kitchen open noon-10pm). Th night jazz jam sessions, F-Sa rock and funk acts. 24hr. reception. Breakfast included. Singles from €35; doubles from €60. ❸

Nelly's Hostel, Warmoesstr. 115/117 (☎638 01 25; nellys@xs4all.nl). Cozy hostel above an Irish pub. Clean, mixed-sex dorms. Guests drink after hours in the bar. Breakfast and sheets included. Locker deposit €10. Reception 24hr. Dorms Su-Th €20, F-Sa €25. ❷

Hotel Rokin, Rokin 73 (☎626 74 56; www.rokinhotel.com), well-located just a few blocks south of Dam Sq. A tad upscale, but well worth the extra cash for rooms with TV and VCR. Breakfast included. Singles €50-60; doubles €60-75; triples €110-145; quads €140-185; 6-person rooms €195-255. AmEx/MC/V. ❹

Hotel Brian, Singel 69 (☎624 46 61). From Centraal Station, turn right at the Victoria Hotel, then turn left onto Singel. Basic communal digs in a friendly, low-key atmosphere. Liberal drug policy. Clean rooms with an effort made at decoration. Picturesque canalside location puts you near the action in Nieuwendijk, the Shipping Quarter, and Spui. Breakfast included. Key deposit €10. Reception daily 8am-11pm. Dorms €27. ❷

The Shelter, Barndesteeg 21 (☎625 32 30; www.shelter.nl), off the Nieuwmarkt. Finding virtue amid red lights, with clean rooms and a friendly staff. Religious slogans abound, but everyone is welcome. Breakfast and sheets included. No drugs. Locker deposit €5. Curfew Su-Th midnight, F-Sa 1am. Dorms €13-17. MC/V with 5% surcharge. ❶

Young Budget Hotel Kabul, Warmoesstr. 38-42 (☎623 71 58; kabulhotel@hotmail.com). 4-16 person dorms have comfortable beds in carpeted, spacious rooms. Breakfast and sheets included. Internet €1 per 17min. No curfew. Max. stay 1 week. €5 key deposit. Dorms €21-29. AmEx/MC/V. ❷

De Witte Tulp Hostel, Warmoesstr. 87 (☎625 59 74; fax 422 08 85). Low-key, budget digs in a sociable, youthful environment. Downstairs pub serves drinks and snacks; hotel guests receive a 10% discount and 50% off breakfast. Sheets included. Dorms and singles €20-35 per person. AmEx/MC/V. ❷

Hotel Continental, Damrak 40-41 (☎622 33 63; www.hotelcontinental.nl). Small but comfy rooms, each with TV and phone. Continental breakfast €5. Reception 24hr. Singles Su-Th €65, F-Sa €80; doubles €90/€115, with bath €105/€135. AmEx/MC/V with 5% surcharge. ❺

Hotel Nova, Nieuwezijds Voorburgwal 276 (☎623 00 66; novahotel@wxs.nl). Exceptionally large, clean accommodations a stone's throw from the city center, all with bath, TV, phone, and refrigerator. Breakfast included. High-season singles €100; doubles €140; triples €170. Off-season singles €75; doubles €93; triples €113. AmEx/MC/V. ❺

The Greenhouse Effect Hotel, Warmoesstr. 55 (☎624 49 74; www.the-greenhouse-effect.com). Reasonably priced theme rooms 5min. from Centraal Station. Hotel guests are treated to an all-day Happy Hour at the downstairs bar (beer €2.30). Check website for discounts. Singles €50, with bath €60; doubles with bath €85; triples with bath €100. AmEx/MC/V. ❹

SHIPPING QUARTER, CANAL RING WEST, AND THE JORDAAN

Hotel Clemens, Raadhuisstr. 39 (☎624 60 89; www.clemenshotel.nl). Take tram #13, 17, or 20 to Westermarkt. Fridge, TV, Internet connection, safe, and hairdryer in all rooms. Deluxe rooms have private bath and more space than budget rooms. Breakfast €7. Key deposit €20. Book well in advance. 3-night min. stay on weekends. Singles €55; budget doubles €70-75, deluxe €110; budget triples with bath €125, deluxe €150. ❹

Ramenas Hotel, Haarlemmerdijk 61 (☎624 69 60 30; www.amsterdamhotels.com). Walk from Centraal Station along Nieuwendijk as it turns into Haarlemmerstr. and then Haarlemmerdijk. Ascetic rooms get the job done. Breakfast included. Doubles, triples, and quints €28 per person, with bath €34. Cash only. ❷

The Shelter Jordan, Bloemstr. 179 (☎624 47 17; www.shelter.nl). Take tram #13 or 17 to Marnixstr., then follow Lijnbaansgr. (off Rozengr.) for 5min., and turn right on Bloemstr.; it's on the right. Hostel has a friendly, English-speaking staff in a quiet corner of the Jordaan. Nightly Bible study groups. Internet €1 per 40min. Breakfast included. Locker deposit €5. Curfew 2am. Single-sex dorms. No smoking, no alcohol. Age limit 35. Arrive by 11am to get a room. Dorms €14-17. ❶

Frederic Rent a Bike, Brouwersgr. 78 (☎624 55 09; www.frederic.nl). In addition to bikes, Frederic also rents rooms, some of which you'll find in the back of his rental shop, others located throughout the city in varying places and in all different price ranges. Amenities vary with the rooms. Singles €50-60; doubles €60-70; apartments available for short-term stays as well. Cash only, credit card required for reservation. ❹

Wiechmann Hotel, Prinsengr. 328-332 (☎626 33 21; www.hotelwiechmann.nl). Take tram #1, 2, or 5 to Prinsengr.; turn right and walk along the left side of the canal. Three restored canal houses. Sizeable rooms, many with canal views. All rooms with bath. Breakfast included. Key deposit €20. 2-night min. stay on weekends. Singles €70-90; doubles €125-135; triples and quads €170-230. ❺

Westertoren Hotel, Raadhuisstr. 35b (☎624 46 39). Take tram #13, 17, or 20 to Westermarkt. Perfect for groups, as this hotel has a few rooms that sleep up to 6 persons. Clean rooms and friendly staff. Not all rooms have shower and toilet. Breakfast included. Tea and coffee in room. 3-night min. stay on weekends. Rooms in summer €40-50; off-season €30-45. ❷

Hotel van Onna, Bloemgr. 104 (☎626 58 01; www.netcentrum.com/onna). Take tram #13 or 17 from Centraal Station to Westermarkt, or tram #10 to Bloemgracht. Visitors get a peaceful night's rest on the nicest canal in the Jordaan. All rooms have bath. Breakfast included. Reception daily 8am-11pm. Dorms and singles €40. ❸

Hotel Belga, Hartenstr. 8 (☎624 90 80; hotelbelga@zonnet.nl). Take tram #1, 2, or 5 to Dam Sq. Walk away from the palace on Raadhuisstr. Turn left at Herengracht and take the 1st right on Hartenstr. Rooms are sunny if bland, all with TV, phone, and safe. Breakfast included. 2-night min. stay on weekends in summer. Singles €41-57; doubles €62-84, with bath €77-118; triples €95-140; quads €134-188; quints €147-204. MC/V. ❸

LEIDSEPLEIN AND MUSEUMPLEIN

NJHC City Hostel Vondelpark (HI), Zandpad 5 (☎589 89 96; www.njhc.org/vondelpark). Take tram #1, 2, or 5 to Leidseplein, walk to the Marriott, and take a left. Walk a block and turn right onto Zandpad just before the park; it's on the right. Exceptionally clean, 10- to 20-person single-sex rooms. Smaller, mixed rooms with bath also available.

Bikes €5.50 per day. Breakfast and sheets included. Lockers €2.50. Reception daily 7:30am-midnight. Dorms €19-23; doubles €54-71; quads €96-108. IYHF members €2.50 less. ❷

Quentin Hotel, Leidsekade 89 (☎626 21 87; fax 622 01 21). You don't have to sacrifice style to get budget accommodations. Hallway walls are plastered with vintage music posters, and each room has its own distinct motif and cable TV. Singles €35, with bath €75; doubles €90; triples €133. AmEx/MC/V with 5% surcharge. ❸

The Flying Pig Palace, Vossiusstr. 46-47 (☎400 41 87; www.flyingpig.nl). Take tram #1, 2, or 5 from Centraal Station to Leidsepl., walk to the Marriott and turn left; go past the entrance to the park and take the first right onto Vossuistr. Fun and friendly hostel geared toward backpackers. All rooms mixed gender. Free Internet and kitchen. Breakfast included. Key deposit €10. Reception daily 8am-9pm. Ages 18-35 only. Call or stop by at 8am to reserve a room. Dorms €16-23; doubles €54-58, with bath €58-62. For long stays, ask about the option of doing work in exchange for rent. AmEx/MC/V. ❶

Hotel Bema, Concertgebouw 19b (☎679 13 96; www.bemahotel.com). Take tram #16 to Museumplein. Facing the Concertgebouw, take a left and cross the street; it's on the left. Seven-room hotel with more style than most. Free breakfast delivered to the room. Reception daily 8am-midnight. Singles €45-55; doubles €55-85; triples €85, with shower €95; quads €115. ❸

Hotel Europa 92, 1e Constantijn Huygenstr. 103-105 (☎618 88 08; www.europa92.nl), between. Vondelstr. and Overtoom. Take tram #1 or 6 to 1e Constantijn Huygenstr. Converted from 2 adjacent houses into 1 labyrinthine hotel. All rooms with bath. Breakfast included. Singles €65-90; doubles €100-125; triples €115-150; quads €135-170. ❺

Hotel de Lantaerne, Leidsekade 111 (☎623 22 21; www.hotellantaerne.com), right by Leidseplein. Lovely accommodations in two converted houses. Stylish rooms have TV, phone, and hairdryer. Breakfast included. Singles €65, with bath €75; doubles €80/€110; triples €105/€140. ❺

Hotel de la Haye, Leidsegr. 114 (☎624 40 44; www.hoteldelahaye.com). Take tram #1, 2, or 5 to Leidseplein. Walk up Marnixstr. 1 block and turn right. Conveniently located hotel combines the activity of Leidseplein with the serenity of a canal view. Breakfast included. Reception daily 8am-10pm. Singles €35-59; doubles €65-82, with bath €75-95; triples €100-130; quads €120-168; quints €150-185. ❸

Hans Brinker Hotel, Kerkstr. 136 (☎622 06 87; www.hansbrinker.com). Take tram #1, 2, or 5 from Centraal Station and get off at Kerkstr.; it's one block down on the left. All-you-can-eat breakfast buffet included. Key deposit €5. Safe €0.50. Reception 24hr. Dorms €21; singles €52; doubles €58-75; triples €90; quads €96. AmEx/MC/V. ❷

International Budget Hostel, Leidsegr. 76-1 (☎624 27 84; www.internationalbudgethostel.com). Tram #1, 2, or 5 to Prinsengracht, turn right and walk along Prinsengracht to Leidsegracht. Like sleepover camp from the 70s. Breakfast €2-4. 2-night min. stay on weekends in summer. Dorms €24-27. ❷

CENTRAL CANAL RING

Euphemia Budget Hotel, Fokke Simonszstr. 1-9 (☎622 90 45; www.euphemiahotel.com), 10min. from Rembrandtplein or Leidseplein. Take tram #16, 24, or 25 to Weteringcircuit, backtrack on Vijzelstr. for about 200m, and turn right on Fokke Simonszstr. Quiet hotel in a former monastery. Rooms are basic but clean. Internet €1. Breakfast €5. Reception daily 8am-11pm. Dorms, doubles and triples €23-55 per person. Discounts for reservations made on their website. AmEx/MC/V with 5% surcharge. ❷

The Golden Bear, Kerkstr. 37 (☎624 47 85; www.goldenbear.nl). Take tram #1, 2, or 5 to Prinsengr. and backtrack one block to Kerkstr. Open since 1948, the Golden Bear is the oldest gay hostel in Amsterdam. Mainly male couples frequent these digs, though lesbians are welcome as well. All rooms include phone, safe, and cable TV. Breakfast included. Singles from €50; doubles from €61, with bath €102. ❹

Hotel Kap, Den Texstr. 5b (☎624 59 08; fax 627 12 89; www.kaphotel.nl). Tram #16, 24, or 25 to Weteringcircuit. Go left down Weteringschans, then right at 2e Weteringplantsoen, and left at Den Texstr.; it's on the left. Personable staff rents comfortable rooms on a residential street. Breakfast included. Reception daily 8am-10:30pm. Check-out 11am. Singles €57; doubles €86-109; triples €109-118; quads €136. AmEx/MC/V with 5% surcharge. ❹

DE PIJP, JODENBUURT, AND THE PLANTAGE

Bicycle Hotel, Van Ostadestr. 123 (☎679 34 52; www.bicyclehotel.com). From Centraal Station, take tram #24 or 25 to Ceintuurbaan, continue south along Ferdinand Bolstr. for one block, then turn left on Van Ostadestr.; the hotel will be half a block down on the left. Clean rooms. Bikes €5 per day; maps of recommended bike trips outside Amsterdam available. All rooms have TV. Breakfast included. Doubles €68-70, with bath €99; triples €90/€120; quads with bath €130. ❺

Hotel Pension Kitty, Plantage Middenlaan 40 (☎622 68 19). Take tram #9 or 14 to Plantage Kerklaan. From there, take Plantage Middenlaan southeast; the unmarked Hotel Pension Kitty is on the right. Laid-back and comfortable, and the staff asks guests to maintain the quiet atmosphere. Singles €50; doubles €60-70. ❹

Hotel Fantasia, Nieuwe Keizersgr. 16 (☎623 82 59; www.fantasia-hotel.com). Take tram #9, 14, or 20 to Waterlooplein and turn left on Nieuwe Keizersgracht. A clean, family-owned establishment in an 18th-century house on a quiet canal in the center of Amsterdam. Most rooms have bath. Breakfast included. Singles €50-58; doubles €75-85; triples €105; quads €125. Closed Dec. 16-26 and Jan. 6-Feb. 21. ❹

FOOD

Many cheap restaurants cluster around **Leidseplein, Rembrandtplein,** and the **Spui.** Cafes, especially in the Jordaan, serve inexpensive sandwiches (€1.50-4) and good meat-and-potatoes fare (€5.50-9). Bakeries line **Utrechtsestraat,** south of Prinsengr. Fruit, cheese, flowers, and even live chickens fill the **markets** on **Albert Cuypstraat,** behind the Heineken brewery. (Open M-Sa 9am-6pm.)

NIEUWE ZIJD AND OUDE ZIJD

In de Waag, Nieuwmarkt 4 (☎452 77 72; www.indewaag.nl.) In the late 1400s, this castle served as the eastern entrance to the city. Today, sandwiches and salads (€4-6) are served on the patio for lunch. At night, the restaurant lights 250 candles and patrons pack the medieval space to enjoy some of the city's tastiest Italian fare. Entrees €17-22. Open Su-Th 10am-midnight, F-Sa 10am-1am. ❸

Pannenkoekenhuis Upstairs, Grimburgwal 2 (☎626 56 03). A tiny nook with the best pancakes (€4-9) in the city. Open M-F noon-7pm, Sa noon-6pm, Su noon-5pm. ❶

Ristorante Caprese, Spuistr. 259-261 (☎620 00 59). Enjoy excellent Italian food while listening to jazz in a candlelight setting. Open daily 5-10:45pm. ❸

Stereo Sushi, Jonge Roelensteeg 4 (☎777 30 10), between Kalverstr. and Nieuwezijds Voorburgwal, south of Dam Sq. One of the city's unique hot spots. Sushi (€4-9) and big noodle soups (€10-12). Open Su and Tu-Th 6pm-1am, F-Sa 6pm-3am. ❷

Aneka Rasa, Warmoesstr. 25-29 (☎626 15 60). Find elegance amidst the seediness of the Red Light District. Indonesian *rijsttafel* (rice table) €16-27 per person. Open daily 5-10:30pm. AmEx/MC/V. ❸

Foodism, Oude Leliestr. 8 (☎427 51 03). Cool and casual, on one of the city's finest side streets. Sandwiches from €5, soups and salads from €4, pasta dishes from €8. Open Su-Th 11am-10pm, F-Sa 11am-11pm. ❶

CANAL RING WEST, JORDAAN, AND THE SHIPPING QUARTER

Harlem: Drinks and Soulfood, Haarlemmerstr. 77 (☎330 14 98), at the Herenmarkt. Soul food, mixed with Amsterdam's finest nouvelle cuisine. Relax to cool jazz inside, or get some fresh air on the patio. Dinner €11-16. Open M-Th 10am-1am, F-Sa 10am-3am, Su 11am-1am. ❷

Bolhoed, Prinsengr. 60-62 (☎626 18 03). Serves the city's best vegetarian and vegan fare in a bright, funky setting. Dinner menu includes a vegan special for €13. Mexican dishes, pasta, and casserole €12-15. Reserve in advance for dinner. Open daily 4-11:30pm; kitchen closes at 10:45pm. ❷

hein, Berenstr. 20 (☎623 10 48). It's a one-woman-show at this refined and relaxed lunchery. Everything is homemade by Hein herself with the freshest of ingredients. Lunch menu includes crepes and *croques monsieurs*. Snacks and sandwiches €2-10. Open W-M 9:30am-6pm. ❶

Padi, Haarlemmerdijk 50 (☎625 12 80). Locals rave about this Indonesian *eethuis*. Try the *lontong opor* (coconut-simmered chicken; €8). Open daily 5-10pm. ❶

Wolvenstraat 23, Wolvenstr. 23 (☎320 08 43). At this trendy spot, lunch is sandwiches, while dinner is strictly Chinese cuisine. Open M-Th 8am-1am, F 8am-2am, Sa 9am-2am, Su 10am-1am. ❷

Manzano, Rozengr. 106 (☎624 57 52). A nice retreat from the hectic Rozengr., this restaurant serves reasonably-priced *tapas* with a wide variety of meat, fish, and vegetable selections. Dips and veggie *tapas* from €4-8. Entrees €9-27. Restaurant open Tu-Su 5:30pm-midnight; shop open noon-10pm. AmEx/MC/V. ❸

LEIDSEPLEIN AND THE CENTRAL CANAL RING

Bojo, Lange Leidsedwarsstr. 51 (☎622 74 34). Bamboo walls, a sassy waitstaff, and excellent Javanese cuisine make for an unforgettable experience. Mini *rijsttafel* €10. **Bojo Speciaal,** just around the corner to the left on Leidsekruisstr., offers the same menu, plus mixed drinks and a larger *rijsttafel* dish (€15). Open M-Th 4pm-2am, F 4pm-4am, Sa noon-4am, Su noon-2am. ❸

Santa Lucia, Leidsekruisstr. 20-22 (☎623 46 39). Great location puts you in the middle of the action. Pizza €4. Open daily noon-11pm. MC/V. ❶

Axum, Utrechtsedwarsstr. 85-87 (☎622 83 89). Tram #4 or 20 to Frederikspl., go north on Utrechtsestr. for a block, then turn right on Utrechtsedwarsstr. Family-run eatery serves traditional Ethiopian fare. Entrees €10. Open M-F 5:30-11pm, Sa-Su 11:30. ❷

SIGHTS AND MUSEUMS

Amsterdam is fairly compact, so tourists can easily explore the area from the Rijksmuseum to the Red Light District on foot. **Circle Tram 20,** geared toward tourists, stops at 30 attractions throughout the city (every 10min. 9am-7pm; day-pass €5, buy on the tram or at VVV offices). The more peaceful **Museumboot Canal Cruise** allows you to hop on and off along its loop from the VVV to the Anne Frank Huis, the Rijksmuseum, the Bloemenmarkt, Waterloopl., and the old shipyard. (Every 30min. 10am-5pm; day-pass €14, after 1pm €11. Buy tickets at any stop. Pass also gives 20% off some museums.) Rent a canal bike to power your own way through the canals. (Deposit €50. 1-2 people €7 per person per hr., 3 or more people €6; pick-up and drop-off points at Rijksmuseum, Leidsepl., Keizergr. at Leidsestr., and Anne Frank Huis. Open daily 10am-10pm.)

MUSEUMPLEIN

VAN GOGH MUSEUM. This architecturally breathtaking museum houses the largest collection of van Goghs in the world (mostly from his family's private collection) and a diverse group of 19th-century paintings by his contemporaries. *(Paulus Potterstr.*

7. Take tram #2, 5, or 20 from the station. ☎570 52 52. Open daily 10am-6pm. €7, ages 13-17 €2.50, under 12 free.)

STEDELIJK MUSEUM OF MODERN ART. The outstanding collection includes Picasso, Pollock, de Kooning, Malevich, and up-and-coming contemporary work. Unfortunately, the museum will close for renovations and expansion on Dec. 31, 2002 and remain closed for three years. During this time, the museum will show some of its collection at the **COBRA** museum and the **Nieuwe Kerk** (p. 783). See its website for more information. *(☎573 27 45; www.stedelijk.nl. Open daily 11am-5pm. €5.)*

RIJKSMUSEUM AMSTERDAM (NATIONAL MUSEUM). If you've made it to Amsterdam, it would be sinful to leave without seeing the Rijksmuseum's impressive collection of works by Rembrandt, Vermeer, Hals, and Steen. With thousands of Dutch Old Master paintings, it can be an overwhelming place—a good approach is to follow the crowds to Rembrandt's famed militia portrait *The Night Watch*, in the Gallery of Honor, and then proceed into **Aria,** the interactive computer room, which can create a personalized map of the museum. Don't miss the dollhouse exhibits, chronicling the boredom of rich married women in 18th-century Holland. In October 2003, the main building of the museum will close for renovations until 2008. The Phillips Wing will remain open to show masterpieces of 17th-century painting. *(On Stadhouderskade. Take tram #2 or 5 from the station. ☎674 70 00; www.rijksmuseum.nl. Open daily 10am-5pm. €8.50, under 18 free.)*

HEINEKEN EXPERIENCE. Every day, busloads of tourists discover that no beer is made in the Heineken Brewery. Plenty is served, however. Your visit includes three beers and a souvenir glass, all of which is well worth the price of admission. The brewery itself has been transformed and renamed the "Heineken Experience," an alcohol-themed amusement park. Highlights include the "bottle ride," which replicates the experience of becoming a Heineken beer. Guide yourself past holograms, virtual reality machines, and other multimedia treats. *(Stadhouderskade 78, at the corner of Ferdinand Bolstr. ☎523 96 66; www.heinekenexperince.com. Open Tu-Su 10am-6pm, last entry at 5pm. under 18 must be accompanied by a parent. €7.50.)*

JODENBUURT AND THE PLANTAGE

VERSETZMUSEUM & HOLLANDSCHE SCHOUWBERG. It didn't take the Dutch military very long to fall to the crushing power of the Nazis in 1940. Despite this, The Netherlands maintained an active resistance throughout the war. **The Versetzmuseum (Resistance Museum)** focuses on the members of this secret army, providing visitors with the details of their lives and struggles. It's housed in the Plancius Building, originally built in 1876 as the social club for a Jewish choir. *(Plantage Kerklaan 61. Tram #9 or 20 to Plantage Kerklaan; #6 or 14 to Plantage Middenlaan/Kerklaan. ☎620 25 35; www.verzetsmuseum.org. Open Tu-F 10am-5pm, Sa-M noon-5pm; public holidays reduced hours; closed Jan. 1, Apr. 30, and Dec. 25. €4.50, ages 7-15 €2.50, under 7 free.)* **The Hollandsche Schouwberg** was originally one of the city's most popular theaters. After Nazi invasion, however, it became the only place that Jews were allowed to congregate. Not long after that, the building was changed into an assembly point for Dutch Jews who were to be deported to Westerbork, the transit camp to the north. The majority of those in transit there met their end in Auschwitz, Bergen-Belsen, or Sobibor. Today, the Hollandsche Schouwberg is a monument to the 104,000 Dutch Jews who were deported and killed during the Holocaust. *(Plantage Middenlaan 24. ☎626 99 45; www.jhm.nl. Open daily 11am-4pm; closed Yom Kippur. Free.)*

MUSEUM HET REMBRANDT. Recently restored in 17th-century fashion, this museum was the home of Rembrandt until the city confiscated the house for taxes. It holds 250 of his etchings and dry points as well as many of his tools and plates. *(Jodenbreestr. 4-6, at the corner of the Oudeschans Canal. Take tram #9, 14, or 20. Open M-Sa 10am-5pm, Su 1-5pm. €7, ISIC holders €5.)*

TIME: 2-3 hours

DISTANCE: 4.7km

SEASON: Year Round

WHERE: Canal Ring West, dipping into The Jordaan and the Nieuwe Zijd.

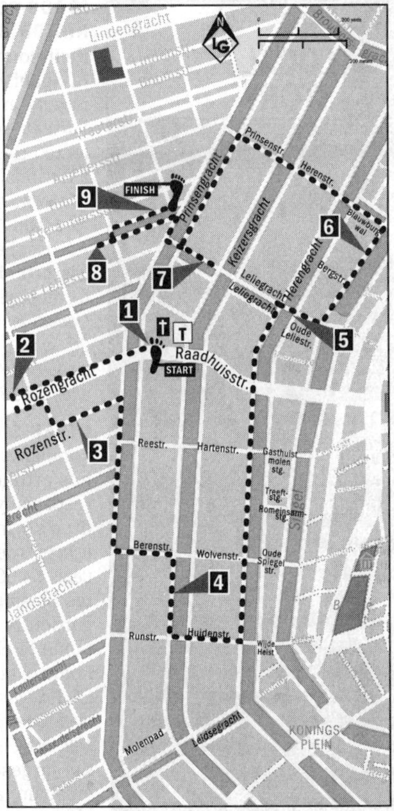

This tour will show you some of the lesser known sights on and around the Western Canal Ring.

1 WESTERKERK. Begin with a sweeping view of the city by climbing the Westetrkerkstoren, Westerkerk's tower.

2 REMBRANDT'S HOUSE. Not to be confused with the Museum Het Rembrandt, Rozengracht 184 is the house where the great artist died penniless. It's marked only by a plaque. On your way there, be sure to window shop along the Rozengracht, a street with boutiques from all over the world.

3 STEDELIJK MUSEUM BUREAU AMSTERDAM. Rozenstraat 59 (☎422 04 71). Not to be confused with the Stedelijk museum itself, this art space, run by the Stedelijk, shows the latest in Dutch art. It's free, so you won't feel bad if the particular exhibit is just too cutting-edge for the man on the street.

4 FELIX MERITIS. Keizersgracht 324 (☎624 93 68). Soak up intellectual headiness at Felix Meritis, the home of the society of arts and sciences in the 18th and early 20th centuries, and the headquarters of the Dutch Communist Party for a few years after World War II. Its canal-side café serves as a forum for impromptu political and intellectual conversations.

5 THEATER INSTITUUT NEDERLAND. Herengracht 168-174 (☎551 33 00). A fascinating museum but, perhaps more interestingly, the city's best 17th-century architectural display. The red "Bartolotti" building on the left was built in 1617 in the Amsterdam Renaissance Style. The grey house on the right was completed in 1638 and was meant to oppose the Renaissance with a new Classicist style, and the city's first neck gable– it's sweeping, rather than stepped.

6 CAPTAIN BANNING COCQ'S HOUSE. Singel 140-142. You may have never heard of Captain Cocq, but if you've been to the Rijksmuseum, you've almost certainly seen him. He's front and center in Rembrandt's *Night Watch.* His opulent home is a stark contrast to that of the painter who immortalized him.

7 GREENPEACE BUILDING. Keizersgracht 174-6. A smashing example of art deco, at the south-eastern-most corner of Leliegracht and Keizersgracht.

8 CLAES CLAESZOON HOFJE. Give your legs a rest at this medieval courtyard, which stands at the corner of Egelantiersgracht and 1e Egelantiersdwarsstraat.

9 SINT ANDRIESHOF. Egelantiersgracht 107-145. One *hofje* is never enough. Step behind the non-descript green door that separates Sint Andrieshof from the street and take a slow stroll around the lush greenery and the quirky architecture of the sloping roofs.

THE LOCAL STORY

POT QUIZ

Mark has owned The Rookies coffeeshop in Leidseplein for over 10 years. He's a "second-generation cannabis retailer" and on the board of two cannabis unions.

LG: What do you like about working in a coffeeshop?
M: It's not aggressive, it's a very tolerant atmosphere and people from all over the world come in.
LG: What do you think it is about Dutch culture that makes cannabis permissible here and nowhere else?
M: Well, it originally started because they needed to separate the soft and hard drugs markets. If a young person wants to get high, then he goes to a coffeeshop and he doesn't get involved with other stuff. In other countries, the same person who sells cannabis will sell ecstasy, pills, cocaine, and other drugs. The coffeeshops are very clean; there are no hard drugs here. Coffeeshops are still here because it's really working. Neighboring countries are beginning to follow our system. The Christian Democrats Party wants to get rid of everything, but it's unrealistic to think you can get rid of drugs in general; there's always going to be people who use them. It's much better to leave it in the open instead of shoving it under the carpet, because then if it's still in the open you have more social control on it.

JOODS-PORTUGUESE SYNAGOGUE AND JOODS HISTORISCH MUSEUM. After being expelled from their countries in the 15th century, a sizable number of Spanish and Portuguese Jews established a community in Amsterdam and built the handsome **Joods-Portuguese Synagogue.** The Dutch government protected the building from Nazi torches by declaring it a national historic site. *(Mr. Visserplein 1-3. ☎624 53 51; www.esnoga.com. Open Su-F 10am-4pm; Nov.-Mar. Su-Th 10am-4pm., F 10am-3pm. €4.50, children €3.50.)* Across the street, the **Joods Historisch Museum (Jewish Historical Museum),** housed in three connected former synagogues, traces the history of Dutch Jews. *(Jonas Daniel Meijerpl., at Waterloopl. Take tram #9, 14, or 20. ☎626 99 45; www.jhm.nl. Open daily 11am-5pm; closed on Yom Kippur. €4.50, over 65 and ISIC holders €3, ages 13-18 €2.50, ages 6-12 €1.50.)*

OTHER SIGHTS. Thanks to the Dutch East India company, the **Museum of the Tropics (Tropenmuseum)** has artifacts from Asia, Africa, and Latin America (especially fine Indonesian art) and an engaging children's wing. *(Linnaeusstr. 2. Tram #9 and bus #22 stop right outside the museum. Open daily 10am-5pm. €6.80, students €4.50.)* Enjoy a respite from the city in the **Hortus Botanicus.** Founded in 1638, this former medical garden is the oldest of its kind in the world. Once home to Europe's first coffee plant, the garden now holds over 6000 species of plants. *(Plantage Middenlaan 2A. Take tram #7, 9, or 14 to the Waterlooplein/Plantage Parklaan. Open Apr.-Oct. M-F 9am-5pm, Sa-Su 11am-5pm; Dec.-Mar. M-F 9am-4pm, Sa-Su 11am-4pm. €5.)* The **Artis Zoo,** the largest zoo in the country, houses a zoological museum, a museum of geology, an aquarium, and a planetarium. *(Plantage Kerklaan 38-40. Tram #9 or 20 to Waterlooplein. Open daily 9am-5pm. €13.50.)*

NIEUWE ZIJD AND OUDE ZIJD

BEGIJNHOF. This stunning courtyard full of little gardens and surrounded by handsome gabled houses provides a quiet escape from the excesses of the city. Begijnhof was founded in 1346 as a convent for Beguines, free-thinking religious women who did not take vows but still lived dedicated to religious contemplation, charity, and manual work. Make sure to visit **Het Houten Huys (the Wooden House),** the oldest house in Amsterdam, the **Engelsekerk,** and the **Begijnhofkapel.** *(Begijnhof open daily 10am-5pm. Free. Het Houten Huys open M-F 10am-4pm. Engelsekerk, at Begijnhof 48. Open for public prayer Su 10:30am. Begijnhofkapel, at Begijnhof 30. Open M-F 9am-5pm, Sa 9am-7pm.)*

DAM SQUARE AND KONINKLIJK PALACE. Completed as the town hall in 1655, the palace's indisputable highlight is the beautiful Citizen's Hall, designed to replicate the universe in a single room. Across from Dam Sq. is the Dutch **Nationaal Monument,** unveiled in 1956 to honor Dutch victims of World War II. Inside the 21m white stone obelisk is soil from all twelve of Holland's provinces as well as the Dutch East Indies. *(Palace open June-Aug. daily 12:30-5pm; Sept.-May hours vary. €4.50.)*

NIEUWE KERK. The Nieuwe Kerk, which has been rebuilt after several fires, is still used for coronations and royal weddings. It also hosts modern and contemporary art. In early 2003, it will open its doors to rotating exhibits from the Stedelijk collection while that museum is being renovated. *(Adjacent to Dam Sq., beside Koninklijk Palace. Open daily 10am-6pm. Organ recitals July-Sept. Su 8pm; €8.)*

OUR LORD IN THE ATTIC. A secret enclave of virtue and piety hides in the 17th-century **Museum Amstelkring, Ons' Lieve Heer op Solder** ("Our Lord in the Attic"), where a Catholic priest, forbidden to practice his faith in public during the Reformation, established a surprisingly grand chapel in his attic. *(Oudezijds Voorburgwal 40, at the corner of Oudezijds Armstr., 5min. from Centraal Station. Open M-Sa 10am-5pm, Su and holidays 1-5pm. €4.50, students €3.40.)*

THE VICES. If it's weed that interests you, far and away your best bet is the staggeringly informative **Cannabis College,** Oudezijds Achterburgwal 124. The center for "higher" education offers info on everything from the uses of medicinal marijuana to facts about the War on Drugs to the creative applications of industrial hemp. For a curated taste of the seaminess that runs down Amsterdam's underbelly, your best bet is to get your jollies right off the train at the **Amsterdam Sex Museum,** Damrak 18, less than a five-minute walk from Centraal Station. The low admission fee won't leave you feeling burned if you find that walls plastered with pictures of such colorful themes as bestiality and S&M are not your thing. *(Cannabis College open daily 11am-7pm. Free. Sex Museum open daily 10am-11:30pm. €2.50.)*

THE RED LIGHT DISTRICT

The Red Light District is surprisingly liveable. Pushers, porn shops, and live sex theaters do run a brisk business, but a surprising number of people there have nothing to do with the debauchery; in many ways the area is less outrageous and seedy than you might have expected. During the day, the Red Light District is comparatively flaccid, with tourists milling about and consulting their maps. As the sun goes down, people get braver and the area comes to life. Cops from the police station on Warmoesstr. patrol the district until midnight, but women may feel uncomfortable walking through this area, and tourists are targets for pickpockets.

LG: When the laws on marijuana were first relaxed in the early 1970s, were there any groups that protested the new legislation?

M: Of course; it's only 10% of the Dutch population that smokes. Even now if you want to open a coffeeshop a lot of people are against it. It's still somehow a conservative country.

LG: 10%?

M: More youngsters smoke in England than in The Netherlands. Maybe 1.5% of users have a problem with cannabis but with alcohol it's as high as 20%. A lot of people are pointing at the 1.5%–I think it's ridiculous.

LG: Since cannabis isn't legal here, just tolerated, how socially accepted is it? Would employers ever hesitate to hire someone who had worked in a coffeeshop?

M: Not really, but it depends on the person. I had a manager who worked here for four years and is now a policeman.

LG: How do you think membership in the EU will affect the status of coffeeshops?

M: It's a minor thing, I think. They just made a law that allows a French policeman to arrest someone here if he committed a felony. But there are two exceptions that they can't hurt somebody: one is for coffeeshops selling soft drugs and the other is euthanasia. Only France and Sweden are giving us problems about it, France especially. But their alcoholism rate is so high; it's really ridiculous that they're complaining about the drug issue. They complain that drugs come from Holland, but so many drugs come from Morocco. And if it comes from Morocco, then it has to come through France.

CANAL RING AND THE JORDAAN

You haven't seen Amsterdam until you've spent some time wandering in the Canal Ring. It's the city's highest rent district and, arguably, its most beautiful. Four main waterways encircle the western and southern sides of the old city. Inside the crescent is most of the tourist traffic of the city center, while the ring itself is a quieter, more picturesque place. Collectively, **Prinsengracht** (Prince's canal), **Keizersgracht** (Emperor's canal), and **Herengracht** (Gentlemen's canal) are known as the *grachtengordel* (literally "canal girdle"). The Ring is home to some of Amsterdam's most important and beautiful architecture. **The Jordaan** is the neighborhood next door—it's less touristed, but still filled with galleries, markets, and great nightlife.

ANNE FRANK HUIS. A visit to the Anne Frank House is a must for everyone, whether or not you've read the famous diary. The museum chronicles the two years the Frank family and four other Jews spent hiding in the annex of this warehouse on the Prinsengr. The rooms are no longer furnished, but personal objects in display cases and text panels with excerpts from the diary bring the story of the eight inhabitants to life, and the magazine clippings and photos that Anne used to decorate her room still hang on the wall. Footage of interviews with her father, Otto Frank, Miep Gies (who supplied the family with food and other necessities), and childhood friends of Anne provide further information and details. *(Prinsengr. 267. Tram #13, 14, 17, or 20 to Westermarkt. Open Apr.-Aug. daily 9am-9pm; Sept.-Mar. 9am-7pm. Last admission 30min. before closing. €6.50, ages 10-17 €3.)*

OTHER SIGHTS. The stately Herengr. leads to the **Museum Willet-Holthuysen,** a richly decorated 18th-century canal house with a peaceful, pristine garden. *(Herengr. 605, between Reguliersgr. and Vijzelstr., 3min. from Rembrandtpl. Open M-F 10am-5pm, Sa-Su 11am-5pm. €3.40.)* Near the Anne Frank Huis is the city's stately **Westerkerk,** a Protestant church built in 1631. Climb the church's tower for the best view in the city. *(Raadhuisstr. between Keizersgr. and Prinsengr. Tram #13, 17, or 20 to Westermarkt. Open Apr.-Sept. M-F 11am-3pm; July-Aug. also Sa. Tours every hr. €3.)*

ENTERTAINMENT

Amsterdam in the summertime is like a love affair: often alluring, sometimes confusing, but always deliciously entertaining. The **Amsterdams Uit Buro (AUB),** Leidsepl. 26, is stuffed with fliers, pamphlets, and guides to help you sift through current events; pick up the free monthly *UITKRANT* at any AUB office to see what's on. The AUB also sells tickets and makes reservations for just about any cultural event. (☎621 13 11; www.uitlijn.nl. Open F-W 10am-6pm, Th 10am-9pm.) The VVV **tourist office,** Stationspl. 10, has a theater desk that can also make reservations. (Open M-Sa 10am-5pm.) If you're thirsty for more info on bars, coffeeshops, and the latest events, pick up *Shark* (www.underwateramsterdam.com; print versions available throughout the city).

CONCERTS

In the summer, the Vondelpark Openluchttheater hosts free performances of all sorts every Wednesday through Sunday. (☎673 14 99; www.openluchttheater.nl.) The **Royal Concertgebouw Orchestra** is one of the world's finest. It plays in the **Concertgebouw,** Concertgebouwplein 2-6. Take tram #316 to Museumplein. (☎671 83 45; www.concertgebouw.nl. Tickets from €7. Guided tours Su at 9:30am; €7. Sept.-June, those under 27 can get last minute tickets for anything that isn't sold out for €7. Free lunchtime concert W 12:30pm, no tickets necessary. Ticket office open daily 10am-7pm.)

FILM AND THEATER

Check out the free www.movieguide.nl for movie listings. When you're in the Vondelpark, head left from the main entrance on Stadhouderskade to see what's on at the stately **Filmmuseum** independent movie theater. (☎589 14 00. Info center open M-F from 10am; Sa-Su box office opens 1hr. prior to first showing. €6.25, students €3.50.) **The Movies,** Haarlemmerstr. 159, is the city's oldest movie theater. (☎624 57 90. Open M-Tu and Th 4:15-10:15pm, W 2-10:15pm, F 4:15pm-12:30am, Sa 2pm-12:30am, Su 11:30am-10:15pm. €7.50, students €6.50). For American improv comedy, go to **Boom! Chicago,** Leidsepl. 12. These expats promise a wry look at life on the continent. (☎423 01 01. Su-F at 8:15pm, Sa at 7:30pm and 10:45pm. Tickets Su-Th €16, F-Sa €18.50)

COFFEESHOPS AND SMART SHOPS

COFFEESHOPS

Marijuana and hashish are tolerated in The Netherlands; coffeeshops sell pot or hash or will let you buy a drink and smoke your own stuff. Look for the green-and-white "Coffeeshop BCD" sticker that means that the shop is reputable. Although Amsterdam is known as the **hash** capital of the world, **marijuana** is increasingly popular. You can legally possess up to 5g of marijuana or hash. Pick up a free copy of the *BCD Official Coffeeshop Guide* for the pot-smoker's map of Amsterdam. For info on legal ins and outs, call the **Jellinek clinic** (☎570 23 55). **Never buy drugs from street dealers.** Don't get too caught up in Amsterdam's narcotic quirk; use common sense, and remember that any experimentation with drugs can be dangerous. If you choose to indulge, you will find that coffeeshops carry a range of products, described below.

Spacecakes, Spaceshakes, and **Space Sweets** are cakes and sweets made with hash or weed; hash chocolate, popsicles, and bonbons are also available. Because they need to be digested, they take longer to affect you and longer to rinse out; they produce a body stone that can take up to an hour to start, so don't gobble down another brownie just because you don't feel effects immediately. Be very careful who you buy from—hard drugs may be mixed in, which have been known to cause permanent side effects such as paralysis and impotence. **Hash** comes in two varieties, black (like Afghani and Nepali) and blonde (like Moroccan). Black tends to be heavier and hits harder. It's grown at high elevations in the mountains; the higher the elevation, the better the hash. Any **marijuana** with white in its name, such as white widow, white butterfly, or white ice, is guaranteed to be strong. It's not a good idea to drink very much while smoking, since getting high can disarm the body's ability to monitor the amount of alcohol consumed, and alcohol poisoning can be much more severe if your gag reflex is hindered. The Dutch tend to mix tobacco with their pot, so joints are harsher on your lungs; ask at coffeeshops if pre-rolled joints are rolled with tobacco or pure cannabis. Dutch marijuana costs €5-22 per gram. Staff at coffeeshops can explain the different kinds of pot on the menu to tourists. Most places will supply rolling papers and filter tips. Almost no one smokes out of pipes; while some places provide bongs, usually only tourists use them. When you move from one coffeeshop to another, it is courteous to buy a drink in the next coffeeshop even if you already have weed.

SMART SHOPS

Smart shops, which peddle a variety of **"herbal enhancers"** and **hallucinogens** that walk the line between soft and hard drugs, are also legal. Some shops are alcohol-free. **All hard drugs are illegal** and possession is treated as a serious crime.

Magic mushrooms start to work thirty minutes to an hour after consumption, and act on your system for four to eight hours, often causing panic or a faster heartbeat. Never look for mushrooms in the wild and never buy from a street dealer; it's extremely difficult to tell the difference between poisonous mushrooms and hallucinogenic mushrooms. Don't mix hallucinogens such as shrooms with alcohol; if you have a bad trip, call ☎112 to go to the hospital or ask someone for help—you won't be arrested, and they've seen it all before.

WHERE TO GO...

Barney's Coffeeshop, Haarlemmerstr. 102. Eat a huge greasy breakfast with your big fat joint. Open daily 7am-8pm.

Kadinsky, Rosmarijnsteeg 9. Stylish spot hidden off an alley near Spui is one of the city's friendliest, hip stoneries. 20min. free Internet with purchase. Open daily 10am-1am.

Grey Area, Oude Leliestr. 2. Where coffeeshop owners go for the best. One of the only owner-operated spots left in the city. The Yankee expat behind the counter will be happy to lend one of the coffeeshop's bongs. Open Tu-Su noon-8pm.

The Rookies, Korte Leidsedwarsstr. 145-147. One of the few remaining places outside of the Red Light District that serves both liquor and marijuana. Open Su-Th 10am-1am, F-Sa 10am-3am.

Abraxas, J. Roelensteeg 12-14. Swanky, casual, no-pressure atmosphere. 12min. free Internet access with drink. Open daily 10am-1am.

Siberie, Brouwersgr. 11. Snacks (*tosti* €1.60) and Internet (€1.15 per 30min.) also available. Open Su-Th 11am-11pm, F-Sa 11am-midnight.

Hill Street Blues, Warmoesstr. 52. A rock 'n' roll vibe permeates this coffeeshop and bar. Open 9am-1am, F-Sa 9am-3am.

Rusland, Ruslandstr. 16. One of the city's oldest coffeeshops. An intimate, comfy nook with an extensive menu. Open Su-Th 10am-midnight, F-Sa 10am-1am.

The Magic Mushroom, Spuistr. 249. At this museum of a smartshop, procure all the mushrooms, herbal XTC, energy and smart drinks, smart drugs, and stoner art you've ever dreamed existed. Open daily 11am-10pm.

Dutch Flowers, Singel 387. The long line is evidence of this hangout's quality hash. Outside seating on the beautiful Singel canal. Open Su-Th 10am-1am, F-Sa 10am-2am.

Paradox, 1e Bloemdwarsstr. 2. The owners match the feel of this place: colorful, free, and ready to have a good time. Weed, hash, and awesome veggie burgers (€3.50). Open daily 10am-8pm, kitchen closes at 4pm.

Tatanka, Korte Leidsedwarstr. 151a. Feels more like a museum than a smartshop. Start your trip in the chill-out room upstairs. Open daily 11am-10pm.

Bluebird, Sint Antoniebreestr. 71. Two stories of azure chill-space, including quiet alcoves for a thoughtful smoke. Open daily 9:30am-1am.

NIGHTLIFE

CAFES AND BARS

Amsterdam's finest cafes are the old, dark, wood-paneled *bruine cafes* (brown cafes) of the **Jordaan,** so named because of the years of cigarette smoke accumulated on the ceilings. Many have outdoor seating lining the canal on **Prinsengracht.** The **Leidseplein** and **Rembrandtplein** are the liveliest nightspots, with crazy coffeeshops, loud bars, and tacky clubs galore. Gay bars line **Reguliersdwarsstraat,** which connects Muntpl. and Rembrandtspl., and **Kerkstraat,** five blocks north of Leidsepl.

Café de Engelbewaarder, Kloveniersburgwal 59. A great atmosphere any time of the week, especially on Su when the cafe hosts live jazz (4:40-7pm). Beer €2. Open M-Th noon-1am, F-Sa noon-3am, Su 2pm-1am. Kitchen open daily 5:30-10pm.

Absinthe, Nieuwezijds Voorburgwal 171, just south of Dam Sq. Draws a young, hip crowd with a mellow vibe. The bar is known for its house drink, a variant called "smart absinthe" with 10% wormwood (€10). Open Su-Th 8pm-3am, F-Sa 8pm-4am.

Lux, Marnixstr. 403. More a lounge than a bar, Lux has a distinctive retro design that sets it apart from its peers. There's not much dancing, but the candles, wave lamps, and DJ (W-Su) will get you pumped to hit the clubs. Beer €2, mixed drinks €4. Open Su-Th 8pm-3am, F-Sa 8pm-4am.

M Bar, Reguliersdwarsstr. 13-15, just off Leidsestr. Take tram #1, 2, or 5 to Koningspl. Sleek, slippery minimalist bar, located on a famously gay street but drawing a mainly straight crowd. DJs spin house, club, and techno Th-Su. Beer €2, wine €3, mixed drinks €6. Open W-Th and Su 6pm-3am, F-Sa 6pm-4am.

Montmartre, Halvemaarsteg 17. Rococo interior bedecked with flowers and rich draperies houses some of the wildest parties in the city. Voted best gay bar in Amsterdam by local gay magazine *Gay Krant*. Open Su-Th 5pm-1am, F-Sa 5pm-3am.

The Tara, Rokin 85-89, a few blocks south of Dam Sq. Irish-themed watering hole with a maze-like interior. DJs or bands usually F-Sa. Beer €2, pints €4. Open Su-Th 11am-1am, F-Sa 11am-3am.

Maximiliaan, Kloveniersburgwal 6-8. Stop in for the fabulous home-brews. Alcohol content can get to a heady 7%. Open Tu-Th and Su 3pm-1am, F-Sa 3pm-3am.

Arc Bar, Reguliersdwarsstr. 44. Lounge in a beige leather chair and watch discreet projections of clouds on the wall. On weekends, the black table-tops in the front are lowered to become platforms for dancing. Open Su-M 10am-1am, F-Sa 10am-3am.

Bamboo Bar, Lange Leidsedwarsstr. 64. *Noir* decorations, a disco ball, and a slick hardwood bar share space with tiki torches. Beer €2, mixed drinks €4-7.50. Open Su-Th 8pm-3am, F-Sa 8pm-4am.

Bar 8, Berenstr. 8. It's unadulterated trendiness at this bar that serves a hip, if touristy, crowd. Beer €3, mixed drinks €9. Open Tu-Th 6pm-1am, F-Sa 6pm-3am.

Proust, Noordermarkt 3. Come for a pre-party drink before hitting the late-night clubs. Open daily 11am-1am, F-Sa 11am-2am.

Wijnand Fockink, 31 Pijlsteeg, on an alleyway just off Dam Sq. They've been brewing the city's best *fockink* liquor for 400 years. Open daily 3-9pm.

Café De Jaren, Nieuwe Doelenstr. 20-22. The cafe's air of sophistication doesn't quite go with its budget-friendly prices. Full hot meals €11. Beer €2-3. Open Su-Th 10am-1am, F-Sa 10am-2am; kitchen open Su-Th till 11pm, F-Sa until midnight.

LIVE MUSIC

Paradiso, Weteringschans 6-8 (☎626 45 21; www.paradiso.nl). When big-name rock, punk, new-wave, hip-hop, and reggae bands come to Amsterdam, they almost invariably play at this converted church. Grace the spot where Lenny Kravitz got his big break and the Stones taped their latest live album. Tickets €5-25.

Bourbon Street Jazz & Blues Club, Leidsekruisstr. 6-8 (☎623 34 40; www.bourbonstreet.nl). Blues, soul, funk, and rock bands keep the crowds coming every night. Mostly smaller bands play this intimate venue, although in the past they have drawn the Stones and Sting. Cover Su and Th €3, F-Sa free if you enter 10-10:30pm. Open Su-Th 10pm-4am, F-Sa 10pm-5am.

Melkweg, Lijnbaansgr. 234a (☎624 17 77; www.melweg.nl), off Leidsepl. Legendary nightspot where bands, theater, films, shows, an art gallery, and discotheque make for sensory overload. Concert tickets €10-22. Box office open M-F 1-5pm, Sa-Su 4-6pm.

Casablanca, Zeedijk 24-26 (☎625 56 85; www.casablanca-amsterdam.nl), between Oudezijds Kolk and Vredenburgersteeg. Casablanca has been around since 1946, and it's still one of the best spots to hear live jazz. Jazz Su-W nights, Th-Sa DJ-hosted dance parties. Open Su-Th 8pm-3am, F-Sa 8pm-4am.

CLUBS AND DISCOS

Many clubs charge a membership fee in addition to normal cover, so the tab can get high. Be prepared for cocky doormen who love to turn away tourists; show up early or hope the bouncer thinks you're cute. It's customary to tip bouncers €1-2 on the way out. There are pricey discos aplenty on **Prinsengracht,** near **Leidsestraat,** and on **Lange Leidsedwarsstraat.** Gay discos almost exclusively for men line **Amstelstraat** and **Reguliersdwarsstraat.** Pick up a wallet-sized *Clu* guide, free at cafes and coffeeshops, for a club map of the city, and *Gay and Night,* a free monthly magazine, for info on gay parties.

Escape, Rembrandtpl. 11. People pour into this massive venue for a night at one of Amsterdam's hottest clubs. 2 floors with 6 bars and an enormous dance floor. Scenesters groove to house, trance, disco, and dance classics. Be sober, well-dressed, and female to increase your chances of entry. Open Th-Su 11pm-4am, F-Sa 11pm-5am.

Arena, Gravesandestr. 51-53, in the Oost. Former chapel throws wild parties. Open F-Sa 11pm-4am, Su 6pm-3am.

Dansen Bij Jansen, Handboogstr. 11-13, near Konigsplein. The hottest student dance club in Amsterdam, popular with backpackers and local students. Show student ID to enter or be accompanied by a student. Open Su-Th 11pm-4am, F-Sa 11pm-5am.

Cockring, Warmoestr. 90. Somewhere between a sex club and a disco. Dark room in the back where anything goes. Men only. No cover, except for special parties, when it runs around €5. Open Su-Th 11pm-4am, F-Sa 11pm-5am.

Item, Nieuwezijds Voorburgwal 163-165, just south of Dam Sq. Young, trendy, and tourist-oriented. In an area with few late-night discos, Item stands out. Cover €10-15. Open Su-Th 11pm-4am, F-Sa 11pm-5am.

De Beetles, Lange Leidsedwarsstr. 81. Find an ideal mix of cool and crazy at this hip drink house. F-Sa 9pm-12:30am 6 beers for €2. Open Su-Th 9pm-4am, F-Sa 9pm-5am.

The Ministry, Reguliersdwarsstr. 12. The very popular Ministry is upscale enough to be classy and hip, but without any attitude. Cover €5-12; look for fliers for free admittance. Open Su-Th 11pm-4am, F-Sa 11pm-5am.

Mazzo, Rozengracht 114. Even the bouncers are nice. The usual black walls, colored spotlights, and plenty of well-dressed singles. W, Th, and Su cover €5-10; F €8-10; Sa €10. Open W, Th, Su 11pm-4am; F-Sa 11pm-5am.

Exit, Reguliersdwarsstr. 42, just west of the intersection with Vijzelstr. Enter Exit to find one of the most popular gay discos in The Netherlands. Mostly men, though female friends often appear. Cover F-Sa €7, Th and Su €3. Open Su-Th midnight-4am, F-Sa midnight-5am.

You II, Amstel 178. F men only; Sa women only; Th and Su are mixed, straight men are allowed only when accompanied by a female friend. Fun theme nights prevail. Cover Sa €7. Open Th and Su 10pm-4am, F-Sa 10pm-5am.

DAYTRIPS FROM AMSTERDAM

TULIP COUNTRY: AALSMEER AND LISSE. Easily accessible by bus (or even bike), old-fashioned **Aalsmeer** is home to the world's largest flower auction. The **Bloemenveiling Aalsmeer,** Legmeerdijk 313, is the world's largest trade building with 878,000 square meters of floor space; the worldwide price of flowers is largely determined here. (☎297 39 21 85; www.vba-aalsmeer.nl. Open M-F 7:30-11am. €4.) From Amsterdam's Centraal Station, take bus #172 (45min., every 15min., 5 strips). For the best action, get there early; buses begin leaving Amsterdam at 6:10am.

For even more flowers, check out the town of **Lisse** in late spring. The **Keukenhof Gardens** become a kaleidoscope of color as over 5 million bulbs come to life. (www.keukenhof.nl. In 2003, open Mar. 21-May 18 daily 8am-7:30pm; tickets on sale until 6pm. €11.) **The Zwarte Tulip Museum** details the history and science of "bulbiculture," or tulip raising. Many call the ongoing quest for the *zwarte* (black) tulip impossible, since the color does not exist naturally. (☎025 241 79 00. Open Tu-Su 1-5pm. €3.) Take a train from Amsterdam's Centraal Station to Leiden (20min., every 30min. until 2:45am, €11), then catch bus #50 or 51 to Lisse (5 strips).

ZAANSE SCHANS. Duck-filled canals, working windmills, and restored houses make Zaanse Schans feel like a museum village, although a handful of people actually live and work here. The **De Kat Windmill** has been grinding plants into artists' pigments since 1782. (Open Apr.-Oct. daily 9am-5pm; Nov.-Mar. Sa-Su 9am-5pm. €2.) The oldest oil mill in the world is the **De Zoeker Windmill.** (Open Mar.-Oct. daily 9:30am-4:30pm. €2.) The **Cheesefarm Catharina Hoeve** offers free samples of its homemade wares as well as a tour of its workshop. (Open daily 8am-6pm.) Watch craftsmen mold blocks of wood into comfy clogs at **Klompenmakerij de Zaanse Schans,** or see where the ubiquitous Albert Heijn supermarket craze started at the original shop, now the **Albert Heijn Museumwinkel.** Next door you can stop by the **Museum van het Nederlandse Uurwerk (Museum of the Dutch Clock),** Kalverringdijk 3, to view the oldest working pendulum clock in the world. (Open Apr.-Oct. daily 10am-5pm. €2.30.) The pint-sized **Museum Het Noorderhuis** features original costumes from the Zaan region. (Open July-Aug. daily 10am-5pm; Mar.-June and Sept.-Oct. Tu-Su 10am-5pm; Nov.-Feb. Sa-Su 10am-5pm. €1.)

From Amsterdam, take the *stoptrein* heading to Alkmaar and get off at Koog Zandijk (20min., €2.25). From there, follow the signs across a bridge to Zaanse Schans (12min.). An **information center** is at Schansend 1. (☎616 82 18; www.zaanse-schans.nl. Open daily 8:30am-5pm.)

EDAM. Discover quaint cottages, peaceful parks, and lots of cheese in the pleasant village of Edam. The best way to get around is on foot, although you can rent bikes at **Ronald Schot,** Grote Kerkstraat 7/9. (€5.50 per day.) From the bus stop, follow Schepenmakersdijk to the Kwakelbrug bridge, then take Lingerzijde to reach the towering 16th-century **Speeltoren;** keep walking to reach the center of town. Directly ahead and over the bridge is **Edam's Museum,** Damplein 8, which chronicles the town's history. (Open Apr.-Sept. M-Sa 10am-4:30pm, Su 1-4:30pm. €2.) From the museum, head toward the **cheese market,** where farmers still bring their famed cheese to the town center by horse and boat. (July-Aug. W 10am-12:30pm.) On the left of the market is the 16th-century **Kaas Waag (Cheese Weigh House).** From the Waag, walk straight on Eilandsgracht and turn left on Nieuw Vaartje to the **Grote of St. Nicolaaskerk.** (Open May-Sept. daily 2-4:30pm. Free.) The truly grand **Grote Kerk** is the largest three-ridged church in Europe; don't forget to look up at the roof, which was made of timber from ships used by the Dutch East India Company.

From Amsterdam, take buses #114 (30min.) or #110, 112, or 116 (45min., 5 strips). In the town hall, the VVV **tourist office** helps arrange accommodations. (☎31 51 25; info@vvv-edam.nl. Open M-Sa 10am-5pm, July-Aug. also open Su 1-4:30pm.) **Hof van Holland ❷,** Lingerzijde 69, prepares cheap Dutch fare, some vegetarian. (Lunch €4, dinner €10-19. Open Tu-F 10:30am-10:30pm, Sa-Su 11am-10:30pm.)

THE NETHERLANDS

HAARLEM ☎023

With narrow cobblestone streets, calm canals, and fields of tulips, it's clear how Haarlem inspired native Frans Hals and other Golden Age Dutch artists. Most visitors come to take in the city's amazing artistic and historic sights.

TRANSPORTATION AND PRACTICAL INFORMATION. Reach Haarlem from Amsterdam by **train** (20min.; €2.90, same-day round-trip €5.20) from Centraal Station or by **bus** #80 (every 30min., 2 strips) from Marnixstr., near Leidsepl. The VVV **tourist office,** Stationspl. 1, to your right when you walk out of the train station, finds rooms (from €18.50) for a €5 fee. (☎090 06 16 16 00; www.vvvzk.nl. Open in summer M-F 9:30am-5:30pm, Sa 10am-4pm; off-season Sa 10am-2pm.)

ACCOMMODATIONS AND FOOD. Walk to the Grote Markt and take a right to reach **Joops Intercity Apartments ❹,** Oude Groenmarkt 20. (☎532 20 08; joops@easynet.nl. Reception daily 7:30am-9pm. Singles €28-65; doubles €55-100. AmEx/MC/V.) **Hotel Carillon ❷,** Grote Markt 27, is ideally located on the town square, to the left of the Grote Kerk. (☎531 05 91; www.hotelcarillon.com. Breakfast included. Reception 7:30am-midnight. Singles €29, with bath €55; doubles €55/€71; triples €92. MC/V.) Take bus #2 (dir.: Haarlem-Noord; every 10min. until 6pm, then every 15min. until 12:30am), then a cab from Haarlem station (about €12) to Jeugdherberg to stay at the **NJHC-Hostel Haarlem (HI) ❷,** Jan Gijzenpad 3. (☎537 37 93; www.njhc.org/haarlem. Breakfast included. Dorms €19-25. AmEx/MC/V.) To **camp** at **De Liede ❶,** Lie Over 68, take bus #2 (dir.: Zuiderpolder) and walk 10min. from the bus stop. (☎535 86 66. €3.50 per person, €2.75 per tent or per car. For cheap meals, try cafes in the **Grote Markt** or **Botermarkt,** many of which offer outdoor patios. To the right of the Grote Kerk, **Grand Café Doria ❶,** Grote Houtstraat 1a, specializes in Italian fare, including pizza margherita (€6) and pasta bolognese (€8.50). (☎531 33 35; www.doria.nl. Open M-W 11am-7:30pm, Th 11am-9pm, F 11am-midnight, Sa 1-11pm.)

SIGHTS AND MUSEUMS. The action centers on the **Grote Markt,** Haarlem's vibrant main square. To get there from the train station, head south along Kruisweg, which becomes Kruisstraat and then Barteljorisstraat. The **Grote Kerk,** at the opposite end of the Grote Markt, houses the mammoth Müller organ once played by an 11-year-old Mozart. (www.bavo.nl. Open M-Sa 10am-4pm. €1.50.) From the front of the church, take a right on to Warmoestraat and walk three blocks to the **Frans Hals Museum,** Groot Heiligland 62, which houses a collection of Golden Age paintings by several masters, including work by Haarlem resident Frans Hals himself. (Open Tu-Sa 11am-5pm, Su noon-5pm. €5.40, under 19 free.) A 2min. walk toward the train station from the Grote Markt is the moving **Corrie Ten Boomhuis,** Barteljorisstraat 19, which served as the headquarters of Corrie ten Boom's movement to protect Jews during World War II. The savior of an estimated 800 lives, Corrie was caught and sent to a concentration camp, but survived to write *The Hiding Place* which was later made into a film. The **Teyler's Museum,** Spaarne 16, is The Netherlands' oldest museum, and contains an eclectic assortment of scientific instruments, fossils, paintings, and drawings, including works by Raphael, Michelangelo, and Rembrandt; from the church, turn left onto Damstr. and follow it until Spaarne. (Open Tu-Sa 10am-5pm, Su noon-5pm. €4.50.) The **De Hallen Museum,** Grote Markt 16, displays rotating exhibits of modern art and is housed in the old 17th-century Dutch Renaissance *vleeshal* (indoor meat market). (www.franshalsmuseum.com. Open M-Sa 11am-5pm, Su 1-5pm. €4, under 19 free.) Dedicated to the many uses of hemp, the **Global Hemp Museum,** Spaarne 94, has everything from hemp denim to a hemp snowboard. (www.globalhempmuseum.com. Open daily 11am-8pm, Su noon-8pm. €2.50.)

DAYTRIPS FROM HAARLEM: ZANDVOORT AND BLOEMENDAAL. Just seven miles from Haarlem, the seaside town of **Zandvoort** draws sun-starved Nederlanders to its miles of sandy beaches. To get to the shore from the train station, follow the signs to the Raadhuis, and then head west along Kerkstraat. For a different feel, walk 30min. to hip **Bloemendaal,** which has been transformed from a quiet, family-oriented beach town to one of the best beach parties in Holland. The hippie-style club **Woodstock 69** hosts **Beach Bop** the last Sunday of every month (www.beachbop.info), although lower-profile parties go on other nights of the week. The town's clubs, including **Republic, De Zomer,** and **Solaris,** are only open in summer, generally from April to September.

Trains arrive in Zandvoort from Haarlem (10min., round-trip €2.75). The VVV **tourist office,** Schoolplein 1, is just east of the town square, off Louisdavidstraat. (☎571 79 47; www.vvvzk.nl. Open M-Sa 9am-5pm.) The **Hotel Noordzee,** Hogeweg 15, has cheerful rooms just 100m from the beach. (☎571 31 27; www.hotel-nordzee.nl. Breakfast included. Doubles €47-60.)

LEIDEN ☎071

Home to one of the oldest and most prestigious universities in Europe, Leiden brims with bookstores, bicycles, windmills, gated gardens, hidden walkways, and some truly outstanding museums. Rembrandt's birthplace and the site of the first **tulips,** the Netherlands' third-largest city offers visitors a gateway to flower country. Follow signs from the train station to the spacious and modern **Museum Naturalis,** which explores the history of our earth and its inhabitants, providing scientific and anthropological explanations of fossils, minerals, animals, evolution, and even astronomy. (www.naturalis.nl. Open Sept.-June Tu-Su 10am-6pm; July-Aug. daily 10am-6pm. €6.) The **Rijksmuseum voor Volkenkunde** (National Museum of Ethnology), Steenstr. 1, is one of the world's oldest anthropological museums, with a fantastic collection from the Dutch East Indies. (www.rmv.nl. Open Tu-Su 10am-5pm. €6.50.) The **Rijksmuseum van Oudheden** (National Antiquities Museum), Rapenburg 28, holds the restored Egyptian Temple of Taffeh, a gift removed from the reservoir basin of the Aswan Dam. (www.rmo.nl. Open Tu-F 10am-5pm, Sa-Su noon-5pm. €6.50.) Sharing a main gate with the Academy building is the university's 400-year-old garden, the **Hortus Botanicus,** Rapenburg 73, where the first Dutch tulips were grown. Its grassy knolls alongside the **Witte Singel** canal make it an ideal picnic spot. (www.hortusleiden.nl. Open Mar.-Nov. daily 10am-6pm; Dec.-Feb. Su-F 10am-4pm. €4.) Scale steep staircases to inspect the inside of a functioning windmill at the **Molenmuseum ("De Valk"),** 2e Binnenvestgracht 1. (Open Tu-Sa 10am-5pm, Su 1pm-5pm. €2.50.) The **Museum De Lakenhal,** Oude Singel 32, exhibits works by Rembrandt and Jan Steen. (Open Tu-Sa 10am-5pm, Su noon-5pm. €4.)

Leiden is easily reached by **train** from Amsterdam's Centraal Station (20min., every 30min. until 2:45am, €11) or The Hague (20min., every 30min. until 3:15am, €4.50). The VVV **tourist office,** Stationsweg 2d, a 5min. walk from the train station, sells maps (€1.15) and walking tour brochures (€2) and helps find hotel rooms (€2.50 fee). (☎090 02 22 23 33; www.leiden.nl. Open M-F 10am-6:30pm, Sa 10am-4:30pm; Apr.-May and July-Aug. also open Su 11am-3pm.) The **Hotel Pension Witte Singel ❷,** Witte Singel 80, 5min. from Hortus Botanicus, has immaculate rooms. Take bus #43 to Merenwijk and tell the driver your destination. (☎512 45 92; fax 514 78 90; wvanvriel@pensione-ws.demon.nl. Singles from €31; doubles from €47.) Especially on weekend nights, locals and students pack into the popular **de Oude Harmonie ❶,** Breestr. 16, just off Rapenburg. (Entrees €6-13. Open Su 3pm-1am, M-Th noon-1am, F-Sa 3pm-3am.) The **Super de Boer supermarket,** Stationsweg 40, is opposite the train station. (Open M-F 7am-9pm, Sa 9am-8pm, Su noon-7pm.)

DAYTRIP FROM LEIDEN: NOORDWIJK. Beautiful white-sand beaches lie 18km away from Leiden in the town of **Noordwijk.** In addition to many outdoor activities, Noordwijk features the **Space Expo,** Keperlaan 3, at the visitors' center for ESTEC (the European Space Agency's largest technical branch). The permanent exhibit attracts thousands of space fanatics each year with simulated rocket launches and interactive astronaut games. (Open Tu-Su 10am-5pm. €6.80.) To get to Noordwijk, take a bus from the Leiden Centraal Station (€3.40). The VVV **tourist office,** De Grent 8 (☎071 361 93 21; www.vvvnoordwijk.nl) has accommodations info. The **Flying Pig Beach Hostel ❶,** Parallel Bvd. 208, is in the center of town.

Take bus #40 or 42 to Vuurtorenplein (20min.); face south and the Pig will be 100m down on your left side. (☎071 362 25 33; www.flyingpig.nl. Bodyboard, surfboard, mountain bike, and inline skate rental. Free Internet. Required key deposit €10. Reception daily 9am-midnight. Open Mar.-Oct. Dorms €14; doubles €25-31.) A variety of restaurants line **Hoofdstraat** near the beach. For cafes and bars, try **Koningin Wilhelmina Boulevard,** where most establishments overlook the North Sea.

THE HAGUE (DEN HAAG) ☎070

William II moved the royal residence to the Hague in 1248, prompting the creation of parliament buildings, museums, and sprawling parks. Today, countless diplomats frequent designer stores, merging rich history with a bustling metropolis.

TRANSPORTATION AND PRACTICAL INFORMATION. **Trains** roll in from Amsterdam (50min., €8) and Rotterdam (25min., €3.50) to both of The Hague's major stations, Centraal Station and Holland Spoor. Trams #1, 9, and 12 connect the two stations. The VVV **tourist office,** Kon. Julianapl. 30, just outside the north entrance to Centraal Station and right next to the Hotel Sofitel, books rooms for a €2 fee and sells detailed city maps. A hotel booking by computer is available 24hr. (☎090 03 40 35 05; www.denhaag.com. Open M and Sa 10am-5pm, Tu-F 9am-5:30pm, Su 11am-5pm.) Most foreign **embassies** are in The Hague: **Australia,** Carnegielaan 4, 2517 KH (☎310 82 00; open M-F 8:45am-4:30pm); **Canada,** Sophialaan 7, 2514 JP (☎311 16 00; open M-F 9am-1pm and 2-5:30pm); **Ireland,** 9 Dr. Kuyperstr., 2514 BA (☎363 09 93; call for hours); **New Zealand,** Carnegielaan 10, 2517 KH (☎346 93 24; open M-F 9am-12:30pm and 1:30-5:30pm); **South Africa,** Wassenaarseweg 40, 2596 CJ (☎392 45 01; open daily 9am-noon); **UK,** Lange Voorhout 10, 2514 ED (☎427 04 27; call for hours); and **US,** Lange Voorhout 102, 2514 EJ (☎310 92 09; open M-F 8am-4:30pm).

ACCOMMODATIONS AND FOOD. The **NJHC City Hostel ❷,** Scheepmakerstr. 27, is near Holland Spoor; turn right from the station, follow the tram tracks, turn right at the big intersection, and Scheepmakerstr. is 3min. down on the right. From Centraal Station, take tram #1 (dir.: Delft), 9 (dir.: Vrederust), or 12 (dir.: Duindrop) to Rijswijkseplein (2 strips); cross to the left in front of the tram, cross the big intersection, and Scheepmakerstr. is straight ahead. (☎315 78 88; www.njhc.org/denhaag. In-house restaurant-bar. Breakfast included. Dorms €23; singles €47; doubles €61. Nonmembers add €2.50.) Budget takeaway places line **Lage Poten** and **Korte Poten** near the Binnenhof.

SIGHTS AND ENTERTAINMENT. The Hague has served as the seat of Dutch government for 800 years, and has of late become headquarters for the international criminal justice system. Andrew Carnegie donated the **Peace Palace (Het Vredespaleis),** the opulent home of the International Court of Justice at Carnegiepl., 3min. on tram #7 or 8 north from the Binnenhof. (www.vredespaleis.nl. Tours M-F 10, 11am, 2, 3pm. Book through the tourist office. €3.50, under 13 €2.30.) For snippets of Dutch politics, visit the **Binnenhof,** the Hague's Parliament complex. Just outside the north entrance of the Binnenhof, the 17th-century **Mauritshuis,** Korte Vijverberg 8, features an impressive collection of Dutch paintings, including works by Rembrandt and Vermeer. (www.mauritshuis.nl. Open Tu-Sa 10am-5pm, Su 11am-5pm. €7, under 18 free.) Guided tours leave from Binnenhof 8a and visit the 13th-century **Ridderzaal** (Hall of Knights) as well as the chambers of the States General. (Open M-Sa 10am-4pm, last tour leaves at 3:45pm. Entrance to courtyard free, tour €5.) The impressive modern art collection at the **Gemeentemuseum,** Stadhouderslaan 41, displays Piet Mondrian's *Victory Boogie Woogie*. Take tram #7 from Holland Spoor or bus #4 from Centraal Station. (www.gemeentemuseum.nl. Open Tu-Su 11am-5pm. €7.) For vibrant nightlife, prowl the Strandweg in nearby **Scheveningen** (see below).

DAYTRIP FROM THE HAGUE: SCHEVENINGEN. Just 5km from The Hague, **Scheveningen** (SCHAYVE-uhn-ing-un; so difficult to say that it was used as a code word by the Dutch in WWII) features family-oriented North Sea beaches by day and crazy dance parties by night. The **Strandweg** is the main drag along the beach, packed with restaurants and nightclubs. Fish vendors sell fresh cod, calamari, perch, and pike, as well as tasty *broodjes*. In the center of the Strandweg, the 100-year-old **Scheveningen Pier** houses music festivals and art exhibitions. (www.pier.nl. €1) The VVV **tourist office,** Gevers Deynootweg 1134, has info on rooms. (☎090 03 40 35 05; €0.40 per min. Open M 11am-6pm, Tu-F 9:30am-6pm, Sa 10am-5pm, Su 1-5pm.) To reach **Hotel Hage,** Seinpostduin 22-23, take tram #8 to Gevers Deynootweg, cross the street toward the sea; Seinpostduin is ahead on the left. This hotel is one of the better deals in town, and just a hop from the beach. (☎351 46 96; fax 358 58 51. Singles €49; doubles €88; triples €110.)

DELFT ☎015

Delft's lilied canals and stone footbridges offer the same images that native Johannes Vermeer immortalized in paint over 300 years ago. It's best to visit on Thursdays and Saturdays, when townspeople flood the marketplace. The town is renowned for **Delftware,** blue-on-white china developed in the 16th century. Watch Delftware made from scratch at **De Candelaer,** Kerkstraat 13a-14, located in the center of town. (www.candelaer.nl. Open daily 9am-6pm.) To see a larger factory, take tram #1 to Vrijenbanselaan and enjoy a free demonstration at **De Delftse Pauw,** Delftweg 133. (www.delftsepauw.com. Open Apr.-Oct. daily 9am-4:30pm; Nov.-Mar. M-F 9am-4:40, Sa-Su 11am-1pm.) Built in 1381, the **Nieuwe Kerk** hosts the restored mausoleum of Dutch liberator Willem of Orange. Climb the tower, which holds a 48-bell carillon, for a view of old Delft. (Church open Apr.-Oct. M-Sa 9am-6pm; Nov.-Mar. M-F 11am-4pm, Sa 11am-5pm. €2. Tower closes 1hr. earlier and can be climbed for €1.60.) Founded in 1200, the **Oude Kerk,** a Dutch Reformed church, has a rich history and a 75m tower that leans 2m out of line. (Open Apr.-Oct. M-Sa 9am-6pm; Nov.-Mar. M-F 11am-4pm, Sa 11am-5pm. €2. Hourly tours.) **Rondvaart Delft,** Koormarkt 113, offers canal rides and rents water bikes. (☎212 63 85. Open Mar.-Oct. daily 10am-6pm.)

The easiest way into Delft is the 15min. ride on **tram** #1 from The Hague (2 strips) to Delft station. **Trains** also arrive from Amsterdam (1hr., €9). From the station, cross the bridge, turn left, turn right at the first light, and follow signs to the Markt for the VVV **tourist office,** Markt 85. (☎213 01 00; www.vvvdelft.nl. Open M-Sa 9am-5:30pm; Apr.-Sept. also open Su 11am-3pm.) While the tourist office will help with room booking, your best bet is to sleep in the Hague; it's 15min. away and has much better deals. **Delftse Hout Recreation Area** ❷ has campsites and cabins. (☎213 00 40; www.tours.nl/delftsehout. Sheets not included. Reception May to mid-Sept. 9am-10pm; mid-Sept. to Apr. 9am-6pm. 2-person tent €22; 4-person camping hut €30.) Restaurants line **Volderstraat** and **Oude Delft.** **Stads Pannekoeckhuys** ❶, Oude Delft 113-115, has giant pancakes with sweet fillings (€4-9). (Open Apr.-Sept. Tu-Su 11am-9pm; Nov.-Mar. W-Su 11am-9pm.) **De Nonnerie** ❶, St. Agathaplein, across the canal from Oude Kerk and through the gate, has a stunning courtyard and sandwiches starting at €3. (Open Tu-F 11am-5pm, Sa-Su noon-5pm.)

THE NETHERLANDS

ROTTERDAM ☎010

The second-largest city in the Netherlands and the busiest port city in the world, Rotterdam lacks the quaint feel that characterizes much of the Netherlands. After it was bombed in 1940, experimental architects replaced the rubble with striking (some say strikingly ugly) buildings, creating an urban, industrial conglomerate. Artsy and innovative, yet almost decrepit in its hyper-modernity, the Rotterdam that arose from the ashes—rife with museums, parks, and ground-breaking architecture—is today one of Europe's biggest centers of cultural activity.

TRANSPORTATION AND PRACTICAL INFORMATION. **Trains** run from: Amsterdam (1¼hr., €11); The Hague (25min., €3.40); and Utrecht (45min., €7). The VVV **tourist office,** Coolsingel 67, opposite the *Stadhuis*, books rooms for a €2 fee. (Open M-Th 9:30am-6pm, F 9:30am-9pm, Sa 9:30am-5pm.) **Postal code:** 3016.

ACCOMMODATIONS AND FOOD. To reach the **NJHC City-Hostel Rotterdam (HI) ❷,** Rochussenstr. 107-109, take the metro to Dijkzigt; at the top of the metro escalator, exit onto Rochussentr and turn left. (☎436 57 63. Breakfast and sheets included. Reception daily 7am-midnight. Dorms €22; singles €31; doubles €52.) To get from the station to the **Hotel Bienvenue ❸,** Spoorsingel 24, exit through the back and walk straight along the canal for 5min.; it's on the right. (☎466 93 94. Breakfast included. Reception M-F 7:30am-9pm, Sa-Su 8am-9pm. Singles €43; doubles €70; triples €90.) Turn onto Schilderstraat from Schiedamse Dijk and follow the street until it turns into Witte de Withstraat to reach **Hotel Bazar ❺,** Witte de Withstraat 16, and escape to the Middle East or South America in one of 18 themed rooms. (☎206 51 51; fax 206 51 59. All include bath, TV, minibar, and breakfast. Singles €65; doubles €75.) Chinese food and schwarma await along **Witte de Withstraat** where you can easily grab a meal for under €5, or try **Lijbaan** for its array of pubs, bars, and all their accompanying culinary charm.

SIGHTS AND ENTERTAINMENT. For a dramatic example of Rotterdam's eccentric designs, check out the **Kijk-Kubus** (Cube Houses) by Piet Blom. Take tram #1 or the metro to Blaak, turn left, and look up. (Open Mar.-Dec. daily 11am-5pm; Jan.-Feb. F-Su only. €1.75.) Try to decipher the architectural madness at the **Netherlands Architecture Institute,** Museumpark 25. (Open Tu-Sa 10am-5pm. €5, under 17 €3.) Then, refresh yourself with Rubens, van Gogh, Rembrandt, Rubinstein, Rothko, and Magritte across the street at the **Museum Boijmans van Beuningen,** Museumpark 18-20. (M: Eendractspl. or tram #5. Open Tu-Sa 10am-5pm, Su 11am-5pm. €6.) Restored to its medieval splendor after the bombing, **St. Laurenskerk,** Grote Kerkplein 15, is one of the most remarkable churches in the country, and home to the largest mechanical organ in Europe. (Open Tu-Sa 10am-4pm. Su services free.) Step aboard the *De Buffel*, a restored 19th-century turret ship at the **Maritiem Museum,** Leeuvehaven 1, or peruse hundreds of intricately detailed model ships. (Open July-Aug. M-Sa 10am-5pm, Su 11am-5pm; Sept.-June closed M. €3.50.) Make sure to swing by the powerful **Zadkine Monument,** to the left of the museum. Known as the Monument for the Destroyed City and erected only 11 years after the bombing, it depicts a man with a hole in his heart writhing in agony. **Museumpark** features sculptures, mosaics, and monuments designed by some of the world's foremost artists and architects; take tram #5 to reach the outdoor exhibit.

Coffeeshop-hop along **Oude Binnenweg** and **Nieuwe Binnenweg,** or dance the night away at **Night Town,** West Kruiskade 26-28. (Cover for dancing €8, bands €11-25. Open F-Sa 11pm-5am.)

DAYTRIP FROM ROTTERDAM: GOUDA. Gouda (HOW-da) is the quintessential Dutch town, with canals, a windmill, and well-known cheese. A regional **cheese market** is held weekly in summer (Th 10am-12:30pm). If you've ever wanted to see a

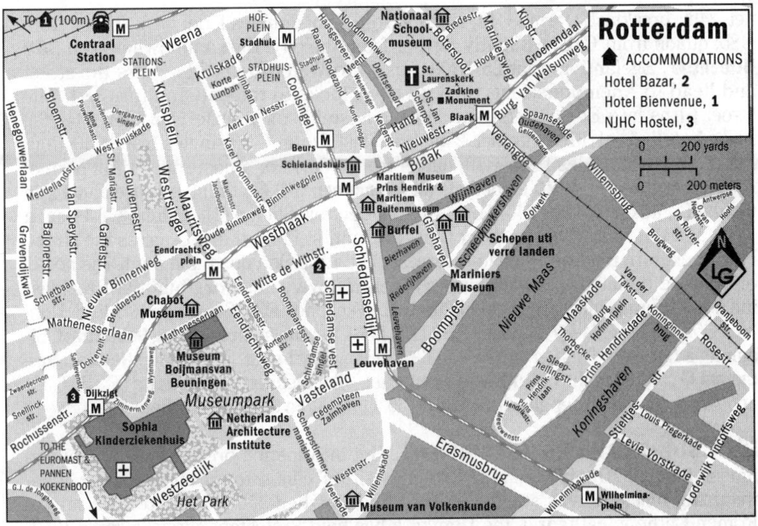

pile of cheese that weighs as much as you, head to **Kaaswaag Gouda (Weigh House Gouda),** Markt 35-36, which features a permanent exhibition about Gouda's cheese trade. (Open Apr.-Oct. Tu-W 1-5pm, Th 10am-5pm, F-Su 1-5pm. Entrance free during the cheese market.) Those with less interest in cheese can try **De Vlaam,** Markt 69, a bakery famous for its take on *sirupwafels.* (Open M-W and F 8:30am-6pm, Th 8:30am-9pm, Sa 8am-5pm.) The gargantuan, late Gothic **Sint Janskerk** has managed to maintain its collection of 16th-century stained-glass windows, despite attacks by both lightning and Reformation iconoclasts. (Open Mar.-Oct. M-Sa 9am-5pm; Nov.-Feb. M-Sa 10am-4pm. €1.90.) The **Goudse Pottenbakkerij "Adrie Moerings,"** Peperstraat 76, has produced the famous Gouda clay smoking pipes since the 17th century. (Open M-F 9am-5pm, Sa 11am-5pm. Free.) Around the corner on Oosthaven, the **Museum het Catharina Gasthuis,** Achter de Kerk 14, houses a wonderful collection of everything from Flemish art and early surgical instruments to period furniture, dolls, and weaponry. (Open M-Sa 10am-5pm, Su noon-5pm. €6.50.) **Trains** roll into town from Rotterdam (15min., round-trip €6) and Amsterdam (1hr., €8). From the station, cross the bridge and walk straight on Kleiweg, which turns into Hoogstr. and leads to the Markt and the VVV **tourist office.** (☎0900 468 32 888; www.vvvgouda.nl. Open M-Sa 9am-5pm; in summer also open Su noon-3pm.)

UTRECHT ☎030

With winding canals, a Gothic cathedral, a prestigious university, numerous museums, and a crazy nightlife, Utrecht (pop. 250,000) has something for everyone.

TRANSPORTATION AND PRACTICAL INFORMATION. **Trains** arrive in the **Hoog Catharijne** from Amsterdam (30min., 3-6 per hr., round-trip €9.50). To get to the VVV **tourist office,** Vinkenbrugstraat 19, follow the signs to Vredenberg, which leads to the town center. (☎0900 128 87 32; info@vvvutrecht.nl. Open M-W and F 9:30am-6:30pm, Th 9:30am-9pm, Sa 9:30am-5pm, Su 10am-2pm.)

ACCOMMODATIONS AND FOOD. Near the corner of Lucasbolwerk and Nobelstraat, **B&B Utrecht City Centre ❶,** Lucasbolwerk 4, offers a kitchen, sauna, piano, and home video system. (☎0650 434 884; www.hostelutrecht.nl. Free Internet. 24hr. breakfast. Dorms €16; singles from €55; doubles from €65; triples from €85; quads from €100.) Slightly farther from the city, the same owners run **B&B Utrecht ❶**, Egelantierstraat 25. Take bus #3 to Watertoren (€1), cross the street and head to Anemoonstraat, then go two blocks to the end and turn left. The street turns into Egelantierstraat and the hostel is on your left. (☎0650 434 884; www.hotelinfo.nl. Free Internet. 24hr. breakfast. Dorm €12; singles from €40; doubles from €45; triples from €70; quads from €85.) For a pastoral setting perfect for recharging, try **NJHC Ridderhofstad Rhijnauwen (HI) ❷**, Rhijnauwenselaan 14, in nearby Bunnik. Take bus #40, 41, or 43 from Centraal Station (10-15min., €2.10 each way) and tell the driver to let you off at Bunnik. From the stop, cross the street, backtrack, turn right on Rhijnauwenselaan, and it's 0.5km down the road. The hostel offers bike rental and a small bar. (☎656 12 77; www.njhc.org/bunnik. Breakfast included. Dorms July-Aug. weeknights €21, weekends €23; Sept.-June €2 less. Doubles €52; triples €64-€77; quads €78-€94.) Look for cheap meals along **Nobelstraat.** Sit among a hip crowd, either by the canal or in the cozy lounge area inside **Het Nachtrestaurant ❶**, Oudegracht 158, a "night restaurant." Try Mediterranean *tapas* (€2.50-6.50) and *sangría* (€3.10 per glass). (☎230 20 36. Open M-Sa 6pm-late, Su 3pm-late.)

SIGHTS AND ENTERTAINMENT. Get information on churches and museums at **RonDom,** Domplein 9, the Utrecht visitors' center for cultural history. Awe-inspiring **Domkerk** was started in 1254 and finished 250 years later. Initially a Roman Catholic cathedral, the Domkerk has held Protestant services since 1580. (Open M-Sa 10am-5pm, Su 2-4pm. Free.) The **Domtoren,** blown off the cathedral during a medieval tornado, is the highest tower in the Netherlands. (Tickets for tours sold at RonDom. Tours July-Aug. daily every 30min. 10am-4:30pm; Sept.-Jun. every hr. 10am-4pm. €6, children €3.60.) The Museum Quarter contains the core of Utrecht's extended family of museums, with something for absolutely everyone. The **Nationaal Museum Van Speelklok tot Pierement,** Buurkerkhof 10, traces the history of mechanical musical instruments. (☎231 27 89. Open Tu-Sa 10am-5pm, Su noon-5pm. Tours every hr. €6, under 12 €4.) At the nearby **Aboriginal Art Museum,** Oude Gracht 176, view ceremonial art from Australian Aborigines. (☎238 01 00. Open Tu-F 10am-5pm, Sa-Su 11am-5pm. €7, under 13 €5.) **Centraal Museum,** Nicolaaskerkhof 10, houses the largest collection of works by de Stijl designer Gerrit Reitveld. (☎236 23 62. Open Tu-Su 11am-5pm. €8, under 13 free.) If Reitveld's work inspires you, take bus #4 from Centraal Station to the **Reitveld Schroder House,** Prins Hendriklaan 50; it's like a Mondrian painting sprung to life. (☎236 23 10. Open W-Sa 11am-4:30pm, Su 12:30-4:30pm. Last tour 3:30pm. €8, under 14 €4) Visit **Museum Catherijnconvent,** Lange Nieuwstr. 38, located at the site of a medieval convent, to view an extensive collection of Christian art. (☎231 72 96. Open Tu-F 10am-5pm, Sa-Su 11am-5pm. €6, family ticket €15.)

Nightlife in Utrecht thrives seven days a week. **'t Oude Pothuys,** Oudegracht 279, has live music every night until 3am. At **Kafe Belgie,** Oudegracht 196, 196 different beers (€1.60 each) are sold. (Open F-Sa until 5am, Th 4am, Su-W 3am.) Students party at **Woolloo Moollo** on Janskerkhof 14. (Student ID required. Open W-Sa 11pm-late.) Find a similar crowd at **De Beurs,** Neude 35-37. (Open daily 10am-late.)

DE HOGE VELUWE NATIONAL PARK ☎0318

The impressive **Hoge Veluwe National Park** (HO-geh VEY-loo-wuh) is a 13,565-acre preserve of woods, heath, dunes, red deer, and wild boars. (☎59 16 27; www.hogeveluwe.nl. Park open June-July daily 8am-10pm; May and Aug. 8am-9pm; Sept. 9am-8pm; Apr. 8am-8pm; Oct. 9am-7pm; Nov.-Mar. 9am-5:30pm. €5, children 6-12 €2.50; 50% discount May-Sept. after 5pm.) Deep in the park, the **Rijksmuseum Kröller-Müller** has troves of van Goghs from the Kroller-Muller family's outstanding collection, as well as key works by Seurat, Mondrian, Picasso, and Brancusi. The museum's striking **sculpture garden,** one of the largest in Europe, has exceptional works by Rodin, Bourdelle, and Hepworth. (www.kmm.nl. Museum open Tu-Su 10am-5pm. Sculpture garden closes at 4:30pm. €5, children €2.75.) Take one of the free **bikes** in the park and get a map (€2) at the **Visitor's Center** to explore over 33km of paths. (☎055 378 81 19. Open daily 10am-5pm.)

ARNHEM. Home to several good restaurants and nightclubs, Arnhem makes a good base for exploring the national park. To get to the VVV **tourist office,** Willemsplein 8, exit the train station, turn left, and walk one block. (☎0900 202 40 75; www.vvvarnhem.nl. Open M 11am-5:30pm, Tu-F 9am-5:30pm, Sa 10am-4pm.) Stay at the **NJHC Herberg Alteveer (HI) ❷,** Diepenbrocklaan 27. Take bus #3 from the station to Rijnstate Hospital; as you face the hospital, turn right, then left on Cattepoelseweg; about 150m ahead, turn right up the brick steps, and at the top turn right to reach the hostel. (☎026 442 01 14; arnhem@njhc.org. Breakfast included. Reception 8am-11pm. Dorms €20-22; singles €28-30; doubles €50-53; triples €69-73; quads €87-93. Nonmembers add €2.50.) Take bus #2 (dir.: Haedaveld; 20min., 3 strips) to **Camping Arnhem ❶,** Kemperbergerweg 771. (☎026 443 16 00; www.holiday.nl/arnhem. Showers free. Open Apr.-Oct. €11 per person.) **Pizzeria Pinoccio ❶,** Korenmarkt 25b, has good pizza (€6-11), a great location, and even better prices. (Open M-W 5pm-9:30pm, Th-F 5pm-10pm, Sa-Su 4pm-10pm.) The nightlife in Arnhem can be surprisingly good. Join the 20-somethings at **Luther Danscafe,** Korenmarkt 26, for three floors of fun. (Beer €2. Open Th-Sa 6pm-2am; in summer W 1pm-1am, Th-F 1pm-2am, Su 1pm-1am.) **Speak Easy,** on Varkensstraat, is a chill coffeeshop. (Joints from €2.50; free coffee or tea with purchase. Open M-T 9am-11pm, W-Su 9am-midnight.)

NEAR ARNHEM: NATIONAAL PARK VELUWEZOOM AND APELDOORN. From the Arnhem train station, take bus #43b and ask the driver to let you off at Groenenstraat (20min., 4 strips) to visit the **Nationaal Park Veluwezoom,** a pine-forest nature preserve with bike and footpaths. (☎495 30 50; www.natuurmonumenten.nl. €2.75). Within the park, the **Kasteel Rosendael** is a furnished 18th-century castle with an 800 year-old tower. (Open T-Su 10am-5pm. €3.60.)

Apeldoorn is another good jumping off place for De Hoge Veluwe. The town is home to the magnificent **Museum Paleis Het Loo,** a 17th-century palace that was home to the many King Willems of Orange. (Open Tu-Su 10am-5pm. €3.) Bus #2 or 3 (10min., 2 strips) to nearby **Apenheul,** or "apes' refuge," an interactive zoo with 30 different species of apes. (www.apenheul.nl. Open Apr.-Aug. daily 9:30am-6pm; Sept.-Oct. 9:30am-5pm. €12.) The VVV **tourist office,** Stationstraat 72, 5min. straight ahead from the station, sells bike maps (€4). (☎0 900 168 16 36. Open M-F 9am-5:30pm, Sa 9am-5pm.) To stay at the lively **NJHC: De Grote Beer ❷,** Asselsestraat 330, take bus #4 or 7 (dir.: Orden) from the station, get off at Chamavenlaan, cross the street, turn left, walk past the intersection and the hostel will be 150m ahead, on the right. (☎355 31 18; apeldoorn@njhc.org. Dorms €22.50; nonmembers add €2.50.) For food, head to the Apeldoorn city center, which is north of the train station. Take Stationsstraat two blocks past the VVV and into the **Marktplein.**

MAASTRICHT ☎043

Situated on a narrow strip of land between Belgium and Germany, Maastricht (pop. 120,000) is one of the oldest cities in The Netherlands. It has been a symbol of European unity since the 1991 Maastricht Treaty, which established the European Union. Home of the prestigious **Jan van Eyck Academie of Art,** Maastricht is also known for its abundance of art galleries and antique stores. The striking **Bonnefantenmuseum,** Av. Ceramique 250, contrasts Maastricht's traditional Dutch brickwork with its futuristic rocketship design. The museum houses permanent collections of archaeological artifacts, medieval sculpture, Northern Renaissance painting, and contemporary art. (www.bonnefanten.nl. Open Tu-Su 11am-5pm. €7; students €6.) Despite its contemporary status as the birthplace of modern European unity, Maastricht has seen its share of interstate rivalries—centuries of foreign threats culminated in an innovative subterranean defense system. The **Mount Saint Peter Caves'** 20,000 underground passages were used as a siege shelter as late as WWII, and contain inscriptions and artwork by generations of inhabitants. Access to the caves is possible only with a tour guide at two locations: the **Northern System** (Grotten Noord), Luikerweg 71 (tours in Dutch, and English available depending on guide; €3); and the **Zonneberg Caves,** Slavante 1 (tours in English July-Aug. daily 2:45pm; €3). Maastricht's above-ground marvels include the **Basilica of Saint Servatius,** Keizer Karelpl., off the central Vrijthof Square, which contains ornate ecclesiastical crafts, 11th-century crypts, and the country's largest bell, affectionately known as **Grameer** (Grandmother). (Open July-Aug. daily 10am-6pm; Sept.-June 10am-5pm. €2.) The medieval **Basilica of Our Dear Lady,** O.L. Vrouwepl., honors Mary with a dark interior and colorful stained glass windows. (Open daily 11am-5pm. Free.) The **Natuurhistorich Museum,** De Bosuetpl. 6-7, features the remains of a newly discovered ancient species, the Montasaurus dinosaur, and giant turtles found fossilized in the sandstone of the St. Pietersberg caves. (www.nhmmaastricht.nl. Open M-F 10am-5pm, Sa-Su 2-5pm. €3.) The **Derlon Museum Cellar,** Planckstr. 21, displays 2nd- to 4th-century Roman artifacts discovered during construction of the Derlon Hotel. (Open Su noon-4pm. Free.)

The train station is on the eastern side of town, across the river from most of the action. **Trains** arrive from Amsterdam (2½hr., €24). To get from the train station to the VVV **tourist office,** Kleine Staat 1, walk straight on Station Str., cross the bridge, go one more block, take a right, and walk down a block; the office will be on the right. (☎325 21 21. Open May-Oct. M-Sa 9am-6pm, Su 11am-3pm; Nov.-Apr. M-F 9am-6pm, Sa 9am-5pm.) Spend the night on the centrally located **Botel ❷,** Maasboulevard 95, a boat with tiny cabins and a cozy deckroom lounge. (☎321 90 23. Reception 24hr. Singles €27-30; doubles €41-43; triples €60.) **Le Virage ❺,** Cortenstraat 2-2b, has four spacious suites with a bedroom, living room, kitchenette, and bathroom. (☎321 66 08; www.levirage.nl. Doubles €90; triples €113; quads €136.) To get from the train station to **City-Hostel de Dousberg (HI) ❷,** Dousbergweg 4, take bus #11 on weekdays, bus #33 on weeknights after 6pm, and bus #8 or 18 on weekends. (☎346 67 77; www.dousberg.nl. Breakfast included with HI membership. Dorms €20; triples €75.) Cheap food can be found around the central **Vrijthof** area. **De Blindgenger ❶,** Koestraat 3, is a warm cafe with tasty *dagschotel* (€8) and antique mirrors. (Open daily 11am-11pm.) Enjoy the view at hilltop **Chalet Bergrust ❶,** Luikerweg 71, a low-priced Dutch cafe. (Open daily in summer 10am-10pm; otherwise open W and F-Su 11am-6pm.) For entertainment info, check out the free *Uit in Maastricht.* Grab a tasty brew (€1.60) at **Falstaff,** Amorspl. 6. (Open Su-Th 11am-2am, F and Sa 11am-3am.) **Night Live,** Kesselkade 43, is a church converted to a disco. (Cover €4-6. Open Th-Sa 11pm-6am.)

GRONINGEN ☎050

With 35,000 students and the nightlife to prove it, Groningen (pop. 175,000) ranks as perhaps the most happening city in the northern region of the Netherlands. The town's spectacular **Groninger Museum,** a unique pastel assemblage of squares, cylinders, and metal, forms a bridge between the station and the city center. The multicolored galleries create a futuristic laboratory atmosphere for their contemporary art exhibits. (www.groninger-museum.nl. Open Tu-Su 10am-5pm; July and Aug. also open M 1-5pm. €6, seniors €5, ages 5-15 €3, under 5 free.) Admire the city from atop the Grote Markt's **Martinitoren Tower,** which weathered the German attacks during World War II. (Open daily Apr.-Oct. 11am-5pm; Nov.-Mar. noon-4pm. €2.20, under 13 €1.20.) Relax in the serene 16th-century **Prinsenhoftuin** (Princes' Court Gardens); the entrance is on the canal 10min. away from the Martinitorin. (Open Apr. to mid-Oct. daily 10am-dusk.) Inside the gardens, the tiny **Theeschenkerij Tea Hut** offers 130 kinds of tea (€0.80). Cool off at **Noorderplantsoen,** a fountain-filled park that serves as host space to the huge **Noorderzon (Northern Sun) Festival** of art in late August, Groningen's annual cultural climax.

Trains roll in from Amsterdam (2½hr., every 30min., €23.80). To reach the VVV **tourist office,** Grote Markt 25, turn right as you exit the station, walk along the canal, turn left at the first bridge, head straight through the Hereplein on Herestr., cross Gedempte Zuiderdiep, and keep on Herestr. until it hits the Grote Markt. (☎(0900) 202 30 50; www.vvvgroningen.nl. Open M-W and F 9am-6pm, Th 9am-8pm, Sa 10am-5pm; July-Aug. also Su 11am-3pm.) A fun crowd hangs out at **Simplon Youthhotel ❶,** Boterdiep 73-2. Take bus #1 from the station (dir.: Korrewegwijk) to Boterdiep; the hostel is through the yellow- and white-striped entranceway. (☎313 52 21; www.xs4all.nl/~simplon. Breakfast €3.40. Free lockers. Sheets €2.50, included in private rooms. Lockout noon-3pm. All-female dorm available. Dorms €10.90; singles €28.35; doubles €41.30; triples €59; quads €76.) For cheap pitchers of beer and shoulder-to-shoulder packed bars, head to the southeastern corner of Grote Markt on Poelestraat and Peperstraat. The intimate, candlelit **de Spieghel Jazz Café,** Peperstr. 11, has two floors of live jazz, funk, or blues every night. (Wine €2 per glass. Open daily 8pm-4am.) **Postal code:** 9725.

WADDEN ISLANDS (WADDENEILANDEN)

Wadden means "mudflat" in Dutch, but sand is the defining characteristic of these islands, with gorgeous beaches hidden behind ridges covered in golden grass. Deserted, tulip-lined bike trails carve through vast, flat stretches of grazing land to the sea. Sleepy and isolated, the islands are truly Holland's best-kept secret.

TRANSPORTATION. The islands arch clockwise around the northwestern coast of Holland: Texel (closest to Amsterdam), Vlieland, Terschelling, Ameland, and Schiermonnikoog. To reach Texel, take the **train** from Amsterdam to Den Helder (1½hr., €11), **bus** #33 (2 strips), and a **ferry** to 't Hoorntje, the southernmost town on Texel (20min., every hr. 6:30am-9:30pm, round-trip €4). **Buses** depart from the ferry dock to various locales throughout the island, though the best way to travel is to rent a **bike** from **Verhuurbedrijf Heijne,** opposite the ferry dock. (From €4.50 per day. Open Apr.-Oct. daily 9am-8pm; Nov.-Mar. 9am-6pm.) To reach the other islands from Amsterdam, grab a **train** from Centraal station to Harlingen (3hr., €25). From Harlingen, **ferries** (☎0517 49 15 00; www.rederij-doeksen.nl) depart for Terschelling (1-2 hr., 3-5 per day, €18).

TEXEL. The southernmost and largest of the Wadden Islands, Texel boasts stunning beaches and delightful museums. The most popular **beaches** lie near De Koog, on the western side of the island. Head farther north or south from town to reach the less crowded sands. **Nude beaches** beckon the uninhibited; you can bare it all near paal 9 (2km southwest of Den Hoorn) or paal 27 (5km west of De Cocksdorp). Say hi to the playful *zeehonden* (seals) at the **Ecomare Museum and Aquarium,** Ruijslaan 92, in De Koog. (www.ecomare.nl. Open daily 9am-5pm. €7, under 13 €3.50.) The staff can also arrange a tour of the surrounding **nature reserves;** ask for an English-speaking guide. A working windmill marks the site of the **Maritime and Beachcomber's Museum,** Barentzstr. 21, in Oudeschild. The museum has a creepy selection of relics scavenged from shipwrecks and an artful presentation of washed-ashore detritus. Don't miss its recreation of a sunken ship; step inside to experience creaky decks and underwater noises. (☎0222 31 49 56; www.texelsmaritiem.nl. Open July-Aug. M-Sa 10am-5pm; Sept.-June Tu-Sa 10am-5pm. €4.)

A **Texel Ticket** (€3.50) allows unlimited one-day travel on the island's bus system. (Runs mid-June to mid-Sept.). The VVV **tourist office,** Emmaln 66, is located just outside Den Burg, about 300m south of the main bus stop; look for the blue signs. (☎0222 31 47 41; www.texel.net. Open M-Th 9am-6pm, F 9am-9pm, Sa 9am-5:30pm; July-Aug. also Su 10am-1:30pm.) Rent a **bike** from **Verhuurbedrijf Heijne,** opposite the 't Horntje ferry dock in Texel. (From €4.50 per day. Open Apr.-Oct. daily 9am-8pm;

Nov.-Mar. 9am-6pm.) To get to **Panorama (HI) ❶**, Schansweg 7, take bus #29 and tell the driver your destination. The hostel is snuggled amid sheep pastures, 7km from the dock at 't Hoorntje and 3km from Den Burg's center. (☎0222 31 54 41. Bikes from €4 per day. Breakfast and sheets included. Reception daily 8:30am-10:30pm. Dorms €15-19, nonmembers add €2.50.) The tiny **Hotel de Merel ❸**, Warmoerstr. 22, is in the center of Den Burg. From the bus stop in Den Burg Square, turn left on Elemert and left again on Warmoerstr. (☎0222 31 31 32. Breakfast included. Reception daily 8am-10pm. Singles from €47; doubles from €64.) **Campgrounds** cluster south of De Koog and near De Cocksdorp; ask at the tourist office. The **De 12 Balcken Tavern,** Weverstr. 20 in Den Burg, serves up giant portions of spare ribs with french fries and salad for €12. Try a shot of *'t Jutterje*, the island's popular licorice-flavored schnapps, for €2. (Open M-Sa 10am-2am, Su 5pm-2am. Kitchen open until 10pm.) Grab groceries at **Albert Heijn,** Waalderstr. 48, in De Burg. (Open M-Sa 8am-8pm.)

At night, the young and sunburned head to shoreside De Koog for its sprightly **nightlife;** check out the wild **Cafe Sam-Sam,** Dorpstr. 146. (70s parties every Th night in summer. Beer €1.50, mixed drinks €4.50. Open daily 9pm-3am.) For a slightly more sophisticated, but no less lively crowd, try **Le Berry,** Dorpstr. 3. (Open daily noon-3am, no entry after 2am.) **Den Burg** is an up-and-coming hot spot; dance the night away with a teen crowd at **Question Plaza,** Kantoorstr. 1. (Cover €6. Open daily 9pm-3am; no entry after 2am.) For live music and locally-brewed beer, join the 20-somethings at **De Pilaar,** Kantoorstr. 5. (Beer €1.80. Open daily 8pm-3am; no entry after 2am.)

TERSCHELLING. With 80% of the island covered by a European Nature Reserve, Terschelling offers secluded **beaches** and green pastures spotted with cows and horses. Don't miss the view from the western tip of the island; at the ferry landing, turn left and walk till you can walk no further—at the statue of the sailor is an unparalleled view of infinite blue waves, lilting sailboats, and sandy stretches. To explore the rest of the island's striking scenery, rent a **bike** from **Tijs Knop,** Torenstr. 10-12, one block up from the pier. (☎0562 44 20 52. From €4.50 per day, €20 per week.) **JOBA Sports** runs rugged off-road bike tours through the nature reserve. (☎0562 44 93 24; www.joba-sports.nl. Tours €27.) Meet the seals of the Waddenzee on a harbor tour with **Stella Maris Zeehonden.** (☎0562 44 40 85. 2½hr.; departure times depend on weather and season; call ahead to reserve a spot.)

Both tours can also be booked at the VVV **tourist office,** W. Barentzkade 19, which sits opposite the ferry landing. (☎0562 44 30 00. Open M-Sa 9:30am-5:30pm.) The **Terschelling Hostel (HI) ❶,** van Heusdenweg 39, is located just out of town on the waterfront. With your back to the harbor, take a right, walk along the pier, and continue 1.5km on the bike path to Midland; it's on the left, when the paved road curves away from the ocean. (☎0562 44 23 38; www.njhc.org/terschelling. Breakfast and sheets included. Laundry €7. Reception daily 9am-10pm. Dorms €18-21; ask for the backpacker special.) Campgrounds abound on Terschelling, especially along the Midslander Hoofdweg on the southwest coast. **Camping Cupido ❶,** Hee 8, is located 3km east of Terschelling West; turn left at the second blue "Hee" sign. (☎0562 44 22 19. Reception daily 9am-7pm. €3 per person; €2-2.75 per tent.) The best place to grab a bite is in the island's main village, **Terschelling West.** At **Amsterdamsche Koffijuis ❷,** Willem Barentszstr. 21, around the corner from the tourist office, munch on a variety of tasty *tapas* during lunch or dinner; then groove to world music after 9pm. (Open daily 11am-2am; dinner served 5-9:30pm.) **Zeezicht ❷,** Wm. Barentszkade 20, has enormous dinner portions (€12-16.50) and a sweeping view of the ocean. (Open daily 10am-midnight; kitchen closes at 9:30pm.) Pick up food and camping supplies at **Supermarkt Spanjer,** Boomstr. 13. (Open M-F 8am-8pm, Sa 8am-5pm.) Young people flood Terschelling on summer nights; head to **Braskoer,** Torenstr. 32, to join a younger crowd on a sweaty, packed dance floor. (Beer €2.50. Cover €5. Open 10am-2am, dancing from 9pm.) For a more relaxed evening, kick back at **Cafe De Zeevaart,** Torenstr. 22. (Beer €1.80. Open daily 10am-2am.)

PORTUGAL

In the era of Christopher Columbus, Vasco da Gama, and Magellan, Portugal was one of the world's most powerful nations, ruling a wealthy empire that stretched from America to Asia. Today, it is often overshadowed by its larger neighbor Spain. But while it shares the beaches, nightlife, and strong architectural heritage of the Iberian Peninsula, Portugal is culturally and geographically quite unique. It contains the most pristine wilderness areas in all of Europe, and some villages in the northeast have barely changed in over 800 years. Despite ongoing modernization, Portugal's rich, age-old traditions seem destined to stay—rows of olive trees give way to ancient castles, and Porto's wines are as fine as ever.

SYMBOL	❶	❷	❸	❹	❺
ACCOMMODATIONS	under €15	€16-25	€26-35	€36-50	over €50
FOOD	under €6	€6-10	€11-15	€16-25	over €25

For Portugal, prices are indicated in food and accommodations listings using the system of icons and price ranges above. Prices for accommodations are based on the lowest cost for one person, excluding special deals or discounts. For restaurants, prices are based on the average entree price.

SUGGESTED ITINERARIES

THREE DAYS Make your way through **Lisbon**'s (1 day; p. 808) famous Moorish district, the **Alfama,** up to the **Castelo de São Jorge,** and to the futuristic **Parque das Nações.** By night, listen to *fado* and hit the clubs in **Barrio Alto.** Daytrip to **Sintra**'s fairy tale castles (p. 818) before sipping sweet port in **Porto** (1 day; p. 830).

ONE WEEK From **Lisbon** (2 days) and **Sintra** (1 day), lounge on the beaches of **Lagos** (1 day; p. 824) and **Praia da Rocha** (1 day; p. 826), then move on to the university town of **Coimbra** (1 day; p. 827), and end your week in **Porto** (1 day).

BEST OF PORTUGAL, TWO WEEKS After the sights, sounds, and cafes of **Lisbon** (2 days), daytrip to **Sintra** (1 day). Head down to the infamous beach-and-bar town **Lagos** (2 days), where hordes of visitors dance the night away, and take an afternoon in **Sagres** (p. 826), once considered the end of the world. Check out the bone chapel in **Évora** (1 day; p. 822) and the mysterious convent in **Tomar** (1 day; p. 819). Head north to **Coimbra** (2 days) and **Porto** (2 days), then finish your tour in the impressive squares of **Viana do Castelo** (1 day; p. 832).

LIFE AND TIMES

HISTORY

EARLY HISTORY. The first clearly identifiable inhabitants of the Iberian peninsula were the **Celts,** who began to settle in northern Portugal and Spanish Galicia in the 8th century BC. The **Greeks** and **Carthaginians** followed them, settling the coasts. After their victory over Carthage in the **Second Punic War** (218-201 BC) and their defeat of the Celts in 140 BC, the **Romans** gained control of central and southern Portugal. Six centuries of Roman rule, which introduced the *Pax Romana* and "Latinized" Portugal's language and customs, paved the way for Christianity.

VISIGOTHS AND ARABIAN KNIGHTS (469-1139). The Iberian Peninsula felt the effects of the Roman Empire's decline in the 3rd and 4th centuries AD. By AD 469, the **Visigoths,** a tribe of migrating Germanic people, had crossed the Pyrenees, and for the next two centuries they dominated the peninsula. In AD 711, however, the Muslims (also known as the **Moors**) invaded Iberia, toppling the Visigoth monarchy. Although these invaders centered their new kingdom of *al-Andalus* in Córdoba, smaller Muslim communities settled along Portugal's southern coast, an area they called the *al-Gharb* (now the Algarve); through nearly four centuries of rule, the Muslims left a significant legacy of agricultural advances, architectural landmarks, and linguistic and cultural customs.

THE CHRISTIAN RECONQUISTA AND THE BIRTH OF PORTUGAL (1139-1415). Though the *Reconquista* officially began in 718, it didn't pick up steam until the 11th century, when Fernando I united Castilla and León and provided a strong base from which to reclaim territory. In 1139, **Afonso Henriques** (Afonso I), a noble from the frontier territory of Portucale (a region centered around Porto), declared independence from Castilla and León. Soon thereafter he named himself the first King of Portugal, though the papacy did not officially recognize the title until 1179.

With the help of Christian military groups like the Knights Templar, the new monarchy battled Muslim forces, capturing Lisbon in 1147. By 1249, the *Reconquista* defeated the last remnants of Muslim power with successful campaigns in the Alentejo and the Algarve. The Christian kings, led by **Dinis I** (Dom Dinis; 1279-1325), promoted use of the Portuguese language (instead of Spanish) and with the **Treaty of Alcañices** (1297) settled border disputes with neighboring Castilla, asserting Portugal's identity as the first unified, independent nation in Europe.

THE AGE OF DISCOVERY (1415-1580). The reign of **João I** (1385-1433), the first king of the House of Aviz, ushered in unity and prosperity never before seen in Portugal. João increased the power of the crown and in doing so established a strong base for future Portuguese expansion and economic success.

The 15th century was one of the greatest periods in the history of maritime travel and naval advances. Under the leadership of João's son, **Prince Henry the Navigator,** Portugal established itself as a world leader in maritime science and exploration. Portuguese adventurers captured the Moroccan city of Ceuta in 1415, discovered the Madeiras Islands in 1419, happened upon the uninhabited Azores in 1427, and began to exploit the African coast for slaves and riches a few years later.

Bartolomeu Dias changed the world forever when he rounded Africa's Cape of Good Hope in 1488. Dias opened the route to the East and paved the way for Portuguese entrance into the spice trade. The Portuguese monarchs may have turned down **Christopher Columbus,** but they did fund a number of momentous voyages. In 1497, they supported **Vasco da Gama,** who led the first European naval expedition to India; successive expeditions added numerous East African and Indian colonies

to Portugal's empire. Three years after da Gama's voyage, **Pedro Álvares Cabral** claimed Brazil for Portugal, and Portugal established a far-flung empire.

Portugal's monarchy reached its peak with **Manuel the Fortunate** (1495-1521) on the throne. Known to foreigners as "the King of Gold," Manuel controlled a spectacular commercial empire. However, before the House of Aviz lost power in 1580, signs of future decline were already becoming evident, and it was not long before competition from other commercial powers took its toll.

THE HOUSES OF HABSBURG AND BRAGANÇA (1580-1807). In 1580, Habsburg King of Spain **Felipe II** forcibly affirmed his quasi-legitimate claim to the Portuguese throne, and the Iberian Peninsula was briefly ruled by one monarch. For

60 years, the Habsburg family dragged Portugal into several ill-fated wars, including the **Spanish-Portuguese Armada**'s crushing loss to England in 1588. But by the end of Habsburg rule, Portugal had lost much of its once vast empire. In 1640, during a rebellion against King Felipe IV, the **House of Bragança** assumed control, once again asserting Portuguese independence from Spain.

The momentous **earthquake of 1755** devastated Lisbon and southern Portugal, killing over 15,000 people. Despite the damage, dictatorial minister **Marquês de Pombal** was able to rebuild Lisbon while instituting national economic reform.

NAPOLEON'S CONQUEST AND ITS AFTERMATH (1807-1910). Napoleon took control of France in 1801 and had grand designs on much of Europe. His army met little resistance when it invaded Portugal in 1807. Rather than risk death, the Portuguese royal family fled to Brazil. The **Constitution of 1822,** drawn up during the royal family's absence, severely limited the power of the monarchy, and after 1826, the ultimate sibling rivalry exploded into the **War of the Two Brothers** (1826-1834) between constitutionalists (supporting Pedro, the new king of Brazil) and monarchists (supporting Miguel, Pedro's brother), which reverberated through Portugal.

FROM THE "FIRST REPUBLIC" TO SALAZAR (1910-1974). Portugal spent the first few years of the 20th century trying to recover from the political discord of the previous century. On October 5, 1910, 20-year-old King **Manuel II** fled to England. The new government, known as the **First Republic,** earned worldwide disapproval for its expulsion of the Jesuits and other religious orders, and the conflict between the government and labor movements heightened tensions at home. Portugal's decision to enter **World War I** (even though on the side of the victorious Allies) proved economically fatal and internally divisive. The weak republic wobbled and eventually fell in a 1926 military coup. General **António Carmona** took over as leader of the provisional military government, and in the face of financial crisis appointed **António de Oliveira Salazar,** a prominent economics professor, his minister of finance. In 1932 Salazar became prime minister, but he soon evolved into a dictator. His *Estado Novo* (New State) granted suffrage to women, but did little else to end the country's authoritarian tradition. While Portugal's international economic standing improved, the regime laid the cost of progress squarely on the shoulders of the working class, the peasantry, and colonial subjects in Africa. A terrifying secret police (PIDE) crushed all opposition to Salazar's rule, and African rebellions were quelled in bloody battles that drained the nation's economy.

REVOLUTION AND REFORM (1974-2000). The slightly more liberal **Marcelo Caetano** dragged on the increasingly unpopular African wars after Salazar's death in 1970. On April 25, 1974, a left-wing military coalition calling itself the **Armed Forces Movement,** under **Francisco da Costa Gomes,** overthrew Caetano in a quick coup. The **Revolution of the Carnations** sent Portuguese dancing into the streets; today, every town in Portugal has its own **Rua 25 de Abril.** The Marxist-dominated armed forces established a variety of civil and political liberties and withdrew Portuguese claims on African colonies by 1975. The landmark year 1986 brought Portugal into the European Community (now the **European Union**), ending its age-old isolation from affluent northern Europe.

TODAY

The European Union declared Portugal a full member of the EU Economic and Monetary Union (EMU) in 1999, and the nation continues in its quest to catch up economically with the rest of Western Europe. In 1999, Macau, Portugal's last overseas territory, was ceded to the Chinese.

Portugal has been a republic since 1910. The President represents the nation, is commander of armed forces, and appoints the Prime Minister in accordance with the results of parliamentary elections. **President Jorge Fernando Branco de Sampaio,** of the center-left Socialist Party, won a second term in January of 2001. However, like many European countries, Portugal has recently swung to the right. Socialist Prime Minister Antonio Guterres resigned in December of 2001 after his party suffered heavy losses in parliamentary elections, in which the conservative Popular Party joined with the center-right Social Democratic Party and won the majority. President Sampaio then appointed **Prime Minister Jose Manuel Durao Barroso** as the representative of the newly merged parties. Barroso has pledged to strengthen the Portuguese economy and reduce government spending.

CULTURE

FOOD & DRINK

Dishes are seasoned with olive oil, garlic, herbs, and sea salt, but few spices. The fish selection includes **chocos grelhados** (grilled cuttlefish), **linguado grelhado** (grilled sole), and **peixe espada** (swordfish). **Sandes** (cheese sandwiches) come on delectable bread. For dessert, try **pudim** or **flan** (caramel custard). The hearty **almoço** (lunch) is eaten between noon and 2pm, **jantar** (dinner) between 8pm and midnight. **Meia dose** (half-portions) are often adequate; full portions may satisfy two. The **prato do dia** (special of the day) or **ementa** (menu) of appetizer, bread, entree, and dessert are also filling. **Vinho do porto** (port) is a dessert in itself. **Madeira** wines have a unique "cooked" flavor. **Coffee** is *bica* (black espresso), *galão* (with milk, served in a glass), or *café com leite* (with milk, in a cup).

CUSTOMS & ETIQUETTE

Much like Spaniards, Portuguese are generally friendly, easygoing, and receptive to foreign travelers. If you greet a local with a smile and forgive them for their recurrent lack of punctuality, you'll fit right in. Even if your Portuguese is a little rusty, a wholehearted attempt at speaking the native tongue will be appreciated.

TABOOS. Be cautious of shorts and flip-flops; they may be seen as disrespectful in some public establishments or in more rural areas, even during a heat wave. Though dress in Portugal is more casual in the hot summer months than in the cold of winter, strapless tops on women and collarless t-shirts on men are generally unacceptable. Skimpy clothes are always a taboo in churches.

PUBLIC BEHAVIOR. On any list of Portuguese values, politeness would be at the top. Be sure to address people as *senhor* (Mr.), *senhora* (Mrs.), or *senhora dona* followed by the first name (for older and respected women). You'll be welcomed openly and made to feel at home if you mention who you are, where you're from, and what you are doing in Portugal.

THE ARTS

PAINTING. The Age of Discovery (1415-1580) was an era of vast cultural exchange with Renaissance Europe and beyond. High Renaissance artist **Jorge Afonso,** King Manuel's favorite, created realistic portrayals of human anatomy. Afonso's best works hang at the Convento de Cristo in **Tomar** (see p. 819) and the **Convento da Madre de Deus** in Lisbon (see p. 808). In the 20th century, Cubism, Expressionism and Futurism trickled into Portugal. More recently, **Maria Helena Vieira da Silva** has won international recognition for her abstract works, and **Carlos Botelho** has become world-renowned for his wonderful vignettes of Lisbon life.

ARCHITECTURE. Portugal's signature **Manueline** style celebrates the prosperity and imperial expansion of King Manuel I's reign. Manueline pieces routinely merge Christian images and maritime motifs. Their rich and lavish ornaments reflect a hybrid of Northern Gothic, Spanish Plateresque, and Moorish influences. The Manueline style found its most elaborate expression in the church and tower at Belém (see p. 816), built to honor Vasco da Gama. Close seconds are the **Mosteiro dos Jerónimos** in Belém and the **Abadia de Santa Maria de Vitória** in Batalha (see p. 819).

LITERATURE. Modernist poet **Fernando Pessoa** was Portugal's most famous author at the turn of the 20th century. **José Saramago,** winner of the 1998 Nobel Prize for Literature, is perhaps Portugal's most important living writer. He is best known for *Baltasar and Blimunda* (1982), the story of lovers who escape the Inquisition in a time machine, and *The Stone Raft* (1986), a satire about Iberia's isolation from the rest of Europe.

HOLIDAYS AND FESTIVALS

Holidays: New Year's Day (Jan. 1); Good Friday (Apr. 18); Easter (Apr. 20); Liberation Day (Apr. 25); Labor Day (May 1); Feast of the Assumption (Aug. 15); Republic Day (Oct. 5); All Saints' Day (Nov. 1); Feast of the Immaculate Conception (Dec. 8); Christmas (Dec. 25).

Festivals: All of Portugal celebrates **Carnival** March 4 and the **Holy Week** Apr. 13-20. Coimbra holds the **Burning of the Ribbons** festival in early May, and Lisbon hosts the **Feira Internacional de Lisboa** in June. Coimbra's **Feira Popular** takes place the 2nd week of July. For more information on Portuguese festivals, see www.portugal.org.

ESSENTIALS

FACTS AND FIGURES	
Official Name: Portuguese Republic.	**Land Area:** 91,951 sq. km.
Capital: Lisbon.	**Time Zone:** GMT.
Major Cities: Porto, Coimbra.	**Language:** Portuguese.
Population: 10 million.	**Religion:** Roman Catholic (94%).

WHEN TO GO

Summer is high season, but the southern coast draws tourists March through November. In the off-season, many hostels cut their prices by 50% or more, and reservations are seldom necessary. But while Lisbon and some of the larger towns (especially Coimbra, with its university) burst with vitality year-round, many smaller towns virtually shut down, and sights cut their hours nearly everywhere.

DOCUMENTS AND FORMALITIES

South Africans need a visa for stays of any length. Citizens of Australia, Canada, the EU, New Zealand, and the US do not need a visa for stays of up to 90 days.

Portuguese Embassies at Home: Australia, 23 Culgoa Circuit, O'Malley, ACT 2603. Mailing address P.O. Box 9092, Deakin, ACT 2600 (☎62 90 17 33; emb-port@mail2me.com.au). **Canada,** 645 Island Park Dr., Ottawa, ON K1Y 0B8 (☎613 729 0883). **South Africa,** 599 Leyds St., Muckleneuk, Pretoria (☎12 341 2340; portemb@satis.co.ca). **UK,** 11 Belgrave Sq., London SW1X 8PP (☎020 7581 8722). **US,** 2125 Kalorama Rd. NW, Washington D.C. 20008 (☎202-328-8610). **New Zealanders** should refer to the Australian embassy.

Foreign Embassies in Portugal: Most foreign embassies are in **Lisbon** (p. 810).

TRANSPORTATION

BY PLANE. Most international airlines serve Lisbon; some serve Porto, Faro, and the Madeiras. **TAP Air Portugal** (in Lisbon ☎218 43 11 00, in US and Canada ☎800-221-7370, in UK ☎0845 601 09 32; www.tap.pt) is Portugal's national airline, serving all domestic locations and many major international cities. **Portugália** (www.pga.pt) is a smaller Portuguese airline that flies between Porto, Faro, Lisbon, all major Spanish cities, and other Western European destinations.

BY TRAIN. Caminhos de Ferro Portugueses (www.cp.pt) is Portugal's national railway, but buses are much better for long-distance travel outside of the Braga-Porto-Coimbra-Lisbon line. The exception is around Lisbon, where local trains are fast and efficient. Trains often leave at irregular hours, and posted schedules *(horarios)* aren't always accurate; check station ticket booths upon arrival. Unless you own a Eurail, **round-trip tickets** must be used before 3am the following day. Don't ride without a ticket; if you're caught *sem bilhete* you'll be fined exorbitantly. Though there is a Portugal Flexipass, it is not worth buying.

BY BUS. Buses are cheap, frequent, and connect just about every town in Portugal. **Rodoviária** (national info ☎213 54 57 75), the national bus company, has recently been privatized. Each company name corresponds to a particular region of the country, such as Rodoviária Alentejo or Minho e Douro, with notable exceptions such as EVA in the Algarve. Be wary of non-express buses in small regions like Estremadura and Alentejo, which stop every few minutes. Express coach service *(expressos)* between major cities is especially good; inexpensive city buses often run to nearby villages.

BY CAR. Portugal has the highest rate of automobile accidents per capita in Western Europe. The new highway system (IP) is quite good, but off the main arteries, the narrow, twisting roads are difficult to negotiate. Speed limits are ignored, recklessness is common, and lighting and road surfaces are often inadequate. Buses are safer options. Moreover, parking space in cities borders on nonexistent. **Gas** prices run about €0.60-0.90 per liter. Portugal's national automobile association, the **Automóvel Clube de Portugal (ACP),** R. Rosa Araújo 42, 1250 Lisbon (☎123 18 01 00), provides breakdown and towing service (M-F 9am-5pm) and first aid (24hr.).

BY THUMB. Hitchers are rare in Portugal. Rides are easiest to come by at gas stations near highways and rest stops. *Let's Go* does not recommend hitchhiking.

TOURIST SERVICES AND MONEY

EMERGENCY	Dial ☎**112** for police, medical, or fire.

TOURIST OFFICES. The official tourism website is www.portugalinsite.pt. When in Portugal, stop by municipal and provincial tourist offices for maps and advice.

BUSINESS HOURS. Official banking hours are Monday through Friday 8:30am to 3pm, but play it safe by giving yourself extra time.

MONEY. Taxes are included in all prices in Portugal and are not redeemable like those in Spain, even for EU citizens. **Tips** are customary only in fancy restaurants or hotels. Some cheaper restaurants include a 10% service charge; if they don't and you'd like to leave a tip, round up and leave the change. Taxi drivers do not expect a tip unless the trip was especially long. **Bargaining** is not customary in shops.

ACCOMMODATIONS AND CAMPING

Movijovem, Av. Duque de Ávila 137, 1069 Lisbon (☎707 20 30 30; www.pousadasjuventude.pt), oversees Portugal's HI hostels. All bookings can be made through them. A bed in a *pousada da juventude* (not to be confused with plush *pousadas*) costs €10-15 per night, slightly less in the off-season. To reserve a bed in the high season, obtain an **International Booking Voucher** from Movijovem (or your country's HI affiliate) and send it from home to the desired hostel four to eight weeks in advance. In the off-season (Oct.-Apr.), double-check to see if the hostel is open. **Hotels** tend to be pricey. When business is weak, try bargaining down in advance. **Quartos** are rooms in private residences; these rooms may be the only option in smaller towns (particularly in the south) or the cheapest one in bigger cities; tourist offices can usually help you. There are over 150 official **campgrounds** *(parques de campismo)* with lots of amenities. Police are strict about illegal camping—especially near official campgrounds. Tourist offices stock the free *Portugal: Camping and Caravan Sites*, an official campgrounds guide. Or, write the **Federação Portuguesa de Campismo e Caravanismo,** Av. Coronel Eduardo Galhardo 24D, 1199-007 Lisbon (☎218 12 68 90; www.fpcampismo.pt).

COMMUNICATION

PHONE CODES	**Country code:** 351. **International dialing prefix:** 00. From outside Portugal, dial int'l dialing prefix (see inside back cover) + 351 + local number.

TELEPHONES. Pay phones are either coin-operated or require a phone card. The basic unit for all calls is €0.10. Telecom phone cards are most common in Lisbon and Porto. Credifone cards are sold at drugstores, post offices, and locations posted on phone booths, and are most useful outside these two big cities. City codes all begin with a 2, and local calls do not require dialing the city code. **Calling cards** probably remain the best method of making international calls.

MAIL. **Air mail** *(via aerea)* can take from one to two weeks (or longer) to reach the US or Canada. It is slightly quicker for destinations in Europe and longer for Australia, New Zealand, and South Africa. **Surface mail** *(superficie)*, for packages only, takes up to two months. **Registered** or **blue mail** takes five to eight business days but costs roughly three times the price of air mail. **EMS** or **Express Mail** will probably get there in three to four days for more than double the blue mail price.

INTERNET. Cybercafes are common in cities and most smaller towns. When in doubt, try the library; they often have at least one computer with Internet access.

LANGUAGE. Portuguese is a Romance language similar to Spanish. English, Spanish, and French are also widely spoken. For basic Portuguese words and phrases, see p. 1029.

LISBON (LISBOA) ☎21

Once the center of the world's richest and farthest-reaching empire, Lisbon hit its peak at the end of the 15th century when Portuguese navigators pioneered explorations of Asia, Africa, and South America. The city has seen more than its share of changes over the course of the 20th century. During World War II, Lisbon's neutrality and its Atlantic connections made it a rendezvous place for spies on both sides. In 1974, when Mozambique and Angola won independence, hundreds of thousands of refugees converged upon the Portuguese capital. In 1998, Lisbon hosted the World Expo, which gave the city the impetus for massive construction projects and a citywide face-lift. Since then, the revival has continued, as more tourist hot spots and sites of cultural interest emerge. Like Portugal itself, Lisbon has managed to preserve its traditions, continually renovating its historic monuments and meticulously maintaining its black-and-white mosaic sidewalks, pastel facades, and cobbled medieval alleys.

TRANSPORTATION

Flights: Aeroporto de Lisboa (LIS; ☎218 41 35 00). Walk out of the terminal, turn right, and follow the road around the curve to the bus stop. From there take **bus** #44 or 45 (15-20min., every 12-15min., €0.90) to Pr. dos Restauradores and the Rossio; the bus stops directly in front of the tourist office. Alternatively, take the express **AeroBus** (#91; 15min., every 20min. 7am-9pm, €2.30) to Pr. dos Restauradores; this bus, which leaves directly from the airport exit, is a better option during rush hour. A **taxi** to the downtown area costs about €11, plus a €1.50 luggage fee.

Trains: Caminhos de Ferro Portuguêses (☎800 20 09 04; www.cp.pt). 4 main stations, each serving different destinations. Portuguese trains are usually quite slow; buses are often a better choice.

Estação Barreiro, across the Rio Tejo, goes south. Station accessible by ferry (included in train ticket) from the Terreiro do Paço dock off Pr. Comércio (30min., every 30min.). Trains to **Évora** (2½hr., 7 per day 6:50am-11:50pm, €6) and **Lagos** (5½hr., 5 per day 7:35am-7:45pm, €14).

Estação Cais do Sodré (☎213 47 01 81), to the right of Pr. Comércio when walking from Baixa. M: Cais do Sodré. To **Estoril** and **Cascais** (30min., every 20min., €1.10).

Estação Rossio (☎213 46 50 22), serves points west. M: Rossio or Restauradores. To **Sintra** (45min., every 15-30min. 6am-2am, €1.10) via **Queluz** (€0.70).

Estação Santa Apolónia (☎218 88 40 25), on Av. Infante D. Henrique, east of the Alfama on the Rio Tejo, runs the international, northern, and eastern lines. Take bus #9, 39, 46, or 90 to Pr. dos Restauradores and Estação Rossio. To: **Coimbra** (2½hr., 7 per day 8am-8pm, €8-13); **Madrid** (10hr., 10pm, €41); **Porto** (4½hr., 12 per day 7:45am-8pm, €10-19).

Buses: Arco do Cego, Av. João Crisóstomo, around the block from the M: Saldanha. All "Saldanha" buses (#36, 44, 45) stop in the *praça* (€0.60). Fast **Rede Expressos** (☎213 54 54 39; www.rede-expressos.pt) go to many destinations, including: **Coimbra** (2½hr., 16 per day 7am-12:15am, €9); **Évora** (2hr., 13 per day 7am-9:30pm, €8); **Lagos** (5hr., 9 per day 5am-1am, €15); **Porto** (4hr., 7 per day 7am-12:15am, €12).

Public Transportation: CARRIS (☎213 61 30 00; www.carris.pt) runs the buses, trams, and funiculars in Lisbon. Fare €0.90 within the city; pay on the bus. Consider investing in a *passe turístico* (tourist pass), good for unlimited travel on all CARRIS transports. 1-day pass €2.30, 3-day €5.50, 4-day €9, 7-day €13. The **metro** (☎213 55 84 57; www.metrolisboa.pt) covers downtown and the modern business district with 4 color-coded lines. Individual tickets €0.55; book of 10 tickets €4.50. Trains run daily 6:30am-1am, though some stations close earlier. **Trams** offer views of the harbor and service older neighborhoods. Line #28 is great for sight-seeing in the Alfama and Mouraria (stop in Pr. Comércio); line #15 heads from Pr. Comércio or Pr. Figueira to Belém and nightlife districts Av. 24 de Julho and Docas Santo Amaro. Tickets €0.90.

Taxis: Rádio Táxis de Lisboa (☎218 11 90 00), **Autocoope** (☎217 93 27 56), and **Teletáxis** (☎218 11 11 00) all line up along Av. da Liberdade and the Rossio.

ORIENTATION AND PRACTICAL INFORMATION

The city center is made up of three main *bairros* (neighborhoods): the **Baixa** (low district, resting in the valley), the **Bairro Alto** (high district), and the **Alfama.** The Baixa is the center of town, sandwiched between Bairro Alto and Alfama; its grid of small, mostly pedestrian streets begins at the **Praça Dom Pedro IV** (better known as the **Rossio**) and ends at the **Praça do Comércio** on the **Rio Tejo.**

Along the river are the Expo '98 grounds, now called the **Parque das Nações** (Park of Nations), and the fast-growing **Alcântara** and **Docas** (docks) regions. Alfama, a labyrinth of narrow alleys and stairways beneath the Castelo de São Jorge, is the city's oldest district. Across the Baixa from Alfama is Bairro Alto, and its upscale shopping district, the **Chiado,** which is traversed by R. do Carmo and R. Garrett, near much of the city's nightlife.

Tourist Offices: Palácio da Foz, Pr. dos Restauradores (☎213 46 33 14). M: Restauradores. This is the mother of all Portuguese tourist offices; it houses information about the entire country. The **Welcome Center,** Pr. Comécio (☎210 31 28 10), is the office for the city of Lisbon. Both offices open daily 9am-8pm. Office at the **Aeroporto de Lisboa** (☎218 45 06 06) is just outside the baggage claim area. Open daily 6am-2am.

American Express: Top Tours, Av. Duque de Loulé 108 (☎213 19 42 90). M: Marquês de Pombal. Exit the metro stop and walk up Av. da Liberdade toward the Marquês de Pombal statue, then turn right; the office is 2 blocks up on the left side of the street. Handles all AmEx functions. English spoken. Open M-F 9:30am-1pm and 2:30-6:30pm.

Embassies: Australia, Av. da Liberdade 200-2 (☎213 10 15 00; austemb@oninet.pt). **Canada,** Av. da Liberdade 198-200, 3rd fl. (☎213 16 46 00; lsbon-cs@dfait-maeci.gc.ca). **Ireland,** R. Imprensa à Estrela, 4th fl. (☎213 92 94 40; fax 97 73 63). **New Zealand** (consulate) R. do S. Felix 13-2 (☎213 50 96 90; fax 21 572 004). **South Africa,** Av. Luis Bivar 10 (☎213 19 22 00; Safrica@mail.EUnet.pt). **UK,** R. São Bernardo 33 (☎213 92 40 00; www.uk-embassy.pt). **US,** Av. das Forças Armadas (☎217 27 33 00; www.american-embassy.pt).

Luggage Storage: Estação Rossio. Lockers €3 for 48hr. Open daily 8:30am-11:30pm. Also available at **Estação Sta. Apolónia.**

English-Language Bookstore: Livraria Britânica, R. Luis Fernandes 14-16 (☎213 42 84 72), in the Bairro Alto. Walk up R. São Pedro de Alcântara and go straight as it becomes R. Dom Pedro V and then R. Escola Politécnica. Turn left on R. São Marcal, then right after 2 blocks onto R. Luis Fernandes. Open M-F 9:30am-7pm.

Laundromat: Lavatax, R. Francisco Sanches 65A (☎218 12 33 92). 1 block from M: Arroios. Wash, dry, and fold €5.50 per 5kg. Open M-F 8:30am-1pm and 3-7pm, Sa 8:30am-1pm.

Emergency: ☎112. **Police:** R. Capelo 13 (☎213 46 61 41). **Ambulance:** (☎219 42 11 11).

Late-night Pharmacy: ☎118 (directory assistance). Rotates; check the list posted on the door of any pharmacy.

Medical Services: British Hospital, R. Saraiva de Carvalho 49 (☎213 95 50 67). **Cruz Vermelha Portuguesa,** R. Duarte Galvão 54 (☎217 71 40 00).

Internet Access: Web C@fe, R. Diário de Notícias 126 (☎213 42 11 81). €2 per 15min., €2.50 per 30min., €4 per hr. Open daily 4pm-2am. **Abracadabra,** Pr. Dom Pedro IV 66. €1 per 15min., €2 per 30min., €3 per hr. Open M-Sa 8am-8pm. **Ciber Chiado,** Largo Picadeiro 10 (☎213 22 57 64), down R. Raiva de Andrade. Upstairs in the National Cultural Center building. Ring the bell to enter. €1.50 per 15min., €2 per 30min., €3 per 1hr., €4 per 2hr. Open M-F 4pm-midnight, Sa 8pm-midnight.

Post Office: Marked by red *Correios* signs. **Main office** (☎213 23 89 71), Pr. dos Restauradores. Open M-F 8am-10pm, Sa-Su 9am-6pm. **Branch office** (☎213 22 09 21) at Pr. Comércio. Open M-F 8:30am-6:30pm. Cash only. **Postal Code:** 1100.

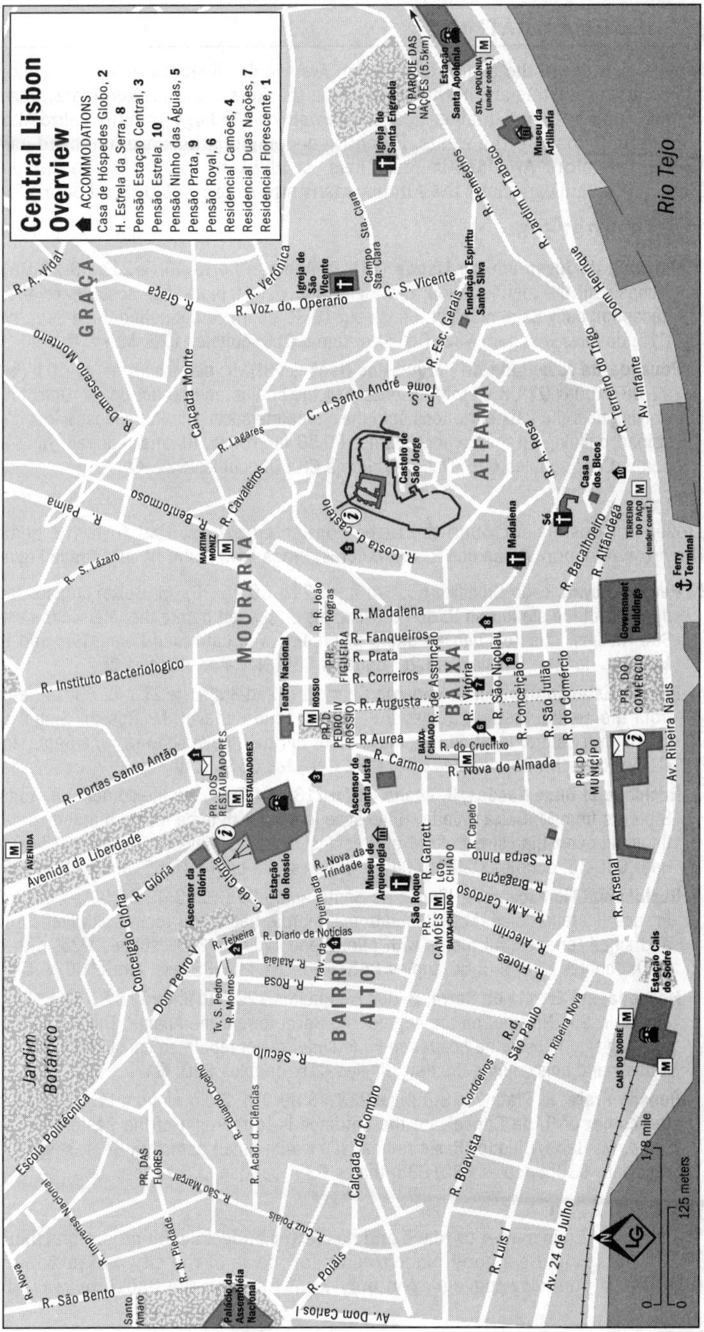
Central Lisbon Overview
ACCOMMODATIONS
Casa de Hóspedes Globo, 2
H. Estrela da Serra, 8
Pensão Estaçao Central, 3
Pensão Estrela, 10
Pensão Ninho das Águias, 5
Pensão Prata, 9
Pensão Royal, 6
Residencial Camões, 4
Residencial Duas Nações, 7
Residencial Florescente, 1
GRAÇA
MOURARIA
ALFAMA
BAIXA
BAIRRO ALTO
Castelo de São Jorge
Igreja de São Vicente
Igreja de Santa Engrácia
Estação Santa Apolónia
STA. APOLÓNIA (under const.)
Museu da Artilharia
TO PARQUE DAS NAÇÕES (5.5km)
Fundação Espiritu Santo Silva
Madalena
Sé
Casa a dos Bicos
TERREIRO DO PAÇO (under const.)
Ferry Terminal
Government Buildings
PR. DO COMÉRCIO
PR. DO MUNICÍPIO
Teatro Nacional
ROSSIO
PR. D. PEDRO IV (ROSSIO)
PR. FIGUEIRA
MARTIM MONIZ
RESTAURADORES
PR. DOS RESTAURADORES
AVENIDA
Estação do Rossio
Ascensor da Glória
Ascensor de Santa Justa
Museu de Arqueologia
São Roque
LGO. CHIADO
BAIXA-CHIADO
PR. CAMÕES
Estação Cais do Sodré
CAIS DO SODRÉ
Jardim Botânico
PR. DAS FLÔRES
Palácio da Assembléia Nacional
Santo Amaro
Rio Tejo
Avenida da Liberdade
R. Portas Santo Antão
R. Instituto Bacteriologico
R. S. Lázaro
R. Palma
R. Benformoso
R. Cavaleiros
R. Lagares
Calçada Monte
R. Damasceno Monteiro
R. Graça
R. A. Vidal
R. Verónica
R. Voz. do. Operario
Campo Sta. Clara
C. S. Vicente
C. d.Santo André
R. Esc. Gerais
R. S. Tomé
R. Remédios
R. Jardim d. Tabaco
Dom Henrique
R. Terreiro do Trigo
Av. Infante
R. A. Rosa
R. Costa d. Castelo
R. Bacalhoeiro
R. Alfândega
R. Madalena
R. Fanqueiros
R. Prata
R. Correiros
R. Augusta
R.Aurea
R. de Assunção
R. Vitória
R. São Nicolau
R. Conceição
R. São Julião
R. do Comércio
R. do Crucifixo
R. Nova do Almada
R. Carmo
R. Garrett
R. Capelo
R. Serpa Pinto
R. Bragança
R. A.M. Cardoso
R. Alecrim
R. Flores
R. Arsenal
Av. Ribeira Naus
R. R. João Regras
R. Nova da Trindade
R. Glória
C. da Glória
Conceição Glória
Dom Pedro V
R. Teixeira
R. Diario de Notícias
R. Atalaia
R. Rosa
Trav. da Queimada
Tv. S. Pedro
R. Monros
R. Século
R. d. São Paulo
R. Ribeira Nova
Cordoeiros
Calçada de Combro
R. Boavista
R. Luís I
Av. 24 de Julho
Av. Dom Carlos I
R. Poiais
R. Cruz Poiais
R. São Marçal
R. Acad. d. Ciências
R. Eduardo Coelho
Escola Politécnica
R. Imprensa Nacional
R. N. Piedade
R. Nova
R. São Bento
1/8 mile
125 meters
LG

PORTUGAL

ACCOMMODATIONS

Most hotels are in the center of town on **Avenida da Liberdade,** while many convenient budget hostels are in the **Baixa** along the **Rossio** and on **Rua Prata, Rua Correeiros,** and **Rua Ouro.** Lodgings near the **Castelo de São Jorge** or in the **Bairro Alto** are quieter and closer to the sights. If central accommodations are full, head east to the hostels along **Avenida Almirante Reis.** At night, be careful in the Baixa, the Bairro Alto, and especially the Alfama; many streets are isolated and poorly lit.

YOUTH HOSTELS

Pousada da Juventude de Lisboa (HI), R. Andrade Corvo 46 (☎213 53 26 96). M: Picoas. Exit the metro station, turn right, and walk 1 block; the hostel is on the left. Reception daily 8am-midnight. Check-out 10:30am. HI card required. June-Sept. dorms €15; doubles with bath €33. Oct.-May dorms €10; doubles €25. MC/V. ❷

Pousada da Juventude de Parque das Nações (HI), R. de Moscavide 47-101 (☎218 92 08 90; fax 92 08 91). M: Oriente. Exit the station and go left on Av. Dom João II, walking past the Park of Nations until the street intersects with R. de Moscavide; it's the striped building on the corner. Internet €0.50 for 15min. HI card required. June-Sept. dorms €11; doubles €26. Oct.-May dorms €8.50; doubles €22. ❶

BAIXA

Dozens of hostels surround the three connected *praças* that form the heart of downtown Lisbon: **Praça dos Restauradores, Praça Dom Pedro IV,** and **Praça Figueira.**

Pensão Royal, R. do Crucifixo 50, 3rd fl. (☎218 86 95 06). M: Baixa/Chiado. Take a right out of the station on R. do Crucifixo; it's on the left before the intersection with R. São Nicolas. This new *pensão* offers airy rooms with hardwood floors, TVs, and bath. May-Oct. dorms €15; singles €20; doubles €30. Nov.-Apr. €5 less. ❷

Pensão Estação Central, Calçada da Carmo 17, 2nd-3rd fl. (☎213 42 33 08), a block from the central station, across the Largo Duque Cadaval. M: Rossio. Small, plain rooms in a central location. Rooms without full bath have shower. June-Sept. singles €15, with bath €20; doubles €30/€35. Oct.-May €5 less. ❷

Residencial Duas Nações, R. Vitória 41 (☎213 46 07 10), on the corner of R. Augusta, 3 blocks from M: Baixa-Chiado. Hotel-style lodging with large rooms that look out onto the main pedestrian street of Baixa. Breakfast included. May-Sept. singles €15-20, with bath €30-35; doubles €20-25/€40-45; triples with bath €45-55. AmEx/MC/V. ❷

Residencial Florescente, R. Portas de Santo Antão 99 (☎213 42 66 09), 1 block from Pr. dos Restauradores. M: Restauradores. Marble baths and rooms with French doors and small terraces. All rooms with phone and TV. June-Sept. singles €25, with bath €40; doubles €30/€45-60; triples €45/€60. Oct.-May €5 less. AmEx/MC/V. ❸

Hospedagem Estrela da Serra, R. dos Fanqueiros 122, 4th fl. (☎218 87 42 51), at the end of R. São Nicolau, on the edge of the Baixa toward the Alfama. The rest of the old building that houses the *hospedagem* is under major repair, so construction can make it dusty and noisy during the day. Singles €15; doubles €20. ❷

Pensão Prata, R. Prata 71, 3rd fl. (☎213 46 89 08), 2 blocks from Pr. Comércio near the corner of R. da Conceição; the entrance is to the right of the Pastelaria Flor da Prata. M: Baixa/Chiado. Basic rooms; some with small bath. July-Sept. singles €25, with bath €30; doubles €30/€35; triples €35. Oct.-June €5-10 less. ❸

BAIRRO ALTO

The Bairro Alto is harder to reach and has fewer budget accommodations than the Baixa, but it can be a good place to stay for views of the city and proximity to nightlife. If you have luggage, you may want to reach the Bairro by way of the

Ascensor Glória from Pr. dos Restauradores; the hike up the stairways and steep streets is a long one from most public transportation stops.

Casa de Hóspedes Globo, R. Teixeira 37 (☎/fax 213 46 22 79), on a small street across from the Parque São Pedro de Alcântara, at the top of the funicular. From the park entrance, cross the street and go one block on Trav. da Cara, then turn right onto R. Teixeira. A popular spot for young travelers. All rooms newly renovated with phones, most with TV, and all but 2 with bath. Laundry €10 per load. Singles €15, with bath €25; doubles with bath €25-35; triples with bath €40. ❷

Residencial Camões, Tr. Poço da Cidade 38, 1st fl. (☎213 47 75 10), off R. Misericórdia. From the top of Ascensor Glória, turn left onto R. São Pedro, which becomes R. Misericórdia; Tr. Poço da Cidade is the 5th right. In the heart of the party district–it may get noisy at night. TV lounge. Breakfast included. Singles €18, with bath €30; doubles €37.50/€47.50; triples with bath €50. ❷

ALFAMA

The Alfama has steep prices (and streets), but staying there can be a nice change of pace, especially after a day or two in the Baixa grid.

Pensão Ninho das Águias, R. Costa do Castelo 74 (☎218 85 40 70), right behind the Castelo. From Pr. Figueira take R. Madalena to Largo Adelino Costa, then head uphill to R. Costa do Castelo. Canary-filled garden looks out over the old city. Singles €25; doubles €30-38, with bath €40; triples €50. ❸

Pensão Estrela, R. dos Bacalhoeiros 8 (☎218 86 95 06). An under appreciated option in the lower part of Alfama. Breezy rooms with just the basic amenities look out onto the busy square below. Check-out 11am. June-Sept. singles €20; doubles €30; one triple €45. Oct.-May singles €13-15; doubles €20-25; triple €38. The similar **Pensão Verandas** (☎218 87 05 19), a floor up, has comparable rooms and prices. ❷

FOOD

Lisbon has some of the best wine and least expensive restaurants of any European capital. A full dinner costs about €9-11 per person; the *prato do dia* (daily special) is often a great deal. Head to the **Calçada de Santa Ana** and **Rua dos Correeiros** to find small, authentic restaurants that cater to locals. Specialties include *amêjoas à bulhão pato* (steamed clams), *creme de mariscos* (seafood chowder with tomatoes), and *bacalhau cozido com grão e batatas* (cod with chick-peas and boiled potatoes, doused in olive oil). Snack on a surprisingly filling, incredibly cheap, and sinfully delicious Portuguese pastry; *pastelarias* (pastry shops) are everywhere. For groceries, look for any **Pingo Doce** supermarket; there's one a block off the Rossio on the corner of Rua 1 de Dezembro and Calçada de Carmo. (Open M-Sa 10am-7pm.)

Lua da Mel, R. Prata 242, on the corner of R. Santa Justa. If it can be caramelized, this diner-style pastry shop has done it. Pastries €0.55-1. Try the house specialty *Lua da Mel*. They also serve affordable meals (€5-7), and the daily specials are a great value (€4-5). Open M-F 7:30am-9pm, Sa 7:30am-7pm. ❶

Restaurante Tripeiro, R. dos Correeiros 70A, serves some of the best Portuguese meals on the lower streets of Baixa. Busy during lunch. Specializes in fish but also offers large portions of non-seafood dishes. Entrees €5-8. Open M-Sa noon-10pm. ❷

Churrasqueira O Cofre, R. dos Bacalhoeiros 2C-D, at the foot of the Alfama near Pensão Estrela. A display case at the entrance shows everything available for grilling. Outside seating in the summer. Entrees €6.50-11. Open daily 9am-midnight, meals noon-4pm and 7-11:30pm. AmEx/MC/V. ❷

Sul, R. do Norte 13. Dark wood paneling and candles give this restaurant and wine bar a romantic feel. Food tastes as good as it looks. Converts to a bar at 10pm. Spanish-themed entrees €7.50-13.50. Open Tu-Su noon-3pm and 7pm-1am. ❸

Restaurante Ali-a-Papa, R. da Atalaia 95. Serves generous helpings of traditional Moroccan food in a quiet atmosphere. Vegetarian options. Entrees €7.50-12. Open M-Sa 7-11pm. ❷

Restaurante Calcuta, R. do Norte 17, near Lg. Camões. Indian restaurant with wide selection of vegetarian options. Vegetarian entrees €5-7. Meat entrees €6-8.50. Fixed price *menú* €12.50. Open M-Sa noon-3pm and 6:30-11pm. ❷

A Brasileira, R. Garrett 120-122. Considered by many to be "the best café in Portugal," it has an after-dinner scene enjoyed by locals and tourists alike. Mixed drinks €5. Restaurant downstairs; specialty is *bife à brasileira* (€11). Open daily 8am-2am. ❸

SIGHTS

BAIXA

Although the Baixa features few historic sights, a lively atmosphere surrounding the neighborhood's three main *praças* makes it a monument in its own right.

AROUND THE ROSSIO. The best place to embark upon your tour of Lisbon's Enlightenment-era center is from its heart—the **Rossio.** The city's main square, also known as the **Praça Dom Pedro IV,** was once a cattle market and home to a public execution stage, bullfighting arena, and carnival ground. Adjoining the Rossio is the elegant **Praça Figueira,** which lies on the border of the Alfama district.

AROUND PRAÇA DOS RESTAURADORES. Just past the Rossio train station, an obelisk and a sculpture of the "Spirit of Independence" commemorate Portugal's independence from Spain in 1640. Pr. dos Restauradores is also the start of **Avenida da Liberdade,** Lisbon's most imposing, yet elegant promenade. Modeled after the wide boulevards of 19th-century Paris, this 1.6km thoroughfare ends at **Praça do Marquês do Pombal;** from here, an 18th-century statue of the Marquês, who supervised Lisbon's reconstruction after the 1755 earthquake, overlooks the city.

BAIRRO ALTO

In the Bairro, pretentious intellectuals mix with insecure teens and idealistic university students. It's the only place in Lisbon that never sleeps; there's as much to do at night as during the day. At the center of the neighborhood is **Praça Camões,** which adjoins **Largo Chiado** at the top of R. Garrett, a good place to rest and orient yourself while sightseeing. To reach **Rua Garret** and the heart of the chic **Chiado** neighborhood, turn left when exiting the elevator and walk one block; Rua Garret is on the right.

THE ASCENSOR DE SANTA JUSTA. The Ascensor de Santa Justa, a historic elevator built in 1902 inside a Gothic wrought-iron tower, once served as transportation up to the Bairro Alto but now just takes tourists up to see the view and then back down again. *(Elevator runs M-F 7am-11pm, Sa-Su 9am-11pm.)*

MUSEU NACIONAL DE ARTE ANTIGA. This museum hosts a large collection of Portuguese art as well as a survey of European painting dating back as far as the 12th century and ranging from Gothic primitives to 18th-century French masterpieces. *(R. das Janelas Verdes, Jardim 9 Abril, 30min. down Av. Infante Santo from the Ascensor de Santa Justa. Buses #40 and 60 stop to the right of the museum exit and head back to the Baixa. Tram #15, from Pr. Figueria or Pr. Comercio, also stops nearby. ☎213 91 28 00. Open Tu 2-6pm, W-Su 10am-6pm. €3, students €1.50. Free Su before 2pm.)*

PARQUE DE SÃO PEDRO DE ALCÂNTARA. The Castelo de São Jorge rests on the cliff opposite this shady park; come here to find a perfect picnic spot. *(On the right off R. São Pedro de Alcântara, the continuation of R. Misericórdia. It's a 5min. walk up R. Misericórdia from Pr. Camões; the park is right next to C. Glória.)*

BASÍLICA DA ESTRÊLA. Half-mad Maria I, desiring a male heir, made fervent religious vows promising God everything if she were granted a son. When a baby boy was finally born, she built this church. Ask the sacristan to show you the gigantic 10th-century manger scene. *(On Pr. Estrela. Accessible by tram #28 from Pr. Comércio. ☎213 96 09 15. Open daily 8am-12:30pm and 3-7:30pm. Free.)*

ALFAMA

The Alfama, Lisbon's medieval quarter, was the only neighborhood to survive the 1755 earthquake. The neighborhood slopes in tiers from the Castelo de São Jorge. Between the Alfama and the Baixa is the **Mouraria** (Moorish quarter), established after the Moors were expelled in 1147.

THE LOWER ALFAMA. While any of the small, uphill streets a few blocks east of the Baixa lead to the Alfama, the least confusing way to see the neighborhood is by climbing up R. Madalena, which begins two blocks away from Pr. Comércio (take R. Alfandega from the *praça*). Turn right when you see the **Igreja da Madalena** in the Largo Madalena on the right. Take R. Santo António da Sé and follow the tram tracks to the cleverly designed and ornamented **Igreja de Santo António,** built in 1812 over the beloved saint's alleged birthplace. The construction was funded with money collected by the city's children, who placed miniature altars bearing images of the saint on doorsteps—a custom reenacted annually on June 13, the saint's feast day. *(☎218 86 91 45. Open daily 8am-7pm. Mass daily 11am, 5, and 7pm.)*

CASTELO DE SÃO JORGE. Near the top of the Alfama lies the must-see Castelo de São Jorge, which offers spectacular views of Lisbon and the ocean. Built in the 5th century by the Visigoths and enlarged by 9th-century Moors, this castle was a playgound for the royal family between the 14th and 16th centuries. Now, anyone can wander around the ruins, soak in the view of the cityscape below, explore the ponds, or gawk at the exotic bird population of the castle gardens. *(From the cathedral, follow the brown and yellow signs for the castle on a winding uphill walk. Castle open daily Apr.-Sept. 9am-9pm; Oct.-Mar. 9am-6pm. Free.)*

ALONG TR. SÃO VICENTE. From the far side of the castle, follow the main tram tracks along Tr. São Tomé (which becomes R. São Vicente as it winds uphill) to Largo São Vicente and the **Igreja de São Vicente de Fora,** built between 1582 and 1629 and dedicated to Lisbon's patron saint. In the church's backyard is the **Feira da Ladra** (flea market), where a lively social scene drowns out cries of merchants hawking used goods. *(From the bottom of R. Correeiros in the Baixa, take bus #12 or tram #28 (€0.90). Church open Tu-Sa 9am-6pm, Su 9am-12:30pm and 3-5pm. Free. Flea market open Tu and Sa 7am-3pm.)* The **Igreja de Santa Engrácia (National Pantheon)** is farther down toward the coast. This church, with its impressive dome, took almost 300 years to complete (1682-1966), giving rise to the famous Portuguese expression, "Endless like the construction of Santa Engrácia." *(Walk along R. São Vicente and keep left as the road branches. Open Tu-Su 10am-5pm.)*

SALDANHA

The modern district of Saldanha, Lisbon's business center, has two excellent museums. The **Museu Calouste Gulbenkian** houses oil tycoon Calouste Gulbenkian's collection, including an extensive array of ancient art as well as more modern European pieces. *(Av. Berna 45. M: S. Sebastião. Bus #18, 46, or 56.*

www.gulbenkian.pt. Open Tu-Su 10am-5pm. €3, students free.) The adjacent **Museu do Centro de Arte Moderna** has a sizeable modern art collection as well as beautiful gardens. *(On R. Dr. Nicolau Bettencourt. Open Tu-Su 10am-5pm. €3, students free.)*

BELÉM

A number of well-maintained museums and historical sites showcase the former opulence and extravagance of the Portuguese empire. To get to Belém, take tram #15 from Pr. Comércio (15min., €0.90), bus #28 or 43 from Pr. Figueira (15min., €0.90), or the train from Estação Cais do Sodré (10min., every 15min., €0.70). From the train station, cross over the tracks, then cross the street and go left. From the bus station, follow the avenue straight ahead.

MOSTEIRO DOS JERÓNIMOS. The Mosteiro dos Jerónimos rises from the banks of the Tejo behind a lush public garden. Established by King Dom Manuel I in 1502 to give thanks for the success of navigator Vasco da Gama's voyage to India, this monastery showcases Portugal's native Manueline style, combining Gothic forms with early Renaissance details. Inside, the symbolic tombs of Luís de Camões and Vasco da Gama lie in two opposing transepts. *(Open Tu-Su 10am-5pm. €3, students €1.50. Cloisters open Tu-Su 10am-5pm. Free.)*

TORRE DE BELÉM. The Torre de Belém rises from the north bank of the Tejo and is surrounded by the ocean on three sides due to the receding shoreline. Today, it is only accessible by a small bridge, offering spectacular panoramic views of Belém, the Tejo, and the Atlantic. *(A 10min. walk along the water from the monastery in the opposite direction from Lisbon. Take the underpass by the gardens to cross the highway. Open Tu-Su 10am-6pm. €3, students and seniors €1.50.)*

PARQUE DAS NAÇÕES. The government took a chance on the former Expo '98 grounds, spending millions to convert it into the Parque das Nações. The gamble paid off—the futuristic park is constantly packed. Enter the park through the **Centro Vasco de Gama** shopping mall to reach the center of the grounds. The biggest attraction is the **Pavilhão dos Oceanos,** the largest oceanarium in Europe, which showcases the four major oceans right down to their sounds, smells, and climates. The four ocean tanks connect to the main tank, which houses fish, sharks, and other sea creatures. The 145m **Torre Vasco de Gama** offers spectacular views of the city. *(M: Oriente. www.parquedasnacoes.pt. Shopping mall open daily 10am-midnight. Oceanarium open daily Apr.-Sept. 10am-7pm; Oct.-Mar. 10am-6pm. €9, under 18 €5. Torre open daily 10am-8pm. €2.50, under 18 €1.25.)*

THE LOCAL STORY

RUNNING FROM FAME

Let's Go met up with Ábilio Ferro at Ta Bar Es in Nazaré to talk about his experience as a musician in Portugal. Look for Ábilio's debut CD, scheduled for release in December 2002.

Q: What kind of music do you play?
A: All types of music—jazz, bossa nova, *fado*, blues, rock-n-roll. I'm 46 and I am still trying to discover myself. I have all kinds of influences and I am not sure which to follow.

Q: Where did you pick up these musical influences—here in Portugal?
A: Both here in Portugal, and when I turned 16 and sailed all over the world. I've been to 70 countries. When I went to Canada and the United States, I met a lot of good musicians. I've already played with Nick McGrain from Iron Maiden and with Nellie Furtado. I know all the star music artists here in Portugal. I've learned a lot, but my base is here. My friends like to hear me play. I've just been running away from fame.

Q: Where do you play?
A: Here in the bars and then I did a few tours through Europe, to the Azores, to Canada. Finally, I came back [to Portugal] four years ago and I've played all over the country. But now I need to rest my voice.

Q: How do you see yourself fitting into the live music scene here in Nazaré?
A: I see what the audience wants. If they want more *fado* or reggae, then I'll play more *fado* or more reggae. It's easy—I like all kinds of music.

ENTERTAINMENT AND NIGHTLIFE

Agenda Cultural and *Follow Me Lisboa* have information on arts events and bullfights; get either for free at kiosks in the Rossio, on R. Portas de Santo Antão, or at the tourist office.

FADO

Lisbon's trademark is the heart-wrenching *fado*, an expressive art that combines elements of singing and narrative poetry. *Fadistas*, cloaked in black dresses and shawls, perform emotional tales of lost loves and faded glory. The Bairro Alto has many *fado* joints off R. Misericórdia and on side streets radiating from the Museu de São Roque, but the prices alone may turn a knife in your heart. To avoid these, try exploring nearby streets; various bars and other small venues often offer free performances. **Machado,** R. Norte 91, is one of the larger *fado* restaurants. (Entrees €20-68. Min. consumption €15. Open Tu-Su 8pm-3am; *fados* start at 9:15pm. AmEx/MC/V.)

BARS AND CLUBS

The first place to go for nightlife is the **Bairro Alto,** where a plethora of small bars and clubs invites exploring the side streets. In particular, **Rua Norte, Rua Diário Notícias,** and **Rua Atalaia** have many small clubs packed into three short blocks, making club-hopping as easy as crossing the street. Most gay and lesbian clubs are found between Pr. Camões and Trav. da Queimada, as well as in the **Rato** area near the edge of Bairro Alto. **Avenida 24 de Julho** and the **Rua das Janelas Verdes** in the **Santos** area above have some of the most popular bars and clubs. Newer expansions include the area along the river across from the **Santa Apolo'nia** train station. There's no reason to arrive before midnight; crowds flow in around 2am.

Lux/Fra'gil, Av. Infante D. Henrique, A. In a class and location of its own, 3 years after its opening Lux continues to be the newest big thing in Lisbon. Take a taxi to the area across from the Sta. Apolo'nia train station to get to this imaginative mix of lights and boxes. Beer €1.50-2.50. Min. consumption €10. Open Tu-Sa 6pm-6am; arrive after 2am if you want company.

Litro e Meio (1,5 Lt.), R. das Janelas Verdes 27, in the Santos area above the clubs on Av. 24 de Julho. This unpretentious bar attracts a young crowd and plays house and Latin music. Most popular from 1-2:30am before clubbing on the street below. Beer €1.50, mixed drinks €3.50. Min. consumption usually €5. Open M-Sa 10pm-4am.

Resto, R. Costa do Castelo 7, in the Alfama, is located at the site of an old circus school. Huge outdoor patio has one of the best views of the city. Filled with a young crowd, especially 10pm-midnight. Live guitar F-Su. *Caipirinha* €4. Beer €1.25. Open daily 7:30pm-2am.

Trumps, R. Imprensa Nacional 104B, in the Bairro Alto. Lisbon's biggest gay club features several bars in addition to a massive dance floor. Min. consumption €5. Open F-Sa 11:30pm-6:30am, Tu-Th and Su 11:30pm-4:30am.

Clandestino, R. da Barroca 99. Cavernous bar with messages sprawled by former patrons covering its rock walls. Rock plays in the background as groups of young people chat at low tables. Beer €2, mixed drinks €4. Open Tu-Su 10pm-2am.

A Capella, R. Atalaia 45. A spacious bar with gold walls and red velvet cushions. Popular in the late hours. Large beers €3, mixed drinks €5. Open daily 9pm-2am.

DAYTRIPS FROM LISBON

SINTRA

Trains (☎219 23 26 05) arrive on Av. Dr. Miguel Bombarda from Lisbon's Estação Rossio (45min., every 15min. 6am-2am, €1.10). Stagecoach buses leave from outside the train station for Cascais (#417; 40min., every hr. 6:30am-7pm, €2.60) and Estoril (#418; 40min., every hr. €2.30). Mafrense buses (down the street) run to Ericeira (50min., every hr. 7:25am-8:25pm, €2).

British Romantic poet Lord Byron described Sintra as a "glorious Eden." His adulation made Sintra (pop. 20,000) a chic destination for 19th-century European aristocrats. These days, Sintra is a favorite among foreign tour groups and backpackers alike, all of whom drool over its fairy-tale castles and mountain vistas. Perched on the peak overlooking the old town, the **Castelo dos Mouros** provides stunning views of the mountains and coast. Follow the blue signs 3km up the mountain or take bus #434 (15min., every 30min., daypass €3.60), which runs to the top from the tourist office. The awestruck are usually sun-struck; a bottle of water is recommended. (Open June-Sept. daily 9am-8pm; Oct.-May 9am-7pm. €3, seniors €1.) A mix of Moorish, Gothic, and Manueline styles, the **Palácio Nacional de Sintra,** in Pr. República, was once the summer residence of Moorish sultans and their harems. (☎219 10 68 40. Open Th-Tu 10am-5:30pm, closed bank holidays. Buy tickets by 5pm. €3, seniors €1.50.) Farther uphill is the **Palácio Nacional da Pena,** a Bavarian castle decorated with Arabic minarets, Gothic turrets, Manueline windows, and a Renaissance dome. (Open July-Sept. Tu-Su 10am-6:30pm; Oct.-June Tu-Su 10am-5pm. €5, seniors and students €1.50.)

The **tourist office,** Sintra-Vila Pr. República 23, is in the historic center. From the bus station, turn left on Av. Bombarda, which becomes the winding Volta do Duche. Continue straight into the Praça da República; the Palácio Nacional de Sintra is ahead, and the tourist office is to the left. (☎219 23 11 57. Open June-Sept. daily 9am-8pm; Oct.-May 9am-7pm.) To reach the **Pousada da Juventude de Sintra (HI) ❶,** on Sta. Eufémia, take bus #434 from the train station to the Palácio da Pena. Look for signs to the hostel. (☎219 24 12 10. Reservations recommended. HI membership required. Dorms €8.50-10.50; doubles €20-24.)

QUELUZ

Take the train toward Sintra from Lisbon's Estação Rossio (M: Rossio) and get off at the Queluz-Belas stop. (25min., every 15min., €0.80.)

Queluz, just 12km west of Lisbon, is the home of the amazing **Palácio Nacional de Queluz,** a pink-and-white Rococo wedding cake of a palace. In the mid-18th century, Dom Pedro III turned an old hunting lodge into this summer residence—check out the **Sala dos Embaixadores,** with its gilded thrones and Chinese vases and the *azulejo*-lined canal in the garden. Exit the station through the ticket office, go left on Av. Antonio Ennes, and follow the signs to the palace. (Open W-M 10am-5pm. Palace €3, garden €0.50. Seniors and students €1.50.)

ESTORIL AND CASCAIS

Trains from Lisbon's Estação do Sodré (M: Cais do Sodré) stop in Cascais (30min., every 20min. 5:30am-2:30am, €1.10) via Estoril (30min., every 20min. 5:30am-2:30am, €1.10). Estoril and Cascais are only a 20min. stroll along the coast or Av. Marginal from each other.

Beautiful beaches, stately vistas, and a bustling casino make Estoril a land of opulence. **Praia Estoril Tamariz** beach greets visitors on arrival. For the beach-weary, the marvelous (and air-conditioned) **Casino Estoril,** Europe's largest casino, is a welcome relief. (☎214 66 77 00; www.casino-estoril.pt. No swimwear, tennis shoes, jeans, or shorts. Slots and game room 18+. Passport required. Open daily 3pm-3am.) From the train station, cross Av. Marginal and head to the **tourist office,** which is left of the casino on Arcadas do Parque, for a free map of both towns. (☎214 66 38 13. Open M-Sa 9am-7pm, Su 10am-6pm.)

Once the summer vacation resort of the royal family, Cascais still caters to a well-to-do crowd. Four popular **beaches** draw throngs of locals and tourists. The **tourist office,** Av. dos Combatantes 25, can help book rooms. To get there, turn right at the fork in the promenade, follow the train tracks to the station, cross the Largo de Estaçaño square, and turn right at the McDonald's on Av. Valbom. (☎214 86 82 04. Open M-Sa 9am-7pm, Su 10am-6pm.)

MAFRA AND ERICEIRA

Frequent Mafrense buses run from Lisbon's Campo Grande (M: Campo Grande) to Mafra (1-1½hr., every hr., €2.75) and Ericeira (1½hr., every hr. 6:30am-11:20pm, €3.80). These buses also run from Mafra to Ericeira. (20min., every hr., €1.25).

Sleepy Mafra is home to one of Portugal's most impressive sights and one of Europe's largest historical buildings, the **Palácio Nacional de Mafra.** The massive 2000-room palace, including a cathedral-sized church, a monastery, and a library, took 50,000 workers 13 years to complete. (Open W-M 10am-5:30pm; last entrance 4:30pm. Daily 45min. tours in English 11am and 2:30pm. €3, students and seniors €1.50, under 14 free.) To reach the **tourist office,** Av. 25 de Abril, take a right off the main steps of the palace onto Terreiro D. João and bear left, passing the post office on your left; the office will be on the right down the road, behind the fountain. (☎261 81 20 23. Open M-F 9am-7pm, Sa-Su 9:30am-1pm and 2:30-6pm.)

Primarily a fishing village, Ericeira is known for its spectacular beaches and surfable waves. The main beaches, **Praia do Sol** and **Praia do Norte,** crowd quickly; for something more secluded, stroll down the Largo da Feira toward Ribamar until you reach the stunning sand dunes of **Praia da Ribeira d'Ilhas.** If you stay, ask about rooms at the **tourist office,** R. Eduardo Burnay 46. (☎261 86 31 22. Open July-Sept. daily 9:30am-midnight; Oct.-June Sa 9:30-10pm, Su-M 9:30am-7pm.)

OTHER DAYTRIPS FROM LISBON

COIMBRA. Party or people-watch in this vibrant university town (see p. 827).

ÉVORA. Peruse the halls of the "museum city," including the cathedral—perhaps Portugal's finest—and the uniquely grotesque Capela dos Ossos (see p. 822).

CENTRAL PORTUGAL

Jagged cliffs and whitewashed fishing villages line the Costa de Prata of **Estremadura,** with beaches that rival even those in the Algarve. In the fertile region of the **Ribatejo** (Banks of the Tejo), lush greenery surrounds historic sights.

LEIRIA ☎244

Capital of the surrounding district and an important transport hub, prosperous and industrial Leiria fans out from a fertile valley, 22km from the coast. Chosen to host the Euro 2004 soccer finals, Leiria is busy preparing itself for the crowds that will flood the city. Leiria's most notable sight is its **Castelo de Leiria,** a granite fort built by Dom Afonso Henriques atop the crest of a volcanic hill after he snatched the town from the Moors. The terrace opens onto a panoramic view of the town and river. (Castle open Apr.-Sept. M-F 9am-6:30pm, Sa-Su 10am-6:30pm; Oct.-Mar. M-F 9am-5:30pm, Sa-Su 10am-5:30pm. €1.) Nearby **beaches,** including **Vieira, Pedrógão,** and **São Pedro de Muel,** are all accessible via buses from the bus station.

Leiria makes a practical base for exploring the nearby region. **Trains** (☎244 88 20 27) run from the station 3km outside town to Coimbra (1½hr., 10 per day 2am-10:15pm, €6) and Lisbon (2hr., 9 per day 3am-11pm, €7). **Buses** (☎244 81 15 07), just off Pr. Paulo VI, next to the main park and close to the tourist office, run to: Batalha (20min., 9 per day 7:15am-7pm, €1.50); Coimbra (1hr., 11 per day 7:15am-2am, €5.80); Lisbon (2hr., 11 per day 7:15am-11pm, €7); Porto (3½hr., 10 per day 7:15am-2am, €9); Santarém (2hr., 5 per day 7:15am-7pm, €4.50-8); and Tomar (1½hr.; M-F 7:15am and 5:45pm, Sa 6:15pm; €3-6). Buses also run between the train station and the **tourist office** (15min., every hr. 7am-7pm, €0.75), in the Jardim Luís de Camões. (☎244 82 37 73. Open May-Sept. daily 10am-1pm and 3-7pm; Oct.-Apr. 10am-1pm and 2-6pm.) If you're going to spend the night, go to **Pousada da Juventude de Leiria (HI) ❶,** on Largo Cândido dos Reis 9. (☎/fax 244 83 18 68. Dorms €8.50-10.50; doubles €21-27.) **Largo Cândido dos Reis** is lined with bars.

TOMAR ☎249

For centuries, the arcane Knights Templar—made up of monks and warriors—plotted crusades from a celebrated convent-fortress high above this small town. The **Convento de Cristo** complex was the Knights' powerful and mysterious head-quarters. The first structure was built in 1160, but some cloisters, convents, and buildings were added later. The **Claustro dos Felipes** is a Renaissance masterpiece. (☎249 31 34 81. Complex open June-Sept. daily 9am-6pm; Oct.-May 9am-5pm. €3, under 14 free.) **Trains** (☎249 31 28 15) run from Av. Combatentes da Grande Guerra, at the southern edge of town, to: Coimbra (2½hr., 6 per day 6an-6pm, €5-6); Lisbon (2hr., 18 per day 5am-10pm, €5-10); Porto (4½hr., 7 per day 8am-8pm, €8-11); and Santarém (1hr., 12 per day 5am-10pm, €2.60-4.20). Rodoviaria Tejo **buses** (☎249 31 27 38) leave from Av. Combatentes Grande Guerra, by the train station, for: Coimbra (2½hr., 7am, €8.25); Leiria (1hr.; M-F 7:15am and 5:45pm, Sa 7am; €3-6); Lisbon (2hr., 4 per day 9:15am-6pm, €6); Porto (4hr., 7am, €10.50); and Santarém (1hr., 9:15am and 6pm, €6). From the bus or train station, take a right onto Av. Combatentes de Grande Guerra and then a left onto Av. Torres Pinheiro and continue past the traffic circle on R. Everaro; the **tourist office** is on the left just past the bridge. (☎249 32 24 27. Open July-Sept. daily 10am-8pm; Oct.-June 10am-6pm.) **Postal code:** 2300.

BATALHA ☎244

The centerpiece of Batalha is the gigantic **Mosteiro de Santa Maria da Vitória.** Built by Dom João I in 1385 to commemorate his victory over the Castilians, the complex of cloisters and chapels remains one of Portugal's greatest monuments. Through the Claustro de Dom Afonso V, out the door and to the right are the impressive **Capelas Imperfeitas (Unfinished Chapels),** with massive buttresses designed to support a large dome that was never actually constructed. Napoleon's troops sacrilegiously turned the nave into a brothel. To get to the monastery, enter through the church. (Open Apr.-Sept. daily 9am-6pm; Oct.-Mar. 9am-5pm. €3, under 25 €1.50.) **Buses** run from the street across from the monastery to: Leiria (20min., 10 per day 7:50am-8:25pm, €1.10); Lisbon (2hr., 6 per day 7:25am-6:55pm, €6); and Tomar (1½hr.; 8am, noon, 6pm; €2.60). The **tourist office,** on Pr. Mouzinho de Albuquerque along R. Nossa Senhora do Caminho, stands opposite the monastery. (☎244 76 51 80. Open May-Sept. daily 10am-1pm and 3-7pm; Oct.-Apr. 10am-1pm and 2-6pm.)

SANTARÉM ☎243

Perhaps the most charming of Ribatejo's cities, Santarém (pop. 30,000) presides over the calm Rio Tejo and its soft green pastures from atop a rocky mound. The austere facade of the **Igreja do Seminário dos Jesuítas** dominates **Praça Sá da Bandeira,** Santarém's main square. (Open Tu-Su 9:30am-12:30pm and 2-5:30pm. Free.) Take R. Serpa Pinto from Pr. Sá da Bandeira to the **Praça Visconde de Serra Pilar,** where Christians, Moors, and Jews gathered centuries ago for social and business affairs. The 12th-century **Igreja de Marvilha,** off the *praça*, has a 17th-century *azulejo* interior. (Open Tu-Su 9:30am-12:30pm and 2-5:30pm. Free.) Nearby is the early Gothic **Igreja da Graça;** within the chapel lies Pedro Alvares Cabral, the explorer who discovered Brazil. (Church and chapel open Tu-Su 9:30am-12:30pm and 2-5:30pm. Free.) From there, take R. Cons. Figueiredo Leal, which becomes Av. 5 de Outubro, to the **Portas do Sol,** a paradise of flowers and fountains surrounded by old Moorish walls. (Open daily 8am-11pm. Free.)

The **train station** (☎243 32 11 99), 2km from town, serves: Coimbra (2hr., 11 per day 6:25am-1:10am, €5.25-7); Lisbon (1hr., 37 per day 4:40am-3:55am, €3.35-5.25); Porto (4hr., 4 per day 9:55am-9pm, €8.50-12); and Tomar (1hr., every hr. 6:20am-1:25am, €2.60). Buses (10min., every 30min-1hr., €1.10) connect the train station with the **bus station** (☎243 33 32 00), on Av. Brasil, near the main praça. **Buses** serve: Coimbra (2hr., 10:45am and 6:45pm, €7.25); Lisbon (1-1½hr., 10 per day 7am-7:15pm, €5.50); and Porto (4hr., 10:45am and 6:45pm, €11). The **tourist office,** R. Capelo Ivêns 63, is nearby. (☎243 30 44 37. Open M 9am-12:30pm and 2-5:30pm, Tu-F 9am-7pm, Sa-Su 10am-12:30pm and 2:30-5:30pm.) **Pousada da Juventude de Santarém (HI) ❶,** Av. Grp. Forcados Amadores de Santarém 1, is near the bullring. (☎/fax 243 39 19 14. Reception 8am-noon and 6pm-midnight. Check-in after 6pm and check-out before 11am. Lockout 11am-6pm. Dorms €7.50-9.50; doubles with bath €19-23.) **Postal code:** 2000.

NAZARÉ ☎262

In Nazaré, it's hard to tell where authenticity stops and tourism begins. Fishermen in traditional garb go barefoot while the day's catch dries in the hot sun. But if Nazaré is part theater, at least it puts on a good show—and everyone gets front row seats on its glorious **beach.** For an evening excursion, take the **funicular** (3min., every 15min. 7:15am-9:30pm, €0.60), which runs from R. Elevador off Av. República to the **Sítio,** a clifftop area replete with uneven cobbled streets, weathered buildings, and wonderful views of the town and ocean. Around 6pm, fishing boats return to the **port** beyond the far left end (facing the ocean) of the beach; head over to watch fishermen at work and eavesdrop as local restaurateurs bid for the most promising catches at the **fish auction** (M-F 6-10pm). **Cafes** in Pr. Souza Oliveira teem with people after midnight. The intimate bar **Ta Bar Es,** R. de Rio Maior 20-22, just off R. Mouzinho Albuquerque, hosts live music most summer nights. (Beer €0.75-2.50, mixed drinks €2.50-3.50. Open daily 2pm-4am. Closed first 2 weeks of Nov.) Nazaré is on the revolving schedule that brings **bullfights** to a different city in the province each summer weekend. (Usually Sa 10pm; tickets start at €24.50.)

Nazaré is only accessible by **bus** (☎262 55 11 72). Buses run to: Coimbra (2hr., 5 per day 6:25am-7:25pm, €7); Lisbon (2hr., 8 per day 6:50am-8pm, €6.50); Porto (3½hr., 5 per day 6:25am-7:25pm, €11); and Tomar (1½hr. 3 per day 7am-5pm, €4.50). The **tourist office** is beachside on Av. República. (☎262 56 11 94. Open July-Aug. daily 10am-10pm; Sept. 10am-8pm; Oct.-Mar. 9:30am-1pm and 2:30-6pm; Apr.-June 10am-1pm and 3-7pm.) Look along Pr. Dr. Manuel de Arriaga and Pr. Sousa Oliveira for the best deals on accommodations. **Vila Turística Conde Fidalgo ❸,** Av. da Independência Nacional 21-A, is three blocks uphill from Pr. Sousa Oliveira. (☎/fax 262 55 23 61. July singles €30; doubles €35. Aug. singles €40; doubles €45. Sept.-June singles €15-20; doubles €20.) For **camping,** head to **Vale Paraíso ❶,** on Estrada Nacional 242, 2.5km out of town. They also rent bungalows and apartments. Take the bus (15min., 8 per day 7am-7pm) to Alcobaça or Leiria. (☎262 56 18 00. June-Sept. €2.70-3.25 per person, per tent, or per car; Nov.-March €1.75-2.50.) Supermarkets line **Rua Sub-Vila,** parallel to Av. República. **Postal code:** 2450.

ÉVORA ☎266

Designated a UNESCO World Heritage site, Évora is justly known as the "Museum City." Moorish arches line the winding streets of this picture-perfect town, which boasts a Roman temple, an imposing cathedral, and a 16th-century university.

■■ **TRANSPORTATION AND PRACTICAL INFORMATION. Trains** (☎266 70 21 25) run from Av. dos Combatentes de Grande Guerra to Lisbon (3hr., 5 per day, €4-6) and Porto (6½hr., 3 per day, €14). **Buses** (☎266 76 94 10) go from Av. Sebastião to Lisbon (2-2½hr., every 1-1½hr., €8) and Faro (5hr., 4 per day, €9.50). The **tourist office** is at Pr. Giraldo 65. (☎266 70 26 71. Open Apr.-Sept. M-F 9am-7pm, Sa-Su 9am-12:30pm and 2-5:30pm; Oct.-Mar. daily 9am-12:30pm and 2-5:30pm.) Free **Internet** access is available at **Instituto Portuguese da la Juventude,** R. República 105, but during the afternoon there's often a long line. (Open M-F 9am-11pm.) Alternatively, **Oficin@,** R. Moeda 27, is off Pr. Giraldo. (€2.50 per hr. Open Tu-F 8pm-3am, Sa 9pm-2am.) **Postal code:** 7000.

■■ **ACCOMMODATIONS AND FOOD.** *Pensões* cluster around **Praça Giraldo.** From the tourist office, cross Pr. Giraldo and take a right on R. República, then turn left on R. Miguel Bombarda to reach **Pousada da Juventude (HI) ❶,** R. Miguel Bombarda 40. (☎266 74 48 48; fax 74 48 43. Dorms €10-12.50; doubles with bath €25-30.) Or, take a right out of the tourist office, then the first right onto R. Bernardo Mato to get to **Casa Palma ❷,** R. Bernardo Mato 29-A. (☎266 70 35 60. Singles €20, with bath €25; doubles €30/€40.) Many budget restaurants are near Pr. Giraldo, particularly along **Rua Mercadores.** Locals flock to **Adega do Neto ❶,** R. Mercadores 46, off Pr. Giraldo, for typical Alentejan dishes. (Entrees €3.50-5. Open M-Sa noon-3:30pm and 7-10pm.) From Pr. Giraldo, walk up R. 5 de Outubro and take a right onto R. Diogo Cão to reach the only real Italian restaurant in Évora, **Pane & Vino ❷,** Páteo do Salema. (Pizza €5-11, pasta €8-15. Open Tu-Su noon-3pm, 6:30-11pm.)

■■ **SIGHTS AND ENTERTAINMENT.** The city's most famous monument is the second-century **Roman temple,** on Largo Conde do Vila Flor. Facing the temple is the **Igreja de São João Evangelista;** its interior is covered with dazzling tiles. Ask to see the hidden chambers. (Open Tu-Su 10am-12:30pm and 2-6pm. €2.50.) From Pr. Giraldo, head up R. 5 de Outubro to the colossal 12th-century **cathedral;** the 12 apostles on the doorway are masterpieces of medieval Portuguese sculpture. The **Museu de Arte Sacra,** above the nave, has religious artifacts. (Cathedral open daily 9am-12:30pm and 2-5pm. Free. Cloisters open daily 9am-noon and 2-4:30pm. Museum open Tu-Su 9am-noon and 2-4:30pm. Cloisters and museum €2.50.) Attached to the pleasant **Igreja Real de São Francisco,** the bizarre ▣**Capela dos Ossos** (Chapel of Bones) was built by three Franciscan monks using the bones of 5000 people. From Pr. Giraldo, follow R. República; the church is on the right and the chapel is around back to the right of the main entrance. (Open M-Sa 9am-1pm and 2:30-5:30pm, Su 10am-1pm. €1.) After sunset, head to ▣**Jonas,** R. Serpa Pinta 67, to discover a warm, cavernous underground lounge and a mellow bar upstairs. (☎964 82 16 47. Open M-Sa 10:30am-3am.) A country fair accompanies the **Feira de São João** festival the last week of June.

BEJA ☎284

Standing out amidst the vast, monotonous wheat fields of southern Alentejo, Beja is a town of remarkable architecture and truly scorching temperatures. Its name, pronounced like the Portuguese word for "kiss" (beijo), is highly appropriate; besides being a summertime oven, it's a prime getaway destination for romantic exploits. The city is also a haven for traditional Portugese food, music, and handcrafts. The **Museu Rainha Dona Leonor,** Lg. da Conceiçao, was built on the site of Sister Mariana Alcoforado's famed indiscretion with a French officer. The museum features a replica of the cell window through which the lovers exchanged secret passionate vows. The *azulejos* (tiles) and Persian-style ceiling make the house look like a mini-mosque. (Open Tu-Su 9:30am-12:30pm and 2-5:15pm. €0.50, Su free.) One block downhill is the 13th-century **Igreja de Santa María da Feira,** transformed into a mosque during the Moorish invasion and back into a church when the city reverted to Portuguese control. A miniature bull on its corner column symbolizes the city's spirit. (Open daily 10am-1pm and 3-7pm. Free.) From here, R. Aresta Branco leads past handsome old houses to the **Castelo de Beja,** built around 1300 on the remnants of a Roman fortress. (Open May-Sept. Tu-Su 10am-1pm and 2-6pm; Oct.-Apr. 9-11:30am and 1-3:30pm. Free.) The castle's **Torre de Menagem** has an impressive view of the vast Alentejan plains (€0.50 to ascend).

Trains run from the station (☎284 32 50 56), about 1km outside of town, to Évora (1½hr., 5 per day 7:45am-8:30pm, €6.50) and Lisbon (2½-3hr., 4 per day 5am-7:20pm, €8.50). The **bus station** (☎284 31 36 20) is on R. Cidade de São Paulo, near the corner of Av. Brasil. **Buses** go to: Évora (1hr., 5 per day 7am-7:15pm, €7.20); Faro (3½hr., 3 per day 10am-7:20pm, €9); and Lisbon (3-3½hr., 6 per day 7am-3pm, €9.40). To get to the town center, turn right onto R. Afonso de Albuquerque and left on R. Capitão J. F. de Sousa, where the **tourist office,** R. Capitão J. F. de Sousa 25, is located. (☎/fax 284 31 19 13. Open May-Sept. M-F 9am-8pm, Sa 10am-1pm and 2-6pm; Oct.-Apr. M-Sa 10am-1pm and 2-6pm). Beja has excellent accommodations. Try **Pousada de Juventude de Beja ❶,** R. Professor Janeiro Acabado, which offers a living room with a TV and games, a laundry room, and a kitchen. (☎284 32 54 58. June 16-Sept. 15 dorms €10; doubles €21. Sept. 16-June 15 dorms €8; doubles €18.) **Residencial Rosa do Campo ❸,** R. Liberdade 12, is an extremely nice, newly-renovated private home. (☎284 32 35 78. Singles €27.50; doubles €35-40.) Beja is one of the best places to taste authentic (and affordable) Alentejo cuisine. Try **Restaurante Casa de Risto o Saiote ❶,** R. Biscainha 6. (*Calhamares* €4.25. Open M-Sa noon-3:30pm and 7-10:30pm). **Postal Code:** 7800.

ALGARVE

Behold the Algarve—a freak of nature, a desert on the sea, an inexhaustible vacationland where happy campers from all over the world bask in the sun. Nearly 3000 hours of sunshine per year have transformed this one-time fishermen's backwater into one of Europe's favorite vacation spots. In July and August, tourists mob the Algarve's resorts in search of perfect tans on the beaches and wild nights in the bars and discos. In the off-season, a less intense sun presides over tranquil grotto beaches at the bases of rugged cliffs. The westernmost town of Sagres offers isolated beaches and steep cliffs, while the eastern border near Tavira features floating flamingo wetlands.

LAGOS ☎282

As the town's countless expatriates will attest, Lagos is a black hole: come for two days and you'll be tempted to stay a month. For as long as anyone in Lagos can remember, this modest-sized town (pop. 22,000) has played host to swarms of sun-worshipping foreigners. Although there isn't much more than beaches and bars, between soaking in the view from the cliffs, soaking in the sun on the beach, and soaking in drinks at the bars, you won't find anyone complaining.

TRANSPORTATION AND PRACTICAL INFORMATION

Running the length of the channel, **Avenida Descubrimentos** is the main road to and from Lagos. From the train station, walk through the pastel pink marina and cross over the channel on the pedestrian suspension bridge, then turn left onto Av. Descubrimentos. Exiting the bus station, walk straight until you hit Av. Descubrimentos, then turn right. Take another right onto R. Porta de Portugal to reach **Praça Gil Eanes,** the center of the old town.

Trains: (☎282 76 29 87), across the river (over the pedestrian suspension bridge) from the main part of town. To **Évora** (6hr., 8:20am and 5:15pm, €11) and **Lisbon** (4-4½hr., 5-6 per day, €13).

Buses: The **EVA** bus station (☎282 76 29 44), off Av. Descubrimentos, is across the channel from the train station. To: **Lisbon** (5hr., 12 per day, €14.50); **Sagres** (1hr., 17 per day, €2.40); **Sevilla, Spain** (5-6hr., 7:30am and 2pm, €15).

Tourist Office: Marques de Pombal Square (☎282 76 41 11), on the corner of R. Lima Leitão. Open July-Aug. M-Sa 10am-10pm; June and Sept. M-Sa 10am-8pm; Oct.-May M-F 10am-6pm.

Emergency: ☎112. **Police:** (☎282 76 29 30), R. General Alberto Silva.

Medical Services: Hospital (☎282 77 01 00), R. Castelo dos Governadores.

Internet Access: The Em@il Box (Ciaxa de Correieo), R. Cândido dos Reis 112 (☎282 76 89 50). €3.50 per hr. Open M-F 9:30am-8pm, Sa-Su 10am-3pm.

Post Office: R. Portas de Portugal (☎282 77 02 50), between Pr. Gil Eanes and the river. Open M-F 9am-6pm. **Postal Code:** 8600.

ACCOMMODATIONS

In the summertime, *pensões* fill up quickly and cost a bundle. Reserve rooms at least a week in advance. Rooms in *casas particulares* run around €10-15 per person in summer; for reduced rates, try haggling with owners.

Pousada da Juventude de Lagos (HI), R. Lançarote de Freitas 50 (☎282 76 19 70; www.hostalbooking.com), off R. 25 de Abril. Friendly staff and lodgers congregate in the courtyard. Breakfast included. In summer, book through the central **Movijovem** office (☎213 59 60 00). June 16-Sept. 15 dorms €15; doubles with bath €42. Sept. 16-June 15 dorms €10; doubles with bath €28. MC/V. ❶

Olinda Teresa Maria Quartos, R. Lançarote de Freitas 37, 2nd fl. (☎282 08 23 29), across the street from the youth hostel. Offers rooms with shared kitchen, terrace, and bath. If the owner is not in, check at the youth hostel. June 16-Sept. 15 dorms €15; doubles €24. Sept. 16-June 15 dorms €10; doubles €30. ❶

Residencial Rubi Mar, R. Barroca 70 (☎282 76 31 65; fax 76 77 49), off Pr. Gil Eanes toward Pr. Infante Dom Henrique. July-Oct. doubles €40, with bath €45; quads €75. Nov.-June doubles €28, with bath €33; quads €50. ❹

Residencial Lagosmar, R. Dr. Faria da Silva 13 (☎282 76 37 22), up from Pr. Gil Eanes. 24hr. reception. July-Aug. singles €60; doubles €70; extra bed €22. June and Sept. singles €35; doubles €40; extra bed €13. Nov.-Feb. singles €22; doubles €25; extra bed €9. Mar.-May and Oct. singles €30; doubles €35; extra bed €11. ❺

Residencial Caravela, R. 25 de Abril 8 (☎282 76 33 61), just up the street from Pr. Gil Eanes. Singles €24; doubles €33, with bath €36; triples €50. ❷

Camping Trindade (☎282 76 38 93), just outside of town. Follow Av. Descubrimentos toward Sagres. The way most Europeans experience the Algarve. €2.90 per person, €3.20 per tent, and €3.50 per car. ❶

Camping Valverde (☎282 78 92 11), 6km outside Lagos and 1.5km west of Praia da Luz. Showers, grocery, and pool. €4.75 per person, €4.75 per tent, or €4 per car. ❶

FOOD

Tourists can peruse multilingual menus around **Praça Gil Eanes** and **Rua 25 de Abril.** For authentic Portuguese seafood, try **Praça Luis Camoes.** The cheapest option is the **market,** on Av. Descubrimentos 5min. from the town center. **Supermercado São Toque,** R. Portas de Portugal 61, is opposite the post office. (☎282 76 28 55. Open July-Sept. M-F 9am-8pm, Sa 9am-7pm; Oct.-June M-F 9am-7:30pm, Sa 9am-7pm.)

Casa Rosa, R. Ferrador 22. Enjoy huge, cheap meals (from €3.50) with hordes of backpackers. Wide-ranging menu with many vegetarian options (€3.50-7). M is all-you-can-eat spaghetti night (€5). Open daily 7pm-2am. ❶

Mediterraneo, R. Senhora da Graça 2 (☎282 76 84 76). Mediterranean and Thai cuisine, including seafood and meat dishes, great salads, and desserts. Indoor and outdoor dining. Entrees €9-13.50. ❸

Snack-Bar Caravela, R. 25 de Abril 14, just off Pr. Gil Eanes. Well-touristed, but for good reason—it's a great place to people-watch and the pizza is the best in town. Outdoor seating on a pedestrian street. Pizzas €4.50-7. Open June-Sept. daily 9am-midnight; Oct.-March 9am-10pm. AmEx/MC/V. ❷

SIGHTS AND ENTERTAINMENT

Flat, smooth, sunbathing sand can be found at **Meia Praia,** across the river from town. Hop on the 30-second ferry near Pr. República (€0.50). For beautiful cliffs with less-crowded beaches and caves, follow Av. Descubrimentos toward Sagres to the **Praia de Pinhão** (20min.). A bit farther, **Praia Dona Ana** features the sculpted cliffs and grottos that grace most Algarve postcards.

Although sunbathing and non-stop debauchery have long erased memories of Lagos's rugged, sea-faring past, most of the city is still surrounded by a nearly intact 16th-century wall. The **Fortaleza da Ponta da Bandeira,** a 17th-century fortress holding maritime exhibitions, overlooks the marina. (☎282 76 14 10. Open Tu-Sa 10am-1pm and 2-6pm, Su 10am-1pm. €1.85, students €1.) Also on the waterfront is the old **Mercado de Escravos** (slave market). Legend has it that in 1441 the first sale of African slaves on Portuguese ground took place here. Today, the waterfront and marina offer jet-ski rentals, scuba diving lessons, sailboat trips, and motorboat tours of the coastal rocks and grottoes.

The streets of Lagos pick up as soon as the sun dips down, and by midnight the city's walls are shaking. The area between **Praça Gil Eanes** and **Praça Luis de Camões** is filled with cafes. For late-night bars and clubs, try R. Cândido dos Reis, R. do Ferrador, and the intersection of R. 25 de Abril, R. Silva Lopes, and R. Soeiro da Costa. Staggered Happy Hours make drinking easy, even on the tightest of budgets. **Eddie's,** R. 25 de Abril 99, is an easy-going bar popular with backpackers and seasonal workers. (Beer €2. Open M-Sa 4pm-2am, Su 8pm-2am.) **Taverna Velha (The Old Tavern),** R. Lançarote de Freitas 34, down the street from Pousada da Juventude, is the only air-conditioned bar in Lagos. (Beer €1.25-2.50. Open M-Sa 4pm-2am, Su 8pm-2am.) Fraternity posters and occasional streakers decorate **The Red Eye,** R. Cândido dos Reis 63. (Mixed drinks €2.50-3.50. Open daily 8pm-2am.) **Joe's Garage,** R. 1 de Maio 78, is the rowdiest, and possibly raunchiest, bar in town. (Beer €2. 2-for-1 beers or drinks 10pm-midnight. Open daily 10pm-2am.)

DAYTRIPS FROM LAGOS

SAGRES. Marooned atop a bleak desert plateau in Europe's southwesternmost corner, desolate Sagres and its cape were once considered the edge of the world. Near the town lurks the **Fortaleza de Sagres,** the fortress where Prince Henry stroked his beard, decided to map the world, and founded his famous **school of navigation.** (Open May-Sept. daily 10am-8:30pm; Oct.-Apr. 10am-6:30pm. €3.) Six kilometers west lies the dramatic **Cabo de São Vicente,** where the second-most powerful lighthouse in Europe shines over 100km out to sea. To get there on weekdays, take the bus from the bus station on R. Comandante Matoso near the tourist office (10min.; 11:15am, 12:30pm, 4:15pm; €1). Alternatively, hike 1hr. or bike past the several fortresses perched atop the cliffs. The most notable **beach** in the area is **Mareta,** at the bottom of the road from the town center. Just west of town, **Praia de Martinhal** and **Praia da Baleeira** have great windsurfing. The nearby coves of **Salema** and **Luz** are intimate and picturesque. At night, a young crowd fills lively **Rosa dos Ventos** in Pr. República. (Beer €1. Open Su-Tu and Th-Sa 10am-2am.)

EVA **buses** (☎282 76 29 44) run from Lagos (1hr., 17 per day 7:15am-8:30pm, €2.80). The **tourist office,** on R. Comandante Matoso, is up the street from the bus stop. (☎282 62 48 73. Open Tu-Sa 9:30am-1pm and 2-5:30pm.)

PRAIA DA ROCHA. A short jaunt from Lagos, this grand **beach** is perhaps the very best the Algarve has to offer. With vast expanses of sand, surfable waves, rocky red cliffs, and plenty of secluded coves, Praia da Rocha has a well-deserved reputation and the crowds to match. From Lagos, take a bus to Portimão (40min., 14 per day 7:15am-8:15pm, €1.80), then switch to the Praia da Rocha bus (10min., every 30min. 7:30am-8:30pm, €1.30). The **tourist office** is at the end of R. Tomás Cabreina. (☎282 41 91 32. Open May-Sept. daily 9:30am-7pm; Oct.-Apr. M-F 9:30am-12:30pm and 2-5:30pm, Sa-Su 9:30am-12:30pm.)

TAVIRA ☎281

Farmers tease police by riding their motor scooters over the Roman pedestrian bridge, but that's about as crazy as Tavira gets. For most visitors to this relaxing haven—speckled with white houses, palm trees, and Baroque churches—that's just fine. From the central Pr. República, steps lead up to the 16th-century **Igreja da Misericórdia.** (Open Tu-Th 9:30am-12:30pm and 2-5:30pm. Free.) Just beyond the church, the remains of the city's **Castelo Mouro** (Moorish Castle) sit next to **Santa Maria do Castelo.** (Castle open M-F 8am-5pm and Sa-Su 10am-5pm. Church open daily 9:30am-12:30pm and 2-5pm. Free.) Local beaches, including **Araial do Barril,** are accessible year-round by the bus to Pedras D'el Rei (10min., 8 per day, €0.90). To reach the golden shores of **Ilha da Tavira,** an island 2km away, take the ferry from the end of Estrada das 4 Aguas (round-trip €1.20).

Trains (☎281 32 23 54) leave Tavira for Faro (40min., 10-17 per day, €1.60) and Vila Real de Santo António (30min., 9-13 per day, €1.20). **EVA buses** (☎281 32 25 46) leave from the station upriver from Pr. República for Faro (1hr., 12-13 per day, €2.25). From the train station it's a short 5-10min. walk down Av. Dr. Teixeira de Azevedo, or you can catch the local **TUT bus** to the town center (10min., every

30min. 8am-8pm, €0.80). **Pensão Residencial Lagôas Bica ❷,** R. Almirante Cândido dos Reis 24, has a hospitable owner and well-furnished rooms. (☎281 32 22 52. Singles €16-18; doubles €26-28, with bath €36-38.) Cafes line Pr. República. **Restaurante Bica ❷,** R. Almirante Candido dos Reis, offers home-style Portuguese cooking. (Four-course *menú toristico* €7.50. Entrees €4-9.) **Postal code:** 8800.

FARO ☎289

The Algarve's capital, largest city, and transportation hub is untouristed despite its charm. Its **old town,** a medley of museums, handicraft shops, and ornate churches, begins at the **Arco da Vila,** a stone arch. In Largo Carmo is the **Igreja de Nossa Senhora do Carmo** and its **Capela dos Ossos** (Chapel of Bones), a macabre bonanza of bones and skulls "borrowed" from the adjacent cemetery. (Open May-Sept. daily 10am-1pm and 3-6pm, Oct.-April M-F 10am-1pm and 3-5pm, Sa 10am-1pm. Church free, chapel €0.75.) Faro's **beach** hides on an islet off the coast. Take bus #16 from the bus station or the stop in front of the tourist office (5-10min., every hr., €0.90).

Trains (☎289 80 17 26) run from Largo Estação to: Évora (5hr., 9am and 5:30pm, €10); Lagos (2hr., 6 per day 8am-9pm, €4); and Lisbon (5-6hr., 6 per day 7:20am-11pm, €13). **EVA buses** (☎289 89 97 00) go from Av. República to: Beja (3-3½hr., 7 per day 7:45am-4pm, €8); Lagos (2hr., 8 per day 7:30am-5:30pm, €4); and Tavira (1hr., 11 per day 7:15am-7:30pm, €3). **Renex** (☎289 81 29 80), across the street, provides express long-distance service to: Braga (8½hr., 9 per day 5:30am-1:30am, €20); Lisbon (4hr., 11-15 per day 5:30am-1:30am, €14); and Porto (7½hr., 6-13 per day 5:30am-1:30am, €19). **Intersul** (☎289 89 97 70) runs to Sevilla, Spain (2 per day, €15) with connecting buses to France and Germany. From the stations, turn right down Av. República along the harbor, then turn left past the garden to reach the **tourist office,** R. Misericórdia 8, at the entrance to the old town. (☎289 80 36 04. Open June-Aug. daily 9:30am-7pm; Sept.-May daily 9:30am-5:30pm.) Travelers sleep easy at **Pousada da Juventude (HI) ❶,** R. Polícia de Segurança Pública, opposite the police station. (☎/fax 289 82 65 21. Dorms €7.50-9.50; doubles €18-23, with bath €21-26.50. AmEx/MC/V.) Enjoy coffee and the local marzipan at cafes along **R. Conselheiro Bívar,** off Pr. Gomes.

NORTHERN PORTUGAL

Although their landscapes and Celtic history invite comparison with the northwest of Spain, the Douro and Minho regions of northern Portugal are wealthier, more populated, and more developed than Spanish Galicia. Hundreds of trellised vineyards for *porto* and *vinho verde* wines beckon connoisseurs, while *azulejo*-lined houses draw visitors to charming, quiet streets. The Three Beiras region offers a sample of the best of Portugal: the unspoiled Costa da Prata (Silver Coast), the plush greenery of the interior, and the rugged peaks of the Serra Estrela.

COIMBRA ☎239

Home to the country's only university from the mid-16th to the early-20th century, vibrant Coimbra continues to be a mecca for youth from around the world. A slew of cheap cafes and bars filled with students keep Coimbra swinging from September to May. The city's charm has long since blotted out Coimbra's infamous role as center of the Portuguese Inquisition and the site of former dictator António Salazar's education.

TRANSPORTATION

Trains: (info ☎239 83 49 98). **Estação Coimbra-A (Nova)** is 2 blocks from the lower town center. **Estação Coimbra-B (Velha)** is 3km northwest of town. Regional trains stop at both Coimbra-B and Coimbra-A. Trains arriving from/departing for cities outside the region stop in Coimbra-B only. If your train only stops at Coimbra-B, it is easiest to take a connecting train to Coimbra-A (4min., immediately after trains arrive, €0.70). Trains run to **Lisbon** (3hr., 23 per day 5:30am-2:20am, €8-14) and **Porto** (2hr., 21 per day 5am-3am, €5-9.50).

Buses: (☎239 82 70 81). To reach the bus station, go from Av. Fernão Magalhães, on the university side of the river, past Coimbra-A. Buses to **Lisbon** (2½hr., 17 per day 7:30am-2:15am, €9) and **Porto** (1½hr., 10 per day 8:30am-9:30pm, €7).

ORIENTATION AND PRACTICAL INFORMATION

There are three major areas of town, all on the same side of the river. The most central is the **Baixa** (also known as lower town, site of the tourist office and Coimbra-A train station), **Largo da Portagem,** and **Praça 8 de Maio.** Coimbra's **university district** is atop the steep hill overlooking the Baixa. On the other side of the university, **Praça da República** hosts cafes and the youth hostel.

Tourist Office: (☎239 85 59 30), off Largo Portagem, in a yellow building 2 blocks up the river from Coimbra-A. From the bus station, turn right, follow the avenue to Coimbra-A, then walk to Largo Portagem (15min.). Open June-Sept. M-F 9am-7pm, Sa-Su 10am-1pm and 2:30-5:30pm; Oct.-May M-F until 6pm. **University branch office** (☎239 83 25 91), in Lg. Dom Dinis. Open M-F 9am-6pm, Sa-Su 9am-12:30pm and 2-5:30pm.

Emergency: ☎112. **Police:** ☎239 82 95 65. Special division for foreigners *(Serviço de Estrangeiros)*, R. Venâncio Rodrigues 25 (☎239 82 37 67).

Hospital: Hospital da Universidade de Coimbra (☎239 40 04 00), Lg. Professor Mota Pinto. Take the #7 or 29 bus to the "Hospital" stop.

Internet Access: Central Modem, Escada de Quebra Costas, down the stairs from Lg. da Sé Velha. €0.55 for 15min. Open M-F 10am-10pm. **Post Net,** R. Antero de Quental 73, between Pr. República and the youth hostel. €0.75 for 15min., €2.50 per hr. Open M-F 10am-midnight, Sa 2pm-midnight, Su 7pm-midnight. **@ caffé,** Lg. da Sé Velha 4-8, across from the old cathedral. €1.50 per hr.

Post Office: Central office (☎239 85 07 70), on Av. Fernão de Magalhães. Open M-F 8:30am-6:30pm. **Postal Code:** 3000.

ACCOMMODATIONS

Pensão Santa Cruz, Pr. 8 de Maio 21, 3rd fl. (☎/fax 239 82 61 97; www.pensaosantacruz.com), directly across from the Igreja da Santa Cruz. Comfortable rooms, most with cable TV, some with bath. July-Sept. singles or doubles €20, with bath €30; triples €25/€35. Oct.-June €5 less. ❷

Pousada da Juventude de Coimbra (HI), R. Henrique Seco 14 (☎239 82 29 55). From the tourist office, walk up R. Ferreira Borges to Pr. 8 de Maio, then walk 20min. uphill along R. Olímpio Nicolau Rui Fernandes to Pr. República, then up R. Lourenço Azevedo (to the left of the park). Take the 2nd right; the hostel is on the right. Laundry €5 per load. Reception daily 8am-noon and 6pm-midnight. Lockout noon-6pm. June 16-Sept. 15 dorms €10.50; doubles with bath €29. Sept. 16-June 15 €3-5 less. ❶

Residencial Vitória, R. da Sota 11-19 (☎239 82 40 49; fax 84 28 97), across from Coimbra-A. Rooms and prices to suit any budget. Reception 24hr. New rooms: singles €25; doubles €35; triples €45. Older rooms: singles €15, with shower €18; doubles €20/€25. MC/V. ❷

FOOD

The best cuisine in Coimbra lies off Pr. 8 de Maio around **Rua Direita,** on the side streets between the river and Largo Portagem, and around **Praça República** in the university district. **Supermercado Minipreço,** R. António Granjo 6C, is in the lower town center. (Open M-Sa 8:30am-8pm, Su 9am-1pm and 3-7pm.)

Porta Romana, R. Martins de Carvalho 10 (☎239 82 84 58), just up from the Igreja da Santa Cruz in Pr. 8 de Maio. Amiable staff serves surprisingly affordable Italian dishes. Pizzas €4-7. Pastas €4.70-7.50. Salads €3.50-4. Open July-Aug. M-Sa 7am-midnight, Su 6pm-midnight; Sept.-June M-F 7am-midnight. ❶

Pastelaria Arco Iris, Av. Fernão de Magalhães 22 (☎239 83 33 04), across from Coimbra-A. Choose from a colorful variety of pastries (€0.50-0.80). Coffee €0.90. Large variety of sandwiches (€1-2.50). Open M-Sa 7:15am-8:30pm, Su 8am-8:30pm. ❶

SIGHTS AND ENTERTAINMENT

Take in the old-town sights by climbing from the river up the narrow stone steps to the university. Begin your ascent at the **Arco de Almedina,** a remnant of the Moorish town wall, one block uphill from Largo Portagem. At the top is the looming 12th-century Romanesque **Sé Velha** (Old Cathedral), complete with tombs, Gregorian chants, and a cloister. (Open M-Th 10am-noon and 2-7:30pm, F-Su 10am-1pm. Cloister €0.75.) Follow signs to the late 16th-century **Sé Nova** (New Cathedral), built for the Jesuits (open Tu-Sa 9am-noon and 2-6:30pm; free), just a few blocks from the 16th-century **University of Coimbra.** The **Porta Férrea** (Iron Gate), off R. São Pedro, opens onto the old university, whose buildings constituted Portugal's royal palace when Coimbra was the kingdom's capital. (Open May-Sept. daily 9am-7:30pm; Oct.-Apr. 9:30am-12:30pm and 2-5:30pm.) The stairs to the right lead to the **Sala dos Capelos,** which houses portraits of Portugal's kings, six of them Coimbra-born. (Open daily 9:30am-12:30pm and 2-5:30pm. €2.50.) The **university chapel** and the mind-boggling, entirely gilded 18th-century **Biblioteca Joanina** (University Library) lie past the Baroque clock tower. (Open May-Sept. daily 9am-7:30pm; Oct.-Apr. 9:30am-noon and 2-5:30pm. €2.50, students free. Ticket for all university sights €4; buy tickets from the office in the main quad.) Cross the bridge in front of Largo Portagem to find the 14th-century **Convento de Santa Clara-a-Velha** and the 17th-century **Convento de Santa Clara-a-Nova.** (Interior closed until summer 2003 for massive renovation. Both open M-Sa 9am-noon and 2-6pm. Cloisters and sacristy €1.)

Nightlife in Coimbra gets highest honors. **Café Tropical,** Pr. República 35, is a great place to start. (Beer €0.70-1.25. Mixed drinks €3.50. Open M-Sa 9am-2am.) **Diligência Bar,** R. Nova 30, off R. Sofia, is known for its *fado*. (*Sangría* €9.20 per liter. Open M-Sa 6pm-2am, Su 7pm-2am.) **Hups!,** R. Castro Matoso 11, is one of the newest dance clubs in town. (Beer €1.50. Open Tu-Su 10pm-5am.) **Via Latina,** R. Almeida Garrett 1, around the corner and uphill from Pr. República, is hot in all senses of the word. (Beer €1.50. Open M-Sa 11pm-7am.) **The English Bar,** R. Lourenço de Almeida Azevedo 24, is new and hip. (Beer €1.50-2. Mixed drinks €3-4. Open M-Sa 10pm-4am.) Dance *and* check email at **@caffé,** Lg. da Sé Velha 4-8. (Open June to mid-Sept. M-Sa 11am-4am; mid-Sept. to May M-Sa 9pm-4am.) In early May, graduates burn the narrow ribbons they got as first-years and get wide ones in return during Coimbra's week-long **Queima das Fitas.**

PORTO (OPORTO) ☎22

Porto is famous for its namesake—strong, sugary port wine. Developed by English merchants in the early 18th century, the port industry is at the root of the city's successful economy. But there's more to Porto than just port. The country's second-largest city retains old school charm with granite church towers, orange-tiled houses, and graceful bridges, but also hosts the sophisticated and modern lifestyle that won Porto its position as a Cultural Capital of Europe in 2001.

TRANSPORTATION. Most trains pass through Porto's main station, **Estação Campanhã** (☎225 36 41 41), on R. da Estação. Trains run to: Coimbra (2hr., 17 per day 5am-12am, €5.30); Lisbon (3½-4½hr., 14 per day 6am-8pm, €11-19); and Madrid (13-14hr., 6:10pm, €48). **Estação São Bento** (☎222 00 27 22), Pr. Almeida Garrett, centrally located one block off Pr. Liberdade, is the terminus for trains with local and regional routes. Rede Expresso **buses,** R. Alexandre Herculano 366 (☎222 05 24 59), in the Garagem Atlântico, has buses to Coimbra (1½hr., 11 per day 7:15am-12:45am, €7) and Lisbon (4hr., 12 per day 7:15am-12:45am, €12). REDM, R. Dr. Alfredo Magalhães 94 (☎222 00 31 52), two blocks from Pr. República, sends buses to Braga (1hr.; M-F 26 per day 6:45am-8pm, Sa-Su 9-12 per day 7:15am-8pm; €3.30). Buy tickets for the **intracity buses** and **trams** from small kiosks around the city, or at the **STCP office,** Pr. Almeida Garrett 27, downhill and across the street from Estação de São Bento (pre-purchased single ticket €0.40; day pass €2.50).

PRACTICAL INFORMATION. The **tourist office,** R. Clube dos Fenianos 25, is off Pr. Liberdade. (☎223 39 34 72. Open July-Sept. daily 9am-7pm; Oct.-June M-F 9am-5:30pm, Sa-Su 9:30am-4:30pm.) Check **email** at **Portweb,** Pr. Gen. Humberto Delgado 291, by the tourist office. (10am-4pm €0.50 per hr., 4pm-2am €1.20 per hr. Open M-Sa 10am-2am, Su 3pm-2am.) The **post office** is on Pr. Gen. Humberto Delgado. (☎223 40 02 00. Open M-F 8:30am-9pm, Sa-Su 9am-6pm.) **Postal code:** 4000.

ACCOMMODATIONS AND FOOD. For good accommodation deals, look west of **Avenida Aliados** or on **Rua Fernandes Tomás** and **Rua Formosa,** perpendicular to Av. dos Aliados. Popular with young travelers from around the world, **Pensão Duas Nações ❷** offers a variety of rooms at low rates. (☎222 08 96 21. Internet €0.50 per 15min. Reserve ahead. Singles €15; doubles €25-30; triples €30, with bath €35.) A few blocks away from the city center, **Pensão Portuguesa ❶,** Tr. Coronel Pacheco 11, has cheap rooms on a quiet street. (☎222 00 41 74. July-Aug. singles €12.50, with bath €15; doubles €15/€20. Sept.-June singles €10; doubles €13.) Take bus #35 from Estação Campanha to **Pousada de Juventude do Porto (HI) ❷,** R. Paulo da Gama 551, which is in a somewhat dodgy neightborhood—women should be cautious walking around at night. (☎226 17 72 57. Reception daily 8am-midnight. June-Sept. dorms €15; doubles with bath €42. Oct.-May €12.50/€35.)

THAT TOOK GUTS When native son Henry the Navigator geared up to conquer Cueta in the early 15th century, Porto's residents slaughtered their cattle, gave the meat to Prince Henry's fleet, and kept only the entrails. This dramatic generosity came in the wake of the Plague, when food supplies were crucial. The dish *tripàs a moda do Porto* commemorates their culinary sacrifice; to this day, the people of Porto are known as *tripeiros* (tripe-eaters). If you're feeling adventurous, try some of the tripe dishes, which locals–and few others–consider quite a delicacy.

Take bus #6, 50, 54, or 87 from Pr. Liberdade (only #50 and 54 run at night) to **camp** at **Prelada ❶,** on R. Monte dos Burgos, in Quinta da Prelada, 3km from the town center. (☎228 31 26 16. Reception 8am-11pm. €2.50-3.30 per person, per tent, or per car.) Look near the river in the **Ribeira** district on C. Ribeira, R. Reboleira, and R. Cima do Muro for great restaurants. The **Majestic Café ❷,** R. de Santa Catarina 112, is the oldest, most famous cafe in Porto. (Open M-Sa 9:30am-midnight.) Across the street, **Confeitaria Império ❶,** R. de Santa Catarina 149-151, serves excellent pastries and inexpensive lunch specials. (Open M-Sa 7:30am-8:30pm.)

SIGHTS AND ENTERTAINMENT. For many, the first brush with Porto's rich stock of fine artwork is the celebrated collection of *azulejos* (tiles) in the **São Bento train station.** Walk past the station and uphill on Av. Afonso Henriques to reach Porto's pride and joy, the 12th- to 13th-century Romanesque **cathedral.** (Open M-Sa 9am-12:30pm and 2:30-6pm, Su 2:30-6pm. Cloister €1.25.) From the station, follow signs downhill on R. Mouzinho da Silveira to R. Ferreira Borges and the **Palácio da Bolsa** (Stock Exchange), the epitome of 19th-century elegance. The ornate **Sala Árabe** (Arabic Hall) took 18 years to decorate. (Open daily 9am-7pm. Tours every 30min., €4.) Next door, the Gothic **Igreja de São Francisco** glitters with an elaborately gilded wooden interior. Thousands of human bones are stored under the floor. (Open daily 9am-6pm. €2.50, students €1.25.) From Pr. Liberdade up R. dos Clérigos rises the **Torre dos Clérigos** (Tower of Clerics), adjacent to the **Igreja dos Clérigos.** (Tower open June-July daily 10am-7pm; Aug. 10am-10pm; Sept.-May 10am-noon and 2-5pm. €1. Church open M-Th 10am-noon and 2-5pm, Sa 10am-noon and 2-8pm, Su 10am-1pm. Free.) From there, head up R. Restauração, turn right on R. Alberto Gouveia, and go left on R. Dom Manuel II to reach the **Museu Nacional Soares dos Reis,** R. Dom Manuel II 44. This former royal residence now houses an exhaustive collection of 19th-century Portuguese painting and sculpture. (Open Tu 2-6pm, W-Su 10am-6pm. €3, students €1.50.) Bus #78 from Av. dos Aliados runs several kilometers out of town to the **Museu de Arte Contemporânea,** which hosts contemporary art and an impressive park with sculpted gardens and fountains. (Museum open Tu-Th 10am-10pm, Sa-Su 10am-8pm. Park closes at sundown. €4, Su before 2pm free.) To get to Porto's rocky and polluted (but popular) **beach,** in the ritzy Foz district, take bus #1 from the São Bento train station or tram #1 from Igreja de São Francisco.

But we digress—back to the port. Fine and bounteous port wines are available for tasting at more than 20 **port wine lodges,** usually *gratuito* (free). The lodges are all across the river in **Vila Nova da Gaia;** from the Ribeira district, cross the lower level of the large bridge. **Sandeman,** with its costumed guides, is a good place to start (entrance €2.50). **Ferreira,** one block up from the end of Av. Ramos Pinto, has a memorable atmosphere (entrance €2.50). **Taylor's,** R. do Choupelo 250, has a terrace with views of the city (free). (Most open daily 10am-6pm.)

BRAGA ☎253

Braga (pop. 160,000) originally served as the capital of a region founded by Celtic tribes in 300 BC. The city's beautiful gardens, plazas, museums, and markets earned it the nickname "Portuguese Rome." In Portugal's oldest **cathedral,** the treasury showcases the archdiocese's most precious paintings and relics, including a collection of *cofres cranianos* (brain boxes), one of which contains the 6th-century cortex of São Martinho Dume, Braga's first bishop. (Cathedral and treasury open June-Aug. daily 8:30am-6pm; Sept.-May 8:30am-5pm. Cathedral free. Treasury €2.) Braga's most famous landmark, **Igreja do Bom Jesús,** is actually 5km outside of town. To visit Bom Jesús, either take the 285m ride on the antique funicular (8am-8pm, €1), or walk 25-30min. up the granite-paved pathway that forks into two zig-zagging 565-step stairways.

Buses (☎253 61 60 80) leave Central de Camionagem for: Coimbra (3hr., 6-9 per day, €8); Guimarães (1hr., every 30min., €2); Lisbon (5¼hr., 8-9 per day, €12); and Porto (1¾ hr., every 45min., €3.80). The **tourist office,** Av. Central 1, is on the corner of Av. Liberdade in Pr. República. (☎253 26 25 50. Open July-Sept. M-F 9am-7pm, Sa-Su 9am-12:30pm and 2-5:30pm; Oct.-June closed Su.) From the tourist office, take a right and follow Av. Combatentes; turn left at R. Santa Margarida to reach the **Pousada da Juventude de Braga (HI) ❶,** R. Santa Margarida 6. (☎/fax 253 61 61 63. Reception daily 8am-midnight. Mid-June to mid-Sept. dorms €9.50.)

DAYTRIP FROM BRAGA: GUIMARÃES. Ask Portugese natives about the city of Guimarães (pop. 60,000), and they will tell you it was the birthplace of the nation. The city is home to one of Portugal's most gorgeous palatial estates, the **Paço dos Duques de Bragança** (Ducal Palace), which is modeled after the manor houses of northern Europe. Overlooking the city is the **Monte da Pena,** home to an excellent **campsite** as well as picnic areas, mini-golf, and cafes. To get there, take the **teleférico** from Lg. das Hortas. (☎253 51 50 85. Closed Oct.-May. Open Aug. daily 10am-8pm; June-July and Sept. M-F 11am-7pm, Sa-Su 10am-8pm. €1.50, round-trip €2.50.) The **tourist office** is on Alameda de São Dámaso 83, facing Pr. Toural. (☎253 41 24 50. Open June-Sept. M-Sa 9:30am-7pm; Oct.-May M-Sa 9:30am-6pm.) Guimarães is best reached by **bus** from Braga. REDM buses (☎253 51 62 29) run frequently between the cities until 8pm (1hr., €2).

VIANA DO CASTELO ☎258

Situated in the northwestern corner of the country, Viana do Castelo (pop. 20,000) is one of the loveliest coastal cities in all of Portugal. Visited mainly as a beach resort, Viana also has a lively historic district centered around the **Praça da República.** Diagonally across the plaza, granite columns support the flowery facade of the **Igreja da Misericórdia.** Known for its *azulejo* interior, the **Monte de Santa Luzia,** overlooking the city, is crowned by magnificent Celtic ruins and the **Templo de Santa Luzia,** an early 20th-century neo-Byzantine church. The view of Viana from the hill is fantastic. For more views of the harbor and ocean, visit the **Castelo de São Tiago da Barra,** built by Felipe I of Spain. Viana do Castelo and the surrounding coast feature excellent beaches. Most convenient are **Praia Norte,** at the end of Av. do Atlántico at the west end of town, and **Praia da Argaçosa,** on Rio Lima.

Trains (☎258 82 13 15) run from the top of Av. Combatentes da Grande Guerra to Porto (2hr., 13-14 per day 5am-9:25pm, €4). **Buses** run to: Braga (1½hr.; M-Sa 6-8 per day 7am-6:35pm, Su 4 per day 8:15am-6:35pm; €3.50); Lisbon (5½hr.; Su-F 3 per day 8am-11:45pm, Sa 7am and 12:30pm; €18); and Porto (2hr.; M-F 9 per day 6:45am-6:30pm, Sa-Su 4-6 per day 8:20am-6:30pm; €3.50-5.25). The **tourist office,** R. do Hospital Velho, at the corner of Pr. Erva, has a helpful English-speaking staff and offers maps and accommodation listings. (☎258 82 26 20. Open Aug. daily 9am-7pm; May-July and Sept. M-Sa 9am-1pm and 2:30-6pm, Su 9:30am-1pm; Oct.-Apr. M-Sa 9am-12:30pm and 2:30-5:30pm.) The **Pousada de Juventude de Viana do Castelo (HI) ❶,** R. da Argaçosa (Azenhas D. Prior), is right on the marina, off Pr. de Galiza. (☎258 80 02 60; fax 82 08 70. Reception daily 8am-midnight. Check-out 10am. Reservations recommended. Mid-June to mid-Sept. dorms €12.50; doubles with bath €30. Mid-Sept. to mid-June dorms €10; doubles with bath €25.

SPAIN (ESPAÑA)

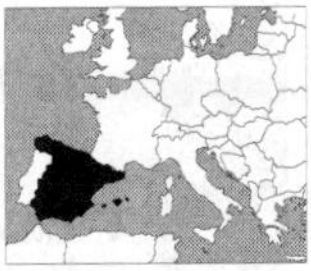

Fiery flamenco dancers, noble bullfighters, and a rich history blending Christian and Islamic culture set Spain apart from the rest of Europe, not to mention drawing almost 50 million tourists each year. The raging nightlife of Madrid, Barcelona, and the Balearic Islands has inspired the popular saying "Spain never sleeps," yet the afternoon siestas of Andalucía exemplify the country's laid-back, easy-going approach to life. Spain houses stunning Baroque, Mudejar, and Mozarabic cathedrals and palaces, hangs the works of Velasquez, Dalí, and Picasso on its hallowed walls, and offers up a backyard of beauty with long, sunny coastlines, snowy mountain peaks, and the dry, golden plains wandered by Don Quixote. You can do Spain in one week, one month, or one year. But you must do it at least once.

SYMBOL	❶	❷	❸	❹	❺
ACCOMMODATIONS	under €15	€16-25	€26-35	€36-50	over €50
FOOD	under €6	€6-10	€11-15	€16-25	over €25

For Spain, prices are indicated in food and accommodations listings using the system of icons and price ranges above. Prices for accommodations are based on the lowest cost for one person, excluding special deals or discounts. For restaurants, prices are based on the average entree price.

SUGGESTED ITINERARIES

THREE DAYS Soak in **Madrid's** (p. 846) blend of art and cosmopolitan life. Walk through the **Retiro's** gardens, peruse the famed halls of the **Prado, Thyssen-Bornemisza,** and **Nacional Centro de Arte Reina Sofia.** By night, move from the *tapas* bars of **Santa Anna** to **Malasaña** and **Chueca.** Daytrip to **Segovia** (p. 871) or somber **Valle de los Caídos** (p. 866).

ONE WEEK Begin in southern Spain, exploring the Alhambra's Moorish palaces in **Granada** (1 day; p. 897) and the mosque in **Córdoba** (1 day; p. 889). After two days in **Madrid** (p. 846), travel east to **Barcelona** (2 days; p. 907) and the beaches of **Costa Brava** (1 day; p. 929).

BEST OF SPAIN, THREE WEEKS Begin in **Madrid** (3 days), with daytrips to **El Escorial** (p. 866) and **Valle de los Caídos** (p. 866). Take the high-speed train to **Córdoba** (2 days), and on to **Sevilla** (2 days; p. 879). Catch the bus to the white town of **Arcos de la Frontera** (1 day; p. 888) before heading south on the Costa del Sol, **Marbella** (1 day, p. 903). Head inland to **Granada** (2 days). Move along the coast to **Valencia** (1 day; p. 905) and escape to **Gandía** (1 day; p. 906). Then it's up the coast to **Barcelona** (2 days), where worthwhile daytrips in Cataluña include **Tossa de Mar** (1 day; p.675), **Montserrat** (p. 927), or **Figueres** (p. 930). From Barcelona, head to the beaches and *tapas* of **San Sebastián** (2 days; p. 937) and **Bilbao** (1 day; p. 942), home of the world-famous Guggenheim Museum.

Ortigueira
Ribadeo
La Coruña
GALICIA
Cabo de Finisterre
Santiago de Compostela
Pontevedra
Vigo
Orense
La Guardia
Miño
Oviedo
ASTURIAS
Cangas de Onís
Llanes
Picos de Europa
Santander
CANTABRIA
Potes
Bilbao
León
Astorga
Carrion de los Condes
Burgos
Santo Domingo
CASTILLA Y LEON
Palencia
El Burgo de Osma
Valladolid
Duero
Zamora
Medina del Campo
Salamanca
Arévalo
Segovia
Alba de Tormes
Ciudad Rodrigo
Ávila
Guadalajara
El Escorial
Madrid
MADRID
Béjar
PORTUGAL
Toledo
Aranjuez
Tajo
Guadalupe
Consuegra
Cáceres
Trujillo
CASTILLA-LA MANCHA
EXTREMADURA
Guadiana
Ciudad Real
Mérida
Badajoz
Almagro
Zafra
Ubeda
Baeza
Aracena
Córdoba
Jaén
Cazorla
Guadalquivir
ANDALUCIA
Ecija
Sevilla
Carmona
Huelva
Guadix
Granada
Osuna
Antequera
Golfo de Cádiz
Arcos de la Frontera
Ronda
Nerja
Chipiona
Málaga
ATLANTIC OCEAN
Jerez de la Frontera
Almuñécar
Cádiz
Marbella
Algeciras
Gibraltar
Spain
Strait of Gibraltar
Ceuta
MOROCCO

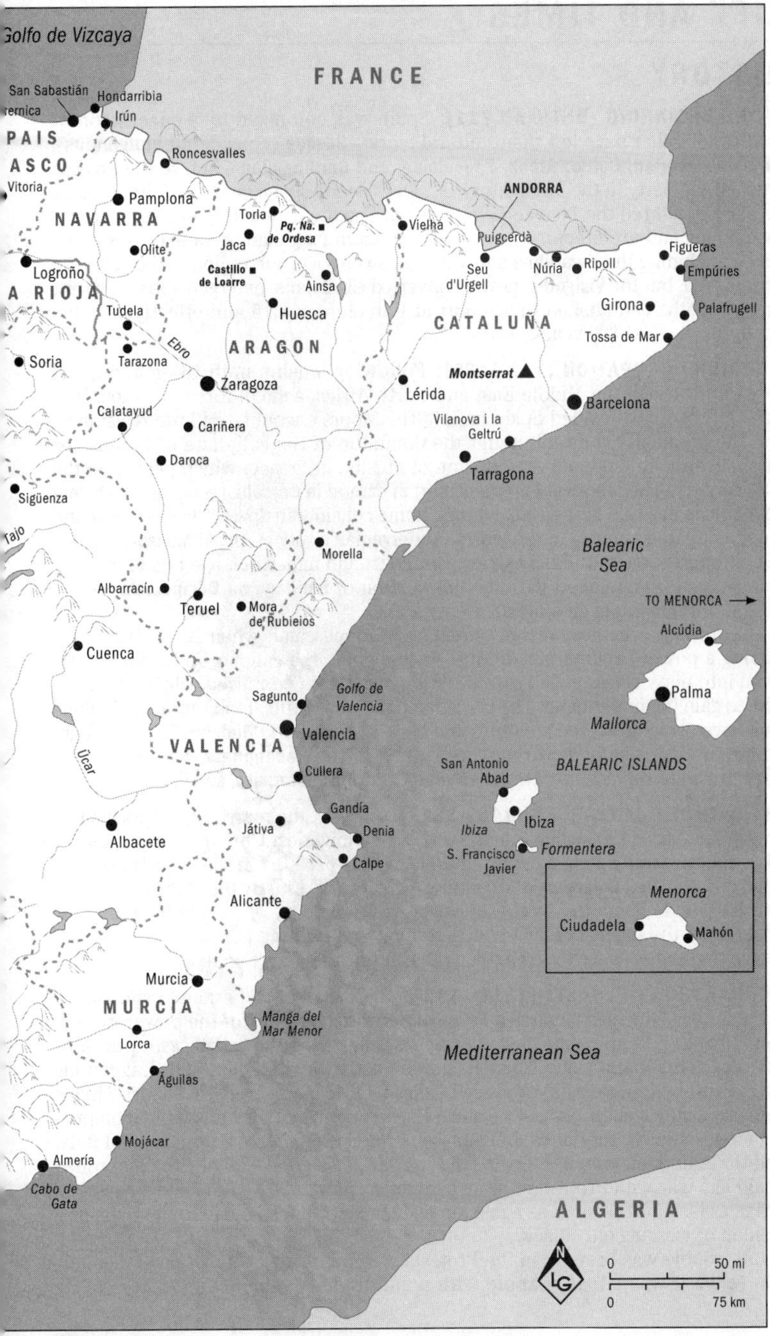
Golfo de Vizcaya
FRANCE
San Sebastián
Hondarribia
Irún
PAIS
VASCO
Vitoria
Roncesvalles
Pamplona
NAVARRA
ANDORRA
Torla
Pq. Na. de Ordesa
Jaca
Vielha
Puigcerdà
Olite
Castillo de Loarre
Ainsa
Seu d'Urgell
Núria
Ripoll
Figueras
Empúries
Logroño
LA RIOJA
Girona
Palafrugell
Tudela
Huesca
CATALUÑA
Tossa de Mar
Ebro
ARAGON
Soria
Tarazona
Montserrat
Zaragoza
Lérida
Barcelona
Calatayud
Cariñera
Vilanova i la Geltrú
Daroca
Tarragona
Sigüenza
Tajo
Morella
Balearic Sea
Albarracín
Teruel
Mora de Rubielos
TO MENORCA
Alcúdia
Cuenca
Sagunto
Golfo de Valencia
Palma
Valencia
Mallorca
VALENCIA
Úcar
San Antonio Abad
BALEARIC ISLANDS
Cullera
Gandía
Ibiza
Játiva
Denia
Ibiza
Albacete
S. Francisco Javier
Formentera
Calpe
Menorca
Alicante
Ciudadela
Mahón
Murcia
MURCIA
Manga del Mar Menor
Lorca
Mediterranean Sea
Águilas
Mojácar
Almería
Cabo de Gata
ALGERIA
N
LG
0
50 mi
0
75 km

LIFE AND TIMES

HISTORY

IN THE BEGINNING (UNTIL AD 711). Spain was colonized by a succession of civilizations that have left their cultural mark—**Basque** (considered indigenous), **Tartesian, Iberian, Celtic, Greek, Phoenician,** and **Carthaginian**—before the **Romans** crashed the party in the 3rd century BC. Over nearly seven centuries, the Romans drastically altered the face and character of Spain, introducing their agricultural techniques and architecture, as well as the Latin language. A slew of Germanic tribes, including the Swabians and Vandals, swept over the region in the early 5th century AD, but the **Visigoths,** newly converted Christians, emerged above the rest. The Visigoths established their court at Barcelona in 415 and effectively ruled Spain for the next 300 years.

MOORISH OCCUPATION (711-1469). Following Muslim unification and a victory tour through the Middle East and North Africa, a small force of Arabs, Berbers, and Syrians invaded Spain in 711. The Moors encountered little resistance, and the peninsula soon fell under the dominion of the caliphate of Damascus. These events precipitated the infusion of Muslim influence, which peaked in the 10th century. The Moors set up their Iberian capital in **Córdoba** (see p. 889). During **Abderramán III**'s rule in the 10th century, some considered Spain the wealthiest and most cultivated country in the world. Abderramán's successor, **Al Mansur,** snuffed out all opposition within his extravagant court and undertook a series of military campaigns that climaxed with the destruction of **Santiago de Compostela** (see p. 947), a Christian holy city, in 997.

The turning point in Muslim-Christian relations came when Al Mansur died, leaving a power vacuum in Córdoba. At this point, the caliphate's holdings shattered into petty states called *taifas.* With power less centralized, Christians were able to gain the upper hand. The Christian policy was official toleration of Muslims and Jews, which fostered a culture and even a style of art, **Mudéjar.** Later, though, countless Moorish structures were ruined in the **Reconquest,** and numerous mosques were replaced by churches (like Córdoba's **Mezquita,** see p. 893).

THE CATHOLIC MONARCHS (1469-1516). In 1469, the marriage of **Fernando de Aragón** and **Isabel de Castilla** joined Iberia's two mightiest Christian kingdoms. By 1492, the dynamic duo had captured **Granada** (see p. 897), the last Moorish stronghold, and shuttled **Columbus** off to explore the New World. By the 16th century, the pair had made Spain the world's most powerful empire. The Catholic monarchs introduced the **Inquisition** in 1478, executing and burning heretics. The Spanish Inquisition's aims were to strengthen the Church and unify Spain.

THE HABSBURG DYNASTY (1516-1713). The daughter of Fernando and Isabel, **Juana la Loca** (the Mad), married **Felipe el Hermoso** (the Fair) of the powerful Habsburg dynasty. Felipe (who died playing a Basque ball game called *cesta punta* or *jai-alai*) and Juana (who refused to believe that he had died and dragged his corpse through the streets) produced **Carlos I.** Carlos, who went by **Charles V** in his capacity as the last official Holy Roman Emperor, reigned over an empire comprising modern-day Netherlands, Belgium, Austria, Spain, parts of Germany and Italy, and the American colonies. Carlos did his part: as a good Catholic, he embroiled Spain in a war with Protestant France; as an art patron of superb taste, he nabbed Titian as his court painter; as a fashion plate, he introduced Spain to the Habsburg fashion of wearing only black.

But trouble was brewing in the Protestant Netherlands. After Carlos I died, his son **Felipe II** was left to grapple with a multitude of rebellious territories. He annexed Portugal after its ailing King Henrique died in 1580. One year later the Dutch declared their independence from Spain, and Felipe began warring with the Protestants, spurring further tensions with England. The war with the British ground to a halt when **Sir Francis Drake** and bad weather buffeted the not-so-invincible **Invincible Armada** in 1588. His enthusiasm and much of his European empire sapped, Felipe retreated to his grim, newly built palace, **El Escorial** (see p. 866), and remained there through the last decade of his reign.

Felipe III, preoccupied with both religion and the finer aspects of life, allowed his favorite adviser, the **Duque de Lerma,** to hold the governmental reins. In 1609, Felipe III and the Duke expelled nearly 300,000 of Spain's remaining Moors. **Felipe IV** painstakingly held the country together through his long, tumultuous reign. Emulating his great-grandfather Carlos I, Felipe IV patronized the arts and architecture. Then the **Thirty Years' War** (1618-1648) broke out over Europe, and defending Catholicism drained Spain's resources; the war ended with the marriage of Felipe IV's daughter, María Teresa, and Louis XIV of France. Felipe's successor **Carlos II,** the *"hechizado"* (bewitched), was epileptic and impotent, the product of inbreeding. From then on, little went right: Carlos II died, Spain fell into a depression, and cultural bankruptcy ensued.

KINGS, LIBERALS, AND DICTATORS (1713-1931). The 1713 **Treaty of Utrecht** seated **Felipe V,** a Bourbon family member and grandson of French King Louis XIV, on the Spanish throne. Felipe built huge, showy palaces (to mimic Versailles in France) and cultivated a flamboyant, debauched court. Despite his undisciplined example, the Bourbons who followed Felipe administered the Empire well, at last beginning to regain control of Spanish-American trade. They also constructed scores of new canals, roads, and organized settlements, and instituted agricultural reform and industrial expansion. **Carlos III** was probably Madrid's finest leader, founding academies of art and science and generally beautifying the capital. Spain's global standing recovered enough for it to team up with France to help the American colonies gain independence from Britain.

In 1808, **Napoleon** invaded Spain. The invasion's battles were particularly bloody. The French occupation ended when the Protestant Brits defeated the Corsican's troops at Waterloo (1814). This victory led to the restoration of arch-reactionary **Fernando VII.** Galvanized by Fernando's ineptitude and inspired by liberal ideas in the new constitution, most of Spain's Latin American empire soon threw off its yoke, and declared independence. Lingering dreams of an empire were further curbed by the loss of the Philippines, Puerto Rico, and Cuba to the US in the **Spanish-American War** of 1898. Upon Fernando VII's death, parliamentary liberalism was restored and would dominate Spanish politics until **Primo de Rivera** came along in 1923. Rivera was brought to power in a military coup d'état, after which he promptly dissolved parliament and suspended the constitution. For almost a decade, he ruled Spain as dictator, but in 1930, having lost the support of his own army, he resigned.

SECOND REPUBLIC AND THE CIVIL WAR (1931-1939). In April 1931, **King Alfonso XIII,** disgraced by his support for Rivera, shamefully fled Spain, thus giving rise to the **Second Republic** (1931-1936). Republican Liberals and Socialists established safeguards for farmers and industrial workers, granted women's suffrage, assured religious tolerance, and chipped away at traditional military dominance. National euphoria, however, faded fast. The 1933 elections split the Republican-Socialist coalition, in the process increasing the power of right-wing and Catholic parties. By 1936, radicals, anarchists, Socialists, and Republicans had formed a loosely federated alliance to win the next elections. But the victory was short-lived. Once **Generalísimo Francisco Franco** snatched control of the Spanish army, militarist uprisings ensued, and the nation plunged into war. The three-year **Civil War** (1936-1939) ignited worldwide ideological passions. Germany and Italy dropped troops, supplies, and munitions into Franco's lap, while the stubbornly isolationist US and the war-weary European states were slow to aid the Republicans. The Soviet Union called for a **Popular Front** of Communists, Socialists, and other leftist sympathizers to battle Franco's fascism. Soon, however, aid from the Soviet Union waned as Stalin began to see the benefits of an alliance with Hitler. Without international aid, Republican forces were cut off from supplies. Bombings, executions, combat, starvation, and disease took nearly 600,000 lives, and in 1939 Franco's forces marched into Madrid and ended the war.

FRANCO AND THE TRANSITION TO DEMOCRACY (1939-1998). Brain drain (as leading scientists, artists, and intellectuals emigrated or were assassinated en masse), worker dissatisfaction, student unrest, and international isolation characterized the first few decades of Franco's dictatorship. In his old age, Franco tried to smooth international relations by joining **NATO** and encouraging tourism, but the "national tragedy" (as it was later called) did not officially end until Franco's death in 1975. **King Juan Carlos I,** grandson of Alfonso XIII and a nominal Franco protégé, carefully set out to undo Franco's damage. In 1978, Spain adopted a constitution that led to the restoration of parliamentary government and regional autonomy.

After serving five years, Prime Minister Adolfo Suárez resigned in 1981, leaving the country vulnerable for an attempted coup d'etat on February 23, when a group of rebels took over Congress in an effort to impose a military-backed government. King Juan Carlos used his personal influence to convince the rebels to stand down, and order was restored. Charismatic **Felipe González** led the **Spanish Socialist Worker's Party** (PSOE) to victory in the 1982 elections. González opened the Spanish economy and championed consensus policies, overseeing Spain's integration into the European Community (now the **European Union**) in 1986. The years 1986 to 1990 were outstanding for Spain's economy, as the nation enjoyed an average annual growth rate of 3.8%. By the end of 1993, however, recession had set in, and González and the PSOE only barely maintained a majority in Parliament over the increasingly popular conservative **Partido Popular** (PP). Revelations of large-scale corruption led to a defeat of the Socialist party at the hands of the PP in 1994.

TODAY

The last several years have seen mixed progress in one of Spain's most pressing areas of concern, Basque nationalism and terrorism. The militant Euskadi Ta Askatasuma (ETA) has committed numerous acts of terror in what they say is an effort to secure autonomy for Basque Country. On September 12, 1998, the federal government called for an open dialogue between all parties and was endorsed by the Basque National Party (PNV). Six days later, ETA publicly declared a truce with the national government. On December 3, 1999, however, ETA announced an end to the 14-month cease-fire due to lack of progress with negotiations. The past years have since seen a return of periodic terrorist murders of PP and PSOE members, and journalists and army officers, as well as instances of arson. In June 2002, authorities seized 288 pounds of dynamite near Valencia, charging that ETA was planning to strike tourist spots along the Mediterranean coast. That same month, controversy ensued when the Spanish parliament moved to ban Batasuna, a pro-independence Basque political party that Aznar claims is allied with ETA.

On a brighter note, the Spanish economy is currently improving. Over the past several years, unemployment has dropped drastically. Aznar talks of visions of "a new Spain" and plans to reduce unemployment even further, draw more women into the workforce, and improve the faltering birthrate by restructuring family and work arrangements.

CULTURE

FOOD & DRINK

Spanish food has tended to receive less international attention than the country's beaches, bars, and discos. Taste often ranks above appearance, preparation is rarely complicated, and many of the best meals are served not in expensive restaurants but in private homes or streetside bars. All of this has begun to change as Spanish food becomes increasingly sophisticated and cosmopolitan, but fresh local ingredients are still an integral part of the cuisine; consequently, it varies according to each region's climate, geography, and history. Most experts, in fact, argue that one can speak of Spanish food only in local terms. Spaniards **breakfast** lightly and wait for a several-course **lunch,** served between 2 and 3pm. **Supper,** a light meal, begins at around 10pm. Some restaurants are "open" from 8am until 1 or 2am, but most serve meals only from 1 to 4pm and from 8pm until midnight. Prices for a full meal start at about €4 in the cheapest *bar-restaurantes*. Many places offer a **plato combinado** (main course, side dishes, bread, and sometimes a beverage) or a **menú del día** (two or three set dishes, bread, beverage, and dessert) for roughly €5-9. If you ask for a *menú*, this is what you may receive; the word for menu is *carta*. **Tapas** (savory meats and vegetables cooked according to local recipes) are truly tasty. **Raciones** are large *tapas* served as entrees. **Bocadillos** are sandwiches on hunks of bread. Specialties include **tortilla de patata** (potato omelette), **jamón serrano** (smoked ham), **calamares fritos** (fried squid), **arroz** (rice), **chorizo** (spicy sausage), **gambas** (shrimp), **lomo** (pork), **paella** (steamed saffron rice with seafood, chicken, and vegetables), and **gazpacho** (cold tomato-based soup). **Vegetarians** should learn the phrase *"yo soy vegetariano"* (I am a vegetarian) and specify that means no *jamón* (ham) or *atún* (tuna). *Vino blanco* is white wine and *tinto* is red. Beer is **cerveza;** Mahou and Cruzcampo are the most common brands. **Sangría** is red wine, sugar, brandy, and fruit.

CUSTOMS & ETIQUETTE

Although Spaniards are known for being proud, they are generally polite, courteous, and kind to foreigners. Attempts at 'correct behavior' will not go unnoticed; you'll be treated with cooperative friendliness if you make the extra effort.

TABOOS. Though dress in Spain is more casual in the hot summer months than in winter, strapless tops on women and collarless t-shirts on men are generally unacceptable. Be cautious of shorts and flip-flops; they may be seen as disrespectful in some public establishments.

PUBLIC BEHAVIOR. Strongly individualistic, Spaniards are formally polite in mannerisms and social behavior. To blend in, it's a good idea to be as formal as possible upon a first meeting. Introduce yourself in detail, giving more than just your *nombre* (name). You'll be welcomed openly and made to feel at home if you mention who you are, where you're from, and what you are doing in Spain. Be sure to address Spaniards as *Señor* (Mr.), *Señora* (Mrs.), or *Señorita* (Ms.), and don't be surprised if you get kissed on both cheeks instead of receiving a handshake. Also, don't yawn or stretch in public; this is considered disrespectful, and your actions could garner some glares and grimaces from Spaniards.

TABLE MANNERS. The key to acceptance at a Spanish *mesa* is not imitating *how* Spaniards eat, but rather eating *when* they do. You'll encounter odd looks if you demand an evening meal at six o'clock. If you'd like to pick up a few Spanish table manners, be sure to eat with both your fork *and* your knife in hand at all times, and make sure both hands are visible during the meal.

THE ARTS

FINE ARTS. Residents of the Iberian peninsula were creating art as early as 13,000 BC, the birthdate of the fabulous cave paintings at **Altamira.** In the 11th and 12th centuries AD, fresco painters and manuscript illuminators decorated churches and their libraries along the **Camino de Santiago** (see p. 949) and in **León** (see p. 876) and **Toledo** (see p. 867). **Pedro Berruguete**'s use of traditional gold backgrounds in his religious paintings exemplifies the Italian-influenced style of early Renaissance works. Berruguete's style is especially evident in his masterpiece, the altarpiece of San Tomás in **Ávila** (1499-1503; see p. 873). Not until after Spain's imperial ascendancy in the 16th century did painting reach its **Golden Age** (roughly 1492-1650). Felipe II imported foreign art and artists in order to jump-start native production and embellish his palace, El Escorial. Although he came to Spain seeking a royal commission, **El Greco** was rejected by Felipe II for his shocking and intensely personal style. Setting up camp in Toledo, El Greco graced the **Iglesia de Santo Tomé** with his masterpiece *The Burial of Count Orgaz* (1586-1588; see p. 867).

Felipe IV's foremost court painter, **Diego Velázquez,** is considered one of the world's greatest artists. Whether depicting Felipe IV's family or lowly court jesters and dwarves, Velázquez painted with the same naturalistic precision. Nearly half of this Sevillian artist's works reside in the **Prado,** including his famous *The Maids of Honor* (1656, see p. 861).

Francisco de Goya, official court painter under the degenerate Carlos IV, ushered European painting into the modern age. Goya's depictions of the royal family come close to caricature, as Queen María Luisa's cruel jawline in the famous *The Family of Charles IV* (1800) can attest. Goya's later paintings graphically protest the lunacy of warfare. The Prado museum houses an entire room of his chilling *Black Paintings* (1820-1823, see p. 861).

It is hard to imagine an artist who has had as profound an effect upon 20th-century painting as Andalucían-born **Pablo Picasso.** A child prodigy, Picasso headed for Barcelona, which was a breeding ground of Modernist architecture and political activism. Picasso's **Blue Period,** beginning in 1900, was characterized by somber depictions of society's outcasts. His permanent move to Paris in 1904 initiated his **Rose Period,** during which he probed into the curiously engrossing lives of clowns and acrobats. With his French colleague Georges Braque, he founded **Cubism,** a method of painting objects simultaneously from multiple perspectives.

Catalán painter and sculptor **Joan Miró** created simplistic, almost child-like shapes in bright primary colors. His haphazard, undefined creations became a statement against the authoritarian society of Fascist Spain. By contrast, fellow Catalán **Salvador Dalí** scandalized both high society and leftist intellectuals in France and Spain by supporting the Fascists. Dalí's name is virtually synonymous with **Surrealism.** The painter tapped into dreams and the unconscious for images like the melting clocks in *The Persistence of Memory* (1931). His haunting *Premonition of the Civil War* (1936) envisioned war as a distorted monster of putrefying flesh. A shameless self-promoter (he often spoke of himself only in the 3rd person), Dalí founded the **Teatre-Museo Dalí** (see p. 930) in Figueres, which defines Surrealism in its collection, its construction, and its very existence.

Since Franco's death in 1975, a new generation of artists, including the unorthodox collage artist **Antonio Tapieshas** and hyperrealist painter **Antonio Lopez Garcia,** have thrived. With impressive museums in Madrid, Barcelona, Valencia, Sevilla, and Bilbao, Spanish artists once again have a national forum for their work.

ARCHITECTURE. Scattered **Roman ruins** testify to six centuries of colonization. The **aqueduct** in Segovia (see p. 871) is one of the finest examples of remaining ruins. After the invasion of 711, the **Moors** constructed mosques and palaces throughout southern Spain. Because the Koran forbade representations of humans and animals, architects lavished buildings with stylized geometric designs, red-and-white horseshoe arches, ornate tiles called *azulejos*, courtyards, pools, and fountains. The spectacular 14th-century **Alhambra** in Granada (see p. 897) and the **Mezquita** in Córdoba (see p. 893) epitomize the Moorish style.

The combination of Islam and Christianity created two architectural movements unique to Spain: **Mozarabic** and **Mudéjar.** The former describes Christians under Muslim rule (Mozarabs) who adopted Arab devices like the horseshoe-shaped arch and the ribbed dome. The more common Mudéjar architecture was created by Moors during their occupation. Extensive use of brick and elaborately carved wooden ceilings typify Mudéjar style, which reached its height in the 14th century with **alcázars** (palaces) in Sevilla (see p. 879) and Segovia (see p. 871) and **synagogues** in Toledo (see p. 867) and Córdoba (see p. 889).

The first Gothic cathedral in Spain was built in Burgos (1221, see p. 877), followed closely by cathedral construction in Toledo and León. The **Spanish Gothic** style brought pointed arches, flying buttresses, slender walls, airy spaces, and stained-glass windows. New World riches inspired the **Plateresque** style, an embellishment of Gothic that transformed wealthier parts of Spain. Intricate stonework and extravagant use of gold and silver splashed 15th- and 16th-century buildings, most notably in **Salamanca** (see p. 874), where the university practically drips with ornamentation. In the late 16th century, **Italian Renaissance** innovations in perspective and symmetry arrived in Spain to sober up the Plateresque style. **El Escorial,** Felipe II's palace, was designed by **Juan de Herrera,** one of Spain's most prominent architects, and best exemplifies unadorned Renaissance style (see p. 866).

Opulence took over in 17th- and 18th-century **Baroque** Spain. The **Churriguera** brothers pioneered this style—called, appropriately, **Churrigueresque**—which is equal parts ostentatious, ornamental, and difficult to pronounce. Elaborate works with extensive detail and twisted columns, like the altar of the **Toledo cathedral** (see p. 867), help distinguish this period in Spanish architecture.

In the late 19th and early 20th centuries, Catalán's **Modernistas** burst onto the scene in Barcelona, led by the eccentric genius of **Antoni Gaudí, Luis Domènech i Montaner,** and **José Puig i Caldafach.** Modernista structures defy previous standards with their voluptuous curves and abnormal textures. Spain's outstanding architectural tradition continues to this day with such new buildings as the Guggenheim (see p. 942) in Bilbao, designed by **Santiago Calatrava.**

LITERATURE. Spain's literary tradition first blossomed in the late Middle Ages (1000-1500). **Fernando de Rojas**'s *The Celestina* (1499), a tragicomic dialogue most noted for its folkloric witch character, helped pave the way for picaresque novels like *Lazarillo of Tormes* (1554) and *Guzmán of Alfarache* (1599), rags-to-riches stories about mischievous boys with good hearts. This literary form surfaced during Spain's **Golden Age** (1492-1650). Poetry particularly thrived in this era. Some consider the sonnets and romances of **Garcilaso de la Vega** the most perfect ever written in Castilian. This period also produced outstanding dramas, including works from **Calderón de la Barca** and **Lope de Vega,** who wrote nearly 2000 plays combined. Both espoused the **Neoplatonic** view of love, claiming that love always changes one's life dramatically and eternally. **Miguel de Cervantes**'s two-part *Don Quixote de la Mancha* (1605-15), which relates the satiric parable of the hapless Don Quixote and his sidekick, Sancho Panza, who think themselves bold *caballeros* (knights) out to save the world, is the most famous work of Spanish literature.

The 19th century bred a multiplicity of styles, from **José Zorrilla**'s romantic poems such as *Don Juan Tenorio* (1844) to the naturalistic novels of **Leopoldo Alas ("Clarín").** The modern literary era began with the **Generación del 1898,** a group led by essayist **Miguel de Unamuno** and cultural critic **José Ortega y Gasset.** These nationalistic authors argued, through essays and novels, that each individual must spiritually and ideologically attain internal peace before society can do the same. The **Generación del 1927,** a clique of experimental lyric poets who used Surrealist and vanguard poetry to express profound humanism included **Jorge Guillén, Federico García Lorca** (assassinated at the start of the Civil War), **Rafael Alberti,** and **Luis Cernuda.** In the 20th century, the Nobel Committee has honored playwright and essayist **Jacinto Benavente y Martínez** (1922), poet **Vicente Aleixandre** (1977), and novelist **Camilo José Cela** (1989). Since the fall of the Fascist regime in 1975, an avant-garde spirit—known as *La Movida*—has been reborn in Madrid. **Ana Rossetti** and **Juana Castro** led a new generation of erotic poets into the 80s. With this newest group of poets, women are at the forefront of Spanish literature for the first time.

FILM. Franco's regime (1939-75) defined Spanish film during and after his rule. Censorship stifled most creative tendencies and left the public with nothing to watch but cheap westerns and bland spy flicks. As government supervision slacked in the early 1970s, Spanish cinema began to show signs of life, led by **Carlos Saura**'s subversive hits such as *The Garden of Delights* (1970).

In 1977, when domestic censorship laws were revoked in the wake of Franco's death, depictions of the exuberant excesses of liberated Spain found increasing international attention. **Pedro Almodovar**'s *Law of Desire* (1986), featuring **Antonio Banderas** as a homosexual, perhaps best captures the risqué themes of transgression most often treated by contemporary Spanish cinema. Almodovar's *All About My Mother* claimed the Best Foreign Film Oscar in 2000. Other directors to look for in Spain include **Bigas Luna,** director of the controversial *Jamón Jamón* (1992), and **Fernando Trueba,** whose *Belle Epoque* won an Oscar in 1994.

BULLFIGHTING. The national spectacle that is bullfighting dates, in its modern form, back to the early 1700s. A bullfight is divided into three principal stages: in the first, *picadors* (lancers on horseback) pierce the bull's neck; next, assistants on foot thrust *banderillas* (decorated darts) into the back; and finally, the matador performs the kill. If a matador has shown special skill and daring, the audience waves white handkerchiefs to implore the bullfight's president to reward the coveted ears (and, very rarely, the tail) to the matador. Although bullfighting has always had its critics—the Catholic church in the 17th century felt that the risks made it equivalent to suicide—the late 20th century has seen an especially strong attack from animal rights' activists. Whatever its faults, however, bullfighting is an essential element of the Spanish national consciousness.

HOLIDAYS & FESTIVALS

Holidays: New Year's Day (Jan. 1); Epiphany (Jan. 6); Maundy Thursday (Apr. 17); Good Friday (Apr. 18); Easter (Apr. 20); Labor Day (May 1); La Asunción (Aug. 15); National Day (Oct. 12); All Saints' Day (Nov. 1); Constitution Day (Dec. 6); Feast of the Immaculate Conception (Dec. 8); Christmas (Dec. 25).

Festivals: Just about everything closes down during festivals. Almost every town has several, and in total there are more than 3000. All of Spain celebrates **Carnaval** from Feb. 9 to 13; the biggest parties are in Cataluña and Cádiz. Valencia hosts the annual **Las Fallas** in mid-March. From April 13-20, the entire country honors the Holy Week, or **Semana Santa.** Sevilla's **Feria de Abril** takes place in late April. Pamplona's **San Fermines** (Running of the Bulls) will break out from July 6 to 14. For more fiesta info, see www.tourspain.es, www.SiSpain.org, or www.cyberspain.es.

ESSENTIALS

FACTS AND FIGURES

Official Name: Kingdom of Spain.

Capital: Madrid.

Major Cities: Barcelona, Valencia, Sevilla, Granada, and Madrid.

Population: 40 million.

Land Area: 499,542 sq. km.

Time Zone: 1hr. ahead of GMT.

Language: Spanish (Castilian); Catalan, Valencian, Basque, Galician dialects.

Religions: Roman Catholic (though it's no longer the official religion).

WHEN TO GO

Summer is high season for the coastal and interior regions. In many parts of the country, high season includes *Semana Santa* (Holy Week; mid-April) and festival days. Tourism peaks in August; the coastal regions overflow while inland cities empty out, leaving behind closed offices, restaurants, and lodgings. Traveling in the off-season has the advantage of noticeably lighter crowds and lower prices, but smaller towns virtually shut down, and tourist offices and sights cut their hours nearly everywhere.

DOCUMENTS AND FORMALITIES

Citizens of Australia, Canada, the EU, New Zealand, South Africa, and the US do not need a visa for stays of up to 90 days.

Spanish Embassies at Home: Australia, 15 Arkana St., Yarralumla, ACT 2600. Mailing address: P.O. Box 9076, Deakin, ACT 2600 (☎02 62 73 35 55; www.embaspain.com). **Canada,** 74 Stanley Ave., Ottawa, ON K1M 1P4 (☎613-747-2252; www.docuweb.ca/SpainInCanada). **Ireland,** 17A Merlyn Park, Ballsbridge, Dublin 4 (☎(01) 269 1640). **South Africa,** 169 Pine St., Arcadia, P.O. Box 1633, Pretoria 0083 (☎(012) 344 3875). **UK,** 39 Chesham Pl., London SW1X 8SB, (☎207 235 5555). **US,** 2375 Pennsylvania Ave. NW, Washington D.C. 20037 (☎202-738-2330; www.spainemb.org).

Foreign Embassies in Spain: Foreign embassies are in **Madrid** (p. 851); all countries have consulates in **Barcelona** (p. 907). Australia, UK, and US also have consulates in **Sevilla** (p. 879). Another Canadian consulate is in Málaga; UK consulates are also in Bilbao, Palma de Mallorca, Ibiza, Alicante, and Málaga; more US consulates are in Las Palmas and Valencia.

TRANSPORTATION

BY PLANE. All major international airlines offer service to Madrid and Barcelona, most serve the Balearic and Canary Islands, and many serve Spain's smaller cities. **Iberia** (in US and Canada ☎800-772-4642; in UK ☎45 601 28 54; in Spain ☎902 40 05 00; in South Africa ☎11 884 92 55; in Ireland ☎1 407 30 17; www.iberia.com) serves all domestic locations and all major international cities. **Aviaco,** a subsidiary of Iberia, covers mostly domestic routes, with a few connections to London and Paris. Some fares purchased in the US require a 21-day minimum advance purchase. Iberia's two less-established domestic competitors often offer cheaper fares and are worth looking into. **Air Europa** (in US ☎888-238-7672 or 718-244-6016; in Spain ☎902 30 06 00; www.air-europa.com) flies out of New York City and most European cities to Madrid, Málaga, Tenerife, and Santiago de Compostela. Discounts available for youth and senior citizens. No service Wednesdays or Sundays during the summer. **SpanAir** (in US ☎888-545-5757; in Spain ☎902 13 14 15; fax 971 49 25 53; www.spanair.com) offers international and domestic flights.

BY TRAIN. Spanish trains are clean, relatively punctual, and reasonably priced, but tend to bypass many small towns. Spain's national railway is **RENFE** (www.renfe.es). Avoid *transvía, semidirecto,* or *correo* trains—they are very slow. *Alta Velocidad Española* (AVE) trains are the fastest between Madrid, Córdoba, and Seville. *Talgos* are almost as fast; there are four lines from Madrid to Málaga, Algeciras, Cádiz, and Huelva. *Intercity* is cheaper, but still fairly fast. *Estrellas* are slow night trains with bunks. *Cercanías* (commuter trains) go from cities to suburbs and nearby towns.

There is absolutely no reason to buy a **Eurail** if you are planning on traveling only within Spain and Portugal. Trains are cheap, so a pass saves little money; moreover, buses are an easier and more efficient means of traveling around Spain. However, there are several **RailEurope** passes that cover travel within Spain. You must purchase railpasses at least 15 days before departure. (US ☎1-800-4EURAIL; www.raileurope.com.) **Spain Flexipass** offers three days of unlimited travel in a two-month period (first-class €211; 2nd-class €164). The **Iberic Railpass** is good for three days of unlimited first-class travel in Spain and Portugal (€217). The **Spain Rail 'n' Drive Pass** is good for three days of unlimited first-class train travel and two days of unlimited mileage in a rental car (€250-345).

BY BUS. In Spain, ignore romanticized visions of European train travel—buses are cheaper, run more frequently, and are sometimes faster than trains. Bus routes also provide the only public transportation to many isolated towns. Spain has numerous private companies; the lack of a centralized bus company may make itinerary planning an ordeal. **ALSA** (☎902 42 22 42; www.alsa.es) serves Madrid, Galicia, Asturias, and Castilla y León, as well as international destinations in Portugal, Morocco, France, Italy, and Poland. **Auto-Res/Cunisa, S.A.** (☎902 02 09 99; www.auto-res.net), serves Madrid, Castilla y León, Extremadura, Galicia, and Valencia. See the practical information sections in individual cities for more information on additional regional carriers.

BY CAR. Gas prices average €1.40-1.50 per liter. Speeders beware: police can "photograph" the speed and license plate of your car and issue a ticket without pulling you over. **Renting a car** in Spain is cheaper than in many other Western European countries. International rental companies offer services throughout the country, but you may want to check with **Atesa** (☎902 10 01 01; www.atesa.es), Spain's largest national rental agency. The Spanish automobile association is **Real Automóbil Club de España (RACE),** C. José Abascal 10, Madrid (☎915 94 74 75).

BY BIKE AND BY THUMB. With hilly terrain and extremely hot summer weather, biking is difficult. Renting a bike should be easy, especially in the flatter southern region. Hitchers report that Castilla, Andalucía, and Madrid offer little more than a long, hot wait. The Mediterranean Coast and the islands are much more promising, but *Let's Go* does not recommend hitchhiking.

TOURIST SERVICES AND MONEY

EMERGENCY	**Emergency:** ☎112. **Local Police:** ☎092. **National Police:** ☎091. **Ambulance:** ☎124.

TOURIST OFFICES. The Spanish Tourist Office operates an extensive official website (www.tourspain.es) and has 29 offices abroad. Municipal tourist offices, called *oficinas de turismo,* are a good stop to make upon arrival in a town; they usually have free maps and region-specific advice for travelers.

MONEY. **Banks** are everywhere in Spain, and often have good exchange rates. **Tipping** is not very common in Spain. In restaurants, all prices include service charge. Satisfied customers occasionally toss in some spare change—usually no more than 5%—but this is purely optional. Many people give train, airport, and hotel porters €1 per bag; taxi drivers sometimes get 5-10%. **Bargaining** is common only at flea markets and with street vendors.

Spain has a 7% **Value Added Tax,** known as IVA, on all restaurants and accommodations. The prices listed in *Let's Go* include IVA unless otherwise mentioned. Retail goods bear a much higher 16% IVA, although listed prices are usually inclusive. Non-EU citizens who have stayed in the EU fewer than 180 days can claim back the tax paid on purchases at the airport. Ask the shop where you made the purchase to supply you with a tax return form.

BUSINESS HOURS. **Banking hours** from June through September are generally Monday through Friday 9am to 2pm; from October to May, banks are also open Saturday 9am to 1pm. Some banks are also open in the afternoon. Most **shops** are open 9am to 6pm, although many in the south close in the afternoon for *siesta.*

HEALTH AND SAFETY

While Spain is a relatively stable country, travelers should beware that there is some terrorist activity; the militant Basque separatist group **ETA** has carried out attacks on government officials and tourist destinations. Though the attacks are ongoing, the threat is relatively small. Travelers should be aware of current levels of tension in the region and exercise appropriate caution. Recreational **drugs** are illegal in Spain. Possession of small amounts of marijuana sometimes goes unpunished, but any attempt to buy or sell could land you in jail or with a heavy fine.

ACCOMMODATIONS AND CAMPING

The cheapest and barest options are **casas de huéspedes** and **hospedajes,** while **pensiones** and **fondas** tend to be a bit nicer. All are basically just boarding houses. Higher up the ladder, **hostales** generally have sinks in bedrooms and provide linens and lockers, while **hostal-residencias** are similar to hotels in overall quality. The government rates *hostales* on a two-star system; even establishments receiving one star are typically quite comfortable. The system also fixes *hostales* prices, posted in the lounge or main entrance. **Red Española de Albergues Juveniles (REAJ),** C. Galera 1a, Sevilla 41001 (☎954 216 803; www.reaj.com), the Spanish Hostelling International (HI) affiliate, runs 165 youth hostels year-round. Prices depend on location (typically some distance away from town center) and services offered, but are generally €9-15 for guests under 26 and higher for those 26 and over. Breakfast is usually included; lunch and dinner are occasionally offered at an additional charge. Hostels usually lock guests out around 11:30am and have curfews between midnight and 3am. As a rule, don't expect much privacy—rooms typically have four to 20 beds in them. To reserve a bed in high season (July-Aug. and during *fiestas*), call in advance. A national **Youth Hostel Card** is usually required. **Campgrounds** are generally the cheapest choice for two or more people. Most charge separate fees per person, per tent, and per car; others charge for a *parcela*—a small plot of land—plus per-person fees. Tourist offices provide information, including the *Guía de campings.*

COMMUNICATION

PHONE CODES	**Country code:** 34. **International dialing prefix:** 00. From outside Spain, dial int'l dialing prefix (see inside back cover) + 34 + local number.

MAIL. Air mail (*por avión*) takes five to eight business days to reach the US or Canada; service is faster to the UK and Ireland and slower to Australia and New Zealand. Standard postage is €0.70 to North America. Surface mail (*por barco*), while less expensive than air mail, can take over a month, and packages take two to three months. Registered or express mail (*registrado* or *certificado*) is the most reliable way to send a letter or parcel home and takes four to seven business days. To send mail *Poste Restante* to Spain, address the letter as follows: SURNAME, First Name; Lista de Correos; City Name; Postal Code; SPAIN; AIR MAIL.

TELEPHONES. The central Spanish phone company is *Telefónica*. The best way to make local calls is with a phone card, issued in denominations of €6 and €12 and sold at tobacconists (*estancos* or *tabacos*) and most post offices. You can also ask tobacconists for calling cards known as *Phonepass* (62min. to US €6, 212min. €12.). American Express and Diner's Club cards now work as phone card substitutes in most pay phones. The best way to call home is with an international calling card issued by your phone company.

INTERNET. The Internet is easily accessible within Spain. An increasing number of bars offer Internet access for a fee of €1-4.50. Cybercafes are listed in most towns and all cities. In small towns, if Internet access is not listed, check the library or the tourist office. The website www.tangaworld.com lists nearly 200 cybercafes in Spain.

LANGUAGE. Catalán is spoken in Cataluña, Valencian in Valencia. The Basque language (Euskera) is common in north-central Spain, Galician (Gallego, related to Portuguese) in the once-Celtic northwest. Spanish (Castilian, or *castellano*) is spoken everywhere. Some English is spoken in large cities. For basic Spanish words and phrases, see p. 1031.

MADRID ☎91

After Franco's death in 1975, young *madrileños* celebrated their liberation from totalitarian repression with raging, nocturnal parties in bars and on streets across the city. This partying became so widespread that it defined an era, and *la Movida* (the Movement) is recognized as a world-famous nightlife renaissance. While the newest generation is too young to recall the Franco years, it has kept the spirit of *la Movida* alive—neither cognizant of the city's historic landmarks nor preoccupied with the future, young people have taken over the streets, shed their parents' decorous reserve, and captured the present. Bright lights and a perpetual stream of cars and people blur the distinction between 4pm and 4am, and infinitely energized party-goers crowd bars and discos until dawn.

The city continues to serve as Spain's political, intellectual, and cultural center; it epitomizes the mix of rich history and passion for the present that defines the country. Madrid's sights and culture equal its rival European capitals and have twice the intensity.

INTERCITY TRANSPORTATION

Flights: All flights land at **Aeropuerto Internacional de Barajas** (MAD), 20min. northeast of Madrid. The **Barajas metro line** connects the airport to all of Madrid (€0.95). From the airport, follow signs to the metro. Another option is the green **Bus-Aeropuerto #89** (look for EMT signs just outside the airport doors), which leaves from the national and international terminals and runs to the city center (every 12min. 4:45am-2am, €2.50). The bus stops underground beneath the Jardines del Descubrimiento in **Plaza de Colón** (M: Colón). Fleets of **taxis** swarm the airport. Taxi fare to central Madrid should be around €15-18, including the €4 airport surcharge. Serving national and international destinations, **Iberia** is at Santa Cruz de Marcenado 2. M: San Bernardo. (Office ☎915 87 47 47. Open M-F 9:30am-2pm and 4-7pm. 24hr. reservations and info ☎902 40 05 00).

Trains: Two *Largo Recorrido* (long distance) **RENFE** stations, **Madrid-Chamartín** and **Madrid-Atocha,** connect Madrid to the rest of the world. Call RENFE (☎913 28 90 20; www.renfe.es) for reservations and info. Try the **RENFE Main Office,** C. Alcalá 44, at Gran Vía (M: Banco de España) for schedules.

Estación Chamartín, Agustín de Foxá (24hr. info for international destinations ☎934 90 11 22; domestic ☎902 24 02 02, Spanish only). M: Chamartín. Bus #5 runs to Sol (45min.). Ticket windows open 8am-10:30pm. *Cercanías* (local) trains stop at Atocha and Chamartín. To: **Barcelona** (7-10hr., 10 per day, €40-42); **Lisbon** (10hr., 10:45pm, €48); **Paris** (13hr., 7pm, €117).

Estación Atocha (☎913 28 90 20). M: Atocha-Renfe. Ticket windows open 7:15am-10pm. Trains to: Andalucía, Castilla y León, Castilla-La Mancha, El Escorial, Extremadura, Sierra de Guadarrama, Toledo, and Valencia. AVE service (☎915 34 05 05) to **Córdoba** (1¾hr., 20 per day, €39-46) and **Sevilla** (2½hr., 20 per day, €53-62). For **luggage storage** (€2.40-4.50), follow signs for *cosignas automaticas.*

Buses: Numerous private companies, each with its own station and set of destinations, serve Madrid; many buses pass through the **Estación Sur de Autobuses.**

Estación Sur de Autobuses, C. Méndez Álvaro (☎914 68 42 00). M: Méndez Álvaro. Info booth open daily 7am-11pm. **Continental-Auto** (☎915 27 29 61) to **Toledo** (1½hr.; M-Sa every 30min. 6:30am-10pm, Su 8:30am-midnight; €3.75).

Estación Auto Res, Pl. Conde de Casal 6 (☎902 02 09 99). M: Conde de Casal. To: **Cuenca** (3hr.; M-F 8-10 per day 6:45am-10pm, Sa-Su 5-6 per day 8am-8pm; €8.50); **Salamanca** (3-3¼hr., 7 per day 8:30am-10pm, €10); **Trujillo** (3¼hr., 11-12 per day 8am-1am, €13); **Valencia** (5hr., 4 per day 1am-2pm, €19).

Estación La Sepulvedana, Po. Frontera 16 (☎915 30 48 00). M: Príncipe Pío (via extension from M: Ópera). To **Segovia** (1½hr., every 30min. 6:30am-10:15pm, €5); and **Ávila** (1½hr.; M-F 8 per day 6am-7pm, Sa-Su 3 per day 10am-7pm; €5.60).

ORIENTATION

Marking the epicenter of both Madrid and Spain, **"Kilometro 0"** in **Puerta del Sol** ("Sol" for short) is within walking distance of most sights. To the west is the **Plaza Mayor,** the **Palacio Real,** and the **Ópera** district. East of Sol lies the heart of cafe, theater, and museum life, **Huertas,** which is centered around Pl. Santa Ana and bordered by C. Alcalá to the north, Po. Prado to the east, and C. Atocha to the south. The area north of Sol is bordered by **Gran Vía,** which runs northwest to **Plaza de España.** North of Gran Vía are three club and bar-hopping districts, linked by Calle de Fuencarral: **Malasaña, Bilbao,** and **Chueca.** Modern Madrid is beyond Gran Vía and east of Malasaña and Chueca. East of Sol, the tree-lined thoroughfares **Paseo de la Castellana, Paseo de Recoletos,** and **Paseo del Prado** split Madrid in two, running from Atocha in the south to **Plaza Castilla** in the north, passing the Prado, the fountains of **Plaza Cibeles,** and **Plaza Colón.** Use the **color map** of Madrid's metro in

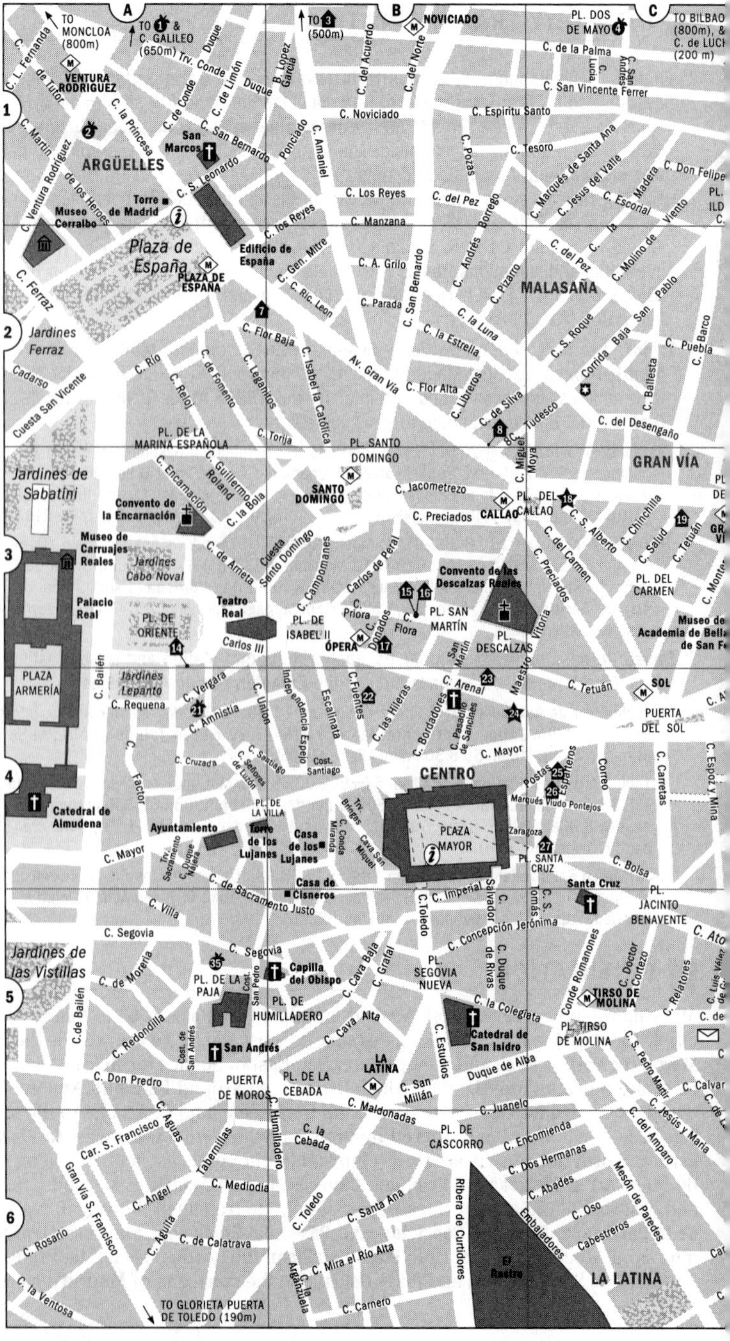
A
B
C
1
2
3
4
5
6
TO MONCLOA (800m)
TO 1 & C. GALILEO (650m)
TO 3 (500m)
NOVICIADO
PL. DOS DE MAYO 4
TO BILBAO (800m), & C. de LUCH (200 m)
VENTURA RODRIGUEZ
C. L. Fernanda
de Tutor
C. Martín
ARGÜELLES
C. Ventura Rodríguez
de los Heroes
Museo Cerralbo
Torre de Madrid
C. la Princesa
C. de Conde
C. de Limón
Trv. Conde Duque
Duque
B. López García
San Marcos
C. San Bernardo
C. S. Leonardo
Ponciado
C. Amaniel
C. del Acuerdo
C. del Norte
C. Noviciado
C. Espiritu Santo
C. de la Palma
C. Lucia
C. San Andrés
C. San Vincente Ferrer
C. Pozas
C. Tesoro
C. Marqués de Santa Ana
C. Jesús del Valle
C. Don Felipe
C. Los Reyes
C. del Pez
C. Borrego
C. Escorial
C. la Madera
C. Viento
C. los Reyes
C. Manzana
Plaza de España
PLAZA DE ESPAÑA
Edificio de España
C. Gen. Mitre
C. A. Grilo
C. San Bernardo
C. Andrés
C. Pizarro
C. del Pez
C. Molino de
MALASAÑA
C. Ferraz
C. Ric. Leon
C. Parada
C. la Luna
C. la Estrella
C. S. Roque
Corrida Baja San Pablo
C. Barco
C. Puebla
Jardines Ferraz
Cadarso
Cuesta San Vicente
C. Rio
C. Reloj
C. de Fomento
C. Flor Baja
C. Leganitos
C. Isabel la Católica
Av. Gran Via
C. Flor Alta
C. Libreros
C. de Silva
C. Tudesco
C. Ballesta
C. del Desengaño
PL. DE LA MARINA ESPAÑOLA
C. Torija
PL. SANTO DOMINGO
C. Miguel Moya
GRAN VÍA
Jardines de Sabatini
C. Encarnación
C. Guillermo Roland
C. la Bola
SANTO DOMINGO
C. Jacometrezo
PL. DEL CALLAO
CALLAO
C. S. Alberto
C. Chinchilla
C. Salud
C. Tetuán
Convento de la Encarnación
C. Preciados
C. del Carmen
Museo de Carruajes Reales
Jardines Cabo Noval
C. de Arrieta
Cuesta Santo Domingo
C. Campomanes
Carlos de Peral
Convento de las Descalzas Reales
C. Preciados
PL. DEL CARMEN
C. Montera
Palacio Real
PL. DE ORIENTE
Teatro Real
PL. DE ISABEL II
C. Priora
C. Donados
C. Flora
PL. SAN MARTÍN
PL. DESCALZAS
Maestro Vitoria
Museo de Academia de Bellas de San F
Carlos III
ÓPERA
C. San Martín
PLAZA ARMERÍA
C. Bailén
Jardines Lepanto
C. Requena
C. Vergara
C. Amnistia
C. Unión
Independencia
Escalinata
C. Fuentes
C. las Hileras
C. Arenal
C. Bordadores
C. Pasadizo de Sanciñes
C. Tetuán
SOL
PUERTA DEL SOL
C. Cruzada
C. Señores de Luzón
C. Santiago
C. Espejo
Cost. Santiago
C. Mayor
CENTRO
Postas
Esparteros
Correo
C. Carretas
C. Espoz y Mina
Catedral de Almudena
C. Factor
PL. DE LA VILLA
Trv. Bringas
Marqués Viudo Pontejos
Ayuntamiento
Torre de los Lujanes
Casa de los Lujanes
C. Conde Miranda
Cava San Miguel
PLAZA MAYOR
Zaragoza
PL. SANTA CRUZ
C. Bolsa
C. Mayor
Trv. Sacramento
C. Duque Nájera
C. de Sacramento
Casa de Cisneros
Justo
C.Toledo
C. Imperial
Salvador
C.S. Tomás
Santa Cruz
PL. JACINTO BENAVENTE
C. Villa
C. Segovia
C. Concepción Jerónima
C. Atocha
Jardines de las Vistillas
C. Segovia
Capilla del Obispo
C. Cava Baja
C. Grafal
PL. SEGOVIA NUEVA
de Rivas
C. Duque
Conde Romanones
C. Doctor Cortezo
C. Relatores
C. de Moreria
PL. DE LA PAJA
Cost. San Pedro
PL. DE HUMILLADERO
C. Cava Alta
C. la Colegiata
TIRSO DE MOLINA
C.de Bailén
C. Redondilla
Cost. de San Andrés
San Andrés
C. Estudios
Catedral de San Isidro
PL. TIRSO DE MOLINA
C. S. Pedro Martir
LA LATINA
C. Don Pedro
PUERTA DE MOROS
PL. DE LA CEBADA
C. San Millán
Duque de Alba
C. Calvario
C. Maldonadas
C. Juanelo
C. Jesús y María
Car. S. Francisco
C. Aguas
Tabernillas
C. Humilladero
C. la Cebada
PL. DE CASCORRO
C. Encomienda
C. del Amparo
C. Dos Hermanas
Gran Via S. Francisco
C. Angel
C. Mediodia
C. Toledo
C. Santa Ana
Ribera de Curtidores
C. Abades
Mesón de Paredes
C. Oso
C. Rosario
C. Aguila
C. de Calatrava
C. Mira el Río Alta
Embajadores
Cabestreros
C. la Arganzuela
El Rastro
LA LATINA
C. la Ventosa
TO GLORIETA PUERTA DE TOLEDO (190m)
C. Carnero

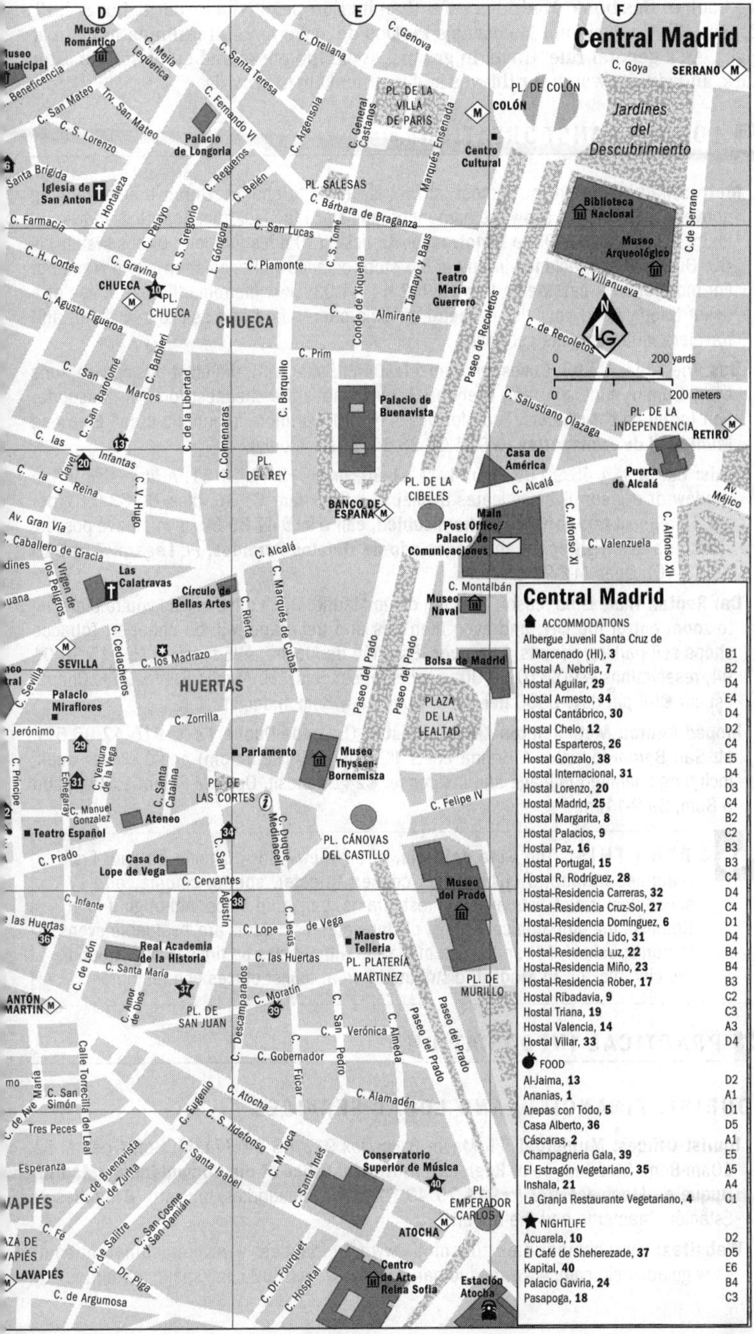

Central Madrid

ACCOMMODATIONS

Albergue Juvenil Santa Cruz de Marcenado (HI), **3**	B1
Hostal A. Nebrija, **7**	B2
Hostal Aguilar, **29**	D4
Hostal Armesto, **34**	E4
Hostal Cantábrico, **30**	D4
Hostal Chelo, **12**	D2
Hostal Esparteros, **26**	C4
Hostal Gonzalo, **38**	E5
Hostal Internacional, **31**	D4
Hostal Lorenzo, **20**	D3
Hostal Madrid, **25**	C4
Hostal Margarita, **8**	B2
Hostal Palacios, **9**	C2
Hostal Paz, **16**	B3
Hostal Portugal, **15**	B3
Hostal R. Rodríguez, **28**	C4
Hostal-Residencia Carreras, **32**	D4
Hostal-Residencia Cruz-Sol, **27**	C4
Hostal-Residencia Domínguez, **6**	D1
Hostal-Residencia Lido, **31**	D4
Hostal-Residencia Luz, **22**	B4
Hostal-Residencia Miño, **23**	B4
Hostal-Residencia Rober, **17**	B3
Hostal Ribadavia, **9**	C2
Hostal Triana, **19**	C3
Hostal Valencia, **14**	A3
Hostal Villar, **33**	D4

FOOD

Al-Jaima, **13**	D2
Ananias, **1**	A1
Arepas con Todo, **5**	D1
Casa Alberto, **36**	D5
Cáscaras, **2**	A1
Champagneria Gala, **39**	E5
El Estragón Vegetariano, **35**	A5
Inshala, **21**	A4
La Granja Restaurante Vegetariano, **4**	C1

NIGHTLIFE

Acuarela, **10**	D2
El Café de Sheherezade, **37**	D5
Kapital, **40**	E6
Palacio Gaviria, **24**	B4
Pasapoga, **18**	C3

the back of this book. Madrid is safer than its European counterparts, but Sol, Pl. España, Pl. Chueca, and Malasaña's Pl. Dos de Mayo are still intimidating late at night. As a general rule, travel in groups, avoid the parks and quiet streets after dark, and always watch for thieves and pickpockets in crowds.

LOCAL TRANSPORTATION

Metro: Madrid's metro puts most subway systems to shame. Green timers hanging above most platforms show the amount of time since the last train departed. Individual metro tickets cost €0.95; a **bonotransporte** ticket (10 rides for metro or bus system) is €5. Buy both at machines in any metro stop, *estanco* (tobacco shop), or newsstand. For more details, call **Metro Info** (☎902 44 44 03; www.metromadrid.es) or ask at a ticket booth. Keep your ticket–metro officials often board and ask to see them, and travelers without tickets get fined.

Bus: The fare is €0.95. Buses run 6am-11:30pm. *Buho* (owl), the night bus service, runs every 20min. midnight-3am, every hr. 3-6am, and is the cheapest form of transportation for late-night revelers. Look for buses N1-20. For more information, call **Empresa Municipal de Transportes** (☎914 06 88 10; Spanish only).

Taxis: Call ☎914 45 90 08, ☎914 47 51 80, or ☎913 71 21 31. A *libre* sign in the window or a green light indicates availability. Base fare €1.35, plus €0.63-0.81 per km. To request **taxi service for the disabled,** call ☎915 47 85 00. If you leave possessions in a taxi, visit or call the **Negociado de Objetos Perdidos,** Pl. Legazpi 7 (☎915 88 43 46). Open M-F 9am-2pm.

Car Rental: There is no reason to rent a car in Madrid. Don't drive unless you're planning to zoom out of the city, and even then bus and train fares will be cheaper. Tobacco shops sell parking permits. **Europcar,** Estación de Atocha, AVE terminal (☎915 30 01 94; reservations ☎902 10 50 30; www.europcar.com). M: Atocha Renfe. 21+. Cheapest car €54 per day, €300 per week. Open daily 8am-midnight.

Moped Rental: Motocicletas Antonio Castro, C. Conde Duque 13 (☎915 42 06 57). M: San Bernardo. 18+. A Honda costs €27 per day (8am-8pm) or €117 per week, including unlimited mileage and insurance. €241 deposit. Open M-F 8am-1:30pm and 5-8pm, Sa 9-11am.

READ THIS. The **Guía del Ocio,** at any news kiosk, should be your first purchase in Madrid (€1). It has concert, theater, sports, cinema, and TV schedules. It also lists exhibits, restaurants, bars, and clubs. Although it is in Spanish, the alphabetical listings of clubs and restaurants are invaluable even to non-speakers. For an English magazine with articles on finds in and around the city, pick up **In Madrid,** distributed free at tourist offices and restaurants.

PRACTICAL INFORMATION

TOURIST, FINANCIAL, AND LOCAL SERVICES

Tourist Offices: Municipal, Pl. Mayor 3 (☎/fax 913 66 54 77). M: Sol. Open M-Sa 10am-8pm, Su 10am-3pm. **Regional/Provincial Office of the Comunidad de Madrid,** Duque de Medinacelia 2 (☎914 29 49 51; www.comadrid.es/turismo). **Branches** at Estación Chamartín and the airport.

Websites: www.comadrid.es/turismo; www.tourspain.es; www.cronicamadrid.com; www.guiadelocio.com; www.madridman.com; www.red2000.com/spain/madrid.

General Info Line: ☎901 30 06 00. Run by the Ayuntamiento. They'll tell you anything about Madrid, from police locations to zoo hours. Ask for *inglés* and you'll be transferred to an English-speaking operator.

Embassies: Australia, Pl. Descubridor Diego de Ordás 3 (☎914 41 60 25; www.embaustralia.es). **Canada,** C. Núñez de Balboa 35 (☎914 23 32 50; www.canada-es.org). **Ireland,** Po. Castellana 46, 4th fl. (☎914 36 40 93; fax 914 35 16 77). **New Zealand,** Pl. Lealtad 2, 3rd fl. (☎915 23 02 26; fax 915 23 01 71). **South Africa,** Claudio Coello 91, 6th fl. (☎914 36 37 80; fax 915 77 74 14). **UK,** C. Fernando el Santo 16 (☎917 00 82 00; fax 917 00 82 72). **US,** C. Serrano 75 (☎915 87 22 00; www.embusa.es).

Budget Travel: Viajes TIVE, C. Fernando el Católico 88 (☎915 43 74 12; fax 915 44 00 62). M: Moncloa. Exit the metro at C. Isaac Peral, walk straight down C. Arcipreste de Hita, and turn left on C. Fernando el Católico; it'll be on your left. Organizes group excursions and language classes. Lodgings and student residence info. ISIC €4.25, HI card €11. Open M-F 9am-2pm, Sa 9am-noon. Arrive early to avoid long lines.

Currency Exchange: In general, credit and ATM cards offer the best exchange rates. Avoid changing money at airport and train station counters; they tend to charge exorbitant commissions on horrible rates. **Banco Central Hispano** charges no commission on cash or traveler's checks up to €500. **Main branch,** Pl. Canalejas 1 (☎915 58 11 11). M: Sol. Follow C. San Jeronimo to Pl. Canalejas. Open Apr.-Sept. M-F 8:30am-2:30pm, Sa 8:30am-1pm; Oct.-Mar. M-Th 8:30am-4:30pm, F 8:30am-2pm, Sa 8:30am-1pm.

American Express: Pl. Cortés 2 (Traveler services ☎913 22 54 40; currency exchange ☎917 43 77 83). M: Sevilla. From the metro stop, take a right on C. Alcala, another right down C. Cedacero, and a left on C. San Jerónimo; the office is on the left. Traveler services open M-F 9am-5:30pm, Sa 9am-noon; currency exchange M-F 9am-7:30pm, Sa 9am-2:00pm. 24hr. Express Cash machine outside.

Luggage Storage: Barajas Airport. Follow the signs to *consigna*. One day €3; 2-15 days €3-5 per day; after day 15 €0.60-1.25 per day. **Estación Chamartín** and **Estación Atocha.** Lockers €2.40-5 per day. Open daily 6:30am-10:15pm.

Bi-Gay-Lesbian Resources: Most establishments in the Chueca area carry **Shanguide,** a free guide to gay nightlife in Spain. **Colectivo de Gays y Lesbianas de Madrid (COGAM),** C. Fuencarral 37 (☎/fax 915 23 00 70). M: Gran Vía. Provides a wide range of services and activities, including an HIV support group (☎915 22 45 17; M-F 6-10pm). Reception daily M-Sa 5:30-9pm. Free counseling M-Th 7-9pm.

Laundromat: Lavandería, C. Cervantes 1. M: Puerta del Sol or Banco de España. From Pl. Santa Ana follow C. Prado, turn right on C. Leon, and then go left onto C. Cervantes. Wash €4, dry €1 per 9min. Open M-Sa 9am-8pm.

EMERGENCY AND COMMUNICATIONS

Emergency: All emergencies: ☎112. **Medical:** ☎061. **National police:** ☎091. **Local police:** ☎092.

Police: C. de los Madrazo 9 (☎915 41 71 60). M: Sevilla. From C. Arenal, make a right onto C. Cedacneros and a left onto C. los Madrazo. To report crimes committed in the **metro,** go to the office in the Sol station (☎915 21 09 11). Open daily 8am-11pm.

Lost or stolen credit cards: American Express (☎915 72 03 03); Visa (☎900 97 44 45); Mastercard (☎915 19 21 00); any credit card (☎915 81 18 11).

Rape Hotline: ☎915 74 01 10. Open M-F 10am-2pm and 4-7pm.

Late-Night Pharmacy: Dial ☎098, Madrid's general information line, to find the nearest one. Or try **C. Mayor 59** (☎915 48 00 14), near M: Sol. Listings of the nearest on-duty pharmacy are also posted in all pharmacy windows.

Hospitals: For non-emergency concerns, **Anglo-American Medical Unit,** Conde de Aranda 1, 1st fl. (☎914 35 18 23), is quick and friendly. M: Serrano or Retiro. Doctors, dentists, and optometrists. Run partly by Brits and Americans. Initial visit €54 for students, €60-90 for non-students. AmEx/MC/V. Embassies and consulates also keep lists of English-speaking doctors in private practice. **Hospital Clínico San Carlos** (☎913 30 30 00/01), on Pl. Cristo Rey. M: Moncloa. Open 24hr.

Emergency Clinics: In a **medical emergency,** dial ☎061 or ☎112. **Hospital de Madrid,** Pl. Conde del Valle Suchil 16 (☎914 47 66 00). **Equipo Quirúrgico Municipal No. 1,** C. Montesa 22 (☎915 88 51 00). M: Manuel Becerra. **Hospital Ramón y Cajal,** Ctra. Colmenar Viejo (☎913 36 80 00). Bus #135 from Pl. Castilla. **Red Cross** ☎915 22 22 22; info ☎902 22 22 92.

Internet Access: New Internet cafes are surfacing everywhere. For the establishments below, prices fall between €.80-€1.50 per 30min. and €1.30-€2.50 per hr.

Easy Everything, C. Montera 10 (☎915 23 29 44; www.easyeverything.com). M: Sol. From the Plaza del Sol, look for C. Montera, which goes toward Gran Vía. Hundreds of computers, fast connections, good music, and a cafe. Access from €0.50. Open 24hr.

Conéctate, C. Hilarión Eslava 27 (☎915 44 54 65; www.conectate.es). M: Moncloa. Over 300 flatscreens and some of the lowest prices in Madrid. Open 24hr.

Yazzgo Internet, Gran Vía 84 & 69 (☎915 22 11 20; www.yazzgo.com). M: San Bernado or Pl. de España. Locations at Puerta del Sol 6, Gran Vía 60, Estación Chamartín, and Estación Méndez Álvaro. A growing chain; check their website for new locations. Open daily 8:30am-10:30pm, except Gran Vía 69, open 8:30am-1am.

Post Office: Palacio de Comunicaciones, C. Alcala 51 (☎902 19 71 97), on Pl. Cibeles. M: Banco de España. Windows for stamp purchases, certified mail, telex, and fax service open M-Sa 8:30am-9:30pm, Su 9am-2pm. **Poste Restante** (Lista de Correos) at windows 80-82; passport required. **Postal Code:** 28080.

ACCOMMODATIONS

The demand for rooms is always high and increases dramatically in summer. But never fear—Madrid is rife with hostels. Prices average from €17 to €50 per person depending on location, amenities, and season. However, higher prices do not necessarily translate into nicer accommodations. Reservations are strongly recommended at the top choices listed in the sections below.

EL CENTRO: SOL, ÓPERA, AND PLAZA MAYOR

Prices and locations in El Centro are as good as they get, especially if you are planning to brave the nightlife. The streets that form the inner triangle between M: Sol, Pl. Mayor, and Pl. Santa Ana are packed with hostels. The following listings fall in the area between the Sol and Ópera metro stops. Buses #3, 25, 39, and 500 serve Ópera; buses #3, 5 (from Atocha), 15, 20, 50-53, and 150 serve Sol.

Hostal Paz, C. Flora 4, 1st and 4th fl. (☎915 47 30 47). M: Ópera. Don't be deterred by the dark street, parallel to C. Arenal, off C. Donados or C. Hileras. Peaceful rooms with large windows are sheltered from street noise and lavished with amenities: wonderful owners, satellite TV, A/C, and spotless, spacious bathrooms. Reservations recommended. Laundry €8. Singles €17; doubles €27-32; triples €40. MC/V. ❷

Hostal-Residencia Luz, C. Fuentes 10, 3rd fl. (☎915 42 07 59; fax 915 42 07 59), off C. Arenal. M: Ópera. Neck-and-neck with Hostal Paz for the best digs in Madrid. Twelve sunny rooms exude comfort with hardwood floors, elegant furniture, beautiful curtains and cozy bedspreads. Laundry €6. Singles €15; doubles €28-33; triples €33-39. ❶

Hostal-Residencia Rober, C. Arenal 26, 5th fl. (☎915 41 91 75). M: Ópera. Brilliant balcony views down Arenal. Singles with double bed and shower €25, with bath €33; doubles with bath €38; triples with bath €58. Discounts for longer stays. ❸

Hostal Valencia, Pl. Oriente 2, 3rd fl. (☎915 59 84 50). M: Ópera. Narrow glass elevator leads to elegant rooms. Singles €42; doubles €60; master suite €78. ❹

Hostal Esparteros, C. Esparteros 12, 4th fl. (☎/fax 915 21 09 03). M: Sol. Cheap, small, sparkling rooms with a balcony or large windows. Hospitable, English-speaking owner ensures a terrific stay. Laundry €7. Singles €20; doubles €35; triples €42. ❷

Hostal Cantabrico, C. de la Cruz 5 (☎915 31 01 30 or 915 21 33 03), near Pl. Canalejas. M: Sol. Spacious rooms, all with complete bath, some with nice balcony views. Over 100 years in operation. Singles €31; doubles €46; triples €61. ❸

Hostal-Residencia Cruz-Sol, Pl. Santa Cruz 6, 3rd fl. (☎915 32 71 97; info@hostalcruzsol.com). M: Sol. Modern rooms with parquet floors, double-paned windows, safes, heat, phones, Internet jacks, and A/C. Laundry €11. Singles with bath €36; doubles €48; triples €60; quads €72. ❹

Hostal Portugal, C. Flora 4, 1st fl. (☎915 59 40 14). M: Ópera. Mediocre rooms with TV and bath. Great location. Doubles €33; triples €45. ❸

Hostal-Residencia Miño, C. Arenal 16, 2nd fl. (☎915 31 50 79). M: Ópera. Don't be deterred by the deer head at the entrance. Nice rooms, some with hardwood floors and balconies. Singles €21-29; doubles €36-39; triples with bath €51. ❷

Hostal Madrid, C. Esparteros 6, 2nd fl. (☎915 22 00 60; www.hostal-madrid.com). M: Sol. Off C. Mayor. Average *hostal* with TVs, safes, A/C, new bathrooms, and high prices. Reserve ahead. Singles €48-55; doubles €66; triple with balcony €84. ❺

HUERTAS

Although *madrileños* have never settled on a nickname for this neighborhood, the area between C. San Jeronimo and C. de las Huertas is generally referred to as Huertas. Once a seedy neighborhood—and a Hemingway hangout—Huertas has shaped up into a hotbed of food and drink. Sol, Pl. Mayor, *el triángulo del arte* (the area bounded by Madrid's three major museums), and the Atocha train station are all within walking distance. Sol-bound buses stop on C. Príncipe, C. Nuñez de Arce, and C. San Jerónimo; buses #14, 27, 37, and 45 run along Po. del Prado. The metro stops are Sol, Sevilla, and Antón Martín.

Hostal Gonzalo, C. Cervantes 34, 3rd fl. (☎914 29 27 14; fax 914 20 20 07). M: Antón Martín. Off C. León, which is off C. Atocha. A traveler's dream–pristine baths, firm beds, TVs, and fans in the summer. Singles €35; doubles €43; triples €55. ❹

Hostal Internacional, C. Echegaray 5, 2nd fl. (☎914 29 62 09). M: Sol or Sevilla. Rooms are newly renovated. Nice common room. Singles €30; doubles €36. ❸

Hostal-Residencia Lido, C. Echegaray 5, 2nd fl. (☎914 29 62 07). M: Sol or Sevilla. Across the hall from Internacional, Lido recently finished a makeover. New rooms have comfy beds, TVs, and complete baths. Singles €18; doubles €30. ❷

Hostal Villar, C. Príncipe 18, 1st-4th fl. (☎915 31 66 00; www.arrakis.es/~h-villar). M: Sol. From the metro, walk down C. San Jerónimo and turn right on C. Príncipe. A secluded feeling despite its busy location. The 1970s stormed through this building, leaving in their wake 46 decidedly brown rooms. Common area attracts young crowd. Singles €20, with bath €23; doubles €27/€35; triples €37/€49. ❷

Hostal Armesto, C. San Agustín 6, 1st fl. (☎914 29 90 31). M: Antón Martín. In front of Pl. Cortés. Offers exceptional hospitality and a quiet night's sleep. All rooms with private bath and A/C. Older crowd. Singles €39; doubles €45; triples €53. ❹

Hostal-Residencia Carreras, C. Príncipe 18, 3rd fl. (☎/fax 915 22 00 36). M: Sol or Sevilla. Off C. San Jerónimo, between Pl. Santa Ana and Canalejas. Ask for a room with a balcony–they tend to be larger. Singles €21, with bath €48; doubles €36/€42-48; triples €54/€60. ❷

Hostal Aguilar, C. San Jerónimo 32, 2nd fl. (☎914 29 59 26; www.hostalaguilar.com). M: Sol or Sevilla. More than 50 clean, expansive rooms with large bathrooms, telephones, A/C, safes, and TVs. Elegant lounge with deep couches serves as a meeting ground for clubbers. Singles €30; doubles €42; triples €47; quads €69. ❸

Hostal R. Rodríguez, C. Núñez de Arce 9, 3rd fl. (☎915 22 44 31), off Pl. Santa Ana. M: Sol or Sevilla. Reception decor makes even the cheapest of travelers feel like royalty. Clean shared baths and spacious rooms. 24hr. reception. English spoken. Singles €25; doubles €42-47; triples €65. ❸

GRAN VÍA

The neon lights of Broadway and the Champs-Élysées have met their match in Gran Vía. *Hostal* signs scatter the horizon, but accommodations here tend to be pricier and less comfortable than in other areas. Have your wits about you when returning late at night. El Centro and Huertas provide safer bargains. Buses #1, 2, 44, 46, 74, 75, 133, 146, 147, and 148 reach Callao; buses #1, 2, 3, 40, 46, 74, 146, and 149 service both Pl. España and Callao. The closest metro stops are Gran Vía, Callao, Santo Domingo, and Banco de España.

Hostal A. Nebrija, Gran Vía 67, 8th fl., elevator A (☎915 47 73 19). M: Pl. España. A grandson continues tradition with pleasant, spacious rooms offering magnificent views of the city landscape. Singles €26; doubles €36; triples €49. AmEx/MC/V. ❸

Hostal Margarita, Gran Vía 50, 5th fl. (☎/fax 915 47 35 49). M: Callao. Simple rooms with large windows and TVs; most with street views. Singles €25; doubles €36, with bath €38; triples with bath €48. MC/V. ❸

Hostal Triana, C. de la Salud 13, 1st fl. (☎915 32 68 12; www.hostaltriana.com). M: Callao or Gran Vía. From Gran Vía, turn onto C. Salud; the sign is quite visible. Catering to those seeking a little more comfort than the standard *hostal*. Reserve 2 weeks ahead. Singles €35; doubles €41. ❹

MALASAÑA AND CHUECA

Split down the middle by C. Fuencarral, Malasaña and Chueca host an outrageous nightlife, great shopping, and excellent dining. Hostels and *pensiones* tend to be a bit pricier here, even though many are located in old, sometimes dilapidated, buildings. Don't be deterred by the occasional sketchy street—Chueca is hip and fun. It is the center of Madrid's large gay population, but offers something for everybody. Buses #3, 40, and 149 run along C. Fuencarral and Hortaleza. Metro stops Chueca, Gran Vía, and Tribunal serve the area.

Hostal-Residencia Domínguez, C. Santa Brígida 1, 1st fl. (☎/fax 915 32 15 47). M: Tribunal. Go down C. Fuencarral toward Gran Vía, and turn left on C. Santa Brígida, and climb up a flight. Hospitable young owner ready with tips on local nightlife. English spoken. Singles €21, with bath €30; doubles with bath and A/C €40. ❷

Hostal Chelo, C. Hortaleza 17, 3rd fl. (☎915 32 70 33; www.chelo.com). M: Gran Vía. Hospitable staff and a great location. Rooms are spacious, with complete baths. Singles €30; doubles €36. ❸

Hostal Lorenzo, C. Clavel 8 (☎915 21 30 57; fax 915 32 79 78). M: Gran Vía. From the metro, walk up C. Clavel; it's on the corner of the plaza. New furniture and modern bathrooms. Reservations recommended. Singles €45; doubles €65-80. AmEx/MC/V. ❹

Hostal Palacios and **Hostal Ribadavia,** C. Fuencarral 25, 1st-3rd fl. (☎915 31 10 58 or 915 31 48 47). M: Gran Vía. Both run by the same cheerful family. Singles €20, with bath €27; doubles €28/€35; triples €45/€48. AmEx/MC/V. ❷

ELSEWHERE AND CAMPING

Budget lodgings are rare near the **Chamartín** train station, as is the case in most of the residential districts located away from the city center. Near the **Madrid-Atocha** train station are a handful of hostels, the closest of which are down Po. Santa María de la Cabeza. Tourist offices can provide info about the 13 campsites within 50km of Madrid. Similar info is in the *Guía Oficial de Campings* (official camping guide), a large book they'll gladly let you peruse. For further camping info, contact the **Consejería de Educación de Juventud** (☎915 22 29 41).

Albergue Juvenil Santa Cruz de Marcenado (HI), C. Santa Cruz de Marcenado 28 (☎915 47 45 32; fax 915 48 11 96). M: Argüelles. From the metro, walk 1 block down C. Alberto Aguilera away from C. Princesa, turn right on C. Serrano Jóve, then left on C. Santa Cruz de Marcenado. Lounge is great for late-night card playing. The 72 beds fill quickly. Rooms have cubbies; recommended lockers are outside the rooms (€2 extra). Breakfast included. Sheets (but no towels) provided. 3-day max. stay. Quiet hours after midnight. Reception daily 9am-10pm. 1:30am curfew is strictly enforced. Reserve a space (by mail, fax, or in person only) in advance, or arrive early. Closed Christmas and New Year's. HI (YHA) members only; cards €12. Dorms €8; over 26 €11.50. ❶

Camping Alpha (☎916 95 80 69; fax 916 83 16 59), on a tree-lined site 12.4km down the Ctra. de Andalucía in Getafe. M: Legazpi. From the metro station, take bus #447, which stops next to the Nissan dealership. Ask the driver to let you off at the pedestrian overpass for the campsite. Cross the bridge and walk 1.5km back toward Madrid along a busy highway; camping signs lead the way. Pool, showers, and laundry. €4 per person, per tent, and per car. ❶

FOOD

In Madrid, it's not hard to fork it down without forking over too much. Most restaurants offer a *menú del día* (€7-9), which includes bread, one drink, and one choice from each of the day's selection of appetizers, main courses, and desserts. Many small eateries line **Calles Echegaray, Bentura de la Vega,** and **Manuel Fernández González** in Huertas. **Calle Agurrosa** at Lavapiés has some funky outdoor cafes, and there are good restaurants up the hill toward Huertas. **Calle Fuencarral** in Gran Vía is lined with cheap eats. **Bilbao,** the area north of Glorieta de Bilbao, is the place to go for ethnically diverse culinary choices. Bars along **Calle Hartzenbusch** and **Calle Cisneros** offer cheap *tapas*. Keep in mind the following essential buzz words for quicker, cheaper *madrileño* fare: *bocadillo* (a sandwich on a long, hard roll; €2-2.75); *ración* (a large *tapa*, served with bread; €1.85-3.75); and *empanada* (a puff pastry with meat fillings; €1.25-1.85). Vegetarians should check out the *Guía del Ocio*, which has a complete listing of Madrid's vegetarian havens under the section *"Otras Cocinas,"* or the website www.mundovegetariano.com. For groceries, **%Dia** and **Simago** are the cheapest supermarket chains. More expensive are **Mantequerías Leonesas, Expreso,** and **Jumbo.**

Inshala, C. Amnistia 10 (☎915 48 26 32). M: Ópera. Eccentric menu filled with delicious Spanish, Mexican, Japanese, Italian, and Moroccan dishes. Weekday lunch *menú* €7.25. Dinner *menú* €8-€15. Reservations strongly recommended for both lunch and dinner. Open M-Sa 2-6pm and 9pm-1am, Su 2-5pm. ❸

Champagneria Gala, C. Moratín 22 (☎91 429 25 62). Down the hill from C. Atocha on C. Moratín. The *paella* buck stops here, with decor as colorful and varied as its specialty. *Menú* €11. Reserve on weekends. Open daily 1:30-5pm and 9pm-12:30am. ❸

El Estragón Vegetariano, Pl. de la Paja 10 (☎91 365 89 82). M: La Latina. Perhaps the best medium-priced restaurant in Madrid, with vegetarian food that could turn the most die-hard carnivores into switch-hitters. Try the delicious *menú (*M-F €9, Sa-Su and evenings €18). Open daily 1:30-4:30pm and 8pm-1am. AmEx/MC/V. ❸

Cáscaras, C. Ventura Rodríguez 7 (☎915 42 83 36). M: Ventura Rodríguez. From the metro, take your first right off C. Princesa. Popular for *tapas, pinchos,* and ice-cold Mahou beer in the early afternoon and evening. Exotic vegetarian entrees €5-6. Open M-F 7am-1am, Sa-Su 10am-1am. AmEx/MC/V. ❶

Ananias, C. Galileo 9 (☎914 48 68 01). M: Argüelles. From C. Alberto Aguilera, take a left onto C. Galileo. Swirling waiters serve Castilian dishes with a flourish. Entrees €9-15. Open Su-Tu and Th-F 1-4pm and 9-11:30pm, Sa 9-11:30pm. AmEx/MC/V. ❸

Arepas con Todo, C. Hartzenbusch 19 (☎91 448 75 45), off C. Cardenal Cisneros, from C. Luchana. Hanging gourds and waitresses in festive dress fill this classic Colombian restaurant. A rotating *menú* (€10-12) for every night of the month, and 60 fixed dishes (€11-15). Only the live music acts repeat themselves. Open daily 2pm-1am. MC/V. ❸

Al-Jaima, Cocina del Desierto, C. Barbieri 1 (☎915 23 11 42). M: Gran Vía or Chueca. Lebanese, Moroccan, and Egyptian food in intimate N. African setting. Specialties include pastela, couscous, shish kebabs, and tayin. Entrees €4-8. Reservations recommended. Open daily 1:30-4pm and 9pm-midnight. ❷

La Granja Restaurante Vegetariano, C. San Andrés 11 (☎915 32 87 93), off Pl. 2 de Mayo. M: Tribunal or Bilbao. Dimmed yellow lights glow above intricately tiled walls in this Arab-themed restaurant. Lunchtime *menú* €7.25. Open W-M 1:30-4:30pm and 9pm-midnight. Closed Su in summer. ❷

Restaurante Casa Botin, C. de Cuchilleros 17 (☎913 66 42 17). The "oldest restaurant in the world," founded in 1725, serves a variety of filling Spanish dishes (€7-20). Reservations recommended. Lunch daily 1-4pm, dinner 8pm-midnight. ❸

La Finca de Susana, C. Arlaban 4 (☎913 69 35 57). M: Sevilla. Probably the most popular lunch place in Madrid; fine dining at an extremely low price (*menú* €6.50). Be prepared to wait in line for lunch. Open daily 1-4pm and 8-11:30pm. ❷

Pizzeria Vesuvio, C. Hortaleza 4 (☎915 21 51 71). M: Gran Vía. Mix and match pasta and sauce or try the 30+ combinations of personal pizzas. Delicious food and fast service. Counter seating only. Try the pasta fresca. Take-out available. Meals €3.30-€5. Open M-Sa 1-4pm and 8pm-midnight, F-Sa until 1am. ❶

Anatolia, C. de la Cruz 10. M: Sol. Turkish restaurant serving succulent Doner Kebab (chicken or lamb gyro sandwiches). Tavuk Kebab with all the trimmings (€3) and other Turkish specialties (€2.70-4.50). Closed Su. ❶

Al Natural, C. Zorrilla 11 (☎913 69 47 09). M: Sevilla. From the metro stop, take a left off C. de Cedaceros; it's behind the Congress building. Vegetarian Mediterranean dishes (€8-12) served in a lively atmosphere. Open daily 1-4pm, M-Sa also 7pm-midnight. ❷

El 26 de Libertad, C. Libertad 26 (☎915 22 25 22), off C. las Infantas. M: Chueca. Innovative Spanish cuisine in an elegant, spacious setting. *Paella* specialties. Order a la carte (€10-16) or try the *menú* (lunch €12, dinner €21). Open M-Th 1-4pm and 8pm-midnight, F-Sa 1-4pm and 9pm-midnight; Sept.-June also Su 1-4pm. ❹

TAPAS

Not so long ago, bartenders in Madrid used to *tapar* (cover) drinks with saucers to keep the flies out. Later, servers began putting little sandwiches on top of the saucers, and there you have it: *tapas*. Hopping from bar to bar gobbling *tapas* is an active alternative to a full sit-down meal. Huertas and the La Latina area are full of *tapas* bars. Try those on **Calle Baja, Plaza Mayor, Plaza Santa Anna,** and around the San Pedro church on **Calle Cuchillos.**

TAPAS *Tapas* menus can often be cryptic and indecipherable—and that's if the bar bothered to print them in the first place. To make sure you don't end up eating the stewed parts of the ox you rode in on, just keep the following words in mind. Servings come in three sizes: *pincho* (normally eaten with toothpicks between sips of beer), *tapa* (small plate), and *ración* (sizable meal portion). *Aceitunas* (olives), *albondingas* (meatballs), *anchoas* (anchovies), *callos* (tripe), *chorizo* (sausage), *croquetas* (breaded and fried combos), *gambas* (shrimp), *jamón* (ham), *patatas alioli y bravas* (potatoes with sauces), *pimentos* (peppers), *pulpo* (octopus), and *tortilla* (potato omelette) comprise any basic menu.

Casa Alberto, C. Huertas 18 (☎914 29 93 56). M: Antón Martín. Interior dining room decorated with bullfighting and Cervantine relics; Cervantes wrote the second part of *El Quijote* here. The *tapas* are all original house recipes. Get the feel of their *gambas al ajillo* (shrimp with garlic and hot peppers; €7.50) or the filled *canapés* (€1.75-2). Sit-down dinner is a bit pricey. Open Tu-Sa noon-5:30pm and 8pm-1:30am. ❸

La Toscana, C. Manuel Fernández González 10-12 (☎914 29 60 31), at C. Ventura de la Vega. M: Sol or Sevilla. A local crowd hangs out over *mocillo asado* (€8). Despite the antique lettering and wrought iron, the range of dishes is anything but medieval. Spacious bar area jam-packed on weekends. Most *tapas* around €5. Open Tu-Sa 1-4pm and 8pm-midnight. ❷

Los Gabrieles, C. Echegaray 17 (☎914 29 62 61), near Villa Madrid. The tiled mural at the back depicts Spain's famous artists—from Velázquez to Goya—as stumbling drunks. Tu is flamenco night. Open daily 1pm-late. ❷

Casa Amadeo, Pl. de Cascorro 18 (☎913 65 94 39). M: La Latina. Jovial owner of 60 years supervises the preparation of *chorizo* (sausage) made with snails (€4.50). Open M-F 10:30am-4pm and 7-10:30pm, Su 7-11pm. ❷

CLASSIC CAFES

Even when chilling, Madrileños like to watch the frenzied streets. It's customary to linger for an hour or two in Madrid's classic cafes. Soak up culture, rest weary legs, and check out passersby from behind your coffee cup.

Café de Oriente, Pl. Oriente 2 (☎915 47 15 64). M: Ópera. A beautiful, old-fashioned café catering to a ritzy, older crowd. Spectacular view of the Palacio Real from the *terraza,* especially at night when a spotlight illuminates the palace. Prices are significantly cheaper inside than on the patio. Specialty coffees (€2-6) live up to their price. Meals also served. Open daily 8:30am-1:30am.

Café Gijón, Po. Recoletos 21 (☎915 21 54 25). M: Colón. In 1988, on its 100th anniversary, Gijón was designated a historic site for its intellectual significance. Check out how smart you look in the mirrors and forget how much that cup of coffee costs; it's well worth the price. Coffees from €3.75. Open daily 9am-1:30am.

Café Comercial, Glorieta de Bilbao 7 (☎915 21 56 55). M: Bilbao. Founded in 1887, Madrid's oldest café has high ceilings, cushioned chairs, and huge mirrors perfect for people-watching. The first anti-Franco protests took place here. Coffee €1 at the bar, €1.55 at a table. Open M-Th 7:30am-1:30am, F-Sa 8am-2am, Su 10am-1am.

Eucalipto, C. Argumosa 4. M: Lavapiés. Take a break from the normal coffee fare and head for refreshing *zumos tropicales* (fresh fruit drinks; €2.40-3.30). Spike up the night with a *daiquiri* (€3.75-4) and enjoy a fantastic fruit salad for 2 (€6). Lively sidewalk seating. Open daily M-Th 6pm-2am, F-Sa 6pm-3am, Su 2pm-midnight.

SIGHTS

Madrid, as large as it may seem, is a walker's city. The word *paseo* refers to a major avenue, but literally means "a stroll." From Sol to Cibeles and from the Plaza Mayor to the Palacio Real, sights will kindly introduce themselves. The municipal tourist office's *Plano de Transportes*—which marks monuments as well as bus and metro lines—is indispensable. In the following pages, sights are arranged by neighborhood, offering opportunities for extensive walking tours in each. Each section has a designated center from which all directions are given.

EL CENTRO

The area known as El Centro, spreading out from the Puerta del Sol ("Door of the Sun"), is the gateway to the history and spirit of Madrid. Although several rulers carved the winding streets, the Habsburg and Bourbon families left behind El Centro's most celebrated monuments. As a result, El Centro is divided into two major sections: Madrid de los Habsburgs and Madrid de los Borbones. All directions are given from the Puerta del Sol.

HABSBURG MADRID

"Old Madrid," the city's central neighborhood, is densely packed with both monuments and tourists. In the 16th century, the Habsburgs built **Plaza Mayor** and the **Catedral de San Isidro.** When Felipe II moved the seat of Castilla from Toledo to Madrid in 1561, he and his descendants commissioned the court architects (including Juan de Herrera) to update many of Madrid's buildings to the latest styles. In 1620, the plaza was completed for Felipe III; his statue, installed in 1847, still graces the plaza's center. Toward evening, Pl. Mayor awakens as *madrileños* resurface, tourists multiply, and cafe tables fill with lively patrons. Live performances of flamenco and music are a common treat. *(M: Sol. From Sol, walk down C. Mayor; the plaza is on the left.)*

CATEDRAL DE SAN ISIDRO. Designed in the Jesuit Baroque style at the beginning of the 17th century, the cathedral received San Isidro's remains in 1769. During the Civil War, rioting workers burned the exterior and damaged much of the cathedral—only the primary nave and a few Baroque decorations remain from the original. *(M: Latina. From Pta. Sol, take C. Mayor to Pl. Mayor, cross the plaza, and exit onto C. Toledo. Open for mass only. Mass daily 9, 10, 11am, and noon.)*

PLAZA DE LA VILLA. Plaza de la Villa marks the heart of what was once old Madrid. Though only a few medieval buildings remain, the plaza still features a stunning courtyard (surrounding the statue of Don Alvara de Bazón), beautiful tile-work, and eclectic architecture. Across the plaza is the 17th-century **Ayuntamiento (Casa de la Villa),** designed in 1640 by Juan Gomez de Mora as both the mayor's home and the city jail. *(M: Sol. From Pta. Sol, go down C. Mayor, past Pl. Mayor.)*

BOURBON MADRID

Weakened by plagues and political losses, the Habsburg era in Spain ended with the death of Carlos II in 1700. Felipe V, the first of Spain's Bourbon monarchs, ascended the throne in 1714 after the 12-year War of the Spanish Succession. Bankruptcy, industrial stagnation, and widespread disillusionment compelled Felipe V to embark on a crusade of urban renewal. The lavish palaces, churches, and parks that remain are the most touristed in Madrid.

PALACIO REAL. The luxurious Palacio Real lies at the western tip of central Madrid, overlooking the Río Manzanares. Felipe V commissioned Giovanni Sachetti to replace the Alcázar, which had burned down in 1734, with a palace that would dwarf all others—he succeeded. Today, the unfinished palace is only used by King

Juan Carlos and Queen Sofía on special occasions. The palace's most impressive rooms are decorated in the Rococo style. The **Salón de Gasparini,** site of the king's ceremonial dressing before the court, houses Goya's portrait of Carlos IV and a Mengs ceiling fresco. The **Salón del Trono** (Throne Room) also contains a ceiling fresco, painted by Tiepolo, that outlines the qualities of the quintessential ruler. The **Biblioteca** shelves first editions of *Don Quixote.* Also open to the public is the **Real Armería** (Armory), which displays the armor of Carlos V and Felipe II. *(From Pta. Sol, take C. Mayor and turn right on C. Bailén. M: Sol. Open Apr.-Sept. M-Sa 9am-6pm, Su 9am-3pm; Oct.-Mar. M-Sa 9:30am-5pm, Su 9am-2pm. €6, students €3; with tour €6.90. W free for EU citizens.)* Next door to the palace is the **Cathedral de la Almudena,** begun in 1879 and finished a century later. The cathedral's modern interior stands in contrast to the gilded Palacio Real. *(M: Sol. From Pta. Sol, go down C. Mayor and it's just across C. Bailén. Open M-Sa 1-7pm. Closed during mass. Free.)*

PLAZA DE ORIENTE. A minor architectural miscalculation was responsible for this sculpture park. Most of the statues here were designed for the palace roof, but because they were too heavy (and the queen had a nightmare about the roof collapsing), they were placed in this shady plaza instead. Elegant *terrazas* encompass the plaza, presenting an opportunity to treat yourself to an overpriced coffee (see p. 857). The **Jardines de Sabatini,** just to the right as you face the palace, is the romantic's park of choice. *(From Pta. Sol, take C. Arenal to the plaza. Free.)*

PARQUE DE LAS VISTILLAS. This park was named for its gorgeous *vistillas* (views) of Palacio Real, Nuestra Señora de la Almudena, and the surrounding countryside. Be careful at night, as it can be dangerous. *(In Pl. Gabriel Miró. Facing the palace, turn left on C. Bailén, and then right on C. Don Pedro into the plaza.)*

HUERTAS

The area east of Sol is a wedge bounded by C. de Alcalá to the north, C. Atocha to the south, and Po. Prado to the east. Huertas's sights, from authors' houses to famous cafes, reflect its artistic focus. Home to Cervantes, Góngora, Quevedo, Calderón, and Moratín in the "Siglo de Oro" (Golden Age), Huertas enjoyed a fleeting return to literary prominence when Hemingway frequented the neighborhood in the 1920s. **Plaza Santa Ana** and its *terrazas* are the center of this old literary haunt. **Casa de Lope de Vega** is the home where the prolific playwright and poet spent the last 25 years of his life and wrote over two-thirds of his plays. The highlights include the simple garden described in his works and the library filled with crumbling, aromatic books. Among the more interesting tidbits revealed on the mandatory tour are the tangible signs of affection Vega would leave for his young daughters. *(C. Cervantes 11. With your back to Pl. Santa Ana, turn left on C. Prado, right on C. León, and left on C. Cervantes. ☎914 29 92 16. Open Tu-F 9:30am-2pm, Sa 10am-2pm. €1.50, students €0.90. Sa free.)*

GRAN VÍA

Urban planners paved the Gran Vía in 1910 to link C. Princesa with Pl. Cibeles. After Madrid became wealthy as a neutral supplier during World War I, the city funneled much of its earnings into making the Gran Vía one of the world's great thoroughfares. At Gran Vía's highest elevation in **Plaza de Callao** (M: Callao), C. Postigo San Martín splits off southward, where you'll find the famed **Monasterio de las Descalzas Reales.** Westward from Pl. Callao, the Gran Vía makes its descent toward **Plaza de España** (M: Pl. España), where a statue commemorates Spain's most prized fictional duo: Cervantes' Don Quixote and Sancho Panza, riding horseback and muleback respectively.

MALASAÑA AND CHUECA

Void of the numerous historic monuments and palaces that characterize most of Madrid, the labyrinthine streets of Malasaña and Chueca house countless undocumented "sights," from platform-shoe stores to spontaneous street performances. Chueca in particular remains an ideal area for people-watching and fabulous boutique shopping. While the area between **Calle de Fuencarral** and **Calle de San Bernardo** contains some of Madrid's most avant-garde architecture and contemporary art exhibitions, most of this neighborhood's scenery lies in the people.

ARGÜELLES

The area known as Argüelles and the zone surrounding Calle San Bernardo form a cluttered mixture of elegant middle-class houses, student apartments, and bohemian hangouts, all brimming with cultural activity. Heavily bombarded during the Civil War, Argüelles inspired Chilean poet Pablo Neruda, then a resident, to write *España en el corazón.* By day, families and joggers roam the city's largest park, **Casa del Campo;** night brings curious but unsafe activity.

The **Parque de la Montaña** is home to Spain's only Egyptian temple. Built by Pharaoh Zakheramon in the 4th century BC, the **Temple de Debod** was a gift from the Egyptian government commemorating the Spanish archaeologists who helped rescue monuments in the Aswan dam floods. From the metro, walk down C. Ventura Rodríguez into the Parque de la Montaña; the temple is on the left. (M: Ventura Rodríguez. Open Tu-F 9:45am-1:15pm and 4:15-5:45pm; Sa-Su 10am-1:45pm. €1.80, students €0.90. W and Su free.) Although out of the way, the **Ermita de San Antonio de la Florida** is worth the trouble. From the metro, go left on C. de Buen Altamirano, walk through the park, and turn left on Po. Florida; it's at the end of this street. The Emita contains Goya's pantheon—a frescoed dome arches above his buried corpse. Goya's skull, apparently stolen by a phrenologist, was missing when the corpse arrived from France. (M: Príncipe Pío. ☎915 42 07 22. Open Tu-F 10am-2pm and 4-8pm, Sa-Su 10am-2pm. €1.80, students €.90; W and Sa free.) The **Faro de Moncloa** is a 92m-tall metal tower that offers astounding views of the city. (M: Av. Arco de la Victoria. Open M-Su 10am-1:45pm and 5-8:45pm. €1.50 to ascend.)

OTHER SIGHTS

RETIRO. Join an array of vendors, palm-readers, soccer players, and sunbathers in what Felipe IV once intended to be a hunting ground, or a *buen retiro* (nice retreat). The finely landscaped 300-acre Parque del Buen Retiro is centered around a rectangular lake and a magnificent monument to King Alfonso XII. Dubbed **Estanque Grande,** this central location is popular among casual rowers. Built by Ricardo Velázquez to exhibit Filipino flowers, the exquisite steel-and-glass **Palacio de Cristal** hosts a variety of art shows. *(Open Apr.-Sept. M and W-Sa 11am-8pm, Su 11am-6pm; Oct.-Mar. M and W-Sa 10am-6pm, Su 10am-4pm. Free.)* Artists dream of having their art displayed in the **Palacio de Velázquez,** with its billowing ceilings, marble floors, and ideal lighting. Avoid venturing into the park alone after dark. *(Past the Estanque, turn left on Paseo del Venezuela. Open Apr.-Sept. M and W-Sa 11am-8pm, Su 11am-6pm; Oct.-Mar. M and W-Sa 10am-6pm, Su 10am-4pm. Free.)*

EL PARDO. Built as a hunting lodge for Carlos I in 1547, El Pardo was enlarged by generations of Habsburgs and Bourbons. El Pardo gained attention in 1940 when Franco made it his home; he resided here until his death in 1975. While renowned for its collection of tapestries—several of which were designed by Goya—the palace also holds paintings by Velázquez and Ribera. *(M: Moncloa. Take bus #601 (15min., €1) from the stop in front of the Ejército del Aire building. Open Apr.-Sept. M-F 10:30am-6pm, Su 9:30am-1:40pm; Oct.-Mar. M-F 10:30am-5pm, Su 10am-1:40pm. Mandatory 45min. guided tour in Spanish. €4.80, students €1.50; W free for EU citizens.)*

EL RASTRO (FLEA MARKET). For hundreds of years, El Rastro has been a Sunday morning tradition. The market begins in La Latina at Pl. Cascorro off C. Toledo and ends at the bottom of C. Ribera de Curtidores. Get lost in the insanity and find anything from jewelry and jeans to antique tools and pet birds. The flea market is a pickpocket paradise, so leave your camera in the room and watch your backpack. *(Open Su and holidays 9am to 2pm.)*

MUSEUMS

Madrid's great museums hardly need an introduction. The worthwhile **Paseo del Arte** ticket grants admission to the Museo del Prado, Museo Thyssen-Bornemisza, and Centro de Arte Reina Sofía (€8). The pass is available at all three museums.

MUSEO DEL PRADO

Po. Prado at Pl. Cánovas del Castillo. M: Banco de España or Atocha. ☎/fax 91 330 28 00; http://museoprado.mcu.es. Open Tu-Sa 9am-7pm, Su 9am-2pm. €3; students €1.50; Sa after 2:30pm, Su, and holidays free.

The Prado is Spain's pride and joy, as well as one of Europe's finest museums. Its 7000 pieces from the 12th-17th centuries are the result of hundreds of years of Bourbon art collecting. Each room is numbered and described in the museum's free guide. On the second floor, keep an eye out for unforgiving realism and use of light in the works of **Diego Velázquez** (1599-1660), which resonate even in the 20th century. Several of his most famous paintings are here, including *Los borrachos (The Drunkards)* and *Las lanzas (The Spears* or *The Surrender of Breda)*. Velazquez's technique, called illusionism, climaxed in his magnum opus *Las Meninas (The Maids of Honor)*, since dubbed an "encounter."

The court portraitist **Francisco de Goya y Lucientes** (1746-1828) created the stark *Dos de Mayo* and *Fusilamientas de Tres de Mayo*, which depict the terrors of the Revolution of 1808. Goya painted the *Pinturas Negras (Black Paintings)* at the end of his life, deaf and alone. *Saturno devorando a su hijo (Saturn Devouring His Son)* stands out among the *Pinturas Negras*, a reminder from an ailing artist that time eventually destroys its creations. The Prado also displays many of **El Greco**'s religious paintings. *La Trinidad (The Trinity)* and *La adoración de los pastores (The Adoration of the Shepherds)* are characterized by luminous colors, elongated figures, and mystical subjects. On the second floor are other works by Spanish artists, including **Murillo, Ribera,** and **Zurbarán.**

The Prado also has a formidable collection of **Italian** works, including pieces by Titian, Raphael, Tintoretto, Botticelli, and Rubens. As a result of the Spanish Habsburgs' control of the Netherlands, the **Flemish** holdings are also top-notch. Works by **van Dyck** and **Albrecht Durer** are here. Especially harrowing is **Peter Breugel the Elder**'s *The Triumph of Death*, in which death drives a carriage of skulls on a decaying horse. **Hieronymus Bosch**'s moralistic *The Garden of Earthly Delights* depicts hedonism and the destiny that awaits its practitioners.

MUSEO THYSSEN-BORNEMISZA

On the corner of Po. Prado and C. San Jerónimo. M: Banco de España. Bus #6, 14, 27, 37, or 45. ☎ 913 69 01 51. Open Tu-Su 10am-7pm. Last entry 6:30pm. €4.20, seniors and ISIC holders €2.40, under 12 free.

Unlike the Prado and the Reina Sofía, the Thyssen-Bornemisza covers a wide range of periods and media, with exhibits ranging from 14th-century canvases to 20th-century sculptures. Baron Heinrich Thyssen-Bornemisza donated his collection in 1993, and today the museum, with over 775 pieces, is the world's most extensive private showcase. To view the collection in chronological order and observe the evolution of styles and themes, begin on the top floor and work your

IN RECENT NEWS

NO MORE BULL?

There is nothing in Spanish culture as ingrained or controversial as the bullfight. Although the sport also takes place in France, Portugal, and Latin America, it has long been the emblem of Spanish culture, though not without vocal protest. Even in its early days, this spectacle of life versus death and man against nature faced considerable opposition. Pope Pius V forbade the bullfight in 1567, claiming it was "contrary to Christian piety." Still, the ritual continued.

Today, bullfighting is under attack by animal rights activists across the world. They lobby politicians, stage massive protests, and besiege the Vatican with postcards. They believe the bullfight is not a fight at all, but the staged torture and killing of an innocent animal. Their efforts have met with some success. In 1992, 400 Spaniards protested the sport in Madrid, and in 1993, an anti-bullfighting petition garnered over one million signatures; recent polls show that younger generations are less captivated by the sport.

As Europe unifies, the bullfight, which supporters call a form of art, has become a strong point of contention between northern and southern Europe. Portuguese laws that ban the killing of the bull continue to be defied by southern cities, which have more in common culturally with their Spanish neighbors. Even now, funds are being pumped into revitalizing and ensuring the preservation of the sport, and tourists arrive everyday believing they haven't experienced Spain if they haven't seen a bullfight.

way down—the organization of the Thyssen-Bornemisza provokes natural comparisons across centuries. The top floor is dedicated to the **Old Masters** collection, which includes such notables as Hans Holbein's austere *Portrait of Henry VIII* and El Greco's *Annunciation.* In both variety and quality, the Thyssen-Bornemisza's **Baroque** collection, including pieces by Caravaggio, José de Ribera, and Claude Lorraine, outshines that of the Prado. The **Impressionist** and **Post-Impressionist** collections explode with texture and color—look for works by Renoir, Manet, Pisarro, Degas, Monet, van Gogh, Toulouse-Lautrec, Cézanne, and Matisse. Though less well-known, **Expressionist** artists are also well represented, with noteworthy works by Nolde, Marc, and Beckmann. The highlight of the museum is the **20th-century** collection, on the first floor. The modern artists showcased include Chagall, Dalí, Ernst, Gorky, Hopper, Kandinsky, Klee, Léger, Miró, Mondrian, O'Keefe, Picasso, Pollack, and Rothko, among others.

MUSEO NACIONAL CENTRO DE ARTE REINA SOFÍA

C. Santa Isabel 52, opposite Estación Atocha at the south end of Po. Prado. M: Atocha. ☎ 914 67 50 62. Open M and W-Sa 10am-9pm, Su 10am-2:30pm. €3, students €1.50; Sa after 2:30pm, Su, and holidays free.

Since Juan Carlos I decreed this renovated hospital the national museum in 1988, the Reina Sofía's collection of **20th-century art** has grown steadily. Rooms dedicated to Juan Gris, Joan Miró, and Salvador Dalí display Spain's vital contributions to the Surrealist movement. Picasso's masterwork **Guernica** is the centerpiece of the Reina Sofía's permanent collection. It depicts the Basque town (see p. 943) bombed by the Germans at Franco's request during the Spanish Civil War. Picasso denounced the bloodshed in a huge, colorless work of contorted, agonized figures. When asked by Nazi officials whether he was responsible for this work, Picasso answered, "No, you are." He gave the canvas to New York's Museum of Modern Art on the condition that they return it to Spain when democracy was restored. The subsequent move to the Reina Sofía sparked an international controversy—Picasso's other stipulation had been that the painting hang only in the Prado, to affirm his equivalent status with artists like Titian and Velázquez.

OTHER MUSEUMS

MUSEO DE LA REAL ACADEMIA DE BELLAS ARTES DE SAN FERNANDO. This beautiful museum contains a collection of Old Masters surpassed only by the Prado, including Goya's La Tirana and Velázquez's portrait of Felipe IV. Other attractions include 17th-century canvases by Ribera, Murillo, Zurbarán, and Rubens. The top floor has Picasso sketches. *(M: Sol. C. Alcalá 13. Open Tu-F 9am-7pm, Sa-M 9am-2:30pm. €2.50, students €1.25; W free.)*

MUSEO DE AMÉRICA. This underappreciated museum documents the cultures of America's pre-Columbian civilizations and the legacy of the Spanish conquest. *(M: Moncloa. Av. Reyes Católicos 6, next to the Faro de Moncloa. Open Tu-Sa 10am-3pm, Su 10am-2:30pm. €3, students €1.50; Su free.)*

ENTERTAINMENT

Anyone interested in the latest live entertainment—from music to dance to theater—should stop by the **Círculo de Bellas Artes,** C. Alcala 42 (☎913 60 54 00), at M: Sevilla or Banco de España. The six-floor building not only houses performance venues and art exhibits, but also serves as an organizing center for events throughout Madrid; it has virtually all information on current performances. Their monthly magazine, *Minerva*, is indispensable.

FLAMENCO. Flamenco in Madrid is tourist-oriented and expensive. A few nightlife spots are authentic, but pricey. **Casa Patas,** C. Cañizares 10, is good quality for less than usual. (☎913 69 04 96; www.casapatas.com.) At **Corral de la Morería,** C. Morería 17, shows start at 9:45pm and last until 2am. (☎913 65 84 46. M: Ópera. Cover €24, includes one drink.)

FÚTBOL. Spaniards obsess over *fútbol* (soccer). If either Real Madrid or Atlético de Madrid wins a match, count on streets clogged with honking cars. Every Sunday and some Saturdays between September and June, one of these teams plays at home. **Real Madrid** plays at Estadio Santiago Bernebéu, Po. Castellana 104 (☎91 457 11 12; M: Lima). **Atlético de Madrid** plays at Estadio Vicente Calderón, C. Virgen del Puerto 67 (☎91 366 47 07; M: Pirámides). Tickets cost €18-42.

BULLFIGHTING. Bullfighters are either loved or loathed. So too are the bullfights themselves. Nevertheless, bullfights are a Spanish tradition, and locals joke that they are the only things in Spain ever to start on time. Hemingway-toting Americans and other fans clog Pl. de Ventas for the heart-pounding, albeit gruesome events. From May 15 to 22 every year, the Fiestas de San Isidro provide a *corrida* (bulfight) every day with top *toreros* and the fiercest bulls. **Plaza de las Ventas,** C. Alcalá 237, east of central Madrid, is the biggest ring in Spain. (☎913 56 22 00. M: Ventas.) A seat runs €5.70-92, depending on whether it's in the *sol* (sun) or *sombra* (shade); shade is more expensive. **Plaza de Toros Palacio de Vista Alegre,** a new ring in town, hosts bullfights and other cultural events. (☎914 22 07 80. M: Vista Alegre. Ticket window open M-F 10am-2pm and 5-8pm.)

FESTIVALS. The brochure *Las Fiestas de España*, available at tourist offices and bigger hotels, contains historical background and general information on Spanish festivals. Madrid's **Carnaval** was inaugurated in the Middle Ages but prohibited during Franco's dictatorship. Today, the city bursts with street fiestas, dancing, and processions during the February holiday. The **Fiesta de San Isidro,** in May, honors Madrid's patron saint, bringing concerts, parades, and Spain's best bullfights. Throughout the summer, the city sponsors the **Veranos de la Villa,** an outstanding set of cultural activities. On November 1, **Todos los Santos** (All Saints' Day), Madrid hosts an International Jazz Festival that attracts famous musicians.

NIGHTLIFE

Spaniards average one hour less sleep a night than other Europeans, and *madrileños* claim to need even less than that. Proud of their nocturnal offerings—they'll say with a straight face that Paris or New York bored them—they don't retire until they've "killed the night" (and a good part of the morning). As the sun sets, *terrazas* and *chiringuitos* (outdoor cafes/bars) spill out onto the sidewalks. An average night makes the most of countless offerings, usually starting in the bars of Huertas, moving to Malasaña's youthful scene, and ending at the crazed parties of Chueca or the after-hours clubs of Gran Vía. Most clubs and discos don't liven up until around 2am; don't be surprised if there's still a line at 5:30am. For the most up-to-date info on what's going on, scan Madrid's entertainment guides (see **Read This,** p. 850).

EL CENTRO: SOL, ÓPERA, AND PLAZA MAYOR

In the middle of Madrid and at the heart of the action are the grandiose and flamboyant clubs of El Centro. The mainstream clubs found among these streets are often tourist hotspots; as a result, a night of fun here is the most expensive in the city. El Centro includes more territory than Madrid's other neighborhoods, so make a plan and bring a map or follow the sleekly dressed.

Palacio Gaviria, C. Arenal 9. M: Sol or Ópera. A grand red carpet leads to two huge ballrooms turned clubs with dancers and blazing light show. The most exceptional of Madrid's grandiose *discotecas*. Cover varies depending on the night (€7-15). Open M-Th 10:30pm-late, F-Sa 11:30pm-late, Su 9pm-late.

Pasapoga, Gran Vía 37. M: Callao. Around the corner from Pl. de Callao. Gay nightlife explodes here on the weekends, especially on Saturdays. Beautiful interior, beautiful people. F-Sa are gay nights. Cover €15. Open daily midnight-late.

Suite, Virgen de los Peligros 4, off C. de Alcalá. M: Sevilla. Classy restaurant, bar, and club boasts nouveau *tapas* by day and sleek drinks (€6) by night. Mixed crowd, gay friendly. Open daily 11am-6pm and 8pm-3:30am.

Joy Madrid, C. Arenal 11. M: Sol or Ópera. Just next to the Palacio Gaviria. Well-dressed crowd parties the night away to disco, techno, and R&B on a three-tiered dance floor. Cover Su-Th €12, F-Sa €15. Open daily 11:30pm-5:30am.

El Barbu, C. Santiago 3. M: Sol or Ópera. Chill to lounge music in a brick 3-room interior. Sunday transforms the bar to "8th," a rave-like setting with popular local DJs (cover €8). Open Tu-Sa 8pm-3am, Su 7pm-5:30am.

HUERTAS

In Huertas lies **Plaza Santa Ana,** which brims with *terrazas*, bars, and live music. Many bars convert to clubs as the night unfolds, spinning house and techno on intimate dance floors. With its variety of styles, Huertas is one of the best places to party. Be sure to check out the *discotecas* on **Calle Atocha.** Most locals begin their evenings here and emerge from El Centro and Chueca (see p. 865) in the morning.

Kapital, C. Atocha, 125. M: Atocha. One of the most extreme results of *La Movida,* this *macro-discoteca* tries even harder than its glittered 20-something clientele. *Thumba la casa* (bring down the house) on 7 floors of *discoteca* insanity. Dress to impress the bouncer. Drinks €9. Cover €12, includes 1 drink. Open Th-Su midnight-6am, Sa-Su also 5:30-11pm.

El Café de Sheherezade, C. Santa María 18, a block from C. Huertas. M: Antón Martín. Recline on opulent pillows while sipping exotic infusions in a bohemian atmosphere. Surrounded by Middle Eastern music and decor, groups cluster around *pipas* (€7-10) that filter sweet, incense-like smoke through whiskey or water. Open daily 7pm-5am.

Cardamomo, C. Echegaray 15. M: Sevilla. Flamenco music spins all night. A local crowd dances flamenco occasionally; come W to see professionals. M bumps with Brazilian and other exotic beats. Open daily 9pm-4am.

No Se Lo Digas a Nadie, C. Ventura de la Vega 7 (☎913 69 17 27), next to Pl. Santa Ana. M: Sevilla. Head through garage doors onto the packed dance floor. Mixed drinks €3-5. Open W-Sa until 3:30am.

Azúcar, Po. Reina Cristina 7 (☎915 01 61 07). M: Atocha. Sweet, sweet salsa. Su-Th cover €6, includes 1 drink; F-Sa €10, includes 1 drink. Open M-Su 11pm-5:30am.

Trocha, C. Huertas 55 (☎914 29 78 61). M: Antón Martín or Sol. Come here for Brazilian *capirinhas* (lime, ice, rum, and sugar drinks; €4.50) in a chill setting with jazz tunes and cushioned wicker couches. Open Su-Th 8pm-3am, F-Sa 8pm-4am.

GRAN VÍA

At the stroke of midnight, deep beats begin to pound through the boisterous landmark clubs of Gran Vía. Most of these clubs are large venues packed with drunk and high club hoppers determined to party until sunrise.

Sugar Hill, C. Fundadores 7. M: Manuel Becerra or O'Donell. Named after the original, this is the only real hip-hop club in town. The dance floor doesn't really get packed until 3:30am. Cover €9, includes 1 drink. Mixed drinks €6. Open Sa only 12:45-5:30am.

Cool, Isabela La Catolica 6. M: Santo Domingo. Heavenly drag performances and occasional underwordly goth parties for a wild, mixed crowd. Mixed drinks €5-8. F-Sa midnight-late. Su is the **Shangay Tea Dance,** primarily gay event; 9pm-late.

MALASAÑA AND CHUECA

Malasaña and Chueca come to life in the early evening, especially in Plaza de Chueca and Plaza Dos de Mayo. By sunset, these plazas are social meccas: places to hang out, meet your friends, and get drunk. The area is ideal for bar-hopping until 2 or 3am, when its time to hit the clubs near Sol, Centro, and Gran Vía.

Acuarela, C. Gravina 10. M: Chueca. A welcome alternative to the club scene. Buddhas and candles surround antique furniture, inspiration for good conversation and a good buzz. Coffees and teas €3-5. Liqueur €4. Open M-Su 3pm-3am.

Why Not? C. San Bartolome 7. M: Chueca. Small, downstairs bar packed almost every night of the week with a wild, mixed crowd. Open daily 10pm-4am.

Star's Café, C. Marqués de Valdeiglesias 5 (☎915 22 27 12). M: Chueca. A stylish cafe during the week and a vivacious dance club on the weekends. Come well-dressed. Open M-Th 1pm-2am, F-Sa 1pm-4am.

Liquid, C. Barquillo 8 (☎915 32 74 28). M: Chueca or Banco de España. Video bar plays English songs by pop divas. Clientele quite refined and mostly gay. Open Tu-Su 9pm-3am, F-Sa until 3:30am.

BILBAO

In the student-filled streets off **Glorieta de Bilbao,** it's easy to find a cheap drink and even easier to find someone to drink it with. Boisterous customers sip icy Mahou on **Plaza Olavide, Calle Fuencarral,** and **Calle Luchana.**

Barnon, C. Santa Engracia 17 (☎914 47 38 37). M: Alonso Martínez or Tribunal. A hip-hop scene as cool as the owner, Real Madrid's stud *fútbol* forward. Tu is salsa night, free lessons 11pm-midnight. Mixed drinks €10. Open daily 9pm-6am.

Clamores Jazz Club, C. Albuquerque 14 (☎914 45 79 38), off C. Cardenal Cisneros. M: Bilbao. Swanky, pink neon setting. The cover (€3-9) gets slipped into the bill if you're there for the live jazz, starting around 10:30 every night except Monday. Check the posters outside and arrive early for a seat. Open Su-Th 6pm-3am, F-Sa 6pm-4am.

Big Bamboo, C. Barquillo 42. M: Alonso Martínez. Walk 3 blocks east of C. Pelayo on C. Gravina and turn left on C. Barquillo. International club jams to smooth reggae. Theater shows W-Th. Mixed drinks €3. Open daily 10:30pm-6am.

DAYTRIPS FROM MADRID

EL ESCORIAL

Complex ☎918 90 59 03. Open Apr.-Sept. Tu-Su 10am-6pm; Oct.-Mar. Tu-Su 10am-5pm. Last admission 1hr. before closing. Monastery €6, students and seniors €3. Autocares Herranz buses arrive from Madrid's Moncloa Metro station (50min.; every 15min. M-F 7am-11:30pm, Sa 9am-10pm, Su 9am-11pm; last return 1hr. earlier; €3).

The **Monasterio de San Lorenzo del Escorial** was a gift from Felipe II to God, the people, and himself, commemorating his victory over the French at the battle of San Quintín in 1557. Near the town of **San Lorenzo,** El Escorial is filled with artistic treasures, two palaces, two pantheons, a church, and a magnificent library. Don't come on Monday, when the complex and most of the town shut down. To avoid crowds, enter via the gate on the west side on C. Florida Blanca. The adjacent **Museos de Arquitectura and Pintura** chronicle the construction of El Escorial and include masterpieces by Bosch, El Greco, Titian, Tintoretto, Velázquez, Zurbarán, and Van Dyck. The **Palacio Real,** lined with 16th-century *azulejos* (tiles), includes the **Salón del Trono** (Throne Room), Felipe II's spartan 16th-century apartments, and the luxurious 18th-century rooms of Carlos III and Carlos IV. The macabre **Panteón Real** is filled with tombs of monarchs and glitters with intricate gold and marble designs.

EL VALLE DE LOS CAÍDOS

El Valle de los Caídos is accessible only via El Escorial. Mass M-Sa 11am; Su 11am, 12:30, 1, and 5:30pm. Entrance gate open Tu-Su 10am-6pm; basilica open 10am-6:30pm. €5, seniors and students €2.50. W free for EU citizens. Funicular to the cross €2.50. Autocares Herranz runs 1 bus to the monument (20min., leaves El Escorial Tu-Su 3:15pm and returns 5:30pm, round-trip plus admission €7).

In a valley of the Sierra de Guadarrama, 8km north of El Escorial, Franco built the overpowering monument of **Santa Cruz del Valle de los Caídos** (Valley of the Fallen) as a memorial to those who gave their lives in the Civil War. The massive granite cross was meant to honor only those who died "serving *Dios* and *España*" (i.e. the Fascist Nationalists). Non-fascist prisoners of war were forced to build the monument, and thousands died during its construction. Although Franco lies buried beneath the high altar, there is no mention of his tomb in tourist literature—testimony to modern Spain's view of the late dictator.

OTHER DAYTRIPS FROM MADRID

TOLEDO. To the architecture-loving tourist, Toledo, the glorious former capital of the Holy Roman, Visigoth, and Muslim empires (see p. 867).

SEGOVIA. The impressive Alcázar and hulking aqueduct merit a spot on any tour, and the town's twisted alleys, fruit stands, and *paseos* represent Castilla y León at its finest (see p. 871).

ÁVILA. Stand on Ávila's medieval walls, 2.5km of magnificently preserved 12th-century stone that encircle the old city (see p. 873).

CENTRAL SPAIN

Castilla La Mancha, surrounding Madrid to the east and south, is one of Spain's least-developed regions; medieval cities and olive groves fill the land. To the west, **Castilla y León's** dramatic cathedrals stand testament to its glorious history. Farther west, bordering Portugal, stark **Extremadura** is home to Roman ruins and birthplace to hundreds of world-famous explorers.

CASTILLA LA MANCHA

You don't need Don Quixote's imagination to fall in love with the battered, windswept plateaus of Castilla La Mancha—its austere beauty surfaces through its tumultuous history, gloomy medieval fortresses, and awesome crags.

TOLEDO ☎925

Cossío called Toledo "the most brilliant and evocative summary of Spain's history." Toledo (pop. 66,000) may today be marred by armies of tourists and caravans of kitsch, but this former capital of the Holy Roman, Visigoth, and Muslim empires remains a treasure trove of Spanish culture. The city's numerous churches, synagogues, and mosques share twisting alleyways, emblematic of a time when Spain's three religions coexisted peacefully.

TRANSPORTATION

Trains: Po. Rosa 2 (RENFE info ☎902 24 02 02), in an exquisite neo-Mudéjar station just over the Puente de Azarquiel. To **Madrid** (1½hr., 9-10 per day, €5).

Buses: (☎925 21 58 50), 5min. from the city gate. **Continental-Auto** (☎925 22 36 41) runs to **Madrid** (1½hr.; every 30min. M-F 6am-10pm, Sa 6:30am-10pm, Su 8:30am-11:30pm; €3.75). **ALSINA** (☎925 21 58 50 in Toledo or 963 49 72 30 in Valencia) runs to **Valencia** (5½hr., M-F 3pm, €17, buy the ticket on the bus).

ORIENTATION AND PRACTICAL INFORMATION

Toledo is an almost unconquerable maze of narrow streets where pedestrians and cars battle for sovereignty. To get to **Plaza de Zocodóver** in the town center, take bus #5 or 6 (€0.78) from the stop on the right after you exit the train station. On foot from the train station, turn right after leaving the station and follow the left fork uphill to a smaller bridge, Puente de Alcántara. Cross the bridge to the stone staircase (through a set of arches); after climbing the stairs, turn left and continue upward, veering right at C. Cervantes to Pl. Zocodóver. Despite the well-labeled streets, you will probably get lost in Toledo.

Tourist Office: (☎925 22 08 43), just outside the Puerta Nueva de Bisagra, on the north side of town. Open July-Sept M-Sa 9am-7pm, Su 9am-3pm; Oct.-June M-F 9am-6pm, Sa 9am-7pm, Su 9am-3pm. There is a **branch office** in Pl. Ayuntamiento (☎925 25 40 30), opposite the cathedral. Open Tu-Su 10:30am-2:30pm and 4:30-7pm.

Currency Exchange: Banco Central Hispano, C. Comercio 47 (☎925 22 98 00). Open Apr.-Sept. M-F 8:30am-2:30pm; Oct.-Mar. M-F 8:30am-2:30pm, Sa 8:30am-1pm.

Luggage Storage: At the **bus station** (€0.60-1.20). Open daily 7am-11pm. At the **train station** (€3). Open daily 7am-9:30pm.

Emergency: ☎112. **Police:** ☎092, where Av. Reconquista and Av. Carlos III meet.

Pharmacy: Pl. Zocodóver (☎925 22 17 68). List of late-night pharmacies posted.

Hospital: Hospital Virgen de la Salud, Av. Barber (☎925 26 92 00).

Internet Access: Punto Com, C. Armas 4, 2nd fl. (☎925 25 62 08), in Pl. Zocodóver, on the right, just as you begin to walk downhill. €0.90 per 15min., €1.50 per 30min., €2.40 per hr. Open M-Sa 11:30am-10pm, Su 4-10pm.

Post Office: C. Plata 1 (☎925 22 36 11), off Pl. Zocodóver via C. Comercio. Lista de Correos. Open M-F 8:30am-8:30pm, Sa 9am-2pm. **Postal Code:** 45070.

ACCOMMODATIONS

Toledo is chock-full of accommodations, but finding a bed during the summer can be a hassle, especially on weekends. If you run into trouble, try the tourist office for suggestions.

Residencia Juvenil San Servando (HI), Castillo San Servando (☎925 22 45 54), uphill from the train station (10min). Attractive, monumental building has 38 rooms, each with 2-4 bunk beds and a private bath. Gorgeous pool in summer. TV room. Free sheets. Reception open 7am-midnight. Dorms €8.50, over 26 €11. Must have HI card. ❶

Hostal Centro, C. Nueva 13 (925 25 70 91), on the Northwest corner of Pl. Zocodover. Centrally located for discovering the city. Clean, spacious rooms with all the amenities: TV, bath, A/C, and phone. Friendly staff. Singles €30; doubles €42; triples €60. ❸

Pensión Descalzos, C. Descalzos 30 (☎925 22 28 88), down the steps off Po. del Tránsito, near the Sinagoga de Tránsito. Recently refurbished hostel in a quiet part of town with stunning views of the surrounding hills. Small pool and big jacuzzi. Apr.-Oct. singles €24; doubles €39-44. Oct.-Mar. €23/€34-39. MC/V. ❷

Pensión Castilla, C. Recoletos 6 (☎925 25 63 18). Take C. Armas downhill from Pl. Zocodóver, then the first left up C. Recoletos (opposite the Caja Madrid bank); hostel is up the stairs in the corner. Singles €15; doubles with bath €25. ❷

Camping El Greco, (☎925 22 00 90). 1.5km from town on the road away from Madrid (C-502). Bus #7 (from Pl. Zocodóver) stops at the entrance. €4 per person, €3.90 per tent, €3.90 per car. ❶

FOOD

Toledo grinds almonds into marzipan of every shape and size, from colorful fruity nuggets to half-moon cookies; *pastelerías* beckon on every corner. If your pocket permits, dining out in Toledo can be a pleasurable culinary experience (*menús* €8-10). Alternatively, buy fresh fruit and the basics at **Alimentación Pantoja,** C. Arrabal 30, just on the inside of Puerta de Bisagra across from the tourist office. (Open June-Aug. M-Sa 9am-11pm, Su 9am-3pm; Sept.-May M-Sa 9am-10pm, Su 9am-3pm.)

La Abadía, Pl. San Nicolás 3 (☎925 25 11 40). From Pl. Zocodóver, take C. Sillería, then bear left when the road splits until you reach a small plaza; Abadía is to your right. This maze of connected underground cave-like rooms is a great place to start the evening. The delicious *menú* is a steal (€8.30). Open M-Th 8am-midnight, F 8am-1:30am, Sa noon-2:30am, Su noon-midnight. AmEx/MC/V. ❷

Pastucci, C. Sinagoga 10 (☎925 21 48 66). From Pl. Zocodóver take C. Comercio; keep to the right and turn right through the underpass. Pastas €5-6. Over 30 kinds of pizza (€6). 10% discount with your *Let's Go* guide. Open daily 12:15pm-midnight. MC/V. ❷

Restaurante-Mesón Palacios, C. Alfonso X El Sabio 3 (☎925 21 59 72), off C. Nuncio Viejo, the street opposite the tourist office in Pl. Ayuntamiento. Toledo's famous partridge dish is an option in the *menú* (€6-10). Entrees €7-12. Open M-Sa 1-4pm and 7-11pm, Su noon-4pm. AmEx/MC/V. ❷

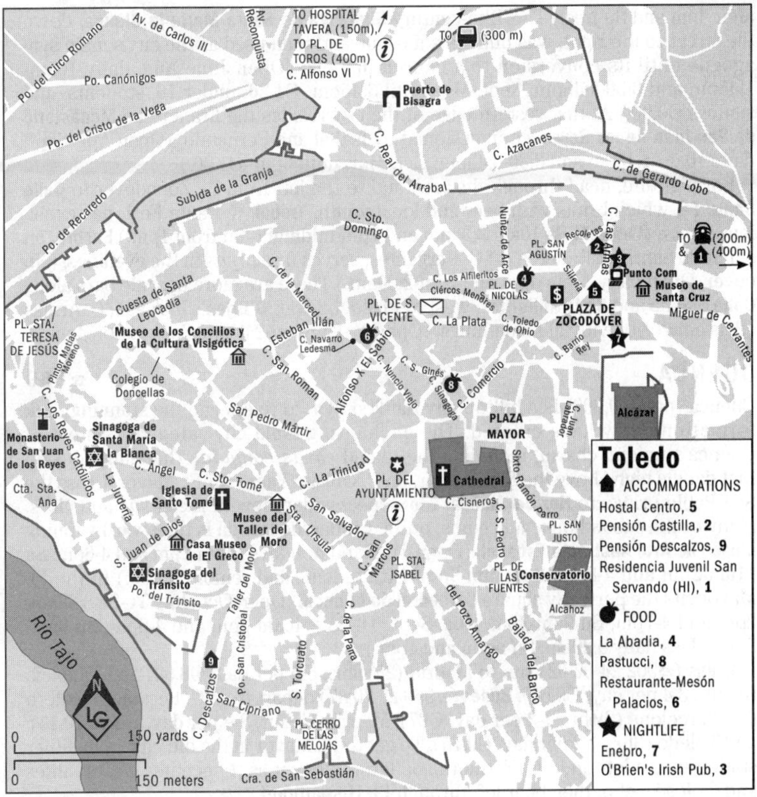

SIGHTS AND ENTERTAINMENT

Toledo's grandiose **cathedral,** southwest of Pl. Zocodóver at the Arco de Palacioz, boasts five naves, delicate stained glass, and unapologetic ostentation. (Open June-Aug. daily 10am-noon and 4-7pm; Sept.-May 10am-noon and 4-6pm.) The city's most formidable landmark, the **Alcázar,** Cuesta Carlos V 2, uphill from Pl. Zocodóver, has been a stronghold of Romans, Visigoths, Moors, and Spaniards. Today, it houses a national military museum. (Open Tu-Su 9:30am-2pm. €2, W free.) El Greco spent most of his life in Toledo, and many of his works are displayed here. On the west side of town, his famous *El Entierro del Conde de Orgaz (Burial of Count Orgaz)* is in the **Iglesia de Santo Tomé,** Pl. Conde. (Open Mar.-Oct. 15 daily 10am-6:45pm; Oct. 16-Feb. daily 10am-5:45pm. €1.20; under 18, students, and seniors €0.90.) Downhill lies the **Casa Museo de El Greco,** C. Samuel Levi 2, which houses 19 works by the master. (Open Tu-Sa 10am-2pm and 4-6pm, Su 10am-2pm. €1.20; under 18, students, and over 65 free. Sa-Su afternoons free.)

The simple exterior of the 14th-century **Sinagoga del Tránsito,** on C. Samuel Levi, hides ornate Mudéjar plasterwork and an intricate wooden ceiling. Inside, the **Museo Sefardí** is packed with artifacts, including a Torah (parts of which are over 400 years old) and a beautiful set of Sephardic wedding costumes. (Open Tu-Sa 10am-1:45pm and 4-5:45pm, Su 10am-2pm. €2.40, under 18 and students €1.20. Sa after 4pm and Su free.) The 12th-century **Sinagoga de Santa María la Blanca,** down the street to the right, was built as a mosque and then used as the city's main synagogue until its conversion to a church in 1492. (Open June-Aug. daily 10am-1:45pm and 3:30-6:45pm; Sept.-May until 5:45pm. €1.20; under 16, students, and seniors €0.90.) At the western edge of the city resides the Franciscan **Monasterio de San Juan de los Reyes,** commissioned by Isabel and Fernando. (Open Apr.-Sept. daily 10am-1:45pm and 3:30-6:45pm; Oct.-Mar. until 6pm. €1.20.)

For nightlife, head through the arch and to the left from Pl. Zocodóver to **Calle Santa Fé,** which brims with beer and local youth. **Trébol,** C. Sante Fe 1, has excellent *tapas*. (Open M-Sa 10am-3:30pm and 7pm-midnight, Su from 1pm.) **Enebro,** on small Pl. Santiago Balleros off C. Cervantes, serves free *tapas* in the evenings. (No cover. Open daily 11am-4pm and 7pm-2:30am.) There are more upscale bars along **Calle Sillería** and **Calle Alfileritos,** west of Pl. Zocodóver. **O'Brien's Irish Pub,** C. Armas 12, is a favorite with 20-somethings. (Open M-Th noon-2:30am, Sa-Su noon-4am.)

CUENCA ☎969

Cuenca (pop. 50,000) is a hilltop city flanked by two rivers and the stunning rock formations they have created. The enchanting ■**old city** safeguards most of Cuenca's unique charm, including the famed *casas colgadas* (hanging houses) that dangle high above the Río Huécar, on C. Obispo Vaero off Pl. Mayor. Cross the San Pablo bridge to **Hoz del Huécar** for a spectacular view of the *casas* and cliffs. Many of the *casas* house museums; on Pl. Ciudad de Ronda is the award-winning **Museo de Arte Abstracto Español.** (Open Tu-F and holidays 11am-2pm and 4-6pm, Sa 11am-2pm and 4-8pm, Su 11am-2pm. €3, students and seniors €1.50.) In the Pl. Mayor sits the perfectly square **Cathedral de Cuenca.** (Open Oct.-July Tu-Sa 8:45am-2pm and 4-7pm, Su 9am-2pm; Aug.-Sept. Tu-Sa 8:45am-2pm and 4-6pm, Su 9am-2pm. Mass daily 9:20am, Su noon and 1pm.)

Trains (☎902 24 02 02) run to Madrid (2½-3hr., 5-6 per day, €8.60) and Valencia (3-4hr., 3-4 per day, €9.50). **Buses** (☎969 22 70 87) depart from C. Fermín Caballero for: Barcelona (3½hr., 1-2 per day, €27); Madrid (2½hr., 8-9 per day, €8.20-10.15); and Toledo (3hr., 1-2 per day, €9.75). To get to Pl. Mayor in the old city from either station take a left on to C. Fermín Caballero, follow it as it becomes C. Cervantes and C. José Cobo, then bear left through Pl. Hispanidad.

From either station, go left to the first bus shelter and take bus #1 (every 20min., €0.50) to the last stop in the old city to reach the **tourist office** in Pl. Mayor. (☎969 23 21 19. Open July-Sept. M-Sa 9am-9pm, Su 9am-2pm; Oct.-June M-Sa 9am-2pm and 4-6pm, Su 9am-2pm.) ■**Hostal-Residencia Posada de San José ❷,** C. Julián Romero 4, a block up from the left side of the cathedral, has gorgeous views worth cashing that extra traveler's check. (☎969 21 13 00. Singles €18, with full bath €39; doubles €29/€57. Prices drop Sept.-June.) To reach **Pensión Tabanqueta ❸,** C. Trabuco 13, head up C. San Pedro from the cathedral past Pl. Trabuco. (☎969 21 12 90. Doubles €30; triples €45.) In the new city, take C. Fermín Caballero from the

BULLBOARDS Gazing out the window of your preferred mode of transportation, you may notice rather unusual monuments along the highway: massive black paper silhouettes of solitary bulls. Once upon a time (in the 1980s) these cutouts were advertisements for Osborne Sherry. In the early 1990s, however, billboards were prohibited on national roads. A plan was drafted to take the bulls down, but Spaniards protested, as the lone bull towering along the roadside had become an important national symbol. After considerable clamoring and hoofing, the bulls were painted black and left to loom proudly against the horizon. The familiar shape now decorates t-shirts and pins in souvenir shops, but the real thing is still impressive.

bus station, turn left on C. Hurtado de Mendoza, and continue on Av. República Argentina to **Pensión Cuenca ❶**, #8, 2nd fl. (☎969 21 25 74. Singles €12, with shower €14; doubles €18/€24.) Budget eateries line **Calle Cervantes** and **Calle República Argentina.** Grab groceries at **%Día,** Av. Castilla La Mancha and Av. República Argentina. (Open M-Th 9:30am-2pm and 5:30-8:30pm, F-Sa 9am-2:30pm and 5:30-9pm.) **Postal Code:** 16004.

CASTILLA Y LEÓN

Castilla y León's cities rise like green oases from a desert of burnt sienna. The majestic Gothic cathedrals of Burgos and León, the slender Romanesque belfries along Camino de Santiago, the sandstone of Salamanca, and the city walls of Ávila have emblazoned themselves as regional and national images.

SEGOVIA ☎921

Legend has it that the devil built Segovia's famed aqueduct in one night, in an effort to win the soul of a Segovian water-seller named Juanilla. When the shocked Juanilla woke up to find the aqueduct almost completed, she prayed to the Virgin Mary, who made the sun rise a bit earlier in order to foil the Devil's scheme. In the 12th and 13th centuries Segovia (pop. 55,000) had more Romanesque monuments than anywhere else in Europe. Today, its remaining cathedrals and castles represent Castilla at its finest—a labyrinthine town of twisted alleys and sharp aromas. However, pleasure has its price: food and accommodations are more expensive than in Madrid. In the Sierra de Guadarrama, 88km northwest of Madrid, Segovia is close enough to the capital to be a daytrip but definitely warrants a longer stay.

TRANSPORTATION AND PRACTICAL INFORMATION. Trains (☎921 42 07 74), Po. Obispo Quesada, run to Madrid (2hr.; 7-9 per day M-F 5:55am-8:55pm, Sa-Su 8:55am-8:55pm; €5). **Buses** run from **Estacionamiento Municipal de Autobuses,** Po. Ezequiel González 12, at the corner of Av. Fernández Ladreda. **La Sepulvedana** (☎921 42 77 07) sends buses to Madrid (1½hr., M-F every 30min. 6-11am and 8:30-11:30pm, €6). **Renfe-Iñigo** (☎921 44 12 52) sends buses to Ávila (1hr.; M-F 10:30am, 2, and 7:30pm; Sa 2pm; Su 7:45pm; €4); and **Linecar** (☎921 42 77 06) sends buses to Salamanca (3hr.; 4 per day M-F 8:50am-5:45pm; Sa 8:50am, 1:30, 5:45pm; Su 5:45pm; €9). Locals describe the city as the "Stone Ship." The **Alcázar** is the bow, the aqueduct the stern, and the cathedral towers are the mainmast. From the train station, take any bus (€0.65) to reach the **Plaza Mayor,** the city's historic center and site of the regional **tourist office.** Segovia is impossible to navigate without a map, so pick one up here. (Open June-Aug. Su-Th 9am-8pm, F-Sa 9am-9pm; Sept.-May M-F 9am-2pm and 5-7pm, Sa-Su 10am-2pm and 5-8pm.) The Po. del Salón **bus** (M-F every 30min. 7:45am-10:15pm) runs directly to the steps of **Puerta del Sol.** From Pl. Azoguejo, follow the aqueduct up C. Teodosio el Grande, then turn right on C. Santa Isabel to access the **Internet** at **Neociber,** C. Santa Isabel 10. (€0.50 per 15min. Open daily M-Th 11am-2pm and 4:30-10:30pm, F 11am-2pm and 4:30-11:30pm; June-Aug. also Sa 6pm-midnight, Su 6-10:30pm; Sept.-May also Sa 11am-2pm and 5pm-midnight, Su 5-10:30pm.)

ACCOMMODATIONS AND FOOD. Reservations are a must for any of Segovia's hotels, especially those in or around major plazas. Budget travelers should prepare to pay €21 or more for a single and arrive early to ensure space. The *pensiones* are significantly cheaper, but rooms tend to be on the less comfortable side of "basic." **Hotel Las Sirenas ❸**, C. Juan Bravo 30, down C. Cervantes, has luxurious rooms with TV, shower, telephone, and A/C. (☎921 46 26 63; fax 921 46 26 57. Singles €35-40, with bath €40-45; doubles with bath €50-60. AmEx/MC/V.) For a fortifying experience, try the stone walls and rustic rooms of the **Pensión Ferri ❶**, C. Escuderos 10, off Pl. Mayor. (☎921 46 09 57. Showers €2. Singles €12; doubles €18.) From Pl. Azoguejo, follow the aqueduct down C. Teodosio and turn left; around the bend and up the slope is **Hostal Don Jaime ❷**, Ochoa Ondategui 8. This *hostal* has rooms with wood paneling and large mirrors. (☎921 44 47 87. Singles €22, with bath €30; doubles €30/€38; triples with bath €48. MC/V.) **Camping Acueducto**, C. Borbón 49/Ctra. Nacional 601 km 112, is 2km toward La Granja. Take the Autobus Urbano (€0.65) from Pl. Azoguejo to Nueva Segovia. (☎/fax 921 42 50 00. Open *Semana Santa*-Sept. €4 per person, per tent, and per car.)

Sample Segovia's famed lamb, *croquetas*, or *sopa castellana* (soup with bread, eggs, and garlic), but steer clear of pricey Pl. Mayor and Pl. Azoguejo. Buy groceries at **%Día**, C. Gobernador Fernández Giménez 3, off C. Fernández Ladreda. (Open M-Th 9:30am-8:30pm, F-Sa 9am-9pm). At **Mesón El Cordero ❸**, C. El Carmen 4-6, spreads of wine, meats, and other specials are a feast for the eyes and the stomach. (Selection of *menús* €11-12. Entrees €9-15. Open M-Sa 12:30-4:30pm and 8pm-midnight, Su 12:30-6pm.) **Restaurante La Almuzara ❷**, C. Marqués del Arco 3, past the cathedral, has tasty vegetarian options (€3.60-9) as well as meat entrees (€6-10). (Open W-Su 12:45-4pm and 8pm-midnight, Tu 8pm-midnight.)

SIGHTS AND ENTERTAINMENT. Segovia rewards the wanderer. Whether palace, church, house, or sidewalk, almost everything deserves close observation. Look for *esgrafía*, lacy patterns on the facades of buildings. The serpentine **roman aqueduct** commands the entrance to the old city. Supported by 128 pillars that span 813m and reach a height of 28.9m near Pl. Azoguejo, the two tiers of 163 arches were constructed out of some 20,000 blocks of granite—without any mortar to hold them together—by the Romans in 50 BC. This spectacular feat of engineering, restored by the monarchy in the 15th century, can transport 30 liters of water per second and was used until the late 1940s. The **cathedral,** commissioned by Carlos I in 1525, towers above Pl. Mayor. Inside, the **Sala Capitular** displays intricate tapestries. The **museum** has a series of 17th-century paintings on marble depicting the Passion of Christ. (Open Apr.-Oct. daily 9am-6:30pm; Nov.-Mar. 9:30am-6pm. €2.) The **Alcázar,** a late-medieval castle and site of Isabel's coronation in 1474, dominates the northern end of the old quarter. In the **Sala de Solio** (throne room), an inscription reads: *tanto monta, monta tanto* ("she mounts, as does he"). Get your mind out of the gutter—this means simply that Fernando and Isabel had equal authority as sovereigns. The 140 steps up a nausea-inducing spiral staircase to the top of the *Torre de Juan II* (80m high) afford a marvelous view of Segovia and the surrounding plains. The **Sala de Armas** holds an arsenal of medieval weaponry. (Open Apr.-Sept. daily 10am-7pm; Oct.-Mar. 10am-6pm. €3.)

Though the city isn't known for its sleepless nights, when it comes to partying, native Segovians go all out. Packed with bars and cafes, the **Plaza Mayor** is the center of nightlife. Club headquarters are on **Calle Ruiz de Alda,** off Pl. Azoguejo. You can count on a party every night of the week at **La Luna,** C. Puerta de la Luna 8, where a young crowd downs cheap shots and Heineken. (Shots €1. Beer €1.35. Open daily 5pm-4am.) From June 24-29, Segovia celebrates a **fiesta** in honor of San Juan and San Pedro. According to local lore, the sun reflects the general joy and intoxication by rising in circles.

DAYTRIP FROM SEGOVIA: LA GRANJA DE SAN ILDEFONSO. The royal palace and grounds of **La Granja,** 9km southeast of Segovia, were commissioned by Philip V, the first Bourbon King. Of the four royal summer retreats (the others being El Pardo, El Escorial, and Aranjuez), this "Versailles of Spain" is by far the most extravagant. Marble, lace curtains, lavish crystal chandeliers, and a world-class collection of Flemish tapestries enliven the palace, while manicured gardens and a forest surround it. (Open Apr.-Sept. Tu-Su 10am-6pm; Oct.-Mar. Tu-Sa 10am-1:30pm and 3-5pm, Su 10am-2pm. Mandatory guided tours in Spanish depart every 15min. €4.80, students and EU seniors €2.40. W free for EU citizens.) **Buses** run to La Granja from Segovia (20min., 9-12 per day, round-trip €1.40).

ÁVILA ☎920

Oh, if walls could talk, what stories Ávila's medieval *murallas* could tell. The 2.5km of magnificent 12th-century stone are even better preserved than the various body parts of Santa Teresa that grace the city's shrines and museums. Santa Teresa would have been pleased with the peaceful life Ávila offers. The inner walls are a time warp, untouched by pollution, advertisements, or the blare of tourist traffic. Ávila (pop. 50,000) is well worth at least a daytrip from Segovia or Madrid.

TRANSPORTATION AND PRACTICAL INFORMATION. **Trains** run from the station at Av. José Antonio (☎920 24 02 02) to Madrid (1½-2hr., 15-19 per day, €7). **Buses,** Av. Madrid 2 (☎920 22 01 54), go to Madrid (1½hr., 4-8 per day, €6) and Segovia (1hr.; M-F 9:30am, 12:45, and 6:30pm; Sa 9am; Su 6:45pm; €4). The tangled city has two main squares: **Plaza de la Victoria** (known to locals as Pl. del Mercado Chico), inside the city walls, and **Plaza de Santa Teresa,** just outside. From the bus station, cross the street and follow C. Duque de Alba to reach Pl. de Santa Teresa. To continue on to Ávila's **tourist office,** Pl. Catedral 4, walk through the main gate and take the second right onto C. Alemania. (☎920 21 13 87. Open Su-Th 9am-8pm, F-Sa 9am-9pm.) Access the **Internet** at **Arroba@25,** C. Ferreol Hernandez 1. (€0.60 per 15min.) **Postal Code:** 05001.

ACCOMMODATIONS AND FOOD. Ávila's walls surround numerous comfortable, affordable accommodations. Those near the cathedral and Pl. Santa Teresa fill up in the summer, so call early. Next to the tourist office, a winding wooden staircase leads to cavernous rooms at **Pensión Continental ❷,** Pl. Catedral 6. (☎920 21 15 02. Singles €15; doubles €26, with bath €33; triples €39.) Behind the pleasant front garden from which its name is derived, **Hostal Jardin ❷,** C. San Segundo 38, offers large rooms with TVs and phones. (☎920 21 10 74. June-Oct. singles €21, with bath €28; doubles €27/€38; Nov.-May €3-5 less.)

The city has won fame for its *chuleton de Ávila* (veal) and *mollejas* (sweetbread). The *yemas de Santa Teresa* or *yemas de Ávila,* local confections made of egg yolk and honey, are delectable. Budget sandwich shops circle **Plaza Victoria**. The most affordable restaurant area is **Calle San Segundo,** off of Pl. Santa Teresa, while the plaza itself holds the more expensive fare. **La Taberna del Lagartijo ❷,** C. Martin Carramolino 4, is named in honor of the great bullfighter Rafael Molina and commemorates the profession with bullfighting paraphernalia. (*Menú* €9. Open M-Th 1:30-3:30pm and 8-10:30pm.) The **supermarket,** C. Juan José Martín 6, stocks all the basics. From Pl. Teresa, turn left off C. Duque de Alba after the Monasterio de San José. (Open M-Sa 9:45am-2pm and 5-8pm.)

SIGHTS AND ENTERTAINMENT. Ávila's **medieval walls,** the oldest and best-preserved walls in Spain, date from 1090. Eighty-eight massive towers reinforce the 3m thick walls; the most imposing of the towers, **Cimorro,** is also the cathedral's bold apse. To walk along the walls, start with the Puerta del Alcázar directly before you and your back to the Pl. de la Teresa. Inside the walls, the profile of the **cathedral** looming over the watchtowers is believed to have inspired Santa Teresa's metaphor of the soul as a diamond castle. View the **Altar de La Virgen**

de la Caridad, where 12-year-old Santa Teresa prostrated herself after the death of her mother. From Pl. Santa Teresa, walk through the Puerta; take the first right onto C. Cruz Vieja, which leads to the cathedral. (Open June-Oct. M-Sa 10am-7pm, Su noon-7pm; Nov.-Apr. daily 10am-1:30pm and 3:30-5:30pm. €2.50.) Santa Teresa's admirers built the 17th-century **Convento de Santa Teresa** on the site of her birthplace and childhood home. From Pl. Santa Teresa, go left on C. San Segundo, right on Po. Rastro, and right through Pta. Santa Teresa. (Open daily 8:30am-1:30pm and 3:30-9pm.) To the right of the convent, the **Sala de Reliquias** holds Santa Teresa relics, including her right ring finger and the cord with which she flagellated herself. (Open Apr.-Oct. daily 9:30am-1:30pm and 3:30-7:30pm; Nov.-Mar. Tu-Su 10am-1:30pm and 3:30-5:30pm. Free.) A short distance outside the city walls on Po. Encarnación is the **Monasterio de la Encarnación,** where Santa Teresa lived for 30 years. The mandatory 15min. guided tour in Spanish visits Santa Teresa's tiny cell and the staircase where she had her mystical encounter with the child Jesus. (Open June-Aug. daily 9:30am-1pm and 4-7pm; Sept.-May 9:30am-1:30pm and 3:30-6pm. €1.20.) The best view of the walls and of Ávila itself is from the **Cuatro Postes,** a four-pillared structure past the Río Adaja on the highway to Salamanca, 1.5km northwest of the city. From Pl. Santa Teresa, walk through the inner city and out the Puerta del Puente. Cross the bridge and follow the road to the right for about 1km. It was at this spot that Santa Teresa was caught by her uncle while she and her brother were trying to flee to the Islamic south.

SALAMANCA ☎923

For centuries, the gates of Salamanca have welcomed scholars, saints, rogues, and royals. The bustling city is famed for its golden sandstone architecture as well as its university—the oldest in Spain, and once one of the "four leading lights of the world" along with the universities of Bologna, Paris, and Oxford.

TRANSPORTATION. From Po. de la Estación (☎923 12 02 02), **trains** run to: Ávila (1¾hr., 3-4 per day 7:45am-7:30pm, €5.30); Lisbon (6hr., 1 per day, €33); and Madrid (2½hr., 4 per day 7:45am-7:30pm, €13). **Buses** run from Av. Filiberto Villalobos 71-85 (☎923 23 67 17) to: Ávila (1½hr.; M-Sa 4 per day 6:30am-8:30pm, Su 3:30pm and 8:30pm; €4.50); León (2½hr.; M-F 3 per day 11am-6:30pm, Sa 11am, Su 10pm; €11); Madrid (3hr., M-Sa 15 per day, €10); and Segovia (3hr., 2 per day, €8).

PRACTICAL INFORMATION. The **tourist office** is at Pl. Mayor 14. (☎923 21 83 42. Open M-Sa 9am-2pm and 4:30-6:30pm, Su 10am-2pm and 4:30-6:30pm.) Access the **Internet** at **Informática Abaco Bar,** C. Zamora 7. (€1.20 per hr. Open M-F 9:30am-2am, Sa-Su 11am-2am.) The **post office** sits at Gran Vía 25-29. (☎923 28 09 02. Open M-F 8:30am-8:30pm, Sa 9:30am-2pm.) **Postal Code:** 37080.

ACCOMMODATIONS AND FOOD. Reasonably priced *hostales* and *pensiones* cater to the floods of student visitors, especially off Pl. Mayor and C. Meléndez. **Pensión Las Vegas ❷,** C. Meléndez 13, 1st fl., has TVs and friendly owners. (☎923 21 87 49. Doubles €24; triples with bath €36. MC/V.) At **Pensión Villanueva ❶,** C. San Justo 8, 1st fl., Sra. Manuela shares local lore and gossip. Exit Pl. Mayor via Pl. Poeta Iglesias, cross the street, and take the first left. (☎923 26 88 33. Singles €12; doubles €24.) **Pensión Estefanía ❷,** C. Jesús 3-5, off Pl. Mayor, has a prime location and comfortable rooms. (☎923 21 73 72. Doubles with shower €22; triples with shower €30.) **Hostal Anaya ❷,** C. Jesús 18, is steps away from Pl. Mayor. (☎923 27 17 73. Singles €24; doubles €42; triples €54; quads €72.) Albetur buses shuttle **campers** from Gran Vía (every 30min.) to the first-class **Regio ❶,** 4km toward Madrid on Ctra. Salamanca. (☎923 13 88 88. €2.70 per person, €5.11 per tent, €2.70 per car.) **Champion,** C. Toro 64, has a downstairs supermarket. (Open

M-Sa 9:15am-9:15pm.) Cafes and restaurants surround **Plaza Mayor;** full meals in cheaper back alley spots run about €8. **El Patio Chico ❷,** C. Meléndez 13, is crowded at lunch time, but the large and delicious portions are worth the wait. (*Menú* €11, entrees €4-8, *bocadillos* €2-3. Open daily 1-4pm and 8pm-midnight.) **Mesón Las Conchas ❷,** Rua Mayor 16, is the quintessential *bar español.* (*Menú* €10.50, *raciones* €6-14. Open daily 1-4pm and 8pm-midnight. MC/V.) **Restaurante El Bardo ❷,** C. Compañía 8, between the Casa de Conchas and the Clerecía, is a traditional Spanish restaurant with veggie options and a lively bar downstairs. (*Menú* €9. Open daily 1:30-4pm and 9-11:30pm. MC/V.)

SIGHTS. The **Plaza Mayor,** designed by Alberto Churriguera, is one of the most beautiful squares in Spain. Between its nearly 100 sandstone arches hang medallions with bas-reliefs of famous Spaniards, from El Cid to Franco. Walk down Rua Mayor to Pl. San Isidro to reach the 15th-century **Casa de las Conchas** (House of Shells), one of Salamanca's most famous landmarks, adorned with over 300 rows of scallop shells chiseled in sandstone. Go down Patio de las Escuelas, off C. Libreros (which leads south from Pl. San Isidro), to enter the **Universidad,** founded in 1218. The university's 16th-century entryway is one of the best examples of Spanish Plateresque, named for the delicate filigree work of *plateros* (silversmiths). Hidden in the sculptural work lies a tiny frog; according to legend, those who can spot the frog without assistance will be blessed with good luck and even marriage. Inside the Patio de Escuelas Menores, the **University Museum** contains the Cielo de Salamanca, a 15th-century fresco of the zodiac. (Open M-F 9:30am-1:30pm and 4-7:30pm, Sa 9:30am-1:30pm and 4-7pm, Su 10am-1:30pm. €2.40, students and seniors €1.20.) Continue down Rua Mayor to Pl. Anaya to reach the *vieja* (old) and *nueva* (new) cathedrals. Begun in 1513 to accommodate the growing tide of Catholics, the spindly spired late-Gothic **Catedral Nueva** wasn't finished until 1733. The **Catedral Vieja,** built in 1140, has a striking cupola with depictions of apocalyptic angels separating the sinners from the saved. The **museum** in the back houses a Mudéjar Salinas organ, one of the oldest organs in Europe. (Nueva open Apr.-Sept. daily 9am-2pm and 4-8pm; Oct.-Mar. 9am-1pm and 4-6pm. Free. Vieja cloister and museum open Apr.-Sept. daily 10am-1:30pm and 4-7:30pm. €3, students €2.25, children €1.50.) **Casa Lis Museo Art Nouveau Y Art Deco,** C. Gibraltar 14, behind the cathedrals, houses the oddities of Miguel de Lis's art collection. Exhibits range from elegant fans signed by such noteworthies as Salvador Dalí to the racy sculptures of animals and people in compromising positions. (Open Apr.-Oct. 15 Tu-F 11am-2pm and 5-9pm, Sa-Su 11am-9pm; Oct. 16-Mar. Tu-F 11am-2pm and 4-7pm, Sa-Su 11am-8pm. €2.10, students €1.50, Tu mornings free.)

ENTERTAINMENT AND NIGHTLIFE. According to Salamantinos, Salamanca is the best place in Spain to party; they say there is one bar for every one hundred people living in the city. There are *chupiterias* (shot bars), *bares*, and *discotecas* on nearly every street, and while some close at 4am, others go all night. Nightlife centers on **Plaza Mayor** and spreads out to Gran Vía, C. Bordadores, and side streets. **Calle Prior** and **Rua Mayor** are also full of bars. Locals gather in the terrazas on **Plaza de la Fuente,** off Av. Alemánia. Intense partying occurs off **Calle Varillas.** Begin at **El Ochavo**, Pl. San Juan Bautista 7, for *litros* of beer or *sangría* (€3 each). Students also pregrame at **La Chupitería,** Pl. Monterrey (at the intersection of C. Prior and Bordadores), which serves inexpensive shots (€0.90 each) and slightly larger *chupas* (€1 each). Drink to modern funk and jazz at **Birdland,** C. Azafranal 57. At **Cum Laude,** C. Prior 5, the dance floor is a replica of the Pl. Mayor. Try **Camelot,** C. Bordadores 3, a monastery-turned-club. Swing to Top-40 songs at the popular **Café Moderno,** Gran Vía, 75. A mixed clientele grooves under blacklights at **Submarino,** C. San Justo 27.

DAYTRIP FROM SALAMANCA: ZAMORA. Perched atop a rocky cliff over the Rio Duero, Zamora (pop. 65,000) is an intriguing mix of the modern and medieval: 15th-century palaces harbor Internet cafes and luxury hotels. Zamora's foremost monument is its Romanesque **cathedral,** built between the 12th and 15th centuries. Highlights are its intricately carved choir stalls (complete with seated apostles laughing and singing) and the main altar, an ornate structure of marble, gold, and silver. Inside the cloister, the **Museo de la Catedral** features the priceless 15th-century black tapestries, which tell the story of the Trojan War and Achilles's defeat. (Cathedral and museum open Tu-Su 10am-2pm and 5-8pm. Mass daily at 10am, also Sa 6pm and Su 1pm. Cathedral free, museum €1.80.) All in all, twelve handsome Romanesque churches remain within the walls of the old city, gleaming in the wake of recent restoration. Most visitors follow the **Romanesque Route,** a self-guided tour of all of the churches available from the **tourist office,** C. Santa Clara 20. (☎980 53 18 45. Open M-Sa 9am-2pm and 5-7pm.) The **Museo de Semana Santa,** in sleepy Pl. Santa María La Nueva 9, is a rare find. Hooded mannequins stand guard over elaborately sculpted floats, dating back to the early 17th century. (Open M-Sa 10am-2pm and 5-8pm, Su 10am-2pm. €2.70.) **Buses** depart from Salamanca, Av. Filiberto Villalobos 71-85 (☎923 23 67 17), to Zamora (1hr.; M-F 22 per day 6:40am-10:35pm, Sa 10 per day 7:45am-8:30pm; €3.50).

LEÓN ☎987

Formerly the center of Christian Spain, today León (pop. 300,000) is best known for its 13th-century Gothic **cathedral,** arguably the most beautiful cathedral in Spain. Its spectacular stained-glass windows have earned the city the nickname *La Ciudad Azul* (The Blue City) and alone warrant a trip to León. The cathedral's **museum** displays gruesome wonders, including a sculpture depicting the skinning of a saint. (Cathedral open in summer daily 8:30am-2:30pm and 5-7pm; off-season 8:30am-1:30pm and 4-7pm. Free. Museum open in summer daily 9:30am-1:30pm and 4-6:30pm; off-season M-F 9:30am-1pm and 4-6pm, Sa 9:30am-1:30pm. €3.50.) The **Basílica San Isidoro,** dedicated in the 11th century to San Isidoro of Sevilla, houses the bodies of countless royals in the impressive *Panteón Real.* From Pl. Santo Domingo, walk up C. Ramon y Cajal; the basilica is up the flight of stairs on the right just before C. La Torre. (Open M-Sa 9am-1:30pm and 4pm-6:30pm, Su 9am-1:30pm. €3.) For bars, discos, and techno music, head to the *barrio húmedo* (drinker's neighborhood) around **Plaza de San Martín** and **Plaza Mayor.** After 2am, the crowds weave to **Calle Lancia** and **Calle Conde de Guillén,** both heavily populated with discos and bars.

Trains (☎(902) 24 02 02) run from Av. Astorga 2 to Madrid (4½hr., M-Sa 7 per day 1am-6pm, €27.50). **Buses** (☎987 21 00 00) leave from Po. Ingeniero Sáenz de Miera for Madrid (4½hr.; M-F 12 per day 2:30am-10:30pm, Sa-Su 8 per day 2:30am-7:30pm; €16.10). Turn left out of the main entrance of the bus station or right out of the main entrance of the train station onto Av. Palencia and cross the river to Plaza Glorieta Guzmán el Bueno, where, after the rotary, it becomes **Avenida de Ordoño II** and leads to León's cathedral and the adjacent **tourist office,** Pl. Regla 3. (☎987 23 70 82. Open M-F 9am-2pm and 5-7pm, Sa-Su 10am-2pm and 5-8pm.) Many accommodations cluster on **Av. de Roma, Av. Ordoño II,** and Av. República Argentina, which lead into the old town from Pl. Glorieta Guzmán el Bueno. From the plaza, follow Av. República Argentina to reach **Hostal Orejas ❹,** C. Villafranca 6, 2nd fl. Each brand-new room comes with bath, shower, and cable TV. (☎987 25 29 09; janton@usarios.Retecal.es. Free Internet. Su-W singles €28, doubles €34; Th-Sa singles €39, doubles €47.) Inexpensive eateries fill the area near the cathedral and on the small streets off C. Ancha; also check **Plaza San Martín,** near Pl. Mayor.

DAYTRIP FROM LEÓN: ASTORGA. Astorga's fanciful **Palacio Episcopal,** designed by Antoni Gaudí in the late-19th century, now houses the **Museo de los Caminos.** (☎987 61 88 82. Open M-Sa 10am-1:30pm and 4-7:30pm, Su 10am-1:30pm. €1.50.) Opposite the *palacio* is Astorga's cathedral and museum. (Both open daily 10am-2pm and 4-8pm. Cathedral free; museum €1.50.) Astorga is most easily reached by **bus** from Po. Ingeniero Saenz de Miera in León (45min.; M-F 16 per day 6:15am-9:30pm, Sa-Su 6-7 per day 8:30am-8:30pm; €2.58).

BURGOS ☎947

During its 500 years as capital of Castile, Burgos (pop. 346,000) witnessed the birth of not only its magnificent Gothic cathedral but also Rodrigo Díaz de Vivar, better known as El Cid Campeador, Spain's greatest national hero. Nine centuries after El Cid's banishment, General Franco stationed his headquarters here. Today, from its duck-filled riverbanks to its elegant denizens sipping *sangría* in sidewalk cafes, Burgos emits an aura of vivacity and prosperity. Officially named a UNESCO world heritage sight and unofficially called the most beautiful cathedral in Spain, the **Catedral Santa Iglesia** is deserving of its notoriety. Its magnificent spires tower over every view of the city, and its Gothic interior is equally remarkable. Devout visitors can enter the **Chapel of Christ,** the cathedral's holiest segment, and its most infamous: the crucified Jesus is constructed of real human body parts. Other highlights include the beautiful 16th-century stained-glass dome of the Capilla Mayor, the eerily lifelike *papamoscas* (fly-catcher), and, under the transept and marked only by a small brick, the remains of El Cid and Doña Jiménez. (☎947 20 47 12. Open M-Sa 9:30am-1pm and 4-7pm, Su 9:30-11:45am and 4-7pm. Cathedral free. Museum €3.60, students €2.40. Recorded histories in English €0.50.) The **Museo-Monasterio de las Huelgas Reales,** built by King Alfonso VIII in 1188, is slightly out of the way, but certainly worth the trip. Chambers, chapels, and cloisters adorned with rare Arabic tapestries and ornate mosaics shelter sepulchres of deceased royalty, including several heirs to the throne. Their burial wardrobes can be viewed in the **Museo de Telas** (Textile Museum). Take the "Barrio del Pilar" bus (€0.50) from Pl. España to the Museo stop. (☎947 20 56 87. Open Tu-Sa 10am-1:15pm and 3:45-5:45pm. €5, students and under 14 €2.50, W free. Obligatory tours in Spanish every 30min.)

Trains (☎947 20 35 60) run from the end of Av. Conde de Guadalhorce, across the river from the town center, to: Barcelona (9-13¾hr., 4 per day, €32); Bilbao (2½-4hr., 3-5 per day, €14); and Madrid (3-5½hr., 9-10 per day, €22-28). **Buses** (☎947 28 88 55) leave C. Miranda 4, off Pl. Vega south of the river, for: Barcelona (7½hr., 5 per day, €28); Bilbao (2-3hr., M-F 4 per day, €9); Madrid (2¾hr., M-F 12 per day, €13); and Salamanca (4hr., M-Sa 10:45am, €13). From the train station, follow Av. Conde de Guadalhorce across the river and take the first right on Av. Generalísimo Franco, which turns into Po. Espolón, to reach the town center. From the main entrance of the bus station, turn left onto C. Miranda, right onto C. Madrid, then cross the river to reach the cathedral.

The **tourist office** is at Pl. Alonso Martínez 7. (☎947 20 31 25. Open M-F 9am-2pm and 5-7pm, Sa-Su 10am-2pm and 5-8pm.) To get from Puerte de Santa María to the family-run **Pensión Peña ❷,** C. Puebla 18, 2nd. fl., turn right onto C. Vitoria, then left at Pl. del Cid. Cross Pl. de la Libertad to your right, and C. La Puebla will be directly in front of you. (☎947 20 63 23. Doubles €18.) **Hostal Joma ❷,** C. San Juan 26, 2nd fl., has spotless rooms and low rates. From Puente de Santa María, turn right onto C. Vitoria, and at Pl. del Cid, turn left onto C. Santander. (☎947 20 33 50. Singles €15; doubles €20.) **Plaza Alonso Martínez** teems with restaurants, while **Calle San Lorenzo** is the place to go for *tapas*. **Mercado de Abastos (Sur),** on C. Miranda next to the bus station, sells fresh meat and bread. (Open M-Sa 7am-3pm.)

By midnight, **Calle Avellanos** (opposite Pl. Alonso Martínez) is at full boil. Crowds bubble over into nearby **Calle Huerto del Rey,** then steam it up at *discotecas* along Calle San Juan. Dance to techno at **Twenty,** Pl. Huerto del Rey 20. (Open M-Sa 7pm-5am, Su 7pm-midnight.) **Postal Code:** 09070.

EXTREMADURA

In Extremadura, arid plains bake under an intense sun, relieved only by scattered patches of sunflowers. This land of harsh beauty and cruel extremes hardened New World conquistadors such as Hernán Cortés and Francisco Pizarro. But for the traveler who braves the Extremaduran plains, the reward is stunning ruins and peaceful towns. Compared to the hectic pace of nearby Madrid, life here is slow and less modern, as the region's rich history dominates its present character.

TRUJILLO ☎927

The gem of Extremadura, hilltop Trujillo (pop. 10,000) is an unspoiled joy. It's often called the "Cradle of Conquistadors" because the city produced over 600 explorers and plunderers of the New World. Scattered with medieval palaces, Roman ruins, Arabic fortresses, and churches of all eras, Trujillo is a glorious hodgepodge of histories and cultures. Its most impressive monument is its highest, the 10th-century **Moorish castle** which offers a stunning panoramic view of surrounding plains. The **Plaza Mayor** was the inspiration for the Plaza de Armas in Cusco, Peru. Festooned with stork nests, **Iglesia de San Martín** dominates the northeastern corner of the plaza. (All churches open June-Sept. daily 10am-2pm and 5-8:30pm; Oct.-May 9:30am-2pm and 4:30-7:30pm. €1.20-€1.25 each; €4.20 all.)

Buses run from Madrid (2½hr., 12-14 per day, €13). To get to the Plaza Mayor, turn left as you exit the station (up C. de las Cruces), right on C. de la Encarnación (following signs to the tourist office), then left on C. Chica; turn left on C. Virgen de la Guia and right on C. Burgos, continuing on to the plaza (15min.). The **tourist office** is across the plaza and posts information in its windows when closed. (☎927 32 26 77. Open June-Sept. 9:30am-2pm and 4:30-7:30pm; Oct.-May 9:30am-2pm and 4-8pm.) **Pensión Boni ❶,** C. Mingo de Ramos, 117, is off Pl. Mayor to the right of the church. (☎927 32 16 04. Singles €12; doubles €21, with bath €30.) **Hostal Trujillo ❷,** C. de Francisco Pizarro, 4-6. From the bus station, turn left on C. de las Cruces, right on C. de la Encarnación, then right again onto C. de Francisco Pizarro. (☎927 32 26 61; ☎/fax 32 22 74. Singles €21; doubles €39.) The Plaza Mayor teems with tourist eateries. **Meson Alberca ❸,** C. Victoria, 8, has a shaded interior garden and an excellent three-course *menú* for €15. (Open Su-T and Th-Sa 11am-1am.)

SOUTHERN SPAIN (ANDALUCÍA)

Andalucía derives its spirit from an intoxicating amalgam of cultures. Under Moorish rule, which lasted from AD 711 until 1492, Sevilla and Granada reached the pinnacle of Islamic arts, and Córdoba matured into the most culturally influential Islamic city. The Moors preserved, perfected, and blended Roman architectural techniques with their own, creating a style that became distinctively and uniquely Andalucian. Intriguing patios, garden oases with fountains and fish ponds, and alternating red brick and white stone were its hallmarks.

Andalucía has been bequeathed as the convergence point of popular images of Spanish culture, sent the world over by advertising campaigns. Bullfighting, flamenco, white-washed villages, sherry *bodegas*, sandy beaches, and the blazing sun are what the region offers tourists, but beyond those outstanding elements lie vivacious and warm-hearted residents who believe their most important job is the art of living well. Despite living in one of the poorest regions of Spain, Andalucians retain an unshakable faith in the good life. The never-ending *festivales*, *ferias*, and *carnavales* of Andalucía are world famous.

SEVILLA ☎954

Site of a small Roman acropolis founded by Julius Caesar, capital of the Moorish empire, focal point of the Spanish Renaissance, and guardian angel of traditional Andalusian culture, Sevilla never disappoints. Flamenco, *tapas*, and bullfighting are at their best here, and the city's cathedral is among the most impressive in Spain. But it is the city's infectious, vivacious spirit that defines it. During the annual *Semana Santa* and *Feria de Abril*, two of the most extravagant festivals in Europe, Sevilla's jasmined balconies and exotic parks spring to life, with matadors, flamenco dancers, and virgins leading the town in endless celebration.

TRANSPORTATION

Flights: All flights arrive at **Aeropuerto San Pablo** (SVQ; ☎954 44 90 00), 12km out of town on Ctra. Madrid. A taxi ride to the town center costs about €13. **Los Amarillos** (☎954 98 91 84) runs a bus to the airport from outside the Hotel Alfonso XIII at the Pta. Jerez (1-2 per hr. 6:15am-11pm, €2.25).

Trains: All train services are centralized in the modern **Estación Santa Justa** (☎954 41 41 11), on Av. Kansas City. In town, the **RENFE** office, C. Zaragoza 29 (☎954 54 02 02), is near Pl. Nueva. Open M-F 9am-1:15pm and 4-7pm. **AVE** trains run to **Córdoba** (45min., 18-20 per day 6:30am-9pm, €15-17) and **Madrid** (2½hr., 18-20 per day 6:30am-9pm, €62). **Talgo** trains run to: **Barcelona** (12hr.; M-F 8, 9:40am, 8:20pm; €53); **Cádiz** (2hr.; 7-12 per day M-F 6:35am-9:25pm, Sa-Su 9am-9:25pm; €8); **Córdoba** (1½hr., 6 per day 6:30am-9pm, €8); **Granada** (3hr., 5 per day 7am-5:40pm, €17); **Málaga** (2½hr., 4-7 per day 7:40am-8pm, €14); **Valencia** (8½hr., 4 per day 8am-9:50pm, €36).

Buses: The old bus station at Prado de San Sebastián (☎954 41 71 11), C. Manuel Vazquez Sagastizabal, mainly serves Andalucía.

- **Transportes Alsina Graells** (☎954 41 88 11). To: **Córdoba** (2hr., 10-12 per day 7am-10pm, €8); **Granada** (3hr., 10 per day 8am-11pm, €16); **Málaga** (3hr., 11 per day 7am-midnight, €13).
- **Transportes Comes** (☎954 41 68 58). To **Cádiz** (1½hr., 11-13 per day 7am-10pm, €9) and **Jerez de la Frontera** (2hr., 6 per day 8:30am-10pm, €6).
- **Los Amarillos** (☎954 98 91 84). To **Arcos de la Frontera** (2hr., 8am and 4:30pm, €6) and **Marbella** (3hr., 3 per day 8am-8pm, €7).
- **Enatcar-Bacoma** (☎902 42 22 42). To **Barcelona** (12-17hr., 9:30am and 5:30pm, €61-73) and **Valencia** (9-11hr., 9:30am and 5:30pm, €40-47).
- **Socibus** (☎954 90 11 60). To **Madrid** (6hr., 11 per day 9am-1am, €17).

Public Transportation: TUSSAM (☎900 71 01 71), the city bus network. Most lines run every 10min. 6am-11:15pm and converge on Pl. Nueva, Pl. Encarnación, or in front of the cathedral. Night service departs from Pl. Nueva (every hr. midnight-2am). Fare €0.90, *bonobús* (10 rides) €4.50. Particularly useful are C3 and C4, which circle the center, and #34, which hits the youth hostel, university, cathedral, and Pl. Nueva.

Taxis: TeleTaxi (☎954 62 22 22). **Radio Taxi** (☎954 58 00 00). Base rate €2.15, Su 25% surcharge. Extra charge for luggage and night service.

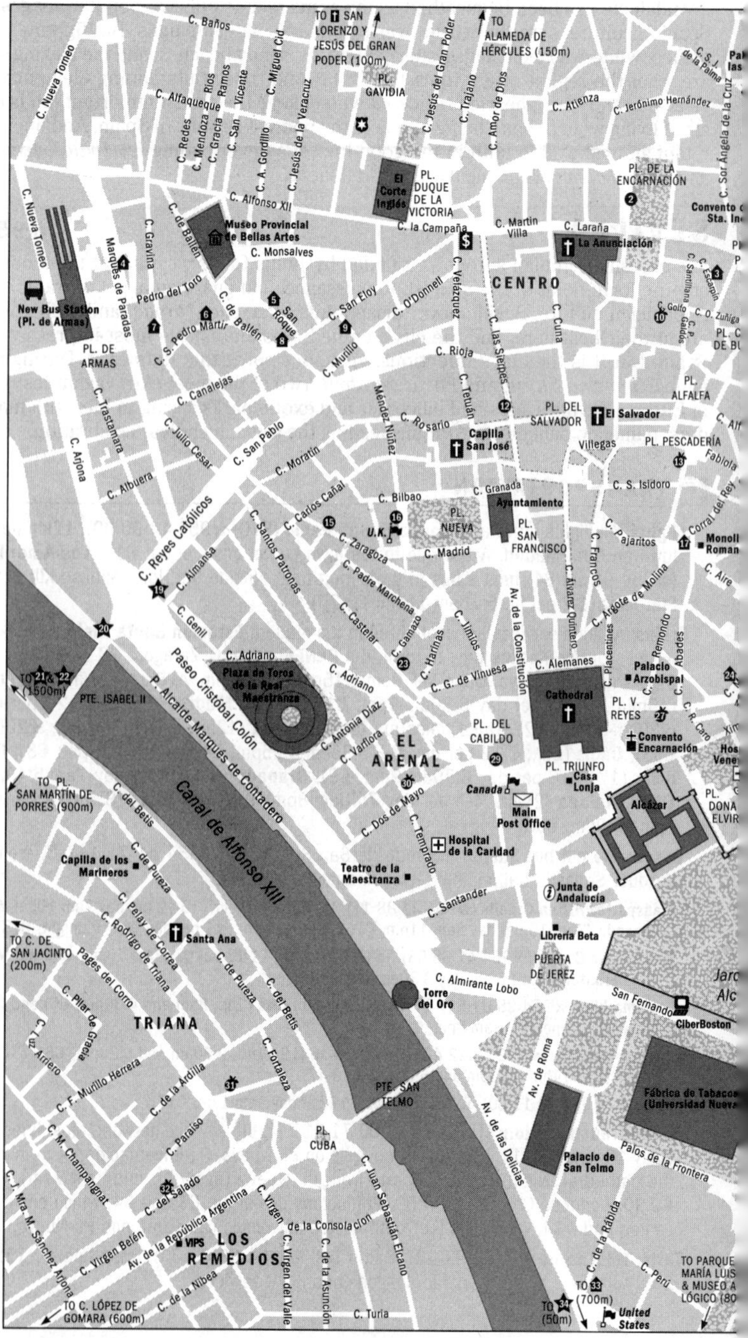
TO SAN LORENZO Y JESÚS DEL GRAN PODER (100m)
TO ALAMEDA DE HÉRCULES (150m)
PL. GAVIDIA
El Corte Inglés
PL. DUQUE DE LA VICTORIA
PL. DE LA ENCARNACIÓN
Museo Provincial de Bellas Artes
New Bus Station (Pl. de Armas)
PL. DE ARMAS
La Anunciación
CENTRO
Convento de Sta. Inés
PL. ALFALFA
PL. DEL SALVADOR
El Salvador
PL. PESCADERÍA
Capilla San José
Ayuntamiento
PL. NUEVA
PL. SAN FRANCISCO
U.K.
Monolito Romano
Plaza de Toros de la Real Maestranza
PTE. ISABEL II
TO (1500m)
TO PL. SAN MARTÍN DE PORRES (900m)
Canal de Alfonso XIII
EL ARENAL
PL. DEL CABILDO
Cathedral
Palacio Arzobispal
PL. V. REYES
Convento Encarnación
PL. TRIUNFO
Casa Lonja
Alcázar
Canada
Main Post Office
Hospital de la Caridad
Teatro de la Maestranza
Capilla de los Marineros
Junta de Andalucía
Librería Beta
PUERTA DE JEREZ
Torre del Oro
CiberBoston
TO C. DE SAN JACINTO (200m)
Santa Ana
TRIANA
PTE. SAN TELMO
PL. CUBA
Palacio de San Telmo
Fábrica de Tabacos (Universidad Nueva)
VIPS
LOS REMEDIOS
TO C. LÓPEZ DE GOMARA (600m)
TO (50m)
TO (700m)
United States
TO PARQUE MARÍA LUISA & MUSEO ARQUEOLÓGICO
C. Baños
C. Nueva Torneo
C. Alfaqueque
C. Redes
C. Mendoza Ríos
C. Gracia Ramos
C. San Vicente
C. Miguel Cid
C. A. Gordillo
C. Jesús de la Veracruz
C. Jesús del Gran Poder
C. Trajano
C. Amor de Dios
C. Atienza
C. Jerónimo Hernández
C. Alfonso XII
C. de Bailén
C. Gravina
Marqués de Paradas
C. Monsalves
C. la Campaña
C. Martín Villa
C. Laraña
Pedro del Toro
C. S. Pedro Mártir
San Roque
C. San Eloy
C. O'Donnell
C. Velázquez
C. las Sierpes
C. Cuna
C. Rioja
C. Murillo
C. Canalejas
C. Trastamara
C. Arjona
C. Julio César
C. San Pablo
C. Moratín
Méndez Núñez
C. Tetuán
C. Rosario
Villegas
C. S. Isidoro
C. Albuera
C. Reyes Católicos
C. Carlos Cañal
C. Bilbao
C. Granada
C. Santos Patronas
C. Zaragoza
C. Madrid
C. Pajaritos
C. Francos
C. Almansa
C. Padre Marchena
Av. de la Constitución
C. Álvarez Quintero
C. Argote de Molina
C. Aire
C. Genil
C. Castelar
C. Gamazo
C. Jimios
C. Harinas
C. Adriano
C. G. de Vinuesa
C. Alemanes
C. Placentines
C. Remondo
C. Abades
Paseo Cristóbal Colón
P. Alcalde Marqués de Contadero
C. Antonia Díaz
C. Varflora
C. Dos de Mayo
C. Temprado
C. del Betis
C. de Pureza
C. Pelay de Correa
C. Rodrigo de Triana
Pages del Corro
C. Santander
C. Almirante Lobo
San Fernando
C. Pilar de Gracia
C. Luz Arriero
C. F. Murillo Herrera
C. de la Ardilla
C. Fortaleza
Av. de Roma
Av. de las Delicias
Palos de la Frontera
C. Paraíso
C. M. Champagnat
C. del Salado
Av. de la República Argentina
C. Virgen de Luján
de la Consolación
C. Juan Sebastián Elcano
C. de la Rábida
C. Perú
C. J. Mra. M. Sánchez Arjona
C. Virgen Belén
C. de la Nibea
C. Virgen del Valle
C. de la Asunción
C. Turia

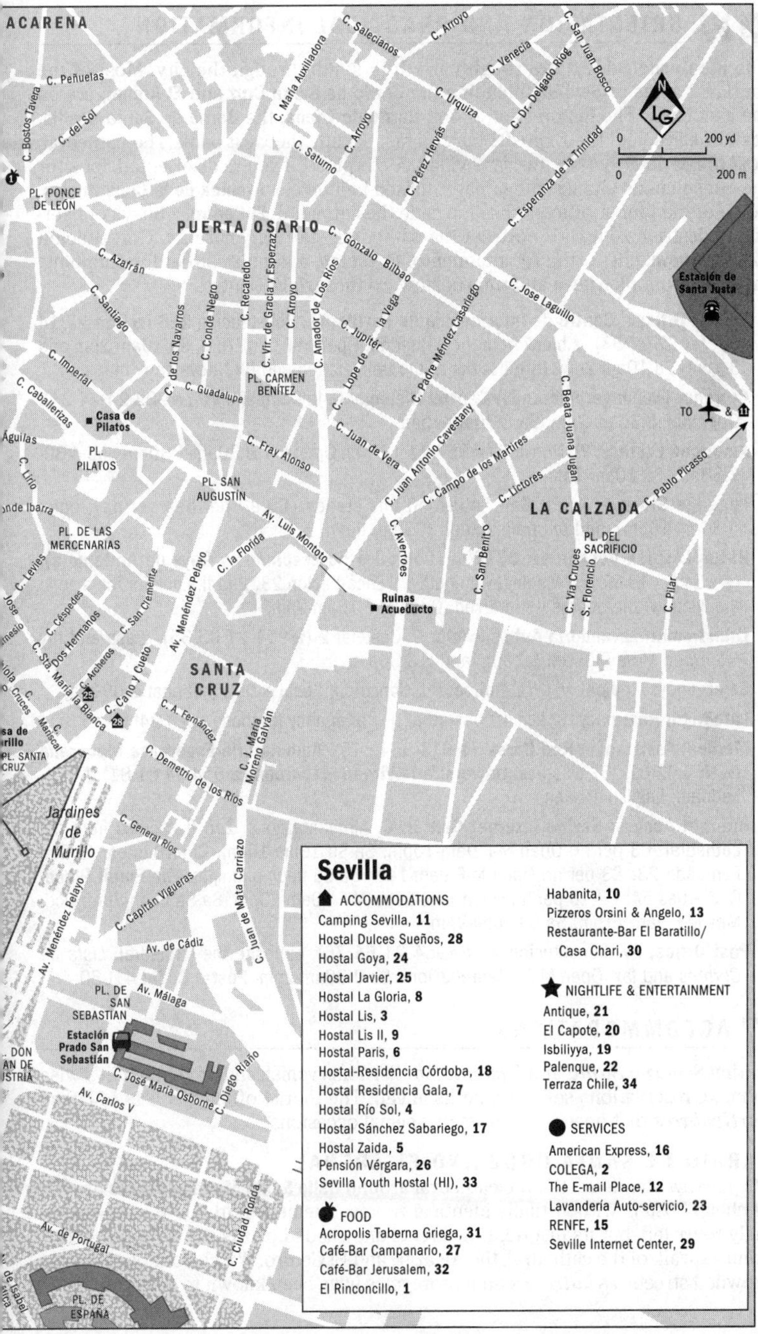

Sevilla

ACCOMMODATIONS

Camping Sevilla, **11**
Hostal Dulces Sueños, **28**
Hostal Goya, **24**
Hostal Javier, **25**
Hostal La Gloria, **8**
Hostal Lis, **3**
Hostal Lis II, **9**
Hostal Paris, **6**
Hostal-Residencia Córdoba, **18**
Hostal Residencia Gala, **7**
Hostal Río Sol, **4**
Hostal Sánchez Sabariego, **17**
Hostal Zaida, **5**
Pensión Vérgara, **26**
Sevilla Youth Hostal (HI), **33**

FOOD

Acropolis Taberna Griega, **31**
Café-Bar Campanario, **27**
Café-Bar Jerusalem, **32**
El Rinconcillo, **1**
Habanita, **10**
Pizzeros Orsini & Angelo, **13**
Restaurante-Bar El Baratillo/ Casa Chari, **30**

NIGHTLIFE & ENTERTAINMENT

Antique, **21**
El Capote, **20**
Isbiliyya, **19**
Palenque, **22**
Terraza Chile, **34**

SERVICES

American Express, **16**
COLEGA, **2**
The E-mail Place, **12**
Lavandería Auto-servicio, **23**
RENFE, **15**
Seville Internet Center, **29**

ORIENTATION AND PRACTICAL INFORMATION

The **Río Guadalquivir** flows roughly north to south through the city. Most of the touristed areas of Sevilla, including the **Barrio de Santa Cruz** and **El Arenal,** are on the east bank. The historic and proud **Barrio de Triana,** the **Barrio de Santa Cecilia, Los Remedios,** and the Expo '92 fairgrounds occupy the west bank. The cathedral, next to Barrio de Santa Cruz, is Sevilla's centerpiece. If you're disoriented, look for the conspicuous **Giralda** (the minaret-turned-belltower). **Avenida de la Constitución,** home of the tourist office, runs alongside the cathedral. **El Centro,** a busy commercial pedestrian zone, lies north of the cathedral, starting where Av. Constitución hits **Pl. Nueva,** site of the Ayuntamiento. **C. Tetuan,** a popular street for shopping, takes off from Pl. Nueva and runs northward through El Centro.

Tourist Offices: Centro de Información de Sevilla, Av. Constitución 21B (☎954 22 14 04; fax 22 97 53), 1 block from the cathedral. Open M-F 9am-7pm, Sa 10am-2pm and 3-7pm, Su 10am-2pm. **Info booths** at the train station and Pl. Nueva carry maps.

Currency Exchange: Santander Central Hispano, C. la Campaña 19 (☎902 24 24 24). Open M-F 8:30am-2pm, Sa 8:30am-1pm.

American Express: Pl. Nueva 7 (☎954 21 16 17). Open M-F 9:30am-1:30pm and 4:30-7:30pm, Sa 10am-1pm.

Luggage Storage: At Pr. San Sebastián bus station (€0.90 per bag per day; open 6:30am-10pm), and the train station (€3 per day).

Bi-Gay-Lesbian Resources: COLEGA (Colectiva de Lesbianas y Gays de Andalucía), (☎954 50 13 77; www.colegaweb.net). Pl. Encarnación 23, 2nd fl. Look for the sign in the window; the door is not marked. Open M-F 10am-2pm.

Laundromat: Lavandería Auto-servicio, C. Castelar 2 (☎954 21 05 35). Wash and dry €6. Open M-Sa 9:30am-1:30pm and 5-8:30pm.

Emergency: Medical: ☎061. **Police:** Po. Concordia (local ☎092; national ☎091).

Late-Night Pharmacy: Check list posted at any pharmacy for those open 24hr.

Medical Assistance: Red Cross: (☎913 354 545). **Ambulatorio Esperanza Macarena** (☎954 42 01 05). **Hospital Universitario Virgen Macarena** (☎954 24 81 81), Av. Dr. Fedriani. English spoken.

Internet Access: Seville Internet Center, C. Almirantazgo 2, 2nd fl., across from the cathedral. €3 per hr. Open M-F 9am-10pm, Sa-Su 10am-10pm. **CiberBoston,** C. San Fernando 23. €3 per hr. Open M-F 9am-1am, Sa-Su noon-midnight. **The Email Place,** C. Sierpes 54. €2.20 per hr. Open June-Sept. M-F 10am-10pm, Sa-Sa noon-8pm; Oct.-May M-F 9am-11pm, Sa-Su noon-9pm.

Post Office: Av. Constitución 32 (☎954 21 64 76), opposite the cathedral. *Lista de Correos* and fax. Open M-F 10am-8:30pm, Sa 9:30am-2pm. **Postal Code:** 41080.

ACCOMMODATIONS

During *Semana Santa* and *Feria de Abril*, rooms vanish and prices soar; it's wise to make reservations several months ahead. The tourist office has lists of *casas particulares* that open for visitors on special occasions.

BARRIO DE SANTA CRUZ AND EL ARENAL

The narrow streets east of the cathedral around **Calle Santa María la Blanca** are full of cheap hostels with virtually identical rooms. The neighborhood is overwhelmingly touristed, but its disorienting streets and shaded plazas are all within a few minutes walk of the cathedral, the Alcázar, and El Centro. Watch your bags on less crowded streets, as *ladrones* on motorcycles have been known to snatch them.

Pensión Vergara, C. Ximénez de Enciso 11, 2nd fl. (☎954 21 56 68), at C. Mesón del Moro. Beautiful rooms of varying size with lace bedspreads, antique-style furniture, and a sitting room with book swap. Singles, doubles, triples, and quads available. All rooms have fans. Towels provided on request. €15-18 per person. ❷

Hostal Dulces-Sueños, Santa Maria la Blanca 21 (☎954 41 93 83). Comfortable rooms, all with A/C. Singles €20; doubles €40, with bath €50; one triple with bath €60. ❷

Hostal Sánchez Sabariego, C. Corral del Rey 23 (☎954 21 44 70). Nice rooms with unique furnishings. A/C upstairs, fans in all other rooms. Singles €15-30; doubles with bath €30-60; triples with bath €40-90. ❷

Hostal Goya, C. Mateos Gago 31 (☎954 21 11 70; fax 56 29 88), 3 blocks from the cathedral. Spacious and sparkling clean rooms with A/C and showers. Doubles €51, with bath €57; triples €72, with bath €80. MC/V. ❸

Hostal-Residencia Córdoba, C. Farnesio 12 (☎954 22 74 98), off C. Fabiola. Run by a friendly and helpful family, this *hostal* offers immaculate and spacious air-conditioned rooms. Curfew 3am. Singles €25, with shower €33; doubles €40/€51. ❷

Hostal Javier, C. Archeros 16 (☎954 41 23 25). Rooms with framed prints and floral-patterned bed sheets. Singles €21, with bath €30; doubles €33/€39-42. MC/V. ❷

EL CENTRO

El Centro, a mess of narrow streets radiating from Pl. Encarnación, is a bustling shopping district during the day, but most streets are deserted at night.

Hostal Lis, C. Escarpín 10 (☎954 21 30 88), on an alley near Pl. Encarnación. Nice-sized rooms, with traditional Spanish tile. Owner is in the process of adding TV and A/C to all rooms, free Internet access, laundry service, and a rooftop terrace. Singles with shower €21; doubles with bath €42; triples with bath €63. MC/V. ❷

Hostal Lis II, C. Olavide 5 (☎954 56 02 28), off the busy shopping street San Eloy. Pleasant, good-sized rooms all with fans. Internet access. May 16-Mar.14 singles €19-22; doubles €32-35, with bath €35-42; triples with shower €45-51, with bath €48-55. Mar. 15-May 15 singles €39/€71; doubles €77/€90; triples €98. MC/V. ❷

Hotel Zaida, C. San Roque 26 (☎954 21 36 12; fax 21 88 10). Huge lobby. All rooms have bath, TV, and A/C. Mar. 16-Oct. singles €42; doubles €55. *Semana Santa* and *Feria de Abril* €51/€110. Nov.-Mar. 15 €35/€48. MC/V. ❹

Hostal La Gloria, C. San Eloy 58, 2nd fl. (☎954 22 26 73), at the end of a lively shopping street. Faded white rooms. Singles €18; doubles €30, with bath €36. ❷

NEAR ESTACIÓN PLAZA DE ARMAS

Most hostels around the Pl. de Armas bus station center around **Calle Gravina,** parallel to C. Marqués de las Paradas and two blocks from the station. These are the most convenient for exploring El Centro and C. Betis on the west bank of the river.

Hostal Río Sol, C. Márquez de Parada 25 (☎954 22 90 38), 1 block from Pl. de Armas bus station. Singles €15; with bath €18; with bath, TV, and fan €21; doubles with bath, TV, and A/C €42. MC/V. ❷

Hostal Paris, C. San Pedro Mártir 14 (☎954 22 98 61; fax 21 96 45), off C. Gravina. Pricey but comfortable. All rooms have bath, A/C, phones, and TVs. Mar.-Oct. singles €39, doubles €52, triples €73; Nov.-Feb. €32/€45/€63. AmEx/MC/V. ❸

Hostal Residencia Gala, C. Gravina 52 (☎954 21 45 03). Clean rooms with framed prints and spacious bathrooms. Singles €25, with bath €30; doubles €50/€60; limited triples available. All prices double during *Semana Santa* and *Feria.* ❸

ELSEWHERE AND CAMPING

Sevilla Youth Hostel (HI), C. Isaac Peral 2 (☎954 61 31 50; reservas@inturjoven.junta-andalucia.es). Take bus #34 across from the tourist office near the cathedral; the 5th stop is behind the hostel. Isolated and difficult to find. A/C. Many private baths. Breakfast included. Dorms Mar.-Oct. €13, over 26 €17; Nov.-Feb. €11/€15. ❶

Camping Sevilla, Ctra. Madrid-Cádiz km 534 (☎954 51 43 79), near the airport. From Pr. San Sebastián, take bus #70 (stops 800m away at Parque Alcosa). Hot showers, supermarket, and pool. €3 per person, €3 per car, or €2.50 per tent. ❶

FOOD

Sevilla is a city of *tapas;* locals spend their evenings relaxing and socializing over plates of *caracoles* (snails), *cocido andaluz* (a thick soup of chick peas), *pisto* (tomato and eggplant hash), *espinacas con garbanzos* (spinach with chick peas), and all manner of fresh seafood. *Pescado frito,* lightly fried fish, is a particular specialty of Sevilla. For those on a stricter budget, there are plenty of markets such as **Mercado del Arenal,** near the bullring on C. Pastor y Leandro, between C. Almansa and C. Arenal, which has fresh meat and produce (open M-Sa 9am-2pm). For a supermarket, try **%Día,** C. San Juan de Ávila, near El Corte Inglés. (Open M-F 9:30am-2pm and 6:30-9pm, Sa 9am-1pm.)

BARRIO DE SANTA CRUZ AND EL ARENAL

Restaurants near the cathedral cater almost exclusively to tourists. Beware the unexceptional, omnipresent *menús* featuring *gazpacho* and *paella* for €7. Food and prices improve along side streets in the Barrio Santa Cruz and in the back-street establishments between the cathedral and the river in El Arenal.

Restaurante-Bar El Baratillo/Casa Chari, C. Pavía 12 (☎954 22 96 51), on a tiny street off C. Dos de Mayo. Hospitable owner will help you practice your Spanish. Call or ask at least an hour in advance for the tour-de-force: homemade *paella* (vegetarian options available) with a jar of wine, beer, or *sangría* (€18 for 2). *Menú* €4-9. Open M-F 10:30am-11pm, Sa noon-5pm; stays open later when busy. ❷

Historico Horno, S.A., Av. de la Constitución 16 (☎954 22 18 19), across from the cathedral. Excellent pastries, cookies, and cakes. Open daily 7:30am-11pm. MC/V. ❷

Café-Bar Campanario, C. Mateos Gago 8 (☎954 56 41 89), half a block from the cathedral. Mixes the best (and strongest) jugs of *sangría* around (.05L €7.25, 1L €10). *Tapas* €1.50-2, *raciones* €6-9. Open daily 11am-midnight. ❷

EL CENTRO

This area belongs to professionals and shoppers by day and young people by night. Inexpensive *tapas* bars line the streets off **Plaza Alfalfa.**

Pizzeros Orsini & Angelo, C. Luchana 2 (☎954 21 61 64), 2 blocks from Pl. del Salvador. Crisp and filling pizza served straight from the oven. Romantic outdoor seating in front of a Baroque church. Pizzas €3.60-6.61, pasta €4.81-7.21, salads €3.61-5.11, and Italian desserts €2.40. Open daily 1-4pm and 8pm-1am. ❷

Habanita Bar Restaurant, C. Golfo 3 (☎606 71 64 56), on a tiny street off C. Perez Galdos. This popular cafe serves Cuban fare, pasta, salads, and Caribbean drinks. Many vegetarian and vegan options. Meals €5-10. Open M-Su 12:30-4:30pm. MC/V. ❷

El Rinconcillo, C. Gerona 40 (☎954 22 31 83), behind the Church of Santa Catalina. Founded in 1670 when Spain's empire stretched from the Philippines to America, this *bodega* continues to attract loyal patrons. *Tapas* €1.25-3.70, *raciones* €3.90-13.15; *media-raciones* available. Open Th-Tu 1pm-2am. AmEx/MC/V. ❷

TRIANA AND BARRIO DE SANTA CECILIA

This old maritime neighborhood, on the far side of the river, was once a separate village. Avoid overpriced C. Betis and plunge down the less expensive side streets, where fresh seafood and *caracoles* abound. *Tapas* bars cluster around **Plaza San Martín** and along **Calle San Jacinto.**

Acropolis Taberna Griega, C. Rosario Vega 10 (☎954 28 46 85), 2 blocks from the Pl. Cuba. This small restaurant serves delicious Greek food. Many vegetarian options. Entrees and appetizers €2.50-4. Open Aug.-June M 8:30-11:30pm, Tu-Sa 1:30-3:30pm and 8:30-11:30pm. MC/V. ❶

Café-Bar Jerusalém, C. Salado 6, at C. Virgen de las Huertas. Bar with an international crowd and creative *tapas*. Chicken, lamb, or pork and cheese *shwarma* (€3-4.50) called a *bocadillo hebreo*–it's not kosher, but it sure is tasty. Open daily 8pm-3am ❶.

SIGHTS

CATHEDRAL. With 44 individual chapels, Seville's cathedral is the third largest in the world, after St. Peter's Basilica in Rome and St. Paul's Cathedral in London, and is the biggest Gothic edifice ever constructed. Not surprisingly, it took more than a century to build. In 1401, Christians destroyed a 12th-century Almohad mosque to clear space—all that remains of the former mosque is the **Patio de Los Naranjos** and the famed minaret **La Giralda,** built in 1198. The tower and its twins in Marrakesh and Rabat, Morocco, are the oldest and largest surviving Almohad minarets. The 35 ramps inside lead to the top of the tower and offer amazing views.

In the center of the cathedral, the **Capilla Real** and its altar stand opposite the dark wooden **choir stalls** made of mahogany recycled from a 19th-century Austrian railway. The **retablo mayor** (altarpiece), one of the largest in the world, is a golden wall of intricately wrought saints and disciples. Circle the choir to see the **Sepulcro de Cristóbal Colón** (Columbus's tomb). There is mystery surrounding the actual whereabouts of Columbus's remains, since he has four alleged resting places throughout the world. The **Sacristía Mayor** holds works by Ribera and Murillo and a glittering Corpus Christi icon, La Custodia Processional. In the corner of the cathedral are the architecturally stunning **Sala de Las Columnas** and **Cabildo.** *(☎954 21 49 71. Open M-Sa 9:30am-4:30pm, Su 2:30-7pm. Tickets sold until 1hr. before closing. €6, seniors and students €1.50, under 12 and Su free. Mass held in the Capilla Real M-F 8:30, 9, 10am; Sa 8:30, 10am, 8pm; Su 8:30, 10, 11am, noon, 1pm.)*

IN RECENT NEWS

DISCOVERING COLUMBUS

For well over a century, historians in both Spain and the Americas have been puzzled by the question: "Where is Columbus buried?"

Spain has always claimed that the remains of the celebrated discoverer of the New World–who sailed under the Spanish flag–are buried under a magnificent altar in the cathedral of Seville. However, authorities in Santo Domingo, in the Dominican Republic, hold that Columbus rests within a large cross on their island known as the *Faro a Colon* (Columbus lighthouse). Despite the lengthy duration of this argument, there has been no scientific evidence to substantiate either side's claims.

Two Spanish high school teachers want to change that. In what is perhaps the most controversial scientific, moral, and cultural debate currently being discussed in Spain, the proposal to exhume, and with the assistance of the Laboratory of Genetic Identification at the University of Granada, test the remains at both sites has excited many who wish to resolve this question once and for all.

But it has also alarmed many, particularly in the Spanish Roman Catholic church, who see it as a disturbance of religious grounds and an infringement of cultural patrimony.

For now, the issue remains unresolved. As Spain struggles to build its image as a progressive, modernized nation, it finds itself torn between scientific advancement and a strong history of tradition.

ALCÁZAR. The Moorish architecture and numerous gardens of Sevilla's Alcázar are nothing short of magnificent. Visitors enter through the **Patio de la Montería,** directly across from the intricate Almohad facade of the Moorish palace. Through the archway lies the **Patio del Yeso** and the exquisitely carved **Patio de las Muñecas** (Patio of the Dolls), named for its miniature proportions. Court life revolved around the **Patio de las Doncellas** (Maids' Court), encircled by archways adorned with glistening tilework. The astonishing golden-domed **Salón de los Embajadores** is allegedly the site where Fernando and Isabel welcomed Columbus back from America. Nearby, the **Corte de las Muñecas** contains the palace's private quarters, decorated with the building's most exquisite carvings. Peaceful gardens stretch from the residential quarters in all directions. *(Pl. Triunfo 7. ☎954 50 23 23. Open Tu-Sa 9:30am-7pm, Su 9:30am-5pm. €5; students, seniors, and under 16 free. Audio guides €3.)*

MUSEO PROVINCIAL DE BELLAS ARTES. This museum contains Spain's finest collection of works by painters of the Sevilla school, notably Murillo, Valdés Leal, and Zurbarán, as well as El Greco and Dutch master Jan Breugel. The building itself is a work of art—take time to sit in its shady gardens. *(Pl. Museo 9, off C. Alfonso XII. ☎954 22 07 90. Open Tu 3-8pm, W-Sa 9am-8pm, Su 9am-2pm. €1.50, EU citizens free.)*

PLAZA DE TOROS DE LA REAL MAESTRANZA. Plaza de Toros de la Real Maestranza is home to one of the two great bullfighting schools (the other is in Ronda). The plaza fills to capacity for the 13 *corridas* of the *Feria de Abril* as well as for weekly fights. The museum inside has costumes, paintings, and antique posters. *(Open non-bullfight days 9:30am-2pm and 3-7pm, bullfight days 9:30am-3pm. Tours every 30min. €3.)*

BARRIO DE SANTA CRUZ. King Fernando III forced Jews fleeing Toledo to live in the Barrio de Santa Cruz, now a neighborhood of winding alleys, wrought-iron gates, and fountained courtyards. Beyond C. Lope de Rueda, off C. Ximénez de Enciso, is the charming and fragrant Plaza de Santa Cruz. South of the plaza are the **Jardines de Murillo,** a shady expanse of shrubbery and benches. The **Convento de San José** in Pl. Santa Cruz houses the grave of the artist Murillo, who died in what is now known as the **Casa Murillo** after falling from a scaffold. The **Iglesia de Santa María la Blanca** was built in 1391 on the foundation of a synagogue and features Murillo's *Last Supper*. *(Church open M-Sa 10-11am and 6:30-8pm, Su 9:30am-2pm and 6:30-8pm. Free.)*

SIERPES AND THE ARISTOCRATIC QUARTER. Originating from Pl. Duque de Victoria, **Calle de Sierpes,** a bustling commercial street, cuts through the Aristocratic Quarter. A plaque marks the spot where the royal prison once loomed—scholars believe Cervantes began writing *Don Quixote* there. The 15th-century **Casa de Pilatos** is a typical Andalucian palace with a mix of medieval and Renaissance elements, including several courtyards. *(Casa open daily 9am-7pm. €8.)*

LA MACARENA. This area northwest of El Centro is named for the Virgin of Sevilla. A stretch of 12th-century **murallas** (walls) runs between the Pta. Macarena and the Pta. Córdoba on the Ronda de Capuchinos. At the west end is the **Basílica Macarena,** whose venerated image of *La Virgen de la Macarena* is paraded through town during *Semana Santa*. A **treasury** within glitters with the virgin's jewels and other finery. *(Basilica open daily 9:30am-1pm and 5-9pm. Free. Treasury open daily 9:30am-1pm and 5-8pm. €2.70.)* Toward the river is the **Iglesia de San Lorenzo y Jesús del Gran Poder,** with Montañés's remarkably lifelike sculpture *El Cristo del Gran Poder*. Worshipers kiss Jesus's ankle through an opening in the bulletproof glass for good luck. *Semana Santa* culminates in a procession honoring the statue. *(Open Sa-Th 8am-1:45pm and 6-9pm, F 7:30-10pm. Free.)*

OTHER SIGHTS. Lovely tropical gardens and innumerable courtyards abound in the monstrous **Parque de María Luisa,** southeast of the city center. *(Open daily 8am-10pm. Boat rides €4.25 for 1-3 people.)* Bordering the park, in the neighboring **Plaza de España,** horse-drawn carriages still clatter in front of the plaza and rowboats can be rented to navigate its narrow moat. Mosaics depicting every provincial capital in Spain line the crumbling colonnade, which is currently undergoing a much-needed restoration. **Triana,** the neighborhood west of the cathedral and across the river, was Sevilla's chaotic 16th- and 17th-century mariners' quarter.

ENTERTAINMENT AND FESTIVALS

The tourist office distributes *El Giraldillo*, a free monthly magazine with complete listings of music, art exhibits, theater, dance, fairs, and film. Get your flamenco fix at **Los Gallos,** Pl. Santa Cruz 11, on the west edge of Barrio Santa Cruz. (Cover €27, includes 1 drink. Shows daily 9pm and 11:30pm.) If you're going to see a **bullfight** somewhere in Spain, Sevilla is probably the best place to do it; the bullring here is generally considered the most beautiful in the country. The cheapest place to buy bullfight tickets is at the ring on Po. Marqués de Contadero, or try the booths on C. Sierpes, C. Velázquez, or Pl. Toros (€18-75). Sevilla's world-famous **Semana Santa** (Holy Week) festival, during which penitents in hoods guide candle-lit processionals, lasts from Palm Sunday to Good Friday. During the last week of April, the city rewards itself for its Lenten piety with the **Feria de Abril.**

NIGHTLIFE

Sevilla's reputation for gaiety is tried and true—most clubs don't get going until well after midnight, and the real fun often starts after 3am. Popular bars can be found around **Calle Mateos Gago** near the cathedral, **Calle Adriano** by the bullring, and **Calle Betis** across the river in Triana.

Terraza Chile, Po. de las Delicias, at the intersection of Av. Uruguay and Av. Chile. Loud salsa and Spanish pop keep this small club packed and pounding through the early morning hours. Beer €2. Open in summer daily 9pm-6am.

La Carbonería, C. Levies 18, off C. Santa María La Blanca. Popular bar with free live flamenco and a massive outdoor patio replete with banana trees, picnic tables, and guitar-strumming Romeos. Beer €2.50. Open M-Sa 8pm-3:30am, Su 8pm-2:30am.

Isbiliyya, Po. de Colon 2, across from Pte. Isabell II. Friendly mixed bar with outdoor seating and a good dance floor. Beer €2-2.50. Open M-W 7pm-4am, Th-Su 7pm-5am.

Palenque, Av. Blas Pascal, on the grounds of Cartuja '93. Once a stadium-sized auditorium, now the largest dance club in Sevilla. Beer €2, mixed drinks €4.20. Cover €6 for men, €4 for women. Open in summer Th-Sa midnight-7am.

El Capote, next to Pte. Isabel II, at the intersection of C. Arjona and C. Reyes Católicos. A hugely popular outdoor bar with live music performances throughout the summer. Open in summer daily 11pm-3am.

Antique, C. Materatico Rey Pastor. Decorated entirely in white, with swirling spotlights and Ottoman pavilions doubling as bars in the yard and patio. Plays mostly Spanish pop-house. Cover for men €7, no cover for women. Open Th-Sa midnight-7am.

DAYTRIPS FROM SEVILLA

CÁDIZ

RENFE trains (☎956 25 43 01) arrive at Pl. Sevilla, off Av. Puerto, from Córdoba (3hr., 4 per day 8am-8:25pm, €25) and Sevilla (2hr., 12 per day 5:55am-7:55pm, €8). Transportes Generales Comes buses (☎956 22 78 11) arrive at Pl. Hispanidad from Sevilla (2hr., 11 per day 7am-10pm, €9).

Founded by the Phoenicians in 1100 BC, Cádiz (pop. 155,000) is thought to be the oldest inhabited city in Europe. **Carnaval** is perhaps Spain's most dazzling party (Feb. 27-Mar. 9 in 2003), but year-round the city offers golden sand **beaches** that put its pebble-strewn eastern neighbors to shame. **Playa de la Caleta** is the most convenient, but better sand awaits in the new city; take bus #1 from Pl. España to Pl. Glorieta Ingeniero (€0.80) to reach **Playa de la Victoria,** which has earned the EU's *bandera azul* for cleanliness. Back in town, the gold-domed, 18th-century **cathedral** is considered the last great cathedral built by colonial riches. To get there from Pl. San Juan de Dios, follow C. Pelota. (Museum open Tu-F 10am-12:45pm and 4:30-6:45pm, Sa 10am-12:45pm. €3. Cathedral open W and F 7-8pm, Su 11am-1pm. Free.) From the train station, walk two blocks past the fountain, with the port on your right, and look left for **Plaza San Juan de Dios,** the town center.

The **tourist office** is at Pl. San Juan de Dios #11. (☎/fax 956 24 10 01. Office open M-F 9am-2pm and 5-8pm. Kiosk in front of office open Sa-Su and holidays 10am-1pm and 5-7:30pm.) Most *hostales* huddle in Pl. San Juan de Dios, just behind it on C. Marqués de Cádiz, and around the harbor. **Quo Qádis ❶,** C. Diego Arias 1, one block from Pl. Falla, offers flamenco classes, planned excursions, and vegetarian dinners. (☎/fax 956 22 19 39. Dorms €6; singles €13; doubles €24.)

JEREZ DE LA FRONTERA

Buses (☎956 34 52 07) come from: Arcos (30min., 8 per day 9am-8:15pm, €2); Cádiz (1hr., 19 per day 7am-11:15pm, €3); Sevilla (1½hr., 7-8 per day 8:30am-7:45pm, €5).

Jerez de la Frontera (pop. 200,000) is the cradle of three staples of Andalucían culture: flamenco, Carthusian horses, and, of course, *jerez* (sherry). Most *bodegas* (wine cellars) offer tours in English, but many are closed in August. Founded in 1730, **Domecq** is the oldest and largest *bodega* in town. Tours include an informative 15min. video followed by a stroll through some of the many warehouses and gardens that comprise the sprawling complex. With unlimited sampling from three sherries (including Harveys Cream) and two brandies, Domecq's wine tasting is by far the most generous and varied in Jerez. Celebrity visitors have included Franco and Alexander Fleming. (☎956 15 15 00. English tours M-F 10am-1pm, €5.) The **tourist office,** Pl. Arenal, has free maps and info on sherry production, *bodega* tours, and horse shows. (☎956 35 96 54. Open June-Sept. M-F 9am-2:30pm and 4:30-6:30pm, Sa-Su 9:30am-3:30pm; Oct.-May M-F 8am-3pm and 4-7pm, Sa-Su 10am-2pm. Look for accommodations along **Calle Medina,** near the bus station, and on **Calle Arcos,** which intersects C. Medina at Pl. Romero Martínez. Take bus L8 from the bus station or bus L1 from Pl. Arenal (10min.) to reach the **Albergue Juvenil (HI) ❶,** Av. Carrero Blanco 30. (☎956 14 39 01. Dorms €16, under 27 €11.) *Tapas*-hoppers bounce around **Plaza Arenal, Calle Larga,** and in the old town around **Plaza del Banco.** Supermarket **Cobreros** is on the second floor of the Centro Comercial, C. Larga. (Open daily 9am-2pm and 5:30-9:30pm.)

ARCOS DE LA FRONTERA

Buses *(☎956 70 20 15), C. Corregidores, come from Cádiz (1½hr., 6 per day 7:20am-7:25pm, €4.45); Jerez (30min.; M-F 8-18 per day 6:30am-8:15pm, Sa-Su 8am-6:30; €2); Sevilla (2hr., 7am and 5pm, €6). Los Amarillos buses (☎956 70 02 57) go to*

Jerez (30min.; M-F 8-18 per day 6:30am-8:15pm, Sa-Su 8am-6:30; €2) and Sevilla (2hr., 7am and 5pm, €6).

With castles and Roman ruins at every turn, Arcos (pop. 33,000) is in essence a historical monument. Travelers wander the alleys, ruins, and hanging flowers of the **old quarter** and marvel at the stunning view from **Plaza Cabildo.** In the square is the **Iglesia de Santa María,** a mix of Baroque, Renaissance, and Gothic styles. To reach the old quarter from the bus station, exit left, turn left on C. Muñoz Vásquez and continue 20min. uphill as it changes names. The **tourist office** is on Pl. Cabildo. (☎956 70 22 64. Open Mar. 15-Oct. 15 M-Sa 10am-2pm and 4-8pm; Oct. 16-Mar. 14 M-Sa 10am-2pm and 3:30-7:30pm.) **Hostal San Marcos ❷,** C. Marqués de Torresoto 6, past C. Dean Espinosa and Pl. Cabildo, is run by a friendly, young family and crowned by a scenic rooftop terrace. (☎956 70 07 21. Singles €25; doubles €36.) Restaurants huddle at the bottom end of **Calle Corredera,** while *tapas* nirvana can be found uphill in the old quarter.

RONDA

Buses (☎952 18 70 61) go from Pl. Concepción García Redondo 2, near Av. Andalucía, to: Málaga (2½hr.; M-F 5 per day 6am-7:30pm, fewer on weekends; €8); Marbella (1½hr., 4 per day 6:30am-7:45pm, €5); Sevilla (2½hr.; M-F 5 per day 7am-7pm, Sa-Su 3-4 per day 7am-7pm; €9).

Most people's strongest impression of Ronda (pop. 38,000), the birthplace of modern bullfighting, is the stomach-churning ascent to get there. A precipitous gorge, carved by the Río Guadalevín, dips below the **Puente Nuevo,** opposite Pl. España. Bullfighting aficionados charge over to Ronda's **Plaza de Toros,** Spain's oldest bullring (est. 1785) and cradle of the modern *corrida.* For something just as bloody, visit the **Museo del Bandolero,** C. Armiñán 59, dedicated to presenting "pillage, theft, and rebellion in Spain since Roman times." (☎952 87 77 85. Open in summer daily 10am-8:30pm; off-season 10am-6pm. €2.70.) The **tourist office** is at Pl. España 1. (☎952 87 12 72. Open M-F 9am-7pm, Sa-Su 10am-2pm.) The best budget deal in town is **Hostal González ❶,** C. San Vincente de Paul 3. (☎952 87 14 45. Singles €10; doubles €16.) **Postal code:** 29400.

CÓRDOBA ☎957

The light of the Dark Ages, Córdoba (pop. 310,000) was built on religious tolerance and intellectual achievement. Once the largest city in Western Europe, its prestigious university (founded in the 12th century) and paved streets welcomed Jews, Christians, and Arabs alike; the city's synagogues, cathedrals, and mosques stand testament to its incredible legacy of tolerance. Today, springtime festivals, flower-filled patios, and a steady nightlife make it one of Spain's most beloved cities.

TRANSPORTATION

Trains: Plaza de las Tres Culturas, Av. América (☎957 40 02 02). To: **Barcelona** (10-11hr., 3 per day 9:45am-10:20pm, €46-60); **Cádiz** (AVE 2¾hr., 12:15am and 6pm, €22; regular 3-4hr., 5 per day 6am-8pm, €15-22); **Madrid** (AVE 2hr., 18 per day 7am-9:40pm, €38-45); **Málaga** (AVE 2¼hr., 6 per day 9am-10pm, €12-13.50; regular 3hr., 9 per day 6:40am-10pm, €10-18); **Sevilla** (AVE 45min., 18 per day 8:40am-11:40pm, €14-18). For international tickets, contact **RENFE,** Ronda de los Tejares, 10 (☎957 49 02 02).

Buses: Estación de Autobuses, Glorieta de las Tres Culturas (☎957 40 40 40; fax 40 44 15), across from the train station. **Alsina Graells Sur** (☎957 27 81 00) covers most of Andalucía. To: **Algeciras** (5hr., 2 per day, €17.50); **Almería** (5hr., 8am, €18); **Ante-**

quera (2½hr., 3 per day 9am-7pm, €6.50); **Cádiz** (4-5hr., 10am and 6pm, €17) via Los Amarillos or Comes Sur; **Granada** (3hr., 8-9 per day 8am-8:30pm, €10); **Málaga** (3-3½hr., 5 per day 8am-7pm, €10); **Sevilla** (2hr., 10-12 per day 5:30am-9:30pm, €8). **Bacoma** (☎957 45 65 14) goes to: Baeza, Ubeda, Valencia, and **Barcelona** (10hr., 6:25pm, €51). **Secorbus** (☎902 22 92 92) provides exceptionally cheap service to **Madrid** (4½hr., 6 per day 1-8pm, €11), departing from Camino de los Sastres in front of Hotel Melía.

Public Transportation: 12 bus lines (☎957 25 57 00) cover the city, running daily until 11pm. **Bus #3** makes a loop from the bus and train stations through Pl. Tendillas, along the river, and up C. Doctor Flemming. **Bus #10** runs from the train station to Barrio Brillante. Purchase tickets onboard for €0.80.

Taxis: Radio Taxi (☎957 76 44 44) has stands at most busy intersections. From the Judería to the bus and train stations about €3-€5; to Barrio Brillante €4-6.

Car Rental: Hertz (☎957 40 20 60), in the train station. Min. age 25. Small car €62 per day. Open M-F 8:30am-9pm, Sa 9am-1pm and 3:30-7pm, Su 9am-1pm.

ORIENTATION AND PRACTICAL INFORMATION

Córdoba is split into two parts: the **old city** and the **new city.** The modern and commercial northern half extends from the train station on Avenida América down to **Plaza de las Tendillas,** the center of the city. The old section in the south is a medieval maze known as the **Judería** (Jewish quarter). The easiest way to reach the old city from the adjacent train and bus stations is to take bus #3 to **Campo Santo de los Mártires** (€0.80). To walk (20min.), exit left from the station, cross the parking plaza, and make a right onto Av. de los Mozarabes. When you reach the Roman columns, turn left and cross Gta. Sargentos Provisionales. Make a right on Paseo de la Victoria and continue until you reach Puerto Almodovar and the old city.

Tourist Offices: Oficina Municipal de Turismo y Congresos, Pl. Judá Leví (☎957 20 05 22), next to the youth hostel, has maps and free event brochures. Open M-F 8:30am-2:30pm. **Tourist Office of Andalucía,** C. Torrijos 10 (☎957 47 12 35), in the Junta de Andalucía, across from the Mezquita. Open May-Sept. M-F 9:30am-8pm, Sa 10am-7pm, Su 10am-2pm; Oct.-Apr. M-Sa 9:30am-6pm, Su 10am-2pm.

Currency Exchange: CajaSur, Ronda de los Tejares 18-24 (☎957 21 42 42), across from El Corte Ingles. Charges 10% commission, €4.50 minimum. Open M-F 8:30am-2:30pm. Banks and **ATMs** dot Pl. Tendillas.

Emergency: ☎092. **Police:** Av. Doctor Flemming, 2 (☎957 59 45 80).

Medical Assistance: Emergencies ☎061. **Red Cross Hospital,** Paso de la Victoria (urgent ☎957 22 22 22, main line 957 42 06 66). Open M-F 9am-1:30pm and 4:30-5:30pm. **Ambulance:** urgent ☎902 505 061, main line ☎957 767 359.

Late-Night Pharmacy: On a rotating basis. Refer to the list posted outside the pharmacy in Pl. Tendillas or the local newspaper.

Internet Access: e-Net, C. Garcia Lovera 10 (☎957 48 14 62). Leave Pl. Tendillas on C. Claudio Marcelo, take second left. €1.20 per hr. Open daily 9am-2pm and 5-10pm.

Post Office: C. Cruz Conde 15 (☎957 47 97 96), 2 blocks up from Pl. Tendillas. *Lista de Correos*. Open M-F 8:30am-8:30pm, Sa-Su 9:30am-2pm. **Postal Code:** 14070.

ACCOMMODATIONS

Hostels in Córdoba are quite impressive: charming, well-maintained, and affordable. Córdoba is especially crowded during *Semana Santa* (the week before Easter) and from May through September; you may have to call two to three months

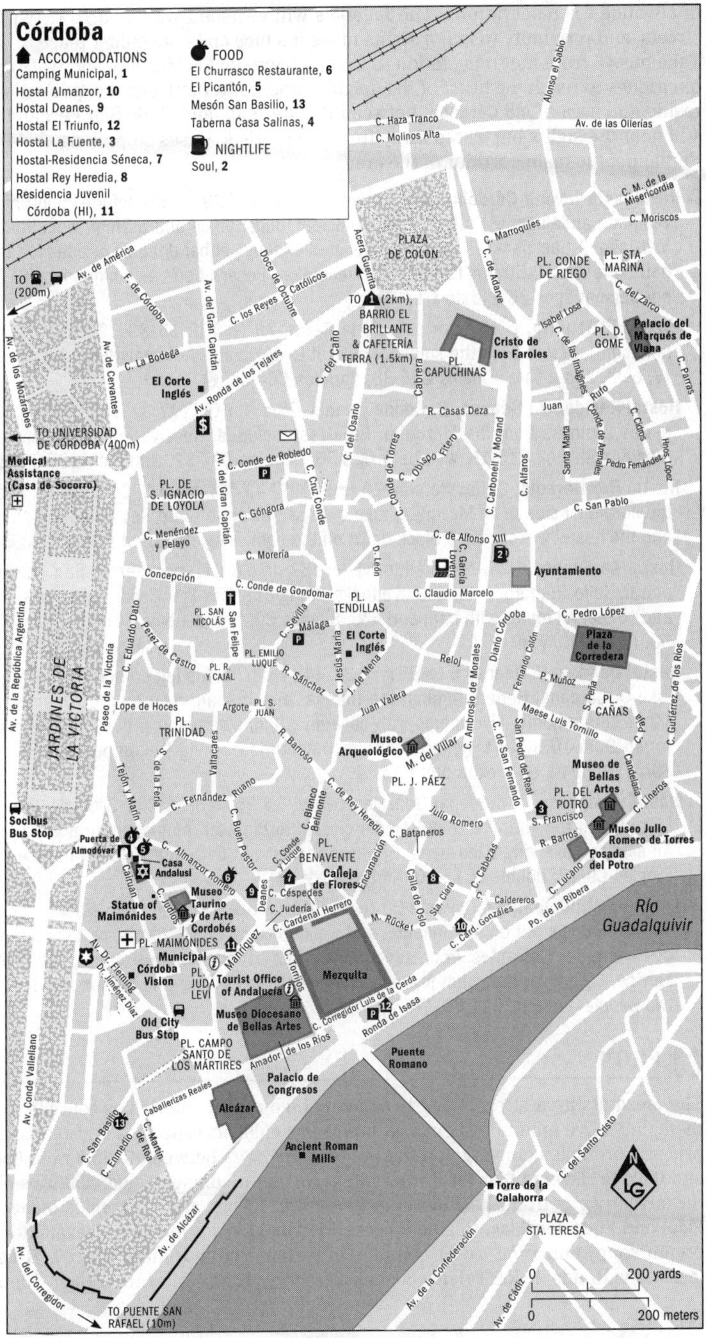
Córdoba
ACCOMMODATIONS
Camping Municipal, 1
Hostal Almanzor, 10
Hostal Deanes, 9
Hostal El Triunfo, 12
Hostal La Fuente, 3
Hostal-Residencia Séneca, 7
Hostal Rey Heredia, 8
Residencia Juvenil Córdoba (HI), 11
FOOD
El Churrasco Restaurante, 6
El Picantón, 5
Mesón San Basilio, 13
Taberna Casa Salinas, 4
NIGHTLIFE
Soul, 2
PLAZA DE COLON
Cristo de los Faroles
PL. CAPUCHINAS
Palacio del Marqués de Viana
PL. CONDE DE RIEGO
PL. STA. MARINA
PL. D. GOME
El Corte Inglés
PL. DE S. IGNACIO DE LOYOLA
Ayuntamiento
PL. TENDILLAS
Plaza de la Corredera
PL. CAÑAS
PL. SAN NICOLÁS
PL. EMILIO LUQUE
PL. R. Y CAJAL
PL. S. JUAN
PL. TRINIDAD
JARDINES DE LA VICTORIA
Museo Arqueológico
PL. J. PÁEZ
Museo de Bellas Artes
PL. DEL POTRO
Museo Julio Romero de Torres
Posada del Potro
Socibus Bus Stop
Puerta de Almodóvar
Casa Andalusí
Statue of Maimónides
Museo Taurino y de Arte Cordobés
PL. BENAVENTE
Calleja de Flores
PL. MAIMÓNIDES
Municipal
Córdoba Vision
PL. JUDA LEVÍ
Tourist Office of Andalucía
Mezquita
Museo Diocesano de Bellas Artes
Old City Bus Stop
PL. CAMPO SANTO DE LOS MÁRTIRES
Palacio de Congresos
Puente Romano
Alcázar
Ancient Roman Mills
Torre de la Calahorra
PLAZA STA. TERESA
Río Guadalquivir
Medical Assistance (Casa de Socorro)
TO UNIVERSIDAD DE CÓRDOBA (400m)
TO (200m)
TO 1 (2km), BARRIO EL BRILLANTE & CAFETERÍA TERRA (1.5km)
TO PUENTE SAN RAFAEL (10m)
Av. de América
Av. de las Ollerías
C. Haza Tranco
C. Molinos Alta
Alonso el Sabio
C. M. de la Misericordia
C. Moriscos
C. Marroquíes
C. de Adarve
C. del Zarco
Isabel Losa
C. de las Imágenes
Rufo
Juan
Santa Marta
Conde de Arenales
C. Cidros
Pedro Fernández
Hnos. López
C. Parras
C. San Pablo
C. Alfaros
C. Carbonell y Morand
R. Casas Deza
Cabrera
C. del Osario
C. del Caño
Acera Guerrita
Doce de Octubre
C. los Reyes Católicos
F. de Córdoba
Av. del Gran Capitán
Av. Ronda de los Tejares
C. La Bodega
Av. de Cervantes
Av. de los Mozárabes
C. Conde de Robledo
C. Cruz Conde
C. Conde de Torres
C. Obispo Fitero
C. Góngora
C. Menéndez y Pelayo
C. Morería
Concepción
C. Conde de Gondomar
D. León
C. de Alfonso XIII
C. García Lovera
C. Claudio Marcelo
C. Pedro López
Diario Córdoba
Fernando Colón
P. Muñoz
S. Peña
C. Gutiérrez de los Ríos
Maese Luis Tornillo
C. Pedro
Candelaria
C. Lineros
San Pedro del Real
C. de San Fernando
C. Ambrosio de Morales
Reloj
C. Sevilla
Málaga
San Felipe
C. Eduardo Dato
Perez de Castro
R. Sánchez
C. Jesús María
J. de Mena
Juan Valera
Paseo de la Victoria
Av. de la República Argentina
Lope de Hoces
Argote
R. Barroso
M. del Villar
Vallacares
S. de la Feria
Tejón y Marín
C. Fernández Ruano
C. Buen Pastor
C. Blanco Belmonte
C. de Rey Heredia
Encarnación
C. Conde y Luque
C. Bataneros
Julio Romero
S. Francisco
R. Barros
C. Lucano
C. Cabezas
Calle de Osio
Sta. Clara
Caldereros
C. Card. Gonzáles
M. Rücker
Po. de la Ribera
C. Almanzor Romero
Cairuan
C. Judíos
C. Céspedes
Deanes
C. Judería
C. Cardenal Herrero
Manríquez
C. Torrijos
Av. Dr. Fleming
Dr. Jiménez Díaz
C. Corregidor Luis de la Cerda
Ronda de Isasa
Amador de los Ríos
Caballerizas Reales
C. San Basilio
C. Enmedio
C. Martín de Roa
Av. Conde Vallellano
Av. del Corregidor
Av. de Alcázar
Av. de la Confederación
Av. de Cádiz
C. del Santo Cristo
0
200 yards
0
200 meters
LG

in advance for reservations. The **Judería's** whitewashed walls, narrow, twisting streets, and proximity to major sights make it a nice and convenient place to stay. Take bus #3 from the train station to Campo Santo de los Mártires and walk up C. Manríques to reach the heart of the neighborhood. Alternatively, the quieter, more residential area of **old Córdoba,** between the Mezquita and C. de San Fernando, is still near the sights but a step away from the tourists. Buses stop along C. de San Fernando, the main corridor of the area.

Residencia Juvenil Córdoba (HI), Pl. Judá Leví (☎957 29 01 66; informacion@inturjoven.junta.andalucia.es), next to the municipal tourist office and a 2min. walk from the Mezquita. A backpacker's utopia. Large, sterile rooms, either doubles or quads, all with bath. Internet €0.50 per 12min. 24hr. reception. Reservations recommended. €12.90 per person; ages 26 and up €17. ❶

Hostal El Triunfo, Corregidor Luis de la Cerda 79 (☎902 15 83 92; reservas@htriunfo.com), across from the southern side of La Mezquita. All rooms have A/C, phone, TV, bath, and a safe. Singles €25-38; doubles €44-57. ❸

Hostal-Residencia Séneca, C. Conde y Luque 7 (☎/fax 957 47 32 34). Follow C. Céspedes 2 blocks from the Mezquita. Breakfast included. Reservations recommended. Singles with sink €15-18, with bath €26-30; doubles €27-32, with bath €35-39. ❷

Hostal Rey Heredia, C. Rey Heredia 26 (☎957 47 41 82). From C. Cardenal Herrero on the northeast side of La Mezquita, take C. Encarnación to C. de Rey Heredia; turn right and the hostel will be half a block down on the right. Singles €12; doubles €24. ❶

Hostal La Fuente, C. San Fernando 51 (☎957 48 78 27), between C. San Francisco and C. Julio Romero. A terrace overlooks the Iglesia San Francisco. Cafe serves beer and coffee. All rooms with bath and A/C. Singles €20-24; doubles €36-40; triples €48-50. AmEx/MC/V. ❷

Hostal Deanes, C. Deanes 6 (☎957 29 37 44). From the top left corner of the Mezquita take C. Cardenal Herrero through the Judería, then a sharp right onto C. Deanes. In a 16th-century home. Five rooms with cavernous baths surround a busy courtyard cafe (open 9am-10:30pm). Reservations recommended during December and *Semana Santa*. Doubles €31, extra bed €10. ❸

Hostal Almanzor, C. Cardenal González 10 (☎/fax 957 48 54 00), 3 blocks from the Mezquita at the end of C. Rey Heredía closest to the river. Ambience for a good price. All singles have king-sized beds. Spotless rooms with bath and A/C. 24hr. reception. Singles €9-12; doubles €18-30. AmEx/MC/V. ❶

Camping Municipal, Av. Brillante 50 (☎957 40 38 36). From the train station, turn left on Av. América, left on Av. Brillante, and walk uphill for about 20min; or, take bus #10 or 11 from Av. Cervantes. Pool, supermarket, free hot showers, restaurant, and laundry service. Camping equipment for rent. Wheelchair accessible. One person and tent €8; two people and tent €11.60. ❶

FOOD

The Mezquita area attracts nearly as many high-priced eateries as tourists to fill them, but a five-minute walk in any direction yields local specialties at reasonable prices. Córdobans converge on the outdoor *terrazas* between **Calle Severo Ochoa** and **Calle Dr. Jimenez Diaz** for drinks and *tapas* before dinner. Cheap eateries cluster farther away from the Judería in **Barrio Cruz Conde,** around **Avenida Menéndez Pidal** and **Plaza Tendillas.** Regional specialties include *salmorejo* (a gazpacho-like cream soup) and *rabo de toro* (bull's tail simmered in tomato sauce). **El Corte Ingles,** Av. Ronda de los Tejeres 30, has a grocery store. (Open M-Sa 10am-10pm.)

El Picantón, C. F. Ruano 19, 1 block from the Puerta de Almódovar. From the right corner of the Mezquita, walk up Romero and turn left. Take ordinary *tapas*, pour on *salsa picante,* stick it in a roll, and you've got lunch (€1.50-2.25). There's nothing else as cheap or as filling. Open daily 10am-3:30pm and 8pm-midnight. ❶

El Churrasco Restaurante, C. Almanzor Romero 16. From the top left side of the Mezquita follow C. Cardinal Herrero through C. Judería, take a right onto C. Deanes and a quick left onto C. Romero; it's near the Pl. Card. A complimentary aperitif and excellent service start the meal off right. Delicious dishes. *Menú* €22, meat and fish dishes €10-38. Open daily 1-4pm and 8:30-11:30pm. Closed in Aug. MC/V. ❹

Casa Dona Vicenta, C. Gonzalo Xicueuea de Quesada 17. C. Gonzalo X. de Quesada runs parallel to the Jardines de la Victoria; walk through the *jardines* to C. Antonio Maura, make a right onto C. Gonzalo X. de Quesda. Excellent food, great prices, and friendly service. Entrees €6-18. Vegetarian options. Open Tu-Su 9am-11pm. MC/V. ❸

Mesón San Basilio, C. San Basilio 19. From Campo Santo de los Mártires, take Caballerizas Reales until the end, turn right onto C. Martin de Roa and then left onto C. San Basilio. The locals love it, and so will you. Dine on one of two floors surrounding a breezy patio or have a drink at the bar. *Menú* M-F €6, Sa-Su €9. Entrees €6-14. Open daily 1-4pm and 8pm-midnight. AmEx/MC/V. ❸

Taberna Casa Salinas, Puerto Almodóvar (☎957 29 08 46). A few blocks from the synagogue, up C. Judíos and to the right. Pepe Salinas has been running this place for over 35 years and it's quite popular. Eschew the jam-packed bar and request a table on the romantic outdoor patio. *Raciones* €4-9. Open M-Sa 11:30am-4:30pm and 8:30pm-12:30am, Su 11:30am-4:30pm. Closed Aug. ❷

SIGHTS

LA MEZQUITA

☎957 47 05 12. Open July-Oct. daily 10am-7pm; Apr.-June M-Sa 10am-7:30pm, Su and holidays 2-7:30pm; Nov.-Mar. daily 10am-6pm. €6.50, under 10 free. Wheelchair accessible. Last entrance 30min. before closing. Opens M-Sa 8:30am for mass starting at 9:30am; Su mass 11am, noon, and 1pm.

Built in 784 on the site of a Visigoth basilica, this architectural masterpiece is considered the most important Islamic monument in the Western world. Carved from granite and marble, the 850 pillars within the Mezquita are capped by brick-and-stone arches of different heights, creating a sense of height and spaciousness.

Visitors enter through the **Patio de los Naranjos,** an arcaded courtyard featuring carefully spaced orange trees and fountains, where the dutiful would wash before prayer. The **Torre del Alminar** encloses remains of the original minaret. Added in the 10th century, the dazzling **mihrab** (prayer niche) once housed a gilt copy of the Koran; worn stones mark where pilgrims knelt in reverence. Estimated at close to 35 tons, the intricate gold, pink, and blue marble Byzantine mosaics shimmering across the arches were given by Emperor Constantine VII to the *cordobés* caliphs.

In 1523, Bishop Alonso Manrique, an ally of Carlos V, proposed the construction of a cathedral in the center of the mosque. The town rallied violently against the idea, promising painful death to any worker who helped tear down the Mezquita. Nevertheless, a towering **crucero** (transept) and **coro** (choir stalls) were eventually erected, incongruously planting a richly adorned baroque cathedral amidst far more austere environs. The townspeople were less than pleased, and even Carlos V regretted the changes to the Mezquita, lamenting, "You have destroyed something unique to create something commonplace." What remains, though, is far from commonplace.

IN AND AROUND THE JUDERÍA

A combined ticket for the Alcázar, Museo Taurino y de Arte Cordobés, and Museo Julio Romero is available at all 3 locations. €7, students €4.

ALCÁZAR. Along the river on the left side of the Mezquita lies the Alcázar. Built in 1328 during the *Reconquista*, the building was both a fortress and a residence for Alfonso XI. Fernando and Isabel bade Columbus farewell here, and from 1490 to 1821 it served as a headquarters for the Inquisition. Its walls enclose a magnificent garden with terraced flower beds, fish ponds, and fountains. Inside, the museum displays first-century Roman mosaics and a third-century Roman marble sarcophagus. *(☎957 42 01 51. Open July-Aug. 8:30am-2:30pm; May-June and Sept. Tu-Sa 10am-2pm and 5:30-7:30pm, Su and holidays 9:30am-2:30pm; Oct.-Apr. Tu-Sa 10am-2pm and 4:30-6:30pm, Su and holidays 9:30am-2:30pm. €2, students €1.)*

MUSEO TAURINO Y DE ARTE CORDOBÉS. Dedicated to the history and lore of the bullfight, the museum features a replica of the tomb of Manolete, Spain's most famous matador, and the hide of the bull that killed him. *(Pl. Maimonides. ☎957 20 10 56. Last entrance 15min. before close. Open July-Aug. Tu-Sa 8:30am-2:30pm, Su 9:30am-2:30pm. Sept.-June Tu-Sa 10am-2pm and 5:30-7:30pm, Su 9:30am-2:30pm. €3, students €1.50, seniors and F free.)*

MUSEO DIOCESANO DE BELLAS ARTES. See where Córdoba's bishops lived as the Inquisition raged from within the Alcázar. This 17th-century ecclesiastical palace houses a modest collection of Renaissance and Baroque religious art. *(C. Torrijos 12, across from the Mezquita in the Palacio de Congresos. ☎/fax 957 49 60 85. Open July-Aug. M-F 9:30am-3pm, Sa 9:30am-1:30pm; Sept-June M-F 9:30am-1:30pm and 2-6pm, Sa 9:30am-1:30pm. €1.20, under 12 free, free with admission to Mezquita.)*

OUTSIDE THE JUDERÍA

MUSEO JULIO ROMERO DE TORRES. Spice up your life with a visit to an exhibit of Romero's sensual portraits of Cordoban women, located in the artist's former home. Only the Andalucian sun gets any hotter than this. *(Pl. Potro, 5-10min. from the Mezquita. ☎957 49 19 09. Open May-Sept. Tu-Sa 10am-2pm and 5:30-7:30pm, Su and holidays 9:30am-2:30pm. Last entrance 30min. before closing. €3, students €1.50, F free.)*

PALACIO DEL MARQUÉS DE VIANA. This elegant 14th-century palace displays 12 quintessential Córdoban patios complete with sprawling gardens and majestic fountains, as well as tapestries, furniture, and porcelain. *(Pl. Don Gome 2. 20min. walk from the Mezquita. ☎957 49 67 41. Open mid-June to Sept. M-Sa 9am-2pm; Oct.-May M-F 10am-1pm and 4-6pm, Sa 10am-1pm; closed June 1-16. Complete tour €6, garden and courtyards only €3. Guided group tours included with admission.)*

OTHER SIGHTS. Near the Palacio del Marqués de Viana, in Pl. Capuchinos (a.k.a. Pl. Dolores) and next to the monastery is the **Cristo de los Faroles** (Christ of the Lanterns). This is one of the most famous religious icons in Spain and is the site of frequent all-night vigils. The eight lanterns that are lit at night symbolize the eight provinces of Andalucía. Facing the Museo Julio Romero de Torres is the **Posada del Potro,** a 14th-century inn mentioned in *Don Quixote.* Crossing the river from the Mezquita is the Puente Romano, a restored Roman bridge used by pedestrians. It passes through a natural bird sanctuary on its way to the **Torre de la Calahorra,** a Muslim military tower built in 1369 to protect the bridge; the tower now houses a museum dedicated to Córdoban culture during the Middle Ages. (Open daily 10am-2pm and 4:30-8:30pm. €3.60, students €2.40, audio-tour €3.60.)

ENTERTAINMENT AND NIGHTLIFE

For the latest cultural events, pick up a free copy of the *Guía del Ocio* at the tourist office. Hordes of tourists flock to see the flamenco dancers at the **Tablao Cardenal,** C. Torrijos 10, facing the Mezquita. The price is high, but a bargain compared to similar shows in Sevilla and Madrid. (€18, includes 1 drink. Shows M-Sa 10:30pm.) **La Bulería,** C. Pedro López 3, is even less expensive. (€11, includes 1 drink. Daily 10:30pm.) Close to town is **Soul,** C. Alfonso XIII 3, a hip and relaxed bar with cozy tables and dreadlock-sporting bartenders. (Beer €1.20, mixed drinks €3.60. Open daily 9am-3am; closed July-Aug.) Starting in June, the **Barrio Brillante,** uphill from Av. de América, is packed with young, well-dressed *Cordobeses* hopping between packed outdoor bars and dance clubs. Bus #10 goes to Brillante from the train station until about 11pm, but the bars don't wake up until around 1am (most stay open until 4am); a taxi ride should cost €3-6. If you're walking, head up Av. Brillante, passing along the way **Pub BSO,** C. Llanos de Pretorio, with **Brujas Bar** right around the corner. Once in Barrio Brillante, where C. Poeta Emilia Prados meets C. Poeta Juan Ramón Jiménez, stop at **Cafetería Terra** before hitting the bars. Along Av. Brillante runs a string of popular nightclubs, including **Pub La Moncloa, Club Don Luis,** and **Club Kachoamba.** During the winter months, nightlife shifts to the pubs surrounding the Universidad de Córdoba, mostly on C. Antonio Maura and C. Camino de los Sastres.

Of Córdoba's festivals, floats, and parades, **Semana Santa** in early April is the most extravagant. During the **Festival de los Patios** in the first two weeks of May, the city erupts with classical music concerts, flamenco dances, and a city-wide patio-decorating contest. Late May brings the **Feria de Nuestra Señora de la Salud** *(La Feria)*, a week of colorful garb, live dancing, and nonstop drinking.

DAYTRIPS FROM CÓRDOBA

MADINAT AL-ZAHRA

Reaching Madinat Al-Zahra takes some effort if you don't go with an organized tour. The O-1 bus leaves from Av. República Argentina in Córdoba for Cruce Medina Azahara; from there you can walk 45min. to the palace. (☎957 25 57 00; 10min. past every hr., €0.80.) On the way back, the bus stop is along the highway at the cross, on the opposite side of the street from the gas station. A complete tour of the ruins takes 20-45min. depending on your level of interest. (☎957 32 91 30. Open May to mid-Sept. Tu-Sa 10am-8:30pm, Su 10am-2pm; mid-Sept. to Apr. Tu-Su 10am-2pm. €1.50, EU citizens free.) ***Córdoba Vision,*** *Av. Doctor Flemming 10, offers transportation and a 2½hr. guided visit to the site in English. (☎957 76 02 41. €18.)*

Built in the **Sierra Morena** mountain range by Abderramán III for his favorite wife, Azahara, this 10th-century medina was considered one of the greatest palaces of its time. The site, long thought to be mythical, was discovered in the mid-19th century and excavated in the early 20th-century. Today it's one of Spain's most impressive archaeological finds. The Medina Azahara is divided into three terraces: one for the nobility, another for servants, and a third for an enclosed garden and almond grove. After moving from Granada, Azahara missed the Sierra Nevada. To appease her, Abderramán planted the white-blossoming almond groves as a substitute for her beloved snow.

OTHER DAYTRIPS FROM CÓRDOBA

CÁDIZ. This city offers a little of everything to its visitors—a metropolis trimmed by golden sand beaches (see p. 888).

MÁLAGA. Known more for its bars than its untouched sands, Málaga has the requisite beachtown monuments and a welcoming modern atmosphere (see p. 903).

SPAIN

GIBRALTAR

PHONE CODE	☎350 from the UK or the US; ☎9567 from Spain.

From the morning mist just off the southern shore of Spain emerges the Rock of Gibraltar. Bastion of empire, Jerusalem of Anglophilia, this rocky peninsula is among history's most contested plots of land. Ancient seafarers called "Gib" one of the Pillars of Hercules, believing it marked the end of the world. After numerous squabbles between Moors, Spaniards, and Turks, the English successfully stormed Gibraltar in 1704 and have remained in possession ever since.

TRANSPORTATION AND PRACTICAL INFORMATION. **Buses** arrive in the Spanish border town of **La Línea** from: Algeciras (40min., every 30min., €1.50); Cádiz (3hr., 4 per day, €10); and Granada (5-6hr., 2 per day, €17). From the bus station, walk directly toward the Rock; the border is 5min. away. After bypassing the line of motorists, Spanish customs, and Gibraltar's passport control, catch bus #9 or 10 or walk across the airport tarmac and along the highway into town (20min.). Stay left on Av. Winston Churchill when the road forks at Corral Lane; Gibraltar's **Main Street,** a commercial strip lined with most services, begins at the far end of a square, on the left.

The **tourist office,** Duke of Kent House, Cathedral Sq., is across the park from the Gibraltar Museum. (☎450 00; tourism@gibraltar.gi. Open M-F 9am-5:30pm.) Although **euros** are accepted most everywhere (except pay phones and public establishments), the **pound sterling (£)** is preferred. Merchants sometimes charge a higher price in euros than in the pound's exchange equivalent. Change is often given in English currency rather than euros. As of press date, **1£ = €1.58.**

SIGHTS. About halfway up the Rock is the infamous **Apes' Den,** where barbary monkeys cavort on the sides of rocks, the tops of taxis, and the heads of tourists. At the northern tip of the Rock facing Spain are the **Great Siege Tunnels.** Originally used to fend off a combined Franco-Spanish siege at the end of the American Revolution, the underground tunnels were later expanded during World War II to span 33 miles. The eerie chambers of **St. Michael's Cave,** located 0.5km from the siege tunnels, were cut into the rock by thousands of years of water erosion. (Cable car to above sights every 10min. 9:30am-5:15pm. Combined ticket, including one-way cable car ride £7/€11, children £5/€8.15.)

ACCOMMODATIONS AND FOOD. Gibraltar is best done as a daytrip. The few accommodations in the area are often full, especially in the summer, and camping is illegal. **Emile Youth Hostel Gibraltar ❷,** Montague Bastian, off Line Wall Rd., has cramped bunkbeds in cheerfully painted rooms with clean communal bathrooms. (☎511 06. Breakfast included. Lock-out 10:30am-4:30pm. Dorms £12/€19; singles £15/€24; doubles £27/€44.) International restaurants are easy to find, but you may choke on the prices. **The Viceroy of India ❸** serves fabulous Indian food. (Entrees £4-10. Open M-F noon-3pm and 7-11pm, Sa 7-11pm. MC/V). As a back-up, there's the **Checkout** supermarket on Main St., next to Marks & Spencer. (Open M-F 8:30am-8pm, Sa 10am-6pm, Su 1am-3pm. MC/V.)

ALGECIRAS ☎956

Hidden beyond Algeciras's seedy port is a more serene old neighborhood, worthy of a visit for those with a few hours to spare. However, for most itinerary-bound travelers, this is a city seen only in transit. RENFE **trains** (☎902 24 02 02) run from C. Juan de la Cierva to Granada (4hr., 3 per day, €15) and Ronda (1½hr., 4 per day,

€6). Empresa Portillo **buses** (☎956 65 43 04) leave from Av. Virgen del Carmen 15 for: Córdoba (6hr., 3-4 per day, €18); Granada (5hr., 4 per day, €16); Málaga (3hr., 8-9 per day, €8.70); and Marbella (1hr., 8-9 per day, €5). Transportes Generales Comes (☎956 65 34 56) goes from C. San Bernardo 1 to Cádiz (2½hr., 6 per day, €8). La Línea runs to: Gibraltar (45min., every 30min. 7am-9:30pm, €1.50); Madrid (8hr., 4 per day, €22); and Sevilla (4hr., 4 per day, €14). To get to the **ferries** from the bus and train stations, follow C. San Bernardo to C. Juan de la Cierva and turn left at the end of the street; the port entrance will be on your right. The **tourist office** is on C. Juan de la Cierva. (☎956 57 26 36. Open M-F 9am-2pm.) Hostels cluster around **Calle José Santacana.** To get to **Hostal Rif ❶,** C. Rafael de Muro 11, follow C. Santacana into the market square, bear left around the kiosk, and continue one block up C. Rafael del Muro. (☎956 65 49 53. Singles €8; doubles €17.) **Postal code:** 11203.

GRANADA ☎958

Legend says that in 1492, when Moorish ruler Boabdil fled Granada, the last Muslim stronghold in Spain, his mother berated him for casting a longing look back at the Alhambra. Today, the spectacular palace celebrated by poets and artists throughout the ages continues to inspire melancholy in those who must leave its timeless beauty. Although Christians torched all the mosques and much of the lower city, embers of Granada's Arab essence still linger. The Albaicín, an enchanting maze of Moorish houses and twisting alleys, is Spain's best-preserved Arab quarter and the only part of the Muslim city to survive the *Reconquista*.

TRANSPORTATION

Flights: Airport (☎958 24 52 37), 17km west of the city. An **Autocares J. Gonzales** bus (☎958 13 13 09) runs to the airport from Gran Vía, in front of the cathedral (5 per day 8am-7pm, €3). A **taxi** to the airport costs €15.

Trains: RENFE Station, Av. Andaluces (☎902 24 02 02). To: **Algeciras** (5-7hr., 3 per day 7:15am-5:50pm, €16); **Madrid** (5-6hr., 8am and 4:40pm, €26-32); **Sevilla** (4-5hr., 4 per day 8am-8pm, €16).

Buses: Major bus routes originate at the **bus station** on the outskirts of Granada on Ctra. Madrid, near C. Arzobispo Pedro de Castro. **Alsina Graells** (☎958 18 54 80) runs to **Córdoba** (3hr., 10 per day 7:30am-8pm, €10) and **Sevilla** (3hr., 9 per day 8am-3am, €15). **La Línea** runs to **Algeciras** (5hr., 6 per day 9am-8pm, €16) and **Madrid** (5hr., 14 per day 7am-1:30am, €12.50). **Bacoma** (☎958 15 75 57) goes to **Alicante** (6hr., 5 per day, €21); **Barcelona** (14hr., 3 per day, €50); and **Valencia** (8hr., 4 per day, €30). All Bacoma buses run 10:15am-1:45am.

Public Transportation: From the bus station, bus #10 runs to the youth hostel, C. de Ronda, C. Recogidas, and C. Acera de Darro; bus #3 goes to Av. Constitución, Gran Vía, and Pl. Isabel la Católica. From Pl. Nueva catch #30 to the Alhambra or #31 to the Albaicin. Rides €0.85, *bonobus* (10 tickets) €5. Free map at tourist office.

Car Rental: Atasa, Pl. Cuchilleros 1 (☎958 22 40 04). Cheapest car €276 per week with unlimited mileage and insurance. Prices rise with shorter rentals. Must be at least 20 and have had a license for at least 1 year.

ORIENTATION AND PRACTICAL INFORMATION

The geographic center is the small **Plaza de Isabel la Católica,** at the intersection of the city's two main arteries, **Calle de los Reyes Católicos** and **Gran Vía de Colón.** To reach Gran Vía and the **cathedral** from the train station, walk three blocks up Av. Andaluces and take bus #3-6, 9, or 11 from Av. Constitución; from the bus station, take bus #3.

Two blocks uphill on C. Reyes Católicos sits **Plaza Nueva.** Downhill on C. Reyes Católicos lies Pl. Carmen, site of the **Ayuntamiento** and Puerta Real. The **Alhambra** commands the steep hill above Pl. Nueva.

Tourist Office: Oficina Provincial, Pl. Mariana Pineda 10 (☎958 24 71 28; www.dipgra.es). From Pta. Real, turn right onto C. Angel Ganivet, then take a right 2 blocks later to reach the plaza. Open M-F 9am-8pm, Sa 10am-7pm, Su 10am-4pm.

American Express: C. Reyes Católicos 31 (☎958 22 45 12), between Pl. Isabel la Católica and Pta. Real. Open M-F 9am-1:30pm and 2-9pm, Sa 10am-2pm and 3-7pm.

Luggage Storage: At the train and bus stations. €2.40. Open daily 4-9pm.

Laundromat: C. La Paz 19. From Pl. Trinidad, take C. Alhóndiga, turn right on C. La Paz, and walk 2 blocks. Wash €3, dry €0.90 per 15min. Open M-F 9:30am-2pm and 4:30-8:30pm, Sa 9am-2pm.

Emergency: ☎112. **Police:** C. Duquesa 21 (☎958 24 81 00). English spoken.

Pharmacy: Farmacia Gran Vía, Gran Vía 6 (☎958 22 29 90). Open M-F 9:30am-2pm and 5-8:30pm.

Medical Assistance: Clínica de San Cecilio, C. Dr. Oloriz 16 (☎958 28 02 00 or 27 20 00), on the road to Jaén. **Ambulance:** ☎958 28 44 50.

Internet Access: Net (☎958 22 69 19) has 3 locations: C. Santa Escolástica 13, up C. Pavaneras from Pl. Isabel la Católica; Pl. de los Girones 3, 1 block from the first locale; and C. Buensucesco 22, 1 block from Pl. Trinidad. €1.20 per hr. All open M-Sa 9am-1am, Su 3pm-1am.

Post Office: Pta. Real (☎958 22 48 35; fax 22 36 41), on the corner of Carrera del Darro and C. Angel Ganinet. **Lista de Correos** and **fax** service. Open M-F 8am-9pm, Sa 9:30am-2pm. Wires money M-F 8:30am-2:30pm. **Postal Code:** 18009.

ACCOMMODATIONS

Near **Plaza Nueva,** hostels line Cuesta de Gomérez, the street leading uphill to the Alhambra. The area around C. Mesones and C. Alhóndiga is close to the cathedral; hostels cluster around **Plaza Trinidad,** at the end of C. Mesones as you approach from Pta. Real. More hostels are along **Gran Vía.** Call ahead during *Semana Santa.*

Hostal Venecia, Cuesta de Gomérez 2, 3rd fl. (☎958 22 39 87). Wake up to a soothing cup of tea, candles, and a hint of incense. Singles €14; doubles, triples, and quads €13 per person. ❶

IN RECENT NEWS

GITANO GENES

Ever since *Gitanos* (gypsies) arrived in Spain from India in the 15th century, they have faced discrimination, assimilation, and expulsion.

About 600,000 *Gitanos* (who are credited with the creation of flamenco) reside in Spain, nearly half of them in Andalucía. Most live in rural areas below the poverty line; an average *Gitano* is five times poorer than the rest of the population. School absenteeism is common, and the group's literacy rate is among the lowest in Spain. Unfortunately, slow transfer of funds for reform programs and a lack of cooperation among officials have largely stymied efforts to change the status quo.

The *Gitano* situation has improved only slightly since the 1978 constitution, which granted equal rights to the group. It's a sensitive issue because the government hopes to integrate *Gitanos* into modern Spanish life without compromising their traditions; a task that could prove difficult.

In 1999, a new parliamentary commission was created to address the issue, and results have been promising. *Gitanos* are pursuing vocational educations, and programs fostering better relations among all Spanish people has had some success.

However, a recent influx of immigrants from North Africa has negatively impacted the *Gitano;* these immigrants have adopted Spanish ways and risen up the socioeconomic ladder quickly, which has left many *Gitanos* feeling frustrated about their prospects for advancement.

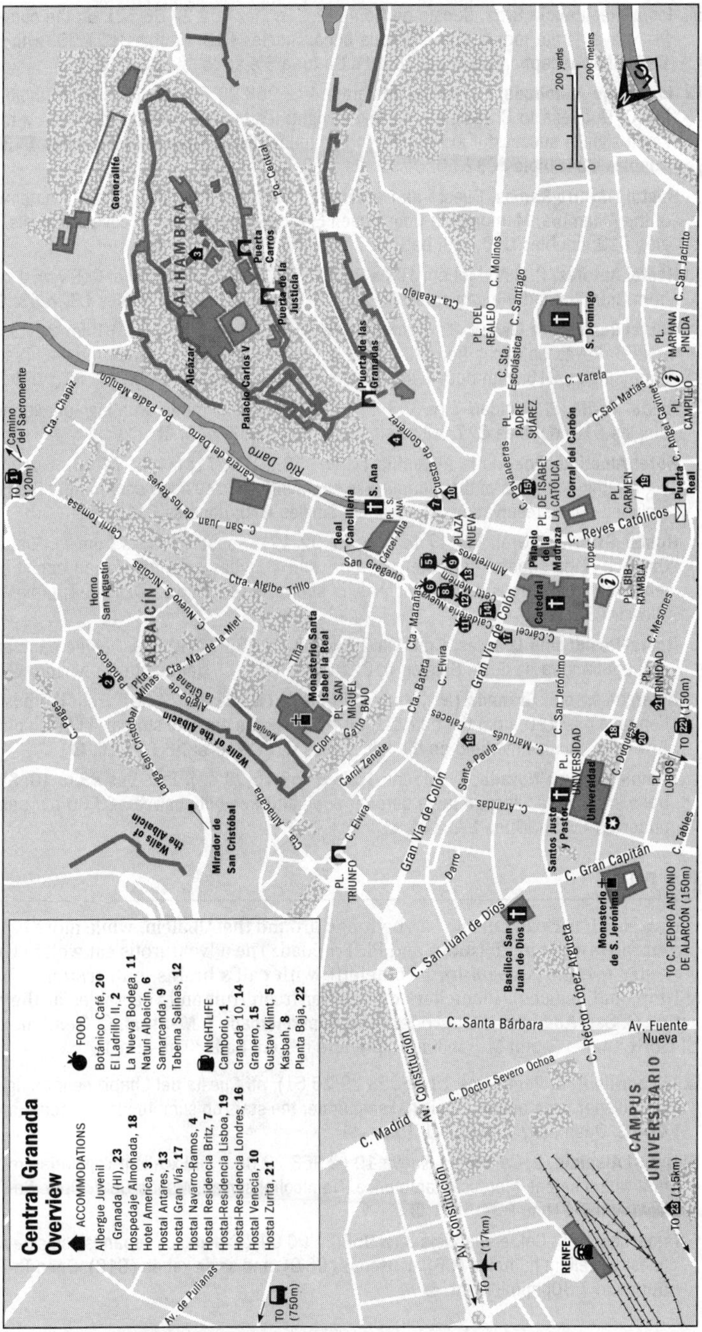
Central Granada Overview
ACCOMMODATIONS
Albergue Juvenil Granada (HI), 23
Hospedaje Almohada, 18
Hotel America, 3
Hostal Antares, 13
Hostal Gran Vía, 17
Hostal Navarro-Ramos, 4
Hostal Residencia Britz, 7
Hostal-Residencia Lisboa, 19
Hostal-Residencia Londres, 16
Hostal Venecia, 10
Hostal Zurita, 21
FOOD
Botánico Café, 20
El Ladrillo II, 2
La Nueva Bodega, 11
Naturi Albaicín, 6
Samarcanda, 9
Taberna Salinas, 12
NIGHTLIFE
Camborio, 1
Granada 10, 14
Granero, 15
Gustav Klimt, 5
Kasbah, 8
Planta Baja, 22
ALHAMBRA
Generalife
Alcázar
Palacio Carlos V
Puerta Carros
Puerta de la Justicia
Puerta de las Granadas
ALBAICÍN
Walls of the Albaicín
Mirador de San Cristóbal
Monasterio Santa Isabel la Real
Real Cancillería
S. Ana
PLAZA NUEVA
Catedral
Palacio de la Madraza
Corral del Carbón
S. Domingo
Basílica San Juan de Dios
Monasterio de S. Jerónimo
Santos Justo y Pastor
Universidad
Puerta Real
CAMPUS UNIVERSITARIO
RENFE
Río Darro
Gran Vía de Colón
C. Reyes Católicos
C. San Juan de Dios
C. Gran Capitán
Av. Constitución
C. Madrid
C. Doctor Severo Ochoa
C. Rector López Argueta
C. Santa Bárbara
Av. Fuente Nueva
Av. de Pulianas
Camino del Sacromonte
Cuesta de Gomérez
Carrera del Darro
TO C. PEDRO ANTONIO DE ALARCÓN (150m)
0 200 yards
0 200 meters

Hostal Residencia Britz, Cuesta de Gomérez 1 (☎/fax 958 22 36 52), on the corner of Pl. Nueva. Large rooms with luxurious beds. Singles €18; doubles €27.50, with bath €38. Show reception your copy of Let's Go for a 6% discount. MC/V. ❷

Hospedaje Almohada, C. Postigo de Zarate 4 (☎958 20 74 46). From Pl. Trinidad, follow C. Duquesa to C. Málaga and take a right; it's the red door on your right with the small sign. A successful experiment in communal living. Dorms €11; singles €13.50; doubles €24; triples €32.50. Discounts available for stays over 1 week. ❶

Hostal Navarro-Ramos, Cuesta de Gomérez 21 (☎958 25 05 55), near the outer walls of the Alhambra. Memorabilia from Queen Elizabeth's silver jubilee cover the walls. Singles €10; doubles €16, with bath €27; triples with bath €36. ❶

Hostal Antares, C. Cetti Meriém 10 (☎958 22 83 13), on the corner of C. Elvira, 1 block from Gran Vía and the cathedral. Singles €18; doubles €30-45; triples €32-€63. ❷

Hostal-Residencia Lisboa, Pl. Carmen 29 (☎958 22 14 13 or 22 14 14; fax 22 14 87). Take C. Reyes Católicos from Pl. Isabel la Católica; Pl. Carmen is on the left. TVs and fans. Singles €16, with bath €24; doubles €24/€35; triples €32/€47. MC/V. ❷

Hostal Zurita, Pl. Trinidad 7 (☎958 27 50 20). Beautiful rooms with high-quality beds. Singles €15; doubles €27, with bath €33; triples €39/€45. ❷

Hotel America, Real de la Alhambra 53 (☎958 22 74 71; fax 22 74 70). Spend the night within the walls of the Alhambra in charming, spacious and cozy rooms. Breakfast included. Make reservations in advance. Singles €70; doubles €110. ❺

Hostal Gran Vía, Gran Vía 17 (☎958 27 92 12), about 4 blocks from Pl. Isabel la Católica. Pink sheets, polyester curtains, and religious art make for an eclectic but remarkably congruous decor. Singles with shower €18; doubles €21/€24; triples with shower €36. ❷

Hostal-Residencia Londres, Gran Vía 29, 6th fl. (☎958 27 80 34). Golden panoramas of the Alhambra by dusk. Singles €18; doubles €21; €9 per additional person. ❷

Albergue Juvenil Granada (HI), Ramón y Cajal 2 (☎958 00 29 00). From the bus station take bus #10, from the train station #11; ask the driver to stop at "El Estadio de la Juventud." Across the field on the left. Dorms €10-12, over 26 €14-16. ❶

Camping: Sierra Nevada, Av. Madrid 107 (☎958 15 00 62). Take bus #3 or 10. Shady trees, modern facilities, a large outdoor pool, and free hot showers. €3.80 per person, under 10 €3.15. Open Mar.-Oct. ❶

FOOD

Cheap North African cuisine can be found around the Albaicín, while more typical *menú* fare awaits in Pl. Nueva and Pl. Trinidad. The adventurous eat well in Granada—try *tortilla sacromonte* (omelette with calf's brains, bull testicles, ham, shrimp, and veggies). Picnickers can gather fresh fruit and vegetables at the **market** on C. San Augustín. Get groceries at **Supermercado T. Mariscal,** C. Genil, next to El Corte Inglés (open M-F 9:30am-2pm and 5-9pm, Sa 9:30am-2pm).

El Ladrillo II, C. Panaderos 13 (☎958 29 26 51), off Cuesta del Chapiz near the Iglesia El Salvador, high on the Albaicín. Feast under the stars on sumptuous seafood. Entrees €6-12. Open daily 12:30pm-1:30am. ❸

Naturi Albaicín, C. Calderería Nueva 10 (☎958 22 06 27). Excellent vegetarian restaurant with a serene Moroccan ambience. No alcohol served. *Menús* €5-7. Open Sa-Th 1-4pm and 7-11pm, F 7-11pm. ❷

Samarcanda, C. Caldereria Vieja 3 (☎958 21 00 04). Experience Lebanese cuisine at its finest. Excellent hummus (€6), couscous (€6-9), and shish kebab (€10). Open Th-Tu 1-5pm and 7:30pm-midnight. ❷

Taberna Salinas, C. Elvira 13 (☎958 22 14 11). Choose from a wide selection of grilled meats and seafood (€9-11) at this rustic tavern. Open daily 12:30pm-2am. ❸

Botánico Café, C. Málaga 3 (☎958 27 15 98), 2 blocks from Pl. Trinidad. Student hangout where a fusion of Manhattan minimalism and Spanish modernity brings new life to old favorites. Entrees €5-9. Open M-Th 10am-3am, Su noon-1am. ❷

La Nueva Bodega, C. Cetti Meriém 9 (☎958 22 59 34), out of Pl. Nueva on a small side street off C. Elvira. Dine on hearty and well-priced traditional cuisine. *Menús* €6-7. *Bocadillos* €1.65. Open daily noon-midnight. ❶

SIGHTS

THE ALHAMBRA. From the streets of Granada, the Alhambra appears simple, blocky, and faded; up close, it's an elaborate and detailed piece of architecture, magically uniting water, light, wood, stucco, and ceramics to create a fortress-palace of rich aesthetics and symbolic grandeur. The age-old saying holds true: "If you have died without seeing the Alhambra, you have not lived." The first Nasrid King Alhamar built the fortress **Alcazaba,** to protect his city from highwaymen and Christian raiders. A dark, spiraling staircase leads to the **Torre de la Vela** (watchtower), where visitors get a 360-degree view of Granada and the surrounding mountains. Follow signs to the *Palacio Nazaries* to see the stunningly ornate **Alcázar,** a 14th-century royal palace full of dripping stalactite archways, multicolored tiles, and sculpted fountains. Fernando and Isabel restored the Alcázar after they drove the Moors from Spain, but two generations later, Emperor Carlos V demolished part of it to make way for his **Palacio de Carlos V;** although glaringly incongruous with such Moorish splendor, many consider it one of the most beautiful Renaissance buildings in Spain. Over a bridge are the vibrant blossoms, towering cypresses, and streaming waterways of **El Generalife,** the sultan's vacation retreat. *(To reach the Alhambra, take C. Cuesta de Gomérez off Pl. Nueva, and be prepared to pant (20min.; no unauthorized cars 9am-9pm). Or take the cheap, quick Alhambra-Neptuno microbus (every 5min., €0.80) from Pl. Nueva. ☎958 22 15 03. Open Apr.-Sept. daily 8:30am-8pm; Oct.-Mar. M-Sa 9am-5:45pm. Nighttime visits June-Sept. Tu, Th, and Sa 10-11:30pm; Oct.-May Sa 8-10pm. All visits €7. Limited to 7700 visitors per day June-Sept., 6300 Oct.-May, so get there early to stand in line. Enter the Palace of the Nasrids (Alcázar) during the time specified on your ticket. It is possible to reserve tickets a few days in advance at banks for a €0.75 service charge. Reservations are also possible by phone ☎902 22 44 60.)*

THE ALBAICÍN. A labyrinth of steep streets and narrow alleys, the Albaicín was the only Moorish neighborhood to escape the torches of the *Reconquista,* and it remains a quintessential part of Granada. After the fall of the Alhambra, a small Muslim population remained here until their expulsion in the 17th century. The abundance of North African cuisine and the recent construction of a mosque near Pl. San Nicolás attests to the persistence of Islamic influence in Andalucía. Spectacular sunsets over the surrounding mountains can be seen from C. Cruz de Quirós, above C. Elvira. Although generally safe, the Albaicín is disorienting and should be approached with caution at night. *(Bus #12 runs from beside the cathedral to C. Pagés at the top of the Albaicín.)*

OTHER SIGHTS. Downhill from the Alhambra's Arab splendor, the **Capilla Real,** Fernando and Isabel's private chapel, exemplifies Christian Granada. The sacristy shelters Isabel's private art collection, the first Christian banner to flutter in triumph over the Alhambra, and the glittering royal jewels. *(Both open daily M-Sa 10:30am-1pm and 2-7pm, Su 11am-1pm and 4-7pm. €2.50.)* Fernando and Isabel began the construction of the adjacent **cathedral** in 1523 upon the foundation of an Arab mosque. It wasn't completed, however, until 1704. The first purely Renaissance cathedral in Spain, its Corinthian pillars support an astonishing 45m vaulted nave. *(Open Apr.-Sept. M-Sa 10:45am-1:30pm and 4-7pm, Su 4-7pm; Oct.-Mar. M-Sa 10:30am-1:30pm and 3:30-6:30pm, Su 11am-1:30pm. €2.50.)*

ENTERTAINMENT AND NIGHTLIFE

Entertainment listings are at the back of the daily paper, the *Ideal,* under *Cine y Espectáculos;* the Friday supplement lists bars and special events. The *Guía del Ocio*, sold at newsstands (€0.85), lists clubs, pubs, and cafés. The most boisterous nightspots can be found on **Calle Pedro Antonio de Alarcón,** running from Pl. Albert Einstein to Ancha de Gracia, while hip new bars and clubs line **Calle Elvira** from Cárcel to C. Cedrán. The most "authentic" flamenco performances, which change monthly, are advertised on posters around town. Gay bars cluster around Carrera del Darro; a complete list of gay clubs and bars is available at the tourist office.

Camborio, Camino del Sacromonte 48, a 20min. walk uphill from Pl. Nueva. Gypsies and highwaymen once roamed the caves of Sacromonte; now scantily clad clubbers do the same. €4.20 cover F-Sa. Beer €1.80-3. Open Tu-Sa 11pm-dawn.

Granero, Pl. Luis Rosales, near Pl. Isabel Católica. A New Age loft filled with grooving Spanish yuppies. Salsa and Spanish pop pervade. Beer €2.40, mixed drinks €3-4.20. Open daily 10pm-dawn.

Planta Baja, C. Horno de Abad 11. Live bands play regularly within the concrete confines of this techno dance club. Open from fall until early July, Th-Sa 10pm-6am.

Granada 10, C. Carcel Baja 3. Movie theater by evening, raging dance club by night. Cover Th-Sa €6, includes 1 drink. Open daily.

Kasbah, C. Caldereria Nueva 4. Relax amidst Oriental comforts and scented candles. Silky pillows and romantic nooks abound. Arab pastries compliment an exhaustive selection of Moroccan teas (€0.80). Open daily 3pm-3am.

Gustav Klimt, C. Imprenta 3. Post-impressionist decor with posters of "The Kiss" on all the walls make this a popular "pick-up" place. Beer €2. Open daily 4pm-4am.

Eshavira, C. Postigo de la Cuna. A smoky, intimate setting awaits. The place to go for flamenco and jazz. Call ☎958 29 08 29 for a schedule. 1 drink min.

HIKING AND SKIING NEAR GRANADA: SIERRA NEVADA

The peaks of **Mulhacén** (3481m) and **Veleta** (3470m), Spain's highest, sparkle with snow and buzz with tourists for most of the year. **Ski** season runs from December to April. The rest of the year, tourists hike, parasail, and take jeep tours. Call **Cetursa** (☎958 24 91 11) for information on outdoor activities. The Autocares Bonal bus (☎958 27 31 00) runs between the bus station in Granada and Veleta. (9am departure, 5pm return; €5.40).

COSTA DEL SOL

The Costa del Sol mixes natural beauty with chic promenades and swank hotels. While some spots have been over-developed and can be hard on the wallet, the coast's stunning natural beauty has been left untouched in lesser-known areas. Summer brings swarms of tourists, but nothing takes away from the main attraction: eight months of spring and four months of summer. June is the best time to visit, after summer has hit the beach but tourists haven't.

MARBELLA ☎952

Like your vacation spots shaken, not shtirred? Scottish smoothie Sean Connery and a host of other jet-setters choose Marbella (pop. 100,000) as their vacation home. With gorgeous beaches that stretch for kilometers and a decidedly more sophisticated atmosphere than much of the Costa del Sol, it's no wonder that Marbella attracts the rich and famous. While primarily a chic resort, Marbella has a long history as an important merchant town utilized by the Phoenicians, Greeks, Romans, and Arabs. Remnants of this history can be felt in the well-preserved architecture and streets of the *casco antiguo.* Although there are more yachts than hostels, it's still possible to have a good time on a budget. The beaches beckon with 320 days of sunshine per year, but no visit would be complete without a stroll through the **casco antiguo** (old town), a maze of cobblestone streets and white-washed facades trimmed with wild roses. With 22km of **beach,** Marbella offers a variety of settings. Beaches to the east of the port are popular with British backpackers; those to the west attract a more posh crowd. City buses along Av. Richard Soriano (dir.: San Pedro; €0.90) run to chic and trendy **Puerto Banús,** where beautiful, clean beaches are buffered by white yachts. The **Museo del Grabado Español Contemporáneo,** on C. Hospital Bazán, displays engravings by Miró, Picasso, Dalí, and Goya. (Open M 10am-2pm, Tu-Sa 10am-2pm and 6-9pm; €2.50.)

Accessible only by **bus,** the station atop Av. Trapiche (☎952 76 44 00) goes to: Algeciras (1½hr., 7 per day, €5); Cádiz (4hr., 6 per day, €14); Granada (4hr., 8 per day, €12); Madrid (7½hr., 10 per day, €19); Málaga (1½hr., every 30min., €4); and Sevilla (4hr., 2-3 per day, €13). The **tourist office** is on Pl. Naranjos. (☎952 82 35 50. Open June-Aug. M-F 9:30am-9pm, Sa 10am-2pm.) The area in the *casco antiguo* around Pl. Naranjos is packed with quick-filling hostels. **Hostal del Pilar ❶,** C. Mesoncillo 4, is off C. Peral. (☎952 82 99 36. Dorms €15-20; roof mattresses €12.) The excellent **Albergue Juvenil (HI) ❶,** Av. Trapiche 2, downhill from the bus station, feels more like a hotel than a hostel. (☎952 77 14 91. Dorms €10-13, over 26 €11-17.) A **24hr. minimarket** is on the corner of C. Pablo Casals and Av. Fontanilla. Nightlife in Marbella begins and ends late. The rowdiest corner of the *casco antiguo* is where C. Mesoncillo meets C. Peral. Loud music and cheery Spaniards spill from **El Güerto,** C. Peral 9, while a mixed crowd of backpackers and locals enjoy the **The Tavern,** C. Peral 7. (Both open at 8:30pm; El Güerto opens only on weekends.) A mellow ambience suffuses the **Townhouse Bar,** C. Alamo, tucked down an alley off C. Nueva. Ask for a shot of apple pie—it ain't mama's. (Open daily at 10pm.) Many clubs and bars are located down by the port at the bottom of Av. Miguel Cano, including the waterfront **House of Silk,** and the more grungy **Loco's;** both play dance hits. **Postal Code:** 29600.

EASTERN SPAIN

Valencia's rich soil and famous orange groves, fed by Moorish irrigation systems, have earned it the nickname *Huerta de España* (Spain's Orchard). Dunes, sandbars, jagged promontories, and lagoons mark the grand coastline, while lovely fountains and pools grace carefully landscaped public gardens in Valencian cities. The famed rice dish *paella* was born in this region.

ALICANTE (ALACANT) ☎965

Sun-drenched Alicante has it all: relaxing beaches, fascinating historical sites, and an unbelievable collection of bars and port-side discos. High above the rows of bronzed beach-goers, the ancient *castillo*, spared by Franco, guards the tangle of streets in the cobblestone *casco antiguo*.

TRANSPORTATION AND PRACTICAL INFORMATION. RENFE **trains** (☎902 24 02 02) run from Estación Término on Av. Salamanca, at the end of Av. Estación, to: Barcelona (4½-6hr., 9 per day 6:55am-6:30pm, €36-62); Madrid (4hr., 9 per day 7am-8pm, €34-52); and Valencia (2hr., 10 per day 6:55am-10:20pm, €9-32). Trains from **Ferrocarriles de la Generalitat Valenciana,** Estació Marina, Av. Villajoyosa 2 (☎965 26 27 31), on Explanada d'Espanya, serve the Costa Blanca. **Buses** run from C. Portugal 17 (☎965 13 07 00), to: Barcelona (7hr., 11 per day 1am-10:30pm, €28); Granada (6hr., 7 per day 1:15am-10:45pm, €21); and Madrid (5hr., 9 per day 8am-midnight, €20-30). The **tourist office** is on Rbla. de Méndez Nuñez 23. (☎965 20 00 00. Open June-Aug. M-F 10am-8pm; Sept.-May M-F 10am-7pm, Sa 10am-2pm and 3-7pm.) Check **email** at **Yazzgo,** Explanada 3. (8am-4pm €1.50 per hr.; 4-11pm €3 per hr. Open M-Sa 8am-11pm, Su 9am-11pm.) **Postal code:** 03070.

ACCOMMODATIONS AND FOOD. The **Habitaciones México ❶,** C. General Primo de Rivera 10, off the end of Av. Alfonso X El Sabio, has a friendly atmosphere and small, cozy rooms. (☎965 20 93 07. Free Internet. Singles €12-15; doubles €27; triples €33.) **Hostal Les Monges Palace ❷,** C. San Augustín 4, behind the Ayuntamiento, in the center of the historic district, is one of the most luxurious hostels in Spain. (☎965 21 50 46. Singles €18-30; doubles €33-78; triples €42-90.) Take bus #21 to **camp** at **Playa Mutxavista ❶.** (☎965 65 45 26. June-Sept. €4 per person, €11 per tent; Oct.-May €2 per person, €7.50 per tent.)

Try the family-run *bar-restaurantes* in the *casco antiguo*, between the cathedral and the castle steps. **Kebap ❷,** C. Italia 2, serves heaping entrees of Middle Eastern cuisine. (Open daily 1-4pm and 8pm-midnight.) Buy basics at **Supermarket Mercadona,** C. Alvarez Sereix 5, off Av. Federico Soto. (Open M-Sa 9am-9pm.)

SIGHTS AND ENTERTAINMENT. The ancient Carthaginian **Castell de Santa Bárbara,** complete with drawbridges, dark passageways, and hidden tunnels, keeps silent guard over Alicante's beach. A paved road from the old section of Alicante leads to the top, but most people take the **elevator** from a hidden entrance at the end of the tunnel that begins on Av. Jovellanos, across the street from Playa Postiguet. (Castle open daily Apr.-Sept. 10am-7:30pm; Oct.-Mar. 9am-6:30pm. Free. Elevator €2.40.) Valencian Modernist art resides along with works by Miró, Picasso, Kandinsky, and Calder in the **Museu de Arte del Siglo XX La Asegurada,** Pl. Santa María 3, at the east end of C. Mayor. (Open mid-May to mid-Sept. M-F 10am-2pm and 5-9pm, Sa-Su 10:30am-2:30pm; mid-Sept. to mid-May M-F 10am-2pm and 4-8pm, Sa-Su 10:30am-2:30pm. Free.) Alicante's **Playa del Postiguet** attracts beach lovers, as do nearby **Playa de San Juan** (take TAM bus #21, 22, or 31) and **Playa del Mutxavista** (take TAM bus #21; all buses depart every 15min., €0.75). Most everyone begins the night bar-hopping in the *casco antiguo;* the complex of bars that overlook the water in Alicante's **main port** tends to fill up a little later. For an even crazier night, the **Trensnochador** night train (July-Aug. F-Sa every hr. 9pm-5am, Su-Th 4 per night 9pm-5am; round-trip €0.90-4.20) runs from Estació Marina to discotecas and other stops along the beach, where places are packed until dawn. Try **Pachá, KU, KM,** and **Space** (open nightly until 9am) at the Disco Benidorm stop. During the hedonistic **Festival de Sant Joan** (June 20-29), *fogueres* (symbolic or satiric effigies) are erected around the city and then burned in the streets.

VALENCIA ☎963

Stylish, cosmopolitan, and business-oriented, Valencia is a striking contrast to the surrounding orchards and mountain ranges. Parks and gardens soothe the city's congested environment, and nearby beaches complement its frenetic pace.

TRANSPORTATION AND PRACTICAL INFORMATION. Trains arrive at C. Xàtiva 24 (☎963 52 02 02). RENFE (24hr. ☎902 24 02 02) runs to: Alicante (2hr., 9 per day 10am-9pm, €9-25); Barcelona (3hr., 12 per day 6:35am-8:05pm, €31); and Madrid (3½hr., 9 per day 6:45am-8:15pm, €28). **Buses** (☎963 49 72 22) go from Av. Menéndez Pidal 13 to: Alicante via the Costa Blanca (4½hr., 13 per day 6:30am-6pm, €12); Barcelona (4½hr., 15 per day 1am-10pm, €19); Madrid (4hr., 13 per day 7am-3am, €21); and Sevilla (11hr., 4 per day 2:45-10:30pm, €40). Bus #8 (€0.80) connects to Pl. Ayuntamiento and the train station. Transmediterránea **ferries** (☎902 45 46 45) sail to the Balearic Islands (see p. 943).

The main **tourist office,** C. Paz 46-48, has branches at the train station and Pl. Ayuntamiento. (☎963 98 64 22. Open M-F 10am-6pm, Sa 10am-2pm.) **Internet** access is at **Ono,** C. San Vicente 22, around the corner from Pl. Ayuntamiento. (☎963 28 19 02. €1.20 per hr. Open daily 9am-1am.) The **post office** is at Pl. Ayuntamiento 24. (Open M-F 8:30am-8:30pm, Sa 9:30am-2pm.) **Postal Code:** 46080.

ACCOMMODATIONS AND FOOD. The best lodgings are around **Plaza Ayuntamiento** and **Plaza Mercado.** The **Home Youth Hostel ❶,** C. Lonja 4, is directly behind the Lonja, on a side street off Pl. Dr. Collado. Brightly painted rooms, a spacious common living room, and a kitchen create a homey atmosphere for road-weary guests. (☎963 91 62 29; www.likeathome.net. Internet €0.50 for 15min. Laundry €4. Dorms €14; singles €21; doubles €30; triples €43; quads €54.) As central as it gets, **Hostal Alicante ❷,** C. Ribera 8, is on the pedestrian street off Pl. Ayuntamiento. Its clean, well-lit rooms and firm beds are hugely popular with backpackers. (☎963 51 22 96. Singles €19, with bath €24; doubles €27/€36. MC/V.) To get to **Hostal Antigua Morellana ❸,** C. En Bou 2, walk past Pl. Dr. Collado; it's on the small streets behind the Lonja. Quiet and comfortable rooms with bath and A/C cater to an older crowd. (☎/fax 963 91 57 73. Singles €29; doubles €42.) *Paella* is the most famous of Valencia's 200 rice dishes; try as many of them as you can before leaving. Buckets of fresh fish, meat, and fruit (including Valencia's famous oranges) are sold at the **Mercado Central,** on Pl. Mercado. (Open M-F 7am-3pm.) For groceries, stop by the basement of **El Corte Inglés,** C. Colon, or the fifth floor of the C. Pintor Sorilla building. (Open M-Sa 10am-10pm.)

SIGHTS. Touring Valencia on foot is a good test of stamina. Most of the sights line Río Turia or cluster near Pl. Reina, which is linked to Pl. Ayuntamiento by C. San Vicente Mártir. EMT bus #5, dubbed the **Bus Turistic,** makes a loop around the old town sights (€0.80; 1-day pass €3). Head toward the beach along the riverbed off C. Alcalde Reig. or take bus #35 from Pl. Ayuntamiento to reach the modern, airy, and thoroughly fascinating **Ciudad de las artes y las ciencias** (City of arts and sciences). This mini-city has created quite a stir; it's become the fourth biggest tourist destination in Spain. The complex is divided into four large attractions, only two of which are currently completed: **Palau de les Arts** and **L'Oceanografic** will not open until at least 2004. The **Museu de Les Ciencias Principe Felipe** is an interactive playground for science and technology fiends; **L'Hemisfèric** has an IMAX theater and planetarium. (www.cac.es. Museum open daily 10am-8pm. €6, M-F students €4.20. IMAX shows €6.60, M-F students €4.80.) The 13th-century **cathedral,** in Pl. Reina, was built on the site of an Arab mosque. The **Museo de la Catedral** squeezes a great many treasures into three tiny rooms. (Cathedral open in summer daily 8am-2pm and 5-8pm; in off-season closes earlier. Free. Tower open daily 10am-1pm and 4:30-7pm. €1.20. Museum open June-Sept. M-F 10am-1pm and 4:30-6pm, Sa-Su 10am-1pm; Oct.-May closes 1hr. earlier. €1.20.) Across the river, the **Museu Provincial de Belles Artes,** on C. Sant Pius V, displays superb 14th- to 16th-century Valencian art. Its collection includes El Greco's *San Juan Bautista,* Velázquez's self-portrait, and a slew of Goyas. (Open Tu-Sa 10am-2:15pm and 4-7:30pm, Su 10am-7:30pm. Free.) West across the old river, the **Instituto València de Arte Moderno (IVAM),** C. Guillem de Castro 118, has works by 20th-century sculptor Julio González. (Open Tu-Su 10am-7pm. €2.10, students €1, Su free.)

ENTERTAINMENT AND NIGHTLIFE. The most popular **beaches** are **Las Arenas** and **Malvarrosa**—buses #20, 21, 22, and 23 all pass through. To get to the more attractive **Salér,** 14km from the center of town, take an Autobuses Buñol **bus** (☎963 49 14 25) from the corner of Gran Vía Germanias and C. Sueca (25min., every 30min. 7am-10pm, €0.90). Bars and pubs abound in the **El Carme district.** Follow C. Bolsería out of Pl. Mercado, bearing right at the fork, to guzzle *agua de Valencia* (orange juice, champagne, and vodka) in **Pl. Tossal.** The loud **Cafe Negrito,** Pl. del Negrito 1, off C. Caballeros, is wildly popular with locals. (Pitcher of *agua de Valencia* €6. Open daily 10pm-3am.) **Rumbo 144,** Av. Blasco Ibañez 144, plays a wide variety of music, from Spanish pop to house. (Cover €6-8. Open F-Su midnight-7am.) For more information, consult the *Qué y Dónde* weekly magazine (€0.90), available at newsstands, or the weekly entertainment supplement *La Cartelera* (€0.75). The most famed festival in Valencia is **Las Fallas** (Mar. 12-19), which culminates with the burning of gigantic (up to 30m) papier-maché effigies of Spanish political figures.

COSTA BLANCA

You could while away a lifetime touring the charming resort towns of the Costa Blanca. The "white coast" that extends through Dénia, Calpe, and Alicante derives its name from its fine white sands. ALSA **buses** (☎902 42 22 42) run from Valencia to: Alicante (4½hr., 13 per day 6:30am-6pm, €12); Altea and Calpe (3-3½hr., 12 per day 6:30am-6pm, €8); and Gandía (1hr., 13 per day 6:30am-9:15pm, €5). From Alicante, buses run to Altea (1¼hr., 18 per day 6:30am-9pm, €4) and Calpe (1½hr., 18 per day 6:30am-9pm, €4). Going to **Calpe** (Calp) is like stepping into a Dalí landscape. The town cowers beneath the **Peñó d'Ifach** (327m), which drops straight to the sea, making it one of the most picturesque coastal settings in Spain. Peaceful **Gandía** has fine sand beaches. The **tourist office,** Marqués de Campo, is opposite the train station. (☎962 87 77 88. Open June-Aug. M-F 9:30am-1:30pm and 4:30-7:30pm, Sa 10am-1:30pm; Sept.-May M-F 9:30am-1:30pm and 4-7pm, Sa 10am-1pm.) Buses depart from outside the train station for **Platja de Piles** (M-Sa 4-5 per day 8:45am-8:30pm, €0.75). To sleep at the fantastic **Alberg Mar i Vent (HI)** ❶ in Platja, follow the signs down C. Dr. Flemming. The beach is out the back door. (☎962 83 17 48. 3-day max. stay, flexible if uncrowded. Sheets €1.80. Curfew Su-F 2am, Sa 4am. Open mid-Feb. to mid-Dec., but will be closed Oct. 2002-Jan. 2003 for renovations. Dorms €7, over 26 €10.)

NORTHEAST SPAIN

Northeastern Spain encompasses the country's most avidly regionalistic areas and is home to some of its best cuisine. Cataluña is justly proud of its treasures, from mountains to beaches to hip Barcelona. However, Cataluña isn't the only reason to head northeast. The area is also home to the glorious mountains of the Pyrenees, the running bulls of Navarra, the industrious cities of Aragón, the beautiful coasts of Basque Country, and the crazy parties of the Balearic Islands.

CATALUÑA

From rocky Costa Brava to chic Barcelona, Cataluña is a vacation in itself. Graced with the nation's richest resources, it is one of Spain's most prosperous regions. Catalán is the region's official language (though most everyone is bilingual), and local cuisine is lauded throughout Spain.

BARCELONA ☎93

Barcelona loves to indulge in the fantastic. From the urban carnival that is Las Ramblas to buildings with no straight lines, and from wild festivals to even wilder nightlife, the city pushes the limits of style and good taste in everything it does—and with amazing results. The center of the whimsical and daring *Modernisme* architectural movement, and once home to the most well-known Surrealist painters, even Barcelona's art is grounded in an alternate reality. In the quarter-century since Spain was freed from Franco's oppressive regime, Barcelona has led the autonomous region of Cataluña in a resurgence of a culture so esoteric and unique it is puzzling even to the rest of Spain. The result is a vanguard city where rooftops drip toward the sidewalk, serpentine park benches twist past fairy-tale houses, and and an unfinished cathedral captures imaginations around the world.

INTERCITY TRANSPORTATION

Flights: All domestic and international flights land at **El Prat de Llobregat Airport** (BNC; ☎932 98 38 38; www.aena.es/ae/bcn/homepage), 12km southwest of Barcelona. The **Aerobus** links the airport to Pl. Catalunya, the center of town (approx. 40min.; every 15min.; to Pl. Catalunya M-F 6am-midnight, Sa-Su 6:30am-midnight; to the airport M-F 5:30am-11:15pm, Sa-Su 6am-11:20pm; €3.30). **RENFE** (24hr. info ☎934 91 31 83; www.renfe.es) trains provide cheaper airport transport (43min.; every 30min.; 6:13am-11:15pm from airport, 5:43am-11:24pm from Estació Barcelona-Sants; €2.15). Three **national airlines** serve all domestic and major international destinations. **Iberia/Aviaco,** Diputación 258 (☎902 40 05 00), has extensive coverage and student discounts. **Air Europa** (☎902 40 15 01; www.air-europa.com) and **Spanair** (☎902 13 14 15) offer cheaper fares.

Trains: Barcelona has 2 main train stations. For general info about trains and train stations, call ☎902 24 02 02. **Estació Barcelona-Sants,** in Pl. Països Catalans. M: Sants-Estació. Barcelona-Sants is the main terminal for domestic and international traffic. **Estació França,** on Av. Marquès de l'Argentera. M: Barceloneta. Services regional destinations, including Girona Tarragona and Zaragoza, and some international arrivals.

Ferrocarrils de la Generalitat de Cataluña (FGC) (☎93 205 15 15; www.fgc.catalunya.net), has commuter trains with main stations at Pl. Catalunya and Pl. Espanya.

RENFE: (☎902 24 02 02, international ☎934 90 11 22; www.renfe.es). RENFE has extensive service in Spain and Europe. Popular connections include: **Bilbao** (8-9hr., 5 per day, €30-32); **Madrid** (7-8hr., 7 per day, €31-42); **San Sebastian** (8-9hr., 5 per day, €31); **Sevilla** (11-12hr., 6 per day, €47-51); **Valencia** (3-5hr., 15 per day 7am-9pm, €28-32). International destinations include **Milan,** Italy (via Figueres and Nice) and **Montpellier,** France with connections to Geneva, Paris, and various stops along the French Riviera. 20% discount on round-trip tickets.

Buses: Most buses arrive at the **Barcelona Nord Estació d'Autobuses,** C. Ali-bei 80 (☎932 65 61 32; info office open daily 7am-9pm). M: Arc de Triomf (exit to Nàpols).

Alsa Enatcar (☎902 42 22 42; www.alsa.es). To: **Alicante** (9hr., 3 per day, €33); **Madrid** (8hr., 13 per day, €22); **Naples** (24hr., 5:15pm, €113); **Valencia** (4hr., 16 per day, €21); **Zaragoza** (3½-4½hr., 20 per day, €18).

Eurolines (☎902 40 50 40; www.eurolines.es). To **London** (25hr., 8:45am and 5:45pm, €92).

Linebús (☎932 65 07 00). Open M-F 8am-8pm, Sa 8:30am-1pm and 5-8pm. To **Paris** (13hr., M-Sa 8pm, €80), southern France, and Morocco. Discounts for travelers under 26 and over 60.

Sarfa (☎902 30 20 25; www.sarfa.com). Sarfa buses stop at many beach towns along the Costa Brava, north of Barcelona. Open daily 8am-9pm. To: **Cadaqués** (2½hr., 11:15am and 8:25pm, €15); **Palafrugell** (2hr., 13 per day, €12); **Tossa del Mar** (1½hr., 10 per day, €7.50).

Ferries: For details on ferries to the Balearic Islands, see **Balearic Islands,** p. 943. **Trasmediterránea** (☎902 45 46 45), in Estació Marítima-Moll Barcelona, Moll de Sant Bertran. In the summer months only, to: **Ibiza** (10-11hr., 1 per day M-Sa, €46); **Palma** (3½hr., 1 per day, €63); **Mahón** (10½hr., 1 per day, €46).

ORIENTATION

Barcelona's layout is simple. Imagine yourself perched on Columbus's head at the **Monument a Colom** (on **Passeig de Colom,** along the shore), viewing the city with the sea at your back. From the harbor, the city slopes upward to the mountains. From the Columbus monument, **Las Ramblas,** the main thoroughfare, runs from the harbor up to **Plaça de Catalunya** (M: Catalunya), the city's center. The **Ciutat Vella** (Old City) is a heavily-touristed historical neighborhood which centers around Las Ramblas and includes the Barri Gòtic, La Ribera, and El Raval. The **Barri Gòtic** is east of Las Ramblas (to the right, with your back to the sea), enclosed on the other side by **Via Laietana.** East of Via Laietana lies the maze-like neighborhood of **La Ribera,** which borders Parc de la Ciutadella and the Estació França train station. To the west of Las Ramblas (to the left, with your back to the sea) is **El Raval.** Beyond La Ribera (farther east, outside the Ciutat Vella), is the **Poble Nou** neighborhood and the **Vila Olímpica,** with its twin towers (the tallest buildings in Barcelona) and an assortment of discos and restaurants. Beyond El Raval (to the west) rises **Montjuïc,** crammed with gardens, museums, the 1992 Olympic grounds, Montjuïc castle, and other attractions. Directly behind the Monument a Colom is the **Port Vell** (Old Port) development, where a wavy bridge leads across to the ultra-modern shopping and entertainment complexes **Moll d'Espanya** and **Maremagnum.** Beyond the Ciutat Vella is **l'Eixample,** the gridded neighborhood created during the expansion of the 1860s, which runs from Pl. Catalunya toward the mountains. **Gran Via de les Corts Catalanes** defines its lower edge and the **Passeig de Gràcia,** l'Eixample's main street, bisects the neighborhood. **Avinguda Diagonal** marks the border between l'Eixample and the **Zona Alta** (Uptown), which includes Pedralbes, Gràcia, and other older neighborhoods in the foothills. The peak of **Tibidabo,** the northwest border of the city, offers the most comprehensive view of Barcelona.

LOCAL TRANSPORTATION

Metro and Buses: Barcelona's public transportation system (☎010) is quick, cheap, and extensive. The useful *Guía d'Autobusos Urbans de Barcelona,* free at tourist offices and in metro stations, maps out all of the city's bus routes and its 5 metro lines. If you plan to use the metro and bus systems, consider buying a **T1 Pass** (€5.60), valid for 10 rides on the bus, metro, and most FGC trains (multiple people can share 1 pass), or a **T-DIA** Card, which entitles you to unlimited bus and metro travel (1-day €4.20, 3-days €10.80). The **T-Mes** (€36.30) offers unlimited travel for 1 month.

Metro: (☎934 86 07 52; www.tmb.net). Vending machines and ticket windows sell Metro passes. Hold on to your ticket until you leave the Metro—riding without a ticket carries a €40 fine. Trains run M-Th 5am-midnight, F-Sa 5am-2am, Su and holidays 6am-midnight. €1 per *sencillo* (ride).

Buses: Go just about anywhere, usually from 5am-10pm. €1.

Nitbus: (☎901 511 151). 16 different lines run every 20-30min. 10:30pm-4:30am; a few run until 5:30am. Buses depart from Pl. Catalunya and stop in front of most of the club complexes.

Bus Turístic: The Bus Turístic stops at 27 sites along 2 routes (red for the north-bound buses, blue for south-bound); a ticket comes with an info guide in 6 languages about each sight. A full ride on both routes takes about 3½ hours, but you can get on and off as often as you wish. The easiest place to hop on the Bus Turístic is Pl. Catalunya, in front of El Corte Inglés. Many sights covered are closed on Mondays. Purchase tickets on the bus, the Pl. Catalunya tourist office, or at Estació Barcelona-Sants. Runs daily except Dec. 25 and Jan. 1; every 10-30min. 9am-9:30pm; 1-day €14, 2-days €18.

Taxis: ☎933 30 03 00. A *libre* sign in the windshield or a lit green light on the roof means they are vacant; yellow means they are occupied.

Car Rental: Avis/Auto Europe, Casanova 209 (☎932 09 95 33). Will rent to ages 21-25 for an additional fee of about €5 a day. **Budget,** Av. Josep Tarradellas 35 (☎934 10 25 08). Min. age 25. **Branch** in El Prat de Llobregat airport. **Docar,** C. Montnegre 18 (24hr. ☎934 39 81 19). M: Les Corts. Free delivery and pickup. From €14 per day plus €9 insurance and €0.15 per km. Open M-F 8:30am-2pm and 3:30-8pm, Sa 9am-2pm.

Bicycle and Moped Rental: Vanguard Rent a Car, C. Viladomat 297, between Londres and París (☎934 39 38 80). Min. age 19 (ID required). Mopeds start at €33-37 per day. More expensive, 2-person *motos* also available. Insurance, helmet, and IVA included. Open M-F 8am-1:30pm and 4-7:30pm, Sa-Su 9am-1pm.

PRACTICAL INFORMATION

TOURIST, FINANCIAL, AND LOCAL SERVICES

Tourist Info: (☎010, ☎906 30 12 82 or ☎933 04 34 21; www.barcelonaturisme.com).

Informació Turística Plaça Catalunya, Pl. Catalunya 17S (☎907 30 12 82), below Pl. Catalunya. M: Catalunya. Open daily 9am-9pm.

Informació Turística Plaça Sant Jaume, Pl. Sant Jaume 1, off C. Ciutat. M: Jaume I. Open M-Sa 10am-8pm, Su 10am-2pm.

Oficina de Turisme de Catalunya, Pg. Gràcia 107 (☎932 38 40 00; www.gencat.es/probert). M: Diagonal. Open M-Sa 10am-7pm, Su 10am-2pm.

Estació Barcelona-Sants, Pl. Països Catalans. M: Sants-Estació. Open M-F 4:30am-midnight, Sa-Su 5am-midnight.

Aeroport El Prat de Llobregat (☎934 78 05 65), international terminal. English-speaking agents offer information, maps, and hotel reservations. Open daily 9am-9pm.

Budget Travel Offices: usit UNLIMITED, Ronda Universitat 16 (☎934 12 01 04; www.unlimted.es). Open M-F 10am-8:30pm, Sa 10am-1:30pm.

Centre d'Informació Assesorament per a Joves, C. Ferrán 32 (☎934 02 78 00; www.bcn.es/ciaj). M: Liceu. One block off Las Ramblas. Free advice and youth opportunities. Library of travel guides. Open M-F 10am-2pm and 4-8pm.

Consulates: Australia, Gran Via Carlos III 98, 9th fl. (☎933 30 94 96). **Canada,** Elisenda de Pinos 8 (☎932 04 27 00). **New Zealand,** Traversa de Gràcia 64, 4th fl. (☎932 09 03 99). **South Africa,** Teodora Lamadrid 7-11 (☎934 18 64 45). **US,** Pg. Reina Elisenda 23 (☎932 80 22 27).

Currency Exchange: As always, **ATMs** give the best rates (with no commission). The next best rates are available at banks. General banking hours M-F 8:30am-2pm.

American Express, Pg. Gràcia 101 (☎933 01 11 66). M: Diagonal. Open M-F 9:30am-6pm, Sa 10am-noon. Also Las Ramblas 74 (☎933 01 11 66). Open daily 9am-8pm.

Luggage Storage: Estació Barcelona-Sants. M: Sants-Estació. Large lockers €4.50 per 24hr., small €3. Open daily 5:30am-11:00pm. **Estació França.** M: Barceloneta. Open daily 7am-10pm.

Department Store: El Corte Inglés, Pl. Catalunya 14 (☎933 06 38 00). M: Catalunya. Behemoth department store. **Free map** of Barcelona at the information desk. Also has

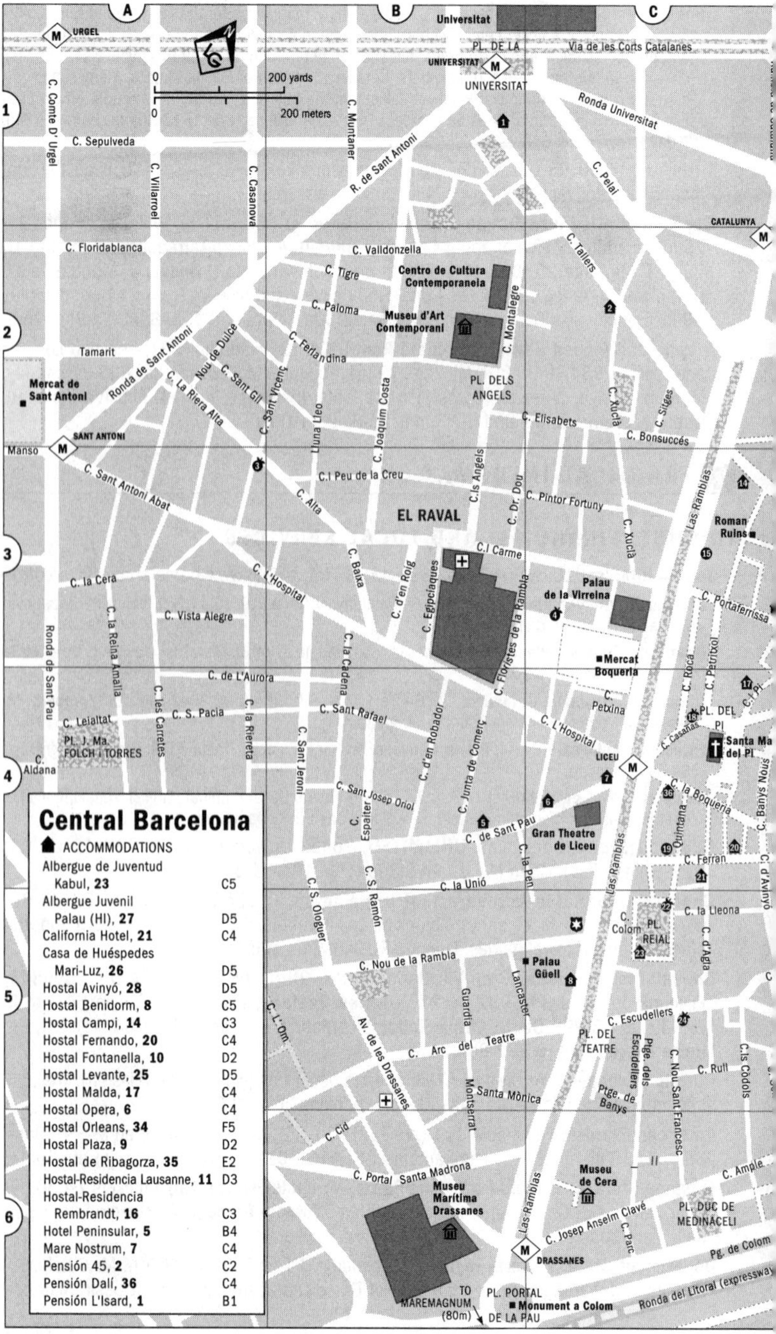
Central Barcelona
ACCOMMODATIONS
Albergue de Juventud Kabul, 23 C5
Albergue Juvenil Palau (HI), 27 D5
California Hotel, 21 C4
Casa de Huéspedes Mari-Luz, 26 D5
Hostal Avinyó, 28 D5
Hostal Benidorm, 8 C5
Hostal Campi, 14 C3
Hostal Fernando, 20 C4
Hostal Fontanella, 10 D2
Hostal Levante, 25 D5
Hostal Malda, 17 C4
Hostal Opera, 6 C4
Hostal Orleans, 34 F5
Hostal Plaza, 9 D2
Hostal de Ribagorza, 35 E2
Hostal-Residencia Lausanne, 11 D3
Hostal-Residencia Rembrandt, 16 C3
Hotel Peninsular, 5 B4
Mare Nostrum, 7 C4
Pensión 45, 2 C2
Pensión Dalí, 36 C4
Pensión L'Isard, 1 B1
A
B
C
1
2
3
4
5
6
0
200 yards
0
200 meters
URGEL
Universitat
PL. DE LA UNIVERSITAT
UNIVERSITAT
Via de les Corts Catalanes
Ronda Universitat
C. Comte D'Urgel
C. Sepulveda
C. Villarroel
C. Casanova
C. Muntaner
R. de Sant Antoni
C. Pelai
CATALUNYA
C. Floridablanca
C. Valldonzella
C. Tigre
C. Paloma
C. Tallers
Centro de Cultura Contemporaneia
Museu d'Art Contemporani
C. Montalegre
C. Ferlandina
Tamarit
Ronda de Sant Antoni
Nou de Dulce
C. Sant Gil
C. La Riera Alta
C. Sant Vicenç
Lluna Lleo
C. Joaquim Costa
PL. DELS ANGELS
C. Xucla
C. Sitges
C. Elisabets
C. Bonsuccés
Mercat de Sant Antoni
SANT ANTONI
Manso
C. Sant Antoni Abat
C.l Peu de la Creu
C. Alta
C.ls Angels
C. Dr. Dou
C. Pintor Fortuny
Las Ramblas
EL RAVAL
Roman Ruins
C.l Carme
C. la Cera
C. L'Hospital
C. Baixa
C. d'en Roig
C. Egipciaques
C. Floristes de la Rambla
Palau de la Virreina
C. Portaferrissa
C. Vista Alegre
C. la Reina Amalia
Ronda de Sant Pau
C. la Cadena
Mercat Boqueria
C. Petritxol
C. Roca
C. de L'Aurora
C. les Carretes
C. S. Pacia
C. la Riereta
C. Sant Rafael
C. d'en Robador
C. Petxina
PL. DEL PI
C. Leialtat
PL. J. Ma. FOLCH i TORRES
C. Sant Jeroni
C. Junta de Comerç
C. Casanas
Santa Ma del Pi
C. Aldana
LICEU
C. Sant Josep Oriol
C. la Boqueria
C. Banys Nous
C. Espalter
C. de Sant Pau
Gran Theatre de Liceu
Quintana
C. la Pen
C. Ferran
C. la Unió
C. S. Ramón
C. S. Ologuer
C. Colom
PL. REIAL
C. la Lleona
C. d'Avinyó
C. d'Agla
C. Nou de la Rambla
Palau Güell
Lancaster
Guardia
C. L'Om
Av. de les Drassanes
C. Escudellers
PL. DEL TEATRE
Ptge. dels Escudellers
C. Nou Sant Francesc
C. Arc del Teatre
C. Rull
C.ls Còdols
Santa Mònica
Montserrat
Ptge. de Banys
C. Cid
C. Portal Santa Madrona
Museu Marítima Drassanes
Museu de Cera
C. Ample
PL. DUC DE MEDINACELI
Las-Ramblas
C. Josep Anselm Clavé
C. Parc
DRASSANES
Pg. de Colom
TO MAREMAGNUM (80m)
PL. PORTAL DE LA PAU
Monument a Colom
Ronda del Litoral (expressway)

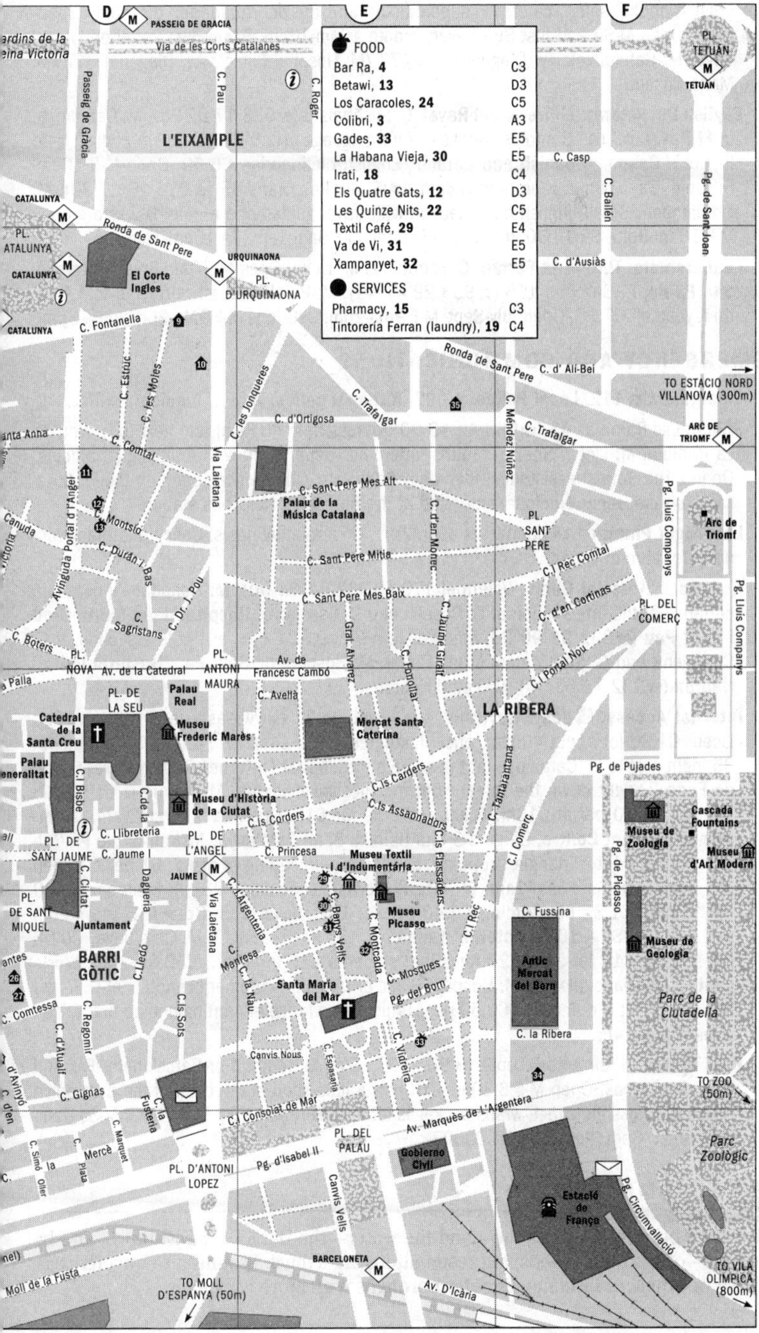
FOOD
Bar Ra, 4 C3
Betawi, 13 D3
Los Caracoles, 24 C5
Colibri, 3 A3
Gades, 33 E5
La Habana Vieja, 30 E5
Irati, 18 C4
Els Quatre Gats, 12 D3
Les Quinze Nits, 22 C5
Tèxtil Café, 29 E4
Va de Vi, 31 E5
Xampanyet, 32 E5
SERVICES
Pharmacy, 15 C3
Tintorería Ferran (laundry), 19 C4
D
E
F
PASSEIG DE GRACIA
Via de les Corts Catalanes
Passeig de Gràcia
C. Pau
C. Roger
L'EIXAMPLE
PL. TETUAN
TETUAN
C. Casp
C. Bailén
Pg. de Sant Joan
C. d'Ausiàs
CATALUNYA
PL. CATALUNYA
Ronda de Sant Pere
URQUINAONA
PL. D'URQUINAONA
El Corte Ingles
C. Fontanella
C. Estruc
C. les Moles
C. les Jonqueres
C. d'Ortigosa
C. Trafalgar
C. d' Alí-Bei
TO ESTACIO NORD VILLANOVA (300m)
ARC DE TRIOMF
C. Méndez Núñez
C. Comtal
Via Laietana
C. Sant Pere Mes Alt
Palau de la Música Catalana
C. d'en Monec
PL. SANT PERE
Arc de Triomf
Pg. Lluís Companys
C. Montsio
C. Duran i Bas
Avinguda Portal d'l'Angel
C. Dr. J. Pou
C. Sant Pere Mitja
C. Sant Pere Mes Baix
C. l Rec Comtal
C. d'en Cortines
PL. DEL COMERÇ
C. Sagristans
C. Boters
PL. NOVA
Av. de la Catedral
PL. ANTONI MAURA
Av. de Francesc Cambó
Grat. Alvarez
C. Fonollar
C. Jaume Giralt
C. l Portal Nou
PL. DE LA SEU
Palau Real
C. Avellà
LA RIBERA
Catedral de la Santa Creu
Museu Frederic Marès
Mercat Santa Caterina
C. Tantarantana
Pg. de Pujades
Palau Generalitat
C. l Bisbe
C. de la
Museu d'Història de la Ciutat
C.ls Carders
C.ls Assaonadors
C.ls Corders
Museu de Zoologia
Cascada Fountains
Museu d'Art Modern
PL. DE SANT JAUME
C. Llibreteria
C. Jaume I
PL. DE L'ANGEL
C. Princesa
Museu Textil i d'Indumentária
C. l Comerç
Pg. de Picasso
JAUME I
C. Ciutat
Daguería
C. l'Argentería
C. Banys Vells
C. Montcada
Museu Picasso
C.ls Flassaders
C. l Rec
C. Fussina
PL. DE SANT MIQUEL
Ajuntament
Museu de Geologia
BARRI GÒTIC
C. Lledó
C. Manresa
C. la Nau
C. Mosques
Antic Mercat del Born
Pg. del Born
Santa Maria del Mar
Parc de la Ciutadella
C. Comtessa
C. Regomir
C.ls Sots
C. d'Atualf
C. Vidrieria
C. la Ribera
Canvis Nous
C. Espasería
TO ZOO (50m)
C. Gignas
C. la Fustería
C. l Consolat de Mar
Av. Marquès de L'Argentera
PL. DEL PALAU
Parc Zoològic
C. Mercè
C. Marquet
C. Simó Oller
C. Plata
Pg. d'Isabel II
Gobierno Civil
PL. D'ANTONI LOPEZ
Canvis Vells
Estació de França
Pg. Circumvallació
BARCELONETA
Moll de la Fusta
TO MOLL D'ESPANYA (50m)
Av. D'Icària
TO VILA OLIMPICA (800m)

English books, salon, cafeteria, supermarket, and the *oportunidades* discount department. Open M-Sa and first Su of every month 10am-10pm. **Branches:** Portal de l'Angel 19-2 (M: Catalunya); Av. Diagonal 471-473 (M: Hospital Clinic); Av. Diagonal 617 (M: Maria Cristina).

English Bookstores: Llibreria del Raval, C. Elisabets 6 (☎933 17 02 93). M: Catalunya, in **El Raval,** off Las Ramblas. Books in four languages (Catalán, Spanish, English, and French). Catalán/Spanish and Catalán/English dictionaries €6.60. Open M-F 10am-8:30pm, Sa 10am-2:30pm and 5-8pm. **LAIE,** Av. Pau Claris 85 (☎933 18 17 39). M: Urquinaona. Small English book section with travel guides and a cafe. Bookstore open M-F 10am-9pm, Sa 10:30am-9pm. Cafe open M-F 9am-1am, Sa 10am-1am.

Laundromats: Tintorería Ferrán, C. Ferrán 11. M: Liceu. Open M-F 9am-8pm. **Tintorería San Pablo,** C. San Pau 105 (☎933 29 42 49). M: Paral·lel. Wash, dry, and fold €10; do-it-yourself €7.25. Open July-Sept. M-F 9am-2pm; Oct.-June M-F 9am-2pm and 4-8pm.

EMERGENCY AND COMMUNICATIONS

Emergency: ☎112. **Local Police:** ☎092. **National police:** ☎091. **Medical:** ☎061.

Police: Las Ramblas 43 (☎933 44 13 00), across from Pl. Reial and next to C. Nou de La Rambla. M: Liceu. Special "Tourist attention" department with multilingual officers. Open 24hr., tourist assistance open daily 8am-2am. Other offices beneath the Pl. Catalunya on the Banco Nacional side, and at the Barcelona-Nord bus station.

Late-Night Pharmacy: Pharmacies open 24hr. on a rotating basis. Check pharmacy windows for current listings.

Hospitals: Hospital Clinic, Villarroel 170 (☎932 27 54 00). M: Hospital Clinic. Main entrance at the intersection of C. Roselló and C. Casanova. **Hospital de la Santa Creu i Sant Pau** (☎932 91 90 00, emergency ☎932 91 91 91), at the intersection of C. Cartagena and C. Sant Antoni Moria Claret. M: Hospital de Sant Pau. **Hospital Vall d' Hebron** (☎932 74 60 00). M: Vall d'Hebron.

Internet Access: ■ **easyEverything,** Las Ramblas 31 (www.easyeverything.com). M: Liceu. €1.20 for about 40min.; price fluctuates. Open 24hr. Also on Ronda Universitat 35, right next to Pl. Catalunya, at the same prices. **bcnet (Internet Gallery Café),** Barra de Ferro 3, right down the street from the Picasso museum. M: Jaume I. €1.50 per 15min., €3.60 per hr.; 10hr. ticket available for €18. Open daily 10am-1am. **Cybermundo Internet Centre,** Bergara 3 and Balmes 8. M: Catalunya. Just off of the Pl. Catalunya, behind the Triangle shopping mall. Allows uploading of disks. €1 per hr. Open M-F 9am-1am, Sa 10am-1am. **El Pati d'Internet,** C. Astúries 78. M: Fontana. €0.90 per 15min., €1.35 per 30min., €2.40 per hr., 10hr. ticket €15. Open M-F 11am-2pm and 4-10pm, Su 4-10pm. **Internet Exchange,** Las Ramblas 130. M: Catalunya. €0.06 per minute; €12 for 5hr., €27 for 20hr.; students €15 for 10hr., €30 for 30hr. **Workcenter,** Av. Diagonal 441. M: Hospital Clinic or Diagonal. Another **branch** is at C. Roger de Lluria 2. M: Urquinaona. €0.50 per 10min. Large range of printing and computer services. Open 24hr.

Post Office: Pl. de Antoni López (☎902 197 197). M: Jaume I or Barceloneta. Fax and **lista de correos.** Open M-F 8:30am-9:30pm. A little shop in the back of the post office building, across the street, wraps packages for mailing (about €2). Shop open M-Sa 9am-2pm and 5-8pm. **Postal Code:** 08003.

ACCOMMODATIONS

The area between Pl. Catalunya and the water—the Barri Gòtic, El Raval, and La Ribera—offers budget beds, but reservations are a must. Last-minute travelers can crash in Gràcia or l'Eixample, outer boroughs with more vacancies.

LOWER BARRI GÒTIC

The following hostels are between C. Ferran and the water. Backpackers flock here to be close to hip Las Ramblas; be careful in the Pl. Reial and below C. Escudellers.

Hostal Levante, Baixada de San Miguel 2 (☎933 17 95 65; www.hostallevante.com). M: Liceu. Walk down C. Ferran, turn right onto C. Avinyó, and take the 1st left onto Baixada de San Miguel (you'll see the sign from C. Avinyó). The best deal in lower Barri Gòtic. Singles €27; doubles €46, with bath €52. MC/V. ❸

Hostal Fernando, C. Ferran 31 (☎/fax 933 01 79 93; www.barcelona-on-line.es/fernando). M: Liceu. Fills from walk-in requests. Dorms with lockers. High season dorms €17, with bath €18; doubles €40/€54; triples with bath €60. MC/V. ❷

Hostal Benidorm, Las Ramblas 37 (☎933 02 20 54). M: Drassanes. The best value on Las Ramblas, with phones and complete baths in each of the very clean rooms, balconies overlooking Las Ramblas, and excellent prices. Singles €25-29; doubles €33-45; triples €50-60; quads €65-70; quints €75. ❸

Casa de Huéspedes Mari-Luz, C. Palau 4 (☎/fax 933 17 34 63). M: Liceu. Tidy dorm rooms for 4-6 people and a few comfortable doubles. Reservations require a credit card. In summer dorms €16; doubles €37. Off-season prices lower. MC/V. ❷

Hostal Avinyó, C. Avinyó 42 (☎933 18 79 45; www.hostalavinyo.com). M: Drassanes. Rooms with couches, high ceilings, fans, safes, and stained-glass windows. Singles €16; doubles €28, with bath €40; triples €42/€60. ❷

Albergue Juvenil Palau (HI), C. Palau 6 (☎934 12 50 80). M: Liceu. A tranquil refuge in the heart of the Barri Gòtic. Kitchen, dining room, and 45 clean dorm rooms with lockers (3-8 people each). Breakfast included. Showers available 8am-noon and 4-10pm. Linen €1.50. Reception daily 7am-3am. Curfew 3am. No reservations. Dorms €13. ❶

Albergue de Juventud Kabul, Pl. Reial 17 (☎933 18 51 90; www.kabul-hostel.com). M: Liceu. Legendary among backpackers; squeezes in up to 200 frat boys at a time. Key deposit €10. Laundry €2.50. No reservations. Dorms €20. ❷

California Hotel, C. Rauric 14 (☎933 17 77 66). M: Liceu. Enjoy one of the 31 clean, sparkling rooms, all with TV, phone, full bath, and A/C. Take the price plunge, and add comfort to the convenient location. Singles €47; doubles €76; triples €95. ❹

UPPER BARRI GÒTIC

Between C. Fontanella and C. Ferran, accommodations are pricier, but more serene than the lower Barri Gòtic. Early reservations are obligatory in summer.

Hostal Plaza, C. Fontanella 18 (☎/fax 933 01 01 39; www.plazahostal.com). M: Catalunya. Savvy, super-friendly Texan owners plus brightly painted rooms in a great location make this place unbeatable. Laundry €9. Singles €52, with bath €65; doubles €58/€67; triples €68/€86. Nov. and Feb. 12% discount. AmEx/MC/V. ❺

Hostal Campi, C. Canuda 4 (☎/fax 933 01 35 45; hcampi@terra.es). M: Catalunya. The first left off Las Ramblas (bear right at the fork). A great bargain. Call ahead to reserve 9am-8pm. Prices vary, but generally doubles €40, with bath €48; triples €60. ❹

Hostal-Residencia Rembrandt, C. Portaferrissa 23 (☎/fax 933 18 10 11). M: Liceu. Ask for a room with a balcony. Fans €2 per night. Singles €25; doubles €42, with bath €50; triples €52/€60. ❸

Pensión Dalí, C. Boquería 12 (☎933 18 55 90; pensiondali@wanadoo.es). M: Liceu. Designed as a religious house by Domènech i Montaner, the architect of the Palau de la Música Catalana. All rooms have TVs. In the high season, doubles €45, with bath €51; triples with bath €69; quads with bath €83. AmEx/MC/V. ❹

Mare Nostrum, Las Ramblas 67 (☎933 18 53 40; fax 934 12 30 69). M: Liceu. The swankiest hostel on the strip. All rooms with A/C and satellite TV. Prices vary by season, but in summer (with breakfast included) doubles €57, with bath €67; triples €77/€87; quads €93/€107. ❺

Hostal-Residencia Lausanne, Av. Portal de l'Angel 24 (☎933 02 11 39). M: Catalunya. Main entrance framed by two Zara display windows. Basic rooms and a posh living room. Doubles €45, with bath €55. ❹

Hostal Fontanella, Via Laietana 71 (☎/fax 933 17 59 43). M: Urquinaona. Tastefully decorated and clean, with a floral waiting room, wood furniture, and fans. Singles €26, with bath €31; doubles €41, with shower €47, with bath €55; triples €58, with shower €66, with bath €66; quads €72, with shower €82. AmEx/MC/V. ❸

Hostal Malda, C. Pi 5 (☎933 17 30 02). M: Liceu. Go down C. Casañas from Las Ramblas, walk through Pl. del Pi, and make a left on C. Pi; the stairwell up to the hostel is inside a shopping center. Same quality as elsewhere in the Barri Gòtic at half the price. Doubles with shower €24-26; triples with shower €36. ❷

LA RIBERA

Hostal de Ribagorza, C. Trafalgar 39 (☎933 19 19 68). M: Urquinaona. Ornate Modernist building. Rooms have TVs and fans. Doubles only. Oct.-Feb. €26.50, with bath €38.50; Mar.-Sept. €35.50/€47.50. ❸

Hostal Orleans, Av. Marqués de l'Argentera 13 (☎933 19 73 82). M: Barceloneta. Spotless, newly renovated hostel with comfortable common area. Singles with TV €31, with bath €39.50; doubles €53, with A/C €54; triples €60-67; quads €80. ❸

EL RAVAL

Be careful in the areas nearer to the port and farther from Las Ramblas.

Pensión L'Isard, C. Tallers 82 (☎933 02 51 83; fax 933 02 01 17). M: Universitat. Simple, elegant, and clean. Singles €19; doubles €33, with bath €42; triples €48. ❷

Hostal Opera, C. Sant Pau 20 (☎933 18 82 01). M: Liceu. Sunny rooms feel like new. All rooms come with bath, phone, and A/C. Singles €31; doubles €50. MC/V. ❸

Pensión 45, C. Tallers 45 (☎933 02 70 61). M: Catalunya. Classic, simple charm. Singles €20; doubles €33, with bath €40. Cash only. ❷

Hotel Peninsular, C. Sant Pau 34 (☎933 02 31 38). M: Liceu. Now one of the 50 sights on the Ruta del Modernisme, this building served as the monastery for the Augustine order of priests in the mid-1800s. Rooms all come with phones and A/C, and most have baths. Breakfast included. Singles €25, with bath €45; doubles €45/€65; triples with bath €80. MC/V. ❷

L'EIXAMPLE

Pensión Fani, València 278 (☎932 15 36 45). M: Catalunya. Charmingly quirky. Rooms are generally rented by the month but can be used for a single night as well. Singles €276 per month; doubles €490 per month; triples €760 per month. One-night stay €20 per person. ❷

Hostal Ciudad Condal, C. Mallorca 255 (☎932 15 10 40). M: Diagonal. Prices reflect the generous amenities and prime location. Singles €65; doubles €90. Prices often drop in winter. MC/V. ❺

Hostal Residencia Oliva, Pg. Gràcia 32 (☎934 88 01 62). M: Pg. Gràcia. Classy rooms have TVs, and some overlook the Manzana de la Discòrdia. Reservations necessary. Laundry €12. Singles €24; doubles €45, with bath €52; triple with bath €72. ❷

Hostal Eden, C. Balmes 55 (☎934 52 66 20; www.eden.iberica.com). M: Pg. Gràcia. Modern rooms equipped with TVs and fans; most have big, new bathrooms. May-Oct. singles €29, with bath €39; doubles €39/€55. Nov.-Apr. singles €23/€32; doubles €29/€45. AmEx/MC/V. ❸

Hostal Hill, C. Provença 323 (☎934 57 88 14; hostalhill@apdo.com), between C. Girona and C. Bailen. M: Verdaguer. Funky, modern furniture. Reservations with a credit card. Singles €25, with bath €32.50; doubles €41/€49. V. ❷

Hostal Qué Tal, C. Mallorca 290 (☎/fax 934 59 23 66; www.hotelsinbarcelona.net/hostalquetal), near C. Bruc. M: Pg. Gràcia or Verdaguer. This high-quality gay- and lesbian-friendly hostel has one of the best interiors of all the hostels in the city. Singles €35; doubles €55, with bath €66. ❸

GRÀCIA

Gràcia is Barcelona's "undiscovered" quarter, but natives have definitely discovered its lively nightlife. Last-minute arrivals may find vacancies here.

Hostal Lesseps, C. Gran de Gràcia 239 (☎932 18 44 34). M: Lesseps. Spacious, classy rooms sport red velvet wallpaper. All 16 rooms have a TV and bath, 4 have A/C (€5.60 extra per day). Singles €34; doubles €52; triples €70; quads €90. MC/V. ❸

Pensión San Medín, C. Gran de Gràcia 125 (☎932 17 30 68; www.sanmedin.com). M: Fontana. Embroidered curtains and ornate tiling adorn this family-run *pensión*. Common room with TV. Singles €30, with bath €39; doubles €48/€60. MC/V. ❸

Hostal Bonavista, C. Bonavista 21 (☎932 37 37 57). M: Diagonal. Well-kept rooms. TV lounge. Showers €1.50. No reservations. Singles €18; doubles €25, with bath €34. ❷

Albergue Mare de Déu de Montserrat (HI), Pg. Mare de Déu del Coll 41-51 (☎932 10 51 51; www.tujuca.com), beyond Parc Güell. Bus #28 from Pl. Catalunya or Nitbus N4. Absolutely gorgeous but way out there. Sheets €2.10. Flexible 3-day max. stay. Reception daily 8am-3pm and 4:30pm-11:30pm. Lockout 10am-1:30pm. HI members only. Dorms €15, over 25 €19; prices drop approx. €5 in the winter. Full and half board available. AmEx/MC/V. ❷

CAMPING

For info, contact **Associació de Càmpings de Barcelona,** Gran Vía 608 (☎934 12 59 55).

El Toro Bravo, Autovía de Castelldefells km 11 (☎936 37 34 62; www.eltorobravo.com). Take bus L95 (€1.50) from Pl. Catalunya to the campsite. Offers beach access, laundry facilities, currency exchange, 3 pools, 2 bars, a restaurant, and a supermarket. Possibility for long-term stays. Reception daily 8am-7pm. Sept.-June 14 €5 per person, €5 per site, €5 per car, €3.65 electricity charge. IVA tax not included. AmEx/MC/V. ❶

Filipinas, Autovía de Castelldefells km 12 (☎936 58 28 95), 1km down the road from El Toro Bravo, accessible by bus L95. Same prices and services as El Toro Bravo. ❶

FOOD

The *Guia del Ocio* (available at newsstands) is an invaluable source of culinary suggestions. **Barceloneta, Port Vell,** and **Port Olímpic** are known for seafood. The restaurants on **Calle Aragó** by Pg. Gràcia have great lunchtime *menús*, and the **Passeig de Gràcia** has beautiful outdoor dining. Gràcia's **Plaça Sol** and La Ribera's **Santa Maria del Mar** are the best places to head for *tapas.* If you want to live cheap and do as Barceloneses do, buy your food fresh at a *mercat* (marketplace). For wholesale fruit, cheese, and wine, head to **La Boqueria** (Mercat de Sant Josep), outside M: Liceu. For groceries, try **Champion Supermarket,** Las Ramblas 11. (M: Liceu. Open M-Sa 10am-10pm.)

BARRI GÒTIC

Great restaurants are scattered on C. Escudellers and C. Clave. Lively hangouts surround Santa Maria del Pi.

Les Quinze Nits, Pl. Reial 6 (☎933 17 30 75). M: Liceu. One of the most popular restaurants in Barcelona, with nightly lines. Delicious Catalán entrees at unbelievable prices (€3-7). No reservations. Open daily 1-3:45pm and 8:30-11:30pm. MC/V. ❶

Els Quatre Gats, C. Montsió 3 (☎933 02 41 40). M: Catalunya. Take the 2nd left off Av. Portal de l'Angel. Picasso's old Modernist hangout. *Tapas* €2-4. Live piano and violin 9pm-1am. Open M-Sa 9am-2am, Su 5pm-2am. Closed Aug. AmEx/MC/V. ❷

Irati, C. Cardenal Casañas 17 (☎933 02 30 84). M: Liceu. An excellent Basque *tapas* bar. Keep your toothpicks to figure out your bill. Bartenders also pour Basque *sidra* (cider) behind their backs. Entrees €15-18. Open daily noon-1am. AmEx/MC/V. ❹

Los Caracoles, C. Escudellers 14 (☎933 01 20 41). M: Drassanes. Started as a snail shop in 1835; specialties include, of course, *caracoles* (snails; €7), half of a rabbit (€10), and chicken (€9). Open daily 1pm-midnight. AmEx/MC/V. ❷

Betawi, C. Montsió 6 (☎934 12 62 64). M: Catalunya. Coming from the Metro, take the 2nd left off Portal de l'Angel. A peaceful Indonesian restaurant with food that verges on gourmet. *Menú* €8. Open M 1-4pm, Tu-Sa 1-4pm and 8-11pm. AmEx/MC/V. ❷

LA RIBERA

East of Via Laietana, La Ribera is home to numerous bars and small restaurants. The few tourists who walk over are well rewarded. The area around Santa Maria del Mar and the Mercat del Born is crawling with *tapas* bars.

La Habana Vieja, Carrer dels Banys Vells 2 (☎932 68 25 04). M: Jaume I. Cuban music sets the mood for large portions, great for sharing. Cuban rice €4-5; meat dishes €10-12. Open M 10am-4:30pm and 8:30-11pm, Tu-Su 10am-4:30pm and 8:30pm-1am. ❷

Xampanyet, C. Montcado 22 (☎933 19 70 03). M: Jaume I. Cross Via Laietana, walk down C. Princesa, and turn right on C. Montcado. Xampanyet is on the right after the Museu Picasso. The house special *cava* is served at the bar. Glasses €1. Bottles €5 and up. Open Tu-Sa noon-4pm and 7-11:30pm, Su 7-11:30pm. Closed Aug. MC/V. ❷

Va de Vi, C. Banys Vells 16 (☎933 19 29 00). M: Jaume I. Romantic, medieval wine bar in a 16th-century building. Wine €1.60-4 per glass, cheeses €3-7, *tapas* €3-5.40. Open Su-W 6pm-1am, Th 6pm-2am, F-Sa 6pm-3am. ❷

Tèxtil Café, C. Montcada 12 (☎932 68 25 98). M: Jaume I. Set in the picturesque courtyard of the Museu Tèxtil i d'Indumentària. Weekday lunch *menú* €9. Wine and *cava* €1.50-2 per glass. Open Tu-Su 10am-midnight. ❷

Gades, C. L'Esparteria 10 (☎933 10 44 55). M: Jaume I. Get your "dip" on in the romantic, dark stone walls of this fondue heaven. Open M-Th 10:30pm-12:30am, F-Sa 10:30pm-1:30am. ❷

EL RAVAL

Students and blue-collar workers congregate in Catalán joints west of Las Ramblas. Restaurants are fairly inexpensive: most have simple decor, basic food, and lots of noise, although trendier places have started to move in as well.

Bar Ra, Pl. Garduña (☎933 01 41 63). M: Liceu. Everything about Ra exudes cool. A mix of traditional Spanish and trendy Californian cuisine. Duck magret with mango and pumpkin sauce €10. Open M-Sa 1:30-4pm and 9:30pm-2am. Dinner by reservation. ❸

Colibri, C. Riera Alta 33-35 (☎934 43 23 06). M: Sant Antoni. From the Metro, head down C. Riera Alta; it will be on your right at the intersection with C. Sant Vincenç. Every evening the finest and freshest ingredients are turned into divine dishes. The pistachio vinaigrette sea bass filet (€25) is unbelievable. Call ahead for reservations. Open M-F 1:30-3:30pm and 8:30-11:30pm. ❺

L'EIXAMPLE

El Racó d'en Baltá, C. Aribau 125 (☎934 53 10 44), at the intersection with C. Roselló. M: Hospital Clínic. Eccentric, colorful restaurant offers creative and flavorful Mediterranean-style dishes. Fish and meat entrees €9.90-15.50. Bottles of wine and *cava* €4-15.50. Open M 9-10:45pm, Tu-Sa 1-3:45pm and 9-10:45pm. AmEx/D/MC/V. ❸

Thai Gardens, C. Diputació 273 (☎934 87 98 98). M: Catalunya. Extravagant decor, complete with a wooden bridge entrance, lush greenery, and colorful pillows. Weekday lunch *menú* €11. Pad thai €6. Entrees €9-13.50. Open Su-Th 1:30-4pm and 8:30pm-midnight, F-Sa 1:30-4pm and 8:30pm-1am. Wheelchair accessible. ❸

Comme-Bio, C. Gran Via 603 (☎933 01 03 76). M: Catalunya or Universitat. On the corner of Gran Via and Rambla de Catalunya. If you've started to wonder if vegetable harvests actually make it to Spain, come here for fresh salad, tofu, yogurt, or juice. Pasta, rice, and veggie pizzas around €6. Open daily 9am-11:30pm; dinner starts at 8pm. ❷

Laie Llibreria Café, C. Pau Claris 85 (☎933 18 17 39; www.laie.es). M: Urquinaona. An ultra-cool lunch spot; offers a fresh buffet lunch (€8.90) in an open, bamboo-draped room with a glass ceiling. Grab a praline cappuccino (€2.30) at the bar on the way out. Vegetarian dinner *menú* €15. Open M-F 9am-1am, Sa 10am-1am. AmEx/MC/V. ❷

Mandalay Café, C. Provença 330 (☎934 58 60 17). M: Verdaguer. Exotic pan-Asian cuisine served in sultanesque luxury. F-Sa night trapeze artist around 11pm; variable extra cover for shows. Entrees €10-18. Open Tu-Sa 9-11pm. MC/V. ❸

Txapela (Euskal Taberna), Pg. Gràcia 8-10 (☎934 12 02 89). M: Catalunya. This Basque restaurant is a godsend for the *tapas*-clueless traveler who wants to learn. *Tapas* €1. Open M-Th 8am-1:30am, F-Su 10am-2am. Wheelchair accessible. ❶

GRÀCIA

La Buena Tierra, C. Encarnació 56 (☎932 19 82 13). M: Joanic. Follow C. Escorial for 2 blocks and turn left on C. Encarnació. Vegetarian delicacies with a Catalán twist. Get back to nature on the backyard terrace. Entrees €4.50-7. Open Tu-F 1-4pm and 8-11pm, F 1-4pm and 8pm-midnight, Su 1-4pm. ❷

La Gavina, C. Ros de Olano 17 (☎934 15 74 50), at the corner of C. St. Joaquím. Funky Italian pizzeria complete with a life-size patron saint. Pizzas €7.50-16. Open F-Sa 2pm-2am, Tu-Th and Su 2pm-1am, . Wheelchair accessible. ❸

SIGHTS

Barcelona is defined by its unique Modernist architecture. The traditional tourist areas are Las Ramblas, a bustling avenue smack in the city center, and the Barri Gòtic, Barcelona's "old city." But don't neglect vibrant La Ribera and El Raval, the upscale avenues of l'Eixample, the panoramic city views from Montjuïc and Tibidabo, Gaudí's Park Güell, and the harbor-side Port Olímpic.

RUTA DEL MODERNISME

For those with a few days and an interest in seeing all the biggest sights, the **Ruta del Modernisme,** a ticket that gives discounted entrance to Modernist sites, is the cheapest and most flexible option. Passes (€3; students, over 65, and groups over 10 people €2) are good for a month and give holders a 50% discount on entrance to Palau Güell, La Sagrada Família, Casa Milà, Palau de la Música Catalana, Casa-Museu Gaudí, Fundació Tàpies, the Museu d'Art Modern, a tour of El Hospital de la Santa Creu i Sant Pau, tours of the facades of La Manzana de la Discòrdia (Casas Amatller, Lleó Morera, and Batlló), and other attractions. Purchase passes at **Casa Amatller,** Pg. Gràcia 41. (M: Pg. Gràcia. ☎934 88 01 39.)

LAS RAMBLAS

Las Ramblas' pedestrian-only median strip is a veritable urban carnival, where street performers dance, fortune-tellers divine, human statues shift poses, and vendors sell birds—all, of course, for a small fee. The sights below are arranged beginning with Pl. Catalunya in the north, continuing to the port in the south.

UPPER LAS RAMBLAS. A port-ward journey begins at the **Font de Canaletes** (more a pump than a fountain), where visitors who wish to eventually return to Barcelona are supposed to sample the water. The upper part of Las Ramblas has been dubbed "Rambla de las Flores" for the numerous flower vendors that inhabit it. Halfway down Las Ramblas, **Joan Miró**'s pavement mosaic brightens up the street.

GRAN TEATRE DEL LICEU. Once one of Europe's leading stages, the Liceu has been ravaged by anarchists, bombs, and fires. It is adorned with palatial ornamentation, gold facades, sculptures, and grand side rooms—including a Spanish hall of mirrors. *(Las Ramblas 51-59, by C. Sant Pau. Office open M-F 2-8:30pm and 1hr. before performances. ☎934 85 99 13. Guided tours M-F 10am by reservation only. €5.)*

MONUMENT A COLOM. Ruis i Taulet's Monument a Colom towers at the port end of Las Ramblas. Ninteenth-century Renaixença enthusiasts convinced themselves that Columbus was Catalán, from a town near Girona. The fact that Columbus points proudly toward Libya, not the Americas, doesn't help the claim; historians agree that Columbus was from Italy. Take the elevator to the top and enjoy a stunning view. *(Portal de la Pau. M: Drassanes. Elevator open June-Sept. 9am-8:30pm; Oct.-Mar. M-F 10am-1:30pm and 3:30-6:30pm, Sa-Su 10am-6:30pm; Apr.-May 10am-2pm and 3:30-7:30pm, Sa-Su 10am-7:30pm. €1.80, children and over 65 €1.20.)*

BARRI GÒTIC

The Barcelona Tourist Office leads professional walking tours of the Barri Gótic (Gothic Quarter); buy tickets there or at the Ajuntament in Pl. St. Jaume. *(For walking tours, call ☎906 30 12 82. Sa-Su at 10am in English and noon in Catalán and Spanish. Buy tickets in advance. €7.)*

ESGLÉSIA CATEDRAL DE LA SANTA CREU. One of Barcelona's most popular monuments. Beyond the **choir** are the altar with the bronze **cross** designed by Frederic Marès in 1976, and the sunken **Crypt of Santa Eulalia,** one of Barcelona's patron saints. The **cathedral museum** holds Bartolomé Bermejo's *Pietà*, the image of Christ dying in the arms of his mother. Catch a performance of the **sardana,** the traditional Catalán dance, in front of the cathedral. Performances take place Sunday after mass (at noon and 6:30pm). *(M: Jaume I. In Pl. Seu, up C. Bisbe from Pl. St. Jaume. Cathedral open daily 8am-1:30pm and 4-7:30pm. Cloister open 9am-1:15pm and 4-7pm. Elevator to the roof open M-Sa 10:30am-12:30pm and 4:30-6pm. €1.35. Choir area open M-F 9am-1pm and 4-7pm, Sa-Su 9am-1pm. €0.90. English audioguide €1.)*

PLAÇA DE SANT JAUME. Plaça de Sant Jaume has been Barcelona's political center since Roman times. Two of Cataluña's most important buildings have dominated the square since 1823: the **Palau de la Generalitat,** the headquarters of Cataluña's autonomous government, and the **Ajuntament,** the city hall. *(Open the 2nd and 4th Su of every month 10:30am-1:30pm. Closed Aug. Mandatory tours in Catalán, Spanish, or English every 30min. starting at 10:30am. Free. Ajuntament open Su 10am-1:45pm. Free.)*

LA RIBERA

This neighborhood has recently evolved into Barcelona's bohemian nucleus, with art galleries, chic eateries, and exclusive bars.

LAS RAMBLAS WALKING TOUR

Suggested Time: 5hr.

Distance: 3.2km or 2mi.

When to go: A weekday morning.

Start: M: Liceu

End: M: Drassanes

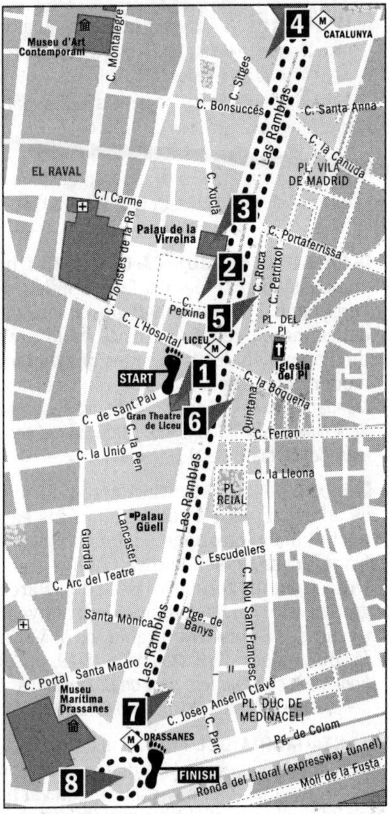

No visit to Barcelona is complete (or even possible) without traversing the famous Las Ramblas first. This promenade is actually a string of five individual Ramblas strung together; each has its own distinct character and plenty of built-in entertainment.

1 GRAN TEATRE DEL LICEU. Start your morning with the 10am guided tour of Barcelona's premier stage, and bask in the history of one of Europe's greatest opera houses (tours M-F).

2 LA BOQUERÍA. Check out the famous all-steel Modernist market and grab a late-morning snack at this wondrous bazaar of fresh and exotic food.

3 PALAU DE LA VIRREINA. Wander in the courtyard of this 18th-century rococo building and see if any exhibitions are going on; if not, visit the building's Cultural Events Office or admire the upscale souvenirs in the giftshop.

4 PLAÇA CATALUNYA. Now you've come to the city's main hub. Every tourist wanders through at least once; can you tell by the crowds? The busy *plaça* makes a great place to people-watch or just relax. It is also where the old city meets the new; turn south to catch the rest of this walking tour, but if you continue farther north you begin the l'Eixample walking tour.

5 MUSEU DE L'ERÒTICA. Swing back around and, if you dare, check out Spain's only erotica museum. Unless you're with your parents. In that case, spare yourself the embarrassment and pretend you didn't notice the place.

6 CAFÉ DE L'OPERA. Enjoy a cup of coffee at the famous cafe. But don't expect to order to go; Europeans like to enjoy their coffee by sipping it leisurely.

7 MUSEU DE CERA. Enjoy some of Barcelona's still life at this wax museum. There are almost as many statues in here as there are living statues along the street you just walked down; only these don't move when you drop a euro in their hat. If they do, that's a bad sign.

8 MONUMENT A COLOM. End your tour with the man Spanish cities love to claim as their own. Sevilla purports that he is buried in their city (he's not); Barcelona claims that he was born in Catalunya (he wasn't). Christopher Columbus may have been elusive in birth and death, but at least Barcelona has captured the prophet in a moment of inspiration, pointing valiantly, heroically, epically . . . the wrong way.

SPAIN

MATING GAME Some call him Snowflake, but in his native Catalán he's Floquet de Neu, the world's only white gorilla in captivity. Taken from the forest in west Africa in the 60s, Floquet has been the toast of Barcelona ever since. With gorillas and other apes in endangered species status, zoos are making concerted efforts to aid breeding. Because of Floquet's dashing good looks, special measures are taken in his case. In an effort to breed another white gorilla, he has been encouraged to mate with his daughters. With over a dozen offspring to date, there's still no Floquet Jr.; Floquet de Neu may be the last of his kind, all the more reason for a pilgrimage to Barcelona.

PALAU DE LA MÚSICA CATALANA. In 1891, the Orfeó Catalán choir society commissioned Modernist Luis Domènech i Montaner to design this must-see concert venue. The music hall glows with tall stained-glass windows, an ornate chandelier, marble reliefs, intricate woodwork, and ceramic mosaics. Concerts given at the Palau include all varieties of symphonic and choral music in addition to more modern pop, rock, and jazz. *(C. Sant Francese de Paula 2. ☎932 95 72 00. M: Jaume I. Mandatory tours in English on the hr. Reserve 1 day in advance. Open daily Aug. 10am-6pm, Sept.-July 10am-3:30pm. €5, students and seniors €4. Check the Guía del Ocio for concert listings. Concert tickets €9-125. MC/V.)*

MUSEU PICASSO. This incredible museum traces the development of Picasso as an artist, with a collection of his early works that weaves through five connected mansions once occupied by nobility. Although the museum offers little from Picasso's well-known middle years, it boasts the world's best collection of work from his formative period in Barcelona. The collection also includes lithographs and pencil sketches by an 11-year-old Picasso, and an excellent display of the artist's Cubist interpretations of Velázquez's *Las Meninas*, which hangs in the Prado in Madrid. *(C. Montcada 15-19. ☎933 19 63 10. M: Jaume I. Walk down C. Princesa from the Metro and turn right on C. Montcada. Open Tu-Sa 10am-8pm, Su 10am-3pm. €5, students and seniors €2.40, under 16 free. First Su of each month free.)*

SANTA MARIA DEL MAR. This architectural wonder was built in the 14th century in a quick 55 years. At a distance of 13m apart, the supporting columns span a width greater than any other medieval building in the world. A fascinating example of the limits of Gothic architecture—were it 2ft. taller, it would have collapsed from structural instability. *(Pl. Santa Maria 1. M: Jaume 1. ☎933 10 23 90. Open M-Sa 9am-1:30pm and 4:30-8pm, Su 9am-2pm and 5-8:30pm. Free.)*

PARC DE LA CIUTADELLA. Host of the 1888 Universal Exposition, the park harbors several museums, well-labeled horticulture, the wacky Cascada fountains, a pond, and a zoo. Buildings of note include Domènech i Montaner's Modernista **Castell dels Tres Dragons** (now Museu de Zoología), the geological museum, and Josep Amergós's Hivernacle. **Floquet de Neu** (a.k.a. *Copito de Nieve;* Little Snowflake), the world's only known albino gorilla, lounges in the Parc Zoològic, on the end of the park closer to the sea. *(M: Ciutadella. Open May-Aug. 9:30am-7:30pm; Apr. and Sept. 10am-7pm; Mar. and Oct. 10am-6pm; Nov.-Feb. 10am-5pm. €10.)* In the center of the park, the **Museu d'Art Modern** houses a potpourri of works by 19th-century Catalán artists. *(Pl. D'Armes. Open Tu-Sa 10am-7pm, Su 10am-2:30pm. €3. Free first Th of every month.)*

EL RAVAL

PALAU GÜELL. Gaudí's Palau Güell (1886)—the Modernist residence built for patron Eusebi Güell of Park Güell fame—has one of Barcelona's most spectacular interiors. Güell and Gaudí spared no expense. The 20 unique rooftop chimneys display Gaudí's first use of the *trencadis*—the covering of surfaces with irregular shards of ceramic, a technique seen in his later work. *(C. Nou de La Rambla 3-5. M: Liceu. Mandatory tour every 15min. Open Mar.-Oct. M-Sa 10am-8pm, Su 10am-2pm, last tour at 6:15pm; Nov.-Dec. M-Sa 10am-6pm. €3, students €1.50.)*

MUSEU D'ART CONTEMPORANI (MACBA). This monstrosity of a building was constructed by American architect Richard Meier with the idea that sparse decor would allow the art to speak for itself. And it does—the MACBA has received worldwide acclaim for its focus on avant-garde art between the two world wars, as well as surrealism and contemporary art. *(Pl. dels Angels 1. M: Catalunya. Open July-Sept. M, W, and F 11am-8pm; Th 11am-9:30pm; Sa 10am-8pm; Su 10am-3pm. Oct.-June M and W-F 11am-7:30pm, Sa 10am-8pm, Su 10am-3pm. €6, students €4, under 17 free.)*

L'EIXAMPLE

The Catalán Renaissance and the growth of Barcelona during the 19th century pushed the city past its medieval walls and into modernity. Ildefons Cerdà drew up a plan for a new neighborhood where people of all social classes could live side by side. However, l'Eixample (pronounced luh-SHOMP-luh) did not thrive as a utopian community but rather as a playground for the bourgeois.

LA SAGRADA FAMÍLIA. Although Antoni Gaudí's unfinished masterpiece is barely a shell of the intended finished product, La Sagrada Família is without a doubt the world's most visited construction site. Despite the fact that only eight of the church's eighteen planned towers have been completed (and those the shortest, at that) and the church still doesn't have an "interior," millions of people make the touristic pilgrimage to witness its work-in-progress majesty. Of the three proposed facades, only the Nativity Facade was finished under Gaudí. A furor has arisen over recent additions, especially sculptor Josep Subirachs's Cubist Passion Facade on C. Sardenya, which is criticized for being inconsistent with Gaudí's plans. *(C. Mallorca 401. M: Sagrada Família. Open Oct.-Mar. daily 9am-6pm, elevator open 9:30am-5:45pm; Apr.-Sept. 9am-8pm, elevator open 9:30am-7:45pm. Entrance €6, students and those with the Ruta pass €4. Guided tours Apr.-Sept. daily 11am, 1, 3, and 5:30pm; Oct. 11am, 1, and 3pm; Nov.-Mar. F-M 11am and 1pm. €3. Cash only.)*

FAR-OUT FACADE Gaudí was a religious man, and his plans for La Sagrada Família called for elaborate and deliberate symbolism in almost every single decorative element of the church. The cypress tree on the **Nativity Facade,** according to one theory, symbolizes the stairway to heaven (cypress trees do not put down deeper roots with time but only grow increasingly taller); the tree is crowned with the word "Tau," the Greek word for God. Similarly, the top of each of the eight finished towers carries the first letter of one of the names of the apostles (and the words "Hosanna" and "Excelsis" are written in a spiral up the sides of the towers). Inside, on the **Portal of the Rosary,** overt references to modern life lurk amongst more traditional religious imagery: the Temptation of Man is represented in one carving by the devil handing a bomb to a terrorist and in another by his waving a purse at a prostitute.

Suberachs, Gaudí's successor, continued the religious symbolism in his **Passion Facade.** To the left, a snake lurks behind Judas, symbolizing the disciple's betrayal of Jesus. The 4x4 box of numbers next to Him contains 310 possible combinations of four numbers, each of which adds up to 33, Christ's age when He died. The faceless woman in the center of the facade, **Veronica,** represents the Biblical woman with the same name and the miraculous appearance of Christ's face on the cloth with which she compassionately wiped his face.

CASA MILÀ (LA PEDRERA). Modernism buffs argue that the spectacular Casa Milà apartment building, an undulating mass of granite popularly known as *La Pedrera* (the Stone Quarry), is Gaudí's most refined work. Note the intricate ironwork around the balconies and the irregularity of the front gate's egg-shaped window panes. The roof sprouts chimneys that resemble armored soldiers, one of which is decorated with broken champagne bottles. Rooftop tours provide a closer look at the "Prussian helmets." The winding brick attic has been transformed into the **Espai Gaudí,** a multimedia presentation of Gaudí's life and works. *(Pg. Gràcia 92. Open daily 10am-8pm. €6; students and over 65 €3, with Ruta del Modernisme pass €4.20. Free guided tours in English M-F 4pm, Sa-Su 11am.)*

LA MANZANA DE LA DISCÒRDIA. A short walk from Pl. Catalunya, the odd-numbered side of Pg. Gràcia between C. Aragó and Consell de Cent is popularly known as *la manzana de la discòrdia* (block of discord), referring to the stylistic clashing of three buildings. Regrettably, the bottom two floors of **Casa Lleó i Morera,** by Domènech i Montaner, were destroyed to make room for a leather store, but you can still buy the **Ruta del Modernisme pass** (see p. 917) there. Puig i Cadafalch opted for a geometric, Moorish-influenced pattern on the facade of **Casa Amatller** at #41. Gaudí's balconies ripple like skulls, and tiles sparkle in blue-purple glory on **Casa Batlló** #43. The most popular interpretation of Casa Batlló is that the building represents Cataluña's patron Sant Jordi (St. George) slaying a dragon; the chimney plays the lance, the scaly roof is the dragon's back, and the bony balconies are the remains of his victims.

WATERFRONT

L'AQUÀRIUM DE BARCELONA. Barcelona's aquarium—Europe's largest—is an aquatic wonder, featuring a large number of octopi and penguins. The highlight is an 80m glass tunnel through an ocean tank of sharks and sting rays, as well as a two-dimensional fish. *(Moll d'Espanya, next to Maremàgnum. M: Drassanes. Open daily July-Aug. 9:30am-11pm; Sept.-June 9:30am-9pm. €11, under 12 and seniors €8, students 10% off.)*

TORRE SAN SEBASTIÀ. One of the easiest and best ways to view the city is on these cable cars, which span the entire Port Vell, connecting beachy Barceloneta with mountainous Montjuïc. The full ride, which takes about 10min. each way and makes an intermediate stop at the Jaume I tower near Colom, gives an aerial perspective of the entire city. *(Pg. Joan de Borbo. M: Barceloneta. In Port Vell, as you walk down Joan de Borbo and see the beaches to the left, stay right and look for the high tower. Open daily 11am-8pm. To Jaume round-trip €7.50; to Montjuïc one-way €7.50, round-trip €9.50.)*

VILA OLÍMPICA. The Vila Olímpica, beyond the east side of the zoo, was built on top of what was once a working-class neighborhood to house 15,000 athletes and entertain millions of tourists for the 1992 Summer Olympics. These days, it's home to several public parks, a shopping center, and business offices. In the area called **Barceloneta,** beaches stretch out from the port. *(M: Ciutadella/Vila Olímpica. Walk along the waterfront on Ronda Litoral toward the two towers.)*

MONTJUÏC

Throughout Barcelona's history, whoever controlled Montjuïc (Hill of the Jews) controlled the city. Dozens of rulers have modified the **fortress,** built atop an ancient Jewish cemetery; Franco made it one of his "interrogation" headquarters, rededicating it to the city in 1960—a huge stone monument expresses Barcelona's (forced) gratitude for its return. The three statues in the monument symbolize the three seas surrounding Spain. *(M: Espanya, then catch bus #50 (every 10min.) at Av. Reina María Cristina.)*

CASTELL DE MONTJUÏC. A visit to this historic fortress and its **Museum Militar** is a great way to get an overview of the city—both of its layout and its history. From the castle's exterior *mirador*, gaze over the city. Enjoy coffee at the cafe while cannons stare you down. *(From M: Paral·lel, take the funicular (every 10min.) to Av. Miramar and then the Teleféric de Montjuïc cable car to the castle. Teleféric open M-Sa 11:15am-9pm. One-way €3.20, round-trip €4.50. Or, walk up the steep slope on C. Foc, next to the funicular station. Open Mar. 21-Nov. 14 Tu-Su 9:30am-7:30pm; Nov. 15-Mar. 20 Tu-Su 9:30am-5pm.)*

FONTS LUMINOSES. The Illuminated Fountains, dominated by the huge central **Font Mágica** (Magic Fountain), are visible from Pl. Espanya up Av. Reina María Cristina. During the summer, they are employed in a weekend music and laser show that illuminates the mountainside and the **Palau Nacional,** located behind the fountains. *(Shows June-Sept. Th-Su every 30min. 9:30pm-12:30am; Oct.-May F-Sa 7-8:30pm. Free.)* The **Museu Nacional d'Art de Cataluña,** behind the fountains, houses an impressive collection of paintings of brutal martyrings. *(M: Espanya, walk up Av. Reina María Cristina to the escalators. Open Tu–Sa 10am-7pm, Su 10am-2:30pm. €4.80, €6 with temporary exhibits; students €3.30. Free first Th of every month.)*

ANELLA OLÍMPICA. The "Olympic Ring" is the area of Olympic facilities Barcelona inaugurated in 1929 with the **Estadi Olímpic de Montjuïc** in its failed bid for the 1932 Games. Over 50 years later, architects Federic Correa and Alfons Milà finished the esplanade in preparation for the 1992 Olympics. *(Open daily 10am-8pm. Free.)* The **Palau d'Esports Sant Jordi** is the most technologically sophisticated of the Olympic structures. *(☎934 26 20 89. You must call in advance to visit.)* Test your swimming mettle in the **Olympic pools** or visit the **Galeria Olímpica** exposition on the games at the south end of the stadium. *(Open M-F 10am-2pm and 4-6pm. €2.40.)*

FUNDACIÓ MIRÓ. Designed by Miró's friend Josep Luís Sert and tucked into the side of Montjuïc, the Fundació links interior and exterior spaces with massive windows and outdoor patios. Skylights illuminate an extensive collection of statues and paintings from Miró's career. Some of the most stunning include the Barcelona Series, which depicts Miró's personal reaction to the Spanish Civil War, and several works from Miro's *Las Constelaciones* series, a reaction to Nazi invasion during World War II. His best-known pieces in the museum include *El Carnival de Arlequin*, *La Masia*, and *L'or de L'azuz*. Room 13 displays experimental work by young artists. The Fundació also sponsors music and film festivals. *(Av. Miramar 71-75. Take the funicular from M: Paral·lel. Turn left out of the funicular station; the museum is a 5min. walk up on the right. Open July-Aug. Tu-W and F-Sa 10am-8pm, Th 10am-9:30pm, Su 10am-2:30pm; Oct.-June Tu-W and F-Sa 10am-7pm, Th 10am-9:30pm, Su 10am-2:30pm. €7.20, students and seniors €4.)*

GRÀCIA

Just beyond L'Eixample, this neighborhood charms and confuses with its narrow alleys and numerous plazas. In August, Gràcia hosts one of Barcelona's best festivals, **Fiesta Mejor.**

PARK GÜELL. This fantastic park was designed entirely by Gaudí, and—in typical Gaudí fashion—was not completed until after his death. Gaudí intended Park Güell to be a garden city, and its multicolored dwarfish buildings and sparkling ceramic-mosaic stairways were designed to house the city's elite. Two mosaic staircases flank the park, leading to a towering Modernist pavilion that Gaudí originally designed as an open-air market. The longest park bench in the world, a multicolored serpentine wonder made of tile shards, decorates the top of the pavilion. In the midst of the park is the **Casa-Museu Gaudí.** *(Bus #24 from Pl. Catalunya stops at the upper entrance. Open May-Sept. daily 10am-9pm; Mar.-Apr. and Oct. 10am-7pm; Nov.-Feb. 10am-6pm. Park free.)*

CASA VICENS. One of Gaudí's earliest projects, Casa Vicens is decorated with cheerful ceramic tiles. The *casa* shows the influence of Arabic architecture and a rigidness that is uncharacteristic of Gaudí's later works. The hard lines contrast with Gaudí's trademark fluid ironwork on the balconies and facade. *(C. Carolines 24-26. M: Fontana. Walk down Gran de Gràcia and turn left onto C. Carolines.)*

PEDRALBES

MUSEU DEL FÚTBOL CLUB BARCELONA. Barcelona's second most visited museum, the FCB museum merits all the attention it gets. Sports fans will appreciate the storied history of the team. The high point is the chance to enter the stadium and take in the enormity of Camp Nou. *(C. Aristides Maillol, next to the stadium. M: Collblanc. Enter through access gates 7 or 9. Open M-Sa 10am-6:30pm, Su 10am-2pm. €5.)*

ENTERTAINMENT

ART GALLERIES

One of the capitals of cutting-edge art, Barcelona showcases many of the latest artistic trends. Many private showings display the works of both budding artists and renowned masters. Most of Barcelona's galleries are located in **La Ribera** around C. Montcada. Three of the best-known in the La Ribera area include: **Gallery Surrealista, Galeria Maeght,** and **Galeria Montcada.** For more in-depth gallery information, check the *Guía del Ocio*. The **Palau de la Virreina** also has information on cultural events. *(Las Ramblas 99, between La Boquería market and C. Carme. M: Liceu. ☎933 01 77 75. Open Tu-Sa 11am-8:30pm and Su 11am-3pm.)*

FÚTBOL

For the record, the lunatics covered head to toe in red and blue didn't just escape from an asylum—they are **F.C. Barcelona** fans. Grab some face paint and head to **Nou Camp,** which has a box office on C. Aristedes Maillol 12-18. Get tickets early. **R.C. Deportivo Espanyol,** a.k.a. *los periquitos* (parakeets), Barcelona's second professional soccer team, spreads its wings at **Estadi Olímpic,** Pg. Olímpic 17-19. This team is not as renowned as the FCB, but it is a great time, and it's free. Obtain tickets for both from Banca Catalana or by phoning TelEntrada (24hr. ☎902 10 12 12).

BULLFIGHTS

Although the best bullfighters rarely venture out of Madrid, Sevilla, and Málaga, Barcelona's **Plaza de Toros Monumental,** Gran Via de les Corts Catalans 743, is an excellent facility, complete with Moorish influences. (☎932 45 58 04. M: Monumental.) Bullfights take place during the summer tourist season (June-Oct. Su at 7pm; doors open at 5:30pm). Tickets are available at travel agencies or ServiCaixa. ("La Caixa" banks. ☎902 33 22 11. €15-69.) The box office also sells tickets before the start of the fight. The cheapest seats are in the *Andanada* section, in the sun.

FESTIVALS

Fiestas abound in Barcelona. Before Christmas, the **Feria de Santa Llúcia** fills Pl. Catedral and the area around the Sagrada Familia with stalls and booths. City residents celebrate **Carnaval** February 27 to March 5, but many head to even more raucous celebrations in Sitges and Vilanova i la Geltrù. Soon thereafter, the **Festa de Sant Jordi** (St. George), April 24, brings feasts in honor of Cataluña's patron saint. This is Barcelona's St. Valentine's Day: men give women roses, and women give men books. Barcelona erupts on June 23, the night before **Día de Sant Joan.** Bonfires roar throughout the city, and the fountains of Pl. Espanya and Palau Reial light up in anticipation of fireworks on Montjuïc. On August 15-21, city folk jam at

Gràcia's **Fiesta Mayor.** Lights blaze in the plazas and streets, and rock bands play all night. On September 11, the **Fiesta Nacional de Cataluña** brings traditional costumes and dancing, and Catalán flags hanging from balconies. The **Feria de Cuina i Vins de Cataluña** draws wine and *butifarra* (sausage) producers to the Rbla. Cataluña. The beginning of November marks the **Fiesta del Sant Çito,** when locals and tourists alike roll up their sleeves and party on Las Ramblas. Finally, from October through November, the **Festival Internacional de Jazz** hits the city's streets and clubs. For information on all festivals, call ☎933 01 77 75 (open M-F 10am-2pm and 4-8pm).

NIGHTLIFE

The whole world knows that Madrid sleeps less than any other city in Europe. Clearly, whoever's counting forgot to take their survey to Barcelona; as in Madrid, nightlife here begins with a 5pm stroll and doesn't wind down until nearly 14 hours later—if even then. Following the afternoon *siesta,* the masses stroll to their favorite *tapas* bars, crowded *plaças,* or outdoor cafés for drinks or a snack with friends. Most people dine between 9 and 11pm, the bar scene picks up around 10pm, and discos start to fill around 2am. Places on Las Ramblas tend to be tourist-dominated, as do the Maremàgnum Mall and most portside establishments. **L'Eixample** is famous for its gay nightlife, and **Poble Nou** (the neighborhood inland from Port Olímpic) has a good alternative music scene.

BARRI GÒTIC

Here, cookie-cutter *cervecerías* and *bar-restaurantes* can be found every five steps. The Barri Gótic is perfect for chit-chatting your night away, sipping *sangría,* or scoping out your next dance partner.

Schilling, C. Ferran 23. M: Liceu. The fancy exterior conceals a surprisingly diverse and chill bar. Mixed gay and straight crowd. Excellent *sangría* (pitcher €14). Beer €2, mixed drinks €5. Open daily 10am-2:30am. Cash only.

Jamboree, Pl. Reial 17. M: Liceu. In the corner immediately to your right coming from Las Ramblas. What was once a convent now serves as one of the city's most popular live music venues. Daily jazz or blues performances. Cover M-F €6, Sa-Su €9-12; includes one drink. Open daily 11pm-1am. Upstairs, the attached club **Tarantos** hosts flamenco shows (€25). Open M-Sa 9:30pm-midnight.

Vildsvin, C. Ferran 38. M: Liceu. On your right as you go down C. Ferran from Las Ramblas. Oysters and international beers (€4-7.50) are the specialties. *Tapas* €3-5, desserts €3.50-10, entrees €8-26.50. Open Su-Th 9am-2am, F-Sa 9am-3am.

El Bosq de les Fades, M: Drassanes. A fairy-tale world, complete with gnarly trees, waterfalls, gnomes, a small bridge, and plush side rooms. Overheard: "Dude, check out that fly honey hanging out at the corner table...oh damn, she's made of wax." Open M-Th until 1:30am, F-Sa until 2:30am.

Molly's Fair City, C. Ferran 7. M: Liceu. With blaring music, fast-flowing imported beer, and a prime location next to the Pl. Reial, Molly's is the place to go if you're looking to meet English-speakers. Guinness on tap €5. Mixed drinks €6. Open M-F 8pm-2:30am, Sa-Su 7pm-3am.

LA RIBERA

In La Ribera, crowds gather at *tapas* bars to soak up artsy flavor.

Plàstic Café, Pg. del Born 19. M: Jaume I. Hyper-trendy bar. Beer €2.40-3, mixed drinks €3 and up. Open Su-Th 10pm-2:30am, F-Sa 10pm-3am.

El Copetin, Pg. del Born 19. M: Jaume I. Cuban rhythm infuses everything in this casual nightspot. Open Su-Th 6pm-2am, F-Sa 6pm-3am.

EL RAVAL

Though El Raval has traditionally been home to a local, unpretentious set of bars, this neighborhood to the west of Las Ramblas is rapidly becoming a hotspot for funky new lounge-style hangouts.

La Oveja Negra, C. Sitges 5. M: Catalunya. The most touristed tavern in town. Open M-Th 9am-3am, F 9am-3:30am, Sa 5pm-3:30am, Su 5pm-3am.

(El Café que pone) Muebles Navarro, Riera Alta 4-6. A mature local crowd is drawn here by a mellow ambience ideal for conversation. Beer and wine €2.50, mixed drinks €3.60-9. Open Tu-Th 6pm-2am, F-Sa 6pm-3am.

London Bar, C. Nou de la Rambla 34, off Las Ramblas. M: Liceu. Rub shoulders with unruly, fun-loving expats. Live music nightly. Beer €3, wine €2, absinthe €3. Open Tu-Th and Su 7:30pm-4:30am, F-Sa 7:30pm-5am.

L'EIXAMPLE

L'Eixample has upscale bars and some of the best gay nightlife in Europe.

La Fira, C. Provença 171. M: Hospital Clinic or FGC: Provença. A bar like no other, La Fira is a hodgepodge of fun-house and circus castaways. Bartenders pour drinks for a hip crowd dangling from carousel swings. DJs spin a mix of funk, disco, and oldies. Open M-Th 10pm-3am, F-Sa 10pm-4:30am, Su 6pm-1am.

Buenavista Salsoteca, C. Rosselló 217. FGC: Provença. This over-the-top salsa club manages to attract a laid-back, mixed crowd. The dancers are not shy. Free salsa and merengue lessons W-Th at 10:30pm. F-Sa cover €9, includes 1 drink. Open W-Th 11pm-4am, F-Sa 11pm-5am, Su 8pm-1am.

Dietrich, C. Consell de Cent 255. M: Pg. Gràcia. A rather unflattering painting of Marlene Dietrich in the semi-nude greets a mostly gay crowd. Beer €3.50, mixed drinks €5-8. Open Su-Th 10:30pm-2:30am, F-Sa 10:30pm-3am.

Fuse, C. Roger de Llúria 40. M: Tetuán or Pg. Gràcia. A cutting-edge Japanese-Mediterranean restaurant, cocktail bar, and dance club. Mixed gay and straight crowd. Beer €3, mixed drinks €6. Restaurant open M-Sa 8:30pm-1am. Bar open Th-Sa 1-3am.

Les Gens que J'Aime, C. València 286. M: Pg. Gràcia. Intimate bar dripping with chandeliers, mirrors, old paintings, plush corner sofas, and arm chairs. Beer €3, mixed drinks €5. Open daily 7pm-2:30am.

PORT OLÍMPIC

Tracing the coast and marked by a gigantic metallic fish structure, the Olympic Village brims with glitzy restaurants and throngs of European dance fiends. Nearly 20 bars and clubs occupy the strip. Revelry begins at midnight and winds down at 6am. From M:Ciutadella-Vila Olímpica, walk down C. Marina toward the towers.

Luna Mora, C. Ramón Trias Fargas, on the corner with Pg. Marítim. This planetarium-like disco with a more mature crowd is one of the best places for late-night dancing on the beach. The mostly local crowd doesn't arrive until 3am. Beer €5, mixed drinks €8. Cover €12. Open F midnight-6am, Sa midnight-6:30am.

El El, Pg. Marítim 36. Hidden behind the Greek restaurant Dionisos; enter from above. Colored strobe lights, fog machines, and techno beats entrance the wild crowd. Beer €4, mixed drinks €7. Cover Th-F and Su €12, Sa €15, free if you eat dinner at Dionisos; includes 2 drinks. Open July-Aug. daily midnight-6am; Sept.-June Th-Su midnight-6am.

MAREMAGNUM

Like Dr. Jekyll, Barcelona's biggest mall has more than one personality. At midnight, the complex turns into a tri-level maze of clubs, complete with escalators to cut down on navigating effort. Each club plays its own music for international students, tourists, and the occasional Spaniard. This is not the most "authentic" experience in Barcelona, but it is an experience. No one charges cover; clubs make their money from exorbitant drink prices. Good luck catching a cab home.

MONTJUÏC

Lower Montjuïc is home to Barcelona's epic "disco theme park," **Poble Espanyol,** Av. Marqués de Comillas (☎933 22 03 26). M: Espanya. Take a cab from the metro and fall in love with the craziest disco experience in all of Barcelona. Some of the most popular (and surreal) discos include: **La Terrrazza** (an outdoor mad house; open July-Aug. Su only; Sept.-June Th-Su midnight-6am); **Torres de Ávila** (with glass elevators; open Th-Sa midnight-6:30am); and **Tinta Roja** (for tango lovers; open July-Aug. Tu-Th 7pm-1:30am, F-Sa 8pm-3am; Sept.-June Tu-Th and Su 7pm-1:30am, F-Sa 8pm-3am). Dancing starts around 1:30am and doesn't end until 9am.

WEST OF GRÀCIA

The area around C. de Marià Cubí has great nightlife, but you'll have to take a taxi. For more accessible fun in Gràcia, head to Pl. Sol.

Otto Zutz, C. Lincoln 15 (ozlistas@hotmail.com). FGC: Pl. Molina. Walk downhill on Via Augusta and take C. Lincoln when it splits off to the right. Groove to house, hip hop, and funk while Japanimation lights up the top floor. Beer €5. Cover €15 (includes 1 drink), but email for a discount. Open Tu-Sa midnight-6:30am.

D_Mer, C. Plató 13. FCG: Muntaner. Walk uphill on C. Muntaner 2 blocks and turn right on C. Plató. A blue-hued heaven for lesbians of all ages. A touch of class, a dash of whimsy, and a ton of fun. Beer €3.50, mixed drinks €6. Cover €6, includes 1 drink. Open Th-Sa 11pm-3:30am.

Bar Fly, C. Plató 15. FGC: Muntaner. Same directions as D_Mer (see above). More popular in the winter. Grab a drink at one of the 2 bars, hit the red-tinted dance floor, or shoot some pool out back. Drinks €6. No cover. Open Th-Sa midnight-3:30am.

DAYTRIPS FROM BARCELONA

MONTSERRAT

FGC trains (☎932 05 15 15) to Montserrat leave from M: Espanya in Barcelona (1hr.; every hr. 8:36am-5:36pm; round-trip including cable car €11.30); get off at Aeri de Montserrat, not Olesa de Montserrat. From the base of the mountain at the other end, the Aeri cable car runs up to the monastery (July-Aug. every 15min. daily 9:25am-6:35pm, Mar. and Oct. 9:25am-1:45pm and 2:20-6:45pm; price included in FCG fare or €6 by itself. Schedules change frequently; call ☎938 77 77 01 to check.)

An hour northwest of Barcelona, the mountain of Montserrat is where a wandering 9th-century mountaineer had a blinding vision of the Virgin Mary. In the 11th century, a monastery was founded to worship the Virgin, and the site has since evolved into a major pilgrimage center. The **monastery**'s ornate **basilica** is above Pl. Creu. To the right of the main chapel is a route through the **side chapels** that leads to the 12th-century Romanesque **La Moreneta** (the black Virgin Mary), Montserrat's venerated icon. (Open Nov.-June M-F 8-10:30am and noon-6:30pm, Sa-Su 8-10:30am and noon-6:30pm; July-Sept. daily 8-10:30am and noon-6:30pm.) In Pl. Santa María, the **Museo de Montserrat** exhibits a sweeping range of art, from an Egyptian mummy to several Picassos. (Open Nov.-June M-F 10am-6pm, Sa-Su 9:30am-6:30pm; July-Sept. M-F 10am-7pm, Sa-Su 9:30am-7pm. €4.50, students €3.50.) The **Santa Cova funicular** descends from Pl. Creu. (Apr.-Oct. daily every 20min. 10am-6pm; Nov.-Mar. Sa-Su 10am-5pm. Round-trip €2.50.) Take the **Saint Joan funicular** up for more inspirational views. (Apr.-Oct. daily every 20min. 10am-6pm; Nov.-Mar. M-F 11am-5pm,

Sa-Su 10am-5pm. Round-trip €6; joint round-trip ticket with the Sta. Cova funicular €7.) The dilapidated **Saint Joan monastery** and **shrine** are only 20min. from the highest station. The real prize is **Saint Jerónim** (1235m), about 2hr. from Pl. Creu (1hr. from the terminus of the St. Joan funicular); take a left at the old chapel.

SITGES

*Cercanías Trains (☎93 490 02 02) link Sitges to Barcelona-Sants Station (*40min., every 15-30min. 5:25am-11:50pm, €2.15*).*

Forty kilometers south of Barcelona, the resort town of Sitges is famous for its prime tanning grounds, lively cultural festivals, international gay community, and wired nightlife. Long considered a watered-down Ibiza, Sitges has better beaches than the notorious Balearic hotspot; you won't find much crazier beach-oriented nightlife on mainland Spain. The **beach** is 10min. from the train station via any street. In town, **Calle Parellades** is the main tourist drag. Late-night foolhardiness clusters around **Calle Primer de Maig,** which runs directly from the beach, and its continuation, **Calle Marques Montroig.** The wild things congregate at the "disco-beach" **Atlántida,** in Sector Terramar. Shuffle your feet at **Pachá,** on Pg. Sant Didac, in nearby Vallpineda. Buses run to the two discos from C. Primer de Maig (midnight-4am). During **Carnaval** (Feb. 27-Mar. 5 in 2003), Spaniards crash the town for a frenzy of dancing, costumes, and alcohol. The **tourist office,** on Pg. Vilafranca, is near the train station. From the station, turn right on C. Artur Carbonell and go downhill. (☎938 94 50 04. Open July-Aug. daily 9am-9pm; Sept.-June W-M 9am-2pm and 4-6:30pm.) If you plan to stay the night, reserve early. **Hostal Parellades ❷,** C. Parellades 11, is close to the beach. (☎938 94 08 01. Singles €20; doubles €32, with bath €38; triples with bath €45.)

NEAR BARCELONA

GIRONA (GERONA) ☎972

A first-class city patiently waiting for the world to notice it, Girona (pop. 70,500) is really two cities in one: a hushed medieval masterpiece on one riverbank and a thriving, modern metropolis on the other. Though founded by the Romans, the city owes more to the renowned *cabalistas de Girona*, who for centuries spread the teachings of Kabbalah (mystical Judaism) in the West. Still a cultural center and university town, Girona is a magnet for artists, intellectuals, and activists.

Most sights are in the old city, across the river from the train station. The **Riu Onyar** separates the new city from the old. The **Pont de Pedra** bridge connects the two banks and heads into the old quarter by way of C. Ciutadans, C. Peralta, and C. Força, which lead to the cathedral and **El Call,** the medieval Jewish neighborhood. A thriving community in the Middle Ages, El Call was virtually wiped out by the 1492 Inquisition and mass expulsion and conversion. The entrance to **Centre Bonastruc Ça Porta,** the site of the last synagogue in Girona (today a museum), is off C. Força, about halfway up the hill. *(☎972 21 67 61. Center and museum open May-Oct. M-Sa 10am-8pm, Su 10am-3pm; Nov.-April M-Sa 10am-6pm, Su 10am-3pm. Museum €2, students €1. The tourist office offers guided tours of El Call in July and Aug. €6 during the day, €12 at night.)* Uphill on C. Força and around the corner to the right, the Gothic **cathedral** rises a record-breaking 90 Rococo steps from the plaza below. The **Tesoro Capitular** within contains some of Girona's most precious possessions, including the **Tapis de la Creació,** a 15th-century tapestry depicting the story of creation. *(Both open July-Sept. Tu-Sa 10am-2pm and 4-7pm, Oct.-Mar. Tu-Sa 10am-2pm and 4-6pm, Mar.-June*

Tu-Sa 10am-2pm and 4-7pm; year-round open Su-M and holidays 10am-2pm. Tesoro and cloister €3.) **La Rambla** and **Plaza de Independéncia** are the places to see and be seen in Girona. The expansive, impeccably designed **Parc de la Devesa** explodes with *carpas*, temporary outdoor bars. Bars in the old quarter draw crowds in the early evening. **Café la Llibreria,** C. Ciutadans 15, serves cocktails (€3.60) and *tapas* (€3) to intellectual types. (Open M-Sa 8:30am-1am, Su 8:30am-midnight. MC/V.)

RENFE **trains** (☎972 24 02 02) depart from Pl. de Espanya to: Barcelona (1½hr., 6:12am and 9:30pm, €5); Figueres (30-40min., 23 per day 6:15am-10:44pm, €2); Madrid (10½hr., 8:20pm, €31); and Paris (11hr.; 10:17pm; €106, under 26 €85). **Buses** (☎972 21 23 19) depart from just around the corner. The **tourist office,** Rambla de la Libertat 1, is directly on the other side. (☎972 22 65 75. Open in summer M-F 9am-3pm, Sa 9am-2pm; off-season M-F 9am-7pm, Sa 9am-2pm.) Most budget accommodations are in the old quarter and are well-kept and reasonably priced. The **Pensió Viladomat ❷**, C. Ciutadans 5, has open, well-furnished rooms. (☎972 20 31 76. Singles €16; doubles €31, with bath €50.) Girona abounds with innovative Cataluñan cuisine; **Calle Cort Reial** is by far the best place to find good, cheap food. **La Crêperie Bretonne ❶,** C. Cort Reial 14, is potent proof of Girona's proximity to France. (☎972 21 81 20. Open Tu-Sa 1-4pm and 8pm-midnight, Su 8pm-midnight.) Pick up groceries at **Caprabo,** C. Sequia 10, a block from C. Nou off the Gran Via. (Open M-Sa 9am-9pm.) **Postal Code:** 17070.

THE COSTA BRAVA

The Costa Brava's jagged cliffs cut into the Mediterranean Sea from Barcelona to the French border. Though rugged by name, the Brave Coast is tamed in July and August by the planeloads of Europeans dumped onto its once tranquil beaches. Unlike its counterparts, Costa Blanca and Costa del Sol, Costa Brava offers more than just high-rises and touristy beaches. Its rocky shores have traditionally attracted artists like Marc Chagall and Salvador Dalí, a Costa Brava native.

TOSSA DE MAR ☎972

Falling in love in (and with) Tossa is easy. The pretty town (pop. 3800), 40km north of Barcelona, is packed with tourists every summer. But Tossa draws on its cliff-studded landscape, its tiny coves, its small-town charm, and its legacy as a 12th-century village to resist becoming the average resort. Inside the walled **Vila Vella** (Old Town), spiraling medieval alleys lead to a tiny plaza, where the **Museu Municipal** displays art from the 20s and 30s. (☎972 34 07 09. Open June 1-15 and Sept. 16-30 M-F 11am-1pm and 3-5pm, Sa-Su 11am-6pm; June 16-Sept. 15 daily 10am-8pm; Oct. M-F 11am-1pm and 3-5pm, Sa-Su 11am-5pm. €3, students €1.80.)

Sarfa **buses** run to Pl. de les Nacions Sense Estat, at Av. de Pelegrí, from Barcelona (1½hr., 18 per day 7:25am-8:10pm, €7.50) and Girona (1hr.; 2 per day, off-season 1 per day; €4). The **tourist office** shares the same building. (☎972 34 01 08. Open June 15-Sept. 15 M-Sa 9am-9pm, Su 10am-2pm and 5-8pm; Apr.-May and Oct. M-Sa 10am-2pm and 5-8pm, Su 10:30am-1:30pm; Mar. and Nov. M-Sa 10am-1pm and 5-7pm; Dec.-Feb. M-F 10am-1pm and 5-7pm, Sa 10am-1pm.) To get to **Fonda/Can Lluna ❶,** C. Roqueta 20, turn right off Pg. Mar onto C. Peixeteras, walk through C. Estalt, turn left at the end, and head straight. (☎972 34 03 65. €12-16 per person.) **Pensión Pepi ❷,** C. Sant Miguel 10, offers cozy rooms with baths. (☎972 34 05 26. Singles €19.50; doubles €39.) The old quarter has the best cuisine and ambience in Tossa. For a great dining atmosphere, try **Restaurant Santa Marta ❸,** C. Tarull 6. (Open daily 12:30-4pm and 7:30-11:30pm.) **Postal Code:** 17320.

FIGUERES ☎972

In 1974, Salvador Dalí chose his native, beachless Figueres (pop. 37,000), 36km north of Girona, as the site to build a museum to house his works, catapulting the city to instant fame. His self-monument is undeniably a masterpiece—and the second most popular museum in Spain. The **Teatre-Museu Dalí** is in Pl. Gala i S. The museum parades the artist's erotically nightmarish landscapes and bizarre installations. From the Rambla, take C. Girona, which becomes C. Jonquera, and climb the steps. (☎972 67 75 00; www.salvador-dali.org. Open July-Sept. daily 9am-7:15pm; Oct.-June daily 10:30am-5:15pm. €9, students and seniors €6.50. Call ahead about night hours during the summer.) **Trains** (☎902 24 02 02) run to Barcelona (2hr., 23 per day 6:10am-9pm, €8) and Girona (30min., 23 per day 6:11am-8:59pm, €2.40). **Buses** (☎972 67 33 54), in Pl. Estació, truck to: Barcelona (2¼hr., 2-6 per day, €13); Cadaqués (1¼hr.; July-Aug. 5 per day, Sept.-June 2-3 per day; €3.50); and Girona (1hr., 2-6 per day, €3.40). The **tourist office** is on Pl. Sol. (☎972 50 31 55. Open July-Aug. M-Sa 9am-8pm, Su 9am-3pm; Apr.-June and Oct. M-F 9am-3pm and 4:30-8pm, Sa 9:30am-1:30pm and 3:30-6:30pm; Sept. M-Sa 9am-8pm; Nov.-Mar. M-F 9am-3pm.) **Hostal La Barretina ❷,** C. Lasauca 13, is a lesson in luxury. (☎972 67 64 12. Singles €22.50; doubles €39.) **Postal Code:** 17600.

CADAQUÉS ☎972

The whitewashed houses and rocky beaches of Cadaqués (pop. 1800) have attracted artists, writers, and musicians—not to mention tourists—ever since Dalí built his summer home here in the 30s. **Casa-Museu Salvador Dalí,** Port Lligat, Dalí's home until 1982, is complete with a lip-shaped sofa and pop-art miniature Alhambra. Follow the signs to Port Lligat (bear right with your back to the statue of liberty) and then to the Casa de Dalí. (☎972 25 10 15. Open June 15-Sept. 15 daily 10:30am-9pm; Sept. 16-Nov. and Mar. 15-June 14 Tu-Su 10:30am-6pm. Tours are the only way to see the house; make reservations 1-2 days in advance. Ticket office closes 45min. before closing. €7.80; students, seniors, and children €4.80.) **Buses** arrive from: Barcelona (2½hr., 11:15am and 4:15pm, €15.20); Figueres (1hr., 5-7 per day, €4.30); and Girona (2hr., 1-2 per day, €7). With your back to the Sarfa office at the bus stop, walk right along Av. Caritat Serinyana; the **tourist office,** C. Cotxe 2, is off Pl. Frederic Rahola opposite the *passeig*. (☎972 25 83 15. Open July-Aug. M-Sa 9:30am-1:30pm and 4-8pm, Su 10:30am-1:30pm; Sept.-June M-Sa 9am-2pm and 4-7pm.) **Hostal Cristina ❸,** C. Riera, is right on the water, to the right of Av. Caritat Serinyana. (☎972 25 81 38. Summer prices include breakfast. May-Sept. singles €26; doubles €40, with bath €52, with TV €57. MC/V.) **Postal Code:** 17488.

THE PYRENEES

The jagged green mountains, Romanesque churches, and tranquil towns of the Pyrenees draw hikers and high-brow skiers in search of outdoor adventures. Spectacular views make driving through the countryside an incredible experience in and of itself. Without a car, transportation is tricky but feasible.

VAL D'ARAN

Some of the Catalán Pyrenees's most dazzling peaks cluster around Val d'Aran, in the northwest corner of Cataluña. The Val d'Aran is best known for its chic ski resorts: the Spanish royal family's favorite slopes are those of **Baquiera-Beret.** The **Albérja Era Garona (HI) ❶,** a few kilometers away in the lovely town of **Salardú,** is accessible by shuttle **bus** in high-season from Vielha. (☎973 64 52 71. Breakfast included. Sheets €2. Dorms €12-15, over 25 €17-19.) While in town, don't miss Salardú's impressive 12th-century **church,** where a colorful mural adorns the ceiling and walls near the altar and one of the valley's most coveted paintings—an image of Santo Christo with the mountains of Salardú in the background—hangs on the back wall. For skiing info, contact the **Oficeria de Baquiera-Beret** (☎973 64 44 55; fax 64 44 88).

The biggest town in the valley, **Vielha** (pop. 7000) welcomes hikers and skiers to its lively streets with every service the outdoorsy type might desire. It's only 12km from Baquiera-Beret; **shuttle buses** connect the two during July and August (schedules at the tourist office). **Alsina Graells buses** (☎973 27 14 70) also run to Barcelona (5½hr., 5:30am and 1:30pm, €23). The **tourist office,** C. Sarriulèra 8, is one block upstream from the *plaça.* (☎973 64 01 10; fax 64 03 72. Open daily 9am-9pm.) Several inexpensive *pensiones* cluster at the end of C. Reiau, off Pg. Libertat (which intersects Av. Casteiro at Pl. Sant Antoni); try **Casa Vicenta ❷** at C. Reiau 3. (☎973 64 08 19. Closed Oct.-Nov. Singles €22; doubles €38.)

PARQUE NACIONAL DE ORDESA

The beauty of Ordesa's Aragonese Pyrenees will enchant even the most seasoned traveler; its well-maintained trails cut across idyllic forests, jagged rock faces, snow-covered peaks, rushing rivers, and magnificent waterfalls. For more info about the park, pay a cyber visit to www.ordesa.net. For assistance beyond the virtual, the **Visitors Center** is on the left, 1.8km past the park entrance. (Open daily Apr. 9am-2pm and 3-6pm; May-Oct. 9am-2pm and 4:30-7pm.) The **Soaso Circle** is the most practical hike; frequent signposts clearly mark the 5hr. journey, which can be cut to a 2hr. loop.

It is easiest to enter the park through the village of **Torla,** where you can buy the indispensable *Editorial Alpina* guide (€7.50). La Oscense (☎974 35 50 60) sends a **bus** from Jaca to Sabiñánigo (20min., 2-3 per day, €1). Sabiñánigo is also easily accessible by **train;** all trains on the Zaragoza-Huesca-Jaca line stop here. From there, Compañía Hudebus (☎974 21 32 77) runs to Torla (55min., 1-2 per day, €2.40). During the high season, a bus shuttles between Torla and Ordesa (15min., 6am-6pm, €2). Off-season, you'll have to hike the 8km to the park entrance or catch a Bella Vista **taxi** (☎974 48 61 53 or 48 62 43; €12). To exit the park area, catch the bus as it passes through Torla at 3:30pm on its way back to Sabiñánigo. In the park, many *refugios* (mountain huts) allow overnight stays. The 120-bed **Refugio Góriz ❶** is a 4hr. hike from the parking lot. (☎974 34 12 01. €9 per person.) In Torla, ascend C. Francia one block to reach **Refugio L'Atalaya ❶,** C. a Ruata 45 (☎974 48 60 22), and **Refugio Briet ❶** (☎974 48 62 21), across the street. (Both €7-9 per person.) Outside Torla are **Camping Río Ara ❶** and **Camping San Anton ❶.** (Ara ☎974 48 62 48, San Anton ☎974 48 60 63. Both €3.50 per person, per tent, and per car. Open Apr.-Oct.) Stock up at **Supermercado Torla,** on C. a Ruata. (Open May-Oct. daily 9am-2pm and 5-8pm; Nov.-Apr. closed Su.)

JACA ☎974

For centuries, pilgrims bound for Santiago would cross the Pyrenees into Spain, spend the night in Jaca (pop. 14,000), and be off the next morning. They had the right idea; the city is best used as a launching pad for the Pyrenees. RENFE **trains** (☎974 36 13 32) run from C. Estación to Madrid (7hr., Su-F 1:45pm, €24) and Zaragoza (3hr., 7:30am and 6:45pm, €9). La Oscense **buses** (☎974 35 50 60) run to Pamplona (2hr., 1 per day, €6) and Zaragoza (2hr., 3-4 per day, €10). The **tourist office,** Av. Regimiento de Galicia 2, is off C. Mayor. (☎974 36 00 98. Open July-Aug. M-F 9am-2pm and 4:30-8pm, Sa 9am-1:30pm and 5-8pm, Su 10am-1:30pm; Sept.-June M-F 9am-1:30pm and 4:30-7pm, Sa 10am-1pm and 5-7pm.) From the bus station, cross the park and head right past the church to the next plaza to find **Hostal Paris ❷,** San Pedro 5, one of the best deals in town. (☎974 36 10 20. Singles €15-16; doubles €23-26; triples €32-35.) Or check out the hip *casa rural* **El Arco ❷,** C. San Nicolas 4, where each room has its own distinct flavor. (☎974 36 44 48. €18 per person.)

NAVARRA

Bordered by Basque Country to the west and Aragón to the east, Navarra's villages—from the rustic Pyrenean pueblos on the French border to bustling Pamplona—are seldom visited apart from the festival of *San Fermines*, and greet non-bullrunning tourists with enthusiasm and open arms.

PAMPLONA (IRUÑA) ☎948

While the lush parks, impressive museums, and medieval churches of Pamplona (pop. 200,000) await exploration, it's an annual, eight-minute event that draws visitors from around the world. Since the publication of Ernest Hemingway's *The Sun Also Rises*, hordes of travelers have come the week of July 6-14 to witness and experience *San Fermines*, the legendary "Running of the Bulls."

TRANSPORTATION AND PRACTICAL INFORMATION. RENFE **trains** (☎902 24 02 02) run from off Av. San Jorge to Barcelona (6-8hr., 3-4 per day 12:25pm-12:55am, €27) and Madrid (5hr., 7:15am and 6:10pm, €34). **Buses** go from C. Conde Oliveto, at C. Yanguas y Miranda, to: Barcelona (5½hr.; 8:30am, 4:30pm and 12:45am; €19); Bilbao (2hr., 4-6 per day 7am-8pm, €10); Madrid (5hr., 4-7 per day 7am-6:30pm, €22); San Sebastián (1hr., 2-9 per day 7am-11pm, €5); and Zaragoza (2-3hr., 6-8 per day 7:15am-8:30pm, €11). From Pl. Castillo, take C. San Nicolás, turn right on C. San Miguel, and walk through Pl. San Francisco to get to the **tourist office,** C. Hilarión Eslava 1. (☎948 20 65 40; www.pamplona.net. Open during *San Fermines* daily 8am-8pm; July-Aug. M-Sa 10am-2pm and 4-7pm, Su 10am-2pm; Sept.-June M-F 10am-2pm and 4-7pm, Sa 10am-2pm.) During *San Fermines*, **store luggage** at the Escuelas de San Francisco, the big stone building at the end of Pl. San Francisco. (€2 per day. Open 24hr.) Check **email** at **Kuria.Net,** C. Curia 15. (€3 per hr. Open M-Sa 10am-10pm, Su 4:30-9:30pm; during *San Fermines* daily 9am-11pm.) **Postal code:** 31001.

ACCOMMODATIONS AND FOOD. Pamplona's accommodations are a lesson in supply and demand: smart *san ferministas* take the bull by the horns and book their rooms up to a year (or at least two months) in advance to avoid paying rates up to four times higher than those listed here. Beware of hawkers at the train and bus stations—quality and prices vary tremendously. Check the newspaper *Diário de Navarra* for **casas particulares.** Many roomless folks are forced to fluff up their sweatshirts and sleep on the lawns of the Ciudadela or on Pl. Fueros, Pl. Castillo, or the banks of the river. Be careful—if you can't store your backpack (storage fills fast), sleep on top of it. During the rest of the year, finding a room in Pamplona is no problem. Budget accommodations line C. San Nicolás and C. San Gregorio off Pl. Castillo. **Hotel Europa ❺,** C. Espoz y Mina 11, off Pl. Castillo, offers bright, luxurious rooms away from the noise of C. San Nicolás. One good night's sleep is worth the price. Reservations are recommended, especially for *San Fermines*. (☎948 22 18 00. Year-round singles €70; doubles €80. MC/V.) To reach the impressive 18th-century mansion of **Pensión Santa Cecilia ❷,** C. Navarrería 17, follow C. Chapitela, take the first right on C. Mercaderes, and make a sharp left. (☎948 22 22 30. *San Fermines* dorms €45. Otherwise singles €15-20; doubles €20-30; triples €30-35. MC/V.) Show up early during the *fiesta* to get a room at **Fonda La Montañesa ❶,** C. San Gregorio 2, which doesn't take reservations. (☎948 22 43 80. *San Fermines* dorms €40. Otherwise dorms €13.) **Hostal Bearán ❹,** C. San Nicolás 25, has squeaky-clean

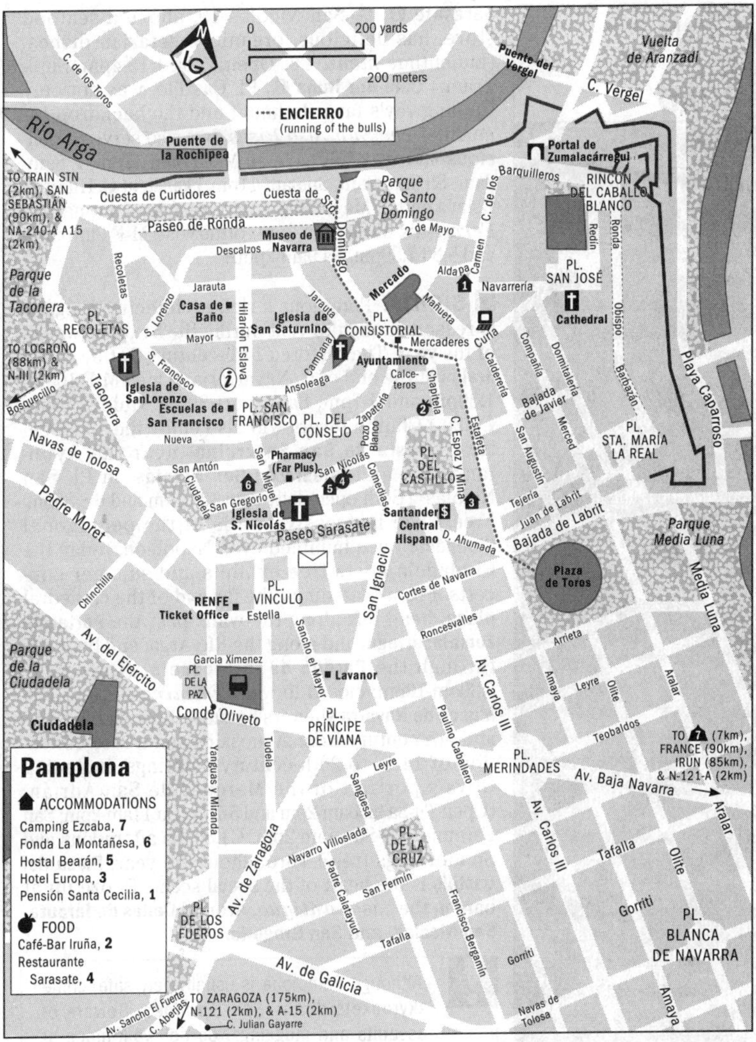

rooms with phone, TV, bath, safebox, and a whopping pricetag. (☎948 22 34 28. *San Fermines* doubles €109; July-Sept. doubles €42; Oct.-June doubles €36.) To get to **Camping Ezcaba** ❼ in Eusa, take city bus line 41 (4 per day, €0.70) from Pl. de las Merindades to the campground. (☎948 33 03 15. *San Fermines* €8.25 per person, per tent, or per car. Otherwise €3.50 per person, per tent or per car. AmEx/MC/V.)

Look for food near Pensión Santa Cecilia, above **Plaza San Francisco,** and around **Paseo Ronda. Calles Navarrería** and **Paseo Sarasate** host *bocadillo* bars. **Restaurante**

Sarasate ❷, C. San Nicolás 19, above a seafood store, has delicious, organic vegetarian dishes. (Lunchtime *menú* €8. Open M-Sa 1:15-4pm, Su 9-11am.) **Café-Bar Iruña ❸**, Pl. Castillo, was not only Hemingway's favorite haunt and the backdrop for much of *The Sun Also Rises*, but also serves a delicious *menú* (€9.60). (Open M-Th 8am-11pm, F 8am-2am, Sa 9am-2am, Su 9am-11pm.) **Vendi,** at C. Hilarión Eslava and C. Mayor, has groceries. (Open during *San Fermines* M-Sa 9am-2pm; otherwise M-F 9am-2pm and 5:30-7:30pm, Sa 9am-2pm.)

SIGHTS. Pamplona's rich architectural legacy is reason enough to visit during the 51 other weeks of the year. The restored 14th-century Gothic **cathedral** is at the end of C. Navarrería. (Open M-F 10am-1:30pm and 4-7pm, Sa 10am-1:30pm. Guided tours €3.20.) Church lovers will also enjoy the 13th-century **Iglesia de San Saturnino,** near the Ayuntamiento, and **Iglesia de San Nicolás,** in Pl. San Nicolás. (Both open daily 9am-12:30pm and 6-8:30pm. Free.) The impressive walls of the pentagonal **Ciudadela** once humbled even Napoleon; today the Ciudadela hosts free exhibits and summer concerts. From C. Redín at the far end of the cathedral plaza, head left along the walls past the **Portal de Zumalacárregui** and along the Río Arga, and bear left through the **Parque de la Taconera.** (Open daily 7:30am-10pm; closed for *San Fermines.* Free.) The **Museo de Navarra** shelters beautifully preserved 4th- and 5th-century Roman mosaics and a nice collection of 14th- to 20th-century paintings, including Goya's portrait of the Marqués de San Adrián. (Open Tu-Sa 9:30am-2pm and 5-7pm, Su 11am-2pm; San Fermines Tu-Su 11am-2pm. €1.80, Sa afternoons and Su mornings free.) Throughout the year, **Plaza del Castillo** is the heart of the social scene. Booze up at bars in the *casco antiguo*, around **Calles de Jarauta, San Nicolás,** and **San Gregorio.**

! Although Pamplona is usually very safe, crime skyrockets during *San Fermines*. Beware of assaults and muggings, do not walk alone at night, and take care in the *casco antiguo.*

LOS SAN FERMINES (JULY 6-14). Visitors overcrowd the city as Pamplona delivers an eight-day frenzy of parades, bullfights, parties, dancing, fireworks, concerts, and wine. Pamplonese, clad in white with red sashes and bandanas, literally throw themselves into the merry-making, displaying obscene levels of both physical stamina and tolerance for alcohol. The "Running of the Bulls,"

FROM THE ROAD

OTRA VEZ?

Cheers and cries of *olé* floated through the window of my pension room in Pamplona's *casco antiguo.* At 6am any other day, this might have been a frustrating wake-up call, but not today. I was was already up. I checked my watch: July 7th. Two hours until the running of the bulls.

I stepped outside, clad in the requisite *San Fermines* garb—all white except the red *faja* encircling my waist and the red *pañuelo* around my neck. Thousands of eager spectators were already planted on, under, and between wooden fences lining the path to the *plaza del toros.* I ducked under one of the gates and made my way up the final stretch of the run, towards the bulls' holding pen. Fences to jump over, or, if need be, roll under, were nearby. Failing that, I told myself, the *capótico de San Fermín* (San Fermin's cape) would shield me; apparently, it's responsible for a few miraculous escapes each year. That morning, I had no idea how much I would need such protection.

Eight o'clock neared. Police passed, dragging runners out of the way; last-minute doubters scaled the sides of storefronts, clambering for the safety of a balcony; the mass slowly drifted away from the holding pen, deciding they'd start a bit closer to the finish line. I began to stampede-proof myself, slipping the loose end of my *faja* into a pocket and scuffing my tennis shoes as best I could to prevent slipping on the champagne- and urine-slicked cobblestone. Murmurs of anticipation resonated in the chilly morning air.

called the *encierro*, is the highlight of *San Fermines;* the first *encierro* of the festival takes place on July 7 at 8am and is repeated at 8am every day for the next seven days. Hundreds of bleary-eyed, hungover, hyper-adrenalized runners flee from large bulls as bystanders cheer from windows, balconies, doorways, and behind barricades. Both the bulls and the mob are dangerous; terrified runners react without concern for those around them. Hemingway had the right idea: don't run. Arrive at the bullring around 6:45am to watch the *encierro*. Tickets for the Grada section of the ring are available before 7am (€4). You can watch for free, but the free section is overcrowded, making it hard to see and breathe. If you want to participate in the bullring excitement, line up by the Pl. Toros well before 7:30am and run in *before* the bulls are in sight. **Be very careful; follow the tourist office's guidelines for running.** To watch a bullfight, wait in the line that forms at the bullring around 8pm (€15-70)). As one fight ends, tickets go on sale for the next day. Once the running ends, insanity spills into the streets and gathers steam until nightfall, when it explodes with singing in bars, dancing in alleyways, spontaneous parades, and a no-holds-barred party in Pl. de Castillo, Europe's biggest open-air dance floor.

RUNNING SCARED So, you're going to run. No one wants to see you end up on evening news programs around the world, so here are a few words of *San Fermines* wisdom:

- Research the *encierro* before you run. The tourist office dispenses a pamphlet that outlines the route of the 3min. run and offers tips for inexperienced runners.
- Do not stay up all night drinking and carousing. Not surprisingly, hung-over foreigners have the highest rate of injury. Experienced runners get lots of sleep the night before. Access to the course closes at 7:30am.
- Give up on getting near the bulls and concentrate on getting to the bullring in one piece. Although some whack the bull with rolled newspapers, runners should never distract or touch the animals; anyone who does is likely to anger the bull and locals alike.
- Try not to cower in a doorway; people have been trapped and killed this way.
- Be particularly wary of isolated bulls–they seek company in the crowds.
- If you fall, **stay down.** Curl up into a fetal position, lock your hands behind your head, and **do not get up** until the clatter of hooves has passed.

Seconds before the signal, a wave of about 50 men rushed toward me, clawing past my startled frame and diving in between the wooden fences. Not a moment later, two blasts shot through the air. I turned and ran.

About halfway through the seven-minute ordeal, I heard the trampling gait of a bull not far behind. Desparate to escape, I tore past the frightened mob in front of me, drilling through the clog of bodies any way I could. I'll admit it–I kicked, I grabbed, I spit, I punched. And so did anyone else who valued his health.

My mad scrambling was to no avail. The *toro* easily advanced alongside me. It jerked its body around and bucked back its head into my left hip, lifting me off the ground. Airborne, I felt something brush against my leg but was so busy readying for the fall that I didn't notice the horn shredding my left pant leg. As my knee hit the ground, I did my best sprinter-start away. The bull's hooves had slipped out from under him, tossing him sidelong to the ground. It wasn't until the next day, when I saw AP photographs of myself contending with the bull in the local and international newspapers, that I realized how much danger I'd been in.

My head ached, my lungs hurt, and the vinegary aftertaste of last night's *kalimotxo* burned my throat, but I had never felt better. I spotted another exhausted runner and gave him a victorious smile.

"Mañana," he wheezed. "Otra vez [again], eh?"

—Nate Gray

ARAGÓN

A striking collage of semi-deserts and lush mountain peaks, Aragón's landscape reflects the influences of both Mediterranean and Continental climates. In the south, sun-baked towns give way to prosperous Zaragoza, while up north the stunning snow-capped peaks of the Pyrenees peer down on tiny medieval towns. The region's harsh terrain and climate, coupled with its strategic location, have produced a martial culture known among Spaniards for its obstinacy.

ZARAGOZA ☎976

Although a popular pilgrimage site since the Virgin Mary dropped in for a visit, Zaragoza (pop. 603,000) has found its charm in its relative international obscurity. Overshadowed by the tourism giants of Madrid and Barcelona, it's just now being pushed to the front of many must-see lists. The massive Baroque **Basílica de Nuestra Señora del Pilar** dominates the **Plaza del Pilar,** filling the skyline with brightly colored tiled domes. The interior is even more incredible, with frescoes by Goya and Velázquez. Don't leave without seeing the panoramic views from one of the towers; take the elevator in the corner, on the left as you face the **Museo del Pilar,** which exhibits the Virgin's glittering jewels. (Basílica open daily 5:45am-9:30pm. Free. Museum open daily 9am-2pm and 4-6pm. €1.50.) The **Palacio de la Aljafería,** on C. Castillo, is the principle relic of Aragón's Moorish era. Take bus # 21 or 33 or head left on C. Coso from Pl. España as you face the *casco viejo*, continue on Conde Aranda, and turn right on Pl. Maria Agustín, then left on C. Aljafería. (Open mid-April to mid-Oct. daily 10am-2pm and 4:30-8pm; mid-Oct. to mid-Apr. closed Tu and F mornings, Su afternoon. €1.80, students €0.90, under 12 free.) The **Museo de Zaragoza,** Pl. Los Sitios 6, houses an extensive collection of artifacts and Aragonese paintings up through the early 20th century. From Pl. España, follow Po. Independencia, turn left on C. Joaquín Costa, and continue 3 more blocks; the museum is on the left. (Open Tu-Sa 10am-2pm and 5-8pm, Su 10am-2pm. Free.)

Trains (☎976 21 11 66) run from Av. Anselmo Clavé to: Barcelona (4hr., 15 per day 1:50am-7pm, €22-28); Madrid (3hr., 12 per day 2:40am-11pm, €21-27); Pamplona (2¼hr., 11:30am and 4:15pm, €8-13); and San Sebastián (4hr., 4 per day 2am-5pm, €21). Agreda Automóvil **buses** (☎976 22 93 43) go from Po. María Agustín 7 to Barcelona (3½hr., 16-21 per day 1-9:30pm, €10) and Madrid (3½hr., 15-18 per day 1:15-10:30pm, €11). The **tourist office** is on Pl. Pilar in the black glass cube across from the basilica. (☎976 20 12 00. Open daily 10am-8pm.) Enjoy TV, A/C, and a built-in radio at **Hostal Belen ❶,** C. Predicadores 2, 2nd fl. A and B. (☎976 28 09 13. Doubles €24, with shower €28.) **Hostal Plaza ❷,** Pl. Pilar 14, has cozy rooms and an unbeatable location. (Singles with shower €24-27; doubles with shower €30-42.) Turn left onto C. San Pablo as you head up Av. Caesar Augusto and walk one block to reach **Hotel Posada de las Almas ❷,** C. San Pablo 22, which offers plain but comfortable rooms with showers. (☎976 43 97 00. Singles €24; doubles €36; triples €50. MC/V.) Take bus #22 from the train station to reach **Albergue-Residencia Juvenil Baltasar Gracián (HI) ❶,** C. Franco y Lopez 4. (☎976 30 66 90. Curfew midnight. Dorms €9, over 26 €11.) The side streets flanking **C. Don Jaime I** and the *tapas* zone known as *El Tubo* (bordered by C. Mártires, C. Cinegio, C. 4 de Agosto, and C. Estébanes) are traditional dinner areas. Get **groceries** at **Consum,** C. San Jorge 22, the continuation of C. Merdeo Nuñez. (Open M-Sa 9am-9pm.) **Postal Code:** 50001.

BASQUE COUNTRY (PAÍS VASCO)

The varied landscape of Basque Country resembles a nation complete unto itself, combining cosmopolitan cities, verdant hills, industrial wastelands, and quaint fishing villages. Many believe that the strongly nationalistic Basques are the native people of Iberia, as their culture and language date back several millennia. Although Castilian Spanish is the predominant language, Basque *euskera* has enjoyed a resurgence of popularity. Basque cuisine is some of Iberia's finest. *Tapas* in País Vasco, considered regional specialties, are called *pintxos;* locals wash them down with *sidra* (cider) and the local white wine, *txakoli*.

SAN SEBASTIÁN (DONOSTIA) ☎943

Glittering on the shores of the Cantabrian Sea, coolly elegant San Sebastián (pop. 180,000) is known for its world-famous beaches, bars, and scenery. Locals and travelers down *pintxos* (tapas) and drinks in the *parte vieja* (old city), which claims the most bars per square meter in the world. Residents and posters are a constant reminder: you are not in Spain, you are in the Basque Country.

TRANSPORTATION

Flights: Airport in Hondarribia (SVQ; ☎943 66 85 00), 20km east of the city. **Interurbanos buses** to Hondarribia pass by the airport (45min., every 15-20min, €1.25). A **taxi** from the airport costs €25. Flights to **Madrid** (1¼hr., 3-6 per day) and **Barcelona** (1¼hr., 1-4 per day). **Iberia** (☎902 40 05 00) has an office at the airport.

Trains: RENFE, Estación del Norte (☎902 24 02 02), on Po. Francia, on the east side of Puente María Cristina. Info office open daily 7am-11pm. To: **Barcelona** (9hr.; Su-F 10:45am and 10:55pm, Sa 10:45am; €30); **Madrid** (8hr., Su-F 10:30pm, €19-22); **Zaragoza** (4hr., daily 10:45am, €19).

Buses: PESA, Av. Sancho el Sabio 33 (☎902 10 12 10), to **Bilbao** (1¼hr., every 30min., €7.50). **Continental Auto,** Av. Sancho el Sabio 31 (☎943 46 90 74), to **Madrid** (6hr., 7-9 per day, €25). **La Roncalesa,** Po. Vizcaya 16 (☎943 46 10 64), to **Pamplona** (1hr., 9 per day, €5.50). **Vibasa,** Po. Vizcaya 16 (☎943 45 75 00), to **Barcelona** (7hr., 3 per day, €22).

Public Transportation: (☎943 28 71 00). Each trip €0.80. **Bus #16** goes from Alameda del Boulevard to the campground and beaches.

Taxis: Santa Clara (☎943 36 46 46), **Vallina** (☎943 40 40 40), or **Donostia** (☎943 46 46 46). Taxis to **Pamplona** take about 45min. and cost around €78.

ORIENTATION AND PRACTICAL INFORMATION

The **Río Urumea** splits San Sebastián. The city center, most monuments, and the two most popular beaches, Playa de la Concha and Playa de Ondaretta, line the peninsula on the west side of the river. The tip of the peninsula is called **Monte Urgull.** On the east side of the river, Playa de la Zurriola attracts a younger surfing and beach crowd. Inland lies the *parte vieja* (old city), San Sebastián's restaurant, nightlife, and budget accommodation nexus, where you'll find the most tourists. South of the *parte vieja*, at the base of the peninsula, is the commercial district. The **bus station** is south of the city on Pl. Pío XII, while the **RENFE station, Barrio de Gros,** and Playa de la Zurriola are east of the city. The river is spanned by four bridges: Puentes Zurriola, Santa Catalina, María Cristina, and de Mundaiz (listed north to south). To get to the *parte vieja* from the train station, head straight to Puente María Cristina, cross the bridge, and turn right at the fountain. Continue four blocks north to Av. Libertad, then take a left and follow it to the port; the *parte vieja* fans out to the right, and Playa de la Concha rests to the left.

Tourist Office: Municipa Centro de Atracción y Turismo, C. Reina Regente 3 (☎943 48 11 66; fax 943 48 11 72), in front of the Puente Zurriola. From the train station, turn right immediately after crossing Puente María Cristina and continue until reaching

Puente Zurriola; the office is on the left. From the bus station, start down Av. Sancho el Sabio. At Pl. Centenario, bear right onto C. Prim and follow the river until the third bridge, Puente Zurriola, and look for the plaza on your left. Open June-Sept. M-Sa 8am-8pm, Su 10am-2pm; Oct.-May M-Sa 9am-1:30pm and 3:30-7pm, Su 10am-2pm.

Hiking Information: Club Vasco de Camping, San Marcial 19 (☎/fax 943 42 84 79), 1 block south of Av. Libertad. Organizes excursions. Open M-F 6-8:30pm. **Izadi,** C. Usandizaga 18 (☎943 29 35 20), off C. Libertad. Sells hiking guides and maps, some in English. Open M-F 10am-1pm, 4-8pm; Sa 10am-1:30pm, 4:30-8pm.

Luggage Storage: Train station (€3 per day; buy tokens at the ticket counter). Open daily 7am-11pm.

Laundromat: Lavomatique, C. Iñigo 14 (☎943 42 38 71), off C. San Juan in the *parte vieja.* 4kg wash €3.75, 6kg wash €5.55 (cold water only); €2.70 dry. Soap €0.45. Open M-F 9:30-2pm and 4-8pm, Sa-Su 10am-2pm.

Emergency: ☎112. **Police: Municipal,** C. Easo (☎943 45 00 00).

Medical Services: Casa de Socorro, Bengoetxea 4 (☎943 44 06 33).

Internet Access: Netline, C. Urdaneta 8 (☎943 44 50 76). €1.80 per 30min., €3 per hr., €18 for 10hr. ticket. Open M-Sa 10am-10pm.

Post Office: Po. De Francia 13 (☎943 44 68 26), near the RENFE station, just over the Santa Catalina bridge and to the right; look for the yellow trim on left side of street. Open M-F 8:30am-8:30pm, Sa 9:30am-2pm. **Postal Code:** 20006.

ACCOMMODATIONS

Desperate backpackers will scrounge for rooms in July and August, particularly during *San Fermines* (July 6-14) and *Semana Grande* (starts Su the week of Aug. 15); September's film festival is just as booked. Budget options center in the *parte vieja* and by the cathedral. The tourist office has lists of accommodations, and most hostel owners know of *casas particulares*.

PARTE VIEJA

The *parte vieja*, where the younger backpackers go for a night's rest, is brimming with reasonably-priced *pensiones* and restaurants. Its proximity to Playa de la Concha and the port makes this area a prime nightspot; scores of places offer a night's sleep above loud *pintxos* (tapas) bars. Call in advance for reservations.

Pensión Amaiur, C. 31 de Agosto 44, 2nd fl. (☎943 42 96 54). From Alameda del Boulevard, follow C. San Jerónimo to its end, turn left, and look for the lower, obscured front. Nine beautiful rooms, five common bathrooms. July-Aug. and *Semana Santa* dorms €24; May-June and Oct. €18; Sept. and Nov-Apr. €13. MC/V. ❷

Pensión Larrea, C. Narrica 21, 2nd fl. (☎943 42 26 94). Spend time with mamá and papá, as the friendly owners are often called, in this comfortable and welcoming *pensión*. July-Aug. singles €21; doubles €34; triples €45. Sept.-June €18/€30/€45. ❷

Pensión San Lorenzo, C. San Lorenzo 2 (☎943 42 55 16), off C. San Juan. All rooms with TV and refrigerators. July-Aug. doubles €45; June-Sept. €30-42; Oct.-May €24. ❷

Pensión Loinaz, C. San Lorenzo 17 (☎943 42 67 14), off C. San Juan. English-speaking owners. Common bathrooms. July-Aug. doubles €40; Sept.-June €25. ❷

Pensión Urgull, Esterlines 10 (☎943 43 00 47). Follow the winding staircase to the 3rd floor. Rooms with sinks. Prices are not set in stone, so bargain away. July-Aug. doubles €36-42; June and Sept. €24-27; Oct.-May €24-30. ❷

Pensión Boulevard, Alameda del Boulevard 24 (☎943 42 94 05). Spacious rooms, all with radios, some with balconies. 2 large shared baths for 8 rooms. July-Aug. doubles €50; June and Sept €36-42; Oct.-May €30. ❸

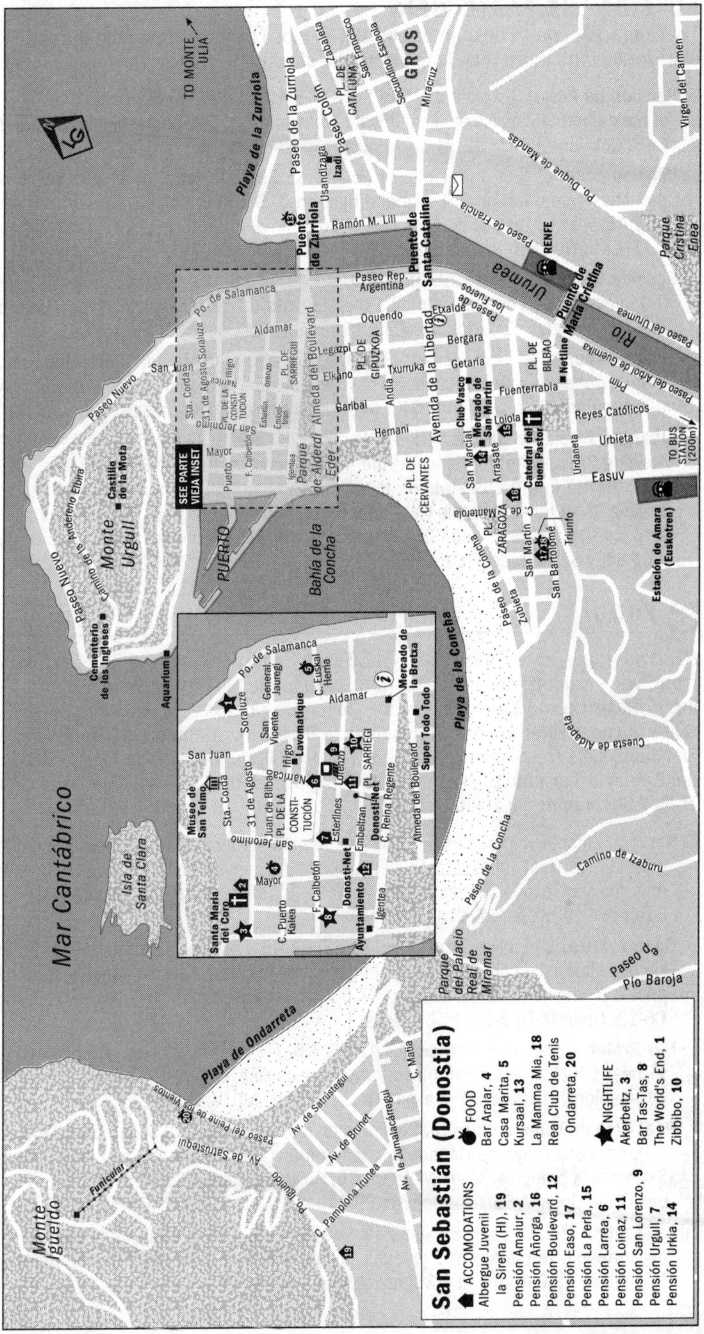
San Sebastián (Donostia)
ACCOMODATIONS
Albergue Juvenil la Sirena (HI), 19
Pensión Amaiur, 2
Pensión Añorga, 16
Pensión Boulevard, 12
Pensión Easo, 17
Pensión La Perla, 15
Pensión Larrea, 6
Pensión Loinaz, 11
Pensión San Lorenzo, 9
Pensión Urgull, 7
Pensión Urkia, 14
FOOD
Bar Aralar, 4
Casa Marita, 5
Kursaal, 13
La Mamma Mia, 18
Real Club de Tenis Ondarreta, 20
NIGHTLIFE
Akerbeltz, 3
Bar Tas-Tas, 8
The World's End, 1
Zibbibo, 10
Mar Cantábrico
Isla de Santa Clara
Monte Urgull
Castillo de la Mota
Cementerio de los Ingleses
Aquarium
Paseo Nuevo
Playa de la Zurriola
TO MONTE ULIA
GROS
Paseo de la Zurriola
Paseo Colón
Puente de Zurriola
Puente de Santa Catalina
Puente de María Cristina
Río Urumea
RENFE
Parque Cristina Enea
Estación de Amara (Euskotren)
TO BUS STATION (200m)
Catedral del Buen Pastor
Mercado de San Martín
Club Vasco
Netline
Avenida de la Libertad
Parque de Alderdi Eder
PUERTO
Bahía de la Concha
Playa de la Concha
Paseo de la Concha
Parque del Palacio Real de Miramar
Playa de Ondarreta
Monte Igueldo
Funicular
Paseo del Peine de los Vientos
Camino de Izaburu
Cuesta de Aldapeta
Paseo de Pío Baroja
SEE PARTE VIEJA INSET
Museo de San Telmo
Santa María del Coro
Ayuntamiento
Donosti-Net
Lavomatique
Mercado de la Bretxa
Super Todo Todo
Alameda del Boulevard
PL. DE LA CONSTITUCIÓN
PL. SARRIEGI

SPAIN

OUTSIDE THE PARTE VIEJA

These places tend to be quieter but just as close to the port, beach, bus and train stations, and no more than 5min. from the old city.

Pensión La Perla, C. Loiola 10, 2nd fl. (☎943 42 81 23), on the street directly ahead of the cathedral. English spoken. Private baths and TVs. July-Sept. singles €30; doubles €46. Oct.-June €24/€32. ❸

Pensión Easo, C. San Bartolomé 24 (☎943 45 39 12). Head toward the beach on C. San Martín, turn left on C. Easo, and right on C. San Bartolomé. July-Sept. 15 singles €32.45, with bath €48; doubles €41/€60. June and Sept. singles €27/€40; doubles €33/€45. Oct.-May singles €25/€33; doubles €30/€40. ❸

Pensión Urkia, C. Urbieta 12, 3rd fl. (☎943 42 44 36), located on C. Urbieta between C. Marcial and C. Arrasate. Borders the Mercado de San Martín. All rooms with bath. July-Sept. singles €30; doubles €39; triples €54. Oct.-June €24/€30/€40. ❸

Pensión Añorga, C. Easo 12 (☎943 46 79 45), at C. San Martín. Shares entryway with 2 other *pensiones*. Spacious rooms have wood floors and comfy beds. July-Aug. singles €25; doubles €32, with bath €43. Sept.-June singles €19; doubles €25/€32. ❷

Albergue Juvenil la Sirena (HI), Po. Igueldo 25 (☎943 31 02 68), a large, light-pink building 3min. from the beach at the far west end of the city. Bus #24 and #27 run from the train and bus stations to Av. Zumalacárregui; from there, take the street angling toward the mountain (Av. Brunet) and turn left at its end. Clean rooms, multilingual staff. HI members and ISIC-carriers only. Breakfast included. Sheets €2.50. Curfew Sept.-May Su-Th midnight, F-Sa 2am. Dorms €11-13, over 25 €13-15. MC/V. ❶

FOOD

Pintxos (tapas; rarely more than €1.50 each), chased down with the fizzy regional white wine *txacoli*, are a religion here; bars in the old city serve an array of enticing *pintxos* on toothpicks or bread. The entire *parte vieja* seems to exist for no other purpose than to feed. **Mercado de la Bretxa,** on Alameda del Boulevard at C. San Juan, sells fresh produce. (Open M-Sa 9am-9pm.) **Super Todo Todo,** on Alameda del Boulevard around the corner from the tourist office, also sells groceries. (Open M-Sa 8:30am-9pm, Su 10am-2pm.)

Kursaal, Zurriola, 1 (☎943 00 31 62), in an ultra-modern building across the river from the Old City. Treat yourself to an elegant lunch on their breezy patio. The chef, who also runs the very expensive restaurant upstairs, is a legend among locals. *Menú* M-F 1-3:30pm €10.50, Sa-Su €14. MC/V. ❷

Casa Marita, C. Euskal Herria (☎943 43 04 43), off Po. Salamanca. The talented kitchen staff uses only fresh, natural ingredients to create satisfying meals at moderate prices. Try the homemade lasagna (€7.50) or smoked salmon (€7). *Menú* €15, entrees €6-13. Open Th-Tu 8-11pm. MC/V. ❷

Bar Aralar, C. Puerto Kalea (☎943 42 63 78). Fresh, tasty *pintxos* (€1.50) and sandwiches (€1-2). An excellent place to try local cuisine. Open F-Sa 11am-2:30am, Su-Th 11am-midnight. Closed 3 weeks in Nov. and May. MC/V. ❶

Real Club de Tenis Ondarreta, Po. Peine de los Vientos (☎943 31 11 50 or 943 31 41 18), on along Playa de Ondarreta. Escape the crowded *parte vieja to* mingle with San Sebastián's preppies. *Menú* M-Sa €9.35, Su €15; entrees €10-15. Call ahead for reservations. Open M-Sa 1-3:30pm and 9-11pm, Su 1-3:30pm. AmEx/MC/V. ❸

La Mamma Mia, C. San Bartolomé 18 (☎943 46 52 93). Freshly-made pastas, including tortellini, fettucine, and lasagna dishes (€5.75-6.50). M-F luncheon *menú* €7. Open daily 1:30-4pm and 8:30pm-12:30am. MC/V. ❷

SIGHTS AND BEACHES

San Sebastián's most attractive sight is the city itself, filled with green walks, grandiose buildings, and the placid bay. The views from **Monte Igueldo,** west of the center, are the best in town: by day, the countryside meets the ocean in a line of white and blue, and by night the flood-lit **Isla de Santa Clara** (island) seems to float on a ring of light. The walk up the mountain is not too strenuous, but there is a funicular (round-trip €1.50). Across the bay from Monte Igueldo, the gravel paths on **Monte Urgull** wind through shady woods, monuments, and stunning vistas. The overgrown **Castillo de Santa Cruz de la Mota** tops the summit with 12 cannons, a chapel, and the statue of the *Sagrado Corazón de Jesús* blessing the city. (Open daily May-Sept. 8am-8pm; Oct.-Apr. 8am-6pm.) Directly below the hill, on Po. Nuevo in the *parte vieja*, the serene **Museo de San Telmo** resides in a Dominican monastery strewn with Basque funerary relics, and the main museum beyond the cloister displays a fascinating array of pre-historic Basque artifacts, a few dinosaur skeletons, and a piece of contemporary art. (Open Tu-Sa 10:30am-8:30pm, Su 10:30am-2pm. Free.) The gorgeous **Playa de la Concha** curves from the port to the **Pico del Loro,** the beak-shaped promontory home to the Palacio de Miramar. The virtually flat beach disappears during high tide, which comes in a matter of minutes. Sunbathing crowds jam onto the smaller and steeper **Playa de Ondarreta,** beyond Miramar, and surfers flock to **Playa de la Zurriola,** across the river from Mt. Urguel. Picnickers head for the alluring **Isla de Santa Clara** in the center of the bay, either by rented rowboat or public motorboat ferry (5min., June-Sept. every 30min., round-trip €1.95).

ENTERTAINMENT AND NIGHTLIFE

For info on **theater** and special events, pick up the weekly *Kalea* (€1.40) from tobacco stands or newsstands. World-class jazz musicians arrive in Vitoria-Gasteiz the second or third week of July for the week-long **Festival de Jazz de Vitoria-Gasteiz** (☎945 14 19 19; www.jazzvitoria.com). Rockets mark the start of the **Fiesta de la Virgen Blanca** (Aug. 4-9) at 6pm on the 4th in Pl. Virgen Blanca. The *parte vieja* pulls out all the stops in July and August, particularly on **Calle Fermín Calbetón,** three blocks in from Alameda del Boulevard. During the year, when students outnumber backpackers, nightlife tends to move beyond the *parte vieja.* Keep an eye out for discount coupons on the street. A favorite pub among expats and young travelers, **The World's End,** Po. de Salamanca 14, is a block from the *parte vieja* toward the beach. (Open Su-Th 2pm-2:30am, F-Sa 2pm-3:30am.) **Zibbibo,** Plaza Sarriegi 8, is a hip club with a dance floor and a blend of hits and techno. (Open daily 2pm-4am.) **Bar Tas-Tas,** C. Fermín Calbetón 35, attracts backpackers. (Open daily 3pm-4am.) **Akerbeltz,** C. Koruko Andra Mari 10, is a sleek, cavernous bar. (Open M-Th 3pm-2:30am, F-Sa 3pm-3:30am.)

DAYTRIP FROM SAN SEBASTIÁN: HONDARRIBIA

Interurbanos buses (☎943 64 13 02) arrive on C. Zuluaga from San Sebastián (45min.; every 20min. M-Sa 7:30am-10:35pm, Su 7:45am-9:45pm; €2).

Refreshingly simple Hondarribia (pop. 15,000) flaunts a silky-smooth **beach** as well as a gorgeous stone-and-timber *casco antiguo*, centered around Carlos V's imposing **palace** in Pl. Armas, that provides welcome relief from Coppertone fumes. Six kilometers up Av. Monte Jaizkibel, **Monte Jaizkibel,** the highest mountain on the Costa Cantábrica, guards the **Santuario de Guadalupe** and offers incredible views of the coast. **Jolaski Boats** shuttle travelers 5km to **Hendaye,** a French town with a bigger beach. The boats leave from the pier at the end of C. Domingo Egia, off La

Marina (every 15min., €1.40). The **tourist office,** C. Javier Ugarte 6, is off Pl. San Cristóbal. (☎943 64 54 58. Open July-Sept. M-Sa 10am-2pm and 3-8pm; Oct.-June M-F 9am-1:30pm and 4-6:30pm, Sa 10am-2pm). Several **markets** spill onto **Calle San Pedro,** three blocks inland from the port.

BILBAO (BILBO) ☎944

Bilbao (pop. 370,000) is a city transformed; what was once all industry—bourgeois, business-minded, and ugly—is now new, avant-garde, and futuristic. Twentieth-century success showered the city with a new subway system, a stylish riverwalk, and other additions all designed by renowned international architects. But above all else, it is the shining Guggenheim Museum that has most powerfully fueled Bilbao's rise to international prominence.

TRANSPORTATION AND PRACTICAL INFORMATION. **Trains** (☎944 23 86 23) arrive at the **Estación del Norte,** Pl. Circular 2, from: Barcelona (9-11hr., Su-F 10am and 10:45pm, €32); Madrid (6-8hr.; Su-F 4:30pm and 11pm, Sa 9:50am; €28-36); and Salamanca (5½hr., 2pm, €23). From Pl. Circular, head right around the station and cross the Puente del Arenal to reach Pl. Arriaga, the entrance to the *casco viejo*. Most **bus** companies leave from the **Termibús terminal,** C. Gurtubay 1 (☎944 39 52 05; M: San Mamés), on the west side of town, for: Barcelona (7¼hr., 4 per day, €34); Madrid (4-5hr.; M-F 10-18 per day, Su 2 per day; €22); Pamplona (2hr., 4-6 per day, €11); and San Sebastián (1¼hr., every hr., €7.50.) The **tourist office** is on Pl. Arenal 1. (☎944 79 57 60; www.bilbao.net. Open M-F 9am-2pm and 4-7:30pm, Sa 9am-2pm, Su 10am-2pm.) Surf the **Internet** at **Ciberteca,** C. José Maria Escuza 23, on the corner of C. Simón Bolívar. (€0.60 per 10min., €2.10 per hr. Open M-Th 8am-10pm, F-Sa 8am-midnight, Su 10am-10pm.) **Postal code:** 48008.

ACCOMMODATIONS AND FOOD. During **Semana Grande** (August 17-25), rates are higher than those listed below. **Plaza Arriaga** and **Calle Arenal** have budget accommodations galore, while upscale hotels line the river or are in the new city off **Gran Vía.** For large, lavish rooms with private bath and A/C, try **Hotel Arriaga ❹,** C. Ribera 3. (☎944 79 00 01; fax 944 79 05 16. Singles €39; doubles €60; triples €72. AmEx/V.) **Pensión Méndez ❷,** C. Santa María 13, 4th fl., is insulated from the raging nightlife below. From the Puente del Arenal, take C. Bidebbarrieta; after two blocks, take a right onto C. Perro, then turn right on C. Santa María. (☎944 16 03 64. Singles €25; doubles €33.) To get to **Pensión Ladero ❷,** C. Lotería 1, 4th fl., from the Puente del Arenal, take C. Corre; after three blocks, take a right onto C. Lotería. This pensión has modern common bathrooms and winter heating. (☎944 15 09 32. Singles €18; doubles €30.) **Restaurante Vegetariano Garibolo ❷,** C. Fernández del Campo 7, serves delicious and creative vegetarian meals. (*Menú* €9.75. Open M-Sa 1-4pm. MC/V.) At **Restaurante Beroki ❸,** Pl. Circular 2, an elegant upstairs dining room is decorated with flowers and wine bottles. (Creamy chowder €8, entrees €9-15. Open Su-Th 1-4pm, F-Sa 1-4pm and 9-11:30pm.) **Mercado de la Ribera,** on the bank of the river at the bottom of the old city, is the biggest indoor **market** in Spain. (Open M-Th and Sa 8am-2:30pm; F 8am-2:30pm and 4:30-7:30pm.) Pick up groceries at **Champión,** Pl. Santos Juanes. (Open M-Sa 9am-9:30pm.)

SIGHTS AND ENTERTAINMENT. Frank O. Gehry's **Guggenheim Museum Bilbao,** Av. Abandoibarra 2, can only be described as breathtaking. Lauded by the international press, it has catapulted Bilbao into cultural stardom. The building's undulating curves of glistening titanium, limestone, and glass resemble an iridescent scaly fish. The museum currently hosts rotating exhibits culled from the Guggenheim Foundation's collection. (☎944 35 90 00; www.guggenheim-bilbao.es.

Audioguides €4. Guided tours in English Tu-Su 11am, 12:30, 4:30, and 6:30pm. Sign up 30min. before tour at the info desk. Open daily July-Aug. 9am-9pm; Sept.-June Tu-Su 10am-8pm. €8.40, students €4.20, under 12 free.) The often overshadowed **Museo de Bellas Artes,** Pl. Museo 2, has an impressive collection of 12th- to 20th-century art. To get there, take C. Elcano to Pl. Museo, or bus #10 from Pte. Arenal. (Audioguides €2. Open Tu-Sa 10am-8pm, Su 10am-2pm. €4.50, students €3, under 12 free. W free.)

Revelers in the *casco viejo* spill into the streets, especially on **Calle Barrencalle** (Barrenkale). A young crowd jams at **Calle Licenciado Poza** on the west side of town. For a more mellow scene, people-watch at the elegant 19th-century **Café Boulevard,** C. Arenal 3. **The Cotton Club,** C. Gregorio de la Revilla 25, decorated with over 30,000 beer caps, draws a huge crowd on Friday and Saturday nights. (Open M-Th 4:30pm-3am, F 4:30pm-6am, Sa 6:30pm-6am, Su 6:30pm-3am.) The massive blowout fiesta in honor of *Nuestra Señora de Begoña* takes place during **Semana Grande,** a nine-day party beginning the Sunday after Aug. 15.

DAYTRIP FROM BILBAO: GUERNICA (GERNIKA). On April 26, 1937, the Nazi "Condor Legion" released an estimated 29,000kg of explosives on Guernica, obliterating 70% of the city in three hours. The nearly 2000 people who were killed in the bombings were immortalized in Pablo Picasso's stark masterpiece *Guernica,* now in Madrid's Reina Sofía gallery (see p. 862). To reach the **tourist office,** C. Artekalea 8, from the train station, walk three blocks up C. Adolfo Urioste and turn right on C. Artekalea. At the first crosswalk on the road, take a right into the alleyway; the office will be on your right. (☎946 25 58 92; www.gernika-lumo.net. Open July-Sept. M-Sa 10am-7:30pm, Su 10:am-2:30pm; Oct.-June M-Sa 10am-1:30pm and 4-7pm, Su 11am-2pm.) The office can direct you to several memorial sites, including the modest **Museo de la Paz de Gernika,** Pl. Foru 1, which features an exhibition chronicling the bombardment. **Trains** (☎902 543 210; www.euskotren.es) roll in from Bilbao (45min., every 45min., €2).

BALEARIC ISLANDS

Every year, discos, ancient history, and beaches—especially beaches—draw nearly two million of the hippest Europeans to the *Islas Baleares,* 100km off the east coast of Spain. Culture-philiacs and shopaholics will fall for the high-class act and stunning natural beauty of **Mallorca.** A counterculture haven since the 1960s, **Ibiza** offers some of the best nightlife in all of Europe. The smaller islands **Formentera** and **Menorca** rest upon unspoiled sands, hidden coves, and mysterious Bronze Age megaliths.

TRANSPORTATION

Flights to the islands prove the easiest way to get there. Those under 26 often get discounts from **Iberia** (☎902 40 05 00; www.iberia.com), which flies to Palma de Mallorca and Ibiza from: Barcelona (40min., €60-120); Madrid (1hr., €150-180); and Valencia. **Air Europa** (☎902 24 00 42) and **SpanAir** (☎902 13 14 15; www.spanair.com) offer budget flights to and between the islands. Most cheap round-trip **charters** include a week's stay in a hotel; some companies called *mayoristas* sell leftover spots on package-tour flights as "seat-only" deals. Look for newspaper ads or inquire at travel agencies.

Ferries to the islands are less popular, but slightly cheaper. **Trasmediterránea** (☎902 45 46 45; www.trasmediterranea.com) departs from Barcelona's Estació Marítima Moll and Valencia's Estació Marítima for Mallorca, Menorca, and Ibiza

(€43-58). **Buquebus** (☎902 41 42 42) goes from Barcelona to Palma (4hr., 2 per day, €49). Book airplane or ferry tickets through a travel agency.

Between islands, **ferries** are the most cost-efficient way to travel. **Trasmediterránea** (see above) sails between Palma and Mahón (6½hr., Su only, €23) and between Palma and Ibiza (2½hr., 7am, €37). **Car** rental costs around €36 per day, **mopeds** €18, and **bikes** €6-10.

MALLORCA ☎971

A favorite with Spain's royal family, Mallorca has been a popular member of the in-crowd since Roman times. Lemon groves and olive trees adorn the jagged cliffs of the northern coast, and lazy beaches sink into calm bays to the east. The capital of the Balearics, **Palma** (pop. 323,000) pleases with its well-preserved old quarter, colonial architecture, and local flavor.

TRANSPORTATION. **Bus** travel to and from Palma is not very difficult, but travel between most other areas is inefficient and restrictive. Nearly all buses stop at the main stop on C. Eusebi Estada, several blocks down from Pl. Espanya; buy tickets on the bus. The tourist office has a schedule of all buses. Some of the more popular destinations include: Covetes/Es Trenc (M-F 3 per day 10am-5pm, Sa-Su 10:30am; €4); Cuevas Drach (M-F 4 per day 10am-1:30pm, Sa-Su 10am; €5.40); and Sóller and Port Sóller (45min.; M-F every hr. 7am-7pm, Sa-Su 1 and 4:30pm; €2).

PRACTICAL INFORMATION. From the airport, take bus #17 or 25 to **Plaza Espanya** (15min., every 20min., €1.80). To continue to the **tourist office,** C. Sant Dominic 11, take Pg. Marítim (a.k.a. Av. Juan Roca) to Av. Antoni Maura, follow C. Conquistador out of Pl. de la Reina, and continue on C. Sant Dominic. (☎971 72 40 90. Open M-F 9am-8pm, Sa 9am-1:30pm.) The **island tourist office,** Pl. Reina 2, offers info on the other islands, a good city map, bus and train schedules, hiking info, and lists of all sporting and cultural events on Mallorca. (☎971 71 22 16. Open M-F 9am-8pm, Sa 10am-2pm.) Check email at **La Red,** C. Concepció 5. (☎971 71 35 74. €2.40 for 30min. Open daily 10am-midnight.)

ACCOMMODATIONS AND FOOD. Accommodations are scarce and often packed in Mallorca; your best bet is to book ahead and use Palma as a base for exploring the island. Centrally located **Hostal Ritzi ❷,** C. Apuntadores 6, above "Big Byte" cyber cafe, has cheerful rooms overlooking an interior patio. (☎971 71 46 10. Laundry €7. Singles €23; doubles €34, with bath €49.) **Hostal Brondo ❷,** C. Can Brondo 1, off Pl. Rei Joan Carles I, is an old, converted house that exudes character. (☎971 71 90 43. Reception M-Sa 9am-2pm and 6-8pm, Su 10am-1:30pm. Singles €21; doubles €33.) **Hostal Apuntadores ❶,** C. Apuntadores 8, is in the middle of the action, less than a block from Pl. Reina. (☎971 71 34 91. Dorms €12; singles €18; doubles €30.) Somewhat pricey but popular outdoor restaurants fill the **Plaza Mayor** and **Plaza Llotja,** but true budget eaters tend to head to the side streets off **Passeig Born,** to the plethora of cheap cafes along **Avenida Joan Miró,** or to the carbon-copy pizzerias along **Passeo Marítimo.** For groceries, try **Servicio y Precios,** on C. Felip Bauzà, near Pl. Reina. (Open M-F 8:30am-8:30pm, Sa 9am-2pm.)

SIGHTS AND ENTERTAINMENT. The capital of the Balearics, Palma does not shy from conspicuous consumption, but it provides plenty of old quarter charm and local flavor. The **Catedral o la Sea,** off Pl. Reina, is one of the world's largest cathedrals and towers over Palma and its bay. (Cathedral and museum open Apr.-Oct. M-F 10am-6pm, Sa 10am-2pm; Nov.-Mar. M-F 10am-3pm. €3.) Built by the Moors, the **Palau Del'Almudaina,** C. Palau Reial, just off Pl. Reina, was at one point a stronghold of *Los Reyes Católicos*, Fernando and Isabel. (Open M-F 10am-

6:30pm, Sa 10am-2pm. Guided visits €4, unguided €3.) The tourist office distributes a list of over 40 nearby **beaches,** many a mere bus ride from Palma; one popular choice is **El Arenal** (Platja de Palma; bus #15), 11km southeast toward the airport.

While a good many party-goers still start their night in the *casco viejo*, nearly everyone ends up by the waterfront at Po. Marítimo come 1am. **La Bodeguita del Medio,** C. Vallseca 18, keeps its crowd dancing to Cuban rhythms. (Open Th-Sa 8pm-3am, Su-W 8pm-1am.) Follow the Aussie accents down C. Apuntadores to the popular **Bar Latitude 39,** C. Felip Bauza 8, a self-proclaimed "yachtie" bar. (Open M-Sa 7pm-3am.) Palma's clubbers start their night along the **Paseo Marítimo** strip, in *bares-musicales* such as salsa-happy **Made in Brasil,** Po. Marítimo 27 (open daily 8pm-4am) and dance-crazy **Salero,** Po. Marítimo 31 (open daily 8pm-6am). The bars and clubs around **El Arenal** overflow with fashion-conscious German disco-fiends, but braving them is well worth the price at **Riu Palace,** one block from the beach. (Cover €15, includes unlimited free drinks. Open M-Su 10pm-6:30am.) **Tito's Palace,** Po. Marítimo, is Palma's hippest disco. (Cover €15-18. Open daily 11pm-6am.)

DAYTRIPS ON MALLORCA. The west coast of Mallorca is one of the most beautiful landscapes in the Mediterranean. The small town of **Sóller** basks in a fertile valley lined with orange groves. The town, with a backdrop of spectacular mountains, is a pleasant change from Las Palmas's more touristed beaches. From Sóller, a 30min. walk down the valley will bring you to **Puerto de Sóller,** a pebble and sand beach where windsurfers zip back and forth. Old-fashioned trolleys also connect the two (every 30min. 7am-9pm, €0.75). On the southeast coast, scalloped fringes of bays and caves are investors' most recent discovery. The **Cuevas Drach,** near Porto Cristo in the southeast, are among the most dramatic natural wonders in Mallorca. The caves amaze with their droopy, finger-like rock formations, illuminating the cave in a spectrum of red and pink color. A 30min. walk into the depths of the cave lies one of the largest underground lakes in the world. The performances given by classical musicians boating across the lake can be classified somewhere between absurd and bizarre; audience members can take free boat rides at the concert's end. A bus runs from Palma to the caves, leaving from the main station by Pl. Espanya (M-Sa 4 per day 10am-1:30pm, Su 10am; €5.40).

IBIZA ☎971

Perhaps nowhere on Earth does style rule over substance (or substances over style) more than on the island of Ibiza (pop. 84,000). Once a 60s hippie enclave, Ibiza has long forgotten her roots in a new-age decadence. Although a thriving gay community still lends credence to its image as a center of "tolerance," the island's high price tags preclude economic diversity. As shocking as it may sound, there is more to Ibiza than just nightlife—its beaches and mountains are some of the most spectacular in the Balearics.

TRANSPORTATION. The **bus** system in Ibiza is much more organized than those of her Balearic sisters. The three main stops in the capital Eivissa are Av. Isidor Macabich 42, Av. Isidor Macabich 20, and Av. Espanya (Voramar buses). For an exact schedule, check the tourist office or *El Diario de Ibiza.* Intercity buses run from Av. Isidor Macabich 42 (☎971 31 21 17) to San Antonio (M-Sa every 15min., Su every 30min. 7am-11:30pm; €1.80). Buses to the beaches cost €0.75 and leave from Av. Isidor Macabich 20.

PRACTICAL INFORMATION. The local paper *Diario de Ibiza* (www.diariodeibiza.es; €0.75) features an *Agenda* page with everything you need to know about Ibiza. The **tourist office,** C. Antoni Riquer 2, is on the water. (☎971 30 19 00; www.ibizaonline.com. Open M-F 9:30am-1:30pm and 5-8pm, Sa 10:30am-1pm.)

Email friends about your crazy night while washing the beer out of your clothes at **Wash and Dry,** Av. España 53. (☎971 39 48 22. Wash and dry €4.20 each. Internet €5.40 per hr. Open M-F 10am-3pm and 5-10pm, Sa 10am-5pm.)

ACCOMMODATIONS AND FOOD. The letters "CH" *(casa de huespedes)* mark many doorways; call the owners at the phone number on the door to see about room availability. Upstairs from Pizzeria de Franco, **Hostal Residencia Sol y Brisa ❷,** Av. B. V. Ramón 15, parallel to Pg. Vara de Rey, has clean rooms, a central location, and a social atmosphere. (☎971 31 08 18; fax 30 30 32. Singles €21; doubles €36.) **Hostal La Marina ❸,** Puerto de Ibiza, C. Barcelona 7, is across from Estació Marítima, right in the middle of the raucous bar scene. (☎971 31 01 72. Singles €27-48; doubles €42-96.) **Hostal Residencia Ripoll ❸** is at C. Vicente Cuervo 14. (☎971 31 42 75. Open July-Sept. Singles €27; doubles €39; 3-person apartments with TV, patio, and kitchen €72.) In a pleasant square close to the edge of the Dalt Vila, **Hostal Parque ❹,** Plaza del Parque 4, has spotless rooms and an attentive staff. (☎971 30 13 58. Singles €48-54; doubles €100.) For a supermarket, try **Hiper Centro,** C. Ignacio Wallis, near C. Juan de Austria. (Open M-Sa 9am-2pm and 5-9pm.) **Mama Pat's Curry y Más,** C. Espanya 43, is Caribbean, creative, and cheap. (Menú €6. Open M-Sa 8am-3am.)

SIGHTS AND ENTERTAINMENT. Wrapped in 16th-century walls, **Dalt Vila** (High Town) hosts 20th-century urban bustle in the city's oldest buildings. Its twisting, sloping streets lead up to the 14th-century cathedral and superb views of the city and ocean. None of Ibiza's beaches is within quick walking distance of **Eivissa (Ibiza City),** but **Platja de Talamanca, Platja des Duros, Platja d'en Bossa,** and **Platja Figueredes** are at most a 20min. bike ride away; buses also leave from Av. Isidor Macabich 20 for Platja d'en Bossa (every 30min., €0.75). One of the most beautiful beaches near Eivissa is **Playa de Las Salinas,** where the nude sunbathers are almost as perfect as the crystal-blue water and silky sand.

The crowds return from the beaches by nightfall, arriving at the largest party on Earth. The bar scene centers around **Calle Barcelona** and spins outward from there into a myriad of sidestreets. **Calle Virgen** is the center of gay nightlife. The island's **discos** (virtually all a mixed gay/straight crowd) are world-famous—veterans claim that you will never experience anything half as wild or fun. Refer to *Ministry in Ibiza* or *DJ,* free at many hostels, bars, and restaurants, for a full list of nightlife options. The **Discobus** runs to and from all the major hotspots (leaves Eivissa from A. Isidoro Macabich every hr. 12:30am-6:30am, schedule for other stops available at tourist office and hotels; €1.50). According to the Guinness Book of World Records, wild, wild **Privilege** is the world's largest club. The club can fit up to 30,000 people, has more than a few bars, and is the place to be Monday nights. (Cover €30-48, includes 1 drink. Open daily June-Sept. midnight-7am.) At **Amnesia,** on the road to San Antonio, you can forget who you are and who you came with at what may just be the craziest disco scene ever. (Cream and MTV Dance Present parties Th; foam parties W and Su. Open daily midnight-7am.) Elegant **Pachá,** on Pg. Perimitral, is a 15min. walk from the port, or a 2min. cab ride. (Cover €30-42. Open daily midnight-7:30am.) Cap off your night in **Space,** which starts hopping around 8am, peaks mid-afternoon, and doesn't wind down until 5pm. (Cover €30 and up.)

MENORCA

Menorca's 200km coastline of raw beaches, rustic landscapes, and well-preserved ancient monuments draws ecologists, photographers, and wealthy young families. Unfortunately, the island's unique qualities and ritzy patrons have resulted in elevated prices. Perched atop a steep bluff, **Mahón** (pop. 23,300) is the main gateway to the island. The more popular **beaches** outside Mahón are accessible by bus.

Transportes Menorca **buses** (7 per day; €1.65) leave from C. Josep Quadrado for **Platges de Son Bou,** which offers 4km of gorgeous beaches on the southern shore. Autocares Fornells buses (2-7 per day; €1.60) leave C. Vasallo in Mahón for the breathtaking views of sandy **Arenal d'en Castell,** while TMSA buses (7 per day; €1) go to touristy **Cala en Porter** and its whitewashed houses, orange stucco roofs, and red sidewalks. A 10min. walk away, the **Covas d'en Xoroi,** caves residing on cliffs high above the sea, are inhabited by a network of bars during the day, and a popular disco at night. (Bars open Apr.-Oct. daily 10:30am-9pm. Cover €3.50. Disco open daily 11pm-late. Cover €15.)

The **tourist office** is at Sa Rovellada de Dalt 24. (☎971 36 37 90. Open M-F 9am-1:30pm and 5-7pm, Sa 9am-1pm.) Off Pl. Miranda, **Hostal-Residencia Jume ❷,** C. Concepció 6, offers rooms in tip-top shape, all with full bath. (☎971 36 32 66; fax 36 48 78. Breakfast included. Closed Dec. 15-Jan. 5. Singles €18; doubles €32-35.) To get to **Hostal La Isla ❷,** C. Santa Catalina 4, take C. Concepció from Pl. Miranda. (☎/fax 971 36 64 92. Singles €15; doubles €30.) **Hostal Orsi ❷** is at C. Infanta 19; from Pl. s'Esplanada, take C. Moreres, which becomes C. Hannover, turn right at Pl. Constitució; follow C. Nou through Pl. Reial. (☎971 36 47 51. Breakfast included. Singles €15-21; doubles €26-35.)

NORTHWESTERN SPAIN

Northwestern Spain is the country's best-kept secret; its seclusion is half its charm. Rainy **Galicia** hides mysterious Celtic ruins, and on the northern coast, tiny **Asturias** allows access to the dramatic Picos de Europa mountain range.

GALICIA (GALIZA)

If, as the Galician saying goes, "rain is art," then there is no gallery more beautiful than the northwest's misty skies. Often veiled in silvery drizzle, it is an area of fern-laden eucalyptus woods, slate-roofed fishing villages, and endless white beaches. Locals speak *gallego*, a linguistic hybrid of Castilian and Portuguese. While newspapers and street signs alternate between languages, most conversations are conducted in Spanish.

SANTIAGO DE COMPOSTELA ☎981

Ever since the remains of the Apostle St. James were discovered here in 813 AD, Santiago (pop. 130,000) has long drawn pilgrims eager to gaze at one of Christianity's holiest cities. The cathedral marks the end of the *Camino de Santiago*, a pilgrimage believed to halve one's time in purgatory. Today, sunburnt pilgrims, street musicians, and hordes of tourists fill the granite streets. In addition to the religious monuments, visitors enjoy the modern art gallery, the state-of-the-art concert hall, and a happening nightlife.

TRANSPORTATION

Trains: R. Horreo (☎981 52 02 02 and 24 02 02). To: **Bilbao** (10¾hr., 9am, €33) via **León** (6½hr., €23) and **Burgos** (8hr., €29); **Madrid** (8hr., 1-3 per day, €35).

Buses: Estación Central de Autobuses, R. de Rodriquez (☎981 58 77 00), a 20min. walk from downtown. Bus #10 and bus C Circular leave from the R. Montero Ríos side of Pr. Galicia for the station (every 15-20min. 6:30am-10pm, €0.66). **ALSA** (☎981 58

61 33) runs to: **Bilbao** (11¼hr., 9am and 9:30pm, €39); **Madrid** (8-9hr., 4 per day 8am-9:30pm, €31); **San Sebastián** (13½hr., 8am and 5:30pm, €44).

Public Transportation: (☎981 58 18 15). Bus #6 to the train station (10am-10:30pm), #9 to the campgrounds (10am-8pm), #10 to the bus station. In the city center, almost all buses stop at Pr. Galicia–check the signs to see which side. Except for buses #6 and 9, buses run every 20min. 6:30am-10:30pm (€0.66).

ORIENTATION AND PRACTICAL INFORMATION

The **cathedral** marks the center of the old city, which sits on a hill above the new city. The **train station** is at the southern end of town. To reach the old city, either take bus #6 to Pr. Galicia or walk up the stairs across the parking lot from the main entrance of the station, cross the street, and bear right onto R. do Horreo, which leads to Pr. Galicia. The bus station is at the northern end of town; the walk is over 20min., take bus #10 to Pr. Galicia. In the old city, three main streets lead to the cathedral: **Rúa de Franco, Rúa de Vilar,** and **Rúa Nova.**

Tourist Offices: Municipal: R. do Vilar 63 (☎981 55 51 29; www.santiagoturismo.com). Open daily 9am-9pm. **Regional:** R. do Vilar 43 (☎981 58 40 81). Open M-F 10am-2pm and 4-7pm, Sa 11am-2pm and 5-7pm, Su and festivals 11am-2pm.

Emergency: ☎112 or 900 44 42 22. **Local Police:** ☎981 54 23 23.

24hr. Pharmacies: Farmacia M. Jesús Valdés Cabo, Cantón del Toral 1. (☎981 58 58 95). **Farmacia R. Bescanses,** Plaza del Toral 1 (☎981 58 59 90).

Medical Assistance: Hospital Xeral, R. das Galeras (☎061 or 981 54 00 00).

Internet Access: Nova 50, R. Nova 50 (☎981 56 01 00). 26 fast computers. €1.20 per hr., €0.45 per min. Open daily 9am-1am.

Post Office: Travesa de Fonseca (☎981 58 12 52; fax 981 56 32 88), on the corner of R. Franco. **Lista de Correos** (around the corner, R. Franco 6) and fax service. Open M-F 8:30am-8:30pm, Sa 9:30am-2pm. **Postal Code:** 15701.

ACCOMMODATIONS

Nearly every street in the old city houses at least one or two *pensiones.* The liveliest and most popular streets are **R. Vilar** and **R. Raíña.** Call ahead in winter when university students occupy most rooms.

Hospedaje Ramos, C. Raíña 18, 2nd fl. (☎981 58 18 59), above O Papa Una restaurant in the center of the *ciudad vieja.* Small, simple rooms. Singles €12, with bath €13; doubles €22/€23.50. ❶

Hospedaje Santa Cruz, R. Vilar 42, 2nd fl. (☎981 58 28 15). Big windows overlook the most popular street in Santiago. Reserve ahead in summer. Singles €15; doubles €25, with bath €30. ❷

Hospedaja Fonseca, R. Fonseca 1, 2nd fl. (☎981 57 24 79). Colorful, sunny rooms across the street from the cathedral. Open July-Sept. Singles, doubles, triples, and quads €12 per person. ❶

Hostal Barbantes, R. do Franco (☎981 58 17 93). Spacious rooms with bath. Singles €26; doubles €39. ❸

Camping As Cancelas, R. 25 de Xullo 35 (☎981 58 02 66), 2km from the cathedral on the northern edge of town; take bus #6 or 9 from the train station or Pr. Galicia. Laundry, supermarket, and pool. €4 per person, per car, and per tent. Electricity €3. ❶

FOOD

Tapas-weary budget travelers will appreciate Santiago's selection of restaurants. Bars and cafeterias line the streets with a variety of inexpensive *menús;* most restaurants are on **R. Vilar, R. Franco, R. Nova,** and **R. Raíña.** In the new city, look near **Pl. Roxa.** Round-off your meal with a *tarta de Santiago*, a rich almond cake emblazoned with a sugary St. James cross. The **market,** between Pl. San Felix and Convento de San Augustín, is an experience in and of itself. (Open M-Sa 7:30am-2pm.) **Supermercado Lorenzo Froiz,** Pl. Toural, is one block from Pr. Galicia. (Open M-Sa 9am-3pm and 4:30-9pm, Sa 9am-3pm and 5-9pm. MC/V.)

Hamburguesería Raíña, C. Raíña 18. Feeding the tired, the hungry, the poor: this joint is a backpacker's dream. Huge hamburgers (€1-2.15), entrees (€3.80-€4.25), and a *menú* that includes bread and wine (€4.30). Open daily 1-4pm and 8pm-1am. ❶

O Cabaliño do Demo, R. Aller Ulloa 7. Walk to Porta Do Camino, where R. Cerca meets R. San Pedro; R. Aller Ulloa is at the end of R. Cerca before the Porta. Enjoy a variety of global vegetarian entrees. *Menú* €6.65. Open M-Sa 2-4pm and 9pm-midnight. Cafe downstairs open 8am-midnight. ❷

Restaurante Le Crêpe, Pr. de Quintana 1, across from the cathedral. Dine on authentic, perfectly thin crepes in this airy, techno-filled eatery. A beautiful terrace makes it perfect for lunch on a sunny day. Open daily 1-4pm and 8pm-midnight. ❷

SIGHTS AND NIGHTLIFE

Offering a cool, quiet sanctuary to priest, pilgrim, and tourist alike, Santiago's **cathedral** rises above the lively old city center. Each of its four facades is a masterpiece from a different time period, and entrances open up onto four different plazas: Platerías, Quintana, Obradoiro, and Azabaxería. The southern **Praza de Platerías** is the oldest of the four facades; the 18th-century Baroque **Obradoiro** facade encases the Maestro Mateo's **Pórtico de la Gloria,** considered the crowning achievement of Spanish Romanesque sculpture. The revered remains of **St. James** lie beneath the high altar in a silver coffer. Inside the **museum** are gorgeous 16th-century tapestries and two poignant statues of the pregnant Virgin Mary. (Cathedral open daily 7am-7pm. Museum open June-Sept. M-Sa 10am-1:30pm and 4-7:30pm, Su 10am-1:30pm; Oct.-Feb. M-Sa

THESE BOOTS WERE MADE FOR WALKING

One night in AD 813, a hermit trudged through the hills on the way to his hermitage. Suddenly, miraculously, bright visions revealed the long-forgotten tomb of the Apostle James ("Santiago" in Spanish). Around this *campus stellae* (field of stars) the cathedral of Santiago de Compostela was built, and around this cathedral a world-famous pilgrimage was born. Since the 9th century, thousands of pilgrims have traveled the 900km of the Camino de Santiago. Clever Benedictine monks built monasteries to host *peregrinos* (pilgrims) along the *camino,* helping to make Santiago's cathedral the most frequented Christian shrine in the world. The scalloped conch shell has become a symbol of the Camino de Santiago, and help distinguish a pilgrim, as do crook-necked walking sticks and sunburned faces. Shelters along the way offer free lodging to pilgrims and stamp "pilgrims' passports" to prove that they were there. At 30km per day, the entire *camino* takes about a month. For inspiration, keep in mind that you are joining the ranks of such illustrious pilgrims as Fernando and Isabel, Francis of Assisi, Pope John Paul II, and Shirley MacLaine. For more info, contact the Officinal de Acogida del Peregrino, C. Vilar 1 (☎981 56 24 19).

SPAIN

11am-1pm and 4-6pm, Su 11am-1pm; Mar.-June M-Sa 10:30am-1:30pm and 4-6:30pm, Su 10:30am-1:30pm. Museum and cloisters €3.) Those curious about the Camino de Santiago can head to the **Museo das Peregrinacións,** Pl. San Miguel. (Open Tu-F 10am-10pm, Sa 10:30am-1:30pm and 5-8pm, Su 10:30am-1:30pm. €2.50; free most of the summer.) The expansive galleries and rooftop *terraza* of the sparkling **Centro Gallego de Arte Contemporáneo (CGAC),** R. Ramon del Valle Inclán, house cutting-edge exhibitions of boundary-bending artists from around the world. (www.cgac.org. Open Tu-Su 11am-8pm. Free.)

At night, crowds looking for post-pilgrimage consumption flood cellars throughout the city. To party with local students, take C. Montero Ríos to the bars and clubs off **Praza Roxa.** **Casa das Crechas,** Vía Sacra 3, just off Pl. Quintana, is a smoky pub with a witchcraft theme. (Beer €3. Open M-F noon-2am, Sa-Su noon-4am.) **Xavestre,** Rua de San Paolo de Antaltares 31, is packed with 20-somethings. (Mixed drinks €5. Open daily noon-late.) Students dance the night away at **La Quintana Cafe,** Pr. Quintana 1. (Beer €3-5. Open daily from 11pm-late.)

DAYTRIP FROM SANTIAGO: O CASTRO DE BAROÑA

Castromil buses from Santiago to Muros stop in Noia (1hr.; M-F 15 per day, Sa 10 per day, Su 8 per day; €3). Hefsel buses from Noia to Riveira stop at O Castro; tell the driver your destination (30min.; M-F 14 per day, Sa 7 per day, Su 11 per day; €1.50).

South of the town of **Noia** is a little-known treasure of historical intrigue and mesmerizing natural beauty: the seaside remains of the 5th-century Celtic fortress of **O Castro de Baroña.** Its foundations dot the isthmus, ascending to a rocky promontory above the sea and then descending to a crescent **beach,** where clothing is optional.

ASTURIAS

Spaniards call the tiny land of Asturias a *paraíso natural* (natural paradise). Surrounded by centuries of civilization, its impenetrable peaks and dense alpine forests have remained untouched. Unlike the rest of the country, travelers don't come here to see the sights; they come here to brave them.

PICOS DE EUROPA

God bless tectonic folding and contracting—300 million years ago, a mere flapping of Mother Nature's limestone bedsheet erected the Picos de Europa, a mountain range of varying and chaotic beauty. This range is home to **Picos de Europa National Park,** the largest national park in Europe. The most popular trails and peaks lie near the **Cares Gorge** (Garganta del Cares). For a list of mountain *refugios* (cabins with bunks but not blankets) and general park info, contact the **Picos de Europa National Park Visitors' Center** in Cangas de Onís. (☎/fax 985 84 86 14. Open daily 9am-2pm and 5-6:30pm.)

CANGAS DE ONÍS. During the summer months, the streets of Cangas are packed with mountaineers and vacationing families looking to spelunk and hang-glide in the Picos de Europa National Park. Cangas itself is a relaxing, if not particularly thrilling, town with its placid, nearly deserted beach, **Praia de Rodeira.** For **buses,** try **ALSA,** Av. Covadonga 18 (☎985 84 81 33), in the Picaro Inmobiliario building across from the tourist office, which runs to Madrid (7hr., 2:35pm, €25) via Valladolid (5hr., €14). The **tourist office,** Jardines del Ayuntamiento 2, is just off Av. Covadonga across from the bus stop. (☎985 84 80 05. Open May-Sept. daily 10am-10pm; Oct.-Apr. 10am-2pm and 4-7pm.)

SWITZERLAND

(SCHWEIZ, SUISSE, SVIZZERA)

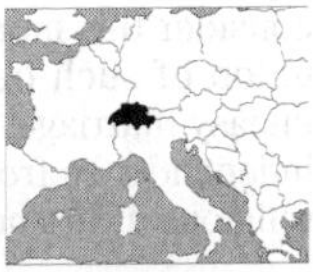

The unparalleled natural beauty of Switzerland entices outdoor enthusiasts from all over the globe to romp in its Alpine playground. Three-fifths of the country is dominated by mountains: the Jura cover the northwest region bordering France; the Alps stretch gracefully across the entire lower half of Switzerland; and the eastern Rhaetian Alps border Austria. While the stereotypes of Switzerland as a "Big Money" banking and watch-making mecca are to some extent true, its energetic youth culture belies its staid reputation. Although the country is not known for being cheap, the best things—warm Swiss hospitality and sublime vistas—always come with no charge.

SYMBOL	❶	❷	❸	❹	❺
ACCOMMODATIONS	under 16SFr	16-35SFr	36-60SFr	61-120SFr	over 120SFr
FOOD	under 9SFr	9-15SFr	16-24SFr	25-34SFr	over 34SFr

For Switzerland, prices are indicated in food and accommodations listings using the system of icons and price ranges above. Prices for accommodations are based on the lowest cost for one person, excluding special deals or discounts. For restaurants, prices are based on the average entree price.

SUGGESTED ITINERARIES

THREE DAYS Experience the great outdoors by spending a day at **Interlaken** (p. 971). Then head to **Lucerne** (1 day, p. 962) for the perfect combination of city culture and natural splendor before jetting to **Geneva** (1 day, p. 976).

ONE WEEK Begin in **Lucerne** (1 day), where your images of a Swiss city will be revealed. Then head to the capital, **Bern** (1 day, p. 958), before getting your adventure thrills in **Interlaken** (1 day). Get a taste of Italian Switzerland in **Locarno** (1 day, p. 985), then traverse northern Italy to reach **Zermatt** (1 day, p. 974). End your trip in the cosmopolitan city of **Geneva** (2 days).

TWO WEEKS Start in **Geneva** (2 days), then check out **Lausanne** (1 day, p. 981) and **Montreux** (1 day, see p. 983). Unwind on the less-touristed path to **Gryon** (1 day, see p. 980), before tackling the Matterhorn in **Zermatt** (1 day) and hiking the Alps at **Interlaken** (1 day). Bask in **Locarno**'s Mediterranean climate (1 day) then explore the **Swiss National Park** (1 day, p. 971). Head to **Zurich** (2 days, p. 964) and nearby **Lucerne** (1 day), before concluding your journey in the capital, **Bern** (2 days).

LIFE AND TIMES

HISTORY

AGAINST THE EMPIRE (500-1520). Switzerland had been loosely united since 1032 as part of the **Holy Roman Empire,** but when Emperor **Rudolf of Habsburg** tried to assert control over their land in the late 13th century, the Swiss decided to rebel. Three of the Alemanni communities (the Forest Cantons) signed an **Everlasting Alliance** in 1291, agreeing to defend each other from outside attack. The Swiss consider this moment to be the beginning of the **Swiss Confederation.** However, a union of such fiercely independent and culturally distinct states made for an uneasy marriage. The **Swabian War** (1499-1500) against the empire brought virtual independence from the Habsburgs, but domestic struggles based on cultural and religious differences continued.

REFORMATION TO REVOLUTION (1520-1800). With no strong central government to settle quibbles between cantons of different religious faith, the Swiss were split even further by the **Protestant Reformation.** Lutheran **Ulrich Zwingli** of Zurich and **John Calvin** of Geneva instituted reforms, but the rural cantons remained loyal to the Catholic faith. When religious differences between the Protestant city cantons and the Catholic rural cantons escalated into full-fledged battle in the mid-16th century, the Confederation intervened, granting Protestants freedom but prohibiting them from imposing their faith on others. The Confederation remained neutral during the **Thirty Years' War,** escaping the devastation wrought on the rest of Europe. The **Peace of Westphalia,** which ended the war in 1648, granted the Swiss independence from the empire, resolving 350 years of international strife. However, Swiss independence was short lived: **Napoleon** invaded in 1798 and established the **Helvetic Republic.** After Napoleon's defeat at Waterloo in 1815, Swiss neutrality was again officially recognized.

NEUTRALITY AND DIPLOMACY (1815 TO THE 20TH CENTURY). With neutrality established by the **Treaty of Vienna** in 1815, Switzerland could turn its attention to domestic issues. Industrial growth brought relative material prosperity, but religious differences continued to create tension between Catholic and all other cantons. A **civil war** broke out in 1847, but it lasted only 25 days. The Protestant forces were victorious, and the country wrote a new constitution modeled after that of the United States. Once stabilized, Switzerland cultivated its reputation for resolving international conflicts. The **Geneva Convention of 1864** established international laws for conduct during war, and Geneva became the headquarters for the **International Red Cross** (see p. 981).

Switzerland's neutrality was tested in **World War I** as French- and German-speaking Switzerland claimed different cultural loyalties. In 1920, Geneva served as the headquarters of the ill-fated **League of Nations,** solidifying Switzerland's reputation as the center for international mediation. During **World War II,** both sides found it useful to have Switzerland (and its banks) as neutral territory. As the rest of Europe cleaned the rubble of two global wars, Switzerland nurtured its already sturdy economy. Zurich emerged as a banking and insurance center. Although Geneva became the world's most prominent diplomatic headquarters, Switzerland remained isolationist in its relations with the rest of Europe, declining membership in the United Nations (until 2002), NATO, and the European Economic Community.

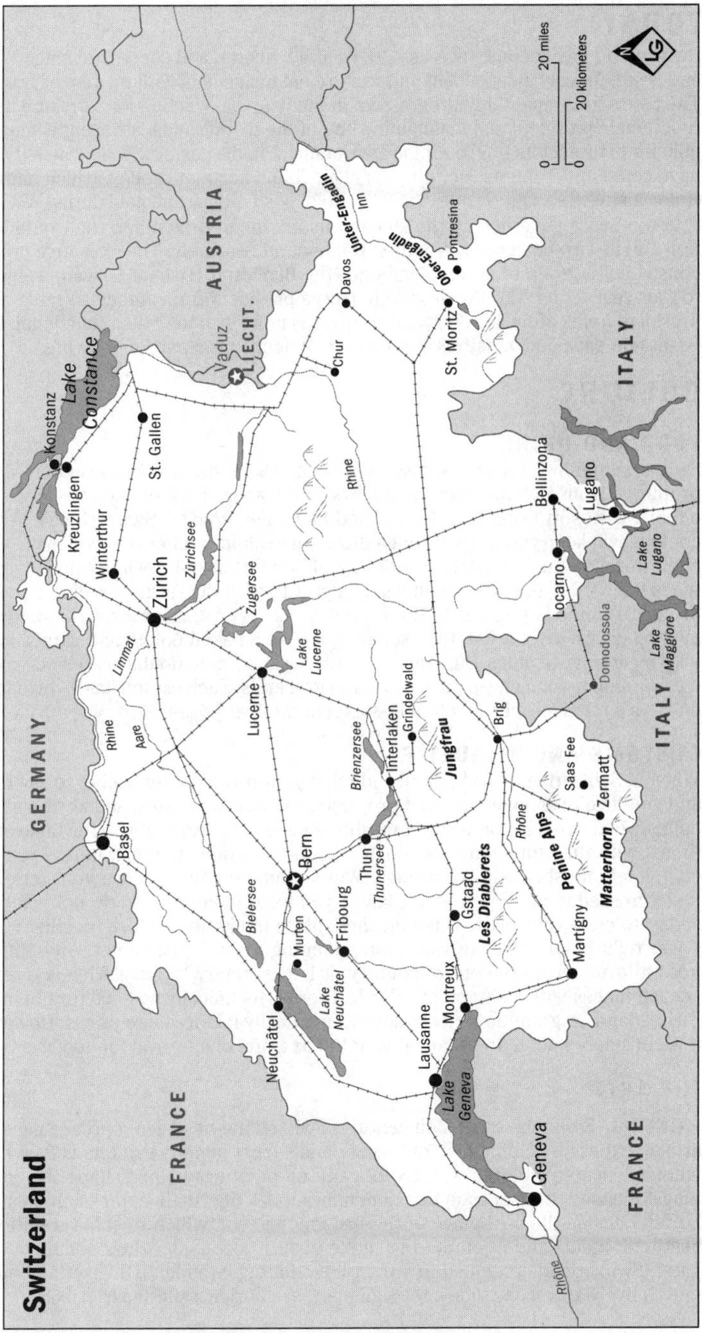

SWITZERLAND

TODAY

Switzerland has become increasingly wealthy, liberal, and successful since WWII and is still fiercely independent and wary of entanglements with the rest of Europe. The Swiss are remarkably progressive in many areas, electing **Ruth Dreifuss** as its first female president and maintaining one of the world's most stringent ecological policies to protect its fragile Alpine environment. In the past few years, Swiss banks have come under intense scrutiny for their "blind account" policy, which allowed Holocaust victims and Nazi leaders alike to deposit money and gold during WWII.

In the Swiss government, the 26 cantons are incorporated into the Confederation and its two-chamber legislature, the Federal Assembly. The executive branch consists of a group of seven members—the **Bundesrat (Federal Council)**—elected to four-year terms. The Bundesrat chooses a president from among its ranks. The president holds office for one year; the post is more symbolic than functional. Frequent **referenda** and **initiatives** make political decisions a part of daily life.

CULTURE

FOOD AND DRINK

Switzerland is not for the lactose intolerant. The Swiss are serious about dairy products, from rich and varied cheeses to decadent milk chocolate—even the major Swiss soft drink is a dairy-based beverage, *rivella*. Switzerland's hearty cooking will keep you warm through those frigid alpine winters but will make your cholesterol skyrocket. Bernese *Rösti*, a plateful of hash-brown potatoes (sometimes flavored with bacon or cheese), is prevalent in the German regions; cheese or meat fondue is popular in the French ones. Try Valaisian *raclette*, made by melting cheese over a fire, then scraping it onto a baked potato and garnishing it with meat or vegetables. Supermarkets Migros and Co-op double as self-serve cafeterias; stop in for a cheap meal as well as groceries. Each canton has its own local beer—it's relatively cheap, often less expensive than Coca-Cola.

CUSTOMS AND ETIQUETTE

When in Switzerland, be punctual and mind your manners: remember to say hello and goodbye to shopkeepers and proprietors of bars and cafes, and always shake hands when being introduced. At mealtime keep both hands above the table at all times, with the knife and fork "open" (apart from one another), unless you are completely finished with your meal. When dining in public, leave your fork and knife crossed in an "X" on your plate if you need to get up and do not want the server to clear your plate; when finished, place the knife and fork together in the lower right hand corner of your plate, pointing towards the center. And, though not uniform across the entire country, it is customary to greet friends or even acquaintances with a kiss on the cheek. There is technically no need for tipping in Switzerland, as gratuities are already automatically factored into prices. However, it is considered polite to round up your bill as a nod of approval for good service.

THE ARTS

PAINTING. Since the early 20th century, Switzerland has been a prime space for artistic experimentation. One of Switzerland's most famous painters is **Paul Klee**, whose delicately colored watercolors and oil paintings helped shape the beginnings of abstraction, questioning dominant modes of artistic expression. In 1916, Zurich became the birthplace of the **Dada** movement, which rejected traditional aesthetic ideals and attempted to make people reconsider their social values. Later, Switzerland continued to attract liberal artistic thinkers. Switzerland maintains a lively arts scene today; for a glimpse, see Zurich's **Kunsthaus,** p. 968.

LITERATURE. Jean-Jacques Rousseau, best known for his *Social Contract* (1762), which inspired the French Revolution, was born in Geneva in 1712 and was always proud of his Swiss background—despite the fact that he spent most of his time outside the country and that the Swiss burned his books. When Romanticism caught on in Switzerland, **J.J. Bodmer** and **J.J. Breitinger** advocated literature in the Swiss-German language, and **Gottfried Keller** penned the *Bildungsroman* (coming-of-age novel) *Green Henry* (1855). **Conrad Ferdinand Meyer** was a highly influential Swiss poet whose writings united characteristics of Romanticism and Realism.

Carl Jung, whose psychiatric practice in Zurich led him to write the famous *Symbols of Transformation* (1916), is considered to be the founder of analytical psychology. Switzerland has also produced several respected modern playwrights: critics laud **Max Frisch** for his Brechtian style and thoughtful treatment of Nazi Germany in works such as *Andorra* (1961), and **Friedrich Dürrenmatt** won renown for his tragicomedic portrayal of human corruptibility in *The Physicists* (1962).

HOLIDAYS AND FESTIVALS

Holidays: New Year's Day (Jan. 1-2); Good Friday (Apr. 18); Easter Monday (Apr. 20); Labor Day (May 1); Swiss National Day (Aug. 1); Christmas (Dec. 25-26).

Festivals: Two raucous festivals are the **Fasnacht** (March; see p. 962) in Basel and the **Escalade** (early December; see p. 981) in Geneva. Music festivals occur throughout the summer, including the **Montreux Jazz Festival** (July; see p. 983) and **Open-Air St. Gallen** (late June; see p. 969).

ESSENTIALS

FACTS AND FIGURES

Official Name: Swiss Confederation.
Capital: Bern.
Major Cities: Geneva, Zurich, Basel.
Population: 7,283,300.
Land Area: 41,290 sq. km.
Time Zone: GMT + 1.
Language: German, French, Italian.
Religions: Roman Catholic (46.1%), Protestant (40%), other (5%), none (8.9%).

DOCUMENTS AND FORMALITIES

Citizens of Australia, Canada, the EU, New Zealand, South Africa, and the US do not need a visa for stays up to 90 days.

Swiss Embassies at Home: Australia, 7 Melbourne Ave., Forrest, Canberra, ACT 2603 (☎02 62 73 39 77). **Canada,** 5 Marlborough Ave., Ottawa, Ontario KIN 8E6 (☎613-235-1837). **Ireland,** 6 Ailesbury Rd., Ballsbridge, Dublin 4 (☎01 218 63 82). **New Zealand,** 22 Panama St., Wellington (☎04 472 15 93). **South Africa,** P818 George Ave., Arcadia 0083, 0001 Pretoria (☎012 430 67 07). **UK,** 16-18 Montague Pl., London W1H 2BQ (☎020 76 16 60 00). and **US,** 2900 Cathedral Ave. NW, Washington D.C. 20008-3499 (☎202-745-7900).

Foreign Embassies in Switzerland: Most foreign embassies are in **Bern** (p. 958).

TRANSPORTATION

BY PLANE. Major international airports for overseas connections are in Bern (BRN), Geneva (GVA), and Zurich (ZRH). From the UK, **easyJet** (☎0870 600 00 00; www.easyjet.com) has flights from London to Geneva and Zurich (UK£47-136). From Ireland, **Aer Lingus** (☎01 886 88 88; www.aerlingus.ie) has round-trip tickets from Dublin, Cork, Galway, Kerry, and Shannon to Zurich for €105-300.

BY TRAIN. Federal **(SBB, CFF)** and private railways connect most towns, with trains running frequently. **Eurail, Europass,** and **Interrail** passes are all valid on Swiss trains. The **SwissPass,** which is sold worldwide, offers five options for unlimited rail travel: 4, 8, 15, 21, or 30 consecutive days. In addition to rail travel, it entitles you to unlimited urban transportation in 36 cities and unlimited travel on certain private railways and lake steamers (2nd-class 4-day pass 242SFr, 8-day 340SFr, 15-day 408SFr, 21-day 476SFr, 1-month 529SFr). The **Swiss Flexipass** entitles you to any 3-8 days of unlimited rail travel within a 1-month period, with the same benefits as the Swiss Pass (2nd-class 3-day pass 236SFr, 5-day 278SFr, 6-day 362SFr, 8-day 426SFr.)

BY BUS. PTT Post Buses, a barrage of government-run banana-colored coaches, connect rural villages and towns where trains don't run. SwissPasses are valid on many buses; Eurailpasses are not. Even with the SwissPass, you might have to pay a bit extra (5-10SFr) if you're riding one of the direct, faster buses.

BY CAR. With armies of mechanized road crews ready to remove snow at a moment's notice, roads at altitudes of up to 1500m generally remain open throughout winter. The speed limit is 50kph in cities, 80kph on open roads, and 120kph on Swiss highways. Many small Swiss towns forbid cars to enter; some forbid only visitors' cars, require special permits, or restrict driving hours. Call ☎140 for roadside assistance.

BY BIKE. Cycling, though strenuous, is a splendid way to see the country; most train stations rent bikes and allow you to return them at another station. The **Touring Club Suisse,** chemin de Blandonnet 4, Case Postale 820, 1214 Vernier (☎(022) 417 27 27; fax 417 20 20), is a good source of information.

TOURIST SERVICES AND MONEY

EMERGENCY	**Police:** ☎117. **Ambulance:** ☎144. **Fire:** ☎118.

TOURIST OFFICES. The **Swiss National Tourist Office,** marked by a standard blue **"i"** sign, is represented in nearly every town in Switzerland; most have English speaking staff. The tourist information website for Switzerland is www.myswitzerland.ch.

Tourist Boards at Home: UK: London, Swiss Centre, Swiss Court, London W1V 8EE (☎0171 734 1921). **US and Canada:** New York, 608 Fifth Ave., New York, NY 10020 (☎877-794-8034; 212-757-5944; fax 262-6116; info.usa@switzerland.com); additional offices in San Francisco (☎415-362-2260) and Los Angeles (☎310-640-8900). In **Canada,** call toll-free (☎800-002-0030) to be transferred to New York.

MONEY. The Swiss monetary unit is the **Swiss Franc (SFr),** divided into 100 *centimes* (called *Rappen* in German Switzerland). Coins come in 5, 10, 20, and 50 *centimes* and 1, 2, and 5SFr; bills come in 10, 20, 50, 100, 500, and 1000SFr. Currency exchange is easiest at ATMs, train stations, and post offices, where rates are the same as or close to bank rates. Though Switzerland is not the cheapest destination, there are ways to experience it on a tight budget. If you stay in hostels and

SWISS FRANC (SFR)		
	AUS$1 = 1.51SFR	1SFR = AUS$1.21
	CDN$1 = 0.97SFR	1SFR = CDN$1.03
	EUR€1 = 1.47SFR	1SFR = EUR€0.68
	NZ$1 = 0.71SFR	1SFR = NZ$1.41
	ZAR1 = 0.14SFR	1SFR = ZAR7.12
	US$1 = 1.51SFR	1SFR = US$0.66
	UK£1 = 2.41SFR	1SFR = UK£0.43

prepare most of your own food, expect to spend anywhere from 45-100SFr per person per day. There is **no value-added tax (VAT)** in Switzerland, though there are frequently tourist taxes of a few SFr per night at hostels.

ACCOMMODATIONS AND CAMPING

HOSTELS AND CAMPING. There are **hostels** (*Jugendherbergen* in German, *Auberges de Jeunesse* in French, *Ostelli* in Italian) in all big cities and in most small towns. *Schweizer Jugendherbergen* (SJH, or Swiss Youth Hostels) runs HI hostels in Switzerland and has a website with contact information for member hostels (www.youthhostel.ch). Hostel beds are usually 20-34SFr. Non-HI members can stay in all of these hostels but are frequently charged a surcharge. The smaller, more informal **Swiss Backpackers (SB)** organization (www.backpacker.ch) has 28 hostels for the young, foreign traveler interested in socializing. Most Swiss **camping sites** are not isolated areas but large plots with many camper vans and cars; camping in Switzerland is less about getting out into nature and more about having a cheap place to sleep. Most sites are open in the summer only. Prices average 6-9SFr per person and 4-10SFr per tent site.

HOTELS AND PRIVATZIMMER. Hotels and pensions tend to charge at least 50-75SFr for a single room, 80-150SFr for a double. The cheapest have Gasthof, Gästehaus, or Hotel-Garni in the name. Privatzimmer (rooms in a family home) run about 25-60SFr per person. Breakfast is included at most accommodations.

HIKING AND SKIING. Nearly every town has **hiking trails;** consult the local tourist office. Lucerne, Interlaken, Grindelwald, and Zermatt offer particularly good hiking opportunities. Trails are usually marked with either red-white-red markers (only sturdy boots and hiking poles needed) or blue-white-blue markers (mountaineering equipment needed). **Skiing** in Switzerland is often less expensive than in North America if you avoid pricey resorts. **Ski passes** run 30-50SFr per day, 100-300SFr per week; a week of lift tickets, equipment rental, lessons, lodging, and *demi-pension* (breakfast plus one other meal) averages 475SFr. **Summer skiing** is less common than it once was but is still available in a few towns, such as Zermatt and Saas Fee.

COMMUNICATION

PHONE CODES	**Country code:** 41. **International dialing prefix:** 00. From outside Switzerland, dial int'l dialing prefix (see inside back cover) + 41 + city code + local number.

TELEPHONES. Wherever possible, use a calling card for international phone calls, as the long-distance rates for national phone services are often exorbitant. Most pay phones in Switzerland accept only prepaid phone cards. Phone cards are available at kiosks, post offices, or train stations. Direct dial access numbers include: **AT&T,** ☎0800 89 00 11; **British Telecom,** ☎0800 55 25 44; **Canada Direct,** ☎0800 55 83 30; **Ireland Direct,** ☎0800 40 00 00; **MCI,** ☎0800 89 02 22; **Sprint,** ☎0800 89 97 77; **Telecom New Zealand,** ☎0800 55 64 11; **Telkom South Africa,** ☎0800 55 85 35.

MAIL. Airmail from Switzerland averages 4-7 days to North America, although times are more unpredictable from smaller towns. Domestic letters take 1-3 days.

LANGUAGES. German, French, and Italian are the national languages. Most urban Swiss speak English fluently. For basic German words and phrases, see p. 1022; for French, see p. 1020; for Italian, see p. 1027.

CENTRAL (GERMAN) SWITZERLAND

The cantons in northwest Switzerland are gently beautiful, with excellent museums, a rich Humanist tradition, and charming old town centers. Previously thought of as a financial mecca, the region has begun to change its image with the growing popularity of Interlaken and the cultural attractions of Lucerne.

BERN

☎031

The city has been Switzerland's capital since 1848, but don't expect fast tracks, power politics, or men in black—Bern prefers to focus on the lighter things in life, such as local Toblerone chocolate and sumptuous flower gardens, and the city, named a world treasure by UNESCO, has a decidedly relaxed atmosphere.

TRANSPORTATION

Flights: The **airport** (BRN; ☎960 21 11) is 20min. from the city. An airport **bus** runs from the train station 50min. before each flight (10min., 14SFr).

Trains: From the **station** at Bahnhofpl. in front of the tourist office, to: **Basel** (1¼hr., every hr., 34SFr); **Berlin** (8hr., 3 per day, 245SFr); **Geneva** (2hr., every hr., 47SFr); **Interlaken** (50min., every hr., 23SFr); **Lausanne** (1¼hr., every 30min., 32SFr); **Lucerne** (1½hr., every 30min., 32SFr); **Milan** (3½hr., 6 per day, 72SFr); **Munich** (6hr., 4 per day, 117SFr); **Paris** (4½hr., 4 per day, 109SFr); **Salzburg** (7¼hr., 5 per day, 130SFr); **Vienna** (10½hr., 4 per day, 157SFr); **Zurich** (1¼hr., every 30min., 45SFr). 25% discount on international fares for ages 26 and under.

Bike Rental: The small blue **Bernrollt Kiosk** outside the train station loans bikes for **free**. A 20SFr deposit plus ID are required. Bikes must be returned on the same day. Open May-Oct. 7:30am-9:30pm.

ORIENTATION AND PRACTICAL INFORMATION

Most of medieval Bern lies in front of the train station and along the Aare River. Bern's main **train station** is a stressful tangle of essential services and extraneous shops. Take extra **caution** around the Parliament park, especially at night.

Tourist Office: (☎328 12 12), on the street level of the train station. In summer, daily **city tours** (8-35SFr) are available by bus, on foot, or by raft. Open June-Sept. daily 9am-8:30pm; Oct.-May M-Sa 9am-6:30pm, Su 10am-5pm.

Embassies: Canada, Kirchenfeldstr. 88 (☎357 32 00). **Ireland,** Kirchenfeldstr. 68 (☎352 14 42). **South Africa,** Alpenstr. 29 (☎350 13 13). **UK,** Thunstr. 50 (☎359 77 00). **US,** Jubiläumstr. 93 (☎357 70 11).

Bi-Gay-Lesbian Resources: Homosexuelle Arbeitsgruppe die Schweiz (HACH), Mühlenpl. 11, is the headquarters of Switzerland's largest gay organization.

Emergency: Police: ☎117. **Ambulance:** ☎144.

Internet Access: Medienhaus, Zeughausg. 14, to the right of Waisenhauspl. **Free** terminal. Open M-F 8am-6pm, Sa 9am-11pm. Basement of **Jäggi Bücher,** Spitalg. on Bubenbergpl. 47-51, in the Loeb department store. Two computers which allow 20min. of **free** access. Four other terminals cost 5SFr for 30min.

Post Office: Schanzenpost 1, a block from the train station. Open M-F 7:30am-6:30pm, Sa 8am-noon. **Poste Restante:** Postlagernde Briefe für Firstname SURNAME, Schanzenpost 3000, Bern 1. **Postal Code:** CH-3000 to CH-3030.

ACCOMMODATIONS

Bern has responded to the influx of backpackers with several new hostels. All offer clean beds with varying services, prices, and personal touches. If the cheaper options are all full, check the tourist office's list of private rooms.

Backpackers Bern/Hotel Glocke, Rathausg. 75 (☎311 37 71). From the train station, cross the tram lines, turn left on Spitalg., continuing on Marktg; turn left at Kornhauspl., then right on Rathausg. The hostel will be on your right. Clean, new, and ideally located. Internet and kitchen access. Laundry 3.80SFr. Reception June-Aug. 8-11am and 3-10pm; Sept.-May 8-11am and 3-8pm. Dorms 32SFr 1st night, 27SFr subsequent nights; singles 75SFr; doubles 120SFr, with bath 160SFr. Apr.-May and Sept.-Oct. dorms 2SFr less, private rooms 5SFr less; Nov.-Mar. 4SFr less/10SFr less. MC/V. ❷

Jugendherberge (HI), Weiherg. 4 (☎311 63 16). From the station, cross the tram lines and go down Christoffelg; take the stairs to the left of the park entrance gates and go down the steep slope, turn left on Weiherg. Breakfast included. Laundry 7SFr. 3-night max. stay. Reception June-Sept. daily 7-10am and 3pm-midnight; Oct.-May 7-10am and 5pm-midnight. Check-out 10am. Closed 2nd and 3rd weeks in Jan. Dorms 28SFr; overflow mattresses 20SFr. Nonmembers add 6SFr. MC/V. ❷

Hotel Nydeck, Gerechtigkeitsg. 1 (☎311 86 86), sits above the busy Junkere bar. Take tram #12 to Nydegg. Bright, modern rooms include TV, telephone, and bathrooms. Breakfast 15SFr. Reception 8am until bar closes. Singles 110SFr; doubles 160SFr. ❹

FOOD

Almost every locale ending in "-platz" overflows with cafes and restaurants, though the bigger ones tend to be pricier and more touristy. Try one of Bern's hearty specialties: *Gschnätzlets* (fried veal, beef, or pork), *Suurchabis* (a kind of sauerkraut), *Gschwellti* (steamed potatoes), or the local Toblerone chocolate. **Fruit and vegetable markets** sell fresh produce daily on Bärenpl. and every Tuesday and Saturday on Bundespl. (open May-Oct. 8am-6pm).

Café des Pyrenées, Kornhauspl. 17, has conservative spaghetti plates (13SFr) and a short list of appetizers. Open M-F 9am-12:30am, Sa 8am-5pm. ❷

Manora, Bubenbergpl. 5A, over the tram lines from the station. This self-service chain tends to be crowded, but serves big platefuls that are nutritious and cheap. Open M-Sa 6:30am-10:45pm, Su 8:30am-10:45pm. ❶

Restaurant Marzilibrücke, Gaßstr. 8. Divided into a classy restaurant and less than classy pizzeria. Gourmet pizzas 16-26SFr. Restaurant open M-Th 11:30am-10:30pm, F 11:30am-11:50pm, Sa 4pm-12:30am, Su 10am-10:30pm. Pizzeria open M-F 5:30-11pm, Sa-Su 4-11pm. ❸

Migros, Marktg. 46, has a restaurant and take-away counters in addition to the supermarket. Open M 9am-6:30pm, T-W and F 8am-6:30pm, Th 8am-9pm, Sa 7am-4pm. ❶

SIGHTS

THE OLD TOWN. The massive **Bundeshaus,** where the Swiss government is centered, dominates the Aare. *(45min. tour every hr. M-Sa 9-11am and 2-4pm. Free.)* From the Bundeshaus, turn left off Kocherg. at Theaterpl. to reach the 13th-century

GRIN AND BEAR IT Legend has it that Duke Berchtold V of Zähringen, founder of Bern, wanted to name the city after the first animal he caught when hunting on the site. The animal was a you-know-what, and Bern (derived from *Bären*, or "bears") was born. The *Bärengraben* themselves weren't built until the Bernese victory at the Battle of Nouana in 1513, when they dragged home a live bear as part of the war booty. A hut was erected for the beast in what is now Bärenplatz (Bear Square) and his descendents have been Bern's collective pets ever since.

Zytglogge (clock tower). Four minutes before each hour, figures on the tower creak to life, but it's more entertaining to watch the tourists ooh and aah. Continue down Kocherg. to the 15th-century Protestant **Münster** (cathedral); inside is a sculpture of the Last Judgment, where the damned shuffle off to Hell on God's left. For a fantastic view of the city, climb the Münster's 100m spire. *(Open Easter-Oct. Tu-Sa 10am-5pm, Su 11:30am-5pm; Nov.-Easter Tu-F 10am-noon and 2-4pm, Sa 10am-noon and 2-5pm, Su 11am-2pm. Tower closes 30min. earlier. 3SFr.)* Several walkways lead steeply down from the Bundeshaus to the **Aare River;** on hotter days, locals dive from the banks to take a brisk ride on its swift currents, but only experienced swimmers should join in.

BEAR PITS AND ROSE GARDEN. Across the Nydeggbr. lie the **Bärengraben** (bear pits), which were recently renovated to provide the bears with trees and rocks to clamber over—perhaps an attempt to make up for the indignity of being on display for gawking crowds. *(Open June-Sept. daily 9am-5:30pm; Oct.-May 10am-4pm.)* The tourist office here presents **The Bern Show,** a slick recap of Bernese history. *(Every 20min. Free.)* The path snaking up the hill to the left leads to the **Rosengarten** (Rose Garden), which provides one of the best views of Bern's *Altstadt.*

KUNSTMUSEUM. Bern's Kunstmuseum includes the world's largest Paul Klee collection and a smattering of 20th-century big names: Picasso, Giacometti, Ernst Kirchner, and Pollock. *(Hodlerstr. 8-12, near Lorrainebrücke. Open Tu 10am-9pm, W-Su 10am-5pm. 15SFr, students and seniors 10SFr, 7SFr/5SFr for Klee collection only.)*

BERNISCHES HISTORISCHE MUSEUM. Anything and everything relating to Bern's lengthy history is displayed in this jam-packed museum, from technology to religious art to 15th-century sculptures. *(Helvetiapl. 5. Open Tu and Th-Su 10am-5pm, W 10am-8pm. 13SFr, students 8SFr, under 16 4SFr.)*

ALBERT EINSTEIN'S HOUSE. This small apartment where Einstein conceived the theory of general relativity is now filled with his photos and letters. *(Kramg. 49. Open Feb.-Nov. Tu-F 10am-5pm, Sa 10am-4pm. 3SFr, students 2SFr.)*

ENTERTAINMENT AND NIGHTLIFE

July's **Gurten Festival** (www.gurtenfestival.ch) has attracted such luminaries as Bob Dylan, Elvis Costello, and Björk, while jazz-lovers arrive in early May for the **International Jazz Festival** (www.jazzfestivalbern.ch). However, Bern's best-known festival is probably the off-the-wall **onion market** on the fourth Monday in November. The orange grove at **Stadgärtnerei Elfnau** (take tram #19 to Elfnau) has free Sunday concerts in summer. From mid-July to mid-August, **OrangeCinema** (www.orangecinema.ch) screens recently released films in the open air; tickets are available from the tourist office in the train station.

At night, the fashionable folk linger in the Altstadt's bars and cafes while a seedier crowd gathers under the gargoyles of the Lorrainebrücke, behind and to the left of the station down Bollwerk. Rablaus Bar, Schmiedenpl. 3, is a popular nightspot. (Open M-W 5pm-1:30am, Th 5pm-2:30am, F-Sa 5pm-3:30am.) Sous le Pont is a den of alternative culture, serving a colorful and diverse crowd. From Bollwerk, head left before Lorrainebrücke through the cement park. (Open Tu 11:30am-12:30am, W-F 11:30am-2:30pm and 6pm-12:30am, Sa 6pm-2:30am.)

BASEL (BÂLE) ☎061

Situated on the Rhine near France and Germany, Basel is home to a large medieval quarter as well as one of the oldest universities in Switzerland—graduates include Erasmus and Nietzsche. Visitors can view art from Roman times to the 20th century and be serenaded by musicians on every street corner year-round.

TRANSPORTATION AND PRACTICAL INFORMATION. Basel has three **train stations:** the French (SNCF) and Swiss (SBB) stations on Centralbahnpl., near the Altstadt, and the German (DB) station across the Rhine. **Trains** leave from the SBB to: Bern (1¼hr., every hr. 5:50am-11:50pm, 34SFr); Geneva (3hr., every hr. 6:20am-8:45pm, 71SFr); Lausanne (2½hr., every hr. 6am-10:30pm, 60SFr); Zurich (1hr., every 15-30min. 4:40am-midnight, 30SFr). Make international connections at the French (SNCF) or German (DB) stations. 25% discount on international trips for ages 16-25. To reach the **tourist office,** Schifflände 5, from the SBB station, take tram #1 to Schifflände; the office is on the river, near the Mittlere Rheinbrücke. (☎268 68 68. Open M-F 8:30am-6pm, Sa-Su 10am-4pm.) For information on **bi, gay, and lesbian** establishments, stop by **Arcados,** Rheing. 69, at Clarapl. (☎681 31 32. Open Tu-F noon-7pm, Sa 11am-4pm.) To reach the **post office,** Rüdeng 1., take tram #1 or 8 to Marktpl. and backtrack one block, away from the river. (Open M-W and F 7:30am-6:30pm, Th 7:30am-8pm, Sa 8am-noon.) **Poste Restante:** Postlagernde Briefe für Firstname SURNAME, Rüdengasse, CH-4001 Basel, Switzerland.

ACCOMMODATIONS AND FOOD. Basel's shortcoming is its lack of cheap lodgings. Call ahead to ensure a spot at the only hostel in town, the **Jugendherberge (HI) ❷,** St. Alban-Kirchrain 10. To get there, take tram #2 to Kunstmuseum; turn right on St. Alban-Vorstadt, then follow the signs. (☎272 05 72. Internet 10SFr per hr. Breakfast included. Laundry 7SFr. Reception Mar.-Oct. 7-10am and 2-11pm; Nov.-Feb. 2-11pm. Check-out 10am. Dorms 29-31SFr; singles 79SFr; doubles 98SFr. Jan.-Feb. 19 and Nov.-Dec. 2.50SFr less. Nonmembers add 6SFr. AmEx/MC/V.) For **Hotel Steinenschanze ❹,** Steinengraben 69, turn left on Centralbahnstr. from the SBB and follow signs for Heuwaage; go up the ramp under the bridge to Steinengraben and turn left. (☎272 53 53. Breakfast included. Reception 24hr. Singles 110-180SFr, under-25 with ISIC 60SFr for up to 3 nights; doubles with shower 160-250SFr, 100SFr. AmEx/MC/V.)

Barfüsserpl., Marktpl., and the streets connecting them are especially full of restaurants. **Wirtshaus zum Schnabel ❷,** Trillengässlein 2, serves tasty German fare. (Open M-Sa 9am-midnight. AmEx/MC/V.) Vegetarians can dine at **Restaurant Gleich ❸,** Leonhardsberg 1. (Open M-F 9am-9:30pm.) Head to **Migros supermarket,** in the SBB station, for groceries. (Open M-F 6am-10pm, Sa-Su 7:30am-10pm.)

SIGHTS. *Groß-Basel* (Greater Basel) and the train station are separated from *Klein-Basel* (Lesser Basel) by the Rheine. The very red **Rathaus** brightens Marktpl. in *Groß-Basel* with its blinding façade and gold and green statues. Behind the Marktpl. is the 775-year-old **Mittlere Rheinbrücke** (Middle Rhine Bridge) which connects the two halves of Basel. At the other end of Marktpl. is a spectacular **Jean Tinguely Fountain,** also known as the **Fasnachtsbrunnen.** Behind Marktpl. stands the red sandstone **Münster,** where you can visit the tomb of Erasmus or climb the tower for a spectacular view of the city. (Open Easter-Oct.15 M-F 10am-5pm, Sa 10am-4pm, Su 1-5pm; Oct. 16-Easter M-Sa 11am-4pm, Su 2-4pm. Free. Tower closes 30min. before the church. 3SFr.)

MONSTER MADNESS In 1529, Basel's residents spiritedly joined the Reformation and ousted the bishop, keeping his *crozier* (staff) as the town's emblem. The staff shares this honor with the basilisk (Basel-isk), a creature part serpent, part dragon, and part rooster, which caused what may be the world's first and only public trial and execution of a chicken. In 1474, a hen allegedly laid an egg on a dung heap under a full moon, an action sure to hatch the horrible creature. The bird was tried, found guilty, and beheaded, and the egg was ceremonially burnt.

MUSEUMS AND ENTERTAINMENT. Basel has over 30 museums; pick up the comprehensive museum guide at the tourist office. The **Basel Card,** available at the tourist office, provides admission to all museums as well as discounts around town. (24hr. card 25SFr, 48hr. card 33SFr, 72hr. card 45SFr.) The **Kunstmuseum** (Museum of Fine Arts), St. Alban-Graben 16, houses outstanding collections of old and new masters; admission also gives access to the **Museum für Gegenwartskunst** (Modern Art), St. Alban-Rheinweg 60. (Kunstmuseum open Tu and Th-Su 10am-5pm, W 10am-7pm. Gegenwartskunst open Tu-Su 11am-5pm. 10SFr, students 8SFr, first Su of every month free.) At **Museum Jean Tinguely,** Grenzacherstr. 214a, everything rattles and shakes in homage to the Swiss sculptor's vision of metal and movement. Take tram #2 or 15 to Wettsteinpl. and bus #31 or 36 to Museum Tinguely. (Open W-Su 11am-7pm. 7SFr, students 5SFr.) The **Fondation Beyeler,** Baselstr. 101, is one of Europe's finest private art collections, housing works by nearly every major artist. Take tram #6 to Fondation Beyeler. (Open daily 9am-8pm. M-F 16SFr, Sa-Su 20SFr; students 5SFr; 12SFr after 6pm.)

In a year-round party town, Basel's carnival, or **Fasnacht,** still manages to distinguish itself. The festivities commence the Monday before Lent with the *Morgestraich*, a not-to-be-missed, 600-year-old, 72hr. parade beginning at 4am. The goal is to scare away winter (it rarely succeeds). During the rest of the year, head to **Barfüsserplatz** for an evening of bar-hopping. **Atlantis,** Klosterberg 10, is a multi-level, sophisticated bar with reggae, jazz, and funk. (Open Tu-Th 11am-midnight, F 11:30am-4am, Sa 6pm-4am.) **Brauerei Fischerstube,** Rheing. 45, brews the delectably sharp *Hell Spezial* ("light special") beer. (Open M-Th 10am-midnight, F-Sa 10am-1am, Su 5pm-midnight. Full dinner menu from 6pm.)

LUCERNE (LUZERN) ☎041

Lucerne is the Swiss traveler's dream come true. The city is small but cosmopolitan, satisfying sophisticated culture lovers and also providing outdoor opportunities for the adventurous. Sunrise over the famous **Mt. Pilatus** has hypnotized hikers and artists—including Twain, Wagner, and Goethe—for centuries.

TRANSPORTATION. Trains leave Bahnhofpl. for: Basel (1¼hr., 1-2 per hr. 4:40am-11:50pm, 29SFr); Bern (1½hr., 1-2 per hr. 4:40am-11:50pm, 30SFr); Geneva (3½hr., every hr. 4:40am-9:55pm, 64SFr); Interlaken (2hr., every hr. 6:30am-7:35pm, 26SFr); Lausanne (2½hr., every hr. 4:40am-9:55pm, 56SFr); Lugano (3hr., every hr. 6:40am-10:15pm, 56SFr); and Zurich (1hr., 2 per hr. 4:55am-11:10pm, 20SFr.) **VBL buses** depart from in front of the station and provide extensive coverage of Lucerne (1 zone 2.40SFr; 2 zones 3.60SFr; 3 zones 5.60SFr; day pass 9SFr; Swiss Pass valid); **route maps** are available at the tourist office.

PRACTICAL INFORMATION. The **tourist office,** in the station, has free city guides, makes hotel reservations for free, and sells the **Visitor's Card,** which, with a hotel or hostel stamp, gives discounts at museums, stores, bars, and more. (☎227

17 17. Open May-Oct. M-F 8:30am-7:30pm, Sa-Su 9am-7:30pm; Nov.-Apr. M-F 8:30am-6pm, Sa-Su 9am-6pm.) **C+A Clothing,** on Hertensteinstr. at the top of the Altstadt, has two free, but busy **Internet** terminals. (Open M-W 9am-6:30pm, Th-F 9am-9pm, Sa 8:30am-4pm.) The **post office** is on the corner of Bahnhofstr. and Bahnhofpl. Address mail to be held: Postlagernde Briefe für NAME, Hauptpost, **CH-6000** Luzern 1. (Open M-F 7:30am-6:30pm, Sa 8am-noon.)

ACCOMMODATIONS AND FOOD. Relatively inexpensive beds are limited in Lucerne, so call ahead to ensure a roof over your head. To reach **Backpackers ❷,** Alpenquai 42, turn right from the station on Inseliquai and follow it until it turns into Alpenquai (20min.); the hostel is on the right (☎360 04 20. Laundry 8SFr. Internet 10SFr per hr. Reception 7:30-10am and 4-11pm. 2- to 4-bed dorms 27-33SFr.) Until 1998, **Hotel Löwengraben ❷,** Löwengraben 18, was a prison, but it was converted into a trendy, clean hostel with a bar, restaurant, Internet (15SFr per hr.), and all-night dance parties for guests every summer Saturday. (☎417 12 12. Breakfast 11SFr. 3- to 4-bed dorms 30SFr; doubles with shower 140-165SFr.) **Tourist Hotel Luzern ❸,** St. Karliquai 12, on the Alstadt side of the Spreuerbrücke, has cheap, clean rooms with views of the river and Mt. Pilatus. (☎410 24 74. Internet 12SFr per hr. Breakfast included. Laundry 10SFr. Reception 7am-10pm. Dorms 35-40SFr; doubles 98-112SFr; quads 156-180SFr. Dec.-May dorms 2-7SFr less; rooms 10-20SFr less.) **Markets** along the river sell fresh and cheap goods on Tuesday and Saturday mornings. Additionally, there's a **Migros supermarket** at the station. (Open M-W and Sa 6:30am-8pm, Th-F 6:30am-9pm, Sa-Su 8am-8pm.)

SIGHTS AND NIGHTLIFE. The *Altstadt*, across the river over Spreuerbrücke from the station, is famous for its frescoed houses, especially those on Hirschenpl. The 660-year-old **Kapellbrücke,** a wooden-roofed bridge, runs from left of the train station to the Altstadt and is ornately decorated with Swiss historical scenes; further down the river, the **Spreuerbrücke** is decorated by Kaspar Meglinger's eerie *Totentanz* (Dance of Death) paintings. On the hills above the river, the **Museggmauer** and its towers are all that remain of the city's medieval ramparts. Three of the towers are accessible to visitors and provide panoramas of the city; walk along St. Karliquai, turn right (uphill), and follow the brown castle signs. (Open daily 8am-7pm.) To the east is the magnificent **Löwendenkmal** (Lion Monument), the dying lion of Lucerne, which is carved into a cliff on Denkmalstr. The **Picasso Museum,** Am Rhyn Haus, Furreng. 21, displays 200 intimate photographs of Picasso as well as a large collection of his unpublished works. From Schwanenpl., take Rathausquai to Furreng. (Open Apr.-Oct. daily 10am-6pm; Nov.-Mar. 11am-4pm. 8SFr, with guest card 7SFr, students 5SFr.) The **Verkehrshaus der Schweiz** (Swiss Transport Museum), Lidostr. 5, has interactive displays on all kinds of vehicles, but the real highlight is the trains. Take bus #6, 8, or 24 to Verkehrshaus. (Open daily Apr.-Oct. 10am-6pm; Nov.-Mar. 10am-5pm. 21SFr, students 19SFr; with SwissPass 16SFr, with Eurail 14SFr.)

Lucerne's nightlife is more about lingering than club-hopping. **Club 57,** Haldenstr. 57, is filled with candlelight and billows of red Moroccan fabric. (Open 8pm-2:30am.) **The Loft,** Haldenstr. 21, is a smoky club with hip-hop and house. (No cover W and Su, Th 10SFr, F 12SFr, Sa 15SFr. Open W-Th 10pm-3am and F-Su 9pm-4am.) Lucerne attracts big names for its **Blue Balls Festival** (3rd week in July) and **Blues Festival** (2nd week in Nov.).

DAYTRIPS FROM LUCERNE

MT. PILATUS AND RIGI KULM

The view of the Alps from the top of **Mt. Pilatus** (2132m) is absolutely phenomenal. For the most memorable trip, catch a boat from Lucerne to Alpnachstad (90min.), ascend by the world's steepest **cogwheel train,** then descend by cable car to Krienz and take the bus back to Lucerne (entire trip 78.40SFr; with Eurail or Swisspass 40-43SFr). For less money and more exercise, take a train or boat to Hegiswil and hike up to Fräkmüntegg (3hr.), a halfway point on the cable car (23SFr, 25% off with Eurail or Swisspass). Across the sea from Pilatus soars the **Rigi Kilm,** which has a magnificent view of the lake and its neighbor. Ferries run from Lucerne to Vitznau, where you can catch a cogwheel train to the summit. You can also conquer Rigi on foot; it's 5hr. from Vitznau to the top, and anyone who tires out halfway can pick up the train at Rigi Kaltbad (3hr. up the hill) and ride the rest of the way. Return by train, take the cable car from Rigi Kaltbad to Weggis, and return to Lucerne by boat (round-trip 87SFr, with Eurail or Swisspass 29SFr).

ZURICH (ZÜRICH) ☎01

Zurich contains a disproportionate number of Switzerland's many banks, but there's more to Zurich than money. The city was once the focal point of the Reformation, led by Ulrich Zwingli, in German Switzerland. In the 20th century, Zurich's Protestant asceticism succumbed to avant-garde artistic and philosophical radicalism: James Joyce toiled away at *Ulysses* in one corner of the city, while Russian exile Vladimir Lenin read Marx and dreamed of revolution in another. Meanwhile, a group of raucous artists calling themselves the Dadaists founded the seminal proto-performance art collective, the Cabaret Voltaire. A walk through Zurich's *Altstadt* and student quarter will immerse you in the energetic youth counter-culture that spawned these subversive thinkers just steps away from the rabid capitalism of the famous Bahnhofstraße shopping district.

TRANSPORTATION

Flights: Kloten Airport (ZRH; ☎816 25 00) is the main hub for **Swiss International Airlines** (☎(084) 885 20 00) with daily connections to Frankfurt, Paris, London, and New York. Trains to the *Hauptbahnhof* (main train station) leave every 10-20min. (5.40SFr).

Trains: From the **Hauptbahnhof** at Bahnhofpl. to: **Basel** (1¼hr., 1-3 per hr., 30SFr); **Bern** (1¼hr., 1-2 per hr., 45SFr); **Geneva** via Bern (3hr., every hr., 76SFr); **Lucerne** (1hr., 2 per hr., 19.80SFr); **Lugano** (3hr., 1-3 per hr., 60SFr); **Milan** (4½hr., every hr., 72SFr); **Munich** (4hr., 4 per day, 86SFr); **Paris** (6-8hr., 2 per day, 133SFr); **Salzburg** (6hr., 5 per day, 97SFr); **Vienna** (9hr., 4 per day, 124SFr). Under-26 discount on international trains.

Public Transportation: Public buses, trams, and trolleys run 5:30am-midnight. **Short rides** (under 5 stops) 2.10SFr (yellow button on ticket machine); **long rides** 3.60SFr (blue button). Buy tickets before boarding and validate in machine or face a fine (from 50SFr). A **Tageskarte** (7.20SFr) is valid for 24hr. of unlimited public transport. **Nightbuses** run from the center of the city to outlying areas F-Sa at 1, 1:30, 2, and 3am.

Bike Rental: Globus (☎(079) 336 36 10); **Enge** (☎(079) 336 36 12); **Hauptbahnhof** (☎210 13 88). All have **free** bike rental. Passport and 20SFr deposit required. Open daily 7:30am-9:30pm.

ORIENTATION AND PRACTICAL INFORMATION

The **Limmat River** splits the city down the middle on its way to the **Zürichsee.** On the west side of the river is the **Hauptbahnhof** and **Bahnhofstraße,** which begins just outside the Hauptbahnhof and runs parallel to the Limmat. Halfway down Bahnhofstr. lies **Paradeplatz,** the town center; **Bürkliplatz** is at the far end of Bahnhofstr. On the east side of the river is the University district, which stretches above the narrow **Niederdorfstraße** and pulses with bars, restaurants, and hostels.

Tourist Offices: Main office (☎215 40 00), in the train station. Offers current information, as well as an electronic hotel reservation board. The staff finds rooms after 10:30am. Open Apr.-Oct. M-Sa 8am-8:30pm, Su 8:30am-6:30pm; Nov.-Mar. M-F 8:30am-7pm, Sa-Su 8:30am-6:30pm. For bikers and backpackers, the **Touring Club des Schweiz** (TCS), Alfred-Escher-Str. 38 (☎286 86 86), offers maps and travel info.

Currency Exchange: At the main train station. Cash advances with MC/V and photo ID; 200SFr min. Open daily 6:30am-10pm. **Credit Suisse,** Bahnhofstr. 53. 2.50SFr commission. Open daily 6am-10pm.

Luggage Storage: At the *Hauptbahnhof.* Lockers 5-8SFr per day. Luggage watch 5SFr at the *Gepäck* counter. Open daily 6am-10:50pm.

Bi-Gay-Lesbian Resources: Homosexuelle Arbeitsgruppe Zürich (HAZ), (☎271 22 50), Sihlquai 67, P.O. Box 7088, CH-8023. Offers library, meetings, and the free newsletter *InfoSchwül.* Open Tu-F 7:30-11pm, Su noon-2pm and 6-11pm.

Laundromat: Speed Wash Self Service Wascherei, Müllerstr. 55. Wash and dry 5kg for 10.20SFr. Open M-Sa 7am-10pm, Su 10:30am-10pm.

Emergency: Police: ☎117. **Ambulance:** ☎144. **Fire:** ☎118.

Rape Crisis Line: ☎291 46 46.

24-Hour Pharmacy: Theaterstr. 14 (☎252 5600), on Bellevuepl.

Internet Access: The **ETH Library,** Ramistr. 101, in the *Hauptgebäude,* has 3 free computers. Take tram #6, 9, or 10 to ETH, enter the main building, and take elevator to fl. H. Open M-F 8:30am-9pm, Sa 9am-2pm. **Telefon Corner,** downstairs in the station next to Marché Mövenpick. 6SFr per hr. Open daily 8am-10pm.

Post Office: Main office, Sihlpost, Kasernestr. 97, just behind the station. Open M-F 6:30am-10:30pm, Sa 6am-8pm. Address *Poste Restante* to: Firstname SURNAME, Sihlpost, Postlagernde Briefe, **CH-8021** Zürich, SWITZERLAND.

ACCOMMODATIONS

The few budget accommodations in Zurich are easily accessible via Zurich's public transportation. Reserve at least a day in advance, especially during the summer.

Martahaus, Zähringerstr. 36 (☎251 45 50). From the station, cross Bahnhofbrücke, and take the 2nd right after Limmatquai at the Seilgraben sign. Sparkling clean rooms in a great location. Breakfast and internet access included. Reception 24hr. Partitioned dorms 37SFr; singles 75-80SFr; doubles 98-110SFr; triples 129SFr. AmEx/MC/V. The owners also run the nearby **Luther Pension,** a women-only residence that shares reception facilities with Martahaus and has slightly lower prices (single 50SFr). ❸

The City Backpacker-Hotel Biber, Niederdorfstr. 5 (☎251 90 15). From the station, cross Bahnhofbrücke; turn right on Niederdorfstr. Tightly packed rooms are balanced by the great location. Internet 12SFr per hr. Kitchen available. Sheets 3SFr. Laundry 10SFr. Key deposit 20SFr or passport. Reception 8am-noon and 3-10pm. Checkout

10am. 4- to 6-bed dorms 29SFr; singles 65-66SFr; doubles 88-92SFr. MC/V. ❷

Justinus Heim Zürich, Freudenbergstr. 146 (☎361 38 06). Take tram #9 or 10 to Seilbahn Rigiblick, then take the hillside tram (by the Migros) uphill to the end. Quiet and spacious. Breakfast and kitchen access included. Reception daily 8am-noon and 5-9pm. Checkout 10am. Singles 50SFr, with shower 60SFr; doubles 80SFr/100SFr; triples 135SFr/165SFr; all rates reduced for multiple-week stays. V. ❸

Hotel Otter, Oberdorfstr. 7 (☎251 22 07), and the swanky **Wurste Bar** below it attract an eclectic and artsy crowd. All rooms have TV and phone. Breakfast included. Reception 8am-5pm. Check-out noon. Singles 100SFr; doubles 130-160SFr. AmEx/MC/V. ❹

Jugendherberge Zürich (HI), Mutschellenstr. 114 (☎482 35 44). Take tram #7 (dir.: Wollishofen) to Morgental and walk 5min. back toward the Migros. An enormous, basic hostel. Internet 1SFr for 4min. Breakfast included. Laundry 8SFr. 24hr. reception, except noon-1pm. Check-in after 2pm. Check-out 10am. Dorms 32SFr; doubles with toilet and shower 90SFr. Nonmembers add 6SFr. AmEx/MC/V. ❶

Camping Seebucht, Seestr. 559 (☎482 16 12). Take tram #11 to Bürklipl., then catch bus #161 or 165 to Stadtgrenze. Showers 2SFr. Reception M-Sa 7:30am-noon and 3-10pm, Su 8am-noon. Open May-Sept. 8SFr per person, 12SFr per tent. 1.50SFr tax. ❶

FOOD

Zurich's specialty is *Geschnetzeltes mit Rösti*, slivered veal in a cream sauce with hash-brown potatoes. The cheapest meals (around 6SFr) are along **Niederdorfstraße.** Try the **farmer's market,** Burklipl. (Tu and F 6-11am), or stop by the **Co-op Super-Center,** next to the train station, for groceries (open M-F 7am-8pm, Sa 7am-4pm). **Manor ❷,** Bahnhofstr. 75 (corner of Uraniastr.), has a self-service restaurant with cheap meals on the 5th floor. (Open M-F 9am-8pm, Sa 9am-4pm.) Check out *Swiss Backpacker News* (at the tourist office and Hotel Biber) for more information on budget meals in Zurich.

Bodega Española, Münsterg. 15. Catalán delights such as potato tortilla dishes (15.50SFr) and tapas (4.80SFr). Open daily 10am-12:30am. AmEx/MC/V. ❷

Gran-Café, Limmatquai 66. Sit right by the Limmat and enjoy some of the tastiest meals around. Daily *Menü* from 13.80SFr. Open M-Th 6am-11:30pm, F 6am-midnight, Sa 7am-midnight, Su 7:30am-11:30pm. AmEx/MC/V. ❸

IN RECENT NEWS

RECLAIMING THE PAST

Unlike most countries, Switzerland did not have banking dormancy laws until 2001. In the period between the two world wars, Switzerland, a stable country amid Europe in turmoil, was a logical safe destination for money. The Nazi era turned Europe upside down. If account owners did not survive to collect their assets, the accounts just sat there. Finally, under increasing pressure, a tribunal was established in Zurich to deal with accounts left over from before 1945. Between 1998 and 2001, we arbitrated over 10,000 claims to 2500 dormant accounts. The stimulus came from the fact that many accounts were owned by victims of the Holocaust and had found their rightful heirs.

The work was long and often emotionally draining. In my most rewarding case, I got to reunite cousins who each had thought that no one in their family had survived. For the survivors, it was not about the money. Many just wanted their relatives to be remembered. It was rewarding to receive thank-you notes, even from claimants who had been denied. They were grateful for our listening to their stories and for treating them like human beings. No amount of money can put the past right, but we can restore money to entitled heirs, and, in all cases record memories.

—Charles Ehrlich is a former Researcher-Writer for *Let's Go: Spain and Portugal.* As Senior Staff Attorney at the Claims Resolution Tribunal, he adjudicated claims to Nazi-era Swiss bank accounts.

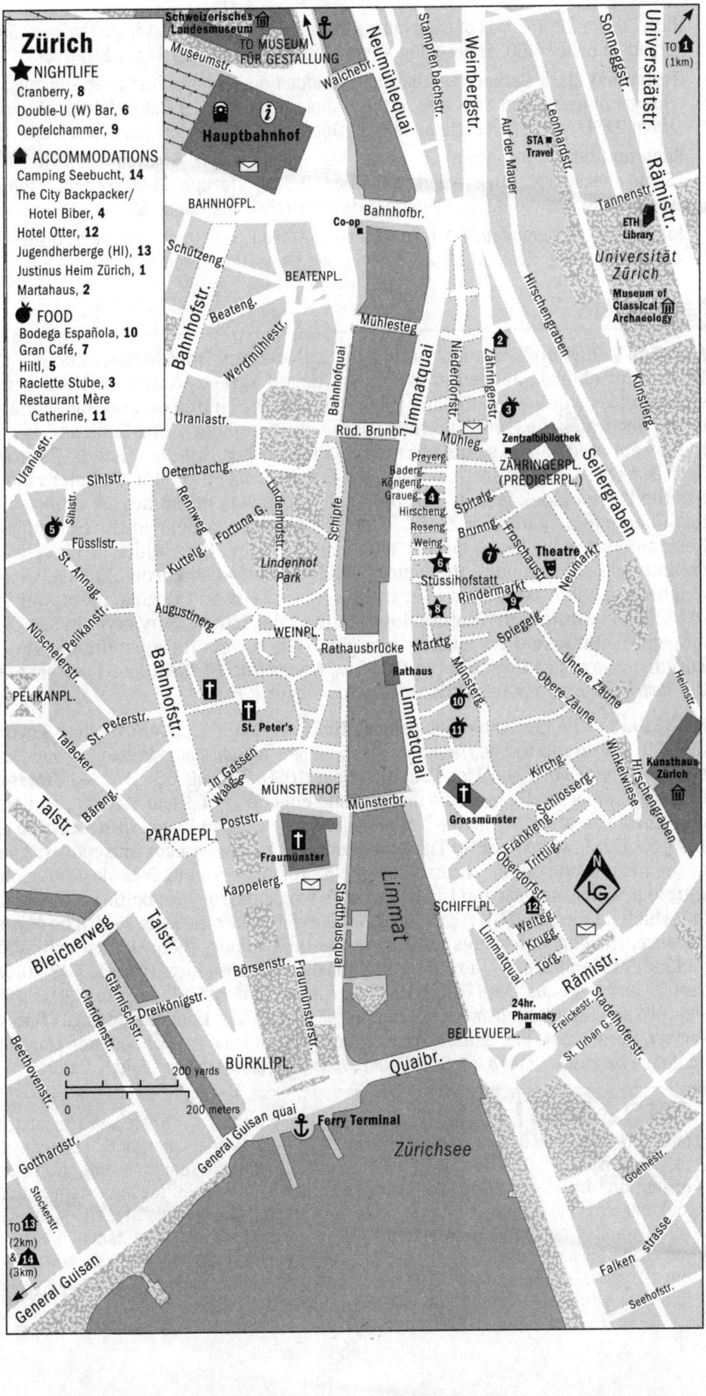

SWITZERLAND

Hiltl, Sihlstr. 28. The lack of meat makes this a surprisingly cheap vegetarian joint. Salad or Indian buffet 4.60SFr per 100g. Open M-Sa 7am-11pm, Su 11am-11pm. ❶

Restaurant Mere Catherine, Nägelihof 3, hidden on a small street near Großmünster. Hoards of locals find their way to this yuppie restaurant for delightful French dishes (from 21SFr) and an upscale ambience. Open daily 11am-midnight. AmEx/MC/V. ❸

Raclette Stube, Zähringerstr. 16. Serves high-quality, classic Swiss fare in an authentic Swiss atmosphere. Large *raclette* appetizer 12.50SFr, fondue 39.50SFr per person, all-you-can-eat *raclette* 32.50SFr per person. Open daily from 6pm. ❺

Johanniter, Niederdorfstr. 70. A favorite among locals, with traditional Swiss dishes and outdoor seating. Rösti 13.80-20.50SFr. Open daily 10am-4am. ❷

SIGHTS

ALTSTADT. Right off Paradepl. stands the 13th-century **Fraumünster;** although it's a Protestant church, Jewish artist Marc Chagall agreed to design the beautiful stained-glass windows in the late 1960s. Outside the church on Fraumünsterstr., a mural decorates the Gothic archway in the courtyard, picturing Felix and Regula, the decapitated patron saints of Zurich, with their heads in their hands. *(Open May-Sept. 9am-6pm; Oct., Mar.-Apr. 10am-5pm; Nov.-Feb. 10-4pm.)* Next door, **St. Peter's Church** has the largest clock face in Europe. The twin towers of the nearby **Großmünster** have become a symbol of Zurich. Ulrich Zwingli spearheaded the Reformation here, and one of his bibles lies in a case near the pulpit from which he preached. A column tells the legend of the church: while chasing a stag from Aachen, Charlemagne supposedly stumbled over the graves of Felix and Regula, prompting him to build *Großmünster*. Venture downstairs to the 12th-century crypt to see Charlemagne's statue and 2m sword, then climb the towers for a panoramic view of Zurich. *(Church open Mar. 15 to Oct. 9am-6pm; Nov. to Mar. 14 10am-5pm. Tower open Mar.-Oct. daily 1:30-5pm, Nov.-Feb. Sa-Su 9:15am-5pm. Tower 2SFr.)*

MUSEUMS. The incredible **Kunsthaus Zürich,** Heimpl. 1, covers Western art from the 15th century to today. *(Take tram #3, 5, 8, or 9 to Kunsthaus. Multilingual audio tours available. Open Tu-Th 10am-9pm, F-Su 10am-5pm. 10SFr, students 6SFr; W free.)* **Museum Rietberg,** Gablerstr. 15, presents an exquisite collection of Asian, African, and other non-European art. *(Take tram #7 to Museum Rietberg. Open Tu and Th-Su 10am-5pm, W 10am-8pm. 6SFr, students 3SFr.)* The **Schweizerisches Landesmuseum,** Museumstr. 2, next to the main train station, encapsulates Swiss history; exhibits include 16th-century astrological instruments and Ulrich Zwingli's weapons from the Battle of Kappel during which he died in 1531. *(Open Tu-Su 10:30am-5pm. 5SFr, students 3SFr.)* The **Museum Bellerive,** Höschg. 3, features rotating out-of-the-ordinary themes. Past exhibitions include "Made in Japan" (a room full of plastic Japanese meals). *(☎383 43 76. Take tram #2 or 4 to Höschg. Open Tu-Th 10am-8pm, F 10am-5pm, Sa-Su 11am-5pm. 6SFr, students and children 3SFr. Closes between exhibits, so call ahead.)* The **Lindt and Sprüngli Chocolate Factory,** Seestr. 204, has exhibits in German only, but the free chocolates transcend language barriers. *(Tram #1 or 8 to Kilburn. Open W-F 10am-noon and 1-4pm. Free.)*

CHOCOHOLICS The Swiss have long had a love affair with chocolate–milk chocolate was first concocted here in 1876, and Nestlé, Lindt, and Toblerone all call Switzerland home. But has this seemingly innocuous romance turned into an obsession? In May of 2001, the Swiss government introduced postage stamps that look and smell like squares of chocolate. (The original design called for chocolate-*flavored* stamps, but the idea was dropped for hygienic reasons.) The stamps are even packaged on paper designed to look like foil wrappers. Officially, they commemorate the centennial of Chocosuisse, the association of chocolate makers and importers, but it might just be evidence that the Swiss truly are addicted.

ENTERTAINMENT AND NIGHTLIFE

Niederdorfstraße rocks as the epicenter of Zurich's nightlife (although women may not want to walk alone in this area at night), and **Münsterg.** and **Limmatquai** are lined with cafes and bars. Pick up *ZüriTip* for more information. On Friday and Saturday nights in summer, **Hirschenpl.** (on Niederdorfstr.) hosts an assortment of impressive street performers. Locals and students guzzle beer (from 10SFr) on the terrace at **Double-U (W) Bar,** Niederdorfstr. 21. (Open M-Th 4pm-2am, F-Su until 4am.) **Oepfelchammer,** Rindermarkt 12, is a popular Swiss wine bar (3-5SFr per glass. Open Tu-Sa 11am-12:30am.) **Cranberry,** Metzgerg. 3 is a gay-friendly bar right off Limmatquai. (Open Su-Tu 5pm-midnight, W-Th until 1am, F-Sa until 2am.)

ST. GALLEN ☎071

St. Gallen's main draw is the **Stiftsbibliothek (Abbey Library),** a Baroque library designated a World Heritage Treasure by UNESCO. Visitors in fuzzy protective slippers glide across exquisite parquet floors and marvel at the lavishly carved and polished shelves, rows of gilt-spined books, and ancient manuscripts. (☎227 34 16. Open M-Sa 10am-5pm, Su 10am-4pm. Closed Nov.-Dec. English tours can be arranged through the tourist office. 7SFr, students 5SFr.) Often overshadowed by the library, but no less beautiful, is the **Kathedrale St. Gallen,** which has enormous stained-glass windows, intricately carved confessionals, and impressive murals. (☎227 33 88. Open daily 7am-6pm, except during mass.) Follow the Marktplatz away from the train station to reach **Museumstraße,** which holds St. Gallen's four museums. The best are the small but fascinating **Natural History Museum** (☎242 06 70), with rotating exhibits, and the slightly disorganized **Historisches Museum** (☎242 06 42), which covers traditional Swiss culture. Although all the exhibits are in German, the detailed displays and varied themes still make a trip to Museumstr. interesting for non-German-speakers. (All museums open Tu-F 10am-noon and 2-5pm, Sa-Su 10am-5pm. Admission to all four museums 6SFr, students 2SFr.) In late June, the **Open-Air St. Gallen Music Festival** features over 20 live bands. Past headliners have included Red Hot Chili Peppers, Cypress Hill, B.B. King, and James Brown. (☎(087) 887 79 94; www.openairsg.ch. Tickets 104-134SFr.)

Trains run to: Bern (2½hr.; 5am-10:40pm; 63-65SFr); Geneva (4½hr.; 5am-8:40pm; 94SFr); Munich (3hr.; 4 per day 8:30am-6:30pm; 62SFr, under 26 51SFr); and Zurich (1hr.; 5am-10:40pm; 26-34SFr). To get to the **tourist office,** Bahnhofpl. 1a, from the train station, cross the bus stop and pass the fountain on the left; the office is on the right. (☎227 37 37. Open M-F 9am-6pm, Sa 9am-noon. City tours June-Sept. M, W, and F 2pm. 15SFr.) **Internet** is available at **Media Lounge,** Katherineng. 10. (☎244 30 90. 2SFr for 10min. Open M-F 9am-9pm, sporadic hours Sa-Su.) The impeccably clean **Jugendherberge St. Gallen (HI) ❷,** Jüchstr. 25, has a TV room, library, and Internet access (1SFr for 4min.). From the Appenzeller/Trogener station next to the main station, take the orange train from track #12 (dir.: Trogen) to Schülerhaus; from the stop, walk uphill, turn left across the tracks, and head downhill. (☎245 47 77. Reception daily 7-10am and 5-10:30pm. Check-out 10am. Closed Dec.-Feb. Dorms 26SFr; singles 46SFr; doubles 72SFr; nonmembers add 6SFr. AmEx/MC/V.) Perched high above the hostel, **Restaurant Scheitlinsbüchel ❸,** Scheitlinsbüchelweg 10, offers a sublime view and traditional Swiss meals. (Open Tu-Su 9am-late.) The **Migros supermarket,** St. Leonhardstr., and adjoining buffet restaurant are one block behind the train station. (Open M-W and F 8am-6:30pm, Th 8am-9pm, Sa 8am-5pm.) **Postal code:** CH-9000.

GRAUBÜNDEN

The largest, least populous, and most alpine of the Swiss cantons, Graubünden's rugged gorges, fir forests, and eddying rivers give the region a wildness seldom found in ultra-civilized Switzerland. Visitors should plan their trips carefully, especially in ski season, when reservations are absolutely required. Beware, almost everything shuts down in May and June.

CHUR ☎081

Chur is the capital of Graubünden and, at 11,000 years old, Switzerland's oldest settlement. Despite the area's rich history and diverse culture, the city attracts few tourists. Since Chur is the transportation hub of Graubünden, you'll probably experience it only as the gateway to other towns. The cavernous 12th-century **Dom,** at the top of the old town, displays eight altarpieces and the **Hochaltar,** a flamboyant 15th-century masterpiece of gold and wood. (Open Tu-Sa 10am-noon and 2-4pm.) The **Bündner Kunstmuseum,** Bahnhofstr. 35, displays the art of the three Giacomettis—Giovanni, Alberto, and Augusto—along with works by Swiss artists. (Open Tu-W and F-Su 10am-noon and 2-5pm, Th 10am-noon and 2-8pm. 7SFr, students 4SFr.) The **Rætisches Museum,** Hofstr. 1, houses a collection of archaeological finds that documents the development of Graubünden. (Open Tu-Su 10am-noon and 2-5pm. 5SFr, students 2SFr.)

Trains connect Chur to Arosa (1hr., every hr. 5:35am-11pm, 13.40SFr); Basel (2¾hr., 1-2 per hr. 4:45am-10:15pm, 60SFr); St. Gallen (1½hr., every hr. 4:45am-10:15pm, 34SFr); and Zurich (1½hr., 1-2 per hr. 4:45am-10:15pm, 35SFr). To get to the **tourist office,** Grabenstr. 5, follow Bahnhofstr. two blocks to Postpl., then turn left on Grabenstr. The office finds rooms for free. (☎252 18 18. Open M 1:30-6pm, Tu-F 8:30am-noon and 1:30-6pm, Sa 9am-noon.) No luxurious budget accommodations await in Chur. If you need to stay in Chur, try **Hotel Schweizerhaus ❷,** Kasernenstr. 10. From the Postpl., turn right on Grabenstr. and follow as it becomes Engadinestr. and crosses the bridge; continue for 300m along Kasernenstr. through Chur's red-light district. (☎252 10 96. Breakfast 10SFr. Reception daily 7am-midnight. 35SFr per person.) Chur has a number of trendy eating establishments; **Valentino's Grill ❶,** Untereg. 5, is the best budget option. From Postpl., turn right on Grabenstr., then head left under the arches. (Open M-Th 11:45am-2pm and 5-11:30pm, F 11:45am-2pm and 5pm-2am, Sa noon-2am.) **Postal code:** CH-7000.

AROSA ☎081

A squeaking train ride from Chur twists and turns through rugged peaks and above lush valleys to reach the secluded town of Arosa. Offering affordable ski-and-stay packages, Arosa caters to budget-conscious **skiers** and **snowboarders.** Developed ski trails dominate one side of the valley; on the other, **hiking** trails stretch to isolated valleys. A **free shuttle bus** (every hr. in summer, every 20min. in winter) transports visitors nearly everywhere. Stops include the ski lifts and the **tourist office,** which arranges hiking trips and ski lessons and makes free hotel reservations. (☎378 70 20. Open Dec. 7 to Apr. 13 M-F 9am-6pm, Sa 9am-5:30pm, Su 4-6:30pm; Apr. 14 to Dec. 6 M-F 8am-noon and 1:30-6pm, Sa 9am-1pm; June 29 to Aug. 17 M-F 8am-noon and 1:30-6pm, Sa 9am-1pm and 2-4pm.)

Arosa is accessible only by way of a scenic **train** route from Chur (1hr., every hr. 5:35am-11pm, 13.40SFr). **Haus Florentium ❸,** run by the ski-lift company Arosa Bergbahnen, is a former convent hidden in the woods. From the tourist office, follow the cobblestone path down the hill and as it bends left and zigzags up the hill. At the top, continue right towards Hotel Hohe Promenade, then left at the gravel path for Pension Suveran, and right at the dirt path through the woods in front of the pension. (☎377 13 97. Breakfast included. Dec.-Apr. 2-night stay and 2-day ski pass 246SFr; 6-night stay and 6-day ski pass 588SFr. Groups only in summer.) **Jugendherberge (HI) ❷,** Seewaldstr., is a better choice in the summer. Walk past the tourist office and follow the signs down the hill. (☎377 13 97. Breakfast included. Showers 0.50SFr for 3min. Reception in summer daily 7-10am and 5-10pm; in winter 7am-noon and 4-10pm. Open mid-June to mid-Oct. and mid-Dec. to mid-Apr. Dorms 29SFr; doubles 70SFr. In winter with dinner included, dorms 44SFr, doubles 108SFr.) **Pension Suveran ❸,** on the way to the Haus Florentium (see above), is a homey, wood-paneled chalet. (☎377 19 69. Breakfast included. Singles 46-60SFr; doubles 82-110SFr. Add 10SFr per person in winter for stays shorter than 3 nights.) **Groceries** are available at the **Co-op,** near the tourist office on Poststr. (Open M-F 8am-12:30pm and 2-6:30pm, Sa 8am-4pm.) **Postal Code:** CH-7050.

THE SWISS NATIONAL PARK

The Swiss National Park offers hikes that rival the best in Switzerland, but no other area can match the park's isolation from man-made constructs, which allows hikers to experience the undiluted wildness of the natural terrain. A network of 20 hiking trails runs throughout the park, mostly concentrated in the center. Few of the trails are level; most involve a lot of climbing, often into snow-covered areas. However, all trails are clearly marked, and it is against park rules to wander off the designated trails. Trails that require no mountaineering gear are marked with white-red-white blazes. The Swiss, however, are practically mountain goats, so even some of the no-gear routes can be tricky.

Zernez is the main gateway to the park, and home to the main headquarters of the park, the **National Parkhouse.** The staff provides helpful trail maps as well as up-to-date information on which trails are navigable—take their advice seriously; when they say a trail is too dangerous, they mean it. (☎856 13 78. Open June-Oct. Tu 8:30am-10pm, W-Su 8:30am-6pm.) From Zernez, **trains** and **post buses** run to other towns in the area, including Scuol, Samedan, and S-chanf. The park is closed November through May. The Swiss National Park is one of the most strictly regulated nature preserves in the world. Camping and campfires are prohibited in the park, as is collecting flowers and plants. A team of wardens patrols the park at all times, so it's better not to test the rules. Zernez, Scuol, and S-chanf have campsites right outside the park boundaries. **Phone code:** ☎081

JUNGFRAU REGION

The most famous (and most-visited) region of the Bernese Oberland, the Jungfrau area has attracted tourists for hundreds of years with glorious hiking trails and permanently snow-capped peaks. From Interlaken, the valley splits at the foot of the Jungfrau: the eastern valley contains Grindelwald, with easy access to two glaciers, while the western valley hosts many smaller towns, each with unique hiking opportunities. The two valleys are divided by an easily hikeable ridge.

INTERLAKEN ☎033

Interlaken lies between the Thunersee and the Brienzersee at the foot of the largest mountains in Switzerland. With easy access to these natural playgrounds, Interlaken has earned its rightful place as one of Switzerland's prime tourist attractions and its top outdoor adventure spot.

TRANSPORTATION AND PRACTICAL INFORMATION. The Westbahnhof (☎826 47 50) and Ostbahnhof (☎828 73 19) have **trains** to: Basel (5:30am-10:30pm, 56SFr); Bern (6:35am-10:30pm, 24SFr); Geneva (5:30am-9:30pm, 63SFr); Lucerne

IN RECENT NEWS

SO YOU SAY YOU WANT A (BIO)REVOLUTION?

The environmentally conscious Swiss are putting their money where their mouths are when it comes to the fight against abusing and altering Mother Nature's world. It's not just clean air and litter-free streets that the Swiss fight for—it's the very food on their shelves that is the current hot issue for businesses, farmers, and consumers alike.

From the recent boom of vegetarian restaurants to the bio-revolution, the Swiss have added many earth-friendly characteristics to their diets. "Bio" products—ones that are produced without human modification—have invaded supermarkets and restaurants alike. The Swiss even passed a food ordinance law in 2001 that says that GMOs (food with genetically modified organisms) cannot be marketed until they pass government inspection and have proper labeling. Other procedures are underway to prevent GMO imports from crossing the border into Switzerland. Today, over 10% of farms in Switzerland are organic, which means that GMOs are absent from the seeds and animal feed used.

Currently, the two largest Swiss supermarket chains, Co-op and Migros, dominate the bio market, with over 600 organic products on their shelves. Of course, the decision to move away from GMO products comes at a price. Their environmentally sound counterparts can add up to 10% to the cost of foods.

(5:30am-8:35pm, 26SFr); Lugano/Locarno (5:30am-4:35pm, 87SFr); and Zurich (5:30am-10:30pm, 62SFr). The Ostbahnhof also sends trains to Grindelwald (June-Sept. every 30min., Sept.-May every hr. 6:35am-10:35pm; 9.80SFr).

The **tourist office,** Höheweg 37, in the Hotel Metropole, offers free maps. (☎826 53 00. Open July-Aug. M-F 8am-6pm, Sa 8am-5pm, Su 10am-noon and 4-6pm; Sept.-June M-F 8am-noon and 1:30-6pm, Sa 9am-noon.) Rent **bikes** at either train station. (30SFr per day. Open daily 6am-7pm.) For **snow and weather information,** call ☎828 79 31. In case of emergency, call the **police** ☎117 or the **hospital** ☎826 26 26. **YESS** on Centralstr. has 5 terminals for **Internet** access. (4SFr for 20min. Open daily 11am-11pm.) **Postal Code:** CH-3800.

ACCOMMODATIONS AND FOOD. **Backpackers Villa Sonnenhof ❷,** Alpenstr. 16, diagonally across the Höhenmatte from the tourist office, is friendly and low-key. (☎826 71 71. Internet 10SFr per hr. Mountain bikes 28SFr per day. Laundry 10SFr. Breakfast and lockers included. Reception 7:30-11am and 4-10pm. Check-out 9:30am. 4- to 7-bed dorms 29-32SFr; doubles 82-88SFr; triples 111-120SFr. 5SFr extra for balcony. AmEx/MC/V.) **Swiss Adventure Hostel ❷,** in the tiny town of Boltigen, provides access to all of Interlaken's activities with beds far from the craziness of the town. A free shuttle runs to and from Interlaken each day (40min.); call for times and availability. The adventure company run out of this hostel offers the same activities as the Interlaken companies, but with a more personal touch. (☎773 73 73. 4- to 10-bed dorms 20SFr; doubles with shower 70SFr; quads with shower 100SFr. Special deals if combined with adventure sports.) **Happy Inn ❷,** Rosenstr. 17, lives up to its name with a friendly staff. From Westbahnhof, turn left towards the tourist office, then right on Rosenstr. at Centralpl. (☎822 32 25. Breakfast 8SFr. Reception daily 7am-6pm. Reserve far in advance. Dorms 22SFr; singles 38SFr; doubles 76SFr.) To reach **Hotel Alphorn ❹,** Rugenstr. 8, take a right out of the station onto Bahnhofstr., then left onto Rugenstr., then another right onto Rothornstr. The Alphorn boasts newly remodelled rooms with sparkling bathrooms. (☎822 30 51. Breakfast included. Doubles 100-150SFr.)

Most hostels serve cheap food. **Migros supermarket ❶,** across from the Ostbahnhof or behind the Westbahnhof, and its restaurant are also convenient. (Open M-Th 8am-7pm, F 8am-9pm, Sa 7:30am-5pm). **Confiserie Schuh ❶,** across from the tourist office, has been an Interlaken institution since the 19th century. The Chocolate medallions (1SFr) are extremely popular. (Open daily 8am-11pm.)

DEATH-(UN)DEFYING. Interlaken's adventure sports are thrilling, but accidents do happen. On July 27, 1999, 19 tourists were killed by a flash flood while canyoning. Be aware that you participate in all activities at your own risk.

OUTDOORS AND HIKING. Interlaken offers a wide range of adrenaline-pumping activities. **Alpin Raft** (☎823 41 00), the most established company in Interlaken, has qualified, personable guides and offers: paragliding (150SFr); canyoning (110-195SFr); river rafting (95-109SFr); skydiving (380SFr); bungee jumping (125-165SFr); and hang gliding (180SFr). All prices include transportation to and from any hostel in Interlaken. A number of horseback and hiking tours, as well as rock-climbing lessons, are also available upon request. **Outdoor Interlaken** (☎826 77 19) offers rock-climbing lessons (89SFr per half-day) and kayaking tours (155SFr per half-day). The owner of **Skydiving Xdream,** Stefan Heuser, has been on the Swiss skydiving team for 17 years. (Skydiving 380SFr. ☎(079) 759 34 83. Open Apr.-Oct.)

Interlaken's most traversed trail climbs to the **Harder Kulm** (1310m). From the Ostbahnhof, head toward town, take the first road-bridge right across the river, and follow the yellow signs that later give way to white-red-white markings on the rocks. From the top, signs lead back to the Westbahnhof. A funicular runs from the trailhead near the Ostbahnhof to the top from May to October. (2½hr. up, 1½hr. down. May to mid-Oct. 13.40SFr, round-trip 21SFr; 25% Eurailpass and SwissPass discount.) For flatter **trails,** turn left from the train station and left before the bridge, then follow the canal over to the nature reserve on the shore of the Thunersee. The trail winds up the Lombach river and through pastures at the base of the Harder Kulm back toward town (3hr.).

ENTERTAINMENT. **Balmer's Herberge,** Hauptstr. 23-25, offers live music—usually reggae—on most nights. (Bar open 9pm-1am.) **Buddy's,** Höheweg 33, is a small, crowded English-style pub with cheap beer. (Open daily 10am-12:30am.) **Johnny's Dancing Club,** Höheweg 92, located in the basement of the Hotel Carlton, is Interlaken's oldest disco. (Open Tu-Su 9:30pm-3am).

GRINDELWALD ☎036

Grindelwald, launching point for the only glaciers accessible by foot in the Bernese Oberland, crouches beneath the north face of the Eiger. Although it only has two streets, Grindelwald is the most developed part of the Jungfrau Region. The town has all kinds of hikes, from easy valley walks to challenging peaks for top climbers. The **Bergführerbüro** (Mountain Guides Office), 200m past the tourist office, sells hiking maps and coordinates glacier walks, ice climbing, and mountaineering. (☎853 52 00. Open June-Oct. M-Sa 9am-noon and 3-6pm, Su 4-6pm.) The 5hr. **Lower Glacier** *(Untere Grindelwaldgletscher)* hike is moderately steep and can be done in sneakers. To reach the trailhead, walk up the main street away from the station and follow the signs downhill to Pfinstegg. Hikers can either walk

MOUNTAIN MANN The face in the Harder Mountain is known as the Harder Mann. According to legend, a strolling monk became possessed, chased a small girl off a cliff, and was turned to stone as punishment. It might make sense if he hadn't been given the best view in Interlaken. Local lore says that the Harder Mann returns every year to fight off winter. On January 2, residents celebrate with wooden "Harder Mann" masks and a large carnival. If you decide to hike this landmark, *do not leave the marked paths.* Every summer people die attempting to climb roped-off areas.

the first forested section of the trail (1hr.), following signs up to Pfinstegg., or take a funicular to the Pfinstegg. hut (8am-4pm, July to mid-Sept. until 7pm; 9.80SFr). From the hut, signs lead to Stieregg., a hut that offers food.

The **Jungfraubahn** runs to Grindelwald from Interlaken's *Ostbahnhof* (40min., 6:35am-10:30pm, 9.80SFr). The **tourist office,** located in the Sport-Zentrum to the right of the station, provides chairlift information and a list of free guided excursions. (☎854 12 12. Open July-Aug. M-F 8am-7pm, Sa 8am-6pm, Su 9-11am and 3-5pm; Sept.-June M-F 8am-noon and 2-6pm, Sa 8am-noon and 2-5pm). For **weather forecasts,** call ☎162; for **medical assistance,** call ☎853 11 53. Access the **Internet** at the tourist office (15SFr per hr.) or at **Ernst Schudel's,** across the street. (Open M-Sa 9am-noon and 2-6:30pm.) **Hotel Hirschen ❹,** to the right of the tourist office, offers clean, bright rooms with comfortable beds. (☎854 84 84. Breakfast included. Reception daily 8am-10pm. Singles 90-135SFr; doubles 150-220SFr.) To reach the **Jugendherberge (HI) ❷,** head left out of the train station for 400m, then cut uphill to the right just before Chalet Alpenblume and follow the steep trail all the way up the hill. (☎853 10 09. Breakfast and lockers included. Reception daily 7:30-10am and 3pm-midnight. Dorms 27.50-29.50SFr; doubles 69SFr, with toilet and shower 101SFr. Nonmembers add 6SFr. AmEx/MC.) For **Gletscherdorf Camping ❶,** take a right out of the station; after 250m, by the ski school, turn right and head downhill. Follow the road as it weaves through a residential neighborhood toward the RV-filled field below. (☎853 14 29. Showers included. Reception daily 8-10am and 5-8pm; come anytime. Open May-Oct. 6.90SFr per person; 6-12SFr per tent. Electricity 4SFr.) **Tea Room Riggenburg ❶,** past the tourist office away from the station, offers soups, salads, lasagna, and fresh-baked desserts. (Open Tu-Sa 7am-10pm, Su 8am-6pm.) There's a **Co-op supermarket** on Hauptstr., across from the tourist office. (Open M-F 8am-6:30pm, Sa 8am-4pm.)

VALAIS

The Valais occupies the deep, wide, glacial gorge traced by the Rhône river. Though mountain resorts can be over-touristed, the region's spectacular peaks and the skiing, hiking, and climbing make fighting traffic worthwhile. Zermatt has the most to offer skiers and hikers, although some small towns have great appeal. Note: Eurail is not valid on the BVZ train line, which serves many regional towns.

ZERMATT AND THE MATTERHORN ☎027

The valley blocks out the great Alpine summits that ring Zermatt, allowing the **Matterhorn** (4478m) to rise alone above the town. Spectacular, well-marked ski paths are accessible to all visitors, including **Europe's longest run,** the 13km trail from Klein Matterhorn to Zermatt. A one-day **ski pass** for any of the area's regions runs 60-77SFr. The **Zermatt Alpin Center,** which houses both the **Bergführerbüro** (Guide's Office; ☎966 24 60) and the **Skischulbüro** (Ski School Office; ☎966 24 66), is located past the post office from the station; here you can pick up detailed four-day weather forecasts, ski passes, and info on guided climbing expeditions. (Open July-Sept. M-F 8:30am-noon and 3:30-7pm, Sa 3:30-7pm, Su 10am-noon and 3:30-7pm; late Dec. to mid-May daily 5-7pm.) Rental prices for **skis** and **snowboards** are set throughout Zermatt (28-50SFr per day, 123-215SFr per week). Try **Slalom Sport,** on Kirchstr. (☎966 23 66. Open M-Sa 8am-noon and 2-6:30pm), or **Bayard Sports,** directly across from the station. (☎966 49 60. Open daily 8am-noon and 2-7pm.) **Freeride Film Factory** (☎213 38 07) offers custom **hiking, biking,** and **climbing** expeditions (160-250SFr) and will even give you a videotape of your trek.

Cars and buses are illegal in Zermatt to preserve the Alpine air—the only way in is the hourly **BVZ** (Brig-Visp-Zermatt) rail line. Connect from Brig (1½hr.; 6am-9pm; 34SFr, round-trip 67SFr) and from Lausanne (73SFr/140SFr) via Visp. The **tourist office,** on Bahnhofpl. in the station complex, sells the **Wanderkarte** (hiking map) for 25.90SFr. (☎966 81 00. Open mid-June to mid-Oct. M-F 8:30am-6pm, Sa 8:30am-6:30pm, Su 9:30am-noon and 4-6:30pm; mid-Oct. to mid-Dec. and May to mid-June M-F 8:30am-noon and 1:30-6pm, Sa 8:30am-noon; mid-Dec. to Apr. 8:30am-noon and 1:30-6:30pm, Sa 8:30am-6:30pm, Su 9:30am-noon and 4-6:30pm.) **Hotel Bahnhof ❷,** on Bahnhofstr. to the left of the station, provides hotel housing at hostel rates. (☎967 24 06. Dorms 30SFr; singles 54-56SFr, with shower 64-68SFr; doubles 84-86SFr/94-96SFr. MC/V.) **Walliserkanne ❸,** on Bahnhofstr. next to the post office, offers filling Swiss fare at reasonable prices. (Open daily 9am-midnight. AmEx/DC/MC/V.) **Café du Pont ❷,** on Bahnhofstr, is Zermatt's oldest restaurant and has multilingual menus burned into slabs of wood hanging on the wall. (Open June-Oct. and Dec.-Apr. daily 9am-11pm, food served 11am-10pm.) Pick up groceries at the **Co-op Center** opposite the station. (Open M-F 8:15am-12:15pm and 1:45-6:30pm, Sa 8:15am-12:15pm and 1:45-6pm.) **Postal code:** CH-3920.

SAAS FEE ☎027

Nicknamed "the pearl of the Alps," Saas Fee (1800m) is in a hanging valley above the Saastal, snuggled among thirteen 4000m peaks. The glacial ice of the **Feegletscher** ("fairy glacier") comes so low that you can visit the frozen giant on a 30min. evening stroll. To protect its Alpine glory, the town is closed to cars, and town officials prohibit disturbing "the fairy-like charm of Saas Fee" after 10pm (noisemakers fined 200SFr). Summer **skiers** enjoy 20km of runs, and in winter an immense network of lifts opens (daypass 59SFr, 6-day 270SFr, 13-day 480SFr). The **Ski School,** across the street from church, offers group skiing and snowboarding lessons from mid-Dec. to Apr. (☎957 23 48. 43-46SFr for 2hr, 158-172SFr per week.) Stores in the **Swiss Rent-A-Sport System** (look for the black and red logo) offer three grades of equipment (skis and snowboards 28-50SFr per day, 109-190SFr for 6 days; boots 15-19SFr/56-80SFr). The **Bergführerbüro** (Mountain Guides' Office), in the same building as the ski school, leads **climbs** of varying difficulty levels. (☎957 44 64. Open M-Sa 9am-noon and 3-6pm Closed May-June.)

A **post bus** runs to Visp (50min.; every hr. 5:35am-7:35pm; 15.20SFr, round-trip 30.40SFr), where trains connect to Lausanne and Zermatt. Reserve a seat on all buses at least 2hr. before departure; call ☎958 11 45 or drop by the bus station. (Open 7:30am-12:35pm and 1:15-6.35pm.) The **tourist office,** opposite the bus station, dispenses hiking advice and town maps. (☎958 18 58. Open July to mid-Sept. and mid-Dec. to mid-Apr. M-F 8:30am-noon and 2-6:30pm, Sa 8am-7pm, Su 9am-noon and 2-6pm; mid-Sept. to mid-Dec. and mid-Apr. to June M-Sa 8:30am-noon and 2-6pm, Su 10am-noon and 4-6pm.) **Hotel Garni Bergheimat ❸,** in the center of town, offers clean mid-sized rooms with showers at reasonable rates. (☎957 20 30. Breakfast included. 60SFr per person in summer, 70SFr in winter, 50SFr in shoulder season.) There are several **grocery stores** sprinkled around town, most open during the same hours. (Open M-F 8:30am-12:15pm and 2:15-6:30pm, Sa 8:15am-12:15pm and 2:15-5pm.) **Postal code:** CH-3906.

WESTERN (FRENCH) SWITZERLAND

All around Lac Léman, hills sprinkled with villas and blanketed by patchwork vineyards seem tame and settled—until the haze clears. From behind the hills surge rough-hewn mountain peaks with the energizing promise of unpopulated wilderness and wide lonely expanses.

GENEVA (GENÈVE) ☎022

A stay in Geneva will likely change your definition of diversity. As the most international city in Switzerland, Geneva is a brew of 178,000 unlikely neighbors: wealthy businessmen speed past dreadlocked skaters in the street while nuclear families stroll past hardworking artists squatting in abandoned factories. Part of Geneva's malleability comes from its strongly international component; only one-third of the city's residents are natives of the canton. Today, multinational organizations, including the Red Cross and the United Nations, continue to give the city an international feel.

INTERCITY TRANSPORTATION

Flights: Cointrin Airport (GVA; ☎717 71 11, flight info ☎799 31 11) is a hub for **Swiss Airlines** (☎(0848) 85 20 00) and also serves **Air France** (☎827 87 87) and **British Airways** (☎(0848) 80 10 10). Several direct flights per day to Amsterdam, London, New York, Paris, and Rome. Bus #10 runs to the Gare Cornavin (15min., every 5-10min., 2.20SFr). The train provides a shorter trip (6min., every 10min., 4.80SFr).

Trains: Trains run approximately 4:30am-1am. **Gare Cornavin,** pl. Cornavin, is the main station. To: **Basel** (2¾hr., every hr., 63-71SFr); **Bern** (2hr., every hr., 47SFr); **Interlaken** (3hr., every hr., 63SFr); **Lausanne** (40min., every 20-30min., 19SFr); **Montreux** (1hr., 2 per hr., 29SFr); **Zurich** (3½hr., every hr., 76SFr). Ticket counter open M-F 8:30am-6:30pm, Sa 9am-5pm. **Gare des Eaux-Vives** (☎736 16 20), on av. de la Gare des Eaux-Vives (tram #12 to Amandoliers SNCF), connects to France's regional rail through **Annecy** (1½hr., 6 per day, 14SFr) or **Chamonix** (2½hr., 4 per day, 24SFr). Ticket office open M-F 9am-6pm, Sa 11am-5:45pm.

LOCAL TRANSPORTATION

Carry your passport with you at all times; the French border is never more than a few minutes away and buses frequently cross it. Ticket purchasing is largely on the honor system, but you may be fined 60SFr for evading fares. Much of the city can be walked in good weather.

Public Transportation: Geneva has an efficient bus and tram network. **Transport Publics Genevois** (☎308 34 34), next to the tourist office in Gare Cornavin, provides *Le Réseau* (a free map of bus routes) and inexpensive timetables. Open M-Sa 7am-7pm, Su 10am-6pm. **Day passes** 6SFr-12SFr. Stamp multi-use tickets before boarding. Buses run roughly 5:30am-midnight. **Noctambus** (1:30-4:30am; 3SFr) runs when the others don't. SwissPass valid on all buses; Eurail not valid.

Taxis: Taxi-Phone (☎331 41 33). 6.80SFr plus 2.90SFr per km. Taxi from airport to city 30SFr., max. 4 passengers (15-20min.).

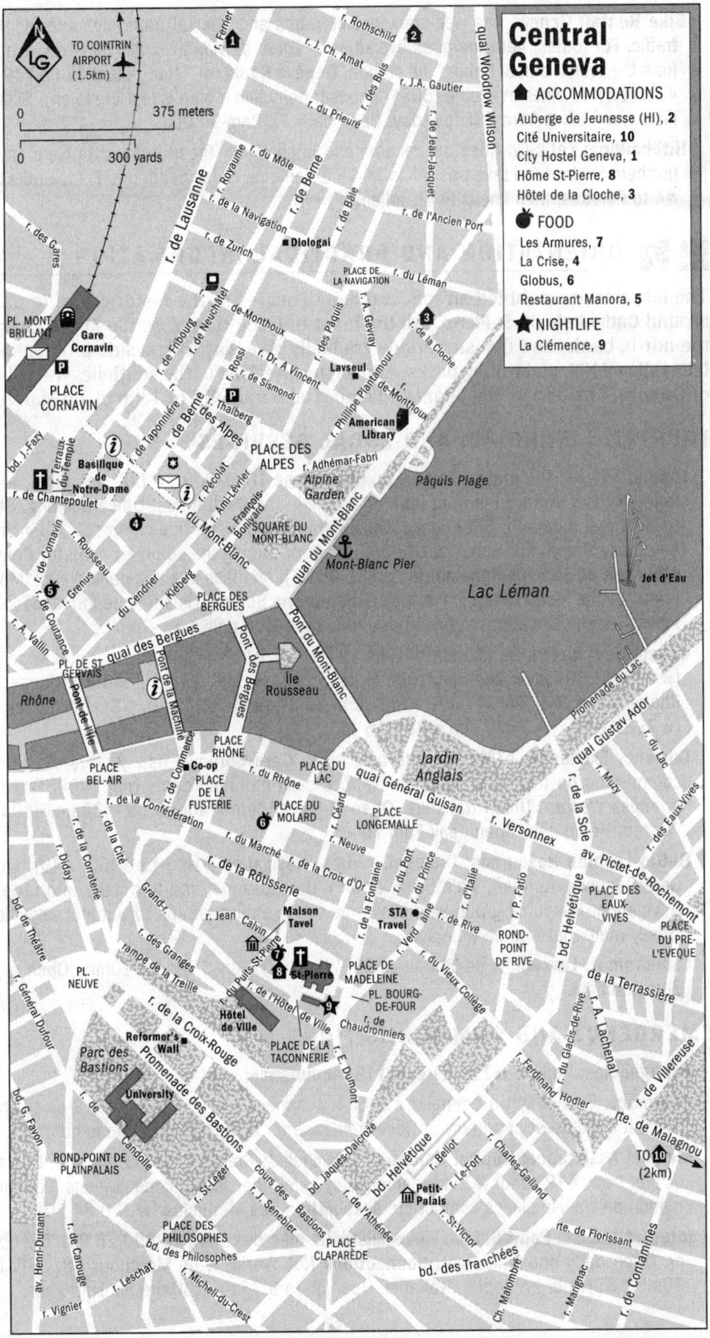
Central Geneva
ACCOMMODATIONS
Auberge de Jeunesse (HI), 2
Cité Universitaire, 10
City Hostel Geneva, 1
Hôme St-Pierre, 8
Hôtel de la Cloche, 3
FOOD
Les Armures, 7
La Crise, 4
Globus, 6
Restaurant Manora, 5
NIGHTLIFE
La Clémence, 9
TO COINTRIN AIRPORT (1.5km)
0
375 meters
0
300 yards
r. Ferrier
r. Rothschild
r. J. Ch. Amat
r. des Buis
r. J.A. Gautier
quai Woodrow Wilson
r. du Prieuré
r. de Jean-Jacquet
r. Royaume
r. du Môle
r. de Berne
r. de Lausanne
r. de la Navigation
r. de Bâle
r. de l'Ancien Port
r. des Gares
r. de Zurich
Diologai
PLACE DE LA NAVIGATION
r. du Léman
r. de Neuchâtel
de-Monthoux
r. A. Gevray
r. des Pâquis
r. de la Cloche
PL. MONT-BRILLANT
Gare Cornavin
r. de Fribourg
r. Dr. A Vincent
r. Rossi
r. de Sismondi
Lavseul
r. Philippe Plantamour
r. de-Monthoux
PLACE CORNAVIN
r. Thalberg
American Library
r. de Berne
r. des Alpes
r. de Taponnière
PLACE DES ALPES
bd. J.-Fazy
r. Terraux-du-Temple
Basilique de Notre-Dame
r. Adhémar-Fabri
Alpine Garden
Pâquis Plage
r. de Chantepoulet
r. Pécolat
r. Ami-Lévrier
r. du Mont-Blanc
r. François Bonivard
SQUARE DU MONT-BLANC
quai du Mont-Blanc
Mont-Blanc Pier
r. de Cornavin
r. Rousseau
r. Grenus
r. du Cendrier
r. Kléberg
PLACE DES BERGUES
Jet d'Eau
Lac Léman
r. de Coutance
r. A. Vallin
quai des Bergues
Pont des Bergues
Pont du Mont-Blanc
PL. DE ST GERVAIS
Rhône
Pont de l'Ile
Pont de la Machine
Île Rousseau
Promenade du Lac
quai Gustav Ador
PLACE BEL-AIR
PLACE RHÔNE
Co-op
r. de Commerce
PLACE DE LA FUSTERIE
r. du Rhône
PLACE DU LAC
quai Général Guisan
Jardin Anglais
r. du Lac
r. Muzy
r. de la Confédération
r. de la Cité
r. de la Corraterie
r. Diday
PLACE DU MOLARD
r. Céard
PLACE LONGEMALLE
r. Versonnex
r. de la Scie
r. des Eaux-Vives
r. du Marché
r. Neuve
r. de la Croix d'Or
av. Pictet-de-Rochemont
r. de la Rôtisserie
r. de la Fontaine
r. du Port
r. du Prince
r. d'Italie
r. P. Fatio
bd. Helvétique
PLACE DES EAUX-VIVES
bd. de Théâtre
Grand-r.
r. Jean Calvin
Maison Tavel
STA Travel
r. Verdaine
r. de Rive
ROND-POINT DE RIVE
PLACE DU PRE-L'EVEQUE
r. des Granges
rampe de la Treille
r. du Puits-St-Pierre
St-Pierre
PLACE DE MADELEINE
r. du Vieux Collège
r. de la Terrassière
PL. NEUVE
r. Général Dufour
r. de l'Hôtel de Ville
PL. BOURG-DE-FOUR
Hôtel de Ville
r. de Chaudronniers
r. du Glacis-de-Rive
r. A. Lachenal
r. de la Croix-Rouge
Reformer's Wall
PLACE DE LA TACONNERIE
r. E. Dumont
Parc des Bastions
Promenade des Bastions
r. Ferdinand Hodler
r. de Villereuse
University
bd. G. Favon
r. de Candolle
bd. Jaques-Dalcroze
bd. Helvétique
r. Bellot
r. Charles-Galland
rte. de Malagnou
TO 10 (2km)
ROND-POINT DE PLAINPALAIS
r. St-Léger
cours des Bastions
r. J. Senebier
r. de l'Athénée
r. Le-Fort
Petit-Palais
r. St-Victor
rte. de Florissant
PLACE DES PHILOSOPHES
bd. des Philosophes
PLACE CLAPARÈDE
bd. des Tranchées
av. Henri-Dunant
r. de Carouge
r. Leschat
r. Micheli-du-Crest
r. Vignier
Ch. Malombre
r. Marignac
r. de Contamines

Bike Rental: Geneva has well-marked bike paths and special traffic lights for spoked traffic. For routes, get *Itineraires cyclables* or *Tours de ville avec les vélos de location* from the tourist office. Behind the station, **Genève Roule,** pl. Montbrillant 17 (☎740 13 43), has free bikes available (50SFr deposit; hefty fine if bike is lost or stolen). Slightly nicer neon bikes from 5SFr per day. Open daily 7:30am-9:30pm.

Hitchhiking: *Let's Go* does not recommend hitchhiking. Those headed to Germany or northern Switzerland take bus #4 to Jardin Botanique. Those headed to France take bus #4 to Palettes, then line D to St. Julien.

ORIENTATION AND PRACTICAL INFORMATION

The labyrinthine cobbled streets and quiet squares of the historic *vieille ville*, around **Cathédrale de St-Pierre,** are the heart of Geneva. Across the **Rhône River** to the north, banks and five-star hotels gradually give way to lakeside promenades, **International Hill,** and rolling parks. Across the **Arve River** to the south lies the village of **Carouge,** home to student bars and clubs (take tram #12 or 13 to pl. du Marché).

TOURIST, FINANCIAL, AND LOCAL SERVICES

Tourist Offices: The **main office,** r. du Mont-Blanc 18 (☎909 70 00), lies 5min. away from Cornavin toward the pont du Mont-Blanc in the Central Post Office Building. Staff books hotel rooms for 5SFr, leads walking tours, and offers free city maps. Open July-Aug. daily 9am-6pm; Sept.-June M-Sa 9am-6pm. During the summer, head for **Centre d'Accueil et de Renseignements** (☎731 46 47), an office-in-a-bus parked in pl. Mont-Blanc, by the Metro Shopping entrance to Cornavin Station. Lists free performances and makes hotel reservations. Open mid-June to mid-Sept. daily 9am-9pm.

Consulates: Australia, chemin des Fins 2 (☎799 91 00). **Canada,** av. de l'Ariana 5 (☎919 92 00). **New Zealand,** chemin des Fins 2 (☎929 03 50). **South Africa,** r. de Rhône 65 (☎849 54 54). **UK,** r. de Vermont 37 (☎918 24 26). **US,** r. Versonnex 5 (☎798 16 05; recorded info ☎798 16 15).

Currency Exchange: ATMs offer the best rates. **Gare Cornavin** has good rates and no commission on traveler's checks, advances cash on credit cards (min. 200SFr), and arranges Western Union transfers. Open M-Sa 6:50am-7:40pm, Su 6:50am-6:40pm. Western Union desk open daily 7am-7pm.

Bi-Gay-Lesbian Resources: Diologai, r. de la Navigation 11-13 (☎906 40 40). From Gare Cornavin, turn left, walk 5min. down r. de Lausanne, and turn right onto r. de la Navigation. Resource group with programs from support groups to outdoor activities. Mostly male, but women welcome.

Laundromat: Lavseul, r. de-Monthoux 29. Wash 5SFr, dry 1SFr per 10min. Open daily 7am-midnight.

EMERGENCY AND COMMUNICATIONS

Emergencies: Police: ☎117. **Fire:** ☎118. **Ambulance:** ☎144.

Pharmacy: Every night a changing set of 4 pharmacies stays open late (9 or 11pm). Consult the closest pharmacy or *Genève Agenda* for addresses and phone numbers.

Medical Assistance: Hôpital Cantonal, r. Micheli-du-Crest 24 (☎372 33 11). Bus #1 or 5 or tram #12. Door #2 is for emergency care, door #3 for consultations. For information on walk-in clinics contact the **Association des Médecins** (☎320 84 20).

Internet Access: Point 6, r. de Vieux-Billard 7a, off r. des Bains (☎800 26 00). 5SFr per hr. Open daily noon-midnight. **Connections Net World,** r. de Monthoux 58. 3SFr for 30min., 5SFr per hr. Copier available. Open M-Sa 9:30am-2:30am, Su 1pm-2am.

Post Office: Poste Centrale, r. de Mont-Blanc 18, a block from Gare Cornavin in the stately Hôtel des Postes. Open M-F 7:30am-6pm, Sa 8:30am-noon. Address mail to be held: *Poste Restante,* Firstname SURNAME, Genève 1 Mont-Blanc, **CH-1211,** Geneva.

ACCOMMODATIONS

The seasonal influx of university students has created a network of decently priced hostels, pensions, and university dorms moonlighting as summer hotels. The indispensable *Info Jeunes* lists about 50 options; the highlights are below. Even for short stays, reservations are a must. For longer stays, check *Tribune de Genève*'s weekly supplement of apartment classifieds or the tourist office board.

City Hostel Geneva, r. Ferrier 2 (☎901 15 00). From the station, turn left on r. de Lausanne, walk 5min., then left onto r. de Prieuré, and right onto r. Ferrier. TV room, kitchen, and Heinekens sold at the desk. Internet 8SFr per hr. Sheets 3SFr. Reception 7:30am-noon and 1pm-midnight. Check-out 10am. Single-sex, 4-bed dorms 25SFr; singles 55SFr; doubles 80SFr. MC/V. ❷

Auberge de Jeunesse (HI), r. Rothschild 28-30 (☎732 62 60). Walk left from the station down r. de Lausanne for 10min., then turn right on r. Rothschild. Restaurant, kitchen facilities (1SFr for 30min.), TV room, library, and 3 Internet stations (7SFr per hr.) Breakfast included. Laundry 6SFr. Special facilities for disabled guests. 6-night max. stay. Reception June-Sept. daily 6:30-10am and 2pm-midnight; Oct.-May 6:30-10am and 4pm-midnight. Lockout 10am-3pm. Dorms 25SFr; doubles 70SFr, with toilet and shower 80SFr; quads 110SFr. MC/V. ❷

Cité Universitaire, av. Miremont 46 (☎839 22 11). Take bus #3 (dir.: Crets-de-Champel) from the station to the last stop. TV rooms, restaurant, disco (Th and Sa, free to residents), and a small grocery shop. Hall showers included. Reception M-F 8am-noon and 2-10pm, Sa 8am-noon and 6-10pm, Su 9-11am and 6-10pm. Check-out 10am. Dorm lockout 11am-6pm. Dorm curfew 11pm. Dorms (July-Sept. only) 20SFr; singles 49SFr; doubles 66SFr; studios with kitchenette and bathroom 75SFr. ❷

Hôme St-Pierre, Cour St-Pierre 4 (☎310 37 07). Take bus #5 to pl. Neuve. Mere seconds from the west entrance of the cathedral, this 150-year-old home has comfortable beds and a convenient location. Breakfast (M-Sa) 7SFr. Lockers 5SFr. Reception M-Sa 9am-noon and 4-8pm, Su 9am-noon. Dorms 23SFr; singles 36-45SFr; doubles 50-60SFr. MC/V. ❷

Hôtel de la Cloche, r. de la Cloche 6 (☎732 94 81), off quai du Mont-Blanc across from the Noga Hilton. Breakfast included. Reception daily 8am-10pm. Singles 65-70SFr; doubles 85-95SFr; triples 110SFr-140SFr; quads 140SFr. AmEx/MC/V. ❹

Camping Pointe-à-la-Bise, Chemin de la Bise (☎752 12 96). Take bus #8 to Rive, then bus E (north) to Bise and walk 10min. to the lake. Reception daily 8am-noon and 2-9pm. Open Apr.-Sept. 6.20SFr per person, 9SFr per tent space. No tents provided. Beds 15SFr; 4-person bungalows 60SFr. ❶

FOOD

You can find anything from sushi to *paella* in Geneva, but you may need a banker's salary to foot the bill. Do-it-yourselfers can pick up basics at *boulangeries*, *pâtisseries*, or at the ubiquitous supermarkets. Many supermarkets also have attached cafeterias; try the **Co-op** on the corner of r. du Commerce and r. du Rhône, in the Centre Rhône Fusterie. (Open M 9am-6:45pm, Tu-W and F 8:30am-6:45pm, Th 8:30am-8pm, Sa 8:30am-5pm.) There are cheap restaurants in the *vieille ville* near the cathedral. To the south, the village of **Carouge** is known for its cozy pizzerias and funky, chic brasseries. Around **place du Cirque** and **plaine de Plainpalais,** cheap, student-oriented tea rooms offer traditional fare at reasonable prices.

Le Rozzel, Grand-Rue 18. Take bus #5 to pl. Neuve, then walk up the hill past the cathedral on r. Jean-Calvin to Grand-Rue. Large dinner crêpes (4-18SFr) and dessert crêpes (5-9SFr). Open M 7am-4pm, Tu-W 7am-7pm, Th-F 7am-10pm, Sa 9am-10pm. ❷

Restaurant Manora, r. de Cornavin 4, to the right of the station in the Placette department store. This huge self-serve restaurant has a fresh, varied, high-quality selection and free water (rare in Switzerland). Open M-Sa 7:30am-9:30pm, Su 9am-9:30pm. ❶

Les Armures, r. due Puits-St-Pierre 1, near the main entrance to the cathedral. One small step up in price, one giant leap up in atmosphere. Fondue 24-26SFr. Pizza 14-17SFr. Open M-F 8am-midnight, Sa 11am-midnight, Su 11am-11pm. ❹

Globus, r. de Rhône 48, on pl. du Molard. Inexpensive gourmet delights, including fresh seafood. Open M-W and F 7:30am-6:45pm, Th 7:30am-8pm, Sa 8am-5:45pm. ❷

Chez Ma Cousine, r. de la Fontaine 6, in the *vieille ville.* Their specialty is chicken (13.90SFr). Open M-F 7am-midnight, Sa 11am-midnight, Su 11am-11pm. ❷

La Crise, r. de Chantepoulet 13. From the station, turn right on r. de Cornavin and left on r. de Chantepoulet. This small but popular snack bar dishes out tasty and veggie-friendly meals at reasonable prices. Open M-F 6am-3pm and 5-8pm, Sa 6am-3pm. ❷

SIGHTS

The city's most interesting historical sites are in a dense, easily walkable space. The tourist office offers 2hr. **walking tours.** (Mid-June to Sept. M-Sa 10am; Oct.-May Sa 10am. 12SFr, students and seniors 8SFr.)

VIEILLE VILLE. From 1536 to 1564, Calvin preached at the **Cathédrale de St-Pierre.** The north tower provides a commanding view of the old town. *(Open June-Sept. daily 9am-7pm; Oct.-May M-Sa 10am-noon and 2-5pm, Su 11am-12:30pm and 1:30-5pm. Tower 3SFr.)* Ruins, including a Roman sanctuary and a 4th-century basilica, rest in an **archaeological site** below the cathedral. *(Open June-Sept. Tu-Sa 11am–5pm, Su 10am-5pm; Oct.-May Tu-Sa 2-5pm, Su 10am-noon and 2-5pm. 5SFr, students 3SFr.)* At the west end of the *vieille ville* sits the 14th-century **Maison Tavel,** which now houses a history **museum.** *(Open Tu-Su 10am-5pm. Free.)* Across the street is the **Hôtel de Ville** (town hall), where world leaders met on August 22, 1864, to sign the Geneva Convention that still governs war conduct today. The **Grand-Rue,** which begins at the Hôtel de Ville, is crammed with clustered medieval workshops and 18th-century mansions; plaques commemorate famous residents,

THE HIDDEN DEAL

THE SWISS ALP RETREAT

A gem unknown to most travelers, the town of **Gryon** provides a tranquil mountain setting within reach of the *Dents du Midi* and *Les Diablerets* glaciers. The real reason to visit Gryon, however, is the popular Swiss Alp Retreat, housed in Chalet Martin. Owners Robyn and Bertrand (and a friendly young staff) provide backpackers a temporary family and various activities to fill their days. New arrivals are immediately welcomed into the bohemian community. Happy to "take a vacation from their vacation," world travelers passing through Gryon have been know to stay long and return often.

Amenities include discounted ski rentals, Internet access (10SFr per hr.), DVD rental (4SFr), and large kitchen facilities. The hostel has daily sign-ups for paragliding, thermal baths, guided overnight hikes, cheese-farm tours, and various other excursions like trips to Montreux and Zermatt.

Gryon is accessible by cog railway from Bex (30min.; every hr., last train 8:20pm; 5.80SFr; Eurail and Swiss-Pass valid), which lies on the main rail line connecting Geneva, Lausanne, and Montreux. From the cog rail station in Gryon, follow the tracks uphill to find the hostel; you'll see backpackers signs to your left. (☎(024) 498 33 21. Laundry 3-5SFr. Check-in 9am-9pm. Call ahead. Dorms 18-25SFr; doubles 50-75SFr. Discounted prices for longer stays. Cash only; the closest ATM is a 45min. walk away.) ❷ including **Jean-Jacques Rousseau,** born at #40. Below the cathedral, along r. de la Croix-Rouge, the **Parc des Bastions** stretches from pl. Neuve to pl. des Philosophes and includes **Le Mur des Réformateurs (Reformers' Wall),** a sprawling collection of bas-relief figures of the Reformers themselves. The park's center walkway leads to the **Petit-Palais,** Terrasse St-Victor 2, a beautiful mansion containing art by Picasso, Renoir, Gauguin, and Chagall, as well as themed exhibitions. *(Bus #36 to Petit Palais or #1, 3, or 5 to Claparède. Open M-F 10am-6pm, Sa-Su 10am-5pm. 10SFr, students 5SFr.)*

WATERFRONT. As you descend from the cathedral to the lake, medieval lanes give way to wide quays and chic boutiques. Down quai Gustave Ardor, the **Jet d'Eau,** the world's highest fountain, spews a spectacular plume of water 140m into the air. The **floral clock** in the nearby **Jardin Anglais** pays homage to Geneva's watch industry. It's probably Geneva's most overrated attraction and was also the most hazardous: the clock had to be moved back almost 1m because tourists, intent on taking the perfect photograph, continually backed into oncoming traffic. On the north shore, **Pâquis Plage,** a beach on quai du Mont-Blanc 30, is popular with locals. *(Open 9am-8:30pm. 2SFr.)*

INTERNATIONAL HILL. The International Red Cross building contains the moving **International Red Cross and Red Crescent Museum,** Av. de la Paix 17. *(Bus #8 or F to Appia or bus V or Z to Ariana. Open W-M 10am-5pm. 10SFr, students 5SFr.)* The nearby European headquarters of the **United Nations** is in the same building that sheltered the now-defunct League of Nations. The constant traffic of international diplomats (often in handsome non-Western dress) provides more excitement than the dull guided tour. *(Open July-Aug. daily 10am-5pm; Apr.-June and Sept.-Oct. 10am-noon and 2-4pm; Nov.-Mar. M-F 10am-noon and 2-4pm. 8.50SFr, seniors and students 6.50SFr.)*

ENTERTAINMENT AND NIGHTLIFE

Genève Agenda, available at the tourist office, is your guide to fun, with event listings ranging from major festivals to movies (be warned—a movie runs about 16SFr). In July and August, the **Cinelac** turns *Genève Plage* into an open-air cinema screening mostly American films. **Free jazz concerts** take place in July and August in *Parc de la Grange.* Geneva hosts the biggest celebration of the **American Independence Day** (July 4) outside the US, and the **Fêtes de Genève** in early August is filled with international music and fireworks. The best party is **L'Escalade** in early December, which lasts a full weekend and commemorates the dramatic repulsion of invading Savoyard troops.

Place Bourg-de-Four, in the *vieille ville* below the cathedral, attracts students and professionals to its charming terraces and old-world atmosphere. **Place du Molard,** on the right bank by the pont du Mont-Blanc, offers terrace cafes and big, loud bars and clubs. **Les Paquis,** near Gare Cornavin and pl. de la Navigation, is the city's red-light district, but it also has a wide array of rowdy, low-lit bars, many ethnically themed. **Carouge,** across the river Arve, is a student-friendly locus of nightlife activity. Generations of students have eaten at the famous **La Clémence,** pl. du Bourg-de-Four 20. (Open M-Th 7am-12:30am, F-Sa 7am-1:30am.)

LAUSANNE ☎021

Lausanne's unique museums, distinctive neighborhoods, and lazy waterfront make it well worth a visit. In the *vieille ville,* two flights of medieval stairs lead to the Gothic **Cathédrale.** (Open July to mid-Sept. M-F 7am-7pm, Sa-Su 8am-7pm; mid-Sept. to June closes 5:30pm.) Below the cathedral, the **Hôtel de Ville** (city hall), on pl. de la Palud, is the meeting point for guided tours of the town. (Tours M-Sa 10am and 3pm. English available. 10SFr, students free.) The **Collection de l'Art Brut,** av.

FROM THE ROAD

TERRIBLY EXCITING

I once read that terror and excitement feel exactly the same, with the only difference being the stimulus. On a wild morning in Locarno, I discovered firsthand that this is true.

Canyoning day. I had passed up the opportunity to jump off cliffs and slide down rocks four years ago and had been regretting it ever since. Then, a guide for a local outdoor adventure company offered me a bargain I could hardly refuse, and before I knew what was happening, I was digging through my pack for a swimsuit.

After suiting up in my Neoprene wetsuit uniform, I felt ready for war and wondered how close that was to what my canyoning team and I were about to face. Our first task was a six-foot rock slide at 60 degrees—"Just to get your feet wet," our guide informed us lightly. And they did indeed get wet, along with the rest of me.

Everything else was history. By the end of the morning I had rapelled behind a waterfall, jumped from a 15ft. cliff into a pool of whirling water scarcely 8ft. in diameter, and slid down 20 vertical feet of rock worn smooth by the continuous flow of water. Each challenge was thrust upon me so quickly I had no time to feel fear, which was fortunate. That way, the screams of what was most likely terror, came out as excitement.

—Jocelyn Beh

Bergières 11, is filled with disturbing and beautiful sculptures, drawings, and paintings by artists on the fringe—including institutionalized schizophrenics, poor and uneducated peasants, and convicted criminals. Take bus #2 or 3 to Jomini. (Open Sept.-June Tu-F 11am-1pm and 2-6pm, Sa-Su 11am-6pm; July-Aug. daily 11am-6pm. 6SFr, students 4SFr.) The **Musée Olympique,** Quai d'Ouchy 1, is a high-tech temple to modern Olympians with an extensive video collection, allowing visitors to relive almost any Olympic moment. Take bus #2 to Ouchy. (Open May-Sept. M-W and F-Su 9am-6pm, Th 9am-8pm; Oct.-Apr. Tu-W and F-Su 9am-6pm, Th 9am-8pm. 14SFr, students 9SFr.) In Ouchy, several booths along quai de Belgique and pl. de la Navigation rent **pedal boats** (10SFr per 30min.) and offer water skiing or wake boarding on **Lake Léman** (30SFr for 15min.).

Trains leave from pl. de la Gare 9 to: Basel (2½hr., every hr. 5:25am-9:25pm, 68SFr); Geneva (50min., every 20min. 4:55am-12:45am, 19SFr); Montreux (20min., every 30min. 5:25am-2:25am, 10SFr); Paris (4hr., 4 per day 7:35am-5:50pm, 71SFr); and Zurich (2½hr., 3 per hr. 5:25am-10:25pm, 65SFr). The **tourist office,** in the train station, reserves rooms. (☎613 73 73. Open daily 9am-5pm.) **Lausanne Guesthouse & Backpacker ❷,** Chemin des Epinettes 4, is conveniently located and has comfortable rooms. Head left and downhill out of the station on ave. W. Fraise; take the first right on Chemin des Epinettes. (☎601 80 00. Sheets for dorms 5SFr. Laundry 5SFr. Reception daily 7am-noon and 3-10pm. 4-bed dorms 29SFr; singles 80SFr, with bathroom 88SFr; doubles 86SFr/98SFr. MC/V.) To reach the large and gleaming **Jeunotel (HI) ❷,** Chemin du Bois-de-Vaux 36, take bus #2 (dir.: Bourdonnette) to Bois-de-Vaux, cross the street, and follow the signs. Courtyards with ping-pong tables, a bowling alley next door, an in-house bar and restaurant, and a mostly young backpacker crowd enliven its concrete sterility. (☎626 02 22. Breakfast included. Call ahead in summer. Reception 24hr. 8-bed dorms 25SFr; singles 53SFr, with shower 77SFr; doubles 78SFr/94SFr; triples 90SFr; quads 120SFr. AmEx/MC/V.) **Camping de Vidy ❶,** chemin du Camping 3, has a restaurant (open May-Sept. daily 7am-11pm), supermarket, and playground. Take bus #2 (dir.: Bourdonnette) to Bois-de-Vaux, cross the street, follow chemin du Bois-de-Vaux past Jeunotel and under the overpass, and it's straight ahead across rte. de Vidy. (☎622 50 00. Showers included. Electricity 3-4SFr. Reception Sept.-June daily 8am-12:30pm and 5-8pm; July-Aug.

8am-9pm. Open year-round. 6.50SFr per person, students 6SFr; 8-12SFr per tent. 1- to 2-person bungalow 54SFr; 3- to 4-person bungalow 86SFr. Cash only.) Restaurants, cafes, and bars cluster around **place St.-François** and the *vieille ville*, while *boulangeries* sell cheap sandwiches on every street and grocery stores abound. **Manora ❶**, pl. St-François 17, beneath the Zürich Bank sign, offers fresh food and "the longest buffet in Lausanne." (Hot food 11am-10pm. Buffet 10:45am-10:30pm. Open daily 7am-10:30pm.)

MONTREUX ☎021

Montreux is scenic Switzerland at its swanky, genteel best. The crystal-blue water of Lac Léman (Lake Geneva) and the snow-capped Alps are a photographer's dream. The gloomy medieval fortress, the **Château de Chillon,** on a nearby island, is one of the most visited attractions in Switzerland. It features all the comforts of home—including prison cells, a torture chamber, and a weapons room. The priest François de Bonivard spent four years manacled in the dungeon for preaching Reformation doctrine and inspired Lord Byron's *The Prisoner of Chillon* as well as works by Rousseau, Hugo, and Dumas. Take the CGN **ferry** (13.80SFr) or bus #1 (2.80SFr) to Chillon. (Open Apr.-Sept. daily 9am-6pm; Mar. and Oct. 9:30am-5pm; Nov.-Feb. 10am-4pm. 8.50SFr, students 6.50SFr.) The **Montreux Jazz Festival,** world famous for exceptional musical talent and one of the biggest parties in Europe, pushes everything aside for 15 days starting the first Friday in July. Write to the tourist office or check out www.montreuxjazz.com for info and tickets (39-69SFr). If you can find a room but no tickets, come anyway for the **Jazz Off,** 500 hours of free, open-air concerts by new bands and musicians.

Trains leave the station, on av. des Alpes, for: Bern (1½hr., 2 per hr. 5:35am-11pm, 37SFr); Geneva (1hr., 2 per hr. 5:35am-11:35pm, 26SFr); and Lausanne (20min., 3-5 per hr. 5:25am-midnight, 9.80SFr). Descend the stairs opposite the station, head left on Grand Rue for 5-10min., and look to the right for the **tourist office,** on pl. du Débarcadère. (☎962 84 84. Open mid-June to mid-Sept. M-F 9:30am-6pm, Sa-Su 10am-5pm; mid-Sept. to mid-June M-F 8:30am-5pm, Sa-Su 10am-3pm.) Cheap rooms are scarce in Montreux and almost nonexistent during the jazz festival; book ahead. **Riviera Lodge ❷**, pl. du Marché 5, in the neighboring town of Vevey, is the best budget accommodation—and it's amazingly convenient. Take bus #1 to Vevey (20min., every 10min., 2.80SFr); from the bus stop, head away from the train station on the main road to the open square on the waterfront; the hostel is on the right. (☎923 80 40. Sheets 5SFr. Laundry 7SFr. Reception daily 8am-noon and 5-8pm. Call if arriving late. 4- to 8-bed dorms 24SFr; doubles 80SFr. MC/V.) To get to **Auberge de Jeunesse Montreux (HI) ❷**, passage de l'Auberge 8, walk 20min. along the lake past the Montreux Tennis Club. (☎963 49 34. Breakfast included. Lockers 2SFr deposit. Reception daily 7:30-10am and 5-10pm. Check-out 10am. 6- to 8-bed dorms 30SFr; doubles 38SFr, with shower and toilet 42SFr. Nonmembers add 6SFr per night. AmEx/MC/V.) For **Hôtel Pension Wilhelm ❸**, r. du Marché 13-15, take a left on av. des Alpes from the station, walk up 3min., and take a left on r. du Marché. (☎963 14 31. Breakfast included. Reception daily 7am-10pm. Closed Oct.-Feb. Singles 60SFr, with shower 70SFr; doubles 100SFr/120SFr.) **Grand Rue** and **Avenue de Casino** have reasonably priced markets. **Marché de Montreux,** pl. du Marché, is an outdoor food market. (Open F 7am-1pm.) There's a **Co-op supermarket** at Grand Rue 80. (Open M-F 8am-12:15pm and 2-6:30pm, Sa 8am-5pm.)

NEUCHÂTEL ☎032

Alexandre Dumas once said that Neuchâtel appeared to be carved out of butter. He was referring to its yellow stone architecture, but his comment could easily be taken as a reference to the rich treats in its famous *pâtisseries*. Aside from its gastronomic delights, Neuchâtel also glows with remarkable medieval beauty. The heart of town (the *vieille ville*) is a block to the right of **Place Plury,** centered on **Place des Halles;** r. de Château leads to up to the **Collégiale** church and the **château.** (Church open Oct.-Mar. daily 9am-6:30pm; Apr.-Sept. 9am-8pm). You can only enter the château on free but dull guided tours. (Apr.-Sept. M-F every hr. 10am-noon and 2-4pm, Sa 10-11am and 2-4pm, Su 2-4pm.) The nearby **Tour des Prisons (Prison Tower),** on r. Jehanne-de-Hochberg, has a magnificent view. (Open Apr.-Sept. daily 8am-6pm. 1SFr.) The **Musée d'Histoire Naturelle,** off r. de l'Hôpital, is a more innovative version of the standard natural history museum. To get there, turn right from pl. des Halles onto Croix du Marché, which becomes r. de l'Hôpital. (Open Tu-Su 10am-6pm. 6SFr, students 3SFr.) The **Musée d'Art et d'Histoire,** Esplanade Léopold-Robert 1, houses an eclectic collection of coins, weapons, and textiles. (Open Apr.-May daily 10am-6pm; June-Mar. Tu-Su 10am-6pm. 7SFr, students 4SFr; W free.)

Trains run to: Basel (1¾hr., every hr. 5:30am-10:20pm, 34SFr); Bern (45min., every hr. 5:15am-11:20am, 17.20SFr); and Geneva (1½hr., every hr. 5:55am-11:35pm, 40SFr). An underground tram runs from the station to the shore area, where you can catch bus #1 to pl. Plury and the **tourist office,** in the same building as the post office. (☎889 68 90. Open M-F 9am-noon and 1:30-6pm, Sa 9am-noon.) To reach **Oasis Neuchâtel ❷,** r. du Suchiez 35, take bus #1 (dir.: Cormondrèche) to Vauseyon; continue walking in the same direction on the smaller uphill road and follow the bend; look for the yellow happy face affixed to the hostel on the left side about 100m up the hill. (☎731 31 90. Breakfast 7SFr. Reception 8-10am and 5-9pm. 4- to 6-bed dorms 30SFr; doubles 70SFr; 2-person garden teepee in summer 40SFr.) To find **Hotel des Arts ❹,** rue Pourtales 3, from the underground tram exit, walk a block towards the city center on ave. du Premier Mars and turn left on rue Pourtales. (☎727 61 61. Breakfast included. Reception 24hr. Check-out noon. Singles 80SFr, with bath 98-130SFr; doubles 100SFr/140-176SFr.) **Crêperie Chez Bach et Buck ❷,** av. du Premier-Mars 22, near the underground tram exit, has an extensive menu of sweet and savory crêpes. (Open M-Th 11:30am-2pm and 5:30-10pm, F 11:30am-2pm and 5:30-11:30pm, Sa 11am-11:30pm, Su noon-10pm.) **Migros,** r. de l'Hôpital 12, has groceries. (Open M-W 8am-7pm, Th 8am-9pm, F-Sa 7:30am-7pm.)

SOUTHEAST (ITALIAN) SWITZERLAND

Ever since Switzerland won the Italian-speaking canton of Ticino (Tessin in German and French) from Italy in 1512, the region has been renowned for its mix of Swiss efficiency and Italian *dolce vita*—no wonder the rest of Switzerland vacations here among jasmine-laced villas painted the bright colors of Italian *gelato*.

LUGANO ☎091

Set in a valley between two mountains, Lugano draws plenty of visitors with its seamless blend of religious beauty, artistic flair, and natural spectacle. The frescoes of the 16th-century **Cattedrale San Lorenzo,** just below the train station, are still magnificently vivid. The national monument **Basilica Sacro Cuore,** on Corso Elevezia, has frescoes featuring Swiss hikers walking alongside the disciples. The most spectacular fresco in town, however, is the gargantuan *Crucifixion* that adorns the **Chiesa Santa Maria degli Angiuli,** on the waterfront to the right of the tourist office. The **Belvedere,** on quai riva Caccia, is an enormous sculpture garden with an emphasis on Modernist metalwork. Armed with topographic maps and trail guides (sold at the tourist office), hikers can tackle the nearby mountains, **Monte Bré** (933m) and **Monte San Salvatore** (912m). Alpine guides at the **ASBEST Adventure Company,** V. Basilea 28 (☎966 11 14), offer everything from snowshoeing and skiing (full-day 90SFr) to paragliding (165SFr), canyoning (from 90SFr), rock-climbing (90SFr), and mountain biking (prices vary; bike not included).

Trains leave P. della Stazione for: Locarno (1hr., every 30min. 5:30am-midnight, 16.60SFr); Milan (45min., every hr. 7am-9:45pm, 21SFr); and Zurich (3½hr., 1-2 per hr. 5:55am-8:35pm, 60SFr). To reach the **tourist office** from the station, cross the footbridge labeled Centro and head down Via Cattedrale through P. Cioccaro as it bears right and turns into Vie Pessina; turn left on Via dei Pesci and continue through P. Riforma toward the Polizei Communale building. The office is across the street from the ferry launch. (Open July-Aug. M-Th 9am-7:30pm, F-Sa 9am-10pm, Su 10am-4pm; Apr.-May and Sept.-Oct. M-F 9am-7:30pm, Sa 9am-5:30pm, Su 10am-4pm; Nov.-Mar. M-F 9am-12:30pm and 1:30-5pm.) **Hotel Montarina ❷,** 1 Via Montarina, is a palm-tree-enveloped hostel with a swimming pool, kitchen, and terrace. (☎966 72 72. Parking available. Breakfast 12SFr. Sheets 4SFr. Laundry 4SFr. Reception daily 8am-10pm. Open Mar.-Oct. Call 2 weeks in advance for reservations July-Aug. Dorms 25SFr; singles 70-80SFr; doubles 100SFr, with bath 120SFr.) The **Migros ❶,** 15 Via Pretoria, two blocks left from the post office, has a food court. (Open M-W and F 8am-6:30pm, Th 8am-9pm, Sa 7:30am-5pm.)

LOCARNO ☎091

A Swiss vacation spot, Locarno gets over 2200 hours of sunlight per year—the most of any place in Switzerland. For centuries, visitors have journeyed to Locarno solely to see the orange-yellow **Church of Madonna del Sasso** (Madonna of the Rock), founded in 1487. A 20min. walk up the smooth stones of the Via al Sasso passes life-size wooden niche statues along the way to the top. Hundreds of silver heart-shaped medallions on the church walls commemorate acts of Mary's intervention in the lives of worshipers who have made pilgrimages here. (Grounds open 6:30am-7pm.) Each August, Locarno swells with pilgrims of a different sort: its world-famous **film festival** draws visitors from all over the globe.

Trains run frequently from P. Stazione to: Lucerne (2½hr., every 30min. 6am-9pm, 54SFr); Lugano (50min., every 30min. 5:30am-midnight, 16.60SFr); Milan via Bellinzona (2hr., every hr. 5am-9:25pm, 34SFr); and Zermatt (4hr., every hr. 7:50am-7pm, 84SFr; change trains in Domodossola, Italy). The **tourist office,** on P. Grande in the *Kursaal* (casino), makes hotel reservations. (☎791 00 91. Open M-F 9am-6pm, Sa 10am-5pm, Su 3-6pm.) **Baracca Backpacker ❷,** in the nearby town of Aurigeno, is perhaps the best reason to come to Locarno. From the train station in Locarno, take bus #10 (dir.: Valle Maggia) to Ronchini. (25min., every hr. 7am-8:10pm and 11:35pm, 7.20SFr.) Cross the street, continue along the road, then turn left, following the hostel signs through the forest (15min.), crossing the big metal bridge, and into the town. Follow the road until the end and turn left; the hostel is beside the church. What this hostel lacks in size (only 10 beds) is made up for in comfort and local hiking, biking, and swimming information. (☎(079) 207 15 54. Kitchen access. Bike rental 10SFr per day. Reception 9-11am and 5-8pm. Open Apr.-Oct. Dorms 25SFr.) To reach **Pensione Città Vecchia ❷,** Via Toretta 13, turn right onto Via Toretta from P. Grande. (☎751 45 54. Breakfast included. Reception 8am-9pm. Check-in 1-6pm; call ahead if arriving after 6pm. Dorms 30SFr; doubles 80SFr; triples 111SFr; quads 140SFr.) **Ristorante Manor ❶,** 1 Via della Stazione, left of the station, provides quality food in a cafeteria-style environment. (Open M-Sa 7:30am-9pm, Su 8am-9pm; Mar.-Oct. open until 10pm.) For groceries, there's an **Aperto** at the station. (Open daily 6am-10pm.) **Postal code:** CH-6900.

HEADING EAST: PRAGUE AND BUDAPEST

During the Cold War, Westerners imposed the name "Eastern Europe" on the Soviet satellites east of the Berlin Wall. The label has always been somewhat of a misnomer, capturing a political rather than geographical reality: Vienna lies farther east than Prague, Croatia sits on the Mediterranean, and most of Russia is really in Asia. However, the term Eastern Europe is not merely a Western construction; communism has fallen throughout Europe and the Soviet Union no longer exists, but the region is still united by an arduous history of political upheaval and disillusionment, as well as by a more optimistic but uncertain future. In order to understand the remarkable complexity of Central and Eastern Europe, imagine a map from 1989, when there were a total of seven countries behind the Iron Curtain; today, 19 independent states comprise the same area, and the region has undergone astounding political and cultural transformations.

With the exception of the tumultuous Balkans, the former Soviet satellites are progressing, with varying degrees of success, toward democracy and a market economy. In March 1999, the Czech Republic, Hungary, and Poland joined NATO, and 11 countries including the Czech Republic and Hungary are currently vying to become the next members of the EU. With the EU's next round of member selection, the countries of Central and Eastern Europe will be drawn even farther westward, perhaps as early as 2004.

The region has also recently become the darling of budget travelers. Cities lacking tourist throngs, pristine national parks, and ridiculously cheap beer lure backpackers seeking bargains and adventure. Prague and Budapest in particular have exploded onto the scene as destinations rivalling the great capitals of Western Europe. If Eastern Europe intrigues you further, pick up a copy of *Let's Go Eastern Europe 2003* or *Let's Go Europe 2003*.

CZECH REPUBLIC ESSENTIALS

CZECH KORUNY		
	AUS$1 = 17.3KČ	10KČ = AUS$0.58
	CDN$1 = 20.1KČ	10KČ = CDN$0.50
	EUR€1 = 30.7KČ	10KČ = EUR€0.33
	NZ$1 = 14.7KČ	10KČ = NZ$0.68
	ZAR1 = 3KČ	10KČ = ZAR3.37
	UK£1 = 31.3KČ	10KČ = UK£0.21
	US$1 = 31.3KČ	10KČ = US$0.32

DOCUMENTS AND FORMALITIES

VISAS

Citizens of Ireland, New Zealand, and the US may visit the Czech Republic without visas for up to 90 days, UK citizens 180 days. Australians, Canadians, and South Africans must obtain 30-day tourist visas. Visas (see p. 18) are available at embassies or consulates, but not at the border. Travelers on a visa must **register** with the Czech Immigration Police within three days of arrival; hotels usually register their guests automatically.

EMBASSIES AND CONSULATES

Czech embassies at home include: **Australia,** 8 Culgoa Circuit, O'Malley, Canberra, ACT 2606 (☎02 6290 1386; canberra@embassy.mzv.cz); **Canada,** 251 Cooper St., Ottawa, ON K2P OGZ (☎613-562-3875; www.czechembassy.org); **Ireland,** 57 Northumberland Rd., Ballsbridge, Dublin 4 (☎01 668 1135; dublin@embassy.mzv.cz); **New Zealand** (consulate), 48 Hair St., Wainuiomata, Wellington (☎04 939 1610; fax 04 564 9022); **South Africa,** 936 Pretorius St., Arcadia 0083, Pretoria; P.O. Box 3326, Pretoria 0001 (☎012 342 3477; www.icon.co.za/~czmzv); **UK,** 26 Kensington Palace Gardens, London W8 4QY (☎020 7243 1115; london@embassy.mzv.cz); and **US,** 3900 Spring of Freedom St. NW, Washington, D.C. 20008 (☎202-274-9103; www.mzv.cz/washington).

HUNGARY ESSENTIALS

FORINTS		
	AUS$1 = 138FT	100FT = AUS$0.73
	CDN$1 = 160FT	100FT = CDN$0.63
	EUR€1 = 245FT	100FT = EUR€0.41
	NZ$1 = 117FT	100FT = NZ$0.86
	ZAR1 = 24FT	100FT = ZAR4.27
	UK£1 = 386FT	100FT = UK£0.26
	US$1 = 249FT	100FT = US$0.40

DOCUMENTS AND FORMALITIES

VISAS

Citizens of Canada, Ireland, South Africa, the UK, and the US may visit Hungary without visas for 90 days, provided their passport does not expire within six months of their journey's end. Australians and New Zealanders must obtain 90-day tourist visas from a Hungarian embassy or consulate.

EMBASSIES AND CONSULATES

Hungarian embassies at home include: **Australia,** 17 Beale Crescent, Deakin, ACT 2600 (☎02 6282 2226; www.matra.com.au/~hungemb); **Canada,** 299 Waverley St., Ottawa, ON K2P 0V9 (☎613-230-2717; www.docuweb.ca/Hungary); **Ireland,** 2 Fitzwilliam Pl., Dublin 2 (☎01 661 2903; fax 01 661 2880); **New Zealand,** 151 Orangi Kaupapa Rd., Wellington, 6005 (☎644 938 0427; www.geocities.com/hu-consul-nz); **South Africa,** 959 Arcadia St., Hatfield, Arcadia; P.O. Box 27077, Sunnyside 0132 (☎012 430 3020; hunem@cis.co.za); **UK,** 35B Eaton Pl., London SW1X 8BY (☎020 7235 5218; www.huemblon.org.uk); and **US,** 3910 Shoemaker St. NW, Washington, D.C. 20008 (☎202-362-6730; www.hungaryemb.org).

PRAGUE (PRAHA) ☎02

In August 2002, extreme weather conditions caused massive flooding along the Vltava River. As of press time, the ultimate extent of the damage was not known. Many establishments we list may have been forced to shut down or may have altered opening times; additionally, train routes may be disrupted or changed. Make sure to check ahead thoroughly: call hostels and hotels in advance, and confirm the feasibility of your itinerary with CKM (www.ckm-praha.cz).

According to legend, Countess Libuše stood above the Vltava and declared, "I see a grand city whose glory will touch the stars." Medieval kings, benefactors, and architects fulfilled the prophecy, building soaring cathedrals and lavish palaces that reflected Prague's status as capital of the Holy Roman Empire. Prague's maze of alleys spawned legends of demons and occult forces and imbued this "city of dreams" with a dark mystique that inspired Franz Kafka's tales of paranoia. Yet since the fall of the Iron Curtain, hordes of foreigners have flooded the city; in summer, tourists pack streets so tightly that crowd-surfing seems a viable way to travel. Walk a few blocks away from the major sights, though, and you'll be lost among cobblestone alleys and looming churches; at outlying Metro stops you'll find haggling *babičky* and sublime natives, without a backpack in sight.

PHONE MAYHEM. Prague is continuously updating its phone system, often giving businesses extremely short notice. Be aware that numbers change quickly, and some of the four- to eight-digit numbers provided in these listings may unfortunately be obsolete by the time you read this. Information ☎14111.

HEADING EAST

TRANSPORTATION

Flights: Ruzyně Airport (PRG; ☎20 11 32 59), 20km northwest of the city. Take bus #119 to Metro A: Dejvická (daily 5am-midnight; 12Kč, luggage 6Kč); buy tickets from kiosks or machines. **Airport buses** (☎20 11 42 96) leave every 30min. from outside Metro stops at Nám. Republiky (90Kč) and Dejvická (60Kč). Taxis to the airport are extremely expensive (400-600Kč); try to settle a price before starting out.

Trains: ☎24 22 42 00; international ☎24 61 52 49; www.cdrail.cz.

Hlavní station (☎24 22 42 00; Metro C: Hlavní nádraží) is the largest. **BIJ Wasteels** (☎24 61 74 54; www.wasteels.cz), 2nd fl., to the right of the stairs, sells general bus tickets and discount international tickets to those under 26. Open summer M-F 7:30am-8pm, Sa 8-11:30am and 12:30-3pm; off season M-F 8:30am-6pm.

Holešovice station (☎24 61 32 49; Metro C: Nádraží Holešovice) serves international routes. BIJ Wasteels and regular train tickets sold at the **Czech Railways Travel Agency** (☎24 23 94 64; fax 24 22 36 00). Open M-F 9am-5pm, Sa-Su 8am-4pm. To: **Berlin** (5hr., 5 per day, 1400Kč); **Bratislava** (5½hr., 7 per day, 400Kč); **Budapest** (10hr., 5 per day, 1300Kč); **Kraków** (8½hr., 1 per day, 730Kč); **Moscow** (30hr., 1 per day, 2500Kč); **Munich** (6hr., 3 per day, 1700Kč); **Vienna** (4½hr., 3 per day, 750Kč); **Warsaw** (9½hr., 3 per day, 870Kč).

Masarykovo station at the corner of Hybernská and Havlíčkova (☎24 61 51 54; Metro B: Nám. Republiky) has domestic trains.

Smíchovské station opposite Vyšehrad (☎24 61 72 55; Metro B: Smíchovské nádraží) also has domestic service.

Buses: Schedules ☎1034 (daily 6am-9pm; www.jiznirday.cz). Timetables are confusing; first look up the bus stop number for your destination. **ČSAD** has several terminals. The biggest is **Florenc,** Křižíkova 4 (☎24 21 49 90; Metro B, C: Florenc). Office open daily 6am-9pm. Buy tickets in advance. To: **Berlin** (8hr., 1 per day, 850Kč); **Budapest** (8hr., 1 per day, 1050Kč); **Paris** (18hr., 1 per day, 2200Kč); **Sofia** (26hr., 4 per day, 1600Kč); **Vienna** (8½hr., 1 per day, 800Kč). Students may get 10% discount. The **Tourbus** office upstairs (☎24 21 02 21; www.eurolines.cz) sells tickets for Eurolines and airport buses. Open M-F 7am-7pm, Sa 8am-7pm, Su 9am-7pm.

Public Transportation: Buy tickets for the **Metro, tram,** or **bus** from newsstands and *tabák* kiosks, machines in stations, or **DP** (*Dopravní Podnik;* transport authority) kiosks. The basic 8Kč ticket is good for 15min. on a tram (or 4 stops on the Metro); 12Kč is valid for 1hr. during the day, with unlimited connections between bus, tram, and Metro in any one direction. Large bags and bikes require extra 6Kč ticket. Validate tickets in machines above escalators or face a 400Kč fine. Before paying a fine, look for the officer's badge and get a receipt. The three **Metro** lines run daily 5am-midnight: A is green on maps, B is yellow, C is red. **Night trams** #51-58 and **buses** run all night after the last Metro; look for dark blue signs with white lettering at bus stops. The tourist office in Old Town Hall sells **multi-day passes** valid for the entire network (24hr. 70Kč, 3-day 200Kč, 7-day 250Kč; student 30-day pass 210Kč).

Taxis: RadioTaxi (☎24 91 66 66) or **AAA** (☎140 14). Both open 24hr. Prague's set rates are a 30Kč flat rate plus 22Kč per km, but taxi drivers are notorious scam artists. Check that the meter is set to zero, and ask the driver to start it *("Zapněte taximetr").* Always ask for a receipt *("Prosím, dejte mi paragon")* with distance traveled and price paid. If the driver doesn't comply, you aren't obligated to pay.

HEADING EAST

ORIENTATION

Straddling the river **Vltava,** Prague is a mess of labyrinthine medieval streets and suburbs. Fortunately, most sights lie within the compact, walkable downtown. The Vltava runs south-northeast through central Prague and separates the **Staré Město** (Old Town) and the **Nové Město** (New Town) from **Malá Strana** (Lesser Side). On the right bank of the river, the Old Town's **Staroměstské náměstí** (Old Town Square) is the focal point of the city. From the square, the elegant **Pařížská ulice** (Paris Street) leads north into **Josefov,** the old Jewish ghetto. In the opposite direction from Josefov, Nové Město houses **Václavské náměstí** (Wenceslas Square), the administrative and commercial heart of the city. West of Staroměstské nám., **Karlův most** (Charles Bridge) spans the Vltava and connects the Old Town with **Malostranské náměstí** (Lesser Town Square). **Pražský Hrad** (Prague Castle) sits on the Hradčany hilltop above Malostranské nám.

All train and bus terminals are on or near the excellent Metro system. To get to Staroměstské nám., take the Metro A line to Staroměstská and walk down Kaprova away from the river. *Tabák* stands and bookstores sell the essential *plán města* (map), along with the English-language weekly *The Prague Post.*

PRACTICAL INFORMATION

TOURIST AND FINANCIAL SERVICES

Tourist Offices: Green "i"s mark tourist agencies, which book rooms and sell maps, bus tickets, and guides. **Pražská Informační Služba** (Prague Info Service) is in the Old Town Hall (☎24 48 20 18; English ☎54 44 44). Branches at Na příkopě 20, Hlavní nádraží, and in the tower on the Malá Strana side of the Charles Bridge. All open in summer M-F 9am-7pm, Sa-Su 9am-6pm; off-season M-F 9am-6pm, Sa-Su 9am-5pm.

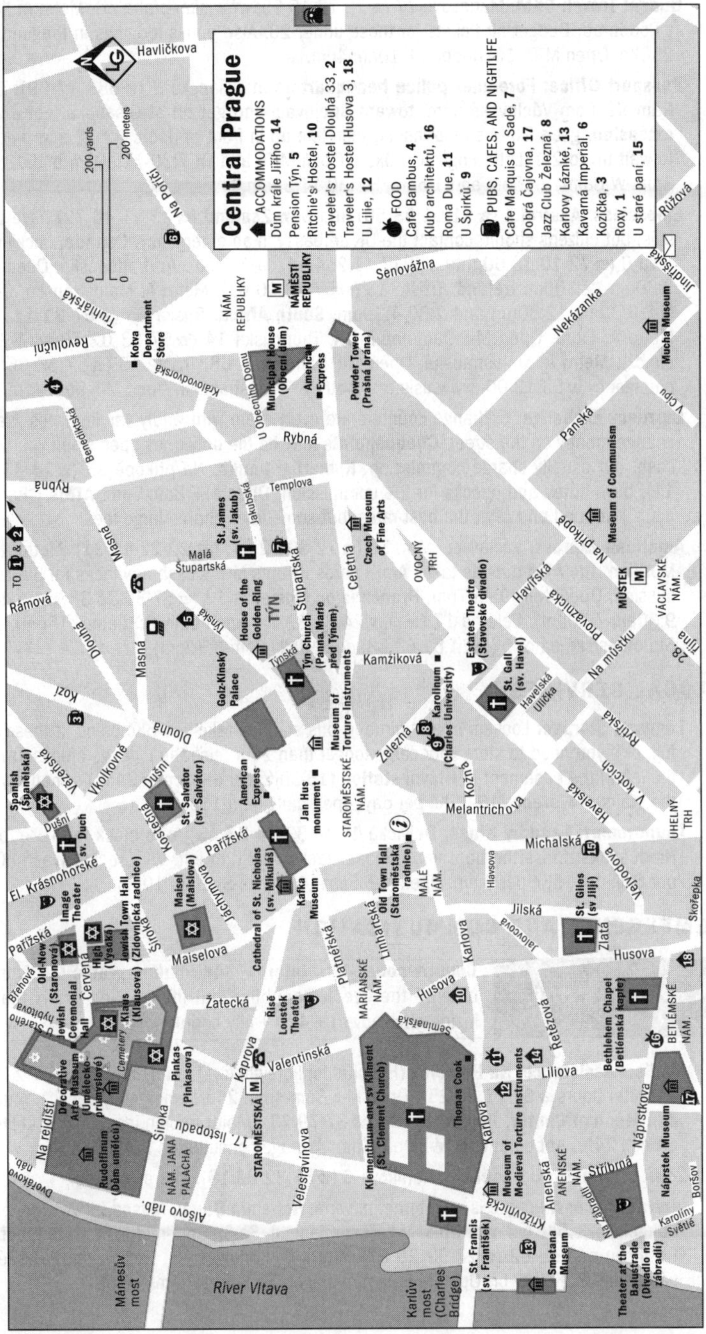
Central Prague
ACCOMMODATIONS
Dům krále Jiřího, 14
Pension Týn, 5
Ritchie's Hostel, 10
Traveler's Hostel Dlouhá 33, 2
Traveler's Hostel Husova 3, 18
U Lilie, 12
FOOD
Cafe Bambus, 4
Klub architektů, 16
Roma Due, 11
U Špirků 9
PUBS, CAFES, AND NIGHTLIFE
Cafe Marquis de Sade, 7
Dobrá Čajovna, 17
Jazz Club Železná, 8
Karlovy Lázně, 13
Kavarná Imperial, 6
Kozička, 3
Roxy, 1
U staré paní, 15
200 yards
200 meters
Havlíčkova
Na Poříčí
Truhlářská
Revoluční
Kotva Department Store
Králodvorská
NÁM. REPUBLIKY
NÁMĚSTÍ REPUBLIKY
Municipal House (Obecní dům)
U Obecního Domu
American Express
Powder Tower (Prašná brána)
Senovážna
Jindřišská
Růžová
Nekázanka
Mucha Museum
V Cípu
Panská
Benediktská
Rybná
Templova
Jakubská
St. James (sv. Jakub)
TO 1 & 2
Rámová
Masná
Malá Štupartská
Štupartská
Týnská
House of the Golden Ring
TÝN
Týn Church (Panna Marie před Týnem)
Celetná
Czech Museum of Fine Arts
OVOCNÝ TRH
Museum of Communism
Na příkopě
MŮSTEK
VÁCLAVSKÉ NÁM.
Havířská
Provaznická
Na můstku
28. října
Estates Theatre (Stavovské divadlo)
Kamžiková
Dlouhá
Kozí
Golz-Kinský Palace
Museum of Torture Instruments
St. Gall (sv. Havel)
Havelská Ulička
Karolinum (Charles University)
Železná
Rytířská
V. kotcích
Havelská
UHELNÝ TRH
Spanish (Španělská)
Vězeňská
Vkolkovně
Dušní
St. Salvator (sv. Salvátor)
Kostečná
American Express
Jan Hus monument
STAROMĚSTSKÉ NÁM.
Melantrichova
Kožná
Michalská
Hlavsova
Vejvodova
sv. Duch
El. Krásnohorské
Pařížská
Image Theater
Cathedral of St. Nicholas (sv. Mikuláš)
Kafka Museum
Old Town Hall (Staroměstská radnice)
MALÉ NÁM.
Jilská
St. Giles (sv Jiljí)
Skořepka
Old-New (Staronová)
High (Vysoká)
Jewish Town Hall (Židovnická radnice)
Maisel (Maislova)
Jáchymova
Široká
Maiselova
Červená
Břehová
Jewish Ceremonial Hall
Klaus (Klausová)
U Starého hřbitova
Cemetery
Žatecká
Platnéřská
Linhartská
MARIÁNSKÉ NÁM.
Karlova
Husova
Zlatá
Jalovcova
Řetězová
Bethlehem Chapel (Betlémská kaple)
BETLÉMSKÉ NÁM.
Decorative Arts Museum (Uměleckoprůmyslové)
Pinkas (Pinkasova)
Kaprova
Valentinská
Seminářská
Klementinum and sv Kliment (St. Clement Church)
Thomas Cook
Liliova
Na rejdišti
Rudolfinum (Dům umělců)
Široka
17. listopadu
STAROMĚSTSKÁ
Veleslavínova
NÁM. JANA PALACHA
Dvořákovo náb.
Alšovo náb.
Museum of Medieval Torture Instruments
Anenská
ANENSKÉ NÁM.
Náprstkova
Stříbrná
Náprstek Museum
Boršov
Mánesův most
River Vltava
Karlův most (Charles Bridge)
St. Francis (sv. František)
Křižovnická
Smetana Museum
Na Zábradlí
Theater at the Balustrade (Divadlo na zábradlí)
Karoliny Světlé

Budget Travel: CKM, Manesove 77 (☎22 72 15 95; www.ckm-praha.cz). Metro A: Jiřího z Poděbrad. Budget air tickets for those under 26. Also books lodgings in Prague from 250Kč. Open M-Th 10am-6pm, F 10am-4pm.

Passport Office: Foreigner police headquarters at Olšanská 2 (☎683 17 39). Take tram #9 from Václavské nám. toward Spojovací and get off at Olšanská. For a **visa extension,** get a 90Kč stamp inside, then line up in front of doors #2-12 and prepare to wait up to 2hr. Little English spoken. Open M-Tu and Th 7:30-11:30am and 12:15-3pm, W 8am-12:15pm and 1-5pm, F 7:30-11:30am.

Embassies: Australia (☎51 01 83 50) and **New Zealand** (☎22 51 46 72) have consuls, but citizens should contact the UK embassy in an emergency. **Canada,** Mickiewiczova 6 (☎72 10 18 00; http://217.11.254.44/ca/). Metro A: Hradčanská. Open M-F 8:30am-12:30pm. **Ireland,** Tržiště 13 (☎57 53 00 61). Metro A: Malostranská. Open M-F 9:30am-12:30pm and 2:30-4:30pm. **South Africa,** Ruská 65 (☎67 31 11 14). Metro A: Flora. Open M-F 9am-noon. **UK,** Thunovská 14 (☎57 53 02 78; www.britain.cz). Metro A: Malostranská. Open M-F 9am-noon. **US,** Tržiště 15 (☎57 53 06 63; emergency ☎53 12 00; www.usis.cz). Metro A: Malostranská. Open M-F 9am-4pm.

Currency Exchange: Exchange counters are everywhere with wildly varying rates. Never change money on the street. **Chequepoints** may be the only ones open when you need cash, but usually charge commission. **Komerční banka,** Na příkopě 33 (☎24 43 21 11), buys notes and checks for 2% commission. Open M-F 8am-5pm. **ATMs** ("Bankomats") abound and offer the best rates, but sometimes charge large fees.

American Express: Václavské nám. 56 (☎22 80 02 37; fax 22 21 11 31). Metro A, C: Muzeum. The **ATM** outside takes AmEx cards. Grants MC/V cash advances for 3% commission. Open daily 9am-7pm. **Branches** on Mostecká 12 (☎57 31 36 38; open daily 9:30am-7:30pm), Celetná 17 (☎/fax 24 81 82 74; open daily 8:30am-7:15pm), and Staroměstské nám. 5 (☎24 81 83 88; open daily 9am-8:30pm).

LOCAL SERVICES

Luggage Storage: Lockers in all train and bus stations take two 5Kč coins. If these are full, or if you need to store your cargo longer than 24hr., use the luggage offices toward the left in the basement of **Hlavní station** (15-30Kč per day; open 24hr.) or halfway up the stairs at **Florenc** (10-25Kč per day; open daily 5am-11pm).

Laundromat: Laundry Kings, Dejvická 16 (☎33 34 37 43), one block from Metro A: Hradčanská. Cross the tram and railroad tracks, and turn left. Very social. Wash 60Kč per 6kg; dry 15Kč per 8min. Open M-F 6am-10pm, Sa-Su 8am-10pm.

EMERGENCY AND COMMUNICATION

PHONE CODE	**Country code:** 420. **International dialing prefix:** 00. From outside the Czech Republic, dial int'l dialing prefix (see inside back cover) + 420 + city code + local number.

Medical Assistance: Na Homolce (Hospital for Foreigners), Roentgenova 2 (☎57 27 11 11; after-hours ☎57 77 20 25). Open M-F 8am-4pm. 24hr. emergency service. **American Medical Center,** Janovského 48 (☎87 79 73). Major foreign insurance accepted. On call 24hr. Appointments M-F 9am-4pm. Average consultation 50-200Kč.

24hr. Pharmacy: U Anděla, Štefánikova 6 (☎57 32 09 18). Metro B: Anděl.

Internet Access: Prague is an Internet nirvana. **Bohemia Bagel,** Masna 2 (www.bohemiabagel.cz). 1.5Kč per min. Open M-F 7am-midnight, Sa-Su 8am-midnight. **Cafe Electra,** Rašínovo nábřeží 62 (☎24 92 28 87). Metro B: Karlovo nám. Exit on the Palackého nám. side. 80Kč per hr. Open M-F 9am-midnight, Sa-Su 11am-midnight.

Telephones: Phone cards sell for 175Kč per 50 units and 320Kč per 100 units at kiosks, post offices, and some exchange places; don't let kiosks rip you off.

Post Office: Jindřišská 14. Metro A, B: Můstek (☎21 13 14 45). Airmail to the US takes 7-10 days. For *Poste Restante*, address mail to be held: Firstname SURNAME, *Poste Restante,* Jindřišská 14, Praha 1 **110 00,** CZECH REPUBLIC. Open daily 2am-midnight.

ACCOMMODATIONS AND CAMPING

Although hotel prices are through the roof, rates in the glutted hostel market have stabilized at around 300-500Kč per night. Reservations are a must at hotels, which can be booked solid months in advance, and a good idea at the few hostels that accept them. Most accommodations have 24hr. reception and require check-out by 10am. A growing number of Prague residents rent out affordable rooms.

CZECH REPUBLIC	❶	❷	❸	❹	❺
ACCOMMODATIONS	under 300Kč	301-500Kč	501-800Kč	801-1200Kč	over 1200Kč

ACCOMMODATIONS AGENCIES

Many room hawkers at the train station offer legitimate deals, but some will rip you off. Apartments go for around 600-1200Kč per day, depending on proximity to the city center. Haggling is possible. If you don't want to bargain on the street, try a **private agency.** Ask where the nearest tram, bus, or Metro stop is, and don't pay until you know what you're getting; ask for details in writing. You can often pay in euros or US dollars, but prices are lower if you pay in Czech crowns. Some travel agencies book lodgings as well. **Ave.,** Hlavní nádraží, on the 2nd floor of the train station, books rooms starting at 800Kč per person and hostels from 290Kč. (☎24 22 352 26; ave@avetravel.cz. Open daily 6am-11pm. (Also see p. 992.).

HOSTELS

If you tote a backpack in Hlavní nádraží or Holešovice, expect to be bombarded by hostel runners. Many hostels are university dorms that free up from June to August, and often you'll be offered free transportation to the hostel. These rooms are convenient options for those arriving in the middle of the night without reservations. If you prefer more than just a place to sleep, smaller places are better alternatives. It's a good idea to call as soon as you know your plans, even if only the night before you arrive or at 10am when they know who's checking out. In Prague, the staff typically speaks English, and hostels have no curfews.

Hostel Boathouse, Lodnická 1 (☎41 77 00 57; www.aa.cz/boathouse), south of the city center. Take tram #21 from Národni south toward Sídliště. Get off at Černý Kůň (20min.) and follow the signs. As Věra the owner says, "This isn't a hostel, it's a crazy-house." Summer camp vibe. Hot breakfast or dinner 70Kč. Dorms 300-320Kč. ❶

Penzion v podzámčí, V podzámčí 27 (☎ 41 44 46 09; evacib@yahoo.com), south of the city center. From Metro C: Budějovická, take bus #192 to the 3rd stop (Nad Rybníky). Homey, with kitchen and laundry. Dorms 280Kč; doubles 640Kč; triples 900Kč. ❶

Ritchie's Hostel, Karlova 9 (☎22 22 12 29; www.mujweb.cz/www/praguehostel.) in Staré Město. Metro A: Staroměstská, down Karlova from the Charles Bridge. Enter through souvenir shop. Great facilities and location; reduced rates for stays longer than 4 nights. Dorms 380-555Kč; doubles 1330-1480Kč; triples 1780-1960Kč. ❷

Hostel U Melounu, Ke Karlovu 7 (☎/fax 24 91 83 22; pus.praha@worldline.cz.), in Nové Město. Metro C: I.P. Pavlova; follow Sokolská to Na Bojišti; continue and turn left onto Ke Karlovu. A historic building with great facilities. Breakfast included. Reservations accepted. Dorms 380Kč; singles 500Kč; doubles 840Kč. 30Kč ISIC discount. ❷

Pension Týn, Týnská 19 (☎/fax 24 80 83 33; backpacker@razdva.cz), in Staré Město. Metro A: Staroměstská. From Old Town Square, head down Dlouhá, bear right at Masná then right onto Týnská. A quiet getaway located in the center of Staré Město. Immaculate facilities. Dorms 400Kč; doubles 1100Kč. 30Kč ISIC discount on doubles. ❷

Traveler's Hostels, in Staré Město (☎24 82 66 62; www.travellers.cz). These summertime big-dorm specialists round up travelers at bus and train stations and shuttle herds to one of their central hostels for lots of beds and beer. Breakfast included.

Dlouhá 33 (☎24 82 66 62). Metro B: Nám. Republiky. Follow Revoluční toward the river, turn left on Dlouhá. Unbeatable location; in the same building as the Roxy (see p. 1002), but soundproof. Open year-round. Dorms 370-430Kč; doubles 1240Kč; triples 1440Kč. ❷

Husova 3 (☎22 22 00 78). Metro B: Národní třída; turn right on Spálená (which becomes Na Perštýně after Národní), and again on Husova. Open July-Aug. Classy dorms 400Kč. ❷

Střelecký ostrov (☎24 91 01 88), on an island off Most Legií bridge. Metro B: Národní třída. Open mid-June to mid-Sept. Spacious dorms 300Kč. ❶

Ujezd (☎57 31 24 03), across Most Legií bridge. Metro B: Národní třída. Sports facilities and park. Open June-Sept. Dorms 220Kč. ❶

Welcome Hostel, Zíkova 13 (☎24 32 02 02; www.bed.cz), outside the center. Metro A: Dejvická. Cheap, tidy, spacious, and convenient university dorm. Breakfast included. Singles 400Kč; doubles 540Kč. ISIC 10% discount. ❷

Welcome Hostel at Strahov Complex, Vaníčkova 5 (☎33 35 92 75), outside the center. Take bus #217 or 143 from Metro A: Dejvická to Koleje Strahov. Newly renovated high-rise dorms next to the stadium. A little far, but there's always space, not to mention free beer at check-in. Singles 300Kč; doubles 480Kč. ISIC 10% discount. ❶

HOTELS AND PENSIONS

With so much tourist traffic in Prague, budget hotels have become scarce. Many of the cheaper places require reservations up to a month in advance, but some don't accept them at all. You may want to call several months ahead if you plan to visit during the summer (call first, then confirm by fax with a credit card). If you can't book a room, try an agency or a hostel (above). Make sure the hotel doesn't bill you for a more expensive room than the one you stayed in.

Dům krále Jiřího, Liliová 10 (☎22 22 09 25; www.kinggeorge.cz), in Staré Město. Metro A: Staroměstská. Exit onto Nám. Jana Palacha, walk down Křížovnická toward the Charles Bridge, turn left onto Karlova; Liliová is the first right. Gorgeous rooms with private baths. Breakfast included. Singles 1500-2000Kč; doubles 2700-3350Kč. ❺

U Lilie, Liliová 15 (☎22 22 04 32; fax 22 22 06 41; pensionulilie@centrum.cz), in Staré Město. Metro A: Staroměstská. See directions for Dům krále Jiřího (above). Lovely courtyard. Breakfast included. Singles with shower 1850Kč; doubles 2150-2800Kč. ❺

Hotel Kafka, Cimburkova 24 (☎22 78 13 33; fax 22 78 04 31), outside the center. From Metro C: Hlavní nádraží, take tram #5 (dir.: Harfa), #9 (dir.: Spojovací), or #26 (dir.: Nádraží Hostivař); get off at Husinecká. Head uphill along Seifertova then go left on Cimburkova. Brand-new hotel amid 19th-century buildings. Breakfast included. Apr.-Oct. singles 1700Kč; doubles 2200Kč. Nov.-Mar. singles 1200Kč; doubles 1600Kč. ❺

Pension Unitas/Cloister Inn, Bartolomějská 9 (☎232 77 00; fax 232 77 09; cloister@cloister-inn.cz), in Staré Město. Metro B: Národní třída. Cross Národní, head up Na Perštýně away from Tesco, and turn left on Bartolomějská. Renovated rooms in the cells of the former Communist prison where Václav Havel was incarcerated. Breakfast included. Singles 1100Kč; doubles 1400Kč; triples 1750Kč. ❹

CAMPING

Campsites can be found in both the outskirts and the centrally located Vltava islands. Bungalows must be reserved in advance, but tent space is generally available without prior notice. Tourist offices sell a guide to sites near the city (15Kč).

Sokol Troja, Trojská 171 (☎/fax 33 54 29 08), north of the center in the Troja district. Metro C: Nádraží Holešovice. Take bus #112 to Kazanka. Similar places line the road. 130Kč per person, 90-180Kč per tent. Dorms 270Kč; bungalow 230Kč per person. ❶

Na Vlachovce, Zenklova 217 (☎/fax 688 02 14). Take bus #102 or 175 from Nádraží Holešovice toward Okrouhlická, then walk up the hill. Reserve a week ahead. Beds in romantic 2-person beer barrels 400Kč; doubles with bath 975Kč. ❶

FOOD

The nearer you are to the center, the more you'll pay. Away from the center, you can get pork, cabbage, dumplings, and a half-liter of beer for 50Kč. You will be charged for everything the waiter brings to the table; check your bill carefully. Most restaurants accept only cash. Outlying Metro stops become markets in the summer. **Tesco,** Národní 26, has **groceries** right next to Metro B: Národní třída. (Open M-F 7am-10pm, Sa 8am-8pm, Su 9am-9pm.) Look for the **daily market** in Staré Město where Havelská and Melantrichova intersect. After a night out, grab a *párek v rohlíku* (hot dog) or a *smažený sýr* (fried cheese sandwich) from a Václavské nám. vendor, or a gyro from a stand on Spálená or Vodíčkova.

CZECH REPUBLIC	❶	❷	❸	❹	❺
FOOD	under 80Kč	81-100Kč	101-140Kč	141-200Kč	over 200Kč

RESTAURANTS

U Sádlů, Klimentskà 2 (☎24 81 38 74). Metro B: Nám. Republiky. From the square, walk down Revoluční toward the river, then go right on Klimentskà. Medieval theme restaurant with bountiful portions; call ahead. Czech-only menu lists traditional meals (115-230Kč). Open daily 11am-midnight and 1-2am. ❸

Klub architektů, Betlémské nám. 52, in Staré Město. Metro B: Národní třída. A 12th-century cellar thrust into the 20th century. Veggie options 90-100Kč; meat dishes 140-150Kč. Open daily 11:30am-midnight. ❸

Radost FX, Bělehradská 120, is a both a dance club (see p. 1002) and a late-night cafe with an imaginative menu. Metro C: I.P. Pavlova. Entrees 150Kč. Brunch Sa-Su 95-140Kč. Open daily 11am-late. See also Clubs and Discos, p. 1002. ❹

U Švejků, Újezd 22, in Malá Strana. Metro A: Malostranská. Head down Klárov and go right onto Letenská. Bear left through Malostranské nám. and follow Karmelitská until it becomes Újezd. Named after the lovable Czech cartoon hero from Hasek's novel, *The Good Soldier Svejk,* and decorated with scenes from the book. Nightly accordion music after 7pm. Main dishes 98-158Kč. Open daily 11am-midnight. ❸

Velryba (The Whale), Opatovická 24, in Nové Město. Metro B: Národní třída. Cross the tram tracks and follow Ostrovní, then go left onto Opatovická. Relaxed cafe-restaurant with a gallery downstairs. Main dishes 80-140Kč. Open M-Th 11am-midnight, F 11am-2am. Cafe and gallery open M-F noon-midnight, Sa 5pm-midnight, Su 3-10pm. ❷

Kajetanka, Hradcanské nám., in Malá Strana. Metro A: Malostranská. Walk down Letenská through Malostranské nám.; climb Nerudova until it curves to Ke Hradu, continue up the hill. Terrace cafe with a spectacular view. Meat dishes 129-289Kč, salads 49-69Kč. Open winter daily 10am-6pm, spring and summer daily 10am-9pm. ❹

THE LOCAL STORY

LIFE ON THE CHARLES

Prague's Charles Bridge (Karlův Most) is filled with portrait artists who set up shop every day, contributing to the bridge's lively atmosphere. Many, such as Ivan, who has worked on the bridge for over a decade, occupy the same spot for years.

LG: Where did you get your start?
I: Oh, I went to a school of drawing, so I made drawings all the time. I started on the bridge after the Revolution. I came here just for weekends and was selling pictures of Prague. Then I saw people painting portraits here and I tried to make portraits too.

LG: Do you need a permit?
I: Yes, we have to have a permit, and every year we have to go through an exam. Last year it was a practical exam. You have to show your work and make portraits in a certain time. And then if you pass, you pay for one square meter here. Those two men in black uniforms are our agency; we pay, and they patrol the bridge every day to make sure no other portraitists are here without permission. The rules must be followed.

LG: Have you ever drawn a portrait for someone famous?
I: Not much, but I do caricatures of Ozzy Osbourne and sometimes I sell them, and ones of Ozzy Osbourne's band. Ozzy Osbourne was in Prague three or four times, and he has bought some of my pieces.

Cafe Bambus, Benediktska 12, in Staré Město. Metro B: Nám. Republiky. An African oasis with an international menu. Main dishes 80-140Kč; sandwiches 45Kč. Open M-F 9am-midnight, Sa-Su 11am-midnight. ❷

U Špirků, ul. Kožná 12, in Staré Město. Metro A: Staroměstská. Authentic Czech decor and some of the city's best and cheapest food. Main dishes about 100Kč. Open daily 11am-midnight. ❶

El Centro Bar y Bodega, Maltezska nám. 9, in Malá Strana. Metro A: Malostranská. Walk towards Charles Bridge and take a right onto Mostecka then left on Lazenska. Spanish-themed restaurant with international cuisine (85-245Kč) and veggie options (95-140Kč). Open daily 11am-midnight. ❸

Roma Due, Liliová 18. Metro A: Staroměstská. Perfect to cap off a night out. Pasta (119-179Kč) until 11pm; pizza (99-150Kč) until 5am. Open 24hr. ❸

CAFES AND TEAHOUSES

Dobrá Čajovna U Čajovníka (Good Tearoom), Boršov 2. Metro A: Staroměstská. Mysterious tea house and Moroccan saloon, with over 90 kinds of international tea (12-150Kč). Open M-Sa 10am-midnight, Su noon-midnight.

Kavarná Imperial, Na Poříčí 15. Metro B: Nám. Republiky. Pillared cafe with a courtly air. Live jazz F-Sa 9pm. Open M-Th 9am-midnight, F-Sa 9am-1am, Su 9am-11pm.

Kavárna Medúza, Belgická 17. Metro A: Nám. Míru. Walk down Rumunská and turn left at Belgická. Cafe masquerading as an antique shop. Fluffed-up Victorian seats and lots of coffee (19-30Kč). Open M-F 11am-1am, Sa-Su noon-1am.

U Malého Glena, Karmelitská 23. Metro A: Malostranská. Take tram #12 to Malostranské nám. Their motto is: "Eat, Drink, Drink Some More." Killer margaritas 90Kč. Nightly jazz or blues 9pm. Cover 100-150Kč. Open daily 10am-2am.

The Globe Coffeehouse, Pštrossova 6. Metro B: Národní třída. At the Globe Bookstore. Exit Metro left on Spálená, turn right on Ostrovní, then left to Pštrossova. Tasty, strong black coffee (20Kč), gazpacho (35Kč), and English speakers trying to make a love connection (priceless). Open daily 10am-midnight.

U zeleného čaje, Nerudova 19. Metro A: Malostranská. Follow Letenská to Malostranské nám.; stay right of the church. Over 60 varieties of fragrant tea (28-62Kč) to please the senses and calm the mind. Sandwiches 25Kč. Open daily 11am-10pm.

Propaganda, Pštrossova 29. Metro B: Národní třída. See directions to The Globe (above). Comfy, low-slung chairs and sunny yellow interior. Serves cheap *Budvar* (25Kč) and espresso (19Kč). Open M-F 3pm-2am, Sa-Su 5pm-2am.

SIGHTS

The only city in Central Europe left unscathed by World War II, Prague at its center is a blend of tangled alleys and Baroque architecture. You can easily escape the packs by venturing away from **Staroměstské náměstí, Karlův Most** (Charles Bridge), and **Václavské náměstí.** Compact central Prague is best explored on foot. There are plenty of opportunities for exploration in the back alleys of **Josefov,** the hills of **Vyšehrad,** and the maze of streets in **Malá Strana.**

NOVÉ MĚSTO (NEW TOWN)

Established in 1348 by Charles IV, Nové Město has become the commercial center of Prague, complete with American chain stores.

WENCESLAS SQUARE. Not so much a square as a broad boulevard running through the center of Nové Město, Wenceslas Square (Václavské náměstí) is named for the Czech ruler and saint **Wenceslas** (Václav), whose statue sits in front of the National Museum (Národní muzeum). Wenceslas has presided over a century of turmoil and triumph, witnessing no fewer than five revolutions from his pedestal: the declaration of the new Czechoslovak state in 1918, the invasion by Hitler's troops in 1939, the arrival of Soviet tanks in 1968, Jan Palach setting himself on fire to protest the Soviet invasion, and the bloodless 1989 Velvet Revolution. The square stretches from the statue past department stores, discos, posh hotels, sausage stands, and trashy casinos. **Radio Free Europe,** which gives global news updates, and advocates peace, has been broadcasting from its glass building behind the National Museum since World War II. *(Metro A, C: Muzeum.)*

FRANCISCAN GARDEN AND VELVET REVOLUTION MEMORIAL. Monks somehow manage to preserve the immaculate and serene **rose garden** (Františkánská zahrada) in the heart of Prague's bustling commercial district. *(Metro A, B: Můstek. Enter through the arch to the left of Jungmannova and Národní, behind the statue. Open daily mid-Apr. to mid-Sept. 7am-10pm; mid-Sept. to mid-Oct. 8am-8pm; mid-Oct. to mid-Apr. 8am-7pm. Free.)* A plaque under the arcades halfway down Národní, across from the Black Theatre, memorializes the hundreds of citizens beaten by police on November 17, 1989. A subsequent wave of mass protests led to the total collapse of communism in Czechoslovakia during the Velvet Revolution.

THE DANCING HOUSE. American architect Frank Gehry (of Guggenheim-Bilbao fame; see p. 942) built the undulating "Dancing House" (Tanečni dům) at the corner of Resslova and Rašínovo nábřeží. Since its 1996 unveiling, it has been called an eyesore by some, and a shining example of postmodern design by others. *(Metro B: Karlovo nám. As you walk down Resslova toward the river, the building is on the left.)*

STARÉ MĚSTO (OLD TOWN)

Losing yourself among the narrow roads and Old-World alleys of Staré Město is the best way to appreciate the 1000-year-old neighborhood's charm.

CHARLES BRIDGE. Thronged with tourists and the hawkers who feed on them, the Charles Bridge (Karlův Most) is Prague's most recognizable landmark. On each side of the bridge, defense towers offer splendid views of the city and of the river. *(30Kč, students 20Kč. Open daily 10am-10pm.)* Five stars and a cross mark the spot where the saint Jan Nepomucký was tossed over the side of the bridge for guarding the queen's extramarital secrets from a suspicious King Wenceslas IV.

OLD TOWN SQUARE. The heart of Staré Město is **Staroměstské náměstí** (Old Town Square), surrounded by eight magnificent towers. Next to the grassy knoll is **Old Town Hall** (Staroměstské radnice), which has a bit blown off the front where the building was partially demolished by the Nazis in the final week of World War II. Crowds gather on the hour to watch the **astronomical clock** chime, releasing a procession of apostles accompanied by a skeleton symbolizing Death. *(Metro A: Staroměstská; Metro A, B: Můstek. Town hall open summer M 11am-5:30pm, Tu-Su 9am-5:30pm. Clock tower open daily 10am-6pm. 30Kč, students 20Kč. Last chime 9pm.)* Opposite the Old Town Hall, the spires of **Týn Church** (Matka Boží před Týnem) rise above a mass of medieval homes. The famous astronomer Tycho Brahe is buried inside. Brahe died when he overindulged at one of Emperor Rudolf's lavish dinner parties, where it was unacceptable to leave the table unless the Emperor himself did so. Because he was forced to stay seated, his bladder burst. The bronze statue of theologian **Jan Hus,** the country's most famous martyr, stands in the middle of the square. In front of the Jan Hus statue sits the flowery **Goltz-Kinský Palace,** the finest of Prague's Rococo buildings. *(Open Tu-F 10am-6pm; closes early in summer for daily concerts.)*

POWDER TOWER AND MUNICIPAL HOUSE. One of the original eight city gates, the Gothic **Powder Tower** (Prašná Brána) looms at the edge of Nám. Republiky as the entrance to Staré Město. A steep climb to the top rewards you with expansive views. Next door, on the site of a former royal court, the **Municipal House** (Obecnídům) showcases music and art. On October 28, 1918, the Czechoslovak state declared independence here. *(Nám. Republiky 5. Metro B: Nám. Republiky. Tower open Apr.-Oct. daily 10am-6pm. House open 10am-6pm. Guided tours Sa noon and 2pm. 150Kč.)*

JOSEFOV

Metro A: Staroměstská. Synagogues and museum open Su-F 9am-6pm. Closed for Jewish holidays. Admission to all six synagogues except Starnová 300Kč, students 200Kč. Starnová Synagogue 200Kč, students 140Kč. Museum only 300Kč, students 200Kč.

Josefov, the oldest Jewish settlement in Central Europe, lies north of Staroměstské nám., along Maiselova. In 1180, Prague's citizens built a 12ft. wall around the area. The closed neighborhood bred exotic tales, many of which centered around Rabbi Loew ben Bezalel (1512-1609) and his legendary *golem*—a mud creature that supposedly came to life to protect Prague's Jews. The city's Jews remained clustered in Josefov until WWII, when the ghetto was vacated as the residents were deported to death camps. Ironically, Hitler's wish to create a "museum of an extinct race" sparked the preservation of Josefov's cemetery and synagogues. Although it is only a fraction of its former size, there is still a Jewish community living in Prague today.

THE SYNAGOGUES. The **Maisel Synagogue** (Maiselova synagoga) displays artifacts from the Jewish Museum's collections. *(On Maiselova, between Široká and Jáchymova.)* Turn left down Široká to reach the 16th-century **Pinkas Synagogue** (Pinkasova), a sobering memorial to the 80,000 Czech Jews killed in the Holocaust. Upstairs is an exhibit of drawings made by children in the Terezín camp. Backtrack up Široká and go left on Maiselova to visit the oldest operating synagogue in Europe, the 700-year-old **Old-New Synagogue** (Staronová). Further up Široká on Dušní is the **Spanish Synagogue** (Španělská), which has an ornate Moorish interior.

OLD JEWISH CEMETERY. The Old Jewish Cemetery (Starý židovský hřbitov) remains Josefov's most-visited site. Between the 14th and 18th centuries, 20,000 graves were laid in 12 layers. The striking clusters of tombstones result from a process in which the older stones rose from underneath. Rabbi Loew is buried by the wall directly opposite the entrance. *(At the corner of Široká and Žatecká.)*

MALÁ STRANA

A seedy hangout for criminals and counter-revolutionaries for nearly a century, the cobblestone streets of Malá Strana have become prized real estate. The Malá Strana is centered around **Malostranské náměstí** and its centerpiece, the Baroque **St. Nicholas's Cathedral** (Chrám sv. Mikuláše), whose towering dome is one of Prague's most prominent landmarks. *(Metro A: Malostranská; follow Letenská to Malostranské nám. Open daily 9am-4pm. 50Kč, students 25Kč.)* Along Letenská, a wooden gate opens through a 10m wall into the beautiful **Wallenstein Garden** (Valdštejnská zahrada), one of Prague's best-kept secrets. *(Letenská 10. Metro A: Malostranská. Open Apr.-Oct. daily 10am-6pm.)* **Church of Our Lady Victorious** (Kostel Panna Marie Vítězné) is known for the famous wax statue of the **Infant Jesus of Prague,** said to bestow miracles on the faithful. *(Metro A: Malostranská. Follow Letecká through Malostranské nám. and continue onto Karmelitská. Open M-F 9:30am-5:30pm, Sa 9:45am-8pm, Su open for mass.)*

PRAGUE CASTLE (PRAŽSKÝ HRAD)

Metro A: Malostranská. Take trams #22 or 23 to Pražský Hrad and go down U Prašného Mostu. Open Apr.-Oct. daily 9am-5pm; Nov.-Mar. 9am-4pm. Buy tickets opposite St. Vitus's Cathedral, inside the castle walls. 3-day ticket valid at Royal Crypt, Cathedral and Powder Tower, Old Royal Palace, and the Basilica. 220Kč, students 110Kč.

Prague Castle has been the seat of the Bohemian government for over 1000 years. From Metro A: Hradčanská, cross the tram tracks and turn left onto Tychonova, which leads to the newly renovated **Royal Summer Palace.** The main castle entrance is at the other end of the lush **Royal Garden** (Královská zahrada), where the Singing Fountain spouts and chimes. Before exploring, pass the main gate to see the **Šternberský Palace,** which houses art from the National Gallery.

ST. VITUS'S CATHEDRAL. Inside the castle walls stands the colossal St. Vitus's Cathedral (Katedrála sv. Víta), which looks Gothic but was in fact finished in 1929, 600 years after construction began. To the right of the high altar stands the **tomb of St. Jan Nepomuc,** 3m of solid, glistening silver weighing 1800kg. In the main church, the walls of **St. Wenceslas's Chapel** (Svatováclavská kaple) are lined with precious stones and a painting cycle depicting the legend of Wenceslas. Climb the 287 steps of the **Cathedral Tower** for the best view of the city, or descend underground to the **Royal Crypt,** which holds the tomb of Charles IV.

OLD ROYAL PALACE. The Old Royal Palace (Starý Královský Palác) is to the right of the cathedral, behind the Old Provost's House and the statue of St. George. The lengthy **Vladislav Hall** once hosted jousting competitions. Upstairs is the **Chancellery of Bohemia,** where the Second Defenestration of Prague took place (see below).

WINDOW OF INOPPORTUNITY At decisive points in European history, unlucky men tend to fall from Prague's window ledges. The Hussite wars began in 1419 after Catholic councillors were thrown to the mob from the New Town Hall on Karlovo nám. The Thirty Years' War devastated Europe after Habsburg officials were tossed from the windows of Prague Castle into a heap of manure in 1618. Two more falls this century have continued the tradition. In 1948, liberal foreign minister Jan Masaryk fell to his death from the top floor of his ministry just two weeks after the Communist takeover; murder was always suspected, but never proven. In 1997, Bohumil Hrabal, popular author of *Closely-Observed Trains,* fell from the fifth floor of his hospital window and died in his pajamas. Nothing unusual here, except that two of his books describe people killing themselves—by jumping out of fifth-floor windows.

THE INSIDER'S CITY

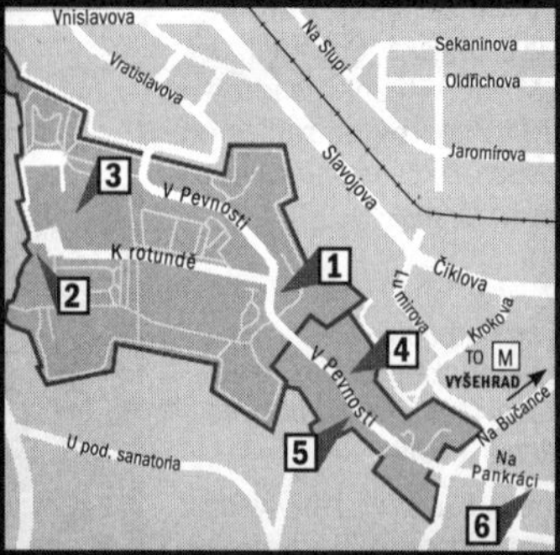

VYŠEHRAD

Vyšehrad is a storehouse of nationalist myths and imperial legends. Quiet paths wind among the crumbling stone walls of this historic settlement, offering respite from Prague's busy streets. (Metro C: Vyšehrad.)

1. Begin by strolling by the city's oldest building, the Romanesque **St. Martin Rotunda.**
2. For lunch, indulge in an elegant Czech meal at **Na Vyšehradě.** (Open daily 10am-10pm.)
3. Visit Vyšehrad's **cemetery,** which holds the remains of the Czech Republic's most famous citizens.
4. Relax in the sun with ice cream from **Obcerstveni Penguin.** (Open daily 11am-7pm.)
5. Peruse the small **gallery** that exhibits the work of local disabled children. (Open daily 10am-5pm.)
6. Pass through **Tábor Gate** and end your day by winding down at **Nad Vyšehradem,** a beer hall packed with locals. (Open M-Th 10am-10pm, F-Su 11am-11pm.)

ST. GEORGE'S BASILICA AND ENVIRONS. Behind the cathedral and across the courtyard from the Old Royal Palace stands St. George's Basilica (Bazilika sv. Jiří). The **National Gallery of Bohemian Art,** which has art ranging from Gothic to Baroque, is inside the adjacent convent. *(Open Tu-Su 9am-5pm. 40Kč, students 20Kč.)* **Jiřská** street begins to the right of the basilica. Halfway down, tiny **Golden Lane** (Zlatá ulička) heads off to the right; alchemists once worked here, and Kafka later lived at #22.

OUTER PRAGUE

The city's outskirts are packed with greenery, churches, and panoramic vistas, all peacefully tucked away from tourist hordes. **Vyšehrad** (see Insider's City, left) is the former haunt of Prague's 19th-century Romantics; one of the Czech Republic's most celebrated sites is **Vyšehrad Cemetery,** which holds the remains of composer Antonin Dvořák. The oldest monastery in Bohemia, **Břevnov Monastery,** was founded in 993 by King Boleslav II and St. Adalbert, each of whom was guided by a divine dream to build a monastery atop a bubbling stream. The stream leads to a pond to the right of **St. Margaret's Church** (Kostel sv. Markéty). *(From Metro A: Malostranská, take tram #22 uphill to Břevnovský klášter. Church open daily 7am-6pm.)* The traditional **Prague Market** (Pražskátrznice) has acres of stalls selling all kinds of wares. *(Take tram #3 or 14 from Nám. Republiky to Vozovna Kobylisy and get off at Pražskátrznice.)*

MUSEUMS

The city's museums often have striking facades but mediocre collections. Still, a few quirky museums are worth mentioning.

MUCHA MUSEUM. The museum is devoted entirely to the work of Alfons Mucha, the country's most celebrated artist, who composed some of the pioneering strokes of the Art Nouveau Movement. *(Panská 7. Metro A, B: Můstek. Walk up Václavské nám. toward the St. Wenceslas statue. Go left onto Jindřišská and again onto Panská. ☎62 84 162; www.mucha.cz. Open daily 10am-6pm. 120Kč, students 60Kč.)*

MUSEUM OF MEDIEVAL TORTURE INSTRUMENTS. The collection and highly detailed explanations are guaranteed to nauseate. *(Staroměstské nám. 20, in Old Town Square. Metro A: Staroměstská. Open daily 10am-10pm. 140Kč.)* Across the hall, the **Exhibition of Spiders and Scorpions** shows live venomous spiders and scorpions in their natural habitats. *(Open daily 10am-10pm. 100Kč, children 80Kč.)*

NATIONAL GALLERY. The massive collection of the National Gallery (Národní Galerie) is kept in nine locations; the notable Šternberský palác and Klášter sv. Jiří are in the **Prague Castle** (see p. 999). The other major branch is at St. Agnes's Cloister (Klášter sv. Anežky), which is undergoing renovation. The Cloister's collection of 19th-century Czech art has been moved to the **Trade Fair Palace and the Gallery of Modern Art** (Veletržní palác a Galerie moderního umwní), which also exhibits 20th-century Czech art. *(Dukelských hrinů 47. Metro C: Vltavská. All open Tu-Su 10am-6pm. 150Kč, students 70Kč.)*

COMMUNISM MUSEUM. This new gallery is committed to exposing the flaws of the Communist system that suppressed the Czech people from 1948-1989. It features 3-D objects, a model factory, and an interrogation office. *(Na Příkopě 10. Metro A: Můstek. Open daily 9am-9pm. 180Kč, students 90Kč.)*

ENTERTAINMENT

For concerts and performances, consult *Threshold* or *Do města-Downtown*, both free at many cafes and restaurants, or *The Prague Post.* Most performances start at 7pm and offer stand-by tickets 30min. beforehand. Between mid-May and early June, the **Prague Spring Festival** draws classical musicians from around the world. For tickets, try **Bohemia Ticket International,** Malé nám. 13, next to Čedok. (☎24 22 78 32; www.ticketsbti.cz. Open M-F 9am-5pm, Sa 9am-2pm.) The **National Theater** (Národní divadlo), Národní 2/4, stages drama, opera, and ballet. (☎24 92 15 28. Metro B: Národní třída. Box office open M-F 10am-6pm, Sa-Su 10am-12:30pm and 3-6pm.) **Estates Theater** (Stavovské divadlo), Ovocný trh 1, is to the left of the pedestrian Na Příkopě. (Metro A, B: Můstek.) Mozart's *Don Giovanni* premiered here; shows today are mostly classic theater. Use the National Theater box office, or show up 30min. before showtime. The **Marionette Theater** (Říše loutek), Žatecká 1, stages a hilarious marionette version of *Don Giovanni.* (Metro A: Staromwstská. Performances June-July Th-Tu 8pm. Box office open daily 10am-8pm. 490Kč, students 390Kč.)

NIGHTLIFE

With some of the best beers in the world on tap, it's no surprise that pubs and beer halls are Prague's most popular nighttime hangouts. Tourists have overrun the city center, so authentic pub experiences are now largely restricted to the suburbs and outlying Metro stops. Although dance clubs abound, Prague is not a clubbing city—locals prefer the many jazz and rock clubs.

BARS

Vinárna U Sudu, Vodičkova 10. Metro A: Můstek. Cross Václavské nám. to Vodičkova and follow the curve left. Infinite labyrinth of cavernous cellars. Red wine 120Kč per 1L. Open M-F noon-midnight, Sa-Su 2pm-midnight.

U Fleků, Křemencova 11. Metro B: Národní třída. Turn right on Spálená away from Národní, right on Myslíkova, and then right again on Křemencova. The oldest brewhouse in Prague. Home-brewed beer 49Kč. Open daily 9am-11pm.

Kozička (The Little Goat), Kozí 1. Metro A: Staroměstská. This giant cellar bar is always packed; you'll know why after your first 0.5L of *Krušovice* (18Kč). Czech 20-somethings stay all night. Open M-F noon-4am, Sa-Su 6pm-4am.

Molly Malone's, U obecního dvora 4. Metro A: Staroměstská. Overturned sewing machines serve as tables in this pub. Small groups can head to the loft. Guinness 80Kč—cheaper than in Ireland. Open Su-Th 11am-1am, F-Sa 11am-2am.

HEADING EAST

ABSINTHE-MINDED Shrouded in Bohemian mystique, this turquoise fire-water has been banned in all except three countries due to allegations of opium-lacing and fatal hallucinations. Nonetheless, Czechs have an attachment to the drink, which has been the mainstay spirit of the Prague intelligentsia since Kafka's days; during World War II every Czech adult was rationed a half-liter per month. Today's backpackers (who will apparently drink anything) have discovered the liquor, which at its strongest can be 160 proof. The bravest and most seasoned ex-pats sip it on the rocks, but you can douse a spoonful of sugar in the alcohol, torch it with a match until the sugar caramelizes and the alcohol burns off, and dump the residue into your glass.

Cafe Marquis de Sade, Melnicka 5. Metro B: Nám. Republiky. Spacious bar decorated in rich red velvet. Happy Hour M-F 4-6pm. Velvet beer 27-35Kč. Open daily noon-2am.

Pivnice u Sv. Tomáše, Letenská 12. Metro A: Malostranská. Walk downhill on Letenská. While meat roasts on a spit, the mighty dungeons echo with boisterous revelry and gushing toasts. Order meats a day in advance. Beer 40Kč. Live brass band nightly 7-11pm. Open daily 11:30am-midnight.

Jo's Bar and Garáž, Malostranské nám. 7. Metro A: Malostranská. All-Anglophone with foosball, darts, cards, and a DJ. Beer 20Kč and under during Happy Hour (daily 6pm-10pm). Open daily 11am-2am.

Újezd, Újezd 18. Metro B: Národní třída. Exit onto Národní, turn left toward the river, cross the Legií bridge, continue straight on Vítězná, and turn right on Újezd. Decorated with gremlins and filled with hidden corners. Beer just 25Kč. Open daily 11am-4am.

Zanzibar, Saská 6. Metro A: Malostranská. Head down Mostecká toward the Charles Bridge, turn right on Lázeňská, and turn left on Saská. The classiest place to see and be seen. Cocktails 110-150Kč. Open daily 5pm-3am.

CLUBS AND DISCOS

Radost FX, Bělehradská 120 (www.radostfx.cz). Metro C: I.P. Pavlova. Plays intense techno, jungle, and house. Creative drinks. Cover 80-150Kč. Open M-Sa 10pm-late.

Jazz Club Železná, Železná 16. Metro A, B: Staroměstská. Vaulted cellar bar showcases live jazz nightly. Beer 30Kč. Cover 80-150Kč. Shows 9-11:30pm. Open daily 3pm-1am.

Roxy, Dlouhá 33. Metro B: Nám. Republiky. In the same building as the Dlouhá 33 Traveler's Hostel (see p. 994). Experimental DJs and theme nights. Crowds hang out on the huge staircases. Cover 100-350Kč. Open M-Tu and Th-Sa 9pm-late.

Palác Akropolis, Kubelíkova 27 (www.palacakropolis.cz). Metro A: Jiřího z Poděbrad. Head down Slavíkova and turn right onto Kubelíkova. Live bands several times a week. Top Czech act *Psí vojáci* is an occasional visitor. Open daily 10pm-5am.

Karlovy Láznkě, Novotného lávka 1. Four floors of themed dance floors under the Charles Bridge. Cover 100Kč, 50Kč before 10pm. Open nightly 9pm-late.

Ungelt, Tyn 2. Metro A, B: Staroměstská. Subterranean vault with live jazz daily from 9pm-midnight. Cover 150Kč. Or, listen from the pub for free. Open daily noon-midnight.

U staré paní, Michalská 9. Metro A, B: Můstek. Some of Prague's finest jazz vocalists in a tiny yet classy venue. Shows nightly W-Sa 9pm-midnight. Cover 160Kč, includes one drink. Open for shows 7pm-1am.

GAY NIGHTLIFE

At any of the places below, you can pick up a copy of *Amigo* (40Kč), the most thorough guide to gay life in the Czech Republic and Slovakia, with a lot in English, or *Gayčko* (59Kč), a glossier piece of work, written mostly in Czech.

U střelce, Karolíny Světlé 12. Metro B: Národní třída. Under the archway on the right, this gay club draws a diverse crowd for its cabarets. Cover 80Kč. Open W-Sa 9:30pm-5am, with shows after midnight.

A Club, Milíčova 25. Metro C: Hlavní nádraží. Take tram #3, 5, 9, 26, or 55 uphill and get off at Lipsanká. Prague's only lesbian nightspot. Men are free to enter, but expect funny looks. Beer 20Kč. Open nightly 7pm-dawn.

Tom's Bar, Pernerova 4. Metro B, C: Florenc. Walk down Křižíkova past the Karlin Theater, pass under the tracks, and go right on Prvního pluků. Follow the tracks as they veer left to become Pernerova. Dance floor and video screening rooms. Men only. Clothing optional Th. Open Tu-Th 8pm-4am, F-Sa 8pm-late.

DAYTRIPS FROM PRAGUE

TEREZÍN (THERESIENSTADT)

A bus runs from Prague-Florenc station (45min., 9 per day, 59Kč); get off at the second Terezín stop, where the tourist office sells a 25Kč map. (Open Tu-Su 9am-4pm.)

In 1941, when Terezín became a concentration camp, Nazi propaganda films touted the area as a resort where Jews would live a normal life. In reality, over 30,000 died here, some of starvation and disease, others in death chambers; another 85,000 Jews were transported to death camps further east. The **Ghetto Museum,** on Komenského in town, sets Terezín in the wider context of WWII. (Open Apr.-Sept. daily 9am-6pm; Oct.-Mar. 9am-5:30pm. Tickets to museum, barracks, and small fortress 160Kč, students 120Kč.) Across the river is the **Small Fortress** (Malá Peunost), which was used as a Gestapo prison. (Open Apr.-Sept. daily 8am-6pm; Oct.-Mar. 8am-4:30pm.) The **cemetery** and the furnaces of the **crematorium** are as they were 50 years ago, with the addition of tributes left by the victims' descendants. Men should cover their heads. (Open Mar.-Nov. Su-F 10am-5pm.) Terezín has been repopulated since the war to about half of its former size; families now live in the barracks and supermarkets occupy former Nazi offices.

KARLŠTEJN

A bus runs from Praha-Smíchov station (45min., every hr., round-trip 50Kč). Turn right out of the station and go left over the modern bridge; turn right, then walk through the village.

A gem of the Bohemian countryside, Karlštejn is a turreted fortress built by Charles IV to store his crown jewels and holy relics. (Open July-Aug. Tu-Su 9am-6pm; May-June and Sept. 9am-5pm; Apr. and Oct. 9am-4pm; Nov.-Mar. 9am-3pm. English tours 200Kč, students 100Kč; 7-8 per day.) The **Chapel of the Holy Cross** is inlaid with precious stones and 129 apocalyptic paintings by medieval artist Master Theodorik. (☎(02) 74 00 81 54; reservace@spusc.cz. Open Tu-Su 9am-5pm. Tours by reservation only; 600Kč, students 200Kč.) The area also has many beautiful trails for **hiking** and **biking.**

KUTNÁ HORA

Take a bus (1½hr., 6 per day, 60Kč) from Prague-Florenc station. Exit left onto Benešova, continue through the rotary until it becomes Vítězná, then go left on Zámecká (2km).

The former mining town of Kutná Hora (Mining Mountain) has a history as morbid as the **bone church** that has made the city famous. In the 13th century, 100,000 silver-crazed diggers were hit by the Black Plague. When the graveyard became overcrowded, the Cistercian Order built a chapel to hold bodies. In a fit of whimsy (or insanity), one monk began designing floral shapes out of pelvi and crania; he never finished, but the artist František Rint eventually completed the project in 1870 with the bones of over 400,000 people, including femur crosses and a grotesque chandelier made from every kind of bone in the human body. (Open Apr.-Oct. daily 8am-6pm; Nov.-Mar. 9am-noon and 1-4pm. 30Kč, students 20Kč.)

ČESKÝ KRUMLOV ☎ 0380

Curving medieval streets, an enormous 13th-century castle, and outdoor activities in the surrounding hills have made UNESCO-protected Český Krumlov one of the most popular spots in Central Europe. The stone courtyards of the **castle**, perched high above the town, are free to the public. Two tours cover different parts of the lavish interior, including a frescoed ballroom, a splendid Baroque theater, and Renaissance-style rooms. The eerie galleries of the **crypts** showcase distorted sculptures. Ascend the 162 steps of the tower for a fabulous view. Castle open June-Aug. Tu-Su 9am-6pm; May and Sept. 9am-5pm; Apr. and Oct. 9am-4pm. 1hr. English tour 140Kč, students 70Kč. Crypts open June-Aug. daily 10am-5pm; 20Kč, students 10Kč. Tower open June-Aug. daily 9am-5:30pm; May and Sept. 9am-6pm; Apr. and Oct. 9:30am-4:30pm. 30Kč, students 20Kč.) The Austrian painter Egon Schiele (1890-1918) lived in Český Krumlov—until residents ran him out for painting burghers' daughters in the nude. The ☒**Egon Schiele International Cultural Center,** Široká 70-72, displays his work, along with paintings by other 20th-century Central European artists. (Open daily 10am-6pm. 150Kč, students 75Kč.) Borrow an **inner tube** from your hostel to spend a lazy day drifting down the Vltava, or hike up into the hills to go horseback riding.

Frequent **buses** arrive from České Budějovice (30-45min., 8-24 per day, 25Kč), which is accessible by bus from Prague (2½hr., 10 per day, 120-144Kč). To get to the main square, **Náměstí Svornosti,** head up the path from the back of the terminal, near stops #20-25. Go downhill at its intersection with Kaplická, then cross the highway and head onto Horní, which leads into the square. The **tourist office,** Nám. Svornosti 1, books pension rooms (from 600Kč) as well as cheaper private rooms. (☎ 70 46 22; www.ckrumlov.cz/infocentrum. Open July-Aug. daily 9am-8pm; May-June and Sept. 9am-7pm; Oct.-Apr. 9am-6pm.) To reach ☒**Krumlov House ❶,** Rooseveltova 68, which is run by an American expat couple, follow the directions to the square from the station; turn left from Horní onto Rooseveltova after the light, just before the bridge, then follow the signs. (☎ 71 19 35; krumlovhostels@sendme.cz. Dorms 250Kč; doubles 600Kč; suites 750Kč.) From the right-hand corner of Nám. Svornosti, across from the tourist office, angle left onto Kájovská. Just down the street is **Na louži ❸,** Kájovská 66, which serves generous portions of Czech dishes. (85-135Kč. Open daily 10am-10pm.) **Rybárška** is lined with lively bars and cafes, including **U Hada** (Snake Bar), Rybárška 37 (open M-Th 7pm-3am, F-Sa 7pm-4am, Su 7pm-2am) and **Babylon,** Rybárška 6 (open daily noon-late).

BUDAPEST

☎1

Ten times larger than any other Hungarian city, Budapest is reassuming its place as a major European capital. Originally two separate cities, Budapest was created in 1872 with the joining of Buda and Pest, soon becoming the most important Habsburg city after Vienna. World War II ravaged the city, but the Hungarians rebuilt it from rubble with the same pride they retained while weathering the Soviet occupation. Neon lights and legions of tourists may draw attention away from the city's cultural and architectural gems—but beneath it all beats a truly Hungarian heart.

TRANSPORTATION

Flights: Ferihegy Airport (BUD; ☎296 96 96). Malév (Hungarian Airlines) flight reservations ☎296 72 11 and 296 78 31. The cheapest way to reach the city center is to take the **BKV Plusz Reptér Busz** (20min.; every 15min. 4:55am-11:20pm; 106Ft), followed by the M3 at Köbanya-Kispest (15min. to Deák tér in downtown Pest).

Trains: There are 3 main stations *(pályaudvar)*: Keleti pu., Nyugati pu., and Déli pu. (☎461 55 00; www.mav.hu). Most international trains arrive at **Keleti Pályaudvar,** but some from Prague go to Nyugati pu. Each station has schedules for the others. To: **Berlin** (12hr., 1 per day, 22,900Ft; night train 15hr., 1 per day, 36,400Ft); **Bucharest** (14hr., 7 per day, 17,400Ft); **Prague** (8hr., 4 per day, 14,000Ft; night train 9hr., 1 per day, 14,000Ft); **Vienna** (3hr., 17 per day, 7000Ft); **Warsaw** (11hr., 2 per day, 13,950Ft). Reservation fees 700-2000Ft. The daily **Orient Express** stops on its way from Paris to İstanbul. Prices vary widely. Purchase train tickets at the **International Ticket Office,** Keleti pu. (Open daily 8am-6pm); or **MÁV Hungarian Railways,** VI, Andrássy út 35 (☎/fax 322 84 05); and at all stations. Open M-F 9am-5pm. For student or under 26 discount on tickets, indicate *diák* (student).

Buses: ☎117 29 66. Most buses to Western Europe leave from **Volánbusz main station,** V, Erzsébet tér (international ticket office ☎485 21 00, ext. 211). M1-3: Deák tér. Open M-F 6am-6pm, Sa 6:30am-4pm. Buses to much of Eastern Europe depart from **Népstadion,** Hungária körút 48/52 (☎252 18 96). M2: Népstadion. To: **Berlin** (14½hr., 5 per week, 19,900Ft); **Prague** (8hr., 4 per week, 6990Ft); **Vienna** (3-3½hr., 5 per day, 5790Ft). **Domestic buses** are cheap but slower than trains.

Commuter Trains: The **HÉV commuter railway** station is at Batthyány tér. Trains head north through Óbuda to **Szentendre** (40min., every 15min. 5am-9pm, 268Ft). Purchase tickets at the station for transport beyond Budapest city limits.

Public Transportation: Subways, buses, and **trams** are cheap, convenient, and easy to navigate. The **Metro** has three lines: yellow (M1), red (M2), and blue (M3). Pick up free **route maps** from hostels, tourist offices, and train stations. Night transit ("É") runs midnight-5am along major routes; buses #7É and 78É follow the M2 route, #6É follows the 4/6 tram line, and #14É and 50É follow the M3 route. **Single-fare tickets** for all public transport (one-way on one line 106Ft) are sold in Metro stations, in *Träfik* shops, and by some sidewalk vendors. Punch them in the orange boxes at the gate of the Metro or on buses and trams; punch a new ticket when you change lines, or face a 1500-3000Ft fine. **Day pass** 850Ft; **3-day** 1750Ft; **1-week** 2100Ft.

Taxis: Beware of scams; check that the meter is on, and inquire about the rates. **Budataxi** (☎233 33 33) charges 135Ft per km if you call. **Főtaxi** (☎222 22 22), **6x6 Taxi** (☎266 66 66), and **Tele 5 Taxi** (☎355 55 55) are also reliable.

ORIENTATION

Originally Buda and Pest, two cities separated by the **Duna River** (Danube), modern Budapest preserves the distinctive character of each. On the west bank, **Buda** has winding streets, breathtaking vistas, a hilltop citadel, and the Castle District. On the east bank is the city's bustling commercial center, **Pest,** home to shopping boulevards, theaters, Parliament (Országház), and the Opera House. Three main bridges join the two halves: **Széchenyi Lánchíd,** slender **Erzsébet híd,** and green **Szabadság híd.** Just down the north slope of Várhegy (Castle Hill) is **Moszkva tér,** the tram and local bus hub. **Batthyány tér,** opposite Parliament in Buda, is the starting point of the HÉV commuter railway. They city's Metro lines converge at **Deák tér,** next to the main international bus terminal at **Erzsébet tér.** Two blocks west toward the river lies **Vörösmarty tér** and the main pedestrian shopping zone **Váci utca.**

Addresses in Budapest begin with a Roman numeral representing one of the city's 23 **districts.** Central Buda is I; central Pest is V. To navigate Budapest's often-confusing streets, an up-to-date **map** is essential. The American Express and Tourinform offices have good free tourist maps, as do most hostels and hotels.

PRACTICAL INFORMATION

TOURIST AND FINANCIAL SERVICES

Tourist Offices: All sell the **Budapest Card** (Budapest Kártya), which provides discounts, unlimited public transport, and museum admission (2-day 3700Ft, 3-day 4500Ft). Your first stop should be **Tourinform,** V, Vigadó u. 6 (☎235 44 81; www.hungarytourism.hu). M1: Vörösmarty tér. Walk toward the river from the Metro. Open 24hr. **Vista Travel Center,** Paulay Ede 7 (☎429 99 50; www.vista.hu). M1-3: Deák tér; exit on Bajcsy-Zsilinszky út. The multilingual staff arranges lodgings and books transportation tickets. Open M-F 9am-6:30pm, Sa 9am-2:30pm. **Budapest in Your Pocket** (www.inyourpocket.com; 750Ft) is a great resource, with maps and reviews.

Embassies: Australia, XII, Királyhágo tér 8/9 (☎457 97 77; www.ausembbp.hu). M2: Déli pu., then bus #21 or tram #59 to Királyhágo tér. Open M-F 9am-noon. **Canada,** XII, Budakeszi út 32 (☎392 33 60; www.canadaeuropa.gc.ca/hungary), entrance at Zugligeti út. 51-53. Take bus #158 from Moszkva tér to the last stop. Open M-F 8:30-11am and 2-3:30pm. **South Africa,** II, Gárdonyi Géza út 17 (☎392 09 99; emergency ☎(0620) 955 80 46; www.sa-embassy.hu). **UK,** V, Harmincad u. 6 (☎266 28 88), near the intersection with Vörösmarty tér. M1: Vörösmarty tér. Open M-F 9:30am-noon and 2:30-4pm. **US,** V, Szabadság tér 12 (☎475 44 00; emergency ☎475 47 03; www.usis.hu). M2: Kossuth tér. Walk 2 blocks down Akademia and turn on Zoltán. Open M-F 8:15am-5pm. **New Zealand** and **Irish** nationals should contact the UK embassy.

Currency Exchange: The best rates are in **ATMs** and banks. **Citibank,** V, Vörösmarty tér 4 (☎374 50 00). M1: Vörösmarty tér. Cashes traveler's checks for no commission and provides MC/V cash advances (passport required).

American Express: V, Deák Ferenc u. 10 (☎235 43 30; travel@amex.hu). M2, 3: Deák tér. Open M-F 9am-5:30pm, Sa 9am-2pm.

LOCAL SERVICES

Luggage storage: Lockers at all three train stations. 140-300Ft.

English-Language Bookstore: Bestsellers KFT, V, Október 6 u. 11 (☎312 12 95; www.bestsellers.hu), near the intersection with Arany János u. M1-3: Deák tér, or M3: Arany János u. Open M-F 9am-6:30pm, Sa 10am-5pm, Su 10am-4pm.

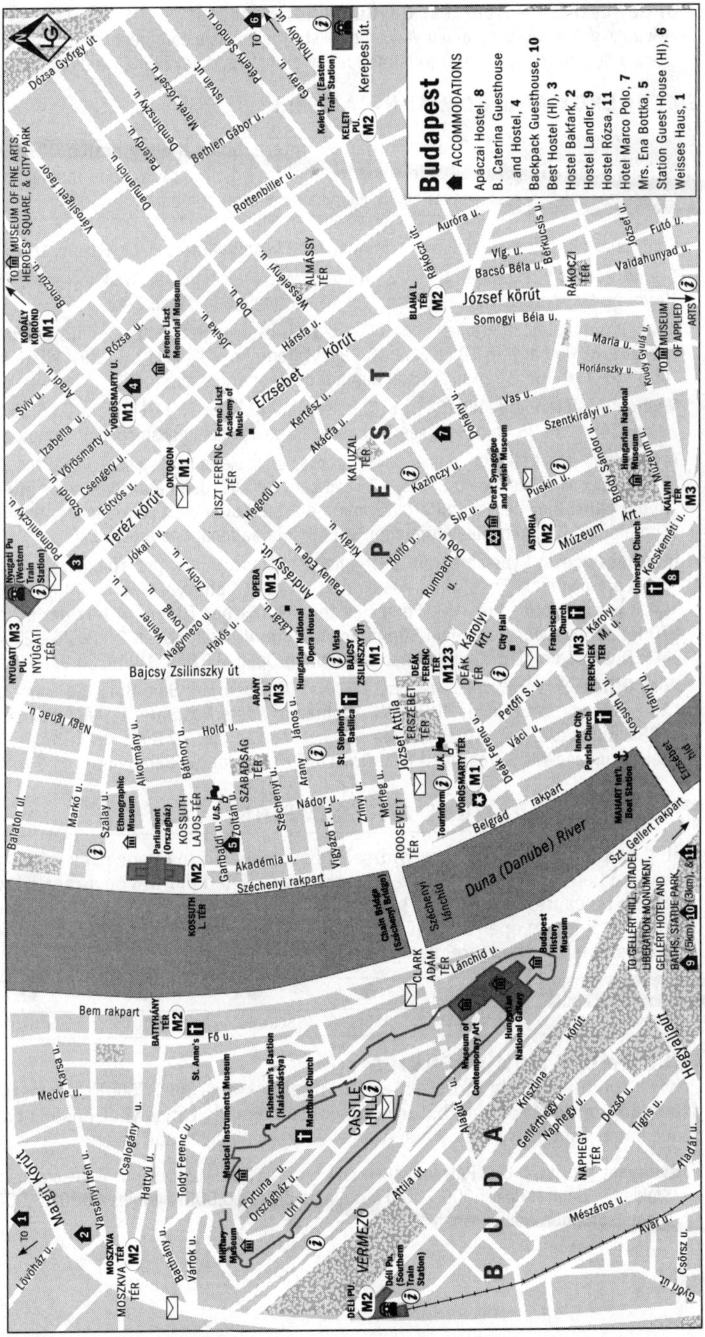
Budapest
ACCOMMODATIONS
Apáczai Hostel, 8
B. Caterina Guesthouse and Hostel, 4
Backpack Guesthouse, 10
Best Hostel (HI), 3
Hostel Bakfark, 2
Hostel Landler, 9
Hostel Rózsa, 11
Hotel Marco Polo, 7
Mrs. Ena Bottka, 5
Station Guest House (HI), 6
Weisses Haus, 1
Duna (Danube) River
BUDA
PEST
CASTLE HILL
József körút
Erzsébet körút
Teréz körút
Andrássy út
Bajcsy Zsilinszky út
Múzeum krt.
Károlyi krt.
Kerepesi út
Rákóczi út
Chain Bridge (Széchenyi Bridge)
Parliament (Országház)
St. Stephen's Basilica
Hungarian National Opera House
Great Synagogue and Jewish Museum
Hungarian National Museum
Budapest History Museum
Hungarian National Gallery
Matthias Church
Fisherman's Bastion (Halászbástya)
Keleti Pu. (Eastern Train Station)
Nyugati Pu (Western Train Station)
Déli Pu. (Southern Train Station)

Bi-Gay-Lesbian Resources: GayGuide.net Budapest (☎(0630) 932 33 34; www.gayguide.net/europe/hungary/budapest), maintains a comprehensive website and runs a hotline (daily 4-8pm) with info for gay tourists and gay-friendly lodging lists.

EMERGENCY AND COMMUNICATIONS

PHONE CODE	**Country code:** 36. **International dialing prefix:** 00. From outside Hungary, dial int'l dialing prefix (see inside back cover) + 36 + city code + local number.

Emergency: ☎112 connects to all. **Police:** ☎107. **Ambulance:** ☎04. **Fire:** ☎105.

Tourist Police: V, Vigadó u. 6 (☎235 44 79). M1: Vörösmarty tér. Walk toward the river from the Metro to reach the station, just inside Tourinform. Open 24hr.

24hr. Pharmacies: II, Frankel Leó út 22 (☎212 44 06); III, Szentendrei út 2/A (☎388 65 28); IV, Pozsonyi u. 19 (☎389 40 79); VI, Teréz krt. 41 (☎311 44 39); VII, Rákóczi út 39 (☎314 36 95). At night, call number on door or ring the bell.

Medical Assistance: Falck (SOS) KFT, II, Kapy út 49/B (☎200 01 00 and 275 15 35). Open 24hr. The US embassy (see Embassies, above) lists English-speaking doctors.

Telephones: Most phones require **phone cards,** available at newsstands, post offices, and Metro stations. 50-unit card 800Ft, 120-unit card 1800Ft. Use card phones for **international calls;** they cut you off after 20min., but are better than coin phones. Domestic operator ☎191; domestic information ☎198; international operator ☎190.

Internet Access: Cybercafes are everywhere, but access can get expensive and long waits are common. Try a wired hostel. **Ami Internet Coffee,** V, Váci u. 40 (☎267 16 44; www.amicoffee.hu). M3: Ferenciek tere. 200Ft per 10min., 400Ft per 30min., 700Ft per hr. Open daily 9am-10pm. **Eckermann,** VI, Andrássy út 24 (☎269 25 42). M1: Opera. Free. Call a week ahead in summer. Open M-F 8am-10pm, Sa 9am-10pm.

Post Office: V, Városház u. 18 (☎318 48 11). Open M-F 8am-8pm, Sa 8am-2pm. Address mail to be held: SURNAME Firstname, *Poste Restante,* V, Városház u. 18, **1052** Budapest, Hungary. **Branches** include: Nyugati pu.; VI, Teréz krt. 105/107 and Keleti pu.; and VIII, Baross tér 11/C. Open M-F 8am-9pm, Sa 8am-2pm.

ACCOMMODATIONS AND CAMPING

Call ahead in summer, or save yourself blisters by storing your pack while you seek out a bed for the night. Travelers arriving at Keleti pu. will be swarmed with hawkers; be cautious and don't believe all promises of free rides or special discounts, but keep an open mind if you need a place to stay. For those who are willing to spend more, there are plenty of Western chain hotels.

HUNGARY	❶	❷	❸	❹	❺
ACCOMMODATIONS	under 1000Ft	1001-3000Ft	3001-6000Ft	6001-10,000Ft	over 10,000Ft

ACCOMMODATION AGENCIES

Private rooms, slightly more expensive than hostels (3000-7500Ft per person, depending on location and bathroom quality), usually offer what hostels can't: peace, quiet, and private showers. Arrive early, bring cash, and haggle.

Budapest Tourist, I, Deli Pályaudvar (☎/fax 212 46 25). M2: Déli pu. Well-established. Singles in Central Pest 5000-7000Ft; doubles 6000-10,000Ft; triples 6000-12,000Ft. Off-season prices lower. Open M-F 9am-5pm. ❸

IBUSZ, V, Ferenciek tere (☎485 27 67 or 485 27 69; accomodations@ibusz.hu). M3: Ferenciek tere. Doubles 5000Ft; triples 5000-6000Ft. 1800Ft surcharge if staying fewer than 4 nights. Open M-Th 8:15am-4pm, F 8:15am-3pm. ❸

Non-Stop Hotel Service, V, Apáczai Csere J. u. 1 (☎266 80 42; tribus.hotel.service@mail.datanet.hu). M1-3: Deák tér. Singles, doubles, triples, and quads vary greatly in price, starting at 6000Ft. Open 24hr. ❹

YEAR-ROUND HOSTELS

Hostels act as social centers, with no curfews and beer- and music-filled common rooms that rival the city's bars and clubs. Most belong to the Hungarian Youth Hostels Association, whose representatives wear HI t-shirts. Although they are legitimate, don't rule out more convenient independent hostels or guesthouses. Unless otherwise noted, all hostels have luggage storage, kitchens, and TV.

Backpack Guesthouse, XI, Takács Menyhért u. 33 (☎/fax 385 89 46; www.backpackbudapest.hu), in Buda, 12min. from central Pest. From Keleti pu., take bus #7 or 7A toward Buda; get off at Tétenyi u. (5 stops past the river), walk back under the railway bridge, turn left at Hamzsabégi út., and go down the 3rd street on the right. Bathrooms are busy but clean. Superb CD and video collections. Internet 15Ft per min. Reception 24hr. Reserve ahead. Dorms 2300Ft; doubles 5600Ft. ❷

Hotel Marco Polo, VII, Nyár u. 6 (☎413 25 55; www.hotelmarcopolo.com), in Pest. M2: Astoria or M2: Blaha Lujza tér. Newly renovated, luxurious, and spotless. Internet 500Ft per 20min. Reception 24hr. Book 1-2 weeks in advance in summer. Dorms 4700Ft; singles 13,000Ft; doubles 17,000Ft. 10% HI and ISIC discount. ❸

Station Guest House (HI), XIV, Mexikói út 36/B (☎221 88 64; station@matavnet.hu; www.stationguesthouse.hu), in Pest. From Keleti pu., take bus #7 or night bus #78É 4 stops to Hungária Körút, walk under the railway pass, and take an immediate right on Mexikói út. Free billiards, live music, and a friendly staff. Internet 20Ft per min. Reserve ahead or end up in the attic. Attic 1700Ft; dorms 2200Ft; doubles 6000Ft; triples 9000Ft. All prices drop 100Ft with each night you stay, up to 5 nights. ❷

Best Hostel (HI), VI, Podmaniczky u. 27, 1st fl. (☎332 49 34; www.besthostel.hu), in Pest. Ring bell 33 in building across from Nyugati pu. Quiet, with spacious dorms. Common room and kitchen close nightly at 11pm. Breakfast included. Internet 10Ft per min. Dorms 2800Ft; doubles 8000Ft. 10% HI discount. ❷

SUMMER HOSTELS

Many university dorms, mostly near Móricz Zsigmond Körtér in District XI, act as hostels in July and August. They usually have kitchens, luggage storage, and a common room TV, and tend to be quieter than year-round hostels. Many summer hostels are run by the same companies, so they can easily find open beds.

Hostel Bakfark, I, Bakfark u. 1/3 (☎329 86 44), in Buda. M2: Moszkva tér. Walk on Margit krt., with Burger King to the right, and take the 1st right after Mammut. Comfortable dorms with lofts instead of bunks. Sparkling showers. Check-out 10am. Call ahead. Open mid-June to late-Aug. Dorms 3300Ft; 10% HI discount. ❸

Apáczai Hostel, V, Papnövelde 4/6 (☎267 03 11), in Pest. Great location, clean rooms, and a warm, friendly staff. Open late-June to mid-Aug. Dorms 3600Ft; doubles 4300Ft. 10% HI discount. ❸

Hostel Landler, XI, Bartók Béla út 17 (☎463 36 21), in Buda. Take bus #7 or 7A across the river and get off at Géllert; take Bartók Béla út away from the river. Comfy dorms. Free ride from the bus or train station. Check-out 9am. Open July 5-Sept. 5. Singles 5850Ft; doubles, triples, and quads 3900Ft per person. 10% HI discount. ❸

HEADING EAST

Hostel Rózsa, XI, Bercsényi u. 28/30 (☎463 42 50), in Buda. M2: Blaha Lujza tér or M3: Nyugati pu. Take tram #4 south toward Blaha Lujza tér to Buda; get off at the last stop, backtrack one block, then go left on Bercsényi ul. Clean (but curtainless) showers. Open July-Sept. Singles 5750Ft; doubles 7800Ft. 10% HI discount. ❸

GUESTHOUSES

Guesthouses and private rooms add a personal touch for about the same price as hostels. Owners will usually pick travelers up from the train station or airport.

Mrs. Ena Bottka, V, Garibaldi u. 5 (☎/fax 302 34 56; garibaldiguest@hotmail.com). M2: Kossuth tér. Heading away from Parliament on Nádor u., take first right on Garibaldi u. Charming Ena lets spacious rooms in her family's apartment, along with other suites in the building, some with kitchenette, TV, showers, and towels. Rooms from 3500Ft per person; apartments 6000-10,000Ft. All prices decrease with longer stays. ❸

B. Caterina Guesthouse and Hostel, VI, Andrássy út 47, 3rd fl., apt. #18, in Pest; ring bell #11. (☎342 08 04; caterina@mail.inext.hu). M1: Oktogon; or trams #4 and 6. Across from Burger King. Grandmother-style house—no curfew, but quiet after 10pm. Free Internet. Reception 24hr. Check-out 9am. Lockout 10am-2pm. Reserve by email. Dorms 2400Ft; doubles 2900Ft; triples 3500Ft. ❷

Weisses Haus, III, Erdőalja út 11 (☎/fax 387 82 36). M3: Árpád híd. Take tram #1 (dir.: Béci ut.) to Floriantér, then bus #137 to Iskola. A family-owned villa in a nice neighborhood 30min. from the city center. Some English spoken. No curfew, but bus #137 stops running at 11:30pm. Doubles US$30, off-season $20. ❹

CAMPING

For a full listing, pick up the pamphlet *Camping Hungary* at tourist offices.

Zugligeti "Niche" Camping, XII, Zugligeti út 101 (☎/fax 200 83 46; camping.niche@matavnet.hu). Take bus #158 from Moszkva tér to Laszállóhely, the last stop. Communal showers, a safe, and an on-site restaurant. Electricity 450Ft. 850Ft per person, 500-900Ft per tent, 700Ft per car. ❶

Római Camping, III, Szentendrei út 189 (☎368 62 60). M2: Batthyány tér. Take HÉV to Római fürdő; walk 100m toward river. Huge site with swimming pool (300Ft). Tents 1990Ft; bungalow 1690-15,000Ft. 3% tourist tax. 10% HI discount. ❷

THE INSIDER'S CITY

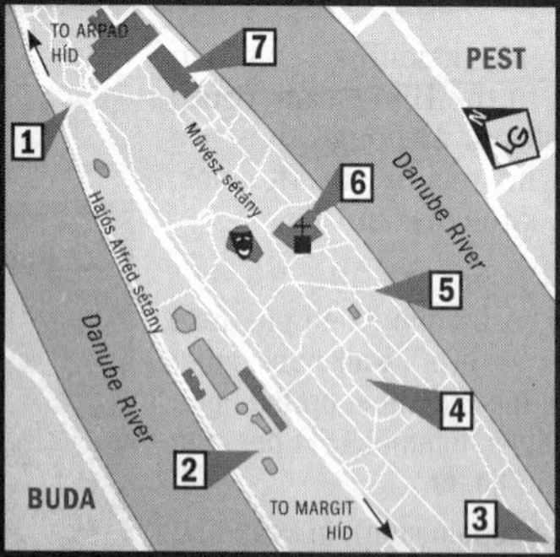

MARGIT ISLAND

Outdoor enthusiasts will revel in the gorgeous scenery of this oasis north of the city. From Nyugati pu in Pest., catch the #26 or 26A bus to the famous Grand Hotel on the island.

1. Rent bikes, in-line skates, or pedal carts at Bringóvár. (☎329 27 46. Open daily 8am-dusk.)
2. Get respite from the heat at the huge pools and waterslides of Palatinus Strandfürdo, known as Budapest's Beach.
3. Stop and have a bite to eat at Europe Grill Kert. (Open daily 11am-10pm.)
4. Stroll or bike through the island's beautiful Rose Garden.
5. Next to the garden is the Artist's Walk, a sculpture park dedicated to Hungary's cultural icons.
6. King Béla IV once bet on his daughter's freedom and lost; St. Margaret's Monastery Ruins are named after the unfortunate girl, who was forced to become a nun.
7. End with a tour of the historical Grand Hotel.

FOOD

Restaurants abound in Pest; the newest trendy area to dine is **Radáy út.** Food at family joints (*kifőzés* or *vendéglő*) is often tastier than in big restaurants. **Non-Stop** corner markets stock the basics. The **Grand Market Hall,** IX, Fövamtér 1/3, next to Szabadság híd (M3: Kálvin Tér), is a tourist attraction in itself.

HUNGARY	❶	❷	❸	❹	❺
FOOD	under 400Ft	401-800Ft	801-1300Ft	1301-2800Ft	over 2800Ft

RESTAURANTS

Gandhi, V, Vigyázó Ferenc u. 4, in Pest. New menu daily at this superior veggie eatery. Herbal teas and wheat beers. Main dishes 980-1680Ft. Open M-Sa noon-10:30pm. ❸

Gundel, XIV, Állatkerti út 2 (☎468 40 40), behind the Museum of Fine Arts. M1: Hősök tere. Hungary's most highly regarded restaurant. Seven-course dinners 13,000-17,500Ft; Su brunch buffet 3900Ft; cafe sandwiches 400-600Ft. Reservation only; jackets required in the evening. Open daily noon-4pm and 6:30pm-midnight. Bar open daily 9am-midnight. Su brunch 11:30am-3pm. ❺

Marquis de Salade, VI, Hajós u. 43, in Pest. M3: Arany János. Corner of Bajscy-Zsilinszky út. Subterranean dining rooms with huge international menu. Main dishes 1300-2300Ft. Open daily 11am-1am. ❹

Fatâl Restaurant, V, Váci u. 67 (☎266 26 07), in Pest. M3: Ferenciek tere or M3: Kálvin tér. Extremely popular. Large and hearty Hungarian meals. Giant, carefully garnished main courses 1070-2790Ft. Reservations only. Open daily 11am-2am. ❹

Robinson Mediterranean-Style Restaurant and Café, Városligeti tó. A spectacular, scenic view on City Park Lake. Veggie options. Main dishes 2300-6000Ft. Open daily noon-4pm and 6pm-midnight. ❹

Söröző a Szent Jupáthoz, II, Retek u. 16, in Buda. M2: Moszkva tér. Huge Hungarian menu and huge Hungarian portions. Main dishes 1090-2590Ft. Open 24hr. ❸

CAFES

Once the haunts of the literary, intellectual, and cultural elite—as well as political dissidents—the city's cafes boast histories as rich as the pastries they serve today.

Gerbeaud, V, Vörösmarty tér 7. M1: Vörösmarty tér. This cafe has been serving its signature layer cakes (520Ft) and homemade ice cream (95Ft) since 1858. The terrace dominates the northern end of Vörösmarty tér. Open daily 9am-9pm.

Művész Kávéház, VI, Andrássy út 29. M1: Opera. Across from the Opera. A crowd of mostly artsy people lounges around polished stone tables. Enjoy a cappuccino (260Ft) on the terrace. Open daily 9am-midnight.

Ruszwurm, I, Szentháromság u. 7, just off the square on Várhegy in the Castle District. This tiny cafe has been making sweets ever since it started catering to Habsburg tastes in 1827. Pastries and cake 120-220Ft. Open daily 10am-7pm.

SIGHTS

In 1896, Hungary's 1000th anniversary prompted the construction of what are today Budapest's most prominent sights. Among the works commissioned by the Habsburgs were **Heroes' Square** (Hősök tér), **Liberty Bridge** (Szbadság híd), **Vajdahunyad Castle** (Vajdahunyad vár), and continental Europe's first subway system. The domes of **Parliament** (Országház) and **St. Stephen's Basilica** (Szent István Bazilika) are both 96m high—vertical references to the historic date. Slightly grayer for wear, war, and Communist occupation, these monuments attest to the optimism of a capital at the peak of its Golden Age. **Absolute Walking & Biking Tours** (☎211 88 61; www.budapestours.com) meets on the steps of the yellow church in Deák tér (mid-May to Sept. daily 9:30am and 1:30pm; 3500Ft, under 26 3000Ft) and at Heroes' Square (daily 10am and 2pm).

BUDA

On the east bank of the Danube, **Buda** sprawls between the base of **Castle Hill** and southern **Gellért Hill,** rambling into Budapest's main residential areas. Older than Pest, Buda is filled with parks, lush hills, and islands.

CASTLE DISTRICT. Towering above the Danube on Castle Hill, the Castle District has been razed three times in its 800-year history, most recently in 1945. With its winding, statue-filled streets, breathtaking views, and hodge-podge of architectural styles, the UNESCO-protected district now appears much as it did in Habsburg times. Although the reconstructed **Buda Castle** *(vár)* now houses a number of fine museums (see p. 1013), bullet holes in the palace facade still recall the 1956 Uprising. *(M2: Moszkva tér. Walk up to the hill on Várfok u. and enter at Vienna Gate (Becsi kapu). Alternatively, from Deák tér, take bus #16 across the Danube and get off at the base of the Széchenyi Chain Bridge. Take the funicular* (sikló) *up the hill. (Runs daily 9:30am-5:30pm; closed 2nd and 4th M of the month; 400Ft.) The upper lift station sits inside the castle walls near the National Gallery.)* Beneath Buda castle are the **Budvári Labirinths,** caverns that allow for spooky trips through the subterranean world of the city. *(Úri u. 9. ☎212 02 07. Open daily 9:30am-7:30pm. 900Ft, students 700Ft.)*

MATTHIAS CHURCH AND FISHERMAN'S BASTION. The multi-colored roof of Matthias Church (Mátyás templom) is one of Budapest's most popular sights. The church was converted into a mosque when Ottoman armies seized Buda in 1541, then reconverted 145 years later when the Habsburgs defeated the Turks. Ascend the spiral staircase to reach the gold-heavy exhibits of the **Museum of Ecclesiastical Art.** *(On Castle Hill. Open M-Sa 9am-5pm, Su 1pm-5pm. 600Ft, students 300Ft. High mass 7am, 8:30am, 6pm; Su also 10am and noon. Free. Concerts W and F 7:30pm. Free.)* Behind Matthias Church is the **Fisherman's Bastion** (Halászbástya), and an equestrian monument of King Stephen bearing his trademark double cross. The view across the Danube from the Bastion's fairy-tale **tower** is stunning. *(240Ft, students 120Ft.)*

GELLÉRT HILL. When King Stephen, the first Christian Hungarian monarch, was coronated, the Pope sent Bishop Gellért to convert the Magyars. The hill got its name (Gellért-hegy) when those unconvinced by his message hurled the good bishop to his death. The **Liberation Monument** (Szabadság Szobor), created to honor Soviet soldiers who died "liberating" Hungary, sits atop the hill. The view from the adjoining **Citadel,** built as a symbol of Habsburg power after the foiled 1848 revolution, is especially spectacular at night. At the base of the hill sits the **Gellért Hotel and Baths,** Budapest's most famous Turkish bath (see p. 1015). *(Take tram #18 or 19 to Hotel Gellért; follow Szabó Verjték u. to Jubileumi Park, continuing on the marked paths to the summit. Or, take bus #27 to the top; get off at Búsuló Juhász and walk 5min. to the peak.)*

PEST

Laid in the 19th century, Pest's winding streets now host cafes, corporations, and monuments. The crowded **Belváros** (Inner City) is based around the swarming boulevards **Váci utca** and **Vörösmarty tér.**

PARLIAMENT. Pest's riverbank sports a string of luxury hotels leading to its magnificent Gothic Parliament (Országház), modeled after Britain's. The massive palatial structure has always been too big for Hungary's government; today, the legislature uses only 12%. *(M2: Kossuth Lajos tér. English-language tours daily 10am and 2pm; come early. 1700Ft, students 800Ft. Purchase tickets at gate #10 and enter at gate #12.)*

ST. STEPHEN'S BASILICA. The city's largest church (Sz. István Bazilika) was decimated by Allied bombs in World War II. Its neo-Renaissance facade is still undergoing reconstruction, but the ornate interior attracts both tourists and worshippers. The **Panorama Tower** offers an amazing 360° view. The oddest attraction is St. Stephen's mummified right hand, one of Hungary's most revered religious relics; a 100Ft donation dropped in the box will light up the hand for two minutes. *(M1-3: Deák tér. Mass M-Sa 7, 8am, 6pm; Su 8:30, 10am, noon, 6pm. Basilica and museum open May-Oct. M-Sa 9am-6pm; Nov.-Apr. M-Sa 10am-4pm. Tower open June-Aug. daily 9:30am-6pm; Sept.-Oct. 10am-5:30pm; Apr.-May 10am-4:30pm. Tower 500Ft, students 400Ft.)*

GREAT SYNAGOGUE. The largest synagogue in Europe and the second-largest in the world after Temple Emmanuel in New York City, Pest's Great Synagogue (Zsinagóga) was designed to hold 3000 worshippers. The Moorish building has been under renovation since 1988, and much of its artwork is blocked from view. In the garden is a **Holocaust Memorial** that sits above a mass grave for thousands of Jews killed near the end of the war. The Hebrew inscription reads "Whose pain can be greater than mine?" with the Hungarian words "Let us Remember" beneath. Each leaf of this enormous metal tree bears the name of a family that perished, but the memorial represents only a fraction of those who suffered. Next door, the **Jewish Museum** (Zsidó Múzeum) documents Hungary's rich Jewish past. *(M2: Astoria. At the corner of Dohány u. and Wesselényi u. Open May-Oct. M-Th 10am-5pm, F 10am-3pm, Su 10am-2pm; Nov.-Apr. M-F 10am-3pm, Su 10am-1pm. Synagogue and museum 600Ft.)*

ANDRÁSSY ÚT AND HEROES' SQUARE. Hungary's grandest boulevard, Andrássy út, extends from Erzsébet tér in downtown Pest to **Heroes' Square** (Hősök tere) to the northeast. The **Hungarian State Opera House** (Magyar Állami Operaház), whose gilded interior glows on performance nights, is a vivid reminder of Budapest's Golden Age. If you can't see an opera, take a tour. *(Andrássy út 22. M1: Opera. Daily English-language tours 3 and 4pm; 1500Ft, students 600Ft. 20% Budapest card discount.)* At the Heroes' Square end of Andrássy út, the **Millenium Monument** (Millenniumi emlékmű) commemorates the nation's most prominent leaders. Right off Heroes' Square is the **Museum of Fine Arts** (see below).

CITY PARK. The City Park (Városliget) is home to a zoo, a circus, a run-down amusement park, and the lakeside **Vajdahunyad Castle,** whose collage of Romanesque, Gothic, Renaissance, and Baroque styles is intended to chronicle the history of Hungarian architecture. Outside the castle broods the hooded statue of King Béla IV's **anonymous scribe,** to whom we owe much of our knowledge of medieval Hungary. Rent a **rowboat** or **ice skates** on the lake next to the castle, or a **bike-trolley** to navigate the shaded paths. The main road through the park is closed to automobiles on weekends, making the park especially peaceful. *(M1: Széchenyi Fürdő. Park open Apr.-Aug. daily 9am-6pm; Sept.-Mar. 9am-3pm. Pedal boat rentals May-Aug. daily 10am-8pm; 980Ft per hr. Rowboat rental May-Aug. daily 10am-9:30pm; 500Ft per hr. Ice skate rental Oct.-Feb. daily 10am-2pm and 4-8pm; 500Ft per 4hr.)*

MUSEUMS

MUSEUM OF FINE ARTS. (Szépművészeti Múzeum). A spectacular collection of European art is housed in the magnificent building. These are paintings you've never seen in books, but should not miss, especially those in the El Greco room. *(XIV, Dózsa György út 41. M1: Hősök tere. Open Tu-Su 10am-5:30pm. 500Ft, students 200Ft. Tours for up to five people 2000Ft.)*

THE BIG SPLURGE

BUCK-NAKED IN BUDAPEST

The city's baths were first built in 1565 by a Turkish ruler who feared that a siege would prevent the population from bathing. Thanks to his anxiety, there's nothing to keep budget travelers from bathing, either: the range of services—from mud baths to massage—are cheap enough to warrant indulgence without guilt.

Although virgin bathers may be intimidated at first, guests at Budapest's baths always receive the royal treatment. Upon arrival, you will probably be handed a bizarre apron no bigger than a dish-rag (and no less dingy), which modesty requires that you tie around your waist. In general, women set the apron aside as a towel, while men keep theirs on; bring a bathing suit just in case. Customs vary greatly by establishment, so just do as the locals do—nothing is more conspicuous than a Speedo-clad tourist among naked natives.

Cycle through the sauna and thermal baths a couple times, then enter the massage area. For a good scrubbing, try the sanitary massage *(vízi)*; if you're a traditionalist, stick to the medical massage *(orvosi)*. Most baths provide a much-needed rest area once the process is complete. Refreshed, smiling, and somewhat sleepy, tip the attendant, lounge over mint tea, and savor your afternoon of guilt-free pampering. *(Baths and pools 700-2000Ft, massages 1000-7500Ft.)*

STATUE PARK. (Szoborpark Múzeum). After the collapse of Soviet rule, the open-air Statue Park Muzeum was created from a collection of communist statuary removed from Budapest's parks and squares. The indispensable English guidebook explains the statues' past and present positions. *(XXII, on the corner of Balatoni út and Szabadkai u. www.szoborpark.hu. Take the express red bus #7 from Keleti pu. to Étele tér, then take the yellow Volán bus from terminal #2 (dir.: Diósd.). Open in good weather Mar.-Nov. daily 10am-dusk; Dec.-Feb. weekends and holidays only. 300Ft, students 200Ft.)*

MUSEUM OF APPLIED ARTS. (Iparművészeti Múzeum). The Art Nouveau building of the Museum of Applied Arts was designed for Hungary's 1896 millennium celebration. Inside is an eclectic collection of impressive hand-crafted objects, including Tiffany glass and furniture, as well as excellent temporary exhibits highlighting specific crafts. *(IX, Üllői út 33-37. M3: Ferenc körút. Open Mar. 15-Oct. Tu-Su 10am-6pm; Nov.-Mar. Tu-Su 10am-4pm. 500Ft, students 250Ft.)*

BUDA CASTLE. Leveled by the Nazis and by the Soviets, the reconstructed Buda Castle (see Castle District, p. 1012) now houses several museums. Wing A contains the **Museum of Contemporary Art** (Kortárs Művészeti Múzeum), as well as the smaller **Ludwig Museum** upstairs, which is devoted to Warhol, Lichtenstein, and other masters of modern art. Wings B-D hold the **Hungarian National Gallery** (Magyar Nemzeti Galéria), a definitive collection of the best in Hungarian painting and sculpture. *(Wings A-D open Tu-Su 10am-6pm. Wing A 400Ft, students 200Ft. Wings B-D 600Ft total, students 300Ft.)* Artifacts from the 1242 castle, unearthed by WWII bombings, lie in the **Budapest History Museum** (Budapesti Történéti Múzeum) in Wing E. *(I, Szent György tér 2. M1-3: Deák tér. Take bus #16 across the Danube to the top of Castle Hill. Wing E open mid-May to mid-Sept. daily 10am-6pm; mid-Sept. to Oct. and Mar. to mid-May W-M 10am-6pm; Nov.-Feb. W-M 10am-4pm. 600Ft, students 300Ft.)*

HUNGARIAN NATIONAL MUSEUM. (Magyar Nemzeti Múzeum). Two extensive exhibits chronicle Hungarian history; a cheery Stalin welcomes you to rooms devoted to Soviet propaganda. Room descriptions have English translations and helpful historical maps. *(VIII, Múzeum krt. 14/16. www.origo.hnm.hu. M3: Kálvin tér. Open Mar. 15-Oct. 15 Tu-Su 10am-6pm; Oct. 16-Mar. 14 Tu-Su 10am-5pm. 600Ft, students 300Ft.)*

ENTERTAINMENT

Budapest Program, *Budapest Panorama*, *Pesti Est* and the essential *Budapest in Your Pocket* (750Ft) are the best English-language entertainment guides, listing everything from festivals to cinemas to art showings. All are available at most tourist offices and hotels. The "Style" section of the *Budapest Sun* (www.budapestsun.com; 300Ft), has a comprehensive 10-day calendar and film reviews. (Tickets 550-1000Ft; cinema schedules change on Th.)

THEATER, MUSIC, AND DANCE. Ticket Express, VI, Andrássy út 15, next to the Opera House, and throughout the city, sells tickets to most shows for no commission. (☎312 00 00. Open M-F 10am-6pm.) For 3000-9800Ft you can enjoy an opera in the splendor of the gilded, neo-Renaissance **Hungarian State Opera House** (see **Andrássy út,** p. 1013). The box office on the left side of the building sells cheaper stand-by tickets 30min. before showtime. (Box office ☎353 01 70. Open M-Sa 11am-5pm, Su 4-5pm; cashier open until 7pm on performance days.) The **Philharmonic Orchestra** has performances almost nightly Sept.-June. Buy tickets at V, Mérleg u. 10. (☎318 02 81. Open daily 9am-3pm. Tickets 2000-5000Ft, same-day discount available.) In late summer, the Philharmonic and Opera take a break, but performances continue at Budapest's acclaimed theaters. Buy tickets at the **Madách Theater Box Office,** VII, Madách tér 6. (☎322 20 15. Open M-Sa 2:30-7pm.) Many big musical acts pass through Budapest. **Music Mix 33 Ticket Service,** V, Váci ú. 33, has reasonably priced tickets. (☎317 77 36. Open M-F 10am-6pm, Sa 10am-1pm.)

THERMAL BATHS. To soak away the city grime, sink into a hot, relaxing thermal bath. First built in 1565, their services—from mud baths to massage—are quite cheap. Some baths are meeting spots for Budapest's gay community. **Széchenyi,** XIV, Állatkerti u. 11/14, is a welcoming bath with beautiful pools. (M1: Hősök tere. 1000Ft deposit on entry; keep your receipt. 15min. massage 1200Ft. Open May-Sept. daily 6am-7pm; Oct.-Apr. M-F 6am-7pm, Sa-Su 6am-5pm.) **Gellért,** XI, Kelenhegyi út 4/6, one of the most elegant baths, has a rooftop sundeck and an outdoor wave pool. Take bus #7 or tram #47 or 49 to Hotel Gellért, at the base of Gellérthegy. (Bath and pool 2000Ft. 15min. massage 1100Ft. Open May-Sept. M-F 6am-6pm, Sa-Su 6am-4pm; Oct.-Apr. closes 1pm weekends.)

NIGHTLIFE

All-night outdoor parties, elegant after-hours clubs, the nightly thump and grind—Budapest has it all. Although pubs and bars bustle until 4am, the streets themselves are surprisingly empty and poorly lit. Upscale cafes and restaurants in **VI, Liszt Ferenc tér** (M1: Oktogon) attract Budapest's hip youth. In summer, the Buda side of the park **Peötlfi híd** becomes a nightly party. Gay life in Budapest is just becoming visible; it's still safer to be discreet. If you have concerns, call the **gay hotline** (see **Bi-Gay-Lesbian Resources,** p. 1008).

Undergrass, VI, Liszt Ferenc tér 10. M1: Oktogon. The hottest spot in Pest's trendiest area. A soundproof glass door divides a hip bar from a packed disco. Open daily 8pm-4am; disco Tu-Su 10pm-4am.

Piaf, VI, Nagymező u. 25. A much-loved lounge, and a good place to meet fellow travelers. Knock on the door to await the approval of the club's matron. Cover 500Ft, includes 1 beer. Open daily 11pm-6am, but don't come before 1am.

Capella, V, Belgrád rakpart 23 (www.extra.hu/capellacafe). With glow-in-the-dark graffiti and an underground atmosphere, this spot draws a mixed gay and straight crowd. Cover 1000-1500Ft. Open Tu-Su 9pm-5am. The owners also run the three-level **Limo Cafe** down the street. Beer 350-700Ft. Open daily noon-5am.

Club Seven, Akácfa u. 7. M2: Blaha Lajos tér. This upscale underground music club is a local favorite. M-F no cover; Sa-Su 1000Ft, women free. Coffeehouse open daily 9pm-4am, restaurant 6pm-midnight, dance floor 10pm-5am.

Old Man's Music Pub, VII, Akácfa u. 13. M2: Blaha Lujza tér. Arrive early for nightly blues and jazz from 9-11pm, then relax in the restaurant (open 3pm-3am) or hit the dance floor (11pm-late). No cover. Open M-Sa 3pm to 4:30 or 5am.

Jazz Garden, V, Veres Páiné u. 44a. Although the "garden" is actually a vaulted cellar with Christmas lights, the effect works well. Live jazz nightly at 10:30pm. Beer 420-670Ft. Open Su-F noon-1am, Sa noon-2am.

Fat Mo's Speakeasy, V, Nyári Pal u. 11. M3: Kálvin tér. 14 varieties of draft beer (350-750Ft). Live jazz Su-M and Th 9-11pm. Th-Sa DJ from 11:30pm. Open M-F noon-2am, Sa noon-4am, Su 6pm-4am.-

NIGHTLIFE SCAM. There have been reports of a mafia-organized scam involving English-speaking Hungarian women who approach foreign men, suggest meeting elsewhere, ask for a drink, then leave. The bill, accompanied by imposing men, can be US$1000 for a single drink. The US Embassy (see Embassies, p. 1006) has advised against patronizing a number of establishments in the Váci u. area. The names of these establishments change faster than a two-bit hustle. For the most current list of establishments about which complaints have been received, check with the US Embassy in Budapest or view their list on the web at www.usembassy.hu/conseng/announcements.html. If you are taken in, call the police. You'll probably still have to pay, but get a receipt to issue a complaint formally at the Consumer Bureau.

APPENDIX

CZECH

ENGLISH	CZECH	PRONOUNCE	ENGLISH	CZECH	PRONOUNCE
yes/no	Ano/ne	AH-no/neh	**departure**	odjezd	OD-yezd
please	Prosím	PROH-seem	**one-way**	jen tam	yen tam
thank you	Děkuji	DYEH-koo-yih	**round-trip**	zpáteční	SPAH-tech-nyee
Hello	Dobrý den	DO-bree den	**reservation**	místenka	mis-TEN-kah
Goodbye	Nashedanou	NAH sleh-dah-noh-oo	**ticket**	lístek	LIS-tek
Sorry/excuse me	Promiňte	PROH-mihn-teh	**train/bus**	vlak/autobus	vlahk/OUT-oh-boos
Help!	Pomoc!	POH-mots	**station**	nádraží	NA-drah-zhee
police	policie	PO-lits-iye	**airport**	letiště	LEH-tish-tyeh
passport	cestovní pas	TSE-stov-neeh	**taxi**	taxi	TEHK-see
hotel	hotel	HOH-tel	**bank**	banka	BAN-ka
single room	jednolůžkový pokoj	YED-noh-luu-zhko-veeh PO-koy	**exchange**	směnárna	smyeh-NAR-na
double room	dvoulůžkový pokoj	DVOU-luu-zhko-veeh PO-koy	**grocery**	potraviny	PO-tra-vee-nee
with bath	s koupelnou	SKOH-pel-noh	**pharmacy**	lékárna	LEE-khaar-nah
with shower	se sprchou	SE SPR-khou	**tourist office**	turistické informace	TOO-rist-it-skeh IN-for-mat-tseh
bathroom	WC	VEE-TSEE	**post office**	pošta	POSH-ta
open/closed	otevřeno/zavřeno	O-te-zheno/ZAV-rzhen-o	**vegetarian**	vegetariánský	VEHG-eh-tah-rih-aan-skee-ee
left/right	vlevo/vpravo	VLE-voh/VPRA-voh	**kosher**	košer	KOH-sher
straight	běžte rovně	BYEZH-teh ROHV-nye	**nuts/milk**	ořech/mléko	OH-rekch/MLEH-koh
center of town	centrum měšţă	MNEHST-skeh TSEN-troom	**menu**	lístek	LIS-tek
castle	hrad	KHRAD	**beer**	pivo	PEE-voh
church	kostel	KO-stel	**market**	trh	TH-rh
square	náměstí	NAH-mye-stee	**bakery**	pekařství	PE-karzh-stvee

ENGLISH	CZECH	PRONOUNCE
Where is...?	Kde je...?	k-DEH
How do I get to...?	Jak se dostanu do...?	YAK seh dohs-TAH-noo doh
How much does this cost?	Kolik to stojí?	KOH-lihk STOH-yee
Do you have...?	Máte...?	MAH-teh
Do you speak English?	Mluvíte anglicky?	MLOO-vit-eh ahng-GLIT-ski
I'd like to order...?	Prosím...	PROH-seem

Every letter is pronounced, and stress is always placed on the first syllable. Letters with certain diacriticals (á, é, í, ó, ú, ů, ý) should be held longer. "C" is pronounced "ts"; "g" is always hard; "č" is pronounced "ch"; "ch" is considered one letter (alphabetized after h) and is pronounced like a guttural "h"; "j" is pronounced "y"; "r" is slightly rolled; "ř" is "rzh"; "š" is "sh"; "w" is proncounced "v"; and "ž" is "zh." The letter "ě" sounds like "ye" or "nye" (e.g., "ně" is "nyeh," "mě" is "mnyeh").

DANISH

ENGLISH	DANISH	PRONOUNCE	ENGLISH	DANISH	PRONOUNCE
yes/no	ja/nej	ya/nai	**departure**	afgang	OW-gahng
please (may I ask for...)	må jeg bede om...	mo yai BEE-the awm	**one-way**	enkeltbillet	ENK-elt bee-LET
thank you	tak	tahk	**round-trip**	returbillet	rih-TOUR bee-LET
Hello	Goddag	go-DAY	**reservation**	reservation	rez-er-vah-SHONE
Goodbye	Farvel	fah-VEL	**ticket**	billet	bee-LET
Sorry/excuse me	Undskyld	OON-skool	**train/bus**	tog/bus	toh/boos
Help!	Hjælp!	yelp	**station**	station	STAH-shone
police	politi	PO-lee-tee	**airport**	lufthavn	LOOFT-hown
embassy	ambassade	AHM-ba-sa-the	**taxi**	taxa	TAHX-a
passport	pas	pass	**ferry**	færge	FA-wuh
hotel/hostel	hotel/vandre-hjem	HO-tel/VAHN-dru-yem	**bank**	bank	bahnk
single room	enkeltværelse	ENG-kult-ver-el-suh	**exchange**	veksling	VEX-ling
double room	dobbeltværelse	DOB-elt-ver-el-suh	**grocery**	supermarked	SOO-per-mah-kuth
with shower	med brusebad	meth BROO-suh-bath	**tourist office**	turistkontor	too-REEST KON-tor
bathroom	badeværelse	BAH-the-ver-el-suh	**vegetarian**	vegetar	VEH-geh-tah
open/closed	åben/lukket	OH-ben/LOO-kuth	**kosher**	kosher	KO-shaw
left/right	venstre/højre	VEN-struh/HOY-ruh	**halal**	halal	hal-AL
straight	ligeud	lee-uh-OOTH	**nuts**	nødder	NER-the
turn	dreje	DRAI-yuh	**milk**	mælk	mehlk

ENGLISH	DANISH	PRONOUNCE
Where is...?	Hvor er...?	vaw a
How do I get to...?	Hvordan kommer jeg til...?	vaw-DAN KO-muh yai till
How much does this cost?	Hvor meget koster det?	vaw MAI-uth KO-stuh deh
Do you have...?	Har du...?	hah doo
Do you speak English?	Snakker du engelsk?	SNAHK-uh doo ENG-uhlsk
I'd like to order...?	Jeg vil gerne bestille...?	yai vill GA-nuh bi-STILL-uh
I'm allergic to...	Jeg er allergisk over for...	yai a al-A-geesk OH-uh for

In Danish, stress is usually placed on the first syllable of the word. Unfortunately, there are no firm rules for pronouncing the alphabet. Danish is a North Germanic language and thus resembles Swedish, Norweigan, Faeroese, and Icelandic.

APPENDIX

DUTCH

ENGLISH	DUTCH	PRONOUNCE
yes/no	ja/nee	ya/nay
please	alstublieft	AL-stoo-bleeft
thank you	dank u wel	dank oo vel
Hello	Hallo	hal-LO
Goodbye	Tot ziens	tot zeens
Sorry/excuse me	Neemt u mij niet/pardon	naymt oo mi neet/par-DON
Help!	Help!	help
police	politie	po-LEET-see
embassy	ambassade	am-bass-AH-duh
passport	paspoort	PAS-pohrt
hotel/hostel	hotel	ho-TEL
single room	eenpersoon-skamer	AYN–persohns-kahmer
double room	tweepersoon-skamer	TVAY-persohns-kahmer
bed	bed	bed
with shower	met douche	met doosh
bathroom	badkamer	BAT-kah-mer
open/closed	openen/geslo-ten	OH-pen-uh/ke-SLO-tuh
left/right	links/rechts	links/rekhts
straight	recht	rekht
turn	ga naar	KHa nahr
alarm clock	wekker	VE-kker
bicycle	fiets	feets
moped	bromfiets	BROM-feets
car	auto	OW-to
church	kerk	lerk
laundromat	wasserette	vass-er-ETT-uh
library	bibliotheek	bib-lee-oh-TAYK

ENGLISH	DUTCH	PRONOUNCE
departure	vertrek	ver-TREK
one-way ticket	enkele reis naar	EN-kel-uh rees-nahr
round-trip ticket	retourtje	ret-OORT-yuh
reservation	reservering	rays-air-VAY-ring
ticket	kaartje	KAHRT-yuh
train/bus	trein/bus	trin/boos
station	station	stash-on
airport	vliegveld	vel-EE-khvelt
taxi	taxi	TAX-ee
ferry	veerboot	VAYR-boht
bank	bank	bank
exchange rate	wisselkoers	VI-ssel-koors
grocery	kruidenier	krow-duh-EER
pharmacy	apotheek	ah-po-TAYK
tourist office	toeristen-bureau	toor-IST-uh-BOO-roh
hospital	ziekenhuis	ZEE-ken-hows
vegetarian	vegetariër	vay-khet-AH-ri-er
meat	vlees	vlays
cheese	kaas	kahs
nuts/milk	noten/melk	NOH-tuh/melk
dessert	nagerecht	NAH-ker-ekht
bread	brood	broot
beer	bier	beer
fish	vis	viss
cigarette	sigaret	see-kha-RET
birthday	verjaardag	ver-YAHRD-ka
reception	receptie	re-SEP-see

ENGLISH	DUTCH	PRONOUNCE
Where is...?	Waar is...?	vaar is
How do I get to...?	Hoe kom ik in...?	hoo kom ik in
How much does this cost?	Wat kost het?	vat kost het
Do you have...?	Heeft u...?	hayft oo
Do you speak English?	Sprekt u Engels?	spraykt oo EN-gels
What time is it?	Hoe laat is het?	hoo laht is uht
Can I have a...?	Mag ik een...?	mahk ik uhn

In Dutch, "j" is pronounced like the "s" in treasure. A guttural "g" sound is used for both "g" and "ch." The Dutch "ui" is pronounced "ow," and the dipthong "ij" is best approximated in English as "ah" followed by a long "e." There are two plural endings for nouns: -en, more common, and -s.

FRENCH

ENGLISH	FRENCH	PRONOUNCE
departure	le départ	DAY-par
one-way	aller simple	al-AY-samp
round-trip	aller retour	al-AY-re-TOOR
reservation	la résérvation	rez-er-va-SEE-on
ticket	le billet	BEE-AY
passport	le passeport	pass-POR
luggage	la valise	vah-LEEZ
station	la gare	gahr
train/bus	le train/le bus	trah/boos
airport	l'aéroport	AYH-o-port
airplane	l'aéro	AYH-o
taxi	le taxi	tax-EE
ferry	le bac	bak
hotel	l'hôtel	LO-tel
single room	une chambre simple	oon-SHAM-bra-samp
double room	une chambre pour deux	oon-SHAM-bra-poor-doo
dorm	le dortoir	DOR-twar
with shower	avec la douche	a-VEK-la-DOO-sh
bathroom	la salle de bain	SAL-de-BAHN
zero	zéro	ser-OH
one	un	AHN
two	deux	DOO
three	trois	TWAH
four	quatre	KATR
five	cinq	SANK
six	six	SEES
seven	sept	SET
eight	huit	HWEET
nine	neuf	noof
ten	dix	DEES
twenty	vingt	VENT
thirty	trente	TRAHNT
forty	quarante	KAR-ahnt
fifty	cinquante	SANK-ahnt
sixty	soixante	SWAZ-ant
seventy	soixante-dix	SWAZ-ant-DEES
eighty	quatre-vingt	KATR-vent
ninety	quatre-vingt-dix	KATR-vent-DEES
one hundred	cent	SAHT
one thousand	mille	MEEL

ENGLISH	FRENCH	PRONOUNCE
open	ouvert	OO-vert/fer-MAY
closed	fermé	fuhr-MAY
bank	la banque	bahnk
exchange	l'échange	lay-SHAN-juh
tourist office	le bureau de tourisme	byur-O-de-toor-EES-muh
grocery	l'épicerie	lep-EES-er-ee
restaurant	le restaurant	res-tahr-AWNT
post office	la poste	pawst
police	la police	po-LEES
embassy	l'ambassade	lam-bas-SAHD
pharmacy	la pharmacie	far-ma-SEE
doctor	un médecin	MAY-dsen
breakfast	le pétit-déjeuner	puh-TEET DAY-zhun-AY
lunch	le déjeuner	DAY-zhun-AY
dinner	le dîner	dee-NAY
menu	le menu	mehn-YOO
vegetarian	le végétarien	veh-JAY-tehr-REE-unh
vegan	le végétaliene	veh-JAY-tal-EE-en
kosher/halal	kascher/halal	ka-SHER/ha-lal
nuts/milk	les caca-houètes/ le lait	CAK-a-hwets/ LAY
left/right	à gauche/ à droite	a-GOSH/a-DWAH
straight	tout droit	TOO-dwah
turn	tournez	toor-NAY
near to	près de	PRAY-duh
far from	loin de	LWEN-duh
north	nord	NOR
south	sud	SOOD
east	est	est
west	ouest	OO-est
yesterday	hier	EE-ayhr
today	aujourd'hui	oh-JOORD-WEE
tomorrow	demain	duh-MEN
morning	le matin	mat-EN
afternoon	l'aprés-midi	luh-PRAY-mee-dee
evening	le soir	SWAR
night	la nuit	NWEE
money	l'argent	lar-JAUNT
change/coins	la monnaie	mon-AY
tip	la service	ser-VEES
waiter	le garçon	gar-SOHN

ENGLISH	FRENCH	PRONOUNCE
Yes/no	oui/non	wee/nohn
Please	S'il vous plaît.	see-voo-PLAY
Thank you	Merci.	mehr-SEE
You're welcome	C'est rien.	SAY-REE-en
Sorry/excuse me	Excusez-moi!	ex-KU-zay-MWAH
Hello	Bonjour.	bohn-ZHOOR
Goodbye	Au revoir.	oh re-VWAHR
What is your name?	Comment appellez-vous?	kaw-MONT-uh-pel-LAY-VOO
My name is	Je m'appelle...	zhe-mahp-PELL
How are you?	Comment allez-vous?	kaw-MONT-ah-LAY-VOO
Do you speak English?	Parlez-vous anglais?	par-LAY-VOO-an-GLAY
I don't speak French	Je ne parle pas français	zhe-nuh-parl-pah-frawn-SAY
I don't understand	Je ne comprends pas	zhe-nuh-kawm-PRAWN-pah
Could you repeat that?	Repetez s'il-vous-plaît	reh-pet-AY sil-VOO-PLAY
Where is...?	Où se trouve...?	OOH-AY
How do I get to...?	Comment peut on aller à...?	KAW-mont-puht-on-a-LAY-a
Help!	Au secours!	oh-sek-OOR
I'm lost	Je suis perdu.	zh'SWEE pehr-DOO
Leave me alone	Laissez-moi tranquille	luh-SAY-mwah-tran-KEEL
How much does this cost?	Ça fait combien?	sa-FAY-com-BEE-uhn
Do you have...?	Avez vous...?	ah-VAY-VOO
I'd like to order	Je voudrais...	zhe-VOO-DRAY
I'm allergic to...	Je suis allergique à...	zhe-SWEE-al-er-ZHEEK-ah
I'd like to pay	L'addition, s'il-vous-plaît	lahd–EE-ohn see-VOO-play
Do you have a vacancy?	Avez-vous une chambre dis-ponible?	ah-VAY-VOO oon-SHAM-brah DEES-pawn-EE-bl
I'd like a room	Je voudrais une chambre	zhe-VOO-DRAY oon-SHAM-brah
May I see the room?	Peut-je vois la chambre?	POO-zh VWAH la-SHAM-brah
No, I don't like it	Non, je ne l'aime pas.	nawn, zhe-nuh lem-pah
Yes, I'll take it	D'accord	da-KORD
Is this the train/bus to...?	Ç'est le train/l'autobus à...	SAY luh-tren/LAW-toh-BOOS ah
I want a ticket to...	Je voudrais un billet à...	zhe-VOO-DRAY uhn BEE-AY ah
What time does the... leave?	À quelle heure départ...	ah-KEL-uyr DAY-par
When?	Quand?	KAWN
What time is it?	Quelle heure est-il?	KEL-uyr-ayh-TEEL
It's 11am.	Il est (onze) heures	eel-ay (AWNZ) uyr

Le is the masculine singular definite article (the); *la* the feminine; both are abbreviated to *l'* before a vowel, while *les* is the plural definite article for both genders. *Un* is the masculine singular indefinite article (a or an), *une* the feminine; while *des* is the plural indefinite article for both genders ("some").

APPENDIX

GERMAN

ENGLISH	GERMAN	PRONOUNCE
departure	Abfahrt	AHB-fart
one-way	einfache	EYN-fahk-uh
round-trip	hin- und zurück	HIHN und tsur-OOK
reservation	reservierung	rez-eyr-VEER-oong
ticket	Karte	KAR-tuh
passport	Reisepass	RY-zuh-pass
luggage	Gepäck	geh-PECK
station	Bahnhof	BAHN-hohf
train/bus	Zug/Bus	tsug/boos
airport	Flughafen	FLOOG-hahf-en
airplane	Flugzeug	FLOOG-tsoyg
taxi	Taxi	TAHK-zee
port	Hafen	HAHF-en
ferry	Fährschiff	FAYR-shif
hotel/hostel	Hotel/ Jugendherberge	ho-TEL/ YOO-gend-hayr-BER-guh
single room	Einzelzimmer	EYN-tsel-tsim-muh
double room	Doppelzimmer	DOPP-pehl-tsim-muh
dorm	Schlafsaal	shlaf-zahl
with shower	mit Düsche	mit DOO-shuh
bathroom	Badezimmer	BAH-deh-tsim-muh
zero	null	nool
one	eins	eynz
two	zwei	tsvai
three	drei	dry
four	vier	feer
five	fünf	foonf
six	sechs	zeks
seven	sieben	ZEE-ben
eight	acht	ahkt
nine	neun	noyn
ten	zehn	tseyn
twenty	zwanzig	TSVAN-tsig
thirty	dreizig	DRY-tsig
forty	vierzig	FEER-zig
fifty	fünfzig	FOONF-zig
sixty	sechzig	ZEK-tsig
seventy	siebzig	SEEB-zig
eighty	achtzig	AHKT-zig
ninety	neunzig	NOYN-tsig

ENGLISH	GERMAN	PRONOUNCE
open	geöffnet	geh-ERF-net
closed	geschlossen	geh-SHLOS-sen
bank	Bank	bahnk
exchange	Wechseln	VECK-zeln
tourist office	Reisebüro	RY-zuh-byur-roh
grocery	Lebensmittel	LAY-benz-mit-tel
restaurant	Restaurant	res-tar-AHNT
post office	Postamt	POST-amt
police	Polizei	poh-lit-tsai
embassy	Botschaft	BOT-shaft
pharmacy	Apotheke	AH-poh-TAY-kuh
doctor	Artz	arts
breakfast	Frühstück	FROO-shtook
lunch	Mittagessen	MIT-tag-es-en
dinner	Abendessen	AH-bend-es-en
menu	Menü	MEN-yoo
vegetarian	vegetarier	veg-eh-TAYR-ee-er
vegan	veganer	VAY-gahn-er
kosher/halal	koscher/halaal	KOH-sher/hah-LAAL
nuts/milk	Nüsse/Milch	NYUOO-suh/ milch
left/right	links/rechts	links/rekts
straight	geradeaus	geh-rah-deh-OWS
(to) turn	drehen	DREY-hen
near to	in der nähe von	in dayr nay-eh fon
far from	weit von	vyt fon
north	Nord	nord
south	Süd	zood
east	Öst	erst
west	West	vest
yesterday	gerstern	GES-tayrn
today	heute	HOY-tuh
tomorrow	morgen	MOR-gen
morning	Morgen	MOR-gen
afternoon	Nachmittag	NAHK-mit-tahg
evening	Abend	AH-bend
night	Nacht	nakt
here	hier	heer
good/bad	gut/schlect	goot/shlekt
many	viel(e)	feel(eh)

ENGLISH	GERMAN	PRONOUNCE
Yes/no/maybe	ja/nein/vielleicht	yah/nine/feel-eykt
Please	bitte	BIH-tuh
Thank you	danke	DAHNG-keh
You're welcome	bitte sehr	BIH-tuh ZAYR
Sorry/excuse me	Entschuldigung	ent-SHOOL-dih-goong
Hello	Hallo	HAH-loh
Goodbye	Auf Wiedersehen/Tschüss (informal)	owf-VEE-dayr-zayn/choos
What is your name?	Wie heißen Sie?	vee HY-sen zee
My name is...	Ich heiße...	ish HY-seh
How are you?	Wie geht's?	vee gayts
I am well.	Es geht mir gut.	es gayt meer goot
Do you speak English?	Sprechen Sie Englisch?	SHPREK-en zee ENG-lish
I don't speak German.	Ich spreche Deutsch nicht.	ish SHPREK-eh doych nikt
I don't understand	Ich verstehe nicht	ish fehr-SHTAY-eh nikt
Could you repeat that?	Wiederholen Sie, bitte?	VEE-dayr-HOH-len zee BIH-tuh
Where is...?	Wo ist...?	voh ist
How do I get to...?	Wie komme ich nach...?	vee KOM-muh ish nock
Help!	Hilfe!	HIL-fuh
I'm lost	Ich habe mich verloren	ish HAB-uh mish feyr-LOR-en
Leave me alone!	Lass mich in Rühe!	lahs mich in ROO-uh
How much does this cost?	Wieviel kostet das?	VEE-feel kost-et das
Do you have...?	Haben Sie...?	HAB-en zee
I'd like to order...	Ich möchte...	ish MERK-tuh
I'm allergic to...	Ich bin zu ___ allergisch.	ish bihn tsoo ___ ah-LEYR-gish
I'd like to pay	Zahlen, bitte.	TSAL-en BIH-tuh
Do you have a vacancy?	Haben Sie einen Platz?	HAH-ben zee eyn-en platz
I'd like a room	Ich möchte ein Zimmer.	ish MERK-tuh eyn TSIM-muh
May I see the room?	Darf ich das Zimmer sehen?	darf ish dahs ZIM-muh SEY-en
No, I don't like it	Nein, es gefällt mir nicht	nine es geh-FELT meer nikt
Yes, I'll take it	Ja, ich nehme es	ya ish NAY-meh es
Is this the train/bus to...?	Geht dieser Zug/Bus nach...?	gayt DEEZ-ayr tsug/boos nock
I want a ticket to...	Ich möchte eine Karte nach...	ish MERK-tuh EYN-eh KAR-teh nock
What time does the... leave?	Um wieviel Uhr geht...	oom VEE-feel oor gayt...
How long does the trip take?	Wieviel Uhr dauert die Reise?	vee-feel oor DOW-ert dee RY-zuh
When?	Wann?	vahn
What time is it?	Wieviel Uhr ist es jetzt?	VEE-feel oor ist es yetz
It's 11am.	Es ist elf Uhr.	es ist elf oor.

Every letter is pronounced. Consonants are pronounced as in English with the following exceptions: "j" is pronounced as "y"; "qu" is pronounced "kv"; a single "s" is pronounced "z"; "v" is pronounced "f"; "w" is pronounced as "v"; and "z" is pronounced "ts." "Sch" is "sh"; "st" is "sht"; and "sp" is "shp." The "ch" sound, as in "ich" ("I") and "nicht" ("not"), is tricky; you can substitute a "sh." The letter ß (esstset) is a symbol for a double-S and is pronounced "ss."

GREEK

ENGLISH	GREEK	PRONOUNCE
departure	αναχωρηση	ah-nah-HO-ree-see
one-way ticket	μονο εισιτηριο	mon-NO ee-see-TEE-ree-o
round-trip ticket	εισιτηριο με επιστροψη	ee-see-TEE-ree-o me e-PEE-stro-FEE
reservation	κρατηση	KRA-tee-see
passport	διαβατηριο	dhee-ah-vah-TEE-ree-o
station	σταθμοζ	stath-MOS
train/bus	τραινο/ λεωφορειο	TREH-no/leh-o-fo-REE-o
airport	αεροδρομειο	ah-e-ro-DHRO-mee-o
port	λιμανι	lee-MAH-nee
ferry	πλοιο	PLEE-o
hotel	ξενοδοχειο	kse-no-dho-HEE-o
single room	μονο δωματιο	mon-NO do-MA-shee-o
double room	δηιπλο δωματιο	dheep-LO do-MA-shee-o
room to let	δωματια	do-MA-shee-ah
with shower	υε ντουζ και τουαλεττα	me dous ke tou-ah-LET-ta
bathroom	τουαλεττα	tou-ah-LET-ta
zero		
one	ενα	EN-ah
two	δυο	DHEE-o
three	τρια	TREE-ah
four	τεσσερα	TEH-ser-ah
five	πεντε	PEN-deh
six	εξη	EHX-ee
seven	εψτα	ef-TAH
eight	οχτω	oh-TO
nine	εννεα	ee-NEE-ah
ten	δεκα	DHEY-kah
twenty	εικοσι	EE-ko-see
thirty	τριαντα	tree-AHN-dah
forty	σαρανδα	sar-AHN-dah
fifty	πενηνδα	pe-NEEN-dah
sixty	εξηντα	ex-EEN-dah
seventy	εβδομηντα	ev-dhom-EEN-dah
eighty	ογδοντα	ogh-DHON-dah
ninety	ενενηντα	eh-neh-NEEN-dah
one hundred	εκατο	eh-kah-TO
one thousand	χιλια	HEE-lee-ah

ENGLISH	GREEK	PRONOUNCE
open	ανοικτο	ah-nee-KTO
closed	κλειστο	klee-STO
bank	τραπεζα	TRAH-peh-zah
exchange	ανταλλασσω	an-da-LAS-so
tourist office	τουριστικο γραψειο	tou-ree-stee-KO graf-EE-o
market	αγορα	ah-go-RAH
restaurant	εστιατοριο	es-tee-ah-TO-ree-o
post office	ταχυδρομειο	ta-hee-dhro-MEE-o
police	αστυνομεια	as-tee-no-MEE-a
embassy	πρεσβεια	prez-VEE-ah
pharmacy	φαρμακειο	fahr-mah-KEE-o
doctor	ιατροσ	yah-TROS
breakfast	πρωινο	pro-ee-NO
lunch	μεσημβρινο	mes-eem-vreen-O
dinner	δειπνο	DHEEP-no
menu	μενου	men-O-UH
vegetarian	χορτοψαγουζ	hor-to-FUH-gos
nuts	ζηροσ καρποσ	zhros kar-POS
milk	γαλα	gah-LAH
left/right	αριστερα/ δεξια	ah-rees-teh-RAH/dhek-see-AH
straight	ευθεια	ef-THEE-ah
turn	στριψτε	STREEP-ste
near	κοντα	kon-DAH
far	μακρια	mah-kree-AH
mineral water	μεταλλικο νερο	me-tal-lee-KO ne-RO
yesterday	χθες	KTHES
today	σημερα	SEE-mer-a
tomorrow	αυριο	AV-ree-o
morning	πρωι	pro-EE
evening	βραδυ	VRAD-hy
later tonight	αποψε	ah-PO-pseh
night	νυχτα	NYH-tah
acropolis	ακροπολη	ah-KROP-o-lee
cathedral	μητροπολη	mee-TROP-o-lee
monastery	μοναστηρι	mon-ah-STEE-ree
ruins	αρχαια	ar-HEE-ah
museum	μουσειο	mou-SEE-o

ENGLISH	GREEK	PRONOUNCE
Yes/no/maybe	ναι/οχι	NEH/OH-hee
Please	παρακαλω	pah-rah-kah-LO
Thank you	ευχαριστω	ef-khah-ree-STO
Sorry/excuse me	Συγνομη	sig-NO-mee
Hello/Goodbye (polite)	Γεια σας	YAH-sas
Hello/Goodbye (familiar)	Γεια σου	YAH-soo
What is your name?	Πωζ σαζ λενε;	pos sas LEH-neh
My name is	Με λενε	meh LEH-neh
How are you?	Τι κανετε;	tee KAH-neh-teh
Do you speak English?	Μιλας αγγλικα;	mee-LAHS ahn-glee-KAH
I don't understand	Δεν καταλαβαινω	den kah-tah-lah-VEHN-o
I don't speak Greek	δεν μιλαω ελληνικα	dhen mee-LAHO el-leen-ee-KAH
Where is...?	Που ειναι...;	pou-EE-neh
How do I get to...?	Πωζ θα παω στο...;	pos tha PA-o sto
Help!	Βοητηεια!	vo-EE-thee-ah
I'm lost	Εχω χαθει	EH-o ha-THEE
Leave me alone	ασεμε	AH-se-me
How much does this cost?	Πσπο κανει;	PO-so KAH-nee
Do you have...?	Εχετε...;	Eh-khe-teh
I'd like to order	Θα ηθελα...	tha EE-thel-ah
I don't eat dairy products.	Δεν τρωω γαλακτοκοηικα προιοντα.	dhen DRO-o gha-lak-to-ko-mee-kah pro-EEON-dah
Can I see a room?	Μπορω να δω ενα δωματιο;	bo-RO nah-DHO E-nah dho-MAH-tee-o
What time is it?	Τι ωρα ειναι;	tee-O-rah EE-neh

GREEK ALPHABET

SYMBOL	LETTER	PRONOUNCE
α Α	alpha	*a* as in father
β Β	beta	*v* as in velvet
γ Γ	gamma	*y* as in yo, *g* as in go
δ Δ	delta	*th* as in there
ε Ε	epsilon	*e* as in jet
ζ Ζ	zeta	*z* as in zebra
η Η	eta	*ee* as in queen
θ Θ	theta	*th* as in health
ι Ι	iota	*ee* as in tree
κ Κ	kappa	*k* as in cat
λ Λ	lambda	*l* as in land
μ Μ	mu	*m* as in moose

SYMBOL	LETTER	PRONOUNCE
ν Ν	nu	*n* as in net
ξ Ξ	ksi	*x* as in mix
ο Ο	omicron	*o* as in row
π Π	pi	*p* as in peace
ρ Ρ	rho	*r* as in roll
σ (ς) Σ	sigma	*s* as in sense
τ Τ	tau	*t* as in tent
υ Υ	upsilon	*ee* as in green
φ (ϕ) Φ	phi	*f* as in fog
χ Χ	xi	*ch (h)* as in horse
ψ Ψ	psi	*ps* as in oops
ω Ω	omega	*o* as in row

The Greek alphabet has 24 letters; the chart above can help decipher signs. The left column gives the name of each letters in Greek, the middle column shows lower case and capital letters, and the right column shows the pronunciation.

APPENDIX

HUNGARIAN

ENGLISH	HUNGARIAN	PRONOUNCE
yes/no	Igen/nem	EF-ghen/nem
please	Kérem	KAY-rem
thank you	Köszönöm	KUH-suh-num
Hello	Szervusz	SAIR-voose
Goodbye	Viszontlátásra	Vi-sont-lah-tah-shraw
Excuse me	Elnézést	EL-nay-zaysht
Help!	Segítség!	SHee-gee-shayg
police	rendőrséget	REN-dur-shay-get
passport	az útlevelemet	oz OOT-lev-el-met
hotel	szálloda	SAH-law-dah
single	ühelist	EW-hel-ist
double	kahelist	KA-hel-ist
with bath	fürdőszobás	FEWR-dur-saw-baash
with shower	zuhanyzós	ZOO-hon-yaw-yawsh
toilet	W.C.	VAY-tsay
open/closed	nyitott/csukott	NYEE-tot/CHOO-kawt
left/right	balra/jobbra	bol-rah/yowb-rah
straight ahead	egyenesen tovább	EH-dyen-esh-en TOV-ahb
water	víz	veez
juice	gyümölcslé	DYEW-murl-chlay
coffee	kávé	KAA-vay
milk	tej	tay
beer	sör	shurr
wine	bor	bawr

ENGLISH	HUNGARIAN	PRONOUNCE
departure	indulás	IN-dool-ahsh
one-way	csak oda	chok AW-do
round-trip	oda-viss	AW-do-VEES-do
seat reservation	potegy	poh-tej
ticket	jegyet	YED-et
train	vonat	VAW-not
bus	autobussz	auto-boos
station	pályaudvar	pa-yo-OOT-var
airport	repúlőtér	rep-ewlu-TAYR
bank	bank	bonk
exchange	valutabeválto	OH-loo-tob-bee-vaal-taw
grocery	élelmiszerbolt	ay-lel-mes-er-balt
pharmacy	gyógyszertár	DYAW-dyser-tar
tourist office	utazási iroda	UH-toh-zah-see EE-raw-dah
post office	posta	PAWSH-toh
vegetarian	vegetáriánus	VEH-geh-tah-ree-ah-nush
kosher	kóser	KWAW-shehr
nuts	smafu	SHMOH-fuh
menu	étlap	ATE-lop
bread	kenyér	KEN-yair
vegetables	zöldségek	ZULD-segek
beef	marhahús	MOR-ho-hoosh
pork	disznóhús	disnow-hoosh
fish	hal	hull

ENGLISH	HUNGARIAN	PRONOUNCE
Where is...?	Hol van...?	hawl von
How much does this cost?	Mennyi ideig tart?	MEN-yee EE-deeg tort
Can I have...?	Kaphatok...?	KAH-fot-tok
Do you speak English?	Beszél angolul?	BAY-sayl ON-gaw-lool
I'm lost.	Eltèvedtem	elle-taav-e-te

The letter "c" is pronounced "ts"; "cs" is "ch"; "g" is always hard; "j" is pronounced "y"; "ly" is "y"; "s" is "sh"; "zs" is "zh." There are no silent letters in Hungarian; double consonants are pronounced long. Vowels standing next to each other are pronounced separately. Stress generally falls on the first syllable of the word.

ITALIAN

ENGLISH	ITALIAN	PRONOUNCE
departure	partenza	par-TEN-zuh
one-way	solo andata	SO-lo ahn-DAH-tah
round-trip	andata e ritorno	ahn-DAH-tah ey ree-TOHR-noh
reservation	prenotazione	pray-no-taht-see-YOH-neh
ticket	biglietto	beel-YEHT-toh
passport	passaporto	pahs-sah-POHR-toh
luggage	bagaglio	ba-GAHL-lee-oh
station	stazione	staht-see-YOH-neh
train/bus	treno/autobus	TRAY-no/aow-toh-BOOS
airport	aeroporto	AIR-o-PORT-o
airplane	aereo	air-EE-oh
taxi	tassi	tass-EE
port	babordo	bab-OR-doh
ferry	traghetto	tra-GHEHT-toh
hotel/hostel	albergo	al-BER-go
single room	camera singola	CAH-meh-rah SEEN-goh-lah
double room	doppia	DOH-pee-yah
with shower	con doccia	kohn DOH-cha
bathroom	gabinetto	gah-bee-NEHT-toh
zero	zero	ZAY-roh
one	uno	OO-no
two	due	DOO-ay
three	tre	TRAY
four	quattro	KWAT-ro
five	cinque	CHEEN-kway
six	sei	SAI
seven	sette	SET-eh
eight	otto	O-toh
nine	nove	NOH-vay
ten	dieci	dee-AY-chee
twenty	venti	VEN-tee
thirty	trenta	TREN-tah
forty	quaranta	kar-AWNT-ah
fifty	cinquanta	sin-KANT-ah
one hundred	cento	CHEN-toh
one thousand	mille	MEE-le

ENGLISH	ITALIAN	PRONOUNCE
open	aperto	ah-PAIR-toh
closed	chiuso	KYOO-zoh
bank	banca	BAHN-kah
exchange	scambiare	skam-bee-AR-ay
tourist office	Azienda Promozione Turistica	a-zi-EN-da pro-mo-tzi-O-nay toor-EES-ti-ka
grocery	alimentari	ah-li-men-TA-ri
restaurant	ristorante	ree-sto-RAWN-tay
post office	l'ufficio postale	loo-FEE-choh poh-STAH-leh
police	polizia	po-LEET-ZEE-ah
embassy	ambasciata	am-ba-shi-AH-ta
pharmacy	farmacia	far-ma-TZI-ah
doctor	dottore	do-TORE-ay
breakfast	la colazione	lah coh-laht-see-YO-neh
lunch	il pranzo	PRAHND-zoh
dinner	la cena	lah CHEH-nah
menu	menu	MAY-nyoo
vegetarian	vegetariano	ve-ge-tar-i-AN-o
kosher/halal	kasher/halal	KA-sher/HA-lal
nuts/milk	noce/latte	NO-chay/LA-tay
left/right	sinistra/destra	see-NEE-strah/DEH-strah
straight	sempre diritto	SEHM-pray DREET-toh
turn	gira a	JEE-rah ah
near to	vicino	vee-CHEE-noh
far from	lontano	lohn-TAH-noh
north	nord	NORD
south	sud	SOOD
east	est	EST
west	ovest	OH-vest
yesterday	ieri	YAYR-ee
today	oggi	OHJ-jee
tomorrow	domani	doh-MAH-nee
morning	mattino	mat-TEEN-oh
afternoon	pomeriggio	poh-meh-REEJ-yoh
evening	sera	SAY-rah
night	notte	NO-teh
cathedral	duomo	DWO-mo

ENGLISH	ITALIAN	PRONOUNCE
Yes/no	Sì/No	see/no
Please	Per favore/Per piacere	pehr fah-VOH-reh/pehr pyah-CHEH-reh
Thank you	Grazie	GRAHT-see-yeh
You're welcome	Prego	PREY-goh
Sorry/excuse me	Scusi	SKOO-zee
Hello	Ciao	chow
Goodbye	Arrivederci/ArrivederLa (formal)	ah-ree-veh-DAIR-chee/ah-ree-veh-DAIR-lah
What is your name?	Come ti chiami?	COH-meh tee key-YAH-mee
My name is	Mi chiamo...	mee key-YAH-moh
How are you?	Come stai/Come sta	COH-meh st-EYE/stah
I am well.	Sto bene	stoh BEH-neh
Do you speak English?	Parla inglese?	PAHR-lah een-GLAY-zeh
I don't speak (Langauge)	Non parlo italiano	non PAHR-loh EE-tal-EE-an-OH
I don't understand	Non capisco	nohn kah-PEES-koh
Could you repeat that?	Potrebbe ripetere?	poh-TREHB-beh ree-peh-TEH-reh
Where is...?	Dov'è...?	doh-VEH
How do I get to...?	Come si arriva a...	KOH-meh see ahr-REE-vah ah
Help!	Aiuto!	ah-YOO-toh
I'm lost	Mi sono perso	mee SOH-noh PAIR-soh
Leave me alone	Lasciami stare!	LAH-shah-mee STAH-reh
How much does this cost?	Quanto costa?	KWAN-toh CO-stah
Do you have...?	Hai...	AI
I'd like to order	Vorrei...	voh-RAY
I'm allergic to...	Ho delle allergie...	OH DEHL-leh ahl-lair-JEE-eh
I'd like to pay	il conto	eel COHN-toh
Do you have a vacancy?	C'è un posto libero stasera?	chay oon POHS-toe LEE-ber-oh sta-SER-ah
I'd like a room	Potrei prenotare una camera	POH-tray pray-noh-TAH-reh OO-nah CAH-meh-rah
Yes, I'll take it	Va bene, la prendo	vah BEHN-eh, lah PREHN-doh
I want a ticket to...	Vorrei un biglietto	voh-RAY oon beel-YEHT-toh
What time does the... leave?	A che ora parte...?	ah kay OH-rah PAHR-tay
When?	quando	KWAN-doh
What time is it?	Che ore sono?	keh OHR-ay SOH-noh
It's 3:30pm.	Sono le tre e mezzo.	SOH-noh leh tray eh MEHD-zoh

In many Italian words, stress falls on the next-to-last syllable. When stress falls on the last syllable, accents indicate where stress falls: *città* (cheet-TAH) or *perchè* (pair-KAY). Stress can fall on the first syllable, but this occurs less often.

PORTUGUESE

ENGLISH	PORTUGUESE	PRONOUNCE
departure	partida	par-TEE-dah
one-way	ida	EE-dah
round-trip	ida e volta	EE-da ee VOHL-tah
reservation	reservação	reh-sehr-vah-SOW
ticket	bilhete	beel-YEHT
passport	passaporte	pah-sah-PORT
station	estação	esh-tah-SOW
train/bus	comboio/auto-carro	kom-BOY-yoo/ow-toh-KAH-roo
airport	aeroporto	aye-roh-POR-too
airplane	avião	ahv-YOW
taxi	taxi	TAHK-see
hotel	hotel	oh-TEHL
single room	quarto individual	KWAR-too een-dee-vee-DWAHL
double room	quarto duplo	KWAR-too DOOP-loo
dorm	dormitório	dor-mee-TOR-yoo
bathroom	banheiro	bahn-YAY-roo
one	um/uma	OOM/OO-mah
two	dois/duas	DOYSH/DOO-ahsh
three	três	TRAYSH
four	quatro	KWAT-roo
five	cinco	SEEN-koo
six	seis	SAYSH
seven	sete	SET
eight	oito	OY-too
nine	nove	NOHV
ten	dez	DAYZ
twenty	vinte	VEENT
thirty	trinta	TREEN-tah
forty	quarenta	kwa-RAYN-tah
fifty	cinqüenta	sin-KWAYN-tah
sixty	sesenta	seh-SAYN-tah
seventy	setenta	se-TAYN-tah
eighty	oitenta	oy-TAYN-tah
ninety	noventa	noh-VAYN-tah
one hundred	cem	SAYM

ENGLISH	PORTUGUESE	PRONOUNCE
open	aberto	ah-BAYR-too
closed	fechado	fay-SHAH-doo
bank	banco	BAHN-koo
exchange	câmbio	KAHM-byoo
tourist office	posto de turismo	POSH-too deh too-REES-moo
grocery	mercearia	mehr-say-ah-REE-ah
restaurant	restaurante	res-tow-RAHNT
post office	correio	koh-RAY-oo
police	polícia	poh-LEE-see-ah
embassy	embaixada	aym-bye-SHAH-dah
pharmacy	farmácia	far-MAHS-yah
doctor	médico	MEH-dee-koo
breakfast	café da manhã	kah-FEH dah man-YAH
lunch	almoço	ahl-MOH-soo
dinner	jantar	zhahn-TAR
menu	menú	meh-NOO
vegetarian	vegetariano	veh-zheh-tar-YAH-noo
vegan	vegan	veh-GAHN
kosher/halal	kosher/halal	koh-SHER/ah-LAHL
nuts/milk	nozes/leite	noh-ZESH/LAYT
left/right	direita/esquerda	dee-RAY-tah/esh-KAYR-dah
straight	em frente	ayn FRAYNT
turn	vire	VEER
near to	perto a	PAYR-too ah
far from	longe de	LONZH deh
north	norte	NORT
south	sul	SOOL
east	leste	LEST
west	oeste	WEST
yesterday	ontem	OHN-tem
today	hoje	OH-zheh
tomorrow	amanhã	ah-mahn-YAH
morning	manhã	mahn-YAH
afternoon	tarde	TARD
night	noite	NOYT

APPENDIX

ENGLISH	PORTUGUESE	PRONOUNCE
Yes/no/maybe	Sim/não/talvez	SEEN/NOW/tahl-VAYZ
Please	Por favor	por fah-VOR
Thank you	Obrigado (m)/Obrigada (f)	oh-bree-GAH-doo/dah
You're welcome	De nada	deh NAH-dah
Sorry/excuse me	Desculpe	desh-KOOLP
Hello	Olá	oh-LAH
Goodbye	Adeus	ah-DAY-oosh
What is your name?	Como se chama?	Koh-moh seh SHAH-mah
My name is	Chamo-me...	SHAH-moo-mee
How are you?	Como está	KOH-moh esh-TAH
I am well.	Estou bem.	esh-TOW BAYN
Do you speak English?	Fala inglês?	FAH-lah een-GLAYSH
I don't speak (language)	Não falo...	now FAH-loo
I don't understand	Não entendo	now ayn-TAYN-doo
Could you repeat that?	Pode repetir isso?	POH-deh reh-peh-TEER EE-soo
Where is...?	Onde é que fica...?	ON-deh ay kay FEE-kah
How do I get to...?	Como posso chegar a...	KOH-moh PO-soo sheh-GAR a
Help!	Socorro!	soh-KOH-roo
I'm lost	Estou perdido.	esh-TOH per-DEE-doo
Leave me alone	Deixe-me em paz!	DAY-shee-mee aym PAHZ
How much does this cost?	Quanto custa?	KWAHN-too KOOSH-tah
Do you have...?	Tem...?	taym
I'd like to order	Quiser encomendar.	kee-SEHR ayn-koh-mayn-DAR
I'm allergic to...	Sou alérgico a...	soh ah-LAYR-zhee-koo a
I'd like to pay	Quiser pagar.	kee-SEHR pah-GAR
Do you have a vacancy?	Tem quartos vagos?	taym KWAR-toosh VAH-goosh
I'd like a room	Quiser um quarto.	kee-SEHR oon KWAR-too
May I see the room?	Posso ver o quarto?	POH-soo vehr oo KWAR-too
No, I don't like it	Não, não gosto dele.	NOW, now GOSH-too DAY-leh
Yes, I'll take it	Sim, fico com ele.	SEEN, FEE-koh kom AY-leh
Is this the train/bus to...?	É este o comboio/autocarro para...?	AY esh-teh oo kom-BOY-yoo/ow-toh-KAH-roo PAH-rah
I want a ticket to...	Quiser um bilhete para...	kee-SEHR oom beel-YEH-teh pah-rah
What time does the... leave?	A que hora parte o...?	a kay OH-rah PART oo
How long does the trip take?	Quanto tempo demora a viagem?	KWAHN-too TAYM-poo deh-MOH-rah ah vee-AH-zhayn
When?	Quando?	KWAHN-doo
What time is it?	Que horas são?	kay OH-rahsh sow
It's 11am.	São as onze na manhã.	sow ahs OHN-zay nah mahn-YAH

Vowels with a *til* (*ã*, *õ*, etc.) or those that come before an *m* or *n* are pronounced with a nasal twang. At the end of a word, *o* is pronounced *oo* as in *room*, and *e* is sometimes silent (usually after a *t* or *d*). The consonant *s* is pronounced *sh* or *zh* when it occurs before another consonant. The consonants *ch* and *x* are pronounced *sh*, although the latter is sometimes pronounced as in English; *j* and *g* (before an *e* or *i*) are pronounced *zh*. The combinations *nh* and *lh* are pronounced "ny" as in *canyon* and "ly" as in *billion*.

SPANISH

ENGLISH	SPANISH	PRONOUNCE
departure	salida	sah-LEE-dah
one-way	ida	EE-dah
round-trip	ida y vuelta	EE-dah ee VOO-ehl-tah
reservation	reservación	ray-sahr-vah-see-OHN
ticket	boleto	boh-LAY-to
luggage	equipaje	eh-kee-PAH-hay
station	estación	eh-sta-see-OHN
train/bus	tren/autobús	trayn/ow-toh-BUS
airport	aeropuerto	ay-roh-PWAYR-to
taxi	taxi	TAH-ksee
port	puerto	PWAYR-toh
ferry	transbordador	trahns-BOR-dah-dohr
hotel/hostel	hotel/hostal	oh-TEHL/OH-stahl
single room	cuarto solo	KWAR-toh SOH-loh
double room	cuarto doble	KWAR-toh DOH-blay
dorm	dormitorio	dohr-mee-TOHR-ee-oh
with shower	con ducha	cohn doo-chah
bathroom	baño	BAHN-yoh
zero	cero	SAY-roh
one	uno	OO-noh
two	dos	dose
three	tres	trace
four	cuatro	KWAH-troh
five	cinco	SEEN-coh
six	seis	sace
seven	siete	see-AY-tay
eight	ocho	OH-choh
nine	nueve	noo-AY-vay
ten	diez	dee-ACE
twenty	vente	VAYN-tay
thirty	treinta	TRAYN-tah
forty	cuarenta	kwahr-EN-tah
fifty	cincuenta	seen-KWEN-tah

ENGLISH	SPANISH	PRONOUNCE
open	abierto(a)	ah-bee-AYR-toh
closed	cerrado(a)	sayr-RAH-doh
bank	banco	BAHN-coh
exchange	intercambio	een-tayr-CAM-bee-oh
tourist office	oficina de turismo	oh-fee-SEE-nah day too-REES-moh
grocery	supermercado	soo-payr-mayr-CAH-doh
restaurant	restaurante	ray-stow-RAHN-tay
post office	correo	cohr-RAY-oh
police	policía	poh-lee-SEE-ah
embassy	embajada	ehm-bah-HAH-dah
pharmacy	farmácia	fahr-mah-SEE-ah
doctor	doctor	dohk-TOR
breakfast	desayuno	day-sai-OON-oh
lunch	almuerzo	ahl-MWAYR-soh
dinner	cena	SAY-nah
menu	menú	may-NOO
vegetarian	vegetariano	vay-hay-tahr-ee-AHN-oh
nuts	nuezes	noo-AY-sace
milk	leche	LAY-chay
left	izquierda	ees-kee-AYR-dah
right	derecha	day-RAY-chah
straight	derecho	day-RAY-choh
turn	dobla	DOH-blah
near to	cerca de	SAYR-cah day
far from	lejos de	LAY-hoce day
yesterday	ayer	ah-YAYR
today	hoy	oy
tomorrow	mañana	mahn-YAH-nah
morning	mañana	mahn-YAH-nah
afternoon	tarde	TAHR-day
evening	tarde	TAHR-day
night	noche	NOH-chay

APPENDIX

ENGLISH	SPANISH	PRONOUNCE
Yes/no/maybe	Si/no/quizás	see/noh/kee-SAHS
Please	Por favor	pohr fah-VOHR
Thank you	Gracias	GRAH-see-ahs
You're welcome	De nada	day NAH-dah
Sorry/excuse me	perdón	payr-DOHN
Hello	Hola	OH-lah
Goodbye	Adiós	ah-dee-OHS
What is your name?	¿Cómo se llama Usted?	COH-moh say YAH-mah ooh-STED
My name is	Me llamo	may YAH-moh
How are you?	¿Cómo está Usted?	COH-moh eh-STAH ooh-STEHD?
I am well.	Estoy bien.	eh-STOY bee-AYN.
Do you speak English?	¿Usted habla inglés?	ooh-STEHD AH-blah een-GLACE?
I don't speak (Langauge)	No hablo	noh Ah-bloh
I don't understand	No entiendo	noh en-tee-EN-doh
Could you repeat that?	¿Repita, por favor?	ray-PEE-tah, pohr fah-VOHR?
Where is...?	¿Dónde está...?	DOHN-day eh-STAH...?
How do I get to...?	¿Cómo voy a...?	COH-moh voy ah...?
Help!	¡Ayuda!	ah-YOO-dah!
I'm lost	Estoy perdido	eh-STOY payr-DEE-doh
Leave me alone	Déjame solo	DAY-hah-may SOH-loh
How much does this cost?	¿Cuánto cuesta?	KWAHN-toh KWES-tah?
Do you have...?	¿Usted tiene...?	ooh-STEHD tee-AYN-ay...?
I'd like to order	Me gustaría	may goo-stah-REE-ah
I'm allergic to...	Soy alérgico a	soy ah-LAYR-hee-coh ah
I'd like to pay	Me gustaría pagar	may goo-stah-REE-ah pah-GAHR
Do you have a vacancy?	¿Usted tiene espacio?	ooh-STEHD tee-AYN-ay eh-SPAH-see-oh
I'd like a room	Me gustaría un cuarto	may goo-stah-REE-ah oon KWAR-toh
May I see the room?	¿Puedo ver el cuarto?	PWAY-doh vayr el KWAR-toh?
No, I don't like it	No, no me gusta	noh, noh may GOO-stah
Yes, I'll take it	Sí, lo quiero	see, lo kee-AYR-oh
Is this the train/bus to...?	¿Es esto el tren/autobús a...?	ace AY-stoh el trayn/ow-toh-BOOS ah...?
I want a ticket to...	Quiero un boleto a...	kee-AYR-oh oon boh-LAY-toh ah...
What time does the busleave?	¿Cuándo sale el autobús...?	KWAHN-doh SAH-lay el ow-toh-BOOS?
How long does the trip take?	¿Cuánto tiempo es el viaje?	KWAHN-toh tee-EM-poh es el vee-AH-hay
When?	¿Cuándo?	KWAHN-doh?
What time is it?	¿Qué hora es?	cay OH-rah es?
It's 11am.	Son las once de la mañana.	sohn lahs OHN-say day lah mahn-YAH-nah.

Vowels are always pronounced in the same way: "a" ("ah" in father); "e" ("eh" in egg); "i" ("ee" in eat); "o" ("oh" in oat); "u" ("oo" in boot). The letter "j" is pronounced "h"; "ll" is pronounced "y"; "ñ" is pronounced "ny"; and "rr" is a trilled "r." The letter "y" by itself is pronounced "ee," and "h" is always silent.

GOT CHANGE FOR A EURO?

A Quick Guide to the New International Currency

Cleaning out one's pack at the end of a trip through Europe used to turn into a comparison between the small change picked up in each country—whose bills looked the most like Monopoly money, whose national engravings were the corniest, or who had the most uselessly small denominations. This game has become a fair bit less interesting, though, now that the euro has been put into circulation in 12 member states of the EU. The euro has been hailed as a turning point in the future of European prosperity, both a symbol of and a step toward a cohesive, long-lasting alliance of autonomous countries. Its introduction into everyday life on January 1, 2002, was all but flawless, silencing critics and, incidentally, making multi-country travel infinitely more convenient.

The transition to the euro has been a long, carefully planned process. The European Economic Community was founded in 1958; the first suggestion of a common currency was made 11 years later, in response to dangerously fluctuating exchange rates. The specific steps of the euro's introduction were outlined in 1989, culminating in fixed exchange rates in 1999 and the establishment of the euro as the sole currency of all 12 eurozone states in 2002. Design contests were held in the mid-1990s to determine the look of the currency, resulting in a comfortable mix of international unity and national representation. The face of each of the seven bills depicts an architectural period from Europe's history, progressing from a Roman facade on the 5 euro to a 20th-century office building on the 500 euro. The backside of each note bears a bridge from the same period, symbolizing connection and communication between the countries. After a bit of contention as to whose landmarks would grace the more valuable bills—and the discovery that the pontoon bridge on the five was actually in India—it was decided that the images would be stylized creations rather than existing structures. The eight coins, which range in value from one-cent pieces to one- and two-euro coins, bear maps of Europe on their faces; their tails, on the other hand, have been designed separately by each of the eurozone countries. As a result, distinct emblems of national pride are shared across borders, as images of the Grand Duke of Luxembourg are tendered in Ireland and coins bearing Finnish cloudberries circulate through German banks.

Although all 15 European Union countries meet or come close to eurozone's stringent financial criteria, only 12 countries joined in for the fledgling currency's debut. Denmark, Sweden, and the UK have all chosen to stay out of the eurozone indefinitely. Although national identity plays a role in their choices, economic factors may be more influential; the UK, for one, is wary of tying its strong economy to the fortunes of a dozen continental countries. Euro-skeptics forecasted a rough transition due to a number of possible hitches, such as hidden price increases due to retailers rounding prices up to the nearest euro and heavy counterfeiting while the general public was still unfamiliar with the security features of the new notes. Some went so far as to predict an anti-integrationist backlash that would jeopardize the EU as a whole.

In practice, however, the transition has been surprisingly smooth. Extensive preparation included massive public education efforts and the monstrous task of converting all printed signs and coin-operated machines to the euro. In many towns and cities, the first few days brought dozens of confusions and inconveniences, as stores ran out of change and consumers struggled to remember the relative value of the new denominations. Prices did jump slightly, but economists attribute the increases to higher food costs stemming from bad weather. On the whole, the European public was quickly satisfied with the transition. Although pockets of discontent remain strong in The Netherlands and in many rural areas, surveys by the European Commission in April 2002 found that 81% of people throughout the eurozone judged the changeover successful.

Tobie Whitman was a Researcher-Writer for Let's Go: London 1999 and 2001, as well as Let's Go: Britain & Ireland 1998. After an internship with the EU, she entered the University of Cambridge to pursue a Master's Degree in European Studies.

WITH OR WITHOUT EU

The Current Candidates for EU Enlargement

Thirteen countries have applied to join the 15-strong EU; ten of them may enter as early as January 1, 2004, uniting almost the entire continent into one big, happy, free-market economy. Yet despite real enthusiasm and a widespread sense of the importance of the project, enlargement does have its opponents. The countries that joined the original six-member EU in the past were relatively well-off at the time and came to the table in small, easy-to-digest bites rather than as a ten-course meal. It's proving difficult for the current members to contemplate dividing the spoils of the Union—agricultural subsidies, regional development funds, and chairs at the EU's tables of power—with their neighbors to the east and south. The candidate countries themselves are not without a number of concerns that make a match with the EU questionable.

The enlargement process began philosophically after the fall of the Berlin Wall but took a decade to pick up any real steam. The hot favorites from the beginning were the large countries closest to the EU—Poland, Hungary, and the former Czechoslovakia—but a little-known contender has taken the lead in the race to the finish line: Slovenia, which was nearly 100% EU-compliant at the end of 2002. The plucky little country is already looking and acting like the newest member of the club, with new international superhighways and a GDP per capita that's higher than any other applicant in Central or Eastern Europe—higher, even, than some of them combined. While Hungary and the Czech Republic have made great strides in the race, the Slovak Republic has fallen behind due to some messy domestic politics, and Poland has proven a bit stubborn; as the largest country likely to join the EU in this round of enlargement, Poland has been holding out in some negotiations in hope of a better accession package.

After a slow start, Lithuania and Latvia have made good progress toward readiness, but still lag behind their Baltic sister-state, Estonia. Yet despite booming growth and one of Europe's freest economies, Estonian public opinion regarding accession has been cooling off fast. The most recent Eurobarometer survey showed public support for EU membership at a mere 38%—compared to 85% in Romania and 70% in Hungary, for instance. Some of this is due to public exhaustion in the wake of the EU's much-delayed plans for their accession, but good old-fashioned scepticism plays a role as well. As one Estonian-on-the-street put it, "We just left a Union, and look where that one got us..."

Romania and Bulgaria are still a bit shy of EU criteria, and analysts say it will be 2010 before they make it to the finish line. Turkey, it seems, has limited prospects for the time being, producing a bit of a quandary over Cyprus. Although the island—divided since 1974 into Greek and Turkish zones of influence—is as prepared a candidate as Slovenia, its accession has become quite controversial. Greece insists that it will veto everyone if Cyprus doesn't join in the first wave, while Turkey has quietly threatened to do the same in the concurrent NATO enlargement if the EU doesn't consider its own application more seriously. The EU, for its part, has always felt that rapid accession may be the best—if not only—solution to the divided island's persistent ethnic problems.

Malta has come back in on the action, having defrosted its earlier application. While it had made headway in the last enlargement round, it pulled out of the race before it was over due to a lack of support at home. Norway, though having been officially accepted for membership, never took up the EU's offer, twice holding referenda in which the Norwegian public rejected membership. Referenda—as the Estonian opinion polls show—may prove to be enlargement's Achilles' heel. Indeed, this entire project hangs on the consent of, well... the Irish. Until Ireland ratifies the enlargement-centered Treaty of Nice from 2001, no new countries can be admitted to the EU.

And what of that most geographically and linguistically European of nations, Switzerland? Having voted to join the UN this year, some speculate that the EU may be nearing the Swiss horizon. If nothing else, Switzerland's accession would fill the lake-like gap in the map on the front of the €2 coin—although some wags point out that, with Norway still missing from the picture, Sweden and Finland give an altogether different kind of impression. Take a look for yourself the next time you have a jingle in your pocket...

Jeremy Faro is a former Senior Consultant at Interbrand and has worked in the past on Let's Go: Britain & Ireland. *He is currently a master's student in European Studies at Cambridge University.*

EUROPE IN BLACK AND WHITE

The Prevalence of Xenophobia in Modern Europe

In Europe as in America, cultural racism has long been a tale of bodies told as a story about minds—an evaluation of hair and skin behind claims about culture and language. This is evident to every child who, though born and raised in Europe, is perceived as an immigrant because she "looks Middle Eastern" or "looks African."

Anti-immigrant agitators have caused several recent electoral earthquakes. In 1999, the ultra-nationalist party of Jörg Haider shocked the European Union by attracting more than one-fourth of Austria's voters and becoming part of the country's governing coalition. Regimes in Italy, Portugal, and Denmark also depend on the extreme right to maintain parliamentary majorities. Osama bin Laden's September 11th gift to reactionary forces worldwide aided the Dutch Muslim-baiting party of the late Pim Fortuyn as well as France's Jean-Marie Le Pen, who was supported by 17% of the electorate in the first round of the 2002 presidential election.

Political entrepreneurs of the far right fan xenophobic fires by framing immigrants and native workers as rival claimants to material resources and social respect. In a western Europe of advanced general-welfare policies, resources for health-care, education, and housing, as well as unemployment benefits, have been squeezed during recent decades of retrenchment. Some politicians portray immigrants as getting something for nothing, receiving social support without having contributed to society. The immigrants themselves are in a catch-22: they are resented if they are unemployed (and thus seen as living off other people's taxes), but also if they find jobs (seen as taking them from natives).

Support for anti-immigrant parties comes largely from the working classes; bourgeois racism also exists, but wealthy citizens often value the inexpensive labor provided by immigrants even while looking down on them. Working-class opposition to immigration arises above all from the humiliations that workers have suffered. A man who welds fenders eight hours a day at a Renault factory, barely supporting his family in a dreary suburban flat—then finds himself unemployed when production is shifted abroad—is unlikely to welcome a Rwandan refugee, much less to empathize with her own biography of humiliations.

Immigration is also debated as part of Europe's ongoing cultural globalization. Multinational products perceived as American—from food to news to movies—have saturated the continent. Citizens of many countries (not least France) see this development as jeopardizing national integrity. Non-European immigrants may be framed as further eroding an imagined cultural homogeneity due to their different diets, clothing, religion, and language.

The more extreme right-wing politicians supplement economic and cultural discourses with imagery of bodily and sexual danger. As in racisms the world over, men of the disfavored groups are presented as violent, criminal, and predatory toward women—invaders, Le Pen once said, "who want to sleep in my bed, with my wife." In fact, it is the immigrants who are often the victims of crimes, committed largely by the underemployed sons of marginalized workers. Here racism is at its most obvious: those targeted may not be "foreign" at all, but native citizens who happen not to be white.

A politician who opposes anti-immigrant parties and the violence they sometimes condone faces a political obstacle course. How to protect asylum seekers arriving from a war-torn world while at the same time reassuring the public that the nation is strictly guarding its borders? How to reduce unemployment while also encouraging immigration of needed workers in such sectors as high technology and care of the expanding elderly population? How to balance respect for cultural and religious differences with the need to socialize new arrivals in the values and habits of the host society? In the hard-won answers to these questions lies the fate of the European Dream, a vision of an inclusive and egalitarian society extending across a continent.

Dr. Brian Palmer lectures on ethnography and ethics, and Kathleen Holbrook researches globalization and human values. They were voted Harvard's best young faculty member and teaching fellow, respectively, for a course which the New York Times nicknamed "Idealism 101."

INDEX

A

B

INDEX

C

D

E

F

INDEX

G

H

I

INDEX

INDEX

P

Q

R

S

INDEX

INDEX

W

Y

Z

Go the distance
with Hostelling International
A Hostelling International membership card gives you access to friendly and affordable accommodations at over 4,000 hostels in 60 countries, including across Europe.
Get your card today and join millions of members worldwide, who save money and have more fun every time they travel.
Join Now!
USA:www.hiayh.org
Canada:www.hihostels.ca
HOSTELLING INTERNATIONAL®
4000 locations • 60 countries • one card

AMERICA'S FAVORITE
LUCKY BRAND
REG. DUNGAREES T.M.
LUCKY BRAND
AMERICA'S FINEST
BLUE JEANS
HANDMADE WITH THE FINEST DENIM FABRICS
BUY A PAIR
DO IT TODAY
RTM
RN:80318
WWW.LUCKYBRANDJEANS.COM
L. B. Mfg. Co.
AMERICAN DENIM STANDARD LA Ca.
LB

© 2002 Yahoo! Inc.
Book your air, hotel, and transportation all in one place.
Hotel or hostel? Cruise or canoe? Car? Plane? Camel? Wherever you're going, visit Yahoo! Travel and get total control over your arrangements. Even choose your seat assignment. So. One hump or two? travel.yahoo.com
powered by hp
YAHOO!
Travel
DO YOU YAHOO!?

MAP INDEX

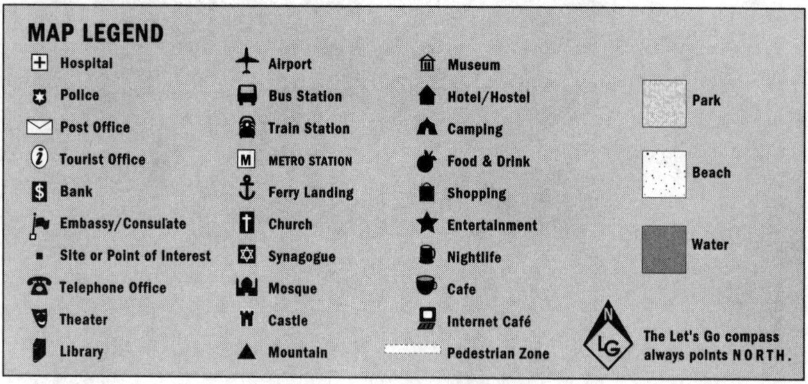

MAP LEGEND
Hospital
Police
Post Office
Tourist Office
Bank
Embassy/Consulate
Site or Point of Interest
Telephone Office
Theater
Library
Airport
Bus Station
Train Station
METRO STATION
Ferry Landing
Church
Synagogue
Mosque
Castle
Mountain
Museum
Hotel/Hostel
Camping
Food & Drink
Shopping
Entertainment
Nightlife
Cafe
Internet Café
Pedestrian Zone
Park
Beach
Water
The Let's Go compass always points NORTH.